漢英詞典

# The Pinyin CHINESE-ENGLISH DICTIONARY

## EDITORIAL STAFF

EDITOR IN CHIEF: Wu Jingrong

DEPUTY EDITORS IN CHIEF: Wang Zuoliang, Liu Shimu, Wei Dongya, Wang Ban

EDITORIAL BOARD: Ying Manrong, Wang Jingxi, Gao Houkun, Zheng Rongcheng, Wu Qianzhi, Zhuang Yichuan, Zhao Mu'ang, Lin Yi, Lin Xuehong, Wang Guilin

ENGLISH CONSULTANT: David Crook

EDITORS (ENGLISH): Du Bingzhou, Chen Wenbo, Wang Shaofang, Zhang Zhi, Wang Guang, Liu Guoyun, Yang Guangci, Lü Xia, Zhang Shifa

EDITORS (CHINESE): Liu Mo, Ma Yaohui, Zhong Shangjun, Lin Xingguang, Chen Dunquan

EDITORS (SCIENCE): Guan Pinshu, Wang Xuehua, Liang Youde, Fang Tingyu, Shang Dianyuan

漢英詞典

# The Pinyin CHINESE-ENGLISH DICTIONARY

**Editor-in-chief**
**Professor Wu Jingrong**
**Beijing Foreign Languages Institute**

The Commercial Press
Beijing · Hong Kong
and
Pitman Advanced Publishing Program
San Francisco · London · Melbourne

The Commercial Press Limited
35 Queen's Road Central
Hong Kong

Pitman Publishing Limited
39 Parker Street
London WC2B 5PB



Library of Congress Cataloging in Progress Number: 79–2477



ISBN 0 273 08454 2 Europe, Australia, New Zealand, Africa
ISBN 0 471 27557 3 N. America & Canada (John Wiley & Sons Inc)

Printed by
The Commercial Press, Limited
Hong Kong Printing Works
75, Pau Chung Street,
Kowloon, Hong Kong

# Contents

# 目录

# Guide to the Use of the Dictionary

## I. Arrangement of Entries

1. All entries are divided into single-character and compound-character entries. The former are set in large, boldface type, the latter are placed in boldface square brackets "【 】"

2. Single-character entries are listed in strict alphabetical order. Characters with the same pronunciation but different tone are arranged according to tone. Characters with both the same pronunciation and tone are arranged according to number of strokes.

3. Compound-character entries are arranged by first character under the respective single-character entries. Where there is more than one compound-character entry under a single-character entry, listing is done according to the alphabetical order of the second character in the compound. If the second character is the same in the two entries then listing is done according to the third character, and so on.

4. Separate entries are made for characters that are the same but have two or more pronunciations or different tones. For example:

"合" hé 和 "合" gě; 【温和】wēnhé 和【温和】wēnhuo; 【播种】bōzhǒng 和【播种】bōzhòng。

5. Characters with the same form and pronunciation but with different meanings are dealt with in subentries in the same single-character entry.

6. Characters with no tone are listed after characters with the same form which have tones. Thus "出" chu is listed after "出" chū ; 【大方】dàfang after【大方】dàfāng. However, "了" le, "着" zhe, and other characters without tones are listed after characters with a fourth tone (去声).

7. In listing character-compounds that have slightly different usages, only the more common form is given. Variant forms are placed at the end of the entry with the words "also read" ("又作") preceding them. Thus: ( 差之毫厘, 谬以千里 )－chā zhī háolí, miù yǐ qiānlǐ (an error the breadth of a single hair can lead you a thousand *li* astray), 又作"差之毫厘, 失之千里"。

## II. Phonetics

1. All entries are recorded in Chinese Phonetics (hanyupinyin).

2. Tonal changes within compound words are not generally marked.

3. Characters with no tones have no marking. Thus: (喇叭) lǎba.

4. "R" endings are marked by the addition of "r" to the phonetic form of the character. This does not signify the actual phonetic change. Thus,【冰棍儿】bīnggùnr;【刘海儿】liúhǎir. Words that do not necessarily take "r" endings in colloquial usage are not listed with "r" endings.

5. An apostrophe (') is used to separate syllables in compound-character entries that may be confused. Thus :【木耳】mù'ěr; 【海鸥】hǎi'ōu;【阴暗】yīn'àn.

6. The first letter of special names and surnames is capitalized. Thus: "鲁" Lǔ;【中国】Zhōngguó. Common objects named after countries, places or people are not capitalized. Thus: 【英尺】 yīngchǐ; 【京剧】 jīngjù; 【本生灯】běnshēngdēng.

## III. Definitions and Examples

1. Specialized entries generally note the names of the specialty or science to which they refer. These names or their abbreviations are put in angle brackets "〈 〉". All specialized or scientific terms that are in common use, or whose relation to a specialized field or science is obvious from the Chinese characters, are not separately annotated.

2. Annotations explaining figures of speech, parts of speech (such as adverbs, prepositions, conjunctions, auxiliaries, exclamations and onomatopes) and some classifiers are also placed in angle brackets "〈 〉".

3. Explantions of the peculiaritis of Chinese grammar, the scope of use of certain words or phrases or their implication are put in square brackets "〔 〕". All words without an equivalent word, words or expression in English are annotated in this way. Thus:

吧…〈助〉①〔在句末表示商量、提议、请求、命令〕: 咱们走～。Let's go.

【关于】…〈介〉〔引进某种行为或事物的关系者，组成介词结构〕 about; on; with regard to; concerning

4. If an entry is an abbreviation, the full word is put in brackets after it. Thus:

干… ②〈简〉(干部)

【革委会】… 〈简〉(革命委员会)

5. Entries generally use equivalent English definitions. Words and expressions that do not have an appropriate English definitions are explained in English. When two or more explanations are necessary, a semicolon ";" is used to divide them. The different meanings of an entry are listed numerically①②③. When finer divisions are required, ⓐⓑⓒ and so on are used. Thus:

家… ① family; household… ② home… ③ a person or family engaged in a certain trade… ④ a specialist in a certain field…

把… ⑦〈量〉 ⓐ〔用于有柄的器具〕: 一～刀 a knife… ⓑ〔指一手抓起的数量〕: 一～米 a handful of rice

6. An explanation is made in English in brackets when an English equivalent has a wider meaning or different meanings than the Chinese. Thus:

嫁… ① (of a woman) marry

【机舱】… ① engine room (of a ship) ② passenger compartment (of an aircraft); cabin

【历次】… all previous (occasions, etc.)

7. Where necessary, further explanations of the background or origin of a term or name are made in English in brackets or marked off by a comma. Thus:

【巴黎公社】… the Paris Commune (the world's first dictatorship of the proletariat established by the French working class after smashing the old state machine, 1871)

【嫦娥】… the goddess of the moon (the lady in the legend who swallowed elixir stolen from her husband and flew to the moon)

【假名】… ② *kana*, a Japanese syllabary

8. Latin or scientific symbols are put in brackets after the English definition where applicable.

【半夏】… 〈中药〉 the tuber of pinellia *(Pinellia ternata)*

钡… 〈化〉 barium (Ba)

9. Where necessary, examples of usage have been given after the definition or explanation of a word or expression. All examples are preceded by a colon ":", and the word or words in the examples that are the same as the entry are represented by a wave line "～". When there is more than one English translation for an example then they are divided by a semicolon ";". If, however, the different translation is an independent sentence, the division is marked by the word "or" ("或"). Examples themselves are divided by a vergule "/". Thus:

【程度】…: 觉悟～ level of political consciousness/ 文化～ level of education; degree of literacy

【电话】…: 有你的～。There's a phone call for you. 或 You're wanted on the phone.

10. If there are sections of the example that

can be substituted by another word or words, then the word or words are placed in brackets in both the Chinese and in the English. Thus:

界…：动(植、矿)物～ the animal (vegetable, mineral) kingdom

【工程】…：土木(机械、电机、采矿)～ civil (mechanical, electrical, mining) engineering

11. If deletions of a word or words can be made in the definitions of the entries or the translations of the examples then these are marked by brackets "( )" Thus:

户…：存～ (bank) depositor

【更新世】… the Pleistocene (Epoch)

12. If there are English words or phrases that can replace other words or phrases in the definitions or examples, these are put in brackets and the word "or" ("或") is put before it. Thus:

【改观】… change the appearance (或 face) of

搞…：～运动 carry on a movement (或 campaign)

13. If there are more than one English definition or example, then a Chinese explanation is placed in brackets in front of the English definition or example. Thus:

【国会】… parliament; (美) Congress; (日) the Diet

【来历】…：～不明 (指事物) of unknown origin; (指人) of dubious background or of questionable antecedents

【陛下】… (直接称呼) Your Majesty; (间接称呼) His or Her Majesty

14. If there are specialized names or words in the English definitions or examples, an explanation is made in Chinese. Thus:

【阿斗】… ① the infant name of Liu Shan (刘禅, 207-271), last emperor of Shu Han (蜀汉, 221-263), known for his want of ability and weakness of character

【八纲】… 〈中医〉 the eight principal syndromes: *yin* and *yang* (阴阳), exterior and interior (表里), cold and heat (寒热), hypofunction and hyperfunction (虚实)

15. English abbreviations are added in brackets after the English definitions or translation of examples. Thus:

【公斤】… kilogram (kg.)

【背面】…：请阅～ please turn over (P.T.O.)

16. Additional explanations of definitions or examples of four-character idioms, proverbs, idiomatic usage or other expressions are placed after a dash "—". Thus:

【画蛇添足】… draw a snake and add feet to it — ruin the effect by adding sth. superfluous

【并蒂莲】… twin lotus flowers on one stalk — a devoted married couple

17. All Chinese personal names, place names, and the names of things peculiar to China are spelt in the Chinese Phonetic Alphabet (hanyupinyin). Thus:

【毛泽东思想】… Mao Zedong Thought

【北京】… Beijing (Peking)

【大字报】… *dazibao*; big-character poster

【人民】… ◇ ～币 Renminbi (RMB)

亩… *mu*, a unit of area (= 0.0667 hectares): ～产量 per *mu* yield

## IV. Compound Words and Set Phrases

The majority of compound words and set phrases that are preceded by compound-character entries are listed according to alphabetical (Chinese Phonetic Alphabet) order after the definitions or examples of their respective entries and are preceded by a diamond "◇" All other symbols used in these listings are the same as those used in the examples. If there are many compound words or set phrases, they are listed on a separate line. Specialized or scientific annotations are added to specialized words and phrases. Thus:

【二元】… ①〈数〉 duality ②〈化〉 binary ◇ ～酸 binary acid

【玻璃】… ① glass: 雕花～ cut glass/ 彩色～ stained glass/ 泡沫～ cellular glass ②〈口〉 nylon; plastic

◇ ～板 glass plate; plate glass; glass top (of a desk)/ ～版 〈印〉 collotype/ ～杯 glass; tumbler/ ～布 glass cloth

# Table of Abbreviations

| | |
|---|---|
| 〈贬〉 | derogatory sense |
| 〈测〉 | mapping |
| 〈地〉 | geology; geography |
| 〈电〉 | electricity; electrical engineering |
| 〈动〉 | animal; zoology |
| 〈法〉 | law |
| 〈方〉 | dialect |
| 〈纺〉 | textile and dyeing |
| 〈讽〉 | satirical term |
| 〈副〉 | adverb |
| 〈工美〉 | arts and crafts |
| 〈化〉 | chemistry; chemical industry |
| 〈化纤〉 | chemical fibre |
| 〈环保〉 | environmental protection |
| 〈机〉 | machinery |
| 〈简〉 | abbreviation |
| 〈建〉 | construction |
| 〈交〉 | transportation |
| 〈教〉 | education |
| 〈介〉 | preposition |
| 〈经〉 | economics |
| 〈敬〉 | polite expression |
| 〈旧〉 | archaic expression |
| 〈剧〉 | drama |
| 〈军〉 | military |
| 〈口〉 | colloquial |
| 〈矿〉 | mineral; mining |
| 〈连〉 | conjunction |
| 〈量〉 | classifier |
| 〈林〉 | forestry |
| 〈逻〉 | logic |
| 〈骂〉 | abusive language |
| 〈牧〉 | animal husbandry |
| 〈农〉 | agriculture |
| 〈气〉 | meteorology |
| 〈谦〉 | self-depreciatory expression |
| 〈商〉 | commerce |
| 〈摄〉 | cinematography |
| 〈生〉 | biology |
| 〈生化〉 | bio-chemistry |
| 〈生理〉 | physiology; anatomy |
| 〈史〉 | history |
| 〈书〉 | literary language |
| 〈数〉 | mathematics |
| 〈水〉 | irrigation |
| 〈叹〉 | exclamation |
| 〈套〉 | polite formula |
| 〈体〉 | sports |
| 〈天〉 | astronomy |
| 〈外〉 | diplomacy |
| 〈婉〉 | euphemism |
| 〈微〉 | microbiology |
| 〈无〉 | radio |
| 〈物〉 | physics |
| 〈象〉 | onomatope |
| 〈心〉 | psychology |
| 〈讯〉 | telecommunications |
| 〈谚〉 | proverb |
| 〈药〉 | pharmaceutical; pharmacology |
| 〈冶〉 | metallurgy |
| 〈医〉 | medicine |
| 〈印〉 | printing |
| 〈邮〉 | postal service |
| 〈渔〉 | fishery |
| 〈宇航〉 | astronavigation |
| 〈语〉 | linguistics |
| 〈原〉 | atomic energy |
| 〈乐〉 | music |
| 〈哲〉 | philosophy |
| 〈植〉 | botanical, botany |
| 〈纸〉 | papermaking |
| 〈助〉 | auxiliary word |
| 〈自〉 | automatic control |
| 〈宗〉 | religion |
| 〈尊〉 | respectful form of address |

**Note: Unabbreviated terms such as 〈铁道〉〈乒乓球〉and〈伊斯兰教〉 have not been included in this table.**

# 用 法 说 明

# Guide to the Use of the Dictionary

## 一 条目安排

1. 本词典所收条目分单字条目和多字条目。前者用大字排印，后者加鱼尾号“【 】”。

2. 单字条目按汉语拼音字母顺序排列。同音异调的汉字按声调顺序排列。同音同调的汉字，按笔划多少排列。

3. 多字条目按第一个字分列于单字条目之下。同一单字条目下的多字条目不止一条时，按第二个字的汉语拼音字母顺序和笔划多少排列。第二个字相同时，按第三个字排列，依此类推。

4. 汉字字形相同而音或调不同者，分立条目。如：“合”hé 和“合”gě；【温和】wēnhé 和【温和】wēnhuo；【播种】bōzhǒng 和【播种】bōzhòng。

5. 汉字字形及字音相同而意义不同者，作为同一条目的不同义项处理。

6. 轻声字一般紧接在同形的非轻声字后面。如：“出”chu 排在“出”chū 之后；【大方】dàfang 排在【大方】dàfāng 之后。但是，“了”le、“着”zhe 等轻声字排在去声音节之后。

7. 在同一单字条目下，多字条目意义相同，仅在用字上略有差异，一般只收录其中较常见者。在该条最后，加“又作…”。如：【差之毫厘，谬以千里】… 又作“差之毫厘，失之千里”。

## 二 注 音

1. 条目用汉语拼音字母注音。

2. 声调一般只注原调，不注变调。

3. 轻声不加调号。如：【喇叭】lǎba。

4. 儿化音只在基本形式后面加 r，不标出语音的实际变化。如：【冰棍儿】bīnggùnr；【刘海儿】liúhǎir。口语中可儿化可不儿化的，一律不加“儿”，不注 r。

5. 多字条目的注音中，音节界限有可能混淆时，加隔音号“'”。如：【木耳】mù'ěr；【海鸥】hǎi'ōu；【阴暗】yīn'àn。

6. 专有名词和姓氏的注音，第一个字母大写。如：“鲁”Lǔ；【中国】Zhōngguó。根据国名、地名、人名等命名的普通事物名称，第一个字母小写。如：【英尺】yīngchǐ；【京剧】jīngjù；【本生灯】běnshēngdēng。

## 三 释义和例证

1. 专业条目一般注明所属专业或学科名称。名称或其略语，放在尖括号“‹ ›”内。凡日常生活中习见或汉字本身能表明所属专业或学科，不致引起误解者，不另加注释。

2. 一般条目根据需要注明修辞特征和六种虚词(副词、介词、连词、助词、叹词、象声词)及部分量词的词类，所用略语也放在尖括号“‹ ›”内。

3. 有关语法特征、使用范围、内容涵义等方面的简略汉语说明，放在方括号“〔 〕”内。凡英语中无适当对应词语或概念不完全相符合者，酌加此类注释。如：

吧…‹助› ①〔在句末表示商量、提议、请求、命令〕：咱们走～。Let's go.

【关于】…‹介›〔引进某种行为或事物的关系者，组成介词结构〕about; on; with regard to; concerning

4. 条目如系简称，一般注出全称。如：

干… ②‹简›(干部)

【革委会】… ‹简›(革命委员会)

5. 条目一般用对应的英语释义；无适当对应词语时，用英语解释。同一义项下有两个或两个以上的英语释义时，用分号“;”隔开。一个条目有两个或两个以上不同意义时，分立义项，用①②③等数码标出顺序；某一义项需再细分时，用ⓐⓑⓒ等字母标出顺序。如：

家… ① family; household… ② home… ③ a person or family engaged in a certain trade… ④ a specialist in a certain field…

把… ⑦〈量〉ⓐ〔用于有柄的器具〕：一～刀 a knife… ⓑ〔指一手抓起的数量〕：一～米 a handful of rice

6. 如英语对应词语的含义比汉语条目广泛或一词多义，则在圆括号"( )"内用英语作限定性说明。如：

嫁… ① (of a woman) marry

【机舱】… ① engine room (of a ship) ② passenger compartment (of an aircraft); cabin

【历次】… all previous (occasions, etc.)

7. 某些条目在英语释义后，根据需要，就有关背景、典故或其他方面加补充性说明，放在圆括号"( )"内或用逗号"，"隔开。如：

【巴黎公社】… the Paris Commune (the world's first dictatorship of the proletariat established by the French working class after smashing the old state machine, 1871)

【嫦娥】… the goddess of the moon (the lady in the legend who swallowed elixir stolen from her husband and flew to the moon)

【假名】… ② *kana*, a Japanese syllabary

8. 某些专业条目在英语释义后，加拉丁语学名或符号。如：

【半夏】…〈中药〉 the tuber of pinellia *(Pinellia ternata)*

钡…〈化〉 barium (Ba)

9. 条目释义(或注释)后，根据需要，收入词、词组或句子作为例证。例证前面加冒号"："。例证中与本条目相同的部分，用代字号"～"表示。例证英语译文不止一个时，如果是词或词组，用分号"；"隔开；如果是句子，则用"或"字隔开。例证与例证之间，用斜线号"/"隔开。如：

【程度】…：觉悟～ level of political consciousness/ 文化～ level of education; degree of literacy

【电话】…：有你的～。There's a phone call for you. 或 You're wanted on the phone.

10. 例证中如有可以替换的部分，这部分及其译文都用圆括号"( )"括出。如：

界…：动(植、矿)物～ the animal (vegetable, mineral) kingdom

【工程】…：土木(机械、电机、采矿)～ civil (mechanical, electrical, mining) engineering

11. 条目释义或例证译文中，如有可以省略的部分，用圆括号"( )"括出。如：

户…：存～ (bank) depositor

【更新世】… the Pleistocene (Epoch)

12. 条目释义或例证译文中，如有可以替换的英语词语时，也用圆括号"( )"括出，另加"或"字。如：

【改观】… change the appearance (或 face) of

搞…：～运动 carry on a movement (或 campaign)

13. 如条目释义或例证译文不止一个，适用范围各不相同，则在释义或译文前，用汉语加限定性说明，也放在圆括号"( )"内。如：

【国会】… parliament; (美) Congress; (日) the Diet

【来历】…：～不明 (指事物) of unknown origin; (指人) of dubious background or of questionable antecedents

【陛下】… (直接称呼) Your Majesty; (间接称呼) His or Her Majesty

14. 在条目释义和例证译文中，出现某些专有名词或比较特殊的词语时，用汉语酌加注释。如：

【阿斗】… ① the infant name of Liu Shan (刘禅, 207-271), last emperor of Shu Han (蜀汉, 221-263), known for his want of ability and weakness of character

【八纲】…〈中医〉 the eight principal syndromes: *yin* and *yang* (阴阳), exterior and interior (表里), cold and heat (寒热), hypofunction and hyperfunction (虚实)

15. 某些条目释义或例证译文后，加英文缩写。如：

【公斤】… kilogram (kg.)

【背面】…：请阅～ please turn over (P.T.O.)

16. 在某些成语、谚语、习语及其他词语的条目释义或例证译文之后，加点明实质的补充性说明，用破折号"—"隔开。如：

【画蛇添足】… draw a snake and add feet to it — ruin the effect by adding sth. superfluous

【并蒂莲】… twin lotus flowers on one stalk — a devoted married couple

17. 中国人名、地名以及某些中国特有事物的名称，按汉语拼音方案音译。如：

【毛泽东思想】… Mao Zedong Thought

【北京】… Beijing (Peking)

【大字报】… *dazibao*; big-character poster

【人民】… ◇ ～币 Renminbi (RMB)

亩… *mu*, a unit of area (= 0.0667 hectares): ～产量 per *mu* yield

## 四 合成词和词化短语

以多字条目领头的大多数合成词和词化短语，不按义项分列，而按汉语拼音字母顺序，集中排列在该条目释义或例证之后，前加一菱形号"◇"，其他符号的用法与例证部分相同。如数量较多，则另起一行排列。专业词语也酌加专业或学科注释。如：

【二元】… ①〈数〉 duality ②〈化〉 binary ◇ ～酸 binary acid

【玻璃】… ① glass: 雕花～ cut glass/ 彩色～ stained glass/ 泡沫～ cellular glass ②〈口〉 nylon; plastic

◇ ～板 glass plate; plate glass; glass top (of a desk)/ ～版〈印〉 collotype/ ～杯 glass; tumbler/ ～布 glass cloth

# 略 语 表

(按汉语拼音字母顺序排列)

| | |
|---|---|
| 〈贬〉 | 贬义 |
| 〈测〉 | 测绘 |
| 〈地〉 | 地质学；地理学 |
| 〈电〉 | 电学；电工 |
| 〈动〉 | 动物；动物学 |
| 〈法〉 | 法律 |
| 〈方〉 | 方言 |
| 〈纺〉 | 纺织印染 |
| 〈讽〉 | 讽刺语 |
| 〈副〉 | 副词 |
| 〈工美〉 | 工艺美术 |
| 〈化〉 | 化学；化工 |
| 〈化纤〉 | 化学纤维 |
| 〈环保〉 | 环境保护 |
| 〈机〉 | 机械 |
| 〈简〉 | 简称 |
| 〈建〉 | 建筑 |
| 〈交〉 | 交通运输 |
| 〈教〉 | 教育 |
| 〈介〉 | 介词 |
| 〈经〉 | 经济 |
| 〈敬〉 | 敬辞 |
| 〈旧〉 | 旧时用语 |
| 〈剧〉 | 戏剧 |
| 〈军〉 | 军事 |
| 〈口〉 | 口语 |
| 〈矿〉 | 矿物；矿业 |
| 〈连〉 | 连词 |
| 〈量〉 | 量词 |
| 〈林〉 | 林业 |
| 〈逻〉 | 逻辑学 |
| 〈骂〉 | 骂人的话 |
| 〈牧〉 | 畜牧业 |
| 〈农〉 | 农业 |
| 〈气〉 | 气象学 |
| 〈谦〉 | 谦辞 |
| 〈商〉 | 商业 |
| 〈摄〉 | 摄影 |
| 〈生〉 | 生物 |
| 〈生化〉 | 生物化学 |
| 〈生理〉 | 生理学；解剖学 |
| 〈史〉 | 历史 |
| 〈书〉 | 文言书面语 |
| 〈数〉 | 数学 |
| 〈水〉 | 水利 |
| 〈叹〉 | 叹词 |

〈套〉 套语
〈体〉 体育
〈天〉 天文学
〈外〉 外交
〈婉〉 婉辞
〈微〉 微生物
〈无〉 无线电
〈物〉 物理学
〈象〉 象声词
〈心〉 心理学
〈讯〉 电信
〈谚〉 谚语
〈药〉 药物；药物学
〈冶〉 冶金
〈医〉 医学
〈印〉 印刷
〈邮〉 邮政
〈渔〉 渔业
〈宇航〉 宇宙航行
〈语〉 语言学
〈原〉 原子能
〈乐〉 音乐
〈哲〉 哲学
〈植〉 植物；植物学
〈纸〉 造纸
〈助〉 助词
〈自〉 自动控制
〈宗〉 宗教
〈尊〉 尊称

说明：未经缩略者不收入本表，如〈铁道〉〈乒乓球〉〈伊斯兰教〉等。

# 部 首 检 字

# Radical Index

## (一) 部首目录

部首左边的号码表示部首的次序

| | | | | | | | | | | | | | |
|---|---|---|---|---|---|---|---|---|---|---|---|---|---|
| 一画 | | 35 | 又 | 70 | ヨ(彐彑) | 105 | 中 | 140 | 业 | 175 | 缶 | 209 | 金 |
| 1 | 丶 | 36 | 廴 | 71 | 弓 | 106 | 贝 | 141 | 目 | 176 | 耒 | 210 | 鱼 |
| 2 | 一 | 37 | 厶 | 72 | 己(巳) | 107 | 见 | 142 | 田 | 177 | 舌 | 九画 | |
| 3 | 丨 | 38 | 凵 | 73 | 女 | 108 | 父 | 143 | 由 | 178 | 竹(⺮) | 211 | 音 |
| 4 | 丿 | 39 | 匕 | 74 | 子(孑) | 109 | 气 | 144 | 申 | 179 | 臼 | 212 | 革 |
| 5 | 乛 | 三画 | | 75 | 马 | 110 | 牛(牜) | 145 | 罒 | 180 | 自 | 213 | 是 |
| 6 | 𠃌 | 40 | 氵 | 76 | 幺 | 111 | 手 | 146 | 皿 | 181 | 血 | 214 | 骨 |
| 7 | 乙(⺄乚) | 41 | 忄 | 77 | 纟(糸) | 112 | 毛 | 147 | 钅 | 182 | 舟 | 215 | 香 |
| 二画 | | 42 | 丬(爿) | 78 | 巛 | 113 | 攵 | 148 | 矢 | 183 | 羽 | 216 | 鬼 |
| 8 | 冫 | 43 | 亡 | 79 | 小(⺌) | 114 | 片 | 149 | 禾 | 184 | 艮(㫐) | 217 | 食 |
| 9 | 亠 | 44 | 广 | 四画 | | 115 | 斤 | 150 | 白 | 七画 | | 十画 | |
| 10 | 讠 | 45 | 宀 | 80 | 灬 | 116 | 爪(爫) | 151 | 瓜 | 185 | 言 | 218 | 高 |
| 11 | 二 | 46 | 门 | 81 | 心 | 117 | 尺 | 152 | 鸟 | 186 | 辛 | 219 | 鬲 |
| 12 | 十 | 47 | 辶 | 82 | 斗 | 118 | 月 | 153 | 皮 | 187 | 辰 | 220 | 髟 |
| 13 | 厂 | 48 | 工 | 83 | 火 | 119 | 殳 | 154 | 癶 | 188 | 麦 | 十一画 | |
| 14 | 𠂇 | 49 | 土(士) | 84 | 文 | 120 | 欠 | 155 | 矛 | 189 | 走 | 221 | 麻 |
| 15 | 匚 | 50 | 卝 | 85 | 方 | 121 | 风 | 156 | 疋 | 190 | 赤 | 222 | 鹿 |
| 16 | 卜(⺊) | 51 | 廾 | 86 | 户 | 122 | 氏 | 六画 | | 191 | 豆 | 十二画 | |
| 17 | 刂 | 52 | 大 | 87 | 礻 | 123 | 比 | 157 | 羊(⺶⺷) | 192 | 束 | 223 | 黑 |
| 18 | 冖 | 53 | 尢 | 88 | 王 | 124 | 肀 | 158 | 类 | 193 | 酉 | 十三画 | |
| 19 | 冂 | 54 | 寸 | 89 | 圭 | 125 | 水 | 159 | 米 | 194 | 豕 | 224 | 鼓 |
| 20 | 𠂉 | 55 | 扌 | 90 | 天(夭) | 五画 | | 160 | 齐 | 195 | 里 | 225 | 鼠 |
| 21 | 亻 | 56 | 弋 | 91 | 韦 | 126 | 立 | 161 | 衣 | 196 | 足 | 十四画 | |
| 22 | 𠂆 | 57 | 巾 | 92 | 耂 | 127 | 疒 | 162 | 亦(亦) | 197 | 采 | 226 | 鼻 |
| 23 | 人(入) | 58 | 口 | 93 | 廿(卄) | 128 | 穴 | 163 | 耳 | 198 | 豸 | —— | |
| 24 | 八(丷) | 59 | 囗 | 94 | 木 | 129 | 衤 | 164 | 臣 | 199 | 谷 | 227 | 余类 |
| 25 | 乂 | 60 | 山 | 95 | 不 | 130 | 𡗗 | 165 | 戋 | 200 | 身 | | |
| 26 | 勹 | 61 | 屮 | 96 | 犬 | 131 | 玉 | 166 | 襾(覀) | 201 | 角 | | |
| 27 | 刀(⺈) | 62 | 彳 | 97 | 歹 | 132 | 示 | 167 | 束 | 八画 | | | |
| 28 | 力 | 63 | 彡 | 98 | 瓦 | 133 | 去 | 168 | 亚 | 202 | 青 | | |
| 29 | 儿 | 64 | 夕 | 99 | 牙 | 134 | 此 | 169 | 而 | 203 | 卓 | | |
| 30 | 几(⺇) | 65 | 夂 | 100 | 车 | 135 | 甘 | 170 | 页 | 204 | 雨 | | |
| 31 | マ | 66 | 丸 | 101 | 戈 | 136 | 石 | 171 | 至 | 205 | 非 | | |
| 32 | 卩 | 67 | 尸 | 102 | 止 | 137 | 龙 | 172 | 光 | 206 | 齿 | | |
| 33 | 阝(在左) | 68 | 饣 | 103 | 日 | 138 | 戊 | 173 | 虍 | 207 | 黾 | | |
| 34 | 阝(在右) | 69 | 犭 | 104 | 曰 | 139 | 业 | 174 | 虫 | 208 | 隹 | | |

# （二）检字表

字右边的号码指词典正文的页码

(46)

## 门部



(47)

## 辶部



(48)

## 工部



(49)

## 土（士）部



(50)

## 艹部

# 汉语拼音音节索引

# Index of Syllables of Hanyupinyin (the Phonetic Transcriptions of Chinese Characters)

## A (1—8 页)

ā 阿啊锕腌 á 啊 ǎ 啊 à 啊 a 啊
āi 哎哀埃挨唉锿 ái 呆挨骇捱皑癌 ǎi 欸矮嗳蔼霭 ài 艾砹唉爱隘碍嗳暧
ān 安桉氨谙庵鹌鮟鞍 ǎn 俺铵埯揞 àn 岸按案胺暗黯
āng 肮 áng 昂 àng 盎
āo 凹熬 áo 敖遨嗷熬獒螯聱翱鳌鏖 ǎo 拗袄媪 ào 坳拗傲奥骜澳懊鏊

## B (9—59 页)

bā 八巴扒叭芭吧疤粑捌笆 bá 拔菝跋魃 bǎ 把钯靶 bà 把坝爸耙罢鲅霸 ba 吧
bāi 掰 bái 白 bǎi 百伯佰柏捭摆 bài 败拜稗
bān 扳班般颁斑搬瘢瘢 bǎn 阪板版 bàn 办半扮伴拌绊瓣
bāng 邦帮浜梆 bǎng 绑榜膀 bàng 蚌谤傍棒蒡磅镑
bāo 包苞孢炮胞剥龅褒 báo 雹薄 bǎo 宝饱保鸨葆堡褓 bào 报刨抱豹鲍暴爆
bēi 杯卑背悲碑鹎 běi 北 bèi 贝狈备背钡悖被倍焙辈惫蓓褙鞴 bei 呗臂
bēn 奔贲锛 běn 本苯畚 bèn 奔笨
bēng 崩绷嘣 béng 甭 běng 绷 bèng 迸泵蚌绷镚蹦
bī 逼 bí 荸鼻 bǐ 匕比吡妣彼秕笔俾鄙 bì 币必闭毕庇毖哔陛贲毙铋秘敝婢愎弼筚跸痹裨萞睥辟滗碧箅蔽弊薜篦避壁臂髀璧襞
biān 边边砭编煸蝙鳊鞭 biǎn 贬窆扁匾褊 biàn 卞弁忭汴苄变便遍緶辨辩辫
biāo 标彪膘瘭镖飙镳 biǎo 表婊裱 biào 鳔
biē 憋瘪鳖 bié 别蹩 biě 瘪 biè 别
bīn 宾彬傧滨缤槟镔濒 bìn 摈膑殡髌鬓
bīng 并冰兵槟 bǐng 丙秉炳柄饼屏禀 bìng 并病摒
bō 波拨玻剥钵饽菠播 bó 伯驳泊帛勃钹铂舶脖渤博鹁搏魄箔膊镈薄礴 bǒ 跛簸 bò 柏薄檗擘簸 bo 卜
bū 逋 bú 醭 bǔ 卜卟补捕哺鹔 bù 不布步怖钚部埠瓿簿

## C (60—119 页)

cā 拆擦嚓 cǎ 礤
cāi 猜 cái 才材财裁 cǎi 采彩睬踩 cài 采菜蔡
cān 参餐 cán 残蚕惭 cǎn 惨穇 càn 灿孱粲璨
cāng 仓伧沧苍舱 cáng 藏
cāo 糙操 cáo 曹漕嘈槽螬 cǎo 草
cè 册厕侧测恻策筴
cēn 参 cén 岑涔
céng 层曾 cèng 蹭
chā 叉杈差插喳馇锸嚓 chá 叉茬茶查搽楂槎察碴檫 chǎ 叉衩蹅镲 chà 汊杈岔诧衩刹姹差
chāi 拆钗差 chái 侪柴豺 chǎi 䏧 chài 虿瘥
chān 觇搀 chán 单婵谗馋孱禅缠蝉廛潺蟾巉 chǎn 产谄铲阐蒇 chàn 忏颤韂
chāng 伥昌菖猖娼鲳 cháng 长场肠尝常偿徜裳嫦 chǎng 厂场昶敞氅 chàng 怅畅倡唱
chāo 抄吵钞绰焯超剿 cháo 晁巢朝潮嘲 chǎo 吵炒 chào 耖
chē 车砗 chě 尺扯 chè 彻坼掣澈撤
chēn 抻琛嗔瞋 chén 尘臣沉忱辰陈晨谌橙 chèn 衬称龀趁榇谶 chen 伧碜
chēng 柽称蛏铛撑瞠 chéng 丞成呈诚承城乘盛程惩塍酲澄橙 chěng 逞骋 chèng 秤
chī 吃哧蚩鸱眵笞痴嗤媸魑 chí 池弛驰迟持匙踟 chǐ 尺齿侈耻豉褫 chì 彳叱斥赤饬炽翅敕啻
chōng 冲充忡茺舂憧 chóng 虫重崇 chǒng 宠 chòng 冲铳
chōu 抽 chóu 仇俦惆绸畴愁稠酬筹踌 chǒu 丑瞅 chòu 臭
chū 出出初 chú 刍除鸰厨锄蜍雏橱踞蹰 chǔ 处杵础楮储褚楚 chù 亍处怵绌畜搐触憷黜矗
chuā 欻
chuāi 揣搋 chuǎi 揣 chuài 揣踹
chuān 川氚穿 chuán 传船遄椽 chuǎn 舛喘 chuàn 串钏
chuāng 创疮窗 chuáng 床幢 chuǎng 闯 chuàng 创怆
chuī 吹炊 chuí 垂陲捶槌锤箠
chūn 春椿蝽 chún 纯唇莼淳鹑醇 chǔn 蠢
chuō 戳 chuò 啜绰辍龊
cī 刺差呲疵 cí 词祠茨瓷辞慈磁雌鹚糍 cǐ 此 cì 次伺刺赐
cōng 从匆囱苁枞锹葱聪 cóng 从丛淙琮
còu 凑辏
cū 粗 cù 促猝酢蔟醋簇蹙蹴
cuān 氽撺镩蹿 cuán 攒 cuàn 窜篡爨
cuī 崔催摧 cuǐ 璀 cuì 脆淬悴萃啐毳瘁粹翠
cūn 村皴 cún 存 cǔn 忖 cùn 寸
cuō 搓磋撮蹉 cuó 痤矬 cuò 挫厝措锉错

## D (120—174 页)

dā 吖耷搭嗒答褡 dá 打达沓答瘩靼鞑 dǎ 打 dà 大 da 垯瘩
dāi 呆待 dǎi 歹逮傣 dài 大代岱迨甙玳带殆待贷怠袋逮戴黛
dān 丹单担眈耽殚箪 dǎn 胆疸掸 dàn 石旦但担诞淡啖蛋弹惮氮
dāng 当珰裆铛 dǎng 挡党谠 dàng 当宕荡挡档菪
dāo 刀叨氘 dǎo 导岛倒捣祷蹈 dào 到倒悼盗道稻纛
dé 得锝德 de 地的得
děi 得
dèn 扽
dēng 灯登噔蹬 děng 等戥 dèng 邓凳澄瞪镫蹬
dī 氐低堤提滴嘀镝 dí 狄的籴迪荻敌涤笛觌嘀嫡镝 dǐ 诋邸底抵砥骶 dì 地弟的帝递谛第棣蒂缔睇碲
diān 掂滇颠巅癫 diǎn 典点碘踮 diàn 电佃甸店玷垫钿淀惦奠殿靛癜
diāo 刁叼凋貂碉雕鲷 diào 吊钓调掉铞
diē 爹跌 dié 迭谍堞喋牒叠碟蝶鲽
dīng 丁仃叮玎疔盯钉耵酊 dǐng 顶酊鼎 dìng 订钉定啶腚碇锭
diū 丢铥
dōng 东冬咚氡 dǒng 董懂 dòng 动冻侗洞恫峒栋胨

dōu 都兜 dǒu 斗抖陡蚪 dòu 斗豆逗痘读窦
dū 都督嘟 dú 毒独读渎椟犊牍黩髑 dǔ 肚笃堵赌睹 dù 杜肚妒度渡镀蠹
duān 端 duǎn 短 duàn 段断缎煅椴锻簖
duī 堆 duì 队对兑怼敦碓
dūn 吨敦墩蹲 dǔn 盹趸 dùn 沌囤炖盾钝顿遁
duō 多咄哆掇 duó 夺度铎踱 duǒ 朵垛躲 duò 驮剁垛舵堕惰跺

## E (175—179 页)

ē 阿屙婀 é 讹俄哦峨娥鹅锇蛾额 ě 恶 è 厄扼呃苊轭垩恶饿鄂愕萼遏腭鹗锷颚噩鳄 ē 欸 é 欸 ě 欸 è 欸
éi 欸 ěi 欸 èi 欸
ēn 恩蒽 èn 摁
ér 儿而鸸 ěr 尔耳迩饵洱珥铒 èr 二贰

## F (180—214 页)

fā 发 fá 乏伐垡罚阀筏 fǎ 法砝 fà 发珐
fān 帆番幡藩翻 fán 凡矾钒烦蕃樊繁 fǎn 反返 fàn 犯泛饭范贩畈梵
fāng 方坊芳妨钫 fáng 防坊妨房肪鲂 fǎng 访仿纺舫 fàng 放
fēi 飞妃非菲啡绯扉蜚霏鲱 féi 肥淝腓 fěi 诽匪悱菲斐蜚翡榧 fèi 吠沸废狒肺费剕痱镄
fēn 分芬吩纷氛酚 fén 汾坟焚棼鼢 fěn 粉 fèn 分份奋忿粪愤
fēng 丰风枫疯砜封峰烽锋蜂酆 féng 冯逢缝 fěng 讽 fèng 凤奉俸缝
fó 佛
fǒu 缶否
fū 夫呋肤麸趺孵敷 fú 夫弗伏凫扶芙孚佛拂绋服茯氟俘浮袱菔符匐幅福辐蜉蝠蝠 fǔ 父甫抚府斧拊釜俯脯辅腑腐簠 fù 父讣付负妇附阜服驸赴复副富赋傅腹缚鲋赙蝮覆馥 fu 咐

## G (215—261 页)

gā 夹旮伽咖嘎 gá 轧钆 gà 尬
gāi 该赅 gǎi 改 gài 丐芥钙盖溉概
gān 干甘杆肝泔矸坩苷柑竿疳酐尴 gǎn 杆秆赶敢感橄擀 gàn 干绀赣
gāng 冈扛刚纲肛缸钢 gǎng 岗港 gàng 杠钢
gāo 高羔膏睾糕篙 gǎo 杲搞缟槁稿镐 gào 告郜诰锆膏
gē 戈仡圪疙咯哥胳袼鸽割搁歌 gé 革阁格胳葛蛤搁隔嗝膈镉骼 gě 个合舸葛 gè 个各虼铬硌
gěi 给
gēn 根跟 gén 哏 gěn 艮 gèn 亘茛
gēng 更庚耕羹 gěng 埂耿哽梗颈鲠 gèng 更
gōng 工弓公功红攻供肱宫恭蚣躬龚觥 gǒng 巩汞拱珙 gòng 共贡供
gōu 勾沟佝钩篝鞲 gǒu 苟狗枸 gòu 勾构购诟垢够媾彀觏
gū 估沽咕呱孤姑轱骨鸪菇蛄菰辜觚菁箍 gú 骨 gǔ 古汩诂谷股牯骨贾钴蛄蛊鹄鼓毂臌瞽 gù 固故顾梏雇痼锢
guā 瓜呱刮胍栝鸹 guǎ 剐寡 guà 卦挂褂
guāi 乖掴 guǎi 拐 guài 怪
guān 关观官冠倌棺鳏 guǎn 馆管 guàn 观贯冠惯掼盥灌鹳罐
guāng 光桄胱 guǎng 广犷 guàng 桄逛
guī 归圭龟规皈闺硅瑰鲑鬶 guǐ 宄轨庋诡匦癸鬼晷簋 guì 刽刿柜贵桂桧跪鳜鳜
gǔn 衮绲辊滚磙 gùn 棍
guō 过郭埚聒锅蝈 guó 国掴帼腘 guǒ 果椁裹 guò 过 guo 过

## H (262—306 页)

hā 哈铪 há 蛤 hǎ 哈 hà 哈
hāi 咳嗨 hái 还孩骸 hǎi 海胲 hài 亥骇害氦嗐
hān 犴顸蚶酣憨鼾 hán 汗含函涵焓琀寒韩 hǎn 罕喊锨 hàn 汉汗旱悍捍焊颔憾撼翰瀚
hāng 夯 háng 行吭杭绗航 hàng 沆巷
hāo 蒿薅嚆 háo 号蚝毫嗥貉豪壕嚎 hǎo 好郝 hào 号好耗浩皓
hē 诃呵喝嗬 hé 禾合纥何河和劾饸曷阂荷核涸盒颌阖貉翮 hè 吓和贺荷喝褐赫鹤壑
hēi 黑嘿
hén 痕 hěn 很狠 hèn 恨
hēng 亨哼脝 héng 恒珩桁鸻横衡蘅 hèng 横
hng 哼
hōng 轰哄訇烘薨 hóng 弘红宏泓洪虹缸鸿 hǒng 哄 hòng 讧哄
hōu 齁 hóu 侯喉猴瘊篌骺 hǒu 吼 hòu 后厚逅候鲎
hū 乎幠呼忽烀惚糊 hú 囫狐弧胡壶核斛湖葫猢煳鹕煳瑚鹕糊槲蝴醐 hǔ 虎浒唬琥 hù 户互沪护怙戽祜笏扈瓠糊
huā 化花哗 huá 划华哗铧滑猾 huà 化划华话画桦
huái 怀徊淮槐踝 huài 坏
huān 欢獾 huán 还环桓锾寰圜鹮鬟 huǎn 缓 huàn 幻宦浣涣换唤焕患痪豢鲩
huāng 肓荒慌 huang 慌 huáng 皇黄凰隍惶徨煌潢璜蝗篁磺蟥簧鳇 huǎng 恍晃谎幌 huàng 晃
huī 灰诙恢咴挥晖辉麾徽隳 huí 回洄茴蛔 huǐ 悔毁 huì 汇卉会讳诲荟绘烩贿彗晦秽惠喙溃慧蕙蟪
hūn 昏荤婚阍 hún 浑珲混馄魂 hùn 诨混
huō 耠劐嚄豁攉 huó 和活 huǒ 火伙钬夥 huò 或和货获祸惑霍豁藿蠖

## J (307—378 页)

jī 几讥击叽饥圾芨机玑乩肌矶鸡奇迹唧积屐姬勣基绩犄嵇期缉跻畸箕稽齑畿激羁 jí 及汲吉岌级极即亟佶急疾脊棘殛集楫戢辑蒺嫉瘠鹡藉籍 jǐ 几己纪虮济挤给脊戟麂 jì 计记纪伎技芰系忌际妓季剂济荠既觊继寄寂悸祭蓟霁暨鲚稷鲫髻冀鲚骥
jiā 加夹伽佳迦茄枷浃家家痂袈笳傢葭嘉镓 jiá 夹荚戛蛱颊 jiǎ 甲岬胛贾钾假斝瘕 jià 价驾架假嫁稼
jiān 尖奸间歼坚肩艰兼监笺渐菅犍缄煎缣鲣鳒 jiǎn 拣茧柬俭捡检剪减硷睑锏简碱翦 jiàn 见件间饯建剑荐贱涧舰监健谏渐溅践腱毽鉴键槛僭箭
jiāng 江将姜豇浆僵缰螀礓疆 jiǎng 讲奖桨蒋耩膙 jiàng 匠降绛将浆弶强酱犟糨
jiāo 艽交郊茭浇娇骄姣胶教蛟焦椒鲛蕉礁鹪 jiáo 矫嚼 jiǎo 角侥佼狡绞饺皎铰脚矫搅湫剿缴 jiào 叫觉校较轿教窖酵藠醮
jiē 节阶疖皆结接秸揭嗟街 jié 孑节讦劫杰诘洁拮结桔桀捷睫竭截碣羯 jiě 姐解 jiè 介芥戒届疥诫界借解 jie 价家
jīn 巾今斤金津矜筋禁襟 jǐn 仅尽卺紧堇锦谨馑槿 jìn 尽进近妗劲荩浸烬晋靳禁觐噤
jīng 泾京茎经荆旌惊猄菁晶腈粳睛精兢鲸鼱 jǐng 井阱刭肼颈景儆憬警 jìng 劲净径经胫痉竞竟敬靖境静镜
jiōng 坰扃 jiǒng 迥炯窘
jiū 纠究鸠赳阄揪啾鬏 jiǔ 九久玖灸韭酒 jiù 旧臼疚咎柩桕救厩就舅鹫
jū 车拘狙居驹疽掬据锔趄裾鞠 jú 局桔菊锔橘 jǔ 沮咀举枸矩蒟龃榉踽 jù 巨句讵拒苣具炬钜俱剧倨惧据距飓锯聚踞遽
juān 涓捐娟圈鹃镌 juǎn 卷 juàn 卷倦绢隽眷圈
juē 撅 jué 孓决诀抉角玦珏觉绝倔掘崛厥谲蕨獗橛噱爵蹶矍嚼

攫镢 juě 蹶 juè 倔
jūn 军均君龟钧菌皲 jùn 俊郡浚峻骏菌竣

## K（379—401 页）

kā 咖喀揢 kǎ 卡咔咯胩
kāi 开揩锎 kǎi 凯剀铠慨楷 kài 忾
kān 刊看勘龛堪戡 kǎn 坎侃砍莰槛 kàn 看瞰
kāng 康慷糠糠鱇 káng 扛 kàng 亢伉抗炕钪
kāo 尻 kǎo 考拷烤栲 kào 铐犒靠
kē 坷苛珂柯科疴砢钶棵颏窠稞颗榼磕瞌蝌髁 ké 壳咳揢 kě 可坷渴 kè 可克刻客恪课氪骒缂锞嗑溘
kēi 剋
kěn 肯垦恳啃
kēng 坑吭铿
kōng 空箜 kǒng 孔恐倥 kòng 空控
kōu 芤抠眍 kǒu 口 kòu 叩扣寇筘蔻
kū 刳枯哭窟骷 kǔ 苦 kù 库裤酷
kuā 夸 kuǎ 侉垮 kuà 挎胯跨
kuǎi 擓蒯 kuài 会快块侩脍筷鲙
kuān 宽髋 kuǎn 款
kuāng 匡诓哐框筐 kuáng 狂诳鵟 kuàng 邝况旷矿框眶
kuī 亏岿盔窥 kuí 奎隗逵馗揆葵喹暌魁睽蝰 kuǐ 傀 kuì 匮溃馈愦喟愧聩篑
kūn 坤昆醌鲲 kǔn 捆 kùn 困
kuò 扩括蛞阔廓

## L（402—451 页）

lā 拉垃啦邋 lá 旯拉喇 lǎ 拉喇 là 刺落腊辣蜡瘌蝲鬎镴 la 啦蓝
lái 来來莱徕梾铼 lài 赉睐赖癞籁
lán 兰岚拦栏婪阑蓝谰澜褴篮斓镧 lǎn 览揽缆榄罱懒 làn 烂滥
lāng 啷 láng 郎狼廊琅榔锒鎯螂 lǎng 朗 làng 郎浪莨
lāo 捞 láo 牢劳唠痨铹醪 lǎo 老佬姥栳铑 lào 涝烙落酪
lè 乐勒鳓 le 了饹
lēi 勒擂 léi 累雷擂镭羸罍 lěi 垒累磊蕾儡 lèi 肋泪类累酹擂
léng 棱楞 lěng 冷 lèng 愣睖
lī 哩 lí 厘离狸骊梨犁喱鹂蜊漓璃犛黎鲡罹篱藜黧蠡 lǐ 礼李里里俚娌逦理锂鲤醴鳢 lì 力历立厉吏沥丽励利呖戾例隶枥疠疬栎荔俐郦俪莉莅砺鬲栗猁砾粒笠唳蛎雳痢傈 li 哩
liǎ 俩
lián 连奁帘怜涟莲联裢廉鲢臁镰蠊 liǎn 敛脸 liàn 练炼恋殓链楝
liáng 良凉莨梁椋量粱粮 liǎng 两俩魉 liàng 亮凉谅辆晾量踉
liāo 撩 liáo 辽疗聊寥僚寮撩嘹獠缭燎鹩 liǎo 了钌蓼潦燎 liào 了尥钌料撂廖镣
liē 咧 liě 咧 liè 列劣冽洌烈趔捩猎裂趔躐鬣
lín 邻林临淋啉琳粼遴嶙霖辚磷鳞麟 lǐn 凛廪檩 lìn 吝赁淋蔺膦躏
līng 拎 líng 〇伶灵苓囹玲瓴凌铃鸰陵羚聆菱棂蛉翎绫零龄鲮櫺 lǐng 令岭领 lìng 另令呤
liū 溜熘 liú 刘浏流留琉硫馏榴瘤镏鹠鎏 liǔ 柳绺 liù 六陆溜碌遛馏鹨
lo 咯
lōng 隆 lóng 龙茏咙珑昽栊胧眬砻聋笼隆癃窿 lǒng 陇垄拢笼 lòng 弄
lōu 搂 lóu 娄偻喽楼蝼耧髅 lǒu 搂篓 lòu 陋漏瘘镂露 lou 喽
lū 噜 lú 卢庐芦炉胪栌轳鸬铲颅舻鲈 lǔ 芦卤虏掳鲁橹镥 lù 陆录赂鹿绿禄碌路漉辘戮璐鹭麓露 lu 氇 lǘ 驴闾榈 lǚ 吕侣旅捋铝偻屡缕褛膂履 lǜ 律虑率绿氯葎滤
luán 峦孪栾挛鸾脔銮 luǎn 卵 luàn 乱
lüè 掠略
lūn 抡 lún 仑伦论沦囵纶轮 lùn 论
luō 罗捋 luó 罗猡萝椤逻椤锣箩骡螺 luǒ 裸瘰 luò 荦洛咯络骆珞落摞

## M（452—485 页）

ḿ 呣 m̀ 呣
mā 妈抹麻摩嬷 má 吗麻痲蟆 mǎ 马吗犸玛码蚂 mà 骂蚂 ma 吗嘛
mái 埋霾 mǎi 买荬 mài 迈麦卖脉
mān 颟 mán 埋蛮谩蔓馒瞒鳗 mǎn 满螨 màn 曼谩漫蔓慢幔嫚镘
máng 忙芒杧盲氓茫硭 mǎng 莽蟒
māo 猫 máo 毛矛茅牦猫锚髦蝥蟊 mǎo 卯铆 mào 茂冒贸耄袤帽瑁貌懋
me 么
méi 没玫枚眉莓梅猸媒煤楣酶鹛镅霉糜 měi 每美镁 mèi 妹袂昧寐谜媚魅
mēn 闷 mén 门扪钔 mèn 闷焖懑 men 们
mēng 蒙 méng 氓虻萌蒙盟濛獴檬曚朦矇 měng 猛蒙锰蜢艋蠓懵 mèng 孟梦
mī 咪眯 mí 弥迷谜猕醚糜縻靡蘼醾 mǐ 米弭脒眯靡 mì 泌宓觅秘密幂谧蜜嘧
mián 眠绵棉 miǎn 免勉娩冕湎缅腼鮸 miàn 面
miāo 喵 miáo 苗描瞄鹋 miǎo 杪秒渺淼缈邈藐 miào 妙庙缪
miē 乜咩 miè 灭蔑篾
mín 民 mǐn 皿闵泯抿闽悯敏鳖
míng 名明鸣茗冥铭溟盟暝瞑螟 mǐng 酩 mìng 命
miù 谬缪
mō 摸 mó 谟馍麽摹模膜摩磨蘑魔 mǒ 抹 mò 万末没沫茉抹殁陌脉莫秣漠寞蓦墨默磨貘
mōu 哞 móu 牟谋眸蛑缪 mǒu 某
mú 模 mǔ 母亩牡拇姆 mù 木目仫沐苜牧钼募墓幕睦慕暮穆

## N（486—503 页）

nā 那 ná 拿镎 nǎ 哪 nà 那呐纳肭衲钠捺 na 哪
nǎi 乃艿奶氖迺 nài 奈柰耐萘鼐
nān 囡 nán 男南难喃楠 nǎn 赧腩蝻 nàn 难
nāng 囔 náng 囊馕 nǎng 曩攮馕 nàng 齉
nāo 孬 náo 呶挠硇铙蛲猱 nǎo 恼脑瑙 nào 闹淖
nè 讷那 ne 呢
něi 哪馁 nèi 内那
nèn 恁嫩
néng 能
ńg 嗯 ňg 嗯 ǹg 嗯
nī 妮 ní 尼泥呢怩倪铌霓鲵 nǐ 拟你旎 nì 泥逆昵匿溺睨腻
niān 拈蔫 nián 年粘鲇黏 niǎn 捻辇碾撵 niàn 廿念埝
niáng 娘酿 niàng 酿
niǎo 鸟茑袅 niào 尿脲
niē 捏 nié 苶 niè 聂涅臬啮嗫镊镍颞蹑孽蘖
nín 您
níng 宁拧咛苎狞柠聍凝 nǐng 拧 nìng 宁佞泞拧
niū 妞 niú 牛 niǔ 忸扭纽狃钮 niù 拗
nóng 农侬浓哝脓秾 nòng 弄
nòu 耨
nú 奴孥驽 nǔ 努弩胬 nù 怒 nǚ 女钕 nǜ 衄
nuǎn 暖
nüè 疟虐

nuó 挪娜傩 nuò 诺喏搦锘懦糯

## O（504 页）

ō 喔噢 ó 哦 ǒ 嚄 ò 哦
ōu 区讴欧瓯殴鸥 ǒu 呕偶耦藕 òu 沤怄

## P（505—529 页）

pā 趴啪葩 pá 扒杷爬耙琶筢筢 pà 怕帕
pāi 拍 pái 排徘牌 pǎi 迫排 pài 派哌湃
pān 潘攀 pán 爿胖盘槃磐蹒蟠 pàn 判叛盼袢畔襻
pāng 乓滂膀 páng 彷庞旁膀磅螃鳑 pǎng 耪髈 pàng 胖
pāo 抛泡脬 páo 刨庖咆狍炮袍 pǎo 跑 pào 泡炮疱
pēi 呸胚 péi 陪培赔锫裴 pèi 沛佩帔配旆辔霈
pēn 喷 pén 盆 pèn 喷
pēng 怦抨砰烹澎 péng 朋棚彭蓬硼鹏澎篷膨蟛 pěng 捧 pèng 碰
pī 丕批纰坯披砒劈噼霹 pí 皮枇吡铍疲蚍啤琵脾裨鲏蜱罴貔鼙 pǐ 匹圮仳否痞劈擗癖 pì 屁辟媲僻譬䴙
piān 片扁偏犏翩篇 pián 便骈胼蹁 piǎn 谝 piàn 片骗
piāo 剽漂缥飘薸螵 piáo 朴嫖瓢 piǎo 殍漂瞟 piào 票漂骠嘌
piē 氕撇瞥 piě 苤撇
pīn 拼姘 pín 贫频嫔蘋颦 pǐn 品 pìn 牝聘
pīng 乒娉 píng 平评坪苹凭屏瓶萍鲆
pō 朴钋泊坡泼颇 pó 婆鄱皤 pǒ 叵钷笸 pò 朴迫珀破粕魄 po 桲
pōu 剖 póu 抔 pǒu 掊
pū 仆扑铺噗 pú 仆匍菩脯葡蒲璞镤 pǔ 朴浦埔圃普溥谱氆镨蹼 pù 铺瀑曝

## Q（530—567 页）

qī 七沏妻柒凄栖桤萋戚期欺漆嘁槭蹊 qí 齐祁芪祈其奇歧荠俟耆脐淇萁畦崎骑琪琦棋蛴旗蜞鳍鲯麒 qǐ 乞岂企启杞起起绮稽 qì 气讫迄汽弃泣亟契砌跂葺碛器憩
qiā 掐袷葜 qiǎ 卡 qià 洽恰髂
qiān 千仟阡扦迁钎牵悭铅谦签愆 qián 前钤荨钳虔钱掮乾潜黔 qiǎn 浅遣谴缱 qiàn 欠纤芡茜倩堑嵌歉
qiāng 抢呛羌枪戗戕腔蜣锵镪 qiáng 强墙蔷樯 qiǎng 抢羟强襁 qiàng 呛炝戗跄
qiāo 悄硗跷跻敲劁锹缲橇 qiáo 乔侨荞桥翘谯憔樵瞧 qiǎo 巧悄雀愀 qiào 壳俏诮窍峭翘撬鞘
qiē 切 qié 茄 qiě 且 qiè 切妾怯窃挈惬趄箧锲
qīn 亲侵钦衾 qín 芹秦琴覃禽勤嗪擒噙檎 qǐn 锓寝 qìn 沁
qīng 青轻氢倾卿清蜻鲭 qíng 情晴氰擎 qǐng 苘顷请 qìng 庆亲磬罄
qióng 穷穹茕琼
qiū 丘邱秋蚯湫楸鳅 qiú 仇囚犰求泅酋球遒裘
qū 区曲岖驱屈祛蛆蛐躯趋蛐麴黢 qú 劬鸲渠蕖磲瞿鼩癯衢蠼 qǔ 曲苣取娶龋 qù 去去阒趣觑
quān 悛圈 quán 权全诠泉拳痊筌蜷醛鬈颧 quǎn 犬绻 quàn 劝券
quē 炔缺阙 qué 瘸 què 却雀阕确阙鹊榷
qūn 逡 qún 裙群麇

## R（568—583 页）

rán 然髯燃 rǎn 冉苒染
rāng 嚷 ráng 禳瓤 rǎng 壤攘嚷 ràng 让
ráo 荛饶娆桡 rǎo 扰绕 rào 绕
rě 惹 rè 热
rén 人壬仁任 rěn 忍荏稔 rèn 刃认仞任妊纫韧轫饪葚
rēng 扔 réng 仍
rì 日
róng 戎荣茸绒容嵘溶蓉熔榕蝾融 rǒng 冗
róu 柔揉糅蹂鞣 ròu 肉
rú 如茹铷儒濡薷嚅孺蠕颥 rǔ 汝乳辱 rù 入溽缛蓐褥
ruǎn 阮朊软
ruǐ 蕊 ruì 芮枘蚋锐瑞睿
rùn 闰润
ruò 若偌弱箬

## S（584—659 页）

sā 仨挲撒 sǎ 洒撒 sà 卅飒脎萨
sāi 塞腮噻鳃 sài 塞赛
sān 三叁 sǎn 伞散 sàn 散
sāng 丧桑 sǎng 搡嗓颡 sàng 丧
sāo 搔骚缫臊 sǎo 扫嫂 sào 扫臊
sè 色涩啬铯塞瑟穑
sēn 森
sēng 僧
shā 杀沙纱杉刹砂痧裟煞鲨 shǎ 傻 shà 啥厦歃煞霎
shāi 筛 shǎi 色 shài 晒
shān 山芟杉删衫苫姗钐珊栅舢扇跚煽潸膻 shǎn 闪陕睒 shàn 讪疝单苫扇善禅骟缮擅膳嬗赡蟮鳝
shāng 伤殇商觞墒熵 shǎng 上垧晌赏 shàng 上上尚绱 shang 裳
shāo 烧捎梢稍筲艄鞘 sháo 勺芍杓韶 shǎo 少 shào 少邵劭绍捎哨潲
shē 奢猞赊畲 shé 舌折佘蛇 shě 舍 shè 设社舍涉射赦摄慑麝
shéi 谁
shēn 申伸身呻绅参砷莘娠深鲹 shén 什甚神钟 shěn 沈审哂谂婶 shèn 肾甚胂渗葚慎蜃瘆
shēng 升生声牲笙甥 shéng 绳 shěng 省 shèng 圣胜乘盛剩
shī 尸失师虱诗狮鸸施湿蓍嘘鲺鲺 shí 十什石识时实拾食蚀鲥 shǐ 史矢豕使始驶屎 shì 士氏市示世仕式似试势事侍视饰室恃拭柿是适逝莳铈弑释嗜誓噬螫 shi 匙
shōu 收 shǒu 手守首 shòu 寿受狩兽授售绶瘦
shū 书殳抒枢叔殊倏淑菽梳舒疏输蔬 shú 秫孰赎塾熟 shǔ 黍属暑署数蜀鼠薯曙 shù 术戍束述树竖恕庶数漱墅澍
shuā 刷 shuǎ 耍 shuà 刷
shuāi 衰摔 shuǎi 甩 shuài 帅率蟀
shuān 闩拴栓 shuàn 涮
shuāng 双霜孀鹴 shuǎng 爽
shuí 谁 shuǐ 水 shuì 说税睡
shǔn 吮 shùn 顺舜瞬
shuō 说 shuò 烁铄朔硕数蒴
sī 司丝私咝思鸶蛳斯缌澌厮澌撕嘶 sǐ 死 sì 巳四寺似祀伺饲驷食俟笥耜嗣肆 si 厕
sōng 忪松凇嵩 sǒng 怂悚耸 sòng 讼宋送诵颂
sōu 溲搜嗖馊飕艘螋 sǒu 叟嗾薮擞 sòu 嗽
sū 苏酥窣稣 sú 俗 sù 夙诉肃素速宿粟溯塑嗉愫鹔僳簌
suān 酸 suàn 蒜算
suī 尿虽荽睢 suí 绥隋随遂 suǐ 髓 suì 岁祟遂碎隧燧邃穗
sūn 孙狲 sǔn 笋损隼榫
suō 娑莎唆挲桫梭睃羧蓑缩 suǒ 所索唢琐锁 suo 嗦

## T（660—703 页）

tā 它他她铊趿褟塌遢踏 tǎ 溚塔獭鳎 tà 拓沓闼挞嗒榻踏蹋
tāi 苔胎 tái 台邰抬苔骀炱鲐薹 tài 太汰态肽钛泰酞
tān 坍贪滩摊瘫 tán 坛昙谈弹覃痰谭潭檀 tǎn 忐坦袒钽毯 tàn 叹炭探碳
tāng 汤铴嘡羰蹚 táng 唐堂棠溏塘搪樘膛糖镗螳 tǎng 帑倘淌耥躺 tàng 烫趟

tāo 叨涛绦掏滔韬饕　táo 逃桃陶淘萄啕　tǎo 讨　tào 套
tè 忒忑特铽
tēi 忒
tēng 腾熥鼟　téng 疼誊腾滕藤縢
tī 体剔梯锑踢䴘　tí 绨提啼缇鹈题醍蹄鳀　tǐ 体　tì 屉剃涕悌绨惕替嚏
tiān 天添黇　tián 田恬钿甜填　tiǎn 忝殄腆觍舔
tiāo 佻挑祧　tiáo 条苕迢调笤髫　tiǎo 挑窕　tiào 眺粜跳
tiē 帖贴萜　tiě 帖铁　tiè 帖餮
tīng 厅汀听烃桯　tíng 廷亭庭莛停蜓婷霆　tǐng 挺铤艇
tōng 通　tóng 同佟彤茼桐铜童酮瞳　tǒng 统捅桶筒　tòng 同恸通痛
tōu 偷　tóu 头头投　tòu 透
tū 凸秃突葖　tú 图涂荼途徒屠酴　tǔ 土吐钍　tù 吐兔堍菟
tuān 湍　tuán 团抟
tuī 忒推　tuí 颓　tuǐ 腿　tuì 退煺蜕褪
tūn 吞暾　tún 屯囤饨豚鲀臀　tǔn 氽　tùn 褪
tuō 托拖脱　tuó 驮陀驼沱坨柁砣鸵跎酡橐鼧鼍　tuǒ 妥庹椭 tuò 拓柝唾箨魄箨

## W（704—734 页）

wā 洼挖哇蛙　wá 娃　wǎ 瓦佤　wà 瓦袜腽　wa 哇
wāi 歪㖞　wǎi 崴　wài 外
wān 弯剜湾蜿豌　wán 丸纨完玩顽烷　wǎn 宛莞挽惋菀晚脘婉绾皖碗　wàn 万萬腕蔓
wāng 汪　wáng 亡王芒忘　wǎng 网枉罔往惘辋魍　wàng 妄忘旺往望
wēi 危委威逶萎偎隈煨微薇巍　wéi 为韦圩违围闱桅惟唯维帷嵬　wěi 伪伟苇纬尾炜玮委娓诿萎唯猥痿韪鲔　wèi 卫为未位味畏胃谓尉遗喂渭猬蔚慰魏鳚
wēn 温榅瘟鳁　wén 文纹闻蚊　wěn 刎抆吻紊稳　wèn 问汶璺
wēng 翁嗡鹟　wěng 蓊　wèng 瓮蕹齆
wō 挝涡倭莴窝喔蜗踒　wǒ 我　wò 沃肟卧渥握硪幄斡龌
wū 乌污邬巫呜诬屋钨　wú 无毋吾芜吴梧鹀蜈鼯　wǔ 五午伍妩忤武侮捂鹉舞　wù 兀乌勿戊务芴坞物误悟恶晤焐痦骛雾寤鹜

## X（735—788 页）

xī 夕兮汐西吸希穸昔析矽郗唏奚牺息浠惜烯硒晞欷悉晰翕稀腊犀溪锡裼皙傒熄豨熙蜥嘻膝嬉螅熹螅歙蹊蟋豀曦鼷　xí 习席袭媳檄　xǐ 洗玺徙铣喜葸屣禧鳍　xì 戏系细阋隙
xiā 呷虾瞎　xiá 匣狎侠峡狭遐瑕暇辖霞黠　xià 下下吓夏厦罅
xiān 仙先纤氙籼莶掀锨跹酰鲜　xián 闲贤弦涎咸娴舷衔鹇痫嫌　xiǎn 冼险显铣跣鲜藓　xiàn 见苋县现限线宪陷馅羡献腺霰
xiāng 乡相香厢湘葙箱襄镶　xiáng 详降祥翔　xiǎng 享响饷鲞想鲞　xiàng 向巷项相象像橡
xiāo 肖枭枵削哓骁哮消宵逍鸮萧硝销蛸潇箫霄魈嚣　xiáo 淆　xiǎo 小晓筱　xiào 孝肖效校笑啸
xiē 些揳楔歇蝎　xié 协邪胁挟谐偕斜携鞋撷　xiě 写血　xiè 写泻泄卸屑械谢亵解榭懈邂蟹瀣
xīn 心芯辛欣锌新薪馨　xín 寻　xìn 芯信衅
xīng 兴星惺猩腥　xíng 刑邢行形型　xǐng 省醒擤　xìng 兴杏性幸姓悻
xiōng 凶兄芎匈汹胸　xióng 雄熊
xiū 休咻修脩羞鸺馐貅　xiǔ 朽宿　xiù 秀岫袖绣臭宿锈溴嗅
xū 圩戌吁胥须虚需嘘墟歔　xú 徐　xǔ 许诩栩醑　xù 旭序恤叙畜酗绪续絮婿蓄煦　xu 蓿
xuān 轩宣萱喧暄煊　xuán 玄旋悬　xuǎn 选烜癣　xuàn 泫券炫绚眩眩旋渲楦
xuē 削靴薛　xué 穴学噱　xuě 雪鳕　xuè 血谑
xūn 勋埙熏薰曛醺　xún 旬驯寻巡询洵峋浔荀循鲟　xùn 讯训汛迅逊徇殉熏蕈

## Y（789—860 页）

yā 丫压呀押哑鸦桠鸭　yá 牙伢芽蚜涯崖睚衙　yǎ 哑雅　yà 轧亚压讶迓砑垭娅氩揠　ya 呀
yān 咽恹烟殷胭淹阉焉湮腌鄢嫣燕　yán 延言严芫妍沿炎岩研盐阎筵蜒颜檐　yǎn 奄俨衍掩眼偃演魇鼹　yàn 厌沿砚咽彦宴晏艳唁验谚焰雁堰酽餍燕赝
yāng 央泱殃秧鸯　yáng 羊阳扬杨佯疡洋徉烊　yǎng 仰养氧痒　yàng 怏恙样漾
yāo 幺夭吆约妖要腰邀　yáo 尧肴姚珧窑谣遥摇徭瑶鳐　yǎo 杳咬窈舀　yào 疟药要钥鹞曜耀
yē 耶倻掖椰噎　yé 爷耶揶　yě 也冶野　yè 业叶页曳夜咽烨晔液掖谒腋靥
yī 一衣伊医依咿铱猗揖壹漪噫繄黟　yí 匜仪圯夷沂诒宜怡迤饴迻贻荑咦姨胰痍移蛇遗颐疑嶷彝　yǐ 乙已以钇矣尾苡迤蚁舐倚椅旖　yì 弋义亿忆艺刈艾议亦屹异译抑呓邑佚役诣易驿绎弈奕弈疫轶益谊挹悒逸翌翊勚溢意裔肄缢蜴瘗镒毅薏劓臆翼翳癔镱懿
yīn 因阴音茵洇姻荫氤殷铟堙喑　yín 吟垠狺淫寅银龈夤　yǐn 尹引饮蚓隐瘾　yìn 印饮茚荫胤鲫窨
yīng 应英莺婴罂嘤缨樱鹦膺鹰　yíng 迎茔盈荧莹营萤萦滢楹潆蝇赢瀛　yǐng 郢颖影瘿　yìng 应映硬媵
yō 育哟唷　yo 哟
yōng 佣拥痈邕庸雍慵墉壅臃鳙　yóng 喁　yǒng 永甬泳咏俑勇涌恿蛹踊鲬　yòng 用佣
yōu 优忧攸呦幽悠　yóu 尤由邮犹油疣柚莜铀蚰游鱿蝣蝤蝣　yǒu 友有卣酉莠铕牖黝　yòu 又右幼有佑侑宥柚囿诱蚴釉鼬
yū 迂淤瘀　yú 与于予余欤盂臾鱼俞竽谀娱狳隅喁萸渔渝腴愉逾揄愚瑜榆觎虞舆窬蝓　yǔ 与予宇屿羽伛雨语禹圄圉庾瘐龉窳　yù 与玉驭芋吁妪育郁语昱狱浴峪预欲域谕尉阈寓裕遇喻御鹆誉蓣煜愈蜮豫鹬鬻
yuān 鸢冤鸳渊　yuán 元芫园员垣爰原袁圆湲援鼋源猿缘辕塬螈橼　yuǎn 远　yuàn 苑怨院垸愿
yuē 曰约　yuè 月乐刖岳钥悦阅钺跃越粤
yūn 晕氲　yún 云匀芸纭昀耘　yǔn 允陨殒　yùn 孕运郓恽晕酝愠韵熨蕴

## Z（861—947 页）

zā 扎匝砸拶臜　zá 杂咂　zǎ 咋
zāi 灾甾哉栽　zǎi 仔宰载崽　zài 再在载
zān 糌簪　zán 咱　zǎn 拶噆攒趱　zàn 暂錾赞　zan 咱
zāng 赃脏臧　zǎng 驵　zàng 脏葬藏
zāo 遭糟　záo 凿　zǎo 早枣蚤澡藻　zào 灶皂造慥簉噪燥躁
zé 则责泽择啧帻舴箦赜　zè 仄
zéi 贼鲗
zěn 怎　zèn 谮
zēng 曾憎增缯罾　zèng 综锃甑赠
zhā 扎咋查喳渣喳揸猹楂　zhá 扎札轧闸炸铡　zhǎ 拃眨砟鲊　zhà 乍诈咋咤炸栅痄蚱榨
zhāi 斋摘　zhái 宅择翟　zhǎi 窄　zhài 债砦寨
zhān 占沾毡粘詹谵瞻　zhǎn 斩展盏崭搌辗黵　zhàn 占战栈站绽湛颤蘸
zhāng 张章彰嫜獐璋樟蟑　zhǎng 长涨掌礃　zhàng 丈仗杖帐胀涨障幛嶂瘴
zhāo 钊招昭着啁朝　zháo 着　zhǎo 爪找沼　zhào 召兆诏赵笊棹照罩肇
zhē 折蜇遮　zhé 折哲辄蛰詟蜇谪磔辙　zhě 者锗赭褶　zhè 这柘浙蔗鹧　zhe 着
zhèi 这
zhēn 贞针侦珍胗祯桢真砧斟甄榛箴臻鱵　zhěn 诊枕轸疹眕缜

zhèn 阵鸩振朕赈震镇
zhēng 丁正争怔征挣峥狰症钲睁铮筝蒸 zhěng 拯整 zhèng 正证诤郑政挣帧阐症
zhī 之支汁只卮芝吱枝知肢织指祇胝栀脂搘蜘 zhí 执直侄指值职植殖跖摭踯蹠 zhǐ 止只旨址芷纸祉指枳咫趾黹酯徵 zhì 至忮识志豸治帜炙帙郅质制栉峙桎轾致秩摰贽掷窒鸷痔滞痣蛭智彘锧置雉稚觯踬
zhōng 中忠终盅钟衷螽 zhǒng 肿种冢踵 zhòng 中众仲种重
zhōu 州舟诌周洲啁粥 zhóu 妯轴碡 zhǒu 肘帚 zhòu 纣宙绉咒胄昼轴皱骤籀
zhū 朱诛侏茱珠株诸猪铢蛛潴 zhú 术竹竺烛逐筑舳蠋躅 zhǔ 主拄渚属煮嘱瞩 zhù 伫苎助住注杼贮驻炷祝柱疰著蛀筑铸翥箸
zhuā 抓 zhuǎ 爪
zhuāi 拽 zhuǎi 跩 zhuài 拽
zhuān 专砖 zhuǎn 转 zhuàn 传转啭赚馔撰篆
zhuāng 妆庄桩装 zhuǎng 奘 zhuàng 壮状撞幢戆
zhuī 追椎锥 zhuì 坠缀惴缒赘
zhūn 肫窀谆 zhǔn 准
zhuō 拙卓捉桌 zhuó 灼茁浊斫酌诼着啄琢斲濯擢镯
zī 仔吱孜咨姿兹资赀缁滋孳辎趑锱龇鲻髭 zǐ 子子仔姊籽梓紫滓訾 zì 字自恣渍眦
zōng 宗综棕踪鬃 zǒng 总偬 zòng 纵粽
zōu 邹陬 zǒu 走 zòu 奏揍
zū 租 zú 足卒族镞 zǔ 阻诅组祖俎
zuān 钻躜 zuǎn 缵纂 zuàn 钻赚攥
zuǐ 嘴 zuì 最罪醉
zūn 尊遵樽鳟 zǔn 撙
zuō 作嘬 zuó 作昨琢 zuǒ 左佐撮 zuò 坐作柞胙座唑做酢凿

# A

## ā

**阿** ā 〈方〉〔用于小名、姓、排行或亲属名称前〕：～宝 A Bao/ ～唐 A Tang; Tang/ ～大 the eldest/ ～哥 elder brother/ ～爹 dad/ ～婆 granny
另见 ē

【阿昌族】 Āchāngzú the Achang nationality, living in Yunnan

【阿的平】 ādìpíng 〈药〉 atabrine

【阿斗】 Ā Dǒu ① the infant name of Liu Shan（刘禅，207–271）, last emperor of Shu Han（蜀汉，221–263）, known for his want of ability and weakness of character ② a weak-minded person; fool: 扶不起的～ a disappointing person; a hopeless case/ 不要把群众看作～。Don't treat the masses as if they were fools.

【阿尔巴尼亚】 Ā'ěrbāníyà Albania ◇ ～人 Albanian/ ～语 Albanian (language)

【阿尔卑斯山】 Ā'ěrbēisīshān the Alps

【阿尔法】 ā'ěrfǎ alpha ◇ ～粒子〈物〉 alpha particle/ ～射线〈物〉 alpha ray

【阿尔及利亚】 Ā'ěrjílìyà Algeria ◇ ～人 Algerian

【阿飞】 āfēi a youth given to rowdy behaviour and queer dress; Teddy boy

【阿伏伽德罗定律】 Āfújiādéluó dìnglǜ 〈化〉 Avogadro's law

【阿富汗】 Āfùhàn Afghanistan ◇ ～人 Afghan

【阿根廷】 Āgēntíng Argentina ◇ ～人 Argentine

【阿訇】 āhōng ahung; imam

【阿基米德原理】 Ājīmǐdé yuánlǐ 〈物〉 Archimedes' principle

【阿Q】 Ā Kiū 或 Ā Qiū A Q, the main character in Lu Xun's *The True Story of A Q* (《阿Q正传》), a backward peasant who interprets his defeats as moral victories

【阿拉伯】 Ālābó Arabian; Arabic; Arab
◇ ～半岛 the Arabian Peninsula; Arabia/ ～国家 Arab countries (或 states)/ ～国家联盟 the League of Arab States; the Arab League/ ～胶 gum arabic; gum acacia/ ～人 Arab/ ～数字 Arabic numerals/ ～语 Arabic

【阿曼】 Āmàn Oman ◇ ～人 Omani

【阿芒拿】 āmángná 〈化〉 ammonal

【阿门】 āmén 〈宗〉 amen

【阿米巴】 āmǐbā 〈动〉 amoeba ◇ ～痢疾 amoebic dysentery

【阿米妥】 āmǐtuǒ 〈药〉 amytal

【阿摩尼亚】 āmóníyà 〈化〉 ammonia

【阿姆哈拉语】 Āmǔhālāyǔ Amharic

【阿尼林】 ānílín 〈化〉 aniline ◇ ～油 aniline oil

【阿片】 āpiàn 〈药〉 opium ◇ ～制剂 opiate

【阿朴吗啡】 āpǔmǎfēi 〈药〉 apomorphine

【阿是穴】 āshìxué 〈中医〉 *Ashi* Point, any nerve point on the affected part of the body other than those specified for acupuncture and moxibustion

【阿司匹林】 āsīpǐlín 〈药〉 aspirin

【阿嚏】 ātì 〈象〉 atishoo

【阿托品】 ātuōpǐn 〈药〉 atropine

【阿伊马拉语】 Āyīmǎlāyǔ Aymara

【阿姨】 āyí ①〈方〉 one's mother's sister; auntie ② a child's form of address for any woman of its mother's generation; auntie ③ nurse (in a family)

【阿扎尼亚】 Āzāníyà Azania ◇ ～人 Azanian

**啊** ā 〈叹〉〔表示惊异或赞叹〕：～！庄稼长得真好哇！ Oh, what a wonderful crop!/ ～！黄河，你是中华民族的摇篮。 O! Huanghe, cradle of the Chinese nation.

**锕** ā 〈化〉 actinium (Ac)

【锕系元素】 ā xì yuánsù 〈化〉 actinides

**腌** ā
另见 yān

【腌臜】 āza 〈方〉 filthy; dirty

## á

**啊** á 〈叹〉〔表示追问或要求再说一遍〕：～？你说什么？ Eh? 或 Pardon?/ ～，你明儿倒是去不去呀？ Well, are you going tomorrow or not?

## ǎ

**啊** ǎ 〈叹〉〔表示惊疑〕：～！这条铁路只用两年就修成啦？ What! This railway took only two years to build?

## à

**啊** à 〈叹〉 ①〔表示应诺，音较短〕：～，我就来。All right, I'm coming. ②〔表示明白过来，音较长〕：～，原来是你！ Ah, so it's you.

## a

**啊** a 〈助〉 ①〔用于句末，表示赞叹、肯定、嘱咐等语气〕：多好的天儿～！ What a fine day!/ 这次参观收获不小～！ What a lot of things we've learned during this visit!/ 你这话说得是～。What you say is quite true./ 你可要小心～！ Do be careful! ②〔用于句末，表示疑问的语气〕：这消息是真的～？ Is this really true? ③〔用于句中，稍作停顿，让人注意下面的话〕：你～，老这样下去可不行！ Look! You can't go on like this. ④〔用于列举的事项之后〕：茄子～，黄瓜～，洋白菜～，西红柿～，各种蔬菜摆满了货架。The shelves were filled with all sorts of vegetables — eggplants, cucumbers, cabbages, tomatoes.

## āi

**哎** āi 〈叹〉〔表示惊讶、提醒或不满意〕：～！是老刘啊！ Why, it's Lao Liu!/ ～，大伙儿来喝口水吧！ Hey, come and have a drink of water, everyone!/ ～，别把凳子碰倒了！ Look out! Don't knock the stool over./ ～，你怎么不早跟我说呢？ But why didn't you tell me sooner?

【哎呀】 āiyā 〈叹〉〔表示惊叹〕：～！我把钥匙弄断了。Damn, I've broken the key!/ ～，这水真甜哪！ Ah, this water is really sweet!/ ～！好不容易见面哪！ So we meet again./ ～，好大的雨呀！ My God! It's raining like hell! 或 It's pouring!

【哎哟】 āiyō 〈叹〉〔表示惊讶、痛苦等〕：～，壶漏啦！ Hey, the kettle leaks!/ ～，真烫。Ouch! (或 Ow!) It's hot.

**哀** āi ① grief; sorrow: 喜怒～乐 joy, anger, grief and happiness — the gamut of human feeling/ ～哭 wail ② mourning: 志～ express one's mourning for the deceased ③ pity: 乞～告怜 piteously beg for help
【哀兵必胜】 āibīng bì shèng an army burning with righteous indignation is bound to win
【哀愁】 āichóu sad; sorrowful
【哀辞】 āicí lament
【哀悼】 āidào grieve (或 mourn) over sb.'s death; lament sb.'s death: 向死者家属表示深切的～ express one's heartfelt condolences to the family of the deceased
【哀告】 āigào beg piteously; supplicate
【哀歌】 āigē a mournful song; dirge; elegy
【哀号】 āiháo cry piteously; wail
【哀鸿遍野】 āihóng biàn yě a land swarming with famished refugees; disaster victims everywhere
【哀怜】 āilián feel compassion for; pity
【哀鸣】 āimíng a plaintive whine; wail: 没落阶级的～ lamentations of the declining classes
【哀求】 āiqiú entreat; implore: 苦苦～ piteously entreat
【哀伤】 āishāng grieved; sad; distressed
【哀思】 āisī sad memories (of the deceased); grief: 寄托～ give expression to one's grief
【哀叹】 āitàn lament; bewail; bemoan: 西方报纸～资本主义世界危机重重。The Western press bewails the crises of the capitalist world.
【哀痛】 āitòng grief; deep sorrow
【哀怨】 āiyuàn sad; plaintive
【哀乐】 āiyuè funeral music; dirge

**埃** āi ① dust ② 〈物〉 angstrom (Å)
【埃及】 Āijí Egypt ◇ ～人 Egyptian
【埃米尔】 āimǐ'ěr emir
【埃塞俄比亚】 Āisài'ébǐyà Ethiopia ◇ ～人 Ethiopian

**挨** āi ① get close to; be next to: ～着窗口坐 sit by the window/ 那两家铺子紧～着。The two shops are next to each other. ② in sequence; by turns: ～门～户给小孩打预防针 go from door to door to give children inoculations/ 还没～到我吧? It isn't my turn yet, is it?
另见 ái
【挨次】 āicì one after another; in turn; one by one: ～上车 get on the bus one after another/ ～入场 file in
【挨个儿】 āigèr 〈口〉 one by one; in turn: ～检查身体 have medical check-ups in turn
【挨近】 āijìn get close to; be near to: 我们村～火车站。Our village is close to the railway station./ 侦察员悄悄地～敌人哨所。The scouts stole up to the enemy sentry post.

**唉** āi 〈叹〉 ①〔答应的声音〕: 快开门去。——～。Open the door, quick. — Right./ 小王! ——～! I say, Xiao Wang! — Yes? ②〔叹息的声音〕 alas
另见 ài
【唉声叹气】 āishēng-tànqì heave deep sighs; sigh in despair; moan and groan: 不要受了一点挫折就～。Don't moan and groan because of a little setback.

**锿** āi 〈化〉 einsteinium (Es)

## ái

**呆** ái
另见 dāi
【呆板】 áibǎn stiff; rigid; inflexible; stereotyped: 动作～ stiff and awkward movements/ ～的公式 a rigid formula/ 这篇文章写得太～。This article is rather hackneyed.

**挨** ái ① suffer; endure: ～饿 suffer from hunger; go hungry/ ～骂 get a scolding; get a dressing down/ ～浇 be caught in the rain/ ～批评 be criticized ② drag out: ～日子 suffer day after day; drag out a miserable existence ③ delay; stall; play for time: 别～时间了。Stop dawdling. 或 Quit stalling./ 为什么非要～到下个月不可? Why must we put it off till next month?
另见 āi
【挨打】 áidǎ take a beating; get a thrashing; come under attack: 处于被动～的地位 be passive and vulnerable to attack/ 侵略军到处～。The invaders took a beating wherever they went.
【挨尅】 áikēi 〈口〉 ① get a talking-to; be told off; get a dressing down ② take a beating; get licked

**骏** ái 〈书〉 stupid; idiotic: 痴～ idiotic

**捱** ái 见"挨" ái

**皑** ái 〈书〉 pure white; snow white
【皑皑】 ái'ái pure white: 白雪～ an expanse of white snow/ ～的雪山 a snowcapped mountain

**癌** ái 〈医〉 cancer; carcinoma: 肝(肺、胃)～ cancer of the liver (lung, stomach)/ 致～物质 carcinogenic substance; carcinogen
【癌扩散】 áikuòsàn 〈医〉 metastasis (或 proliferation) of cancer
【癌细胞】 áixìbāo 〈医〉 cancer cell
【癌症】 áizhèng 〈医〉 cancer

## ǎi

**欸** ǎi
另见 ē; é; ě; è
【欸乃】 ǎinǎi 〈书〉〈象〉 the creak of an oar

**矮** ǎi ① short (of stature): 他比他哥哥～一头。He's a head shorter than his brother. ② low: ～墙 a low wall/ ～一级 a grade lower/ 往日穷人～三分,如今当家作主人。In the old days we poor people were treated as inferiors; today we are masters of our country.
【矮凳】 ǎidèng low stool
【矮墩墩】 ǎidūndūn pudgy; dumpy; stumpy
【矮秆品种】 ǎigǎn pǐnzhǒng 〈农〉 short-stalked variety; short-straw variety
【矮个儿】 ǎigèr a person of short stature; a short person
【矮林】 ǎilín coppice; brushwood
【矮胖】 ǎipàng short and stout; dumpy; roly-poly
【矮小】 ǎixiǎo short and small; low and small; undersized: 身材～ short and slight in figure/ ～的房屋 a small, low house
【矮星】 ǎixīng 〈天〉 dwarf (star)
【矮壮素】 ǎizhuàngsù 〈农〉 cycocel
【矮子】 ǎizi a short person; dwarf: 言语的巨人,行动的～ a giant in words, a dwarf in deeds
【矮子里拔将军】 ǎizili bá jiāngjūn pick a general from among the dwarfs — choose the best person available

**嗳** ǎi 〈叹〉〔表示不同意或否定〕: ～,别客气了。Come

on. Don't be so polite./ ～,你搞混啦。No, no, you're all mixed up.
另见 ài

【嗳气】 ǎiqì 〈医〉 belch; eructation

**蔼** ǎi friendly; amiable

【蔼然可亲】 ǎirán kěqīn kindly; amiable; affable

**霭** ǎi 〈书〉 mist; haze: 暮～ evening haze

## ài

**艾** ài ① 〈植〉 Chinese mugwort (*Artemisia argyi*) ② 〈书〉end; stop: 方兴未～ be just unfolding ③(Ài) a surname
另见 yì

【艾绒】 àiróng moxa

【艾炷】 àizhù moxa cone ◇ ～灸 moxibustion

**砹** ài 〈化〉 astatine (At)

**唉** ài 〈叹〉〔表示伤感或惋惜〕: ～,要是老张在这儿该多好啊! Oh, if only Lao Zhang were here./ ～,谁能想到啊! Well, who'd have thought of that?/ ～,真可惜! What a pity!
另见 āi

**爱** ài ① love; affection: ～祖国 love one's country/ 母～ maternal love/ 他们俩相～已经多年。They have been in love for a number of years./ 她～上了大草原。She's fallen in love with the grasslands. ② like; be fond of; be keen on: ～游泳 be fond of swimming/ 只～听恭维话,不～听批评话,早晚要犯错误。Those who like flattery but not criticism are bound to go astray. ③ cherish; treasure; hold dear; take good care of: ～社胜家 hold the people's commune dearer than one's family/ 军～民,民拥军。The army cherishes the people, and the people support the army. ④ be apt to; be in the habit of: ～发脾气 be apt to lose one's temper; be short-tempered/ 铁～生锈。Iron rusts easily.

【爱…不…】 ài...bù... 〔用于相同的动词前面,表示听便的意思〕: 爱信不信 believe it or not/ 他爱去不去。He can go or not, for all I care.

【爱不释手】 ài bù shìshǒu fondle admiringly

【爱称】 àichēng term of endearment; pet name; diminutive

【爱戴】 àidài love and esteem: 受到人民的～ enjoy the love and esteem of the people; enjoy popular support

【爱尔兰】 Ài'ěrlán Ireland ◇ ～人 the Irish; Irishman/ ～语 Irish

【爱抚】 àifǔ show tender care for

【爱国】 àiguó love one's country; be patriotic: ～一家,～不分先后。All patriots belong to one big family, whether they rally to the common cause early or late.
◇～华侨 patriotic overseas Chinese/ ～人士 patriotic personage/ ～同胞 patriotic fellow-countryman/ ～卫生运动 patriotic health campaign/ ～心 patriotic feeling; patriotism/ ～者 patriot/ ～主义 patriotism

【爱好】 àihào ① love; like; be fond of; be keen on: ～和平 love peace; be peace-loving/ ～京剧 be keen on Beijing opera ② interest; hobby: 你在文娱方面有什么～? What kind of recreation do you go in for?

【爱好者】 àihàozhě lover (of art, sports, etc.); amateur; enthusiast; fan: 音乐～ music-lover/ 无线电～ radio amateur/ 体育～ sports enthusiast; sports fan

【爱护】 àihù cherish; treasure; take good care of: ～群众的积极性 cherish the initiative of the masses/ ～公物 take good care of public property/ ～儿童 take good care of children; bring up children with loving care/ ～祖国的一草一木 cherish every tree and every blade of grass in our country

【爱克斯光】 àikèsīguāng X ray; Roentgen ray
◇ ～机 X-ray apparatus/ ～透视 fluoroscopy; X-ray examination/ ～照片 roentgenogram/ ～诊断 X-ray diagnosis; roentgen diagnosis

【爱理不理】 àilǐ-bùlǐ look cold and indifferent; be standoffish

【爱丽舍宫】 Àilìshě Gōng the Elysée Palace

【爱怜】 àilián show tender affection for

【爱恋】 àiliàn be in love with; feel deeply attached to: 对乡土的～ attachment to one's native soil

【爱面子】 ài miànzi be concerned about face-saving; be sensitive about one's reputation

【爱莫能助】 ài mò néng zhù willing to help but unable to do so

【爱慕】 àimù adore; admire: 相互～ adore each other/ ～虚荣 be vain

【爱情】 àiqíng love (between man and woman)

【爱人】 àiren ① husband or wife ② sweetheart

【爱斯基摩人】 Àisījīmórén Eskimo

【爱屋及乌】 ài wū jí wū 〈书〉 love for a person extends even to the crows on his roof; love me, love my dog

【爱惜】 àixī cherish; treasure; use sparingly: ～我们集体的荣誉 cherish the good name of our collective/ ～人力物力 use manpower and material sparingly/ ～时间 be economical of one's time; make the best use of one's time

【爱因斯坦方程】 Àiyīnsītǎn fāngchéng 〈物〉 Einstein equation

【爱憎】 ài-zēng love and hate: ～分明 be clear about what to love and what to hate/ 阶级立场不同,～也不同。People with different class stands have different standards of love and hate.

**隘** ài ① narrow: ～巷 a narrow lane; alley ② pass: 要～ a strategic pass

【隘路】 àilù defile; narrow passage

【隘口】 àikǒu (mountain) pass

**碍** ài hinder; obstruct; be in the way of: 在这儿呆着吧,你～不着我。Stay where you are. You're not in my way./ 有～团结 be harmful (或 detrimental) to unity/ ～于情面 for fear of hurting sb.'s feelings; just to spare sb.'s feelings

【碍口】 àikǒu be too embarrassing to mention: 这事有点～,不好说。It's rather embarrassing; I don't know how to bring it up.

【碍难】 àinán 〔旧时公文用语〕find it difficult (to do sth.): ～照办 find it difficult to comply/ ～照准 cannot approve

【碍事】 àishì ① be in the way; be a hindrance: 这桌子放在门口太～了。This table is too close to the door, it gets in the way. ② be of consequence; matter: 这不～。It doesn't matter. 或 It's of no consequence./ 受了点凉,不～。It's just a slight cold, nothing serious.

【碍手碍脚】 àishǒu-àijiǎo be in the way; be a hindrance

【碍眼】 àiyǎn be unpleasant to look at; offend the eye; be an eyesore

**嗳** ài 〈叹〉〔表示悔恨、懊恼〕: ～,早知道就好了。Oh! If only I'd known earlier.
另见 ǎi

**暧** ài 〈书〉 (of daylight) dim

【暧昧】 àimèi ① ambiguous; equivocal: 态度～ assume an ambiguous attitude ② shady; dubious: ～关系 dubious relationship

## ān

**安** ān ① peaceful; quiet; tranquil; calm: ～睡 sleep peacefully/ 心神不～ feel uneasy or perturbed ② set (sb.'s mind) at ease; calm: ～神 calm (或 soothe) the nerves ③ rest content; be satisfied: ～于现状 be content with things as they are; be satisfied with the existing state of affairs ④ safe; secure; in good health: ～抵拉萨 arrive in Lhasa safely (或 safe and sound)/ ～不忘危 mindful of possible danger in time of peace/ 欠～〈书〉 be slightly indisposed; be unwell ⑤ place in a suitable position; find a place for: 把我～在哪儿都行。I'll be happy with any job I'm assigned to. ⑥ install; fix; fit: ～电灯 install electric lights/ ～窗玻璃 put in a windowpane/ 门上～锁 fit a lock on the door/ 村里～了广播喇叭。Loudspeakers have been set up in the village. ⑦ bring (a charge against sb.); give (sb. a nickname): ～罪名 bring charges against ⑧ harbour (an intention): ～坏心 harbour evil intentions/ 他们～的是什么心？ What are they up to? ⑨〈书〉 where: 其故～在？Wherein lies the cause? ⑩〈书〉 how: ～能袖手旁观？How can one stand by and do nothing? ⑪〈电〉 ampere ⑫ (Ān) a surname

【安步当车】 ān bù dàng chē walk over leisurely instead of riding in a carriage; walk rather than ride

【安瓿】 ānbù 〈药〉 ampoule

【安插】 ānchā place in a certain position; assign to a job; plant: 新徒工就～在我们车间好吗？Could the new apprentice be assigned to our shop?/ 作者在这里～了一段倒叙。At this point the writer puts in (或 inserts) a flashback./ ～亲信 put one's trusted followers in key positions/ 资本家在工会里～了坐探。The boss planted a stool pigeon in the union.

【安道尔】 Āndào'ěr Andorra ◇ ～人 Andorran

【安的列斯群岛】 Āndìlièsī Qúndǎo the Antilles Islands

【安第斯山】 Āndìsīshān the Andes (Mountains)

【安定】 āndìng ① stable; quiet; settled: ～团结 stability and unity/ ～的生活 a stable (或 settled) life/ 职业～ security of employment; job security ② stabilize; maintain: ～社会秩序 maintain social order/ ～人心 reassure the public; set people's minds at rest

【安顿】 āndùn ① find a place for; help settle down; arrange for: 先把同志们～好。First let's help the comrades to settle in./ 家里都～好了吗？Have you got everything settled at home? ② undisturbed; peaceful: 病人吃了药，睡觉～多了。The patient slept much better after taking the medicine.

【安放】 ānfàng lay; place; put in a certain place: 烈士墓前～着花圈。Wreaths were laid at the martyr's tomb./ 把仪器～好。Put the instruments in their proper places.

【安分】 ānfèn not go beyond one's bounds; be law-abiding

【安分守己】 ānfèn-shǒujǐ abide by the law and behave oneself; know one's place

【安抚】 ānfǔ 〈书〉 placate; pacify; appease

【安哥拉】 Āngēlā Angola ◇ ～人 Angolan

【安哥拉兔】 āngēlātù Angora rabbit

【安好】 ānhǎo safe and sound; well: 全家～，请勿挂念。You will be pleased to know that everyone in the family is well.

【安徽】 Ānhuī Anhui (Province)

【安家】 ānjiā settle down; set up a home: 哪里艰苦哪～。We'll go and settle down where conditions are hardest. ◇ ～费 allowance for setting up a home in a new place; settling-in allowance; family allowance

【安家落户】 ānjiā-luòhù make one's home in a place; settle: 他们已经在农村～。They have settled in the countryside.

【安静】 ānjìng quiet; peaceful: 病人需要～。The patient needs peace and quiet./ 保持～。Keep quiet!

【安居乐业】 ānjū-lèyè live and work in peace and contentment

【安康】 ānkāng good health: 祝您～ wishing you the best of health

【安乐】 ānlè peace and happiness ◇ ～窝 cosy nest/ ～椅 easy chair

【安谧】 ānmì 〈书〉 tranquil; peaceful

【安眠】 ānmián sleep peacefully ◇ ～药 sleeping pill (或 tablet); soporific

【安眠酮】 ānmiántóng 〈药〉 methaqualone; hyminal

【安民告示】 ānmín gàoshì ① a notice to reassure the public ② advance notice (of an agenda, etc.)

【安乃近】 ānnǎijìn 〈药〉 analgin

【安宁】 ānníng ① peaceful; tranquil: 确保两国边境～ ensure tranquillity on the border of the two countries/ 超级大国争霸是世界不得～的根源。The contention for hegemony between the superpowers is the cause of the world's intranquillity. ② calm; composed; free from worry: 心里很不～ feel rather worried

【安宁片】 ānníngpiàn 〈药〉 meprobamate

【安排】 ānpái arrange; plan; fix up: 为外宾～参观游览 arrange visits and sightseeing trips for foreign guests/ ～本年度的生产 plan this year's production/ 长计划，短～ long-term plans with short-term arrangements/ 每周～一个下午的政治学习 set aside one afternoon a week for political study/ 合理～人力 rational disposition of manpower/ 一生交给党～ place one's whole life at the disposal of the Party/ ～好社员的生活 make adequate arrangements for the daily life of the commune members/ 重新～河山 reshape rivers and mountains; remake nature

【安培】 ānpéi 〈电〉 ampere ◇ ～计 ammeter; amperemeter/ ～小时 ampere-hour

【安全】 ānquán safe; secure: ～到达 arrive safely/ ～第一 safety first/ 交通～ traffic safety/ 保证～生产 ensure safety in production/ ～行车 safe driving
◇ ～玻璃 safety glass/ ～操作 safe operation/ ～措施 safety measures (或 precautions)/ ～带 safety belt (或 strap); seat belt/ ～岛〈交〉 safety (或 pedestrian) island/ ～阀 safety valve/ ～感 sense of security/ ～高度〈航空〉 safe altitude/ ～规程 safety regulations (或 rules, code)/ ～胶片〈电影〉 safety film/ ～角〈军〉 safety angle/ ～界〈军〉 safety limit/ ～帽 safety helmet/ ～门 exit/ ～设施 safety devices (或 equipment, installations)/ ～梯 emergency staircase; fire escape/ ～停车距离 safe stopping distance/ ～停止装置〈机〉 safety stop/ ～通行证 safe-conduct/ ～网〈建〉 safety netting/ ～系数 safety coefficient (或 factor)/ ～正点 safe and punctual running (of a train or bus)

【安全灯】 ānquándēng ①〈矿〉 safety lamp ②〈摄〉 safelight

【安全理事会】 Ānquán Lǐshìhuì the (U.N.) Security Council

【安然】 ānrán ① safely: ～脱险 be out of danger/ ～无恙 safe and sound; (escape) unscathed ② peacefully; at rest: ～入睡 go to sleep peacefully

【安如磐石】 ān rú pánshí as solid as a rock

【安如泰山】 ān rú Tàishān as secure as Mount Taishan; as solid as a rock

【安山岩】 ānshānyán 〈地〉 andesite

【安设】 ānshè install; set up: 在山顶上～一个气象观测站 set up a weather station at the top of the hill

【安身】 ānshēn make one's home; take shelter: 无处～ have nowhere to make one's home/ 地主霸占了我家的房子，逼得

我们只得在破庙里～。The landlord seized our house, and we had to take shelter in a dilapidated temple.

【安身立命】ānshēn-lìmìng settle down and get on with one's pursuit

【安神】ānshén ① calm (或 soothe) the nerves ②〈中医〉relieve uneasiness of body and mind ◇ ～药 sedative; tranquillizer

【安生】ānshēng ① peaceful; restful: 叫敌人不得～ leave the enemy no peace/ 为了抢修机器，他几天没有吃过一顿～饭。To get the machine repaired quickly, he didn't enjoy a leisurely meal for several days. ② quiet; still: 这孩子一会儿也不～。The child simply will not keep quiet for a moment.

【安适】ānshì quiet and comfortable: ～的生活 a quiet and comfortable life; a life of ease and comfort

【安提瓜岛】Āntíguādǎo Antigua

【安替比林】āntìbǐlín〈药〉antipyrine

【安土重迁】ān tǔ zhòng qiān hate to leave a place where one has lived long; be attached to one's native land and unwilling to leave it

【安妥】āntuǒ antu (a rat poison)

【安危】ān-wēi safety and danger; safety: 不顾个人～ heedless of one's personal safety/ 把矿工们的～冷暖时刻挂在心上 always have the safety and well-being of the miners at heart

【安慰】ānwèi comfort; console: ～他几句 say a few words to comfort him; give him a few words of comfort/ 同志们的关怀给了我很大的～。The comrades' solicitude was a great comfort (或 consolation) to me. ◇ ～赛〈体〉consolation event (或 match)

【安稳】ānwěn smooth and steady: 船走得很～。The boat sailed smoothly./ 睡得很～ sleep peacefully (或 soundly)

【安息】ānxī ① rest; go to sleep ② rest in peace: 烈士们，～吧！May the revolutionary martyrs rest in peace! ③ (Ānxī)〈史〉Parthia (an ancient country southeast of the Caspian Sea)

【安息日】ānxīrì〈宗〉Sabbath (day)

【安息香】ānxīxiāng〈药〉benzoin ◇ ～酸 benzoic acid

【安闲】ānxián peaceful and carefree; leisurely: ～自在 leisurely and carefree/ ～的心情 a relaxed mood

【安详】ānxiáng serene; composed; unruffled: 举止～ behave with composure

【安歇】ānxiē go to bed; retire for the night

【安心】ānxīn ① feel at ease; be relieved; set one's mind at rest: 春播还没完成，大家都安不下心来。None of us could feel at ease until the spring sowing was finished./ 听到这个消息，她就～了。She was relieved at the news./ 希望你～休养。You just get better and don't worry. ② keep one's mind on sth.: ～工作 keep one's mind on one's work; work contentedly/ 回乡～生产 go home and settle down to productive work

【安逸】ānyì easy and comfortable; easy: ～的生活 an easy life/ 贪图～ seek an easy life; love comfort

【安营】ānyíng pitch a camp; camp

【安营扎寨】ānyíng-zhāzhài pitch a camp; camp: 社员们在工地上～。The commune members camped at the worksite.

【安葬】ānzàng bury (the dead)

【安之若素】ān zhī ruò sù ① bear (hardship, etc.) with equanimity ② regard (wrongdoing, etc.) with equanimity

【安置】ānzhì find a place for; help settle down; arrange for: 把行李～好 put the luggage in the right place/ 复员军人得到了适当的～。Proper arrangements have been made for the placement of demobilized soldiers. ◇ ～费 settlement allowance

【安装】ānzhuāng install; erect; fix; mount: ～电话 install a telephone/ ～机器 install machinery/ ～扩音器 set up a microphone/ ～蒸馏塔 erect a distillation column/ 推进器的叶片已经～好了。The propeller blade has been mounted.

**桉** ān〈植〉eucalyptus

【桉树】ānshù eucalyptus

**氨** ān〈化〉ammonia: 合成～ synthetic ammonia

【氨苯磺胺】ānběn huáng'àn〈药〉sulphanilamide

【氨茶硷】ānchájiǎn〈药〉aminophylline

【氨化】ānhuà ammoniation ◇ ～过磷酸钙〈农〉ammoniated superphosphate

【氨基】ānjī〈化〉amino; amino-group ◇ ～塑料 amino-plastic/ ～酸 amino acid

【氨基比林】ānjībǐlín〈药〉aminopyrine

【氨碱法】ānjiǎnfǎ〈化〉ammonia soda process

【氨硫脲】ānliúniào〈药〉thiacetazone

【氨水】ānshuǐ〈化〉ammonia water; aqua ammoniae

**谙** ān〈书〉know well: 素～水性 be a skilful swimmer

【谙练】ānliàn〈书〉conversant; skilled; proficient

**庵** ān ①〈书〉hut: 草～ a thatched hut ② nunnery; Buddhist convent

**鹌** ān

【鹌鹑】ānchún quail

**鮟** ān

【鮟鱇】ānkāng〈动〉angler; fishing frog

**鞍** ān saddle

【鞍部】ānbù saddle (of a hill or mountain)

【鞍鞯】ānchàn a saddle with saddle cloth

【鞍钢宪法】Āngāng xiànfǎ the Charter of the Anshan Iron and Steel Company (a set of guiding principles approved by Chairman Mao for running socialist enterprises, viz., keep politics firmly in command; strengthen Party leadership; launch vigorous mass movements; have cadre participation in productive labour and worker participation in management; reform irrational and outdated rules and regulations; maintain close cooperation among cadres, workers and technicians; and go all out with technical innovation and revolution)

【鞍马】ānmǎ ①〈体〉pommelled horse; side horse ②〈书〉saddle and horse: ～生活 life on horseback/ ～劳顿 travel-worn

【鞍子】ānzi saddle

## ǎn

**俺** ǎn〈方〉I; we: ～爹 my father/ ～村 our village

**铵** ǎn〈化〉ammonium: ～矾 ammonium alum

**埯** ǎn ① a hole to sow seeds in ② dibble: ～豆 dibble beans ③〈量〉〔用于点种的作物〕: 一～花生 a cluster of peanut seedlings

**揞** ǎn apply (medicinal powder to a wound)

## àn

**岸** àn ① bank; shore; coast: 江～ the bank of a river; a river bank/ 海～ coast; seashore/ 上～ go ashore ② 〈书〉 lofty: 傲～ haughty

【岸标】 ànbiāo shore beacon

【岸然】 ànrán in a solemn manner: 道貌～ be sanctimonious

**按** àn ① press; push down: ～电钮 press (或 push) a button/ ～门铃 ring a doorbell/ ～手印 put one's thumbprint (on a document, etc.) ② leave aside; shelve: ～下此事不提 leave this aside for the moment ③ restrain; control: ～不住心头怒火 be unable to restrain (或 control) one's anger ④ keep one's hand on; keep a tight grip on: ～住操纵杆 keep a tight grip on the control lever ⑤ according to; in accordance with; in the light of; on the basis of: 反对形而上学，～辩证法办事。 Oppose metaphysics and act in accordance with dialectics./ ～质定价 fix the price according to the quality/ ～比例发展 develop in proportion; proportional development/ ～人口平均 per capita; per head/ ～年代顺序 in chronological order/ ～姓氏笔划为序 in the order of the number of strokes in the surnames/ ～我的意思 in my opinion ⑥〈书〉 check; refer to: 有原文可～。 There's the original to refer to. ⑦ note: 编者～ editor's note

【按兵不动】 àn bīng bù dòng not throw the troops into battle; bide one's time; take no action: 大家都动起来了，你怎么还～呢？ Everybody else has started work. Why do you sit there doing nothing?

【按部就班】 ànbù-jiùbān follow the prescribed order; keep to conventional ways of doing things

【按劳分配】 àn láo fēnpèi distribution according to work 参见"各尽所能，按劳分配" gè jìn suǒ néng, àn láo fēnpèi

【按理】 ànlǐ according to reason; in the ordinary course of events; normally: 他们队遭了灾，～可以少交公粮，可他们就是不干。As a team hit by natural calamity, they were entitled to a grain-tax reduction, but they rejected it./ 这种病～不该有并发症。 Normally there are no complications with this illness.

【按脉】 ànmài feel (或 take) the pulse

【按摩】 ànmó 〈医〉 massage ◇ ～疗法 massotherapy

【按捺】 ànnà restrain; control: ～不住激动的心情 be unable to hold back one's excitement

【按钮】 ànniǔ push button ◇ ～控制 push-button control; dash control

【按期】 ànqī on schedule; on time: ～交货 deliver goods on schedule/ ～出版 come out on time

【按时】 ànshí on time; on schedule: ～到达 arrive on time

【按说】 ànshuō in the ordinary course of events; ordinarily; normally: ～这时候该下雪了。 Ordinarily it should be snowing at this time of the year./ ～现在是蔬菜的淡季，可是你们这里供应还不错。This is supposed to be an off season for vegetables but you seem to have enough here.

【按图索骥】 àn tú suǒ jì look for a steed with the aid of its picture — try to locate sth. by following up a clue

【按蚊】 ànwén anopheles; malarial mosquito

【按下葫芦浮起瓢】 ànxià húlu fúqǐ piáo hardly has one gourd been pushed under water when another bobs up — solve one problem only to find another cropping up

【按需分配】 àn xū fēnpèi distribution according to need 参见"各尽所能，按需分配" gè jìn suǒ néng, àn xū fēnpèi

【按验】 ànyàn 见"案验" ànyàn

【按语】 ànyǔ note; comment

【按照】 ànzhào according to; in accordance with; in the light of; on the basis of: ～党章规定 according to the rules of the Party Constitution/ ～实际情况决定工作方针 determine working policies in the light of actual conditions/ ～自愿原则 on a voluntary basis/ ～贡献大小，分别给以奖励 award people according to their contributions/ 计划已～群众的意见修改了。The plan has been revised in accordance with the opinions of the masses./ ～计划，我们应于四月中旬出发。We were scheduled to leave in mid-April.

**案** àn ① table; desk: 条～ a long narrow table ② case; law case: 办～ handle a case/ 破～ clear up (或 solve) a criminal case ③ record; file: 有～可查 be on record (或 file)/ 声明在～ have a statement placed on record ④ a plan submitted for consideration; proposal: 提～ proposal; motion/ 决议草～ a draft resolution

【案板】 ànbǎn kneading or chopping board

【案秤】 ànchèng counter scale

【案件】 ànjiàn law case; case: 反革命～ a counterrevolutionary case/ 刑事～ a criminal case

【案卷】 ànjuàn records; files; archives

【案情】 ànqíng details of a case; case: 了解～ investigate the details of a case

【案头】 àntóu on one's desk: ～放着一套《毛泽东选集》。There is a set of *Selected Works of Mao Zedong* on the desk. ◇ ～剧 closet drama/ ～日历 desk calendar

【案文】 ànwén text: 协商～ negotiating text

【案验】 ànyàn 〈书〉 investigate the evidence of a case

【案由】 ànyóu main points of a case; brief; summary

【案子】 ànzi ① long table; counter: 乒乓球～ ping-pong table/ 肉～ meat counter ②〈口〉 case; law case

**胺** àn 〈化〉 amine

【胺化】 ànhuà amination

【胺盐】 ànyán amine salt

**暗** àn ① dark; dim; dull: 天色渐～。It's getting dark./ 灯光很～。 The light is rather dim./ ～紫色 dull purple/ ～绿 dark green ② hidden; secret: 我们在明处，敌人在～处，要提高警惕。We're in the open while the enemy is hidden; we must be vigilant./ 明人不做～事。A person who is aboveboard does nothing underhand. ③ unclear; hazy: 对情况若明若～ have only a vague idea of the situation

【暗暗】 àn'àn secretly; inwardly; to oneself: ～跟踪 secretly follow sb./ ～吃了一惊 be startled but not show it/ 侦察员～记住了敌人的火力部署。The scout made a mental note of the disposition of enemy fire./ 他～发誓要为牺牲的同志报仇。He vowed to himself to avenge his martyred comrade.

【暗堡】 ànbǎo bunker

【暗藏】 àncáng hide; conceal: ～枪枝 conceal firearms; illegally possess firearms/ ～的反革命分子 a hidden counterrevolutionary

【暗娼】 ànchāng unlicensed (或 unregistered) prostitute

【暗潮】 àncháo undercurrent

【暗袋】 àndài 〈摄〉 camera bag (for changing film)

【暗淡】 àndàn dim; faint; dismal; gloomy: ～的颜色 a dull colour/ ～的景象 a dismal picture/ 屋里灯光～。The room is dimly lit.

【暗地里】 àndìlì secretly; inwardly; on the sly: ～捣鬼 secretly make trouble/ 我们～替他高兴。We inwardly rejoiced for him.

【暗渡陈仓】 àn dù Chéncāng 见"明修栈道，暗渡陈仓" míng

xiū zhàndào, àn dù Chéncāng
【暗害】 ànhài ① kill secretly ② stab in the back
【暗含着】 ànhánzhe imply: 他的回答～对我们工作的批评。His reply implied a criticism of our work.
【暗号】 ànhào secret signal (或 sign); countersign; cipher
【暗合】 ànhé agree without prior consultation; (happen to) coincide
【暗河】 ànhé underground river
【暗盒】 ànhé 〈摄〉 magazine; cassette
【暗花儿】 ànhuār a veiled design incised in porcelain or woven in fabric
【暗疾】 ànjí unmentionable disease; a disease one is ashamed of
【暗记儿】 ànjìr secret mark
【暗间儿】 ànjiānr inner room
【暗箭】 ànjiàn an arrow shot from hiding; attack by a hidden enemy; a stab in the back: ～伤人 stab sb. in the back; injure sb. by underhand means
【暗礁】 ànjiāo submerged reef (或 rock)
【暗井】 ànjǐng 〈矿〉 blind shaft; winze
【暗流】 ànliú undercurrent
【暗杀】 ànshā assassinate
【暗伤】 ànshāng ① internal (或 invisible) injury ② internal (或 invisible) damage
【暗示】 ànshì ① drop a hint; hint; suggest: 他～要我走开。He hinted that he wanted me to leave./ 她没有懂我的～。She didn't take my hint. ② 〈心〉 suggestion
【暗室】 ànshì 〈摄〉 darkroom
【暗适应】 ànshìyìng 〈心〉 dark adaptation
【暗送秋波】 àn sòng qiūbō make eyes at sb. while others are not looking; stealthily give sb. the glad eye; make secret overtures to sb.
【暗算】 ànsuàn plot against: 遭人～ fall a prey to a plot
【暗锁】 ànsuǒ built-in lock
【暗滩】 àntān hidden shoal
【暗探】 àntàn secret agent; detective
【暗无天日】 àn wú tiānrì complete darkness; total absence of justice: 旧社会～。The old society was an abyss of darkness.
【暗线光谱】 ànxiàn guāngpǔ 〈物〉 dark-line spectrum
【暗箱】 ànxiāng 〈摄〉 camera bellows; camera obscura
【暗笑】 ànxiào laugh in (或 up) one's sleeve; snigger; snicker
【暗影】 ànyǐng ① shadow ② 〈天〉 umbra
【暗语】 ànyǔ code word
【暗中】 ànzhōng ① in the dark: ～摸索 grope in the dark ② in secret; on the sly; surreptitiously: ～操纵 pull strings from behind the scenes/ ～支持 give secret support to/ ～串通 collude with; conspire
【暗转】 ànzhuǎn 〈剧〉 blackout
【暗自】 ànzì inwardly; to oneself; secretly: ～庆幸 congratulate oneself; consider oneself lucky

**黯** àn dim; gloomy
【黯淡】 àndàn 见"暗淡" àndàn
【黯然】 ànrán 〈书〉 ① dim; faint: ～失色 be overshadowed; be eclipsed; pale into insignificance ② dejected; low-spirited; downcast: ～神伤 feel dejected (或 depressed)

## āng

**肮** āng
【肮脏】 āngzāng dirty; filthy: ～的阴沟 a filthy sewer/ ～的勾当 dirty work; a foul deed/ ～的政治交易 a dirty political deal

## áng

**昂** áng ① hold (one's head) high: ～首挺胸 hold up one's head and throw out one's chest; chin up and chest out ② high; soaring: 战天斗地志气～ battle against nature with high resolve
【昂昂】 áng'áng high-spirited; brave-looking: 雄赳赳，气～ fearless and militant
【昂贵】 ángguì expensive; costly
【昂然】 ángrán upright and unafraid
【昂首阔步】 ángshǒu-kuòbù stride forward with one's chin up; stride proudly ahead
【昂扬】 ángyáng high-spirited: 斗志～ have high morale; be full of fight; be militant/ ～的歌声 spirited singing

## àng

**盎** àng an ancient vessel with a big belly and a small mouth
【盎格鲁撒克逊人】 Ànggélǔ-Sākèxùnrén Anglo-Saxon
【盎然】 àngrán abundant; full; overflowing; exuberant: 趣味～ full of interest/ 生机～ overflowing with vigour; exuberant/ 春意～。Spring is in the air.
【盎司】 àngsī ounce 又作"盎斯"

## āo

**凹** āo concave; hollow; sunken; dented: ～凸不平 full of bumps and holes; uneven
【凹岸】 āo'àn 〈地〉 concave bank
【凹版】 āobǎn 〈印〉 intaglio; gravure: 照相～ photogravure ◇ ～印刷 intaglio (或 gravure) printing/ ～印刷机 intaglio (或 gravure) press/ ～制版 gravure plate-making
【凹度】 āodù concavity
【凹面镜】 āomiànjìng concave mirror
【凹透镜】 āotòujìng concave lens
【凹凸轧花】 āotū yàhuā 〈纺〉 embossing
【凹凸印刷】 āotū yìnshuā embossing; die stamping ◇ ～机 embossing (或 die stamping) press
【凹陷】 āoxiàn hollow; sunken; depressed: 双颊～ sunken (或 hollow) cheeks/ 地面～。The ground caved in.

**熬** āo cook in water; boil: ～白菜 stewed cabbage
另见 áo

## áo

**敖** Áo a surname

**遨** áo stroll; saunter
【遨游】 áoyóu roam; travel: 我国的人造卫星～太空。Our man-made satellites are travelling through space.

**嗷** áo
【嗷嗷】 áo'áo 〈象〉〔表示动物或人的叫声〕: 疼得～叫 scream with pain/ 雁群～地飞过。Flocks of honking geese flew past.
【嗷嗷待哺】 áo'áo dài bǔ cry piteously for food

**熬** áo ①boil; stew; decoct: ～粥 cook gruel/ ～药 decoct medicinal herbs ②endure; hold out: ～过苦难的岁月 go through years of suffering and privation/ 直到解放,苦日子才算～出了头。It was liberation that brought an end to those long years of suffering./ ～红了眼睛 stay up till one's eyes become bloodshot
另见 āo

【熬煎】 áojiān suffering; torture: 受尽～ be subjected to all kinds of suffering

【熬夜】 áoyè stay up late or all night

**獒** áo 〈动〉 mastiff

**螯** áo chela; pincers

**謷** áo 见"佶屈謷牙" jíqū áoyá

**翱** áo 〈书〉 take wing

【翱翔】 áoxiáng hover; soar: 海鸥在惊涛骇浪上～。Seagulls hover over the surging waves./ ～长空的女飞行员 women pilots soaring in the skies ◇ ～飞行 soaring flight/ ～机 sailplane; soaring glider

**鳌** áo a huge legendary turtle

**鏖** áo 〈书〉 engage in fierce battle

【鏖战】 áozhàn 〈书〉 fight hard; engage in fierce battle

## ǎo

**拗** ǎo 〈方〉 bend so as to break: 把甘蔗～断 break a piece of sugarcane in two
另见 ào; niù

**袄** ǎo a short Chinese-style coat or jacket: 皮～ a fur coat/ 棉～ a cotton-padded jacket

**媪** ǎo 〈书〉 old woman

## ào

**坳** ào a depression in a mountain range; col: 珠峰北～ the North Col of Mount Qomolangma

**拗** ào
另见 ǎo; niù

【拗口】 àokǒu hard to pronounce; awkward-sounding ◇ ～令 tongue twister

【拗陷】 àoxiàn 〈地〉 depression

**傲** ào ①proud; haughty ②refuse to yield to; brave; defy: 红梅～雪凌霜开。Braving snow and frost, the plum trees blossomed defiantly.

【傲岸】 ào'àn 〈书〉 proud; haughty: ～不群 proud and aloof/ ～的青松 a proud and towering pine

【傲骨】 àogǔ lofty and unyielding character

【傲慢】 àomàn arrogant; haughty: 态度～ adopt an arrogant attitude; put on airs

【傲气】 àoqì air of arrogance; haughtiness: ～十足 full of arrogance; extremely haughty

【傲然】 àorán loftily; proudly; unyieldingly: ～挺立的山峰 a mountain peak towering proudly into the skies

【傲视】 àoshì turn up one's nose at; show disdain for; regard superciliously

**奥** ào ①profound; abstruse; difficult to understand ②〈物〉 oersted

【奥得河】 Àodéhé the Oder River

【奥地利】 Àodìlì Austria ◇ ～人 Austrian

【奥林匹克运动会】 Àolínpǐkè Yùndònghuì the Olympic Games

【奥秘】 àomì profound mystery: 探索宇宙的～ probe the mysteries of the universe

【奥妙】 àomiào profound; subtle; secret: 神奇～ mysterious and profound/ ～无穷 extremely subtle/ 不难明白其中的～。It's not difficult to see what's behind it./ 其中定有～。There must be more to it than meets the eye.

【奥氏体】 àoshìtǐ 〈冶〉 austenite ◇ ～钢 austenitic steel

【奥斯曼帝国】 Àosīmàn Dìguó the Ottoman Empire (1290-1922)

【奥斯特】 àosītè 〈物〉 oersted (Oe)

【奥陶纪】 Àotáojì 〈地〉 the Ordovician period

【奥匈帝国】 Ào-Xiōng Dìguó Austro-Hungary (1867-1918)

**骜** ào 〈书〉 ①a good horse; steed ②见"桀骜不驯" jié'ào bù xún

**澳** ào ①〔多用于地名〕an inlet of the sea; bay: 三都～ Sandu Bay ②(Ào) short for Aomen

【澳大利亚】 Àodàlìyà Australia ◇ ～人 Australian

【澳门】 Àomén Aomen (Macao)

**懊** ào ①regretful; remorseful ②annoyed; vexed

【懊悔】 àohuǐ feel remorse; repent; regret: 我～不该错怪了她。I regretted having blamed her unjustly.

【懊恼】 àonǎo annoyed; vexed; upset: 他工作没做好,心里很～。He was quite upset at not having done his work well.

【懊丧】 àosàng dejected; despondent; depressed

**鏊** ào

【鏊子】 àozi griddle

# B

## bā

**八** bā eight

注意 "八"字在第四声(去声)字前念第二声(阳平)，如"八月" báyuè，"八岁" básuì。本词典为简便起见，条目中的"八"字，都注第一声(阴平)。

【八宝】 bābǎo eight treasures (choice ingredients of certain special dishes) ◇ ～菜 eight-treasure pickles; assorted soy-sauce pickles/ ～饭 eight-treasure rice pudding (steamed glutinous rice with bean paste, lotus seeds, preserved fruit, etc.)

【八倍体】 bābèitǐ 〈生〉 octoploid

【八成】 bāchéng ① eighty per cent: ～新 eighty per cent new; practically new/ 事情有了～啦。It's almost as good as settled. 或 There's a fair chance of success. ② most probably; most likely: ～他不来了。Most probably he isn't coming.

【八带鱼】 bādàiyú octopus

【八度】 bādù 〈乐〉 octave

【八方】 bāfāng the eight points of the compass; all directions: 一方有难，～支援。When trouble occurs at one spot, help comes from all quarters.

【八分音符】 bāfēn yīnfú 〈乐〉 quaver; eighth note

【八纲】 bāgāng 〈中医〉 the eight principal syndromes: *yin* and *yang* (阴阳), exterior and interior (表里), cold and heat (寒热), hypofunction and hyperfunction (虚实) ◇ ～辨证 analysis and differentiation of pathological conditions in accordance with the eight principal syndromes

【八哥儿】 bāgēr 〈动〉 myna

【八股】 bāgǔ ① eight-part essay (a literary composition prescribed for the imperial civil service examinations, known for its rigidity of form and poverty of ideas) ② stereotyped writing

【八卦】 bāguà the Eight Diagrams (eight combinations of three whole or broken lines formerly used in divination)

【八国联军】 Bāguó Liánjūn the Eight-Power Allied Forces, aggressive troops sent by Britain, the United States, Germany, France, tsarist Russia, Japan, Italy and Austria in 1900, to suppress the anti-imperialist Yihetuan Movement (义和团运动) of the Chinese people

【八会穴】 bāhuìxué 〈中医〉 the Eight Strategic Nerve Points

【八级风】 bājífēng 〈气〉 force 8 wind; fresh gale

【八级工】 bājígōng eighth-grade worker (highest on the eight-grade wage scale); top-grade worker

【八级工资制】 bā jí gōngzīzhì eight-grade wage scale (或 system)

【八角】 bājiǎo ① 〈植〉 anise; star anise ② aniseed ③ octagonal ◇ ～帽 octagonal cap/ ～形 octagon

【八角枫】 bājiǎofēng 〈植〉 alangium

【八九不离十】 bā jiǔ bù lí shí 〈口〉 pretty close; very near; about right: 猜个～ make a very close guess

【八开】 bākāi 〈印〉 octavo; 8vo ◇ ～本 octavo

【八路军】 Bālùjūn the Eighth Route Army (led by the Chinese Communist Party during the War of Resistance Against Japan)

【八面玲珑】 bāmiàn línglóng be smooth and slick (in establishing social relations)

【八旗】 bāqí the "Eight Banners" (military-administrative organizations of the Man nationality in the Qing Dynasty)

【八仙】 Bāxiān the Eight Immortals (in the legend): ～过海，各显神通 like the Eight Immortals crossing the sea, each one showing his or her special prowess

【八仙桌】 bāxiānzhuō old-fashioned square table for eight people

【八小时工作制】 bā xiǎoshí gōngzuòzhì eight-hour day

【八一建军节】 Bā Yī Jiànjūnjié Army Day (August 1, anniversary of the founding of the Chinese People's Liberation Army)

【八一南昌起义】 Bā Yī Nánchāng Qǐyì the August 1 Nanchang Uprising (1927), which fired the first shot against the KMT reactionaries and marked the beginning of the Chinese Communist Party's independent leadership of the revolutionary war

【八月】 bāyuè ① August ② the eighth month of the lunar year; the eighth moon ◇ ～节 the Mid-Autumn Festival (15th day of the 8th lunar month)

【八字】 bāzì ① character 八: ～还没见一撇儿。Not even the first stroke of the character 八 is in sight—there's not the slightest sign of anything happening yet. ② Eight Characters (in four pairs, indicating the year, month, day and hour of a person's birth, each pair consisting of one Heavenly Stem and one Earthly Branch, formerly used in fortune-telling) ◇ ～步 a measured gait with the toes pointing outwards/ ～脚 splayfoot

【八字宪法】 bā zì xiànfǎ 见"农业八字宪法" nóngyè bā zì xiànfǎ

**巴** bā ① hope earnestly; wait anxiously: ～望 look forward to ② cling to; stick to: 爬山虎～在墙上。The ivy clings to the wall./ 粥～锅了。The porridge has stuck to the pot. ③ be close to; be next to: 前不～村，后不着店 with no village ahead and no inn behind—stranded in an uninhabited area ④ 〈物〉 bar: 毫～ millibar/ 微～ microbar ⑤ (Bā) a surname

【巴巴多斯】 Bābāduōsī Barbados ◇ ～人 Barbadian

【巴比合金】 bābǐ héjīn babbitt (metal)

【巴比伦】 Bābǐlún Babylon

【巴比妥】 bābǐtuǒ 〈药〉 barbitone; barbital

【巴布亚新几内亚】 Bābùyà Xīnjǐnèiyà Papua New Guinea ◇ ～人 Papua New Guinean

【巴不得】 bābude 〈口〉 be only too anxious (to do sth.); eagerly look forward to; earnestly wish: 他～立刻回到工作岗位。He is only too anxious to get back to work right away./ 我～天快晴。I wish it would clear up soon.

【巴豆】 bādòu 〈植〉 (purging) croton ◇ ～霜〈中药〉 defatted croton seed powder

【巴尔干】 Bā'ěrgàn Balkan ◇ ～半岛 the Balkan Peninsula/ ～国家 Balkan states; the Balkans

【巴哈马】 Bāhāmǎ the Bahamas ◇ ～人 Bahamian

【巴基斯坦】 Bājīsītǎn Pakistan ◇ ～人 Pakistani

【巴结】 bājie fawn on; curry favour with; make up to

【巴克夏猪】 bākèxiàzhū Berkshire (swine)

【巴枯宁主义】 Bākūníngzhǔyì Bakuninism

【巴拉圭】 Bālāguī Paraguay ◇ ～人 Paraguayan

【巴勒斯坦】 Bālèsītǎn Palestine ◇ ～解放组织 the Palestine

Liberation Organization (PLO)/ ～人 Palestinian
【巴黎公社】 Bālí Gōngshè the Paris Commune (the world's first dictatorship of the proletariat, established by the French working class after smashing the old state machine, 1871)
【巴黎绿】 bālílǜ 〈化〉 Paris green
【巴林】 Bālín Bahrain ◇ ～人 Bahraini
【巴龙霉素】 bālóngméisù 〈药〉 paromomycin
【巴拿马】 Bānámǎ Panama ◇ ～人 Panamanian/ ～运河 the Panama Canal
【巴儿狗】 bārgǒu ① pekingese (a breed of dog) ② sycophant; toady
【巴士底狱】 Bāshìdǐyù the Bastille
【巴松管】 bāsōngguǎn 〈乐〉 bassoon
【巴望】 bāwàng 〈方〉 look forward to
【巴西】 Bāxī Brazil ◇ ～人 Brazilian
【巴掌】 bāzhang palm; hand: 拍～ clap hands/ 打他一～ give him a slap/ 一个～拍不响。 One hand alone can't clap — it takes two to make a quarrel.

**扒** bā ① hold on to; cling to: 孩子们～着窗台看游行队伍。Holding on to the window sill, the children watched the parade. ② dig up; rake; pull down: ～土 rake earth/ ～了旧房盖新房 pull down the old house to build a new one in its place/ 城墙～了个豁口。A breach was made in the city wall. ③ push aside: ～开芦苇 push aside the reeds ④ strip off; take off: ～兔皮 skin a rabbit/ 他把棉袄一～就干起活来。Stripping off his padded coat, he set to work at once.
另见 pá
【扒钉】 bādīng cramp
【扒拉】 bāla push lightly: 把压在苗上的土～开 flick the earth off the seedlings/ ～算盘子儿 move the beads of an abacus up and down; click away at an abacus

**叭** bā 见"吧" bā

**芭** bā
【芭蕉】 bājiāo 〈植〉 *bajiao* banana
【芭蕉扇】 bājiāoshàn palm-leaf fan
【芭蕾舞】 bālěiwǔ ballet ◇ ～女演员 ballerina/ ～设计 choreography/ ～演员 ballet dancer

**吧** bā ①〈象〉: ～的一声，弦断了。 The string broke with a snap./ ～～两声枪响。 Crack! Crack! Two shots rang out. ②〈口〉 draw on (或 pull at) one's pipe, etc.
另见 ba
【吧嗒】 bādā 〈象〉: ～一声，门关上了。 The door clicked shut.
【吧嗒】 bāda ① smack one's lips (in surprise, alarm, etc.): 他～了一下嘴，一声也不言语。He smacked his lips but did not utter a word. ②〈方〉 pull at (a pipe, etc.)
【吧唧】 bājī 〈象〉: 她光着脚～～地在泥里走。She squelched barefoot through the mud.

**疤** bā scar
【疤痕】 bāhén scar

**粑** bā 〈方〉 cake

**捌** bā eight (used for the numeral 八 on cheques, etc. to avoid mistakes or alterations)

**笆** bā basketry
【笆斗】 bādǒu round-bottomed basket

## bá

**拔** bá ① pull out; pull up: ～草 pull up weeds; weed/ ～麦子 harvest wheat (by pulling it up)/ ～牙 pull out (或 extract) a tooth/ ～剑 draw one's sword/ 把剥削根子全～掉 remove the roots of exploitation ② suck out; draw: 把火～一～。Put a chimney on the stove to make the fire draw. ③ choose; select; pick: 选～ select (from candidates) ④ lift; raise: ～起嗓子直嚷 shout at the top of one's voice ⑤ stand out among; surpass: 出类～萃 stand out among one's fellows; be out of the common run ⑥ capture; seize: 连～敌人五个据点 capture five enemy strongholds in succession ⑦ 〈方〉 cool in water: 把西瓜放在冰水里～一～ cool a watermelon in ice water ⑧ 〈机〉 drawing: 冷～ cold drawing / 热～ hot drawing
【拔除】 báchú pull out; remove: ～敌军哨所 wipe out an enemy sentry post
【拔钉锤】 bádīngchuí claw hammer
【拔顶】 bádǐng 〈石油〉 topping
【拔毒】 bádú 〈中医〉 draw out pus by applying a plaster to the affected part
【拔罐子】 bá guànzi 〈中医〉 cupping
【拔海】 báhǎi elevation (above sea level): ～五千米 at an elevation of 5,000 metres; 5,000 metres above sea level
【拔河】 báhé 〈体〉 tug-of-war
【拔火罐儿】 báhuǒguànr detachable stove chimney
【拔尖儿】 bájiānr 〈口〉 ① tiptop; top-notch: 他的学习成绩是～的。He is a top-notch student. ② push oneself to the front
【拔脚】 bájiǎo 见"拔腿"
【拔节】 bájié 〈农〉 jointing ◇ ～期 jointing (或 elongation) stage
【拔锚】 bámáo weigh anchor
【拔苗助长】 bá miáo zhù zhǎng try to help the shoots grow by pulling them upward — spoil things by excessive enthusiasm
【拔染】 bárǎn 〈纺〉 discharge ◇ ～剂 discharging agent; discharge
【拔丝】 básī ① 〈机〉 wire drawing: ～机 wire drawing bench (或 machine) ② candied floss: ～山药 hot candied yam
【拔腿】 bátuǐ 〔多用于〕: ～就跑 start running away at once; immediately take to one's heels/ ～就追 give instant chase
【拔秧】 báyāng 〈农〉 pull up seedlings (for transplanting)
【拔营】 báyíng 〈军〉 strike camp

**菝** bá
【菝葜】 báqiā 〈植〉 chinaroot greenbrier

**跋** bá ① cross mountains: ～山涉水 scale mountains and ford streams; travel across mountains and rivers ② postscript
【跋扈】 báhù domineering; bossy
【跋涉】 báshè trudge; trek: 长途～ trudge over a long distance; trek a long way; make a long and difficult journey

**魃** bá 见"鼧魃" tuóbá

## bǎ

**把** bǎ ① hold; grasp: ～住栏杆 hold on to a railing/ ～着手教 take sb. by the hand and teach him how to do

sth./ ～犁 handle a plough ② hold (a baby while it relieves itself): 给孩子～尿 hold a baby out to let it urinate ③ control; monopolize; dominate: 要充分发挥群众的积极性，不要什么都～着不放手。You must give full play to the initiative of the masses and not keep such a tight control on things. ④ guard; watch: ～门 guard a gate ⑤ handle (of a pushcart, etc.): 自行车～ the handlebar of a bicycle ⑥ bundle; bunch: 草～ a bundle of straw ⑦ 〈量〉 ⓐ〔用于有柄的器具〕: 一～刀 a knife/ 一～茶壶 a teapot/ 一～椅子 a chair ⓑ〔指一手抓起的数量〕: 一～米 a handful of rice/ 一～花 a bunch of flowers ⓒ〔用于某些抽象事物〕: 有一～年纪 be getting on in years/ 有～力气 be quite strong/ 加～劲 make an extra effort; put on a spurt ⓓ〔用于手的动作〕: 拉他一～ give him a tug; give (或lend) him a hand ⑧ about; or so: 个～月 about a month; a month or so/ 百～人 some hundred people ⑨ 〈介〉 ⓐ〔宾语是后面动词的受事者，整个格式有处置的意思〕: ～衣服洗洗 wash the clothes/ ～头一扭 toss one's head/ ～方便让给别人，～困难留给自己 take difficulties on oneself and leave what is easy to others/ ～水搅浑 muddy the water; create confusion ⓑ〔宾语后面接"忙""累""急""气"等词，加上表示结果的补语，整个格式有致使的意思〕: 这一趟可～他累坏了。That trip really tired him out.
另见 bà

【把柄】 bǎbǐng handle: 给人抓住～ give sb. a handle (against oneself)

【把持】 bǎchí control; dominate; monopolize: ～一切 monopolize everything/ ～一部分权力 seize a certain amount of power

【把舵】 bǎduò hold the rudder; hold (或take, be at) the helm; steer

【把风】 bǎfēng keep watch (for one's partners in a clandestine activity); be on the lookout

【把关】 bǎguān ① guard a pass ② check on: 层层～ make checks at all levels/ 把好政治关 ensure political soundness/ 把好质量关 guarantee the quality (of products)

【把酒】 bǎjiǔ ① raise one's wine cup ② fill a wine cup for sb.

【把式】 bǎshi 〈口〉 ① *wushu* (武术): 练～ practise *wushu* ② person skilled in a trade: 车～ carter ③ skill: 学会木工的全套～ learn all the skills of carpentry 又作"把势"

【把守】 bǎshǒu guard: ～城门 guard a city gate/ 分兵～ divide up one's forces for defence

【把手】 bǎshou handle; grip; knob

【把头】 bǎtóu labour contractor; gangmaster

【把稳】 bǎwěn 〈方〉 trustworthy; dependable: 办事～ be dependable in what one does

【把握】 bǎwò ① hold; grasp: 透过现象，～本质 see through the phenomena to grasp the essence/ ～时机 seize the opportunity; seize the right time ② assurance; certainty: 没有成功的～ have no certainty of success/ 他很有～地回答了所有的问题。He answered all the questions with assurance./ 做这项工作，他很有～。He's quite sure he can do this job./ 不打无准备之仗，不打无～之仗。Fight no battle unprepared, fight no battle you are not sure of winning.

【把戏】 bǎxì ① acrobatics; jugglery ② cheap trick; game: 耍鬼～ play dirty tricks

【把兄弟】 bǎxiōngdì sworn brothers

## 钯

bǎ 〈化〉 palladium (Pd)

## 靶

bǎ target: 打～ shooting (或 target) practice

【靶场】 bǎchǎng shooting range; range

【靶船】 bǎchuán target ship

【靶机】 bǎjī target drone

【靶心】 bǎxīn bull's-eye

【靶纸】 bǎzhǐ target sheet

【靶子】 bǎzi target

# bà

## 把

bà ① grip; handle: 茶壶～儿 the handle of a teapot/ 枪～儿 rifle butt ② stem (of a leaf, flower or fruit)
另见 bǎ

【把子】 bàzi handle: 刀～ the handle of a knife/印～ (the handle of) an official seal

## 坝

bà ① dam ② dyke; embankment ③ 〈方〉 sandbar ④〔多用于地名〕 flatland; plain

## 爸

bà pa; dad; father

【爸爸】 bàba papa; dad; father

## 耙

bà ① harrow ② draw a harrow over (a field); harrow
另见 pá

## 罢

bà ① stop; cease: 欲～不能 try to stop but cannot; cannot refrain from carrying on ② dismiss: ～职 remove from office; dismiss ③ finish: 说～，他就走了。With these words he left.

【罢黜】 bàchù 〈书〉 ① dismiss from office ② ban; reject

【罢工】 bàgōng strike; go on strike

【罢官】 bàguān dismiss from office

【罢教】 bàjiào teachers' strike

【罢课】 bàkè students' strike

【罢了】 bàle 〈助〉〔用在句末，有"仅此而已"的意思〕: 这没有什么，我不过做了我应该做的事～。It's nothing. I've only done what I ought to do./ 你就是不想去～。You just don't want to go, that's all.

【罢了】 bàliǎo 〔表示容忍，有勉强放过暂不深究的意思〕: 他不肯也～，连个回信也不给。I wouldn't have minded his refusing, but he didn't even answer my letter.

【罢论】 bàlùn abandoned idea: 此事已作～。The idea has already been dropped.

【罢免】 bàmiǎn recall: 常委会由代表大会选举或者～。Members of the standing committee are elected and subject to recall by the congress. ◇ ～权 right of recall; recall

【罢市】 bàshì shopkeepers' strike

【罢手】 bàshǒu give up: 不试验成功，我们决不～。We will never stop until the experiment succeeds.

【罢休】 bàxiū give up; let the matter drop: 不达目的，决不～。We'll not stop until we reach our goal.

## 鲅

bà

【鲅鱼】 bàyú Spanish mackerel

## 霸

bà ① chief of feudal princes; overlord ② tyrant; despot; bully: 恶～ local tyrant (或 despot) ③ hegemonist power; hegemonism; hegemony: 反～斗争 the struggle against hegemonism/ 超级大国争～世界。The superpowers are contending for world hegemony. ④ dominate; lord it over; tyrannize over: 军阀割据，各～一方。The country was torn by warlordism, with each warlord dominating a region.

【霸道】 bàdào (feudal) rule by force

【霸道】 bàdao ① overbearing; high-handed ② (of liquor, medicine, etc.) strong; potent

【霸权】 bàquán hegemony; supremacy ◇ ～主义 hegemonism

【霸王】 bàwáng ①(Bàwáng) Xiang Yu the Conqueror (项羽, 232-202 B.C.) ② overlord: despot
【霸王鞭】 bàwángbiān ① a rattle stick used in folk dancing ② rattle stick dance
【霸占】 bàzhàn forcibly occupy; seize: ～别国领土 forcibly occupy the territory of another country
【霸主】 bàzhǔ ① a powerful chief of the princes of the Spring and Autumn Period (770-476 B.C.) ② overlord; hegemon: 海上～ maritime overlord

## ba

**吧** ba 〈助〉①〔在句末表示商量、提议、请求、命令〕: 咱们走～。Let's go./ 你好好儿想想～! Just think it over. ②〔在句末表示同意或认可〕: 明天就明天～。All right, let's make it tomorrow. ③〔在句末表示疑问或不肯定〕: 他会来～? He'll come, won't he?/ 他好象是这么说的～。That's what he said, it seems. ④〔在句中表示停顿,带假设的语气〕: 打～, 打不下去,跑～,跑不了,敌人只好投降。Unable to fight on or to escape, the enemy were forced to surrender.
另见 bā

## bāi

**掰** bāi break off with the fingers and thumb: 把饼～成两半 break the cake in two/ ～玉米 break off corncobs/ 一分钱～成两半花 watch every penny/ ～着手指算 count on one's fingers
【掰腕子】 bāi wànzi hand wrestling

## bái

**白** bái ① white: 几根～发 a few white (或 grey) hairs/ 皮肤～ have a fair complexion ② clear: 真相大～。Everything is clear now. 或 The whole truth has come out. ③ pure; plain; blank: ～开水 plain boiled water/ ～纸 a blank sheet of paper ④ in vain; for nothing: ～忙了半天 go to a lot of trouble for nothing/ ～跑一趟 make a fruitless trip/ 烈士们的鲜血没有～流。The martyrs did not shed their blood in vain. ⑤ free of charge; gratis: ～送 give away free (of charge)/ ～给我也不要。I wouldn't take it even as a gift. ⑥ White (as a symbol of reaction): ～军 the White army ⑦ (of a Chinese character) wrongly written or mispronounced: 念～字 mispronounce a character ⑧ spoken part in opera, etc.: 独～ soliloquy; monologue/ 对～ dialogue ⑨ state; explain: 自～ confessions ⑩ dialect: 苏～ Suzhou dialect ⑪ (Bái) a surname
【白矮星】 bái'ǎixīng 〈天〉 white dwarf
【白白】 báibái in vain; to no purpose; for nothing: 不要让时光～过去。Don't let time slip by.
【白班儿】 báibānr 〈口〉 day shift
【白报纸】 báibàozhǐ newsprint
【白璧微瑕】 báibì wēi xiá a flaw in white jade — a slight blemish
【白璧无瑕】 báibì wú xiá flawless white jade — impeccable moral integrity
【白醭】 báibú mould (on the surface of vinegar, soy sauce, etc.)
【白卜鲔】 báibǔwěi 〈动〉 wavyback skipjack
【白布】 báibù plain white cloth; calico
【白菜】 báicài Chinese cabbage
【白痴】 báichī ① idiocy ② idiot
【白炽】 báichì white heat; incandescence ◇ ～灯 incandescent lamp
【白搭】 báidā 〈口〉 no use; no good: 和他辩也是～。It's no use arguing with him.
【白带】 báidài 〈医〉 leucorrhoea; whites
【白蛋白】 báidànbái 〈生化〉 albumin
【白道】 báidào 〈天〉 moon's path
【白癜风】 báidiànfēng 〈医〉 vitiligo
【白垩】 bái'è chalk
【白垩纪】 Bái'èjì 〈地〉 the Cretaceous period
【白矾】 báifán alum
【白饭】 báifàn plain cooked rice; rice with nothing to go with it
【白匪】 báifěi White bandits
【白费】 báifèi waste: ～力气(唇舌) waste one's energy (breath)/ ～心思 bother one's head for nothing
【白粉病】 báifěnbìng 〈农〉 powdery mildew
【白干儿】 báigānr 见"白酒"
【白宫】 Bái Gōng the White House
【白姑鱼】 báigūyú white Chinese croaker
【白骨】 báigǔ bones of the dead ◇ ～精 the White Bone Demon (in the novel *Pilgrimage to the West*《西游记》)
【白骨顶】 báigǔdǐng 〈动〉 coot
【白果】 báiguǒ 〈植〉 ginkgo; gingko
【白鹤】 báihè 〈动〉 white crane
【白喉】 báihóu 〈医〉 diphtheria
【白狐】 báihú arctic fox
【白花花】 báihuāhuā shining white: ～的胡子 silky white beard/ ～的银子 gleaming silver (coins)/ ～的流水 foaming water
【白花蛇】 báihuāshé long-noded pit viper (*Agkistrodon acutus*)
【白化病】 báihuàbìng albinism ◇ ～人 albino
【白话】 báihuà vernacular ◇ ～诗 free verse written in the vernacular/ ～文 writings in the vernacular
【白桦】 báihuà 〈植〉 white birch
【白芨】 báijī 〈中药〉 the tuber of hyacinth bletilla (*Bletilla striata*)
【白僵蚕】 báijiāngcán 〈中药〉 the larva of a silkworm with batrytis
【白金】 báijīn platinum
【白金汉宫】 Báijīnhàn Gōng Buckingham Palace
【白净】 báijing (of skin) fair and clear
【白酒】 báijiǔ spirit usu. distilled from sorghum or maize; white spirit
【白卷】 báijuàn blank examination paper: 交～ hand in a blank examination paper; hand in an examination paper unanswered
【白开水】 báikāishuǐ plain boiled water
【白口铁】 báikǒutiě white iron
【白蜡】 báilà white wax; insect wax ◇ ～虫 wax insect
【白镴】 báilà solder
【白兰地】 báilándì brandy
【白痢】 báilì ①〈中医〉 dysentery characterized by white mucous stool ②〈牧〉 white diarrhoea
【白鲢】 báilián silver carp
【白脸】 báiliǎn white face, face painting in Beijing opera, etc., traditionally for the villain: 唱～ play the villain; pretend to be harsh and severe
【白磷】 báilín 〈化〉 white phosphorus
【白蛉】 báilíng sand fly ◇ ～热〈医〉 sand-fly fever
【白令海】 Báilìnghǎi the Bering Sea
【白榴石】 báiliúshí 〈矿〉 leucite
【白鹭】 báilù 〈动〉 egret
【白露】 Báilù White Dew (15th solar term)

【白茫茫】 báimángmáng (of mist, snow, floodwater, etc.) a vast expanse of whiteness: 下了一场大雪，田野上～一片。After the heavy snow, the fields were a vast expanse of whiteness.
【白茅】 báimáo 〈植〉 cogongrass (*Imperata cylindrica*) ◇ ～根〈中药〉 cogongrass rhizome
【白煤】 báiméi ①〈方〉 anthracite; hard coal ② white coal; waterpower
【白米】 báimǐ (polished) rice ◇ ～饭 (cooked) rice
【白棉纸】 báimiánzhǐ stencil tissue paper
【白面】 báimiàn wheat flour; flour
【白面儿】 báimiànr heroin
【白面书生】 báimiàn shūshēng pale-faced scholar
【白描】 báimiáo ①〈美术〉 line drawing in traditional ink and brush style ② simple, straightforward style of writing
【白木耳】 báimù'ěr tremella
【白内障】 báinèizhàng 〈医〉 cataract ◇ ～摘除术 cataract extraction
【白砒】 báipī 〈化〉 white arsenic; arsenic trioxide
【白皮书】 báipíshū white paper; white book
【白皮松】 báipísōng lacebark pine
【白旗】 báiqí white flag
【白区】 báiqū White area (the Kuomintang-controlled area during the Second Revolutionary Civil War, 1927-1937)
【白屈菜】 báiqūcài 〈植〉 greater celandine
【白热】 báirè white heat; incandescence
【白热化】 báirèhuà turn white-hot: 争论达到了～的程度。The debate became white-hot.
【白人】 báirén white man or woman
【白刃】 báirèn naked sword ◇ ～战 bayonet charge; hand-to-hand combat
【白日做梦】 báirì zuòmèng daydream; indulge in wishful thinking
【白肉】 báiròu plain boiled pork
【白色】 báisè ① white (colour) ② White (as a symbol of reaction)
◇ ～据点 White stronghold; stronghold of reaction/ ～恐怖 White terror/ ～政权 White regime
【白色人种】 báisè rénzhǒng the white race
【白色体】 báisètǐ 〈植〉 leucoplast
【白芍】 báisháo 〈中药〉 (peeled) root of herbaceous peony (*Paeonia lactiflora*)
【白手起家】 báishǒu qǐjiā build up from nothing; start from scratch
【白薯】 báishǔ sweet potato
【白水泥】 báishuǐní 〈建〉 white cement
【白苏】 báisū 〈植〉 common perilla
【白糖】 báitáng (refined) white sugar
【白陶】 báitáo 〈考古〉 white pottery (of the Shang Dynasty, c. 16th-11th century B.C.)
【白体】 báitǐ 〈印〉 lean type
【白天】 báitiān daytime; day
【白铁】 báitiě galvanized iron
【白厅】 Bái Tīng Whitehall
【白铜】 báitóng copper-nickel alloy
【白头】 báitóu hoary head; old age
【白头偕老】 báitóu xiélǎo live to ripe old age in conjugal bliss; remain a devoted couple to the end of their lives
【白头翁】 báitóuwēng ①〈中药〉 the root of Chinese pulsatilla ②〈动〉 Chinese bulbul
【白文】 báiwén ① the text of an annotated book ② an unannotated edition of a book ③ intagliated characters (on a seal)
【白钨矿】 báiwūkuàng scheelite
【白细胞】 báixìbāo 〈生理〉 white blood cell; leucocyte
【白鲜】 báixiān 〈植〉 shaggy-fruited dittany (*Dictamnus dasycarpus*) ◇ ～皮〈中药〉 the root bark of shaggy-fruited dittany
【白鹇】 báixián 〈动〉 silver pheasant
【白熊】 báixióng polar bear; white bear
【白血病】 báixuèbìng leukaemia
【白血球】 báixuèqiú 〈生理〉 white blood cell; leucocyte
【白鲟】 báixún Chinese paddlefish
【白眼】 báiyǎn supercilious look: ～看人 treat people superciliously; look upon people with disdain/ 遭人～ be treated with disdain
【白眼珠】 báiyǎnzhū 〈口〉 the white of the eye
【白杨】 báiyáng 〈植〉 white poplar
【白药】 báiyào 〈中药〉 *baiyao*, a white medicinal powder for treating haemorrhage, wounds, bruises, etc.
【白夜】 báiyè 〈天〉 white night
【白衣战士】 báiyī zhànshì warrior in white; medical worker
【白蚁】 báiyǐ termite; white ant
【白银】 báiyín silver
【白鱼】 báiyú whitefish
【白云苍狗】 báiyún-cānggǒu white clouds change into grey dogs — the changes in human affairs often take freakish forms
【白云母】 báiyúnmǔ 〈矿〉 muscovite; white mica
【白云石】 báiyúnshí 〈矿〉 dolomite
【白芷】 báizhǐ 〈中药〉 the root of Dahurian angelica
【白纸黑字】 báizhǐ-hēizì (written) in black and white
【白种】 báizhǒng the white race
【白昼】 báizhòu daytime
【白术】 báizhú 〈中药〉 the rhizome of large-headed atractylodes (*Atractylodes macrocephala*)
【白字】 báizì wrongly written or mispronounced character: ～连篇 pages and pages of wrongly written characters
【白族】 Báizú the Bai (Pai) nationality, living in Yunnan

## bǎi

**百** bǎi ① hundred ② numerous; all kinds of: ～花盛开 a hundred flowers in bloom/ ～忙之中 in the midst of pressing affairs; despite many claims on one's time/ ～问不厌，～拿不烦 (of a shop assistant) patiently answer any questions the customers ask and show them any goods they want to see
【百般】 bǎibān in a hundred and one ways; in every possible way; by every means: ～咒骂 abuse in every possible way; heap abuse on/ ～抵赖 try by every means to deny/ ～刁难 create all sorts of obstacles; put up innumerable obstacles/ ～奉承 flatter sedulously/ ～照顾 show sb. every consideration
【百倍】 bǎibèi a hundredfold; a hundred times: 展望未来，信心～ look to the future with full confidence
【百步穿杨】 bǎi bù chuān yáng shoot an arrow through a willow leaf a hundred paces away; shoot with great precision
【百部】 bǎibù 〈中药〉 the tuber of stemona (*Stemona japonica* 或 *Stemona sessilifolia*)
【百尺竿头，更进一步】 bǎi chǐ gāntóu, gèng jìn yī bù make still further progress
【百川归海】 bǎi chuān guī hǎi all rivers flow to the sea; all things tend in one direction
【百读不厌】 bǎi dú bù yàn be worth reading a hundred times: 这本书～。You never get tired of reading this book.
【百端待举】 bǎi duān dài jǔ a thousand things remain to be done; numerous tasks remain to be undertaken

【百儿八十】 bǎi'erbāshí 〈口〉 about a hundred; a hundred or so
【百发百中】 bǎifā-bǎizhòng a hundred shots, a hundred bull's-eyes; every shot hits the target; shoot with unfailing accuracy; be a crack shot
【百废俱兴】 bǎi fèi jù xīng all neglected tasks are being undertaken — full-scale reconstruction is under way
【百分比】 bǎifēnbǐ percentage: 按～计算 in terms of percentage
【百分率】 bǎifēnlǜ percentage; per cent
【百分数】 bǎifēnshù percentage
【百分之百】 bǎifēn zhī bǎi a hundred per cent; out and out; absolutely: 有～的把握 be a hundred per cent sure; be absolutely certain/ 这是～的谎话。That's an out-and-out lie!
【百分制】 bǎifēnzhì hundred-mark system
【百感交集】 bǎi gǎn jiāojí all sorts of feelings well up in one's heart
【百合】 bǎihé 〈植〉 lily
【百花齐放，百家争鸣】 bǎihuā qífàng, bǎijiā zhēngmíng let a hundred flowers blossom and a hundred schools of thought contend (a policy set forth by Chairman Mao for promoting the progress of the arts and the sciences and the development of a flourishing socialist culture)
【百花齐放，推陈出新】 bǎihuā qífàng, tuīchén-chūxīn let a hundred flowers blossom, weed through the old to bring forth the new (a policy set forth by Chairman Mao for transforming and developing theatrical art)
【百货】 bǎihuò general merchandise: 日用～ articles of daily use ◇ ～商店 department store; general store
【百家争鸣】 bǎijiā zhēngmíng ① contention of a hundred schools of thought (during the Spring and Autumn and Warring States Periods, 770-221 B.C.) ② let a hundred schools of thought contend 参见"百花齐放，百家争鸣"
【百科全书】 bǎikē quánshū encyclopaedia
【百孔千疮】 bǎikǒng-qiānchuāng riddled with gaping wounds; afflicted with all ills
【百里挑一】 bǎi lǐ tiāo yī one in a hundred; cream of the crop
【百炼成钢】 bǎi liàn chéng gāng be tempered into steel: 在革命斗争中～ be tempered in revolutionary struggle
【百灵】 bǎilíng 〈动〉 lark
【百米赛跑】 bǎi mǐ sàipǎo 100-metre dash
【百慕大】 Bǎimùdà Bermuda ◇ ～人 Bermudan
【百乃定】 bǎinǎidìng 〈药〉 panadin
【百年】 bǎinián ① a hundred years; a century: ～不遇的大水灾 the biggest flood in a century ② lifetime: ～之后〈婉〉 when sb. has passed away; after sb.'s death ◇ ～纪念 centenary; centennial
【百年大计】 bǎinián dàjì a project of vital and lasting importance: 基本建设是～，要求质量第一。Capital construction projects, which are to last for generations, call for good quality above everything else.
【百日咳】 bǎirìké whooping cough; pertussis ◇ ～疫苗 pertussis vaccine
【百十】 bǎishí a hundred or so: ～户人家 about a hundred households
【百事通】 bǎishìtōng ① knowledgeable person ② know-all
【百思不解】 bǎi sī bù jiě remain puzzled after pondering over sth. a hundred times; remain perplexed despite much thought
【百听不厌】 bǎi tīng bù yàn worth hearing a hundred times: 这个故事～。You never get tired of hearing this story.
【百万】 bǎiwàn million: ～雄师 a million bold warriors ◇ ～吨级 megaton/ ～富翁 millionaire
【百闻不如一见】 bǎi wén bùrú yī jiàn it is better to see once than hear a hundred times; seeing for oneself is a hundred times better than hearing from others
【百无聊赖】 bǎi wú liáolài bored to death; bored stiff; overcome with boredom
【百无一失】 bǎi wú yī shī no danger of anything going wrong; no risk at all
【百姓】 bǎixìng common people
【百叶窗】 bǎiyèchuāng shutter; blind; jalousie
【百叶箱】 bǎiyèxiāng 〈气〉 thermometer screen
【百依百顺】 bǎiyī-bǎishùn docile and obedient; all obedience
【百战百胜】 bǎizhàn-bǎishèng fight a hundred battles, win a hundred victories; emerge victorious in every battle; be ever-victorious
【百折不挠】 bǎi zhé bù náo keep on fighting in spite of all setbacks; be undaunted by repeated setbacks; be indomitable 又作"百折不回"
【百足之虫，死而不僵】 bǎi zú zhī chóng, sǐ ér bù jiāng a centipede does not topple over even when dead; a centipede dies but never falls down; old institutions die hard

**伯** bǎi 见"大伯子" dàbǎizi
另见 bó

**佰** bǎi hundred (used for the numeral 百 on cheques, etc. to avoid mistakes or alterations)

**柏** bǎi cypress
另见 bò
【柏树】 bǎishù cypress
【柏油】 bǎiyóu pitch; tar; asphalt ◇ ～混凝土 tar concrete/ ～路 asphalt road/ ～喷洒机 tar sprayer
【柏子仁】 bǎizǐrén 〈中药〉 the seed of Oriental arborvitae

**捭** bǎi 见"纵横捭阖" zònghéng-bǎihé

**摆** bǎi ① put; place; arrange: 把药瓶～在架子上 put the medicine bottles on the shelf/ 把碗筷～好 set (或 lay) the table/ 各种标本～了一桌子。The table was loaded with all kinds of specimens./ ～在我们面前的任务 the task confronting us/ 把问题～到桌面上来 place the problem on the table; bring the issue out into the open/ ～正个人和集体的关系 put oneself in a correct relationship to the collective/ 水库工地～战场。The reservoir construction site was like a battlefield, seething with activity. ② lay bare; state clearly: ～矛盾 lay bare the contradictions/ 把有利和不利的条件～一～ set forth the advantages and disadvantages ③ put on; assume: ～威风 give oneself airs; put on airs/ ～出一副吓人的架势 assume an intimidating posture/ ～老资格 flaunt one's seniority; put on the airs of a veteran ④ sway; wave: 他～手叫我走开。He waved me away. ⑤ 〈物〉 pendulum: 单～ simple pendulum/ 复～ compound pendulum
【摆布】 bǎibu order about; manipulate: 任人～ allow oneself to be ordered about; be at the mercy of others
【摆荡吊环】 bǎidàng diàohuán 〈体〉 swinging rings
【摆动】 bǎidòng swing; sway: 柳条迎风～。The willows swayed in the breeze./ 指示针来回～。The pointer flickered.
【摆渡】 bǎidù ferry
【摆架子】 bǎi jiàzi put on airs; assume great airs
【摆阔】 bǎikuò parade one's wealth; be ostentatious and extravagant

【摆龙门阵】 bǎi lóngménzhèn 〈方〉 chat; gossip; spin a yarn
【摆轮】 bǎilún balance (of a watch or clock); balance wheel
【摆门面】 bǎi ménmiàn keep up appearances
【摆弄】 bǎinòng ① move back and forth; fiddle with: 你别来回～那几盆花了。Don't move those flower pots back and forth. ② order about; manipulate
【摆设】 bǎishè furnish and decorate (a room): 屋里～得很雅致。The room is tastefully furnished.
【摆设儿】 bǎisher ornaments; furnishings: 小～ knick-knacks
【摆事实，讲道理】 bǎi shìshí, jiǎng dàoli present the facts and reason things out
【摆摊子】 bǎi tānzi ① set up a stall ② maintain a large staff or organization
【摆脱】 bǎituō cast off; shake off; break away from; free (或 extricate) oneself from: ～殖民主义的桎梏 cast off the yoke of colonialism/ ～贫穷落后的状态 be lifted out of poverty and backwardness/ 有助于妇女～繁重的家务劳动 help to free women from household chores/ ～困境 extricate oneself from a predicament
【摆样子】 bǎi yàngzi do sth. for show: 他的自我批评是认真的，不是～的。His self-criticism was serious and not made for show.
【摆钟】 bǎizhōng pendulum clock
【摆子】 bǎizi 〈方〉 malaria: 打～ have malaria

## bài

**败** bài ① be defeated; lose: ～军之将 a defeated general/ ～下阵来 lose a battle/ 主队以二比三～于客队。The home team lost to the visitors 2 to 3. ② defeat; beat: 大～侵略军 inflict a severe defeat on the invading troops ③ fail: 成～ success or failure ④ spoil: 事情可能就～在他手里。He may spoil the whole show. ⑤ counteract: ～毒 counteract a toxin ⑥ decay; wither: 枯枝～叶 dead twigs and withered leaves/ 大寨红花开不～。The red flowers of Dazhai will never fade.
【败北】 bàiběi 〈书〉 suffer defeat; lose a battle
【败笔】 bàibǐ ① a faulty stroke in calligraphy or painting ② a faulty expression in writing
【败坏】 bàihuài ruin; corrupt; undermine: ～名誉 discredit; defame/ 道德～ morally degenerate/～风俗 corrupt morals; exert a bad moral influence/ ～社会风气 corrupt social values
【败火】 bàihuǒ 〈中医〉 relieve inflammation or internal heat
【败绩】 bàijī 〈书〉 be utterly defeated; be routed
【败家子】 bàijiāzǐ spendthrift; wastrel; prodigal
【败局】 bàijú lost game; losing battle
【败类】 bàilèi scum of a community; degenerate: 民族～ scum of a nation
【败露】 bàilù (of a plot, etc.) fall through and stand exposed: 阴谋终于～。In the end the conspiracy was brought to light.
【败落】 bàiluò decline (in wealth and position): 这部小说反映了一个封建家庭的～。This novel reflects the decline of a feudal family.
【败诉】 bàisù lose a lawsuit
【败退】 bàituì retreat in defeat: 敌军节节～。Again and again the enemy retreated in defeat.
【败胃】 bàiwèi spoil one's appetite
【败兴】 bàixìng disappointed: ～而归 come back disappointed
【败血症】 bàixuèzhèng 〈医〉 septicaemia
【败仗】 bàizhàng lost battle; defeat: 打～ be defeated in battle; suffer a defeat
【败阵】 bàizhèn be defeated on the battlefield; be beaten in a contest: ～而逃 lose the field and take to flight
【败子回头】 bàizǐ huítóu return of the prodigal son

**拜** bài ① do obeisance: ～佛 prostrate oneself before the image of Buddha; worship Buddha ② make a courtesy call: 回～ pay a return visit ③ acknowledge sb. as one's master, godfather, etc.: ～贫下中农为老师 take the poor and lower-middle peasants as one's teachers ④ 〈敬〉〔用于动词之前〕: ～读大作 have the pleasure of perusing your work/ ～谢 express one's thanks
【拜把子】 bài bǎzi become sworn brothers
【拜别】 bàibié 〈敬〉 take leave of
【拜倒】 bàidǎo prostrate oneself; fall on one's knees; grovel: ～在帝国主义脚下的买办文人 comprador scholars who grovel (或 lie prostrate) at the feet of the imperialists
【拜访】 bàifǎng pay a visit; call on: 正式～ formal visit/专诚～ make a special trip to call on sb.
【拜会】 bàihuì 〔多用于外交场合〕 pay an official call; call on: 告别～ farewell call/ 礼节性～ courtesy call/ 私人～ personal visit (或 call)
【拜火教】 Bàihuǒjiào Zoroastrianism; Mazdaism
【拜见】 bàijiàn ① pay a formal visit; call to pay respects ② meet one's senior or superior
【拜金主义】 bàijīnzhǔyì money worship
【拜年】 bàinián pay a New Year call; wish sb. a Happy New Year: 给军属～ pay New Year calls to servicemen's families/ 大妈，我们给您～来啦！Auntie, we've come to wish you a Happy New Year.
【拜寿】 bàishòu congratulate an elderly person on his birthday; offer birthday felicitations
【拜托】 bàituō 〈敬〉 request sb. to do sth.: ～您捎个信给他。Would you be kind enough to take a message to him?
【拜望】 bàiwàng 〈敬〉 call to pay one's respects; call on
【拜物教】 bàiwùjiào fetishism: 商品～ commodity fetishism
【拜谒】 bàiyè ① pay a formal visit; call to pay respects ② pay homage (at a monument, mausoleum, etc.)
【拜占庭帝国】 Bàizhàntíng Dìguó the Byzantine Empire (395-1453)

**稗** bài ① barnyard grass ② 〈书〉 insignificant; unofficial
【稗官野史】 bàiguān-yěshǐ books containing anecdotes
【稗子】 bàizi 〈植〉 barnyard grass; barnyard millet

## bān

**扳** bān pull; turn: ～倒 pull down/ ～枪栓 pull back the bolt of a rifle/ ～道岔 pull railway switches/ ～着指头算 count on one's fingers/ ～成平局 equalize the score
【扳不倒儿】 bānbùdǎor 〈口〉 tumbler; roly-poly
【扳道员】 bāndàoyuán 〈交〉 pointsman; switchman
【扳机】 bānjī trigger
【扳手】 bānshou ① spanner; wrench ② lever (on a machine)
【扳子】 bānzi spanner; wrench

**班** bān ① class; team: 学习～ study class/ 作业～ work team ② shift; duty: 三～倒 work in three shifts/ 上夜～ be on night shift/ 轮～护理病人 take turns tending the sick ③ 〈军〉 squad ④ 〈量〉 ⓐ〔用于人群〕: 这～青年人真了不起。They're a fine bunch of young people. ⓑ〔用于定时开行的交通运输工具〕: 搭下一～火车 take the next train/ 末～车 last bus, train, etc. (of the day)/ 一路公共汽车每隔三分钟就有一～。There's a Number One bus every three minutes. ⑤ regularly-run; regular; scheduled: ～机 regular air service ⑥ (Bān) a surname

【班巴拉语】 Bānbālāyǔ Bambara (language)

【班车】 bānchē regular bus (service)

【班次】 bāncì ① order of classes or grades at school: 在学校时，她～比我高。At school she was in a higher class than me. ② number of runs or flights: 增加货车～ increase the number of runs of freight trains

【班底】 bāndǐ ordinary members of a theatrical troupe

【班房】 bānfáng 〈口〉 jail: 坐～ be (put) in jail

【班机】 bānjī airliner; regular air service: 京沪～ scheduled flights between Beijing and Shanghai

【班级】 bānjí classes and grades in school

【班轮】 bānlún regular passenger or cargo ship; regular steamship service

【班门弄斧】 Bān mén nòng fǔ show off one's proficiency with the axe before Lu Ban (鲁班) the master carpenter—display one's slight skill before an expert

【班期】 bānqī schedule (for flights, voyages, etc.) ◇ ～表 a table of scheduled flights, voyages, etc.; timetable

【班师】 bānshī 〈书〉 withdraw troops from the front; return after victory

【班图人】 Bāntúrén Bantu

【班图语】 Bāntúyǔ Bantu (language)

【班务会】 bānwùhuì a routine meeting of a squad, team or class

【班长】 bānzhǎng ① class monitor ② 〈军〉 squad leader ③ (work) team leader

【班主任】 bānzhǔrèn a teacher in charge of a class

【班子】 bānzi ① 〈旧〉 theatrical troupe ② organized group: 领导～ a leading body (或 group)/ 生产～ a team in charge of production/ 专业～ a special, full-time group

【班组】 bān-zǔ teams and groups (in factories, etc.) ◇ ～竞赛 emulation between teams or groups; emulation at the team or group level

**般** bān sort; kind; way: 百～ in every possible way/ 这～ such; this kind of/ 暴风雨～的掌声 stormy (或 thunderous) applause/ 兄弟～的情谊 fraternal feelings

**颁** bān promulgate; issue

【颁布】 bānbù promulgate; issue; publish: ～法令 promulgate (或 issue) a decree

【颁发】 bānfā ① issue; promulgate: ～嘉奖令 issue an order of commendation ② award: ～奖章 award a medal

【颁行】 bānxíng issue for enforcement

**斑** bān ① spot; speck; speckle; stripe: 油～ oil stains; grease spots ② spotted; striped

【斑白】 bānbái grizzled; greying: 两鬓～ greying at the temples

【斑斑】 bānbān full of stains or spots: 血迹～ bloodstained

【斑驳】 bānbó 〈书〉 mottled; motley

【斑驳陆离】 bānbó-lùlí variegated

【斑翅山鹑】 bānchì shānchún partridge

【斑点】 bāndiǎn spot; stain; speckle

【斑鸠】 bānjiū turtledove

【斑斓】 bānlán gorgeous; bright-coloured; multicoloured: 五彩～ a riot of colour

【斑羚】 bānlíng goral

【斑马】 bānmǎ zebra

【斑蝥】 bānmáo 〈动〉 Chinese blister beetle; cantharides

【斑铜矿】 bāntóngkuàng bornite

【斑纹】 bānwén stripe; streak

【斑岩】 bānyán 〈地〉 porphyry

【斑疹】 bānzhěn 〈医〉 macula ◇ ～伤寒 typhus

【斑竹】 bānzhú mottled bamboo

**搬** bān ① take away; move; remove: 把桌子～走 take the table away/ ～山填沟 raze hills to fill gullies/ ～掉绊脚石 remove a stumbling block/ ～起石头打自己的脚 lift a rock only to drop it on one's own feet/ 把工农兵英雄人物形象～上舞台 present worker, peasant and soldier heroes on the stage/ ～救兵 call in reinforcements; ask for help ② move (house): 他早就～走了。He moved out long ago. ③ apply indiscriminately; copy mechanically: 生～硬套 copy mechanically and apply indiscriminately

【搬家】 bānjiā move (house): 我们下星期～。We're moving next week.

【搬弄】 bānnòng ① move sth. about; fiddle with: 别～枪栓。Don't fiddle with the rifle bolt. ② show off; display: ～学问 show off one's erudition

【搬弄是非】 bānnòng shìfēi sow discord; tell tales; make mischief

【搬运】 bānyùn carry; transport: ～货物 transport goods ◇ ～工人（车站等）porter;（码头）docker

**瘢** bān scar

【瘢痕】 bānhén scar

**癍** bān abnormal pigmentary deposits on the skin; flecks

## bǎn

**阪** bǎn 〈书〉 slope

**板** bǎn ① board; plank; plate: 切菜～ chopping block/ 混凝土～ concrete slab/ 玻璃～ plate glass; glass top (of a desk)/钢～ steel plate ② shutter: 上～儿 put up the shutters ③（乒乓球）bat;（板羽球）battledore ④ 〈乐〉 clappers ⑤ an accented beat in traditional Chinese music; time; measure: 一～三眼 one accented beat and three unaccented beats in a bar ⑥ hard: 地～了，锄不动。The ground is too hard to hoe. ⑦ stiff; unnatural: 我这张照片照得太～了。I look too stiff in this picture. ⑧ stop smiling; look serious: ～起面孔 put on a stern expression/ ～着脸 keep a straight face

【板板六十四】 bǎnbǎn liùshí sì unaccommodating; rigid

【板壁】 bǎnbì wooden partition

【板擦儿】 bǎncār blackboard eraser

【板锉】 bǎncuò flat file

【板凳】 bǎndèng wooden bench or stool

【板斧】 bǎnfǔ broad axe

【板鼓】 bǎngǔ 〈乐〉 a small drum for marking time

【板规】 bǎnguī 〈机〉 plate gauge

【板胡】 bǎnhú 〈乐〉 a bowed stringed instrument with a thin wooden soundboard

【板结】 bǎnjié harden: ～的土壤 hardened and impervious soil

【板栗】 bǎnlì Chinese chestnut

【板梁桥】 bǎnliángqiáo plate girder bridge

【板皮】 bǎnpí 〈林〉 slab

【板上钉钉】 bǎnshàng dìng dīng that clinches it; that's final; no two ways about it

【板书】 bǎnshū writing on the blackboard

【板刷】 bǎnshuā scrubbing brush

【板条】 bǎntiáo 〈建〉 lath

【板条箱】 bǎntiáoxiāng crate

【板鸭】 bǎnyā pressed (或 dried) salted duck
【板牙】 bǎnyá ① 〈方〉 front tooth; incisor ② 〈方〉 molar ③ 〈机〉 screw die; threading die ◇ ～扳手 stock and die
【板烟】 bǎnyān plug (of tobacco)
【板岩】 bǎnyán 〈地〉 slate
【板眼】 bǎnyǎn ① measure in traditional Chinese music ② orderliness: 他说话有板有眼。Whatever he says is well presented./ 她做事很有～。She is very methodical in her work.
【板油】 bǎnyóu leaf fat; leaf lard
【板羽球】 bǎnyǔqiú ① battledore and shuttlecock ② shuttlecock
【板纸】 bǎnzhǐ paperboard; board: 草～ strawboard/ 牛皮～ kraft board
【板滞】 bǎnzhì stiff; dull
【板桩】 bǎnzhuāng 〈建〉 sheet pile
【板子】 bǎnzi ① board; plank ② bamboo or birch for corporal punishment

**版** bǎn ① printing plate (或 block): 铜～ copperplate/ 制～ plate making ② edition: 初～ first edition/ 绝～ out of print ③ page (of a newspaper): 头～新闻 front-page news
【版本】 bǎnběn edition
【版次】 bǎncì the order in which editions are printed
【版画】 bǎnhuà a picture printed from an engraved or etched plate; print
【版刻】 bǎnkè carving; engraving
【版面】 bǎnmiàn ① space of a whole page ② layout (或 makeup) of a printed sheet ◇ ～设计 layout
【版权】 bǎnquán copyright: ～所有 all rights reserved ◇ ～页 copyright page; colophon
【版式】 bǎnshì format
【版税】 bǎnshuì royalty (on books)
【版图】 bǎntú domain; territory: ～辽阔 vast in territory

## bàn

**办** bàn ① do; handle; manage; tackle; attend to: 大～农业 go in for agriculture in a big way/ 群众发动起来，事情就好～了。Once the masses are mobilized, things can be done easily./ 这点事她一个人～得了。She can handle (或 tackle) this by herself./ 我有点事得～一～。I have something to attend to./ 在中央的统一计划下，让地方～更多的事。Let the localities undertake more work under unified central planning. ② set up; run: 县～工厂 a county-run factory/ ～学习班 run (或 organize) a study class/ 勤俭～社 run the people's communes industriously and thriftily/ 村里新～了一所中学。A new middle school has been set up in the village. ③ buy a fair amount of; get sth. ready: ～年货 do New Year shopping; do shopping for the Spring Festival/ ～酒席 prepare a feast ④ punish (by law); bring to justice: 严～ punish severely
【办案】 bàn'àn handle a case
【办报】 bànbào run a newspaper
【办到】 bàndào get sth. done; accomplish: 原来认为办不到的事，现在～了。What was thought impossible has now been done./ 时代不同了，男女都一样。男同志能～的事情，女同志也能办得到。Times have changed, and today men and women are equal. Whatever men comrades can accomplish, women comrades can too.
【办法】 bànfǎ way; means; measure: 找出克服困难的～ find a way to overcome a difficulty/ 用切实的～来改进我们的工作 adopt effective measures to improve our work
【办公】 bàngōng handle official business; work (usu. in an office)
◇ ～费 administrative expenses/ ～时间 office hours/ ～室 office/ ～厅 general office/ ～桌 desk; bureau
【办理】 bànlǐ handle; conduct; transact: ～进出口业务 handle imports and exports/ ～手续 go through the formalities (或 procedure)/ 这些事情你可以斟酌～。You may handle these matters as you see fit.
【办事】 bànshì handle affairs; work: ～公正 be fair and just in handling affairs/ ～认真 be conscientious in one's work/ 按原则～ act according to principles
◇ ～处 office; agency/ ～机构 administrative body; working body/ ～员 office worker/ ～组 administrative group
【办学】 bànxué run a school ◇ ～方针 guiding principle for running a school
【办罪】 bànzuì punish

**半** bàn ① half; semi-: ～小时 half an hour/ 一个～月 a month and a half; one and a half months/ ～年 six months/ 增加一倍～ increase by 150%/ ～机械化 semi-mechanized ② in the middle; halfway: ～夜 midnight/ ～山腰 halfway up a hill ③ very little; the least bit: 他连～句话都不说。He wouldn't breathe a word. ④ partly; about half: ～开玩笑地说 say sth. half jokingly/ 房门～开着。The door was left half open./ 给打了个～死 be beaten within an inch of one's life
【半百】 bànbǎi fifty (years of age): 年近～ getting on for fifty; approaching fifty
【半…半…】 bàn...bàn... 〔分别用在意义相反的两个词或词素前面，表示相对的两种性质或状态同时存在〕: 半文半白 half literary, half vernacular/ 半饥半饱 underfed/ 半推半就 yield with a show of reluctance/ 半心半意 half-hearted/ 半信半疑 half-believing, half-doubting; not quite convinced/ 半真半假 half-genuine, half-sham; partly true, partly false/ 半嗔半喜 half-annoyed, half-pleased
【半半拉拉】 bànbanlālā 〈口〉 incomplete; unfinished: 这点活儿干完算了，别剩下～的。Let's finish the job off. Don't leave a lot of loose ends hanging over.
【半辈子】 bànbèizi half a lifetime
【半壁江山】 bànbì jiāngshān half of the country (usu. referring to the unoccupied part of an invaded country)
【半边】 bànbiān half of sth.; one side of sth.
【半边莲】 bànbiānlián 〈中药〉 Chinese lobelia (*Lobelia chinensis*)
【半边天】 bànbiāntiān ① half the sky: 妇女能顶～。Women hold up half the sky. ② women of the new society; womenfolk
【半…不…】 bàn...bù... 〔意思和"半…半…"相同〕: 半生不熟 half cooked/ 半死不活 half-dead; more dead than alive/ 半新不旧 no longer new; showing signs of wear
【半场】 bànchǎng 〈体〉 ① half of a game or contest ② half-court: ～紧逼〈篮球〉 half-court press
【半成品】 bànchéngpǐn semi-manufactured goods; semi-finished articles; semi-finished products
【半导体】 bàndǎotǐ semiconductor
◇ ～存储器 semiconductor store (或 memory)/ ～集成电路 semiconductor integrated circuit/ ～收音机 transistor radio (或 receiver)
【半岛】 bàndǎo peninsula
【半道儿】 bàndàor 见"半路"
【半点】 bàndiǎn the least bit: 没有～慌张 not the least bit flurried/ 原则问题～也不能动摇。One should never waver on matters of principle.
【半吊子】 bàndiàozi ① dabbler; smatterer ② tactless and impulsive person

【半封建】 bànfēngjiàn semi-feudal
【半复赛】 bànfùsài 〈体〉 eighth-finals
【半工半读】 bàngōng-bàndú part work, part study; work-study programme
【半公开】 bàngōngkāi semi-overt; more or less open
【半官方】 bànguānfāng semi-official: 据～人士称 according to semi-official sources
【半规管】 bànguīguǎn 〈生理〉 semicircular canal
【半价】 bànjià half price: ～出售 sell at half price
【半截】 bànjié half (a section): ～香肠 half of a sausage/ 话只说了～儿 finish only half of what one has to say/ ～子革命 one who gives up the cause of revolution halfway
【半斤八两】 bànjīn-bāliǎng six of one and half a dozen of the other — not much to choose between the two; tweedledum and tweedledee
【半径】 bànjìng radius
【半决赛】 bànjuésài 〈体〉 semifinals
【半空中】 bànkōngzhōng in mid air; in the air: 悬在～ hang in midair
【半拉】 bànlǎ 〈口〉 half: ～苹果 half an apple
【半劳动力】 bànláodònglì one able to do light manual labour only; semi-ablebodied or part-time (farm) worker 又作"半劳力"
【半流体】 bànliútǐ semifluid
【半路】 bànlù halfway; midway; on the way: 走到～,天就黑了。We had got only halfway when it began to get dark./ ～上遇到熟人 run into a friend on the way
【半路出家】 bànlù chūjiā become a monk or nun late in life — switch to a job one was not trained for
【半票】 bànpiào half-price ticket; half fare
【半瓶醋】 bànpíngcù dabbler; smatterer
【半旗】 bànqí half-mast: 下～ fly a flag at half-mast
【半球】 bànqiú hemisphere: 东～ the Eastern Hemisphere/ 北～ the Northern Hemisphere
【半人马座】 bànrénmǎzuò 〈天〉 Centaurus
【半日制学校】 bànrìzhì xuéxiào half-day (或 double-shift) school
【半晌】 bànshǎng 〈方〉 ① half of the day: 前～ morning/ 后～ afternoon/ 晚～ dusk ② a long time; quite a while: 他想了～才想起来。It took him a long time to recall it.
【半身不遂】 bànshēn bùsuí 〈医〉 hemiplegia
【半身象】 bànshēnxiàng ① half-length photo or portrait ② bust
【半生】 bànshēng half a lifetime: 前～ first half of one's life
【半失业】 bànshīyè semi-employed; partly employed; underemployed
【半熟练】 bànshúliàn semi-skilled
【半数】 bànshù half the number; half: ～以上 more than half
【半衰期】 bànshuāiqī 〈物〉 half-life
【半天】 bàntiān ① half of the day: 前～ morning/ 后～ afternoon ② a long time; quite a while: 他～说不出话来。He remained tongue-tied for a long time.
【半透明】 bàntòumíng translucent; semitransparent ◇ ～体 〈物〉 translucent body/ ～纸 onionskin
【半途】 bàntú halfway; midway: ～拆伙 part company halfway
【半途而废】 bàntú ér fèi give up halfway; leave sth. unfinished
【半脱产】 bàntuōchǎn partly released from productive labour; partly released from one's regular work
【半文盲】 bànwénmáng semiliterate
【半无产阶级】 bànwúchǎnjiējí semi-proletariat
【半夏】 bànxià 〈中药〉 the tuber of pinellia (*Pinellia ternata*)
【半硝革】 bànxiāogé crust leather
【半夜】 bànyè midnight; in the middle of the night: 会议一直开到～。The meeting went on far into the night.
【半夜三更】 bànyè-sāngēng in the depth of night; late at night: ～的,你起来干什么? Why are you getting up at this time of night?
【半音】 bànyīn 〈乐〉 semitone ◇ ～音阶 chromatic scale
【半影】 bànyǐng 〈物〉 penumbra ◇ ～锥 penumbra cone
【半元音】 bànyuányīn 〈语〉 semivowel
【半圆】 bànyuán semicircle
【半月瓣】 bànyuèbàn 〈生理〉 semilunar valve
【半月刊】 bànyuèkān semimonthly; fortnightly
【半载】 bànzài 〈交〉 half load
【半支莲】 bànzhīlián 〈植〉 sun plant
【半殖民地】 bànzhímíndì semi-colony ◇ ～半封建社会 semi-colonial, semi-feudal society
【半制浆】 bànzhìjiāng 〈纸〉 half stuff; semi-pulp
【半制品】 bànzhìpǐn 见"半成品"
【半中腰】 bànzhōngyāo 〈口〉 middle; halfway: 他的话说到～就停住了。He broke off in the middle of a sentence./ 山的～有一座亭子。A pavilion is halfway up the hill.
【半自动】 bànzìdòng semi-automatic ◇ ～步枪 semi-automatic rifle
【半自耕农】 bànzìgēngnóng semi-tenant peasant; semi-owner peasant

**扮** bàn ① be dressed up as; play the part of; disguise oneself as: 他在戏里～一位老贫农。In the opera he plays the part of an old poor peasant./ 侦察员～作一个商人。The scout disguised himself as a merchant. ② put on (an expression): ～鬼脸 make grimaces; make faces
【扮相】 bànxiàng the appearance of an actor or actress in costume and makeup
【扮演】 bànyǎn play the part of; act : 她在《白毛女》里～喜儿。She played the part of (或 acted) Xi'er in *The White-Haired Girl*.
【扮装】 bànzhuāng makeup

**伴** bàn ① companion; partner: 旅～ a travelling companion/ 作～ keep sb. company ② accompany: 行政命令必须～之以说服教育。Administrative regulations must be accompanied by persuasion and education.
【伴唱】 bànchàng ① vocal accompaniment ② accompany (a singer)
【伴侣】 bànlǚ companion; mate; partner
【伴生气】 bànshēngqì 〈石油〉 associated gas
【伴随】 bànsuí accompany; follow: ～着生产的大发展,必将出现一个文化高潮。An upsurge in culture is bound to follow the rapid advance in production.
【伴星】 bànxīng 〈天〉 companion (star)
【伴奏】 bànzòu accompany (with musical instruments): 钢琴～ piano accompaniment/ 手风琴～:张小芳 Accompanied on the accordion by Zhang Xiaofang ◇ ～者 accompanist

**拌** bàn mix: ～匀 mix thoroughly/ ～饲料 mix fodder/ ～鸡丝 shredded chicken salad
【拌和】 bànhuo mix and stir; blend
【拌面】 bànmiàn noodles served with soy sauce, sesame butter, etc.
【拌种】 bànzhǒng 〈农〉 seed dressing ◇ ～机 seed dresser
【拌嘴】 bànzuǐ bicker; squabble; quarrel

**绊** bàn (cause to) stumble; trip: ～手～脚 be in the way/ 他被树根～了一下。He stumbled over the root of a tree./ 差点儿～了我一交。I tripped and almost fell./ 别让日常事务把你～住了。Don't get yourself bogged down in routine work.

【绊脚石】 bànjiǎoshí stumbling block; obstacle

**瓣** bàn ① petal ② segment or section (of a tangerine, etc.); clove (of garlic) ③ valve; lamella: 三尖～ tricuspid valve/ 鳃～ gill lamella ④ fragment; piece: 摔成几～儿 be broken into several pieces

【瓣膜】 bànmó 〈生理〉 valve

## bāng

**邦** bāng nation; state; country: 邻～ a neighbouring country

【邦交】 bāngjiāo relations between two countries; diplomatic relations: 建立(断绝,恢复)～ establish (sever, resume) diplomatic relations

【邦联】 bānglián confederation

**帮** bāng ① help; assist: 互～互学 help each other and learn from each other/ ～他搬行李 help him with his luggage/ 她今天要～大夫做手术。She's going to assist the doctor in an operation today./ 你能～我们弄点白菜籽吗? Could you get some cabbage seeds for us? ② side (of a boat, truck, etc.); upper (of a shoe) ③ outer leaf (of cabbage, etc.) ④ gang; band; clique: 匪～ bandit gang ⑤ 〈量〉〔用于人〕: 来了一～孩子。Here comes a group of children.

【帮办】 bāngbàn ① assist in managing: ～军务 assist in handling military affairs ② deputy: 副国务卿～ Deputy Under Secretary (of the U.S. Department of State)/ 助理国务卿～ Deputy Assistant Secretary (of the U.S. Department of State)

【帮厨】 bāngchú help in the mess kitchen

【帮倒忙】 bāng dàománg be more of a hindrance than a help

【帮工】 bānggōng ① help with farm work ② helper

【帮会】 bānghuì secret society; underworld gang

【帮忙】 bāngmáng help; give (或 lend) a hand; do a favour; do a good turn: 帮大忙 be a big help; give a lot of help/ 来找人～ come for help/ 请你帮个忙。Will you give me a hand?/ 他帮过我们的忙。He once did us a good turn.

【帮派】 bāngpài faction ◇ ～体系 factionalist setup

【帮腔】 bāngqiāng ① 〈乐〉 vocal accompaniment in some traditional Chinese operas ② speak in support of sb.; echo sb.; chime in with sb.

【帮手】 bāngshou helper; assistant

【帮闲】 bāngxián hang on to and serve the rich and powerful by literary hack work, etc. ◇ ～文人 literary hack

【帮凶】 bāngxiōng accomplice; accessary

【帮助】 bāngzhù help; assist: 没有多大～ be of little help; not be much help/ 他～我学外文。He helped me learn a foreign language./ 希望你从思想上多给我～。I hope you will give me as much help as you can to improve myself.

【帮子】 bāngzi ① outer leaf (of cabbage, etc.) ② upper (of a shoe)

**浜** bāng 〈方〉 creek; streamlet

**梆** bāng ① watchman's clapper ② 〈象〉〔敲打木头的声音〕 rat-tat; rat-a-tat

【梆子】 bāngzi ① watchman's clapper ② 〈乐〉 wooden clappers with bars of unequal length ③ 见"梆子腔"

【梆子腔】 bāngziqiāng ① a general term for local operas in Shanxi, Shaanxi, Henan, Hebei, Shandong, etc. performed to the accompaniment of *bangzi* (梆子) ② the music of such operas

## bǎng

**绑** bǎng ① bind; tie: ～个三脚架 tie three sticks together to make a tripod ② bind sb.'s hands behind him; truss up

【绑匪】 bǎngfěi kidnapper

【绑架】 bǎngjià ① kidnap ② 〈农〉 staking: 下午咱们给黄瓜～。We're going to stake the cucumbers this afternoon.

【绑票】 bǎngpiào kidnap (for ransom)

【绑腿】 bǎngtuǐ leg wrappings; puttee

**榜** bǎng ① a list of names posted up: 光荣～ honour roll/ 发～ publish the list of successful candidates ② announcement; notice

【榜样】 bǎngyàng example; model: 以大庆为～ take Daqing as the model/ ～的力量是无穷的。A fine example has boundless power.

**膀** bǎng ① upper arm; arm ② shoulder: ～阔腰圆 broad-shouldered and solidly-built; hefty; husky ③ wing (of a bird)

另见 pāng; páng

【膀臂】 bǎngbì ① 〈方〉 upper arm; arm ② reliable helper; right-hand man

【膀子】 bǎngzi ① upper arm; arm: 光着～ stripped to the waist ② wing: 鸭～ duck wings

## bàng

**蚌** bàng freshwater mussel; clam

另见 bèng

**谤** bàng 〈书〉 slander; defame; vilify

**傍** bàng draw near; be close to: 船～了岸。The boat drew alongside the bank./ 依山～水 be situated at the foot of a hill and beside a stream

【傍晚】 bàngwǎn toward evening; at nightfall; at dusk

**棒** bàng ① stick; club; cudgel: 垒球～ softball bat ② 〈口〉 good; fine; excellent; strong: 字写得～ write a good hand/ 庄稼长得真～。The crops are excellent./ ～小伙子 a strong young fellow/ 你干得～极了。You've done a first-rate job.

【棒槌】 bàngchui wooden club (used to beat clothes in washing)

【棒硫】 bàngliú 〈化〉 roll sulphur

【棒磨机】 bàngmòjī 〈矿〉 rod mill

【棒球】 bàngqiú baseball ◇ ～场 baseball field

【棒糖】 bàngtáng sucker; lollipop

【棒子】 bàngzi ① stick; club; cudgel ② 〈方〉 maize; corn ③ 〈方〉 ear of maize (或 corn); corncob ◇ ～面 cornmeal; corn flour/ ～面粥 cornmeal porridge (或 mush)

**蒡** bàng 见"牛蒡" niúbàng

**磅** bàng ①pound ②scales: 把行李搁在～上看有多重。Put the luggage on the scales and see how much it weighs. ③weigh: ～体重 weigh oneself or sb. on the scales ④〈印〉point (type): 六～字太小了。6-point type is too small.

另见 páng

【磅秤】 bàngchèng platform scale; platform balance

**镑** bàng pound (a currency)

## bāo

**包** bāo ①wrap: 把东西～起来 wrap things up/ 头上～着一条白毛巾 with a white towel wrapped round one's head/ ～书 wrap up a book in a piece of paper; put a jacket (或 cover) on a book/ ～饺子 make dumplings/ 纸～不住火。You can't wrap fire in paper. ②bundle; package; pack; packet; parcel: 邮～ postal parcel (或 packet) ③bag; sack: 书～ satchel; school bag ④〈量〉[用于成包的东西]: 一大～衣服 a big bundle of clothes/ 一～香烟 a packet (或 pack) of cigarettes/ 两～大米 two sacks of rice/ 一～棉纱 a bale of cotton yarn ⑤protuberance; swelling; lump: 脑门上碰了个～ have (或 get) a bump on one's forehead/ 腿上起了个～ have a swelling in the leg ⑥surround; encircle; envelop: 浓雾～住了群山。The hills were enveloped in dense fog. ⑦include; contain: 无所不～ all-inclusive; all-embracing ⑧undertake the whole thing: 这事由我～了吧。Just leave it all to me. ⑨assure; guarantee: ～你满意。You'll like it, I assure you. 或 Satisfaction guaranteed. ⑩hire; charter: ～一只船 hire (或 charter) a boat/ ～机 a chartered plane ⑪(Bāo) a surname

【包办】 bāobàn ①take care of everything concerning a job: 这件事你一个人～了吧。You'd better do the whole job yourself. ②run the whole show; monopolize everything: ～代替 take on what ought to be done by others; run things all by oneself without consulting others ◇ ～婚姻 arranged marriage

【包背装】 bāobèizhuāng 〈印〉wrapped-ridge binding

【包庇】 bāobì shield; harbour; cover up: 互相～ shield each other/ ～坏人坏事 harbour evildoers and cover up their evil deeds

【包藏】 bāocáng contain; harbour; conceal: 大海～着许多秘密。The sea contains many mysteries./ ～祸心 harbour evil intentions (或 malicious intent)

【包产】 bāochǎn make a production contract; take full responsibility for output quotas ◇ ～合同 contract for fixed output/ ～指标 targets stated in a contract for fixed output

【包产到户】 bāochǎn dào hù fixing of farm output quotas for each household 参见"三自一包" sānzì yībāo

【包场】 bāochǎng book a whole theatre or cinema; make a block booking

【包抄】 bāochāo outflank; envelop: 从两翼～逃敌 outflank the fleeing enemy on both wings/ 骑兵分三路～过去。The cavalry closed in on the enemy in a three-pronged attack.

【包乘制】 bāochéngzhì 〈交〉responsible crew system

【包乘组】 bāochéngzǔ 〈交〉(responsible) crew

【包虫病】 bāochóngbìng echinococcosis; hydatid disease

【包饭】 bāofàn get or supply meals at a fixed rate; board: 在附近的饭馆里～ board at a nearby restaurant

【包袱】 bāofu ①cloth-wrapper ②a bundle wrapped in cloth ③millstone round one's neck; load; weight; burden: 思想～ a load (或 weight) on one's mind/ 不要把成绩当～ not allow one's merits to become a hindrance to one's progress

【包干】 bāogān be responsible for a task until it is completed: 分片～ divide up the work and assign a part to each individual or group

【包干制】 bāogānzhì a system of payment partly in kind and partly in cash 参见"供给制" gōngjǐzhì

【包工】 bāogōng ①undertake to perform work within a time limit and according to specifications; contract for a job ②contractor ◇ ～头 labour contractor

【包谷】 bāogǔ 〈方〉maize; corn

【包管】 bāoguǎn assure; guarantee: 这件活三天完成，～没问题。We'll finish this job in three days without fail./ ～退换。Merchandise will be exchanged if found unsatisfactory.

【包裹】 bāoguǒ ①wrap up; bind up ②bundle; package; parcel: 邮政～ postal parcel (或 packet) ◇ ～单 parcel form

【包含】 bāohán contain; embody; include: 没有什么事物是不～矛盾的。There is nothing that does not contain contradiction./ 他的建议～不少合理的因素。His proposal contains much that is reasonable./ 群众的意见常常～着许多深刻的道理。The opinions of the masses often embody profound truths.

【包涵】 bāohan 〈套〉excuse; forgive; bear with: 我唱得不好，请多多～。Excuse (me for) my poor singing.

【包伙】 bāohuǒ 见"包饭"

【包金】 bāojīn cover with gold leaf; gild

【包括】 bāokuò include; consist of; comprise; incorporate: 房租每月四元，水电费～在内。The rent is 4 *yuan* a month, including water and electricity./ 这个政策～联合和斗争两个方面。The policy embraces (或 comprises) two aspects, unity and struggle./ 委员会中～老、中、青三部分人。The committee consists of old, middle-aged and young people./ 我们的设计已经～了你们的意见。Our design has incorporated your suggestions.

【包揽】 bāolǎn undertake the whole thing; take on everything: 这样多的事，一个人～不了。No one person can take on so much work./ ～词讼 engage in pettifoggery

【包罗】 bāoluó include; cover; embrace: 民间艺术～甚广。Folk art covers a wide range.

【包罗万象】 bāoluó wànxiàng all-embracing; all-inclusive

【包赔】 bāopéi guarantee to pay compensations

【包皮】 bāopí ①wrapping; wrapper ②〈生理〉prepuce; foreskin ◇ ～环切术 circumcision

【包容】 bāoróng ①pardon; forgive: 大度～ magnanimous ②contain; hold

【包身工】 bāoshēngōng indentured labourer

【包围】 bāowéi surround; encircle: 以农村～城市，最后夺取城市 encircle the cities from the rural areas and then capture them ◇ ～圈 ring of encirclement

【包厢】 bāoxiāng box (in a theatre or concert hall)

【包销】 bāoxiāo ①have exclusive selling rights ②be the sole agent for a production unit or a firm

【包圆儿】 bāoyuánr 〈口〉①buy the whole lot ②finish up (或 off): 剩下的活儿我一个人～了。I'll finish off what's left of the work.

【包扎】 bāozā wrap up; bind up; pack: ～伤口 bind up (或 dress) a wound/ 待运的自行车已经～好了。The bicycles to be transported are packed.

【包治百病】 bāozhì bǎibìng guarantee to cure all diseases: ～的药方 remedy for all ills; panacea; cure-all

【包装】 bāozhuāng pack; package ◇ ～车间 packing department/ ～清单 packing list/ ～设计 packing design/ ～箱 packing box (或 case)/ ～纸

wrapping (或 packing) paper

【包子】 bāozi steamed stuffed bun

【包租】 bāozū 〈旧〉 ① rent land or a house for subletting ② fixed rent for farmland (to be paid no matter how bad the harvest might be)

**苞** bāo ① bud ② 〈书〉 luxuriant; profuse; thick: 竹～松茂 bamboos and pines growing in profusion

**孢** bāo

【孢子】 bāozǐ 〈植〉 spore ◇ ～生殖 sporogony/ ～体 sporophyte/ ～植物 cryptogam

**炮** bāo ① quick-fry; *sauté*: ～羊肉 quick-fried mutton ② dry by heat: 湿衣服搁在热炕上，一会儿就～干了。Put the damp clothes on a hot *kang* and they'll soon dry.

另见 páo; pào

**胞** bāo ① afterbirth ② born of the same parents: ～兄弟 full (或 blood) brothers

【胞衣】 bāoyī 〈中医〉 afterbirth

**剥** bāo shell; peel; skin: ～花生 shell peanuts/ ～香蕉 peel a banana/ ～兔皮 skin a rabbit

另见 bō

**龅** bāo

【龅牙】 bāoyá bucktooth

**褒** bāo praise; honour; commend

【褒贬】 bāo-biǎn pass judgment on; appraise: ～人物 pass judgment on people/ 不加～ make no comment, complimentary or otherwise; neither praise nor censure

【褒贬】 bāobian speak ill of; cry down: 别在背地里～人。Don't speak ill of anybody behind his back.

【褒奖】 bāojiǎng praise and honour; commend and award

【褒扬】 bāoyáng praise; commend

【褒义】 bāoyì commendatory ◇ ～词 commendatory term

## báo

**雹** báo hail

【雹暴】 báobào hailstorm

【雹灾】 báozāi disaster caused by hail

【雹子】 báozi hail; hailstone

**薄** báo ① thin; flimsy: ～纸 thin paper/ 复写用的～纸 flimsy ② weak; light: 酒味很～。This is a light wine. ③ lacking in warmth; cold: 待他不～ treat him quite well ④ infertile; poor: ～地 poor land

另见 bó; bò

【薄板】 báobǎn 〈冶〉 sheet metal; sheet: 不锈钢～ stainless sheet steel ◇ ～轧机 sheet rolling mill

【薄饼】 báobǐng thin pancake

【薄脆】 báocuì crisp fritter

【薄壳结构】 báoqiào jiégòu 〈建〉 shell structure

【薄纱织物】 báoshā zhīwù muslin

【薄页纸】 báoyèzhǐ tissue paper

## bǎo

**宝** bǎo ① treasure: 粮食是～中之～。Grain is the treasure of treasures. ② precious; treasured: ～刀 a treasured sword ③ 〈敬〉〔旧时用于称别人的家眷等〕: ～眷 your wife and children; your family

【宝宝】 bǎobǎo 〔对小孩的爱称〕 darling; baby

【宝贝】 bǎobèi ① treasured object; treasure ② darling; baby ③ cowry: 虎斑～ tiger cowry ④ 〈讽〉 good-for-nothing or queer character: 这人真是个～！What a fellow!

【宝贵】 bǎoguì ① valuable; precious: ～意见 valuable suggestion/ ～经验 valuable experience/ ～文物 precious cultural relics ② value; treasure; set store by: 世间一切事物中，人是第一个可～的。Of all things in the world, people are the most precious.

【宝剑】 bǎojiàn a double-edged sword

【宝库】 bǎokù treasure-house: 中国医药学是一个伟大的～。Chinese medicine and pharmacology are a great treasure-house.

【宝蓝】 bǎolán sapphire blue

【宝石】 bǎoshí precious stone; gem

【宝书】 bǎoshū treasured book

【宝塔】 bǎotǎ pagoda ◇ ～菜〈植〉 Chinese artichoke/ ～筒子〈纺〉 cone

【宝物】 bǎowù treasure

【宝藏】 bǎozàng precious (mineral) deposits: 发掘地下～ unearth buried treasure; tap mineral resources

【宝座】 bǎozuò throne

**饱** bǎo ① have eaten one's fill; be full: 吃～喝足 eat and drink one's fill/ 我～了，一点也吃不下了。I've had enough. I can't eat any more./ ～汉不知饿汉饥。〈谚〉 The well-fed don't know how the starving suffer. ② full; plump: 谷粒很～。The grains are quite plump. ③ fully; to the full: ～尝旧社会的辛酸 taste to the full the bitterness of life in the old society/ ～览海岛的美丽风光 drink in the beauty of the island scenery/ 她的眼眶里～含着幸福的热泪。Her eyes filled with tears of joy./ 旧中国～经忧患。Old China suffered untold tribulations. ④ satisfy: 一～眼福 have the opportunity to feast one's eyes on sth.; enjoy to the full watching a scene, show, etc.

【饱嗝儿】 bǎogér belch; burp

【饱和】 bǎohé saturation ◇ ～差〈气〉 saturation deficit (或 deficiency)/ ～点 saturation point/ ～轰炸 saturation bombing/ ～剂〈化〉 saturant/ ～器 saturator/ ～溶液〈化〉 saturated solution/ ～压力 saturation pressure

【饱经风霜】 bǎo jīng fēngshuāng weather-beaten; having experienced the hardships of life: ～的面容 a weather-worn face/ 一位在旧社会～的老渔民 an old fisherman who has survived the hardships of life in the old society

【饱满】 bǎomǎn full; plump: 颗粒～的小麦 plump-eared wheat/ 精神～ full of vigour; energetic ◇ ～度〈农〉 plumpness (of seeds)

【饱食终日，无所用心】 bǎoshí zhōngrì, wú suǒ yòngxīn eat three square meals a day and do no work; be sated with food and remain idle

【饱学】 bǎoxué learned; erudite; scholarly: ～之士 an erudite person; a learned scholar; a man of learning

**保** bǎo ① protect; defend: ～家卫国 protect our homes and defend our country ② keep; maintain; preserve: 这种热水瓶能～暖二十四小时。This kind of thermos flask keeps water hot for 24 hours./ ～水～肥 preserve moisture and fertility (in the soil) ③ guarantee; ensure: ～质～量 guarantee both quality and quantity/ 旱涝～收 ensure stable yields despite drought or waterlogging ④ stand guarantor (或 surety) for sb.: ～外就医〈法〉 be released on bail for medical treatment/ ～外执行〈法〉 serve a sentence on bail ⑤ guarantor: 作～ stand guarantor (或 surety) for sb.

【保安】 bǎo'ān ① ensure public security ② ensure safety (for workers engaged in production)
◇ ～措施 security measures/ ～队 peace preservation corps (under KMT and warlord rule)/ ～规程 safety regulations/ ～人员 security personnel/ ～装置 protective device

【保安族】 Bǎo'ānzú the Bonan (Paoan) nationality, living in Gansu

【保镖】 bǎobiāo bodyguard

【保不住】 bǎobuzhù most likely; more likely than not; may well: ～会下雨。Most likely it's going to rain./ 他～把这事儿全给忘了。He may well have forgotten all about it.

【保藏】 bǎocáng keep in store; preserve: 食品～ food preservation

【保持】 bǎochí keep; maintain; preserve: ～安静 keep quiet/ ～冷静的头脑 keep a cool head; keep cool/ 跟群众～密切联系 keep close to the masses/ ～中立 remain neutral; maintain neutrality/ ～警惕 maintain vigilance; be on the alert/ ～艰苦奋斗的作风 preserve (或 keep up) the style of plain living and hard struggle/ ～跳高记录 retain the high jump record

【保存】 bǎocún preserve; conserve; keep: ～实力 preserve one's strength; conserve one's forces/ ～自己，消灭敌人 preserve oneself and destroy the enemy/ 这批文物～得很完好。These cultural relics are well preserved./ 他还～着长征时戴的那顶帽子。He still keeps the cap he wore on the Long March.

【保单】 bǎodān guarantee slip

【保管】 bǎoguǎn ① take care of: 负责～农具 take care of farm tools/ 图书～工作 the care of library books ② certainly; surely: 他～不知道。He certainly doesn't know.
◇ ～费 storage charges; storage fee/ ～室 storeroom/ ～员 storeman; storekeeper

【保护】 bǎohù protect; safeguard: ～环境，防止污染 protect the environment against pollution/ ～人民的利益 safeguard the people's interests/ ～现场 keep intact the scene of a crime or accident/ 体操运动员都学会了互相～和自我～。The gymnasts have all learnt to protect each other and themselves against injuries.
◇ ～地 protectorate; dependent territory/ ～关税 protective tariff/ ～国 protectorate/ ～贸易政策 policy of protection; protectionism/ ～鸟 protected birds/ ～人 guardian/ ～伞 umbrella/ ～色〈动〉 protective coloration/ ～涂剂 protective coating/ ～性拘留 protective custody; protective detention

【保皇党】 bǎohuángdǎng royalists

【保加利亚】 Bǎojiālìyà Bulgaria ◇ ～人 Bulgarian/ ～语 Bulgarian (language)

【保甲制度】 bǎojiǎ zhìdù the *Bao-Jia* system (an administrative system organized on the basis of households, each *Jia* being made up of 10 households, and each *Bao* of 10 *Jia*, by which the KMT reactionary clique enforced its fascist rule at the primary level after 1932)

【保驾】 bǎojià 〔现多作诙谐语用〕 escort the Emperor: 放心吧，我给你～。Don't worry. I'll escort you.

【保健】 bǎojiàn health protection; health care: 妇幼～ maternal and child hygiene; mother and child care
◇ ～按摩 keep-fit massage/ ～操 setting-up exercises/ ～费 health subsidies/ ～事业 public health work/ ～网 health care network/ ～箱 medical kit/ ～员 health worker/ ～站 health station (或 centre)/ ～组织 health (care) organization

【保洁箱】 bǎojiéxiāng litter-bin

【保留】 bǎoliú ① continue to have; retain: 他还～着战争年代的革命朝气。He still retains the revolutionary fervour of the war years. ② hold (或 keep) back; reserve: 无～地同意 agree unreservedly (或 without reservation)/ ～以后再答复的权利 reserve the right to reply at a later date/ 持～意见 have reservations/ 票给你～到明天中午。We'll reserve the ticket for you till tomorrow noon./ 有意见都谈出来，不要～。Don't hold back anything you want to say.
◇ ～地 reservation/ ～剧目 repertory; repertoire/ ～条款 reservation clause

【保密】 bǎomì maintain secrecy; keep sth. secret: 这事绝对～。This must be kept absolutely secret. 或 This is strictly confidential.
◇ ～级别 security classification/ ～条例 security regulations/ ～文件 classified document

【保苗】 bǎomiáo 〈农〉 keep a full stand of seedlings

【保姆】 bǎomǔ ① (children's) nurse ② housekeeper

【保全】 bǎoquán ① save from damage; preserve: ～革命力量 preserve revolutionary strength/ 由于战士们的抢救，这一批物资终于～了。Thanks to the soldiers' rescue operations, the supplies were finally saved./ ～面子 save face ② maintain; keep in good repair ◇ ～工 maintenance worker

【保人】 bǎorén 见"保证人"

【保墒】 bǎoshāng 〈农〉 preservation of soil moisture

【保释】 bǎoshì 〈法〉 release on bail; bail: 准予（不准）～ accept (refuse) bail

【保守】 bǎoshǒu ① guard; keep: ～党和国家机密 guard Party and state secrets ② conservative: ～观点 conservative point of view/ ～思想 conservative ideas (或 thinking)
◇（英国）～党 the Conservative Party/ ～疗法〈医〉 conservative treatment/ ～派 conservatives/ ～主义 conservatism

【保送】 bǎosòng recommend sb. for admission to school, etc.

【保泰松】 bǎotàisōng 〈药〉 phenylbutazone

【保卫】 bǎowèi defend; safeguard: ～祖国 defend one's country/ ～国家主权和领土完整 safeguard state sovereignty and territorial integrity
◇ ～部门 public security bodies/ ～工作 security work/ ～科 security section

【保温】 bǎowēn heat preservation
◇ ～材料 thermal insulation material/ ～层〈建〉 (thermal) insulating layer/ ～车〈铁道〉 refrigerator wagon (或 car)/ ～瓶 vacuum flask (或 bottle); thermos

【保险】 bǎoxiǎn ① insurance: 人寿(海损)～ life (maritime) insurance ② safe: 骑车太快可不～。It's not safe to cycle too fast./ 你还是带上雨衣吧，～点儿。You'd better take your raincoat just to be on the safe side. ③ be sure; be bound to: 他明天～会来。He is sure to come tomorrow./ ～能行。It's bound to work.
◇ ～带 safety belt/ ～单 insurance policy/ ～刀 safety razor/ ～费 insurance premium/ ～粉〈纺〉 sodium hydrosulphite/ ～杠〈汽车〉 bumper/ ～公司 insurance company/ ～柜 safe/ ～机 safety (of a firearm)/ ～箱 safe; strongbox/ ～装置 safety device

【保险丝】 bǎoxiǎnsī 〈电〉 fuse; fuse-wire: ～烧断了。The fuse has blown.

【保修】 bǎoxiū guarantee to keep sth. in good repair: 这只表～一年。There is a year's guarantee with this watch. 或 This watch is guaranteed for a year.

【保养】 bǎoyǎng ① take good care of (或 conserve) one's health ② maintain; keep in good repair: 机器～ maintenance (或 upkeep) of machinery/ 这条路～得很好。This road is in good repair. ◇ ～费 maintenance cost; upkeep/ ～工 maintenance worker

【保佑】 bǎoyòu bless and protect: 我们相信人定胜天，不靠老天～。We believe in man's conquest of nature and don't rely on blessings from heaven.

【保育】 bǎoyù child care; child welfare ◇ ～员 child-care worker; nurse/ ～院 nursery school

【保障】 bǎozhàng ensure; guarantee; safeguard: ～人民言论自由 guarantee freedom of speech for the people/ 在新社会职业有～。In the new society jobs are secure.

【保真度】 bǎozhēndù 〈电子〉 fidelity: 高～ high fidelity

【保证】 bǎozhèng pledge; guarantee; assure; ensure: ～完成任务 pledge (或 guarantee) to fulfil a task/ ～不再发生类似事件 guarantee against the occurrence of similar incidents/ 党的领导是我们胜利的～。Party leadership is the guarantee of our victory./ ～妇女在产前产后有充分的休息。Adequate rest is ensured for women during pregnancy and after childbirth. ◇ ～书 written pledge; guarantee; guaranty; letter of guarantee

【保证金】 bǎozhèngjīn ① earnest money; cash deposit ② 〈法〉 bail

【保证人】 bǎozhèngrén 〈法〉 ① guarantor ② bail

【保重】 bǎozhòng 〔用于希望别人注意身体〕 take care of oneself: 多多～。Take good care of yourself. 或 Look after yourself.

**鸨** bǎo ① 〈动〉 bustard ② procuress

**葆** bǎo 〈书〉 ① luxuriant growth ② preserve; nurture: 继续革命，永～青春 continue to make revolution and keep alive the fervour of youth

**堡** bǎo fort; fortress

【堡垒】 bǎolěi fort; fortress; stronghold; blockhouse: ～是最容易从内部攻破的。The easiest way to capture a fortress is from within./ 把党支部建设成坚强的战斗～ build the Party branch into a powerful fighting force ◇ ～战 blockhouse warfare

**褓** bǎo 见"襁褓" qiǎngbǎo

## bào

**报** bào ① report; announce; declare: ～火警 report a fire/ ～上级批准 report (或 submit) sth. to the higher authorities for approval ② reply; respond; reciprocate: ～友人书 a (letter in) reply to a friend/ ～以热烈的掌声 respond with warm applause ③ recompense; requite: 无以为～ be unable to repay a kindness/ 以怨～德 requite kindness with ingratitude; return evil for good ④ newspaper ⑤ periodical; journal: 画～ pictorial/ 周～ weekly/ 学～ college journal ⑥ bulletin; report: 喜～ report of success, a happy event, etc.; glad tidings; good news/ 战～ war bulletin ⑦ telegram; cable: 发～ transmit (或 send) a telegram

【报案】 bào'àn report a case to the security authorities

【报表】 bàobiǎo forms for reporting statistics, etc.; report forms

【报偿】 bàocháng repay; recompense

【报仇】 bàochóu revenge; avenge: 为阶级兄弟～ avenge one's class brothers/ 干革命不是为了报私仇，而是为了解放全人类。Revolution is not for personal vengeance, it's for the emancipation of all mankind.

【报酬】 bàochou reward; remuneration; pay: 不计～ not concerned about pay; irrespective of remuneration/ 在发展生产的基础上逐步提高劳动～ gradually increase payment for labour on the basis of increased production

【报答】 bàodá repay; requite: 以实际行动～党的关怀 repay the Party's kindness with one's deeds

【报单】 bàodān taxation form; declaration form

【报到】 bàodào report for duty; check in; register: 向部里～ report for duty at the ministry/ 向大会秘书处～ check in at the secretariat of the congress/ 新生已开始～。The new students have started registering.

【报道】 bàodào ① report (news); cover: ～考古新发现 report new archaeological finds/ ～会议情况 cover the conference/ 据～ it is reported that/ 据新华社三月二日自北京～ according to a Xinhua News Agency dispatch datelined Beijing, March 2/ 各报都在第一版～了这条消息。This was front-paged in all the papers. ② news report; story

【报恩】 bào'ēn pay a debt of gratitude

【报废】 bàofèi ① report sth. as worthless ② discard as useless; reject; scrap: 使～矿井复生 reopen an abandoned mine/ 这架机器太旧，快～了。This machine is so old it will soon have to be scrapped.

【报分】 bàofēn 〈体〉 call the score

【报复】 bàofù make reprisals; retaliate: 图谋～ nurse thoughts of revenge ◇ ～性打击 vindictive blow; retaliatory strike

【报告】 bàogào ① report; make known: 向上级～ report to the higher authorities/ ～大家一个好消息。Here's a piece of good news for us all./ 现在～新闻。Here is the news./ 国务院对全国人民代表大会负责并～工作。The State Council is responsible and accountable to the National People's Congress./ ～! Reporting! ② report; speech; talk; lecture: 作～ give a talk or lecture/ 总结～ summing-up report/ 动员～ mobilization speech

◇ ～会 public lecture/ ～人 speaker; lecturer/ ～文学 reportage

【报关】 bàoguān declare sth. at customs; apply to customs: 你有什么东西要～吗? Have you got anything to declare? ◇ ～表 declaration form; customs declaration

【报馆】 bàoguǎn 〈旧〉 newspaper office

【报国】 bàoguó dedicate oneself to the service of one's country

【报户口】 bào hùkǒu apply for a residence permit: 报临时户口 apply for a temporary residence permit/ 给新生婴儿～ register the birth of a child

【报话机】 bàohuàjī handie-talkie

【报价】 bàojià 〈经〉 quoted price

【报捷】 bàojié report a success; announce a victory

【报界】 bàojiè the press; journalistic circles; the journalists: 向～发表谈话 make a statement to the press

【报警】 bàojǐng ① report (an incident) to the police ② give an alarm: 鸣钟～ sound the alarm bell

【报刊】 bàokān newspapers and periodicals; the press

【报考】 bàokǎo enter oneself for an examination

【报名】 bàomíng enter one's name; sign up: ～参加百米赛跑 enter one's name for the 100-metre dash/ ～下乡 sign up for work in the countryside/ ～参加比赛的共有五十人。There are fifty entries (或 entrants) altogether.

【报幕】 bàomù announce the items on a (theatrical) programme ◇ ～员 announcer

【报社】 bàoshè general office of a newspaper; newspaper office

【报失】 bàoshī report the loss of sth. to the authorities concerned

【报时】 bàoshí give the correct time ◇ ～器 chronopher/ ～台 (telephone) time inquiry service

【报数】 bàoshù number off: ～!（口令）Count off!

【报税】 bàoshuì declare dutiable goods; make a statement of dutiable goods

【报摊】 bàotān news-stand; news stall
【报头】 bàotóu masthead (of a newspaper, etc.); nameplate
【报务员】 bàowùyuán telegraph operator; radio operator
【报喜】 bàoxǐ announce good news; report success: ～不报忧 report only the good news and not the bad; hold back unpleasant information
【报系】 bàoxì newspaper chain; syndicate
【报销】 bàoxiāo ① submit an expense account; apply for reimbursement: 向财务科～ submit an expense account to the treasurer's office/ 旅费凭票～。Travelling expenses can be reimbursed on handing in the tickets. ② hand in a list of expended articles ③ 〈口〉 write off; wipe out: 敌人马上～了。This enemy force was wiped out right away.
【报晓】 bàoxiǎo (of a cock, bell, etc.) herald the break of day; be a harbinger of dawn
【报效】 bàoxiào render service to repay sb.'s kindness
【报信】 bàoxìn notify; inform
【报应】 bàoyìng 〈宗〉 retribution; judgment
【报章】 bàozhāng newspapers ◇ ～杂志 newspapers and magazines
【报帐】 bàozhàng render an account; submit an expense account; apply for reimbursement: 修理费用可以～。Costs of repairs may be reimbursed.
【报纸】 bàozhǐ ① newspaper ② newsprint ◇ ～夹 newspaper holder

**刨** bào ① plane sth. down; plane: ～木板 plane a board ② plane; planer; planing machine
另见 páo
【刨冰】 bàobīng water ice (powdered or in shavings)
【刨程】 bàochéng 〈机〉 planing length
【刨齿】 bàochǐ 〈机〉 gear-shaping ◇ ～机 gear shaper
【刨床】 bàochuáng planer; planing machine
【刨刀】 bàodāo 〈机〉 planer tool
【刨工】 bàogōng ① planing ② planing machine operator; planer
【刨花】 bàohuā wood shavings ◇ ～板〈建〉 shaving board
【刨刃儿】 bàorènr plane iron
【刨子】 bàozi plane

**抱** bào ① hold or carry in the arms; embrace; hug: 把小孩子～起来 take a child in one's arms/ 不要～住错误观点不放。Don't stick to your wrong views. ② have one's first child or grandchild: 她快～孙子了。She'll soon be a grandmother. ③ adopt (a child): 他的女儿是～的。His daughter is adopted. ④ 〈方〉 hang together: ～成一团 gang up; hang together ⑤ cherish; harbour: ～很大希望 entertain high hopes/ ～正确的态度 adopt (或 take) a correct attitude/ 不～幻想 cherish no illusions ⑥ 〈量〉〔表示两臂合围的量〕: 一～草 an armful of hay/ 这棵树有一～粗。You can just get your arms around this tree trunk. ⑦ hatch (eggs); brood
【抱病】 bàobìng be ill; be in bad health: ～工作 go on working in spite of ill health
【抱不平】 bào bùpíng be outraged by an injustice (done to another person): 打～ defend sb. against an injustice
【抱残守缺】 bàocán-shǒuquē cherish the outmoded and preserve the outworn — be conservative
【抱粗腿】 bào cūtuǐ latch on to the rich and powerful
【抱佛脚】 bào fójiǎo clasp Buddha's feet — profess devotion only when in trouble; make a hasty last-minute effort: 平时不烧香,急来～ never burn incense when all is well but clasp Buddha's feet when in distress; do nothing until the last minute
【抱负】 bàofù aspiration; ambition: 很有～ have high aspirations; cherish high ambitions
【抱恨】 bàohèn have a gnawing regret: ～终天 regret sth. to the end of one's days
【抱愧】 bàokuì feel ashamed
【抱歉】 bàoqiàn be sorry; feel apologetic; regret: 叫你久等了,很～。Very sorry to have kept you waiting.
【抱屈】 bàoqū feel wronged
【抱头鼠窜】 bàotóu shǔcuàn cover the head and sneak away like a rat; scurry (或 scamper) off like a frightened rat
【抱头痛哭】 bàotóu tòngkū weep in each other's arms; cry on each other's shoulder
【抱窝】 bàowō sit (on eggs); brood; hatch: 母鸡～了。The hen is sitting.
【抱薪救火】 bào xīn jiùhuǒ carry faggots to put out a fire — adopt a wrong method to save a situation and end up by making it worse
【抱养】 bàoyǎng adopt (a child)
【抱怨】 bàoyuàn complain; grumble: 不要总是～别人对你帮助不够。Don't always complain that you haven't been given enough help.

**豹** bào leopard; panther
【豹猫】 bàomāo leopard cat

**鲍** Bào a surname
【鲍鱼】 bàoyú ① abalone ② 〈书〉 salted fish: 如入～之肆,久而不闻其臭。It's like staying in a fish market and getting used to the stink — long exposure to a bad environment accustoms one to evil ways.

**暴** bào ① sudden and violent: ～雷 violent thunderclaps/ ～饮～食 eat and drink too much at one meal ② cruel; savage; fierce: 残～ brutal ③ short-tempered; hot-tempered: 脾气～ have a hot temper ④ stick out; stand out; bulge: 急得头上的青筋都～出来了 be so agitated that the veins on one's forehead stand out
【暴病】 bàobìng sudden attack of a serious illness: 得～ be suddenly seized with a severe illness
【暴跌】 bàodiē steep fall (in price); slump
【暴动】 bàodòng insurrection; rebellion: 革命是～,是一个阶级推翻一个阶级的暴烈的行动。A revolution is an insurrection, an act of violence by which one class overthrows another.
【暴发】 bàofā ① break out: 山洪～。Torrents of water rushed down the mountain. ② suddenly become rich or important; get rich quick ◇ ～户 upstart
【暴风】 bàofēng ① storm wind ② storm (force 11 wind)
【暴风雪】 bàofēngxuě snowstorm; blizzard
【暴风雨】 bàofēngyǔ rainstorm; storm; tempest: 革命的～ a storm of revolution; a revolutionary tempest/ ～般的掌声 thunderous applause
【暴风骤雨】 bàofēng-zhòuyǔ violent storm; hurricane; tempest: 其势如～ with the force of a hurricane
【暴光】 bàoguāng 〈摄〉 exposure ◇ ～表 exposure meter/ ～宽容度 exposure latitude
【暴洪】 bàohóng a sudden, violent flood; flash flood
【暴君】 bàojūn tyrant; despot
【暴力】 bàolì violence; force: 以革命的～反对反革命的～ oppose counterrevolutionary violence with revolutionary violence/ ～是每一个孕育着新社会的旧社会的助产婆。Force is the midwife of every old society pregnant with a new one. ◇ ～革命 violent revolution/ ～机关 organ of violence
【暴利】 bàolì sudden huge profits: 牟取～ reap staggering

(或 colossal) profits
【暴戾】 bàolì 〈书〉 ruthless and tyrannical; cruel and fierce
【暴戾恣睢】 bàolì-zìsuī 〈书〉 extremely cruel and despotic
【暴烈】 bàoliè violent; fierce: 性情～ have a fiery temper
【暴露】 bàolù expose; reveal; lay bare: ～思想 lay bare one's thoughts/ ～目标 give away one's position/ ～无遗 be thoroughly exposed/ ～在光天化日之下 be exposed to the light of day/ 矛盾还没有充分～。The contradictions have not yet been fully revealed. ◇ ～文学 literature of exposure
【暴乱】 bàoluàn riot; rebellion; revolt: 平定反革命～ suppress (或 put down, quell) a counterrevolutionary rebellion
【暴怒】 bàonù violent rage; fury
【暴虐】 bàonüè brutal; tyrannical
【暴殄天物】 bàotiǎn tiānwù a reckless waste of grain, etc.
【暴跳如雷】 bàotiào rú léi stamp with fury; fly into a rage
【暴徒】 bàotú ruffian; thug
【暴行】 bàoxíng savage act; outrage; atrocity
【暴雨】 bàoyǔ torrential rain; rainstorm
【暴躁】 bàozào irascible; irritable
【暴涨】 bàozhǎng (of floods, prices, etc.) rise suddenly and sharply: 河水～。The river suddenly rose./ 物价～。Prices soared (或 skyrocketed).
【暴政】 bàozhèng tyranny; despotic rule
【暴卒】 bàozú die of a sudden illness; die suddenly

**爆** bào ① explode; burst: 车胎～了。The tyre's burst./ 子弹打在石头上,～起许多火星。The bullet hit the rock and sent sparks flying from it. ② quick-fry; quick-boil: 油～肚儿 quick-fried tripe
【爆发】 bàofā erupt; burst out; break out: 火山～ volcanic eruption/ 战争～。War broke out./ 人群中～出一片欢呼声。The crowd burst into cheers. ◇ ～力 〈体〉 explosive force/ ～音 〈语〉 plosive
【爆管】 bàoguǎn cartridge igniter; squib
【爆裂】 bàoliè burst; crack: 豌豆过熟就会～。Pea pods burst open when overripe.
【爆米花】 bàomǐhuā puffed rice
【爆破】 bàopò blow up; demolish; dynamite; blast: 连续～ successive demolitions
◇ ～弹 blasting cartridge/ ～手 dynamiter/ ～筒 bangalore (torpedo)/ ～音 〈语〉 plosive/ ～英雄 demolition hero; ace dynamiter/ ～组 demolition team
【爆音】 bàoyīn 〈航空〉 sonic boom; shock-wave noise
【爆炸】 bàozhà explode; blow up; detonate: 炸弹～了。A bomb exploded./ 敌人的军火库～了。The enemy ammunition dump blew up./ ～一个核装置 detonate a nuclear device/ ～性的局势 an explosive situation
◇ ～极限 explosive limit/ ～力 explosive force/ ～物 explosive
【爆竹】 bàozhú firecracker: 放～ let off firecrackers/ ～没响。The firecracker didn't go off.

## bēi

**杯** bēi ① cup: 茶～ teacup/ 一～茶 a cup of tea/ 玻璃～ glass ② (prize) cup; trophy: 银～ silver cup
【杯弓蛇影】 bēigōng-shéyǐng mistaking the reflection of a bow in the cup for a snake — extremely suspicious
【杯水车薪】 bēishuǐ-chēxīn trying to put out a burning cartload of faggots with a cup of water — an utterly inadequate measure
【杯子】 bēizi cup; glass

**卑** bēi ① low: 地势～湿 low-lying and damp ② inferior: ～不足道 not worth mentioning ③ 〈书〉 modest; humble: ～辞厚礼 humble words and handsome gifts
【卑鄙】 bēibǐ base; mean; contemptible; despicable: ～行为 a base (或 mean) action; sordid conduct; abject behaviour/ ～手段 contemptible means; dirty tricks/ ～勾当 a dirty deal
【卑躬屈节】 bēigōng-qūjié bow and scrape; cringe; act servilely (或 obsequiously)
【卑贱】 bēijiàn ① lowly: ～者最聪明,高贵者最愚蠢。The lowly are most intelligent; the *élite* are most ignorant. ② mean and low
【卑劣】 bēiliè base; mean; despicable: ～行径 base conduct/ ～手法 a mean (或 despicable) trick
【卑怯】 bēiqiè mean and cowardly; abject: ～行为 abject behaviour
【卑微】 bēiwēi petty and low
【卑污】 bēiwū despicable and filthy; foul
【卑下】 bēixià base; low

**背** bēi ① carry on the back: ～着孩子 carry a baby on one's back ② bear; shoulder: 我怕～不起这样的责任。I'm afraid I can't shoulder such a responsibility.
另见 bèi
【背包】 bēibāo ① knapsack; rucksack; infantry pack; field pack ② 〈军〉 blanket roll
【背包袱】 bēi bāofu have a weight (或 load) on one's mind; take on a mental burden: 你不要因此～。Don't let it weigh on your mind.
【背带】 bēidài ① braces; suspenders ② sling (for a rifle); straps (for a knapsack)
【背负】 bēifù bear; carry on the back; have on one's shoulder
【背黑锅】 bēi hēiguō 〈口〉 be made a scapegoat; be unjustly blamed
【背篓】 bēilǒu a basket carried on the back ◇ ～商店 a mobile shop with shop assistants carrying goods in baskets on their backs to sell in mountain areas; mobile shop with goods carried in baskets; pack-basket shop
【背债】 bēizhài be in debt; be saddled with debts

**悲** bēi ① sad; sorrowful; melancholy: ～不自胜 be overcome with grief/ 处于可～的境地 be in a deplorable state; be in a sorry plight ② compassion: 慈～ compassionate; merciful
【悲哀】 bēi'āi grieved; sorrowful
【悲惨】 bēicǎn miserable; tragic: ～的遭遇 a tragic experience/ ～的过去 the bitter past/ 我们永远不会忘记在旧社会的～生活。We'll never forget our miserable life in the old society.
【悲悼】 bēidào mourn; grieve over sb.'s death
【悲愤】 bēifèn grief and indignation: ～填膺 be filled with grief and indignation
【悲歌】 bēigē ① sad melody; stirring strains ② elegy; dirge; threnody ③ sing with solemn fervour
【悲观】 bēiguān pessimistic: ～情绪 pessimism/ 感到～失望 feel disheartened/ 持～看法 take a pessimistic (或 gloomy) view ◇ ～主义 pessimism
【悲欢离合】 bēi-huān-lí-hé joys and sorrows, partings and reunions — vicissitudes of life
【悲剧】 bēijù tragedy
【悲鸣】 bēimíng utter sad calls; lament: 让反华小丑～去吧! Let the anti-China buffoons bemoan their fate!
【悲泣】 bēiqì weep with grief
【悲切】 bēiqiè 〈书〉 mournful

【悲伤】 bēishāng sad; sorrowful
【悲叹】 bēitàn sigh mournfully; lament
【悲天悯人】 bēitiān-mǐnrén bemoan the state of the universe and pity the fate of mankind: 装出一副～的样子 pretend to bewail the times and pity the people; be sanctimonious; assume a compassionate tone
【悲痛】 bēitòng grieved; sorrowful: 感到深切的～ be deeply grieved; be filled with deep sorrow/ 化～为力量 turn grief into strength
【悲喜交集】 bēi-xǐ jiāojí mixed feelings of grief and joy; grief and joy intermingled; joy tempered with sorrow
【悲喜剧】 bēi-xǐjù tragicomedy
【悲壮】 bēizhuàng solemn and stirring; moving and tragic: ～的歌曲 a solemn and stirring song

**碑** bēi an upright stone tablet; stele: 人民英雄纪念～ the Monument to the People's Heroes/ 墓～ tombstone/ 西安～林 the Forest of Steles in Xi'an
【碑额】 bēi'é the top part of a tablet
【碑记】 bēijì a record of events inscribed on a tablet
【碑碣】 bēijié 〈书〉 an upright stone tablet; stele
【碑帖】 bēitiè a rubbing from a stone inscription (usu. as a model for calligraphy)
【碑文】 bēiwén an inscription on a tablet

**鹎** bēi bulbul

## běi

**北** běi ① north: ～风 a north wind/ 城～ north of the city/ 华～ north China/ ～屋 a room with a southern exposure ② 〈书〉 be defeated: 敌军连战皆～。The enemy were defeated in one battle after another. 或 The enemy suffered repeated defeats.
【北半球】 běibànqiú the Northern Hemisphere
【北冰洋】 Běibīngyáng the Arctic (Ocean)
【北朝】 Běi Cháo the Northern Dynasties (386-581), namely, the Northern Wei Dynasty (北魏, 386-534), the Eastern Wei Dynasty (东魏, 534-550), the Western Wei Dynasty (西魏, 535-556), the Northern Qi Dynasty (北齐, 550-577) and the Northern Zhou Dynasty (北周, 557-581)
【北大荒】 Běidàhuāng the Great Northern Wilderness (in northeast China)
【北大西洋公约组织】 Běi Dàxīyáng Gōngyuē Zǔzhī the North Atlantic Treaty Organization (NATO)
【北斗星】 běidǒuxīng the Big Dipper; the Plough
【北伐军】 Běifájūn the Northern Expeditionary Army
【北伐战争】 Běifá Zhànzhēng the Northern Expedition (1926-1927) 参见"第一次国内革命战争" Dìyī Cì Guónèi Gémìng Zhànzhēng
【北方】 běifāng ① north ② the northern part of the country, esp. the area north of the Huanghe River; the North ◇ ～话 northern dialect/ ～人 Northerner
【北国】 běiguó 〈书〉 the northern part of the country; the North: 好一派～风光! What magnificent northern scenery!
【北海】 Běihǎi the North Sea
【北海道】 Běihǎidào Hokkaido
【北寒带】 běihándài the north frigid zone
【北回归线】 běihuíguīxiàn 〈地〉 the Tropic of Cancer
【北极】 běijí ① the North Pole; the Arctic Pole ② the north magnetic pole
◇ ～光 〈天〉 northern lights; aurora borealis/ ～狐 Arctic fox/ ～圈 the Arctic Circle/ ～星 Polaris; the North Star; the polestar/ ～熊 polar bear
【北京】 Běijīng Beijing (Peking)
【北京人】 Běijīngrén 〈考古〉 Peking Man (*Sinanthropus pekinensis*)
【北美洲】 Běi Měizhōu North America
【北齐】 Běi Qí the Northern Qi Dynasty (550-577), one of the Northern Dynasties
【北宋】 Běi Sòng the Northern Song Dynasty (960-1127)
【北纬】 běiwěi north (或 northern) latitude
【北魏】 Běi Wèi the Northern Wei Dynasty (386-534), one of the Northern Dynasties
【北温带】 běiwēndài the north temperate zone
【北洋】 Běiyáng the Qing Dynasty name for the coastal provinces of Liaoning, Hebei and Shandong
【北洋军阀】 Běiyáng Jūnfá the Northern Warlords (1912-1927)
【北周】 Běi Zhōu the Northern Zhou Dynasty (557-581), one of the Northern Dynasties

## bèi

**贝** bèi ① shellfish ② cowrie: 虎斑～ tiger cowrie ③ (Bèi) a surname
【贝雕】 bèidiāo 〈工美〉 shell carving ◇ ～画 shell carving picture
【贝加尔湖】 Bèijiā'ěrhú Lake Baikal
【贝壳】 bèiké shell ◇ ～学 conchology
【贝类】 bèilèi shellfish; molluscs
【贝母】 bèimǔ 〈中药〉 the bulb of fritillary (*Fritillaria thunbergii*)
【贝宁】 Bèiníng Benin ◇ ～人 Beninian
【贝丘】 bèiqiū 〈考古〉 shell mound

**狈** bèi 见"狼狈" lángbèi

**备** bèi ① be equipped with; have: 各种农业机械无一不～ be equipped with all sorts of farm machinery ② prepare; get ready: 把料～齐 get all the materials ready ③ provide (或 prepare) against; take precautions against: 以～万一 prepare against all eventualities ④ equipment: 军～ military equipment; armaments ⑤ fully; in every possible way: ～受虐待 be subjected to every kind of maltreatment/ 艰苦～尝 suffer untold hardships/ ～受欢迎 enjoy great popularity; be very popular
【备案】 bèi'àn put on record (或 on file); enter (a case) in the records: 报上级党委～ report to the next higher Party committee for the record
【备查】 bèichá for future reference: 所有重要文件都要存档～。All important documents should be kept on file for reference.
【备而不用】 bèi ér bù yòng have sth. ready just in case; keep sth. for possible future use
【备耕】 bèigēng make preparations for ploughing and sowing
【备荒】 bèihuāng prepare against natural disasters
【备件】 bèijiàn spare parts
【备考】 bèikǎo (an appendix, note, etc.) for reference
【备课】 bèikè (of a teacher) prepare lessons
【备料】 bèiliào ① get the materials ready ② prepare feed (for livestock)
【备品】 bèipǐn machine parts or tools kept in reserve; spare parts
【备取】 bèiqǔ be on the waiting list (for admission to a school)
【备忘录】 bèiwànglù ① 〈外〉 memorandum; aide-mémoire ② memorandum book

【备用】 bèiyòng reserve; spare; alternate ◇ ～航空站 alternate airport/ ～机器 standby machine/ ～款项 reserve funds/ ～轮胎 spare tyre/ ～燃油箱 reserve fuel tank

【备战】 bèizhàn ① prepare for war: 扩军～ arms expansion and war preparations ② be prepared against war: ～、备荒、为人民。Be prepared against war, be prepared against natural disasters, do everything for the people.

【备至】 bèizhì to the utmost; in every possible way: 关怀～ show sb. every consideration/ 颂扬～ praise profusely

【备注】 bèizhù remarks ◇ ～栏 remarks column

**背** bèi ① the back of the body: ～痛 backache ② the back of an object: 手～ the back of the hand/ 刀～儿 the back of a knife/ 椅～ the back of a chair ③ with the back towards: ～着太阳坐 sit with one's back to the sun/ ～山面海 with hills behind and the sea in front ④ turn away: 把脸～过去 turn one's face away ⑤ hide sth. from; do sth. behind sb.'s back: ～着人说话 talk behind sb.'s back/ 没有什么～人的事 have nothing to hide from anyone ⑥ recite from memory; learn by heart (或 by rote): ～台词 speak one's lines ⑦ act contrary to; violate; break: ～约 violate an agreement; break one's promise; go back on one's word ⑧ out-of-the-way: ～街 back street; side street ⑨ hard of hearing: 耳朵有点～ be a bit hard of hearing ⑩ 〈口〉 unlucky
另见 bēi

【背城借一】 bèi chéng jiè yī make a last-ditch stand before the city wall; fight to the last ditch; put up a desperate struggle

【背道而驰】 bèi dào ér chí run in the opposite direction; run counter to

【背地里】 bèidìli behind sb.'s back; privately; on the sly

【背风】 bèifēng out of the wind; on the lee side; leeward ◇ ～处 lee side; sheltered side

【背光】 bèiguāng be in a poor light; do sth. with one's back to the light; stand in one's own light

【背后】 bèihòu ① behind; at the back; in the rear: 门～ behind the door/ 房子～ at the back of the house/ 从～袭击敌人 attack the enemy from the rear ② behind sb.'s back: 当面不说，～乱说 say nothing to people to their faces but gossip about them behind their backs/ ～捣鬼 plot (或 scheme) behind the scenes; play underhand tricks/ ～下毒手 stab in the back

【背脊】 bèijǐ the back of the human body

【背井离乡】 bèijǐng-líxiāng leave one's native place (esp. against one's will)

【背景】 bèijǐng background; backdrop: 历史～ historical background (或 setting)

【背静】 bèijing quiet and secluded

【背离】 bèilí deviate from; depart from: ～革命路线 deviate from the revolutionary line/ ～社会主义的言论 views departing from socialism

【背面】 bèimiàn the back; the reverse side; the wrong side: 信封的～ the back of an envelope/ 请阅～ please turn over (P.T.O.); see overleaf

【背叛】 bèipàn betray; forsake: 现代修正主义者～了马克思主义。The modern revisionists have betrayed Marxism./ 忘记过去就意味着～。Forgetting the past means betrayal./ ～原来的阶级 forsake one's original class; rebel against one's own class

【背鳍】 bèiqí 〈动〉 dorsal fin

【背弃】 bèiqì abandon; desert; renounce: ～原来的立场 abandon one's original stand/ ～自己的诺言 go back on one's word

【背时】 bèishí 〈方〉 ① behind the times ② unlucky

【背书】 bèishū ① recite a lesson from memory; repeat a lesson ② 〈经〉 endorsement (on a cheque)

【背水一战】 bèi shuǐ yī zhàn fight with one's back to the river — fight to win or die

【背诵】 bèisòng recite; repeat from memory

【背斜】 bèixié 〈地〉 anticline ◇ ～层 anticlinal strata

【背心】 bèixīn a sleeveless garment: 西服～ waistcoat/ 汗～ vest; singlet/ 毛～ sleeveless woollen sweater/ 棉～ cotton-padded waistcoat

【背信弃义】 bèixìn-qìyì break faith with sb.; be perfidious: ～的行为 a breach of faith; perfidy/ ～地撕毁协定和合同 perfidiously tear up agreements and contracts

【背阴】 bèiyīn in the shade; shady ◇ ～处 shady spot

【背影】 bèiyǐng a view of sb.'s back; a figure viewed from behind: 凝望着他逐渐消失的～ gazing at his receding figure

【背约】 bèiyuē break an agreement; go back on one's word; fail to keep one's promise

【背着手】 bèizhe shǒu with one's hands clasped behind one's back

**钡** bèi 〈化〉 barium (Ba)

【钡餐】 bèicān 〈医〉 barium meal

**悖** bèi 〈书〉 ① be contrary to; go against: ～理 contrary to reason/ 并行不～ parallel and not contrary to each other; not mutually exclusive ② perverse; erroneous

【悖谬】 bèimiù 〈书〉 absurd; preposterous

【悖入悖出】 bèirù-bèichū ill-gotten, ill-spent

**被** bèi ① quilt: 棉～ cotton-wadded quilt ② 〈介〉〔在被动式里引进主动者〕: 他爸爸是～地主害死的。His father was murdered by a landlord. ③ 〈助〉〔用在动词前，表示主语是被动者〕: ～捕 be arrested; be under arrest/ ～选为主席 be elected chairman

【被剥削阶级】 bèibōxuējiējí exploited class

【被乘数】 bèichéngshù 〈数〉 multiplicand

【被除数】 bèichúshù 〈数〉 dividend

【被袋】 bèidài bedding bag

【被单】 bèidān (bed) sheet ◇ ～布 sheeting

【被动】 bèidòng passive: 陷于～地位 land oneself in a passive position; be thrown into passivity/ 变～为主动 regain the initiative ◇ ～式 〈语〉 passive form/ ～语态 〈语〉 passive voice

【被服】 bèifú bedding and clothing (esp. for army use) ◇ ～厂 clothing factory

【被俘】 bèifú be captured; be taken prisoner ◇ ～人员 captured personnel

【被告】 bèigào 〈法〉 defendant; the accused ◇ ～席 defendant's seat; dock

【被管制分子】 bèiguǎnzhìfènzǐ a person under the surveillance of the masses

【被害人】 bèihàirén 〈法〉 the injured party; the victim

【被加数】 bèijiāshù 〈数〉 summand

【被减数】 bèijiǎnshù 〈数〉 minuend

【被里】 bèilǐ the underneath side of a quilt

【被面】 bèimiàn the facing of a quilt: 绣花～ an embroidered quilt cover

【被难】 bèinàn be killed in a disaster, political incident, etc.

【被迫】 bèipò be compelled; be forced; be constrained: 敌人～放下武器。The enemy were compelled to lay down their arms.

【被侵略者】 bèiqīnlüèzhě victim of aggression

【被褥】 bèirù bedding; bedclothes

【被上诉人】 bèishàngsùrén 〈法〉 appellee

【被套】 bèitào ① bedding bag ② (bag-shaped) quilt cover ③ cotton wadding for a quilt
【被统治者】 bèitǒngzhìzhě the ruled
【被窝儿】 bèiwōr a quilt folded to form a sleeping bag
【被选举权】 bèixuǎnjǔquán the right to be elected
【被压迫民族】 bèiyāpò mínzú oppressed nation
【被子植物】 bèizǐ zhíwù angiosperm
【被子】 bèizi quilt

**倍** bèi ① times; -fold: 四～ four times; fourfold/ 二的五～是十。Five times two is ten./ 十是五的两～。Ten is twice as much as five./ 大一～ twice as big; twice the size/ 增长了五～ increase by 500%; register a 500% increase; be six times as much/ 战胜了两～于我的敌人。We defeated an enemy outnumbering us two to one./ 产量成～增长。Output has doubled and redoubled. ② double; twice as much: 勇气～增 with redoubled courage
【倍频器】 bèipínqì 〈电子〉 frequency multiplier
【倍数】 bèishù 〈数〉 multiple
【倍塔】 bèitǎ beta ◇ ～粒子 〈物〉 beta particle/ ～射线 〈物〉 beta ray
【倍增器】 bèizēngqì 〈电子〉 multiplier: 光电～ photoelectric multiplier

**焙** bèi bake over a slow fire: ～干 dry over a fire/ ～制 cure sth. by drying it over a fire
【焙烧】 bèishāo roast; bake ◇ ～炉 roaster

**辈** bèi ① people of a certain kind; the like: 无能之～ people without ability ② generation: 他比我长(小)一～。He's one generation my senior (junior)./ 他俩同～。They belong to the same generation./ 老一～的无产阶级革命家 proletarian revolutionaries of the older generation ③ lifetime: 后半～儿 the latter part of one's life
【辈出】 bèichū come forth in large numbers: 人材～ people of talent coming forth in large numbers/ 英雄～的时代 an age of heroes
【辈分】 bèifen seniority in the family or clan; position in the family hierarchy: 她的～比我小。She ranks as my junior in the clan.
【辈子】 bèizi all one's life; lifetime: 他给地主扛了一～的活。He worked for a landlord all his life./ 改造世界观是一～的事。The remoulding of one's world outlook is a lifelong affair./ 她家三～都当工人。Hers has been a working-class family for three generations.

**惫** bèi exhausted; fatigued

**蓓** bèi
【蓓蕾】 bèilěi bud

**褙** bèi stick one piece of cloth or paper on top of another

**鞴** bèi 见"鞲鞴"gōubèi

## bei

**呗** bei 〈助〉 ①〔表示事实或道理明显,很容易了解〕: 你不会骑车就学～。You can't ride a bike? Well, learn to. ②〔表示勉强同意的语气〕: 你一定要去,就去～。Well, go if you insist.

**臂** bei 见"胳臂"gēbei

另见 bì

## bēn

**奔** bēn ① run quickly: ～马 a galloping horse ② hurry; hasten; rush: ～赴前线 hurry to the front/ ～向共产主义明天 march on towards the Communist future ③ flee: 东～西窜 flee in all directions
另见 bèn
【奔波】 bēnbō rush about; be busy running about: 两地～ shuttle back and forth between two places
【奔驰】 bēnchí run quickly; speed: 骏马在草原上～。Sturdy steeds gallop on the grasslands./ 火车向前～。The train sped on.
【奔放】 bēnfàng bold and unrestrained; untrammelled: ～不羁的风格 a bold and flowing style/ 热情～ overflowing with enthusiasm
【奔流】 bēnliú ① flow at great speed; pour: ～入海 flow into the sea/ 铁水～ molten iron pouring out in a stream ② racing current
【奔忙】 bēnmáng be busy rushing about; bustle about: 为革命日夜～ be busy day and night working for the revolution
【奔命】 bēnmìng rush about on errands; be kept on the run: 疲于～ be tired out by too much running around; be kept constantly on the run
另见 bènmìng
【奔跑】 bēnpǎo run
【奔丧】 bēnsāng hasten home for the funeral of a parent or grandparent
【奔逃】 bēntáo flee; run away: 四散～ flee in all directions; flee helter-skelter; stampede
【奔腾】 bēnténg ① gallop: 犹如万马～ like ten thousand horses galloping ahead ② surge forward; roll on in waves: 革命的洪流～向前。The tide of revolution is surging ahead./ 浩浩长江,～不息。The mighty waters of the Changjiang roll on incessantly.
【奔袭】 bēnxí 〈军〉 long-range raid
【奔泻】 bēnxiè (of torrents) rush down; pour down: 怒涛滚滚,～千里。An angry torrent rolls thunderously on for a thousand *li*.
【奔走】 bēnzǒu ① run ② rush about; be busy running about: ～呼号 go around campaigning for a cause/ ～相告 run around spreading the news; lose no time in telling each other the news

**贲** bēn
另见 bì
【贲门】 bēnmén 〈生理〉 cardia

**锛** bēn ① adze ② cut with an adze
【锛子】 bēnzi adze

## běn

**本** běn ① the root or stem of a plant: 水有源,木有～。A stream has its source; a tree has its root. ② foundation; basis; origin: 兵民是胜利之～。The army and the people are the foundation of victory. ③ capital; principal: 还～付息 pay back the capital (或 principal) plus interest/ ～小利微 have tiny funds and small earnings ④ original: ～意 original idea; real intention/ 我～想不去。Originally I didn't want to go. ⑤ one's own; native: ～厂 this factory/

～乡～土 native soil; home village ⑥ this; current; present: ～周(月) this week (month); the current week (month)/ ～决议 this resolution ⑦ according to; based on: ～着政策办事 act according to policy/ 每句话都有所～。Every statement is well-founded. ⑧ book: 帐～儿 account book/ 日记～ diary/ 照相～ photograph album ⑨ edition; version: 普及～ popular edition/ 马克思《资本论》英译～ the English translation (或 version) of Marx's *Capital* ⑩〈量〉[用于书籍、簿册等]: 两～书 two books/ 这部电影有十二～。This is a twelve-reel film.

【本本主义】 běnběnzhǔyì book worship; bookishness

【本草】 běncǎo a book on Chinese (herbal) medicine; Chinese materia medica ◇《～纲目》*Compendium of Materia Medica*

【本初子午线】 běnchū zǐwǔxiàn the first meridian; the prime meridian

【本底】 běndǐ 〈物〉 background: 放射性～ radioactive background ◇ ～噪声 background noise

【本地】 běndì this locality: ～风光 local colour/ ～口音 local accent/ ～货 local (或 native) goods/ 我是～人。I'm a native of this place. 或 I was born here.

【本笃会】 Běndǔhuì 〈天主教〉 the Benedictine Order

【本分】 běnfèn one's duty: 尽～ do one's duty (或 bit)/ 为人民服务是我们的～。To serve the people is our duty.

【本固枝荣】 běn gù zhī róng when the root is firm, the branches flourish

【本国】 běnguó one's own country: ～资源 national resources ◇ ～语 native language; mother tongue

【本行】 běnháng one's line; one's own profession: 搞建筑是他的～。Architecture is his line.

【本家】 běnjiā a member of the same clan; a distant relative with the same family name

【本届】 běnjiè current; this year's: ～联合国大会 the current session of the U.N. General Assembly/ ～毕业生 this year's graduates

【本金】 běnjīn capital; principal

【本科】 běnkē undergraduate course; regular college course ◇ ～学生 undergraduate

【本来】 běnlái ① original: ～的意思 original meaning (或 intention)/ 事物～的辩证法 the dialectics inherent in things ② originally; at first: 大会～定星期五举行。The meeting was originally fixed for Friday. ③ it goes without saying; of course: ～就该这样办。Of course it should be handled that way./ 你～用不着着急。You needn't have worried about it./ 这样的事～不应该发生。Such a thing should never have been allowed to happen in the first place.

【本来面目】 běnlái miànmù true colours; true features: 认清修正主义者的～ see the revisionists in their true colours/ 恢复历史的～ restore historical truth/ 按照历史的～ according to what actually occurred in history

【本垒】 běnlěi 〈棒、垒球〉 home base

【本领】 běnlǐng skill; ability; capability: 组织生产的～ ability to organize production/ 苦练杀敌～ train hard to increase one's combat efficiency/ 掌握为人民服务的～ master the skills needed for serving the people

【本末】 běn-mò ① the whole course of an event from beginning to end; ins and outs: 详述～ tell the whole story from beginning to end ② the fundamental and the incidental

【本末倒置】 běn mò dàozhì take the branch for the root; put the incidental before the fundamental; put the cart before the horse

【本能】 běnnéng instinct: 阶级～ class instinct

【本年度】 běnniándù this year; the current year: ～计划 this year's plan/ ～国家预算 the national budget for this fiscal year

【本票】 běnpiào cashier's cheque

【本钱】 běnqián capital

【本人】 běnrén ① I (me, myself) ② oneself; in person: 我想见政委～。I'd like to see the commissar himself./ 必须你～来。You must come in person./ ～成分 one's class status

【本色】 běnsè true (或 inherent) qualities; distinctive character: 劳动人民的～ the true qualities of the labouring people/ 他们战天斗地,显示了贫下中农的～。In combating nature the poor and lower-middle peasants showed their sterling qualities.

【本色】 běnshǎi natural colour ◇ ～布 grey (cloth)

【本身】 běnshēn itself; in itself: 运动～就是矛盾。Motion itself is a contradiction./ 广交会～标志着我国对外贸易的发展。The Guangzhou Trade Fair is in itself a symbol of the growth of China's foreign trade./ 条约～ the treaty *per se*

【本生灯】 běnshēngdēng Bunsen burner

【本事】 běnshì source material; original story

【本事】 běnshi 见"本领"

【本题】 běntí the subject under discussion; the point at issue: 请不要离开～。Please keep (或 stick) to the point./ 这跟～无关。This has nothing to do with the point at issue. 或 This is quite irrelevant.

【本体】 běntǐ 〈哲〉 noumenon; thing-in-itself ◇ ～论 ontology

【本土】 běntǔ ① one's native country (或 land) ② metropolitan territory

【本位】 běnwèi ① standard: 金～ gold standard ② one's own department or unit: ～工作 the work of one's own department; one's own job (或 work) ◇ ～号 〈乐〉 natural

【本位主义】 běnwèizhǔyì selfish departmentalism; departmental selfishness

【本文】 běnwén ① this text, article, etc. ② the main body of a book

【本性】 běnxìng natural instincts (或 character, disposition); nature; inherent quality: ～难移。It is difficult to alter one's character. 或 The leopard can't change his spots./ 帝国主义、社会帝国主义的～就是战争。By their very nature imperialism and social-imperialism mean war.

【本义】 běnyì 〈语〉 original meaning; literal sense: "兵"字的～是武器。The original meaning of "兵" is weapon./ 这个词不能按～去理解。This word should not be taken in its literal sense.

【本意】 běnyì original idea; real intention

【本影】 běnyǐng 〈物〉 umbra

【本源】 běnyuán origin; source

【本着】 běnzhe in line with; in conformity with; in the light of: ～我们一贯的立场 in line with our consistent stand/ ～为人民服务的精神 motivated by a desire to serve the people/ ～增进两国之间友好关系的愿望 actuated by a desire to promote friendly relations between our two countries/ ～平等互利、互通有无的原则 adhering to the principles of equality, mutual benefit and helping to meet each other's needs/ 办一切事业都要～节约的原则。In running all enterprises we should observe the principle of frugality.

【本职】 běnzhí one's job (或 duty): 做好～工作 do one's own job well

【本质】 běnzhì essence; nature; innate character; intrinsic quality: ～方面 an essential aspect/ 非～方面 a non-essential aspect/ ～差别 an essential distinction/ 透过现象看～ see through the appearance to the essence/ 一切反动派～上是虚弱的。All reactionaries are intrinsically weak.

【本州】 Běnzhōu Honshu

【本子】 běnzi ① book; notebook: 笔记～ notebook/ 改～

go over students' written exercises; correct papers ② edition
【本族语】 běnzúyǔ native language; mother tongue

**苯** běn 〈化〉 benzene; benzol: ～中毒 benzene poisoning; benzolism
【苯胺】 běn'àn 〈化〉 aniline
◇ ～革 aniline leather/ ～染料 aniline dyes/ ～印刷 aniline printing; flexography/ ～紫 mauve
【苯巴比妥】 běnbābǐtuǒ 〈药〉 phenobarbital; phenobarbitone; luminal
【苯酚】 běnfēn 〈化〉 phenol
【苯海拉明】 běnhǎilāmíng 〈药〉 diphenhydramine; benadryl
【苯甲酸】 běnjiǎsuān 〈化〉 benzoic acid
【苯妥英纳】 běntuǒyīngnà 〈药〉 phenytoin sodium; dilantin
【苯乙烯】 běnyǐxī 〈化〉 styrene: 聚～ polystyrene

**畚** běn 〈方〉 scoop up with a dustpan
【畚箕】 běnjī 〈方〉 ① a bamboo or wicker scoop ② dustpan

## bèn

**奔** bèn ① go straight towards; head for: 直～实验室 head straight for the laboratory/ 这条路～天津。This road goes (或 leads) to Tianjin./ 咱们是一心～共产主义。Our minds are set on the goal of communism. ② approach; be getting on for: 他是～六十的人了。He's getting on for sixty.
另见 bēn
【奔命】 bènmìng 〈口〉 be in a desperate hurry
另见 bēnmìng
【奔头儿】 bèntour sth. to strive for; prospect: 大有～ have a bright prospect

**笨** bèn ① stupid; dull; foolish: ～人 a stupid person; fool/ 脑子～ stupid; slow-witted ② clumsy; awkward: 他这人～手～脚。He is clumsy. 或 His fingers are all thumbs. ③ cumbersome; awkward; unwieldy: 这把锄头太～。This is an awkward hoe.
【笨蛋】 bèndàn 〈骂〉 fool; idiot
【笨口拙舌】 bènkǒu-zhuōshé awkward in speech
【笨鸟先飞】 bèn niǎo xiān fēi clumsy birds have to start flying early — the slow need to start early
【笨重】 bènzhòng heavy; cumbersome; unwieldy: ～的家具 heavy (或 cumbersome) furniture/ 通过技术革新,我们车间摆脱了～的体力劳动。Through technical innovations, our workshop has got rid of heavy manual labour.
【笨拙】 bènzhuō clumsy; awkward; stupid: 动作～ clumsy (或 awkward) in movement/ ～的伎俩 stupid tricks

## bēng

**崩** bēng ① collapse: 山～ landslide; landslip ② burst: 把气球吹～了 burst a balloon/ 他们谈～了。Their negotiations broke down. ③ be hit by sth. bursting: 爆竹～了他的手。The firecracker went off in his hand. ④〈口〉 execute by shooting; shoot ⑤〈旧〉 (of an emperor) die
【崩溃】 bēngkuì collapse; crumble; fall apart: 殖民主义的～ the collapse of colonialism/ 旧世界正在～。The old world is crumbling./ 敌军全线～。The enemy collapsed all along the line.
【崩裂】 bēngliè burst (或 break) apart; crack: 炸药轰隆一声,山石～。Boom! The dynamite sent the rocks flying.
【崩龙族】 Bēnglóngzú the Benglong (Penglung) nationality, living in Yunnan
【崩漏】 bēnglòu 〈中医〉 uterine bleeding
【崩塌】 bēngtā collapse; crumble
【崩陷】 bēngxiàn fall in; cave in

**绷** bēng ① stretch (或 draw) tight: 弓弦～得很紧。The bowstring is stretched taut./ 在绷子上～块绸子 stretch a piece of silk on an embroidery frame/ 阶级斗争这根弦一定要～紧。The bowstring of class struggle must be drawn tight — we must be on the alert in class struggle. ② spring; bounce: 盒子一打开,弹簧就～出来了。When the box was opened, the spring jumped out. ③ baste; tack; pin
另见 běng; bèng
【绷带】 bēngdài bandage
【绷簧】 bēnghuáng 〈方〉 spring
【绷子】 bēngzi embroidery frame; hoop; tambour

**嘣** bēng 〈象〉〔东西跳动或爆裂的声音〕: 我心里～～直跳。My heart is thumping./ 爆竹～地一响。The firecracker went bang.

## béng

**甭** béng 〈方〉 don't; needn't: ～再说了。Don't say any more./ 有这样好的徒工,老师傅～提有多高兴了。Needless to say, the old master worker was happy to have such good apprentices.

## běng

**绷** běng 〈口〉 ①〔多用于〕: ～着脸 look displeased; pull a long face ② strain oneself: 咬住牙～住劲 clench one's teeth and strain one's muscles
另见 bēng; bèng

## bèng

**迸** bèng spout; spurt; burst forth: 火星乱～ sparks flying in all directions/ 他怎么突然～出这句话来? What made him blurt out such a remark?
【迸发】 bèngfā burst forth; burst out: 大厅里～出一阵笑声。There was an outburst of laughter in the hall./ 热烈的掌声,有如春雷～。Applause broke out like spring thunder.
【迸裂】 bèngliè split; burst (open): 脑浆～ have one's brains dashed out

**泵** bèng pump: 离心～ centrifugal pump/ 高扬程～ high lift pump
【泵房】 bèngfáng pump house
【泵排量】 bèngpáiliàng pumpage; pump delivery

**蚌** Bèng short for Bengbu (蚌埠)
另见 bàng

**绷** bèng ① split open; crack: 玻璃～了一条缝儿。The glass has a crack in it. ②〈口〉〔用于某些形容词前面表示程度深〕 very: ～脆 very crisp/ ～硬 hard as a rock; stiff as a board
另见 bēng; běng

**镚** bèng small coin
【镚子】 bèngzi 〈口〉 small coin: 他干了一年,地主连个～也

没给。The landlord didn't give him a single penny for a whole year's work.

**蹦** bèng leap; jump; spring: 他使劲一～就过了沟。With one powerful leap he crossed the ditch./ 这件事还没处理完，那件事又～出来了。One problem had scarcely been solved when another cropped up.

【蹦蹦跳跳】 bèngbèng-tiàotiào bouncing and vivacious

## bī

**逼** bī ① force; compel; drive: ～使对方采取守势 force one's opponent onto the defensive/ 敌人～他招供，他一句话也不说。The enemy tried to force him to talk, but he wouldn't say a word./ 旧社会～得她走投无路。The old society left her no way out. ② press for; extort: ～租 press for payment of rent ③ press on towards; press up to; close in on: 直～城下 press up to the city wall

【逼宫】 bīgōng (of ministers, etc.) force the king or emperor to abdicate

【逼供】 bīgòng extort a confession

【逼供信】 bī-gòng-xìn obtain confessions by compulsion and give them credence: 要重证据，重调查研究，严禁～。Stress should be laid on the weight of evidence and on investigation and study, and it is strictly forbidden to obtain confessions by compulsion and to give them credence.

【逼近】 bījìn press on towards; close in on; approach; draw near: 我军已～运河。Our troops were pressing on towards the canal./ ～敌主力 close in on the main force of the enemy

【逼迫】 bīpò force; compel; coerce: 国民党匪军～老百姓迁移。The KMT bandit troops forced the inhabitants to abandon their homes.

【逼人】 bīrén pressing; threatening: 形势～。The situation spurs us on./ 寒气～。There is a cold nip in the air.

【逼上梁山】 bī shàng Liángshān be driven to join the Liangshan Mountain rebels; be driven to revolt; be forced to do sth. desperate

【逼视】 bīshì look at from close-up; watch intently: 光采夺目，不可～ shine with dazzling brilliance

【逼死】 bīsǐ hound sb. to death

【逼肖】 bīxiào 〈书〉 bear a close resemblance to; be the very image of

【逼仄】 bīzè 〈书〉 narrow; cramped

【逼债】 bīzhài press for payment of debts; dun

【逼真】 bīzhēn ① lifelike; true to life: 这幅湘竹画得十分～。This painting of mottled bamboos is really true to life. ② distinctly; clearly: 听得～ hear distinctly ◇ ～度〈电子〉 fidelity

## bí

**荸** bí

【荸荠】 bíqi water chestnut (*Eleocharis tuberosa*)

**鼻** bí nose

【鼻窦】 bídòu 〈生理〉 paranasal sinus ◇ ～炎 nasosinusitis

【鼻镜】 bíjìng 〈医〉 rhinoscope: 电光～ nasoscope

【鼻孔】 bíkǒng nostril

【鼻梁】 bíliáng bridge of the nose

【鼻牛儿】 bíniúr 〈方〉 hardened mucus in nostrils

【鼻衄】 bínǜ 〈医〉 nosebleed; epistaxis

【鼻腔】 bíqiāng 〈生理〉 nasal cavity

【鼻青脸肿】 bíqīng-liǎnzhǒng a bloody nose and a swollen face; badly battered: 打得～ have one's face bashed in; be beaten black and blue

【鼻儿】 bír 〈方〉 ① a hole in an implement, utensil, etc., for sth. to be inserted into; eye: 针～ the eye of a needle/ 门～ bolt staple ② 〈口〉 whistle: 火车拉～了。The engine is whistling.

【鼻塞】 bísè have a stuffy nose

【鼻饲法】 bísìfǎ 〈医〉 nasal feeding

【鼻涕】 bítì nasal mucus; snivel: 流～ have a running nose

【鼻息】 bíxī breath: 听见均匀的～声 hear sb.'s regular and even breathing/ 仰人～ be slavishly dependent on others

【鼻烟】 bíyān snuff ◇ ～盒 snuffbox/ ～壶 snuff bottle

【鼻炎】 bíyán 〈医〉 rhinitis

【鼻音】 bíyīn 〈语〉 nasal sound: 说话带～ speak with a twang ◇ ～化 nasalization

【鼻渊】 bíyuān 〈中医〉 nasosinusitis

【鼻韵母】 bíyùnmǔ 〈语〉 (of Chinese pronunciation) a vowel followed by a nasal consonant

【鼻针疗法】 bízhēn liáofǎ 〈中医〉 nose-acupuncture therapy

【鼻中隔】 bízhōnggé 〈生理〉 nasal septum

【鼻子】 bízi nose: 高～ high-bridged nose; high nose/ 塌～ snub nose; pug nose/ 鹰钩～ aquiline nose; Roman nose/ 牵着～走 lead by the nose/ 他把这事说得有～有眼的。He made the story sound quite convincing./ 不要只顾～底下的小事。Don't get bogged down in trivial matters.

【鼻祖】 bízǔ the earliest ancestor; originator (of a tradition, school of thought, etc.)

## bǐ

**匕** bǐ an ancient type of spoon

【匕首】 bǐshǒu dagger

**比** bǐ ① compare; contrast: ～得上 can compare with; compare favourably with/ 想想过去的苦，～～今天的甜 recall past bitterness and contrast it with present happiness/ 不～不知道，一～吓一跳。If you don't compare, you're in the dark; the moment you do, you get a start. ② emulate; compete; match: ～革命干劲 emulate (或 compete with) each other in revolutionary drive/ 咱俩～～谁先跑到。Let's have a race and see who gets there first. ③ draw an analogy; liken to; compare to: 列宁把帝国主义～做泥足巨人。Lenin likened imperialism to a colossus with feet of clay. ④ gesture; gesticulate: 连说带～ gesticulate as one talks ⑤ copy; model after: ～着旧衣裁新衣 pattern a new garment on an old one ⑥ 〈介〉〔用来比较性状和程度的差别〕: 许多同志都～我干得好。Many comrades have done better than I./ 人民的生活一年～一年好。The life of the people is getting better and better each year. ⑦ ratio; proportion: 反～ inverse ratio (或 proportion)/ 这里小麦同水稻的年产量约为一与三之～。Here the annual yield of wheat and rice is in a ratio of about one to three. ⑧ to (in a score): 甲队以二～一胜乙队。Team A beat team B (by a score of) two to one./ 现在几～几？ What's the score? ⑨ 〈书〉 close together; next to

【比比皆是】 bǐbǐ jiē shì can be found everywhere

【比方】 bǐfang analogy; instance: 打～ draw an analogy/ 拿盖房子作～ take for instance the building of a house/ 这不过是个～。This is only by way of analogy.

【比分】 bǐfēn 〈体〉 score: 场上～是三比二。The score is 3 to 2./ 双方～十分接近。It's a close game.

【比画】 bǐhua gesture; gesticulate: 他～着讲。He made himself understood with the help of gestures.

【比价】 bǐjià price relations; parity; rate of exchange: 工农业产品～ the price parities between industrial and agricultural products/ 英镑和美元的～ the rate of exchange between the pound sterling and the U.S. dollar/ 粮棉～ the price ratios between grain and cotton
【比较】 bǐjiào ① compare; contrast: 把译文和原文～一下 check the translation against the original/ 真理是跟谬误相～,并且同它作斗争发展起来的。Truth stands in contrast to falsehood and develops in struggle with it./ 社员的生活水平同去年～又有所提高。The living standard of the commune members is higher than it was last year. ②〈介〉〔用来比较性状和程度的差别〕: ～去年有显著的增长 show a marked increase over last year ③〈副〉fairly; comparatively; relatively; quite; rather: 两个都可以,不过这个～好一点儿。Either will do, but this one is a bit better./ 这里条件～艰苦。Conditions are rather tough here. ◇ ～级〈语〉comparative degree
【比利时】 Bǐlìshí Belgium ◇ ～人 Belgian
【比例】 bǐlì ① proportion: 正(反)～ direct (inverse) proportion/ 不合～ out of proportion/ 按～发展 develop in proportion; proportionate development/ 安排积累和消费的适当～ establish a proper ratio between accumulation and consumption ② scale: 按～绘制 be drawn to scale/ 这个模型是按准确的～做的。This model is made exactly to scale. ◇ ～税〈经〉proportional tax
【比例尺】 bǐlìchǐ ①〈测〉scale: 这张地图的～是四十万分之一。The scale of the map is 1:400,000. ② architect's scale; engineer's scale
【比量】 bǐliang take rough measurements (with the hand, a stick, string, etc.)
【比邻】 bǐlín ① neighbour; next-door neighbour ② near; next to: 跟车站～的那个工厂 the factory next to the railway station
【比率】 bǐlǜ ratio; rate
【比目鱼】 bǐmùyú flatfish; flounder
【比拟】 bǐnǐ ① compare; draw a parallel; match: 无可～ beyond compare; incomparable; matchless ② analogy; metaphor; comparison: 这种～是不恰当的。It is inappropriate to draw such a parallel.
【比热】 bǐrè〈物〉specific heat
【比容】 bǐróng〈物〉specific volume
【比如】 bǐrú for example; for instance; such as
【比赛】 bǐsài match; competition: 友谊第一,～第二。Friendship first, competition second./ 足球～ football match/ 自行车～ bicycle race/ 射击～ shooting contest/ 象棋～ chess tournament ◇ ～规则 rules of the game; rules of a contest/ ～项目 event
【比色分析】 bǐsè fēnxī〈化〉colorimetric analysis
【比色计】 bǐsèjì〈化〉colorimeter
【比上不足,比下有余】 bǐ shàng bù zú, bǐ xià yǒu yú fall short of the best but be better than the worst; can pass muster
【比湿】 bǐshī〈气〉specific humidity
【比试】 bǐshi ① have a competition: 不信咱俩～～。If you don't believe me, let's have a competition and see. ② measure with one's hand or arm; make a gesture of measuring: 两个小演员拿长枪一～,就开始对打起来。With a flourish of their spears, the two little performers started sparring with each other.
【比学赶帮超】 bǐ-xué-gǎn-bāng-chāo emulate, learn from, catch up with, help and in turn surpass each other
【比翼】 bǐyì fly wing to wing: ～双飞 pair off wing to wing; fly side by side ◇ ～鸟 a pair of lovebirds — a devoted couple
【比喻】 bǐyù metaphor; analogy; figure of speech: 这只是一个～的说法。This is just a figure of speech./ 人们常用青松来～坚贞不屈的革命者。Steadfast revolutionaries are often likened to pine trees.
【比照】 bǐzhào ① according to; in the light of: 我们可以～其它厂的做法拟定计划。We can draw up our plan in the light of the experience of other factories. ② contrast: 两相～ contrasting the two
【比值】 bǐzhí specific value; ratio
【比重】 bǐzhòng ① proportion: 工业在整个国民经济中的～ the proportion of industry in the national economy as a whole/ 农业～大的省 predominantly agricultural provinces ②〈物〉specific gravity ◇ ～计〈物〉hydrometer/ ～选种〈农〉specific gravity selection (of seeds)

## 吡 bǐ

【吡啶】 bǐdìng〈化〉pyridine
【吡咯】 bǐluò〈化〉pyrrole

## 妣 bǐ

〈书〉deceased mother: 先～ my deceased mother

## 彼 bǐ

① that; those; the other; another: ～时 at that time/ 由此及～ proceed from one to the other ② the other party: 要知己知～。You must know both your opponent and yourself.
【彼岸】 bǐ'àn〈佛教〉the other shore; Faramita
【彼此】 bǐcǐ ① each other; one another: ～呼应 support each other; act in coordination with each other ②〈套〉〔常叠用做答话,表示大家一样〕: 您辛苦啦! — ～～! You must have taken a lot of trouble about it. — So must you!
【彼一时,此一时】 bǐ yīshí, cǐ yīshí that was one situation, and this is another — times have changed

## 秕 bǐ

(of grain) not plump; blighted
【秕糠】 bǐkāng ① chaff ② worthless stuff
【秕子】 bǐzi blighted grain

## 笔 bǐ

① pen: 圆珠～ ball-point pen/ 蘸水～ pen/ 钢～ fountain pen/ 毛～ writing brush/ 下～ set (或 put) pen to paper ② technique of writing, calligraphy or drawing: 文～ style of writing ③ write: 代～ write sth. for sb./ ～之于书 put down in black and white ④ stroke; touch: "天"字有四～。The character 天 has four strokes./ 这里再添几～,情节就更生动了。Add a few touches here and the episode will be more lively./ 你给他写信时,替我带一～。Please remember me to him when you write. ⑤〈量〉〔用于款项、书画等〕: 一～钱 a sum of money; a fund/ 我们有三～帐要算。We have three scores to settle./ 写得一～好字 write a good hand
【笔触】 bǐchù brush stroke in Chinese painting and calligraphy; brushwork; style of drawing or writing: 简洁的～ simple, light touches; a succinct style
【笔底下】 bǐdǐxia ability to write: ～不错 write well/ ～来得快 write with ease (或 facility)
【笔调】 bǐdiào (of writing) tone; style: 讽刺的～ a satirical tone/ 他用通俗的～写了许多科学读物。He wrote many books on science in a popular style.
【笔法】 bǐfǎ technique of writing, calligraphy or drawing
【笔锋】 bǐfēng ① the tip of a writing brush ② vigour of style in writing; stroke; touch: ～犀利 write in an incisive style; wield a pointed pen
【笔杆】 bǐgǎn ① the shaft of a pen or writing brush; penholder ② pen: 耍～〈口〉wield the pen
【笔杆子】 bǐgǎnzi ① pen ② an effective writer: 他是我们理论组的～。He is one of the most effective writers of our theoretical study group.
【笔画】 bǐhuà strokes of a Chinese character

【笔迹】 bǐjì a person's handwriting; hand: 对～ identify sb.'s handwriting
【笔记】 bǐjì ① take down (in writing) ② notes: 记～ take notes ③ a type of literature consisting mainly of short sketches ◇ ～本 notebook/ ～小说 literary sketches; sketchbook
【笔架】 bǐjià pen rack; penholder
【笔尖】 bǐjiān ① nib; pen point ② the tip of a writing brush or pencil
【笔力】 bǐlì vigour of strokes in calligraphy or drawing; vigour of style in literary composition: ～雄健 powerful strokes/ 这篇文章没有表现出作者平素的～。This essay lacks the vigour and vitality which characterize the author's usual style.
【笔录】 bǐlù ① put down (in writing); take down ② notes; record
【笔帽】 bǐmào the cap of a pen, pencil or writing brush
【笔名】 bǐmíng pen name; pseudonym
【笔墨】 bǐmò pen and ink; words; writing: 我们激动的心情难以用～来形容。Words can hardly describe how excited we were./ 把无关紧要的话删去,不要浪费～。To save space leave out superfluous words and sentences. ◇ ～官司 written polemics (或 controversy); a battle of words
【笔石】 bǐshí 〈古生物〉 graptolite
【笔试】 bǐshì written examination
【笔顺】 bǐshùn order of strokes observed in calligraphy
【笔算】 bǐsuàn ① do a sum in writing ② written calculation
【笔谈】 bǐtán ① conversation by writing ②〔多用于书名〕 sketches and notes
【笔套】 bǐtào ① the cap of a pen, pencil or writing brush ② the sheath of a pen (made of cloth, silk or thread)
【笔挺】 bǐtǐng ① (standing) very straight; straight as a ramrod; bolt upright ② well-ironed; trim: 穿着一身～的制服 be dressed in a trim uniform
【笔筒】 bǐtǒng pen container; brush pot
【笔头】 bǐtóu ① 见"笔尖" ② ability to write; writing skill: 你～快,你写吧。You're good at writing. You do it. ③ written; in written form: ～练习 written exercises
【笔误】 bǐwù a slip of the pen
【笔下】 bǐxià ① 见"笔底下" ② the wording and purport of what one writes: 对于反动派,鲁迅是从来不讲什么～留情的。In his writings, Lu Xun was never sparing in his criticism of the reactionaries.
【笔心】 bǐxīn ① pencil lead ② refill (for a ball-point pen)
【笔译】 bǐyì written translation
【笔战】 bǐzhàn written polemics
【笔者】 bǐzhě 〔多用于作者自称〕 the author; the writer
【笔直】 bǐzhí perfectly straight; straight as a ramrod; bolt upright: ～的马路 straight avenues/ ～走 go straight on (或 ahead)/ 身子挺得～ stand straight as a ramrod; draw oneself up to one's full height

**俾** bǐ 〈书〉 in order to; so that: 对该项工程应予大力支持,～能按期完成。We should give this project every support so that it may be completed on schedule./ ～众周知 for the information of all; so as to make it known to everyone

**鄙** bǐ ① low; mean; vulgar: 粗～ coarse; vulgar/ 卑～ mean; despicable ②〈谦〉 my: ～意 my humble opinion; my idea ③〈书〉 despise; disdain; scorn: 可～ despicable ④〈书〉 an out-of-the-way place: 边～ remote districts
【鄙薄】 bǐbó despise; scorn: 不应～技术工作。One should not despise technical work.
【鄙俚】 bǐlǐ 〈书〉 vulgar; philistine
【鄙吝】 bǐlìn 〈书〉 ① vulgar ② stingy; miserly; mean
【鄙陋】 bǐlòu superficial; shallow: ～无知 shallow and ignorant
【鄙弃】 bǐqì disdain; loathe: ～这种庸俗作风 disdain such vulgar practices
【鄙人】 bǐrén 〈谦〉 your humble servant; I
【鄙视】 bǐshì despise; disdain; look down upon: ～体力劳动是剥削阶级思想的表现。To despise manual labour is an expression of the ideology of the exploiting classes.
【鄙俗】 bǐsú vulgar; philistine

## bì

**币** bì money; currency: 外～ foreign currency/ 银～ silver coin
【币值】 bìzhí currency value: 人民币～稳定。Renminbi is a stable currency.
【币制】 bìzhì currency (或 monetary) system ◇ ～改革 currency (或 monetary) reform

**必** bì ① certainly; surely; necessarily: 你们这次访问～将增强两国人民之间的友谊。Your visit will certainly strengthen the friendship between our two peoples./ 骄兵～败。An army puffed up with pride is bound to lose. ② must; have to: ～读书目 a list of required reading
【必不可少】 bì bùkě shǎo absolutely necessary; indispensable; essential
【必得】 bìděi must; have to: 你～去一趟。You simply must go.
【必定】 bìdìng be bound to; be sure to: 明天我们～把图纸送到。We'll be sure to send you the blueprints tomorrow.
【必恭必敬】 bìgōng-bìjìng reverent and respectful; extremely deferential
【必然】 bìrán ① inevitable; certain: ～结果 inevitable outcome/ ～趋势 inexorable trend/ 反动派～要和我们作拼死的斗争。The reactionaries are bound to struggle desperately against us. ②〈哲〉 necessity
◇ ～规律 inexorable law/ ～王国 realm of necessity/ ～性 necessity; inevitability; certainty
【必修课】 bìxiūkè a required (或 obligatory) course
【必须】 bìxū must; have to: ～指出 it must be pointed out that/ 共产党员～勇于批评和自我批评。A Communist must be bold in criticism and self-criticism./ ～厉行节约。It is imperative to practise economy./ 学习～刻苦。Study demands diligence.
【必需】 bìxū essential; indispensable: 发展工业所～的原料 raw materials essential for industrial development/ 应该把国家建设资金用在最～的地方。Our national construction funds should be spent where they are most needed.
【必需品】 bìxūpǐn necessities; necessaries
【必要】 bìyào necessary; essential; indispensable: 国家为这个国营农场提供了～的资金。The state provided the requisite capital for this state farm./ 没有～再讨论了。There's no need to discuss it any more.
◇ ～产品〈经〉 necessary product/ ～劳动〈经〉 necessary labour/ ～前提 prerequisite; precondition/ ～条件 essential condition; prerequisite/ ～性 necessity
【必由之路】 bì yóu zhī lù the road one must follow or take; the only way

**闭** bì ① shut; close: ～上眼 close one's eyes/ ～口不谈 refuse to say anything about; avoid mentioning/ ～口

无言 remain silent; be tongue-tied; be left speechless/ ～嘴! Hold your tongue! 或 Shut up! ②stop up; obstruct: ～住气 hold one's breath

【闭关政策】 bìguān zhèngcè closed-door policy

【闭关自守】 bìguān zì shǒu close the country to international intercourse

【闭合】 bìhé close

◇ ～电路 closed circuit/ ～度〈地〉closure/ ～生态〈宇航〉closed ecology

【闭会】 bìhuì close (或 end, adjourn) a meeting: 委员会～期间 when the committee is not in session

【闭经】 bìjīng 〈医〉amenorrhoea

【闭门羹】 bìméngēng 〔多用于〕: 飨以～ slam the door in sb.'s face/ 吃～ be denied entrance; find the door slammed in one's face

【闭门思过】 bì mén sī guò shut oneself up and ponder over one's mistakes: 有错误要在实践中改正,不要～。When we have made a mistake, we should correct it in practice and not ponder over it in seclusion.

【闭门造车】 bì mén zào chē make a cart behind closed doors; work behind closed doors; divorce oneself from the masses and from reality and act blindly

【闭目塞听】 bì mù sè tīng shut one's eyes and stop up one's ears — be out of touch with reality

【闭幕】 bìmù ①the curtain falls; lower the curtain: 在观众热烈掌声中～。The curtain fell to the loud applause of the audience. ②close; conclude: 会议已胜利～。The conference has come to a successful close. ◇ ～词 closing address (或 speech)/ ～式 closing ceremony

【闭塞】 bìsè ①stop up; close up: 鼻孔～ with one's nose stuffed up ②hard to get to; out-of-the-way; inaccessible: 以前这一带交通～。In the past this district was very hard to get to. ③unenlightened: 消息～ ill-informed/ 耳目～ uninformed; ignorant ④〈电〉blocking ◇ ～信号〈铁道〉block signal

【闭塞眼睛捉麻雀】 bìsè yǎnjing zhuō máquè try to catch sparrows with one's eyes blindfolded — act blindly

【闭音节】 bìyīnjié 〈语〉closed syllable

【闭元音】 bìyuányīn 〈语〉close vowel

## 毕

bì ①finish; accomplish; conclude: 阅～请放回原处。Please replace after reading. ②〈书〉fully; altogether; completely: 原形～露 show one's true colours ③(Bì) a surname

【毕恭毕敬】 bìgōng-bìjìng 见"必恭必敬" bìgōng-bìjìng

【毕竟】 bìjìng 〈副〉after all; all in all; when all is said and done; in the final analysis: 她的缺点同她的成绩相比,～是第二位的。Compared with her achievements, her shortcomings are, after all, only secondary.

【毕其功于一役】 bì qí gōng yú yī yì accomplish the whole task at one stroke

【毕生】 bìshēng all one's life; lifetime: ～事业 lifework; work of a lifetime/ 他～为共产主义事业奋斗。He fought all his life for the cause of communism.

【毕肖】 bìxiào 〈书〉resemble closely; be the very image of: 画得神情～ paint a lifelike portrait of sb.

【毕业】 bìyè graduate; finish school

◇ ～班 graduating class/ ～典礼 graduation (ceremony); commencement/ ～分配 job assignment on graduation/ ～论文 graduation thesis (或 dissertation)/ ～设计 graduation project/ ～生 graduate/ ～实习 graduation field work/ ～证书 diploma; graduation certificate

## 庇

bì shelter; protect; shield

【庇护】 bìhù shelter; shield; put under one's protection; take under one's wing ◇ ～权 right of asylum/ ～所 sanctuary; asylum

【庇荫】 bìyìn ①(of a tree, etc.) give shade ②shield

【庇佑】 bìyòu bless; prosper

## 毖

bì caution

## 哔

bì

【哔叽】 bìjī 〈纺〉serge

## 陛

bì 〈书〉a flight of steps leading to a palace hall

【陛下】 bìxià (直接称呼) Your Majesty; (间接称呼) His or Her Majesty

## 贲

bì 〈书〉beautifully adorned

另见 bēn

【贲临】 bìlín 〈书〉(of distinguished guests) honour my house, firm, etc. with your presence

## 毙

bì ①die; get killed: 倒～ drop dead ②〈口〉kill or execute by shooting; shoot: 愤怒的群众要求～了这个反革命杀人犯。The angry masses demanded that the counterrevolutionary murderer be shot.

【毙命】 bìmìng meet violent death; get killed: 两名匪徒当场～。Two of the bandits were killed on the spot.

## 铋

bì 〈化〉bismuth (Bi)

## 秘

bì 见"便秘" biànbì

另见 mì

【秘鲁】 Bìlǔ Peru ◇ ～人 Peruvian

## 敝

bì ①〈书〉shabby; worn-out; ragged: ～衣 ragged clothing; shabby (或 worn-out) clothes ②〈谦〉my; our; this: ～处 my place/ ～校 my school/ ～姓陈。My name is Chen.

【敝屣】 bìxǐ 〈书〉worn-out shoes; a worthless thing: 弃之如～ cast away like a pair of worn-out shoes

【敝帚自珍】 bìzhǒu zì zhēn value one's own old broom — cherish sth. of little value simply because it is one's own

## 婢

bì slave girl; servant-girl

【婢女】 bìnǚ slave girl; servant-girl

## 愎

bì wilful; self-willed

## 弼

bì 〈书〉assist

## 箄

bì a bamboo or wicker fence: 蓬门～户 a house with a door of wicker and straw — a humble abode

【箄路蓝缕】 bìlù-lánlǚ 〈书〉drive a cart in ragged clothes to blaze a new trail — endure great hardships in pioneer work

## 跸

bì 见"驻跸" zhùbì

## 痹

bì 〈中医〉pain or numbness caused by cold, damp, etc.; rheumatism

## 裨

bì 〈书〉benefit; advantage: 无～于事。It won't help matters. 或 It won't do any good.

另见 pí

【裨益】 bìyì 〈书〉benefit; advantage; profit: 大有～ be of great benefit

**蓖** bì

【蓖麻】 bìmá 〈植〉 castor-oil plant ◇ ～蚕 castor silkworm/ ～油 castor oil/ ～子 castor bean

**睥** bì

【睥睨】 bìnì 〈书〉 look at sb. disdainfully out of the corner of one's eye: ～一切 consider everyone and everything beneath one's notice; be overweening

**辟** bì ①〈书〉 monarch; sovereign: 复～ restore a monarchy; restoration ②〈书〉 ward off; keep away

另见 pì

【辟邪】 bìxié exorcise evil spirits

**滗** bì decant; strain; drain: 别把壶里的茶～干了。Don't drain the teapot dry.

**碧** bì ①〈书〉 green jade ②bluish green; blue: ～海 the blue sea/ ～空 a clear blue sky; an azure sky/ ～草如茵 a carpet of green grass

【碧蓝】 bìlán dark blue

【碧绿】 bìlǜ dark green

【碧瓦】 bìwǎ green, glazed tile

【碧血】 bìxuè blood shed in a just cause

【碧玉】 bìyù jasper

**箅** bì

【箅子】 bìzi grate; grating; grid: 炉～ fire grate/ 竹～ bamboo grid (to be put in a pot for steaming food)

**蔽** bì cover; shelter; hide: ～风雨 shelter from the wind and rain/ 衣不～体 be dressed in rags; have nothing but rags on one's back

**弊** bì ①fraud; abuse; malpractice: 舞～ practise fraud; engage in corrupt practices ②disadvantage; harm: 有利有～。There are both advantages and disadvantages./ ～多利少。The disadvantages outweigh the advantages.

【弊病】 bìbìng ①malady; evil; malpractice: 资本主义所固有的社会～ social evils inherent in capitalism ②drawback; disadvantage: 这种做法～不少。This method has quite a few drawbacks (或 disadvantages).

【弊端】 bìduān malpractice; abuse; corrupt practice

**薜** bì

【薜荔】 bìlì 〈植〉 climbing fig

**篦** bì comb with a double-edged fine-toothed comb: ～头 comb one's hair with such a comb

【篦子】 bìzi a double-edged fine-toothed comb

**避** bì ①avoid; evade; shun: ～而不谈 evade the question; avoid the subject; keep silent about the matter/ ～而不答 avoid making a reply/ ～雨 seek shelter from the rain/ ～开敌人岗哨 keep clear of enemy sentries ②prevent; keep away; repel: ～蚊剂 mosquito repellent

【避弹坑】 bìdànkēng 〈军〉 foxhole

【避风】 bìfēng ①take shelter from the wind ②lie low; stay away from trouble ◇ ～港 haven; harbour

【避讳】 bìhuì taboo on using the personal names of emperors, one's elders, etc.

【避讳】 bìhui ①a word or phrase to be avoided as taboo; taboo ②evade; dodge: ～这个问题 evade the issue

【避坑落井】 bì kēng luò jǐng dodge a pit only to fall into a well; out of the frying pan into the fire

【避雷器】 bìléiqì lightning arrester

【避雷针】 bìléizhēn lightning rod

【避免】 bìmiǎn avoid; refrain from; avert: ～错误 avoid mistakes/ ～轻率行动 refrain from any rash action/ 设法～了一场事故 succeed in averting an accident/ ～挫伤群众的积极性 see that the enthusiasm of the masses is not dampened

【避难】 bìnàn take refuge; seek asylum ◇ ～港 port of refuge/ ～所 refuge; sanctuary; asylum; haven

【避其锐气,击其惰归】 bì qí ruìqì, jī qí duò guī avoid the enemy when he is fresh and strike him when he is tired and withdraws

【避实就虚】 bì shí jiù xū stay clear of the enemy's main force and strike at his weak points

【避暑】 bìshǔ ①be away for the summer holidays; spend a holiday at a summer resort ②prevent sunstroke ◇ ～胜地 summer resort/ ～药 medicine for preventing sunstroke; preventive against sunstroke

【避嫌】 bìxián avoid doing anything that may arouse suspicion; avoid arousing suspicion

【避孕】 bìyùn contraception ◇ ～栓 contraceptive suppository/ ～套 condom/ ～丸药 the pill/ ～药膏 contraceptive jelly/ ～用品 contraceptives

【避重就轻】 bì zhòng jiù qīng avoid the important and dwell on the trivial; keep silent about major charges while admitting minor ones

**壁** bì ①wall ②sth. resembling a wall: 细胞～ cell wall ③cliff: 峭～ a precipitous cliff; precipice ④rampart; breastwork: 作～上观 watch the fighting from the ramparts — be an onlooker

【壁报】 bìbào wall newspaper

【壁橱】 bìchú a built-in wardrobe or cupboard; closet

【壁灯】 bìdēng wall lamp; bracket light

【壁挂】 bìguà 〈工美〉 (wall) hanging

【壁虎】 bìhǔ 〈动〉 gecko; house lizard

【壁画】 bìhuà mural (painting); fresco: 敦煌～ the Dunhuang frescoes

【壁龛】 bìkān niche

【壁垒】 bìlěi rampart; barrier: 关税～ tariff wall/ 贸易～ trade barrier/ ～分明 be diametrically opposed; be sharply divided/ 哲学中的两大～ two rival camps in philosophy; two diametrically opposed philosophical theories

【壁垒森严】 bìlěi sēnyán ①closely guarded; strongly fortified ②sharply divided

【壁立】 bìlì (of cliffs, etc.) stand like a wall; rise steeply: ～千尺 a sheer rise of a thousand feet/ ～的山峰 a sheer cliff

【壁炉】 bìlú fireplace ◇ ～台 mantelpiece

【壁虱】 bìshī 〈动〉 ①tick ②〈方〉 bedbug

【壁毯】 bìtǎn tapestry (used as a wall hanging)

**臂** bì ①arm: 左～ the left arm/ 助一～之力 give sb. a hand ②upper arm

另见 bei

【臂膀】 bìbǎng arm

【臂纱】 bìshā (black) armband: 戴～ wear a black armband

【臂章】 bìzhāng ①armband; armlet ②〈军〉 shoulder emblem (或 patch)

【臂助】 bìzhù 〈书〉 ①help ②assistant

**髀** bì 〈书〉 ①thigh ②thighbone

**璧** bì a round flat piece of jade with a hole in its

centre (used for ceremonial purposes in ancient China)
【璧还】 bìhuán 〈敬〉 ①return (a borrowed object) with thanks ② decline (a gift) with thanks
【璧谢】 bìxiè 〈敬〉 decline (a gift) with thanks

**襞** bì ①〈书〉folds in a garment ②〈生理〉folds (of the stomach, intestines, etc.)

## biān

**边** biān ①side: 三角形的一～ one side of a triangle/ 街道两～ both sides of the street/ 站在劳动人民一～ side with the labouring people ②margin; edge; brim; rim: 每页～上都有批注。There are notes in the margin on every page./ 湖～有座扬水站。There is a pumping station on the edge of the lake./ 田～地头 edges of fields/ 碗～儿 the rim of a bowl/ 宽～草帽 a straw hat with a broad brim/ 衬衣的～ the hem of a shirt ③border; frontier; boundary: 戍～ garrison a border region/ ～城 border (或 frontier) town/ ～寨 borderland village ④limit; bound: 无～的大海 a boundless sea/ 这话可太没～儿了。That's just absurd. ⑤by the side of; close by: 老师傅身～有两个好徒弟。The veteran worker has two good apprentices working with him./ 党的教导在她耳～回响。The Party's teachings were ringing in her ears./ 手～没有纸笔 have no pen or paper at hand ⑥(Biān) a surname

**边** bian 〔方位词后缀〕: 这～ here/ 东～ in the east/ 左～ on the left/ 前～ in front/ 里～ inside
【边币】 biānbì Border Region currency (consisting of the currency notes issued by the Border Region governments during the War of Resistance Against Japan and the War of Liberation)
【边…边…】 biān...biān... 〔分别用在动词前,表示动作同时进行〕: 边干边学 learn while working; learn on the job/ 边读边议 read sth. and discuss it as one goes along/ 边发展边巩固 expand while consolidating
【边陲】 biānchuí 〈书〉 border area; frontier
【边地】 biāndì border district; borderland
【边防】 biānfáng frontier (或 border) defence ◇ ～部队 frontier guards/ ～检查条例 frontier inspection regulations/ ～检查站 frontier inspection station/ ～军 frontier force/ ～哨 border sentry/ ～战士 frontier guard/ ～站 frontier station
【边锋】 biānfēng 〈足球〉 wing; wing forward: 左(右)～ left (right) wing
【边际】 biānjì limit; bound; boundary: 漫无～ rambling; discursive/ 不着～ wide of the mark; not to the point; irrelevant ◇ ～效用论〈经〉the theory of marginal utility
【边疆】 biānjiāng border area; borderland; frontier; frontier region: 支援～建设 support the construction of the border areas/ 保卫～ guard the frontier
【边角料】 biānjiǎoliào leftover bits and pieces (of industrial material)
【边界】 biānjiè boundary; border: 划定～ delimit boundaries/ 标定～ demarcate boundaries/ 越过～ cross a boundary; cross the border ◇ ～实际控制线 line of actual control on the border/ ～事件 border incident/ ～现状 *status quo* on the border; *status quo* of the boundary/ ～线 boundary line/ ～协定 boundary agreement/ ～争端 boundary dispute/ ～走向 alignment of the boundary line
【边境】 biānjìng border; frontier: 封锁～ close the frontiers; seal off the borders ◇ ～冲突 border clash (或 conflict)/ ～贸易 frontier trade/ ～市镇 border town
【边框】 biānkuàng frame; rim: 镜子的～ the rim of a mirror
【边门】 biānmén side door; wicket door (或 gate)
【边民】 biānmín people living on the frontiers; inhabitants of a border area
【边卡】 biānqiǎ border checkpoint
【边区】 biānqū border area (或 region): 陕甘宁～ the Shaanxi-Gansu-Ningxia Border Region
【边塞】 biānsài frontier fortress
【边线】 biānxiàn ①〈体〉sideline ②〈棒、垒球〉foul line
【边沿】 biānyán edge; fringe: 森林～ the edge (或 fringe) of a forest
【边音】 biānyīn 〈语〉 lateral (sound)
【边缘】 biānyuán ①edge; fringe; verge; brink; periphery: 在解放区的～ on the border of the liberated area/ 悬崖的～ the edge of a precipice/ 经济破产的～ the verge of economic bankruptcy/ 战争～政策 brink-of-war policy; brinkmanship ②marginal; borderline ◇ ～地区 border district; borders/ ～海 marginal sea/ ～科学 frontier science
【边远】 biānyuǎn far from the centre; remote; outlying: ～省份 remote border provinces/ ～地区 an outlying district

**砭** biān ①〈中医〉a stone needle used in acupuncture in ancient China ②pierce: 冷风～骨。The cold wind cuts one to the marrow.

**编** biān ①weave; plait: ～柳条筐 weave wicker baskets/ ～辫子 plait one's hair ②organize; group; arrange: ～班 group into classes/ 把他～在我们组吧。Put him in our group. ③edit; compile: ～教材 compile teaching material/ ～杂志 edit a magazine; work in the editorial department of a magazine ④write; compose: ～剧本 write a play/ ～儿童歌曲 compose songs for children ⑤fabricate; invent; make up; cook up: 这事儿是他～出来的。He made the whole thing up. ⑥part of a book; book; volume: 上～ Book I; Volume I; Part I
【编次】 biāncì order of arrangement
【编导】 biāndǎo ①write and direct (a play, film, etc.): 这个话剧是由两位青年作家～的。The play was written and directed by two young writers. ②(戏剧) playwright-director; (舞剧) choreographer-director; (电影) scenarist-director
【编队】 biānduì ①form into columns; organize into teams ②formation (of ships or aircraft) ◇ ～飞行 formation flight (或 flying)/ ～轰炸 formation bombing
【编号】 biānhào ①number: 给树苗～ number the saplings ②serial number
【编辑】 biānjí ①edit; compile: ～图书索引 compile an index (of books) ②(assistant) editor; compiler: 总～ editor-in-chief ◇ ～部 editorial department/ ～人员 editorial staff/ ～委员会 editorial board
【编剧】 biānjù ①write a play, scenario, etc. ②(戏剧) playwright; (电影) screenwriter; scenarist
【编码】 biānmǎ coding
【编目】 biānmù ①make a catalogue; catalogue: 新到的图书正在～。The new books are being catalogued. ②catalogue; list ◇ ～部 cataloguing department/ ～员 cataloguer
【编年史】 biānniánshǐ annals; chronicle
【编年体】 biānniántǐ annalistic style (in historiography)
【编排】 biānpái arrange; lay out: 文字和图片的～ the layout of pictures and articles/ 课文要按难易程度～。The texts should be graded in order of difficulty.

【编遣】 biānqiǎn reorganize (troops, etc.) and discharge surplus personnel
【编审】 biānshěn ① read and edit ② copy editor
【编舞】 biānwǔ ① choreography ② choreographer
【编写】 biānxiě ① compile: ～教科书 compile a textbook ② write; compose: ～歌剧 compose an opera/ ～剧本 write a play
【编选】 biānxuǎn select and edit; compile
【编译】 biānyì translate and edit
【编印】 biānyìn compile and print; publish
【编造】 biānzào ① compile; draw up; work out: ～预算 draw up a budget/ ～表册 compile statistical tables ② fabricate; invent; concoct; make up; cook up: ～谎言 fabricate lies/ ～情节 falsify the details of an event; invent (或 make up) a story ③ create out of the imagination: 古代人民～的神话 myths invented by the ancients
【编者】 biānzhě editor; compiler ◇ ～按 editor's note; editorial note
【编织】 biānzhī weave; knit; plait; braid: ～地毯 weave a rug/ ～草席 weave a straw mat/ ～毛衣 knit a sweater
【编制】 biānzhì ① weave; plait; braid: ～竹器 weave bamboo articles ② work out; draw up: ～生产计划 work out a production plan/ ～教学大纲 draw up a teaching programme ③ authorized strength; establishment: 部队～ establishment (for army units)/ 战时～ wartime establishment/ 政府机关的～ authorized size of a government body/ 缩小～ reduce the staff
【编著】 biānzhù compile; write
【编组】 biānzǔ ① organize into groups ② 〈铁道〉 marshalling ◇ ～场 marshalling (或 classification) yard
【编纂】 biānzuǎn compile: ～词典 compile a dictionary

**煸** biān stir-fry before stewing

**蝙** biān
【蝙蝠】 biānfú bat

**鳊** biān
【鳊鱼】 biānyú bream

**鞭** biān ① whip; lash ② an iron staff used as a weapon in ancient China ③ sth. resembling a whip: 教～ (teacher's) pointer ④ a string of small firecrackers ⑤〈书〉 flog; whip; lash: ～马 whip a horse
【鞭策】 biāncè spur on; urge on: 要经常～自己，为革命努力学习。We should constantly urge ourselves on to study hard for the revolution./ 领导的表扬是对我们的～。The leadership's praise will spur us on.
【鞭长莫及】 biān cháng mò jí beyond the reach of one's power (或 authority); too far away for one to be able to help
【鞭笞】 biānchī 〈书〉 flog; lash
【鞭虫】 biānchóng whipworm
【鞭打】 biāndǎ whip; lash; flog; thrash
【鞭痕】 biānhén welt; whip scar; lash mark
【鞭毛】 biānmáo 〈动〉 flagellum ◇ ～虫 flagellate
【鞭炮】 biānpào ① firecrackers ② a string of small firecrackers
【鞭辟入里】 biān pì rù lǐ penetrating; trenchant; incisive
【鞭挞】 biāntà 〈书〉 lash; castigate: 影片对吃人的旧社会进行了无情的～。The film mercilessly castigates the cannibalistic old society.
【鞭子】 biānzi whip

## biǎn

**贬** biǎn ① demote; relegate ② reduce; devalue: ～价出售 sell at a reduced price ③ censure; depreciate: ～得一钱不值 condemn as worthless
【贬斥】 biǎnchì ① 〈书〉 demote ② denounce
【贬词】 biǎncí derogatory term; expression of censure
【贬低】 biǎndī belittle; depreciate; play down: ～其重要性 belittle the importance of sth./ 企图～这一文件的意义 try to play down the significance of the document
【贬义】 biǎnyì derogatory sense ◇ ～词 derogatory term
【贬抑】 biǎnyì belittle; depreciate
【贬谪】 biǎnzhé banish from the court; relegate
【贬值】 biǎnzhí 〈经〉 ① devalue; devaluate ② depreciate

**窆** biǎn 〈书〉 bury

**扁** biǎn flat: 一只～盒子 a flat case; a shallow box/ ～体字 squat-shaped handwriting/ 纸箱子压～了。The cardboard box was crushed./ 别把人看～了。Don't underestimate people.
另见 piān
【扁虫】 biǎnchóng flatworm
【扁蝽】 biǎnchūn flat bug
【扁担】 biǎndan carrying pole; shoulder pole: ～没扎，两头打塌。〈谚〉 When the carrying pole is not secured at both ends, its loads slip off — try to grab both but end up getting neither.
【扁豆】 biǎndòu hyacinth bean: 小～ lentil
【扁坯】 biǎnpī 〈冶〉 slab
【扁骨】 biǎngǔ 〈生理〉 flat bone
【扁桃】 biǎntáo ① almond tree ② almond ③ 〈方〉 flat peach
【扁桃体】 biǎntáotǐ 〈生理〉 tonsil
◇ ～肥大 〈医〉 hypertrophy of tonsils/ ～切除术 tonsillectomy/ ～炎 tonsillitis 又作"扁桃腺"
【扁圆】 biǎnyuán oblate

**匾** biǎn ① a horizontal inscribed board ② a silk banner embroidered with words of praise: 绣金～ embroidering a silk banner with words of gold ③ a big round shallow basket
【匾额】 biǎn'é a horizontal inscribed board

**褊** biǎn 〈书〉 narrow; cramped
【褊急】 biǎnjí 〈书〉 narrow-minded and short-tempered
【褊狭】 biǎnxiá 〈书〉 narrow; cramped: 居处～ live in cramped quarters/ 气量～ small-minded

## biàn

**卞** biàn ① 〈书〉 impetuous ② (Biàn) a surname

**弁** biàn ① a man's cap used in ancient times ② a low-ranking military officer in old China
【弁言】 biànyán 〈书〉 foreword; preface

**忭** biàn 〈书〉 glad; happy: 不胜欣～ be overjoyed

**汴** Biàn another name for Kaifeng

**苄** biàn 〈化〉 benzyl

【苄基】 biànjī 〈化〉 benzyl

**变** biàn ① change; become different: 情况～了。The situation has changed./ 人～,地～,产量～。When people change, the land changes and output changes too./ 多～的战术 varied tactics ② change into; become: 后进队～先进队。Less advanced production teams have become advanced ones./ 旱地～水田。Dry land has been turned into paddy fields. ③ transform; change; alter: ～废为宝 change waste material into things of value; recycle waste material/ ～害为利 turn bane into boon ④ an unexpected turn of events: 事～ incident/ 政～ *coup d'état*/ 兵～ mutiny

【变本加厉】 biàn běn jiā lì become aggravated; be further intensified: 资本家～地剥削工人。The capitalists are intensifying their efforts to exploit the workers.

【变成】 biànchéng change into; turn into; become: 物质可以～精神,精神可以～物质。Matter can be transformed into consciousness and consciousness into matter./ 贫穷落后的旧中国已经～了初步繁荣昌盛的社会主义国家。Poor and backward old China has changed into a socialist country with the beginnings of prosperity./ 在一定的条件下,坏事能够～好事。Under given conditions, bad things can be turned into good things.

【变电站】 biàndiànzhàn (transformer) substation

【变调】 biàndiào 〈语〉 ①modified tone ②tonal modification

【变动】 biàndòng change; alteration: 文字上作一些～ make some changes (或 alterations) in the wording/ 人事～ personnel changes

【变法】 biànfǎ 〈史〉 political reform ◇ ～维新 Constitutional Reform and Modernization (1898)

【变法儿】 biànfǎr try different ways

【变分法】 biànfēnfǎ 〈数〉 calculus of variations

【变革】 biàngé transform; change: ～自然 transform nature/ 社会～ social change/ 你要有知识,你就得参加～现实的实践。If you want knowledge, you must take part in the practice of changing reality.

【变更】 biàngēng change; alter; modify: 所有制方面的～ changes in the system of ownership/ ～作息时间 alter the daily timetable/ 我们的计划稍有～。We have modified our plan.

【变工】 biàngōng exchange work (或 labour) ◇ ～队 work-exchange team (an agricultural producers' mutual-aid organization)

【变故】 biàngù an unforeseen event; accident; misfortune: 发生了～。Something quite unforeseen has happened.

【变卦】 biànguà go back on one's word; break an agreement: 昨天说得好好的,怎么～了? Yesterday you agreed. What made you change your mind?

【变化】 biànhuà change; vary: 化学～ chemical change/ 气温的～ variations (或 fluctuations) of temperature/ 我家乡有了很大的～。Great changes have taken place in my home village./ 他发球～多端。He's always changing his way of serving./ 高山天气～无常。In high mountains the weather is changeable.

【变幻】 biànhuàn change irregularly; fluctuate: ～莫测 changeable; unpredictable/ 风云～ unexpected gathering of clouds; constant change of events

【变换】 biànhuàn vary; alternate: ～手法 vary one's tactics/ ～位置 shift one's position

【变价】 biànjià appraise at the current rate: ～出售 sell at the current price

【变焦距镜头】 biànjiāojù jìngtóu 〈摄〉 zoom lens

【变节】 biànjié make a political recantation; turn one's coat ◇ ～分子 recanter; turncoat

【变脸】 biànliǎn suddenly turn hostile

【变量】 biànliàng 〈数〉 variable

【变流器】 biànliúqì 〈电〉 converter

【变乱】 biànluàn turmoil; social upheaval

【变卖】 biànmài sell off (one's property)

【变频】 biànpín 〈电子〉 frequency conversion ◇ ～管 converter tube

【变迁】 biànqiān changes; vicissitudes: 煤乡的～ changes in a coal-mining district

【变色】 biànsè ①change colour; discolour: 这种墨水不会～。This ink will not change colour./ 脸不～心不跳 one's face does not change colour, nor does one's heart beat faster — without a trace of fear/ 保证我国社会主义江山永不～ ensure that socialist China will never change her political colour ② change countenance; become angry: 勃然～ suddenly change countenance

【变色龙】 biànsèlóng chameleon

【变数】 biànshù 〈数〉 variable

【变速】 biànsù 〈机〉 speed change; gearshift ◇ ～比 〈汽车〉 gear ratio/ ～器 gearbox; transmission/ ～运动 〈物〉 variable motion

【变态】 biàntài ① 〈生〉 metamorphosis ② abnormal; anomalous ◇ ～反应〈医〉 allergy/ ～心理 abnormal psychology/ ～心理学 abnormal psychology

【变天】 biàntiān ① change of weather: 太闷热了,看来要～。The weather is bound to change soon, it's so close. ②restoration of reactionary rule: 被推翻的阶级总是妄想～。The overthrown classes are always dreaming of a restoration of their rule. ◇ ～帐 restoration records (of usurious loans, former land holdings, etc., kept secretly by members of the overthrown classes dreaming of a comeback)

【变通】 biàntōng be flexible; accommodate (或 adapt) sth. to circumstances: ～办法 accommodation; adaptation/ 根据不同情况作适当的～ make appropriate adaptations in the light of specific conditions

【变温动物】 biànwēn dòngwù poikilothermal (或 cold-blooded) animal

【变文】 biànwén a popular form of narrative literature flourishing in the Tang Dynasty (618-907), with alternate prose and rhymed parts for recitation and singing (often on Buddhistic themes)

【变戏法】 biàn xìfǎ perform conjuring tricks; conjure; juggle

【变相】 biànxiàng in disguised form; covert: ～体罚 corporal punishment in disguised form/ ～的剥削行为 a covert act of exploitation

【变心】 biànxīn cease to be faithful

【变星】 biànxīng 〈天〉 variable (star)

【变形】 biànxíng be out of shape; become deformed: 这箱子压得～了。The box has been crushed out of shape./ 病人的脊椎骨已经～。The patient has a deformed spine.

【变形虫】 biànxíngchóng amoeba

【变形体】 biànxíngtǐ 〈生〉 plasmodium

【变性】 biànxìng 〈化〉 denaturation: ～酒精 denatured alcohol/ ～蛋白质 denatured protein

【变修】 biànxiū go revisionist

【变压器】 biànyāqì 〈电〉 transformer

【变异】 biànyì 〈生〉 variation ◇ ～性 variability

【变质】 biànzhì ① go bad; deteriorate: 这肉～了。The meat has gone bad./ 蜕化～ become morally degenerate ② 〈地〉 metamorphism ◇ ～岩 metamorphic rock

【变种】 biànzhǒng ① 〈生〉 mutation; variety ② variety; variant: 机会主义的～ a variety of opportunism

【变奏】 biànzòu 〈乐〉 variation ◇ ～曲 variations

【变阻器】 biànzǔqì 〈电〉 rheostat

便 biàn ①convenient; handy: 日夜服务,顾客称～。Customers find the 24-hour service very convenient. ②when an opportunity arises; when it is convenient: 悉听尊～ suit your own convenience/ 得～请来一趟。Come whenever it's convenient. ③informal; plain; ordinary: ～宴 an informal dinner/ ～装 ordinary (或 everyday) clothes ④relieve oneself: 小～ piss; urinate/ 大～ shit; defecate ⑤piss or shit; urine or excrement: 粪～ excrement; night soil ⑥〈副〉〔表示事情发生或结束得早及某种情况带来的结果等〕: 天一亮她～下地去了。She went to the fields as soon as it was light./ 没有一个人民的军队,～没有人民的一切。Without a people's army the people have nothing. ⑦〈连〉〔表示假设的让步〕: ～是剩下我一个人,也要战斗下去。Even if I'm the only one left alive, I will fight on.
另见 pián

【便秘】 biànbì 〈医〉 constipation

【便步走】 biànbùzǒu 〈军〉 march at ease; route step: ～!(口令) At ease, march! 或 Route step, march!

【便池】 biànchí urinal

【便当】 biàndang convenient; handy; easy: 房子里家具不多,收拾起来很～。There isn't too much furniture in the room. We can easily tidy it up.

【便道】 biàndào ①shortcut: 抄～走 take a shortcut ②pavement; sidewalk: 行人走～。Pedestrians walk on the pavement. ③makeshift road

【便饭】 biànfàn a simple meal; potluck: 跟我们一块儿吃顿～吧。Come along and take potluck with us.

【便服】 biànfú ①everyday clothes; informal dress ②civilian clothes

【便函】 biànhán an informal letter sent by an organization

【便壶】 biànhú (bed) urinal; chamber pot

【便笺】 biànjiān notepaper; memo; memo pad

【便览】 biànlǎn brief guide: 交通～ roadbook/ 旅游～ guidebook

【便利】 biànlì ①convenient; easy: 交通～ have convenient communications; have good transport facilities; be conveniently located ②facilitate: 水库建成后大大～了农田灌溉。The completion of the reservoir greatly facilitated irrigation./ 为～居民,新盖了一个副食商场。A new food market has been built for the convenience of the residents./ 为对方建立使馆提供～ provide the other side with facilities for the establishment of its embassy

【便帽】 biànmào cap

【便门】 biànmén side door; wicket door

【便盆】 biànpén bed pan

【便桥】 biànqiáo temporary (或 makeshift) bridge

【便人】 biànrén somebody who happens to be on hand for an errand: 如有～,请把那本书捎来。Please send the book by anyone who happens to come this way.

【便士】 biànshì penny

【便条】 biàntiáo (informal) note

【便桶】 biàntǒng chamber pot

【便鞋】 biànxié cloth shoes; slippers

【便血】 biànxiě 〈医〉 having (或 passing) blood in one's stool

【便宴】 biànyàn informal dinner: 设～招待 give a dinner for sb.

【便衣】 biànyī ①civilian clothes; plain clothes: ～公安人员 plainclothes public security personnel; public security personnel in plain clothes ②plainclothesman

【便宜行事】 biànyí xíng shì act at one's discretion; act as one sees fit

【便于】 biànyú easy to; convenient for: ～携带 easy to carry

【便中】 biànzhōng at one's convenience; when it's convenient: 我替你捎来一双鞋,望～来取。I've brought you a pair of shoes. Please come for them whenever it's convenient.

遍 biàn ①all over; everywhere: 走～全省 have travelled all over the province/ 我们的朋友～天下。We have friends all over the world. ②〈量〉〔表示动作从开始到结束的整个过程〕: 这本书我从头到尾看过两～。I've read the book twice from cover to cover./ 请再说一～。Please say it again.

【遍布】 biànbù be found everywhere; spread all over: 大寨式社队～全国。Dazhai-type communes and brigades can be found all over the country.

【遍地开花】 biàndì kāihuā blossom everywhere; spring up all over the place: 合作医疗已在广大农村～。Cooperative medical service has sprung up all over the vast rural areas.

【遍及】 biànjí extend (或 spread) all over

【遍体鳞伤】 biàntǐ línshāng covered all over with cuts and bruises; beaten black and blue; be a mass of bruises

缏 biàn 见"草帽缏" cǎomàobiàn

辨 biàn differentiate; distinguish; discriminate: 不～真伪 fail to distinguish between truth and falsehood; be unable to tell the true from the false

【辨别】 biànbié differentiate; distinguish; discriminate: ～真假马克思主义 distinguish true Marxism from sham/ ～香花毒草 differentiate between fragrant flowers and poisonous weeds/ ～方向 take one's bearings

【辨认】 biànrèn identify; recognize: 他的笔迹容易～。His handwriting is easy to identify./ 相片已经模糊,不能～。The photo has faded beyond recognition.

【辨析】 biànxī differentiate and analyse; discriminate: 同义词～ synonym discrimination

【辨证施治】 biànzhèng shīzhì 〈中医〉 diagnosis and treatment based on an overall analysis of the illness and the patient's condition

辩 biàn argue; dispute; debate: 真理愈～愈明。The more truth is debated, the clearer it becomes.

【辩白】 biànbái offer an explanation; plead innocence; try to defend oneself

【辩驳】 biànbó dispute; refute: 无可～ beyond all dispute; indisputable; irrefutable

【辩才】 biàncái 〈书〉 eloquence: 颇有～ be quite eloquent; have a silver tongue

【辩护】 biànhù ①speak in defence of; argue in favour of; defend: 不要替他～了。Don't try to defend him. ②〈法〉 plead; defend: 为被告人～ plead for the accused/ 出庭～(of a lawyer) defend a case in court/ 被告人有权获得～。The accused has the right to defence.
◇ ～权 right to defence/ ～人 defender; counsel/ ～士 apologist

【辩解】 biànjiě provide an explanation; try to defend oneself: 错了就错了,不要～。A mistake is a mistake. Don't try to explain it away.

【辩论】 biànlùn argue; debate: ～个水落石出 argue the matter out ◇ ～会 a debate

【辩难】 biànnàn retort with challenging questions; debate

【辩证】 biànzhèng dialectical: ～的统一 dialectical unity/ ～地看问题 look at things dialectically/ 事物发展的～规律 the dialectical law of the development of things ◇ ～法 dialectics/ ～逻辑 dialectical logic

【辩证唯物主义】 biànzhèng wéiwùzhǔyì dialectical materialism: ～的认识论 the dialectical materialist theory of knowledge/ ～观点 a dialectical materialist point of view ◇ ～者 dialectical materialist

**辫** biàn plait; braid; pigtail: 梳小～儿 wear pigtails/ 蒜～ a braid of garlic

【辫子】 biànzi ① plait; braid; pigtail: 梳～ wear one's hair in braids/ 把问题梳梳～ sort out and classify the problems ② a mistake or shortcoming that may be exploited by an opponent; handle: 揪～ seize on sb.'s mistake or shortcoming; capitalize on sb.'s vulnerable point

## biāo

**标** biāo ① mark; sign: 商～ trade mark/ 路～ road sign/ 音～ phonetic symbol ② put a mark, tag or label on; label: ～上号码 put a number on/ ～界 demarcate a boundary/ 商品都～了价格。Every article has a price tag on it. ③ prize; award: 夺～ compete for the first prize; win the championship ④ outward sign; symptom: 治～ seek temporary relief ⑤ tender; bid: 招～ invite tenders/ 投～ make (或 put in) a tender

【标榜】 biāobǎng ① flaunt; advertise; parade: ～自由平等 flaunt the banner of liberty and equality ② boost; excessively praise: 互相～ boost each other; exchange excessive praise/ 自我～ blow one's own trumpet; sing one's own praises

【标本】 biāoběn ① specimen; sample: 昆虫～ insect specimen ② 〈中医〉 the root cause and symptoms of a disease: ～同治 treat a disease by looking into both its root cause and symptoms

【标本虫】 biāoběnchóng 〈动〉 spider beetle

【标兵】 biāobīng ① parade guards (usu. spaced out along parade routes) ② example; model; pacesetter: 树立～ set a good example/ 石油战线上的～ a pacesetter on the oil production front

【标尺】 biāochǐ ① 〈测〉 surveyor's rod; staff ② 〈水〉 staff gauge ③ 〈军〉 rear sight

【标灯】 biāodēng beacon light; beacon

【标点】 biāodiǎn ① punctuation ② punctuate ◇ ～符号 punctuation mark

【标定】 biāodìng demarcate: ～边界线 demarcate a boundary by setting up boundary markers (done jointly by the two parties concerned)

【标杆】 biāogān 〈测〉 surveyor's pole

【标高】 biāogāo 〈测〉 elevation; level

【标号】 biāohào grade: 水泥～ grade of cement/ 高～水泥 high-grade cement

【标记】 biāojì sign; mark; symbol: 探清地雷，作出～ locate the landmines and mark their location

【标价】 biāojià ① mark a price ② marked price

【标量】 biāoliàng 〈物〉 scalar quantity

【标明】 biāomíng mark; indicate: 货箱上～"小心轻放"。The crate is marked "Handle with care"./ 在这幅地图上北京是用一颗红星～的。Beijing is indicated on the map by a red star.

【标签】 biāoqiān label; tag: 贴上～ stick on a label/ 价目～ price tag

【标枪】 biāoqiāng javelin: 掷～ javelin throw

【标题】 biāotí title; heading; headline; caption: 通栏大字～ banner headline; banner/ 小～ subheading; crosshead ◇ ～音乐 programme music

【标新立异】 biāoxīn-lìyì start something new in order to be different; do something unconventional or unorthodox; create something new and original

【标语】 biāoyǔ slogan; poster: 张贴～ put up slogans (或 posters) ◇ ～牌 placard/ ～塔 slogan pylon

【标志】 biāozhì ① sign; mark; symbol: 兴旺发达的～ a sign of vigour and prosperity ② indicate; mark; symbolize: 中华人民共和国的成立，～着我国社会主义历史阶段的开始。The founding of the People's Republic of China marked the beginning of the historical period of socialism in our country.

【标致】 biāozhi (usu. of women) beautiful; handsome

【标桩】 biāozhuāng (marking) stake

【标准】 biāozhǔn standard; criterion: 合乎～ up to standard/ 按我们的～来看 by our standards/ 用高～要求自己 set high demands on oneself/ 真理的～只能是社会的实践。Only social practice can be the criterion of truth. ◇ ～层〈地〉 key bed/ ～大气压〈物〉 standard atmosphere/ ～化 standardization/ ～时 standard time/ ～像 official portrait/ ～音 standard pronunciation/ ～语 standard speech

**彪** biāo 〈书〉 young tiger

【彪炳】 biāobǐng 〈书〉 shining; splendid: ～千古 shining through the ages/ ～显赫的历史功绩 splendid achievements in history

【彪形大汉】 biāoxíng dàhàn burly chap; husky fellow

**膘** biāo fat (of an animal): 长～ get fat; put on flesh; flesh out/ 社里的牲口～肥体壮。The commune's animals are plump and sturdy.

**瘭** biāo

【瘭疽】 biāojū 〈中医〉 pyogenic infection of the pad of a finger

**镖** biāo a dartlike weapon

【镖客】 biāokè 〈旧〉 armed escort (of travellers or merchants' caravans)

**飙** biāo violent wind; whirlwind

**镳** biāo ① 〈书〉 bit (of a bridle) ② 见"镖" biāo

## biǎo

**表** biǎo ① surface; outside; external: 由～及里 proceed from the outside to the inside ② show; express: 深～同情 show deep sympathy/ ～决心 express (或 declare) one's determination ③ model; example ④ 〈中医〉 administer medicine to bring out the cold ⑤ table; form; list: 时间～ timetable; schedule/ 登记～ registration form/ 价目～ price list ⑥ meter; gauge: 温度～ thermometer ⑦ watch: 手～ (wrist) watch ⑧ the relationship between the children or grandchildren of a brother and a sister or of sisters: ～兄 cousin 参见"姑表" gūbiǎo; "姨表" yíbiǎo ⑨ memorial to an emperor

【表白】 biǎobái vindicate: ～诚意 assert one's sincerity/ 我们看一个人，不是根据他的～，而是根据他的行动。We judge a person not by what he says but by what he does.

【表报】 biǎobào statistical tables and reports

【表册】 biǎocè statistical forms; book of tables or forms: 公文报告～ documents, written reports and statistical forms

【表层】 biǎocéng surface layer

【表尺】 biǎochǐ 〈军〉 rear sight ◇ ～座 rear sight base

【表达】 biǎodá express; convey; voice: 我激动的心情难以用语言来～。Words can hardly express my excitement./ ～

群众的感情 voice the feelings of the masses/ ～人民的坚强意志 demonstrate the firm will of the people
【表带】 biǎodài watchband; watch strap
【表格】 biǎogé form; table: 填写～ fill in a form
【表观】 biǎoguān 〈物〉 apparent ◇ ～运动 apparent motion/ ～质量 apparent mass
【表记】 biǎojì 〈书〉 something given as a token; souvenir
【表决】 biǎojué decide by vote; vote: 付～ put to the vote; take a vote/ 投票～ vote by ballot/ 举手～ vote by a show of hands/ 唱名～ vote by roll call; roll-call vote/ 口头～ voice vote/ 起立～ vote by sitting and standing/ ～通过 be voted through
◇ ～程序 voting procedure/ ～机器 voting machine/ ～指示牌 vote indicator
【表决权】 biǎojuéquán right to vote; vote: 行使～ exercise the right to vote/ 有(无)～ have the right (no right) to vote
【表里】 biǎo-lǐ ① the outside and the inside; one's outward show and inner thoughts: ～不一 think in one way and behave in another/ ～如一 think and act in one and the same way ② 〈中医〉 exterior and interior
【表露】 biǎolù show; reveal: 他很着急,但并没有～出来。He was very worried, but didn't show it.
【表蒙子】 biǎoméngzi watch glass; crystal
【表面】 biǎomiàn surface; face; outside; appearance: 地球的～ the surface of the earth/ 你不能只看事情的～。You must not look only at the surface of things./ 他那番话不过是～文章。He was merely paying lip service./ ～上气壮如牛,实际上胆小如鼠 outwardly fierce as a bull but inwardly timid as a mouse
◇ ～处理 surface treatment/ ～价值 face value/ ～现象 superficial phenomenon/ ～硬化 〈冶〉 case-hardening/ ～张力 〈物〉 surface tension
【表面化】 biǎomiànhuà come to the surface; become apparent: 矛盾～了。The contradiction has become apparent.
【表明】 biǎomíng make known; make clear; state clearly; indicate: ～立场 make known one's position; declare one's stand/ 有迹象～会谈即将恢复。There are indications that the talks will be resumed soon.
【表盘】 biǎopán dial plate; dial
【表皮】 biǎopí 〈生〉 epidermis; cuticle
【表亲】 biǎoqīn ① cousin ② cousinship
【表情】 biǎoqíng ① express one's feelings ② expression: 面部～ facial expression/ ～不自然 look awkward; wear an unnatural expression
【表示】 biǎoshì show; express; indicate: ～关切 show concern/ ～愤慨 voice (或 express) one's indignation/ ～热烈欢迎 extend a warm welcome/ 友好的～ a manifestation of friendship; a friendly gesture/ 我们谨向你们～衷心的祝贺。We wish to convey to you our hearty congratulations./ 这只不过～敌人的虚弱而已。This only indicates the enemy's weakness.
【表率】 biǎoshuài example; model: 雷锋是全心全意为人民服务的～。Lei Feng set an example of wholehearted service to the people.
【表态】 biǎotài make known one's position; declare where one stands: 明确～ take a clearcut stand/ 她没有～。She didn't say which side she was on./ 作～性发言 make a statement of one's position
【表土】 biǎotǔ 〈农〉 surface soil; topsoil
【表现】 biǎoxiàn ① expression; manifestation: 经济是基础,政治则是经济的集中的～。Economics is the base and politics the concentrated expression of economics./ 反对大国沙文主义的各种～ combat great-nation chauvinism in all its manifestations ② show; display; manifest: ～出极大的勇敢和智慧 display immense courage and wisdom/ 他在工作中～很好。He is doing very well in his work./ 一贯～积极 be always active; always show great initiative/ ～革命战争的文学作品 literary works depicting revolutionary war/ 阶级敌人是一定要寻找机会～他们自己的。The class enemy will invariably seek opportunities to assert himself. ③ show off: 好～ like to show off ◇ ～手法 technique of expression/ ～形式 form of expression; manifestation
【表现型】 biǎoxiànxíng 〈生〉 phenotype
【表象】 biǎoxiàng 〈心〉 idea
【表演】 biǎoyǎn ① perform; act; play: ～节目 give a performance; put on a show/ 她～得很好。She performed very well. ② performance; exhibition: 杂技～ acrobatic performance/ 体育～ sports exhibition/ 航空模型～ model planes exhibition/ 阶级敌人的丑恶～ the antics of the class enemy ③ demonstrate: ～新操作方法 demonstrate new techniques of operation ◇ ～唱 singing with actions/ ～赛 exhibition match
【表扬】 biǎoyáng praise; commend: ～好人好事 praise good people and good deeds/ 大会～了十个先进集体。The conference commended ten advanced units./ 工人们的革命干劲得到了～。These workers have been praised for their revolutionary drive. ◇ ～信 commendatory letter
【表意文字】 biǎoyì wénzì 〈语〉 ideograph
【表语】 biǎoyǔ 〈语〉 predicative
【表彰】 biǎozhāng cite (in dispatches); commend: 六连的出色战功得到～。The 6th Company was cited for its distinguished service in the battle./ 大庆是毛主席～的一面红旗。Daqing is a red banner commended by Chairman Mao./ 为了～他生前的事迹 in recognition of his deeds in his lifetime
【表证】 biǎozhèng 〈中医〉 illness that has not attacked the vital organs of the human body

**婊** biǎo
【婊子】 biǎozi prostitute; whore: 又想当～,又想立牌坊 lead the life of a whore and expect a monument to one's chastity

**裱** biǎo mount (a picture, etc.): 把画拿去～一下 have the painting mounted
【裱褙】 biǎobèi mount (a picture, etc.)
【裱糊】 biǎohú paper (a wall, ceiling, etc.)

## biào

**鳔** biào 〈动〉 ① swim bladder; air bladder ② fish glue
【鳔胶】 biàojiāo isinglass; fish glue

## biē

**憋** biē ① suppress; hold back: ～不住 be unable to hold oneself back; can't contain oneself/ ～住气 hold one's breath/ ～了一肚子火 be filled with pent-up anger/ ～着一肚子气 have pent-up grievances/ ～足了劲儿 be bursting with energy ② suffocate; feel oppressed: 心里～得慌 feel very much oppressed/ 屋里太闷,～得人透不过气来。The room was so stuffy, one could hardly breathe.
【憋闷】 biēmen feel oppressed; be depressed; be dejected
【憋气】 biēqì ① feel suffocated (或 oppressed) ② choke with resentment; feel injured and resentful

**瘪** biē

另见 biě
【瘪三】 biēsān 〈方〉 a wretched-looking tramp who lives by begging or stealing

**鳖** biē soft-shelled turtle
【鳖甲】 biējiǎ 〈中药〉 turtle shell
【鳖裙】 biēqún calipash

## bié

**别** bié ① leave; part: ～故乡 leave one's native place/ 临～赠言 parting advice/ 久～重逢 meet after a long separation ② other; another: ～人 other people; others/ ～处 another place; elsewhere ③ difference; distinction: 天渊之～ a world of difference/ 性～ sex distinction; sex ④ differentiate; distinguish: ～其真伪 determine whether it's true or false ⑤ fasten with a pin or clip: 把表格～在一起 pin (或 clip) the forms together/ 胸前～着大红花 with a big red flower pinned on one's breast ⑥ stick in: 腰里～着旱烟袋 with a pipe stuck in one's belt ⑦ don't: ～忘了。Don't forget./ ～忙! No hurry. 或 Take your time./ ～管我,救火要紧! Don't bother about me! Put out the fire first. ⑧〔跟"是"字合用,表示揣测〕: 约定的时间都过了,～是他不来了吧? It's past the appointed time. Maybe he isn't coming.
另见 biè
【别称】 biéchēng another name; alternative name: 湘是湖南的～。Xiang is another name for Hunan.
【别出心裁】 bié chū xīncái adopt an original approach; try to be different
【别动队】 biédòngduì ① special detachment; commando ② an armed secret agent squad
【别管】 biéguǎn 〈连〉 no matter (who, what, etc.): ～是谁,一律按原则办事。No matter who it is, we'll act according to principle.
【别号】 biéhào alias
【别具一格】 bié jù yī gé having a unique (或 distinctive) style: 这个舞蹈刚健清新,～。There is something unique about the liveliness and vigour of the dance.
【别开生面】 bié kāi shēngmiàn start something new (或 original); break a new path; break fresh ground: 一次～的现场会 an entirely new sort of on-the-spot meeting
【别离】 biélí take leave of; leave: ～家乡,踏上征途 leave home and start on a long journey
【别名】 biémíng another name: 铁牛是拖拉机的～。Iron-ox is another name for tractor.
【别人】 biéren other people; others; people: 认真考虑～的意见 consider other people's suggestions seriously
【别树一帜】 bié shù yī zhì set up a new banner; found a new school of thought; have a style of one's own
【别墅】 biéshù villa
【别提】 biétí 〈口〉〔表示程度之深不必细说〕: 他那个高兴劲儿,就～了。He was indescribably happy./ 你爷爷小时候～有多苦了。You can hardly imagine what a hard time your grandpa had when he was a child.
【别有风味】 bié yǒu fēngwèi have a distinctive flavour
【别有天地】 bié yǒu tiān-dì a place of unique beauty; scenery of exceptional charm
【别有用心】 bié yǒu yòngxīn have ulterior motives; have an axe to grind
【别针】 biézhēn ① safety pin; pin ② brooch
【别致】 biézhì unique; unconventional: 天坛的建筑结构非常～。The architecture of the Temple of Heaven is unique.
【别字】 biézì wrongly written or mispronounced character: 读～ mispronounce a character/ 写～ write a character wrongly

**蹩** bié 〈方〉 sprain (one's ankle or wrist)
【蹩脚】 biéjiǎo inferior; shoddy: ～的宣传家 an incompetent propagandist/ 演了一出～的滑稽戏 enact a clumsy farce ◇ ～货 inferior goods; poor stuff; shoddy work

## biě

**瘪** biě shrivelled; shrunken: 干～ dry and shrivelled; wizened/ ～花生 blighted peanuts/ 车胎～了。The tyre is flat.
另见 biē
【瘪螺痧】 biěluóshā 〈中医〉 cholera (with dehydration)

## biè

**别** biè
另见 bié
【别扭】 bièniu ① awkward; uncomfortable; difficult: 她刚来牧区的时候,生活上感到有点～。When she first came to this pastoral area, she found life here a bit difficult to get used to./ 这个人真～。That chap is really difficult to deal with. ② cannot see eye to eye: 闹～ be at odds ③ (of speech or writing) unnatural; awkward: 这句话听起来有点～。This sentence sounds a bit awkward.

## bīn

**宾** bīn guest: 贵～ distinguished guest/ 国～ state guest
【宾词】 bīncí 〈逻〉 predicate
【宾馆】 bīnguǎn guesthouse
【宾客】 bīnkè guests; visitors
【宾语】 bīnyǔ 〈语〉 object: 直接～ direct object/ 间接～ indirect object
【宾至如归】 bīn zhì rú guī guests feel at home (in a hotel, guesthouse, etc.); a home from home

**彬** bīn
【彬彬有礼】 bīnbīn yǒu lǐ refined and courteous; urbane

**傧** bīn
【傧相】 bīnxiàng 〈旧〉 attendant of the bride or bridegroom at a wedding: 男～ best man/ 女～ bridesmaid

**滨** bīn ① bank; brink; shore: 海～ seashore/ 湖～ lakeshore; lakeside/ 湘江之～ on the banks of the Xiangjiang River ② be close to (the sea, a river, etc.); border on: ～海 border on the sea/ ～海地区 coastal region/ ～江公园 riverside park

**缤** bīn
【缤纷】 bīnfēn 〈书〉 in riotous profusion: 五彩～ a riot of colour/ 落英～ petals falling in riotous profusion

**槟** bīn
另见 bīng
【槟子】 bīnzi 〈植〉 *binzi*, a species of apple which is slightly sour and astringent

**镔** bīn

【镔铁】 bīntiě wrought iron

**濒** bīn ① be close to (the sea, a river, etc.); border on: 东～大海 face the sea on the east ② be on the brink of; be on the point of: ～死 on the brink (或 verge) of death; dying/ ～行 on the point of going

【濒临】 bīnlín be close to; border on; be on the verge of: ～黄海 border on the Huanghai Sea/ 春秋末期奴隶社会～瓦解。By the end of the Spring and Autumn Period (770-476 B.C.) slave society was on the verge of disintegration.

【濒危】 bīnwēi ① be in imminent danger ② be critically ill

【濒于】 bīnyú be on the brink of: ～破产 be on the brink of bankruptcy/ ～崩溃 verge on collapse/ ～绝境 face an impasse/ ～灭亡 near extinction

## bìn

**摈** bìn 〈书〉 discard; get rid of: ～而不用 reject/ ～诸门外 shut (或 lock) sb. out

【摈斥】 bìnchì reject; dismiss: ～异己 dismiss those who hold different opinions

【摈除】 bìnchú discard; get rid of; dispense with: ～繁文缛节 dispense with all unnecessary formalities

【摈弃】 bìnqì abandon; discard; cast away: ～剥削阶级的道德观念 cast away the moral values of the exploiting classes

**膑** bìn 见"髌" bìn

**殡** bìn ① lay a coffin in a memorial hall ② carry a coffin to the burial place

【殡车】 bìnchē hearse

【殡殓】 bìnliàn encoffin a corpse and carry it to the grave

【殡仪馆】 bìnyíguǎn the undertaker's; funeral parlour (或 home)

【殡葬】 bìnzàng funeral and interment

**髌** bìn ① kneecap; patella ② chopping off the kneecaps (a punishment in ancient China)

【髌骨】 bìngǔ 〈生理〉 kneecap; patella

**鬓** bìn temples; hair on the temples

【鬓发】 bìnfà hair on the temples: ～灰白 greying at the temples

【鬓角】 bìnjiǎo temples; hair on the temples

## bīng

**并** Bīng another name for Taiyuan
另见 bìng

**冰** bīng ① ice ② put on the ice; ice: 把那瓶啤酒～上。Ice the bottle of beer. ③ feel cold: 这水～手。This water is freezing cold.

【冰雹】 bīngbáo hail; hailstone

【冰场】 bīngchǎng skating (或 ice) rink; ice stadium; ice arena

【冰川】 bīngchuān glacier
◇ ～湖 glacial lake/ ～舌 glacier tongue/ ～学 glaciology/ ～作用 glaciation

【冰醋酸】 bīngcùsuān 〈化〉 glacial acetic acid

【冰镩】 bīngcuān ice chisel

【冰袋】 bīngdài 〈医〉 ice bag

【冰蛋】 bīngdàn frozen eggs

【冰刀】 bīngdāo 〈体〉 (ice) skates

【冰岛】 Bīngdǎo Iceland ◇ ～人 Icelander/ ～语 Icelandic (language)

【冰点】 bīngdiǎn 〈物〉 freezing point ◇ ～测定器 cryoscope

【冰冻】 bīngdòng freeze: ～三尺,非一日之寒。It takes more than one cold day for the river to freeze three feet deep — the trouble has been brewing for quite some time.
◇ ～季节 freezing season/ ～区 frost zone/ ～食物 frozen food

【冰盖】 bīnggài 〈地〉 ice sheet

【冰糕】 bīnggāo 〈方〉 ① ice cream ② 见"冰棍儿"

【冰棍儿】 bīnggùnr ice-lolly; popsicle; ice-sucker; frozen sucker

【冰河】 bīnghé glacier ◇ ～时代 glacial epoch

【冰窖】 bīngjiào icehouse

【冰晶】 bīngjīng 〈气〉 ice crystal

【冰晶石】 bīngjīngshí cryolite

【冰冷】 bīnglěng ice-cold

【冰凉】 bīngliáng ice-cold

【冰凝器】 bīngníngqì 〈物〉 cryophorus

【冰排】 bīngpái ice raft; ice floe

【冰片】 bīngpiàn 〈中药〉 borneol

【冰期】 bīngqī 〈地〉 glacial epoch; ice age

【冰淇淋】 bīngqílín ice cream

【冰碛】 bīngqì 〈地〉 moraine ◇ ～物 till/ ～岩 tillite

【冰橇】 bīngqiāo sled; sledge; sleigh

【冰球】 bīngqiú 〈体〉 ① ice hockey ② puck

【冰染染料】 bīngrǎn rǎnliào azoic dyes

【冰山】 bīngshān iceberg

【冰上运动】 bīngshàng yùndòng ice-sports ◇ ～会 ice-sports meet

【冰释】 bīngshì 〈书〉 (of misgivings, misunderstandings, etc.) disappear; vanish; be dispelled: 涣然～ be instantly dispelled (或 removed)

【冰霜】 bīngshuāng ① moral integrity ② austerity: 凛若～ severe-looking

【冰塔】 bīngtǎ 〈地〉 serac

【冰炭不相容】 bīng-tàn bù xiāngróng as incompatible (或 irreconcilable) as ice and hot coals

【冰糖】 bīngtáng crystal sugar; rock candy ◇ ～葫芦 candied haws on a stick

【冰天雪地】 bīngtiān-xuědì a world of ice and snow

【冰隙】 bīngxì 〈地〉 crevasse

【冰箱】 bīngxiāng icebox; refrigerator; freezer

【冰消瓦解】 bīngxiāo-wǎjiě melt like ice and break like tiles; disintegrate; dissolve

【冰鞋】 bīngxié skating boots; skates

【冰镇】 bīngzhèn iced: ～西瓜 iced watermelon

【冰洲石】 bīngzhōushí Iceland spar

【冰柱】 bīngzhù icicle

【冰砖】 bīngzhuān ice-cream brick

**兵** bīng ① weapons; arms: 坚甲利～ strong armour and sharp weapons ② soldier: 当～ be a soldier; serve (或 enlist) in the armed forces/ 新～ recruit/ 老～ seasoned soldier; veteran/ 实现全民皆～ turn the whole nation into soldiers ③ rank-and-file soldier; private: 官～一致 unity between officers and men ④ army; troops ⑤ military ⑥ pawn, one of the pieces in Chinese chess

【兵变】 bīngbiàn mutiny

【兵不血刃】 bīng bù xuè rèn the edges of the swords not being stained with blood—win victory without firing a shot

【兵不厌诈】 bīng bù yàn zhà there can never be too much deception in war; in war nothing is too deceitful; all's fair in war

【兵部】 Bīngbù the Ministry of War in feudal China
【兵船】 bīngchuán man-of-war; naval vessel; warship
【兵法】 bīngfǎ art of war; military strategy and tactics
【兵戈】 bīnggē 〈书〉 ① weapons; arms: 不动～ without resorting to force ② fighting; war: ～扰攘 war-torn
【兵工厂】 bīnggōngchǎng munitions (或 ordnance) factory; arsenal
【兵贵神速】 bīng guì shénsù speed is precious in war
【兵荒马乱】 bīnghuāng-mǎluàn turmoil and chaos of war
【兵家】 bīngjiā ① military strategist in ancient China ② military commander; soldier: 胜败乃～常事。For a military commander, winning or losing a battle is a common occurrence./ ～必争之地 a place contested by all strategists; strategic point
【兵舰】 bīngjiàn warship
【兵力】 bīnglì military strength; armed forces; troops: ～对比 relative military strength/ 分散～ disperse one's troops; spread one's forces too thin/ ～不足 be short of men (或 armed forces)/ ～转移 transfer of troops/ ～部署 troop disposition; battle array
【兵连祸结】 bīnglián-huòjié ravaged by successive wars; war-torn; war-ridden
【兵临城下】 bīng lín chéngxià the attacking army has reached the city gates; the city is under siege
【兵马】 bīngmǎ troops and horses; military forces: ～未动，粮草先行。Food and fodder should go before troops and horses — proper preparations should be made in advance. ◇ ～俑 〈考古〉 wood or clay figures of warriors and horses buried with the dead
【兵痞】 bīngpǐ army riffraff; army ruffian; soldier of fortune
【兵器】 bīngqì weaponry; weapons; arms
【兵强马壮】 bīngqiáng-mǎzhuàng strong soldiers and sturdy horses — a well-trained and powerful army
【兵权】 bīngquán military leadership; military power
【兵戎】 bīngróng arms; weapons: ～相见 resort (或 appeal) to arms
【兵士】 bīngshì ordinary soldier
【兵书】 bīngshū a book on the art of war
【兵团】 bīngtuán ① large (military) unit; formation; corps: 主力～ main force/ 地方～ regional formation/ 生产建设～ production and construction corps ② army
【兵蚁】 bīngyǐ soldier ant; dinergate
【兵役】 bīngyì military service: 服～ serve in the army; perform military service ◇ ～法 military service law/ ～制 system of military service
【兵营】 bīngyíng military camp; barracks
【兵员】 bīngyuán soldiers; troops
【兵源】 bīngyuán manpower resources (for military service); sources of troops
【兵站】 bīngzhàn army service station; military depot
【兵种】 bīngzhǒng arm of the services: 技术～ technical arms

**槟** bīng
另见 bīn
【槟榔】 bīnglang areca; betel palm ◇ ～子 〈中药〉 betel (或 areca) nut

## bǐng

**丙** bǐng ① the third of the ten Heavenly Stems ② third: ～等 the third grade; grade C/ ～种维生素 vitamin C
【丙纶】 bǐnglún 〈纺〉 polypropylene fibre
【丙酮】 bǐngtóng 〈化〉 acetone ◇ ～树脂 acetone resin
【丙烯酸】 bǐngxīsuān 〈化〉 acrylic acid ◇ ～绘画 acrylic painting
【丙种射线】 bǐngzhǒng shèxiàn 〈物〉 gamma ray

**秉** bǐng 〈书〉 ① grasp; hold: ～烛夜游 take an evening stroll with a lantern ② control; preside over: ～政 hold political power; be in power
【秉承】 bǐngchéng 〈书〉 take (orders); receive (commands): ～其主子的旨意 act on the orders of one's master
【秉公】 bǐnggōng justly; impartially: ～办理 handle a matter impartially

**炳** bǐng 〈书〉 bright; splendid; remarkable: 彪～ shining; splendid

**柄** bǐng ① handle: 刀～ the handle of a knife/ 斧～ the shaft of an axe; helve ② stem (of a flower, leaf or fruit) ③ 〈书〉 power; authority

**饼** bǐng ① a round flat cake: 月～ moon cake/ 烙～ unleavened pancake; flapjack ② sth. shaped like a cake: 豆～ soybean cake/ 铁～ 〈体〉 discus
【饼铛】 bǐngchēng baking pan
【饼饵】 bǐng'ěr cakes; pastry
【饼肥】 bǐngféi cake (fertilizer)
【饼干】 bǐnggān biscuit; cracker
【饼子】 bǐngzi (maize or millet) pancake

**屏** bǐng ① hold (one's breath) ② reject; get rid of; abandon
另见 píng
【屏除】 bǐngchú get rid of; dismiss; brush aside: ～杂念 dismiss distracting thoughts
【屏气】 bǐngqì hold one's breath
【屏弃】 bǐngqì discard; reject; throw away; abandon
【屏息】 bǐngxī hold one's breath: ～静听 listen with bated breath

**禀** bǐng ① report (to one's superior); petition ② receive; be endowed with
【禀承】 bǐngchéng 见"秉承" bǐngchéng
【禀赋】 bǐngfù natural endowment; gift: ～聪明 be gifted with keen intelligence
【禀告】 bǐnggào report (to one's superior)
【禀性】 bǐngxìng natural disposition: ～纯厚 be simple and honest by nature

## bìng

**并** bìng ① combine; merge; incorporate: 把几个小厂～成一个大厂 combine several small factories into a big one ② simultaneously; equally; side by side: 两者～重 lay equal stress on; pay equal attention to ③ 〈副〉 〔用于否定词之前以加强语气〕: 所谓团结，～非一团和气。When we speak of unity, we do not mean unprincipled peace. ④ 〈连〉 and: 我完全同意～拥护这个报告。I fully agree with and endorse this report.
另见 Bīng
【并蒂莲】 bìngdìlián twin lotus flowers on one stalk — a devoted married couple
【并发】 bìngfā be complicated by; erupt simultaneously ◇ ～症 〈医〉 complication
【并激】 bìngjī 〈电〉 shunt excitation ◇ ～电动机 shunt

motor/ ～绕组 shunt winding
【并驾齐驱】 bìngjià-qíqū run neck and neck; keep abreast of (或 keep pace with, be on a par with) one another
【并肩】 bìngjiān shoulder to shoulder; side by side; abreast: ～作战 fight side by side/ 四人～而行。The four of them walked abreast./ 互帮互学，～前进 help and learn from each other and advance together
【并举】 bìngjǔ develop simultaneously: 土洋～ employ both simple and sophisticated methods; employ both indigenous and foreign methods
【并卷机】 bìngjuǎnjī 〈纺〉 ribbon lap machine
【并立】 bìnglì exist side by side; exist simultaneously
【并联】 bìnglián 〈电〉 parallel connection ◇ ～电路 parallel circuit
【并列】 bìngliè stand side by side; be juxtaposed: ～第二名 be both runners-up; tie for second place ◇ ～分句 〈语〉 coordinate clauses/ ～句 〈语〉 compound sentence
【并排】 bìngpái side by side; abreast: 不要～骑车。Don't all cycle abreast.
【并且】 bìngqiě 〈连〉 and; besides; moreover; furthermore: 任务艰巨，～时间紧迫。The task is difficult and, moreover, time is pressing./ 这本书内容好，～写得很生动。This book is sound in content and lively in style.
【并入】 bìngrù merge into; incorporate in
【并纱】 bìngshā 〈纺〉 doubling ◇ ～机 doubling winder
【并条】 bìngtiáo 〈纺〉 drawing ◇ ～机 drawing frame
【并吞】 bìngtūn swallow up; annex; merge: 大垄断资本集团～中小企业。Big monopoly capitalist groups swallow up medium and small enterprises.
【并行不悖】 bìngxíng bù bèi both can be implemented without coming into conflict; not be mutually exclusive; run parallel
【并重】 bìngzhòng lay equal stress on; pay equal attention to: 两者～ lay equal stress on both

**病** bìng ①ill; sick: 生～ fall ill; be taken ill/ 他～了三天。He was ill for three days. ②disease: 心脏～ heart trouble; heart disease/ 流行～ epidemic disease ③fault; defect: 语～ ill-chosen expression/ 不足为～ can't count as a fault
【病包儿】 bìngbāor 〈口〉 a person who is always falling ill; chronic invalid
【病变】 bìngbiàn pathological changes
【病程】 bìngchéng course of disease
【病虫害】 bìng-chónghài plant diseases and insect pests
【病床】 bìngchuáng ①hospital bed: 这所医院有三百张～。The hospital has three hundred beds. ②sickbed: 她躺在～上还坚持学习马列主义。She carried on with her study of Marxism-Leninism even while ill in bed.
【病从口入】 bìng cóng kǒu rù illness finds its way in by the mouth
【病倒】 bìngdǎo be down with an illness; be laid up
【病毒】 bìngdú 〈医〉 virus ◇ ～病 virosis/ ～学 virology
【病笃】 bìngdǔ 〈书〉 be critically ill; be terminally ill
【病房】 bìngfáng ward (of a hospital); sickroom: 隔离～ isolation ward/ 内科～ medical ward
【病夫】 bìngfū sick man
【病根】 bìnggēn ①an incompletely cured illness; an old complaint ②the root cause of trouble: 他犯错误的～在于私心太重。His error stems from selfishness.
【病故】 bìnggù die of an illness
【病害】 bìnghài (plant) disease
【病号】 bìnghào sick personnel; person on the sick list; patient: 老～ one who is always ill; chronic invalid ◇ ～饭 patient's diet; special food for patients
【病机】 bìngjī 〈中医〉 interpretation of the cause, onset and process of an illness; pathogenesis
【病急乱投医】 bìng jí luàn tóu yī turn to any doctor one can find when critically ill — try anything when in a desperate situation
【病家】 bìngjiā a patient and his family
【病假】 bìngjià sick leave: 请～ ask for sick leave/ 休～ be on sick leave/ 给三天～ grant three days' sick leave ◇ ～条 certificate for sick leave
【病菌】 bìngjūn pathogenic bacteria; germs
【病况】 bìngkuàng state of an illness; patient's condition
【病理】 bìnglǐ pathology ◇ ～学 pathology
【病历】 bìnglì medical record; case history ◇ ～室 records room
【病例】 bìnglì case (of illness): 流感～ a case of influenza
【病脉】 bìngmài 〈中医〉 abnormal pulse
【病魔】 bìngmó serious illness: ～缠身 be afflicted with a lingering disease
【病情】 bìngqíng state of an illness; patient's condition: 孩子的～有好转。The child's condition took a favourable turn. 或 The child's condition was improving. ◇ ～公报 medical bulletin
【病人】 bìngrén patient; invalid: 重～ a serious case
【病容】 bìngróng sickly look: 面带～ look ill; look unwell
【病入膏肓】 bìng rù gāohuāng the disease has attacked the vitals — beyond cure
【病势】 bìngshì degree of seriousness of an illness; patient's condition: 针灸以后，～略为减轻。The patient became a bit better after the acupuncture treatment.
【病榻】 bìngtà 〈书〉 sickbed
【病态】 bìngtài morbid (或 abnormal) state ◇ ～心理 morbid psychology (或 mentality)
【病痛】 bìngtòng slight illness; indisposition; ailment
【病危】 bìngwēi be critically ill; be terminally ill
【病象】 bìngxiàng symptom (of a disease)
【病因】 bìngyīn cause of disease; pathogeny
【病友】 bìngyǒu a friend made in hospital or people who become friends in hospital; wardmate
【病愈】 bìngyù recover (from an illness)
【病员】 bìngyuán sick personnel; person on the sick list; patient
【病原】 bìngyuán cause of disease; pathogeny ◇ ～体 pathogen/ ～学 aetiology
【病院】 bìngyuàn a specialized hospital: 精神～ mental hospital/ 传染～ infectious diseases hospital; isolation hospital
【病灶】 bìngzào focus (of infection)
【病征】 bìngzhēng symptom (of a disease)
【病症】 bìngzhèng disease; illness
【病株】 bìngzhū diseased or infected plant
【病状】 bìngzhuàng symptom (of a disease)

**摒** bìng get rid of; dismiss; brush aside
【摒挡】 bìngdàng 〈书〉 arrange; put in order; get ready: ～行李 get one's luggage ready

## bō

**波** bō ①wave: 微～ ripples ②〈物〉 wave: 声(光、电)～ sound (light, electric) wave/ 纵(横)～ longitudinal (transverse) wave ③an unexpected turn of events: 风～ storm; disturbance
【波长】 bōcháng wavelength ◇ ～计 wavemeter; cymometer
【波茨坦公告】 Bōcítǎn Gōnggào Potsdam Proclamation

(1945)
【波荡】 bōdàng heave; surge: 海水～。The sea surges.
【波导】 bōdǎo 〈物〉 wave guide ◇ ～管 wave guide/ ～通信 wave guide communication
【波动】 bōdòng ① undulate; fluctuate: 物价～ price fluctuation/ 情绪～ in an anxious state of mind ② 〈物〉 wave motion ◇ ～说〈物〉 wave theory
【波段】 bōduàn 〈无〉 wave band ◇ ～开关 band switch; waver
【波多黎各】 Bōduōlígè Puerto Rico ◇ ～人 Puerto Rican
【波尔多液】 bō'ěrduōyè 〈农〉 Bordeaux mixture
【波峰】 bōfēng 〈物〉 wave crest
【波幅】 bōfú 〈物〉 amplitude ◇ ～失真 amplitude distortion
【波谷】 bōgǔ 〈物〉 trough
【波及】 bōjí spread to; involve; affect: 经济危机～整个资本主义世界。The economic crisis affected the entire capitalist world.
【波兰】 Bōlán Poland ◇ ～人 Pole/ ～语 Polish (language)
【波澜】 bōlán great waves; billows
【波澜起伏】 bōlán qǐfú (of a piece of writing) with one climax following another
【波澜壮阔】 bōlán zhuàngkuò surging forward with great momentum; unfolding on a magnificent scale: ～的民族解放运动 the surging national liberation movement/ 一首～、气势磅礴的史诗 an epic of magnificent sweep
【波浪】 bōlàng wave: ～式前进 advance wave upon wave
【波利尼西亚】 Bōlíníxīyà Polynesia ◇ ～人 Polynesian/ ～语 Polynesian (language)
【波罗的海】 Bōluódìhǎi the Baltic (Sea)
【波美比重计】 bōměibǐzhòngjì Baumé hydrometer 又作"波美表"
【波美度】 bōměidù 〈化〉 Baumé degrees
【波谱】 bōpǔ 〈物〉 spectrum
【波束】 bōshù 〈物〉 beam
【波涛】 bōtāo great waves; billows: ～汹涌 roaring waves/ ～滚滚的大海 rolling seas
【波特】 bōtè 〈讯〉 baud
【波纹】 bōwén ① ripple ② corrugation ◇ ～管〈机〉 bellows; corrugated pipe/ ～铁 corrugated iron/ ～纸板 corrugated cardboard
【波音】 bōyīn 〈乐〉 mordent: 逆～ inverted mordent
【波折】 bōzhé twists and turns: 事情发生了～。Events took an unexpected turn.
【波状热】 bōzhuàngrè 〈医〉 undulant fever; brucellosis
【波状云】 bōzhuàngyún 〈气〉 undulatus

**拨** bō ① move with hand, foot, stick, etc.; turn; stir; poke: ～火 poke a fire/ ～钟 set a clock/ ～电话号码 dial a telephone number/ ～到北京电台 tune in to Radio Beijing/ ～转马头 turn the horse round ② set aside; assign; allocate: ～两间房子给理论组 set aside two rooms for the theoretical study group/ ～了五名青年工人到我们车间。Five young workers have been assigned to our workshop./ 国家～出大批资金，发展支农工业。The state allocates huge funds for the development of aid-agriculture industries. ③〈量〉〔用于人的分组等〕group; batch: 社员分成两～儿挖渠道。The commune members divided themselves into two groups for digging the channel./ 轮～儿休息 take rest by turns
【拨付】 bōfù appropriate (a sum of money)
【拨号盘】 bōhàopán (telephone) dial
【拨火棍】 bōhuǒgùn poker
【拨款】 bōkuǎn ① allocate funds ② appropriation: 军事～ military appropriations/ 财政～ financial allocation
【拨刺】 bōla 〈象〉 splash (of a fish)
【拨浪鼓】 bōlanggǔ a drum-shaped rattle (used by pedlars or as a toy); rattle-drum
【拨乱反正】 bō luàn fǎn zhèng bring order out of chaos; set to rights things which have been thrown into disorder
【拨弄】 bōnong ① move to and fro (with hand, foot, stick, etc.); fiddle with: ～算盘子儿 move the beads of an abacus/ ～火盆里的木炭 poke the charcoal in the brazier/ ～琴弦 pluck the strings of a fiddle ② stir up: ～是非 stir things up
【拨冗】 bōrǒng 〈套〉 find time in the midst of pressing affairs: 务希～出席。Your presence is cordially requested.
【拨弦乐器】 bōxián yuèqì plucked string (或 stringed) instrument; plucked instrument
【拨云见日】 bō yún jiàn rì dispel the clouds and see the sun — restore justice: 咱家乡自从来了共产党，～得解放。The Communist Party came to our home village, swept away the clouds and brought us the sunlight of liberation.
【拨正】 bōzhèng set right; correct: ～航向 correct the course
【拨子】 bōzi 〈乐〉 plectrum
【拨奏】 bōzòu 〈乐〉 *pizzicato*

**玻** bō
【玻利维亚】 Bōlìwéiyà Bolivia ◇ ～人 Bolivian
【玻璃】 bōli ① glass: 雕花～ cut glass/ 彩色～ stained glass/ 泡沫～ cellular glass ②〈口〉 nylon; plastic ◇ ～板 glass plate; plate glass; glass top (of a desk)/ ～版〈印〉 collotype/ ～杯 glass; tumbler/ ～布 glass cloth/ ～厂 glassworks/ ～刀 glass cutter; glazier's diamond/ ～粉 glass dust/ ～钢 glass fibre reinforced plastic/ ～棉(绒) glass wool/ ～片 sheet glass/ ～纱〈纺〉 organdy/ ～丝 glass silk/ ～体〈生理〉 vitreous body/ ～纤维 glass fibre/ ～纸 cellophane; glassine/ ～砖 glass block
【玻意耳定律】 Bōyì'ěr dìnglǜ 〈物〉 Boyle's law

**剥** bō
另见 bāo
【剥采比】 bōcǎibǐ 〈矿〉 stripping-to-ore ratio; stripping ratio
【剥夺】 bōduó deprive; expropriate; strip: ～政治权利 deprive sb. of political rights/ 被～的阶级 the expropriated classes/ ～权力 divest sb. of his power
【剥离】 bōlí (of tissue, skin, covering, etc.) come off; peel off; be stripped: 表土～ topsoil stripping
【剥落】 bōluò peel off: 门上的漆已～了。The paint on the door has peeled off.
【剥蚀】 bōshí denude; corrode: 由于风雨～，碑文已无法辨认。Owing to the ravages of wind and rain, the inscription on the stone tablet is already undecipherable. ◇ ～作用〈地〉 denudation
【剥削】 bōxuē exploit: 消灭人～人的制度 abolish the system of exploitation of man by man/ 把～根子全拔掉 uproot exploitation/ 贫雇农受到地主的残酷～。The poor peasants and farm labourers were cruelly exploited by the landlords. ◇ ～阶级 exploiting class/ ～收入 income from exploitation/ ～者 exploiter
【剥啄】 bōzhuó 〈书〉〈象〉 tap (on a door or window)

**钵** bō ① earthen bowl ② alms bowl (of a Buddhist monk): 沿门托～ begging alms from door to door
【钵盂】 bōyú alms bowl

**饽** bō
【饽饽】 bōbo 〈方〉 ① pastry ② (steamed) bun; cake: 玉米～ maize cake

**菠** bō
【菠菜】 bōcài spinach
【菠萝】 bōluó pineapple

**播** bō ①sow; seed: 夏～ summer sowing/ 撒～ broadcast sowing/ ～下革命的种子 sow the seeds of revolution ②broadcast: ～出《东方红》乐曲 broadcast the music of *The East Is Red*
【播弄】 bōnong ①order sb. about ②stir up: ～是非 stir things up; stir up trouble; sow dissension
【播送】 bōsòng broadcast; transmit; beam: ～新闻 broadcast news/ ～电视节目 broadcast a T. V. programme/ 向东南亚～的节目 programme beamed to Southeast Asia
【播音】 bōyīn transmit; broadcast: 这次～到此结束。That concludes our programme for this transmission. ◇ ～室 broadcasting studio/ ～员 announcer
【播种】 bōzhǒng sow seeds; sow; seed ◇ ～机 seeder; planter; grain drill
【播种】 bōzhòng sowing; seeding ◇ ～面积 sown area; seeded area/ ～期 sowing (或 seeding) time

## bó

**伯** bó ①father's elder brother; uncle ②the eldest of brothers ③earl; count
另见 bǎi
【伯伯】 bóbo father's elder brother; uncle
【伯父】 bófù father's elder brother; uncle
【伯爵】 bójué earl; count ◇ ～夫人 countess
【伯劳】 bóláo 〈动〉 shrike
【伯力】 Bólì 见"哈巴罗夫斯克" Hābāluófūsīkè
【伯利兹】 Bólìzī Belize
【伯母】 bómǔ wife of father's elder brother; aunt
【伯仲】 bó-zhòng 〈书〉〔多用于〕: 相～ be much the same/ ～之间 almost on a par
【伯仲叔季】 bó-zhòng-shū-jì eldest, second, third and youngest of brothers; order of seniority among brothers

**驳** bó ①refute; contradict; gainsay: 真理不怕人～。Truth fears no refutation. ②barge; lighter: 铁～ iron barge/ 油～ oil barge ③transport by lighter: ～卸 unload by lighter ④〈书〉 of different colours: 斑～ parti-coloured; variegated
【驳岸】 bó'àn a low stone wall built along the water's edge to protect an embankment; revetment
【驳斥】 bóchì refute; denounce
【驳船】 bóchuán barge; lighter
【驳倒】 bódǎo demolish sb.'s argument; refute; outargue
【驳回】 bóhuí reject; turn down; overrule: ～上诉 reject an appeal/ 法院～了他的无理要求。The court overruled his unreasonable claim.
【驳壳枪】 bókéqiāng Mauser pistol
【驳运】 bóyùn transport by lighter; lighter ◇ ～费 lighterage
【驳杂】 bózá heterogeneous: 内容～ heterogeneous in content

**泊** bó be at anchor; moor; berth: 停～ lie at anchor/ ～岸 anchor alongside the shore
另见 pō
【泊位】 bówèi 〈交〉 berth: 深水～ deepwater berth

**帛** bó 〈书〉 silks: 布～ cottons and silks/ ～画 painting on silk/ ～书 (ancient) book copied on silk

**勃** bó suddenly
【勃勃】 bóbó thriving; vigorous; exuberant: 生气～ full of vitality; alive with activity/ 兴致～ full of enthusiasm; in high spirits/ 野心～ driven by wild ambition; overweeningly ambitious
【勃发】 bófā ①thrive; prosper ②break out: 游兴～ be seized with a desire to travel
【勃然】 bórán ①agitatedly; excitedly: ～变色 agitatedly change colour; be visibly stung/ ～大怒 fly into a rage; flare up ②vigorously: 第三世界在反帝、反殖、反霸斗争中～兴起。In the struggle against imperialism, colonialism and hegemonism, the third world has risen as a vigorous new force.
【勃谿】 bóxī 〈书〉 family quarrel; tiff; squabble
【勃兴】 bóxīng rise suddenly; grow vigorously: 一个工业城市的～ the vigorous growth of an industrial town

**钹** bó 〈乐〉 cymbals

**铂** bó 〈化〉 platinum (Pt)

**舶** bó oceangoing ship

**脖** bó neck
【脖颈儿】 bógěngr back of the neck; nape
【脖子】 bózi neck

**渤** bó
【渤海】 Bóhǎi the Bohai Sea

**博** bó ①rich; abundant; plentiful: 地大物～ vast in territory and rich in natural resources/ ～而不精 have wide but not expert knowledge; know something about everything ②win; gain: 聊～一笑 just for your entertainment
【博爱】 bó'ài universal fraternity (或 brotherhood); universal love
【博茨瓦纳】 Bócíwǎnà Botswana ◇ ～人 (单数) Motswana; (复数) Batswana
【博得】 bódé win; gain: ～同情 win sympathy/ ～全场喝采 draw loud applause from the audience; bring the house down/ ～好评 have a favourable reception
【博古通今】 bógǔ-tōngjīn conversant with things past and present — erudite and informed
【博览】 bólǎn read extensively: ～群书 well-read
【博览会】 bólǎnhuì (international) fair
【博取】 bóqǔ try to gain; court: ～同情 seek (或 enlist) sb.'s sympathy/ ～欢心 curry favour/ ～信任 try to win sb.'s confidence
【博士】 bóshì ①doctor: 哲学～ Doctor of Philosophy (Ph. D.) ②court academician (in feudal China) ◇ ～学位 doctor's degree; doctorate
【博闻强记】 bówén-qiángjì have wide learning and a retentive memory; have encyclopaedic knowledge
【博物】 bówù natural science ◇ ～学家 naturalist
【博物馆】 bówùguǎn museum: 历史～ the Museum of History/ 中国革命～ the Museum of the Chinese Revolution ◇ ～学 museology
【博学】 bóxué learned; erudite: ～之士 learned scholar; erudite person
【博雅】 bóyǎ learned: ～之士 a scholar of profound knowledge

**鹁** bó

【鹁鸽】 bógē pigeon

**搏** bó ① wrestle; fight; combat; struggle: 肉～ hand-to-hand fight (或 combat) ② pounce on: 恶狼～羊。The wolf pounced on the sheep. ③ beat; throb: 脉～ pulse

【搏动】 bódòng beat rhythmically; throb; pulsate

【搏斗】 bódòu wrestle; fight; struggle: 与风浪～ battle with the winds and waves/ 生死的～ a life-and-death struggle

**魄** bó 见"落泊(魄)" luòbó

另见 pò; tuò

**箔** bó ① screen (of reeds, sorghum stalks, etc.): 苇～ reed screen ② bamboo tray for rearing silkworms ③ foil; tinsel: 金～ gold foil (或 leaf) ④ paper tinsel burnt as offerings to the dead

**膊** bó arm: 赤～ bare to the waist

**镈** bó a large bell used in ancient times

**薄** bó ① slight; meagre; small: ～技 〈谦〉 my slight skill/ ～酬 small reward; meagre remuneration ② ungenerous; unkind; mean: ～待 treat ungenerously ③ frivolous: 轻～ frivolous; given to philandering ④ despise; belittle: 鄙～ despise/ 厚此～彼 favour one and slight the other ⑤ 〈书〉 approach; near: 日～西山。The sun is setting behind the western hills. ⑥ (Bó) a surname

另见 báo; bò

【薄利】 bólì small profits: ～多销 small profits but quick turnover

【薄命】 bómìng 〈旧〉 (usu. of women) born under an unlucky star; born unlucky

【薄膜】 bómó ① membrane ② film: 塑料～ plastic film ◇ ～电阻 film resistor

【薄暮】 bómù 〈书〉 dusk; twilight

【薄片】 bópiàn thin slice; thin section ◇ ～分析 〈地〉 thin section analysis

【薄情】 bóqíng inconstant in love; fickle

【薄弱】 bóruò weak; frail: 意志～ weak-willed/ 能力～ lacking in ability/ 技术力量～ lack qualified technical personnel ◇ ～环节 weak link; vulnerable spot

【薄胎瓷器】 bótāi cíqì 〈工美〉 eggshell china

【薄雾】 bówù mist; haze

【薄油层】 bóyóucéng 〈石油〉 oil sheet

**礴** bó 见"磅礴" pángbó

## bǒ

**跛** bǒ lame: ～了一只脚 lame in one leg/ 一颠一～ walk with a limp; limp along

【跛子】 bǒzi lame person; cripple

**簸** bǒ winnow with a fan; fan: ～谷 winnow away the chaff; fan the chaff

另见 bò

【簸荡】 bǒdàng roll; rock: 船～得很厉害。The ship was rolling heavily.

【簸扬】 bǒyáng winnow

## bò

**柏** bò 见"黄檗(柏)" huángbò

另见 bǎi

**薄** bò

另见 báo; bó

【薄荷】 bòhe 〈植〉 field mint; peppermint ◇ ～醇 〈化〉 menthol; peppermint camphor/ ～糖 peppermint drops/ ～酮 menthone/ ～油 peppermint oil

**檗** bò 见"黄檗(柏)" huángbò

**擘** bò 〈书〉 thumb: 巨～ an authority in a certain field

【擘画】 bòhuà 〈书〉 plan; arrange: 此事尚待～。This has yet to be planned. 又作"擘划"

**簸** bò

另见 bǒ

【簸箕】 bòji ① dustpan ② winnowing fan ③ loop (of a fingerprint)

## bo

**卜** bo 见"萝卜" luóbo

另见 bǔ

## bū

**逋** bū 〈书〉 flee: ～逃 flee; abscond

【逋逃薮】 būtáosǒu 〈书〉 refuge for fugitives

## bú

**醭** bú mould (on the surface of soy sauce, vinegar, etc.)

## bǔ

**卜** bǔ ① divination; fortune-telling: ～卦 divine by the Eight Diagrams ② 〈书〉 foretell; predict: 生死未～ hard to tell whether the person is alive or not/ 胜败可～。Victory or defeat can be predicted. 或 We can forecast the outcome. ③ 〈书〉 select; choose: ～居 choose a place for one's home/ 行期未～。The date of departure remains undecided. ④ (Bǔ) a surname

另见 bo

【卜辞】 bǔcí oracle inscriptions of the Shang Dynasty (c. 16th-11th century B. C.) on tortoiseshells or animal bones

【卜筮】 bǔshì divination

**吥** bǔ

【吥吩】 bǔfēn 〈化〉 porphin

**补** bǔ ① mend; patch; repair: ～衣服 mend (或 patch) clothes/ ～鞋 repair (或 mend) shoes/ ～袜子 darn socks/ ～车胎 mend a puncture/ 修桥～路 build bridges and repair roads ② fill; supply; make up for: 弥～损失 make up for a loss/ 把漏了的字～上 supply the missing words/ 我们还得～两个人。We have two vacancies to be filled. 或 We need two more people. ③ nourish: ～血 enrich the blood/ ～身体 build up one's health (with nourishing food or tonics) ④ 〈书〉 benefit; use; help: 不无小～ not be without some advantage; be of some help/ 无～于事 not help matters

【补白】 bǔbái filler (in a newspaper or magazine)

【补报】 bǔbào ①make a report after the event; make a supplementary report ②repay a kindness
【补偿】 bǔcháng compensate; make up: ～所受的损失 compensate sb. for a loss/ ～差额 make up a deficiency ◇～电容器 compensation condenser/ ～费 compensation
【补充】 bǔchōng ① replenish; supplement; complement; add: ～人力 replenish manpower/ ～兵员 fill up (an army unit) to full strength; replace losses/ ～库存 replenish the stock/ ～两点意见 have two points to add/ 互相～ complement each other; be mutually complementary ② additional; complementary; supplementary
◇～读物 supplementary reading material/ ～规定 additional regulations/ ～说明 additional remarks
【补丁】 bǔding patch: 打～ put (或 sew) a patch on; patch up
【补发】 bǔfā supply again (sth. lost, etc.); reissue; pay retroactively: 材料丢失,不予～。The material will not be reissued if lost./ ～增加的工资 pay increased wages retroactively/ 上次没领到工作服的,现由总务处～。Those who were not issued workclothes last time can get them at the general affairs office now.
【补法】 bǔfǎ 〈中医〉① treatment involving the use of tonics to restore the patient's health ② reinforcing method (in acupuncture)
【补花】 bǔhuā 〈工美〉*appliqué*
【补给】 bǔjǐ 〈军〉supply
◇～点 supply point/ ～品 supplies/ ～线 supply line/ ～站 depot
【补角】 bǔjiǎo 〈数〉supplementary angle
【补救】 bǔjiù remedy: ～办法 remedial measure; remedy/ 无可～ be past (或 beyond) remedy; irremediable; irreparable
【补考】 bǔkǎo make-up examination
【补课】 bǔkè make up a missed lesson: 教师给学生～。The teacher helped his pupils make up the lessons they had missed.
【补炉】 bǔlú 〈冶〉fettling
【补苗】 bǔmiáo 〈农〉fill the gaps with seedlings
【补偏救弊】 bǔpiān-jiùbì remedy defects and rectify errors; rectify (或 remedy) abuses
【补票】 bǔpiào buy one's ticket after the normal time
【补品】 bǔpǐn tonic
【补缺】 bǔquē fill a vacancy; supply a deficiency ◇～选举 by-election
【补色】 bǔsè complementary colour
【补税】 bǔshuì ① pay a tax one has evaded ② pay an overdue tax
【补体】 bǔtǐ 〈医〉complement (in blood serum) ◇～结合试验 complement fixation test
【补贴】 bǔtiē subsidy; allowance: 粮食～ grain subsidy/ 出口～ export subsidy/ 生活～ living allowances/ 由国家给予～ be subsidized by the state ◇～工分 subsidiary workpoints
【补习】 bǔxí take lessons after school or work ◇～学校 continuation school
【补泻】 bǔxiè 〈中医〉reinforcing and reducing methods (in acupuncture)
【补选】 bǔxuǎn by-election: ～人民代表 hold a by-election for a people's deputy
【补血】 bǔxuè enrich the blood ◇～剂 blood (或 haematic) tonic
【补牙】 bǔyá 〈医〉 fill a tooth; have a tooth stopped
【补养】 bǔyǎng take a tonic or nourishing food to build up one's health
【补药】 bǔyào tonic
【补液】 bǔyè 〈医〉fluid infusion
【补遗】 bǔyí addendum
【补益】 bǔyì 〈书〉 benefit; help: 有所～ be of some help (或 benefit)
【补语】 bǔyǔ 〈语〉complement
【补种】 bǔzhòng reseed; resow; replant
【补助】 bǔzhù subsidy; allowance: 煤火～ heating allowance ◇～金 grant-in-aid; subsidy
【补缀】 bǔzhuì mend (clothes); patch: 缝连～ mend and darn/ ～成文 put together some sort of an article; produce a patchwork of an article
【补足】 bǔzú bring up to full strength; make up a deficiency; fill (a vacancy, gap, etc.)

**捕** bǔ catch; seize; arrest: ～鱼 catch fish/ 被～ be arrested; be under arrest
【捕虫叶】 bǔchóngyè 〈植〉insect-catching leaf
【捕风捉影】 bǔfēng-zhuōyǐng chase the wind and clutch at shadows — make groundless accusations; speak or act on hearsay evidence
【捕俘】 bǔfú 〈军〉capture enemy personnel (for intelligence purposes)
【捕获】 bǔhuò catch; capture; seize: 当场～ catch sb. redhanded ◇～量 catch (of fish, etc.)/ ～法〈法〉law of prize
【捕鲸船】 bǔjīngchuán whaler; whale catcher
【捕捞】 bǔlāo fish for (aquatic animals and plants); catch: ～对虾 catch prawns ◇～能力 fishing capacity
【捕拿】 bǔná arrest; capture; catch
【捕食】 bǔshí catch and feed on; prey on: 蜻蜓～蚊蝇。The dragonfly feeds on mosquitoes and flies.
【捕鼠器】 bǔshǔqì mousetrap
【捕鱼】 bǔyú catch fish; fish: 出海～ go fishing on the sea
【捕捉】 bǔzhuō catch; seize: ～昆虫 catch insects/ ～战机 seize the opportunity for battle; seize the right moment to strike/ ～镜头 seize the right moment to get a good shot (或 to take a picture)

**哺** bǔ ①feed (a baby); nurse ②〈书〉the food in one's mouth
【哺乳】 bǔrǔ breast-feed; suckle; nurse
◇～动物 mammal/ ～动物学 mammalogy/ ～室 nursing room (where mothers leave their babies when at work and breast-feed them during breaks)
【哺养】 bǔyǎng 〈书〉 feed; rear
【哺育】 bǔyù ① feed: ～雏鸟 (of mother birds) feed little birds ② nurture; foster: 青年一代在毛泽东思想～下茁壮成长。Nurtured by Mao Zedong Thought, the younger generation is growing up strong and healthy.

**鹔** bǔ 见"地鹔" dìbǔ

## bù

**不** bù 〈副〉①〔表示否定〕: ～严重 not serious/ ～必要 unnecessary/ ～正确 incorrect/ ～合法 illegal/ ～可能 impossible/ ～规则 irregular/ ～小心 careless/ 拿～动 find sth. too heavy to carry/ 睡～好 not sleep well/ 她～走了。She's not going. 或 She's decided to stay./ 互～侵犯 mutual nonaggression ②〔单用,表示否定对方的话〕: 他知道吧? —～,他不知道。He knows, doesn't he? — No, he doesn't./ 他不知道吧? —～,他知道。He doesn't know, does he? — Yes, he does. ③〔用在句末表示疑问〕: 你明儿来～? Are you coming tomorrow? ④〔在"不"字前后,叠用相同的词,前面常加"什么",表示不在乎或不相干〕: 什么难学～难

学，我保证学会。No matter how hard it is, I'll learn how to do it. ⑤〔跟"就"搭用，表示选择〕他这会儿～是在车间就是在实验室。He's either in the workshop or in the laboratory.

注意 "不"字在第四声（去声）字前念第二声（阳平），如"不必"búbì；"不是" búshì。本词典为简便起见，条目中的"不"字，都注第四声。

【不安】 bù'ān ① intranquil; unpeaceful; unstable: 世界局势动荡～。The world situation is characterized by turbulence and intranquility. ② uneasy; disturbed; restless: 坐立～ restless; on pins and needles/ 听了这消息我心里很～。I was rather disturbed by the news./ 老来麻烦您，真是～。I'm sorry to trouble you so often.

【不白之冤】 bù bái zhī yuān unrighted wrong; unredressed injustice

【不败之地】 bù bài zhī dì invincible position: 立于～ be in an invincible position

【不备】 bùbèi unprepared; off guard: 乘其～ catch sb. off guard/ 伺其～ watch for a chance to take sb. by surprise

【不比】 bùbǐ unlike: 北方～南方，春天老刮风。The north of China, unlike the south, is windy in spring.

【不必】 bùbì 〈副〉 need not; not have to: ～担心（惊慌）。There is no need to worry (panic)./ 你～去了。You don't have to go now.

【不避艰险】 bù bì jiānxiǎn shrink (或 flinch) from no difficulty or danger; make light of difficulties and dangers

【不变价格】 bùbiàn jiàgé 〈经〉 fixed price; constant price

【不变资本】 bùbiàn zīběn 〈经〉 constant capital

【不便】 bùbiàn ① inconvenient; inappropriate; unsuitable: 交通～ have poor transport facilities; not be conveniently located/ 给治疗带来～ hamper medical treatment/ 在场的人很多，～同他长谈。With so many people around, it wasn't convenient to have a long talk with him./ 如果对你没有什么～的话，我想把时间提早一点。I'd like to make it earlier, if that's not inconvenient to you. ② 〈口〉 short of cash: 手头～ be short of cash; be hard up

【不辨菽麦】 bù biàn shū-mài be unable to tell beans from wheat — have no knowledge of practical matters

【不…不…】 bù ... bù ... ①〔用于意思相同或相近的词或词素之前，表示否定，稍强调〕：不骄不躁 not conceited or rash; free from arrogance and rashness/ 不慌不忙 unhurried; calm; leisurely/ 不声不响 quiet; silent/ 不理不睬 ignore; take no notice of ②〔用于意思相对的词或词素之前，表示"既不…又不…"〕：不大不小 neither too big nor too small; just right/ 不多不少 not too much and not too little; just right/ 不死不活 neither dead nor alive; lifeless; lethargic/ 不上不下 suspended in mid air; in a fix/ 不盈不亏 break even ③〔用于意思相对的词或词素之前，表示"如不…就不…"〕：不破不立，不塞不流，不止不行。There is no construction without destruction, no flowing without damming and no motion without rest.

【不测】 bùcè accident; mishap; contingency: 以防～ be prepared for any contingency/ 如有～ if anything untoward should happen/ 险遭～ have a narrow escape

【不曾】 bùcéng never (have done sth.): 我～到过那里。I have never been there.

【不成】 bùchéng ① won't do: 只说不做，那是～的。Mere talk and no action won't do./ 任凭资产阶级思想泛滥是～的。Bourgeois ideas must not be allowed to spread unchecked. ② 〈助〉〔用在句末，表示揣度或反问的语气，前面常有"难道""莫非"等词相呼应〕：难道就这样算了～？How can we let it go at that?/ 莫非说起重机不到，大家就坐等～？Are we going to sit back and do nothing until the cranes arrive?

【不成材】 bùchéngcái good-for-nothing; worthless; ne'er-do-well 又作"不成器"

【不成文法】 bùchéngwénfǎ 〈法〉 unwritten law

【不承认主义】 bùchéngrènzhǔyì policy of nonrecognition

【不逞之徒】 bùchěng zhī tú desperado

【不齿】 bùchǐ 〈书〉 despise; hold in contempt: 为革命人民所～ held in contempt by the revolutionary people/ ～于人类的狗屎堆 filthy and contemptible as dog's dung

【不耻下问】 bù chǐ xià wèn not feel ashamed to ask and learn from one's subordinates

【不啻】 bùchì 〈书〉 ① not less than: 工程所需，～万金。The project requires a tremendous amount of money. ② as; like; as good as: ～沧海一粟 like a drop in the ocean/ ～是当头一棒 like a blow on the head/ 人民盼望解放军，～大旱之望云霓。The people longed for the coming of the People's Liberation Army as one longs for rain during a drought.

【不出所料】 bù chū suǒ liào as expected: ～，敌人果然自投罗网。As was expected, the enemy walked right into the trap.

【不揣冒昧】 bù chuǎi màomèi 〈套〉 venture to; presume to; take the liberty of

【不辞而别】 bù cí ér bié leave without saying good-bye

【不辞辛苦】 bù cí xīnkǔ make nothing of hardships

【不错】 bùcuò ① correct; right: 一点儿～ perfectly correct; quite right ②〔单用，表示肯定对方的话〕：～，他是这么说的。Yes, that's what he said. ③〈口〉 not bad; pretty good: 庄稼长得挺～。The crops are doing quite well./ 这本小说～。This novel is pretty good.

【不打不相识】 bù dǎ bù xiāngshí 〈谚〉 from an exchange of blows friendship grows; no discord, no concord

【不打自招】 bù dǎ zì zhāo confess without being pressed; make a confession without duress

【不大】 bùdà ① not very; not too: ～好 not very good/ ～清楚 not too clear ② not often: 他最近～来。He hasn't been coming around much recently.

【不大离儿】 bùdàlír 〈口〉 ① pretty close; just about right: 你这个子打篮球还～。You're about the right height for a basketball player. ② not bad: 这块地的麦子长得～。The wheat on this field is not bad.

【不待说】 bùdài shuō needless to say; it goes without saying

【不丹】 Bùdān Bhutan ◇ ～人 Bhutanese/ ～语 Bhutanese (language)

【不单】 bùdān ① not the only: 超产的～是这几个生产大队。These are not the only production brigades that have overfulfilled the output quota. ② not merely; not simply: 人民解放军～是战斗队，也是工作队和生产队。The PLA is not merely a fighting force, but a working force and a production corps as well.

【不但】 bùdàn 〈连〉 not only: 我们的产品～要求数量多，而且要求质量好。In production, we demand not only quantity but also quality.

【不当】 bùdàng unsuitable; improper; inappropriate: 处理～ not be handled properly/ 措词～ wrong choice of words

【不倒翁】 bùdǎowēng tumbler; roly-poly

【不到黄河心不死】 bù dào Huánghé xīn bù sǐ 〈谚〉 not stop until one reaches the Huanghe River — not stop until one reaches one's goal; refuse to give up until all hope is gone

【不道德】 bùdàodé immoral

【不得】 bùdé must not; may not; not be allowed: ～将参考书携出阅览室。Reference books may not be taken out of the reading room.

【不得】 bude 〔用在动词后面，表示不可以或不能够〕：去～ must not go/ 马虎～ mustn't (或 can't afford to) be careless/ 这件事你做～。You must never do this.

【不得不】 bùdé bù have no choice (或 option) but to; cannot but; have to: 铁证如山，那个坏家伙～低头认罪。Confronted with ironclad evidence the scoundrel had to plead guilty.

【不得而知】 bùdé ér zhī unknown; unable to find out: 作者是谁，～。The name of the author is unknown./ 情况如何，～。We are unable to find out how the situation stands.

【不得劲】 bù déjìn 〈口〉 ① awkward; unhandy: 这把铁锹使起来～。This is an awkward spade. ② be indisposed; not feel well: 我今天有点～儿。I'm not feeling too well today.

【不得了】 bùdéliǎo ① desperately serious; disastrous: 没有什么～的事。There's nothing really serious./ 成绩不夸跑不了，缺点不找～。If we don't speak of our achievements, they won't run away. If we don't find out our faults, we'll be in a bad way. ②〔用在"得"后作补语〕 extremely; exceedingly: 高兴得～ be extremely happy; be wild with joy/ 坏得～ couldn't be worse; be very bad

【不得人心】 bù dé rénxīn not enjoy popular support; be unpopular

【不得要领】 bù dé yàolǐng fail to grasp the main points: 他讲了半天我还是～。He talked at great length, but I just couldn't see what he was driving at.

【不得已】 bùdéyǐ act against one's will; have no alternative but to; have to: ～而求其次 have to be content with the second best/ 实在～，她只好请几天假。She had no alternative but to ask for a few days' leave./ 非万～不要用这种药。Don't take this medicine unless it's absolutely necessary.

【不登大雅之堂】 bù dēng dàyǎ zhī táng 〈书〉 not appeal to refined taste; be unrefined; be unpresentable

【不等】 bùděng vary; differ: 数量～ vary in amount/ 大小～ differ (或 vary) in size/ 每包的重量从三斤到十斤～。The packages vary in weight from 3 to 10 *jin*.

【不等边三角形】 bùděngbiān sānjiǎoxíng 〈数〉 scalene triangle

【不等号】 bùděnghào 〈数〉 sign of inequality

【不等价交换】 bùděngjià jiāohuàn 〈经〉 exchange of unequal values

【不等式】 bùděngshì 〈数〉 inequality

【不抵抗主义】 bùdǐkàngzhǔyì policy of nonresistance

【不迭】 bùdié 〔用于动词之后〕 ① cannot cope; find it too much: 忙～ hasten (to do sth.)/ 后悔～ too late for regrets ② incessantly: 叫苦～ complain incessantly; pour out endless grievances/ 称赞～ praise profusely

【不定】 bùdìng ① 〈副〉〔表示不肯定〕: 他一天～来多少次。He comes I don't know how many times a day./ 我明天还～去不去呢。It's not at all certain whether I'll go tomorrow./ 事情还～怎样呢。It's hard to predict how things will turn out. ② indefinite ③〈生〉 adventitious; indeterminate ◇ ～变异〈生〉 indeterminate variation/ ～方程 〈数〉 indeterminate equation/ ～根 〈植〉 adventitious root/ ～冠词 〈语〉 indefinite article/ ～积分 〈数〉 indefinite integral/ ～式 〈语〉 infinitive/ ～芽〈植〉 adventitious bud

【不动产】 bùdòngchǎn real estate; immovable property; immovables

【不动声色】 bù dòng shēngsè maintain one's composure; stay calm and collected; not turn a hair; not bat an eyelid

【不冻港】 bùdònggǎng ice-free port; open port

【不独】 bùdú not only: 养猪～可以改善人民生活，还能多积肥料。Pig-breeding not only improves the people's diet; it makes more manure available.

【不端】 bùduān improper; dishonourable: 品行～ dishonourable behaviour; bad conduct

【不断】 bùduàn unceasing; uninterrupted; continuous; constant: 促进生产力的～发展 promote the uninterrupted (或 continuous) growth of the productive forces/ 人类社会总是～进步的。Human society makes unceasing progress./ 先进单位～涌现。Advanced units are constantly emerging./ 使针刺麻醉～完善 bring about steady improvement in acupuncture anaesthesia

【不断革命论】 bùduàn gémìnglùn the theory of uninterrupted revolution

【不对】 bùduì ① incorrect; wrong: 这样做～。It's wrong to act like that. ②〔单用，表示否定对方的话〕: ～，我没有那么说。No, I didn't say that. ③ amiss; abnormal; queer: 这机器声音～。The machine makes a queer noise./ 她今天神色有点～。She doesn't quite look her usual self today.

【不对碴儿】 bùduìchár 〈口〉 not proper; not fit for the occasion: 他觉得自己说的话～，就停住了。He found what he was saying was not proper for the occasion and he stopped short.

【不对头】 bù duìtóu 见"不对"①③

【不…而…】 bù … ér … 〔表示虽不具有某条件或原因而产生某结果〕: 不战而胜 win without fighting a battle; win hands down/ 不教而诛 punish without prior warning

【不二法门】 bù èr fǎmén the one and only way; the only proper course to take

【不乏】 bùfá 〈书〉 there is no lack of: ～先例。There is no lack of precedents./ ～其人。Such people are not rare.

【不法】 bùfǎ lawless; illegal; unlawful: ～之徒 a lawless person/ ～行为 unlawful practice; an illegal act/ ～资本家 a lawbreaking capitalist

【不凡】 bùfán out of the ordinary; out of the common run: 自命～ consider oneself a person of no ordinary talent; have an unduly high opinion of oneself

【不妨】 bùfāng there is no harm in; might as well: 你～现在就告诉他。You might as well tell him right now./ ～一试。There is no harm in trying./ 你～同他联系一下。You might get in touch with him.

【不费吹灰之力】 bù fèi chuī huī zhī lì as easy as blowing off dust — not needing the slightest effort

【不分彼此】 bù fēn bǐ-cǐ make no distinction between what's one's own and what's another's; share everything; be on very intimate terms

【不分青红皂白】 bù fēn qīng-hóng-zào-bái indiscriminately

【不分胜负】 bù fēn shèng-fù tie; draw; come out even: 一场～的比赛 a drawn game/ 两队～。The two teams tied. 或 The two teams came out even.

【不服】 bù fú refuse to obey (或 comply); refuse to accept as final; remain unconvinced by; not give in to: ～输 refuse to take defeat lying down/ ～罪 not admit one's guilt; plead not guilty/ ～老 refuse to give in to old age/ ～指导 refuse to obey instructions/ ～裁判 refuse to accept the referee's ruling/ 对同志们的批评表示～ express disagreement with the criticism of one's comrades

【不服水土】 bù fú shuǐtǔ (of a stranger) not accustomed to the climate of a new place; not acclimatized

【不符】 bùfú not agree (或 tally, square) with; not conform to; be inconsistent with: 言行～ deeds not matching words/ 名实～ have an undeserved reputation/ 与事实～ be inconsistent (或 at variance) with the facts/ 他说话前后～。What he said was self-contradictory. 或 What he said didn't hang together.

【不干不净】 bùgān-bùjìng unclean; filthy: 嘴里～ be foul-mouthed

【不干涉】 bù gānshè noninterference; nonintervention ◇ ～政策 policy of noninterference (或 nonintervention)

【不甘】 bùgān unreconciled to; not resigned to; unwilling: ～落后 unwilling to lag behind/ ～示弱 not to be outdone

【不甘心】 bù gānxīn not reconciled to; not resigned to: 阶级敌人决～于他们的失败。The class enemy will not take his defeat lying down.

【不敢当】 bùgǎndāng 〈谦〉〔表示承当不起对方的招待、夸奖等〕: I really don't deserve this; you flatter me

【不敢越雷池一步】 bùgǎn yuè Léichí yī bù dare not go one step beyond the prescribed limit

【不公】 bùgōng unjust; unfair: 办事～ be unfair in handling matters

【不攻自破】 bù gōng zì pò collapse of itself: 这种谣言在事实面前将～。Facts will eventually scotch these rumours.

【不恭】 bùgōng disrespectful: 言词～ use disrespectful language/ 却之～ it would be disrespectful to decline (a gift, an invitation, etc.)

【不共戴天】 bù gòng dài tiān will not live under the same sky (with one's enemy) — absolutely irreconcilable: ～的敌人 sworn enemy/ ～之仇 inveterate hatred

【不苟】 bùgǒu not lax; not casual; careful; conscientious: 工作一丝～ work most conscientiously/ ～言笑 serious in speech and manner

【不够】 bùgòu not enough; insufficient; inadequate: 我做得很～。I haven't done nearly enough./ 他们人力～。They haven't enough manpower./ 分析～深入。The analysis lacks depth./ 准备～ be inadequately prepared

【不顾】 bùgù in spite of; regardless of: ～后果 regardless of the consequences/ ～事实 fly in the face of the facts; have no regard for the truth/ ～大局 show no consideration for the general interest; ignore the larger issues/ ～信义 be guilty of bad faith

【不管】 bùguǎn no matter (what, how, etc.); regardless of: ～结果如何 whatever the consequences/ ～怎样 in any case; anyway/ ～工作多忙，我们都挤时间学习毛主席著作。No matter how busy we are, we always find time to study Chairman Mao's works./ 在党的领导下，～多大的困难，我们都能克服。Under the leadership of the Party, we can overcome any difficulty, however great.

【不管部部长】 bùguǎnbù bùzhǎng minister without portfolio

【不管三七二十一】 bù guǎn sān qī èrshí yī casting all caution to the winds; regardless of the consequences; recklessly

【不光】 bùguāng 〈口〉 ① not the only one: 报名参加的～是他一个人。He was not the only one to sign up. ② not only: 我们县～出煤，而且出铁。Our county produces not only coal, but iron.

【不规则】 bùguīzé irregular ◇ ～动词 〈语〉 irregular verb

【不轨】 bùguǐ against the law or discipline: 图谋～ engage in conspiratorial activities

【不过】 bùguò ① 〔用在形容词性的词组或双音形容词后面，表示程度最高〕: 那就再好～了! It couldn't be better! 或 That would be superb! ② 〈副〉 only; merely; no more than: 她参军的时候～十七岁。She was only seventeen when she joined the army. ③ 〈连〉 but; however; only: 病人精神还不错，～胃口不大好。The patient feels pretty well, but he hasn't much of an appetite.

【不过尔尔】 bùguò ěr'ěr 〈书〉 merely mediocre; just middling

【不过意】 bù guòyì be sorry; feel apologetic: 叫您受累了，真～。I'm terribly sorry to have given you such a lot of trouble.

【不含糊】 bù hánhu 〈口〉 ① unambiguous; unequivocal; explicit: 以毫～的语言作出回答 answer in clear and unequivocal terms; answer in explicit language/ 在原则问题上绝～ stand firm on matters of principle/ 党叫干啥就干啥，她一点～! She'll do whatever the Party tells her to and no two ways about it. ② not ordinary; really good: 他那手乒乓球可～。He is a very good table-tennis player./ 他这活儿做得真～。He's really made a good job of it.

【不寒而栗】 bù hán ér lì shiver all over though not cold; tremble with fear; shudder

【不好惹】 bù hǎorě not to be trifled with; not to be pushed around; stand no nonsense

【不好意思】 bù hǎoyìsi ① feel embarrassed; be ill at ease: 她被夸得～了。She felt embarrassed by so much praise. ② find it embarrassing (to do sth.): ～推辞 find it difficult to refuse/ ～再问 hesitate to ask again

【不合】 bùhé ① not conform to; be unsuited to; be out of keeping with: ～规定 not conform to the rules/ ～当前的需要 be unsuited to present needs/ ～客观情况 be out of keeping with the objective conditions/ ～标准 not up to the (required) standard; below the mark/ 脾气～ be temperamentally incompatible/ ～她的口味 not be to her taste; not appeal to her/ ～时宜 be out of keeping with the times; be incompatible with present needs ② 〈书〉 should not; ought not: 早知如此，当初～叫他去。Had we foreseen that, we would not have let him go.

【不和】 bùhé ① not get along well; be on bad terms; be at odds ② discord: 制造～ sow discord

【不怀好意】 bù huái hǎoyì harbour evil designs; harbour malicious intentions

【不欢而散】 bùhuān ér sàn part on bad terms; (of a meeting, etc.) break up in discord

【不讳】 bùhuì 〈书〉 ① without concealing anything: 供认～ candidly confess; confess everything; make a clean breast of everything/ 直言～ speak bluntly; be outspoken; call a spade a spade ② 〈婉〉 die

【不会】 bùhuì ① be unlikely; will not (act, happen, etc.): 她～不知道。It's not likely that she doesn't know./ 人～多的。There won't be too many people. ② have not learned to; be unable to: 我～抽烟。I don't smoke. ③〔表示责备语气〕: 你就～打个电话问一问? Couldn't you have phoned up and asked?

【不羁】 bùjī 〈书〉 unruly; uninhibited

【不及】 bùjí ① not as good as; inferior to: 我学习～他刻苦。I don't study as hard as he does. ② find it too late: 躲避～ too late to dodge/ 后悔～ too late for regrets

【不及物动词】 bùjíwù dòngcí 〈语〉 intransitive verb

【不即不离】 bùjí-bùlí be neither too familiar nor too distant; keep sb. at arm's length

【不急之务】 bù jí zhī wù a matter of no great urgency

【不计其数】 bù jì qí shù countless; innumerable

【不记名投票】 bùjìmíng tóupiào secret ballot

【不济】 bùjì 〈口〉 not good; of no use: 我眼力～了。My eyesight is failing.

【不济事】 bùjìshì no good; of no use; not of any help: 这是项突击任务，人少了～。This is a shock task. It'll be no good to be short of hands.

【不假思索】 bù jiǎ sīsuǒ without thinking; without hesitation; readily; offhand 又作"不加思索"

【不简单】 bù jiǎndān ① not simple; rather complicated: 这事～，需要进一步调查。The matter is not so simple; it requires further investigation. ② remarkable; marvellous: 他有这么大的进步真～。It's remarkable he's made such good progress.

【不见】 bùjiàn not see; not meet: 好久～。Haven't seen you for a long time./ 这孩子一年～，长这么高了。It's only a year since I last saw the child and he's grown so tall./ 咱们两点钟在大门口碰头，～不散。Let's meet at the gate around two o'clock and not leave without seeing each other.

【不见得】 bù jiànde not necessarily; not likely: ～对 not necessarily correct/ 他今晚～会来。He's not likely to come tonight.

【不见棺材不落泪】 bù jiàn guāncai bù luò lèi not shed a tear until one sees the coffin — refuse to be convinced until one is faced with grim reality

【不见经传】 bù jiàn jīngzhuàn not to be found in the classics — not authoritative; unknown: 此人名～。He was not a well-known figure. 或 He was a nobody.

【不见了】 bùjiànle disappear; be missing: 我的钢笔～。My pen's disappeared.

【不结盟】 bùjiéméng nonalignment ◇ ～国家 nonaligned countries/ ～政策 nonalignment policy

【不解】 bùjiě ⑴ not understand: ～其意 not understand what he means/ 迷惑～ be puzzled; be bewildered/ ～之谜 an unsolved riddle; enigma; mystery ⑵ indissoluble: ～之缘 an indissoluble bond

【不禁】 bùjīn can't help (doing sth.); can't refrain from: ～哑然失笑 can't help laughing

【不仅】 bùjǐn ⑴ not the only one: 这～是我一个人的看法。I'm not the only one who holds this view. ⑵ not only: ～如此 not only that; nor is this all; moreover

【不近人情】 bù jìn rénqíng not amenable to reason; unreasonable

【不经一事,不长一智】 bù jīng yī shì, bù zhǎng yī zhì you can't gain knowledge without practice; wisdom comes from experience

【不经意】 bù jīngyì carelessly; by accident: 他～把茶杯碰倒了。He accidentally knocked over a cup.

【不经之谈】 bù jīng zhī tán absurd statement; cock-and-bull story

【不景气】 bù jǐngqì ① 〈经〉 depression; recession; slump ② depressing state

【不胫而走】 bù jìng ér zǒu get round fast; spread like wildfire

【不久】 bùjiǔ ⑴ soon; before long: 水库～就能完工。The reservoir will soon be completed. ⑵ not long after; soon after: 插完秧～就下了一场雨。It rained soon after we had transplanted the rice seedlings.

【不咎既往】 bù jiù jìwǎng not censure sb. for his past misdeeds; overlook sb.'s past mistakes; let bygones be bygones

【不拘】 bùjū ⑴ not stick to; not confine oneself to: ～小节 not bother about small matters; not be punctilious/ 字数～。No limit is set on the length (for an article). ⑵ whatever: ～什么任务，只要对人民有益的，我都愿意接受。I'm ready to accept any job whatever, so long as it is in the interest of the people.

【不拘一格】 bùjū yī gé not stick to one pattern

【不倦】 bùjuàn tireless; untiring; indefatigable: 诲人～ be tireless in teaching; teach with tireless zeal

【不绝如缕】 bù jué rú lǚ ⑴ hanging by a thread; very precarious; almost extinct ⑵ (of sound) linger on faintly

【不堪】 bùkān ⑴ cannot bear; cannot stand: ～回首 cannot bear to look back; find it unbearable to recall/ ～设想 dreadful to contemplate/ ～入耳 intolerable to the ear; revolting; disgusting/ ～一击 cannot withstand a single blow; collapse at the first blow ⑵ utterly; extremely: 疲惫～ extremely tired; exhausted; dog-tired/ 狼狈～ be in an extremely awkward position; be in a sorry plight/ 穿得破烂～ be dressed in rags

【不亢不卑】 bùkàng-bùbēi neither haughty nor humble; neither overbearing nor servile; neither supercilious nor obsequious 又作"不卑不亢"

【不可】 bùkě ⑴ cannot; should not; must not: 两者～偏废。Neither can be neglected./ ～一概而论 must not make sweeping generalizations/ ～剥夺的权利 an inalienable right/ ～抗拒的历史潮流 an irresistible historical trend ⑵ [与"非"搭配，表示必须或一定]: 今天这个会很重要，我非去～。Today's meeting is very important. I simply must go.

【不可多得】 bùkě duō dé hard to come by; rare: ～的佳作 a rare specimen of good writing

【不可告人】 bùkě gào rén not to be divulged; hidden: ～的动机 ulterior motives/ ～的勾当 a sinister trick

【不可估量】 bùkě gūliàng inestimable; incalculable; beyond measure

【不可救药】 bùkě jiù yào incurable; incorrigible; beyond cure; hopeless

【不可开交】 bùkě kāijiāo [只做"得"后的补语，表示无法摆脱或结束]: 忙得～ be up to one's eyes in work; be awfully (或 terribly) busy/ 打得～ be locked in a fierce struggle/ 争得～ be engaged in a heated argument

【不可抗力】 bùkěkànglì 〈法〉 force majeure

【不可理喻】 bùkě lǐyù be impervious to reason; won't listen to reason

【不可名状】 bùkě míng zhuàng indescribable; beyond description 又作"不可言状"

【不可磨灭】 bùkě mómiè indelible: ～的印象 indelible impressions/ ～的贡献 an indelible contribution/ ～的功绩 everlasting merit

【不可侵犯权】 bùkě qīnfàn quán 〈外〉 inviolability

【不可胜数】 bùkě shèngshǔ countless; innumerable: 缴获的武器装备～。The military equipment captured was beyond counting.

【不可收拾】 bùkě shōushi irremediable; unmanageable; out of hand; hopeless

【不可思议】 bùkě sīyì inconceivable; unimaginable

【不可同日而语】 bùkě tóngrì ér yǔ cannot be mentioned in the same breath

【不可一世】 bùkě yīshì consider oneself unexcelled in the world; be insufferably arrogant

【不可逾越】 bùkě yúyuè impassable; insurmountable; insuperable: ～的鸿沟 an impassable chasm/ ～的障碍 an insurmountable (或 insuperable) barrier

【不可知论】 bùkězhīlùn 〈哲〉 agnosticism ◇ ～者 agnostic

【不可终日】 bùkě zhōng rì be unable to carry on even for a single day; be in a desperate situation

【不克】 bùkè be unable to; cannot: ～胜任 be unequal to the job

【不客气】 bù kèqi ⑴ impolite; rude; blunt: 说句～的话 to put it bluntly/ 你再这样，我可就要～了。If you go on like this, I won't be so easy on you. ⑵ 〈套〉 [回答别人的感谢] you're welcome; don't mention it; not at all ⑶ 〈套〉 [感谢别人的好意] please don't bother; I'll help myself

【不快】 bùkuài ⑴ be unhappy; be displeased; be in low spirits ⑵ be indisposed; feel under the weather; be out of sorts

【不愧】 bùkuì be worthy of; deserve to be called; prove oneself to be: ～为建设社会主义的积极分子 be worthy of the title of activist in socialist construction/ 他们～为中国人民的好儿女。They have proved themselves to be fine sons and daughters of the Chinese people.

【不赖】 bùlài 〈方〉 not bad; good; fine: 今年的庄稼可真～。This year's crops are really fine.

【不稂不莠】 bùláng-bùyǒu useless; worthless; good-for-nothing 又作"不郎不秀"

【不劳而获】 bù láo ér huò reap without sowing; profit by other people's toil

【不离儿】 bùlír 〈方〉 ⑴ not bad; pretty good ⑵ pretty close

【不理】 bùlǐ refuse to acknowledge; pay no attention to; take no notice of; ignore: 见了人～ cut sb. dead/ 别～他，要帮助他。Don't ignore him; help him./ 我才～那些闲话呢。I don't pay attention to such gossip.

【不力】 bùlì not do one's best; not exert oneself: 办事～ not do one's best in one's work; be slack in one's work/ 领导～ not exercise effective leadership

【不利】 bùlì ① unfavourable; disadvantageous; harmful; detrimental: 化～因素为有利因素 turn unfavourable factors into favourable ones ② unsuccessful: 首战～ lose the first battle

【不良】 bùliáng bad; harmful; unhealthy: ～倾向 harmful trends/ ～现象 unhealthy tendencies/ ～影响 harmful (或 adverse) effects/ 存心～ harbour evil intentions; have ulterior motives

【不了】 bùliǎo 〔多用于动词加"个"之后〕 without end: 一天到晚忙个～ busy from morning till night/ 大雨下个～。The rain kept pouring down.

【不了了之】 bùliǎo liǎo zhī settle a matter by leaving it unsettled; end up with nothing definite

【不料】 bùliào unexpectedly; to one's surprise: 早上天气还好好的，～下午竟下起雹子来了。It was so fine this morning. Who would have thought it would hail in the afternoon!

【不吝】 bùlìn 〈套〉〔用于征求意见时〕 not stint; not grudge; be generous with: 尚希～指教。We hope that you will not stint your criticism.

【不灵】 bùlíng not work; be ineffective: 这机器～了。The machine doesn't work./ 老太太手脚有点～了。The old lady has trouble moving about.

【不露声色】 bù lù shēngsè not show one's feelings, intentions, etc.

【不伦不类】 bùlún-bùlèi neither fish nor fowl; nondescript: ～的比喻 an inappropriate metaphor; a far-fetched analogy

【不论】 bùlùn 〈连〉〔下文多用"都""总"等副词跟它呼应〕 no matter (what, who, how, etc.); whether... or...; regardless of: ～性别年龄 regardless (或 irrespective) of sex and age/ 全村～男女老幼，都参加了抗旱斗争。All the villagers, men and women, old and young, took part in the battle against the drought./ 政治，～革命的和反革命的，都是阶级对阶级的斗争，不是少数个人的行为。Politics, whether revolutionary or counterrevolutionary, is the struggle of class against class, not the activity of a few individuals.

【不落窠臼】 bù luò kējiù not follow the beaten track; have an original style

【不买账】 bù mǎizhàng not buy it; not go for it: 你摆架子，群众就不买你的账。If you put on airs, the masses just won't go for it.

【不满】 bùmǎn resentful; discontented; dissatisfied: 心怀～ nurse a grievance

【不忙】 bùmáng there's no hurry; take one's time: 这件事你先去调查一下，～表态。Don't be in a hurry to say what you think about this. First find out the facts.

【不毛之地】 bù máo zhī dì barren land; desert

【不免】 bùmiǎn unavoidable: 这段路太窄，交通有时～堵塞。This section of the road is so narrow that there are bound to be traffic jams now and then.

【不妙】 bùmiào (of a turn of events) not too encouraging; far from good; anything but reassuring

【不名数】 bùmíngshù 〈数〉 abstract number

【不名一文】 bù míng yī wén without a penny to one's name; penniless; stony-broke

【不名誉】 bùmíngyù disreputable; disgraceful

【不明】 bùmíng ① not clear; unknown: 失踪的渔船至今下落～。The whereabouts of the missing fishing boat is still unknown./ ～国籍的飞机 a plane of unidentified nationality; an unidentified aircraft ② fail to understand: ～事理 lack common sense/ ～是非 confuse right and wrong/ ～真相 be unaware of the truth; be ignorant of the facts

【不摸头】 bù mōtóu 〈口〉 not acquainted with the situation; not up on things

【不谋而合】 bù móu ér hé agree without prior consultation; happen to hold the same view: 我们的意见～。Our views happened to coincide.

【不能】 bùnéng cannot; must not; should not: 我们决～一见成绩就自满起来。We must not become complacent the moment we have some success.

【不能不】 bùnéng bù have to; cannot but: ～表示惋惜 cannot but express regret/ ～指出 it must be pointed out that/ 我们～提到某些历史事实。We cannot very well avoid mentioning certain historical facts.

【不偏不倚】 bùpiān-bùyǐ even-handed; impartial; unbiased

【不平】 bùpíng ① injustice; unfairness; wrong; grievance ② indignant; resentful: 愤愤～ very indignant; deeply resentful/ 消除心中的～ allay one's resentment

【不平等条约】 bùpíngděng tiáoyuē unequal treaty

【不平衡】 bùpínghéng disequilibrium: 工农业发展～ the disequilibrium between the development of industry and agriculture

【不平则鸣】 bùpíng zé míng where there is injustice, there will be an outcry; man will cry out against injustice

【不破不立】 bù pò bù lì without destruction there can be no construction

【不期而遇】 bù qī ér yù meet by chance; have a chance encounter

【不期然而然】 bù qī rán ér rán happen unexpectedly; turn out contrary to one's expectations

【不巧】 bùqiǎo unfortunately; as luck would have it: 我到那儿，～他刚走。As luck would have it, he had just left when I arrived.

【不切实际】 bùqiè shíjì unrealistic; unpractical; impracticable: ～的计划 an impracticable plan/ ～的幻想 unrealistic notions; fanciful ideas

【不情之请】 bù qíng zhī qǐng 〈套〉 my presumptuous request

【不求甚解】 bù qiú shèn jiě not seek to understand things thoroughly; be content with superficial understanding

【不屈】 bùqū unyielding; unbending: 坚强～ iron-willed and unyielding

【不屈不挠】 bùqū-bùnáo unyielding; indomitable

【不然】 bùrán ① not so: 其实～。Actually this is not so. ②〔用在句子开头，表示否定对方的话〕 no: ～，事情没有那样简单。No, it's not as simple as that. ③〈连〉 or else; otherwise; if not: 我得早点去，～就赶不上火车了。I've got to leave a bit early, otherwise I'll miss the train./ 要去就别迟到，～，就甭去了。Either be there on time, or don't go at all.

【不人道】 bùréndào inhuman

【不仁】 bùrén ① not benevolent; heartless: 为富～ in the pursuit of riches there is no benevolence; the heartless rich ② numb: 麻木～ insensitive; apathetic

【不忍】 bùrěn cannot bear to: ～坐视 cannot bear to stand idly by

【不日】 bùrì 〈书〉 within the next few days; in a few days' time

【不容】 bùróng not tolerate; not allow; not brook: ～外国干涉 tolerate no foreign interference/ ～耽搁 allow of no delay/ ～置喙 not allow others to butt in; brook no intervention

【不如】 bùrú ① not equal to; not as good as; inferior to: 论手巧，一般人都～她。Few can equal (或 compare with) her in manual dexterity. ② it would be better to: 我看～派老王去。I think it would be better to send Lao Wang instead.

【不入虎穴，焉得虎子】 bù rù hǔxué, yān dé hǔzǐ how can

you catch tiger cubs without entering the tiger's lair; nothing venture, nothing gain (或 have)

【不三不四】 bùsān-bùsì ① dubious; shady: ～的人 a person of dubious (或 shady) character ② neither one thing nor the other; neither fish nor fowl; nondescript: 自己生造的～的词句 nondescript expressions of one's own coinage/ 说些～的话 make frivolous remarks

【不善】 bùshàn ① bad; ill: 来意～ come with ill intent/ 处理～ not handle properly; mishandle ② not good at: ～管理 not good at managing things ③ 〈方〉 not to be pooh-poohed; quite impressive: 别看他身体不强，干起农活来可～。He does not look strong, but he does all right in farm work.

【不设防城市】 bùshèfáng chéngshì open city

【不胜】 bùshèng ① cannot bear (或 stand); be unequal to: 体力～ be physically unequal to (a task); be physically incapable of coping with (a job)/ ～其烦 be pestered beyond endurance ②〔前后重复同一动词，表示不能做或做不完〕: 防～防 be difficult or impossible to prevent (或 ward off) ③〔用于感情方面〕 very; extremely: ～遗憾 be very sorry; much to one's regret/ ～感激 be very much obliged; be deeply grateful

【不胜枚举】 bùshèng méi jǔ too numerous to mention individually (或 one by one)

【不失时机】 bù shī shíjī seize the opportune moment; lose no time

【不失为】 bùshīwéi can yet be regarded as; may after all be accepted as: 这～一个办法。This, after all, is one way of doing it.

【不识大体】 bù shí dàtǐ fail to see the larger issues; ignore the general interest

【不识时务】 bù shí shíwù ① show no understanding of the times ② be insensible

【不识抬举】 bù shí táiju fail to appreciate sb.'s kindness; not know how to appreciate favours

【不时】 bùshí ① frequently; often ② at any time

【不时之需】 bùshí zhī xū a possible period of want or need: 以备～ for emergency needs; to provide against a rainy day

【不是玩儿的】 bùshì wánrde 〈口〉 it's no joke: 你正在养伤，受了寒可～！ It's no joke catching a chill when you are recovering from an injury.

【不是味儿】 bùshì wèir 〈口〉 ① not the right flavour; not quite right; a bit off: 这个菜炒得～。This dish doesn't taste quite right./ 他的京剧唱得～。The way he sings Beijing opera is a bit off. ② fishy; queer; amiss: 他的作风，我越看越～。I feel more and more that there's something wrong with his way of doing things. ③ feel bad; be upset: 听了他的话，我心里感到～。I was upset by what he said.

【不是】 bùshi fault; blame: 落个～ get blamed in the end/ 这就是你的～了。It's your fault. 或 You're to blame.

【不适】 bùshì unwell; indisposed; out of sorts: 胃部～ have a stomach upset/ 略感～ feel a bit unwell

【不受欢迎的人】 bù shòu huānyíng de rén 〈外〉 persona non grata

【不受理】 bù shòulǐ ① 〈法〉 reject a complaint ② 〈外〉 refuse to entertain (a proposal)

【不爽】 bùshuǎng ① not well; out of sorts; in a bad mood ② without discrepancy; accurate: 丝毫～ not deviate a hair's breadth; be perfectly accurate; be right in every detail/ 屡试～。It comes out right every time.

【不死心】 bù sǐxīn unwilling to give up; unresigned: 敌人失败了，还～。The enemy is not reconciled to his defeat.

【不送】 bùsòng 〈套〉 don't bother to see me out

【不送气】 bù sòngqì 〈语〉 unaspirated ◇ ～音 unaspirated sound

【不速之客】 bù sù zhī kè uninvited (或 unexpected) guest

【不随意肌】 bùsuíyìjī 〈生理〉 involuntary muscle

【不遂】 bùsuì 〈书〉 fail; fail to materialize

【不碎玻璃】 bùsuì bōli shatterproof (或 safety) glass

【不特】 bùtè 〈书〉 not only

【不通】 bùtōng ① be obstructed; be blocked up; be impassable: 管子～。The pipe is blocked./ 此路～。Not a Through Road./ 电话～。The line's dead./ 想～ cannot figure out why; remain unconvinced/ 行～ won't work ② not make sense; be illogical; be ungrammatical: 文章写得～。The article is badly written.

【不同】 bùtóng not alike; different; distinct: 两个～的革命阶段 two distinct revolutionary stages/ 在～的程度上 to varying degrees

【不同凡响】 bùtóng fánxiǎng outstanding; out of the ordinary; out of the common run

【不痛不痒】 bùtòng-bùyǎng scratching the surface; superficial; perfunctory: ～的批评 superficial criticism/ 讲些～的话 make some perfunctory remarks

【不透明】 bù tòumíng opaque ◇ ～色 body colour/ ～体 opaque body/ ～性 opacity

【不透气】 bù tòuqì airtight

【不透水】 bù tòushuǐ waterproof; watertight; impermeable ◇ ～层 〈地〉 impermeable stratum; impervious bed

【不吐气】 bù tǔqì 〈语〉 unaspirated ◇ ～音 unaspirated sound

【不妥】 bùtuǒ not proper; inappropriate: 这样处理，恐怕～。I'm afraid this isn't the proper way to handle the case./ 没有调查研究就作决定是～的。It's not right to make a decision without investigation and study./ 觉得有些～ feel that something is amiss

【不外】 bùwài not beyond the scope of; nothing more than: ～两种可能。There are only two possibilities.

【不完全叶】 bùwánquányè 〈植〉 incomplete leaf

【不完全中立】 bùwánquán zhōnglì 〈法〉 imperfect neutrality

【不为已甚】 bù wéi yǐ shèn refrain from going to extremes in meting out punishment, etc.; not be too hard on sb.

【不违农时】 bùwéi nóngshí not miss the farming season; do farm work in the right season

【不惟】 bùwéi 〈书〉 not only

【不闻不问】 bùwén-bùwèn not bother to ask questions or listen to what's said; show no interest in sth.; be indifferent to sth.: 同志们有困难我们不能～。We can't remain indifferent when any comrade is in difficulty.

【不稳平衡】 bùwěn pínghéng 〈物〉 unstable equilibrium

【不问】 bù wèn ① pay no attention to; disregard; ignore: ～年龄大小 irrespective of age/ ～事实真相 ignore the facts/ ～是非曲直 make no distinction between right and wrong; not look into the rights and wrongs of the case ② let go unpunished; let off: 胁从～。Those who acted under duress shall go unpunished.

【不无小补】 bùwú xiǎobǔ not be without some advantage; be of some help

【不务正业】 bù wù zhèngyè ① not engage in honest work ② ignore one's proper occupation; not attend to one's proper duties

【不惜】 bùxī ① not stint; not spare: ～工本 spare neither labour nor money; spare no expense/ ～一切代价 at all costs; at any cost ② not hesitate (to do sth.); not scruple (to do sth.): 为革命～牺牲自己的一切 not hesitate to sacrifice one's all for the revolution

【不暇】 bùxiá have no time (for sth.); be too busy (to do sth.): ～顾及 be too busy to attend to sth.

【不下于】 bùxiàyú ① as many as; no less than: 展出的新产品～二百种。There are as many as 200 new products on show./ 参加五一节游园活动的～五十万人。No less than half a million people took part in the May Day festivities in the parks. ②not inferior to; as good as; on a par with: 这个街道小厂的产品，质量～一些国营大厂。The products of this small neighbourhood factory are as good as those turned out by some large state-run plants.

【不相干】 bù xiānggān be irrelevant; have nothing to do with: ～的话 irrelevant remarks/ 那件事跟你～。That has nothing to do with you.

【不相容】 bù xiāngróng incompatible: 水火～ incompatible as fire and water; mutually antagonistic

【不相上下】 bù xiāng shàng-xià equally matched; about the same: 能力～ of about the same ability; equally able/ 这两种水稻都是良种，产量～。Both rice seeds are good strains and will give about the same yield.

【不详】 bùxiáng 〈书〉①not in detail: 言之～ not be given in detail; be stated too briefly ②not quite clear: 历史情况～。Little is known about the historical background.

【不祥】 bùxiáng ominous; inauspicious: ～之兆 an ill omen

【不像话】 bù xiànghuà ①unreasonable: 要你们自己掏钱就～了。It would be unreasonable for you to pay out of your own pockets. ②shocking; outrageous: 这种行为真～。Such behaviour is really shocking.

【不像样】 bù xiàngyàng ①in no shape to be seen; unpresentable: 这活儿～，拿不出手。This is a shoddy piece of work, it's hardly presentable. ②〔用在"得"后作补语〕 beyond recognition: 瘦得～ extremely thin; worn to a mere shadow/ 破得～ worn to shreds

【不肖】 bùxiào 〈书〉unworthy: ～子孙 unworthy descendants

【不屑】 bùxiè disdain to do sth.; think sth. not worth doing; feel it beneath one's dignity to do sth.: ～隐瞒自己的观点 disdain to conceal one's views

【不谢】 bùxiè 〈套〉don't mention it; not at all

【不懈】 bùxiè untiring; unremitting; indefatigable: 作～的努力 make unremitting efforts; make a sustained effort/ 坚持～ persevere unremittingly

【不信任案】 bùxìnrèn'àn no-confidence motion

【不信任投票】 bùxìnrèn tóupiào vote of no-confidence

【不兴】 bùxīng ①out of fashion; outmoded: 我们现在～做生日了。Few people give birthday parties now. 或 Birthday parties are on the way out. ②impermissible; not allowed: ～这样做。That's not allowed. ③〔用于反问句〕can't: 你干吗嚷嚷，就～小点儿声吗？Why shout? Can't you lower your voice a little?

【不行】 bùxíng ①won't do; be out of the question: 学大寨不首先抓路线～。Without first grasping the political line, learning from Dazhai is out of the question. ②be no good; not work: 这个方法～。This method just doesn't work./ 他干这种工作身体～。He is physically unfit for this kind of work. ③〔用于"得"后作补语〕 awfully; extremely: 高兴得～ awfully happy

【不行了】 bùxíngle on the point of death; dying: 病人怕～。The patient won't pull through, I'm afraid.

【不省人事】 bù xǐng rénshì be unconscious; be in a coma

【不幸】 bùxìng ①misfortune; adversity: 遭～ meet with a misfortune ②unfortunate; sad: ～的消息 sad news ③unfortunately: ～而言中。The prediction has unfortunately come true./ 他～以身殉职。To our great sorrow he died at his post.

【不休】 bùxiū 〔用做补语〕 endlessly; ceaselessly: 争论～ argue endlessly; keep on arguing

【不修边幅】 bù xiū biānfú not care about one's appearance; be slovenly

【不朽】 bùxiǔ immortal: ～的著作 an immortal masterpiece/ ～的功勋 immortal deeds/ 人民英雄永垂～！Eternal glory to the people's heroes!

【不锈钢】 bùxiùgāng stainless steel

【不虚此行】 bù xū cǐ xíng the trip has not been made in vain; the trip has been well worthwhile; it's been a worthwhile trip

【不许】 bùxǔ ①not allow; must not: ～说谎。You mustn't tell lies./ 熄灯后～说话。No talking after lights out. ②〔用于反问句〕can't: 何必非等我，你就～自己去吗？Why wait for me? Can't you go yourself?

【不宣而战】 bù xuān ér zhàn open hostilities without declaring war; start an undeclared war

【不学无术】 bùxué-wúshù have neither learning nor skill; be ignorant and incompetent

【不逊】 bùxùn 〈书〉rude; impertinent: 出言～ make impertinent remarks

【不雅观】 bù yǎguān offensive to the eye; unbecoming

【不言而喻】 bù yán ér yù it goes without saying; it is self-evident

【不厌】 bùyàn not mind doing sth.; not tire of; not object to: ～其烦 not mind taking all the trouble; take great pains; be very patient/ ～其详 go into minute details; dwell at great length

【不要】 bùyào don't: ～麻痹大意。Don't slacken your vigilance./ ～总是以为自己对。Don't think you are always right.

【不要紧】 bù yàojǐn ①unimportant; not serious: 有点伤风，～。Just a slight cold, nothing serious. ②it doesn't matter; never mind: 路远也～，我们可以骑车去。It doesn't matter how far it is; we can go by bike. ③it looks all right, but: 你这一嚷～，把大家都吵醒了。You may think it's all right for you to shout, but you've woken everybody up.

【不要脸】 bù yàoliǎn 〈骂〉have no sense of shame; shameless: 只有～的人才能做出这样～的事。Only those who have no sense of shame can do such shameful things./ 真～！What a nerve!

【不一】 bùyī vary; differ: 质量～ vary in quality/ 长短～ differ in length

【不一而足】 bùyī'érzú by no means an isolated case; numerous: 凡此种种～。Similar cases are numerous.

【不依】 bùyī ①not comply; not go along with: 我们劝他休息，他怎么也～。We advised him to have a rest, but he simply wouldn't hear of it. ②not let off easily; not let sb. get away with it: 你要是再这样，我可～你。If you do this again, I won't let you off so easily.

【不宜】 bùyí not suitable; inadvisable: ～操之过急。It's no good being overhasty./ 这一点～过分强调。It's inadvisable to overemphasize this point./ 这种土壤～种花生。This kind of soil is not suitable for growing peanuts.

【不遗余力】 bù yí yúlì spare no pains (或 effort); do one's utmost

【不已】 bùyǐ endlessly; incessantly: 赞叹～ praise again and again

【不以为然】 bù yǐ wéi rán object to; take exception to; not approve

【不义之财】 bùyì zhī cái ill-gotten wealth (或 gains)

【不亦乐乎】 bùyìlèhū 〔用在"得"后作补语〕extremely; awfully: 忙得～ awfully (或 terribly) busy

【不易之论】 bù yì zhī lùn perfectly sound proposition; unalterable truth; irrefutable argument

【不意】 bùyì 〈书〉①unexpectedly: ～大雨如注，无法启程。Unexpectedly it poured with rain and it was impossible to start off. ②unawareness; unpreparedness: 出其～，攻其无备 catch sb. unprepared; take sb. by surprise/ 利

用敌人的错觉和 ～ 来争取自己的主动 exploit the enemy's misconceptions and unpreparedness to gain the initiative

【不翼而飞】 bù yì ér fēi ① disappear without trace; vanish all of a sudden ② spread fast; spread like wildfire

【不用】 bùyòng need not: ～着急。You needn't worry. 或 There is no need to worry./ ～说 it goes without saying; needless to say

【不由得】 bùyóude can't help; cannot but: 他说得这么透彻，～你不信服。He spoke so cogently that you couldn't help being convinced.

【不由自主】 bù yóu zìzhǔ can't help; involuntarily: ～地流下了眼泪 couldn't help shedding tears; couldn't hold back one's tears

【不虞】 bùyú <书> ① unexpected: ～之誉 unexpected praise ② eventuality; contingency: 以备～ provide against any contingency ③ not worry about: ～匮乏 fear no shortage of material resources; not worry about running out of supplies

【不予】 bùyǔ not grant: ～批准 not grant approval/ ～考虑 refuse to take into consideration; will not consider

【不育性】 bùyùxìng <农> sterility 又作"不孕性"

【不育症】 bùyùzhèng <医> sterility; barrenness

【不远千里】 bù yuǎn qiān lǐ make light of travelling a thousand *li*; go to the trouble of travelling a long distance

【不约而同】 bù yuē ér tóng take the same action or view without prior consultation; happen to coincide: 她一讲完，大家～都鼓起掌来。Spontaneous applause broke out as soon as she finished speaking./ 他们都～地提出了这个问题。They all raised the question as if by prior agreement.

【不在】 bù zài not be in; be out: 你找老王吗？他～。Are you looking for Lao Wang? He's out.

【不在乎】 bùzàihu not mind; not care: 满～ not care a pin/ 铁姑娘队的队员挑百斤重的担子毫～。It's nothing for a member of the Iron Girls' Team to shoulder a load of 100 *jin*./ ～他怎么说，要看他怎么做。Never mind what he says, let's see what he does.

【不在话下】 bù zài huà xià be nothing difficult; be a cinch: 两个月拿下这项任务，～。It will be a cinch to get the job done in two months./ 她摩托车都会骑，自行车更～了。She can ride a motorcycle, to say nothing of a bicycle./ 有这样的决心，再大的困难也～。For people with such determination, no difficulty amounts to much.

【不在了】 bùzàile <婉> be dead: 他爷爷早就～。His grandfather has been dead a long time.

【不在意】 bù zàiyì ① pay no attention to; take no notice of; not mind: 别人背后议论，他毫～。He doesn't care at all what people say behind his back. ② negligent; careless: 人家托你的事，你别～。When people ask you to do something, you should take it seriously.

【不赞一词】 bù zàn yī cí <书> keep silent; make no comment: 我对这个问题不清楚，只能～。I'm not clear about this matter, so I had better keep quiet.

【不择手段】 bù zé shǒuduàn by fair means or foul; by hook or by crook; unscrupulously

【不怎么】 bù zěnme not very; not particularly: 这块地～大。This plot isn't very big./ 我～想去。I'm not particularly keen on going.

【不怎么样】 bù zěnmeyàng not up to much; very indifferent: 这幅画画得～。This isn't much of a painting.

【不战不和】 bùzhàn-bùhé no war, no peace: ～的局面 a stalemate of "no war, no peace"

【不折不扣】 bùzhé-bùkòu ① a hundred per cent; to the letter: ～地贯彻党的政策 implement the Party's policies to the letter ② out-and-out: ～的修正主义分子 an out-and-out revisionist; a revisionist, pure and simple

【不争气】 bù zhēngqì be disappointing; fail to live up to expectations: 他这个人真～。This chap has let us down./ 我这腿～，最后一圈跑不动了。My legs failed me and I wasn't able to run the last lap.

【不正之风】 bù zhèng zhī fēng unhealthy tendency

【不知不觉】 bùzhī-bùjué unconsciously; unwittingly: ～已过了三个月。Three months had passed before we knew it.

【不知凡几】 bù zhī fán jǐ can't tell how many there are — there are numerous similar cases

【不知好歹】 bù zhī hǎo-dǎi not know what's good for one

【不知死活】 bù zhī sǐ-huó act recklessly

【不知所措】 bù zhī suǒ cuò be at a loss; be at one's wits' end

【不知所云】 bù zhī suǒ yún not know what sb. is driving at; be unintelligible: 这篇文章写得太乱，使人看了～。This is such a chaotic piece of writing that it is practically unintelligible.

【不知天高地厚】 bù zhī tiāngāo-dìhòu not know the immensity of heaven and earth — have an exaggerated opinion of one's abilities

【不值】 bùzhí not worth: ～一文 not worth a penny; worthless/ ～一驳 not worth refuting/ ～识者一笑 beneath the contempt of the discerning/ 我看～那么多。I don't think it's worth that much.

【不止】 bùzhǐ ① incessantly; without end: 树欲静而风～。The tree craves calm but the wind will not drop. ② more than; not limited to: 他恐怕～六十岁了。He is probably over sixty./ 这水库给公社带来的好处～是在农业方面。The benefit which the reservoir brings to the commune is not limited to agriculture.

【不只】 bùzhǐ not only; not merely

【不至于】 bùzhìyú cannot go so far; be unlikely: 他～连这一点道理也不明白。He must have more sense than that./ 如果你事先作好准备，也～那么被动。If you had prepared in advance, you wouldn't be in such an awkward position.

【不治之症】 bùzhì zhī zhèng incurable disease

【不置可否】 bù zhì kě-fǒu decline to comment; not express an opinion; be noncommittal; hedge: 你是负责人，你怎么能对这个问题～？You are in charge of the job. How could you evade the issue?

【不中用】 bù zhōngyòng unfit for anything; no good; useless: 这铁锹～，我去换一把吧。This spade is no good. I'll go and get another one.

【不中意】 bù zhòngyì not to one's liking

【不周延】 bù zhōuyán <逻> undistributed

【不准】 bùzhǔn not allow; forbid; prohibit: 此处～吸烟。Smoking is not allowed here. 或 No Smoking!/ ～停车！No parking!/ ～入内。No admittance.

【不着边际】 bù zhuó biānjì not to the point; wide of the mark; neither here nor there; irrelevant: ～的长篇大论 a long rambling talk/ 他越讲越～。The more he talked, the further he strayed from the point.

【不着陆飞行】 bùzhuólù fēixíng nonstop flight

【不赀】 bùzī <书> immeasurable; incalculable: 工程浩大，所费～。The project is on such a gigantic scale that the cost is hard to calculate.

【不自量】 bù zìliàng not take a proper measure of oneself; overrate one's own abilities: 蚍蜉撼大树，可笑～ ridiculously overrate oneself like an ant trying to topple a giant tree

【不足】 bùzú ① not enough; insufficient; inadequate: 资源～ inadequate resources/ 给养～ be short of supplies/ 人手～ be shorthanded; be understaffed/ 估计 ～ underestimate/ 信心～ lack confidence/ ～之处 deficiency; inadequacy/ ～一千 less than a thousand/ ～以引起人们的注

意 not enough to attract attention ② not worth: ～道 inconsiderable; of no consequence/ ～为奇 not at all surprising/ ～挂齿 not worth mentioning; nothing to speak of ③ cannot; should not: ～为凭 not to be taken as evidence

【不足为训】 bù zú wéi xùn not to be taken as an example; not an example to be followed; not to be taken as authoritative: 书本上讲的也有～的。 What is taught in books is not always authoritative.

【不做声】 bù zuòshēng keep silent; not say a word

**布** bù ① cloth: ～鞋 cloth shoes/ 花～ cotton prints ② declare; announce; publish; proclaim: 公～于众 make known to the public; make public ③ spread; disseminate: 控制疾病传～ check the spread of disease ④ dispose; arrange; deploy: ～好阵势 deploy the troops in battle formation/ ～下天罗地网 cast an escape-proof net ⑤ an ancient Chinese copper coin

【布帛】 bùbó cloth and silk; cotton and silk textiles

【布帛菽粟】 bù-bó-shū-sù cloth, silk, beans and grain; food and clothing; daily necessities

【布达拉宫】 Bùdálā Gōng the Potala Palace

【布道】 bùdào 〈宗〉 preach

【布店】 bùdiàn cloth store; draper's; piece-goods store

【布丁】 bùdīng pudding

【布尔什维克】 Bù'ěrshíwéikè Bolshevik

【布尔什维主义】 Bù'ěrshíwéizhǔyì Bolshevism

【布防】 bùfáng place troops on garrison duty; organize a defence

【布告】 bùgào notice; bulletin; proclamation: 张贴～ paste up a notice ◇ ～栏 notice board; bulletin board

【布谷鸟】 bùgǔniǎo cuckoo

【布景】 bùjǐng ① composition (of a painting) ② 〈剧〉 setting ◇ ～设计师 set designer

【布局】 bùjú ① overall arrangement; layout; distribution: 新市区的～ layout of a new urban district/ 工业的合理～ rational distribution of industry/ ～整齐的工农村 neatly arranged worker-peasant villages/ 我们一定要建成～合理，相互配套的科研体系。 We are determined to set up a complete, rationally distributed scientific and technological research system. ② composition (of a picture, piece of writing, etc.) ③ position (of pieces on a chessboard)

【布朗基主义】 Bùlǎngjīzhǔyì Blanquism

【布朗运动】 Bùlǎng yùndòng 〈物〉 Brownian movement

【布朗族】 Bùlǎngzú the Blang (Pulang) nationality, living in Yunnan

【布雷】 bùléi lay mines; mine: 在港口～ mine a harbour ◇ ～舰艇 minelayers/ ～区 minefield

【布列斯特和约】 Bùlièsītè Héyuē the Treaty of Brest-Litovsk (1918)

【布隆迪】 Bùlóngdí Burundi ◇ ～人 Burundian

【布鲁氏菌病】 bùlǔshìjūnbìng brucellosis; undulant fever

【布面】 bùmiàn cloth cover ◇ ～精装本 clothbound *de luxe* edition

【布匹】 bùpǐ cloth; piece goods ◇～染色 piece dyeing

【布票】 bùpiào cloth coupon; clothing coupon

【布施】 bùshī 〈佛教〉 alms giving; donation

【布头】 bùtóu leftover of a bolt of cloth; odd bits of cloth

【布网船】 bùwǎngchuán 〈军〉 netlayer

【布纹纸】 bùwénzhǐ 〈摄〉 wove paper

【布线】 bùxiàn 〈电〉 wiring ◇ ～图 wiring diagram

【布依族】 Bùyīzú the Bouyei (Puyi) nationality, living in Guizhou

【布置】 bùzhì ① fix up; arrange; decorate: ～会场 fix up a place for a meeting/ ～展品 arrange exhibits/ 礼堂～得很漂亮。 The auditorium was beautifully decorated. ② assign; make arrangements for; give instructions about: ～工作 assign work; give instructions about an assignment/ ～政治学习和业务学习 make arrangements for political and vocational study

**步** bù ① step; pace: 只有几～路了。 It's only a few steps away./ 快～走 walk at a quick pace/ 大～前进 advance with big strides ② stage; step: 下一～怎么办？ What's the next step (或 move)?/ 这只好一～一～地去做。 This will have to be done step by step. ③ condition; situation; state: 事情怎么发展到这一～？ How did things get into such a state? ④ walk; go on foot: 学～ learn to walk/ 散～ take a walk ⑤ 〈书〉 tread: ～其后尘 follow in sb.'s footsteps ⑥ an old unit for measurement of length, equivalent to 5 *chi* (尺) ⑦ pace off: ～测二十米的距离 pace off a distance of 20 metres

【步兵】 bùbīng ① infantry; foot ② infantryman; foot soldier

【步步】 bùbù step by step; at every step: ～进逼 press forward steadily

【步步为营】 bùbù wéi yíng advance gradually and entrench oneself at every step; consolidate at every step

【步测】 bùcè pacing

【步调】 bùdiào pace; step: ～一致 keep in step/ 统一～ concert action

【步伐】 bùfá step; pace: 加快～ quicken one's steps (或 pace)/ ～整齐 (march) in step/ 跟上时代的～ keep pace with the times

【步法】 bùfǎ 〈体〉〈舞蹈〉 footwork

【步话机】 bùhuàjī walkie-talkie 又作"步谈机"

【步进制】 bùjìnzhì 〈邮〉 step-by-step system

【步犁】 bùlí walking plough

【步履维艰】 bùlǚ wéi jiān 〈书〉 have difficulty walking; walk with difficulty

【步枪】 bùqiāng rifle

【步人后尘】 bù rén hòuchén follow in other people's footsteps; trail along behind others

【步哨】 bùshào sentry; sentinel

【步行】 bùxíng go on foot; walk

【步行虫】 bùxíngchóng 〈动〉 ground beetle

【步韵】 bùyùn use the rhyme sequence of a poem (when replying to it)

【步骤】 bùzhòu step; move; measure: 有计划有～地进行工作 carry on the work step by step in a planned way/ 采取适当的～ take proper steps/ 这是增产的一个具体～。 This is a practical move to increase production.

【步子】 bùzi step; pace: ～轻快 walk with springy steps/ 技术革新的～越迈越大。 Technical innovations are being made at a faster and faster pace.

**怖** bù fear; be afraid of: 恐～ terror; horror/ 可～ horrible; frightful

**钚** bù 〈化〉 plutonium (Pu)

**部** bù ① part; section: 分为三～ divide into three parts (或 sections)/ 南～ the southern part ② unit; ministry; department; board: 解放军某～ a certain PLA unit/ 国防～ the Ministry of National Defence/ 编辑～ editorial board (或 office) ③ headquarters: 师～ division headquarters/ 前沿指挥～ advance command post ④ troops; forces ⑤ 〈书〉 command: 所～ troops under one's command ⑥ 〈量〉: 一～电影 a film/ 两～机器 two machines/ 一～好作品 a fine work of literature

【部队】 bùduì ① army; armed forces ② troops; force; unit: 通讯兵～ signal troops/ 人民解放军北京～ PLA units under the Beijing Command/ ～就要出发了。The troops are about to set out./ 这是一支野战～。This is a field army unit. ◇ ～代号 code designation (of a military unit)

【部分】 bùfen part; section; share: 我们看问题,不但要看到～,而且要看到全体。In approaching a problem we should see the whole as well as the parts./ 他完成了自己的那～工作以后,又去帮助别人。After finishing his share of the work he went to help the others./ 我们～地改变了原计划。We've altered the original plan to some extent. ◇ ～禁止核试验条约 the Partial Nuclear Test Ban Treaty

【部件】 bùjiàn parts; components; assembly ◇ ～分解图 exploded view

【部类】 bùlèi category; division

【部落】 bùluò tribe ◇ ～社会 tribal society

【部门】 bùmén department; branch: 政府各～ various government departments/ 主管～ the department responsible for the work/ 工业和农业是国民经济的两个重要～。Industry and agriculture are the two important sectors of the national economy.

【部首】 bùshǒu 〈语〉radicals by which characters are arranged in traditional Chinese dictionaries

【部属】 bùshǔ ① 见"部下" ② affiliated to a ministry: ～机构 organizations affiliated to the ministry

【部署】 bùshǔ dispose; deploy: ～兵力 dispose (或 deploy) troops for battle/ 战略～ a strategic plan; strategic deployment/ 为实现祖国的社会主义现代化,五届人大作出了进行新的长征的重大～。The Fifth People's Congress drew up an important plan for a new Long March towards the socialist modernization of our country.

【部委】 bùwěi ministries and commissions: 国务院各～ ministries and commissions under the State Council

【部位】 bùwèi position; place: 发音时舌的～ the position of the tongue in pronunciation; tongue position/ 受伤～ the location of an injury

【部下】 bùxià ① troops under one's command ② subordinate

【部长】 bùzhǎng minister; head of a department (under the Party Central Committee): 外贸部～ Minister of Foreign Trade/ 对外联络部～ Head of the International Liaison Department/ 省委宣传部～ Director of the Propaganda Department of a provincial Party committee ◇ ～会议 Council of Ministers/ ～级会议 conference at ministerial level/ ～助理 assistant minister

**埠** bù ① wharf; pier ② port: 本～ this port/ 外～ other ports/ 商～ a commercial (或 trading) port

**瓿** bù 〈书〉vase

**簿** bù book: 练习～ exercise book/ 账～ account book/ 登记～ register

【簿册】 bùcè books for taking notes or keeping accounts

【簿籍】 bùjí account books, registers, records, etc.

【簿记】 bùjì bookkeeping: 复(单)式～ double-entry (single-entry) bookkeeping

【簿子】 bùzi notebook; book

# C

## cā

**拆** cā
另见 chāi
【拆烂污】 cā lànwū 〈方〉 do slovenly work; leave things in a mess; be irresponsible

**擦** cā ①rub: ～伤了膝盖 rub the skin off one's knee; graze one's knee/ ～根火柴 strike a match/ 没关系,就～破了一点皮。Nothing serious. Just a scratch. ②wipe: ～桌子 wipe the table/ ～地板 mop (或 scrub) the floor/ ～汗 wipe the sweat away/ ～背 scrub one's or sb.'s back/ ～枪 clean a gun/ ～皮鞋 polish shoes ③spread on; put on: 给伤口～碘酒 apply iodine to a wound/ ～粉 powder one's face ④brush; shave: ～肩而过 brush past sb./ 飞机～着山顶飞过。The plane shaved the hilltops. ⑤scrape (into shreds): 把萝卜～成丝儿 shred turnips
【擦棒球】 cābàngqiú 〈棒、垒球〉 foul tip
【擦边球】 cābiānqiú 〈乒乓球〉 edge ball; touch ball
【擦黑儿】 cāhēir 〈方〉 dusk
【擦亮眼睛】 cāliàng yǎnjīng remove the scales from one's eyes; sharpen one's vigilance
【擦拭】 cāshì clean; cleanse: ～武器 clean weapons
【擦网球】 cāwǎngqiú 〈体〉 net ball
【擦音】 cāyīn 〈语〉 fricative
【擦澡】 cāzǎo rub oneself down with a wet towel; take a sponge bath

**嚓** cā 〈象〉: 汽车～的一声停住了。The car screeched to a stop.
另见 chā

## cǎ

**磜** cǎ
【磜床儿】 cǎchuángr shredder (for vegetables)

## cāi

**猜** cāi ①guess; conjecture; speculate: 你～谁来了? Guess who's here./ 他准～不着。He's sure to guess wrong./ 这个谜语真难～。This riddle is really difficult to solve. ②suspect: 我～他和这件事有点牵连。I suspect that he is more or less involved in the affair.
【猜测】 cāicè guess; conjecture; surmise: 那都是～。That's pure conjecture. 或 That's all guesswork./ 考古新发现否定了过去对这个问题的～。The new archaeological finds have disproved previous conjectures on this subject.
【猜度】 cāiduó surmise; conjecture
【猜忌】 cāijì be suspicious and jealous of
【猜谜儿】 cāimèir ①guess a riddle ②guess: 快说吧,别让我们～了。Now out with it. Don't keep us guessing.
【猜拳】 cāiquán a finger-guessing game; mora
【猜想】 cāixiǎng suppose; guess; suspect: 我～她又练投弹去了。I suppose she's gone to practise grenade throwing again./ 我～他病了。I suspect he is ill.
【猜疑】 cāiyí harbour suspicions; be suspicious; have misgivings

## cái

**才** cái ①ability; talent; gift: 德～兼备 have both ability and political integrity ②capable person: 人～ a person of talent; talent ③people of a certain type: 奴～ flunkey ④〈副〉 ⓐ〔表示事情刚发生,或发生得晚〕: 比赛～开始。The match has just started./ 怎么,～来了就走? Why leave so soon? You've only just arrived./ 你怎么～来? Why are you so late? ⓑ〔表示事情取决于某种条件〕: 我们只有依靠群众～有力量。Only by relying on the masses can we become strong./ 老马总要把办公室打扫干净了～走。Lao Ma never leaves the office until he has given it a good cleaning./ 非要等起重机来了～能装运吗? Must we wait till the crane arrives before we start loading? ⓒ〔表示对比之下数量小,次数少等〕: 他参加长征的时候～十四岁。He was only fourteen when he went on the Long March./ 解放前全国钢年产量最高～九十多万吨。Before liberation, China's highest annual output of steel was only just over 900,000 tons. ⓓ〔表示强调〕: 麦子长得～好呢! The wheat is coming along fine./ 他要是不知道～怪呢! It would be strange if he didn't know.
【才干】 cáigàn ability; competence: 在三大革命运动中增长～ enhance one's abilities by taking part in the three great revolutionary movements
【才华】 cáihuá literary or artistic talent: 他是一位很有～的作家。He is a gifted writer.
【才略】 cáilüè ability and sagacity (in political and military affairs)
【才能】 cáinéng ability; talent
【才气】 cáiqì literary talent: ～横溢 brim with talent; have superb talent
【才识】 cáishí ability and insight: ～过人 be gifted with talent and insight far beyond the average person
【才疏学浅】 cáishū-xuéqiǎn 〈谦〉 have little talent and less learning
【才思】 cáisī 〈书〉 imaginative power; creativeness: ～敏捷 have a facile imagination
【才学】 cáixué talent and learning; scholarship
【才智】 cáizhì ability and wisdom: 充分发挥人民群众的聪明～ give full play to the wisdom and creativeness of the people
【才子】 cáizǐ gifted scholar: ～佳人 gifted scholars and beautiful ladies (in Chinese romances)

**材** cái ①timber: 木～ timber; lumber ②material: 教～ teaching material/ 钢～ steel products/ 就地取～ obtain material from local sources; draw on local resources ③ability; talent; aptitude: 因～施教 teach students in accordance with their aptitude ④capable person: 人～难得 a person of rare talent ⑤coffin
【材积】 cáijī 〈林〉 volume (of timber)
【材料】 cáiliào ①material: 建筑～ building material/ 原～ raw material ②data; material: 学习～ material for study/ 档案～ archival material/ 调查～ data; findings/ 搜集～

gather material; collect data/ 熟悉一下～ acquaint oneself with the facts/ 根据现有～还不能得出肯定的结论。We cannot draw any definite conclusion from the available data. ③ makings; stuff: 她不是演戏的～。She hasn't the makings of an actress. ◇ ～科学 materials science/ ～力学 mechanics of materials

**财** cái wealth; money

【财宝】 cáibǎo money and valuables
【财帛】 cáibó wealth; money
【财产】 cáichǎn property: 公共～ public property/ 国家～ state property/ 保护人民的生命～ protect the life and property of the people ◇ ～权 property right/ ～税 property tax
【财东】 cáidōng 〈旧〉 ① shopowner ② moneybags
【财阀】 cáifá financial magnate; plutocrat; tycoon
【财富】 cáifù wealth; riches: 自然～ natural wealth/ 精神～ spiritual wealth/ 毛泽东思想是马克思列宁主义理论宝库的最新～。Mao Zedong Thought is the newest acquisition enriching the treasure-house of Marxist-Leninist theory.
【财经】 cái-jīng finance and economics
【财礼】 cáilǐ 见"彩礼" cǎilǐ
【财力】 cáilì financial resources (或 capacity)
【财贸】 cáimào finance and trade (或 commerce)
【财迷】 cáimí moneygrubber; miser
【财神】 cáishén the God of Wealth
【财团】 cáituán financial group: 国际～ consortium
【财务】 cáiwù financial affairs ◇ ～报告 financial statement (或 report)/ ～科 finance section/ ～行政 financial administration
【财物】 cáiwù property; belongings: 个人～ personal effects
【财源】 cáiyuán financial resources; source of revenue
【财政】 cáizhèng (public) finance: ～金融危机 financial and monetary crisis/ ～收支平衡 balance of revenue and expenditure ◇ ～部 the Ministry of Finance/ ～赤字 financial deficits/ ～机关 financial organ (或 administration); fiscal organ (或 administration)/ ～年度 financial (或 fiscal) year/ ～收入 revenue/ ～政策 financial (或 fiscal) policy/ ～支出 expenditure
【财主】 cáizhu rich man; moneybags

**裁** cái ① cut (paper, cloth, etc.) into parts: 把一张纸～成条儿 cut a sheet of paper into strips/ ～件新衣服 cut out a new garment/ 这块料子可以～两套衣服。Two suits can be cut out of this piece of material. ② reduce; cut down; dismiss: 他刚一有病，资本家就把他～掉了。The boss fired him the moment he fell ill. ③ judge; decide: ～夺 consider and decide ④ check; sanction: 经济制～ economic sanction ⑤ mental planning: 别出心～ adopt an original approach; try to be different

【裁并】 cáibìng cut down and merge (organizations)
【裁撤】 cáichè dissolve (an organization)
【裁定】 cáidìng 〈法〉 ruling
【裁断】 cáiduàn consider and decide
【裁夺】 cáiduó consider and decide
【裁缝】 cáifeng tailor; dressmaker
【裁减】 cáijiǎn reduce; cut down: ～机关工作人员 reduce (或 cut down) the staff of an organization/ ～军备 reduction of armaments
【裁剪】 cáijiǎn cut out: ～衣服 cut out garments
【裁决】 cáijué ruling; adjudication: 依法～ adjudicate according to law/ 会议主席作出了～。A ruling was given by the chairman.
【裁军】 cáijūn disarmament
【裁判】 cáipàn ① 〈法〉 judgment ② 〈体〉 act as referee; referee ③ 〈体〉 referee; umpire; judge ◇ ～权 jurisdiction/ ～员 referee; judge; umpire/ ～长 head judge; chief judge; (乒乓球、网球等) referee
【裁员】 cáiyuán 〈旧〉 cut down the number of persons employed; reduce the staff
【裁纸机】 cáizhǐjī (paper) trimmer; paper cutter

## cǎi

**采** cǎi ① pick; pluck; gather: ～茶 pick tea/ ～药 gather medicinal herbs/ ～珍珠 dive for pearls ② mine; extract: ～煤 mine coal/ ～油 extract oil ③ adopt; select: ～取一系列措施 adopt a series of measures ④ complexion; spirit: 兴高～烈 in high spirits
另见 cài

【采办】 cǎibàn buy on a considerable scale; purchase
【采场】 cǎichǎng 〈矿〉 stope
【采伐】 cǎifá fell; cut: ～原始森林 open up a primeval forest ◇ ～迹地 cutover/ ～量 cut
【采访】 cǎifǎng (of a reporter) gather material; cover: ～新闻 gather news; cover/ ～全国运动会消息 cover the National Games/ 向一位名演员进行～ interview a famous actor
【采风】 cǎifēng collect folk songs (as in ancient China)
【采购】 cǎigòu make purchases for an organization or enterprise; purchase: ～建筑材料 purchase building materials ◇ ～员 purchasing agent/ ～站 purchasing station
【采光】 cǎiguāng 〈建〉 (natural) lighting; daylighting
【采集】 cǎijí gather; collect: ～标本 collect specimens/ 原始部落靠渔猎～为生。Primitive tribes lived by fishing, hunting and gathering.
【采掘】 cǎijué 〈矿〉 excavate ◇ ～设备 equipment for excavation
【采矿】 cǎikuàng mining: 露天～ opencut (或 opencast) mining/ 地下～ underground mining ◇ ～工程 mining engineering
【采录】 cǎilù collect and record: ～民歌 collect and record folk songs
【采买】 cǎimǎi purchase; buy
【采煤】 cǎiméi coal mining; coal extraction; coal cutting ◇ ～工作面 coal face/ ～回收率 coal recovery
【采棉机】 cǎimiánjī cotton picker
【采纳】 cǎinà accept; adopt: ～群众建议 accept suggestions made by the masses
【采暖】 cǎinuǎn 〈建〉 heating: 蒸气～ steam heating ◇ ～设备 heating equipment (或 facilities)
【采取】 cǎiqǔ adopt; take: ～紧急措施 take emergency measures/ ～主动 take the initiative/ ～攻势 take the offensive/ ～一项新政策 adopt a new policy/ ～说服教育的办法 use the method of persuasion and education/ ～拖延战术 employ stalling tactics/ ～强制手段 resort to compulsion
【采石场】 cǎishíchǎng stone pit; quarry
【采收率】 cǎishōulǜ 〈石油〉 recovery ratio
【采撷】 cǎixié 〈书〉 ① pick; pluck ② gather
【采样】 cǎiyàng 〈矿〉 sampling
【采用】 cǎiyòng adopt; use; employ: ～新技术 adopt new techniques
【采油】 cǎiyóu 〈石油〉 oil extraction; oil recovery: 气举～ air-lift recovery/ 二次～ secondary recovery ◇ ～队 oil production crew
【采择】 cǎizé select and adopt: 提出几种办法，以供～ propose several measures for you to choose from

【采摘】 cǎizhāi pluck; pick: ～苹果 pick apples
【采脂】 cǎizhī 〈林〉 (resin) tapping
【采制】 cǎizhì collect and process: ～中草药 gather medicinal herbs and prepare them for use
【采种】 cǎizhǒng 〈农〉 seed collecting

**彩** cǎi ①colour: 五～ of different colours; multicoloured/ ～云 rosy clouds ②coloured silk; variegated silk: 张灯结～ decorate with lanterns and coloured ribbons ③applause; cheer: 喝～ acclaim; cheer/ ～声 acclamation; applause ④variety; splendour: 丰富多～ rich and colourful; rich and varied ⑤prize: 中～ win a prize (in a lottery, etc.) ⑥blood from a wound: 挂～ be wounded in battle
【彩蚌】 cǎibàng 〈工美〉 painted shell; painting on shell
【彩车】 cǎichē float (in a parade)
【彩绸】 cǎichóu coloured silk
【彩带】 cǎidài coloured ribbon (或 streamer)
【彩蛋】 cǎidàn 〈工美〉 painted eggshell; painting on eggshell
【彩调】 cǎidiào 〈剧〉 a local opera of the Guangxi Zhuang Autonomous Region
【彩号】 cǎihào wounded soldier
【彩虹】 cǎihóng rainbow
【彩绘】 cǎihuì coloured drawing or pattern: ～磁器 porcelain decorated with coloured drawings/ ～乐俑群 painted pottery figurines of musicians
【彩礼】 cǎilǐ betrothal gifts (from the bridegroom to the bride's family); bride-price: 破除订婚受～的旧习 reject the old custom of accepting betrothal gifts
【彩练】 cǎiliàn coloured ribbon
【彩门】 cǎimén decorated gateway (erected on festive occasions)
【彩排】 cǎipái dress rehearsal
【彩棚】 cǎipéng decorated tent (set up on festive occasions); marquee
【彩票】 cǎipiào lottery ticket
【彩旗】 cǎiqí coloured flag; bunting
【彩色】 cǎisè multicolour; colour: ～缤纷 a riot of colour ◇ ～电视 colour television/ ～胶片 colour film/ ～铅笔 colour pencil; crayon/ ～印刷 colour printing/ ～影片 colour film
【彩塑】 cǎisù colour modelling; painted sculpture: ～泥人 painted clay figurine
【彩陶】 cǎitáo ancient painted pottery
【彩陶文化】 cǎitáo wénhuà 〈考古〉 Painted-Pottery Culture 参见"仰韶文化" Yǎngsháo wénhuà
【彩霞】 cǎixiá rosy (或 pink) clouds
【彩釉陶】 cǎiyòutáo glazed coloured pottery

**睬** cǎi pay attention to; take notice of: 不要～他。Take no notice of him. 或 Ignore him.

**踩** cǎi step on; trample: 当心～坏了庄稼。Mind you don't tread on the crops./ 一切困难～脚下 trample all difficulties underfoot; surmount all difficulties
【踩水】 cǎishuǐ 〈体〉 tread water
【踩线】 cǎixiàn step on the line; footfault

## cài

**采** cài
另见 cǎi
【采邑】 càiyì fief; benefice

**菜** cài ①vegetable; greens: 种～ grow vegetables/ 咸～ pickles ②(non-staple) food: 上街买～ go to the market to buy food ③dish; course: 荤～ meat dish/ 素～ vegetable dish/ 一道～ a course/ 川～ Sichuan dishes; Sichuan cuisine/ 做～ prepare the dishes; do the cooking
【菜帮儿】 càibāngr outer leaves (of a cabbage, etc.)
【菜场】 càichǎng food market
【菜单】 càidān menu; bill of fare
【菜刀】 càidāo kitchen knife
【菜地】 càidì vegetable plot
【菜豆】 càidòu kidney bean
【菜粉蝶】 càifěndié cabbage butterfly
【菜瓜】 càiguā snake melon
【菜花】 càihuā ①cauliflower ②rape flower
【菜窖】 càijiào vegetable cellar; clamp
【菜码儿】 càimǎr 〈方〉 shredded or sliced vegetables to go with noodles
【菜牛】 càiniú beef cattle
【菜农】 càinóng vegetable grower
【菜圃】 càipǔ vegetable garden; vegetable farm
【菜畦】 càiqí small sections of a vegetable plot; vegetable bed
【菜青】 càiqīng dark greyish green
【菜青虫】 càiqīngchóng cabbage caterpillar
【菜色】 càisè famished (或 emaciated) look: 面有～ look famished
【菜市】 càishì food market
【菜蔬】 càishū ①vegetables; greens ②dishes at a meal
【菜苔】 càitái bolt (of rape, mustard, etc.)
【菜摊】 càitān vegetable stall
【菜心儿】 càixīnr heart (of a cabbage, etc.)
【菜肴】 càiyáo cooked food (usu. meat dishes)
【菜油】 càiyóu rapeseed oil; rape oil
【菜园】 càiyuán vegetable garden; vegetable farm
【菜籽】 càizǐ ①vegetable seeds ②rapeseed ◇ ～饼 rapeseed cake/ ～油 rape (或 rapeseed) oil

**蔡** Cài a surname

## cān

**参** cān ①join; enter; take part in: ～战 enter a war ②refer; consult: ～阅 see; consult; compare ③call to pay one's respects to: ～谒烈士陵园 pay homage at the mausoleum of the martyred heroes ④impeach an official before the emperor
另见 cēn; shēn
【参半】 cānbàn half; half-and-half: 疑信～ half believing, half doubting/ 毁誉～ get both praise and blame; be as much praised as blamed
【参观】 cānguān visit; look around: ～工厂 visit a factory/ ～名胜古迹 go on sightseeing trips to scenic spots and historical monuments/ ～游览 visit places of interest; go sightseeing/ 欢迎～。Visitors are welcome. ◇ ～团 visiting group
【参加】 cānjiā ①join; attend; take part in: ～革命 join the revolutionary ranks/ ～党 join the Party; be admitted into (或 to) the Party/ 积极～社会主义建设 take an active part in socialist construction/ ～集体生产劳动 participate in collective productive labour/ ～管理国家大事 participate in the management of state affairs/ ～会议 attend a meeting/ ～会谈 take part in talks ②give (advice, suggestion, etc.): 这件事你也来～点儿意见吧。Come and give

us your view on the matter, won't you?
【参见】 cānjiàn ①see also; cf.: ～第九章。See also Chapter 9. ②pay one's respects to (a superior, etc.)
【参军】 cānjūn join the army; join up; enlist
【参看】 cānkàn ①see (also): ～下面注释 see note below/ ～第二十二页 see page 22 ②consult: 他～了不少有关书刊。He consulted a number of relevant books and periodicals. ③read sth. for reference: 学习时事可以～这篇文章。In studying current affairs you might read this article for reference.
【参考】 cānkǎo ①consult; refer to: ～历史文献 consult historical documents ②reference: 仅供～ for reference only
◇ ～书 reference book/ ～书目 a list of reference books; bibliography/ ～资料 reference material
【参谋】 cānmóu ①staff officer ②give advice: 这事可以让老张给你～一下。You might ask Lao Zhang for advice on this matter. ◇ ～长 chief of staff
【参事】 cānshì counsellor; adviser
【参数】 cānshù 〈数〉 parameter
【参天】 cāntiān reaching to the sky; towering; very tall: ～古树 towering old trees
【参谒】 cānyè ①pay one's respects to (a superior) ②pay homage to sb. (before his tomb or image) 又作"参拜"
【参议员】 cānyìyuán senator
【参议院】 cānyìyuàn senate
【参与】 cānyù participate in; have a hand in: ～其事 have a hand in the matter/ ～制订规划 participate in the drawing up of a plan
【参赞】 cānzàn counsellor: 商务～ commercial counsellor/ 文化～ cultural attaché
【参战】 cānzhàn enter a war; take part in a war ◇ ～国 belligerent state
【参照】 cānzhào consult; refer to: 我们～原文作了必要的修改。We consulted the original and made some necessary changes./ 这个句子要～上下文来译。We can't translate this sentence without reference to the context./ ～具体情况作出适当安排。Make proper arrangements in the light of the specific situation.
【参政】 cānzhèng participate in government and political affairs
【参酌】 cānzhuó consider (a matter) in the light of actual conditions; deliberate

**餐** cān ①eat: 聚～ dine together/ 野～ go on a picnic; picnic ②food; meal: 中～ Chinese food/ 西～ Western food/ 午～ lunch ③regular meal: 一日三～ three meals a day
【餐车】 cānchē restaurant car; dining car; diner
【餐风宿露】 cānfēng-sùlù 见"风餐露宿" fēngcān-lùsù
【餐巾】 cānjīn table napkin ◇ ～纸 napkin paper; paper napkin
【餐具】 cānjù tableware; dinner service (或 set)
【餐厅】 cāntīng ①dining room (或 hall) ②restaurant

## cán

**残** cán ①incomplete; deficient: ～稿 an incomplete manuscript ②remnant; remaining: ～敌 remnants of the enemy forces/ ～冬 the last days of winter ③injure; damage: 身～志不～ broken in health but not in spirit ④savage; barbarous; ferocious: 凶～ cruel
【残暴】 cánbào cruel and ferocious; ruthless; brutal; savage
【残兵败将】 cánbīng-bàijiàng remnants of a routed army
【残存】 cáncún remnant; remaining; surviving: 大熊猫是一种～的古动物。The giant panda is one of the surviving ancient animals.
【残废】 cánfèi ①maimed; crippled; disabled: ～军人 disabled armyman ②a maimed person; cripple ◇ ～证 〈军〉 certificate of disability
【残羹剩饭】 cángēng-shèngfàn remains of a meal; leftovers; crumbs from the table
【残骸】 cánhái remains; wreckage: 敌机～ the wreckage of an enemy plane
【残害】 cánhài cruelly injure or kill: ～肢体 cause bodily injury/ 侵略者到处～老百姓。Wherever they went, the invaders slaughtered the local people.
【残货】 cánhuò shopworn goods; damaged or substandard goods
【残迹】 cánjì a remaining trace, sign, etc.; vestiges
【残疾】 cánji deformity
【残局】 cánjú ①the final phase of a game of chess ②the situation after the failure of an undertaking or after social unrest: 收拾～ clear up the mess; pick up the pieces
【残酷】 cánkù cruel; brutal; ruthless: ～的剥削 cruel (或 ruthless) exploitation/ ～的殖民统治 brutal colonial rule/ ～斗争,无情打击 ruthless struggle and merciless blows/ ～的阶级斗争现实教育了我们。The harsh reality of class struggle educated us./ ～地杀害 kill sb. in cold blood
【残留】 cánliú remain; be left over
【残年】 cánnián ①the last days of the year ②the evening of life; declining years: 风烛～ old and ailing like a candle guttering in the wind
【残篇断简】 cánpiān-duànjiǎn fragments of ancient texts
【残品】 cánpǐn damaged article; defective goods
【残破】 cánpò broken; dilapidated: 有些器皿在出土时已经～。Some utensils were in a state of decay when they were unearthed.
【残缺】 cánquē incomplete; fragmentary: 一套～不全的茶具 an incomplete tea set/ 迄今仍未发现竹简～的部分。The missing parts of the inscribed bamboo slips have not yet been discovered.
【残忍】 cánrěn cruel; ruthless
【残杀】 cánshā murder; massacre; slaughter: 反动统治阶级内部自相～,是经常发生的。Mutual slaughter was a common occurrence within the reactionary ruling classes.
【残生】 cánshēng one's remaining years
【残阳】 cányáng the setting sun
【残余】 cányú remnants; remains; survivals; vestiges: 封建～ survivals of feudalism/ ～势力 remaining (或 surviving) forces/ 剥削阶级思想～ vestiges of the ideology of the exploiting classes
【残渣余孽】 cánzhā-yúniè evil elements from the old society; dregs of the old society
【残照】 cánzhào the setting sun: 西风～ the sun setting in the wild west wind

**蚕** cán silkworm: 家～ Chinese silkworm/ 野～ wild silkworm/ 养～ raise silkworms; silkworm breeding; sericulture
【蚕箔】 cánbó a bamboo tray for raising silkworms
【蚕蔟】 cáncù a small bundle of straw, etc., for silkworms to spin cocoons on
【蚕豆】 cándòu broad bean
【蚕蛾】 cán'é silk moth
【蚕茧】 cánjiǎn silkworm cocoon
【蚕眠】 cánmián the inactive state of the silkworm before it sheds its skin

【蚕农】 cánnóng silkworm raiser; sericulturist
【蚕沙】 cánshā silkworm excrement
【蚕食】 cánshí nibble ◇ ～政策 the policy of "nibbling" at another country's territory
【蚕食鲸吞】 cánshí-jīngtūn nibble away like a silkworm or swallow like a whale — seize another country's territory by piecemeal encroachment or wholesale annexation
【蚕丝】 cánsī natural silk; silk
【蚕蚁】 cányǐ newly-hatched silkworm
【蚕蛹】 cányǒng silkworm chrysalis
【蚕纸】 cánzhǐ paper with silkworm eggs
【蚕子】 cánzǐ silkworm seed (或 egg)

**惭** cán feel ashamed: 大言不～ be shamelessly boastful; brazenly brag
【惭愧】 cánkuì be ashamed: 我没有完成任务,感到很～。I feel quite ashamed that I have not fulfilled the task.

## cǎn

**惨** cǎn ① miserable; pitiful; tragic: ～不忍睹 too horrible to look at/ ～遭不幸 die a tragic death/ ～遭反动派杀害 be murdered in cold blood by the reactionaries ② cruel; savage: ～无人道 inhuman; brutal ③ to a serious degree; disastrously: 敌人愈是捣乱,就失败得愈～。The more trouble the enemy makes, the worse will be his defeat.
【惨案】 cǎn'àn ① massacre (as suffered by oppressed peoples or classes in struggle against reactionary rulers or foreign invaders) ② murder case
【惨白】 cǎnbái pale: 脸色～ look deathly pale
【惨败】 cǎnbài crushing (或 disastrous) defeat
【惨淡】 cǎndàn gloomy; dismal; bleak: 天色～。It was gloomy weather./ 在～的星光下 in the dim starlight
【惨淡经营】 cǎndàn jīngyíng keep (an enterprise, etc.) going by painstaking effort; take great pains to carry on one's work under difficult circumstances
【惨祸】 cǎnhuò horrible disaster; frightful calamity
【惨境】 cǎnjìng miserable condition; tragic circumstances; dire straits
【惨剧】 cǎnjù tragedy; calamity
【惨绝人寰】 cǎn jué rénhuán tragic beyond compare in this human world; extremely tragic: ～的暴行 atrocity of unparalleled savagery
【惨然】 cǎnrán saddened; grieved: 他听到这个不幸的消息,不禁感到～。He felt deeply grieved at this sad news
【惨杀】 cǎnshā massacre; murder
【惨死】 cǎnsǐ die a tragic death
【惨痛】 cǎntòng deeply grieved; painful; bitter: ～的教训 a bitter lesson
【惨笑】 cǎnxiào a wan smile
【惨重】 cǎnzhòng heavy; grievous; disastrous: 损失～ suffer heavy (或 grievous) losses/ ～失败 a disastrous defeat/ 伤亡～ suffer heavy casualties
【惨状】 cǎnzhuàng miserable condition; pitiful sight

**穇** cǎn
【穇子】 cǎnzi 〈植〉 billion-dollar grass

## càn

**灿** càn
【灿烂】 cànlàn magnificent; splendid; resplendent; bright: ～的阳光 the bright sun; brilliant sunshine/ ～的民族文化 splendid national culture/ 祖国前途光辉～。Our country's prospects are magnificent.

**孱** càn
另见 chán
【孱头】 càntou 〈方〉 weakling; coward

**粲** càn 〈书〉 ① bright; beaming ② smile: 以博一～ just for your amusement
【粲然】 cànrán ① bright; beaming ② smiling broadly: ～一笑 give a beaming smile; grin with delight

**璨** càn 见"璀璨" cuǐcàn

## cāng

**仓** cāng storehouse; warehouse: 谷～ barn/ 粮食满～。The granary is bursting with grain.
【仓储】 cāngchǔ keep grain, goods, etc. in a storehouse: 尽量避免商品在～过程中的损耗 avoid so far as possible the spoilage of goods during storage
【仓促】 cāngcù hurriedly; hastily; all of a sudden: 走得～ leave in a hurry/ ～应战 accept battle in haste/ 不要～下结论。Don't jump to conclusions. 又作"仓猝""仓卒"
【仓房】 cāngfáng warehouse; storehouse
【仓皇】 cānghuáng in a flurry; in panic: ～失措 be scared out of one's wits; be panic-stricken/ ～逃窜 flee in confusion; flee in panic; flee helter-skelter/ ～退却 retreat in haste
【仓库】 cāngkù warehouse; storehouse; depository: 清理～ take stock; check warehouse stocks ◇ ～保管员 warehouseman
【仓廪】 cānglǐn granary
【仓鼠】 cāngshǔ hamster
【仓租】 cāngzū warehouse storage charges

**伧** cāng rude; rough
另见 chen
【伧俗】 cāngsú vulgar

**沧** cāng (of the sea) dark blue
【沧海】 cānghǎi the blue sea; the sea
【沧海桑田】 cānghǎi-sāngtián seas change into mulberry fields and mulberry fields into seas — time brings great changes to the world
【沧海一粟】 cānghǎi yī sù a drop in the ocean: 个人的力量和群众的力量相比,不过是～。The strength of an individual, as compared with that of the masses, is but a drop in the ocean.
【沧桑】 cāngsāng 〔"沧海桑田"的略语〕: 饱经～ have experienced many vicissitudes of life

**苍** cāng ① dark green: ～松 green pines ② blue: ～天 the blue sky ③ grey; ashy: ～髯 a grey beard
【苍白】 cāngbái pale; pallid; wan: 脸色～ look pale/ ～无力 pale and weak; feeble
【苍苍】 cāngcāng ① grey: 两鬓～ greying at the temples ② vast and hazy: 天～,野茫茫。Vast is the sky, boundless the wilds.
【苍翠】 cāngcuì dark green; verdant: ～的山峦 verdant hills
【苍耳子】 cāng'ěrzǐ 〈中药〉 the achene of Siberian cocklebur (*Xanthium sibiricum*)
【苍黄】 cānghuáng ① greenish yellow: 面色～ have a sallow

complexion/ ～的天空 a sombre sky ②〈书〉black or yellow (as in the Mohist saying: "White silk can be dyed either black or yellow.") — changeable ③ 见"仓皇" cānghuáng

【苍劲】 cāngjìng ① old and strong: ～挺拔的青松 hardy, old pines ② (of calligraphy or painting) vigorous; bold: 笔力～ (write or paint) in bold, vigorous strokes

【苍老】 cānglǎo ① old; aged: 他显得～了。He looks old. ② (of calligraphy or painting) vigorous; forceful

【苍凉】 cāngliáng desolate; bleak: 过去这一带满目～,现在却有了无数的工厂。Numerous factories have sprung up in this once desolate area.

【苍鹭】 cānglù 〈动〉 heron

【苍茫】 cāngmáng ① vast; boundless: ～大地 boundless land ② indistinct: 暮色～ deepening shades of dusk/ 一片～的海天景色 a vast expanse of sea and sky

【苍穹】 cāngqióng 〈书〉 the vault of heaven; the firmament

【苍生】 cāngshēng 〈书〉 the common people

【苍天】 cāngtiān ① the blue sky ② Heaven

【苍鹰】 cāngyīng goshawk

【苍蝇】 cāngying fly ◇ ～拍子 flyswatter

【苍郁】 cāngyù 〈书〉 verdant and luxuriant

【苍术】 cāngzhú 〈中药〉 the rhizome of Chinese atractylodes (*Atractylodes chinensis*)

**舱** cāng ① cabin: 客～ (passenger) cabin/ 货～ hold ②〈宇航〉 module: 指挥～ command module

【舱壁】 cāngbì bulkhead

【舱口】 cāngkǒu hatchway; hatch ◇ ～盖 hatch door; hatch cover

【舱单】 cāngdān 〈交〉 manifest

【舱面】 cāngmiàn deck ◇ ～货 deck cargo

【舱内货】 cāngnèihuò underdeck cargo

【舱室】 cāngshì cabin

【舱位】 cāngwèi ① cabin seat or berth ② shipping space

## cáng

**藏** cáng ① hide; conceal: 老大娘把八路军伤员～在自己家里。Grandma hid the wounded Eighth Route Army man in her house./ 这人肚子里～不住话。This chap can't keep anything to himself. ② store; lay by: ～粮于民 store grain among the people

另见 zàng

【藏垢纳污】 cánggòu-nàwū shelter evil people and countenance evil practices: ～之地 a sink of iniquity

【藏猫儿】 cángmāor 〈口〉 (play) hide-and-seek

【藏匿】 cángnì conceal; hide; go into hiding

【藏身】 cángshēn hide oneself; go into hiding: 无处～ no place to hide/ ～之处 hiding-place; hideout

【藏书】 cángshū ① collect books ② a collection of books; library

【藏头露尾】 cángtóu-lùwěi show the tail but hide the head — tell part of the truth but not all of it

【藏掖】 cángyē try to cover up: ～躲闪 dodge and hide

【藏拙】 cángzhuō hide one's inadequacy by keeping quiet

## cāo

**糙** cāo rough; coarse: ～纸 rough paper/ 这活儿做得太～。This is very slipshod work.

【糙米】 cāomǐ brown rice; unpolished rice

【糙皮病】 cāopíbìng pellagra

**操** cāo ① grasp; hold: ～刀 hold a sword, cleaver, etc. in one's hand/ ～胜算 find success within one's grasp; be sure to win ② act; do; operate: ～之过急 act with undue haste/ 重～旧业 resume one's old profession; take up one's old trade again ③ speak (a language or dialect): ～本地口音 speak with a local accent/ ～着一口流利的英语 speak fluent English ④ drill; exercise: 战士们在上～。The soldiers are drilling./ 大家去做～吧。Let's go and do exercises. ⑤ conduct; behaviour: 节～ one's moral principles; personal integrity

【操场】 cāochǎng playground; sports ground; drill ground

【操持】 cāochi manage; handle: ～家务 manage household affairs/ 这件事由你～一下。I'll leave the matter in your hands.

【操典】 cāodiǎn 〈军〉 drill regulations (或 manual); drill book

【操舵室】 cāoduòshì wheelhouse; pilothouse; steering room

【操法】 cāofǎ methods and rules for military drill or physical exercise

【操课】 cāokè 〈军〉 ① military drill ② lecture as part of military training: ～时间 time for drill or lecture

【操劳】 cāoláo ① work hard: ～过度 overwork (或 strain) oneself/ 终年为集体～ work hard for the collective all the year round ② take care; look after: 这事请您多～。Would you mind looking after this?

【操练】 cāoliàn drill; practice

【操切】 cāoqiè rash; hasty: ～从事 act with undue haste

【操守】 cāoshǒu personal integrity

【操心】 cāoxīn ① worry about; trouble about; take pains: 这件事,你不必～了。You needn't worry about it. ② rack one's brains: 为了抗旱,支书可没少～。The Party secretary has put his heart and soul into the task of combating the drought.

【操行】 cāoxíng behaviour or conduct of a student

【操演】 cāoyǎn demonstration; drill

【操纵】 cāozòng ① operate; control: 培养～新机器的工人 train workers to operate new machines/ 无线电～ radio control ② rig; manipulate: ～市场 rig the market/ ～表决机器 tamper with the voting machine; manipulate the voting/ 幕后～ manipulate from behind the scenes; pull strings ◇ ～杆 operating lever; control rod; control stick/ ～台 control panel (或 board)

【操作】 cāozuò operate; manipulate: 避免～上的疏忽 avoid carelessness in manipulation/ 在老师傅的指导下,青年徒工很快就学会独立～了。Guided by the master workers, the young apprentices quickly learned to operate the machines. ◇ ～程序 operation sequence/ ～程序图 flow diagram; flow chart/ ～方法 method of operation/ ～规程 operating rules (或 instructions)/ ～说明书 operating manual/ ～性能〈机〉 serviceability

## cáo

**曹** cáo ①〈书〉 people of the same kind: 尔～ all of you; you ② (Cáo) a surname

【曹白鱼】 cáobáiyú Chinese herring

**漕** cáo water transport (esp. of grain)

【漕运】 cáoyùn water transport of grain to the capital (in feudal times)

**嘈** cáo noise; din

【嘈杂】 cáozá noisy: 人声～ a hubbub of voices

**槽** cáo ①trough: 马～ manger/ 水～ water trough ②〈机〉groove; slot: 开～ slotting/ 键～ key groove
【槽坊】 cáofang brewery; distillery
【槽钢】 cáogāng 〈冶〉channel (iron) 又作"槽铁"
【槽谷】 cáogǔ 〈地〉trough valley
【槽距】 cáojù 〈机〉slot pitch
【槽口】 cáokǒu 〈机〉notch
【槽探】 cáotàn 〈矿〉trenching
【槽头】 cáotóu trough (in a livestock shed): ～兴旺 a manger full of sturdy livestock
【槽牙】 cáoyá molar

**螬** cáo 见"蛴螬" qícáo

## cǎo

**草** cǎo ①grass; straw: ～绳 straw rope ②careless; hasty; rough: 字写得很～。The handwriting is very sloppy. ③draft: 起～文件 draft a document ④见"草书" ⑤〈口〉female (of certain domestic animals or fowls): ～驴 jenny ass/ ～鸡 hen
【草案】 cǎo'àn draft (of a plan, law, etc.): 决议～ a draft resolution
【草包】 cǎobāo ①straw bag; straw sack ②idiot; blockhead; good-for-nothing
【草本】 cǎoběn herbaceous ◇ ～植物 herb
【草草】 cǎocǎo carelessly; hastily: ～地看过一遍 read through roughly; give a cursory reading; skim through/ ～收场 hastily wind up the matter/ ～了事 get through with sth. any old way
【草测】 cǎocè preliminary survey
【草叉】 cǎochā pitch-fork
【草虫】 cǎochóng 〈美术〉grass-and-insect painting
【草创】 cǎochuàng start (an enterprise, etc.): ～时期 initial (或 pioneering) stage
【草丛】 cǎocóng a thick growth of grass
【草地】 cǎodì ①grassland; meadow ②lawn
【草甸子】 cǎodiànzi 〈方〉grassy marshland
【草垫子】 cǎodiànzi straw mattress; pallet
【草垛】 cǎoduò haystack; hayrick
【草房】 cǎofáng thatched cottage
【草稿】 cǎogǎo rough draft; draft
【草菇】 cǎogū straw mushroom
【草果】 cǎoguǒ 〈植〉*caoguo (Amomum tsao-ko)*
【草荒】 cǎohuāng farmland running to weeds; more weeds than crops
【草菅人命】 cǎojiān rénmìng treat human life as if it were not worth a straw; act with utter disregard for human life
【草荐】 cǎojiàn pallet
【草浆】 cǎojiāng 〈纸〉straw pulp
【草芥】 cǎojiè trifle; mere nothing: 视如～ regard as worthless; treat like dirt
【草寇】 cǎokòu ①robbers in the greenwood ②bandits (a smear word applied by feudal rulers to peasant rebels)
【草兰】 cǎolán cymbidium; orchid
【草料】 cǎoliào forage; fodder
【草履虫】 cǎolǚchóng paramecium
【草绿】 cǎolǜ grass green
【草莽】 cǎomǎng ①a rank growth of grass ②uncultivated land; wilderness ◇ ～英雄 a hero of the bush; greenwood hero
【草帽】 cǎomào straw hat
【草帽缏】 cǎomàobiàn plaited straw (for making hats, baskets, etc.) 又作"草帽辫"
【草莓】 cǎoméi strawberry
【草木灰】 cǎomùhuī 〈农〉plant ash
【草木皆兵】 cǎo mù jiē bīng every bush and tree looks like an enemy — a state of extreme nervousness
【草木犀】 cǎomùxi 〈植〉sweet clover
【草拟】 cǎonǐ draw up; draft: ～一个计划 draft a plan
【草棚】 cǎopéng thatched shack; straw shed
【草皮】 cǎopí sod; turf
【草坪】 cǎopíng lawn
【草器】 cǎoqì 〈工美〉articles woven of straw; straw articles
【草签】 cǎoqiān initial: ～协定 initial an agreement
【草石蚕】 cǎoshícán 〈植〉Chinese artichoke (*Stachys sieboldii*)
【草食动物】 cǎoshí dòngwù plant-eating animal; herbivore
【草书】 cǎoshū (in Chinese calligraphy) characters executed swiftly and with strokes flowing together; cursive hand
【草率】 cǎoshuài careless; perfunctory; rash: 不宜～从事 should not take any hasty action
【草酸】 cǎosuān 〈化〉oxalic acid
【草体】 cǎotǐ ①见"草书" ②running hand
【草头王】 cǎotóuwang king of the bushes (a euphemism for bandit chief)
【草图】 cǎotú sketch (map); draft
【草席】 cǎoxí straw mat
【草鞋】 cǎoxié straw sandals: ～没样，边打边像。Straw sandals need no last; the shape comes with the weaving — work things out as you go along.
【草药】 cǎoyào medicinal herbs
【草鱼】 cǎoyú grass carp
【草原】 cǎoyuán grasslands; prairie
【草约】 cǎoyuē draft treaty; draft agreement; protocol
【草泽】 cǎozé grassy marsh; swamp
【草纸】 cǎozhǐ ①rough straw paper ②toilet paper
【草子】 cǎozǐ grass seed
【草字】 cǎozì a Chinese character written in the cursive hand

## cè

**册** cè ①volume; book: 这部书一共六～。This book is in six volumes./ 装订成～ bind into book form/ 画～ an album of paintings ②〈量〉copy: 这本书已销售十万～。100,000 copies of the book have been sold.
【册页】 cèyè an album of paintings or calligraphy
【册子】 cèzi book; volume: 小～ pamphlet; booklet; brochure

**厕** cè lavatory; toilet; washroom; W.C.: 公～ public lavatory/ 男～ men's (room, toilet)/ 女～ women's (room, toilet)
另见 si
【厕所】 cèsuǒ lavatory; toilet; W.C.

**侧** cè ①side: 左(右)～ the left (right) side/ 公路两～种着杨树。Poplars are planted on both sides of the highway. ②incline; lean: ～耳细听 incline the head and listen attentively; prick up one's ears/ ～着身子睡 sleep on one's side
【侧柏】 cèbǎi 〈植〉oriental arborvitae
【侧吹】 cèchuī 〈冶〉side-blown ◇ ～转炉 side-blown converter
【侧根】 cègēn 〈植〉lateral root

【侧航】 cèháng 〈航空〉 crabbing
【侧击】 cèjī flank attack
【侧记】 cèjì sidelights: 《出口商品交易会～》 *Sidelights on the Export Commodities Fair*
【侧力】 cèlì side (或 lateral) force
【侧门】 cèmén side door; side entrance
【侧面】 cèmiàn side; aspect; flank: 从～进攻敌人 make a flank attack on the enemy/ 从～了解 find out from indirect sources/ 这部小说反映了农村阶级斗争的一个～。The novel presents one aspect of the class struggle in the countryside. ◇ ～像 profile
【侧目】 cèmù sidelong glance: ～而视 look askance at sb. (with fear or indignation)
【侧身】 cèshēn on one's side; sideways: ～匍匐前进 crawl ahead on one's side
【侧石】 cèshí 〈交〉 curbstone; curb
【侧视图】 cèshìtú 〈机〉 side view
【侧手翻】 cèshǒufān 〈体〉 cartwheel; turn a cartwheel
【侧卫】 cèwèi 〈军〉 flank guard
【侧线】 cèxiàn ①〈铁道〉 siding ②〈动〉 lateral line
【侧旋】 cèxuán 〈乒乓球〉 sidespin
【侧压力】 cèyālì 〈物〉 lateral pressure
【侧芽】 cèyá 〈植〉 lateral bud
【侧翼】 cèyì 〈军〉 flank
【侧影】 cèyǐng silhouette; profile
【侧泳】 cèyǒng sidestroke
【侧重】 cèzhòng lay particular emphasis on: 他～抓宣传工作。His job is to pay particular attention to propaganda work.

**测** cè ① survey; fathom; measure: ～雨量 gauge (或 measure) rainfall/ 我国测绘工作者精确～得珠穆朗玛峰海拔高程为八千八百四十八点一三米。Chinese cartographers determined the exact height of Mount Qomolangma to be 8,848.13 metres above sea level. ② conjecture; infer: 变化莫～ unpredictable; constantly changing
【测程仪】 cèchéngyí 〈交〉 log
【测电笔】 cèdiànbǐ test pencil
【测定】 cèdìng determine: ～船只的方位 take a ship's bearings/ 放射性碳素～年代 radiocarbon dating/ 示踪～ tracer determination
【测度】 cèdù 〈数〉 measure
【测度】 cèduó estimate; infer: 根据风向～，今天不会下雨。Judging by the direction of the wind, it won't rain today.
【测风经纬仪】 cèfēng jīngwěiyí pilot balloon theodolite
【测风气球】 cèfēng qìqiú pilot balloon
【测杆】 cègān measuring staff; surveying rod
【测候】 cèhòu astronomical and meteorological observation ◇ ～网 〈气〉 reseau
【测绘】 cèhuì survey and drawing; mapping ◇ ～板 plotting board/ ～部队 mapping unit; topographic troops/ ～飞机 air-mapping plane/ ～员 surveyor; cartographer
【测井】 cèjǐng 〈石油〉 (well) logging: 井径～ caliper logging/ 电～ electric logging/ 放射性～ radioactivity logging
【测距】 cèjù range finding ◇ ～仪 range finder
【测力计】 cèlìjì 〈物〉 dynamometer
【测量】 cèliáng survey; measure; gauge: ～地形 survey the topography/ 大地～ geodetic survey/ 航空～ aerial survey; air survey
◇ ～队 survey party/ ～学 surveying/ ～仪表 instrumentation/ ～仪器 surveying instrument/ ～员 surveyor
【测漏】 cèlòu track down a leak; leak hunting
【测深仪】 cèshēnyí fathometer; depth-sounder; echo sounder
【测图摄影机】 cètú shèyǐngjī mapping camera
【测向计】 cèxiàngjì goniometer
【测斜仪】 cèxiéyí inclinometer
【测验】 cèyàn test: 算术～ arithmetic test (或 quiz)/ ～机械性能 test the performance of a machine
【测云气球】 cèyún qìqiú ceiling balloon
【测云器】 cèyúnqì 〈气〉 nephoscope
【测震学】 cèzhènxué seismometry
【测字】 cèzì fortune-telling by analysing the component parts of a Chinese character; glyphomancy

**恻** cè sorrowful; sad: 凄～ sad; grieved
【恻隐】 cèyǐn compassion; pity: ～之心 sense of pity

**策** cè ① plan; scheme; strategy: 决～ policy making ② whip: ～马前进 whip a horse on ③ bamboo or wooden slips used for writing on in ancient China ④ a type of essay in ancient China: ～论 discourse on politics
【策动】 cèdòng instigate; engineer; stir up: 阴谋～政变 plot to stage a *coup d'état*
【策反】 cèfǎn instigate rebellion within the enemy camp; incite defection
【策划】 cèhuà plan; plot; scheme; engineer: ～阴谋 hatch a plot/ 幕后～ plot behind the scenes
【策励】 cèlì encourage; spur on: 时时刻刻～自己 constantly spur oneself ahead
【策略】 cèlüè ① tactics: 研究对敌斗争的～ study the tactics of our struggle against the enemy ② tactful: 这个提法不～。It's not tactful to couch the statement in such terms.
【策应】 cèyìng 〈军〉 support by coordinated action
【策源地】 cèyuándì source; place of origin: 战争～ a source of war; a hotbed of war/ 北京是五四运动的～。Beijing was where the May 4th Movement started.

**筴** cè 见"竹筴鱼" zhúcèyú

## cēn

**参** cēn
另见 cān; shēn
【参差】 cēncī irregular; uneven: ～不齐 uneven; not uniform

## cén

**岑** cén ①〈书〉 high hill ② (Cén) a surname

**涔** cén 〈书〉 rainwater in puddles
【涔涔】 céncén 〈书〉 dripping; streaming: 汗～下 sweat streaming down; dripping with sweat

## céng

**层** céng ① layer; tier; stratum: 一～油漆 a coat of paint/ 一～薄冰 a thin sheet (或 layer) of ice ② storey; floor: 五～大楼 a five-storey building/ 我住在一～。I live on the ground floor (美: first floor)./ 他住在二～。He lives on the first floor (美: second floor). ③ a component part in a sequence: 他这话还有一～意思。What he said has further implications.
【层层】 céngcéng layer upon layer; ring upon ring; tier upon tier: ～梯田 tier upon tier of terraced fields/ ～包围 surround ring upon ring/ ～设防 set up successive lines of defence; erect defensive works in depth/ ～把关 check at each level

【层出不穷】 céng chū bù qióng emerge in an endless stream: 社会主义新生事物～。Newborn socialist things are emerging one after another.
【层次】 céngcì ① administrative levels: 减少～，精简人员 simplify the administrative structure and reduce the staff ② arrangement of ideas (in writing or speech): 这篇文章～不清。This article lacks unity and coherence.
【层见迭出】 céngjiàn-diéchū occur frequently; appear repeatedly
【层理】 cénglǐ ‹地› bedding; stratification
【层峦迭嶂】 céngluán-diézhàng peaks rising one higher than another
【层压】 céngyā ‹化› lamination: ～玻璃 laminated glass
【层云】 céngyún ‹气› stratus
【层子】 céngzǐ ‹物› straton: ～模型 straton model

**曾** céng ‹副›〔表示有过某些行为或情况〕: 几年前我～见过她一面。I met her once several years ago./ 我未～听说过这样的事。I've never heard of such a thing.
另见 zēng
【曾几何时】 céng jǐ hé shí before long; not long after: 猖獗一时的反革命匪帮，～，遭到了彻底覆灭。The counterrevolutionary gang was on the rampage for a time, but before long it was completely overthrown.
【曾经】 céngjīng ‹副›〔表示有过某些行为或情况〕: 她～参加过石油大会战。She has taken part in a major battle for oil./ 这顶军帽是他爸爸长征时～戴过的。This army cap was worn by his father on the Long March.
【曾经沧海】 céng jīng cānghǎi have sailed the seven seas; have experienced great things; have seen much of the world: ～难为水。To a sophisticated person there is nothing new under the sun.

## cèng

**蹭** cèng ① rub: 把手～破了 have the skin rubbed off one's hand ② be smeared with: 小心～油漆。Mind the fresh paint. ③ dillydally; loiter: 磨～ dawdle; dillydally/ 你走这么慢，哪辈子才能～到家呀？You'll never get home if you drag along like this./ 一点点往前～ inch one's way forward
【蹭蹬】 cèngdèng ‹书› meet with setbacks; be down on one's luck

## chā

**叉** chā ① fork: 钢～ (steel) fork/ 干草～ hayfork; pitchfork/ 餐～ (table) fork ② work with a fork; fork: ～草上垛 fork hay onto a stack/ ～鱼 spear fish ③ cross: 在每个错别字上打个～ put a cross above each wrongly written word
另见 chá; chǎ
【叉丝】 chāsī ‹物› cross hair; spider line
【叉腰】 chāyāo akimbo: 双手～ with arms akimbo
【叉子】 chāzi fork: 粪～ dung fork

**杈** chā wooden fork; hayfork; pitchfork
另见 chà

**差** chā ① difference; dissimilarity: 时～ time difference ② mistake: 偏～ deviation ③ ‹数› difference
另见 chà; chāi; cī
【差别】 chābié difference; disparity: 年龄～ disparity in age/ 数(质)量上的～ quantitative (qualitative) difference/ 二者之间～很大。There is a world of difference between the two. ◇ ～关税 differential rates of duty; differential duties/ ～阈限‹心› difference limen (或 threshold)
【差错】 chācuò ① mistake; error; slip: 工作认真负责，就会少出～。If we work conscientiously, we won't make many mistakes./ 这笔账目里有～。There's an accounting error in this entry./ 几个月来这部机器一直运转正常，没有出过～。This machine has been running without a hitch for months. ② mishap; accident: 万一这孩子出了～怎么办？What if anything should happen to the child?
【差动】 chādòng ‹机› differential ◇ ～齿轮 differential gear/ ～滑轮 differential pulley
【差额】 chā'é difference; balance; margin: 补足～ make up the balance (或 difference)
【差价】 chājià price difference: 地区～ regional price differences/ 季节～ seasonal price differences ◇ ～关税 variable import levy
【差距】 chājù ① gap; disparity: 比大庆，找～。Let's compare ourselves with Daqing and see where we lag behind./ 在成绩面前找～。Try to find out where you fall short when you have achieved success./ 我们和先进单位比还有很大的～。Compared with advanced units, we still have a long way to go. ② ‹机› difference: 测定工件与设计标准之间的～ measure the difference between the workpiece and the designed standard
【差强人意】 chā qiáng rényì just passable
【差异】 chāyì difference; divergence; discrepancy; diversity: 这两个地区气候～很大。These two regions differ greatly in climate.
【差之毫厘，谬以千里】 chā zhī háolí, miù yǐ qiānlǐ an error the breadth of a single hair can lead you a thousand *li* astray 又作"差之毫厘，失之千里"

**插** chā ① stick in; insert: 把插头～上 insert the plug in a socket; plug in/ 把双手～在口袋里 put one's hands in one's pockets/ 把门～上 bolt the door/ 山峰高～入云 peaks penetrating into the clouds/ 把红旗～上峰顶 plant a red flag on the mountain top/ 似尖刀直～敌人心脏 like a dagger stuck into the enemy's heart ② interpose; insert: 这本书再版时～入了新的一章。A new chapter is included in the second edition./ 他说个没完，别人半句话也～不进。He talked on and on and nobody else could get a word in edgeways.
【插班】 chābān join a class in the middle of the course
【插翅难飞】 chā chì nán fēi unable to escape even if given wings
【插床】 chāchuáng ‹机› slotting machine; slotter: 齿轮～ gear slotter
【插刀】 chādāo ‹机› slotting tool
【插队】 chāduì go to live and work in a production team: ～锻炼 work in a production team to temper oneself ◇ ～知识青年 a school graduate who has gone to live and work in the countryside
【插队落户】 chāduì-luòhù go and settle in the countryside
【插管】 chāguǎn ‹医› intubate ◇ ～法 intubation
【插花地】 chāhuādì land belonging to one production unit but enclosed in that of another
【插话】 chāhuà ① interpose (a remark, etc.); chip in: 这时老张插了话，补充了一些新例子。At this point Lao Zhang chipped in with some fresh examples./ 支书的发言和大队长的～都很鼓舞人心。The Party branch secretary's speech and the occasional remarks added by the brigade leader were both very inspiring. ② digression; episode: 这一段～使她的报告生动多了。This digression added to the liveli-

ness of her talk.
【插科打诨】 chākē-dǎhùn ①(of an actor) make impromptu comic gestures and remarks ②jesting; buffoonery
【插口】 chākǒu 〈电〉 socket; jack
【插屏】 chāpíng 〈工美〉 table plaque
【插曲】 chāqǔ ①〈乐〉 interlude ②songs in a film or play ③episode; interlude: 双方谈判中的一个～ an episode in the negotiations between the two parties
【插入】 chārù ①insert ②〈电〉 plug in: ～部件 plug-in unit
【插入语】 chārùyǔ 〈语〉 parenthesis
【插身】 chāshēn ①squeeze in; edge in: 很难～ difficult to squeeze in ②take part in; get involved in: 他不想～在这场纠纷中间。 He doesn't want to get involved in this dispute. 或 He's trying to keep out of this quarrel.
【插手】 chāshǒu ①take part; lend a hand: 人够多了，您就不用～了。You don't have to join in, there are more than enough people on the job already./ 想帮忙又插不上手 be ready to help but not know how to ②have a hand in; poke one's nose into; meddle in: 想不到她会插上一手。We never thought she would poke her nose into this.
【插条】 chātiáo 〈植〉 ①transplant a cutting ②cutting
【插头】 chātóu 〈电〉 plug: 三脚～ three-pin plug
【插图】 chātú illustration; plate: 书中有几幅彩色～。The book has several colour plates. ◇ ～本 illustrated edition
【插销】 chāxiāo ①bolt (for a door, window, etc.) ②〈电〉 plug
【插叙】 chāxù narration interspersed with flashbacks
【插秧】 chāyāng transplant rice seedlings (或 shoots) ◇～机 rice transplanter
【插页】 chāyè inset; insert
【插足】 chāzú ①put one's foot in: 这儿几乎没有～的地方。There's not even standing room. ②participate (in some activity)
【插嘴】 chāzuǐ interrupt; chip in: 插不上嘴 cannot get a word in edgeways
【插座】 chāzuò 〈电〉 socket; outlet: 弹簧～ cushion socket

## 喳

chā
另见 zhā
【喳喳】 chāchā whispering sound
【喳喳】 chācha whisper: 她在她妈妈耳边～了两句。 She whispered a few words in her mother's ear.

## 馇

chā cook and stir: ～猪食 cook and stir feed for pigs

## 锸

chā spade

## 嚓

chā 见"咯嚓" kāchā; "啪嚓" pāchā
另见 cā

# chá

## 叉

chá 〈方〉block up; jam: 游行队伍把路口全都～住了。Traffic was completely held up by the procession (或 paraders).
另见 chā; chǎ

## 茬

chá ①stubble: 麦～ wheat stubble ②crop; batch: 二～韭菜 the second crop of Chinese chives/ 换～ change crops/ 这块菜地一年种几～? How many crops can this vegetable plot produce a year?/ 又一～新干部成长起来了。Still another batch of new cadres has matured.
【茬口】 chákǒu ①crops for rotation: 选好～，实行合理轮作 select the right crops and rotate them rationally ②soil on which a crop has been planted and harvested:西红柿～壮，种白菜挺合适。A crop of tomatoes enriches the soil and makes it suitable for growing cabbage.

## 茶

chá ①tea: 沏～ make tea/ 浓(淡)～ strong (weak) tea/ 红(绿)～ black (green) tea ②certain kinds of drink or liquid food: 杏仁～ almond paste
【茶杯】 chábēi teacup
【茶场】 cháchǎng tea plantation
【茶匙】 cháchí teaspoon
【茶炊】 cháchuī tea-urn
【茶底儿】 chádǐr tea dregs
【茶点】 chádiǎn tea and pastries; refreshments
【茶碟儿】 chádiér saucer
【茶房】 cháfáng 〈旧〉 waiter; steward
【茶缸子】 chágāngzi mug
【茶馆】 cháguǎn teahouse
【茶褐色】 cháhèsè dark brown
【茶壶】 cháhú teapot
【茶花】 cháhuā camellia
【茶话会】 cháhuàhuì tea party
【茶会】 cháhuì tea party
【茶几】 chájī tea table; teapoy; side table
【茶巾】 chájīn tea cloth
【茶晶】 chájīng citrine; yellow quartz
【茶具】 chájù tea set; tea-things; tea service
【茶卤儿】 chálǔr strong tea (to be diluted before drinking)
【茶末】 chámò tea dust
【茶农】 chánóng tea grower
【茶盘】 chápán tea tray; teaboard
【茶钱】 cháqian ①payment for tea (in a teahouse) ②〈旧〉 tip
【茶色】 chásè dark brown
【茶食】 cháshi cakes and sweetmeats
【茶树】 cháshù tea tree
【茶水】 cháshuì tea or boiled water (supplied to walkers, trippers, etc.) ◇ ～站 tea-stall
【茶亭】 chátíng tea-booth; tea-stall; tea-kiosk
【茶托】 chátuō saucer
【茶碗】 cháwǎn teacup
【茶味儿】 cháwèir tea flavour: 这种茶冲两次～才出来。The flavour of this kind of tea doesn't come out till after the second watering.
【茶锈】 cháxiù tea stain
【茶叶】 cháyè tea; tea-leaves: 买二两～ buy two *liang* of tea/ 把茶壶里的～倒掉 empty the old tea-leaves out of the pot ◇ ～罐 tea caddy; canister
【茶油】 cháyóu tea-seed oil; tea oil
【茶余酒后】 cháyú-jiǔhòu over a cup of tea or after a few glasses of wine — at one's leisure
【茶园】 cháyuán ①tea plantation ②a place where tea and soft drinks are served; tea garden
【茶砖】 cházhuān brick tea
【茶座】 cházuò ①teahouse ②seats in a teahouse or tea garden

## 查

chá ①check; examine: ～卫生 make a public health and sanitation check (或 inspection)/ ～血 have a blood test ②look into; investigate: ～一～事故的原因 find out the cause of an accident/ ～个水落石出 get to the bottom of a matter; investigate sth. thoroughly ③look up; consult: ～字典 look up a word in the dictionary; consult a dictionary/ ～资料 read up the literature (on a special

subject)/ ～档案 look into the archives
另见 zhā

【查办】 chábàn investigate and deal with accordingly: 撤职～ dismiss a person and have him prosecuted

【查抄】 cháchāo make an inventory of a criminal's possessions and confiscate them

【查点】 chádiǎn check the number or amount of; make an inventory of: ～人数 check the number of people present; check the attendance/ ～存货 make an inventory of the goods in stock; take stock

【查对】 cháduì check; verify: ～材料 check the data/ ～原文 check against the original (text, manuscript, etc.)/ ～数字 verify the figures/ ～无误 examined and found correct; verified

【查房】 cháfáng (of doctors) make (或 go) the rounds of the wards

【查访】 cháfǎng go around and make inquiries; investigate: 经过公安人员到处～，他终于和失散多年的亲人重新团聚了。Thanks to the security personnel going around and making inquiries, he was at long last reunited with his family.

【查封】 cháfēng seal up; close down: ～伪政府大楼 seal up the office building of the puppet government/ ～敌产 seal up and confiscate enemy property/ 反动派常常以莫须有的罪名～进步报社。The reactionaries often close down progressive newspapers on false charges.

【查号台】 cháhàotái 〈讯〉 directory inquiries; information

【查户口】 chá hùkǒu check residence cards; check on household occupants

【查获】 cháhuò hunt down and seize; ferret out; track down: ～一部敌人的秘密电台 discover and seize a secret enemy transmitter/ ～逃犯 track down a fugitive criminal

【查禁】 chájìn ban; prohibit

【查究】 chájiū investigate and ascertain (cause, responsibility, etc.): ～责任 find out who should be held responsible

【查勘】 chákān survey; prospect: ～地界 survey the boundaries of a piece of land/ ～矿产资源 prospect for mineral deposits

【查看】 chákàn look over; examine: ～帐目 examine the accounts/ ～水情 look into the water (或 flood) situation/ ～机器运转的情况 see how the machine is working

【查考】 chákǎo examine; do research on; try to ascertain: ～中国古时有关地震的全部文献 study all available literature about earthquakes in ancient China/ ～一批新出土文物的年代 try to ascertain the date of a new lot of unearthed relics

【查明】 chámíng prove through investigation; find out; ascertain: ～事实真相 find out the truth; ascertain the facts/ 现已～ it has been established that; investigation reveals that

【查票】 chápiào examine (或 check) tickets

【查铺】 chápù 〈军〉 go the rounds of the beds at night; bed check: 干部坚持～制度。The officers make it a regular practice to go the rounds of the men's beds at night.

【查讫】 cháqì checked

【查清】 cháqīng make a thorough investigation of; check up on: ～某人的来历 find out sb.'s background; check up on sb./ ～一件事情的来龙去脉 find out how sth. started and developed

【查哨】 cháshào 〈军〉 go the rounds of guard posts; inspect the sentries

【查收】 cháshōu 〔多用于书信〕 please find: 寄上样品两种，请～。Please find two samples enclosed herewith.

【查税】 cháshuì tax inspection

【查问】 cháwèn question; interrogate: ～证人 interrogate a witness/ ～口令 challenge (for a password)

【查无实据】 chá wú shíjù investigation reveals no evidence (against the suspect)

【查询】 cháxún inquire about: ～地址 inquire sb.'s address/ ～行李下落 inquire about (the whereabouts of) the luggage

【查验】 cháyàn check; examine: ～护照 examine a passport

【查夜】 cháyè ① go the rounds at night ② night patrol

【查阅】 cháyuè consult; look up: ～技术资料 consult technical data; look up technical literature

【查帐】 cházhàng check (或 audit, examine) accounts

【查照】 cházhào 〔旧时公文用语〕 please note: 希～办理。Please note and take appropriate action.

【查证】 cházhèng investigate and verify; check: ～属实 be checked and found to be true; be verified

**搽** chá put (powder, ointment, etc.) on the skin; apply: ～雪花膏 put on vanishing cream/ ～药 apply ointment, lotion, etc./ ～粉 powder

**楂** chá ① short, bristly hair or beard; stubble: 胡子～ a stubbly beard ② 见"茬" chá
另见 zhā

**槎** chá ①〈书〉 raft ② 见"茬" chá

**察** chá examine; look into; scrutinize: ～其言，观其行 examine his words and watch his deeds; check what he says against what he does

【察觉】 chájué be conscious of; become aware of; perceive: ～到反革命分子的阴谋 discover the plot of the counterrevolutionaries/ 开始我没有～到他有病。At first I wasn't aware that he was ill.

【察看】 chákàn watch; look carefully at; observe: ～风向 watch which way the wind is blowing/ ～地形 survey the terrain/ ～杀虫药的治虫效果 check the effectiveness of the insecticide/ ～四周的动静 peer in all directions to see if anything is afoot/ 支书仔细～了庄稼的生长情况。The Party branch secretary looked carefully to see how the crops were coming along.

【察言观色】 cháyán-guānsè carefully weigh up a person's words and closely watch his expression; watch a person's every mood

**碴** chá 〈方〉 be cut (by broken glass, china, etc.): 小心别让碎玻璃～了手！Mind you don't cut yourself on the broken glass!

【碴儿】 chár ① broken pieces; fragments: 冰～ small pieces of ice/ 玻璃～ fragments of glass ② sharp edge of broken glass, china, etc.: 碗～ the sharp edge of a broken bowl ③ the cause of a quarrel; quarrel: 找～打架 pick a quarrel (with sb.) ④ sth. just said or mentioned: 答～ make a reply/ 接不上～ cannot take the cue

**檫** chá sassafras

## chǎ

**叉** chǎ part so as to form a fork; fork: ～着腿站着 stand with one's legs apart
另见 chā; chá

**杈** chǎ 见"裤衩" kùchǎ
另见 chà

**踏** chǎ trudge (in mud, snow, etc.) 我的鞋都～湿了。My shoes got soaked as I trudged along.

**镲** chǎ 〈乐〉 small cymbals

## chà

**汊** chà branch of a river

**杈** chà branch (of a tree)
另见 chā

【杈子】 chàzi branch: 树～ a branch of a tree

**岔** chà ① branch off; fork: 这条路过了桥就分～了。The road forks on the other side of the bridge./ ～路 branch road/ 三～路口 a fork in the road; a junction of three roads ② turn off: 自行车下了公路～上了小道。The cyclist turned off the highway onto a side road. ③ 见"岔子"

【岔开】 chàkāi ① branch off; diverge: 线路在这儿～了。The line branches here. ② diverge to (another topic); change (the subject of conversation): 两个人正要争吵,我给～了。A quarrel was starting between the two of them, but I headed it off. ③ stagger: 把休假日～ stagger the days of rest

【岔口】 chàkǒu fork (in a road): 他们把他送到～。They saw him to a fork in the road.

【岔路】 chàlù branch road; byroad; side road 又作"岔道儿"

【岔气】 chàqì feel a pain in the chest when breathing

【岔子】 chàzi ① accident; trouble: 拖拉机出了什么～? What's wrong with the tractor?/ 他开了好几年卡车,从没有出过～。He has been driving a truck for years and never had an accident./ 你放心吧,出不了～。Don't worry, everything will be all right. ② 见"岔路"

**诧** chà be surprised

【诧异】 chàyì be surprised; be astonished: ～的神色 a surprised look/ 听了这个突如其来的消息,我们都十分～。We were all astonished at the unexpected news.

**衩** chà vent (或 slit) in the sides of a garment
另见 chǎ

**刹** chà Buddhist temple (或 monastery)
另见 shā

【刹地利】 Chàdìlì Kshatriya

【刹那】 chànà instant; split second: 一～ in an instant; in a flash; in the twinkling of an eye

**姹** chà 〈书〉 beautiful

【姹紫嫣红】 chàzǐ-yānhóng brilliant purples and reds — beautiful flowers: 公园里～,十分绚丽。With lovely flowers everywhere, the park is a blaze of colour.

**差** chà ① differ from; fall short of: 我们离党的要求还～得远。We still fall far short of what the Party expects of us. ② wrong: 这你可说～了。You're wrong there. ③ wanting; short of: 一个月～两天 two days less than a month/ ～七天不到一年 seven days short of a year/ ～十分四点 ten (minutes) to four/ ～两个人 two people short/ 我还～你两块钱。I still owe you two *yuan*./ 还～一道工序。There's still one more step in the process./ 木料还～多少?——～不了多少了。How much more timber is needed? — Not much. ④ not up to standard; poor: 成绩不算太～。The results are by no means poor./ 这个街道工厂设备～,可是产品并不～。The neighbourhood factory's equipment is not up to much, but its products are not at all bad.
另见 chā; chāi; cī

【差不多】 chàbuduō ① almost; nearly: ～五点了。It's nearly five o'clock./ 她离开延安～三十年了。It's almost thirty years since she left Yan'an./ 这座大楼～快完工了。The building is nearing completion. ② about the same; similar: 他们俩高矮～。They two are about the same height./ 这两种观点～。These two views are similar. ③ just about right (或 enough); not far off; not bad: 我们应该力争上游,而不应该有"～"的思想。We should aim high and not think "That's good enough".

【差不多的】 chàbuduōde the average person: 这包大米二百斤重,～还扛不起来。This sack of rice weighs 200 *jin*; no ordinary person can carry it.

【差不离】 chàbulí 见"差不多"

【差点儿】 chàdiǎnr ① not quite up to the mark; not good enough: 她的技术还～。Her technique is not quite up to the mark./ 这块布质量挺好,就是颜色～。The quality of this cloth is fine, but the colour is not quite right. 或 The cloth is quite good except for the colour. ② 〈副〉〔表示某种事情接近实现或勉强实现〕 almost; nearly; on the verge of: ～没赶上车 very nearly miss the bus/ 这盘棋他～赢了。He nearly won the chess game./ ～(没)哭出来 be on the verge of tears/ ～(没)触电 narrowly escape getting a shock

【差劲】 chàjìn no good; disappointing: 这条路坑坑洼洼的,太～了。The road is no good, it's rough and full of holes./ 真～,麦子刚上场就下起雨来了! Too bad! We'd just got the wheat to the threshing ground when it started to rain.

## chāi

**拆** chāi ① tear open; take apart: ～信 open a letter/ ～机器 disassemble a machine; take a machine apart; strip a machine/ 把这个组～了 break up the group ② pull down; dismantle: ～房子 pull down a house/ ～桥 dismantle a bridge/ ～帐篷 strike tents/ 把旧毛衣～了重新织一下 unravel an old sweater and reknit it
另见 cā

【拆除】 chāichú demolish; dismantle; remove: ～城墙 remove (或 demolish) a city wall/ ～障碍物 remove obstacles/ ～军事基地 dismantle military bases

【拆穿】 chāichuān expose; unmask: ～骗局 expose a fraud/ ～西洋镜 strip off the camouflage; expose sb.'s tricks

【拆东墙,补西墙】 chāi dōngqiáng, bǔ xīqiáng tear down the east wall to repair the west wall — resort to a makeshift solution

【拆毁】 chāihuǐ demolish; pull down: 侵略军强行～民房。The invading troops tore down the people's houses.

【拆伙】 chāihuǒ dissolve a partnership; part company

【拆开】 chāikāi take apart; open; separate: 把机器～ disassemble a machine/ 这两个字构成一个词,不能～。The two characters form a single word, they cannot be separated./ 他能摸着黑儿把机枪～再装上。He can strip and reassemble a machine gun in the dark.

【拆模】 chāimú 〈建〉 form removal; form stripping

【拆墙脚】 chāi qiángjiǎo undermine; pull away a prop: 投机倒把是拆社会主义的墙脚。Speculation undermines socialism.

【拆散】 chāisǎn break (a set): 这些家具是一整套,别～了。These pieces of furniture belong together. Don't break the set.

【拆散】 chāisàn break up (a marriage, family, etc.)

【拆台】 chāitái cut the ground (或 pull the rug) from under sb.'s feet; pull away a prop: 工作要互相支持，不要互相～。Our work calls for mutual support. We shouldn't counteract each other's efforts./ 你一定来，可别拆我的台。Be sure to come. Don't let me down.

【拆息】 chāixī a daily interest rate on private loans or deposits

【拆洗】 chāixǐ ① wash (padded coats, quilts, etc.) after removing the padding or lining; unpick and wash ② strip and clean: ～打字机 strip and clean a typewriter

【拆线】 chāixiàn 〈医〉 take out stitches

【拆卸】 chāixiè dismantle; disassemble; dismount

【拆字】 chāizì 见"测字" cèzì

**钗** chāi hairpin (formerly worn by women for adornment)

**差** chāi ① send on an errand; dispatch: ～人去送封信 send a letter by messenger/ ～他去办件事 send (或 dispatch) him on an errand/ 因公出～ be away on official business ② errand; job: 兼～ hold more than one job concurrently

另见 chā; chà; cī

【差遣】 chāiqiǎn send sb. on an errand or mission; dispatch; assign: 听候～ await assignment; be at sb.'s disposal

【差使】 chāishǐ send; assign; appoint

【差使】 chāishi 〈旧〉 official post; billet; commission

【差事】 chāishi ① errand; assignment: 给你们一件～。Here's a job for you. ② 见"差使" chāishi

【差役】 chāiyì 〈旧〉 ① corvée ② runner or bailiff in a feudal *yamen*

## chái

**侪** chái 〈书〉 fellows; associates: 吾～ we; people like us

**柴** chái ① firewood ② (Chái) a surname

【柴草】 cháicǎo firewood; faggot

【柴胡】 cháihú 〈中药〉 the root of Chinese thorowax (*Bupleurum chinense*)

【柴火】 cháihuo firewood; faggot

【柴米油盐】 chái-mǐ-yóu-yán fuel, rice, oil and salt — chief daily necessities

【柴油】 cháiyóu diesel oil ◇ ～机车 diesel locomotive

【柴油机】 cháiyóujī diesel engine: 船用～ marine diesel engine/ 陆用～ stationary diesel engine

**豺** chái jackal

【豺狼】 cháiláng jackals and wolves — cruel and evil people: 在那～当道的旧社会，劳动人民生活在水深火热之中。In the old society, jackals and wolves held sway and the working people lived in utter misery.

【豺狼成性】 cháiláng chéng xìng wolfish; rapacious and ruthless

## chǎi

**踹** chǎi ground beans or maize

## chài

**虿** chài ancient name for a kind of scorpion

**瘥** chài 〈书〉 be recovered: 久病初～ have just recovered from a long illness

## chān

**觇** chān 〈书〉 observe; survey

【觇标】 chānbiāo 〈测〉 surveyor's beacon

**搀** chān ① help by the arm; support sb. with one's hand: 把老大娘～进屋 help the old lady into the room/ ～着他点。Help him along. ② mix: 往沙子里～石灰 mix lime into sand/ 油和水～不到一块儿。Oil and water do not mix.

【搀扶】 chānfú support sb. with one's hand

【搀和】 chānhuo mix: 细粮粗粮～着吃 have a mixed diet of fine and coarse grain

【搀假】 chānjiǎ adulterate

【搀杂】 chānzá mix; mingle: 别把这两种菜籽～在一起。Don't mix up the two kinds of vegetable seeds.

## chán

**单** chán

另见 dān; Shàn

【单于】 chányú chief of the Xiongnu (匈奴) in ancient China

**婵** chán

【婵娟】 chánjuān 〈书〉 ① lovely (used in ancient writings to describe women) ② the moon

**谗** chán slander; backbite

【谗害】 chánhài calumniate or slander sb. in order to have him persecuted; frame sb. up

【谗言】 chányán slanderous talk; calumny

**馋** chán greedy; gluttonous: 嘴～ greedy; fond of good food/ 看见下棋他就～得慌。His fingers itch at the sight of a game of chess.

【馋涎欲滴】 chánxián yù dī mouth drooling with greed: 使他～ make his mouth water

【馋嘴】 chánzuǐ gluttonous

**孱** chán frail; weak

另见 càn

【孱弱】 chánruò frail (of physique); delicate (in health)

**禅** chán 〈佛教〉 ① prolonged and intense contemplation; deep meditation; dhyana: 坐～ sit in meditation ② Buddhist: ～堂 a room in a Buddhist monastery set apart for meditation; meditation room/ ～杖 Buddhist monk's staff

另见 shàn

【禅机】 chánjī Buddhist allegorical word or gesture

【禅林】 chánlín Buddhist temple

【禅师】 chánshī honorific title for a Buddhist monk

【禅宗】 chánzōng the Chan sect; Dhyana; Zen

**缠** chán ①twine; wind: ～线轴 wind thread onto a reel/ 他手上～着绷带。His hand was bandaged. ②tangle; tie up; pester: 这两股线～在一起了。The two threads got tangled up./ 他被事情～住了，没能来。He couldn't come because he was tied up./ 她～住指导员不放，要求参加战斗。She kept pestering the political instructor to let her join in the battle./ 干吗老～着我？Why do you keep worrying me? ③〈方〉deal with: 这人真难～。This fellow is really hard to deal with.

【缠绵】chánmián ①lingering: ～病榻 be bedridden with a lingering disease/ 乡思～ be tormented by nostalgia ②touching; moving

【缠绵悱恻】chánmián-fěicè (of writing) exceedingly sentimental

【缠绕】chánrǎo ①twine; bind; wind: 大树上～着藤萝。There is a wisteria twining round the big tree. ②worry; harass ◇ ～植物 twining plant; twiner

【缠手】chánshǒu troublesome; hard to deal with: 这件事有些～。That's a rather troublesome matter./ 这病真～。This is a very difficult case.

【缠足】chánzú foot-binding

**蝉** chán cicada

【蝉联】chánlián continue to hold a post or title: 多次～全国冠军 win the national championship several times running

【蝉蜕】chántuì〈中药〉cicada slough

【蝉翼】chányì cicada's wings: 薄如～的轻纱 gauze as thin as a cicada's wings ◇ ～纱〈纺〉organdie

**廛** chán ①ancient name for ground allotted to a household ②a market place

**潺** chán

【潺潺】chánchán〈象〉murmur; babble; purl: ～流水 a murmuring stream

【潺湲】chányuán〈书〉flow slowly: 秋水～。Gently flow the autumn streams.

**蟾** chán

【蟾蜍】chánchú〈书〉①toad ②the fabled toad in the moon ③the moon

【蟾宫】chángōng〈书〉the moon

【蟾酥】chánsū〈中药〉the dried venom of toads; toad-cake

**巉** chán〈书〉dangerously steep; precipitous

## chǎn

**产** chǎn ①give birth to; be delivered of: 助～ midwifery/ 熊猫每胎～仔一、二只。Pandas have only one or two young at a birth. ②produce; yield: ～油 produce oil; oil-producing/ ～棉区 cotton-producing area/ 水稻亩～超千斤。The per *mu* yield of rice is over 1,000 *jin*. ③product; produce: 土特～ local and special products ④property; estate: 房地～ real estate; real property/ 家～ family possessions

【产蛋鸡】chǎndànjī laying hen; layer

【产地】chǎndì place of production (或 origin); producing area: 甘蔗～ a sugarcane growing area/ 原料～ sources of raw materials/ 金丝猴～ the native haunt of the golden monkey ◇ ～证明书 certificate of origin

【产犊】chǎndú〈牧〉calving

【产儿】chǎn'ér newborn baby

【产房】chǎnfáng delivery room

【产妇】chǎnfù lying-in woman

【产羔】chǎngāo〈牧〉lambing; kidding

【产后】chǎnhòu postpartum ◇ ～出血〈医〉postpartum haemorrhage

【产假】chǎnjià maternity leave

【产驹】chǎnjū〈牧〉foaling

【产科】chǎnkē ①obstetrical (或 maternity) department ②obstetrics

◇ ～病房 obstetrical (或 maternity) ward/ ～学 obstetrics/ ～医生 obstetrician/ ～医院 maternity (或 lying-in) hospital

【产量】chǎnliàng output; yield: 煤～ output of coal/ 亩～ per *mu* yield

【产卵】chǎnluǎn (鸟、家禽) lay eggs; (鱼、蛙) spawn; (昆虫) oviposit

【产品】chǎnpǐn product; produce: 农～ farm produce/ 畜～ livestock products/ 工业～ industrial products

【产前】chǎnqián antenatal: ～检查 antenatal examination

【产钳】chǎnqián〈医〉obstetric forceps

【产权】chǎnquán property right ◇ ～要求 property claim

【产褥期】chǎnrùqī〈医〉puerperium

【产褥热】chǎnrùrè〈医〉puerperal fever

【产生】chǎnshēng ①produce; engender: ～好的结果 produce good results/ ～很大的影响 exert a great influence/ 实践使我们的认识～了新的飞跃。Practice brings about a new leap in our knowledge. ②emerge; come into being: 现代战争～于帝国主义。Modern war is born of imperialism./ 正确的路线是在斗争中～和发展起来的。A correct line emerges and develops only in the course of struggle./ 革命事业的接班人，是在群众斗争中～的。Successors to the revolutionary cause of the proletariat come forward in mass struggles.

【产物】chǎnwù outcome; result; product: 经济危机是资本主义制度的必然～。Economic crises are an inevitable outcome of capitalism./ 这个方案是领导意见和群众意见相结合的～。This plan is the result of combining the ideas of the leadership with those of the masses.

【产销】chǎn-xiāo production and marketing: ～平衡 coordination of production and marketing/ ～两旺。Both production and marketing thrive./ ～直接挂钩 direct contact between the producing and marketing departments

【产业】chǎnyè ①estate; property ②industrial ◇ ～革命 the Industrial Revolution/ ～工人 industrial worker/ ～后备军 industrial reserve army; reserve army of labour

【产值】chǎnzhí value of output; output value

【产仔】chǎnzǐ〈牧〉farrowing

**谄** chǎn flatter; fawn on

【谄媚】chǎnmèi flatter; fawn on; toady

【谄上欺下】chǎnshàng-qīxià be servile to one's superiors and tyrannical to one's subordinates; fawn on those above and bully those below

【谄笑】chǎnxiào ingratiating smile

【谄谀】chǎnyú flatter

**铲** chǎn ①shovel: 煤～ coal shovel/ 锅～ slice ②lift or move with a shovel; shovel: ～煤 shovel coal/ 把地～平 scrape the ground even; level the ground with a shovel or spade

【铲车】chǎnchē〈机〉forklift (truck)

【铲齿车床】chǎnchǐ chēchuáng relieving lathe; backing-off lathe

【铲除】 chǎnchú root out; uproot; eradicate: ～毒草 uproot poisonous weeds
【铲运机】 chǎnyùnjī scraper; carry-scraper
【铲子】 chǎnzi shovel

## 阐

chǎn explain
【阐发】 chǎnfā elucidate: 这篇文章～了普及大寨县的意义。This article elucidates the significance of building Dazhai-type counties all over the country.
【阐明】 chǎnmíng expound; clarify: 精辟地～社会发展规律 brilliantly expound the laws of social development/ ～观点 clarify one's views/ 支持声明中所～的正义立场 support the just stand expounded in the statement
【阐释】 chǎnshì explain; expound; interpret: 她对各项规定作了明确的～。She gave a clear explanation of each of the rules and regulations.
【阐述】 chǎnshù expound; elaborate; set forth: 各方～了自己对这一问题的立场。Each side set forth its position on this question./ 对辩证唯物主义进行系统的～ make a systematic exposition of dialectical materialism/ ～人民群众在历史上的伟大作用 expound the great role played in history by the masses of the people
【阐扬】 chǎnyáng expound and propagate

## 蒇

chǎn 〈书〉 finish; complete: ～事 have finished the work; be through with the job

# chàn

## 忏

chàn repent
【忏悔】 chànhuǐ ① repent; be penitent ②〈宗〉 confess (one's sins)

## 颤

chàn quiver; tremble; vibrate: 他激动得说话声音都发～了。He was so overcome with emotion that his voice quivered.
另见 zhàn
【颤动】 chàndòng vibrate; quiver: 声带～ vibration of the vocal chords/ 树叶在微风中～。The leaves quivered in the breeze.
【颤抖】 chàndǒu shake; tremble; quiver; shiver: 冻得全身～ shiver all over with cold/ 吓得两腿～ shake in one's shoes
【颤巍巍】 chànwēiwēi tottering; faltering: 控诉会上老贫农～地走上台去。The old poor peasant went tottering onto the platform at the accusation meeting.
【颤音】 chànyīn ①〈语〉 trill ②〈乐〉 trill; shake: 逆～ inverted trill
【颤悠】 chànyou shake; quiver; flicker: ～的灯光 a flickering light/ 这块桥板直～。This board on the bridge is shaky./ 他挑起担子～～地走了。He shouldered the loaded carrying pole and walked off with a swing.

## 韂

chàn 见"鞍韂" ānchàn

# chāng

## 伥

chāng 见"为虎作伥" wèi hǔ zuò chāng

## 昌

chāng prosperous; flourishing
【昌明】 chāngmíng flourishing; thriving; well-developed: 科学～。Science is flourishing.
【昌盛】 chāngshèng prosperous: 建设一个繁荣～的社会主义国家 build a prosperous socialist country

## 菖

chāng
【菖蒲】 chāngpú 〈植〉 calamus

## 猖

chāng
【猖獗】 chāngjué be rampant; run wild: 旧中国～多年的天花，解放后灭迹了。Smallpox, rampant in old China, was eliminated soon after liberation./ 这个地区过去风沙～。The area used to be struck by raging sandstorms.
【猖狂】 chāngkuáng savage; furious: ～的挑衅 reckless provocation/ ～的攻击 a furious attack/ 打退敌人的～进攻 beat back (或 smash) the enemy's savage onslaught

## 娼

chāng prostitute
【娼妇】 chāngfù 〔旧时多用于骂人〕 bitch; whore
【娼妓】 chāngjì prostitute; streetwalker

## 鲳

chāng
【鲳鱼】 chāngyú silvery pomfret; butterfish

# cháng

## 长

cháng ① long: 这条河很～。This is a long river./ 夏季昼～夜短。In summer the days are long and the nights short. ② length: 南京长江大桥全～六千七百多米。The overall length of the Changjiang River Bridge at Nanjing is more than 6,700 metres. ③ of long duration; lasting: 与世～辞 pass away ④ steadily; regularly ⑤ strong point; forte: 取人之～，补己之短 overcome one's shortcomings by learning from others' strong points/ 她～于绘画。She is good at painting. 或 Painting is her forte.
另见 zhǎng
【长安】 Cháng'ān Chang'an, capital of China in the Han and Tang dynasties
【长臂猿】 chángbìyuán gibbon
【长波】 chángbō long wave ◇ ～通信 long-wave communication
【长城】 Chángchéng ① the Great Wall ② impregnable bulwark: 人民解放军是我们祖国的钢铁～。The People's Liberation Army is China's great wall of steel.
【长虫】 chángchong 〈口〉 snake
【长抽短吊】 chángchōu-duǎndiào 〈乒乓球〉 combine long drives with drop shots
【长处】 chángchu good qualities; strong (或 good) points: 他有许多～。He has many good qualities./ 有联系群众的～ have the strong point of maintaining close contact with the masses/ 国无论大小，都各有～和短处。Every nation, big or small, has its strong and weak points.
【长川】 chángchuān 见"常川" chángchuān
【长春】 Chángchūn Changchun
【长蝽】 chángchūn 〈动〉 chinch bug: 高粱～ sorghum chinch bug
【长此以往】 cháng cǐ yǐ wǎng if things go on like this; if things continue this way
【长存】 chángcún live forever
【长笛】 chángdí flute
【长度】 chángdù length
【长短】 chángduǎn ① length: 这两条扁担～差不多。The two carrying poles are about the same length./ 这件上衣～不合适。This coat is not the right length. ② accident; mishap: 万一这孩子的母亲有个～，怎么办？What if anything should happen to the child's mother? ③ right and wrong; strong and weak points: 背地里议论别人～是不应该的。It is not

right to gossip about a person behind his back.

【长短句】 chángduǎnjù ① 见"词" cí③ ② a kind of classical poetry consisting chiefly of seven-character lines interspersed with shorter or longer ones 参见"古体诗" gǔtǐshī

【长吨】 chángdūn long ton

【长方体】 chángfāngtǐ cuboid; rectangular parallelepiped

【长方形】 chángfāngxíng rectangle

【长庚】 chánggēng 〈天〉 ancient Chinese name for Venus

【长工】 chánggōng farm labourer hired by the year; long-term hired hand

【长骨】 chánggǔ 〈生理〉 long bone

【长鼓】 chánggǔ a long drum, narrowing towards the middle, used by the Chaoxian and Yao nationalities

【长号】 chánghào 〈乐〉 trombone

【长河】 chánghé long river — endless flow: 历史的～ the long process of history/ 在绝对真理的～中有无数相对真理。In the endless flow of absolute truth there are innumerable relative truths.

【长活】 chánghuó long-term job (of a farm labourer): 他早先给地主扛过～。He used to be a long-term labourer for a landlord.

【长江】 Chángjiāng the Changjiang (Yangtze) River: ～后浪推前浪，一代更比一代强。As in the Changjiang River the waves behind drive on those before, so each new generation excels the last one.

【长颈鹿】 chángjǐnglù giraffe

【长久】 chángjiǔ for a long time; permanently: 他打算在这儿～住下去。He is thinking of living here permanently. 或 He is thinking of settling down here./ 不是～之计 not a permanent solution; just a makeshift arrangement

【长距离】 chángjùlí long distance: ～赛跑 a long-distance race

【长空】 chángkōng vast sky

【长裤】 chángkù trousers; slacks; pants

【长廊】 chángláng ① a covered corridor or walk; gallery ② the Long Corridor (of the Summer Palace in Beijing)

【长毛绒】 chángmáoróng plush

【长眠】 chángmián 〈婉〉 eternal sleep; death: ～地下 dead and buried

【长年】 chángnián all the year round: 筑路工人～奋战在风雪高原。The road builders brave the wind and snow on the plateaus all the year round.

【长年累月】 chángnián-lěiyuè year in year out; over the years: 勘探队员～在各地寻找地下宝藏。Year in year out, our prospectors travel far and wide, looking for mineral deposits./ ～没修理，墙上的灰泥都剥落了。The plaster on the wall had peeled off through years of neglect.

【长袍】 chángpáo long gown; robe

【长跑】 chángpǎo long-distance race; long-distance running

【长篇大论】 chángpiān-dàlùn a lengthy speech or article

【长篇小说】 chángpiān xiǎoshuō novel

【长期】 chángqī over a long period of time; long-term: ～规划 a long-term plan/ ～天气预报 a long-range weather forecast/ ～存在的问题 a long-standing problem/ ～无息贷款 a long-term loan without interest/ ～战争 a long-drawn-out war; a protracted war/ ～观点 a long-term view/ 作～打算 take a long view; make long-term plans/ 同资产阶级思想进行～的斗争 wage a protracted struggle against bourgeois ideology/ 反修防修是我们～的战斗任务。Combating and preventing revisionism will remain our fighting task for a long time to come. ◇ ～性 protracted nature

【长崎】 Chángqí Nagasaki

【长枪】 chángqiāng ① spear ② long-barrelled gun

【长驱】 chángqū (of an army) make a long drive; push deep: ～千里 make a long drive of 1,000 *li*/ 我军～直入，所向披靡。Our army drove straight in, carrying everything before it.

【长沙】 Chángshā Changsha

【长衫】 chángshān (unlined) long gown

【长舌】 chángshé fond of gossip

【长蛇阵】 chángshézhèn single-line battle array: 排成一字～ deploy the troops in a long line; string out in a long line

【长蛇座】 chángshézuò 〈天〉 Hydra

【长生果】 chángshēngguǒ 〈方〉 peanut

【长石】 chángshí 〈矿〉 feldspar

【长时记忆】 chángshí jìyì 〈心〉 long-term memory

【长逝】 chángshì pass away; be gone forever

【长寿】 chángshòu long life; longevity: 祝您健康～。I wish you good health and a long life.

【长丝】 chángsī 〈纺〉 filament

【长叹】 chángtàn deep sigh: ～一声 heave a deep sigh

【长条校样】 chángtiáo jiàoyàng 〈印〉 galley proof

【长统袜】 chángtǒngwà stockings

【长途】 chángtú long-distance: ～跋涉 make a long, arduous journey
◇ ～奔袭 long-distance raid/ ～电话 long-distance (或 trunk) call/ ～电话局 long-distance exchange; trunk-line exchange/ ～飞行 long-range flight/ ～汽车 long-distance bus; coach/ ～运输 long-distance transport

【长网】 chángwǎng 〈纸〉 fourdrinier wire ◇ ～造纸机 fourdrinier (machine)

【长尾鹟】 chángwěiwēng 〈动〉 paradise flycatcher

【长物】 chángwù anything that may be spared; surplus: 别无～ have nothing other than daily necessities; have no valuable personal possessions

【长效磺胺】 chángxiào huáng'àn 〈药〉 sulphamethoxypyridazine (SMP)

【长吁短叹】 chángxū-duǎntàn sighs and groans; moan and groan

【长须鲸】 chángxūjīng finback

【长阳人】 Chángyángrén Changyang Man (a type of primitive man of about 100,000 years ago whose fossil remains were found in Changyang, Hubei Province, in 1956 and 1957)

【长夜】 chángyè long (或 eternal) night

【长元音】 chángyuányīn 〈语〉 long vowel

【长远】 chángyuǎn long-term; long-range: ～的利益 long-term interests/ ～规划 a long-term (或 long-range) plan/ 从～的观点看问题 from a long-term point of view

【长斋】 chángzhāi (Buddhists') permanent abstention from meat, fish, etc.

【长征】 chángzhēng ① expedition; long march ② the Long March (a major strategic movement of the Chinese Workers' and Peasants' Red Army which succeeded in reaching the revolutionary base in northern Shaanxi after traversing eleven provinces and covering 25,000 *li*, or 12,500 kilometres, 1934-1935)

【长足】 chángzú 〈书〉 by leaps and bounds: 取得～的进步 make rapid progress; make great strides forward/ 有了～的进展 have made considerable progress

**场** cháng ① a level open space; threshing ground: 打～ threshing ② 〈方〉 country fair; market: 赶～ go to market ③〈量〉〔用于事情的经过〕: 一～大雨 a downpour/ 一～硬仗 a hard battle/ 大干一～ go in for sth. in a big way; go all out/ 害了一～病 be ill for a while
另见 chǎng

【场院】 chángyuàn threshing ground

**肠** cháng intestines: 大(小)～ large (small) intestine
【肠梗阻】 chánggěngzǔ 〈医〉 intestinal obstruction
【肠激酶】 chángjīméi 〈生化〉 enterokinase
【肠结核】 chángjiéhé 〈医〉 tuberculosis of the intestines
【肠扭转】 chángniǔzhuǎn volvulus
【肠儿】 chángr 〈食品〉 sausage
【肠套叠】 chángtàodié 〈医〉 intussusception
【肠胃】 cháng-wèi intestines and stomach; stomach; belly: ～不好 suffer from indigestion ◇ ～炎 enterogastritis
【肠炎】 chángyán enteritis
【肠衣】 chángyī casing (for sausages)
【肠痈】 chángyōng 〈中医〉 appendicitis
【肠子】 chángzi intestines

**尝** cháng ① taste; try the flavour of: ～～咸淡 have a taste and see if it's salty enough/ ～到甜头 become aware of the benefits of; come to know the good of/ 艰苦备～ have experienced all the hardships ② ever; once: 未～见过此人 have never seen the person/ 何～不想去，只是没时间。I meant to go, only I didn't have the time.
【尝试】 chángshì attempt; try: 他们为了增产，曾～过各种方法。They have tried various things to increase production./ 巴黎公社是建立无产阶级专政的第一次英勇～。 The Paris Commune was the first heroic attempt to establish the dictatorship of the proletariat.
【尝新】 chángxīn have a taste of what is just in season

**常** cháng ① ordinary; common; normal: 人情之～ natural and normal/ 反～ unusual; abnormal/ 习以为～ be used (或 accustomed) to sth. ② constant; invariable: 冬夏～青 remain green throughout the year; evergreen ③ frequently; often; usually: ～来～往 exchange frequent visits; pay frequent calls/ 她～去听音乐会。 She goes to concerts quite often./ 我们～见面。 We see quite a lot of each other. ④ (Cháng) a surname
【常备不懈】 cháng bèi bù xiè always be on the alert; be ever prepared (against war): 人民解放军～地守卫着祖国边疆。The People's Liberation Army, ever on the alert, guards the borders of our country.
【常备军】 chángbèijūn standing army
【常常】 chángcháng frequently; often; usually; generally: 她～工作到深夜。She often works far into the night./ 年终时，人们～总结过去，展望将来。At the end of the year, people usually sum up their experience and make plans for the future.
【常川】 chángchuān frequently; constantly: ～往来 keep in constant touch/ ～供给 keep sb. constantly supplied
【常春藤】 chángchūnténg 〈植〉 Chinese ivy
【常规】 chángguī ① convention; rule; common practice; routine: 按照～办事 follow the old routine/ 打破～ break with convention ② 〈医〉 routine: 血(尿)～ routine blood (urine) test
◇ ～疗法 routine treatment/ ～武器 conventional weapons/ ～战争 conventional war
【常轨】 chángguǐ normal practice (或 course)
【常衡】 chánghéng avoirdupois
【常会】 chánghuì regular meeting (或 session)
【常见】 chángjiàn common: 现在拖拉机在这里是很～的。Nowadays tractors are a common sight here. ◇ ～病 common disease; common ailment
【常例】 chánglì common practice
【常绿树】 chánglǜshù evergreen (tree)
【常年】 chángnián ① throughout the year; perennial: ～坚持体育锻炼 persist in physical training all the year round ② year in year out: ～战斗在农业生产第一线 work hard on the agricultural production front year in year out ③ average year: 这儿小麦～亩产五百斤。In this area the per *mu* yield of wheat for an average year is 500 *jin*.
【常青】 chángqīng evergreen
【常情】 chángqíng reason; sense: 按照～，他会提出这个问题同你讨论的。 It stands to reason that he will take up the matter with you.
【常人】 chángrén ordinary person; the man in the street
【常任】 chángrèn permanent; standing: 安理会～理事国 permanent member of the Security Council ◇ ～代表 permanent delegate (或 representative)
【常山】 chángshān 〈中药〉 the root of antipyretic dichroa (*Dichroa febrifuga*)
【常设】 chángshè standing; permanent
◇ ～机构 standing body; permanent organization/ ～秘书处 permanent secretariat/ ～委员会 permanent committee
【常识】 chángshí ① general (或 elementary) knowledge: 卫生～ elementary knowledge of hygiene and sanitation/ 安全用电，在我们村已经成了～。How to use electricity safely has become general knowledge in our village. ② common sense: 天冷了要穿得暖一点儿，这是～。It's common sense to dress more warmly when it gets cold. ◇ ～课 general knowledge course
【常数】 chángshù 〈数〉 constant
【常态】 chángtài normality; normal behaviour or conditions: 一反～ contrary to one's normal behaviour; contrary to the way sb. usually behaves ◇ ～曲线 〈统计〉 normal curve
【常委】 chángwěi 〈简〉(常务委员) member of the standing committee
【常温】 chángwēn ① normal atmospheric temperature (between 15° and 25°C) ② homoiothermy ◇ ～动物 homoiothermal (或 warm-blooded) animal
【常务】 chángwù day-to-day business; routine: 主持～ in charge of day-to-day business ◇ ～委员 member of the standing committee/ ～委员会 standing committee
【常压塔】 chángyātǎ 〈化〉 atmospheric tower
【常言】 chángyán saying: ～道 as the saying goes/ ～说得好 it is well said that
【常用】 chángyòng in common use: ～词语 everyday expressions/ ～药材 medicinal herbs most in use
【常驻】 chángzhù resident; permanent
◇ ～大使 resident ambassador/ ～记者 resident correspondent/ ～联合国代表 permanent representative to the United Nations/ ～联合国代表团 permanent mission to the United Nations

**偿** cháng ① repay; compensate for: ～债 pay (或 discharge) a debt/ 补～损失 compensate for the loss ② meet; fulfil: 得～夙愿 have fulfilled one's long-cherished wish
【偿付】 chángfù pay back; pay: 延期～ 〈法〉 moratorium
【偿还】 chánghuán repay; pay back: ～债务 pay a debt/ 如数～ pay back the exact amount
【偿命】 chángmìng pay with one's life (for a murder); a life for a life
【偿清】 chángqīng clear off: ～债务 clear off one's debts

**徜** cháng
【徜徉】 chángyáng 〈书〉 wander about unhurriedly

**裳** cháng skirt (worn in ancient China)
另见 shang

**嫦** cháng
【嫦娥】 Cháng'é the goddess of the moon (the lady in the legend who swallowed elixir stolen from her husband and flew to the moon)

## chǎng

**厂** chǎng ① factory; mill; plant; works: 鞋～ shoe factory/ 面粉～ flour mill/ 机床～ machine tool plant/ 钢铁～ iron and steel works/ 制糖～ sugar refinery/ 造船～ shipyard/ ～办大学 factory-run college ② yard; depot: 煤～ coal yard
【厂房】 chǎngfáng ① factory building ② workshop
【厂矿】 chǎng-kuàng factories and mines ◇ ～企业 factories, mines and other enterprises; industrial enterprises
【厂礼拜】 chǎnglǐbài day of rest for factory workers (usu. on a weekday); workers' day off
【厂商】 chǎngshāng firm: 承包～ contractor
【厂史】 chǎngshǐ the history of a factory
【厂丝】 chǎngsī 〈纺〉 filature silk
【厂校挂钩】 chǎng-xiào guàgōu establish a hookup between school and factory; link schools with factories
【厂长】 chǎngzhǎng factory director
【厂址】 chǎngzhǐ the site (或 location) of a factory: 选择～ choose a site for building a factory
【厂主】 chǎngzhǔ factory owner; millowner
【厂子】 chǎngzi ①〈口〉 factory; mill ②〈旧〉 yard; depot: 木～ timberyard

**场** chǎng ① a place where people gather: 会～ meeting-place/ 战～ battlefield/ 篮球～ basketball court (或 pitch)/ 运动员入～ athletes enter the arena (或 sports field)/ 观众进～ spectators enter the stadium, etc. ② farm: 国营农～ state farm/ 养鸭～ duck farm/ 种马～ stud farm ③ stage: 出～ come on the stage; appear on the scene ④〈剧〉 scene: 第二幕第三～ Act II, Scene iii ⑤〈量〉〔用于文娱体育活动〕: 一～电影 a film show/ 一～球赛 a match; a ball game/ 加演一～ give an extra performance or show/ 第二～两点开始。The second show starts at two. ⑥〈物〉 field: 电(磁)～ electric (magnetic) field
另见 cháng
【场磁铁】 chǎngcítiě 〈电〉 field magnet
【场次】 chǎngcì the number of showings of a film, play, etc.
【场地】 chǎngdì space; place; site: 比赛～ competition arena; ground; court/ 施工～ construction site/ 由于～有限,他们只展出了部分产品。They displayed only a part of their products because space was limited.
【场合】 chǎnghé occasion; situation: 外交～ a diplomatic occasion
【场记】 chǎngjì 〈剧〉〈电影〉 ① log ② log keeper
【场界灯】 chǎngjièdēng 〈航空〉 boundary lights
【场论】 chǎnglùn 〈物〉 field theory
【场面】 chǎngmiàn ① scene (in drama, fiction, etc.); spectacle: 老工人讲家史的～很感人。The scene in which the old worker tells about his family's history is most moving./ 油画再现了红军过雪山的雄伟～。 The painting conjures up the grand spectacle of the Red Army crossing the snowcapped mountains./ 作者很善于描写大的～。The author is adept in depicting vast scenes. ② occasion; scene: 盛大的～ a grand occasion/ 热烈友好的～ a scene of warm friendship ③ appearance; front; façade: 撑～ keep up appearances
【场所】 chǎngsuǒ place; arena: 公共～ a public place/ 娱乐～ place of recreation/ 帝国主义角逐的～ an arena of imperialist rivalry/ 蚊蝇孳生的～ a breeding ground of flies and mosquitoes
【场子】 chǎngzi a place where people gather for various purposes (e.g. theatre, hall, sports ground, etc.)

**昶** chǎng 〈书〉 long day

**敞** chǎng ① spacious: 宽～ spacious; roomy ② open; uncovered: ～着门 leave the door open; with the door open/ ～着怀 with one's coat or shirt unbuttoned
【敞车】 chǎngchē 〈铁道〉 ① open wagon; open freight car ② flatcar
【敞开】 chǎngkāi open wide: 把门～ open the door wide/ ～思想 say what's in (或 on) one's mind; get things off one's chest
【敞开儿】 chǎngkāir 〈口〉 unlimited; unrestricted: 开水有的是,大家～喝吧。There's plenty of boiled water. Drink all you want./ ～供应 unlimited (或 open-ended) supply
【敞亮】 chǎngliàng ① light and spacious: 这间屋子很～。This room is light and spacious. ② clear (in one's thinking): 学习了这篇社论,心里更～了。After I studied the editorial, things seemed much clearer.
【敞喷】 chǎngpēn 〈石油〉 open flow
【敞篷车】 chǎngpéngchē open car
【敞着口儿】 chǎngzhekǒur ① uncovered; unsealed; unsettled: 他的伤还～呢。His wound hasn't healed up yet./ 这个问题还～呢。This is still an open question. ②〈方〉 unrestrained; as much as one likes: 生活好了,也不能～过日子。Things are much better than they were, but still we mustn't spend too freely.

**氅** chǎng cloak: 大～ overcoat

## chàng

**怅** chàng disappointed; sorry: 走访不遇为～。Sorry not to have found you at home.
【怅然】 chàngrán disappointed; upset: ～而返 come away disappointed
【怅惘】 chàngwǎng distracted; listless

**畅** chàng ① smooth; unimpeded: ～行无阻 pass unimpeded/ 流～ easy and smooth; fluent ② free; uninhibited: ～饮 drink one's fill
【畅达】 chàngdá fluent; smooth: 译文～。The translation reads smoothly./ 交通～ have a good transport and communications network; be easily accessible
【畅快】 chàngkuài free from inhibitions; carefree: 心情～ have ease of mind
【畅所欲言】 chàng suǒ yù yán speak without any inhibitions; speak one's mind freely; speak out freely
【畅谈】 chàngtán talk freely and to one's heart's content; speak glowingly of: ～国内外大好形势 speak glowingly of the excellent situation at home and abroad
【畅通】 chàngtōng unimpeded; unblocked: 前面道路～无阻 open road ahead/ 这里过去是穷乡僻壤,现在铁路公路都～了。 This formerly inaccessible place can now be reached by road and rail.
【畅销】 chàngxiāo be in great demand; sell well; have a ready market: 中国丝绸～国外。Chinese silk fabrics sell well on foreign markets./ 秋天是毛织品～的季节。Autumn is a lively season for the wool market. ◇ ～书 best seller
【畅叙】 chàngxù chat cheerfully (usu. about old times): ～

革命友情 relive an old revolutionary friendship

【畅游】 chàngyóu ① have a good swim: ～长江 have a good swim in the Changjiang River ② enjoy a sightseeing tour: ～名胜古迹 enjoy a trip to places of historic interest

**倡** chàng initiate; advocate: 首～ initiate; start

【倡导】 chàngdǎo initiate; propose: ～和平共处五项原则 initiate the Five Principles of Peaceful Coexistence

【倡言】 chàngyán 〈书〉 propose; initiate

【倡议】 chàngyì propose: ～召开国际会议 propose the calling of an international conference/ 在他的～下 at his suggestion/ 提出利用废料的～ put forward a proposal to make use of waste material

◇ ～权 〈外〉 initiative/ ～书 written proposal; proposal/ ～者 initiator

**唱** chàng ① sing: ～《国际歌》 sing *The Internationale*/ 颂歌一曲～北京 sing a song in praise of Beijing/ ～～农村新面貌 sing of the new look of the countryside ② call; cry: 鸡～三遍。The cock has crowed for the third time. ③ a song or a singing part of a Chinese opera

【唱白脸】 chàng báiliǎn wear the white makeup of the stage villain; play the villain; pretend to be harsh and severe

【唱本】 chàngběn the libretto or script of a ballad-singer

【唱词】 chàngcí libretto; words of a ballad

【唱段】 chàngduàn aria: 京剧～ an aria from a Beijing opera

【唱对台戏】 chàng duìtáixì put on a rival show; enter into rivalry

【唱反调】 chàng fǎndiào sing a different tune; deliberately speak or act contrary to

【唱高调】 chàng gāodiào use high-flown words; affect a high moral tone

【唱歌】 chànggē sing (a song): 她很会～。She is a good singer.

【唱工】 chànggōng 〈剧〉 art of singing; singing ◇ ～戏 Chinese opera featuring singing (rather than acrobatics, etc.) 又作"唱功"

【唱和】 chànghè ① one singing a song and the others joining in the chorus: 此唱彼和。When one starts singing, another joins in. ② one person writing a poem to which one or more other people reply, usu. using the same rhyme sequence

【唱红脸】 chàng hóngliǎn wear the red makeup of the stage hero; play the hero; pretend to be generous and kind: 一个～,一个唱白脸 one coaxes, the other coerces

【唱机】 chàngjī gramophone; phonograph: 电～ record player

【唱名】 chàngmíng ① roll call: ～表决 vote by roll call ② 〈乐〉 sol-fa syllables

【唱名法】 chàngmíngfǎ 〈乐〉 sol-fa; solmization: 固定～ fixed-do system/ 首调～ movable-do system

【唱片】 chàngpiàn gramophone (或 phonograph) record; disc: 放～ play a gramophone record/ 灌～ cut a disc

【唱票】 chàngpiào call out the names of those voted for while counting ballot-slips ◇ ～人 teller

【唱腔】 chàngqiāng 〈剧〉 music for voices in a Chinese opera

【唱诗班】 chàngshībān choir

【唱双簧】 chàng shuānghuáng ① give a two-man comic show, with one speaking or singing while hiding behind the other who does the acting; one sings while the other acts ② collaborate with each other

【唱头】 chàngtóu pickup

【唱戏】 chàngxì 〈口〉 act in an opera

【唱针】 chàngzhēn gramophone needle; stylus

【唱做念打】 chàng-zuò-niàn-dǎ 〈剧〉 singing, acting, recitation and acrobatics

## chāo

**抄** chāo ① copy; transcribe: 请把稿件～一下。Please make a fair copy of the manuscript./ 照～原文 make a verbatim transcription of the original ② plagiarize; lift ③ search and confiscate; make a raid upon: ～土匪的老窝 destroy the bandits' den ④ go (或 walk) off with: 谁把我的字典～走了? Who's gone off with my dictionary? ⑤ take a shortcut: ～到敌人前面 outstrip the enemy by taking a shortcut ⑥ fold (one's arms): ～着手站在一边 stand by with folded arms ⑦ grab; take up: ～起一把铁锹就干 take up a spade and plunge into the job

【抄本】 chāoběn hand-copied book; transcript: 《红楼梦》～ a handwritten copy of *A Dream of Red Mansions*

【抄道】 chāodào ① take a shortcut ② 〈口〉 shortcut: 走～去要近二里路。If you take the shortcut, it will be two *li* closer.

【抄后路】 chāo hòulù outflank the enemy and attack him in the rear; turn the enemy's rear

【抄获】 chāohuò search and seize; ferret out

【抄家】 chāojiā search sb.'s house and confiscate his property

【抄件】 chāojiàn duplicate; copy: 现将报告的～转发给你们。A copy of the report is forwarded herewith.

【抄录】 chāolù make a copy of; copy: 这段引文是从报上～来的。This quotation is taken from a newspaper article.

【抄身】 chāoshēn search sb.; frisk

【抄送】 chāosòng make a copy for; send a duplicate to

【抄网】 chāowǎng 〈渔〉 dip net

【抄袭】 chāoxí ① plagiarize; lift: ～行为 (an act of) plagiarism ② borrow indiscriminately from other people's experience ③ launch a surprise attack on the enemy by making a detour

【抄写】 chāoxiě copy; transcribe ◇ ～员 copyist

**吵** chāo

另见 chǎo

【吵吵】 chāochao make a row; kick up a racket: 一个一个说,别～。Speak one at a time. Don't make such a row.

**钞** chāo ① bank note; paper money: 现～ cash ② collected writings: 诗～ collected poems

【钞票】 chāopiào bank note; paper money; bill: 五元一张的～ a five-*yuan* bill ◇ ～纸 bank-note paper

**绰** chāo grab; take up: ～起一根棍子 grab a stick/ ～起活儿就干 plunge right into the job

另见 chuò

**焯** chāo scald (as a way of cooking)

**超** chāo ① exceed; surpass; overtake: ～《纲要》 overfulfil the targets set by the National Programme for Agricultural Development/ 赶先进,～先进 catch up with and surpass the advanced/ 亩产～千斤 produce over 1,000 *jin* per *mu*; exceed 1,000 *jin* in per *mu* yield ② ultra-; super-; extra-: ～高温 superhigh temperature/ ～显微镜 ultramicroscope ③ transcend; go beyond: 在阶级社会中,没有～阶级的文艺。In class society there is no such thing as art and literature transcending classes.

【超产】 chāochǎn overfulfil a production target (或 quota) ◇ ～粮 grain output in excess of a production target

【超车】 chāochē overtake other cars on the road: 不准～! No overtaking!

【超出】 chāochū overstep; go beyond; exceed: ～范围 go beyond the scope (或 bounds)/ ～定额 exceed the quota/ ～预料 exceed one's expectations

【超导】 chāodǎo 〈物〉 superconduction ◇ ～电性 superconductivity/ ～体 superconductor

【超等】 chāoděng of superior grade; extra fine: ～质量 extra good quality; superfine

【超低空飞行】 chāodīkōng fēixíng minimum altitude flying; hedgehopping

【超低量喷雾器】 chāodīliàng pēnwùqì ultra-low-volume sprayer

【超低温】 chāodīwēn ultralow temperature

【超帝国主义论】 chāodìguózhǔyìlùn the theory of ultra-imperialism (或 supra-imperialism) — a reactionary theory put forward by K. J. Kautsky

【超度】 chāodù 〈宗〉 release souls from purgatory; expiate the sins of the dead

【超短波】 chāoduǎnbō ultrashort wave

【超短裙】 chāoduǎnqún miniskirt

【超额】 chāo'é above quota: ～完成生产指标 overfulfil the production quota; surpass the production target ◇ ～利润 superprofit/ ～剩余价值 excess surplus value

【超负荷】 chāofùhè excess load; overload

【超高】 chāogāo 〈水〉 freeboard

【超高频】 chāogāopín 〈电〉 ultrahigh frequency ◇ ～变压器 ultrahigh-frequency transformer

【超高压】 chāogāoyā ① 〈物〉 superhigh pressure ② 〈电〉 extrahigh voltage (或 tension): ～线路带电作业 working on live extrahigh tension power lines

【超高真空】 chāogāo zhēnkōng ultrahigh vacuum

【超过】 chāoguò outstrip; surpass; exceed: ～规定的速度 exceed the speed limit/ ～限度 go beyond the limit/ ～历史最高水平 top all previous records/ ～世界先进水平 surpass advanced world levels/ 有利条件～困难条件。The favourable conditions outweigh the difficulties./ 到会的代表已～百分之九十。More than 90 per cent of the delegates to the conference have arrived.

【超级】 chāojí super ◇ ～大国 superpower/ ～公路 superhighway/ ～间谍 superspy/ ～商场 supermarket/ ～油轮 supertanker

【超假】 chāojià overstay one's leave

【超阶级】 chāojiējí transcending classes; supra-class: ～的"全民国家"是不存在的。There has never been a supra-class "state of the whole people"

【超经济剥削】 chāojīngjì bōxuē 〈经〉 extraeconomic exploitation

【超巨星】 chāojùxīng 〈天〉 supergiant (star)

【超绝】 chāojué unique; superb; extraordinary: 技艺～ extraordinary skill; superb performance

【超龄】 chāolíng overage: ～团员 overage Youth League member

【超期服役】 chāoqī fúyì 〈军〉 extended active duty; extended service in the army

【超前】 chāoqián 〈电〉 lead ◇ ～角 angle of lead

【超群】 chāoqún head and shoulders above all others; preeminent: 武艺～ extremely skilful in martial arts

【超然】 chāorán aloof; detached: 在激烈的阶级斗争中,任何人都不可能是～的。It is impossible for anybody to stand aloof in the midst of acute class struggle.

【超然物外】 chāorán wù wài hold aloof from the world; be above worldly considerations; stay away from the scene of contention

【超人】 chāorén ① be out of the common run: ～的记忆力 exceptionally good memory ② superman (as defined by Nietzsche)

【超深井】 chāoshēnjǐng 〈石油〉 extradeep well

【超声波】 chāoshēngbō ultrasonic (wave); supersonic (wave) ◇ ～探伤仪 ultrasonic flaw detector/ ～疗法 ultrasonic therapy

【超声物理学】 chāoshēng wùlǐxué ultrasonic physics

【超声学】 chāoshēngxué ultrasonics

【超速】 chāosù ① exceed the speed limit ② hypervelocity ◇ ～粒子 〈物〉 hypervelocity particle

【超脱】 chāotuō ① unconventional; original: 他的字,信笔写来,十分～。His effortless calligraphy has an unconventional grace of its own. ② be detached; stand (或 hold, keep) aloof: ～现实是不可能的。It's impossible to detach oneself from reality.

【超外差】 chāowàichā 〈电子〉 superheterodyne; superhet ◇ ～收音机 superheterodyne (radio set)

【超细纤维】 chāoxì xiānwéi superfine fibre

【超现实主义】 chāoxiànshízhǔyì surrealism

【超小型管】 chāoxiǎoxíngguǎn 〈电子〉 subminiature tube

【超新星】 chāoxīnxīng 〈天〉 supernova

【超逸】 chāoyì unconventionally graceful; free and natural

【超音速】 chāoyīnsù supersonic speed ◇ ～喷气机 superjet/ ～战斗机 supersonic fighter-plane; supersonic fighter

【超铀元素】 chāoyóu yuánsù transuranic (或 transuranium) element

【超越】 chāoyuè surmount; overstep; transcend; surpass: ～障碍 surmount an obstacle/ ～职权范围 go beyond one's terms of reference; overstep one's authority ◇ ～射击 〈军〉 overhead fire

【超载】 chāozài 〈交〉 overload ◇ ～能力 overload capacity

【超支】 chāozhī overspend: 从不～ never live beyond one's income

【超重】 chāozhòng ① overload ② overweight: ～信件 overweight letter/ ～行李 excess luggage

【超重量级】 chāozhòngliàngjí 〈举重〉 super-heavyweight

【超重氢】 chāozhòngqīng tritium (T 或 $H^3$)

【超轴】 chāozhóu 〈铁道〉 over haulage ◇ ～牵引 trains hauling above-normal tonnage

【超子】 chāozǐ 〈物〉 hyperon

【超自然】 chāozìrán supernatural

**剿** chāo 〈书〉 plagiarize

另见 jiǎo

【剿袭】 chāoxí plagiarize

## cháo

**晁** Cháo a surname

**巢** cháo nest: 鸟～ bird's nest/ 匪～ nest (或 den) of robbers; bandits' lair

【巢菜】 cháocài common vetch

【巢蛾】 cháo'é ermine moth

【巢鼠】 cháoshǔ harvest mouse

【巢穴】 cháoxué lair; den; nest; hideout: 敌人的～ the enemy's lair/ 反动政权的～ a hideout of the reactionary regime

**朝** cháo ① court; government: 上～ go to court/ 在～党 party in power; ruling party ② dynasty: 唐～ the

Tang Dynasty/ 改～换代 dynastic changes ③ an emperor's reign: 康熙～ during the reign of Emperor Kangxi ④ have an audience with (a king, an emperor, etc.); make a pilgrimage to ⑤ facing; towards: 坐东～西 with a western exposure; facing west/ ～着共产主义目标前进 advance towards the goal of communism/ 迈开大步～前走 march ahead with great strides/ ～敌人开火 fire at the enemy/ ～南走 go southward/ 这门～里开还是～外开？ Does this door open inwards or outwards?

另见 zhāo

【朝拜】 cháobài pay respects to (a sovereign); pay religious homage to; worship

【朝臣】 cháochén courtier

【朝代】 cháodài dynasty

【朝贡】 cháogòng pay tribute (to an imperial court); present tribute

【朝见】 cháojiàn have an audience with (a king, an emperor, etc.): 进宫～ be presented at court

【朝觐】 cháojìn ① 〈书〉见"朝见" ② 〈宗〉 go on a pilgrimage (to a shrine or a sacred place)

【朝山】 cháoshān 〈佛教〉 make a pilgrimage to a temple on a famous mountain

【朝圣】 cháoshèng 〈宗〉 pilgrimage; hadj

【朝廷】 cháotíng ① royal or imperial court ② royal or imperial government

【朝鲜】 Cháoxiān Korea ◇ ～人 Korean/ ～语 Korean (language)

【朝鲜族】 Cháoxiānzú ① the Chaoxian (Korean) nationality, distributed over Jilin, Heilongjiang and Liaoning ② the Korean people (of Korea)

【朝阳】 cháoyáng ① exposed to the sun; sunny ② with a sunny, usu. southern, aspect: 这间屋～。The room has a southern exposure.

另见 zhāoyáng

【朝野】 cháo-yě ① 〈旧〉 the court and the commonalty ② the government and the public

**潮** cháo ① tide: 早～ morning tide/ 大(小)～ spring (neap) tide/ 涨(落)～了。The tide is flowing (ebbing)./ 歌声如～ the sound of songs rising and falling like waves ② (social) upsurge; current; tide: 工～ workers' strike/ 思～ trend of thought/ 革命高～ a revolutionary high tide/ 低～ low tide/ 怒～ raging tide ③ damp; moist: 火柴受～了。The matches have got damp./ 雨季里东西容易返～。In the rainy season things get damp easily.

【潮呼呼】 cháohūhū damp; dank; clammy: 接连下了七八天雨，屋子里什么都是～的。After a week's rain, everything in the house became damp and clammy.

【潮解】 cháojiě 〈化〉 deliquescence

【潮流】 cháoliú ① tide; tidal current ② trend: 历史～ historical trend/ 顺应世界之～ adapt oneself to (或 go along with) world trends

【潮气】 cháoqì moisture in the air; damp; humidity: 仓库里～太大，粮食就容易发霉。The grain is liable to mildew when the humidity in the barn is too high.

【潮热】 cháorè 〈中医〉 hectic fever

【潮湿】 cháoshī moist; damp

【潮水】 cháoshuǐ tidewater; tidal water: 欢乐的人群象～般地涌向天安门广场。Crowds of joyous people streamed into Tian'anmen Square from all directions.

【潮汐】 cháoxī morning and evening tides; tide ◇ ～表 tide table/ ～测站 tide station/～能 tidal energy

【潮汛】 cháoxùn spring tide

**嘲** cháo ridicule; deride: 解～ try to explain things away when ridiculed/ 冷～热讽 freezing irony and burning satire

【嘲讽】 cháofěng sneer at; taunt

【嘲弄】 cháonòng mock; poke fun at: ～历史的人必将被历史所～。Those who mock history will be mocked by history.

【嘲笑】 cháoxiào ridicule; deride; jeer at; laugh at

## chǎo

**吵** chǎo ① make a noise: 别～！ Don't make so much noise! 或 Be quiet!/ ～得慌 terribly noisy/ 瞧，孩子被你们～醒了。Look! You've woken the child with your noise./ 别～他。Don't disturb him. ② quarrel; wrangle; squabble: 不要为一点小事就～起来。Don't squabble over trifles./ ～翻了天 kick up a terrific row

另见 chāo

【吵架】 chǎojià quarrel; wrangle; have a row

【吵闹】 chǎonào ① wrangle; kick up a row ② din; hubbub: 院子里一片～声。A hubbub was heard in the courtyard.

【吵嚷】 chǎorǎng make a racket; shout in confusion; clamour

【吵嘴】 chǎozuǐ quarrel; bicker

**炒** chǎo stir-fry; fry; *sauté*: ～肉丝 stir-fried shredded pork/ ～黄瓜 *sautéed* cucumber/ ～鸡蛋 scrambled eggs/ 蛋～饭 rice fried with eggs/ 糖～栗子 chestnuts roasted in sand with brown sugar

【炒菜】 chǎocài ① stir-fry; *sauté* ② a fried dish ③ a dish cooked to order

【炒货】 chǎohuò roasted seeds and nuts

【炒冷饭】 chǎo lěngfàn heat leftover rice — say or do the same old thing; rehash

【炒米】 chǎomǐ ① parched rice ② millet stir-fried in butter (staple food of the Monggol nationality) ◇ ～花 puffed rice

【炒面】 chǎomiàn ① *chow mein*; fried noodles ② parched flour

【炒勺】 chǎosháo round-bottomed frying pan

## chào

**耖** chào ① a harrow-like implement for pulverizing soil ② level land with such an implement

## chē

**车** chē ① vehicle: 汽～ motor vehicle; automobile/ 火～ train/ 军用～ army vehicle ② wheeled machine or instrument: 纺～ spinning wheel/ 滑～ pulley/ 水～ waterwheel ③ machine: 开～ set the machine going; start the machine/ 停～ stop the machine/ 试～ trial (或 test) run ④ lathe; turn: ～机器零件 lathe a machine part/ ～光 smooth sth. on a lathe ⑤ lift water by waterwheel: 把河里的水～到稻田里 lift water from a river into paddy fields ⑥ (Chē) a surname

另见 jū

【车把】 chēbǎ handlebar (of a bicycle, motor cycle, etc.); shaft (of a wheelbarrow, etc.)

【车把式】 chēbǎshi cart-driver; carter 又作"车把势"

【车床】 chēchuáng lathe: 多刀～ multicut lathe

◇ ～顶尖 lathe centre/ ～卡盘 lathe chuck/ ～拖板 lathe carriage
【车次】 chēcì ①train number ②motorcoach number (indicating order of departure)
【车刀】 chēdāo lathe tool; turning tool: 沉割～ undercutting turning tool/ 木工～ wood turning tool
【车到山前必有路】 chē dào shānqián bì yǒu lù the cart will find its way round the hill when it gets there — things will eventually sort themselves out
【车道】 chēdào (traffic) lane
【车队】 chēduì motorcade
【车费】 chēfèi fare
【车工】 chēgōng ①lathe work ②turner; lathe operator ◇ ～车间 turning shop
【车钩】 chēgōu 〈铁道〉 coupling
【车轱辘】 chēgūlu 〈口〉 wheel (of a vehicle)
【车轱辘话】 chēgūluhuà 〈方〉 repetitious talk
【车祸】 chēhuò traffic (或 road) accident
【车技】 chējì 〈杂技〉 trick-cycling
【车架】 chējià frame (of a car, bicycle, etc.)
【车间】 chējiān workshop; shop: 装配～ assembly shop
【车库】 chēkù garage
【车辆】 chēliàng vehicle; car: 来往～ traffic/ 铁路机车及～ rolling stock ◇ ～周转率 〈铁道〉 average turnround rate of rolling stock
【车裂】 chēliè tearing a person asunder by five carts (a punishment in ancient China)
【车轮】 chēlún wheel (of a vehicle)
【车轮战】 chēlúnzhàn the tactic of several persons taking turns in fighting one opponent to tire him out
【车马费】 chēmǎfèi travel allowance
【车马坑】 chēmǎkēng 〈考古〉 chariot pit
【车皮】 chēpí railway wagon or carriage
【车票】 chēpiào train or bus ticket; ticket
【车前草】 chēqiáncǎo 〈中药〉 Asiatic plantain (*Plantago asiatica*)
【车身】 chēshēn automobile body
【车水马龙】 chēshuǐ-mǎlóng incessant stream of horses and carriages — heavy traffic: 门前～。The courtyard is thronged with visitors.
【车速】 chēsù speed of a motor vehicle
【车胎】 chētāi tyre
【车厢】 chēxiāng railway carriage; railroad car
【车削】 chēxiāo 〈机〉 turning
【车辕子】 chēyuánzi shaft (of a cart, etc.)
【车载斗量】 chēzài-dǒuliáng enough to fill carts and be measured by the *dou* — common and numerous: 在我们那里象我这样的人～，不可胜数。Where I come from, people like me come by the bushel.
【车闸】 chēzhá brake (of a car, bicycle, etc.)
【车站】 chēzhàn station; depot; stop
【车照】 chēzhào licence (of a car, bicycle, etc.)
【车辙】 chēzhé rut
【车轴】 chēzhóu axletree; axle
【车子】 chēzi small vehicle (such as a car, pushcart, etc.)

**砗** chē
【砗磲】 chēqú 〈动〉 giant clam; tridacna

## chě

**尺** chě 〈乐〉 a note of the scale in *gongchepu* (工尺谱), corresponding to 2 in numbered musical notation 另见 chǐ

**扯** chě ① pull: 没等他说完，我～着他就走。Without letting him finish what he had to say, I pulled him away./ ～着嗓子喊 shout at the top of one's voice/ 这是两个问题，不能往一块儿～。These two questions should not be lumped together. ②tear: 把信～得粉碎 tear a letter to pieces/ ～下假面具 tear off the mask ③buy (cloth, thread, etc.): ～点儿布 buy some cloth ④chat; gossip: 咱俩好好～一～。Let's have a good chat./ ～家常 chat about everyday family affairs; chitchat/ 别～远了。Don't wander from the subject. 或 Stick to the point.
【扯淡】 chědàn 〈方〉 ①talk nonsense ②nonsense
【扯后腿】 chě hòutuǐ hold sb. back (from action); be a drag on sb.; be a hindrance to sb.
【扯谎】 chěhuǎng tell a lie; lie
【扯皮】 chěpí dispute over trifles; argue back and forth; wrangle

## chè

**彻** chè thorough; penetrating: ～夜工作 work all night/ 透～的了解 thorough understanding/ 响～云霄 resounding across the skies
【彻底】 chèdǐ thorough; thoroughgoing: ～革命精神 thoroughgoing revolutionary spirit/ 进行～调查 make a thorough investigation/ ～推翻资产阶级和一切剥削阶级 completely overthrow the bourgeoisie and all other exploiting classes/ ～地为人民的利益工作 work entirely in the people's interests ◇ ～性 (degree of ) thoroughness
【彻骨】 chègǔ to the bone: 寒风～。The bitter wind chills one to the bone.
【彻头彻尾】 chètóu-chèwěi out and out; through and through; downright: ～的骗局 a downright (或 sheer) fraud; deception from beginning to end/ ～的修正主义纲领 an out-and-out revisionist programme/ ～的谎言 an absolute lie
【彻夜】 chèyè all night; all through the night: ～不眠 lie awake all night/ 工地上灯火～通明。The lights were ablaze at the worksite all through the night.

**坼** chè 〈书〉 split open; crack

**掣** chè ①pull; tug ②draw: 他赶紧～回手去。He quickly drew back his hand./ ～签 draw lots
【掣肘】 chèzhǒu hold sb. back by the elbow; impede; handicap: 这件事办得很顺利，没有人～。As there was no one making things difficult for us, we settled the matter smoothly.

**澈** chè (of water) clear; limpid

**撤** chè ①remove; take away: 把障碍物～了 remove the barrier/ 把盘子、碗～了 clear away the dishes ②withdraw; evacuate: 向后～ withdraw; retreat/ 主动～出 withdraw on one's own initiative/ ～伤员 evacuate the wounded
【撤兵】 chèbīng withdraw troops
【撤除】 chèchú remove; dismantle: ～军事设施 dismantle military installations
【撤防】 chèfáng withdraw a garrison; withdraw from a defended position
【撤换】 chèhuàn dismiss and replace; recall; replace
【撤回】 chèhuí ①recall; withdraw: ～代表 recall a representative/ ～步哨 withdraw the guard ②revoke; retract; withdraw: ～起诉 withdraw charges; revoke a court

action/ ～声明 retract a statement
【撤离】 chèlí withdraw from; leave; evacuate: ～阵地 abandon a position/ ～城市 evacuate a city
【撤退】 chètuì withdraw; pull out: ～方向 the line of withdrawal/ 安全～ make good one's retreat
【撤销】 chèxiāo cancel; rescind; revoke: ～其职务 dismiss a person from his post/ ～一项决议 annul a decision/ ～处分 rescind (或 annul) a penalty/ ～原计划 rescind the original plan/ ～命令 countermand an order/ ～法令 repeal a decree/ ～邀请 withdraw an invitation
【撤职】 chèzhí dismiss (或 discharge) sb. from his post; remove sb. from office: ～查办 discharge sb. from his post and prosecute him
【撤走】 chèzǒu withdraw

## chēn

**抻** chēn 〈口〉 pull out; stretch: 把衣裳～～再晾起来。Stretch the clothes before hanging them up to dry.
【抻面】 chēnmiàn ①make noodles by drawing out the dough by hand ②hand-pulled noodles

**琛** chēn 〈书〉 treasure

**嗔** chēn ①be angry; be displeased: 生～ get angry ②be annoyed (with sb.): 他～着我说错了话。He was annoyed with me for having said the wrong thing.
【嗔怪】 chēnguài blame; rebuke
【嗔怒】 chēnnù get angry
【嗔色】 chēnsè angry or sullen look: 微露～ look somewhat displeased

**瞋** chēn 〈书〉 stare angrily; glare
【瞋目】 chēnmù stare angrily; glare: ～而视 stare at sb. angrily

## chén

**尘** chén ①dust; dirt: 一～不染 not stained with a particle of dust; spotless ②this world: ～俗 this mortal world
【尘埃】 chén'āi dust ◇ ～传染〈医〉dust infection
【尘暴】 chénbào 〈气〉 dust storm
【尘肺】 chénfèi 〈医〉 pneumoconiosis
【尘封】 chénfēng covered with dust; dust-laden
【尘垢】 chéngòu dust and dirt; dirt
【尘寰】 chénhuán 见"尘世"
【尘世】 chénshì 〈宗〉 this world; this mortal life
【尘土】 chéntǔ dust: 卡车过处，～飞扬。The truck sped past raising a cloud of dust.
【尘嚣】 chénxiāo hubbub; uproar

**臣** chén official under a feudal ruler; subject: 君～ the monarch and his subjects
【臣服】 chénfú 〈书〉submit oneself to the rule of; acknowledge allegiance to
【臣民】 chénmín subjects of a feudal ruler
【臣子】 chénzǐ official in feudal times

**沉** chén ①sink: 船～了。The boat has sunk./ ～底儿 sink to the bottom/ 月落星～。The moon is down and the stars have set. ②〔多指抽象事物〕keep down; lower: ～下心来 settle down (to one's work, etc.); concentrate (on one's work, study, etc.)/ 把脸一～ put on a grave expression; pull a long face ③deep; profound: 睡得很～ be in a deep sleep; be fast asleep; sleep like a log ④heavy: 这只箱子真～！ This trunk is heavy!/ 我头有点发～。My head feels heavy (或 fuzzy)./ 胳膊～ have a stiff arm
【沉沉】 chénchén ①heavy: 穗子～地垂下来。The ears hang heavy on the stalks. ②deep: ～入睡 sink into a deep sleep/ 暮气～ lifeless; lethargic; apathetic/ 暮霭～。Dusk is falling.
【沉甸甸】 chéndiāndiān heavy: ～的一口袋稻种 a heavy sack of rice seed/ ～的谷穗 heavy ears of millet/ 任务还没有完成，我心里老是～的。The thought of the unfinished task weighed heavily on my mind.
【沉淀】 chéndiàn sediment; precipitate: 墨水～了。There is some sediment in the ink./ 水太浑啦，～一下再用。The water is muddy; let it settle for a while.
◇ ～池〈环保〉precipitating tank/ ～剂〈化〉precipitating agent/ ～物 sediment; precipitate
【沉积】 chénjī 〈地〉 deposit: 陆(海)相～ continental (marine) deposit/ 泥沙～河底。The silt is deposited in the riverbed.
◇ ～物 deposit; sediment/ ～旋回 cycle of sedimentation/ ～岩 sedimentary rock/ ～作用 deposition; sedimentation
【沉寂】 chénjì ①quiet; still: ～的深夜 in the still of (the) night/ 傍晚，暴风雨已经过去，四周开始～下来。By evening the storm had subsided and all was quiet again. ②no news: 消息～。There has been no news whatsoever.
【沉降】 chénjiàng subside: 地面～ earth subsidence ◇ ～缝〈建〉settlement joint
【沉浸】 chénjìn immerse; steep: ～在幸福的回忆中 be immersed in happy memories/ 整个首都～在节日的欢乐气氛中。The entire capital was permeated with a festive atmosphere.
【沉井】 chénjǐng 〈建〉 open caisson
【沉静】 chénjìng ①quiet; calm: 夜深了，村子里～下来。It was late at night, and all was quiet in the village. ②calm; serene; placid: ～的神色 a serene look/ 心情～ be in a placid mood
【沉疴】 chénkē severe and lingering illness
【沉沦】 chénlún sink into (vice, degradation, depravity, etc.)
【沉脉】 chénmài 〈中医〉 deep pulse (which can be felt only by pressing hard)
【沉闷】 chénmèn ①(of weather, atmosphere, etc.) oppressive; depressing ②depressed; in low spirits: 心情～ feel depressed ③not outgoing; withdrawn: 他这个人很～。He's rather withdrawn.
【沉迷】 chénmí indulge; wallow: ～在幻想里 indulge in illusions
【沉湎】 chénmiǎn 〈书〉 wallow in; be given to: ～于酒 be given to heavy drinking
【沉没】 chénmò sink: 敌舰被鱼雷击中，立即～。The enemy warship was torpedoed and sank at once.
【沉默】 chénmò ①reticent; taciturn; uncommunicative: ～寡言的人 a reticent person; a person of few words ②silent: 保持～ remain silent/ 他～了一会又继续说下去。After a moment's silence he went on speaking.
【沉溺】 chénnì indulge; wallow: ～于声色 wallow in sensual pleasures/ ～于享乐是资产阶级人生观的一种表现。Indulgence in worldly pleasure is an expression of the bourgeois outlook on life.
【沉砂池】 chénshāchí 〈环保〉 grit chamber
【沉睡】 chénshuì be sunk in sleep; be fast asleep
【沉思】 chénsī ponder; meditate; be lost in thought: 为这个问题，她坐在那里～了好久。She sat there pondering over

the problem for a long time.

【沉痛】 chéntòng ①deep feeling of grief or remorse: 怀着～的心情 be deeply grieved/ 表示～的哀悼 express profound condolences/ 他对自己的错误感到十分～。He felt deep remorse for his error. ②deeply felt; bitter: 应该接受这个～的教训。It is necessary to learn a lesson from this bitter experience.

【沉陷】 chénxiàn ①sink; cave in: 地震后路基～了。The earthquake made the roadbed cave in. ②〈建〉settlement: 不均匀～ unequal settlement

【沉香】 chénxiāng 〈植〉agalloch eaglewood

【沉箱】 chénxiāng 〈建〉caisson

【沉吟】 chényín mutter to oneself, unable to make up one's mind

【沉郁】 chényù depressed; gloomy

【沉冤】 chényuān gross injustice; unrighted wrong: 解放前，多少劳动人民～莫白。Countless working people suffered grievous wrongs before liberation.

【沉渣】 chénzhā sediment; dregs

【沉重】 chénzhòng ①heavy: ～的脚步 heavy steps/ ～的打击 a heavy blow/ 心情～ with a heavy heart ②serious; critical: 病情～ critically ill

【沉舟】 chénzhōu sunken boat; shipwreck: ～侧畔千帆过，病树前头万木春。A thousand sails pass by the shipwreck; ten thousand saplings shoot up beyond the withered tree.

【沉住气】 chénzhuqì keep calm; keep cool; be steady: ～，等敌人靠近了再打。Steady, don't fire till the enemy come closer./ 不要一听到不同意见就沉不住气。Don't get excited the moment you hear a differing opinion.

【沉着】 chénzhuó cool-headed; composed; steady; calm: 勇敢～ brave and steady/ ～应战 meet the attack calmly

【沉子】 chénzǐ 〈渔〉sinker

【沉醉】 chénzuì get drunk; become intoxicated: ～在节日的欢乐里 be intoxicated with the spirit of the festival

**忱** chén 〈书〉sincere feeling; true sentiment: 谢～ thankfulness/ 热～ zeal; warmheartedness

**辰** chén ①celestial bodies: 星～ stars ②the fifth of the twelve Earthly Branches ③any of the traditional twelve two-hour periods of the day 参见"时辰" shíchen ④time; day; occasion: 诞～ birthday

【辰砂】 chénshā cinnabar; vermillion

【辰时】 chénshí the period of the day from 7 a.m. to 9 a.m.

**陈** chén ①lay out; put on display ②state; explain: 此事当另函详～。The matter will be explained in detail in a separate letter. ③old; stale ④(Chén) a surname ⑤(Chén) the Chen Dynasty (557-589), one of the Southern Dynasties

【陈兵】 chénbīng mass (或 deploy) troops: ～边境 mass troops along the border/ ～百万 deploy a million troops

【陈陈相因】 chén chén xiāng yīn follow a set routine; stay in the same old groove

【陈词滥调】 chéncí-làndiào hackneyed and stereotyped expressions; *clichés*

【陈醋】 chéncù mature vinegar

【陈腐】 chénfǔ old and decayed; stale; outworn: ～的词句 stale phrases/ 批判男尊女卑的～观念 criticize the outworn concept that men are superior to women

【陈规】 chénguī outmoded conventions: 打破～，大胆创造 break with outmoded conventions and make bold innovations

【陈规陋习】 chénguī-lòuxí outmoded conventions and bad customs; bad customs and habits

【陈货】 chénhuò old stock; shopworn goods

【陈迹】 chénjī a thing of the past

【陈酒】 chénjiǔ old wine; mellow wine

【陈旧】 chénjiù outmoded; obsolete; old-fashioned; out-of-date: ～的观点 an outmoded notion/ ～的设备 obsolete equipment/ ～的词语 obsolete words and expressions

【陈列】 chénliè display; set out; exhibit: 玻璃柜里～着各种矿物标本。Ore specimens are on display in showcases. ◇ ～馆 exhibition hall/ ～柜 showcase/ ～品 exhibit/ ～室 exhibition room; showroom

【陈皮】 chénpí 〈中药〉dried tangerine or orange peel

【陈皮梅】 chénpíméi preserved prune

【陈设】 chénshè ①display; set out: 屋子里～着几件工艺品。There is some artware set out in the room. ②furnishings: 房间里的～朴素大方。The room was furnished simply and in good taste.

【陈氏定理】 Chénshì dìnglǐ 〈数〉Chen's theorem: any sufficiently large even number can be represented as one prime plus the product of at most two primes

【陈胜吴广起义】 Chén Shèng Wú Guǎng Qǐyì the Chen Sheng-Wu Guang Uprising (209 B.C.), the first large-scale peasant uprising in China's history

【陈述】 chénshù state: ～自己的意见 state one's views ◇ ～句〈语〉declarative sentence

【陈说】 chénshuō state; explain: ～利害 explain the advantages and disadvantages (of a situation, course of action, etc.)

【陈诉】 chénsù state; recite: ～委屈 state one's grievances

**晨** chén morning: 清～ early morning; dawn

【晨光】 chénguāng the light of the early morning sun; dawn: ～熹微 first faint rays of dawn

【晨曦】 chénxī first rays of the morning sun

【晨星】 chénxīng ①stars at dawn: 寥若～ as few as stars at dawn ②〈天〉morning star

**谌** Chén a surname

**橙** chén
另见 chéng

【橙子】 chénzi orange

## chèn

**衬** chèn ①line; place sth. underneath: ～着驼绒的大衣 a fleece-lined overcoat/ ～上一层纸 put a piece of paper underneath/ 里面～一件背心 wear a vest underneath ②lining; liner: 领～ collar lining/ 袖～ cuff lining/ 钢～ steel liner/ ～管 liner tube ③set off: 白雪～着红梅，景色十分美丽。The red plum blossoms set off by the white snow were a beautiful sight.

【衬布】 chènbù lining cloth

【衬层】 chèncéng 〈机〉lining: 炉壁～ furnace lining

【衬垫】 chèndiàn 〈机〉liner: 接合～ joint liner

【衬裤】 chènkù underpants; pants

【衬里】 chènlǐ lining: 水泥～〈机〉cement lining

【衬裙】 chènqún underskirt; petticoat

【衬衫】 chènshān shirt

【衬套】 chèntào 〈机〉bush; bushing: 隔离～ dividing bushing/ 减震～ shock absorbing bushing

【衬托】 chèntuō set off; serve as a foil to

【衬衣】 chènyī underclothes; shirt

【衬纸】 chènzhǐ slip sheet; interleaving paper

【衬字】 chènzì word inserted in a line of verse for balance

or euphony

**称** chèn fit; match; suit: 颜色相～ well matched in colour

另见 chēng

【称身】 chènshēn fit: 这件衣服你穿了挺～的。This coat fits you perfectly.

【称心】 chènxīn find sth. satisfactory; be gratified: 这辆自行车买得很～。This bicycle is quite satisfactory — just the thing I want./ 这老人在年青时吃过很多苦，晚年过得很～。The old man who had suffered greatly in his youth spent his old age in contentment./ 这个问题解决得好，双方都～如意。The problem was solved to the satisfaction of both parties.

【称愿】 chènyuàn be gratified (esp. at the misfortune of a rival)

【称职】 chènzhí fill a post with credit; be competent

**龀** chèn 〈书〉 grow permanent teeth

**趁** chèn ① take advantage of; avail oneself of: 我想～这个机会讲几句话。I'd like to take this opportunity to say a few words. ② while: ～他在这儿，请他跟我们讲讲家乡的变化吧。While he's here, let's ask him to tell us about the changes in our hometown./ 这面～热吃吧。Eat the noodles while they are hot./ 咱们～亮儿走吧。Let's start while it is still light./ ～风起帆 set sail when the wind is fair ③ 〈方〉 be possessed of; be rich in: ～钱 have pots of money

【趁便】 chènbiàn when it is convenient; at one's convenience: 你回去的时候，～给我带个口信。When you go back would you take a message for me?/ 我在回来的路上～去他家看了看。I dropped in on him on my way home.

【趁火打劫】 chèn huǒ dǎjié loot a burning house; take advantage of sb.'s misfortune to do him harm

【趁机】 chènjī take advantage of the occasion; seize the chance: ～捣乱 seize the opportunity to make trouble

【趁空】 chènkòng use one's spare time; avail oneself of leisure time

【趁热打铁】 chèn rè dǎtiě strike while the iron is hot

【趁势】 chènshì take advantage of a favourable situation: 他越过对方后卫，～把球踢入球门。He dribbled past the full-back and scored a goal.

【趁早】 chènzǎo as early as possible; before it is too late; at the first opportunity: 我们还是～把场打完，免得雨淋。We'd better finish the threshing as soon as possible, in case it rains./ 你脸色不好，～去看看吧。You don't look well. You'd better go and see a doctor right away.

**榇** chèn 〈书〉 coffin

**谶** chèn 〈书〉 augury

【谶纬】 chènwěi divination combined with mystical Confucianist belief (prevalent during the Eastern Han Dynasty, 25-220)

【谶语】 chènyǔ a prophecy believed to have been fulfilled

## chen

**伧** chen 见"寒伧" hánchen

另见 cāng

**碜** chen 见"牙碜" yáchen

## chēng

**柽** chēng

【柽柳】 chēngliǔ 〈植〉 Chinese tamarisk

**称** chēng ① call: 自～ call (或 style) oneself/ 我们都～解放军为工农子弟兵。We all call the PLA the workers' and peasants' own army. ② name: 俗～ popular name/ 青藏高原素有世界屋脊之～。The Qinghai-Xizang Plateau has long been known as the roof of the world. ③ 〈书〉 say; state: 连声～好 say "good, good" again and again/ 据外交部发言人～ according to the Foreign Ministry spokesman ④ 〈书〉 commend; praise: 这支部队以善于夜战著～。This unit is famous for night fighting. ⑤ weigh: 用秤～一～。Weigh it in the balance./ 给我～二斤梨。I'd like two *jin* of pears, please.

另见 chèn

【称霸】 chēngbà seek hegemony; dominate: 超级大国妄图～世界。The superpowers vainly attempt to dominate the world./ 深挖洞，广积粮，不～。Dig tunnels deep, store grain everywhere, and never seek hegemony.

【称便】 chēngbiàn find sth. a great convenience: 商店日夜服务，群众无不～。Shops that stay open twenty-four hours a day are a great convenience to the public.

【称病】 chēngbìng plead illness

【称道】 chēngdào speak approvingly of; commend: 值得～ be praiseworthy

【称得起】 chēngdeqǐ deserve to be called; be worthy of the name of: 他真～我们车间的标兵。He really deserves to be called the pacesetter of our workshop.

【称孤道寡】 chēnggū-dàoguǎ style oneself king — act like an absolute ruler

【称号】 chēnghào title; name; designation: 她获得了先进工作者的～。She has won the title of advanced worker.

【称呼】 chēnghu ① call; address: 我该怎么～她？ What should I call her? 或 How should I address her? ② form of address

【称快】 chēngkuài express one's gratification: 拍手～ clap one's hands with satisfaction

【称量体重】 chēngliáng tǐzhòng 〈举重〉 weighing-in

【称赏】 chēngshǎng extol; speak highly of

【称颂】 chēngsòng praise; extol; eulogize: 人人～他的崇高品德。Everyone extols his noble qualities.

【称王称霸】 chēngwáng-chēngbà act like an overlord; lord it over; domineer

【称谓】 chēngwèi appellation; title

【称羡】 chēngxiàn express one's admiration; envy: ～不已 express profuse admiration

【称谢】 chēngxiè express one's thanks; thank: ～不止 thank sb. again and again

【称兄道弟】 chēngxiōng-dàodì call each other brothers; be on intimate terms

【称雄】 chēngxióng hold sway over a region; rule the roost: 割据～ break away from central authority and exercise local power; set up separationist rule

【称许】 chēngxǔ praise; commendation: 他的工作博得广大群众的～。His work won the praise of the broad masses.

【称誉】 chēngyù sing the praises of; praise; acclaim: 《国际歌》被列宁～为全世界无产阶级之歌。*The Internationale* was acclaimed by Lenin as the song of the world proletariat.

【称赞】 chēngzàn praise; acclaim; commend: 我们都～她的革命精神。We all praise her for her revolutionary spirit./ 他们获得全国人民的～。They have won the acclaim of the people all over the country.

**蛏** chēng razor clam

【蛏干】 chēnggān dried razor clam

【蛏子】 chēngzi razor clam

**铛** chēng shallow, flat pan; griddle
另见 dāng

**撑** chēng ① prop up; support: 他一手～起身子，一手投弹。He propped himself up on one hand and threw a grenade with the other./ 两手～着下巴 hold one's chin in one's hands ② push or move with a pole: ～船 pole a boat; punt ③ maintain; keep up: 他～不住，笑了。He could not help laughing./ 他连着打了两场球，再打恐怕～不住劲儿了。I'm afraid he won't be able to go on with another game; he's played two in a row already. ④ open; unfurl: ～伞 open an umbrella/ 把麻袋～开 hold open the sack ⑤ fill to the point of bursting: 我肚子有点～。I'm rather full./ 别装得太多，把口袋～破了。Don't stuff the sack too full or it'll burst. ⑥〈机〉brace; stay: 角～ corner brace

【撑臂】 chēngbì 〈机〉brace

【撑场面】 chēng chǎngmiàn keep up appearances 又作"撑门面"

【撑持】 chēngchí prop up; shore up; sustain: ～局面 shore up a shaky situation

【撑竿跳高】 chēnggān tiàogāo pole vault; pole jump

【撑条】 chēngtiáo 〈机〉stay: 斜～ diagonal stay/ 横～ cross stay

【撑腰】 chēngyāo support; back up; bolster up: ～打气 bolster and pep up

**瞠** chēng 〈书〉stare

【瞠乎其后】 chēng hū qí hòu stare helplessly at the vanishing back of the runner ahead — despair of catching up

【瞠目结舌】 chēngmù-jiéshé stare tongue-tied (或 dumbfounded)

## chéng

**丞** chéng ① assist ② assistant officer (in ancient China): 县～ county magistrate's assistant

【丞相】 chéngxiàng prime minister (in ancient China)

**成** chéng ① accomplish; succeed: 事～之后 after this is achieved ② become; turn into: 雪化～水。Snow melts into water./ 磨～粉末 be ground into powder/ 绿树～荫。The trees give welcome shade. /他～了水稻专家了。He's become an expert on paddy rice. ③ achievement; result: 怎能坐享其～？How can one sit idle and enjoy the fruits of others' labour? ④ fully developed; fully grown: ～人 adult ⑤ established; ready-made: 既～事实 established fact; *fait accompli*/ 现～服装 ready-made clothes ⑥ in considerable numbers or amounts: ～千上万的人 tens of thousands of people/ ～排的新房 row upon row of new houses/产量～倍增长。Output has doubled and redoubled. ⑦ all right; O.K.: ～！就这么办吧。All right. Let's do it that way. 或 O.K. Go ahead./ 你不去可不～。No, you must go. ⑧ able; capable: 说起庄稼活，他可真～！When it comes to farm work, he really knows his job. ⑨ one tenth: 增产两～ a 20% increase in output; output increased by 20 per cent ⑩ (Chéng) a surname

【成败】 chéng-bài success or failure: ～在此一举。Success or failure hinges on this one action./ ～利钝尚难逆料。Whether this will be successful or not is still difficult to predict.

【成本】 chéngběn cost: 生产～ production cost/ 固定～ fixed cost/ 可变～ variable cost/ 直接(间接)～ direct (indirect) cost
◇～核算 cost accounting/ ～价格 cost price/ ～会计 cost accounting/ ～帐 cost accounts

【成材】 chéngcái ① grow into useful timber; grow to full size ② become a useful person: 不让孩子经风雨见世面，怎么能～呢？How can a child grow up to be useful if he is not allowed to face the world and brave the storm? ◇～林 standing (或 mature) timber

【成虫】 chéngchóng 〈动〉imago; adult

【成都】 Chéngdū Chengdu

【成堆】 chéngduī form a pile; be in heaps: 菜市场门外摆着～的蔬菜。Vegetables are piled (或 heaped) up outside the food market./ 我们不要等问题成了堆才去解决。We shouldn't wait until problems pile up before we try to solve them.

【成方】 chéngfāng 〈中医〉set prescription

【成分】 chéngfèn ① composition; component part; ingredient: 化学～ chemical composition/ 肥料的～ the composition of a fertilizer/ 军队是国家政权的主要～。The army is the chief component of state power. ② one's class status; one's profession or economic status (before one joins the revolutionary ranks): 定～ determine sb.'s class status/ 改变～ change sb.'s class status/ 个人～好，出身也好 (person) of good class status and family background 又作"成份"

【成风】 chéngfēng become a common practice; become the order of the day: 学习马列著作和毛主席著作蔚然～。Studying Marxist-Leninist works and works by Chairman Mao has become a common practice./ 勤俭～。Diligence and frugality are now the order of the day.

【成个儿】 chénggèr ① be well formed; grow to a good size: 苹果已经～了。The apples have grown to a good size. ② be in the proper form: 他的字写得不～。His handwriting lacks form.

【成功】 chénggōng succeed; success: 大会开得很～。The congress was a great success./ 试验～了吗？Did the experiment come off all right?/ 这项革新一定能够～。The innovation is bound to be a success.

【成规】 chéngguī established practice; set rules; groove; rut: 墨守～ stick to conventions; get into a rut

【成果】 chéngguǒ achievement; fruit; gain; positive result: 科研～ achievements in scientific research/ 每一粒粮食都是辛勤劳动的～。Every single grain is the fruit of hard work./ 会谈取得了一些～。The talks have yielded some positive results.

【成婚】 chénghūn get married

【成活】 chénghuó survive: 新栽的树苗百分之九十五都已～。Ninety-five per cent of the new seedlings have survived. ◇～率 survival rate

【成绩】 chéngjī result; achievement; success: 取得了很大的～ have achieved great successes/ 在比赛中取得良好的～ get good results in a tournament/ 学习～优异 do exceedingly well in one's studies/ 在我们的工作中间～是主要的。Our achievements are the main aspect of our work./ 他们的工作是有～的。Their work has been fruitful. ◇～单 school report; report card

【成家】 chéngjiā (of a man) get married: 他才二十五岁，还没有～。He's not married yet, he's only twenty-five./ ～立业 get married and start one's career

【成见】 chéngjiàn preconceived idea; prejudice: 消除～

dispel prejudices/ 固执～ prejudiced; biased; opinionated
【成交】 chéngjiāo strike a bargain; conclude a transaction; clinch a deal ◇ ～额 volume of business
【成就】 chéngjiù ① achievement; accomplishment; attainment; success: 取得很大的～ achieve great successes/ 他是一个很有～的农民科学家。He is an accomplished peasant scientist./ 剧本的艺术～ artistic merits of a play ② achieve; accomplish: ～革命大业 accomplish a great revolutionary task
【成矿作用】 chéngkuàng zuòyòng mineralization
【成立】 chénglì ① found; establish; set up: 一九四九年十月一日毛主席庄严宣告中华人民共和国～。On October 1, 1949, Chairman Mao solemnly proclaimed the founding of the People's Republic of China./ 一九五八年农村中～了人民公社。People's communes were set up in the countryside in 1958./ ～革命委员会 establish a revolutionary committee/ 举行～大会 hold an inaugural meeting ② be tenable; hold water: 这个论点不能～。That argument is untenable (或 does not hold water).
【成例】 chénglì precedent; existing model: 这件事没有～可援。There is no precedent for this.
【成粒器】 chénglìqì 〈机〉 granulator
【成殓】 chéngliàn encoffin
【成龙配套】 chénglóng-pèitào fill in the gaps to complete a chain (of equipment, construction projects, etc.); link up the parts to form a whole: 使排灌设备～ complete a drainage and irrigation network/ 大小沟渠,～。The canals and ditches formed a complete irrigation system.
【成眠】 chéngmián 〈书〉 fall asleep; go to sleep: 夜不～ lie awake all night
【成名】 chéngmíng become famous; make a name for oneself
【成名成家】 chéngmíng-chéngjiā establish one's reputation as an authority
【成命】 chéngmìng order already issued: 收回～ countermand (或 retract) an order; revoke a command
【成年】 chéngnián ① grow up; come of age: 未～ be under age/ 解放前,他还没有～就给地主扛长活去了。Before liberation, he was compelled to work as a farmhand before he was grown up./ 在我国,年满十八岁为～。In China, a person comes of age at eighteen. ② adult; grown-up: ～人 an adult; a grown-up ③ 〈口〉 year after year: ～在外 be away all year/ ～累月 year in year out; for years on end
【成批】 chéngpī group by group; in batches: ～的新钢材 batches of new-type steel products/ ～生产 serial production; mass production
【成品】 chéngpǐn end (或 finished) product
【成气候】 chéng qìhou 〔多用于否定〕 make good: 成不了什么气候 will not get anywhere
【成器】 chéngqì grow up to be a useful person
【成亲】 chéngqīn get married
【成全】 chéngquán help (sb. to achieve his aim)
【成群】 chéngqún in groups; in large numbers: 三五～ in threes and fours; in small groups/ ～结队 in crowds; in throngs/ ～的牛羊 herds of cattle and sheep/ ～的蜜蜂 swarms of bees/ ～的对虾 shoals of prawns
【成人】 chéngrén ① grow up; become full-grown: 长大～ be grown to manhood ② adult; grown-up ◇ ～教育 adult education
【成人之美】 chéng rén zhī měi help sb. to fulfil his wish; aid sb. in doing a good deed
【成仁】 chéngrén 〈书〉 die for a righteous cause
【成日】 chéngrì 〈方〉 the whole day; all day long
【成色】 chéngsè ① the percentage of gold or silver in a coin, etc.; the relative purity of gold or silver ② quality: 看～定价钱 fix the prices according to the quality
【成事】 chéngshì accomplish sth.; succeed: ～不足,败事有余 unable to accomplish anything but liable to spoil everything
【成熟】 chéngshú ripe; mature: 桃子～了。The peaches are ripe./ 革命条件已经～。Conditions were ripe for revolution. 或 Conditions for a revolution have matured./ 时机～。The time is ripe./ 政治上～的党 a politically mature party/ ～的经验 ripe experience/ ～的意见 well-considered opinion/ 我的意见还不～。I haven't thought this idea through. ◇ ～林 mature forest/ ～期 〈农〉 mature period
【成说】 chéngshuō accepted theory or formulation: 进行科学研究,不能囿于～,要敢于创新。In scientific research, one should break new paths and not be fettered by accepted theories.
【成诵】 chéngsòng able to recite; able to repeat from memory: 熟读～ read again and again until one knows by heart; learn by rote
【成套】 chéngtào ① form a complete set: 这些仪器是～的,不要拆散。These instruments form a complete set. Don't separate them. ② whole (或 complete) set: ～设备 complete sets of equipment/ ～唱腔 a complete score for voices (in an opera)/ 提供～项目和技术援助 supply whole plants as well as technical aid
【成体】 chéngtǐ 〈动〉 adult
【成天】 chéngtiān 〈口〉 all day long; all the time
【成为】 chéngwéi become; turn into: 她已经～一个出色的拖拉机手。She's become an excellent tractor driver./ 把我国建设～社会主义的现代化强国 build China into a powerful modern socialist country
【成文】 chéngwén ① existing writings: 抄袭～ copy existing writings; follow a set pattern ② written ◇ ～法 written law; statute law
【成问题】 chéng wèntí be a problem; be open to question (或 doubt, objection): 雨再不停,明天的比赛就要～了。If the rain doesn't stop, I doubt if we can have the game tomorrow./ 这活干得这样粗,真～。The job has been done very carelessly; this is really serious./ 完成生产指标不～。We will fulfil the quota without fail./ 在我国大学毕业生就业不～。Getting a job is no problem for college graduates in our country.
【成象】 chéngxiàng 〈物〉 formation of image; imagery
【成效】 chéngxiào effect; result: ～显著 produce a marked effect; achieve remarkable success/ ～甚少 achieve little/ 初见～ win initial success/ 这种药连着吃下去一定会有～。This medicine will be effective if you keep on taking it for a time./ 几年来计划生育收到了巨大的～。Family planning has had marked success during the last few years.
【成心】 chéngxīn intentionally; on purpose; with deliberate intent: 他不是～让你难堪。He didn't mean to embarrass you.
【成形】 chéngxíng ① take shape: 我们的计划开始～了。Our plan is beginning to take shape. ② shaping; forming: 爆炸～ explosive forming/ 冷滚～ cold roll forming
【成性】 chéngxìng by nature; become sb.'s second nature: 帝国主义侵略～。Imperialism is aggressive by nature./ 这家伙盗窃～。Stealing has become that rascal's second nature.
【成药】 chéngyào medicine already prepared by a pharmacy
【成衣】 chéngyī ① 〈旧〉 tailoring ② ready-made clothes ◇ ～铺 tailor's shop; tailor's
【成因】 chéngyīn cause of formation; contributing factor
【成鱼】 chéngyú adult fish

【成语】 chéngyǔ 〈语〉 set phrase; idiom: «英语～词典» *A Dictionary of English Idioms*

【成员】 chéngyuán member: 领导小组～ a member of the leading group ◇ ～国 member state (或 country)

【成灾】 chéngzāi cause disaster: 暴雨～。The heavy rainstorm caused a disastrous flood.

【成长】 chéngzhǎng grow up; grow to maturity: 新栽的果树正在茁壮～。The young fruit trees are growing well./ 关心年轻一代的健康～ take an active interest in the healthy growth of the younger generation/ 大批少数民族干部已经～起来。 Many members of minority nationalities have become mature cadres.

【成竹在胸】 chéngzhú zài xiōng 见"胸有成竹" xiōng yǒu chéngzhú

**呈** chéng ① assume (form, colour, etc.): 叶～椭圆形。The leaf is oval in shape. ② submit; present ③ petition; memorial

【呈报】 chéngbào submit a report; report a matter: ～上级机关备案 report the matter to the higher level for the record

【呈递】 chéngdì present; submit: ～国书 present credentials (或 letter of credence)

【呈请】 chéngqǐng apply (to the higher authorities for consideration or approval)

【呈文】 chéngwén document submitted to a superior; memorial; petition

【呈现】 chéngxiàn present (a certain appearance); appear; emerge: 我国各条战线～着一片大好形势。A good situation prevails on all fronts in our country./ 全厂～出生动活泼的政治局面。A lively political situation has emerged in the factory./ 广大农村～出一派繁荣的景象。The countryside is one vast scene of prosperity.

【呈献】 chéngxiàn respectfully present

**诚** chéng ① sincere; honest: 开～相见 treat sb. openheartedly ②〈书〉 really; actually; indeed: ～非易事 be by no means easy/ ～有此事。There actually was such a thing.

【诚惶诚恐】 chénghuáng-chéngkǒng with reverence and awe; in fear and trepidation

【诚恳】 chéngkěn sincere: 作～的自我批评 make a sincere self-criticism/ ～听取群众的意见 listen to the criticisms of the masses with an open mind

【诚朴】 chéngpǔ honest; sincere and simple: 一个～的青年 an honest youth

【诚然】 chéngrán true; indeed; to be sure: 旱情～是严重的，但是它吓不倒我们。True, the drought is serious, but it can't scare us./ ～，武器是战争的重要因素，但决定的因素是人不是物。To be sure, weapons are an important factor in war, but it is people, not things, that are decisive.

【诚实】 chéngshí honest: ～可靠 honest and dependable

【诚心】 chéngxīn sincere desire; wholeheartedness: 一片～ in all sincerity/ ～诚意 earnestly and sincerely

【诚意】 chéngyì good faith; sincerity: 表明～ show one's good faith/ 缺乏～ lack sincerity

【诚挚】 chéngzhì sincere; cordial: ～友好的气氛 a sincere and friendly atmosphere/ ～的谢意 heartfelt thanks/ ～的接待 a cordial reception

**承** chéng ① bear; hold; carry: 那木桥～得住这样重的卡车吗？ Can that wooden bridge carry such heavy trucks? ② undertake; contract (to do a job): ～印 undertake the printing of/ ～制棉衣。We accept orders for padded clothes. ③〈套〉 be indebted (to sb. for a kindness); be granted a favour: ～您过奖。You flatter me. ④ continue; carry on: 继～ inherit; carry on

【承办】 chéngbàn undertake: ～土木工程 undertake civil engineering projects

【承包】 chéngbāo 〈旧〉 contract: ～桥梁工程 contract to build a bridge/ ～一万吨水泥的订货 contract for ten thousand tons of cement ◇ ～商 contractor

【承保】 chéngbǎo accept insurance ◇ ～范围 insurance coverage/ ～人 insurer/ ～通知书 cover note

【承担】 chéngdān bear; undertake; assume: ～一切费用 bear all the costs/ ～由此而产生的一切严重后果 bear responsibility (或 be held responsible) for all the serious consequences arising therefrom/ ～新设备的全部安装任务 undertake to install all the new equipment/ ～不首先使用核武器的义务 commit oneself not to be the first to use nuclear weapons/ ～额外工作 take on extra work/ 对一切损失～全部责任 be held fully responsible for all losses; answer for all the losses incurred

【承当】 chéngdāng take; bear: ～责任 bear the responsibility

【承兑】 chéngduì 〈商〉 honour; accept: 此处～旅行支票。Traveller's cheques (are) cashed here. ◇ ～人 accepter

【承继】 chéngjì ① be adopted as heir to one's uncle ② adopt one's brother's son (as one's heir)

【承接】 chéngjiē ① hold out a vessel to have liquid poured into it ② continue; carry on: ～上文 continued from the preceding paragraph

【承揽】 chénglǎn contract to do a job

【承梁】 chéngliáng 〈机〉 bolster: 防松～ check bolster

【承蒙】 chéngméng 〈套〉 be indebted (to sb. for a kindness); be granted a favour: ～热情招待，十分感激。I am very grateful to you for the cordial hospitality you accorded me.

【承诺】 chéngnuò promise to undertake; undertake to do sth.: 双方～为进一步开展文化交流创造便利条件。Both sides undertake to facilitate further cultural exchanges.

【承平】 chéngpíng 〈书〉 peaceful: ～年月 piping times of peace; time of peace

【承情】 chéngqíng 〈套〉 be much obliged; owe a debt of gratitude

【承认】 chéngrèn ① admit; acknowledge; recognize: ～错误 admit one's mistake; acknowledge one's fault/ 大家都～这个规划还很不完善。Everybody agreed that the plan was far from perfect./ 只有～阶级斗争、同时也～无产阶级专政的人，才是马克思主义者。Only he is a Marxist who extends the recognition of the class struggle to the recognition of the dictatorship of the proletariat./ ～党的章程 accept the Constitution of the Party ② give diplomatic recognition; recognize: ～中华人民共和国政府为中国的唯一合法政府 recognize the Government of the People's Republic of China as the sole legal government of China

【承上启下】 chéngshàng-qǐxià form a connecting link between the preceding and the following (as in a piece of writing, etc.)

【承受】 chéngshòu ① bear; support; endure: 这桥能～很大的重量。The bridge can bear a tremendous weight./ ～种种考验 endure every kind of trial ② inherit (a legacy, etc.)

【承望】 chéngwàng 〔多用于否定式〕 expect

【承袭】 chéngxí ① adopt; follow (a tradition, etc.) ② inherit (a peerage, etc.) ◇ ～海 patrimonial sea

【承先启后】 chéngxiān-qǐhòu inherit the past and usher in the future; serve as a link between past and future

【承运人】 chéngyùnrén carrier

【承载】 chéngzài bear the weight of ◇ ～能力 bearing capacity; load-bearing capacity

【承重】 chéngzhòng bearing; load-bearing ◇ ～墙 〈建〉

bearing (或 load-bearing) wall
【承转】 chéngzhuǎn forward (a document to the next level above or below)

**城** chéng ① city wall; wall: 长～ the Great Wall/ ～外 outside the city wall; outside the city ② city: 内(外)～ inner (outer) city/ 东～ the eastern part of the city ③ town: ～乡差别 the difference between town and country
【城邦】 chéngbāng city-state
【城堡】 chéngbǎo castle
【城池】 chéngchí city wall and moat; city
【城堞】 chéngdié battlements
【城垛口】 chéngduǒkǒu battlements
【城防】 chéngfáng the defence of a city: ～巩固。The city is closely guarded. ◇ ～部队 city garrison/ ～工事 defence works of a city
【城府】 chéngfǔ 〈书〉 shrewdness; subtlety: ～很深 shrewd and deep; subtle/ 胸无～ artless; simple and candid
【城根】 chénggēn sections of a city close to the city wall
【城关】 chéngguān the area just outside a city gate
【城郭】 chéngguō inner and outer city walls; city walls
【城壕】 chéngháo moat
【城隍】 Chénghuáng 〈道教〉 town god ◇ ～庙 town god's temple
【城郊】 chéngjiāo outskirts of a town
【城里】 chénglǐ inside the city; in town: ～人 city dwellers; townspeople
【城楼】 chénglóu a tower over a city gate; gate tower: 在天安门～上 on the rostrum of Tian An Men
【城门】 chéngmén city gate
【城门失火，殃及池鱼】 chéngmén shīhuǒ, yāng jí chí yú when the city gate catches fire, the fish in the moat suffer — in a disturbance innocent bystanders get into trouble
【城墙】 chéngqiáng city wall
【城区】 chéngqū the city proper: ～和郊区 the city proper and the suburbs
【城阙】 chéngquè 〈书〉 the watch tower on either side of a city gate
【城市】 chéngshì town; city
◇ ～规划 city planning/ ～环境 urban environment/ ～建设 urban construction/ ～居民 city dwellers; urban population/ ～贫民 urban (或 city) poor
【城头】 chéngtóu on top of the city wall: ～飘扬着红旗。Red flags are flying on top of the city wall.
【城下之盟】 chéng xià zhī méng a treaty concluded with the enemy who have reached the city wall; terms accepted under duress; a treaty signed under coercion
【城厢】 chéngxiāng the city proper and areas just outside its gates
【城垣】 chéngyuán 〈书〉 city wall
【城镇】 chéngzhèn cities and towns

**乘** chéng ① ride: ～公共汽车 ride in a bus; go by bus/ ～出租汽车到火车站去 take a taxi to the railway station/ ～火车(飞机、海轮、船)旅行 travel by train (plane, ship, boat)/ 代表团～车前往宾馆。The delegation drove to the guesthouse. ② take advantage of; avail oneself of: ～夜出击 attack under cover of night/ ～敌不备 take the enemy unawares ③ 〈数〉 multiply: 五～三等于十五。Five times three is fifteen. 或 5 multiplied by 3 is 15.
另见 shèng
【乘便】 chéngbiàn when it is convenient; at one's convenience: 请你～把那本书带给我。Please bring me the book whenever it's convenient.
【乘法】 chéngfǎ 〈数〉 multiplication ◇ ～表 multiplication table
【乘方】 chéngfāng 〈数〉 ① involution ② power: $n$ 的五次～ the fifth power of $n$; $n$ (raised) to the power of 5; $n^5$
【乘风破浪】 chéngfēng-pòlàng ride the wind and cleave the waves; brave the wind and the waves: 舰艇～巡逻在祖国的海疆。Braving the wind and the waves, the warships patrol our territorial waters./ 让我们沿着毛主席的革命路线，～，奋勇前进！Let us surmount all difficulties and forge ahead along Chairman Mao's revolutionary line!
【乘机】 chéngjī seize the opportunity: ～反攻 seize the opportunity to counterattack
【乘积】 chéngjī 〈数〉 product
【乘客】 chéngkè passenger
【乘凉】 chéngliáng enjoy the cool; relax in a cool place
【乘幂】 chéngmì 〈数〉 power
【乘人之危】 chéng rén zhī wēi take advantage of sb.'s precarious position
【乘胜】 chéngshèng exploit (或 follow up) a victory: ～追击 follow up a victory with hot pursuit/ ～前进 advance on the crest of a victory; push on in the flush of victory
【乘数】 chéngshù 〈数〉 multiplier
【乘务员】 chéngwùyuán attendant on a train
【乘隙】 chéngxì take advantage of a loophole; turn sb.'s mistake to one's own account: 乘敌之隙 exploit the enemy's blunder
【乘兴】 chéngxìng while one is in high spirits: ～作了一首诗 improvise a poem while in a joyful mood/ ～而来，兴尽而返 arrive in high spirits and depart after enjoying oneself to one's heart's content/ ～而来，败兴而归 set out cheerfully and return disappointed
【乘虚】 chéngxū take advantage of a weak point (或 an opening) in an opponent's defence; act when sb. is off guard: 在一营佯攻的时候，我们～而人，拿下了敌军司令部。While the first battalion created a diversion, we broke through and captured the enemy headquarters.
【乘晕宁】 chéngyùnníng 〈药〉 dramamine

**盛** chéng ① fill; ladle: ～饭 fill a bowl with rice/ 把菜～出来 ladle food from the pot; dish out food/ ～汤 ladle out soup/ 缸里～满了酒。The crock is filled with wine. ② hold; contain: 这麻袋可以～一百多斤粮食。This sack can hold more than 100 *jin* of grain./ 这间屋子太小，～不了这么多东西。The room is too small to hold all these things./ 这个礼堂能～一千人。This hall is big enough for a thousand people.
另见 shèng
【盛器】 chéngqì vessel; receptacle

**程** chéng ① rule; regulation: 章～ rules; constitution/ 规～ rules ② order; procedure: 议～ agenda ③ journey; stage of a journey: 启～ set out on a journey/ 送他一～ accompany him part of the way/ 送了一～又一～ accompany (a guest, traveller, etc.) league after league before parting ④ distance: 行～ distance of travel/ 射～ range (of fire) ⑤ (Chéng) a surname
【程度】 chéngdù ① level; degree: 觉悟～ level of political consciousness/ 文化～ level of education; degree of literacy ② extent; degree: 在很大(一定)～上 to a great (certain) extent/ 在不同～上 in varying degrees
【程式】 chéngshì form; pattern; formula: 公文～ forms and formulas of official documents ◇ ～动作 stylized movements (as in Beijing opera)/ ～化 stylization
【程序】 chéngxù ① order; procedure; course; sequence: 工作～ working procedure/ 法律～ legal procedure/ ～事项 procedural matters/ ～问题 point of order/ 符合～ be in

order/ ～性动议 procedural motion ②〈自〉programme ◇ ～法〈法〉law of procedure; procedural law/ ～教学 programmed instruction or learning/ ～控制〈自〉programme control/ ～设计〈自〉programming

**惩** chéng punish; penalize: 严～敢于入侵之敌 severely punish any enemy that dares to intrude

【惩办】 chéngbàn punish: 依法～反革命分子 punish counterrevolutionaries according to law/ ～和宽大相结合 combine punishment with leniency

【惩处】 chéngchǔ penalize; punish: 依法～ punish in accordance with the law

【惩罚】 chéngfá punish; penalize: 受到一次严厉的～ pay a severe penalty/ 侵略者受到了应得的～。The aggressors got what they deserved.

【惩戒】 chéngjiè punish sb. to teach him a lesson; discipline sb. as a warning; take disciplinary action against: 吊销执照,以示～ revoke sb.'s licence as a punishment

【惩前毖后,治病救人】 chéngqián-bìhòu, zhìbìng-jiùrén learn from past mistakes to avoid future ones, and cure the sickness to save the patient (a consistent policy of our Party towards cadres who have erred)

【惩一儆百】 chéng yī jǐng bǎi punish one to warn a hundred; make an example of sb.

【惩治】 chéngzhì punish; mete out punishment to

**塍** chéng 〈方〉a path between fields

**酲** chéng 〈书〉hangover

**澄** chéng clear; transparent: ～空 a clear, cloudless sky
另见 dèng

【澄清】 chéngqīng ① clear; transparent: 湖水碧绿～。The water of the lake is green and clear. ② clear up; clarify: ～误会 clear up a misunderstanding/ ～事实 clarify some facts/ 要求～ demand clarification
另见 dèngqīng

**橙** chéng ① orange ② orange colour: ～黄 orange (colour)
另见 chén

## chěng

**逞** chěng ① show off; flaunt: ～英雄 pose as a hero/ ～威风 show off one's strength or power; swagger about ② carry out (an evil design); succeed (in a scheme): 得～ succeed in one's schemes ③ indulge; give free rein to: ～性子 be wayward

【逞能】 chěngnéng show off one's skill or ability; parade one's ability: 他的缺点是好～。The trouble with him is that he likes to show off.

【逞强】 chěngqiáng flaunt one's superiority: ～好胜 parade one's superiority and strive to outshine others

【逞凶】 chěngxiōng act violently; act with murderous intent

**骋** chěng 〈书〉① gallop: 驰～ gallop about; dash about ② give free rein to

【骋怀】 chěnghuái 〈书〉give free rein to one's thoughts and feelings

【骋目】 chěngmù 〈书〉look into the distance: ～远眺 scan distant horizons

## chèng

**秤** chèng balance; steelyard: 杆～ steelyard; lever scales/ 台～ platform balance (或 scale)

【秤锤】 chèngchuí the sliding weight of a steelyard

【秤杆】 chènggǎn the arm (或 beam) of a steelyard

【秤钩】 chènggōu steelyard hook

【秤纽】 chèngniǔ the lifting cord of a steelyard 又作"秤毫"

【秤盘】 chèngpán the pan of a steelyard

【秤砣】 chèngtuó 〈口〉the sliding weight of a steelyard

【秤星】 chèngxīng gradations marked on the beam of a steelyard

## chī

**吃** chī ① eat; take: ～苹果 eat an apple/ ～药 take medicine/ ～糖 have some sweets ② have one's meals; eat: ～馆子 eat in a restaurant; dine out/ ～食堂 have one's meals in the mess ③ live on (或 off): ～利钱 live on interest ④ annihilate; wipe out: 又～掉敌军一个师 annihilate another enemy division/ ～一个子儿 take a piece (in chess) ⑤ exhaust; be a strain: 感到～力 feel the strain (of work, etc.); find a job difficult ⑥ absorb; soak up: 这种纸不～墨。This kind of paper does not absorb ink. ⑦ suffer; incur: 腿上～了一枪 get shot in the leg/ 连～败仗 suffer one defeat after another

【吃不服】 chībufú not be accustomed to eating sth.; not be used to certain food: 生冷的东西我总～。Cold and raw things never agree with me.

【吃不开】 chībukāi be unpopular; won't work: 这种工作作风到哪儿都～。Such a work style is unpopular anywhere./ 在新社会请客送礼、吹吹拍拍那一套可～了。The new society frowns upon such old practices as lavish private parties, expensive gifts, fulsome flattery and the like.

【吃不来】 chībulái not be fond of certain food: 芥末我～。I'm not especially fond of mustard./ 他～生蒜。He doesn't eat raw garlic.

【吃不了兜着走】 chībuliǎo dōuzhe zǒu get more than one bargained for; land oneself in serious trouble

【吃不上】 chībushàng ① be unable to get something to eat: 解放前你爷爷从来也～一顿饱饭。Before liberation your grandfather never got enough to eat. ② miss a meal: 快走吧,再晚了就～饭了。Hurry up, or we'll be too late to get anything to eat.

【吃不下】 chībuxià not feel like eating; be unable to eat any more: 他不太舒服,～。He's not very well; he doesn't feel like eating./ 谢谢,我实在～了。Thanks, but I really can't eat any more. 或 Thanks, I've really had enough.

【吃不消】 chībuxiāo be unable to stand (exertion, fatigue, etc.): 走这么多的路恐怕你～。It may be too much for you to walk such a long way./ 这文章写得又长又难懂,真让看的人～。No reader can put up with such a long and difficult article.

【吃不住】 chībuzhù be unable to bear or support: 机器太沉,这个架子～。The stand is not strong enough for this heavy machine./ 在我军强大攻势下,敌人～了。In the face of our strong attack, the enemy couldn't stand their ground.

【吃穿】 chī-chuān food and clothing: ～不愁 not have to worry about food and clothing

【吃醋】 chīcù be jealous (usu. of a rival in love)

【吃大户】 chī dàhù mass seizure and eating of food in the homes of landlords during famines before liberation

【吃刀】 chīdāo 〈机〉 penetration of a cutting tool

【吃得开】 chīdekāi be popular; be much sought after: 这种人在旧社会～，在新社会可不行。This sort of person could get along all right in the old society, but not in the new.

【吃得来】 chīdelái be able to eat; not mind eating: 辣椒我～，但不特别喜欢。I can eat red pepper, though I'm not overfond of it.

【吃得上】 chīdeshàng ① can afford to eat: 咱们家解放前吃糠咽菜，现在也～大米白面了。Before liberation our family lived on chaff and wild herbs, but now we can afford rice and wheat flour. ② be in time for a meal; be able to get a meal: 十二点半以前赶回去还～饭。If we get back before twelve thirty, we won't be too late for lunch./ 工人们不管什么时候到食堂去，都～热饭。The workers can get a hot meal any time they go to the canteen.

【吃得下】 chīdexià be able to eat: 还有一点，你～吗？There's still a bit left. Can you eat some more?/ 她已经好多了，饭也～了。She's much better; she's got an appetite now.

【吃得消】 chīdexiāo be able to stand (exertion, fatigue, etc.): 再干一个夜班，我也完全～。I can easily stand working another night shift. 或 I'm certainly good for another night shift./ 高空飞行，要身体结实才～。One needs a strong physique for high altitude flying.

【吃得住】 chīdezhù be able to bear or support: 再重的卡车，这座桥也能～。This bridge can bear the weight of the heaviest lorry.

【吃饭】 chīfàn ① eat; have a meal: 吃了饭再走吧！Don't go. Stay for dinner. ② keep alive; make a living: 靠打猎～ make a living by hunting/ 革命加生产即能解决～问题。Revolution plus production can solve the problem of feeding the population.

【吃喝玩乐】 chī-hē-wán-lè eat, drink and be merry — idle away one's time in pleasure-seeking

【吃喝儿】 chīher 〈口〉 food and drink: 他过去把钱都花在～上，现在可节省了。He used to spend all his money on food and drink; now he lives a simple life.

【吃紧】 chījǐn be critical; be hard pressed: 形势～。The situation was critical./ 前后方都～ be hard pressed both at the front and in the rear

【吃劲】 chījìn entail much effort; be a strain: 他挑一百五十斤也不～。He can carry 150 *jin* on a pole without straining himself.

【吃惊】 chījīng be startled; be shocked; be amazed; be taken aback: 大吃一惊 be flabbergasted/他那坚强的毅力使人～。His will power is amazing.

【吃苦】 chīkǔ bear hardships: ～耐劳 bear hardships and stand hard work/ ～在前，享乐在后 be the first to bear hardships and the last to enjoy comforts/ 决不再吃二遍苦 never allow oneself to be thrown back into the misery of the old society

【吃苦头】 chī kǔtou suffer: 蛮干是要～的。If you act rashly you'll suffer for it./ 要给敌人吃点苦头。We'll make the enemy suffer.

【吃亏】 chīkuī ① suffer losses; come to grief; get the worst of it: 有备才能无患，无备必定～。If one is prepared, one will be safe; if not, one will suffer. 或 Preparedness ensures security; unpreparedness invites disaster./ 有的人～，就在于不老实。Some people come to grief on account of their dishonesty./ 机械地搬用外国的东西是要吃大亏的。Mechanical copying of things foreign would be disastrous./ 吃眼前亏 immediately get the worst of it ② at a disadvantage; in an unfavourable situation: 他跑得不快，踢足球～。He can't run fast and that puts him at a disadvantage as a footballer.

【吃老本】 chī lǎoběn live off one's past gains; rest on one's laurels

【吃里爬外】 chīlǐ-páwài live off one person while secretly helping another

【吃力】 chīlì entail strenuous effort; be a strain: 他身体好，干这点儿活不算～。He's strong; this bit of work won't be too much for him./ 热情帮助学习上感到～的同学 warmheartedly help classmates who have difficulty in their studies/ ～不讨好的差使 a thankless task

【吃零嘴】 chī língzuǐ take snacks between meals; nibble between meals

【吃奶】 chīnǎi suck the breast: ～的孩子 sucking child; suckling/ 使尽～的力气 strain every muscle

【吃请】 chīqǐng accept an invitation to dinner (extended as a bribe)

【吃软不吃硬】 chīruǎn bù chīyìng be open to persuasion, but not to coercion

【吃水】 chīshuǐ ① drinking water: 过去这里～很困难。It used to be difficult to get drinking water here. ② absorb water: 这块地不～。This plot of land absorbs little water./ 这种大米～。You need a lot of water in cooking this kind of rice. ③〈航海〉 draught; draft: 满（空）载～ load (light) draught/ 这船～三米。The ship has a draught of 3 metres. ◇ ～线 waterline

【吃素】 chīsù abstain from eating meat; be a vegetarian

【吃透】 chītòu have a thorough grasp: ～文件精神 understand a document thoroughly; grasp the spirit of a document

【吃闲饭】 chī xiánfàn lead an idle life; be a loafer or sponger

【吃香】 chīxiāng 〈口〉 be very popular; be much sought after; be well-liked: 这种花布在群众中很～。This kind of cotton print is very popular.

【吃一堑，长一智】 chī yī qiàn, zhǎng yī zhì a fall into the pit, a gain in your wit

【吃斋】 chīzhāi practise abstinence from meat (as a religious exercise); be a vegetarian for religious reasons

【吃重】 chīzhòng ① arduous; strenuous: 这个任务很～。This is a hard job. 或 The task is arduous. ② carrying (或 loading) capacity: 这辆卡车～多少？ What's the carrying capacity of this truck?

**哧** chī 〈象〉: ～的一声撕下一块布来 rip off a piece of cloth with a sharp tearing sound/ ～～地笑 titter

**蚩** chī 〈书〉 ignorant; stupid

**鸱** chī

【鸱鸺】 chīxiū 〈动〉 owl

**眵** chī 见"眼眵" yǎnchī

**笞** chī 〈书〉 beat with a stick, cane, etc.: 鞭～ flog; whip

**痴** chī ① silly; idiotic: 白～ idiot ② crazy about: 书～ bookworm ③〈方〉 insane; mad: ～子 madman

【痴呆】 chīdāi ① dull-witted; stupid ②〈医〉 dementia: 老年性～ senile dementia

【痴肥】 chīféi abnormally fat; obese

【痴迷】 chīmí infatuated; obsessed; crazy

【痴情】 chīqíng unreasoning passion; infatuation

【痴人说梦】 chīrén shuō mèng idiotic nonsense; lunatic ravings

【痴想】 chīxiǎng wishful thinking; illusion

【痴心】 chīxīn infatuation: 一片～ sheer infatuation
【痴心妄想】 chīxīn-wàngxiǎng wishful thinking; fond dream

**嗤** chī sneer
【嗤笑】 chīxiào laugh at; sneer at
【嗤之以鼻】 chī zhī yǐ bí give a snort of contempt; despise

**媸** chī 〈书〉 ugly; unsightly; hideous

**魑** chī
【魑魅魍魉】 chīmèi-wǎngliǎng 〈书〉 evil spirits; demons and monsters

## chí

**池** chí ① pool; pond: 游泳～ swimming pool/ 养鱼～ fishpond ② an enclosed space with raised sides: 花～ flower bed/ 舞～ dance floor/ 乐～ orchestra pit ③ stalls (in a theatre): ～座 the stalls ④〈书〉 moat: 城～ city wall and moat; city ⑤ (Chí) a surname
【池汤】 chítāng a big pool in a bathhouse
【池塘】 chítáng pond; pool
【池盐】 chíyán lake salt
【池沼】 chízhǎo pond; pool
【池子】 chízi 〈口〉 ① pond ② a big pool in a bathhouse ③〈旧〉 dance floor

**弛** chí 〈书〉 relax; slacken: 一张一～ tension alternating with relaxation
【弛缓】 chíhuǎn relax; calm down: 他听了这一番话,紧张的心情渐渐～下来。On hearing this he calmed down.
【弛禁】 chíjìn 〈书〉 rescind a prohibition; lift a ban
【弛张热】 chízhāngrè 〈医〉 remittent fever

**驰** chí ① speed; gallop: 一辆汽车飞～而过。A car sped past. ② spread: ～名 well-known ③〈书〉 turn eagerly towards: 心～神往 let one's thoughts fly to (a place or person); long for
【驰骋】 chíchěng 〈书〉 gallop: ～在辽阔的原野上 gallop across the vast plain/ ～文坛 play an outstanding role in the literary world; bestride the literary stage
【驰名】 chímíng known far and wide; well-known; famous; renowned: 世界～的万里长城 the world-famous Great Wall/ ～中外 renowned at home and abroad
【驰驱】 chíqū ① gallop ② do one's utmost in sb.'s service
【驰援】 chíyuán rush to the rescue

**迟** chí ① slow; tardy: ～于作复,歉甚。I'm sorry I have not been able to reply sooner. ② late: 对不起,来～了。I'm sorry I'm late. ③ (Chí) a surname
【迟迟】 chíchí slow; tardy: ～不表态 not state one's position even after stalling for a long time/ 他为什么～不来? Why is he taking so long to come?
【迟到】 chídào be (或 come, arrive) late: ～五分钟 be five minutes late/ 上班从不～ never be late for work
【迟钝】 chídùn slow (in thought or action); obtuse: 反应～ be slow in reacting; react slowly
【迟缓】 chíhuǎn slow; tardy; sluggish: 进展～ make slow progress/ 行动～ act slowly/ 这件事要赶快办,不能～。This must be done at once. There must be no delay.
【迟脉】 chímài 〈中医〉 retarded pulse (less than 60 beats per minute)
【迟慢】 chímàn slow; tardy
【迟暮】 chímù 〈书〉 past one's prime; late in one's life
【迟误】 chíwù delay; procrastinate: 不得～ admit of no delay
【迟延】 chíyán delay; retard: 毫不～地执行命令 carry out orders without delay
【迟疑】 chíyí hesitate: ～不决 hesitate to make a decision; be irresolute; be undecided/ 毫不～地接受了任务 accept an assignment without hesitation
【迟早】 chízǎo sooner or later
【迟滞】 chízhì ① slow-moving; sluggish: 河道淤塞,水流～。The river is silted up and the water flows sluggishly. ②〈军〉 delaying (action)

**持** chí ① hold; grasp: ～枪 hold a gun/ ～相反意见 hold a contrary opinion/ ～保留态度 have reservations/ ～不同政见者 dissident ② support; maintain: 支～ support; sustain/ 维～ keep; maintain ③ manage; run: 主～ take charge of; manage/ 操～ manage; handle ④ oppose: 相～不下 be locked in stalemate
【持家】 chíjiā run one's home; keep house: 勤俭～ be industrious and thrifty in running one's home
【持久】 chíjiǔ lasting; enduring; protracted: 作～打算 plan on a long-term basis/ 没有正确的领导,群众的积极性就不可能～。Without correct leadership, the enthusiasm of the masses cannot be sustained./ 只要帝国主义存在,就不可能有～和平。So long as imperialism exists, there can never be lasting peace. ◇ ～力 staying power; stamina; endurance /～战 protracted war; protracted warfare
【持论】 chílùn present an argument; put a case; express a view: ～公平 state a case fairly/ ～有据 put forward a well-grounded argument
【持平】 chípíng unbiased; fair: ～之论 a fair argument; an unbiased view
【持枪】 chíqiāng ① hold a gun ②〈军〉 port arms: ～!(口令) Port arms!
【持球】 chíqiú 〈排球〉 holding
【持续】 chíxù continued; sustained: 生产～跃进 continued leap forward in production/ 使原油产量～稳定上升 keep up a steady increase in the output of crude oil/ 两国的文化交流已经～了一千多年。Cultural interchange between the two countries has gone on for more than a thousand years. ◇ ～射击 sustained fire
【持有】 chíyǒu hold: ～护照 hold a passport/ ～不同意见 hold differing views
【持之以恒】 chí zhī yǐ héng persevere: 刻苦学习,～ study assiduously and perseveringly
【持之有故】 chí zhī yǒu gù have sufficient grounds for one's views
【持重】 chízhòng prudent; cautious; discreet: 老成～ experienced and prudent

**匙** chí spoon: 汤～ soup spoon/ 茶～ teaspoon
另见 shi
【匙子】 chízi spoon

**踟** chí
【踟蹰】 chíchú hesitate; waver: ～不前 hesitate to move forward

## chǐ

**尺** chǐ ① *chi*, a unit of length (=1/3 metre) ② rule; ruler: 折～ folding rule/ 丁字～ T-square ③ an instrument in the shape of a ruler: 计算～ slide rule/ 镇～ bronze

paperweight
另见 chě

【尺寸】 chǐcun measurement; dimensions; size: 衣服的～ measurements of a garment/ 量～ take sb.'s measurements/ 这块木板～正好。This board is just the right size./ 轮廓～ overall size/ 名义～ nominal size/ 加工～ finish size ◇ ～比例尺<机> dimension scale

【尺动脉】 chǐdòngmài <生理> ulnar artery

【尺牍】 chǐdú ① a model of epistolary art ② correspondence (of an eminent writer)

【尺度】 chǐdù yardstick; measure; scale: 只有千百万人民的革命实践，才是检验真理的～。The only yardstick of truth is the revolutionary practice of millions of people.

【尺短寸长】 chǐ duǎn cùn cháng sometimes a *chi* may prove short while a *cun* may prove long — everyone has his strong and weak points

【尺幅千里】 chǐfú qiānlǐ a panorama of a thousand *li* on a one-*chi* scroll—rich content within a small compass

【尺骨】 chǐgǔ <生理> ulna

【尺蠖】 chǐhuò <动> looper; inchworm; geometer: 桑～ mulberry looper ◇ ～蛾 <动> geometrid moth

【尺码】 chǐmǎ size; measures: 你穿多大～的鞋子？ What size shoes do you wear?

【尺子】 chǐzi rule; ruler

## 齿

chǐ ① tooth ② a tooth-like part of anything: 梳～儿 the teeth of a comb/ 锯～儿 the teeth of a saw ③ <书> age: 稚～ very young ④ <书> mention: 不足挂～ not worth mentioning

【齿冷】 chǐlěng <书> laugh sb. to scorn: 令人～ arouse one's scorn

【齿轮】 chǐlún gear wheel; gear: 正～ spur gear/ 斜～ helical gear/ 伞～ bevel gear
◇ ～传动 gear drive/ ～间隙 gear clearance/ ～箱 gear box/ ～组 gear cluster

【齿条】 chǐtiáo <机> rack

【齿舞】 Chǐwǔ Habomai

【齿龈】 chǐyín <生理> gums

## 侈

chǐ <书> ① wasteful; extravagant ② exaggerate

【侈谈】 chǐtán talk glibly about; prate about; prattle about: ～永久和平 prate about eternal peace/ 不能脱离生产实际去～技术革新。One should not prattle about technical innovations and disregard actual production.

## 耻

chǐ shame; disgrace; humiliation: 知～ have a sense of shame/ 引以为～ regard as a disgrace

【耻骨】 chǐgǔ <生理> pubic bones; pubis

【耻辱】 chǐrǔ shame; disgrace; humiliation

【耻笑】 chǐxiào hold sb. to ridicule; sneer at; mock

## 豉

chǐ 见"豆豉" dòuchǐ

## 褫

chǐ <书> strip; deprive: ～职 deprive sb. of his post; remove sb. from office

【褫夺】 chǐduó strip; deprive: ～公权 deprive sb. of civil rights

# chì

## 彳

chì

【彳亍】 chìchù <书> walk slowly: 独自在河边～ take a solitary walk along a river

## 叱

chì <书> loudly rebuke; shout at: 怒～ shout angrily at sb.

【叱喝】 chìhè shout at; bawl at

【叱骂】 chìmà scold roundly; curse; abuse

【叱责】 chìzé scold; upbraid; rebuke

【叱咤风云】 chìzhà fēngyún commanding the wind and the clouds; shaking heaven and earth; all-powerful: ～的英雄气概 earthshaking heroism

## 斥

chì ① upbraid; scold; denounce; reprimand: 痛～ vehemently denounce ② repel; exclude; oust: ～逐 expel; oust; drive away/ 同电相～。Two like electric charges repel each other. ③ <书> open up; expand: ～地 expand territory ④ <书> reconnoitre; scout: ～候 reconnoitre

【斥力】 chìlì <物> repulsion

【斥骂】 chìmà reproach; upbraid; scold

【斥退】 chìtuì ① <旧> dismiss sb. from his post ② <旧> expel from a school ③ shout at sb. to go away

【斥责】 chìzé reprimand; rebuke; denounce: 厉声～ severely reprimand; excoriate

## 赤

chì ① red: 面红耳～ get red in the face; be flushed (with excitement, shame or shyness) ② loyal; sincere; single-hearted: ～心 loyalty; sincerity ③ bare: ～背 barebacked/ ～身露体 naked

【赤膊】 chìbó barebacked: 打～ be stripped to the waist

【赤膊上阵】 chìbó shàngzhèn ① go into battle stripped to the waist ② throw away all disguise; come out into the open

【赤诚】 chìchéng absolute sincerity: ～待人 treat people with absolute sincerity

【赤胆忠心】 chìdǎn-zhōngxīn utter devotion; wholeheartedness; loyalty: ～为人民 serve the people with utter devotion

【赤道】 chìdào ① the equator ② <天> the celestial equator ◇ ～面 the equatorial plane/ ～无风带 the equatorial calm belt/ ～仪 equatorial telescope

【赤道几内亚】 Chìdào Jǐnèiyà Equatorial Guinea ◇ ～人 Equatorial Guinean

【赤地千里】 chìdì qiānlǐ a thousand *li* of barren land — a scene of utter desolation (after drought, pests, etc.)

【赤豆】 chìdòu red bean

【赤褐色】 chìhèsè russet

【赤红】 chìhóng crimson

【赤脚】 chìjiǎo barefoot: 社员们赤着脚在稻田里干活。The commune members worked barefooted in the paddy fields. ◇ ～医生 barefoot doctor

【赤金】 chìjīn pure gold; solid gold

【赤经】 chìjīng <天> right ascension

【赤痢】 chìlì <中医> dysentery characterized by blood in the stool

【赤磷】 chìlín red phosphorus

【赤露】 chìlù bare: ～着胸口 with bared chest

【赤裸裸】 chìluǒluǒ ① without a stitch of clothing; stark-naked ② undisguised; naked; out-and-out: ～的勾结 undisguised collusion/ ～的强盗行径 plain robbery/ ～的侵略 naked aggression

【赤霉素】 chìméisù <生化> gibberellin

【赤贫】 chìpín in abject poverty; utterly destitute

【赤芍】 chìsháo <中药> the (unpeeled) root of herbaceous peony (*Paeonia lactiflora*)

【赤手空拳】 chìshǒu-kōngquán bare-handed; unarmed

【赤松】 chìsōng <植> Japanese red pine

【赤陶】 chìtáo terra-cotta
【赤条条】 chìtiáotiáo have not a stitch on; be stark-naked
【赤铁矿】 chìtiěkuàng red iron ore; hematite
【赤铜矿】 chìtóngkuàng red copper ore; cuprite
【赤纬】 chìwěi 〈天〉 declination
【赤尾屿】 Chìwěiyǔ Chiweiyu
【赤卫队】 chìwèiduì Red Guards (armed units of the masses in the revolutionary base areas during the Second Revolutionary Civil War, 1927-1937)
【赤血盐】 chìxuèyán 〈化〉 potassium ferricyanide; red prussiate of potash
【赤眼蜂】 chìyǎnfēng trichogramma
【赤子】 chìzǐ a newborn baby: ～之心 the pure heart of a newborn babe — utter innocence
【赤字】 chìzì deficit: ～开支 deficit spending/ 财政(贸易)～ financial (trade) deficit/ 弥补～ make up (或 meet) a deficit
【赤足】 chìzú barefoot

**饬** chì 〈书〉 ① put in order; readjust: 整～ put in order; strengthen (discipline, etc.) ② orderly; well-behaved: 谨～ sober and well-behaved ③〔旧时公文用语〕 order: 严～ issue strict orders

**炽** chì flaming; ablaze
【炽烈】 chìliè burning fiercely; flaming; blazing: 炉火～。The stove is burning fiercely./ ～的气氛 a fervent atmosphere
【炽热】 chìrè ① red-hot; blazing: ～的钢水 red-hot molten steel/ 中国工人在～的阳光下与非洲兄弟共同劳动。The Chinese workers laboured under a blazing sun side by side with their African brothers. ② passionate: ～的情感 passionate feelings
【炽盛】 chìshèng flaming; ablaze; flourishing: 火势～。The fire is blazing.

**翅** chì ① wing ② shark's fin
【翅膀】 chìbǎng wing
【翅果】 chìguǒ 〈植〉 samara
【翅脉】 chìmài 〈动〉 vein (of the wings of an insect)

**敕** chì imperial order; edict

**啻** chì 〈书〉 only

## chōng

**冲** chōng ① pour boiling water on: ～茶 make tea ② rinse; flush: 把盘子～一～ rinse the plates/ 便后～水。Flush the toilet after use./ 秧苗给大水～走了。The seedlings were washed away by the flood. ③ charge; rush; dash: 向敌人～去 charge the enemy/ 哪里有困难就～向哪里。Rush to wherever there are difficulties to tackle./ 指导员～进着火的房子,救出了两个小孩。The political instructor dashed into the burning house and rescued two children. ④ clash; collide: ～突 conflict ⑤ thoroughfare; important place: 要～ hub ⑥ 〈方〉 a stretch of flatland in a hilly area ⑦〈摄〉 develop: ～胶卷 develop a roll of film ⑧〈天〉 opposition: 大～ favourable opposition
另见 chòng
【冲程】 chōngchéng 〈机〉 stroke: 四～发动机 four-stroke engine
【冲冲】 chōngchōng in a state of excitement: 怒气～ in a great rage/ 兴～ bursting with enthusiasm; in high spirits
【冲刺】 chōngcì 〈体〉 spurt; sprint: 向终点线～ make a spurt (或dash) towards the tape/ 最后～ a final sprint; a sprint at the finish ◇ ～速度 dash speed
【冲淡】 chōngdàn ① dilute: 把溶液～ dilute the solution ② water down; weaken; play down: 资产阶级报纸故意～这次罢工的意义。The bourgeois press played down the significance of the strike./ ～戏剧效果 weaken the dramatic effect/ 不要因次要问题而～了中心任务。Don't stress minor issues at the expense of the central task.
【冲动】 chōngdòng ① impulse: 出于一时～ act on impulse ② get excited; be impetuous: 他很容易～。He easily gets excited.
【冲断层】 chōngduàncéng 〈地〉 thrust fault
【冲犯】 chōngfàn offend; affront
【冲锋】 chōngfēng charge; assault: 打退敌人的～ beat back the enemy assault/ 为革命,他总是～在前。He is always in the van fighting for the revolution. ◇ ～号 bugle call to charge/ ～枪 submachine gun; tommy gun
【冲锋陷阵】 chōngfēng-xiànzhèn charge and shatter enemy positions; charge the enemy lines; charge forward
【冲服】 chōngfú take (medicine) after mixing it with water, wine, etc.
【冲沟】 chōnggōu 〈军〉 stormed crack
【冲昏头脑】 chōnghūn tóunǎo turn sb.'s head: 胜利～ dizzy with success
【冲击】 chōngjī ① lash; pound: 海浪～着礁石,飞起象珠子般的水花。The waves lashed at the rocks, sending up pearly spray./ 各国人民的革命斗争～着旧世界。The revolutionary struggles of the people of various countries are pounding at the old world. ②〈军〉 charge; assault: 向敌人阵地发起～ charge an enemy position ◇ ～波 〈物〉 shock wave; blast wave
【冲积】 chōngjī 〈地〉 alluviation
◇ ～层 alluvium/ ～平原 alluvial plain/ ～土 alluvial soil
【冲剂】 chōngjì 〈中药〉 medicine to be taken after being mixed with boiling water, wine, etc.
【冲决】 chōngjué burst; smash: ～堤防 burst the dykes/ ～束缚他们的罗网 smash the trammels that bind them
【冲口而出】 chōng kǒu ér chū say sth. unthinkingly; blurt sth. out
【冲垮】 chōngkuǎ burst; shatter: ～敌军防线 shatter the enemy lines
【冲力】 chōnglì impulsive force; momentum
【冲量】 chōngliàng 〈物〉 impulse
【冲破】 chōngpò break through; breach: ～重重障碍 break through one barrier after another; surmount all obstacles/ ～敌军包围 break through the enemy encirclement/ ～传统观念的束缚 smash the bonds of tradition
【冲散】 chōngsàn break up; scatter; disperse: ～人群 disperse a crowd
【冲杀】 chōngshā charge; rush ahead: 没有革命先辈在枪林弹雨中～,怎能有我们今天的幸福生活? If our revolutionary predecessors had not charged head-on against a hail of bullets, how could we enjoy the happy life of today?
【冲沙闸】 chōngshāzhá 〈水〉 scouring sluice
【冲晒】 chōngshài 〈摄〉 develop and print
【冲绳】 Chōngshéng Okinawa
【冲刷】 chōngshuā erode; scour; wash out (或 away): 垒起石坝,防止雨水～梯田。Stone banks were built to prevent erosion of the terraced fields./ 用劳动汗水～资产阶级思想 wash away bourgeois ideas in the sweat of one's brow; get rid of bourgeois ideas through manual labour/ ～旧社会遗留下来的污泥浊水 wash away the dirt and filth left over from the old society ◇ ～作用 〈水〉 scouring

【冲塌】 chōngtā (of floodwater, etc.) cause to collapse; burst: ～堤坝 burst dykes and dams/ ～房屋 dash against the houses and wash them away

【冲天】 chōngtiān towering; soaring: ～干劲 boundless enthusiasm/ 怒气～ in a towering rage

【冲突】 chōngtū conflict; clash: 武装～ an armed conflict/ 边境～ a border clash/利害～ conflict of interests/ 这两个会的时间～了。The two meetings clash.

【冲洗】 chōngxǐ ① rinse; wash: 用消毒药水～伤口 wash a wound with a disinfectant ② 〈摄〉 develop

【冲要】 chōngyào strategically important (place)

【冲帐】 chōngzhàng 〈会计〉 ① strike a balance ② reverse an entry

【冲撞】 chōngzhuàng ① collide; bump; ram: 渔船遭到敌舰的～。The fishing boat was rammed by an enemy warship. ② give offence; offend: 我没想到这句话竟～了他。I didn't expect him to take offence at that remark.

## 充

chōng ① sufficient; full: 供应～分 have ample supplies ② fill; charge: ～电 charge (a battery) ③ serve as; act as: ～向导 serve as a guide ④ pretend to be; pose as; pass sth. off as: ～内行 pretend to be an expert/ ～好汉 pose as a hero

【充斥】 chōngchì flood; congest; be full of: 解放前,上海市场上～着外国商品。Before liberation, Shanghai was flooded with foreign goods.

【充当】 chōngdāng serve as; act as; play the part of: ～翻译 act as interpreter/ ～辩护士 play the part of an apologist/ 好些知识青年现在在农村～拖拉机手。Many school graduates now work as tractor drivers in the countryside.

【充电】 chōngdiàn charge (a battery) ◇ ～器 charger

【充耳不闻】 chōng ěr bù wén stuff one's ears and refuse to listen; turn a deaf ear to

【充分】 chōngfèn full; ample; abundant: ～协商 full consultation/ ～证据 ample evidence/ ～利用 fully utilize; make full use of; turn to full account/ ～发动群众 fully arouse the masses/ 我们有～理由相信这消息是可靠的。We have every reason to believe that the news is true.

【充公】 chōnggōng confiscate

【充饥】 chōngjī allay (或 appease) one's hunger: 解放前我爷爷奶奶常靠野菜～。Before liberation my grandparents often allayed their hunger with wild herbs.

【充军】 chōngjūn 〈旧〉 be transported to a distant place for penal servitude; banish

【充满】 chōngmǎn full of; brimming with; permeated (或 imbued) with: 屋子里～着阳光。The room is full of sunshine./ 大厅里～了孩子们的欢笑声。The hall resounded with the laughter of children./ ～热情的讲话 a speech brimming with warmth/ 这首诗～革命乐观主义。This poem is imbued with revolutionary optimism.

【充沛】 chōngpèi plentiful; abundant; full of: 雨水～abundant rainfall/ 精力～ full of vim and vigour; vigorous; energetic/ ～的革命热情 unflagging revolutionary enthusiasm

【充其量】 chōngqíliàng at most; at best: 这点给养～只够维持三天。 The provisions can last three days at most./ ～十天就可以完成这项任务。The job will be finished in ten days at most.

【充任】 chōngrèn fill the post of; hold the position of: 聘请老工人～顾问 ask veteran workers to be our advisers/ 挑选政治觉悟高的青年人～民兵干部 recruit militia cadres from among young people with high political consciousness

【充塞】 chōngsè fill (up); cram

【充实】 chōngshí ① substantial; rich: 内容～ substantial in content ② substantiate; enrich; replenish: ～论据 substantiate one's argument/ ～库存 replenish the stocks/ 下放干部，～基层 transfer cadres to strengthen organizations at the grass roots

【充数】 chōngshù make up the number; serve as a stopgap

【充血】 chōngxuè 〈医〉 hyperaemia; congestion

【充溢】 chōngyì full to the brim; exuberant; overflowing: 孩子们的脸上～着幸福的笑容。The children's faces beamed with happy smiles./ 祖国大地～着春意。There is spring in the air all over our country.

【充盈】 chōngyíng plentiful; full: 仓廪～。The granaries are full.

【充裕】 chōngyù abundant; ample; plentiful: 时间～ have ample (或 plenty of) time/ 经济～ well-off

【充足】 chōngzú adequate; sufficient; abundant; ample: 经费～ have sufficient (或 ample) funds/ 阳光～ full of sunshine; sunny

【充足理由律】 chōngzúlǐyóulǜ 〈逻〉 the law of sufficient reason

## 忡

chōng

【忡忡】 chōngchōng laden with anxiety; careworn: 忧心～ heavyhearted; deeply worried

## 茺

chōng

【茺蔚】 chōngwèi 〈植〉 motherwort

## 舂

chōng pound; pestle: ～米 husk rice with mortar and pestle/ ～药 pound medicinal herbs in a mortar

## 憧

chōng

【憧憧】 chōngchōng flickering; moving: 树影～ flickering shadows of trees/ 人影～ shadows of people moving about

【憧憬】 chōngjǐng long for; look forward to: 我们～着四个现代化的实现。We look forward to the realization of the "four modernizations"

# chóng

## 虫

chóng insect; worm

【虫草】 chóngcǎo 〈中药〉 Chinese caterpillar fungus (*Cordyceps sinensis*)

【虫害】 chónghài insect pest

【虫积】 chóngjī 〈中医〉 parasitic diseases (mainly in the stomach or intestines)

【虫胶】 chóngjiāo shellac ◇ ～清漆 shellac (varnish)

【虫媒花】 chóngméihuā 〈植〉 entomophilous flower

【虫情】 chóngqíng insect pest situation ◇ ～测报站 pest forecasting station

【虫牙】 chóngyá carious (或 decayed) tooth

【虫瘿】 chóngyǐng 〈植〉 gall

【虫灾】 chóngzāi plague of insects

【虫豸】 chóngzhì 〈书〉 insects

【虫子】 chóngzi insect; worm

## 重

chóng ① repeat; duplicate: 这两个例子～了。These two examples duplicate each other./ 书买～了。Two copies of the same book have been bought by mistake. ② again; once more: ～启战端 renew hostilities/ ～访延安 revisit Yan'an ③ layer: 越过万～山 climb over countless mountains/ 双～领导 dual leadership/ 新旧社会两～天。The old and new societies are two entirely different worlds.

另见 zhòng
【重版】 chóngbǎn republication
【重唱】 chóngchàng 〈乐〉 an ensemble of two or more singers, each singing one part: 二～ duet
【重重】 chóngchóng layer upon layer; ring upon ring: 敌人陷入～包围之中。The enemy was encircled ring upon ring./ 克服～困难 overcome one difficulty after another; surmount numerous difficulties/ 受到～剥削 be fleeced right and left/ 顾虑～ full of misgivings
【重蹈覆辙】 chóng dǎo fùzhé follow the same old disastrous road
【重迭】 chóngdié one on top of another; overlapping: 山峦～ range upon range of mountains/ 精简～的行政机构 simplify overlapping administrative organizations
【重发球】 chóngfāqiú 〈体〉 let service; let
【重返】 chóngfǎn return: ～前线 go back to the front/ ～家园 return to one's homeland ◇ ～大气层运载工具 reentry vehicle
【重犯】 chóngfàn repeat (an error or offence): 吸取教训,避免～错误 draw a lesson from past errors so as to prevent their recurrence
【重逢】 chóngféng meet again; have a reunion: 久别～ meet again after a long separation/ 旧友～ reunion of old friends
【重复】 chóngfù repeat; duplicate: 避免不必要的～ avoid unnecessary repetition/ 任何历史现象都不会是简单的～。No historical phenomenon is a mere repetition of the past.
【重合】 chónghé 〈数〉 coincide
【重婚】 chónghūn 〈法〉 bigamy
【重见天日】 chóng jiàn tiānrì once more see the light of day — be delivered from oppression or persecution
【重建】 chóngjiàn rebuild; reconstruct; reestablish; rehabilitate: 战后的～工作 postwar reconstruction/ ～家园 rehabilitate one's homeland; rebuild one's home village or town
【重九】 Chóngjiǔ 见"重阳"
【重起炉灶】 chóng qǐ lúzào begin all over again; make a fresh start
【重庆谈判】 Chóngqìng Tánpàn the Chongqing Negotiations (August-October 1945, peace talks between the representatives of the Chinese Communist Party led by Comrade Mao Zedong, and those of the Kuomintang)
【重申】 chóngshēn reaffirm; reiterate; restate: ～前令 reaffirm an existing decree/ ～党的纪律 affirm anew the discipline of the Party/ ～我国政府的一贯立场 reiterate the consistent stand of our government
【重施故技】 chóng shī gùjì play the same old trick; repeat a stock trick
【重孙】 chóngsūn great-grandson
【重孙女】 chóngsūnnǚ great-granddaughter
【重弹老调】 chóng tán lǎodiào harp on the same string; sing the same old tune
【重提】 chóngtí bring up again: 旧事～ bring up an old case; recall past events
【重围】 chóngwéi tight encirclement: 杀出～ break through a tight encirclement
【重温】 chóngwēn review: ～两条路线斗争的历史 review the history of the two-line struggles/ ～毛主席关于统一战线的教导 study again Chairman Mao's teachings on the united front
【重温旧梦】 chóng wēn jiùmèng revive an old dream; relive an old experience
【重现】 chóngxiàn reappear: 当年的战斗场面又～在他眼前。The battle scenes of those years reappeared in his mind's eye.
【重新】 chóngxīn 〈副〉 again; anew; afresh: ～做人 begin one's life anew; turn over a new leaf/ ～考虑 reconsider/ ～部署 rearrange; redeploy/ ～发起进攻 launch a fresh offensive
【重修旧好】 chóng xiū jiùhǎo renew cordial relations; become reconciled; bury the hatchet
【重檐】 chóngyán 〈建〉 double-eaved roof
【重演】 chóngyǎn ① put on an old play, etc. ② recur; reenact; repeat: 历史的错误不许～。Past mistakes should not be repeated.
【重阳】 Chóngyáng the Double Ninth Festival (9th day of the 9th lunar month)
【重洋】 chóngyáng the seas and oceans: 远涉～ travel across the oceans/ 远隔～ be separated by seas and oceans
【重译】 chóngyì retranslate
【重印】 chóngyìn reprint ◇ ～本 reprint
【重振军威】 chóng zhèn jūnwēi restore the prestige of an army; make an army's might felt once again
【重整旗鼓】 chóng zhěng qígǔ rally one's forces (after a defeat)
【重奏】 chóngzòu 〈乐〉 an ensemble of two or more instrumentalists, each playing one part: 四～ quartet

**崇** chóng ① high; lofty; sublime: ～山峻岭 high mountain ridges ② esteem; worship: ～洋迷外 worship and have blind faith in things foreign ③ (Chóng) a surname
【崇拜】 chóngbài worship; adore: ～偶像 worship of idols; idolatry
【崇奉】 chóngfèng believe in (a religion); worship
【崇高】 chónggāo lofty; sublime; high: ～的理想 a lofty ideal/ ～的威望 high prestige/ 顺致最～的敬意。I avail myself of this opportunity to renew to you the assurances of my highest consideration.
【崇敬】 chóngjìng esteem; respect; revere: 怀着十分～的心情 cherish a feeling of great reverence for/ 革命英雄永远受到人民的～。Revolutionary heroes will always be held in esteem by the people.
【崇尚】 chóngshàng uphold; advocate: ～勤俭 advocate industry and thrift

## chǒng

**宠** chǒng dote on; bestow favour on: 得～ find favour with sb.; be in sb.'s good graces/ 失～ fall out of favour/ 别把孩子～坏了。Don't spoil the child.
【宠爱】 chǒng'ài make a pet of sb.; dote on
【宠儿】 chǒng'ér pet; favourite
【宠辱不惊】 chǒng-rǔ bù jīng remain indifferent whether granted favours or subjected to humiliation
【宠信】 chǒngxìn be specially fond of and trust unduly (a subordinate)

## chòng

**冲** chòng 〈口〉 ① with vim and vigour; with plenty of dash; vigorously: 这小伙子干活儿真～。This young fellow does his work with vim and vigour./ 水流得很～。The water flows with great force./ 他说话很～。He speaks bluntly. ② (of smell) strong: 这药味很～。This medicine has a strong smell. ③ facing; towards: 窗户～南开。The window faces south./ 这话是～他说的。That remark was aimed at him. ④ on the strength of; on the basis of; because: ～他们这股子干劲儿,没有克服不了的困难。With such

drive, there's no difficulty that they can't overcome. ⑤ 〈机〉 punching
另见 chōng
【冲床】 chòngchuáng 〈机〉 punch (press); punching machine
【冲孔】 chòngkǒng 〈机〉 ①punching ②punched hole
【冲模】 chòngmú 〈机〉 die ◇ ～插床 die slotting machine
【冲头】 chòngtóu 〈机〉 drift; punch pin
【冲压】 chòngyā 〈机〉 stamping; punching ◇ ～机 punch
【冲子】 chòngzi punching pin

**铳** chòng blunderbuss

## chōu

**抽** chōu ① take out (from in between): 从文件夹里～出一份申请书 take an application out of the file ② take (a part from a whole): ～出一部分劳力去抗旱 release part of the labour force from other work to combat the drought/ 把他～出来管仓库 release him from his job and put him in charge of the warehouse/ 开会前请～时间把文件看一下。Try and find time to read the document before the meeting. ③ (of certain plants) put forth: ～枝 branch out; sprout/ 小树～出了嫩芽。The saplings are budding. ④ obtain by drawing, etc.: ～水 pump water/ ～血 draw blood (for a test or transfusion) ⑤ shrink: 这种布一洗就～。This cloth shrinks in the wash. ⑥ lash; whip; thrash: ～陀螺 whip a top/ ～牲口 lash a draught animal
【抽查】 chōuchá selective examination; spot check (或 test)
【抽搐】 chōuchù ① twitch ②〈医〉 tic
【抽打】 chōudǎ lash; whip; thrash: 狠毒的农奴主用皮鞭～农奴。The vicious serf owner lashed the serf with a whip.
【抽搭】 chōuda 〈口〉 sob: 抽抽搭搭地哭了起来 break into sobs
【抽调】 chōudiào transfer (personnel or material): ～部分兵力向北增援 move part of the troops to the north as reinforcements/ ～干部支援农业 transfer cadres to strengthen the agricultural front
【抽丁】 chōudīng press-gang
【抽动】 chōudòng twitch; spasm; spasmodic jerk
【抽斗】 chōudǒu 〈方〉 drawer
【抽肥补瘦】 chōuféi-bǔshòu take from the fat to pad the lean; take from those who have too much and give to those who have too little
【抽风】 chōufēng 〈医〉 convulsions
【抽筋】 chōujīn ① pull out a tendon ②〈口〉 cramp: 腿～ have a cramp in the leg
【抽空】 chōukòng manage to find time: 他工作很忙，可是还～学习英语。Despite the pressure of work, he manages to find time to study English./ 抽不出空来 be unable to find time 又作"抽功夫"
【抽冷子】 chōu lěngzi do sth. when people are off guard: 医生让他在医院里再呆几天，他却～跑回了工地。The doctor had told him to stay in hospital a few more days, but he slipped back to the worksite.
【抽搦】 chōunuò 〈医〉 tic; twitch
【抽气机】 chōuqìjī air exhauster; air extractor; air pump
【抽泣】 chōuqì sob
【抽签】 chōuqiān draw (或 cast) lots
【抽球】 chōuqiú 〈体〉 drive
【抽纱】 chōushā 〈工美〉 drawnwork
【抽身】 chōushēn leave (one's work); get away: 我七点钟以前恐怕抽不出身来。I'm afraid I'll be tied up until 7 o'clock. 或 I'm afraid I won't be free until 7 o'clock. /及早～ hasten to sever one's connection with (a corrupt clique, etc.)
【抽水】 chōushuǐ draw (或 pump) water: 从河里～ pump water from a river
◇ ～机 water pump/ ～马桶 flush toilet; water closet/ ～站 pumping station
【抽税】 chōushuì levy a tax
【抽丝】 chōusī reel off raw silk from cocoons
【抽穗】 chōusuì heading; earing: 小麦正在～。The wheat is in the ear. ◇ ～期 heading stage (或 period)
【抽缩】 chōusuō shrink; contract
【抽薹】 chōutái bolting: 油菜～了。The rape has bolted.
【抽提】 chōutí 〈化〉 extraction: ～蒸馏 extractive distillation
【抽屉】 chōuti drawer
【抽头】 chōutóu ① take a percentage (或 cut) of the winnings in gambling ②〈电〉 tap: ～电路 tap circuit
【抽象】 chōuxiàng abstract: ～的概念 an abstract concept/ 科学的～ scientific abstraction/ 不要这样～地谈问题。Don't speak in such abstract terms./ 从客观事物中～出正确的结论 draw a correct conclusion from objective facts
◇ ～劳动〈经〉 abstract labour/ ～派 abstractionist school; abstractionism/ ～数 〈数〉 abstract number/ ～思维 abstract thought
【抽薪止沸】 chōuxīn-zhǐfèi take out the firewood to stop the pot boiling — take drastic measures to stop sth.
【抽绣】 chōuxiù punchwork
【抽芽】 chōuyá put forth buds; bud; sprout
【抽烟】 chōuyān smoke (a cigarette or a pipe): 你～吗？Do you smoke?/ 请～。Have a smoke./ 抽一袋烟 smoke a pipe
【抽样】 chōuyàng 〈统计〉 sample; sampling: 随机～ random sampling
【抽噎】 chōuyē sob
【抽印】 chōuyìn offprint ◇ ～本 offprint
【抽壮丁】 chōu zhuàngdīng press-gang

## chóu

**仇** chóu ① enemy; foe: 亲痛～快 sadden one's friends and gladden one's enemies ②hatred; enmity: 阶级～ class hatred/ 有～ have a score to settle/ 记～ nurse a grievance
另见 Qiú
【仇敌】 chóudí foe; enemy
【仇恨】 chóuhèn hatred; enmity; hostility: 满腔～ seething with hatred
【仇人】 chóurén personal enemy: ～相见，分外眼红。When enemies come face to face, their eyes blaze with hate.
【仇杀】 chóushā kill in revenge
【仇视】 chóushì regard as an enemy; look upon with hatred; be hostile to
【仇隙】 chóuxì 〈书〉 bitter quarrel; feud

**俦** chóu 〈书〉 companion

**惆** chóu
【惆怅】 chóuchàng disconsolate; melancholy

**绸** chóu silk fabric; silk: ～伞 silk parasol
【绸缎】 chóuduàn silks and satins
【绸缪】 chóumóu ① sentimentally attached: 情意～ be head over heels in love ② 见"未雨绸缪" wèi yǔ chóumóu
【绸子】 chóuzi silk fabric

**畴** chóu 〈书〉 ① farmland: 平～千里 a vast expanse

of cultivated land ②kind; division: 范～ category
【畴昔】 chóuxī 〈书〉 in former times

**愁** chóu worry; be anxious: 不～吃,不～穿 not have to worry about food and clothing/ 你别～,病人很快会好的。Don't worry. The patient will soon recover./ 只要依靠群众,不～完不成任务。As long as we rely on the masses, we will certainly fulfil our task.
【愁肠】 chóucháng pent-up feelings of sadness: ～百结 weighed down with anxiety; with anxiety gnawing at one's heart
【愁苦】 chóukǔ anxiety; distress
【愁眉】 chóuméi knitted brows; worried look: ～不展 with a worried frown/ ～苦脸 have a worried look; pull a long face
【愁闷】 chóumèn feel gloomy; be in low spirits; be depressed
【愁容】 chóuróng worried look; anxious expression: ～满面 look extremely worried
【愁绪】 chóuxù 〈书〉 gloomy mood

**稠** chóu ①thick: 粥很～。The porridge is very thick. ②dense: 地窄人～ small in area but densely populated
【稠密】 chóumì dense: 人烟～ densely populated; populous/ 交通网～ a dense communications network
【稠人广众】 chóurén-guǎngzhòng large crowd; big gathering: 在～面前说话,她还是第一回呢。It was the first time she had ever spoken before such a big audience.

**酬** chóu ①〈书〉 propose a toast; toast ②reward; payment: 稿～ payment for an article or book written ③friendly exchange ④fulfil; realize: 壮志未～ with one's lofty aspirations unrealized
【酬报】 chóubào requite; reward; repay; recompense
【酬答】 chóudá ①thank sb. with a gift ②respond with a poem or speech
【酬和】 chóuhè respond (to a poem) with a poem
【酬金】 chóujīn monetary reward; remuneration
【酬劳】 chóuláo recompense; reward
【酬谢】 chóuxiè thank sb. with a gift
【酬应】 chóuyìng social intercourse: 不善～ socially inept
【酬载】 chóuzài 〈航空〉 payload
【酬酢】 chóuzuò 〈书〉 ①exchange of toasts ②friendly intercourse

**筹** chóu ①chip; counter: 竹～ bamboo chips ②prepare; plan: 统～ over-all planning/ ～款 raise money (或 funds)
【筹办】 chóubàn make preparations; make arrangements: 这次越野赛跑由我们厂负责～。Our factory is to make arrangements for the cross-country race.
【筹备】 chóubèi prepare; arrange: ～建校事宜 make preparations for the setting up of a school
◇～工作 preparatory work; preparations/ ～会议 preparatory (或 preliminary) meeting/ ～委员会 preparatory committee
【筹措】 chóucuò raise (money): ～旅费 raise money for travelling expenses
【筹划】 chóuhuà plan and prepare: 合作医疗站正～种植中草药。The cooperative medical service centre is planning to grow medicinal herbs./ 这里正在～建设一座水力发电站。Plans are being drawn up to build a hydroelectric station here.
【筹集】 chóují raise (money): ～基金 raise funds
【筹建】 chóujiàn prepare to construct or establish sth.: 这个车间从去年开始～。Preparations were started last year for the construction of the workshop./ ～研究所 make preparations for the setting up of a research institute
【筹码】 chóumǎ chip; counter: 政治交易的～ bargaining counters in political deals
【筹募】 chóumù collect (funds)
【筹商】 chóushāng discuss; consult: ～对策 discuss what countermeasures to take

**踌** chóu
【踌躇】 chóuchú hesitate; shilly-shally: ～不前 hesitate to move forward; hesitate to make a move
【踌躇满志】 chóuchú mǎn zhì enormously proud of one's success; smug; complacent

## chǒu

**丑** chǒu ①ugly; unsightly; hideous: 长得不～ not bad-looking ②disgraceful; shameful; scandalous: 出～ make a fool of oneself ③clown in Beijing opera, etc. ④the second of the twelve Earthly Branches
【丑八怪】 chǒubāguài 〈口〉 a very ugly person
【丑表功】 chǒubiǎogōng brag shamelessly about one's deeds
【丑恶】 chǒu'è ugly; repulsive; hideous: ～灵魂 an ugly soul/ ～面目 ugly features/ ～表演 a disgusting performance/揭露叛徒的～嘴脸 expose the hideous features of a renegade
【丑化】 chǒuhuà smear; uglify; defame; vilify: 这出坏戏～了劳动人民的形象。This play is notorious for vilifying the working people.
【丑剧】 chǒujù farce
【丑角】 chǒujué clown; buffoon
【丑陋】 chǒulòu ugly
【丑时】 chǒushí the period of the day from 1 a.m. to 3 a.m.
【丑事】 chǒushì scandal
【丑态】 chǒutài ugly (或 ludicrous) performance; buffoonery: ～百出 act like a buffoon; cut a contemptible figure
【丑闻】 chǒuwén scandal

**瞅** chǒu 〈方〉 look at: 让我～～。Let me have a look./ ～了一眼 take a look (或 glance) at
【瞅见】 chǒujiàn 〈方〉 see

## chòu

**臭** chòu ①smelly; foul; stinking: ～味 stink; offensive odour; foul smell/ ～鸡蛋 a rotten egg/ ～不可闻 give off an unbearable stink ②disgusting; disgraceful: 摆～架子 put on nauseating airs/ 买办资产阶级的名声早就～了。The comprador-bourgeoisie has long been discredited.
另见 xiù
【臭虫】 chòuchóng bedbug
【臭椿】 chòuchūn 〈植〉 tree of heaven (*Ailanthus altissima*)
【臭豆腐】 chòudòufu strong-smelling preserved bean curd
【臭烘烘】 chòuhōnghōng stinking; foul-smelling
【臭骂】 chòumà curse roundly; scold angrily and abusively: 挨了一顿～ get a tongue-lashing; get a dressing down
【臭名远扬】 chòumíng yuǎn yáng notorious
【臭名昭著】 chòumíng zhāozhù of ill repute; notorious
【臭皮囊】 chòupínáng 〈佛教〉 the vile skin-bag; the human body; this mortal flesh
【臭气】 chòuqì bad (或 offensive) smell; stink: ～熏天 stink

to high heaven
【臭氧】 chòuyǎng 〈化〉 ozone ◇ ～层 ozonosphere
【臭鼬】 chòuyòu 〈动〉 skunk

## chū

**出** chū ① go or come out: ～城 go out of town/ ～狱 be released from prison ② exceed; go beyond: ～月 after this month; next month/ 不～三年 within three years ③ issue; put up: ～证明 issue a certificate/ ～考题 set the paper; set the examination questions/ ～主意 offer advice; supply ideas; make suggestions/ ～布告 post an announcement; put up a notice/ ～大字报 put up a *dazibao* (或 big-character poster)/ 县委决定每个公社～一百个民工参加水库建设。It was decided by the County Party Committee that each commune was to send a hundred workers to help build the reservoir./ 今晚比赛,你们～谁? Who's going to play for your side in tonight's match? ④ produce; turn out: 多～煤,～好煤 produce more coal and good coal, too/ 实践～真知。Genuine knowledge comes from practice./ 我们部队～过不少战斗英雄。Our unit has produced quite a few combat heroes. ⑤ arise; happen: 这事～在三十年前。It happened thirty years ago./ ～问题 go wrong; go amiss/ 防止～事故 prevent accidents ⑥ rise well (with cooking): 这种米～饭。This kind of rice rises well when it's cooked. ⑦ put forth; vent: ～芽 put forth buds; sprout/ ～气 vent one's spleen/ ～疹子 have measles ⑧ pay out; expend: 量入为～ keep expenditures within the limits of income; cut one's coat according to one's cloth/ 入不敷～ one's income falling short of one's expenditure; unable to make both ends meet ⑨ a dramatic piece: 一～戏 an opera; a play

**出** chu 〔用于动词之后,表示向外、显露或完成〕: 从大厅里走～ come out of the hall/ 拿～证件 produce one's papers/ 派～代表团参加会议 send a delegation to attend a conference/ 选～新的中央委员会 elect a new central committee/ 看～问题 see where the problem lies; realize that there's something wrong/ 做～成绩 achieve (good) results

【出版】 chūbǎn come off the press; publish; come out: 这本书什么时候～? When will the book be published? ◇ ～社 publishing house/ ～物 publication/ ～自由 freedom of the press
【出榜】 chūbǎng ① publish a list of successful candidates or examinees ② 〈旧〉 put up a notice
【出殡】 chūbìn carry a coffin to the cemetery; hold a funeral procession
【出兵】 chūbīng dispatch troops
【出操】 chūcāo (go out to) drill or do exercises: 民兵今天下午～。The militia will have drill this afternoon.
【出岔子】 chū chàzi go wrong: 希望别～。I hope nothing goes wrong.
【出差】 chūchāi be away on official business; be on a business trip ◇ ～费 allowances for a business trip
【出产】 chūchǎn produce; manufacture: 江西景德镇～精美的瓷器。Jingdezhen in Jiangxi Province produces fine porcelain.
【出厂】 chūchǎng (of products) leave the factory ◇ ～价格 producer price; ex-factory price/ ～日期 date of production (或 manufacture)
【出场】 chūchǎng ① come on the stage; appear on the scene: 他们是今晚～的演员。They are the actors and actresses appearing tonight. ② enter the arena: ～的运动员名单 list of players for the match
【出超】 chūchāo favourable balance of trade
【出车】 chūchē ① dispatch a vehicle: 公共汽车早五点～。Bus service starts at 5 a.m. ② be out driving a vehicle: 老王～了。Lao Wang is out with the car.
【出丑】 chūchǒu make a fool of oneself; bring shame on oneself: 当众～ make a fool of oneself before others
【出处】 chūchù source (of a quotation or allusion): 注明～ indicate the source; give references
【出错】 chūcuò make mistakes: 他管帐很少～。He seldom makes a mistake in the accounts.
【出点子】 chū diǎnzi offer advice; make suggestions: 咱们怎么干,大家来～。What's to be done? Let's put our heads together./ 有人在背后出坏点子。Someone is directing the show from behind the scenes.
【出动】 chūdòng ① set out; start off: 小分队提前～了。The detachment set off ahead of schedule./ 待命～ await orders to set out (或 go into action)/ 全连～扫雪。The whole company turned out to sweep the snow. ② send out; dispatch: ～军舰 dispatch warships/ ～飞机二十架次 fly 20 sorties/ 反动当局～军队镇压罢工。The reactionary authorities called out troops to put down the strike. ◇ ～机场 departure airfield
【出尔反尔】 chū ěr fǎn ěr go back on one's word; contradict oneself
【出发】 chūfā ① set out; start off: 巡回医疗队今晚就要～了。The mobile medical team is leaving tonight. ② start from; proceed from: 一切从人民的利益～。Proceed in all cases from the interests of the people./ 从长远的观点～ from a long-term point of view ◇ ～点 starting point; point of departure/ ～港 port of departure
【出风头】 chū fēngtou seek or be in the limelight: 喜欢～ like to be in the limelight; seek the limelight
【出伏】 chūfú ending of the dog days
【出钢】 chūgāng 〈冶〉 tapping (of molten steel)
【出港】 chūgǎng clear a port; leave port ◇ ～呈报表 bill of clearance/ ～证 clearance (papers)
【出阁】 chūgé (of a woman) get married; marry
【出格】 chūgé exceed what is proper: 你这话有点～了。That's going a bit too far.
【出工】 chūgōng go to work; show up for work: 大忙季节,社员天不亮就～了。During the busy seasons the commune members go to work before dawn.
【出恭】 chūgōng go to the lavatory (for a bowel movement)
【出乖露丑】 chūguāi-lùchǒu make an exhibition of oneself
【出轨】 chūguǐ ① be derailed; go off the rails ② overstep the bounds: ～行为 improper behaviour
【出国】 chūguó go abroad
【出海】 chūhǎi go to sea; put out to sea: ～捕鱼 go fishing on the sea
【出汗】 chūhàn perspire; sweat: 出一身汗 break into a sweat; sweat all over
【出航】 chūháng ① set out on a voyage; set sail ② set out on a flight; take off ◇ ～航线 outbound course
【出乎意料】 chūhū yìliào exceeding one's expectations; contrary to one's expectations; unexpectedly: 试验结果～地好。The experiment turned out to be even more successful than was expected.
【出活】 chūhuó yield results in work; be efficient: 这样干,很～。This is an efficient way to work./ 新式农具既轻巧,又～。The improved farm tools are efficient as well as easy to handle./ 我们下午虽然只干了两个钟头,可是很～。We worked only two hours in the afternoon, but we accomplished a lot.

【出击】 chūjī launch an attack; hit out; make a sally: 不要四面～。Don't hit out in all directions.
【出家】 chūjiā become a monk or nun
【出价】 chūjià offer a price; bid
【出嫁】 chūjià (of a woman) get married; marry
【出界】 chūjiè 〈体〉 out-of-bounds; outside
【出借】 chūjiè lend; loan
【出境】 chūjìng leave the country: 递解～ send out of the country under escort/ 驱逐～ deport/ 办理～手续 go through exit formalities
◇ ～登记 departure registration/ ～签证 exit visa/ ～许可证 exit permit
【出局】 chūjú 〈棒、垒球〉 out
【出口】 chūkǒu ①speak; utter: ～伤人 speak bitingly ②exit: 会场的～ the exits of a conference hall ③export: ～大米 export rice
◇ ～补贴 export subsidy/ ～货 exports; outbound freight; exportation/ ～检疫 export quarantine/ ～贸易 export trade/ ～商品 export commodities/ ～税 export duties/ ～信贷担保 export credit guarantee/ ～许可证 export licence
【出口成章】 chū kǒu chéng zhāng words flow from the mouth as from the pen of a master
【出来】 chūlai come out; emerge: 太阳～了。The sun has come out./ 大伙儿都～欢迎子弟兵。We all turned out to welcome our soldiers.
【出来】 chulai ①〔用在动词后,表示动作由里向外朝着说话的人〕: 从屋里走出一个人来。Someone came out of the room. ②〔用在动词后,表示动作完成或实现〕: 他们终于把这种优质钢炼～了。They finally succeeded in making the high-grade steel. ③〔用在动词后,表示由隐蔽到显露〕: 有什么困难说～,大家帮助解决。If you have any difficulty, just let us know and we'll help you out./ 我一眼就认出他来了。I recognized him the moment I saw him.
【出类拔萃】 chūlèi-bácuì stand out from one's fellows; be out of the common run: ～的人物 an outstanding figure
【出力】 chūlì put forth one's strength; exert oneself: 他为我们公社的医疗卫生工作出过不少力。He has done quite a lot for the medical and health work of our commune./ 每人多出把力,任务就可以提前完成。If everyone puts in a bit more effort, the job will be finished ahead of time./ 垄断资本家强迫工人为他们～卖命。The monopoly capitalists force the workers to sweat their guts out.
【出列】 chūliè 〈军〉 leave one's place in the ranks: ～! (口令) Fall out!
【出猎】 chūliè go hunting
【出溜】 chūliu 〈方〉 slide; slip: 他脚底下一～,摔了一交。He slipped and fell.
【出笼】 chūlóng ①come out of the steamer: 刚～的包子 hot stuffed buns just out of the steamer ②〈贬〉 come forth; appear: 这部反党影片一～,立即受到群众的有力批判。As soon as the anti-Party film came out, it met with sharp criticism from the masses.
【出路】 chūlù way out; outlet: 河道淤塞,水无～。The riverbed is silted up, so there's no outlet for the floodwater./ 给以生活～ provide sb. with the opportunity to earn a living/ 农业的根本～在于机械化。The fundamental way out for agriculture lies in mechanization.
【出乱子】 chū luànzi go wrong; get into trouble
【出落】 chūluo grow (prettier, etc.): 一年不见,小姑娘～得更漂亮了。The girl has grown prettier than ever since I saw her a year ago.
【出马】 chūmǎ go into action; take the field: 亲自～ take up the matter oneself; attend to the matter personally; take personal charge of the matter
【出卖】 chūmài ①offer for sale; sell ②sell out; betray: ～原则 barter away principles/ 机会主义者～工人阶级的利益。Opportunists betray the interests of the working class.
【出毛病】 chū máobing be or go out of order: 机器～了。The machine is out of order./ 汽车～了。Something has gone wrong with the car./ 一路上没出什么毛病。Nothing went wrong on the journey.
【出门】 chūmén be away from home; go on a journey; go out: 他刚～,一会儿就回来。He's just gone out, he'll be back soon.
【出门子】 chū ménzi 〈口〉(of a woman) get married; marry
【出面】 chūmiàn act in one's own capacity or on behalf of an organization; appear personally: ～调停 act as a mediator/ 部长亲自～向大使们说明情况。The minister personally explained the matter to the ambassadors./ 双方由民间团体～商谈贸易。Trade talks are to be held by nongovernmental organizations of both sides./ 为什么你自己不～? Why didn't you take up the matter yourself?
【出苗】 chūmiáo 〈农〉 (of seedlings) emerge; come out ◇～率 rate of emergence
【出名】 chūmíng ①famous; well-known: 这儿是战争时期～的游击区。This was a famous guerrilla zone during the war./ 哈密瓜～地甜。Hami melons are known for their sweetness. ②lend one's name (to an occasion or enterprise); use the name of: 今晚由学生会～,召开迎新晚会。This evening the Students' Union will give a party to welcome the new students.
【出没】 chūmò appear and disappear; haunt: ～无常 appear and disappear unexpectedly; come and go unpredictably/ 川西的王朗自然保护区是大熊猫～的地方。The Wanglang Preserve in western Sichuan is the haunt of the giant panda.
【出谋划策】 chūmóu-huàcè give counsel; mastermind a scheme: 躲在背后～ mastermind a scheme from behind the scenes
【出纳】 chūnà ①receive and pay out money or bills ②cashier; teller ③receive and lend books, etc. ◇ ～台(图书馆) circulation desk; (银行等) cashier's (或 teller's) desk/ ～员 cashier; teller
【出品】 chūpǐn ①produce; manufacture; make: 光明化工厂～ manufactured (或 made) by Guangming Chemical Plant ②product: 新～ a new product
【出其不意】 chū qí bù yì take sb. by surprise; catch sb. unawares
【出奇】 chūqí unusually; extraordinarily: 今年夏天热得～。It's unusually hot this summer./ 那天清晨,大海～地宁静。The sea was extraordinarily calm that morning./ 机会主义者往往忽而右得要命,忽而"左"得～。Opportunists can be extremely Right at one time and extraordinarily "Left" at another.
【出奇制胜】 chū qí zhì shèng defeat one's opponent by a surprise move
【出气】 chūqì give vent to one's anger; vent one's spleen: 镇压了这个恶霸,可给乡亲们出了一口气! The villagers felt avenged when they saw the local despot shot. ◇ ～筒〈方〉 a person against whom sb.'s anger is wrongly vented; the undeserved target of sb.'s anger
【出气口】 chūqìkǒu gas outlet; air vent
【出勤】 chūqín ①turn out for work: 全体～ full attendance ②be out on duty ◇ ～率 rate of attendance; attendance
【出去】 chūqu go out; get out: ～走走 go out for a walk/ 门口太拥挤,一时出不去。The exit is too crowded for us to get out yet.
【出去】 chuqu 〔用在动词后,表示动作由里向外离开说话的人〕: 走～向工农群众征求意见 go out among the workers and

peasants to ask for their opinions/ 把侵略者赶～ drive the invaders out
【出圈儿】 chūquānr 〈方〉 overstep the bounds; go too far: 说话出了圈儿 go too far in what one says
【出缺】 chūquē (of a high post) fall vacant
【出让】 chūràng sell (one's own things): 自行车减价～ sell one's bicycle at a reduced price
【出人头地】 chū rén tóu dì rise head and shoulders above others; stand out among one's fellows
【出人意表】 chū rén yìbiǎo exceeding all expectations; beyond all expectations: 疗效之佳～。The curative effect far exceeded all expectations.
【出任】 chūrèn 〈书〉 take up the post of
【出入】 chūrù ① come in and go out: 骑自行车～请下车。Cyclists please dismount at the gate. ② discrepancy; divergence: 他说的和你说的有～。There's some discrepancy between your account and his./ 现款跟帐上的数目没有～。Cash on hand tallies with the figure in the accounts. ◇ ～证 pass (identifying a staff member, etc.)
【出色】 chūsè outstanding; remarkable; splendid: 干得很～ do a remarkable job; acquit oneself splendidly
【出身】 chūshēn ① class origin; family background: ～好 be of good class origin; have a good class background/ 贫农～的干部 cadres of poor-peasant origin/ 他是工人家庭～。He comes from a worker's family./ 咱们都是穷苦～。We're all from poor families. ② one's previous experience or occupation: 工人～的技术员 a technician promoted from among the workers/ 我们的游击队长是石匠～。Our guerrilla leader began life as a stonemason.
【出神】 chūshén be spellbound; be in a trance; be lost in thought: 青年钢琴家的演奏使她听得～。She was held spellbound by the performance of the young pianist./ 他坐在那里～。He sat there, lost in thought.
【出神入化】 chūshén-rùhuà reach the acme of perfection; be superb: ～的表演艺术 superb performance
【出生】 chūshēng be born: ～在一个下中农家庭里 be born into a lower-middle peasant family ◇ ～登记 registration of birth/ ～地 birthplace/ ～率 birthrate/ ～日期 date of birth/ ～证 birth certificate
【出生入死】 chūshēng-rùsǐ go through fire and water; brave untold dangers
【出师】 chūshī ① finish one's apprenticeship ② dispatch troops to fight; send out an army
【出使】 chūshǐ serve as an envoy abroad; be sent on a diplomatic mission
【出示】 chūshì show; produce: ～证件 produce one's papers
【出世】 chūshì ① come into the world; be born ② renounce the world; stand aloof from worldly affairs
【出事】 chūshì meet with a mishap; have an accident: 出了什么事？What's wrong? 或 What's happening?/ 放心吧，出不了事。Don't worry. Nothing will go wrong. ◇ ～地点 site of an accident
【出手】 chūshǒu ① get (hoarded goods, etc.) off one's hands; dispose of; sell: 货物已经～了。The goods have been disposed of. ② skill displayed in making opening moves: ～不凡 make skilful (或 masterly) opening moves (in *wushu*, chess, etc.) ③ length of sleeve
【出售】 chūshòu offer for sale; sell
【出数儿】 chūshùr 〈口〉 (of rice) rise well with cooking
【出粜】 chūtiào sell (grain)
【出挑】 chūtiao ① 见"出落" ② develop (in skill, etc.): 不满一年，他就～成一个好司机。In less than a year he developed into a good driver.
【出铁】 chūtiě 〈冶〉 tap a blast furnace; tapping: 出一炉铁 tap a heat of molten iron ◇ ～口 taphole; iron notch
【出庭】 chūtíng appear in court: ～作证 appear in court as a witness
【出头】 chūtóu ① lift one's head; free oneself (from misery, persecution, etc.): 打倒了地主，农民才有了～之日。It was not until the landlords were overthrown that the peasants could hold up their heads. ② appear in public; come forward: 教唆犯自己不～，专唆使青少年干坏事。Abettors of crime put youngsters up to all sorts of evil while staying in the background themselves. ③〔用在整数之后〕 a little over; odd: 他三十刚～。He's just a little over thirty./ 三百～ three hundred odd
【出头露面】 chūtóu-lùmiàn appear in public; be in the limelight: ～的人物 a public figure/ 喜欢～ fond of being in the limelight
【出土】 chūtǔ ① be unearthed; be excavated: ～文物展览 exhibition of unearthed artifacts; exhibition of archaeological finds ② come up out of the ground: 小苗刚～。The sprouts have just come up./ 只有让毒草～，才便于铲除。Only when poisonous weeds are allowed to come up out of the ground can they be uprooted.
【出脱】 chūtuō ① manage to sell; dispose of ② 见"出落" ③ acquit; absolve: 在旧社会，只要有钱，天大的罪名也～得了。In the old society, a person could get away with the most heinous crime so long as he was rich.
【出亡】 chūwáng flee; live in exile
【出席】 chūxí attend; be present: ～会议 attend a meeting/ ～宴会 be present at a banquet/ ～人数 number of persons present; attendance
【出息】 chūxi promise; prospects; future: 只要对人民有利，干什么工作都有～。Any job that benefits the people has a future./ 她自愿到最艰苦的地方去，真是个有～的姑娘。She wants to go where conditions are hardest. She's really a high-minded girl./ 满足于现状，不求上进是最没～的。To be content with things as they are and not strive to make progress is spineless and sterile./ 这个人真没～。This chap is a good-for-nothing.
【出险】 chūxiǎn ① be or get out of danger: 掩护游击队员～ help the guerrillas to escape from danger ② be in danger; be threatened: 河堤～，全村的人都赶去抢修。When the dyke was in danger, the whole village rushed out to repair it.
【出现】 chūxiàn appear; arise; emerge: 数百名手举鲜花的儿童～在运动场上。Several hundred children carrying bouquets came out onto the sports ground./ 工地上～了你追我赶的社会主义竞赛场面。The construction site presented an exciting scene of each one vying with the other in the socialist emulation campaign./ 旧的矛盾解决了，又会～新的矛盾。New contradictions will arise as old ones are resolved./ 我们将以一个具有高度文化的民族～于世界。We shall take our place in the world as a nation with an advanced culture.
【出项】 chūxiàng item of expenditure; expenses; outlay
【出血】 chūxuè 〈医〉 haemorrhage; bleeding: 大(内、胃)～ massive (internal, gastric) haemorrhage
【出巡】 chūxún ① royal progress ② tour of inspection
【出言不逊】 chūyán bù xùn make impertinent remarks; speak insolently
【出洋】 chūyáng 〈旧〉 go abroad: ～留学 go abroad to pursue one's studies; study abroad
【出洋相】 chū yángxiàng make an exhibition of oneself
【出以公心】 chū yǐ gōngxīn keep the public interest in mind; act without any selfish considerations
【出迎】 chūyíng go or come out to meet
【出油井】 chūyóujǐng 〈石油〉 producing well

【出游】 chūyóu go on a (sightseeing) tour
【出于】 chūyú start from; proceed from; stem from: ～对工作的责任感 proceed from a sense of duty/ ～对同志的关怀 out of concern for one's comrades/ ～不可告人的目的 actuated by ulterior motives/ ～无奈 as it cannot be helped; there being no alternative/ ～自愿 on a voluntary basis; of one's own accord
【出院】 chūyuàn leave hospital: 病愈～ be discharged from hospital after recovery ◇ ～证明 hospital discharge certificate
【出渣口】 chūzhākǒu 〈冶〉 slag notch; cinder notch
【出帐】 chūzhàng ① enter an item of expenditure in the accounts ② 〈方〉 items of expenditure
【出诊】 chūzhěn (of a doctor) visit a patient at home; pay a home visit; make a house call
【出征】 chūzhēng go on an expedition; go out to battle: ～的战士 soldiers sent on an expedition
【出众】 chūzhòng be out of the ordinary; be outstanding: 人才～ a person of exceptional ability
【出走】 chūzǒu leave; run away; flee: 仓卒～ leave in a hurry
【出租】 chūzū hire; let: 游船按小时～。Rowboats for hire by the hour./ 房屋～。Houses to let./ 连环画～处 picture book lending library ◇ ～汽车 taxicab; taxi; cab

**初** chū ① at the beginning of; in the early part of: 年～ at the beginning of the year/ ～夏 early summer/ 八月～ early in August; in early August ② first (in order): ～雪 first snow/ ～战 first battle/ ～五 the fifth day (of a lunar month) ③ for the first time: 感冒～起 with the first symptoms of a cold/ ～具规模 begin to take shape/ ～上阵的战士同老战士一样,也打得英勇顽强。Soldiers going into action for the first time fought just as bravely and stubbornly as the veterans. ④ elementary; rudimentary: ～级班 elementary course ⑤ original: ～愿 one's original intention/ 和好如～ become reconciled ⑥ (Chū) a surname
【初版】 chūbǎn first edition
【初步】 chūbù initial; preliminary; tentative: ～设想(方案) a tentative idea (programme)/ ～估计 preliminary estimates/ ～繁荣昌盛的社会主义国家 a socialist country with the beginnings of prosperity/ 获得～成果 reap first fruits; get initial results/ ～交换意见 have a preliminary exchange of views
【初出茅庐】 chū chū máolú just come out of one's thatched cottage — at the beginning of one's career; young and inexperienced: ～的作家 fledgling writer
【初创】 chūchuàng newly established: ～阶段 initial stage
【初次】 chūcì the first time: ～见面 see sb. for the first time/ ～登台 appear for the first time on the stage; make one's *dêbut*
【初等】 chūděng elementary; primary ◇ ～教育 primary education/ ～数学 elementary mathematics
【初犯】 chūfàn ① first offender ② first offence
【初伏】 chūfú ① the first of the three ten-day periods of the hot season ② the first day of the first period of the hot season
【初稿】 chūgǎo first draft
【初婚】 chūhūn first marriage
【初级】 chūjí elementary; primary ◇ ～产品 primary products/ ～读本 primer/ ～线圈 〈电〉 primary coil/ ～小学 lower primary school/ ～中学 junior middle school
【初级农业生产合作社】 chūjí nóngyè shēngchǎn hézuòshè elementary agricultural producers' cooperative (in which distribution was according to the amount of work each member did and the amount of land he contributed)
【初级社】 chūjíshè 〈简〉 (初级农业生产合作社) elementary agricultural producers' cooperative
【初交】 chūjiāo new acquaintance
【初亏】 chūkuī 〈天〉 first contact (of an eclipse)
【初恋】 chūliàn first love
【初馏塔】 chūliútǎ 〈石油〉 primary tower
【初露锋芒】 chū lù fēngmáng display one's talent for the first time
【初期】 chūqī initial stage; early days: 战争～ in the early days of the war/ 解放～ during the initial post-liberation period; just (或 right) after liberation
【初审】 chūshěn 〈法〉 trial of first instance; first trial ◇ ～案件 case of first instance/ ～法庭 court of first instance
【初生之犊】 chū shēng zhī dú newborn calf: ～不畏虎。〈谚〉 Newborn calves are not afraid of tigers — young people are fearless.
【初试】 chūshì ① first try ② preliminary examination
【初速度】 chūsùdù 〈物〉 initial velocity
【初小】 chūxiǎo 〈简〉 (初级小学) lower primary school
【初选】 chūxuǎn primary election
【初学】 chūxué begin to learn: 我是～,还不会拉曲子。I'm just a beginner; I can't play a tune yet.
【初叶】 chūyè early years (of a century): 二十世纪～ early in the twentieth century
【初诊】 chūzhěn first visit (to a doctor or hospital)
【初值】 chūzhí 〈数〉 initial value
【初中】 chūzhōng 〈简〉 (初级中学) junior middle school
【初衷】 chūzhōng original intention: 不改～ not change one's original intention

## chú

**刍** chú 〈书〉 ① hay; fodder: ～秣 fodder/ 反～ ruminate; chew the cud ② cut grass
【刍荛】 chúráo 〈书〉 ① cut grass and firewood ② one who gathers grass and firewood ③ 〈谦〉 bumpkin; boor; rustic: ～之言 my superficial remarks
【刍议】 chúyì 〈谦〉 my humble opinion

**除** chú ① get rid of; eliminate; remove: 为民～害 rid the people of a scourge/ 战天灾,～人祸 fight natural disasters and conquer human evils/ ～恶务尽 one must be thorough in exterminating an evil ② except: ～此而外 with the exception of this; excepting this ③ besides: ～水稻外,我们还种棉花和小麦。Besides rice, we grow cotton and wheat. ④ 〈数〉 divide: 八～以四得二。8 divided by 4 is 2./ 二～六得三。2 goes into 6 three times./ 十能被五～尽。10 divides by 5. 或 5 goes into 10. ⑤ 〈书〉 steps to a house; doorsteps: 洒扫庭～ sweep the courtyard
【除草】 chúcǎo weeding ◇～机 weeder/ ～剂 weed killer; herbicide
【除尘器】 chúchénqì dust remover
【除虫菊】 chúchóngjú 〈植〉 Dalmatian chrysanthemum
【除法】 chúfǎ 〈数〉 division
【除非】 chúfēi 〈连〉 ①〔常跟"才""否则""不然"等合用,表示唯一的条件〕 only if; only when: ～在这里修个水库,才能解决灌溉问题。Only when a reservoir is built here can we solve our irrigation problem./ 若要人不知,～己莫为。If you don't want people to know, you'd better not do it. ②〔表示不计算在内〕 unless: 他不会不来,～他病了。He'll certainly come unless he is ill.
【除根】 chúgēn dig up the roots; cure once and for all; root out: 斩草必须～。When you're weeding, you must

dig up the roots./ 这病很难～。It's difficult to find a permanent cure for this disease.

【除旧布新】 chújiù-bùxīn get rid of the old to make way for the new; do away with the old and set up the new

【除了】 chúle ① except: 那条山路，～这位老猎人，谁也不熟悉。Nobody knows the mountain path well except the old hunter. ② besides; in addition to: 他～教课，还负责学校里共青团的工作。Besides teaching, he's in charge of the school's Youth League work.

【除名】 chúmíng remove sb.'s name from the rolls; take sb.'s name off the books; expunge sb.'s name from a list

【除数】 chúshù 〈数〉 divisor

【除四害】 chú sì hài eliminate the four pests (i.e. rats, bedbugs, flies and mosquitoes)

【除外】 chúwài except; not counting; not including: 展览会每天开放，星期一～。The exhibition is open every day except Monday./ 一共五件行李，药箱～。There are five pieces of luggage, not counting the medical kit.

【除夕】 chúxī New Year's Eve

【除莠剂】 chúyǒujì herbicide

**鸲** chú 见"雏" chú

**厨** chú kitchen

【厨房】 chúfáng kitchen ◇ ～用具 kitchen (或 cooking) utensils

【厨师】 chúshī cook; *chef*

【厨子】 chúzi 〈旧〉 cook

**锄** chú ① hoe ② work with a hoe; hoe: ～玉米地 hoe the cornfields/ ～草 hoe up weeds; weed with a hoe ③ uproot; eliminate; wipe out

【锄奸】 chújiān eliminate traitors; ferret out spies: ～工作 elimination of traitors; anti-espionage work/ 为党～ remove a bunch of hidden traitors from the Party

【锄头】 chútou hoe

**蜍** chú 见"蟾蜍" chánchú

**雏** chú ① young (bird): ～燕 young swallow/ ～鸡 chicken ② nestling; fledgling

【雏鸟】 chúniǎo nestling; fledgling

【雏儿】 chúr 〈口〉 a young, inexperienced person; fledgling

【雏形】 chúxíng embryonic form; embryo: 龙山文化时期已产生了阶级的～。Classes appeared in an embryonic form as early as the age of the Longshan Culture.

**橱** chú cabinet; closet: 壁～ built-in cabinet/ 衣～ wardrobe/ 书～ bookcase/ 碗～ cupboard

【橱窗】 chúchuāng ① show (或 display) window; showcase; shopwindow ② glass-fronted billboard

【橱柜】 chúguì ① cupboard ② a cupboard that also serves as a table; sideboard

**躇** chú 见"踌躇" chóuchú

**蹰** chú 见"踟蹰" chíchú

## chǔ

**处** chǔ ① get along (with sb.): 容易相～ easy to get along with/ 他们俩～得很好。They get along quite well./ 这个人不好～。This fellow is hard to get along with. ② be situated in; be in a certain condition: 昔阳县地～太行山区。Xiyang County is located in the Taihang Mountains./ 我们正～在一个伟大的历史时代。We are living in a great historic era. ③ manage; handle; deal with: ～事 handle affairs; manage matters ④ punish; sentence: ～以两年徒刑 sentence sb. to two years' imprisonment ⑤ 〈书〉 dwell; live: 穴居野～ live in the wilds and dwell in caves

另见 chù

【处罚】 chǔfá punish; penalize

【处方】 chǔfāng ① write out a prescription; prescribe ② prescription; recipe

【处分】 chǔfèn take disciplinary action against; punish: 免予～ exempt sb. from punishment/ 按情节轻重予以～ punish a person according to the seriousness of his case/ 予以警告～ give sb. disciplinary warning/ 党内～ disciplinary action within the Party/ 行政～ administrative disciplinary measure

【处境】 chǔjìng unfavourable situation; plight: ～困难 be in a sorry plight; be in a predicament; be in a difficult situation/ ～危险 be in a dangerous (或 precarious) situation; be in peril

【处决】 chǔjué put to death; execute: 依法～ put to death in accordance with the law

【处理】 chǔlǐ ① handle; deal with; dispose of: 正确～人民内部矛盾 correctly handle contradictions among the people/ 必须严加～ should be dealt with sternly/ ～国家大事 conduct state affairs/ ～日常事务 handle day-to-day work; deal with routine matters/ 我回去～一下家务就来。I'll go home and come back as soon as I'm through with my chores./ 这事请保卫科～。Please refer the matter to the security section./ 垃圾～ garbage disposal ② treat by a special process: 用硫酸～ treat with sulphuric acid/ 热～ heat treatment ③ sell at reduced prices: ～积压商品 sell old stock at reduced prices ◇ ～价格 reduced price; bargain price/ ～品 goods sold at reduced prices; shopworn or substandard goods

【处女】 chǔnǚ virgin; maiden ◇ ～地 virgin land (或 soil)/ ～航 maiden voyage or flight/ ～膜 〈生理〉 hymen/ ～作 maiden work; first effort

【处世】 chǔshì conduct oneself in society: 批判资产阶级的～哲学 criticize the bourgeois philosophy of life

【处暑】 Chǔshǔ the Limit of Heat (14th solar term)

【处死】 chǔsǐ put to death; execute

【处心积虑】 chǔxīn-jīlǜ deliberately plan (to achieve evil ends); incessantly scheme: ～地破坏革命队伍的团结 be bent on undermining the unity of the revolutionary ranks

【处刑】 chǔxíng 〈法〉 condemn; sentence

【处于】 chǔyú be (in a certain condition): ～有利的地位 find oneself in an advantageous position/ ～平等地位 be on an equal footing/ ～优势 have the advantage/ ～高潮 be at high tide/ 今天世界上还有许许多多被压迫被剥削的人们～水深火热之中。In the world today there are still millions of oppressed and exploited people living in the abyss of suffering.

【处之泰然】 chǔ zhī tàirán take things calmly; remain unruffled

【处治】 chǔzhì punish

【处置】 chǔzhì ① handle; deal with; manage; dispose of: 妥善地～各种复杂情况 handle complex situations aptly/ ～失当 mismanage; mishandle ② punish

**杵** chǔ ① pestle: ～臼 mortar and pestle ② a stick used to pound clothes in washing ③ poke: 用手指头～他一下 give him a poke/ 把纸～个窟窿 poke a hole in the paper

【杵臼时代】 chǔjiù shídài the mortar-and-pestle age; the age of the hand-pestle

【杵状指】 chǔzhuàngzhǐ 〈医〉 clubbed finger

**础** chǔ plinth: ~石 the stone base of a column; plinth

**楮** chǔ ①〈植〉 paper mulberry ②〈书〉 paper

【楮实】 chǔshí 〈中药〉 paper mulberry fruit

**储** chǔ ① store up: ~粮备荒 store up grain against natural disasters/ 冬~白菜 cabbages stored for the winter ② (Chǔ) a surname

【储备】 chǔbèi ① store for future use; lay in; lay up: ~过冬饲料 lay up fodder for the winter/ ~粮食 store up grain; build up supplies of grain ② reserve: 黄金~ gold reserve/ 外汇~ foreign exchange reserve ◇ ~基金 reserve fund/ ~粮 grain reserves

【储藏】 chǔcáng ① save and preserve; store; keep: 鲜果~ preservation (或 storage) of fresh fruit ② deposit: 我国有丰富的石油~。Our country abounds in oil deposits. ◇ ~量〈矿〉 reserves/ ~室 storeroom

【储存】 chǔcún lay in; lay up; store; stockpile: ~余粮 store up surplus grain/ ~战略物资 stockpile strategic materials

【储户】 chǔhù depositor

【储集层】 chǔjícéng 〈石油〉 reservoir (bed)

【储君】 chǔjūn crown prince

【储量】 chǔliàng 〈矿〉 reserves: 远景~ prospective reserves/ 探明~ proved reserves/ 可采~ recoverable (或 workable) reserves ◇ ~等级 ore reserve classification

【储气】 chǔqì gas storage ◇ ~构造 gas-bearing structure/ ~罐 gas tank

【储蓄】 chǔxù save; deposit: 活期(定期)~ current (fixed) deposit/ 提倡~ encourage saving/ 城乡~迅速增加。Savings deposits in both urban and rural areas have shown a rapid increase. ◇ ~存款 savings deposit/ ~额 total savings deposits/ ~所 savings bank

【储油】 chǔyóu 〈石油〉 oil storage ◇ ~构造 oil-bearing structure

【储油罐】 chǔyóuguàn 〈石油〉 oil storage tank; oil tank: 浮顶~ floating roof tank/ 球形~ spherical tank

**褚** Chǔ a surname

**楚** chǔ ① clear; neat: 一清二~ perfectly clear ②〈书〉 pang; suffering: 苦~ distress; suffering ③ (Chǔ) a name for the region covering Hunan and Hubei, esp. Hubei ④ (Chǔ) a surname

【楚楚】 chǔchǔ clear; tidy; neat: 衣冠~ immaculately dressed

【楚剧】 chǔjù Chu opera (popular in Hubei and part of Jiangxi)

## chù

**亍** chù 见"彳亍" chìchù

**处** chù ① place: 住~ dwelling place; quarters/ 别~ another place; elsewhere/ 停车~ parking place (或 lot); car park ② point; part: 长~ strong point; forte/ 有相同之~ bear a resemblance; have something in common ③〈量〉: 几~人家 several homesteads/ 发现两~印刷错误 find two misprints ④ department; office: 人事~ personnel section/ 总务~ general affairs department/ 联络~ liaison office

另见 chǔ

【处处】 chùchù everywhere; in all respects: ~严格要求自己 set strict demands on oneself in all respects/ ~以革命利益为重 always put the interests of the revolution first/ 祖国~有亲人。All over our country one can find friends and dear ones.

【处所】 chùsuǒ place; location

【处长】 chùzhǎng the head of a department or office; section chief

**怵** chù fear: ~惕 feel apprehensive

**绌** chù 〈书〉 inadequate; insufficient: 相形见~ prove definitely inferior; pale by comparison

**畜** chù domestic animal; livestock: ~群 a herd of livestock

另见 xù

【畜肥】 chùféi animal manure

【畜类】 chùlèi domestic animals

【畜力】 chùlì animal power ◇ ~车 animal-drawn cart/ ~农具 animal-drawn farm implements

【畜生】 chùsheng ① domestic animal ②〈骂〉 beast; dirty swine

【畜疫】 chùyì epidemic disease of domestic animals

**搐** chù 见"抽搐" chōuchù

**触** chù ① touch; contact: 请勿~摸展品。Please don't touch the exhibits./ ~到痛处 touch a sore spot; touch sb. to the quick ② strike; hit: ~雷 strike (或 touch off) a mine ③ move sb.; stir up sb.'s feelings

【触电】 chùdiàn get an electric shock: 小心~! Danger! Electricity! 或 Danger! Live wire!

【触动】 chùdòng ① touch sth., moving it slightly: 他在暗中摸索着，忽然~了什么东西。Groping in the dark, he suddenly touched something./ 敌人的诽谤~不了我们一根毫毛。The enemy's slanders can't do us the slightest harm. ② move sb.; stir up sb.'s feelings: 有所~ be somewhat moved/ 这句话~了他的心事。That remark reminded him of something he'd had on his mind for a long time./ 群众的批评对我们~很大。The masses' criticisms shook us up a lot.

【触发】 chùfā detonate by contact; touch off; spark; trigger: ~热核聚变 trigger thermonuclear fusion/ ~乡思 touch off a train of home thoughts; provoke nostalgic longing ◇ ~地雷 contact mine/ ~电路 trigger circuit/ ~器 trigger

【触犯】 chùfàn offend; violate; go against: ~法律 violate (或 break) the law/ ~人民利益 encroach on the interests of the people/ 我什么地方~了你? What have I done to offend you?

【触感】 chùgǎn tactile impression

【触击】 chùjī 〈棒、垒球〉 bunt

【触及】 chùjí touch: ~人们的灵魂 touch people to their very souls/ ~事物的本质 get to the essence of a matter/ 这本书仅仅~而没有深刻揭示封建社会的主要矛盾。The book merely touches on the main contradiction of feudal society; it does not go into it deeply.

【触礁】 chùjiāo run (up) on rocks; strike a reef (或 rock)

【触角】 chùjiǎo 〈动〉 antenna; feeler

【触景生情】 chù jǐng shēng qíng the sight strikes a chord in one's heart
【触觉】 chùjué 〈生理〉 tactile (或 tactual) sensation; sense of touch ◇ ～器官 tactile organ
【触类旁通】 chù lèi páng tōng grasp a typical example and you will grasp the whole category; comprehend by analogy
【触媒】 chùméi 〈化〉 catalyst; catalytic agent
【触霉头】 chù méitóu 〈方〉 have a stroke of bad luck; be unfortunate; come to grief
【触目】 chùmù meet the eye: ～皆是 can be seen everywhere
【触目惊心】 chùmù-jīngxīn startling; shocking: ～的阶级斗争现实 the grim realities of class struggle
【触怒】 chùnù make angry; infuriate; enrage
【触杀剂】 chùshājì 〈农〉 contact insecticide
【触手】 chùshǒu 〈动〉 tentacle
【触痛】 chùtòng ① touch a tender (或 sore) spot; touch sb. to the quick ② 〈医〉 tenderness
【触网】 chùwǎng 〈体〉 touch net
【触须】 chùxū 〈动〉 cirrus: 鱼类～ barbel/ 无脊椎动物～ palp
【触诊】 chùzhěn 〈医〉 palpation

**憷** chù fear; shrink from: 这孩子～见生人。The child is afraid of strangers.
【憷场】 chùchǎng 〈方〉 feel nervous before a large audience
【憷头】 chùtóu 〈方〉 shrink from difficulties; be timid

**黜** chù 〈书〉 remove sb. from office; dismiss
【黜免】 chùmiǎn 〈书〉 dismiss (a government official)

**矗** chù 〈书〉 stand tall and upright
【矗立】 chùlì stand tall and upright; tower over sth.: 人民英雄纪念碑～在天安门广场上。The Monument to the People's Heroes towers aloft in Tian'anmen Square.

## chuā

**欻** chuā 〈象〉: 一队队民兵～～地走过去，非常整齐。Tramp, tramp, tramp, columns of militiamen marched by in perfect step.
【欻拉】 chuālā 〈象〉: ～一声，把菜倒进了滚油锅里。The vegetables dropped into the boiling oil with a sizzle.

## chuāi

**揣** chuāi hide or carry in one's clothes: ～在怀里 hide in the bosom; tuck into the bosom/ 这封信一直～在我口袋里。The letter has been in my pocket all this time.
另见 chuǎi; chuài
【揣手儿】 chuāishǒur tuck each hand in the opposite sleeve

**搋** chuāi rub; knead: ～面 knead dough/ 这衣服没洗干净，再～两下。These clothes haven't been washed clean. Let me give them another rub or two.

## chuǎi

**揣** chuǎi 〈书〉 estimate; surmise; conjecture
另见 chuāi; chuài
【揣测】 chuǎicè guess; conjecture: 据我～，他已经离开太原了。My guess is that he's already left Taiyuan.
【揣度】 chuǎiduó estimate; appraise; conjecture: ～敌情 make an appraisal of the enemy's situation
【揣摩】 chuǎimó try to fathom; try to figure out: 我始终～不透他的用意。I simply couldn't figure out his intention.

## chuài

**揣** chuài 见"挣揣" zhèngchuài
另见 chuāi; chuǎi

**踹** chuài ① kick: 一脚把门～开 kick the door open ② tread; stamp: 一脚～在水坑里 step in a puddle

## chuān

**川** chuān ① river: 高山大～ high mountains and big rivers ② plain: 一马平～ a vast expanse of flat land; a great stretch of land ③ (Chuān) short for Sichuan Province
【川贝】 chuānbèi 〈中药〉 tendril-leaved fritillary bulb
【川剧】 chuānjù Sichuan opera
【川流不息】 chuān liú bù xī flowing past in an endless stream; never-ending: 顾客～。Customers came in an endless stream. 或 Customers kept pouring in.
【川芎】 chuānxiōng 〈中药〉 the rhizome of *chuanxiong* (*Ligusticum wallichii*)
【川资】 chuānzī travelling expenses

**氚** chuān 〈化〉 tritium (T 或 $H^3$)
【氚核】 chuānhé 〈物〉 triton

**穿** chuān ① pierce through; penetrate: ～个窟窿 pierce (或 bore) a hole/ 看～ see through ② pass through; cross: ～过地道 pass through a tunnel/ ～过马路 cross a street/ 从人群中～过去 thread one's way through the crowd/ 飞机～云下降。The plane descended through the clouds./ 咱们从操场～过去吧。 Let's take the shortcut across the sports field. ③ wear; put on; be dressed in: ～上工作服 put on work clothes/ ～灰大衣的那个同志 the comrade in a grey overcoat/ 衣服～旧了。The clothes show signs of wear./ 这种鞋小点不要紧，～～就大了。It doesn't matter if the shoes feel a bit tight. They'll stretch with wearing./ ～得这么少，不冷吗？ Aren't you cold with so little on?
【穿插】 chuānchā ① alternate; do in turn: 施肥和除草～进行 do manuring and weeding in turn ② weave in; insert: 他在报告中～了一些生动的例子。 His talk was spiced with vivid examples. ③ subplot; interlude; episode ④ 〈军〉 thrust deep into the enemy forces: ～营 deep-thrust battalion/ 打～ fight a deep-thrust battle/ ～分割敌人 penetrate and cut up the enemy forces
【穿刺】 chuāncì 〈医〉 puncture: 肝(腰椎)～ liver (lumbar) puncture
【穿戴】 chuāndài apparel; dress: ～整齐 be neatly dressed/ 不讲究～ not be particular about one's dress
【穿甲弹】 chuānjiǎdàn armour-piercing projectile; armour-piercing shell or bullet; armour piercer
【穿孔】 chuānkǒng ① bore (或 punch) a hole; perforate ② 〈医〉 perforation: 胃(阑尾)～ gastric (appendicular) perforation
◇ ～机 punch; perforator/ ～卡片 punched card/ ～纸带 punched tape

【穿筘机】 chuānkòujī 〈纺〉 reeding machine
【穿山甲】 chuānshānjiǎ ①〈动〉 pangolin ②〈中药〉 pangolin scales
【穿梭】 chuānsuō shuttle back and forth ◇ ～轰炸 shuttle bombing
【穿堂】 chuāntáng hallway (connecting two courtyards in an old-style Chinese compound) ◇ ～风 draught
【穿小鞋】 chuān xiǎoxié 〔多用于〕: 给某人～ give sb. tight shoes to wear — make things hard for sb. by abusing one's power
【穿孝】 chuānxiào be in mourning; wear mourning
【穿心莲】 chuānxīnlián 〈中药〉 creat
【穿衣镜】 chuānyījìng full-length mirror
【穿窬】 chuānyú 〈书〉 cut through a wall or climb over it (in order to rob the house): 口谈道德,而志在～ contemplate burglary while mouthing morality; talk of virtue but think of vice/ ～之盗 burglar
【穿越】 chuānyuè pass through; cut across: 铁路～原始森林。The railway cuts through a primeval forest.
【穿针】 chuānzhēn thread a needle
【穿针引线】 chuānzhēn-yǐnxiàn act as a go-between
【穿着】 chuānzhuó dress; apparel: ～朴素整洁 be plainly but neatly dressed
【穿凿】 chuānzuò give a farfetched (或 strained) interpretation; read too much into sth.: ～附会 give strained interpretations and draw farfetched analogies

## chuán

**传** chuán ① pass; pass on: ～球 pass a ball/ 此件请按名单顺序速～。Please pass on this document without delay, in the order of the name list. ② hand down: 家～秘方 a secret recipe handed down in the family/ 革命传统代代～。Revolutionary traditions will be handed down from generation to generation. ③ pass on (knowledge, skill, etc.); impart; teach: 老中医把自己的医术～给赤脚医生。The old man passed on his knowledge of traditional Chinese medicine to the barefoot doctors. ④ spread: 消息很快～开了。The news spread quickly. 或 The news soon got around./ 捷报频～。Good news keeps pouring in./ 喜讯～来,欢声雷动。The glad tidings gave rise to thunderous cheers. ⑤ transmit; conduct: ～热 transmit heat/ 铜～电。Copper conducts electricity. ⑥ convey; express: 眉目～情 flash amorous glances ⑦ summon: ～证人 summon a witness ⑧ infect; be contagious: 小心别让你孩子～上流感。Mind that your children don't catch the flu. 另见 zhuàn
【传帮带】 chuán-bāng-dài pass on experience, give help and set an example (in training new hands)
【传播】 chuánbō ① disseminate; propagate; spread: ～马列主义 propagate (或 disseminate) Marxism-Leninism/ ～知识 spread knowledge/ 制止病菌的～ check the spread of germs ②〈物〉 propagation: 直线～ rectilinear propagation/ 散射～ scatter propagation
【传布】 chuánbù disseminate; spread
【传抄】 chuánchāo make private copies (of a manuscript, document, etc. which is being circulated)
【传出神经】 chuánchū shénjīng 〈生理〉 efferent nerve
【传达】 chuándá ① pass on (information, etc.); transmit; relay; communicate: ～命令 transmit an order/ 听～报告 hear a relayed report/ 把上级指示～到党员群众中去 communicate the instructions of a higher leading body to the Party rank and file; relay to Party members the directive of the higher level ② reception and registration of callers at a public establishment ③ janitor ◇ ～室 reception office; janitor's room
【传单】 chuándān leaflet; handbill
【传导】 chuándǎo 〈物〉 conduction: 热的～ conduction of heat
【传道】 chuándào ①〈旧〉 propagate doctrines of the ancient sages ②〈宗〉 preach; deliver a sermon
【传递】 chuándì transmit; deliver; transfer: ～信件 deliver mail/ ～信息 transmit messages
【传动】 chuándòng 〈机〉 transmission; drive: 变速～ change drive/ 齿轮～ gear drive (或 transmission) ◇ ～齿轮 transmission (或 drive) gear/ ～带 transmission belt/ ～箱 transmission case/ ～轴 transmission shaft/ ～装置 gearing
【传粉】 chuánfěn 〈植〉 pollination ◇ ～媒介 pollination medium
【传感器】 chuángǎnqì 〈电〉 sensor; transducer: 激光～ laser sensor
【传呼】 chuánhū (of a trunk-line operator or public telephone custodian) notify sb. of a phone call; pass on a message left by phone ◇ ～电话 neighbourhood telephone service
【传话】 chuánhuà pass on a message
【传唤】 chuánhuàn 〈法〉 summon to court; subpoena
【传家宝】 chuánjiābǎo ① family heirloom ② cherished tradition (或 heritage): 我们一定要把毛主席的伟大旗帜当作～,世世代代传下去。We must cherish the great banner of Chairman Mao as our precious heritage, and hand it on from generation to generation.
【传教】 chuánjiào 〈宗〉 do missionary work ◇ ～士 missionary
【传经送宝】 chuánjīng-sòngbǎo pass on one's valuable experience: 热烈欢迎六连指导员来～。We extend a warm welcome to the political instructor of the sixth company for coming to pass on his valuable experience.
【传令】 chuánlìng transmit (或 dispatch) orders: ～嘉奖 cite sb. in a dispatch
【传票】 chuánpiào ①〈法〉 (court) summons; subpoena: 发出～ issue a summons ②〈会计〉 voucher
【传奇】 chuánqí ① short stories of the Tang and Song dynasties (618-1279) ② poetic dramas of the Ming and Qing dynasties (1368-1911) ③ legend; romance: ～式的人物 legendary figure; legend
【传染】 chuánrǎn infect; be contagious: 接触～ contagion/ 空气～ infection through air/ 水～ waterborne infection/ 这病不～。This disease is not contagious (或 infectious). ◇ ～病 infectious (或 contagious) disease/ ～病院 hospital for infectious diseases/ ～性肝炎 infectious hepatitis
【传入神经】 chuánrù shénjīng 〈生理〉 afferent nerve
【传神】 chuánshén vivid; lifelike: ～之笔 a vivid touch (in writing or painting)
【传声器】 chuánshēngqì microphone
【传声清晰度】 chuánshēng qīngxīdù 〈无〉 articulation
【传声筒】 chuánshēngtǒng ① megaphone; loud hailer ② one who parrots another; sb.'s mouthpiece
【传世】 chuánshì be handed down from ancient times: ～珍宝 a treasure handed down from ancient times
【传授】 chuánshòu pass on (knowledge, skill, etc.); impart; teach: ～技术 pass on (或 impart) one's technical skill/ 向青年～培育良种的经验 teach young people how to cultivate good strains of seed
【传输】 chuánshū 〈电〉 transmission ◇ ～损耗 transmission loss/ ～线 transmission line
【传说】 chuánshuō ① it is said; they say: ～如此。So the story goes./ 这只不过是～而已。That's only hearsay. ②

legend; tradition: 民间～ folklore; popular legend

【传诵】 chuánsòng be on everybody's lips; be widely read: 为世人所～ be read with admiration by people all over the world/ 当地群众中～着工农红军的英雄事迹。The heroic deeds of the Workers' and Peasants' Red Army are continually on the lips of the local inhabitants.

【传送】 chuánsòng convey; deliver ◇ ～带〈机〉 conveyer belt

【传统】 chuántǒng tradition: 革命～ revolutionary tradition/ ～友谊 traditional (ties of) friendship/ ～观念 traditional ideas ◇ ～剧目 traditional theatrical pieces

【传闻】 chuánwén ① it is said; they say ② hearsay; rumour; talk

【传讯】 chuánxùn 〈法〉 summon for interrogation or trial; subpoena; cite

【传言】 chuányán ① hearsay; rumour: ～非虚。It's not just hearsay. ② pass on a message

【传扬】 chuányáng spread (from mouth to mouth): ～四方 spread far and wide

【传阅】 chuányuè pass round (或 circulate) for perusal: 这篇稿子请大家～并提出意见。Please pass the draft round and make suggestions./ 文件正在党委成员中～。The document is being circulated among the members of the Party committee.

【传真】 chuánzhēn ① portraiture ② 〈讯〉 facsimile: 无线电～ radio facsimile; radiophotography ◇ ～电报 phototelegraph/ ～照片 radiophoto

【传种】 chuánzhǒng propagate; reproduce

**船** chuán boat; ship: 上～ board a ship; go on board; embark/ 下～ disembark/ 乘～去大连 go to Dalian by boat; embark (on a ship) for Dalian

【船帮】 chuánbāng ① the side of a ship; shipboard ② merchant fleet

【船舶】 chuánbó shipping; boats and ships ◇ ～登记证书 certificate of registry/ ～证书 ship's papers

【船埠】 chuánbù wharf; quay

【船舱】 chuáncāng ① ship's hold ② cabin

【船到江心补漏迟】 chuán dào jiāngxīn bǔ lòu chí it's too late to plug the leak when the boat is in midstream

【船东】 chuándōng 〈旧〉 shipowner

【船队】 chuánduì fleet; flotilla

【船方】 chuánfāng 〈商〉 the ship: ～不负担装货费用 free in (F.I.)/ ～不负担卸货费用 free out (F.O.)/ ～不负担装、卸、理仓费用 free in and out and stowed (F.I.O.S.)

【船夫】 chuánfū 〈旧〉 boatman ◇ ～曲 boatmen's song

【船工】 chuángōng boatman; junkman

【船棺葬】 chuánguānzàng 〈考古〉 boat-coffin burial

【船户】 chuánhù ① 见"船家" ② 〈方〉 boat dweller

【船级】 chuánjí ship's classification (或 class) ◇ ～证书 classification certificate

【船级社】 chuánjíshè classification society: 劳氏～ Lloyd's Register of Shipping

【船籍港】 chuánjígǎng port of registry; home port

【船家】 chuánjia 〈旧〉 one who owns a boat and makes a living as a boatman; boatman

【船壳】 chuánké hull

【船老大】 chuánlǎodà 〈方〉 ① the chief crewman of a wooden boat ② boatman

【船篷】 chuánpéng ① the mat or wooden roofing of a boat ② sail

【船票】 chuánpiào steamer ticket: 预定去青岛的～ book one's passage to Qingdao

【船期】 chuánqī sailing date ◇ ～表 sailing schedule

【船桥】 chuánqiáo (ship's) bridge

【船蛆】 chuánqū 〈动〉 shipworm

【船首】 chuánshǒu stem; bow; prow ◇ ～楼 forecastle

【船台】 chuántái (building) berth; shipway; slipway; slip: 干式～ dry shipway ◇ ～周期 berth period

【船体】 chuántǐ the body of a ship; hull

【船尾】 chuánwěi stern ◇ ～部 quarter/ ～楼 poop/ ～轴 stern shaft

【船位】 chuánwèi ① accommodation (on a ship): 订～ book one's passage (on a ship) ② ship's position: 测定～ fix a ship's position (at sea); position finding ◇ ～推算法 dead reckoning

【船坞】 chuánwù dock; shipyard: 浮～ floating dock/ 干～ dry (或 graving) dock ◇ ～费 dockage

【船舷】 chuánxián side (of a ship or boat)

【船用油】 chuányòngyóu bunker oil

【船员】 chuányuán (ship's) crew

【船闸】 chuánzhá (ship) lock

【船长】 chuánzhǎng captain; skipper

【船只】 chuánzhī shipping; vessels: 往来～ shipping traffic/ 载货～ carrying vessels/ ～失事 shipwreck

**遄** chuán 〈书〉 quickly: ～返 return quickly

**椽** chuán rafter

【椽条】 chuántiáo rafter 又作"椽子"

## chuǎn

**舛** chuǎn 〈书〉 ① error; mishap: 命途多～ suffer many a setback during one's life ② run counter

【舛误】 chuǎnwù 〈书〉 error; mishap

**喘** chuǎn ① breathe heavily; gasp for breath; pant ② 〈医〉 asthma

【喘气】 chuǎnqì ① breathe (deeply); pant; gasp: 喘不过气来 gasp for breath; be out of breath/ 喘粗气 puff and blow ② take a breather: 喘口气儿再干。Let's take a breather before we go on.

【喘息】 chuǎnxī ① pant; gasp for breath: ～未定 before regaining one's breath; before one has a chance to catch one's breath ② breather; breathing spell; respite: 乘胜追击，不让敌人有～的机会 follow up the victory with pursuit so as not to allow the enemy a breathing spell

【喘吁吁】 chuǎnxūxū puff and blow

## chuàn

**串** chuàn ① string together: 把鱼～起来 string the fish together ② conspire; gang up: ～骗 gang up and swindle sb. ③ get things mixed up: 电话～线 get the (telephone) lines crossed/ (收音机)～台 get two or more (radio) stations at once/ 字印得太小，很容易看～行。The print is too small, you can easily miss (或 skip) a line. ④ go from place to place; run about; rove: 走村～寨 go from village to village/ ～亲戚 go visiting one's relatives ⑤ play a part (in a play); act: 客～ be a guest performer ⑥ 〈量〉〔用于连贯起来的东西〕 string; bunch; cluster: 一～珠子 a string of beads/ 一～钥匙 a bunch of keys/ 一～葡萄 a cluster of grapes

【串并联】 chuàn-bìnglián 〈电〉 series-parallel connection

【串供】 chuàngòng act in collusion to make each other's confessions tally

【串话】 chuànhuà 〈讯〉 cross talk

【串激】 chuànjī 〈电〉 series excitation ◇ ～电动机 series motor/ ～发电机 series generator; series dynamo
【串讲】 chuànjiǎng construe
【串联】 chuànlián ① establish ties; contact: 革命～ establish revolutionary ties; exchange revolutionary experience/ 一九五一年秋，他～了几户贫农，组织起一个互助组。In the autumn of 1951 he contacted several poor peasant families and organized a mutual-aid team. ② 〈电〉 series connection ◇ ～电池组 series battery/ ～电阻 series resistance
【串门子】 chuànménzi 〈口〉 call at sb.'s home; drop in: 有空来～。Drop in when you're free. 又作"串门儿"
【串通】 chuàntōng gang up; collaborate; collude: 两人～一气，互相包庇。Acting in collaboration, the two of them shielded each other.
【串演】 chuànyǎn play (或 act) the role of
【串秧儿】 chuànyāngr 〈口〉 crossbreed; interbreed
【串珠】 chuànzhū a string of beads

**钏** chuàn bracelet

## chuāng

**创** chuāng wound: 予以重～ inflict heavy casualties (on the enemy)/ ～巨痛深 badly injured and in great pain — in deep distress
另见 chuàng
【创痕】 chuānghén scar
【创口】 chuāngkǒu wound; cut
【创伤】 chuāngshāng wound; trauma: 精神上的～ a mental scar; a traumatic experience/ 医治战争的～ heal the wounds of war

**疮** chuāng ① sore; skin ulcer: 褥～ bedsore/ 头上长～，脚底流脓——坏透了 with boils on the head and feet running with pus — rotten from head to foot; rotten to the core ② wound: 刀～ a sword wound
【疮疤】 chuāngbā scar: 脸上的～ a scar on the face/ 揭他的～ pull the scab right off his sore — touch his sore spot/ 咱们不能好了～忘了痛。We mustn't forget the pain after the wound is healed. 或 We mustn't forget the bitter past when we are relieved of our suffering.
【疮痂】 chuāngjiā 〈医〉 scab
【疮口】 chuāngkǒu the open part of a sore
【疮痍满目】 chuāngyí mǎnmù everywhere a scene of devastation meets the eye

**窗** chuāng window: 花格～ lattice window/ 气～ transom/ 纱～ screen window
【窗玻璃】 chuāngbōli windowpane
【窗洞】 chuāngdòng an opening in a wall (to let in light and air)
【窗格子】 chuānggézi window lattice
【窗户】 chuānghu window; casement
【窗花】 chuānghuā paper-cut for window decoration
【窗口】 chuāngkǒu ① window: 坐在～ sit at (或 by) the window ② wicket; window: 去上海的火车票在那个～卖。Train tickets to Shanghai are sold at that window.
【窗框】 chuāngkuàng window frame
【窗帘】 chuānglián (window) curtain
【窗棂子】 chuānglíngzi 〈方〉 window lattice
【窗明几净】 chuāngmíng-jījìng with bright windows and clean tables; bright and clean
【窗纱】 chuāngshā gauze for screening windows; window screening
【窗扇】 chuāngshàn casement
【窗台】 chuāngtái windowsill
【窗子】 chuāngzi window

## chuáng

**床** chuáng ① bed: 单人～ single bed/ 双人～ double bed/ 小孩～ child's cot; baby's crib/ 帆布～ camp bed; cot/ 折叠～ folding bed/ 卧病在～ take to one's bed; be laid up in bed ② sth. shaped like a bed: 车～ lathe/ 河～ riverbed ③ 〈量〉: 一～被 one quilt/ 两～铺盖 two sets of bedding
【床单】 chuángdān sheet
【床垫】 chuángdiàn mattress
【床架】 chuángjià bedstead
【床铺】 chuángpù bed
【床身】 chuángshēn 〈机〉 lathe bed
【床头】 chuángtóu the head of a bed; bedside ◇ ～灯 bedside lamp/ ～柜 bedside cupboard
【床头箱】 chuángtóuxiāng 〈机〉 headstock
【床位】 chuángwèi berth; bunk; bed
【床罩】 chuángzhào bedspread; counterpane

**幢** chuáng ① pennant or streamer used in ancient China ② a stone pillar inscribed with Buddha's name or Buddhist scripture
另见 zhuàng
【幢幢】 chuángchuáng flickering; dancing: 人影～ shadows of people moving about

## chuǎng

**闯** chuǎng ① rush; dash; charge: ～进来 rush in; break in; force one's way in/ 横冲直～ charge about furiously; run amuck ② temper oneself (by battling through difficulties and dangers): 他这几年～出来了。He has hewed out his path in life during these past few years./ 我们必须～出一条新路子。We must break a new path.
【闯关东】 chuǎng Guāndōng brave the journey to the Northeast (to eke out an existence in the old society)
【闯祸】 chuǎnghuò get into trouble; bring disaster: 你～了！Look what you've done!/ 你开车要小心，千万别～。Drive carefully and be sure not to have an accident.
【闯江湖】 chuǎng jiānghu make a living wandering from place to place (as a fortune-teller, acrobat, quack doctor, etc.)
【闯将】 chuǎngjiàng daring general; pathbreaker: 革命的先锋，生产的～ a pioneer in revolution and pathbreaker in production
【闯劲】 chuǎngjìn the spirit of a pathbreaker; pioneering spirit: 搞技术革新就要有一股不怕困难的～。To go in for technical innovation, one must have the fearless spirit of a pathbreaker.
【闯练】 chuǎngliàn leave home to temper oneself; be tempered in the world: 让青年人到三大革命运动中去～～。Let young people temper themselves in the three great revolutionary movements.

## chuàng

**创** chuàng start (doing sth.); achieve (sth. for the first time): 排万难，～高产 surmount all difficulties and achieve higher output/ ～记录 set a record/ 该厂钢产量～历史最高水平。The plant's steel output was an all-time high.

另见 chuāng

【创办】 chuàngbàn establish; set up: ～农具修理厂 set up a farm tool repair shop

【创见】 chuàngjiàn original idea: 有～的思想家 an original thinker

【创建】 chuàngjiàn found; establish: ～马列主义的党 found a Marxist-Leninist party/ 这所五七干校是一九六八年冬～的。This May 7 cadre school was set up in the winter of 1968.

【创举】 chuàngjǔ pioneering work (或 undertaking): 伟大的～ a great beginning

【创刊】 chuàngkān start publication: 《人民日报》于一九四八年六月十五日～。*Renmin Ribao* started publication on June 15, 1948. ◇ ～号 first issue (或 number)

【创立】 chuànglì found; originate: 马克思和恩格斯～了科学社会主义理论。Marx and Engels founded the theory of scientific socialism./ ～新学派 found a new academic school

【创设】 chuàngshè found; create; set up: ～一个新的研究所 set up a new research institute

【创始】 chuàngshǐ originate; initiate: 处在～阶段 be in the initial stage/ 中国是联合国的～会员国之一。China is a founding member of the United Nations. ◇ ～人 founder; originator

【创世记】 Chuàngshìjì Genesis

【创新】 chuàngxīn bring forth new ideas; blaze new trails: 在艺术上不断～ constantly bring forth new ideas in the arts/ 勇于实践，大胆～。Be bold in putting things into practice and blazing new trails.

【创业】 chuàngyè start an undertaking; do pioneering work: 为社会主义～，为共产主义奠基 be builders of socialism and foundation layers of communism/ 扎根农村创大业 strike roots in the countryside and pioneer a great cause

【创造】 chuàngzào create; produce; bring about: ～有利条件 create favourable conditions/ ～优异成绩 produce excellent results/ ～奇迹 create miracles; work wonders; achieve prodigious feats/ 人民，只有人民，才是～世界历史的动力。The people, and the people alone, are the motive force in the making of world history. ◇ ～力 creative power (或 ability)/ ～性 creativeness; creativity

【创制】 chuàngzhì formulate; institute; create: ～拼音文字 formulate an alphabetic system of writing

【创作】 chuàngzuò ① create; produce; write: ～反映现实斗争的美术作品 produce works of art that reflect present-day struggles ② creative work; creation: 文艺～ literary and artistic creation/ 划时代的～ epoch-making creative work

◇ ～技巧 artistic technique; craftsmanship/ ～经验 creative experience/ ～思想 ideas guiding artistic or literary creation

**怆** chuàng 〈书〉 sorrowful: ～然泪下 burst into sorrowful tears

## chuī

**吹** chuī ① blow; puff: ～火 blow a fire/ 把灯～灭 blow out the lamp/ ～一口气 give a puff/ 雨打风～ be exposed to the weather/ 门～开了。The door blew open./ 什么风把你给～来了? What brings you here?/ ～起床号 sound the reveille ② play (wind instruments): ～笛子 play the flute ③ 〈口〉 boast; brag: 先别～，做出具体成绩来再说。Don't brag about what you're going to do. Get something done./ 自～自擂 blow one's own trumpet/ ～得天花乱坠 boast in the most fantastic terms ④ 〈口〉 break off; break up; fall through: 他们俩～了。That couple have broken up./ 原来的计划～了。The original plan has fallen through.

【吹吹打打】 chuīchuī-dǎdǎ beating drums and blowing trumpets; piping and drumming

【吹吹拍拍】 chuīchuī-pāipāi boasting and toadying: ～，拉拉扯扯 resort to boasting, flattery and touting

【吹打乐】 chuīdǎyuè 〈乐〉 an ensemble of Chinese wind and percussion instruments

【吹风】 chuīfēng ① be in a draught; catch a chill: 你病还没有好，不要～。Don't get in a draught, you aren't well yet. ② dry (hair, etc.) with a blower ③ 〈口〉 let sb. in on sth. in advance: 下次会要讨论什么，你给我们吹吹风吧。Will you give us some idea of what will be taken up at the next meeting? ◇ ～会 briefing/ ～机 blower (for drying hair); drier

【吹拂】 chuīfú sway; stir: 晨风～着垂柳。The morning breeze is swaying the weeping willows.

【吹鼓手】 chuīgǔshǒu trumpeter; bugler: 议会道路的～ a eulogist of the parliamentary road

【吹管】 chuīguǎn 〈机〉 blowpipe: 氢氧～ oxyhydrogen blowpipe/ 氧乙炔～ oxyacetylene blowpipe

【吹胡子瞪眼】 chuīhúzi-dèngyǎn froth at the mouth and glare with rage; foam with rage

【吹灰之力】 chuī huī zhī lì the effort needed to blow away a speck of dust; just a small effort: 不费～ as easy as blowing away dust; without the least effort

【吹冷风】 chuī lěngfēng blow a cold wind over; throw cold water on

【吹炼】 chuīliàn 〈冶〉 blowing

【吹毛求疵】 chuī máo qiú cī find fault; pick holes; nitpick

【吹牛】 chuīniú boast; brag; talk big: ～拍马 boast and flatter

【吹捧】 chuīpěng flatter; laud to the skies; lavish praise on: 互相～ flatter each other

【吹蚀】 chuīshí 〈地〉 deflation

【吹台】 chuītái 〈口〉 break off; fall through; fizzle out

【吹嘘】 chuīxū lavish praise on oneself or others; boast: 自我～ self-praise

【吹奏】 chuīzòu play (wind instruments) ◇ ～乐 band music; wind music

**炊** chuī cook a meal

【炊具】 chuījù cooking utensils

【炊事】 chuīshì cooking; kitchen work

◇ ～班 cookhouse (或 mess, kitchen) squad/ ～用具 cooking utensils/ ～员 a cook or the kitchen staff

【炊烟】 chuīyān smoke from kitchen chimneys

【炊帚】 chuīzhou a brush for cleaning pots and pans; pot-scouring brush

## chuí

**垂** chuí ① hang down; droop; let fall: ～泪 shed tears; weep/ ～手站着 stand with one's hands at one's sides ② 〈书〉 bequeath to posterity; hand down: 功～竹帛 be recorded in history in letters of gold/ ～法后世 set an example for posterity ③ 〈书〉 nearing; approaching: ～老 approaching old age; getting on in years ④ 〈书〉〈敬〉〔多用于称长辈、上级对自己的行动〕 condescend: ～询 condescend to inquire/ ～念 show kind concern for (me)

【垂钓】 chuídiào fish with a hook and line; go angling
【垂帘听政】 chuí lián tīng zhèng (of an empress or empress dowager) hold court from behind a screen; attend to state affairs
【垂柳】 chuíliǔ 〈植〉 weeping willow
【垂暮】 chuímù 〈书〉 dusk; towards sunset; just before sundown: ～之年 in old age
【垂盆草】 chuípéncǎo 〈中药〉 stringy stonecrop (*Sedum sarmentosum*)
【垂青】 chuíqīng 〈书〉 show appreciation for sb.; look upon sb. with favour
【垂死】 chuísǐ moribund; dying: ～挣扎 be in one's death throes; put up a last-ditch (或 deathbed) struggle/ 帝国主义无法挽救其～的命运。Imperialism cannot save itself from its approaching doom.
【垂体】 chuítǐ 〈生理〉 hypophysis; pituitary body (或 gland) ◇ ～后叶素 〈药〉 pituitrin
【垂髫】 chuítiáo 〈书〉 early childhood
【垂头丧气】 chuítóu-sàngqì crestfallen; dejected
【垂危】 chuíwēi critically ill; at one's last gasp
【垂涎】 chuíxián drool; slaver; covet: ～三尺 spittle three feet long — drool with envy
【垂直】 chuízhí perpendicular; vertical: ～平面 vertical plane/ ～发射 vertical firing (或 launching)/ ～俯冲 steep dive; nose dive/ ～起飞 vertical takeoff/ 两线～相交。The two lines meet at right angles. ◇ ～贸易 vertical trade/ ～起落飞机 vertical takeoff and landing aircraft; VTOL aircraft/ ～天线 vertical antenna/ ～线 perpendicular line; vertical line

**陲** chuí 〈书〉 frontiers; borders

**捶** chuí beat (with a stick or fist); thump; pound: ～背 pound sb.'s back (as in massage)/ ～鼓 beat a drum/ ～门 bang on the door
【捶打】 chuídǎ beat; thump: ～衣服 beat clothes (when washing them)/ ～凸纹 hammer *repoussé*
【捶胸顿足】 chuíxiōng-dùnzú beat one's breast and stamp one's feet (in deep sorrow, etc.)

**槌** chuí mallet; beetle: 碾～ pestle/ 鼓～儿 drumstick

**锤** chuí ①hammer: 铁～ iron hammer/ 大～ sledgehammer ②mace ③hammer into shape: ～金箔 hammer gold into foil ④weight: 秤～ steelyard weight/ 调节～ 〈机〉 governor weight/ 平衡～ 〈机〉 balance weight
【锤骨】 chuígǔ 〈生理〉 malleus
【锤光】 chuíguāng 〈机〉 planish
【锤炼】 chuíliàn ①hammer into shape ②temper: ～一颗对革命事业的忠心 temper one's loyalty to the revolutionary cause ③polish: ～词句 polish a piece of writing
【锤子】 chuízi hammer

**箠** chuí 〈书〉 ①whip ②flog with a whip; whip

## chūn

**春** chūn ①spring: 温暖如～ as warm as spring ②love; lust: ～情 stirrings of love ③life; vitality: 枯木逢～。A withered tree comes to life again. ④(Chūn) a surname
【春饼】 chūnbǐng spring pancake
【春播】 chūnbō spring sowing ◇ ～作物 spring-sown crops
【春分】 Chūnfēn the Spring Equinox (4th solar term)
【春风】 chūnfēng spring breeze: 满面～ (a face) beaming with smiles
【春风化雨】 chūnfēng huà yǔ life-giving spring breeze and rain — salutary influence of education
【春风满面】 chūnfēng mǎnmiàn beaming with satisfaction; radiant with happiness
【春耕】 chūngēng spring ploughing: ～大忙季节 busy spring ploughing season
【春灌】 chūnguàn 〈农〉 spring irrigation
【春光】 chūnguāng sights and sounds of spring; spring scenery: ～明媚 a sunlit and enchanting scene of spring
【春化】 chūnhuà 〈农〉 vernalization
【春季】 chūnjì spring; springtime
【春假】 chūnjià spring vacation; spring holidays
【春节】 Chūnjié the Spring Festival
【春卷】 chūnjuǎn spring roll (a thin sheet of dough, rolled, stuffed and fried)
【春雷】 chūnléi spring thunder
【春雷霉素】 chūnléiméisù 〈药〉 kasugarnycin
【春联】 chūnlián Spring Festival couplets (pasted on gateposts or door panels); New Year scrolls
【春令】 chūnlìng ①spring ②spring weather: 冬行～ a springlike winter; a very mild winter
【春梦】 chūnmèng spring dream; transient joy
【春秋】 chūnqiū ①spring and autumn; year: ～多佳日。There are many fine days in spring and autumn. ②age: ～正富 in the prime of youth/ ～已高 be advanced in years ③(Chūnqiū) the Spring and Autumn Period (770-476 B.C.) ④(Chūnqiū) *The Spring and Autumn Annals* 参见"五经" wǔjīng ⑤annals; history
【春色】 chūnsè spring scenery: 水乡～ spring in a waterside village/ ～满园 a garden full of the beauty of spring
【春上】 chūnshang 〈口〉 in spring: 今年～雨水多。We have had plenty of rain this spring.
【春笋】 chūnsǔn bamboo shoots in spring: 雨后～ springing up like mushrooms
【春天】 chūntiān spring; springtime
【春小麦】 chūnxiǎomài spring wheat
【春汛】 chūnxùn ①〈水〉 spring flood ②〈渔〉 spring (fishing) season
【春意】 chūnyì ①spring in the air; the beginning (或 awakening) of spring: ～盎然。Spring is very much in the air. ②thoughts of love
【春游】 chūnyóu spring outing
【春装】 chūnzhuāng spring clothing

**椿** chūn 〈植〉 ①Chinese toon ②tree of heaven
【椿白皮】 chūnbáipí 〈中药〉 the bark of the root or stem of the tree of heaven
【椿象】 chūnxiàng 〈动〉 stinkbug; shieldbug

**蝽** chūn 〈动〉 stinkbug; shieldbug

## chún

**纯** chún ①pure; unmixed: ～毛 pure wool/ ～金 pure (或 solid) gold/ ～白 pure white/ ～黑 all black ②simple; pure and simple: ～属捏造 sheer fabrication ③skilful; practised; well versed: 功夫不～ not skilful enough
【纯粹】 chúncuì pure; unadulterated: 一个～的人 a pure person/ ～是浪费时间 a sheer waste of time
【纯度】 chúndù purity; pureness
【纯化】 chúnhuà purification
【纯碱】 chúnjiǎn 〈化〉 soda ash; sodium carbonate
【纯洁】 chúnjié pure; clean and honest: 保持马克思主义的

～性 preserve the purity of Marxism/ ～党的组织 purify the Party organization
【纯净】 chúnjìng pure; clean
【纯利】 chúnlì net profit
【纯朴】 chúnpǔ honest; simple; unsophisticated: ～敦厚 simple and honest/ ～爽朗 honest and frank/ 文风～ simplicity of style
【纯收入】 chúnshōurù net income
【纯熟】 chúnshú skilful; practised; well versed: 技术～ highly skilled
【纯损】 chúnsǔn net loss
【纯一】 chúnyī single; simple: 目标～ singleness of purpose
【纯音】 chúnyīn 〈物〉 pure (或 simple) tone
【纯真】 chúnzhēn pure; sincere: ～无邪 pure and innocent
【纯正】 chúnzhèng pure; unadulterated: 动机～ have pure motives
【纯种】 chúnzhǒng purebred: ～牛 purebred cattle; pedigree cattle

**唇** chún lip: 上～ upper lip/ 下～ lower lip
【唇齿相依】 chún-chǐ xiāngyī be as close as lips and teeth; be closely related and mutually dependent: ～的兄弟邻邦 fraternal neighbour countries as closely related as lips and teeth
【唇齿音】 chúnchǐyīn 〈语〉 labiodental (sound)
【唇膏】 chúngāo lipstick
【唇裂】 chúnliè 〈医〉 harelip; cleft lip
【唇枪舌剑】 chúnqiāng-shéjiàn cross verbal swords; engage in a battle of words
【唇舌】 chúnshé words; argument: 费一番～ take a lot of explaining or arguing/ 徒费～ a waste of breath
【唇亡齿寒】 chúnwáng-chǐhán if the lips are gone, the teeth will be cold; if one (of two interdependent things) falls, the other is in danger; share a common lot
【唇音】 chúnyīn 〈语〉 labial (sound)

**莼** chún
【莼菜】 chúncài 〈植〉 water shield

**淳** chún 〈书〉 pure; honest
【淳厚】 chúnhòu pure and honest; simple and kind
【淳朴】 chúnpǔ honest; simple; unsophisticated: ～的阶级感情 simple class sentiments/ ～的庄稼人 an honest peasant; unsophisticated countryfolk
【淳于】 Chúnyú a surname

**鹑** chún quail
【鹑衣】 chúnyī 〈书〉 ragged clothes: ～百结 in rags

**醇** chún ① 〈书〉 mellow wine; good wine ② 〈书〉 pure; unmixed ③ 〈化〉 alcohol: ～醛 alcohol aldehyde
【醇厚】 chúnhòu ① mellow; rich: 酒味～。The wine is (或 tastes) mellow. ② pure and honest; simple and kind
【醇化】 chúnhuà ① refine; purify; perfect ② 〈化〉 alcoholization ◇ ～物 alcoholate
【醇解】 chúnjiě 〈化〉 alcoholysis
【醇酸】 chúnsuān 〈化〉 alcohol (或 alcoholic) acid ◇ ～树脂 alkyd resin

## chǔn

**蠢** chǔn ① stupid; foolish; dull; clumsy ② 〈书〉 wriggle
【蠢笨】 chǔnbèn clumsy; awkward; stupid
【蠢材】 chǔncái idiot; fool
【蠢蠢欲动】 chǔnchǔn yù dòng ready to start wriggling — ready to make trouble: 敌人又在～。The enemy is going to start something again.
【蠢动】 chǔndòng ① wriggle ② create disturbances; carry on disruptive activities
【蠢货】 chǔnhuò blockhead; dunce; idiot
【蠢驴】 chǔnlǘ idiot; donkey; ass
【蠢人】 chǔnrén fool; blockhead
【蠢猪】 chǔnzhū idiot; stupid swine; ass

## chuō

**戳** chuō ① jab; poke; stab: 小心！你的竹竿儿别～了他的眼睛。Be careful! Don't jab his eye out with your bamboo pole./ 在纸上～了一个洞 poke a hole in the paper/ 一～就破 break at the slightest touch ② 〈方〉 sprain; blunt: 打排球～了手 sprain one's wrist while playing volleyball/ 钢笔尖儿～了。The nib is blunted. ③ 〈方〉 stand sth. on end: 把秫秸～起来 stand the bundle of sorghum stalks on end ④ 〈口〉 stamp; seal
【戳穿】 chuōchuān puncture; lay bare; expose; explode: ～谣言和诡辩 lay bare sb.'s lies and sophistry/ ～纸老虎 punch holes in the paper tiger; expose sb. or sth. as a paper tiger
【戳记】 chuōjì stamp; seal
【戳子】 chuōzi 〈口〉 stamp; seal: 在文件上盖个～ put a seal (或 stamp) on a document/ 橡皮～ rubber stamp

## chuò

**啜** chuò 〈书〉 ① sip; suck: ～茗 sip tea ② sob
【啜泣】 chuòqì sob

**绰** chuò 〈书〉 ample; spacious: ～有余裕 enough and to spare
另见 chāo
【绰绰有余】 chuòchuò yǒu yú more than sufficient; enough and to spare
【绰号】 chuòhào nickname
【绰约】 chuòyuē 〈书〉 (of a woman) graceful

**辍** chuò 〈书〉 stop; cease: ～工 stop work/ 时作时～ on and off; by fits and starts
【辍笔】 chuòbǐ stop in the middle of writing or painting
【辍学】 chuòxué discontinue one's studies

**龊** chuò 见"龌龊" wòchuò

## cī

**刺** cī 〈象〉: ～的一声，他滑了一个跟头。 Wham! He slipped and fell./ 花炮点着后，～～地直冒火星。 The firecracker spattered sparks the moment it was lit.
另见 cì
【刺棱】 cīlēng 〈象〉〔动作迅速的声音〕: 猫～一下跑了。The cat scampered away.
【刺溜】 cīliū 〈象〉〔脚底下滑动的声音或东西迅速滑过的声音〕: ～一下滑倒了 slip and fall/ 子弹～～地从他耳边擦过去。The bullets whistled past his ears.

**差** cī 见"参差" cēncī
另见 chā; chà; chāi

**呲** cī 〈口〉 give a talking-to; give a tongue-lashing: 挨了一顿～儿 get a good talking-to

**疵** cī flaw; defect; blemish: 小～ a trifling defect/ 无～ flawless; impeccable

【疵点】 cīdiǎn flaw; fault; defect

【疵毛】 cīmáo defective wool

## cí

**词** cí ①〈语〉word; term: 贬义～ derogatory term/ 同义～ synonym ②speech; statement: 开幕～ opening speech/ 台～ lines of an opera or play/ 各执一～。Each holds to his own statement./ 我说了几句就没～儿了。After a few sentences I became tongue-tied. ③*ci*, poetry written to certain tunes with strict tonal patterns and rhyme schemes, in fixed numbers of lines and words, originating in the Tang Dynasty (618-907) and fully developed in the Song Dynasty (960-1279)

【词不达意】 cí bù dá yì the words fail to convey the idea

【词典】 cídiǎn dictionary ◇ ～学 lexicography

【词调】 cídiào tonal patterns and rhyme schemes of *ci* poetry 参见"词"③

【词法】 cífǎ 〈语〉 morphology

【词干】 cígàn 〈语〉 stem

【词根】 cígēn 〈语〉 root

【词话】 cíhuà ①notes and comments on *ci* poetry 参见"词"③ ②storytelling interspersed with songs and ballads, popular in the Song Dynasty (960-1279) ③novel with parts in verse, common in the Ming Dynasty (1368-1644)

【词汇】 cíhuì 〈语〉 vocabulary; words and phrases: 常用～ common words ◇ ～表 word list; vocabulary; glossary/ ～学 lexicology

【词句】 cíjù words and phrases; expressions: 空洞的～ empty phrases

【词类】 cílèi 〈语〉 parts of speech

【词牌】 cípái names of the tunes to which *ci* poems are composed 参见"词"③

【词谱】 cípǔ a collection of tunes of *ci* poems 参见"词"③

【词曲】 cíqǔ a general term for *ci* (词) and *qu* (曲) 参见"词"③; "曲" qǔ①

【词讼】 císòng legal cases

【词素】 císù 〈语〉 morpheme

【词头】 cítóu 〈语〉 prefix

【词尾】 cíwěi 〈语〉 suffix

【词形】 cíxíng 〈语〉 morphology ◇ ～变化 morphological changes; inflections

【词性】 cíxìng 〈语〉 syntactical functions and morphological features that help to determine a part of speech

【词序】 cíxù 〈语〉 word order

【词义】 cíyì 〈语〉 the meaning (或 sense) of a word

【词语】 cíyǔ words and expressions; terms

【词源】 cíyuán 〈语〉 the origin of a word; etymology

【词韵】 cíyùn ①rhyme of *ci* poems ②rhyming dictionary (of *ci* poems) 参见"词"③

【词缀】 cízhuì 〈语〉 affix

【词组】 cízǔ 〈语〉 word group; phrase

**祠** cí ancestral temple: 宗～ clan hall

【祠堂】 cítáng ancestral hall (或 temple); memorial temple

**茨** cí 〈书〉 ①thatch (a roof) ②〈植〉 puncture vine

**瓷** cí porcelain; china: ～碗 china bowl/ 细～ fine china

【瓷雕】 cídiāo 〈工美〉 porcelain carving

【瓷漆】 cíqī enamel paint; enamel

【瓷器】 cíqì porcelain; chinaware: 薄胎～ eggshell china

【瓷实】 císhi 〈方〉 solid; firm; substantial: 他身体很～。He is solidly built./ 打夯以后，地基就～了。The foundation becomes solid after tamping.

【瓷土】 cítǔ porcelain clay; china clay

【瓷砖】 cízhuān ceramic tile; glazed tile

**辞** cí ①diction; phraseology: 修～ rhetoric ②a type of classical Chinese literature: 《楚～》 *The Songs of Chu* ③a form of classical poetry: 《木兰～》 *The Ballad of Mulan* ④take leave: 告～ take one's leave/ 不～而别 leave without saying good-bye ⑤decline: 固～ firmly decline ⑥dismiss; discharge ⑦shirk: 不～劳苦 spare no effort; take pains

【辞别】 cíbié bid farewell; say good-bye; take one's leave

【辞呈】 cíchéng (written) resignation: 提出～ submit (或 hand in) one's resignation

【辞典】 cídiǎn dictionary

【辞令】 cílìng language appropriate to the occasion: 外交～ diplomatic language/ 善于～ gifted with a silver tongue

【辞让】 círàng politely decline: 他～了一番，才在前排就座。After first politely declining, he eventually took a seat in the front row.

【辞色】 císè 〈书〉 one's speech and facial expression: ～严厉 severe in speech and countenance/ 假以～ look at sb. encouragingly/ 他欣喜之情，形于～。There was joy in his speech and countenance.

【辞书】 císhū dictionary; lexicographical work (e.g. wordbook, etc.)

【辞岁】 císuì bid farewell to the outgoing year; celebrate the lunar New Year's Eve

【辞退】 cítuì dismiss; discharge

【辞谢】 cíxiè politely decline; decline with thanks

【辞行】 cíxíng say good-bye (to one's friends, etc.) before setting out on a journey

【辞藻】 cízǎo flowery language; rhetoric; ornate diction: 堆砌～ string together ornate phrases

【辞章】 cízhāng ①poetry and prose; prose and verse ②art of writing; rhetoric

【辞职】 cízhí resign; hand in one's resignation

**慈** cí ①kind; loving: 心～ tenderhearted; kindhearted ②〈书〉 mother: 家～ my mother

【慈爱】 cí'ài love; affection; kindness

【慈悲】 cíbēi mercy; benevolence; pity: 发～ have pity; be merciful/ 对敌人的～就是对人民的残忍。Kindness to the enemy means cruelty to the people.

【慈姑】 cígu 〈植〉 arrowhead

【慈和】 cíhé kindly and amiable

【慈母】 címǔ loving mother; mother

【慈善】 císhàn charitable; benevolent; philanthropic ◇ ～机关 charitable institution (或 organization)/ ～家 philanthropist/ ～事业 charities; good works; philanthropy

【慈祥】 cíxiáng kindly: ～的面容 a kindly face

**磁** cí ①〈物〉 magnetism: 起～ magnetization/ 地～ terrestrial magnetism ②porcelain; china

【磁暴】 cíbào 〈物〉 magnetic storm ◇ ～记录器 magnetic storm monitor

【磁北】 cíběi the magnetic north

【磁场】 cíchǎng 〈物〉 magnetic field ◇ ～强度 magnetic

field intensity
【磁畴】 cíchóu magnetic domain
【磁带】 cídài (magnetic) tape ◇ ～录音机 tape recorder
【磁感应】 cígǎnyìng 〈物〉 magnetic induction
【磁钢】 cígāng magnet steel
【磁化】 cíhuà 〈物〉 magnetization ◇ ～率 magnetic susceptibility/ ～器 magnetizer
【磁极】 cíjí 〈物〉 magnetic pole ◇ ～强度 magnetic pole strength
【磁力】 cílì 〈物〉 magnetic force ◇ ～测定 magnetometry/ ～勘探 magnetic prospecting/ ～探矿仪 magnetic detector (for ore deposits)/ ～探伤器 magnetic flaw detector; magnetic fault finder/ ～线 magnetic line of force/ ～选矿 magnetic dressing/ ～仪 magnetometer
【磁流体】 cíliútǐ 〈物〉 magnetic fluid ◇ ～力学 magnetofluid dynamics
【磁盘存储器】 cípán cúnchǔqì 〈计算机〉 magnetic disc store
【磁偏角】 cípiānjiǎo 〈物〉 magnetic declination
【磁石】 císhí ①〈矿〉 magnetite ②〈电〉 magnet: ～发电机 magneto/ ～检波器 magneto detector
【磁体】 cítǐ 〈物〉 magnetic body; magnet
【磁铁】 cítiě 〈物〉 magnet: 马蹄形～ horseshoe magnet/ 永久～ permanent magnet/ 电～ electromagnet ◇ ～矿 magnetite
【磁通量】 cítōngliàng 〈物〉 magnetic flux
【磁心】 cíxīn magnetic core ◇ ～储存器 magnetic core memory
【磁性】 cíxìng 〈物〉 magnetism; magnetic: 顺～ paramagnetism/ 抗～ diamagnetism/ 铁～ ferromagnetism ◇ ～水雷 magnetic mine/ ～炸弹 magnetic bomb
【磁选】 cíxuǎn 〈矿〉 magnetic separation: 湿法～ wet magnetic separation ◇ ～厂 magnetic ore dressing plant
【磁针】 cízhēn magnetic needle
【磁子】 cízǐ 〈物〉 magneton

**雌** cí female
【雌花】 cíhuā 〈植〉 female (或 pistillate) flower
【雌黄】 cíhuáng ①〈矿〉 orpiment ②见"信口雌黄" xìnkǒu cíhuáng
【雌蕊】 círuǐ 〈植〉 pistil
【雌性】 cíxìng female
【雌雄】 cí-xióng ① male and female ② victory and defeat: 决一～ have a showdown; see who's master ◇ ～同体〈动〉 hermaphroditism; monoecism/ ～同株〈植〉 monoecism/ ～异体〈动〉 gonochorism; dioecism/ ～异株〈植〉 dioecism

**鹚** cí 见"鸬鹚" lúcí

**糍** cí
【糍粑】 cíbā cooked glutinous rice pounded into paste; glutinous rice cake

## cǐ

**此** cǐ this: ～处 this place; here/ ～等 this kind; such as these/ 由～往南 go south from here
【此岸】 cǐ'àn 〈佛教〉 this shore; temporality
【此辈】 cǐbèi people of this type (或 ilk); such people: 勿与～来往。Don't associate with such people.
【此地】 cǐdì this place; here: ～人 local people
【此地无银三百两】 cǐdì wú yín sānbǎi liǎng No 300 taels of silver buried here (the sign put up by the man in the folk tale over the place where he had hidden some money) — a guilty person gives himself away by conspicuously protesting his innocence; protest one's innocence too much
【此后】 cǐhòu after this; hereafter; henceforth: 她一九五八年到农村去，～一直在那儿工作。She went to the countryside in 1958 and has worked there ever since.
【此间】 cǐjiān around here; here: ～已有传闻。It has been so rumoured here.
【此刻】 cǐkè this moment; now; at present
【此路不通】 cǐ lù bù tōng dead end; blind alley: ～！(路牌) Not a Through Road.
【此起彼伏】 cǐqǐ-bǐfú as one falls, another rises; rise one after another: ～的农民起义 repeated peasant uprisings/ 欢呼声～。Loud cheers rang out continuously. 又作"此伏彼起"
【此时】 cǐshí this moment; right now: ～此刻 at this very moment/ ～此地 here and now
【此外】 cǐwài besides; in addition; moreover: ～，还要讨论一下分工问题。In addition, we'll discuss the question of division of labour./ 我们公社新买了一台拖拉机，～还买了几台水泵。Our commune has just bought a tractor, and some pumps as well.
【此一时，彼一时】 cǐ yīshí, bǐ yīshí this is one situation and that was another — times have changed
【此致】 cǐzhì 〔信末套语〕: ～革命敬礼 With revolutionary greetings

## cì

**次** cì ①order; sequence: 依～ in due order; in succession; one by one/ 席～ seating arrangement/ 车～ train number ②second; next: ～子 second son/～日 next day ③second-rate; inferior: ～棉 poor quality cotton/ 真～ really no good; terrible/ 我的字写得可～了。My handwriting is terrible. ④〈化〉 hypo-: ～氯酸 hypochlorous acid ⑤〈量〉: 三～ three times/ 首～ first time; first/ 二十一～列车 No. 21 train/ 进行几～会谈 hold several talks ⑥〈书〉stopping place on a journey; stopover: 旅～ at a stopover; at a hotel
【次大陆】 cìdàlù subcontinent
【次等】 cìděng second-class; second-rate; inferior
【次第】 cìdì ① order; sequence ② one after another: ～入座 take seats one after another
【次货】 cìhuò inferior goods; substandard goods
【次级线圈】 cìjí xiànquān 〈电〉 secondary coil
【次品】 cìpǐn substandard products; defective goods
【次轻量级】 cìqīngliàngjí 〈举重〉 featherweight
【次生】 cìshēng secondary: ～矿床 secondary deposit
【次声】 cìshēng 〈物〉 infrasonic sound
【次数】 cìshù number of times; frequency: ～不多 not very often/ 练习的～越多，熟练的程度越高。The more you practise, the more skilful you'll become.
【次序】 cìxù order; sequence: ～颠倒 not in the right order/ 按农、轻、重～安排国民经济计划 work out the national economic plan in this order of priorities: agriculture, light industry, heavy industry
【次要】 cìyào less important; secondary; subordinate; minor: ～问题 secondary questions/ ～矛盾 secondary contradiction/ 使这个问题退居～地位 relegate the problem to a secondary position
【次之】 cìzhī take second place: 该省矿藏，以锡最多，铜～。Among the mineral deposits of the province, tin occupies first place; copper comes second.
【次中音号】 cìzhōngyīnhào 〈乐〉 tenor horn

【次重量级】 cìzhòngliàngjí 〈举重〉 middle heavyweight
【次最轻量级】 cìzuìqīngliàngjí 〈举重〉 flyweight

# 伺

cì
另见 sì
【伺候】 cìhou wait upon; serve: 难～ hard to please; fastidious

# 刺

cì ① thorn; splinter: 手上扎了个～ get a thorn (或 splinter) in one's hand/ 他说话总带～儿。There's always a sting in his words. ② stab; prick: ～伤 stab and wound ③ assassinate: 被～ be assassinated ④ irritate; stimulate: ～鼻 irritate the nose; assail one's nostrils ⑤ criticize: 讽～ satirize ⑥〈书〉 visiting card
另见 cī
【刺刺不休】 cìcì bù xiū talk incessantly; chatter on and on
【刺刀】 cìdāo bayonet: 上～!(口令) Fix bayonets!/ 下～!(口令) Unfix bayonets!/ 拼～ bayonet-fighting
【刺耳】 cì'ěr grating on the ear; jarring; ear-piercing; harsh: 这声音太～。The sound is too piercing./ ～的话 harsh words; sarcastic remarks
【刺骨】 cìgǔ piercing to the bones; piercing; biting: 寒风～。The cold wind chills one to the bone.
【刺槐】 cìhuái 〈植〉 locust (tree)
【刺激】 cìjī ① stimulate: 物质～ material incentive/ 强～ strong stimulus ② provoke; irritate; upset: 这一不幸的消息给了她很大的～。She was badly upset by the sad news. ◇ ～物 stimulus; stimulant/ ～性毒剂 irritant agent
【刺客】 cìkè 〈旧〉 assassin
【刺挠】 cìnao 〈口〉 itchy
【刺配】 cìpèi tattoo the face of a criminal and send him into exile (a punishment in feudal China)
【刺杀】 cìshā ① assassinate ②〈军〉 bayonet charge: 练～ practise bayonet fighting
【刺史】 cìshǐ feudal provincial or prefectural governor
【刺探】 cìtàn make roundabout or secret inquiries; pry; spy: ～军情 spy out military secrets; gather military intelligence
【刺铁丝】 cìtiěsī barbed wire 又作"刺丝"
【刺网】 cìwǎng 〈渔〉 gill net: 三层～ trammel net
【刺猬】 cìwei hedgehog
【刺绣】 cìxiù ① embroider ② embroidery ◇ ～品 embroidery
【刺眼】 cìyǎn dazzling; offending to the eye: 亮得～ dazzlingly bright/ 打扮得～ be loudly dressed
【刺痒】 cìyang 〈口〉 itchy
【刺鱼】 cìyú stickleback

# 赐

cì grant; favour; gift: 赏～ grant (或 bestow) a reward/ 请即～复。Please favour me with an early reply./ 厚～受之有愧。I feel unworthy of the precious gift you have bestowed on me.
【赐教】 cìjiào 〈敬〉 condescend to teach; grant instruction: 不吝～ please favour (或 enlighten) me with your instructions; be so kind as to give me a reply
【赐予】 cìyǔ grant; bestow

## cōng

# 从

cōng
另见 cóng
【从容】 cōngróng ① calm; unhurried; leisurely: ～不迫 calm and unhurried/ ～就义 go to one's death unflinchingly; meet one's death like a hero ② plentiful: 时间很～。There's still plenty of time.

# 匆

cōng hastily; hurriedly
【匆匆】 cōngcōng hurriedly: ～吃了一顿饭 take a hurried meal; hurry through a meal/ 行色～ be in a rush getting ready for a journey; be pressed for time on a journey
【匆促】 cōngcù hastily; in a hurry: ～起程 set out hastily/ 时间～ be pressed for time
【匆忙】 cōngmáng hastily; in a hurry: ～作出决定 make a hasty decision/ 临行～,未能向你告别。I left in such a hurry that I didn't have time to say good-bye to you./ 他匆匆忙忙吃了几口东西,又回车间去了。He bolted down a few mouthfuls of food and hurried back to the workshop.

# 囱

cōng 见"烟囱" yāncōng

# 苁

cōng
【苁蓉】 cōngróng 〈中药〉 desert cistanche (*Cistanche deserticola*)

# 枞

cōng 〈植〉 fir

# 锹

cōng short spear (a weapon used in ancient times)

# 葱

cōng ① onion; scallion: 大～ green Chinese onion/ 小～ shallot/ 洋～ onion ② green
【葱白】 cōngbái very light blue
【葱白儿】 cōngbáir scallion stalk
【葱翠】 cōngcuì fresh green; luxuriantly green: ～的竹林 a green bamboo grove
【葱花】 cōnghuā chopped green onion ◇ ～饼 green onion pancake
【葱茏】 cōnglóng verdant; luxuriantly green: 草木～ luxuriant vegetation
【葱绿】 cōnglǜ pale yellowish green; light green; verdant: ～的田野 verdant fields/ 麦苗一片～。The wheat shoots are a lush green.
【葱头】 cōngtóu onion
【葱郁】 cōngyù verdant; luxuriantly green: ～的松树林 a verdant pine wood

# 聪

cōng ①〈书〉 faculty of hearing: 左耳失～ become deaf in the left ear ② acute hearing: 耳～目明 able to see and hear clearly
【聪慧】 cōnghuì bright; intelligent
【聪明】 cōngming intelligent; bright; clever: ～能干 bright and capable/ ～才智 intelligence and wisdom/ ～反被～误。Clever people may be victims of their own cleverness. 或 Cleverness may overreach itself./ ～一世,糊涂一时 clever all one's life but stupid this once; smart as a rule, but this time a fool
【聪颖】 cōngyǐng intelligent; bright; clever

## cóng

# 从

cóng ①〈介〉〔表示起于或经过〕 from; through: ～群众中来,到群众中去 from the masses, to the masses/ ～现在起 from now on/ ～这儿往西 go west from here; west of here/ ～战争中学习战争 learn warfare through warfare/ ～党的要求来看 judged by the requirements of the Party/ ～全局出发 proceed from the situation as a whole/ ～根本上说 essentially; in essence/ ～路线上分清是非 distinguish between right and wrong in the light of the two-line struggle ②〈副〉〔用在否定词前面〕 ever: 她在成绩和荣誉

面前～不骄傲。Her head was never turned by achievements or honours./ ～不计较个人的名誉地位 never give any consideration to personal fame and position ③ follow; comply with; obey: ～俗 follow the general custom; conform to custom/ ～命 comply with sb.'s wish; obey an order/ ～征 go on a military expedition ④ join; be engaged in: ～军 join the army; enlist ⑤ in a certain manner or according to a certain principle: 批判～严，处理～宽 criticize strictly, handle leniently/ 训练要～难、～严、～实战出发。Training should be hard, strict and geared to the needs of actual combat. ⑥ follower; attendant: 随～ attendant; retainer; retinue/ ～者如云 have a large following ⑦ secondary; accessary: 主～ the primary and the secondary/ 分别首～ distinguish between the chief culprit and the accessary ⑧ relationship between cousins, etc. of the same paternal grandfather, great-grandfather or a yet earlier common ancestor; of the same clan: ～兄 first, second or distant cousin of the same clan; cousin

另见 cōng

【从长计议】 cóng cháng jìyì give the matter further thought and discuss it later

【从此】 cóngcǐ from this time on; from now on; from then on; henceforth; thereupon

【从…到…】 cóng ... dào ... from... to...: 从上到下 from top to bottom; from the higher levels to the grass roots/ 从无到有 grow out of nothing/ 从早到晚 from dawn to dusk; from morning till night/ 从古到今 from ancient times to the present; from time immemorial/ 革命力量的发展总是从弱到强，从小到大。The development of revolutionary forces is always from weak to strong and from small to large.

【从动】 cóngdòng 〈机〉driven: ～齿轮 driven gear/ ～构件 driven member

【从而】 cóng'ér 〈连〉 thus; thereby: 农业迅速发展，～为轻工业提供了充足的原料。Agriculture has developed rapidly, thus providing light industry with ample raw materials.

【从犯】 cóngfàn accessary criminal; accessary

【从价税】 cóngjiàshuì 〈经〉 *ad valorem* duties

【从简】 cóngjiǎn conform to the principle of simplicity: 一切～ dispense with all unnecessary formalities

【从句】 cóngjù 〈语〉 subordinate clause

【从军】 cóngjūn join the army; enlist

【从来】 cónglái always; at all times; all along: 世界各国人民的革命斗争～都是互相支持的。The people of all countries have always supported each other in their revolutionary struggle./ 我～没有见过他。I've never seen him before.

【从量税】 cóngliàngshuì 〈经〉specific duties

【从略】 cónglüè be omitted: 此处引文～。The quotation is omitted here.

【从前】 cóngqián before; formerly; in the past: 咱们村跟～大不一样了。Our village is very different from what it was before./ ～，有一个老人，名叫"愚公"。 Once upon a time, there lived an old man called Yu Gong.

【从权】 cóngquán as a matter of expediency: ～处理 do what is expedient

【从戎】 cóngróng 〈书〉 join the army; enlist: 投笔～ throw aside the writing brush and join the army — renounce the pen for the sword

【从善如流】 cóng shàn rú liú follow good advice as naturally as a river follows its course; readily accept good advice

【从事】 cóngshì ① go in for; be engaged in: ～科学研究工作 be engaged in scientific research/ ～文学创作 take up writing as a profession; be engaged in literary work/ ～技术革新 work on technical innovations/ ～群众工作 do mass work ② deal with: 慎重～ act cautiously; steer a cautious course/ 军法～ deal with according to military law; court-martial

【从属】 cóngshǔ subordinate: ～地位 subordinate status/ 文艺是～于政治的，但又反转来给予伟大的影响于政治。Literature and art are subordinate to politics, but in their turn exert a great influence on politics.

【从速】 cóngsù as soon as possible; without delay: ～处理 deal with the matter as soon as possible; settle the matter quickly/ 存书无多，欲购～。Only a few copies left. Buy now, while they last.

【从头】 cóngtóu ① from the beginning: ～儿做起 start from the very beginning ② anew; once again: ～儿再来 start afresh; start all over again

【从小】 cóngxiǎo from childhood; as a child: 他～热爱劳动。He has loved labour ever since he was a child.

【从刑】 cóngxíng 〈法〉 accessary punishment

【从中】 cóngzhōng out of; from among; therefrom: ～渔利 profit from; cash in on/ ～调解 mediate between two sides/ ～吸取有益的教训 draw a salutary lesson from it

## 丛

cóng ① crowd together: ～生 grow thickly ② clump; thicket; grove: 草～ a patch of grass/ 树～ a clump of trees; grove ③ crowd; collection: 人～ a crowd of people/ 论～ a collection of essays; collected essays ④ (Cóng) a surname

【丛集】 cóngjí crowd together; pile up: 百感～ all sorts of feelings welling up/ 债务～ debts piling up

【丛刊】 cóngkān a series of books; collection

【丛林】 cónglín ① jungle; forest ② Buddhist monastery ◇ ～热〈医〉 jungle fever/ ～战 jungle warfare

【丛生】 cóngshēng ① (of plants) grow thickly: 荆棘～ be overgrown with brambles ② (of diseases, evils, etc.) break out: 百病～ all kinds of diseases and ailments breaking out

【丛书】 cóngshū a series of books; collection: 知识青年自学～ school-leavers' self-study series

【丛杂】 cóngzá motley

## 淙

cóng

【淙淙】 cóngcóng 〈象〉 gurgling: 流水～ a gurgling stream

## 琮

cóng a long hollow piece of jade with rectangular sides

# còu

## 凑

còu ① gather together; pool; collect: ～钱 pool money/ ～足人数 gather together enough people; get a quorum/ ～情况 pool information ② happen by chance; take advantage of: 正～上是个星期天。It happened to be a Sunday./ ～空儿 try to find time (to do sth.) ③ move close to; press near: ～近点儿。Move closer, please.

【凑份子】 còu fènzi club together (to present a gift to sb.)

【凑合】 còuhe ① gather together; collect; assemble: 昨天下班后大伙儿～在一起练歌。 Yesterday we gathered after work to practise singing. ② improvise: 请大家会前作好发言准备，不要临时～。Please prepare before coming to the meeting. Don't speak offhand. ③ make do: 我这件棉袄～着还能穿一冬。I can make this padded jacket do for another winter./ 他没有学过会计，但还能～着记记帐。 He isn't a trained accountant, but he manages to keep simple accounts. ④ passable; not too bad: 这本小说怎么样？——还～。What do you think of this novel? — Not too bad.

【凑集】 còují gather together: ～图书以建立街道儿童阅览室 pool books to form a neighbourhood children's reading room/ 晚饭后工人们～在一起研究技术革新问题。After supper the workers got together to discuss technical innovations.

【凑巧】 còuqiǎo luckily; fortunately; as luck would have it: 搬家的那一天,～赶上下雨。As luck would have it, it rained the day we moved./ 真不～! 他出去了。What bad luck! He's not at home.

【凑趣儿】 còuqùr ① join in (a game, etc.) just to please others: 他也说了几句玩笑话,凑了个趣儿。He also cracked a few jokes to make everybody happy. ② make a joke about; poke fun at: 别拿我～。Don't poke fun at me.

【凑热闹】 còu rènào ① join in the fun ② add trouble to: 我们够忙的,别再来～了。We're busy enough as it is, don't give us more trouble.

【凑手】 còushǒu at hand; within easy reach: 一时不～,我拿不出那么多钱来。It happens I haven't got so much money on me at the moment.

【凑数】 còushù make up the number or amount; serve as a stopgap

**辏** còu 见"辐辏" fúcòu

## cū

**粗** cū ① wide (in diameter); thick: ～绳 a thick rope/ 这棵树很～。This tree has a thick trunk./ ～眉大眼 bushy eyebrows and big eyes ② coarse; crude; rough: ～沙 coarse sand; grit/ ～盐 crude salt/ ～黑的手 rough, work-soiled hands ③ gruff; husky: ～嗓子 a husky voice/ ～声大气 a deep, gruff voice ④ careless; negligent: ～中有细 usually careless, but quite sharp at times; crude in most matters, but subtle in some ⑤ rude; unrefined; vulgar: 说话很～ speak rudely; use coarse language ⑥ roughly; slightly: ～知一二 have a rough idea; know a little/ ～具规模 be roughly in shape

【粗暴】 cūbào rude; rough; crude; brutal: ～态度 a rude attitude/ ～行为 crude behaviour/ ～违反国际惯例 gross violation of international practice/ ～干涉别国内政 wantonly interfere in the internal affairs of other countries/ ～践踏别国主权 brutally trample on the sovereignty of another country

【粗笨】 cūbèn clumsy; unwieldy: 动作～ clumsy/ ～的家具 unwieldy furniture

【粗鄙】 cūbǐ vulgar; coarse: 言语～ vulgar in speech

【粗布】 cūbù coarse cloth

【粗糙】 cūcāo coarse; rough; crude: 皮肤～ rough skin/ 手工～ crudely made; of poor workmanship

【粗茶淡饭】 cūchá-dànfàn plain tea and simple food; homely fare

【粗大】 cūdà ① thick; bulky: ～的手 big strong hands ② loud: ～的嗓门 a loud voice/ ～的鼾声 thunderous snoring

【粗放】 cūfàng 〈农〉 extensive: ～耕作 extensive cultivation

【粗犷】 cūguǎng ① rough; rude; boorish ② straightforward and uninhibited; bold and unconstrained; rugged

【粗豪】 cūháo forthright; straightforward

【粗花呢】 cūhuāní 〈纺〉 tweed

【粗话】 cūhuà vulgar language

【粗活】 cūhuó heavy manual labour; unskilled work

【粗加工】 cūjiāgōng 〈机〉 rough machining; roughing

【粗粮】 cūliáng coarse food grain (e. g. maize, sorghum, millet, etc. as distinct from wheat and rice)

【粗劣】 cūliè of poor quality; cheap; shoddy: ～的赝品 a cheap imitation

【粗陋】 cūlòu coarse and crude: 这所房子盖得很～。This is a crudely built house.

【粗鲁】 cūlǔ rough; rude; boorish: 态度～ rude

【粗略】 cūlüè rough; sketchy: ～估计 a rough estimate/ ～一看 on cursory examination

【粗麻布】 cūmábù burlap; gunny; sacking

【粗毛羊】 cūmáoyáng coarse-wooled sheep; coarse wool

【粗浅】 cūqiǎn superficial; shallow; simple: ～的体会 a superficial understanding/ ～的道理 a simple truth

【粗人】 cūrén rough fellow; boor; unrefined person: 我是个～,说话直来直去,你可别见怪。I'm a bit of a boor, so I hope you won't mind if I speak bluntly.

【粗鞣革】 cūróugé rough-tanned leather; crust leather

【粗纱机】 cūshājī 〈纺〉 fly frame

【粗梳毛纺】 cūshū máofǎng 〈纺〉 woollen spinning

【粗梳棉纱】 cūshū miánshā 〈纺〉 carded yarn

【粗疏】 cūshū careless; inattentive

【粗率】 cūshuài rough and careless; ill-considered: ～的决定 an ill-considered decision

【粗饲料】 cūsìliào coarse fodder; roughage

【粗俗】 cūsú vulgar; coarse: 说话～ use coarse or vulgar language

【粗细】 cūxì ① (degree of) thickness: 碗口～的钢管 steel tubes as big as the mouth of a bowl/ 这样～的沙子最合适。Sand this fine will be just right. ② crudeness or fineness; degree of finish; quality of work: 庄稼长得好坏,也要看活的～。Whether the crops grow well or badly depends also on how the work is done.

【粗线条】 cūxiàntiáo ① thick lines; rough outline: ～的描写 a rough sketch ② rough-and-ready; slapdash

【粗心】 cūxīn careless; thoughtless: ～大意 negligent; careless; inadvertent

【粗野】 cūyě rough; boorish; uncouth: 举止～ behave boorishly/ 比赛中动作～ play rough

【粗轧】 cūzhá 〈冶〉 roughing (down) ◇ ～机 roughing mill

【粗支纱】 cūzhīshā 〈纺〉 coarse yarn

【粗枝大叶】 cūzhī-dàyè crude and careless; sloppy; slapdash: ～的工作作风 a crude and careless style of work

【粗制滥造】 cūzhì-lànzào manufacture in a rough and slipshod way

【粗制品】 cūzhìpǐn semifinished product

【粗重】 cūzhòng ① (of voice, etc.) loud and jarring: ～的嗓音 a gruff voice/ ～的喘息声 loud breathing ② big and heavy; bulky: ～的钢管 big and heavy steel tubes ③ thick and heavy: 眉毛浓黑～ bushy black eyebrows ④ strenuous; heavy: ～的活计 heavy work; heavy manual labour

【粗壮】 cūzhuàng ① sturdy; thickset; brawny: ～的小伙子 a sturdy lad/ ～的胳臂 brawny arms ② thick and strong: ～的树干 a thick tree trunk ③ deep and resonant: 声音～ have a deep, resonant voice

## cù

**促** cù ① (of time) short; hurried; urgent: 气～ breathe quickly; be short of breath; pant ② urge; promote: 催～ urge; hurry/ 抓革命,～生产 grasp (或 keep a tight hold on) revolution and promote production/ 大批～大干,大干～大变。Mass criticism inspires great drive, and that brings about great changes. ③ 〈书〉 close to; near: ～膝 sit knee to knee; sit close together

【促成】 cùchéng help to bring about; facilitate: ～双方取得协议 help to bring about an agreement between the two parties ◇ ～栽培〈农〉 forcing culture

【促进】 cùjìn promote; advance; accelerate: 互相～ help each other forward/ ～两国关系的正常化 promote the normalization of relations between the two countries/ ～工农业生产的大发展 bring about a great advance in industrial and agricultural production ◇ ～剂〈化〉promoter/ ～派 promoter of progress
【促染剂】 cùrǎnjì 〈纺〉accelerant
【促使】 cùshǐ impel; urge; spur: 生产的发展～我们不断地钻研技术。The development of production impels us continuously to study technique./ 革命斗争的需要～我们去刻苦地学习马列主义。The demands of revolutionary struggle spur us on to study Marxism-Leninism diligently.
【促膝谈心】 cù xī tánxīn sit side by side and talk intimately; have a heart-to-heart talk
【促狭】 cùxiá 〈方〉mischievous ◇ ～鬼 a mischievous person; mischief
【促织】 cùzhī 〈动〉cricket

**猝** cù 〈书〉sudden; abrupt; unexpected: ～不及防 be taken by surprise
【猝倒病】 cùdǎobìng 〈农〉damping off: 松苗～ damping off of pine seedlings
【猝然】 cùrán suddenly; abruptly; unexpectedly: ～决定 make a sudden decision

**酢** cù vinegar
另见 zuò
【酢浆草】 cùjiāngcǎo 〈植〉creeping oxalis (*Oxalis corniculata*)

**蔟** cù 见"蚕蔟" cáncù

**醋** cù ① vinegar ② jealousy (as in love affair): 吃～ feel jealous/ ～意 (feeling of) jealousy
【醋精】 cùjīng 〈食品〉vinegar concentrate
【醋栗】 cùlì 〈植〉gooseberry
【醋酸】 cùsuān 〈化〉acetic acid ◇ ～酐 acetic oxide/ ～盐 acetate
【醋酯纤维】 cùzhǐ xiānwéi acetate fibre

**簇** cù ①〈书〉form a cluster; pile up: 花团锦～ bouquets of flowers and piles of brocades — rich multicoloured decorations ②〈量〉cluster; bunch: 一～鲜花 a bunch of flowers/ 一～～灿烂的礼花 clusters of brilliant fireworks
【簇射】 cùshè 〈物〉shower: 宇宙线～ cosmic-ray shower/ 高能～ energetic shower
【簇新】 cùxīn brand new
【簇拥】 cùyōng cluster round: 前后～着一大群人 escorted by big crowds in front and behind/ 工人们～着自己的代表,热烈地欢呼着。The workers gathered round their own representative, cheering lustily.

**蹙** cù 〈书〉① pressed; cramped: 穷～ in dire straits ② knit (one's brows): ～额 knit one's brows; frown

**蹴** cù 〈书〉① kick ② tread: 一～而就 reach the goal in one step; accomplish one's aim in one move

## cuān

**汆** cuān quick-boil: ～丸子 quick-boiled meat balls with soup
【汆子】 cuānzi a small, cylindrical metal pot which can be thrust into a fire to make the water in it boil quickly

**撺** cuān 〈方〉① throw; fling ② do in a hurry: 临时现～ improvise ③ fly into a rage: 他～儿了。He flared up.
【撺掇】 cuānduo 〈口〉urge; egg on: 你自己不干,为什么～他呢? Why do you egg him on to do what you won't do yourself?

**镩** cuān cut or break (ice) with an ice pick
【镩子】 cuānzi ice pick

**蹿** cuān leap up: 他往上一～,把球接住。He leapt up and caught the ball.

## cuán

**攒** cuán collect together; assemble: 自己～一辆自行车 assemble a bicycle oneself
另见 zǎn
【攒聚】 cuánjù gather closely together
【攒三聚五】 cuánsān-jùwǔ (of people) gather in little knots; gather in threes and fours

## cuàn

**窜** cuàn ① flee; scurry: 东逃西～ flee in all directions/ 鼠～ scurry like rats; run away like frightened rats ②〈书〉exile; expel ③ change (the wording in a text, manuscript, etc.); alter: 点～ make some alterations (in wording)
【窜犯】 cuànfàn raid; make an inroad into: ～边境的匪徒已全部就歼。All the bandits that invaded the border area have been wiped out.
【窜改】 cuàngǎi alter; tamper with; falsify: ～原文 alter the original text/ ～记录 tamper with the minutes/ ～帐目 falsify accounts
【窜扰】 cuànrǎo harass: ～活动 harassment/ 一架～我领空的敌机被击落了。An enemy plane that had intruded into our air space was shot down.
【窜逃】 cuàntáo flee in disorder; scurry off

**篡** cuàn usurp; seize: ～权 usurp power
【篡夺】 cuànduó usurp; seize: 妄图～党和国家的最高领导权 vainly attempt to usurp the supreme Party leadership and state power
【篡改】 cuàngǎi distort; misrepresent; tamper with; falsify: ～历史 distort history/ ～马列主义 distort (或 falsify) Marxism-Leninism/ 事实不容～,谎言必须戳穿。Facts cannot be altered; lies must be exposed.
【篡位】 cuànwèi usurp the throne

**爨** cuàn 〈书〉① cook: 分～ have separate kitchens — divide up the household (between brothers) ② an earthen cooking stove

## cuī

**崔** Cuī a surname
【崔巍】 cuīwēi 〈书〉lofty; towering: 山势～。The mountains stand tall and imposing.
【崔嵬】 cuīwéi 〈书〉① rocky mound ② high; towering

**催** cuī ①urge; hurry; press: ～办 press sb. to do sth./ 扬鞭～马 urge one's horse on with a whip; whip one's horse on/ 去～他一下。Go and hurry him up. ②hasten; expedite; speed up: 春风～绿。The spring wind speeds the greening of the plants.

【催逼】 cuībī press (for payment of debt, etc.)

【催产】 cuīchǎn expedite child delivery; hasten parturition 又作"催生"

【催促】 cuīcù urge; hasten; press: 我们～她尽快来成都。We urged her to come to Chengdu as soon as possible.

【催肥】 cuīféi 〈牧〉 fatten

【催化】 cuīhuà 〈化〉 catalysis ◇ ～促进剂 catalytic promoter/ ～反应 catalytic reaction/ ～剂 catalyst; catalytic agent/ ～裂化〈石油〉 catalytic cracking

【催泪弹】 cuīlèidàn tear bomb; tear-gas grenade

【催眠】 cuīmián lull (to sleep); hypnotize; mesmerize ◇ ～曲 lullaby; cradlesong/ ～术 hypnotism; mesmerism

【催奶】 cuīnǎi stimulate the secretion of milk; promote lactation ◇ ～剂 galactagogue

【催青】 cuīqīng 〈农〉 hasten the hatching of silkworms (by adjusting temperature and humidity)

【催熟】 cuīshú 〈农〉 accelerate the ripening (of fruit)

【催吐剂】 cuītùjì 〈药〉 emetic

【催醒剂】 cuīxǐngjì 〈药〉 analeptic: 中药～ herbal analeptic

**摧** cuī break; destroy: ～折 break; snap/ 无坚不～ capable of destroying any stronghold; all-conquering

【摧残】 cuīcán wreck; destroy; devastate: ～身体 ruin one's health/ ～民主 trample on democracy/ 反动派总想～革命力量。The reactionaries always try to destroy revolutionary forces.

【摧毁】 cuīhuǐ destroy; smash; wreck: ～敌人据点 destroy enemy strongholds/ ～旧的国家机器 smash the old state machinery

【摧枯拉朽】 cuīkū-lāxiǔ (as easy as) crushing dry weeds and smashing rotten wood

## cuǐ

**璀** cuǐ

【璀璨】 cuǐcàn 〈书〉 bright; resplendent: ～夺目 dazzling

## cuì

**脆** cuì ①fragile; brittle: 这纸太～。This kind of paper is too fragile./ ～金属 brittle metal ②crisp: 这种梨又甜又～。These pears are sweet and crisp. ③(of voice) clear; crisp: 听她的嗓音多～! What a crisp voice she has! ④〈方〉 neat: 这件事办得很～。That was a neat job.

【脆骨】 cuìgǔ gristle (as food)

【脆弱】 cuìruò fragile; frail; weak: 感情～ be easily upset

【脆生】 cuìsheng 〈口〉 ①crisp: 这黄瓜～爽口。The cucumbers are crisp and refreshing. ②(of sound) clear and sharp

【脆性】 cuìxìng 〈冶〉 brittleness

**淬** cuì temper by dipping in water, oil, etc.; quench

【淬火】 cuìhuǒ quench ◇ ～剂 hardening agent; quenching liquid/ ～硬化 quench hardening

【淬砺】 cuìlì 〈书〉 temper oneself through severe trials

**悴** cuì 见"憔悴" qiáocuì

**萃** cuì 〈书〉 ①come together; assemble: 荟～ assemble ②a gathering of people or a collection of things: 出类拔～ outstanding

【萃取】 cuìqǔ 〈化〉 extraction

**啐** cuì spit; expectorate: ～他一口 spit at him

**毳** cuì 〈书〉 fine hair on animals; down

**瘁** cuì 〈书〉 overworked; tired: 心力交～ be physically and mentally tired

**粹** cuì ①pure: ～白 pure white/ ～而不杂 pure and unadulterated ②essence; the best: 精～ essence; quintessence

**翠** cuì ①emerald green; green: ～竹 green bamboos ②kingfisher: 点～ handicraft using kingfisher's feathers for ornament ③jadeite: 珠～ pearls and jade jewellery

【翠菊】 cuìjú 〈植〉 China aster (*Callistephus chinensis*)

【翠绿】 cuìlǜ emerald green; jade green

【翠鸟】 cuìniǎo kingfisher

【翠微】 cuìwēi 〈书〉 a shady retreat on a green hill

## cūn

**村** cūn ①village; hamlet ②rustic; boorish: ～野 boorish

【村落】 cūnluò village; hamlet

【村史】 cūnshǐ village history

【村长】 cūnzhǎng village head

【村镇】 cūnzhèn villages and small towns

【村庄】 cūnzhuāng village; hamlet

【村子】 cūnzi village; hamlet

**皴** cūn ①(of skin) chapped (from the cold); cracked: 孩子的手～了。The child's hands were chapped from the cold. ②〈美术〉 the method of showing the shades and texture of rocks and mountains by light ink strokes in traditional Chinese landscape painting

## cún

**存** cún ①exist; live; survive: 父母均～。Both parents are still living. ②store; keep: ～粮 store up grain/ 新水库～了大量的水。A large quantity of water is stored in the new reservoir./ 天气热，西红柿～不住。Tomatoes won't keep in hot weather. ③accumulate; collect: 一下雨，洼地里就～了好些水。Whenever it rains, a lot of water accumulates in the low-lying land. ④deposit: 把钱～在银行里 deposit money in a bank ⑤leave with; check: 行李先～在这里，回头再来取。Let's check our luggage here and come back for it later./ ～自行车 leave one's bicycle in a bicycle park ⑥reserve; retain: 求同～异 seek common ground while reserving differences/ 他有什么说什么，肚子里～不住话。He always says what he thinks; he can't hold anything back. ⑦remain on balance; be in stock: 收支相抵，净～两千元。The accounts show a surplus of 2,000 *yuan*. ⑧cherish; harbour: ～着很大的希望 cherish high hopes/ 不～幻想 harbour no illusions

【存案】 cún'àn register with the proper authorities

【存查】 cúnchá file for reference

【存车处】 cúnchēchù parking lot (for bicycles); bicycle park (或 shed)
【存储】 cúnchǔ 〈电子〉 memory; storage
◇ ～二极管 storage diode/ ～器 memory; storage/ ～容量 memory capacity/ ～元件 memory element
【存单】 cúndān deposit receipt: 定期～ time certificate (bearing specific maturity date)
【存档】 cúndàng keep in the archives; place on file; file
【存底儿】 cúndǐr keep the original draft; keep a file copy
【存而不论】 cún ér bù lùn leave the question open
【存放】 cúnfàng ①leave with; leave in sb.'s care: 我把箱子～在朋友那里了。I've left my suitcase with a friend of mine. ② deposit (money)
【存根】 cúngēn counterfoil; stub: 支票～ cheque stub
【存户】 cúnhù depositor
【存货】 cúnhuò goods in stock; existing stock
【存款】 cúnkuǎn deposit; bank savings: 个人～ personal savings account/ 活期～ current deposit; demand deposit/ 定期～ fixed deposit; time deposit
【存栏】 cúnlán 〈牧〉 amount of livestock on hand: 牲畜～总头数比去年增加了一倍。The amount of livestock is twice as large as it was last year.
【存身】 cúnshēn take shelter; make one's home: 无处～ find no shelter; have no place to call one's home
【存食】 cúnshí suffer from indigestion
【存亡】 cún-wáng live or die; survive or perish: 抗日战争是关系中华民族生死～的战争。The War of Resistance Against Japan was a life-and-death struggle for the Chinese nation./ 与阵地共～ defend one's position to the death/ ～绝续的关头 at a most critical moment
【存项】 cúnxiàng credit balance; balance
【存心】 cúnxīn ① cherish certain intentions: ～不良 cherish evil designs (或 intentions)/ 他说这番话,不知存什么心。It's hard to say what his intentions were in saying that. ② intentionally; deliberately; on purpose: 我不是～这么做的。I didn't do it on purpose.
【存疑】 cúnyí leave a question open; leave a matter for future consideration: 这件事情暂时～吧。Let's put this matter aside for the time being.
【存在】 cúnzài exist; be: 只要阶级～，就有阶级斗争。So long as classes exist there will always be class struggle./ 人们的社会～决定人们的思想。It is man's social being that determines his thinking./ 矛盾～于一切事物发展的过程中。Contradiction is present in the process of development of all things.
【存折】 cúnzhé deposit book; bankbook
【存执】 cúnzhí counterfoil; stub

## cǔn

**忖** cǔn turn over in one's mind; ponder; speculate
【忖度】 cǔnduó speculate; conjecture; surmise
【忖量】 cǔnliàng ① think over; turn over in one's mind: 她～了半天，还拿不定主意。She turned the matter over in her mind for a long while but still could not come to a decision. ② conjecture; guess: 我一边走，一边～着他说的那番话的意思。As I walked along I kept wondering what he really meant.

## cùn

**寸** cùn ①*cun*, a unit of length (= 1/3 decimetre) ② very little; very short; small: ～进 a little progress/ ～功 small contribution; meagre achievement/ ～草不留 leave not even a blade of grass; be devastated/ ～土必争 fight for every inch of land
【寸步】 cùnbù a tiny step; a single step: ～不离 follow sb. closely; keep close to/ ～不让 refuse to yield an inch/ 离开了群众我们就～难行。Without the masses we can't move a single step.
【寸关尺】 cùn-guān-chǐ 〈中医〉 *cun*, *guan* and *chi*, three places at the wrist where the pulse is usually taken
【寸金难买寸光阴】 cùn jīn nán mǎi cùn guāngyīn 〈谚〉 money can't buy time; time is more precious than gold
【寸心】 cùnxīn feelings: 聊表～ as a small token of my feelings; just to show my appreciation
【寸阴】 cùnyīn 〈书〉 time indicated by a shadow moving a *cun* — a very short time

## cuō

**搓** cuō rub with the hands: ～手取暖 rub one's hands together to warm them/ ～麻绳 make cord by twisting hemp fibres between the palms/ ～纸捻 roll paper spills/ 这件上衣太脏了,洗时要多～～。This jacket is very dirty; give it a good scrubbing.
【搓板】 cuōbǎn washboard
【搓球】 cuōqiú 〈乒乓球〉 chop: 一板一板地把球搓过去 return every shot with a chop
【搓手顿脚】 cuōshǒu-dùnjiǎo wring one's hands and stamp one's feet — get anxious and impatient
【搓澡】 cuōzǎo give sb. a rubdown with a damp towel (in a public bathhouse)

**磋** cuō consult
【磋商】 cuōshāng consult; exchange views: 与各有关部门进行～ hold consultations with all departments concerned

**撮** cuō ①〈书〉 gather; bring together ② scoop up (with a dustpan or shovel): ～走一簸箕土 scoop up a dustpan of dirt ③〈方〉 take up with the fingers: ～一点盐 take a pinch of salt ④ extract; summarize: ～要 make extracts ⑤ *cuo*, a unit of capacity (= 1 millilitre) ⑥〈量〉 pinch: 一～盐 a pinch of salt/ 一小～法西斯匪徒 a handful of fascist bandits
另见 zuǒ
【撮合】 cuōhe make a match; act as go-between
【撮弄】 cuōnòng ① make fun of; play a trick on; tease ② abet; instigate; incite
【撮要】 cuōyào ① make an abstract; outline essential points: 把工作情况～上报 submit an outline report on one's work ② abstract; synopsis; extracts: 论文～ abstract of a thesis

**蹉** cuō
【蹉跎】 cuōtuó waste time: ～岁月 let time slip by without accomplishing anything; idle away one's time/ 一再～ let one opportunity after another slip away

## cuó

**痤** cuó
【痤疮】 cuóchuāng 〈医〉 acne

**矬** cuó 〈方〉 short: ～个儿 a short person
【矬子】 cuózi 〈方〉 a short person; dwarf

## cuò

**挫** cuò ①defeat; frustrate: 受～ suffer a setback ② subdue; lower: ～敌人的锐气，长自己的威风 deflate the enemy's arrogance and boost our own morale/ ～其锋芒 blunt the edge of one's advance

【挫败】 cuòbài frustrate; foil; defeat: 遭到严重的～ suffer a serious defeat/ ～侵略计划 frustrate plans for aggression/ ～新、老殖民主义者的阴谋 foil the schemes of the old and new colonialists

【挫伤】 cuòshāng ①〈医〉contusion; bruise ② dampen; blunt; discourage: 不要～群众的积极性。Don't dampen the enthusiasm of the masses.

【挫折】 cuòzhé setback; reverse: 遭受～ suffer setbacks (或 reverses)

**厝** cuò 〈书〉①lay; place ②place a coffin in a temporary shelter pending burial

【厝火积薪】 cuò huǒ jī xīn put a fire under a pile of faggots — a hidden danger

**措** cuò ①arrange; manage; handle: 惊慌失～ be seized with panic; be frightened out of one's wits/ 不知所～ be at a loss what to do; be at one's wit's end ②make plans: 筹～款项 raise funds

【措辞】 cuòcí wording; diction: ～不当 inappropriate wording/ ～严厉 couched in harsh terms/ ～强硬 strongly worded

【措施】 cuòshī measure; step: 采取重大～ adopt an important measure/ 十分指标，十二分～。If the target is ten, take measures to achieve twelve — make ample preparations to guarantee success.

【措手不及】 cuò shǒu bù jí be caught unprepared; be caught unawares: 打他个～ make a surprise attack on them

【措置】 cuòzhì handle; manage; arrange: ～得当 be handled properly

**锉** cuò ①file: 方～ square file/ 圆～ round file/ 木～ (wood) rasp ②make smooth with a file; file: ～光 file sth. smooth

【锉刀】 cuòdāo file

【锉屑】 cuòxiè filing

**错** cuò ①interlocked and jagged; intricate; complex: 犬牙交～ jigsaw-like; interlocking ②grind; rub: ～牙 grind one's teeth (in one's sleep) ③alternate; stagger: 这两个会不能同时开，得～一下。We can't hold the two meetings at the same time; we must stagger them. ④ wrong; mistaken; erroneous: 你弄～了。You've got it wrong./ 拿～东西 take sth. by mistake ⑤fault; demerit: 这是他的～，不怨你。You are not to blame; it is his fault. ⑥〔用于否定式〕bad; poor: 今年的收成～不了。This year's harvest is sure to be good./ 他们感情不～。They are on good terms. ⑦〈书〉inlay or plate with gold, silver, etc. ⑧〈书〉grindstone for polishing jade: 他山之石，可以为～。Stones from other hills may serve to polish the jade of this one — advice from others may help one overcome one's shortcomings.

【错爱】 cuò'ài 〈谦〉undeserved kindness

【错案】 cuò'àn 〈法〉misjudged case

【错别字】 cuò-biézì wrongly written or mispronounced characters

【错车】 cuòchē one vehicle gives another the right of way

【错处】 cuòchu fault; demerit

【错怪】 cuòguài blame sb. wrongly

【错过】 cuòguò miss; let slip: ～机会 miss an opportunity/ ～这趟汽车，今天就走不成了。If we miss this bus, we won't be able to go today.

【错角】 cuòjiǎo 〈数〉alternate angle

【错金】 cuòjīn inlaying gold: ～器皿 gold-inlaid ware; metal-inlaid ware

【错觉】 cuòjué illusion; misconception; wrong impression: 这样会给人造成～。This will give people a false impression.

【错开】 cuòkāi stagger: 把公休日子～ stagger the days off

【错乱】 cuòluàn in disorder; in confusion; deranged: 颠倒～ topsy-turvy/ 精神～ mentally deranged; insane

【错落】 cuòluò strewn at random: ～不齐 scattered here and there/ 苍松翠柏～其间 dotted with green pines and cypresses

【错误】 cuòwù ①wrong; mistaken; erroneous: ～思想 wrong thinking; a mistaken idea/ ～的结论 wrong conclusion/ ～路线 an erroneous line ②mistake; error; blunder: 犯～ make a mistake; commit an error/ ～百出 riddled with errors; full of mistakes

【错杂】 cuòzá mixed; heterogeneous; jumbled; of mixed content

【错字】 cuòzì ①wrongly written character ②misprint

【错综复杂】 cuòzōng-fùzá intricate; complex: 这部小说的情节～，引人入胜。The plot of the novel is intricate and fascinating.

# D

## dā

**哒** dā 〔发音短促，吆喝牲口前进的声音〕 gee; gee-up; giddyap

**耷** dā 〈书〉 big-eared

【耷拉】 dāla droop; hang down: ～着脑袋 hang one's head

**搭** dā ① put up; build: ～一个临时舞台 put up a makeshift stage/ ～桥 build a bridge/ ～帐篷 pitch a tent ② hang over; put over: 把洗好的衣服～在绳上 hang the washing on a line/ 他肩膀上～着一块毛巾。He had a towel over his shoulder. ③ come into contact; join: 那两根电线～上了。The two wires are touching./ ～上关系 strike up a relationship with; establish contact with/ 前言不～后语 speak incoherently; mumble disconnected phrases ④ throw in more (people, money, etc.); add: 你忙不过来，给你～个人吧。You're terribly busy. We'll send someone to help you. ⑤ lift sth. together: 帮我把这包大米～上卡车。Help me lift the bag of rice onto the truck./ 咱们俩把这筐土～走。Let's carry this basket of earth away. ⑥ take (a ship, plane, etc.); travel (或 go) by: ～轮船去上海 go to Shanghai by boat/ ～飞机 go by plane/ ～长途汽车 travel by coach/ ～他们的车走 get a lift in their car

【搭伴】 dābàn join sb. on a trip; travel together: 他也到新疆去，你们搭个伴儿吧。He's going to Xinjiang too, so you may as well travel together.

【搭乘】 dāchéng travel by (plane, car, ship, etc.)

【搭档】 dādàng ① cooperate; work together: 咱俩～吧。Let us two team up. ② partner: 老～ old partner; old workmate

【搭伙】 dāhuǒ ① join as partner: 他们明天去参观故宫，我也想～去。They're going to visit the Palace Museum tomorrow and I'd like to join them. ② eat regularly in (a mess, etc.): 我们都在厂里食堂～。We all eat in the factory canteen.

【搭架子】 dā jiàzi build a framework; get (an undertaking, etc.) roughly into shape: 先搭好架子，再充实内容。First make an outline, then fill in the content.

【搭救】 dājiù rescue; go to the rescue of

【搭客】 dākè 〈方〉 take on passengers

【搭配】 dāpèi ① arrange in pairs or groups: 这几种肥料要～着用。These fertilizers should be used in proper proportions./ 她和小王～参加混合双打。She paired up with Xiao Wang in the mixed doubles. ② 〈语〉 collocation: 这两个词～不当。These two words don't go together.

【搭腔】 dāqiāng ① answer; respond: 我问了两遍，没人～。I repeated my question, but nobody answered. ② talk to each other: 以前他俩合不来，彼此不～。In the past the two of them did not get on at all well; they weren't even on speaking terms.

【搭讪】 dāshàn strike up a conversation with sb.; say something to smooth over an embarrassing situation: 他很尴尬，～着走开了。Feeling embarrassed, he muttered a few words and walked off.

**嗒** dā 〈象〉: ～～的马蹄声 clatter of horses' hoofs/ 机枪～～地响着。The machine guns rattled away.
另见 tà

**答** dā
另见 dá

【答碴儿】 dāchár 〈方〉 pick up the thread of a conversation and take part in it: 这问题我还没有仔细考虑，没法～。I haven't thought over the matter, so I can't say anything.

【答理】 dāli 〔多用于否定句〕 acknowledge (sb.'s greeting, etc.); respond; answer: 我跟他打招呼，他没～我。I greeted him but he didn't respond.

【答应】 dāying ① answer; reply; respond: 敲了半天门没人～。I knocked again and again but there was no answer. ② agree; promise; comply with: 我们请他来参加座谈会，他已经～了。We asked him to attend our discussion, and he agreed to come./ 他～八点半到。He promised to be here at 8:30./ 生产队长一口～了我们的要求。The production team leader readily complied with our request.

**褡** dā

【褡包】 dābao a long, broad girdle

【褡裢】 dālian ① a long, rectangular bag sewn up at both ends with an opening in the middle (usu. worn round the waist or across the shoulder) ② a jacket, made of several layers of cloth, worn by wrestlers

## dá

**打** dá 〈量〉 dozen: 一～铅笔 a dozen pencils/ 论～出售 sell by the dozen
另见 dǎ

**达** dá ① extend: 这里铁路四通八～。Here you find railways extending in all directions./ 这是开往昆明的直～火车。This is a through train to Kunming. ② reach; attain; amount to: 全县粮食平均亩产～千斤。The per *mu* grain yield for the whole county has reached 1,000 *jin*./ 我们不～目的决不罢休。We will never cease our efforts until we achieve our aim./ 听众鼓掌～两分钟之久。The audience applauded for two whole minutes./ 灌溉面积共～五十万亩。The irrigated area amounts to 500,000 *mu*. ③ understand thoroughly: 通情～理 be understanding and reasonable; be sensible ④ express; communicate: 上级的重要指示要立即下～。Important directives from the higher authorities should be handed down immediately. ⑤ eminent; distinguished: ～官 ranking official

【达卜】 dábǔ a small drum similar to the tambourine, used by the Uygur nationality

【达成】 dáchéng reach (agreement): 双方就会议议程～协议。The two parties reached agreement on the agenda of the meeting./ ～交易 strike a bargain

【达旦】 dádàn until dawn: 通宵～ all through the night

【达到】 dádào achieve; attain; reach: ～目的 achieve (或 attain) the goal/ ～高潮 reach a high tide; come to a climax/ ～世界先进水平 come up to advanced world standards/ 通过批评和自我批评在新的基础上～新的团结 arrive at a new unity on a new basis through criticism and self-criticism/ 货物运输量将～四千万吨。The volume of freight handled will amount to 40 million tons./ 天下大乱，～天下大治。Great disorder across the land leads to great order.

【达尔文主义】Dá'ěrwénzhǔyì Darwinism

【达观】dáguān take things philosophically

【达官贵人】dáguān-guìrén high officials and noble lords; VIPs

【达姆弹】dámǔdàn 〈军〉 dumdum (bullet)

【达斡尔族】Dáwò'ěrzú the Daur (Tahur) nationality, distributed over Heilongjiang Province and the Xinjiang Uygur Autonomous Region

【达意】dáyì express (或 convey) one's ideas: 词不～。The words fail to convey the idea./ 抒情～ express one's thoughts and feelings

【达因】dáyīn 〈物〉 dyne

**沓** dá 〈量〉 pile (of paper, etc.); pad: 一～报纸 a pile of newspapers/ 一～信纸 a pad of letter paper/ 一～钞票 a wad of bank notes

另见 tà

**答** dá ① answer; reply; respond: ～非所问 an irrelevant answer ② return (a visit, etc.); reciprocate: ～礼 return a salute

另见 dā

【答案】dá'àn answer; solution; key: 找不到问题的～ find no solution to the problem/ 练习的～ key to an exercise

【答辩】dábiàn reply (to a charge, query or an argument): 保留公开～的权利 reserve the right of public reply

【答词】dácí thank-you speech; answering speech; reply

【答对】dáduì 〔多用于否定句〕answer sb.'s question; reply: 被问得没法～ be baffled by the question

【答复】dáfù answer; reply: ～他的询问 reply to his inquiry

【答话】dáhuà 〔多用于否定句〕answer; reply: 你怎么不～？ Why don't you answer?

【答谢】dáxiè express appreciation (for sb.'s kindness or hospitality); acknowledge ◇ ～宴会 a return banquet

**瘩** dá

另见 da

【瘩背】dábèi 〈中医〉 carbuncle on the back

**靼** dá 见"鞑靼" Dádá

**鞑** dá

【鞑靼】Dádá Tartar

## dǎ

**打** dǎ ① strike; hit; knock: ～门 knock at the door/ 敲锣～鼓 beat gongs and drums/ ～稻子 thresh rice ② break; smash: 窗玻璃～了。The windowpane is broken. ③ fight; attack: ～硬仗 fight a hard battle/ 你们～得好。You're putting up a good fight. ④ construct; build: ～坝 construct a dam/ ～田埂 build low ridges between paddy fields ⑤ make (in a smithy); forge: ～一把刀 forge a knife ⑥ mix; stir; beat: ～鸡蛋 beat eggs/ ～糨子 mix paste ⑦ tie up; pack: ～成一捆 tie (things) up in a bundle/ ～行李 pack one's luggage; pack up ⑧ knit; weave: ～草鞋 weave straw sandals/ ～毛衣 knit a sweater ⑨ draw; paint; make a mark on: ～方格儿 draw squares/ ～手印 put one's fingerprint on a document/ ～一个问号 put a question mark; put a query ⑩ spray; spread: ～农药 spray insecticide/ 在地板上～蜡 wax the floor ⑪ open; dig: ～井 dig (或 sink) a well/ ～炮眼 drill a blasting hole ⑫ raise; hoist: ～伞 hold up an umbrella/ ～着"缓和"的幌子 use *détente* as a camouflage/ ～起精神来 raise one's spirits; cheer up ⑬ send; dispatch; project: ～电报 send a telegram/ ～电话 make a phone call/ ～信号 signal; give a signal/ ～炮 fire a cannon/ ～手电 flash a torch ⑭ issue or receive (a certificate, etc.): ～介绍信 write a letter of introduction (for sb.); get a letter of introduction (from one's organization) ⑮ remove; get rid of: ～旁杈 prune the side branches/ ～蛔虫 take medicine to get rid of roundworms; take worm medicine ⑯ ladle; draw: ～粥 ladle gruel/ ～一盆水 fetch a basin of water/ 从井里～水 draw water from a well ⑰ gather in; collect; reap: ～柴 gather firewood/ ～了八百斤麦子 get in 800 *jin* of wheat ⑱ buy: ～酱油 buy soy sauce/ ～票 buy a (train, bus, etc.) ticket ⑲ catch; hunt: ～鱼 catch fish/ ～野鸭 go duck-hunting ⑳ estimate; calculate; reckon: 成本～二百块钱 estimate (或 reckon) the cost at 200 *yuan* ㉑ work out: ～草稿 work out a draft ㉒ do; engage in: ～短工 work as a day or seasonal labourer; be a temporary worker/ ～夜班 go on night shift ㉓ play: ～篮球 play basketball/ ～扑克 play cards/ ～秋千 have a swing ㉔〔表示身体上的某些动作〕: ～个跟斗 turn (或 do) a somersault/ ～手势 make a gesture; gesticulate/ ～喷嚏 sneeze ㉕ adopt; use: ～个比方 draw an analogy ㉖ from; since: 你～那儿来？ Where did you come from?/ ～那以后 since then/ ～心眼里热爱社会主义制度 love the socialist system from the bottom of one's heart

另见 dá

【打靶】dǎbǎ target (或 shooting) practice ◇ ～场 target range

【打摆子】dǎ bǎizi 〈方〉 suffer from malaria

【打败】dǎbài ① defeat; beat; worst ② suffer a defeat; be defeated

【打板子】dǎ bǎnzi flog; cane

【打扮】dǎban dress up; make up; deck out: 节日的天坛～得格外壮丽。The Temple of Heaven was magnificently decked out for the festive occasion./ 孩子们～得象春天的花朵一样。The gaily-dressed children looked like spring flowers./ 她虽然在城里工作多年，还是那副农村妇女的朴素～。Although she has worked in the city a long time, she still dresses in the simple style of a countrywoman./ 把自己～成英雄 pose as a hero

【打包】dǎbāo ① bale; pack ② unpack ◇ ～机 baling press/ ～费 packing charges

【打包票】dǎ bāopiào vouch for; guarantee: 我敢～，机器一定准时送到。I guarantee that the machines will be delivered on time.

【打苞】dǎbāo (of wheat, sorghum, etc.) form ears; ear up

【打抱不平】dǎ bàobùpíng take up the cudgels for the injured party; defend sb. against an injustice

【打草惊蛇】dǎ cǎo jīng shé beat the grass and frighten away the snake — act rashly and alert the enemy

【打喳喳】dǎchācha 〈方〉 whisper

【打杈】dǎchà pruning: 给棉花～ prune cotton plants

【打岔】dǎchà interrupt; cut in: 他们在谈正经事儿，别～。Don't interrupt them; they're talking business.

【打场】dǎcháng thresh grain (on the threshing ground)

【打成一片】dǎchéng yīpiàn become one with; identify oneself with; merge with: 和群众～ be (或 become) one with the masses/ 知识分子应同工人农民～。Intellectuals should identify themselves with the workers and peasants.

【打倒】dǎdǎo overthrow: ～帝国主义！ Down with imperialism!

【打得火热】dǎde huǒrè be on terms of intimacy; be as

thick as thieves
【打底】 dǎdǐ 〈纺〉 bottoming ◇ ～机 padding machine
【打底子】 dǎ dǐzi ① sketch (a plan, picture, etc.) ② lay a foundation
【打点】 dǎdian get (luggage, etc.) ready
【打掉】 dǎdiào destroy; knock out; wipe out: 把敌人的探照灯～ knock out the enemy's searchlight/ ～敌人一个师 wipe out an enemy division
【打动】 dǎdòng move; touch: 这番话～了他的心。He was moved (或 touched) by these words.
【打赌】 dǎdǔ bet; wager: 我敢～他明天准来。I bet he'll come tomorrow.
【打短儿】 dǎduǎnr 〈口〉 work as a casual labourer
【打断】 dǎduàn ① break: 我爸爸的腿是被地主～的。It was the landlord who broke my father's leg. ② interrupt; cut short: ～思路 interrupt sb.'s train of thought/ 别～他,让他说完。Don't cut him short; let him finish./ 他的讲话不时被热烈的掌声～。His speech was punctuated with warm applause.
【打盹儿】 dǎdǔnr doze off; take a nap
【打耳光】 dǎ ěrguāng box sb.'s ears; slap sb. in the face
【打发】 dǎfa ① send; dispatch: 赶快～人去请大夫。Send for a doctor at once. ② dismiss; send away: 他把孩子们～走了,坐下来工作。He sent the children away and sat down to work. ③ while away (one's time)
【打翻】 dǎfān overturn; strike down: 一个大浪把小船～了。A huge wave overturned the boat./ 将恶霸地主～在地 strike despotic landlords down to the dust
【打榧子】 dǎ fěizi 〈方〉 snap the fingers
【打更】 dǎgēng sound the night watches
【打埂】 dǎgěng 〈农〉 ridging
【打嗝儿】 dǎgér 〈口〉 ① hiccup ② belch; burp
【打躬作揖】 dǎgōng-zuōyī fold the hands and make deep bows; do obeisance; beg humbly
【打谷场】 dǎgǔcháng threshing ground (或 floor)
【打鼓】 dǎgǔ ① beat a drum ② feel uncertain (或 nervous): 心里直～ feel extremely diffident
【打官腔】 dǎ guānqiāng talk like a bureaucrat; stall with official jargon
【打官司】 dǎ guānsi ① go to court (或 law); engage in a lawsuit ② 〈口〉 squabble: 打不完的官司 endless squabbles
【打滚】 dǎgǔn roll about: 小驴子在地上～。The little donkey rolled on the ground./ 疼得直～ writhe with pain
【打棍子】 dǎgùnzi come down with the big stick (upon sb.); bludgeon
【打哈哈】 dǎ hāha make fun; crack a joke: 别拿我～。Don't make fun of me./ 这是正经事,可别～。This is a serious matter; let's not joke about it.
【打哈欠】 dǎ hāqian yawn
【打鼾】 dǎhān snore
【打夯】 dǎhāng ramming; tamping ◇ ～机 ramming machine; rammer; tamper
【打火】 dǎhuǒ strike sparks from a flint; strike a light ◇ ～机 lighter
【打击】 dǎjī hit; strike; attack: ～投机倒把活动 crack down on speculation and profiteering/ ～歪风 take strong measures against unhealthy tendencies/ ～反动派的气焰 puncture the arrogance of the reactionaries/ ～报复 retaliate/ 狠狠～敌人 strike relentless blows at the enemy
【打击乐器】 dǎjī yuèqì percussion instrument
【打家劫舍】 dǎjiā-jiéshè loot; plunder
【打架】 dǎjià come to blows; fight; scuffle
【打尖】 dǎjiān ① stop for refreshment when travelling; have a snack (at a rest stop) ② 〈农〉 topping; pinching
【打浆】 dǎjiāng 〈纸〉 beating ◇ ～机 beating engine; beater
【打交道】 dǎ jiāodao come into (或 make) contact with; have dealings with: 两个厂经常～。The two factories maintain frequent contacts./ 我没跟他打过交道。I've never had any dealings with him.
【打搅】 dǎjiǎo disturb; trouble: 人家正在工作,别去～他了。He's working. Don't disturb him./ 对不起,～您了! Sorry to have bothered you./ ～您一下。May I trouble you a minute?
【打劫】 dǎjié rob; plunder; loot: 趁火～ loot a burning house
【打结】 dǎjié tie a knot ◇ ～器 〈化纤〉 knotter
【打开】 dǎkāi ① open; unfold: 把门～ open the door/ ～盖子 take off the lid/ ～包袱 untie a bundle/ ～缺口 make a breach/ ～眼界 widen one's horizon ② turn on; switch on: ～收音机(电灯) turn on the radio (light)
【打开天窗说亮话】 dǎkāi tiānchuāng shuō liànghuà frankly speaking; let's not mince matters
【打瞌睡】 dǎ kēshuì doze off; nod
【打捞】 dǎlāo ① get out of the water; salvage: ～沉船 salvage a sunken ship/ ～尸体 retrieve a corpse from the water ② 〈石油〉 fishing: ～工具 fishing tool
【打量】 dǎliang ① measure with the eye; look sb. up and down; size up: 门卫上下～着那个陌生人。The sentry looked the stranger up and down. ② think; suppose; reckon: 你～她这点事都干不了? Do you think she can't do a little job like that?
【打猎】 dǎliè go hunting
【打乱】 dǎluàn throw into confusion; upset: ～敌人的阵脚 throw the enemy into confusion/ ～计划 disrupt a plan; upset a scheme
【打落水狗】 dǎ luòshuǐgǒu beat a drowning dog — completely crush a defeated enemy
【打马虎眼】 dǎ mǎhuyǎn 〈方〉 pretend to be ignorant of sth. in order to gloss it over; act dumb
【打埋伏】 dǎ máifu ① lie in ambush; set an ambush; ambush ② hold sth. back for one's own use
【打磨】 dǎmo polish; burnish; shine
【打屁股】 dǎ pìgu ① beat on the buttocks; spank ② 〈口〉 take sb. to task
【打破】 dǎpò break; smash: ～僵局 break a deadlock; find a way out of a stalemate/ ～记录 break a record/ ～界线 break down barriers/ ～平衡 upset a balance/ ～超级大国的核垄断 break the nuclear monopoly of the superpowers/ ～洋框框 break with foreign conventions/ ～常规,尽量采用先进技术。Break free from conventions and use advanced techniques as much as possible.
【打破沙锅问到底】 dǎpò shāguō wèn dàodǐ insist on getting to the bottom of the matter
【打破碗花花】 dǎpòwǎnhuāhuā 〈植〉 Hubei anemone (*Anemone hupehensis*)
【打气】 dǎqì ① inflate; pump up: 给车胎～ inflate (或pump up) a tyre ② bolster up (或 boost) the morale; encourage; cheer up ◇ ～筒 inflater; tyre pump
【打钎】 dǎqiān drill a blasting hole in rock with a hammer and a drill rod
【打前站】 dǎ qiánzhàn act as an advance party; set out in advance to make arrangements
【打趣】 dǎqù banter; tease; make fun of
【打圈子】 dǎ quānzi circle: 飞机在机场上空～。The plane circled over the airfield./ 不要在枝节问题上～。Don't get bogged down in minor issues.
【打拳】 dǎquán shadowboxing
【打群架】 dǎ qúnjià engage in a gang fight
【打扰】 dǎrǎo 见"打搅"

【打入】 dǎrù ① throw into; banish to: 被～地下 be driven underground/ ～十八层地狱 banish sb. to the lowest depths of hell ② infiltrate: ～匪巢 infiltrate the bandits' den

【打散】 dǎsǎn break up; scatter: 把原来的组～重编 break up the existing groups to form new ones

【打扫】 dǎsǎo sweep; clean: ～房间 clean a room/ ～垃圾 sweep away rubbish/ ～战场 clean up the battlefield/ 把院子～干净 sweep the courtyard clean

【打手】 dǎshou hired roughneck (或 thug); hatchet man: 充当反动派的～ serve as a hatchet man for the reactionaries

【打算】 dǎsuàn plan; intend: 代表团～去延安访问。The delegation plans to visit Yan'an./ 他～当教师。He intends to become a teacher./ 作最坏的～ be prepared for the worst/ 各有各的～。Each has a plan of his own. 或 Each has his own calculations.

【打算盘】 dǎ suànpan calculate on an abacus; calculate: 打小算盘 be calculating; be petty and scheming/ 打错算盘 miscalculate

【打碎】 dǎsuì break into pieces; smash; destroy: 玻璃杯～了。The glass is smashed to pieces./ ～旧的国家机器 smash (或 destroy) the old state machinery

【打胎】 dǎtāi have an (induced) abortion

【打铁】 dǎtiě forge iron; work as a blacksmith: ～先得本身硬。〈谚〉 If you want to work with iron, you must be tough yourself — one must be ideologically sound and professionally competent to do arduous work.

【打听】 dǎting ask about; inquire about: 跟您～一件事。I'd like to ask you about something./ ～战友的消息 inquire about one's comrades-in-arms

【打通】 dǎtōng get through; open up: 电话打不通 be unable to get through (on the telephone)/ 两家的院墙～了。An opening has been made in the wall between the two courtyards./ ～思想 straighten out sb.'s thinking; talk sb. round

【打头】 dǎtóu ① take the lead: 老师傅～,青年人跟着上。The old worker took the lead and the youngsters followed suit. ② 〈方〉 from the beginning: 咱们再～儿来。Let's do the job all over again.

【打头炮】 dǎ tóupào fire the first shot; be the first to speak or act

【打头阵】 dǎ tóuzhèn fight in the van; spearhead the attack; take the lead

【打退】 dǎtuì beat back (或 off); repulse: ～敌人的进攻 repulse an enemy attack

【打退堂鼓】 dǎ tuìtánggǔ beat a retreat; back out: 不能遇到点困难就～呀。You can't back out the moment you run up against a little difficulty.

【打碗花】 dǎwǎnhuā 〈中药〉 ivy glorybind (*Calystegia hederacea*)

【打围】 dǎwéi encircle and hunt down (animals)

【打先锋】 dǎ xiānfēng fight in the van; be a pioneer

【打响】 dǎxiǎng ① start shooting; begin to exchange fire: 先头部队～了。The advance detachment has engaged the enemy./ 南昌起义～了反对国民党反动派的第一枪。The Nanchang Uprising fired the first shot against the Kuomintang reactionaries. ② win initial success: 这一炮～了,下一步就好办了。Success at this stage will make the next step easier./ ～了春耕第一炮。The spring ploughing got off to a good start.

【打消】 dǎxiāo give up (an idea, etc.); dispel (a doubt, etc.): 她～了春节回家的念头。She gave up the idea of going home for the Spring Festival./ ～顾虑 dispel misgivings

【打雪仗】 dǎ xuězhàng have a snowball fight; throw snowballs

【打鸭子上架】 dǎ yāzi shàng jià drive a duck onto a perch — make sb. do sth. entirely beyond him

【打牙祭】 dǎ yájì 〈方〉 have sth. special to eat

【打眼】 dǎyǎn ① punch (或 bore) a hole; drill ② 〈方〉 catch the eye; attract attention

【打掩护】 dǎ yǎnhù provide cover for; shield: 为主力部队～ provide cover for the main force/ 你这样做,实际上是给敌人打了掩护。By doing that, you were actually shielding the enemy.

【打样】 dǎyàng ① draw a design ② 〈印〉 make a proof ◇ ～机 proof press

【打印】 dǎyìn ① put a seal on; stamp ② cut a stencil and mimeograph; mimeograph

【打油诗】 dǎyóushī doggerel; ragged verse

【打游击】 dǎ yóujī ① fight as a guerrilla: 上山～ join the guerrillas in the mountains; wage guerrilla warfare in the mountains ② 〈口〉 work (eat, sleep, etc.) at no fixed place

【打圆场】 dǎ yuánchǎng mediate a dispute; smooth things over

【打援】 dǎyuán attack (或 ambush) enemy reinforcements: 围点～ besiege an enemy stronghold in order to strike at the reinforcements

【打砸抢】 dǎ-zá-qiǎng beating, smashing and looting: 严禁～。Acts of smashing and grabbing are strictly forbidden. ◇ ～者 smash-and-grabber

【打杂儿】 dǎzár do odds and ends

【打战】 dǎzhàn shiver; tremble; shudder: 浑身～ shiver all over

【打仗】 dǎzhàng fight; go to war; make war: 要准备～。Be ready to fight in a war./ 大打矿山之仗。Go all out to develop mining.

【打招呼】 dǎ zhāohu ① greet sb.; say hello ② notify; let sb. know: 你什么时候去开封,给我打个招呼。When you go to Kaifeng, please let me know. ③ warn; remind: 事先已跟他们打过招呼了。I've already warned them.

【打折扣】 dǎ zhékòu ① sell at a discount; give a discount ② fall short of a requirement or promise: 说到做到,不～ carry out one's pledge to the letter

【打针】 dǎzhēn give or have an injection

【打制石器】 dǎzhì shíqì 〈考古〉 chipped stone implement

【打肿脸充胖子】 dǎzhǒng liǎn chōng pàngzi slap one's face until it's swollen in an effort to look imposing — puff oneself up to one's own cost

【打中】 dǎzhòng hit the mark (或 target); hit: ～一艘敌舰 hit an enemy vessel/ ～要害 hit on the vital spot; hit where it really hurts

【打主意】 dǎ zhǔyi ① think of a plan; evolve an idea: 打定主意 make up one's mind/ 打错主意 miscalculate; make a wrong decision ② try to obtain; seek: 他们正在打你的主意,要你帮忙呢。They are thinking of asking you to help.

【打住】 dǎzhù come to a halt; (in speech or writing) stop

【打转】 dǎzhuàn spin; rotate; revolve: 卡车轮子在烂泥里直～。The truck's wheels kept spinning in the mud./ 不要老在个人利益的小圈子里～。Don't keep going round and round pursuing your own selfish interests.

【打桩】 dǎzhuāng pile driving; piling ◇ ～机 pile driver

【打字】 dǎzì typewrite; type
◇ ～带 typewriter ribbon/ ～稿 typescript/ ～机 typewriter/ ～员 typist/ ～纸 typing-paper

【打坐】 dǎzuò (of a Buddhist or Taoist monk) sit in meditation

## dà

**大** dà ①big; large; great: ～城市 a big city/ ～救星 the great liberator/ 这张照片不够～。The picture isn't large enough. ②heavy (rain, etc.); strong (wind, etc.) ③loud: 声音太～ too loud/ 收音机开～点。Turn the radio up a bit louder. ④general; main; major: ～路 main road; highway/ ～问题 major issue; big problem/ ～手术 major operation/ ～反攻 general counteroffensive ⑤size: 那间屋子有这间两个～。That room is twice the size of this one./ 你穿多～的鞋？What size shoes do you wear? ⑥age: 你的孩子多～了？How old is your child? ⑦greatly; fully: ～吃一惊 be greatly surprised; be quite taken aback/ ～长革命人民的志气 greatly heighten the morale of the revolutionary people ⑧in a big way; on a big (或 large) scale; with all-out efforts; vigorously: ～学解放军 go all out to learn from the PLA/ ～搞农田水利 go all out with irrigation and water conservancy/ ～揭～批 do a thorough job in exposing and criticizing sb. or sth. ⑨eldest: ～哥 eldest brother/ ～房 senior branch of a family ⑩〈敬〉 your: ～札 your letter/ ～作 your writing ⑪〔用在时间或节日前表示强调〕: ～白天 in broad daylight/ ～清早 early in the morning
另见 dài

【大白】 dàbái ①come out; become known: 真相已～于天下。The truth has become known to all. ②〈方〉 whiting ◇ ～浆〈建〉 whitewash
【大白菜】 dàbáicài Chinese cabbage
【大伯子】 dàbǎizi husband's elder brother; brother-in-law
【大败】 dàbài ①defeat utterly; put to rout: ～敌军 inflict a crushing defeat on the enemy ②suffer a crushing defeat
【大班】 dàbān the top class in a kindergarten
【大阪】 Dàbǎn Osaka
【大板车】 dàbǎnchē large handcart
【大办】 dàbàn go in for sth. in a big way: ～农业 go in for agriculture in a big way; make great efforts to develop agriculture/ ～民兵师 organize contingents of the people's militia on a big scale
【大半】 dàbàn ①more than half; greater part; most: ～天 the greater part of a day; most of the day/ 这个突击队的队员～是青年人。Most of the members of this shock team are young. ②very likely; most probably: 他～不来了。Most probably he isn't coming.
【大棒】 dàbàng big stick — means of intimidation: 帝国主义的"～加胡萝卜"政策 the imperialists' stick-and-carrot policy; the imperialists' policy of the stick and the carrot
【大本营】 dàběnyíng ①supreme headquarters ②base camp: 登山队～ the base camp of a mountaineering expedition
【大笔】 dàbǐ ①pen: ～一挥 with one stroke of the pen ②〈敬〉 your writing; your handwriting: 这是您的～吧？Isn't this your handwriting?
【大便】 dàbiàn ①defecate; have a bowel movement; shit: ～不通 (suffer from) constipation ②stool; human excrement; shit; faeces: 去化验～ have one's stool examined
【大辩论】 dàbiànlùn great (或 mass) debate 参见"四大"sìdà
【大兵】 dàbīng 〈旧〉 common soldier
【大兵团】 dàbīngtuán large troop formation ◇ ～作战 large formation warfare; grand (或 major) tactics
【大饼】 dàbǐng a kind of large flatbread
【大伯】 dàbó ①father's elder brother; uncle ②uncle (a polite form of address for an elderly man)
【大不列颠】 Dàbùlièdiān Great Britain
【大不了】 dàbuliǎo ①at the worst; if the worst comes to the worst: ～我们走着回去。If the worst comes to the worst, we'll walk back. ②〔多用于否定式〕 alarming; serious: 划破点皮，没有什么～的。It's nothing serious, just a scratch.
【大步流星】 dàbù liúxīng with vigorous strides; at a stride
【大部】 dàbù greater part: 歼敌～ annihilate the greater part of the enemy
【大材小用】 dàcái xiǎo yòng put fine timber to petty use; use talented people for trivial tasks; waste one's talent on a petty job
【大肠】 dàcháng 〈生理〉 large intestine ◇ ～杆菌 colon bacillus
【大氅】 dàchǎng overcoat; cloak; cape
【大潮】 dàcháo spring tide
【大车】 dàchē ①cart ②chief engineer (of a ship) ③engine driver ◇ ～店 an inn for carters
【大臣】 dàchén minister (of a monarchy)
【大冲】 dàchōng 〈天〉 favourable opposition
【大虫】 dàchóng 〈方〉 tiger
【大出血】 dàchūxuè 〈医〉 massive haemorrhage
【大处落墨】 dàchù luò mò concentrate on the key points
【大处着眼，小处着手】 dàchù zhuó yǎn, xiǎochù zhuó shǒu keep the general goal in sight and take the daily tasks in hand
【大吹大擂】 dàchuī-dàlèi make a great fanfare; make a big noise
【大锤】 dàchuí sledgehammer
【大醇小疵】 dàchún-xiǎocī sound on the whole though defective in details
【大词】 dàcí 〈逻〉 major term
【大慈大悲】 dàcí-dàbēi 〔佛教用语，现多用于讽刺〕 infinitely merciful
【大葱】 dàcōng green Chinese onion
【大打出手】 dà dǎ chūshǒu strike violently; attack brutally
【大大】 dàdà greatly; enormously: 生产效率～提高。Productivity has risen greatly./ 革命～推动了社会生产力的发展。The revolution has given an enormous impetus to the social productive forces./ 今年的棉花产量～超过了去年。This year's cotton production exceeded last year's by a big margin.
【大…大…】 dà...dà... 〔分别用在名词、动词或形容词的前面，表示规模大、程度深〕: 大鱼大肉 plenty of meat and fish; rich food/ 大红大绿 loud colours/ 大吵大闹 kick up a row; make a scene/ 大吃大喝 eat and drink extravagantly
【大大咧咧】 dàdaliēliē 〈方〉 (of a person) careless; casual
【大袋鼠】 dàdàishǔ kangaroo
【大胆】 dàdǎn bold; daring; audacious: ～的革新 a bold innovation
【大刀】 dàdāo broadsword
【大刀阔斧】 dàdāo-kuòfǔ bold and resolute; drastic
【大道理】 dàdàolǐ major principle; general principle; great truth: 这些～人人都懂，真正做到可不容易啊！These general principles are widely known, but it isn't easy to live up to them./ 小道理要服从～。Minor principles should be subordinated to major ones.
【大灯】 dàdēng 〈汽车〉 headlight
【大敌】 dàdí formidable enemy; archenemy: ～当前 faced with a formidable foe
【大抵】 dàdǐ generally speaking; in the main; on the whole
【大地】 dàdì earth; mother earth: 共产主义的光芒必将普照～。The radiance of communism will illuminate every corner of the earth./ ～回春。Spring returns to the earth. 或 Spring is here again./ 走遍祖国～ travel all over the land
◇ ～测量学 geodesy/ ～构造学 geotectology; tectonics/

～水准面 geoid
【大典】 dàdiǎn ① grand ceremony: 开国～ the ceremony to proclaim the founding of a state ② a body of classical writings; canon: 《永乐～》 *Yongle Canon*
【大殿】 dàdiàn ① audience hall ② main hall of a Buddhist temple
【大调】 dàdiào 〈乐〉 major: C～奏鸣曲 sonata in C major
【大动脉】 dàdòngmài 〈生理〉 main artery; aorta: 南北交通的～ the main artery of communications between north and south
【大豆】 dàdòu soybean; soya bean
【大都】 dàdū for the most part; mostly: 这些诗歌～是工农兵写的。Most of these poems were written by workers, peasants and soldiers.
【大肚子】 dàdùzi 〈口〉 ① pregnant ② big eater ③ potbelly
【大度】 dàdù 〈书〉 magnanimous: ～包容 magnanimous and tolerant
【大端】 dàduān 〈书〉 main aspects (或 features); salient points: 仅举其～ merely point out the main features
【大队】 dàduì ① a military unit corresponding to the battalion or regiment; group ② production brigade (of a rural people's commune); brigade ③ a large body of: ～人马 a large contingent of troops; a large body of marchers, paraders, etc.
【大多】 dàduō for the most part; mostly: 出席大会的代表～是先进工作者。The representatives present at the meeting are mostly advanced workers.
【大多数】 dàduōshù great majority; vast majority; the bulk: 团结～ unite with the great majority/ 人口的～ the bulk of the population/ 为中国和世界的～人谋利益 work for the interests of the vast majority of the people of China and of the whole world
【大而无当】 dà ér wú dàng large but impractical; unwieldy: ～的计划 a grandiose but impractical plan
【大发雷霆】 dà fā léitíng be furious; fly into a rage; bawl at sb. angrily
【大凡】 dàfán generally; in most cases: ～坚持锻炼的,身体抵抗力都比较强。Generally those who exercise regularly have high resistance to disease.
【大方】 dàfāng 〈书〉 expert; scholar: 贻笑～ incur the ridicule of experts
【大方】 dàfang ① generous; liberal ② natural and poised; easy; unaffected: 举止～ have an easy manner; have poise; carry oneself with ease and confidence ③ in good taste; tasteful: 这种料子的颜色和花样很～。The pattern and colour of this fabric are in good taste.
【大方向】 dàfāngxiàng general orientation: 牢牢掌握斗争的～ keep firmly to the general orientation of the struggle
【大放厥词】 dà fàng jué cí talk a lot of nonsense; spout a stream of empty rhetoric
【大分子】 dàfēnzǐ 〈化〉 macromolecule
【大粪】 dàfèn human excrement; night soil
【大风】 dàfēng ① 〈气〉 fresh gale ② gale; strong wind: 外面刮着～。There's a gale blowing. 或 It's blowing hard.
【大风大浪】 dàfēng-dàlàng wind and waves; great storms: ～也不可怕。人类社会就是从～中发展起来的。 Even great storms are not to be feared. It is amid great storms that human society progresses.
【大风子】 dàfēngzǐ 〈植〉 chaulmoogra (*Hydnocarpus anthelmintica*) ◇ ～油 chaulmoogra oil
【大夫】 dàfū a senior official in feudal China
另见 dàifu
【大副】 dàfù first (或 chief) mate; mate; chief officer
【大腹贾】 dàfùgǔ potbellied merchant; rich merchant
【大腹皮】 dàfùpí 〈中药〉 the shell of areca nut
【大腹便便】 dàfù piánpián potbellied; big-bellied
【大概】 dàgài ① general idea; broad outline: 我只知道个～。I have only a general idea. ② general; rough; approximate: 作一个～的分析 make a general analysis/ ～的数字 an approximate figure/ ～的估计 a rough estimate ③ probably; most likely; presumably: 会议～要延期。The meeting will probably be postponed.
【大干】 dàgàn work energetically; go all out; make an all-out effort: ～社会主义 work energetically for socialism/ ～快上 get going and go all out/ 天大旱,人～。Let the heavens bring drought. We'll go all out.
【大纲】 dàgāng outline: 世界史～ an outline history of the world/ 《土地法～》 *Outline Land Law*
【大哥】 dàgē ① eldest brother ② elder brother (a polite form of address for a man about one's own age)
【大革命】 dàgémìng ① great revolution: 无产阶级文化～ the Great Proletarian Cultural Revolution/ 法国～ the French Revolution ② the Great Revolution in China (1924-1927)
【大公】 dàgōng grand duke ◇ ～国 grand duchy
【大公无私】 dàgōng-wúsī ① selfless; unselfish: 工人阶级最～。It is the working class that is most selfless. ② perfectly impartial
【大功】 dàgōng great merit; extraordinary service: 立了～ have performed exceptionally meritorious services
【大功告成】 dàgōng gàochéng (of a project, work, etc.) be accomplished; be crowned with success
【大功率】 dàgōnglǜ 〈电〉 high-power: ～可控硅 high-power silicon controlled rectifier
【大姑子】 dàgūzi husband's elder sister; sister-in-law
【大骨节病】 dàgǔjiébìng Kaschin-Beck disease
【大鼓】 dàgǔ ①〈乐〉 bass drum ②〈曲艺〉 *dagu*, versified story sung to the accompaniment of a small drum and other instruments
【大褂】 dàguà unlined long gown
【大观】 dàguān grand sight; magnificent spectacle: 蔚为～ present a magnificent spectacle
【大管】 dàguǎn 〈乐〉 bassoon
【大规模】 dàguīmó large-scale; extensive; massive; mass: ～生产 large-scale production/ ～兴修水利 launch a large-scale (或 extensive) water conservancy project/ ～进攻 launch a massive attack/ 举行～罢工 stage a massive strike/ ～毁灭性武器 weapon of mass destruction
【大锅饭】 dàguōfàn food prepared in a large canteen cauldron; mess: 吃～ eat in the canteen the same as everyone else; mess together
【大国沙文主义】 dàguó shāwénzhǔyì great-nation chauvinism 又作"大国主义"
【大过】 dàguò serious offence: 记～一次 record a serious mistake
【大海捞针】 dàhǎi lāo zhēn fish for a needle in the ocean; look for a needle in a haystack
【大寒】 Dàhán Great Cold (24th solar term)
【大喊大叫】 dàhǎn-dàjiào ① shout at the top of one's voice ② conduct vigorous propaganda
【大汉】 dàhàn big (或 hefty, burly) fellow
【大汉族主义】 dà-Hànzúzhǔyì Han chauvinism
【大旱望云霓】 dàhàn wàng yúnní long for a rain cloud during a drought — look forward to relief from distress
【大好】 dàhǎo very good; excellent: 形势～。The situation is very good./ ～河山 beautiful rivers and mountains of a country; one's beloved motherland/ ～时机 opportune moment; golden opportunity; finest hour
【大号】 dàhào ① large size: ～的鞋 large-size shoes ②〈乐〉 tuba; bass horn ③ 〈敬〉 your (given) name
【大合唱】 dàhéchàng cantata; chorus: 《黄河～》 *The Yellow*

*River Cantata*

【大河】 dàhé ① great river: ～有水小河满，～无水小河干。The small streams rise when the main stream is high; when the main stream is low, the small streams run dry — individual well-being depends on collective prosperity. ② the Huanghe River (Yellow River)

【大亨】 dàhēng big shot; bigwig; magnate

【大轰大嗡】 dàhōng-dàwēng make a terrific din; raise a hue and cry

【大红】 dàhóng bright red; scarlet

【大后方】 dàhòufāng ① rear area ② the area under KMT rule during the War of Resistance Against Japan

【大后年】 dàhòunián three years from now

【大后天】 dàhòutiān three days from now

【大户】 dàhù ① rich and influential family ② large family

【大话】 dàhuà big (或 tall) talk; boast; bragging: 说～ talk big; brag

【大黄蜂】 dàhuángfēng hornet

【大黄鱼】 dàhuángyú large yellow croaker

【大茴香】 dàhuíxiāng 〈植〉 anise; star anise

【大会】 dàhuì ① plenary session; general membership meeting: 党支部～ a general membership meeting of a Party branch/ 社员～ a general meeting of (people's) commune members ② mass meeting; mass rally

【大伙儿】 dàhuǒr 〈口〉 we all; you all; everybody

【大惑不解】 dà huò bù jiě be extremely puzzled; be unable to make head or tail of sth.

【大戟】 dàjǐ 〈中药〉 the root of Beijing euphorbia (*Euphorbia pekinensis*)

【大计】 dàjì a major programme of lasting importance; a matter of fundamental importance: 百年～ a matter of fundamental importance for generations to come; a major project affecting future generations/ 共商～ discuss matters of vital importance

【大蓟】 dàjì 〈植〉 setose thistle (*Cephalanoplos setosum*)

【大家】 dàjiā ① great master; authority: 书法～ a great master of calligraphy; a noted calligrapher ② all; everybody: ～知道，中国是一个发展中国家。As everybody knows, China is a developing country./ ～的事～管。Everybody's business should be everybody's responsibility./ 我报告～一个好消息。I have some good news for you all.

【大家庭】 dàjiātíng big family; community: 革命～ the big revolutionary family

【大建】 dàjiàn a lunar month of 30 days

【大江】 dàjiāng ① great river ② the Changjiang River (Yangtze River)

【大将】 dàjiàng ① senior general ② high-ranking officer

【大教堂】 dàjiàotáng cathedral

【大街】 dàjiē main street; street: 逛～ go window-shopping; go for a walk in the street/ ～小巷红旗飘扬。The streets and lanes are decked with red flags.

【大节】 dàjié political integrity

【大捷】 dàjié great victory

【大姐】 dàjiě ① eldest sister ② elder sister (a polite form of address for a woman about one's own age)

【大解】 dàjiě have a bowel movement

【大襟】 dàjīn the front of a Chinese garment which buttons on the right

【大尽】 dàjìn 见"大建"

【大惊小怪】 dàjīng-xiǎoguài be surprised or alarmed at sth. perfectly normal; make a fuss: 有什么值得～的？What's there to be surprised at?

【大净】 dàjìng 〈伊斯兰教〉 Ghusl

【大静脉】 dàjìngmài 〈生理〉 vena cava

【大舅子】 dàjiùzi 〈口〉 wife's elder brother; brother-in-law

【大局】 dàjú overall (或 general, whole) situation: 顾全～ take the whole situation into account; take the interests of the whole into account/ 事关～。It's an issue that concerns the overall situation./ ～已定。The outcome is a foregone conclusion.

【大举】 dàjǔ carry out (a military operation) on a large scale: ～进攻 mount a large-scale offensive; attack in force

【大军】 dàjūn ① main forces; army: 我们是先头部队，～随后就到。We are the advance detachment. The main forces will be here soon./ ～过处，秋毫无犯。Wherever the troops went, they never infringed on the people's interests. ② large contingent: 筑路～ a large contingent of road builders/ 百万～ an army a million strong

【大卡】 dàkǎ 〈物〉 kilocalorie; large (或 great) calorie

【大楷】 dàkǎi ① regular script in big characters, as used in Chinese calligraphy exercises ② block letters; blockwriting

【大考】 dàkǎo end-of-term examination; final exam

【大课】 dàkè a lecture given to a large number of students; enlarged class

【大跨径桥】 dàkuàjìngqiáo long-span bridge

【大快人心】 dà kuài rénxīn (of the punishment of an evildoer) affording general satisfaction; most gratifying to the people; to the immense satisfaction of the people

【大牢】 dàláo 〈口〉 prison; jail

【大老粗】 dàlǎocū uncouth fellow; uneducated person; rough and ready fellow

【大礼拜】 dàlǐbài alternate Sunday on which one has a day off; fortnightly holiday: 休～ have every other Sunday off

【大理石】 dàlǐshí marble

【大力】 dàlì energetically; vigorously: ～支援农业 give energetic support to agriculture/ ～发展教育事业 devote major efforts to developing education

【大力士】 dàlìshì a man of unusual strength

【大丽花】 dàlìhuā 〈植〉 dahlia

【大殓】 dàliàn encoffining ceremony

【大量】 dàliàng ① a large number; a great quantity: 为国家积累～资金 accumulate large funds for the state/ ～生产拖拉机 mass-produce tractors/ ～杀伤敌人 inflict heavy casualties on the enemy/ 收集～科学资料 collect a vast amount of scientific data/ ～财富 enormous wealth; large fortune/ ～事实 a host of facts/ ～库存 huge stocks ② generous; magnanimous: 宽宏～ magnanimous; large-minded

【大料】 dàliào 〈方〉 aniseed

【大楼】 dàlóu multi-storied building: 居民～ apartment house; block of flats

【大陆】 dàlù continent; mainland
◇ ～隆〈地〉 continental rise/ ～架 continental shelf/ ～漂移说 the theory of continental drift/ ～坡 continental slope/ ～性气候 continental climate

【大路货】 dàlùhuò popular goods of dependable quality

【大略】 dàlüè ① general idea; broad outline: 我只知道个～。I have only a general idea. ② generally; roughly; approximately: ～相同 roughly the same/ 时间不多了，你～说说吧。There isn't much time left. Could you speak just briefly?

【大妈】 dàmā ① father's elder brother's wife; aunt ② aunt (an affectionate or respectful form of address for an elderly woman)

【大麻】 dàmá ① hemp ② marijuana

【大麻哈鱼】 dàmáhǎyú chum salmon; dog salmon 又作"大马哈鱼"

【大麦】 dàmài barley

【大忙】 dàmáng very busy: ～季节 rush (或 busy) season

【大猫熊】 dàmāoxióng giant panda
【大毛】 dàmáo long-haired pelt
【大帽子】 dàmàozi an exaggerated epithet used to categorize a person; unwarranted charge; political label: 别拿～压人。Don't you try to intimidate people by pinning political labels on them.
【大门】 dàmén entrance (或 front) door; gate
【大米】 dàmǐ (husked) rice
【大面儿】 dàmiànr 〈方〉 general appearance; surface: ～上还过得去。It's basically all right.
【大民主】 dàmínzhǔ great democracy: 实行无产阶级领导下的～ practise great democracy under the leadership of the proletariat
【大民族主义】 dàmínzúzhǔyì big-nationality chauvinism
【大名】 dàmíng ① one's formal personal name ②〈敬〉 your (given) name
【大名鼎鼎】 dàmíng dǐngdǐng famous; celebrated; well-known
【大鸣大放】 dàmíng-dàfàng free airing of views 参见"四大" sìdà
【大螟】 dàmíng pink rice borer (*Sesamia inferens*)
【大谬不然】 dà miù bùrán entirely wrong; grossly mistaken
【大模大样】 dàmú-dàyàng in an ostentatious manner; with a swagger
【大拇指】 dàmuzhǐ 〈口〉 thumb: 竖起～叫好 hold up one's thumb in approval
【大拿】 dàná 〈口〉 person with power; boss
【大难】 dànàn catastrophe; disaster: ～临头 be faced with imminent disaster
【大脑】 dànǎo 〈生理〉 cerebrum
◇ ～半球 cerebral hemisphere/ ～脚 cerebral peduncle/ ～皮层 cerebral cortex
【大鲵】 dàní 〈动〉 giant salamander
【大逆不道】 dà nì bù dào treason and heresy; worst offence; greatest outrage: 封建统治者常给那些反抗他们的人加上～的罪名。Feudal rulers often branded those who rebelled against them as traitors and heretics.
【大年】 dànián ① good year; bumper year; (of fruit trees) on-year ② a lunar year in which the last month has 30 days
【大年初一】 dàniánchūyī 〈口〉 first day of the lunar year; lunar New Year's Day
【大年夜】 dàniányè 〈方〉 lunar New Year's Eve
【大娘】 dàniáng 〈口〉 ① wife of father's elder brother; aunt ② aunt (a respectful form of address used for elderly women)
【大炮】 dàpào ① artillery; big gun; cannon ②〈口〉 one who speaks boastfully or forcefully; one who noisily overstates things
【大批】 dàpī ① large quantities (或 numbers, amounts) of: ～轻工业品运往农村。Large quantities of light industrial products are transported to the countryside./ ～干部深入基层。Large numbers of cadres go to the grass-roots level. ② mass criticism
【大批判】 dàpīpàn mass criticism; mass criticism and repudiation ◇ ～专栏 mass criticism column (in a publication); display of mass criticism posters/ ～组 mass criticism group
【大辟】 dàpì capital punishment (in feudal times); decapitation 参见"五刑" wǔxíng
【大薸】 dàpiāo 〈植〉 water lettuce; water cabbage
【大谱表】 dàpǔbiǎo 〈乐〉 great stave
【大谱儿】 dàpǔr general idea: 究竟怎么做，心里应该先有个～。Before you start anything, you ought to have a general idea of what you're going to do.
【大气】 dàqì ①〈气〉 atmosphere; air ② heavy breathing: 跑得直喘～ breathe heavily from running/ 吓得连～也不敢出 catch (或 hold) one's breath in fear
◇ ～层 atmospheric layer; atmosphere/ ～电 atmospheric electricity/ ～干扰 atmospheric interference/ ～环流 atmospheric circulation; general circulation of atmosphere/ ～科学 atmospheric sciences/ ～污染 air (或 atmospheric) pollution/ ～压 atmospheric pressure; atmosphere/ ～折射 atmospheric (或 astronomical) refraction
【大气候】 dàqìhòu 〈气〉 macroclimate
【大器晚成】 dàqì wǎn chéng great minds mature slowly
【大千世界】 dàqiān shìjiè 〈佛教〉 the boundless universe
【大前年】 dàqiánnián three years ago
【大前提】 dàqiántí 〈逻〉 major premise
【大前天】 dàqiántiān three days ago
【大钳】 dàqián tongs
【大庆】 dàqìng ① grand celebration of an important event; great occasion: 十年～ the festive occasion of the 10th anniversary ②〈敬〉〔用于老年人〕 birthday: 七十～ seventieth birthday ③ (Dàqìng) Daqing Oilfield, the pacesetter on China's industrial front: 工业学～。In industry, learn from Daqing.
◇ ～红旗 the red banner of Daqing/ ～精神 the Daqing spirit/ ～式企业 Daqing-type enterprise
【大秋】 dàqiū ① harvest season in autumn ② crops harvested in autumn; autumn harvest ◇ ～作物 crops sown in spring and reaped in autumn; autumn-harvested crops
【大曲】 dàqū ① yeast for making hard liquor ② a hard liquor made with such yeast
【大权】 dàquán power over major issues; authority: ～在握 hold power in one's hands/ ～独揽 centralize power in one man's hands to deal with major issues; arrogate all authority to oneself/ ～旁落。Power has fallen into the hands of others.
【大犬座】 dàquǎnzuò 〈天〉 Canis Major
【大人】 dàrén 〈敬〉〔旧时多用于书信〕: 父亲～ Dear Father
【大人】 dàren ① adult; grown-up ②〈旧〉(直接称呼) Your Excellency; (间接称呼) His Excellency
【大人物】 dàrénwù important person; great personage; big shot; VIP
【大扫除】 dàsǎochú general cleaning; thorough cleanup: 节日～ thorough cleanup before a holiday
【大嫂】 dàsǎo ① eldest brother's wife; sister-in-law ② elder sister (a polite form of address for a woman about one's own age)
【大厦】 dàshà large building; mansion
【大少爷】 dàshàoyé ① eldest son (of a rich family) ② a spoilt son of a rich family; spendthrift: ～作风 behaviour typical of the spoilt son of a rich family; extravagant ways
【大舌头】 dàshétou 〈口〉 a thick-tongued person; one who lisps; lisper
【大赦】 dàshè amnesty; general pardon
【大婶儿】 dàshěnr aunt (an affectionate or respectful form of address for a woman about one's mother's age)
【大声疾呼】 dàshēng jíhū raise a cry of warning; loudly appeal to the public
【大牲口】 dàshēngkou draught animal
【大乘】 dàshèng 〈佛教〉 Mahayana; Great Vehicle
【大失所望】 dà shī suǒ wàng greatly disappointed; to one's great disappointment
【大师】 dàshī ① great master; master: 国画～ a great master of traditional Chinese painting ②〈佛教〉 Great Master, a courtesy title used to address a Buddhist monk
【大师傅】 dàshīfu cook; *chef*
【大使】 dàshǐ ambassador: 特命全权～ ambassador extra-

ordinary and plenipotentiary
◇ ～馆 embassy/ ～级会谈 talks at ambassadorial level; ambassadorial talks/ ～衔 ambassadorial rank

【大事】 dàshì ① great (或 major) event; important matter; major issue: 头等～ a matter of prime (或 paramount) importance/ 关心国家～ concern oneself with affairs of state/ 当前国际政治中的一件～ a major event in current international politics/ 完成了一桩～ have accomplished an important task/ 党委要抓～。Party committees should grasp major issues. ② overall (或 general) situation: ～不好。A disaster is imminent. ③ in a big way: ～渲染 enormously exaggerate; play up ◇ ～记 chronicle of events

【大事化小，小事化了】 dàshì huà xiǎo, xiǎoshì huà liǎo turn big problems into small problems and small problems into no problem at all

【大势】 dàshì general trend of events: ～所趋，人心所向 the trend of the times and the desire of the people; the general trend and popular feeling/ ～已去。The game is as good as lost. 或 Not much can be done about it now.

【大是大非】 dàshì-dàfēi major issues of principle; cardinal questions of right and wrong: 分清～ draw clear distinctions concerning cardinal issues of right and wrong

【大手大脚】 dàshǒu-dàjiǎo wasteful; extravagant

【大叔】 dàshū ① younger brother of one's father; uncle ② uncle (a polite form of address for a man about one's father's age)

【大暑】 Dàshǔ Great Heat (12th solar term)

【大肆】 dàsì without restraint; wantonly: ～攻击 wantonly vilify; launch an unbridled (或 all-out) attack against/ ～鼓吹 noisily advocate/ ～宣扬 indulge in unbridled propaganda for; give enormous publicity to

【大苏打】 dàsūdá 〈化〉 sodium thiosulfate; sodium hyposulfite; hypo

【大蒜】 dàsuàn garlic: 一头～ a head of garlic

【大踏步】 dàtàbù in big strides: ～前进 stride along

【大…特…】 dà...tè... 〔分别用在同一个词前面，表示规模大，程度深〕: 大错特错 make a gross error; be grievously mistaken/ 大书特书 record in letters of gold; write volumes about

【大提琴】 dàtíqín violoncello; cello

【大体】 dàtǐ ① cardinal principle; general interest: 识～，顾大局 have the cardinal principles in mind and take the overall situation into account ② roughly; more or less; on the whole; by and large; for the most part: ～相同 more or less alike; about the same/ 收支～平衡。Income and expenditure roughly balance./ 我～上同意你的看法。On the whole I agree with you.

【大天白日】 dàtiān-báirì 〈口〉 broad daylight

【大田】 dàtián land for growing field crops ◇ ～作物 field crop

【大厅】 dàtīng hall

【大庭广众】 dàtíng-guǎngzhòng (before) a big crowd; (on) a public occasion: ～之中 in public; on a public occasion

【大同】 dàtóng Great Harmony (an ideal or perfect society)

【大同小异】 dàtóng-xiǎoyì largely identical but with minor differences; alike except for slight differences; very much the same

【大头菜】 dàtóucài 〈植〉 rutabaga

【大头针】 dàtóuzhēn pin

【大团圆】 dàtuányuán ① happy reunion ② happy ending

【大腿】 dàtuǐ thigh

【大王】 dàwáng king; magnate: 煤油～ oil king; oil magnate

【大尉】 dàwèi senior captain

【大无畏】 dàwúwèi dauntless; utterly fearless; indomitable: ～的英雄气概 dauntless heroism

【大西洋】 Dàxīyáng the Atlantic (Ocean)

【大喜】 dàxǐ 〈口〉 great rejoicing: 在这～的日子里 in these days of great rejoicing

【大喜过望】 dàxǐ guò wàng be delighted that things are better than one expected; be overjoyed

【大虾】 dàxiā prawn

【大显身手】 dà xiǎn shēnshǒu display one's skill to the full; give full play to one's abilities; distinguish oneself; give a good account of oneself

【大显神通】 dà xiǎn shéntōng give full play to one's remarkable skill (或 abilities)

【大相径庭】 dà xiāng jìng tíng 〈书〉 be widely divergent

【大小】 dàxiǎo ① big or small: ～水库十座 ten reservoirs of varying sizes/ 国家不论～，应该一律平等。All countries, big or small, should be equal. ② size: 这双鞋我穿上～正合适。These shoes are just my size. ③ degree of seniority: 说话没个～ speak impolitely to elderly people ④ adults and children: 全家～五口。There are five people in the family altogether.

【大校】 dàxiào senior colonel

【大协作】 dàxiézuò large-scale cooperation; a major pooling of efforts: 社会主义～ large-scale socialist cooperation

【大写】 dàxiě ① the capital form of a Chinese numeral: ～金额 amount in words ② capitalization: ～字母 capital letter

【大兴】 dàxīng go in for sth. in a big way: ～土木 go in for large-scale construction/ ～调查研究之风 energetically encourage the practice of conducting investigations and studies/ ～问罪之师 angrily point an accusing finger at sb.; condemn scathingly

【大猩猩】 dàxīngxing gorilla

【大行星】 dàxíngxīng 〈天〉 major planet

【大型】 dàxíng large-scale; large: ～企业 large enterprise/ ～彩色记录片 full-length colour documentary film/ ～运输机 giant transport aircraft; air freighter/ ～轧钢厂 heavy steel rolling plant

【大熊猫】 dàxióngmāo giant panda

【大熊座】 dàxióngzuò 〈天〉 Ursa Major; the Great Bear

【大修】 dàxiū 〈机〉 overhaul; heavy repair

【大选】 dàxuǎn general election

【大学】 dàxué ① university; college ② *The Great Learning* 参见"四书" sìshū ◇ ～生 university (或 college) student

【大雪】 dàxuě ① heavy snow ② (Dàxuě) Great Snow (21st solar term)

【大循环】 dàxúnhuán 〈生理〉 systemic circulation

【大牙】 dàyá ① molar ② front tooth: 你这样会叫人笑掉～的。That would only make you a laughingstock.

【大雅】 dàyǎ 〈书〉 elegance; refinement; good taste: 不登～之堂 not appeal to refined taste; not in good taste

【大烟】 dàyān opium ◇ ～鬼 opium addict

【大言不惭】 dàyán bù cán brag unblushingly; talk big

【大盐】 dàyán crude salt

【大雁】 dàyàn wild goose

【大洋】 dàyáng ① ocean ② silver dollar

【大洋洲】 Dàyángzhōu Oceania; Oceanica

【大样】 dàyàng ① 〈印〉 full-page proof ② 〈建〉 detail drawing

【大摇大摆】 dàyáo-dàbǎi strutting; swaggering

【大要】 dàyào main points; gist: 文章的～ the gist of an article

【大业】 dàyè great cause; great undertaking: 革命～ the great cause of revolution/ 创～ become pioneers in a great undertaking

【大爷】 dàye 〈口〉 ① father's elder brother; uncle ② uncle

(a respectful form of address for an elderly man)
【大衣】 dàyī overcoat; topcoat
【大姨】 dàyí 〈口〉 mother's eldest sister; aunt
【大姨子】 dàyízi 〈口〉 wife's elder sister; sister-in-law
【大义】 dàyì cardinal principles of righteousness; righteous cause: 深明～ be deeply conscious of the righteousness of a cause
【大义凛然】 dàyì lǐnrán inspiring awe by upholding justice
【大义灭亲】 dàyì miè qīn place righteousness above family loyalty
【大意】 dàyì general idea; main points; gist; tenor: 段落～ the gist of a paragraph/ 把他讲话的～记下来就行了。Just jot down the main ideas (或 points) of what he says.
【大意】 dàyi careless; negligent; inattentive: 千万不可粗心～ must never on any account be negligent
【大音阶】 dàyīnjiē 〈乐〉 major scale
【大印】 dàyìn great seal—the seal of power
【大油】 dàyóu 〈口〉 lard
【大有可为】 dà yǒu kě wéi be well worth doing; have bright prospects: 淡水养鱼～。There are bright prospects for freshwater fish farming.
【大有人在】 dà yǒu rén zài there are plenty of such people; such people are by no means rare
【大有文章】 dà yǒu wénzhāng there's something behind all this; there's more to it than meets the eye
【大有作为】 dà yǒu zuòwéi there is plenty of scope for one's talents; be able to develop one's ability to the full: 农村是一个广阔的天地，在那里是可以～的。The countryside is a vast world where much can be accomplished.
【大雨】 dàyǔ heavy rain: ～如注。The rain came down in sheets.
【大元帅】 dàyuánshuài generalissimo
【大员】 dàyuán 〈旧〉 high-ranking official: 委派～ appoint high-ranking officials
【大院】 dàyuàn courtyard; compound: 居民～ residential compound
【大约】 dàyuē 〈副〉 ① approximately; about: ～一小时的路程。It's about an hour's journey. ② probably: 他～是到车间去了。He has probably gone to the workshop.
【大月】 dàyuè ① a solar month of 31 days ② a lunar month of 30 days
【大跃进】 dàyuèjìn great leap forward: 我国国民经济出现了～的局面。China's national economy is making a great leap forward.
【大运河】 Dàyùnhé the Grand Canal
【大杂烩】 dàzáhuì hodgepodge; hotchpotch
【大杂院儿】 dàzáyuànr a compound occupied by many households
【大灶】 dàzào ordinary mess
【大寨】 Dàzhài Dazhai, a production brigade in Xiyang County, Shanxi Province, the pacesetter on China's agricultural front: 农业学～。In agriculture, learn from Dazhai. ◇ ～精神 the Dazhai spirit/ ～县 Dazhai-type county
【大张旗鼓】 dà zhāng qí-gǔ on a grand scale; in a big way: ～地宣传新时期的总任务 give wide publicity to the general task in the new period
【大丈夫】 dàzhàngfu 〈旧〉 true man; real man; man
【大指】 dàzhǐ thumb
【大志】 dàzhì high aim; lofty aim; exalted ambition; high aspirations
【大治】 dàzhì great order: ～之年 a year of great order
【大致】 dàzhì roughly; approximately; more or less: ～相同 roughly the same/ 这项工程～两年可以完工。This project will take about two years to complete.
【大智若愚】 dàzhì ruò yú a man of great wisdom often appears slow-witted
【大众】 dàzhòng the masses; the people; the public; the broad masses of the people ◇ ～歌曲 popular songs/ ～文艺 art and literature for the masses; popular literature
【大众化】 dàzhònghuà popular; in a popular style: ～的饭菜 popular low-priced dishes/ 语言～ use the language of the ordinary people
【大洲】 dàzhōu continent
【大主教】 dàzhǔjiào archbishop
【大专院校】 dà-zhuān yuàn-xiào universities and colleges; institutions of higher education
【大篆】 dàzhuàn an ancient style of calligraphy, current in the Zhou Dynasty (c. 11th century-256 B.C.)
【大资产阶级】 dàzīchǎnjiējí the big bourgeoisie
【大字报】 dàzìbào *dazibao*; big-character poster 参见"四大" sìdà
【大字本】 dàzìběn 〈印〉 large-character edition; large-type edition
【大自然】 dàzìrán nature: 征服～ conquer nature
【大宗】 dàzōng ① a large amount (或 quantity): ～款项 a large amount of money; large sums ② staple: 本地出产以棉花为～。Cotton is the staple crop here.

## da

**垯** da 见"圪垯" gēda

**瘩** da 见"疙瘩" gēda
另见 dá

## dāi

**呆** dāi ① slow-witted; dull: ～头～脑 dull-looking ② blank; wooden: ～～地望着 stare at sth. blankly/ 吓得发～ be stupefied; be scared stiff; be dumbstruck ③ stay: ～在家里 stay at home
另见 ái
【呆若木鸡】 dāi ruò mùjī dumb as a wooden chicken; dumbstruck; transfixed (with fear or amazement)
【呆小症】 dāixiǎozhèng 〈医〉 cretinism
【呆性物质】 dāixìng wùzhì 〈化〉 inert material
【呆帐】 dāizhàng bad debt
【呆滞】 dāizhì ① dull: 两眼～无神 with a dull look in one's eyes ② idle: 避免资金～ prevent capital from lying idle
【呆子】 dāizi idiot; simpleton; blockhead

**待** dāi 〈口〉 stay: 他在广州～了三天。He stayed in Guangzhou for three days.
另见 dài

## dǎi

**歹** dǎi bad; evil; vicious: 为非作～ do evil
【歹徒】 dǎitú scoundrel; ruffian; evildoer

**逮** dǎi capture; catch: 猫～老鼠。Cats catch mice.
另见 dài

**傣** Dǎi
【傣族】 Dǎizú the Dai (Tai) nationality, living in Yunnan

## dài

**大** dài
另见 dà

【大夫】 dàifu 〈口〉 doctor; physician

【大黄】 dàihuáng 〈植〉 Chinese rhubarb

**代** dài ① take the place of; be in place of: 主任不在时由老王～。Lao Wang acts for the director during his absence./ ～人受过 suffer for the faults of another; bear the blame for somebody else/ 请～我向他致意。Please give him my regards. ② acting: ～部长 acting minister ③ historical period: 古～ ancient times/ 汉～ the Han Dynasty ④ 〈地〉 era: 古生～ the Palaeozoic Era ⑤ generation: ～～相传 pass on (或 hand down) from generation to generation/ 一～新人在成长。A generation of people of a new type is growing up.

【代办】 dàibàn ① do sth. for sb.; act on sb.'s behalf: 这件事请你～吧。Could you do this for me? 或 Could you act on my behalf? ② 〈外〉 chargé d'affaires: 临时～ chargé d'affaires ad interim ◇ ～处 Office of the Chargé d'Affaires

【代办所】 dàibànsuǒ agency: 储蓄～ savings agency/ 邮政～ postal agency

【代笔】 dàibǐ write on sb.'s behalf

【代表】 dàibiǎo ① deputy; delegate; representative: 全国人大～ deputy to the National People's Congress/ 党代会～ delegate to the Party Congress/ 双方～ representatives from both sides/ 常驻～ permanent representative (或 delegate) ② represent; stand for: ～无产阶级利益 represent the interests of the proletariat/ 这三个人～三种不同性格。These three persons represent three different types of character./ ～时代精神 embody the spirit of the era ③ on behalf of; in the name of: ～我国政府表示衷心的感谢 express heartfelt thanks on behalf of our government/ ～全厂工人讲话 speak in the name of the workers of the factory
◇ ～权 representation/ ～人物 representative figure (或 personage); typical representative; leading exponent/ ～团 delegation; mission; deputation/ ～资格 qualifications of a representative/ ～资格审查委员会 (delegates') credentials committee/ ～作 representative work

【代表大会】 dàibiǎo dàhuì congress; representative assembly (或 conference): 中国共产党全国～ the National Congress of the Communist Party of China/ 公社社员～ the commune members' representative assembly

【代步】 dàibù 〈书〉 ride instead of walk

【代词】 dàicí 〈语〉 pronoun

【代购】 dàigòu buy on sb.'s behalf; act as a purchasing agent ◇ ～代销点 purchasing and marketing agency

【代号】 dàihào code name

【代价】 dàijià price; cost: 不惜任何～ prepared to pay any price; at any cost; at all costs

【代课】 dàikè take over a class for an absent teacher

【代劳】 dàiláo do sth. for sb.; take trouble on sb.'s behalf: 这事请你老李～吧。Will you do this for us, Lao Li?

【代理】 dàilǐ ① act on behalf of someone in a responsible position: 公社党委书记病了，工作由他～。He acted for the commune Party secretary who was ill./ ～厂长 acting manager of a factory ② act as agent (或 proxy, procurator)

【代理人】 dàilǐrén ① agent; deputy; proxy ② 〈法〉 procurator; attorney

【代脉】 dàimài 〈中医〉 slow, intermittent pulse

【代名词】 dàimíngcí ① 〈语〉 pronoun ② synonym: 诸葛亮在民间传说中成了智慧的～。Zhuge Liang is a synonym for wisdom in folklore.

【代庖】 dàipáo do what is sb. else's job; act in sb.'s place

【代乳粉】 dàirǔfěn milk powder substitute

【代售】 dàishòu be commissioned to sell sth. (usu. as a sideline)

【代数】 dàishù algebra ◇ ～方程 algebraic equation/ ～式 algebraic expression/ ～数论 algebraic theory of numbers

【代替】 dàitì replace; substitute for; take the place of: 社会主义制度终究要～资本主义制度。The socialist system will eventually replace the capitalist system./ 无产阶级国家～资产阶级国家，非通过暴力革命不可。It is impossible for the proletarian state to supersede the bourgeois state without a violent revolution./ 好些外科手术都可用针麻～药麻。In many surgical operations, acupuncture anaesthesia may be used instead of medicinal anaesthetics.

【代销】 dàixiāo sell goods (for the state) on a commission basis; be commissioned to sell sth. (usu. as a sideline); act as a commission agent ◇ ～店 shop commissioned to sell certain goods; commission agent

【代谢】 dàixiè ① supersession: 新旧事物的～ the supersession of the old by the new ② 〈生〉 metabolize: 分解～ catabolism/ 组成～ anabolism
◇ ～期 metabolic stage/ ～物 metabolite/ ～作用 metabolism

【代行】 dàixíng act on sb.'s behalf: ～职权 function in an acting capacity

【代序】 dàixù an article used in lieu of a preface (或 by way of introduction)

【代言人】 dàiyánrén spokesman; mouthpiece

【代议制】 dàiyìzhì the representative system (of government) ◇ ～机构 representative institution

【代营食堂】 dàiyíng shítáng neighbourhood canteen

【代用】 dàiyòng substitute: ～材料 substitute (或 ersatz) materials ◇ ～品 substitute; ersatz

【代字号】 dàizìhào swung dash (～)

**岱** Dài another name for Taishan Mountain

**迨** dài 〈书〉 ① wait till ② before sth. happens: ～天之未阴雨 before it rains

**甙** dài 〈化〉 glucoside

**玳** dài

【玳瑁】 dàimào 〈动〉 hawksbill turtle

**带** dài ① belt; girdle; ribbon; band; tape: 皮～ leather belt/ 丝～ silk ribbon/ 录音～ recording tape/ 腰～ waist band/ 鞋～ shoelaces; shoestrings ② tyre: 自行车～ bicycle tyre ③ zone; area; belt: 热～ the torrid zone/ 绿化地～ greenbelt/ 他在这一～打过游击。He was once a guerrilla fighter in these parts. ④ take; bring; carry: 我可以～多少行李？How much luggage can I take?/ 别忘了～雨衣。Don't forget to take your raincoat along./ 连队走到哪里，就把老红军的传统～到哪里。Wherever it goes, the company passes on to the people the glorious tradition of the Red Army./ 请人～个话儿给她。Ask somebody to take her a message./ 我没有～钱。I haven't any money on me. ⑤ do sth. incidentally: 上街时给～点茶叶来。When you go out, get me some tea./ 你在信上给我～一笔，问你父亲好。Remember me to your father in your letter./ 你出去请把门～上。Please pull the door to when you go out. ⑥ bear; have: ～有时代的特点 bear the imprint of the times/ 面～笑容

wear a smile/说话别～刺儿。Don't be sarcastic./一项～根本性的措施 a measure of fundamental importance ⑦ having sth. attached; simultaneous: ～叶的橘子 tangerines with their leaves on/ 这几个茶杯是～碟儿的。There are saucers to go with these cups./ 连说～笑地走进来 enter laughing and talking/ 放牛～割草 cut grass while tending cattle/ 玉米地里～着种点黄豆 grow some soybeans in the maize field ⑧ lead; head: ～队 lead (或 be the leader of) a group of people/ ～兵 lead (或 be in command of) troops/ 书记亲自～班。The Party secretary took personal charge of the shift. ⑨ look after; bring up; raise: ～孩子 look after children/ 他是由一位贫农大娘～大的。He was brought up by a poor peasant woman.

【带病】 dàibìng in spite of illness: 他～坚持工作。He went on working in spite of his illness.

【带材】 dàicái 〈冶〉 strip

【带电】 dàidiàn electrified; live; charged ◇ ～导线 live wire/ ～粒子 〈物〉 charged particle/ ～体 charged (或 electrified) body/ ～作业 live-wire work

【带动】 dàidòng drive; spur on; bring along: 用拖拉机上的发动机～打谷机 use the tractor motor to power the thresher/ 先进～后进。The more advanced bring along the less advanced./ 抓好典型，～全局 take firm hold of typical examples to promote the work as a whole/ 革命～了生产。The revolution has given an impetus to production.

【带钢】 dàigāng strip steel

【带劲】 dàijìn ① energetic; forceful: 他干起活来可～了。He works like a horse./ 这篇大字报批得真～。This is a hard-hitting *dazibao*. ② interesting; exciting; wonderful: 这场比赛真～。This is really a terrific match./ 下棋不～，咱们游泳去吧。Chess is no fun; let's go swimming./ 什么时候我学会开拖拉机，那才～呢。It'll be wonderful if I can drive a tractor some day.

【带锯】 dàijù 〈机〉 band saw

【带菌者】 dàijūnzhě 〈医〉 carrier

【带累】 dàilěi implicate; involve

【带领】 dàilǐng lead; guide: 队长～社员出海捕鱼。The team leader led commune members out to sea to catch fish./ ～群众朝着正确的方向前进 guide the masses in the correct direction

【带路】 dàilù show (或 lead) the way; act as a guide: 老猎户给我们～。The old hunter acted as our guide. ◇ ～人 guide

【带头】 dàitóu take the lead; be the first; take the initiative; set an example: ～冲锋 lead the charge/ 起～作用 play a leading role/ ～发言 be the first to speak; break the ice/ ～斗私批修 set an example in fighting selfishness and repudiating revisionism/ 老干部～参加集体生产劳动。Veteran cadres take the lead in doing collective productive labour.

【带徒弟】 dài túdi train (或 take on) an apprentice

【带下】 dàixià 〈中医〉 morbid leucorrhoea

【带孝】 dàixiào wear mourning for a parent, relative, etc.; be in mourning

【带音】 dàiyīn 〈语〉 voiced

【带鱼】 dàiyú hairtail

【带子】 dàizi belt; girdle; ribbon; band; tape

## 殆

dài 〈书〉 ① danger: 危～ in great danger ② nearly; almost: 敌人伤亡～尽。The enemy were practically wiped out.

## 待

dài ① treat; deal with: ～人诚恳 treat people sincerely; be sincere with people/ 宽～俘虏 treat prisoners of war leniently ② entertain: ～客 entertain a guest ③ wait for; await: ～机 await an opportunity; bide one's time/ 尚～解决的问题 a problem awaiting solution; an outstanding issue/ 有～改进 have yet to be improved ④ need: 自不～言。This goes without saying. 或 This is taken for granted. ⑤ going to; about to: 我正～出门，有人来了。I was about to go out when someone came.

另见 dāi

【待价而沽】 dài jià ér gū wait for the right price to sell; wait for the highest bid

【待考】 dàikǎo need checking; remain to be verified

【待命】 dàimìng await orders: ～出发 await orders to set off/ 原地～ stay where one is, pending orders; stand by

【待人接物】 dàirén-jiēwù the way one gets along with people

【待续】 dàixù to be continued

【待遇】 dàiyù ① treatment: 最惠国～ most-favoured-nation treatment/ 政治～ political treatment ② remuneration; pay; wages; salary: 优厚～ excellent pay and conditions

## 贷

dài ① loan: 农～ agricultural loans ② borrow or lend: 向银行～款 get a bank loan/ 银行～给公社大量款项。The bank granted a large loan to the commune. ③ shift (responsibility); shirk: 责无旁～ be one's unshirkable responsibility; be duty-bound ④ pardon; forgive: 严惩不～ punish without mercy

【贷方】 dàifāng 〈簿记〉 credit side; credit

【贷款】 dàikuǎn ① provide (或 grant) a loan; extend credit to; make an advance to ② loan; credit: 无息～ interest-free loans/ 未偿～ outstanding loans

## 怠

dài idle; remiss; slack

【怠惰】 dàiduò idle; lazy; indolent

【怠工】 dàigōng slow down; go slow: 资本主义国家的工人以～作为斗争的一种方式。Workers in capitalist countries go slow as a form of struggle.

【怠慢】 dàimàn ① cold-shoulder; slight: 不要～了客人。See that none of the guests are neglected. ② 〈套〉〔表示招待不周〕: ～了! I'm afraid I have been a poor host.

## 袋

dài ① bag; sack; pocket; pouch: 旅行～ travelling bag/ 邮～ mailbag/ 工具～ tool kit/ 衣～ pocket ② 〈量〉: 一～面粉 a sack of flour/ 一～烟的功夫 time needed to smoke a pipe

【袋兽】 dàishòu marsupial

【袋鼠】 dàishǔ kangaroo

【袋装】 dàizhuāng in bags ◇ ～奶粉 milk powder in bags

【袋子】 dàizi sack; bag

## 逮

dài 〈书〉 reach: 力有未～ beyond one's reach (或 power)

另见 dǎi

【逮捕】 dàibǔ arrest; take into custody: ～法办 arrest and deal with according to law; bring to justice ◇ ～证 arrest warrant

## 戴

dài ① put on; wear: ～上手套 put on one's gloves/ ～眼镜 wear glasses ② respect; honour: 爱～ love and respect ③ (Dài) a surname

【戴帽小学】 dàimào xiǎoxué a primary school with first-year middle school classes attached

【戴胜】 dàishèng 〈动〉 hoopoe

【戴孝】 dàixiào wear mourning for a parent, relative, etc.; be in mourning

【戴罪立功】 dàizuì lìgōng atone for one's crimes by doing

good deeds; redeem oneself by good service

**黛** dài a black pigment used by women in ancient times to paint their eyebrows

【黛绿】 dàilǜ 〈书〉 dark green

## dān

**丹** dān ① red ② 〈中药〉 pellet or powder

【丹顶鹤】 dāndǐnghè red-crowned crane

【丹毒】 dāndú 〈医〉 erysipelas

【丹方】 dānfāng folk prescription; home remedy

【丹桂】 dānguì 〈植〉 orange osmanthus

【丹麦】 Dānmài Denmark ◇ ～人 Dane/ ～语 Danish (language)

【丹皮】 dānpí 〈中药〉 the root bark of the tree peony

【丹青】 dānqīng 〈书〉 painting: ～妙笔 superb artistry (in painting); the superb touch of a great painter

【丹砂】 dānshā cinnabar

【丹参】 dānshēn 〈中药〉 the root of red-rooted salvia (*Salvia miltiorrhiza*)

【丹田】 dāntián the pubic region: ～之气 deep breath controlled by the diaphragm

【丹心】 dānxīn a loyal heart; loyalty

**单** dān ① one; single: ～扇门 single-leaf door/ ～丝不成线，独木不成林。One strand of silk doesn't make a thread; one tree doesn't make a forest. ② odd: ～日 odd-numbered days/ ～只袜子 an odd sock ③ singly; alone: ～人独马 single-handed/ 把这几件东西～放在一个地方。Keep these things in a separate place. ④ only; alone: 不～ not only/ 不要～凭热情去工作。Don't work by enthusiasm alone. ⑤ simple: 简～ simple; plain ⑥ thin; weak ⑦ unlined (clothing) ⑧ sheet: 床～ bed sheet ⑨ bill; list: 名～ name list/ 菜～ menu; bill of fare/ 价目～ price list

另见 chán; Shàn

【单摆】 dānbǎi 〈物〉 simple pendulum

【单板】 dānbǎn 〈林〉 veneer

【单帮】 dānbāng 〈旧〉 a travelling trader working on his own: 跑～ travel around trading on one's own

【单倍体】 dānbèitǐ 〈生〉 monoploid; haploid

【单本位制】 dānběnwèizhì 〈经〉 monometallic standard; monometallism

【单边】 dānbiān 〈经〉 unilateral: ～进(出)口 unilateral import (export)

【单兵教练】 dānbīng jiàoliàn 〈军〉 individual drilling

【单兵装备】 dānbīng zhuāngbèi 〈军〉 individual equipment

【单薄】 dānbó ① (of clothing) thin: 穿得～ be thinly clad ② thin and weak; frail: 身体～ have a poor physique ③ insubstantial; flimsy; thin: 论据～ a feeble argument

【单产】 dānchǎn per unit area yield

【单车】 dānchē 〈方〉 bicycle

【单程】 dānchéng one way ◇ ～车票 one-way (或 single) ticket/ ～清棉机 〈纺〉 single process scutcher

【单纯】 dānchún ① simple; pure: 问题决不象我们当初想象的那么～。The problem is by no means as simple as we first thought. ② alone; purely; merely: 不～追求数量 not concentrate on quantity alone ◇ ～词 〈语〉 single-morpheme word/ ～技术观点 exclusive concern about technique; putting technique above everything else

【单词】 dāncí 〈语〉 ① individual word; word ② single-morpheme word

【单打】 dāndǎ 〈体〉 singles: 男子(女子)～ men's (women's) singles/ 少年男子(女子)～ boys' (girls') singles/ 她只参加～。She's only playing in the singles.

【单打一】 dāndǎyī ① concentrate on one thing only ② have a one-track mind

【单单】 dāndān only; alone: 别人都来了，～他没来。He's the only one absent. Everybody else is here. 或 Everybody has come except him.

【单刀】 dāndāo ① short-hilted broadsword ② 〈武术〉 single-broadsword event

【单刀直入】 dāndāo zhí rù come straight to the point; speak out without beating about the bush

【单调】 dāndiào monotonous; dull; drab: 声音～ in a monotonous tone/ 色彩～ dull colouring/ 昨天的节目比较～。Yesterday's programme was rather dull.

【单独】 dāndú alone; by oneself; on one's own; single-handed; independent: ～一个人干不了这个活儿。Nobody can do this job alone (或 by himself)./ 采取～行动 take independent action/ 她～住一间屋子。She has a room to herself./ 我要和他～谈一谈。I want to have a talk with him alone.

【单发】 dānfā 〈军〉 single shot ◇ ～射击 single shot

【单方】 dānfāng folk prescription; home remedy

【单方面】 dānfāngmiàn one-sided; unilateral: ～撕毁协定 unilaterally tear up an agreement

【单飞】 dānfēi 〈航空〉 solo flight

【单峰驼】 dānfēngtuó 〈动〉 one-humped camel; dromedary; Arabian camel

【单幅】 dānfú 〈纺〉 single width

【单干】 dāngàn ① work on one's own; go it alone; work by oneself; do sth. single-handed ② individual farming ◇ ～风 the tendency to return to individual farming; the trend towards going it alone/ ～户 a peasant family still farming on its own after agricultural cooperation

【单杠】 dāngàng 〈体〉 ① horizontal bar ② horizontal bar gymnastics

【单个儿】 dāngèr ① individually; alone: 最好集体去，不要～去。We'd better go in a group, not individually. ② an odd one: 这副手套只剩下～了。There's only an odd glove left.

【单轨】 dānguǐ single track

【单号】 dānhào odd numbers (of tickets, seats, etc.)

【单簧管】 dānhuángguǎn 〈乐〉 clarinet

【单级火箭】 dānjí huǒjiàn single-stage rocket

【单季稻】 dānjìdào single cropping of rice

【单价】 dānjià ① 〈经〉 unit price ② 〈化〉〈生〉 univalent

【单间儿】 dānjiānr separate room (in a hotel, restaurant, etc.)

【单键】 dānjiàn 〈化〉 single bond

【单交】 dānjiāo 〈农〉 single cross

【单脚跳】 dānjiǎotiào 〈体〉 hop

【单晶硅】 dānjīngguī 〈电子〉 monocrystalline silicon

【单晶体】 dānjīngtǐ 〈物〉 monocrystal

【单句】 dānjù 〈语〉 simple sentence

【单据】 dānjù documents attesting to the giving or receiving of money, goods, etc., such as receipts, bills, vouchers and invoices: 货运～ shipping documents

【单孔目】 dānkǒngmù 〈动〉 Monotremata ◇ ～动物 monotreme

【单跨】 dānkuà 〈建〉 single span

【单利】 dānlì 〈经〉 simple interest

【单轮射箭】 dānlún shèjiàn 〈体〉 single round archery: 女子三十米～ women's 30-metre single round archery event

【单宁酸】 dānníngsuān 〈化〉 tannic acid

【单片眼镜】 dānpiàn yǎnjìng monocle

【单枪匹马】 dānqiāng-pǐmǎ single-handed; all by oneself; alone

【单人床】 dānrénchuáng single bed
【单人舞】 dānrénwǔ solo dance: 跳～ dance a solo
【单日】 dānrì odd-numbered days (of the month)
【单弱】 dānruò thin and weak; frail
【单色】 dānsè monochromatic ◇ ～电视 monochrome television/ ～光 ‹物› monochromatic light/ ～画 monochrome/ ～胶印机 single-colour offset press/ ～性 monochromaticity
【单身】 dānshēn ① unmarried; single ② not be with one's family; live alone: ～在外 live alone away from home ◇ ～汉 bachelor/ ～宿舍 quarters for single men or women; bachelor quarters
【单生花】 dānshēnghuā ‹植› solitary flower
【单式】 dānshì ‹簿记› single entry
【单数】 dānshù ① odd number ② ‹语› singular number
【单丝】 dānsī ‹纺› monofilament
【单瘫】 dāntān ‹医› monoplegia
【单糖】 dāntáng ‹化› monose; monosaccharide
【单体】 dāntǐ ‹化› monomer
【单位】 dānwèi ① unit (as a standard of measurement): 长度～ a unit of length/ 货币～ monetary unit/ ～面积产量 yield per unit area/ 以秒为～计算时间 measure time by the second ② unit (as an organization, department, division, section, etc.): 行政～ administrative unit/ 生产～ production unit/ 基层～ basic (或 grass-roots) unit ◇ ～圆‹数› unit circle/ ～制 system of unit
【单细胞】 dānxìbāo unicellular ◇ ～动物 unicellular animal
【单弦儿】 dānxiánr *danxianr*, story-telling to musical accompaniment
【单线】 dānxiàn ① single line ② one-way (contact); single-line (link): 做地下工作时，他和我～联系。When we were doing underground work, he was my only contact. ③ ‹交› single track ◇ ～铁路 single-track railway; single-track line
【单相思】 dānxiāngsī unrequited love
【单向】 dānxiàng one-way; unidirectional ◇ ～电路 one-way circuit/ ～交通 one-way traffic
【单项】 dānxiàng ‹体› individual event ◇ ～比赛 individual competition
【单相】 dānxiàng single-phase; monophase ◇ ～电动机 single-phase motor/ ～合金 single-phase alloy
【单斜】 dānxié ‹地› monocline ◇ ～层 monoclinal stratum
【单行本】 dānxíngběn ① separate edition ② offprint
【单行法规】 dānxíng fǎguī special (或 separate) regulations
【单行条例】 dānxíng tiáolì specific regulations
【单行线】 dānxíngxiàn one-way road
【单性花】 dānxìnghuā ‹植› unisexual flower
【单性生殖】 dānxìng shēngzhí ‹生› parthenogenesis; parthenogenetic propagation (或 reproduction)
【单眼】 dānyǎn ‹动› simple eye
【单叶】 dānyè ‹植› simple leaf
【单一】 dānyī single; unitary: ～的生产资料全民所有制 a unitary system of the ownership of the means of production by the whole people ◇ ～经济 single-product economy/ ～种植 monoculture; one-crop farming
【单衣】 dānyī unlined garment
【单翼机】 dānyìjī monoplane
【单音词】 dānyīncí ‹语› monosyllabic word; monosyllable
【单元】 dānyuán unit: 运算～ arithmetic unit/ 三号楼丙～四号 No.4, Entrance C, Building 3
【单渣操作】 dānzhā cāozuò ‹冶› single-slag practice
【单质】 dānzhì ‹化› simple substance
【单子】 dānzǐ ‹哲› monad
【单子】 dānzi ① list; bill; form: 开个～ make out a list/ 菜～ bill of fare; menu/ 填写～ fill in a form ② bed sheet
【单子叶植物】 dānzǐyè zhíwù monocotyledon
【单字】 dānzì individual character; separate word
【单座飞机】 dānzuò fēijī single-seater (aeroplane)

**担** dān ① carry on a shoulder pole: ～水 carry water (with a shoulder pole and buckets) ② take on; undertake: 咱们把任务～起来。Let's take on the job./ 不怕～风险 ready to face any danger; not be afraid of running risks
另见 dàn
【担保】 dānbǎo assure; guarantee; vouch for: 这事交给她办，～错不了。I assure you that she can be trusted to do the work well. 或 I'll vouch for her as the best person for the job./ 出口信贷～ export credit guarantees ◇ ～人 guarantor; guarantee
【担不是】 dān bùshi take the blame
【担当】 dāndāng take on; undertake; assume: ～重任 take on heavy responsibilities
【担负】 dānfù bear; shoulder; take on; be charged with: ～责任 shoulder responsibility/ ～费用 bear an expense/ ～领导工作 hold a leading post
【担架】 dānjià stretcher; litter ◇ ～队 stretcher-team/ ～员 stretcher-bearer
【担惊受怕】 dānjīng-shòupà feel alarmed; be in a state of anxiety
【担任】 dānrèn assume the office of; hold the post of: ～工会主席 be the chairman of a trade union/ ～革委会委员 be on the revolutionary committee/ ～会议主席 take the chair/ 请他们～校外辅导员 invite them to be advisers on after-school activities
【担心】 dānxīn worry; feel anxious: ～她的健康 worry about her health/ 快给老大娘写信，免得她～。Write to the old lady at once so as to set her mind at rest.
【担忧】 dānyōu worry; be anxious: 不要为我的身体～。Don't worry about my health.

**眈** dān 见"虎视眈眈" hǔ shì dāndān

**耽** dān ① delay ② ‹书› abandon oneself to; indulge in: ～乐 indulge in pleasure
【耽搁】 dānge ① stop over; stay: 我去天津途中可能在济南～一下。I may have a stopover at Jinan on my way to Tianjin./ 我不打算在这里～多久。I won't be here for long. ②delay: 毫不～ without delay/ 不得～ admit of no delay/ 一分钟也不能～。Not a single minute is to be lost.
【耽误】 dānwu delay; hold up: ～了整个工程 hold up (或 delay) the whole project/ ～功夫 waste time/ 把～的时间夺回来 make up for lost time/ 她从不为个人事情～生产。She never allows her private affairs to interfere with production.

**殚** dān ‹书› exhaust: ～思极虑 rack one's brains

**箪** dān ‹书› a bamboo utensil for holding cooked rice
【箪食壶浆】 dānsì-hújiāng welcome (an army) with food and drink

## dǎn

**胆** dǎn ① gallbladder ② courage; guts; bravery: 壮～ boost sb.'s courage ③ a bladder-like inner container: 热水瓶～ the glass liner of a vacuum flask/ 球～ the rubber bladder of a ball
【胆大】 dǎndà bold; audacious: ～心细 bold but cautious/ ～包天 audacious in the extreme/ ～妄为 reckless

【胆矾】 dǎnfán 〈化〉 chalcanthite; blue vitriol
【胆敢】 dǎngǎn dare; have the audacity to: 敌人～来侵犯，就坚决消灭它。If the enemy dare to invade us, we'll resolutely wipe them out.
【胆固醇】 dǎngùchún 〈生化〉 cholesterol
【胆管】 dǎnguǎn 〈生理〉 bile duct ◇ ～炎 cholangitis/ ～造影 cholangiography
【胆寒】 dǎnhán be terrified; be struck with terror
【胆红素】 dǎnhóngsù 〈生化〉 bilirubin
【胆碱】 dǎnjiǎn 〈生化〉 choline
【胆量】 dǎnliàng courage; guts; pluck; spunk: 很有～ have plenty of guts (或 spunk)
【胆略】 dǎnlüè courage and resourcefulness: ～过人 have unusual courage and resourcefulness
【胆囊】 dǎnnáng 〈生理〉 gallbladder ◇ ～炎 cholecystitis
【胆瓶】 dǎnpíng a vase with a slender neck and a bulging belly
【胆怯】 dǎnqiè timid; cowardly
【胆石】 dǎnshí 〈医〉 cholelith; gallstone ◇ ～病 cholelithiasis
【胆识】 dǎnshí courage and insight
【胆酸】 dǎnsuān 〈生化〉 cholic acid
【胆小】 dǎnxiǎo timid; cowardly: ～如鼠 as timid as a mouse; chicken-hearted ◇ ～鬼 coward
【胆战心惊】 dǎnzhàn-xīnjīng tremble with fear; be terror-stricken: 使人～ strike terror into sb.; be terrifying
【胆汁】 dǎnzhī 〈生理〉 bile
【胆子】 dǎnzi courage; nerve: 放开～ pluck up courage; stop being afraid/ 好大的～！What a nerve!

**疸** dǎn 见"黄疸" huángdǎn

**掸** dǎn brush lightly; whisk: ～掉身上的雪花 brush (或 whisk) the snow off one's coat/ ～～衣服 brush the dust off one's clothes
【掸子】 dǎnzi duster (usu. made of chicken feathers or strips of cloth): 鸡毛～ feather duster

## dàn

**石** dàn *dan*, a unit of dry measure for grain (= 1 hectolitre)
另见 shí

**旦** dàn ① 〈书〉 dawn; daybreak ② day: 元～ New Year's Day ③ the female character type in Beijing opera, etc. ④ 〈纺〉 denier
【旦夕】 dànxī 〈书〉 this morning or evening — in a short while: 危在～ in imminent danger/ ～之间 in a day's time; overnight

**但** dàn ① 〈连〉 but; yet; still; nevertheless: 他早已年过六十，～毫不见老。He's well over sixty, but he doesn't look at all old. ② only; merely: 在辽阔的原野上，～见麦浪随风起伏。On the vast fields, one sees nothing but the wheat billowing in the wind.
【但凡】 dànfán in every case; without exception; as long as: ～过路的人，没有一个不停下来欣赏这儿的风景的。Whoever passes here stops to admire the scenery./ ～同志们有困难，他没有不热情帮助的。Whenever a comrade needs help, he is ready to give it.
【但是】 dànshì 〈连〉 but; yet; still; nevertheless
【但书】 dànshū 〈法〉 proviso
【但愿】 dànyuàn if only; I wish: ～天气赶快放晴。If only it would clear up soon!/ ～如此。I wish it were true! 或 Let's hope so.

**担** dàn ① *dan*, a unit of weight (＝50 kilograms) ② a carrying pole and the loads on it; load; burden: 货郎～ loads of goods carried on a shoulder pole by an itinerant pedlar/ 为革命勇挑重～ ready to shoulder heavy tasks for the revolution ③ 〈量〉〔用于成担的东西〕: 一～水 two buckets of water (carried on a shoulder pole)
另见 dān
【担担面】 dàndànmiàn Sichuan noodles with peppery sauce
【担子】 dànzi a carrying pole and the loads on it; load; burden: ～拣重的挑 ready to shoulder the heaviest loads

**诞** dàn ① birth ② birthday ③ absurd; fantastic: 荒～ fantastic
【诞辰】 dànchén birthday
【诞生】 dànshēng be born; come into being; emerge: 新中国的～ the birth of New China/ 在斗争的烈火中～ emerge from the flames of struggle

**淡** dàn ① thin; light: ～酒 light wine/ 云～风轻。The clouds are pale and a light breeze is blowing. ② tasteless; weak: ～茶 weak tea/ ～而无味 tasteless; insipid/ 这个菜太～。 This dish is not salty enough. ③ light; pale: ～黄 light yellow/ ～紫 pale purple; lilac ④ indifferent: ～然处之 treat with indifference; take things coolly/ ～～地答应了一声 answer drily ⑤ slack; dull: 生意清～。Business is slack. ⑥ 〈方〉 meaningless; trivial: 扯～ talk nonsense
【淡泊】 dànbó not seek fame and wealth
【淡薄】 dànbó ① thin; light: 朝雾渐渐地～了。The morning mist gradually thinned. ② become indifferent; flag: 他对象棋的兴趣逐渐～了。His interest in chess has begun to flag. ③ faint; dim; hazy: 时间隔得太久，印象也就～了。With the passage of time, these impressions became dim./ 必须提醒他，他的阶级斗争观念～了。We must warn him that his sense of class struggle is getting blunted.
【淡菜】 dàncài 〈动〉 mussel
【淡出】 dànchū 〈电影〉 fade out
【淡化】 dànhuà desalination: 海水～ desalination of sea water
【淡积云】 dànjīyún 〈气〉 cumulus humilis
【淡季】 dànjì slack (或 dull, off) season: 争取做到蔬菜～不淡，旺季不烂 strive for an ample supply of vegetables in the off seasons and avoid waste in the peak periods
【淡漠】 dànmò ① indifferent; apathetic; nonchalant ② faint; dim; hazy: 这件事在我脑子里已很～了。 The event has left only faint memories in my mind.
【淡青】 dànqīng light greenish blue
【淡入】 dànrù 〈电影〉 fade in
【淡水】 dànshuǐ fresh water
◇ ～湖 freshwater lake/ ～养鱼 freshwater fish-farming/ ～鱼 freshwater fish
【淡忘】 dànwàng fade from one's memory
【淡雅】 dànyǎ simple and elegant; quietly elegant: 刺绣品有的鲜艳，有的～。Some of the embroideries are in bold, bright colours; others are quietly elegant.
【淡竹】 dànzhú 〈植〉 henon bamboo (*Phyllostachys nigra* var. *henonis*)

**啖** dàn 〈书〉 ① eat ② feed ③ entice; lure

**蛋** dàn ① egg ② an egg-shaped thing: 泥～儿 mud ball
【蛋白】 dànbái ① egg white; albumen ② protein ◇ ～酶〈生化〉 protease; proteinase/ ～尿〈医〉 albuminuria

【蛋白石】 dànbáishí 〈地〉 opal
【蛋白质】 dànbáizhì protein ◇ ～塑料 protein plastics
【蛋粉】 dànfěn powdered eggs; egg powder
【蛋糕】 dàngāo cake
【蛋黄】 dànhuáng yolk
【蛋壳】 dànké eggshell
【蛋品】 dànpǐn egg products
【蛋清】 dànqīng 〈口〉 egg white
【蛋用鸡】 dànyòngjī layer

**弹** dàn ① ball; pellet ② bullet; bomb: 燃烧～ incendiary bomb/ ～尽粮绝 run out of ammunition and food supplies
另见 tán
【弹道】 dàndào trajectory
◇ ～导弹 ballistic missile/ ～弧线 ballistic curve/ ～火箭 ballistic rocket
【弹道学】 dàndàoxué ballistics: 内(外)～ interior (exterior) ballistics
【弹弓】 dàngōng catapult; slingshot
【弹痕】 dànhén bullet or shell hole; shot mark
【弹夹】 dànjiā (cartridge) clip; charger
【弹壳】 dànké shell case; cartridge case
【弹坑】 dànkēng (shell) crater
【弹幕】 dànmù barrage
【弹盘】 dànpán cartridge drum; magazine
【弹片】 dànpiàn shell fragment (或 splinter); shrapnel
【弹膛】 dàntáng chamber
【弹头】 dàntóu bullet; projectile nose; warhead
【弹丸】 dànwán ① pellet; shot; bullet ② 〈书〉〔多用于〕: ～之地 a tiny area; a small bit of land
【弹匣】 dànxiá 〈军〉 magazine
【弹药】 dànyào ammunition
◇ ～库 ammunition depot (或 storehouse)/ ～手 ammunition man (或 bearer)/ ～所 ammunition supply (或 refilling) point/ ～箱 ammunition chest; cartridge box
【弹着】 dànzhuó 〈军〉 impact
◇ ～点 point of impact; hitting point/ ～观察 spotting/ ～观察兵 spotter/ ～角 angle of impact/ ～区 impact (或 objective) area
【弹子】 dànzi ① a pellet shot from a slingshot ② marble: 打～ play marbles ③ 〈方〉 billiards ◇ ～房 billiard room

**惮** dàn 〈书〉 fear; dread

**氮** dàn 〈化〉 nitrogen (N)
【氮肥】 dànféi nitrogenous fertilizer

## dāng

**当** dāng ① equal: 实力相～ well-matched in strength ② ought; should; must: 能省的就省，～用的还是得用。Save what you can, but use what you must. ③ in sb.'s presence; to sb.'s face: ～着大家谈一谈。Speak out in the presence of everyone. ④ just at (a time or place): ～时 at that time/ ～场 on the spot ⑤ work as; serve as; be: 我长大要～解放军。I want to be a PLA man when I grow up./ 他解放前～长工。He worked as a farmhand before liberation./ ～官做老爷 act like an overlord/ 选他～组长 elect him group leader ⑥ bear; accept; deserve: 我可～不起这样的夸奖。I just don't deserve such praise. ⑦ direct; manage; be in charge of: ～家 manage household affairs ⑧〈象〉〔金属器物撞击声〕: ～～的钟声 the tolling of a bell; the ding-dong of bells
另见 dàng
【当兵】 dāngbīng be a soldier; serve in the army
【当场】 dāngchǎng on the spot; then and there: ～拒绝他们的要求 turn down their request on the spot/ 他～表演了这种新的操作方法。He gave a demonstration of the new technique then and there./ ～抓住 catch red-handed (或 in the act)
【当场出彩】 dāngchǎng chūcǎi ① make a spectacle of oneself ② give the whole show away on the spot
【当初】 dāngchū originally; at the outset; in the first place; at that time: ～打算在这儿盖一座大楼。It was originally planned to put up a big building here./～这儿是一片荒野，如今工厂林立。Factories now stand where there used to be a wilderness./ 我～怎么对你讲的？What did I tell you, eh?/ ～你就不该这么做。You should never have acted the way you did in the first place./ 早知今日，何必～？If I had known it would come to this, I would have acted differently.
【当代】 dāngdài the present age; the contemporary era: 毛泽东同志是～最伟大的马克思列宁主义者。Comrade Mao Zedong was the greatest Marxist-Leninist of our time.
【当道】 dāngdào ① blocking the way: 别在～站着。Don't stand in the way. ② 〈贬〉 be in power; hold sway: 坏人～，好人受害。When evildoers are in power, good people suffer.
【当地】 dāngdì at the place in question; in the locality; local: ～贫下中农 the poor and lower-middle peasants of the locality/～人民 local people/ ～时间 local time
【当归】 dāngguī 〈中药〉 Chinese angelica
【当机立断】 dāng jī lì duàn decide promptly and opportunely; make a prompt decision
【当即】 dāngjí at once; right away: ～表示同意 give one's consent right away
【当家】 dāngjiā manage (household) affairs: 她是队里的好～。She does a good job as leader of the production team. 或 She is a good manager of the brigade's affairs.
【当家的】 dāngjiāde ① 〈口〉 the head of a family ② 〈方〉 husband
【当家作主】 dāngjiā zuòzhǔ be master in one's own house; be the master of one's own affairs (或 destiny): 在我们国家里，劳动人民～。In our country the working people are the masters
【当街】 dāngjiē ① facing the street ② 〈方〉 in the street
【当今】 dāngjīn now; at present; nowadays: ～之世 in the world of today; at the present time
【当局】 dāngjú the authorities: 政府(学校)～ the government (school) authorities
【当局者迷，旁观者清】 dāngjúzhě mí, pángguānzhě qīng the spectators see the chess game better than the players; the onlooker sees most of the game
【当空】 dāngkōng high above in the sky: 明月～。A bright moon is shining in the sky.
【当口儿】 dāngkour 〈口〉 this or that very moment: 就在这～ at the very moment; just at that time
【当啷】 dānglāng 〈象〉 clank; clang
【当量】 dāngliàng 〈化〉 equivalent (weight): 电化～ electrochemical equivalent/ 克～ gram equivalent ◇ ～比例定律 the law of equivalent proportions/ ～浓度 equivalent concentration
【当令】 dānglìng in season: 现在是伏天，西瓜正～。These are the dog days; watermelons are just in season.
【当面】 dāngmiàn to sb.'s face; in sb.'s presence: ～撒谎 tell a barefaced lie/ ～弄清楚 straighten things out face to face/ ～说好话，背后下毒手 say nice things to sb.'s face, then stab him in the back/ 信是我～交给主任的。I handed

the letter to the director personally.

【当年】 dāngnián ① in those years (或 days): ～家里穷,无力抚养孩子。In those years we were too poor to bring up our children properly./ 想～，这里还没有火车呢! Well, in those days there was no railway here./ 他的精力不减～。He is as energetic as ever. ② the prime of life: 他正在～。He is in his prime.

另见 dàngnián

【当前】 dāngqián ① before one; facing one: 大敌～。A formidable enemy stands before us./ 一事～，应该先想到革命的利益。Whenever something crops up, one should first think of the interests of the revolution. ② present; current: ～的中心任务 the central task at present/ ～世界的主要倾向 the main trend in the world today/ ～利益 immediate interests/ ～的国际形势 the current (或 present) international situation

【当权】 dāngquán be in power; hold power ◇ ～派 person in power; people in authority

【当然】 dāngrán ① as it should be; only natural: 理所～。That is just as it should be. 或 That's only natural. ② without doubt; certainly; of course; to be sure: 同志有困难～要帮助。It goes without saying that we should help a comrade in difficulty. ③ natural: ～同盟军 natural ally

【当仁不让】 dāng rén bù ràng not pass on to others what one is called upon to do; not decline to shoulder a responsibility

【当时】 dāngshí then; at that time: ～我并不知道。I didn't know then.

另见 dàngshí

【当事人】 dāngshìrén ①〈法〉party (to a lawsuit); litigant ② person (或 party) concerned; interested parties

【当头】 dāngtóu ① right overhead; right on sb.'s head; head on: 烈日～照。The hot sun is shining right overhead./ 给他～一瓢冷水 pour cold water on him/ ～一棒 a head-on blow ② facing (或 confronting) one; imminent: 那时候正是国难～，爱国青年都纷纷到抗敌前线去。The country was in imminent danger, and large numbers of patriotic young people left for the front to fight the enemy.

另见 dàngtou

【当头棒喝】 dāngtóu bànghè a blow and a shout — a sharp (或 severe) warning

【当务之急】 dāng wù zhī jí a pressing matter of the moment; a task of top priority; urgent matter

【当下】 dāngxià instantly; immediately; at once: 我一听这话,～就警惕起来了。Hearing this, I was instantly on the alert.

【当先】 dāngxiān in the van; in the front ranks; at the head: 奋勇～ fight bravely in the van/ 一马～ gallop at the head — take the lead

【当心】 dāngxīn take care; be careful; look out: ～别把试管打碎了。Take care not to break the test tube./ ～别踩了庄稼。Be careful not to step on the crops./ ～!汽车来了。Look out! There's a car coming. 或 Mind that car./ ～路滑。Watch your step. The road is slippery.

【当选】 dāngxuǎn be elected: 他～为全国人大代表。He was elected a deputy to the National People's Congress.

【当政】 dāngzhèng be in power; be in office

【当之无愧】 dāng zhī wúkuì fully deserve (a title, an honour, etc.); be worthy of: 劳动英雄的称号,他～。He is worthy of the title of labour hero.

【当中】 dāngzhōng ① in the middle; in the centre: 河～水流最急。The current is swiftest in the middle of the river./ 坐在主席台～ be seated in the centre of the rostrum ② among: 工人～出现了许多技术革新能手。 Many technical innovators have emerged from among the workers.

【当众】 dāngzhòng in the presence of all; in public: ～认错 acknowledge one's mistakes in public/ ～出丑 make an exhibition of oneself

**珰** dāng 见"玎珰" dīngdāng

**裆** dāng ① crotch (of trousers) ②〈生理〉crotch

**铛** dāng 〈象〉clank; clang

另见 chēng

## dǎng

**挡** dǎng ① keep off; ward off; block: ～雨 keep off the rain; shelter one from the rain/ ～风 shelter sth. from (或 keep out) the wind/ 防护林带～住了风沙。The shelterbelt kept the sand in check./ 喝一口～～夜里的寒气。Have a drop. It'll ward off the cold of the night. ② block; get in the way of: ～路 be (或 get) in the way/ ～光 be (或 get) in the light/ 山高～不住太阳。The highest mountains can't shut out the sun./ 绝不能让私利～住了眼睛。Never be blinded by private interests. ③ fender; blind: 炉～儿 (fire) fender; fire screen/ 窗～子 window blind (或 shade) ④〈汽车〉gear: 前进(倒)～ forward (reverse) gear/ 高速(低速)～ top (bottom) gear

另见 dàng

【挡驾】 dǎngjià 〈婉〉turn away a visitor with some excuse; decline to receive a guest

【挡箭牌】 dǎngjiànpái ① shield ② excuse; pretext

【挡泥板】 dǎngníbǎn 〈汽车〉mudguard; fender

【挡土墙】 dǎngtǔqiáng 〈建〉retaining wall

**党** dǎng ① political party; party ② the Party (the Communist Party of China): 入～ join the Party/ ～的生活 Party life ③ clique; faction; gang: 死～ sworn follower ④〈书〉be partial to; take sides with: ～同伐异 defend those who belong to one's own faction and attack those who don't ⑤〈书〉kinsfolk; relatives: 父～ father's kinsfolk ⑥ (Dǎng) a surname

【党八股】 dǎngbāgǔ stereotyped Party writing; Party jargon

【党报】 dǎngbào ① party newspaper (或 organ) ② the organ of the Chinese Communist Party; the Party organ

【党代表】 dǎngdàibiǎo Party representative (a political worker of the Chinese Communist Party in the Red Army before 1929) ◇ ～制 the system of Party representatives

【党的基本路线】 Dǎng de jīběn lùxiàn the Party's basic line for the entire historical period of socialism (formulated by Chairman Mao in 1962 as follows: Socialist society covers a considerably long historical period. In the historical period of socialism, there are still classes, class contradictions and class struggle, there is the struggle between the socialist road and the capitalist road, and there is the danger of capitalist restoration. We must recognize the protracted and complex nature of this struggle. We must heighten our vigilance. We must conduct socialist education. We must correctly understand and handle class contradictions and class struggle, distinguish the contradictions between ourselves and the enemy from those among the people and handle them correctly. Otherwise a socialist country like ours will turn into its opposite and degenerate, and a capitalist restoration will take place.)

【党费】 dǎngfèi party membership dues

【党纲】 dǎnggāng party programme

【党籍】 dǎngjí party membership: 开除～ expel from the

party
【党纪】 dǎngjì party discipline
【党课】 dǎngkè Party class; Party lecture: 听(讲)～ attend (give) a Party lecture
【党魁】 dǎngkuí 〈贬〉 party chieftain (或 chief, boss)
【党龄】 dǎnglíng party standing: 多年～的老党员 a Communist Party member of many years' standing
【党内】 dǎngnèi within (或 inside) the party; inner-party ◇ ～两条路线斗争 inner-Party struggle between two lines; two-line struggle within the Party/ ～民主 democracy within the Party; inner-Party democracy/ ～走资本主义道路的当权派 those in power within the Party taking the capitalist road; capitalist-roaders within the Party
【党派】 dǎngpài political parties and groups; party groupings: ～关系 party affiliation
【党旗】 dǎngqí party flag
【党参】 dǎngshēn 〈中药〉 *dangshen (Codonopsis pilosula)*
【党同伐异】 dǎng tóng fá yì defend those who belong to one's own faction and attack those who don't; be narrowly partisan
【党徒】 dǎngtú 〈贬〉 ① member of a clique or a reactionary political party ② henchman
【党团】 dǎng-tuán ① political parties and other organizations ② the Chinese Communist Party and the Chinese Communist Youth League; the Party and the League: ～员 Party and League members ③〔多用于外国议会〕: 议会～ parliamentary group of a political party
【党外】 dǎngwài outside the party ◇ ～人士 non-Party personages
【党委】 dǎngwěi Party committee ◇ ～制 the Party committee system (a system for ensuring collective leadership in the Party)
【党务】 dǎngwù party work; party affairs
【党小组】 dǎng-xiǎozǔ Party group (a small group under a branch committee in the Party)
【党校】 dǎngxiào Party school
【党性】 dǎngxìng Party spirit; Party character: ～不纯的表现 a sign of impurity in Party spirit
【党羽】 dǎngyǔ 〈贬〉 members of a clique; adherents; henchmen
【党员】 dǎngyuán party member ◇ ～大会 general membership meeting of a party organization; meeting of all party members
【党章】 dǎngzhāng party constitution
【党证】 dǎngzhèng party card
【党支部】 dǎng-zhībù Party branch ◇ ～书记 Party branch secretary
【党中央】 Dǎng-zhōngyāng the Party Central Committee; the central leading body of the Party
【党总支】 dǎng-zǒngzhī general Party branch
【党组】 dǎngzǔ leading Party group (in a state organ or people's organization)

**谠** dǎng (of advice or comment) honest; unbiased

## dàng

**当** dàng ① proper; right: 用词不～ inappropriate choice of words ② match; equal to: 他一个人能～两个人用。He can do the work of two persons put together. ③ treat as; regard as; take for: 不要把支流～主流。Don't take minor aspects for major ones. ④ think: 我～你不知道。I thought you didn't know. ⑤ that very (day, etc.): ～月 the same month; that very month ⑥ pawn: ～衣服 pawn one's clothes; put one's clothes in pawn ⑦ sth. pawned; pawn; pledge: 赎～ take sth. out of pledge; redeem sth. pawned
另见 dāng
【当年】 dàngnián the same year; that very year: 这个水库一修成,～就受益。The reservoir provided benefits the same year it was completed.
另见 dāngnián
【当票】 dàngpiào pawn ticket
【当铺】 dàngpù pawnshop ◇ ～老板 pawnbroker
【当日】 dàngrì the same day; that very day: ～有效 good for the date of issue only
【当时】 dàngshí right away; at once; immediately: 他一接到电报，～就赶回去了。He hurried back the moment he received the telegram.
另见 dāngshí
【当天】 dàngtiān the same day; that very day: 你可以～来回。 You can go and come back on the same day./ ～的事～做完。Today's work must be done today.
【当头】 dàngtou 〈口〉 sth. pawned; pawn; pledge
另见 dāngtóu
【当真】 dàngzhēn ① take seriously: 我只是开个玩笑，何必～呢？I was only joking. Why take it seriously? ② really true; really: 这话～？Is it really true?/ 他说要来，～来了。He said he would come and, sure enough, he did.
【当做】 dàngzuò treat as; regard as; look upon as: 农奴主把农奴～会说话的牲口。Serf owners regarded their serfs as animals that could talk./ 我们把雷锋～学习的榜样。We take Lei Feng as our model./ 退休老工人把教育下一代～自己应尽的责任。The retired workers regard it as their duty to educate the younger generation./ 白求恩把中国人民的解放事业～他自己的事业。Norman Bethune adopted the cause of the Chinese people's liberation as his own.

**宕** dàng 〈书〉 delay: 延～ procrastinate; put off

**荡** dàng ① swing; sway; wave: ～秋千 play on a swing/ ～桨 pull on the oars ② loaf: 游～ loaf about ③ rinse: 冲～ rinse out; wash away ④ clear away; sweep off: 扫～ mopping up; mopping-up operation/ ～平 wipe out; quell; stamp out ⑤ loose in morals: 放～ dissolute; dissipated/ 淫～ lustful; lascivious ⑥ shallow lake; marsh; 芦苇～ a reed marsh
【荡船】 dàngchuán swingboat
【荡涤】 dàngdí cleanse; clean up; wash away: ～旧社会遗留下来的污泥浊水 clean up the filth and mire left over from the old society
【荡然无存】 dàngrán wú cún 〈书〉 all gone; nothing left
【荡漾】 dàngyàng ripple; undulate: 湖水～。There were ripples on the lake./ 歌声～。The song rose and fell like waves./ 金黄的小麦在微风中～。The golden wheat rippled in the breeze.

**挡** dàng 见"摒挡" bìngdàng
另见 dǎng

**档** dàng ① shelves (for files); pigeonholes: 把文件归～ file a document; place a document on file ② files; archives: 查～ consult the files ③ crosspiece (of a table, etc.) ④ grade: 高(低)～商品 high-grade (low-grade) goods
【档案】 dàng'àn files; archives; record; dossier ◇ ～馆 archives/ ～管理员 archivist/～柜 filing cabinet

**菪** dàng 见"莨菪" làngdàng

## dāo

**刀** dāo ①knife; sword ②sth. shaped like a knife: 冰～ ice skates ③〈量〉one hundred sheets (of paper)

【刀把子】dāobàzi ①(sword) hilt ②military power; power: 旧社会劳动人民受压迫就是因为没有掌握～、印把子。It was because they had neither arms nor power that the working people were oppressed in the old society. ③sth. that may be used against one; a handle

【刀背】dāobèi the back of a knife blade

【刀笔】dāobǐ writing of indictments, appeals, etc.; pettifoggery ◇～吏 petty official who draws up indictments, etc.; pettifogger

【刀兵】dāobīng ①weapons; arms ②fighting; war: 动～ resort to arms; resort to force

【刀叉】dāo-chā knife and fork

【刀豆】dāodòu sword bean

【刀锋】dāofēng the point or edge of a knife

【刀耕火种】dāogēng-huǒzhòng slash-and-burn cultivation

【刀光剑影】dāoguāng-jiànyǐng the glint and flash of cold steel

【刀架】dāojià 〈机〉tool carrier; tool carriage

【刀具】dāojù 〈机〉cutting tool; tool

【刀口】dāokǒu ①the edge of a knife ②where a thing can be put to best use; the crucial point; the right spot: 把劲儿使在～上 bring efforts to bear on the right spot/ 钱要花在～上。Use your money where it's needed most. ③cut; incision

【刀片】dāopiàn ①razor blade ②〈机〉(tool) bit; blade

【刀枪】dāo-qiāng sword and spear; weapons: 拿起笔作～ take up one's pen as a weapon/ ～入库，马放南山 put the weapons back in the arsenal and graze the war horses on the hillside — relax vigilance against war

【刀鞘】dāoqiào sheath; scabbard

【刀刃】dāorèn ①the edge of a knife ②where a thing can be put to best use; the crucial point: 好钢用在～上 use the best steel to make the knife's edge — use resources, etc., where they are needed most

【刀山火海】dāoshān-huǒhǎi a mountain of swords and a sea of flames; most dangerous places; most severe trials: 为革命～也敢闯 dare to climb a mountain of swords or plunge into a sea of flames for the sake of the revolution; be ready to undergo the most severe trials for the revolution

【刀子】dāozi 〈口〉small knife; pocketknife

【刀俎】dāozǔ 〈书〉butcher's knife and chopping block

**叨** dāo
另见 tāo

【叨唠】dāolao talk on and on; chatter away: 他～了半天，人都不爱听。He chattered for a long time and bored everybody. 又作"叨叨"

**氘** dāo 〈化〉deuterium ($H^2$ 或 D)

【氘核】dāohé deuteron

## dǎo

**导** dǎo ①lead; guide: ～淮入海 channel the Huaihe River into the sea ②transmit; conduct: ～电 transmit electric current; conduct electricity ③instruct; teach; give guidance to: 教～ teach; instruct

【导弹】dǎodàn guided missile ◇～发射场 missile (launching) site; launching site/ ～发射井 launching silo/ ～发射器 missile launcher/ ～发射台 (missile) launching pad/ ～核潜艇 nuclear submarine armed with guided missiles/ ～基地 missile base/ ～驱逐舰 guided missile destroyer/ ～巡洋舰 guided missile cruiser

【导电】dǎodiàn electric conduction ◇～性 electric conductivity

【导风板】dǎofēngbǎn 〈航空〉baffle

【导管】dǎoguǎn ①〈机〉conduit; pipe; duct: 冷却～ cooling duct/ 金属～ metal conduit ②〈生〉vessel; duct

【导轨】dǎoguǐ 〈机〉slideway; guide: 刀架～ tool guide ◇～磨床 slideway grinder

【导航】dǎoháng navigation: 无线电(雷达，天文)～ radio (radar, celestial) navigation ◇～台 guidance station; nondirection radio beacon (NDB)

【导火索】dǎohuǒsuǒ 〈军〉(blasting) fuse

【导火线】dǎohuǒxiàn ①(blasting) fuse ②a small incident that touches off a big one: 战争的～ an incident that touches off a war

【导流】dǎoliú 〈水〉diversion ◇～隧洞 diversion tunnel

【导轮】dǎolún 〈机〉guide pulley; pilot wheel

【导尿】dǎoniào 〈医〉catheterization

【导盘】dǎopán 〈化纤〉godet

【导热】dǎorè 〈物〉heat conduction ◇～系数 thermal conductivity

【导师】dǎoshī ①tutor; teacher ②guide of a great cause; teacher: 无产阶级的伟大～ great teacher of the proletariat

【导数】dǎoshù 〈数〉derivative

【导体】dǎotǐ 〈物〉conductor: 非～ nonconductor/ 超～ superconductor

【导线】dǎoxiàn 〈电〉lead; (conducting) wire: 玻璃纤维～ fibreglass wire ◇～管 conduit

【导言】dǎoyán introduction (to a piece of writing); introductory remarks

【导演】dǎoyǎn ①direct (a film, play, etc.) ②director

【导游】dǎoyóu ①conduct a sightseeing tour ②guidebook ◇～图 tourist map

【导源】dǎoyuán ①(of a river) have its source: 黄河～于青海。The Huanghe River rises in Qinghai Province. ②originate; derive: 认识～于实践。Knowledge derives from practice.

【导致】dǎozhì lead to; bring about; result in; cause: 阶级斗争必然要～无产阶级专政。The class struggle necessarily leads to the dictatorship of the proletariat.

**岛** dǎo island

【岛国】dǎoguó country consisting of one or more islands; island country

【岛屿】dǎoyǔ islands and islets; islands

**倒** dǎo ①fall; topple: 摔～ fall over/ 风把树刮～了。The gale uprooted the tree./ 我～在床上就睡着了。I threw myself down on the bed and fell asleep immediately./ 一个英雄～下去，千百个英雄站起来。One hero falls, a thousand rise./ 一边～ lean to one side ②collapse; fail: 内阁～了。The cabinet collapsed. ③close down; go bankrupt; go out of business ④(of voice) become hoarse: 他的嗓子～了。He has lost his voice. ⑤change; exchange: ～车 change trains or buses/ ～肩 shift a burden from one shoulder to the other/ 请你们两位把座位～一下。Will you two please swop (或 change) seats? ⑥move around: 地方太小，～不开身。There is no room to move around.
另见 dào

【倒把】 dǎobǎ engage in profiteering; speculate
【倒班】 dǎobān change shifts; work in shifts; work by turns: 昼夜～ work in shifts round the clock
【倒闭】 dǎobì close down; go bankrupt; go into liquidation: 企业～ bankruptcy of an enterprise
【倒仓】 dǎocāng ① take grain out of a granary to sun it ② transfer grain from one granary to another
【倒茬】 dǎochá 〈农〉 rotation of crops
【倒伏】 dǎofú (of crops) lodging: 抗～力强的稻种 a strain of rice with strong resistance to lodging
【倒戈】 dǎogē change sides in a war; turn one's coat; transfer one's allegiance
【倒换】 dǎohuàn ① rotate; take turns: 几种作物～着种 rotate several crops/ ～着看护伤员 take turns looking after the wounded ② rearrange (sequence, order, etc.); replace
【倒卖】 dǎomài resell at a profit
【倒霉】 dǎoméi have bad luck; be out of luck; be down on one's luck: 真～,赶到车站车刚开走。What lousy luck! When I reached the station, the train had just left. 又作"倒楣"
【倒嗓】 dǎosǎng (of a singer) lose one's voice
【倒手】 dǎoshǒu (of merchandise, etc.) change hands
【倒塌】 dǎotā collapse; topple down
【倒台】 dǎotái fall from power; downfall
【倒头】 dǎotóu touch the pillow; lie down: ～就睡 tumble into bed
【倒胃口】 dǎo wèikou spoil one's appetite
【倒牙】 dǎoyá 〈方〉 set (或 put) one's teeth on edge
【倒运】 dǎoyùn ① profiteer by buying cheap and selling dear ② 〈方〉 be unlucky; be out of luck

**捣** dǎo ① pound with a pestle, etc.; beat; smash: ～药 pound medicine in a mortar/ ～米 husk rice with a pestle and mortar/ ～衣 beat clothes (in washing)/ 直～匪巢 drive straight on to the bandits' den ② harass; disturb
【捣蛋】 dǎodàn make trouble: 调皮～ be mischievous
【捣固】 dǎogù make firm by ramming or tamping
【捣鬼】 dǎoguǐ play tricks; do mischief
【捣毁】 dǎohuǐ smash up; demolish; destroy: ～敌军据点 destroy enemy strongpoints
【捣乱】 dǎoluàn make trouble; create a disturbance: 叔叔忙着呢,你别～。Uncle's busy. Don't disturb him./ 不管什么地方出现反革命分子～,就应当坚决消灭他。Counterrevolutionaries must be rooted out with a firm hand wherever they are found making trouble. ◇ ～分子 trouble-maker
【捣碎】 dǎosuì pound to pieces

**祷** dǎo ① pray ② 〔旧时书信用语〕 ask earnestly; beg
【祷告】 dǎogào pray; say one's prayers

**蹈** dǎo ① 〈书〉 tread; step: 赴汤～火 go through fire and water—defy all difficulties and dangers/ 循规～矩 not step out of bounds; toe the line; stick to convention ② skip; trip: 舞～ dance
【蹈常袭故】 dǎocháng-xígù go on in the same old way; get into a rut
【蹈袭】 dǎoxí follow slavishly: ～前人 slavishly follow one's predecessors

## dào

**到** dào ① arrive; reach: 火车～站了。The train has arrived at the station./ ～了多少人? How many people were present?/ ～! (点名时的回答) Here! ② go to; leave for: ～兰州去 go to Lanzhou/ ～群众中去 go among the masses; go into the midst of the masses ③ up until; up to: 从星期三～星期五 from Wednesday to Friday/ ～目前为止 up to the present; until now; so far ④〔用作动词的补语,表示动作有结果〕: 办得～ can be done/ 说～做～ be as good as one's word/ 想不～你来了。I didn't expect you would come. ⑤ thoughtful; considerate: 不～之处请原谅。Please excuse me if I have been inconsiderate in any way.
【到岸价格】 dào'àn jiàgé cost, insurance and freight (C.I.F.)
【到场】 dàochǎng be present; show up; turn up
【到处】 dàochù at all places; everywhere: 侵略者～挨打。The invaders were attacked wherever they went./ 烟头不要～乱扔。Don't drop cigarette ends about.
【到达】 dàodá arrive; get to; reach: 代表团于今晨～广州。The delegation arrived in Guangzhou this morning. ◇ ～港 port of arrival/ ～站 destination
【到底】 dàodǐ ① to the end; to the finish: 将革命进行～。Carry the revolution through to the end./ 打～ fight to the finish ② 〈副〉 at last; in the end; finally: 新方法～试验成功了。The new method has finally proved to be a success. ③ 〈副〉 〔用于问句,加强语气〕: 你～是什么意思? What on earth do you mean? ④ 〈副〉 after all; in the final analysis: 他～是新手,干活还不熟练。After all, he's new to the work and isn't very skilful at it yet.
【到顶】 dàodǐng reach the summit (或 peak, limit); cannot be improved: 增产～的想法是错误的。The idea that production has reached its peak and can't go any higher is wrong.
【到会】 dàohuì be present at a meeting; attend a meeting: ～人数很多。There was a large attendance.
【到家】 dàojiā reach a very high level; be perfect; be excellent: 把思想工作做～ do ideological work really well/ 这活儿做得很～。This is excellent workmanship./ 他这笔字写得还不～。His calligraphy is far from perfect.
【到来】 dàolái arrival; advent: 迎接革命新高潮的～ hail the arrival of a new high tide of the revolution/ 一个社会主义的文化建设高潮正在～。A new high tide in the development of socialist culture is in the offing.
【到期】 dàoqī become due; mature; expire: 这本书已经～了。This book is due for return./ 这张票据什么时候～? When does this bill mature (或 become due)?/ 签证下月～。The visa expires next month. ◇ ～日 date due
【到手】 dàoshǒu in one's hands; in one's possession: 眼看就要～的粮食,决不能让洪水冲走。The grain is nearly in our hands. We mustn't allow the flood to carry it away.
【到头】 dàotóu to the end; at an end: 这条街走～就有一个邮局。There's a post office at the end of the street.
【到头来】 dàotóulai 〈副〉 in the end; finally: 不老实的人～总是要栽跟头的。Dishonest people are bound to come a cropper in the end.
【到职】 dàozhí take office; arrive at one's post

**倒** dào ① upside down; inverted; inverse; reverse: 次序～了。The order is reversed./ 小孩把画挂～了。The child hung the picture upside down. ② move backward; turn upside down: 火车～回去了。The train backed up. ③ pour; tip: ～一杯茶 pour a cup of tea/ ～垃圾 tip (或 dump) rubbish/ 他把一肚子冤屈都～了出来。He poured out all his grievances. ④ 〈副〉 ⓐ〔表示跟意料相反〕: 本想省事,没想～费事了。We wanted to save ourselves trouble but actually we gave ourselves more./ 你还有什么要说的,

我～要听听。I'd like to hear what else you've got to say. ⓑ〔表示事情不是那样〕：你说得～容易，做起来可不容易。It's easy for you to say that, but it's not so easy to do it. 或 That's easier said than done. ⓒ〔表示让步〕：我跟他认识～认识，就是不太熟。I know him, but not very well. ⓓ〔表示催促或追问〕：你～去不去呀！Do you want to go or don't you?
另见 dǎo
【倒背如流】 dào bèi rú liú can even recite sth. backwards fluently — know sth. thoroughly by heart
【倒背手】 dàobèishǒu with one's hands behind one
【倒彩】 dàocǎi booing; hooting; catcall: 喝～ make catcalls; boo and hoot
【倒车】 dàochē back a car: 开历史～ turn back the wheel of history; put the clock back
【倒刺】 dàocì hangnail; agnail
【倒打一耙】 dào dǎ yī pá make unfounded countercharges; put the blame on one's victim; recriminate: 他自己错了不承认，反而～。So far from admitting his own mistake, he falsely accused his critic.
【倒挡】 dàodǎng reverse gear
【倒飞】 dàofēi 〈航空〉 inverted (或 upside down) flight
【倒粪】 dàofèn turn over a heap of manure or a compost heap and pile it up afresh
【倒挂金钟】 dàoguàjīnzhōng 〈植〉 fuchsia
【倒好儿】 dàohǎor booing; hooting; catcall: 叫～ make catcalls; boo and hoot
【倒睫】 dàojié 〈医〉 trichiasis
【倒立】 dàolì ① stand upside down: 宝塔的影子～在水里。The pagoda is reflected upside down in the water. ② 〈体〉 handstand
【倒流】 dàoliú flow backwards: 防止商品运输上的～ avoid transporting goods back to their place of origin
【倒片】 dàopiàn 〈电影〉 rewind ◇ ～机 rewinder
【倒摄遗忘】 dàoshè yíwàng 〈心〉 retroactive (或 retrograde) amnesia
【倒收付息】 dàoshōu fùxī 〈经〉 negative interest
【倒数】 dàoshǔ count backwards: ～第三行 the third line from the bottom/ 我住在这条胡同里～第二家。I live in the last house but one in this lane.
【倒数】 dàoshù 〈数〉 reciprocal
【倒算】 dàosuàn seize back confiscated property 参见"反攻倒算" fǎngōng-dàosuàn
【倒退】 dàotuì go backwards; fall back: 坚持进步，反对～ persist in progress and oppose retrogression
【倒象】 dàoxiàng 〈物〉 inverted image
【倒行逆施】 dàoxíng-nìshī ① go against the historical trend; try to put the clock back; push a reactionary policy ② perverse acts: 国民党反动派的～从反面教育了人民。The perverse acts of the KMT reactionaries taught the people by negative example.
【倒叙】 dàoxù flashback
【倒悬】 dàoxuán 〈书〉 hang by the feet — be in sore straits
【倒因为果】 dào yīn wéi guǒ reverse cause and effect; take cause for effect
【倒影】 dàoyǐng inverted image; inverted reflection in water
【倒栽葱】 dàozāicōng fall head over heels; fall headlong: 敌机被击中，一个～掉到海里了。The enemy plane was hit and fell headlong into the sea.
【倒置】 dàozhì place upside down; invert: 轻重～ place the unimportant before the important
【倒转】 dàozhuǎn ① turn the other way round; reverse: ～来说，也是这样。The same is true the other way round. ② 〈方〉 contrary to reason or one's expectation: 你把事情搞糟了，～来怪我。You messed up the whole thing yourself and now you put the blame on me.
【倒装词序】 dàozhuāngcíxù 〈语〉 inverted word order

**悼** dào mourn; grieve: 哀～死者 mourn for the dead
【悼词】 dàocí memorial speech
【悼念】 dàoniàn mourn; grieve over: 沉痛～ mourn with deep grief

**盗** dào ① steal; rob ② thief; robber
【盗匪】 dàofěi bandits; robbers: 肃清～ exterminate banditry
【盗汗】 dàohàn 〈医〉 night sweat
【盗卖】 dàomài steal and sell (public property)
【盗墓】 dàomù rob a tomb (或 grave) ◇ ～人 grave robber
【盗窃】 dàoqiè steal: ～国家机密 steal state secrets ◇ ～犯 thief/ ～罪 〈法〉 larceny
【盗取】 dàoqǔ steal; embezzle
【盗用】 dàoyòng embezzle; usurp: ～公款 embezzle public funds/ ～名义 usurp a name
【盗贼】 dàozéi robbers; bandits

**道** dào ① road; way; path: 山间小～ a mountain path ② channel; course: 黄河改～ change of course of the Huanghe River ③ way; method: 养生之～ the way to keep fit/ 以其人之～，还治其人之身 deal with a man as he deals with you; pay sb. back in his own coin ④ doctrine; principle: 批判孔孟之～ criticize the doctrines of Confucius and Mencius ⑤ Taoism; Taoist: ～观 a Taoist temple/ 老～ a Taoist priest ⑥ superstitious sect: 会～门 superstitious sects and secret societies ⑦ line: 画一条斜～儿 draw a slanting line ⑧ 〈量〉 ⓐ〔用于某些长条的东西〕：一～河 a river/ 万～金光 myriads of golden rays/ 一～缝儿 a crack ⓑ〔用于门、墙等〕：两～门 two successive doors/ 三～防线 three lines of defence ⓒ〔用于命令、题目等〕：一～命令 an order/ 出五～题 set five questions (for an examination, etc.) ⓓ〔表示"次"〕：上四～菜 serve four courses/ 省一～手续 save one step in the process ⑨ say; talk; speak: 能说会～ have a glib tongue; have the gift of the gab/ 常言～ as the saying goes ⑩ think; suppose: 我～是老周呢，原来是你。So it's you! I thought it was Lao Zhou.
【道白】 dàobái spoken parts in an opera
【道班】 dàobān railway or highway maintenance squad
【道不拾遗】 dào bù shí yí no one pockets anything found on the road — honesty prevails throughout society
【道岔】 dàochà 〈铁道〉 switch; points
【道场】 dàochǎng ① Taoist or Buddhist rites (performed to save the souls of the dead) ② place where such rites are performed
【道床】 dàochuáng 〈铁道〉 roadbed: 整体～ monolithic roadbed
【道道儿】 dàodaor 〈方〉 way; method: 找到增产的新～ find new ways of increasing production/ 说出个～来 give a convincing explanation
【道德】 dàodé morals; morality; ethics: ～品质 moral character/ 旧～观念 old moral concepts/ 共产主义～ communist morality (或 ethics)/ 体育～ sportsmanship/ ～败坏 degenerate/ 永恒的、超阶级的～是根本不存在的。There is no such thing as eternal morality transcending classes.
【道地】 dàodì 〈方〉 见"地道" dìdao①
【道钉】 dàodīng 〈铁道〉 (dog) spike
【道姑】 dàogū Taoist nun
【道贺】 dàohè congratulate
【道家】 Dàojiā Taoist school (a school of thought in the Spring and Autumn and Warring States Periods, 770-221

B.C.); Taoists
【道教】 Dàojiào 〈宗〉Taoism (one of the chief religions in old China)
【道具】 dàojù 〈剧〉stage property; prop
【道口】 dàokǒu ① road junction ② level crossing
【道理】 dàoli ① principle; truth; hows and whys: 讲解深耕细作的～ explain the principles of deep ploughing and intensive cultivation/ 言语不多～深。The words were few, but they contained profound truth. ② reason; argument; sense: 你的话很有～。What you said is quite reasonable (或 right)./ 讲不出一点～ unable to come up with any convincing argument; unable to justify oneself in any way
【道林纸】 dàolínzhǐ glazed printing paper
【道路】 dàolù road; way; path: ～泥泞。The road is muddy./ 社会主义同资本主义两条～的斗争 the struggle between the socialist road and the capitalist road/ 走前人没有走过的～ break paths none have explored before/ 为两国首脑会谈铺平～ pave the way for summit talks between the two countries
【道貌岸然】 dàomào ànrán pose as a person of high morals; be sanctimonious
【道木】 dàomù 〈铁道〉sleeper
【道破】 dàopò point out frankly; lay bare; reveal: 一语～其中奥秘 lay bare its secret with one remark
【道歉】 dàoqiàn apologize; make an apology
【道情】 dàoqíng 〈曲艺〉chanting folk tales to the accompaniment of simple percussion instruments
【道人】 dàoren a respectful form of address for a Taoist priest
【道士】 dàoshi Taoist priest
【道听途说】 dàotīng-túshuō hearsay; rumour; gossip
【道统】 dàotǒng Confucian orthodoxy
【道喜】 dàoxǐ congratulate sb. on a happy occasion
【道谢】 dàoxiè express one's thanks; thank
【道学】 dàoxué ① a Confucian school of philosophy of the Song Dynasty (960-1279); Neo-Confucianism ② affectedly moral: 假～ canting moralist; hypocrite ◇ ～先生 Confucian moralist
【道义】 dàoyì morality and justice: ～上的支持 moral support
【道藏】 dàozàng collected Taoist scriptures
【道砟】 dàozhǎ 〈铁道〉ballast

**稻** dào rice; paddy
【稻白叶枯病】 dàobáiyèkūbìng bacterial blight of rice
【稻苞虫】 dàobāochóng rice plant skipper
【稻草】 dàocǎo rice straw ◇ ～人 scarecrow
【稻恶苗病】 dào'èmiáobìng Bakanae disease of rice
【稻谷】 dàogǔ paddy
【稻糠】 dàokāng rice chaff
【稻壳】 dàoké rice husk (或 hull)
【稻烂秧】 dàolànyāng seedling blight of rice
【稻螟虫】 dàomíngchóng rice borer
【稻田】 dàotián (rice) paddy; rice field; paddy field ◇ ～皮炎〈医〉paddy-field dermatitis
【稻瘟病】 dàowēnbìng rice blast 又作"稻热病"
【稻纹枯病】 dàowénkūbìng sheath and culm blight of rice
【稻秧】 dàoyāng rice seedlings; rice shoots
【稻子】 dàozi 〈口〉rice; paddy
【稻纵卷叶螟】 dàozòngjuǎnyèmíng rice leaf roller

**纛** dào a big army banner used in ancient times

## dé

**得** dé ① get; obtain; gain: 取～经验 gain experience/ ～了结核病 have (或 contract) tuberculosis/ 今天的幸福生活～来不易。The happy life we have today was not easily won. ② (of a calculation) result in: 二三～六。Twice three is six. ③ fit; proper: ～用 fit for use; handy ④〈书〉satisfied; complacent: 自～ pleased with oneself; self-satisfied ⑤〈口〉be finished; be ready: 饭～了。Dinner is ready. ⑥〈口〉〔表示同意或禁止〕: ～,就这么办。All right! Just go ahead./ ～了,别再说了。That's enough. Let it go at that. ⑦〈口〉〔用于情况变坏时,表示无可奈何〕: ～,又搞错了! Look! I've got it wrong again! ⑧〔用在别的动词前,表示许可〕: 这笔钱非经批准不～动用。This fund may not be drawn on without permission.
另见 de; děi
【得便】 débiàn when it's convenient: 这几样东西,请你～捎给他。Please take these things to him whenever it's convenient.
【得不偿失】 dé bù cháng shī the loss outweighs the gain; the game is not worth the candle: 不打～的消耗战。Avoid battles of attrition in which we lose more than we gain.
【得逞】 déchěng 〈贬〉have one's way; prevail; succeed: 如果修正主义者的阴谋～,革命人民就要遭殃。If the revisionists' plot should succeed, the revolutionary people would suffer.
【得宠】 déchǒng 〈贬〉find favour with sb.; be in sb.'s good graces
【得出】 déchū reach (a conclusion); obtain (a result)
【得寸进尺】 dé cùn jìn chǐ reach out for a yard after taking an inch; give him an inch and he'll take an ell; be insatiable
【得当】 dédàng apt; appropriate; proper; suitable: 安排～ be properly arranged/ 措词～ aptly worded; appropriate wording
【得到】 dédào get; obtain; gain; receive: ～及时治疗 get timely medical treatment/ ～群众的支持 enjoy the support of the masses/ 退休工人～很好的照顾。Retired workers are all well provided for.
【得道多助,失道寡助】 dé dào duō zhù, shī dào guǎ zhù a just cause enjoys abundant support while an unjust cause finds little support
【得法】 défǎ do sth. in the proper way; get the knack: 管理～ be properly managed/ 讲授不甚～ not teach in the right (或 proper) way
【得分】 défēn score: 客队的六号～最多。Player No. 6 of the visiting team scored the most points./ 连得四分 win four points in a row
【得过且过】 dé guò qiě guò muddle along; drift along
【得计】 déjì succeed in one's scheme: 自以为～ think oneself clever
【得奖】 déjiǎng win (或 be awarded) a prize ◇ ～人 prizewinner/ ～单位 prizewinning unit
【得劲】 déjìn ① feel well: 他这几天身体不大～。He hasn't been feeling well for the last few days. ② fit for use; handy: 这把锹我用起来很～。This spade is just right for me.
【得空】 dékòng have leisure; be free: 老想来看你,总不～。I've been meaning to come and see you but haven't had the time.
【得力】 délì ① benefit from; get help from: ～于平时勤学苦练 profit from diligent study and practice/ 我得他的力很不小。I benefited a lot from his help. ② capable; competent: ～助手 capable assistant; right-hand man/ ～干部 competent cadre/ 办事～ do things efficiently
【得陇望蜀】 dé Lǒng wàng Shǔ covet Sichuan after capturing Gansu — have insatiable desires

【得气】 déqì 〈中医〉bring about the desired sensation (in acupuncture treatment)
【得胜】 déshèng win a victory; triumph: ～归来 return in triumph; return with flying colours
【得失】 dé-shī ① gain and loss; success and failure: ～相当 gains and losses balance each other; break even/ 从不计较个人～ never give a thought to personal gain or loss ② advantages and disadvantages; merits and demerits: 两种办法各有～。Each of the two methods has its advantages and disadvantages.
【得势】 déshì ① be in power ② get the upper hand; be in the ascendant
【得手】 déshǒu go smoothly; come off; do fine; succeed: 歼敌左翼，～后，迅速扩大战果 wipe out the enemy's left flank and, this accomplished, swiftly exploit the victory
【得体】 détǐ befitting one's position or suited to the occasion; appropriate: 讲话～ speak in appropriate terms
【得天独厚】 dé tiān dú hòu be richly endowed by nature; abound in gifts of nature; enjoy exceptional advantages
【得悉】 déxī hear of; learn about: ～病体康复，不胜欣慰。I rejoice to hear of your recovery.
【得闲】 déxián have leisure; be at leisure
【得心应手】 déxīn-yìngshǒu ① with facility; with high proficiency ② serviceable; handy
【得宜】 déyí proper; appropriate; suitable: 措置～ handle properly
【得以】 déyǐ so that... can (或 may)...: 放手发动群众，让群众的意见～充分发表出来 boldly mobilize the masses so that they can fully express their opinions
【得益】 déyì benefit; profit: 读者的意见使他～不少。He benefits considerably from the readers' comments.
【得意】 déyì proud of oneself; pleased with oneself; complacent: ～扬扬 be immensely proud; look triumphant
【得意忘形】 déyì wàngxíng get dizzy with success; have one's head turned by success
【得鱼忘筌】 dé yú wàng quán forget the trap as soon as the fish is caught; forget the means by which the end is attained; forget the things or conditions which bring one success
【得志】 dézhì achieve one's ambition; have a successful career: 少年～ enjoy success when young/ 小人～ villains holding sway
【得罪】 dézuì offend; displease: 不怕～人 not be afraid of giving offence

**锝** dé technetium (Tc)

**德** dé ① virtue; morals; moral character: 品～ moral character ② heart; mind: 同心同～ be of one heart and one mind ③ kindness; favour: 以怨报～ return evil for good; repay kindness with ingratitude; bite the hand that feeds you
【德才兼备】 dé-cái jiānbèi have both ability and political integrity
【德高望重】 dégāo-wàngzhòng be of noble character and high prestige; enjoy high prestige and command universal respect
【德国】 Déguó Germany ◇ ～人 German
【德行】 déxíng moral integrity; moral conduct
【德行】 déxing 〈方〉disgusting; shameful: 那个家伙真～。That fellow is really disgusting.
【德语】 Déyǔ German (language)
【德育】 déyù moral education
【德政】 dézhèng benevolent rule
【德治】 dézhì rule of virtue

## de

**地** de 〔用在状语的后面〕: 实事求是～处理问题 handle problems in a practical and realistic way/ 天渐渐～冷了。The weather is getting cold.
另见 dì

**的** de ①〔用在定语的后面〕: 铁～纪律 iron discipline/ 已经站起来～中国人民 the Chinese people who have stood up/ 我～母亲 my mother/ 无产阶级～政党 a party of the proletariat ②〔用来造成没有中心词的"的"字结构〕: 赶大车～ a carter/ 我爱吃辣～。I like hot (或 peppery) food./ 菊花开了，有红～，有黄～。The chrysanthemums are in bloom; some are red and some yellow./ 他说他～，我干我～。Let him say what he likes; I'll just get on with my work./ 火车上看书～看书，聊天～聊天。On the train some people were reading and some were chatting. ③〔用在谓语动词后面，强调动作的施事者、时间、地点等〕: 是我打～稿子，他上～色。I made the sketch; he filled in the colours./ 他是昨天进～城。He went to town yesterday./ 我是在车站打～票。I bought the ticket at the station. ④〔用在陈述句末尾，表示肯定的语气〕: 你们这两天真够辛苦～。You've really been working hard the past few days. ⑤〈口〉〔用在两个数量词中间，表示相乘或相加〕: 这间屋子是五米～三米，合十五平方米。This room is five metres by three, or fifteen square metres.
另见 dí; dì
【的话】 dehuà 〈助〉〔用在表示假设的分句后面，引起下文〕: 如果你有事～，就不要来了。Don't come if you're busy.

**得** de ①〔用在动词后面，表示能够或可以〕: 咱们可粗心不～。We can't afford to be careless./ 她去～，我为什么去不～? If she can go, why can't I? ②〔用在动词和补语中间，表示可能〕: 我拿～动。I can carry it./ 那办～到。That can be done. ③〔用在动词或形容词后面，连接表示程度或结果的补语〕: 写～非常好 very well written/ 唱～不好 not sing well/ 冷～打哆嗦 shiver with cold/ 笑～肚子痛 laugh till one's sides split
另见 dé; děi

## děi

**得** děi 〈口〉① need: 这个工程～三个月才能完。This project will take three months to complete. ② must; have to: 有错误就～批评。Wherever mistakes occur, they must be criticized. ③〔表示揣测的必然〕: 要不快走，我们就～迟到了。We'll be late if we don't hurry.
另见 dé; de

## dèn

**扽** dèn pull with sharp tugs; yank

## dēng

**灯** dēng ① lamp; lantern; light: 煤油～ kerosene lamp/ 电～ electric light/ 宫～ palace lantern ② valve; tube: 五～收音机 a five-valve radio set ③ burner: 酒精～ alcohol burner; spirit lamp
【灯彩】 dēngcǎi ① coloured-lantern making ② coloured lanterns (formerly used on the stage)

【灯草】 dēngcǎo rush (used as lampwick)
【灯船】 dēngchuán lightship; light vessel
【灯光】 dēngguāng ① the light of a lamp; lamplight ② (stage) lighting: ～渐暗 lights slowly dim; lights fade to dark/ 舞台～ stage lights; lighting ◇ ～球场 floodlit (或 illuminated) court, field, etc.
【灯红酒绿】 dēnghóng-jiǔlǜ red lanterns and green wine — scene of debauchery
【灯花】 dēnghuā snuff (of a candlewick)
【灯火】 dēnghuǒ lights: ～辉煌 brilliantly illuminated; ablaze with lights ◇ ～管制 blackout
【灯节】 Dēngjié the Lantern Festival (15th of the first lunar month)
【灯具】 dēngjù lamps and lanterns
【灯笼】 dēnglong lantern
【灯笼裤】 dēnglongkù knee-length or ankle-length sports trousers; knickerbockers
【灯谜】 dēngmí riddles written on lanterns; lantern riddles
【灯泡】 dēngpào 〈口〉(electric) bulb; light bulb: 螺口(卡口)～ screw (bayonet) socket bulb/ 乳白～ opal bulb
【灯丝】 dēngsī filament (in a light bulb or valve)
【灯塔】 dēngtǎ lighthouse; beacon
【灯台】 dēngtái lampstand
【灯头】 dēngtóu ① lamp holder; electric light socket: 螺口～ screw socket/ 开关～ switch socket ② a holder for the wick and chimney of a kerosene lamp
【灯心】 dēngxīn lampwick; wick
【灯心草】 dēngxīncǎo 〈植〉 rush
【灯心绒】 dēngxīnróng 〈纺〉 corduroy
【灯油】 dēngyóu lamp-oil; kerosene; paraffin oil
【灯语】 dēngyǔ lamp signal
【灯罩】 dēngzhào (电灯) lampshade; (油灯) lamp-chimney

**登** dēng ① ascend; mount; scale (a height): ～岸 go ashore/ ～上讲台 mount the platform/ ～上峰顶 reach the summit/ 在旧社会，穷孩子上大学比～天还难。In the old society, for poor children to go to college was harder than climbing to heaven. ② publish; record; enter: ～帐 enter an item in an account book/ ～广告 advertise (in a newspaper)/ 最近一期《红旗》～了几篇有关四个现代化的文章。The latest issue of *Hongqi* carries several articles about the four modernizations./ 他的名字～上了光荣榜。 His name appeared on the honour roll. ③ be gathered and taken to the threshing ground: 五谷丰～ reap a bumper grain harvest ④ press down with the foot; pedal; treadle: ～三轮车 pedal a pedicab ⑤ step on; tread: ～在窗台儿上擦玻璃 step onto the sill to clean the window ⑥ 〈方〉 wear (shoes, etc.)
【登报】 dēngbào publish in the newspaper: ～声明 make a statement in the newspaper
【登场】 dēngcháng be gathered and taken to the threshing ground: 小麦已经～。The wheat has been carried to the threshing ground.
【登场】 dēngchǎng come on stage ◇ ～人物 characters in a play; *dramatis personae*
【登程】 dēngchéng start (off) on a journey; set out
【登峰造极】 dēngfēng-zàojí reach the peak of perfection; have a very high level (of scholastic attainment or technical skill); reach the limit
【登高】 dēnggāo ascend a height: ～远眺 ascend a height to enjoy a distant view
【登革热】 dēnggérè 〈医〉 dengue fever
【登基】 dēngjī ascend the throne; be enthroned
【登记】 dēngjì register; check in; enter one's name: 结婚～ marriage registration/ 向有关部门～ register with the proper authorities/ 在旅馆～住宿 check in at a hotel ◇ ～簿 register; registry/ ～处 registration (或 registry) office
【登临】 dēnglín ① climb a hill, a tall building, etc. which commands a broad view ② visit famous mountains, places of interest, etc.
【登陆】 dēnglù land; disembark ◇ ～部队 landing force/ ～场 beachhead/ ～地点 debarkation (或 landing) point/ ～舰(艇) landing ship (boat)/ ～母舰 landing-craft carrier/ ～作战 landing operations
【登门】 dēngmén call at sb.'s house: ～拜访 pay sb. a visit
【登山】 dēngshān 〈体〉 mountain-climbing; mountaineering ◇ ～队 mountaineering party (或 expedition)/ ～运动 mountaineering/ ～运动员 mountaineer
【登时】 dēngshí 〔多用于叙述过去的事情〕 immediately; at once; then and there
【登台】 dēngtái mount a platform; go up on the stage: 想～表演一番 strive to take the stage and perform
【登堂入室】 dēngtáng-rùshì pass through the hall into the inner chamber — reach a higher level in one's studies or become more proficient in one's profession
【登载】 dēngzǎi publish (in newspapers or magazines); carry: 各报在显著位置～了这条消息。The newspapers gave prominent coverage to the news.

**噔** dēng 〈象〉 thump; thud: 听见楼梯上～～～的脚步声 hear heavy footsteps on the stairs

**蹬** dēng 见"登" dēng④⑤⑥
另见 dèng
【蹬技】 dēngjì 〈杂技〉 juggling with the feet

## děng

**等** děng ① class; grade; rank: 分为三～ classify into three grades/ 一～品 top quality goods ② equal: 长短相～ be equal in length ③ wait; await: ～车 wait for a train, bus, etc./ ～上级批准 await approval by the higher authorities/ 请～一下。Would you mind waiting a minute, please./ 别～我吃饭。Don't wait dinner for me. ④ when; till: ～我做完再走。Stay till I'm through. ⑤ 〈助〉〔用在人称代词或指人的名词后面，表示复数〕: 我～ we ⑥ 〈助〉 and so on; and so forth; etc.: 购置书籍、纸张、文具～ buy books, stationery and so on/ 赴沈阳、鞍山～地视察 go to Shenyang, Anshan and other places on a tour of inspection ⑦ 〈助〉〔列举后煞尾〕: 长江、黄河、黑龙江、珠江～四大河流 the four large rivers — the Changjiang, the Huanghe, the Heilongjiang and the Zhujiang
【等边】 děngbiān 〈数〉 equilateral ◇ ～三角形 equilateral triangle
【等次】 děngcì place in a series; grade: 产品按质量划分～。The products are graded according to quality.
【等待】 děngdài wait; await: ～时机 await a favourable opportunity; wait for a chance; bide one's time/ 抓紧时间，不要～。Don't waste time. Go ahead.
【等到】 děngdào by the time; when: ～敌军赶到，游击队已经转移了。By the time the enemy troops arrived, the guerrilla force had already disappeared.
【等等】 děngděng and so on; and so on and so forth; etc.
【等等】 děngdeng waite a minute
【等而下之】 děng ér xià zhī from that grade down; lower down: 最好的尚且如此，～的就不必谈了。Even the best of the bunch is not worth much, to say nothing of those

lower down.

【等风速线】 děngfēngsùxiàn 〈气〉 isotach

【等高线】 děnggāoxiàn 〈地〉 contour (line) ◇ ～地图 contour map

【等号】 děnghào 〈数〉 equal-sign; equality sign

【等候】 děnghòu wait; await; expect: ～命令 wait for instructions; await orders

【等级】 děngjí ① grade; rank: 棉花按～收购 pay for cotton according to its grade ② order and degree; social estate; social stratum: 封建社会～森严。Feudal society was rigidly stratified. ◇ ～制度 hierarchy; social estate system

【等价】 děngjià of equal value; equal in value ◇ ～交换 exchange of equal values; exchange at equal value/ ～物 〈经〉 equivalent

【等距离】 děngjùlí equidistance ◇ ～外交 equidistant diplomacy

【等离子体】 děnglízǐtǐ 〈物〉 plasma
◇ ～激光器 plasma laser/ ～加速器 plasmatron/ ～物理学 plasma physics

【等量齐观】 děngliàng-qíguān equate; put on a par: 这两部小说差得太远了，怎么能～呢？There is a world of difference between these two novels. How can you equate one with the other?

【等日照线】 děngrìzhàoxiàn 〈气〉 isohel

【等熵面】 děngshāngmiàn 〈气〉 isentropic surface

【等深线】 děngshēnxiàn 〈地〉 isobath; bathymetric contour

【等式】 děngshì 〈数〉 equality

【等同】 děngtóng equate; be equal: 你不能把现象和本质～起来。You must not equate the appearance with the essence. ◇ ～语 equivalent

【等外】 děngwài substandard ◇ ～品 substandard product

【等温线】 děngwēnxiàn 〈气〉 isotherm

【等闲】 děngxián ① ordinary; unimportant: ～视之 regard as unimportant; treat lightly (或 casually) ② aimlessly; thoughtlessly: 大好时光，不可～度过。Don't fritter away your precious time.

【等效】 děngxiào 〈电〉 equivalent ◇ ～电抗 equivalent reactance/ ～天线 equivalent antenna

【等压面】 děngyāmiàn 〈气〉 isobaric surface; constant pressure surface

【等压线】 děngyāxiàn 〈气〉 isobar; isobaric line

【等腰】 děngyāo 〈数〉 isosceles ◇ ～三角形 isosceles triangle

【等因奉此】 děngyīn-fèngcǐ 〔旧时公文用语〕 ① in view of the above, we therefore ② officialese

【等音】 děngyīn 〈乐〉 enharmonic

【等于】 děngyú ① equal to; equivalent to: 一公里～二华里。One kilometre is equal to two *li*./ 三加二～五。Three plus two is five./ 我们厂去年的产量～一九六五年的五倍。Last year our factory produced five times as much as in 1965. ② amount to; be tantamount to: 这～拒绝执行命令。This is tantamount to refusal to carry out orders./ 抓而不紧，～不抓。Not to grasp firmly is not to grasp at all./ 没有正确的政治观点，就～没有灵魂。Not to have a correct political orientation is like not having a soul.

【等雨量线】 děngyǔliàngxiàn 〈气〉 isohyet

【等值线】 děngzhíxiàn 〈气〉 isopleth ◇～图 isogram

**戥** děng weigh with a small steelyard

【戥子】 děngzi a small steelyard for weighing precious metal, medicine, etc.

## dèng

**邓** Dèng a surname

**凳** dèng stool; bench: 方～ square stool/ 长～ bench

**澄** dèng (of a liquid) settle
另见 chéng

【澄清】 dèngqīng (of a liquid) settle; become clear: 这水太浑，等～了再用。This water is too muddy. Wait till it has settled before you use it.
另见 chéngqīng

【澄沙】 dèngshā sweetened bean paste

**瞪** dèng open (one's eyes) wide; stare; glare: 我生气地～了他一眼。I gave him an angry stare.

【瞪眼】 dèngyǎn ① open one's eyes wide; stare; glare: 干～ look on helplessly/ 别瞪着眼叫敌人溜了。Don't let the enemy get away from right under your nose. ② glower and glare at sb.; get angry with sb.: 你怎么老爱跟人～？Why are you always glowering at people?

**镫** dèng stirrup

【镫骨】 dènggǔ 〈生理〉 stapes; stirrup bone

**蹬** dèng 见"蹭蹬" cèngdèng
另见 dēng

## dī

**氐** Dī Di (Ti), an ancient nationality in China

**低** dī ① low: ～水位 low water level/ ～声 in a low voice/ ～年级学生 students of the junior years (或 lower grades)/ 我比他～一年级。I am one grade below him. ② let droop; hang down: ～头 hang one's head

【低产】 dīchǎn low yield
◇ ～井〈石油〉 stripper well; stripped well/ ～田 low-yield (或 low-yielding) land/ ～作物 low-yielding crop

【低潮】 dīcháo low tide; low ebb: 处于～ be at a low tide; be at a low ebb

【低沉】 dīchén ① overcast; lowering: ～的天空 an overcast sky ② (of voice) low and deep ③ low-spirited; downcast

【低地】 dīdì lowland

【低调】 dīdiào low-key

【低估】 dīgū underestimate; underrate: 反动派总是高估自己的力量，～人民的力量。The reactionaries invariably overestimate their own strength and underestimate the strength of the people.

【低合金钢】 dīhéjīngāng 〈冶〉 low-alloy steel

【低级】 dījí ① elementary; rudimentary; lower ② vulgar; low: ～趣味 vulgar interests; bad taste

【低贱】 dījiàn low and degrading; humble

【低空】 dīkōng low altitude; low level
◇ ～飞行 low-altitude (或 low-level) flying/ ～轰炸 low-level bombing/ ～扫射 low-level strafing; ground strafing

【低栏】 dīlán 〈体〉 low hurdles

【低廉】 dīlián cheap; low: 物价～。Prices are low.

【低劣】 dīliè inferior; low-grade

【低落】 dīluò low; downcast: 情绪～ be low-spirited

【低能】 dīnéng mental deficiency; feeble-mindedness ◇ ～儿 imbecile; retarded child

【低频】 dīpín low frequency ◇ ～变压器 low-frequency transformer/ ～放大器 low-frequency amplifier

【低气压】 dīqìyā 〈气〉 low pressure; depression

【低人一等】 dī rén yī děng inferior to others: 在我们的社会里没有～的工作。In our society there are no inferior

jobs.
【低三下四】 dīsān-xiàsì ①lowly; mean; humble ②servile; obsequious; cringing
【低烧】 dīshāo 〈医〉 low fever; slight fever
【低声】 dīshēng in a low voice; under one's breath; with bated breath
【低声波】 dīshēngbō 〈物〉 infrasonic wave
【低声下气】 dīshēng-xiàqì soft-spoken and submissive; meek and subservient
【低首下心】 dīshǒu-xiàxīn obsequiously submissive
【低碳钢】 dītàngāng 〈冶〉 low-carbon steel
【低头】 dītóu ①lower (或 bow, hang) one's head: ～认罪 hang one's head and admit one's guilt; plead guilty/ ～默哀 bow one's head in silent mourning ②yield; submit: 决不向困难～ never bow to difficulties/ 叫高山～,河水让路 make the mountains bow their heads and the rivers give way
【低洼】 dīwā low-lying ◇ ～地 low-lying land
【低微】 dīwēi ①(of a voice or sound) low: ～的呻吟 low groans ②lowly; humble
【低温】 dīwēn ①low temperature ②〈气〉 microtherm: ～气候 microthermal climate ③〈医〉 hypothermia
◇ ～恒温器 〈物〉 cryostat/ ～麻醉 hypothermic anaesthesia/ ～生物学 cryobiology/ ～学 cryogenics
【低息】 dīxī low interest
【低下】 dīxià (of status or living standards) low; lowly: 经济地位～ be of low economic status
【低消耗】 dīxiāohào low consumption (of raw materials, fuel, etc.): 保持高产、优质、～ maintain a record of high production, good quality and low consumption
【低血糖】 dīxuètáng 〈医〉 hypoglycemia
【低压】 dīyā ①〈物〉 low pressure ②〈电〉 low tension; low voltage ③〈气〉 low pressure; depression ④〈医〉 minimum pressure
◇ ～槽 〈气〉 trough/ ～气流 〈气〉 low-pressure air current/ ～水银蒸气灯 low-tension mercury-vapour lamp
【低音提琴】 dīyīn tíqín double bass; contrabass
【低云】 dīyún 〈气〉 low clouds

**堤** dī dyke; embankment
【堤岸】 dī'àn embankment
【堤坝】 dībà dykes and dams
【堤防】 dīfáng dyke; embankment: 加固～ strengthen the dykes ◇ ～工程 dyke building; embankment project

**提** dī
另见 tí
【提防】 dīfang take precautions against; be on guard against; beware of: ～坏人破坏 guard against sabotage by bad elements

**滴** dī ①drip: 他脸上的汗水直往下～。Sweat kept dripping from his face./ 往轴承里～油 put a few drops of lubricating oil in the bearings; oil the bearings/ ～眼药 put drops in one's eyes ②〈量〉 drop: 一～水 a drop of water
【滴虫】 dīchóng trichomonad ◇ ～病 trichomoniasis
【滴答】 dīdā 〈象〉 tick; ticktack; ticktock: 夜很静,只有钟摆～～地响。The night was very quiet except for the ticktack of the clock./ 发报机滴滴答答不停地发出电报。The transmitter ticked (或 tapped) out message after message./ 雨～～地下个不停。The rain kept pitter-pattering.
【滴答】 dīda drip: 屋顶上的雪化了,～着水。The snow on the roof melted and dripped down.
【滴滴涕】 dīdītì DDT (dichloro-diphenyl-trichloroethane)
【滴定】 dīdìng 〈化〉 titration: 比浊～ heterometric titration/ 碘量～ iodometry
◇ ～度 titre/ ～管 burette/ ～剂 titrant
【滴管】 dīguǎn dropper
【滴灌】 dīguàn 〈农〉 drip irrigation; trickle irrigation
【滴滤池】 dīlǜchí 〈环保〉 trickling filter
【滴水成冰】 dī shuǐ chéng bīng (so cold that) dripping water freezes; freezing cold: ～的天气 freezing weather
【滴水穿石】 dī shuǐ chuān shí water constantly dripping wears holes in stone; little strokes fell great oaks
【滴水石】 dīshuǐshí dripstone

**嘀** dī
另见 dí
【嘀嗒】 dīda tick; ticktack; ticktock

**镝** dī 〈化〉 dysprosium (Dy)
另见 dí

## dí

**狄** Dí a surname

**的** dí
另见 de; dì
【的确】 díquè indeed; really: 我～不知道。I really don't know.
【的确良】 díquèliáng 〈纺〉 dacron; terylene

**籴** dí buy in (grain)

**迪** dí 〈书〉 enlighten; guide

**荻** dí a kind of reed

**敌** dí ①enemy; foe: 劲～ a formidable enemy; a foe worthy of one's steel; a worthy opponent/ ～机 an enemy plane ②oppose; fight; resist: 以寡～众 fight against heavy odds/ 所向无～ carry all (或 everything) before one; be all-conquering/ 与人民为～的人绝不会有好下场。Those who oppose the people will come to no good end. ③match; equal: 军民团结如一人,试看天下谁能～? If the army and the people are united as one, who in the world can match them?
【敌百虫】 díbǎichóng 〈农〉 dipterex
【敌稗】 díbài 〈农〉 Stam F-34 (dichloropropionanilide)
【敌敌畏】 dídíwèi DDVP; dichlorvos
【敌对】 díduì hostile; antagonistic: ～阶级 antagonistic (或 hostile) classes/ ～行为 a hostile act/ ～行动 hostilities/ ～分子 a hostile element/ ～情绪 hostility; enmity/ ～双方 opposing sides; parties to hostilities
【敌国】 díguó enemy state
【敌后】 díhòu enemy's rear area: 深入～ penetrate into the enemy's rear area/ 建立～根据地 establish base areas behind the enemy lines
【敌军】 díjūn enemy troops; the enemy; hostile forces
【敌忾】 díkài hatred towards the enemy
【敌情】 díqíng the enemy's situation: 侦察～ make a reconnaissance of the enemy's situation/ ～的变化 changes on the enemy's side/ ～严重。Enemy activities present a serious threat.
【敌情观念】 díqíng guānniàn alertness to the presence of the enemy: ～强 be keenly aware of the enemy's presence/ 要有～ must not relax our vigilance against the enemy

【敌人】 dírén enemy; foe
【敌视】 díshì be hostile (或 antagonistic) to; adopt a hostile attitude towards
【敌手】 díshǒu ①match; opponent; adversary ②enemy hands: 落入～ fall into enemy hands
【敌台】 dítái enemy broadcasting station
【敌探】 dítàn enemy spy
【敌特】 dítè enemy spy; enemy agent
【敌伪】 díwěi the enemy and the puppet regime (during the War of Resistance Against Japan) ◇ ～人员 enemy and puppet personnel/ ～时期 the period of Japanese occupation; during the Japanese occupation
【敌我矛盾】 dí-wǒ máodùn contradictions between ourselves and the enemy
【敌意】 díyì hostility; enmity; animosity

**涤** dí 〈书〉wash; cleanse
【涤除】 díchú wash away; do away with; eliminate: ～旧习 do away with old customs
【涤荡】 dídàng wash away; cleanse: ～剥削阶级遗留下来的污泥浊水 clean up the filth left behind by the exploiting classes
【涤纶】 dílún 〈纺〉polyester fibre

**笛** dí ①bamboo flute ②whistle: 汽～ steam whistle
【笛子】 dízi *dizi*, bamboo flute

**觌** dí 〈书〉meet: ～面 meet each other

**嘀** dí
另见 dī
【嘀咕】 dígu ①whisper; talk in whispers: 两个女孩子嘀嘀咕咕地不知谈些什么。The two girls were talking in whispers. I couldn't hear a word. ②have misgivings about sth.; have sth. on one's mind: 我心里直～这件事。It's been on my mind all the while.

**嫡** dí ①of or by the wife (as distinguished from a concubine under the feudal-patriarchal system): ～长子 the wife's eldest son ②of lineal descent; closely related
【嫡传】 díchuán handed down in a direct line from the master
【嫡派】 dípài ①见"嫡系" ②disciples taught by the master himself
【嫡亲】 díqīn blood relations; close paternal relations: ～弟兄 blood brothers; whole brothers
【嫡系】 díxì ①direct line of descent ②one's own clique ◇ ～部队 troops under one's direct control

**镝** dí 〈书〉arrowhead: 鸣～ whistling arrow
另见 dī

## dǐ

**诋** dǐ 〈书〉slander; defame
【诋毁】 dǐhuǐ slander; vilify; calumniate; defame

**邸** dǐ the residence of a high official: 官～ official residence

**底** dǐ ①bottom; base: 井～ the bottom of a well/ ～价 base price ②the heart of a matter; ins and outs: 这一下就露了～儿了。And so the whole thing came out./ 心里没～ feel unsure of sth./ 刨根问～ get to the bottom of sth.; get to the root of things ③rough draft ④a copy kept as a record: 留个～儿 keep a copy on file; duplicate and file (a letter, etc.) ⑤end: 年～ the end of a year ⑥ground; background; foundation: 白～红花 red flowers on a white background ⑦〈书〉end up with; come to: 终～于成 succeed in the end
【底版】 dǐbǎn negative; photographic plate
【底本】 dǐběn ①a copy for the record or for reproduction; master copy ②a text against which other texts are checked
【底册】 dǐcè a bound copy of a document kept on file
【底层】 dǐcéng ①〈建〉(英) ground floor; (美) first floor ②bottom; the lowest rung: 旧中国劳动妇女被压在社会的最～。In old China working women were kept at the bottom of society.
【底肥】 dǐféi 〈农〉base fertilizer
【底稿】 dǐgǎo draft; manuscript
【底火】 dǐhuǒ ①the fire in a stove before fuel is added ②〈军〉primer; ignition cartridge
【底架】 dǐjià 〈机〉chassis
【底孔】 dǐkǒng 〈水〉bottom outlet
【底牌】 dǐpái cards in one's hand; hand: 亮～ show one's hand
【底盘】 dǐpán 〈汽车〉chassis
【底片】 dǐpiàn negative; photographic plate
【底栖生物】 dǐqī shēngwù benthon
【底漆】 dǐqī priming paint; primer
【底色】 dǐsè 〈纺〉bottom
【底墒】 dǐshāng 〈农〉soil moisture (before sowing or planting)
【底视图】 dǐshìtú 〈机〉bottom view
【底数】 dǐshù ①the truth or root of a matter; how a matter actually stands: 心中有～ know how the matter stands ②〈数〉base number
【底图】 dǐtú 〈地〉base map
【底细】 dǐxi ins and outs; exact details: 我们不了解这件事的～。We don't know the ins and outs of the matter.
【底下】 dǐxia ①under; below; beneath: 树～ under the tree/ 手～工作多 have one's hands full/ 笔～不错 write well ②next; later; afterwards: 他们～说的话我就听不清了。I didn't catch what they said next./ ～再交换意见吧。We can exchange views after the meeting.
【底蕴】 dǐyùn 〈书〉inside information; details
【底止】 dǐzhǐ 〈书〉end; limit
【底子】 dǐzi ①bottom; base: 鞋～ the sole of a shoe ②foundation: ～薄 have a poor foundation to start with/ 他的英文～好。He has a good grounding in English. ③rough draft or sketch: 画画儿要先打个～。When drawing a picture, first make a rough sketch. ④a copy kept as a record: 发出的文件要留个～。Keep a copy of each document sent out. ⑤remnant: 货～ remnants of stock
【底座】 dǐzuò base; pedestal; foundation

**抵** dǐ ①support; sustain; prop: 用手～着下巴颏儿 prop one's chin in one's hands/ 用东西把门～住,别让风刮开。Prop something against the door so that it won't blow open. ②resist; withstand: ～住来自外面的压力 withstand the pressure from outside ③compensate for; make good: ～命 pay with one's life (for a murder, etc.); a life for a life ④mortgage: 用房屋做～ mortgage a house ⑤balance; set off: 收支相～。Income balances expenditure. ⑥be equal to: 干活他一个能～我们两个。He can do the work of two of us. ⑦〈书〉reach; arrive at: 日内～京 arrive in Beijing in a day or two
【抵偿】 dǐcháng compensate for; make good; give sth. by way of payment for

【抵触】 dǐchù conflict; contradict: 在个人利益和集体利益有～的时候,应服从集体利益。When individual and collective interests conflict, those of the collective should prevail./ 与法律相～ contravene (或 go against) the law/ ～情绪 resentment; resistance

【抵达】 dǐdá arrive; reach

【抵挡】 dǐdǎng keep out; ward off; check; withstand: ～风寒 keep out the wind and the cold/ ～洪水 keep the flood in check

【抵换】 dǐhuàn substitute for; take the place of

【抵近射击】 dǐjìn shèjī 〈军〉 point-blank firing

【抵抗】 dǐkàng resist; stand up to: 奋起～ rise in resistance/ 增强对疾病的～力 build up one's resistance to disease

【抵赖】 dǐlài deny; disavow: 不容～ brook no denial/ 事实是～不了的。Denying the facts is futile. 或 Facts cannot be denied.

【抵消】 dǐxiāo offset; cancel out; counteract: ～影响 offset an influence/ ～药物的作用 counteract the effect of a medicine

【抵押】 dǐyā mortgage: 以某物作～ raise a mortgage on sth.; leave sth. as a pledge ◇ ～放款 mortgage loan; secured loan/ ～品 security; pledge

【抵御】 dǐyù resist; withstand: ～侵略 resist aggression/ ～自然灾害 withstand natural calamities/ 建立防风林带～风沙的侵袭 build a shelter belt against sandstorms

【抵债】 dǐzhài pay a debt in kind or by labour

【抵制】 dǐzhì resist; boycott: ～资产阶级思想的侵蚀 resist the corrosive influence of bourgeois ideology

【抵罪】 dǐzuì be punished for a crime

**砥** dǐ 〈书〉 whetstone

【砥砺】 dǐlì ① temper: ～革命意志 temper one's revolutionary will ② encourage: 互相～ encourage each other

**骶** dǐ

【骶骨】 dǐgǔ 〈生理〉 sacrum

## dì

**地** dì ① the earth ② land; soil: 山～ hilly land/ 盐碱～ saline and alkaline land (或 soil) ③ fields: 下～干活儿 go and work in the fields/ 麦～ wheat field ④ ground; floor: 水泥～ cement floor ⑤ place; locality: 每到一～ wherever one goes/ 各～党组织 Party organizations of all localities/ ～处山区 be located in a mountain area ⑥ position; situation: 立于不败之～ be in an invincible position ⑦ background; ground: 一块白～黑字的木牌 a board with black characters on a white background/ 白～红花的大碗 a big white bowl with a pattern of red flowers on it ⑧〔用于里数、站数后〕distance: 学校离村子有一里～。The school is one *li* away from the village./ 我家离工厂只有两站～。My home is only a couple of bus stops from the factory.

另见 de

【地巴唑】 dìbāzuò 〈药〉 dibazol

【地板】 dìbǎn ① floor board ② floor: 水泥～ cement floor

【地堡】 dìbǎo 〈军〉 bunker; blockhouse; pillbox

【地表】 dìbiǎo the earth's surface ◇ ～水 〈地〉 surface water

【地鳖虫】 dìbiēchóng 〈中药〉 ground beetle (*Eupolyphage sinensis*)

【地鹔】 dìbǔ 〈动〉 bustard

【地步】 dìbù ① condition; plight: 你怎么闹到这样的～?How did you get into such a mess?/ 事情到了不可收拾的～。The situation got out of hand. ② extent: 发展到公开对抗的～ develop to the point of an open clash/ 兴奋到不能人睡的～ be so excited that one can't get to sleep ③ room for action: 留～ leave room for manoeuvre; have some leeway; give oneself elbowroom

【地财】 dìcái valuables buried by landlords or rich peasants

【地蚕】 dìcán cutworm

【地槽】 dìcáo 〈地〉 geosyncline ◇ ～学说 theory of geosyncline

【地层】 dìcéng 〈地〉 stratum; layer

◇ ～层序 stratigraphic succession (或 sequence)/ ～对比 stratigraphic correlation/ ～图 stratigraphic map/ ～学 stratigraphy

【地产】 dìchǎn landed estate; landed property; real estate

【地秤】 dìchèng weighbridge

【地磁】 dìcí 〈物〉 terrestrial magnetism; geomagnetism

◇ ～场 terrestrial magnetic field; geomagnetic field/ ～极 geomagnetic pole/ ～记录仪 magnetograph/ ～仪 magnetometer/ ～异常 magnetic anomaly

【地大物博】 dìdà-wùbó vast territory and abundant resources; a big country abounding in natural wealth

【地带】 dìdài district; region; zone; belt: 沙漠(森林)～ a desert (forest) region/ 危险～ a danger zone/ 无人～ no man's land

【地道】 dìdào tunnel ◇ ～战 tunnel warfare

【地道】 dìdao ① from the place noted for the product; genuine: ～的吉林人参 genuine Jilin ginseng ② pure; typical: 她的上海话说得真～。She speaks pure Shanghai dialect./ 讲一口～的英语 speak idiomatic English/ 地地道道的伪君子 a thoroughgoing hypocrite ③ well-done; thorough: 他干的活儿真～。He does excellent work.

【地点】 dìdiǎn place; site; locale: 开会～ place for a meeting; venue/ 故事发生的～ the locale (或 scene) of a story/ 在这里建个百货商店,～倒适中。This would be a suitable site for a new department store.

【地电】 dìdiàn terrestrial electricity

【地动】 dìdòng 〈口〉 quake; earthquake ◇ ～仪 seismograph as invented by the Chinese scientist Zhang Heng (张衡) in A.D. 132

【地洞】 dìdòng a hole in the ground; burrow

【地段】 dìduàn a sector (或 section) of an area

【地对地导弹】 dì duì dì dǎodàn ground-to-ground (guided) missile; surface-to-surface missile

【地对空导弹】 dì duì kōng dǎodàn ground-to-air (guided) missile; surface-to-air missile

【地盾】 dìdùn 〈地〉 shield

【地方】 dìfāng ① locality (as distinct from the central administration): 党的～组织 Party organizations in the localities/ 民族自治～ national autonomous area/ 充分发挥中央和～两个积极性 give full play to the initiative of both central and local authorities ② local: ～武装 local armed forces

◇ ～病 endemic disease/ ～观念 localistic way of thinking; localism/ ～军 local forces; regional troops/ ～民族主义 local nationalism; local-nationality chauvinism/ ～时间 local time/ ～税 local taxes/ ～戏 local opera; local drama/ ～志 local chronicles; annals of local history

【地方】 dìfang ① place; space; room: 你是什么～人?Where are you from?/ 这张桌子太占～。That desk takes up too much space./ 我这个～有点疼。I've got a pain here. ② part; respect: 你说的话有对的～,也有不对的～。What you say is partly right and partly wrong.

【地方国营】 dìfāng guóyíng state-owned but locally-administered: ～企业 locally-administered state enterprise/ ～农场 state farm under local administration

【地肤】 dìfū 〈植〉 summer cypress (*Kochia scoparia*) ◇ ~子 〈中药〉 the fruit of summer cypress
【地高辛】 dìgāoxīn 〈药〉 digoxin
【地骨皮】 dìgǔpí 〈中药〉 the root bark of Chinese wolfberry (*Lycium chinense*)
【地瓜】 dìguā 〈方〉 ① yam bean ② sweet potato
【地光】 dìguāng flashes of light preceding an earthquake
【地滚球】 dìgǔnqiú 〈棒、垒球〉 ground ball; grounder
【地核】 dìhé 〈地〉 the earth's core
【地黄】 dìhuáng 〈植〉 glutinous rehmannia (*Rehmannia glutinosa*)
【地积】 dìjī measure of land; area
【地基】 dìjī ① ground ② foundation
【地极】 dìjí 〈地〉 terrestrial pole
【地脚】 dìjiǎo lower margin (of a page)
【地脚螺栓】 dìjiǎo luóshuān 〈机〉 foundation bolt
【地窖】 dìjiào cellar
【地界】 dìjiè the boundary of a piece of land
【地锦】 dìjǐn 〈植〉 humid euphorbia (*Euphorbia humifusa*)
【地块】 dìkuài 〈地〉 massif
【地蜡】 dìlà 〈矿〉 earth wax; ozocerite: 纯~ ceresin wax
【地牢】 dìláo dungeon
【地老虎】 dìlǎohǔ cutworm
【地雷】 dìléi (land) mine: 埋~ plant (或 lay) mines/ 防坦克~ antitank mine ◇ ~场 minefield/ ~战 (land) mine warfare
【地垒】 dìlěi 〈地〉 horst
【地理】 dìlǐ ① geographical features of a place: 熟悉~民情 be familiar with the place and its people ② geography: 自然(经济)~ physical (economic) geography
◇ ~发现 geographical discovery/ ~分布 geographical distribution/ ~环境 geographical conditions/ ~特点 geographical features/ ~位置 geographical position/ ~学 geography/ ~学家 geographer/ ~坐标 geographical coordinates
【地力】 dìlì soil fertility
【地利】 dìlì ① favourable geographical position; topographical advantages ② land productivity
【地沥青】 dìlìqīng asphalt; bitumen
【地龙】 dìlóng 〈中药〉 earthworm
【地龙墙】 dìlóngqiáng 〈建〉 sleeper wall
【地漏】 dìlòu 〈建〉 floor drain
【地幔】 dìmàn 〈地〉 (the earth's) mantle
【地貌】 dìmào the general configuration of the earth's surface; landforms
◇ ~图 geomorphologic map/ ~学 geomorphology/ ~学家 geomorphologist
【地面】 dìmiàn ① the earth's surface; ground: 高出~两米 two metres above ground level ② 〈建〉 ground; floor: 水磨石~ *terrazzo* floor ③ 〈口〉 region; area; territory: 这里已经进入山东~。We're now in the Province of Shandong.
◇ ~部队 ground forces/ ~沉降 〈地〉 surface subsidence/ ~辐射 〈气〉 terrestrial surface radiation/ ~灌溉 surface irrigation/ ~炮兵 ground artillery/ ~卫星站 ground satellite station/ ~遥测装置 ground telemetering equipment/ ~砖 〈建〉 floor tile
【地名】 dìmíng place name ◇ ~辞典 dictionary of place names; gazetteer/ ~学 toponomy; toponymy
【地盘】 dìpán territory under one's control; domain: 军阀互相争夺~。The warlords competed for spheres of influence.
【地皮】 dìpí ① land for building ② ground: 雨停了,~还没有干。The ground is still wet after the rain.
【地痞】 dìpǐ local ruffian; local riffraff
【地平俯角】 dìpíng fǔjiǎo 〈测〉 dip of the horizon
【地平经度】 dìpíng jīngdù 〈天〉 azimuth
【地平经纬仪】 dìpíng jīngwěiyí 〈天〉 altazimuth
【地平纬度】 dìpíng wěidù 〈天〉 altitude
【地平线】 dìpíngxiàn horizon
【地平坐标】 dìpíng zuòbiāo 〈天〉 horizontal coordinates
【地铺】 dìpù shakedown
【地契】 dìqì title deed for land
【地堑】 dìqiàn 〈地〉 graben
【地壳】 dìqiào 〈地〉 the earth's crust ◇ ~均衡 isostasy/ ~运动 crustal movement
【地勤】 dìqín 〈航空〉 ground service ◇ ~人员 ground crew; ground personnel
【地球】 dìqiú the earth; the globe
◇ ~化学 geochemistry/ ~科学 geoscience/ ~卫星 earth satellite/ ~物理学 geophysics/ ~仪 (terrestrial) globe
【地区】 dìqū ① area; district; region: 北京~ the Beijing area/ 多山~ a mountainous district/ 这个~最适宜种小麦。This area is most suitable for growing wheat. ② prefecture: 河北省保定~ the Baoding Prefecture of Hebei Province ◇ ~差价 regional price differences
【地权】 dìquán land ownership: 平均~ equalization of land ownership
【地热】 dìrè 〈地〉 the heat of the earth's interior; terrestrial heat
◇ ~电力 geothermal power/ ~能源 geothermal energy resources/ ~学 geothermics
【地声】 dìshēng earthquake sounds
【地史学】 dìshǐxué historical geology
【地势】 dìshì physical features of a place; relief; terrain; topography: ~险要。The terrain is strategically situated and difficult of access.
【地台】 dìtái 〈地〉 platform
【地毯】 dìtǎn carpet; rug
【地头】 dìtóu ① edge of a field: 开个~会 have a meeting at the edge of the field ② 〈方〉 destination ③ 〈方〉 the place: 你~熟悉,联系起来方便。You know the place well, so you can easily make contacts there. ④ lower margin (of a page)
【地头蛇】 dìtóushé a snake in its old haunts — local villain (或 bully)
【地图】 dìtú map
◇ ~集 atlas/ ~投影 map projection/ ~学 cartography
【地委】 dìwěi prefectural Party committee
【地位】 dìwèi ① position; standing; place; status: 政治~ political position (或 standing)/ 国际~ international standing/ 经济~ economic status/ 社会~ social position (或 status)/ ~平等 equal in status; on an equal footing/ 一定的历史~ a proper or definite place in history/ 他~变了,但普通劳动者的本色没有变。His status has changed but he's kept the fine qualities of an ordinary labourer. ② place (as occupied by a person or thing)
【地温】 dìwēn 〈气〉 ground (或 earth) temperature ◇ ~表 ground (或 earth) thermometer/ ~梯度 geothermal gradient
【地文学】 dìwénxué physical geography; physiography
【地物】 dìwù surface features (usu. man-made features of a region)
【地峡】 dìxiá isthmus: 巴拿马~ the Isthmus of Panama
【地下】 dìxià ① underground; subterranean: ~仓库 underground storehouse ② secret (activity); underground: 转入~ go underground/ 搞~工作 do underground work
◇ ~党 underground Party; underground Party organization/ ~宫殿 underground palace/ ~河流 subterranean river (或 stream)/ ~核试验 underground nuclear test/ ~茎 〈植〉 subterranean stem/ ~渗流 underground percola-

tion/ ～室 basement; cellar/ ～水 groundwater/ ～水位 groundwater level; water table/ ～铁道 underground (railway); tube; subway

【地下】 dìxia on the ground: 掉在～ fall on the ground/ 从～拣起 pick up from the ground

【地线】 dìxiàn 〈电〉 ground (或 earth) wire

【地心】 dìxīn 〈地〉 the earth's core ◇ ～引力 terrestrial gravity; gravity

【地形】 dìxíng topography; terrain: ～优越 enjoy topographical advantages/ 中国～复杂。China has a varied topography.

◇ ～测量 topographic survey/ ～图 topographic map; relief map/ ～学 topography/ ～雨 〈气〉 orographic rain/ ～云 〈气〉 orographic cloud/ ～侦察 terrain reconnaissance

【地衣】 dìyī 〈植〉 lichen

【地应力】 dìyìnglì 〈地〉 crustal stress ◇ ～场 (crustal) stress field

【地榆】 dìyú 〈植〉 garden burnet

【地舆图】 dìyútú 〈旧〉 atlas

【地狱】 dìyù hell; inferno

【地域】 dìyù region; district: ～辽阔 vast in territory ◇ ～观念 regionalism

【地缘政治学】 dìyuán zhèngzhìxué geopolitics 又作"地理政治学"

【地震】 dìzhèn earthquake; seism: 国家～局 the State Bureau of Seismology/ 这次～为七点一级。The shock was of 7.1 magnitude.

◇ ～波 seismic (或 earthquake) wave/ ～波曲线 seismogram/ ～带 seismic belt/ ～工作者 seismologist/ ～观测 seismological observation/ ～海啸 seismic sea wave; tsunami/ ～活动 seismic activity/ ～检波器 geophone/ ～烈度 earthquake intensity/ ～区 seismic area (或 region)/ ～台站 seismograph (或 seismic) station/ ～学 seismology/ ～仪 seismograph/ ～预报 earthquake prediction; earthquake forecasting/ ～震级 (earthquake) magnitude

【地支】 dìzhī the twelve Earthly Branches, used in combination with the Heavenly Stems to designate years, months, days and hours

【地址】 dìzhǐ address: 回信～ return address

【地志学】 dìzhìxué 〈地〉 topology

【地质】 dìzhì geology

◇ ～博物馆 geological museum/ ～调查 geological survey/ ～构造 geological structure/ ～勘探 geological prospecting/ ～勘探队 geological prospecting party (或 team)/ ～力学 geomechanics/ ～年代学 geochronology/ ～时代 geologic age; geologic period/ ～图 geologic map/ ～学 geology/ ～学家 geologist

【地中海】 Dìzhōnghǎi the Mediterranean (Sea)

【地轴】 dìzhóu the earth's axis

【地主】 dìzhǔ ① landlord: 逃亡恶霸～ a runaway (或 fugitive) despotic landlord ② host: 尽～之谊 perform the duties of the host ◇ ～阶级 the landlord class

【地啄木】 dìzhuómù 〈动〉 wryneck

【地租】 dìzū land rent; ground rent; rent: ～剥削 exploitation through land rent

## 弟

dì ① younger brother ②〔男性朋友相互间的谦称,多用于旧时书信中〕I

【弟弟】 dìdi younger brother; brother

【弟妇】 dìfù younger brother's wife; sister-in-law

【弟妹】 dìmèi ① younger brother and sister ②〈口〉 younger brother's wife; sister-in-law

【弟兄】 dìxiong brothers: 亲～ blood brothers/ 阶级～ class brothers/ 他就～一个。He is the only son of the family.

【弟子】 dìzǐ disciple; pupil; follower

## 的

dì target; bull's-eye

另见 de; dí

## 帝

dì ①〈宗〉 the Supreme Being: 玉皇大～ the Jade Emperor (supreme ruler of Heaven in Taoism)/ 上～ God ② emperor: 称～ proclaim oneself emperor ③〈简〉 (帝国主义) imperialism: 美～ U.S. imperialism

【帝俄】 Dì É tsarist Russia

【帝国】 dìguó empire: 英～ the British Empire

【帝国主义】 dìguózhǔyì imperialism ◇ ～分子 imperialist element; imperialist/ ～者 imperialist

【帝王】 dìwáng emperor; monarch

【帝汶岛】 Dìwèndǎo Timor

【帝制】 dìzhì autocratic monarchy; monarchy

## 递

dì ① hand over; pass; give: 把报～给我。Hand me the paper, please./ ～眼色 tip sb. the wink; wink at sb./ 给他～个口信 take a message to him ② successively; in the proper order: ～升 promote to the next rank

【递补】 dìbǔ fill vacancies in the proper order

【递加】 dìjiā progressively (或 successively) increase; increase by degrees

【递减】 dìjiǎn decrease progressively (或 successively); decrease by degrees: 产品的成本随着生产率提高而～。Increase in productivity is accompanied by a progressive decrease in production costs.

【递交】 dìjiāo hand over; present; submit: ～国书 (of an ambassador) present one's credentials/ ～抗议书 lodge a protest/ ～一份声明 send in a statement/ ～入党申请书 submit an application for Party membership

【递解】 dìjiè 〈旧〉 escort (a criminal) from one place to another: ～回籍 send (a convict, etc.) to his native place under escort

【递送】 dìsòng send; deliver: ～情报 send out (或 pass on) information/ ～信件 deliver letters

【递推公式】 dìtuī gōngshì 〈数〉 recurrence formula

【递增】 dìzēng increase progressively; increase by degrees: 产量平均每年～百分之十五。The output increased at an average rate of 15 per cent a year. 或 The output showed a yearly average increase of 15 per cent.

## 谛

dì 〈书〉 ① carefully; attentively: ～听 listen attentively/ ～视 examine closely; scrutinize ② meaning; significance: 真～ true significance; truth

## 第

dì ①〔用在数词前面,表示次序〕: ～一 the first/ 党章～三条 Article 3 of the Party Constitution ②〈书〉 grades into which successful candidates in the imperial examinations were placed: 及(落)～ pass (fail in) the imperial examinations ③〈旧〉 the residence of a high official

【第二次国内革命战争】 Dì'èr Cì Guónèi Gémìng Zhànzhēng the Second Revolutionary Civil War or the Agrarian Revolutionary War (1927-1937), waged by the Chinese people under the leadership of the Chinese Communist Party against the reactionary KMT rule

【第二次世界大战】 Dì'èr Cì Shìjiè Dàzhàn the Second World War (1939-1945); World War II

【第二国际】 Dì'èr Guójì the Second International (1889-1914)

【第二审】 dì'èrshěn 〈法〉 second instance ◇ ～法院 court of second instance

【第二声】 dì'èrshēng 〈语〉 rising tone, the second of the four tones in modern standard Chinese pronunciation

【第二世界】 dì'èr shìjiè the second world (composed of developed countries other than the two superpowers)
【第二信号系统】 dì'èr xìnhào xìtǒng 〈生理〉 the second signal system
【第二性】 dì'èrxìng 〈哲〉 secondary
【第三次国内革命战争】 Dìsān Cì Guónèi Gémìng Zhànzhēng the Third Revolutionary Civil War or the War of Liberation (1945-1949), in which the Chinese people, under the wise leadership of the Chinese Communist Party and Chairman Mao Zedong, finally overthrew the reactionary KMT rule and founded the People's Republic of China
【第三国际】 Dìsān Guójì the Third International (1919-1943)
【第三纪】 Dìsānjì 〈地〉 the Tertiary Period
【第三声】 dìsānshēng 〈语〉 falling-rising tone, the third of the four tones in modern standard Chinese pronunciation
【第三世界】 dìsān shìjiè the third world (composed of the developing countries in Asia, Africa, Latin America and elsewhere)
【第三者】 dìsānzhě a third party (to a dispute, etc.)
【第四纪】 Dìsìjì 〈地〉 the Quaternary Period
【第四声】 dìsìshēng 〈语〉 falling tone, the fourth of the four tones in modern standard Chinese pronunciation
【第五纵队】 dìwǔ zòngduì fifth column
【第一】 dìyī first; primary; foremost: 党委～书记 the first secretary of the Party committee/ 做出～等的工作 do first-rate work/ ～号种子选手 No.1 seeded player/ 获得～名 win first place; get a first; win a championship/ 他跑百米得了～。He came in first in the 100-metre dash./ 把坚定正确的政治方向放在～位 attach primary importance to a firm and correct political orientation/ 以革命利益为～生命 look upon the interests of the revolution as one's very life/ 把劳动看作生活的～需要 regard labour as life's prime want
【第一把手】 dìyī bǎ shǒu first in command; number one man; a person holding primary responsibility
【第一次国内革命战争】 Dìyī Cì Guónèi Gémìng Zhànzhēng the First Revolutionary Civil War (1924-1927), waged by the Chinese people under the leadership of the Chinese Communist Party against the imperialists and the Northern warlords
【第一次世界大战】 Dìyī Cì Shìjiè Dàzhàn the First World War (1914-1918); World War I
【第一国际】 Dìyī Guójì the First International (1864-1876)
【第一审】 dìyīshěn 〈法〉 first instance ◇ ～法院 court of first instance
【第一声】 dìyīshēng 〈语〉 high and level tone, the first of the four tones in modern standard Chinese pronunciation
【第一世界】 dìyī shìjiè the first world (composed of the two superpowers, the Soviet Union and the United States)
【第一手】 dìyīshǒu firsthand: ～材料 firsthand material
【第一线】 dìyīxiàn forefront; front line; first line: 战斗在三大革命运动的～ fight in the forefront of the three great revolutionary movements ◇ ～飞机 first-line aircraft
【第一信号系统】 dìyī xìnhào xìtǒng 〈生理〉 the first signal system
【第一性】 dìyīxìng 〈哲〉 primary: 物质是～的,意识是第二性的。Matter is primary and consciousness is secondary.

**棣** dì 〈书〉 younger brother
【棣棠】 dìtáng 〈植〉 kerria

**蒂** dì the base of a fruit

**缔** dì form (a friendship); conclude (a treaty)
【缔交】 dìjiāo ① establish diplomatic relations ② form (或 contract) a friendship
【缔结】 dìjié conclude; establish: ～条约 conclude a treaty/ ～邦交 establish diplomatic relations
【缔约】 dìyuē conclude (或 sign) a treaty: ～双方 both contracting parties ◇ ～国 signatory (state) to a treaty; party to a treaty; (high) contracting party
【缔造】 dìzào found; create: 毛主席亲自～和培育了伟大的中国共产党。Chairman Mao founded and nurtured the great Chinese Communist Party. ◇ ～者 founder

**睇** dì 〈书〉 look askance; cast a sidelong glance

**碲** dì 〈化〉 tellurium (Te)

## diān

**掂** diān weigh in the hand: ～～这有多重。Weigh this in your hand.
【掂斤播两】 diānjīn-bōliǎng engage in petty calculations; be calculating in small matters 又作"掂斤簸两"
【掂量】 diānliang 〈方〉 ① weigh in the hand ② think over; weigh up: 你～着办得了。Just do as you think fit./ 听到什么话要～～,看它代表哪个阶级的利益。We must weigh up what we hear and see which class interests it represents.
【掂算】 diānsuàn estimate; calculate; weigh

**滇** Diān another name for Yunnan Province

**颠** diān ① crown (of the head) ② top; summit: 山～ mountain top/ 塔～ the top of a pagoda ③ jolt; bump: 路不平,卡车～得厉害。As the road was rough, the truck jolted badly. ④ fall; turn over; topple down: ～覆 overturn; subvert ⑤ 〈方〉 run; go away: 整天跑跑～～ be on the go all day long/ 对不起,我得～儿了。Sorry, I've got to be on my way.
【颠簸】 diānbǒ jolt; bump; toss: 卡车在土路上～着前进。The truck bumped along the dirt road./ 风更大了,船身～起来。As the wind grew stronger, the boat was tossed about by the waves.
【颠倒】 diāndǎo ① put (或 turn) upside down; transpose; reverse; invert: 这一头朝上,别放～了。This is the top; don't put it upside down./ 把这两个字～过来句子就顺了。Transpose these two words and the sentence will read right./ 主次～ reverse the order of importance/ 把被～的历史再～过来 reverse the reversal of history; set the record of history straight/ ～敌我关系 take enemies for comrades and comrades for enemies ② confused; disordered: 神魂～ be in a confused state of mind; be infatuated
【颠倒黑白】 diāndǎo hēi-bái confound black and white; confuse right and wrong; stand facts on their heads
【颠倒是非】 diāndǎo shì-fēi confound right and wrong; confuse truth and falsehood; turn things upside down
【颠覆】 diānfù overturn; subvert: 警惕帝国主义、社会帝国主义的～和侵略 guard against subversion and aggression by imperialism and social-imperialism
【颠来倒去】 diānlái-dǎoqù over and over: 就那么点事,他～地说个没完。It was just a small matter but he kept harping on it./ 如果一篇文章～总是那么几个词,人家就不愿看。No one cares to read an article that merely rings the changes on a few terms.
【颠连】 diānlián ① hardship; trouble; difficulty ② peak upon peak
【颠沛流离】 diānpèi-liúlí drift from place to place, homeless

and miserable; wander about in a desperate plight; lead a vagrant life
【颠扑不破】 diānpū bù pò be able to withstand heavy battering; irrefutable; indisputable: ～的真理 irrefutable truth
【颠茄】 diānqié 〈药〉 belladonna
【颠三倒四】 diānsān-dǎosì incoherent; disorderly; confused

**巅** diān mountain peak; summit: 泰山之～ the summit of Taishan Mountain

**癫** diān mentally deranged; insane
【癫狂】 diānkuáng ① demented; mad; insane ② frivolous
【癫痫】 diānxián 〈医〉 epilepsy

## diǎn

**典** diǎn ① standard; law; canon ② standard work of scholarship: 词～ dictionary/ 药～ pharmacopoeia ③ allusion; literary quotation: 用～ use allusions ④ ceremony: 盛～ a grand ceremony (或 occasion) ⑤〈书〉 be in charge of: ～狱 prison warden ⑥ mortgage
【典当】 diǎndàng mortgage; pawn
【典范】 diǎnfàn model; example; paragon
【典故】 diǎngù allusion; literary quotation
【典籍】 diǎnjí ancient codes and records; ancient books and records: 先秦～ pre-Qin books and records
【典礼】 diǎnlǐ ceremony; celebration
【典型】 diǎnxíng ① typical case (或 example); model; type: 抓～ grasp typical cases/ 理论与实践相结合的～ a model of the integration of theory and practice/ 大庆式企业的～ a typical example of a Daqing-type enterprise ② typical; representative: ～人物 a typical character/ ～事例 a typical instance (或 case)/ ～的中国村庄 a representative Chinese village/ 文艺作品所反映的生活应该比实际生活更～。Life as reflected in works of art and literature ought to be more typical than actual everyday life. ◇ ～性 typicalness; representativeness
【典押】 diǎnyā mortgage; pawn
【典雅】 diǎnyǎ (of diction, etc.) refined; elegant
【典章】 diǎnzhāng institutions; decrees and regulations

**点** diǎn ① drop (of liquid): 雨～ raindrops ② spot; dot; speck: 墨～ ink spots/ 污～ stain ③ dot stroke (in Chinese characters) ④〈数〉 point: 基准～ datum point (或 mark)/ 两线的交～ the point of intersection of two lines ⑤ decimal point; point: 三～五 three point five (3.5) ⑥ a little; a bit; some: 给我～纸。Give me some paper, will you?/ 读～鲁迅 read some of Lu Xun's works/ 他今天好～了。He's feeling a bit better today./ 人的认识一～也不能离开实践。Human knowledge can in no way be separated from practice. ⑦〈量〉〔用于事项〕: 我有几～不成熟的想法。I have some tentative suggestions. ⑧ place; point: 突破一～ make a breakthrough at one point/ 沸～ boiling point/ 居民～ residential area/ 以～带面 promote work in all areas by drawing upon experience gained at key points ⑨ aspect; feature: 特～ characteristic feature/ 从这～上去看 viewed from this aspect/ 对这一～没人怀疑。Nobody has any doubt about that. ⑩ put a dot: ～三个点表示省略 put three dots to show that something has been omitted ⑪ touch on very briefly; skim: 蜻蜓～水 dragonflies skimming (over) the water/ 他用篙一～就把船撑开了。He pushed the boat off with a shove of the pole./ 她发言时～了这件事。She touched on the matter in her speech. ⑫ drip: ～眼药 put drops in the eyes ⑬ sow in holes; dibble: ～豆子 dibble beans ⑭ check one by one: 请你把钱～一～。Please check and see if the money is right./ ～货 check over goods; take stock ⑮ select; choose: ～菜 order dishes (in a restaurant) ⑯ hint; point out: 一～他就明白了。He quickly took the hint. ⑰ light; burn; kindle: ～灯 light a lamp/ 他是火爆性子，一～就着。He's got a fiery temper and flares up at the slightest provocation. ⑱ o'clock: 上午九～钟 nine o'clock in the morning/ 现在几～了? What time is it now? ⑲ appointed time: 误～ behind time; delayed; late/ 到～了，咱们开会吧。It's time. Let's start the meeting. ⑳ refreshments: 茶～ tea and cake; tea/ 早～ breakfast ㉑〈印〉 point, a unit of measurement for type
【点播】 diǎnbō 〈农〉 dibble seeding; dibbling ◇ ～器 dibbler
【点补】 diǎnbu have a snack to stave off hunger; have a bite: 这里有点吃的，谁饿了可以先～～。Here's a bite to eat if anyone's hungry.
【点菜】 diǎncài choose dishes from a menu; order dishes (in a restaurant)
【点滴】 diǎndī ① a bit: 这批资料是点点滴滴积累起来的。This fund of information has been accumulated bit by bit. ②〈医〉 intravenous drip: 打葡萄糖～ have an intravenous glucose drip
【点焊】 diǎnhàn spot (或 point) welding
【点火】 diǎnhuǒ ① light a fire ② ignition ③ stir up trouble
【点饥】 diǎnjī have a snack to stave off hunger
【点将】 diǎnjiàng ① (in traditional operas) call the muster roll of officers and assign them tasks ② name a person for a particular job
【点交】 diǎnjiāo hand over item by item
【点卯】 diǎnmǎo (in *yamen*) call the roll in the morning
【点名】 diǎnmíng ① call the roll: 晚～ evening roll call ② mention sb. by name: 他～要你去。He named you as the one he wanted./ ～攻击 attack sb. by name/ ～批判 criticize sb. by name ◇ ～册 roll book; roll
【点明】 diǎnmíng point out; put one's finger on: ～问题所在 put one's finger on the cause of the trouble
【点破】 diǎnpò bring sth. out into the open; lay bare; point out bluntly: 我没有～他的真实意图。I didn't point out what he was really after.
【点燃】 diǎnrán light; kindle; ignite: ～火把 light a torch/ ～革命之火 kindle the flames of revolution
【点染】 diǎnrǎn ①〈美术〉 add details to a painting ② touch up (或 polish) a piece of writing
【点射】 diǎnshè 〈军〉 ① fixed fire ② firing in bursts
【点石成金】 diǎn shí chéng jīn touch a stone and turn it into gold — turn a crude essay into a literary gem
【点收】 diǎnshōu check and accept: 按清单～货物 acknowledge receipt of goods after checking them against a list
【点数】 diǎnshù check the number (of pieces, etc.); count
【点题】 diǎntí bring out the theme
【点头】 diǎntóu nod one's head; nod: ～同意 nod assent/ ～打招呼 nod to sb. (as a greeting)/ ～示意 signal by nodding/ ～之交 nodding (或 bowing) acquaintance/ 他已经～了。He's already given the go-ahead. 或 He's already OK'd it.
【点头哈腰】 diǎntóu-hāyāo 〈口〉 bow unctuously; bow and scrape
【点心】 diǎnxin light refreshments; pastry
【点验】 diǎnyàn examine item by item
【点阵】 diǎnzhèn 〈物〉 lattice
【点种】 diǎnzhǒng dibble in the seeds
【点种】 diǎnzhòng dibbling
【点缀】 diǎnzhuì ① embellish; ornament; adorn: 几株红梅

把雪后的园林～得格外美丽。Embellished with the red blossoms of the plum trees, the garden looked more beautiful than ever after the snow. ② use sth. merely for show
【点字】 diǎnzì braille
【点子】 diǎnzi ① drop (of liquid) ② spot; dot; speck: 油～ grease spot ③ beat (of percussion instruments): 鼓～ drumbeat ④ key point: 工作抓到～上 get to grips with the essentials in one's work; put one's finger on the right spot/ 这话说到～上了。This remark gets to the heart of the matter. ⑤ idea; pointer: 他～多。He's full of ideas.

**碘** diǎn 〈化〉 iodine (I)
【碘酊】 diǎndīng 〈药〉 tincture of iodine
【碘仿】 diǎnfǎng 〈化〉 iodoform
【碘酒】 diǎnjiǔ 〈药〉 tincture of iodine

**踮** diǎn stand on tiptoe: 护士～着脚走到伤员床边。The nurse tiptoed to the bedside of the wounded soldier.

## diàn

**电** diàn ① electricity ② give or get an electric shock: 电门有毛病，～了我一下。 There was something wrong with the switch and I got a shock. ③ telegram; cable: 急～ urgent telegram/ ～上级请示 telegraph the higher authorities for instructions/ ～复 reply by telegraph/ ～贺 telegraph one's congratulations to sb.; cable a message of congratulations
【电棒】 diànbàng 〈方〉 (electric) torch; flashlight
【电报】 diànbào telegram; cable: 无线～ radiotelegram/ 有线～ wire telegram/ 打～ send a telegram/ 打～让他回来 wire him to come back
◇ ～等级 telegram message precedence/ ～挂号 cable address; telegraphic address/ ～机 telegraph/ ～音响器 telegraph sounder
【电表】 diànbiǎo ① any meter for measuring electricity, such as ammeter or voltmeter ② kilowatt-hour meter; watt-hour meter; electric meter
【电冰箱】 diànbīngxiāng (electric) refrigerator; fridge; freezer
【电波】 diànbō electric wave
【电铲】 diànchǎn power shovel
【电场】 diànchǎng electric field ◇ ～强度 electric field intensity
【电唱机】 diànchàngjī electric gramophone (或 phonograph); record player
【电唱头】 diànchàngtóu pickup
【电唱针】 diànchàngzhēn (gramophone) stylus; needle
【电车】 diànchē ① tram; tramcar; streetcar ② trolleybus; trolley
【电池】 diànchí (electric) cell; battery: 干～ dry cell/ 太阳能～ solar cell ◇ ～组 battery
【电传打字电报机】 diànchuán dǎzì diànbàojī teletypewriter; teleprinter
【电磁】 diàncí electromagnetism
◇ ～波 electromagnetic wave/ ～感应 electromagnetic induction/ ～铁 electromagnet/ ～学 electromagnetics
【电导】 diàndǎo conductance ◇ ～仪 conductivity gauge
【电灯】 diàndēng electric lamp; electric light: 偏僻的山村现在有了～。Electric light has now reached remote mountain villages. ◇ ～泡 electric (light) bulb
【电动】 diàndòng motor-driven; power-driven; power-operated; electric
◇ ～泵 motor-driven pump; electric pump/ ～车 electrically operated motor car/ ～发电机 motor generator/ ～割草机 power-operated mower/ ～葫芦 〈机〉 electric hoist (或 block)/ ～回转罗盘 electric gyro-compass/ ～机 (electric) motor/ ～记分牌 electric scoreboard/ ～势 electromotive force (EMF)
【电动力学】 diàndònglìxué electrodynamics
【电度表】 diàndùbiǎo kilowatt-hour meter; watt-hour meter; electric meter
【电镀】 diàndù electroplate: 无氰～ electroplating without using cyanide
【电法勘探】 diànfǎ kāntàn 〈矿〉 electrical prospecting
【电感】 diàngǎn inductance ◇ ～电桥 inductance bridge
【电工】 diàngōng ① electrical engineering ② electrician
◇ ～技术 electrotechnics/ ～器材厂 electrical appliances factory/ ～学 electrical engineering; electrotechnics
【电功率】 diàngōnglǜ electric power ◇ ～计 electrodynamometer
【电灌站】 diànguànzhàn electric pumping station (或 house)
【电光】 diànguāng light produced by electricity; lightning
◇ ～工艺 〈纺〉 schreinering
【电焊】 diànhàn electric welding
◇ ～工 electric welder/ ～机 electric welding machine; electric welder/ ～条 welding electrode; welding rod
【电荷】 diànhè electric charge; charge: 正(负)～ positive (negative) charge
【电弧】 diànhú electric arc
◇ ～割切机 arc cutting machine/ ～焊接 arc welding/ ～炉 arc furnace
【电化当量】 diànhuà dāngliàng electrochemical equivalent
【电化教育】 diànhuà jiàoyù education with electrical audio-visual aids; audio-visual education programme
【电化学】 diànhuàxué electrochemistry
【电话】 diànhuà ① telephone; phone: 无线～ radio (或 wireless) telephone/ 自动～ automatic telephone/ 市内～ local call/ 请别把～挂上。Hold the line, please./ 他把～挂了。He's hung up. ② phone call: 打～ make a phone call; phone sb.; call (或 ring) sb. up; give sb. a ring/ 他正在打～。He's on the phone./ 有你的～。There's a phone call for you. 或 You're wanted on the phone.
◇ ～簿 telephone directory (或 book)/ ～分机 extension (telephone)/ ～号码 telephone number/ ～机 telephone (set)/ ～间 telephone box (或 booth, kiosk); call box/ ～交换台 telephone exchange (或 switchboard)/ ～局 telephone office (或 exchange)/ ～用户 telephone subscriber/ ～增音机 telephone repeater
【电汇】 diànhuì telegraphic money order; remittance by telegram; telegraphic transfer ◇ ～汇率 rate for telegraphic transfer
【电火花】 diànhuǒhuā electric spark ◇ ～加工 electric spark machining
【电机】 diànjī electrical machinery ◇ ～厂 electrical machinery plant/ ～工程 electrical engineering
【电机车】 diànjīchē electric locomotive
【电积】 diànjī 〈冶〉 electrodeposition
【电极】 diànjí electrode: 阳～ anode; positive electrode/ 阴～ cathode; negative electrode
【电价键】 diànjiàjiàn 〈化〉 electrovalent bond
【电键】 diànjiàn telegraph key; key; button
【电解】 diànjiě electrolysis ◇ ～质 electrolyte
【电介质】 diànjièzhì dielectric
【电锯】 diànjù electric saw
【电抗】 diànkàng reactance ◇ ～器 reactor
【电缆】 diànlǎn electric cable; cable: 同轴～ coaxial cable
【电烙铁】 diànlàotiě ① electric iron ② electric soldering iron

【电离】 diànlí ionization ◇ ～层〈气〉ionosphere
【电力】 diànlì electric power; power
◇ ～工程 electric power project/ ～工业 power industry/ ～供应 supply of electricity/ ～机械 electrical power equipment/ ～网 power network/ ～系统 power system/ ～线 power line; electric line of force/ ～消耗 power consumption
【电疗】 diànliáo 〈医〉 electrotherapy: 短波～ shortwave therapy/ 超短波～ ultrashort-wave therapy
【电料】 diànliào electrical materials and appliances
【电铃】 diànlíng electric bell
【电流】 diànliú electric current: 载波～ carrier current/ 反向～ reverse current ◇ ～计 galvanometer/ ～强度 current intensity
【电溜子】 diànliùzi 〈矿〉 chain conveyor; face conveyor
【电炉】 diànlú ①(家用) electric stove; hot plate ②(工业用) electric furnace ◇ ～钢 electric steel/ ～炼钢法 electric furnace process
【电路】 diànlù (electric) circuit ◇ ～图 circuit diagram
【电码】 diànmǎ (telegraphic) code: 莫尔斯～ Morse code ◇ ～本 code book
【电鳗】 diànmán 〈动〉 electric eel
【电门】 diànmén (electric) switch
【电木】 diànmù 〈化〉 bakelite ◇ ～粉 phenolic moulding powder
【电纳】 diànnà 〈物〉 susceptance
【电钮】 diànniǔ push button; button: 按～ press (或 push) a button
【电耙】 diànpá 〈矿〉 scraper
【电瓶】 diànpíng storage battery; accumulator ◇ ～车 storage battery car; electromobile
【电气】 diànqì electric ◇ ～机车 electric locomotive/ ～设备 electrical equipment
【电气化】 diànqìhuà electrification: 农业～ electrification of agriculture ◇ ～铁路 electric railway
【电气石】 diànqìshí 〈矿〉 tourmaline
【电器】 diànqì electrical equipment (或 appliance)
【电热】 diànrè electric heat; electrothermal ◇ ～丝 heating wire
【电容】 diànróng electric capacity; capacitance ◇ ～率 permittivity/ ～器 condenser; capacitor
【电熔炼】 diànróngliàn 〈冶〉 electric smelting
【电扇】 diànshàn electric fan
【电渗析】 diànshènxī 〈化〉 electrodialysis
【电石】 diànshí 〈化〉 calcium carbide ◇ ～气 acetylene
【电势】 diànshì 见"电位"
【电视】 diànshì television; TV: 看～ watch television/ 彩色(黑白,立体)～ colour (black-and-white, stereoscopic) television
◇ ～电话 video telephone; video-phone/ ～电影 telecine/ ～发射机 television transmitter/ ～广播 television broadcasting; telecasting; videocast/ ～讲座 telecourse/ ～接收机 television receiver; television set/ ～雷达导航仪 teleran/ ～屏幕 television screen/ ～摄影机 television camera; telecamera/ ～塔 television tower/ ～台 television station/ ～网 television network/ ～影片 telefilm/ ～转播 television relay/ ～转播卫星 television transmission satellite
【电枢】 diànshū armature ◇ ～绕组 armature winding
【电刷】 diànshuā 〈机〉 brush ◇ ～触点 brush contact
【电台】 diàntái ①transmitter-receiver; transceiver ②broadcasting (或radio) station
【电烫】 diàntàng permanent hair styling (或 waving); permanent wave; perm
【电梯】 diàntī lift; elevator ◇ ～司机 lift operator; elevator runner
【电筒】 diàntǒng (electric) torch; flashlight
【电网】 diànwǎng electrified wire netting; live wire entanglement
【电位】 diànwèi (electric) potential ◇ ～差 potential difference
【电文】 diànwén text (of a telegram)
【电线】 diànxiàn (electric) wire ◇ ～杆子 (wire) pole
【电信】 diànxìn telecommunications ◇ ～局 telecommunication bureau/ ～业务 telecommunication service
【电学】 diànxué electricity (as a science)
【电讯】 diànxùn ①(telegraphic) dispatch: 世界各地发来的～ dispatches from all parts of the world ②telecommunications ◇ ～设备 telecommunication equipment
【电压】 diànyā voltage ◇ ～表 voltmeter
【电眼】 diànyǎn electric eye; magic eye
【电唁】 diànyàn send a telegram (或 message) of condolence
【电冶金】 diànyějīn electrometallurgy
【电椅】 diànyǐ electric chair
【电影】 diànyǐng film; movie; motion picture: 有声(无声)～ sound (silent) film/ 彩色(黑白)～ colour (black-and-white) film/ 立体～ three-dimensional film; stereoscopic film
◇ ～发行公司 film distribution corporation/ ～放映队 film projection unit (或 team)/ ～放映机 (film) projector; cine-projector/ ～放映网 film projection network/ ～剪辑机 film editing machine/ ～胶片 cinefilm; motion-picture film/ ～节 film festival/ ～剧本 scenario/ ～摄影机 cinecamera; film camera/ ～摄影师 cinematographer; cameraman/ ～说明书 film synopsis/ ～演员 film actor or actress/ ～译制厂 film dubbing studio/ ～院 cinema; movie (house)/ ～招待会 film reception/ ～制片厂 (film) studio/ ～周 film week/ ～字幕 film caption
【电泳】 diànyǒng 〈物〉 electrophoresis
【电玉粉】 diànyùfěn 〈化〉 urea-formaldehyde moulding powder
【电源】 diànyuán power supply; power source; mains: 接上～ connect with the mains ◇ ～变压器 power transformer; mains transformer
【电灶】 diànzào electric cooking stove (或 range)
【电渣焊】 diànzhāhàn electroslag welding
【电渣炉】 diànzhālú 〈冶〉 electroslag furnace
【电针疗法】 diànzhēn liáofǎ 〈中医〉 acupuncture with electric stimulation; galvano-acupuncture
【电针麻醉】 diànzhēn mázuì 〈中医〉 galvano-acupuncture anaesthesia
【电铸版】 diànzhùbǎn 〈印〉 electrotype
【电子】 diànzǐ electron: 热～ thermal electron/ 正～ positron/ 负～ negatron
◇ ～称 electronic-weighing system/ ～伏特 electron-volt/ ～工业 electronics industry/ ～管 electron tube; valve/ ～管收音机 valve radio set/ ～光学 electron optics/ ～回旋加速器 betatron/ ～计算机 electronic computer/ ～刻版机 〈印〉 electronic engraving machine/ ～器件 electronic device/ ～枪 electron gun/ ～壳层 electron shell/ ～人工喉 artificial electronic larynx/ ～束 electron beam/ ～望远镜 electron telescope/ ～物理学 electron physics/ ～学 electronics/ ～云 electron cloud/ ～照相术 electrophotography
【电子显微镜】 diànzǐ xiǎnwēijìng electron microscope: 八十万倍～ an electron microscope with a magnification of 800,000 times
【电阻】 diànzǔ resistance
◇ ～对焊 〈机〉 upset butt welding/ ～炉 〈冶〉 resistance

furnace/ ～率 resistivity; specific resistance
【电钻】 diànzuàn electric drill

**佃** diàn rent land (from a landlord)
【佃户】 diànhù tenant (farmer)
【佃农】 diànnóng tenant-peasant; tenant farmer
【佃契】 diànqì tenancy contract
【佃权】 diànquán tenant right
【佃租】 diànzū land rent

**甸** diàn 〔多用于地名〕 pasture

**店** diàn ① shop; store: 服装～ clothing store/ 书～ bookshop; bookstore/ 文具～ stationer's ② inn: 住～ stop at an inn
【店铺】 diànpù shop; store
【店员】 diànyuán shop assistant; salesclerk; clerk; salesman or saleswoman

**玷** diàn ① a flaw in a piece of jade ② blemish; disgrace
【玷辱】 diànrǔ bring disgrace on; be a disgrace to
【玷污】 diànwū stain; sully; tarnish: 他这种行为～了共产党员的光荣称号。By such behaviour he has sullied the honour of a Communist.

**垫** diàn ① put sth. under sth. else to raise it or make it level; fill up; pad: ～路 repair a road by filling the holes/ 桌子腿底下～点儿纸就平了。Put a wad of paper under the leg of the table to make it level. ② pad; cushion; mat: 椅～ chair cushion/ 鞋～ inner sole; insole/ 床～ mattress ③ pay for sb. and expect to be repaid later: 你先给我～上,以后再还你。Would you mind paying for me? I'll pay you back later.
【垫付】 diànfù pay for sb. and expect to be repaid later
【垫肩】 diànjiān shoulder pad (或 padding)
【垫脚石】 diànjiǎoshí stepping-stone
【垫圈】 diànjuàn bed down the livestock; spread earth in a pigsty, cowshed, etc.
另见 diànquān
【垫款】 diànkuǎn money advanced for sb. to be paid back later
【垫密片】 diànmìpiàn 〈机〉 gasket: 气缸～ cylinder gasket
【垫片】 diànpiàn 〈机〉 ① spacer: 绝缘～ insulation spacer ② shim: 轴承～ bearing shim
【垫平】 diànpíng level up: 把篮球场～ level a basketball court
【垫圈】 diànquān 〈机〉 washer: 毡～ felt washer/ 锁紧～ locking washer/ 开口～ snap washer
另见 diànjuàn
【垫上运动】 diànshàng yùndòng 〈体〉 mat tumbling; mat work
【垫子】 diànzi mat; pad; cushion: 蹭鞋～ doormat/ 体操～ gym mat/ 沙发～ sofa cushion/ 弹簧～ spring mattress/ 茶杯～ teacup mat; coaster

**钿** diàn 见"螺钿" luódiàn
另见 tián

**淀** diàn ① form sediment; settle; precipitate ② 〔多用于地名〕 shallow lake: 白洋～ Baiyangdian Lake (in Hebei Province)
【淀粉】 diànfěn starch; amylum ◇ ～酶〈生化〉 amylase
【淀积作用】 diànjī zuòyòng 〈地〉 illuviation

**惦** diàn remember with concern; be concerned about; keep thinking about: 我一直～着这件事。I've been thinking about that all the time.
【惦记】 diànjì remember with concern; be concerned about; keep thinking about: 老支书躺在病床上,还～着队里的工作。Although ill in bed, the old Party secretary was still concerned about the work of the brigade./ 她老～着给孩子打件毛衣。She's always thinking of knitting a sweater for her child.
【惦念】 diànniàn keep thinking about; be anxious about; worry about: 我一切都好,请您不要～。Everything's fine with me. Don't worry.

**奠** diàn ① establish; settle ② make offerings to the spirits of the dead
【奠定】 diàndìng establish; settle: ～基础 lay a foundation
【奠都】 diàndū establish (或 found) a capital: 太平天国～南京。The Taiping Heavenly Kingdom made Nanjing its capital.
【奠基】 diànjī lay a foundation
◇ ～礼 foundation stone laying ceremony/ ～人 founder/ ～石 foundation stone; cornerstone
【奠仪】 diànyí a gift of money made on the occasion of a funeral

**殿** diàn ① hall; palace; temple: 太和～ the Hall of Supreme Harmony ② at the rear
【殿后】 diànhòu bring up the rear
【殿军】 diànjūn ① rearguard ② a person who comes last in a contest or last among the winners; the last of the successful candidates
【殿试】 diànshì final imperial examination (presided over by the emperor)
【殿下】 diànxià (直接称呼) Your Highness; (间接称呼) His or Her Highness

**靛** diàn ① indigo ② indigo-blue
【靛蓝】 diànlán indigo ◇ ～色 indigo-blue
【靛青】 diànqīng ① indigo-blue ② 〈方〉 indigo

**癜** diàn purplish or white patches on the skin: 紫～ purpura/ 白～风 vitiligo

## diāo

**刁** diāo ① tricky; artful; sly ② (Diāo) a surname
【刁悍】 diāohàn cunning and fierce
【刁滑】 diāohuá cunning; crafty; artful
【刁难】 diāonàn create difficulties; make things difficult: 故意～ deliberately make things difficult for others/ 百般～ create obstructions of every description; raise all manner of difficulties; put up innumerable obstacles
【刁钻】 diāozuān cunning; artful; wily: 发球～ tricky service/ ～古怪 sly and capricious

**叼** diāo hold in the mouth: 嘴里～着烟卷 with a cigarette dangling from one's lips/ 黄鼠狼～走一只小鸡。A weasel ran off with a chick in its mouth.

**凋** diāo wither: 苍松翠柏,常绿不～。The pine and the cypress remain green all the year round.
【凋敝】 diāobì ① (of life) hard; destitute: 民生～。The people lived in destitution. ② (of business) depressed: 百业～。All business languished.
【凋零】 diāolíng withered, fallen and scattered about

【凋落】 diāoluò wither and fall
【凋谢】 diāoxiè ① wither and fall ② die of old age: 老成～ the passing away of worthy old people

**貂** diāo marten
【貂皮】 diāopí fur or pelt of marten; marten
【貂裘】 diāoqiú marten coat
【貂熊】 diāoxióng glutton

**碉** diāo
【碉堡】 diāobǎo pillbox; blockhouse
【碉楼】 diāolóu watchtower

**雕** diāo ① carve; engrave: 石～ stone carving/ 瓷～ carved porcelain/ 浮～ relief ② <动> vulture
【雕虫小技】 diāo chóng xiǎojì insignificant skill (esp. in writing); the trifling skill of a scribe; literary skill of no high order
【雕花】 diāohuā ① carve patterns or designs on woodwork ② carving: ～家具 carved furniture
【雕刻】 diāokè carve; engrave: 玉石～ jade carving/ 整个成昆铁路的模型是用四根象牙～成的。The entire model of the Chengdu-Kunming Railway is carved out of four pieces of ivory.
◇ ～刀 carving tool; burin/ ～品 carving/ ～工艺 artistic carving
【雕梁画栋】 diāoliáng-huàdòng carved beams and painted rafters — a richly ornamented building
【雕漆】 diāoqī <工美> carved lacquerware
【雕砌】 diāoqì write in a laboured and ornate style
【雕塑】 diāosù sculpture
【雕像】 diāoxiàng statue: 大理石～ marble statue/ 半身～ bust/ 小～ statuette
【雕琢】 diāozhuó ① cut and polish (jade, etc.); carve ② write in an ornate style

**鲷** diāo porgy

## diào

**吊** diào ① hang; suspend: 门前～着两盏红灯。There were two red lanterns hanging over the door./ ～打 hang up and beat sb. ② lift up or let down with a rope, etc.: 把和好的水泥～上去。Hoist up the mixed cement. ③ condole; mourn: ～丧 pay a condolence call ④ put in a fur lining: ～皮袄 line a coat with fur ⑤ revoke; withdraw: ～销 revoke (a licence, etc.) ⑥ <旧> a string of 1,000 cash ⑦ crane: 塔～ tower crane
【吊钹】 diàobó <乐> suspension cymbal
【吊车】 diàochē crane; hoist ◇ ～梁 crane beam
【吊床】 diàochuáng hammock
【吊灯】 diàodēng pendent lamp
【吊斗】 diàodǒu cableway bucket
【吊儿郎当】 diào'erlángdāng careless and casual; slovenly
【吊杆】 diàogān <机> boom; jib: 起重机～ crane boom/ (船用)起重～ derrick
【吊杠】 diàogàng <体> trapeze
【吊钩】 diàogōu <机> (lift) hook; hanger
【吊环】 diàohuán <体> rings: 摆荡(静止)～ swinging (still) rings
【吊货盘】 diàohuòpán platform (或 tray) sling
【吊货网】 diàohuòwǎng cargo net
【吊架】 diàojià <机> hanger: 平衡～ balance hanger
【吊景】 diàojǐng <剧> drop scenery
【吊卡】 diàokǎ <石油> elevator: 油管～ tubing elevator
【吊雷】 diàoléi <军> hanging mine
【吊链】 diàoliàn chain sling; sling chain
【吊楼】 diàolóu <方> house projecting over the water
【吊铺】 diàopù hanging bed; hammock
【吊桥】 diàoqiáo ① suspension bridge ② drawbridge
【吊丧】 diàosāng visit the bereaved to offer one's condolences; pay a condolence call
【吊嗓子】 diào sǎngzi train (或 exercise) one's voice
【吊死】 diàosǐ hang by the neck; hang oneself
【吊索】 diàosuǒ sling: 钢丝～ wire sling/ 绳～ rope sling
【吊桶】 diàotǒng well-bucket; bucket
【吊袜带】 diàowàdài garters; suspenders
【吊线】 diàoxiàn plumb-line
【吊销】 diàoxiāo revoke; withdraw: ～驾驶执照 revoke a driving licence/ ～护照 withdraw a passport
【吊唁】 diàoyàn condole; offer one's condolences: ～函电 messages of condolence
【吊装】 diàozhuāng <建> hoisting

**钓** diào fish with a hook and line; angle
【钓饵】 diào'ěr bait
【钓竿】 diàogān fishing rod
【钓钩】 diàogōu fishhook
【钓具】 diàojù fishing tackle
【钓鱼】 diàoyú angle; go fishing
【钓鱼岛】 Diàoyúdǎo Diaoyu Island

**调** diào ① transfer; shift; move: ～干部 transfer cadres/ ～挡 shift gears/ ～军队 move troops/ 改变南粮北～的局面 put an end to the state of affairs in which grain has to be sent from the south to the north/ 她～到这个小组来了。She has been transferred to this group. ② accent: 这人说话带山东～儿。This person speaks with a Shandong accent. ③ <乐> key ④ air; tune; melody: ～寄《沁园春》to the tune of *Qinyuanchun* ⑤ <语> tone; tune: 升～ rising tone (或 tune)/ 降～ falling tone (或 tune)
另见 tiáo
【调兵遣将】 diàobīng-qiǎnjiàng move troops; deploy forces
【调拨】 diàobō allocate and transfer (goods or funds); allot: ～款项购置图书 allocate funds for books/ 国家给他们～了大量化肥。The state allotted them large quantities of chemical fertilizer.
【调查】 diàochá investigate; inquire into; look into; survey: 作社会～ make a social investigation/ ～原因 investigate the cause/ 农村～ rural survey
◇ ～报告 findings report/ ～会 fact-finding meeting/ ～提纲 outline for investigation; questionnaire/ ～团 fact-finding mission
【调车场】 diàochēchǎng <铁道> switchyard
【调动】 diàodòng ① transfer; shift: ～工作 transfer sb. to another post ② move (troops); manoeuvre; muster: ～十万军队，一千辆坦克 muster a hundred thousand troops and a thousand tanks/ 部队～频繁。There have been numerous troop movements. ③ bring into play; arouse; mobilize: ～一切积极因素 bring every positive factor into play/ ～群众的社会主义积极性 arouse (或 mobilize) the socialist enthusiasm of the masses
【调度】 diàodù ① dispatch (trains, buses, etc.) ② dispatcher: 他是电车公司的～。He is a dispatcher at the trolleybus company. ③ manage; control: 生产～ production management ◇ ～室 dispatcher's office; control room/ ～员 dispatcher; controller
【调防】 diàofáng <军> relieve a garrison
【调干学员】 diàogàn xuéyuán a college student enrolled

from among cadres; cadre student
【调号】 diàohào ①〈语〉tone mark ②〈乐〉key signature
【调虎离山】 diào hǔ lí shān lure the tiger out of the mountains — lure the enemy away from his base
【调换】 diàohuàn exchange; change; swop
【调回】 diàohuí recall (troops, etc.)
【调集】 diàojí assemble; muster: ～兵力 assemble forces/ ～二十个师 concentrate twenty divisions
【调类】 diàolèi 〈语〉tone category
【调令】 diàolìng transfer order: 她的～已到。The order for her transfer has arrived.
【调门儿】 diàoménr 〈口〉pitch: 请把～定低点儿。Please pitch the tune in a lower key./ 他说话～高。He has a high-pitched voice.
【调派】 diàopài send; assign: ～大批干部下乡 assign large numbers of cadres to the countryside
【调配】 diàopèi allocate; deploy: ～原材料 allocation of raw materials/ 合理～劳动力 rational deployment of manpower
另见 tiáopèi
【调遣】 diàoqiǎn dispatch; assign: ～军队 dispatch troops/ 听从～ (be ready to) accept an assignment
【调任】 diàorèn be transferred to another post: 他已～车间主任。He has been transferred to be head of a workshop.
【调式】 diàoshì 〈乐〉mode
【调头】 diàotou tune; tone
【调用】 diàoyòng transfer (under a unified plan): ～干部 transfer cadres (to a specific job)
【调运】 diàoyùn allocate and transport: ～大批工业品到农村 allocate and ship large quantities of industrial products to the rural areas
【调值】 diàozhí 〈语〉tone pitch
【调职】 diàozhí be transferred to another post
【调子】 diàozi ① tune; melody: 这个～倒挺熟的。The tune is quite familiar./ 新老修正主义者唱的是一个～。New and old revisionists all sing the same tune. ② tone (of speech); note: 定～ set the tone (或 keynote)

**掉** diào ① fall; drop; shed; come off: ～下几滴眼泪 shed a few tears/ 被击伤的敌机～在海里了。The damaged enemy plane dropped into the sea./ 镐头～了。The pick-head has come off./ 正确的思想不是从天上～下来的。Correct ideas don't fall from the skies. ② lose; be missing: 我把钥匙～了。I've lost my key./ 这本书～了两页。Two pages are missing from the book./ 他害了一场大病，体重～了十多斤。During his serious illness he lost over ten *jin*. ③ fall behind: 他脚上打了泡，～在后面了。He got blisters on his feet, so he lagged behind. ④ change; exchange: ～座位 change (或 exchange) seats; swop places with sb. ⑤ turn: 把车头～过来 turn the car round ⑥〔用在某些动词后，表示动作的完成〕: 洗～ wash out/ 扔～ throw away/ 擦～ wipe off/ 改～坏习气 correct bad habits
【掉包】 diàobāo stealthily substitute one thing for another
【掉点儿】 diàodiǎnr 〈口〉start to rain: ～了。It's starting to rain.
【掉队】 diàoduì drop out (或 off); fall behind: 在三天的急行军中，没有一个～的。No one dropped out in the three days' forced march./ 继续革命，永不～ continue to make revolution and never fall behind
【掉换】 diàohuàn exchange; change; swop: 咱们俩的上班时间～一下好吗？Would you mind swopping shifts with me?/ ～工作 be assigned a new job; be transferred to another post
【掉色】 diàoshǎi lose colour; fade: 这种料子不～。This material won't fade. 或 This material is colourfast.
【掉头】 diàotóu turn round; turn about: 这地方太窄，汽车不好～。The place is too narrow for the truck to turn around./ 敌人见势不妙，～就跑。Seeing that the situation was getting hot for them, the enemy turned tail and fled.
【掉以轻心】 diào yǐ qīngxīn lower one's guard; treat sth. lightly: 虎狼在前，我们决不可～。With wolves and tigers pacing before us, we must not lower our guard.
【掉转】 diàozhuǎn turn round: ～身子 turn round/ ～枪口 turn one's gun (against one's superiors or old associates)

**铞** diào 见"钌铞儿" liàodiàor

## diē

**爹** diē 〈口〉father; dad; daddy; pa: ～娘 father and mother; mum and dad; ma and pa; parents
【爹爹】 diēdie 〈方〉father; dad; daddy; pa

**跌** diē ① fall; tumble: 他～伤了。He fell down and injured himself./ ～进修正主义泥坑 fall into the quagmire of revisionism ② drop; fall: 物价下～。Prices have dropped.
【跌打损伤】 diē-dǎ sǔnshāng injuries from falls, fractures, contusions and strains
【跌宕】 diēdàng ① free and easy; bold and unconstrained ② flowing rhythm
【跌倒】 diēdǎo fall; tumble: 在哪儿～就从哪儿爬起来。Pick yourself up from where you fell — correct your mistake where you made it.
【跌跌撞撞】 diēdiēzhuàngzhuàng dodder along; stagger along
【跌价】 diējià go down in price: 收音机～了。The prices of radio sets have gone down.
【跌交】 diējiāo ① trip (或 stumble) and fall; fall: 跌了一交 have a fall ② make a mistake; meet with a setback
【跌落】 diēluò fall; drop
【跌水】 diēshuǐ 〈水〉drop
【跌足】 diēzú 〈书〉stamp one's foot (in bitter remorse, sorrow or despair)

## dié

**迭** dié ① alternate; change ② repeatedly; again and again: ～挫强敌 inflict repeated reverses on a formidable enemy/ 文化大革命以来，地下文物～有发现。Since the Cultural Revolution, archaeological finds have been made one after another.
【迭次】 diécì repeatedly; again and again: ～磋商 repeatedly consult each other
【迭起】 diéqǐ occur repeatedly; happen frequently

**谍** dié ① espionage ② intelligence agent; spy
【谍报】 diébào information obtained through espionage; intelligence report; intelligence ◇ ～员 intelligence agent; spy

**堞** dié battlements

**喋** dié
【喋喋不休】 diédié bù xiū chatter away; rattle on, talk endlessly
【喋血】 diéxuè bloodshed; bloodbath

**牒** dié an official document or note; certificate: 最后

通～ ultimatum

**叠** dié ①pile up; repeat: 层峦～嶂 peaks rising one higher than another ②fold: 把信～好 fold the letter/ ～被子 fold up a quilt

【叠床架屋】 diéchuáng-jiàwū pile one bed upon another or build one house on top of another — needless duplication: 这样～，文章就太罗嗦了。So much needless repetition makes the article long-winded.

【叠句】 diéjù 〈语〉 reiterative sentence

【叠罗汉】 dié luóhàn 〈体〉 pyramid

【叠韵】 diéyùn 〈语〉 two or more characters with the same vowel formation (e.g. 阑干 lángān); vowel rhyme

【叠字】 diézì 〈语〉 reiterative locution (e.g. 坛坛罐罐 tántánguànguàn); reduplication

**碟** dié small plate; small dish: 一～炒黄豆 a dish of fried soya beans

【碟子】 diézi small dish; small plate

**蝶** dié butterfly

【蝶骨】 diégǔ 〈生理〉 sphenoid bone

【蝶形花】 diéxínghuā papilionaceous flower

【蝶泳】 diéyǒng butterfly stroke

**鲽** dié right-eyed flounder; flatfish

## dīng

**丁** dīng ① man: 壮～ able-bodied man/ 成～ reach manhood ②members of a family; population: 添～ have a baby born into the family/ ～口 population ③ a person engaged in a certain occupation: 园～ gardener ④the fourth of the ten Heavenly Stems ⑤fourth: ～等 the fourth grade; grade D/ ～种维生素 vitamin D ⑥ small cubes of meat or vegetable; cubes: 黄瓜～ diced cucumber ⑦(Dīng) a surname

另见 zhēng

【丁坝】 dīngbà 〈水〉 spur dike; spur

【丁苯橡胶】 dīngběn xiàngjiāo butadiene styrene rubber

【丁村人】 Dīngcūnrén Dingcun Man, a type of primitive man of about 100,000 years ago whose fossil remains were found in Dingcun, Shanxi Province, in 1954

【丁当】 dīngdāng 〈象〉 ding-dong; jingle; clatter: 碟子碗碰得丁丁当当的。The dishes and bowls slid together with a clatter.

【丁点儿】 dīngdiǎnr 〈方〉 a tiny bit: 这套茶具连一～毛病都没有。There isn't the slightest flaw in this tea set./ 这～事不必放在心上。Don't bother about such trifles.

【丁东】 dīngdōng 〈象〉〔形容玉石撞击的声音〕 tinkle 又作"丁冬"

【丁零】 dīnglíng 〈象〉 tinkle; jingle: ～～的自行车铃声 the jingling of bicycle bells

【丁零当郎】 dīnglingdānglāng 〈象〉 jinglejangle; cling-clang

【丁宁】 dīngníng urge again and again; warn; exhort: 她一再～儿子向贫下中牧学习。She repeatedly urged her son to learn from the poor and lower-middle herdsmen.

【丁是丁，卯是卯】 dīng shì dīng, mǎo shì mǎo keep *ding* (a Heavenly Stem) distinct from *mao* (an Earthly Branch) — be conscientious and meticulous

【丁烷】 dīngwán 〈化〉 butane ◇ ～气 butagas

【丁烯】 dīngxī 〈化〉 butene

【丁香】 dīngxiāng 〈植〉 ①lilac ②clove ◇ ～油 clove oil

【丁字】 dīngzì T-shaped ◇ ～尺 T-square/ ～钢 T-steel/ ～街 T-shaped road junction/ ～形 T-shaped

**仃** dīng 见"伶仃" língdīng

**叮** dīng ①sting; bite: 腿上叫蚊子～了一下 get a mosquito bite on the leg ②say or ask again to make sure: 我～了他一句，他才说了真话。I asked him again, and at last he came out with the truth.

【叮当】 dīngdāng 见"丁当" dīngdāng

【叮咛】 dīngníng 见"丁宁" dīngníng

【叮嘱】 dīngzhǔ urge again and again; warn; exhort: 支书再三～我们要谦虚谨慎。The Party secretary urged us again and again to be modest and prudent.

**玎** dīng

【玎珰】 dīngdāng 见"丁当" dīngdāng

【玎玲】 dīnglíng 〈象〉〔多形容玉石撞击声〕 clink; jingle; tinkle

**疔** dīng malignant boil (或 furuncle)

【疔疽】 dīngjū miliary vesicle under the nose or on either side of the mandible

**盯** dīng fix one's eyes on; gaze at; stare at: 他两眼～着雷达萤光屏。His eyes were fixed on the radar screen./ ～住这个坏蛋。Keep a close watch on the scoundrel.

【盯梢】 dīngshāo shadow sb.; tail sb.

**钉** dīng ①nail; tack ②follow closely; tail: 紧紧～住敌长机 keep on the tail of the enemy's lead plane ③ urge; press: 你要～着他吃药，别让他忘了。You must remind him to take his medicine, in case he forgets. ④见"盯" dīng

另见 dìng

【钉齿耙】 dīngchǐbà spike-tooth harrow

【钉锤】 dīngchuí nail hammer; claw hammer

【钉螺】 dīngluó 〈动〉 oncomelania (a kind of freshwater snail, which is the intermediate host of the blood fluke); snail

【钉帽】 dīngmào the head of a nail

【钉耙】 dīngpá (iron-toothed) rake

【钉人】 dīngrén 〈体〉 watch (或 mark) an opponent in a game ◇ ～防守 man-for-man (或 man-to-man) defence

【钉梢】 dīngshāo shadow sb.; tail sb.

【钉鞋】 dīngxié spiked shoes; spikes

【钉子】 dīngzi ①nail ②snag: 碰～ hit (或 strike, run against) a snag; meet with a rebuff/ 警惕敌人在革命队伍内部安插黑～。Be on guard against the enemy planting saboteurs in the revolutionary ranks.

【钉子精神】 dīngzi jīngshén the spirit of the nail — grasping every available minute, as Lei Feng did, to delve into revolutionary theory like a nail being driven into a piece of wood

**耵** dīng

【耵聍】 dīngníng earwax; cerumen

**酊** dīng tincture

另见 dǐng

【酊剂】 dīngjì 〈药〉 tincture

## dǐng

**顶** dǐng ①the crown of the head: 秃～ be bald ②

top：山～ mountaintop; hilltop/ 屋～ roof/ 到～ reach the limit (或 peak) ③ carry on the head：头上～着一罐水 carry a pitcher of water on one's head/ 社员们～着月亮抢收稻子。The commune members did a rush job reaping the rice in the moonlight. ④ gore; butt：这牛爱～人。This bull gores people. ⑤ go against：～风雪，战严寒 face blizzards and brave severe cold ⑥ push from below or behind; push up; prop up：嫩芽把土～起来了。The sprouts have pushed up the earth./ 用千斤顶把汽车～起来 jack up a car ⑦ retort; turn down：我～了他几句。I said a few words to him in retort./ 把抗议～回去 reject a protest ⑧ cope with; stand up to：负担虽重，他们两个也～下来了。The load was heavy, but the two of them coped with it all right. ⑨ take the place of; substitute; replace：～别人的名字 assume sb. else's name ⑩ equal; be equivalent to：一台收割机能～几十个人。One harvester can do the work of scores of people. ⑪〈量〉〔用于某些有顶的东西〕：一～帽子 a cap; a hat/ 一～帐子 a mosquito net ⑫ very; most; extremely：～有用 very useful/ ～小的那个孩子 the youngest (或 smallest) child

【顶班】 dǐngbān work on regular shifts; work full time：领导干部经常下车间～劳动。Leading cadres often go to the workshops to work regular shifts.

【顶板】 dǐngbǎn 〈矿〉 roof：直接～ immediate (或 nether) roof/ ～下沉 roof-to-floor convergence; roof convergence

【顶吹】 dǐngchuī 〈冶〉 top-blown ◇ ～转炉 top-blown converter

【顶灯】 dǐngdēng 〈汽车〉 dome light

【顶点】 dǐngdiǎn ① apex; zenith; acme; pinnacle ② 〈数〉 vertex; apex

【顶端】 dǐngduān top; peak; apex

【顶多】 dǐngduō at (the) most; at best

【顶风】 dǐngfēng ① against the wind：～骑车 cycle against the wind/ 开～船 sail against the wind/ ～冒雨 brave wind and rain ② head wind

【顶峰】 dǐngfēng peak; summit; pinnacle

【顶骨】 dǐnggǔ 〈生理〉 parietal bone

【顶呱呱】 dǐngguāguā tip-top; first-rate; excellent

【顶花坛】 dǐng huātán 〈杂技〉 balancing a jar on the head

【顶尖】 dǐngjiān ① tip ② 〈机〉 centre：死～ dead centre

【顶交】 dǐngjiāo 〈农〉 topcross

【顶角】 dǐngjiǎo 〈数〉 vertex angle

【顶礼】 dǐnglǐ 〈佛教〉 prostrate oneself before sb. and press one's head against his feet (a Buddhist salute of the highest respect)

【顶礼膜拜】 dǐnglǐ-móbài prostrate oneself in worship; make a fetish of; pay homage to

【顶梁柱】 dǐngliángzhù pillar; backbone

【顶牛儿】 dǐngniúr lock horns like bulls; clash; be at loggerheads：他们两人一谈就～。The two of them began to wrangle the moment they got talking.

【顶棚】 dǐngpéng ceiling

【顶球】 dǐngqiú 〈足球〉 head (a ball)

【顶少】 dǐngshǎo at least

【顶事】 dǐngshì be useful; serve the purpose：这孩子可～啦！The boy is a great help!

【顶替】 dǐngtì take sb.'s place; replace：他走了谁来～他？Who's going to take his place after he leaves?

【顶天立地】 dǐngtiān-lìdì of gigantic stature; of indomitable spirit：做一个～的英雄汉 be a hero of indomitable spirit

【顶头】 dǐngtóu ① coming directly towards one：～风 head wind ② top; end：这条胡同的～有个公用电话。There is a public telephone (booth) at the end of this lane.

【顶头上司】 dǐngtóu shàngsi one's immediate (或 direct) superior

【顶碗】 dǐngwǎn 〈杂技〉 balancing a stack of bowls on the head; pagoda of bowls

【顶芽】 dǐngyá 〈植〉 terminal bud

【顶用】 dǐngyòng be of use (或 help); serve the purpose：我去也不～。I can't be of any help even if I go./ 你干着急顶什么用？What's the use of just worrying and doing nothing about it?

【顶针】 dǐngzhen thimble

【顶住】 dǐngzhù withstand; stand up to; hold out against：～压力 withstand pressure/ ～逆流 stand up against an adverse current/ ～风浪 weather a storm

【顶撞】 dǐngzhuàng contradict (one's elder or superior)

【顶嘴】 dǐngzuǐ reply defiantly; answer back; talk back

**酊** dǐng 见"酩酊大醉" mǐngdǐng dàzuì
另见 dīng

**鼎** dǐng an ancient cooking vessel with two loop handles and three or four legs：三足～ tripod/ 四足～ quadripod

【鼎鼎大名】 dǐngdǐng dàmíng a great reputation

【鼎沸】 dǐngfèi like a seething cauldron; noisy and confused：人声～ a hubbub of voices

【鼎力】 dǐnglì 〈套〉 your kind effort：多蒙～协助，无任感谢。We are extremely grateful to you for the trouble you have taken on our behalf.

【鼎立】 dǐnglì (of three antagonists confronting one another) stand like the three legs of a tripod; tripartite confrontation; tripartite balance of forces

【鼎盛】 dǐngshèng in a period of great prosperity; at the height of power and splendour：春秋～ in the prime of manhood

【鼎足】 dǐngzú the three legs of a tripod — three rival powers：～之势 a situation of tripartite confrontation

## dìng

**订** dìng ① conclude; draw up; agree on：～条约 conclude a treaty/ ～合同 enter into (或 make) a contract/ ～计划 draw up (或 work out) a plan/ ～日期 fix (或 agree on) a date/ ～生产指标 set a production target ② subscribe to (a newspaper, etc.); book (seats, tickets, etc.); order (merchandise, etc.) ③ make corrections; revise：修～ revise ④ staple together

【订单】 dìngdān order for goods; order form

【订费】 dìngfèi subscription (rate)

【订购】 dìnggòu order (goods); place an order for sth.

【订户】 dìnghù ① subscriber (to a newspaper or periodical) ② a person or household with a standing order for milk, etc.

【订婚】 dìnghūn be engaged (to be married); be betrothed

【订货】 dìnghuò order goods; place an order for goods ◇ ～确认书 confirmation of order

【订立】 dìnglì conclude (a treaty, agreement, etc.); make (a contract, etc.)

【订书机】 dìngshūjī stapler; stapling-machine

【订阅】 dìngyuè subscribe to (a newspaper, periodical, etc.)

【订正】 dìngzhèng make corrections; emend：～了第一版中的错误。Corrections have been made to the first edition.

**钉** dìng ① nail：～马掌 nail on horseshoes/ ～钉子 drive in a nail/ 把窗子～死 nail up a window ② sew on：～扣子 sew a button on

另见 dīng

**定** dìng ①calm; stable: 心神不～ be ill at ease; feel restless/ 天下大～。General stability has been achieved in the country. ②decide; fix; set: 开会时间～在明天上午。The meeting is fixed for tomorrow morning./ 代表团～于今日离京。The delegation is due to leave Beijing today./ ～方针 decide on a policy/ ～计划 make a plan ③fixed; settled; established: ～数 fixed number/ ～评 accepted opinion ④subscribe to (a newspaper, etc.); book (seats, tickets, etc.); order (merchandise, etc.) ⑤〈书〉surely; certainly; definitely: ～可取胜 be sure to win

【定案】dìng'àn ①decide on (或 pass) a verdict; reach a conclusion on a case ②verdict; final decision

【定本】dìngběn definitive edition

【定比定律】dìngbǐ dìnglǜ 〈化〉the law of definite (或 constant) proportions

【定产】dìngchǎn a system of fixed quotas for grain production 参见"三定" sāndìng

【定单】dìngdān order for goods; order form

【定都】dìngdū choose a site for the capital; establish a capital: ～北京 make Beijing the capital; decide on Beijing as the capital

【定夺】dìngduó make a final decision; decide: 讨论后再行～。We won't make any decision until after the discussion.

【定额】dìng'é quota; norm: 生产～ production quota

【定稿】dìnggǎo ①finalize a manuscript, text, etc. ②final version or text

【定购】dìnggòu ①order (goods); place an order for sth. ②a system of fixed quotas for purchasing 参见"三定" sāndìng

【定冠词】dìngguàncí 〈语〉definite article

【定规】dìngguī ①established rule or practice; set pattern: 并无～。There's no hard and fast rule. ②〈方〉be bent on; be determined

【定户】dìnghù 见"订户" dìnghù

【定婚】dìnghūn be engaged (to be married); be betrothed

【定货】dìnghuò order goods; place an order for goods

【定计】dìngjì devise a stratagem; work out a scheme

【定价】dìngjià ①fix a price ②fixed price; list price

【定见】dìngjiàn definite opinion; set view

【定睛】dìngjīng fix one's eyes upon: ～细看 look fixedly and scrutinize

【定居】dìngjū settle down: 牧民～点 herdsmen's settlement

【定局】dìngjú ①foregone conclusion; inevitable outcome: 今年丰收已成～。It's a foregone conclusion that we'll have a bumper harvest this year. ②settle finally: 事情还没有～，明天可以再议。The matter isn't settled yet. We can take it up again tomorrow.

【定理】dìnglǐ theorem: 基本～ fundamental theorem

【定例】dìnglì usual practice; set pattern; routine

【定量】dìngliàng ①fixed quantity; ration ②determine the amounts of the components of a substance ◇ ～分析〈化〉quantitative analysis/ ～供应 rationing

【定律】dìnglǜ law: 万有引力～ the law of universal gravitation

【定论】dìnglùn final conclusion: 这个问题尚无～。No final conclusion has yet been reached on this matter. 或 This is still an open question.

【定苗】dìngmiáo 〈农〉final singling (of seedlings)

【定名】dìngmíng name; denominate: 这个厂～为东风造船厂。It was named Dongfeng Shipyard.

【定期】dìngqī ①fix (或 set) a date ②regular; at regular intervals; periodical: ～体格检查 regular physical check-ups/ ～轮换 rotate at regular intervals/ ～汇报工作 regularly report back on one's work/ ～刊物 periodical publication; periodical/ 不～刊物 nonperiodic publication ◇ ～存款 fixed deposit; time deposit/ ～租船 time charter

【定钱】dìngqian deposit; earnest (money)

【定亲】dìngqīn engagement (arranged by parents); betrothal

【定然】dìngrán certainly; definitely

【定神】dìngshén ①collect oneself; compose oneself; pull oneself together ②concentrate one's attention: 听见有人叫我，～一看原来是小李。I heard someone calling me and, looking hard, saw that it was Xiao Li.

【定时炸弹】dìngshí zhàdàn time bomb

【定位】dìngwèi ①fixed position; location; orientation ②orientate; position ◇ ～器〈矿〉positioner

【定息】dìngxī fixed interest (an annual rate of interest paid by the state to the national bourgeoisie on the money value of their assets for a given period of time, after the 1956 conversion of capitalist industry and commerce into joint state-private enterprises)

【定弦】dìngxián tune a stringed instrument

【定向】dìngxiàng directional
◇ ～爆破 directional blasting/ ～地雷 oriented mine/ ～广播 directional broadcasting/ ～培育〈农〉directive breeding/ ～天线 directional antenna/ ～仪〈气〉direction finder/ ～钻井 directional drilling; directed drilling

【定销】dìngxiāo a system of fixed quotas for marketing 参见"三定" sāndìng

【定心】dìngxīn 〈机〉centering ◇ ～装置 centering device

【定心丸】dìngxīnwán sth. capable of setting sb.'s mind at ease: 吃了～ be reassured

【定形】dìngxíng ①〈化纤〉setting: 热～ heat setting ②〈针织〉boarding ◇ ～机 boarding machine

【定型】dìngxíng finalize the design; fall into a pattern: 这种插秧机正在试制，尚未～。This type of rice transplanter is being trial-produced; the design hasn't been finalized.

【定性】dìngxìng ①determine the nature (of an offence or a case) ②determine the chemical composition of a substance ◇ ～分析〈化〉qualitative analysis

【定义】dìngyì definition: 下～ give a definition; define

【定音鼓】dìngyīngǔ kettledrums; timpani

【定影】dìngyǐng 〈摄〉fixing; fixation
◇ ～罐 fixing tank/ ～剂 fixer/ ～液 fixing bath

【定语】dìngyǔ 〈语〉attribute ◇ ～从句 attributive clause

【定员】dìngyuán fixed number of staff members or passengers: 这节车厢～一百二十人。This carriage has a seating capacity of 120 people.

【定则】dìngzé 〈物〉rule: 左手(右手)～ left-hand (right-hand) rule

【定植】dìngzhí 〈植〉field planting (或 setting)

【定制】dìngzhì have sth. made to order; have sth. custom-made: ～家具 have furniture made to order/ 欢迎选购和～。Orders for ready-made or custom-made articles are welcome.

【定置网】dìngzhìwǎng 〈渔〉set (或 fixed) net

【定子】dìngzǐ 〈电〉stator ◇ ～绕组 stator winding

【定罪】dìngzuì declare sb. guilty; convict sb. (of a crime)

【定做】dìngzuò have sth. made to order (或 measure): ～的衣服 tailor-made clothes; clothes made to measure/ 这双鞋是～的。This pair of shoes was made to order.

**啶** dìng 见"吡啶" bǐdìng

**腚** dìng 〈方〉buttocks

**碇** dìng a heavy stone used as an anchor; killick

**锭** dìng ① ingot-shaped tablet (of medicine, Chinese ink, etc.) ② 〈纺〉 spindle

【锭剂】 dìngjì 〈药〉 lozenge; pastille; troche

【锭模】 dìngmú 〈冶〉 ingot mould

【锭子】 dìngzi 〈纺〉 spindle

## diū

**丢** diū ① lose; mislay: 这套书～了一本。There's a book missing from the set./ 我把钳子～哪儿了？ Where have I left my pliers? ② throw; cast; toss: 把菜帮子～给小兔吃 throw the outer leaves to the rabbit/ 劳动人民的本色不能～。We mustn't lose the good qualities of the labouring people. ③ put (或 lay) aside: ～在脑后 let sth. pass out of one's mind; clean forget; completely ignore/ 我的法语～了好几年了，都忘得差不多了。I haven't used my French for years and have forgotten almost all of it./ 只有这件事～不开。That's the one thing that keeps worrying me. 或 That's my only worry.

【丢丑】 diūchǒu lose face; be disgraced: 简直是～！ It's really a disgrace!

【丢掉】 diūdiào ① lose: 我～了一支笔。I've lost my pen. ② throw away; cast away; discard: ～幻想，准备斗争。Cast away illusions, prepare for struggle./ ～错误观点 discard mistaken views/ ～官气 shed one's bureaucratic airs

【丢盔卸甲】 diūkuī-xièjiǎ throw away one's helmet and coat of mail; throw away everything in headlong flight

【丢脸】 diūliǎn lose face; be disgraced: 这不是～的事。There's nothing to be ashamed of.

【丢面子】 diū miànzi lose face: 有了错误要作自我批评，不要怕～。Criticize yourself when you've made a mistake. Don't be afraid of losing face.

【丢弃】 diūqì abandon; discard; give up

【丢人】 diūrén lose face; be disgraced

【丢三落四】 diūsān-làsì forgetful; scatterbrained

【丢失】 diūshī lose

【丢手】 diūshǒu wash one's hands of; give up: 他～不管了。He washed his hands of the matter.

【丢眼色】 diū yǎnsè wink at sb.; tip sb. the wink

【丢卒保车】 diū zú bǎo jū give up a pawn to save a chariot — sacrifice minor things to save major ones

**铥** 〈化〉 diū 〈化〉 thulium (Tm)

## dōng

**东** dōng ① east: 城～ east of the city/ ～城 the eastern part of the city/ ～郊 eastern suburbs ② master; owner: 房～ landlord ③ host: 做～ stand treat; stand host; play the host

【东半球】 dōngbànqiú the Eastern Hemisphere

【东北】 dōngběi ① northeast ② (Dōngběi) northeast China; the Northeast

【东北抗日联军】 Dōngběi Kàng Rì Liánjūn the Anti-Japanese Amalgamated Army of the Northeast (organized and led by the Communist Party of China after the September 18th Incident of 1931)

【东奔西跑】 dōngbēn-xīpǎo run around here and there; bustle about; rush about (或 around)

【东不拉】 dōngbùlā 见"冬不拉" dōngbùlā

【东道】 dōngdào one who treats sb. to a meal; host: 做～ play the host; stand treat ◇ ～国 host country/ ～主 host

【东方】 dōngfāng ① the east: ～欲晓。Dawn is breaking./ 《～红》的乐曲声 the strains of *The East Is Red* ② (Dōngfāng) the East; the Orient ③ (Dōngfāng) a surname

【东风】 dōngfēng ① east wind ② driving force of revolution; the East Wind: ～压倒西风。The East Wind prevails over the West Wind./ ～劲吹，捷报频传。The East Wind is strong. News of victory keeps pouring in. ◇ ～带 〈气〉 easterlies

【东风吹马耳】 dōngfēng chuī mǎ'ěr like the east wind blowing at the ear of a horse — go in one ear and out the other

【东郭先生】 Dōngguō Xiānsheng Master Dongguo, the foolish, softhearted scholar who narrowly escaped being eaten by a wolf which he had helped to hide from a hunter — a naive person who gets into trouble through being softhearted to evil people

【东海】 Dōnghǎi the Donghai Sea; the East China Sea

【东汉】 Dōng Hàn the Eastern Han Dynasty (25-220)

【东家】 dōngjia a form of address formerly used by an employee to his employer or a tenant-peasant to his landlord; master; boss

【东晋】 Dōng Jìn the Eastern Jin Dynasty (317-420)

【东经】 dōngjīng 〈地〉 east longitude: 北京位于～116度，北纬40度。Beijing is located at 40°N and 116°E.

【东拉西扯】 dōnglā-xīchě drag in all sorts of irrelevant matters; talk at random; ramble

【东鳞西爪】 dōnglín-xīzhǎo odds and ends; bits and pieces; fragments

【东南】 dōngnán ① southeast ② (Dōngnán) southeast China; the Southeast

【东南亚】 Dōngnán Yà Southeast Asia ◇ ～国家联盟 the Association of Southeast Asian Nations (ASEAN)

【东欧】 Dōng Ōu Eastern Europe

【东拼西凑】 dōngpīn-xīcòu scrape together; knock together: 那篇文章是～的。That article is scissors-and-paste work.

【东沙群岛】 Dōngshā Qúndǎo the Dongsha Islands

【东山再起】 Dōngshān zài qǐ stage a comeback

【东施效颦】 Dōngshī xiào pín Dong Shi, an ugly woman, knitting her brows in imitation of the famous beauty Xi Shi (西施), only to make herself uglier — blind imitation with ludicrous effect

【东魏】 Dōng Wèi the Eastern Wei Dynasty (534-550), one of the Northern Dynasties

【东西】 dōng-xī ① east and west ② from east to west: 这地方～三里，南北五里。This district is three *li* across from east to west and five *li* from north to south.

【东西】 dōngxi ① thing: 他收拾好～就走了。He packed his things and left./ 一成不变的～是没有的。Nothing is immutable./ 她买～去了。She's out shopping./ 分析形势要注意全局性的～。In analysing a situation, pay attention to things that concern the situation as a whole. ②〔指人或动物，多含喜爱或厌恶的感情〕thing; creature: 这小～真可爱。What a sweet little thing!/ 真不是～！ What a despicable creature!

【东…西…】 dōng ... xī ... here ... there: 东一榔头，西一棒子 hammer here and batter there; act or speak haphazardly/ 东一个，西一个 (of things) be scattered here and there/ 东一句，西一句 talk incoherently

【东乡族】 Dōngxiāngzú the Dongxiang (Tunghsiang) nationality, living in Gansu

【东亚】 Dōng Yà East Asia

【东张西望】 dōngzhāng-xīwàng gaze (或 peer) around

【东正教】 Dōngzhèngjiào the Orthodox Eastern Church
【东周】 Dōng Zhōu the Eastern Zhou Dynasty (770-256 B.C.)

**冬** dōng ① winter: 变～闲为～忙 turn the "slack winter season" into the "busy winter season" ②〈象〉 rub-a-dub; rat-tat; rat-a-tat
【冬不拉】 dōngbùlā 〈乐〉 a plucked stringed instrument, used by the Kazak nationality
【冬菜】 dōngcài preserved, dried cabbage or mustard greens
【冬虫夏草】 dōngchóng-xiàcǎo 〈中药〉 Chinese caterpillar fungus (*Cordyceps sinensis*)
【冬耕】 dōnggēng winter ploughing
【冬菇】 dōnggū dried mushrooms (picked in winter)
【冬瓜】 dōngguā wax gourd; white gourd
【冬灌】 dōngguàn 〈农〉 winter irrigation
【冬烘】 dōnghōng shallow but pedantic ◇ ～先生 pedant
【冬候鸟】 dōnghòuniǎo winter bird
【冬季】 dōngjì winter
◇ ～施工 winter construction/ ～体育运动 winter sports/ ～作物 winter crops
【冬眠】 dōngmián 〈生〉 winter sleep; hibernation
【冬青】 dōngqīng 〈植〉 Chinese ilex
【冬笋】 dōngsǔn winter bamboo shoots
【冬天】 dōngtiān winter
【冬小麦】 dōngxiǎomài winter wheat
【冬汛】 dōngxùn 〈渔〉 winter fishing season
【冬衣】 dōngyī winter clothes
【冬至】 Dōngzhì the Winter Solstice (22nd solar term)
【冬装】 dōngzhuāng winter dress (或 clothes)

**咚** dōng 见"冬"dōng②

**氡** dōng 〈化〉 radon (Rn)

## dǒng

**董** dǒng ①〈书〉 direct; superintend; supervise: ～其成 supervise the project until its completion ② director; trustee ③ (Dǒng) a surname
【董事】 dǒngshì director; trustee ◇ ～会 (企业) board of directors; (学校等) board of trustees/ ～长 chairman of the board

**懂** dǒng understand; know: ～英语 know English/ ～礼貌 have good manners/ 不要不～装～。Don't pretend to know (或 understand) when you don't./ 干部必须～政策。Cadres must have a good grasp of policy.
【懂得】 dǒngde understand; know; grasp: ～革命道理 understand revolutionary principles/ 用群众所熟悉和～的词句 use words which are familiar and intelligible to the masses/ 这一事件使大家更清楚地～了阶级斗争的长期性和复杂性。This incident brought home to us the protracted and complex nature of class struggle.
【懂行】 dǒngháng know the business; know the ropes
【懂事】 dǒngshì sensible; intelligent: ～的孩子 a sensible child/ 你怎么这样不～? How can you be so thoughtless?

## dòng

**动** dòng ① move; stir: 他扭了腰,～不了。He's strained his back and can't move./ 微风吹～树叶。A breeze stirred the leaves./ 这东西一个人拿不～。No one can carry that single-handed./ 你～一～,我就开枪。Move one step, and I fire. ② act; get moving: 经过动员,群众普遍地～起来了。After the mobilization meetings, the masses all got moving. ③ change; alter: 这句话只要～一两个字就顺了。Just change one or two words and the sentence will read smoothly. ④ use: ～脑筋 use one's head ⑤ touch (one's heart); arouse: ～了公愤 have aroused public indignation/ ～感情 be carried away by emotion; get worked up/ ～肝火 flare up/ 不为甜言蜜语所～ not be swayed by fine words ⑥〈方〉〔多用于否定式〕eat or drink: 不～荤腥 never touch meat or fish; be a vegetarian
【动笔】 dòngbǐ take up the pen; start writing: 他最近很少～。He hasn't done much writing recently./ 想清楚了再～。Think it all out before you start writing.
【动宾词组】 dòng-bīn cízǔ 〈语〉 verb-object word group
【动兵】 dòngbīng send out troops to fight
【动不动】 dòngbudòng easily; frequently; at every turn: ～就感冒 catch cold easily/ ～就发脾气 be apt to lose one's temper; often get into a temper
【动产】 dòngchǎn movable property; movables; personal property
【动词】 dòngcí 〈语〉 verb ◇ ～不定式 infinitive
【动荡】 dòngdàng turbulence; upheaval; unrest: ～的局势 a turbulent situation/ 世界在～中前进。The world advances amidst turbulence.
【动电学】 dòngdiànxué electrokinetics
【动工】 dònggōng begin construction; start building
【动画片】 dònghuàpiàn animated cartoon (或 drawing); cartoon
【动火】 dònghuǒ 〈口〉 get angry; flare up
【动机】 dòngjī motive; intention: 出于自私的～ be actuated by selfish motives/ ～不纯 have impure motives/ 他的～是好的。His intentions are good. 或 He means well.
【动静】 dòngjing ① the sound of sth. astir: 屋子里静悄悄的,一点～也没有。It was quiet in the room; nothing was stirring. ② movement; activity: 发现可疑～ spot something suspicious/ 一有～就来报告。Report as soon as anything happens.
【动觉】 dòngjué 〈心〉 kinaesthesia
【动力】 dònglì ① motive power; power ② motive (或 driving) force; impetus: 社会发展的～ the motive force of the development of society ◇ ～设备 power plant/ ～学 dynamics; kinetics
【动量】 dòngliàng 〈物〉 momentum: 广义～ generalized momentum ◇ ～矩 moment of momentum/ ～守恒定律 the law of conservation of momentum
【动令】 dònglìng 〈军〉 command of execution
【动乱】 dòngluàn turmoil; disturbance; upheaval; turbulence: ～时期 a time of turmoil; a time of storm and stress/ 社会～ social upheaval/ ～年代 years of upheaval
【动脉】 dòngmài 〈生理〉 artery
◇ ～弓 arch of aorta/ ～脉搏 arterial pulse/ ～血压 arterial pressure/ ～炎 arteritis/ ～硬化 arteriosclerosis/ ～粥样硬化 atherosclerosis
【动名词】 dòngmíngcí 〈语〉 gerund
【动能】 dòngnéng 〈物〉 kinetic energy
【动怒】 dòngnù lose one's temper; flare up
【动气】 dòngqì 〈口〉 take offence; get angry
【动情】 dòngqíng ① get worked up; become excited ② become enamoured; have one's (sexual) passions aroused
【动人】 dòngrén moving; touching: ～的情景 a moving scene/ ～的事迹 stirring deeds
【动容】 dòngróng 〈书〉 change countenance; be visibly moved

【动身】 dòngshēn go (或 set out) on a journey; leave (for a distant place)
【动手】 dòngshǒu ① start work; get to work: 早点儿～,早点儿完成。The sooner we start, the sooner we finish./ ～修建一座高炉 start building a blast furnace/ 大家～干了起来。Everyone set to work. ② touch; handle: 爱护展品,请勿～。Please don't touch the exhibits. ③ raise a hand to strike; hit out: 谁先动的手? Who struck the first blow?
【动手术】 dòngshǒushù ① perform an operation; operate on sb. ② have an operation; be operated on
【动态】 dòngtài ① trends; developments: 科技新～ recent developments in science and technology/ 了解敌军的～ find out about enemy troop movements/ 油井～ behaviour (或 performance) of an oil well ② dynamic state
◇ ～电阻 dynamic resistance/ ～平衡 〈物〉dynamic equilibrium/ ～特性 〈电〉 dynamic characteristic
【动弹】 dòngtan move; stir: 车里太挤,～不得。The bus was so crowded that nobody could move./ 机器不～了。The machine has stopped.
【动听】 dòngtīng interesting or pleasant to listen to: 他能把极平常的事儿说得很～。He can make ordinary things sound interesting./ 她唱得很～。She sings beautifully.
【动土】 dòngtǔ break ground; start building
【动窝儿】 dòngwōr 〈方〉 start moving; make a move: 不管你说什么,他就是不～。No matter what you say, he just won't stir.
【动武】 dòngwǔ use force; start a fight; come to blows
【动物】 dòngwù animal
◇ ～胶 〈化〉 animal size (或 glue)/ ～界 the animal kingdom/ ～区系 fauna/ ～生态学 animal ecology/ ～学 zoology/ ～油 animal oil/ ～园 zoological garden; zoo/ ～志 fauna
【动向】 dòngxiàng trend; tendency: 新～ new trends/ 密切注意敌人～。Keep a close watch on the enemy's movements.
【动心】 dòngxīn one's mind is perturbed; one's desire, enthusiasm or interest is aroused
【动刑】 dòngxíng subject sb. to torture; torture
【动眼神经】 dòngyǎn shénjīng oculomotor nerve
【动摇】 dòngyáo shake; vacillate; waver: 威逼利诱不能～一个革命战士的坚强意志。No coercion or cajolery can shake the iron will of a revolutionary fighter./ 人民的革命斗争～了反动派的统治基础。The people's revolutionary struggle shook the rule of the reactionaries to its very foundations./ 风吹浪打不～ never waver in the storm and stress of struggle ◇ ～分子 wavering element; vacillating element
【动议】 dòngyì motion: 紧急～ an urgent motion/ 提出一项～ put forward a motion
【动用】 dòngyòng put to use; employ; draw on: ～大量人力 employ a tremendous amount of manpower/ ～库存 draw on stock
【动员】 dòngyuán mobilize; arouse: 总～ general mobilization/ 全国～,大办农业 mobilize the whole nation and go in for agriculture in a big way/ 作一番～ give a mobilization (或 pep) talk/ 整个医院都～起来,抢救伤员。The whole hospital was galvanized into action to save the wounded.
◇ ～报告 mobilization speech/ ～大会 mobilization meeting/ ～令 mobilization order
【动辄】 dòngzhé 〈书〉 easily; frequently; at every turn: ～发怒 fly into a rage on the slightest provocation/ ～得咎 be frequently taken to task; be blamed for whatever one does
【动作】 dòngzuò ① movement; motion; action: ～敏捷(缓慢) quick (slow) in one's movements/ 优美的舞蹈～ graceful dance movements ② act; start moving: 且看他下一步如何～。Let's see how he acts next.

## 冻

dòng ① freeze: ～肉 frozen meat/ 不能让这些白菜～坏。We mustn't let the cabbages be damaged by frost. ② jelly: 肉～儿 jellied meat ③ feel very cold; freeze; be frostbitten: 多穿些,别～着了。Put on more clothes so you don't catch cold./ 她手都～了。Her hands were frostbitten./ 真～得够戗! Brr, I'm freezing!
【冻冰】 dòngbīng freeze: 河上～了。The river is frozen.
【冻疮】 dòngchuāng chilblain: 生～ have chilblains
【冻豆腐】 dòngdòufu frozen bean curd
【冻害】 dònghài 〈农〉 freeze injury
【冻僵】 dòngjiāng frozen stiff; numb with cold
【冻结】 dòngjié ① freeze; congeal ② (of wages, prices, etc.) freeze: 工资～ wage freeze/ ～的资产 frozen assets
【冻馁】 dòngněi cold and hunger
【冻凝】 dòngníng congeal ◇ ～点 congealing point
【冻伤】 dòngshāng frostbite
【冻死】 dòngsǐ freeze to death; freeze and perish; die of frost
【冻土】 dòngtǔ frozen earth (或 ground, soil) ◇ ～学 cryopedology
【冻雨】 dòngyǔ 〈气〉 sleet

## 侗

Dòng
【侗族】 Dòngzú the Dong (Tung) nationality, distributed over Guizhou, Hunan and the Guangxi Zhuang Autonomous Region

## 洞

dòng ① hole; cavity: 衬衣破了一个～ have a hole in one's shirt/ 山～ mountain cave/ 城门～儿 archway of a city gate ② penetratingly; thoroughly: ～见症结 see clearly the crux of the matter; get to the heart of the problem
【洞察】 dòngchá see clearly; have an insight into: ～是非 see clearly the rights and wrongs of the case/ ～一切 have a keen insight into matters ◇ ～力 insight; discernment; acumen
【洞彻】 dòngchè understand thoroughly; see clearly
【洞达】 dòngdá understand thoroughly: ～事理 be sensible
【洞房】 dòngfáng bridal (或 nuptial) chamber: ～花烛 wedding festivities; wedding
【洞若观火】 dòng ruò guān huǒ see sth. as clearly as a blazing fire
【洞悉】 dòngxī know clearly; understand thoroughly
【洞箫】 dòngxiāo *dongxiao*, a vertical bamboo flute
【洞晓】 dòngxiǎo have a clear knowledge of: ～其中利弊 have a clear understanding of the advantages and disadvantages
【洞穴】 dòngxué cave; cavern ◇ ～墓 catacomb
【洞烛其奸】 dòng zhú qí jiān see through sb.'s tricks

## 恫

dòng fear
【恫吓】 dònghè threaten; intimidate: 虚声～ bluff; bluster

## 峒

dòng 〔多用于地名〕 cave; cavern

## 栋

dòng ① 〈书〉 ridgepole ② 〈量〉: 一～楼房 a building
【栋梁】 dòngliáng ridgepole and beam — pillar of the state

## 胨

dòng 〈生化〉 peptone

## dōu

**都** dōu 〈副〉①all: 大家～到了吗? Is everybody here?/ 我们的干部～是人民的勤务员。Our cadres are all servants of the people./ 不管做什么,～应该考虑到人民的利益。Whatever we do, we should take the interests of the people into consideration. ②〔跟"是"字合用,说明理由〕: ～是你老磨蹭,害得我们迟到了。It was all because of your dawdling that we were late./ ～是党的领导,我们才有今天幸福的生活。Thanks to the leadership of the Party, we are leading a happy life today. ③even: 今天天气真怪,中午比早晨～冷。Strange weather we're having today. It's even colder at noon than it was early in the morning. ④already: 他～八十岁了,身子骨还那么硬朗。He's already eighty but still going strong.
另见 dū

**兜** dōu ①pocket; bag: 裤～儿 trouser pocket/ 网～儿 string bag ②wrap up in a piece of cloth, etc.: 用毛巾～着几个鸡蛋 carry a few eggs wrapped up in a towel ③move round: 我们乘车在城里～了一圈。We went for a drive around in town. ④canvass; solicit: ～售 peddle ⑤take upon oneself; take responsibility for sth.: 没关系,出了问题我～着。Don't worry. If anything goes wrong, I'll take responsibility for it.

【兜捕】 dōubǔ surround and seize; round up

【兜抄】 dōuchāo close in from the rear and both flanks; round up

【兜底】 dōudǐ reveal all the details (of a person's disreputable background, etc.); disclose the whole inside story

【兜兜】 dōudou 〈口〉见"兜肚"

【兜兜裤儿】 dōudoukùr sunsuit (for a child)

【兜肚】 dōudu an undergarment covering the chest and abdomen

【兜风】 dōufēng ①catch the wind: 帆破了,兜不住风。The sails are torn; they won't catch the wind. ②〈方〉go for a drive, ride or sail; go for a spin

【兜揽】 dōulǎn ①canvass; solicit: ～生意 solicit custom; drum up trade ②take upon oneself (sb. else's work, etc.)

【兜圈子】 dōu quānzi ①go around in circles; circle: 飞机在森林上空～。The aeroplane circled over the forest. ②beat about the bush

【兜售】 dōushòu peddle; hawk

【兜子】 dōuzi pocket; bag

## dǒu

**斗** dǒu ①*dou*, a unit of dry measure for grain (=1 decalitre) ②a *dou* measure ③an object shaped like a cup or dipper: 烟～ (tobacco) pipe/ 漏～ funnel ④whorl (of a fingerprint) ⑤〈天〉the Big Dipper: ～柄 the handle of the Dipper
另见 dòu

【斗车】 dǒuchē trolley (in a mine or at a construction site); tram

【斗胆】 dǒudǎn 〈谦〉make bold; venture: 我～说一句,这件事您做错了。May I make bold to suggest that you were wrong to do so.

【斗拱】 dǒugǒng 〈建〉*dougong*, a system of brackets inserted between the top of a column and a crossbeam (each bracket being formed of a double bow-shaped arm, called *gong*, which supports a block of wood, called *dou*, on each side)

【斗箕】 dǒuji fingerprint

【斗笠】 dǒulì bamboo hat

【斗篷】 dǒupeng cape; cloak

【斗渠】 dǒuqú 〈水〉lateral canal

【斗式提升机】 dǒushì tíshēngjī 〈机〉bucket elevator

【斗室】 dǒushì 〈书〉a small room

【斗烟丝】 dǒuyānsī pipe tobacco

**抖** dǒu ①tremble; shiver; quiver: 浑身直～ tremble all over/ 冷得发～ shiver with cold/ 气得发～ quiver with anger ②shake; jerk: 把衣服上的雪～掉 shake the snow off one's clothes/ ～一～缰绳 give the reins a jerk/ ～开棉被 spread the quilt with a flick ③rouse; stir up: ～起精神 pluck up one's spirits ④〈讽〉get on in the world

【抖动】 dǒudòng shake; tremble; vibrate

【抖搂】 dǒulou 〈方〉①shake off; shake out of sth.: 把包里的东西～出来 shake a bag to empty it ②expose; bring to light: 把她干的那些坏事给大伙～～。Let everyone know all the wicked things she has done. ③waste; squander: 别把钱～光了。Don't waste all the money.

【抖擞】 dǒusǒu enliven; rouse: ～精神 brace up; pull oneself together/ 精神～ full of energy; full of beans

【抖威风】 dǒu wēifēng throw one's weight about

**陡** dǒu ①steep; precipitous: 山～路险。The hill is steep, and the climb is dangerous. ②suddenly; abruptly: 天气～变。The weather changed suddenly.

【陡槽】 dǒucáo 〈水〉chute

【陡度】 dǒudù 〈物〉gradient: 压力～ pressure gradient

【陡峻】 dǒujùn high and precipitous

【陡立】 dǒulì rise steeply

【陡峭】 dǒuqiào precipitous

【陡然】 dǒurán suddenly; unexpectedly: ～下降 fall suddenly

**蚪** dǒu 见"蝌蚪" kēdǒu

## dòu

**斗** dòu ①fight; tussle: 拳～ fist fight; fisticuffs ②struggle against; denounce: ～地主 struggle against the landlords; settle scores with the landlords ③contest with; contend with: 狐狸再狡猾也～不过好猎手。The craftiest fox can't escape the skilled hunter. ④make animals fight (as a game): ～蛐蛐 cricketfight ⑤fit together: ～榫 fit the tenon into the mortise; dovetail/ 大家～一～情况。Let's pool our information and size up the situation.
另见 dǒu

【斗鸡】 dòujī ①gamecock ②cockfighting

【斗批改】 dòu-pī-gǎi struggle-criticism-transformation (important tasks of the Great Proletarian Cultural Revolution)

【斗气】 dòuqì quarrel or contend with sb. on account of a personal grudge

【斗私批修】 dòu sī pī xiū fight selfishness, repudiate revisionism

【斗眼】 dòuyǎn cross-eye 又作"斗鸡眼"

【斗争】 dòuzhēng ①struggle; fight; combat: 跟修正主义作坚决的～ fight resolutely against revisionism/ 同一切不正确的思想和行为作不疲倦的～ wage a tireless struggle against all incorrect ideas and actions/ 新与旧的～ conflict between the new and the old ② accuse and denounce at a meeting: ～恶霸地主 publicly denounce (或 struggle against) a despotic landlord ③ strive for; fight for: 为完成五年计划而～ strive for the fulfilment of the five-year plan ◇ ～会 public accusation meeting/ ～性 fighting spirit; militancy

【斗志】 dòuzhì will to fight; fighting will: 鼓舞群众的～ arouse the fighting will of the masses/ ～昂扬 have high morale

【斗智】 dòuzhì battle of wits

**豆** dòu ① legumes; pulses; beans; peas: 蚕～ broad beans/ 豌～ peas/ 扁～ hyacinth beans ② an ancient stemmed cup or bowl

【豆瓣酱】 dòubànjiàng thick broad-bean sauce

【豆包】 dòubāo steamed bun stuffed with sweetened bean paste

【豆饼】 dòubǐng 〈农〉 soya-bean cake; bean cake

【豆豉】 dòuchǐ fermented soya beans, salted or otherwise

【豆腐】 dòufu bean curd ◇ ～房 bean-curd plant/ ～干 dried bean curd/ ～脑儿 jellied bean curd/ ～乳 fermented bean curd

【豆腐皮】 dòufupí ① skin of soya-bean milk ② 〈方〉 thin sheets of bean curd

【豆荚】 dòujiá pod

【豆浆】 dòujiāng soya-bean milk

【豆角儿】 dòujiǎor 〈口〉 fresh kidney beans

【豆科】 dòukē 〈植〉 the pulse family; bean or pea family ◇ ～植物 legume; leguminous plant

【豆蔻】 dòukòu 〈植〉 round cardamom (*Amomum cardamomum*)

【豆绿】 dòulǜ pea green 又作"豆青"

【豆面】 dòumiàn bean flour

【豆娘】 dòuniáng 〈动〉 damselfly

【豆萁】 dòuqí 〈方〉 beanstalk

【豆蓉】 dòuróng fine bean mash, used as stuffing in cakes

【豆沙】 dòushā sweetened bean paste

【豆薯】 dòushǔ yam bean

【豆象】 dòuxiàng 〈动〉 bean weevil

【豆芽儿】 dòuyár bean sprouts

【豆雁】 dòuyàn 〈动〉 bean goose

【豆油】 dòuyóu soya-bean oil

【豆渣】 dòuzhā residue from beans after making soya-bean milk; bean dregs

【豆汁】 dòuzhī a fermented drink made from ground beans

【豆制品】 dòuzhìpǐn bean products

【豆子】 dòuzi beans or peas

**逗** dòu ① tease; play with: ～孩子玩 play with a child ② provoke (laughter, etc.); amuse: 这小女孩～人喜欢。She's a charming little girl. ③ 〈方〉 funny: 这话真～! What a funny remark! ④ stay; stop ⑤ a slight pause in reading

【逗号】 dòuhào comma (,)

【逗留】 dòuliú stay; stop: 他们中途在西安～了几天。They stopped over in Xi'an for several days./ 禁止～! No loitering!

【逗弄】 dòunong tease; kid; make fun of: 他～你呢。He's kidding you.

【逗趣儿】 dòuqùr 〈方〉 set people laughing (by funny remarks, etc.); amuse: 他真会～! He's really very amusing!

【逗笑儿】 dòuxiàor 〈方〉 amusing

【逗引】 dòuyǐn tease

**痘** dòu ① smallpox ② smallpox pustule

【痘苗】 dòumiáo (bovine) vaccine

**读** dòu a slight pause in reading
另见 dú

**窦** dòu ① hole ② 〈生理〉 sinus: 鼻旁～ paranasal sinus ③ (Dòu) a surname

## dū

**都** dū ① capital ② big city; metropolis: 鞍山是我国的钢～。Anshan is our country's steel metropolis.
另见 dōu

【都城】 dūchéng capital

【都会】 dūhuì city; metropolis

【都市】 dūshì city; metropolis

**督** dū superintend and direct: ～战 supervise operations

【督察】 dūchá superintend; supervise

【督促】 dūcù supervise and urge: ～大家及时归还工具 urge everybody to return the tools on time/ 已经布置了的工作，应当认真～检查。We must supervise and speed up fulfilment of assigned tasks.

【督励】 dūlì urge and encourage

【督学】 dūxué 〈旧〉 educational inspector

**嘟** dū ① 〈象〉 toot; honk: 汽车喇叭～～响。The car tooted. ② 〈方〉 pout: ～起了嘴 pout

【嘟噜】 dūlu 〈口〉 ① 〈量〉 bunch; cluster: 一～葡萄 a bunch of grapes ② hang down in a bunch ③ trill: 打～儿 pronounce with a trill; trill

【嘟囔】 dūnang mutter to oneself; mumble 又作"嘟哝"

## dú

**毒** dú ① poison; toxin: 服～ take poison ② narcotics: 吸～ take drugs/ 贩～ traffic in drugs ③ poisonous; noxious; poisoned: ～蜘蛛 poisonous spider/ 有～气体 noxious gas/ ～箭 a poisoned arrow ④ kill with poison; poison ⑤ malicious; cruel; fierce: 地主的心肠真～! How cruel the landlords are!/ 那时太阳正～，晒得他汗珠直往下滚。The sun was at its fiercest and beads of sweat kept rolling down his face./ ～打 beat up

【毒扁豆】 dúbiǎndòu 〈植〉 calabar bean ◇ ～碱 〈药〉 physostigmine; eserine

【毒草】 dúcǎo poisonous weeds — harmful speech, writing, etc.

【毒蛾】 dú'é tussock moth

【毒饵】 dú'ěr poison bait

【毒谷】 dúgǔ poison grains (planted with seeds to kill harmful insects)

【毒害】 dúhài poison (sb.'s mind): 用资产阶级思想～青年 poison young people with bourgeois ideology

【毒化】 dúhuà poison; spoil: ～会谈的气氛 poison the atmosphere of the talks

【毒计】 dújì venomous scheme; deadly trap

【毒剂】 dújì toxic; toxicant

【毒辣】 dúlà sinister; diabolic

【毒瘤】 dúliú malignant tumour; cancer

【毒品】 dúpǐn narcotic drugs; narcotics

【毒气】 dúqì poisonous (或 poison) gas ◇ ～弹 gas shell;

gas bomb/ ～室 gas chamber
【毒区】 dúqū contaminated area (in chemical warfare); gassed area
【毒杀】 dúshā kill with poison
【毒杀芬】 dúshāfēn 〈农〉 toxaphene; octachlorocamphene
【毒砂】 dúshā 〈矿〉 arsenopyrite; mispickel
【毒蛇】 dúshé poisonous (或 venomous) snake; viper
【毒手】 dúshǒu violent treachery; murderous scheme: 下～ resort to violent treachery; lay murderous hands on sb.
【毒死】 dúsǐ kill with poison; poison
【毒素】 dúsù ①〈生〉 toxin ② poison: 清除封建～ eliminate feudal poison
【毒瓦斯】 dúwǎsī poisonous (或 poison) gas
【毒物】 dúwù poisonous substance; poison
【毒腺】 dúxiàn 〈动〉 poison gland
【毒刑】 dúxíng cruel corporal punishment; horrible torture
【毒性】 dúxìng toxicity; poisonousness
【毒蕈】 dúxùn poisonous fungus; toadstool
【毒牙】 dúyá poison (或 venom) fang
【毒药】 dúyào poison; toxicant
【毒液】 dúyè venom
【毒汁】 dúzhī venom: 一篇～四溅的反党文章 a poisonous anti-Party article

**独** dú ① only; single: ～子 only son/ 大家都到了，～有他还没来。 He's the only one who isn't here yet. ② alone; by oneself; in solitude: ～居 live a solitary existence/ ～坐 sit alone ③ old people without offspring; the childless
【独霸】 dúbà dominate exclusively; monopolize: ～一方 lord it over a district; be a local despot
【独白】 dúbái soliloquy; monologue
【独裁】 dúcái dictatorship; autocratic rule ◇ ～者 autocrat; dictator/ ～政治 autocracy
【独唱】 dúchàng (vocal) solo ◇ ～会 recital (of a vocalist)
【独出心裁】 dú chū xīncái show originality; be original
【独创】 dúchuàng original creation: ～一格 create a style all one's own ◇ ～精神 creative spirit/ ～性 originality
【独词句】 dúcíjù 〈语〉 one-member sentence
【独当一面】 dú dāng yī miàn take charge of a department or locality: 他成长很快，已经可以～了。 He's matured quickly. He can now take charge of the whole locality.
【独到】 dúdào original: ～的见解 original view/ ～之处 originality
【独断】 dúduàn arbitrary; dictatorial
【独断独行】 dúduàn-dúxíng make arbitrary decisions and take peremptory actions; act arbitrarily
【独夫】 dúfū a bad ruler forsaken by all; autocrat: ～民贼 autocrat and traitor to the people
【独孤】 Dúgū a surname
【独角戏】 dújiǎoxì monodrama; one-man show: 唱～ put on a one-man show; go it alone
【独居石】 dújūshí 〈矿〉 monazite
【独具匠心】 dú jù jiàngxīn show ingenuity; have originality
【独具只眼】 dú jù zhī yǎn be able to see what others cannot; have exceptional insight
【独揽】 dúlǎn arrogate; monopolize: ～大权 arrogate all powers to oneself
【独力】 dúlì by one's own efforts; on one's own: ～经营 manage affairs on one's own
【独立】 dúlì ① stand alone: ～山巅的苍松 a pine tree standing alone on a mountain peak ② independence: 宣布～ proclaim independence ③ independent; on one's own: ～营(团、师) independent battalion (regiment, division)/ ～分析问题和解决问题的能力 ability to analyse and solve problems on one's own
◇ ～成分 〈语〉 independent element/ ～国 independent state/ ～核算单位 independent accounting unit
【独立王国】 dúlì wángguó independent kingdom: 头脑里资产阶级思想的～ the realm of bourgeois ideology in one's mind
【独立性】 dúlìxìng independent character; independence: 闹～ assert one's "independence" — refuse to obey the leadership
【独立自主】 dúlì-zìzhǔ maintain independence and keep the initiative in one's own hands; act independently and with the initiative in one's own hands
【独龙族】 Dúlóngzú the Drung (Tulung) nationality, living in Yunnan
【独轮车】 dúlúnchē wheelbarrow
【独门儿】 dúménr special skill (of an individual or a family)
【独木不成林】 dú mù bù chéng lín one tree does not make a forest — one person alone cannot accomplish much
【独木难支】 dú mù nán zhī one log cannot prop up a tottering building — one person alone cannot save the situation
【独木桥】 dúmùqiáo ① single-plank (或 single-log) bridge ② difficult path
【独木舟】 dúmùzhōu dugout canoe
【独幕剧】 dúmùjù one-act play
【独辟蹊径】 dú pì xījìng open a new road for oneself; develop a new style or a new method of one's own
【独善其身】 dú shàn qí shēn pay attention to one's own moral uplift without thought of others
【独身】 dúshēn ① separated from one's family: ～在外 be away from home and family ② unmarried; single ◇ ～主义 celibacy
【独生女】 dúshēngnǚ only daughter
【独生子】 dúshēngzǐ only son
【独树一帜】 dú shù yī zhì fly one's own colours — develop a school of one's own
【独特】 dútè unique; distinctive: ～的风格 a unique style
【独舞】 dúwǔ solo dance
【独眼龙】 dúyǎnlóng a person blind in one eye; one-eyed person
【独一无二】 dúyī-wú'èr unique; unparalleled; unmatched
【独占】 dúzhàn have sth. all to oneself; monopolize
【独占鳌头】 dú zhàn áotóu come out first; head the list of successful candidates; be the champion
【独占资本】 dúzhàn zīběn 〈经〉 monopoly capital
【独自】 dúzì alone; by oneself
【独奏】 dúzòu (instrumental) solo: 钢琴～ piano solo ◇ ～会 recital (of an instrumentalist)

**读** dú ① read; read aloud: 这部小说值得一～。 This novel is worth reading. ② attend school: ～完大学 finish college
另见 dòu
【读本】 dúběn reader; textbook: 汉语～ a Chinese reader
【读书】 dúshū ① read; study: ～是学习，使用也是学习，而且是更重要的学习。 Reading is learning, but applying is also learning and the more important kind of learning at that./ 她～很用功。 She studies hard. ② attend school
◇ ～班 study class/ ～笔记 reading notes/ ～人 a scholar; an intellectual
【读数】 dúshù reading: 温度计～ thermometer reading/ 标度～ scale reading
【读图】 dútú interpret blueprints; interpret drawings
【读物】 dúwù reading matter (或 material): 儿童～ chil-

dren's books/ 通俗～ popular literature
【读音】 dúyīn pronunciation
【读者】 dúzhě reader ◇ ～来信 readers' letters; letters to the editor

**渎** dú 〈书〉 ① show disrespect or contempt: 亵～ blaspheme; profane ② ditch; drain
【渎职】 dúzhí malfeasance; dereliction of duty

**椟** dú 〈书〉 casket; case; box

**犊** dú calf

**牍** dú ① wooden tablets or slips for writing (in ancient times) ② documents; archives; correspondence

**黩** dú ① blacken; defile ② act wantonly
【黩武】 dúwǔ militaristic; warlike; bellicose: 穷兵～ engage in unjust military ventures ◇ ～主义 militarism/ ～主义者 militarist

**髑** dú
【髑髅】 dúlóu 〈书〉 skull (of a dead person)

## dǔ

**肚** dǔ tripe: 拌～丝儿 slices of tripe and cucumber in soy sauce
另见 dù
【肚子】 dǔzi tripe
另见 dùzi

**笃** dǔ ① sincere; earnest ② (of an illness) serious; critical: 病～ be dangerously ill; be in a critical condition; be terminally ill
【笃厚】 dǔhòu sincere and magnanimous
【笃实】 dǔshí ① honest and sincere ② solid; sound: 学问～ sound scholarship
【笃信】 dǔxìn sincerely believe in; be a devout believer in
【笃学】 dǔxué diligent in study; devoted to study; studious

**堵** dǔ ① stop up; block up: 把老鼠洞～死 stop up mouseholes/ 别～着门! Don't stand in the doorway!/ 黄继光舍身～枪眼。Defying death, Huang Jiguang threw himself against the embrasure of the enemy's blockhouse./ ～不住资本主义的路，就迈不开社会主义的步。If you don't block the way to capitalism, you can't move a step along the socialist road. ② stifled; suffocated; oppressed: 胸口～得慌 feel suffocated; feel a tightness in the chest/ 心里～得难受 have a load on one's mind ③〈书〉 wall: 观者如～。There was a crowd of spectators. ④〈量〉: 一～墙 a wall
【堵击】 dǔjī intercept and attack: ～逃敌 intercept the fleeing enemy
【堵塞】 dǔsè stop up; block up: 交通～ traffic jam/ ～漏洞 stop up a loophole; plug a hole
【堵嘴】 dǔzuǐ gag sb.; silence sb.

**赌** dǔ ① gamble: 禁～ ban gambling ② bet: 打～ make a bet; bet
【赌本】 dǔběn money to gamble with
【赌博】 dǔbó gambling
【赌场】 dǔchǎng gambling house
【赌棍】 dǔgùn hardened (或 professional) gambler
【赌具】 dǔjù gambling paraphernalia; gambling device
【赌窟】 dǔkū gambling-den
【赌气】 dǔqì feel wronged and act rashly: 他觉得受了委屈，一～就走了。Feeling he had been wronged, he went off in a fit of pique.
【赌钱】 dǔqián gamble
【赌徒】 dǔtú gambler
【赌咒】 dǔzhòu take an oath; swear
【赌注】 dǔzhù stake

**睹** dǔ see: 目～ see with one's own eyes; be an eyewitness to
【睹物思人】 dǔ wù sī rén seeing the thing one thinks of the person — the thing reminds one of its owner

## dù

**杜** dù ① birch-leaf pear ② shut out; stop; prevent: ～门谢客 close one's door to visitors/ 以～流弊 so as to put an end to abuses ③ (Dù) a surname
【杜蘅】 dùhéng 〈植〉 wild ginger 又作"杜衡"
【杜鹃】 dùjuān ① 〈动〉 cuckoo ② 〈植〉 azalea
【杜绝】 dùjué stop; put an end to: ～弊端 stop all corrupt practices/ ～浪费 put an end to waste
【杜梨】 dùlí birch-leaf pear
【杜灭芬】 dùmièfēn 〈药〉 domiphen
【杜宇】 dùyǔ 〈动〉 cuckoo
【杜仲】 dùzhòng 〈中药〉 the bark of eucommia (*Eucommia ulmoides*) ◇ ～胶 gutta-percha
【杜撰】 dùzhuàn fabricate; make up: 他讲的是真有其事，不是～的。The story he told is true, not made up.

**肚** dù belly; abdomen; stomach
另见 dǔ
【肚带】 dùdài bellyband; girth
【肚皮】 dùpí 〈方〉 belly
【肚脐】 dùqí navel; belly button
【肚子】 dùzi belly; abdomen: ～痛 have a stomachache; suffer from abdominal pain/ 笑得～痛 laugh till one's sides split/ 一～气 absolutely exasperated; full of pent-up anger
另见 dǔzi

**妒** dù be jealous (或 envious) of; envy
【妒忌】 dùjì be jealous (或 envious) of; envy

**度** dù ① linear measure ② degree of intensity: 硬～ hardness/ 湿～ humidity ③ a unit of measurement for angles, temperature, etc.; degree: 直角为九十～。A right angle is an angle of 90 degrees./ 北纬三十八～ latitude 38° N./ 水的沸点是摄氏一百～。The boiling point of water is 100 degrees centigrade./ 这种酒五十～。This spirit contains 50 per cent alcohol./ 您的眼镜多少～? What's the strength of the lenses of your glasses? ④ 〈电〉 kilowatt-hour (kwh) ⑤ limit; extent; degree: 劳累过～ be overworked/ 将玻璃管加热，以能弯曲为～。Heat the glass tube to the point that it can bend./ 长短适～ be the right length/ 高～的无产阶级政治觉悟 a high degree (或 level) of proletarian political consciousness ⑥ tolerance; magnanimity: 大～包容 regard with kindly tolerance; be magnanimous ⑦ consideration: 把生死置之～外 give no thought to personal safety ⑧ 〈量〉 occasion; time: 再～ a second time; once more/ 一年一～ once a year ⑨ spend; pass: 在农村～过童年 spend one's childhood in the countryside/ 欢～节日 joyously celebrate a festival
另见 duó

【度荒】 dùhuāng tide over a lean year
【度假】 dùjià spend one's holidays (或 vacation); go vacationing
【度冷丁】 dùlěngdīng 〈药〉 dolantin
【度量】 dùliàng tolerance; magnanimity: ～大 broad-minded; magnanimous/ ～小 narrow-minded
【度量衡】 dùliànghéng length, capacity and weight; weights and measures ◇ ～学 metrology
【度命】 dùmìng drag out a miserable existence: 靠糠菜～ manage to keep oneself alive with bran and wild herbs
【度日】 dùrì subsist (in hardship); eke out an existence: 过去他靠什么～的？What did he do for a living in the old days?
【度日如年】 dù rì rú nián one day seems like a year; days wear on like years
【度数】 dùshu number of degrees; reading: 那个表上的～是多少？What does that meter read?

**渡** dù ① cross (a river, the sea, etc.): ～河 cross a river/ 飞～太平洋 fly (across) the Pacific/ 红军强～大渡河。The Red Army forced its way across the Dadu River. ② tide over; pull through: ～过难关 tide over a difficulty; pull through ③ ferry (people, goods, etc.) across ④〔多用于地名〕 ferry crossing
【渡槽】 dùcáo aqueduct
【渡场】 dùchǎng 〈军〉 crossing site
【渡船】 dùchuán ferryboat; ferry
【渡河点】 dùhédiǎn point of crossing
【渡口】 dùkǒu ferry
【渡鸦】 dùyā 〈动〉 raven

**镀** dù plating: 电～ electroplating; galvanizing/ ～镍 nickel-plating/ ～铝钢 aluminium-plated steel
【镀金】 dùjīn ① gold-plating; gilding ② get gilded (formerly said of students who went abroad to study in order to enhance their social status)
【镀锡】 dùxī tin-plating; tinning ◇ ～铁皮 tinplate
【镀锌】 dùxīn zinc-plating; galvanizing
【镀银】 dùyín silver-plating; silvering

**蠹** dù ① a kind of insect that eats into books, clothing, etc.; moth: 书～ bookworm ② moth-eaten; worm-eaten: 流水不腐，户枢不～。Running water is never stale and a door-hinge never gets worm-eaten.
【蠹虫】 dùchóng ① 见"蠹"① ② a harmful person; vermin
【蠹鱼】 dùyú silverfish; fish moth

## duān

**端** duān ① end; extremity: 两～ both ends/ 岛的南～ the southern tip (或 end) of the island ② beginning: 开～ beginning ③ point; item: 举其一～ for instance; just to mention one example ④ reason; cause: 无～ without rhyme or reason; unwarranted/ 借～ use sth. as a pretext ⑤ upright; proper: ～坐 sit up straight/ 品行不～ improper behaviour; misconduct ⑥ hold sth. level with both hands; carry: ～盘子 carry a tray/ ～饭上菜 serve a meal/ ～进两杯茶来 bring in two cups of tea/ 给病人～大小便 carry bedpans for the patients/ 有什么想法都～出来。Whatever you think, come out with it.
【端量】 duānliáng look sb. up and down
【端木】 Duānmù a surname
【端倪】 duānní clue; inkling: 略有～ have an inkling of the matter
【端午节】 Duānwǔjié the Dragon Boat Festival (the 5th day of the 5th lunar month)
【端线】 duānxiàn 〈体〉 end line
【端详】 duānxiáng ① details: 细说～ give a full and detailed account; give full particulars ② dignified and serene: 举止～ behave with serene dignity
【端详】 duānxiang look sb. up and down
【端绪】 duānxù inkling; clue: 我们谈了半天，仍然毫无～。We talked the matter over for quite some time but didn't get anywhere.
【端砚】 duānyàn a kind of high-quality ink-slab made in Duanxi (端溪), Guangdong Province
【端阳】 Duānyáng 见"端午节"
【端正】 duānzhèng ① upright; regular: 五官～ have regular features/ 把画像端端正正地挂起来 hang the portrait straight ② proper; correct: 品行～ correct in behaviour ③ rectify; correct: ～思想 correct one's thinking; straighten out one's ideas/ ～学习态度 take a correct attitude towards study
【端庄】 duānzhuāng dignified; sedate

## duǎn

**短** duǎn ① short; brief: 这条路最～。This is the shortest way./ 冬季日～夜长。In winter the days are short and the nights long./ 我给他写了封～信。I dropped him a few lines./ 开个～会 have a brief meeting ② lack; owe: 理～ lack sound argument/ ～斤缺两 give short measure/ 一个月～两天 two days short of a month; a month less two days/ 别人都来了，就～他一个。All the others are here; he's the only one missing. ③ weak point; fault: 揭人的～儿 pick on sb.'s weakness/ 说长道～ gossip
【短兵相接】 duǎnbīng xiāng jiē fight at close quarters; engage in hand-to-hand fight (或 close combat)
【短波】 duǎnbō shortwave
【短不了】 duǎnbuliǎo ① cannot do without: 人～水。Man cannot do without water. ② cannot avoid; have to: 以后～还要请你帮忙。Most likely I'll have to ask you for help again.
【短程】 duǎnchéng short distance; short range
【短处】 duǎnchu shortcoming; failing; fault; weakness
【短传】 duǎnchuán 〈体〉 short pass
【短促】 duǎncù of very short duration; very brief: 呼吸～ be short of breath; gasp; pant
【短打】 duǎndǎ ①〈剧〉 hand-to-hand fight in tights ② 见"短装"
【短大衣】 duǎndàyī short overcoat
【短笛】 duǎndí 〈乐〉 piccolo
【短吨】 duǎndūn short ton
【短工】 duǎngōng casual labourer; seasonal labourer
【短骨】 duǎngǔ 〈生理〉 short bone
【短号】 duǎnhào 〈乐〉 cornet
【短见】 duǎnjiàn ① shortsighted view ② suicide: 寻～ attempt suicide; commit suicide
【短角牛】 duǎnjiǎoniú shorthorn
【短距离】 duǎnjùlí short distance ◇ ～赛跑 short-distance run; dash; sprint
【短裤】 duǎnkù shorts
【短路】 duǎnlù 〈电〉 short circuit
【短命】 duǎnmìng die young; be short-lived: ～的军阀政权 a short-lived warlord regime
【短跑】 duǎnpǎo dash; sprint ◇ ～运动员 dash man; sprinter
【短篇小说】 duǎnpiān xiǎoshuō short story

【短片】 duǎnpiàn 〈电影〉 short film; short
【短评】 duǎnpíng short commentary; brief comment
【短期】 duǎnqī short-term: 在～内 in a short time; in a brief space of time ◇ ～贷款 short-term loan/ ～轮训 short-term training in rotation
【短浅】 duǎnqiǎn narrow and shallow: 目光～ shortsighted/ 见识～ lacking knowledge and experience; shallow
【短欠】 duǎnqiàn ① owe; be in arrears ② be short of
【短枪】 duǎnqiāng short arm; handgun
【短球】 duǎnqiú 〈乒乓球〉 short ball; drop shot
【短缺】 duǎnquē shortage
【短少】 duǎnshǎo deficient; short; missing: ～一页。There is one page missing./ 你们需要的钢材我们保证供应，一吨也不～。We guarantee to supply the steel you need, and not fall short by a single ton.
【短时记忆】 duǎnshí jìyì 〈心〉 short-term memory
【短视】 duǎnshì ① nearsightedness; myopia ② lack foresight; be shortsighted
【短统靴】 duǎntǒngxuē ankle boots
【短途】 duǎntú short distance ◇ ～运输 short-distance transport; short haul
【短袜】 duǎnwà socks
【短尾猴】 duǎnwěihóu stump-tailed macaque (或 monkey)
【短纤维】 duǎnxiānwéi ① short-staple: ～棉花 short-staple cotton ② 〈纺〉 staple (fibre) ◇ ～切断器 staple cutter
【短小】 duǎnxiǎo short and small; short; small: 身材～ of small stature/ ～的序幕 a brief prologue
【短小精悍】 duǎnxiǎo jīnghàn ① not of imposing stature but strong and capable ② (of a piece of writing) short and pithy; terse and forceful
【短训班】 duǎnxùnbān short-term training course
【短语】 duǎnyǔ 〈语〉 phrase
【短元音】 duǎnyuányīn 〈语〉 short vowel
【短暂】 duǎnzàn of short duration; transient; brief: 她的一生是～而光荣的一生。Her life was short but glorious.
【短装】 duǎnzhuāng be dressed in a Chinese-style jacket and trousers

## duàn

**段** duàn ① 〈量〉 section; segment; part: 一～铁路 a section of railway/ 一～衣料 a length of dress material/ 这～历史 this phase of history/ 一～时间 a period of time/ 边界东～ the eastern sector of the boundary ② paragraph; passage ③ (Duàn) a surname
【段落】 duànluò ① paragraph: 这篇文章～清楚。This article is well paragraphed. ② phase; stage: 第一期工程已经告一～。The first phase of the project has been completed.

**断** duàn ① break; snap: 喀嚓一声，～成两截 break in two with a snap/ 他给小提琴调弦的时候，E 弦～了。When he was tuning his violin, the E string snapped. ② break off; cut off; stop: ～水 cut off the water supply/ ～敌退路 cut off the enemy's retreat/ 与指挥部的联系～了 lose contact with headquarters ③ give up; abstain from: ～烟 give up (或 quit) smoking ④ judge; decide: 当机立～ decide promptly and opportunely; make a prompt decision ⑤ 〈书〉〈副〉〔只用于否定式〕absolutely; decidedly: ～不可信 absolutely incredible/ ～无此理 absolutely untenable (或 unreasonable); the height of absurdity
【断案】 duàn'àn ① settle a lawsuit ② 〈逻〉 conclusion (of a syllogism)
【断编残简】 duànbiān-cánjiǎn stray fragments of text 又作"断简残编"
【断层】 duàncéng 〈地〉 fault: 倾向(走向)～ dip (strike) fault ◇ ～带 fault zone/ ～地震 fault earthquake/ ～面 fault plane/ ～作用 faulting
【断肠】 duàncháng heartbroken
【断炊】 duànchuī run out of rice and fuel; can't keep the pot boiling; go hungry
【断代】 duàndài division of history into periods ◇ ～史 dynastic history
【断定】 duàndìng conclude; form a judgment; decide; determine: 我们有理由可以～，会议推迟了。We may reasonably conclude that the meeting has been postponed./ 他～机器出了毛病了。He came to the conclusion that the machine was out of order.
【断断】 duànduàn 〔只用于否定式〕 absolutely: ～使不得。That will never do. 或 That simply won't do.
【断断续续】 duànduànxùxù off and on; intermittently: ～读过四年书 had four years of schooling off and on/ ～地说 speak disjointedly
【断顿】 duàndùn can't afford the next meal; go hungry
【断根】 duàngēn be completely cured; effect a permanent cure
【断后】 duànhòu ① bring up the rear; cover a retreat ② have no progeny
【断乎】 duànhū 〔只用于否定式〕 absolutely: ～不可 absolutely impermissible
【断交】 duànjiāo ① break off a friendship ② sever (或 break off) diplomatic relations
【断句】 duànjù ① make pauses in reading unpunctuated ancient writings ② punctuate
【断绝】 duànjué break off; cut off; sever: ～外交关系 sever (或 break off) diplomatic relations/ ～交通 stop traffic ◇ ～地 〈军〉 broken terrain (或 ground)
【断粮】 duànliáng run out of grain (或 food)
【断流器】 duànliúqì 〈电〉 cutout: 安全～ safety cutout
【断路】 duànlù 〈电〉 open circuit; broken circuit ◇ ～器 circuit breaker
【断面】 duànmiàn 〈测〉 section ◇ ～图 sectional drawing; section
【断奶】 duànnǎi weaning
【断气】 duànqì ① breathe one's last; die ② cut off the gas
【断然】 duànrán ① absolutely; flatly; categorically: ～不能接受 absolutely inacceptable/ ～拒绝 flatly refuse/ ～否认 categorically deny ② resolute; drastic: 采取～措施 take drastic measures
【断送】 duànsòng forfeit (one's life, future, etc.); ruin
【断头】 duàntóu 〈纺〉 ① broken end ② end breaking ◇ ～率 end breakage rate
【断头台】 duàntóutái guillotine
【断尾】 duànwěi 〈牧〉 docking
【断线风筝】 duànxiàn fēngzhēng a kite with a broken string — a person or thing gone beyond recall
【断言】 duànyán say (或 state) with certainty; assert categorically; affirm
【断语】 duànyǔ conclusion; judgment: 遽下～ jump to conclusions
【断垣残壁】 duànyuán-cánbì (a desolate scene of) broken walls; debris
【断章取义】 duàn zhāng qǔ yì quote out of context; garble a statement, etc.
【断肢再植】 duànzhī zàizhí 〈医〉 replantation of a severed limb
【断子绝孙】 duànzǐ-juésūn 〈骂〉 may you die without sons; may you be the last of your line

【断奏】 duànzòu 〈乐〉 *staccato*

**缎** duàn satin

【缎纹】 duànwén satin weave

【缎子】 duànzi satin

**煅** duàn ① forge: ～铁 forge iron ② calcine

【煅烧】 duànshāo calcine

**椴** duàn 〈植〉 (Chinese) linden

**锻** duàn forge

【锻锤】 duànchuí forging hammer

【锻工】 duàngōng ① forging ② forger; blacksmith ◇ ～车间 forging shop; forge/ ～钳 band jaw tongs

【锻件】 duànjiàn forging

【锻接】 duànjiē forge welding

【锻炼】 duànliàn ① take exercise; have physical training: 每天～半小时 take half an hour's exercise every day/ ～身体，保卫祖国 build up a good physique to defend the country/ 在大江大海中游泳，既可以～身体，又可以～意志。Swimming in big rivers and seas helps to build up both physical strength and willpower. ② temper; steel; toughen: 在三大革命运动中～自己 temper (或 steel) oneself in the three great revolutionary movements

【锻炉】 duànlú forge

【锻模】 duànmú forging die

【锻铁】 duàntiě wrought iron

【锻压机】 duànyājī forging press

【锻造】 duànzào forging; smithing: 压力～ press forging

**簖** duàn bamboo weir (for catching fish, etc.)

## duī

**堆** duī ① pile up; heap up; stack: 把麦秸～在场上 stack the wheat-stalks on the threshing ground/ 桌上～满了书。The desk was piled with books./ 粮食～满仓，果子～成山。Storehouses are bursting with grain, and fruit is piled high on the ground. ② heap; pile; stack: 柴火～ a pile (或 stack) of firewood/ 土～ mound/ 粪～ manure (或 dung) heap; dunghill/ 草～ haystack ③〈量〉heap; pile; crowd: 一～垃圾 a garbage (或 rubbish) heap/ 一～人 a crowd of people ④〔多用于地名〕hillock; mound

【堆存】 duīcún store up

【堆垛机】 duīduòjī (hay) stacker

【堆放】 duīfàng pile up; stack: 库房里～着许多农具。A lot of farm tools are piled in the storehouse.

【堆肥】 duīféi 〈农〉 compost

【堆积】 duījī ① pile up; heap up: 工地上建筑材料～如山。Building materials are piled up mountain-high on the construction site. ② 〈地〉 accumulation

【堆垒数论】 duīlěishùlùn 〈数〉 additive theory of numbers

【堆漆】 duīqī 〈工美〉 embossed lacquer

【堆砌】 duīqì ① load one's writing with fancy phrases ② pile up (hewn rocks, etc. to build sth.)

【堆石坝】 duīshíbà 〈水〉 rock-fill dam

【堆栈】 duīzhàn storehouse; warehouse

## duì

**队** duì ① a row of people; line: 排成两～ fall into two lines ② team; group: 篮球～ basketball team/ 军乐～ military band/ 游击～ guerrilla forces; guerrillas/ 钻井～ drilling crew

【队部】 duìbù the office or headquarters of a team, etc.: 生产队～ the office of a production team

【队列】 duìliè formation ◇ ～教练 〈军〉 (military) drill; formation drill

【队旗】 duìqí 〈体〉 team pennant: 互赠～ exchange team pennants

【队伍】 duìwǔ ① troops ② ranks; contingent: 革命～ the revolutionary ranks; battalions of the revolution/ 马克思主义理论～ a contingent of Marxist theoretical workers/ 游行～ contingents of marchers; procession; parade

【队形】 duìxíng formation: 成战斗～ in battle formation/ 以密集(散开)～前进 advance in close (open) order ◇ ～变换 evolution

【队员】 duìyuán team member

【队长】 duìzhǎng ① 〈体〉 captain ② team leader: 生产队～ production team leader

**对** duì ① answer; reply: 无言以～ have nothing to say in reply ② treat; cope with; counter: 刀～刀，枪～枪 sword against sword and spear against spear/ ～事不～人 concern oneself with facts and not with individuals/ 上海队～北京队 the Shanghai team versus the Beijing team ③ be trained on; be directed at: 枪口～着敌人 train the gun on the enemy/ 她的话不是～着你的。What she said was not directed at you. ④ mutual; face to face: ～骂 call each other names/ ～坐 sit facing each other/ ～饮 (two people) have a drink together ⑤ opposite; opposing: ～岸 the opposite bank; the other side of the river ⑥ bring (two things) into contact; fit one into the other: ～暗号 exchange code words/ ～个火儿。Give me a light, please./ 这个榫头～不上。This tenon won't fit. ⑦ suit; agree; get along: ～心眼儿 suit one down to the ground/ ～胃口 suit one's taste ⑧ compare; check; identify: ～笔迹 identify the handwriting/ ～号码 check numbers ⑨ set; adjust: ～表 set one's watch; synchronize watches/ ～好望远镜的距离 adjust the focus of a telescope ⑩ right; correct: 猜～了 guess right/ ～，就这么办。All right, just go ahead./ 他今天神色不～。He doesn't look himself today. ⑪ mix; add: 茶太浓了，给我～点儿水。Add some water to the tea, it's too strong for me. ⑫ divide into halves: ～股劈 go halves; split fifty-fifty ⑬ antithetical couplet; couplet: 喜～ wedding couplet ⑭ 〈量〉 pair; couple: 一～花瓶 a pair of vases/ 一～夫妇 a married couple ⑮ 〈介〉〔引进对象或事物的关系者〕: ～敌狠，～己和 ruthless to the enemy, kind to one's comrades/ ～这个问题的不同意见 different views on this question/ ～青少年的教育工作 educational work among young people/ ～无产阶级革命事业的必胜信念 a firm belief in the ultimate triumph of the proletarian revolution/ ～反革命分子实行无产阶级专政 exercise proletarian dictatorship over counterrevolutionaries

【对氨水杨酸钠】 duì'ān shuǐyángsuānnà 〈药〉 sodium para-aminosalicylate (PASNa)

【对案】 duì'àn 〈外〉 counterproposal

【对白】 duìbái dialogue

【对半】 duìbàn ① half-and-half; fifty-fifty: ～儿分 divide half-and-half; go halves ② double: ～儿利 a double profit

【对比】 duìbǐ ① contrast; balance: 今昔～ contrast the present with the past/ 构成鲜明的～ form a sharp contrast/ 阶级力量的～ the balance of class forces/ 敌我力量的～ the relative strength of the enemy forces and our own ② ratio: 双方人数～是一对四。The ratio between the two sides (或 parties) is one to four. ◇ ～剂 〈医〉 contrast medium

【对不起】 duìbuqǐ ①〈套〉I'm sorry; sorry; excuse me; pardon me; I beg your pardon: ～，给你添麻烦了。Sorry to have given you so much trouble./ ～，是我的错。Pardon me. It was my fault./ ～，我得走了。Excuse me, but I'll have to go now./ ～，请你再讲一遍好吗？I beg your pardon, but would you repeat what you said? 或 I beg your pardon? ②let sb. down; be unworthy of; do a disservice to; be unfair to 又作"对不住"

【对策】 duìcè the way to deal with a situation; countermeasure; countermove ◇ ～论〈数〉game theory

【对唱】 duìchàng musical dialogue in antiphonal style; antiphonal singing

【对称】 duìchèn symmetry

【对答】 duìdá answer; reply: ～如流 answer fluently; answer the questions without any hitch

【对待】 duìdài treat; approach; handle: ～同志象春天般的温暖 treat one's comrades with the warmth of spring/ 用无产阶级观点～一切问题 approach all problems from the proletarian point of view/ 正确地～群众 adopt a correct attitude towards the masses

【对得起】 duìdeqǐ not let sb. down; treat sb. fairly; be worthy of 又作"对得住"

【对等】 duìděng reciprocity; equity: 在～的基础上 on the basis of reciprocity; on a reciprocal basis

【对调】 duìdiào exchange; swop: ～工作 exchange jobs/ ～座位 exchange (或 swop) seats

【对顶角】 duìdǐngjiǎo 〈数〉vertical angles

【对方】 duìfāng the other (或 opposite) side; the other party

【对付】 duìfu ①deal with; cope with; counter; tackle: 沉着机智地～敌人 deal with the enemy calmly and resourcefully/ 用人民战争～侵略战争 counter a war of aggression with people's war/ 他只学了几个月的文化，写信也能～了。He has had only a few months' schooling, but he can manage to write a letter. ②make do: 这把锹你先～着用吧。Try to make do with this spade for now.

【对歌】 duìgē singing in antiphonal style

【对光】 duìguāng 〈摄〉set (或 focus) a camera

【对过】 duìguò opposite; across the way: 他就住在～。He lives just across the way./ 我家～就是邮局。The post office is just opposite my house.

【对号】 duìhào ①check the number: ～入座 take one's seat according to the number on the ticket; sit in the right seat ②fit; tally: 这张图纸有几个数据对不上号。There are a few figures on this blueprint that don't tally./ 他说的和做的不～。His deeds don't match his words. ③check mark (√); tick

【对话】 duìhuà dialogue: 两国政府已开始～。The two governments have opened a dialogue.

【对角线】 duìjiǎoxiàn 〈数〉diagonal (line)

【对接焊】 duìjiēhàn 〈机〉butt welding

【对襟】 duìjīn a kind of Chinese-style jacket with buttons down the front

【对劲儿】 duìjìnr ①be to one's liking; suit one: 这把锄我使着很～。This hoe suits me very well. ②normal; right: 这件事我越想越觉得不～。The more I think of it, the more I'm convinced there's something fishy about it. ③get along (well): 他们俩一向很～。The two of them have always got along very well.

【对进突击】 duìjìn tūjī 〈军〉two-pronged assault from opposite directions

【对局】 duìjú play a game of chess, etc.

【对开】 duìkāi ①(of trains, buses or ships) run from opposite directions ②divide into two halves; go fifty-fifty ③〈印〉folio

【对抗】 duìkàng ①antagonism; confrontation: 阶级～ class antagonism/ 两国之间的～ confrontation between two states ②resist; oppose ◇ ～赛〈体〉dual meet

【对抗性】 duìkàngxìng antagonism ◇ ～矛盾 antagonistic contradiction

【对空监视哨】 duìkōng jiānshìshào antiaircraft lookout (或 scout); ground observer; aircraft spotter

【对空射击】 duìkōng shèjī 〈军〉antiaircraft firing

【对口】 duìkǒu ①(of two performers) speak or sing alternately ②be geared to the needs of the job; fit in with one's vocational training or speciality: ～训练 training geared to the needs of the job/ 专业～ a job suited to one's special training
◇ ～唱 musical dialogue in antiphonal style; antiphonal singing/ ～词〈曲艺〉rhymed dialogue/ ～会谈〈外〉talks between representatives of similar organizations of two countries; counterpart conversations/ ～赛 emulation between counterpart organizations/ ～相声 cross talk; comic dialogue

【对口疮】 duìkǒuchuāng 〈中医〉a boil on the nape

【对垒】 duìlěi stand facing each other, ready for battle; be pitted against each other: 两军～ two armies pitted against each other

【对立】 duìlì oppose; set sth. against; be antagonistic to: 两条～的路线 two sharply contrasting lines; two diametrically opposed lines/ 消灭城乡～ abolish the antithesis between town and country/ ～情绪 antagonism/ 不要把学习和工作～起来。Don't think of study as conflicting with work./ 把依靠群众和加强领导～起来是错误的。It is wrong to set reliance on the masses against strengthening the leadership. ◇ ～物 opposite; antithesis

【对立面】 duìlìmiàn 〈哲〉opposite; antithesis: 矛盾着的～ the opposites in a contradiction/ 为自己树立～ create one's own antithesis

【对立统一】 duìlì tǒngyī 〈哲〉unity of opposites: ～规律是宇宙的根本规律。The law of the unity of opposites is the fundamental law of the universe.

【对联】 duìlián antithetical couplet (written on scrolls, etc.)

【对流】 duìliú 〈物〉convection ◇ ～层〈气〉troposphere/ ～雨〈气〉convective rain

【对硫磷】 duìliúlín 〈农〉parathion

【对路】 duìlù ①satisfy the need: 这种货到农村正～。These goods are the very thing the countryside needs. ②be to one's liking; suit one

【对门】 duìmén ①(of two houses) face each other ②the building or room opposite: 农具厂～是大队部。Opposite the farm tool factory is the office of the production brigade.

【对面】 duìmiàn ①opposite: 他家就在我家～。His house is opposite mine. ②right in front: ～来了一位解放军。A PLA man came towards us. ③face to face: 这事儿得他们本人～儿谈。They should talk about this face to face./ 他俩～坐着。The two of them sat facing each other.

【对内】 duìnèi internal; domestic; at home ◇ ～政策 domestic (或 internal) policy

【对牛弹琴】 duì niú tánqín play the lute to a cow—choose the wrong audience

【对偶】 duì'ǒu ①〈语〉antithesis 参见"对仗" ②〈数〉dual ◇ ～原理 principle of duality/ ～运算 dual operations

【对瓶】 duìpíng 〈工美〉twin vases

【对日照】 duìrìzhào 〈天〉counterglow

【对生】 duìshēng 〈植〉opposite ◇ ～叶 opposite leaf

【对手】 duìshǒu ①opponent; adversary ②match; equal: 他不是你的～ He's no match for you.

【对数】 duìshù 〈数〉logarithm ◇ ～表 logarithmic table/

～函数 logarithmic function
【对台戏】 duìtáixì rival show: 唱～ put on a rival show
【对头】 duìtóu ①correct; on the right track: 方法～,效率就高。When the method is correct, efficiency is high. 或 Good methods make for high efficiency./ 你的思想不～。Your thinking is not on the right track. 或 You're not thinking along the right lines. ②〔多用于否定〕 normal; right: 你的脸色不～。You're not looking well. ③〔多用于否定〕 get on well; hit it off: 过去他俩不大～,现在却合得来了。The two didn't get along in the past but now they hit it off well.
【对头】 duìtou ①enemy: 死～ sworn enemy ②opponent; adversary
【对外】 duìwài external; foreign ◇ ～工作 external work; work in the field of external relations/ ～关系 external (或 foreign) relations/ ～援助 aid to foreign countries/ ～政策 external (或 foreign) policy
【对外贸易】 duìwài màoyì foreign trade: ～逆差 foreign trade deficit; unfavourable balance of trade/ ～顺差 foreign trade surplus; favourable balance of trade
【对位】 duìwèi 〈乐〉 counterpoint
【对味儿】 duìwèir ①to one's taste; tasty ②〔多用于否定〕 seem all right: 他的发言不大～。What he said didn't sound quite right.
【对虾】 duìxiā prawn
【对象】 duìxiàng ①target; object: 革命～ targets of the revolution/ 研究～ an object of study/ 党的发展～ a prospective Party member/ 这本书的～是中学生。This book is intended for middle school students./ 讲话或写文章要看～。One should not speak or write without considering one's audience. ②boy or girl friend: 找～ look for a partner in marriage
【对消】 duìxiāo offset; cancel each other out
【对眼】 duìyǎn cross-eye
【对应】 duìyìng corresponding; homologous ◇ ～物 homologue/ ～原理〈物〉 correspondence principle
【对于】 duìyú 〈介〉〔引进对象或事物的关系者〕: ～每个具体问题要进行具体分析。We should make a concrete analysis of each specific question./ 革命文化,～人民大众,是革命的有力武器。Revolutionary culture is a powerful revolutionary weapon for the broad masses of the people./ ～一个革命者来说，为人民服务就是最大的幸福。Nothing makes a revolutionary happier than serving the people.
【对仗】 duìzhàng (in poetry, etc.) a matching of both sound and sense in two lines, sentences, etc. usu. with the matching words in the same part of speech; antithesis
【对照】 duìzhào contrast; compare: 形成鲜明的～ form a sharp contrast/ 用共产党员标准～检查自己 measure oneself by the standards of a Communist/ ～原文修改译文 check the translation against the original and make corrections/ 英汉～读本 an English-Chinese bilingual textbook
【对折】 duìzhé 50% discount
【对证】 duìzhèng verify; check: ～事实 verify the facts
【对症下药】 duì zhèng xià yào suit the medicine to the illness; suit the remedy to the case
【对质】 duìzhì confrontation (in court): 让被告与原告～ confront the accused with his accuser
【对峙】 duìzhì stand facing each other; confront each other: 两山～。The two mountains stand facing each other./ 武装～ military confrontation
【对准】 duìzhǔn ①aim at: 把枪口～敌人 aim a gun at the enemy ②〈机〉 alignment: 轴～ shaft alignment
【对子】 duìzi ①a pair of antithetical phrases, etc.: 对～ supply the antithesis to a given phrase, etc. 参见"对仗" ②见"对联"

**兑** duì ①exchange; convert ②add (water, etc.): 这酒是～了水的。The wine has been watered.
【兑付】 duìfù cash (a cheque, etc.)
【兑换】 duìhuàn exchange; convert: 把外币～成人民币 exchange foreign money for Renminbi ◇ ～率 rate of exchange
【兑现】 duìxiàn ①cash (a cheque, etc.) ②honour (a commitment, etc.); fulfil; make good: 他们的声明是不准备～的。They had no intention of carrying out what they had publicly undertaken to do./ 说话不～ not live up to one's promise; fail to make good one's promise

**怼** duì 〈书〉 rancour; resentment

**敦** duì 〈考古〉 grain receptacle
另见 dūn

**碓** duì a treadle-operated tilt hammer for hulling rice

## dūn

**吨** dūn ton (t.)
【吨公里】 dūngōnglǐ ton kilometre
【吨海里】 dūnhǎilǐ ton sea (或 nautical) mile
【吨时】 dūnshí ton hour
【吨位】 dūnwèi tonnage

**敦** dūn honest; sincere: ～请 cordially invite; earnestly request
另见 duì
【敦促】 dūncù urge; press: ～他早日启程 urge him to start on his journey early
【敦厚】 dūnhòu honest and sincere
【敦煌石窟】 Dūnhuáng Shíkū the Dunhuang Caves, Gansu Province, dating from 366 A.D., containing Buddhist statues, frescoes, and valuable manuscripts
【敦睦】 dūnmù promote friendly relations
【敦实】 dūnshi 〈方〉 stocky

**墩** dūn ①mound: 土～ mound ②a block of stone or wood: 树～ stump/ 桥～ pier (of a bridge) ③〈量〉 cluster: 栽稻秧三万～ transplant 30,000 clusters of rice seedlings
【墩布】 dūnbù mop; swab
【墩子】 dūnzi a block of wood or stone: 菜～ chopping block

**蹲** dūn ①squat on the heels: 两人～下就聊起来了。Squatting down, the two of them started to have a chat. ②stay: 他在实验室里一～就是好几个小时。He would stay for hours at a stretch in the laboratory.
【蹲膘】 dūnbiāo (of cattle, etc.) fatten in the shed
【蹲点】 dūndiǎn (of cadres) stay at a selected grass-roots unit to help improve its work and gain firsthand experience for guiding overall work: 县委书记到一个生产大队～去了。The county Party secretary has gone to stay in a production brigade to gain firsthand experience.
【蹲苗】 dūnmiáo 〈农〉 restrain the growth of seedlings (for root development)

## dǔn

**盹** dǔn doze: 打～儿 doze off

**趸** dǔn ① wholesale ② buy wholesale: ～货 buy goods wholesale

【趸船】 dǔnchuán landing stage; pontoon

【趸批】 dǔnpī wholesale: ～买进(卖出) buy (sell) wholesale

## dùn

**沌** dùn 见"混沌" hùndùn

**囤** dùn a grain bin
另见 tún

**炖** dùn ① stew: ～鸡 stewed chicken/ 清～ boil sth. in its own soup without soy sauce ② warm sth. by putting the container in hot water: ～酒 warm (up) wine

**盾** dùn shield

【盾牌】 dùnpái ① shield ② pretext; excuse

**钝** dùn ① blunt; dull: 刀～了。The knife is blunt. ② stupid; dull-witted: 迟～ dull-witted; slow

【钝化】 dùnhuà 〈化〉 passivation; inactivation ◇ ～剂 passivator

【钝角】 dùnjiǎo 〈数〉 obtuse angle ◇ ～三角形 obtuse triangle

【钝性物质】 dùnxìng wùzhì 〈化〉 inactive substance

**顿** dùn ① pause: 他～了一下,又接着往下说。After a short pause, he went on. ② (in Chinese calligraphy) pause in writing in order to reinforce the beginning or ending of a stroke ③ arrange; settle: 安～ arrange for; help settle down ④ touch the ground (with one's head) ⑤ stamp (one's foot) ⑥ suddenly; immediately: ～悟 suddenly realize the truth, etc.; attain enlightenment ⑦〈量〉:一天三～饭 three meals a day/ 说了他一～ give him a dressing down ⑧ fatigued; tired: 劳～ tired out; exhausted

【顿挫】 dùncuò pause and transition in rhythm or melody: 抑扬～ modulation in tone

【顿号】 dùnhào a slight-pause mark used to set off items in a series (、)

【顿河】 Dùnhé the Don

【顿开茅塞】 dùn kāi máo sè suddenly see the light

【顿时】 dùnshí immediately; at once; forthwith: 喜讯传来,人们～欢呼起来。People broke into cheers as soon as they heard the good news.

【顿足捶胸】 dùnzú-chuíxiōng stamp one's foot and beat one's breast

【顿钻钻井】 dùnzuàn zuànjǐng churn drilling; percussion drilling; cable tool drilling

**遁** dùn escape; flee; fly

【遁词】 dùncí subterfuge; quibble

## duō

**多** duō ① many; much; more: 要办的事情很～。There are many things to attend to./ 请你～～帮助。Please give me all the help you can./ 南方～水,利于灌溉。Irrigation is easy in the South because of the abundance of water./ 人～议论～,热气高,干劲大。More people mean a greater ferment of ideas, more enthusiasm and more energy. ② more than the correct or required number; too many: 这个句子～了一个字。There is one word too many in this sentence./ 他～喝了一点儿。He's had a drop too much./ 我们大队比原计划～打了十口井。Our production brigade has sunk 10 wells more than the plan called for./ 我在那里～住了几天。I stayed there a few days longer. ③ excessive; too much: ～疑 oversensitive; oversuspicious; given to suspicion ④ more; over; odd: 三个～月 more than three months; three months and more/ 六十～岁 over sixty years old/ 全书一千～页。It's a book of 1,000-odd pages. ⑤ much more; far more: 病人今天好～了。The patient is much better today. ⑥〈副〉〔表示程度〕:他～大年纪了?How old is he?/ 看她～精神! Look how energetic she is!/ 给我一根绳子,～长都行。Give me a piece of rope; any length will do./ 有～大劲使～大劲。Use all your strength.

【多半】 duōbàn ① the greater part; most: 这支足球队的成员～是工人。Most of the members of this football team are workers. ② probably; most likely: 他这会儿还不来,～不来了。Since he hasn't come yet, he probably isn't coming.

【多倍体】 duōbèitǐ 〈生〉 polyploid ◇ ～植物 polyploid plant

【多臂机】 duōbìjī 〈纺〉 dobby

【多边】 duōbiān multilateral: ～会谈 multilateral talks/ ～贸易 multilateral trade/ ～条约 multilateral treaty

【多边形】 duōbiānxíng 〈数〉 polygon

【多变】 duōbiàn changeable; changeful; varied: ～的气候 a changeable climate/ ～的战术 varied tactics

【多才多艺】 duōcái-duōyì versatile; gifted in many ways

【多吃多占】 duōchī-duōzhàn eat or take more than one is entitled to; take more than one's share

【多愁善感】 duōchóu-shàngǎn sentimental

【多此一举】 duō cǐ yī jǔ make an unnecessary move: 何必～? Why take the trouble to do that?

【多次】 duōcì many times; time and again; repeatedly; on many occasions: 她曾～访问中国。She's visited China many times./ 他在部队里～立功。He repeatedly distinguished himself in the PLA.

【多弹头】 duōdàntóu multiple warhead ◇ ～导弹 multiple warhead missile/ ～分导重返大气层运载工具 multiple independently targeted reentry vehicle (MIRV)

【多刀切削】 duōdāo qiēxiāo 〈机〉 multiple cut; multicut

【多多益善】 duōduō yì shàn the more the better

【多发病】 duōfābìng frequently-occurring disease

【多方】 duōfāng in many ways; in every way: ～设法 try all possible means; make every effort/ ～协助 render all manner of help

【多方面】 duōfāngmiàn many-sided; in many ways: 这条水渠给公社带来的好处是～的。The canal has proved useful to the commune in many ways.

【多哥】 Duōgē Togo ◇ ～人 Togolese

【多寡】 duō-guǎ number; amount: ～不等 vary in amount or number

【多管】 duōguǎn 〈军〉 multibarrel
◇ ～高射机关炮 pompom/ ～火箭炮 multibarrel (rocket) launcher/ ～炮 multibarreled gun

【多国公司】 duōguó gōngsī multinational corporation

【多核苷酸】 duōhégānsuān 〈生化〉 polynucleotide

【多铧犁】 duōhuálí multishare (或 multifurrow) plough

【多会儿】 duōhuìr 〈口〉 ① when: 你是～来的? When did you come? ② ever; at any time: 我～有空～去。I'll go there when I'm free.

【多级火箭】 duōjí huǒjiàn multistage rocket

【多极】 duōjí 〈电〉 multipolar ◇ ～发电机 multipolar generator

【多晶硅】 duōjīngguī 〈电子〉 polycrystalline silicon
【多晶体】 duōjīngtǐ 〈物〉 polycrystal
【多孔】 duōkǒng porous ◇ ～动物 sponge/ ～砖 porous brick; perforated brick
【多口词】 duōkǒucí 〈曲艺〉 rhymed dialogue performed by more than two persons
【多口相声】 duōkǒu xiàngsheng cross talk (或comic dialogue) performed by more than two persons
【多跨】 duōkuà 〈建〉 multispan ◇ ～结构 multispan structure/ ～桥 multiple span bridge
【多快好省】 duō-kuài-hǎo-shěng achieve greater, faster, better and more economical results
【多亏】 duōkuī thanks to; luckily: ～你的帮助 thanks to your help/ ～你给我们带路。We were lucky to have you as our guide.
【多么】 duōme 〈副〉〔表示程度〕how; what: ～新鲜的水果啊！How fresh the fruit is! 或 What fresh fruit!/ 这是～高尚的精神！What a noble spirit this is!/ 不管天～冷，他都坚持户外锻炼。However cold it was, he never stopped taking outdoor exercise.
【多米尼加】 Duōmǐníjiā Dominica
【多米诺骨牌】 duōmǐnuò gǔpái dominoes ◇ ～理论 the domino theory
【多面手】 duōmiànshǒu a many-sided person; a versatile person; an all-rounder
【多面体】 duōmiàntǐ 〈数〉 polyhedron
【多民族国家】 duōmínzú guójiā multinational country
【多明我会】 Duōmíngwǒhuì 〈天主教〉 the Dominican Order
【多谋善断】 duōmóu-shànduàn resourceful and decisive; sagacious and resolute
【多幕剧】 duōmùjù a play of many acts; a full-length drama
【多难兴邦】 duō nàn xīng bāng much distress regenerates a nation
【多瑙河】 Duōnǎohé the Danube
【多年生】 duōniánshēng 〈植〉 perennial ◇ ～植物 perennial plant
【多尿症】 duōniàozhèng polyuria
【多普勒效应】 Duōpǔlè xiàoyìng 〈物〉 Doppler effect
【多情】 duōqíng full of tenderness or affection (for a person of the opposite sex)
【多刃刀具】 duōrèn dāojù 〈机〉 multiple-cutting-edge tool; multipoint tool
【多色】 duōsè polychrome ◇ ～染料 polygenetic dyes/ ～印刷 polychrome printing
【多少】 duōshǎo ① number; amount: ～不等 vary in amount or number ② somewhat; more or less; to some extent: ～有点失望 feel somewhat disappointed/ 他讲的～有点道理。There's something in what he says.
【多少】 duōshao ① how many; how much: 这一班有～学生？How many pupils are there in this class?/ 这药我每次吃～？How much of the medicine do I take each time?/ 这里的粮食亩产量是～？What is the per *mu* yield of grain here? ②〔表示不定的数量〕: 我跟你说过不知～次了。I've told you I don't know how many times./ 我知道～说～。I'll tell all I know./ 不论有～困难，都不能阻止我们前进。No matter what the difficulties, nothing can stop our advance.
【多神教】 duōshénjiào polytheism
【多时】 duōshí a long time: 等候～ have waited a long time
【多事】 duōshì ① meddlesome: 怪我～。I shouldn't have poked my nose into this. 或 I shouldn't have interfered. ② eventful: ～之秋 an eventful period or year; troubled times
【多数】 duōshù majority; most: 绝大～ an overwhelming majority/ 微弱的～ a small majority/ 必要的～ the requisite majority/ 三分之二的～ a two-thirds majority/ 我们是～。We are in the majority./ 少数服从～。The minority is subordinate to the majority./ 团结～，孤立少数 unite with the many and isolate the few ◇ ～表决 decision by majority/ ～票 majority vote
【多肽】 duōtài 〈生化〉 polypeptide ◇ ～酶 polypeptidase
【多糖】 duōtáng 〈化〉 polysaccharide; polysaccharose ◇ ～酶 polysaccharase; polyase
【多头】 duōtóu (on the stock exchange) bull; long
【多细胞生物】 duōxìbāo shēngwù multicellular organism
【多相】 duōxiàng 〈化〉 heterogeneous ◇ ～催化 heterogeneous catalysis/ ～聚合 heterogeneous polymerization
【多项式】 duōxiàngshì 〈数〉 multinomial; polynomial
【多谢】 duōxiè 〈套〉 many thanks; thanks a lot
【多心】 duōxīn oversensitive; suspicious
【多芯电缆】 duōxìn diànlǎn multicore cable
【多样化】 duōyànghuà diversify; make varied: 使农作物～ diversify the crops/ ～的艺术风格 a variety of artistic styles
【多义词】 duōyìcí 〈语〉 polysemant
【多余】 duōyú unnecessary; surplus; superfluous; uncalled-for: 删掉～的词语 cut out superfluous words and phrases/ 把～的农产品卖给国家 sell surplus farm products to the state/ 事实证明我们的担心是～的。Facts proved that our worries were uncalled-for.
【多元论】 duōyuánlùn 〈哲〉 pluralism ◇ ～历史观 the pluralistic concept of history
【多元酸】 duōyuánsuān 〈化〉 polybasic acid
【多云】 duōyún 〈气〉 cloudy
【多咱】 duōzan 〈方〉 what time; when: 咱们～走？When are we leaving?/ 这是～的事？When did that happen? 或 When was that?
【多种多样】 duōzhǒng-duōyàng varied; manifold: 满足人民群众～的需要 meet the manifold needs of the people/ 阶级斗争的形式是～的。The forms of class struggle are many and varied.
【多种经营】 duōzhǒng jīngyíng diversified economy; diversification: 以粮为纲，～，全面发展。Take grain as the key link, develop a diversified economy and ensure an all-round development.
【多足动物】 duōzú dòngwù myriopod
【多嘴】 duōzuǐ speak out of turn; shoot off one's mouth: ～多舌 gossipy and meddlesome; long-tongued/ 要不是他～，事情也不至于搞僵。If he hadn't shot his mouth off, things wouldn't have been so awkward./ 你不了解情况，别～！You don't know the facts, so keep your mouth shut!

**咄** duō tut-tut
【咄咄逼人】 duōduō bī rén overbearing; aggressive
【咄咄怪事】 duōduō guàishì monstrous absurdity

**哆** duō
【哆嗦】 duōsuo tremble; shiver: 气得直～ tremble with rage/ 冷得打～ shiver with cold

**掇** duō pick up: 拾～ tidy up

## duó

**夺** duó ① take by force; seize; wrest: 从暴徒手上～下刀子 wrest a knife from a hooligan/ ～印 seize the seal —seize power ② force one's way: ～门而出 force open the door and rush out; force one's way out/ 眼泪～眶而出。Tears started from one's eyes. ③ contend for; compete for; strive for: ～红旗 contend for the red banner/ ～高产 strive for high yields/ ～得冠军 carry off the first prize ④ deprive: 剥～ deprive ⑤〈书〉decide: 定～ make a final decision ⑥〈书〉omission (in a text): 讹～ errors and omissions

【夺佃】 duódiàn eviction of peasants from land leased to them by landlords or rich peasants

【夺回】 duóhuí recapture; retake; seize back: ～阵地 recapture a position/ ～一局 win a game (after losing one or more); pull up by a game/ ～被野心家窃取的权力 seize back the power usurped by the careerists/ ～失去的时间 make up for lost time

【夺目】 duómù dazzle the eyes: 光彩～ with dazzling brightness; brilliant; resplendent

【夺取】 duóqǔ ① capture; seize; wrest: ～敌人的据点 capture an enemy stronghold/ ～主动权 seize the initiative/ 武装～政权 seize state power by armed force ② strive for: ～社会主义建设的新胜利 strive for new victories in socialist construction

【夺权】 duóquán seize power; take over power

**度** duó〈书〉surmise; estimate
另见 dù

【度德量力】 duódé-liànglì estimate one's own moral and material strength; make an appraisal of one's own position

**铎** duó a kind of bell used in ancient China when issuing proclamations or in times of war

**踱** duó pace; stroll: ～来～去 pace to and fro; pace up and down/ ～方步 walk with measured tread

## duǒ

**朵** duǒ〈量〉: 一～花 a flower/ 一～云 a cloud

【朵儿】 duǒr flower

**垛** duǒ ① buttress ② battlements
另见 duò

【垛口】 duǒkǒu crenel

【垛子】 duǒzi ① buttress ② battlements: 城～ battlements on a city wall

**躲** duǒ ① hide (oneself): ～进深山老林 hide in a mountain forest ② avoid; dodge: 你怎么老～着他? Why do you keep avoiding him?/ 车来了,快～开! Look out! A truck's coming! Get out of the way./ ～雨 take shelter from the rain

【躲避】 duǒbì ① hide (oneself) ② avoid; elude; dodge: 阶级斗争是客观存在的,是～不了的。Class struggle is an objective fact which cannot be avoided.

【躲藏】 duǒcáng hide (或 conceal) oneself; go into hiding

【躲懒】 duǒlǎn shy away from work; shirk

【躲闪】 duǒshǎn dodge; evade: 小王～不及,和我撞了个满怀。It was too late for Xiao Wang to dodge and I bumped into him./ 躲躲闪闪 be evasive; hedge; equivocate

【躲债】 duǒzhài avoid a creditor

## duò

**驮** duò
另见 tuó

【驮子】 duòzi a load carried by a pack-animal; pack

**剁** duò chop; cut: 把柳条～成三段 chop a willow branch into three pieces/ ～肉馅 chop up (或 mince) meat

**垛** duò ① pile up neatly; stack: 把木头～起来 pile up the logs ② pile; stack: 柴火～ a pile of faggots/ 麦～ a stack of wheat
另见 duǒ

**舵** duò rudder; helm

【舵轮】 duòlún steering wheel

【舵手】 duòshǒu steersman; helmsman

**堕** duò fall; sink: ～地 fall on the ground

【堕落】 duòluò degenerate; sink low: 走上～、犯罪的道路 embark on the road of degeneration and crime/ 政治上～ be politically degenerate/ ～成为新生的资产阶级分子 degenerate into a new bourgeois element

【堕入】 duòrù sink (或 lapse) into; land oneself in: ～陷阱 fall into a trap

【堕胎】 duòtāi ① induced abortion ② have an (induced) abortion

**惰** duò lazy; indolent: 懒～ lazy

【惰性】 duòxìng inertia ◇ ～气体 inert gas/ ～元素 inert element

**跺** duò stamp (one's foot): 气得直～脚 stamp one's foot with fury

# E

## ē

**阿** ē play up to; pander to: ～其所好 pander to sb.'s whims
另见 ā
【阿附】 ēfù 〈书〉 fawn on and echo; toady to and chime in with
【阿胶】 ējiāo 〈中药〉 donkey-hide gelatin
【阿弥陀佛】 Ēmítuófó 〈佛教〉 ① *Amitabha; Amitayus* ② may Buddha preserve us; merciful Buddha
【阿魏】 ēwèi 〈植〉 asafoetida
【阿谀】 ēyú fawn on; flatter

**屙** ē 〈方〉 discharge (excrement or urine)

**婀** ē
【婀娜】 ēnuó (of a woman's bearing) graceful

## é

**讹** é ① erroneous; mistaken: ～字 wrong words (in a text)/ 以～传～ spread an error or a falsehood ② extort; blackmail; bluff: ～人 blackmail sb.; bluff sb.
【讹传】 échuán false (或 unfounded) rumour
【讹误】 éwù error (in a text)
【讹诈】 ézhà extort under false pretences; blackmail: ～钱财 extort money under false pretences/ 核～ nuclear blackmail

**俄** é very soon; presently; suddenly: ～而日出。Presently the sun emerged.
【俄罗斯族】 Éluósīzú ① the Eluosi (Russian) nationality, distributed over the Xinjiang Uygur Autonomous Region and Heilongjiang Province ② the Russians (of the U.S.S.R.)
【俄顷】 éqǐng 〈书〉 in a moment; presently
【俄语】 Éyǔ Russian (language)

**哦** é 〈书〉 softly chant (a poem)
另见 ó; ò

**峨** é 〈书〉 high: 巍～ towering; lofty

**娥** é pretty young woman: 宫～ palace maid; maid of honour
【娥眉】 éméi ① delicate eyebrows ② beautiful woman

**鹅** é goose
【鹅黄】 éhuáng light yellow
【鹅颈管】 éjǐngguǎn 〈机〉 gooseneck
【鹅口疮】 ékǒuchuāng 〈医〉 thrush
【鹅卵石】 éluǎnshí cobblestone; cobble
【鹅毛】 émáo goose feather: 下了一场～大雪。Snow fell in big flakes.
【鹅绒】 éróng goose down
【鹅掌风】 ézhǎngfēng 〈中医〉 fungal infection of the hand; tinea manuum
【鹅掌楸】 ézhǎngqiū 〈植〉 Chinese tulip tree

**锇** é 〈化〉 osmium (Os)

**蛾** é moth
【蛾眉】 éméi 见"娥眉" éméi
【蛾子】 ézi moth

**额** é ① forehead ② a horizontal tablet ③ a specified number or amount: 贸易～ volume of trade/ 超～ above quota
【额定】 édìng specified (number or amount); rated: ～的人数 the maximum number of persons allowed; the stipulated number of personnel ◇ ～功率 rated power/ ～马力 rated horsepower
【额骨】 égǔ 〈生理〉 frontal bone
【额角】 éjiǎo frontal eminence
【额手称庆】 éshǒu chēng qìng put one's hand on one's forehead in jubilation; be overjoyed
【额外】 éwài extra; additional; added: ～开支 extra expenses/ ～收入 additional income/ ～负担 added burden

## ě

**恶** ě
另见 è; wù
【恶心】 ěxin ① feel like vomiting; feel nauseated; feel sick ② nauseating; disgusting

## è

**厄** è 〈书〉 ① strategic point: 险～ a strategic pass ② adversity; disaster; hardship: 遭～ meet with disaster ③ be in distress; be stranded: 渔船～于风暴。The fishing boat was caught in a storm.
【厄瓜多尔】 Èguāduō'ěr Ecuador ◇ ～人 Ecuadorian
【厄运】 èyùn adversity; misfortune

**扼** è 〈书〉 ① clutch; grip: ～住他的咽喉 clutch at his throat ② guard; control
【扼流圈】 èliúquān 〈电〉 choke
【扼杀】 èshā strangle; smother; throttle: ～在摇篮里 strangle in the cradle/ ～在萌芽状态中 nip in the bud
【扼守】 èshǒu hold (a strategic point); guard
【扼死】 èsǐ strangle; throttle
【扼要】 èyào to the point: 简明～ brief and to the point/ 请～说明。Please explain the main points briefly.

**呃** è
【呃逆】 ènì 〈医〉 hiccup

**苊** è 〈化〉 acenaphthene

**轭** è yoke

**垩** è chalk

**恶** è ①evil; vice; wickedness: 无～不作 stop at nothing in doing evil/ 罪大～极 guilty of the most heinous crimes ②fierce; ferocious: 一场～战 a fierce battle/ ～骂 vicious abuse/ ～狗 a ferocious (或 vicious) dog; cur ③bad; evil; wicked: ～行 evil (或 wicked) conduct/ ～势力 evil force
另见 ě; wù

【恶霸】 èbà local tyrant (或 despot) ◇ ～地主 despotic landlord

【恶报】 èbào retribution for evildoing; judgment

【恶病质】 èbìngzhì 〈医〉 cachexia

【恶臭】 èchòu foul smell; stench

【恶毒】 èdú vicious; malicious; venomous: ～的诬蔑 venomous slander/ ～攻击 viciously attack

【恶感】 ègǎn ill feeling; malice: 我对他并无～。I bear him no malice.

【恶贯满盈】 è guàn mǎnyíng have committed countless crimes and deserve to come to judgment; face retribution for a life of crime

【恶棍】 ègùn ruffian; scoundrel; bully

【恶果】 èguǒ evil consequence; disastrous effect

【恶狠狠】 èhěnhěn fierce; ferocious: ～地瞪了他一眼 give him a ferocious stare

【恶化】 èhuà worsen; deteriorate; take a turn for the worse: 他的病情～了。His condition has worsened./ 两国关系不断～。The relations between the two countries have steadily deteriorated.

【恶疾】 èjí foul (或 nasty) disease

【恶劣】 èliè odious; abominable; disgusting: ～作风 abominable behaviour/ ～行径 disgusting conduct/ ～手段 mean (或 dirty) tricks/ ～环境 adverse circumstances/ ～气候 harsh climate; vile weather/ 品质～ unprincipled; base/ 影响～ make a very bad impression/ 作案的情节十分～。The way in which the crime was committed was absolutely vile.

【恶露】 èlù 〈中医〉 lochia

【恶魔】 èmó demon; devil; evil spirit

【恶人】 èrén evil person; vile creature; villain: ～先告状。The villain sues his victim before he himself is prosecuted. 或 The guilty party files the suit.

【恶少】 èshào 〈旧〉 young ruffian

【恶习】 èxí bad (或 pernicious) habit: 染上～ contract a bad habit; fall into evil ways

【恶性】 èxìng malignant; pernicious; vicious: ～贫血 pernicious anaemia/ ～通货膨胀 galloping (或 runaway) inflation/ ～循环 vicious circle/ ～肿瘤 malignant tumour

【恶意】 èyì evil (或 ill) intentions; ill will; malice: ～攻击 malicious attack/ 并无～ bear no ill will

【恶语中伤】 èyǔ zhòngshāng viciously slander; calumniate

【恶兆】 èzhào ill (或 bad) omen

【恶浊】 èzhuó foul; filthy

【恶阻】 èzǔ 〈中医〉 vomiting during early pregnancy

【恶作剧】 èzuòjù practical joke; prank; mischief

**饿** è ①hungry: 挨～ go hungry ②starve: 别～着小猪。Don't starve the piglets.

【饿饭】 èfàn 〈方〉 go hungry; go without food

【饿虎扑食】 èhǔ pū shí like a hungry tiger pouncing on its prey

【饿殍】 èpiǎo bodies of the starved: ～遍野 strewn with bodies of the starved everywhere

**鄂** È ①another name for Hubei Province ②a surname

【鄂伦春族】 Èlúnchūnzú the Oroqen (Olunchun) nationality, living in Heilongjiang Province

【鄂温克族】 Èwēnkèzú the Ewenki (Owenk) nationality, living in Heilongjiang Province

**愕** è stunned; astounded

【愕然】 èrán stunned; astounded: ～四顾 look around in astonishment/ 消息传来，大家为之～。Everyone was stunned by the news.

**萼** è 〈植〉 calyx

【萼片】 èpiàn 〈植〉 sepal

**遏** è check; hold back: 怒不可～ be in a towering rage; be overcome with indignation; boil with anger

【遏止】 èzhǐ check; hold back: 不可～的革命洪流 the irresistible tide of revolution

【遏制】 èzhì keep within limits; contain: ～愤怒的情绪 check one's anger ◇ ～政策 policy of containment

**腭** è 〈生理〉 palate: 硬(软)～ hard (soft) palate

【腭裂】 èliè 〈医〉 cleft palate

**鹗** è osprey; fish hawk; sea eagle

**锷** è the blade of a sword

**颚** è ①jaw: 上(下)～ upper (lower) jaw ②palate

【颚骨】 ègǔ jawbone

【颚针鱼】 èzhēnyú needlefish

**噩** è shocking; upsetting

【噩耗】 èhào sad news of the death of one's beloved: ～传来，犹如晴天霹雳。The grievous news came like a bolt from the blue.

【噩梦】 èmèng frightening (或 horrible) dream; nightmare

**鳄** è crocodile; alligator

【鳄鱼】 èyú crocodile; alligator: ～的眼泪 crocodile tears

## ē

**欸** ē 〈叹〉〔表示招呼〕: ～，你快来！ Hey! Come over here.
另见 ǎi; é; ě; è

## é

**欸** é 或 éi 〈叹〉〔表示诧异〕: ～，他怎么走了！ Why, he's gone!
另见 ǎi; ē; ě; è

## ě

**欸** ě 或 ěi 〈叹〉〔表示不以为然〕: ～，你这话可不对呀！ Now, you can't say that.
另见 ǎi; ē; é; è

## è

**欸** è 或 èi 〈叹〉〔表示答应或同意〕: ～，我这就来！ Yes, I'll come in a minute. 或 Coming./ ～，就这么办！ All

right. That's settled.
另见 ǎi; ē; é; ě

## ēn

**恩** ēn kindness; favour; grace: 施～ bestow favours/ 报～ requite a kindness; pay a debt of gratitude
【恩爱】 ēn'ài conjugal love ◇ ～夫妻 an affectionate couple
【恩赐】 ēncì ① bestow (favours, charity, etc.): 独立是被压迫民族斗争得来的，不是什么人～的。Independence is won by the oppressed nations through struggle; it is not bestowed as a favour./ 在土改中，我们党发动群众自己起来进行斗争，坚决反对～观点。During the land reform our Party mobilized the masses to struggle for their rights, and firmly opposed the idea of bestowing land as a favour. ② favour; charity
【恩德】 ēndé favour; kindness; grace
【恩典】 ēndiǎn favour; grace
【恩惠】 ēnhuì favour; kindness; grace; bounty
【恩将仇报】 ēn jiāng chóu bào requite kindness with enmity
【恩情】 ēnqíng loving-kindness: 天大地大不如党的～大。Heaven and earth are great but greater still is the kindness of the Party./ 共产党的～说不完。We can never say enough about our gratitude to the Party.
【恩人】 ēnrén benefactor
【恩怨】 ēn-yuàn ① feeling of gratitude or resentment ② resentment; grievance; old scores: 不计较个人～ not allow oneself to be swayed by personal feelings
【恩泽】 ēnzé 〈旧〉 bounties bestowed by a monarch or an official

**蒽** ēn 〈化〉 anthracene: ～酸 anthroic acid

## èn

**摁** èn press (with the hand or finger): ～电钮 press (或 push) a button/ ～住不放 press sth. down and hold it there/ ～电铃 ring an electric bell
【摁钉儿】 èndīngr 〈口〉 drawing pin; thumbtack
【摁扣儿】 ènkòur 〈口〉 snap fastener

## ér

**儿** ér ① child: 小～ little child ② youngster; youth: 英雄～女 young heroes and heroines ③ son: 他有一～一女。He has a son and a daughter. ④ male: ～马〈口〉 stallion ⑤〔后缀〕: 小猫～ kitten/ 有门～。There's a chance. 或 Things are opening up./ 屋里有亮～。There's a light in the room./ 他火～了。He got angry. 参见"儿化"
【儿茶】 érchá 〈中药〉 catechu
【儿歌】 érgē children's song; nursery rhymes
【儿化】 érhuà 〈语〉 suffixation of a nonsyllabic r to nouns and sometimes verbs, causing a retroflexion of the preceding vowel, typical of the pronunciation of standard Chinese and of some dialects 参见"儿"⑤
【儿皇帝】 érhuángdì puppet emperor
【儿科】 érkē (department of) paediatrics ◇ ～医生 paediatrician
【儿女】 ér-nǚ ① sons and daughters; children: 中国人民的优秀～ fine sons and daughters of the Chinese people/ ～都已长大成人。The children have all grown up. ② young man and woman (in love): ～情长 be immersed in love
【儿孙】 ér-sūn children and grandchildren; descendants; posterity
【儿童】 értóng children
◇ ～保育事业 child care/ ～读物 children's books/ ～节 (International) Children's Day (June 1)/ ～团 the Children's Corps/ ～文学 children's (或 juvenile) literature/ ～医院 children's hospital
【儿媳妇儿】 érxífur daughter-in-law
【儿戏】 érxì trifling matter: 这样重要的工作可不能当～。You shouldn't regard such important work as a trifling matter.
【儿韵】 éryùn 〈语〉 r-ending retroflexion
【儿子】 érzi son

**而** ér 〈连〉 ①〔连接语意相承的成分〕: 伟大～艰巨的任务 a great and arduous task/ 战～胜之 fight and defeat the enemy ②〔连接肯定和否定互相补充的成分〕: 华～不实 flashy without substance/ 有其名～无其实 in name but not in reality/ 他们的错误在于只看到事情的支流，～没有看到事情的主流。Their mistake is that they see only the nonessentials but not the essence of the matter. ③〔连接语意相反的成分，表示转折〕: 大～无当 large but impractical; unwieldy ④〔连接事理上前后相因的成分〕: 为工农兵～创作 create literature and art for the workers, peasants and soldiers/ 疗效因人～异。The effect of the treatment varies with different individuals. ⑤〔表示"到"的意思〕: 由南～北 from south to north/ 自远～近 approach from a distance/ 一～再，再～三 again and again; time and again ⑥〔把表示时间或方式的成分连接到动词上面〕: 匆匆～来 come hastening/ 盘旋～上 spiral up ⑦〔插在主语谓语中间，有"如果"的意思〕: 作家～不深入群众，那就不会写出好的作品来。If a writer does not go deep among the masses, he cannot expect to turn out good works.
【而后】 érhòu after that; then: 先小组酝酿～由大会讨论。First exchange ideas in small groups and then hold a general discussion.
【而今】 érjīn now; at the present time
【而且】 érqiě 〈连〉 ①〔表示平列〕: 这屋子很宽敞，～光线充足。The room is spacious and bright. ②〔表示进一层〕: 大寨人民不但战胜了灾害，～获得了丰收。The Dazhai people not only overcame the effects of the natural adversity, but won a bumper harvest.
【而已】 éryǐ 〈助〉 that is all; nothing more: 如此～，岂有他哉！ That's all there is to it!

**鸸** ér
【鸸鹋】 érmiáo 〈动〉 emu

## ěr

**尔** ěr 〈书〉 ① you ② like that; so: 果～ if so/ 不过～～ just middling ③ that: ～日 that day/ ～时 at that time ④〔形容词后缀〕: 率～而对 give a hasty reply; reply without thinking
【尔曹】 ěrcáo 〈书〉 you people; you and your kind: ～身与名俱灭，不废江河万古流。Your bodies and names will perish, but the river will flow on for ever — the names of mediocre writers will be forgotten, but those of the great masters will live.
【尔格】 ěrgé 〈物〉 erg
【尔后】 ěrhòu 〈书〉 thereafter; subsequently: ～的战斗 the subsequent battles
【尔虞我诈】 ěryú-wǒzhà each trying to cheat or outwit the other

**耳** ěr ①ear: 外(中、内)～ the outer (middle, inner) ear ②any ear-like thing; ear of a utensil: 银～ tremella/ 鼎～ ears of a tripod ③on both sides; flanking; side: ～房 side rooms/ ～门 side doors ④〈书〉〈助〉only; just: 距此不过五里～。It's only five *li* from here.

【耳背】 ěrbèi hard of hearing

【耳鼻喉科】 ěr-bí-hóukē ①E.N.T. (ear-nose-throat) department; otolaryngological department ②otolaryngology ◇～医生 E.N.T. specialist; otolaryngologist

【耳边风】 ěrbiānfēng a puff of wind passing the ear — unheeded advice: 当作～ let sth. in at one ear and out the other; turn a deaf ear to sth.

【耳沉】 ěrchén 〈方〉 hard of hearing

【耳垂】 ěrchuí 〈生理〉 earlobe

【耳聪目明】 ěrcōng-mùmíng ①(of old people) have good ears and eyes; can hear and see well ②have a thorough grasp of the situation

【耳朵】 ěrduo ear: ～尖 have sharp ears/ ～软 credulous; easily influenced; susceptible to flattery

【耳垢】 ěrgòu earwax

【耳光】 ěrguāng a slap on the face; a box on the ear: 打～ slap sb.'s face; box sb.'s ear

【耳环】 ěrhuán earrings

【耳机】 ěrjī earphone

【耳镜】 ěrjìng 〈医〉 otoscope

【耳孔】 ěrkǒng earhole

【耳廓】 ěrkuò 〈生理〉 auricle 又作"耳郭"

【耳轮】 ěrlún 〈生理〉 helix

【耳鸣】 ěrmíng 〈医〉 tinnitus

【耳目】 ěrmù ①what one sees and hears; knowledge; information: ～所及 from what one sees and hears; from what one knows/ ～闭塞 ill-informed ②one who spies for sb. else: ～众多 eyes and ears everywhere; too many people around

【耳目一新】 ěr-mù yī xīn find everything fresh and new: 归国侨胞一到广州就感到～。The returned overseas Chinese found themselves in an entirely new world the moment they arrived in Guangzhou.

【耳屏】 ěrpíng 〈生理〉 tragus

【耳濡目染】 ěrrú-mùrǎn be imperceptibly influenced by what one constantly sees and hears

【耳软心活】 ěrruǎn-xīnhuó credulous and pliable

【耳塞】 ěrsāi earplug

【耳生】 ěrshēng unfamiliar to the ear; strange-sounding: 外面说话的声音听着～。The voice outside sounds unfamiliar to me.

【耳屎】 ěrshǐ 〈口〉 earwax

【耳熟】 ěrshú familiar to the ear

【耳提面命】 ěrtí-miànmìng pour (或 din) exhortations into sb.'s ear; give earnest exhortations

【耳挖子】 ěrwāzi earpick

【耳闻】 ěrwén hear of (或 about): 这事曾经～，详细情况不很清楚。I've heard about it, but I don't know the details./ ～不如目见。Seeing for oneself is better than hearing from others.

【耳闻目睹】 ěrwén-mùdǔ what one sees and hears

【耳蜗】 ěrwō 〈生理〉 cochlea; acoustic labyrinth

【耳咽管】 ěryānguǎn Eustachian tube; auditory tube

【耳语】 ěryǔ whisper in sb.'s ear; whisper

【耳针疗法】 ěrzhēn liáofǎ 〈中医〉 auriculotherapy; ear-acupuncture therapy

【耳坠子】 ěrzhuìzi eardrop

**迩** ěr 〈书〉 near: 名闻遐～ be known far and near

**饵** ěr ①cakes; pastry: 果～ candies and cakes; confectionery ②bait ③〈书〉 entice: ～以重利 use great wealth as a bait; entice sb. with prospects of great wealth

**洱** ěr 见"普洱茶" pǔ'ěrchá

**珥** ěr earring made of jade or pearl

**铒** ěr 〈化〉 erbium (Er)

## èr

**二** èr ①two: ～两茶叶 two *liang* of tea/ ～～得四。Twice two is four./ 中共七届～中全会 the Second Plenary Session of the Seventh Central Committee of the CPC/ ～路公共汽车 No. 2 bus/ ～嫂 wife of one's second elder brother; sister-in-law/ ～层楼(英) first floor; (美) second floor/ 一百～ a hundred and twenty/ 三千～ three thousand two hundred/ ～者必居其一 either one or the other ②different: ～心 disloyalty; half-heartedness

【二把刀】 èrbǎdāo 〈方〉 ①have a smattering of a subject ②smatterer

【二百二】 èrbǎi'èr 〈口〉〈药〉 mercurochrome

【二百五】 èrbǎiwǔ 〈口〉 ①a stupid person: 他是个～。He's a rather stupid person. 或 He's not all there. ②dabbler; smatterer

【二倍体】 èrbèitǐ 〈生〉 diploid

【二遍苦，二茬罪】 èr biàn kǔ, èr chá zuì 〔多用于〕: 吃二遍苦，受二茬罪 suffer oppression and exploitation all over again

【二部制】 èrbùzhì 〈教〉 two-shift system; two part-time shifts ◇～学校 school with two part-time shifts; two-shift school

【二重唱】 èrchóngchàng 〈乐〉 (vocal) duet

【二重性】 èrchóngxìng dual character (或 nature); duality

【二重奏】 èrchóngzòu 〈乐〉 (instrumental) duet

【二次方程】 èrcì fāngchéng 〈数〉 quadratic equation

【二次曲面】 èrcì qūmiàn 〈数〉 quadratic surface

【二等】 èrděng second-class; second-rate: ～残废军人 disabled soldier, second class ◇～舱 second-class cabin/ ～功 Merit Citation Class II; second-class merit/ ～奖 second prize/ ～秘书〈外〉 Second Secretary/ ～品 goods of second quality; seconds

【二地主】 èrdìzhǔ sub-landlord

【二叠纪】 Èrdiéjì 〈地〉 the Permian (Period)

【二·二八起义】 Èr Èrbā Qǐyì the Uprising of February 28, 1947 (an armed revolt in Taiwan Province against the reactionary rule of the Kuomintang)

【二房东】 èrfángdōng sublessor (of a room or house); sub-landlord

【二分点】 èrfēndiǎn 〈天〉 the equinoxes

【二分裂】 èrfēnliè 〈生〉 binary fission

【二分音符】 èrfēn yīnfú 〈乐〉 minim; half note

【二副】 èrfù 〈航海〉 second mate; second officer

【二锅头】 èrguōtóu a strong spirit usu. made from sorghum

【二胡】 èrhú *erhu*, a two-stringed bowed instrument with a lower register than *jinghu*（京胡）

【二化螟】 èrhuàmíng striped rice borer (*Chilo suppressalis*)

【二话】 èrhuà 〔多用于否定〕 demur; objection: ～不说 without demur/ 革命需要他干什么，他就干什么，从来没有～。Whatever job the revolution requires him to do, he does it readily.

【二黄】 èrhuáng 〈剧〉 *erhuang*, one of the two chief types of music in traditional Chinese operas 又作"二簧"
【二级风】 èrjífēng 〈气〉 force 2 wind; light breeze
【二极管】 èrjíguǎn 〈电子〉 diode
【二尖瓣】 èrjiānbàn 〈生理〉 mitral valve ◇ ～狭窄 mitral stenosis
【二进制】 èrjìnzhì 〈数〉 binary system ◇ ～标度 binary scale/ ～数 binary number/ ～数字 binary digit
【二郎腿】 èrlángtuǐ 〔多用于〕: 跷起～ sit cross-legged or with ankle on knee
【二愣子】 èrlèngzi rash fellow
【二硫化物】 èrliúhuàwù bisulphide
【二流子】 èrliúzi loafer; idler; bum
【二面角】 èrmiànjiǎo 〈数〉 dihedral angle
【二名法】 èrmíngfǎ 〈生〉 binomial nomenclature
【二年生】 èrniánshēng 〈植〉 biennial ◇ ～植物 biennial plant
【二七大罢工】 Èr Qī Dà Bàgōng· the Great Strike of February 7, 1923 (an anti-imperialist, anti-warlord strike of the Beijing-Hankou Railway workers led by the Chinese Communist Party)
【二全音符】 èrquán yīnfú 〈乐〉 breve
【二人台】 èrréntái a popular Nei Monggol song-and-dance duet
【二人转】 èrrénzhuàn a song-and-dance duet popular in the Northeast
【二十八宿】 èrshí bā xiù 〈天〉 the lunar mansions
【二十四节气】 èrshí sì jiéqì the 24 solar terms 参见"节气" jiéqi
【二十四史】 èrshí sì shǐ ① the Twenty-Four Histories (dynastic histories from remote antiquity till the Ming Dynasty) ② a long intricate story: 一部～，不知从何说起。It's such a long and complicated story, I hardly know where to start.
【二四滴】 èrsìdī 〈农〉 2,4-D; 2,4-dichlorophenoxyacetic acid
【二踢脚】 èrtījiǎo 〈方〉 double-bang firecracker
【二五眼】 èrwuyǎn 〈方〉 ① of inferior ability or quality ② an incompetent person
【二项式】 èrxiàngshì 〈数〉 binomial
【二象性】 èrxiàngxìng 〈物〉 dual property; duality: 物质的～ the dualistic nature of matter/ 波粒～ wave-particle duality
【二心】 èrxīn disloyalty; halfheartedness
【二氧化物】 èryǎnghuàwù dioxide (e.g. 二氧化碳 carbon dioxide)
【二元】 èryuán ①〈数〉 duality ②〈化〉 binary ◇ ～酸 binary acid
【二元论】 èryuánlùn 〈哲〉 dualism
【二月】 èryuè ① February ② the second month of the lunar year; the second moon
【二至点】 èrzhìdiǎn 〈天〉 the solstices

**贰** èr two (used for the numeral 二 on cheques, banknotes, etc. to avoid mistakes or alterations)
【贰臣】 èrchén an official who retains his position after capitulating to the new dynasty; turncoat official
【贰心】 èrxīn 见"二心" èrxīn

# F

## fā

**发** fā ① send out; issue; deliver; distribute: ～电报 send a telegram/ ～货 deliver goods/ ～传单 distribute leaflets/ ～信号 give a signal/ ～工资 pay out wages ② utter; express: 有五个同志在会上～了言。 Five comrades spoke at the meeting. ③ discharge; shoot; emit: 万箭齐～。Ten thousand arrows shot at once./ ～光～热 emit light and heat ④ develop; expand: ～育 growth; development ⑤ (of foodstuffs) rise or expand when fermented or soaked: 面～起来了。The dough has risen./ ～豆芽 raise bean sprouts; sprout beans ⑥ come or bring into existence: ～电 generate electricity/ 旧病复～ have an attack of a recurrent sickness; have a recurrence of an old illness; have a relapse ⑦ open up; discover; expose: ～现 find; discover/ 揭～ expose ⑧ get into a certain state; become: 树叶开始～黄。The leaves are beginning to turn yellow./ 脸色～白 lose colour; become pale/ 肉～臭了。The meat smells a bit off. 或 The meat smells bad. ⑨ show one's feeling: ～怒 get angry/ ～笑 laugh ⑩ feel; have a feeling: 有点～冷 feel a bit chilly/ 嘴里～苦 have a bitter taste in the mouth/ ～麻 tingle/ ～痒 itch ⑪ start; set out; begin an undertaking: 车船齐～。All the boats and carts started off at the same time./ 朝～夕至 set off in the morning and arrive in the evening ⑫ 〈量〉: 一～炮弹 one shell/ 两百～子弹 two hundred rounds of ammunition; two hundred cartridges

另见 fà

【发榜】 fābǎng publish a list of successful candidates or applicants

【发报】 fābào transmit messages by radio, telegraphy, etc. ◇ ～机 transmitter

【发背】 fābèi 〈中医〉 carbuncle on the back

【发表】 fābiǎo publish; issue: ～文章 publish an article/～声明 issue (或 make) a statement/ ～意见 express an opinion; state one's views/ ～演说 make (或 deliver) a speech/ ～社论 carry an editorial

【发病】 fābìng (of a disease) come on

【发病率】 fābìnglǜ incidence of a disease: 近几年这种病的～大大降低了。The incidence of this disease has dropped considerably in the past few years.

【发布】 fābù issue; release: ～命令 issue orders/ ～新闻 release news

【发财】 fācái get rich; make a fortune; make a pile

【发潮】 fācháo become damp: 衣服有点儿～。The clothes feel a bit damp.

【发车场】 fāchēchǎng 〈铁道〉 departure track (或 yard)

【发愁】 fāchóu worry; be anxious: 不要为这事～。Don't worry about it.

【发出】 fāchū issue; send out; give out: ～指示 issue a directive/ ～警告 send out a warning/ ～阵阵清香 send forth wafts of delicate fragrance/ ～警报 sound the alarm/ 原子反应堆～大量的热能。The atomic reactor generates enormous amounts of thermal energy.

【发憷】 fāchù 〈方〉 feel timid; grow apprehensive

【发达】 fādá developed; flourishing: 肌肉～ have well-developed muscles/ 工商业很～。Industry and commerce are flourishing. ◇ ～国家 developed country

【发呆】 fādāi stare blankly; be in a daze; be in a trance: 他话也不说,坐在那里～。He said nothing but sat there staring blankly. 或 He said nothing but sat there as if in a trance.

【发电】 fādiàn generate electricity (或 electric power) ◇ ～量 generated energy; electric energy production/ ～站 power station

【发电厂】 fādiànchǎng power plant; power station: 水力(火力)～ hydraulic (thermal) power plant/ 地热～ geothermal power plant/ 原子能～ atomic power plant ◇ ～容量 station capacity

【发电机】 fādiànjī generator; dynamo: 双水内冷汽轮～ turbogenerator with inner water-cooled stator and rotor/ 永磁～ magneto generator ◇ ～容量 generator capacity/ ～组 generating set

【发动】 fādòng ① start; launch: ～机器 start a machine; set a machine going/ ～战争 launch (或 unleash) a war ② call into action; mobilize; arouse: ～群众 arouse the masses to action; mobilize the masses ◇ ～机 engine; motor

【发抖】 fādǒu shiver; shake; tremble: 冷得～ shiver (或 shake) with cold/ 吓得～ tremble with fear; shake in one's shoes

【发端】 fāduān make a start

【发凡】 fāfán 〈书〉 introduction (to a subject or a book)

【发放】 fāfàng provide; grant; extend: ～农业贷款 grant (或 extend) agricultural credits/ 救灾物资很快～到灾区人民手里。Relief goods were quickly handed out to the people in the stricken area.

【发粉】 fāfěn baking powder

【发奋】 fāfèn ① work energetically ② 见"发愤"

【发愤】 fāfèn make a firm resolution; make a determined effort: ～工作 put all one's energies into one's work/ ～图强 work with a will to make the country strong/ ～忘食 be so immersed in work as to forget one's meals

【发疯】 fāfēng go mad; go crazy; become insane; be out of one's mind: 发酒疯 be roaring drunk

【发福】 fāfú grow stout; put on weight

【发绀】 fāgàn 〈医〉 cyanosis

【发糕】 fāgāo steamed sponge cake (usu. sweetened)

【发稿】 fāgǎo ① distribute news dispatches ② send manuscripts to the press

【发给】 fāgěi issue; distribute; grant: ～护照 issue a passport/ ～复员费 issue (或 give) demobilization pay/ ～社员学习材料 distribute study material among the commune members

【发光】 fāguāng ① give out light; shine; be luminous: 群星闪闪～。The stars twinkled./ 有一分热，发一分光 give as much light as the heat can produce — do one's best, however little it may be ② 〈物〉 luminescence: 场致～ electroluminescence

◇ ～度 luminosity/ ～漆 luminous paint/ ～体 luminous body; luminary; luminophor

【发汗】 fāhàn induce perspiration (as by drugs); diaphoresis ◇ ～药 sudorific; diaphoretic

【发号施令】 fāhào-shīlìng issue orders; order people about: 干部要深入群众，不要只是坐在办公室里～。Cadres should go deep among the masses, not just sit in their offices issuing orders.

【发狠】 fāhěn ①make a determined effort: 他们一～,三天的任务一天就完成了。With a determined effort, they finished the three-day task in a single day. ②be angry
【发花】 fāhuā (of the eyes) grow dim; see things in a blur
【发还】 fāhuán return sth. (usu. to one's subordinate); give (或 send) back: 把作业～给学生 return the homework to the pupils/ 把计划～原单位去讨论修改 send the plan back where it came from for discussion and revision
【发慌】 fāhuāng feel nervous; get flustered; get flurried:她虽是第一次当众讲话，却一点都不～。She didn't feel a bit nervous though it was the first time she'd spoken in public.
【发挥】 fāhuī ①bring into play; give play to; give free rein to: 充分～群众的积极性 bring the initiative of the masses into full play/ ～共产党员的模范作用 play the exemplary role of a Communist/ ～专长 give full play to sb.'s professional knowledge or skill/ ～水利设施的最大效益 make the most of the water conservancy works/ 在运动中～主力军作用 play the part of the main force in the movement/ ～集体智慧 give full play to collective wisdom/ ～想象力 give the rein to one's imagination ②develop (an idea, a theme, etc.); elaborate: 这一论点有待进一步～。This point needs further elaboration.
【发昏】 fāhūn ①feel giddy (或 dizzy): 我的头有点儿～。I feel a bit giddy. ②lose one's head; become confused: 你～啦！Are you out of your mind?
【发火】 fāhuǒ ①catch fire; ignite ②detonate; go off: 他打了一枪,没有～。He pulled the trigger but the gun didn't go off. ③get angry; flare up; lose one's temper ④〈方〉(of a stove) draw well ◇～点〈物〉ignition point
【发货】 fāhuò send out goods; deliver goods ◇～单 dispatch list/ ～人 consignor; shipper
【发迹】 fājī (of a poor man) gain fame and fortune; rise to power and position
【发急】 fājí become impatient: 等得～ waiting impatiently
【发家】 fājiā build up a family fortune: 走集体富裕的道路,不搞个人～致富 take the road of collective prosperity instead of trying to build up family fortunes
【发奖】 fājiǎng award prizes ◇～仪式 prize-giving ceremony
【发酵】 fājiào ferment ◇～饲料 fermented feed
【发觉】 fājué find; detect; discover: 错误一经～,就应改正。Mistakes should be corrected as soon as they are discovered.
【发掘】 fājué excavate; unearth; explore: ～古墓 excavate an ancient tomb/ ～文物 unearth cultural relics/ ～人才 seek gifted (或 talented) people/ ～祖国的医药学遗产 explore the legacy of traditional Chinese medicine and pharmacology
【发刊词】 fākāncí foreword (或 introduction) to a periodical: «共产党人»～ Introducing *The Communist*
【发狂】 fākuáng go mad; go crazy
【发困】 fākùn 〈口〉feel sleepy (或 drowsy)
【发懒】 fālǎn feel lazy (或 languid)
【发冷】 fālěng feel cold (或 chilly)
【发愣】 fālèng 〈口〉stare blankly; be in a daze; be in a trance
【发亮】 fāliàng shine: 把机器擦得～ polish the machine till it shines/ 东方～了。The gleam of dawn shimmered in the east.
【发令枪】 fālìngqiāng 〈体〉starting gun (或 pistol)
【发聋振聩】 fālóng-zhènkuì 见"振聋发聩" zhènlóng-fākuì
【发落】 fāluò deal with (an offender): 从轻～ deal with sb. leniently
【发毛】 fāmáo ①〈口〉be scared; get gooseflesh ②〈方〉lose one's temper
【发霉】 fāméi go mouldy; become mildewed
【发蒙】 fāmēng 〈口〉get confused; get into a muddle
【发蒙】 fāméng 〈旧〉teach a child to read and write; teach a child his ABC
【发面】 fāmiàn ①leaven dough ②leavened dough ◇～饼 leavened pancake
【发明】 fāmíng ①invent: 印刷术是中国首先～的。Printing was first invented by the Chinese. ②invention: 最新～ the latest invention ③〈书〉expound ◇～权 inventor's patent right
【发难】 fānàn rise in revolt; launch an attack
【发排】 fāpái send a manuscript to the compositor
【发胖】 fāpàng put on (或 gain) weight; get fat
【发泡剂】 fāpàojì 〈化〉foaming (或 blowing) agent
【发脾气】 fā píqi lose one's temper; get angry: 有理慢慢儿说,何必～。Speak calmly if you think you're in the right; there's no need to get angry.
【发票】 fāpiào bill; receipt: 开～ make out a bill; write a receipt
【发起】 fāqǐ ①initiate; sponsor: 这次会议是由十四个国家～的。The meeting was sponsored by 14 countries./ 这个歌咏队是我们大队的知识青年～成立的。This singing group was formed on the initiative of the school graduates in our brigade. ②start; launch: ～反攻 launch a counterattack ◇～国 sponsor nation/ ～人 initiator; sponsor
【发情】 fāqíng 〈动〉①oestrus: 同步～ synchronization of oestrus ②be in heat ◇～期 heat period; oestrus/ ～周期 oestrous cycle
【发球】 fāqiú serve a ball: 该谁～？Whose service is it?/ 换～！Change service!/ 他～发得好。He has a very good serve./ 巧妙的～ a tricky serve/ ～得分 ace/ ～犯规 fault ◇～区 service area
【发热】 fārè ①give out heat; generate heat ②have (或 run) a fever: 我好象有点儿～。I feel as if I'm running a fever. ③be hotheaded ◇～量〈化〉calorific capacity
【发人深省】 fā rén shēn xǐng set people thinking; call for deep thought; provide food for thought
【发轫】 fārèn 〈书〉set sth. afoot; commence an undertaking
【发散】 fāsàn ①(of rays, etc.) diverge ②〈中医〉disperse the internal heat with sudorifics: 吃点药～一下 take a sudorific to sweat out a cold ◇～度〈物〉divergency/ ～透镜 divergent lens; diverging lens
【发色团】 fāsètuán 〈纺〉chromophore
【发痧】 fāshā 〈方〉have a heatstroke
【发烧】 fāshāo have (或 run) a fever; have (或 run) a temperature
【发射】 fāshè ①launch; project; discharge; shoot; fire:～导弹 launch (或 project) a guided missile/ ～人造卫星 launch a man-made satellite/ ～炮弹 fire shells ②〈物〉transmit; emit
◇～场 launching site/ ～光谱 emission spectrum/ ～架 launcher/ ～井 launching silo/ ～台 launching stand; launching (或 firing) pad
【发身】 fāshēn puberty
【发生】 fāshēng happen; occur; take place: ～了意外。Something unexpected happened./ 那里～了强烈地震。A violent earthquake occurred there./ ～了巨大的变化。Tremendous changes have taken place./ ～新的困难。New difficulties cropped up (或 arose)./ 机器～故障。The machine broke down./ 故事～在一九六二年秋天。The story is set in the autumn of 1962.
【发生器】 fāshēngqì 〈化〉generator: 氨～ ammonia generator
【发声】 fāshēng sound production

【发誓】 fāshì vow; pledge; swear: 他们～要为死难烈士报仇。They vowed to avenge the martyrs.

【发售】 fāshòu sell; put on sale: 这些杂志在全国各地书店均有～。These magazines are sold at bookstores throughout the country./ 新的纪念邮票将于下星期～。The new commemorative stamps will be put on sale next week.

【发抒】 fāshū express; voice: ～己见 express one's personal views/ ～革命豪情 voice lofty revolutionary sentiments

【发水】 fāshuǐ flood: 过去一下暴雨，这条河就发大水。This river used to get flooded whenever there was a rainstorm.

【发送】 fāsòng ① transmit by radio: ～密码电报 transmit a coded message ② dispatch (letters, etc.)

【发酸】 fāsuān ① turn sour: 牛奶～了。The milk has turned sour. ② ache slightly: 腰有点～ have a slight backache

【发条】 fātiáo 〈机〉 spiral power spring; clockwork spring

【发文】 fāwén outgoing message; dispatch ◇ ～簿 register of outgoing documents, letters, etc.

【发问】 fāwèn ask (或 put, pose, raise) a question

【发现】 fāxiàn find; discover: ～一些线索 find some clues/ ～问题，解决问题 discover problems and solve them/ ～敌炮艇一艘 spot an enemy gunboat/ 敌机被我们的雷达～了。Enemy planes were picked up by our radar./ 文化大革命以来在考古方面有许多重大的～。Many important archaeological finds have been made since the Great Proletarian Cultural Revolution./ 我没有～什么情况。I didn't notice anything.

【发祥地】 fāxiángdì place of origin; birthplace: 我国古代文化的～ the birthplace of China's ancient culture

【发饷】 fāxiǎng 〈旧〉 issue pay (esp. to soldiers)

【发笑】 fāxiào laugh: 令人～ make one laugh; provoke laughter; be ridiculous

【发泄】 fāxiè give vent to; let off: ～个人情绪 give vent to one's personal feelings/ ～不满 air (或 express) one's grievances

【发信】 fāxìn post a letter ◇ ～人 addresser

【发行】 fāxíng (of currency, bonds, books, etc.) issue; publish; distribute; put on sale: ～纸币 issue paper money/ ～书刊 publish books and magazines/ ～影片 release a film/ 由新华书店～ distributed by Xinhua Bookstore/ 将在全国各地～ will be put on sale throughout the country ◇ ～银行 bank of issue/ ～者 publisher

【发芽】 fāyá germinate; sprout: 种子还没有～。The seeds haven't sprouted (或 come up) yet. ◇ ～率 germination percentage/ ～试验 germination test

【发言】 fāyán speak; make a statement or speech; take the floor: 他在会上～了吗？Did he speak at the meeting?/ 要求～ ask to be heard; ask for the floor/ 他的～很精彩。He made a brilliant speech. ◇ ～稿 the text of a statement or speech

【发言权】 fāyánquán right to speak: 我们对这事当然有～。Of course we have a say in this matter./ 他们对这个问题最有～。They are best qualified to speak on this question.

【发言人】 fāyánrén spokesman: 政府～ government spokesman

【发炎】 fāyán 〈医〉 inflammation: 伤口～了。The wound has become inflamed.

【发扬】 fāyáng ① develop; carry on (或 forward): ～民主作风 develop a democratic style of work/ ～艰苦奋斗的作风 keep up the practice of plain living and hard struggle/ ～我党我军的优良传统 carry forward the fine tradition of our Party and Army/ ～成绩，纠正错误，以利再战。Add to your achievements and correct your mistakes to do still better in future struggles./ ～正气，打击歪风。Encourage healthy trends and combat unhealthy ones./ 他们～了一不怕苦、二不怕死的彻底革命精神。They displayed their revolutionary spirit in their utter disregard of hardship and danger. ② make the most of; make full use of: ～火力，消灭敌人 make full use of firepower to destroy the enemy

【发扬光大】 fāyáng guāngdà carry forward; develop; enhance: 延安精神～。Carry forward the Yan'an spirit.

【发疟子】 fā yàozi have an attack of malaria; suffer from malarial fever

【发音】 fāyīn pronunciation; enunciation; articulation: 这个字怎么～？How do you pronounce this word?/ 这个字母不～。This letter is silent (或 not pronounced)./ 她～清晰。She enunciates her words clearly./ 他～不清楚。His articulation is poor.
◇ ～部位 points of articulation/ ～困难 〈医〉dysphonia/ ～器官 vocal (或 speech) organs

【发育】 fāyù growth; development: ～健全 physically well developed/ 婴儿～情况良好。The baby is coming on well.
◇ ～不全 〈医〉hypoplasia/ ～异常 〈医〉dysplasia

【发源】 fāyuán rise; originate: 长江～于青海。The Changjiang River rises in Qinghai Province./ 一切真知都是从直接经验～的。All genuine knowledge originates in direct experience. ◇ ～地 place of origin; source; birthplace

【发晕】 fāyùn feel dizzy (或 giddy)

【发展】 fāzhǎn ① develop; expand; grow: ～经济，保障供给。Develop the economy and ensure supplies./ ～革命力量 expand revolutionary forces/ ～大好形势 make further advances on the already very good situation/ 用～的眼光看人 look at a person with an eye on the course of his development/ 我国社会主义建设事业蓬勃～。China's socialist construction is forging rapidly ahead./ 第三世界国家的力量迅速～壮大。The third world countries are rapidly going from strength to strength. ② recruit; admit: ～新党员 recruit new Party members

【发展中国家】 fāzhǎnzhōng guójiā developing country

【发胀】 fāzhàng ① swell: 肚子～ feel bloated/ 头脑～ have a swelled head ② 〈针灸〉 feel distended

【发作】 fāzuò ① break out; show effect: 她的心脏病又～了。She's had another heart attack./ 酒性开始～。The liquor began to show its effect. ② have a fit of anger; flare up: 他有些生气，但当着大家的面不好～。He was angry, but with everybody present, he kept his temper under control./ 歇斯底里大～ have a bad fit of hysterics

## fá

**乏** fá ① lack: 不～其人。There's no lack of such people./ 回天～术 unable to save the situation ② tired; weary: 走～了 be tired from a long walk ③ 〈方〉 exhausted; worn-out: ～地 exhausted soil; poor land/ ～走狗 a decrepit (或 broken-down) running dog/ 火～了，该续煤了。The fire's going out, put on some more coal.

【乏货】 fáhuò 〈方〉 good-for-nothing; ne'er-do-well

【乏味】 fáwèi dull; insipid; drab; tasteless: 语言～ dull (或 drab) language

**伐** fá ① fell; cut down: ～了几棵树 cut down a few trees ② send an expedition against; strike; attack: 讨～ send a punitive expedition

【伐木】 fámù lumbering; felling; cutting ◇ ～工 lumberman/ ～业 lumbering

【伐区】 fáqū 〈林〉 cutting (或 felling) area

**垡** fá ① turn up soil ② upturned soil

**罚** fá punish; penalize: ～不当罪 be unduly punished/

赏～分明 be fair in meting out rewards or punishments
【罚出场】 fá chūchǎng 〈体〉 be ordered off the field for foul play; foul out
【罚金】 fájīn fine; forfeit: 处以～ impose a fine on sb.; fine sb.
【罚酒】 fájiǔ be made to drink as a forfeit
【罚款】 fákuǎn ① impose a fine or forfeit ② fine; forfeit; penalty ◇ ～条款 penalty clause
【罚球】 fáqiú (篮球) penalty shot; (足球) penalty kick

**阀** fá ① a powerful person or family: 军～ warlord/ 财～ financial magnate; plutocrat ② 〈机〉 valve: 安全～ safety valve/ 止回～ check valve
【阀门】 fámén 〈机〉 valve

**筏** fá raft: 橡皮～ rubber raft
【筏道】 fádào log chute; logway
【筏子】 fázi raft

## fǎ

**法** fǎ ① law: 守～ observe the law; be law-abiding/ 违～ break the law ② method; way; mode: 教～ teaching method/ 表达～ mode of expression ③ follow; model after: 效～ take as model; follow ④ standard; model: ～书 model calligraphy ⑤ Legalists; the Legalist School ⑥ Buddhist doctrine; the dharma ⑦ magic arts: 戏～ conjuring tricks
【法案】 fǎ'àn proposed law; bill
【法办】 fǎbàn deal with according to law; punish by law; bring to justice
【法宝】 fǎbǎo a magic weapon: 战胜敌人的～ magic weapon for defeating the enemy/ 祭起"缓和"～，妄图欺骗世界人民 try to use "*détente*" as a talisman to deceive the people of the world
【法币】 fǎbì paper currency issued by the reactionary KMT government from 1935 onwards
【法场】 fǎchǎng execution ground; place of execution
【法典】 fǎdiǎn code; statute book
【法定】 fǎdìng legal; statutory
◇ ～代理人 legal representative/ ～汇率 official rate (of exchange); pegged rate of exchange; pegged exchange parity/ ～货币 legal tender/ ～年龄 lawful (或 legal) age/ ～期限 legal time limit
【法定人数】 fǎdìng rénshù quorum: 已足～。We have a quorum now.
【法度】 fǎdù ① law ② moral standard
【法官】 fǎguān judge; justice
【法规】 fǎguī laws and regulations
【法国】 Fǎguó France
◇ ～大革命 the French Revolution (1789)/ ～人 the French; Frenchman/ ～梧桐 plane tree
【法纪】 fǎjì law and discipline: 目无～ act in utter disregard of law and discipline; flout law and discipline
【法家】 Fǎjiā Legalists (a school of thought in the Spring and Autumn and Warring States Periods, 770-221 B.C.)
【法警】 fǎjǐng bailiff
【法拉】 fǎlā 〈物〉 farad: 微～ microfarad
【法拉第定律】 Fǎlādì dìnglǜ 〈物〉 Faraday's law
【法兰】 fǎlán 〈机〉 flange ◇ ～盘 flange plate
【法兰绒】 fǎlánróng flannel
【法郎】 fǎláng franc
【法理】 fǎlǐ legal principle; theory of law ◇ ～学 jurisprudence
【法力】 fǎlì supernatural power
【法令】 fǎlìng laws and decrees; decree: 政府～ government decree
【法律】 fǎlǜ law; statute
◇ ～保护 legal protection/ ～承认 *de jure* recognition/ ～地位 legal status/ ～根据 legal basis/ ～顾问 legal adviser/ ～规定 legal provisions/ ～手续 legal procedure/ ～效力 legal effect/ ～制裁 legal sanction
【法罗群岛】 Fǎluó Qúndǎo the Faroe Islands
【法螺】 fǎluó ① 〈动〉 triton (shell) ② conch: 自吹～ blow one's own trumpet
【法器】 fǎqì 〈宗〉 musical instruments used in a Buddhist or Taoist mass
【法权】 fǎquán right: 治外～ extraterritoriality
【法人】 fǎrén 〈法〉 legal person; juridical person; *legalis homo* ◇ ～税 corporation tax/ ～团体 body corporate; corporation
【法师】 fǎshī Master, a title of respect for a Buddhist or Taoist priest
【法式】 fǎshì rule; method; model: 《营造～》 *Rules of Architecture*
【法书】 fǎshū ① model calligraphy ② 〈敬〉 your calligraphy
【法术】 fǎshù magic arts
【法庭】 fǎtíng court; tribunal: 军事～ military tribunal; court-martial
【法统】 fǎtǒng legally constituted authority
【法网】 fǎwǎng the net of justice; the arm of the law: 逃不出人民的～ be unable to escape the net of justice spread by the people
【法西斯】 fǎxīsī fascist ◇ ～化 fascistization/ ～主义 fascism
【法线】 fǎxiàn 〈数〉 normal (line)
【法学】 fǎxué the science of law; law ◇ ～家 jurist
【法衣】 fǎyī garments worn by a Buddhist or Taoist priest at a religious ceremony
【法医】 fǎyī legal medical expert ◇ ～学 medical jurisprudence; forensic medicine
【法语】 Fǎyǔ French (language)
【法院】 fǎyuàn court of justice; law court; court: 最高人民～ the Supreme People's Court/ 高级人民～ Higher People's Court
【法则】 fǎzé rule; law: 自然～ law of nature
【法治】 fǎzhì rule by law
【法制】 fǎzhì legal system; legal institutions; legality: 加强社会主义～ strengthen the socialist legal system
【法子】 fǎzi way; method: 我们得想个～解决这个问题。We'll have to think of a way to solve the problem. 或 We must find a way out.

**砝** fǎ
【砝码】 fǎmǎ weight (used on a balance)

## fà

**发** fà hair: 理～ haircut
另见 fā
【发夹】 fàjiā hairpin; bobby pin
【发蜡】 fàlà pomade
【发卡】 fàqiǎ hairpin
【发刷】 fàshuā hairbrush
【发网】 fàwǎng hairnet
【发型】 fàxíng hair style; hairdo; coiffure
【发癣】 fàxuǎn 〈医〉 ringworm of the scalp; tinea capitis
【发油】 fàyóu hair oil

【发指】 fàzhǐ bristle (或 boil) with anger: 敌人的暴行令人～。The enemy's atrocities made one boil with anger.

**珐** fà

【珐琅】 fàláng enamel

【珐琅质】 fàlángzhì 〈生理〉 enamel

## fān

**帆** fān sail: ～樯林立 a forest of masts

【帆布】 fānbù canvas ◇ ～包 canvas bag; kit bag/ ～床 cot; campbed/ ～篷 canvas roof; awning/ ～鞋 plimsolls

【帆船】 fānchuán sailing boat (或 ship); junk

**番** fān 〈量〉〔表示"种""回""次"〕: 别有一～天地 like stepping into a fairyland; an altogether different world/ 三～五次 time and again/ 粮食产量翻了一～。Grain output has doubled./ 费了一～功夫 put in a lot of effort

【番瓜】 fānguā 〈方〉 pumpkin

【番号】 fānhào designation (of a military unit)

【番木瓜】 fānmùguā 〈植〉 papaya

【番木鳖硷】 fānmùbiējiǎn 〈药〉 strychnine

【番茄】 fānqié tomato ◇ ～酱 tomato ketchup/ ～汁 tomato juice

【番薯】 fānshǔ 〈方〉 sweet potato

**幡** fān long narrow flag; streamer

【幡然】 fānrán 见"翻然" fānrán

**藩** fān

【藩篱】 fānlí hedge; fence

【藩属】 fānshǔ vassal state

【藩镇】 fānzhèn Tang Dynasty military governor (usu. in control of outlying prefectures)

**翻** fān ① turn over (或 up): ～谷子 turn over the grain (to dry)/ 船～了。The ship capsized. 或 The ship turned turtle./ 车～了。The cart turned over./ 把饼～个个儿再烙一会儿。Turn the cake over and bake it some more./ 碰～ knock over ② cross; get over: ～过山头 cross a mountaintop/ ～墙 climb over a wall ③ rummage; search: 抽屉我都～遍了,还是找不到。I rummaged all the drawers, but still couldn't find it./ ～参考书 look through reference works ④ translate: 把英文～成中文 translate the English into Chinese/ ～电报 decode a telegram ⑤ reverse: ～案 reverse a verdict ⑥ multiply: 使炼油能力～一番 double the oil-refining capacity ⑦〈口〉 fall out; break up: 他们闹～了。They quarrelled and split up. 或 They fell out.

【翻案】 fān'àn reverse a (correct) verdict

【翻白眼】 fān báiyǎn show the whites of one's eyes (as from emotion or illness)

【翻版】 fānbǎn reprint; reproduction; refurbished version

【翻茬】 fānchá plough under the stubble after the harvest

【翻场】 fāncháng turn over the grain on the threshing ground

【翻车机】 fānchējī 〈矿〉 tipper; dumper; tipple

【翻车鱼】 fānchēyú ocean sunfish; headfish

【翻地】 fāndì turn up the soil

【翻斗】 fāndǒu tipping bucket; skip bucket ◇ ～车 skip car; tipcart/ ～卡车 tipping lorry; tip lorry; tip truck

【翻覆】 fānfù overturn; turn upside down

【翻盖】 fāngài renovate (a house)

【翻杠子】 fān gàngzi 〈体〉 do gymnastics on a horizontal bar or on parallel bars

【翻跟头】 fān gēntou turn a somersault; loop the loop: 飞机连翻了三个跟头。The plane looped the loop three times.

【翻供】 fāngòng withdraw a confession; retract one's testimony

【翻滚】 fāngǔn roll; toss; tumble: 白浪～。The waves rolled and foamed.

【翻花】 fānhuā 〈工美〉 magic flower

【翻悔】 fānhuǐ back out (of a commitment, promise, etc.)

【翻江倒海】 fānjiāng-dǎohǎi overturning rivers and seas — overwhelming; stupendous; terrific: 以～之势 with the momentum of an avalanche

【翻浆】 fānjiāng 〈交〉 frost heave; frost boil

【翻来复去】 fānlái-fùqù ① toss and turn; toss from side to side: 他在床上～睡不着。He tossed and turned in bed, unable to sleep. ② again and again; repeatedly: 这种话,她～不知说过多少遍了。This is what she has been saying over and over again — I don't know how many times.

【翻老帐】 fān lǎozhàng bring up old scores again

【翻脸】 fānliǎn fall out; suddenly turn hostile: ～不认人 turn against a friend/ ～无情 turn against a friend and show him no mercy; be treacherous and ruthless

【翻领】 fānlǐng turndown collar

【翻然】 fānrán (change) quickly and completely: ～悔悟 quickly wake up to one's error

【翻砂】 fānshā 〈机〉 founding; moulding; casting ◇ ～车间 foundry shop/ ～工 foundry worker; caster

【翻山越岭】 fānshān-yuèlǐng cross over mountain after mountain; tramp over hill and dale

【翻身】 fānshēn ① turn over: 他翻了个身又睡着了。He turned over in bed and fell asleep again./ 一～从床上爬起来 roll off the bed ② free oneself; stand up: ～农奴 emancipated serfs/ ～做主人 stand up and be master of one's fate/ ～不忘共产党。We shall never forget the Communist Party now that we've stood up./ 大打造纸工业～仗 work hard to bring about an upswing in the paper industry

【翻绳儿】 fānshéngr cat's cradle

【翻腾】 fānténg 〈跳水〉 tuck dive: 向内(前)～两周半 backward (forward) tuck dive with two-and-a-half somersaults

【翻腾】 fānteng ① seethe; rise; churn: 波浪～ seething (或 turbulent) waves ② turn sth. over and over: 几个箱子都～遍了也没有找到。I rummaged through all the boxes but still could not find it.

【翻天】 fāntiān overturn the heavens; shake the sky: 不许阶级敌人～。We shall never allow the class enemy to wreak vengeance.

【翻天覆地】 fāntiān-fùdì earth-shaking; world-shaking: ～的变化 an earth-shaking change/ ～的时代 an earth-shaking era

【翻蔓儿】 fānwànr turn the vines (of sweet potato, etc.)

【翻胃】 fānwèi gastric disorder causing nausea

【翻箱倒柜】 fānxiāng-dǎoguì rummage through chests and cupboards; ransack boxes and chests

【翻新】 fānxīn renovate; recondition; make over: 旧大衣可以～。Old overcoats can be reconditioned./ ～车胎 retread a tyre/ 花样～ (the same old thing) in a new guise

【翻修】 fānxiū rebuild: ～房屋 have the house rebuilt/ ～地板 relay a wooden floor/ ～马路 repair the roads

【翻译】 fānyì ① translate; interpret: 请你帮我～一下好吗？Would you mind translating (或 interpreting) for me?/ ～电码 decode; decipher ② translator; interpreter ◇ ～本 translation/ ～片 dubbed film

【翻印】 fānyìn reprint; reproduce

【翻阅】 fānyuè browse; look over; glance over; leaf

through: ～报章杂志 look over newspapers and magazines/ ～目录 glance through a catalogue

【翻云覆雨】 fānyún-fùyǔ produce clouds with one turn of the hand and rain with another — given to playing tricks; shifty

## fán

**凡** fán ① commonplace; ordinary: 非～ extraordinary ② this mortal world; the earth: 天仙下～ a celestial beauty come down to earth ③ every; any; all: 在我国，～年满十八岁的公民，都有选举权和被选举权。In China, every citizen who has reached the age of eighteen has the right to vote and stand for election./ ～属我国文化遗产中有用的东西，都应当批判地继承。All of our cultural heritage which is useful should be inherited, but in a critical way./ ～是逆历史潮流而动的人，都没有好下场。Whoever goes against the tide of history will come to no good end. ④〈书〉altogether: 全书～二十卷。The set consists of 20 volumes altogether. ⑤〈书〉outline: 发～ an introduction (to a subject or book) ⑥〈乐〉a note of the scale in *gongchepu* (工尺谱), corresponding to 4 in numbered musical notation

【凡立丁呢】 fánlìdīngní 〈纺〉 valitin

【凡例】 fánlì notes on the use of a book, etc.; guide to the use of a book, etc.

【凡人】 fánrén ① ordinary person ② mortal

【凡士林】 fánshìlín vaseline; petrolatum

【凡事】 fánshì everything: ～应该用脑筋好好想一想。We should always use our brains and think everything over carefully.

【凡是】 fánshì every; any; all: ～正义的事业都是不可战胜的。A just cause is invincible.

【凡庸】 fányōng commonplace; ordinary

**矾** fán 〈化〉 vitriol: 明～ alum/ 胆～ blue vitriol; bluestone/ 绿～ green vitriol; copperas

【矾土】 fántǔ 〈矿〉 alumina ◇ ～水泥 alumina cement

**钒** fán 〈化〉 vanadium (V): ～钢 vanadium steel

**烦** fán ① be vexed; be irritated; be annoyed: 心～ feel vexed/ 真～人！How annoying!/ 你～什么？What are you getting so annoyed about? ② be tired of: 厌～ be fed up with ③ superfluous and confusing: 要言不～ giving the essentials in simple language; pithy; terse ④ trouble: ～交某人 please forward this to so-and-so/ ～您给她捎个信儿。May I trouble you to pass on a message to her?

【烦劳】 fánláo trouble: ～您带几本书给他。Would you mind taking a few books to him?

【烦闷】 fánmèn be unhappy; be worried: 你干吗这样～？Why are you so worried?/ 他一上午都没说话，心里一定很～。There must be something on his mind, he's been so quiet the whole morning.

【烦恼】 fánnǎo be vexed; be worried: 自寻～ worry over for nothing; bring vexation on oneself/ 何必为这些小事～？Why should you fret over such trifles?

【烦扰】 fánrǎo ① bother; disturb ② feel disturbed

【烦冗】 fánrǒng ① (of one's affairs) diverse and complicated ② (of speech or writing) lengthy and tedious; prolix

【烦琐】 fánsuǒ loaded down with trivial details: ～的手续 overelaborate procedure; tedious formalities/ ～的考证 pedantic textual criticism; overelaborate research

【烦琐哲学】 fánsuǒ zhéxué ① scholasticism ②〈口〉over-elaboration; hairsplitting

【烦嚣】 fánxiāo noisy and annoying

【烦躁】 fánzào be fidgety; be agitated: 某些动物～不安可能是地震临震前的预兆。Agitated activity by certain animals may be a sign of an impending earthquake.

**蕃** fán ① luxuriant; growing in abundance: ～茂 luxuriant; lush ② multiply; proliferate: ～衍 multiply; increase gradually in number or quantity

**樊** fán ①〈书〉fence ② (Fán) a surname

【樊篱】 fánlí ① fence ② barriers; restriction: 冲破～ break down barriers; cast off trammels

【樊笼】 fánlóng bird cage — place or condition of confinement

**繁** fán ① in great numbers; numerous; manifold: ～星满天 a starry sky/ 头绪纷～ have too many things to attend to; have too many irons in the fire/ 删～就简 simplify by weeding out superfluities; reduce to bare essentials ② propagate; multiply: 生产大队自～自养的牲畜 livestock propagated and raised by the production brigade itself

【繁多】 fánduō various: 花样～ of all shapes and colours/ 解放前，苛捐杂税，名目～。Before liberation there were exorbitant taxes and levies of every sort under the sun.

【繁分数】 fánfēnshù 〈数〉 complex fraction

【繁复】 fánfù heavy and complicated: 有了计算机，～的计算工作在几秒钟之内就可以完成。A computer does complicated calculations in a few seconds.

【繁华】 fánhuá flourishing; bustling; busy: 城里最～的地区 the busiest section of town; the downtown district

【繁忙】 fánmáng busy: ～的收获季节 the busy harvest season/ 工作～ be very busy with one's work; be busily engaged

【繁茂】 fánmào lush; luxuriant: 草木～ a lush growth of trees and grass/ 枝叶～ with luxuriant foliage

【繁密】 fánmì dense: 林木～ densely wooded

【繁难】 fánnán hard to tackle; troublesome

【繁荣】 fánróng ① flourishing; prosperous; booming: ～的社会主义文化 a flourishing socialist culture/ ～富强 rich, strong and prosperous/ 物价稳定，市场～。Prices are stable and the market is brisk. ② make sth. prosper: ～经济 bring about a prosperous economy; promote economic prosperity

【繁荣昌盛】 fánróng-chāngshèng thriving and prosperous: 祖国日益～。Our country is thriving and prospering day by day./ 祝贵国～，人民幸福。We wish your country prosperity and her people happiness.

【繁冗】 fánrǒng 见"烦冗" fánrǒng

【繁缛】 fánrù overelaborate: ～的礼节 overelaborate formalities

【繁盛】 fánshèng thriving; flourishing; prosperous: 这个城市越来越～了。The city is becoming more and more prosperous.

【繁琐】 fánsuǒ 见"烦琐" fánsuǒ

【繁体字】 fántǐzì the original complex form of a simplified Chinese character

【繁文缛节】 fánwén-rùjié unnecessary and overelaborate formalities; red tape

【繁芜】 fánwú loaded with unnecessary words; wordy; verbose

【繁细】 fánxì overloaded with details; excessively detailed

【繁衍】 fányǎn 〈书〉 multiply; increase gradually in number or quantity

【繁育】 fányù breed: ～优良品种 breed good strains

【繁杂】 fánzá many and diverse; miscellaneous: ～的日常事务 daily chores of all sorts

【繁殖】 fánzhí 〈生〉 breed; reproduce; propagate: 自我～ self-reproduction; autosynthesis/ ～牲畜 breed livestock/ 靠种子～的植物 plants which propagate themselves by seeds ◇ ～力 reproductive capacity; fecundity; fertility/ ～率 rate of reproduction; breeding rate

【繁重】 fánzhòng heavy; strenuous; onerous: ～的劳动 strenuous labour/ 任务～。The tasks are arduous.

## fǎn

**反** fǎn ① turn over: 易如～掌 as easy as turning one's hand over/ ～败为胜 turn defeat into victory; turn the tide ② in an opposite direction; in reverse; inside out: ～面 the reverse side/ ～绑着双手 with one's hands tied behind one's back/ ～其道而行之 act in a diametrically opposite way; do exactly the opposite/ 适得其～。The result is just the contrary./ 穿～了袜子 have one's socks on inside out/ ～科学 contrary to science ③ on the contrary; instead: 这样做不但于事无补，～会把事情弄糟。This won't do any good; on the contrary, it will make things even worse. ④ return; counter: ～问 counter with a question; ask in retort/ ～击 strike back; counterattack ⑤ revolt; rebel: ～叛 revolt; rebel ⑥ oppose; combat: ～修 combat revisionism/ ～法西斯斗争 anti-fascist struggle; struggle against fascism/ 颠覆与～颠覆 subversion and anti-subversion/ ～间谍 counterespionage ⑦ counterrevolutionaries; reactionaries: 肃～ elimination of counterrevolutionaries/ 帝、修、～ imperialism, revisionism and all reaction

【反霸】 fǎnbà ① oppose local despots ② oppose hegemonism: 第三世界国家的～斗争 the struggle of the third world countries against hegemonism

【反比】 fǎnbǐ 〈数〉 inverse ratio (或 proportion)

【反比例】 fǎnbǐlì 〈数〉 inverse proportion: 分数值与分母值成～。The value of a fraction is inversely proportional to that of the denominator.

【反驳】 fǎnbó refute; retort

【反差】 fǎnchā 〈摄〉 contrast

【反常】 fǎncháng unusual; abnormal; perverse; strange: 最近天气有点儿～。The weather is a bit unusual these days./ 他昨天的表现有点儿～。His behaviour yesterday was a bit strange.

【反潮流】 fǎn cháoliú go against the tide: 毛主席讲的～，就是反对搞修正主义、搞分裂、搞阴谋诡计的恶流。By going against the tide Chairman Mao meant going against the adverse tide of revisionism, splittism and conspiracy.

【反衬】 fǎnchèn set off by contrast; serve as a foil to

【反冲】 fǎnchōng 〈物〉 recoil ◇ ～核 recoil nucleus

【反刍】 fǎnchú ruminate; chew the cud ◇ ～动物 ruminant/ ～胃 ruminant stomach

【反唇相讥】 fǎn chún xiāng jī answer back sarcastically

【反导弹导弹】 fǎndǎodàn dǎodàn antimissile missile

【反倒】 fǎndào on the contrary; instead

【反帝】 fǎndì anti-imperialist; against imperialism: ～斗争 anti-imperialist struggle

【反动】 fǎndòng ① reactionary: ～势力 reactionary forces ② reaction: 他弃家出走，是对旧社会婚姻压迫的～。He finally left home in an effort to counter the tyranny of arranged marriage in the old society.
◇ ～分子 reactionary element; reactionary/ ～会道门 reactionary secret societies/ ～派 reactionaries

【反对】 fǎnduì oppose; be against; fight; combat: ～贪污浪费 fight against corruption and waste/ ～官僚主义 combat bureaucracy/ 有～意见吗？Any objection?/ 我们对待世界大战这个问题的态度是，第一，～；第二，不怕。Our attitude on the question of world war is: first, we are against it; second, we are not afraid of it./ 要提倡唯物辩证法，～形而上学和烦琐哲学。Promote materialist dialectics and oppose metaphysics and scholasticism./ 被敌人～是好事而不是坏事。To be attacked by the enemy is a good thing, not a bad thing.
◇ ～党 opposition party; the Opposition/ ～派 opposition faction/ ～票 dissenting vote; negative vote

【反而】 fǎn'ér 〈连〉 on the contrary; instead: 困难吓不倒我们，～激起我们更大的革命干劲。We were not cowed by difficulties. On the contrary, they inspired us to greater efforts for the revolution.

【反封建】 fǎn fēngjiàn anti-feudal; against feudalism

【反复】 fǎnfù ① repeatedly; again and again; over and over again: ～解释 explain over and over again/ ～思考 think a lot about sth.; turn sth. over in one's mind again and again/ ～辩论 argue back and forth/ ～强调思想工作的重要性 repeatedly stress the importance of ideological work/ 这个计划是经过～讨论而产生的。The plan was born out of repeated discussions. ② reversal; relapse: 你的病虽然好了，可要防止～。You are well now, but mind you don't have a relapse./ 思想上有～ have ideological relapses/ 斗争出现了～ meet with a setback in the struggle ◇ ～记号〈乐〉 repeat

【反复无常】 fǎnfù wú cháng changeable; fickle; capricious: 这个人～，很不可靠。This fellow is always chopping and changing; he's very unreliable.

【反感】 fǎngǎn be disgusted with; be averse to; dislike; take unkindly to: 我对他的话很～。I'm disgusted with what he said./ 对这种人极其～ have a strong aversion to such people; feel a repugnance to such people

【反戈一击】 fǎn gē yī jī turn one's weapon around and strike — turn against those one has wrongly sided with

【反革命】 fǎngémìng counterrevolutionary: 镇压～ suppression of counterrevolutionaries
◇ ～分子 a counterrevolutionary/ ～两面派 counterrevolutionary double-dealer/ ～罪 counterrevolutionary crime

【反攻】 fǎngōng counteroffensive; counterattack

【反攻倒算】 fǎngōng-dàosuàn counterattack to settle old scores; launch a vindictive counterattack; retaliate: 决不允许阶级敌人～ never allow the class enemies to retaliate/ 粉碎恶霸地主～的阴谋 frustrate the despotic landlords' scheme of taking reprisals

【反躬自问】 fǎngōng zìwèn examine oneself; examine one's conscience

【反顾】 fǎngù 〈书〉 look back: 义无～ be duty-bound not to turn back

【反光】 fǎnguāng ① reflect light: 白墙～，屋里显得很敞亮。With the white walls reflecting the light, the room looks bright and spacious. ② reflection of light ◇ ～灯 reflector lamp/ ～镜 reflector

【反过来】 fǎnguolai ① conversely; the other way round: ～也是一样。It's the same the other way round./ 这话～说就不一定对。The converse of this statement may not be true. ② in turn: 经济基础决定上层建筑，～上层建筑又作用于经济基础。The superstructure is determined by the economic base and in turn reacts on it.

【反函数】 fǎnhánshù 〈数〉 inverse function

【反话】 fǎnhuà irony

【反悔】 fǎnhuǐ go back on one's word (或 promise): 一言为定，决不～。I give you my word and I'll never go back on it.

【反击】 fǎnjī strike back; beat back; counterattack: 自卫～ counterattack in self-defence/ 对敌人的挑衅给予有力的～ answer the enemy's provocation with a vigorous counterblow
【反剪】 fǎnjiǎn ① with one's hands behind one's back ② with one's hands tied behind one's back
【反间】 fǎnjiàn sow distrust or dissension among one's enemies; set one's enemies at odds (by spreading rumours, etc.) ◇ ～计 stratagem of sowing distrust or discord among one's enemies
【反建议】 fǎnjiànyì counterproposal
【反骄破满】 fǎnjiāo-pòmǎn oppose arrogance and shatter complacency
【反诘】 fǎnjié ask in retort; counter with a question
【反抗】 fǎnkàng revolt; resist: ～精神 spirit of revolt; rebellious spirit/ 那里有压迫，那里就有～。Where there is oppression, there is resistance.
【反客为主】 fǎn kè wéi zhǔ reverse the positions of the host and the guest
【反空降】 fǎnkōngjiàng 〈军〉 anti-airborne defence
【反馈】 fǎnkuì 〈电〉 feedback: 正(负)～ positive (negative) feedback ◇ ～抑制 feedback inhibition
【反粒子】 fǎnlìzǐ 〈物〉 antiparticle
【反面】 fǎnmiàn ① reverse side; wrong side; back: 唱片的～ the reverse side of a disc/ 料子的～ the wrong side of the cloth/ 我们必须学会全面地看问题，不但要看到事物的正面，也要看到它的～。We must learn to look at problems from all sides, seeing the reverse as well as the obverse side of things. ② opposite; negative side: 走向～ change (或 turn) into one's opposite/ ～的教训 a lesson learnt from negative (或 bitter) experience; wisdom won from hard knocks
◇ ～教材 negative example which may serve as a lesson; bad experience which teaches us what not to do/ ～教员 teacher by negative example; negative teacher/ ～人物 villain; negative character; negative role
【反目】 fǎnmù fall out (esp. between husband and wife)
【反派】 fǎnpài villain (in drama, etc.); negative character: 演～人物 act the part of the villain; play a negative role
【反叛】 fǎnpàn revolt; rebel
【反批评】 fǎnpīpíng counter-criticism
【反扑】 fǎnpū pounce on sb. again after being beaten off; launch a counteroffensive to retrieve lost ground: 打退敌人一次又一次的～ repulse the repeated counterattacks of the enemy
【反气旋】 fǎnqìxuán 〈气〉 anticyclone
【反潜机】 fǎnqiánjī antisubmarine plane
【反潜舰艇】 fǎnqián jiàntǐng antisubmarine vessels
【反切】 fǎnqiè 〈语〉 a traditional method of indicating the pronunciation of a Chinese character by using two other Chinese characters, the first having the same consonant as the given character and the second having the same vowel (with or without final nasal) and tone (e.g. the pronunciation of 同 tóng is indicated as 徒红切, meaning a combination of the consonant t from 徒 tú and the vowel plus nasal óng from 红 hóng)
【反求诸己】 fǎn qiú zhū jǐ seek the cause in oneself (instead of in sb. else)
【反射】 fǎnshè ① 〈生〉 reflex: 条件(非条件)～ conditioned (unconditioned) reflex/ 膝腱～ knee jerk reflex ② 〈物〉 reflection
◇ ～比〈物〉 reflectance/ ～测云器 reflecting nephoscope/ ～弧〈生理〉 reflex arc/ ～计 reflectometer/ ～镜 reflector/ ～炉〈冶〉 reverberatory furnace/ ～望远镜 reflecting telescope
【反手】 fǎnshǒu 〈体〉 backhand: ～抽球 backhand drive
【反水】 fǎnshuǐ turn one's coat; defect
【反诉】 fǎnsù 〈法〉 countercharge; counterclaim
【反坦克炮】 fǎntǎnkèpào antitank gun
【反特】 fǎntè anti-espionage ◇ ～影片 spy film; anti-espionage film
【反题】 fǎntí 〈哲〉 antithesis
【反铁电】 fǎntiědiàn 〈物〉 antiferroelectric ◇ ～现象 antiferroelectricity
【反围盘】 fǎnwéipán 〈机〉 reverse repeater (used in steel rolling)
【反胃】 fǎnwèi gastric disorder causing nausea
【反问】 fǎnwèn ① ask (a question) in reply ② 〈语〉 rhetorical question
【反响】 fǎnxiǎng repercussion; echo; reverberation: 在世界上引起广泛的～ evoke worldwide repercussions/ 在很多人心中引起～ find an echo in the hearts of many people
【反向】 fǎnxiàng opposite direction; reverse
◇ ～铲 backhoe/ ～电流 reverse current/ ～卫星 retrograde satellite
【反斜面】 fǎnxiémiàn 〈军〉 reverse slope; rear slope
【反信风】 fǎnxìnfēng 〈气〉 antitrades; countertrades
【反省】 fǎnxǐng introspection; self-questioning; self-examination
【反修】 fǎnxiū anti-revisionist; against revisionism: ～斗争 the struggle against revisionism/ ～防修 combat and prevent revisionism
【反宣传】 fǎnxuānchuán ① counterpropaganda ② slander campaign
【反咬一口】 fǎnyǎo yī kǒu trump up a countercharge against one's accuser; make a false countercharge
【反义词】 fǎnyìcí 〈语〉 antonym
【反应】 fǎnyìng ① reaction: 碱性～〈化〉 alkaline reaction/ 链式～〈物〉 chain reaction/ 过敏～〈医〉 allergic reaction/ 阳性(阴性)～ positive (negative) reaction/ 你打了针以后有什么～？Have you had a reaction to your injection? ② response; repercussion; reaction: ～不一。Reactions vary./ ～冷淡。The response was far from warm./ 作出～ make a response/ 这位青年科学家的研究报告在科学界引起了强烈的～。The young scientist's research paper evoked strong repercussions in scientific circles.
◇ ～本领 reaction capacity/ ～塔 reaction tower/ ～物 reactant
【反应堆】 fǎnyìngduī 〈物〉 reactor: 高温～ high-temperature reactor/ 浓缩铀～ enriched uranium reactor/ 增殖～ breeder reactor/ 石墨减速～ graphite-moderated reactor/ 热中子～ thermal reactor/ 轻水慢化～ light-water-moderated reactor
【反映】 fǎnyìng ① reflect; mirror: 一定的文化是一定社会的政治和经济的～。Any given culture is a reflection of the politics and economics of a given society./ ～新时代的特点 mirror the features of our new age/ ～工农兵的战斗生活 portray (或 depict) the struggle of the workers, peasants and soldiers/ 资产阶级、小资产阶级，他们的思想意识是一定要～出来的。It is inevitable that the bourgeoisie and petty bourgeoisie will give expression to their own ideologies./ 用传统国画手法～祖国的新面貌 use the traditional style of painting to represent the new face of our country/ 社会上的阶级斗争必然会～到党内来。Class struggle in society will inevitably find expression in the Party./ 这个决定～了广大人民的根本利益。This decision represents the fundamental interests of the people. ② report; make known: 向上级～ report to the higher level/ 向他～同志们的意见 let him know the comrades' opinions/ 我将经常向你～进度。I'll keep you informed of the progress made.
【反映论】 fǎnyìnglùn 〈哲〉 theory of reflection: 唯物论的～

the materialist theory of reflection/ 能动的革命的～ the dynamic revolutionary theory of knowledge as the reflection of reality
【反右派斗争】 fǎn yòupài dòuzhēng the Anti-Rightist Struggle (the counterattack in 1957 against the bourgeois Rightists)
【反语】 fǎnyǔ 〈语〉 irony
【反照】 fǎnzhào reflection of light: 夕阳～ evening (或 sunset) glow ◇ ～镜 rearview mirror
【反正】 fǎnzhèng come over from the enemy's side
【反正】 fǎnzheng 〈副〉 anyway; anyhow; in any case: ～得去一个人，就让我去吧！ Since someone has to go anyway, let me go./ 不管怎么样，～工作不能停。Come what may, the work must go on./ 不管晴天雨天，～我们去支援。 We'll go and give a hand, rain or shine.
【反证】 fǎnzhèng disproof; counterevidence
【反证法】 fǎnzhèngfǎ reduction to absurdity; *reductio ad absurdum*
【反之】 fǎnzhī conversely; on the contrary; otherwise: 认为物质是第一性，意识是第二性的，是唯物主义；～，认为意识是第一性，物质是第二性的，则是唯心主义。 To take matter as primary and consciousness as secondary is materialism; conversely, to take consciousness as primary and matter as secondary is idealism.
【反殖】 fǎnzhí anti-colonialist; against colonialism
【反质子】 fǎnzhìzǐ 〈物〉 antiproton
【反治】 fǎnzhì 〈中医〉 treatment by reverse process, e.g. administering medicine of a hot nature to treat a pseudofebrile disease
【反中子】 fǎnzhōngzǐ 〈物〉 antineutron
【反转】 fǎnzhuǎn reverse ◇ ～片〈电影〉 reversal film
【反坐】 fǎnzuò sentence the accuser to the punishment facing the person he falsely accused
【反作用】 fǎnzuòyòng counteraction; reaction: 上层建筑对经济基础的～ the reaction of the superstructure on the economic base ◇ ～力〈物〉 reacting force

**返** fǎn return: ～沪 return to Shanghai/ 流连忘～ linger on without any thought of leaving/ 一去不复～ gone forever; gone never to return
【返潮】 fǎncháo get damp: 每年到这时候就爱～。 Things easily get damp at this time of the year.
【返防】 fǎnfáng 〈军〉 return to stations
【返工】 fǎngōng do poorly done work over again: 这项工作必须～。This job will have to be done over again.
【返航】 fǎnháng return to base or port: 在～途中 on the homebound voyage or flight
【返回】 fǎnhuí return; come or go back: ～原地 return to the starting point/ ～港口 put back to port/ 使人造地球卫星～地面 recover a man-made earth satellite
【返老还童】 fǎnlǎo-huántóng recover one's youthful vigour; feel rejuvenated
【返青】 fǎnqīng 〈农〉 (of winter crops or transplanted seedlings) turn green
【返任】 fǎnrèn return to one's post
【返销】 fǎnxiāo (grain, etc.) resold by the state to the place of production (in cases of natural disaster, etc.): 我们大队学大寨，很快就不再吃～粮了。Learning from Dazhai, our brigade soon stopped eating "resold grain".
【返校】 fǎnxiào ① return to school after the vacation ② return to school during the vacation to have homework checked or to take part in school activities
【返盐】 fǎnyán 〈农〉 accumulation of salt in the surface soil 又作"返碱"
【返照】 fǎnzhào 见"反照" fǎnzhào
【返祖现象】 fǎnzǔ xiànxiàng 〈生〉 atavism

## fàn

**犯** fàn ① violate; offend (against law, etc.): ～纪律 violate discipline/ ～忌讳 offend a person's sensitivity; touch a person's sore spot ② attack; assail; work against: 人不～我，我不～人；人若～我，我必～人。We will not attack unless we are attacked; if we are attacked, we will certainly counterattack. ③ criminal: 战～ war criminal/ 杀人～ murderer ④ have a recurrence of (an old illness); revert to (a bad habit): 他的气喘病又～了。He's got another attack of asthma./ ～脾气 get angry; fly into a temper; be in a bad temper ⑤ commit (a mistake, crime, etc.): ～错误 make a mistake/ ～官僚主义 commit the error of bureaucracy
【犯案】 fàn'àn 〈旧〉 be found out and brought to justice
【犯病】 fànbìng have an attack of one's old illness
【犯不着】 fànbuzháo 〈口〉 not worthwhile: 在枝节问题上～花这么多时间。It isn't worthwhile spending so much time on minor problems.
【犯愁】 fànchóu worry; be anxious
【犯得着】 fàndezháo 〔多用于反问〕 is it worthwhile: 为这么点小事～和他吵吗？ Is it worthwhile quarrelling with him over such a trifling matter?
【犯法】 fànfǎ violate (或 break) the law ◇ ～行为 offence against the law
【犯规】 fànguī ① break the rules ② 〈体〉 foul: 侵人～ personal foul ◇ ～者〈体〉 offender
【犯忌】 fànjì violate a taboo
【犯节气】 fàn jiéqi have an attack of a seasonal illness
【犯禁】 fànjìn violate a ban (或 prohibition)
【犯人】 fànrén prisoner; convict
【犯上】 fànshàng go against one's superiors
【犯嫌疑】 fàn xiányí arouse suspicion; come under suspicion
【犯疑】 fànyí suspect; be suspicious
【犯罪】 fànzuì commit a crime (或 an offence) ◇ ～分子 offender; criminal/ ～行为 criminal offence

**泛** fàn ① 〈书〉 float: ～舟西湖 go boating on the West Lake ② be suffused with: 脸上～出红晕 with one's cheeks suffused with blushes/ 她的脸色黑里～红。She has a tanned and glowing face. ③ flood; inundate: 黄～区 areas formerly flooded by the Huanghe River ④ extensive; general; nonspecific: 广～ wide; extensive/ 空～ containing nothing but generalities
【泛称】 fànchēng general term
【泛泛】 fànfàn general; not deepgoing: ～而谈 talk in generalities/ ～之交 casual acquaintance
【泛光灯】 fànguāngdēng floodlight
【泛函分析】 fànhán fēnxī 〈数〉 functional analysis
【泛滥】 fànlàn ① be in flood; overflow; inundate: 河水～。 The river was in flood. 或 The river overflowed its banks. ② spread unchecked: ～成灾 run rampant; run wild; be swamped by sth.
【泛美主义】 fàn-Měizhǔyì Pan-Americanism
【泛神论】 fànshénlùn 〈哲〉 pantheism
【泛水】 fànshuǐ 〈建〉 flashing
【泛酸】 fànsuān 〈化〉 pantothenic acid
【泛音】 fànyīn 〈乐〉 overtone; harmonic ◇ ～列 harmonic series
【泛指】 fànzhǐ make a general reference; be used in a general sense: 他的发言是～一般情况，不是针对某一个人的。 His statement refers to people in general, not to anyone in particular.

**饭** fàn ① cooked rice or other cereals: 米～ (cooked) rice/ 小米～ (cooked) millet ② meal: 一天三顿饱～ three square meals a day/ ～前洗手。Wash your hands before meals.

【饭菜】 fàncài ① meal; repast: ～可口，服务周到 tasty food and good service ② dishes to go with rice, steamed buns, etc.

【饭店】 fàndiàn ① hotel ②〈方〉restaurant

【饭馆】 fànguǎn restaurant

【饭锅】 fànguō pot for cooking rice; rice cooker

【饭盒】 fànhé lunch-box; mess tin; dinner pail

【饭来张口，衣来伸手】 fàn lái zhāngkǒu, yī lái shēnshǒu have only to open one's mouth to be fed and hold out one's hands to be dressed — lead an easy life, with everything provided; be waited on hand and foot

【饭量】 fànliàng appetite: ～很大 have an enormous appetite; be a big eater/ 她的～比你小多了。She eats much less than you do.

【饭票】 fànpiào meal ticket; mess card

【饭铺】 fànpù (small) restaurant; eating house

【饭食】 fànshi food (esp. with regard to its quality): 那儿的～挺不错。You get pretty good food there.

【饭厅】 fàntīng dining hall; dining room; mess hall

【饭桶】 fàntǒng ① rice bucket ② big eater ③ fathead; good-for-nothing

【饭碗】 fànwǎn ① rice bowl ②〈旧〉job; means of livelihood: 丢～ lose one's job

【饭庄】 fànzhuāng (big) restaurant

【饭桌】 fànzhuō dining table

**范** fàn ①〈书〉pattern ② model; example; pattern: 典～ example/ 示～ demonstrate ③ limits: 就～ submit ④ (Fàn) a surname

【范本】 fànběn model for calligraphy or painting

【范畴】 fànchóu category

【范例】 fànlì example; model: 这是厉行节约的一个出色～。This is an outstanding example of strict economy.

【范围】 fànwéi scope; limits; range: ～狭小 limited in scope/ 国家管辖～ the limits of national jurisdiction/ 在法律许可～内 within the limits permitted by law/ 在协定规定的～内 within the framework of the agreement/ 实际控制～ the extent of actual control/ 势力～ sphere of influence/ 这不属于我们研究的～。This is outside the range of our study./ 作业～ operating range

【范文】 fànwén model essay

【范性】 fànxìng 〈物〉plasticity ◇ ～形变 plastic deformation

**贩** fàn ① buy to resell: ～牲口 buy and sell draught animals/ ～毒 traffic in narcotics ② dealer; monger; pedlar: 小～ vendor; pedlar

【贩卖】 fànmài traffic; peddle; sell: ～皮货 be in the fur trade/ ～军火 traffic in arms/ ～修正主义黑货 peddle revisionist rubbish

【贩运】 fànyùn transport goods for sale; traffic

【贩子】 fànzi dealer; monger: 马～ horse dealer/ 鱼～ fishmonger/ 战争～ warmonger

**畈** fàn 〈方〉〈量〉〔用于大片土地〕: 一～田 a big tract of farmland

**梵** fàn Buddhist: ～宫 Buddhist temple

【梵蒂冈】 Fàndìgāng Vatican

【梵文】 Fànwén Sanskrit

## fāng

**方** fāng ① square: ～桌 square table/ 五米见～ five metres square ②〈数〉involution; power: 二的四次～是十六。The fourth power of 2 is 16./ 二的三次～是八。The cube of 2 is 8. ③〈量〉short for square metre or cubic metre: 一～木材 a cubic metre of lumber/ 土石～ cubic metres of earth or stone work/ 铺地板十五～ lay 15 square metres of wooden floor ④ upright; honest: 品行～正 have an upright character ⑤ direction: 东～ the east/ 前～ the front/ 四面八～ in all directions ⑥ side; party: 我～ our side/ 双～ both sides (或 parties) ⑦ place; region; locality: 远～ a faraway (或 remote) place/ ～音 local accent ⑧ method; way: 千～百计 in a hundred and one ways; by every conceivable means/ 多～ in various ways/ 领导有～ exercise good leadership ⑨ prescription: 处～ make out a prescription ⑩〈副〉just; at the time when: 年～二十 be just twenty years old/ ～今 at present; nowadays ⑪ (Fāng) a surname

【方案】 fāng'àn scheme; plan; programme: 提出初步～ put forward a preliminary plan

【方便】 fāngbiàn ① convenient: 为了～起见 for convenience' sake/ ～群众 make things convenient for the people/ 什么时候～，什么时候来。Drop in whenever it's convenient./ 这儿说话不～。It's not convenient to talk here. 或 This isn't the right place to talk./ 交通～ have a good transport service/ 把～让给别人，把困难留给自己 take the difficulties on oneself and make things easy for others ②〈口〉go to the lavatory: 你要不要～一下？Do you want to use the lavatory (或 wash your hands)? ③〈婉〉have money to spare or lend: 手头不～ have little money to spare

【方步】 fāngbù measured steps: 迈～ walk with measured steps

【方才】 fāngcái just now: ～我到他家去了。I went to his place just now./ 她～还在这儿。She was here just a moment ago.

【方程】 fāngchéng 〈数〉equation: 三次～ cubic equation/ 高次～equation of higher degree/ 线性～ linear equation

【方程式】 fāngchéngshì ①〈数〉equation ②〈化〉equation: 化学～ chemical equation

【方尺】 fāngchǐ square *chi*

【方寸】 fāngcùn ① square *cun* ②〈书〉heart: ～已乱 with one's heart troubled and confused; with one's mind in a turmoil; greatly agitated

【方法】 fāngfǎ method; way; means: 阶级分析的～ the method of class analysis/ 学习～ method of study/ 看问题的～ the way one looks at things/ 用各种～ in all sorts of ways; by every means/ 用某种～ by some means or other; one way or another

【方法论】 fāngfǎlùn 〈哲〉methodology

【方钢】 fānggāng 〈冶〉square steel

【方格】 fānggé check: ～桌布 a check tablecloth/ ～纹 trellis design/ ～纸 squared paper; graph paper

【方根】 fānggēn 〈数〉root

【方剂】 fāngjì 〈中医〉prescription; recipe

【方济各会】 Fāngjìgéhuì 〈天主教〉the Franciscan Order

【方尖碑】 fāngjiānbēi obelisk

【方解石】 fāngjiěshí 〈矿〉calcite

【方块字】 fāngkuàizì Chinese characters

【方括号】 fāngkuòhào square brackets ([ ])

【方略】 fānglüè general plan

【方面】 fāngmiàn respect; aspect; side; field: 在这～ in this respect (或 connection)/ 矛盾的主要～ the principal aspect of a contradiction/ 站在革命人民～ stand on the side of the revolutionary people/ 考虑各～的意见 consider opinions from different quarters/ 在意识形态～的阶级斗争 the class struggle in the ideological field/ 我们两国的关系在各个～都有了显著的发展。The relations between our two countries have improved markedly in every aspect.

【方面军】 fāngmiànjūn front army: 中国工农红军第一～ the First Front Army of the Chinese Workers' and Peasants' Red Army

【方铅矿】 fāngqiānkuàng galena

【方枘圆凿】 fāngruì-yuánzuò like a square tenon for a round mortice—at variance with each other

【方士】 fāngshì ① necromancer ② alchemist

【方式】 fāngshì way; fashion; pattern: 生活～ way (或 mode) of life; life-style/ 斗争～ form of struggle/ 领导～ style of leadership/ 一反过去因袭的～ depart from the formula followed in the past/ 做工作应注意～方法。In doing our work, we must pay attention to ways and means.

【方糖】 fāngtáng cube sugar; lump sugar

【方位】 fāngwèi position; bearing; direction; points of the compass
◇ ～词〈语〉 noun of locality/ ～角 azimuth/ ～罗盘〈测〉 azimuth compass/ ～天文学 positional astronomy/ ～物〈军〉 topographic marker; landmarker

【方向】 fāngxiàng direction; orientation: 朝这个～ in this direction/ 坚持为工农兵服务的～ adhere to the orientation of serving the workers, peasants and soldiers/ 坚定正确的政治～ a firm and correct political orientation/ 马列主义给人类指明了前进的～。Marxism-Leninism has pointed out the way forward for mankind./ 十月革命改变了整个世界历史的～。The October Revolution changed the course of world history. ◇ ～舵〈航空〉 rudder/ ～盘〈汽车〉 steering wheel

【方兴未艾】 fāngxīng-wèi'ài be just unfolding; be in the ascendant: 这场革命运动～。The revolutionary movement is now in the ascendant.

【方形】 fāngxíng square

【方言】 fāngyán 〈语〉 dialect ◇ ～学 dialectology

【方圆】 fāngyuán ① circumference: 那个湖～八百里。The lake has a circumference of 800 *li*. ② neighbourhood: ～左近的人谁不知道他。Who in the neighbourhood doesn't know him?

【方丈】 fāngzhàng square *zhang*

【方丈】 fāngzhang ① Buddhist abbot ② abbot's room

【方针】 fāngzhēn policy; guiding principle: 基本～ fundamental policy (或 principle)/ ～政策 general and specific policies/ 文艺～ guiding principles for literature and art

【方正】 fāngzhèng ① upright and foursquare: 字要写得～。In writing, make the characters square and upright. ② straightforward; upright; righteous: 他为人～。He is an upright man.

【方志】 fāngzhì local records

【方子】 fāngzi ① prescription: 开～ write out a prescription ② directions for mixing chemicals; formula

【方钻杆】 fāngzuàngǎn 〈石油〉 kelly (bar)

**坊** fāng ① lane (usu. as part of a street name): 白纸～ White Paper Lane ② 见"牌坊" páifāng
另见 fáng

【坊本】 fāngběn block-printed edition prepared by a bookshop

【坊间】 fāngjiān ① on the street stalls ② in the bookshops

**芳** fāng ① sweet-smelling; fragrant: ～草 fragrant grass ② good (name or reputation); virtuous: 流～百世 leave a good name to posterity

【芳烃】 fāngtīng 〈化〉 aromatic hydrocarbon

【芳香】 fāngxiāng fragrant; aromatic ◇ ～剂 aromatic

【芳族】 fāngzú 〈化〉 aromatics ◇ ～化合物 aromatic compound; aromatic/ ～酸 aromatic acid

**妨** fāng〔用于否定与疑问〕 harm: 试试又何～? What harm is there in trying?/ 不～早点动身。There's no harm in leaving a little earlier./ 不～同他再谈一次。We might as well have another talk with him.
另见 fáng

**钫** fāng ①〈化〉 francium (Fr) ②〈考古〉 a square-mouthed wine vessel

## fáng

**防** fáng ① guard against; provide against: 预～ prevent sth. from happening; take precautions/ ～病 prevent disease/ ～特 guard against enemy agents/ 以～万一 be prepared for all contingencies; be ready for any eventuality ② defend: 国～ national defence/ 边～ frontier defence/ ～身 defend oneself ③ dyke; embankment

【防备】 fángbèi guard against; take precautions against: ～敌人突然袭击 be prepared for surprise attacks by the enemy/ 采取措施～发生事故 take precautions against accidents

【防波堤】 fángbōdī breakwater; mole

【防不胜防】 fáng bùshèng fáng impossible to defend effectively; very hard to guard against: 他的球路多变，打得对手～。His opponent couldn't stand up to his varied and fast-changing tactics.

【防潮】 fángcháo ① dampproof; moistureproof ② protection against the tide: ～堰堤 tidal barrage
◇ ～层〈建〉 dampproof course; damp course/ ～火药 moistureproof powder; nonhygroscopic powder/ ～纸 moistureproof (或 tarred) paper/ ～砖 moistureproof brick

【防尘】 fángchén dustproof ◇ ～圈〈机〉 dust ring/ ～罩 dust cover

【防除】 fángchú prevent and kill off: ～害虫 prevent and kill off insect pests

【防磁】 fángcí 〈物〉 antimagnetic

【防弹】 fángdàn bulletproof; shellproof ◇ ～背心 bulletproof vest/ ～玻璃 bulletproof glass

【防盗】 fángdào guard against theft; take precautions against burglars

【防地】 fángdì 〈军〉 defence sector; station (of a unit)

【防冻】 fángdòng prevent frostbite ◇ ～药品 frostbite preventive

【防毒】 fángdú gas defence
◇ ～面具 gas mask/ ～器材 gas protection equipment/ ～衣 protective clothing

【防范】 fángfàn be on guard; keep a lookout

【防风】 fángfēng 〈中药〉 the root of *fangfeng* (*Saposhnikovia divaricata*)

【防风林】 fángfēnglín windbreak (forest)

【防辐射】 fáng fúshè radiation protection

【防腐】 fángfǔ antiseptic; anticorrosive ◇ ～材料 antirot material/ ～剂 preservative; antiseptic

【防洪】 fánghóng prevent or control flood: ～措施 flood control measures ◇ ～工程 flood control works

【防护】 fánghù protect; shelter: 人体～〈军〉 physical protection
◇ ～堤 (protection) embankment/ ～林 shelter-forest/ ～林

带 shelterbelt/ ～涂层 protective coating
【防滑链】 fánghuáliàn 〈汽车〉 tyre chain; skid chain
【防化学兵】 fánghuàxuébīng antichemical warfare corps 又作"防化兵"
【防患未然】 fáng huàn wèi rán take preventive measures; provide against possible trouble
【防火】 fánghuǒ fire prevention; fireproof ◇ ～墙 fire wall/ ～隔离线 〈林〉 fire lane
【防己】 fángjǐ 〈中药〉 the root of *fangji* (*Stephania tetrandra*)
【防空】 fángkōng air defence; antiaircraft
◇ ～部队 air defence forces/ ～导弹 air defence missile; interceptor missile/ ～壕 air-raid dugout/ ～警报 air defence warning/ ～演习 air defence exercise (或 practice); air-raid drill
【防空洞】 fángkōngdòng ① air-raid shelter ② a hideout for evildoers ③ a cover for wrong thoughts
【防涝】 fánglào prevent waterlogging
【防凌】 fánglíng reduce the menace of ice run
【防区】 fángqū defence area; garrison area
【防染剂】 fángrǎnjì 〈纺〉 resist
【防守】 fángshǒu defend; guard
【防暑】 fángshǔ heatstroke (或 sunstroke) prevention ◇ ～药 heatstroke preventive
【防水】 fángshuǐ waterproof
◇ ～表 waterproof watch/ ～布 waterproof cloth/ ～层 〈建〉 waterproof layer/ ～水泥 waterproof cement
【防缩】 fángsuō 〈纺〉 shrinkproof: ～整理 shrinkproof finish; shrinkage control finish
【防坦克】 fángtǎnkè antitank defence
◇ ～地雷 antitank mine/ ～壕 tank (或 antitank) ditch/ ～阵地 antitank position
【防特】 fángtè guard against enemy agents
【防微杜渐】 fángwēi-dùjiàn nip an evil in the bud; check erroneous ideas at the outset
【防卫】 fángwèi defend
【防务】 fángwù matters pertaining to defence; defence
【防线】 fángxiàn line of defence
【防修】 fángxiū prevent the emergence of revisionism; prevent revisionism
【防锈】 fángxiù antirust
◇ ～剂 rust inhibitor; antirusting agent/ ～漆 antirust paint/ ～脂 antirust grease
【防汛】 fángxùn flood prevention or control: 组成～大军 organize an army of flood-fighters ◇ ～指挥部 flood-control headquarters
【防疫】 fángyì epidemic prevention ◇ ～站 epidemic prevention station/ ～针 (prophylactic) inoculation
【防雨布】 fángyǔbù waterproof cloth; tarpaulin
【防御】 fángyù defence: 积极（消极）～ active (passive) defence/ 纵深～ defence in depth/ 加强～力量 strengthen defence capabilities/ 由～转入进攻 go over from the defensive to the offensive/ 迫使敌人转入～地位 force the enemy onto the defensive/ ～国家外部敌人的颠覆和侵略 guard against subversion and aggression by external enemies
◇ ～部队 defending force (或 troops, unit)/ ～部署 defensive disposition/ ～工事 defences; fortifications; defence works/ ～战 defensive warfare/ ～阵地 defensive position; defended post/ ～正面 frontage in defence; front of defence
【防灾】 fángzāi take precautions against natural calamities
【防震】 fángzhèn ① take precautions against earthquakes: ～措施 precautions against earthquakes ② shockproof; quakeproof ◇ ～设计 aseismatic design
【防止】 fángzhǐ prevent; guard against; forestall; avoid: ～资本主义复辟 prevent capitalist restoration/ ～煤气中毒 guard against gas poisoning/ ～浪费人力 avoid waste of manpower/ ～骄傲自满 guard against conceit and complacency
【防治】 fángzhì prevention and cure; prophylaxis and treatment: ～血吸虫病 the prevention and cure of schistosomiasis/ ～病虫害 the prevention and control of plant diseases and elimination of pests

**坊** fáng workshop; mill: 染～ dyer's workshop/ 油～ oil mill
另见 fāng

**妨** fáng hinder; hamper; impede; obstruct
另见 fāng

【妨碍】 fáng'ài hinder; hamper; impede; obstruct: ～团结 hinder unity/ ～生产的发展 hamper the growth of production/ ～工作 hinder one's work/ ～交通 block traffic/ 这不～我们按期动工。This won't stop us from starting the work on the project on time./ 这不应～我们两国之间良好关系的发展。This should not present an obstacle to the development of good relations between our two countries.
【妨害】 fánghài impair; jeopardize; be harmful to: ～健康 be harmful to one's health

**房** fáng ① house: 平～ single-storey house/ 楼～ a building of two or more storeys/ 草～ thatched cottage/ 洗澡～ bathhouse ② room: 客～ guest room/ 书～ study/ 病～ sickroom; ward ③ a house-like structure: 蜂～ beehive/ 莲～ lotus pod ④ a branch of a family: 长～ the eldest branch, i.e. the eldest son and his family ⑤ (Fáng) a surname

【房舱】 fángcāng passenger's cabin in a ship
【房产】 fángchǎn house property
【房地产】 fángdìchǎn real estate
【房顶】 fángdǐng roof
【房东】 fángdōng the owner of the house one lives in; landlord or landlady
【房基】 fángjī foundations (of a building)
【房间】 fángjiān room: 一套～ a suite; an apartment; a flat
【房客】 fángkè tenant (of a room or house); lodger
【房契】 fángqì title deed (for a house)
【房事】 fángshì sexual intercourse (between a married couple)
【房屋】 fángwū houses; buildings
【房檐】 fángyán eaves
【房主】 fángzhǔ house-owner
【房子】 fángzi ① house; building ② room
【房租】 fángzū rent (for a house, flat, etc.)

**肪** fáng 见"脂肪" zhīfáng

**鲂** fáng triangular bream (*Megalobrama terminalis*)

【鲂鮄】 fángfú gurnard

## fǎng

**访** fǎng ① visit; call on: ～友 call on a friend/ 互～ exchange visits ② seek by inquiry or search; try to get: ～求民间丹方 search for folk remedies

【访查】 fǎngchá go about making inquiries; investigate
【访问】 fǎngwèn visit; call on; interview: 正式（非正式）～

an official (unofficial) visit/ ～亲友 call on friends and relatives/ ～革命圣地延安 visit Yan'an, sacred place of the revolution/ 记者～了这位战斗英雄。A reporter interviewed the combat hero.

**仿** fǎng ① imitate; copy ② resemble; be like: 相～ be very much alike; be similar

【仿单】 fǎngdān instructions for the use of an article sold (esp. a medicine)

【仿佛】 fǎngfú ① seem; as if: 这事他～已经知道了。He seems to know about it already. ② be more or less the same; be alike: 这两个人的年纪相～。These two persons are about the same age.

【仿古】 fǎnggǔ modelled after an antique; in the style of the ancients: ～青铜器 an imitation of an ancient bronze

【仿生学】 fǎngshēngxué bionics

【仿宋】 fǎngsòng 〈印〉imitation Song-Dynasty-style typeface

【仿效】 fǎngxiào imitate; follow the example of: 她是个好榜样，我们应当～她。We ought to follow her good example.

【仿形】 fǎngxíng 〈机〉 profile modelling ◇ ～车床 copying lathe; repetition lathe/ ～机械 profiling mechanism

【仿造】 fǎngzào copy; be modelled on

【仿照】 fǎngzhào imitate; follow: 这个办法很好，各地可以～办理。This is a good method. It might well be adopted by other localities.

【仿制】 fǎngzhì copy; be modelled on ◇ ～品 imitation; replica; copy

**纺** fǎng ① spin: 把棉花～成纱 spin cotton into yarn ② a thin silk cloth

【纺车】 fǎngchē spinning wheel

【纺绸】 fǎngchóu a soft plain-weave silk fabric

【纺锤】 fǎngchuí spindle

【纺纱】 fǎngshā spinning ◇ ～工人 spinner/ ～机 spinning machine

【纺丝】 fǎngsī 〈化纤〉 spinning

◇ ～泵 spinning pump/ ～罐 spinning box/ ～机 spinning machine/ ～浴 spinning bath

【纺液染色】 fǎngyè rǎnsè 〈化纤〉 dope dyeing ◇ ～纤维 dope-dyed fibre

【纺织】 fǎngzhī spinning and weaving

◇ ～厂 textile mill/ ～工人 textile worker/ ～工业 textile industry/ ～品 textile; fabric

【纺织娘】 fǎngzhīniáng 〈动〉 katydid; long-horned grasshopper

**舫** fǎng boat: 画～ a gaily-painted pleasure-boat/ 石～ the Marble Boat (in the Summer Palace, Beijing)

## fàng

**放** fàng ① let go; set free; release: 不～他走 won't let him go/ 抓住绳子不～ won't let go of the rope/ 把俘虏～了 release the captives/ 把游泳池里的水～掉 let the water out of the swimming pool ② let off; give out: ～枪 fire a gun/ ～焰火 set off fireworks/ ～风筝 fly a kite/ 毛泽东思想永～光芒。Mao Zedong Thought will shine forever. ③ put out to pasture: ～牛 put cattle out to pasture; pasture (或 graze) cattle/ ～鸭 tend ducks ④ let oneself go; give way to: ～声歌唱 sing heartily/ ～声大哭 cry loudly and bitterly ⑤ lend (money) for interest: ～债 lend money at (a certain rate of) interest/ ～高利贷 practise usury ⑥ let out; expand; make larger, longer, etc.: 把裤腰～半寸 let the trousers out half a *cun* at the waist/ 把上衣～长一点 lower the hemline of the jacket a little ⑦ blossom; open: 百花齐～ a hundred flowers in bloom/ 心花怒～ be wild with joy ⑧ put in; add: 菜里多～点酱油。Put a bit more soy sauce in the food (或 dish). ⑨ put; place: 把书～在桌子上。Put the book on the table./ 把人民利益～在个人利益之上 place the interests of the people above personal interests ⑩ leave alone; lay aside: 这事不急，先～一～。It's not an urgent matter. Let's lay it aside for the moment. ⑪ send away: 流～ send into exile ⑫ readjust (attitude, behaviour, etc.) to a certain extent: ～老实点儿！You behave yourself!/ ～明白些。Be sensible./ 脚步～轻些。Tread softly./ 把速度～慢点儿。Slow down a little. ⑬ show: ～电影 show a film/ ～幻灯 show slides/ ～电视 turn on the TV

【放长线，钓大鱼】 fàng chángxiàn, diào dàyú throw a long line to catch a big fish—adopt a long-term plan to secure sth. big

【放出】 fàngchū give out; let out; emit: ～光和热 give out light and heat/ ～清香 exude a delicate fragrance

【放大】 fàngdà enlarge; magnify; amplify: 把照片～ make enlargements of a photograph; have a photograph enlarged/ 本位主义是～了的个人主义。 Departmentalism is magnified individualism.

◇ ～尺 pantograph/ ～机 〈摄〉 enlarger/ ～镜 magnifying glass; magnifier/ ～率 magnifying power/ ～照片 enlarged photograph; enlargement; blowup/ ～纸 enlarging paper; bromide paper

【放大器】 fàngdàqì 〈电子〉 amplifier: 共益～ bootstrap amplifier

【放胆】 fàngdǎn act boldly and with confidence

【放诞】 fàngdàn wild in speech and behaviour

【放荡】 fàngdàng ① dissolute; dissipated ② unconventional: ～不羁 unconventional and unrestrained

【放电】 fàngdiàn 〈物〉 (electric) discharge: 火花～ spark discharge/ 尖端～ point discharge

【放刁】 fàngdiāo make difficulties for sb.; act in a rascally manner

【放毒】 fàngdú ① put poison in food, water, etc.; poison ② make vicious remarks; spread poisonous ideas

【放风】 fàngfēng ① let in fresh air ② let prisoners out for exercise or to relieve themselves ③ leak certain information; spread news or rumours ④ 〈方〉 be on the lookout; act as a lookout

【放工】 fànggōng (of workers) knock off

【放过】 fàngguò let off; let slip: 我们决不冤枉一个好人，也决不～一个坏人。We will never wrong a single good person nor let off a single bad one./ 人民绝不会～这些叛徒。The people will never let these traitors go unpunished./ 这是个好机会，不要～。Don't let slip this good opportunity.

【放虎归山】 fàng hǔ guī shān 见"纵虎归山" zòng hǔ guī shān

【放火】 fànghuǒ ① set fire to; set on fire; commit arson: 游击队～烧了敌人的仓库。The guerrillas burned down the enemy's depot. ② create disturbances ◇ ～犯 arsonist

【放假】 fàngjià have a holiday or vacation; have a day off: 你们什么时候放暑假？When is your summer vacation?/ 三八节女同志～半天。Women comrades have a half-day holiday on March 8./ ～时她常去参加义务劳动。She often does volunteer labour during holidays.

【放空炮】 fàng kōngpào talk big; spout hot air; indulge in idle boasting: 不要～，拿出行动来。Now, none of your empty talk. Let's see how you act.

【放空气】 fàng kōngqì drop a hint; spread word; create an impression: 放出紧张空气 try to create the impression that the situation is tense

【放宽】 fàngkuān relax restrictions; relax: ～尺度 relax the requirements/ ～期限 extend a time limit/ ～条件 soften the terms

【放款】 fàngkuǎn make loans; loan: 短(中,长)期～ short-(medium-, long-) term loan

【放浪】 fànglàng ① unrestrained ② dissolute

【放量】 fàngliàng to the limit of one's capacity (in eating or drinking)

【放牧】 fàngmù put out to pasture; graze; herd: ～牛羊 herd (或 graze) sheep and cattle ◇ ～期 grazing season

【放牛娃】 fàngniúwá child cowherd

【放排】 fàngpái 〈林〉 rafting

【放盘】 fàngpán 〈旧〉 sale at reduced prices; sale

【放炮】 fàngpào ① fire a gun ② blowout (of a tyre, etc.): 车胎～了。The tyre's had a blowout. ③ blasting: 危险,正在～! Danger! Blasting in progress! ④ shoot off one's mouth: 不了解情况不要乱～。Don't shoot off your mouth if you don't know the facts.

【放屁】 fàngpì ① break wind; fart ② 〈骂〉 talk nonsense: ～! Shit! 或 What crap!

【放弃】 fàngqì abandon; give up; renounce: ～原来计划 abandon the original plan/ ～表决权 abstain from voting/ ～原则 forsake one's principles

【放青】 fàngqīng put cattle out to graze

【放青苗】 fàng qīngmiáo (of landlords and merchants in the old society) purchase standing crops at extremely low prices from poor peasants who run short before the harvest; buy standing crops dirt cheap

【放晴】 fàngqíng clear up (after rain): 天一～咱们就开镰收麦子。 We'll begin harvesting the wheat as soon as it clears up.

【放热】 fàngrè 〈化〉 exothermic ◇ ～反应 exothermic reaction

【放任】 fàngrèn ① not interfere; let alone: ～自流 let things drift (或 slide) ② noninterference; *laissez-faire*: 采取～态度 take a *laissez-faire* attitude

【放散】 fàngsàn (of smoke, scent, etc.) diffuse; spread

【放哨】 fàngshào stand sentry (或 sentinel); be on sentry go: 在门口～ be posted as a sentry in front of the house

【放射】 fàngshè radiate: 初升的太阳～出万道金光。The rising sun radiated myriads of golden rays.
◇ ～病 radiation sickness/ ～疗法 radiotherapy/ ～现象 〈物〉 radioactivity/ ～线 radioactive rays

【放射性】 fàngshèxìng 〈物〉 radioactivity
◇ ～示踪物 radioactive tracer/ ～微尘 radioactive dust; fallout/ ～污染 radioactive pollution/ ～元素 radioactive element; radioelement/ ～沾染 radioactive contamination/ ～战剂 radioactive agent

【放射性同位素】 fàngshèxìng tóngwèisù radio isotope: 人造～ induced radio isotope

【放生】 fàngshēng ① free captive animals ② (of Buddhists) buy captive fish or birds and set them free

【放手】 fàngshǒu ① let go; let go one's hold: 你抓紧,我要～了。Hold tight. I'm going to let go. ② have a free hand; go all out: 让他们～工作 give them a free hand in their work/ ～发动群众 go all out to mobilize the masses; fully arouse the masses/ 我们信得过你,你～干吧。We trust you. Just go ahead boldly with your work.

【放水】 fàngshuǐ ① turn on the water ② (of a reservoir) draw off

【放肆】 fàngsì unbridled; wanton: ～的行为 unbridled behaviour/ 胆敢如此～! How dare you take such liberties!/ ～诬蔑 wantonly vilify/ 极为～ throw all restraint to the winds

【放松】 fàngsōng relax; slacken; loosen: ～肌肉 relax one's muscles/ ～警惕 relax one's vigilance/ 我们不能～世界观的改造。We mustn't slacken our efforts to remould our world outlook.

【放送】 fàngsòng broadcast; send out (over a loudspeaker, etc.)

【放下】 fàngxià lay down; put down: ～手头的工作 put aside the work on hand/ 命令敌军～武器 order the enemy to lay down their arms/ ～臭架子,拜群众为师 drop pretentious airs and learn from the masses

【放下屠刀,立地成佛】 fàngxià túdāo, lì dì chéng fó a butcher becomes a Buddha the moment he drops his cleaver — a wrongdoer achieves salvation as soon as he gives up evil: 帝国主义决不会～,这是它的本性所决定的。It is not in the nature of imperialism to lay down its butcher's knife and suddenly become a Buddha.

【放线菌】 fàngxiànjūn 〈微〉 actinomyces

【放心】 fàngxīn set one's mind at rest; be at ease; rest assured; feel relieved: 昨天她来了电报,我们才～。We were worried about her until her telegram came yesterday./ 你～,一切都会安排好的。You can rest assured that everything will be all right./ 对他不大～ not quite trust him/ ～不下 be kept in suspense; feel anxious

【放行】 fàngxíng let sb. pass: 申请～ request clearance

【放学】 fàngxué ① classes are over: 他们学校下午五点～。Their school closes at five p.m. ② 〈旧〉 have summer or winter holidays

【放血】 fàngxuè bloodletting

【放眼】 fàngyǎn take a broad view; scan widely: 胸怀祖国,～世界 have the whole country in mind and the whole world in view/ 他～远望,只见万里长江,奔腾东去。He looked ahead and saw the mighty Changjiang rolling and surging towards the east.

【放养】 fàngyǎng put (fish, etc.) in a suitable place to breed: 水库里～了许多种鱼。 Various kinds of fish are being bred in the reservoir.

【放样】 fàngyàng 〈造船〉 lofting

【放映】 fàngyìng show; project: ～电影 show a film; have a film show/ 今晚新华电影院～《创业》。*The Pioneers* is on at Xinhua Cinema this evening.
◇ ～队 film projection team/ ～机 (film) projector/ ～室 projection room/ ～员 projectionist

【放淤】 fàngyū warping: ～造田 land reclamation by warping

【放之四海而皆准】 fàng zhī sìhǎi ér jiē zhǔn universally applicable; valid everywhere: 马列主义是～的普遍真理。Marxism-Leninism is universally applicable truth.

【放置】 fàngzhì lay up; lay aside: ～不用 lay up (machinery, equipment, etc.); lie idle

【放逐】 fàngzhú send into exile; exile; banish

【放纵】 fàngzòng ① let sb. have his own way; connive at; indulge: 你太～孩子了。 You are too indulgent with your children. ② self-indulgent; undisciplined

## fēi

**飞** fēi ① fly; flit: 鹰～得高。 Eagles fly high./ 乘专机～往乌鲁木齐 fly to Ürümqi by special plane/ 从北京直～广州 make a nonstop flight from Beijing to Guangzhou/ 蜜蜂在花丛中～来～去。Bees are flitting from flower to flower. ② hover or flutter in the air: ～鸢 a hovering kite/ ～絮 willow catkins flying in the air ③ swiftly: ～奔 dash; tear along/ 他沿着大路～跑。He flew down the road. ④ unexpected; accidental: ～来横祸 unexpected disaster ⑤ unfounded; groundless: 流言～语 rumours and slanders ⑥〈口〉disappear through volatilization: 樟脑放久了,都～净了。The camphor has all disappeared; it's been there too long. ⑦〈方〉free wheel (of a bicycle)

【飞白】 fēibái a style of calligraphy characterized by hollow strokes, as if done with a half-dry brush

【飞车走壁】 fēi chē zǒu bì 〈杂技〉 stunt cycling, driving or motorcycling on the inner surface of a cylindrical wall

【飞驰】 fēichí speed along: 火车～而过。A train sped by.

【飞虫】 fēichóng winged insect

【飞船】 fēichuán airship; dirigible

【飞弹】 fēidàn ① missile ② stray bullet

【飞地】 fēidì ① land of one province or county enclosed by that of another ② enclave; exclave

【飞短流长】 fēiduǎn-liúcháng spread embroidered stories and malicious gossip

【飞蛾投火】 fēi'é tóu huǒ a moth darting into a flame—bringing destruction upon oneself; seeking one's own doom

【飞花】 fēihuā 〈纺〉 flyings; fly

【飞黄腾达】 fēihuáng téngdá make rapid advances in one's career; have a meteoric rise

【飞蝗】 fēihuáng migratory locust

【飞机】 fēijī aircraft; aeroplane; plane: 垂直起落～ vertical takeoff and landing aircraft (VTOL)/ 短距起落～ short takeoff and landing aircraft (STOL) ◇ ～场 airfield; airport; aerodrome/ ～库 hangar/ ～制造业 aviation industry; aircraft industry

【飞溅】 fēijiàn splash: 浪花～到甲板上。The waves splashed on the deck./ 钢花～ sparks flying off molten steel

【飞快】 fēikuài ① very fast; at lightning speed: 以～的速度前进 forge ahead at full speed ② extremely sharp; razor-sharp: 把镰刀磨得～。Sharpen the sickles till they are like razors.

【飞轮】 fēilún ①〈机〉flywheel ② free wheel (of a bicycle)

【飞毛腿】 fēimáotuǐ ① fleet-footed ② fleet-footed runner

【飞沫传染】 fēimò chuánrǎn 〈医〉 infection through breathing in flying particles of the saliva or phlegm of a sick person

【飞蓬】 fēipéng 〈植〉 bitter fleabane

【飞禽走兽】 fēiqín-zǒushòu birds and beasts

【飞泉】 fēiquán cliffside spring

【飞绕】 fēirào wind high above: 红旗渠～太行山,宛如长龙。The Red Flag Canal winds like a long dragon through the Taihang Mountains.

【飞虱】 fēishī plant hopper

【飞鼠】 fēishǔ flying squirrel

【飞速】 fēisù at full speed: 列车在～前进。The train is running at full speed./ 这个县轻重工业都在～发展。This county is making rapid strides in both light and heavy industry.

【飞腾】 fēiténg fly swiftly upward; soar

【飞天】 fēitiān 〈美术〉 flying *Apsaras* (as in the frescoes of the Dunhuang Caves)

【飞艇】 fēitǐng airship; dirigible

【飞舞】 fēiwǔ dance in the air; flutter: 雪花～。Snowflakes are dancing in the air./ 蝴蝶在花丛中～。Butterflies fluttered about among the flowers.

【飞翔】 fēixiáng circle in the air; hover: 象雄鹰在空中～ hovering in the air like an eagle

【飞行】 fēixíng flight; flying: 仪表～ blind (或 instrument) flying/ 不着陆～ nonstop flight/ 特技～ stunt flying; aerobatics/ 水平～ level (或 horizontal) flight ◇ ～半径 flying radius/ ～表演 demonstration (或 exhibition) flight/ ～服 flying suit/ ～管制 air traffic control/ ～记录簿 flight log/ ～帽 aviator's helmet/ ～速度 flying speed/ ～员 pilot; aviator; flyer

【飞檐】 fēiyán 〈建〉 upturned eaves

【飞檐走壁】 fēiyán-zǒubì (of swordsmen, etc., in old Chinese novels) leap onto roofs and vault over walls

【飞眼】 fēiyǎn make eyes; ogle

【飞扬】 fēiyáng fly upward; rise: 尘土～ clouds of dust flying up/ 到处～着欢乐的歌声。Songs of joy were floating in the air.

【飞扬跋扈】 fēiyáng-báhù arrogant and domineering

【飞鱼】 fēiyú 〈动〉 flying fish

【飞跃】 fēiyuè ① leap: 我国的石油工业正～地发展。China's oil industry is developing by leaps and bounds. ②〈哲〉 leap: 认识过程的一次～ a leap in the process of cognition

【飞灾】 fēizāi unexpected disaster

【飞贼】 fēizéi ① a burglar who makes his way into a house over walls and roofs ② an intruding enemy airman; air marauder (或 pirate)

【飞涨】 fēizhǎng (of prices, etc.) soar; shoot up; skyrocket: 物价～。Prices were skyrocketing.

【飞针走线】 fēizhēn-zǒuxiàn do needlework very skilfully: 她们～,很快地绣出了韶山美景。They worked quickly and skilfully, and soon produced a beautiful embroidery of Shaoshan.

**妃** fēi ① imperial concubine ② the wife of a prince

【妃色】 fēisè light pink

【妃子】 fēizi imperial concubine

**非** fēi ① wrong; evildoing: 分清是～ distinguish between right and wrong/ 为～作歹 do evil ② not conform to; run counter to: ～分 overstepping one's bounds; assuming; presumptuous ③ censure; blame: 未可厚～ not altogether inexcusable; excusable ④ not; no: 答～所问 give an irrelevant answer/ ～笔墨所能形容 no words can adequately describe; beggar description/ ～比寻常 unusual; out of the ordinary/ ～无产阶级思想 non-proletarian ideology (或 ideas)/ ～党干部 a non-Party cadre ⑤〔跟"不"呼应,表示"必须"〕: 应该坚决镇压反革命,～如此不能巩固无产阶级专政。We must firmly suppress the counterrevolutionaries, otherwise we shall not be able to consolidate the dictatorship of the proletariat./ 难道～你去处理这件事不成? Are you really the only one who can handle the matter? ⑥〈口〉have got to; simply must: 不行,我～去! No, I simply must go. ⑦ (Fēi) short for Africa

【非病原菌】 fēi-bìngyuánjūn nonpathogenic bacteria

【非…不可】 fēi...bùkě ① must; have to: 我非参加这次登山活动不可。I simply must join this mountaineering expedition. 要学好马列主义,非下苦功不可。You can't get a good grasp of Marxism-Leninism without making a painstaking effort. ② will inevitably; be bound to: 一味蛮干的人非碰壁不可。One who acts rashly and arbitrarily is bound to come to grief.

【非常】 fēicháng ① extraordinary; unusual; special: ～会议 extraordinary session/ ～支出 a special expenditure/ ～措施 emergency measures/ ～时期 unusual times ② very; extremely; highly: ～必要 highly necessary/ ～重要 extremely important/ ～精彩 simply marvellous/ ～清楚 perfectly clear/ ～重视 attach great importance to/ ～抱歉 awfully (或 terribly) sorry

【非常任理事国】 fēi-chángrèn lǐshìguó nonpermanent member of the UN Security Council

【非但】 fēidàn not only: 他～自己干得好,还肯帮助别人。He not only does his own work well, but is also ready to help others.

【非得】 fēiděi have got to; must: 干这活儿～仔细才行。You've got to be careful when you do this job./ 这病～马上开刀不可。This disease calls for an immediate operation.
【非独】 fēidú 〈书〉 not merely: ～无益,而且有害 not merely useless, but harmful
【非对抗性】 fēiduìkàngxìng nonantagonistic ◇ ～矛盾 nonantagonistic contradiction
【非法】 fēifǎ illegal; unlawful; illicit: ～活动 unlawful (或 illegal) activities/ ～收入 illicit income/ 被宣布为～ be outlawed; be declared illegal; be illegalized
【非凡】 fēifán outstanding; extraordinary; uncommon: ～的成就 outstanding achievements; extraordinary successes/ ～的革命英雄气概 outstanding revolutionary courage/ 热闹～ bustling with activity
【非…非…】 fēi...fēi... neither... nor...: 非亲非故 neither relative nor friend; neither kith nor kin
【非分】 fēifèn overstepping one's bounds; assuming; presumptuous: ～的要求 presumptuous demands/ ～之想 inordinate ambitions
【非公莫入】 fēi gōng mò rù no admittance except on business
【非官方】 fēiguānfāng unofficial
【非…即…】 fēi...jí... either...or...: 非此即彼 either this or that; one or the other
【非交战国】 fēijiāozhànguó nonbelligerent
【非金属】 fēijīnshǔ nonmetal ◇ ～材料 nonmetallic materials/ ～元素 nonmetallic elements
【非晶质】 fēijīngzhì 〈矿〉 noncrystalline; amorphous ◇ ～体 amorphous body
【非军事化】 fēijūnshìhuà demilitarize
【非军事区】 fēijūnshìqū demilitarized zone
【非军事人员】 fēijūnshì rényuán civilian personnel
【非驴非马】 fēilǘ-fēimǎ neither ass nor horse; neither fish, flesh, nor fowl
【非轮回亲本】 fēi-lúnhuí qīnběn 〈农〉 nonrecurrent parent
【非卖品】 fēimàipǐn (articles) not for sale
【非命】 fēimìng 〔多用于〕: 死于～ die a violent death
【非难】 fēinàn 〔多用于否定式〕 blame; censure; reproach: 无可～ above criticism; not blameworthy
【非人】 fēirén ①〈书〉 not the right person: 所用～ choose the wrong person for a job ② inhuman: ～待遇 inhuman treatment
【非生产部门】 fēishēngchǎn bùmén nonproductive departments
【非生产劳动】 fēishēngchǎn láodòng nonproductive labour
【非生产性】 fēishēngchǎnxìng unproductive; nonproductive: ～开支 nonproductive (或 unproductive) expenditure
【非同小可】 fēi tóng xiǎokě no small (或 trivial) matter
【非刑】 fēixíng brutal torture: ～拷打 torture sb. brutally; subject sb. to brutal torture
【非议】 fēiyì 〔多用于否定式〕 reproach; censure: 无可～ beyond (或 above) reproach; irreproachable
【非约束性条款】 fēi-yuēshùxìng tiáokuǎn permissive provision
【非战斗人员】 fēi-zhàndòu rényuán noncombatant
【非正规军】 fēizhèngguījūn irregular troops; irregulars
【非正式】 fēizhèngshì unofficial; informal: ～译文 unofficial translation/ ～访问 unofficial (或 informal) visit/ ～会议 informal meeting
【非正统】 fēizhèngtǒng unorthodox
【非正义战争】 fēizhèngyì zhànzhēng unjust war
【非洲】 Fēizhōu Africa
【非洲统一组织】 Fēizhōu Tǒngyī Zǔzhī the Organization of African Unity (OAU)
【非主要矛盾】 fēizhǔyào máodùn nonprincipal contradiction

**菲** fēi ① luxuriant ② rich with fragrance ③〈化〉 phenanthrene
另见 fěi
【菲菲】 fēifēi 〈书〉 ① luxuriant and beautiful ② richly fragrant
【菲律宾】 Fēilǜbīn the Philippines ◇ ～人 Filipino

**啡** fēi 见"咖啡" kāfēi; "吗啡" mǎfēi

**绯** fēi red
【绯红】 fēihóng bright red; crimson: 脸羞得～ blush with shame/ ～的晚霞 rosy evening clouds

**扉** fēi door leaf
【扉页】 fēiyè 〈印〉 title page

**蜚** fēi
另见 fěi
【蜚短流长】 fēiduǎn-liúcháng 见"飞短流长" fēiduǎn-liúcháng
【蜚声】 fēishēng 〈书〉 make a name; become famous: 我国的工艺美术品～海外。China's arts and crafts enjoy a high reputation abroad.
【蜚语】 fēiyǔ rumours; gossip: 散布流言～ spread rumours

**霏** fēi
【霏霏】 fēifēi 〈书〉 falling thick and fast: 雨雪～。It was sleeting hard.

**鲱** fēi Pacific herring

## féi

**肥** féi ① fat: ～猪 a big porker/ 这肉太～了。The meat is too fat./ 资本家靠工人的血汗养～了自己。The capitalists fatten on the blood and sweat of the workers. ② fertile; rich: 这里的地～极了。The soil here is extremely fertile. ③ fertilize: ～田 fertilize the soil ④ fertilizer; manure: 化～ chemical fertilizer/ 农家～ farmyard manure/ 绿～ green manure ⑤ loose-fitting; loose; large: 这裤子太～了。These trousers are too baggy.
【肥肠】 féicháng pig's large intestines (used as food)
【肥大】 féidà ① loose; large: ～的衣服 a loose garment ② fat; plump; corpulent: ～的鲤鱼 a fat carp ③〈医〉 hypertrophy: 心脏(扁桃体)～ hypertrophy of the heart (tonsils)
【肥分】 féifèn 〈农〉 (the percentage of) nutriment in a fertilizer
【肥厚】 féihòu plump; fleshy: 果肉～。The pulp is full and fleshy.
【肥力】 féilì 〈农〉 fertility (of soil)
【肥料】 féiliào fertilizer; manure: 有机～ organic fertilizer/ 细菌～ bacterial fertilizer
【肥煤】 féiméi rich coal
【肥美】 féiměi ① fertile; rich: ～的土地 rich soil; fertile land ② luxuriant; plump; fat: 水草～牛羊壮 rich pastures and thriving herds/ ～的北京鸭 fat Beijing ducks
【肥胖】 féipàng fat; corpulent ◇ ～病 〈医〉 obesity
【肥缺】 féiquē 〈旧〉 lucrative post
【肥实】 féishi 〈口〉 fat; stout: 这匹马很～。This is a stout horse.
【肥瘦儿】 féishòur ① the girth of a garment, etc. ② the proportion of fat and lean: 这块肉～正好。This chunk of

meat is not too fat and not too lean.

【肥硕】 féishuò ①(of fruit) big and fleshy ②(of limbs and body) large and firm-fleshed

【肥田】 féitián ①fertilize (或 enrich) the soil: 毒草锄了可以～。Poisonous weeds upturned can fertilize the soil. ②fertile land ◇～粉 ammonium sulphate

【肥沃】 féiwò fertile; rich

【肥效】 féixiào 〈农〉fertilizer efficiency (或 effect)

【肥育】 féiyù 〈牧〉fattening ◇～期 stage of fattening/ ～猪 fattening pig

【肥源】 féiyuán 〈农〉source of manure

【肥皂】 féizào soap

◇～粉 soap powder/ ～泡 soap bubble/ ～片 soap flakes/ ～水 soapsuds

【肥壮】 féizhuàng stout and strong: 牛羊～ thriving herds of sheep and cattle

**淝** Féi the name of a river in Anhui Province

**腓** féi calf (of the leg)

【腓骨】 féigǔ 〈生理〉fibula

## fěi

**诽** fěi slander

【诽谤】 fěibàng slander; calumniate; libel

**匪** fěi ①bandit; brigand; robber ②〈书〉not: 获益～浅 reap no little benefit

【匪帮】 fěibāng bandit gang

【匪巢】 fěicháo bandits' lair

【匪患】 fěihuàn the evil of banditry; banditry

【匪军】 fěijūn bandit troops

【匪窟】 fěikū bandits' lair

【匪首】 fěishǒu bandit chieftain

【匪徒】 fěitú gangster; bandit

【匪夷所思】 fěi yí suǒ sī unimaginably queer; fantastic

**悱** fěi 〈书〉be at a loss for words

【悱恻】 fěicè 〈书〉laden with sorrow; sad at heart: 缠绵～ exceedingly sentimental; extremely sad

**菲** fěi 〈书〉〔多用作谦词〕poor; humble; unworthy: ～酌 a simple meal/ ～材 my humble talent/ ～仪 my small (或 unworthy) gift

另见 fēi

【菲薄】 fěibó ①humble; poor: ～的礼物 a small gift ②belittle; despise: 不可骄傲自满，也不可妄自～。Neither be conceited nor excessively humble.

**斐** fěi

【斐济】 Fěijì Fiji ◇～人 Fijian/ ～语 Fijian (language)

【斐然】 fěirán 〈书〉striking; brilliant: ～成章 show striking literary merit/ 成绩～ (achieve) splendid results

**蜚** fěi

另见 fēi

【蜚蠊】 fěilián 〈动〉cockroach; roach

**翡** fěi

【翡翠】 fěicuì ①jadeite ②〈动〉halcyon

**榧** fěi 〈植〉Chinese torreya

【榧子】 fěizi 〈植〉①Chinese torreya ②Chinese torreya-nut

## fèi

**吠** fèi bark; yap

【吠舍】 Fèishè Vaisya

【吠形吠声】 fèixíng-fèishēng when one dog barks at a shadow all the others join in — slavishly echo others 又作"吠影吠声"

**沸** fèi boil: ～水 boiling water

【沸点】 fèidiǎn 〈物〉boiling point

【沸沸扬扬】 fèifèiyángyáng bubbling with noise; in a hubbub: 大家～地嚷起来。A hubbub arose with everybody taking part./ 消息～地传开了。The news spread like wildfire.

【沸泉】 fèiquán 〈地〉boiling spring

【沸石】 fèishí 〈矿〉zeolite

【沸腾】 fèiténg ①〈物〉boiling; ebullition ②seethe with excitement; boil over: 热血～ one's blood boils/ 工地上一片～。The construction site was seething with excitement./ ～的斗争生活 a life bubbling over with stirring struggles/ 军阀混战，民怨～。Warlords fought one another and popular grievances ran high.

**废** fèi ①give up; abandon; abolish; abrogate: 半途而～ give up halfway/ 秦始皇～封建，设郡县。The First Emperor of Qin abolished principalities and established prefectures and counties./ 不以人～言 not reject an opinion because of the speaker ②waste; useless; disused: ～热 waste heat/ ～棉 cotton waste/ ～油 used oil/ ～井 a disused well/ ～矿 an abandoned mine/ 修旧利～ repair old equipment and make use of waste materials ③disabled; maimed: ～疾 disability

【废弛】 fèichí ①(of a law, custom, etc.) cease to be binding ②(of discipline, etc.) become lax

【废除】 fèichú abolish; abrogate; annul; repeal: ～一切不平等条约 abrogate all unequal treaties/ ～烦琐的礼节 do away with tedious formalities

【废黜】 fèichù dethrone; depose

【废话】 fèihuà superfluous words; nonsense; rubbish: 我说的也可能是～，不过还是请你再考虑考虑。What I said may seem superfluous, but I do hope you'll give it a little more thought./ ～！我还不知道？You're wasting your breath! Do you think I don't know that?/ 少～！No more nonsense!/ ～连篇 pages of nonsense; reams of rubbish

【废料】 fèiliào waste material; waste; scrap ◇～堆 scrap heap; waste heap

【废票】 fèipiào ①invalidated ticket ②invalidated ballot

【废品】 fèipǐn ①waste product; reject ②scrap; waste ◇～回收 waste recovery; salvage of waste material/ ～率 reject rate/ ～收购站 salvage station (where waste materials may be turned in for payment)

【废气】 fèiqì waste gas or steam

【废弃】 fèiqì discard; abandon; cast aside: ～陈规旧习 discard outdated regulations and customs

【废寝忘食】 fèiqǐn-wàngshí (so absorbed or occupied as to) forget food and sleep

【废人】 fèirén ①disabled person ②good-for-nothing

【废水】 fèishuǐ waste water; liquid waste

◇～处理场 waste water processing station/ ～处理池 purification tank for liquid waste/ ～渗透 waste water infiltration

【废丝】 fèisī 〈纺〉waste silk

【废铁】 fèitiě scrap iron
【废物】 fèiwù ① waste material; trash: ～利用 make use of waste material; convert waste into useful material ② good-for-nothing
【废墟】 fèixū ruins: 翻身农奴正在农奴制度的～上建设社会主义的新西藏。The liberated serfs are building a new socialist Xizang on the ruins of serfdom.
【废液】 fèiyè waste liquid; waste liquor
【废渣】 fèizhā waste residue
【废止】 fèizhǐ abolish; annul; put an end to: ～注入式教学法 abolish the cramming method of teaching
【废纸】 fèizhǐ waste paper: 不要乱扔～。Don't litter the place with waste paper./ 他们的那个条约不过是一张～而已。That treaty of theirs is a mere scrap of paper.
【废置】 fèizhì put aside as useless

**狒** fèi
【狒狒】 fèifèi 〈动〉 baboon

**肺** fèi lungs
【肺癌】 fèi'ái carcinoma of the lungs; lung cancer
【肺病】 fèibìng pulmonary tuberculosis (TB)
【肺动脉】 fèidòngmài 〈生理〉 pulmonary artery
【肺腑】 fèifǔ the bottom of one's heart: 出自～ straight from the heart; from the depths of one's heart/ ～之言 words from the bottom of one's heart/ 感人～ move one deeply; touch one to the depths of one's soul
【肺活量】 fèihuóliàng vital capacity
【肺结核】 fèijiéhé pulmonary tuberculosis (TB)
【肺静脉】 fèijìngmài 〈生理〉 pulmonary vein
【肺痨】 fèiláo consumption; tuberculosis
【肺脓肿】 fèinóngzhǒng pulmonary abscess
【肺泡】 fèipào 〈生理〉 pulmonary alveolus
【肺气肿】 fèiqìzhǒng pulmonary emphysema
【肺切除术】 fèiqiēchúshù pneumonectomy
【肺吸虫】 fèixīchóng lung fluke ◇ ～病 paragonimiasis
【肺循环】 fèixúnhuán 〈生理〉 pulmonary circulation
【肺炎】 fèiyán pneumonia
【肺叶】 fèiyè 〈生理〉 a lobe of the lung
【肺鱼】 fèiyú lungfish
【肺脏】 fèizàng lungs

**费** fèi ① fee; dues; expenses; charge: 学～ tuition (或 schooling) fees; tuition/ 会～ membership dues/ 生活～ living expenses/ 水电～ charges for water and electricity/ 报～ subscription for a newspaper/ 车～ fare/ 免～ free of charge ② cost; spend; expend: 买这部电影机～了我们不少钱。This projector cost us a lot of money./ 他为了改革钻头～了不少时间。He spent a lot of time trying to improve the drill bits./ 我们～了两个钟头才把屋子打扫干净。It took us two hours to clean the room. ③ wasteful; consuming too much; expending sth. too quickly: 这种锅炉～煤。This kind of boiler consumes too much coal./ 孩子们穿鞋很～。Children wear out shoes quickly. ④ (Fèi) a surname
【费边主义】 Fèibiānzhǔyì Fabianism
【费工】 fèigōng take a lot of work; require a lot of labour: 这种房子抗震性能好,又不太～。This kind of house stands up to earthquakes well and isn't too hard to build.
【费工夫】 fèi gōngfu take time and energy; be time-consuming: 做思想工作要不怕～。You shouldn't stint your time and energy when doing ideological work./ 这种牙雕很～。This kind of ivory carving is time-consuming.
【费解】 fèijiě hard to understand; obscure; unintelligible: 这段文章实在～。This passage is really hard to understand.
【费尽心机】 fèijìn xīnjī rack one's brains in scheming
【费劲】 fèijìn need or use great effort; be strenuous: 安装这台机器真～。It really took a lot of effort to install this machine./ 这山越往上爬越～。The higher we went up the mountain, the more strenuous the climb became./ 他看英文参考书不～。He can read reference books in English without difficulty.
【费力】 fèilì need or use great effort; be strenuous: ～不讨好 do a hard but thankless job/ 有了这种机器,插秧就不～了。With this kind of machine it is no longer a strain to transplant rice seedlings.
【费钱】 fèiqián cost a lot; be costly: 修这样的水电站不很～。It doesn't cost much to build hydroelectric stations of this kind.
【费神】 fèishén 〈套〉 may I trouble you (to do sth.); would you mind (doing sth.): 这篇稿子您～看看。Would you mind going over this article for us?
【费时】 fèishí take time; be time-consuming
【费事】 fèishì give or take a lot of trouble: 别给我们烧水了,太～了。——一点儿也不～。Don't bother to boil any water for us. — Oh, it's no trouble at all./ 他费了不少事才把材料找齐。He went to a lot of trouble to find all the necessary materials.
【费心】 fèixīn ① give a lot of care; take a lot of trouble: 她为这些孩子可费了不少心。She devoted a lot of care to these children. ② 〈套〉 may I trouble you (to do sth.); would you mind (doing sth.): 您见到他时,～把这封信交给他。Will you be so kind as to give him this letter when you see him?
【费用】 fèiyòng cost; expenses: 生产～ production cost/ 生活～ cost of living; living expenses/ 这笔～由我们负担。We'll bear the expenses.

**剕** fèi amputating the feet (a punishment in ancient China) 参见"五刑" wǔxíng

**痱** fèi
【痱子】 fèizi 〈医〉 prickly heat ◇ ～粉 prickly-heat powder

**镄** fèi 〈化〉 fermium (Fm)

## fēn

**分** fēn ① divide; separate; part: 一年～四季。The year is divided into four seasons./ 难舍难～ cannot bear to part from each other/ ～阶段实行 carry out stage by stage/ ～组讨论 hold discussions in groups/ 这药～三次吃。This medicine is to be taken in three separate doses./ 这里的树木大致～为三类。The trees grown here fall roughly into three categories. ② distribute; assign; allot: 音乐会的票都已经～完了。The tickets for the concert have all been distributed./ 把这个任务～给我们排吧。Assign (或 Give) this task to our platoon, please./ 打土豪,～田地 overthrow the landlords and share out the land ③ distinguish; differentiate: 是非不～ make no distinction between right and wrong ④ branch (of an organization): ～店 branch (of a shop)/ 新华社上海～社 the Shanghai Branch of the Xinhua News Agency ⑤ fraction: 三～之二 two-thirds/ 二～之一 half ⑥ one-tenth: 七～成绩,三～错误 70 per cent achievements, 30 per cent mistakes/ 有十～把握 be hundred-percent sure ⑦ *fen*, a unit of length (=1/3 centimetre): 三尺零五～ three *chi* and half

a *cun* ⑧ *fen*, a unit of area (=66.666 square metres): 两亩四～地 2.4 *mu* of land ⑨ *fen*, a unit of weight (=1/2 gram): 一两五钱三～ 1.53 *liang* ⑩ *fen*, a fractional unit of money in China (=1/100 of a *yuan* or 1/10 of a *jiao*): 六元三角五～ 6.35 *yuan*; six *yuan* thirty-five *fen* ⑪ minute (=1/60 of an hour): 这个电影要演两小时十～。This film lasts two hours and ten minutes./ 六点十～起床 get up at ten past six ⑫ minute (=1/60 of a degree): 东经129度15～ 129 degrees 15 minutes (129° 15′) east longitude/ 成36度30～角 form an angle of 36 degrees 30 minutes (36°30′) ⑬ point; mark: 甲队罚球连得二～。Team A scored two successive points by free throws. ⑭〔指利率〕: 月利一～ 1% interest a month/ 年利一～ 10% interest a year
另见 fèn

【分贝】 fēnbèi 〈物〉 decibel (db)

【分崩离析】 fēnbēng-líxī disintegrate; fall to pieces; come apart

【分辨】 fēnbiàn ① distinguish; differentiate: ～真假 distinguish truth from falsehood/ 在这支劳动大军中,很难～谁是干部谁是社员群众。In this huge labour force you can hardly tell who are cadres and who are rank-and-file commune members. ②〈物〉 resolution ◇ ～率 resolving power

【分辩】 fēnbiàn defend oneself (against a charge); offer an explanation: 不容～ allowing no explanation to be offered

【分别】 fēnbié ① part; leave each other: 他们～不久又见面了。They met again after a short separation. ② distinguish; differentiate: ～善恶 distinguish good from evil/ ～轻重缓急 differentiate the important from the less important and the urgent from the less urgent; do things in order of importance and urgency ③ difference: 两者之间没有任何～。There is no difference between the two. ④ respectively; separately: 他们～代表本国政府在协定上签了字。They signed the agreement on behalf of their respective governments./ 你还是～跟他们谈谈的好。You'd better have a talk with each of them separately./ 县委干部～到基层参加劳动。Cadres of the county Party committee go down to different grass-roots units to take part in manual labour.

【分兵】 fēnbīng divide forces: ～把守 divide the forces for defence

【分布】 fēnbù be distributed (over an area); be dispersed; be scattered: 彝族主要～在云南、四川、贵州三省。The Yi nationality is distributed mainly over Yunnan, Sichuan and Guizhou provinces./ 气象站～在广阔的平原和山区。Weather stations are scattered all over the vast plains and the mountain regions./ 我国石油资源～范围很广。Oil deposits are widely dispersed over our country.

【分册】 fēncè a separately published part of a book; fascicle: 第二～ Book Two

【分杈】 fēnchà 〈农〉 ① branching ② branch

【分词】 fēncí 〈语〉 participle: 现在(过去)～ present (past) participle ◇ ～短语 participial phrase

【分寸】 fēncun proper limits for speech or action; sense of propriety: 他说话很有～。He knows what to say and what not to say./ 不知～ lack tact; have no sense of propriety

【分担】 fēndān share responsibility for: ～费用 shoulder part of the expenses; share the expenses/ 提倡男女～家务劳动。Men and women are encouraged to share household duties.

【分道】 fēndào 〈体〉 lane: 第一～ the first lane

【分道扬镳】 fēndào yángbiāo separate and go different ways; part company, each going his own way

【分等】 fēnděng grade; classify: 产品按质～ grade products according to quality/ 商品～论价 grade commodities and fix prices accordingly; fix prices according to the different grades of commodities

【分度】 fēndù graduation (of a measuring instrument)

【分队】 fēnduì a troop unit corresponding to the platoon or squad; element

【分而治之】 fēn ér zhì zhī divide and rule

【分发】 fēnfā distribute; hand out; issue: 把学习材料～给同志们 hand out study materials to the comrades/ 给优胜者～奖品 distribute prizes to the winners/ ～证件 issue certificates individually

【分肥】 fēnféi share out ill-gotten gains; divide booty

【分封制】 fēnfēngzhì the system of enfeoffment (of the Western Zhou Dynasty, c.11th. century–771 B.C., investing the nobility with hereditary titles, territories and slaves)

【分赴】 fēnfù leave for different destinations: ～各个战场 leave for the various war fronts/ ～不同的工作岗位 go to take up different posts

【分付】 fēnfu 见"吩咐" fēnfu

【分割】 fēngē cut apart; break up; carve up: ～围歼入侵之敌 break up the invading enemy forces into many pockets and wipe them out one by one; carve up and wipe out the invaders/ 民主和集中这两方面,任何时候都不能～开。Democracy and centralism can at no time be separated.

【分隔】 fēngé separate; divide: 把一间房～成两间 partition a room into two

【分工】 fēngōng divide the work; division of labour: ～合作 share out the work and cooperate with one another/ ～负责 division of labour with individual responsibility/ 咱们怎么～? How shall we divide up the work?/ 社会～ social division of labour

【分管】 fēnguǎn be assigned personal responsibility for; be put in charge of: 党委成员中有专人～妇女工作。One of the members of the Party committee is in charge of women's affairs.

【分光计】 fēnguāngjì 〈物〉 spectrometer

【分光镜】 fēnguāngjìng 〈物〉 spectroscope

【分行】 fēnháng branch (of a bank): 国内～ home (或 domestic) branch/ 国外～ overseas branch

【分毫】 fēnháo fraction; iota: 不差～ without the slightest error; just right

【分号】 fēnhào ① semicolon (;) ② branch (of a firm, etc.)

【分红】 fēnhóng 〈旧〉share out bonus; draw extra dividends (或 profits)

【分洪】 fēnhóng flood diversion
◇ ～工程 flood-diversion project/ ～区 flood-diversion area/ ～闸 flood-diversion sluice

【分户帐】 fēnhùzhàng ledger

【分化】 fēnhuà ① split up; become divided; break up: 随着私有制的产生,人类便～为阶级。With the emergence of private ownership, humanity was divided into classes./ 中间派是容易动摇的,并且不可避免地要发生～。The middle-of-the-roaders tend to vacillate and are bound to split up./ 把一部分人从敌人营垒中间～出来 split off a number of people from the enemy camp/ 两极～ polarization/ ～瓦解 disintegrate; divide and demoralize ②〈生〉 differentiation

【分会】 fēnhuì branch (of a society, committee, association, etc.); chapter

【分机】 fēnjī extension (telephone)

【分级】 fēnjí grade; classify: 这几筐苹果还没～。These baskets of apples have not been graded yet.

【分级机】 fēnjíjī 〈农〉 grader; sorter: 水果～ fruit grader/ 马铃薯～ potato sorter

【分家】 fēnjiā divide up family property and live apart; break up the family and live apart

【分解】 fēnjiě ① resolve; decompose; break down: 水可以～为氢和氧。Water can be resolved (或 decomposed) into hydrogen and oxygen./ 力的～ resolution of force ②〔章回小说用语〕recount; disclose: 欲知后事如何,且听下回～。But as to what happened thereafter, that will be disclosed in the ensuing chapter.
◇ ～代谢〈生〉 catabolism/ ～反应 decomposition reaction/ ～热 decomposition heat
【分界】 fēnjiè ① have as the boundary; be demarcated by: 这两个县以运河～。The two counties have the canal as their common boundary. ② dividing line; line of demarcation
【分界线】 fēnjièxiàn line of demarcation; boundary: 军事～ a military demarcation line
【分进合击】 fēnjìn-héjī 〈军〉 concerted attack by converging columns
【分居】 fēnjū (of members of a family) live apart: 他们～两处。They live in two separate places.
【分句】 fēnjù 〈语〉 clause
【分开】 fēnkāi separate; part: 弟兄俩～已经三年了。It is three years since the two brothers parted./ 把好的和坏的～ sort out the good ones from the bad/ 这两个问题咱们～来谈。Let's discuss the two problems separately./ 动机和效果是分不开的。Motive is inseparable from effect.
【分类】 fēnlèi classify: 把这些资料加以～ classify the data ◇ ～法 classification/ ～数字 breakdown figures/ ～索引 classified index/ ～帐 ledger
【分类学】 fēnlèixué taxology; taxonomy; systematics: 植物(动物)～ systematic botany (zoology)
【分离】 fēnlí separate; sever: 从空气中把氮～出来 separate nitrogen from air/ 旧社会害得他卖儿卖女,骨肉～。The old society forced him to sell his children, and severed him from his own flesh and blood. ◇ ～器〈化〉 separator
【分理处】 fēnlǐchù 〈经〉 a small local branch (of a bank)
【分力】 fēnlì 〈物〉 component (of force)
【分列式】 fēnlièshì 〈军〉 march-past
【分裂】 fēnliè ① split; divide; break up: ～革命队伍 split the revolutionary ranks/ 这些人是从反动营垒～出来,加入革命行列的。These people broke away from the reactionary camp to join the revolutionary ranks. ②〈生〉〈物〉 fission; division: 核～ nuclear fission/ 细胞～ cell division
◇ ～主义 splittism/ ～主义分子 splittist/ ～主义路线 splittist line; divisive line
【分馏】 fēnliú 〈化〉 fractional distillation; fractionation ◇ ～塔 fractionating tower; fractional column
【分路】 fēnlù ① along separate routes; from several directions: ～前进 advance along separate routes/ ～出击 attack from several directions ②〈电〉 shunt ◇ ～电流 branch current/ ～电阻 shunt resistance
【分袂】 fēnmèi 〈书〉 leave each other; part
【分门别类】 fēnmén-biélèi put into different categories; classify
【分米】 fēnmǐ decimetre (dm.)
【分泌】 fēnmì 〈生〉 secrete: ～胃液 secrete gastric juice ◇ ～物 secretion
【分娩】 fēnmiǎn childbirth; parturition
【分秒必争】 fēn-miǎo bì zhēng seize every minute and second; every second counts; not a second is to be lost
【分明】 fēnmíng ① clearly demarcated; sharply contoured; distinct: 爱憎～ be clear about what to love and what to hate; know clearly whom to love and whom to hate/ 这件事情是非～,无可争辩。The rights and wrongs of the case are perfectly clear and admit of no dispute. ② clearly; plainly; evidently: ～是强盗,却要装圣贤。He is obviously a gangster, but he pretends to be a saint.
【分母】 fēnmǔ 〈数〉 denominator
【分蘖】 fēnniè 〈农〉 tillering: 有效～ effective tillering ◇ ～节 tillering node/ ～期 tillering stage
【分派】 fēnpài assign (to different persons); apportion: 队长给各个组都～了任务。The team leader has assigned tasks to all the groups.
【分配】 fēnpèi ① distribute; allot; assign: ～土地 distribute land/ ～住房 allot dwelling houses/ 服从组织～ accept the job that the organization assigns to one/ 她被～到公社卫生院工作。She was assigned to work at a commune hospital./ 社员的收入按工分～。The commune members' income is distributed to them according to their workpoints. ②〈经〉 distribution ◇ ～律〈数〉 distributive law/ ～制度 distribution system
【分批】 fēnpī in batches; in turn: ～轮流参加训练班 go to a training course in turn/ 赤脚医生～到县医院学习。Groups of barefoot doctors go in turn for training in county hospitals.
【分片包干】 fēn piàn bāogān divide up the work and assign a part to each individual or group
【分期】 fēnqī by stages: ～实行 implement by stages/ ～分批 by stages and in groups; group after group at different times ◇ ～付款 payment by instalments; hire purchase; instalment plan
【分歧】 fēnqí difference; divergence: 意见～ divergence of views; differences of opinion/ 原则～ a difference in principle/ 制造～ sow discord; create dissension/ 消除～ iron out differences/ 在这个问题上我们的看法有～。Our views are divergent on this question.
【分清】 fēnqīng distinguish; draw a clear distinction between; draw a clear line of demarcation between: ～路线是非 distinguish right from wrong on the question of line/ ～敌我友 draw a distinction between ourselves, our friends and the enemy/ 不学革命理论就分不清真假马克思主义。One cannot distinguish between genuine and sham Marxism without studying revolutionary theory.
【分群】 fēnqún (of bees) hive off
【分散】 fēnsàn disperse; scatter; decentralize: ～的落后的个体经济 a scattered and backward individual economy/ 兵力的～和集中 dispersion and concentration of forces/ 集中领导,～经营 unified leadership and decentralized management/ ～注意力 divert one's attention; take sb.'s mind off sth.
◇ ～剂〈化〉 dispersing agent/ ～染料 disperse dyes/ ～指挥 decentralized command (或 direction)/ ～主义 decentralism
【分色机】 fēnsèjī 〈印〉 colour scanner
【分身】 fēnshēn spare time from one's main work to attend to sth. else: 他实在太忙,无法～。He is really too busy to attend to anything else.
【分神】 fēnshén give some attention to: 请～照顾一下这孩子。Would you mind keeping an eye on the child?
【分手】 fēnshǒu part company; say good-bye: 我们是在车站～的。We said good-bye to each other at the station.
【分数】 fēnshù ①〈数〉 fraction ② mark; grade
【分水岭】 fēnshuǐlǐng ①〈地〉 watershed; divide ② line of demarcation; watershed: 承认不承认无产阶级专政是马列主义和修正主义的～。Recognition or nonrecognition of the dictatorship of the proletariat is the watershed between Marxism-Leninism and revisionism.
【分水闸门】 fēnshuǐzhámén 〈水〉 bifurcation gate
【分说】 fēnshuō〔多用在"不容""不由"等否定语之后〕defend oneself (against a charge); explain matters: 不容～ allow no explanation
【分送】 fēnsòng send; distribute: 把学习材料～给各组。Dis-

tribute the study materials to all the groups.
【分摊】 fēntān share: ～费用 share the expenses
【分庭抗礼】 fēntíng-kànglǐ stand up to sb. as an equal; make rival claims as an equal; act independently and defiantly
【分头】 fēntóu ① separately; severally: 这事咱们～去做吧。Let's go about the work separately. ② parted hair
【分文】 fēnwén a single cent (或 penny): ～不取 not take (或 charge) a single cent; free of charge
【分析】 fēnxī analyse: 培养～问题和解决问题的能力 cultivate the ability to analyse and solve problems/ 善于～形势 be proficient in sizing up a situation ◇ ～化学 analytical chemistry/ ～语〈语〉analytical language
【分线规】 fēnxiànguī dividers
【分享】 fēnxiǎng share (joy, rights, etc.); partake of: ～胜利的喜悦 share the joys of victory
【分相】 fēnxiàng〈电〉split phase ◇ ～电动机 split-phase motor/ ～器 phase splitter
【分销店】 fēnxiāodiàn retail shop
【分晓】 fēnxiǎo ① outcome; solution: 此事明天就见～。We'll know the outcome of the whole affair tomorrow. ② see or understand clearly: 问个～ inquire about and get to the bottom of a matter ③〔多用于否定式〕reason: 没～的话 unreasonable remarks
【分心】 fēnxīn divert (或 distract) one's attention: 她工作起来,什么事也不能使她～。Nothing can divert her attention once she starts working.
【分压器】 fēnyāqì〈电〉voltage divider
【分野】 fēnyě dividing line: 无产阶级世界观和资产阶级世界观的～ the dividing line between a proletarian and a bourgeois world outlook
【分忧】 fēnyōu share sb.'s cares and burdens; help sb. to get over a difficulty
【分赃】 fēnzāng divide the spoils; share the booty (或 loot)
【分针】 fēnzhēn minute hand
【分支】 fēnzhī branch: 银行的～机构 branches of a bank
【分子】 fēnzǐ ①〈数〉numerator (in a fraction) ②〈化〉molecule: 克～ gram molecule
◇ ～病 molecular disease/ ～仿生学 molecular bionics/ ～结构 molecular structure/ ～量 molecular weight/ ～筛 molecular sieve/ ～生物学 molecular biology/ ～式 molecular formula/ ～遗传学 molecular genetics
另见 fènzǐ
【分组】 fēnzǔ divide into groups: ～讨论 discuss in groups; group discussion

**芬** fēn sweet smell; fragrance
【芬芳】 fēnfāng ① sweet-smelling; fragrant ② fragrance
【芬兰】 Fēnlán Finland ◇ ～人 Finn; Finlander/ ～语 Finnish (language)

**吩** fēn
【吩咐】 fēnfu tell; instruct: 张大爷～我好生照看小马驹。Uncle Zhang told me to take good care of the foal.

**纷** fēn ① confused; tangled; disorderly ② many and various; profuse; numerous: 大雪～飞。The snow flakes were falling thick and fast. 或 It was snowing hard.
【纷繁】 fēnfán numerous and complicated: 头绪～ have too many things to take care of; be highly complicated/ 从～的现象中抓住本质的东西 grasp the essentials from a variety of phenomena; sort out the essentials from a mass of detail
【纷纷】 fēnfēn ① one after another; in succession: ～要求参军 volunteer to join the army one after another /世界各地～来电祝贺我国国庆。Telegrams congratulating China on her National Day poured in from every part of the world. ② numerous and confused: 社员对此事议论～。This has become the subject of much discussion among the commune members./ 敌军～逃窜。The enemy troops fled pell-mell.
【纷乱】 fēnluàn numerous and disorderly; helter-skelter; chaotic: ～的脚步声 hurried footsteps/ ～的局面 a state of chaos
【纷扰】 fēnrǎo confusion; turmoil: 内心的～使他无法入睡。His mind was in such a turmoil that he couldn't get to sleep.
【纷纭】 fēnyún diverse and confused: 众说～。Opinions are widely divided.
【纷争】 fēnzhēng dispute; wrangle: ～不已 endless dispute
【纷至沓来】 fēnzhì-tàlái come in a continuous stream; come thick and fast; keep pouring in

**氛** fēn atmosphere
【氛围】 fēnwéi atmosphere

**酚** fēn〈化〉phenol
【酚磺酞】 fēnhuángtài〈药〉phenolsulphonphthalein
【酚醛】 fēnquán〈化〉phenolic aldehyde ◇ ～树脂 phenolic resin/ ～塑料 phenolic plastics; phenolics; phenoplast
【酚酞】 fēntài〈化〉phenolphthalein: ◇ ～试纸 phenolphthalein test paper

## fén

**汾** Fén the name of a river in Shanxi Province
【汾酒】 fénjiǔ a kind of spirit distilled in Fenyang (汾阳)

**坟** fén grave; tomb
【坟地】 féndì graveyard; cemetery
【坟墓】 fénmù grave; tomb
【坟头】 féntóu grave mound
【坟茔】 fényíng ① grave; tomb ② graveyard; cemetery

**焚** fén burn: ～香 burn incense/ 玩火者必自～。He who plays with fire will get burned.
【焚风】 fénfēng〈气〉foehn
【焚化】 fénhuà incinerate; cremate ◇ ～炉 incinerator; cremator
【焚毁】 fénhuǐ destroy by fire; burn down
【焚烧】 fénshāo burn; set on fire: 起义农民～了地主庄园。The peasant rebels burned down the manor houses.

**棼** fén〈书〉confused; tangled

**鼢** fén
【鼢鼠】 fénshǔ zokor

## fěn

**粉** fěn ① powder: 磨成～ grind into powder; pulverize/ 奶～ powdered milk/ 面～ flour/ 爽身～ talcum powder/ 漂白～ bleaching powder ② noodles or vermicelli made from bean or sweet potato starch ③ white: ～墙 whitewashed wall ④ pink: ～色 pink colour ⑤〈方〉whitewash: 墙刚～过。The wall has just been whitewashed.
【粉笔】 fěnbǐ chalk ◇ ～槽 a ledge for chalk on a

blackboard/ ～画 a drawing done with coloured chalk; crayon
【粉彩】 fěncǎi 〈工美〉 famille rose
【粉刺】 fěncì 〈医〉 acne
【粉翠】 fěncuì 〈工美〉 Beijing jade
【粉蝶】 fěndié 〈动〉 white (butterfly): 菜～ cabbage butterfly (或 white)
【粉红】 fěnhóng pink
【粉剂】 fěnjì ①〈药〉 powder ②〈农〉 dust
【粉瘤】 fěnliú 〈医〉 sebaceous cyst
【粉末】 fěnmò powder ◇ ～冶金 powder metallurgy
【粉墨登场】 fěnmò dēngchǎng make oneself up and go on stage; embark upon a political venture
【粉皮】 fěnpí sheet jelly made from bean or sweet potato starch
【粉扑儿】 fěnpūr powder puff
【粉墙】 fěnqiáng ① whitewash a wall ② whitewashed wall
【粉身碎骨】 fěnshēn-suìgǔ have one's body smashed to pieces; die the most cruel death
【粉饰】 fěnshì gloss over; whitewash: ～太平 present a false picture of peace and prosperity
【粉刷】 fěnshuā ①whitewash ②〈方〉 plaster
【粉丝】 fěnsī vermicelli made from bean starch, etc.
【粉碎】 fěnsuì ① smash; shatter; crush: ～经济封锁 smash an economic blockade/ ～军事进攻 shatter a military attack/ ～反动派的阴谋 crush the conspiracy of the reactionaries ② broken to pieces: 茶杯摔得～。The cup was smashed to pieces.
【粉碎机】 fěnsuìjī pulverizer; grinder; kibbler: 饲料～ fodder grinder/ 球磨～ ball mill pulverizer
【粉条】 fěntiáo noodles made from bean or sweet potato starch
【粉线】 fěnxiàn tailor's chalk line

## fèn

**分** fèn ① component: 盐～ salt content ② what is within one's rights or duty: 本～ one's duty/ 过～ exceeding what is proper; going too far; excessive
另见 fēn
【分量】 fènliang weight: 给足～ give full measure/ ～给得不足 give short measure/ 这个铺盖卷没多少～，我拿得动。This bedding roll isn't heavy at all, I can manage it./ 掂掂这个问题的～ consider the significance of the question; weigh the matter carefully/ 他这话说得很有～。What he said should not be taken lightly. 或 What he has said carries a lot of weight.
【分内】 fènnèi one's job (或 duty): 从思想上关心学生是教师～的事。It's a teacher's duty to be concerned about the students' ideology.
【分外】 fènwài ① particularly; especially: ～高兴 particularly happy/ ～香 especially fragrant/ 战友重逢～亲。Meeting again after a long separation, comrades-in-arms are drawn to each other more closely than ever. ② not one's job (或 duty): 革命工作不分分内和～。In revolutionary work there's no such thing as "that's not my job".
【分子】 fènzǐ member; element: 工人阶级一～ a member of the working class/ 积极～ activist/ 知识～ intellectual/ 动摇～ wavering element/ 反动～ reactionary element; reactionary
另见 fēnzǐ

**份** fèn ① share; portion: 股～ stock; share/ 为建设社会主义新农村出一～力 do one's bit in building a new socialist countryside ②〈量〉: 一～儿礼 a gift/ 一～《人民日报》 a copy of *Renmin Ribao*/ 复写三～ make three carbon copies/ 共两～，每～都用汉语和英语写成，两种文本具有同等效力 done in duplicate, in the Chinese and English languages, both texts being equally authentic
【份额】 fèn'é share; portion
【份儿饭】 fènrfàn *table d'hôte*; set meal
【份子】 fènzi one's share of expenses for a joint undertaking, as in buying a gift for a mutual friend: 凑～ club together to present a gift to sb.

**奋** fèn ① exert oneself; act vigorously: 振～ rouse oneself ② raise; lift: ～臂一呼 raise one's hand and issue a rousing call
【奋不顾身】 fèn bù gù shēn dash ahead regardless of one's safety: ～的无产阶级斗志 the proletarian fighting will that defies personal danger/ 他～地抢救遇险同志。Completely disregarding his own safety, he rushed to rescue the comrades in danger.
【奋斗】 fèndòu struggle; fight; strive: ～目标 the objective of a struggle/ 为共产主义事业～终身 fight all one's life for the cause of communism; dedicate one's life to the struggle for communism
【奋发】 fènfā rouse oneself; exert oneself
【奋发图强】 fènfā túqiáng go all out to make the country strong; work hard for the prosperity of the country: 自力更生、～的革命精神 the revolutionary spirit of relying on our own efforts and working hard for the prosperity of the country
【奋力】 fènlì do all one can; spare no effort: 骑兵战士冲入敌群，～砍杀。The cavalrymen charged into the enemy ranks, slashing furiously.
【奋勉】 fènmiǎn make a determined effort
【奋乃静】 fènnǎijìng 〈药〉 perphenazine
【奋起】 fènqǐ rise with force and spirit; rise: ～抗敌 rise against the enemy/ ～自卫 rise in self-defence/ ～直追 do all one can to catch up
【奋勇】 fènyǒng summon up all one's courage and energy: ～前进 advance bravely; forge ahead courageously
【奋战】 fènzhàn fight bravely: ～到底 fight to the bitter end/ ～七天 fight for seven days on end; work without a letup for seven days/ 经过四个月的～，他们修建了一百七十块大寨田。After four months of valiant struggle, they built 170 Dazhai-type plots.

**忿** fèn 见"愤" fèn

**粪** fèn ① excrement; faeces; dung; droppings ②〈书〉 apply manure: ～田 manure the fields
【粪便】 fènbiàn excrement and urine; night soil ◇ ～检查 stool examination
【粪车】 fènchē dung-cart; night-soil cart
【粪池】 fènchí manure pit
【粪堆】 fènduī dunghill; manure pile (或 heap)
【粪肥】 fènféi muck; manure; dung
【粪箕子】 fènjīzi manure basket
【粪坑】 fènkēng manure pit
【粪筐】 fènkuāng manure basket
【粪桶】 fèntǒng night-soil bucket; manure bucket
【粪土】 fèntǔ dung and dirt; muck: ～当年万户侯。We counted the mighty as no more than muck./ 视如～ look upon as dirt

**愤** fèn indignation; anger; resentment: 公～ public indignation/ ～然离去 leave in anger; walk off in a huff

【愤愤不平】 fènfèn bùpíng be indignant; feel aggrieved; be resentful
【愤恨】 fènhèn indignantly resent; detest
【愤激】 fènjī excited and indignant; roused
【愤慨】 fènkǎi (righteous) indignation: 表示～ express one's indignation
【愤懑】 fènmèn depressed and discontented; resentful
【愤怒】 fènnù indignation; anger; wrath: 激起广大人民群众的极大～ rouse the broad masses of the people to great indignation/ ～的烈火在胸中燃烧 burn with anger; boil with rage
【愤世嫉俗】 fènshì-jísú detest the world and its ways

## fēng

**丰** fēng ① abundant; plentiful: ～收 a bumper harvest ② great: ～功伟绩 great achievements ③ fine-looking; handsome ④ (Fēng) a surname
【丰碑】 fēngbēi ① monument: 周总理的光辉业绩在中国人民心中立下了不朽的～。Premier Zhou's illustrious deeds are an everlasting monument in the hearts of the Chinese people. ② monumental work: 这部著作不愧为中国新文化运动的～。This book is a monumental work worthy of China's new cultural movement.
【丰采】 fēngcǎi 见"风采" fēngcǎi
【丰产】 fēngchǎn high yield; bumper crop: ～田 a high-yield plot/ ～经验 experience in getting bumper crops
【丰登】 fēngdēng bumper harvest: 五谷～ a bumper grain harvest
【丰度】 fēngdù 〈物〉 abundance
【丰富】 fēngfù ① rich; abundant; plentiful: 资源～ rich in natural resources/ 积累～的资料 accumulate a wealth of data ② enrich: ～自己的生活经验 enrich one's experience of life
【丰富多彩】 fēngfù duōcǎi rich and varied; rich and colourful: ～的节日活动 varied and colourful festival activities/ 演出了～的节目 present a varied and interesting programme/ ～的传统出口商品 a rich array of traditional products for export
【丰功伟绩】 fēnggōng-wěijì great achievements; signal contributions: 毛主席在革命理论和革命实践上立下的～是永存的。The magnificent contributions Chairman Mao made in revolutionary theory and practice are immortal./ 为祖国的解放事业建立～ make great contributions to the liberation of the country
【丰厚】 fēnghòu ① thick: 绒毛～ rich and thick fur ② rich and generous: ～的礼品 generous gifts
【丰满】 fēngmǎn ① plentiful: 粮仓～。The granaries are full. ② full and round; well-developed; full-grown: ～的脸盘儿 a chubby (或 plump) face/ 羽毛～ full-fledged
【丰茂】 fēngmào luxuriant; lush
【丰美】 fēngměi lush: 水草～ lush pasture
【丰年】 fēngnián bumper harvest year; good year
【丰沛】 fēngpèi plentiful: 雨水～ have plenty of rain
【丰饶】 fēngráo rich and fertile: ～的草原 fertile grassland
【丰润】 fēngrùn plump and smooth-skinned
【丰盛】 fēngshèng rich; sumptuous: ～的酒席 a sumptuous feast
【丰收】 fēngshōu bumper harvest: 连年～ bumper harvests for years running/ ～在望。A good harvest is in sight./ 革命生产双～ brilliant achievements in both revolution and production
【丰硕】 fēngshuò plentiful and substantial; rich: 取得～的成果 reap rich fruits; score great successes
【丰衣足食】 fēngyī-zúshí have ample food and clothing; be well-fed and well-clothed: 过着～的生活 live a life of plenty
【丰盈】 fēngyíng ① have a full figure ② plentiful
【丰腴】 fēngyú 见"丰盈"①
【丰裕】 fēngyù well provided for; in plenty: 生活～ live in plenty; be comfortably off
【丰韵】 fēngyùn 见"风韵" fēngyùn
【丰姿】 fēngzī 见"风姿" fēngzī
【丰足】 fēngzú abundant; plentiful: 衣食～ have plenty of food and clothing

**风** fēng ① wind: ～里来,雨里去 come in the wind and go in the rain; carry out one's task even in the teeth of wind and rain ② put out to dry or air: ～干 air-dry ③ winnow: 晒干～净 sun-dried and well winnowed ④ style; practice; custom: 文～ style of writing/ 节约成～。Thrift has become the prevailing practice./ 纠正不正之～ correct unhealthy tendencies ⑤ scene; view: ～景 scenery; landscape ⑥ news; information: 走～ leak news/ 闻～而动 act without delay upon hearing sth. ⑦ a section in *The Book of Songs* (《诗经》) consisting of ballads: 采～ collect ballads
【风暴】 fēngbào windstorm; storm; tempest: 海上～ a storm at sea/ 革命～ the storm of revolution
【风泵】 fēngbèng ① air pump ② air compressor
【风痹】 fēngbì 〈中医〉 wandering arthritis
【风标】 fēngbiāo weathercock; weather vane
【风波】 fēngbō disturbance: ～迭起。Disturbances arose repeatedly./ 平地起～ a storm out of nowhere
【风采】 fēngcǎi elegant demeanour; graceful bearing
【风餐露宿】 fēngcān-lùsù eat in the wind and sleep in the dew — endure the hardships of an arduous journey or fieldwork
【风潮】 fēngcháo agitation; unrest: 闹～ agitate (for reform, etc.)
【风车】 fēngchē ① windmill ② winnower ③ pinwheel
【风尘】 fēngchén ① travel fatigue: 满面～ travel-stained ② hardships or uncertainties in an unstable society: 沦落～ be driven to prostitution
【风尘仆仆】 fēngchén púpú endure the hardships of a long journey; be travel-stained; be travel-worn and weary
【风驰电掣】 fēngchí-diànchè swift as the wind and quick as lightning
【风传】 fēngchuán hearsay; rumour
【风吹草动】 fēngchuī-cǎodòng the rustle of leaves in the wind — a sign of disturbance or trouble: 不要一有～,就惊慌失措。Don't fly into a panic at the mere rustle of leaves in the wind.
【风挡】 fēngdǎng 〈汽车〉 windscreen; windshield
【风动】 fēngdòng 〈机〉 pneumatic: ～工具 pneumatic tools
【风洞】 fēngdòng 〈航空〉 wind tunnel
【风斗】 fēngdǒu wind scoop
【风度】 fēngdù demeanour; bearing: 有～ have poise/ ～大方 have an easy manner
【风发】 fēngfā ① swift as the wind ② energetic: 意气～ daring and energetic
【风干】 fēnggān air-dry
【风镐】 fēnggǎo 〈矿〉 pneumatic pick; air pick
【风格】 fēnggé style: 公而忘私的共产主义～ the communist style of working selflessly for the public interest/ 散文的～ prose style/ 京剧的独特～ the characteristic style of Beijing opera/ 运动员们赛出了水平,赛出了～。The athletes gave a good account of themselves and displayed fine sportsmanship.

【风骨】 fēnggǔ ① strength of character ② vigour of style
【风光】 fēngguāng scene; view; sight: 北国～ a typical northern scene/ 好～ a wonderful sight
【风害】 fēnghài damage caused by a windstorm; windburn
【风寒】 fēnghán chill; cold: 只是受了点儿～。It's nothing but a chill./ 经常洗冷水澡可以抵御～。Taking cold baths regularly can heighten one's resistance to colds.
【风和日暖】 fēnghé-rìnuǎn bright sunshine and gentle breeze; warm and sunny weather
【风花雪月】 fēng-huā-xuě-yuè wind, flowers, snow and moon — referring originally to the subject matter typical of certain types of feudal literary works and later to the effete and sentimental writings of the exploiting classes
【风华】 fēnghuá elegance and talent: ～正茂 at life's full flowering; in one's prime
【风化】 fēnghuà ① morals and manners; decency: 有伤～ an offence against decency ②〈化〉 efflorescence ③〈地〉 weathering
【风级】 fēngjí 〈气〉 wind scale
【风纪】 fēngjì conduct and discipline; discipline ◇ ～扣 hook and eye (on the collar)
【风井】 fēngjǐng 〈矿〉 ventilating shaft; air shaft
【风景】 fēngjǐng scenery; landscape: 欣赏～ admire the scenery/ 以～优美著称 famous for its scenic beauty/ 西湖～如画。The West Lake is as beautiful as a painting./ 昆明是一座～美丽的城市。Kunming is a picturesque city. ◇ ～画 landscape painting/ ～林 scenic forest/ ～区 scenic spot
【风镜】 fēngjìng goggles
【风卷残云】 fēng juǎn cányún a strong wind scattering the last clouds — make a clean sweep of sth.
【风口】 fēngkǒu ① a place where there is a draught: 别站在～上，小心着凉。Don't stand in the draught. You may catch cold. ②〈地〉 wind gap ③〈冶〉 (blast) tuyere: 渣～ slag tuyere
【风口浪尖】 fēngkǒu-làngjiān where the wind and the waves are highest: 阶级斗争的～ the storm of class struggle
【风浪】 fēnglàng stormy waves; storm: ～大，船颠簸得很利害。There was a heavy sea and the ship tossed terribly./ 久经～ have weathered many a storm
【风雷】 fēngléi wind and thunder; tempest: 反帝斗争，～激荡。Stormy anti-imperialist struggles are raging.
【风力】 fēnglì ① wind-force ② wind power ◇ ～发电机 wind-driven generator; windmill generator/ ～发电站 wind power station/ ～输送机 pneumatic conveyor/ ～提水机 wind-driven water pump; wind pump
【风凉】 fēngliáng cool
【风凉话】 fēngliánghuà irresponsible and sarcastic remarks: 说～ make sarcastic comments
【风铃】 fēnglíng aeolian bells (hung on the eaves of pagodas or temple buildings)
【风流】 fēngliú ① distinguished and admirable: ～人物 truly great men ② talented in letters and unconventional in life style ③ dissolute; loose
【风流云散】 fēngliú-yúnsàn blown apart by the wind and scattered like the clouds — (of old companions) separated and scattered
【风马牛不相及】 fēng mǎ-niú bù xiāng jí have absolutely nothing to do with each other; be totally unrelated
【风帽】 fēngmào ① a cowl-like hat worn in winter ② hood
【风貌】 fēngmào ① style and features: 民间艺术的～ the style and features of folk art ② view; scene: 社会主义农村的新～ the new look of the socialist countryside
【风媒传粉】 fēngméi chuánfěn wind pollination
【风媒花】 fēngméihuā 〈植〉 anemophilous flower
【风门】 fēngmén 〈矿〉 air door; ventilation door
【风门子】 fēngménzi storm door
【风靡】 fēngmǐ fashionable: ～一时 become fashionable for a time; be all the rage at the time
【风鸟】 fēngniǎo 〈动〉 bird of paradise
【风平浪静】 fēngpíng-làngjìng the wind has subsided and the waves have calmed down; calm and tranquil
【风起云涌】 fēngqǐ-yúnyǒng like a rising wind and scudding clouds; rolling on with full force: 全世界人民反霸斗争～。The struggle of the people of the world against hegemonism is surging forward.
【风气】 fēngqì general mood; atmosphere; common (或 established) practice: 促进整个社会～的革命化 help to revolutionize the general mood of society/ 全厂出现了大搞技术革新的～。It has become the regular practice in the factory to go in for technical innovations.
【风琴】 fēngqín organ: 管～ pipe organ; organ/ 簧～ reed organ; harmonium
【风情】 fēngqíng amorous feelings; flirtatious expressions: 卖弄～ play the coquette; coquette
【风趣】 fēngqù humour; wit: 他是一个很有～的人。He is a man of charm and wit./ 她说话很有～。She is a witty talker.
【风圈】 fēngquān solar or lunar halo
【风骚】 fēngsāo ①〈书〉 literary excellence ② coquettish
【风色】 fēngsè how the wind blows: 看～ see which way the wind blows; see how things stand
【风沙】 fēngshā sand blown by the wind: 这里春天～很大。It's very windy and dusty here in spring.
【风扇】 fēngshàn ① electric fan ②〈机〉 fan: 散热～ radiator fan/ 通风～ draught fan
【风尚】 fēngshàng prevailing custom (或 practice, habit): 勤俭节约的新～ a new habit of diligence and frugality
【风声】 fēngshēng rumour: 听到～ get wind of sth./ ～很紧。The situation is getting tense./ 防止走漏～ prevent leakage of information
【风声鹤唳】 fēngshēng-hèlì the sound of the wind and the cry of cranes — a fleeing army's suspicion of danger at the slightest sound
【风湿】 fēngshī 〈医〉 rheumatism ◇ ～性关节炎 rheumarthritis
【风蚀】 fēngshí 〈地〉 wind erosion
【风霜】 fēngshuāng wind and frost — hardships of a journey or of one's life: 饱经～ weather-beaten; having had one's fill of hardships
【风水】 fēngshui the location of a house or tomb, supposed to have an influence on the fortune of a family; geomantic omen: 看～ practise geomancy ◇ ～先生 geomancer
【风俗】 fēngsú custom ◇ ～画 *genre* painting; *genre*
【风速】 fēngsù wind speed; wind velocity ◇ ～表 anemometer/ ～计 anemograph/ ～器 wind gauge
【风瘫】 fēngtān paralysis
【风调雨顺】 fēngtiáo-yǔshùn good weather for the crops; favourable weather
【风头】 fēngtóu the way the wind blows: 船老大仔细观察～和水势。The boatman kept a close watch on the wind and water.
【风头】 fēngtou ① the trend of events (as affecting a person): 避避～ lie low until sth. blows over ② the publicity one receives: 出～ be in the limelight
【风土】 fēngtǔ natural conditions and social customs of a place: ～人情 local conditions and customs
【风土驯化】 fēngtǔ xúnhuà 〈农〉 acclimatization

【风味】 fēngwèi special flavour; local colour (或 flavour): 别有～ have a distinctive flavour/ 家乡～ the pleasing taste of the cooking of one's native place; local flavour ◇ ～菜 typical local dish
【风闻】 fēngwén learn through hearsay; get wind of
【风物】 fēngwù scenery (typical of a place)
【风险】 fēngxiǎn risk; hazard: 冒～ take risks/ 干革命就不怕担～。Those who wage revolution fear no dangers.
【风箱】 fēngxiāng bellows
【风向】 fēngxiàng wind direction ◇ ～标 wind vane/ ～袋 wind sleeve; wind sock/ ～计 registering weather vane/ ～图 wind rose/ ～仪 anemoscope
【风信子】 fēngxìnzǐ 〈植〉 hyacinth
【风行】 fēngxíng be in fashion (或 vogue); be popular: ～一时 be popular for a while; be all the rage for a time
【风选】 fēngxuǎn 〈农〉 selection by winnowing (或 wind) ◇ ～机 winnowing machine; winnower
【风压】 fēngyā 〈气〉 wind pressure
【风雅】 fēngyǎ ① literary pursuits ② elegant; refined: 举止～ have refined manners
【风言风语】 fēngyán-fēngyǔ groundless talk; slanderous gossip
【风雨】 fēngyǔ wind and rain; the elements; trials and hardships: 迎着～去战斗 go into battle braving wind and rain/ 经～，见世面 face the world and brave the storm/ 群众斗争的大～ the mighty storm of mass struggle
【风雨飘摇】 fēng-yǔ piāoyáo swaying in the midst of a raging storm; precarious; tottering
【风雨如晦】 fēng-yǔ rú huì wind and rain sweeping across a gloomy sky — a grim and grave situation
【风雨同舟】 fēng-yǔ tóng zhōu in the same storm-tossed boat — stand together through thick and thin
【风雨无阻】 fēng-yǔ wú zǔ stopped by neither wind nor rain — regardless of the weather; rain or shine
【风云】 fēngyún wind and cloud — a stormy or unstable situation: ～突变。There is a sudden change in the situation./ ～变幻 a changeable situation
【风云人物】 fēngyún rénwù man of the hour
【风韵】 fēngyùn graceful bearing; charm
【风灾】 fēngzāi disaster caused by a windstorm: 遭受～ be hit by a windstorm
【风闸】 fēngzhá 〈机〉 pneumatic brake
【风障】 fēngzhàng 〈农〉 windbreak
【风疹】 fēngzhěn 〈医〉 nettle rash; urticaria
【风筝】 fēngzheng kite: 放～ fly a kite
【风烛残年】 fēngzhú cánnián old and ailing like a candle guttering in the wind
【风姿】 fēngzī graceful bearing; charm
【风钻】 fēngzuàn pneumatic drill

**枫** fēng 〈植〉 ① Chinese sweet gum ② maple
【枫香树】 fēngxiāngshù Chinese sweet gum (*Liquidambar taiwaniana*)

**疯** fēng ① mad; insane; crazy ② (of a plant, grain crop, etc.) spindle
【疯癫】 fēngdiān insane; mad
【疯疯癫癫】 fēngfēngdiāndiān be mentally deranged; act like a lunatic; be flighty
【疯狗】 fēnggǒu mad dog; rabid dog
【疯狂】 fēngkuáng ① insane ② frenzied; unbridled: ～咒骂 frenzied vilification/ ～反扑 a desperate counterattack/ ～掠夺 unbridled plunder/ ～叫嚣 frenzied clamouring
【疯人院】 fēngrényuàn madhouse; lunatic asylum
【疯瘫】 fēngtān paralysis
【疯长】 fēngzhǎng 〈农〉 overgrowth; spindling: 防止～ prevent spindling
【疯子】 fēngzi lunatic; madman

**砜** fēng 〈化〉 sulphone

**封** fēng ① seal: 把信～上 seal a letter/ ～门 seal up a door/ 大雪纷飞，江河冰～。A heavy snow is falling, and the rivers and streams have frozen over. ② bank (a fire): 炉子～了吗？Have you banked up the fire? ③ envelope: 信～ envelope ④〈量〉: 一～信 a letter ⑤ confer (a title, territory, etc.) upon: 分～诸侯 grant titles and territories to the nobles/ ～王 make sb. a prince ⑥〈简〉(封建主义) feudalism: ～资修 feudalism, capitalism and revisionism
【封闭】 fēngbì ① seal: 用蜡～瓶口 seal a bottle with wax ② seal off; close: ～机场 close an airport ◇ ～层〈石油〉 confining bed
【封存】 fēngcún seal up for safekeeping
【封底】 fēngdǐ back cover
【封地】 fēngdì fief; feud; manor
【封冻期】 fēngdòngqī a period of freezing weather; freeze
【封二】 fēng'èr inside front cover
【封官许愿】 fēngguān xǔyuàn 〈贬〉 offer official posts and make lavish promises; promise high posts and other favours
【封罐机】 fēngguànjī tin seamer; can seamer
【封建】 fēngjiàn ① the system of enfeoffment 参见"分封制" fēnfēngzhì ② feudalism: 反～ anti-feudal/ 头脑～ feudal-minded ◇ ～把头 feudal gangmaster/ ～割据 feudal separationist rule/ ～社会 feudal society/ ～主 feudal lord/ ～主义 feudalism
【封口】 fēngkǒu ① seal: 这封信还没～。The letter hasn't been sealed yet. ② heal: 腿上的伤已经～了。The leg wound has healed. ③ say sth. definitive so as to prevent further discussion
【封蜡】 fēnglà sealing wax
【封里】 fēnglǐ ① inside front cover ② inside back cover
【封面】 fēngmiàn ① the title page of a thread-bound book ② the front and back cover of a book ③ front cover
【封泥】 fēngní 〈冶〉 lute
【封皮】 fēngpí 〈方〉 ① 见"封条" ② 见"封面" ③ paper wrapping ④ envelope
【封三】 fēngsān inside back cover
【封山】 fēngshān seal (或 close) a mountain pass: 大雪～。Heavy snow has sealed the mountain passes. ◇ ～育林 close hillsides (to livestock grazing and fuel gathering) to facilitate afforestation
【封四】 fēngsì back cover
【封锁】 fēngsuǒ blockade; block; seal off: ～港口 blockade a port/ ～边境 close the border/ ～消息 block the passage of information/ 经济～ economic blockade ◇ ～线 blockade line; blockade
【封套】 fēngtào big envelope (for holding documents, books, etc.)
【封条】 fēngtiáo a strip of paper used for sealing (doors, drawers, etc.); paper strip seal
【封网】 fēngwǎng 〈排球〉 block
【封檐板】 fēngyánbǎn 〈建〉 eaves board
【封一】 fēngyī front cover
【封印】 fēngyìn 〈邮〉 seal

**峰** fēng ① peak; summit: 山～ mountain peak/ 攀登科学高～ scale the heights of science/ 浪～ the crest of a wave ② hump: 驼～ camel's hump

【峰峦】 fēngluán ridges and peaks
【峰态】 fēngtài 〈数〉 kurtosis
【峰值】 fēngzhí 〈电〉 peak (或 crest) value

**烽** fēng beacon
【烽火】 fēnghuǒ ① beacon-fire (used to give border alarm in ancient China); beacon ② flames of war: ～连天 flames of battle raging everywhere ◇ ～台 beacon tower
【烽烟】 fēngyān beacon-fire; beacon

**锋** fēng ① the sharp point or cutting edge of a sword, etc. ② van: 先～ vanguard ③ 〈气〉 front
【锋钢】 fēnggāng high speed steel; rapid steel
【锋利】 fēnglì ① sharp; keen: ～的钢刀 a sharp knife ② incisive; sharp; poignant: ～泼辣的笔调 a sharp and pungent style
【锋芒】 fēngmáng ① cutting edge; spearhead: 斗争的～ the spearhead of struggle/ ～所向 target of attack ② talent displayed; abilities: 不露～ refrain from showing one's ability; be able but modest/ ～逼人 display one's talent in an aggressive manner
【锋芒毕露】 fēngmáng bìlù make a showy display of one's abilities
【锋面】 fēngmiàn 〈气〉 frontal surface: 暖～ anaphalanx ◇ ～低压 frontal low

**蜂** fēng ① wasp ② bee: 蜜～ honeybee/ 养～场 apiary; bee yard ③ in swarms: ～聚 gather in swarms; swarm together/ ～起 rise in swarms
【蜂巢】 fēngcháo honeycomb
【蜂刺】 fēngcì the sting of a bee or wasp
【蜂毒】 fēngdú bee venom
【蜂房】 fēngfáng any of the six-sided wax cells in a honeycomb
【蜂糕】 fēnggāo steamed sponge cake (made of wheat or rice flour)
【蜂虎】 fēnghǔ 〈动〉 bee eater
【蜂皇精】 fēnghuángjīng 〈药〉 royal jelly
【蜂蜡】 fēnglà beeswax
【蜂蜜】 fēngmì honey
【蜂鸣器】 fēngmíngqì buzzer
【蜂鸟】 fēngniǎo hummingbird
【蜂群】 fēngqún (bee) colony
【蜂乳】 fēngrǔ 〈药〉 royal jelly
【蜂王】 fēngwáng ① queen bee ② queen wasp
【蜂窝】 fēngwō ① honeycomb ② a honeycomb-like thing ◇ ～炉 honeycomb briquet stove/ ～煤 honeycomb briquet/ ～胃〈动〉 honeycomb stomach; reticulum/ ～织炎 〈医〉 phlegmon; cellulitis
【蜂箱】 fēngxiāng beehive; hive
【蜂拥】 fēngyōng swarm; flock: ～而来 come swarming; swarm forward

**酆** Fēng a surname

## féng

**冯** Féng a surname

**逢** féng meet; come upon: 久别重～ meet again after a long separation/ ～人便问 ask whoever happens to come one's way/ ～山开路，遇水搭桥 cut paths through mountains and build bridges across rivers/ ～双(单)日开放 open on even (odd) days of the month
【逢场作戏】 féng chǎng zuò xì join in the fun on occasion
【逢集】 féngjí market day: 我们进村的那天正好～。The day we arrived at the village happened to be market day.
【逢年过节】 féng nián guò jié on New Year's Day or other festivals
【逢凶化吉】 féng xiōng huà jí turn ill luck into good
【逢迎】 féngyíng make up to; fawn on; curry favour with: 阿谀～ flatter and toady

**缝** féng stitch; sew: ～被子 stitch a quilt/ ～扣子 sew on a button
另见 fèng
【缝补】 féngbǔ sew and mend
【缝缝连连】 féngféngliánlián sewing and mending
【缝合】 fénghé 〈医〉 suture; sew up: ～伤口 sew up (或 suture) a wound
【缝纫】 féngrèn sewing; tailoring ◇ ～车间 tailoring workshop/ ～机 sewing machine
【缝线】 féngxiàn 〈医〉 suture: 吸收性～ absorbable suture/ 羊肠～ catgut suture
【缝叶莺】 féngyèyīng tailorbird

## fěng

**讽** fěng ① satirize; mock: 冷嘲热～ burning satire and freezing irony ② 〈书〉 chant; intone
【讽刺】 fěngcì satirize; mock: 这是一部～封建文人的作品。This is a satire on feudal scholars.
◇ ～画 satirical drawing; caricature; cartoon/ ～诗 satirical poem/ ～小品 satirical essay
【讽诵】 fěngsòng 〈书〉 read with intonation and expression
【讽喻】 fěngyù parable; allegory

## fèng

**凤** fèng phoenix
【凤冠】 fèngguān phoenix coronet (worn by empresses or imperial concubines and also as a bride's headdress in feudal China)
【凤凰】 fènghuáng phoenix ◇ ～座 〈天〉 Phoenix
【凤梨】 fènglí pineapple
【凤毛麟角】 fèngmáo-línjiǎo (precious and rare as) phoenix feathers and unicorn horns; rarity of rarities
【凤尾鱼】 fèngwěiyú anchovy
【凤尾竹】 fèngwěizhú fernleaf hedge bamboo (*Bambusa multiplex* var. *nana*)
【凤仙花】 fèngxiānhuā garden balsam

**奉** fèng ① give or present with respect: 双手～上 present respectfully with both hands/ ～上新书一册。I am forwarding you a new book. ② receive (orders, etc.): ～上级指示，暂停开放 temporarily closed on orders from above ③ esteem; revere: ～为典范 look upon as a model ④ believe in: 信～伊斯兰教 believe in Islam ⑤ wait upon; attend to: 侍～老人 attend to aged parents or grandparents ⑥ 〈敬〉 〔用于自己的举动涉及对方时〕: ～访未晤，甚怅。 Much to my regret you weren't at home when I called.
【奉承】 fèngcheng flatter; fawn upon; toady ◇ ～话 flattery
【奉告】 fènggào let sb. know; inform: 详情容后～。I'll give you the details later./ 无可～。No comment.
【奉公守法】 fènggōng-shǒufǎ be law-abiding
【奉还】 fènghuán 〈敬〉 return sth. with thanks

【奉命】 fèngmìng receive orders; act under orders: ～出发 receive orders to set off/ ～于危难之间 be entrusted with a mission at a critical and difficult moment/ 穿插营～来到。The deep-thrust battalion is here as ordered./ 中国代表团～就这一问题阐明中国政府的立场。The Chinese Delegation has been instructed to state the position of the Chinese Government on this question.

【奉陪】 fèngpéi keep sb. company: 恕不～。Sorry, I won't be able to keep you company./ 如果帝国主义或社会帝国主义要打，我们就～到底。If the imperialists or social-imperialists attack us, we'll oblige them and fight to the finish.

【奉劝】 fèngquàn may I offer a piece of advice: ～你还是听听群众的意见为好。You would be well advised to listen to the opinions of the masses.

【奉若神明】 fèng ruò shénmíng worship sb. or sth.; make a fetish of sth.

【奉送】 fèngsòng offer as a gift; give away free

【奉献】 fèngxiàn offer as a tribute; present with all respect

【奉行】 fèngxíng pursue (a policy, etc.): ～不结盟政策 pursue a policy of nonalignment

【奉养】 fèngyǎng support and wait upon (one's parents, etc.)

**俸** fèng pay; salary

【俸禄】 fènglù 〈旧〉 an official's salary

**缝** fèng ① seam: 无～钢管 seamless steel tube ② crack; crevice; fissure: 院墙上裂了一道～儿。There is a crack in the courtyard wall.

另见 féng

【缝隙】 fèngxì chink; crack; crevice

【缝子】 fèngzi 〈口〉 crack; crevice

## fó

**佛** fó ① Buddha ② Buddhism: 信～ believe in Buddhism ③ image of Buddha: 铜～ a bronze statue of Buddha

另见 fú

【佛得角】 Fódéjiǎo Cape Verde ◇ ～人 Cape Verdean

【佛法】 fófǎ ① Buddha dharma; Buddhist doctrine ② power of Buddha

【佛法僧】 fófǎsēng Buddha-dharma-sangha 参见"三宝" sānbǎo

【佛教】 Fójiào Buddhism ◇ ～徒 Buddhist

【佛经】 Fójīng Buddhist Scripture; Buddhist sutra

【佛龛】 fókān niche for a statue of Buddha

【佛兰芒语】 Fólánmángyǔ Flemish (language)

【佛门】 fómén Buddhism ◇ ～弟子 followers of Buddhism; Buddhists

【佛事】 fóshì Buddhist ceremony (或 service)

【佛手】 fóshǒu 〈植〉 fingered citron; Buddha's-hand

【佛堂】 fótáng family hall for worshipping Buddha

【佛陀】 Fótuó Buddha

【佛象】 fóxiàng figure (或 image) of Buddha

【佛学】 Fóxué Buddhism

【佛牙】 Fóyá tooth relic of Buddha

【佛爷】 fóye Buddha

## fǒu

**缶** fǒu ①〈书〉 an amphora-like jar ②〈考古〉 a clay musical instrument

**否** fǒu ① negate; deny: ～认 deny ②〈书〉 nay; no: 这是妥当的办法吗？～。Is that the right way to do it? No. ③〈书〉〔用在句尾表示询问〕: 知其事～？Do you know anything about it? ④〔用于"是否""能否""可否"中〕: 明日能～出发，需视天气而定。Whether or not we can start off tomorrow will depend on the weather.

另见 pǐ

【否定】 fǒudìng ① negate; deny: 事实～了他的看法。Facts have refuted his views./ 采取～一切的态度 adopt an attitude of negating everything/ ～之～ the negation of negation ② negative: ～的答复 a negative answer; an answer in the negative

【否决】 fǒujué vote down; veto; overrule: 提案被大会～了。The motion was voted down at the assembly. 或 The assembly rejected the motion. ◇ ～权 veto power; veto

【否认】 fǒurèn deny; repudiate: 不能～，雹灾给我们大队带来了一些困难。There is no denying the fact that the hailstorm has brought some difficulties to our brigade./ 我们断然～这种无理指责。We categorically reject this groundless charge.

【否则】 fǒuzé 〈连〉 otherwise; if not; or else: 快点走，～要迟到了。Hurry up, or we'll be late.

## fū

**夫** fū ① husband ② man: 匹～ ordinary man/ 一～当关，万～莫开。If one man guards the pass, ten thousand are unable to get through. ③〈旧〉 a person engaged in manual labour: 船～ boatman/ 樵～ woodcutter

另见 fú

【夫妇】 fū-fù husband and wife: 新婚～ newly married couple; newlyweds

【夫妻】 fū-qī man and wife

【夫妻店】 fūqīdiàn small shop run by husband and wife

【夫权】 fūquán authority of the husband: ～是封建宗法制度束缚妇女的一条绳索。The authority of the husband was one of the thick ropes with which the feudal-patriarchal system bound women.

【夫人】 fūren Lady; Madame; Mrs.: 某某～ Madame So-and-so/ 各国使节和～ foreign diplomatic envoys and their wives

【夫子】 fūzǐ ① an ancient form of address to a Confucian scholar or to a master by his disciples ② pedant: 迂～ a pedantic old fogey

【夫子自道】 fūzǐ zì dào the master exposes himself (through strictures on others, which apply to himself)

**呋** fū

【呋喃】 fūnán 〈化〉 furan ◇ ～坦啶〈药〉 nitrofurantoin; furadantin/ ～西林〈药〉 nitrofurazone; furacin

**肤** fū skin

【肤泛】 fūfàn superficial; shallow: ～之论 shallow views

【肤觉】 fūjué 〈生理〉 dermal sensation

【肤皮潦草】 fūpí liáocǎo cursory; casual; perfunctory

【肤浅】 fūqiǎn superficial; shallow: 我对这个问题的认识很～。I have only a superficial understanding of the problem.

【肤色】 fūsè colour of skin: 不同国度、不同～的运动员欢聚一堂。Players from different lands and of different colours were gathered happily in the same hall.

**麸** fū

【麸皮】 fūpí (wheat) bran

【麸子】 fūzi (wheat) bran

# 跗

fū instep

【跗骨】 fūgǔ 〈生理〉 tarsus; tarsal bones

【跗面】 fūmiàn instep

# 孵

fū hatch; brood; incubate: ～小鸡 hatch chickens

【孵化】 fūhuà hatching; incubation: 人工～ artificial incubation ◇ ～场 hatchery

【孵卵】 fūluǎn hatch; brood; incubate ◇ ～鸡 brooding hen/ ～期 incubation period/ ～器 incubator

# 敷

fū ① apply (powder, ointment, etc.): 外～ for external application ② spread; lay out: ～设 lay (pipes, etc.) ③ be sufficient for: 入不～出 unable to make ends meet

【敷料】 fūliào 〈医〉 dressing

【敷设】 fūshè lay: ～管道 lay pipelines/ ～铁轨 lay a railway track

【敷衍】 fūyǎn elaborate; expound 又作"敷演"

【敷衍】 fūyan be perfunctory; go through the motions: 她办事认真,从不～了事。She is very conscientious and never does her work perfunctorily./ 他～了几句就走了。He made a few casual remarks and left.

【敷衍了事】 fūyan liǎoshì muddle through one's work

【敷衍塞责】 fūyan-sèzé perform one's duty in a perfunctory manner

## fú

# 夫

fú 〈书〉〈助〉 ①〔用于议论的开端〕: ～人必自侮而后人侮之。A man must despise himself before others will. ②〔用于句尾,表示感叹〕: 逝者如斯～! Thus do things flow away!

另见 fū

# 弗

fú 〈书〉 not: 自愧～如 feel ashamed of one's inferiority

# 伏

fú ① bend over: ～案读书 bend over one's desk reading ② lie prostrate: ～地不动 lie still on the ground with one's face downward ③ subside; go down: 此～彼起 down here, up there ④ hide: 昼～夜出 hide by day and come out at night/ 设～ lay an ambush ⑤ hot season; dog days ⑥ admit (defeat or guilt) ⑦ 〈电〉 volt

【伏安】 fú'ān 〈电〉 volt-ampere

【伏笔】 fúbǐ a hint foreshadowing later developments in a story, essay, etc.; foreshadowing

【伏兵】 fúbīng (troops in) ambush

【伏打】 fúdǎ 〈电〉 voltaic ◇ ～电池 voltaic cell

【伏尔加河】 Fú'ěrjiāhé the Volga

【伏法】 fúfǎ be executed

【伏击】 fújī ambush: 遭到～ fall into an ambush ◇ ～圈 ambush ring

【伏流】 fúliú 〈地〉 subterranean drainage; underground stream

【伏侍】 fúshi 见"服侍" fúshi

【伏输】 fúshū 见"服输" fúshū

【伏暑】 fúshǔ hot season; dog days

【伏特】 fútè 〈电〉 volt ◇ ～计 voltmeter

【伏特加】 fútèjiā vodka

【伏天】 fútiān hot summer days; dog days

【伏贴】 fútiē fit perfectly: 这身衣服穿着很～。This suit fits perfectly.

【伏帖】 fútiē 见"服帖" fútiē

【伏汛】 fúxùn summer flood (或 freshet)

【伏罪】 fúzuì 见"服罪" fúzuì

# 凫

fú ① wild duck ② swim: ～水 swim

【凫翁】 fúwēng 〈动〉 water cock

# 扶

fú ① support with the hand; place a hand on sb. or sth. for support: ～着栏杆上楼 walk upstairs with one's hand on the banisters/ 你～着点梯子,我上去。Hold the ladder while I climb up. ② help sb. up; straighten sth. up: ～苗 straighten up the seedlings/ 护士～起伤员,给他换药。The nurse propped up the wounded soldier and changed the dressing on his wound. ③ help; relieve: 救死～伤 heal the wounded and rescue the dying

【扶病】 fúbìng in spite of illness: ～出席 be present in spite of illness

【扶持】 fúchí help sustain; give aid to; help sb. to stand or walk; support: 疾病相～。When one is ill, the others take good care of him./ 伤员们互相～着练习走路。Leaning on each other for support, the wounded men practised walking./ 荷花虽好,也要绿叶～。For all its beauty the lotus needs its green leaves to set it off.

【扶乩】 fújī planchette writing 又作"扶鸾"

【扶老携幼】 fúlǎo-xiéyòu holding the old by the arm and the young by the hand; bringing along the old and the young

【扶犁】 fúlí put one's hand to the plough; follow the plough

【扶手】 fúshou ① handrail; rail; banisters ② armrest ◇ ～椅 armchair

【扶疏】 fúshū 〈书〉 luxuriant and well-spaced: 枝叶～。The branches and leaves are luxuriant but well-spaced.

【扶梯】 fútī staircase

【扶养】 fúyǎng provide for; foster; bring up: ～成人 bring up (a child)

【扶摇直上】 fúyáo zhí shàng soar on the wings of a cyclone; rise steeply; skyrocket

【扶掖】 fúyè 〈书〉 support; help

【扶植】 fúzhí foster; prop up: 帝国主义～起来的傀儡政权 a puppet regime propped up by imperialism

【扶助】 fúzhù help; assist; support: ～老弱 help the old and the weak

# 芙

fú

【芙蕖】 fúqú 〈书〉 lotus

【芙蓉】 fúróng 〈植〉 ① cottonrose hibiscus ② lotus

# 孚

fú inspire confidence in sb.: 深～众望 enjoy great popularity; enjoy high prestige

# 佛

fú 见"仿佛" fǎngfú

另见 fó

# 拂

fú ① stroke: 春风～面 a spring breeze stroking the face ② whisk; flick: ～去桌上的尘土 whisk the dust off a desk ③ go against (sb.'s wishes): 不忍～其意 not have the heart to go against sb.'s wishes; not wish to refuse sb.

【拂尘】 fúchén horsetail whisk

【拂拭】 fúshì whisk or wipe off

【拂晓】 fúxiǎo before dawn: ～前发起总攻 start the general offensive before dawn

【拂袖而去】 fú xiù ér qù leave with a flick of one's sleeve — go off in a huff

# 绋

fú a long, thick rope; a long cord guiding the

hearse

**服** fú ①clothes; dress: 工作～ work clothes ② take (medicine): 日～三次，每次两片。To be taken three times a day, two (tablets) each time. ③serve: ～兵役 serve in the army; perform military service/ ～刑 serve a sentence ④be convinced; obey: 你说得有道理，我～了。What you've said is reasonable. I'm convinced./ 以理～人 convince people by force of argument/ 不～指导 refuse to obey directions ⑤be accustomed to: 不～水土 not accustomed to the climate; not acclimatized

另见 fù

【服从】 fúcóng obey; submit (oneself) to; be subordinated to: ～命令 obey orders/ 少数～多数。The minority should submit to the majority. 或 The minority is subordinate to the majority./ 个人利益必须～革命利益。One's personal interests must be subordinated to the interests of the revolution./ 组织形式应当～革命斗争的需要。Organizational forms should serve the needs of revolutionary struggle./ 一切～抓纲治国的战略决策。Everything must accord with the strategic decision to grasp the key link of class struggle and bring about great order across the land.

【服毒】 fúdú take poison

【服气】 fúqì be convinced: 他批评得对，你别不～。His criticism is justified. You shouldn't take it amiss.

【服丧】 fúsāng be in mourning (for the death of a kinsman, etc.)

【服饰】 fúshì dress and personal adornment; dress

【服侍】 fúshi wait upon; attend: ～病人 attend the sick

【服输】 fúshū admit (或 acknowledge) defeat

【服帖】 fútiē ①docile; obedient; submissive: 反动统治阶级总是要人民服服帖帖地忍受剥削和压迫。The reactionary ruling classes always wanted the people to endure exploitation and oppression submissively. ②be convinced: 心里很～ be positively convinced ③fitting; well arranged: 把事情都弄得服服帖帖的 arrange everything smoothly

【服务】 fúwù give service to; be in the service of; serve: 为人民～。Serve the people./ 提高～质量 improve one's service/ ～周到 provide good service

◇ ～行业 service trades/ ～台 service desk (或 counter); information and reception desk/ ～态度 attitude in attending to or waiting on guests, customers, etc./ ～员 attendant/ ～站 neighbourhood service centre

【服刑】 fúxíng serve a sentence: ～期满 complete a term of imprisonment

【服役】 fúyì ①be on active service; enlist in the army: ～期间 during one's term of military service; during the period of enlistment/ ～期满 complete one's term of service ②do corvée labour

【服膺】 fúyīng 〈书〉①bear in mind ②feel deeply convinced: 拳拳～ have sincere belief in

【服用】 fúyòng take (medicine)

【服装】 fúzhuāng dress; clothing; costume: ～整齐 be neatly dressed/ 民族～ national costume/ 她负责保管这出戏的～。She's the wardrobe mistress of this play.

◇～厂 clothing factory/ ～商店 clothes shop; clothing store/ ～设计 dress designing; costume designing

【服罪】 fúzuì plead guilty; admit one's guilt

**茯** fú

【茯苓】 fúlíng 〈中药〉*fuling* (*Poris cocos*)

**氟** fú 〈化〉fluorine (F)

【氟化物】 fúhuàwù 〈化〉fluoride (e.g. 氟化氢 hydrogen fluoride)

【氟利昂】 fúlì'áng 〈化〉freon

**俘** fú ①capture; take prisoner: 敌军长被～。The enemy army commander was taken prisoner. ②prisoner of war; captive: 遣～ repatriate prisoners of war

【俘获】 fúhuò ①capture: ～敌军一千多人 capture over 1,000 enemy troops ②〈物〉capture: 中子～ neutron capture/ 裂变～ fission capture

【俘虏】 fúlǔ ①capture; take prisoner ②captive; captured personnel; prisoner of war (P.O.W.): 执行宽待～的政策 carry out the policy of lenient treatment of prisoners of war/ 成了资产阶级思想的～ fall captive to bourgeois ideology

**浮** fú ①float: 木头～在水上。Wood floats on water./ 潜水员～上来了。The diver has emerged./ 干部要深入群众，不能～在上面。Cadres should go deep among the masses, not remain on the surface./ 她脸上～起了笑容。A faint smile played on her face. ②〈方〉swim: 他一口气～到了对岸。He swam across at one go. ③on the surface; superficial: ～土 dust on the surface ④temporary; provisional: ～支 expenditure not in the regular account ⑤flighty; unstable; superficial: 他这人太～，办事不踏实。He is too superficial to do solid work. ⑥hollow; inflated: ～名 bubble reputation ⑦excessive; surplus: ～额 surplus number/ 人～于事 be overstaffed

【浮报】 fúbào give inflated figures in a report

【浮标】 fúbiāo buoy

【浮冰】 fúbīng floating ice; (ice) floe

【浮财】 fúcái movable property possessed by landlords and rich peasants at the time of the Land Reform (such as cash, grain and clothing)

【浮尘】 fúchén floating dust; surface dust

【浮尘子】 fúchénzǐ 〈动〉leafhopper

【浮沉】 fúchén now sink, now emerge; drift along: 与世～ follow the trend; swim with the tide

【浮船坞】 fúchuánwù floating (dry) dock

【浮袋】 fúdài water wings

【浮荡】 fúdàng float in the air: 歌声在空中～。The air resounded with singing.

【浮雕】 fúdiāo relief (sculpture): ～群像 a relief sculpture of a group of people

【浮吊】 fúdiào 〈机〉floating crane

【浮动】 fúdòng ①float; drift: 树叶在水面上～。Leaves floated on the water. ②be unsteady; fluctuate: 西方世界物价飞涨，人心～。With the soaring of prices, there was a growing feeling of insecurity in the West. ③〈经〉float: 货币共同～ a joint currency float ◇ ～汇率 floating (exchange) rate/ ～轴 〈机〉floating axle

【浮泛】 fúfàn ①〈书〉float about: 轻舟～ a light boat gliding past ②reveal; display: 她的脸上～着愉快的神情。Her face beamed with joy. ③superficial; too abstract: 他的发言内容～。His speech was superficial and full of generalities.

【浮光掠影】 fúguāng-lüèyǐng skimming over the surface; hasty and casual; cursory

【浮华】 fúhuá showy; ostentatious; flashy: 文辞～ florid language; an ornate style/ ～的生活 a showy and luxurious life

【浮记】 fújì keep a tally of a transaction before entering it in the regular accounts; keep a temporary account

【浮夸】 fúkuā be boastful; exaggerate: ～作风 proneness to boasting and exaggeration

【浮雷】 fúléi 〈军〉floating mine

【浮力】 fúlì 〈物〉buoyancy

【浮码头】 fúmǎtou floating pier

【浮脉】 fúmài 〈中医〉 surface pulse which can be felt when touched only lightly
【浮面】 fúmiàn surface: 把～的一层泥铲掉 scrape the mud off the surface
【浮皮蹭痒】 fúpí cèngyǎng scratching the surface; superficial
【浮皮儿】 fúpír ① outer skin ② surface
【浮萍】 fúpíng 〈植〉 duckweed
【浮签】 fúqiān a note pasted on the margin of a page
【浮浅】 fúqiǎn superficial; shallow
【浮桥】 fúqiáo pontoon (或 floating) bridge
【浮石】 fúshí 〈矿〉 pumice (stone)
【浮水】 fúshuǐ 〈方〉 swim
【浮筒】 fútǒng float; pontoon; buoy
【浮头儿】 fútóur 〈方〉 surface
【浮屠】 fútú 〈佛教〉 ① Buddha ② Buddhist monk ③ pagoda; stupa
【浮土】 fútǔ dust collected on furniture, etc.; surface dust
【浮文】 fúwén verbiage; padding
【浮现】 fúxiàn appear before one's eyes: 往事～在我眼前。Scenes of the past rose before my eyes. 或 The past came back to my mind.
【浮想】 fúxiǎng thoughts or recollections flashing across one's mind: ～联翩 thoughts thronging one's mind
【浮选】 fúxuǎn 〈矿〉 flotation ◇ ～剂 flotation agent
【浮游生物】 fúyóu shēngwù plankton
【浮云】 fúyún floating clouds
【浮躁】 fúzào impetuous; impulsive
【浮渣】 fúzhā 〈冶〉 dross
【浮肿】 fúzhǒng 〈医〉 dropsy; edema
【浮舟】 fúzhōu pontoon
【浮子】 fúzi ① 〈渔〉 float ② 〈汽车〉 carburettor float

**祓** fú 见"包袱" bāofu

**菔** fú 见"莱菔" láifú

**符** fú ① a tally issued by a ruler to generals, envoys, etc., as credentials in ancient China ② symbol: 音～ musical notes ③ tally with; accord with: 与事实不～ not tally with the facts ④ magic figures drawn by Taoist priests to invoke or expel spirits and bring good or ill fortune ⑤ (Fú) a surname
【符号】 fúhào ① symbol; mark: 注音～ phonetic symbol/ 标点～ punctuation mark/ 代数～ algebraic symbol/ 文字是记录语言的～。The written word is a symbol for recording human speech. ② insignia
【符合】 fúhé ① accord with; tally with; conform to; be in keeping with: ～要求 accord with the demands/ ～实际情况 tally with the actual situation; conform to reality/ ～斗争大方向 be in line with the general direction of the struggle/ ～阶级斗争的客观规律 conform to the objective laws of class struggle/ ～各国人民的愿望 be in keeping with the aspirations of the people of all countries ② 〈物〉 coincidence: ～摆 coincidence pendulum
【符拉迪沃斯托克(海参崴)】 Fúlādíwòsītuōkè (Hǎishēnwǎi) Vladivostok (Haishenwai)
【符咒】 fúzhòu Taoist magic figures or incantations

**匐** fú 见"匍匐" púfú

**幅** fú ① width of cloth: 单(双)～床单 single-(double-) width bed sheet ② size: 大～照片 a large-sized photo ③ 〈量〉〔用于布帛、呢绒、图画等〕: 一～画 a picture; a painting
【幅度】 fúdù range; scope; extent: 病人血压变化的～不大。The patient's blood pressure fluctuates within a narrow range./ 粮食产量大～增长。There was a big increase in grain production. 或 Grain output increased by a big margin.
【幅面】 fúmiàn width of cloth
【幅员】 fúyuán the area of a country's territory; the size of a country: ～辽阔的国家 a country with a vast territory

**福** fú good fortune; blessing; happiness: 造～人类 promote the well-being of mankind; benefit mankind/ 你可不能身在～中不知～啊! Don't take your good fortune for granted.
【福尔马林】 fú'ěrmǎlín 〈化〉 formalin
【福分】 fúfen 〈口〉 见"福气"
【福建】 Fújiàn Fujian (Province)
【福克兰群岛】 Fúkèlán Qúndǎo the Falkland Islands
【福利】 fúlì material benefits; well-being; welfare: 为人民谋～ work for the well-being of the people
◇ ～费 welfare funds/ ～国家 welfare state/ ～设施 welfare facilities/ ～事业 welfare projects (或 services)
【福气】 fúqi happy lot; good fortune
【福星】 fúxīng lucky star; mascot
【福音】 fúyīn ① 〈基督教〉 Gospel ② glad tidings
【福州】 Fúzhōu Fuzhou

**辐** fú spoke: 轮～ the spoke of a wheel
【辐辏】 fúcòu 〈书〉 converge
【辐散】 fúsàn 〈气〉 divergence ◇ ～场 divergence field
【辐射】 fúshè 〈物〉 radiation: 电磁～ electromagnetic radiation/ 受激～ stimulated radiation/ 自发～ spontaneous radiation
◇ ～带 〈天〉 radiation zone/ ～计 radiometer/ ～剂量 radiation dosage/ ～频率 radiation frequency/ ～容限 radiotolerance/ ～体 radiating body/ ～学 radiology/ ～育种 〈农〉 radioactive breeding/ ～源 radiant
【辐条】 fútiáo 〈口〉 spoke
【辐照】 fúzhào 〈物〉 irradiation ◇ ～度 irradiance

**蜉** fú
【蜉蝣】 fúyóu 〈动〉 mayfly

**蚨** fú 见"鲂蚨" fángfú

**蝠** fú 〈动〉 bat

## fǔ

**父** fǔ a respectful term for an elderly man in ancient times
另见 fù

**甫** fǔ ① 〈书〉 just; only: 年～二十 have just reached the age of twenty ② one's courtesy name: 台～ your name

**抚** fǔ ① comfort; console: 安～ placate; appease; pacify ② nurture; foster: ～养 foster; raise; bring up ③ stroke: ～琴 〈书〉 play the zither
【抚爱】 fǔ'ài caress; fondle
【抚躬自问】 fǔgōng zìwèn 见"反躬自问" fǎngōng zìwèn
【抚今追昔】 fǔjīn-zhuīxī recall the past and compare it with the present; reflect on the past in the light of the present
【抚摩】 fǔmó stroke

【抚弄】 fǔnòng stroke; fondle
【抚慰】 fǔwèi comfort; console; soothe: ～灾区人民 console the people in afflicted areas
【抚恤】 fǔxù comfort and compensate a bereaved family ◇ ～金 pension for the disabled or for the family of the deceased
【抚养】 fǔyǎng foster; raise; bring up: 是党把他～大的。It was the Party that brought him up.
【抚育】 fǔyù foster; nurture; tend: ～烈士子女 bring up the children of revolutionary martyrs/ 森林～ tending of woods

**府** fǔ ① seat of government; government office: 首～ capital ② official residence; mansion: 总统～ presidential palace ③ 〈敬〉 your home: 贵～ your home ④ prefecture (from the Tang to the Qing Dynasty): 济南～ the Prefecture of Jinan
【府绸】 fǔchóu poplin: 山东～ Shandong pongee; shantung
【府邸】 fǔdǐ mansion; mansion house
【府第】 fǔdì mansion; mansion house
【府库】 fǔkù 〈旧〉 government repository
【府上】 fǔshang 〈敬〉 ① your home; your family ② your native place

**斧** fǔ axe; hatchet
【斧头】 fǔtou axe; hatchet
【斧正】 fǔzhèng (please) make corrections
【斧锧】 fǔzhì executioner's block and cleaver (used in ancient China)
【斧子】 fǔzi axe; hatchet

**拊** fǔ 〈书〉 clap
【拊掌】 fǔzhǎng 〈书〉 clap hands

**釜** fǔ a kind of cauldron used in ancient China
【釜底抽薪】 fǔ dǐ chōu xīn take away the firewood from under the cauldron — take a drastic measure to deal with a situation
【釜底游鱼】 fǔ dǐ yóuyú a fish swimming in the bottom of a cauldron — a person whose fate is sealed

**俯** fǔ ① bow (one's head): ～视 overlook ② 〈敬〉〔旧时公文书信中用来称对方的动作〕: ～察 deign to examine/ ～就 condescend to take the post
【俯冲】 fǔchōng 〈航空〉 dive ◇ ～轰炸 dive bombing/ ～角 dive angle
【俯伏】 fǔfú lie prostrate
【俯角】 fǔjiǎo 〈测〉 angle of depression
【俯瞰】 fǔkàn look down at; overlook: 从飞机上～海面 look down at the sea from a plane ◇ ～摄影 crane (或 boom) shot
【俯拾即是】 fǔ shí jí shì can be found everywhere; be extremely common: 这类事例～。Such instances are extremely common.
【俯视】 fǔshì look down at; overlook ◇ ～图〈机〉 vertical view
【俯首】 fǔshǒu bow one's head (in submission): ～就范 meekly submit; surrender without a struggle/ ～帖耳 be docile and obedient; be all obedience; be servile/ ～听命 obey submissively
【俯卧撑】 fǔwòchēng 〈体〉 push-up
【俯仰】 fǔ-yǎng a bending or lifting of the head — a simple move or action: 随人～ be at sb.'s beck and call ◇ ～角〈航空〉 angle of pitch/ ～运动〈机〉 pitching movement
【俯仰由人】 fǔ-yǎng yóu rén be at sb.'s beck and call
【俯仰之间】 fǔ-yǎng zhījiān in the twinkling of an eye; in an instant; in a flash

**脯** fǔ ① dried meat: 鹿～ dried venison ② preserved fruit: 桃～ preserved peaches
另见 pú

**辅** fǔ assist; complement; supplement: 相～相成 complement each other/ 自力更生为主，争取外援为～ rely mainly on our own efforts while making external assistance subsidiary
【辅币】 fǔbì fractional currency (或 money): 硬～ subsidiary coin; minor coin
【辅导】 fǔdǎo give guidance in study or training; coach: 学习这篇文章，你给我们～～好不好？Could you give us some guidance in studying this article?/ ～孩子们练武术 coach the children in *wushu* exercises/ 个别～ individual coaching (或 tutorial) ◇ ～报告 guidance lecture (supplementary lecture on background, study method, etc.)/ ～材料 guidance material
【辅导员】 fǔdǎoyuán (political and ideological) assistant; instructor: 政治～ political assistant/ 理论～ instructor in political theory/ 校外～ after-school activities counsellor
【辅课】 fǔkè subsidiary course
【辅音】 fǔyīn 〈语〉 consonant
【辅助】 fǔzhù ① assist ② supplementary; auxiliary; subsidiary
◇ ～仪器 supplementary instrument/ ～机构 auxiliary body/ ～舰船 auxiliary vessels/ ～劳动 auxiliary labour (或 jobs)/ ～人员 auxiliary staff members/ ～授粉〈农〉 supplementary pollination
【辅佐】 fǔzuǒ assist a ruler in governing a country

**腑** fǔ 见"脏腑" zàngfǔ

**腐** fǔ ① rotten; putrid; stale; corroded: 流水不～。Running water is never stale./ ～肉 rotten meat ② bean curd
【腐败】 fǔbài ① rotten; putrid; decayed: ～的食物 putrid food ② corrupt; rotten: ～无能 corrupt and incompetent
【腐恶】 fǔ'è corrupt and evil: 征～ chastise the corrupt and evil
【腐化】 fǔhuà ① degenerate; corrupt; dissolute; depraved: ～堕落 morally degenerate/ 生活～ lead a dissolute (或 dissipated) life ② rot; decay ◇ ～分子 degenerate; a depraved person
【腐烂】 fǔlàn ① decomposed; putrid ② corrupt; rotten
【腐泥煤】 fǔníméi sapropelic coal
【腐儒】 fǔrú pedantic scholar; pedant
【腐乳】 fǔrǔ fermented bean curd
【腐生】 fǔshēng 〈生〉 saprophytic: ～细菌 saprophytic bacteria/ ～植物 saprophyte
【腐蚀】 fǔshí ① corrode; etch ② corrupt; corrode: 警惕资产阶级思想的～ be on guard against the corrosive influence of bourgeois ideas
◇ ～版〈印〉 etched plate/ ～机〈印〉 etching machine/ ～剂〈化〉 corrosive; corrodent/ ～性 corrosiveness
【腐熟】 fǔshú 〈农〉 (of compost, etc.) become thoroughly decomposed
【腐朽】 fǔxiǔ ① rotten; decayed: 这些木材已经～了。The timber has rotted. ② decadent; degenerate: ～没落的资本主义 decadent and moribund capitalism; decaying capitalism/ 反对～庸俗的作风 oppose decadent and philistine ways

【腐殖煤】 fǔzhíméi humic coal
【腐殖酸】 fǔzhísuān 〈农〉 humic acid: ～类肥料 humic acid fertilizers
【腐殖土】 fǔzhítǔ 〈农〉 humus soil
【腐殖质】 fǔzhízhì 〈地〉 humus
【腐竹】 fǔzhú dried bean milk cream in tight rolls

**簠** fǔ 〈考古〉 a square grain receptacle used at sacrificial ceremonies in ancient China

## fù

**父** fù ①father ② male relative of a senior generation: 伯～ one's father's elder brother; uncle/ 祖～ grandfather 另见 fǔ
【父本】 fùběn 〈植〉 male parent: ～植株 paternal plant
【父老】 fùlǎo elders (of a country or district): ～兄弟 elders and brethren
【父母】 fù-mǔ father and mother; parents
【父亲】 fùqin father
【父权制】 fùquánzhì patriarchy
【父系】 fùxì paternal line; the father's side of the family ◇ ～亲属 relatives on the paternal side/ ～氏族公社 patriarchal clan commune
【父兄】 fù-xiōng ① father and elder brothers ② head of a family

**讣** fù obituary
【讣告】 fùgào ① announce sb.'s death ② obituary (notice)
【讣闻】 fùwén obituary (notice)

**付** fù ① hand (或 turn) over to; commit to: 交～审讯 hand over to the law; commit to trial/ ～表决 put to the vote/ ～诸实施 put into effect/ ～之一笑 dismiss with a laugh ② pay: ～税 pay taxes/ ～息 pay interest
【付出】 fùchū pay; expend: ～代价 pay a price/ 为人类解放事业不惜～自己的生命 be ready to give one's life for the emancipation of mankind/ ～辛勤的劳动 put in a lot of hard work
【付方】 fùfāng credit side; credit
【付款】 fùkuǎn pay a sum of money: 货到～ cash on delivery (C.O.D.)/ 凭单～ cash against documents ◇ ～办法 methods of payment/ ～凭证 payment voucher/ ～人 payer; drawee
【付排】 fùpái send to the compositor
【付讫】 fùqì (of a bill) paid
【付清】 fùqīng pay in full; pay off; clear (a bill): 一次～ pay off in one lump sum
【付托】 fùtuō put sth. in sb.'s charge; entrust: ～得人 have entrusted the matter to the right person/ ～重任 charge sb. with a heavy responsibility
【付息】 fùxī payment of interest
【付现】 fùxiàn pay in cash; cash
【付印】 fùyìn ① send to the press ② turn over to the printing shop (after proofreading)
【付邮】 fùyóu take to the post; post
【付帐】 fùzhàng pay a bill
【付之一炬】 fù zhī yī jù commit to the flames
【付诸东流】 fù zhū dōngliú thrown into the eastward flowing stream — all one's efforts wasted; irrevocably lost

**负** fù ① carry on the back or shoulder; shoulder; bear: ～薪 carry firewood on one's back/ 如释重～ feel as if relieved of a heavy load; feel greatly relieved/ 身～重任 shoulder an important task/ ～主要责任 assume the main responsibility ② have at one's back; rely on: ～险固守 put up a stubborn defence by relying on one's strategic position ③ suffer: ～屈 suffer an injustice; be wronged/ ～伤 get wounded ④ enjoy: 久～盛名 have long enjoyed a good reputation ⑤ owe: ～债 be in debt ⑥ fail in one's duty, obligation, etc.; betray: ～约 break a promise/ 忘恩～义 be ungrateful ⑦ lose (a battle, game, etc.); be defeated: 一比二～于对方 lose the match 1:2/ 该队以二胜一～的成绩取得小组第二名。The team finished second in its group with two wins and one defeat./ 不分胜～ end in a draw; end in a tie; break even ⑧ 〈数〉 minus; negative: ～一点五 minus one point five (-1.5)/ ～号 negative sign ⑨ 〈电〉 negative
【负担】 fùdān ① bear (a burden); shoulder: 旅费由东道国～。All the travelling expenses will be borne by the host country. ② burden; load; encumbrance: 财政～ financial burden/ 家庭～ family burden (esp. financial)/ 工作～ load of work; work load/ 思想～ a load on one's mind; mental burden/ 减轻学生～ lighten the students' load/ 解除精神～ free one's mind of encumbrances
【负电荷】 fùdiànhè negative (electric) charge
【负电极】 fùdiànjí negative electrode; cathode
【负号】 fùhào negative sign
【负荷】 fùhè 见"负载"
【负极】 fùjí 〈电〉 negative pole
【负加速度】 fù-jiāsùdù 〈物〉 negative acceleration
【负荆请罪】 fùjīng qǐngzuì proffer a birch and ask for a flogging — offer a humble apology
【负疚】 fùjiù 〈书〉 feel apologetic; have a guilty conscience
【负离子】 fùlízǐ 〈物〉 anion
【负片】 fùpiàn 〈摄〉 negative
【负气】 fùqì do sth. in a fit of pique: ～而去 leave angrily out of spite
【负伤】 fùshāng be wounded; be injured: 光荣～ be wounded in action
【负数】 fùshù 〈数〉 negative number
【负像】 fùxiàng 〈物〉 negative image
【负隅顽抗】 fùyú wánkàng (of an enemy or a robber) fight stubbornly with one's back to the wall; put up a desperate struggle
【负约】 fùyuē break a promise; go back on one's word
【负载】 fùzài 〈电〉 load: 高峰～ peak load/ 工作～ operating load ◇ ～调整 load regulation
【负责】 fùzé ① be responsible for; be in charge of: 我们的责任,是向人民～。Our duty is to hold ourselves responsible to the people./ 本着对革命～的精神 out of one's sense of responsibility to the revolutionary cause/ 由此产生的一切后果由你方～。Your side will be held responsible for all the consequences arising therefrom./ 他～保卫工作。He is in charge of security affairs. ② conscientious: 她对工作很～。She is very conscientious in her work. ◇ ～干部 cadre in a responsible position; responsible cadre; cadre in charge/ ～人 person in charge; leading cadre
【负债】 fùzhài be in debt; incur debts: ～累累 be heavily in debt; be up to one's eyes in debt/ 资产与～ assets and liabilities

**妇** fù ① woman: ～孺 women and children ② married woman: 少～ young married woman ③ wife: 夫～ husband and wife
【妇产科】 fùchǎnkē (department of) gynaecology and obstetrics
【妇产医院】 fùchǎn yīyuàn a hospital for gynaecology and obstetrics

【妇科】 fùkē (department of) gynaecology ◇ ～医生 gynaecologist
【妇联】 fùlián 〈简〉(妇女联合会) the Women's Federation: 全国～ the All-China Women's Federation
【妇女】 fùnǚ woman
◇ ～病 gynaecological (或 women's) disease/ ～队长 woman leader (in charge of women's affairs in a production team)/ ～节 International Working Women's Day (March 8)
【妇人】 fùrén married woman
【妇幼】 fù-yòu women and children ◇ ～保健站 health centre for women and children; maternity and child care centre/ ～卫生 maternity and child hygiene

**附** fù ① add; attach; enclose: ～上一笔 add a word or two (in a letter, etc.)/ ～表 attached list or chart/ ～寄一张照片 enclosed herewith a photo ② get close to; be near: ～在耳边低声说话 whisper in sb.'s ear ③ agree to: ～议 second a motion
【附带】 fùdài ① in passing: ～说一下 mention in passing; by the way; incidentally ② attach: 我们提供的援助不～任何条件。The aid we provide has no strings attached. ③ subsidiary; supplementary: 从事～劳动 do supplementary labour
【附点】 fùdiǎn 〈乐〉 dot ◇ ～音符 dotted note
【附耳】 fù'ěr move close to sb.'s ear: ～低语 whisper in sb.'s ear
【附睾】 fùgāo 〈生理〉 epididymis ◇ ～炎 epididymitis
【附和】 fùhè echo; chime in with: ～别人的意见 echo other people's views/ 随声～ chime in with others
【附会】 fùhuì draw wrong conclusions by false analogy; strain one's interpretation: 穿凿～ give strained interpretations and draw farfetched analogies
【附加】 fùjiā ① add; attach: 文件后面～两项说明。The document has two explanatory notes attached to it. ② additional; attached; appended
◇ ～费 extra charges; surcharge/ ～税 surtax; additional tax; supertax/ ～条款 additional article; memorandum clause/ ～文件 〈外〉 appended document/ ～议定书 〈外〉 additional protocol
【附件】 fùjiàn ① appendix; annex: 作为调查报告的～ as an appendix to the investigation report ② enclosure ③ 〈机〉 accessories; attachment: 车床～ lathe accessories/ 铲工～ backing-off attachment
【附近】 fùjìn ① nearby; neighbouring: ～地区 nearby regions/ ～的城市 neighbouring (或 adjacent) towns ② close to; in the vicinity of: 住在工厂～ live close to the factory/ ～有没有邮局？Is there a post office near here?
【附录】 fùlù appendix
【附上】 fùshàng enclosed herewith: 随信～商品目录一份。A catalogue of commodities is enclosed herewith./ ～样稿一份，请查收。Enclosed please find a set of sample sheets.
【附设】 fùshè have as an attached institution: 这个学院～一所中学。There is a middle school attached to the institute./ 这个商店～了一个早晚服务部。This store has set up an after-hours department.
【附生植物】 fùshēng zhíwù epiphyte
【附属】 fùshǔ subsidiary; auxiliary; attached; affiliated: 医学院～医院 a hospital attached to a medical college
◇ ～国 dependency/ ～机构 subsidiary body/ ～品 accessory; appendage
【附图】 fùtú attached map or drawing; figure: 见～一。See Figure 1.
【附小】 fùxiǎo 〈简〉(附属小学) attached primary school
【附言】 fùyán postscript (P.S.)
【附议】 fùyì second a motion; support a proposal: 我～！I second that!
【附庸】 fùyōng dependency; vassal; appendage
【附庸风雅】 fùyōng fēngyǎ (of landlords, merchants, etc.) mingle with men of letters and pose as a lover of culture
【附则】 fùzé supplementary articles (appended to a treaty, decree, etc.)
【附肢】 fùzhī 〈动〉 appendage
【附中】 fùzhōng 〈简〉(附属中学) attached middle school
【附注】 fùzhù notes appended to a book, etc.; annotations
【附着】 fùzhuó adhere to; stick to: 这种病菌～在病人使用过的东西上。This germ is found on things used by the patients. ◇ ～力 〈物〉 adhesive force; adhesion
【附子】 fùzǐ 〈中药〉 monkshood

**阜** fù 〈书〉 ① mound ② abundant: 物～民丰。Products abound and the people live in plenty.

**服** fù 〈量〉〔用于中药〕dose: 一～药 a dose of medicine
另见 fú

**驸** fù
【驸马】 fùmǎ emperor's son-in-law

**赴** fù go to; attend: ～约 keep an appointment/ ～宴 attend a banquet/ 离京～渝 leave Beijing for Chongqing
【赴难】 fùnàn go to the aid of one's country; go to help save the country from danger
【赴任】 fùrèn go to one's post; be on the way to one's post
【赴汤蹈火】 fùtāng-dǎohuǒ go through fire and water

**复** fù ① duplicate: ～本 a duplicate ② compound; complex: ～姓 compound surname; two-character surname/ ～光谱 complex spectrum ③ turn round; turn over: 翻来～去睡不着 toss in bed, unable to sleep ④ answer; reply: 请即电～。Cable reply immediately. ⑤ recover; resume: 祝早日康～。Best wishes for an early recovery./ ～职 resume one's post ⑥ revenge: 报～ retaliate; take revenge ⑦ again: 周而～始 go round and begin again/ 一去不～返 gone never to return
【复背斜】 fùbèixié 〈地〉 anticlinorium
【复本】 fùběn duplicate
【复本位制】 fùběnwèizhì 〈经〉 bimetallism
【复辟】 fùbì ① restoration of a dethroned monarch ② restoration of the old order: 防止资本主义～ prevent capitalist restoration/ ～活动 restorationist activities (或 manoeuvres)
【复波】 fùbō 〈物〉 complex wave
【复查】 fùchá check; reexamine: 一个月后到医院～ come back to the hospital for a check in a month's time
【复仇】 fùchóu revenge; avenge: ～心理 vindictiveness; a desire for revenge/ ～的子弹向敌人射去 fire bullets of vengeance at the enemy ◇ ～主义 revanchism
【复电】 fùdiàn telegram in reply (to one received)
【复调音乐】 fùdiào yīnyuè polyphony
【复发】 fùfā have a relapse; recur: 旧病～ have an attack of an old illness; have a relapse/ 他的关节炎～了。He's suffering from arthritis again.
【复方】 fùfāng 〈药〉 medicine made of two or more ingredients; compound ◇ ～阿斯匹林 aspirin compound (APC)/ ～甘草合剂 brown mixture
【复分解反应】 fùfēnjiě fǎnyìng 〈化〉 double decomposition reaction
【复根】 fùgēn 〈化〉 compound radical

【复工】 fùgōng return to work (after a strike or layoff)
【复古】 fùgǔ restore ancient ways; return to the ancients ◇ ～主义 the doctrine of "back to the ancients"
【复合】 fùhé compound; complex; composite
◇ ～词〈语〉compound (word)/ ～电路 compound circuit/ ～肥料 compound fertilizer/ ～句〈语〉compound or complex sentence/ ～量词〈语〉compound classifier/ ～元音〈语〉compound vowel
【复核】 fùhé ① check: 把数字～一下 check the figures ②〈法〉(of the Supreme People's Court) review a case in which a death sentence has been passed by a lower court
【复会】 fùhuì resume a session (或 sitting)
【复活】 fùhuó ① bring back to life; revive: 防止法西斯主义～ guard against the revival of fascism ②〈基督教〉Resurrection ◇ ～节 Easter
【复激】 fùjī 〈电〉compound excitation ◇ ～发电机 compound generator
【复交】 fùjiāo 〈外〉reestablish (或 resume) diplomatic relations
【复旧】 fùjiù restoration (或 revival) of old ways; return to the past
【复句】 fùjù 〈语〉a sentence of two or more clauses
【复卷机】 fùjuǎnjī 〈纸〉rewinding machine; rewinder
【复刊】 fùkān resume publication
【复课】 fùkè resume classes
【复理层】 fùlǐcéng 〈地〉flysch
【复利】 fùlì 〈经〉compound interest
【复捻】 fùniǎn 〈纺〉second twist
【复赛】 fùsài 〈体〉intermediary heat
【复审】 fùshěn ① reexamine ②〈法〉review a case
【复式】 fùshì 〈簿记〉double entry
【复式车床】 fùshì chēchuáng 〈机〉double lathe
【复述】 fùshù ① repeat: ～命令 repeat an order ② retell (in language learning): 把故事～一遍 retell a story
【复数】 fùshù ①〈语〉plural (number) ②〈数〉complex number
【复丝】 fùsī 〈化纤〉multifilament
【复苏】 fùsū ①come back to life or consciousness; resuscitate ② recovery
【复位术】 fùwèishù 〈医〉reduction
【复习】 fùxí review; revise: ～功课 review (或 revise) lessons
【复线】 fùxiàn 〈交〉multiple track
【复向斜】 fùxiàngxié 〈地〉synclinorium
【复写】 fùxiě make carbon copies; duplicate ◇ ～纸 carbon paper
【复信】 fùxìn ① write a letter in reply ② letter in reply; reply
【复兴】 fùxīng revive; resurge; rejuvenate: 民族～ national rejuvenation/ 文艺～ the Renaissance
【复姓】 fùxìng compound surname; two-character surname
【复学】 fùxué go back to school (after prolonged absence for health reasons, etc.); resume one's interrupted studies
【复盐】 fùyán 〈化〉double salt
【复眼】 fùyǎn 〈动〉compound eye
【复叶】 fùyè 〈植〉compound leaf
【复议】 fùyì reconsider (a decision)
【复音】 fùyīn 〈物〉complex tone
【复音词】 fùyīncí 〈语〉disyllabic or polysyllabic word
【复印】 fùyìn 〈印〉duplicate ◇ ～机 duplicator; duplicating machine/ ～纸 duplicating paper
【复员】 fùyuán demobilize
◇ ～费 demobilization pay/ ～军人 demobilized soldier; ex-serviceman/ ～令 demobilization order
【复原】 fùyuán ① recover from an illness; be restored to health: 他身体已经～了。He's already recovered. ② restore; rehabilitate: ～后的金缕玉衣充分显示出中国古代劳动人民的精湛工艺。The restored jade burial suit fully reveals the consummate skill of the labouring people of ancient China.
【复圆】 fùyuán 〈天〉(of an eclipse) fourth contact; last contact
【复杂】 fùzá complicated; complex: 情况～。The situation is complicated./ 故事情节～。The story is very complicated./ ～的心情 mixed feelings/ 使问题～化 make things complicated; complicate matters/ 阶级斗争的～性 the complex nature of class struggle
【复照】 fùzhào 〈外〉a note in reply
【复诊】 fùzhěn further consultation (with a doctor); subsequent visit
【复职】 fùzhí resume one's post; be reinstated
【复制】 fùzhì duplicate; reproduce; make a copy of
◇ ～模型 reconstructed model/ ～片 duplicated film; copy of a film/ ～品 replica; reproduction
【复种】 fùzhòng 〈农〉multiple cropping ◇ ～面积 multiple cropping area/ ～指数 multiple crop index
【复壮】 fùzhuàng 〈农〉rejuvenation

**副** fù ① deputy; assistant; vice-: ～主席 vice-chairman/ ～总理 vice-premier/ ～部长 vice-minister/ ～领事 vice-consul/ ～书记 deputy secretary/ ～秘书长 deputy secretary-general/ ～主任 deputy director/ ～司令员 assistant commanding officer (或 commandant)/ ～教授 associate professor/ (飞机)～驾驶员 copilot ② auxiliary; subsidiary; secondary: ～泵 auxiliary pump ③ correspond to; fit: 名不～实。The name falls short of the reality. ④〈量〉〔用于成套的东西或用于面部表情〕: 一～手套 a pair of gloves/ 装出一～笑脸 put on a false smile; assume a smiling face
【副本】 fùběn duplicate; transcript; copy
【副标题】 fùbiāotí subheading; subtitle
【副产品】 fùchǎnpǐn by-product
【副赤道带】 fùchìdàodài 〈气〉subequatorial belt
【副词】 fùcí 〈语〉①(in Chinese grammar) adverbial word, any of a class of words that are used mainly to modify a verb or an adjective ②(in English grammar) adverb
【副歌】 fùgē 〈乐〉refrain
【副官】 fùguān adjutant; aide-de-camp
【副虹】 fùhóng 〈气〉secondary bow
【副交感神经】 fùjiāogǎn shénjīng 〈生理〉parasympathetic nerve
【副井】 fùjǐng 〈矿〉auxiliary shaft
【副刊】 fùkān supplement: 文学～ literary supplement
【副品】 fùpǐn substandard goods
【副伤寒】 fùshānghán 〈医〉paratyphoid (fever)
【副神经】 fùshénjīng 〈生理〉accessory nerve
【副食】 fùshí non-staple food (或 foodstuffs) ◇ ～品加工厂 non-staple food processing factory/ ～商店 grocer's; grocery
【副手】 fùshǒu assistant
【副署】 fùshǔ countersign
【副业】 fùyè sideline; side occupation: ～生产 sideline (或 supplementary, subsidiary) production/ 家庭～ household sideline production
【副翼】 fùyì 〈航空〉aileron
【副油箱】 fùyóuxiāng 〈航空〉① auxiliary tank ② drop tank
【副职】 fùzhí the position of a deputy to the chief of an office, department, etc.
【副轴】 fùzhóu 〈机〉countershaft; layshaft
【副作用】 fùzuòyòng ① side effect; by-effect: 麻醉药物的～

side effects from the use of anaesthetics ② 〈机〉 secondary action

**富** fù ① rich; wealthy; abundant: ～日子当穷日子过。Be thrifty even in days of abundance./ ～于养分 be rich in nutrition/ ～于自我批评精神 be imbued with the spirit of self-criticism/ ～于创造性 be highly creative ② (Fù) a surname

【富国强兵】 fù guó qiáng bīng make one's country rich and build up its military power
【富贵】 fùguì riches and honour; wealth and rank
【富豪】 fùháo rich and powerful people
【富矿】 fùkuàng 〈矿〉 rich ore; high-grade ore ◇ ～体 ore shoot
【富丽堂皇】 fùlì tánghuáng sumptuous; gorgeous; splendid
【富农】 fùnóng rich peasant
【富强】 fùqiáng prosperous and strong: 使祖国更加繁荣～ make our country more prosperous and powerful
【富饶】 fùráo richly endowed; fertile; abundant: 美丽～的国家 a beautiful and richly endowed country/ ～的土地 fertile land
【富士山】 Fùshìshān Fujiyama
【富庶】 fùshù rich and populous
【富翁】 fùwēng man of wealth
【富有】 fùyǒu ① rich; wealthy ② rich in; full of: ～经验 rich in experience; very experienced/ ～战斗性 very militant/ ～代表性 typical/ 是～生命力的 be full of vitality
【富裕】 fùyù prosperous; well-to-do; well-off ◇ ～中农 well-to-do middle peasant
【富余】 fùyu have more than needed; have enough and to spare: 粮食有～ have a surplus of grain/ 我们还～两张票。We have two tickets to spare.
【富源】 fùyuán natural resources
【富足】 fùzú plentiful; abundant; rich

**赋** fù ① bestow on; endow with; vest with: 消灭人剥削人的制度是历史～予无产阶级的使命。History has entrusted to the proletariat the task of abolishing the exploitation of man by man./ 禀～ natural endowments ② tax: 田～ land tax ③ *fu*, descriptive prose interspersed with verse ④ compose (a poem): ～诗一首 compose a poem

【赋格曲】 fùgéqǔ 〈乐〉 fugue
【赋税】 fùshuì taxes
【赋闲】 fùxián (of an official, etc.) be unemployed
【赋形剂】 fùxíngjì 〈药〉 excipient
【赋性】 fùxìng inborn nature
【赋役】 fùyì taxes and corvée

**傅** fù ① teach; instruct ② teacher; instructor ③ lay on; apply: ～彩 lay on colours/ ～粉 put powder on; powder (the face, etc.) ④ (Fù) a surname

【傅会】 fùhuì 见"附会" fùhuì

**腹** fù belly; abdomen; stomach

【腹背受敌】 fù-bèi shòu dí be attacked front and rear
【腹地】 fùdì hinterland
【腹诽】 fùfěi 〈书〉 unspoken criticism
【腹稿】 fùgǎo a draft worked out in one's mind; mental notes
【腹股沟】 fùgǔgōu 〈生理〉 groin
【腹膜】 fùmó 〈生理〉 peritonaeum ◇ ～炎 peritonitis
【腹鳍】 fùqí 〈动〉 ventral fin
【腹腔】 fùqiāng 〈生理〉 abdominal cavity ◇ ～镜 〈医〉 peritoneoscope
【腹水】 fùshuǐ 〈医〉 ascites: 抽～ tap the abdomen
【腹痛】 fùtòng abdominal pain
【腹泻】 fùxiè diarrhoea
【腹心】 fùxīn ① true thoughts and feelings: 敢布～ venture to air some of my views ② 见"心腹" xīnfù ①
【腹胀】 fùzhàng abdominal distension
【腹足】 fùzú 〈动〉 abdominal foot (或 leg); proleg

**缚** fù tie up; bind fast: 手无～鸡之力 lack the strength to truss a chicken — physically very weak

**鲋** fù crucian carp

**赙** fù

【赙仪】 fùyí 〈书〉 a gift to a bereaved family
【赙赠】 fùzèng 〈书〉 present a gift to a bereaved family

**蝮** fù

【蝮蛇】 fùshé Pallas pit viper

**覆** fù 〈书〉 ① cover ② overturn; upset: ～舟 capsized boat/ 前车之～,后车之鉴。The overturned cart ahead is a warning to the cart behind.

【覆巢无完卵】 fù cháo wú wánluǎn when the nest is overturned no egg stays unbroken — in a great disaster no one can escape unscathed
【覆盖】 fùgài ① cover: 积雪～着地面。The ground is covered with snow. ② plant cover; vegetation ◇ ～层 〈地〉 overburden
【覆灭】 fùmiè destruction; complete collapse: 帝国主义终将逃脱不了最后～的下场。Imperialism will not be able to escape its doom.
【覆没】 fùmò ① 〈书〉 capsize and sink ② be overwhelmed; be annihilated: 敌人全军～。The enemy's whole army was destroyed.
【覆盆之冤】 fù pén zhī yuān irredeemable wrong
【覆盆子】 fùpénzǐ 〈中药〉 Korean raspberry
【覆水难收】 fù shuǐ nán shōu spilt water can't be gathered up — what is done can't be undone
【覆亡】 fùwáng fall (of an empire, nation, etc.)
【覆辙】 fùzhé the track of an overturned cart: 重蹈～ take the same disastrous road

**馥** fù 〈书〉 fragrance

【馥郁】 fùyù 〈书〉 strong fragrance; heavy perfume: ～的花香 the strong scent of flowers

## fu

**咐** fu 见"吩咐" fēnfu; "嘱咐" zhǔfu

# G

## gā

**夹** gā
另见 jiā; jiá
【夹肢窝】 gāzhiwō armpit

**旮** gā
【旮旯儿】 gālár 〈方〉 ① nook; corner: 旮旮旯旯儿都打扫干净了。Every nook and cranny has been swept clean. ② out-of-the-way place: 山～ a mountain recess

**伽** gā
另见 jiā
【伽马】 gāmǎ gamma ◇ ～射线 〈物〉 gamma ray

**咖** gā
另见 kā
【咖喱】 gālí curry: ～牛肉 beef curry ◇ ～粉 curry powder

**嘎** gā
【嘎巴】 gābā 〈象〉〔树枝等折断声〕 crack; snap
【嘎巴】 gāba 〈方〉 ① form into a crust; crust: 瞧，浆糊都～在你袖子上了。Look, the paste has crusted on your sleeve. ② crust: 粥～儿 porridge crust
【嘎嘎】 gāgā 〈象〉〔鸭叫声〕 quack
【嘎吱】 gāzhī 〈象〉 〔物体受压力而发出的声音，多叠用〕 creak: 行李压得扁担～～直响。The shoulder pole creaked under the weight of the luggage.

## gá

**轧** gá 〈方〉 ① press hard against each other ② make friends: ～朋友 make friends with sb. ③ check: ～帐 check the accounts
另见 yà; zhá

**钆** gá 〈化〉 gadolinium (Gd)

## gà

**尬** gà 见"尴尬" gāngà

## gāi

**该** gāi ① ought to; should: 这事你早就～办了！ You ought to have done it long ago./ 本来就～如此。That's just as it should be./ 这会早～开了。The meeting is long overdue./ ～干的都干了。All that needs to be done has been done./ 我们～走了。It's time we were leaving. ② be sb.'s turn to do sth.: 这一回～我了吧？It's my turn now, isn't it?/ 下一个～谁发言？ Who's the next speaker? ③ deserve: 他～受到表扬。He deserves to be commended./ ～！谁叫他不守纪律。It serves him right, he shouldn't have broken the rules. ④ most likely; probably; ought to; should: 再走一个钟头就～到了。We ought to (或 should) be able to get there in another hour./ 你明年春天再来，水库就～完工了。When you come again next spring, the reservoir will have been completed. ⑤〔用在感叹句中加强语气〕: 她的责任～有多重啊！How heavy her responsibilities are!/ 要是水泵今天就运到，～多好哇！ If only the pump could arrive today! ⑥ owe: 我不～他钱。I don't owe him any money./ 没带钱不要紧，先～着吧。It doesn't matter if you haven't brought any money with you. You can have it on credit. ⑦〔多用于公文〕this; that; the said; the above-mentioned: ～厂 this (或 the said) factory/ ～校 that (或 the above-mentioned) school/ ～项工作 the job (或 work) in question
【该当】 gāidāng ① deserve: ～何罪？What punishment do you think you deserve? ② should: 集体的事，我们～尽力。It's for the collective and we should do our best.
【该死】 gāisǐ 〈口〉〔表示厌恶或愤恨的话〕: ～的天气！What wretched weather!/ 这牛又在吃麦子啦！真～！That damned cow's eating the wheat again!/ ～！我又忘了带钥匙了。Oh, no! I've forgotten my key again.
【该帐】 gāizhàng be in debt

**赅** gāi 〈书〉 complete; full: 言简意～ terse but comprehensive

## gǎi

**改** gǎi ① change; transform: 几年没来，这儿完全～样了。I've been away for only a few years, but the place has completely changed./ ～洼地为稻田 transform waterlogged land into paddy fields ② alter; revise: ～灶节煤 make alterations in an oven so that it will burn less coal/ 请把这条裤子～短一些。Please have this pair of trousers shortened./ 这个戏已经～了好多次了。The play has been revised many times. ③ correct; rectify; put right: ～作业 correct students' homework or papers ④〔后接动词〕switch over to (doing sth. else): ～种水稻 switch over to growing rice/ ～乘五路公共汽车 change to a No.5 bus/ ～用良种 begin to use improved varieties/ 他现在～踢左后卫。He's playing left-back now.
【改版】 gǎibǎn 〈印〉 correcting
【改编】 gǎibiān ① adapt; rearrange; revise: 这支歌已～成小提琴曲。The music of the song has been rearranged (或 adapted) for the violin./ 经过～，戏的主题更突出了。The theme of the play stands out even more clearly now that it's been revised./ 根据这本小说～的剧本 a stage version of the novel ② reorganize; redesignate: 把七个师～为六个师 reorganize seven divisions into six/ 抗日战争时期红军～为八路军、新四军。During the War of Resistance Against Japan the Red Army was redesignated as the Eighth Route Army and the New Fourth Army.
【改变】 gǎibiàn change; alter; transform: ～主意 change one's mind/ 人们的精神面貌～了。People's spiritual complexion has changed./ 如果不反修防修，整个中国就会～颜色。If we don't combat and prevent revisionism, the whole of China will change its colour./ 历史发展的总趋势是不可～的。The general trend of history is unalterable.

【改朝换代】 gǎicháo-huàndài change of dynasty or regime; dynastic changes

【改道】 gǎidào ① change one's route: 他们决定～先去延安。They decided to change their route and go to Yan'an first. ② (of a river) change its course: 历史上，黄河曾多次～。The Huanghe River has changed its course many times over the centuries.

【改掉】 gǎidiào give up; drop: ～坏习惯 give up bad habits

【改订】 gǎidìng reformulate; rewrite: ～规章制度 draw up new rules and regulations

【改动】 gǎidòng change; alter; modify: 文字上作少许～ make a few changes in wording

【改恶从善】 gǎi'è-cóngshàn abandon evil and do good; turn over a new leaf; mend one's ways

【改革】 gǎigé reform: 土地～ land (或 agrarian) reform/ 文字～ reform of a writing system/ 工具～ improvement of tools

【改观】 gǎiguān change the appearance (或 face) of: 第二次世界大战后，世界的面貌大大～了。The face of the world has changed greatly since the Second World War./ 这一胜利使战争形势为之～。This victory changed the complexion of the war./ 昔日荒山已经大为～。The barren hills of yesterday have changed considerably.

【改过】 gǎiguò mend one's ways; correct one's mistakes: ～自新 correct one's errors and make a fresh start; mend one's ways; turn over a new leaf

【改行】 gǎiháng change one's profession (或 occupation, trade)

【改换】 gǎihuàn change over to; change: ～一套新的做法 change over to new ways; adopt a new approach/ ～日期 change the date/ ～名称 rename

【改悔】 gǎihuǐ repent: 毫无～之意 show not the least sign of repentance; absolutely unrepentant

【改嫁】 gǎijià (of a woman) remarry

【改建】 gǎijiàn reconstruct; rebuild

【改进】 gǎijìn improve; make better: ～工作作风 improve one's work style/ 有～就好。If you've improved, that's good.

【改口】 gǎikǒu withdraw or modify one's previous remark; correct oneself: 他发现自己说错了，连忙～。He corrected himself as soon as he found he had made a mistake./ 他原来是那么说的，现在～了。That's what he said first, but he's changed it now.

【改良】 gǎiliáng ① improve; ameliorate: ～土壤 improve (或 ameliorate) the soil/ ～家畜品种 improve the breed of domestic animals ② reform ◇ ～派 reformists

【改良主义】 gǎiliángzhǔyì reformism: ～对旧制度主张修修补补，反对革命。Reformism aims at patching up the old system; it is opposed to revolution.

【改判】 gǎipàn 〈法〉 change the original sentence; commute; amend a judgment: 由死刑～无期徒刑 commute the death sentence to life imprisonment

【改期】 gǎiqī change the date: 会议～举行。The meeting has been postponed.

【改任】 gǎirèn change to another post: 他从上月起～车间主任。He has been at his new post as workshop superintendent since last month.

【改日】 gǎirì another day; some other day: 咱们～再商量吧！Let's talk it over another day. 又作"改天"

【改善】 gǎishàn improve; ameliorate: ～劳动条件 improve working conditions/ 两国关系有所～。The relations between the two countries have shown some improvement./ 今天我们～生活。We have something especially good to eat today.

【改天换地】 gǎitiān-huàndì transform heaven and earth; change the world; remake nature: 以～的气概重新安排河山 rearrange the rivers and mountains in a spirit of changing heaven and earth

【改头换面】 gǎitóu-huànmiàn 〈贬〉 change the appearance; dish up in a new form

【改土】 gǎitǔ 〈农〉 improve the soil

【改弦更张】 gǎixián-gēngzhāng change over to new ways; make a fresh start

【改弦易辙】 gǎixián-yìzhé change one's course; strike out on a new path

【改邪归正】 gǎixié-guīzhèng give up evil and return to good; turn over a new leaf

【改写】 gǎixiě rewrite; adapt: 经过～，文章生动多了。Rewriting has livened up the article./ 这篇课文是根据《中国文学》上的一个故事～的。This text is adapted from a story in *Chinese Literature*.

【改性】 gǎixìng 〈化〉 modified ◇ ～剂 modifier/ ～树脂 modified resin

【改选】 gǎixuǎn reelect: 班委会每年～一次。A new class committee is elected every year.

【改元】 gǎiyuán change the designation of an imperial reign; change the title of a reign

【改造】 gǎizào transform; reform; remould; remake: ～思想 remould one's ideology/ ～盐碱地 transform saline-alkali land/ ～自然 remake nature/ 在～客观世界的同时～主观世界 remould one's subjective world while changing the objective world

【改正】 gǎizhèng correct; amend; put right: ～错误 correct one's mistakes

【改装】 gǎizhuāng ① change one's costume or dress ② repackage; repack ③ reequip; refit: ～一辆卡车 refit a truck

【改锥】 gǎizhuī screwdriver

【改组】 gǎizǔ reorganize; reshuffle: ～管理机构 reorganize the management/ ～内阁 reshuffle the cabinet

## gài

**丐** gài 〈书〉 ① beg ② beggar

**芥** gài
另见 jiè

【芥菜】 gàicài 〈植〉 leaf mustard
另见 jiècài

【芥蓝】 gàilán 〈植〉 cabbage mustard

**钙** gài 〈化〉 calcium (Ca)

【钙化】 gàihuà 〈医〉 calcification

【钙镁磷肥】 gàiměilínféi calcium magnesium phosphate

**盖** gài ① lid; cover: 茶壶～ teapot lid/ 轴承～ 〈机〉 bearing cap (或 cover)/ 引擎～ bonnet (或 hood) of an engine ② shell (of a tortoise, crab, etc.) ③ canopy: 亭亭如～ (of a tree) stand towering with a canopy of leaves ④ cover: 用塑料薄膜～住秧苗 cover the seedlings with plastic sheeting/ 箱子没～严。The lid of the box hasn't been put on right. 或 The box isn't closed properly./ 他昨天晚上没～好，着凉了。He didn't cover himself up well last night and now he's got a cold./ 连长象往常一样来给战士们把被子～好。As usual the company commander came to tuck in the lads' bedclothes. ⑤ affix (a seal) ⑥ surpass; top: 大桥通车了，欢庆的锣鼓声～过了江上的浪涛声。When the bridge was opened to traffic, the joyful sounds of gongs and drums drowned the roar of the river./ 他的跳高成绩～过了所有的选手。He excelled all the other contestants in the high jump.

⑦ build: ～新房 build new houses ⑧〈书〉 approximately; about; around: 与会者～一千人。About a thousand people attended the meeting. ⑨〈书〉 for; because; in fact: 有所不知，～未学也。If there are things we do not know, it is because we haven't learnt them. ⑩ (Gài) a surname

【盖菜】 gàicài 〈植〉 leaf mustard

【盖层】 gàicéng 〈石油〉 cap rock

【盖饭】 gàifàn rice served with meat and vegetables on top 又作"盖浇饭"

【盖棺论定】 gài guān lùn dìng final judgment can be passed on a person only when the lid is laid on his coffin

【盖然性】 gàiránxìng 〈逻〉 probability

【盖世】 gàishì unparalleled; matchless; peerless: ～英雄 peerless hero/ ～无双 unparalleled anywhere in the world

【盖世太保】 Gàishìtàibǎo Gestapo

【盖章】 gàizhāng affix one's seal; seal; stamp: 由本人签字～ to be signed and sealed by the recipient or applicant

【盖子】 gàizi ① lid; cover; cap; top: 水壶～ the lid of a kettle/ 瓶～ bottle top/ 揭开两条路线斗争的～ uncover (或 bring to light, reveal) the facts of the two-line struggle/ 捂～ try to cover up the truth (about class struggle, etc.) ② shell (of a tortoise, etc.)

**溉** gài 见"灌溉" guàngài

**概** gài ① general; approximate: ～而论之 generally speaking ② without exception; categorically: ～莫能外 admit of no exception whatsoever/ ～不追究 no action will be taken (against sb. for his past offences)/ 药品售出，～不退换。Once medicines leave the store they may not be returned. ③ the manner of carrying oneself; deportment: 气～ mettle; spirit

【概观】 gàiguān general survey

【概况】 gàikuàng general situation; survey: «非洲～» *A Survey of Africa*/ 我把这里的～介绍一下。I'll give a brief account of how things are in this place.

【概括】 gàikuò ① summarize; generalize; epitomize: 这部小说的优点～起来有以下几方面。The good points of the novel may be summarized as follows./ ～起来说 to sum up/ 高度的艺术～ a highly artistic condensation ② briefly; in broad outline: ～地说 to put it briefly/ 请把你的看法～地讲一讲。Please give your views in broad outline.

【概括性】 gàikuòxìng generality: 最后这段话～很强。The last paragraph is a succinct summary.

【概率】 gàilǜ 〈数〉 probability

【概略】 gàilüè outline; summary: 这只是故事的～。This is only an outline of the story.

【概论】 gàilùn 〔多用于书名〕 outline; introduction: «地质学～» *An Introduction to Geology*

【概貌】 gàimào general picture: 反映人民生活的～ give a general picture of the life of the people

【概念】 gàiniàn concept; conception; notion; idea: 基本～ fundamental conception; basic concept/ 玩弄～游戏 juggle with concepts/ 经过反复实践，人们的脑子里就产生了～。As a result of repeated practice, concepts are formed in man's brains./ 我对这件事只有一点模糊的～。I have only a hazy idea about it.

【概念化】 gàiniànhuà deal in generalities; write or speak in abstract terms: 公式化、～的作品 literary works which tend to formularize and generalize

【概数】 gàishù approximate number; round number

【概算】 gàisuàn 〈经〉 budgetary estimate

【概要】 gàiyào 〔多用于书名〕 essentials; outline: «汉语语法～» *Essentials of Chinese Grammar*

## gān

**干** gān ①〈古〉 shield ②〈书〉 offend: ～犯 offend ③ have to do with; be concerned with; be implicated in: 与你何～? What has this to do with you?/ 这事与我无～。It has nothing to do with me. 或 It's none of my business. ④ dry: 这天气洗衣服～得慢。The washing dries slowly in this weather./ 池塘快～了。The pond is running dry./ 口～ thirsty/ 油漆未～。Wet paint. ⑤ dried food: 豆腐～儿 dried bean curd/ 萝卜～儿 dried radish/ 牛肉～儿 dried beef; jerked beef ⑥ empty; hollow; dry: 外强中～ outwardly strong but inwardly weak/ ～号 cry aloud but shed no tears; affected wailing ⑦ taken into nominal kinship: ～儿子 (nominally) adopted son ⑧ (do sth.) for nothing; futilely: 他们上午不来，咱们别～等了。They're not coming this morning. Let's not waste time waiting for them. ⑨〈方〉 cold-shoulder; leave sb. out in the cold: 主人走了，把他们～在这儿了。The host went off, leaving them out in the cold.

另见 gàn

【干巴】 gānba 〈口〉 dried up; shrivelled; wizened: 枣儿都晒～了。The dates have all dried up in the sun./人老了，皮肤就变得～了。When a person grows old, his skin shrivels.

【干巴巴】 gānbābā dull and dry; insipid; dryasdust; dull as ditchwater: ～的土地 parched land/ 文章写得～的。The article is dull.

【干板】 gānbǎn 〈摄〉 dry plate

【干杯】 gānbēi drink a toast: 我提议为两国人民的友谊～! I now propose a toast to the friendship between our two peoples — to our friendship!/ 为朋友们的健康～! Here's to the health of our friends — to your health!/ 老王，～! Lao Wang, cheers!

【干贝】 gānbèi 〈食品〉 dried scallop (adductor)

【干瘪】 gānbiě shrivelled; wizened

【干冰】 gānbīng 〈化〉 dry ice

【干菜】 gāncài dried vegetable

【干草】 gāncǎo hay ◇ ～垛 haystack

【干脆】 gāncuì ① clear-cut; straightforward: 他回答得很～。His answer was simple and straightforward. 或 He gave a clear-cut reply./ 我～跟你说吧。I'll be frank with you./ ～一点嘛! Make it snappy! 或 Be quick about it! ② simply; just; altogether: 你～说"行"还是"不行"。Just say yes or no./ 她～不承认有这回事。She simply denied that such a thing had ever happened.

【干打雷，不下雨】 gān dǎléi bù xiàyǔ thunder but no rain — much noise but no action

【干打垒】 gāndǎlěi a house with walls of rammed earth; rammed-earth construction

【干瞪眼】 gāndèngyǎn 〈口〉 stand by anxiously, unable to help; look on in despair

【干电池】 gāndiànchí dry cell ◇ ～组 dry battery

【干犯】 gānfàn offend; encroach upon: ～法纪 break the law and violate discipline

【干饭】 gānfàn cooked rice

【干纺】 gānfǎng dry spinning ◇ ～纱 dry-spun yarn

【干戈】 gāngē weapons of war; arms; war: 动～ take up arms; go to war

【干果】 gānguǒ ① dry fruit (e.g. nuts) ② dried fruit

【干旱】 gānhàn (of weather or soil) arid; dry

【干涸】 gānhé dry up; run dry: 河道～。The river dried up.

【干货】 gānhuò dried food and nuts (as merchandise)

【干结】 gānjié dry and hard: 大便～ constipated

【干净】 gānjìng ① clean; neat and tidy: 把院子扫～ sweep

the yard clean/ 屋子收拾得挺～。The room is neat and tidy./ 干干净净过春节 give every place a thorough cleaning for the Spring Festival ②completely; totally: 把谷子扬～ winnow the grain thoroughly/ 忘得干干净净 have completely forgotten; clean forgot

【干净利落】 gānjìng-lìluo neat and tidy; neat; efficient: 这一仗打得～。The battle was neatly won./ 他办事～。He's very efficient.

【干咳】 gānké dry cough

【干枯】 gānkū dried-up; withered; shrivelled; wizened: ～的树木 withered trees/ ～的皮肤 wizened skin/ 小河～了。The stream has dried up.

【干酪】 gānlào cheese ◇ ～素 casein

【干冷】 gānlěng dry and cold (weather)

【干粮】 gānliang solid food (prepared for a journey); field rations; rations for a journey: 明天郊游，请自带～。Bring your own food on tomorrow's outing. ◇ ～袋 haversack; ration bag

【干馏】 gānliú 〈化〉 dry distillation

【干呕】 gān'ǒu 〈医〉 retch

【干亲】 gānqīn nominal kinship

【干扰】 gānrǎo ① disturb; interfere; obstruct: 把收音机开小点儿，别～人家。Turn down the radio, or you'll disturb people./ 修正主义路线的～ disruption caused by the revisionist line/ 排除～，坚持正确路线 overcome obstruction and adhere to the correct line ②〈电〉 interference; jam ◇ ～台 jamming station

【干鞣法】 gānróufǎ 〈皮革〉 dry tannage

【干涉】 gānshè ①interfere; intervene; meddle: 外来～ external interference/ 武装～ armed intervention/ 互不～内政 noninterference in each other's internal affairs ②〈物〉 interference: 相长(相消)～ constructive (destructive) interference ◇ ～仪 interferometer

【干湿表】 gānshībiǎo 〈气〉 psychrometer

【干瘦】 gānshòu skinny; bony

【干洗】 gānxǐ dry-clean; dry cleaning

【干系】 gānxi responsibility; implication: 逃脱不了～ cannot shirk the responsibility/ 他同这桩案子有～。He is involved in the case.

【干舷】 gānxián freeboard

【干笑】 gānxiào hollow laugh

【干薪】 gānxīn salary drawn for a sinecure: 领～ hold a sinecure

【干选】 gānxuǎn 〈矿〉 dry separation

【干血痨】 gānxuèláo 〈中医〉 type of tubercular disease found in women, usu. characterized by menostasis, recurrent low fever and general debility

【干眼症】 gānyǎnzhèng 〈医〉 xerophthalmia

【干预】 gānyù intervene; interpose; meddle: 这是你们内部的事情，我们不便～。This is your internal affair; it is not for us to interfere.

【干燥】 gānzào ①dry; arid: 气候～ arid climate/ 大便～ constipated; costive ②dull; uninteresting: ～无味 dryasdust; dull ◇ ～剂 drier; drying agent; desiccating agent/ ～器 〈化〉 desiccator

【干着急】 gānzháojí be anxious but unable to do anything

【干支】 gān-zhī the Heavenly Stems and Earthly Branches (two sets of signs, with one being taken from each set to form 60 pairs, designating years, formerly also months and days)

# 甘

gān ①sweet; pleasant: ～泉 sweet spring water ② willingly; of one's own accord: ～当群众的小学生 be a willing pupil of the masses/ 不～落后 unwilling to lag behind ③ (Gān) short for Gansu Province ④(Gān) a surname

【甘拜下风】 gān bài xiàfēng candidly admit defeat (in friendly competition, etc.)

【甘草】 gāncǎo 〈中药〉 licorice root

【甘汞】 gāngǒng 〈化〉 calomel; mercurous chloride ◇ ～电池 calomel cell

【甘苦】 gānkǔ ①sweetness and bitterness; weal and woe: 同甘共苦 share the joys and sorrows ②hardships and difficulties experienced in work: 没有搞过这种工作，就不知道其中的～。You don't know how difficult the job is, unless you have done it yourself.

【甘蓝】 gānlán 〈植〉 wild cabbage

【甘霖】 gānlín a good rain after a long drought; timely rainfall

【甘露】 gānlù ①sweet dew ②〈医〉 manna

【甘露子】 gānlùzǐ 〈植〉 Chinese artichoke (*Stachys sieboldii*)

【甘美】 gānměi sweet and refreshing

【甘薯】 gānshǔ sweet potato ◇ ～黑斑病 sweet potato black rot/ ～软腐病 sweet potato soft rot

【甘肃】 Gānsù Gansu (Province)

【甘遂】 gānsuì 〈中药〉 the root of *gansui* (*Euphorbia kansui*)

【甘心】 gānxīn ①willingly; readily: ～情愿 willingly and gladly ②be reconciled to; resign oneself to; be content with: 阶级敌人对于他们的失败是不会～的。The class enemy will not resign themselves to defeat.

【甘休】 gānxiū be willing to give up: 试验不成功，决不～。We won't give up until the experiment succeeds.

【甘油】 gānyóu 〈化〉 glycerine

【甘于】 gānyú be willing to; be ready to; be happy to: ～牺牲个人利益 be ready to sacrifice one's personal interests

【甘愿】 gānyuàn willingly; readily

【甘蔗】 gānzhe sugarcane: ～没有两头甜。A sugarcane is never sweet at both ends — you can't have it both ways. ◇ ～板 〈建〉 cane fibre board/ ～渣 bagasse/ ～渣浆厂 bagasse-pulp mill

【甘之如饴】 gān zhī rú yí enjoy sth. bitter as if it were malt sugar; gladly endure hardships

# 杆

gān pole; staff: 旗～ flagstaff; flagpole/ 电线～ pole (for telephone or electric power lines, etc.)
另见 gǎn

【杆子】 gānzi pole

# 肝

gān liver

【肝癌】 gān'ái 〈医〉 cancer of the liver

【肝胆】 gāndǎn ①liver and gall: ～俱裂 overwhelmed by grief or terror; heart-broken or terror-stricken ②heroic spirit; courage: ～过人 unsurpassed in valour ③openheartedness; sincerity: ～相照 show utter devotion to (a friend, etc.)

【肝功能】 gāngōngnéng liver function ◇ ～试验 liver function test

【肝火】 gānhuǒ irascibility: 动～ get worked up; fly into a rage/ ～旺 hot-tempered; irascible

【肝脑涂地】 gān-nǎo tú dì (ready to) die the cruelest death

【肝气】 gānqì ①〈中医〉 diseases with such symptoms as costal pain, vomiting, diarrhoea, etc. ②irritability

【肝素】 gānsù 〈药〉 heparin

【肝泰乐】 gāntàilè 〈药〉 glucurolactone; glucurone

【肝吸虫】 gānxīchóng 〈动〉 liver fluke

【肝炎】 gānyán 〈医〉 hepatitis

【肝硬变】 gānyìngbiàn 〈医〉 cirrhosis (of the liver)

【肝脏】 gānzàng liver

【肝蛭】 gānzhì liver fluke

【肝肿大】 gānzhǒngdà 〈医〉 hepatomegaly

**泔** gān

【泔水】 gānshuǐ swill; slops; hogwash

**矸** gān

【矸石】 gānshí 〈矿〉 waste (rock)

**坩** gān

【坩埚】 gānguō 〈化〉 crucible: 石墨～ graphite (或 carbon) crucible ◇ ～炉 〈冶〉 crucible furnace

**苷** gān 〈化〉 glucoside

**柑** gān mandarin orange

【柑橘】 gānjú ① oranges and tangerines ② citrus ◇ ～酱 marmalade

【柑子】 gānzi mandarin orange

**竿** gān pole; rod: 竹～ bamboo pole/ 钓鱼～ fishing rod

【竿子】 gānzi bamboo pole: 一～插到底 carry (a task or directive) right down to the grass-roots level

**疳** gān 〈中医〉 infantile malnutrition due to digestive disturbances or intestinal parasites

**酐** gān 〈化〉 anhydride: 醋酸～ acetic anhydride/ 碱～ basic anhydride

**尴** gān

【尴尬】 gāngà awkward; embarrassed: 处境～ in an awkward position; in a dilemma/ 样子十分～ look very much embarrassed

## gǎn

**杆** gǎn ① the shaft or arm of sth.: 秤～ the arm of a steelyard/ 钢笔～儿 penholder/ 枪～ the barrel of a rifle/ 保险～ 〈机〉 bumper bar/ 调整～ 〈机〉 adjusting rod ② 〈量〉〔用于有杆的器物〕: 一～秤 a steelyard/ 一～枪 a rifle/ 一～红旗 a red flag

另见 gān

【杆秤】 gǎnchèng steelyard

【杆菌】 gǎnjūn 〈微〉 bacillus: 结核～ tubercle bacillus ◇ ～载体 bacillus carrier

**秆** gǎn stalk: 高粱～ sorghum stalk/ 麻～ hemp stalk

**赶** gǎn ① catch up with; overtake: ～先进 catch up with the advanced/ 后进的也～上来了。Those who lagged behind have caught up./ 要说摘棉花，可谁也～不上她。Nobody can keep up with her in picking cotton./ 她已经～到大伙儿前头去了。She's shot ahead of all the rest of us. ② try to catch; make a dash for; rush for: ～头班车 catch the first bus/ 火车七点三十分开，我们～得及吗？The train leaves at 7:30. Can we make it? ③ hurry (或 rush) through: ～任务 rush through one's job/ ～前不～后。It's better to hurry at the beginning than to do things in a rush at the last moment./ 他连夜～写了一份大字报。He dashed off a *dazibao* that very night./ ～调了一个团到灾区去帮助救灾。A regiment was rushed to the stricken area to help with relief work. ④ drive: ～大车 drive a cart/ 把羊～到山上去放 drive the sheep up the hill to graze ⑤ drive away; expel: 把敌人～走 drive the enemy away; throw out the enemy/ 辛亥革命～跑了一个皇帝，但是没有摧毁封建统治的基础。The 1911 Revolution sent an emperor packing, but failed to demolish the foundation of feudal rule./ ～苍蝇 whisk the flies off; brush away a fly ⑥ happen to; find oneself in (a situation); avail oneself of (an opportunity): 我去了两趟，正～上他下厂去了。I went there twice, but he happened to be away at the factory each time./ 得～好天把场打完。We've got to finish the threshing while the good weather lasts. ⑦ 〈介〉〔用于时间词前表示等到某个时候〕: 咱俩的婚事～年下再办吧。Let's put off our wedding till the Spring Festival.

【赶集】 gǎnjí go to market; go to a fair

【赶紧】 gǎnjǐn lose no time; hasten: ～刹车 quickly put on the brakes/ ～解释 hasten to explain/ 发现情况，～报告。If you find anything unusual, report at once./ 他～吃了饭就上工地去了。He had a hurried meal and made for the construction site.

【赶尽杀绝】 gǎnjìn-shājué spare none; be ruthless

【赶快】 gǎnkuài at once; quickly: ～跟我走。Come along with me at once./ ～把这块地收完。Let's finish reaping this plot quickly./ ～! Be quick! 或 Hurry up!

【赶浪头】 gǎn làngtou follow the trend

【赶路】 gǎnlù hurry on with one's journey: 快休息吧，明天一早还要～呢。Let's go to bed right away. We must push on with our journey early tomorrow morning./ 赶了一天路，累了吧？Aren't you tired after such a hard day's journey?

【赶忙】 gǎnmáng hurry; hasten; make haste: 趁还没熄灯，他～把最后两页书看完。He hurried through the last two pages before lights-out./ 他～道歉。He hastened to apologize.

【赶明儿】 gǎnmíngr 〈方〉 one of these days; another day

【赶巧】 gǎnqiǎo happen to; it so happened that: 这次进城，～跟张大爷同车。On my way to the city, I happened to ride in the same bus as Grandpa Zhang.

【赶上】 gǎnshàng ① overtake; catch up with; keep pace with: ～先进单位 catch up with the advanced units/ ～时代的发展 keep abreast of the times/ 我们的认识常常赶不上形势的发展。Our knowledge often fails to keep pace with the march of events. ② run into (a situation); be in time for: 我到北京那天正～过国庆。It happened to be National Day when I arrived in Beijing./ 你要～渔汛来，就能跟我们一块儿出海了。If you come during the fishing season, you'll be able to go out to sea with us./ 没～车 miss the bus or the train

【赶时髦】 gǎn shímáo follow the fashion; try to be in the swim

【赶趟儿】 gǎntàngr 〈口〉 be in time for: 我们要不快点儿走，就赶不上趟儿了。We'll be late if we don't hurry.

【赶鸭子上架】 gǎn yāzi shàng jià drive a duck onto a perch — make sb. do sth. entirely beyond him

**敢** gǎn ① bold; courageous; daring: 果～ courageous and resolute; daring ② dare: 要～想、～说、～干。We should dare to think, dare to speak and dare to act./ ～教山河换新装 dare to rearrange the mountains and rivers ③ have the confidence to; be certain: 我不～说他究竟哪一天来。I'm not sure just what day he will come. ④ 〈书〉 make bold; venture: ～问 I venture to ask; may I ask

【敢怒而不敢言】 gǎn nù ér bùgǎn yán be forced to keep one's resentment to oneself; suppress one's rage; choke with silent fury

【敢情】 gǎnqing 〈方〉 〈副〉 ①〔表示发现原来没有发现的情况〕 why; so; I say: ～这屋子都笼上火啦！Oh, so there's a fire in the room already! ②〔表示情理明显〕 of course; indeed; really: 去大寨参观？那～好！Are we going to visit

Dazhai? That'll be really wonderful.

【敢死队】 gǎnsǐduì 〈旧〉 dare-to-die corps

【敢于】 gǎnyú dare to; be bold in; have the courage to: ～斗争,～胜利 dare to struggle and dare to win

**感** gǎn ①feel; sense: 身体略～不适 not feel very well; be under the weather; be out of sorts/ 他～到自己错了。He sensed that he himself was wrong./ 她对草原上的一切都～到新鲜。She found everything on the grasslands new and attractive. ②move; touch; affect: ～人 touching; moving ③be grateful; be obliged: 请早日寄下为～。I should be grateful if you would send it to me at an early date. ④〈中医〉be affected: 外～风寒 be affected by the cold; have a cold ⑤sense; feeling: 责任～ sense of responsibility/ 民族自豪～ sense of national pride/ 读后～ reaction to (或 impressions of) a book or an article/ 给人以一种新鲜～ engender a feeling of freshness

【感触】 gǎnchù thoughts and feelings; feeling: 深有～地说 say with deep feeling

【感动】 gǎndòng move; touch: ～得流下眼泪 be moved to tears/ 深为他的革命精神所～ be deeply touched by his revolutionary spirit

【感恩】 gǎn'ēn feel grateful; be thankful: ～图报 be grateful to sb. and seek ways to return his kindness/ ～戴德 be deeply grateful

【感奋】 gǎnfèn be moved and inspired; be fired with enthusiasm: 老红军的报告令人～。Everybody was moved and inspired by the veteran Red Army man's talk.

【感官】 gǎnguān sense organ; sensory organ

【感光】 gǎnguāng 〈摄〉 sensitization
◇～度 (light) sensitivity/ ～计 sensitometer/ ～性树脂版〈印〉 photopolymer plate/ ～纸 sensitive paper

【感化】 gǎnhuà help (a misguided or erring person) to change by persuasion, setting an example, etc.

【感怀】 gǎnhuái ①recall with emotion: ～往事 recall past events with deep feeling ②reflections; thoughts; recollections: 新春～ thoughts on the Spring Festival

【感激】 gǎnjī feel grateful; be thankful; feel indebted: ～涕零 shed grateful tears; be moved to tears of gratitude/ 不胜～ be deeply grateful; feel very much indebted

【感觉】 gǎnjué ①sense perception; sensation; feeling: 概念同～的区别 the difference between concepts and sense perceptions/ ～和思想只是外部世界的反映。Sensations and ideas are only reflections of the external world./ 这只是我个人的～。That's only my personal feeling./ ～只解决现象问题,理论才解决本质问题。Perception only solves the problem of phenomena; theory alone can solve the problem of essence. ②feel; perceive; become aware of: 你～怎么样? How do you feel now?/ 他～到了问题的严重性。He became aware of the seriousness of the matter.
◇～论〈哲〉 sensualism/ ～器官 sense organ/ ～神经 sensory nerve/ ～阈限〈心〉 sense limen; sense threshold

【感慨】 gǎnkǎi sigh with emotion: ～万端 all sorts of feelings well up in one's mind

【感冒】 gǎnmào common cold: 患～ catch cold; have a cold

【感念】 gǎnniàn remember with gratitude; recall with deep emotion

【感情】 gǎnqíng ①emotion; feeling; sentiment: 动～ be carried away by one's emotions; get worked up/ 伤～ hurt sb.'s feelings/ 小资产阶级～ petty-bourgeois sentiments/ 思想～开始发生变化 experience a change in one's thoughts and feelings ②affection; attachment; love: 我们对延安的一草一木都怀有深厚的～。We cherish a deep affection for every tree and bush in Yan'an.

【感情用事】 gǎnqíng yòngshì be swayed by one's emotions; act impetuously

【感染】 gǎnrǎn ①infect: 细菌～ bacterial infection/ 手术后～ postoperative infection ②influence; infect; affect: 她的革命乐观主义～了周围的人。Her revolutionary optimism was infectious./ 诗人的激情～了每一个读者。The poet's passion affected all his readers./ 艺术～力 artistic appeal (或 power)

【感伤】 gǎnshāng sad; sorrowful; sentimental

【感生】 gǎnshēng 〈电〉 induced: ～电流 induced current

【感受】 gǎnshòu ①be affected by: ～风寒 be affected by the cold; catch cold ②experience; feel: 我才来几天,就～到这个革命集体的温暖。I've been here only a few days and I've already experienced the warmth of this revolutionary collective./ 这次去东北参观～很深。My visit to the Northeast made a deep impression on me. ◇ ～器〈生理〉 receptor

【感叹】 gǎntàn sigh with feeling
◇～词 interjection; exclamation/ ～号 exclamation mark; exclamation point (!)/ ～句 exclamatory sentence

【感想】 gǎnxiǎng impressions; reflections; thoughts: 请你谈谈看了这部影片后的～。Please tell us your impressions of the film. 或 Tell us what you think of the film./ 把～当政策 substitute one's personal feelings for policy

【感谢】 gǎnxiè thank; be grateful: 表示衷心的～ express heartfelt thanks/ 非常～你的帮助。Thank you very much for your help. ◇ ～信 letter of thanks

【感性】 gǎnxìng perceptual: ～认识 perceptual knowledge/ 认识的～阶段 the perceptual stage of cognition ◇ ～运动〈生〉 nastic movement/ ～知觉〈心〉 sense impressions

【感应】 gǎnyìng ①response; reaction; interaction ②〈生〉 irritability ③〈电〉 induction: 电磁～ electromagnetic induction/ 静电～ electrostatic induction
◇～干扰 inductive interference/ ～率 inductivity/ ～式话筒 inductor microphone/ ～线圈 induction coil; inductor

【感召】 gǎnzhào move and inspire; impel: 在党的政策～下 under the influence of the Party's policy

**橄** gǎn

【橄榄】 gǎnlǎn 〈植〉 ① Chinese olive (*Canarium album*); the fruit of the canary tree ② olive
◇～绿 olive green/ ～球〈体〉 Rugby (football)/ ～石〈矿〉 olivine/ ～岩〈地〉 peridotite/ ～油 olive oil/ ～枝 olive branch

**擀** gǎn ①roll (dough, etc.): ～饺子皮 roll out dumpling wrappers/ ～面条 make noodles ②〈方〉 polish; shine: 用湿布把玻璃窗擦完后,再用干布～一～。When you've finished cleaning the windows with a wet towel, polish them with a dry one.

【擀面杖】 gǎnmiànzhàng rolling pin

## gàn

**干** gàn ①trunk; main part: 树～ tree-trunk; trunk/ 骨～ backbone; hard core; mainstay ②〈简〉(干部) cadre: 高～ senior cadre/ ～群关系 relations between cadres and the masses; cadre-mass relations ③do; work: 叫我～什么都行。I'll do any job I may be assigned to./ 咱们～吧! Let's get cracking! 或 Let's get started!/ ～社会主义 build socialism; work for socialism/ ～革命靠毛泽东思想。Making (或 Waging) revolution depends on Mao Zedong Thought. ④ fight; strike: ～到底 fight to the bitter end ⑤capable; able: ～员 a capable official

另见 gān

【干部】 gànbù cadre: 各级领导～ leading cadres at all levels ◇ ～政策 policy towards cadres; cadre policy

【干才】 gàncái ① ability; capability ② capable (或 able) person

【干掉】 gàndiào 〈口〉 kill; get rid of; put sb. out of the way: 先～敌人的哨兵。Get rid of the enemy sentry first.

【干活】 gànhuó work; work on a job: ～去吧。Let's get to work./ 他们都在～呢。They are all at work. 或 They are all on the job./ 今儿你干什么活啊？What's your job for today?

【干架】 gànjià ① quarrel ② come to blows

【干将】 gànjiàng capable person; go-getter

【干劲】 gànjìn drive; vigour; enthusiasm: 鼓～ rouse one's enthusiasm/ ～十足 be full of vigour (或 drive)/ 冲天的革命～ soaring revolutionary enthusiasm

【干了】 gànle 〈方〉 too bad; what a mess: ～，车闸坏了。That's fixed it; the brakes are out of order.

【干练】 gànliàn capable and experienced

【干流】 gànliú trunk stream; mainstream

【干吗】 gànmá 〈口〉 ① why on earth; whatever for: ～这么大规矩？Why all this formality? ② what to do: 今儿下午～？ What are we going to do this afternoon?/ 你想～？What are you up to?

【干渠】 gànqú 〈水〉 trunk canal; main canal

【干什么】 gàn shénme 见"干吗"

【干事】 gànshi a secretary (或 clerical worker) in charge of sth.: 文娱～ person in charge of recreational activities

【干线】 gànxiàn main line; trunk line; artery: 公路～ arterial or main highway/ 交通～ main lines of communication

【干校】 gànxiào 〈简〉(干部学校) a school for cadres; cadre school: 五七～ May 7 cadre school

**绀** gàn dark purple

【绀青】 gànqīng dark purple; prune purple

**赣** Gàn another name for Jiangxi Province

## gāng

**冈** gāng ridge (of a hill): 景阳～ the Jingyang Ridge

【冈比亚】 Gāngbǐyà the Gambia ◇ ～人 Gambian

**扛** gāng ① lift with both hands ② 〈方〉 (of two or more people) carry together

另见 káng

**刚** gāng ① firm; strong; indomitable: 革命人民志气～。The revolutionary people have an indomitable will./ 她的舞蹈柔中有～。There is strength as well as grace in her dancing. ② 〈副〉 just; exactly: 这双鞋大小～合适。This pair of shoes is just the right size. 或 This pair of shoes fits perfectly. ③ 〈副〉 barely; only just: 我参加八路军时，～跟枪一般高。When I joined the Eighth Route Army, I was barely the height of a rifle. ④ 〈副〉 only a short while ago; just: 她～走。She has just gone./ 她～来过。She was here just now./ 他～到农村时，连麦子韭菜都分不清。When he first came to the countryside, he couldn't tell wheat from Chinese chives.

【刚愎自用】 gāngbì zìyòng self-willed; headstrong; opinionated

【刚才】 gāngcái just now; a moment ago: 别把～跟你说的事忘了。Don't forget what I told you just now./ 他～还说要去呢。He was saying only a moment ago that he wanted to go.

【刚刚】 gānggang 〈副〉 ① just; only; exactly: 上次讨论会到现在～一个月。It's only a month since the last discussion./ 那时候天～亮。It was just beginning to get light. ② a moment ago; just now: 报纸～到。The newspaper came just now.

【刚果】 Gāngguǒ the Congo ◇ ～河 the Congo (River)/ ～红 Congo red/ ～人 Congolese/ ～语 Congolese (language)

【刚好】 gānghǎo ① just; exactly: 我们～赶上末班车。We just managed to catch the last bus./ 你们来得～。You've come in the nick of time. ② happen to; it so happened that: 他们两人～编在一个组里。The two of them happened to be in the same group./ ～书记在这儿，你就跟他谈谈吧。The Party secretary happens to be here. You'd better talk it over with him.

【刚架】 gāngjià 〈建〉 rigid frame ◇ ～结构 rigid-framed structure

【刚健】 gāngjiàn vigorous; energetic; robust: ～的舞姿 vigorous movements of a dancer

【刚劲】 gāngjìng bold; vigorous; sturdy: 笔力～ write in a bold hand/ ～的松枝 sturdy boughs of a pine

【刚…就…】 gāng…jiù… 〔表示两件事紧接〕 as soon as; no sooner than; immediately: 他刚开完会回来，就下地干活去了。As soon as he got back from the conference, he went to work in the fields.

【刚毛】 gāngmáo 〈动〉 bristle; seta; chaeta

【刚强】 gāngqiáng firm; staunch; unyielding

【刚巧】 gāngqiǎo 见"刚好"②

【刚体】 gāngtǐ 〈物〉 rigid body

【刚性】 gāngxìng 〈物〉 rigidity ◇ ～结构 rigid structure

【刚毅】 gāngyì resolute and steadfast: 在斗争中表现得非常～和机智 display both fortitude and resourcefulness in the struggle

【刚玉】 gāngyù 〈矿〉 corundum

【刚正】 gāngzhèng upright; honourable; principled: ～不阿 upright and never stooping to flattery

【刚直】 gāngzhí upright and outspoken

**纲** gāng ① the headrope of a fishing net ② key link; guiding principle: 以阶级斗争为～ take class struggle as the key link ③ outline; programme: 党章总～ the general programme of the Party Constitution ④ 〈生〉 class: 哺乳动物～ the class of mammals/ 亚～ subclass ⑤ transportation of goods under convoy (in feudal China): 盐～ salt transported under convoy; salt convoy

【纲常】 gāngcháng 见"三纲五常" sāngāng wǔcháng

【纲举目张】 gāngjǔ-mùzhāng once the headrope of a fishing net is pulled up, all its meshes open: 路线是个纲，～。The line is the key link; once it is grasped, everything falls into place.

【纲领】 gānglǐng programme; guiding principle: 最低(高)～ minimum (maximum) programme/ ～性文件 programmatic document

【纲目】 gāngmù 〔多用于书名〕 detailed outline (of a subject); outline

【纲要】 gāngyào ① outline; sketch: 他把意见写成～，准备在会上发言。He made an outline of his views and got ready to present them at the meeting. ② essentials; compendium: 《英语语法～》 *Essentials of English Grammar* ③ 〈简〉(《全国农业发展纲要》) *The National Programme for Agricultural Development:* 全县粮食上～。The county's grain yield has reached the target set by *The National Programme for Agricultural Development.*

**肛** gāng anus

【肛裂】 gāngliè 〈医〉 anal fissure
【肛瘘】 gānglòu 〈医〉 anal fistula
【肛门】 gāngmén anus

**缸** gāng vat; jar; crock: 水～ water vat/ 一～咸菜 a jar of salted vegetables/ 金鱼～ goldfish bowl
【缸管】 gāngguǎn earthen pipe
【缸盆】 gāngpén glazed earthen basin
【缸瓦】 gāngwǎ a compound of sand, clay, etc. for making earthenware
【缸砖】 gāngzhuān clinker (tile); quarry tile
【缸子】 gāngzi mug; bowl: 茶～ (tea) mug/ 糖～ sugar bowl

**钢** gāng steel: 炼～ steelmaking/ 不锈～ stainless steel
另见 gàng
【钢板】 gāngbǎn ①steel plate; plate: 锅炉～ boiler plate/ 造船～ ship plate ②spring (of a motorcar, etc.) ③stencil steel board
【钢笔】 gāngbǐ pen; fountain pen ◇ ～画 pen-and-ink drawing
【钢材】 gāngcái steel products; steels; rolled steel
【钢尺】 gāngchǐ steel rule
【钢锭】 gāngdìng steel ingot
【钢骨水泥】 gānggǔ shuǐní reinforced concrete
【钢管】 gāngguǎn steel tube (或 pipe): 无缝～ seamless steel tube/ 焊接～ welded steel pipe
【钢轨】 gāngguǐ rail ◇ ～探伤仪 rail flaw detector
【钢号】 gānghào 〈冶〉 steel grade
【钢花】 gānghuā spray (或 sparks) of molten steel
【钢化玻璃】 gānghuà bōli toughened glass
【钢结构】 gāngjiégòu 〈建〉 steel structure
【钢筋】 gāngjīn reinforcing bar ◇ ～混凝土 reinforced concrete
【钢精】 gāngjīng aluminium (as used for utensils) ◇ ～锅 aluminium pan
【钢锯】 gāngjù hacksaw ◇ ～架 hacksaw frame/ ～条 hacksaw blade
【钢筘】 gāngkòu 〈纺〉 reed
【钢盔】 gāngkuī (steel) helmet
【钢坯】 gāngpī 〈冶〉 billet: 大～ bloom
【钢片琴】 gāngpiànqín 〈乐〉 celesta
【钢钎】 gāngqiān drill rod; drill steel
【钢琴】 gāngqín piano: 弹～ play the piano/ 大～ grand piano/ 竖式～ upright piano ◇ ～家 pianist
【钢水】 gāngshuǐ 〈冶〉 molten steel ◇ ～包 steel ladle
【钢丝】 gāngsī (steel) wire: 走～ 〈杂技〉 walk the wire; walk the tightrope; high-wire walking
◇ ～床 spring bed/ ～垫子 spring mattress/ ～锯 fret saw; scroll saw/ ～录音机 wire recorder/ ～钳 combination pliers; cutting pliers/ ～绳 steel cable; wire rope
【钢铁】 gāngtiě iron and steel; steel: ～意志 iron will/ ～运输线 an unbreakable transportation line/ ～战士 a dauntless fighter/ 解放军是保卫祖国的～长城。 The PLA is a great wall of steel guarding our country.
◇ ～厂 steelworks/ ～工业 iron and steel industry/ ～公司 iron and steel company/ ～联合企业 integrated iron and steel works; iron and steel complex
【钢印】 gāngyìn ①steel seal; embossing seal ②embossed stamp
【钢珠】 gāngzhū steel ball (in a ball bearing); ball bearing; ball

## gǎng

**岗** gǎng ①hillock; mound: ～峦起伏 undulating hills ②ridge; welt; wale ③sentry; post: 站～ stand sentry; keep guard/ 布～ post a sentinel/ 下～ come off sentry duty
【岗警】 gǎngjǐng policeman on point duty
【岗楼】 gǎnglóu watchtower
【岗哨】 gǎngshào ①lookout post ②sentry; sentinel: 设置～ post sentries
【岗亭】 gǎngtíng sentry box; police box
【岗位】 gǎngwèi post; station: 战斗～ fighting post; battle station/ 坚守～ stand fast at one's post; stick to one's guns/ 走上新的～ take up a new post; take on a new job ◇ ～责任制 system of personal responsibility (for each section of a production line, etc.)
【岗子】 gǎngzi ①mound; hillock ②ridge; wale; welt

**港** gǎng ①port; harbour: 天然～ natural harbour/ 停靠～ port of call ②(Gǎng) short for Xianggang
【港汊】 gǎngchà branching stream
【港口】 gǎngkǒu port; harbour: 沿海～ coastal port
◇ ～规章 harbour regulations/ ～吞吐量 traffic (of a port)/ ～税 port dues
【港湾】 gǎngwān harbour
【港务费】 gǎngwùfèi harbour dues
【港务监督】 gǎngwù jiāndū harbour superintendency administration
【港务局】 gǎngwùjú port office

## gàng

**杠** gàng ①thick stick; stout carrying pole ②〈体〉 bar: 单～ horizontal bar/ 双～ parallel bars ③thick line (drawn beside or under words in reading, correcting papers, etc.) ④cross out; delete: 她把草稿中不必要的词句都～掉了。She crossed out all the superfluous words and phrases in the draft.
【杠棒】 gàngbàng stout carrying pole
【杠杆】 gànggǎn lever
◇ ～臂 lever arm/ ～原理 lever principle/ ～率 leverage
【杠铃】 gànglíng 〈体〉 barbell ◇ ～片 disc (of a barbell)
【杠子】 gàngzi ①thick stick; stout carrying pole ②〈体〉 bar ③见"杠"③

**钢** gàng ①sharpen; whet; strop: ～菜刀 sharpen a kitchen knife/ ～镰刀 whet a sickle/ ～剃刀 strop a razor ②reinforce the edge (of a knife, etc.) by adding steel and retempering
另见 gāng
【钢刀布】 gàngdāobù (razor) strop

## gāo

**高** gāo ①tall; high: 她比小红～一头。 She's a head taller than Xiao Hong./ 坝～四十米。The dam is 40 metres high (或 in height)./ 这片地中间～起一块。There is a mound in the middle of the field. ②of a high level or degree; above the average: ～年级 higher (或 senior) grades/ ～质量 high (或 good) quality/ ～招 masterstroke/ ～醋 top-quality vinegar/ ～风格 fine style/ ～难度动作 exceedingly difficult movements; operations of extraordinary difficulty/ 他的思想境界比我～。He has nobler thoughts than I./ 这主意真～！What a brilliant idea! ③ loud: 嗓门儿～ have a loud voice/ ～喊 shout loudly; raise a cry ④ high-priced; dear; expensive: 要价太～ ask too high a price ⑤〈敬〉your: ～见 your opinion ⑥ (Gāo) a surname

【高矮】 gāo'ǎi height: 这两棵树～差不多。The two trees are about the same height.

【高昂】 gāo'áng ① hold high (one's head, etc.) ② high; elated; exalted: 情绪～ be in high spirits/ 大会在～的《国际歌》声中结束。The meeting ended with the inspiring strains of *The Internationale*. ③ dear; expensive; exorbitant

【高傲】 gāo'ào supercilious; arrogant; haughty

【高不成,低不就】 gāo bù chéng, dī bù jiù ① be unfit for a higher post but unwilling to take a lower one ② can't have one's heart's desire but won't stoop to less

【高不可攀】 gāo bùkě pān too high to reach; unattainable

【高才生】 gāocáishēng a brilliant (或 outstanding) student

【高层云】 gāocéngyún 〈气〉 altostratus

【高产】 gāochǎn high yield; high production
◇ ～品种 high-yield variety/ ～田 high-yield field/ ～作物 high-yield crop; highly productive crop

【高唱】 gāochàng ① sing loudly; sing with spirit: ～革命战歌 sing revolutionary battle songs ② talk glibly about; call out loudly for: 社会帝国主义一面～"和平"，一面疯狂备战。Social-imperialism is talking glibly about "peace" but frenziedly preparing for war.

【高超】 gāochāo superb; excellent: 技艺～ superb skill

【高超音速】 gāo-chāoyīnsù 〈物〉 hypersonic speed ◇ ～火箭 hypersonic rocket

【高潮】 gāocháo ① high tide; high water ② upsurge; climax; high tide: 全剧的～ the climax of the play/ 迎接社会主义建设的新～ greet the new high tide of socialist construction/ 运动已经达到～。The movement has reached high tide. ◇ ～线 high-water mark (或 line)

【高大】 gāodà ① tall and big; tall: 身材～ be of great stature/ ～的建筑物 tall buildings/ ～明亮的车间 a big, bright, high-ceilinged workshop ② lofty: 革命英雄的～形象 the lofty image of a revolutionary hero

【高蛋白】 gāodànbái high protein

【高档】 gāodàng 〈方〉 top grade; superior quality ◇ ～商品 high-grade goods; expensive goods

【高等】 gāoděng higher
◇ ～哺乳动物 higher mammal/ ～教育 higher education/ ～数学 higher mathematics/ ～院校 institutions of higher learning; colleges and universities

【高低】 gāodī ① height: 山崖的～ the height of a cliff/ 声调的～ the pitch of a voice ② relative superiority or inferiority: 争个～ vie with each other to see who is better/ 难分～ hard to tell which is better ③ sense of propriety; discretion: 不知～ not know what's proper; have no sense of propriety ④〈方〉 on any account; just; simply: 不管大家怎么劝说，他～不听。No matter how hard everyone tried to persuade him, he just wouldn't listen. ⑤〈方〉 at long last: 经过几天的苦战，～把涵洞修好了。After days of hard work, the culvert was at last completed. ◇ ～杠〈体〉 uneven (parallel) bars/ ～角〈军〉 angle of site

【高地】 gāodì ① highland; upland; elevation: ～田 an upland field ②〈军〉 height: 拿下三三二～ capture Height 332

【高调】 gāodiào lofty tone; high-sounding words: 唱～ mouth high-sounding words; say fine-sounding things

【高度】 gāodù ① altitude; height: 飞行～ flying altitude/ 山的～ the height of a mountain/ 应该从路线斗争的～来认识这个问题。We should approach this question from the high plane of two-line struggle. ② a high degree of; highly: ～赞扬 pay high tribute to; speak highly of/ ～政治觉悟 a high level of political consciousness/ 给予～重视 attach great importance to/ ～现代化的工厂 a highly modernized plant/ 没有充分的民主，就不可能有～的集中。Without ample democracy, it is impossible to have a high degree of centralism. ◇ ～表 altimeter

【高尔夫球】 gāo'ěrfūqiú ① golf ② golf ball ◇ ～场 golf course; golf links

【高尔基体】 gāo'ěrjītǐ 〈生〉 golgiosome

【高分子】 gāofēnzǐ 〈化〉 high polymer; macromolecule ◇ ～化合物 macromolecular compound; high-molecular compound/ ～化学 (high) polymer chemistry / ～聚合物 high polymer

【高峰】 gāofēng peak; summit; height: 珠穆朗玛峰是世界第一～。Mount Qomolangma is the world's highest peak./ 攀登科学的～ scale the heights of science

【高高在上】 gāogāo zài shàng stand high above the masses; be far removed from the masses and reality

【高歌猛进】 gāogē měngjìn stride forward singing militant songs; advance triumphantly

【高个儿】 gāogèr a tall person 又作"高个子"

【高根】 gāogēn 〈植〉 coca

【高跟鞋】 gāogēnxié high-heeled shoes

【高官厚禄】 gāoguān-hòulù high position and handsome salary; high posts with salaries to match

【高贵】 gāoguì ① noble; high: ～品质 noble quality ② highly privileged; elitist

【高积云】 gāojīyún 〈气〉 altocumulus

【高级】 gāojí ① senior; high-ranking; high-level; high: ～参谋 senior staff officer/ ～干部 senior cadre/ ～将领 high-ranking general officers/ ～官员 high-ranking official/ 最～会议 summit meeting ② high-grade; high-quality; advanced: ～染料 high-grade dyestuff/ ～墨水 high-quality ink/ ～读本 advanced reader/ 这个旅馆真～！This hotel is really first-class.
◇ ～党校 Higher Party School/ ～人民法院 higher people's court/ ～小学 higher primary school/ ～中学 senior middle school

【高级农业生产合作社】 gāojí nóngyè shēngchǎn hézuòshè advanced agricultural producers' cooperative (in which the land and other chief means of production were collectively owned by the co-op and the distribution system was based on the principle of "from each according to his ability, to each according to his work")

【高级社】 gāojíshè 〈简〉(高级农业生产合作社) advanced agricultural producers' cooperative

【高级神经活动】 gāojí shénjīng huódòng 〈生理〉 higher nervous activity

【高加索山脉】 Gāojiāsuǒ Shānmài the Caucasus Mountains

【高价】 gāojià high price: ～收买 buy over at a high price/ ～货物 expensive goods

【高架桥】 gāojiàqiáo viaduct

【高架铁道】 gāojià tiědào overhead railway; elevated railway

【高见】 gāojiàn 〈敬〉 your brilliant idea; your opinion: 有何～？What do you think about it?/ 不知～以为何如？I wonder if you would be kind enough to enlighten us on this matter.

【高洁】 gāojié noble and unsullied

【高精尖】 gāo-jīng-jiān high-grade, precision and advanced (industrial products)

【高举】 gāojǔ hold high; hold aloft: 华国锋同志一贯～马克思主义、列宁主义、毛泽东思想伟大旗帜，坚决执行毛主席的无产阶级革命路线。Comrade Hua Guofeng has always held high the great banner of Marxism-Leninism-Mao Zedong Thought and steadfastly implemented Chairman Mao's proletarian revolutionary line.

【高聚物】 gāojùwù 〈化〉 high polymer

【高踞】 gāojù stand above; set oneself above; lord it over: 共产党员绝不可～于群众之上。A Communist must never set himself above the masses.

【高峻】 gāojùn high and steep

【高亢】 gāokàng loud and sonorous; resounding: ～的歌声 sonorous singing

【高空】 gāokōng high altitude; upper air
◇ ～病 altitude sickness/ ～飞行 high-altitude flight/ ～核试验 high-altitude nuclear test/ ～气象学 aerology/ ～适应 high-altitude adaptation/ ～作业 work high above the ground

【高栏】 gāolán 〈体〉 high hurdles

【高利贷】 gāolìdài usury; usurious loan: 放～ practise usury ◇ ～者 usurer; loan shark/ ～资本 usurer's capital

【高良姜】 gāoliángjiāng 〈植〉 (lesser) galangal (*Alpinia officinarum*)

【高粱】 gāoliang *kaoliang*; Chinese sorghum ◇ ～米 husked *kaoliang*/ ～饴 sweets (或 candy) made of sorghum syrup; sorghum candy

【高龄】 gāolíng advanced age; venerable age: 八十～ the advanced age of 80

【高岭石】 gāolǐngshí kaolinite

【高岭土】 gāolǐngtǔ kaolin

【高楼大厦】 gāolóu-dàshà high buildings and large mansions

【高炉】 gāolú 〈冶〉 blast furnace
◇ ～利用系数 capacity factor of a blast furnace/ ～煤气 blast furnace gas/ ～寿命 life of a blast furnace

【高氯酸】 gāolǜsuān 〈化〉 perchloric acid

【高论】 gāolùn 〈敬〉 enlightening remarks; brilliant views

【高迈】 gāomài advanced in years

【高帽子】 gāomàozi ① tall paper hat (worn as a sign of humiliation) ② flattery

【高锰酸钾】 gāoměngsuānjiǎ 〈化〉 potassium permanganate

【高妙】 gāomiào ingenious; masterly: 手艺～ masterly craftsmanship

【高明】 gāomíng brilliant; wise: 群众比我们～。The masses are wiser than we are./ 他这一手一点也不～。This move of his is not at all clever./ 另请～。Find someone better qualified (than myself).

【高能燃料】 gāonéng ránliào high-energy fuel

【高能物理学】 gāonéng wùlǐxué high-energy physics

【高攀】 gāopān make friends or claim ties of kinship with someone of a higher social position

【高频】 gāopín high frequency: 甚～ very high frequency (vhf)/ 超～ ultrahigh frequency (uhf)
◇ ～淬火 〈机〉 high-frequency quenching/ ～感应电炉 〈冶〉 high-frequency induction furnace/ ～扬声器 tweeter

【高气压】 gāoqìyā high atmospheric (或 barometric) pressure ◇ ～区 high-pressure area; region of high barometric pressure

【高强】 gāoqiáng excel in; be master of: 武艺～ excel in martial arts

【高强度】 gāoqiángdù high strength: ～钢 high-strength steel; high-tensile steel

【高跷】 gāoqiāo stilts: 踩～ walk on stilts

【高球】 gāoqiú 〈体〉 high ball; lob: 放～ lob

【高人一等】 gāo rén yī děng a cut above other people: 他老以为自己～。He always thinks he's a cut above others.

【高僧】 gāosēng eminent monk

【高山病】 gāoshānbìng mountain sickness

【高山植物】 gāoshān zhíwù alpine plant

【高山族】 Gāoshānzú the Gaoshan (Kaoshan) nationality, living in Taiwan Province

【高尚】 gāoshàng noble; lofty: ～的人 a noble-minded person/ ～的理想 lofty ideals

【高烧】 gāoshāo high fever: 发～ have (或 run) a high fever

【高射机关枪】 gāoshè jīguānqiāng antiaircraft machine gun

【高射炮】 gāoshèpào antiaircraft gun (或 artillery)

【高深】 gāoshēn advanced; profound; recondite: 莫测～ unfathomable

【高视阔步】 gāoshì-kuòbù carry oneself proudly; strut; prance

【高手】 gāoshǒu past master; master-hand; ace: 象棋～ master (Chinese) chess player

【高寿】 gāoshòu ① longevity; long life ② 〈敬〉 your venerable age: 老大爷,您今年～? May I ask how old you are, Grandpa?

【高耸】 gāosǒng stand tall and erect; tower: ～入云 reach to the sky; tower into the clouds/ ～的纪念碑 a towering monument

【高速】 gāosù high speed: ～前进 advance at high speed/ ～发展 develop by leaps and bounds; develop at top speed/ ～转弯很危险。It's dangerous to turn a corner at high speed.
◇ ～档 top gear; high gear/ ～钢 high-speed steel; rapid steel/ ～工具钢 high-speed tool steel/ ～公路 expressway/ ～切削 〈机〉 high-speed cutting

【高台定车】 gāotái dìngchē 〈杂技〉 a bicycle balancing act on an elevated stand

【高谈阔论】 gāotán-kuòlùn indulge in loud and empty talk; talk volubly or bombastically; harangue

【高碳钢】 gāotàngāng 〈冶〉 high-carbon steel

【高汤】 gāotāng ① soup-stock ② thin soup

【高温】 gāowēn high temperature
◇ ～计 〈仪表〉 pyrometer/ ～气候 megathermal climate/ ～切削 〈机〉 high-temperature machining/ ～作业 〈冶〉 high-temperature operation

【高屋建瓴】 gāowū jiàn líng pour water off a steep roof — sweep down irresistibly from a commanding height; operate from a strategically advantageous position

【高下】 gāoxià 见"高低"②

【高小】 gāoxiǎo 〈简〉(高级小学) higher primary school

【高兴】 gāoxìng ① glad; happy; cheerful: 小强高高兴兴地上学去了。Xiao Qiang cheerfully went off to school./ 快把这消息告诉你爷爷,叫他老人家也～～。Tell Grandpa the good news, so that he can share our joy./ 他们～得太早了。They rejoiced too soon. ② be willing to; be happy to: 你不～去就甭去了。You needn't go if you don't feel like it.

【高血压】 gāoxuèyā 〈医〉 hypertension; high blood pressure

【高压】 gāoyā ① 〈物〉 〈气〉 high pressure ② 〈电〉 high tension; high voltage ③ high-handed: 反动政权的～政策 the high-handed policy of a reactionary regime ④ 〈医〉 maximum pressure
◇ ～泵 〈机〉 high-pressure pump/ ～电力网 high-tension network/ ～锅 pressure cooker/ ～锅炉 high-pressure boiler/ ～脊 〈气〉 ridge of high pressure; pressure ridge/ ～灭菌器 autoclave/ ～线 high-tension line (或 wire)

【高眼蝶】 gāoyǎndié 〈动〉 plaice

【高音喇叭】 gāoyīn lǎba tweeter

【高原】 gāoyuán plateau; highland; tableland: 青藏～ the Qinghai-Xizang Plateau

【高瞻远瞩】 gāozhān-yuǎnzhǔ stand high and see far; take a broad and long-term view; show great foresight

【高涨】 gāozhǎng rise; upsurge; run high: 反霸斗争的浪潮空前～。The struggle against hegemonism is rising to an unprecedented height./ 群众热情～。The enthusiasm of the masses ran high.

【高着儿】 gāozhāor 〈口〉 clever move; brilliant idea: 我看他也没有什么～。I don't think he can come up with any clever move./ 你有什么～，快说说。What have you got up your sleeve? Out with it! 又作"高招"

【高枕无忧】 gāo zhěn wú yōu shake up the pillow and have a good sleep; sit back and relax

【高中】 gāozhōng 〈简〉(高级中学) senior middle school

【高姿态】 gāozītài lofty stance; magnanimous attitude

【高足】 gāozú 〈敬〉 your brilliant disciple; your pupil

【高祖】 gāozǔ (paternal) great-great-grandfather

【高祖母】 gāozǔmǔ (paternal) great-great-grandmother

**羔** gāo lamb; kid; fawn

【羔皮】 gāopí lambskin; kidskin; kid

【羔羊】 gāoyáng lamb; kid

【羔子】 gāozi lamb; kid; fawn

**膏** gāo ① fat; grease; oil: 春雨如～。Rain in spring is as precious as oil. ② paste; cream; ointment: 牙～ toothpaste/ 雪花～ vanishing cream/ 软～ ointment

另见 gào

【膏肓】 gāohuāng 见"病入膏肓" bìng rù gāohuāng

【膏剂】 gāojì 〈药〉 medicinal extract; electuary

【膏粱】 gāoliáng fat meat and fine grain; rich food ◇ ～子弟 good-for-nothing sons of the idle rich

【膏药】 gāoyao plaster: 贴～ apply a plaster to

【膏腴】 gāoyú 〈书〉 fertile: ～之地 fertile land

**睾** gāo

【睾丸】 gāowán 〈生理〉 testis; testicle ◇ ～炎 orchitis

**糕** gāo cake; pudding: 年～ New Year cake (made of glutinous rice)/ 蛋～ cake (enriched with eggs)

【糕点】 gāodiǎn cake; pastry

【糕干】 gāogan sweetened rice flour (sometimes fed to infants as a substitute for powdered milk)

**篙** gāo punt-pole

## gǎo

**杲** gǎo 〈书〉 bright

**搞** gǎo ① do; carry on; be engaged in: ～调查研究 do some investigation and study/ ～运动 carry on a movement (或 campaign)/ ～生产 engage in production/ ～阴谋诡计的人注定要失败。Those who go in for intrigues and conspiracy are doomed to failure./ 他是～建筑的。He's in building./ 这是个～不～社会主义的问题。It's a question of whether or not one practises socialism. ② make; produce; work out: ～个计划 draw up a plan/ 我们～一点核武器完全是为了自卫。It is purely for self-defence that we have produced some nuclear weapons./ 我们这个月已经～了两期大批判专栏。This month we have put out two special mass criticism numbers./ 别～那么多菜了。Don't make so many dishes. ③ set up; start; organize: 这个小厂是由几个家庭妇女～起来的。This small factory was started by a few housewives./ 我们打算在这里～个发电站。We're thinking of putting up a power station here. ④ get; get hold of; secure: 你去给我们～点吃的来。Go and get us something to eat. ⑤〔后面接补语〕produce a certain effect or result; cause to become: 把事情～糟了 make a mess of things/ 把某人～臭 make sb.'s name stink; discredit sb./ 把问题～清楚 get a clear understanding of the question/ 别把机器～坏了。Don't break the machine./ 我把你们的名字～混了。I've mixed up your names./ 他思想～通了，精神也就愉快了。Once he straightened out his ideas, he became cheerful again.

【搞好】 gǎohǎo make a good job of; do well: ～团结 strengthen unity/ ～军民关系 build good relations between the army and the people/ 这块地～了，每亩可以收一千斤。If this plot of land is handled well, it can yield 1,000 *jin* per *mu*./ 搞不好还得重来。If things go wrong we'll have to start all over again.

【搞鬼】 gǎoguǐ play tricks; be up to some mischief: 提防阶级敌人暗中～。Beware of the class enemy's tricks.

**缟** gǎo a thin white silk used in ancient China

【缟素】 gǎosù white mourning dress

**槁** gǎo withered

【槁木死灰】 gǎomù-sǐhuī dead trees and cold ashes — complete apathy

**稿** gǎo ①〈书〉 stalk of grain; straw ② draft; sketch: 初～ first draft/ 先打个～儿再画 make a sketch before painting ③ manuscript; original text: 遗～ literary remains; posthumous papers/ 定～ finalize a text/ 来～ contributed article; contribution

【稿本】 gǎoběn manuscript

【稿费】 gǎofèi payment for an article or book written; contribution fee; author's remuneration

【稿件】 gǎojiàn manuscript; contribution

【稿荐】 gǎojiàn straw mattress; pallet

【稿约】 gǎoyuē notice to contributors

【稿纸】 gǎozhǐ squared or lined paper for making drafts or copying manuscripts

【稿子】 gǎozi ① draft; sketch: 起个～ make a draft ② manuscript; contribution: 给黑板报写～ write sth. for the blackboard newspaper ③ idea; plan: 我心里还没个准～。I haven't got any definite plan yet.

**镐** gǎo pick; pickaxe

【镐头】 gǎotou pick; pickaxe

## gào

**告** gào ① tell; inform; notify: 何时启程，盼～。Please inform me of your date of departure. ② accuse; go to law against; bring an action against ③ ask for; request; solicit: ～假 ask for leave ④ declare; announce: 不～而别 go away without taking leave; leave without saying good-bye/ 自～奋勇 volunteer to do sth. ⑤〔宣布或表示某种情况的实现〕: ～一段落 come to the end of a stage; be brought to a temporary close/ 大功～成。The task is at last accomplished.

【告别】 gàobié ① leave; part from: 我们～了这个地方，继续向前进。We left the place and went on with our journey./ 他把信交给了队长，就匆匆～了。He hurried off after giving the letter to the team leader. ② bid farewell to; say good-bye to: 挥手～ wave farewell/ 我向你～来了。I've come to say good-bye to you./ 向遗体～ pay one's last respects to the deceased

◇ ～词 farewell speech; valediction/ ～宴会 farewell ban-

quet/ ～仪式 farewell ceremony
【告吹】 gàochuī fizzle out; fail
【告辞】 gàocí take leave (of one's host)
【告贷】 gàodài ask for a loan
【告发】 gàofā report (an offender); inform against; lodge an accusation against
【告急】 gàojí ①be in an emergency: 洪水猛涨,大坝～。The dam was in danger because of the rising flood. ②report an emergency; ask for emergency help
【告假】 gàojià ask for leave
【告捷】 gàojié ①win victory: 首战～ win in the very first battle or game ②report a victory
【告诫】 gàojiè warn; admonish; exhort: 师长经常～我们要提高警惕。The division commander constantly exhorted us to heighten our vigilance.
【告警】 gàojǐng ①report an emergency ②give (或 sound) an alarm
【告竣】 gàojùn be completed: 治河工程全部～。The whole project for harnessing the river has been completed.
【告老】 gàolǎo retire on account of age: ～还乡 retire on account of old age and return to one's native place
【告密】 gàomì inform against sb.: 他做地下工作时,曾因叛徒～而被捕。When he was doing underground work he was arrested because a renegade informed against him. ◇ ～者 informer
【告罄】 gàoqìng run out; be exhausted: 弹药～。Ammunition has run out.
【告饶】 gàoráo beg for mercy; ask pardon
【告示】 gàoshi official notice; bulletin; placard
【告诉】 gàosu tell; let know: ～他们别等了。Tell them not to wait./ 有什么消息,～我一声。Let me know if there's any news.
【告退】 gàotuì ask for leave to withdraw from a meeting, etc.
【告知】 gàozhī inform; notify
【告终】 gàozhōng come to an end; end up: 以失败～ end in failure/ 以损人开始,以害己～ start with the aim of harming others and end up by harming oneself
【告状】 gàozhuàng ①go to law against sb.; bring a lawsuit against sb. ②lodge a complaint against sb. with his superior

## 郜
Gào a surname

## 诰
gào imperial mandate: ～封 the conferment of honorary titles by imperial mandate
【诰命】 gàomìng imperial mandate

## 锆
gào 〈化〉 zirconium (Zr)
【锆鞣】 gàoróu zirconium tanning ◇ ～革 zirconium tanned leather
【锆石】 gàoshí 〈矿〉 zircon

## 膏
gào ①lubricate: ～车 lubricate the axle of a cart/ 在轴上～点儿油 put some lubricant on the axle ②dip a brush in ink and smooth it on an inkstone before writing
另见 gāo

# gē

## 戈
gē ①dagger-axe (an ancient weapon) ②(Gē) a surname
【戈壁】 gēbì 〈地〉 ①gobi ②the Gobi Desert

## 仡
gē
【仡佬族】 Gēlǎozú the Gelo (Kelao) nationality, living in Guizhou

## 圪
gē
【圪垯】 gēda ①见"疙瘩" gēda ②mound; knoll

## 疙
gē
【疙瘩】 gēda ①a swelling on the skin; pimple; lump ②lump; knot: ～汤 dough drop soup/ 线结成～了。The thread has got tangled (或 got into a knot). ③a knot in one's heart; hang-up: 支书的话解开了我心上的～。The Party secretary got rid of my hang-up./ 我们帮助他们解开了～。We helped to dispel the misunderstanding between them.
【疙疙瘩瘩】 gēgedādā 〈口〉 rough; knotty; bumpy

## 咯
gē
另见 kǎ; lo; luò
【咯噔】 gēdēng 〈象〉 click: ～～的皮靴声 the click of boots (on a floor)
【咯咯】 gēgē 〈象〉 ①〔形容母鸡叫声〕 cluck; chuckle; cackle ②〔形容笑声〕 chuckle; titter
【咯吱】 gēzhī 〈象〉 creak; groan: 扁担压得～～地直响。The carrying pole creaked under the load.

## 哥
gē (elder) brother
【哥瓷】 gēcí porcelain with crackled glaze; crackle-china
【哥德巴赫猜想】 Gēdébāhè cāixiǎng 〈数〉 Goldbach's conjecture
【哥哥】 gēge (elder) brother
【哥伦比亚】 Gēlúnbǐyà Colombia ◇ ～人 Colombian
【哥罗仿】 gēluófǎng 〈化〉 chloroform
【哥儿】 gēr brothers; boys: 你们～几个? How many of you boys are there altogether in your family?/ 他们～仨都是运动员。All three brothers are athletes.
【哥儿们】 gērmen 〈口〉 ①brothers ②buddies; pals: 穷～ we, the poor/ 要讲阶级感情,不能讲～义气。We must go by class feeling, not by brotherhood.
【哥斯达黎加】 Gēsīdálíjiā Costa Rica ◇ ～人 Costa Rican
【哥特式】 gētèshì 〈建〉 Gothic: ～教堂 Gothic cathedral (或 church)
【哥特体】 gētètǐ 〈印〉 gothic

## 胳
gē
另见 gé
【胳臂】 gēbei arm
【胳膊】 gēbo arm ◇ ～腕子 wrist/ ～肘儿 elbow

## 袼
gē
【袼褙】 gēbei pieces of old cloth or rags pasted together to make cloth shoes

## 鸽
gē pigeon; dove: 家～ pigeon/ 野～ wild pigeon; dove/ 通信～ carrier (或 homing) pigeon
【鸽子】 gēzi pigeon; dove ◇ ～笼 dovecote; pigeon house; loft

## 割
gē cut: ～麦子 cut (或 reap) wheat/ ～草 cut grass; mow
【割爱】 gē'ài give up what one treasures; part with some cherished possession: 忍痛～ part reluctantly with what one treasures
【割草机】 gēcǎojī mower

【割除】 gēchú cut off; cut out; excise
【割地】 gēdì cede territory: 帝国主义列强多次强迫清廷～赔款。The imperialist powers repeatedly forced the Qing government to cede territory and pay indemnities.
【割断】 gēduàn sever; cut off: ～联系 sever relations/ ～敌人的电话线 cut enemy telephone wires/ 我们不能～历史看问题。We mustn't consider a question apart from its historical context.
【割鸡焉用牛刀】 gē jī yān yòng niúdāo why use an ox-cleaver to kill a chicken; why break a butterfly on the wheel
【割胶】 gējiāo rubber tapping
【割炬】 gējù 〈机〉 cutting torch
【割据】 gējù set up a separatist regime by force of arms: 封建～ feudal separatist rule/ 军阀～ separatist warlord regimes/ 诸侯～称雄的封建国家 a feudal state torn apart by rival principalities/ 工农武装～ an armed independent regime of workers and peasants (during the Second Revolutionary Civil War)
【割捆机】 gēkǔnjī 〈农〉 self-binder; binder
【割礼】 gēlǐ 〈宗〉 circumcision
【割裂】 gēliè cut apart; separate; isolate: 这两点是互相联系的，不能～。The two points are related and cannot be taken separately./ 不应把这种斗争方式同当时的环境～开来。One must not isolate this type of struggle from its historical context.
【割让】 gēràng cede: ～领土 cession of territory
【割晒机】 gēshàijī 〈农〉 swather; windrower
【割舍】 gēshě give up; part with: 难以～ find it hard to part with
【割线】 gēxiàn 〈数〉 secant

**搁** gē ①put: 把箱子～在行李架上。Put the suitcase on the luggage-rack./ 汤里～点盐。Put some salt in the soup./ 把东西～在这儿吧。Just leave your things here./ 这屋子太热，种子～不住。This room is too hot; the seeds won't keep. ②put aside; leave over; shelve: 这件事得～一～再办。We'll have to put the matter aside for the time being.
另见 gé
【搁浅】 gēqiǎn run aground; be stranded; reach a deadlock: 船～了。The ship got stranded (或 ran aground)./ 谈判～了。The negotiations have come to a deadlock.
【搁置】 gēzhì shelve; lay aside; pigeonhole: ～一项动议 shelve a motion

**歌** gē ①song ②sing: 纵情高～ sing loudly and without constraint
【歌本】 gēběn songbook
【歌唱】 gēchàng sing: ～我们社会主义祖国 sing (in praise) of our socialist land ◇ ～家 singer; vocalist
【歌词】 gēcí words of a song
【歌功颂德】 gēgōng-sòngdé eulogize sb.'s virtues and achievements; sing the praises of sb.
【歌喉】 gēhóu (singer's) voice; singing voice: ～婉转 sing in a beautiful voice
【歌剧】 gējù opera: 小～ operetta
◇ ～剧本 libretto/ ～团 opera troupe/ ～院 opera house
【歌诀】 gējué formulas or directions put into verse: 汤头～ (a handbook of) Chinese herb prescriptions in verse
【歌片儿】 gēpiānr song sheet
【歌谱】 gēpǔ music of a song
【歌曲】 gēqǔ song
【歌手】 gēshǒu singer; vocalist
【歌颂】 gēsòng sing the praises of; extol; eulogize: ～劳动英雄 sing the praises of labour heroes/ ～共产主义风格 extol the communist style of behaviour
【歌舞】 gēwǔ song and dance ◇ ～剧 song and dance drama/ ～团 song and dance ensemble (或 troupe)
【歌舞升平】 gēwǔ shēngpíng sing and dance to extol the good times — put on a false show of peace and prosperity
【歌谣】 gēyáo ballad; folk song; nursery rhyme
【歌咏】 gēyǒng singing ◇ ～比赛 singing contest/ ～队 singing group; chorus

## gé

**革** gé ①leather; hide: ～制品 leather goods/ ～履 leather shoes/ 制～厂 tannery ②change; transform: 洗心～面 turn over a new leaf ③remove from office; expel ④(Gé) a surname
【革除】 géchú ①abolish; get rid of: ～陈规陋习 abolish outmoded regulations and irrational practices ②expel; dismiss; remove from office
【革命】 gémìng revolution: ～到底 carry the revolution through to the end; remain a revolutionary to the end of one's life/ 敢挑～重担 dare to shoulder heavy responsibilities for the revolution/ ～加拼命 revolutionary enthusiasm plus death-defying spirit/ 农民起来革地主的命。The peasants rose in revolt against the landlords.
◇ ～传统教育 education in revolutionary tradition/ ～大批判 revolutionary mass criticism/ ～干部 revolutionary cadre/ ～回忆录 reminiscences of earlier revolutionary times/ ～家 revolutionary; revolutionist/ ～军人 revolutionary armyman/ ～浪漫主义 revolutionary romanticism/ ～乐观主义 revolutionary optimism/ ～烈士 revolutionary martyr/ ～群众歌曲 revolutionary popular song/ ～人道主义 revolutionary humanitarianism/ ～现实主义 revolutionary realism/ ～英雄主义 revolutionary heroism/ ～者 revolutionary
【革命发展阶段论】 gémìng fāzhǎn jiēduànlùn the theory of the development of revolution by stages
【革命化】 gémìnghuà revolutionize; do things in a revolutionary way: 实现机关～ revolutionize government organizations/ 过一个～的春节 spend the Spring Festival in a revolutionary way
【革命军人委员会】 gémìng jūnrén wěiyuánhuì revolutionary armymen's committee (a mass organization of a company, elected by all its members)
【革命性】 gémìngxìng revolutionary character (或 quality, spirit): 无产阶级的～ the revolutionary character of the proletariat/ 这本教科书～和科学性结合得很好。This textbook successfully combines revolutionary spirit with scientific methodology.
【革委会】 géwěihuì 〈简〉(革命委员会) revolutionary committee
【革新】 géxīn innovation: 技术～ technological innovation/ 传统的手工艺技术不断～。Traditional handicraft techniques are being steadily improved.
【革职】 gézhí remove from office; cashier

**阁** gé ①pavilion (usu. two-storeyed) ②cabinet: 组～ form a cabinet/ 倒～ bring down a cabinet
【阁楼】 gélóu attic; loft; garret
【阁下】 géxià 〈敬〉(直接称呼) Your Excellency; (间接称呼) His or Her Excellency: 大使～ Your Excellency Mr. Ambassador; His Excellency the Ambassador
【阁员】 géyuán member of the cabinet

**格** gé ①squares formed by crossed lines; check: 在纸上打方～儿 square off the paper ②division (horizontal or otherwise): 横～纸 ruled paper/ 四～儿的书架 a bookcase with four shelves/ 每服一小～。Dose: one measure each time. ③standard; pattern; style: 合～ up to standard/ 别具一～ have a style of its own ④〈语〉case: 主～ the nominative case/ 宾～ the objective case
【格调】 gédiào ①(literary or artistic) style: ～豪放 a vigorous and flowing style ②〈书〉one's style of work as well as one's moral quality
【格斗】 gédòu grapple; wrestle; fistfight
【格格不入】 gégé bù rù incompatible with; out of tune with; out of one's element; like a square peg in a round hole
【格局】 géjú pattern; setup; structure: 在这场足球比赛中我队始终保持"四三三"的～。Throughout the football match our team kept to the 4-3-3 pattern./ 这几个菜市场的～差不多。These food markets have more or less the same setup.
【格林纳达】 Gélínnàdá Grenada ◇ ～人 Grenadian
【格林威治平时】 Gélínwēizhì píngshí Greenwich mean time (GMT)
【格陵兰】 Gélínglán Greenland
【格律】 gélǜ rules and forms of classical poetic composition (with respect to tonal pattern, rhyme scheme, etc.)
【格杀勿论】 géshā wùlùn kill on the spot with the authority of the law
【格式】 géshi form; pattern: 公文～ the form of an official document
【格外】 géwài 〈副〉especially; all the more: 雪地上骑车要～小心。You've got to be especially careful when you cycle on snow./ 国庆节，天安门显得～壮丽。Tian An Men looks especially magnificent on National Day.
【格言】 géyán maxim; motto; aphorism
【格子】 gézi check; chequer
◇ ～布 checked fabric; check/ ～窗 lattice window/ ～花呢 tartan

**胳** gé
另见 gē
【胳肢】 gézhi 〈方〉tickle sb.

**葛** gé 〈植〉kudzu vine
另见 gě
【葛布】 gébù ko-hemp cloth
【葛根】 gégēn 〈中药〉the root of kudzu vine

**蛤** gé clam
另见 há
【蛤蜊】 géli clam

**搁** gé bear; stand; endure: ～不住压 cannot stand crushing
另见 gē

**隔** gé ①separate; partition; stand or lie between: 把一间屋～成两间 partition a room into two/ 龟蛇二山～江相望。Tortoise and Snake Hills face each other across the river./ ～一座山就是水库。The reservoir is just on the other side of the hill. ② at a distance from; after or at an interval of: 相～千里 be a thousand *li* away from each other/ 每棵树苗要～开五米。The saplings should be five metres apart./ 你～两天再来吧。Come back in two days' time./ ～两周去一次 go there every third week/ 请～行写。Please write on every other line./ ～四小时服一次。To be taken once every four hours.
【隔岸观火】 gé àn guān huǒ watch a fire from the other side of the river — look on at sb.'s trouble with indifference
【隔壁】 gébì next door: ～邻居 next-door neighbour/ 住在～ live next door/ ～第二间 next door but one
【隔断】 géduàn cut off; separate; obstruct: 洪水把村子同县城的交通～了。The flood cut the village off from the county town./ 高山大海隔不断我们两国人民的友好往来。Mountains and seas cannot obstruct the friendly exchanges between our two peoples.
【隔断】 géduan 〈建〉partition (wall, board, etc.)
【隔阂】 géhé estrangement; misunderstanding: 制造～ foment feelings of estrangement/ 经过批评和自我批评，他们消除了～。Through criticism and self-criticism they cleared up their misunderstanding (或 ended their estrangement). ②barrier: 语言的～ language barrier
【隔火墙】 géhuǒqiáng fire division wall; fire wall
【隔绝】 géjué completely cut off; isolated: 和外界～ be cut off from the outside world/ 他走了以后就与我们音信～了。He has never been heard of since he left us.
【隔离】 gélí keep apart; isolate; segregate: 种族～ racial segregation; apartheid/ 病人已经～了一周。The patient has been in isolation for a week. ◇ ～病房 isolation ward
【隔膜】 gémó ①lack of mutual understanding: 他们之间有些～。They are rather estranged from each other. ② unfamiliar with: 我对那里的情况很～。I know very little about the situation there.
【隔片】 gépiàn 〈机〉spacer
【隔墙】 géqiáng 〈建〉partition (wall)
【隔墙有耳】 gé qiáng yǒu ěr walls have ears; beware of eavesdroppers
【隔热】 gérè 〈建〉heat insulation
【隔扇】 géshan partition board
【隔声】 géshēng 〈建〉sound insulation ◇ ～板 sound insulating board/ ～材料 sound insulator
【隔靴搔痒】 gé xuē sāoyǎng scratch an itch from outside one's boot — attempt an ineffective solution
【隔夜】 géyè of the previous night: 把～的菜热一热 warm up last night's leftovers/ 过去那日子，真是家无～粮啊。In the old days, we never had any food at home to tide us over the next day.
【隔音】 géyīn ①sound insulation: ～室 soundproof room ②syllable-dividing: ～符号 syllable-dividing mark

**嗝** gé ① belch ② hiccup

**膈** gé diaphragm
【膈膜】 gémó diaphragm

**镉** gé 〈化〉cadmium (Cd)

**骼** gé 见"骨骼" gǔgé

## gě

**个** gě 见"自个儿" zìgěr
另见 gè

**合** gě *ge*, a unit of dry measure for grain (= 1 decilitre)
另见 hé

**舸** gě barge

**葛** Gě a surname
另见 gé

【葛仙米】 gěxiānmǐ 〈植〉 nostoc

## gè

**个** gè ①〈量〉 ⓐ〔多用于没有专用量词的名词〕: 三～苹果 three apples/ 一～故事 a story/ 两～星期 two weeks; a fortnight/ 一～心眼儿 be of one mind/ 第五～年头 the fifth year ⓑ〔用于约数的前面〕: 这点活儿有～两三天就干完了。This bit of work can easily be finished in a couple of days. ⓒ〔用于带宾语的动词后面〕: 洗～澡 have a bath/ 睡～好觉 have a good sleep/ 他在农村锻炼了两年,扶～犁,赶～车,都拿得起来。After a couple of years in the countryside, he was quite good at handling a plough and driving a cart. ⓓ〔用于动词和补语之间〕: 砸～稀巴烂 smash sth. to smithereens/ 忙～不停 be as busy as a bee ② individual
另见 gě

【个把】 gèbǎ one or two: 多～人也住得下。There is enough room to put up one or two more people.

【个别】 gèbié ① individual; specific: ～辅导 individual coaching/ ～照顾 special consideration for individual cases/ 一般号召和～指导相结合 combine the general call with particular guidance/ 领导找她～谈话。The leading comrade had a private talk with her. ② very few; one or two; exceptional: 只有～人请假。Only one or two people asked for leave./ 这是极其～的事例。Such instances are very rare./ 这是～情况。These are isolated cases. ◇ ～差异〈心〉 individual differences

【个个】 gègè each and every one; all: 这些战士～都是好样儿的。Each and every one of these soldiers has proved his mettle.

【个儿】 gèr ① size; height; stature: 别看她～不大, 劲儿可不小。She's not big, but she's strong./ 瞧这棉桃的～! Look, what huge bolls these are! ② persons or things taken singly: 挨～握手 shake hands with each one/ 论～卖 be sold by the piece

【个人】 gèrén ① individual (person): 关心集体比关心～为重 be more concerned about the collective than about oneself/ ～利益服从革命利益 subordinate one's personal interests to those of the revolution/ 集体领导和～负责相结合 combine collective leadership with individual responsibility/ 用他～的名义 in his own name ② I: ～认为 in my opinion
◇ ～迷信 cult of the individual; personality cult/ ～卫生 personal hygiene/ ～项目〈体〉 individual events/ ～野心 personal ambition/ ～野心家 careerist/ ～英雄主义 individualistic heroism/ ～主义 individualism

【个体】 gètǐ individual
◇ ～经济 individual economy/ ～劳动者 a person who works on his own; self-employed labourer/ ～农业经营 individual farming/ ～生产者 individual producer/ ～所有制 individual ownership

【个头儿】 gètóur 〈方〉 size; height: 这种西瓜～大。This kind of watermelon is remarkable for its size./ 这小伙子～不小。This young chap is very tall.

【个性】 gèxìng individual character; individuality; personality: 共性和～ the general and specific character of sth./ 这孩子～很强。The boy has a strong character.

【个中】 gèzhōng 〈书〉 therein: ～奥妙 the inside story; the secret of it ◇ ～人 a person in the know

【个子】 gèzi height; stature; build: 高～ a tall person/ 小～ a small fellow; a short person

**各** gè each; every; various; different: ～国的事务应当由～国人民自己来管。The affairs of each country should be managed by its own people./ 反对本位主义的～种表现 oppose every manifestation of departmentalism/ 全国～地 in all parts of the country/ ～派政治力量之间的阶级斗争 the class struggle between the different political forces/ ～不相让 neither being ready to give way; each trying to outdo the other/ ～不相同 have nothing in common with each other/ ～就位!〈体〉 On your marks!

【各半】 gèbàn half and half; fifty-fifty: 成败的可能性～。The chances of success are fifty-fifty./ 我们排党员和非党员～。Half of the men in our platoon are Party members.

【各奔前程】 gè bèn qiánchéng each pursues his own course; each goes his own way

【各别】 gèbié ① distinct; different: ～对待 treat differently; treat each on its (his, etc.) own merits ②〈方〉 out of the ordinary; peculiar: 这只闹钟式样很～。This alarm clock is quite unusual-looking. ③ odd; eccentric; funny: 这个人真～! What an odd chap! 或 What a funny fellow!

【各持己见】 gè chí jǐjiàn each sticks to his own view

【各打五十大板】 gè dǎ wǔshí dàbǎn blame both sides without discrimination; punish the innocent and the guilty alike

【各得其所】 gè dé qí suǒ each is in his proper place; each is properly provided for; each has a role to play

【各…各…】 gè ... gè ... ① each ... his own...: 分好了工,就各干各的去吧。Now that the work has been divided up, let each one get on with his job./ 各吹各的号,各唱各的调。Each blows his own bugle and sings his own tune — each does things in his own way./ 各就各位!〈军〉 Man your posts!〈体〉 On your marks! ② all kinds of; all: 各行各业 all trades and professions; all walks of life/ 各式各样的农具 farm tools of all kinds

【各个】 gègè ① each; every; various: ～革命发展阶段 each stage in the development of the revolution/ 社会上的～阶级 the various classes in society ② one by one; separately: ～击破 destroy (或 crush) one by one/ ～解决 piecemeal solution/ 集中优势兵力,～歼灭敌人。Concentrate a superior force to destroy the enemy forces one by one.

【各级】 gèjí all or different levels: ～领导机关 leading organizations at all levels/ ～人民代表大会 the people's congresses at different levels

【各界】 gèjiè all walks of life; all circles: ～人士 personalities of various circles

【各尽所能,按劳分配】 gè jìn suǒ néng, àn láo fēnpèi from each according to his ability, to each according to his work — the socialist principle of distribution

【各尽所能,按需分配】 gè jìn suǒ néng, àn xū fēnpèi from each according to his ability, to each according to his needs — the communist principle of distribution

【各取所需】 gè qǔ suǒ xū each takes what he needs

【各人】 gèrén each one; everyone: ～自扫门前雪,不管他人瓦上霜。〈俗〉 Each one sweeps the snow from his own doorstep and doesn't bother about the frost on his neighbour's roof.

【各色】 gèsè of all kinds; of every description; assorted: 商店里～货物,一应俱全。The shop is well stocked with goods of all kinds.

【各抒己见】 gè shū jǐjiàn each airs his own views

【各位】 gèwèi ① everybody (a term of address): ～请注意! Attention please, everybody. ② every: ～代表 fellow delegates

【各向同性】 gèxiàngtóngxìng 〈物〉 isotropy

【各向异性】 gèxiàngyìxìng 〈物〉 anisotropy

【各行其是】 gè xíng qí shì each does what he thinks is right; each goes his own way
【各有千秋】 gè yǒu qiānqiū each has something to recommend him; each has his strong points
【各有所长】 gè yǒu suǒ cháng each has his own strong points
【各有所好】 gè yǒu suǒ hào each has his likes and dislikes; each follows his own bent
【各执一词】 gè zhí yī cí each sticks to his own version or argument
【各自】 gèzì each; respective: 孩子们帮老大爷挑完了水，就～回家了。After carrying water for the old man, the children went home./ 研究社会各阶级的相互关系和～状况 study the mutual relations and respective conditions of the various classes in society/ 既要～努力，也要彼此帮助。There must be both individual effort and mutual help.
【各自为政】 gèzì wéi zhèng each does things in his own way

## 虼 gè
【虼蚤】 gèzao 〈口〉 flea

## 铬 gè 〈化〉 chromium (Cr)
【铬钢】 gègāng 〈冶〉 chromium steel; chrome steel
【铬镍钢】 gènièɡāng chrome-nickel steel
【铬鞣】 gèróu 〈皮革〉 chrome tanning ◇ ～革 chrome leather
【铬铁】 gètiě ferrochrome ◇ ～矿 chromite

## 硌 gè 〈口〉 (of sth. hard or bulging) press or rub against: 褥子没有铺平，躺在上面～得难受。The rumpled mattress stuck into me most uncomfortably. 或 That rumpled mattress was terribly uncomfortable./ 鞋里有砂子，～脚。There's some grit in the shoe, and it hurts my foot.

# gěi

## 给 gěi ① give; grant: ～他一个星期的假 grant him a week's leave/ 党～了我们勇气和力量。The Party has given us courage and strength./ 这本书是～你的。This book is for you. ②〔用在动词后面，表示交付〕: 信已经交～他了。I've handed the letter to him./ 把锤子递～我。Pass me the hammer./ 我把钥匙留～你。I'll leave the key with you. ③〔表示行为的对象或有关事物〕for; for the benefit of: 她～旅客送水倒茶。She brought drinking water and tea for the passengers./ 大夫～孩子们种牛痘。The doctor vaccinated the children. ④let; allow: ～我看看。Let me have a look. ⑤〔表示被动，相当于"被"〕: 这股敌人全～游击队消灭了。The whole horde of enemy soldiers was wiped out by the guerrillas./ 我们的衣服～汗水湿透了。Our clothes were soaked with sweat. ⑥〈助〉〔常与前面"叫""让""把"相呼应，以加强语气〕: 把纸收起来，别叫风～刮散了。Put away all the paper. Don't let it get blown about./ 我差点儿把这事～忘了。I almost forgot that.
另见 jǐ
【给以】 gěiyǐ 〔多用于抽象事物〕give; grant: ～充分的重视 pay ample attention to/ ～适当照顾 show due consideration for/ 给敌人以迎头痛击 deal the enemy a head-on blow/ 我们不给反动派以任何的民主权利。We will not grant any democratic rights to the reactionaries.

# gēn

## 根 gēn ① root (of a plant): 连～拔 pull up by the root ②〈数〉root: 平方～ square root ③〈化〉radical: 酸～ acid radical ④ root; foot; base: 舌～ the root of the tongue/ 城墙～ the foot (或 base) of a city wall ⑤ cause; origin; source; root: 祸～ the root of trouble or disaster/ 只有坚持走社会主义道路才能挖掉穷～。Only by sticking to the socialist road can we do away with the root cause of poverty. ⑥ thoroughly; completely: ～除 completely do away with; eradicate ⑦〈量〉〔用于细长的东西〕: 一～火柴 a match/ 一～小绳子 a piece of string
【根本】 gēnběn ① basic; fundamental; essential; cardinal: ～原因 basic reason; root cause/ ～原则 cardinal principle/ 一件带～性的大事 a major measure of fundamental importance/ 两种～对立的世界观 two diametrically opposed world outlooks/ 从～上改变农村缺医少药的现象 put an end once and for all to the lack of doctors and medicine in the rural areas/ 千头万绪抓～。Faced with a great variety of problems, one must concentrate on what is of basic importance./ 十月革命的道路，从～上说来，是全人类发展的共同的光明大道。The road of the October Revolution is, fundamentally speaking, the common bright road of development for all humanity. ②〔多用于否定〕at all; simply: 我～就不赞成你的主张。I don't agree with you at all./ 奴隶主～不把奴隶当人看待。The slave owners simply did not treat the slaves as human beings. ③ radically; thoroughly: 必须～改变我们这里的落后面貌。We must thoroughly overcome our backwardness./ 问题已经得到～解决。The problem has been settled once and for all. ◇ ～法 fundamental law
【根除】 gēnchú thoroughly do away with; eradicate; root out; eliminate: ～一切形式的殖民主义 eradicate all forms of colonialism/ ～水患 eliminate the scourge of floods
【根底】 gēndǐ ① foundation: ～浅 have a shaky foundation/ 他的英文～很好。He has a solid foundation in English. ② cause; root: 追问～ inquire into the cause of the matter/ 你了解这个人的～吗? Do you know that fellow's background?
【根腐病】 gēnfǔbìng 〈农〉 root rot
【根冠】 gēnguān 〈植〉 root cap
【根号】 gēnhào 〈数〉 radical sign
【根基】 gēnjī foundation; basis: 打好～ lay a solid foundation
【根茎】 gēnjīng 〈植〉 rhizome 又作"根状茎"
【根究】 gēnjiū make a thorough investigation of; get to the bottom of; probe into: ～缘由 probe into the cause
【根据】 gēnjù ① on the basis of; according to; in the light of; in line with: ～天气预报 according to the weather forecast/ ～具体情况 in the light of specific conditions/ ～两国人民的利益和愿望 in accordance (或 conformity) with the interests and desire of the peoples of the two countries/ ～公报的精神 in the spirit of the *communiqué*/ ～同名小说拍摄的影片 a film based on the novel of the same title ② basis; grounds; foundation: 说话要有～。One should avoid making assertions without good grounds./ 毫无～ utterly groundless ◇ ～地 base area; base
【根绝】 gēnjué stamp out; eradicate; exterminate: ～血吸虫病 stamp out snail fever/ ～事故 eliminate accidents
【根瘤】 gēnliú 〈植〉 root nodule ◇ ～菌 nodule bacteria
【根毛】 gēnmáo 〈植〉 root hair
【根苗】 gēnmiáo ① root and shoot ② source; root ③〈旧〉 offspring
【根深蒂固】 gēnshēn-dìgù deep-rooted; ingrained; inveterate: ～的偏见 deep-rooted (或 ingrained) prejudice
【根深叶茂】 gēnshēn-yèmào have deep roots and luxuriant leaves — be well established and vigorously developing
【根式】 gēnshì 〈数〉 radical (expression)

【根外追肥】 gēnwài zhuīféi foliage dressing; foliage spray
【根由】 gēnyóu cause; origin
【根源】 gēnyuán source; origin; root: 帝国主义是现代战争的～。In modern times imperialism is the source of war./ 分析犯错误的思想～ analyse the ideological roots of the mistakes
【根治】 gēnzhì effect a radical cure; cure once and for all; bring under permanent control: ～支气管炎 effect a radical cure of bronchitis/ ～海河 bring the Haihe River under permanent control; permanently harness the Haihe River ◇ ～手术〈医〉radical operation
【根轴系】 gēnzhóuxì 〈植〉root system
【根子】 gēnzi 〈口〉root; source; origin: 错误是他犯的，～可在阶级敌人那里。He made the mistake, but its source lay with the class enemy./ 这件案子的～很深。It's hard to get to the bottom of this case./ ～正，思想好 be of good class background and have sound ideology

**跟** gēn ①heel: 鞋后～ the heel of a shoe ②follow: ～我来。Come along with me./ ～着党走 follow the Party/ 紧～形势 keep abreast of the current situation/ 请～我念。Please read after me. ③〈介〉〔表示"和""同"〕: 有事要～群众商量。Consult the masses when a problem crops up./ ～社员一起劳动 work with the commune members ④〈介〉〔表示"向""对"〕: 快～大伙说说。Tell us all about it./ ～错误思想作斗争 combat wrong ideas ⑤〈介〉〔引进比较的对象〕: 今天的活儿～往常一样。Our job today is the same as before. ⑥〈连〉and: 种子～农药都准备好了。The seeds and the pesticide are both ready.
【跟班】 gēnbān ①join a regular shift or class: ～劳动 (of a leading comrade) go to work in a workshop for a specified period of time ②〈旧〉footman
【跟脚】 gēnjiǎo 〈口〉①(of shoes) fit well ②close upon sb.'s heels: 你刚走，他～儿就来找你。He came to see you just after you left.
【跟进】 gēnjìn 〈军〉follow-up
【跟前】 gēnqián in front of; close to; near: 他把我叫到～又讲了几句。He told me to come closer and said a few words more./ 桌子～靠着一支猎枪。A shotgun leans against the table.
【跟前】 gēnqian (of one's children) living with one: 他～有一儿一女。He has a son and a daughter living with him.
【跟上】 gēnshang keep pace with; catch up with; keep abreast of: 快～! Close up!/ ～亿万人民前进的步伐 keep pace with the onward march of the millions/ 跟不上形势的需要 fall short of the demands of the times
【跟随】 gēnsuí follow: 这个英雄连队曾经～毛主席长征过。This heroic company was with Chairman Mao on the Long March.
【跟头】 gēntou ①fall: 摔～ have a fall ②somersault: 翻个～ turn a somersault
【跟头虫】 gēntouchóng wiggler; wriggler
【跟着】 gēnzhe follow in the wake of: 我们听完报告～就讨论。We held a discussion right after the speech./ 革命形势变了，革命的策略也必须～改变。When the revolutionary situation changes, revolutionary tactics must change accordingly.
【跟踪】 gēnzōng follow the tracks of: 雪地～ follow sb.'s tracks in the snow/ ～追击 go in hot pursuit of/ ～敌舰 shadow the enemy warships

## gén

**哏** gén 〈方〉①amusing; comical; funny: 这孩子笑的样子有点儿～。The way the child laughs is quite funny. ②clownish speech or behaviour; clowning; antics: 逗～ play the fool

## gěn

**艮** gěn 〈方〉①(of food) tough; leathery ②straightforward; forthright; blunt: 这人真～! That fellow is really blunt./ 他说的话太～。He put it too sharply.

## gèn

**亘** gèn extend; stretch: 绵～数百里 (of a mountain range) extend for hundreds of *li*/ ～古及今 from time immemorial down to the present day

**茛** gèn 见"毛茛" máogèn

## gēng

**更** gēng ①change; replace: 除旧～新 replace the old with the new ②〈书〉experience: 少不～事 young and inexperienced ③one of the five two-hour periods into which the night was formerly divided; watch: 打～ beat the watches/ 三～半夜 in the dead of night
另见 gèng
【更迭】 gēngdié alternate; change: 内阁～ a change of cabinet
【更动】 gēngdòng change; alter: 人事～ personnel changes/ 图案已有所～。The design has been altered.
【更番】 gēngfān alternately; by turns
【更夫】 gēngfū 〈旧〉night watchman
【更改】 gēnggǎi change; alter: 由于天气恶劣，飞机不得不～航线。Owing to bad weather the plane had to change its course./ 不可～的决定 an unalterable decision
【更换】 gēnghuàn change; replace: ～位置 change places/ 农展馆的展品常有～。The exhibits in the agricultural exhibition keep changing.
【更深人静】 gēngshēn-rénjìng deep is the night and all is quiet: 在～的时候 at dead of night; in the quiet of the night
【更生】 gēngshēng ①regenerate; revive: 自力～ regeneration through one's own efforts; self-reliance ②renew: 可～和不可～的海洋资源 renewable and nonrenewable marine resources
【更生霉素】 gēngshēngméisù 〈药〉actinomycin D
【更替】 gēngtì replace: 生产方式的～ the replacement of one mode of production by another
【更新】 gēngxīn renew; replace: 设备～ renewal of equipment/ 万象～。Everything takes on a new look./ 公社的渔船在不断～。The commune's old fishing vessels are continually being replaced by new ones./ 他们采用科学方法～草场。They have adopted scientific methods to rejuvenate the pastures. ◇ ～伐〈林〉regeneration felling (或 cutting)/ ～造林 reforestation
【更新世】 Gēngxīnshì 〈地〉the Pleistocene (Epoch)
【更衣】 gēngyī change one's clothes ◇ ～室 changeroom; locker room
【更正】 gēngzhèng make corrections (of errors in statements or newspaper articles)

**庚** gēng ①the seventh of the ten Heavenly Stems

②age: 同～ of the same age

**耕** gēng plough; till: 春～ spring ploughing/ 深～ deep ploughing/ ～者有其田 land to the tiller

【耕畜】 gēngchù farm animal

【耕地】 gēngdì ①plough; till ②cultivated land: ～面积 area under cultivation; cultivated area

【耕具】 gēngjù tillage implements

【耕牛】 gēngniú farm cattle

【耕耘】 gēngyún ploughing and weeding; cultivation: 一分～,一分收获。The more ploughing and weeding, the better the crop.

【耕种】 gēngzhòng till; cultivate

【耕作】 gēngzuò tillage; cultivation; farming ◇ ～方法 methods of cultivation; farming methods/ ～机械 tillage machinery/ ～技术 farming technique/ ～园田化 garden-style cultivation of farmland; gardenization/ ～制度 cropping system

**羹** gēng a thick soup: 鸡蛋～ egg custard (usu. salty)/ 分得一杯～ take a share of the spoils or profits

【羹匙】 gēngchí soup spoon; tablespoon

## gěng

**埂** gěng ①a low bank of earth between fields ②a long, narrow mound ③an earth dyke (或 embankment)

**耿** gěng ①〈书〉 bright ②dedicated ③honest and just; upright ④(Gěng) a surname

【耿耿】 gěnggěng ①devoted; dedicated: 忠心～为革命 be dedicated heart and soul to the revolution ②have sth. on one's mind; be troubled: ～不寐 lose sleep over sth./ ～于怀 brood on (an injury, one's neglected duty, etc.); take sth. to heart

【耿直】 gěngzhí honest and frank; upright: 秉性～ be upright by nature

**哽** gěng choke (with emotion); feel a lump in one's throat

【哽咽】 gěngyè choke with sobs

**梗** gěng ①stalk; stem: 荷～ lotus stem/ 菠菜～儿 spinach stalk ②a slender piece of wood or metal: 火柴～ matchstick ③straighten: ～着脖子 straighten up one's neck ④obstruct; block: 从中作～ place obstacles in the way; put a spoke in sb.'s wheel

【梗概】 gěnggài broad outline; main idea; gist: 故事的～ the gist of a story; synopsis

【梗塞】 gěngsè ①block; obstruct; clog: 交通～ traffic jam ②〈医〉 infarction: 心肌～ myocardial infarction

【梗直】 gěngzhí honest and frank; upright

【梗阻】 gěngzǔ ①block; obstruct; hamper: 横加～ unreasonably obstruct/ 山川～ be separated by mountains and rivers; be far away from each other ②〈医〉 obstruction: 肠～ intestinal obstruction

**颈** gěng 见"脖颈儿" bógěngr

另见 jǐng

**鲠** gěng ①〈书〉 fishbone ②(of a fishbone) get stuck in one's throat

【鲠直】 gěngzhí honest and frank; upright

## gèng

**更** gèng 〈副〉 ①more; still more; even more: 团结起来,争取～大的胜利! Unite to win still greater victories! ②further; furthermore; what is more: ～进一步 go a step further/ 不能压制批评,～不能打击报复。One must not suppress criticism, still less retaliate on one's critics./ ～有甚者 what is more/ ～上一层楼 climb one storey higher; attain a yet higher goal; scale new heights

另见 gēng

【更加】 gèngjiā 〈副〉 more; still more; even more: 问题～复杂了。The problem became even more complicated./ 经过无产阶级文化大革命,我国的无产阶级专政～巩固。As a result of the Great Proletarian Cultural Revolution, our proletarian dictatorship has been further consolidated. 又作"更其"

## gōng

**工** gōng ①worker; workman; the working class: 女～ woman worker/ 矿～ miner/ ～欲善其事,必先利其器。A workman must first sharpen his tools if he is to do his work well. ②work; labour: 上～ go to work/ 既省料又省～ save both material and labour ③(construction) project: 动～ begin a project/ 竣～ complete a project ④industry: 化～ chemical industry/ ～交战线 the industry and communications front; industry and communications ⑤man-day: 这项工程需要五千个～。This project will take 5,000 man-days to complete. ⑥skill; craftsmanship: 唱～ (art of) singing/ 做～ acting ⑦be versed in; be good at: ～诗善画 be well versed in painting and poetry ⑧〈乐〉 a note of the scale in *gongchepu* (工尺谱), corresponding to 3 in numbered musical notation

【工本】 gōngběn cost (of production): 不惜～ spare no expense

【工笔】 gōngbǐ 〈美术〉 traditional Chinese realistic painting characterized by fine brushwork and close attention to detail

【工兵】 gōngbīng engineer: 坑道～ sapper/ 轻～ pioneer

【工部】 Gōngbù the Ministry of Works in feudal China

【工厂】 gōngchǎng factory; mill; plant; works: 铁～ iron works ◇ ～区 factory district

【工场】 gōngchǎng workshop

【工潮】 gōngcháo workers' demonstration or protest movement; strike movement

【工尺】 gōngchě *gongche*, a traditional Chinese musical scale ◇ ～谱 *gongchepu*, a traditional Chinese muscial notation

【工程】 gōngchéng engineering; project: 土木(机械、电机、采矿)～ civil (mechanical, electrical, mining) engineering/ 水利～ water conservancy project/ ～浩大 a gigantic project; a tremendous amount of work ◇ ～兵 engineer/ ～兵部队 engineer troops (或 units)/ ～地质学 engineering geology/ ～队 construction brigade/ ～技术人员 engineers and technicians/ ～师 engineer/ ～塑料 engineering plastics/ ～验收〈建〉 acceptance of work

【工党】 gōngdǎng the Labour Party

【工地】 gōngdì building site; construction site

【工段】 gōngduàn ①a section of a construction project ②workshop section ◇ ～长 section chief

【工分】 gōngfēn workpoint (a unit indicating the quantity and quality of labour performed, and the amount of

payment earned, in rural people's communes) ◇ ～值 cash value of a workpoint
【工蜂】 gōngfēng worker (bee)
【工夫】 gōngfu ① time: 他三天～就学会了滑冰。It took him only three days to learn to skate./ 她去了没多大～就回来了。She didn't take long to get there and come back./ 明天有～再来吧。Come again tomorrow if you have time. ② workmanship; skill; art: 练～ (of actors, athletes, etc.) practise/ 这位杂技演员可真有～! The acrobat's skill is really superb! ③ work; labour; effort: 花了好大～ put in a lot of work/ 只要～深,铁杵磨成针。〈谚〉 If you work at it hard enough, you can grind an iron rod into a needle.
【工会】 gōnghuì trade union; labour union
【工间操】 gōngjiāncāo work-break exercises
【工件】 gōngjiàn workpiece; work ◇ ～夹具 workpiece holder; (work) fixture/ ～架 work rest
【工匠】 gōngjiàng craftsman; artisan
【工具】 gōngjù tool; means; instrument; implement: 木工～ carpenter's tools/ 生产～ implements of production/ 运输～ means of transport/ 爱护～ take good care of the tools/ ～改革 improvement of tools
◇ ～车床 toolmaker lathe/ ～袋 kit bag; workbag/ ～房 toolhouse/ ～钢 tool steel/ ～书 reference book/ ～箱 toolbox; tool kit; workbox
【工科】 gōngkē engineering course ◇ ～大学 college of engineering
【工力】 gōnglì skill; craftsmanship: ～深厚 remarkable craftsmanship/ 颇见～ show the hand of a master
【工联主义】 gōngliánzhǔyì (trade) unionism
【工龄】 gōnglíng length of service; standing; seniority: 一个有三十年～的老工人 an old worker of thirty years' standing
【工农】 gōng-nóng workers and peasants
◇ ～差别 the difference between industry and agriculture/ ～大众 the broad masses of workers and peasants/ ～干部 cadres of worker-peasant origin; worker and peasant cadres/ ～联盟 alliance of workers and peasants; worker-peasant alliance/ ～子弟 children of workers and peasants/ ～子弟兵 workers' and peasants' own troops
【工农兵】 gōng-nóng-bīng workers, peasants and soldiers: 革命文艺应当为～服务。Revolutionary literature and art should serve the workers, peasants and soldiers. ◇ ～学员 worker-peasant-soldier students
【工农业总产值】 gōng-nóngyè zǒngchǎnzhí gross output value of industry and agriculture
【工棚】 gōngpéng ① builders' temporary shed ② work shed
【工期】 gōngqī time limit for a project
【工钱】 gōngqián ① money paid for odd jobs; charge for a service: 做这套衣服要多少～? How much should I pay for having the suit made? ② 〈口〉 wages; pay
【工巧】 gōngqiǎo exquisite; fine
【工区】 gōngqū work area (a grass-roots unit of an industrial enterprise)
【工人】 gōngrén worker; workman: 产业～ industrial worker
◇ ～干部 worker-cadre/ ～贵族 labour aristocracy/ ～技术员 technician of worker origin; worker-technician/ ～纠察队 workers' pickets/ ～运动 labour (或 workers') movement
【工人阶级】 gōngrénjiējí the working class
【工伤】 gōngshāng injury suffered on the job; industrial injury: ～事故 industrial accident
【工商界】 gōng-shāngjiè industrial and commercial circles; business circles
【工商联】 gōng-shānglián 〈简〉 (工商业联合会) association of industry and commerce
【工商业】 gōng-shāngyè industry and commerce: 私营～ privately owned industrial and commercial enterprises ◇ ～者 industrialists and businessmen (或 merchants)
【工时】 gōngshí man-hour
【工事】 gōngshì fortifications; defence works
【工头】 gōngtóu foreman; overseer
【工团主义】 gōngtuánzhǔyì syndicalism
【工委】 gōngwěi 〈简〉 (工作委员会) working committee
【工效】 gōngxiào work efficiency
【工休日】 gōngxiūrì day off; holiday
【工序】 gōngxù working procedure; process
【工宣队】 gōngxuānduì 〈简〉 (工人毛泽东思想宣传队) workers' Mao Zedong Thought propaganda team; workers' propaganda team
【工业】 gōngyè industry: 轻(重)～ light (heavy) industry/ ～酒精 industrial alcohol
◇ ～大气压 technic atmosphere/ ～革命 the Industrial Revolution/ ～国 industrialized (或 industrial) country/ ～化 industrialization/ ～基地 industrial base/ ～品 industrial products; manufactured goods/ ～企业 industrial enterprise/ ～体系 industrial system/ ～无产阶级 the industrial proletariat/ ～总产值 gross value of industrial output
【工蚁】 gōngyǐ worker (ant)
【工艺】 gōngyì technology; craft: 手～ handicraft
◇ ～流程 technological process/ ～美术 industrial art; arts and crafts/ ～品 handicraft article; handiwork; handicraft/ ～设计 technological design/ ～水平 technological level/ ～要求 technological requirements
【工友】 gōngyǒu 〈旧〉 ① fellow worker ② a manual worker such as janitor, cleaner, etc. in a school or government office
【工贼】 gōngzéi scab; blackleg
【工长】 gōngzhǎng section chief (in a workshop, or on a building site); foreman
【工整】 gōngzhěng carefully and neatly done: 字迹～ neatly lettered/ 他把列宁的语录工工整整地写在书的衬页上。He carefully printed the quotation from Lenin on the flyleaf.
【工种】 gōngzhǒng type of work in production
【工装裤】 gōngzhuāngkù overalls
【工资】 gōngzī wages; pay: 基本～ basic wages/ 附加～ supplementary wages/ 货币～ money wages
◇ ～表 payroll; pay sheet/ ～袋 pay packet/ ～改革 reform of the wage system/ ～级别 wage scale/ ～率 wage rate/ ～制 wage system
【工字钢】 gōngzìgāng I-steel
【工字形】 gōngzìxíng I-shaped
【工作】 gōngzuò work; job: 努力～ work hard/ 分配～ assign jobs (或 work)/ 他是做消防～的。He works in the fire brigade.
◇ ～本 working copy/ ～单位 an organization in which one works; place of work/ ～队 work team; working force/ ～服 work clothes; boiler suit/ ～会议 working conference/ ～量 amount of work; work load/ ～母机 machine tool/ ～人员 working personnel; staff member; functionary/ ～日 workday; working day/ ～台 〈机〉 working table; bench/ ～样片 〈电影〉 rushes/ ～语言 working language/ ～证 employee's card; I.D. card
【工作面】 gōngzuòmiàn ① 〈矿〉 face: 采煤～ coal face/ 回采～ stope ② 〈机〉 working surface ◇ ～运输机〈矿〉 face conveyor
【工作者】 gōngzuòzhě worker: 教育～ educational worker/ 文艺～ literary and art workers; writers and artists/ 美术

～ art worker; artist/ 音乐～ musician/ 新闻～ journalist

**弓** gōng ① bow: ～箭 bow and arrow ② anything bow-shaped ③ wooden land-measuring dividers ④ an old unit of length for measuring land, equal to five *chi* (尺) ⑤ bend; arch; bow: ～着背 arch one's back; bend low

【弓箭步】 gōngjiànbù forward lunge (in *wushu* 武术 or gymnastics)

【弓弦】 gōngxián bowstring ◇ ～乐器 bowed stringed (或 string) instrument; bowed instrument

【弓形】 gōngxíng ①〈数〉 segment of a circle ② bow-shaped; arched; curved

【弓子】 gōngzi ① bow (of a stringed instrument) ② anything bow-shaped

【弓钻】 gōngzuàn bow drill

**公** gōng ① public; state-owned; collective: ～私要分清 make a clear distinction between public and private interests/ 交～ turn over to the authorities/ 立党为～ build a party to serve the interests of the vast majority ② common; general: ～分母 common denominator ③ metric: ～里 kilometre ④ make public: ～之于世 make known to the world; reveal to the public ⑤ equitable; impartial; fair; just: 秉～办理 handle affairs equitably or impartially; be evenhanded ⑥ public affairs; official business: ～余 after work/ 因～外出 be away on official business ⑦ duke ⑧〔旧时对中年以上男子的尊称〕: 张～ the revered Mr. Zhang ⑨ husband's father; father-in-law: ～说～有理，婆说婆有理。Each says he is right. 或 Both parties claim to be in the right. ⑩ male (animal): ～牛 bull/ ～鸡 cock; rooster ⑪ (Gōng) a surname

【公安】 gōng'ān public security ◇～部 the Ministry of Public Security/ ～部队 public security troops/ ～机关 public security organs/ ～局 public security bureau/ ～人员 public security officer (或 man)

【公案】 gōng'àn 〈旧〉 a complicated legal case: 无头～ an intricate case without a clue

【公报】 gōngbào *communiqué*; bulletin: 联合～ joint *communiqué*/ 新闻～ press *communiqué*/ 政府～ (government) bulletin

【公报私仇】 gōng bào sīchóu avenge a personal wrong in the name of public interests; abuse public power to retaliate on a personal enemy

【公倍数】 gōngbèishù 〈数〉 common multiple: 最小～ least (或 lowest) common multiple

【公布】 gōngbù promulgate; announce; publish; make public: ～法令 promulgate a decree/ ～罪状 announce sb.'s crimes/ ～名单 publish a name list

【公差】 gōngchā ①〈数〉 common difference ②〈机〉 tolerance: 制造(安装)～ manufacturing (location) tolerance

【公差】 gōngchāi ① public errand; noncombatant duty: 出～ go on a public errand; go on official business; perform noncombatant duty ② a person on a public errand (或 noncombatant duty): 连里叫咱们班出两个～。The company has assigned two men from our squad to noncombatant duty.

【公产】 gōngchǎn public property

【公称】 gōngchēng nominal ◇ ～尺寸〈机〉 nominal dimension

【公尺】 gōngchǐ metre (m.)

【公出】 gōngchū be away on official business

【公畜】 gōngchù male animal (kept for breeding); stud

【公担】 gōngdàn quintal (q.)

【公道】 gōngdào justice: 主持～ uphold justice

【公道】 gōngdao fair; just; reasonable; impartial: 说句～话 to be fair; in fairness to sb./ 价钱～。The price is reasonable./ 办事～ be evenhanded; be impartial

【公德】 gōngdé social morality; social ethics: 有～心 be public-spirited

【公敌】 gōngdí public enemy: 人民～ an enemy of the people; a public enemy

【公断】 gōngduàn arbitration

【公吨】 gōngdūn metric ton (MT)

【公而忘私】 gōng ér wàng sī so devoted to public service as to forget one's own interests; selfless: ～的共产主义风格 a selfless communist spirit

【公法】 gōngfǎ 〈法〉 public law

【公费】 gōngfèi at public (或 state) expense ◇ ～医疗 free medical service (或 care); public health services

【公分】 gōngfēn ① centimetre (cm.) ② gram (g.)

【公愤】 gōngfèn public indignation; popular anger: 引起～ arouse public indignation

【公干】 gōnggàn business: 有何～? What important business brings you here?

【公告】 gōnggào announcement; proclamation

【公共】 gōnggòng public; common; communal ◇ ～财产 public property/ ～厕所 public conveniences; public latrine/ ～场所 public places/ ～积累 common accumulation; accumulation fund/ ～建筑 public buildings/ ～食堂 canteen; mess/ ～卫生 public health (或 hygiene)/ ～秩序 public order

【公共汽车】 gōnggòng qìchē bus ◇ ～线路 bus line/ ～站 bus stop

【公公】 gōnggong ① husband's father; father-in-law ②〈方〉 grandfather ③〈尊〉 grandpa; grandad

【公股】 gōnggǔ government share (in a joint state-private enterprise)

【公馆】 gōngguǎn 〈旧〉 residence (of a rich or important person); mansion

【公国】 gōngguó duchy; dukedom

【公海】 gōnghǎi high seas

【公害】 gōnghài social effects of pollution; environmental pollution

【公函】 gōnghán official letter

【公积金】 gōngjījīn accumulation fund (of a socialist economic collective)

【公祭】 gōngjì public memorial ceremony

【公家】 gōngjia 〈口〉 the state; the public; the organization: 咱们宁可个人受损失，也决不让～吃亏。We would rather sustain personal losses than let the state suffer./ ～的财产就是人民的财产。Public property is the people's property.

【公检法】 gōng-jiǎn-fǎ public security organs, procuratorial organs and people's courts

【公教人员】 gōng-jiào rényuán 〈旧〉 government employees and teachers

【公斤】 gōngjīn kilogram (kg.); kilo

【公爵】 gōngjué duke ◇ ～夫人 duchess

【公开】 gōngkāi ① open; overt; public: ～论战 open polemics/ ～审判 public (或 open) trial/ ～的秘密 an open secret/ ～的斗争 an overt struggle/ ～的和暗藏的敌人 overt and covert enemies/ ～的场合 a public occasion/ ～指名攻击 attack publicly by name ② make public; make known to the public: 把事情～出去 make the matter known to the public ◇ ～化 come out into the open; be brought into the open/ ～信 open letter

【公款】 gōngkuǎn public money (或 fund)

【公厘】 gōnglí millimetre (mm.)

【公里】 gōnglǐ kilometre (km.)

【公理】 gōnglǐ ① generally acknowledged truth; self-evident

truth ②〈数〉axiom
【公理宗】Gōnglǐzōng 〈基督教〉the Congregational Church
【公历】gōnglì ① the Gregorian calendar ② 见"公元"
【公立】gōnglì established and maintained by the government; public
【公例】gōnglì general rule
【公粮】gōngliáng agricultural tax paid in grain; grain delivered to the state; public grain
【公量】gōngliàng 〈纺〉conditioned weight
【公路】gōnglù highway; road: 高速～ express highway; expressway
◇ ～工程 highway engineering/ ～交通 highway communication (或 traffic)/ ～桥 highway bridge/ ～容量 highway capacity/ ～运输 highway (或 road) transportation
【公论】gōnglùn public opinion; verdict of the masses: 是非自有～。Public opinion will decide which is right and which is wrong. 或 Public opinion is the best judge.
【公民】gōngmín citizen ◇ ～权 civil rights; citizenship; citizen's rights/ ～投票 referendum; plebiscite
【公亩】gōngmǔ are (a.)
【公墓】gōngmù cemetery
【公平】gōngping fair; just; impartial; equitable: ～合理 fair and reasonable/ 买卖～ be fair in buying and selling; buy and sell at reasonable prices/ ～交易 fair deal/ ～的协议 an equitable agreement/ 太不～了。It's grossly unfair.
【公婆】gōng-pó husband's father and mother; parents-in-law
【公仆】gōngpú public servant
【公切线】gōngqiēxiàn 〈数〉common tangent
【公勤人员】gōng-qín rényuán service personnel in an office; office attendants
【公顷】gōngqǐng hectare (ha.)
【公然】gōngrán 〈贬〉openly; undisguisedly; brazenly: ～撕毁协议 brazenly tear up an agreement/ 对马列主义的～背叛 open betrayal of Marxism-Leninism
【公认】gōngrèn generally acknowledged (或 recognized); (universally) accepted; established: ～的领袖 acknowledged leader/ ～的国际关系原则 generally recognized principles governing international relations/ ～的国际法准则 established principles of international law
【公设】gōngshè 〈数〉postulate
【公社】gōngshè ① primitive commune ② commune: 巴黎～ the Paris Commune ③ people's commune
【公社化】gōngshèhuà be organized into people's communes: 我们县在一九五八年实现了～。People's communes were organized throughout our county in 1958.
【公审】gōngshěn 〈法〉public (或 open) trial
【公使】gōngshǐ envoy; minister ◇ ～馆 legation/ ～衔参赞 counsellor with the rank of minister; minister-counsellor
【公式】gōngshì formula
【公式化】gōngshìhuà ① formulism (in art and literature) ② formulistic; stereotyped
【公事】gōngshì public affairs; official business (或 duties): 还是～要紧。Public affairs should come first./ 我还有很多～要办。I still have a lot of official duties to attend to. ◇ ～包 briefcase; portfolio
【公事公办】gōngshì gōng bàn do official business according to official principles; not let personal considerations interfere with one's execution of public duty
【公司】gōngsī company; corporation: 钢铁～ iron and steel company/ 进出口～ import and export corporation
【公私合营】gōng-sī héyíng joint state-private ownership (the principal form of state capitalism adopted during the socialist transformation of capitalist enterprises in China) ◇ ～企业 joint state-private enterprise
【公诉】gōngsù 〈法〉public prosecution: 对罪犯提起～ institute proceedings against a legal offender ◇ ～人 public prosecutor; the prosecution
【公孙】Gōngsūn a surname
【公堂】gōngtáng 〈旧〉law court; tribunal: 私设～ set up a clandestine tribunal
【公推】gōngtuī recommend by general acclaim
【公文】gōngwén official document
◇ ～程式 forms and formulas of official documents/ ～袋 document envelope/ ～纸 paper for copying documents
【公务】gōngwù public affairs; official business
◇ ～护照 service passport/ ～人员 government functionary/ ～员 orderly
【公物】gōngwù public property
【公休】gōngxiū general holiday; official holiday
【公演】gōngyǎn perform in public; give a performance
【公羊】Gōngyáng a surname
【公议】gōngyì public or mass discussion: 自报～ self-assessment and public discussion/ 交由群众～ pass on to the masses for discussion
【公益】gōngyì public good; public welfare: 热心～ public-spirited ◇ ～金 public welfare fund (of a socialist economic collective)
【公意】gōngyì public will; will of the public
【公因子】gōngyīnzǐ 〈数〉common factor: 最大～ greatest common factor (或 divisor)
【公营】gōngyíng publicly-owned; publicly-operated; public ◇ ～经济 the public sector of the economy; public economy/ ～企业 public enterprise
【公用】gōngyòng for public use; public; communal ◇ ～电话 public telephone/ ～事业 public utilities
【公有】gōngyǒu publicly-owned; public: ～财产 public property ◇ ～化 transfer to public ownership; socialization/ ～制 public ownership (of means of production)
【公寓】gōngyù ① flats; apartment house ②〈旧〉lodging house
【公元】gōngyuán the Christian era: ～一二〇〇年 A. D. 1200/ ～前二二一年 221 B. C.
【公园】gōngyuán park
【公约】gōngyuē ① convention; pact: 北大西洋～ the North Atlantic Treaty ② joint pledge: 爱国卫生～ patriotic public health pledge/ 服务～ service pledge (given by workers in the service trades)
【公约数】gōngyuēshù 〈数〉common divisor
【公允】gōngyǔn just and sound; fair and equitable; even-handed: 持论～ be just and fair in argument/ 貌似～ pretend to be just and fair; put on an appearance of impartiality
【公债】gōngzhài (government) bonds: 经济建设～ economic construction bonds
【公章】gōngzhāng official seal
【公正】gōngzhèng just; fair; impartial; fair-minded: ～的舆论 fair-minded public opinion/ 历史将对这些人作出最～的判断。History will pass the fairest judgment on such people.
【公证】gōngzhèng notarization ◇ ～人 notary public; notary
【公职】gōngzhí public office; public employment: 担任～ hold public office/ 开除～ discharge from public employment
【公制】gōngzhì the metric system ◇ ～尺寸 metric size/ ～螺纹〈机〉metric thread
【公众】gōngzhòng the public
【公诸同好】gōng zhū tónghào share enjoyment with those

of the same taste
【公主】 gōngzhǔ princess
【公转】 gōngzhuàn 〈天〉 revolution
【公子】 gōngzǐ son of a feudal prince or high official
【公子哥儿】 gōngzǐgēr a pampered son of a wealthy or influential family

**功** gōng ① meritorious service (或 deed); merit; exploit: 立大～ render outstanding service/ 二等～ Merit Citation Class II/ ～大于过 one's achievements outweigh one's errors ② achievement; result: 事半～倍 yield twice the result with half the effort/ 劳而无～ work hard but to no avail ③ skill: 练～ do exercises in gymnastics, acrobatics, etc.; practise one's skill/ ～到自然成。Constant effort yields sure success. ④〈物〉work: 机械～ mechanical work
【功败垂成】 gōng bài chuí chéng fail in a great undertaking on the verge of success; suffer defeat when victory is within one's grasp
【功臣】 gōngchén a person who has rendered outstanding service: 治淮～ meritorious workers in harnessing the Huaihe River/ 不要以～自居。Don't give yourself the airs of a hero.
【功德】 gōngdé ① merits and virtues ②〈佛教〉charitable and pious deeds; benefaction; beneficence; works: ～无量 boundless beneficence
【功夫】 gōngfu 见"工夫" gōngfu
【功绩】 gōngjì merits and achievements; contribution: 为革命事业建立不朽的～ make immortal contributions to the revolutionary cause
【功课】 gōngkè schoolwork; homework: 做～ do homework
【功亏一篑】 gōng kuī yī kuì fail to build a mound for want of one final basket of earth — fall short of success for lack of a final effort
【功劳】 gōngláo contribution; meritorious service; credit: 她的～可不小啊！She has certainly made no small contribution! 或 She has rendered great service./ 这都是群众的～。All the credit should go to the masses./ 绝不能把一切～归于自己。One must never claim all the credit for oneself.
【功劳簿】 gōngláobù record of merits: 不要躺在自己的～上。Don't rest on your laurels.
【功利】 gōnglì utility; material gain ◇ ～主义 utilitarianism/ ～主义者 utilitarian
【功率】 gōnglǜ 〈物〉power ◇ ～计 dynamometer
【功名】 gōngmíng scholarly honour or official rank (in feudal times)
【功能】 gōngnéng function: ～锻炼 functional training/ ～性障碍 functional disorder/ 肝～正常。The liver is functioning normally.
【功效】 gōngxiào efficacy; effect
【功勋】 gōngxūn exploit; meritorious service: 为革命立下了不朽的～ have performed immortal feats for the revolution
【功业】 gōngyè exploits; achievements
【功用】 gōngyòng function; use

**红** gōng 见"女红" nǚgōng
另见 hóng

**攻** gōng ① attack; take the offensive: ～入敌阵 storm into the enemy position/ 主～方向 the main direction of the offensive/ 全～型选手 an all-out attack player ② accuse; charge: 群起而～之。Everyone points an accusing finger at him. ③ study; specialize in: 他专～考古学。He specializes in archaeology.
【攻城略地】 gōngchéng-lüèdì take cities and seize territory
【攻打】 gōngdǎ attack; assault
【攻读】 gōngdú ① assiduously study; diligently study ② specialize in
【攻关】 gōngguān ① storm a strategic pass ② tackle key problems: 三结合～小组 three-in-one key task team
【攻击】 gōngjī ① attack; assault; launch an offensive: 发起总～ launch a general offensive ② accuse; charge; vilify: 恶毒～ viciously attack/ 无端的～ groundless charges/ 人身～ personal attack ◇ ～点 a point chosen for attack; point of attack/ ～机 attack plane; attacker
【攻坚】 gōngjiān storm fortifications; assault fortified positions
◇ ～部队 assault troops/ ～战 storming of heavily fortified positions/ ～战术 tactics of storming heavily fortified points
【攻讦】 gōngjié 〈书〉 rake up sb.'s past and attack him; expose sb.'s past misdeeds
【攻克】 gōngkè capture; take: ～敌军据点 capture an enemy stronghold/ ～技术难关 surmount (或 overcome) a technical difficulty; solve a difficult technical problem
【攻破】 gōngpò make a breakthrough; breach: ～敌军防线 break through (或 penetrate) the enemy defence lines/ 正义的事业是任何敌人也攻不破的。A just cause is invincible before any enemy.
【攻其不备】 gōng qí bù bèi strike where or when the enemy is unprepared; take sb. by surprise; catch sb. unawares
【攻其一点,不及其余】 gōng qí yī diǎn, bù jí qí yú attack sb. for a single fault without considering his other aspects; seize upon one point and ignore the overall picture
【攻取】 gōngqǔ storm and capture; attack and seize
【攻势】 gōngshì offensive: 采取～ take the offensive/ 政治～ political offensive/ 客队～凌厉。The visiting team maintained a powerful offensive. ◇ ～防御 offensive defence/ ～作战 offensive operation
【攻守同盟】 gōng-shǒu tóngméng ① offensive and defensive alliance; military alliance ② an agreement between partners in crime not to give each other away; a pact to shield each other
【攻丝】 gōngsī 〈机〉 tapping ◇ ～机 tapping machine
【攻无不克】 gōng wú bù kè all-conquering; ever-victorious
【攻下】 gōngxià capture; take; overcome: ～这一关,其他问题就好办了。Once this difficulty is overcome, other problems will be easy to solve.
【攻陷】 gōngxiàn capture; storm: 夺回被敌军～的城镇 recapture towns from enemy hands
【攻心】 gōngxīn make a psychological attack; try to persuade an offender to confess: 政策～ try to win over or obtain a confession from a person by explaining the Party's policy
【攻占】 gōngzhàn attack and occupy; storm and capture

**供** gōng ① supply; feed: ～不上 run out; be in short supply/ 你～砖,我来砌。You pass the bricks to me, and I'll lay them. ② for (the use or convenience of): 仅～参考 for your reference only/ ～批判用 to be criticized and rebutted/ 这个饭厅可～五百人同时用饭。This dining hall can accommodate five hundred people at a time.
另见 gòng
【供不应求】 gōng bù yìng qiú supply falls short of demand; demand exceeds supply
【供电】 gōngdiàn power supply

◇ ～调度员 load dispatcher/ ～干线 supply main/ ～局 power supply bureau

【供给】 gōngjǐ supply; provide; furnish: 原料由国家～。Raw materials are provided by the state.

【供给制】 gōngjǐzhì the supply system — a system of payment in kind (practised during the revolutionary wars and in the early days of the People's Republic, providing working personnel and their dependents with the primary necessities of life)

【供暖】 gōngnuǎn 〈建〉 heating: 热水～ hot water heating/ 蒸气～ steam heating ◇ ～系统 heating system

【供气】 gōngqì 〈机〉 air feed

【供求】 gōng-qiú supply and demand: ～关系 the relation between supply and demand/ ～平衡 balance between supply and demand

【供销】 gōng-xiāo supply and marketing ◇ ～(合作)社 supply and marketing cooperative

【供养】 gōngyǎng provide for (one's parents or elders); support
另见 gòngyǎng

【供应】 gōngyìng supply: 医药品～ medical supplies/ 市场～ supply of commodities; market supplies ◇ ～点 supply centre/ ～线 supply line

## 肱

gōng 〈书〉 the upper arm; arm

【肱骨】 gōnggǔ 〈生理〉 humerus

## 宫

gōng ① palace ② temple (used in a name): 雍和～ the Lama Temple of Peace and Harmony (in Beijing) ③ a place for cultural activities and recreation: 工人文化～ the Workers' Cultural Palace ④〈生理〉 womb; uterus ⑤〈乐〉 a note of the ancient Chinese five-tone scale, corresponding to 1 in numbered musical notation ⑥ (Gōng) a surname

【宫灯】 gōngdēng palace lantern

【宫殿】 gōngdiàn palace ◇ ～式建筑 palatial architecture

【宫调】 gōngdiào 〈乐〉 modes of ancient Chinese music

【宫内节育器】 gōngnèi jiéyùqì intrauterine device (IUD)

【宫女】 gōngnǚ a maid in an imperial palace; maid of honour

【宫阙】 gōngquè 〈书〉 imperial palace

【宫廷】 gōngtíng ① palace ② royal or imperial court; court ◇ ～政变 palace *coup*; *coup*

【宫外孕】 gōngwàiyùn 〈医〉 ectopic pregnancy; extrauterine pregnancy

【宫闱】 gōngwéi 〈书〉 palace chambers

【宫刑】 gōngxíng castration (a punishment in ancient China) 参见"五刑" wǔxíng

## 恭

gōng respectful; reverent

【恭贺】 gōnghè congratulate: ～新禧 Happy New Year

【恭候】 gōnghòu 〈敬〉 await respectfully: ～光临。We request the pleasure of your company.

【恭谨】 gōngjǐn respectful and cautious

【恭敬】 gōngjìng respectful: 恭恭敬敬地向群众学习 learn respectfully from the masses

【恭顺】 gōngshùn respectful and submissive

【恭桶】 gōngtǒng closestool; commode

【恭维】 gōngwei flatter; compliment ◇ ～话 flattery; compliments 又作"恭惟"

【恭喜】 gōngxǐ 〈套〉 congratulations

## 蚣

gōng 见"蜈蚣" wúgong

## 躬

gōng ① 〈书〉 personally: ～行实践 practise what one preaches/ ～逢其盛 be present in person on the grand occasion ② bend forward; bow: ～身 bend at the waist

【躬亲】 gōngqīn attend to personally: 事必～ attend to everything personally

## 龚

Gōng a surname

## 觥

gōng 〈考古〉 an ancient wine vessel made of horn

# gǒng

## 巩

gǒng ① consolidate ② (Gǒng) a surname

【巩固】 gǒnggù ① consolidate; strengthen; solidify: ～阵地 consolidate a position/ ～工农联盟 strengthen the worker-peasant alliance ② consolidated; strong; solid; stable: 建立～的革命根据地 build stable revolutionary base areas/ ～的国防 strong national defence/ 我国无产阶级专政空前～。The dictatorship of the proletariat in our country is more consolidated than ever.

【巩膜】 gǒngmó 〈生理〉 sclera ◇ ～炎〈医〉 scleritis

## 汞

gǒng 〈化〉 mercury (Hg)

【汞弧灯】 gǒnghúdēng 〈电〉 mercury-arc lamp

【汞化】 gǒnghuà 〈化〉 mercuration; mercurization ◇ ～物 mercuride

【汞溴红】 gǒngxiùhóng 〈药〉 mercurochrome

## 拱

gǒng ① cup one hand in the other before the chest ② surround: 众星～月。A myriad of stars surround the moon. ③ hump up; arch: 猫～了～腰。The cat arched its back. ④〈建〉 arch: ～式涵洞 arch culvert/ ～道 archway ⑤ push without using one's hands: 用肩膀把门～开 push open the door with one's shoulder ⑥ (of pigs, etc.) dig earth with the snout; (of earthworms, etc.) wriggle through the earth ⑦ sprout up through the earth

【拱坝】 gǒngbà 〈水〉 arch dam

【拱抱】 gǒngbào surround: 群峰～的山坞 a cove surrounded by cliffs

【拱点】 gǒngdiǎn 〈天〉 apsis; apse

【拱顶】 gǒngdǐng 〈建〉 vault

【拱门】 gǒngmén 〈建〉 arched door

【拱桥】 gǒngqiáo 〈建〉 arch bridge: 双曲～ double-curvature arch bridge

【拱手】 gǒngshǒu ① make an obeisance by cupping one hand in the other before one's chest ② submissively: ～让人 surrender sth. submissively; hand over sth. on a silver platter

【拱卫】 gǒngwèi surround and protect

【拱券】 gǒngxuàn 〈建〉 arch

## 珙

gǒng 〈书〉 a kind of jade

【珙桐】 gǒngtóng 〈植〉 dove tree

# gòng

## 共

gòng ① common; general: ～性 general character ② share: 同呼吸，～命运 share a common fate; throw in one's lot with sb. ③ doing the same thing; together: 各族人民的代表～聚一堂，商讨国家大事。Representatives of different nationalities gather in the same hall to discuss affairs of state./ 两国人民～饮一江水。The people of our two countries drink from the same river. ④ altogether; in all; all told: 这个生产大队全年～打粮食四十万斤。The production brigade harvested altogether 400,000 *jin* of grain that year. ⑤〈简〉(共产党) the Communist Party: 中～ the CPC (the Communist Party of China)

【共产党】 gòngchǎndǎng the Communist Party
◇ ～人 Communist/ «～宣言» *Manifesto of the Communist Party*; *Communist Manifesto*/ ～员 member of the Communist Party; Communist; Party member

【共产国际】 Gòngchǎn Guójì the Communist International (1919-1943); Comintern

【共产主义】 gòngchǎnzhǔyì communism: 我们对～事业充满着必胜的信念。We are fully confident that the cause of communism will triumph.
◇ ～道德 communist morality/ ～风格 communist style (或 spirit)/ ～觉悟 communist consciousness/ ～劳动大学 Communist Labour University/ ～人生观 communist outlook on life/ ～者 communist

【共产主义青年团】 gòngchǎnzhǔyì qīngniántuán the Communist Youth League

【共处】 gòngchǔ coexist

【共存】 gòngcún coexist

【共大】 gòngdà 〈简〉(共产主义劳动大学) Communist Labour University

【共电制】 gòngdiànzhì 〈讯〉 common-battery system ◇ ～电话机 common-battery telephone/ ～电话局 common-battery telephone exchange

【共轭】 gòng'è conjugate ◇ ～象〈物〉 conjugate image/ ～角〈数〉 conjugate angles

【共发射极】 gòngfāshèjí 〈电子〉 common emitter

【共犯】 gòngfàn 〈法〉 accomplice

【共管】 gòngguǎn 〈外〉 condominium

【共和】 gònghé republicanism; republic ◇ ～国 republic

【共基极】 gòngjījí 〈电子〉 common base

【共计】 gòngjì amount to; add up to; total: 两项开支～三十元。These two items of expenditure come to thirty *yuan*./ 解放战争中我们～歼灭八百万国民党反动军队。During the War of Liberation we wiped out a grand total of eight million reactionary KMT troops./ 参观展览会的～二十万人。Altogether 200,000 people visited the exhibition.

【共价】 gòngjià 〈化〉 covalence ◇ ～键 covalent bond

【共聚】 gòngjù 〈化〉 copolymerization ◇ ～物 copolymer

【共勉】 gòngmiǎn mutual encouragement: 愿～之。Let us encourage each other in our endeavours.

【共鸣】 gòngmíng ①〈物〉 resonance ②sympathetic response: 引起～ arouse sympathy; strike a sympathetic chord ◇ ～器 resonator

【共栖】 gòngqī 〈生〉 commensalism

【共青团】 gòngqīngtuán 〈简〉(共产主义青年团) the Communist Youth League ◇ ～员 member of the Communist Youth League; League member

【共生】 gòngshēng ①〈地〉 intergrowth; paragenesis: 矿物～ mineral intergrowth ②〈生〉 symbiosis ◇ ～次序〈地〉 paragenesis/ ～细菌 symbiotic bacteria

【共事】 gòngshì work together (at the same organization); be fellow workers: ～多年 have been colleagues for many years

【共通】 gòngtōng applicable to both or all: 这两者之间有～的道理。The same argument applies to both cases.

【共同】 gòngtóng ①common: ～语言 common language/ ～敌人 common enemy/ ～关心的问题 matters of common concern; issues of common interest/有～之处 have something in common ②together; jointly: ～战斗 fight side by side/ ～努力 make joint efforts/ ～对敌 join forces to oppose the enemy/ ～行动 act in concert
◇ ～点 common ground/ ～纲领 common programme/ ～市场 the Common Market

【共同体】 gòngtóngtǐ community: 欧洲经济～ the European Economic Community/ 加勒比～ the Caribbean Community

【共析】 gòngxī 〈冶〉 eutectoid ◇ ～钢 eutectoid steel

【共享】 gòngxiǎng enjoy together; share: ～胜利的喜悦 share the joys of victory

【共性】 gòngxìng general character; generality

【共振】 gòngzhèn 〈物〉 resonance
◇ ～器 resonator/ ～腔 resonant cavity/ ～示波器 resonoscope

【共轴】 gòngzhóu coaxial

**贡** gòng ①tribute: 进～ pay tribute (to an imperial court) ②(Gòng) a surname

【贡品】 gòngpǐn articles of tribute; tribute

【贡税】 gòngshuì tribute and taxes

【贡献】 gòngxiàn contribute; dedicate; devote: 中国应当对于人类有较大的～。China ought to make a greater contribution to humanity./ 为共产主义事业～自己的一切 dedicate oneself heart and soul to the cause of communism/ 为革命～一份力量 do one's bit for the revolution

**供** gòng ①lay (offerings) ②offerings ③confess; own up: 据该犯～称 as was confessed by the culprit/ 他～出了主犯的名字。He gave the name of the chief culprit. ④confession; deposition: 口～ oral confession
另见 gōng

【供词】 gòngcí a statement made under examination; confession

【供奉】 gòngfèng enshrine and worship; consecrate

【供具】 gòngjù sacrificial vessel

【供品】 gòngpǐn offerings

【供认】 gòngrèn confess: ～不讳 confess everything; candidly confess

【供养】 gòngyǎng make offerings to; offer sacrifices to; enshrine and worship; consecrate
另见 gōngyǎng

【供职】 gòngzhí hold office

【供状】 gòngzhuàng written confession; deposition

【供桌】 gòngzhuō altar

## gōu

**勾** gōu ①cancel; cross out; strike out; tick off: 把他的名字～掉 cross out his name; strike his name off the register/ ～了这笔帐 cancel the debt/ 把重要的项目～出来 tick off the important items ②delineate; draw: ～出一个轮廓 draw an outline ③fill up the joints of brickwork with mortar or cement; point: ～墙缝 point a brick wall ④thicken: ～芡 thicken soup ⑤induce; evoke; call to mind: 这件事～起了我对童年的回忆。This evoked memories of my childhood. ⑥collude with; gang up with: 他们这帮人怎么～上的? How did these people come to gang up? ⑦〔用于中国古代数学〕 the shorter leg of a right triangle
另见 gòu

【勾搭】 gōuda ①gang up with: 这四个坏家伙～上了。The four scoundrels ganged up./ 那家伙跟投机倒把分子勾勾搭搭。That fellow works hand in glove with speculators. ②seduce

【勾股定理】 gōugǔ dìnglǐ 〈数〉 the Pythagorean theorem (或 proposition)

【勾股形】 gōugǔxíng 〔用于中国古代数学〕 right triangle

【勾画】 gōuhuà draw the outline of; delineate; sketch:

寥寥数笔，就把这高利贷者贪婪的嘴脸～出来了。A few words successfully bring out the greediness of the usurer.
【勾结】 gōujié collude with; collaborate with; gang up with: 反动统治者与帝国主义相～。The reactionary rulers colluded with the imperialists.
【勾勒】 gōulè ① draw the outline of; sketch the contours of ② give a brief account of; outline
【勾留】 gōuliú stop over; break one's journey at: 我们回京途中，在保定稍作～。We stopped over at Baoding on our way back to Beijing.
【勾通】 gōutōng collude with; work hand in glove with
【勾销】 gōuxiāo liquidate; write off; strike out: ～债务 liquidate a debt/ 一笔～ write off at one stroke
【勾心斗角】 gōuxīn-dòujiǎo 见"钩心斗角" gōuxīn-dòujiǎo
【勾引】 gōuyǐn tempt; entice; seduce

**沟** gōu ① ditch; channel; trench: 排水～ drainage ditch; drain/ 交通～ communication trench ② groove; rut; furrow: 拖拉机在泥路上轧出两道～。The tractor made ruts in the dirt road./ 开～播种 make furrows for sowing ③ gully; ravine: 七～八梁 seven gullies and eight ridges; full of gullies and ridges/ 乱石～ boulder-strewn gully
【沟灌】 gōuguàn 〈农〉 furrow irrigation
【沟壑】 gōuhè gully; ravine
【沟渠】 gōuqú irrigation canals and ditches: 田野上～纵横。The fields are crisscrossed by irrigation canals and ditches.
【沟通】 gōutōng link up: ～南方各省的新铁路 the new railways that link up the southern provinces/ ～两大洋的运河 an interoceanic canal/ 早在两千年前，著名的"丝绸之路"就～了中国和西亚各国的文化。As far back as 2,000 years ago, the famous Silk Road facilitated the flow of culture between China and the countries of West Asia.
【沟沿儿】 gōuyànr banks of a ditch or canal

**佝** gōu
【佝偻病】 gōulóubìng rickets

**钩** gōu ① hook: 钓鱼～ fishhook/ 挂衣～ clothes-hook ② hook stroke (in Chinese characters) ③ check mark; tick ④ secure with a hook; hook: 杂技演员用脚～住绳圈儿。The acrobat hooked his foot into a loop./ 他的袖子给钉子～住了。His sleeve caught on a nail./ 他把掉到井里的水桶～上来了。He fished up the bucket which had dropped into the well. ⑤ sew with large stitches: ～贴边 sew on an edging ⑥ crochet: ～花边 crochet lace
【钩虫】 gōuchóng hookworm ◇ ～病 hookworm disease; ancylostomiasis
【钩端螺旋体病】 gōuduān-luóxuántǐbìng leptospirosis
【钩吻】 gōuwěn 〈植〉 elegant jessamine
【钩心斗角】 gōuxīn-dòujiǎo intrigue against each other; jockey for position
【钩针】 gōuzhēn crochet hook ◇ ～编织品 crochet
【钩子】 gōuzi hook

**篝** gōu 〈书〉 cage
【篝火】 gōuhuǒ bonfire; campfire

**鞲** gōu
【鞲鞴】 gōubèi piston

## gǒu

**苟** gǒu ① careless; negligent; indifferent (to right or wrong): 一丝不～ be not the least bit negligent; be scrupulous about every detail; be conscientious and meticulous ② 〈书〉 if: ～能坚持，必将胜利。If you can persist, you are sure to win. 或 Given persistence, victory is certain.
【苟安】 gǒu'ān seek momentary ease; be content with temporary ease and comfort
【苟合】 gǒuhé illicit sexual relations
【苟活】 gǒuhuó drag out an ignoble existence; live on in degradation
【苟且】 gǒuqiě ① drift along; be resigned to circumstances: ～偷生 drag out an ignoble existence ② perfunctorily; carelessly: ～了事 dispose of sth. perfunctorily ③ illicit (sexual relations); improper
【苟全】 gǒuquán preserve (one's own life) at all costs: 他为了～性命，无耻地向敌人屈膝投降了。To save his skin, he shamefully threw himself at the feet of the enemy.
【苟同】 gǒutóng 〔用于否定句〕 agree without giving serious thought; readily subscribe to (sb.'s view): 不敢～ beg to differ; cannot agree
【苟延残喘】 gǒuyán-cánchuǎn be on one's last legs; linger on in a steadily worsening condition

**狗** gǒu ① dog ② 〈骂〉 damned; cursed: 那个～地主 that brute of a landlord; that cursed landlord
【狗宝】 gǒubǎo 〈中药〉 the stone of a dog's gallbladder, kidney or bladder
【狗胆包天】 gǒudǎn bāo tiān monstrous audacity
【狗獾】 gǒuhuān badger
【狗急跳墙】 gǒu jí tiào qiáng a cornered beast will do something desperate
【狗脊蕨】 gǒujǐjué 〈植〉 chain fern
【狗拿耗子，多管闲事】 gǒu ná hàozi, duō guǎn xiánshì a dog trying to catch mice — too meddlesome; poke one's nose into other people's business
【狗皮膏药】 gǒupí gāoyào ① 〈中药〉 dogskin plaster (a plaster for rheumatism, strains, contusions, etc., formerly spread on dogskin, but now usu. on cloth) ② quack medicine
【狗屁】 gǒupì 〈骂〉 horseshit; rubbish; nonsense: ～不通 unreadable rubbish; mere trash
【狗屎堆】 gǒushǐduī a heap of dog's droppings; a pile of dog's dung: 不齿于人类的～ filthy and contemptible as dog's dung
【狗头军师】 gǒutóu jūnshī ① a person who offers bad advice; inept adviser ② villainous adviser
【狗腿子】 gǒutuǐzi 〈口〉 hired thug; lackey; henchman
【狗尾草】 gǒuwěicǎo 〈植〉 green bristlegrass
【狗尾续貂】 gǒuwěi xù diāo a wretched sequel to a fine work
【狗窝】 gǒuwō kennel; doghouse
【狗熊】 gǒuxióng ① black bear ② coward
【狗血喷头】 gǒuxuè pēn tóu 〔多用于〕: 骂得～ let loose a stream of abuse against sb.; pour out a flood of invective against sb.
【狗眼看人低】 gǒuyǎn kàn rén dī be damned snobbish; act like a snob
【狗咬狗】 gǒu yǎo gǒu dog-eat-dog: 傀儡集团内部～的斗争 a dog-eat-dog struggle within a puppet clique
【狗咬吕洞宾】 gǒu yǎo Lǚ Dòngbīn snarl and snap at Lü Dongbin (one of the eight immortals in Chinese mythology) — mistake a good man for a bad one
【狗蝇】 gǒuyíng dog louse fly
【狗鱼】 gǒuyú 〈动〉 pike
【狗蚤】 gǒuzǎo dog flea
【狗仗人势】 gǒu zhàng rén shì 〈骂〉 like a dog threatening

people on the strength of its master's power — be a bully under the protection of a powerful person
【狗嘴里吐不出象牙】 gǒuzuǐli tǔbuchū xiàngyá a dog's mouth emits no ivory; a filthy mouth can't utter decent language; what can you expect from a dog but a bark

**枸** gǒu
另见 jǔ
【枸骨】 gǒugǔ 〈植〉 Chinese holly
【枸杞子】 gǒuqǐzǐ 〈中药〉 the fruit of Chinese wolfberry (*Lycium chinense*)

## gòu

**勾** gòu
另见 gōu
【勾当】 gòudang 〈贬〉 business; deal: 罪恶～ criminal activities/ 肮脏～ a dirty deal

**构** gòu ①construct; form; compose: ～词 form a word ②fabricate; make up: 虚～ fabrication ③literary composition: 佳～ a good piece of writing
【构成】 gòuchéng constitute; form; compose; make up: ～威胁 constitute (或 pose) a threat/ ～部分 component part/ 西沙群岛是由珊瑚礁～的。The Xisha Archipelago is formed of coral reefs.
【构词法】 gòucífǎ 〈语〉 word-building; word-formation
【构件】 gòujiàn ①〈建〉 (structural) member; component ②〈机〉 component (part)
【构思】 gòusī ①(of writers or artists) work out the plot of a literary work or the composition of a painting: 故事的～相当巧妙。The plot of the story is ingeniously conceived. ②conception: 大胆的～ boldness of conception
【构图】 gòutú 〈美术〉 composition (of a picture)
【构陷】 gòuxiàn make a false charge against sb.; frame sb. up
【构造】 gòuzào ①structure; construction: 人体～ the structure of the human body/ 这种机器～简单,使用方便。This machine is simple in construction and easy to handle. ②〈地〉 tectonic; structural
◇ ～地震 tectonic earthquake/ ～地质学 structural geology/ ～复合 compounding of structures/ ～体系 structural system/ ～序次 structural generation/ ～要素 structural element/ ～运动 tectonic movement
【构筑】 gòuzhù construct (military works); build: ～工事 construct field works (或 fortifications); build defences; dig in ◇ ～物〈建〉 structures

**购** gòu purchase; buy: ～粮 purchase grain/ 赊～ buy on credit
【购货单】 gòuhuòdān order form; order
【购买】 gòumǎi purchase; buy ◇ ～力 purchasing power
【购销】 gòu-xiāo purchase and sale; buying and selling: ～两旺 brisk buying and selling
【购置】 gòuzhì purchase (durables): ～农具 purchase farm implements

**诟** gòu 〈书〉 ①shame; humiliation ②revile; talk abusively
【诟病】 gòubìng 〈书〉 denounce; castigate: 为世～ become an object of public denunciation
【诟骂】 gòumà revile; abuse; vilify

**垢** gòu ①〈书〉 dirty; filthy: 蓬头～面 with dishevelled hair and a dirty face ②dirt; filth: 油～ grease stain/ 牙～ dental calculus ③〈书〉 disgrace; humiliation: 含～忍辱 endure humiliation and insult; (be forced to) swallow insults

**够** gòu ①enough; sufficient; adequate: 这几个图钉～不～? Will these drawing pins be enough?/ 你们那里人力～不～? Have you got enough manpower?/ 我们大队的储备粮～吃三年。Our brigade has a grain reserve sufficient for three years./ 这里只举一个例子就～了。Here a single example will suffice./ 这活儿～我们忙几天的。This job will keep us busy for several days. ②reach; be up to (a certain standard, etc.): 你～得着那些桑葚儿吗? Can you reach those mulberries?/ 他们交售的棉花全部～得上一级。All the cotton they sold to the state was top grade. ③quite; rather; really: 这儿的土～肥的。The soil here is quite fertile./ 今天你们可～辛苦了。You've really done a hard day's work.
【够本】 gòuběn make enough money to cover the cost; break even
【够格】 gòugé be qualified; be up to standard: 当代表,他满～。He's well qualified to be a representative.
【够劲儿】 gòujìnr 〈口〉 ①(of an onerous task, etc.) almost too much to cope with: 他一个人担任那么多工作,真～。He really has a tough job having to attend to so many things. ②strong (in taste, strength, etc.): 这辣椒真～。This pepper is really hot./ 这茅台酒真～。This *maotai* is certainly powerful stuff.
【够朋友】 gòu péngyou deserve to be called a true friend; be a friend indeed
【够戗】 gòuqiàng 〈方〉 unbearable; terrible: 疼得～ unbearably painful/ 她的脚冻得～。Her feet were terribly frostbitten./ 他的伤势怎么样? ——～! How's his wound? — Pretty bad!/ 这家伙真～! He's simply impossible.
【够瞧的】 gòuqiáode really awful; too much: 天热得真～。The weather is terribly hot. 或 The weather is really scorching.
【够受的】 gòushòude quite an ordeal; hard to bear: 累得～ be dog-tired/ 他这一跤摔得真～。He had a really bad fall.
【够数】 gòushù sufficient in quantity; enough: 你领的镰刀不～。You didn't get enough sickles to go round.
【够味儿】 gòuwèir 〈口〉 just the right flavour; just the thing; quite satisfactory: 最后这两句你唱得真～! The way you sang the last two lines was just superb!
【够意思】 gòu yìsi ①really something; terrific: 这场球赛可真～。That was really a terrific game. ②generous; really kind: 不～ unfriendly; ungrateful

**媾** gòu 〈书〉 ①wed: 婚～ marriage ②reach agreement: ～和 make peace ③coition: 交～ copulate
【媾和】 gòuhé make peace: 单独～ make peace without consulting one's allies; make a separate peace

**彀** gòu a bow drawn to the full
【彀中】 gòuzhōng 〈书〉 shooting range: 尽入～ have all come within shooting range (或 come under control); have all fallen into the trap

**觏** gòu 〈书〉 meet: 罕～ rarely seen

## gū

**估** gū estimate; appraise: 不要低～了群众的社会主义积

极性。Don't underestimate the socialist enthusiasm of the masses./ 你～一～这堆西红柿有几斤。 Can you tell how many *jin* of tomatoes there are in this heap?

【估产】 gūchǎn ① estimate the yield: 这块地～八百斤。The estimated yield of this plot of land is 800 *jin*. ② appraise the assets; assess

【估计】 gūjì estimate; appraise; reckon: 一切过高地～敌人力量和过低地～人民力量的观点，都是错误的。All views that overestimate the strength of the enemy and underestimate the strength of the people are wrong./ ～错误 miscalculate/ 清醒地～当前的形势 make a clearheaded appraisal of the present situation/ 我～他会来。I reckon he will come./ 这种可能性我们必须～到。We must take that possibility into account. 或 That is a possibility to be reckoned with./ ～今年又是一个丰收年。It looks as if there'll be another good harvest this year.

【估价】 gūjià ① appraise; evaluate: 对历史人物的～ evaluation of historical personages/ 对自己要有正确的～。One must have a correct estimate of oneself. ② 〈经〉 appraised price

【估量】 gūliang appraise; estimate; assess: 不可～的损失 an immeasurable loss/ 正确地～阶级力量的对比 correctly assess the balance of class forces

【估摸】 gūmo 〈口〉 reckon; guess: 我～着她月底就能回来。I reckon she'll be back by the end of this month.

## 沽

gū ① buy: ～酒 buy wine ② sell: 待价而～ wait to sell at a good price; wait for the highest bid

【沽名钓誉】 gūmíng-diàoyù fish for fame and compliments

## 咕

gū 〈象〉 (of hens, etc.) cluck; (of turtledoves, etc.) coo

【咕咚】 gūdōng 〈象〉 thud; splash; plump: 大石头～一声掉到水里去了。The rock fell into the water with a splash.

【咕嘟】 gūdū 〈象〉 bubble; gurgle: 泉水～～地往外冒。The spring kept bubbling up./ 他端起一碗水，～～地喝了下去。He took up a bowl of water and gulped it down.

【咕嘟】 gūdu ① boil for a long time: 白菜早就～烂了。The cabbage is overcooked. ② 〈方〉 purse (one's lips): 不高兴地～着嘴 purse one's lips in displeasure

【咕唧】 gūjī 〈象〉 squelch: 水牛拉着犁，在稻田里～～地走着。The water buffalo squelched up and down the paddy fields, pulling the plough.

【咕唧】 gūji whisper; murmur: 他俩～了半天。They whispered to each other for a long time.

【咕隆】 gūlōng 〈象〉 rumble; rattle; roll: 远处雷声～～地响。Thunder rumbled in the distance./ 行李车在月台上～～地跑着。The luggage trolley rattled along the platform.

【咕噜】 gūlū 〈象〉 rumble; roll: 肚子～～直响 one's stomach keeps rumbling/ 粗大的圆木～～地从山坡上滚下来。 Large logs came rolling down the slope.

【咕噜】 gūlu murmur; whisper

【咕哝】 gūnong murmur; mutter; grumble: 他在～些什么? What is he muttering about?

【咕容】 gūrong 〈方〉 (of a snake, etc.) wriggle

## 呱

gū

另见 guā

【呱呱】 gūgū 〈书〉 the cry of a baby: ～坠地 (of a baby) come into the world with a cry; be born

另见 guāguā

## 孤

gū ① (of a child) fatherless; orphaned ② solitary; isolated; alone: ～雁 a solitary wild goose/ ～岛 an isolated island ③ I (used by feudal princes)

【孤傲】 gū'ào proud and aloof: 去掉～习气 rid oneself of aloofness and arrogance

【孤本】 gūběn the only copy extant; the only existing copy

【孤单】 gūdān ① alone: 孤孤单单一个人 all alone; all by oneself; a lone soul ② lonely; friendless

【孤独】 gūdú lonely; solitary: 过着～的生活 live in solitude

【孤儿】 gū'ér orphan

【孤芳自赏】 gūfāng zì shǎng a solitary flower in love with its own fragrance; a lone soul admiring his own purity; indulge in self-admiration

【孤寂】 gūjì lonely

【孤家寡人】 gūjiā-guǎrén a person in solitary splendour; a person who has no mass support; a loner

【孤军】 gūjūn an isolated force: ～深入 an isolated force penetrating deep into enemy territory/ ～作战 fight in isolation

【孤苦伶仃】 gūkǔ-língdīng orphaned and helpless; friendless and wretched

【孤立】 gūlì ① isolated: 处境～ find oneself in an isolated position/ ～无援 isolated and cut off from help/ 任何事物都不是～地存在着的。Nothing exists in isolation. ② isolate: ～敌人 isolate the enemy ◇ ～主义 isolationism

【孤零零】 gūlínglíng solitary; lone; all alone

【孤陋寡闻】 gūlòu-guǎwén ignorant and ill-informed

【孤僻】 gūpì unsociable and eccentric: 性情～ of an uncommunicative and eccentric disposition

【孤掌难鸣】 gūzhǎng nán míng it's impossible to clap with one hand; it's difficult to achieve anything without support

【孤注一掷】 gūzhù yī zhì stake everything on a single throw; risk everything on a single venture; put all one's eggs in one basket

## 姑

gū ① father's sister; aunt ② husband's sister; sister-in-law ③ 〈书〉 husband's mother; mother-in-law ④ nun: 尼～ Buddhist nun/ 道～ Taoist nun ⑤ 〈书〉 tentatively; for the time being

【姑表】 gūbiǎo the relationship between the children of a brother and a sister; cousinship: ～兄弟 cousins (the father of one and the mother of the other being brother and sister)

【姑夫】 gūfu the husband of one's father's sister; uncle 又作"姑父"

【姑姑】 gūgu 〈口〉 father's sister; aunt

【姑母】 gūmǔ father's sister (married); aunt 又作"姑妈"

【姑奶奶】 gūnǎinai ① married daughter ② the sister of one's paternal grandfather; grandaunt

【姑娘】 gūniang ① girl ② 〈口〉 daughter

【姑且】 gūqiě 〈副〉 tentatively; for the moment: ～不谈 leave sth. aside for the moment/ 你～试一试。Have a try, anyhow. 或 Suppose you give it a try.

【姑嫂】 gū-sǎo a woman and her brother's wife; sisters-in-law

【姑妄听之】 gū wàng tīng zhī see no harm in hearing what sb. has to say

【姑妄言之】 gū wàng yán zhī tell sb. sth. for what it's worth

【姑息】 gūxī appease; indulge; tolerate: 不应该～他的错误。We shouldn't be indulgent towards his mistakes. ◇ ～疗法〈医〉 palliative treatment

【姑息养奸】 gūxī yǎng jiān to tolerate evil is to abet it

【姑爷】 gūye 〈口〉 a form of address for a man used by the senior members of his wife's family

# 轱 gū

【轱辘】 gūlu 〈口〉 wheel ◇ ～鞋 roller skates

# 骨 gū

另见 gú; gǔ

【骨朵儿】 gūduor 〈口〉 flower bud

【骨碌】 gūlu roll: 从床上一～爬起来 roll out of bed

# 鸪 gū 见"鹁鸪" bógū; "鹧鸪" zhègū

# 菇 gū mushroom

# 蛄 gū 见"蟪蛄" huìgū; "蝼蛄" lóugū

另见 gǔ

# 菰 gū 〈植〉 wild rice

# 辜 gū ① guilt; crime: 无～ guiltless; innocent/ 死有余～。Even death would not expiate all his crimes. ② (Gū) a surname

【辜负】 gūfù let down; fail to live up to; be unworthy of; disappoint: 我们决不～党的期望。We will never let the Party down. 或 We'll certainly live up to the expectations of the Party./ ～群众的信任 be unworthy of the trust the masses place in one; let the masses down

# 觚 gū 〈考古〉 ① wine vessel; beaker; goblet ② a wooden writing tablet

# 菁 gū

【菁葖】 gūtū 〈植〉 follicle

# 箍 gū ① hoop; band: 铁～ hoop iron ② bind round; hoop: 用铁丝把桶～上 bind a bucket with wire

【箍桶匠】 gūtǒngjiàng cooper; hooper

## gú

# 骨 gú bone

另见 gū; gǔ

【骨头】 gútou ① bone ② character; a person of a certain character: 无产阶级的硬～ a proletarian of unyielding integrity/ 懒～ lazybones/ 软～ a spineless creature

【骨头架子】 gútoujiàzi 〈口〉 skeleton: 瘦得只剩个～ be reduced to a skeleton; be all skin and bone

## gǔ

# 古 gǔ ① ancient; age-old; palaeo-: ～时候 in ancient times; in olden days/ ～画 ancient painting/ ～瓷 old china/ ～气候学 palaeoclimatology ② 见"古体诗" ③ (Gǔ) a surname

【古奥】 gǔ'ào archaic and abstruse

【古巴】 Gǔbā Cuba ◇ ～人 Cuban

【古板】 gǔbǎn old-fashioned and inflexible

【古代】 gǔdài ancient times; antiquity: ～文化 ancient civilization ◇ ～史 ancient history

【古典】 gǔdiǎn ① classical allusion ② classical ◇ ～文学 classical literature/ ～音乐 classical music/ ～主义 classicism/ ～作品 classic

【古董】 gǔdǒng ① antique; curio ② old fogey ◇ ～鉴赏家 connoisseur of curios

【古动物学】 gǔdòngwùxué palaeozoology

【古都】 gǔdū ancient capital

【古尔邦节】 Gǔ'ěrbāngjié 〈伊斯兰教〉 Corban

【古风】 gǔfēng ① ancient customs; antiquities ② 见"古体诗"

【古怪】 gǔguài eccentric; odd; strange: ～脾气 eccentric character/ 样子～ odd-looking

【古话】 gǔhuà old saying: ～说,有志者事竟成。As the old saying goes, where there's a will there's a way.

【古迹】 gǔjì historic site; place of historic interest

【古籍】 gǔjí ancient books

【古今中外】 gǔ-jīn Zhōng-wài ancient and modern, Chinese and foreign; at all times and in all countries: ～,概莫能外。There is no exception to this in modern or ancient times, in China or elsewhere.

【古旧】 gǔjiù antiquated; archaic: ～词语 archaic words and expressions; archaisms

【古柯】 gǔkē 〈植〉 coca ◇ ～碱〈药〉 cocaine

【古来】 gǔlái since time immemorial

【古兰经】 Gǔlánjīng 〈伊斯兰教〉 the Koran

【古老】 gǔlǎo ancient; age-old: ～的传说 legend

【古朴】 gǔpǔ (of art, architecture, etc.) simple and unsophisticated; of primitive simplicity

【古琴】 gǔqín *guqin*, a seven-stringed plucked instrument in some ways similar to the zither

【古人】 gǔrén the ancients; our forefathers

【古人类学】 gǔrénlèixué palaeoanthropology ◇ ～家 palaeoanthropologist

【古色古香】 gǔsè-gǔxiāng antique; quaint

【古生代】 Gǔshēngdài 〈地〉 the Palaeozoic Era

【古生物学】 gǔshēngwùxué palaeontology

【古诗】 gǔshī ① ancient poetry ② 见"古体诗"

【古书】 gǔshū ancient books

【古塔胶】 gǔtǎjiāo 〈化〉 gutta-percha

【古体诗】 gǔtǐshī a form of pre-Tang poetry, usu. having five or seven characters to each line, without strict tonal patterns or rhyme schemes

【古田会议】 Gǔtián Huìyì the Gutian Congress (the 9th Party Congress of the 4th Army of the Chinese Workers' and Peasants' Red Army presided over by Comrade Mao Zedong in December 1929 at Gutian, Shanghang County, Fujian)

【古田会议决议】 Gǔtián Huìyì Juéyì the Gutian Congress Resolution (entitled *On Correcting Mistaken Ideas in the Party*, drawn up by Comrade Mao Zedong, a programme for building the people's armed forces on a Marxist-Leninist basis)

【古铜色】 gǔtóngsè bronze-coloured; bronze

【古玩】 gǔwán antique; curio

【古往今来】 gǔwǎng-jīnlái through the ages; of all ages; since time immemorial

【古为今用】 gǔ wéi jīn yòng make the past serve the present: ～,洋为中用。Make the past serve the present and foreign things serve China.

【古文】 gǔwén ① prose written in the classical literary style; ancient Chinese prose ② Chinese script before the Qin Dynasty (221-207 B.C.)

【古文字】 gǔwénzì ancient writing ◇ ～学 palaeography

【古物】 gǔwù ancient objects; antiquities ◇ ～陈列馆 museum of antiquities

【古稀】 gǔxī seventy years of age: 年近～ getting on for seventy

【古雅】 gǔyǎ of classic beauty and in elegant taste; of classic elegance

【古语】 gǔyǔ ① archaism ② old saying

【古植物学】 gǔzhíwùxué palaeobotany

【古装】 gǔzhuāng ancient costume

# 汩

gǔ

【汩汩】 gǔgǔ gurgle: 渠水～地流入稻田。Gurgling water flowed from the irrigation ditch into the paddy fields.

# 诂

gǔ explain archaic or dialectal words in current language

# 谷

gǔ ① valley; gorge: 深～ a deep valley; gorge ② cereal; grain: ～类作物 cereal crops ③ millet ④〈方〉unhusked rice ⑤ (Gǔ) a surname

【谷氨酸】 gǔ'ānsuān〈药〉glutamic acid

【谷仓】 gǔcāng granary; barn

【谷草】 gǔcǎo ① millet straw ②〈方〉rice straw

【谷蛾】 gǔ'é〈动〉grain moth

【谷坊】 gǔfáng〈水〉check dam

【谷壳】 gǔké husk (of rice)

【谷物】 gǔwù cereal; grain

【谷雨】 Gǔyǔ Grain Rain (6th solar term)

【谷子】 gǔzi ① millet ②〈方〉unhusked rice ◇ ～白发病 downy mildew of millet

# 股

gǔ ① thigh ② section (of an office, enterprise, etc.): 人事～ personnel section ③ strand; ply: 三～的绳子 a rope of three strands/ 三～的毛线 three-ply wool ④ one of several equal parts; share in a company: 分～ divide into equal parts/ 优先～ preference shares; preferred stock ⑤〔用于中国古代数学〕the longer leg of a right triangle ⑥〈量〉ⓐ〔用于成条的东西〕: 一～线 a skein of thread/ 一～泉水 a stream of spring water/ 两～道 two roads (或 paths, tracks)/ 只要大伙儿拧成一～绳,没有克服不了的困难。As long as we are united as one, there is no difficulty we cannot overcome. ⓑ〔用于气体、气味、力气〕: 一～香味 a whiff of fragrance/ 一～热气 a stream (或 puff) of hot air/ 一～劲 a burst of energy ⓒ〈贬〉〔用于成批的人〕: 两～土匪 two gangs of bandits/ 一～敌军 a horde of enemy soldiers; an enemy detachment

【股本】 gǔběn capital stock

【股东】 gǔdōng shareholder; stockholder

【股匪】 gǔfěi gang of bandits

【股份】 gǔfèn share; stock
◇ ～公司 joint-stock company; stock company/ ～有限公司 limited-liability company; limited company (Ltd.)/ ～资本 share capital

【股肱】 gǔgōng〈书〉right-hand man

【股骨】 gǔgǔ〈生理〉thighbone; femur

【股金】 gǔjīn money paid for shares (in a partnership or cooperative)

【股票】 gǔpiào share certificate; share; stock
◇ ～行市 current prices of stocks; quotations on the stock exchange/ ～交易 buying and selling of stocks/ ～交易所 stock exchange/ ～经纪人 stockbroker; stockjobber/ ～市场 stock market

【股息】 gǔxī dividend

【股线】 gǔxiàn〈纺〉plied yarn

【股长】 gǔzhǎng section chief

【股子】 gǔzi ① share ②〈量〉〔用于力量、气味等〕: 这小伙子有一～使不完的劲。The youngster just doesn't know what it is to be tired.

# 牯

gǔ bull

【牯牛】 gǔniú bull

# 骨

gǔ ① bone ② skeleton; framework: 钢～水泥 reinforced concrete ③ character; spirit: 傲～ lofty and unyielding character/ 媚～ obsequiousness
另见 gū; gú

【骨刺】 gǔcì〈医〉spur

【骨顶鸡】 gǔdǐngjī coot

【骨董】 gǔdǒng 见"古董" gǔdǒng

【骨粉】 gǔfěn bone meal; bone dust

【骨干】 gǔgàn ①〈生理〉diaphysis ② backbone; mainstay: 起～作用 be a mainstay/ 科技队伍的～力量 the backbone of the scientific and technological contingents/ 民兵～ key members of the militia/ 治淮的～工程 key projects for harnessing the Huaihe River ◇ ～分子 core member; key member

【骨骼】 gǔgé〈生理〉skeleton ◇ ～肌 skeletal muscle

【骨鲠在喉】 gǔ gěng zài hóu have a fishbone caught in one's throat: 如～,不吐不快 feel as if one has a fishbone in one's throat and cannot rest until one has spat it out; have an opinion one cannot suppress

【骨骺】 gǔhóu〈生理〉epiphysis

【骨化】 gǔhuà〈生理〉ossify

【骨灰】 gǔhuī ① bone ash ② ashes of the dead ◇ ～盒 cinerary casket

【骨架】 gǔjià skeleton; framework: 房屋的～ the framework of a house/ 小说的～已经有了。The framework of the novel has been worked out.

【骨胶】 gǔjiāo〈化〉bone glue

【骨节】 gǔjié〈生理〉joint

【骨科】 gǔkē〈医〉(department of) orthopaedics ◇ ～医生 orthopaedist

【骨刻】 gǔkè〈工美〉bone sculpture (或 carving)

【骨痨】 gǔláo〈中医〉tuberculosis of bones and joints

【骨料】 gǔliào〈建〉aggregate: 轻～ light aggregate

【骨瘤】 gǔliú〈医〉osteoma

【骨膜】 gǔmó〈生理〉periosteum ◇ ～炎 periostitis

【骨牌】 gǔpái dominoes

【骨盆】 gǔpén〈生理〉pelvis

【骨气】 gǔqì strength of character; moral integrity; backbone: 我们中国人是有～的。We Chinese have backbone./ 有～的人 a man of integrity

【骨器】 gǔqì bone object; bone implement

【骨肉】 gǔròu flesh and blood; kindred: 亲生～ one's own flesh and blood/ ～兄弟 blood brothers; one's own brothers/ ～相连 as closely linked as flesh and blood/ ～之亲 blood relations/ ～情谊 kindred feelings; feelings of kinship/ ～团聚 a family reunion/ 台湾人民是我们的～同胞。The people of Taiwan are our own flesh and blood.

【骨软化】 gǔruǎnhuà〈医〉osteomalacia

【骨瘦如柴】 gǔ shòu rú chái thin as a lath; worn to a shadow; a mere skeleton; a bag of bones

【骨髓】 gǔsuǐ〈生理〉marrow ◇ ～炎 osteomyelitis

【骨碎补】 gǔsuìbǔ〈中药〉the rhizome of davallia (*Davallia mariesii*)

【骨炭】 gǔtàn bone black; animal charcoal

【骨学】 gǔxué〈医〉osteology

【骨折】 gǔzhé〈医〉fracture: 粉碎～ comminuted fracture/ 开放～ open (或 compound) fracture

【骨子】 gǔzi frame; ribs: 伞～ umbrella frame; the ribs of an umbrella/ 扇～ the ribs of a fan

【骨子里】 gǔzilǐ in one's heart of hearts: 这家伙从～仇恨社会主义。That fellow hates socialism to the marrow of his bones.

# 贾

gǔ ① merchant ② engage in trade ③〈书〉sell; afford: 余勇可～ still having plenty of fight left in one;

with one's strength not exhausted
另见 jiǎ

**钴** gǔ 〈化〉 cobalt (Co)

**蛄** gǔ 见"蝲蝲蛄" lǎlàgǔ; "蝲蛄" lǎgǔ
另见 gū

**蛊** gǔ a legendary venomous insect

【蛊惑】 gǔhuò poison and bewitch: ～人心 confuse and poison people's minds; resort to demagogy

**鹄** gǔ 〈书〉 target (in archery): 中～ hit the target
另见 hú

**鼓** gǔ ①drum: 打～ beat a drum/ ～声 drumbeats ②beat; strike; sound: ～瑟 play the *se* (an ancient Chinese plucked instrument)/ ～掌 clap one's hands/ ～其如簧之舌 talk glibly ③blow with bellows, etc.: ～风 work a bellows ④rouse; agitate; pluck up: 大～革命干劲 bring one's revolutionary drive into full play/ ～起勇气 pluck up (或 muster) one's courage ⑤bulge; swell: 把口袋装得～～的 fill one's pockets till they bulge/ ～着嘴 pout

【鼓板】 gǔbǎn 〈乐〉 clappers

【鼓吹】 gǔchuī ①advocate: ～革命 advocate revolution ②〈贬〉 preach; advertise; play up: ～阶级斗争熄灭论 preach the theory of the dying out of class struggle

【鼓槌】 gǔchuí drumstick

【鼓捣】 gǔdao 〈方〉 ①tinker with; fiddle with: 他最爱～收音机。He likes to tinker with radios. ②egg on; incite: 在背后～ egg on from behind the scenes/ ～别人去干坏事 incite people to do evil

【鼓点子】 gǔdiǎnzi ①drumbeats ②clapper beats which set the tempo and lead the orchestra in traditional Chinese operas

【鼓动】 gǔdòng ①agitate; arouse: 做宣传～工作 conduct propaganda and agitation/ ～群众 arouse the masses ②instigate; incite: 这些坏事是谁～你干的? Who put you up to all these dirty tricks?

【鼓风】 gǔfēng 〈冶〉 (air) blast: 富氧～ oxygen-enriched (air) blast ◇ ～机 air-blower; blower/ ～炉 blast furnace

【鼓鼓囊囊】 gǔgunāngnāng bulging: 背包里装满了工具,～的。The bag is bulging with tools.

【鼓励】 gǔlì encourage; urge: 精神～和物质～相结合, 而以精神～为主的方针 the policy of combining moral encouragement and material reward, with stress on the former/ 首长对我们讲了许多～的话。The leading comrades said a lot to encourage us.

【鼓楼】 gǔlóu drum-tower

【鼓膜】 gǔmó 〈生理〉 tympanic membrane; eardrum ◇ ～穿孔〈医〉 perforation of the tympanic membrane

【鼓室】 gǔshì 〈生理〉 tympanum

【鼓手】 gǔshǒu drummer

【鼓舞】 gǔwǔ inspire; hearten: 在大好形势～下 inspired by the very good situation/ ～人心的消息 most heartening news/ ～了社员的社会主义积极性 fire the socialist enthusiasm of the commune members/ ～群众的斗志 enhance the morale of the masses

【鼓乐】 gǔyuè strains of music accompanied by drumbeats: ～齐鸣,万众欢腾。The cheers of the jubilant crowds mingled with *crescendos* of music.

【鼓噪】 gǔzào make an uproar; raise a hubbub; clamour: ～一时 make a great to-do about sth. for a time

【鼓掌】 gǔzhǎng clap one's hands; applaud: 热烈～ warmly applaud/ ～通过 approve by acclamation

【鼓足干劲】 gǔzú gànjìn go all out: ～,力争上游,多快好省地建设社会主义。Go all out, aim high and achieve greater, faster, better and more economical results in building socialism.

**毂** gǔ hub

**臌** gǔ

【臌胀】 gǔzhàng 〈中医〉 distension of abdomen caused by accumulation of gas or fluid due to dysfunction of liver and spleen; tympanites

**瞽** gǔ 〈书〉 blind: ～者 blind person

## gù

**固** gù ①solid; firm: 加～ make sth. more solid; strengthen; reinforce/ 本～枝荣。When the root is firm, the branches flourish. ②firmly; resolutely: ～辞 resolutely refuse; firmly decline ③solidify; consolidate; strengthen: ～堤 strengthen the dyke ④〈书〉 originally; in the first place; as a matter of course: ～当如此。It is just as it should be. ⑤〈书〉 admittedly; no doubt: 乘车～可, 乘船亦无不可。Admittedly we can make the journey by train, but there is no harm in our travelling by boat.

【固步自封】 gù bù zì fēng 见"故步自封" gù bù zì fēng

【固氮菌】 gùdànjūn 〈微〉 nitrogen-fixing bacteria; azotobacter

【固氮作用】 gùdàn zuòyòng 〈农〉 nitrogen fixation; azofication

【固定】 gùdìng ①fixed; regular: 电台的～节目 a regular (或 scheduled) radio programme/ ～的作战线 fixed battle lines/ 不要用～眼光看问题。Don't take a static view of things. ②fix; regularize: 把灯座～在车床上 fix the lampstand on the lathe/ 把业务学习时间～下来 set a regular time for vocational study
◇ ～工资制 fixed-wage system/ ～汇率 fixed (exchange) rate/ ～机库 permanent hangar/ ～基金 fixed fund/ ～价格 fixed price/ ～平价 fixed parity/ ～式平炉〈冶〉 stationary open-hearth furnace/ ～职业 permanent occupation/ ～资本 fixed capital/ ～资产 fixed assets

【固化】 gùhuà 〈化〉 solidify ◇ ～酒精 solidified alcohol

【固件】 gùjiàn 〈计算机〉 firmware

【固井】 gùjǐng 〈石油〉 well cementation

【固然】 gùrán 〈副〉 ①〔表示承认某个事实,引起下文转折〕 no doubt; it is true; true: 这里条件～艰苦些,但正是我们锻炼的好地方。True, conditions are tougher here, but that gives us a chance to temper ourselves./ 这样办～稳当些,可就是要慢一些。No doubt it would be safer to do it that way, but it would be slower. ②〔表示承认甲事实, 也不否认乙事实〕 of course; admittedly: 他能来～很好,不来也没关系。If he can come, of course that'll be fine, but if he can't, it doesn't matter.

【固若金汤】 gù ruò jīn tāng strongly fortified; impregnable

【固涩】 gùsè 〈中医〉 astringent or styptic treatment for spontaneous sweating, seminal emission, chronic diarrhoea, anal prolapse, uterine bleeding, etc.

【固沙林】 gùshālín sand-fixation forest; dune-fixing forest

【固守】 gùshǒu defend tenaciously; be firmly entrenched in: ～阵地 tenaciously defend one's position/ ～老一套的办法 stick to the old ways

【固态】 gùtài 〈物〉 solid state ◇ ～物理学 solid-state physics

【固体】 gùtǐ solid body; solid
◇～废物 solid waste/ ～酱油 solidified soy sauce/ ～燃料 solid fuel/ ～燃料火箭发动机 solid propellant (rocket) engine; solid engine
【固有】 gùyǒu intrinsic; inherent; innate: ～的属性 intrinsic attributes/ 资本主义制度～的矛盾 the contradictions inherent in the capitalist system/ 人的正确思想不是自己头脑里～的。 Correct ideas are not innate in the mind.
【固执】 gùzhí ① obstinate; stubborn ② persist in; cling to: ～己见 stubbornly adhere to one's opinions

**故** gù ① incident; happening: 事～ accident/ 变～ unforeseen event; misfortune ② reason; cause: 无～缺勤 be absent without reason (或 cause)/ 托～离开 make an excuse and leave/ 该生不知何～缺席。The reason for the student's absence remains unknown. ③ on purpose; intentionally: 明知～犯 wilfully violate (a law or rule)/ ～作镇静 pretend to be calm/ ～作惊讶 put on a show of surprise; feign surprise ④ hence; therefore; consequently; for this reason: 无私～能无畏。Fearlessness stems from selflessness. ⑤ former; old: ～址 site (of an ancient monument, etc.)/ 黄河～道 the old course of the Huanghe River ⑥ friend; acquaintance: 非亲非～ neither relative nor friend; a perfect stranger ⑦ die: 病～ die of illness
【故步自封】 gù bù zì fēng stand still and refuse to make progress; be complacent and conservative
【故地】 gùdì old haunt
【故都】 gùdū onetime capital
【故宫】 Gùgōng the Imperial Palace ◇～博物院 the Palace Museum
【故伎】 gùjì stock trick; old tactics: ～重演 play the same old trick
【故旧】 gùjiù old friends and acquaintances
【故居】 gùjū former residence (或 home)
【故里】 gùlǐ native place
【故弄玄虚】 gù nòng xuánxū purposely turn simple things into mysteries; be deliberately mystifying
【故去】 gùqù die; pass away
【故人】 gùrén old friend
【故杀】 gùshā 〈法〉 premeditated (或 wilful) murder
【故世】 gùshì die; pass away
【故事】 gùshì old practice; routine: 奉行～ follow established practice mechanically
【故事】 gùshi ① story; tale: 红军长征的～ stories about the Long March of the Red Army/ 民间～ folktale; folk story ② plot: 这部小说～性很强。The novel has an interesting plot.
◇～会 a gathering at which (revolutionary) stories are told; story-telling session/ ～片 feature film/ ～员 storyteller
【故态复萌】 gùtài fù méng slip back into one's old ways
【故土】 gùtǔ native land
【故乡】 gùxiāng native place; hometown; birthplace
【故意】 gùyì intentionally; wilfully; deliberately; on purpose: ～刁难 place obstacles in sb.'s way/ 天气好象～和我们作对似的。It looks as if the weather was purposely making trouble for us./ 对不起,我不是～的。I'm sorry, I didn't do it on purpose. 或 I'm sorry, I didn't mean it.
【故障】 gùzhàng hitch; breakdown; stoppage; trouble: 排除～ fix a breakdown; clear a stoppage/ 发动机出了～。The engine has broken down. 或 The engine is out of order./ 出了什么～? What's gone wrong?
【故纸堆】 gùzhǐduī a heap of musty old books or papers

**顾** gù ① turn round and look at; look at: 环～四周 look around/ 相～一笑 smile at each other knowingly ② attend to; take into consideration: 兼～ give consideration to both/ 不～个人安危 not give a thought to one's safety/ 医生～不得吃饭就去抢救病人。The doctor immediately attended to the emergency case without stopping for a meal./ 这么多事你一个人～得过来吗? You've got so many things to attend to. Can you manage all by yourself? ③ visit; call on: 三～茅芦 call on sb. repeatedly (to enlist his help, etc.) ④ (Gù) a surname
【顾此失彼】 gùcǐ-shībǐ attend to one thing and lose sight of another; have too many things to take care of at the same time
【顾及】 gùjí take into account; attend to; give consideration to: 无暇～ have no time to attend to the matter/ 事前应该～事后的效果。Before taking an action, one should consider what effect it may have./ ～可能产生的后果 take the possible consequences into account
【顾忌】 gùjì scruple; misgiving: 毫无～ without scruple; have no scruples/ 不能不有所～ have to think twice (before doing sth.); be unable to overcome certain misgivings
【顾客】 gùkè customer; shopper; client
【顾虑】 gùlǜ misgiving; apprehension; worry: 打消～ dispel one's misgivings (或 worries)/ ～重重 be full of worries; have no end of misgivings/ 你不必有任何～。You needn't have any misgivings whatsoever./ 他毫无～地谈出了自己的想法。 He spoke his mind without the slightest hesitancy.
【顾名思义】 gù míng sī yì seeing the name of a thing one thinks of its function; just as its name implies; as the term suggests: 变频器,～,它的功能是改变交流电路的频率。The frequency converter, as the term suggests, serves to change the frequency of an alternating-current circuit.
【顾盼】 gùpàn 〈书〉 look around: 左顾右盼 look right and left/ ～自雄 look about complacently
【顾前不顾后】 gù qián bù gù hòu drive ahead without considering the consequences; act rashly
【顾全】 gùquán show consideration for and take care to preserve: ～大局 take the interests of the whole into account; take the situation as a whole into consideration/ ～面子 save sb.'s face; spare sb.'s feelings
【顾问】 gùwèn adviser; consultant ◇ ～委员会 consultative (或 advisory) committee
【顾影自怜】 gù yǐng zì lián ① look at one's reflection and admire oneself ② look at one's shadow and lament one's lot
【顾主】 gùzhǔ 〈旧〉 customer; client; patron

**梏** gù wooden handcuffs: 桎～ fetters; shackles

**雇** gù hire; employ: ～船 hire a boat
【雇工】 gùgōng ① hire labour; hire hands: ～剥削 exploitation through the hiring of labour ② hired labourer (或 hand, worker)
【雇农】 gùnóng farmhand; farm labourer
【雇佣】 gùyōng employ; hire
◇～兵役制 mercenary system/ ～军 mercenary army (或 troops); mercenaries/ ～奴隶 wage slave
【雇佣观点】 gùyōng guāndiǎn hired hand mentality — the attitude of one who will do no more than he is paid for
【雇佣劳动】 gùyōng láodòng wage labour: 资本的生存条件是～。The condition for capital is wage labour. ◇～者 wage labourer
【雇员】 gùyuán employee
【雇主】 gùzhǔ employer

**痼** gù chronic; inveterate

【痼疾】 gùjí chronic (或 obstinate) illness: 经济危机是资本主义制度的~。 Economic crises are a chronic malady of capitalism.
【痼习】 gùxí inveterate (或 confirmed) habit

**锢** gù ① plug with molten metal; run metal into cracks ② 〈书〉 hold in custody; imprison
【锢囚】 gùqiú 〈气〉 occlusion ◇ ~气旋 occluded cyclone

## guā

**瓜** guā melon, gourd, etc.: 冬~ white gourd/ 西~ watermelon/ ~儿离不开秧, 革命群众离不开共产党。 The revolutionary masses cling to the Communist Party as the melon clings to the vine.
【瓜德罗普岛】 Guādéluópǔdǎo Guadeloupe
【瓜分】 guāfēn carve up; divide up; partition: ~别国领土 carve up the territory of another country/ 帝国主义重新~世界的斗争 the imperialists' struggle to redivide the world
【瓜葛】 guāgé connection; implication; association: 他跟投机倒把分子有~。 He's got mixed up with speculators. ◇ ~亲 distant relatives
【瓜皮帽】 guāpímào a kind of skullcap resembling the rind of half a watermelon; skullcap
【瓜熟蒂落】 guāshú-dìluò when a melon is ripe it falls off its stem — things will be easily settled when conditions are ripe
【瓜田李下】 guātián-lǐxià in a melon patch or under a plum tree — in suspicious circumstances or surroundings: 瓜田不纳履,李下不正冠。 Don't pull on your shoe in a melon patch; don't adjust your cap under a plum tree — don't do anything to arouse suspicion.
【瓜子】 guāzǐ melon seeds ◇ ~脸 oval face

**呱** guā
另见 gū
【呱哒】 guādā 〈象〉 clip-clop; clack
【呱哒】 guāda 〈方〉 ①〔多用于〕: ~着脸 pull a long face ② talk foolishly
【呱哒板儿】 guādabǎnr 〈口〉 ① bamboo clappers ② 〈方〉 clogs
【呱呱】 guāguā 〈象〉 (of ducks) quack; (of frogs) croak; (of crows) caw
另见 gūgū
【呱呱叫】 guāguājiào 〈口〉 tiptop; top-notch
【呱唧】 guāji 〈象〉 clap (hands)

**刮** guā ① scrape: ~锅子 scrape a pot clean/ ~鱼鳞 scale a fish/ ~胡子 shave the beard/ 就~破一点皮。 It's only a scratch. ② smear with (paste, etc.): ~糨子 stiffen (cloth) by spreading paste over it ③ plunder; fleece; extort: 从农民身上~来的财富 the wealth extorted from the peasants ④ blow: ~大风了。 It's blowing hard. 或 There's a gale blowing./ 把~倒的树苗扶起来 straighten up the saplings that have been blown down/ ~起一股资本主义妖风 stir up an evil wind of capitalism
【刮刀】 guādāo scraping cutter; scraper: 三角~ triangular scraper
【刮地皮】 guā dìpí batten on extortions
【刮宫】 guāgōng 〈医〉 dilatation and curettage (D. and C.)
【刮脸】 guāliǎn shave (the face) ◇ ~刀 razor
【刮脸皮】 guā liǎnpí 〈方〉 rub the forefinger against one's own cheek (to indicate scorn for sb.); point the finger of scorn at sb.
【刮目相看】 guāmù xiāng kàn look at sb. with new eyes; treat sb. with increased respect
【刮痧】 guāshā 〈中医〉 a popular treatment for sunstroke by scraping the patient's neck, chest or back
【刮削】 guāxiāo scrape ◇ ~器 scraper

**胍** guā 〈化〉 guanidine

**栝** guā
【栝楼皮】 guālóupí 〈中药〉 the fruit-rind of Chinese trichosanthes (*Trichosanthes kirilowii*)

**鸹** guā 见"老鸹" lǎogua

## guǎ

**剐** guǎ ① cut to pieces (a form of capital punishment in ancient times); dismember: 千刀万~ be cut to pieces/ 舍得一身~,敢把皇帝拉下马。 He who fears not being cut to pieces dares to unhorse the emperor. ② cut; slit: 手上~了个口子 cut one's hand

**寡** guǎ ① few; scant: 沉默~言 uncommunicative; taciturn/ 以~敌众 pit a few against many; fight against heavy odds/ 失道~助。 An unjust cause finds scant support. ② tasteless: 清汤~水 watery soup; something insipid ③ widowed: 鳏~ widowers and widows/ 守~ live in widowhood
【寡不敌众】 guǎ bù dí zhòng be hopelessly outnumbered
【寡妇】 guǎfù widow
【寡廉鲜耻】 guǎlián-xiǎnchǐ lost to shame; shameless
【寡人】 guǎrén I, the sovereign; we (used by a royal person in proclamations instead of I)
【寡头】 guǎtóu oligarch: 金融~ financial oligarchy; financial magnates ◇ ~垄断 oligopoly/ ~政治 oligarchy

## guà

**卦** guà divinatory symbols: 占~ divination

**挂** guà ① hang; put up: 把地图~在墙上 put (或 hang) the map up on the wall/ 天上~着一轮明月。 A bright moon hung in the sky./ 把这件事先~一~再说。 Let's leave the matter aside for the moment./ 修正主义分子总是~着马列主义的招牌。 Revisionists always pose as Marxist-Leninists. ② hitch; get caught: 把拖车~上 hitch up the trailer/ 她的衣服给钉子~住了。 Her dress got caught on a nail. ③ ring off: 她已经把电话~了。 She's hung up./ 你先别~, 等我查一下。 Hold the line while I find out. ④ 〈方〉 call (或 phone, ring) up; put sb. through to: 我呆会儿再给他~电话。 I'll ring him up again./ 请给我~拖拉机站。 Give me the tractor station, please. 或 Please put me through to the tractor station. ⑤ 〈方〉 be concerned about: 时刻把群众的利益~在心上 always have the welfare of the masses at heart/ 他总是~着队长的病。 He's very worried about the team leader's illness. ⑥ 〈方〉 be covered with; be coated with: 瓦盆里面~一层釉子。 The earthen pot is glazed inside. ⑦ register (at a hospital, etc.): 我要~外科。 I want to register for surgery. 或 Surgery, please./ 你~的是几号? What's your registration number? ⑧ 〈量〉〔用于成套或成串的东西〕: 一~大车 a horse and cart/ 十多~鞭炮 a dozen strings of firecrackers

【挂彩】 guàcǎi ①decorate with coloured silk festoons; decorate for festive occasions ②be wounded in action
【挂车】 guàchē trailer
【挂齿】 guàchǐ mention: 区区小事，何足～。Such a trifling matter is not worth mentioning.
【挂锄】 guàchú put away the hoe (for the winter); finish hoeing
【挂挡】 guàdǎng put into gear: 挂高速挡 change to (或 put into) high gear/ 挂头挡 engage the first gear
【挂钩】 guàgōu ①〈交〉 couple (two railway coaches); articulate ②link up with; establish contact with; get in touch with: 大学应该与科研单位～。Universities should establish close contact with institutes of scientific research.
【挂号】 guàhào ①register (at a hospital, etc.): 请排队～。Please queue up to register. ②send by registered mail: 你这封信要不要～? Do you want to have this letter registered?
◇ ～处 registration office/ ～费 registration fee/ ～信 registered letter (或 mail)
【挂花】 guàhuā be wounded in action
【挂怀】 guàhuái have sth. weighing on one's mind; be concerned (或 worried) about
【挂火】 guàhuǒ 〈方〉 be furious; flare up
【挂镰】 guàlián 〈农〉 put away the sickle; complete the year's harvest
【挂零】 guàlíng odd: 四十～ forty odd
【挂虑】 guàlǜ be anxious about; worry about
【挂面】 guàmiàn fine dried noodles; vermicelli
【挂名】 guàmíng titular; nominal; only in name
【挂念】 guàniàn worry about sb. who is absent; miss: 十分～ miss sb. very much
【挂牌】 guàpái 〈旧〉 hang out one's shingle; put up one's brass plate
【挂失】 guàshī report the loss of (identity papers, cheques, etc.)
【挂帅】 guàshuài be in command; assume (或 take) command; assume leadership: 无产阶级政治～ put proletarian politics in command/ 书记～ with the Party secretary taking command
【挂锁】 guàsuǒ padlock
【挂毯】 guàtǎn tapestry
【挂图】 guàtú ①wall map ②hanging chart
【挂线疗法】 guàxiàn liáofǎ 〈中医〉 ligating method for treating anal fistula
【挂羊头，卖狗肉】 guà yángtóu, mài gǒuròu hang up a sheep's head and sell dogmeat — try to palm off sth. inferior to what it purports to be
【挂一漏万】 guà yī lòu wàn for one thing cited, ten thousand may have been left out — the list is far from complete
【挂衣钩】 guàyīgōu clothes-hook
【挂钟】 guàzhōng wall clock
【挂轴】 guàzhóu hanging scroll (of Chinese painting or calligraphy)

**褂** guà a Chinese-style unlined garment; gown: 短～儿 short gown/ 大～儿 long gown
【褂子】 guàzi a Chinese-style unlined upper garment; short gown

## guāi

**乖** guāi ①well-behaved (child); good: 真是个～孩子。There's a dear. ②clever; shrewd; alert: 学～了 become a little wiser ③〈书〉 perverse; contrary to reason: 有～常理 run counter to reason
【乖乖】 guāiguāi ①well-behaved; obedient: 孩子们都～儿地坐着听老师讲革命故事。 The children all sat quietly listening to the teacher telling revolutionary stories. ②little dear; darling ③〈叹〉 good gracious
【乖觉】 guāijué alert; quick
【乖戾】 guāilì perverse (behaviour); disagreeable (character)
【乖谬】 guāimiù absurd; abnormal
【乖僻】 guāipì eccentric; odd
【乖巧】 guāiqiǎo ①clever ②cute; lovely
【乖张】 guāizhāng eccentric and unreasonable

**掴** guāi slap; smack: ～耳光 box sb.'s ears; slap sb. on the face
另见 guó

## guǎi

**拐** guǎi ①turn: ～过墙角 turn the corner of a house/ ～进一条胡同 turn into an alley/ 往左～ turn to the left/ 前面走不通了，咱们～回去吧。We can't get through here, let's turn back. ②limp: 一～一～地走 limp along; walk with a limp ③crutch: 走路架着双～ walk with crutches ④abduct; kidnap ⑤swindle; make off with: ～款潜逃 abscond with funds
【拐脖儿】 guǎibór elbow (of a stove pipe)
【拐棍】 guǎigùn walking stick
【拐角】 guǎijiǎo corner; turning: 胡同～有个邮筒。 There is a pillar-box at the street corner.
【拐骗】 guǎipiàn ①abduct ②swindle: ～钱财 swindle money (out of sb.)
【拐弯】 guǎiwān ①turn a corner; turn: ～要慢行。 Slow down when turning a corner./ 往前走向左一～就到了。Go straight ahead, turn left and you'll be there./ 在河水～的地方 at the river bend ②turn round; pursue a new course: 他思想一时还拐不过弯来。He hasn't straightened out his ideas yet.
【拐弯抹角】 guǎiwān-mòjiǎo talk in a roundabout way; beat about the bush: 说话不要～。 Get to the point. Don't beat about the bush.
【拐杖】 guǎizhàng walking stick
【拐子】 guǎizi ①〈口〉 cripple ②abductor ③swindler ④I-shaped reel

## guài

**怪** guài ①strange; odd; queer; bewildering: 你说～不～? Isn't this strange?/ ～现象 something quite unusual/ 出～题 set queer (或 odd) questions (in an examination) ②find sth. strange; wonder at: 那有什么可～的? Is that anything to be surprised at? ③quite; rather: 箱子～沉的。The suitcase is rather heavy./ 瞧，这些葡萄～水灵的。Look, how fresh and juicy those grapes are. ④monster; demon; evil being: 鬼～ demons, ghosts and goblins; forces of evil ⑤blame: 不能～他们。They're not to blame. 或 It's not their fault./ ～我没讲清楚。I'm to blame for not having made it clearer.
【怪不得】 guàibude ①no wonder; so that's why; that explains why: ～多一张票，小张把她的让出来了。So that's why (或 No wonder) there's an extra ticket. Xiao Zhang has given hers up. ②not to blame: 这事～他。He's not to blame for this.

【怪诞】 guàidàn weird; strange: ～不经 weird and uncanny; fantastic
【怪话】 guàihuà cynical remark; grumble; complaint: 说～ make cynical remarks
【怪里怪气】 guàiliguàiqì eccentric; peculiar; queer: ～的人 an eccentric fellow
【怪模怪样】 guàimú-guàiyàng queer-looking; grotesque
【怪僻】 guàipì eccentric: 性情～ eccentric
【怪声怪气】 guàishēng-guàiqì (speak in a) strange voice or affected manner
【怪物】 guàiwu ① monster; monstrosity; freak ② an eccentric person
【怪异】 guàiyì monstrous; strange; unusual

## guān

**关** guān ① shut; close: 请随手～门。Please close the door behind you./ 这扇门～不上。The door won't shut. ② turn off: ～收音机 turn (或 switch) off the radio/ ～电灯 turn off the light ③ lock up; shut in: ～进监狱 lock up (in prison); put behind bars/ 别把孩子们成天～在屋里。Don't keep the children inside all day. ④ close down: 解放前夕，镇上～了好几家店铺。On the eve of the liberation, quite a few shops in the town closed down. ⑤ pass: 把～ guard the pass; check ⑥ customhouse ⑦ barrier; critical juncture: 技术难～ technical barriers ⑧ concern; involve: 这不～他的事。That doesn't concern him./ 这些意见至～重要。These ideas are of extreme importance. ⑨ (Guān) a surname
【关隘】 guān'ài 〈书〉 (mountain) pass
【关闭】 guānbì ① close; shut: ～门窗 close the doors and windows ② (of a shop or factory) close down; shut down
【关岛】 Guāndǎo Guam
【关东】 Guāndōng east of Shanhaiguan; the Northeast; northeast China
【关东糖】 guāndōngtáng a kind of malt candy (originating in the Northeast)
【关怀】 guānhuái show loving care for; show solicitude for: ～备至 show the utmost solicitude/ 在华主席和党中央的深切～下，英雄的唐山人民战胜了地震灾害。Thanks to the profound concern of Chairman Hua and the Party Central Committee, the heroic people of Tangshan successfully overcame the effects of the earthquake./ 党和国家非常～少年儿童的健康成长。The Party and the state pay great attention to the healthy growth of children./ 祖国人民对海外侨胞深为～。The Chinese residents overseas are much in the thoughts of the people at home.
【关键】 guānjiàn hinge; key; crux: 问题的～ the crux (或 heart) of the matter; the key to the question/ ～的一年 a year of crucial importance/ ～时刻 a critical (或 crucial) moment/ ～在于要有决心和信心。What counts is determination and confidence./ 建设大寨县，县委是～。The key to building Dazhai-type counties lies in the county Party committees.
【关节】 guānjié ① 〈生理〉 joint ② key (或 crucial) links; links: 应该注意那些涉及全局的重要～。Attention should be centred on the links that have a bearing on the situation as a whole. ◇ ～炎 arthritis
【关口】 guānkǒu ① strategic pass ② juncture
【关联】 guānlián be related; be connected: 国民经济各部门是互相～互相依存的。The various branches of the national economy are interrelated and interdependent./ 数学和天文学是互相～的科学。Mathematics and astronomy are cognate sciences.
【关门】 guānmén ① close: 展览馆六点半～。The exhibition centre closes at 6:30. ② slam the door on sth.; refuse discussion or consideration: 对方在谈判中还没有～。The other side hasn't yet slammed the door on further negotiations./ 采取～态度 adopt a closed-door attitude ③ behind closed doors: 我们不能～办报。We must not run a newspaper behind closed doors. ◇ ～主义 closed-doorism
【关门打狗】 guānmén dǎ gǒu bolt the door and beat the dog — block the enemy's retreat and then destroy him
【关内】 Guānnèi inside Shanhaiguan
【关卡】 guānqiǎ 〈旧〉 an outpost of the tax office
【关切】 guānqiè be deeply concerned; show one's concern over: 表示严重～ show grave concern over/ 获悉贵国遭受地震，我们极为～。We are deeply concerned at the news that your country has been struck by an earthquake.
【关税】 guānshuì customs duty; tariff: 保护～ protective tariff/ 特惠～ preferential tariff
◇ ～壁垒 tariff barrier/ ～豁免 exemption from customs duties/ ～同盟 customs (或 tariff) union/ ～优惠 tariff preference/ ～自主 tariff autonomy
【关头】 guāntóu juncture; moment: 在革命的重要～ at important junctures of the revolution/ 紧要～ a critical moment
【关外】 Guānwài outside Shanhaiguan; the Northeast; northeast China
【关系】 guānxi ① relation; relationship: 外交～ diplomatic relations/ 社会各阶级的相互～ relations between the various classes in society/ 搞好群众～ build good relations with the masses/ 军民～ relationship between the army and the people/ 两国间的友好合作～ friendly relations and cooperation between the two countries ② bearing; impact; significance: 这一点对今后工作～重大。This has an important bearing on our future work./ 你上午去还是下午去，～不大。It won't make much difference whether you go in the morning or in the afternoon. ③〔泛指原因条件，多与"由于""因为"连用〕: 由于时间～，就谈到这里吧。Since time is limited, I'll have to stop here. ④ concern; affect; have a bearing on; have to do with: 农业～国计民生极大。Agriculture is of vital importance to the nation's economy and the people's livelihood./ 交通运输是～到工农业生产的重要部门。Transport and communications play a very important part in industrial and agricultural production. ⑤ credentials showing membership in or connection with an organization: 党员调动工作时要转党的～。When a Party member is transferred to another place of work, his Party credentials are sent there./ 组织～带来了吗？Have you brought your membership credentials with you?
【关厢】 guānxiāng a neighbourhood outside of a city gate
【关心】 guānxīn be concerned with; show solicitude for; be interested in; care for: 一切革命队伍的人都要互相～，互相爱护，互相帮助。All people in the revolutionary ranks must care for each other, must love and help each other./ 我们要～国家大事。We should concern ourselves with affairs of state./ 双方共同～的问题 matters of interest to both sides
【关押】 guānyā lock up; put in prison: 这就是过去农奴主～农奴的地牢。This is the dungeon where the serf owner used to lock up his serfs.
【关于】 guānyú 〈介〉〔引进某种行为或事物的关系者，组成介词结构〕 about; on; with regard to; concerning: ～修改联合公报稿的具体建议 specific proposals with regard to the rewording of the draft joint *communiqué*/ ～保护森林的若干规定 regulations concerning the protection of forests
【关张】 guānzhāng 〈方〉 close down

【关照】 guānzhào ①look after; keep an eye on: 我走后，这里的工作就靠你多～了。 When I'm gone, you'll have to look after the work here./ 感谢你的～。 Thank you for the trouble you've taken on my behalf. ②notify by word of mouth: 你走的时候请～一声。Please let me know when you're ready to go.
【关中】 Guānzhōng the central Shaanxi plain
【关注】 guānzhù follow with interest; pay close attention to; show solicitude for: 我们对这个地区的情况十分～。We follow with interest the development of the situation in this area. 或 We're paying a good deal of attention to what's going on in this area.

**观** guān ①look at; watch; observe: 登泰山，～日出 ascend Taishan Mountain to see the sunrise/ 从轻处理，以～后效 deal with sb. leniently and see how he behaves in future ②sight; view: 奇～ wonderful sight (或 spectacle)/ 外～ outward appearance ③outlook; view; concept: 世界～ world outlook
另见 guàn
【观测】 guāncè observe: ～气象 make weather observations/ 气球～ balloon observation
【观察】 guānchá observe; watch; survey: ～地形 survey the terrain/ ～动静 watch what is going on/ 用阶级分析的方法～问题和解决问题 study and solve problems with the method of class analysis/ 这个病人需要住院～。This patient should be hospitalized for observation.
◇ ～机 observation aircraft/ ～家 observer/ ～所 observation post/ ～员 observer
【观潮派】 guāncháopài a person who takes a wait-and-see attitude; onlooker; bystander
【观点】 guāndiǎn point of view; viewpoint; standpoint: 阶级～ class viewpoint/ 马克思列宁主义的～ Marxist-Leninist standpoint/ 阐明～ explain one's position
【观风】 guānfēng be on the lookout; serve as a lookout
【观感】 guāngǎn impressions: 对新中国的～ impressions of New China
【观光】 guānguāng go sightseeing; visit; tour ◇ ～团 sightseeing party; visiting group/ ～者 sightseer
【观看】 guānkàn watch; view: ～排球比赛 watch a volleyball match
【观礼】 guānlǐ attend a celebration or ceremony: 国庆～代表 a representative attending National Day celebrations ◇ ～台 reviewing stand; visitors' stand
【观摩】 guānmó inspect and learn from each other's work; view and emulate ◇ ～演出 performance before fellow artists for the purpose of discussion and emulation
【观念】 guānniàn sense; idea; concept: 组织～ sense of organization/ 私有～ private ownership mentality/ 增强党的～ strengthen one's sense of responsibility to the Party ◇ ～形态 ideology
【观赏】 guānshǎng view and admire; enjoy the sight of ◇ ～植物 ornamental (或 decorative) plant
【观通站】 〈军〉 guāntōngzhàn observation and communication post (of the naval service)
【观望】 guānwàng wait and see; look on (from the sidelines): 采取～态度 take a wait-and-see attitude
【观象台】 guānxiàngtái 〈天〉 observatory
【观音】 Guānyīn 〈佛教〉 *Avalokitesvara*; Guanyin (a Bodhisattva) 又作"观世音"
【观音土】 guānyīntǔ a kind of white clay (eaten by famine victims to appease their hunger in the old society)
【观音竹】 guānyīnzhú 〈植〉 fernleaf hedge bamboo (*Bambusa multiplex* var. *nana*)
【观瞻】 guānzhān the appearance of a place and the impressions it leaves; sight; view: 有碍～ be unsightly; be repugnant to the eye; offend the eye
【观众】 guānzhòng spectator; viewer; audience

**官** guān ①government official; officer; officeholder: ～兵一致 unity between officers and men ②〈旧〉 government-owned; government-sponsored; official; public: ～办 run by the government; operated by official bodies ③organ: 感～ sense organ ④(Guān) a surname
【官场】 guānchǎng 〈旧〉 officialdom; official circles
【官邸】 guāndǐ official residence; official mansion: 大使～ ambassador's residence
【官方】 guānfāng 〔旧时通用，现在多用来指资本主义国家的〕 of or by the government; official: ～人士 official quarters/ ～消息 news from government sources; official sources/ 以～身分 in an official capacity
【官府】 guānfǔ 〈旧〉 ①local authorities ②feudal official
【官复原职】 guān fù yuán zhí restore an official to his original post; be reinstated
【官官相护】 guān guān xiāng hù bureaucrats shield one another
【官价】 guānjià 〈旧〉 official price (或 rate)
【官架子】 guānjiàzi the airs of an official; bureaucratic airs
【官阶】 guānjiē official rank
【官吏】 guānlì 〈旧〉 government officials
【官僚】 guānliáo bureaucrat: 封建～ feudal bureaucrat/ 清除～习气 get rid of bureaucratic practices/ 这人真～! What a bureaucrat that fellow is!
◇ ～机构 bureaucratic apparatus/ ～垄断资本 bureaucrat-monopoly capital/ ～买办资产阶级 the bureaucrat-comprador bourgeoisie/ ～资本 bureaucrat capital/ ～资本主义 bureaucrat capitalism/ ～资产阶级 the bureaucrat-capitalist class
【官僚主义】 guānliáozhǔyì bureaucracy ◇ ～者 bureaucrat/ ～作风 bureaucratic style of work; bureaucratic way of doing things
【官能】 guānnéng (organic) function; sense: 视、听、嗅、味、触这五种～ the five senses of sight, hearing, smell, taste and touch ◇ ～团 〈化〉 functional group/ ～症 〈医〉 functional disease
【官气】 guānqì bureaucratic airs: 劳动的汗水冲掉了他身上的～。The sweat of labour washed away his bureaucratic airs.
【官腔】 guānqiāng bureaucratic tone; official jargon: 打～ speak in a bureaucratic tone; stall with official jargon
【官司】 guānsi 〈口〉 lawsuit: 和人打～ go to law against sb.
【官衔】 guānxián official title
【官样文章】 guānyàng wénzhāng mere formalities; officialese
【官员】 guānyuán official: 外交～ diplomatic official
【官职】 guānzhí government post; official position

**冠** guān ①hat: 免～照片 bare-headed photo/ 衣～整齐 be neatly dressed ②corona; crown: 树～ the crown of a tree/ 花～ corolla/ 牙～ the crown of a tooth ③crest; comb: 鸡～ cock's comb; crest
另见 guàn
【冠冕】 guānmiǎn royal crown; official hat
【冠冕堂皇】 guānmiǎn tánghuáng highfalutin; high-sounding: ～的理由 high-sounding excuses
【冠心病】 guānxīnbìng 〈医〉 coronary heart disease
【冠周炎】 guānzhōuyán 〈医〉 pericoronitis
【冠状动脉】 guānzhuàng dòngmài 〈生理〉 coronary artery ◇ ～硬化 coronary arteriosclerosis
【冠子】 guānzi crest; comb

**倌** guān ① a keeper of domestic animals; herdsman: 猪～儿 swineherd/ 羊～儿 shepherd/ 马～儿 groom ②〈旧〉a hired hand in certain trades: 堂～儿 waiter

**棺** guān coffin

【棺材】 guāncai coffin

【棺床】 guānchuáng 〈考古〉coffin platform

【棺椁】 guānguǒ 〈考古〉inner and outer coffins

【棺架】 guānjià bier

**鳏** guān wifeless; widowered

【鳏夫】 guānfū 〈书〉an old wifeless man; bachelor or widower

【鳏寡孤独】 guān-guǎ-gū-dú widowers, widows, orphans and the childless — those who have no kith and kin and cannot support themselves

## guǎn

**馆** guǎn ① accommodation for guests: 旅～ hotel/ 宾～ guesthouse ② embassy, legation or consulate: 办理建～事宜 arrange for the setting up of an embassy ③ (of service trades) shop: 理发～ barbershop/ 茶～ teahouse/ 饭～ restaurant/ 照相～ photo studio ④ a place for cultural activities: 博物～ museum/ 展览～ exhibition hall/ 文化～ cultural centre/ 美术～ art gallery/ 体育～ gymnasium /图书～ library

【馆子】 guǎnzi restaurant; eating house: 下～ eat at a restaurant

**管** guǎn ① tube; pipe: 钢～ steel tube/ 血～ blood vessel/ 输油～ oil pipeline ② wind instrument: 单簧～ clarinet/ 铜～乐器 brass wind ③〈量〉〔用于细长圆筒形的东西〕: 一～毛笔 a writing brush/ 一～牙膏 a tube of toothpaste ④〈电子〉valve; tube: 电子～ electron tube ⑤ manage; run; be in charge of: ～伙食 be in charge of the mess/ ～家务 run the house; keep house/ 他把仓库～得井井有条。He keeps the warehouse in good order./ 每个工人～好几台机器。Each worker minds (或 tends) several machines. ⑥ subject sb. to discipline: 孩子要～，但更要引导。Children need discipline, but they need guidance even more. ⑦ bother about; mind: ～得宽 make everything one's own business/ 别～我！Don't bother about me./ 怎么～不着？对人民不利的事就是要～。Why shouldn't we interfere? It's our duty to interfere with anything that's against the interests of the people. ⑧ provide; guarantee: ～住 provide accommodation/ 质量不合格～换。Substandard products will be exchanged. ⑨〈介〉〔专用于"管…叫…"中〕: 大家～他叫小淘气。People call him "little rogue". 或 He's known as "little rogue". ⑩ (Guǎn) a surname

【管保】 guǎnbǎo ① guarantee; assure: 我～你吃了这药就好。I guarantee that if you take this medicine, you'll soon get well. ② certainly; surely: 他～不知道。I'm sure he doesn't know.

【管道】 guǎndào pipeline; piping; conduit; tubing: 煤气～ gas piping/ ～安装 piping erection

【管风琴】 guǎnfēngqín 〈乐〉pipe organ; organ

【管家】 guǎnjia ①〈旧〉steward; butler ② manager; housekeeper: 生产队的好～ the production team's good manager

【管见】 guǎnjiàn 〈谦〉my humble opinion; my limited understanding: 容陈～。Let me state my humble opinion.

【管教】 guǎnjiào 〈方〉certainly; assuredly; surely: 听他的话，～没错。Surely you won't go wrong if you follow his advice.

【管教】 guǎnjiao subject sb. to discipline

【管井】 guǎnjǐng 〈水〉tube well

【管窥】 guǎnkuī look at sth. through a bamboo tube — have a restricted view: ～所及 in my humble opinion

【管窥蠡测】 guǎnkuī-lícè look at the sky through a bamboo tube and measure the sea with a calabash — restricted in vision and shallow in understanding

【管理】 guǎnlǐ manage; run; administer; supervise: ～生产 manage production/ ～群众生活 look after the everyday life of the masses/ ～华侨事务 administer affairs concerning overseas Chinese/ 加强企业～ strengthen the administration (或 management) of enterprises ◇ ～处 administrative (或 management) office/ ～费 management expenses; costs of administration/ ～人员 administrative (或 managerial) personnel/ ～委员会 management committee; board of management/ ～员 a person managing some aspect of daily work within an organization

【管路】 guǎnlù 〈机〉pipeline ◇ ～铺设 pipe laying/ ～输送能力 carrying capacity of a pipeline; delivery capacity

【管纱】 guǎnshā 〈纺〉cop

【管事】 guǎnshì ① run affairs; be in charge: 这里谁～? Who's in charge here? ②〈口〉efficacious; effective; of use: 这药很～儿。This medicine is very effective./ 找他不～。It's no use asking him. ③〈旧〉manager; steward

【管束】 guǎnshù restrain; check; control: 严加～ keep sb. under strict control

【管辖】 guǎnxiá have jurisdiction over; administer: 在～范围之内 come within the jurisdiction of/ 这个市由中央直接～。This municipality is directly under the Central Government. ◇ ～权 jurisdiction

【管弦乐】 guǎnxiányuè orchestral music ◇ ～队 orchestra/ ～法 orchestration

【管押】 guǎnyā take sb. into custody; keep in custody; detain

【管用】 guǎnyòng 见"管事"②

【管乐队】 guǎnyuèduì wind band; band

【管乐器】 guǎnyuèqì wind instrument

【管制】 guǎnzhì ① control: 军事～ military control/ 外汇～ foreign exchange control ② put under surveillance: 交群众～ put under public surveillance

【管中窥豹】 guǎnzhōng kuī bào look at a leopard through a bamboo tube — have a limited view of sth.

【管中窥豹，可见一斑】 guǎnzhōng kuī bào, kě jiàn yī bān look at one spot on a leopard and you can visualize the whole animal; conjure up the whole thing through seeing a part of it

【管状花】 guǎnzhuànghuā 〈植〉tubular flower

【管子】 guǎnzi tube; pipe ◇ ～工 plumber; pipe fitter

## guàn

**观** guàn Taoist temple
另见 guān

**贯** guàn ① pass through; pierce: 纵～两省的铁路 a railway passing through two provinces from north to south/ 学～古今 well versed in both ancient and modern learning ② be linked together; follow in a continuous line: 鱼～而入 file in ③ birthplace; native place: 籍～ the place of one's birth or origin ④〈旧〉a string of 1,000 cash ⑤ (Guàn) a surname

【贯彻】 guànchè carry out (或 through); implement; put

into effect: ～党的基本路线 implement the Party's basic line/ ～党委的决议 put into effect the Party Committee's decisions/ ～群众路线 follow the mass line/ ～代表大会精神 act in the spirit of the congress/ 艰苦奋斗的精神要～始终。We must always adhere to the principle of plain living and hard struggle.

【贯穿】 guànchuān run through; penetrate: 这条公路～十几个县。This highway runs through a dozen counties./ 农业合作化运动始终～着两个阶级、两条道路、两条路线的斗争。The struggle between the two classes, the two roads and the two lines ran through the movement of agricultural cooperation. ◇ ～辐射 penetrating radiation

【贯串】 guànchuàn run through; permeate: 比赛～着"友谊第一，比赛第二"的精神。The contest was permeated with the spirit of "friendship first, competition second".

【贯通】 guàntōng ① have a thorough knowledge of; be well versed in: ～中西医学 have a thorough knowledge of both Western and traditional Chinese medicine/ 豁然～ suddenly see the light ② link up; thread together: 大运河～五大河流。The Grand Canal links up five big rivers./ 这条铁路已全线～。The whole railway line has been joined up.

【贯众】 guànzhòng 〈中药〉 the rhizome of cyrtomium (*Cyrtomium fortunei*)

【贯注】 guànzhù ① concentrate on; be absorbed in: 把精力～在革命工作上 concentrate one's energy on revolutionary work/ 全神～ be wholly absorbed; be rapt ② be connected in meaning or feeling: 这两句是一气～下来的。These two sentences are closely connected. 或 These two sentences hang together.

## 冠

guàn ①〈书〉 put on a hat ② precede; crown with: 人民公社的名称一般都～以所属县名。The name of a people's commune is usually preceded by the county name. ③ first place; the best: 这里的棉花产量为全国之～。This area ranks first in the whole country for cotton output.

另见 guān

【冠词】 guàncí 〈语〉 article

【冠军】 guànjūn champion

## 惯

guàn ① be used to; be in the habit of: 劳动～了，闲着就不舒服。When you are used to physical labour, you feel uncomfortable if you're idle./ 这里空气比较稀薄，～了就好了。The air is rather thin here, but you'll get used to it in time. ② indulge; spoil: 别把孩子～坏了。Don't spoil the child.

【惯犯】 guànfàn habitual offender; hardened criminal; recidivist; repeater

【惯匪】 guànfěi hardened bandit; professional brigand

【惯技】 guànjì 〈贬〉 customary tactic; old trick

【惯例】 guànlì convention; usual practice: 国际～ international practice

【惯量】 guànliàng 〈物〉 inertia

【惯窃】 guànqiè hardened thief 又作"惯偷"

【惯性】 guànxìng 〈物〉 inertia

◇ ～定律 the law of inertia/ ～飞行导弹 coasting missile; coaster/ ～矩 moment of inertia/ ～领航 inertial navigation

【惯用】 guànyòng ① habitually practise; consistently use: 修正主义者～两面派的手法欺骗群众。The revisionists consistently use double-faced tactics to deceive the masses. ② habitual; customary: ～伎俩 customary tactics; old tricks/ ～手法 habitual practice

## 掼

guàn 〈方〉 hurl; fling

【掼纱帽】 guàn shāmào 〈方〉 throw away one's official's hat in a huff; resign in resentment; quit office

## 盥

guàn 〈书〉 wash (the hands or face)

【盥漱】 guànshù wash one's face and rinse one's mouth

【盥洗】 guànxǐ wash one's hands and face

◇ ～室 washroom/ ～台 washstand/ ～用具 toilet articles

## 灌

guàn ① irrigate: 冬～ winter irrigation/ 引水～田 channel water to irrigate the fields ② fill; pour: 暖瓶都～满了。The thermos flasks have all been filled./ ～药 pour medicine down the throat/ 冷风往屋里直～。The cold air poured into the room./ ～醉 get sb. drunk/ 满堂～ cram students; spoonfeed

【灌肠】 guàncháng 〈医〉 enema; clyster

【灌肠】 guànchang sausage

【灌唱片】 guàn chàngpiàn make a gramophone record; cut a disc

【灌溉】 guàngài irrigate: 提水～ irrigation by pumping

◇ ～面积 irrigated area/ ～渠 irrigation canal/ ～网 irrigation network/ ～系统 irrigation system

【灌浆】 guànjiāng ①〈建〉 grouting ②〈农〉 (of grain) be in the milk ③〈医〉 form a vesicle (during smallpox or after vaccination)

【灌米汤】 guàn mǐtang bewitch sb. by means of flattery

【灌木】 guànmù bush; shrub

【灌输】 guànshū instil into; inculcate; imbue with: 向农民～社会主义思想 imbue the peasants with socialist ideas

【灌音】 guànyīn have one's voice recorded

【灌注】 guànzhù pour into: 把铁水～到砂型里 pour molten iron into a sand mould

## 鹳

guàn stork

## 罐

guàn ① jar; pot; tin: 一～苹果酱 a jar of apple jam/ 茶叶～ tea caddy/ 水～ water pitcher ②〈矿〉 coal tub

【罐车】 guànchē tank car; tank truck; tanker

【罐笼】 guànlóng 〈矿〉 cage

【罐头】 guàntou tin; can: ～牛肉 tinned (或 canned) beef

◇ ～食品 tinned (或 canned) food

【罐子】 guànzi pot; jar; pitcher; jug

# guāng

## 光

guāng ① light; ray: 日～ sunlight/ 爱克斯～ X ray ② brightness; lustre: 红～满面 one's face aglow (with health, etc.)/ 两眼无～ dull-eyed ③ honour; glory: 为祖国争～ win honour for one's country; bring credit to one's country/ 脸上无～ feel ashamed ④ scenery: 春～ sights and sounds of spring; spring scene ⑤ smooth; glossy; polished: 这种纸两面～。This kind of paper is smooth on both sides./ 把工件磨～ polish the workpiece ⑥ used up; nothing left: 墨水用～了。The ink's used up./ 把敌人消灭～ wipe out the enemy ⑦ bare; naked: ～着头 be bareheaded/ ～着膀子 be stripped to the waist ⑧ solely; only; merely; alone: 干革命～凭一股子热情是不够的。It's not enough to rely on enthusiasm alone in waging revolution.

【光斑】 guāngbān 〈天〉 facula

【光板儿】 guāngbǎnr worn-out fur

【光泵】 guāngbèng optical pump

【光波】 guāngbō light wave

【光彩】 guāngcǎi ① lustre; splendour; radiance: ～夺目 dazzlingly brilliant/ ～绚丽的贝雕吸引了许多观众。The brilliant lustre of the shell carving attracted many visitors./ 大庆精神放～。The spirit of Daqing shines with dazzling

splendour. ② honourable; glorious: 扮演一个极不～的角色 play a most inglorious part/ 谁说当修鞋工不～? Who says it's not respectable to be a shoe repairer?
【光电】 guāngdiàn 〈物〉 photoelectricity
◇ ～导体 photoconductor/ ～发射 photoelectric emission; photoemission/ ～管 photocell; phototube
【光电子】 guāngdiànzǐ 〈物〉 photoelectron
【光度】 guāngdù 〈物〉 luminosity ◇ ～计 photometer
【光辐射】 guāngfúshè ray radiation ◇ ～伤害 ray radiation injury
【光复】 guāngfù recover: ～旧物 recover lost territory
【光杆儿】 guānggǎnr ① a bare trunk or stalk ② a man who has lost his family ③ a person without a following: ～司令 a general without an army; a leader without a following
【光顾】 guānggù 〔旧时商家用的敬辞〕 patronize: 如蒙～,无任欢迎。Your patronage is cordially invited.
【光怪陆离】 guāngguài-lùlí grotesque in shape and gaudy in colour; bizarre and motley: ～的广告 grotesque and gaudy advertisements
【光棍儿】 guānggùnr unmarried man; bachelor
【光棍】 guānggun ruffian; hoodlum
【光合作用】 guānghé zuòyòng 〈植〉 photosynthesis
【光华】 guānghuá brilliance; splendour
【光滑】 guānghuá smooth; glossy; sleek
【光化】 guānghuà 〈化〉 ① actinic: ～射线 actinic ray ② photochemical: ～作用 photochemical action
【光环】 guānghuán ① a ring of light: 土星～ Saturn's ring ② 〈宗〉 halo; aureole
【光辉】 guānghuī ① radiance; brilliance; glory: 毛泽东思想的～照耀着我们前进的道路。The radiance of Mao Zedong Thought lights our way forward./ 乌鸦的翅膀挡不住太阳的～。The wings of a crow cannot shut out the rays of the sun./ 敌人的诽谤无损于我党的～。The slanderous attacks of enemies cannot diminish the glory of our Party. ② brilliant; magnificent; glorious: 马列主义的～著作 magnificent works of Marxism-Leninism/ ～榜样 a shining example/ ～的一生 a glorious life
【光洁】 guāngjié bright and clean ◇ ～度 〈机〉 smooth finish
【光介子】 guāngjièzǐ 〈物〉 photomeson
【光景】 guāngjǐng ① scene: 看到这排窑洞,当年延安的～又重现在眼前。The sight of the caves recalled our days at Yan'an. ② circumstances; conditions: 过去我们工人做梦也想不到会有今天这样的好～啊! We workers never dreamed of such a happy life as we enjoy today. ③ about; around: 离这儿有十里～。It's about 10 *li* away from here. ④ very probably; quite likely: 今天太闷热,～是要下雨。The weather is stifling. It looks like rain.
【光刻】 guāngkè 〈物〉 photoetching
【光亮】 guāngliàng bright; luminous; shiny
【光疗】 guāngliáo 〈医〉 phototherapy
【光临】 guānglín 〈敬〉 presence (of a guest, etc.): 敬请～。Your presence is cordially requested./ 欢迎你们～指导。We welcome you and would appreciate your advice.
【光溜溜】 guāngliūliū ① smooth; slippery: ～的大理石地面 a smooth marble floor ② bare; naked: 孩子们脱得～的在河里游泳。The children stripped off their clothes and swam naked in the river.
【光溜】 guāngliu 〈口〉 smooth; slippery
【光芒】 guāngmáng rays of light; brilliant rays; radiance: 旭日东升,～四射。The morning sun rises in the east, shedding its rays in all directions./ 延安精神永放～。The Yan'an spirit will shine for ever.
【光芒万丈】 guāngmáng wàn zhàng shining with boundless radiance; gloriously radiant; resplendent: 总路线如～的灯塔,照耀着我们胜利前进。The Party's general line for building socialism shines like a radiant beacon, guiding us in our victorious march forward.
【光敏】 guāngmǐn 〈物〉 photosensitive ◇ ～电阻 photoresistance/ ～二极管 photodiode
【光明】 guāngmíng ① light: 黑暗中的一线～ a streak of light in the darkness/ 是共产党把中国引向～。It was the Communist Party that led China to the light. ② bright; promising: 世界的前途是～的。The future of the world is bright./ 社会主义的～大道 the bright road of socialism ③ openhearted; guileless: ～磊落 open and aboveboard
【光年】 guāngnián 〈天〉 light-year
【光谱】 guāngpǔ 〈物〉 spectrum: 明(暗)线～ bright-line (dark-line) spectrum/ 太阳～ solar spectrum
◇ ～比较仪 spectrocomparator/ ～分析 spectrum (或 spectral) analysis/ ～学 spectroscopy/ ～学家 spectroscopist
【光气】 guāngqì 〈化〉 phosgene
【光球】 guāngqiú 〈天〉 photosphere
【光圈】 guāngquān 〈摄〉 diaphragm; aperture
【光荣】 guāngróng honour; glory; credit: ～称号 a title of honour/ ～使者 an honoured envoy/ ～军属 the honoured family of a PLA man; soldier's family/ ～传统 a glorious tradition/ 大干社会主义～。It's a glorious thing to go all out for socialism./ ～地加入中国共产党 have the honour of being admitted into the Communist Party of China/ 党把这样艰巨的任务交给我们,这是我们的～。It is an honour for us to have been entrusted with such an arduous task by the Party. ◇ ～榜 honour roll/ ～花 rosette (presented as a mark of honour to combat heroes, model workers, recruits to the army, etc.)
【光润】 guāngrùn (of skin) smooth
【光栅】 guāngshān 〈物〉 grating
【光渗】 guāngshèn 〈物〉 irradiation
【光束】 guāngshù 〈物〉 light beam: 参考～ reference beam
【光速】 guāngsù 〈物〉 velocity of light
【光天化日】 guāngtiān-huàrì broad daylight; the light of day: 把敌人的阴谋暴露在～之下 expose the enemy's plot to the light of day
【光通量】 guāngtōngliàng 〈物〉 luminous flux
【光头】 guāngtóu ① bareheaded ② shaven head; shaven-headed: 剃～ have one's head shaved
【光秃秃】 guāngtūtū bare; bald: ～的山坡 bare hillsides/ ～的树枝 naked branches
【光线】 guāngxiàn light; ray: 别在～不好的地方看书。Don't read in a poor light.
【光行差】 guāngxíngchā 〈天〉 aberration
【光学】 guāngxué optics: 几何～ geometrical optics/ 非线性～ nonlinear optics
◇ ～玻璃 optical glass/ ～录音 optical recording/ ～录音机 photographic sound recorder/ ～谐振腔 optical resonator/ ～仪器 optical instrument/ ～影象 optical image
【光焰】 guāngyàn radiance; flare
【光耀】 guāngyào ① brilliant light; brilliance: ～夺目 dazzling ② glorious; honourable
【光阴】 guāngyīn time: ～似箭。Time flies like an arrow. 或 How time flies.
【光源】 guāngyuán 〈物〉 light source; illuminant
【光泽】 guāngzé lustre; gloss; sheen
【光照】 guāngzhào 〈植〉 illumination ◇ ～阶段 photostage
【光制】 guāngzhì 〈机〉 finishing: 最后～ final finishing ◇ ～品 finished product
【光质子】 guāngzhìzǐ 〈物〉 photoproton
【光子】 guāngzǐ 〈物〉 photon ◇ ～火箭 photon rocket
【光宗耀祖】 guāngzōng-yàozǔ bring honour to one's ancestors

**桄** guāng
另见 guàng
【桄榔】 guāngláng 〈植〉 gomuti palm

**胱** guāng 见"膀胱" pángguāng

## guǎng

**广** guǎng ① wide; vast; extensive: 地～人稀 a vast and thinly populated area/ 见多识～ have wide experience and extensive knowledge/ 我们县这次改造农田,面积之～是前所未有的。Such extensive improvement of farmland is unprecedented in our county./ 丰收不忘～积粮。When we reap a good harvest, we must make a point of storing grain everywhere. ② numerous: 在大庭～众之中 before a large audience; in public ③ expand; spread: 以～流传 so that it may spread far and wide ④ short for Guangzhou: ～交会 the Guangzhou Export Commodities Fair

【广板】 guǎngbǎn 〈乐〉 *largo*

【广播】 guǎngbō broadcast; be on the air: 实况～ live broadcast; live transmissions over the radio or television/ 开始(停止)～ go on (off) the air/ 听北京台～ tune in to Radio Beijing/ 作～讲话 speak over the radio; broadcast a talk/ 现在全文～《人民日报》社论。We now bring you the full text of the *Renmin Ribao* editorial.
◇ ～电台 broadcasting (或 radio) station/ ～稿 broadcast script/ ～讲话 broadcast speech; radio talk/ ～节目 broadcast (或 radio) programme/ ～剧 radio play/ ～喇叭 loudspeaker/ ～体操 setting-up exercises to radio music/ ～网 rediffusion (或 broadcasting) network/ ～员 (radio) announcer; broadcaster/ ～站 broadcasting station (of a factory, school, etc.); rediffusion station

【广博】 guǎngbó (of a person's knowledge) extensive; wide: 知识～ have extensive knowledge; erudite

【广场】 guǎngchǎng public square; square: 天安门～ Tian'anmen Square

【广大】 guǎngdà ① vast; wide; extensive: 幅员～ vast in territory/ ～地区 vast areas; extensive regions/ ～农村 the vast countryside; extensive rural areas ② large-scale; widespread: 合作医疗已经有了～的发展。There is already an extensive cooperative medical service. ③ numerous: ～人民群众 the broad masses of the people/ ～干部 vast numbers of cadres/ ～青年学生 the mass of student youth/ ～官兵 the broad ranks of officers and men/ ～读者 the reading public

【广岛】 Guǎngdǎo Hiroshima

【广东】 Guǎngdōng Guangdong (Province)

【广度】 guǎngdù scope; range: 人类利用自然资源的～将日益扩大。The scope of man's use of natural resources will steadily grow./ 向生产的～和深度进军 develop the range and quality of production

【广而言之】 guǎng ér yán zhī speaking generally; in a general sense

【广泛】 guǎngfàn extensive; wide-ranging; widespread: ～的兴趣 wide interests/ ～而深入的影响 a widespread and profound influence/ ～的统一战线 a broad united front/ 在社会主义制度下,人民享受～的民主和自由。Under the socialist system, the people enjoy extensive democracy and freedom./ 进行～的交谈 have a wide-ranging conversation/ ～征求意见 solicit opinions from all sides/ ～宣传计划生育的好处 give wide publicity to the advantages of family planning

【广柑】 guǎnggān a kind of orange

【广告】 guǎnggào advertisement: 做～ advertise
◇ ～画 poster/ ～栏 advertisement column/ ～牌 billboard/ ～色 poster colour

【广寒宫】 Guǎnghán Gōng the Moon Palace (the mythical palace in the moon)

【广开才路】 guǎng kāi cáilù open all avenues for people of talent

【广开言路】 guǎng kāi yánlù encourage the free airing of views

【广阔】 guǎngkuò vast; wide; broad: ～的国土 a vast country/ ～的前景 broad prospects/ 交游～ have a wide acquaintance; have a large circle of friends/ ～天地,大有作为 a vast world where much can be accomplished; a vast field for using one's talents

【广袤】 guǎng-mào 〈书〉 length and breadth of land: ～千里的黄土高原 a vast expanse of loess plateau a thousand *li* across

【广漠】 guǎngmò vast and bare: 在～的沙滩上 on the bare expanse of the beach

【广木香】 guǎngmùxiāng 〈中药〉 costusroot (*Saussurea lappa*)

【广西】 Guǎngxī Guangxi

【广西壮族自治区】 Guǎngxī Zhuàngzú Zìzhìqū the Guangxi Zhuang Autonomous Region

【广延】 guǎngyán 〈物〉 extension ◇ ～量 extensive quantity

【广义】 guǎngyì ① broad sense: ～地说 in a broad sense; broadly speaking ② 〈物〉 generalized: ～空间 generalized space/ ～坐标 generalized coordinates

【广种薄收】 guǎng zhòng bó shōu extensive cultivation

【广州】 Guǎngzhōu Guangzhou

【广州起义】 Guǎngzhōu Qǐyì the Guangzhou Uprising of Dec. 11, 1927 (organized by the revolutionary soldiers and workers of the city, under the leadership of the Chinese Communist Party — one of the three major uprisings of this period, the other two being the Nanchang and Autumn Harvest Uprisings)

**犷** guǎng 〈书〉 rustic; uncouth; boorish
【犷悍】 guǎnghàn tough and intrepid

## guàng

**桄** guàng ① reel thread or wire on a revolving frame ② reel: 一～线 a reel of thread
另见 guāng
【桄子】 guàngzi reel

**逛** guàng stroll; ramble; roam: 到郊外～～ go for a walk in the suburbs/ ～大街 go window-shopping; stroll around the streets
【逛荡】 guàngdang loiter; loaf about

## guī

**归** guī ① go back to; return: ～期 date of return/ 无家可～ be homeless/ 拉练～来 return from a camping trip (或 route march) ② give back to; return sth. to: 物～原主 return (或 restore) a thing to its rightful owner ③ converge; come together: 千条江河～大海,各族人民心向党。A thousand rivers find their way to the sea; the hearts of all nationalities turn to the Party./ 把性质相同的问题～为一类 group together problems of a similar nature ④ turn over to; put in sb.'s charge: ～集体所有 be turned over to the collective; be owned by the collective/ 颗粒～仓 every grain to the granary/ 消防工作～我们管。We are in charge of fire fighting. ⑤〔用在重叠动词之间，表示不相干或无结果〕: 玩笑～玩笑，事情可得认真去办。It's all right to crack jokes but you must do your job seriously./ 批评～批评，他就是不改。Despite our repeated criticisms, he simply won't mend his ways. ⑥〈数〉division on the abacus with a one-digit divisor ⑦ (Guī) a surname

【归案】 guī'àn bring to justice: 缉拿～ arrest and bring to justice

【归并】 guībìng ① incorporate into; merge into: 这个厂后来～到另一个工厂里去了。This factory was later incorporated into another one./ 把两组～成一组 merge the two groups into one ② lump together; add up: 这三笔帐～起来是四百五十元。The three accounts add up to 450 *yuan*.

【归程】 guīchéng return journey

【归除】 guīchú 〈数〉division on the abacus with a divisor of two or more digits

【归档】 guīdàng place on file; file

【归队】 guīduì ① rejoin one's unit: 他的伤已经好了，可以～了。Now that his wound has healed, he can go back to his unit. ② return to the profession one was trained for

【归附】 guīfù submit to the authority of another: ～国法 obey the law of the state

【归根结底】 guīgēn-jiédǐ in the final analysis: 人类社会的发展，～，是由生产力的发展决定的。The development of human society is, in the final analysis, conditioned by the development of the productive forces.

【归功于】 guīgōng yú give the credit to; attribute the success to: 我们的一切成就都应～毛主席的无产阶级革命路线。We owe all our achievements to Chairman Mao's proletarian revolutionary line.

【归国】 guīguó return to one's country: ～观光 return to one's homeland on a sightseeing tour ◇ ～华侨 returned overseas Chinese

【归航】 guīháng 〈航空〉homing ◇ ～飞行 homing flight/ ～台 homer

【归还】 guīhuán return; revert: 向图书馆借书要按时～。Books borrowed from the library should be returned on time.

【归结】 guījié ① sum up; put in a nutshell: 说来话长，～起来，他们无非要篡党夺权。It is a long story. To put it in a nutshell, their aim was to usurp Party and state power. ② end (of a story, etc.)

【归咎】 guījiù impute to; attribute a fault to; put the blame on: 不要把你的错误都～于客观原因。Don't attribute all your mistakes to objective causes.

【归类】 guīlèi sort out; classify

【归拢】 guīlǒng put together: 你把工具～一下。Please put the tools together.

【归谬法】 guīmiùfǎ reduction to absurdity; *reductio ad absurdum*

【归纳】 guīnà induce; conclude; sum up: 请你把这篇文章的大意～一下。Will you please sum up the main ideas of this article?/ 这是他从大量事实中～出来的结论。This is a conclusion which he has drawn from numerous facts. ◇ ～法 inductive method; induction

【归侨】 guīqiáo 〈简〉(归国华侨) returned overseas Chinese

【归入】 guīrù classify; include: 这些问题可～一类。These questions may be included in the same category.

【归属】 guīshǔ belong to; come under the jurisdiction of: 该岛的～早已确定无疑。The ownership of the island has long been established beyond dispute.

【归顺】 guīshùn come over and pledge allegiance

【归宿】 guīsù a home to return to: 这位流浪多年的老人，到解放后才在我们村找到了～。After long years of wandering, the old man at last found a home in our village after liberation./ 政策是革命政党一切实际行动的出发点，并且表现于行动的过程和～。Policy is the starting point of all the practical actions of a revolutionary party and manifests itself in the process and the end-result of that party's actions.

【归天】 guītiān 〈旧〉pass away; die

【归途】 guītú homeward journey; one's way home

【归向】 guīxiàng turn towards (the righteous side); incline to: 人心～ the inclination of the hearts of the people

【归心似箭】 guīxīn sì jiàn with one's heart set on speeding home; impatient to get back; anxious to return

【归于】 guīyú ① belong to; be attributed to: 光荣～伟大的中国共产党。Glory to the great Communist Party of China. ② result in; end in: 经过长时间的辩论，大家的意见～一致。The long debate finally ended in agreement. 或 Agreement was reached after a long debate.

【归着】 guīzhe 〈口〉put in order; tidy up: ～屋子 tidy up the room/ 行李～好了吗? Have you finished packing? 又作"归置"

【归真反璞】 guīzhēn-fǎnpú (drop all affectation and) return to original purity and simplicity

【归总】 guīzǒng put (items, etc.) together; sum up: ～一句话 to put it in a nutshell/ 大家提的问题我还没来得及～。I haven't had time yet to make a list of all your questions.

【归罪】 guīzuì put the blame on; impute to

**圭** guī an elongated pointed tablet of jade held in the hands by ancient rulers on ceremonial occasions

【圭表】 guībiǎo an ancient Chinese sundial consisting of an elongated dial (*gui*) and one or two gnomons (*biao*), used for measuring the length of the year and of the 24 solar terms

【圭臬】 guīniè 〈书〉criterion; standard: 奉为～ look up to as the standard

【圭亚那】 Guīyànà Guyana ◇ ～人 Guyanese

**龟** guī tortoise; turtle
另见 jūn

【龟板】 guībǎn 〈中药〉tortoise plastron

【龟背】 guībèi 〈中医〉curvature of the spinal column

【龟甲】 guījiǎ tortoise-shell

【龟缩】 guīsuō huddle up like a turtle drawing in its head and legs; withdraw into passive defence; hole up: 敌人～在几个孤立的据点里。The enemy was holed up in a few isolated strongholds.

【龟头】 guītóu 〈生理〉glans penis

**规** guī ① compasses; dividers: 一个圆～ a pair of compasses ② regulation; rule: 校～ school regulations ③ admonish; advise: ～劝 admonish ④ plan; map out: ～划 plan ⑤〈机〉gauge: 线～ wire gauge/ 测隙～ feeler (gauge)

【规避】 guībì evade; dodge; avoid: ～问题的实质 evade the substance of the issue ◇ ～战术 evasion tactics

【规程】 guīchéng rules; regulations: 操作～ rules of operation

【规定】 guīdìng ① stipulate; provide: 遵守党章的～ abide by the stipulations of the Party Constitution/ 法律～的措施 measures provided for by law/ 宪法～妇女享有与男子完全相同的权利。The Constitution stipulates that women enjoy exactly the same rights as men./ ～干部经常参加集体生产劳动 make it a rule that cadres should regularly take part in collective productive labour ② fix; set; formulate: 在～的时间内 within the fixed time/ ～的指标

a set quota/ ～的表格 prescribed forms/ 在～的地点集合 assemble at an assigned spot/ 中国革命的特点～了我党的战略和战术。The characteristics of the Chinese revolution determined the strategy and tactics of our Party. ◇ ～动作〈体〉compulsory exercise/ ～数额〈经〉quota

【规范】 guīfàn standard; norm: 合乎～ conform to the standard/ 这个词的用法不～。This is not the normal way of using the word. ◇ ～化 standardization

【规格】 guīgé specifications; standards; norms: 统一的～ unified standards/ 不合～ not be up to standard; fall short of specifications ◇ ～化 standardization

【规划】 guīhuà programme; plan: 长远～ long-term programme (或 planning)/ 生产～ production plan

【规矩】 guīju ① rule; established practice; custom: 损坏东西要赔，是我们解放军的老～。To pay compensation for damage done is an old rule in our PLA. ② well-behaved; well-disciplined: 守～ abide by the rules; behave oneself/ 没～ have no manners; be impolite/ 规规矩矩 well-behaved; law-abiding/ 他的字写得很～。His handwriting shows care and training.

【规律】 guīlǜ law; regular pattern: 客观～ objective law/ 历史发展的～ law of the development of history/ 摸清阶级敌人活动的～ find out the pattern of activities of the class enemy/ 生活有～ live a regular life ◇ ～性 law; regularity

【规模】 guīmó scale; scope; dimensions: ～宏大 broad in scale (或 scope)/ ～空前的盛会 a grand gathering of unprecedented size

【规劝】 guīquàn admonish; advise: 好意～ give well-meaning advice

【规行矩步】 guīxíng-jǔbù ① behave correctly and cautiously ② stick to established practice; follow the beaten track

【规约】 guīyuē stipulations of an agreement

【规则】 guīzé ① rule; regulation: 交通～ traffic regulations ② regular: 这条河流的水道原来很不～。The course of this river used to be quite irregular.

【规章】 guīzhāng rules; regulations: ～制度 rules and regulations

**皈** guī

【皈依】 guīyī 〈宗〉① the ceremony of proclaiming sb. a Buddhist ② be converted to Buddhism or some other religion

**闺** guī boudoir

【闺房】 guīfáng boudoir

【闺女】 guīnü ① girl; maiden ② 〈口〉 daughter

**硅** guī 〈化〉silicon (Si)

【硅肺】 guīfèi 〈医〉silicosis

【硅钢】 guīgāng 〈冶〉 silicon steel

【硅华】 guīhuá 〈地〉siliceous sinter; silica sinter

【硅胶】 guījiāo 〈化〉silica gel

【硅可控整流器】 guīkěkòng zhěngliúqì 〈电〉silicon controlled rectifier; thyristor

【硅铝带】 guīlǚdài 〈地〉sial

【硅镁带】 guīměidài 〈地〉sima

【硅锰钢】 guīměnggāng silico-manganese steel

【硅石】 guīshí silica

【硅酸】 guīsuān 〈化〉silicic acid ◇ ～钠 sodium silicate

【硅酸盐】 guīsuānyán 〈化〉silicate ◇ ～工业 silicate industry/ ～砖 silicate brick

【硅铁】 guītiě ferrosilicon

【硅藻】 guīzǎo 〈植〉diatom ◇ ～土 diatomaceous earth; diatomite

【硅砖】 guīzhuān silica brick

**瑰** guī 〈书〉rare; marvellous

【瑰宝】 guībǎo rarity; treasure; gem: 敦煌壁画是我国古代艺术中的～。The Dunhuang frescoes are gems of ancient Chinese art.

【瑰丽】 guīlì surpassingly beautiful; magnificent: 南京长江大桥的夜景雄伟～。The view of the Nanjing Changjiang bridge at night is magnificent.

【瑰玮】 guīwěi 〈书〉① remarkable ② (of language or style) ornate

**鲑** guī salmon

**鬶** guī 〈考古〉a pitcher with three legs

## guǐ

**宄** guǐ 见"奸宄" jiānguǐ

**轨** guǐ ① rail; track: 单(双)～ single (double) track/ 出～ be derailed ② course; path: 常～ normal practice/ 走上正～ get onto the right path

【轨道】 guǐdào ① track: 地铁～ underground railway track ② orbit; trajectory: 人造卫星已进入～。The man-made satellite is now in orbit. ③ course; path: 工作已走上～。The work has got onto the right track.

◇ ～变换〈宇航〉orbital transfer/ ～火箭 orbital rocket/ ～衡〈铁道〉track scale/ ～交角〈宇航〉orbit inclination/ ～空间站〈宇航〉orbital space station/ ～平面〈宇航〉orbit plane/ ～运动〈天〉orbital motion

【轨范】 guǐfàn standard; criterion

【轨迹】 guǐjì ①〈数〉locus ②〈天〉orbit

【轨距】 guǐjù 〈铁道〉gauge: 标准～ standard gauge

【轨枕】 guǐzhěn 〈铁道〉 sleeper; tie: 纵向～ longitudinal sleeper ◇ ～板 concrete slab sleeper

**庋** guǐ 〈书〉① shelf ② keep; preserve: ～藏 store up; preserve

**诡** guǐ ① deceitful; tricky; cunning ② 〈书〉weird; eerie

【诡辩】 guǐbiàn sophistry; sophism; quibbling: ～改变不了事实。Sophistry won't alter facts. ◇ ～术 sophistry

【诡称】 guǐchēng falsely allege; pretend: 敌特～自己是公安人员。The enemy agent pretended that he was one of our own security men.

【诡计】 guǐjì crafty plot; cunning scheme; trick; ruse: ～多端 have a whole bag of tricks; be very crafty

【诡谲】 guǐjué 〈书〉strange and changeful; treacherous

【诡雷】 guǐléi 〈军〉booby mine; booby trap

【诡秘】 guǐmì surreptitious; secretive: 行踪～ surreptitious in one's movements

【诡诈】 guǐzhà crafty; cunning; treacherous

**匦** guǐ box: 票～ ballot box

**癸** guǐ the last of the ten Heavenly Stems

**鬼** guǐ ① ghost; spirit; apparition: 不信～，不信神 believe in neither ghosts nor gods ② 〈骂〉: 懒～ lazy bones/ 胆小～ coward/ 酒～ drunkard ③ stealthy; surreptitious ④ sinister plot; dirty trick: 心里有～ have a guilty conscience/ 这里边有～。There's some dirty work going on here. 或 I smell a rat. ⑤ terrible; damnable: ～天气 terrible weather/ ～地方 a damnable place ⑥ 〈口〉 clever; smart;

quick: 这家伙真～。He's an artful devil.
【鬼把戏】 guǐbǎxì sinister plot; dirty (或 underhand) trick
【鬼点子】 guǐdiǎnzi 〈方〉 wicked idea; trick: 出～ give devilish advice; make a wicked suggestion/ 他～多。He's full of wicked ideas. 或 He's always ready with some trick or other.
【鬼斧神工】 guǐfǔ-shéngōng uncanny workmanship; superlative craftsmanship
【鬼怪】 guǐguài ghosts and monsters; monsters of all kinds; forces of evil: 革命的怒涛将冲走一切妖魔～。The raging tide of revolution will sweep away all forces of evil.
【鬼鬼祟祟】 guǐguǐsuìsuì sneaking; furtive; stealthy: 这家伙～的,想干什么? What's that fellow up to, sneaking around like that?
【鬼话】 guǐhuà lie: ～连篇 a pack of lies
【鬼画符】 guǐhuàfú ① scrawly handwriting ② hypocritical talk
【鬼魂】 guǐhún ghost; spirit; apparition
【鬼混】 guǐhùn lead an aimless or irregular existence; fool around: 和不三不四的人～ hang around with shady characters
【鬼火】 guǐhuǒ will-o'-the-wisp; jack-o'-lantern
【鬼哭狼嚎】 guǐkū-lángháo wail like ghosts and howl like wolves; set up wild shrieks and howls
【鬼脸】 guǐliǎn ① funny face; wry face; grimace: 做～ make a wry face; make faces; make grimaces ② mask used as a toy
【鬼魅】 guǐmèi 〈书〉 ghosts and goblins; forces of evil
【鬼门关】 guǐménguān the gate of hell; danger spot; a trying moment: 穷人进了收租院,就象进了～。For the poor peasants, to enter that rent-collecting courtyard was like entering the gate of hell.
【鬼迷心窍】 guǐ mí xīnqiào be possessed; be obsessed
【鬼神】 guǐshén ghosts and gods; spirits; supernatural beings
【鬼使神差】 guǐshǐ-shénchāi doings of ghosts and gods — unexpected happenings; a curious coincidence
【鬼胎】 guǐtāi sinister design; ulterior motive: 心怀～ harbour sinister designs
【鬼头鬼脑】 guǐtóu-guǐnǎo thievish; stealthy; furtive: 有两个人～地从山洞里钻了出来。Two people sneaked out of the cave.
【鬼鲉】 guǐyóu devil stinger; lumpfish
【鬼蜮】 guǐyù evil spirit; demon; treacherous person: ～伎俩 devilish stratagem; evil tactics
【鬼针草】 guǐzhēncǎo 〈植〉 beggar-ticks *(Bidens bipinnata)*
【鬼主意】 guǐzhǔyì evil plan; wicked idea
【鬼子】 guǐzi devil (a term of abuse for foreign invaders)

**晷** guǐ ①〈书〉 a shadow cast by the sun ②〈书〉 time: 余～ spare time ③ sundial

**簋** guǐ 〈考古〉 a round-mouthed food vessel with two or four loop handles

## guì

**刽** guì cut off; chop off
【刽子手】 guìzishǒu ① executioner; headsman ② slaughterer; butcher

**刿** guì stab; cut

**柜** guì cupboard; cabinet: 碗～ kitchen cupboard/ 书～ bookcase/ 衣～ wardrobe
【柜台】 guìtái counter; bar: 站～ serve behind the counter
【柜子】 guìzi cupboard; cabinet

**贵** guì ① expensive; costly; dear: 这本书不～。This book is not expensive. ② highly valued; valuable; precious: 兵～精,不～多。Troops are valued for their quality, not their number./ ～在鼓劲。The important thing is revolutionary drive./ 春雨～如油。Rain in spring is as precious as oil. ③ of high rank; noble ④〈敬〉 your: ～国 your country/ ～姓? May I ask your name? ⑤ (Guì) short for Guizhou Province
【贵宾】 guìbīn honoured guest; distinguished guest ◇ ～席 seats for distinguished guests; distinguished visitors' gallery/ ～休息室 reserved lounge (for honoured guests)
【贵妃】 guìfēi highest-ranking imperial concubine
【贵金属】 guìjīnshǔ noble (或 precious) metal
【贵阳】 Guìyáng Guiyang
【贵重】 guìzhòng valuable; precious: ～物品 valuables/ ～药品 costly (或 expensive) medicines
【贵州】 Guìzhōu Guizhou (Province)
【贵族】 guìzú noble; aristocrat: 封建～ feudal nobles/ 精神～ intellectual aristocrats/ ～老爷式的态度 an aristocratic attitude/ 工人～ labour aristocracy; aristocrats of labour

**桂** guì ① cassiabarktree ② laurel; bay tree ③ sweet-scented osmanthus ④ (Guì) another name for the Guangxi Zhuang Autonomous Region ⑤ (Guì) a surname
【桂冠】 guìguān laurel (as an emblem of victory or distinction)
【桂花】 guìhuā 〈植〉 sweet-scented osmanthus ◇ ～酒 wine fermented with osmanthus flowers
【桂皮】 guìpí cassia bark; Chinese cinnamon
【桂圆】 guìyuán longan ◇ ～肉 dried longan pulp
【桂枝】 guìzhī 〈中药〉 cassia twig

**桧** guì 〈植〉 Chinese juniper

**跪** guì kneel; go down on one's knees
【跪拜】 guìbài worship on bended knees; kowtow
【跪倒】 guìdǎo throw oneself on one's knees; prostrate oneself; grovel: ～在敌人脚下的可耻叛徒 a shameless renegade who prostrated himself before the enemy
【跪射】 guìshè 〈军〉 kneeling fire
【跪姿】 guìzī kneeling position: ～射击 shoot from a kneeling position

**鲹** guì minnow

**鳜** guì mandarin fish

## gǔn

**衮** gǔn ceremonial dress for royalty
【衮衮】 gǔngǔn 〈书〉 ① continual ② numerous
【衮衮诸公】 gǔngǔn zhūgōng 〈讽〉 ① high-ranking officials ② Your Excellencies

**绲** gǔn 〈书〉 ① band; tape ② string; cord

**辊** gǔn 〈机〉 roller
【辊筒印花】 gǔntǒng yìnhuā 〈纺〉 roller printing

**滚** gǔn ① roll; trundle: ～铁环 trundle a hoop/ 一块石

头从山坡上～下来。A stone came rolling down the slope./ 从马背上～下来 tumble from a horse/ 汗珠不停地从她脸上～下来。Drops of sweat coursed (或 trickled) down her face. ② get away; beat it: ～出去! Get out of here! ③〈方〉boil: 水～了。The water is boiling. ④ bind; trim: 袖口上～一条边儿 bind the cuffs/ 裙子～上花边 trim the skirt with lace

【滚槽机】 gǔncáojī 〈机〉 channelling machine

【滚齿机】 gǔnchǐjī 〈机〉 gear-hobbing machine; hobbing machine

【滚蛋】 gǔndàn 〈骂〉 beat it; scram

【滚刀】 gǔndāo 〈机〉 hobbing cutter; hob

【滚动】 gǔndòng roll; trundle ◇ ～摩擦〈物〉rolling friction/ ～轴承〈机〉rolling bearing

【滚翻】 gǔnfān 〈体〉 roll: 侧～ sideward roll

【滚瓜烂熟】 gǔnguā lànshú (recite, etc.) fluently; (know sth.) pat: 背得～ have memorized sth. thoroughly; have sth. pat

【滚滚】 gǔngǔn roll; billow; surge: ～的浓烟 billowing smoke/ 历史车轮～向前。The wheel of history rolls on./ 革命洪流～向前，势不可挡。The revolutionary torrent surges forward with irresistible force.

【滚雷】 gǔnléi 〈军〉 rolling mine

【滚轮】 gǔnlún 〈体〉 gyro wheel

【滚水坝】 gǔnshuǐbà 〈水〉 overflow dam

【滚烫】 gǔntàng boiling hot; burning hot 又作"滚热"

【滚筒】 gǔntǒng cylinder; roll ◇ ～印刷机 cylinder press

【滚圆】 gǔnyuán round as a ball

【滚轧】 gǔnzhá 〈机〉 rolling ◇ ～机 rolling mill

【滚针轴承】 gǔnzhēn zhóuchéng needle bearing

【滚珠】 gǔnzhū 〈机〉 ball ◇～轴承 ball bearing

【滚柱轴承】 gǔnzhù zhóuchéng roller bearing

【滚子链】 gǔnziliàn roller chain

**磙** gǔn ① roller: 石～ stone roller ② level (ground, etc.) with a roller: ～地 roll the ground

【磙子】 gǔnzi ① stone roller ② roller

## gùn

**棍** gùn ① rod; stick ② scoundrel; rascal: 恶～ ruffian; rascal/ 赌～ gambler

【棍棒】 gùnbàng ① club; cudgel; bludgeon ② a stick or staff used in gymnastics

【棍子】 gùnzi rod; stick

## guō

**过** guō ①〈口〉beyond the limit; undue; excessive: ～费 go to undue expense ② (Guō) a surname

另见 guò; guo

**郭** guō ① the outer wall of a city ② (Guō) a surname

**埚** guō 见"坩埚" gānguō

**聒** guō noisy

【聒耳】 guō'ěr grate on one's ears

【聒噪】 guōzào 〈方〉 noisy; clamorous

**锅** guō ① pot, pan, boiler, cauldron, etc.: 沙～ clay pot/ 炒菜～ frying pan/ 两口大～ two cauldrons ② bowl (of a pipe, etc.): 烟袋～儿 the bowl of a pipe; pipe

【锅巴】 guōbā crust of cooked rice; rice crust

【锅炉】 guōlú boiler: 火管～ fire tube boiler/ 水管～ water tube boiler

◇ ～防垢剂 boiler compound/ ～房 boiler room/ ～给水 boiler feedwater

【锅台】 guōtái the top of a kitchen range: 围着～转 be tied to the kitchen sink

【锅贴儿】 guōtiēr lightly fried dumpling

【锅驼机】 guōtuójī portable steam engine; locomobile

【锅烟子】 guōyānzi soot on the bottom of a pan

【锅子】 guōzi ① bowl (of a pipe, etc.) ② chafing dish

**蝈** guō

【蝈蝈儿】 guōguor katydid; long-horned grasshopper

## guó

**国** guó ① country; state; nation: 全～各地 all over the country/ ～营 state-run/ 收归～有 be nationalized; be taken over by the state ② of the state; national: ～旗 national flag ③ of our country; Chinese: ～画 traditional Chinese painting ④ (Guó) a surname

【国宝】 guóbǎo national treasure

【国宾】 guóbīn state guest ◇ ～馆 state guesthouse

【国策】 guócè the basic policy of a state; national policy

【国产】 guóchǎn made in our country; made in China: ～远洋货轮 Chinese-built oceangoing freighter

【国耻】 guóchǐ national humiliation

【国粹】 guócuì the quintessence of Chinese culture

【国都】 guódū national capital; capital

【国度】 guódù country; state; nation

【国法】 guófǎ the law of the land; national law; law

【国防】 guófáng national defence

◇ ～部 the Ministry of National Defence/ ～建设 the building up of national defence/ ～力量 defence capability/ ～生产 defence production/ ～委员会 the National Defence Council/ ～线 national defence line/ ～支出 expenditure on national defence; defence spending

【国歌】 guógē national anthem

【国后岛】 Guóhòudǎo Kunashiri

【国画】 guóhuà traditional Chinese painting

【国徽】 guóhuī national emblem

【国会】 guóhuì parliament; (美) Congress; (日) the Diet

【国货】 guóhuò 〈旧〉 China-made goods; Chinese goods

【国籍】 guójí nationality: 双重～ dual nationality/ 选择～ choose one's nationality/ ～不明的飞机 unidentified aircraft/ 保留中国～ retain one's Chinese citizenship

【国计民生】 guójì-mínshēng the national economy and the people's livelihood

【国际】 guójì international: ～地位 international status (或 standing)/ ～形势 the international (或 world) situation/ ～影响 international repercussions; impact abroad/ 带有～性 have an international character

◇ ～奥林匹克委员会 the International Olympic Committee (IOC)/ ～博览会 international fair/ ～儿童节 International Children's Day (June 1)/ ～法 international law; the law of nations/ ～法院 the International Court of Justice; the World Court/ ～公法 (public) international law/ ～公制 the metric system/ ～关系 international relations/ ～惯例 international practice/ ～航道 international waterway/ ～化 internationalization/ ～货币 convertible foreign exchange; international currency/ ～劳动妇女节 International Working Women's Day (March 8)/ ～劳动节 International Labour Day; May Day (May 1)/ ～联盟 the League of Nations (1920-1946)/ ～列车 international train/ ～贸易

international trade (或 commerce)/ ～日期变更线 (international) date line/ ～市场 international market/ ～事务 international (或 world) affairs/ ～水平 international (或 world) standards/ ～私法 private international law/ ～象棋 chess/ ～行为准则 international code of conduct/ ～音标 〈语〉 the International Phonetic Symbols (或 Alphabet)/ ～友人 foreign friends/ ～舆论 world (public) opinion/ ～争端 international dispute/ ～纵队 the International Brigade (in the Spanish civil war of 1936-1939)

【国际分工论】 guójì fēngōnglùn international division of labour (as preached by the social-imperialists)

【国际歌】 Guójìgē *The Internationale*

【国际共产主义运动】 guójì gòngchǎnzhǔyì yùndòng the international communist movement

【国际收支】 guójì shōuzhī balance of (international) payments: ～不平衡 disequilibrium of balance of payments/ ～逆差 international payments deficit; unfavourable balance of payments/ ～顺差 international payments surplus; favourable balance of payments/ ～危机 international payments crisis

【国际主义】 guójìzhǔyì internationalism ◇ ～义务 internationalist duty/ ～者 internationalist

【国家】 guójiā country; state; nation: ～无非是一个阶级镇压另一个阶级的机器。The state is nothing but a machine for the oppression of one class by another./ 在我国，母亲和儿童受～的保护。In our country, mothers and children are protected by the state.

◇ ～大事 national (或 state) affairs/ ～典礼 state functions/ ～队 national team/ ～法 constitutional law; the law of the state/ ～机关 state organs; government offices/ ～机关工作人员 personnel of organs of state; state personnel/ ～机器 state apparatus (或 machinery)/ ～决算 final accounts of state revenue and expenditure; final state accounts/ ～垄断资本主义 state monopoly capitalism/ ～权力机关 organs of state power/ ～所有制 state ownership/ ～学说 theory of the state/ ～银行 state bank/ ～元首 head of state/ ～政权 state power/ ～职能 functions and powers of the state/ ～资本主义 state capitalism

【国教】 guójiào state religion

【国界】 guójiè national boundaries

【国境】 guójìng territory: 偷越～ cross the border illegally ◇ ～线 boundary line

【国君】 guójūn monarch

【国库】 guókù national (或 state) treasury; exchequer

【国力】 guólì national power (或 strength, might): ～雄厚 have solid national strength

【国立】 guólì 〈旧〉 state-maintained; state-run ◇ ～大学 national university

【国民】 guómín national

◇ ～经济 national economy/ ～生产总值 gross national product (GNP)/ ～收入 national income

【国民党】 Guómíndǎng the Kuomintang (KMT) ◇ ～反动派 the Kuomintang reactionaries

【国难】 guónàn national calamity (caused by foreign aggression)

【国内】 guónèi internal; domestic; home: ～市场 domestic (或 home) market/ ～贸易 domestic trade/ ～新闻 home news/ ～革命战争 revolutionary civil war/ ～外形势一片大好。The situation at home and abroad is very good.

【国旗】 guóqí national flag

【国情】 guóqíng the condition (或 state) of a country; national conditions ◇ ～咨文 (美) State of the Union Message

【国庆】 guóqìng National Day ◇ ～节 National Day (October 1)

【国人】 guórén 〈书〉 compatriots; fellow countrymen; countrymen

【国事】 guóshì national (或 state) affairs ◇ ～访问 state visit

【国手】 guóshǒu national champion (in chess, etc.); grand master

【国书】 guóshū letter of credence; credentials

【国体】 guótǐ ① state system: ～问题就是社会各阶级在国家中的地位问题。The question of the state system is a question of the status of the various social classes within the state. ② national prestige

【国土】 guótǔ territory; land: 神圣～ our sacred land/ 捍卫每一寸～ defend every inch of our territory

【国外】 guówài external; overseas; abroad: ～事务 external affairs/ ～来信 letter from abroad/ ～市场 overseas (或 foreign) market

【国王】 guówáng king

【国务会议】 guówù huìyì state conference: 最高～ the Supreme State Conference

【国务卿】 guówùqīng (美) Secretary of State

【国务院】 guówùyuàn ① the State Council ② (美) the State Department

【国宴】 guóyàn state banquet

【国药】 guóyào traditional Chinese medicines

【国营】 guóyíng state-operated; state-run

◇ ～工商业 state-operated industry and commerce/ ～经济 state sector of the economy; state-owned economy/ ～农场 state farm/ ～企业 state enterprise

【国有化】 guóyǒuhuà nationalization

【国葬】 guózàng state funeral

【国债】 guózhài national debt

【国子监】 guózǐjiàn the Imperial College, the highest educational administration in feudal China

**掴** guó 见"掴" guāi

**帼** guó 见"巾帼" jīnguó

**腘** guó 〈生理〉 the back of the knee

【腘窝】 guówō 〈生理〉 the hollow of the knee

## guǒ

**果** guǒ ① fruit: 开花结～ blossom and bear fruit ② result; consequence: 恶～ a disastrous result; dire consequences ③ resolute; determined: 行必～ be resolute in action ④ really; as expected; sure enough: ～不出所料 just as one expected ⑤ if indeed; if really: ～能如此 if things can really turn out that way; if that is so

【果断】 guǒduàn resolute; decisive: 办事～ handle affairs in a decisive manner/ ～地作出决定 resolutely make a decision

【果脯】 guǒfǔ preserved fruit; candied fruit

【果腹】 guǒfù fill the stomach; satisfy one's hunger: 在旧社会，劳动人民过着衣不蔽体，食不～的生活。In the old society, the labouring people had rags on their backs and never enough food in their bellies.

【果敢】 guǒgǎn courageous and resolute: 采取～的行动 take resolute action/ 她～地跳入水中，救起溺水的孩子。Without hesitation, she leapt into the water and saved the drowning child.

【果酱】 guǒjiàng jam

【果料儿】 guǒliàor raisins, kernels, melon seeds, etc. used in making cakes, buns, etc.

【果木】 guǒmù fruit tree ◇ ～园 orchard

【果皮】 guǒpí the skin of fruit; peel; rind
【果品】 guǒpǐn fruit: 干鲜～ fresh and dried fruit
【果然】 guǒrán 〈副〉 really; as expected; sure enough: ～名不虚传 a really well-deserved reputation/ 敌人～中了我们的埋伏。Just as we expected, the enemy were caught in our ambush.
【果仁儿】 guǒrénr kernel
【果肉】 guǒròu the flesh of fruit; pulp
【果实】 guǒshí ①fruit: ～累累 fruit growing in close clusters; fruit hanging heavy on the trees ②gains; fruits: 劳动～ fruits of labour/ 保卫革命～ guard the gains of the revolution
【果树】 guǒshù fruit tree ◇～栽培 fruit growing; pomiculture
【果糖】 guǒtáng 〈化〉 fructose; levulose
【果园】 guǒyuán orchard
【果真】 guǒzhēn ①见"果然" ②〈连〉if indeed; if really: ～如此,我就放心了。If this is really true, it'll take a load off my mind.
【果汁】 guǒzhī fruit juice
【果枝】 guǒzhī ①fruit-bearing shoot; fruit branch ②boll-bearing branch (of the cotton plant)
【果子】 guǒzi fruit ◇～酒 fruit wine/ ～露 fruit syrup
【果子狸】 guǒzilí masked (或 gem-faced) civet

**椁** guǒ outer coffin

**裹** guǒ bind; wrap: 把伤口～好 bind up (或 bandage) the wound/ 头上～着毛巾 have one's head wrapped in a towel; wear a towel turban
【裹脚】 guǒjiǎo foot-binding — a vile feudal practice which crippled women both physically and spiritually
【裹脚】 guǒjiao bandages used in binding women's feet in feudal China
【裹腿】 guǒtui puttee
【裹胁】 guǒxié force to take part; coerce: 把敌军中被～的人争取过来 win over those who joined the enemy army under duress
【裹足不前】 guǒ zú bù qián hesitate to move forward

## guò

**过** guò ①cross; pass: 长征途中,红军爬雪山,～草地。On the Long March, the Red Army climbed snow-topped mountains and plodded through grasslands./ 野营部队要从咱们村～。The troops will be passing through our village on their camping trip. ②across; past; through; over: 汽艇穿～激流,绕～险滩。The motorboat cut across swift currents and skirted dangerous reefs./ 接～革命先辈手中的枪 take up the guns of the revolutionary pioneers ③spend (time); pass (time): 假期～得怎样? How did you spend your holiday?/ 我们今年春节是在工地上～的。This year we spent the Spring Festival at the construction site./ 退休工人～着幸福的晚年。The retired workers have a happy old age. ④after; past: ～了好几个月我才收到他的信。Several months passed before I heard from him./ ～了夏至,天就开始变短。The days get shorter after the Summer Solstice./ 我～两天再来。I'll come again in a couple of days. ⑤undergo a process; go through; go over: ～了筛子又～箩 sifted again and again; carefully screened/ 咱们把这篇稿子再～一遍。Let's go over the draft once again. ⑥exceed; go beyond: 我们县粮棉都～了长江。Our county's per *mu* yield of grain and cotton has exceeded the norm for north of the Changjiang River./ 亩产～千斤。The yield is over 1,000 *jin* per *mu*./ 小心别坐～了站。Be sure you don't go past your station./ 雪深～膝。The snow is more than knee-deep. ⑦excessively; unduly: 雨水～多 excessive rainfall; too much rain/ ～早 too early; premature/ ～长 too long; unduly long ⑧〈化〉〈物〉 per-; super-; over-: ～氧化物 peroxide/ ～熔 superfusion/ ～伐〈林〉 overcutting ⑨fault; mistake: 勇于改～ be bold in correcting one's mistakes/ 记～ put a person's error on record ⑩〔用在动词后,跟"得"或"不"连用,表示胜过或通过〕: 要说跑,咱们谁也比不～他。None of us can run as fast as he can./ 这样的大学生,我们信得～。We have confidence in college students of this sort./ 小伙子们干起活来,个个赛(得)～小老虎。The lads threw themselves into the work with more vigour than young tigers. ⑪〈量〉 time: 衣服漂了三～儿了。The clothes have been rinsed three times./ 我又重新读了一～儿。I have read it once more.
另见 guō; guo

**过** guo ①〔用在动词后,表示完毕〕: 我吃～午饭就去。I'll go right after lunch./ 桃花都已经开～了。The peach blossoms are over. ②〔用在动词后面,表示行为曾经发生,但并未继续到现在〕: 你去～韶山吗? Have you ever been to Shaoshan?/ 没见～的大旱,没见～的大干 unprecedented drive in combating an unprecedented drought/ 解放战争时期他打～仗,负～伤。He fought in the War of Liberation and was wounded in action.
另见 guō, guò

【过半数】 guòbànshù more than half; majority: 这个工厂～的职工是妇女。More than half the workers and staff members in this mill are women./ ～的同志赞成第一个方案。The majority of the comrades were in favour of the first plan.
【过磅】 guòbàng weigh (on the scales): 行李～了没有? Has the luggage been weighed?
【过饱和】 guòbǎohé 〈化〉 supersaturation; oversaturation ◇～溶液 supersaturated solution
【过不去】 guòbuqù ①cannot get through; be unable to get by; be impassable: 前面正在修路,～。As the road ahead is under repair, you can't get through. ②be hard on; make it difficult for; embarrass: 群众批评你,并不是跟你～。People didn't mean to be hard on you when they criticized you. ③feel sorry: 费了你这么多时间,我心里真～。I'm sorry for having taken up so much of your time.
【过场】 guòchǎng ①〈剧〉 interlude ②〈剧〉 cross the stage ③〔多用于〕: 走～ do sth. as a mere formality; go through the motions
【过程】 guòchéng course; process: 在讨论～中 in the course of the discussion/ 缩短制作～ shorten the process of manufacture
【过秤】 guòchèng weigh (on the steelyard)
【过从】 guòcóng 〈书〉 have friendly intercourse; associate: ～甚密 be in close association with sb.
【过错】 guòcuò fault; mistake: 这不是你的～。That's not your fault.
【过道】 guòdào passageway; corridor
【过得去】 guòdeqù ①be able to pass; can get through: 卡车从这儿～吗? Can the truck get through here? ②passable; tolerable; so-so; not too bad: 我身体还～。My health is not too bad./ 干工作可不能满足于～。No one should be satisfied with just doing a passable job. ③〔多用于反问〕 feel at ease: 叫你一趟一趟地跑,我怎么～呢? I'm terribly sorry to have kept you on the go like this.
【过冬】 guòdōng pass the winter; winter: 把羊群赶到山坳里去～ herd the sheep into the valley for the winter/ 这种鸟在哪儿～? Where do these birds winter?
【过度】 guòdù excessive; undue; over-: 饮酒～对身体有害。

Excessive drinking is harmful to the health./ ～兴奋 be overexcited/ ～疲劳 be overtired

【过渡】 guòdù transition; interim: 从社会主义～到共产主义 transition from socialism to communism ◇ ～措施 interim measure

【过渡时期】 guòdù shíqī transition period

【过渡时期总路线】 guòdù shíqī zǒnglùxiàn the general line for the transition period (put forward by Chairman Mao in 1953, basically to accomplish China's industrialization and the socialist transformation of agriculture, handicrafts and capitalist industry and commerce over a fairly long period of time)

【过分】 guòfèn excessive; undue; over-: ～的要求 excessive demands/ ～强调 put undue stress on; overemphasize/ 做得太～ go too far; overdo sth.

【过关】 guòguān ① pass a barrier; go through an ordeal ② pass a test; reach a standard: 过好社会主义关 pass the test of socialism successfully; be able to stand up to the test of socialist revolution/ 这项新产品的质量已经～。The quality of this new product is up to standard./ 粮食问题还没有～。The problem of adequate grain production has not been solved yet. ◇ ～思想 attitude of just getting by (或 scraping past)

【过河拆桥】 guò hé chāi qiáo remove the bridge after crossing the river — drop one's benefactor as soon as his help is not required; kick down the ladder

【过后】 guòhòu afterwards; later: 他起初同意,～又翻悔了。At first he agreed, but later he backed out.

【过户】 guòhù 〈法〉 transfer ownership; change the name of the owner in a register

【过话】 guòhuà 〈方〉 ① exchange words; talk with one another: 我跟他不在一个单位,所以很少～。We don't work in the same outfit, so we haven't talked much. ② send word; pass on a message: 请你替我过个话,就说我明天不去找他了。Would you mind giving him a message? Just say I won't call tomorrow.

【过活】 guòhuó make a living; live: 解放前他父亲靠拉洋车～。Before liberation his father made a living by pulling a rickshaw.

【过火】 guòhuǒ go too far; go to extremes; overdo: ～的行动 excesses/ 这话说得太～了。It's going too far to say that.

【过激】 guòjī too drastic; extremist: ～的言论 extremist opinions

【过继】 guòjì ① adopt a young relative ② have one's child adopted by a relative

【过奖】 guòjiǎng 〈谦〉 overpraise; undeserved compliment: 您～了。You flatter me.

【过街楼】 guòjiēlóu an overhead building projection spanning a lane

【过节】 guòjié celebrate a festival

【过境】 guòjìng pass through the territory of a country; be in transit
◇ ～贸易 transit trade/ ～签证 transit visa/ ～权 right of passage/ ～税 transit duty

【过客】 guòkè passing traveller; transient guest

【过来】 guòlái 〔用在动词后,多跟"得"或"不"连用,表示时间、能力、数量充分或不足〕: 孩子多了照顾不～。If you have too many children, you won't be able to take good care of them all./ 你一个人忙得～吗? Can you manage by yourself?

【过来】 guòlai come over; come up: 快～! Come over here, quick!/ 一个人～向我打听去火车站的路。A person came up and asked me the way to the railway station.

【过来】 guolai ①〔用在动词后,表示来到自己所在的地方〕: 一队红小兵正朝我们走～。A contingent of Little Red Guards was marching towards us./ 把被敌人占领的阵地夺～ recapture the position seized by the enemy ②〔用在动词后,表示使正面对着自己〕: 把柴火翻～晒晒。Turn the firewood over and sun it./ 请你转～让我量量胸围。Please turn round and let me measure your chest. ③〔用在动词后,表示回到原来的、正常的状态〕: 醒～ wake up; sober up; come to/ 喘不过气来 be out of breath/ 他终于觉悟～了。At last he saw the light.

【过来人】 guòláirén a person who has had the experience: 作为～,我可以讲讲我的体会。As one who has had experience in this respect, let me tell you how I feel about it./ 要知水深浅,须问～。He knows the water best who has waded through it.

【过冷】 guòlěng 〈物〉 super-cooling

【过梁】 guòliáng 〈建〉 lintel

【过量】 guòliàng excessive; over-: 饮食～ excessive eating and drinking/ 这种药千万不能服～。Whatever happens, never take an overdose of this medicine.

【过磷酸钙】 guòlínsuāngài calcium superphosphate

【过路】 guòlù pass by on one's way ◇ ～人 passerby

【过虑】 guòlǜ be overanxious; worry overmuch; worry unnecessarily: 问题会得到解决的,你不必～。The problem wil be solved. You needn't be overanxious.

【过滤】 guòlǜ filter; filtrate ◇ ～器 filter/ ～嘴 filter tip (of a cigarette)

【过门】 guòmén move into one's husband's household upon marriage

【过门儿】 guòménr 〈乐〉 ① opening bars ② short interlude between verses

【过敏】 guòmǐn 〈医〉 allergy ◇ ～性反应 allergic reaction

【过目】 guòmù look over (papers, lists, etc.) so as to check or approve: 名单已经排好,请您～。Here's the list for you to go over.

【过目成诵】 guòmù chéng sòng be able to recite sth. after reading it over once; have a photographic (或 very retentive) memory

【过年】 guònián celebrate the New Year; spend the New Year: 他今年回家～。He'll be home for the New Year holiday./ 快～了。It'll soon be New Year.

【过年】 guònian next year: 这孩子～该上学了。The boy's going to school next year.

【过期】 guòqī exceed the time limit; be overdue: 你借的书已经～。The book you borrowed is overdue./ ～作废 invalid after the specified date
◇ ～胶卷 expired film/ ～提单 stale bill of lading/ ～杂志 back number of a magazine

【过谦】 guòqiān too modest: 这件事你办最合适,不必～了。You are the best person for the job. Don't be so modest.

【过去】 guòqù in or of the past; formerly; previously: 不了解～的苦,就不知道今天的甜。If you don't know the bitterness of the past, you won't appreciate the happiness of the present./ 这个地方～流行的一些疾病已经基本消除。Diseases formerly prevalent here have mostly been eradicated./ ～的荒山坡如今成了果园。The once desolate slopes have been turned into orchards./ 他比～胖多了。He's much fatter than he used to be.

【过去】 guòqu go over; pass by: 你在这里等着,我～看看。You wait here, I'll go over and see./ 一辆公共汽车刚～。A bus has just passed by.

【过去】 guoqu ①〔用在动词后,表示离开或经过自己所在的地方〕: 向敌人阵地冲～ charge at the enemy position/ 一只燕子飞～了。A swallow flew past. ②〔用在动词后,表示使反面对着自己〕: 先别把这一页翻～。Don't turn over the page yet. ③〔用在动词后,表示失去原来的、正常的状态〕: 病人晕～了。The patient has fainted. ④〔用在动词后,表示通过〕:

企图蒙混～ try to get by under false pretences/ 群众的眼睛是雪亮的，他休想骗～。The masses are clear-sighted. He won't fool them.

【过去了】 guòqùle 〈婉〉 pass away; die: 他祖父昨晚～。His grandfather died last night.

【过人】 guòrén surpass; excel: 精力～ surpass many others in energy/ 勇气～ excel in courage/ ～的记忆力 a remarkable memory/ ～之处 the things one excels in; one's forte

【过日子】 guò rìzi live; get along: 勤俭～ live industriously and frugally/ 挺会～ can manage to get along quite well

【过筛】 guòshāi sift out

【过甚】 guòshèn exaggerate; overstate: ～其词 give an exaggerated account; overstate the case

【过剩】 guòshèng excess; surplus: 生产～ overproduction/ 资本～ surplus of capital/ 商品～ a glut of goods

【过失】 guòshī ① fault; slip; error ② 〈法〉 unpremeditated crime; offence ◇ ～杀人 manslaughter

【过时】 guòshí ① out-of-date; outmoded; obsolete; antiquated; out of fashion: ～的设备 outmoded (或 obsolete) equipment/ ～的观念 antiquated ideas ② past the appointed time: 校车六点开车，～不候。The school bus leaves at six sharp and won't wait.

【过手】 guòshǒu take in and give out (money, etc.); receive and distribute; handle: 银钱～，当面点清。Count the money on the spot./ 他～信件千千万，但没有错过一件。He handled thousands and thousands of letters without making a single mistake.

【过熟林】 guòshúlín 〈林〉 overmature forest

【过数】 guòshù count

【过堂】 guòtáng 〈旧〉 appear in court to be tried

【过堂风】 guòtángfēng draught

【过头】 guòtóu go beyond the limit; overdo: 菜煮～了。The food is overcooked./ 批评他是可以的，不过你说得～了。It was all right to criticize him, but you overdid it./ 聪明～ be too clever by half

【过屠门而大嚼】 guò túmén ér dà jué pass the butcher's and start munching — feed oneself on illusions

【过往】 guòwǎng ① come and go: ～的行人 pedestrian traffic/ ～的车辆 vehicular traffic ② have friendly intercourse with; associate with

【过问】 guòwèn concern oneself with; take an interest in; bother about: 亲自～ take up a matter personally; take a personal interest in a matter/ 无人～ not be attended to by anybody; be nobody's business/ 这事你不必～了。You needn't bother about this.

【过细】 guòxì meticulous; careful: ～地做工作 work carefully; work with meticulous care/ 他～地检查了所有的安全设备。He closely examined all the safety equipment.

【过眼云烟】 guò yǎn yúnyān as transient as a fleeting cloud

【过夜】 guòyè pass the night; put up for the night; stay overnight

【过意不去】 guòyì bùqù feel apologetic; feel sorry: 这事给你添不少麻烦，真～。I'm very sorry to have put you to so much trouble.

【过瘾】 guòyǐn satisfy a craving; enjoy oneself to the full; do sth. to one's heart's content: 今天我一口气游了两千米，真～。Today I really swam to my heart's content. I did 2,000 metres at a stretch./ 这段唱腔听起来很～。This aria is a joy to hear.

【过硬】 guòyìng have a perfect mastery of sth.; be really up to the mark; be able to pass the stiffest test: ～的操作技术 a perfect mastery of operational technique/ 苦练～的杀敌本领 train hard to perfect one's combat skill

【过犹不及】 guò yóu bù jí going too far is as bad as not going far enough

【过于】 guòyú 〈副〉 too; unduly; excessively: ～劳累 overtired/ 你不必～为我们担心。You needn't worry too much about us.

【过鱼孔】 guòyúkǒng fish pass; fish way

【过载】 guòzài ① tranship ② overload: ～电平〈电〉 overload level

【过帐】 guòzhàng transfer items (as from a daybook to a ledger); post

【过重】 guòzhòng overweight ◇ ～加费 〈邮〉 overweight charge

# H

## hā

**哈** hā ① breathe out (with the mouth open): 眼镜上～点儿气再擦。Breathe on your glasses before wiping them. ②〈象〉〔形容笑声，大多叠用〕: ～～大笑 laugh heartily; roar with laughter ③〈叹〉〔表示得意或满意，大多叠用〕: ～～,我猜着了。Aha, I've got (或 guessed) it./ ～～,小鬼,这下子可跑不了啦。Aha, you can't get away from me this time, you little devil.
另见 hǎ; hà

【哈巴罗夫斯克(伯力)】 Hābāluófūsīkè (Bólì) Khabarovsk (Boli)
【哈尔滨】 Hā'ěrbīn Harbin
【哈哈镜】 hāhājìng distorting mirror
【哈吉】 hājí 〈伊斯兰教〉 haji (a title of honour for a Moslem who has made a pilgrimage to Mecca)
【哈喇子】 hālázi 〈方〉 dribble; drivel; drool
【哈喇】 hāla 〈口〉 rancid: 这大油～了。The lard has gone rancid.
【哈雷彗星】 Hāléi Huìxīng 〈天〉 Halley's Comet; the Halley Comet
【哈里发】 hālǐfā 〈伊斯兰教〉 caliph
【哈密瓜】 hāmìguā Hami melon (a variety of muskmelon)
【哈乃斐派】 Hānǎifěipài 〈伊斯兰教〉 the Hanafite school
【哈尼族】 Hānízú the Hani nationality, living in Yunnan
【哈欠】 hāqian yawn: 打～ give a yawn
【哈萨克族】 Hāsàkèzú ① the Kazak (Kazakh) nationality, distributed over the Xinjiang Uygur Autonomous Region, Gansu and Qinghai ② the Kazakhs (of U.S.S.R.)
【哈腰】 hāyāo 〈口〉 ① bend one's back; stoop: 我一～把钢笔掉在地上了。As I bent over, my fountain pen fell to the ground. ② bow: 点头～ bow unctuously; bow and scrape

**铪** hā 〈化〉 hafnium (Hf)

## há

**蛤** há
另见 gé
【蛤蟆】 háma ① frog ② toad

## hǎ

**哈** hǎ
另见 hā; hà
【哈巴狗】 hǎbagǒu ① Pekinese (a breed of dog) ② toady; sycophant
【哈达】 hǎdá *hada*, a piece of silk used as a greeting gift among the Zang and Monggol nationalities: 献～ present a *hada*

## hà

**哈** hà
另见 hā; hǎ

【哈什蚂】 hàshimǎ Chinese forest frog (*Rana temporaria chensinensis*) ◇ ～油〈中药〉 the dried oviduct fat of the forest frog

## hāi

**咳** hāi 〈叹〉〔表示伤感、后悔或惊异〕: ～,我怎么这么糊涂! Dammit! How stupid I was!/ ～,真有这种怪事儿! What! That's really strange!
另见 ké

**嗨** hāi
【嗨哟】 hāiyō 〈叹〉: heave ho; yo-heave-ho; yo-ho

## hái

**还** hái 〈副〉 ① still; yet: 夜深了,他～在学习毛主席著作。It was late at night and he was still reading Chairman Mao's works./ ～有一些具体问题要解决。Some specific problems have yet to be solved. ② even more; still more: 今年的收成比去年～要好。This year's harvest is even better than last year's. ③ also; too; as well; in addition: 我们不但参观了大寨大队,～参观了南垴大队。We visited Nannao Brigade as well as Dazhai. ④ passably; fairly: 屋子不大,收拾得倒～干净。The room is small, but it's kept quite tidy. ⑤ even: 你跑那么快～赶不上他,何况我呢? If a good runner like you can't catch up with him, how can I? ⑥〔用以加强语气〕: 这～了得! This is the limit! 或 This is simply atrocious!/ 那～用说! That goes without saying. ⑦〔表示对某件事物没想到如此,而居然如此〕: 他～真有办法。You've got to admit he's resourceful. 或 He really is resourceful.
另见 huán

【还好】 háihǎo ① not bad; passable: 你今天感觉怎样?——～。How are you feeling today? — Not so bad. ② fortunately: ～,这场大水没有把堤坝冲坏。Fortunately, the flood did not break the dyke.
【还是】 háishi ①〈副〉 still; nevertheless; all the same: 尽管下着大雨,社员们～坚持插完了秧。It was raining hard. Nevertheless, the commune members went on working in the fields until they finished transplanting the rice-seedlings. ② had better: 天冷了,你～多穿点儿吧。It's getting cold, you'd better put on more clothes. ③ or: 你去,～他去? Are you going or is he?/ 我们是上午去,～下午去? Shall we go in the morning or in the afternoon? ④〈副〉〔表示对某件事物没想到如此,而居然如此〕: 我没想到这事儿～真难办。I didn't expect it to be so difficult.

**孩** hái child: 小女～儿 a little girl
【孩儿参】 hái'érshēn 〈中药〉 caryophyllaceous ginseng (*Pseudostellaria heterophylla*)
【孩提】 háití 〈书〉 early childhood; infancy
【孩子】 háizi ① child: 男～ boy/ 女～ girl ② son or daughter; children: 她有两个～。She has two children.
【孩子气】 háiziqì childishness: 你已经十六啦,别这么～! You shouldn't be so childish, you're sixteen now!

**骸** hái ① bones of the body; skeleton: 四肢百～ all

the limbs and bones ②body: 形～ the human body/ 病～ ailing body/ 遗～ (dead) body; corpse; remains

【骸骨】 háigǔ human bones; skeleton

## hǎi

**海** hǎi ①sea or big lake: 出～ put out to sea/ 黄～ the Huanghai Sea/ 洱～ Erhai Lake (in Yunnan Province) ②a great number of people or things coming together: 人～ a sea of people; crowds of people/ 林～ a vast stretch of forest ③extra large; of great capacity: ～碗 a very big bowl ④(Hǎi) a surname

【海岸】 hǎi'àn seacoast; coast; seashore
◇ ～炮 coast gun/ ～炮兵 coast (或 seacoast) artillery/ ～炮台 coast battery/ ～线 coastline

【海拔】 hǎibá height above sea level; elevation: ～四千米 4,000 metres above sea level; with an elevation of 4,000 metres

【海百合】 hǎibǎihé 〈动〉 sea lily; crinoid

【海报】 hǎibào playbill

【海豹】 hǎibào seal

【海滨】 hǎibīn seashore; seaside: ～疗养院 a seaside sanatorium

【海波】 hǎibō 〈化〉 hypo

【海菜】 hǎicài edible seaweed

【海产】 hǎichǎn marine products

【海昌蓝】 hǎichānglán 〈纺〉 hydron blue

【海潮】 hǎicháo (sea) tide

【海程】 hǎichéng distance travelled by sea; voyage

【海船】 hǎichuán seagoing vessel

【海带】 hǎidài kelp

【海胆】 hǎidǎn 〈动〉 sea urchin

【海岛】 hǎidǎo island (in the sea)

【海盗】 hǎidào pirate; sea rover ◇ ～船 pirate (ship); sea rover/ ～行为 piracy

【海堤】 hǎidī sea wall

【海底】 hǎidǐ the bottom of the sea; seabed; sea floor
◇ ～采矿 undersea mining; offshore mining/ ～电报 submarine telegraph; cablegram/ ～电缆 submarine cable/ ～勘察 submarine exploration/ ～矿 submarine mine/ ～山 seamount/ ～水雷 ground mine (或 torpedo)/ ～油田 offshore oilfield/ ～资源 seabed resources; submarine resources

【海底捞月】 hǎidǐ lāo yuè try to fish out the moon from the bottom of the sea — strive for the impossible or illusory: ～一场空 be as futile as fishing for the moon in the sea

【海底捞针】 hǎidǐ lāo zhēn fish for a needle in the ocean; look for a needle in a haystack

【海地】 Hǎidì Haiti ◇ ～人 Haitian

【海防】 hǎifáng coast defence
◇ ～部队 coastal defence force/ ～前哨 outpost of coastal defence/ ～前线 coastal front/ ～艇 coastal defence boat

【海风】 hǎifēng sea breeze; sea wind

【海港】 hǎigǎng seaport; harbour ◇ ～设备 harbour installations

【海沟】 hǎigōu (oceanic) trench

【海狗】 hǎigǒu fur seal; ursine seal

【海关】 hǎiguān customhouse; customs
◇ ～人员 customs officer/ ～手续 customs formalities/ ～税则 customs tariff

【海关检查】 hǎiguān jiǎnchá customs inspection (或 examination): 通过～ go through customs ◇ ～站 customs inspection post

【海龟】 hǎiguī green turtle (*Chelonia mydas*)

【海涵】 hǎihán 〈敬〉 be magnanimous enough to forgive or tolerate (sb.'s errors or shortcomings): 招待不周，还望～。Please forgive us if we have not looked after you well.

【海魂衫】 hǎihúnshān sailor's striped shirt

【海货】 hǎihuò marine products

【海鲫】 hǎijì Japanese seaperch

【海疆】 hǎijiāng coastal areas and territorial seas

【海角】 hǎijiǎo cape; promontory

【海进】 hǎijìn 〈地〉 transgression

【海禁】 hǎijìn ban on maritime trade or intercourse with foreign countries (as during the Ming and Qing dynasties)

【海景】 hǎijǐng seascape

【海鸠】 hǎijiū 〈动〉 guillemot

【海军】 hǎijūn navy
◇ ～航空兵 naval air force/ ～基地 naval base/ ～陆战队 marine corps; marines/ ～武官〈外〉naval *attaché*/ ～学校 naval academy/ ～演习 naval manoeuvre (或 exercise)/ ～制服呢 navy cloth

【海口】 hǎikǒu ①seaport ②〔多用于〕: 夸～ boast about what one can do; talk big

【海枯石烂】 hǎikū-shílàn (even if) the seas run dry and the rocks crumble: ～心不变。The sea may run dry and the rocks may crumble, but our hearts will always remain loyal.

【海葵】 hǎikuí 〈动〉 sea anemone

【海阔天空】 hǎikuò-tiānkōng as boundless as the sea and sky; unrestrained and far-ranging: ～地聊个没完 have a rambling chat about everything under the sun

【海蓝宝石】 hǎilán bǎoshí 〈矿〉 aquamarine

【海狸】 hǎilí beaver

【海狸鼠】 hǎilíshǔ coypu; nutria

【海里】 hǎilǐ nautical mile; sea mile

【海力司粗呢】 hǎilìsī cūní 〈纺〉 Harris tweed

【海量】 hǎiliàng ①〈敬〉 magnanimity: 对不住的地方，望您～包涵。I hope you will be magnanimous enough to excuse any incorrect behaviour on my part. ②great capacity for liquor: 您是～，再来一杯。Have another one. You can hold your liquor.

【海流】 hǎiliú ocean current

【海龙】 hǎilóng ①〈口〉 sea otter ②pipefish

【海路】 hǎilù sea route; sea-lane; seaway: 走～ travel by sea

【海轮】 hǎilún seagoing (或 oceangoing) vessel

【海螺】 hǎiluó conch

【海洛因】 hǎiluòyīn heroin

【海绿石】 hǎilǜshí 〈矿〉 glauconite

【海马】 hǎimǎ sea horse

【海鳗】 hǎimán conger pike

【海米】 hǎimǐ dried shrimps

【海绵】 hǎimián ①sponge ②foam rubber or plastic; sponge
◇ ～垫 foam-rubber cushion/ ～球拍 foam-rubber (或 sponge) table-tennis bat/ ～田 mellow-soil field; spongy soil/ ～铁 sponge iron

【海难】 hǎinàn perils of the sea

【海内】 hǎinèi within the four seas; throughout the country

【海鲇】 hǎinián sea catfish

【海牛】 hǎiniú manatee; sea cow

【海鸥】 hǎi'ōu sea gull

【海盘车】 hǎipánchē 〈动〉 starfish

【海泡石】 hǎipàoshí 〈矿〉 sepiolite; sea-foam

【海螵蛸】 hǎipiāoxiāo 〈中药〉 cuttlebone

【海平面】 hǎipíngmiàn sea level

【海区】 hǎiqū 〈军〉 sea area

【海群生】 hǎiqúnshēng 〈药〉 hetrazan
【海鳃】 hǎisāi 〈动〉 sea pen; sea feather
【海商法】 hǎishāngfǎ maritime law
【海上】 hǎishàng at sea; on the sea: ～风暴 a storm at sea/ ～作业 operation on the sea/ ～空间 air space above the sea
◇ ～霸权 maritime (或 naval) hegemony/ ～保险 marine (或 maritime) insurance/ ～补给 sealift; seaborne supply/ ～封锁〈军〉 naval blockade/ ～交通线 sea route; sea-lane/ ～遇险信号 signal of distress; SOS/ ～运输 marine transportation
【海蛇】 hǎishé sea snake
【海参】 hǎishēn sea cucumber; sea slug; trepang
【海参崴】 Hǎishēnwǎi 见"符拉迪沃斯托克" Fúlādíwòsītuōkè
【海狮】 hǎishī sea lion
【海市蜃楼】 hǎishì shènlóu mirage
【海事】 hǎishì maritime affairs ◇ ～法庭 admiralty court; maritime court
【海誓山盟】 hǎishì-shānméng (make) a solemn pledge of love
【海水】 hǎishuǐ seawater; brine; the sea: ～不可斗量。The sea cannot be measured with a bushel — great minds cannot be fathomed. ◇ ～工业 marine industry/ ～浴 seawater bath; sea bathing
【海损】 hǎisǔn 〈商〉 average: 共同(单独)～ general (particular) average ◇ ～理算 average adjustment
【海獭】 hǎitǎ sea otter
【海滩】 hǎitān seabeach; beach
【海棠】 hǎitáng 〈植〉 Chinese flowering crabapple
【海塘】 hǎitáng seawall
【海桐花】 hǎitónghuā tobira
【海图】 hǎitú sea (或 marine, nautical) chart ◇ ～室 chart room (或 house)
【海退】 hǎituì 〈地〉 regression
【海豚】 hǎitún 〈动〉 dolphin ◇ ～泳〈体〉 dolphin butterfly; dolphin fishtail; dolphin
【海外】 hǎiwài overseas; abroad: ～华侨 overseas Chinese/ ～同胞 countryman residing abroad ◇ ～版 overseas edition
【海外奇谈】 hǎiwài qítán strange story from over the seas; traveller's tale; tall story
【海湾】 hǎiwān bay; gulf
【海王星】 hǎiwángxīng 〈天〉 Neptune
【海味】 hǎiwèi choice seafood
【海峡】 hǎixiá strait; channel: 台湾～ the Taiwan Straits/ 英吉利～ the English Channel
【海峡群岛】 Hǎixiá Qúndǎo the Channel Islands
【海鲜】 hǎixiān seafood
【海相】 hǎixiàng 〈地〉 marine (或 sea) facies ◇ ～沉积〈地〉 marine deposit
【海象】 hǎixiàng walrus; morse
【海啸】 hǎixiào tsunami; seismic sea wave
【海星】 hǎixīng 〈动〉 starfish; sea star
【海熊】 hǎixióng fur seal; ursine seal
【海寻】 hǎixún nautical fathom
【海牙】 Hǎiyá The Hague
【海盐】 hǎiyán sea salt
【海蜒】 hǎiyán 〈动〉 anchovy
【海燕】 hǎiyàn (storm) petrel
【海洋】 hǎiyáng seas and oceans; ocean
◇ ～霸权 maritime hegemony/ ～动物 marine animal/ ～法 law of the sea/ ～公约 maritime convention/ ～气象船 ocean weather ship/ ～气象学 marine meteorology/ ～权 maritime rights/ ～生物学 marine biology/ ～性气候 maritime (或 marine) climate/ ～学 oceanography; oceanology/ ～渔业 sea fishery/ ～资源 marine resources/ ～钻井 marine (或 offshore) drilling
【海域】 hǎiyù sea area; maritime space: 南海～ Nanhai Sea waters
【海员】 hǎiyuán seaman; sailor; mariner ◇ ～俱乐部 seamen's club/ ～用语 nautical expression
【海运】 hǎiyùn sea transportation; ocean shipping
【海葬】 hǎizàng sea-burial
【海枣】 hǎizǎo 〈植〉 date palm; date
【海藻】 hǎizǎo marine alga; seaweed
【海战】 hǎizhàn sea warfare; naval battle
【海蜇】 hǎizhé jellyfish
【海震】 hǎizhèn 〈地〉 seaquake
【海子】 hǎizi 〈方〉 lake

**胲** hǎi 〈化〉 hydroxylamine

## hài

**亥** hài the last of the twelve Earthly Branches
【亥时】 hàishí the period of the day from 9 p. m. to 11 p.m.

**骇** hài be astonished; be shocked
【骇怪】 hàiguài be shocked; be astonished
【骇然】 hàirán gasping with astonishment; struck dumb with amazement
【骇人听闻】 hài rén tīngwén shocking; appalling: ～的暴行 horrifying atrocities/ ～的剥削 shocking exploitation
【骇异】 hàiyì be shocked; be astonished

**害** hài ① evil; harm; calamity: 为民除～ rid the people of a scourge/ ～多利少 more disadvantages than advantages; more harm than good/ 灾～ calamity; disaster ② harmful; destructive; injurious: ～鸟 harmful bird ③ do harm to; impair; cause trouble to: ～人不浅 do people great harm/ 你把地址搞错了，～得我白跑一趟。You gave me the wrong address and made me go all that way for nothing. ④ kill; murder: 遇～ be murdered ⑤ contract (an illness); suffer from: ～了一场大病 have a serious attack of illness/ ～了急性病 suffer from an acute illness ⑥ feel (ashamed, afraid, etc.)
【害虫】 hàichóng injurious (或 destructive) insect
【害处】 hàichu harm: 吸烟过多对身体有～。Excessive smoking is harmful to one's health.
【害鸟】 hàiniǎo harmful (或 destructive) bird
【害怕】 hàipà be afraid; be scared: 没有什么可～的。There's nothing to be afraid of./ ～得要命 be scared to death; be mortally afraid
【害群之马】 hài qún zhī mǎ an evil member of the herd; one who brings disgrace on his group; black sheep
【害人虫】 hàirénchóng an evil creature; pest; vermin
【害臊】 hàisào 〈口〉 feel ashamed; be bashful: 替他～ be ashamed of him/ 真不～。You've got some nerve!
【害兽】 hàishòu harmful (或 destructive) animal
【害羞】 hàixiū be bashful; be shy: 她是第一次当众讲话，有些～。This was the first time she had spoken before many people, so she was a bit shy.
【害眼】 hàiyǎn have eye trouble

**氦** hài 〈化〉 helium (He)

**嗐** hài 〈叹〉〔表示伤感或惋惜〕: ～，想不到他病得这么重。Oh, I didn't know he was so seriously ill.

## hān

**犴** hān 〈动〉 elk; moose

**顸** hān 〈方〉 thick: 这线太～了,有细的吗? This thread is too thick. Have you got anything finer?

**蚶** hān 〈动〉 blood clam

【蚶子】 hānzi 〈动〉 blood clam

**酣** hān (drink, etc.) to one's heart's content: 酒～耳热 heated with wine/ 半～ half drunk/ ～歌 sing to one's heart's content

【酣畅】 hānchàng ① merry and lively (with drinking) ② sound (sleep) ③ with ease and verve; fully: ～的笔墨 something written with ease and verve/ 这首诗～淋漓地抒发了作者的革命豪情。This poem fully expresses the author's revolutionary fervour.

【酣梦】 hānmèng sweet dream

【酣睡】 hānshuì sleep soundly; be fast asleep

【酣饮】 hānyǐn drink to the full; carouse

【酣战】 hānzhàn hard-fought battle: 两军～ two armies locked in fierce battle

【酣醉】 hānzuì be dead drunk

**憨** hān ① foolish; silly: ～痴 idiotic ② straightforward; naive; ingenuous: ～态可掬 charmingly naive

【憨厚】 hānhou straightforward and good-natured; simple and honest

【憨笑】 hānxiào smile fatuously; simper

【憨直】 hānzhí honest and straightforward

**鼾** hān snore

【鼾声】 hānshēng sound of snoring: ～如雷 snore thunderously

【鼾睡】 hānshuì sound, snoring sleep

## hán

**汗** hán 见"可汗" kèhán

另见 hàn

**含** hán ① keep in the mouth: 嘴里～着止咳糖 with a cough drop in one's mouth/ 此丸宜～服。This pill is to be sucked, not swallowed. ② contain: ～多种矿物 contain several kinds of minerals/ ～泪 with tears in one's eyes/ ～硫污水 sulphur-bearing waste water/ 这种梨～的水分很多。These pears are very juicy./ ～沙量 silt content ③ nurse; cherish; harbour: ～恨 nurse one's hatred

【含苞】 hánbāo 〈书〉 in bud: ～待放 be in bud

【含垢忍辱】 hángòu-rěnrǔ endure contempt and insults; bear shame and humiliation

【含糊】 hánhu ① ambiguous; vague: ～不清 ambiguous and vague/ ～其词 talk ambiguously/ 在原则问题上不能～。One must not be vague on matters of principle. ② careless; perfunctory: 这事一点儿也不能～。We'll have to handle the matter with meticulous care. 参见"不含糊" bù hánhu

【含混】 hánhùn indistinct; ambiguous: 言词～,令人费解 speak so ambiguously as to be barely intelligible

【含量】 hánliàng content: 牛奶的乳糖～ the lactose content of the milk

【含怒】 hánnù in anger

【含情脉脉】 hánqíng mòmò (soft eyes) exuding tenderness and love

【含沙射影】 hán shā shè yǐng attack by innuendo; make insinuations: 采用～的卑劣手法 resort to insinuation/ ～,恶语中伤 vilify sb. with insidious language

【含漱剂】 hánshùjì 〈药〉 gargle

【含水】 hánshuǐ containing water or moisture ◇ ～层〈地〉 water-bearing stratum; aquifer/ ～率 moisture content

【含笑】 hánxiào have a smile on one's face: ～点头 nod with a smile

【含辛茹苦】 hánxīn-rúkǔ endure all kinds of hardships; put up with hardships

【含羞】 hánxiū with a shy look; bashfully

【含羞草】 hánxiūcǎo 〈植〉 sensitive plant

【含蓄】 hánxù ① contain; embody ② implicit; veiled: ～的批评 implicit criticism ③ reserved

【含血喷人】 hán xuè pēn rén make slanderous accusations

【含义】 hányì meaning; implication: 这个词用在不同场合有不同的～。The meaning of this word varies with different contexts./ 这句话～深刻。This remark has profound implications.

【含油层】 hányóucéng 〈石油〉 oil-bearing formation (或 stratum)

【含冤】 hányuān suffer a wrong: ～死去 die uncleared of a false charge

【含怨】 hányuàn bear a grudge; nurse a grievance

**函** hán ① 〈书〉 case; envelope: 镜～ a case for a mirror ② letter: 公～ official letter/ ～复 reply by letter; write a letter in reply/ ～告 inform by letter

【函购】 hángòu purchase by mail; mail order ◇ ～部 mail-order department

【函件】 hánjiàn letters; correspondence

【函授】 hánshòu teach by correspondence; give a correspondence course ◇ ～部 correspondence department (of a school)/ ～学校 correspondence school

【函数】 hánshù 〈数〉 function

**涵** hán ① contain ② culvert: 桥～ bridges and culverts

【涵洞】 hándòng culvert

【涵蓄】 hánxù 见"含蓄" hánxù

【涵养】 hányǎng ① ability to control oneself; self-restraint: 很有～ know how to exercise self-control ② conserve: 用造林来～水源 conserve water through afforestation

【涵义】 hányì 见"含义" hányì

**焓** hán 〈物〉 enthalpy; total heat

**琀** hán 〈考古〉 a jade piece put in the mouth of the dead upon burial

**寒** hán ① cold: 天～地冻。The weather is cold and the ground is frozen./ 受了一点～ catch a slight cold ② tremble (with fear): 胆～ be terrified ③ poor; needy: 贫～ in indigent circumstances; poverty-stricken ④ 〈谦〉 humble: ～舍 my humble home

【寒痹】 hánbì 〈中医〉 arthritis (aggravated by cold)

【寒潮】 háncháo 〈气〉 cold wave

【寒伧】 hánchen 〈口〉 ① ugly; unsightly: 长得不～ not bad-looking ② shabby; disgraceful: 这有什么～。There's nothing to be ashamed of. ③ ridicule; put to shame: 叫人～了一顿 be ridiculed by sb. 又作"寒碜"

【寒带】 hándài 〈地〉 frigid zone

【寒冬腊月】 hándōng-làyuè severe winter; dead of winter
【寒风】 hánfēng cold wind: ～刺骨。The cold wind chilled one to the bone.
【寒假】 hánjià winter vacation
【寒噤】 hánjìn shiver (with cold or fear): 他打了个～。A shiver ran over his body. 或 A chill shot through him.
【寒苦】 hánkǔ destitute; poverty-stricken
【寒来暑往】 hánlái-shǔwǎng as summer goes and winter comes; with the passage of time
【寒冷】 hánlěng cold; frigid: ～的气候 a cold climate
【寒流】 hánliú 〈气〉 cold current
【寒露】 Hánlù Cold Dew (17th solar term)
【寒毛】 hánmao fine hair on the human body
【寒气】 hánqì cold air; cold draught; cold: ～逼人。There is a nip in the air.
【寒热】 hánrè 〈中医〉 chills and fever ◇ ～往来 alternating spells of fever and chills
【寒暑表】 hánshǔbiǎo thermometer
【寒酸】 hánsuān (of a poor scholar in the old days) miserable and shabby
【寒腿】 hántuǐ 〈口〉 rheumatism in the legs
【寒微】 hánwēi 〈书〉 of low station; of humble origin
【寒武纪】 Hánwǔjì 〈地〉 the Cambrian (Period)
【寒心】 hánxīn be bitterly disappointed: 令人～ bitterly disappointing
【寒暄】 hánxuān exchange of conventional greetings; exchange of amenities (或 compliments): 她同客人～了几句。She exchanged a few words of greeting with the guests.
【寒鸦】 hányā jackdaw
【寒衣】 hányī winter clothing
【寒意】 hányì a nip (或 chill) in the air: 初春季节仍有～。It's spring but there's still a chill in the air.
【寒战】 hánzhàn shiver (with cold or fear) 又作"寒颤"
【寒症】 hánzhèng 〈中医〉 symptoms caused by cold factors (e.g. chill, slow pulse, etc.)

**韩** Hán a surname

## hǎn

**罕** hǎn rarely; seldom: ～闻 seldom heard of
【罕百理派】 Hǎnbǎilǐpài 〈伊斯兰教〉 the Hanbalite school
【罕见】 hǎnjiàn seldom seen; rare: 一场～的洪水 an exceptionally serious flood

**喊** hǎn ① shout; cry out; yell: ～口号 shout slogans/ 把嗓子～哑了 shout oneself hoarse/ ～救命 cry "Help! Help!" ② call (a person): 你走以前～他一声。Give him a shout before you go.
【喊话】 hǎnhuà ① propaganda directed to the enemy at the front line: 对敌人～ shout propaganda at enemy troops across the lines ② communicate by tele-equipment: 向团部～ establish radio contact with the regimental headquarters
【喊叫】 hǎnjiào shout; cry out
【喊冤叫屈】 hǎnyuān-jiàoqū cry out about one's grievances; complain loudly about an alleged injustice

**㲦** hǎn 〈化〉 hahnium (Ha)

## hàn

**汉** Hàn ① the Han Dynasty (206 B.C.-A.D. 220) ② the Han nationality 参见"汉族" ③ Chinese (language): ～英词典 a Chinese-English dictionary ④ (hàn) man: 老～ an old man/ 大～ a big fellow
【汉白玉】 hànbáiyù white marble
【汉奸】 hànjiān traitor (to China): ～卖国贼 traitor and collaborator
【汉人】 Hànrén the Hans; the Han people
【汉学】 Hànxué ① the Han school of classical philology ② Sinology ◇ ～家 Sinologist
【汉语】 Hànyǔ Chinese (language) ◇ ～拼音方案 the Scheme for the Chinese Phonetic Alphabet/ ～拼音字母 the Chinese phonetic alphabet
【汉字】 Hànzì Chinese character ◇ ～改革 reform of Chinese characters/ ～简化方案 the Scheme for Simplifying Chinese Characters/ ～注音 phonetic annotation of Chinese characters
【汉子】 hànzi ① man; fellow ② 〈方〉 husband
【汉族】 Hànzú the Han nationality, China's main nationality, distributed all over the country

**汗** hàn sweat; perspiration: 出～ sweat; perspire/ ～如雨下 dripping with perspiration
另见 hán
【汗斑】 hànbān ① sweat stain ② 〈医〉 tinea versicolor
【汗背心】 hànbèixīn sleeveless undershirt; vest; singlet
【汗碱】 hànjiǎn sweat stain
【汗脚】 hànjiǎo feet that sweat easily; sweaty feet
【汗津津】 hànjīnjīn 〈方〉 sweaty; moist with sweat
【汗流浃背】 hàn liú jiā bèi streaming with sweat (from fear or physical exertion)
【汗马功劳】 hàn mǎ gōngláo ① distinctions won in battle; war exploits: 立下了～ perform deeds of valour in battle ② one's contributions in work
【汗毛】 hànmao fine hair on the human body
【汗牛充栋】 hàn niú chōng dòng enough books to make the ox carrying them sweat or to fill a house to the rafters — an immense number of books
【汗青】 hànqīng ① sweating green bamboo strips — completion of a literary undertaking (reference to the ancient practice of drying green bamboo strips on the fire before writing on them) ② historical records; chronicles; annals: 人生自古谁无死，留取丹心照～。What man was ever immune from death? Let me but leave a loyal heart shining in the pages of history.
【汗衫】 hànshān undershirt; T-shirt
【汗腺】 hànxiàn 〈生理〉 sweat gland
【汗颜】 hànyán 〈书〉 blush with shame; feel deeply ashamed
【汗珠子】 hànzhūzi beads of sweat

**旱** hàn ① dry spell; drought: 抗～ combat drought/ 久～的禾苗逢甘雨。A sweet rain falls on the parched seedlings. ② dryland: ～稻 dry rice ③ on land: ～路 overland route
【旱船】 hànchuán land boat, a model boat used as a stage prop in some folk dances
【旱稻】 hàndào upland rice; dry rice
【旱地】 hàndì nonirrigated farmland; dry land
【旱季】 hànjì dry season
【旱金莲】 hànjīnlián 〈植〉 nasturtium
【旱井】 hànjǐng ① water-retention well ② dry well (used to store vegetables in winter)
【旱涝保收】 hàn-lào bǎo shōu ensure stable yields despite drought or excessive rain
【旱柳】 hànliǔ dryland willow (*Salix matsudana*)
【旱路】 hànlù overland route: 走～ travel by land

【旱年】 hànnián year of drought
【旱桥】 hànqiáo viaduct; overpass; flyover
【旱情】 hànqíng damage to crops by drought; ravages of a drought: ～严重 be afflicted with a severe drought/ ～缓和了。The drought has become less serious.
【旱伞】 hànsǎn 〈方〉 parasol
【旱生动物】 hànshēng dòngwù xerophilous animal
【旱生植物】 hànshēng zhíwù xerophyte
【旱獭】 hàntǎ 〈动〉 marmot: 藏～ Himalayan marmot
【旱田】 hàntián dry farmland; dry land
【旱象】 hànxiàng signs of drought
【旱烟】 hànyān tobacco (smoked in a long-stemmed Chinese pipe) ◇ ～袋 long-stemmed Chinese pipe
【旱灾】 hànzāi drought

**悍** hàn ① brave; bold: 一员～将 a brave warrior ② fierce; ferocious: 凶～ fierce and tough; ferocious
【悍然】 hànrán outrageously; brazenly; flagrantly: ～入侵 outrageously invade/ ～撕毁协议 flagrantly scrap an agreement/ ～不顾 in flagrant defiance of

**捍** hàn defend; guard
【捍卫】 hànwèi defend; guard; protect: ～马列主义的基本原则 defend the fundamental principles of Marxism-Leninism/ 我们一定要高举和～毛主席的伟大旗帜。We must hold high and defend the great banner of Chairman Mao./ ～国家主权 uphold state sovereignty/ ～民族经济权益 protect national economic rights and interests

**焊** hàn weld; solder: 气～ gas welding
【焊缝】 hànfèng welding seam; weld line
【焊工】 hàngōng ① welding; soldering ② welder; solderer
【焊接】 hànjiē welding; soldering: 电弧～ (electric) arc welding ◇ ～钢管 welded steel pipe
【焊料】 hànliào solder
【焊枪】 hànqiāng welding torch; (welding) blowpipe
【焊条】 hàntiáo welding rod
【焊锡】 hànxī soldering tin; tin solder
【焊液】 hànyè welding fluid; soldering fluid
【焊油】 hànyóu soldering paste

**颔** hàn 〈书〉 ① chin ② nod
【颔首】 hànshǒu 〈书〉 nod: ～微笑 nod smilingly

**憾** hàn regret: 引以为～ deem it regrettable/ 为革命而死,死而无～。If we die for the revolution, we shall die without regret.
【憾事】 hànshì a matter for regret

**撼** hàn shake: ～山易,～解放军难。It is easier to rock a mountain than the Liberation Army./ 蚍蜉～树 an ant trying to shake a tree — ridiculously overrating oneself
【撼动】 hàndòng shake; vibrate

**翰** hàn 〈书〉 ① writing brush: 挥～ wield one's writing brush; write (with a brush) ② writing: 华～ 〈敬〉 your letter
【翰林】 hànlín member of the Imperial Academy ◇ ～院 the Imperial Academy (in feudal China)
【翰墨】 hànmò 〈书〉 brush and ink — writing, painting, or calligraphy

**瀚** hàn 〈书〉 vast
【瀚海】 hànhǎi 〈书〉 big desert

## hāng

**夯** hāng ① rammer; tamper ② ram; tamp; pound: 把土～实 ram the earth
【夯歌】 hānggē rammers' work chant
【夯具】 hāngjù rammer; tamper
【夯土机】 hāngtǔjī rammer; tamper

## háng

**行** háng ① line; row: 排成两～ fall into two lines/ 杨柳成～ lined with rows of willows ② seniority among brothers and sisters: 你～几?—我～三。Where do you come among your brothers and sisters? — I'm the third. ③ trade; profession; line of business: 各～各业 all trades and professions; different walks of life/ 改～ change one's profession/ 他干哪～? What's his line?/ 干一～爱一～ love whatever job one takes up ④ business firm: 拍卖～ auctioneer's/ 银～ bank ⑤ 〈量〉: 一～树 a row of trees/ 四～诗句 four lines of verse
另见 xíng
【行帮】 hángbāng 〈旧〉 trade association
【行当】 hángdang ① 〈口〉 trade; profession; line of business ② 〈剧〉 type of role (in traditional Chinese operas)
【行道】 hángdao 〈方〉 trade; profession
【行贩】 hángfàn pedlar
【行规】 hángguī 〈旧〉 guild regulations
【行话】 hánghuà jargon; cant
【行会】 hánghuì 〈旧〉 guild ◇ ～制度 the guild system
【行家】 hángjia expert; connoisseur
【行距】 hángjù 〈农〉 row spacing
【行列】 hángliè ranks: 排成整齐的～ be drawn up in orderly ranks/ 参加革命～ join the ranks of the revolution
【行列式】 hánglièshì 〈数〉 determinant
【行频】 hángpín 〈电视〉 line frequency
【行情】 hángqíng quotations (on the market); prices ◇ ～表 quotations list
【行市】 hángshi quotations (on the market); prices
【行伍】 hángwǔ 〈旧〉 the ranks: ～出身 rise from the ranks
【行业】 hángyè trade; profession; industry: 服务～ service trades ◇ ～语 jargon; cant
【行栈】 hángzhàn 〈旧〉 broker's storehouse
【行长】 hángzhǎng president (of a bank)

**吭** háng throat: 引～高歌 sing lustily
另见 kēng

**杭** Háng ① short for Hangzhou ② a surname
【杭育】 hángyō 〈叹〉 heave ho; yo-heave-ho; yo-ho
【杭州】 Hángzhōu Hangzhou

**绗** háng sew with long stitches: ～被子 sew on the quilt cover with long stitches

**航** háng ① boat; ship ② navigate (by water or air): 夜～ night navigation/ 首～ maiden voyage or flight/ 民～ civil aviation
【航班】 hángbān scheduled flight; flight number
【航标】 hángbiāo navigation mark
【航测】 hángcè 〈简〉(航空测量) aerial survey
【航程】 hángchéng voyage; passage; range ◇ ～记录器 odograph

【航船】 hángchuán boat that plies regularly between inland towns
【航次】 hángcì ① the sequence of voyages or flights; voyage or flight number ② the number of voyages or flights made
【航道】 hángdào channel; lane; course: 主～ the main channel/ 重要的国际～ an important international sea-lane/ 沿着毛主席开辟的革命～奋勇前进 advance courageously along the revolutionary course charted by Chairman Mao
【航海】 hánghǎi navigation
◇ ～法规 navigation law/ ～罗盘 mariner's compass/ ～日志 logbook; log/ ～天文历 nautical almanac/ ～天文学 nautical astronomy/ ～仪器 nautical instrument/ ～用语 nautical term
【航迹】 hángjī 〈航空〉 flight path; track
【航空】 hángkōng aviation: 民用～ civil aviation
◇ ～版 airmail edition/ ～保险 aviation insurance/ ～标塔 airway beacon/ ～测量 aerial survey/ ～磁测 aeromagnetic survey/ ～地图 aeronautical chart; aerial map/ ～电子学 avionics/ ～发动机 aero-engine; aircraft engine/ ～法 air law/ ～港 air harbour/ ～工程 aeronautical engineering/ ～工业 aviation (或 aircraft) industry/ ～公司 airline company; airways/ ～货运 airfreight/ ～机械员 aircraft mechanic/ ～力学 aeromechanics/ ～联运 through air transport/ ～模型 model airplane/ ～母舰 aircraft carrier/ ～气象台 air weather station; aeronautical meteorological station/ ～气象学 aeronautical meteorology/ ～汽油 aviation gasoline/ ～器材 air material/ ～燃料 aviation (或 aircraft) fuel/ ～日志 aircraft logbook/ ～探矿 mineral exploration aviation; aerial prospecting/ ～体育运动 air sports; flying sports/ ～天文历 air almanac/ ～通信 air communications/ ～线 airline; airway/ ～协定 air transport agreement/ ～信 airmail letter; air letter; airmail/ ～学 aeronautics; aviation/ ～学校 aviation (或 flying) school/ ～学院 aeronautical engineering institute/ ～邮件 airmail/ ～运输 air transportation/ ～照相 aerial photography/ ～照相机 aerocamera; aerial camera
【航空兵】 hángkōngbīng ① air arm ② airman ◇ ～部队 air unit
【航路】 hánglù air or sea route ◇ ～标志 route markings
【航速】 hángsù speed of a ship or plane
【航天】 hángtiān spaceflight
◇ ～舱 space capsule/ ～飞机 space shuttle/ ～技术 space technology/ ～通信 space communication (SPACECOM)/ ～站 spaceport
【航图】 hángtú chart
【航务】 hángwù navigational matters
【航线】 hángxiàn air or shipping line; route; course: 内河～ inland navigation line
【航向】 hángxiàng course (of a ship or plane): 改变～ change course ◇ ～指示器 direction (或 heading) indicator
【航行】 hángxíng ① navigate by water; sail: 内河～ inland navigation ② navigate by air; fly: 空中～ aerial navigation ◇ ～半径 navigation radius/ ～灯 navigation light/ ～权 right of navigation
【航运】 hángyùn shipping ◇ ～保险 shipping insurance/ ～公司 shipping company

## hàng

**沆** hàng
【沆瀣】 hàngxiè evening mist
【沆瀣一气】 hàng-xiè yī qì ① act in collusion with; wallow in the mire with ② like attracts like

**巷** hàng
另见 xiàng
【巷道】 hàngdào 〈矿〉 tunnel ◇ ～掘进机 tunnelling machine

## hāo

**蒿** hāo
【蒿子】 hāozi 〈植〉 wormwood; artemisia
【蒿子杆儿】 hāozigānr crown daisy chrysanthemum (as a vegetable)

**薅** hāo pull up (weeds, etc.)
【薅草】 hāocǎo weeding

**嚆** hāo
【嚆矢】 hāoshǐ 〈书〉 ① an arrow with a whistle attached ② forerunner; harbinger; precursor

## háo

**号** háo ① howl; yell: 北风怒～。A north wind is howling. ② wail: 哀～ cry piteously; wail
另见 hào
【号哭】 háokū wail
【号叫】 háojiào howl; yell
【号啕】 háotáo cry loudly; wail: ～大哭 cry one's eyes out

**蚝** háo oyster
【蚝油】 háoyóu oyster sauce

**毫** háo ① fine long hair: 羊～笔 a writing brush made of goat's hair ② writing brush: 挥～ wield one's writing brush; write or draw a picture (with a brush) ③〔用于否定式〕 in the least; at all: ～不足怪 not at all surprising/ ～不动摇 not waver in the least; be unswerving/ ～无道理 utterly unjustifiable; for no reason whatsoever/ ～无顾虑 free from all inhibitions ④ milli-: ～米 millimetre/ ～升 millilitre ⑤ *hao*, a unit of length (=1/3 decimillimetre) ⑥ *hao*, a unit of weight (=0.005 grams)
【毫安】 háo'ān 〈电〉 milliampere ◇ ～表 milliammeter
【毫巴】 háobā 〈气〉 millibar
【毫法】 háofǎ 〈电〉 millifarad
【毫发】 háofà 〈书〉〔多用于否定式〕 a hair; the least bit; the slightest: ～不爽 not deviate a hair's breadth; be perfectly accurate
【毫伏】 háofú 〈电〉 millivolt ◇ ～计 millivoltmeter
【毫克】 háokè milligram (mg.)
【毫厘】 háolí the least bit; an iota: ～不差 without the slightest error; just right
【毫毛】 háomáo soft hair on the body: 敌人的诬蔑无损于我们一根～。The slanders of the enemy can't harm a single hair of our head.
【毫米】 háomǐ millimetre (mm.) ◇ ～波 〈无〉 millimetre wave
【毫秒】 háomiǎo millisecond
【毫升】 háoshēng millilitre (ml.)
【毫微法】 háowēifǎ 〈电〉 millimicrofarad
【毫微米】 háowēimǐ millimicron (mμ)
【毫微秒】 háowēimiǎo nanosecond; millimicrosecond
【毫无二致】 háo wú èr zhì without the slightest difference; just the same; identical

【毫针】 háozhēn filiform needle in acupuncture; acupuncture needle

【毫子】 háozi 〈方〉 silver coin (of small denominations, used in the old days)

**嗥** háo (of a jackal or wolf) howl

**貉** háo
另见 hé

【貉绒】 háoróng racoon dog fur

【貉子】 háozi racoon dog

**豪** háo ① a person of extraordinary powers or endowments: 文～ a literary giant ② bold and unconstrained; forthright; unrestrained: ～气 heroic spirit/ ～饮 unrestrained (或 heavy) drinking/ ～雨 torrential rain ③ despotic; bullying: 土～ local despot/ 巧取～夺 take away by force or trickery

【豪放】 háofàng bold and unconstrained: ～的性格 a bold and uninhibited character

【豪富】 háofù ① powerful and wealthy ② the rich and powerful

【豪横】 háohèng despotic; bullying

【豪华】 háohuá luxurious; sumptuous: ～的饭店 a luxury hotel

【豪杰】 háojié person of exceptional ability; hero

【豪举】 háojǔ ① bold move ② munificent act

【豪迈】 háomài bold and generous; heroic: ～的誓言 a bold pledge/ ～的气概 heroic spirit/ ～地说 say with pride/ 以～的步伐跨入新的一年 stride into the new year with pride and confidence

【豪门】 háomén rich and powerful family; wealthy and influential clan

【豪气】 háoqì heroism; heroic spirit

【豪强】 háoqiáng ① despotic; tyrannical ② despot; bully

【豪情】 háoqíng lofty sentiments: ～满怀 full of pride and enthusiasm/ ～壮志 lofty sentiments and aspirations

【豪绅】 háoshēn despotic gentry

【豪爽】 háoshuǎng straightforward; forthright

【豪侠】 háoxiá 〈旧〉 ① gallant ② gallant man

【豪兴】 háoxìng exuberant spirits; exhilaration; keen interest

【豪言壮语】 háoyán-zhuàngyǔ brave (或 proud) words

【豪猪】 háozhū porcupine

【豪壮】 háozhuàng grand and heroic: ～的事业 a grand and heroic cause/ ～的声音 a firm, strong voice

**壕** háo ① moat ② trench: 掘～ dig trenches; dig in/ 防空～ air-raid dugout

【壕沟】 háogōu ① 〈军〉 trench ② ditch

【壕堑战】 háoqiànzhàn 〈军〉 trench warfare

**嚎** háo howl; wail: 狼～ the howl of a wolf

【嚎啕】 háotáo cry loudly; wail

## hǎo

**好** hǎo ① good; fine; nice: ～看 good-looking; pleasant to the eye; beautiful/ 人民公社～! People's communes are fine./ 祖国的～儿子 a worthy (或 fine) son of our country/ 庄稼长得真～。The crops are doing well. ② friendly; kind: ～朋友 great (或 good) friend/ 他们对我真～。They are really kind to me./ 这两个孩子又～了。The two children have become friends again. ③ be in good health; get well: 我的病～了。I'm well (或 all right) now./ 你～! Hello! ④〔用在动词后,表示完成〕: 工具都准备～了。The tools are ready./ 坐～吧,要开会了。Take your seats please. The meeting is going to begin. ⑤〔表示赞许、结束、不满等语气〕: ～,就这么办。O.K., it's settled./ ～了,不要再说了。All right, no need to say any more./ ～,这下可麻烦了。Well, we're in for trouble now. ⑥ be easy (to do); be convenient: 这个问题～回答。This question is easy to answer./ 这本书可不～买。This book is not easily available./ 暖瓶放在这儿～拿。It's handy to have the thermos here. ⑦ so as to; so that: 今儿早点睡,明儿～早起赶火车。Let's turn in early, so as to get up early tomorrow to catch the train./ 把她的地址告诉我,我～找她。Tell me her address so that I can go and see her. ⑧〔表示程度深、数量多、时间久等〕: ～冷啊! How cold it is!/ ～大的工程! What a huge project!/ ～几个月 several months/ ～半天 quite a while ⑨〔用在形容词前面问数量或程度〕: 火车站离这儿～远? How far is the railway station from here? ⑩〈方〉 may; can; should: 我～进来吗? May I come in?/ 时间不早了,你～走了。It's getting late. You ought to get going. ⑪〔用于套语〕: ～走! Goodbye!
另见 hào

【好办】 hǎobàn easy to handle: 这事不～。This is no easy matter. 或 This is rather a headache./ 这件事～。That can be easily arranged.

【好比】 hǎobǐ can be compared to; may be likened to; be just like: 军民关系～鱼和水的关系。The relationship between the army and the people is like that between fish and water. 或 The people are to the army what water is to fish.

【好不】 hǎobù 〈副〉〔表示程度深,并带感叹语气〕: 人来人往,～热闹! What a busy place, with so many people coming and going./ 他们见了面,～欢喜。How happy they were to see each other./ 他～容易才挤到台前。He had a hard time squeezing through the crowd to get up to the platform.

【好吃】 hǎochī good to eat; tasty; delicious

【好处】 hǎochu ① good; benefit; advantage: 对革命事业有～ be good for the revolution; be of benefit to the revolution/ 计划生育～多。Family planning has many advantages./ 你每天做点户外运动会有～。Some outdoor exercises every day will do you good. ② gain; profit: 敌人从这里捞不到任何～。The enemy can gain nothing from this./ 别上他的当!他给你这点～是为了拉拢你。Don't fall into his trap. He's given you this to win you over.

【好歹】 hǎodǎi ① good and bad; what's good and what's bad: 不知～ unable to tell what's good or bad for one; not appreciate a favour ② mishap; disaster: 万一她有个～,这可怎么办? What if something should happen to her? ③ in any case; at any rate; anyhow: ～试试看。Let's try, anyhow./ 他要是在这里,～也能拿个主意。If he were here he would give us some advice. ④ no matter in what way; anyhow: 别再做什么了,～吃点儿就得了。Don't cook us anything more. We'll have whatever there is.

【好端端】 hǎoduānduān in perfectly good condition; when everything is all right: ～的,怎么生起气来了? Why are you angry when everything is perfectly all right?

【好多】 hǎoduō ① a good many; a good deal; a lot of: 她上街买了～东西。She went shopping and bought quite a few things. ②〈方〉 how many; how much: 今天到会的人有～? How many came to the meeting today?

【好感】 hǎogǎn good opinion; favourable impression: 对他有～ be well disposed towards him; have a good opinion of him/ 给人～ make a good impression on people

【好过】 hǎoguò ① have an easy time; be in easy circumstances: 这几年她家的日子越来越～了。Her family have had an easier and easier time these last few years./ 超级大国

内外交困，日子很不～。Beset with difficulties at home and abroad, the superpowers are having a very hard time. ② feel well: 他吃了药，觉得～一点儿了。He felt a bit better after taking the medicine.

【好汉】 hǎohàn brave man; true man; hero: ～做事～当。A true man has the courage to accept the consequences of his own actions.

【好好儿】 hǎohǎor ① in perfectly good condition; when everything is all right: 电话刚才还是～的，怎么就坏了？Why isn't the phone working now? It was all right a moment ago./ ～的一支笔，叫他给弄折了。He broke a perfectly good pen./ 那棵百年的老树，至今还长得～的。That hundred-year-old tree is still growing well./ 你～地跟他说，别生气。Talk to him nicely. Don't get angry. ② all out; to one's heart's content: ～想一想。Think it over carefully./ 把这房间～打扫一下。Give the room a thorough cleaning./ 我得～谢谢他。I'll really have to thank him./ 咱俩～聊一聊。Let's have a good talk.

【好好先生】 hǎohǎo xiānshēng one who tries not to offend anybody

【好话】 hǎohuà ① a good word; word of praise: 给他说句～ put in a good word for him/ 不要听了一些～就沾沾自喜。Don't become complacent when you hear a few words of praise. ② fine words: ～说尽，坏事做绝 say every fine word and do every foul deed

【好家伙】 hǎojiāhuo 〈叹〉〔表示惊讶或赞叹〕good god; good lord; good heavens: ～，他们一天足足走了一百里！Good lord, they walked a hundred *li* in a day!

【好景不长】 hǎojǐng bù cháng good times don't last long

【好看】 hǎokàn ① good-looking; nice: 你戴那顶帽子很～。That hat looks nice on you. ② interesting: 这本小说很～。This novel is very interesting. ③ honoured; proud: 儿子立了功，我这做娘的脸上也～。My son has won distinction; as his mother, I share the honour. ④ in an embarrassing situation; on the spot: 等着吧，有他的～。You can be sure he'll soon find himself on the spot./ 让我上台表演，这不是要我的～吗？Me, on the stage? Do you want me to make a fool of myself?

【好赖】 hǎo-lài 见"好歹"③

【好评】 hǎopíng favourable comment; high opinion: 对他颇有～ have a rather high opinion of him /博得读者～ be well received by the readers

【好球】 hǎoqiú well played; good shot; bravo

【好人】 hǎorén ① good (或 fine) person: ～好事 good people and good deeds; fine people and fine deeds ② a healthy person ③ a person who tries to get along with everyone (often at the expense of principle) ◇ ～主义 seeking good relations with all and sundry at the expense of principle

【好日子】 hǎorìzi ①〈旧〉 auspicious day ② wedding day ③ good days; happy life: 过～ live a happy life; live well; live in happiness

【好容易】 hǎoróngyì with great difficulty; have a hard time (doing sth.): 他们～才找到我这儿。They had a hard time finding my place. 又作"好不容易"

【好生】 hǎoshēng ① quite; exceedingly: ～奇怪！What an exceedingly strange thing! /这个人～面熟。That person looks quite familiar. ②〈方〉 carefully; properly: ～想一想。Think it over carefully./ ～拿着。Mind how you carry it.

【好声好气】 hǎoshēng-hǎoqì 〈口〉 in a kindly manner; gently

【好使】 hǎoshǐ be convenient to use; work well: 这把剪刀不～。This pair of scissors doesn't work well./ 这架录音机很～。This tape recorder is very reliable./ 这支笔挺～。This pen writes very well.

【好事】 hǎoshì ① good deed; good turn: 为群众做～ do people good turns ②〈旧〉 an act of charity; good works 另见 hàoshì

【好事多磨】 hǎoshì duō mó ① the road to happiness is strewn with setbacks ② the course of true love never did run smooth

【好手】 hǎoshǒu good hand; past master: 做针线活儿，她可是把～。She is adept at needlework.

【好受】 hǎoshòu feel better; feel more comfortable: 我吃了药以后～多了。I felt much better after taking the medicine./ 白天太热，夜里还～点。It's terribly hot during the day but a bit better at night./ 你别说了，他心里正不～呢！Don't say anything more; he's feeling bad enough as it is.

【好说】 hǎoshuō 〈套〉〔用在别人向自己致谢或恭维自己时，表示不敢当〕: ～，～！您太夸奖了。It's very good of you to say so, but I don't deserve such praise. 或 You flatter me. I wish I could deserve such compliments.

【好说歹说】 hǎoshuō-dǎishuō try every possible way to persuade sb.: 我～，他总算答应了。He agreed, but only after I had pleaded with him in every way I could.

【好说话儿】 hǎoshuōhuàr good-natured; open to persuasion: 王大爷～，求求他准行。Uncle Wang is very obliging. He's sure to help if you ask him.

【好似】 hǎosì seem; be like: 大坝～铜墙铁壁，顶住了洪水的冲击。Like an iron bastion, the dam withstood the rushing floodwaters.

【好天儿】 hǎotiānr fine day; lovely weather: 这些衣服～要拿出去晒晒。These clothes should be put out to air on a sunny day.

【好听】 hǎotīng pleasant to hear: ～的话 fine words/ 这支歌很～。This is a very pleasant song./ 他说的比唱的还～。His glib talk sounds as sweet as a song.

【好玩儿】 hǎowánr amusing; interesting: 颐和园～极了。The Summer Palace is a most delightful place./ 这小娃娃挺～。The baby is very cute./ 这可不是～的！This is no joking matter.

【好戏】 hǎoxì ① good play ②〈讽〉 great fun: 这回可有～看了！We're going to see some fun!

【好象】 hǎoxiàng seem; be like: 他们～是多年的老朋友了。They seem to have been close friends for many years./ ～要下雨。It looks like rain./ 她们俩处得～亲姐妹一样。The two of them were as intimate as sisters.

【好笑】 hǎoxiào laughable; funny; ridiculous: 有什么～的？What's so funny? /又好气又～ be annoying and amusing at the same time

【好些】 hǎoxiē quite a lot; a good deal of

【好心】 hǎoxīn good intention: 一片～ with the best of intentions /～当作驴肝肺 take sb.'s goodwill for ill intent

【好样儿的】 hǎoyàngrde 〈口〉 (of a man or woman) fine example; great fellow: 你们个个都抢重活干，真是～！Each one of you wanted to do the hardest job. That's the stuff!/ 是～，就站出来说吧！If you are man enough, come out with what you have to say!

【好一个】 hǎoyīge what a: ～正人君子！An honourable man, indeed!

【好意】 hǎoyì good intention; kindness: ～相劝 give well-intentioned advice/ 谢谢您的～。Thank you for your kindness.

【好意思】 hǎoyìsi 〔多用在反问句中〕have the nerve: 做了这种事，亏他还～说呢！Fancy his doing that sort of thing and then having the nerve to talk about it!

【好在】 hǎozài fortunately; luckily: ～他伤势不重。Luckily he was not very seriously wounded. /我可以再去一趟，～路不远。Luckily it's not very far. I can easily go there again.

【好转】 hǎozhuǎn take a turn for the better; take a favourable turn; improve: 形势～。The situation took a favourable turn./ 病情～。The patient is on the mend.

**郝** Hǎo a surname

## hào

**号** hào ① name: 国～ the name of a dynasty/ 绰～ nickname ② assumed name; alternative name ③ business house: 银～ banking house/ 分～ branch (of a firm, etc.) ④ mark; sign; signal: 问～ question mark/ 加～ plus sign/ 举火为～ light a beacon/ ～房子 mark out houses (as billets, etc.) ⑤ number: 五～楼 Building No. 5/ 编～ serial number ⑥ size: 大(中,小)～ large (medium, small) size/ 这鞋小了两～。These shoes are two sizes too small. ⑦ date: 今天几～? —— 十三～。What date is it today? — The 13th. ⑧ order: 发～施令 issue orders ⑨ <乐> any brass-wind instrument: 军～ bugle/ 小～ trumpet ⑩ anything used as a horn: 螺～ conch-shell trumpet; conch ⑪ bugle call; any call made on a bugle: 熄灯～ taps/ 吹起床～ sound the reveille ⑫ <量>〔用于人数〕: 一百多～人 over a hundred people
另见 háo

【号称】hàochēng ① be known as: 四川～天府之国。Sichuan is known as a land of plenty. ② claim to be: ～五十万大军 an army claiming to be half a million strong/ 一切～强大的反动派都不过是纸老虎。All allegedly powerful reactionaries are merely paper tigers.

【号角】hàojiǎo ① bugle; horn ② bugle call: 吹响战斗的～ sound a bugle call for battle/ 吹响了向科学技术现代化进军的～ sound the clarion call to march towards the modernization of science and technology

【号令】hàolìng verbal command; order

【号码】hàomǎ number: 电话～ telephone number ◇ ～机 numbering machine

【号脉】hàomài <中医> feel the pulse

【号手】hàoshǒu trumpeter; bugler

【号外】hàowài extra (of a newspaper)

【号衣】hàoyī <旧> livery or army uniform

【号召】hàozhào call; appeal: 响应党的～ respond to the Party's call ◇ ～书 appeal

【号子】hàozi a work song sung to synchronize movements, with one person leading

**好** hào ① like; love; be fond of: 虚心～学 be modest and eager to learn/ ～表现 like to show off/ ～管闲事 meddlesome; officious ② be liable to: ～晕船 be liable to seasickness; be a bad sailor/ ～伤风 be subject to colds
另见 hǎo

【好吃懒做】hàochī-lǎnzuò be fond of eating and averse to work; be gluttonous and lazy

【好大喜功】hàodà-xǐgōng crave for greatness and success; have a fondness for the grandiose

【好高务远】hàogāo-wùyuǎn reach for what is beyond one's grasp; aim too high; bite off more than one can chew 又作"好高骛远"

【好客】hàokè be hospitable; keep open house

【好奇】hàoqí be curious; be full of curiosity ◇ ～心 curiosity

【好强】hàoqiáng eager to do well in everything

【好胜】hàoshèng seek to do others down

【好事】hàoshì meddlesome; officious ◇ ～之徒 busybody
另见 hǎoshì

【好恶】hào-wù likes and dislikes; taste: 翻译时不应根据自己的～改变原文意思。In doing translation, one should not alter the meaning of the original to suit one's own taste.

【好逸恶劳】hàoyì-wùláo love ease and hate work

【好战】hàozhàn bellicose; warlike ◇ ～分子 bellicose (或 warlike) elements

【好整以暇】hào zhěng yǐ xiá remain calm and composed while handling pressing affairs

**耗** hào ① consume; cost: ～了不少粮食 have consumed much grain/ ～资百万 cost a million *yuan*/ 锅里的水快～干了。The pot is boiling dry. ② waste time; dawdle: 别～着了,快走吧。Stop dawdling and get going. ③ bad news: 噩～ the sad news of the death of one's beloved

【耗电量】hàodiànliàng power consumption

【耗费】hàofèi consume; expend: ～时间、金钱 expend time and money

【耗竭】hàojié exhaust; use up: 人力～ be drained of manpower

【耗尽】hàojìn exhaust; use up: ～心血 exhaust all one's energies/ ～体力 use up all one's strength

【耗散】hàosàn <物> dissipation: 功率～ power dissipation

【耗损】hàosǔn consume; waste; lose: 减少水果在运输中的～ reduce the wastage of fruit in transit

【耗子】hàozi <方> mouse; rat ◇ ～药 ratsbane

**浩** hào great; vast; grand

【浩大】hàodà very great; huge; vast: ～的工程 a huge (或 vast) project/ 声势～的示威游行 a gigantic (或 huge, mammoth) demonstration

【浩荡】hàodàng vast and mighty: ～的长江 the mighty Changjiang River/ 东风～。The east wind blows with mighty power./ 浩浩荡荡的革命大军 an enormous and powerful revolutionary army; mighty revolutionary contingents/石油工人浩浩荡荡开进了新油田。Oil workers gathered in force at the new oil field.

【浩繁】hàofán vast and numerous: 卷帙～ a voluminous work; a vast collection of books/ ～的开支 heavy expenditure

【浩瀚】hàohàn vast: ～的沙漠 a vast expanse of desert/ 典籍～ a vast accumulation of ancient literature

【浩劫】hàojié great calamity; catastrophe: 空前～ an unheard-of calamity

【浩淼】hàomiǎo (of water) extending into the distance; vast: 洞庭湖上,烟波～。On the Dongting Lake, mists and waves stretch far into the distance. 又作"浩渺"

【浩气】hàoqì noble spirit: ～长存 imperishable noble spirit

【浩如烟海】hào rú yānhǎi (of data, etc.) vast as the open sea; tremendous amount of; voluminous

【浩叹】hàotàn heave a deep sigh; sigh deeply

**皓** hào ① white: ～齿 white teeth ② bright; luminous: ～月当空。A bright moon hung in the sky.

【皓矾】hàofán <化> zinc sulphate

【皓首】hàoshǒu <书> hoary head

## hē

**诃** hē scold

【诃子】hēzǐ <植> myrobalan (*Terminalia chebula*)

**呵** hē ① breathe out (with the mouth open): ～手 breathe on one's hands (to warm them)/ ～一口气 give a puff ② scold: ～责 scold sb. severely; give sb. a dressing

down ③ 见"嗬" hē
【呵斥】 hēchì berate; excoriate
【呵呵】 hēhē 〈象〉: ～大笑 laugh loudly; roar with laughter
【呵欠】 hēqiàn yawn

**喝** hē ① drink: ～茶 drink tea/ ～汤 drink soup ② drink alcoholic liquor: 爱～两盅 be fond of drinking/ ～醉了 be drunk
另见 hè
【喝西北风】 hē xīběifēng drink the northwest wind — have nothing to eat

**嗬** hē 〈叹〉〔表示惊讶〕ah; oh: ～，这小伙子真棒！Oh, what a fine young chap!

## hé

**禾** hé standing grain (esp. rice)
【禾本科】 héběnkē 〈植〉 the grass family ◇ ～植物 grass
【禾场】 hécháng threshing floor
【禾苗】 hémiáo seedlings of cereal crops

**合** hé ① close; shut: ～上眼 close one's eyes/ 笑得～不拢嘴 grin from ear to ear ② join; combine: ～力 combined strength; joint effort ③ whole: ～家团聚 a reunion of the whole family ④ suit; agree: ～胃口 suit one's taste; be to one's taste/ ～得来 get along well/ 正～我意。It suits me fine. ⑤ be equal to; add up to: 一公顷～十五市亩。A hectare is equal to 15 *mu.*/ 这件上衣连工带料～多少钱？How much will this coat cost, including material and tailoring? ⑥〈书〉 proper: 理～声明。I deem it appropriate to make a statement. ⑦〈乐〉 a note of the scale in *gongchepu* (工尺谱), corresponding to 5 in numbered musical notation ⑧〈量〉〔旧小说中指交战的回合〕 round ⑨〈天〉 conjunction
另见 gě
【合瓣】 hébàn 〈植〉 sympetalous; gamopetalous ◇ ～花 sympetalous flower/ ～花类 metachlamydeae; sympetalae
【合抱】 hébào (of a tree, etc.) so big that one can just get one's arms around: ～之木，生于毫末。A huge tree grows from a tiny seedling. 或 Great oaks from little acorns grow.
【合璧】 hébì (of two different things) combine harmoniously; match well: 中西～ a good combination of Chinese and Western elements
【合并】 hébìng merge; amalgamate: 五个组～为两个组了。The five groups have merged into two./ 这三个提议～讨论。The three proposals will be discussed together.
【合唱】 héchàng chorus: 混声～ mixed chorus
◇ ～曲 chorus/ ～团 chorus/ ～团指挥 chorus master
【合成】 héchéng ① compose; compound: 由两部分～ be composed of two parts/ 力的～〈物〉 composition of forces ②〈化〉 synthetize; synthesize
◇ ～氨〈化〉 synthetic ammonia/ ～词〈语〉 compound word/ ～结晶牛胰岛素 synthetic crystalline bovine insulin/ ～军队 combined arms unit/ ～酶〈生化〉 synzyme/ ～树脂 synthetic resin/ ～塔〈化〉 synthetic tower/ ～洗涤剂 synthetic detergent/ ～纤维 synthetic fibre
【合订本】 hédìngběn one-volume edition; bound volume: «毛泽东选集»～ one-volume edition of the *Selected Works of Mao Zedong*/ «红旗»～ a bound volume of *Hongqi*/ «人民日报»～ a file of *Renmin Ribao*
【合二而一】 hé èr ér yī 〈哲〉 two combine into one — a revisionist concept diametrically opposed to the Marxist concept that "one divides into two"
【合法】 héfǎ legal; lawful; legitimate; rightful: 唯一～政府 the sole legal government
◇ ～地位 legal status/ ～斗争 legal struggle/ ～化 legalize; legitimize/ ～继承人 rightful heir/ ～权利 legitimate right; lawful right/ ～权益 legitimate rights and interests/ ～收入 lawfully earned income/ ～途径 legal means
【合肥】 Héféi Hefei
【合格】 hégé qualified; up to standard: ～的司机 a qualified driver/ 产品～。The product is up to standard./ 我们保证质量～。We can vouch for the quality. ◇ ～证 certificate of inspection; certificate of quality
【合股】 hégǔ ① pool capital; form a partnership ②〈纺〉 plying: ～线 ply (或 plied) yarn
【合乎】 héhū conform with (或 to); correspond to; accord with; tally with: ～人民的利益 conform with the interests of the people/ ～实际 conform to the actual situation/ ～历史发展的规律 be in conformity with the law of historical development/ ～事实 tally with the facts/ ～广大群众的需要 meet the needs of the broad masses/ ～规格 up to the specifications/ ～逻辑 logical/ ～情理 reasonable; sensible
【合欢】 héhuān 〈植〉 silk tree
【合伙】 héhuǒ form a partnership: ～经营 run a business in partnership
【合击】 héjī make a joint attack on: 分进～ concerted attack by converging columns
【合计】 héjì amount to; add up to; total: 这两项开支～一千元。The cost of the two items amounts to 1,000 *yuan.*/ 把这一栏的数字～一下。Add up the figures in this column.
【合计】 héji ① think over; figure out: 他心里老～这件事。He kept thinking it over. ② consult: 大家～～该怎么办。Let's put our heads together and see what's to be done.
【合剂】 héjì 〈药〉 mixture
【合金】 héjīn alloy: 二元(三元)～ binary (ternary) alloy
◇ ～结构钢 structural alloy steel/ ～元素 alloying element
【合金钢】 héjīngāng alloy steel: 高～ high-alloy steel
【合刊】 hékān combined issue (of a periodical)
【合口】 hékǒu ① (of a wound) heal up ② (of a dish) be to one's taste
【合理】 hélǐ rational; reasonable; equitable: ～分工 rational division of labour/ ～利用资源 put resources to rational use; make rational use of resources/ ～的价格 a reasonable (或 equitable) price/ ～解决两国之间的争端 equitable settlement of the issues between the two countries/ ～轮作〈农〉 proper rotation of crops/ ～施肥 apply fertilizer rationally
【合理化】 hélǐhuà rationalize: ～建议 rationalization proposal
【合力】 hélì ① join forces; pool efforts: ～修建水库 pool efforts to build a reservoir/ 同心～大干社会主义 unite in spirit and action and go all out to build socialism ②〈物〉 resultant of forces
【合流】 héliú ① flowing together; confluence: 永定河和大清河在天津附近～。The Yongding and Daqing rivers meet near Tianjin. ② collaborate; work hand in glove with sb.
【合龙】 hélóng ① closure (of a dam, dyke, etc.) ② join the two sections of a bridge, etc.
【合霉素】 héméisù 〈药〉 syntomycin
【合谋】 hémóu ① conspire; plot together ②〈法〉 conspiracy
【合拍】 hépāi in time; in step; in harmony: 与时代潮流～ in step with the trend of the times
【合情合理】 héqíng-hélǐ fair and reasonable; fair and sensible: 这个建议～。The proposal is fair and reasonable.
【合群】 héqún ① get on well with others ② be gregarious
【合身】 héshēn fit: 这件上衣很～。This jacket fits well.

【合十】 héshí put the palms together (a Buddhist greeting)
【合适】 héshì suitable; appropriate; becoming; right: 这双鞋我穿着正～。These shoes fit me beautifully./ 星期五对我最～。Friday suits me best./ 你这样说不～。It's not right (或 suitable) for you to say so./ 这个词用在这里不～。This isn't the right word to use here. 又作"合式"
【合算】 hésuàn ① paying; worthwhile ② reckon up
【合题】 hétí 〈哲〉 synthesis
【合同】 hétong contract: 签订～ sign a contract/ 撕毁～ tear up a contract ◇ ～工 contract worker/ ～医院 assigned hospital (to which people from a given organization or area go for treatment)
【合围】 héwéi ① surround ② 〈书〉 见"合抱"
【合页】 héyè hinge
【合议庭】 héyìtíng 〈法〉 collegiate bench (of judges, or of a judge and people's assessors)
【合议制】 héyìzhì 〈法〉 collegiate system (a judicial system according to which justice is administered by a collegiate bench of judges, or by a judge and people's assessors)
【合意】 héyì suit; be to one's liking (或 taste)
【合营】 héyíng jointly owned; jointly operated 参见"公私合营" gōng-sī héyíng
【合影】 héyǐng group photo (或 picture): ～留念 have a group photo taken to mark the occasion
【合辙】 hézhé ① in rhyme ② in agreement: 两人一说就～。The moment they started talking they found themselves in complete agreement.
【合著】 hézhù write in collaboration with; coauthor
【合子】 hézǐ 〈生〉 zygote
【合奏】 hézòu instrumental ensemble
【合作】 hézuò cooperate; collaborate; work together: 互相～ cooperate with each other/ 这幅画是他们～的。This painting is their joint work.
◇ ～经济 cooperative economy; cooperative sector of the economy/ ～商店 cooperative shop (或 store)/ ～社 cooperative; co-op/ ～医疗 cooperative medical service/ ～医疗站 cooperative medical station
【合作化】 hézuòhuà (a movement to) organize cooperatives: 农业～ cooperative transformation of agriculture/ 那时全村已经～了。By then the whole village had gone cooperative./ 通过～，国家对农业和手工业进行了社会主义改造。Through the cooperative movement, the state carried out the socialist transformation of agriculture and handicrafts.

## 纥

hé 见"回纥" Huíhé

## 何

hé 〈书〉 ①〔表示疑问〕: ～人 who/ ～时 what time; when/ ～处 what place; where/ ～往 whither/ 从～而来? Where from? ②〔表示反问〕: ～济于事? Of what avail is it?/ 有～不可? Why not? ③ (Hé) a surname
【何必】 hébì there is no need; why: ～去那么早。There is no need to go so early./ 开个玩笑嘛，～当真呢? I was only joking. Why take it so seriously?
【何不】 hébù why not: ～早说? Why didn't you say so earlier?
【何尝】 hécháng 〔用于反问，表示未曾或并不〕: 我～不想去，只是没工夫罢了。Not that I don't want to go; I just haven't got the time./ 他这样的态度，～有解决问题的诚意呢? If that's his attitude, how can you say he sincerely wants the question settled?
【何等】 héděng ① what kind: 你知道他是～人物? Do you know what kind of person he is? ②〔用于感叹语气，表示不同寻常〕: 这是～高超的技术! What consummate skill!
【何妨】 héfāng why not; might as well: ～一试? Why not have a try? 或 You might as well have a try.
【何苦】 hékǔ why bother; is it worth the trouble: 你～在这些小事上伤脑筋? Why bother your head about such trifles?/ 冒着这么大的雨去看电影，～呢? Going to the movies in this rain — is it worth it?
【何况】 hékuàng 〈连〉 much less; let alone: 这根木头连小伙子都抬不动，～老人呢? The log is too heavy even for a young fellow to lift, let alone an old man.
【何乐而不为】 hé lè ér bù wéi what is there against it: 发展养猪事业，对国家、对集体都有利，～? Pig-breeding is beneficial to both the state and the collective. Why not go ahead with it?
【何其】 héqí how; what: ～相似乃尔! What a striking likeness (或 similarity)!
【何去何从】 héqù-hécóng what course to follow: ～，速作抉择。What course to follow — that is a question you must quickly decide for yourselves.
【何如】 hérú ① how about: 请君一试，～? How about you having a try? ② wouldn't it be better: 与其强攻，～智取。It would be better to use strategy than to attack by force.
【何首乌】 héshǒuwū 〈中药〉 the tuber of multiflower knotweed (*Polygonum multiflorum*)
【何谓】 héwèi 〈书〉 what is meant by; what is the meaning of
【何许】 héxǔ 〈书〉 what kind of; what: ～人 what sort of person
【何以】 héyǐ how; why: ～自解? How are you to explain yourself?/ ～见得? What makes you think so?
【何在】 hézài where: 困难～? Wherein lies the difficulty?/ 原因～? What is the reason for it?
【何止】 hézhǐ far more than: 例子～这些。There are far more instances than we have just enumerated.

## 河

hé ① river ② (Hé) the Huanghe River; the Yellow River
【河岸】 hé'àn river bank
【河北】 Héběi Hebei (Province)
【河汊子】 héchàzi a branch of a river
【河床】 héchuáng riverbed
【河道】 hédào river course
【河防】 héfáng flood-prevention work done on rivers, esp. the Huanghe River
【河沟】 hégōu brook; stream
【河谷】 hégǔ river valley
【河口】 hékǒu river mouth; stream outlet ◇ ～湾 estuary
【河狸】 hélí beaver
【河流】 héliú rivers ◇ ～沉积 fluvial (或 fluviatile) deposit/ ～袭夺 〈地〉 river capture; river piracy
【河马】 hémǎ hippopotamus; hippo; river horse
【河鳗】 hémán river eel
【河南】 Hénán Henan (Province)
【河泥】 héní river silt; river mud
【河曲】 héqū bend (of a river); meander
【河渠】 héqú rivers and canals; waterways: ～纵横 be criss-crossed by rivers and canals
【河山】 héshān rivers and mountains; land; territory: 锦绣～ a land of enchanting beauty
【河滩地】 hétāndì flood land
【河套】 hétào ① the bend of a river ② (Hétào) the Great Bend of the Huanghe River ◇ ～地区 the Hetao area (at the top of the Great Bend of the Huanghe River in the Nei Monggol Autonomous Region and Ningxia)
【河豚】 hétún globefish; balloonfish; puffer
【河外星云】 héwài xīngyún 〈天〉 extragalactic nebula
【河网】 héwǎng a network of waterways ◇ ～化 build a network of waterways

【河蟹】 héxiè river crab
【河源】 héyuán river head (或 source)
【河运】 héyùn river transport

**和** hé ①gentle; mild; kind: 风～日暖 bright sunshine and gentle breeze/ 对敌狠,对己～ ruthless to the enemy, kind to one's comrades ②harmonious; on good terms: 兄弟不～ brothers on bad terms with each other ③peace: 讲～ make peace ④〈体〉 draw; tie: 那盘棋～了。That game of chess ended in a draw. ⑤together with: ～衣而卧 sleep with one's clothes on; sleep in one's clothes ⑥〈介〉〔表示相关、比较等〕: ～这件事没有关系 have nothing to do with the matter; bear no relation to it/ 他～我一样高。He's the same height as I. ⑦〈连〉 and: 工人～农民 workers and peasants ⑧〈数〉 sum: 两数之～ the sum of the two numbers ⑨(Hé) a surname
另见 hè; huó; huò

【和蔼】 hé'ǎi kindly; affable; amiable: ～可亲 affable; genial/ 态度～ amiable
【和畅】 héchàng (of a wind) gentle and pleasant: 惠风～ a gentle and pleasant breeze
【和风】 héfēng ①soft (或 gentle) breeze: ～拂面 a gentle breeze caressing one's face/ ～丽日 a gentle breeze and a bright sun; fine weather ②〈气〉 moderate breeze
【和风细雨】 héfēng-xìyǔ like a gentle breeze and a mild rain —in a gentle and mild way: ～地开展批评和自我批评 make criticism and self-criticism in the manner of "a gentle breeze and a mild rain"
【和服】 héfú *kimono*
【和好】 héhǎo become reconciled: 他们吵过架,现在～了。They had a quarrel but have made it up now./ ～如初 be on good terms again; restore good relations
【和缓】 héhuǎn ①gentle; mild: 水流～ gentle flow of a stream/ 态度～ adopt a mild attitude ②ease up; relax: ～一下气氛 relieve the tension a little
【和会】 héhuì peace conference
【和解】 héjiě become reconciled: 采取～的态度 adopt a conciliatory attitude
【和局】 héjú drawn game; draw; tie
【和睦】 hémù harmony; concord; amity: ～相处 live in harmony/ 民族～ national concord/ 家庭～ family harmony; domestic peace/ 友好～关系 friendly and harmonious relations
【和暖】 hénuǎn pleasantly warm; genial: 天气～ warm, genial weather
【和盘托出】 hé pán tuōchū reveal everything; make a clean breast of everything: 把自己的想法～ reveal everything on one's mind
【和平】 hépíng ① peace: ～倡议 peace proposals/ 克服～麻痹思想 overcome a false sense of peace and security/ ～利用原子能 peaceful utilization of atomic energy; use of atomic energy for peaceful purposes/ ～解决边界争端 peaceful settlement of a boundary dispute ②mild: 药性～。The medicine is mild.
◇ ～攻势 peace offensive/ ～过渡 peaceful transition/ ～竞赛 peaceful competition/ ～谈判 peace negotiations/ ～中立政策 policy of peace and neutrality/ ～主义 pacifism/ ～主义者 pacifist
【和平共处】 hépíng gòngchǔ peaceful coexistence: 被压迫阶级同压迫阶级,被压迫民族同压迫民族,是不能～的。It is impossible for the oppressed classes and nations to coexist peacefully with the oppressor classes and nations.
【和平共处五项原则】 hépíng gòngchǔ wǔ xiàng yuánzé the Five Principles of Peaceful Coexistence (mutual respect for territorial integrity and sovereignty, mutual non-aggression, non-interference in each other's internal affairs, equality and mutual benefit, and peaceful coexistence)
【和平演变】 hépíng yǎnbiàn peaceful evolution (from socialism back to capitalism)
【和棋】 héqí a draw in chess or other board games
【和气】 héqi gentle; kind; polite; amiable: 说话～ speak politely (或 gently); be soft-spoken/ 伤了～ hurt sb.'s feelings/ 和和气气 polite and amiable/ 我们主张积极的思想斗争,反对无原则的一团～。We stand for active ideological struggle and oppose keeping on good terms at the expense of principle.
【和亲】 héqīn 〈史〉 (of some feudal dynasties) attempt to cement relations with rulers of minority nationalities in the border areas by marrying daughters of the Han imperial family to them
【和善】 héshàn kind and gentle; genial
【和尚】 héshang Buddhist monk
【和声】 héshēng 〈乐〉 harmony
【和事老】 héshìlǎo peacemaker (esp. one who is more concerned with stopping the bickering than settling the issue)
【和谈】 hétán peace talks
【和弦】 héxián 〈乐〉 chord
【和谐】 héxié harmonious: ～的气氛 a harmonious atmosphere/ 音调～ in perfect harmony; melodious; tuneful
【和煦】 héxù pleasantly warm; genial: ～的阳光 genial sunshine
【和颜悦色】 héyán-yuèsè with a kind and pleasant countenance
【和约】 héyuē peace treaty
【和衷共济】 hézhōng-gòngjì work together with one heart (in times of difficulty)

**劾** hé expose sb.'s misdeeds or crimes: 弹～ impeach

**饸** hé

【饸饹】 héle a kind of noodles made from buckwheat, sorghum flour, etc.

**曷** hé 〈书〉①how ②why ③when

**阂** hé cut off from; not in communication with: 隔～ misunderstanding; estrangement

**荷** hé lotus
另见 hè

【荷包】 hébao ①small bag (for carrying money and odds and ends); pouch ②pocket (in a garment) ◇ ～蛋 fried eggs
【荷花】 héhuā lotus
【荷兰】 Hélán the Netherlands (Holland) ◇ ～人 the Dutch; Dutchman/ ～语 Dutch (language)
【荷兰牛】 hélánniú Holstein (cattle)
【荷叶】 héyè lotus leaf

**核** hé ①pit; stone: 桃～ peach-pit; peach-stone/ 无～葡萄干 seedless raisins ②nucleus: 细胞～ cell nucleus/ 原子～ atomic nucleus/ ～大国 nuclear power ③examine; check: ～准 check and approve; ratify
另见 hú

【核保护伞】 hébǎohùsǎn nuclear umbrella
【核爆炸】 hébàozhà nuclear explosion
【核打击力量】 hédǎjī lìliàng nuclear strike capability (或 force)
【核蛋白】 hédànbái 〈生化〉 nucleoprotein
【核弹头】 hédàntóu nuclear warhead

【核导弹】 hédǎodàn nuclear missile
【核定】 hédìng check and ratify; appraise and decide
【核动力】 hédònglì nuclear power
【核对】 héduì check: ～数字 check figures/ ～帐单 check a bill/ ～事实 check the facts
【核讹诈】 hé'ézhà nuclear blackmail
【核反应】 héfǎnyìng nuclear reaction ◇ ～堆 nuclear reactor
【核辐射】 héfúshè nuclear radiation
【核苷】 hégān 〈生化〉 nucleoside ◇ ～酸 nucleotide
【核果】 héguǒ 〈植〉 drupe
【核黄素】 héhuángsù 〈药〉 riboflavin; lactoflavin
【核火箭】 héhuǒjiàn nuclear rocket
【核计】 héjì assess; calculate: ～成本 assess the cost
【核聚变】 héjùbiàn nuclear fusion
【核扩散】 hékuòsàn nuclear proliferation
【核裂变】 hélièbiàn nuclear fission
【核垄断】 hélǒngduàn nuclear monopoly
【核能】 hénéng nuclear energy
【核潜艇】 héqiántǐng nuclear-powered submarine
【核燃料】 héránliào nuclear fuel
【核仁】 hérén ①〈生〉 nucleolus ② kernel (of a fruit-stone)
【核实】 héshí verify; check: ～的产量 verified output/ ～的材料 verified materials/ 请把这些数字～一下。Please check these figures.
【核试验】 héshìyàn nuclear test: 大气层(高空,地下)～ atmospheric (high-altitude, underground) nuclear test
【核素】 hésù ①〈化〉 nuclein ②〈物〉 nuclide
【核酸】 hésuān 〈化〉 nucleic acid ◇ ～酶 〈生化〉 nuclease/ ～内切酶 〈生化〉 endonuclease
【核算】 hésuàn business accounting: 成本～ cost accounting
【核算单位】 hésuàn dānwèi accounting unit: 基本～ basic accounting unit/ 独立～ independent accounting unit
【核桃】 hétao walnut
【核糖】 hétáng 〈生化〉 ribose
【核糖核酸】 hétáng hésuān 〈生化〉 ribonucleic acid; RNA: 脱氧～ deoxyribonucleic acid; DNA/ 信息～ messenger ribonucleic acid; m-RNA
【核威慑力量】 héwēishè lìliàng nuclear deterrent (power)
【核威胁】 héwēixié nuclear threat
【核微粒沾染】 héwēilì zhānrǎn contamination from nuclear fallout
【核武器】 héwǔqì nuclear weapon ◇ ～储备 stockpiling of nuclear weapons; nuclear weapons stockpile
【核销】 héxiāo cancel after verification
【核心】 héxīn nucleus; core; kernel: 中国共产党是全中国人民的领导～。The Chinese Communist Party is the core of leadership of the whole Chinese people./ 辩证法的～ the kernel of dialectics/ 党的～小组 leading Party nucleus/ 抓住问题的～ get to the heart of the matter ◇ ～力量 force at the core/ ～人物 key person; key figure
【核战争】 hézhànzhēng nuclear war (或 warfare)
【核装置】 hézhuāngzhì nuclear device
【核子】 hézǐ 〈物〉 nucleon ◇ ～学 nucleonics

**涸** hé 〈书〉 dry up
【涸辙之鲋】 hé zhé zhī fù a fish trapped in a dry rut — a person in a desperate situation

**盒** hé box; case: 一～火柴 a box of matches/ 铅笔～ pencil case; pencil box
【盒子】 hézi box; case; casket
【盒子枪】 héziqiāng 〈方〉 Mauser pistol

**颌** hé 〈书〉 jaw: 上(下)～ the upper (lower) jaw

**阖** hé 〈书〉 ① entire; whole: ～城 the whole town/ ～家 the whole family ② shut; close: ～户 close the door

**貉** hé racoon dog
另见 háo

**翮** hé ① shaft of a feather; quill ② wing (of a bird): 振～高飞 flap the wings and soar high into the sky

## hè

**吓** hè ① threaten; intimidate ②〈叹〉〔表示不满〕: ～, 怎么能干这种事呢? Tut-tut, how could you do that?
另见 xià

**和** hè ① join in the singing: 一唱百～。When one starts singing, all the others join in. ② compose a poem in reply: 奉～一首 write a poem in reply (to one sent by a friend, etc., using the same rhyme sequence)
另见 hé; huó; huò

**贺** hè ① congratulate ② (Hè) a surname
【贺词】 hècí speech (或 message) of congratulation; congratulations; greetings
【贺电】 hèdiàn message of congratulation; congratulatory telegram
【贺礼】 hèlǐ gift (as a token of congratulation)
【贺年】 hènián extend New Year greetings or pay a New Year call ◇ ～片 New Year card
【贺喜】 hèxǐ congratulate sb. on a happy occasion (e.g. a wedding, the birth of a child, etc.)
【贺信】 hèxìn congratulatory letter; letter of congratulation

**荷** hè 〈书〉 ① carry on one's shoulder or back: ～锄 carry a hoe on one's shoulder/ ～枪实弹 carry a loaded rifle ② burden; responsibility: 肩负重～ shoulder heavy responsibilities ③〔多用于书信〕 grateful; obliged: 无任感～。I'll be very much obliged./ 请早日示复为～。An early reply will be appreciated.
另见 hé
【荷载】 hèzài load

**喝** hè shout loudly: ～问 shout a question to/ 大～一声 give a loud shout
另见 hē
【喝彩】 hècǎi acclaim; cheer: 齐声～ cheer in chorus; cheer with one accord/ 博得全场～ bring the house down
【喝倒彩】 hè dàocǎi make catcalls; hoot; boo
【喝令】 hèlìng shout an order (或 command)

**褐** hè ①〈书〉 coarse cloth or clothing ② brown
【褐煤】 hèméi brown coal; lignite
【褐色土】 hèsètǔ drab soil
【褐铁矿】 hètiěkuàng brown iron ore; limonite
【褐藻】 hèzǎo 〈植〉 brown alga

**赫** hè ① conspicuous; grand: 显～ distinguished and influential; illustrious ②〈电〉 hertz: 千～ kilohertz/ 兆～ megahertz ③ (Hè) a surname
【赫赫】 hèhè illustrious; very impressive: ～战功 illustrious military exploits; brilliant military success/ ～有名的人物 an illustrious personage
【赫然】 hèrán ① impressively; awesomely: 一只猛虎～出现

在山坡上。To his consternation, a fierce tiger suddenly appeared on the mountain slope. ② terribly (angry): ～震怒 get into a terrible temper; fly into a violent rage

【赫哲族】 Hèzhézú the Hezhen (Hoche) nationality, living in Heilongjiang Province

【赫兹】 hèzī 〈电〉 hertz

**鹤** hè crane

【鹤发童颜】 hèfà-tóngyán white hair and ruddy complexion; healthy in old age; hale and hearty

【鹤立鸡群】 hè lì jīqún like a crane standing among chickens — stand head and shoulders above others

【鹤嘴锄】 hèzuǐchú pick; pickaxe; mattock

**壑** hè gully; big pool: 千山万～ innumerable mountains and valleys

## hēi

**黑** hēi ① black: ～发 black hair ② dark: 天～了。It's dark. ③ secret; shady: ～会 a clandestine meeting/ ～交易 shady deal ④ wicked; sinister: ～后台 sinister backstage boss/ ～秀才 vicious hack writer/ 修正主义～线 a sinister revisionist line ⑤ (Hēi) short for Heilongjiang Province

【黑暗】 hēi'àn dark: ～的角落 a dark corner/ 在～的旧社会 in the dark old society/ ～统治 dark rule; reactionary rule/ ～面 a dark aspect; the seamy side/ ～势力 forces of darkness; reactionary forces

【黑白】 hēi-bái black and white; right and wrong: ～分明 with black and white sharply contrasted; in sharp contrast/ 颠倒～ confound black and white; confuse right and wrong ◇ ～电视 black-and-white television/ ～片〈电影〉 black-and-white film

【黑板】 hēibǎn blackboard ◇ ～报 blackboard newspaper/ ～擦子 eraser

【黑帮】 hēibāng reactionary gang; sinister gang: 由新老反革命结成的～ a sinister crew of new and old-time counterrevolutionaries/ 反革命～ counterrevolutionary cabal

【黑不溜秋】 hēibuliūqiū 〈方〉 swarthy

【黑潮】 hēicháo 〈地〉 Kuroshio

【黑灯瞎火】 hēidēng-xiāhuǒ 〈口〉 dark; unlighted: ～的，我送你回家吧。It's dark. Let me see you home.

【黑店】 hēidiàn 〔旧小说用语〕 an inn run by brigands

【黑貂】 hēidiāo sable ◇ ～皮 sable fur

【黑鲷】 hēidiāo black porgy

【黑洞洞】 hēidōngdōng pitch-dark

【黑豆】 hēidòu black soya bean

【黑非洲】 Hēi Fēizhōu Black Africa

【黑粪】 hēifèn 〈医〉 melaena

【黑钙土】 hēigàitǔ 〈农〉 chernozem; black earth

【黑更半夜】 hēigēng-bànyè 〈口〉 in the dead of night

【黑咕隆咚】 hēigulōngdōng very dark; pitch-dark: 天还～的，他就起来了。He got up when it was still pitch-dark.

【黑管】 hēiguǎn 〈乐〉 clarinet

【黑光】 hēiguāng black light

【黑海】 Hēihǎi the Black Sea

【黑糊糊】 hēihūhū ① black; blackened: 墙熏得～的。The wall was blackened by smoke. ② rather dark; dusky: 屋子里～的。It's rather dark in the room. ③ indistinctly observable in the distance: 远处是一片～的树林。A dark mass of trees loomed in the distance.

【黑话】 hēihuà ① (bandits') argot; (thieves') cant ② double-talk; malicious words

【黑鲩】 hēihuàn black carp

【黑货】 hēihuò ① smuggled goods; contraband ② sinister stuff; trash

【黑胶布】 hēijiāobù 〈电〉 black tape; friction tape

【黑里康大号】 hēilǐkāng dàhào 〈乐〉 helicon

【黑瘤】 hēiliú 〈医〉 melanoma

【黑龙江】 Hēilóngjiāng ① the Heilongjiang River ② Heilongjiang (Province)

【黑麦】 hēimài rye

【黑面包】 hēimiànbāo black bread; brown bread; rye bread

【黑名单】 hēimíngdān blacklist

【黑幕】 hēimù inside story of a plot, shady deal, etc.: 揭穿～ expose a sinister project; tell the inside story of a plot, etc.

【黑啤酒】 hēipíjiǔ dark beer; stout

【黑漆漆】 hēiqīqī pitch-dark

【黑热病】 hēirèbìng kala-azar

【黑人】 hēirén Black people; Black; Negro: 美国～ Afro-American; Black American

【黑色】 hēisè black
◇ ～火药 black powder/ ～金属 ferrous metal/ ～素〈生化〉 melanin

【黑色人种】 hēisè rénzhǒng the black race

【黑市】 hēishì black market

【黑手】 hēishǒu a vicious person manipulating sb. or sth. from behind the scenes; evil backstage manipulator

【黑死病】 hēisǐbìng the plague

【黑穗病】 hēisuìbìng 〈农〉 smut

【黑陶】 hēitáo 〈考古〉 black pottery ◇ ～文化 black-pottery culture

【黑体】 hēitǐ ①〈物〉 blackbody ②〈印〉 boldface ◇ ～字 boldface type

【黑土】 hēitǔ black earth

【黑钨矿】 hēiwūkuàng wolframite

【黑心】 hēixīn black heart; evil mind

【黑信】 hēixìn 〈口〉 poison-pen letter

【黑猩猩】 hēixīngxing chimpanzee

【黑熊】 hēixióng black bear

【黑压压】 hēiyāyā a dense or dark mass of: 广场上～地挤满了人。The square was thronged with a dense crowd./ 远处～的一片，看不清是些什么东西。One couldn't make out what the dark mass was from a distance.

【黑眼镜】 hēiyǎnjìng sunglasses

【黑曜岩】 hēiyàoyán 〈矿〉 obsidian

【黑油油】 hēiyōuyōu jet-black; shiny black: ～的头发 shiny black hair

【黑黝黝】 hēiyǒuyǒu ① shiny black ② dim; dark: 四周～的。It's dark all around.

【黑鱼】 hēiyú snakeheaded fish; snakehead

【黑云母】 hēiyúnmǔ 〈矿〉 black mica; biotite

【黑枣】 hēizǎo dateplum persimmon (*Diospyros lotus*)

【黑子】 hēizǐ ① 〈书〉 black mole (on the skin) ② 〈天〉 sunspot

**嘿** hēi 〈叹〉 hey: ～！快走吧！Hey, hurry up!/ ～，咱们生产的机器可真不错呀！ Hey, the machine we made is really not bad./ ～，下雪了！ Why, it's snowing!

## hén

**痕** hén mark; trace: 刀～ a mark or scar left by a knife-cut/ 泪～ tear stains/ 伤～ a scar from a wound

【痕迹】 hénjì mark; trace; vestige: 轮子的～ wheel tracks/ 旧社会的～ vestiges of the old society

【痕量】 hénliàng 〈化〉 trace ◇ ～元素 trace elements/ ～杂

质 trace impurity

## hěn

**很** hěn 〈副〉 very; quite; awfully: 好得～ very good/ ～满意 feel very satisfied; feel quite pleased/ ～有道理 contain much truth; be quite correct

**狠** hěn ① ruthless; relentless: 凶～ ferocious and ruthless/ 比豺狼还～ more savage than a wolf ② suppress (one's feelings); harden (the heart) ③ firm; resolute: ～抓革命,猛促生产 vigorously promote revolution and production/ ～～打击歪风邪气 take vigorous measures to counter evil trends/ 就是要有这股～劲。This is the kind of fortitude we must have.

【狠毒】 hěndú vicious; venomous: 用心～ with vicious intent

【狠心】 hěnxīn cruel-hearted; heartless

## hèn

**恨** hèn ① hate: ～之入骨 hate sb. to the very marrow of one's bones/ ～得咬牙切齿 grind one's teeth with hatred/ 怀～在心 nurse hatred in one's heart/ 阶级仇,民族～ class hatred and national enmity ② regret: 遗～ eternal regret

【恨不得】 hènbude how one wishes one could; one would if one could; itch to: 我～一枪把敌机揍下来。How I wished I could bring the enemy plane down with one burst./ 他～马上投入战斗。He itched to plunge into the battle.

【恨事】 hènshì a matter for regret

【恨铁不成钢】 hèn tiě bù chéng gāng wish iron could turn into steel at once — set a high demand on somebody in the hope that he will improve

## hēng

**亨** hēng ① go smoothly ② 〈电〉 henry

【亨利】 hēnglì 〈电〉 henry: 微～ microhenry

【亨通】 hēngtōng go smoothly; be prosperous: 万事～。Everything is going smoothly.

**哼** hēng ① groan; snort: 痛得直～～ groan with pain/ 轻蔑地～了一声 give a snort of contempt ② hum; croon: 他一边走,一边～着曲子。He was humming a tune as he walked along./ ～着歌子哄孩子睡觉 croon the baby to sleep

另见 hng

【哼哧】 hēngchī 〈象〉 puff hard: 他跑得～～地直喘。He was puffing and blowing from running.

【哼儿哈儿】 hēngrhār 〈象〉 hem and haw: 他总是～的,就是不说句痛快话。He hemmed and hawed but wouldn't say anything definite.

【哼声】 hēngshēng 〈电〉 hum

【哼唷】 hēngyō 〈叹〉 heave ho; yo-heave-ho; yo-ho

**脝** hēng 见"膨脝" pénghēng

## héng

**恒** héng ① permanent; lasting: 永～ eternal; everlasting ② perseverance: 持之以～ persevere in (doing sth.) ③ usual; common; constant: ～言 common saying

【恒齿】 héngchǐ 〈生理〉 permanent tooth

【恒等】 héngděng 〈数〉 identically equal; identical ◇～式 identical equation; identity

【恒河沙数】 Hénghé shā shù as numerous as the sands of the Ganges; innumerable; countless

【恒量】 héngliàng 〈物〉 constant

【恒温】 héngwēn constant temperature ◇ ～动物 homoiothermal (或 warm-blooded) animal/ ～器 thermostat

【恒心】 héngxīn perseverance; constancy of purpose: 你要是没有～可学不好。Unless you persevere with a subject you can't hope to master it.

【恒星】 héngxīng 〈天〉 (fixed) star
◇～年(月、日) sidereal year (month, day)/ ～时 sidereal time/ ～天文学 stellar astronomy/ ～物理学 stellar physics/ ～系 stellar system; galaxy/ ～云 star cloud

【恒压器】 héngyāqì barostat

**珩** héng the top gem of a girdle-pendant (as worn by aristocrats and high officials in ancient China)

【珩床】 héngchuáng 〈机〉 honing machine

【珩磨】 héngmó 〈机〉 honing

**桁** héng 〈建〉 purlin

【桁架】 héngjià 〈建〉 truss ◇～桥 truss bridge

**鸻** héng 〈动〉 plover: 金～ golden plover

**横** héng ① horizontal; transverse: 纵～ vertical and horizontal/ 人行～道 (pedestrians') street crossing ② across; sideways: ～写 write words sideways/ ～渡太平洋的飞行 a trans-Pacific flight/ 车间里～挂着一幅大标语。A huge streamer was hung across the workshop. ③ move crosswise; traverse: ～刀跃马 gallop ahead with sword drawn/ 这条铁路～贯五省。The railway traverses five provinces. ④ unrestrainedly; turbulently: 江河～溢 turbulent waters overflowing their banks/ 老泪～流 tears flowing from aged eyes ⑤ violently; fiercely; flagrantly: ～加阻挠 wilfully obstruct/ ～加干涉 flagrantly interfere ⑥ horizontal stroke (in Chinese characters)

另见 hèng

【横波】 héngbō 〈物〉 transverse wave

【横冲直撞】 héngchōng-zhízhuàng push one's way by shoving or bumping; jostle and elbow one's way; dash around madly; barge about

【横断面】 héngduànmiàn cross (或 transverse) section

【横队】 héngduì rank; row: 排成三列～ line up three deep

【横幅】 héngfú ① horizontal scroll of painting or calligraphy ② banner; streamer: 欢迎群众举着～标语。The welcoming crowd carried banners with slogans on them.

【横格纸】 hénggézhǐ lined paper

【横膈膜】 hénggémó 〈生理〉 diaphragm

【横亘】 hénggèn lie across; span: 一座雄伟的大桥～在江上。A magnificent bridge spans the river.

【横巷】 hénghàng 〈矿〉 crosscut

【横结肠】 héngjiécháng 〈生理〉 transverse colon

【横跨】 héngkuà stretch over or across: 一道彩虹～天际。A rainbow arched across the sky.

【横梁】 héngliáng ① 〈建〉 crossbeam ② 〈汽车〉 cross member

【横眉】 héngméi frown; scowl: ～怒目 face others with frowning brows and angry eyes; dart fierce looks of hate/ ～冷对千夫指,俯首甘为孺子牛。Fierce-browed, I coolly defy a thousand pointing fingers, Head-bowed, like a willing ox I serve the children.

【横拍握法】 héngpāi wòfǎ 〈乒乓球〉 tennis grip; handshake grip

【横批】 héngpī a horizontal scroll bearing an inscription (usu. hung over a door and flanked by two vertical scrolls forming a couplet)

【横披】 héngpī a horizontal wall inscription; a horizontal hanging scroll

【横剖面】 héngpōumiàn cross section

【横七竖八】 héngqī-shùbā in disorder; at sixes and sevens; higgledy-piggledy: 院子里～地堆放着许多东西。The yard was cluttered up with all sorts of things.

【横切】 héngqiē crosscut ◇ ～锯 crosscut (saw)/ ～面 cross section

【横肉】 héngròu 〔多用于〕: 一脸～ look ugly and ferocious

【横扫】 héngsǎo sweep away; make a clean sweep of: ～千军如卷席 rolling back the enemy as we would a mat

【横生】 héngshēng ① grow wild: 蔓草～ be overgrown with weeds ② be overflowing with; be full of: 妙趣～ be full of wit and humour ③ happen unexpectedly

【横生枝节】 héngshēng zhījié ① side issues or new problems unexpectedly crop up ② raise obstacles; deliberately complicate an issue

【横竖】 héngshù 〈口〉 in any case; anyway: ～我要去的，不用给他打电话了。No need to ring him up. I'll be going there anyway.

【横挑鼻子竖挑眼】 héng tiāo bízi shù tiāo yǎn find fault in a petty manner; pick holes in sth.; nit-pick

【横尾翼】 héngwěiyì 〈航空〉 tail plane; horizontal stabilizer

【横纹肌】 héngwénjī 〈生理〉 striated muscle

【横向】 héngxiàng crosswise: ～进刀 〈机〉 cross (traverse) feed

【横心】 héngxīn steel one's heart; become desperate: 横下一条心 resolve to do sth. in desperation

【横行】 héngxíng run wild; run amuck; be on a rampage: ～一时 run wild for a time

【横行霸道】 héngxíng-bàdào ride roughshod; play the tyrant; tyrannize; domineer

【横征暴敛】 héngzhēng-bàoliǎn extort excessive taxes and levies; levy exorbitant taxes

【横轴】 héngzhóu 〈机〉 cross axle (或 shaft)

【横坐标】 héngzuòbiāo 〈数〉 abscissa

**衡** héng ① the graduated arm of a steelyard ② weighing apparatus ③ weigh; measure; judge: ～情度理 considering the circumstances and judging by common sense; all things considered

【衡量】 héngliang weigh; measure; judge: ～得失 weigh up the gains and losses/ 用政治标准来～ measure sth. or judge sb. by political criteria/ 请你～一下这件事该怎么办。Will you please consider what to do about it?

【衡器】 héngqì weighing apparatus

**蘅** héng 见"杜蘅" dùhéng

## hèng

**横** hèng ① harsh and unreasonable; perverse: ～话 harsh, unreasonable words/ 发～ act in an unreasonable (或 brutal) way ② unexpected: ～事 an untoward accident
另见 héng

【横暴】 hèngbào perverse and violent

【横财】 hèngcái ill-gotten wealth (或 gains): 发～ get rich by foul means

【横祸】 hènghuò unexpected calamity; sudden misfortune

【横死】 hèngsǐ die a violent death; meet with a sudden death

## hng

**哼** hng 〈叹〉〔表示不满或怀疑〕 humph: ～，谁信你的！Humph! Who believes what you say?
另见 hēng

## hōng

**轰** hōng ① 〈象〉 bang; boom: ～的一声，敌人的碉堡给炸飞了。The enemy pillbox was blown up with a bang./ ～！～！～！一连串爆破声震撼山谷。Boom! Boom! Boom! A series of explosions shook the valley. ② rumble; bombard; explode: 雷～电闪。Thunder rumbled and lightning flashed./ 万炮齐～ ten thousand cannons booming ③ shoo away; drive off: ～麻雀 shoo away the sparrows/ ～下台 hoot sb. off the platform; oust sb. from office or power/ 把他～出去。Throw him out.

【轰动】 hōngdòng cause a sensation; make a stir: ～全国 cause a sensation throughout the country/ ～一时 create a furore/ 全场～ make a stir in the audience (或 in the hall)

【轰轰烈烈】 hōnghōnglièliè on a grand and spectacular scale; vigorous; dynamic: ～的农业学大寨运动 a mighty movement to learn from Dazhai in agriculture

【轰击】 hōngjī shell; bombard: ～敌人阵地 shell enemy positions/ 中子～ 〈物〉 neutron bombardment

【轰隆】 hōnglōng 〈象〉 rumble; roll: 雷声～～地响。Thunder rumbled./ ～的机器声 the hum of machines

【轰鸣】 hōngmíng thunder; roar: 马达～。Motors roared./ 雷声～。There was a peal of thunder.

【轰然】 hōngrán with a loud crash (或 bang)

【轰炸】 hōngzhà bomb
◇ ～机 bomber/ ～瞄准具 bombsight/ ～误差 bombing error

**哄** hōng ① 〈象〉 roars of laughter ② hubbub
另见 hǒng; hòng

【哄传】 hōngchuán (of rumours) circulate widely: 这个消息不久就～开了。It was not long before the news was widely circulated.

【哄动】 hōngdòng cause a sensation; make a stir

【哄然】 hōngrán boisterous; uproarious: ～大笑 burst into uproarious laughter

【哄抬】 hōngtái drive up (prices)

【哄堂大笑】 hōngtáng dàxiào the whole room rocking with laughter

**訇** hōng ① 〈书〉 loud noise: ～然 with a loud crash ② 见"阿訇" āhōng

**烘** hōng ① dry or warm by the fire: ～手 warm one's hands at the fire/ 把湿衣服～一～ dry wet clothes by the fire/ ～面包 bake bread ② set off: ～衬 set off by contrast; serve as a foil to

【烘焙】 hōngbèi cure (tea or tobacco leaves)

【烘干】 hōnggān 〈化〉 stoving

【烘缸】 hōnggāng dryer

【烘烤】 hōngkǎo toast; bake

【烘漆】 hōngqī baking finish; stoving finish

【烘丝机】 hōngsījī cut-tobacco drier

【烘托】 hōngtuō ①(in painting) add shading around an object to make it stand out ②set off by contrast; throw into sharp relief: ～出音乐的主题 set off the *leitmotiv* by contrast
【烘箱】 hōngxiāng oven
【烘相器】 hōngxiàngqì 〈摄〉 print drier
【烘云托月】 hōngyún-tuōyuè paint clouds to set off the moon; provide a foil to set off a character or incident in a literary work: 收到了～的艺术效果 achieve the artistic effect of prominence through contrast

**薨** hōng (of feudal lords or high officials) die; pass away

## hóng

**弘** hóng ①great; grand; magnificent ②enlarge; expand
【弘大】 hóngdà grand

**红** hóng ①red: ～墙 a red ochre wall/ 他的眼睛都熬～了。His eyes become bloodshot from lack of sleep./ 脸上～一阵白一阵 flush and turn pale by turns ②revolutionary; red: ～五月 the red month of May/ 一颗～心永向党 with a red heart always loyal to the Party/ 又～又专 both red and expert; both socialist-minded and professionally proficient ③red cloth, bunting, etc. used on festive occasions: 披～ wear red sashes or cloth as a sign of honour, festivity, etc./ 挂～ hang up red festoons ④symbol of success: 开门～ get off to a good start ⑤bonus; dividend: 分～ distribute or draw dividends
另见 gōng
【红白事】 hóng-báishì weddings and funerals 又作"红白喜事"
【红斑】 hóngbān 〈医〉 erythema ◇ ～狼疮 lupus erythematosus
【红榜】 hóngbǎng honour roll (或 board)
【红宝石】 hóngbǎoshí ruby
【红菜头】 hóngcàitóu beetroot
【红茶】 hóngchá black tea
【红潮】 hóngcháo blush; flush
【红尘】 hóngchén 〈旧〉 the world of mortals; human society: 看破～ see through the vanity of the world; be disillusioned with this human world
【红丹】 hóngdān 〈化〉 red lead; minium ◇ ～漆 red lead paint
【红电气石】 hóngdiànqìshí 〈矿〉 rubellite
【红豆】 hóngdòu ①ormosia ②love pea
【红汞】 hónggǒng 〈药〉 mercurochrome
【红骨顶】 hónggǔdǐng 〈动〉 moorhen
【红光满面】 hóngguāng mǎnmiàn one's face glowing with health; in ruddy health
【红果】 hóngguǒ 〈方〉 the fruit of large Chinese hawthorn; haw
【红海】 Hónghǎi the Red Sea
【红鹤】 hónghè ibis
【红狐】 hónghú red fox
【红花】 hónghuā 〈中药〉 safflower
【红火】 hónghuo 〈方〉 flourishing; prosperous: 这个生产队越办越～。The production team is becoming more and more prosperous.
【红脚鹬】 hóngjiǎoyù redshank
【红军】 Hóngjūn ①〈简〉(中国工农红军) the Chinese Workers' and Peasants' Red Army (1928-1937); the Red Army ②Red Army man
【红利】 hónglì bonus; extra dividend
【红脸】 hóngliǎn ①blush: 这小孩跟生人说话爱～。This child often blushes when speaking to strangers. ②flush with anger; get angry: 他俩从来没有红过脸。There has never been a cross word between the two of them. ③red face, face painting in Beijing opera, etc., traditionally for the heroic or the honest
【红磷】 hónglín red phosphorus
【红铃虫】 hónglíngchóng pink bollworm
【红领巾】 hónglǐngjīn ①red scarf (worn by Young Pioneers) ②Young Pioneer
【红领章】 hónglǐngzhāng red collar tab (as on PLA uniforms)
【红绿灯】 hónglǜdēng traffic light; traffic signal
【红麻】 hóngmá 〈植〉 bluish dogbane (*Apocynum venetum*)
【红霉素】 hóngméisù 〈药〉 erythromycin
【红焖】 hóngmèn stew in soy sauce: ～鸡 stewed chicken
【红米】 hóngmǐ red rice
【红模子】 hóngmúzi a sheet of paper with red characters printed on it, to be traced over with a brush by children learning calligraphy
【红木】 hóngmù padauk
【红娘鱼】 hóngniángyú sea robin; red gurnard
【红旗】 hóngqí red flag or banner (often as a symbol of the proletarian revolution or of an advanced unit): 在～下长大 be brought up under the red flag; grow up in socialist society/ 工业战线上的一面～ a red banner (或 pacesetter) on the industrial front
◇ ～单位 red-banner unit; advanced unit/ ～竞赛 emulation drive with red banners as awards; red banner emulation/ ～手 red-banner pacesetter
【红人】 hóngrén a favourite with sb. in power; fair-haired boy
【红润】 hóngrùn ruddy; rosy: 脸色～ ruddy complexion; rosy cheeks
【红三叶草】 hóngsānyècǎo red clover
【红色】 hóngsè ①red ②revolutionary; red: ～政权 red political power
【红杉】 hóngshān Chinese larch
【红烧】 hóngshāo braise in soy sauce: ～肉 pork braised in brown sauce
【红十字会】 Hóngshízìhuì the Red Cross
【红薯】 hóngshǔ sweet potato
【红树】 hóngshù mangrove
【红松】 hóngsōng Korean pine
【红糖】 hóngtáng brown sugar
【红陶】 hóngtáo red pottery; terra-cotta
【红藤】 hóngténg Sargent gloryvine (*Sargentodoxa cuneata*)
【红通通】 hóngtōngtōng bright red; glowing: ～的火苗 glowing red flames/ 他脸儿晒得～的。His face is aglow from exposure to the sun. 又作"红彤彤"
【红土】 hóngtǔ red soil (或 earth)
【红外激射】 hóngwài jīshè 〈物〉 iraser
【红外线】 hóngwàixiàn 〈物〉 infrared ray
◇ ～辐射 infrared radiation/ ～扫描装置 infrared scanner/ ～探测器 infrared detector/ ～照相 infrared photography
【红卫兵】 Hóngwèibīng ①the Red Guards ②Red Guard
【红细胞】 hóngxìbāo red blood cell; erythrocyte ◇ ～计数 red cell count
【红线】 hóngxiàn red line: 贯穿全书的一条～ a red thread running through the book
【红小兵】 Hóngxiǎobīng ①the Little Red Guards ②Little Red Guard
【红小豆】 hóngxiǎodòu red bean

【红新月会】 Hóngxīnyuèhuì the Red Crescent
【红星】 hóngxīng red star (a symbol of the proletarian revolution): ～帽徽 red star cap insignia (of PLA soldiers)
【红血球】 hóngxuèqiú red blood cell; erythrocyte
【红眼】 hóngyǎn ① pinkeye ② become infuriated; see red
【红艳艳】 hóngyànyàn brilliant red
【红药水】 hóngyàoshuǐ mercurochrome
【红叶】 hóngyè red autumnal leaves (of the maple, etc.)
【红衣主教】 hóngyī zhǔjiào 〈天主教〉 cardinal
【红医工】 hóngyīgōng red medical worker (a name for barefoot doctors in factories, mines, etc.)
【红缨枪】 hóngyīngqiāng red-tasselled spear
【红鱼】 hóngyú (red) snapper
【红运】 hóngyùn good luck
【红晕】 hóngyùn blush; flush: 脸上泛出～ one's face blushing scarlet
【红藻】 hóngzǎo red alga
【红蜘蛛】 hóngzhīzhū red spider (mite); spider mite
【红肿】 hóngzhǒng red and swollen
【红柱石】 hóngzhùshí 〈地〉 andalusite
【红装】 hóngzhuāng 〈书〉 ① gay feminine attire: 中华儿女多奇志，不爱～爱武装。 China's daughters have high-aspiring minds, They love their battle array, not silks and satins. ② young woman

**宏** hóng great; grand; magnificent
【宏大】 hóngdà grand; great: 规模～ on a grand scale/ ～的志愿 great aspirations/ 一支～的马克思主义理论队伍 a mighty contingent of Marxist theoretical workers/ 建设～的科学技术队伍 build a mammoth force of scientific and technical personnel
【宏观】 hóngguān 〈物〉 macroscopic ◇ ～结构 macrostructure/ ～世界 macrocosm
【宏论】 hónglùn informed opinion; intelligent view
【宏图】 hóngtú great plan; grand prospect: 发展国民经济的～ great plans for developing the national economy
【宏伟】 hóngwěi magnificent; grand: ～的人民大会堂 the magnificent Great Hall of the People/ ～的前景 grand prospects/ 共产主义的～目标 the magnificent goal of communism
【宏愿】 hóngyuàn great aspirations; noble ambition
【宏旨】 hóngzhǐ main theme; leading idea of an article: 无关～ insignificant

**泓** hóng ① (of water) deep ② 〈量〉: 一～清泉 a clear spring/ 一～秋水 an expanse of limpid water in autumn

**洪** hóng ① big; vast: ～涛 big waves ② flood: 防～ control or prevent flood ③ (Hóng) a surname
【洪大】 hóngdà loud: ～的回声 resounding echoes
【洪都拉斯】 Hóngdūlāsī Honduras ◇ ～人 Honduran
【洪泛区】 hóngfànqū floodplain; flooded area
【洪峰】 hóngfēng flood peak
【洪亮】 hóngliàng loud and clear; sonorous: 嗓音～ a sonorous voice
【洪量】 hóngliàng ① magnanimity; generosity ② great capacity for liquor
【洪流】 hóngliú mighty torrent; powerful current: 时代的～ the powerful current of the times/ 革命的～ the mighty torrent of the revolution/ 反对霸权主义的～汹涌澎湃。A tidal wave against hegemonism is surging forward.
【洪炉】 hónglú great furnace: 在革命的～里锻炼成长 be tempered in the mighty furnace of revolution
【洪脉】 hóngmài 〈中医〉 pulse beating like waves; full pulse
【洪水】 hóngshuǐ flood; floodwater ◇ ～位 flood level
【洪水猛兽】 hóngshuǐ-měngshòu fierce floods and savage beasts — great scourges
【洪钟】 hóngzhōng 〈书〉 large bell: 声如～ have a stentorian (或 sonorous) voice

**虹** hóng rainbow
【虹膜】 hóngmó 〈生理〉 iris ◇ ～炎 iritis
【虹吸管】 hóngxīguǎn siphon
【虹吸现象】 hóngxī xiànxiàng siphonage
【虹雉】 hóngzhì monal

**魟** hóng stingray

**鸿** hóng ① swan goose ② 〈书〉 letter: 远方来～ a letter from afar ③ great; grand: ～图 great plans; grand prospects
【鸿沟】 hónggōu wide gap; chasm: 不可逾越的～ an unbridgeable gap; an impassable chasm
【鸿鹄之志】 hónghú zhī zhì lofty ambition; high aspirations
【鸿毛】 hóngmáo 〈书〉 a goose feather — something very light or insignificant
【鸿雁】 hóngyàn swan goose

## hǒng

**哄** hǒng ① fool; humbug: 你这是～我，我不信。 You're kidding me; I don't believe it. ② coax; humour: ～孩子吃药 coax a child to take medicine/ 她很会～孩子。 She knows how to handle children. 或 She has a way with children.
另见 hōng; hòng
【哄骗】 hǒngpiàn cheat; humbug; hoodwink

## hòng

**讧** hòng 见"内讧" nèihòng

**哄** hòng uproar; horseplay: 一～而散 break up in an uproar
另见 hōng; hǒng

## hōu

**齁** hōu ① sickeningly sweet or salty: 这个菜咸得～人。 This dish is much too salty. ② 〈方〉 very; awfully: ～苦 very bitter/ 天气～热。 It's awfully hot.
【齁声】 hōushēng the sound of snoring; snore

## hóu

**侯** hóu ① marquis ② a nobleman or a high official: ～门似海。 The mansions of the nobility were inaccessible to the common man. ③ (Hóu) a surname
【侯爵】 hóujué marquis ◇ ～夫人 marquise

**喉** hóu larynx; throat
【喉擦音】 hóucāyīn 〈语〉 guttural fricative
【喉结】 hóujié 〈生理〉 Adam's apple
【喉镜】 hóujìng 〈医〉 laryngoscope
【喉咙】 hóulóng throat: ～痛 have a sore throat
【喉塞音】 hóusèyīn 〈语〉 glottal stop
【喉痧】 hóushā 〈中医〉 scarlet fever

【喉舌】 hóushé mouthpiece: 人民的～ the mouthpiece of the people
【喉头】 hóutóu larynx; throat
【喉炎】 hóuyán laryngitis

**猴** hóu ①monkey ②clever boy; smart chap
【猴面包树】 hóumiànbāoshù 〈植〉 monkey-bread tree; baobab
【猴皮筋儿】 hóupíjīnr 〈口〉 rubber band
【猴头】 hóutóu 〈植〉hedgehog hydnum (*Hydnum erinaceus*)
【猴戏】 hóuxì a show by a performing monkey; monkey show
【猴子】 hóuzi monkey

**瘊** hóu wart
【瘊子】 hóuzi wart

**篌** hóu 见"箜篌" kōnghóu

**骺** hóu epiphysis

## hǒu

**吼** hǒu roar; howl: 狮～ the roar of a lion/ 远方传来大炮的～声。Guns rumbled in the distance./ 石油工人一声～，地球也要抖三抖。The oil workers let out one mighty roar, and the earth shakes three times with fear.

## hòu

**后** hòu ①behind; back; rear: 屋～ behind (或 at the back of) a house/ ～排 back row/ 敌～ the enemy's rear/ ～五名 the last five (persons) ②after; afterwards; later: 课～ after class/ 不久以～ soon afterwards; before long ③offspring: 无～ without male offspring; without issue ④empress; queen
【后半】 hòubàn latter half; second half: ～场球赛 the second half of the game
◇ ～生 the latter half of one's life/ ～天 afternoon/ ～夜 the second half of the night; the small hours
【后备】 hòubèi reserve: 留有～ keep sth. in reserve
◇ ～部队 reserve units/ ～基金 reserve fund/ ～力量 reserve forces
【后备军】 hòubèijūn ①reserves ②reserve force: 产业～ industrial reserve army; industrial reserve; reserve army of labour
【后辈】 hòubèi ①younger generation ②posterity
【后步】 hòubù room for manoeuvre: 留～ leave sufficient room for manoeuvre
【后尘】 hòuchén 〈书〉〔多用于〕: 步人～ follow in sb.'s footsteps
【后处理】 hòuchǔlǐ ①〈化〉aftertreatment ②〈纺〉finishing
【后代】 hòudài ①later periods (in history); later ages ②later generations; descendants; posterity: 为～着想 for the sake of future generations; in the interest of future generations ③〈生〉progeny
【后灯】 hòudēng 〈汽车〉 taillight; tail lamp
【后爹】 hòudiē 〈口〉 stepfather
【后盾】 hòudùn backing; backup force: 坚强的～ powerful backing
【后发制人】 hòu fā zhì rén gain mastery by striking only after the enemy has struck
【后方】 hòufāng rear: ～工作 rear-area work; work in the rear
◇ ～留守处 rear headquarters/ ～医院 base (或 rear) hospital/ ～基地 rear base/ ～勤务 rear service; logistics (service)
【后跟】 hòugēn heel (of a shoe or sock)
【后顾】 hòugù ①turn back (to take care of sth.): 无暇～ have no time to look after things one has left behind/ ～之忧 fear of disturbance in the rear; trouble back at home ②look back (on the past): ～与前瞻 look back to the past and ahead into the future
【后滚翻】 hòugǔnfān 〈体〉 backward roll
【后果】 hòuguǒ consequence; aftermath: 承担～ accept the consequences/ ～不堪设想。The consequences would be too ghastly to contemplate. 或 The consequences would be disastrous./ 检查制度不严，会造成严重的～。A lax checking system may have serious consequences.
【后汉】 Hòu Hàn ①见"东汉" Dōng Hàn ②the Later Han Dynasty (947-950), one of the Five Dynasties
【后患】 hòuhuàn future trouble: 根除～ dig up the root of (或 remove the cause of) future trouble/ ～无穷 no end of trouble for the future
【后悔】 hòuhuǐ regret; repent: ～不已 be overcome with regret/ ～莫及 too late to repent
【后会有期】 hòuhuì yǒu qī we'll meet again some day
【后记】 hòujì postscript
【后继】 hòujì succeed; carry on: 无产阶级革命事业～有人。There is no lack of successors to carry on the revolutionary cause of the proletariat.
【后脚】 hòujiǎo ①the rear foot (in walking): 前脚一滑，～也站不稳。As the front foot slipped, the rear foot became unsteady. ②〔与"前脚"连说表示紧接在别人后面〕: 我前脚到车站，他～就赶到了。Immediately after I got to the station, he arrived.
【后襟】 hòujīn the back of a Chinese robe or jacket
【后进】 hòujìn lagging behind; less advanced; backward: 见～就帮 ready to help those who lag behind/ ～赶先进 the less advanced striving to catch up with the more advanced
◇ ～队 a brigade or team that lags behind
【后劲】 hòujìn ①delayed effect; aftereffect: 这酒～大。This wine has a strong delayed effect. ②reserve strength; stamina: 他干活有～。He has staying power when he's doing a job.
【后晋】 Hòu Jìn the Later Jin Dynasty (936-946), one of the Five Dynasties
【后景】 hòujǐng background
【后空翻】 hòukōngfān 〈体〉 backward somersault
【后来】 hòulái afterwards; later: ～怎么样? What happened afterwards?/ ～的情况好多了。Things got much better later on. ◇ ～人 successors
【后来居上】 hòu lái jū shàng the latecomers surpass the old-timers
【后梁】 Hòu Liáng the Later Liang Dynasty (907-923), one of the Five Dynasties
【后路】 hòulù ①communication lines to the rear; route of retreat: 抄敌人～ attack the enemy from the rear/ 切断敌人～ cut off the enemy's route of retreat ②room for manoeuvre; a way of escape: 留条～ leave oneself a way of escape; leave oneself a way out
【后掠角】 hòulüèjiǎo 〈航空〉 sweep angle; sweepback
【后掠翼】 hòulüèyì 〈航空〉 swept-back wing
【后轮】 hòulún rear wheel
【后妈】 hòumā 〈口〉 stepmother
【后门】 hòumén ①back door (或 gate): 大院的～ the back gate of a compound ②backdoor (或 backstairs) influence: 走～儿 get in by the "back door"; get sth. done through

pull
【后面】 hòumian ①at the back; in the rear; behind: ～还有座位。There are vacant seats at the back. ②later: 这个问题我～还要讲。I'll come back to this question later.
【后脑】 hòunǎo 〈生理〉 hindbrain; rhombencephalon
【后脑勺子】 hòunǎoshǎozi 〈方〉 the back of the head
【后年】 hòunián the year after next
【后娘】 hòuniáng 〈口〉 stepmother
【后怕】 hòupà fear after the event: 事过之后,我倒真有些～。After it was all over, I became really scared.
【后排】 hòupái back row: ～座位 back row seats
【后期】 hòuqī later stage; later period: 解放战争～ the later stage of the War of Liberation/ 十九世纪四十年代～ the late 1840s
【后起】 hòuqǐ (of people of talent) of new arrivals; of the younger generation: ～的乒坛好手 the younger generation of crack table-tennis players/ ～的青年作家 budding young writers/ ～之秀 an up-and-coming youngster; a promising young person
【后桥】 hòuqiáo 〈汽车〉 rear (或 back) axle ◇ ～壳 rear axle housing
【后勤】 hòuqín rear service; logistics
◇ ～部 rear-service department; logistics department (或 command)/ ～部队 rear-service units; rear services/ ～部部长 director of the logistics department/ ～机关 rear-service establishments/ ～基地 logistics base; rear supply base/ ～人员 rear-service personnel/ ～支援 logistic support
【后人】 hòurén ①later generations ②posterity; descendants
【后任】 hòurèn successor
【后三角队形】 hòusānjiǎo duìxíng 〈军〉 V formation
【后晌】 hòushǎng 〈方〉 afternoon
【后晌】 hòushang 〈方〉 evening ◇ ～饭 supper
【后身】 hòushēn ①the back of a person: 我只看见个～,认不清是谁。I couldn't make out who he was as I only saw his back. ②the back of a garment: 这件衬衫的～太长了。The back of the shirt is too long.
【后生可畏】 hòushēng kě wèi a youth is to be regarded with respect — the younger generation will surpass the older
【后生】 hòusheng 〈方〉 ①young man; lad ②having a youthful appearance: 他长得～,看不出是四十岁的人。He's forty but looks much younger.
【后世】 hòushì ①later ages ②later generations ◇ ～子孙 descendants; posterity
【后事】 hòushì ①〔多见于章回小说〕 what happened afterwards: 欲知～如何,且听下回分解。If you want to know what happened afterwards, read the next chapter. ②funeral affairs: 料理～ make arrangements for a funeral
【后视镜】 hòushìjìng 〈汽车〉 rearview (或 rear-vision) mirror
【后视图】 hòushìtú 〈机〉 back view; rearview
【后手】 hòushǒu ①defensive position (in chess) ②room for manoeuvre; a way of escape
【后熟作用】 hòushú zuòyòng 〈农〉 afterripening
【后送】 hòusòng 〈军〉 evacuation
【后台】 hòutái ①backstage ②backstage supporter; behind-the-scenes backer: ～很硬 have very strong backing ◇ ～老板 backstage boss
【后唐】 Hòu Táng the Later Tang Dynasty (923-936), one of the Five Dynasties
【后天】 hòutiān ①day after tomorrow: 大～ three days from today ②postnatal; acquired: 知识是～获得的,不是先天就有的。Knowledge is acquired, not innate. ◇ ～性免疫 acquired immunity
【后头】 hòutou 见"后面"
【后退】 hòutuì draw back; fall back; retreat: 主动～,以便歼灭更多敌人 retreat on one's own initiative in order to wipe out more enemy troops/ 遇到困难决不～ never shrink from difficulties
【后卫】 hòuwèi ①〈军〉 rear guard ②〈足球〉 full back: 左～ left back/ 右～ right back ③〈篮球〉 guard ◇ ～战斗 rear-guard action
【后续部队】 hòuxù bùduì 〈军〉 follow-up units
【后续会议】 hòuxù huìyì follow-up meeting
【后悬】 hòuxuán 〈汽车〉 rear overhang
【后遗症】 hòuyízhèng sequelae: 脑震荡～ sequelae of cerebral concussion
【后裔】 hòuyì descendant; offspring
【后影】 hòuyǐng the shape of a person or thing as seen from the back
【后援】 hòuyuán reinforcements; backup force; backing
【后院】 hòuyuàn backyard
【后者】 hòuzhě the latter
【后肢】 hòuzhī 〈动〉 hind legs
【后周】 Hòu Zhōu the Later Zhou Dynasty (951-960), one of the Five Dynasties
【后轴】 hòuzhóu rear axle
【后缀】 hòuzhuì 〈语〉 suffix
【后坐力】 hòuzuòlì 〈军〉 recoil: 无～炮 recoilless gun
【后座议员】 hòuzuò yìyuán backbencher

厚 hòu ①thick: ～木板 a thick plank/ ～棉衣 a heavy padded coat/ 一尺～的雪 snow one *chi* deep ②deep; profound: 深情～谊 profound friendship ③kind; magnanimous: 忠～ honest and kind ④large; generous: ～利 large profits/ ～礼 generous gifts ⑤rich or strong in flavour: 酒味很～。The wine tastes strong./ ～味 rich (或 greasy) food ⑥favour; stress: ～此薄彼 favour one and be prejudiced against the other
【厚薄】 hòubó thickness: ～合适。It's just the right thickness. ◇ ～规 〈机〉 feeler (gauge)
【厚道】 hòudao honest and kind
【厚度】 hòudù thickness
【厚墩墩】 hòudūndūn very thick: ～的棉大衣 a heavy padded overcoat
【厚古薄今】 hòu gǔ bó jīn stress the past, not the present
【厚今薄古】 hòu jīn bó gǔ stress the present, not the past
【厚脸皮】 hòuliǎnpí thick-skinned; brazen; cheeky: 厚着脸皮说 have the nerve to say
【厚朴】 hòupò 〈中药〉 the bark of official magnolia (*Magnolia officinalis*)
【厚漆】 hòuqī paste paint
【厚实】 hòushi ①〈口〉 thick: 这布挺～。This cloth is very thick./ ～的被褥 thick, heavy quilts and mattresses ②〈方〉 abundant; rich: 储备～ abundant reserves
【厚望】 hòuwàng great expectations: 不负～ live up to sb.'s expectations; not let sb. down
【厚颜无耻】 hòuyán-wúchǐ impudent; brazen; shameless
【厚意】 hòuyì kind thought; kindness: 多谢你的～。Thank you for your kindness.

逅 hòu 见"邂逅" xièhòu

候 hòu ①wait; await: 请稍～一会儿。Please wait a moment./ ～领 to be kept until claimed ②inquire after: 致～ send one's regards ③time; season: 时～ time/ 季～ season ④condition; state: 症～ symptom
【候补】 hòubǔ be a candidate (for a vacancy); be an alternate: 中共中央政治局～委员 an alternate member of the Political Bureau of the Central Committee of the CPC

【候车室】 hòuchēshì waiting room (in a railway or bus station)
【候光】 hòuguāng 〈书〉〈敬〉await the honour of your presence (at a dinner party, etc.)
【候机室】 hòujīshì airport lounge or waiting room
【候教】 hòujiào 〈敬〉await your instructions
【候鸟】 hòuniǎo migratory bird; migrant
【候审】 hòushěn 〈法〉await trial
【候选人】 hòuxuǎnrén candidate: 提出～ nominate candidates ◇ ～名单 list of candidates/ ～资格 qualifications for standing for election
【候诊】 hòuzhěn wait to see the doctor ◇ ～室 waiting room (in a hospital)

**鲎** hòu king (或 horseshoe) crab
【鲎虫】 hòuchóng apus

## hū

**乎** hū ①〈书〉〈助〉〔表示疑问或揣度〕: 一之为甚，其可再～? Once is more than enough. How can you do it again?/ 成败之机，其在斯～? Does not success or failure hinge on this? ②〔动词后缀〕: 合～客观规律 conform to an objective law/ 出～意料 exceed one's expectations; be beyond one's expectations/ 超～寻常 be out of the ordinary ③〔形容词或副词后缀〕: 巍巍～ towering; lofty/ 确～重要 very important indeed

**戏** hū 〈方〉cover: 小苗都快让草～住了，赶快锄吧。Let's start hoeing at once. The young shoots are almost choked by the weeds.

**呼** hū ① breathe out; exhale: ～出二氧化碳 exhale carbon dioxide ② shout; cry out: ～口号 shout slogans ③ call: 直～其名 address sb. disrespectfully (by name)/ ～之即来，挥之即去 have sb. at one's beck and call ④〈象〉: 北风～～地吹。A north wind is whistling.
【呼哧】 hūchī 〈象〉: ～～直喘 puff and blow 又作"呼蚩"
【呼风唤雨】 hūfēng-huànyǔ ① summon wind and rain — control the forces of nature ② stir up trouble
【呼喊】 hūhǎn call out; shout
【呼号】 hūháo wail; cry out in distress: 奔走～ go around crying for help
【呼号】 hūhào ①〈讯〉 call sign; call letters ② catchword (of an organization)
【呼和浩特】 Hūhéhàotè Huhhot (Huhehot)
【呼唤】 hūhuàn call; shout to: 祖国在～我们! Our country is calling us.
【呼叫】 hūjiào ① call out; shout ②〈讯〉 call ◇ ～灯 calling lamp/ ～信号 calling signal
【呼救】 hūjiù call for help
【呼啦】 hūlā 〈象〉: 风卷红旗～～地响。The red flags are flapping in the wind. 又作"呼喇"
【呼噜】 hūlū 〈象〉: 他喉咙里～～地响。He's a bit wheezy.
【呼噜】 hūlu 〈口〉 snore: 打～ snore
【呼朋引类】 hūpéng-yǐnlèi gang up
【呼哨】 hūshào whistle: 打～ give a whistle
【呼声】 hūshēng cry; voice: 群众的～ the voice of the masses/ 被压迫人民的正义～ the just demand of the oppressed people/ 世界舆论的强大～ the powerful voice of world opinion
【呼天抢地】 hūtiān-qiāngdì lament to heaven and knock one's head on earth — utter cries of anguish
【呼吸】 hūxī breathe; respire: ～新鲜空气 have a breath of fresh air/ ～急促 be short of breath/ ～困难 breathe with difficulty; lose one's breath ◇ ～道 respiratory tract/ ～率 respiratory rate/ ～器 respirator/ ～系统 respiratory system
【呼啸】 hūxiào whistle; scream; whizz: 子弹～而过。A bullet whizzed past./ 寒风～。A cold wind is whistling.
【呼延】 Hūyán a surname
【呼应】 hūyìng echo; work in concert with: 遥相～ echo each other over a distance; echo from afar
【呼吁】 hūyù appeal; call on: ～团结 appeal for unity ◇ ～书 letter of appeal; appeal
【呼之欲出】 hū zhī yù chū seem ready to come out at one's call (said of lifelike figures in pictures or characters in novels) — be vividly portrayed

**忽** hū ① neglect; overlook; ignore ② suddenly: ～发奇想 suddenly have a strange idea
【忽而】 hū'ér now..., now...: ～哭，～笑 cry and laugh by turns/ ～主张这个，～主张那个 advocate one thing today and another tomorrow
【忽…忽…】 hū...hū... now..., now...: 情绪忽高忽低 be in high spirits one moment and in low spirits the next; be subject to sudden changes of mood/ 天气忽冷忽热。The weather is cold one minute and hot the next./ 镜头忽远忽近。Sometimes there are long shots, sometimes close-ups./ 灯光忽明忽暗。The lights keep flickering.
【忽略】 hūlüè neglect; overlook; lose sight of: 我们在注意主要矛盾的同时，不可～次要矛盾。While paying attention to the main contradiction, we should not neglect the secondary ones.
【忽然】 hūrán 〈副〉 suddenly; all of a sudden
【忽视】 hūshì ignore; overlook; neglect: 不可～的力量 a force not to be ignored; a force to be reckoned with/ 不应～困难。We should not overlook the difficulties./ 不要强调一面而～另一面。Don't stress one aspect to the neglect of another.
【忽悠】 hūyou 〈方〉 flicker: 渔船上的灯火～～的。Lights flickered on the fishing boats.

**烀** hū stew in shallow water

**惚** hū 见"恍惚" huǎnghū

**糊** hū plaster: 用灰把墙缝～上 plaster up cracks in the wall/ ～一层泥 spread a layer of mud
另见 hú; hù

## hú

**囫** hú
【囫囵】 húlún whole: ～吞下 swallow sth. whole
【囫囵吞枣】 húlún tūn zǎo swallow dates whole — lap up information without digesting it; read without understanding

**狐** hú fox
【狐臭】 húchòu body odour; bromhidrosis
【狐蝠】 húfú fox bat
【狐假虎威】 hú jiǎ hǔ wēi the fox borrows the tiger's terror (by walking in the latter's company) — bully people by flaunting one's powerful connections
【狐狸】 húli fox ◇ ～精 fox spirit — seductive woman
【狐狸尾巴】 húli wěiba fox's tail — something that gives away a person's real character or evil intentions; cloven

hoof: ～总是要露出来的。A fox cannot hide its tail. 或 The devil can't hide his cloven hoof./ 抓住阴谋家的～ seize hold of the evidence which gives the conspirator away
【狐媚】 húmèi bewitch by cajolery; entice by flattery
【狐裘】 húqiú fox-fur robe
【狐群狗党】 húqún-gǒudǎng a pack of rogues; a gang of scoundrels
【狐疑】 húyí doubt; suspicion: 满腹～ be full of misgivings; be very suspicious

**弧** hú 〈数〉 arc
【弧度】 húdù 〈数〉 radian
【弧光】 húguāng arc light; arc ◇ ～灯 arc lamp; arc light
【弧菌】 hújūn vibrio
【弧圈球】 húquānqiú 〈乒乓球〉 loop drive
【弧形】 húxíng arc; curve ◇ ～闸门 〈水〉 radial gate

**胡** hú ①〈史〉non-Han nationalities living in the north and west in ancient times ② introduced from the northern and western nationalities or from abroad: ～萝卜 carrot/ ～桃 walnut ③〈副〉recklessly; wantonly; outrageously: ～吹 boast outrageously; talk big/ ～编 recklessly concoct ④〈书〉why: ～不归? Why not return? ⑤ moustache, beard or whiskers ⑥ (Hú) a surname
【胡扯】 húchě talk nonsense: ～! Nonsense! 或 That's a lie!
【胡蜂】 húfēng wasp; hornet
【胡搞】 húgǎo ① mess things up; meddle with sth. ② carry on an affair with sb.; be promiscuous
【胡话】 húhuà ravings; wild talk: 烧得直说～ be delirious from fever
【胡笳】 hújiā 〈乐〉 a reed instrument used by the northern tribes in ancient China
【胡椒】 hújiāo pepper
【胡椒鲷】 hújiāodiāo 〈动〉 grunt (*Plectorhynchus cinctus*)
【胡搅】 hújiǎo ① pester sb.; be mischievous ② argue tediously and vexatiously; wrangle: ～蛮缠 harass sb. with unreasonable demands; pester sb. endlessly
【胡来】 húlái ① mess things up; fool with sth.: 你要是不会修就别～。If you don't know how to repair it, don't fool with it (或 mess it up). ② run wild; make trouble
【胡噜】 húlu 〈方〉 ① rub: 孩子的头碰疼了,你给他～～。The child's knocked his head against something. Rub it for him./ 他用手巾～了一把脸就上工了。He gave his face a quick rub with a towel and went off to work. ② sweep (away); scrape together: 把瓜子壳～到簸箕里 sweep the melon-seed shells into a dustpan/ 把剥好的豆子～到一堆儿 scrape the hulled beans together
【胡乱】 húluàn carelessly; casually; at random: ～吃了点饭 eat a hasty meal; grab a quick bite/ ～写了几行 scribble a few lines/ ～猜测 make wild guesses
【胡萝卜】 húluóbo carrot ◇ ～素 〈生化〉 carotene
【胡闹】 húnào run wild; be mischievous
【胡琴】 húqin *huqin*, a general term for certain two-stringed bowed instruments, such as *erhu* (二胡), *jinghu* (京胡), etc.
【胡说】 húshuō ① talk nonsense; drivel ② nonsense
【胡说八道】 húshuō-bādào ① talk nonsense ② sheer nonsense; rubbish
【胡思乱想】 húsī-luànxiǎng imagine things; go off into wild flights of fancy; let one's imagination run away with one
【胡同儿】 hútòngr lane; alley
【胡颓子】 hútuízi 〈植〉 thorny elaeagnus (*Elaeagnus pungens*)
【胡须】 húxū beard, moustache or whiskers
【胡言乱语】 húyán-luànyǔ talk nonsense; rave
【胡杨】 húyáng 〈植〉 diversiform-leaved poplar (*Popular diversifolia*)
【胡枝子】 húzhīzi 〈植〉 shrub lespedeza (*Lespedeza bicolor*)
【胡诌】 húzhōu fabricate wild tales; cook up: ～了一大堆理由 cook up a lot of excuses/ 现代修正主义～什么资本主义可以和平过渡到社会主义。The modern revisionists have spun wild yarns about the possibility of peaceful transition from capitalism to socialism.
【胡子】 húzi beard, moustache or whiskers
【胡子拉碴】 húzi lāchā a stubbly beard; a bristly unshaven chin
【胡作非为】 húzuò-fēiwéi act wildly in defiance of the law or public opinion; commit all kinds of outrages

**壶** hú ① kettle; pot: 水～ kettle/ 茶～ teapot/ 油～ oil can ② bottle; flask: 行军～ water bottle; canteen/ 暖～ thermos bottle (或 flask)

**核** hú
另见 hé
【核儿】 húr 〈口〉 ① stone; pit; core: 杏～ apricot stone/ 梨～ pear core ② sth. resembling a fruit stone: 煤～ partly-burnt coals or briquets; cinders

**斛** hú a dry measure used in former times, originally equal to 10 *dou* (斗), later 5 *dou*

**湖** hú ① lake ② (Hú) a name referring to the provinces of Hunan and Hubei
【湖北】 Húběi Hubei (Province)
【湖笔】 húbǐ writing brush produced in Huzhou (湖州), now Wuxing (吴兴), Zhejiang Province
【湖滨】 húbīn lakeside
【湖南】 Húnán Hunan (Province)
【湖泊】 húpō lakes
【湖色】 húsè light green
【湖田】 hútián land reclaimed from a lake; shoaly land
【湖心亭】 húxīntíng a pavilion in the middle of a lake; mid-lake pavilion
【湖沼学】 húzhǎoxué limnology

**葫** hú
【葫芦】 húlu bottle gourd; calabash: 他的～里到底卖的是什么药? What has he got up his sleeve?

**猢** hú
【猢狲】 húsūn macaque: 树倒～散。When the tree falls, the monkeys scatter — when the boss falls from power, his lackeys disperse.

**餬** hú
【餬口】 húkǒu keep body and soul together; eke out one's livelihood

**鹄** hú swan
另见 gǔ
【鹄候】 húhòu 〈书〉 await respectfully; expect: ～回音。I am awaiting your reply.
【鹄望】 húwàng 〈书〉 eagerly look forward to

**煳** hú (of food) burnt: 饭～了。The rice is burnt.

**瑚** hú 见"珊瑚" shānhú

**鹕** hú 见"鹈鹕" tíhú

**糊** hú ①paste: 将面粉加水调成～状 mix flour and water into a paste ②stick with paste; paste: ～窗户 paste a sheet of paper over a lattice window or seal with paper the cracks around a window ③(of food) burnt
另见 hū; hù
【糊精】 hújīng 〈化〉 dextrin; artificial gum
【糊口】 húkǒu 见"餬口" húkǒu
【糊料】 húliào thickener
【糊墙纸】 húqiángzhǐ wall paper
【糊涂】 hútu muddled; confused; bewildered: ～观念 a muddled idea/ 别装～。Don't play the fool./ 他越想越～。The more he thought the more confused he became./ 这个人糊里～的，管帐不行。That chap's no good for bookkeeping, he's so muddleheaded./ 我真～，把信忘在家里了。How careless of me to have left the letter at home. ◇ ～虫 blunderer; bungler/ ～帐 chaotic accounts; a mess

**槲** hú 〈植〉 Mongolian oak (*Quercus dentata*)
【槲寄生】 hújìshēng 〈植〉 mistletoe (*Viscum coloratum*)
【槲栎】 húlì 〈植〉 oriental white oak (*Quercus aliena*)

**蝴** hú
【蝴蝶】 húdié butterfly
◇ ～阀〈水〉 butterfly valve/ ～花 fringed iris/ ～结 bow/ ～鱼 butterfly fish

**醐** hú 见"醍醐" tíhú

## hǔ

**虎** hǔ ①tiger: 小～ a tiger cub ②brave; vigorous: ～将 brave general/ ～～有生气 be full of vigour
【虎耳草】 hǔ'ěrcǎo 〈植〉 saxifrage
【虎伏】 hǔfú 〈体〉 gyro wheel
【虎符】 hǔfú a tiger-shaped tally issued to generals as imperial authorization for troop movement in ancient China
【虎骨酒】 hǔgǔjiǔ tiger-bone liquor
【虎劲】 hǔjìn dauntless drive; dash: 有一股子～ be full of drive and daring; have plenty of dash
【虎踞龙盘】 hǔjù-lóngpán 见"龙盘虎踞" lóngpán-hǔjù
【虎口】 hǔkǒu ①tiger's mouth — jaws of death: 把同志救出～ save one's comrade from the jaws of death/ ～拔牙 pull a tooth from the tiger's mouth — dare the greatest danger; beard the lion in his den/ ～余生 survive a disaster; have a narrow escape ②part of the hand between the thumb and the index finger
【虎钳】 hǔqián vice: 台～ bench vice/ 万能～ universal vice
◇ ～口 vice jaw
【虎鲨】 hǔshā bullhead shark
【虎视眈眈】 hǔ shì dāndān glare like a tiger eyeing its prey; eye covetously
【虎头蛇尾】 hǔtóu-shéwěi in like a lion, out like a lamb; fine start and poor finish
【虎穴】 hǔxué tiger's den: ～追踪 track the tiger to its lair
【虎杖】 hǔzhàng 〈中药〉 giant knotweed (*Polygonum cuspidatum*)

**浒** hǔ waterside

**唬** hǔ 〈口〉 bluff: 你别～人。Quit bluffing./ 她没被～住。She wasn't intimidated.

**琥** hǔ
【琥珀】 hǔpò amber ◇ ～油 amber oil

## hù

**户** hù ①door: 足不出～ never step out of doors; confine oneself within doors/ ～外活动 outdoor activities ②household; family: 全村共三十～。There are thirty households in the village./ 家家～～ each and every family/ 由缺粮～变为余粮～ change from a household short of grain to one with a grain reserve ③(bank) account: 存～ (bank) depositor
【户部】 Hùbù the Ministry of Revenue in feudal China
【户籍】 hùjí ①census register; household register ②registered permanent residence ◇ ～警 policeman in charge of household registration
【户口】 hùkǒu ①number of households and total population ②registered permanent residence: 查～ check residence cards; check on household occupants/ 迁～ report to the local authorities for change of domicile/ 报～ register or apply for residence/ 销～ cancel one's residence registration ◇ ～簿 (permanent) residence booklet/ ～清册 census record
【户枢不蠹】 hùshū bù dù a door-hinge is never worm-eaten
【户头】 hùtóu (bank) account: 开～ open an account
【户限】 hùxiàn 〈书〉 threshold: ～为穿 a threshold worn low by visitors — an endless flow of visitors
【户主】 hùzhǔ head of a household

**互** hù mutual; each other: ～不干涉内政 noninterference in each other's internal affairs/ ～为条件 mutually conditional; interdependent/ ～通情报 exchange information; keep each other informed/ ～派常驻使节 exchange resident envoys; mutually accredit resident envoys
【互不侵犯条约】 hù bù qīnfàn tiáoyuē nonaggression treaty (或 pact)
【互导】 hùdǎo 〈电〉 mutual conductance; transconductance
【互访】 hùfǎng exchange visits: 两国体育代表团的～ exchange of sports delegations between two countries
【互感】 hùgǎn 〈电〉 mutual inductance
【互…互…】 hù...hù... mutual; each other: 互勉互助 encourage and help each other/ 互教互学 teach and learn from each other; teach each other/ 互谅互让 mutual understanding and (mutual) accommodation
【互换】 hùhuàn exchange: ～批准书 exchange instruments of ratification/ ～记者 exchange correspondents
【互惠】 hùhuì mutually beneficial; reciprocal: 在～的基础上 on a mutually beneficial basis/ 贸易～ reciprocity in trade
◇ ～待遇 reciprocal treatment/ ～关税 mutually preferential tariff/ ～条约 reciprocal treaty
【互利】 hùlì mutually beneficial; of mutual benefit
【互通有无】 hù tōng yǒu-wú each supplies what the other needs; help supply each other's needs
【互相】 hùxiāng 〈副〉 mutual; each other: ～依存 depend on each other for existence; be interdependent/ ～排斥 be mutually exclusive/ ～配合 work in coordination/ ～利用 each using the other for his own ends/ ～掣肘 hold each other back/ ～勾结 work in collusion
【互助】 hùzhù help each other: ～合作 mutual aid and cooperation
【互助组】 hùzhùzǔ ①mutual aid group: 学习～ mutual help study group ②mutual aid team (an elementary form of organization in China's agricultural cooperation): 临时～ temporary mutual aid team/ 常年～ all-the-year-round

mutual aid team

**沪** Hù another name for Shanghai: ～宁铁路 the Shanghai-Nanjing Railway

【沪剧】 hùjù Shanghai opera

**护** hù ① protect; guard; shield: ～林 protect a forest/ ～厂 guard a factory/ 在敌机扫射时,她用自己的身子～住伤员。She shielded the wounded soldier from the strafing of the enemy plane with her own body. ② be partial to; shield from censure: 别～着自己的孩子。Don't be partial to your own child.

【护岸】 hù'àn 〈水〉 bank revetment ◇ ～林 protective belt (of trees) along an embankment

【护城河】 hùchénghé city moat

【护持】 hùchí shield and sustain

【护短】 hùduǎn shield a shortcoming or fault

【护耳】 hù'ěr earflaps; earmuffs

【护封】 hùfēng book jacket; jacket

【护航】 hùháng escort; convoy: 由五艘军舰～ be convoyed by five warships; have an escort of five warships ◇ ～部队 escort force/ ～飞机 escort aircraft/ ～舰 convoy ship

【护理】 hùlǐ nurse; tend and protect: ～伤病员 nurse the sick and the wounded/ 重病～组 a team of nurses in charge of serious cases ◇ ～人员 nursing staff

【护路】 hùlù ① patrol and guard a road or railway ②〈交〉 road maintenance ◇ ～林 protective belt (of trees) along a road

【护面】 hùmiàn 〈体〉 mask

【护目镜】 hùmùjìng goggles

【护坡】 hùpō 〈水〉〈交〉 slope protection

【护身符】 hùshēnfú ① amulet; protective talisman ② a person or thing that protects one from punishment or censure; shield

【护士】 hùshi (hospital) nurse ◇ ～学校 nurses' school/ ～长 head nurse

【护手盘】 hùshǒupán 〈击剑〉 hand guard

【护送】 hùsòng escort; convoy: ～伤员去后方医院 escort wounded men to a rear hospital/ ～救灾物资 convoy vehicles bringing relief to a disaster-stricken area

【护腿】 hùtuǐ 〈体〉 shinguard

【护卫】 hùwèi ① protect; guard ②〈旧〉 bodyguard ◇ ～舰 escort vessel; corvette

【护膝】 hùxī 〈体〉 kneepad; kneecap

【护胸】 hùxiōng 〈体〉 chest protector

【护养】 hùyǎng ① cultivate; nurse; rear: ～秧苗 cultivate seedlings; nurse young plants/ ～仔猪 rear (或 look after) piglets ② maintain: ～公路 maintain a highway

【护照】 hùzhào passport: 外交～ diplomatic passport/ 公务～ service passport

**怙** hù 〈书〉 rely on: 失～ have nobody to rely on, one's father being dead; have lost one's father

【怙恶不悛】 hù è bù quān be steeped in evil and refuse to repent

**戽** hù bail: ～水灌田 bail water to irrigate fields

【戽斗】 hùdǒu bailing bucket

**祜** hù 〈书〉 blessing; bliss

**笏** hù a tablet held before the breast by officials when received in audience by the emperor

**扈** hù ①〈书〉 retinue ②(Hù) a surname

【扈从】 hùcóng 〈书〉 retinue; retainer

**瓠** hù

【瓠子】 hùzi a kind of edible gourd

**糊** hù paste: 辣椒～ chilli paste/ 玉米～ (cornmeal) mush

另见 hū; hú

【糊弄】 hùnong 〈方〉 ① fool; deceive; palm sth. off on: 你别～我。Don't try to fool me. ② go through the motions; be slipshod in work: 这可是细活,不能瞎～。This is a delicate job. It mustn't be done carelessly.

## huā

**化** huā spend; expend: ～钱 spend money; cost money/ ～工夫 spend time; take time

另见 huà

**花** huā ① flower; blossom; bloom: 种～儿 cultivate (或 grow) flowers/ 桃～ peach blossom/ 祖国盛开大寨～。The whole country is blooming with the flowers of Dazhai. ② anything resembling a flower: 火～ spark/ 雪～ snowflakes/ 浪～ spray ③ fireworks: 放～ let off fireworks ④ pattern; design: 她织的～儿真好看。The pattern she knitted is really beautiful./ 这被面的～儿很大方。The design on this quilt cover is quite elegant. ⑤ multicoloured; coloured; variegated: ～衣服 bright-coloured clothes/ ～蝴蝶 variegated butterfly/ 小～狗 spotted puppy/ 布染～了。The cloth is dyed unevenly. ⑥ blurred; dim: 看书看得眼睛都～了 read until the print looks blurred ⑦ fancy; florid; flowery; showy: 你的字太～了。Your handwriting is too fancy./ 要练好基本功,别尽学～架子。You should spend time on basic training, not on those flourishes. ⑧ cotton: 轧～ gin cotton ⑨ smallpox: 出～儿 get smallpox/ 种～儿 vaccinate ⑩ wound: 小王在战斗中挂了～。Xiao Wang got wounded in action. ⑪ spend; expend: ～了不少钱 spend a lot of money/ 很～时间 take a lot of time; be time-consuming ⑫ (Huā) a surname

【花白】 huābái grey; grizzled: 头发～ with grey (或 grizzled) hair; grey-haired

【花斑】 huābān piebald: ～马 a piebald horse

【花斑癣】 huābānxuǎn 〈医〉 tinea versicolour

【花瓣】 huābàn petal

【花被】 huābèi 〈植〉 perianth; floral envelope

【花边】 huābiān ① decorative border: 瓶口上有一道～。There is a floral border round the mouth of the vase. ② lace: ～装饰 lace trimmings/ 在衣服上镶一条～ trim a dress with lace ③〈印〉 fancy borders in printing

【花布】 huābù cotton print; print

【花草】 huācǎo flowers and plants

【花茶】 huāchá scented tea: 茉莉～ jasmine tea

【花车】 huāchē festooned vehicle

【花池子】 huāchízi flower bed

【花丛】 huācóng flowering shrubs; flowers in clusters

【花大姐】 huādàjiě 〈动〉 potato ladybird

【花搭着】 huādazhe interspersed; diversified: 细粮粗粮～吃 diversify one's diet by eating both fine and coarse grain

【花灯】 huādēng festive lantern (as displayed on the Lantern Festival)

【花雕】 huādiāo high-grade Shaoxing (绍兴) wine

【花缎】 huāduàn figured satin; brocade

【花朵】 huāduǒ flower
【花萼】 huā'è calyx
【花房】 huāfáng greenhouse
【花费】 huāfèi spend; expend; cost: ～金钱 spend money (on a project,etc.)/ ～时间 spend time; take time/ ～心血 take pains
【花费】 huāfei money spent; expenditure; expenses
【花粉】 huāfěn 〈植〉 pollen ◇ ～管 pollen tube
【花岗岩】 huāgāngyán granite: ～脑袋 a granite-like skull; ossified thinking ◇ ～化〈地〉 granitization
【花格墙】 huāgéqiáng lattice wall
【花梗】 huāgěng pedicel
【花骨朵】 huāgūduo (flower) bud
【花鼓】 huāgǔ flower-drum, a folk dance popular in the Changjiang valley ◇ ～戏 flower-drum opera, popular in Hunan, Hubei, Jiangxi and Anhui
【花冠】 huāguān corolla: 合瓣～ gamopetalous corolla/ 离瓣～ choripetalous corolla
【花好月圆】 huāhǎo-yuèyuán〔旧时多用作新婚的颂词〕blooming flowers and full moon — perfect conjugal bliss
【花红】 huāhóng ①〈植〉Chinese pear-leaved crabapple ②〈旧〉bonus ③〈旧〉gift for a wedding, etc.
【花候】 huāhòu 〈植〉 flowering season
【花花公子】 huāhuā gōngzǐ dandy; coxcomb; fop
【花花绿绿】 huāhuālǜlǜ brightly coloured; colourful: 穿得～的 be colourfully dressed/ ～的招贴画 poster in colour
【花花世界】 huāhuā shìjiè 〈贬〉 the dazzling human world with its myriad temptations; this mortal world
【花环】 huāhuán garland; floral hoop
【花卉】 huāhuì ① flowers and plants ②〈美术〉painting of flowers and plants in traditional Chinese style ◇ ～画 flower-and-plant painting
【花鸡】 huājī bramble finch; brambling
【花甲】 huājiǎ a cycle of sixty years: 年逾～ over sixty years old
【花剑】 huājiàn 〈体〉 foil
【花键】 huājiàn 〈机〉 spline ◇ ～轴 spline shaft/ ～座 splined hub
【花匠】 huājiàng gardener
【花椒】 huājiāo Chinese prickly ash
【花轿】 huājiào 〈旧〉bridal sedan chair
【花秸】 huājiē chopped straw
【花镜】 huājìng presbyopic glasses
【花卷】 huājuǎn steamed twisted roll
【花篮】 huālán ① a basket of flowers ② gaily decorated basket
【花蕾】 huālěi (flower) bud
【花里胡哨】 huālihúshào ① gaudy; garish ② showy; without solid worth
【花鲢】 huālián variegated carp
【花柳病】 huāliǔbìng venereal disease (V.D.)
【花露】 huālù (medicinal) liquid distilled from honeysuckle flowers or lotus leaves
【花露水】 huālùshuǐ toilet water
【花蜜】 huāmì 〈植〉 nectar
【花面狸】 huāmiànlí masked civet; gem-faced civet
【花名册】 huāmíngcè register (of names); membership roster; muster roll
【花木】 huāmù flowers and trees (in parks or gardens)
【花呢】 huāní fancy suiting
【花鸟】 huāniǎo 〈美术〉painting of flowers and birds in traditional Chinese style ◇ ～画 flower-and-bird painting
【花农】 huānóng flower grower
【花盘】 huāpán 〈植〉 ① flower disc ②〈机〉 disc chuck; faceplate
【花炮】 huāpào fireworks and firecrackers
【花盆】 huāpén flowerpot
【花瓶】 huāpíng flower vase; vase
【花圃】 huāpǔ flower nursery
【花枪】 huāqiāng ① a short spear used in ancient times ② trickery: 耍～ play tricks
【花腔】 huāqiāng ① florid ornamentation in Chinese opera singing; *coloratura* ② guileful talk: 耍～ speak guilefully ◇ ～女高音 *coloratura* soprano; *coloratura*
【花青】 huāqīng 〈化〉 cyanine ◇ ～染料 cyanine dyes/ ～素 anthocyanidin
【花圈】 huāquān (floral) wreath
【花蕊】 huāruǐ 〈植〉（雄）stamen;（雌）pistil
【花色】 huāsè ① design and colour: 这布的～很好看。This cloth is beautiful in both design and colour. ②(of merchandise) variety of designs, sizes, colours, etc.: 新的～ latest designs/ ～繁多 a great variety
【花纱布】 huāshābù a collective name for cotton, cotton yarn and cloth
【花哨】 huāshao ① garish; gaudy ② full of flourishes; flowery
【花生】 huāshēng peanut; groundnut ◇ ～饼〈农〉 peanut cake/ ～黑斑病 cercospora black spot of peanut/ ～酱 peanut butter/ ～壳 peanut shell/ ～米 shelled peanut; peanut kernel/ ～糖 peanut brittle/ ～油 peanut oil
【花饰】 huāshì ornamental design
【花鼠】 huāshǔ Siberian chipmunk; chipmunk
【花束】 huāshù a bunch of flowers; bouquet
【花丝】 huāsī ①〈植〉 filament ②〈工美〉 filigree ◇ ～工 filigree work
【花坛】 huātán (raised) flower bed; flower terrace
【花天酒地】 huātiān-jiǔdì indulge in dissipation; lead a life of debauchery
【花团锦簇】 huātuán-jǐncù bouquets of flowers and piles of silks — rich multicoloured decorations
【花托】 huātuō 〈植〉 receptacle
【花纹】 huāwén decorative pattern; figure: 各种～的地毯 carpets of different patterns/ 这些瓷盘的～很别致。These porcelain plates have rather original designs on them. ◇ ～玻璃 figured glass
【花线】 huāxiàn ① coloured thread ②〈电〉 flexible cord; flex
【花消】 huāxiao 〈口〉 cost; expense 又作"花销"
【花序】 huāxù 〈植〉 inflorescence
【花絮】 huāxù titbits (of news); interesting sidelights: 运动会～ sidelights on the sports meet
【花薰】 huāxūn 〈工美〉 a jade vessel for perfuming; jade perfumer
【花芽】 huāyá 〈植〉 (flower) bud
【花言巧语】 huāyán-qiǎoyǔ sweet words; blandishments
【花眼】 huāyǎn presbyopia
【花样】 huāyàng ① pattern; variety: ～繁多 a great variety/ ～翻新 the same old thing in a new guise ② trick: 玩～ play tricks ◇ ～滑冰〈体〉 figure skating
【花药】 huāyào 〈植〉 anther
【花椰菜】 huāyēcài cauliflower
【花叶病】 huāyèbìng 〈农〉 mosaic (disease): 甜菜～ beet mosaic
【花园】 huāyuán flower garden; garden
【花帐】 huāzhàng padded accounts or bills: 开～ make out a padded account; pad accounts
【花招】 huāzhāo ① showy movement in *wushu*（武术）; flourish ② trick; game: 别耍～！ None of your little tricks.
【花枝招展】 huāzhī zhāozhǎn (of women) be gorgeously

dressed
【花轴】 huāzhóu 〈植〉 floral axis
【花柱】 huāzhù 〈植〉 style
【花子】 huāzi 〈旧〉 beggar

**哗** huā 〈象〉: 铁门～的一声拉上了。The iron gate was pulled to with a clang./ 溪水～～地流。The stream went gurgling on.
另见 huá

【哗啦】 huālā 〈象〉: 风吹得树叶～～地响。The leaves rustled in the wind./ 墙～一声倒了。The wall fell with a crash./ 雨～～地下个不停。The rain kept pouring down.

## huá

**划** huá ① paddle; row: ～船 paddle (或 row) a boat; go boating ② be to one's profit; pay: 这么好的地,种饲料～不来。It doesn't pay to grow feed crops on such good soil. ③ scratch; cut the surface of: 她手～破了。Her hands were scratched./ ～玻璃 cut a piece of glass/ ～火柴 strike a match/ 几道闪电～破长空。Flashes of lightning streaked across the sky.
另见 huà

【划拉】 huála 〈方〉 ① brush away ② scrawl
【划拳】 huáquán finger-guessing game — a drinking game at feasts
【划算】 huásuàn ① calculate; weigh: ～来,～去 carefully weigh the pros and cons ② be to one's profit; pay: ～不～,不能只从本单位的利益考虑。One mustn't consider whether or not it pays simply from the standpoint of one's own unit.
【划子】 huázi small rowboat

**华** huá ① magnificent; splendid: ～屋 magnificent house ② prosperous; flourishing: 繁～ flourishing; bustling ③ best part; cream: 精～ the cream; the best part ④ flashy; extravagant: 奢～ extravagant; luxurious/ 朴实无～ simple and unadorned ⑤ grizzled; grey: ～发 grey hair ⑥ 〈敬〉 your: ～翰 your esteemed letter/ ～诞 your birthday ⑦ 〈气〉 corona ⑧ (Huá) China: 来～访问 come to China on a visit/ ～北 north China
另见 Huà

【华表】 huábiǎo ornamental columns erected in front of palaces, tombs, etc.
【华彩乐段】 huácǎi yuèduàn 〈乐〉 *cadenza*
【华达呢】 huádání gabardine
【华灯】 huádēng colourfully decorated lantern; light: ～初上 when the evening lights are lit
【华而不实】 huá ér bù shí ① flashy and without substance ② superficially clever
【华尔街】 Huá'ěrjiē Wall Street ◇ ～财阀 Wall Street magnates
【华盖】 huágài ① 〈书〉 canopy (as over an imperial carriage) ② 〈气〉 aureole
【华贵】 huáguì luxurious; sumptuous; costly: ～的地毯 luxurious carpet
【华里】 huálǐ *li*, a unit of distance (=1/2 kilometre)
【华丽】 huálì magnificent; resplendent; gorgeous: ～的宫殿 a magnificent palace/ 服饰～ gorgeously dressed and richly ornamented/ ～的词藻 flowery language
【华美】 huáměi magnificent; resplendent; gorgeous
【华侨】 Huáqiáo overseas Chinese
【华沙条约】 Huáshā Tiáoyuē the Warsaw Treaty (1955) ◇ ～组织 the Warsaw Treaty Organization
【华氏温度计】 huáshìwēndùjì the Fahrenheit thermometer
【华夏】 Huáxià an ancient name for China
【华夏系构造】 Huáxiàxì gòuzào 〈地〉 Cathaysian (structural) system
【华裔】 Huáyì foreign citizen of Chinese origin
【华章】 huázhāng 〈敬〉 your beautiful writing; your brilliant work

**哗** huá noise; clamour: 寂静无～ silent and still; very quiet
另见 huā

【哗变】 huábiàn mutiny
【哗然】 huárán in an uproar; in commotion: 举座～。The audience burst into an uproar./ 舆论～。There was a public outcry.
【哗笑】 huáxiào uproarious laughter
【哗众取宠】 huá zhòng qǔ chǒng try to please the public with claptrap

**铧** huá ploughshare: 双～犁 double-shared plough; double-furrow plough

**滑** huá ① slippery; smooth: 又圆又～的小石子 smooth, round pebbles/ 路～。The road is slippery. ② slip; slide: ～了一跤 slip and fall/ 在错误的道路上越～越远 slide further and further down the wrong road/ 不要～到唯心论和形而上学方面去。Don't lapse into the quagmire of idealism and metaphysics. ③ cunning; crafty; slippery: 又奸又～ mean and crafty

【滑板】 huábǎn ① 〈机〉 slide ② 〈乒乓球〉 feint play
【滑冰】 huábīng ice-skating; skating ◇ ～场 skating rink
【滑车】 huáchē 〈机〉 pulley; block ◇ ～组 block and tackle; pulley block
【滑车神经】 huáchē shénjīng 〈生理〉 trochlear nerve
【滑道】 huádào chute; slide
【滑动】 huádòng 〈物〉 slide ◇ ～轴承 〈机〉 sliding bearing
【滑竿】 huágān a kind of litter
【滑稽】 huájī ① funny; amusing; comical: 滑天下之大稽 be the biggest joke in the world; be the object of universal ridicule ② 〈曲艺〉 comic talk ◇ ～戏 farce
【滑精】 huájīng 〈中医〉 involuntary emission; spermatorrhoea
【滑溜】 huáliū *sauté* with starchy sauce ◇ ～里脊 *sauté* fillet with thick gravy
【滑溜】 huáliu 〈口〉 slick; smooth; slippery
【滑轮】 huálún pulley; block
【滑脉】 huámài 〈中医〉 smooth pulse
【滑面】 huámiàn 〈机〉 sliding surface; slide face
【滑腻】 huánì (of the skin) satiny; velvety; creamy
【滑坡】 huápō 〈地〉 landslide; landslip
【滑润】 huárùn smooth; well-lubricated
【滑石】 huáshí talcum; talc ◇ ～粉 talcum powder
【滑膛枪】 huátángqiāng smoothbore (gun); musket
【滑梯】 huátī (children's) slide
【滑头】 huátóu ① slippery fellow; sly customer ② slippery; shifty; slick: ～滑脑 crafty; artful; slick
【滑翔】 huáxiáng glide ◇ ～机 glider; sailplane
【滑行】 huáxíng slide; coast: 冰上～ slide on the ice/ ～下坡 coast down a slope/ 飞机在跑道上～。The plane taxied along the runway.
【滑雪】 huáxuě skiing
◇ ～板 skis/ ～鞋 ski boots/ ～杖 ski pole (或 stick)
【滑音】 huáyīn ① 〈语〉 glide ② 〈乐〉 *portamento*
【滑脂枪】 huázhīqiāng 〈机〉 grease gun

**猾** huá cunning; crafty; sly

## huà

**化** huà ①change; turn; transform: ～害为利 turn harm into good; turn a disadvantage into an advantage/ ～公为私 appropriate public property ②convert; influence: 潜移默～ exert a subtle influence on sb.'s character, thinking, etc. ③melt; dissolve: 雪～了。The snow has melted./ 用水～开 dissolve in water/ ～冻 thawing ④digest: ～食 help digestion ⑤burn up: 焚～ burn up; incinerate/ 火～ cremate ⑥〈简〉(化学) chemistry ⑦〔后缀,加在名词或形容词之后构成动词〕-ize; -ify: 工业～ industrialize/ 现代～ modernize/ 简～ simplify/ 工人～的知识分子 worker-intellectual/ 知识分子～的工人 intellectual-worker/ 劳动人民要知识～,知识分子要劳动～。Working people should master intellectual work and intellectuals should integrate themselves with the working people. ⑧(of Buddhist monks or Taoist priests) beg alms: ～斋 beg a (vegetarian) meal ⑨〈宗〉die: 坐～ pass away in a sitting posture
另见 huā

【化肥】 huàféi 〈简〉(化学肥料) chemical fertilizer

【化粪池】 huàfènchí septic tank

【化工】 huàgōng 〈简〉(化学工业) chemical industry ◇～厂 chemical plant/ ～原料 industrial chemicals

【化合】 huàhé 〈化〉chemical combination ◇～反应 combination reaction/ ～价 valence/ ～物 chemical compound

【化境】 huàjìng sublimity; perfection: 这幅山水画已臻～。This landscape painting is a consummate work of art.

【化名】 huàmíng (use an) assumed name; alias

【化脓】 huànóng fester; suppurate: 伤口～了。The wound is festering.

【化身】 huàshēn incarnation; embodiment: 智慧和勇敢的～ the embodiment of wisdom and courage/ 魔鬼的～ the devil incarnate

【化石】 huàshí fossil: 整理～ dress fossils/ 标准～ index fossil/ 指相～ facies fossil/ 微体～ microfossil ◇～作用 fossilization

【化痰】 huàtán reduce phlegm

【化铁炉】 huàtiělú 〈冶〉cupola furnace

【化为乌有】 huà wéi wūyǒu melt into thin air; vanish; come to naught

【化纤】 huàxiān 〈简〉(化学纤维) chemical fibre

【化险为夷】 huà xiǎn wéi yí turn danger into safety; head off a disaster

【化学】 huàxué chemistry: 应用～ applied chemistry/ 理论～ theoretical chemistry
◇～变化 chemical change/ ～成分 chemical composition/ ～当量 chemical equivalent/ ～反应 chemical reaction/ ～方程式 chemical equation/ ～符号 chemical symbol/ ～合成 chemosynthesis; chemical synthesis/ ～化 〈农〉extensive use of chemical fertilizers and other farm chemicals/ ～疗法 chemotherapy/ ～试剂 chemical reagent/ ～武器 chemical weapons/ ～纤维 chemical fibre/ ～性质 chemical property/ ～需氧量〈环保〉chemical oxygen demand/ ～药品 chemicals/ ～元素 chemical element/ ～战争 chemical warfare/ ～作用 chemical action

【化验】 huàyàn chemical examination; laboratory test
◇～单 laboratory test report/ ～室 laboratory/ ～员 laboratory technician (或 assistant)

【化油器】 huàyóuqì 〈机〉carburettor

【化缘】 huàyuán 〈宗〉(of Buddhist monks or Taoist priests) beg alms

【化整为零】 huà zhěng wéi líng break up the whole into parts

【化妆】 huàzhuāng put on makeup; make up ◇～品 cosmetics

【化装】 huàzhuāng ①(of actors) make up ②disguise oneself: ～侦察 go reconnoitring in disguise ◇～师 makeup man/ ～室 dressing room

**划** huà ①delimit; differentiate: ～界 delimit a boundary/ ～成分 determine class status ②transfer; assign: ～款 transfer money/ 生产大队把试验田～给这个小组负责。The production brigade assigned the experimental plot to that group. ③plan: 筹～ plan and prepare ④draw; mark; delineate: ～线 draw a line/ ～十字 mark sth. with a cross/ ～掉一个字 cross out a word ⑤stroke (of a Chinese character)
另见 huá

【划拨】 huàbō transfer: 这笔款子由银行～。The money will be transferred through the bank.

【划定】 huàdìng delimit; designate: ～捕鱼区 delimit fishing areas/ ～边界 delimit a boundary line/ 在～的区域内游泳 swim in the designated areas

【划分】 huàfēn ①divide: ～行政区域 divide a country into administrative areas/ 帝国主义～势力范围的斗争 a struggle among the imperialists to carve out spheres of influence ②differentiate: ～阶级成分 determine class status/ 毛主席关于三个世界～的理论具有重大而深远的意义。Chairman Mao's thesis differentiating the three worlds is of profound and far-reaching significance.

【划归】 huàguī put under (sb.'s administration, etc.); incorporate into: 这个企业已～地方管理。The enterprise has been put under local administration./ 这个县已经～另一个省了。That county has now been incorporated into another province.

【划框框】 huà kuāngkuang set limits; place restrictions

【划清】 huàqīng draw a clear line of demarcation; make a clear distinction: ～是非界限 make a clear distinction between right and wrong/ ～政策界限 draw distinctions in accordance with the Party's policy/ 跟他～界线 make a clean break with him

【划时代】 huàshídài epoch-making: 具有～的意义 have epoch-making significance/ ～的宣言 a declaration that is a landmark in history; an epoch-making declaration

【划一】 huàyī standardized; uniform: 整齐～ uniform

【划一不二】 huà yī bù èr fixed; unalterable; rigid: 价钱～ fixed price (not subject to bargaining)/ 写文章没有～的公式。There's no hard and fast rule for writing.

**华** Huà ①Huashan Mountain (in Shaanxi Province) ②(Huà) a surname
另见 huá

**话** huà ①word; talk: 说几句～ say a few words/ 留～ leave a message; leave word ②talk about; speak about: ～家常 chitchat; exchange small talk/ 忆苦思甜～今昔 talk about the happiness of today in contrast with the misery of the past/ ～不投机半句多。When the conversation gets disagreeable, to say one word more is a waste of breath.

【话本】 huàběn script for story-telling (in Song and Yuan folk literature); text of a story

【话别】 huàbié say a few parting words; say good-bye

【话柄】 huàbǐng subject for ridicule; handle 又作"话把儿"

【话碴儿】 huàchár 〈方〉①thread of discourse: 接上～ take up the thread of a conversation ②tone of one's speech:

听他的～，这件事好办。From what he says, that'll be easily done.

【话锋】 huàfēng thread of discourse; topic of conversation: 把～一转 switch the conversation to some other subject

【话旧】 huàjiù talk over old times; reminisce

【话剧】 huàjù modern drama; stage play ◇ ～团 modern drama troupe; theatrical company

【话里有话】 huàlǐ yǒu huà the words mean more than they say; there's more to it than what is said

【话题】 huàtí subject of a talk; topic of conversation: 转～ change the subject

【话筒】 huàtǒng ① microphone ② telephone transmitter ③ megaphone

【话头】 huàtóu thread of discourse: 打断～ interrupt sb.; cut sb. short/ 拾起～ take up the thread of a conversation

【话务员】 huàwùyuán (telephone) operator

【话匣子】 huàxiázi 〈方〉 ① gramophone ② radio receiving set ③ chatterbox: 这人是个～。That fellow is a chatterbox./ 他打开～就没个完。Once he opens his mouth, he never stops.

【话音】 huàyīn ① one's voice in speech: ～儿未落 when one has hardly finished speaking ② 〈口〉 tone; implication: 听他的～儿，准是另有打算。His tone suggests that he has something else in mind.

**画** huà ① draw; paint: ～画儿 draw a picture/ ～圈儿 draw (或 describe) a circle/ ～一张草图 make a sketch ② drawing; painting; picture: 年～ New Year picture/ 油～ oil painting ③ be decorated with paintings or pictures: ～栋雕梁 painted pillars and carved beams (of a magnificent building) ④ stroke (of a Chinese character): "人"字两～。The character 人 is made up of two strokes.

【画板】 huàbǎn drawing board

【画报】 huàbào illustrated magazine or newspaper; pictorial

【画笔】 huàbǐ painting brush; brush

【画饼充饥】 huà bǐng chōngjī draw cakes to allay hunger — feed on illusions

【画布】 huàbù canvas (for painting)

【画册】 huàcè an album of paintings; picture album

【画地为牢】 huà dì wéi láo draw a circle on the ground to serve as a prison — restrict sb.'s activities to a designated area or sphere

【画法】 huàfǎ technique of painting or drawing: ～新颖 a novel technique in painting or drawing

【画舫】 huàfǎng gaily-painted pleasure-boat

【画幅】 huàfú ① picture; painting ② size of a picture: ～虽然不大，所表现的天地却十分广阔。The picture is small but it shows broad vistas.

【画稿】 huàgǎo rough sketch (for a painting)

【画虎类狗】 huà hǔ lèi gǒu try to draw a tiger and end up with the likeness of a dog — make a poor imitation 又作"画虎不成反类犬"

【画家】 huàjiā painter; artist

【画架】 huàjià easel

【画匠】 huàjiàng ① artisan-painter ② 〈旧〉 inferior painter

【画境】 huàjìng picturesque scene: 如入～ feel as though one were in a landscape painting

【画具】 huàjù painter's paraphernalia

【画卷】 huàjuàn picture scroll

【画绢】 huàjuàn silk for drawing on; drawing silk

【画刊】 huàkān ① pictorial section of a newspaper ② pictorial

【画廊】 huàláng ① painted corridor ② (picture) gallery

【画龙点睛】 huà lóng diǎn jīng ① bring the painted dragon to life by putting in the pupils of its eyes — add the touch that brings a work of art to life; add the finishing touch ② add a word or two to clinch the point

【画眉】 huàméi 〈动〉 a kind of thrush

【画面】 huàmiàn ① general appearance of a picture; tableau ② 〈电影〉 frame

【画皮】 huàpí disguise or mask of an evildoer: 剥～ rip off sb.'s mask

【画片】 huàpiàn a miniature reproduction of a painting

【画屏】 huàpíng 〈工美〉 painted screen

【画谱】 huàpǔ ① 见"画帖" ② a book on the art of drawing or painting

【画蛇添足】 huà shé tiān zú draw a snake and add feet to it — ruin the effect by adding sth. superfluous

【画师】 huàshī painter

【画室】 huàshì studio

【画帖】 huàtiè a book of model paintings or drawings

【画图】 huàtú ① draw designs, maps, etc. ② picture

【画外音】 huàwàiyīn 〈电影〉 offscreen voice

【画像】 huàxiàng ① draw a portrait; portray: 给孩子画个像 draw a portrait of the child/ 让人～ sit for one's portrait ② portrait; portrayal: 巨幅～ huge portrait/ 自～ self-portrait ◇ ～石 〈考古〉 stone relief (on ancient Chinese tombs, shrines, etc.)

【画押】 huàyā make one's cross (或 mark); sign

【画页】 huàyè page with illustrations (in a book or magazine); plate

【画院】 huàyuàn imperial art academy, notably that of the reign of the Emperor Huizong (徽宗) of the Song Dynasty, whose paintings were characterized by delicate brushwork and close attention to detail

【画展】 huàzhǎn art exhibition; exhibition of paintings

【画轴】 huàzhóu painted scroll; scroll painting

**桦** huà 〈植〉 birch

## huái

**怀** huái ① bosom: 小孩儿在妈妈的～里睡着了。The baby fell asleep in its mother's arms. ② mind: 襟～坦白 frank and open-minded ③ keep in mind; cherish: ～着真诚的愿望 cherish sincere hopes/ ～着深厚的感情 with deep feelings/ 不～好意 harbour evil designs ④ think of; yearn for: ～友 think of a friend/ ～乡 yearn for one's native place; be homesick ⑤ conceive (a child): ～了孩子 become pregnant; be with child

【怀抱】 huáibào ① bosom: 回到祖国的～ return to the embrace of one's homeland/ 投入敌人的～ throw oneself into the arms of the enemy ② cherish: ～远大的理想 cherish lofty ideals

【怀表】 huáibiǎo pocket watch

【怀古】 huáigǔ meditate on the past; reflect on an ancient event

【怀恨】 huáihèn nurse hatred; harbour resentment

【怀旧】 huáijiù remember past times or old acquaintances (usu. with kindly thoughts)

【怀恋】 huáiliàn think fondly of (past times, old friends, etc.); look back nostalgically

【怀念】 huáiniàn cherish the memory of; think of: ～革命先烈 cherish the memory of revolutionary martyrs/ ～远方的友人 think of an absent friend who is far away

【怀柔】 huáiróu (of feudal rulers) make a show of conciliation in order to bring other nationalities or states under control ◇ ～政策 policy of control through conciliation;

policy of mollification
【怀胎】 huáitāi be pregnant
【怀想】 huáixiǎng think about with affection (a faraway person, place, etc.); yearn for
【怀疑】 huáiyí doubt; suspect: 引起～ raise doubts; arouse suspicion/ 消除～ dispel doubts; clear up suspicion/ 受到～ come under suspicion/ ～他的动机 suspect his motives/ ～有埋伏 suspect an ambush/ 我～他别有用心。I suspect that he has ulterior motives./ 持～态度 take a sceptical attitude ◇ ～论〈哲〉scepticism
【怀孕】 huáiyùn be pregnant: ～五个月了 be five months pregnant; be five months gone ◇ ～期 period of pregnancy; gestation period

**徊** huái 见"徘徊" páihuái

**淮** Huái the Huaihe River
【淮海战役】 Huái-Hǎi Zhànyì the Huai-Hai Campaign (Nov. 6, 1948–Jan. 10, 1949), the second of the three decisive campaigns in the Chinese People's War of Liberation
【淮剧】 huáijù Huai opera, popular in northern Jiangsu

**槐** huái Chinese scholartree
【槐角】 huáijiǎo 〈中药〉 the pod of Chinese scholartree

**踝** huái ankle: ～骨 anklebone

## huài

**坏** huài ① bad: ～习惯 bad habit/ ～透了 downright bad; rotten to the core/ ～书 a bad (或 harmful) book/ ～天气 foul weather ② go bad; spoil; ruin: 鱼～了。The fish has gone bad./ 他身体～了。His health has broken down./ 他胃口～了。He has lost his appetite. ③ badly; awfully; very: 吓～了 be badly scared/ 气～了 be beside oneself with rage/ 乐～了 be wild with joy/ 累～了 be dead tired; be dog-tired ④ evil idea; dirty trick: 使～ play a dirty trick/ 一肚子～ full of tricks
【坏包儿】 huàibāor 〈口〉 rascal; rogue
【坏处】 huàichu harm; disadvantage: 一点～也没有。There's no harm in it at all. 或 There's nothing bad about it./ 从～着想,往好处努力。Prepare for the worst; strive for the best.
【坏蛋】 huàidàn 〈口〉 bad egg; scoundrel; bastard
【坏东西】 huàidōngxi bastard; scoundrel; rogue
【坏分子】 huàifènzǐ 〈法〉 bad element; evildoer
【坏话】 huàihuà ① malicious remarks; vicious talk: 讲别人～ speak ill of others ② unpleasant words: 好话～都要让人讲完。One should let others finish what they have to say whether it sounds pleasant or unpleasant.
【坏疽】 huàijū 〈医〉 gangrene
【坏人】 huàirén bad person; evildoer; scoundrel
【坏事】 huàishì ① bad thing; evil deed: 向坏人～作斗争 struggle against evildoers and evil deeds ② ruin sth.; make things worse: 急躁只能～。Impetuosity will only make things worse./ ～了! Something terrible has happened.
【坏死】 huàisǐ 〈医〉 necrosis: 局部～ local necrosis/ 牙～ dental necrosis
【坏心眼儿】 huàixīnyǎnr 〈口〉 evil intention; ill will
【坏血病】 huàixuèbìng scurvy

## huān

**欢** huān ① joyous; merry; jubilant: ～跃 jump for joy/ ～唱 sing merrily ②〈方〉 vigorously; with great drive; in full swing: 这些小青年干得可～呢! How vigorously these lads work!/ 春耕闹得正～。Spring ploughing is in full swing./ 雨越下越～。It's raining harder and harder./ 火着得很～。The fire is burning cheerfully.
【欢蹦乱跳】 huānbèng-luàntiào healthy-looking and vivacious: 孩子们～地簇拥着解放军进了村。Dancing and skipping with joy, the children followed the PLA men to the village./ 小马驹和小牛犊围着饲养员～。The colts and calves are gambolling round the stockman.
【欢畅】 huānchàng thoroughly delighted; elated
【欢度】 huāndù spend (an occasion) joyfully: ～佳节 celebrate a festival with jubilation
【欢呼】 huānhū hail; cheer; acclaim: ～毛泽东思想的伟大胜利 hail the great victory of Mao Zedong Thought/ 长时间的～ prolonged cheers (或 ovation)
【欢聚】 huānjù happy get-together; happy reunion: ～一堂 happily gather under the same roof
【欢快】 huānkuài cheerful and light-hearted; lively: ～的曲调 a lively melody/ 随着音乐～地跳舞 dance cheerfully to the music
【欢乐】 huānlè happy; joyous; gay: ～的人群 happy crowds/ ～的景象 a scene of great joy/ 给节日增添了～气氛 add to the gaiety of the festival
【欢庆】 huānqìng celebrate joyously: ～五一 celebrate May Day
【欢声雷动】 huānshēng léidòng cheers resound like rolls of thunder: 全场～。The audience broke into deafening cheers.
【欢送】 huānsòng see off; send off: 热烈～毕业生到祖国需要的地方去 give a warm send-off to graduates going to where the country needs them ◇ ～会 farewell meeting; send-off meeting/ ～仪式 seeing-off ceremony
【欢腾】 huānténg great rejoicing; jubilation: 喜讯传来,举国～。There was nationwide rejoicing at the good news./ 广场上一片～。The square was astir with jubilant crowds.
【欢天喜地】 huāntiān-xǐdì with boundless joy; wild with joy; overjoyed: ～地迎接国庆 greet National Day with boundless joy
【欢喜】 huānxǐ ① joyful; happy; delighted: 满心～ be filled with joy/ 欢欢喜喜过春节 spend a joyful Spring Festival ② like; be fond of; delight in: 她～拉手风琴。She likes to play the accordion.
【欢笑】 huānxiào laugh heartily
【欢心】 huānxīn favour; liking; love: 想博取～ try to win sb.'s favour
【欢欣鼓舞】 huānxīn-gǔwǔ be filled with exultation; be elated: 捷报传来,全国人民无不～。The good tidings filled the whole nation with joy. 或 The good tidings elated the whole nation.
【欢迎】 huānyíng welcome; greet: ～大家批评。Criticisms are welcome./ 夹道～ line the streets to give sb. a welcome/ 到机场～贵宾 meet distinguished guests at the airport/ 这部电影深受群众～。The film has been well received by the masses./ ～老王给我们唱个歌! Let's ask Lao Wang to sing us a song! ◇ ～词 welcoming speech; address of welcome/ ～会 a party (或 meeting) to welcome sb.

**獾** huān 〈动〉 badger
【獾油】 huānyóu 〈药〉 badger fat (for treating burns)

## huán

**还** huán ① go (或 come) back: ～家 return home ② give back; return; repay: 这几本是到期要～的书。These

books are due for return./ 下个月～你钱。I'll pay you back next month. ③ give or do sth. in return
另见 hái

【还本】 huánběn repayment of principal (或 capital): ～付息 repay capital with interest
【还魂】 huánhún ① revive after death; return from the grave ② 〈方〉 reprocessed ◇ ～纸 reprocessed paper
【还击】 huánjī ① fight back; return fire; counterattack: 进行自卫～ fight in self-defence/ ～敌人 hit back at the enemy ② 〈击剑〉 riposte
【还价】 huánjià counter-offer; counter-bid
【还礼】 huánlǐ ① return a salute ② present a gift in return
【还清】 huánqīng pay off: ～债务 pay off one's debts
【还手】 huánshǒu strike (或 hit) back
【还俗】 huánsú (of Buddhist monks and nuns or Taoist priests) resume secular life
【还乡】 huánxiāng return to one's native place ◇ ～团 home-going legion; landlords' restitution corps
【还原】 huányuán ① return to the original condition or shape; restore ② 〈化〉 reduction ◇ ～剂 reducing agent; reductant/ ～酶 reductase
【还愿】 huányuàn ① redeem a vow to a god ② fulfil one's promise: 说话要算数，不能光许愿不～。You should do what you say; you can't go on making promises and not keeping them.
【还债】 huánzhài pay one's debt; repay a debt
【还嘴】 huánzuǐ 〈口〉 answer (或 talk) back; retort

**环** huán ① ring; hoop: 耳～ earring ② link: 一～套一～ all linked with one another; wheels within wheels/ 最薄弱的一～ the weakest link ③ surround; encircle; hem in: 四面～山 be surrounded (或 hemmed in) by mountains ④ 〈体〉 ring: 命中九～ hit the nine-point ring/ 在射箭中取得三百四十二～的成绩 score 342 points in archery

【环靶】 huánbǎ 〈体〉 round target
【环抱】 huánbào surround; encircle; hem in: 群山～的村庄 a village nestling among the hills
【环城】 huánchéng around the city ◇ ～赛跑 round-the-city race
【环带】 huándài 〈动〉 clitellum
【环顾】 huángù 〈书〉 look about (或 round): ～四周 look all round/ ～国际局势 take stock of the world situation
【环礁】 huánjiāo 〈地〉 atoll
【环节】 huánjié ① link: 主要～ a key link/ 生产～ links in the production chain ② 〈动〉 segment ◇ ～动物 annelid
【环颈雉】 huánjǐngzhì 〈动〉 ring-necked pheasant
【环境】 huánjìng environment; surroundings; circumstances: 换换～ have a change of environment/ 在艰苦的～中成长 grow up under tough conditions/ ～顺利 under favourable circumstances/ 如～许可 if circumstances permit ◇ ～保护 environmental protection/ ～改良 environmental improvement/ ～监测系统 environmental monitoring system/ ～科学 environmental science/ ～卫生 environmental sanitation; general sanitation/ ～污染 pollution of the environment
【环流】 huánliú 〈气〉 circulation: 大气～ atmospheric circulation
【环球】 huánqiú ① round the world: ～旅行 travel round the world; a round-the-world tour ② the earth; the whole world
【环绕】 huánrào surround; encircle; revolve around: 大院的四周，绿树～。The compound is surrounded by trees./ 月亮～着地球转动。The moon revolves around the earth./ ～着中心任务 centre around the main task
【环蛇】 huánshé krait
【环食】 huánshí 〈天〉 annular eclipse (of the sun)
【环视】 huánshì look around
【环烃】 huántīng 〈化〉 cyclic hydrocarbon
【环烷】 huánwán 〈化〉 cycloalkanes; cycloparaffin; naphthene
【环行】 huánxíng going in a ring: ～一周 make a circuit ◇ ～公共汽车 bus with a circular route/ ～公路 ring road; belt highway/ ～铁路 circuit railway; belt line
【环形】 huánxíng annular; ringlike ◇ ～山 〈天〉 ring structure; lunar crater
【环氧树脂】 huányǎng shùzhī 〈化〉 epoxy resin
【环子】 huánzi ring; link: 门～ knocker

**桓** Huán a surname

**锾** huán a unit of weight used in ancient China, equal to six *liang* (两)

**寰** huán extensive region: 人～ the world of man

【寰球】 huánqiú the earth; the whole world 又作"寰宇"

**圜** huán 见"转圜" zhuǎnhuán

**鹮** huán 〈动〉 ibis

**鬟** huán 〈书〉 bun (of hair)

## huǎn

**缓** huǎn ① slow; unhurried: ～流 flow slowly/ ～步而行 walk unhurriedly/ ～不济急。Slow action cannot save a critical situation. ② delay; postpone; put off: ～办 postpone doing sth./ ～口气 have a respite/ 这事～几天再说。Let's put it off for a couple of days. ③ not tense; relaxed ④ recuperate; revive; come to: 过了好一阵他才～过来。It was a long time before he came to./ 这场及时雨使受旱的禾苗都～过来了。The timely rain revived the drought-stricken crops./ ～过劲儿来 feel refreshed after a breathing spell

【缓兵之计】 huǎn bīng zhī jì stratagem to gain a respite; stalling tactics
【缓冲】 huǎnchōng ① buffer; cushion: 弹性～ elastic buffer/ 起～的作用 produce a cushioning effect; absorb the shock/ ～的余地 leeway; room for manoeuvre ② 〈化〉 buffer ◇ ～地带 buffer zone/ ～国 buffer state/ ～剂 〈化〉 buffer/ ～器 〈机〉 buffer; bumper
【缓和】 huǎnhé ① relax; ease up; mitigate; alleviate: 风势渐趋～。The wind is subsiding./ ～紧张局势 relax the tension/ ～矛盾 mitigate (或 alleviate) a contradiction ② *détente* ◇ ～剂 〈物〉 moderator
【缓急】 huǎnjí ① pressing or otherwise; of greater or lesser urgency: 分别轻重～ do things in order of importance and urgency ② emergency: ～相助 give mutual help in an emergency; help each other in case of need
【缓颊】 huǎnjiá 〈书〉 intercede for sb.; put in a good word for sb.
【缓慢】 huǎnmàn slow: 行动～ slow in action; slowmoving/ 进展～ make slow progress
【缓坡】 huǎnpō gentle slope
【缓期】 huǎnqī postpone a deadline; suspend: ～付款 delay (或 defer) payment/ 判处死刑，～二年执行 condemned to death with the sentence suspended for two years; sentenced to death with a two-year reprieve
【缓气】 huǎnqì get a breathing space; have a respite; take a breather

【缓刑】 huǎnxíng 〈法〉 temporary suspension of the execution of a sentence; reprieve; probation: ～二年 two years' probation
【缓役】 huǎnyì 〈军〉 deferment (of service)
【缓征】 huǎnzhēng postpone the imposition of a tax or levy

## huàn

**幻** huàn ① unreal; imaginary; illusory: 虚～ unreal; illusory; visionary ② magical; changeable: 变～ change irregularly; fluctuate
【幻灯】 huàndēng ① slide show: 放～ show slides/ 看～ watch a slide show ② slide projector ◇ ～机 slide projector; epidiascope/ ～片 (lantern) slide
【幻景】 huànjǐng illusion; mirage
【幻境】 huànjìng dreamland; fairyland
【幻觉】 huànjué 〈心〉 hallucination
【幻梦】 huànmèng illusion; dream
【幻灭】 huànmiè vanish into thin air: 他的希望～了。His hopes were dashed.
【幻视】 huànshì 〈医〉 photism
【幻术】 huànshù magic; conjuring
【幻听】 huàntīng 〈医〉 phonism
【幻想】 huànxiǎng illusion; fancy; fantasy: 抱有～ cherish illusions/ 丢掉～ cast away illusions/ 沉湎于～ indulge in fantasy; be lost in reverie/ 把～看作现实 regard one's fantasies as reality ◇ ～曲 〈乐〉 fantasia
【幻象】 huànxiàng mirage; phantom; phantasm
【幻影】 huànyǐng unreal image

**宦** huàn ① official ② eunuch ③ (Huàn) a surname
【宦官】 huànguān eunuch
【宦海】 huànhǎi 〈旧〉 officialdom; official circles
【宦途】 huàntú 〈旧〉 official career

**浣** huàn 〈书〉 ① wash: ～衣 wash clothes ② any of the three ten-day divisions of a month: 上～ the first ten days of a month
【浣熊】 huànxióng racoon

**涣** huàn melt; vanish
【涣然】 huànrán melt away; disappear; vanish: 他的疑虑～冰释。His misgivings have all vanished.
【涣散】 huànsàn lax; slack: 纪律～ be lax in discipline/ ～斗志 sap sb.'s morale (或 fighting will)

**换** huàn ① exchange; barter; trade: 以兽皮～工业品 exchange (或 barter) furs for industrial products/ 用鲜血～来的教训 a lesson paid for in blood ② change: ～衣服 change one's clothes/ 带一套～洗的衣服。Take along a change of clothes./ ～乘火车 change to a train/ ～句话说 in other words/ 出去走一下，～～脑筋。Let's go for a walk and give our minds a rest.
【换班】 huànbān ① change shifts ② relieve a person on duty ③ 〈军〉 changing of the guard
【换边】 huànbiān 〈体〉 change sides
【换步】 huànbù 〈军〉 change step
【换茬】 huànchá 〈农〉 change of crops
【换车】 huànchē change trains or buses
【换挡】 huàndǎng 〈机〉 shift gears
【换发球】 huànfāqiú 〈体〉 change of service
【换防】 huànfáng 〈军〉 relieve a garrison
【换俘协定】 huànfú xiédìng agreement for exchange of prisoners; cartel
【换岗】 huàngǎng relieve a sentry (或 guard)
【换工】 huàngōng exchange labour
【换货】 huànhuò exchange goods; barter ◇ ～和付款协定 goods exchange and payments agreement/ ～协定 barter agreement
【换机放映】 huàn jī fàngyìng 〈电影〉 changeover
【换季】 huànjì change garments according to the season; wear different clothes for a new season
【换能器】 huànnéngqì 〈物〉 transducer
【换气】 huànqì take a breath (in swimming)
【换钱】 huànqián ① change money (或 bills) ② sell
【换取】 huànqǔ exchange (或 barter) sth. for; get in return: 用工业品～农产品 exchange (或 barter) industrial products for farm produce/ ～外汇 gain foreign exchange
【换人】 huànrén 〈体〉 substitution (of players)
【换算】 huànsuàn conversion ◇ ～表 conversion table
【换汤不换药】 huàn tāng bù huàn yào the same medicine differently prepared; the same old stuff with a different label; a change in form but not in content (或 essence)
【换文】 huànwén exchange of notes (或 letters): 建立外交关系的～ an exchange of notes on the establishment of diplomatic relations
【换牙】 huànyá (of a child) grow permanent teeth
【换羽】 huànyǔ moulting
【换装站】 huànzhuāngzhàn 〈铁道〉 transshipment station

**唤** huàn call out: 呼～ call; shout
【唤起】 huànqǐ ① arouse: ～民众 arouse the masses of the people ② call; recall: 有必要～人们注意这个事实。It is necessary to call attention to this fact./ ～对往事的回忆 evoke past memories
【唤醒】 huànxǐng wake up; awaken: ～人民 arouse the people

**焕** huàn shining; glowing
【焕发】 huànfā shine; glow; irradiate: 容光～ one's face glowing with health/ ～精神，努力工作 call forth all one's vigour and work with redoubled efforts/ 老干部～出革命青春。Old cadres still radiate the revolutionary vigour of their youth.
【焕然一新】 huànrán yī xīn take on an entirely new look (或 aspect); look brand-new: 自从有了中国共产党，中国革命的面目就～了。With the birth of the Communist Party of China, the face of the Chinese revolution took on an altogether new aspect./ 这个老港经过改造和建设，面貌～。After renovation and reconstruction this old port has changed beyond recognition.

**患** huàn ① trouble; peril; disaster: 防～于未然 take preventive measures; provide against possible trouble/ 有备无～。Preparedness averts peril. ② anxiety; worry: 何～之有。There's no need to worry. ③ contract; suffer from: ～肝炎 contract (或 have) hepatitis/ ～病 suffer from an illness; fall ill; be ill
【患处】 huànchù affected part (of a patient's body)
【患得患失】 huàndé-huànshī worry about personal gains and losses; be swayed by considerations of gain and loss
【患难】 huànnàn trials and tribulations; adversity; trouble: ～之交 friend in adversity; tested friend/ ～与共 go through thick and thin together
【患者】 huànzhě sufferer; patient: 结核病～ a person suffering from tuberculosis; a TB patient

**痪** huàn 见"瘫痪" tānhuàn

**豢** huàn

【豢养】 huànyǎng feed; groom; keep: 资产阶级～的反动文人 reactionary men of letters kept by the bourgeoisie

**鲩** huàn grass carp

## huāng

**肓** huāng 见"病入膏肓" bìng rù gāohuāng

**荒** huāng ① waste: 地～了。The land lies waste. ② wasteland; uncultivated land: 垦～ open up (或 reclaim) wasteland ③ desolate; barren: ～村 deserted village/ ～岛 desert (或 uninhabited) island/ ～山 barren hill ④ famine; crop failure: 储粮备～ store up grain against natural disasters ⑤ neglect; be out of practice: 别把功课～了。Don't neglect your lessons./ 好久不下棋，～了。It's a long time since I played chess. I'm out of practice./ 他的英语丢～了。His English is rusty. ⑥ shortage; scarcity: 房～ housing shortage/ 水～ water shortage ⑦ roughly processed; crude: ～子 〈机〉 blank

【荒诞】 huāngdàn fantastic; absurd; incredible: ～的想法 a fantastic idea/ ～的情节 an incredible plot/ ～无稽之谈 a tall story; a preposterous statement/ ～不经 preposterous; fantastic

【荒地】 huāngdì wasteland; uncultivated (或 undeveloped) land

【荒废】 huāngfèi ① leave uncultivated; lie waste: 我们公社没有一亩地是～的。Not a single *mu* of land in our commune lies waste. ② fall into disuse (或 disrepair): ～了的水渠又利用起来了。The irrigation canals that fell into disrepair are in use again. ③ neglect; be out of practice: ～学业 neglect one's studies

【荒郊】 huāngjiāo desolate place outside a town; wilderness

【荒凉】 huāngliáng bleak and desolate; wild: 一片～ a scene of desolation/ 过去这里是～的穷山沟。This used to be a bleak and barren gully./ ～的景色 wild scenery

【荒乱】 huāngluàn in great disorder; in turmoil

【荒谬】 huāngmiù absurd; preposterous: ～的说法 an absurd formulation/ ～绝伦 absolutely preposterous; utterly absurd

【荒漠】 huāngmò desert; wilderness

【荒年】 huāngnián famine (或 lean) year

【荒僻】 huāngpì desolate and out-of-the-way

【荒歉】 huāngqiàn crop failure; famine

【荒时暴月】 huāngshí-bàoyuè time of dearth; lean year; hard times

【荒疏】 huāngshū out of practice; rusty

【荒唐】 huāngtang ① absurd; fantastic; preposterous: ～可笑 ridiculous; absurd/ ～透顶 absolutely ridiculous; preposterous ② dissipated; loose; intemperate

【荒无人烟】 huāng wú rényān desolate and uninhabited: ～的地带 a region with no sign of human habitation

【荒芜】 huāngwú lie waste; go out of cultivation

【荒野】 huāngyě wilderness; the wilds

【荒淫】 huāngyín dissolute; licentious; debauched: ～无耻 dissipated and unashamed

【荒原】 huāngyuán wasteland; wilderness

**慌** huāng flurried; flustered; confused: 沉住气，别～! Keep calm! Don't panic!/ ～了手脚 be alarmed and confused; be flustered/ ～了神儿 be scared out of one's wits/ ～作一团 be thrown into utter confusion

**慌** huang 〈口〉〔用做补语，前面加"得"〕 awfully; unbearably: 心里闷得～ be bored beyond endurance/ 累得～ be tired out; be dog-tired; be played out

【慌乱】 huāngluàn flurried; alarmed and bewildered: 作好充分准备，免得临时～ make ample preparations so as not to be in a rush at the last moment

【慌忙】 huāngmáng in a great rush; in a flurry; hurriedly: ～赶到现场 rush to the spot/ 不慌不忙 unhurriedly; calmly

【慌张】 huāngzhang flurried; flustered; confused: 神色～ look flurried/ 为什么这样慌慌张张的？ Why are you so flustered?

## huáng

**皇** huáng emperor; sovereign: 女～ empress

【皇带鱼】 huángdàiyú oarfish

【皇帝】 huángdì emperor

【皇甫】 Huángfǔ a surname

【皇宫】 huánggōng (imperial) palace

【皇冠】 huángguān imperial crown

【皇后】 huánghòu empress

【皇家】 huángjiā imperial family (或 house)

【皇历】 huángli 〈旧〉 almanac

【皇权】 huángquán imperial power (或 authority)

【皇上】 huángshang ① the emperor; the throne; the reigning sovereign ②（直接称呼）Your Majesty;（间接称呼）His Majesty

【皇室】 huángshì imperial family (或 house)

【皇太后】 huángtàihòu empress dowager

【皇太子】 huángtàizǐ crown prince

【皇族】 huángzú people of imperial lineage; imperial kinsmen

**黄** huáng ① yellow; sallow: 脸色发～ a sallow face ② short for the Huanghe River: ～泛区 the Huanghe River Inundated Area/ 治～ harness the Huanghe River ③〈口〉 fizzle out; fall through: 那笔买卖～了。The deal is off. ④ (Huáng) a surname

【黄檗(柏)】 huángbò 〈中药〉 the bark of a cork tree (*Phellodendron*)

【黄灿灿】 huángcàncàn bright yellow; golden: ～的稻子 golden rice

【黄刺玫】 huángcìméi 〈植〉 yellow rose (*Rosa xanthina*)

【黄丹】 huángdān 〈化〉 yellow lead

【黄疸】 huángdǎn 〈医〉 jaundice: 肝原性～ hepatogenous jaundice/ 阻塞性～ obstructive jaundice ◇ ～指数 icterus index 又作"黄病"

【黄道】 huángdào 〈天〉 ecliptic
◇ ～带 zodiac/ ～光 zodiacal light/ ～十二宫 the 12 signs of the zodiac; zodiacal signs/ ～星座 zodiacal constellation/ ～座标 ecliptic coordinates

【黄道吉日】 huángdào jírì propitious (或 auspicious) date; lucky day

【黄澄澄】 huángdēngdēng glistening yellow; golden: ～的麦穗儿 golden ears of wheat

【黄鲷】 huángdiāo yellow porgy

【黄豆】 huángdòu soya bean; soybean

【黄蜂】 huángfēng wasp

【黄姑鱼】 huánggūyú spotted maigre

【黄瓜】 huángguā cucumber

【黄海】 Huánghǎi the Huanghai Sea; the Yellow Sea

【黄河】 Huánghé the Huanghe River; the Yellow River
◇ ～象 〈古生物〉 Huanghe River stegodon

【黄褐色】 huánghèsè yellowish-brown; tawny
【黄花】 huánghuā ① chrysanthemum ② day lily
【黄花菜】 huánghuācài day lily
【黄花苜蓿】 huánghuā mùxu 〈植〉(California) bur clover
【黄花鱼】 huánghuāyú yellow croaker
【黄昏】 huánghūn dusk
【黄鹡鸰】 huángjílíng yellow wagtail
【黄酱】 huángjiàng salted and fermented soya paste
【黄巾起义】 Huángjīn Qǐyì 〈史〉the Yellow Turbans Uprising (a large-scale peasant uprising at the close of the Eastern Han Dynasty)
【黄金】 huángjīn gold
◇ ～储备 gold reserve (或 stock)/ ～分割〈数〉golden section/ ～价格 price of gold; gold rate/ ～时代 golden age/ ～市场 gold market/ ～总库 gold pool
【黄荆】 huángjīng 〈植〉five-leaved chaste tree (*Vitex negundo*)
【黄猄】 huángjīng muntjac
【黄精】 huángjīng 〈中药〉sealwort (*Polygonatum sibiricum*)
【黄酒】 huángjiǔ yellow rice or millet wine; Shaoxing (绍兴) wine
【黄鹂】 huánglí oriole: 黑枕～ black-naped oriole
【黄历】 huángli 〈旧〉almanac
【黄连】 huánglián 〈中药〉the rhizome of Chinese goldthread (*Coptis chinensis*)
【黄连木】 huángliánmù 〈植〉Chinese pistache
【黄粱美梦】 huángliáng měimèng Golden Millet Dream (from the story of a poor scholar who dreamt that he had become a high official but awoke to find only the pot of millet still cooking on the fire); pipe dream
【黄磷】 huánglín yellow phosphorus
【黄栌】 huánglú 〈植〉smoke tree (*Cotinus coggygria*)
【黄麻】 huángmá (roundpod) jute ◇ ～袋 gunnysack; gunny-bag; gunny/ ～袋布 gunny (cloth)
【黄毛丫头】 huángmáo yātou a chit of a girl; a silly little girl
【黄梅季】 huángméijì the rainy season, usu. in April and May, in the middle and lower reaches of the Changjiang River 又作"黄梅天"
【黄梅雨】 huángméiyǔ intermittent drizzles in the rainy season in the middle and lower reaches of the Changjiang River
【黄米】 huángmǐ glutinous millet
【黄明胶】 huángmíngjiāo 〈中药〉oxhide gelatin
【黄鸟】 huángniǎo oriole
【黄牛】 huángniú ox; cattle
【黄袍加身】 huángpáo jiā shēn be draped with the imperial yellow robe by one's supporters — be acclaimed emperor
【黄芪】 huángqí 〈中药〉the root of membranous milk vetch (*Astragalus membranaceus*)
【黄芩】 huángqín 〈中药〉the root of large-flowered skullcap (*Scutellaria baicalensis*)
【黄泉】 huángquán netherworld
【黄雀】 huángquè siskin
【黄壤】 huángrǎng yellow earth; yellow soil
【黄热病】 huángrèbìng yellow fever
【黄色】 huángsè ① yellow ② decadent; obscene; pornographic
◇ ～电影 pornographic movie; sex film/ ～工会 yellow union; scab union/ ～书刊 pornographic books and periodicals/ ～小说 pornographic novel/ ～新闻 yellow journalism/ ～音乐 decadent music/ ～炸药 trinitrotoluene (TNT); trinol
【黄色人种】 huángsè rénzhǒng the yellow race
【黄鳝】 huángshàn ricefield eel; finless eel
【黄熟】 huángshú 〈农〉yellow maturity
【黄鼠】 huángshǔ ground squirrel; suslik
【黄鼠狼】 huángshǔláng yellow weasel: ～给鸡拜年,没安好心。The weasel goes to pay his respects to the hen — not with the best of intentions.
【黄水疮】 huángshuǐchuāng impetigo
【黄体】 huángtǐ 〈生理〉corpus luteum ◇ ～酮〈药〉progesterone
【黄铁矿】 huángtiěkuàng pyrite
【黄铜】 huángtóng brass ◇ ～管 brass pipe (或 tube)/ ～矿 chalcopyrite
【黄土】 huángtǔ 〈地〉loess ◇ ～高原 loess plateau
【黄萎病】 huángwěibìng 〈农〉verticillium wilt: 棉～ verticillium wilt of cotton
【黄癣】 huángxuǎn 〈医〉favus
【黄羊】 huángyáng Mongolian gazelle
【黄杨】 huángyáng 〈植〉Chinese littleleaf box
【黄莺】 huángyīng oriole
【黄油】 huángyóu ① butter ②〈化〉grease ◇ ～枪 grease gun
【黄鼬】 huángyòu yellow weasel
【黄鱼】 huángyú yellow croaker
【黄玉】 huángyù 〈矿〉topaz
【黄种】 huángzhǒng the yellow race

**凰** huáng 见"凤凰" fènghuáng

**隍** huáng dry moat outside a city wall

**惶** huáng fear; anxiety; trepidation: ～悚 sudden fear; fright
【惶惶】 huánghuáng in a state of anxiety; on tenterhooks; alarmed: ～不可终日 be in a constant state of anxiety; be on tenterhooks
【惶惑】 huánghuò perplexed and alarmed; apprehensive: ～不安 perplexed and uneasy
【惶遽】 huángjù 〈书〉frightened; scared: 神色～ look scared
【惶恐】 huángkǒng terrified: ～万状 be seized with fear; be frightened out of one's senses

**徨** huáng 见"彷徨" pánghuáng

**煌** huáng bright; brilliant: 明星～～。The stars are sparkling.
【煌斑岩】 huángbānyán 〈地〉lamprophyre

**潢** huáng 见"装潢" zhuānghuáng

**璜** huáng 〈考古〉semi-annular jade pendant

**蝗** huáng locust: ～灾 plague of locusts
【蝗虫】 huángchóng locust
【蝗蝻】 huángnǎn the nymph of a locust

**篁** huáng ① bamboo grove: 幽～ a secluded and restful bamboo grove ② bamboo: 修～ tall bamboos

**磺** huáng sulphur
【磺胺】 huáng'àn 〈药〉sulphanilamide (SN)
◇ ～醋酰 sulphacetamide (SA)/ ～胍 sulphaguanidine (SG)/ ～嘧啶 sulphadiazine (SD)/ ～噻唑 sulphathiazole (ST)/ ～异噁唑 sulphafurazole; gantrisin
【磺化】 huánghuà sulphonating ◇ ～剂 sulphonating agent
【磺酸盐】 huángsuānyán 〈化〉sulphonate
【磺酰胺】 huángxiān'àn 〈化〉sulphonic acid amide

**蟥** huáng 见"蚂蟥" mǎhuáng

**簧** huáng ①〈乐〉reed ② spring: 闹钟的～断了。The main spring of the alarm clock is broken.

【簧风琴】 huángfēngqín reed organ; harmonium

【簧片】 huángpiàn 〈乐〉reed

【簧乐器】 huángyuèqì reed instrument

**鳇** huáng huso sturgeon

## huǎng

**恍** huǎng ① all of a sudden; suddenly ②〔与"如""若"等字连用〕seem; as if: ～如梦境 as if in a dream

【恍惚】 huǎnghū ① in a trance; absentminded: 精神～ be in a trance ② dimly; faintly; seemingly: 我～听见他进屋去了。I was faintly aware that he entered the room.

【恍然大悟】 huǎngrán dàwù suddenly see the light; suddenly realize what has happened: 经他一指点，我才～，原来是我错了。When he dropped the hint, it suddenly dawned on me that I was wrong.

**晃** huǎng ① dazzle: 亮得～眼 dazzlingly bright/ 明～～的刺刀 a shining bayonet ② flash past: 窗外有个人影儿一～就不见了。A figure flashed past the window./ 一～半个月过去了。A fortnight passed in a flash.
另见 huàng

**谎** huǎng lie; falsehood

【谎报】 huǎngbào lie about sth.; give false information; start a *canard*: ～年龄 lie about one's age/ ～军情 make a false report about the military situation

【谎话】 huǎnghuà lie; falsehood: 说～ tell a lie; lie

【谎言】 huǎngyán lie; falsehood: 墨写的～掩盖不了血写的事实。Lies written in ink cannot cover up facts recorded in blood.

**幌** huǎng

【幌子】 huǎngzi ① shop sign; signboard ② pretence; cover; front: 打着"援助"的～ under the pretence of aid; in the guise of aid/ 骗人的～ a facade; a front

## huàng

**晃** huàng shake; sway: 他～～手说: "不去了"。With a sweep of his hand he said, "I won't go."
另见 huǎng

【晃荡】 huàngdang rock; shake; sway: 小船在江面上～。The small boat is rocking on the river./ 桶里水很满，一～就出来了。The bucket was so full that it overflowed at the slightest motion./ 风吹得马灯不停地～。The barn lantern kept swaying in the wind./ 一瓶子不响，半瓶子～。The half-filled bottle sloshes, the full bottle remains still — the dabbler in knowledge chatters away, the wise man stays silent.

【晃动】 huàngdòng rock; sway: 别～这船。Don't rock the boat./ 车轮有点～。The wheels wobble a bit.

【晃梯】 huàngtī 〈杂技〉balancing on an upright ladder

【晃悠】 huàngyou shake from side to side; wobble; stagger: 树枝在风中来回～。The branches of the trees are swaying in the wind./ 他晃晃悠悠地往前走。He was staggering along.

## huī

**灰** huī ① ash: 飞～ fly ash/ 草木～ plant ash (as fertilizer) ② dust: 积了厚厚的一层～ accumulate a thick layer of dust ③ lime; (lime) mortar: ～墙 plastered wall/ 和～ mix mortar ④ grey: ～马 a grey horse ⑤ disheartened; discouraged: 心～意懒 feel disheartened

【灰暗】 huī'àn murky grey; gloomy: ～的天空 a gloomy (或 murky grey) sky

【灰白】 huībái greyish white; ashen; pale: ～的鬓发 greying temples/ 脸色～ look pale

【灰尘】 huīchén dust; dirt: 大风过后，桌上落了一层～。After the wind, there was a layer of dust on the desk./ 掸掉桌上的～ dust the table

【灰分】 huīfèn 〈矿〉ash content

【灰鹤】 huīhè grey crane

【灰黄霉素】 huīhuángméisù 〈药〉griseofulvin

【灰浆】 huījiāng 〈建〉mortar

【灰烬】 huījìn ashes: 化为～ be reduced to ashes

【灰口铁】 huīkǒutiě 〈冶〉grey (pig) iron

【灰溜溜】 huīliūliū gloomy; dejected; crestfallen: 他看起来有点～的样子。He looked a little crestfallen (或 depressed)./ 老李，别那么～的。Cheer up, Lao Li.

【灰蒙蒙】 huīmēngmēng dusky; overcast: ～的夜色 a dusky night scene/ 天色～的。The sky was overcast.

【灰锰氧】 huīměngyǎng potassium permanganate

【灰泥】 huīní 〈建〉plaster

【灰雀】 huīquè bullfinch

【灰壤】 huīrǎng 〈农〉podzol

【灰色】 huīsè ① grey; ashy ② pessimistic; gloomy: ～人生观 a pessimistic (或 grey) outlook on life ③ obscure; ambiguous

【灰沙燕】 huīshāyàn sand martin

【灰鼠】 huīshǔ squirrel

【灰心】 huīxīn lose heart; be discouraged: ～丧气 be utterly disheartened/ 成功不骄傲，失败不～。When you succeed don't get conceited; when you fail don't be dejected.

【灰指甲】 huīzhījia 〈医〉ringworm of the nails; onychomycosis

【灰质】 huīzhì 〈生理〉grey matter

**诙** huī

【诙谐】 huīxié humorous; jocular ◇ ～曲〈乐〉humoresque

**恢** huī extensive; vast

【恢复】 huīfù ① resume; renew: ～邦交 resume diplomatic relations/ ～正常 return to normal ② recover; regain: ～健康 recover one's health/ ～知觉 recover consciousness; come to ③ restore; reinstate; rehabilitate: ～民族权利 restoration of national rights/ ～名誉 rehabilitation (of a person's reputation)/ ～组织生活 be allowed to resume Party activities; be reinstated as a Party member ◇ ～期〈医〉convalescence

【恢恢】 huīhuī 〈书〉extensive; vast: 天网～，疏而不漏。The net of Heaven has large meshes, but it lets nothing through.

**咴** huī

【咴儿咴儿】 huīrhuīr 〈象〉〔马叫声〕neigh; whinny

**挥** huī ① wave; wield: ～刀 wield a sword/ ～笔 wield the brush; put pen to paper ② wipe off: ～泪 wipe away tears; wipe one's eyes/ ～汗如雨 drip with sweat ③ command (an army): ～师南下 command an army to march

south ④ scatter; disperse
【挥动】 huīdòng brandish; wave: ～大棒 brandish a big stick/ ～旗子 wave a flag/ ～拳头 shake one's fist
【挥发】 huīfā volatilize ◇ ～性 volatility/ ～油 volatile oil
【挥戈】 huīgē brandish one's weapons: ～东进 march eastward
【挥毫】 huīháo 〈书〉 wield one's writing brush; write or draw a picture (with a brush)
【挥霍】 huīhuò spend freely; squander: ～无度 spend without restraint
【挥金如土】 huī jīn rú tǔ throw money about like dirt; spend money like water
【挥手】 huīshǒu wave one's hand; wave: ～致意 wave greetings to; wave to sb. in acknowledgment/ ～告别 wave farewell; wave good-bye to sb.
【挥舞】 huīwǔ wave; wield; brandish: ～花束表示欢迎 wave bouquets in welcome/ ～指挥棒 brandish the baton — order sb. about/ ～核武器 brandish nuclear weapons/ 社员们～锄头向荒山开战。Hoes in hand, the commune members battled to reclaim the barren hills.

**晖** huī sunshine; sunlight

**辉** huī ① brightness; splendour ② shine: 与日月同～ shine for ever like the sun and the moon
【辉长岩】 huīchángyán 〈地〉 gabbro
【辉光】 huīguāng 〈电〉 glow
◇ ～灯 glow lamp/ ～放电 glow discharge/ ～放电管 glow discharge tube
【辉煌】 huīhuáng brilliant; splendid; glorious: ～的战果 a brilliant military victory/ ～的文化 splendid civilization/ 灯火～ brilliantly illuminated; ablaze with lights
【辉绿岩】 huīlǜyán diabase
【辉钼矿】 huīmùkuàng molybdenite
【辉砷钴矿】 huīshēngǔkuàng cobaltite
【辉石】 huīshí 〈地〉 pyroxene; augite
【辉锑矿】 huītīkuàng stibnite
【辉铜矿】 huītóngkuàng chalcocite
【辉银矿】 huīyínkuàng argentite
【辉映】 huīyìng shine; reflect: 湖光山色,交相～。The lake and the hills add radiance and beauty to each other.

**麾** huī 〈书〉 ① standard of a commander (used in ancient times) ② command: ～军前进 command an army to march forward
【麾下】 huīxià 〈书〉 ① 〈敬〉 general; commander; your excellency ② those under one's command

**徽** huī emblem; badge; insignia: 国～ national emblem/ 校～ school badge/ 帽～ cap insignia
【徽号】 huīhào title of honour
【徽墨】 huīmò inkstick produced in Huizhou (徽州), Anhui Province
【徽章】 huīzhāng badge; insignia

**隳** huī 〈书〉 destroy; ruin

## huí

**回** huí ① circle; wind: 迂～ winding; circuitous; roundabout/ 峰～路转。The path winds along mountain ridges. ② return; go back: ～到原地 return to where one came from/ ～到生产第一线 go back to one's post on the production front/ 出敌不意,红军～师遵义。The Red Army swung back to Zunyi, taking the enemy by surprise. ③ turn round: ～过身来 turn round ④ answer; reply: ～信 send a letter in reply; write back ⑤ 〈量〉 chapter: 这部小说共一百一十二～。This novel has 112 chapters. ⑥ 〈量〉 〔用于事情,动作的次数〕: 来过一～ have been here once/ 完全是两～事 two entirely different matters/ 一～生,二～熟。First time strangers, second time friends. ⑦ (Huí) the Hui nationality 参见"回族"
【回拜】 huíbài pay a return visit
【回报】 huíbào ① report back on what has been done ② repay; requite; reciprocate: ～他的盛情 repay him for his hospitality or kindness ③ retaliate; get one's own back
【回避】 huíbì evade; dodge; avoid (meeting sb.): ～要害问题 evade (或 sidestep) the crucial question/ ～困难 dodge difficulties
【回禀】 huíbǐng 〈旧〉 report back (to one's superior)
【回波】 huíbō 〈电〉 echo ◇ ～脉冲 echo pulse
【回驳】 huíbó refute
【回采】 huícǎi 〈矿〉 stoping; extraction
◇ ～工作面 stope/ ～率 percentage of recovery; recovery/ ～损失 mining loss
【回肠】 huícháng ① ileum ② 〈书〉 worried; agitated
【回肠荡气】 huícháng-dàngqì (of music, poems, etc.) soul-stirring; heartrending
【回潮】 huícháo resurgence; reversion: 思想～ an ideological relapse (或 retrogression)
【回潮率】 huícháolǜ 〈纺〉 (moisture) regain
【回程】 huíchéng ① return trip ② 〈机〉 return (或 back) stroke
【回春】 huíchūn ① return of spring: 大地～。Spring returns to the earth. 或 Spring is here again. ② bring back to life: ～灵药 a miraculous cure; a wonderful remedy
【回答】 huídá answer; reply; response: 从理论上～了这个问题 furnish a theoretical answer to this question/ 事实是对造谣者最有力的～。Facts are the most powerful rebuff to rumourmongers.
【回荡】 huídàng resound; reverberate: 欢呼声在山谷间～。Shouts of joy reverberated in the valleys.
【回电】 huídiàn wire back: 请即～。Wire reply immediately.
【回动】 huídòng 〈机〉 reverse ◇ ～机构 reversing mechanism
【回访】 huífǎng pay a return visit
【回风道】 huífēngdào 〈矿〉 air return way
【回复】 huífù reply (to a letter)
【回顾】 huígù look back; review: ～长征 look back on the Long March/ ～党内两条路线斗争的历史 review the history of the two-line struggle within the Party / 一九七七年的～ 1977 in retrospect
【回光返照】 huíguāng fǎnzhào ① the last radiance of the setting sun — momentary recovery of consciousness just before death ② a sudden spurt of activity prior to collapse
【回归】 huíguī 〈统计〉 regression
【回归年】 huíguīnián 〈天〉 tropical year
【回归热】 huíguīrè 〈医〉 relapsing fever
【回归线】 huíguīxiàn 〈地〉 tropic: 南～ the Tropic of Capricorn/ 北～ the Tropic of Cancer
【回锅】 huíguō cook again ◇ ～肉 twice-cooked pork often with chilli seasoning
【回合】 huíhé round; bout: 第一个～的胜利 a first-round victory
【回纥】 Huíhé Huihe (Ouigour), an ancient nationality in China
【回话】 huíhuà reply; answer: 请你给他带个～。Please take a message to him by way of reply.
【回火】 huíhuǒ 〈机〉 tempering ◇ ～脆性 temper brittleness
【回击】 huíjī fight back; return fire; counterattack: 给以有

力的～ strike a powerful counterblow; hit back hard
【回见】 huíjiàn 〈套〉 see you later (或 again); cheerio
【回交】 huíjiāo 〈生〉 backcross
【回教】 Huíjiào 〈旧〉 Islam
【回敬】 huíjìng return a compliment; do or give sth. in return: ～一杯 drink a toast in return/ ～一拳 return a blow
【回绝】 huíjué decline; refuse: 一口～ flatly refuse
【回扣】 huíkòu sales commission
【回来】 huílai return; come back; be back: 他马上就～。He'll be back in a minute.
【回来】 huilai 〔用在动词后,表示到原来的地方来〕back: 跑～ run back/ 把借出去的书要～。Recall the books on loan.
【回廊】 huíláng winding corridor
【回礼】 huílǐ ① return a salute ② send a present in return; present a gift in return
【回笼】 huílóng ① steam again: 把凉馒头回回笼。Heat up the cold steamed buns. ② withdrawal (of currency) from circulation
【回炉】 huílú ① melt down: 废铁～ melt down scrap iron; use scrap iron for smelting ② bake (cakes, etc.) again
【回路】 huílù 〈电〉 return circuit; return; loop ◇ ～增益 loop gain
【回落】 huíluò (of water levels, prices, etc.) fall after a rise
【回马枪】 huímǎqiāng back thrust: 杀他个～ give sb. a back thrust; swing round and catch sb. off guard
【回民】 Huímín the Huis; the Hui people
【回暖】 huínuǎn get warm again after a cold spell
【回请】 huíqǐng return hospitality; give a return banquet
【回去】 huíqu return; go back; be back: 他离开家乡十年,从未～过。He has never been back to his birthplace since he left it ten years ago.
【回去】 huiqu 〔用在动词后,表示到原来的地方去〕back: 请把这封信给他退～。Please return the letter to him.
【回扫】 huísǎo 〈电子〉 flyback
【回升】 huíshēng rise again (after a fall); pick up: 气温～。The temperature has gone up again./ 指数～。The index is picking up.
【回生】 huíshēng ① bring back to life: 起死～ bring the dying back to life ② forget through lack of practice; get rusty: 几个月不用,我的法语又～了。I haven't practised my French for months and it's getting rusty.
【回声】 huíshēng echo ◇ ～测深仪 echo sounder; fathometer
【回收】 huíshōu retrieve; recover; reclaim: ～贵重金属 retrieve rare metals/ 余热～ recovery of waste heat ◇ ～率 rate of recovery (或 reclamation)/ ～塔 〈化〉 recovery tower/ ～站 (waste materials) collection depot
【回手】 huíshǒu ① turn round and stretch out one's hand: 他走出了屋子,～把门带上。He went out of the room and closed the door behind him. ② hit back; return a blow
【回首】 huíshǒu ① turn one's head; turn round ② 〈书〉 look back; recollect
【回水】 huíshuǐ 〈水〉 backwater
【回苏灵】 huísūlíng 〈药〉 dimefline
【回溯】 huísù recall; look back upon: ～党内两条路线斗争史 recall the history of the two-line struggle within the Party/ ～革命战争的岁月 look back upon the years of revolutionary war
【回天之力】 huí tiān zhī lì power capable of saving a desperate situation; tremendous power
【回填】 huítián 〈建〉 backfill ◇ ～土 backfill
【回条】 huítiáo a short note acknowledging receipt of sth.; receipt
【回帖】 huítiě a money order receipt to be signed and returned to the sender
【回头】 huítóu ① turn one's head; turn round ② repent: 及早～ repent before it is too late ③ 〈口〉 later: ～再谈。We'll talk it over later./ ～见! See you later!
【回头路】 huítóulù the road back to one's former position; the road of retrogression: 走～ take the road back; backtrack
【回头是岸】 huítóu shì àn repent and be saved: 希望劝说反动派发出善心,～,是不可能的。It is impossible to persuade the reactionaries to show kindness of heart and to turn from their evil ways.
【回味】 huíwèi ① aftertaste ② call sth. to mind and ponder over it: ～他说的话 ponder over what he has said
【回乡】 huíxiāng return to one's home village ◇ ～知识青年 a school graduate who returns to do farm work in his or her home village
【回翔】 huíxiáng circle round; wheel
【回响】 huíxiǎng reverberate; echo; resound: 雷声在山谷里激起了～。Thunder reverberated in the valley./ 他的亲切教导仍在我的耳边～。His earnest instructions still ring in my ears.
【回想】 huíxiǎng think back; recollect; recall: 这首歌使我～起在五七干校的生活。The song brought back to my mind our life at the May 7th cadre school.
【回销】 huíxiāo 见"返销" fǎnxiāo
【回心转意】 huíxīn-zhuǎnyì change one's views; come around
【回信】 huíxìn ① write in reply; write back: 我回了他一封信。I wrote him a reply./ 望早日～。I'm looking forward to hearing from you soon. ② a letter in reply ③ a verbal message in reply; reply: 事情办妥了,我给你个～儿。I'll let you know when I'm through with it.
【回形针】 huíxíngzhēn (paper) clip
【回修】 huíxiū return sth. for repairs
【回旋】 huíxuán ① circle round: 飞机在上空～。The aeroplane is circling overhead. ②(room for) manoeuvre: 这件事还有～余地。The whole thing is not final. 或 It's still possible to make changes. ◇ ～加速器 〈物〉 cyclotron/ ～曲 〈乐〉 *rondo*
【回忆】 huíyì call to mind; recollect; recall: ～对比 recall the past and contrast it with the present/ 战争年代的～ reminiscences of the war years/ 童年的～ recollections of childhood; childhood memories ◇ ～录 reminiscences; memoirs; recollections
【回音】 huíyīn ① echo ② reply: 立候～ hoping for an immediate reply ③ 〈乐〉 turn: 逆～ inverted turn ◇ ～壁 the Echo Wall (in the Temple of Heaven in Beijing)
【回游】 huíyóu 〈动〉 migration: 索饵～ feeding migration/ 产卵～ spawning migration
【回执】 huízhí a short note acknowledging receipt of sth.; receipt
【回注】 huízhù 〈石油〉 recycle
【回柱】 huízhù 〈矿〉 prop drawing ◇ ～机 prop drawer; post puller
【回转】 huízhuǎn turn round
◇ ～半径 〈航海〉 radius of gyration/ ～工作台 〈机〉 rotary table/ ～炉 〈冶〉 rotary furnace/ ～式钻床 rotary drill/ ～体 〈数〉 solid of revolution/ ～仪 〈天〉 gyroscope; gyro
【回族】 Huízú the Hui nationality, mainly distributed over the Ningxia Hui Autonomous Region, Gansu, Henan, Hebei, Qinghai, Shandong, Yunnan, Anhui, the Xinjiang Uygur Autonomous Region, Liaoning, Beijing and Tianjin
【回嘴】 huízuǐ answer (或 talk) back; retort

**洄** huí 〈书〉 (of water) whirl

**茴** huí

【茴香】 huíxiāng 〈植〉 ① fennel ② aniseed ◇ ～豆 beans flavoured with aniseed/ ～油 fennel oil

**蛔** huí

【蛔虫】 huíchóng roundworm; ascarid ◇ ～病 roundworm disease; ascariasis

## huǐ

**悔** huǐ regret; repent

【悔不当初】 huǐ bù dāngchū regret having done sth.: 早知今日，～。If I'd known then what was going to happen, I wouldn't have done as I did.

【悔改】 huǐgǎi repent and mend one's ways: 毫无～之意 have no intention of mending one's ways; show no sign of repentance

【悔过】 huǐguò repent one's error; be repentant: 有～表示 show signs of repentance/ ～自新 repent and turn over a new leaf; repent and make a fresh start ◇ ～书 a written statement of repentance

【悔恨】 huǐhèn regret deeply; be bitterly remorseful

【悔棋】 huǐqí retract a false move in a chess game

【悔悟】 huǐwù realize one's error and show repentance

【悔之无及】 huǐ zhī wú jí too late to repent; too late to regret

【悔罪】 huǐzuì show repentance; show penitence

**毁** huǐ ① destroy; ruin; damage: ～于一旦 be destroyed in a moment/ 这场雹子把庄稼～了。The hailstorm ruined the crops. ② burn up: 焚～ destroy by fire; burn down ③ defame; slander ④ 〈方〉 refashion; make over: 把这件大褂给孩子们～两件上衣。Make two children's jackets out of this gown.

【毁谤】 huǐbàng slander; malign; calumniate: 这纯系～。This is slander, pure and simple./ 敌人对鲁迅的～，更坚定了他的战斗意志。The enemy's calumnies made Lu Xun all the more determined to go on fighting.

【毁坏】 huǐhuài destroy; damage

【毁灭】 huǐmiè destroy; exterminate: 给侵略者以～性打击 deal the aggressors a crushing (或 devastating) blow

【毁弃】 huǐqì scrap; annul

【毁伤】 huǐshāng injure; hurt; damage

【毁损】 huǐsǔn damage; impair

【毁誉】 huǐ-yù praise or blame; praise or condemnation: 不计～ be indifferent to people's praise or blame/ ～参半 (of a person) get both praise and censure; (of a book, etc.) have a mixed reception

【毁约】 huǐyuē ① break one's promise ② scrap a contract or treaty

## huì

**汇** huì ① converge: ～成巨流 converge into a mighty torrent ② gather together: ～印成书 have (articles on a given subject) collected and published in book form ③ things collected; assemblage; collection: 词～ vocabulary ④ remit: 给家里～钱 remit money to one's family/ 电～ telegraphic transfer

【汇报】 huìbào report; give an account of: ～工作 report to sb. on one's work/ ～调查结果 report the findings of an investigation/ 经常向党组织～思想 regularly report to the Party organization on one's ideological progress and problems ◇ ～会 report-back meeting/ ～演出 report-back performance (a dramatic representation of a group's experience in the countryside, a factory, etc.)

【汇编】 huìbiān compilation; collection; corpus: 资料～工作 compilation of reference material/ 文件～ a collection of documents/ 语言学研究资料～ a corpus of philological data

【汇兑】 huìduì remittance: 国内～ domestic remittance ◇ ～网 remittance network

【汇费】 huìfèi remittance fee 又作"汇水"

【汇合】 huìhé converge; join: 这两条河在什么地方～? Where do the two rivers join?/ ～成一支巨大的力量 unite to form a gigantic force/ 五条支流的～口 the confluence of five tributaries

【汇集】 huìjí ① collect; compile: ～材料 collect all relevant data ② come together; converge; assemble: 游行队伍从四面八方～到天安门广场上。The paraders converged on Tian'anmen Square from all directions.

【汇款】 huìkuǎn ① remit money; make a remittance ② remittance: 收到一笔～ receive a remittance/ 邮政～ postal remittance ◇ ～单 money order/ ～人 remitter

【汇流】 huìliú converge; flow together ◇ ～点 〈地〉 confluence/ ～条 〈电〉 busbar

【汇率】 huìlǜ exchange rate: 固定～ fixed (exchange) rate/ 浮动～ floating (exchange) rate/ 中心～ central rate

【汇票】 huìpiào draft; bill of exchange; money order: 银行～ bank draft/ 邮政～ postal money order

【汇演】 huìyǎn 见"会演" huìyǎn

【汇总】 huìzǒng gather; collect; pool: 把材料～上报 collect data for the higher level; present an itemized report to the higher level

**卉** huì (various kinds of) grass: 奇花异～ rare flowers and grasses

**会** huì ① get together; assemble: 明晨七时在门口～齐。We'll assemble at the gate at 7 o'clock tomorrow morning. ② meet; see: 昨天我没有～着他。I didn't see him yesterday. ③ meeting; gathering; party; get-together; conference: 晚上有个全组～。There's going to be a meeting of the whole group tonight./ 欢迎～ welcoming party/ 欢送～ send-off party ④ association; society; union: 帮～ secret society/ 工～ trade union ⑤ 〈旧〉 a temple fair: 赶～ go to a fair ⑥ 〈旧〉 an association of people who regularly contribute to a common fund and draw from it by turns ⑦ chief city; capital: 都～ city; metropolis/ 省～ provincial capital ⑧ opportunity; occasion: 适逢其～ happen to be present on the occasion ⑨ understand; grasp: 误～ misunderstand ⑩ can; be able to: ～滑冰 can skate/ ～英文 know English ⑪ be good at; be skilful in: ～做思想工作 be good at doing ideological work/ ～修各种钟表 be skilful in repairing all kinds of clocks and watches/ 很～这一套 be a past master of this sort of game ⑫ be likely to; be sure to: 不学习辩证唯物主义，就～滑到唯心论和形而上学方面去。If one doesn't study dialectical materialism, one is liable to slip into idealism and metaphysics./ 离开党的基本路线，就～犯错误。One is sure to make mistakes if one deviates from the Party's basic line. ⑬ pay (或 foot) a bill: 饭钱我～过了。I've paid for the meal. ⑭ 〈口〉 a moment: 我去一～儿就回来。I'll be back in a moment.

另见 kuài

【会餐】 huìcān dine together; have a dinner party

【会场】 huìchǎng meeting-place; conference (或 assembly) hall

【会道门】 huì-dàomén superstitious sects and secret societies:

反动～ reactionary secret societies
【会费】 huìfèi membership dues
【会馆】 huìguǎn 〈旧〉 guild hall; provincial or county guild
【会合】 huìhé join; meet; converge; assemble: 成千上万的社员在水坝工地～。Thousands of commune members assembled at the dam site./ 两军～后继续前进。The two armies joined forces and marched on.
【会合点】 huìhédiǎn 〈军〉 meeting point; rallying point; rendezvous
【会话】 huìhuà conversation (as in a language course)
【会籍】 huìjí membership (of an association)
【会见】 huìjiàn meet with (esp. a foreign visitor)
【会聚】 huìjù assemble; flock together: 游园群众～于各个公园,欢庆五一节。Holidaymakers flocked to the parks to celebrate May Day.
【会聚透镜】 huìjù tòujìng 〈物〉 convergent lens
【会刊】 huìkān ① proceedings of a conference, etc. ② the journal of an association, society, etc.
【会客】 huìkè receive a visitor (或 guest): ～时间 the time for receiving visitors; visiting hours/ 现在开会,不～。No visitors. Meeting in progress. ◇ ～室 reception room
【会盟】 huìméng meetings of sovereigns or their deputies in ancient China to form alliances
【会面】 huìmiàn meet: 我约定了星期天和他～。I have an appointment to meet him on Sunday.
【会期】 huìqī ① the time fixed for a conference; the date (或 time) of a meeting ② the duration of a meeting: ～定为三天。The meeting is scheduled to last three days.
【会儿】 huìr 〈口〉 moment: 一～ a little while/ 等～。Wait a moment./ 用不了多大～。It won't be a minute. 或 It won't take long.
【会商】 huìshāng hold a conference or consultation: ～解决办法 consult to find a solution
【会审】 huìshěn ① joint hearing (或 trial) ② make a joint checkup: ～施工图纸 have a joint checkup on the blueprints for a project
【会师】 huìshī join forces; effect a junction
【会谈】 huìtán talks: 双边～ bilateral talks ◇ ～纪要 minutes of talks; notes on talks; summary of a conversation
【会堂】 huìtáng assembly hall; hall: 人民大～ the Great Hall of the People
【会同】 huìtóng (handle an affair) jointly with other organizations concerned
【会晤】 huìwù meet: 两国外长定期～。The foreign ministers of the two countries meet regularly.
【会心】 huìxīn understanding; knowing: ～的微笑 an understanding smile/ 露出～的表情 with a knowing look
【会穴】 huìxué 〈中医〉 crossing point (a point where two or more channels cross each other)
【会演】 huìyǎn joint performance (by a number of theatrical troupes, etc.): 文艺～ theatrical festival
【会厌】 huìyàn 〈生理〉 epiglottis
【会议】 huìyì meeting; conference: 正式～ official meeting/ 全体～ plenary session
◇ ～地点 meeting-place; venue/ ～日程表 the daily agenda of a conference/ ～室 meeting (或 conference) room; council chamber/ ～厅 conference (或 assembly) hall
【会意】 huìyì ① understanding; knowing ② 〈语〉 associative compounds, one of the six categories of Chinese characters (六书), which are formed by combining two or more elements, each with a meaning of its own, to create a new meaning, e.g. 信, a character made up of 人 (man) and 言 (word), meaning a message or something that can be believed or trusted
【会阴】 huìyīn 〈生理〉 perineum
【会员】 huìyuán member: 正式～ full (或 full-fledged) member/ ～人数 membership
◇ ～国 member state (或 nation)/ ～证 membership card/ ～资格 the status of a member; membership
【会战】 huìzhàn ① 〈军〉 meet for a decisive battle ② join in a battle; launch a mass campaign: ～海河工地 join in the battle to harness the Haihe River/ 石油大～ a great battle for oil (as when the Daqing Oil Field was being opened up)
【会章】 huìzhāng ① the constitution (或 statutes) of an association, society, etc. ② the emblem of an association, society, etc.
【会长】 huìzhǎng the president of an association or society
【会帐】 huìzhàng pay (或 foot) a bill
【会诊】 huìzhěn 〈医〉 consultation of doctors; (group) consultation: 中西医～ hold group consultations of doctors practising Chinese and Western medicine
【会址】 huìzhǐ ① the site of an association or society ② the site of a conference or meeting

**讳** huì ① avoid as taboo: 直言不～ speak bluntly; call a spade a spade ② forbidden word; taboo: 犯了他的～了。Something was said that happened to be taboo with him. ③ 〈旧〉 the name, regarded as taboo, of a deceased emperor or head of a family
【讳疾忌医】 huìjí-jìyī hide one's sickness for fear of treatment — conceal one's fault for fear of criticism
【讳莫如深】 huì mò rú shēn closely guard a secret; not breathe a word to a soul; not utter a single word about sth.
【讳言】 huìyán dare not or would not speak up: 毫不～ make no attempt to conceal the truth; confess freely/ 无可～ there's no denying the fact

**诲** huì teach; instruct
【诲人不倦】 huì rén bù juàn be tireless in teaching; teach with tireless zeal
【诲淫诲盗】 huìyín-huìdào、propagate sex and violence; stir up the base passions

**荟** huì 〈书〉 luxuriant growth (of plants)
【荟萃】 huìcuì (of distinguished people or exquisite objects) gather together; assemble: 人才～ a galaxy of talent/ ～一堂 gather together in one hall

**绘** huì paint; draw
【绘画】 huìhuà drawing; painting
【绘声绘色】 huìshēng-huìsè vivid; lively: ～的描述 a vivid description (或 portraiture) 又作"绘影绘声";"绘声绘影"
【绘图】 huìtú 见"制图" zhìtú
【绘制】 huìzhì draw (a design, etc.): 为社会主义新农村～了宏伟的图景 draw up a grand plan for a new socialist countryside

**烩** huì ① braise: ～虾仁 braised shrimp meat ② cook (rice or shredded pancakes) with meat, vegetables and water

**贿** huì bribe: 受～ accept (或 take) bribes/ 行～ practise bribery; bribe
【贿赂】 huìlù ① bribe ② bribery
【贿买】 huìmǎi buy over; suborn
【贿选】 huìxuǎn practise bribery at an election; get elected by bribery

**彗** huì 〈书〉 broom

【彗尾】 huìwěi 〈天〉 the tail of a comet
【彗星】 huìxīng 〈天〉 comet

**晦** huì ① the last day of a lunar month ② dark; obscure; gloomy ③ night
【晦暗】 huì'àn dark and gloomy
【晦气】 huìqì unlucky: 自认～ be resigned to one's bad luck
【晦涩】 huìsè hard to understand; obscure: ～的语言 obscure language (in poetry, drama, etc.)
【晦朔】 huì-shuò the last and first days of a lunar month

**秽** huì ① dirty: 污～ filthy ② ugly; abominable: ～行 abominable behaviour
【秽土】 huìtǔ rubbish; refuse; dirt
【秽闻】 huìwén 〈书〉 ill repute (referring to sexual behaviour); reputation for immorality
【秽行】 huìxíng 〈书〉 abominable behaviour; immoral conduct

**惠** huì ① favour; kindness; benefit: 小恩小～ small favours/ 受～ receive kindness (或 favour); be favoured/ 互～ mutual benefit ② 〈敬〉［用于对方对待自己的行动］: ～鉴 be kind enough to read (the following letter)/ ～书 your letter ③ (Huì) a surname
【惠存】 huìcún 〈敬〉 please keep (this photograph, book, etc. as a souvenir); to so-and-so
【惠顾】 huìgù 〈敬〉 your patronage
【惠临】 huìlín 〈敬〉 your gracious presence: 敬请～。Your presence is requested.

**喙** huì ① beak or snout ② mouth: 百～莫辩。A hundred mouths can't explain it away./ 不容置～ not allow others to butt in; brook no intervention

**殨** huì festering: ～脓 suppuration

**慧** huì intelligent; bright: 智～ wisdom; intelligence
【慧黠】 huìxiá 〈书〉 clever and artful; shrewd
【慧心】 huìxīn wisdom
【慧眼】 huìyǎn ① 〈佛教〉 a mind which perceives both past and future ② mental discernment (或 perception); insight; acumen

**蕙** huì
【蕙兰】 huìlán a species of orchid

**蟪** huì
【蟪蛄】 huìgū a kind of cicada

## hūn

**昏** hūn ① dusk: 晨～ at dawn and dusk ② dark; dim ③ confused; muddled: 利令智～ be blinded by lust for gain/ 以其～～,使人昭昭,是不行的。Those in the dark are in no position to light the way for others. ④ lose consciousness; faint: ～倒 fall into a swoon; go off into a faint; fall unconscious
【昏暗】 hūn'àn dim; dusky: ～的灯光 a dim light
【昏沉】 hūnchén ① murky: 暮色～ murky twilight ② dazed; befuddled: 我昨晚没睡好,头脑昏昏沉沉的。I feel in a daze because I didn't sleep well last night.
【昏黑】 hūnhēi dusky; dark
【昏花】 hūnhuā dim-sighted: 老眼～ dim-sighted from old age
【昏黄】 hūnhuáng pale yellow; faint; dim: 月色～ faint moonlight/ ～的灯光 a dim light
【昏昏欲睡】 hūnhūn yù shuì drowsy; sleepy
【昏厥】 hūnjué faint; swoon: ～过去 fall into a coma; faint away
【昏君】 hūnjūn a fatuous and self-indulgent ruler
【昏聩】 hūnkuì decrepit and muddleheaded
【昏乱】 hūnluàn dazed and confused; befuddled
【昏迷】 hūnmí stupor; coma: 处于～状态 be in a state of unconsciousness; be in a coma/ ～不醒 remain unconscious
【昏睡】 hūnshuì lethargic sleep; lethargy
【昏天黑地】 hūntiān-hēidì ① pitch-dark ② dizzy: 我只觉得一阵～,随即失去了知觉。I suddenly felt dizzy and then fell unconscious. ③ perverted; decadent: ～的生活 a dissipated life ④ dark rule and social disorder
【昏头昏脑】 hūntóu-hūnnǎo ① addleheaded; muddleheaded ② absentminded; forgetful
【昏星】 hūnxīng evening star
【昏眩】 hūnxuàn dizzy; giddy
【昏庸】 hūnyōng fatuous; muddleheaded; stupid

**荤** hūn meat or fish: ～菜 meat dishes/ 她不吃～。She doesn't eat meat. 或 She's a vegetarian.
【荤腥】 hūnxīng meat or fish
【荤油】 hūnyóu lard

**婚** hūn ① wed; marry ② marriage; wedding
【婚嫁】 hūnjià marriage
【婚礼】 hūnlǐ wedding ceremony; wedding
【婚龄】 hūnlíng (legally) marriageable age
【婚期】 hūnqī wedding day
【婚生子女】 hūnshēng zǐnǚ 〈法〉 children born in wedlock; legitimate children: 非～ children born out of wedlock
【婚事】 hūnshì marriage; wedding
【婚姻】 hūnyīn marriage; matrimony: ～自由 freedom of marriage/ 美满的～ a happy marriage/ ～纠纷 matrimonial dispute/ ～状况 marital status ◇ ～法 marriage law
【婚约】 hūnyuē marriage contract; engagement: 解除～ break off one's engagement

**阍** hūn 〈书〉 ① tend or guard a gate: 司～ gatekeeper; janitor ② palace gate
【阍者】 hūnzhě 〈书〉 gatekeeper; janitor

## hún

**浑** hún ① muddy; turbid: ～水 muddy water ② foolish; stupid ③ simple and natural; unsophisticated ④ whole; all over
【浑蛋】 húndàn 〈骂〉 blackguard; wretch; scoundrel; bastard; skunk
【浑厚】 húnhòu ① simple and honest ② (of writing, painting, etc.) simple and vigorous: 笔力～ (of handwriting) bold and vigorous strokes
【浑浑噩噩】 húnhún'è'è ignorant; simple-minded; muddleheaded
【浑金璞玉】 húnjīn-púyù 见"璞玉浑金" púyù-húnjīn
【浑然一体】 húnrán yī tǐ one integrated mass; a unified entity; an integral whole
【浑身】 húnshēn from head to foot; all over: 吓得～发抖 tremble all over with fear/ ～疼痛 aching all over/ ～是劲 brimming with energy; bursting with energy/ ～是胆 be every inch a hero; be the very embodiment of valour/

猪～上下都是宝。Every part of the pig is useful.
【浑水摸鱼】 húnshuǐ mō yú fish in troubled waters
【浑天仪】 húntiānyí 〈天〉 ① armillary sphere ② celestial globe
【浑象】 húnxiàng 〈天〉 celestial globe
【浑仪】 húnyí 〈天〉 armillary sphere
【浑圆】 húnyuán perfectly round
【浑浊】 húnzhuó muddy; turbid

**珲** hún 〈书〉 a kind of jade

**混** hún
另见 hùn
【混蛋】 húndàn 见"浑蛋" húndàn

**馄** hún
【馄饨】 húntun *won ton*; dumpling soup

**魂** hún ① soul ② mood; spirit: 神～不定 be distracted; have the jitters ③ the lofty spirit of a nation: 民族～ national spirit
【魂不附体】 hún bù fù tǐ as if the soul had left the body: 吓得～ be scared out of one's wits
【魂灵】 húnling 〈口〉 soul
【魂魄】 húnpò soul

## hùn

**诨** hùn joke; jest: 打～ make gags
【诨名】 hùnmíng nickname

**混** hùn ① mix; confuse: ～在一起 mix things up/ 这是两码事,不要搞～了。They're two entirely different matters; don't mix them up. ② pass for; pass off as: 鱼目～珠 pass off fish eyes as pearls — pass off the sham as genuine/ ～在革命队伍中的叛徒 renegades lurking in the revolutionary ranks ③ muddle along; drift along: ～日子 drift along aimlessly/ 在旧社会他连口饭都～不上。In the old society he could hardly make a living. ④ get along with sb.: 同他们～得很熟 be quite familiar with them ⑤ thoughtlessly; recklessly; irresponsibly: ～出主意 put forward irresponsible suggestions
另见 hún
【混充】 hùnchōng pass oneself off as; palm sth. off as
【混沌】 hùndùn ① Chaos (the primeval state of the universe according to folklore): ～初开 when earth was first separated from heaven ② innocent as a child
【混纺】 hùnfǎng 〈纺〉 blending ◇ ～织物 blend fabric
【混合】 hùnhé mix; blend; mingle: 客货～列车 mixed train ◇ ～编队 〈军〉 composite formation/ ～面 flour mixed with dirt and other adulterants (sold in the occupied areas during the War of Resistance Against Japan)/ ～器 〈化〉 mixer/ ～色 secondary colour/ ～授粉 〈农〉 mixed pollination/ ～双打 〈体〉 mixed doubles/ ～委员会 mixed committee/ ～物 mixture/ ～岩 〈地〉 migmatite
【混迹】 hùnjì unworthily occupy a place among
【混交林】 hùnjiāolín mixed forest
【混进】 hùnjìn infiltrate; sneak into; worm one's way into: ～革命队伍中的阶级异己分子 alien class elements who have sneaked into the revolutionary ranks
【混乱】 hùnluàn confusion; chaos: 敌军陷于～。The enemy were thrown into confusion./ 思想～ ideological confusion
【混凝剂】 hùnníngjì 〈化〉 coagulant
【混凝土】 hùnníngtǔ concrete ◇ ～搅拌机 concrete mixer/ ～结构 concrete structure/ ～振捣器 (concrete) vibrator
【混频管】 hùnpínguǎn 〈电子〉 mixer tube
【混世魔王】 hùn shì mówáng fiend in human shape; devil incarnate
【混水摸鱼】 hùnshuǐ mō yú fish in troubled waters
【混同】 hùntóng confuse; mix up: 不要把敌我矛盾与人民内部矛盾～起来。We must not confuse contradictions between ourselves and the enemy with those among the people.
【混为一谈】 hùn wéi yī tán lump (或 jumble) together; confuse sth. with sth. else: 把正义战争与非正义战争～ lump together just wars and unjust wars/ 把革命和改良～ confuse revolution with reform
【混响】 hùnxiǎng 〈物〉 reverberation
【混淆】 hùnxiáo obscure; blur; confuse; mix up: ～革命与反革命的界限 obscure the demarcation line (或 blur the distinction) between revolution and counterrevolution/ ～阶级阵线 blur class alignments/ ～敌友 confuse friend with foe/ ～两类不同性质的矛盾 mix up the two different types of contradictions/ ～黑白 mix up black and white/ ～是非 confuse right and wrong/ ～视听 mislead the public; confuse public opinion
【混血儿】 hùnxuè'ér a person of mixed blood; half-breed
【混一】 hùnyī amalgamation
【混杂】 hùnzá mix; mingle: 不要把不同的种子～在一起。Don't mix up different kinds of seeds.
【混战】 hùnzhàn tangled warfare: 军阀～ tangled warfare among warlords; tangled fighting between warlords
【混帐】 hùnzhàng 〈骂〉 scoundrel; bastard; son of a bitch ◇ ～话 impudent remark
【混浊】 hùnzhuó muddy; turbid: ～的水 turbid water/ ～的空气 foul (或 stale) air

## huō

**耠** huō hoeing
【耠子】 huōzi a hoeing implement

**劐** huō 〈口〉 ① slit or cut with a knife: 把鱼肚子～开 slit open the fish ② hoeing

**嚄** huō 〈叹〉〔表示惊讶〕: ～! 好大的鱼! Oh! What a big fish!
另见 ǒ

**豁** huō ① slit; break; crack: 墙上～了一个口子。There is a breach in the wall. ② give up; sacrifice: ～出三天时间,也要把它做好。Even if it takes us three days, we must get the job done.
另见 huò
【豁出去】 huōchuqu go ahead regardless; be ready to risk everything: 工人们～了,决心跟资本家干到底。The workers were resolved to fight it out with the bosses at all costs.
【豁口】 huōkǒu opening; break; breach: 城墙～ an opening in the city wall
【豁嘴】 huōzuǐ ① 〈口〉 harelip ② a harelipped person

**攉** huō shovel coal, ore, etc. from one place to another: ～煤工人 coal shoveller

## huó

**和** huó mix (powder) with water, etc.: ～点儿灰泥

prepare some plaster
另见 hé; hè; huò
【和面】 huómiàn knead dough ◇ ～机 flour-mixing machine

活 huó ①live: 她～到八十岁。She lived to be eighty./ ～到老,学到老。One is never too old to learn. ②alive; living: 在他～着的时候 during his lifetime/ ～捉 capture alive/ ～老虎 a live tiger/ ～字典 a walking dictionary ③save (the life of a person): ～人无算 (of a good doctor, etc.) save countless lives ④vivid; lively: ～画出一副叛徒的嘴脸 give a vivid picture of a renegade/ 思想工作做得很～ do ideological work in a lively way/ 脑子很～ have a quick mind ⑤movable; moving: ～水 flowing water ⑥exactly; simply: ～像 look exactly like; be the spit and image of ⑦work: 干～儿 work/ 重～儿 heavy work/ 针线～儿 needlework ⑧product: 这批～儿做得好。This batch of products is well made.
【活靶】 huóbǎ 〈军〉 manoeuvring target
【活靶子】 huóbǎzi live target: 革命大批判的～ the live target of revolutionary mass criticism
【活版】 huóbǎn 〈印〉 typography; letterpress ◇ ～印刷 typographic printing; typography; letterpress printing/ ～印刷机 letterpress (printing) machine 又作"活字版"
【活瓣】 huóbàn 〈生理〉 valve
【活宝】 huóbǎo a bit of a clown; a funny fellow
【活报剧】 huóbàojù living newspaper; skit; street performance
【活标本】 huóbiāoběn living specimen: 假共产主义、真资本主义的～ a living specimen of sham communism and real capitalism
【活茬】 huóchá 〈口〉 farm work
【活地狱】 huódìyù hell on earth
【活动】 huódòng ①move about; exercise: 站起来～～ stand up and move about/ ～一下筋骨 limber up the joints; limber oneself up ②shaky; unsteady: 这把椅子直～。The chair is rickety./ 这颗牙～了。This tooth's loose. ③movable; mobile; flexible: 口气有点～ sound less adamant; begin to relent a little ④activity; manoeuvre: 户外～ outdoor activities/ 政治～ political activities/ 从事科学～ go in for scientific pursuits/ 游击队在敌人后方～。The guerrilla forces were operating behind the enemy lines./ ～余地 room for manoeuvre ⑤use personal influence or irregular means: 替他～～ put in a word for him; use one's influence on his behalf ⑥〈心〉 behaviour
◇ ～靶 〈军〉 manoeuvring target/ ～坝 〈水〉 movable dam/ ～扳手 〈机〉 adjustable spanner (或 wrench)/ ～家 activist; public figure/ ～资本 liquid capital
【活度】 huódù 〈化〉 activity ◇ ～系数 activity coefficient
【活佛】 huófó 〈宗〉 Living Buddha
【活该】 huógāi 〈口〉 serve sb. right: 这家伙落得如此下场,～。The fellow got what he deserved.
【活荷载】 huóhèzài 〈交〉〈建〉 live load
【活化】 huóhuà 〈化〉 activation ◇ ～剂 activator/ ～吸附 activation absorption
【活活】 huóhuó while still alive: ～烧死 be burnt alive
【活计】 huóji ①handicraft work; manual labour: 把生产队的～统一安排一下。Make an overall arrangement of the work of the production team. ②handiwork; work: 她拿着～给大家看。She showed her work to everybody.
【活见鬼】 huójiànguǐ it's sheer fantasy; you're imagining things
【活结】 huójié a knot that can be undone by a pull; slipknot
【活口】 huókǒu ①a survivor of a murder attempt ②a prisoner who can furnish information
【活扣】 huókòu 〈口〉 见"活结"
【活力】 huólì vigour; vitality; energy: 充满着青春的～ be brimming with youthful vigour
【活灵活现】 huólíng-huóxiàn vivid; lifelike: 说得～ give a vivid description; make it come to life 又作"活龙活现"
【活路】 huólù ①means of subsistence; way out: 旧社会哪有咱穷人的～。What way out was there for us poor folk in the old society? ②workable method
【活络】 huóluò 〈方〉 ①loose: 牙齿有点～。The tooth has become a bit loose. ②noncommittal; indefinite: 他说得很～。He was rather noncommittal.
【活埋】 huómái bury alive
【活门】 huómén 〈机〉 valve
【活命】 huómìng ①earn a bare living; scrape along; eke out an existence: 他在旧社会靠卖艺～。In the old society he scraped along as a street entertainer. ②〈书〉 save sb.'s life: ～之恩 indebtedness to sb. for saving one's life ③life ◇ ～哲学 the philosophy of survival (preached by the modern revisionists)
【活泼】 huópo ①lively; vivacious; vivid: 天真～的孩子 lively children/ 文字～ written in a lively style ②〈化〉 reactive
【活期】 huóqī current ◇ ～储蓄 current deposit; demand deposit/ ～存款帐户 current account
【活塞】 huósāi 〈机〉 piston ◇ ～杆 piston rod/ ～圈 piston ring
【活生生】 huóshēngshēng ①real; living: ～的阶级斗争现实 the living reality of class struggle/ ～的例子 a living example ②while still alive: 万恶的封建礼教把这个年轻的妇女～地折磨死了。The barbarous feudal ethical code literally snuffed out her young life.
【活受罪】 huóshòuzuì 〈口〉 have a hell of a life
【活水】 huóshuǐ flowing water; running water
【活现】 huóxiàn appear vividly; come alive: 黄继光的英雄形象又～在我们眼前。The heroic image of Huang Jiguang once again appeared vividly in our mind's eye.
【活像】 huóxiàng look exactly like; be the spit and image of; be an exact replica of: 这孩子长得～他父亲。The child is the very spit (或 image) of his father.
【活性】 huóxìng 〈化〉 active; activated ◇ ～染料 reactive dyes/ ～碳 〈化〉 active (或 activated) carbon
【活血】 huóxuè 〈中医〉 invigorate the circulation of blood
【活阎王】 huóyánwang devil incarnate; tyrannical ruler
【活页】 huóyè loose-leaf
◇ ～笔记本 loose-leaf notebook/ ～夹 loose-leaf binder; spring binder/ ～文选 loose-leaf selections/ ～纸 paper for a loose-leaf notebook
【活跃】 huóyuè ①brisk; active; dynamic: 市场～。Business is brisk./ 人是生产力中最～的因素。Man is the most active factor among the productive forces. ②enliven; animate; invigorate: ～文娱生活 liven up cultural and recreational activities/ ～会场气氛 enliven the atmosphere of the meeting/ ～城乡物资交流 stimulate the interchange of urban and rural products
【活字】 huózì 〈印〉 type; letter ◇ ～盘 type case; letter board
【活组织检查】 huózǔzhī jiǎnchá 〈医〉 biopsy

## huǒ

火 huǒ ①fire: 生～ make a fire/ 这屋里有～。There's a fire in the room. ②firearms; ammunition: 交～ exchange shots ③〈中医〉 internal heat — one of the six causes of disease 参见"上火" shànghuǒ② ④fiery; flaming: ～红 red as fire; flaming ⑤urgent; pressing: ～速回电。Cable reply immediately. ⑥anger; temper: 心头～起

flare up in anger/ 你怎么这么大的～儿？Why are you in such a temper?/ 他～儿了。He flared up.
【火把】 huǒbǎ torch
【火棒】 huǒbàng lighted torch (used in acrobatics)
【火暴】 huǒbào 〈方〉 fiery; irritable: ～性子 a hot temper
【火并】 huǒbìng open fight between factions: 反动统治阶级内部的～ an open factional fight within the reactionary ruling class
【火柴】 huǒchái match ◇ ～盒 matchbox
【火场】 huǒchǎng the scene of a fire
【火车】 huǒchē train
◇ ～轮渡 train ferry/ ～票 railway ticket/ ～时刻表 railway timetable; train schedule/ ～司机 engine driver; (locomotive) engineer/ ～站 railway station
【火车头】 huǒchētóu (railway) engine; locomotive: 革命是历史的～。Revolutions are the locomotives of history.
【火成岩】 huǒchéngyán 〈地〉 igneous rock
【火法冶金】 huǒfǎ yějīn 〈冶〉 pyrometallurgy
【火夫】 huǒfū 〈旧〉 ① stoker; fireman ② mess cook
【火攻】 huǒgōng fire attack (using fire as a weapon against enemy personnel and installations)
【火罐】 huǒguàn 〈中医〉 cupping jar (或 glass): 拔～ cupping
【火光】 huǒguāng flame; blaze: ～冲天。The flames lit up the sky.
【火锅】 huǒguō chafing dish
【火海】 huǒhǎi a sea of fire: 刀山敢上，～敢闯 dare to climb a mountain of swords and plunge into a sea of flames — ready to undergo the most severe trials
【火红】 huǒhóng red as fire; fiery; flaming: ～的太阳 a flaming sun/ ～的战旗 a flame-red battle flag/ ～的战争年代 fiery years of war
【火候】 huǒhou ① duration and degree of heating, cooking, smelting, etc.: 烧窑得看～。In operating a kiln you must pay attention to temperature control./ 这鸭子烤得正到～。This roast duck is done to a turn. ② level of attainment: 他的书法到～了。He has matured as a calligrapher. ③ a crucial moment: 正在战斗的～上，援军赶到了。Reinforcements rushed up at the crucial moment of the battle.
【火狐】 huǒhú red fox
【火花】 huǒhuā spark: ～四溅 sparks flying off in all directions ◇ ～塞 〈机〉 sparking plug; spark plug; ignition plug
【火化】 huǒhuà cremation
【火鸡】 huǒjī turkey
【火急】 huǒjí urgent; pressing: 十万～ most urgent
【火剪】 huǒjiǎn ① fire-tongs; tongs ② curling tongs; curling irons
【火碱】 huǒjiǎn caustic soda
【火箭】 huǒjiàn rocket: 发射～ fire (或 launch) a rocket
◇ ～部队 rocket troops/ ～弹 rocket projectile; rocket shell/ ～发射场 rocket launching site/ ～发射台 rocket launching pad; rocket mount/ ～技术 rocketry/ ～炮 rocket gun/ ～筒 rocket launcher (或 projector); bazooka
【火井】 huǒjǐng 〈方〉 gas well
【火警】 huǒjǐng fire alarm
【火酒】 huǒjiǔ 〈方〉 alcohol
【火炬】 huǒjù torch ◇ ～赛跑 torch race/ ～游行 torchlight parade
【火炕】 huǒkàng heated *kang*; heated brick bed
【火坑】 huǒkēng fiery pit; pit of hell; abyss of suffering: 跳出～ escape from the living hell
【火筷子】 huǒkuàizi fire-tongs; tongs
【火辣辣】 huǒlālā burning: ～的太阳 a scorching sun/ 疼得～的 a searing pain/ 脸上觉得～的 feel one's cheeks burning (as with shame)/ 心里～的 burning with anxiety
【火老鸦】 huǒlǎoyā 〈方〉 leaping flames (of raging fire)
【火力】 huǒlì 〈军〉 firepower; fire: 发扬～ make full use of firepower
◇ ～点 firing point/ ～发电厂 thermal power plant/ ～控制 control of fire/ ～配系 organization of fire; fire system/ ～突击 fire assault/ ～圈 field of fire/ ～网 network of fire; fire net/ ～掩护 fire cover/ ～侦察 reconnaissance by firing (to observe enemy reactions)/ ～支援 support fire; fire support
【火镰】 huǒlián steel (for flint)
【火烈鸟】 huǒlièniǎo flamingo
【火流星】 huǒliúxīng 〈天〉 bolide; fireball
【火龙】 huǒlóng ① fiery dragon — a procession of lanterns or torches ② 〈方〉 an air channel from a brick kitchen stove to a chimney; flue
【火炉】 huǒlú (heating) stove
【火帽】 huǒmào 〈军〉 detonating cap; percussion cap
【火煤】 huǒméi kindling 又作"火媒"
【火棉】 huǒmián guncotton; pyroxylin
【火苗】 huǒmiáo a tongue of flame; flame
【火捻】 huǒniǎn ① kindling ② fuse
【火炮】 huǒpào cannon; gun
【火盆】 huǒpén fire pan; brazier
【火漆】 huǒqī sealing wax
【火气】 huǒqì ① 〈中医〉 internal heat (as a cause of disease) ② anger; temper: ～很大 have a bad temper
【火器】 huǒqì 〈军〉 firearm
【火钳】 huǒqián fire-tongs; tongs
【火枪】 huǒqiāng firelock
【火墙】 huǒqiáng a wall with flues for space heating
【火热】 huǒrè ① burning hot; fervent; fiery: ～的太阳 a burning sun/ ～的心 a fervent heart/ 投身到～的群众斗争中去 plunge into the fiery struggles of the masses/ 反映工农兵～的斗争生活 portray workers, peasants and soldiers in the thick of their struggle ② intimate: 打得～ carry on intimately with; be as thick as thieves
【火绒】 huǒróng tinder
【火色】 huǒsè 〈方〉 condition of fire (as for cooking); strength of fire: 看～ see if the fire is good enough/ 拿稳了～ make sure that the fire is just right
【火山】 huǒshān volcano: ～喷发 volcanic eruption/ 活(死)～ active (extinct) volcano/ 休眠～ dormant volcano
◇ ～岛 volcanic island/ ～地震 volcanic earthquake/ ～灰 volcanic ash/ ～口 crater/ ～砾 lapillus/ ～作用 volcanism
【火伤】 huǒshāng burn (caused by fire)
【火上加油】 huǒshàng jiā yóu pour oil on the fire; add fuel to the flames
【火烧火燎】 huǒshāo-huǒliǎo ① feeling terribly hot ② restless with anxiety
【火烧眉毛】 huǒ shāo méimao the fire is singeing the eyebrows — a desperate situation; a matter of the utmost urgency
【火烧油层】 huǒshāo yóucéng 〈石油〉 combustion (of oil) in situ
【火烧】 huǒshao 〈食品〉 baked wheaten cake
【火舌】 huǒshé tongues of fire
【火绳】 huǒshéng a rope of plaited plants burnt as a mosquito repellent
【火石】 huǒshí flint
【火树银花】 huǒshù-yínhuā fiery trees and silver flowers — a display of fireworks and a sea of lanterns (on a festival night)
【火速】 huǒsù at top speed; posthaste: 任务十分紧急，必须

～完成。It's an urgent task and must be completed at once./ ～增援 rush up reinforcements

【火头】 huǒtóu ① flame ② duration and degree of heating, cooking, smelting, etc.: ～儿不到，饼就烙不好。You can't bake a cake properly if the fire is not right. ③ anger: 正在～上 at the height of one's anger/ 你先把～压一压，别着急。Don't fly off the handle. Calm down.

【火头军】 huǒtóujūn 〔现用做戏谑的话〕 army cook

【火腿】 huǒtuǐ ham

【火网】 huǒwǎng 〈军〉 network of fire; fire net

【火卫】 huǒwèi 〈天〉〈简〉(火星卫星) Martian satellite

【火险】 huǒxiǎn fire insurance

【火线】 huǒxiàn ① battle (或 firing, front) line: ～入党 join the Party at the battlefront/ 轻伤不下～ refuse to leave the front because of minor wounds/ ～抢救 frontline first aid ②〈电〉 live wire

【火硝】 huǒxiāo 〈化〉 nitre; saltpetre ◇ ～纸 touch paper

【火星】 huǒxīng ① spark: ～迸发 a shower of sparks ②〈天〉 Mars

【火性】 huǒxìng 〈口〉 bad temper; hot temper

【火眼】 huǒyǎn 〈医〉 pinkeye

【火焰】 huǒyàn flame ◇ ～光谱 flame spectrum/ ～喷射器 flamethrower

【火药】 huǒyào gunpowder; powder ◇ ～库 powder magazine/ ～桶 powder keg

【火药味】 huǒyàowèi the smell of gunpowder: 这是一篇充满～的声明。This statement has a strong smell of gunpowder.

【火印】 huǒyìn a mark burned on bamboo or wooden articles; brand

【火油】 huǒyóu 〈方〉 kerosene

【火灾】 huǒzāi fire (as a disaster); conflagration

【火葬】 huǒzàng cremation ◇ ～场 crematorium; crematory

【火纸】 huǒzhǐ touch paper

【火中取栗】 huǒzhōng qǔ lì pull sb.'s chestnuts out of the fire; be a cat's-paw

【火种】 huǒzhǒng ① kindling material; kindling; tinder ② live cinders kept for starting a new fire: 革命的～ sparks of revolution; seeds of revolution

【火烛】 huǒzhú things that may cause a fire: 小心～！ Be careful about fires!

【火主】 huǒzhǔ a house where a fire started

**伙** huǒ ① mess; board; meals: 包～ get or supply meals at a fixed rate; board/ 在学校入～ board at school ② partner; mate ③ partnership; company: 合～ enter into partnership/ 中途拆～ part company halfway ④〈量〉 group; crowd; band: 三个一群，五个一～ in small groups; in knots; in twos and threes/ 一～强盗 a band of robbers ⑤ combine; join: ～买 club together to buy sth./ ～着用 share in the use of sth.

【伙伴】 huǒbàn partner; companion: 我小时候的～ a childhood pal of mine

【伙房】 huǒfáng kitchen (in a school, factory, etc.)

【伙夫】 huǒfū 〈旧〉 mess cook

【伙计】 huǒji ① partner ②〈口〉 fellow; mate: ～，上哪儿去？ Where are you going, mate? ③〈旧〉 salesman; salesclerk; shop assistant ④〈旧〉 farm labourer

【伙食】 huǒshi mess; food; meals: 管理～ handle messing arrangements
◇ ～补助 food allowance/ ～费 money spent on meals; board expenses/ ～节余 mess savings/ ～科 catering office/ ～团 mess

【伙同】 huǒtóng in league with; in collusion with

**钬** huǒ 〈化〉 holmium (Ho)

**夥** huǒ 〈书〉 much; a great deal; many; numerous: 获益甚～ have derived much benefit

## huò

**或** huò ①〈副〉 perhaps; maybe; probably: 代表团明晨～可到达。The delegation may arrive tomorrow morning. ②〈连〉 or; either... or...: 这块地可以种高粱～玉米。We can grow sorghum or maize on this plot. ③〈书〉 someone; some people: ～曰 someone says; some say

【或…或…】 huò...huò... 〈连〉 either... or...; or: 或明或暗 either overt or covert/ 或大或小 big or small/ 或迟或早 sooner or later/ 或多或少 more or less; to a greater or lesser extent; in varying degrees

【或然】 huòrán probable ◇ ～率〈数〉 probability

【或许】 huòxǔ 〈副〉 perhaps; maybe: 他～没有赶上火车。Perhaps he has missed the train./ 她～能来。She might be able to come.

【或者】 huòzhě ①〈副〉 perhaps; maybe: 快点走，～还赶得上他。Be quick, we may catch up with him yet. ②〈连〉 or; either... or...: 请你把这本书交给小王～小李。Please give this book to either Xiao Wang or Xiao Li.

**和** huò ① mix; blend: 豆沙里～点儿糖 mix a little sugar into the bean paste/ 油和水～不到一块儿。Oil and water do not mix. ②〈量〉〔指洗东西换水或煎药加水的次数〕: 衣裳已经洗了三～。The clothes have been rinsed three times./ 二～药 second decoction (of medicinal herbs)
另见 hé; hè; huó

【和稀泥】 huò xīní try to mediate differences at the sacrifice of principle; try to smooth things over

**货** huò ① goods; commodity: 送～上门 sell goods at the customers' doors ② money: 通～ currency ③〈骂〉: 蠢～ blockhead; idiot ④〈书〉 sell

【货币】 huòbì money; currency: 储备～ reserve currency/ 周转～ vehicle currency/ 自由兑换～ convertible currency ◇ ～单位 monetary unit/ ～地租〈经〉 money rent/ ～回笼 withdrawal of currency from circulation/ ～交换 exchange through money/ ～流通量 currency (或 money) in circulation; money supply/ ～平价 currency parity; par value of currency/ ～危机 monetary crisis/ ～政策 monetary policy/ ～资本 money-capital

【货币贬值】 huòbì biǎnzhí ① (currency) devaluation ② (currency) depreciation

【货币升值】 huòbì shēngzhí ① (currency) revaluation ② (currency) appreciation

【货舱】 huòcāng (cargo) hold; cargo bay (of a plane)

【货场】 huòchǎng goods (或 freight) yard

【货车】 huòchē ① goods train; freight train ② goods van (或 wagon); freight car (或 wagon) ③ lorry; truck

【货船】 huòchuán freighter; cargo ship; cargo vessel: 定期～ cargo liner

【货单】 huòdān manifest; waybill; shipping list

【货到付款】 huò dào fù kuǎn cash on delivery (COD)

【货机】 huòjī 〈航空〉 cargo aircraft (或 plane); air freighter

【货价】 huòjià commodity price; price of goods

【货架子】 huòjiàzi goods shelves

【货款】 huòkuǎn money for buying or selling goods; payment for goods

【货郎】 huòláng itinerant pedlar; street vendor ◇ ～担

street vendor's load (carried on a shoulder pole)
【货品】 huòpǐn kinds or types of goods
【货色】 huòsè ① goods: ～齐全。Goods of every description are available./ 上等～ first-class goods; quality goods ② stuff; trash; rubbish: 修正主义～ revisionist rubbish
【货摊】 huòtān stall; stand
【货物】 huòwù goods; commodity; merchandise
【货箱】 huòxiāng packing box
【货样】 huòyàng sample goods; sample
【货源】 huòyuán source of goods; supply of goods: ～充足 an ample supply of goods/ 开辟～ find (或 open up) new sources of goods
【货运】 huòyùn freight transport
◇ ～单 waybill/ ～费 shipping cost; freight (charges)/ ～量 volume of goods transported; volume of rail freight; volume of road haulage/ ～列车 goods train; freight train/ ～业务 cargo service/ ～周转量 rotation volume of goods (或 freight) transport
【货栈】 huòzhàn warehouse
【货真价实】 huòzhēn-jiàshí ① genuine goods at a fair price ② through and through; out-and-out; dyed-in-the-wool: ～的政治骗子 an out-and-out political swindler/ ～的反革命分子 a dyed-in-the-wool counterrevolutionary
【货殖】 huòzhí 〈书〉 engage in trade
【货主】 huòzhǔ owner of cargo

**获** huò ① capture; catch: 捕～ capture ② obtain; win; reap: ～一等奖 win the first prize/ ～救 be rescued/ ～利 make a profit; reap profits/ 喜～丰收 happily reap a bumper harvest/ 不劳而～ enjoy the fruits of other people's labour; reap without sowing
【获得】 huòdé gain; obtain; acquire; win; achieve: ～解放 achieve emancipation; win liberation/ ～独立 gain independence/ ～巨大的成绩 achieve great success/ ～知识 acquire knowledge/ ～好评 win acclaim; earn favourable comment ◇ ～性 〈生〉 acquired character
【获胜】 huòshèng win victory; be victorious; triumph: 革命人民的斗争必将～。The struggles of the revolutionary people will surely triumph./ 甲队以五比二～。Team A won the match five to two.
【获悉】 huòxī 〈书〉 learn (of an event)

**祸** huò ① misfortune; disaster; calamity: 车～ traffic accident; road accident ② bring disaster upon; ruin
【祸不单行】 huò bù dān xíng misfortunes never come singly
【祸端】 huòduān 〈书〉 the source of the disaster; the cause of ruin
【祸根】 huògēn the root of the trouble; the cause of ruin; bane
【祸国殃民】 huòguó-yāngmín bring calamity to the country and the people
【祸害】 huòhai ① disaster; curse; scourge: 黄河在历史上经常引起～。Throughout the ages the Huanghe River was a scourge of the nation. ② damage; destroy: 防止野猪～庄稼。Don't let the boars damage the crops.
【祸患】 huòhuàn disaster; calamity
【祸起萧墙】 huò qǐ xiāoqiáng trouble arises within the family; there is internal strife afoot
【祸事】 huòshì disaster; calamity; mishap
【祸首】 huòshǒu chief culprit (或 offender)
【祸胎】 huòtāi the root of the trouble; the cause of the disaster
【祸兮福所倚，福兮祸所伏】 huò xī fú suǒ yǐ, fú xī huò suǒ fú good fortune lieth within bad, bad fortune lurketh within good
【祸心】 huòxīn evil intent: 包藏～ harbour malicious intentions

**惑** huò ① be puzzled; be bewildered: 大～不解 be greatly puzzled ② delude; mislead: 造谣～众 fabricate rumours to mislead people

**霍** huò ① suddenly; quickly ② (Huò) a surname
【霍地】 huòdì 〈副〉 suddenly: ～立起身来 suddenly stand up; spring to one's feet
【霍霍】 huòhuò ① 〈象〉: ～的磨刀声 the scrape, scrape of a sword being sharpened ② flash: 电光～。The lightning flashed.
【霍乱】 huòluàn ① 〈医〉 cholera ② 〈中医〉 acute gastroenteritis
【霍然】 huòrán ① 〈副〉 suddenly; quickly: 手电筒～一亮。Suddenly somebody flashed an electric torch. ② 〈书〉 (of an illness) be cured quickly: 数日之后，定当～。You will be restored to health in a matter of days.

**豁** huò ① clear; open; open-minded; generous: ～达大度 open-minded and magnanimous ② exempt; remit: ～免 exempt; remit
另见 huō
【豁亮】 huòliàng ① roomy and bright: 这屋子又干净，又～。The room is clean, bright and spacious./ 毛主席著作越学心里越～。The more one studies Chairman Mao's works, the more enlightened one becomes. ② sonorous; resonant: 嗓音～ have a sonorous voice
【豁免】 huòmiǎn exempt (from taxes or from customs inspection, etc.); remit: ～捐税 exempt sb. from taxes; remit taxes/ 外交～权 diplomatic immunity
【豁然贯通】 huòrán guàntōng suddenly see the whole thing in a clear light
【豁然开朗】 huòrán kāilǎng suddenly see the light; be suddenly enlightened

**藿** huò 〈书〉 leaves of pulse plants
【藿香】 huòxiāng 〈中药〉 wrinkled giant hyssop (*Agastache rugosa*)

**蠖** huò 见"尺蠖" chǐhuò

# J

## jī

**几** jī ①a small table: 茶～儿 tea table; teapoy ②〈书〉nearly; almost; practically: 到会者～三千人。Nearly 3,000 people came to the meeting.
另见 jǐ

【几乎】 jīhū nearly; almost; practically: 他～一夜没睡。He lay awake almost the whole night./ 她干得飞快,～谁也赶不上她。She worked so fast that hardly anyone could keep up with her./ 水电站～全部完工。The hydroelectric station is as good as completed./ 故乡变化太大了,我～认不出来了。My home town had changed so much that I could hardly recognize it.

【几率】 jīlǜ 〈数〉probability

【几维鸟】 jīwéiniǎo kiwi

**讥** jī ridicule; mock; satirize

【讥刺】 jīcì 〈书〉ridicule; satirize

【讥讽】 jīfěng ridicule; satirize

【讥诮】 jīqiào 〈书〉sneer at; deride

【讥笑】 jīxiào ridicule; jeer; sneer at; deride: 他毫不理睬某些人的～,继续进行试验。Completely ignoring some people's sneers, he went on with his experiments.

**击** jī ①beat; hit; strike: ～鼓 beat a drum/ ～掌 clap one's hands ②attack; assault: 声东～西 feint in the east and attack in the west ③come in contact with; bump into: 撞～ collide with; ram

【击败】 jībài defeat; beat; vanquish: 以三比一～了对手 beat one's opponent 3 to 1

【击毙】 jībì shoot dead: 四名匪徒被当场～。Four bandits were shot dead on the spot.

【击沉】 jīchén bombard and sink; send (a ship) to the bottom: ～敌舰三艘 sink three enemy warships

【击穿】 jīchuān 〈电〉puncture; breakdown

【击发】 jīfā 〈军〉percussion ◇ ～装置 percussion lock (或 mechanism)

【击毁】 jīhuǐ smash; wreck; shatter; destroy: ～坦克二十四辆 destroy 24 tanks

【击剑】 jījiàn 〈体〉fencing

【击节】 jījié beat time: ～叹赏 show appreciation (of a poem or a piece of music) by beating time with one's hand; greatly admire

【击溃】 jīkuì rout; put to flight

【击落】 jīluò shoot down; bring down; down: ～敌机七架 bring down seven enemy planes

【击破】 jīpò break up; destroy; rout: 各个～ destroy (enemy forces) one by one

【击球】 jīqiú 〈棒、垒球〉batting ◇ ～员 batter; batsman

【击伤】 jīshāng wound (a person); damage (a plane, tank, etc.)

【击退】 jītuì beat back; repel; repulse: ～敌军几次进攻 repulse several enemy assaults

【击弦乐器】 jīxián yuèqì hammered string instrument

【击乐器】 jīyuèqì percussion instrument

【击中】 jīzhòng hit: ～目标 hit the target/ ～要害 hit sb.'s vital point

**叽** jī 〈象〉: 小鸟～～叫。Little birds chirp.

【叽咕】 jīgu talk in a low voice; whisper; mutter: 他们俩叽叽咕咕地说些什么? What are those two whispering to each other about?

【叽叽嘎嘎】 jījigāgā 〈象〉〔形容说笑声等〕: 大家～地笑起来。Everybody started cackling. / 这门老～响。This door always creaks.

【叽叽喳喳】 jījizhāzhā 〈象〉chirp; twitter: 麻雀在外面～地叫。Sparrows are twittering outside./ 别～的了,干点正经事吧。Stop jabbering and get down to business.

【叽里咕噜】 jīligūlū 〈象〉①〔形容说话别人听不清楚或听不懂〕 gabble; jabber: 他们～地说了半天。They gabbled away for a long time. ②〔形容物体滚动的声音〕: 石块～滚下山去。Rocks went tumbling down the hill.

**饥** jī ①be hungry; starve; famish ②famine; crop failure: 大～之年 a year of great famine

【饥不择食】 jī bù zé shí a hungry person is not choosy about his food

【饥肠】 jīcháng 〈书〉empty stomach: ～辘辘 one's stomach rumbling with hunger

【饥饿】 jī'è hunger; starvation: 挣扎在～线上 struggle along on the verge of starvation

【饥寒交迫】 jī-hán jiāopò suffer hunger and cold; live in hunger and cold; be poverty-stricken

【饥荒】 jīhuang ①famine; crop failure ②〈口〉be hard up; be short of money: 解放前我家月月闹～。Before liberation my family ran short of cash month after month. ③〈口〉debt: 拉～ run into debt

【饥馑】 jījǐn famine; crop failure

【饥民】 jīmín famine victim; famine refugee

**圾** jī 见"垃圾" lājī

**芨** jī

【芨芨草】 jījīcǎo splendid achnatherum (*Achnatherum splendens*)

**机** jī ①machine; engine: 挖泥～ dredging machine; dredge/ 内燃～ internal-combustion engine ②aircraft; aeroplane; plane: 客～ passenger plane ③crucial point; pivot; key link: 转～ a turning point; a turn for the better ④chance; occasion; opportunity: 趁～ take advantage of the occasion; seize the opportunity (或 chance)/ 见～行事 do as one sees fit; use one's discretion/ ～不可失,时不再来。Don't let slip an opportunity; it may never come again. 或 Opportunity knocks but once. ⑤organic: 有～体 organism/ 无～化学 inorganic chemistry ⑥flexible; quick-witted: ～巧 adroit; ingenious

【机舱】 jīcāng ①engine room (of a ship) ②passenger compartment (of an aircraft); cabin

【机铲】 jīchǎn mechanical shovel

【机场】 jīchǎng airport; airfield; aerodrome: 国际～ international airport/ 简易～ airstrip/ 军用～ military airfield ◇ ～标志 aerodrome markings/ ～待战 ground alert/ ～灯标 airport beacon

【机车】 jīchē 〈铁道〉locomotive; engine: 内燃(电力,蒸汽)～ diesel (electric, steam) locomotive ◇ ～车辆厂 rolling stock plant/ ～组 locomotive crew

【机床】 jīchuáng machine tool: 木工～ woodworking machine tool/ 金属切削～ metal cutting machine tool/ 数字程序控制～ numerical controlled machine tool ◇ ～工业 machine tool industry

【机动】 jīdòng ① power-driven; motorized: ～车 motor-driven (或 motor) vehicle ② flexible; expedient; mobile: ～处置 deal with sth. flexibly ③ in reserve; for emergency use: ～力量 reserve force/ ～时间 time kept in reserve/ 拨出五十元作为～开支 allot 50 *yuan* for extras
◇ ～粮 grain reserve for emergency use/ ～炮 mobile artillery/ ～性 mobility; manoeuvrability/ ～自行车 moped

【机断】 jīduàn act on one's own judgment in an emergency: ～行事 act promptly at one's own discretion

【机帆船】 jīfānchuán motor sailboat; motorized junk

【机房】 jīfáng ① generator or motor room ② engine room (of a ship)

【机耕】 jīgēng 〈农〉 tractor-ploughing ◇ ～船 boat tractor; wet-field tractor/ ～面积 area ploughed by tractors

【机工】 jīgōng mechanic; machinist

【机构】 jīgòu ① 〈机〉 mechanism: 传动～ transmission mechanism/ 分离～ disengaging mechanism ② organization; setup: 政府～ government organization/ 宣传～ propaganda organ/ 公社的管理～ the administrative setup of a commune ③ the internal structure of an organization: 调整～ adjust the organizational structure

【机关】 jīguān ① 〈机〉 mechanism; gear: 起动～ starting gear ② machine-operated: ～布景 machine-operated stage scenery ③ office; organ; body: 领导～ leading bodies/ 党政～ Party and government organizations/ 文化教育～ cultural and educational institutions/ 公安～ public security organs ④ stratagem; scheme; intrigue: 识破～ see through a trick/ ～算尽太聪明，反算了卿卿性命。All your clever calculations and intrigues have brought you nothing but your doom.
◇ ～报 official newspaper of a party, government, etc.; organ/ ～干部 government functionary; office worker/ ～炮 machine cannon/ ～枪 machine gun

【机会】 jīhuì chance; opportunity: 错过(抓住)～ lose (seize) a chance/ 千载一时的好～ a golden opportunity; the chance of a lifetime/ 能有～到大寨去看看就好了。It would be wonderful if I could go and visit Dazhai./ 我愿借此～向你们表示衷心的感谢。I wish to avail myself of this opportunity to extend to you my heartfelt thanks.

【机会主义】 jīhuìzhǔyì opportunism: "左"、右倾～ Right and "Left" opportunism ◇ ～路线 opportunist line/ ～者 opportunist

【机件】 jījiàn 〈机〉 parts; works: 钟表的～ the works of a clock or watch

【机井】 jījǐng motor-pumped well

【机警】 jījǐng alert; sharp-witted; vigilant: 游击队～地监视敌人的动静。The guerrillas kept a close watch on the movements of the enemy.

【机具】 jījù machines and tools: 农业～ farm implements

【机库】 jīkù hangar

【机理】 jīlǐ mechanism: 腐蚀～ corrosion mechanism/ 结晶～ crystallization mechanism/ 分娩～ 〈医〉 mechanism of labour

【机灵】 jīling ① clever; smart; sharp; intelligent: 这孩子怪～的。This child's very smart./ 她有一双～的大眼睛。She has large, intelligent eyes./ 这个人办事挺～的。This chap manages things quite cleverly. ② 〈方〉 give a start ◇ ～鬼儿 a clever child

【机米】 jīmǐ ① machine-processed rice ② 见"籼米" xiānmǐ

【机密】 jīmì ① secret; classified; confidential: ～文件 classified papers; confidential documents ② secret: 严守党和国家的～ strictly guard Party and state secrets

【机敏】 jīmǐn alert and resourceful: 她在紧急关头总是沉着～。She is calm and resourceful in an emergency.

【机谋】 jīmóu 〈书〉 stratagem; artifice; scheme

【机能】 jīnéng 〈生〉 function

【机器】 jīqì machine; machinery; apparatus: ～保养 machine maintenance/ 安装新～ install new machinery/ 国家～ state apparatus (或 machine)
◇ ～翻译 machine translation/ ～人 robot/ ～油 lubricating oil; lubricant/ ～造型 machine moulding/ ～制造 machine building

【机枪】 jīqiāng machine gun: 轻(重)～ light (heavy) machine gun/ 高射～ antiaircraft machine gun ◇ ～手 machine gunner

【机群】 jīqún a group of planes: 大～ air armada; air fleet

【机上导弹】 jīshang dǎodàn air-launched missile

【机身】 jīshēn fuselage

【机体】 jītǐ ① 〈生〉 organism ② 〈航空〉 airframe

【机头】 jītóu nose (of an aircraft) ◇ ～炮 nose gun

【机尾】 jīwěi tail (of an aircraft)

【机务人员】 jīwù rényuán ① maintenance personnel ② 〈航空〉 ground crew

【机械】 jīxiè ① machinery; machine; mechanism: ～故障 mechanical failure (或 breakdown) ② mechanical; inflexible; rigid: 别人的经验不能～地照搬。Other people's experience should not be applied mechanically.
◇ ～动力学 mechanical kinetics/ ～师 machinist/ ～工程学 mechanical engineering/ ～工业 engineering industry/ ～功 mechanical work/ ～加工 machining/ ～论 〈哲〉 mechanism/ ～能 〈物〉 mechanical energy/ ～唯物主义 〈哲〉 mechanical materialism/ ～运动 〈物〉 mechanical movement/ ～制图 mechanical drawing

【机械化】 jīxièhuà mechanize: 农业～ mechanization of agriculture; mechanization of farm work ◇ ～部队 mechanized force (或 troops, unit)

【机械手】 jīxièshǒu 〈机〉 manipulator: 仿效～ master-slave manipulator/ 万能～ general-purpose manipulator

【机型】 jīxíng ① type (of an aircraft) ② model (of a machine)

【机要】 jīyào confidential
◇ ～部门 departments in charge of confidential or important work/ ～工作 confidential work/ ～秘书 confidential secretary

【机宜】 jīyí principles of action; guidelines: 面授～ brief sb. on how to act

【机翼】 jīyì wing (of an aircraft)

【机油】 jīyóu engine oil; machine oil

【机遇】 jīyù 〈书〉 favourable circumstances; opportunity

【机缘】 jīyuán good luck; lucky chance: ～凑巧 as luck would have it; by chance; by a lucky coincidence

【机长】 jīzhǎng aircraft (或 crew) commander

【机罩】 jīzhào bonnet (of an aircraft)

【机制】 jīzhì ① machine-processed; machine-made: ～糖 machine-processed sugar/ ～纸 machine-made paper ② mechanism: 激发～ 〈物〉 excitation mechanism

【机智】 jīzhì quick-witted; resourceful: ～勇敢的侦察兵 brave and resourceful scouts

【机杼】 jīzhù 〈书〉 ① loom ② conception (of a piece of writing): 自出～ be original in conception

【机子】 jīzi 〈口〉 ① loom ② a small machine (e.g. a sewing machine, a telephone) ③ trigger

【机组】 jīzǔ ① 〈机〉 unit; set: 发电～ generating unit (或 set) ② aircrew; flight crew

**玑** jī 〈书〉①a pearl that is not quite round ②an ancient astronomical instrument

**乩** jī 见"扶乩" fújī

**肌** jī muscle; flesh: 随意～〈生理〉voluntary muscle

【肌肤】 jīfū 〈书〉(human) skin ◇ ～甲错〈中医〉scaly dry skin, a symptom of blood stasis; pellagra

【肌腱】 jījiàn 〈生理〉tendon

【肌理】 jīlǐ 〈书〉skin texture: ～细腻 fine-textured skin

【肌肉】 jīròu muscle: ～发达 muscular ◇ ～注射 intramuscular injection

【肌体】 jītǐ human body; organism: 防止各种政治微生物侵蚀我们党的～ prevent all kinds of political germs from contaminating the body of our Party

【肌萎缩】 jīwěisuō 〈医〉amyotrophy

**矶** jī a rock projecting over the water

**鸡** jī chicken: 公～ cock; rooster/ 母～ hen/ 雏～ chick; chicken/ ～鸣而起 rise at cockcrow

【鸡蛋】 jīdàn (hen's) egg ◇ ～糕 (sponge) cake

【鸡蛋里挑骨头】 jīdànli tiāo gǔtou look for a bone in an egg; look for a flaw where there is none; find fault; nitpick

【鸡蛋碰石头】 jīdàn pèng shítou like an egg striking a rock — attack sb. far stronger than oneself

【鸡飞蛋打】 jīfēi-dàndǎ the hen has flown away and the eggs in the coop are broken — all is lost

【鸡冠】 jīguān cockscomb

【鸡冠花】 jīguānhuā cockscomb

【鸡冠石】 jīguānshí 〈矿〉realgar

【鸡霍乱】 jīhuòluàn fowl cholera

【鸡奸】 jījiān sodomy; buggery

【鸡肋】 jīlèi 〈书〉chicken ribs — things of little value or interest: 味同～ taste like chicken ribs — be of little or no value

【鸡零狗碎】 jīlíng-gǒusuì in bits and pieces; fragmentary

【鸡毛】 jīmáo chicken feather: 拿着～当令箭 take a chicken feather for a warrant to give commands; treat one's superior's casual remark as an order and make a big fuss about it ◇ ～掸子 feather duster/ ～信 a message with a feather attached as a sign of urgency

【鸡毛蒜皮】 jīmáo-suànpí chicken feathers and garlic skins; trifles; trivialities: 这是～的事，不值得计较。This is a trivial matter; it's not worth arguing about.

【鸡鸣狗盗】 jīmíng-gǒudào (ability to) crow like a cock and snatch like a dog — small tricks: ～之徒 people who know small tricks

【鸡内金】 jīnèijīn 〈中药〉the membrane of a chicken's gizzard

【鸡皮疙瘩】 jīpí gēda gooseflesh: 冻得我直起～。It was so cold I was gooseflesh all over./ 想起那可怕的情景，我浑身都起～。The thought of the horrible scene made my flesh creep.

【鸡犬不惊】 jī-quǎn bù jīng even fowls and dogs are not disturbed — excellent army discipline; peace and tranquility

【鸡犬不留】 jī-quǎn bù liú even fowls and dogs are not spared — ruthless mass slaughter

【鸡犬不宁】 jī-quǎn bù níng even fowls and dogs are not left in peace — general turmoil

【鸡肉】 jīròu chicken (as food)

【鸡头米】 jītóumǐ 〈植〉Gorgon fruit

【鸡尾酒】 jīwěijiǔ cocktail ◇ ～会 cocktail party

【鸡瘟】 jīwēn chicken pest

【鸡窝】 jīwō chicken coop; henhouse; roost

【鸡心】 jīxīn ①heart-shaped ②a heart-shaped pendant ◇ ～领 V-neck

【鸡胸】 jīxiōng 〈医〉pigeon breast; chicken breast

【鸡血藤】 jīxuèténg 〈植〉reticulate millettia (*Millettia reticulata*)

【鸡眼】 jīyǎn 〈医〉corn; clavus ◇ ～膏 corn plaster

【鸡杂】 jīzá chicken giblets

【鸡子儿】 jīzǐr 〈方〉(hen's) egg

【鸡子】 jīzi 〈方〉chicken

**奇** jī ①odd (number): ～数 odd number ②〈书〉a fractional amount (over that mentioned in a round number); odd lots: 五十有～ fifty odd
另见 qí

【奇零】 jīlíng 〈书〉a fractional amount (over that mentioned in a round number); odd lots

【奇数】 jīshù 〈数〉odd number

**迹** jì ①mark; trace: 足～ footmark; footprint/ 血～ bloodstain ②remains; ruins; vestige: 古城墙的遗～ the ruins of an old city wall/ 陈～ a thing of the past ③an outward sign; indication: ～近剽窃 an act verging on plagiarism

【迹地】 jìdì 〈林〉slash

【迹象】 jìxiàng sign; indication: 这是一种不寻常的～。This is an unusual sign./ 有～表明两国将改善关系。There are indications that the two countries are going to improve their relations.

**唧** jī spurt; squirt: ～了我一身水。The water squirted all over me.

【唧咕】 jīgu 见"叽咕" jīgu

【唧唧】 jījī 〈象〉[形容虫叫声] chirp: 蟋蟀在草丛里～地叫。Crickets are chirping in the grass.

【唧唧喳喳】 jījizhāzhā 见"叽叽喳喳" jījizhāzhā

【唧哝】 jīnong talk in a low voice; whisper

【唧筒】 jītǒng pump

**积** jī ①amass; store up; accumulate: ～谷防荒 store up grain against a lean year/ ～长期斗争的经验 accumulate experience of struggle over a long period/ ～小胜为大胜。Many small victories add up to a big one. ②long-standing; long-pending; age-old: ～案 a long-pending case ③〈中医〉indigestion: 这孩子有～了。The child is suffering from indigestion. ④〈数〉product: 求～ find the product by multiplication

【积弊】 jībì age-old malpractice; long-standing abuse

【积不相能】 jī bù xiāng néng 〈书〉have always been at variance; have never been on good terms; be always at loggerheads

【积存】 jīcún store up; lay up; stockpile: ～的物资 goods in stock

【积肥】 jīféi collect (farmyard) manure

【积分】 jīfēn 〈数〉integral: 定(不定)～ definite (indefinite) integral
◇ ～方程 integral equation/ ～学 integral calculus/ ～仪 integrator

【积极】 jījí ①positive: 调动一切～因素 mobilize all positive factors/ 作出～贡献 make positive contributions ②active; energetic; vigorous: ～响应党的号召 enthusiastically respond to the Party's call/ ～工作 work hard; work with all one's energy/ 采取～措施 adopt vigorous measures/ 开展～的思想斗争 wage an active ideological struggle/ ～地推进人民的医药卫生事业 take vigorous action to expand the people's medical and health services/ 他锻炼身体一向很～。He has always been very keen on doing physical exercises.

【积极分子】 jījífènzǐ activist; active element; enthusiast: 在斗争中涌现出大批的～。Large numbers of activists have come forward in the course of the struggle./ 体育运动的～ sport enthusiast

【积极性】 jījíxìng zeal; initiative; enthusiasm: 革命的～ revolutionary zeal/ 社会主义～ enthusiasm for socialism/ 调动群众的～ bring into play the initiative of the masses

【积久】 jījiǔ accumulate in the course of time: ～成习 form a habit or custom through long-repeated practice

【积聚】 jījù gather; accumulate; build up: ～革命力量 build up revolutionary strength/ 资本～ concentration of capital

【积劳成疾】 jī láo chéng jí 〈书〉break down from constant overwork

【积累】 jīlěi accumulate: ～了丰富的经验 have accumulated a wealth of experience/ 逐年增加公共～和个人收入 increase public accumulation and personal income year by year/ 我国建设资金是靠发展生产～起来的。Funds for China's construction are accumulated by developing production.

【积木】 jīmù building blocks; toy bricks

【积年】 jīnián 〈书〉for many years: ～旧案 law cases which have piled up over the years

【积欠】 jīqiàn ①have one's debts piling up ②outstanding debts; arrears: 还清～ clear up all outstanding debts

【积少成多】 jī shǎo chéng duō many a little makes a mickle

【积食】 jīshí 〈方〉indigestion

【积习】 jīxí old habit; long-standing practice: ～难除。It is difficult to get rid of deep-rooted habits. 或 Old habits die hard.

【积蓄】 jīxù ①put aside; save; accumulate: ～力量 accumulate strength ②savings: 月月有～ save some money every month

【积压】 jīyā keep long in stock; overstock: 长期～的物资 materials kept too long in stock/ 产品～ overstocking of products/ 不要～国家资金。Don't let state funds lie idle./ 把～的事情做完 clear off arrears of work/ ～在心头的愤怒 pent-up anger

【积羽沉舟】 jī yǔ chén zhōu enough feathers can sink a boat — tiny things may gather into a mighty force; minor offences unchecked may bring disaster

【积雨云】 jīyǔyún 〈气〉cumulonimbus

【积怨】 jīyuàn accumulated rancour; piled-up grievances: ～甚多 have incurred widespread resentment; have many complaints against one

【积云】 jīyún 〈气〉cumulus: 层～ stratocumulus/ 卷～ cirrocumulus/ 高～ altocumulus

【积攒】 jīzǎn 〈口〉save (或 collect) bit by bit: ～邮票 collect stamps/ 集体的家业是一点一滴地～起来的。The collective wealth has been accumulated bit by bit.

【积重难返】 jī zhòng nán fǎn bad old practices die hard

【积铢累寸】 jīzhū-lěicùn save every tiny bit; accumulate bit by bit

**屐** jī ①clogs ②shoes in general: 草～ straw sandals

**姬** jī ①a complimentary term for women used in ancient China ②a name used in ancient China for a concubine ③〈旧〉a professional female singer: 歌～ singing girl; female entertainer ④(Jī) a surname

【姬蜂】 jīfēng 〈动〉ichneumon wasp

**勣** jī achievement; accomplishment; merit

**基** jī ①base; foundation: 坝～ the base of a dam/ 路～ roadbed; bed/ 房～ foundations (of a building)/ 奠～ lay a foundation ②basic; key; primary; cardinal: ～调 keynote/ ～数 cardinal number ③〈化〉radical; base; group: 自由～ free radical/ 石蜡～ paraffin base/ 氨～ amino; amino-group

【基本】 jīběn ①basic; fundamental; elementary: ～原则 basic principles/ ～观点 basic concept/ ～知识 elementary (或 rudimentary) knowledge ②main; essential: ～条件 main conditions ③basically; in the main; on the whole; by and large: 一九五六年我国～上完成了生产资料所有制的社会主义改造。China basically completed the socialist transformation of the ownership of the means of production in 1956./ 这部电影～上是好的。This film is good on the whole.

◇～词汇〈语〉basic vocabulary; basic word-stock/ ～点 main point; fundamental proposition/ ～纲领 basic programme/ ～工资 basic wage (或 salary)/ ～核算单位 basic accounting unit/ ～建设 capital construction/ ～粒子〈物〉elementary particle/ ～路线 basic line/ ～矛盾 basic contradiction

【基本功】 jīběngōng basic training; basic skill; essential technique: 练好～ have a thorough training in basic skills; master the basic skills

【基层】 jīcéng basic level; primary level; grass-roots unit: 深入～ go down to the grass-roots units

◇～单位 basic unit; grass-roots unit; unit at the grass-roots level/ ～干部 cadre at the basic (或 grass-roots) level/ ～领导 leading body at the basic level; basic-level leadership/ ～人民法院 basic-level people's court/ ～选举 elections at the basic level/ ～政权组织 organizations of political power at the grass-roots level/ ～组织 primary organization; organization at the basic level

【基础】 jīchǔ foundation; base; basis: 打～ lay a foundation/ 物质～ material base/ 理论～ theoretical basis/ 经济～ economic base (或 basis)/ 农业是国民经济的～。Agriculture is the foundation of the national economy./ 在原有的～上提高一步 make improvements on what has already been achieved/ 在和平共处五项原则的～上，同各国建立和发展关系 establish and develop our relations with other countries on the basis of the Five Principles of Peaceful Coexistence

◇～处理〈水〉foundation treatment/ ～代谢〈生〉basal metabolism/ ～工业 basic industries/ ～教育 elementary education/ ～科学 basic science/ ～课 basic courses (of a college curriculum)/ ～理论 basic theory/ ～知识 rudimentary (或 elementary) knowledge

【基底细胞癌】 jīdǐxìbāo'ái 〈医〉basal-cell carcinoma

【基地】 jīdì base: 军事～ military base/ 导弹～ missile base/ 工业～ industrial base/ 原料～ source of raw materials

【基点】 jīdiǎn ①basic point; starting point; centre: 建立科研～ set up scientific research centres/ 分析问题是解决问题的～。The analysis of a problem is the starting point for its solution./ 我们的方针要放在自力更生的～上。Our policy should rest on the basis of self-reliance. ②〈测〉base point (BP)

【基调】 jīdiào ①〈乐〉fundamental key; main key ②keynote: 他讲话的～是团结。The keynote of his speech was unity.

【基督】 Jīdū 〈宗〉Christ

◇ ～教 Christianity; the Christian religion/ ～教女青年会 the Young Women's Christian Association (Y.W.C.A.)/ ～教青年会 the Young Men's Christian Association (Y.M.C.A.)/ ～徒 Christian

【基肥】 jīféi 〈农〉 base manure; base fertilizer

【基干】 jīgàn backbone; hard core ◇ ～民兵 primary militia; core members of the militia

【基极】 jījí 〈电子〉 base

【基价】 jījià base price

【基建】 jījiàn capital construction

【基金】 jījīn fund: 积累(消费)～ accumulation (consumption) fund/ 外汇平准～ exchange stabilization fund ◇ ～会 foundation

【基期】 jīqī 〈统计〉 base period

【基石】 jīshí foundation stone; cornerstone: 剩余价值学说是马克思经济理论的～。The doctrine of surplus value is the cornerstone of Marx's economic theory.

【基数】 jīshù ①〈数〉 cardinal number ②〈统计〉 base: 以一九六五年的产量为～ taking the output of 1965 as the base

【基态】 jītài 〈物〉 ground state: 原子的～ atomic ground state

【基线】 jīxiàn 〈测〉 datum line

【基岩】 jīyán bedrock

【基因】 jīyīn 〈生〉 gene: 等位～ allele/ 显性～ dominant gene ◇ ～突变 gene mutation/ ～型 genotype

【基音】 jīyīn 〈乐〉 fundamental tone

【基于】 jīyú because of; in view of: ～目前这种情况,我们不得不修改原来的计划。In view of the present situation, we'll have to revise our original plan./ ～以上理由,我不赞同他的意见。For the above-mentioned reasons, I cannot agree with him.

【基准】 jīzhǔn ①〈测〉 datum ② standard; criterion ◇ ～兵 guide; base marker/ ～点(面,线)〈测〉 datum point (plane, line)

**绩** jī ① twist hempen thread ② achievement; accomplishment; merit: 战～ military achievement (或 exploit)/ 功～ merits and achievements; contributions

**犄** jī

【犄角】 jījiǎo corner: 桌子～ the corner of a table/ 屋子～里有一个衣架。A clothes tree stands in a corner of the room.

【犄角】 jījiao horn: 牛～ ox horn/ 鹿～ antler

**嵇** Jī a surname

**期** jī 〈书〉 anniversary
另见 qī

**缉** jī seize; arrest

【缉捕】 jībǔ seize; arrest

【缉拿】 jīná seize; arrest; apprehend: ～凶手 apprehend the murderer/ ～归案 bring (a criminal) to justice

【缉私】 jīsī seize smugglers or smuggled goods; suppress smuggling ◇～船 anti-smuggling patrol boat; coast guard vessel/ ～人员 anti-contraband personnel

**跻** jī 〈书〉 ascend; mount: 使中国科学～于世界先进科学之列 enable China's science to rank among the world's most advanced

**畸** jī ① lopsided; unbalanced: ～轻～重 attach too much weight to this and too little weight to that; lopsided; now too much, now too little ② irregular; abnormal ③ 〈书〉 a fractional amount (over that mentioned in a round number); odd lots

【畸变】 jībiàn 〈物〉 distortion

【畸零】 jīlíng 〈书〉 a fractional amount (over that mentioned in a round number); odd lots

【畸形】 jīxíng ①〈医〉 deformity; malformation: 先天～ congenital malformation/ 肢体发育～ have deformed limbs ② lopsided; unbalanced; abnormal: ～发展 lopsided development/～现象 abnormal phenomenon

**箕** jī ① dustpan ② winnowing basket; winnowing fan ③ loop (of a fingerprint)

【箕斗】 jīdǒu 〈矿〉 skip

【箕踞】 jījù 〈书〉 sit (on the floor) with one's legs stretched out

**稽** jī ① check; examine; investigate: 有案可～ be on record; be verifiable ②〈书〉 delay; procrastinate: ～延时日 be considerably delayed
另见 qǐ

【稽查】 jīchá ① check (to prevent smuggling, tax evasion, etc.) ② an official engaged in such work; customs officer

【稽核】 jīhé check; examine: ～账目 audit accounts

【稽考】 jīkǎo 〈书〉 ascertain; verify: 无可～ be unverifiable

【稽留】 jīliú 〈书〉 delay; detain: 因事～ be detained by business

【稽留热】 jīliúrè 〈医〉 continued fever

**齑** jī 〈书〉 ① fine; powdery ② finely chopped ginger, garlic, etc.

【齑粉】 jīfěn 〈书〉 fine powder; broken bits: 碾成～ be ground to dust

**畿** jī 见"京畿" jīngjī

**激** jī ① swash; surge; dash: 海水冲击礁石,～起高高的浪花。Swashing against the rocks, the breakers sent up a fountain of spray. ② arouse; stimulate; excite: ～起我们学习科学技术的热情 arouse our enthusiasm for studying science and technology/ ～于义愤 be stirred by righteous indignation ③ sharp; fierce; violent: ～战 fierce fighting ④ fall ill from getting wet: 他叫雨～着了。He caught a chill from getting wet in the rain. ⑤〈方〉 chill (by putting in ice water, etc.): 把西瓜放在冷水里～一～ chill a watermelon in cold water

【激昂】 jī'áng excited and indignant; roused: 群情～。Public feeling was aroused (或 ran high)./ 会场上响起～的口号声。The meeting hall resounded with outbursts of militant slogans.

【激变】 jībiàn violent change; cataclysm

【激波】 jībō 〈物〉 shock wave

【激荡】 jīdàng agitate; surge; rage: 海水～。The sea surged./ 心潮～ thoughts surging in one's mind/ 革命的友谊在他们胸中～。Their hearts were overflowing with revolutionary friendship.

【激动】 jīdòng excite; stir; agitate: 情绪～ be excited; get worked up/ 令人～的场面 an inspiring scene/ ～人心的讲话 a stirring (或 rousing) speech/ ～得流下眼泪 be moved to tears/ 他～地说:"是党救了我一家。" He said with feeling, "It's the Party that has saved my family."

【激发】 jīfā ① arouse; stimulate; set off: 学大寨运动～了社员们改天换地的干劲。The movement to learn from Dazhai has aroused the commune members' enthusiasm for reshaping nature./ ～群众的社会主义积极性 kindle the masses' enthusiasm for socialism ②〈物〉 excitation: 热～

thermal excitation
◇ ～机制 excitation mechanism/ ～能级 excitation level/ ～态 excited state
【激奋】 jīfèn be roused to action
【激愤】 jīfèn wrathful; indignant: 心情～ be filled with indignation
【激光】 jīguāng 〈物〉 laser
◇ ～波束制导武器 laser beam riding weapon/ ～测距仪 laser range finder/ ～测云仪 laser ceilometer/ ～导弹跟踪系统 laser missile tracking system/ ～干涉仪 laser interferometer/ ～光谱学 laser spectroscopy/ ～束 laser beam/ ～显微光谱分析仪 laser microspectral analyser/ ～照明器 laser illuminator/ ～准直仪 laser collimator
【激化】 jīhuà sharpen; intensify; become acute: 当前世界各种基本矛盾进一步～。At present, all the basic contradictions in the world are intensifying./ 斗争进一步～。The struggle became more acute.
【激活】 jīhuó 〈物〉 activation
◇ ～剂 activator/ ～媒质 active medium/ ～能 activation energy
【激将法】 jījiàngfǎ prodding (或 goading) sb. into action (as by ridicule, sarcasm, etc.)
【激进】 jījìn radical ◇ ～派 radicals
【激励】 jīlì ① encourage; impel; urge: 新老干部相互学习，相互～。Old and young cadres learn from each other and encourage each other./ 共产主义理想～我们前进。The ideal of communism impels us forward./ ～斗志 inspire one's fighting will/ 用革命先烈的英雄事迹～自己 draw inspiration from the heroic deeds of the revolutionary martyrs ② 〈电子〉 drive; excitation ◇ ～器 driver; exciter
【激烈】 jīliè intense; sharp; fierce; acute: ～的冲突 sharp conflict/ ～的争论 heated argument/ ～的思想斗争 intense ideological struggle/ ～的阶级斗争 acute (或 sharp) class struggle/ 一场～的比赛 a closely fought game; a gruelling match/ 争吵得很～ quarrel bitterly/ 这一仗打得很～。It was a fierce fight.
【激流】 jīliú torrent; rapids; turbulent current: 闯过～ shoot the rapids
【激怒】 jīnù enrage; infuriate; exasperate: 种族主义者的暴行～了人民。The atrocities committed by the racists enraged the people.
【激起】 jīqǐ arouse; evoke; stir up: ～公愤 arouse public indignation/ ～强烈的反抗 evoke strong opposition/ ～全世界人民的愤怒 incur the wrath of the people of the whole world/ ～了一场风波 cause a commotion
【激切】 jīqiè 〈书〉 impassioned; vehement: 言辞～ impassioned language
【激情】 jīqíng intense emotion; fervour; passion; enthusiasm: 满怀革命～ be full of revolutionary enthusiasm/ 他们的演出充满了革命的～。Their performance was permeated with revolutionary fervour.
【激赏】 jīshǎng 〈书〉 highly appreciate; greatly admire
【激素】 jīsù 〈生理〉 hormone: 生长～ growth hormone/ 性～ sex hormone
【激扬】 jīyáng ① drain away the mud and bring in fresh water; drive out evil and usher in good ② encourage; urge: ～士气 boost the morale
【激越】 jīyuè intense; vehement; loud and strong: 草原上扬起清亮～的歌声。Songs were heard ringing loud and clear over the grasslands.
【激增】 jīzēng increase sharply; soar; shoot up: 化肥的产量～。The output of chemical fertilizer has soared./ 粮食每亩产量从五百斤～至九百斤。The per-*mu* grain yield has jumped from 500 to 900 *jin*./ 经济危机加剧，失业人数～。With the deepening of the economic crisis, unemployment shot up.
【激浊扬清】 jīzhuó-yángqīng drain away the mud and bring in fresh water; drive out evil and usher in good; eliminate vice and exalt virtue
【激子】 jīzǐ 〈物〉 exciton

**羁** jī 〈书〉 ① bridle; headstall: 无～之马 a horse without a bridle ② control; restrain: 放荡不～ unconventional and uninhibited ③ stay; delay; detain: 事务～身 be detained by one's duties
【羁绊】 jībàn 〈书〉 trammels; fetters; yoke: 摆脱殖民主义的～ throw off the yoke of colonialism/ 挣脱旧思想的～ break the fetters of old ideas; smash the shackles of convention
【羁留】 jīliú ① stay; stop over: 在穗～三日 stop over in Guangzhou for three days ② keep in custody; detain
【羁旅】 jīlǚ 〈书〉 stay long in a strange place; live in a strange land
【羁押】 jīyā 〈书〉 detain; take into custody

## jí

**及** jí ① reach; come up to: 目力所～ as far as the eye can reach/ 水深～腰。The water came up to one's waist (或 was waist-deep)./ 由此～彼 proceed from one point to another/ 力所能～ within one's power/ 这辆自行车不～那辆好。This bike is not so good as that one. ② in time for: ～时 timely; in time ③ 〈连〉〔连接并列名词或名词性词组，连接的成分中主要的放在"及"之前〕: 地里种着小麦、油菜～其他作物。The fields are under wheat, rape and other crops.
【及第】 jídì pass an imperial examination
【及格】 jígé pass a test, examination, etc.; pass
【及龄】 jílíng reach a required age: ～儿童 children who have reached school age
【及时】 jíshí ① timely; in time; seasonable: 要～下种。Sowing must be done in good time./ 这场雪很～。This snow has come at the right time. ② promptly; without delay: ～纠正错误 correct a mistake promptly/ ～汇报 report without delay ◇ ～雨 timely rain
【及物动词】 jíwù dòngcí 〈语〉 transitive verb
【及早】 jízǎo at an early date; as soon as possible; before it is too late: ～回头 repent before it is too late; mend one's ways without delay/ 有病要～治。When you are ill, see the doctor as soon as possible.
【及至】 jízhì 〈连〉 up to; until: ～宋代，方有刻本。Block-printed books did not appear until the Song Dynasty (960-1279).

**汲** jí draw (water): 从井里～水 draw water from a well
【汲汲】 jíjí 〈书〉 anxious; avid: ～于个人名利 crave personal fame and gain
【汲取】 jíqǔ draw; derive: 从群众中～丰富的政治营养 derive rich political nourishment from the masses/ 从毛主席著作中～无穷的力量 draw boundless strength from Chairman Mao's works

**吉** jí ① lucky; auspicious; propitious: 万事大～。All is well. ② (Jí) short for Jilin Province ③ (Jí) a surname
【吉卜赛人】 Jíbǔsàirén Gypsy
【吉布提】 Jíbùtí Djibouti ◇ ～人 Djiboutian
【吉光片羽】 jíguāng piàn yǔ a fragment of a highly treasured relic
【吉利】 jílì lucky; auspicious; propitious
【吉林】 Jílín Jilin (Province)

【吉普车】 jípǔchē jeep
【吉期】 jíqī 〈旧〉 wedding day
【吉庆】 jíqìng auspicious; propitious; happy
【吉他】 jítā 〈乐〉 guitar
【吉祥】 jíxiáng lucky; auspicious; propitious
【吉凶】 jí-xiōng good or ill luck: ～未卜。No one knows how it will turn out.
【吉兆】 jízhào good omen; propitious sign

**岌** jí 〈书〉 (of a mountain) lofty; towering
【岌岌】 jíjí 〈书〉 precarious: ～可危 in imminent danger/ ～不可终日 live in constant fear; live precariously

**级** jí ① level; rank; grade: 各～党组织 Party organizations at all levels/ 大使～会谈 talks at ambassadorial level/ 甲～产品 grade A products; first-class products/ 三～工 grade-3 worker/ 一～战备 No. 1 alert/ 七～地震 an earthquake of magnitude 7 (on the Richter scale)/ 七～风 force 7 wind (on the Beaufort scale) ② any of the yearly divisions of a school course; grade; class; form: 同～不同班 be in different classes of the same grade ③ step: 石～ stone steps ④〈量〉 step; stage: 十几～台阶 a flight of a dozen steps/ 多～火箭 multistage rocket ⑤〈语〉 degree: 比较～ the comparative degree/ 最高～ the superlative degree
【级别】 jíbié rank; level; grade; scale: 干部～ the rank of a cadre/ 外交～ diplomatic rank/工资～ wage scale; grade on the wage scale
【级差地租】 jíchā dìzū differential (land) rent
【级间分离】 jíjiān fēnlí 〈宇航〉 stage separation
【级联】 jílián 〈电〉 cascade ◇ ～管 cascade tube
【级数】 jíshù 〈数〉 progression; series

**极** jí ① the utmost point; extreme: 无所不用其～ go to any extreme; stop at nothing/ 愚蠢之～ be the height of folly/ ～而言之 talk in extreme terms ② pole: 北(南)～ the North (South) Pole ③〈副〉 extremely; exceedingly: ～为重要 of the utmost importance/ 高兴～了 extremely happy/ ～少数 a tiny minority; only a few; a handful/ 给予～大的注意 give maximum attention to; pay very close attention to/ ～尽招摇撞骗之能事 bluff and swindle right and left
【极板】 jíbǎn 〈电〉 plate
【极地】 jídì polar region ◇ ～航空 polar aviation/ ～航行 arctic navigation; polar air navigation
【极点】 jídiǎn the limit; the extreme; the utmost: 感动到了～ be extremely moved/ 蛮横无理到了～ reach the height of truculence
【极度】 jídù extreme; exceeding; to the utmost: ～疲劳 be extremely tired; be overcome with fatigue/ ～兴奋 be elated
【极端】 jíduān ① extreme: 走～ go to extremes ② extreme; exceeding: ～仇视 show extreme hatred for/ ～困难 exceedingly difficult/ ～贫困 in dire poverty/ ～腐败 rotten to the core/ 对工作～负责任 have a boundless sense of responsibility in one's work ◇ ～个人主义者 out-and-out egoist/ ～民主化 ultra-democracy
【极光】 jíguāng 〈天〉 aurora; polar lights: 北～ aurora borealis; northern lights/ 南～ aurora australis; southern lights
【极化】 jíhuà 〈物〉 polarization ◇ ～张量 polarization tensor
【极乐鸟】 jílèniǎo bird of paradise
【极乐世界】 jílè shìjiè 〈佛教〉 *Sukhavati*; Pure Land; Western Paradise
【极力】 jílì do one's utmost; spare no effort: ～避免发生事故 do one's utmost (或 best) to avoid accidents/ ～劝阻 try very hard to dissuade sb. from doing sth./ ～吹捧 laud sb. to the skies/ ～鼓吹 vigorously publicize (an erroneous theory, etc.); clamorously advocate/ ～扩大 expand to the maximum/ ～缩小 reduce to the minimum; minimize
【极量】 jíliàng 〈医〉 maximum dose
【极目】 jímù look as far as the eye can see: ～远眺 gaze into the distance
【极品】 jípǐn 〈书〉 highest grade; best quality: ～绿茶 best quality green tea
【极谱】 jípǔ 〈物〉 polarogram ◇ ～分析 polarographic analysis/ ～仪 polarograph
【极其】 jíqí 〈副〉 most; extremely; exceedingly: 一项～光荣的任务 a most glorious task/ 受到～深刻的阶级教育 receive a profound lesson in class education
【极圈】 jíquān 〈地〉 polar circle: 北～ the Arctic Circle/ 南～ the Antarctic Circle
【极权主义】 jíquánzhǔyì totalitarianism
【极盛】 jíshèng heyday; zenith; acme: 在古埃及文明的～时期 at the height of ancient Egyptian civilization/ 在他精力～的时期 in his prime of life/ 唐朝是中国旧诗的～时期。The Tang Dynasty was the golden age of classical Chinese poetry.
【极限】 jíxiàn ① the limit; the maximum: 达到了～ reach the limit ②〈数〉 limit ◇ ～负载〈电〉 limit load/ ～压力〈物〉 limiting pressure
【极刑】 jíxíng capital punishment; the death penalty
【极夜】 jíyè polar night
【极右】 jíyòu ultra-Right ◇ ～分子 ultra-Rightist
【极值】 jízhí 〈数〉 extreme value
【极"左"】 jí"zuǒ" ultra-"Left": 以～的面貌出现 put on an extremely "Left" front/ 貌似～而实质极右 ultra-"Left" in appearance but ultra-Right in essence ◇ ～分子 ultra-"Leftist"/ ～思潮 ultra-"Left" trend of thought

**即** jí ① approach; reach; be near: 可望而不可～ within sight but beyond reach ② assume; undertake: ～位 ascend the throne ③ at present; in the immediate future: ～日 this or that very day/ 成功在～。Success is in sight. ④ prompted by the occasion: ～兴 impromptu ⑤〈书〉 be; mean; namely: 春节～农历新年。The Spring Festival is the lunar New Year./ 非此～彼。It must be either this or that./ 对旧中国的许多大学生来说，毕业～失业。For many college students in old China, graduation meant unemployment./ 元代建都于大都，～今之北京。The Yuan Dynasty established its capital in Dadu, now Beijing. ⑥〈书〉 promptly; at once: 闻过～改 correct one's mistake as soon as it is pointed out/ 招之～来 be on call at any hour ⑦〈书〉 even; even if
【即便】 jíbiàn even; even if; even though: ～你有理，也不应该发火啊！You shouldn't have lost your temper even if you were in the right.
【即或】 jíhuò even; even if; even though
【即将】 jíjiāng be about to; be on the point of: 比赛～开始。The match is about to begin./ 水电站～竣工。The hydroelectric station is nearing completion./ 国庆节～来临。It will soon be National Day./ 胜利～到来。Victory is at hand.
【即景】 jíjǐng 〈书〉 (of a literary or artistic work) be inspired by what one sees: 公社～ glimpses of a people's commune ◇ ～诗 extempore verse
【即景生情】 jíjǐng shēng qíng the scene brings back memories; the scene touches a chord in one's heart
【即刻】 jíkè at once; immediately; instantly
【即令】 jílìng even; even if; even though

【即期】 jíqī 〈经〉 immediate; spot
◇ ～付现 immediate (或 prompt) cash payment/ ～外汇 spot exchange/ ～汇价 spot rate
【即日】 jírì 〈书〉 ① this or that very day: 本条例自～起施行。The regulations come into force as of today. ② within the next few days: 本片～放映。The film will be shown within a few days.
【即若】 jíruò 〈书〉 even; even if; even though
【即时】 jíshí immediately; forthwith
【即使】 jíshǐ 〈连〉 even; even if; even though: ～我们的工作得到了极其伟大的成绩，也没有任何值得骄傲自大的理由。Even if we achieve gigantic successes in our work, there is no reason whatsoever to be conceited and arrogant.
【即位】 jíwèi ascend the throne
【即席】 jíxí 〈书〉 ① impromptu; extemporaneous: ～赋诗一首 compose a poem impromptu; improvise a poem/ ～讲话 speak impromptu; make an impromptu (或 extemporaneous) speech ② take one's seat (at a dinner table, etc.)
【即兴】 jíxìng impromptu; extemporaneous: ～之作 an improvisation ◇ ～曲 〈乐〉 impromptu/ ～诗 extempore verse

**亟** jí 〈书〉 urgently; anxiously; earnestly: ～盼 earnestly hope/ ～欲 desire most ardently; want very much/ ～待解决的重大问题 important problems demanding prompt solution/ ～须纠正 must be speedily put right
另见 qì

**佶** jí 〈书〉 robust and sturdy
【佶屈聱牙】 jíqū áoyá full of difficult, unpronounceable words

**急** jí ① impatient; anxious: ～着要出发 be impatient to set out ② worry: 你怎么来得这么晚，真把人～死啦！Why are you so late? We were worried to death about you. ③ irritated; annoyed; nettled: 我没想到他真～了。I didn't expect him to get angry. ④ fast; rapid; violent: 水流很～。The current is swift. 或 It's a strong current./ 雨下得正～。It's raining hard./ ～病 acute disease ⑤ urgent; pressing: 事情很～，必须立即处理。The matter is pressing (或 urgent) and must be dealt with at once./ 他走得很～。He left in a hurry. ⑥ urgency; emergency: 应～ meet an emergency ⑦ be eager to help: ～人之难 be eager to help those in need/ ～工农兵之所～ be eager to meet the needs of the workers, peasants and soldiers
【急板】 jíbǎn 〈乐〉 *presto*
【急不可待】 jí bùkě dài too impatient to wait; extremely anxious
【急促】 jícù ① hurried; rapid: ～的脚步声 hurried footsteps/ ～的枪声 rapid gunfire/ 呼吸～ be short of breath/ 脉搏～ have a short, quick pulse ② (of time) short; pressing: 时间很～，不要再犹豫了。Time is running short. Stop hesitating (或 dithering). ◇ ～跃进 〈军〉 rush; advance by rushes
【急电】 jídiàn urgent telegram; urgent cable
【急风暴雨】 jífēng-bàoyǔ violent storm; hurricane; tempest: 经历过～的考验 have stood the test of violent storms/ 这场运动如～，势不可挡。This movement carried all before it like a hurricane.
【急腹症】 jífùzhèng 〈医〉 acute abdominal disease; acute abdomen
【急公好义】 jígōng-hàoyì zealous for the common weal; public-spirited
【急功近利】 jígōng-jìnlì eager for quick success and instant benefit
【急件】 jíjiàn urgent document or dispatch
【急进】 jíjìn radical
【急惊风】 jíjīngfēng 〈中医〉 acute infantile convulsions
【急救】 jíjiù first aid; emergency treatment
◇ ～包 first-aid dressing/ ～人员 first-aid personnel/ ～药品 first-aid medicine/ ～药箱 first-aid kit/ ～站 first-aid station
【急就章】 jíjiùzhāng hurriedly-written essay; hasty work; improvisation
【急剧】 jíjù rapid; sharp; sudden: ～的变化 rapid change/ ～上升 steep rise/ ～下降 sudden drop; sharp decline/ ～转折 abrupt turn
【急遽】 jíjù rapid; sharp; sudden
【急流】 jíliú ① torrent; rapid stream; rapids: 闯过～险滩 sweep over rapids and shoals ② 〈气〉 jet stream; jet flow
【急流勇进】 jíliú yǒng jìn forge ahead against a swift current; press on in the teeth of difficulties
【急流勇退】 jíliú yǒng tuì resolutely retire at the height of one's official career
【急忙】 jímáng in a hurry; in haste; hurriedly; hastily: 你干吗这样急急忙忙的？Why are you in such a hurry?/ 她背起药箱，～朝病人家里跑去。She flung the medical kit over her shoulder and hurriedly set out for the patient's home.
【急难】 jínàn 〈书〉 ① misfortune; grave danger ② be anxious to help (those in grave danger)
【急迫】 jípò urgent; pressing; imperative: 这是当前最～的任务。This is the most pressing task at present./ 事情很～，得赶快处理。The matter is urgent and something's got to be done about it at once.
【急起直追】 jíqǐ-zhízhuī rouse oneself to catch up
【急切】 jíqiè ① eager; impatient: 用～的目光注视着 gaze intently at sb. or sth./ ～地盼望 eagerly look forward to; wait impatiently for ② in a hurry; in haste: ～难办 hard to do in a hurry/ ～间找不着适当的人 cannot find the right person at such short notice
【急如星火】 jí rú xīnghuǒ extremely pressing; most urgent; posthaste: 灾区需用医药，～。Medical aid must be sent to the stricken area posthaste.
【急刹车】 jíshāchē ① slam the brakes on ② bring to a halt
【急射】 jíshè 〈军〉 quick fire
【急速】 jísù very fast; at high speed; rapidly: 汽车～地向前行驶。The car was running at high speed./ 他的病情～恶化。His condition rapidly worsened./ 情况～变化。The situation changed quickly.
【急湍】 jítuān swift current
【急弯】 jíwān sharp turn: 拐了个～ made a sharp turn/ 前有～，行车小心。Sharp turn ahead. Drive carefully.
【急务】 jíwù urgent task: 有～在身 have some urgent task on hand
【急先锋】 jíxiānfēng ① daring vanguard ② most aggressive, adventurous henchman
【急行军】 jíxíngjūn rapid march: 部队～，一夜走了一百里。The detachment made a rapid march of 100 *li* in one night.
【急性】 jíxìng acute: ～阑尾炎 acute appendicitis/ ～传染病 acute infectious disease
【急性病】 jíxìngbìng ① 〈医〉 acute disease ② impetuosity: 犯～ become impetuous
【急性子】 jíxìngzǐ 〈中药〉 the seed of garden balsam
【急性子】 jíxìngzi ① of impatient disposition; impetuous ② an impetuous person
【急需】 jíxū ① be badly in need of: ～帮助 be in need of immediate help/ 提供～的资金 provide much-needed funds ② urgent need: 以应～ meet a crying need

【急用】 jíyòng urgent need: 节约储蓄,以备～ practise economy and save money against a rainy day/ 请把材料赶紧送来,有～。Please send us the material at once; it's urgently needed.
【急于】 jíyú eager; anxious; impatient: ～完成任务 eager to fulfil a task/ ～表态 impatient to state one's position/ ～求成 overanxious for quick results; impatient for success/ 没准备好,就不要～开会。Don't call the meeting till we're ready.
【急躁】 jízào ① irritable; irascible ② impetuous; rash; impatient: 防止～情绪 guard against impetuosity/ 产生～情绪 give way to impatience
【急诊】 jízhěn emergency call; emergency treatment ◇ ～病人 emergency case/ ～室 emergency ward
【急智】 jízhì nimbleness of mind in dealing with emergencies; quick-wittedness
【急中生智】 jízhōng shēng zhì suddenly hit upon a way out of a predicament; show resourcefulness in an emergency
【急转直下】 jízhuǎn-zhíxià (of the march of events, etc.) take a sudden turn and then develop rapidly

**疾** jí ① disease; sickness; illness: 痼～ a stubborn illness/ 眼～ eye trouble ② suffering; pain; difficulty: ～苦 sufferings; hardships ③ hate; abhor: ～恶如仇 hate evil like an enemy ④ fast; quick: ～驰而过 speed past
【疾病】 jíbìng disease; illness: 防治～ prevention and treatment of disease
【疾风】 jífēng ① strong wind; gale ② 〈气〉 moderate gale
【疾风劲草】 jífēng jìngcǎo the force of the wind tests the strength of the grass — strength of character is tested in a crisis 又作"疾风知劲草"
【疾苦】 jíkǔ sufferings; hardships: 关心人民的～ be concerned about the weal and woe of the people/ 他总是把群众的～挂在心上。He always has the well-being of the masses at heart.
【疾首蹙额】 jíshǒu-cù'é with aching head and knitted brows — with abhorrence
【疾言厉色】 jíyán-lìsè harsh words and stern looks: 他对人很和蔼,从不～。He is affable and is never brusque with people.

**脊** jí
另见 jǐ
【脊梁】 jíliang back (of the human body)
【脊梁骨】 jílianggǔ backbone; spine: 断了～的癞皮狗 a mangy dog with a broken back (a term of contempt for renegades, etc.)
【脊檩】 jílǐn 〈建〉 ridgepole; ridgepiece
【脊瓦】 jíwǎ 〈建〉 ridge tile

**棘** jí ① sour jujube ② thorn bushes; brambles ③ 〈动〉 spine; spina
【棘轮】 jílún 〈机〉 ratchet (wheel)
【棘皮动物】 jípí dòngwù echinoderm
【棘手】 jíshǒu thorny; troublesome; knotty: ～的问题 a knotty problem/ 这件事情很～。This is a sticky business.
【棘爪】 jízhuǎ 〈机〉 pawl; detent: 止回～ check pawl

**殛** jí 〈书〉 kill: 雷～ be struck dead by lightning

**集** jí ① gather; collect: 聚～ gather together/ 大门口聚～了一大堆人。A crowd gathered at the gate./ ～各家之长 incorporate the strong points of different schools ② country fair; market: 赶～ go to a country fair; go to market ③ collection; anthology: 诗～ a collection of poems/ 画～ an album of paintings ④ volume; part: 这些文章分三～出版。These articles will be published in three volumes./ 这部影片分上、下两～。This film is in two parts.
【集材】 jícái 〈林〉 logging; skidding; yarding: 索道～ cable logging ◇ ～道 skid road/ ～绞盘机 yarder
【集尘器】 jíchénqì 〈机〉 dust arrester; dust collector; duster
【集成电路】 jíchéng diànlù 〈电子〉 integrated circuit ◇ ～晶体管 integrated circuit transistor
【集大成】 jí dàchéng be a comprehensive expression of; be an agglomeration of; epitomize: 他是这一学派思想的～者。He epitomized the thought of this school.
【集电极】 jídiànjí 〈电子〉 collecting electrode; collector
【集管】 jíguǎn 〈机〉 header
【集合】 jíhé gather; assemble; muster; call together: ～! (口令) Fall in!/ 紧急～ emergency muster/ ～地点 assembly place; rendezvous/ 命令全排战士～。Order the whole platoon to fall in./ 民兵～好了。The militiamen have already lined up.
◇ ～号 bugle call for fall-in; assembly/ ～论 〈数〉 set theory/ ～名词 〈语〉 collective noun/ ～体 〈矿〉 aggregate
【集会】 jíhuì assembly; rally; gathering; meeting: ～结社自由 freedom of assembly and association/ 举行群众～ hold a mass rally
【集结】 jíjié mass; concentrate; build up: ～军队 mass troops; concentrate forces/ ～力量 build up strength/ ～待命 assemble and await orders ◇ ～地域 〈军〉 assembly area
【集锦】 jíjǐn a collection of choice specimens: 儿童画～ outstanding examples of children's drawings
【集句】 jíjù a poem made up of lines from various poets
【集聚】 jíjù gather; collect; assemble
【集刊】 jíkān collected papers (of an academic institution)
【集流环】 jíliúhuán 〈电〉 slip ring
【集权】 jíquán centralization of state power: 中央～的封建帝国 a centralized feudal empire
【集日】 jírì market day
【集散地】 jísàndì collecting and distributing centre; distributing centre
【集市】 jíshì country fair; market ◇ ～贸易 country fair trade
【集水】 jíshuǐ 〈水〉 catchment ◇ ～面积 catchment area
【集思广益】 jísī-guǎngyì draw on collective wisdom and absorb all useful ideas; pool the wisdom of the masses
【集体】 jítǐ collective: ～的智慧 collective wisdom/ 一个战斗的～ a militant collective/ 荣立～二等功 gain a Collective Award of Merit, Second Class
◇ ～创作 collective effort in literary or artistic creation/ ～观念 collective spirit/ ～经济 collective economy/ ～领导 collective leadership/ ～农庄 collective farm/ ～生产劳动 collective productive labour/ ～宿舍 dormitory/ ～所有制 collective ownership/ ～舞 group dancing/ ～英雄主义 collective heroism/ ～主义 collectivism
【集体化】 jítǐhuà collectivization: 农业～ the collectivization of agriculture/ 走～的道路 follow (或 take) the road of collectivization
【集团】 jítuán group; clique; circle; bloc: 七十七国～ the Group of 77/ 统治～ the ruling clique; the ruling circle/ 军事～ a military bloc/ 小～ a small clique ◇ ～军 group army
【集训】 jíxùn assemble for training: 干部轮流～。Cadres take turns to receive training at a given place. ◇ ～队 〈体〉 team of athletes in training
【集腋成裘】 jí yè chéng qiú the finest fragments of fox fur, sewn together, will make a robe — many a little makes a mickle
【集邮】 jíyóu stamp collecting; philately ◇ ～簿 stamp-

album/ ～者 stamp-collector; philatelist
【集约】 jíyuē 〈农〉 intensive ◇ ～经营 intensive farming
【集镇】 jízhèn town; market town
【集中】 jízhōng concentrate; centralize; focus; amass; put together: ～精力 concentrate one's energy/ ～火力 concentrate fire (on a target)/ ～目标 concentrate on the same target/ 民主基础上的～, ～指导下的民主 centralism on the basis of democracy and democracy under centralized guidance/ ～大量财富 amass vast fortunes/ ～注意力 focus one's attention on/ ～群众的智慧 pool the wisdom of the masses/ ～指挥 centralized direction (或 command)/ 思想不～ be absent-minded/ ～各方面的正确意见 sum up correct ideas from all quarters
◇ ～管理 centralized management/ ～轰炸 mass bombing/ ～营 concentration camp
【集装箱】 jízhuāngxiāng 〈交〉 container
◇ ～船 container ship/ ～化 containerization/ ～运输 containerized traffic
【集注】 jízhù ① focus: 代表们的眼光都～在大会主席台上。 Every eye at the conference was focused on the rostrum. ② variorum ◇ ～本 variorum edition
【集资】 jízī raise funds; collect money; pool resources
【集子】 jízi collection; collected works; anthology
【集总】 jízǒng 〈电〉 lumped ◇ ～电容 lumped capacitance

**楫** jí 〈书〉 oar

**戢** jí 〈书〉 ① hide; conceal: ～翼 (of a bird) fold its wings ② restrain: ～怒 restrain one's anger; become placated

**辑** jí ① collect; compile; edit: 编～ edit; compile ② part; volume; division: 新闻简报第一～ Newsreel No. 1
【辑录】 jílù compile
【辑要】 jíyào summary; abstract

**蒺** jí
【蒺藜】 jíli 〈植〉 puncture vine

**嫉** jí ① be jealous; be envious ② hate
【嫉妒】 jídù be jealous of; envy
【嫉恨】 jíhèn envy and hate; hate out of jealousy

**瘠** jí 〈书〉 ① lean; thin and weak ② barren; poor; lean: ～土 poor soil; barren land
【瘠薄】 jíbó barren; unproductive: ～的山坡地 barren land on a mountain slope

**鹡** jí
【鹡鸰】 jílíng wagtail

**藉** jí 见"狼藉" lángjí

**籍** jí ① book; record: 古～ ancient books ② registry; roll: 户～ household register; population register ③ native place; home town; birthplace: 回～ return to one's native place/ 祖～ the land of one's ancestors ④ membership: 党～ party membership/ 国～ nationality
【籍贯】 jíguàn the place of one's birth or origin; native place

## jǐ

**几** jǐ ① how many: ～天可以完工? How many days will it take to finish the work?/ ～点钟了? What's the time? 或 What time is it?/ 你～号? What's your number?/ 离这儿有～里地? How far is it from here? ② a few; several; some: 说～句话 say a few words/ 过～天 in a couple of days/ ～十 tens; dozens; scores/ ～万万 several hundred million; hundreds of millions/ 十～岁的孩子 teenager/ 二十～个人 twenty odd people/ 相差无～ not much difference
另见 jī
【几分】 jǐfēn a bit; somewhat; rather: 有～醉意 a bit merry; a bit tipsy/ 让他～ humour him a little/ 她说的有～道理。There's something in what she said./ 对他的意图我有～怀疑。I'm somewhat suspicious of his intentions.
【几何】 jǐhé ① 〈书〉 how much; how many: 不知尚有～ be uncertain how much is left or how many are left ② 〈数〉 geometry ◇ ～级数 〈数〉 geometric progression; geometric series/ ～图形 〈数〉 geometric figure
【几何学】 jǐhéxué 〈数〉 geometry: 解析～ analytic geometry/ 立体～ solid geometry/ 平面～ plane geometry
【几内亚】 Jǐnèiyà Guinea ◇ ～人 Guinean
【几内亚比绍】 Jǐnèiyà Bǐshào Guinea-Bissau
【几儿】 jǐr 〈口〉 what date: 你～来的? When did you get here?/ 今儿是～? What's the date today?
【几时】 jǐshí what time; when: 你们～走? What time are you leaving?/ 不知～咱们能再见面! Who knows when we'll meet again?
【几许】 jǐxǔ 〈书〉 how much; how many: 不知～。No one can tell how much.

**己** jǐ ① oneself; one's own; personal: 舍～为公 make personal sacrifices for the public good/ 引为～任 regard as one's (own) duty/ 各抒～见。Each airs his own views. ② the sixth of the ten Heavenly Stems
【己方】 jǐfāng one's own side

**纪** Jǐ a surname
另见 jì

**虮** jǐ
【虮子】 jǐzi the egg of a louse; nit

**济** jǐ
另见 jì
【济济】 jǐjǐ (of people) many; numerous: 人才～ an abundance of capable people; a galaxy of talent/ 老中青～一堂, 进行了热烈的讨论。The old, the middle-aged and the young gathered together and had a lively discussion.
【济南】 Jǐnán Jinan

**挤** jǐ ① squeeze; press: 把水～掉 squeeze the water out/ ～时间 try and find time to do sth.; find time ② jostle; push against: ～进去 force (或 elbow, shoulder, push) one's way in; squeeze in/ ～上前去 push to the front/ 别～。Don't push./ 人们互相～来～去。People jostled each other. ③ crowd; pack; cram: ～做一团 pressed close together; packed like sardines/ 小屋～不下那么多人。It's impossible to pack so many people into the small room./ 礼堂已经～满了。The assembly hall is filled to capacity./ 几件事～在一块儿了。 Several matters have cropped up at the same time.
【挤兑】 jǐduì a run on a bank
【挤咕】 jǐgu 〈方〉 wink: 我朝他～眼儿, 叫他别开腔。 I winked at him to keep quiet.
【挤挤插插】 jǐjichāchā 〈方〉 very crowded; packed tight; jammed together; packed like sardines

【挤眉弄眼】 jǐméi-nòngyǎn make eyes; wink

【挤奶】 jǐ'nǎi milk (a cow, etc.) ◇～机 milking machine; milker

【挤牙膏】 jǐyágāo squeeze toothpaste out of a tube — be forced to tell the truth bit by bit

【挤压】 jǐyā 〈冶〉 extruding ◇～机 extrusion press; extruder

**给** jǐ ① supply; provide: 这支部队粮食全部自～。This army unit produces all its own food grain. ② ample; well provided for: 家～户足。Every household is well provided for.

另见 gěi

【给水】 jǐshuǐ ①〈建〉 water supply ②〈机〉 feed water: 锅炉～ boiler feed water ◇～工程 water-supply engineering/ ～器〈机〉 water feeder

【给养】 jǐyǎng provisions; victuals: ～充足 be abundantly provisioned/ ～不足 be short of provisions

【给予】 jǐyǔ 〈书〉 give; render: ～支持 give support to/ ～协助 render assistance to/ ～正式承认 give official recognition to/ ～很高的评价 have a very high opinion of; appreciate highly/ ～同情 show sympathy for/ ～适当的纪律处分 take appropriate disciplinary measures against sb.

**脊** jǐ ① spine; backbone ② ridge: 山～ the ridge of a hill or mountain/ 屋～ the ridge of a roof

另见 jí

【脊背】 jǐbèi back (of a human being or any other vertebrate)

【脊鳍】 jǐqí 〈动〉 dorsal fin

【脊神经】 jǐshénjīng spinal nerve

【脊髓】 jǐsuǐ spinal cord ◇～灰质炎 poliomyelitis; polio/ ～炎 myelitis

【脊索】 jǐsuǒ 〈动〉 notochord ◇～动物 chordate (animal)

【脊柱】 jǐzhù spinal column; vertebral column; backbone; spine

【脊椎】 jǐzhuī vertebra ◇～动物 vertebrate/ ～骨 vertebra; spine

**戟** jǐ halberd

**麂** jǐ muntjac

【麂皮】 jǐpí chamois (leather); chammy

## jì

**计** jì ① count; compute; calculate; number: 不～其数 countless; innumerable/ 数以万～ by the tens of thousands; numbering tens of thousands/ 工作不～时间 be ready to work longer hours than required; not mind working extra hours/ 不～报酬 not be concerned about pay/ 大小拖拉机～二十台。The tractors, light and heavy, numbered twenty in all. 或 There were twenty light and heavy tractors in all. ② meter; gauge: 雨量～ rain gauge ③ idea; ruse; stratagem; plan: 退敌之～ a stratagem to repulse the enemy/ 中～ fall into a trap/ 作归～ plan to go home/ 他们一～不成,又生一～。Their first ruse having failed, they tried another./ 为长远～ from a long-term point of view ④ (Jì) a surname

【计策】 jìcè stratagem; plan

【计程仪】 jìchéngyí 〈航海〉 log

【计划】 jìhuà ① plan; project; programme: 切实可行的～ a feasible (或 workable) plan/ 宏伟的～ a magnificent project/ 河流开发～ a river development programme/ 有～地进行 proceed in a planned way ② map out; plan: ～好了再动手干。Map it out before you start./ 我们～下周出发。We plan to leave next week.

◇～供应 planned supply/ ～经济 planned economy/ ～生产 planned production/ ～生育 family planning; birth control

【计件】 jìjiàn reckon by the piece ◇～工资 piece rate wage/ ～工作 piecework

【计较】 jìjiào ① haggle over; fuss about: ～小事 be too particular about trifles/ 他不～个人得失。He gives no thought to personal gains or losses. ② argue; dispute: 我不同你～,等你气平了再说。I won't argue with you now. Let's talk it over when you've calmed down. ③ think over; plan: 先安排一周的活儿,以后再作～。We'll arrange a week's work first and think about the rest afterwards.

【计量】 jìliàng measure; calculate; estimate: 不可～ inestimable ◇～学 metrology

【计谋】 jìmóu scheme; stratagem

【计日程功】 jì rì chéng gōng estimate exactly how much time is needed to complete a project; have the completion of a project well in sight

【计时】 jìshí reckon by time ◇～工资 payment by the hour; time wage/ ～工作 timework

【计数】 jìshù count

【计数器】 jìshùqì 〈物〉 counter: 盖革～ Geiger counter/ 闪烁～ scintillation counter

【计算】 jìsuàn ① count; compute; calculate: ～出席人数 count the number of people present/ ～产值 calculate the output value ② consideration; planning: 做事不能没个～。We shouldn't do anything without a plan. ◇～尺 slide rule

【计算机】 jìsuànjī computer; calculating machine: 机械～ mechanical computer/ 电子～ electronic computer/ 模拟～ analogue computer/ 微型～ microcomputer/ 数字控制～ digital control computer/ 自动数字跟踪分析～ automatic digital tracking analyser computer/ 自动程序控制～ automatic sequence-controlled calculator/ 超高速巨型～ giant ultra-high-speed computer

◇～程序设计 computer programming/ ～存储器 computer storage/ ～代码 computer code/ ～软设备 computer software/ ～硬设备 computer hardware/ ～装置 computer installation

【计议】 jìyì deliberate; talk over; consult: 从长～ take one's time in coming to a decision; think sth. over carefully/ 二人～已定。The two of them settled on a scheme.

**记** jì ① remember; bear in mind; commit to memory: ～错了 remember wrongly/ ～不清 cannot recall exactly; remember only vaguely/ 死～硬背 learn by rote/ 党的教导～在心 bear in mind the Party's teachings/ 我们要～住这个教训。We must keep this lesson in mind. ② write (或 jot, take) down; record: ～在笔记本上 write it down in a notebook/ 把结果～下来 record the results/ ～下电话号码 jot down the telephone number ③ notes; record: 游～ travel notes/ 大事～ a chronicle of events ④ mark; sign: 暗～儿 secret mark ⑤ birthmark: 他左腿有块～。There is a birthmark on his left leg. ⑥〈方〉〈量〉: 一～耳光 a slap in the face

【记仇】 jìchóu bear grudges; harbour bitter resentment: 他可不～。He's not the sort of person to bear a grudge.

【记得】 jìde remember: ～他的模样儿 remember what he looked like/ 我完全记不得了。I simply don't remember it./ 你～住这些数字吗? Can you carry all these figures in your head?

【记分】 jìfēn ①keep the score; record the points (in a game) ②register a student's marks ③record workpoints ◇～册 (teacher's) markbook/ ～牌 scoreboard/ ～员 scorekeeper; scorer; marker
【记工】 jìgōng record workpoints (earned by a commune member) ◇～本 workpoint registration book/ ～员 workpoint recorder
【记功】 jìgōng cite sb. for meritorious service; record a merit: 记一等功 award sb. a Citation for Merit, First Class
【记挂】 jìguà 〈方〉 be concerned about; keep thinking about; miss
【记过】 jìguò record a demerit
【记号】 jìhao mark; sign: 做个～ make a sign; mark out
【记恨】 jìhèn bear grudges
【记录】 jìlù ①take notes; keep the minutes; record: 把发言的主要内容～下来 note down the main points of the speeches ②minutes; notes; record: 会议～ the minutes of a meeting/ 会谈～ a transcript of talks/ 正式～ official record/ 逐字～ verbatim record/ 摘要～ summary record/ 列入会议～ place on record in the minutes; minute ③notetaker: 这次讨论请你做～好吗？ Would you take the minutes of the discussion? ④record: 创～ set a record; chalk up a record/ 打破～ break a record/ 世界～ world record ◇～本 minute book/ ～片〈电影〉 documentary film; documentary
【记名】 jìmíng put down one's name (on a cheque, etc. to indicate responsibility or claim); sign: 无～投票 secret ballot ◇～支票 order cheque
【记谱法】 jìpǔfǎ 〈乐〉 musical notation
【记取】 jìqǔ remember; bear in mind: ～这个血的教训 bear firmly in mind this lesson learned at the cost of blood/ ～正反两方面的经验 draw on experience both positive and negative
【记时仪】 jìshíyí 〈天〉 chronograph
【记事】 jìshì ①keep a record of events; make a memorandum: 刻木结绳～ keep records by notching wood or tying knots ②account; record of events; chronicles
【记事儿】 jìshìr (of a child) begin to remember things: 那时我只有五岁，才～。 I was then only five years old and had just begun to remember things.
【记述】 jìshù record and narrate: 该书前言～了作者生平。 The preface of the book includes an account of the author's life.
【记诵】 jìsòng commit to memory and be able to recite; learn by heart
【记性】 jìxing memory: ～好 have a good memory/ ～坏 have a poor (或 short) memory
【记叙】 jìxù narrate: 这篇文章～了铁人王进喜的先进事迹。 The article tells about the exemplary deeds of Iron Man Wang Jinxi. ◇～文 narration; narrative
【记要】 jìyào 见"纪要" jìyào
【记忆】 jìyì ①remember; recall: 就我～所及 so far as I can remember ②memory: 你们的深情厚谊将永远留在我们的～中。 Your warm friendship will always remain in our memory.
【记忆力】 jìyìlì the faculty of memory; memory: ～衰退 one's memory is failing/ ～强(弱) have a good (poor) memory
【记忆犹新】 jìyì yóu xīn remain fresh in one's memory
【记载】 jìzǎi ①put down in writing; record: 详细地～事情经过 record the incident in detail/ 有文字～的历史 recorded history ②record; account: 地方志中有关于这次旱灾的～。 There is an account of this drought in the local chronicles.
【记帐】 jìzhàng ①keep accounts ②charge to an account: 请把这批化肥记在大队的帐上。 Please charge this batch of chemical fertilizer to the brigade's account.
【记者】 jìzhě reporter; correspondent; newsman; journalist: 新闻～ newspaper reporter; newsman/ 随军～ war correspondent/ 特派～ special correspondent/ 新华社～ Xinhua correspondent; reporter of the Xinhua News Agency
◇～协会 journalists' association/ ～招待会 press conference/ ～证 press card
【记住】 jìzhu remember; learn by heart; bear in mind: 把这首诗～ learn the poem by heart/ 牢牢～党的基本路线 bear firmly in mind the Party's basic line

## 纪

jì ①discipline: 军～ military discipline/ 违法乱～ break the law and violate discipline ②put down in writing; record: ～事 chronicle ③age; epoch: 中世～ the Middle Ages/ 世～ century ④〈地〉 period: 震旦～ the Sinian Period
另见 Jǐ
【纪录】 jìlù 见"记录" jìlù
【纪律】 jìlǜ discipline: ～是执行路线的保证。 Discipline is the guarantee for the implementation of the line./ 遵守～ keep discipline; observe discipline/ 劳动～ labour discipline; labour regulations/ 无～现象 indiscipline/ 加强～性 heighten one's sense of discipline/ ～严明 highly disciplined/ 给予～处分 take disciplinary measures against sb. ◇～检查委员会 commission for inspecting discipline
【纪年】 jìnián ①a way of numbering the years: 阴历用干支～。 In the lunar calendar, the years are designated by the Heavenly Stems and Earthly Branches. ②chronological record of events; annals
【纪念】 jìniàn ①commemorate; mark: 值得～的日子 a memorable day/ ～活动 commemorative activities/ 举行～大会 hold a commemoration meeting/ ～建军节 mark (或 observe) Army Day ②souvenir; keepsake; memento: 留个～ keep sth. as a souvenir/ 给你这张照片作个～。 Have this picture for a souvenir./ 这盏油灯是我们延安生活的～。 This oil lamp is a memento of our days in Yan'an. ③commemoration day; anniversary: 十周年～ the tenth anniversary
◇～册 autograph book; autograph album/ ～品 souvenir; keepsake; memento/ ～日 commemoration day/ ～塔 memorial tower; monument/ ～邮票 commemorative stamp/ ～章 souvenir badge
【纪念碑】 jìniànbēi monument; memorial: 人民英雄～ the Monument to the People's Heroes/ 建立革命烈士～ erect a memorial to the revolutionary martyrs
【纪念馆】 jìniànguǎn memorial hall; museum in memory of sb.: 鲁迅～ the Lu Xun Museum
【纪念堂】 jìniàntáng memorial hall; commemoration hall: 毛主席～ the Chairman Mao Memorial Hall
【纪实】 jìshí record of actual events; on-the-spot report: 动员大会～ an on-the-spot report of the mobilization meeting
【纪事本末体】 jìshì běnmòtǐ 〈史〉 history presented in separate accounts of important events
【纪行】 jìxíng travel notes: 陕北～ notes on a trip to Northern Shaanxi
【纪要】 jìyào summary of minutes; summary: 会谈～ summary of conversations (或 talks)/ 座谈会～ summary of a forum or panel discussion
【纪元】 jìyuán ①the beginning of an era (e.g. an emperor's reign) ②epoch; era: 开辟了世界历史的新～ usher in a new era in world history
【纪传体】 jìzhuàntǐ 〈史〉 history presented in a series of

biographies

**伎** jì ① skill; ability; trick: 故～重演 be up to one's old tricks again; play the same old trick ② a professional female dancer or singer in ancient China

【伎俩】 jìliǎng trick; intrigue; manoeuvre: "分而治之"是帝国主义者惯用的～。"Divide and rule" has long been a favourite trick of the imperialists.

**技** jì skill; ability; trick: 绝～ unique skill/ 一～之长 what one is skilled in; skill/ 使敌人无所施其～ make it impossible for the enemy to play any tricks

【技工】 jìgōng ①〈简〉(技术工人) skilled worker ② mechanic; technician

【技击】 jìjī the art of attack and defence in *wushu*

【技能】 jìnéng technical ability; mastery of a skill or technique: 生产～ skill in production

【技巧】 jìqiǎo skill; technique; craftsmanship: 写作～ writing technique/ 艺术～ artistry/ 精湛的玉雕～ superb skill in jade carving ◇ ～运动 acrobatic gymnastics

【技师】 jìshī technician

【技术】 jìshù technology; skill; technique: 科学～ science and technology/ 提高～水平 increase technical competence/ ～要求很高 demand high-level technology/ 重大～改革 key technological transformations ◇ ～兵种 technical arms (或 troops)/ ～革命 technological revolution/ ～革新 technological innovation; technical innovation/ ～工人 skilled worker/ ～规范 technical specification; technological specification/ ～鉴定 technical appraisement/ ～力量 technical force; technical personnel/ ～名词 technical term/ ～人员 technical personnel (或 staff)/ ～手册 technical manual; technological manual/ ～学校 technical school/ ～研究所 technological research institute/ ～知识 technological know-how; technical knowledge/ ～职称 titles for technical personnel/ ～资料 technical data; technological data

【技术推广站】 jìshù tuīguǎngzhàn technical advice station: 农业～ agrotechnical station

【技术性】 jìshùxìng technical; of a technical nature: ～问题 technical matters/ 这工作～很强。This job is highly technical.

【技术员】 jìshùyuán technician: 农业～ agronomist

【技术指导】 jìshù zhǐdǎo ① technological (或 technical) guidance ② technical adviser

【技痒】 jìyǎng itch to exercise one's skill: 他看到孩子们打乒乓,不觉～。Seeing the children playing ping-pong, he itched to have a go.

【技艺】 jìyì skill; artistry: ～精湛 highly skilled; masterly

**芰** jì 〈书〉 an ancient name for water caltrop

**系** jì tie; fasten; do up; button up: ～鞋带 tie shoe laces/ 把衣服扣子～上 button up a jacket/ 把晾衣绳～在树上 fasten a clothesline between two trees/ 少先队员都～着红领巾。The Young Pioneers all wear red scarves.
另见 xì

【系泊】 jìbó moor (a boat) ◇ ～浮筒 mooring buoy

【系船索】 jìchuánsuǒ mooring rope; mooring line

【系留】 jìliú moor (a balloon or airship) ◇ ～塔 mooring mast; mooring tower

**忌** jì ① be jealous of; envy: ～才 be jealous of other people's talent; resent people more able than oneself/ ～恨 envy and hate ② fear; dread; scruple: 横行无～ ride roughshod; run amuck ③ avoid; shun; abstain from: ～生冷 avoid cold and uncooked food/ 研究问题,～带主观性、片面性和表面性。In studying a problem, we must shun subjectivity, one-sidedness and superficiality. ④ quit; give up: ～酒 give up alcohol; abstain from wine/ ～烟 quit smoking

【忌辰】 jìchén the anniversary of the death of a parent, ancestor, or anyone else held in esteem

【忌惮】 jìdàn dread; fear; scruple: 肆无～ stopping at nothing; unscrupulous

【忌妒】 jìdu be jealous of; envy

【忌讳】 jìhui ① taboo: 犯～ violate (或 break) a taboo ② avoid as taboo: 老张～人家叫他的外号。Lao Zhang resents being called by his nickname. ③ avoid as harmful; abstain from: 得了痢疾～吃生冷油腻。People suffering from dysentery must avoid raw, cold or greasy food.

【忌刻】 jìkè jealous and mean; jealous and malicious

【忌口】 jìkǒu avoid certain food (as when one is ill); be on a diet

【忌日】 jìrì 见"忌辰"

【忌嘴】 jìzuǐ 见"忌口"

**际** jì ① border; boundary; edge: 水～ the edge of a body of water; waterside/ 天～ horizon/ 无边无～ boundless ② between; among; inter-: 春夏之～ between spring and summer/ 国～ international; between nations/ 校～比赛 interschool matches; intercollegiate games ③ inside: 脑～ in one's head (或 mind) ④ occasion; time: 在代表大会召开之～ on the occasion of the convening of the congress/ 临别之～ at the time of parting ⑤ on the occasion of: ～此盛会 on the occasion of this grand gathering ⑥ one's lot; circumstances: 遭～ vicissitudes in one's life; one's lot

【际遇】 jìyù 〈书〉 favourable or unfavourable turns in life; spells of good or bad fortune

**妓** jì prostitute

【妓女】 jìnǚ prostitute

【妓院】 jìyuàn brothel

**季** jì ① season: 一年四～ the four seasons of the year; all the year round/ 雨～ rainy season; wet season ② the yield of a product in one season; crop: 由种一～改为种两～ reap two crops a year instead of one ③ the last month of a season: ～春 the last month of spring ④ the fourth or youngest among brothers: ～弟 the fourth or youngest brother ⑤ (Jì) a surname

【季度】 jìdù quarter (of a year): ～报告 a quarterly report/ 第一～生产指标 the production quota for the first quarter

【季风】 jìfēng 〈气〉 monsoon ◇ ～气候 monsoon climate/ ～雨 monsoon rain 又作"季候风"

【季节】 jìjié season: 农忙～ a busy farming season/ 收获～ harvest season; harvest time
◇ ～差价 seasonal variations in price/ ～工 seasonal worker/ ～回游 seasonal migration (of fish, etc.)

【季节性】 jìjiéxìng seasonal ◇ ～工作 seasonal work; seasonal jobs

【季刊】 jìkān quarterly publication; quarterly

**剂** jì ① a pharmaceutical or other chemical preparation: 针～ injection/ 丸～ pill; bolus/ 片～ tablet/ 麻醉～ narcotic; anaesthetic/ 防腐制～ preservative; antiseptic/ 干燥～ drying agent; desiccant ②〈量〉〔用于汤药〕: 一～中药 a dose of Chinese herbal medicine

【剂量】 jìliàng 〈药〉 dosage; dose

【剂型】 jìxíng 〈药〉 the form of a drug (e.g. liquid, powder,

pill)

**济** jì ①cross a river: 同舟共～ people in the same boat help each other; pull together to tide over difficulties ②aid; relieve; help: ～人之急 relieve sb. in need/ 扶危～困 help the distressed and succour those in peril ③be of help; benefit: 无～于事 not help matters; be of no help 另见 jǐ

【济事】 jìshì 〔多用于否定〕be of help (或 use): 空谈不～。Empty talk doesn't help matters./ 光我们几个不～，要发动群众。Just the few of us are no use; we must mobilize the masses.

**荠** jì
另见 qí

【荠菜】 jìcài 〈植〉 shepherd's purse

【荠苧】 jìníng 〈植〉 Chinese mosla (*Mosla chinensis*)

**既** jì ①already: 盥洗～毕 having performed one's ablutions/ ～得权利 vested right ②〈连〉since; as; now that: ～来之，则安之。Since we are here, we may as well stay and make the best of it./ ～要革命，就要有一个革命党。If there is to be revolution, there must be a revolutionary party. ③〈连〉〔与"且""又""也"等副词连用〕both...and; as well as: 这间屋子～宽敞，又亮堂。The room is both light and spacious./ ～不实用，又不美观 neither useful nor attractive

【既成事实】 jìchéng shìshí accomplished fact; *fait accompli*: 造成～ present a *fait accompli*; make sth. an accomplished fact/ 承认～ accept a *fait accompli*

【既得利益】 jìdé lìyì vested interest ◇ ～集团 vested interests

【既定】 jìdìng set; fixed; established: ～目标 set objective; fixed goal/ ～方案 existing plan

【既而】 jì'ér 〈书〉〈副〉 afterwards; later; subsequently

【既然】 jìrán 〈连〉 since; as; now that: ～如此 since it is so; such being the case; under these circumstances/ 你～表示了决心，就应该见之于行动。Now that you have expressed your determination, you should act.

【既是】 jìshì 〈连〉 since; as; now that: ～天气不好，那就不去了吧。Since the weather is bad, let's call off the trip.

【既遂】 jìsuì 〈法〉 accomplished offence

【既往不咎】 jìwǎng bù jiù forgive sb.'s past misdeeds; let bygones be bygones

**觊** jì

【觊觎】 jìyú 〈书〉 covet; cast greedy eyes on: ～别国领土 covet another country's territory

**继** jì ①continue; succeed; follow: ～踵 follow close on sb.'s heels/ ～位 succeed to the throne/ 前赴后～ advance wave upon wave/ ～成昆铁路之后，我国西南又一条铁路建成通车了。Following the Chengdu-Kunming Railway another new railway in southwest China was completed and opened to traffic. ②then; afterwards: 初感头晕，～又呕吐 feel dizzy and then begin to vomit

【继承】 jìchéng inherit; carry on: ～财产 inherit property/ ～优良传统 carry forward the good traditions/ ～革命事业 carry on the revolutionary cause/ ～毛主席的遗志，把无产阶级革命事业进行到底。Carry out Chairman Mao's behests and carry the proletarian revolutionary cause through to the end.

【继承权】 jìchéngquán right of succession; right of inheritance: 剥夺～ disinherit sb./ 长子～ primogeniture

【继承人】 jìchéngrén heir; successor; inheritor: 直系～ lineal successor/ 王位～ successor to the throne/ 法定～ heir at law; legal heir

【继电器】 jìdiànqì 〈电〉 relay

【继而】 jì'ér 〈副〉 then; afterwards

【继父】 jìfù stepfather

【继母】 jìmǔ stepmother

【继配】 jìpèi 〈旧〉 second wife (taken after the death of one's first wife) 又作"继室"

【继任】 jìrèn succeed sb. in a post: ～首相 succeed sb. as prime minister

【继往开来】 jìwǎng-kāilái carry forward the (revolutionary) cause and forge ahead into the future: 我们正处在承先启后、～的重要历史时刻。We are now at an important juncture in history when we are carrying forward the revolutionary cause pioneered by our predecessors and forging ahead into the future.

【继续】 jìxù continue; go on: ～工作 continue working/ ～有效 remain valid; remain in force/ ～执政 continue in office; remain in power/ 会议～到深夜。The meeting went on till late at night./ 有些问题仍需～研究。Some problems require further study./ 他们第二天又～会谈。They resumed the talks the next day./ 中国革命是伟大的十月革命的～。The Chinese revolution is a continuation of the great October Revolution.

【继续革命】 jìxù géming continue the revolution: 坚持无产阶级专政下的～ persevere in continuing the revolution under the dictatorship of the proletariat/ 他们～的觉悟高。They have a strong sense of the need for continuous revolution.

**寄** jì ①send; post; mail: ～信 post a letter; mail a letter/ ～包裹 send a parcel by post/ ～钱 remit money ②entrust; deposit; place: ～希望于人民 place hopes on the people ③depend on; attach oneself to: ～食 live with a relative, etc. (because of one's straitened circumstances) ④〈旧〉adopted: ～儿 adopted son

【寄存】 jìcún deposit; leave with; check: 把大衣～在衣帽间 check one's overcoat at the cloakroom/ 行李～处 left-luggage office; checkroom

【寄存器】 jìcúnqì 〈计算机〉 register: 变址～ index register/ 进位～ carry storage register

【寄放】 jìfàng leave with; leave in the care of: 把箱子～在朋友家里 leave a suitcase with a friend

【寄件人】 jìjiànrén sender

【寄居】 jìjū live away from home: 从小～在舅父家里 live from childhood with one's uncle ◇ ～蟹 hermit crab

【寄卖】 jìmài consign for sale on commission; put up for sale in a secondhand shop: 把自行车放在委托商店里～ put a bicycle on sale in a secondhand shop ◇ ～商店 commission shop; secondhand shop

【寄人篱下】 jì rén líxià live under another's roof; depend on sb. for a living

【寄生】 jìshēng ①〈生〉 parasitism ②parasitic: ～生活 parasitic life
◇ ～动物 parasitic animal/ ～蜂 parasitic wasp/ ～振荡〈电〉 parasitic oscillation/ ～植物 parasitic plant

【寄生虫】 jìshēngchóng parasite ◇ ～病 parasitic disease; parasitosis/ ～学 parasitology

【寄售】 jìshòu 见"寄卖"

【寄宿】 jìsù ①lodge: ～在朋友家里 lodge (或 put up) at a friend's house ②(of students) board ◇ ～生 resident student; boarder/ ～学校 boarding school; residential college

【寄托】 jìtuō ①entrust to the care of sb.; leave with sb.: 把孩子～在邻居家里 entrust one's child to the care of a neighbour ②place (hope, etc.) on; find sustenance in: 精

神有所～ have spiritual sustenance
【寄信人】 jìxìnrén sender
【寄养】 jìyǎng entrust one's child to the care of sb.; ask sb. to bring up one's child
【寄予】 jìyǔ ① place (hope, etc.) on: 党对青年一代～很大的希望。The Party places great hopes on the youth. ② show; give; express: ～深切的同情 show heartfelt sympathy to
【寄语】 jìyǔ 〈书〉 send word: ～亲人报喜讯。Send our dear ones the happy news.
【寄主】 jìzhǔ 〈生〉 host (of a parasite)

**寂** jì ① quiet; still; silent: 万籁俱～。All is quiet and still. ② lonely; lonesome; solitary: 枯～ bored and lonely
【寂静】 jìjìng quiet; still; silent: 在～的深夜里 in the still of the night/ ～的山村，顿时沸腾起来。The quiet mountain village suddenly became astir./ 一阵阵号子声，打破了森林的～。Work songs broke the silence of the forest.
【寂寥】 jìliáo 〈书〉 solitary; lonesome
【寂寞】 jìmò lonely; lonesome: 我在这里又交了新朋友，一点也不～。I don't feel lonely as I've made new friends here.
【寂然】 jìrán 〈书〉 silent; still

**悸** jì 〈书〉 (of the heart) throb with terror; palpitate: 惊～ palpitate with terror/ 心有余～ have a lingering fear

**祭** jì ① hold a memorial ceremony for ② offer a sacrifice to: ～天 offer a sacrifice to Heaven; worship Heaven ③ wield: ～起法宝 wield a magic wand
【祭奠】 jìdiàn hold a memorial ceremony for
【祭礼】 jìlǐ ① sacrificial rites ② memorial ceremony ③ sacrificial offerings
【祭品】 jìpǐn sacrificial offerings; oblation
【祭器】 jìqì sacrificial utensil
【祭祀】 jìsì offer sacrifices to gods or ancestors
【祭坛】 jìtán sacrificial altar
【祭文】 jìwén funeral oration; elegiac address

**蓟** jì 〈植〉 setose thistle
【蓟马】 jìmǎ 〈动〉 thrips: 烟～ tobacco thrips

**霁** jì 〈书〉 ① cease raining or snowing; clear up after rain or snow: 雪～。It's stopped snowing and is clearing up./ ～月 an unclouded moon; the moon in a cloudless sky ② calm down after being angry: ～颜 calm down after a fit of anger; appear mollified

**暨** jì 〈书〉 ① and ② up to; till: ～今 up till now

**鲚** jì long-tailed anchovy; anchovy

**稷** jì ① millet ② the god of grains worshipped by ancient emperors

**鲫** jì crucian carp

**髻** jì hair worn in a bun or coil

**冀** jì ① 〈书〉 hope; long for; look forward to: 希～ hope for; look forward to/ ～其成功 look forward to the success of sb. or sth. ② (Jì) another name for Hebei Province ③ (Jì) a surname

**鰶** jì gizzard shad

**骥** jì 〈书〉 a thoroughbred horse

## jiā

**加** jiā ① add; plus: 二～三等于五。Two plus three makes five. 或 Two and three is five./ 小米～步枪 millet plus rifles / 苦干～巧干 work arduously and skilfully ② increase; augment: ～工资 increase (或 raise) sb.'s wages/ ～件衣服再出去。Put on more clothes before you go out./ ～大油门 open the throttle; step on the gas/ 为社会主义添砖～瓦 contribute one's bit to the building of socialism ③ put in; add; append: 汤里～点盐 put some salt in the soup/ ～注解 append notes to/ 给人～上种种罪名 level all sorts of charges against sb./ 给自己～上新的头衔 confer a new title on oneself ④〔表示施以某种动作〕: 大～赞扬 praise highly; lavish praise on/ 不～考虑 not consider at all
【加班】 jiābān work overtime; work an extra shift: ～加点 work extra shifts or extra hours; put in extra hours ◇ ～费 overtime pay
【加倍】 jiābèi double; redouble: ～努力 redouble one's efforts/ ～警惕 redouble one's vigilance/ ～注意 be doubly careful/ 明年产量可能～。The output may double next year.
【加车】 jiāchē (put on) extra buses or trains
【加成】 jiāchéng 〈化〉 addition ◇ ～化合物 additive compound; addition compound
【加法】 jiāfǎ 〈数〉 addition
【加工】 jiāgōng ① process: 食品～ food processing/ ～中草药 process medicinal herbs/ 这篇文章需要～。This article needs polishing. ② 〈机〉 machining; working: 冷～ cold working/ 机～ machining ◇ ～厂 processing factory/ ～留量 allowance
【加工订货】 jiāgōng dìnghuò orders placed by the state with private enterprises for processing materials or supplying manufactured goods (an early form of state capitalism adopted to effect the socialist transformation of capitalist industry in China)
【加固】 jiāgù reinforce; consolidate: ～堤坝 reinforce dykes and dams/ ～工事 improve defence works
【加害】 jiāhài injure; do harm to: ～于人 do harm to sb.; do sb. an injury
【加号】 jiāhào 〈数〉 plus sign (+)
【加级鱼】 jiājíyú 〈口〉 (red) porgy
【加急电】 jiājídiàn urgent telegram; urgent cable
【加紧】 jiājǐn step up; speed up; intensify: ～生产 step up production/ ～准备 speed up preparation
【加劲】 jiājìn put more energy into; make a greater effort: 加把劲儿！ Put your back into it!
【加剧】 jiājù aggravate; intensify; exacerbate: ～紧张局势 aggravate tension/ 矛盾正在～。The contradictions are sharpening./ 病势～。The patient's condition has taken a turn for the worse.
【加快】 jiākuài quicken; speed up; accelerate; pick up speed: ～步子 quicken one's step/ ～农业机械化的进程 speed up farm mechanization/ 火车～了速度。The train picked up speed./ 我国社会主义建设的速度大大～了。Our socialist construction is going on at a greatly accelerated pace.
【加宽】 jiākuān broaden; widen: ～路面 widen the road
【加勒比共同体】 Jiālèbǐ Gòngtóngtǐ the Caribbean Community (CARICOM)
【加勒比海】 Jiālèbǐhǎi the Caribbean Sea
【加力】 jiālì 〈航空〉 thrust augmentation; afterburning ◇ ～俯冲 afterburning dive
【加料】 jiāliào ① feed in raw material: 自动～ automatic

feeding ②reinforced: ～药酒 reinforced tonic wine/ ～狼毫 a writing brush reinforced with superfine weasel hair

【加仑】 jiālún gallon

【加榴炮】 jiāliúpào gun-howitzer

【加码】 jiāmǎ ①〈旧〉raise the price of commodities; overcharge ②〈旧〉raise the stakes in gambling ③raise the quota: 层层～ raise the quota at each level

【加冕】 jiāmiǎn coronation ◇ ～日 Coronation Day

【加拿大】 Jiānádà Canada ◇ ～人 Canadian

【加那利群岛】 Jiānàlì Qúndǎo the Canary Islands

【加纳】 Jiānà Ghana ◇ ～人 Ghanaian

【加捻】 jiāniǎn 〈纺〉twisting

【加农炮】 jiānóngpào gun; cannon

【加蓬】 Jiāpéng Gabon ◇ ～人 Gabonese

【加气】 jiāqì 〈建〉air entrainment ◇ ～混凝土 aerocrete/ ～水泥 air entraining cement

【加强】 jiāqiáng strengthen; enhance; augment; reinforce: ～党的领导 strengthen Party leadership/ 对青年～阶级教育 strengthen class education among the youth/ ～纪律性 strengthen discipline/ ～战备 enhance combat preparedness; intensify preparations against war/ ～对运动的领导 give more effective leadership to the movement/ ～军事力量 augment military strength/ ～敌情观念 heighten one's awareness of the enemy's activities/ ～控制 tighten one's control (或 grip) ◇ ～排(连、营) reinforced platoon (company, battalion)

【加氢】 jiāqīng 〈化〉hydrogenization; hydrogenation ◇ ～精制 hydrofining/ ～裂化 hydrocracking

【加权平均值】 jiāquán píngjūnzhí 〈数〉weighted average

【加热】 jiārè heating ◇ ～炉 heating furnace/ ～器 heating apparatus; heater

【加入】 jiārù ①add; mix; put in ②join; accede to: ～共产党 join the Communist Party/ ～条约 accede to a treaty ◇ ～国 acceding state/ ～书 instrument of accession

【加塞儿】 jiāsāir 〈口〉push into a queue out of turn; jump a queue

【加色法】 jiāsèfǎ 〈电影〉additive process

【加深】 jiāshēn deepen: ～河道 deepen the channel of a river/ ～理解 get a deeper understanding

【加数】 jiāshù 〈数〉addend

【加速】 jiāsù quicken; speed up; accelerate; expedite: 队伍～前进。The contingent quickened its advance./ ～发展工业 speed up the development of industry/ ～旧制度的灭亡 hasten the collapse of the old social order

【加速度】 jiāsùdù 〈物〉acceleration: 重力～ acceleration of gravity ◇ ～计 accelerometer

【加速器】 jiāsùqì 〈物〉accelerator: 直线～ linear accelerator/ 回旋～ cyclotron/ 同步～ synchrotron/ 粒子～ particle accelerator/ 微波～ microwave accelerator/ 稳相～ synchrocyclotron

【加线】 jiāxiàn 〈乐〉ledger line; leger line

【加以】 jiāyǐ ①〔表示如何对待或处理前面提到的事物〕: 原计划须～修改。It is necessary to revise the original plan./ 有问题要及时～解决。Problems should be resolved in good time. ②〈连〉in addition; moreover: 这种鞋结实耐穿,～价格便宜,很受群众欢迎。These shoes are very popular. They're sturdy and, what's more, they're cheap.

【加意】 jiāyì with special care; with close attention: ～保护 protect with special care/ ～提防 be particularly watchful

【加油】 jiāyóu ①oil; lubricate: 这台机器该～了。This machine needs oiling. ②refuel: 飞机要在上海降落～。The plane will land in Shanghai for refuelling./ 空中～ in-flight (或 air) refuelling ③make an extra effort: ～干 work with added vigour/ ～! ～! Come on! Come on!/ 观众为运动员～。The spectators cheered the players on. ◇ ～车 refuelling truck; refueller/ ～飞机 tanker aircraft/ ～站 filling (或 petrol, gas) station

【加油添醋】 jiāyóu-tiāncù 见"添油加醋" tiānyóu-jiācù

【加重】 jiāzhòng ①make or become heavier; increase the weight of: ～任务 add to one's tasks/ ～思想负担 add to one's worries/ ～语气 say sth. with emphasis ②make or become more serious; aggravate: ～危机 aggravate the crisis/ 病情～。The patient's condition worsened.

**夹** jiā ①press from both sides; place in between: 把相片～在书里 put the photos in between the leaves of a book/ 用钳子把烧红的铁～住 grip a piece of red-hot iron with a pair of tongs/ 用筷子～菜 pick up food with chopsticks/ ～着皮包 carry a briefcase under one's arm/ 他～在我们两人中间。He was sandwiched between the two of us./ 我的手指头被门～了一下。My fingers got squeezed in the door./ 鞋子～脚。The shoe pinches./ 敌军～起尾巴逃跑了。The enemy troops ran away with their tails between their legs./ 无论什么时候,都要谦虚谨慎,把尾巴～紧一些。We must always be modest and prudent and must, so to speak, tuck our tails between our legs. ②mix; mingle; intersperse: ～在人群里 mingle with the crowd/ ～叙～议 narration interspersed with comments/ 狂风～着暴雨 a violent wind accompanied by a torrential rain ③clip, clamp, folder, etc.: 纸～ paper clip/ 发～ hairpin/ 文件～ folder

另见 gā; jiá

【夹板】 jiābǎn ①boards for pressing sth. or holding things together ②〈医〉splint: 上～ put (a limb, etc.) in splints/ 石膏～ plaster splints

【夹叉射击】 jiāchā shèjī 〈军〉bracket

【夹带】 jiādài ①carry secretly; smuggle: 邮寄包裹不能～信件。Don't put letters into a parcel. ②notes smuggled into an examination hall

【夹道】 jiādào ①a narrow lane; passageway ②line both sides of the street: ～欢迎贵宾 line the street to welcome a distinguished guest

【夹缝】 jiāfèng a narrow space between two adjacent things; crack; crevice

【夹攻】 jiāgōng attack from both sides; converging attack; pincer attack: 受到两面～ be under a pincer attack; be caught in a two-way squeeze/ 前后～ attack from the front and the rear simultaneously

【夹击】 jiājī converging attack; pincer attack

【夹具】 jiājù 〈机〉clamping apparatus; fixture; jig

【夹七夹八】 jiāqī-jiābā incoherent; confused; cluttered (with irrelevant remarks): 他～地说了许多话,我也没听懂是什么意思。He rambled on at great length but I couldn't make head or tail of what he said.

【夹生】 jiāshēng half-cooked ◇ ～饭 half-cooked rice

【夹馅】 jiāxiàn stuffed (pastry, etc.)

【夹心】 jiāxīn with filling: 果酱～糖 sweets with jam centre ◇ ～饼干 sandwich biscuits

【夹杂】 jiāzá be mixed up with; be mingled with: 脱粒机的轰鸣声～着年轻人的欢笑声。The droning of the threshers intermingled with youthful laughter./ 他说话～着南方口音。He speaks with a slight southern accent./ 文章里～着不少生造的词语。The article is cluttered up with unclear coined expressions. ◇ ～物〈冶〉inclusion

【夹竹桃】 jiāzhútáo 〈植〉(sweet-scented) oleander

【夹注】 jiāzhù interlinear notes

【夹子】 jiāzi ①clip; tongs: 弹簧～ spring clip/ 点心～ cake tongs/ 衣服～ clothes-peg; clothespin ②folder; wallet: 文件～ folder; binder/ 皮～ wallet; pocketbook

**伽** jiā 〈物〉 gal
另见 gā
【伽倻琴】 jiāyēqín a plucked stringed instrument, used by the Chaoxian nationality

**佳** jiā good; fine; beautiful: ～景 fine landscape; beautiful view/ 成绩甚～ achieve very good results/ ～宾 a welcome guest/ ～肴 delicacies / 身体欠～ not feel well; be indisposed
【佳话】 jiāhuà a deed praised far and wide; a story on everybody's lips; a much-told tale: 两国运动员互相帮助的事迹一时传为～。Everybody was telling the story of how the athletes of the two countries helped each other.
【佳节】 jiājié happy festival time; festival: 中秋～ the joyous Mid-Autumn Festival/ 欢度国庆～ celebrate the joyous festival of National Day
【佳境】 jiājìng 〈书〉 the most enjoyable or pleasant stage: 渐入～ become more and more delightful
【佳句】 jiājù beautiful line (in a poem); well-turned phrase
【佳偶】 jiā'ǒu 〈书〉 a happily married couple
【佳期】 jiāqī wedding (或 nuptial) day
【佳人】 jiārén 〈书〉 beautiful woman
【佳音】 jiāyīn welcome news; good tidings; favourable reply: 静候～。I am awaiting the news of your success.
【佳作】 jiāzuò a fine piece of writing; an excellent work

**迦** jiā a character used in proper names and in rendering some foreign names, as in 释迦牟尼 (Sakyamuni)

**茄** jiā
另见 qié
【茄克】 jiākè jacket

**枷** jiā cangue
【枷锁】 jiāsuǒ yoke; chains; shackles; fetters: 精神～ spiritual shackles/ 摆脱殖民主义的～ shake off the yoke of colonialism

**浃** jiā 见"汗流浃背" hàn liú jiā bèi

**家** jiā ① family; household: 他全～都是工人。They're all workers in his family./ 张～和王～ the Zhangs and the Wangs /～事 family matters; domestic affairs ② home: 回～ go home/ 不在～ not be in; be out/ 上我～去吧。Come to my place. ③ a person or family engaged in a certain trade: 船～ boatman/ 渔～ fisherman's family ④ a specialist in a certain field: 科学～ scientist/ 政治～ statesman/ 文学～ a man of letters; writer/ 画～ painter ⑤ a school of thought; school: 法～ the Legalist School/ 百～争鸣。A hundred schools of thought contend. ⑥ 〈谦〉〔用于对别人称比自己辈分高或年纪大的亲属〕: ～父 my father/ ～兄 my elder brother ⑦ domestic; tame: ～兔 rabbit ⑧ 〈量〉〔用来计算家庭或企业〕: 三～商店 three shops/ 一～电影院 a cinema/ 两～人家 two families

**家** jia 〈口〉 ①〔后缀,用在名词后,表示属于哪一类人〕: 小孩子～别插嘴! You kids shouldn't interrupt!/ 现在姑娘～也会开飞机啦! Nowadays girls pilot planes, too! ②〔后缀,用在男人姓名后面,指他的妻〕: 水生～ Shuisheng's wife
另见 jie
【家蚕】 jiācán silkworm
【家产】 jiāchǎn family property
【家常】 jiācháng the daily life of a family; domestic trivia: 拉～ engage in small talk ◇ ～话 small talk; chitchat
【家常便饭】 jiācháng biànfàn ① homely food; simple meal ② common occurrence; routine; all in the day's work: 在旧社会当学徒,挨打受骂是～。In the old society it was routine for an apprentice to be cursed and beaten./ 搬家对勘探队员来说,简直是～。To the members of a prospecting team, moving from place to place is all in the day's work.
【家丑】 jiāchǒu family scandal; the skeleton in the cupboard (或 closet): ～不可外扬。Domestic shame should not be made public. 或 Don't wash your dirty linen in public.
【家畜】 jiāchù domestic animal; livestock
【家传】 jiāchuán handed down from the older generations of the family ◇ ～秘方 a secret recipe handed down in the family
【家当】 jiādang 〈口〉 family belongings; property: 我们这个润滑油厂创办的时候,全部～就是三口大锅。When we first set up this lubricant factory, all we had was three cauldrons.
【家道】 jiādào family financial situation: ～小康 be comfortably off
【家底】 jiādǐ family property accumulated over a long time; resources: ～薄 without substantial resources; not financially solid/ 把咱们的～清理清理。Let's take stock of what we've got.
【家法】 jiāfǎ ① domestic discipline exercised by the head of a feudal household ② a rod for punishing children or servants in a feudal household
【家访】 jiāfǎng a visit to the parents of schoolchildren or young workers
【家鸽】 jiāgē pigeon
【家伙】 jiāhuo 〈口〉 ① tool; utensil; weapon: 这把～挺好使。This is a very handy tool. ② fellow; guy: 小～ little chap; kid/ 那个～是谁? Who's that fellow?/ 一帮反动～ a pack of reactionary scoundrels/ 一个极端阴险的～ a most treacherous villain
【家给人足】 jiājǐ-rénzú each family is provided for and every person is well-fed and well-clothed; all live in plenty
【家计】 jiājì 〈书〉 family livelihood
【家家户户】 jiājiā-hùhù each and every family; every household: 做到～有余粮 ensure that every household has surplus grain
【家教】 jiājiào family education; upbringing: 没有～ not properly brought up; ill-bred/ ～严 be strict with one's children
【家境】 jiājìng family financial situation; family circumstances: ～困难 with one's family in straitened circumstances/ ～好 come from a well-to-do family
【家具】 jiāju furniture: 几件～ several pieces of furniture/ 一套～ a set of furniture
【家眷】 jiājuàn ① wife and children; one's family ② wife
【家口】 jiākǒu members of a family; the number of people in a family
【家破人亡】 jiāpò-rénwáng with one's family broken up, some gone away, some dead: 没有共产党,我早已是～。Without the Communist Party, my whole family would have been ruined or dead long ago.
【家谱】 jiāpǔ family tree; genealogical tree; genealogy
【家禽】 jiāqín domestic fowl; poultry
【家史】 jiāshǐ family history: 老贫农血泪斑斑的～ an old poor peasant's family history of blood and tears
【家什】 jiāshi 〈口〉 utensils, furniture, etc.
【家书】 jiāshū ① a letter home ② a letter from home
【家属】 jiāshǔ family members; (family) dependents: 工人～ families of workers/ 军人～ armymen's families ◇ ～工厂 factory run by family members of workers, cadres, armymen, etc.

【家私】 jiāsī 〈口〉 family property

【家庭】 jiātíng family; household
◇ ～背景 family background/ ～成员 family members/ ～出身 class status of one's family; family origin/ ～负担 family responsibilities/ ～妇女 housewife/ ～副业 household sideline production/ ～观念 attachment to one's family/ ～教师 private teacher; tutor/ ～教育 family education; home education/ ～纠纷 family quarrel; domestic discord/ ～生活 home life; family life/ ～作业 homework

【家徒四壁】 jiā tú sì bì have nothing but the bare walls in one's house — be utterly destitute

【家务】 jiāwù household duties ◇ ～劳动 housework; household chores

【家乡】 jiāxiāng hometown; native place ◇ ～话 native dialect

【家小】 jiāxiǎo 〈口〉 wife and children

【家信】 jiāxìn a letter to or from one's family

【家业】 jiāyè family property; property: 不要以为我们厂～大,浪费一点不算啥。Don't think, just because our factory is big and well-off, that we can waste things.

【家蝇】 jiāyíng housefly

【家用】 jiāyòng family expenses; housekeeping money

【家喻户晓】 jiāyù-hùxiǎo widely known; known to all: 做到～ make known to every household/ 王铁人这个名字在中国已是～的了。Iron Man Wang is a household word in China.

【家园】 jiāyuán home; homeland: 重建～ rebuild one's homeland; rebuild one's village or town

【家长】 jiāzhǎng ① the head of a family; patriarch ② the parent or guardian of a child: 学校里明天开～会。There will be a parents' meeting in our school tomorrow.
◇ ～式统治 paternalism; arbitrary rule as by a patriarch/ ～制 patriarchal system/ ～作风 a high-handed way of dealing with people; patriarchal behaviour

【家族】 jiāzú clan; family

**痂** jiā scab; crust: 结～ form a scab; crust

**袈** jiā

【袈裟】 jiāshā *kasaya*, a patchwork outer vestment worn by a Buddhist monk

**笳** jiā 见"胡笳" hújiā

**傢** jiā

【傢伙】 jiāhuo 见"家伙" jiāhuo

【傢具】 jiāju 见"家具" jiāju

【傢什】 jiāshi 见"家什" jiāshi

**葭** jiā 〈书〉 the young shoot of a reed

**嘉** jiā ① good; fine: ～宾 honoured guest; welcome guest ② praise; commend: 精神可～ a praiseworthy spirit

【嘉奖】 jiājiǎng commend; cite: 传令～全连指战员 cite the officers and men of the company for their meritorious service ◇ ～令 citation

【嘉勉】 jiāmiǎn 〈书〉 praise and encourage

【嘉许】 jiāxǔ 〈书〉 praise; approve

**镓** jiā 〈化〉 gallium (Ga)

## jiá

**夹** jiá double-layered; lined: ～袄 lined jacket
另见 gā; jiā

**荚** jiá pod: 结～ bear pods; pod

【荚果】 jiáguǒ 〈植〉 pod; legume

**戛** jiá 〈书〉 knock gently; tap

【戛戛】 jiájiá 〈书〉 ① difficult; hard going ② original: ～独造 have great originality

【戛然】 jiárán 〈书〉 ①〈象〉〔多形容嘹亮的鸟声〕: ～长鸣 long and loud cries ②〔多用于〕: ～而止 (of a sound) stop abruptly

**蛱** jiá

【蛱蝶】 jiádié a kind of butterfly harmful to crop plants; vanessa

**颊** jiá cheek: 两～红润 with rosy cheeks

【颊骨】 jiágǔ 〈生理〉 cheekbone

【颊囊】 jiánáng 〈动〉 cheek pouch

## jiǎ

**甲** jiǎ ① the first of the ten Heavenly Stems ② first: ～级 first rate; Class A/ 桂林山水～天下。The mountains and waters of Guilin are the finest under heaven. ③〔用作代称〕: 某～与某乙 Mr. A and Mr. B/ ～方和乙方 the first party and the second party/ ～队和乙队 team A and team B ④ shell; carapace: 龟～ tortoise shell ⑤ nail: 手指～ fingernail ⑥ armour: 装～车 armoured car/ 丢盔卸～ throw away one's helmet and coat of mail — flee pell-mell ⑦ 见"保甲制度" bǎojiǎ zhìdù

【甲板】 jiǎbǎn deck

【甲苯】 jiǎběn 〈化〉 toluene; methylbenzene

【甲兵】 jiǎbīng 〈书〉 ① armour and weaponry; military equipment ② soldier in armour

【甲虫】 jiǎchóng beetle

【甲醇】 jiǎchún 〈化〉 methyl alcohol; methanol

【甲酚】 jiǎfēn 〈化〉 cresol

【甲睾酮】 jiǎgāotóng 〈药〉 methyltestosterone

【甲沟炎】 jiǎgōuyán 〈医〉 paronychia

【甲骨文】 jiǎgǔwén inscriptions on bones or tortoise shells of the Shang Dynasty (c. 16th—11th century B.C.)

【甲基】 jiǎjī methyl ◇ ～纤维素〈药〉 methylcellulose

【甲壳】 jiǎqiào crust ◇ ～动物 crustacean

【甲醛】 jiǎquán 〈化〉 formaldehyde ◇ ～水 formalin

【甲酸】 jiǎsuān 〈化〉 formic acid; methanoic acid

【甲烷】 jiǎwán 〈化〉 methane

【甲午战争】 Jiǎwǔ Zhànzhēng 〈史〉 the Sino-Japanese War of 1894-1895 (launched by Japanese imperialism to annex Korea and invade China)

【甲癣】 jiǎxuǎn 〈医〉 onychomycosis; ringworm of the nails

【甲氧胺】 jiǎyǎng'àn 〈药〉 methoxamine

【甲鱼】 jiǎyú soft-shelled turtle

【甲胄】 jiǎzhòu 〈书〉 armour

【甲状腺】 jiǎzhuàngxiàn 〈生理〉 thyroid gland
◇ ～机能亢进 hyperthyroidism/ ～素 thyroxine/ ～肿 goitre

【甲子】 jiǎzǐ a cycle of sixty years 参见"干支" gān-zhī

【甲紫】 jiǎzǐ gentian violet

**岬** jiǎ ① cape; promontory ② a narrow passage between mountains

【岬角】 jiǎjiǎo cape; promontory

**胛** jiǎ

【胛骨】 jiǎgǔ 〈生理〉 shoulder blade

**贾** Jiǎ a surname
另见 gǔ

**钾** jiǎ 〈化〉 potassium (K)

【钾肥】 jiǎféi potash fertilizer
【钾碱】 jiǎjiǎn potash
【钾盐】 jiǎyán sylvite

**假** jiǎ ① false; fake; sham; phoney; artificial: ～腿 artificial leg/ ～民主 bogus democracy; sham democracy/ ～和平 phoney peace/ ～检讨 insincere self-criticism/ 以～乱真 create confusion by passing off the spurious as genuine ② borrow; avail oneself of: 久～不归 keep putting off returning sth. one has borrowed; appropriate sth. borrowed for one's own use ③ if; suppose: ～令 in case
另见 jià

【假扮】 jiǎbàn disguise oneself as; dress up as: 小游击队员～放牛娃，骗过了敌人的岗哨。The boy guerrilla fighter disguised himself as a cowherd and got past the enemy sentry.
【假充】 jiǎchōng pretend to be; pose as: ～内行 pretend to be an expert
【假道】 jiǎdào via; by way of: 代表团～欧洲去联合国。The delegation went to the United Nations via Europe.
【假道学】 jiǎdàoxué a sanctimonious person; hypocrite
【假定】 jiǎdìng ① suppose; assume; grant; presume: ～有这么一回事 suppose it really happened/ ～这是真的，也影响不了大局。Even if this is the case, it will not affect the whole situation. ② hypothesis
【假发】 jiǎfà wig
【假分数】 jiǎfēnshù 〈数〉 improper fraction
【假根】 jiǎgēn 〈植〉 rhizoid
【假公济私】 jiǎ gōng jì sī use public office for private gain; jobbery
【假果】 jiǎguǒ 〈植〉 pseudocarp; spurious fruit
【假花】 jiǎhuā artificial flower
【假话】 jiǎhuà lie; falsehood: 说～ tell lies
【假借】 jiǎjiè ① make use of: ～外力 make use of outside forces/ ～名义 under the guise of; in the name of; under false pretences ② 〈语〉 phonetic loan characters, characters adopted to represent homophones, e.g. 求 qiú (fur) for 求 qiú (entreat) — one of the six categories of Chinese characters (六书)
【假冒】 jiǎmào pass oneself off as; palm off (a fake as genuine): 谨防～。Beware of imitations.
【假寐】 jiǎmèi 〈书〉 catnap; doze
【假面具】 jiǎmiànjù mask; false front: 撕下修正主义者的～ unmask the revisionists
【假名】 jiǎmíng ① pseudonym ② *kana*, a Japanese syllabary
【假漆】 jiǎqī varnish
【假仁假义】 jiǎrén-jiǎyì pretended benevolence and righteousness; hypocrisy
【假如】 jiǎrú if; supposing; in case: ～明天开会，准备工作来得及吗？Supposing we hold the meeting tomorrow, will there be enough time to prepare?/ ～我忘了，请提醒我一下。Remind me in case I forget.
【假若】 jiǎruò if; supposing; in case
【假嗓子】 jiǎsǎngzi *falsetto*
【假山】 jiǎshān rockery
【假设】 jiǎshè ① suppose; assume; grant; presume ② hypothesis: 科学～ a scientific hypothesis
【假声】 jiǎshēng 〈乐〉 *falsetto*
【假使】 jiǎshǐ if; in case; in the event that: ～他不同意，那就作罢。If he disagrees, let the matter drop.
【假释】 jiǎshì 〈法〉 release on parole (或 on probation)
【假手】 jiǎshǒu do sth. through sb. else; make a cat's-paw of sb.: ～于人 make sb. else do the work
【假说】 jiǎshuō hypothesis
【假死】 jiǎsǐ ① 〈医〉 suspended animation ② 〈动〉 play dead; feign death; play possum
【假托】 jiǎtuō ① on the pretext of: ～有病 on the pretext of illness ② under sb. else's name: 这篇文章不是他写的，是别人～他的名义发表的。He didn't write the essay; somebody else did, and published it under his name. ③ by means of; through the medium of: 人们～披着羊皮的狼的故事说明要警惕伪装的敌人。The story of the wolf in sheep's clothing is a fable intended to teach people to be on guard against enemies in disguise.
【假想】 jiǎxiǎng ① imagination; hypothesis; supposition ② imaginary; hypothetical; fictitious: 这个故事里的人物都是～的。The characters in this story are all fictitious. ◇ ～敌 〈军〉 imaginary enemy
【假象】 jiǎxiàng ① false appearance: 制造～ create a false impression; put up a false front/ 不要被～所迷惑。Don't be misled by appearances. ② 〈地〉 pseudomorph
【假惺惺】 jiǎxīngxing hypocritically; unctuously: ～地表示愿意支持 hypocritically express willingness to support/ ～地宣称 declare unctuously
【假牙】 jiǎyá dental prosthesis; false tooth; denture
【假眼】 jiǎyǎn ocular prosthesis; artificial eye; glass eye
【假意】 jiǎyì ① unction; insincerity; hypocrisy ② pretend; put on: ～奉承 cheap flattery
【假造】 jiǎzào ① forge; counterfeit: ～证件 forge a certificate/ 这张钞票是～的。This banknote is a forgery. 或 This is a forged banknote. ② invent; fabricate: ～理由 invent an excuse/ ～罪名 cook up a false charge against; frame up
【假…真…】 jiǎ...zhēn... 〔从一假一真的对比中点明实质〕: 假和平，真备战 peace in words, war preparation in deeds; pay lip service to peace but prepare for war/ 假团结，真分裂 unity in name, splitting in reality/ 假支持，真出卖 sham support, real betrayal/ 假批判，真包庇 sham denunciation, real protection
【假肢】 jiǎzhī artificial limb
【假植】 jiǎzhí 〈农〉 heel in
【假装】 jiǎzhuāng pretend; feign; simulate; make believe: ～积极 pretend to be (politically) active; simulate enthusiasm/ ～不知道 feign ignorance/ 孩子们～解放军攻山头。The boys played at being PLA men storming a mountain stronghold.

**斝** jiǎ 〈考古〉 a round-mouthed three-legged wine vessel

**瘕** jiǎ a lump in the abdomen

## jià

**价** jià ① price: 减～ reduce the price/ 要～ ask a price ② value: 等～交换 exchange of equal values/ 估～ estimate the value of; evaluate ③ 〈化〉 valence: 氢是一～的元素。Hydrogen is a one-valence element.
另见 jie

【价格】 jiàgé price: 批发(零售)～ wholesale (retail) price/ 标明～ mark (goods) with a price tag; have goods clearly priced
【价款】 jiàkuǎn money paid for sth. purchased or received for sth. sold; cost

【价目】 jiàmù marked price; price ◇～表 price list
【价钱】 jiàqian price: 讲～ bargain/ ～公道 a fair (或 decent, reasonable) price/ 西红柿什么～? How much are the tomatoes?
【价值】 jiàzhí ①〈经〉value: 剩余～ surplus value/ 使用～ use value ②worth; value: ～五百万元的设备 five million *yuan* worth of equipment; equipment worth (或 valued at) five million *yuan*/ 毫无～ completely worthless/ 这些资料对我们很有～。This data is of great value to us. ◇～尺度 measure of value/ ～规律 law of value/ ～量 magnitude of value/ ～形态 form of value
【价值连城】 jià zhí liánchéng worth several cities — invaluable; priceless

**驾** jià ①harness; draw (a cart, etc.): ～上牲口耕地 harness cattle to plough the fields/ 那匹马没～过车。That horse has never been harnessed to a cart. ②drive (a vehicle); pilot (a plane); sail (a boat) ③〔原指车辆,借用于对人的敬辞〕: 大～ your good self
【驾临】 jiàlín 〈敬〉your arrival; your esteemed presence: 恭候～。Your presence is requested.
【驾轻就熟】 jiàqīng-jiùshú drive a light carriage on a familiar road; be able to handle a job with ease because one has had previous experience; do a familiar job with ease
【驾驶】 jiàshǐ drive (a vehicle); pilot (a ship or plane): ～拖拉机 drive a tractor ◇～舱〈航空〉control cabin; cockpit; pilot's compartment/ ～杆〈航空〉control stick (或 column); joystick/ ～盘 steering wheel/ ～室 driver's cab/ ～台〈航海〉bridge/ ～员 (车辆的) driver; (飞机的) pilot/ ～执照 driving (或 driver's) license
【驾束式导弹】 jiàshùshì dǎodàn beam rider
【驾驭】 jiàyù ①drive (a cart, horse, etc.): 这匹马不好～。This horse is hard to control. ②control; master: ～形势 have the situation well in hand/ ～自然 tame nature
【驾辕】 jiàyuán pull a cart or carriage from between the shafts; be hitched up: 车太重,得用一匹大骡子～。The cart is heavy and we need to hitch up a big mule.

**架** jià ①frame; rack; shelf; stand: 房～ the frame of a house/ 行李～ luggage-rack/ 工具～ tool rack/ 衣～儿 clothes hanger/ 衣帽～ clothes tree/ 书～ bookshelf/ 黄瓜～ cucumber trellis/ 钢～桥 steel-framed bridge ②put up; erect: ～桥 put up (或 build) a bridge/ ～电话线 set up telephone lines/ ～枪 stack rifles/ ～起机枪 mount a machine gun ③fend off; ward off; withstand: 他一刀砍来,我拿枪～住。I fended off his sword thrust with my spear. ④support; prop; help: ～着伤员走路 help a wounded soldier to walk/ ～着拐走 walk on crutches/ 他扭了脚脖子,我们只得把他～回去。He sprained his ankle and had to be helped home. ⑤kidnap; take sb. away forcibly: 强行～走 carry sb. away by force; kidnap ⑥fight; quarrel: 劝～ step in and patch up a quarrel; mediate between quarrelling parties ⑦〈量〉: 一～收音机 a radio set/ 几百～飞机 several hundred planes
【架不住】 jiàbuzhù 〈方〉①cannot sustain (the weight); cannot stand (the pressure); cannot stand up against: 他开始不想来,～我一说,也就来了。At first he didn't feel like coming, but I persuaded him to./ 谁也～这么大的浪费。Nobody can afford to be so extravagant. ②be no match for; cannot compete with: 主队虽然技术不错,也～客队合作得好。The home team displayed great skill but were no match for the visitors in teamwork.
【架次】 jiàcì sortie: 出动四批飞机共六十～ fly sixty sorties in four groups
【架空】 jiàkōng ①built on stilts: 这里的竹楼都是～的。The bamboo huts here are all built on stilts. ②impracticable; unpractical: 不采取相应的措施,计划就会成为～的东西。Unless we adopt the necessary measures the plan will come to nothing. ③make sb. a mere figurehead ◇～管道 overhead pipe
【架设】 jiàshè erect (above ground or water level, as on stilts or posts): 在河上～浮桥 throw a pontoon bridge across the river/ ～输电线路 erect power transmission lines
【架势】 jiàshi 〈口〉posture; stance; manner: 摆出一副海上霸主的～ assume the posture of lord of the seas/ 看他们的～,是要大干一场。They seem to be getting ready for a big effort. 又作"架式"
【架子】 jiàzi ①frame; stand; rack; shelf: 脸盆～ washstand ②framework; skeleton; outline: 写文章要先搭好～。Make an outline before you start writing./ 把新机构的～搭起来 set up the framework of the new organization ③airs; haughty manner: 摆～ put on airs/ 没有～ be modest and unassuming; be easy of approach/ 放下～ get down from one's high horse ④posture; stance: 他拉开～,打起了太极拳。He adopted a stance and began to do *Taiji* shadowboxing. ◇～工〈建〉scaffolder
【架子猪】 jiàzizhū feeder pig

**假** jià ①holiday; vacation: 暑～ summer vacation ②leave of absence; furlough: 事～ leave of absence to attend to personal affairs/ 病～ sick leave/ 休～ be on leave; be on furlough/ 请～ ask for leave/ 超～ overstay one's leave of absence
另见 jiǎ
【假期】 jiàqī ①vacation ②period of leave
【假日】 jiàrì holiday; day off
【假条】 jiàtiáo ①application for leave ②leave permit: 病～ doctor's certificate (for sick leave)

**嫁** jià ①(of a woman) marry: ～人 get married/ ～女儿 marry off a daughter ②shift; transfer
【嫁祸于人】 jià huò yú rén shift the misfortune onto sb. else; put the blame on sb. else
【嫁接】 jiàjiē 〈植〉grafting
【嫁娶】 jiàqǔ marriage
【嫁妆】 jiàzhuang dowry; trousseau

**稼** jià ①sow (grain): 耕～ ploughing and sowing; farm work ②cereals; crops: 庄～ crops; standing grain
【稼穑】 jiàsè 〈书〉sowing and reaping; farming; farm work

## jiān

**尖** jiān ①point; tip; top: 针～ the point of a needle or pin; pinpoint/ 铅笔～ the tip of a pencil/ 指～ fingertip/ 塔～ the pinnacle of a pagoda ②pointed; tapering: ～下巴 a pointed chin/ 把铅笔削～ sharpen a pencil ③shrill; piercing: ～声～气 in a shrill voice/ ～叫 scream ④sharp; acute: 耳朵～ have sharp ears; be sharp-eared/ 眼～ have sharp eyes; be sharp-eyed/ 鼻子～ have an acute (或 sharp) sense of smell ⑤the best of its kind; the pick of the bunch; the cream of the crop: 拔～儿的 top-notch; the pick of the bunch
【尖兵】 jiānbīng ①〈军〉point ②trailblazer; pathbreaker; pioneer; vanguard: 反修防修的～ a vanguard in combating and preventing revisionism/ 科学种田的～ pioneers in scientific farming
【尖刀】 jiāndāo sharp knife; dagger: 象一把～插入敌人心

脏 like a dagger stuck into the enemy's heart ◇ ～班 Dagger Squad

【尖端】 jiānduān ① pointed end; acme; peak: 标枪的～ the point of a javelin ② most advanced; sophisticated ◇ ～产品 highly sophisticated products/ ～放电 point discharge/ ～科学 most advanced branches of science; frontiers of science/ ～武器 sophisticated weapons

【尖刻】 jiānkè acrimonious; caustic; biting: 说话～ speak with biting sarcasm

【尖括号】 jiānkuòhào angle brackets (〈 〉)

【尖利】 jiānlì ① sharp; keen; cutting: ～的钢刀 a sharp knife ② shrill; piercing: ～的叫声 a shrill cry

【尖脐】 jiānqí ① the narrow triangular abdomen of a male crab ② male crab

【尖锐】 jiānruì ① sharp-pointed ② penetrating; incisive; sharp; keen: ～的批评 incisive (或 sharp) criticism/ ～地指出 point out sharply/ 他看问题很～。He sees things with a keen (或 sharp) eye. ③ shrill; piercing: ～的哨声 the shrill sound of a whistle ④ intense; acute; sharp: ～的思想斗争 sharp mental conflicts/ ～对立 be diametrically opposed to each other ◇ ～化 sharpen; intensify; become more acute

【尖酸】 jiānsuān acrid; acrimonious; tart: ～刻薄 tart and mean; bitterly sarcastic

【尖子】 jiānzi ① the best of its kind; the pick of the bunch; the cream of the crop: 他是班上的～。He's one of the top students in the class. ② a sudden rise in pitch (in opera singing)

【尖嘴薄舌】 jiānzuǐ-bóshé have a caustic and flippant tongue

**奸** jiān ① wicked; evil; treacherous: ～计 an evil plot ② traitor: 内～ a secret enemy agent within one's ranks; hidden traitor/ 汉～ traitor to the Chinese nation; traitor/ 锄～ eliminate traitors; weed out enemy agents ③ 〈口〉 self-seeking and wily: 这个人才～哪，总想占便宜。He's a self-seeker; he's always on the make. ④ illicit sexual relations: 通～ have illicit sexual relations; commit adultery

【奸臣】 jiānchén treacherous court official

【奸宄】 jiānguǐ 〈书〉 evildoers; malefactors

【奸猾】 jiānhuá treacherous; crafty; deceitful

【奸佞】 jiānnìng 〈书〉 ① crafty and fawning ② crafty sycophant

【奸商】 jiānshāng unscrupulous merchant; profiteer

【奸污】 jiānwū rape or seduce

【奸细】 jiānxi spy; enemy agent

【奸险】 jiānxiǎn wicked and crafty; treacherous; malicious

【奸笑】 jiānxiào sinister (或 villainous) smile

【奸邪】 jiānxié 〈书〉 ① crafty and evil; treacherous ② a crafty and evil person

【奸雄】 jiānxióng a person who achieves high position by unscrupulous scheming; arch-careerist

【奸淫】 jiānyín ① illicit sexual relations; adultery ② rape or seduce: ～掳掠 rape and loot

【奸贼】 jiānzéi traitor; conspirator

【奸诈】 jiānzhà fraudulent; crafty; treacherous

**间** jiān ① between; among: 同志之～ among comrades ② within a definite time or space: 世～ (in) the world/ 田～ (in) the fields/ 晚～ (in the) evening; (at) night ③ room: 里～ inner room/ 衣帽～ cloakroom ④ 〈量〉: 一～卧室 a bedroom/ 三～门面 a three-bay shop front

另见 jiàn

【间冰期】 jiānbīngqī 〈地〉 interglacial stage; interglacial

【间不容发】 jiān bù róng fà not a hair's breadth in between—the situation is extremely critical

【间架】 jiānjià ① form of a Chinese character ② structure of an essay

【间量】 jiānliang 〈方〉 the area of a room; floor space: 这间屋子～儿太小。This room is not spacious enough.

**歼** jiān annihilate; wipe out; destroy: ～敌五千 annihilate 5,000 enemy troops

【歼击机】 jiānjījī fighter plane; fighter

【歼灭】 jiānmiè annihilate; wipe out; destroy: ～敌人有生力量 wipe out the enemy's effective strength ◇ ～射击 annihilation fire/ ～战 war or battle of annihilation

**坚** jiān ① hard; solid; firm; strong: ～冰 solid ice; hard ice/ 身残志～ broken in body but firm in spirit ② a heavily fortified point; fortification; stronghold: 攻～ storm strongholds ③ firmly; steadfastly; resolutely: ～信 firmly believe/ ～拒 flatly refuse/ ～称 state insistently; insist

【坚壁】 jiānbì hide supplies to prevent the enemy from seizing them; place in a cache; cache: 把粮食～起来 hide grain from the enemy

【坚壁清野】 jiānbì-qīngyě strengthen defence works, evacuate noncombatants, and hide provisions and livestock; strengthen the defences and clear the fields

【坚不可摧】 jiān bùkě cuī indestructible; impregnable

【坚持】 jiānchí persist in; persevere in; uphold; insist on; stick to; adhere to: 我们党～辩证唯物主义和历史唯物主义的世界观。Our Party upholds dialectical materialism and historical materialism as its world outlook./ ～无产阶级国际主义 adhere to proletarian internationalism/ ～党在整个社会主义历史阶段的基本路线 adhere to the Party's basic line for the entire historical period of socialism/ ～无产阶级专政下的继续革命 persist in continuing the revolution under the dictatorship of the proletariat/ ～干部参加集体生产劳动的制度 maintain the system of cadre participation in collective productive labour/ ～原则 adhere (或 stick) to principle/ ～敌后斗争 keep up the struggle behind enemy lines/ ～真理 hold firmly to the truth/ ～上次会议上提出的条件 insist on the terms put forward at the previous session/ ～已见 hold on to one's own views/ ～错误 persist in one's errors/ 再～一会儿 hold out a little longer

【坚持不懈】 jiānchí bù xiè unremitting: 作～的努力 make unremitting efforts

【坚持不渝】 jiānchí bù yú persistent; persevering; unremitting

【坚定】 jiāndìng ① firm; staunch; steadfast: ～不移 firm and unshakable; unswerving; unflinching/ ～的步伐 firm strides/ ～的立场 a firm stand/ ～的意志 constancy of purpose/ ～正确的政治方向 a firm and correct political orientation/ 革命的～性 revolutionary steadfastness (或 staunchness) ② strengthen: ～了攀登科学技术新高峰的决心 strengthen one's resolve to scale new heights of science and technology

【坚固】 jiāngù firm; solid; sturdy; strong: ～耐用 sturdy and durable/ ～的工事 strong fortifications/ 这座桥造得很～。This bridge is very solidly built.

【坚果】 jiānguǒ 〈植〉 nut

【坚决】 jiānjué firm; resolute; determined: ～支持 firmly support; stand firmly by/ ～反对 resolutely oppose/ ～完成任务！We'll carry out the task without fail!/ 他很～。He stood firm. 或 He was determined./ 采取～措施 take resolute measures

【坚苦卓绝】 jiānkǔ zhuōjué showing the utmost fortitude: ～的斗争 an extremely hard and bitter struggle; a most arduous struggle/ ～的战斗 a hard-fought battle

【坚牢度】 jiānláodù 〈纺〉 fastness: 耐日光～ fastness to sunlight; sunfastness/ 耐洗～ washfastness

【坚强】 jiānqiáng ① strong; firm; staunch: ～的决心 strong determination/ 在中国共产党的～领导下 under the firm leadership of the Communist Party of China/ ～的无产阶级党性 staunch proletarian Party spirit/ 一个性格～的人 a person of strong character ② strengthen: ～党的组织 strengthen the Party organizations
【坚忍】 jiānrěn steadfast and persevering (in face of difficulties)
【坚韧】 jiānrèn ① tough and tensile ② firm and tenacious: 运动员在比赛中表现出～的斗志。The athletes displayed great tenacity throughout the contest.
【坚韧不拔】 jiānrèn bù bá firm and indomitable; persistent and dauntless: ～的革命精神 indomitable revolutionary spirit
【坚如磐石】 jiān rú pánshí solid as a rock; rock-firm
【坚实】 jiānshí solid; substantial: ～的基础 a solid foundation/ 迈出～的步子 make solid progress/ 这条公路～平整。This is a smooth, strongly built highway.
【坚守】 jiānshǒu stick to; hold fast to; stand fast: ～岗位 stand fast at one's post/ ～阵地 hold fast to one's position; hold one's ground
【坚挺】 jiāntǐng 〈金融〉 strong
【坚毅】 jiānyì firm and persistent; with unswerving determination; with inflexible will
【坚硬】 jiānyìng hard; solid: ～的岩石 solid rock
【坚贞】 jiānzhēn faithful; constant
【坚贞不屈】 jiānzhēn bù qū remain faithful and unyielding

**肩** jiān ① shoulder: 并～战斗 fight shoulder to shoulder ② take on; undertake; shoulder; bear: 身～重任 shoulder heavy responsibilities
【肩膀】 jiānbǎng shoulder
【肩负】 jiānfù take on; undertake; shoulder; bear: 我们～人民的希望。The people place their hopes on us./ ～着贫下中农的委托 entrusted with a mission by the poor and lower-middle peasants/ ～光荣的任务 undertake a glorious task
【肩胛骨】 jiānjiǎgǔ 〈生理〉 scapula; shoulder blade
【肩摩毂击】 jiānmó-gǔjī shoulder to shoulder and hub to hub — crowded with people and vehicles
【肩章】 jiānzhāng ① shoulder loop ② epaulet

**艰** jiān difficult; hard
【艰巨】 jiānjù arduous; formidable: 一项光荣而～的任务 a glorious but arduous task/ 付出～的劳动 make tremendous efforts/ 这个工程非常～。This is a formidable project.
【艰苦】 jiānkǔ arduous; difficult; hard; tough: ～的生活 hard life/ ～的斗争 arduous struggle/ ～朴素 hard work and plain living/ 做～细致的思想工作 do painstaking ideological work/ 学习大庆人～创业的革命精神 learn from the Daqing people's revolutionary spirit of building an enterprise through arduous effort/ 自愿到最～的地方去 volunteer to go where conditions are hardest/ ～的环境能磨炼人的意志。Difficult circumstances can temper one's will.
【艰难】 jiānnán difficult; hard: 行动～ walk with difficulty/ 生活～ live in straitened circumstances/ 克服～困苦 overcome difficulties and hardships/ 经过无数～曲折 go through countless difficulties and setbacks/ ～险阻 difficulties and obstacles
【艰涩】 jiānsè involved and abstruse; intricate and obscure: 文词～ involved and abstruse writing
【艰深】 jiānshēn difficult to understand; abstruse
【艰危】 jiānwēi difficulties and dangers (confronting a nation)
【艰险】 jiānxiǎn hardships and dangers: 不避～ brave hardships and dangers
【艰辛】 jiānxīn hardships: 历尽～ experience all kinds of hardships

**兼** jiān ① double; twice: ～旬 twenty days ② simultaneously; concurrently: 任县委书记，～县革委会主任 be secretary of the county Party committee and concurrently chairman of the county revolutionary committee/ ～管 be concurrently in charge of; also look after/ ～而有之 have both at the same time ③ hold two or more jobs concurrently: 身～数职 hold several posts simultaneously
【兼备】 jiānbèi have both... and...: 德才～ have both political integrity and ability; combine ability with political integrity
【兼并】 jiānbìng annex (territory, property, etc.)
【兼程】 jiānchéng travel at double speed: ～前进 advance at the double/ 日夜～ travel day and night
【兼顾】 jiāngù give consideration to (或 take account of) two or more things: 发展生产和改善人民生活二者必须～。Consideration must be given to both the development of production and the improvement of the people's livelihood.
【兼课】 jiānkè ① do some teaching in addition to one's main occupation ② hold two or more teaching jobs concurrently
【兼任】 jiānrèn ① hold a concurrent post: 党委副书记～革委会主任。The deputy Party committee secretary is concurrently chairman of the revolutionary committee. ② part-time ◇ ～教师 part-time teacher
【兼容】 jiānróng 〈电视〉 compatible ◇ ～制电视 compatible television
【兼收并蓄】 jiānshōu-bìngxù incorporate things of diverse nature; take in everything
【兼祧】 jiāntiāo 〈书〉 be appointed heir to one's uncle as well as to one's father
【兼听则明，偏信则暗】 jiān tīng zé míng, piān xìn zé àn listen to both sides and you will be enlightened; heed only one side and you will be benighted
【兼之】 jiānzhī 〈书〉 furthermore; besides; in addition; moreover
【兼职】 jiānzhí ① hold two or more posts concurrently: ～过多 hold too many posts at the same time ② concurrent post; part-time job: 辞去～ resign one's concurrent job

**监** jiān ① supervise; inspect; watch ② prison; jail 另见 jiàn
【监测器】 jiāncèqì 〈物〉 monitor: 污染～ contamination monitor
【监察】 jiānchá supervise; control ◇ ～委员会 control commission; supervisory committee/ ～员 supervisor; controller/ ～制度 supervisory system
【监督】 jiāndū ① supervise; superintend; control: 由群众～劳动 do penal labour under surveillance by the masses/ 国际～ international control/ 国家机关工作人员必须接受群众～。The personnel of organs of state must accept supervision by the masses. ② supervisor ◇ ～权 authority to supervise
【监犯】 jiānfàn prisoner; convict
【监工】 jiāngōng ① supervise work; oversee ② overseer; supervisor
【监护】 jiānhù 〈法〉 guardianship ◇ ～人 guardian
【监禁】 jiānjìn take into custody; imprison; put in jail (或 prison)
【监考】 jiānkǎo invigilate ◇ ～人 invigilator
【监牢】 jiānláo prison; jail
【监票】 jiānpiào scrutinize balloting ◇ ～人 scrutineer

【监视】 jiānshì keep watch on; keep a lookout over: ～敌人的行动 keep watch on the movements of the enemy ◇ ～器 monitor/ ～哨 〈军〉 lookout
【监守】 jiānshǒu have custody of; guard; take care of
【监守自盗】 jiānshǒu zì dào steal what is entrusted to one's care; embezzle; defalcate
【监听】 jiāntīng monitor ◇ ～器 monitor/ ～无线电台 monitoring station
【监狱】 jiānyù prison; jail ◇ ～长 warden
【监制】 jiānzhì supervise the manufacture of

**笺** jiān 〈书〉 ① writing paper: 信～ letter paper ② letter ③ annotation; commentary
【笺注】 jiānzhù 〈书〉 notes and commentary on ancient texts

**渐** jiān 〈书〉 ① soak; be saturated with: ～染 be imperceptibly influenced ② flow into: 东～于海 flow east and empty into the sea
另见 jiàn

**菅** jiān 〈植〉 villous themeda (*Themeda gigantea* var. *villosa*)

**犍** jiān
【犍牛】 jiānniú bullock

**缄** jiān seal; close: 信封上写着"刘～"。On the envelope is written: "from Liu".
【缄口】 jiānkǒu 〈书〉 keep one's mouth shut; hold one's tongue; say nothing
【缄默】 jiānmò keep silent; be reticent

**煎** jiān ① fry in shallow oil: ～鸡蛋 fried eggs ② simmer in water; decoct: ～药 decoct medicinal herbs
【煎熬】 jiān'áo suffering; torture; torment
【煎饼】 jiānbing thin pancake made of millet flour, etc.

**缣** jiān 〈书〉 fine silk

**鲣** jiān oceanic bonito; skipjack (tuna)

**鳒** jiān spiny-rayed flounder; big-mouthed flounder

## jiǎn

**拣** jiǎn ① choose; select; pick out: 把最好的西红柿～出来 pick out the best tomatoes/ 担子～重的挑 choose the heavy loads to carry; volunteer to undertake difficult tasks/ ～要紧的说。Say what you think is most urgent. ② 见"捡" jiǎn
【拣选】 jiǎnxuǎn select; choose

**茧** jiǎn ① cocoon: 蚕～ silkworm cocoon ② callus: 老～ thick callus
【茧绸】 jiǎnchóu pongee

**柬** jiǎn card; note; letter: 请～ invitation card
【柬埔寨】 Jiǎnpǔzhài Kampuchea ◇ ～人 Kampuchean
【柬帖】 jiǎntiě note; short letter

**俭** jiǎn thrifty; frugal: 省吃～用 eat sparingly and spend frugally; be economical in everyday spending
【俭朴】 jiǎnpǔ thrifty and simple; economical: 生活～ lead a thrifty and simple life/ 衣着～ dress simply
【俭省】 jiǎnshěng economical; thrifty: 过日子～ live a frugal life; live economically

**捡** jiǎn pick up; collect; gather: ～麦穗 pick up ears of wheat; glean a wheat field/ ～煤核儿 pick out unburnt coal from cinders/ ～粪 collect manure/ ～柴火 gather firewood/ ～到一支钢笔 find a fountain pen
【捡了芝麻，丢了西瓜】 jiǎnle zhīma, diūle xīguā pick up the sesame seeds but overlook the watermelons; mindful of small matters to the neglect of large ones; penny wise and pound foolish
【捡漏】 jiǎnlòu 〈建〉 repair the leaky part of a roof; plug a leak in the roof
【捡破烂儿】 jiǎn pòlànr pick odds and ends from refuse heaps
【检拾压捆机】 jiǎnshíyākǔnjī 〈农〉 pick-up bale; pick-up press

**检** jiǎn ① check up; inspect; examine: ～定 examine and determine ② restrain oneself; be careful in one's conduct: 行为不～ depart from correct conduct
【检波】 jiǎnbō 〈电子〉 detection ◇ ～管 detection tube/ ～器 detector
【检查】 jiǎnchá ① check up; inspect; examine: ～工作 check up on work/ ～质量 check on the quality of sth./ ～护照 inspect sb.'s passport/ ～行李 inspect (或 examine) sb.'s luggage/ ～身体 have a physical examination; have a health check; have a medical check-up/ ～视力 test sb.'s eyesight/ 新闻～ press censorship/ ～自己对群众的态度 examine one's attitude to the masses/ 把练习～一遍再交。Look over your exercises before handing them in. ② self-criticism: 作～ criticize oneself/ 写～ write a self-criticism ◇ ～飞行 check flight/ ～井 〈建〉 inspection shaft; inspection well/ ～哨 checkpost/ ～团 inspection party/ ～站 checkpoint; checkpost; inspection station
【检察】 jiǎnchá procuratorial work
◇ ～官 public procurator (或 prosecutor)/ ～机关 procuratorial organ/ ～院 procuratorate/ ～长 chief procurator; public procurator-general
【检点】 jiǎndiǎn ① examine; check: ～一下行李，看是不是都齐了。Check the luggage and see if everything is there. ② be cautious (about what one says or does): 言行有失～ be careless about one's words and acts; be indiscreet in one's speech and conduct/ 病人对饮食要多加～。Sick people should be careful about their diet.
【检举】 jiǎnjǔ report (an offence) to the authorities; inform against (an offender): ～特务 inform against a secret agent ◇ ～箱 a box for accusation letters/ ～信 letter of accusation; written accusation
【检漏】 jiǎnlòu 〈电〉 leak hunting ◇ ～器 leak detector; leak localizer
【检讨】 jiǎntǎo self-criticism: 作～ make a self-criticism/ ～自己的错误 examine one's mistakes ◇ ～书 written self-criticism
【检修】 jiǎnxiū examine and repair; overhaul: ～自行车 overhaul a bicycle/ ～汽车引擎 overhaul the engine of a car
【检验】 jiǎnyàn test; examine; inspect: 严格～产品质量 strictly examine the quality of the products/ 商品～ commodity inspection/ 社会实践及其效果是～主观愿望或动机的标准。The criterion for judging subjective intention or motive is social practice and its effect.
【检疫】 jiǎnyì quarantine
◇ ～范围 quarantine range/ ～旗 quarantine flag; yellow

flag/ ～员 quarantine officer/ ～站 quarantine station/ ～证明书 quarantine certificate; vaccination certificate

【检阅】 jiǎnyuè review (troops, etc.); inspect: ～仪仗队 review a guard of honour/ 对科研新成果的一次～ a review of recent achievements in scientific research ◇ ～台 reviewing stand

【检字法】 jiǎnzìfǎ 〈语〉 the way in which Chinese characters are arranged and are to be located (as in a dictionary); indexing system for Chinese characters

**剪** jiǎn ① scissors; shears; clippers ② cut (with scissors); clip; trim: 别把头发～得太短了。Don't cut the hair too short./ ～指甲 trim one's nails/ ～羊毛 shear a sheep ③ wipe out; exterminate: ～除 wipe out; annihilate

【剪报】 jiǎnbào newspaper cutting (或 clipping)

【剪裁】 jiǎncái ① cut out (a garment); tailor ② cut out unwanted material (from a piece of writing); prune: 写文章要下一番～的工夫。In writing an essay one must do a lot of pruning.

【剪彩】 jiǎncǎi cut the ribbon at an opening ceremony: 为展览会～ cut the ribbon at the opening of an exhibition

【剪除】 jiǎnchú wipe out; annihilate; exterminate

【剪床】 jiǎnchuáng 〈机〉 shearing machine

【剪刀】 jiǎndāo scissors; shears

【剪刀差】 jiǎndāochā scissors movement of prices; scissors differential (或 difference); price scissors: 我们对于工农业产品的交换是缩小～，而不是扩大～。In the exchange of industrial products for agricultural products, we try to narrow the price scissors, not widen them.

【剪辑】 jiǎnjí ①〈电影〉 montage; film editing: 电影～机 motion-picture editing machine ② editing and rearrangement: 话剧录音～ highlights of a live recording of a play

【剪接】 jiǎnjiē montage; film editing

【剪毛】 jiǎnmáo 〈牧〉 shearing; clipping ◇ ～机 shearing machine

【剪票】 jiǎnpiào punch a ticket ◇ ～铁 conductor's punch

【剪秋萝】 jiǎnqiūluó 〈植〉 senno campion (*Lychnis senno*)

【剪贴】 jiǎntiē ① clip and paste (sth. out of a newspaper, etc.) in a scrapbook or on cards ② cutting out (as schoolchildren's activity) ◇ ～簿 scrapbook

【剪影】 jiǎnyǐng ① paper-cut silhouette ② outline; sketch

【剪应力】 jiǎnyìnglì 〈机〉 shearing stress

【剪纸】 jiǎnzhǐ 〈工美〉 paper-cut; scissor-cut

【剪子】 jiǎnzi scissors; shears; clippers

**减** jiǎn ① subtract: 九～四得五。Nine minus four is five. 或 Four from nine is five. ② reduce; decrease; cut: ～半 reduce by half/ 工作热情有增无～ work with ever increasing zeal/ 他人虽老了，干劲却不～当年。Old as he is, he works just as hard as he did in his younger days.

【减产】 jiǎnchǎn reduction of output; drop in production

【减低】 jiǎndī reduce; lower; bring down; cut: ～速度 lower (或 slacken) speed; slow down/ 耗煤率～了百分之五。Consumption of coal went down by 5%.

【减法】 jiǎnfǎ subtraction

【减号】 jiǎnhào minus sign (－)

【减河】 jiǎnhé 〈水〉 distributary

【减缓】 jiǎnhuǎn retard; slow down: ～进程 slow down the pace (或 progress)

【减价】 jiǎnjià reduce the price; mark down: ～出售 sell at a reduced price/ ～一成 be marked down by 10%

【减免】 jiǎnmiǎn ① mitigate or annul (a punishment) ② reduce or remit (taxation, etc.)

【减摩】 jiǎnmó 〈机〉 antifriction: ～合金 antifriction alloy (或 metal)/ ～轴承 antifriction bearing

【减轻】 jiǎnqīng lighten; ease; alleviate; mitigate: ～国家的负担 lighten the burden on the state/ ～劳动强度 reduce labour intensity/ ～病人的痛苦 alleviate (或 ease) a patient's suffering/ ～处分 mitigate a punishment

【减弱】 jiǎnruò weaken; abate: 体力大大～ be much weakened physically/ 风势～了。The wind has subsided./ 思想政治工作一刻也不能～。Ideological and political work must never for a moment be relaxed.

【减色】 jiǎnsè lose lustre; impair the excellence of; detract from the merit of: 音响效果不好，使演出大为～。Poor acoustics spoilt the performance. ◇ ～法 〈电影〉 subtractive process

【减杀】 jiǎnshā weaken; reduce

【减少】 jiǎnshǎo reduce; decrease; lessen; cut down: ～非生产性开支 reduce nonproductive expenditure/ 精简机构，～层次 simplify the administrative structure and eliminate duplication/ 给他～一些工作 relieve him of some of his work/ 交通事故～了。There has been a decrease in traffic accidents.

【减声器】 jiǎnshēngqì 〈机〉 muffler

【减数】 jiǎnshù 〈数〉 subtrahend

【减数分裂】 jiǎnshù fēnliè 〈生〉 meiosis

【减速】 jiǎnsù slow down; decelerate; retard ◇ ～度 deceleration/ ～副翼 〈航空〉 deceleron/ ～火箭 retro-rocket/ ～剂 〈物〉 moderator/ ～伞 〈航空〉 drag (或 deceleration) parachute/ ～运动 〈物〉 retarded motion

【减缩】 jiǎnsuō reduce; cut down; retrench: ～开支 reduce expenditure

【减退】 jiǎntuì drop; go down: 视力(记忆力)～。One's eyesight (memory) is failing./ 雨后炎热～了许多。After the rain, the heat abated considerably.

【减刑】 jiǎnxíng 〈法〉 reduce a penalty; commute (或 mitigate) a sentence

【减压】 jiǎnyā reduce pressure; decompress ◇ ～器 pressure reducer; decompressor/ ～室 decompression chamber

【减员】 jiǎnyuán depletion of numbers (in the armed forces)

【减震】 jiǎnzhèn shock absorption; damping ◇ ～器 〈机〉 shock absorber; damper

【减租减息】 jiǎnzū-jiǎnxī reduction of rent for land and of interest on loans (the Chinese Communist Party's agrarian policy during the War of Resistance Against Japan); reduction of rent and interest

**硷** jiǎn 见"碱" jiǎn

**睑** jiǎn eyelid

【睑腺炎】 jiǎnxiànyán 〈医〉 sty

**锏** jiǎn mace

**简** jiǎn ① simple; simplified; brief: 从～ conform to the principle of simplicity/ ～而言之 in brief; in short; to put it in a nutshell ② bamboo slips (used for writing on in ancient times) ③ letter: 书～ letters; correspondence ④ 〈书〉 select; choose: ～拔 select and promote

【简报】 jiǎnbào bulletin; brief report: 会议～ conference bulletin; brief reports on conference proceedings

【简编】 jiǎnbiān 〔多用于书名〕 short course; concise edition

【简便】 jiǎnbiàn simple and convenient; handy: ～的方法 a simple and convenient method; a handy way/ 操作～ easy to operate

【简称】 jiǎnchēng ① the abbreviated form of a name; abbreviation: "鞍钢"是鞍山钢铁公司的～。"Angang" is the abbreviation for the Anshan Iron and Steel Company. ② be called sth. for short: 中国共产党党员和中国共产主义

青年团团员～"党团员"。Members of the Chinese Communist Party and the Chinese Communist Youth League are called "Party and League members" for short.

【简单】 jiǎndān ① simple; uncomplicated: ～明了 simple and clear; concise and explicit/ 这机器构造～。The machine is simple in structure./ 不要把复杂的阶级斗争看得太～了。Don't oversimplify the complicated class struggle./ 事情没那么～。There is more to it. ②〔多用于否定式〕commonplace; ordinary: 她的枪法那么准，真不～。She's a marvel to be able to shoot with such accuracy./ 这家伙鬼点子特多，可不～。This fellow is no simpleton. He is full of tricks. ③ oversimplified; casual: ～粗暴 do things in an oversimplified and crude way/ 头脑～ simple-minded; seeing things too simply/ ～地看问题 take a naïve view; oversimplify a problem/ 不能用～的方法去解决这个问题。This matter cannot be settled in a summary fashion./ 这篇文章我只是～地看了看。I only skimmed through this article. ◇ ～多数 simple majority/ ～化 oversimplify/ ～再生产 simple reproduction

【简短】 jiǎnduǎn brief: 他的发言～有力。His speech was brief and forceful.

【简化】 jiǎnhuà simplify: ～工序 simplify working processes

【简化汉字】 jiǎnhuà Hànzì ① simplify Chinese characters (i.e. reduce the number of strokes and eliminate complicated variants) ② simplified Chinese characters

【简洁】 jiǎnjié succinct; terse; pithy: ～生动的语言 terse and lively language/ 文笔～ written in a pithy style

【简捷】 jiǎnjié simple and direct; forthright

【简介】 jiǎnjiè brief introduction; synopsis; summarized account: 剧情～ the synopsis of a drama/ «天坛～» *A Short Guide to the Temple of Heaven*

【简括】 jiǎnkuò brief but comprehensive; compendious

【简历】 jiǎnlì biographical notes; *curriculum vitae*; *résumé*

【简练】 jiǎnliàn terse; succinct; pithy: 内容丰富，文字～ rich in content and succinct in style

【简陋】 jiǎnlòu simple and crude: 设备～ simple and crude equipment

【简略】 jiǎnlüè simple (in content); brief; sketchy: 他提供的材料过于～。The material he supplied is too sketchy.

【简慢】 jiǎnmàn negligent (in attending to one's guest)

【简明】 jiǎnmíng simple and clear; concise: ～扼要 brief and to the point ◇ ～新闻 news in brief

【简朴】 jiǎnpǔ simple and unadorned; plain: 生活～ a simple and frugal life; plain living/ ～的语言 plain language

【简谱】 jiǎnpǔ 〈乐〉 numbered musical notation

【简体字】 jiǎntǐzì simplified Chinese character

【简图】 jiǎntú sketch; diagram

【简谐运动】 jiǎnxié yùndòng 〈物〉 simple harmonic motion

【简写】 jiǎnxiě ① write a Chinese character in simplified form ② simplify a book for beginners ◇ ～本 simplified edition

【简讯】 jiǎnxùn news in brief

【简要】 jiǎnyào concise and to the point; brief: ～的介绍 a brief introduction; briefing

【简仪】 jiǎnyí 〈天〉 abridged armilla

【简易】 jiǎnyì ① simple and easy: ～的办法 a simple and easy method ② simply constructed; simply equipped; unsophisticated
◇ ～病房 simply equipped ward/ ～读物 easy reader/ ～公路 simply-built highway/ ～机场 airstrip

【简约】 jiǎnyuē brief; concise; sketchy

【简章】 jiǎnzhāng general regulations

【简直】 jiǎnzhí 〈副〉 simply; at all: 我～不能想象有这种事。I simply couldn't imagine such a thing./ 这个星期～没有一个好天。We've had no fine weather at all this week./ ～是浪费时间。It's a sheer waste of time./ ～跟新的一样 as good as new

**碱** jiǎn ① alkali ② soda: 纯～ soda (ash)/ 洗涤～ washing soda

【碱地】 jiǎndì alkaline land

【碱化】 jiǎnhuà alkalization; basification

【碱金属】 jiǎnjīnshǔ alkali (或 alkaline) metal

【碱式盐】 jiǎnshìyán 〈化〉 basic salt

【碱土金属】 jiǎntǔ jīnshǔ alkaline-earth metal

【碱性】 jiǎnxìng basicity; alkalinity
◇ ～法 〈冶〉 basic process/ ～反应 alkaline reaction/ ～染料 basic dyes/ ～土 alkaline soil

**翦** Jiǎn a surname

## jiàn

**见** jiàn ① see; catch sight of: 所～所闻 what one sees and hears/ 只～一个人影闪过墙角 catch sight of sb. turning the corner ② meet with; be exposed to: 这种药怕～光。This medicine is not to be exposed to daylight./ 冰～热就化。Ice melts with heat./ ～困难就上，～荣誉就让 dash forward where there are difficulties to overcome and draw back when honours are to be conferred; take the difficulties for oneself and leave the honours to others ③ show evidence of; appear to be: 并不～瘦 not seem to be any thinner/ 病已～轻。The patient's condition has improved./ ～之于行动 be translated into action ④ refer to; see; *vide*: ～第三十六页 see page 36/ ～上 see above; *vide supra*/ ～下 see below; *vide infra*/ ～前 see before; *vide ante*/ ～后 see after; *vide post* ⑤ meet; call on; see: 你～到他了没有? Did you meet him?/ 我不想～他。I don't wish to see him./ 她今天下午要来～你。She'll call on you this afternoon. ⑥ view; opinion: 依我之～ in my opinion; to my mind ⑦〈书〉〈助〉〔用在动词前面表示被动或表示对我怎么样〕: ～责 be blamed/ ～弃 be rejected; be discarded/ 即希～告。Hope to be informed immediately.
另见 xiàn

【见报】 jiànbào appear in the newspapers

【见不得】 jiànbude ① not to be exposed to; unable to stand: ～阳光 not to be exposed to the sunlight ② not fit to be seen or revealed: ～人 shameful; scandalous

【见长】 jiàncháng be good at; be expert in: 她以写作～。She is good at writing.
另见 jiànzhǎng

【见得】 jiànde 〔只用于否定式或疑问式〕seem; appear: 这片稻子不～比那片差。This plot of paddy doesn't seem to be any worse than that one./ 明天不～会下雨。It doesn't look as if it's going to rain tomorrow./ 怎么～他来不了? How do you know he can't come?/ 何以～? How so?

【见地】 jiàndì insight; judgment: 很有～ have keen insight; show sound judgment

【见多识广】 jiànduō-shíguǎng experienced and knowledgeable

【见方】 jiànfāng 〈口〉 square: 这张桌子三尺～。The table is 3 *chi* square.

【见风使舵】 jiàn fēng shǐ duò trim one's sails

【见缝插针】 jiàn fèng chā zhēn stick in a pin wherever there's room — make use of every bit of time or space

【见怪】 jiànguài mind; take offence: 菜做得不好，请不要～。I hope you won't mind my poor cooking./ 批评得不对，可别～。Don't take offence if my criticism is incorrect.

【见怪不怪，其怪自败】 jiàn guài bù guài, qí guài zì bài face

the fearful with no fears, and its fearfulness disappears

【见鬼】 jiànguǐ ① fantastic; preposterous; absurd: 种庄稼不除草不是～吗? Isn't it absurd to plant crops and not weed the fields?/ 手套怎么不见了? 真～! That's funny! What have I done with my gloves? ② go to hell: 让阶级斗争熄灭论～去吧! To hell with the theory of the dying out of class struggle.

【见好】 jiànhǎo (of a patient's condition) get better; mend: 她的病～了。She's on the mend.

【见机】 jiànjī as the opportunity arises; as befits the occasion; according to circumstances: ～行事 act according to circumstances; do as one sees fit

【见教】 jiànjiào 〈套〉 favour me with your advice; instruct me: 有何～? Is there something you want to see me about?

【见解】 jiànjiě view; opinion; understanding: 抱有不同～ hold different views/ 一篇很有～的文章 an article with original ideas/ 对这个问题他没有提出任何新的～。He didn't put forward any new ideas on the subject./ 这只是我个人的～。That's just my own opinion.

【见谅】 jiànliàng 〈书〉 excuse me; forgive me: 务希～。I sincerely hope you'll excuse me.

【见猎心喜】 jiàn liè xīn xǐ thrill to see one's favourite sport and itch to have a go

【见面】 jiànmiàn meet; see: 他俩经常～。They see a lot of each other./ 思想～ each stating frankly what's on his mind ◇ ～礼 a present given to sb. on first meeting him

【见票即付】 jiàn piào jí fù 〈商〉 payable at sight; payable to bearer

【见仁见智】 jiànrén-jiànzhì different people, different views; opinions differ

【见世面】 jiàn shìmiàn see the world; enrich one's experience: 经风雨,～ face the world and brave the storm; see life and stand its tests/ 这回到化工厂去参观,可见了世面了。The trip to the chemical works was a real eye-opener.

【见识】 jiànshi ① widen one's knowledge; enrich one's experience: 到各处走走,～～也是好的。It's not a bad idea to go around a bit and gain experience. ② experience; knowledge; sensibleness: 长～ widen one's knowledge; broaden one's horizons/ 他～很广。He's a man of wide experience./ 他那样对待你是不对的,你别和他一般～。He's behaved badly towards you, but a sensible person like you shouldn't want to take him up on it.

【见树不见林】 jiàn shù bù jiàn lín not see the wood for the trees

【见所未见】 jiàn suǒ wèi jiàn ① see what one has never seen before ② never seen before; unprecedented

【见外】 jiànwài regard sb. as an outsider: 你对我这样客气,倒有点～了。Please don't go to so much trouble about me, or I'll feel I'm being treated as a stranger./ 到了我这儿可别～。Just make yourself at home.

【见微知著】 jiàn wēi zhī zhù from the first small beginnings one can see how things will develop; from one small clue one can see what is coming

【见闻】 jiànwén what one sees and hears; knowledge; information: 增长～ add to one's knowledge/ ～广 well-informed; knowledgeable

【见物不见人】 jiàn wù bù jiàn rén see things but not people; see only material factors to the neglect of human ones

【见习】 jiànxí learn on the job; be on probation
◇ ～技术员 technician on probation/ ～领事 student consul/ ～生 probationer/ ～医生 intern

【见效】 jiànxiào become effective; produce the desired result: 这药吃下去就～。This medicine produces an instant effect.

【见笑】 jiànxiào ① laugh at (me or us): 我刚开始学,您可别～。Now don't laugh at me. I'm only a beginner. ② incur ridicule (by one's poor performance): 写得不好,～,～。Excuse my poor writing.

【见血封喉】 jiànxuèfēnghóu 〈植〉 upas

【见义勇为】 jiàn yì yǒng wéi ready to take up the cudgels for a just cause

【见异思迁】 jiàn yì sī qiān change one's mind the moment one sees something new; be inconstant or irresolute

【见长】 jiànzhǎng grow perceptibly: 下了一场雨,麦苗立刻～。The wheat sprouts grew perceptibly after the rain./ 这孩子不～。The child doesn't seem to be growing.
另见 jiàncháng

【见证】 jiànzhèng witness; testimony ◇ ～人 eyewitness; witness

**件** jiàn ①〈量〉: 一～衬衫 a shirt/ 一～事 a matter; a thing/ 一～工作 a piece of work; a job/ 三～行李 three pieces of luggage ②〔指可以一一计算的事物〕: 工～ workpiece/ 锻～ forged piece; forging/ 案～ (law) case ③ letter; correspondence; paper; document: 来～ a communication, document, etc. received/ 密～ confidential (或 classified) documents; secret papers

**间** jiàn ① space in between; opening: 乘～ seize an opportunity/ 亲密无～ closely united; on intimate terms ② separate: 黑白相～ chequered with black and white/ 晴～多云 fine with occasional clouds ③ sow discord: 离～ sow discord; drive a wedge between ④ thin out (seedlings): ～玉米苗 thin out maize seedlings
另见 jiān

【间壁】 jiànbì next door; next-door neighbour

【间道】 jiàndào 〈书〉 bypath; shortcut

【间谍】 jiàndié spy
◇ ～飞机 spy plane/ ～活动 espionage/ ～网 espionage network/ ～卫星 spy satellite

【间断】 jiànduàn be disconnected; be interrupted: 他坚持锻炼,几年来从不～。He has kept up physical training for several years without interruption./ 斗争一刻也没有～过。Never for a moment has the struggle ceased.

【间断性】 jiànduànxìng 〈哲〉 discontinuity: 不～ continuity

【间隔】 jiàngé interval; intermission: 两次会议～才二十天。There was an interval of only twenty days between the two conferences./ 每两行树苗～三米。There is a space of three metres between each two rows of saplings./ 幼苗～匀整。The seedlings are evenly spaced.

【间隔号】 jiàngéhào 〈语〉 separation dot, a punctuation mark separating the day from the month, as in 一二·九运动 (the December 9th Movement), or separating the parts of a person's name, as in 诺尔曼·白求恩 (Norman Bethune)

【间或】 jiànhuò occasionally; now and then; sometimes; once in a while

【间接】 jiànjiē indirect; secondhand: 这消息我是～听来的。I heard the news indirectly.
◇ ～宾语 〈语〉 indirect object/ ～肥料 indirect fertilizer/ ～接触 〈医〉 mediate contacts/ ～经验 indirect experience/ ～贸易 indirect trade/ ～税 indirect tax/ ～推理 〈逻〉 mediate inference/ ～消费 indirect consumption/ ～选举 indirect election

【间苗】 jiànmiáo ① thin out seedlings (或 young shoots) ② thinning

【间隙】 jiànxì ① interval; gap; space: 利用战斗～进行休整 rest, train and consolidate between battles ② 〈机〉 clearance: 齿轮～ gear clearance

【间歇】 jiànxiē intermittence; intermission ◇ ～泉 〈地〉 geyser; intermittent spring/ ～热 〈医〉 intermittent fever
【间杂】 jiànzá be intermingled; be mixed
【间奏曲】 jiànzòuqǔ 〈乐〉 ① *entr'acte* ② intermezzo
【间作】 jiànzuò 〈农〉 intercropping: 实行玉米和大豆～ intercrop maize and soya beans

**饯** jiàn ① give a farewell dinner ② 见"蜜饯" mìjiàn
【饯别】 jiànbié give a farewell dinner: ～友人 give a friend a farewell dinner
【饯行】 jiànxíng give a farewell dinner

**建** jiàn ① build; construct; erect: ～电站 build a power station/ 新厂房已经～成。The new factory building has been completed./ ～桥工地 the construction site of the bridge/ 重～家园 rebuild one's homeland ② establish; set up; found: ～社 set up a people's commune or a cooperative/ ～新功 make new contributions ③ propose; advocate: 我～个议。I'd like to make a suggestion. ④ of Fujian Province: ～漆 Fujian lacquerware
【建党】 jiàndǎng ① found (或 form) a party ② Party building ◇ ～路线 line for Party building
【建都】 jiàndū found a capital; make (a place) the capital: 唐代～长安。The Tang Dynasty made Chang'an its capital.
【建国】 jiànguó ① found (或 establish) a state: 象这样的大会还是～以来第一次。This congress is the first of its kind since the founding of our People's Republic. ② build up a country: 勤俭～ build up our country through diligence and frugality/ ～宏图 a grand project for national reconstruction
【建交】 jiànjiāo establish diplomatic relations
【建军】 jiànjūn ① found an army ② army building ◇ ～节 Army Day (August 1)/ ～路线 line for army building/ ～原则 principles of army building
【建兰】 jiànlán 〈植〉 sword-leaved cymbidium (*Cymbidium ensifolium*)
【建立】 jiànlì build; establish; set up; found: ～外交关系 establish diplomatic relations/ ～农村根据地 build rural base areas/ ～统一战线 form a united front/ ～"铁人"式的工人队伍 build up contingents of workers of the "Iron Man" type/ ～信心 build up one's confidence/ ～功勋 perform meritorious deeds/ 广大农村～了合作医疗制度。A cooperative medical service has been set up (或 instituted) in the vast rural areas.
【建设】 jiànshè build; construct: 在本世纪内把我国～成为社会主义的现代化强国 build China into a powerful modern socialist country before the end of the century/ 一万多人的～大军 a work force of more than 10,000/ 加强连队～ strengthen the Army at company level/ 加强党的思想～和组织～ strengthen the Party ideologically and organizationally/ 社会主义～ socialist construction
【建设性】 jiànshèxìng constructive: ～的意见 constructive suggestions/ 起～的作用 play a constructive role
【建树】 jiànshù 〈书〉 make a contribution; contribute: 对发展体育事业有所～ contribute to the development of physical culture/ 人类认识史上的重大～ major attainments in the history of human knowledge
【建议】 jiànyì ① propose; suggest; recommend: 他们～休会。They propose that the meeting be adjourned./ 我～你多做点户外运动。I suggest you should have more outdoor exercise. ② proposal; suggestion; recommendation: 反～ counterproposal/ 合理化～ rationalization proposal
【建造】 jiànzào build; construct; make
【建制】 jiànzhì organizational system: 部队～ the organizational system of the army ◇ ～部队 organic unit
【建筑】 jiànzhù ① build; construct; erect: ～桥梁 construct a bridge/ ～高楼 erect a tall building/ ～铁路 build a railway/ 一切剥削者都把自己的幸福～在劳动人民的痛苦之上。All exploiters build their happiness on the suffering of the working people. ② building; structure; edifice: 古老的～ an ancient building/ 宏伟的～ a magnificent structure ③ architecture: 他是学现代～的。His speciality is modern architecture.
◇ ～材料 building materials/ ～工程学 architectural engineering/ ～工地 building site; construction site/ ～工人 building worker; builder/ ～红线 property line/ ～群 architectural complex/ ～设计 architectural design/ ～师 architect/ ～物 building; structure/ ～学 architecture

**剑** jiàn sword; sabre: ～柄 the handle of a sword; hilt/ ～鞘 scabbard
【剑拔弩张】 jiànbá-nǔzhāng with swords drawn and bows bent; at daggers drawn
【剑齿虎】 jiànchǐhǔ 〈古生物〉 sabre-toothed tiger; machairodont
【剑齿象】 jiànchǐxiàng 〈古生物〉 stegodon
【剑麻】 jiànmá 〈植〉 sisal hemp
【剑眉】 jiànméi straight eyebrows slanting upwards and outwards; dashing eyebrows

**荐** jiàn ① recommend ② 〈书〉 grass; straw ③ 〈书〉 straw mat
【荐举】 jiànjǔ propose sb. for an office; recommend

**贱** jiàn ① low-priced; inexpensive; cheap: ～卖 sell cheap ② lowly; humble: 贫～ poor and lowly ③ low-down; base; despicable: 下～ low-down; base ④ 〈谦〉 my: ～恙 my illness
【贱骨头】 jiàngútou 〈骂〉 miserable (或 contemptible) wretch

**涧** jiàn ravine; gully

**舰** jiàn warship; naval vessel; man-of-war
【舰队】 jiànduì fleet; naval force: 东海～ the Dong Hai Sea Fleet
【舰对空导弹】 jiàn duì kōng dǎodàn ship-to-air missile
【舰首炮】 jiànshǒupào bow chaser
【舰艇】 jiàntǐng naval ships and boats; naval vessels
【舰尾炮】 jiànwěipào stern chaser
【舰载】 jiànzài carrier-borne; carrier-based; ship-based ◇ ～导弹 ship-based missile/ ～飞机 shipboard aircraft; deck-landing aircraft
【舰长】 jiànzhǎng captain (of a warship)
【舰只】 jiànzhī warships; naval vessels: 海军～ naval vessels

**监** jiàn an imperial office: 国子～ the Imperial College, the highest educational administration in feudal China 另见 jiān

**健** jiàn ① healthy; strong ② strengthen; toughen; invigorate: ～胃 be good for the stomach/ ～脾 invigorate the function of the spleen ③ be strong in; be good at: ～谈 be a good talker
【健步】 jiànbù walk with vigorous strides: ～如飞 walk as if on wings; walk fast and vigorously
【健儿】 jiàn'ér ① valiant fighter ② good athlete: 乒坛～ skilful ping-pong players
【健将】 jiànjiàng master sportsman; top-notch player: 运动～ master sportsman/ 足球～ top-notch footballer

【健康】 jiànkāng ①health; physique: ～状况 state of health; physical condition/ 人民的～水平有了很大提高。The general level of the people's health has markedly improved. ②healthy; sound: 身体～ be in good health/ 祝你～! I wish you good health./ 运动正在～地发展。The movement is developing healthily./ 情况基本上是～的。The situation is basically sound. ◇ ～证明书 health certificate
【健美】 jiànměi strong and handsome; vigorous and graceful: ～的体操表演 a vigorous and graceful performance of callisthenics
【健全】 jiànquán ①sound; perfect: 身心～ sound in mind and body/ 头脑～的人 a person in his or her right mind ②strengthen; amplify; perfect: ～合理的规章制度 amplify necessary rules and regulations/ 一定要发扬民主,～民主集中制。We must promote democracy and strengthen democratic centralism.
【健身房】 jiànshēnfáng gymnasium; gym
【健谈】 jiàntán be a good talker; be a brilliant conversationalist
【健忘】 jiànwàng forgetful; having a bad memory ◇ ～症 amnesia
【健旺】 jiànwàng healthy and vigorous
【健在】 jiànzài 〈书〉(of a person of advanced age) be still living and in good health
【健壮】 jiànzhuàng healthy and strong; robust: ～的小伙子 a robust young man

**谏** jiàn 〈书〉 remonstrate with (one's superior or friend); expostulate with; admonish: ～止 plead with sb. not to do sth.; admonish against sth.
【谏诤】 jiànzhèng 〈书〉 criticize sb.'s faults frankly

**渐** jiàn gradually; by degrees: 天气～冷。The weather is getting cold.
另见 jiān
【渐变】 jiànbiàn gradual change
【渐次】 jiàncì 〈书〉 gradually; one after another
【渐渐】 jiànjiàn 〈副〉 gradually; by degrees; little by little: 路上的行人～少了。The number of pedestrians gradually dwindled./ 雨～小了。The rain is beginning to let up.
【渐进】 jiànjìn advance gradually; progress step by step: 循序～ advance gradually in due order
【渐缩管】 jiànsuōguǎn 〈机〉 reducing pipe
【渐显】 jiànxiǎn 〈摄〉 fade in
【渐新世】 Jiànxīnshì 〈地〉 the Oligocene Epoch
【渐隐】 jiànyǐn 〈摄〉 fade out

**溅** jiàn splash; spatter: ～一身泥 be spattered with mud/ 钢花四～ sparks of molten steel flying in all directions
【溅落】 jiànluò 〈宇航〉 splash down ◇ ～点 splash point

**践** jiàn ①trample; tread ②act on; carry out: ～诺 keep one's promise (或 word)
【践踏】 jiàntà tread on; trample underfoot: 请勿～草地。Keep off the grass./ 肆意～别国主权 wantonly trample on the sovereignty of other countries
【践约】 jiànyuē keep a promise; keep an appointment

**腱** jiàn 〈生理〉 tendon
【腱鞘】 jiànqiào 〈生理〉 tendon sheath ◇ ～炎 tenosynovitis

**毽** jiàn shuttlecock
【毽子】 jiànzi shuttlecock: 踢～ kick the shuttlecock (as a game)

**鉴** jiàn ①ancient bronze mirror ②reflect; mirror: 水清可～。The water is so clear that you can see your reflection in it. ③warning; object lesson: 引以为～ take warning from it ④inspect; scrutinize; examine: 请～核。Please examine. ⑤〔旧时书信套语,表示请对方看信〕: 某先生台～。 Dear Mr. so-and-so: May I draw your attention to the following.
【鉴别】 jiànbié distinguish; differentiate; discriminate: 有比较才能～。Only by comparing can one distinguish./ ～香花和毒草 distinguish fragrant flowers from poisonous weeds/ ～文物 make an appraisal of a cultural relic ◇ ～器 〈电〉 discriminator
【鉴定】 jiàndìng ①appraisal (of a person's strong and weak points): 毕业～ graduation appraisal ②appraise; identify; authenticate; determine: ～产品质量 appraise the quality of a product/ ～文物年代 determine the date of a cultural relic/ 人民是最好的～人。The people are the best judges.
【鉴戒】 jiànjiè warning; object lesson: 我们应当把这次挫折引为～。We should take warning from this setback.
【鉴赏】 jiànshǎng appreciate: ～能力 ability to appreciate (painting, music, etc.); connoisseurship/ 对音乐颇有～力 have a good ear for music
【鉴于】 jiànyú in view of; seeing that: ～上述情况，我们提出以下建议。In view of the above-mentioned facts, we wish to make the following proposals.

**键** jiàn ①〈机〉key: 轴～ shaft key ②key (of a typewriter, piano, etc.) ③〈化〉bond: 共价～ covalent bond ④〈书〉 bolt (of a door)
【键槽】 jiàncáo 〈机〉 keyway; key slot; key seat
【键盘】 jiànpán keyboard; fingerboard ◇ ～乐器 keyboard instrument

**槛** jiàn ①banisters; balustrade ②cage: ～车 prisoners' van (used in ancient times)
另见 kǎn

**僭** jiàn 〈书〉 overstep one's authority: ～越 overstep one's authority

**箭** jiàn arrow
【箭靶子】 jiànbǎzi target for archery
【箭步】 jiànbù a sudden big stride forward
【箭杆】 jiàngǎn arrow shaft
【箭楼】 jiànlóu an embrasured watchtower over a city gate
【箭石】 jiànshí 〈古生物〉 belemnite
【箭筒】 jiàntǒng quiver
【箭头】 jiàntóu ①arrowhead ②arrow (as a sign)
【箭在弦上】 jiàn zài xián shàng like an arrow on the bowstring — there can be no turning back
【箭猪】 jiànzhū porcupine
【箭镞】 jiànzú metal arrowhead

## jiāng

**江** jiāng ①river ②(Jiāng) the Changjiang River: ～南 south of the lower reaches of the Changjiang River ③(Jiāng) a surname
【江河日下】 jiāng-hé rì xià go from bad to worse; be on the decline
【江湖】 jiānghú ①rivers and lakes ②all corners of the country: 流落～ live a vagabond life
【江湖】 jiānghu ①itinerant entertainers, quacks, etc. ②

trade of such people
◇～骗子 swindler; charlatan/ ～医生 quack; mountebank/ ～艺人 itinerant entertainer
【江轮】 jiānglún river steamer
【江米】 jiāngmǐ polished glutinous rice ◇ ～酒 fermented glutinous rice
【江山】 jiāngshān ①rivers and mountains; land; landscape: ～如画 a picturesque landscape; beautiful scenery/ ～易改,本性难移。It's easy to change rivers and mountains but hard to change a person's nature. ②country; state power: 打～ fight to win state power/ 坐～ rule the country/ 保卫人民的～ safeguard the people's state power/ 保证我国的社会主义～永不变色 ensure that socialist China will never change her political colour
【江苏】 Jiāngsū Jiangsu (Province)
【江豚】 jiāngtún black finless porpoise 又作"江猪"
【江西】 Jiāngxī Jiangxi (Province)
【江洋大盗】 jiāngyáng dàdào an infamous robber or pirate
【江珧】 jiāngyáo 〈动〉 pen shell ◇ ～柱 the dried adductor of a pen shell

**将** jiāng ①〈书〉support; take; bring: ～幼弟而归 bring home one's little brother/ 相～而去 go off supporting each other ②take care of (one's health): ～养 rest; recuperate ③do sth.; handle (a matter): 慎重～事 handle a matter with care ④〈象棋〉check ⑤put sb. on the spot: 我们这一问可把他～住了。Our question certainly put him on the spot. ⑥incite sb. to action; challenge; prod: 他已拿定主意不参加比赛了,你再～他也没用。It's no use egging him on; he's made up his mind not to join in the tournament. ⑦〈介〉〔引进所凭借的工具、材料、方法等,意思跟"用"相同〕with; by means of; by: ～功折罪 expiate one's crime by good deeds ⑧〈介〉〔宾语是后面动词的受事者,整个格式有处置的意思〕: ～他请来 invite him to come over/ ～革命进行到底。Carry the revolution through to the end. ⑨be going to; be about to; will; shall: 船～启碇。The ship is about to weigh anchor./ 我们～制定一个长远规划。We are going to draw up a long-range plan./ ～欲取之,必先与之。Give in order to take./ 必～取得更大胜利 be certain to win still greater victories ⑩〔叠用,表示"又""且"的意思〕: ～信～疑 half believing, half doubting ⑪〈助〉〔用在动词和表示趋向的补语之间〕: 唱～起来 start to sing/ 传～出去 (of news, etc.) spread abroad/ 赶～上去 hurry to catch up
另见 jiàng
【将错就错】 jiāng cuò jiù cuò leave a mistake uncorrected and make the best of it
【将功补过】 jiāng gōng bǔ guò make amends for one's faults by good deeds
【将功赎罪】 jiāng gōng shú zuì atone for a crime by good deeds; expiate one's crime by good deeds
【将计就计】 jiāng jì jiù jì turn sb.'s trick against him; beat sb. at his own game
【将近】 jiāngjìn close to; nearly; almost: ～一百人 close to a hundred people/ ～完成 almost completed
【将就】 jiāngjiu make do with; make the best of; put up with: 这件大衣稍微短一点,你～着穿吧。This coat may be a bit too short for you, but perhaps you could make do with it.
【将军】 jiāngjūn ①general ②〈象棋〉check ③put sb. on the spot; embarrass; challenge: 他们要我唱歌, 这可将了我一军。They embarrassed me by calling on me to sing.
【将来】 jiānglái future: 在不远的～ in the not too distant future; before long/ 在可以预见的～ in the foreseeable future
【将息】 jiāngxī rest; recuperate
【将养】 jiāngyǎng rest; recuperate: 医生说你再～一个礼拜就可以好了。The doctor says you ought to be well again after another week's rest.
【将要】 jiāngyào be going to; will; shall: 他～到西藏去工作。He's going to work in Xizang.

**姜** jiāng ①ginger ②(Jiāng) a surname
【姜黄】 jiānghuáng 〈植〉 turmeric
【姜片虫】 jiāngpiànchóng fasciolopsis ◇ ～病 fasciolopsiasis

**豇** jiāng
【豇豆】 jiāngdòu cowpea

**浆** jiāng ①thick liquid: 糖～ syrup/ 纸～ pulp ②starch: ～衣服 starch clothes
另见 jiàng
【浆板】 jiāngbǎn 〈纸〉 pulp board
【浆度】 jiāngdù 〈纸〉 degree of beating (in making pulp)
【浆果】 jiāngguǒ 〈植〉 berry
【浆纱】 jiāngshā 〈纺〉 sizing ◇ ～机 sizing machine; slasher
【浆洗】 jiāngxǐ wash and starch
【浆液】 jiāngyè 〈纺〉 size
【浆纸机】 jiāngzhǐjī 〈纸〉 coating machine

**僵** jiāng ①stiff; numb: 他的脚冻～了。His feet were numb with cold. ②deadlocked: 他把事情搞～了。He's brought things to a deadlock.
【僵持】 jiāngchí (of both parties) refuse to budge: 双方～好久。For quite some time, neither party was willing to budge from its original position.
【僵化】 jiānghuà become rigid; ossify: 思想～ a rigid (或 ossified) way of thinking
【僵局】 jiāngjú deadlock; impasse; stalemate: 打破～ break a deadlock/ 谈判陷入～。The negotiations have reached an impasse.
【僵尸】 jiāngshī corpse: 政治～ a political mummy
【僵死】 jiāngsǐ dead; ossified
【僵硬】 jiāngyìng ①stiff: 觉得四肢～ feel stiff in the limbs ②rigid; inflexible: ～的公式 a rigid formula

**缰** jiāng reins; halter
【缰绳】 jiāngsheng reins; halter

**鳉** jiāng killifish

**礓** jiāng 见"砂礓" shājiāng

**疆** jiāng boundary; border
【疆场】 jiāngchǎng battlefield
【疆界】 jiāngjiè boundary; border
【疆土】 jiāngtǔ territory
【疆域】 jiāngyù territory; domain

## jiǎng

**讲** jiǎng ①speak; say; tell: ～英语 speak English/ ～故事 tell stories/ 给孩子们～村史 tell the children about the history of the village/ ～几句话 say a few words/ ～几点意见 make a few remarks/ ～的是一套, 做的是另一套 say one thing and do another ②explain; make clear; interpret: 把道理～清楚 state the reasons clearly/ 我来～～今天开会的目的。Let me explain the purpose of today's meeting./ 这本书是～气象的。This is a book about meteorology./ 这个字有几个～法。This word may be interpreted in different ways. ③ discuss; negotiate: ～条件 negotiate the terms; insist on the fulfilment of certain conditions ④ stress; pay attention to; be particular about: ～卫生 pay attention to hygiene/ ～质量 stress quality/ ～排场 go in for ostentation and extravagance; go in for showy display; be ostentatious ⑤ as far as sth. is concerned; when it comes to; as to; as regards: ～干劲，她比谁都足。When it comes to drive, she's got more than any of us.

【讲稿】 jiǎnggǎo the draft or text of a speech; lecture notes

【讲和】 jiǎnghé make peace; settle a dispute; become reconciled

【讲话】 jiǎnghuà ① speak; talk; address: 对着话筒～ speak into a microphone/ 他在会上讲了话。He spoke at the meeting. 或 He addressed the meeting. ② speech; talk: 鼓舞人心的～ an inspiring speech ③〔多用于书名〕guide; introduction: 《政治经济学～》 *A Guide to Political Economy*

【讲价】 jiǎngjià bargain; haggle over the price

【讲解】 jiǎngjiě explain: 他指着示意图给来宾～大队的远景规划。Pointing at a sketch map, he explained the production brigade's long-term plan to the visitors. ◇ ～员 guide

【讲究】 jiǎngjiu ① be particular about; pay attention to; stress; strive for: 不～吃穿 not be too fastidious about one's food or clothing/ ～卫生，减少疾病 pay attention to hygiene and reduce the incidence of disease/ ～实际效果 stress practical results/ 写文章一定要～逻辑。In writing one must have regard for logic. ② exquisite; tasteful: 宾馆布置得很～。The guesthouse is tastefully furnished. ③ careful study: 翻译技巧大有～。The art of translation calls for careful study. 或 Translation is quite an art.

【讲课】 jiǎngkè teach; lecture ◇ ～时数 teaching hours

【讲理】 jiǎnglǐ ① reason with sb.; argue: 咱们跟他～去。Let's go and argue it out with him. ② listen (或 be amenable) to reason; be reasonable; be sensible: 蛮不～ be utterly unreasonable; be impervious to reason

【讲明】 jiǎngmíng explain; make clear; state explicitly: ～我们的立场 explain (或 state) our stand/ 向群众～党的政策 make the Party's policies clear to the masses

【讲评】 jiǎngpíng comment on and appraise: ～学生的作业 comment on the students' work

【讲情】 jiǎngqíng intercede; plead for sb.

【讲求】 jiǎngqiú be particular about; pay attention to; stress; strive for: ～效率 strive for efficiency

【讲师】 jiǎngshī lecturer

【讲授】 jiǎngshòu lecture; instruct; teach ◇ ～提纲 an outline for a lecture; teaching notes

【讲述】 jiǎngshù tell about; give an account of; narrate; relate: ～自己的家史 tell (或 relate) one's family history

【讲台】 jiǎngtái platform; dais; rostrum

【讲坛】 jiǎngtán ① platform; rostrum ② forum

【讲堂】 jiǎngtáng lecture room; classroom

【讲习】 jiǎngxí lecture and study ◇～班 study group/ ～所 institute (for instruction or training)

【讲学】 jiǎngxué give lectures; discourse on an academic subject: 应邀来华～ be invited to give lectures in China

【讲演】 jiǎngyǎn lecture; speech

【讲义】 jiǎngyì (mimeographed or printed) teaching materials

【讲座】 jiǎngzuò a course of lectures: 英语广播～ English lessons over the radio; English by radio

**奖** jiǎng ① encourage; praise; reward: ～许 praise; give encouragement to/ 有功者～。Those who have gained merit will be rewarded. ② award; prize; reward: 发～ give awards; give prizes/ 得～ win a prize

【奖杯】 jiǎngbēi cup (as a prize)

【奖惩】 jiǎng-chéng rewards and punishments ◇ ～制度 system of rewards and penalties

【奖金】 jiǎngjīn money award; bonus; premium

【奖励】 jiǎnglì encourage and reward; award; reward: ～模范工作者 give awards to model workers/ 物质～ material reward/ ～发明创造 encourage innovations by giving awards

【奖品】 jiǎngpǐn prize; award; trophy

【奖券】 jiǎngquàn lottery ticket

【奖赏】 jiǎngshǎng award; reward

【奖学金】 jiǎngxuéjīn scholarship; exhibition

【奖掖】 jiǎngyè 〈书〉 reward and promote; encourage by promoting and rewarding

【奖章】 jiǎngzhāng medal; decoration

【奖状】 jiǎngzhuàng certificate of merit

**桨** jiǎng oar

**蒋** Jiǎng a surname

**耩** jiǎng sow with a drill

【耩子】 jiǎngzi 〈方〉 drill

**膙** jiǎng

【膙子】 jiǎngzi callosity; callus

## jiàng

**匠** jiàng craftsman; artisan: 能工巧～ skilled craftsmen/ 铁～ blacksmith/ 石～ stonemason

【匠人】 jiàngrén artisan; craftsman

【匠心】 jiàngxīn 〈书〉 ingenuity; craftsmanship: 独具～ show ingenuity; have great originality

**降** jiàng fall; drop; lower: ～雨 a fall of rain; rainfall/ ～价 lower prices/ 温度～到摄氏零下十度。The temperature dropped to minus ten degrees centigrade.
另见 xiáng

【降低】 jiàngdī reduce; cut down; drop; lower: ～生产成本 reduce production costs/ ～原料消耗 cut down the consumption of raw materials/ 价格～了，但质量并未～。The price is lower, but the quality is the same.

【降调】 jiàngdiào 〈语〉 falling tune; falling tone

【降格】 jiànggé 〈书〉 lower one's standard or status: ～以求 fall back on sth. inferior to what one originally wanted; accept a second best

【降号】 jiànghào 〈乐〉 flat

【降级】 jiàngjí ① reduce to a lower rank; demote ② send (a student) to a lower grade

【降临】 jiànglín 〈书〉 befall; arrive; come: 夜色～。Night fell.

【降落】 jiàngluò descend; land: 大型飞机的起飞和～ the take-off and landing of big aircraft/ 强迫～ forced landing/ 垂直～ vertical landing
◇ ～场 landing field/ ～辅助设备 landing aid/ ～伞 parachute/ ～设备 landing equipment

【降旗】 jiàngqí lower a flag

【降生】 jiàngshēng 〈书〉 (of the founder of a religion, etc.) be born

【降水】 jiàngshuǐ 〈气〉 precipitation: 人工～ artificial precipitation ◇ ～量 precipitation

【降温】 jiàngwēn ① lower the temperature (as in a workshop) ② 〈气〉 drop in temperature

【降压】 jiàngyā 〈电〉 step-down ◇ ～变电站 step-down substation/ ～变压器 step-down transformer
【降压片】 jiàngyāpiàn 〈药〉 hypertension pill
【降雨量】 jiàngyǔliàng rainfall: 年～ annual rainfall

**绛** jiàng deep red; crimson
【绛紫】 jiàngzǐ dark reddish purple

**将** jiàng ① general ② commander in chief, the chief piece in Chinese chess ③〈书〉 command; lead: ～兵 command troops
另见 jiāng
【将官】 jiàngguān 〈口〉 high-ranking military officer; general
【将领】 jiànglǐng high-ranking military officer; general
【将士】 jiàngshì 〈书〉 officers and men
【将指】 jiàngzhǐ 〈书〉 ① middle finger ② big toe

**浆** jiàng 见"糨" jiàng
另见 jiāng

**弶** jiàng 〈方〉 ① trap; snare: 装～捉鸟 set a trap to catch birds ② catch in a trap; trap

**强** jiàng stubborn; unyielding: 倔～ unbending; unyielding
另见 qiáng; qiǎng
【强嘴】 jiàngzuǐ reply defiantly; answer back; talk back

**酱** jiàng ① a thick sauce made from soya beans, flour, etc. ② cooked or pickled in soy sauce: ～肉 pork cooked in soy sauce; braised pork seasoned with soy sauce ③ sauce; paste; jam: 苹果～ apple jam/ 番茄～ tomato sauce; ketchup
【酱菜】 jiàngcài vegetables pickled in soy sauce; pickles
【酱豆腐】 jiàngdòufu fermented bean curd
【酱色】 jiàngsè dark reddish brown
【酱油】 jiàngyóu soy sauce; soy
【酱园】 jiàngyuán a shop making and selling sauce, pickles, etc.; sauce and pickle shop
【酱紫】 jiàngzǐ dark reddish purple

**犟** jiàng obstinate; stubborn; self-willed: 这人真～。He is a pigheaded (或 bullheaded) person. 或 He is as stubborn as a mule.

**糨** jiàng thick: 粥熬得太～了。The porridge is too thick.
【糨糊】 jiànghu paste
【糨子】 jiàngzi 〈口〉 paste: 打～ make paste

## jiāo

**艽** jiāo 见"秦艽" qínjiāo

**交** jiāo ① hand over; give up; deliver: ～还 give back; return/ ～活 turn over a finished item (或 product)/ ～公粮 deliver tax grain to the state/ ～团费 pay League membership dues/ 把任务～给我们实验室吧。Assign the task to our laboratory. ② (of places or periods of time) meet; join: 井冈山位于四县之～。The Jinggang Mountains stand where the boundaries of four counties meet./ 春夏之～ when spring is changing into summer ③ reach (a certain hour or season): ～冬以后 when winter has set in/ 明天就～夏至了。Tomorrow will be the Summer Solstice./ ～了好运气 have good luck ④ cross; intersect: 圆周内两直径必相～。Any two diameters of a circle intersect each other. ⑤ associate with: ～朋友 make friends ⑥ friend; acquaintance; friendship; relationship: 一面之～ a passing (或 casual) acquaintance/ 知～ bosom friend/ 建～ establish diplomatic relations/ 绝～ sever relations; break off relations ⑦ have sexual intercourse ⑧ mate; breed: 杂～ crossbreed ⑨ mutual; reciprocal; each other: ～换 exchange ⑩ together; simultaneous: 内外～困 be beset with difficulties at home and abroad ⑪ business transaction; deal; bargain: 成～ strike a bargain; conclude a transaction; clinch a deal ⑫ fall: 他脚一滑，摔了一大～。He slipped and fell heavily.
【交白卷】 jiāo báijuàn ① hand in a blank examination paper ② completely fail to accomplish a task: 咱们得把情况摸清楚，要不回去就得～。We must find out exactly how things stand here, or we'll have nothing to report.
【交班】 jiāobān hand over to the next shift
【交臂失之】 jiāo bì shī zhī 见"失之交臂" shī zhī jiāo bì
【交兵】 jiāobīng 〈书〉 (of two or more parties) be at war; wage war
【交叉】 jiāochā ① intersect; cross; crisscross: 两条铁路在此～。The two railways cross here. ② overlapping: 两个提案中～的部分 the overlapping parts of the two proposals ③ alternate; stagger: ～进行 do alternately ◇ ～点 intersect/ ～火力〈军〉 cross fire
【交差】 jiāochāi report to the leadership after accomplishing a task: 你不开收据，我们回去怎么～？If you don't give us a receipt, how are we going to account for it?
【交出】 jiāochū surrender; hand over: ～武器 surrender one's weapons
【交存】 jiāocún deposit; hand in for safekeeping: ～批准书 deposit instruments of ratification
【交错】 jiāocuò ① interlock; crisscross: 沟渠～。Ditches and canals crisscross. ② 〈机〉 staggered ◇ ～气缸 staggered cylinder
【交代】 jiāodài ① hand over: ～工作 hand over work to one's successor; brief one's successor on handing over work ② explain; make clear; brief; tell: ～政策 explain policy/ ～任务 assign and explain a task; brief sb. on his task/ 作者对此未作进一步～。The author makes no further reference to this./ 政委一再～我们要保护群众的利益。The political commissar repeatedly told us to protect the interests of the masses. ③ account for; justify oneself: 这个问题你怎么～？How are you going to account for this?/ ～不过去 be unable to justify an action ④ confess: ～罪行 confess a crime/ 彻底～ make a clean breast of 又作"交待"
【交底】 jiāodǐ tell sb. what one's real intentions are; put all one's cards on the table
【交点】 jiāodiǎn ① 〈数〉 point of intersection ② 〈天〉 node: ～月 nodical month
【交锋】 jiāofēng cross swords; engage in a battle or contest: 敌人不敢和我们正面～。The enemy didn't dare to risk a frontal engagement with us./ 第一次大～ the first great trial of strength/ 思想～ confrontation of ideas/ 这两支足球队将在明天～。The two football teams will face each other tomorrow.
【交付】 jiāofù ① pay: ～租金 pay rent ② hand over; deliver; consign: ～表决 put to the vote/ 新建的楼房已经～使用。The new building has been made available to the users.
【交感神经】 jiāogǎn shénjīng 〈生理〉 sympathetic nerve
【交割】 jiāogē complete a business transaction: 此项货款业

已～。The money for this consignment has already been paid.

【交工】 jiāogōng hand over a completed project

【交公】 jiāogōng hand over to the collective or the state

【交媾】 jiāogòu sexual intercourse

【交好】 jiāohǎo (of people or states) be on friendly terms

【交互】 jiāohù ① each other; mutual: ～校订译文 check each other's translations ② alternately; in turn: 两种策略～使用 use the two tactics alternately/ 他两手～地抓住野藤爬上崖顶。Holding on to the creepers, he climbed hand over hand to the top of the cliff.

【交换】 jiāohuàn exchange; swop: ～意见 exchange views; compare notes/ ～场地〈体〉change of courts, goals or ends/ 商品～ exchange of commodities/ 用小麦～大米 barter wheat for rice
◇ ～齿轮〈机〉change gear/ ～机〈电话〉switchboard; exchange/ ～价值〈经〉exchange value/ ～器〈电〉converter

【交货】 jiāohuò delivery: 即期～ prompt delivery/ 近期～ near delivery/ 远期～ forward delivery/ 分批～ partial delivery/ 仓库～ *ex* warehouse/ 船上～ *ex* ship/ 铁路旁～ *ex* rail
◇ ～港 port of delivery/ ～期 date of delivery/ ～收据 delivery receipt

【交集】 jiāojí (of different feelings) be mixed; occur simultaneously: 悲喜～ mixed feelings of grief and joy; joy and sorrow intermingled

【交际】 jiāojì social intercourse; communication: 语言是人们～的工具。Language is the means by which people communicate with each other./ 他不善于～。He is not a good mixer./ 她～很广。She has a large circle of acquaintances.
◇ ～花 social butterfly/ ～舞 ballroom dancing; social dancing

【交加】 jiāojiā〈书〉(of two things) accompany each other; occur simultaneously: 雷电～ lightning accompanied by peals of thunder; there was thunder and lightning/ 风雪～ a raging snowstorm/ 悔恨～ regret mingled with self-reproach/ 贫病～ be plagued by both poverty and illness

【交接】 jiāojiē ① join; connect: 夏秋～的季节 when summer is changing into autumn ② hand over and take over: ～班 relief of a shift ③ associate with: 他所～的朋友 the people he associates with; the friends he has made
◇ ～手续(仪式) handing over procedure (ceremony)

【交界】 jiāojiè (of two or more places) have a common boundary: 三省～的地方 a place where three provinces meet; the juncture of three provinces/ 江苏北面与山东～。Jiangsu is bounded on the north by Shandong.

【交卷】 jiāojuàn ① hand in an examination paper ② fulfil one's task; carry out an assignment

【交口称誉】 jiāokǒu chēngyù unanimously praise

【交流】 jiāoliú ① exchange; interflow; interchange: ～经验 exchange experience; draw on each other's experience/ 城乡物资～ flow of goods and materials between city and country/ 国际文化～ international cultural exchange/ 经济和技术～ economic and technical interchange ②〈电〉alternating ◇ ～电 alternating current/ ～发电机 alternating current generator; alternator

【交纳】 jiāonà pay (to the state or an organization); hand in: ～会费 pay membership dues

【交配】 jiāopèi mating; copulation ◇ ～期 mating season

【交情】 jiāoqing friendship; friendly relations: 老～ long-standing friendship/ 讲～ do things for the sake of friendship/ 他们两人～不错。The two of them are on very good terms.

【交融】 jiāoróng blend; mingle: 水乳～ blend as well as milk and water; be in perfect harmony

【交涉】 jiāoshè negotiate; make representations: 办～ carry on negotiations with; take up a matter with/ 口头～ verbal representations/ 向有关方面进行过多次～ have made many representations to the quarters concerned; have more than once approached the departments concerned/ 经过～,问题解决了。The problem was solved through negotiations.

【交手】 jiāoshǒu fight hand to hand; be engaged in a hand-to-hand fight; come to grips

【交售】 jiāoshòu sell (to the state): 踊跃向国家～油菜籽 enthusiastically sell rapeseed to the state

【交谈】 jiāotán talk with each other; converse; chat: 自由～ a freewheeling conversation/ 他们就广泛的问题进行了友好的～。They had a friendly conversation on a wide range of subjects.

【交替】 jiāotì ① supersede; replace: 新旧～。The new replaces the old. ② alternately; in turn: ～演奏两国乐曲 play music of the two countries alternately

【交通】 jiāotōng ① traffic; communications: 公路～ highway traffic/ 陆上～ land traffic/ 市区～ urban traffic/ ～便利 have transport facilities/ 妨碍～ interfere with the traffic ② liaison; liaison man
◇ ～安全 traffic safety/ ～标线 traffic marking/ ～标志 traffic sign/ ～部 the Ministry of Communications/ ～干线 main line of communication; main communications artery/ ～高峰 traffic peak/ ～管理 traffic control/ ～管理色灯 traffic lights/ ～规则 traffic regulations/ ～壕〈军〉communication trench/ ～警 traffic police/ ～量 volume of traffic/ ～事故 traffic (或 road) accident/ ～网 network of communication lines/ ～信号 traffic signal/ ～要道 vital communication line/ ～员 liaison man; underground messenger/ ～运输 communications and transportation/ ～阻塞 traffic jam (或 block)

【交头接耳】 jiāotóu-jiē'ěr speak in each other's ears; whisper to each other

【交往】 jiāowǎng association; contact: 我和他～,得益不少。I have gained a lot by associating with him./ 在同各国人民的～中,我们学习到不少有用的东西。In our contacts with people of other countries, we have learned many useful things.

【交尾】 jiāowěi mating; pairing; coupling

【交恶】 jiāowù fall foul of each other; become enemies

【交响曲】 jiāoxiǎngqǔ〈乐〉symphony

【交响诗】 jiāoxiǎngshī〈乐〉symphonic poem; tone poem

【交响乐】 jiāoxiǎngyuè〈乐〉symphony; symphonic music
◇ ～队 symphony orchestra; philharmonic orchestra

【交心】 jiāoxīn lay one's heart bare; open one's heart to: 互相～ have a heart-to-heart talk

【交椅】 jiāoyǐ ① an ancient folding chair ② armchair: 坐第二把～ occupy the second highest post; be second in command

【交易】 jiāoyì business; deal; trade; transaction: 现款～ cash transaction/ 赊帐～ credit transaction/ 做成一笔～ make a deal/ 商品～会 trade fair; commodities fair/ 肮脏的政治～ a dirty political deal/ 决不拿原则做～ never barter away principles ◇ ～额 volume of trade

【交易所】 jiāoyìsuǒ exchange: 证券～ stock exchange/ 商品～ commodity exchange

【交谊】 jiāoyì〈书〉friendship; friendly relations

【交游】 jiāoyóu〈书〉make friends: ～甚广 have a large circle of friends

【交战】 jiāozhàn be at war; fight; wage war: ～状态 state of war; belligerency/ ～的一方 a belligerent/ ～双方 the two belligerent parties ◇ ～国 belligerent countries (或

states, nations)/ ～团体 belligerent; party to a war
【交帐】 jiāozhàng ① hand over the accounts ② account for: 把小孩冻坏了，我们怎么向他母亲～？ If the child catches a chill, what are we going to say to its mother?
【交织】 jiāozhī interweave; intertwine; mingle: 惊异和喜悦的感情～在一起。Joy mingled with surprise.
【交嘴雀】 jiāozuǐquè crossbill

**郊** jiāo suburbs; outskirts: 京～ the suburbs of Beijing/ 西～ the western suburbs/ 远～ the outer suburbs; the remoter outskirts of a city
【郊区】 jiāoqū suburban district; suburbs; outskirts
【郊外】 jiāowài the countryside around a city; outskirts
【郊游】 jiāoyóu outing; excursion

**茭** jiāo
【茭白】 jiāobái 〈植〉 wild rice stem

**浇** jiāo ① pour liquid on; sprinkle water on: 大雨～得他全身都湿透了。He was drenched with rain. ② irrigate; water: ～花 water flowers/ ～地 irrigate the fields ③〈印〉 cast: ～铅字 type casting; type founding
【浇版】 jiāobǎn 〈印〉 casting ◇ ～机 casting machine
【浇灌】 jiāoguàn ① water; irrigate ② pour: ～混凝土 pour concrete
【浇口】 jiāokǒu 〈冶〉 runner
【浇铸】 jiāozhù 〈冶〉 casting; pouring ◇ ～机 casting machine

**娇** jiāo ① tender; lovely; charming: 嫩红～绿 tender blossoms and delicate leaves ② fragile; frail; delicate: 这孩子身体太～。The child's health is fragile. ③ squeamish; finicky: 她才走几里地就叫苦，未免太～了。She started grumbling after walking only a few *li*. She's really too soft. ④ pamper; spoil: 别把你的小女儿～坏了！ Don't pamper your little daughter.
【娇滴滴】 jiāodīdī delicately pretty; affectedly sweet
【娇惯】 jiāoguàn pamper; coddle; spoil: ～孩子 pamper a child
【娇贵】 jiāogui enervated (by good living); pampered
【娇媚】 jiāomèi ① coquettish ② sweet and charming
【娇嫩】 jiāonèn ① tender and lovely ② fragile; delicate: ～的幼苗 delicate seedlings/ ～的身子 delicate health
【娇气】 jiāoqi ① fragile; delicate: 这种菜太～，我们这儿种不了。This kind of vegetable's too delicate to grow here./ 你的身子也太～了，淋这么几滴雨就感冒。You're really too delicate, catching cold from just a few drops of rain. ② squeamish; finicky: 粗粮细粮一样吃，别那么～。Coarse grain is just as good as fine. Don't be so finicky./ 去掉～ get rid of squeamishness
【娇娆】 jiāoráo enchantingly beautiful
【娇生惯养】 jiāoshēng-guànyǎng pampered since childhood
【娇小玲珑】 jiāoxiǎo línglóng delicate and exquisite
【娇艳】 jiāoyàn delicate and charming; tender and beautiful: ～的桃花 delicate and charming peach blossoms
【娇纵】 jiāozòng indulge (a child); pamper; spoil

**骄** jiāo proud; arrogant; conceited: ～兵必败。An army puffed up with pride is bound to lose./ 胜不～，败不馁 not be dizzy with success, nor discouraged by failure
【骄傲】 jiāo'ào ① arrogant; conceited: ～自大 swollen with pride; conceited and arrogant/ 我们永远不能～，不能翘尾巴。We should never become arrogant and cocky. ② be proud; take pride in: 老科学家为青年同志的成就感到～。The old scientist takes pride in the achievements of his young colleagues. ③ pride: 民族的～ the pride of the nation
【骄横】 jiāohèng arrogant and imperious; overbearing
【骄矜】 jiāojīn 〈书〉 self-important; proud; haughty: 他为人谦逊，毫无～之态。He is modest, and never puts on airs.
【骄气】 jiāoqi overbearing airs; arrogance
【骄奢淫逸】 jiāoshē-yínyì lordly, luxury-loving, loose-living and idle; wallowing in luxury and pleasure; extravagant and dissipated
【骄阳】 jiāoyáng 〈书〉 blazing sun: ～似火 scorching sun
【骄纵】 jiāozòng arrogant and wilful

**姣** jiāo 〈书〉 handsome; beautiful-looking

**胶** jiāo ① glue; gum ② stick with glue; glue ③ gluey; sticky; gummy ④ rubber
【胶版】 jiāobǎn offset plate
◇ ～打样机 offset proof press/ ～印刷 offset printing; offset lithography; offset/ ～印刷机 offset press/ ～纸 offset paper
【胶布】 jiāobù ① rubberized fabric ②〈口〉 adhesive plaster
◇ ～带〈电〉 rubberized tape; adhesive tape
【胶合】 jiāohé glue together; veneer ◇ ～板 plywood; veneer board
【胶结】 jiāojié glued; cemented ◇ ～材料 cementing material/ ～剂 cementing agent
【胶卷】 jiāojuǎn roll film; film
【胶料】 jiāoliào 〈化〉 sizing material; size
【胶轮】 jiāolún rubber tyre ◇ ～大车 rubber-tyred cart
【胶木】 jiāomù bakelite
【胶囊】 jiāonáng capsule
【胶泥】 jiāoní ① clay ②〈化〉 daub
【胶粘剂】 jiāoniánjì adhesive
【胶凝作用】 jiāoníng zuòyòng 〈化〉 gelation
【胶皮】 jiāopí ① (vulcanized) rubber ②〈方〉 rickshaw
【胶片】 jiāopiàn film: 正色～ orthochromatic film/ 缩微～ microfiche
【胶乳】 jiāorǔ 〈化〉 latex: 硫化～ vulcanized latex; vultex
【胶水】 jiāoshuǐ mucilage; glue
【胶态】 jiāotài 〈物〉 colloidal state
◇ ～发射药 colloidal propellant/ ～悬浮 colloidal suspension/ ～运动 colloidal movement
【胶体】 jiāotǐ 〈化〉 colloid ◇ ～化学 colloid chemistry
【胶鞋】 jiāoxié ① rubber overshoes; galoshes; rubbers ② rubber-soled shoes; tennis shoes; sneakers
【胶靴】 jiāoxuē high rubber overshoes; galoshes
【胶印】 jiāoyìn offset printing; offset lithography; offset
◇ ～机 offset press; offset (printing) machine
【胶柱鼓瑟】 jiāo zhù gǔ sè play the *se* (an ancient zither-like instrument) with the pegs glued — stubbornly stick to old ways in the face of changed circumstances
【胶着】 jiāozhuó deadlocked; stalemated: ～状态 deadlock; stalemate; impasse

**教** jiāo teach; instruct: 互～互学 teach and learn from each other/ 她～我们做实验。She taught us how to conduct experiments.
另见 jiào
【教书】 jiāoshū teach school; teach: 在小学～ teach in a primary school/ ～育人 impart knowledge and educate people

**蛟** jiāo flood dragon, a mythical creature capable of invoking storms and floods
【蛟龙】 jiāolóng 见"蛟"

**焦** jiāo ① burnt; scorched; charred: 饼烤～了。The pancake is burnt./ 树被烧～了。The trees are charred. ② coke: 炼～ coking ③ worried; anxious: 心～ worried ④ (Jiāo) a surname

【焦比】 jiāobǐ 〈冶〉 coke ratio

【焦点】 jiāodiǎn ①〈物〉 focal point; focus: 主～ principal focus/ 虚～ virtual focus ② central issue; point at issue: 这就是问题的～。That is the heart of the matter./ 争论的～ the point at issue

【焦耳】 jiāo'ěr 〈物〉 joule

【焦黑】 jiāohēi burned black

【焦化】 jiāohuà 〈化〉 coking: 延迟～ delayed coking

【焦黄】 jiāohuáng sallow; brown: 脸色～ a sallow face/ 把馒头烤得～ toast a steamed bun brown

【焦急】 jiāojí anxious; worried: 大家都在～地等着他。Everyone is waiting anxiously for him.

【焦痂】 jiāojiā 〈医〉 eschar

【焦距】 jiāojù 〈物〉 focal distance; focal length

【焦渴】 jiāokě terribly thirsty; parched

【焦枯】 jiāokū shrivelled; dried up; withered

【焦虑】 jiāolǜ feel anxious; have worries and misgivings

【焦煤】 jiāoméi coking coal

【焦炭】 jiāotàn coke: 沥青～ pitch coke

【焦头烂额】 jiāotóu-làn'é badly battered; in a terrible fix: 敌军被打得～,狼狈逃窜。Badly battered, the enemy fled in utter confusion.

【焦土】 jiāotǔ scorched earth — ravages of war ◇ ～政策 scorched earth policy

【焦心】 jiāoxīn 〈方〉 feel terribly worried

【焦油】 jiāoyóu 〈化〉 tar: 煤～ coal tar/ 木～ wood tar

【焦躁】 jiāozào restless with anxiety; impatient: 克服～情绪 curb one's impatience

【焦灼】 jiāozhuó 〈书〉 deeply worried; very anxious

**椒** jiāo any of several hot spice plants: 辣～ chili; red pepper/ 胡～ pepper

【椒盐】 jiāoyán a condiment made of roast prickly ash and salt; spiced salt

**鲛** jiāo shark

**蕉** jiāo any of several broadleaf plants: 香～ banana/ 美人～ canna

【蕉麻】 jiāomá 〈植〉 abaca; Manila hemp

**礁** jiāo reef: 触～ strike a reef; run up on a rock

【礁石】 jiāoshí reef; rock

**鹪** jiāo

【鹪鹩】 jiāoliáo wren

【鹪莺】 jiāoyīng wren warbler

## jiáo

**矫** jiáo

另见 jiǎo

【矫情】 jiáoqing 〈方〉 argumentative; contentious; unreasonable

另见 jiǎoqíng

**嚼** jiáo masticate; chew; munch: 细～慢咽 chew carefully and swallow slowly; chew one's food well before swallowing it

另见 jué

【嚼舌】 jiáoshé ① wag one's tongue; chatter; gossip: 别在背后～。Don't gossip behind people's backs. ② argue meaninglessly; squabble: 没功夫跟你～。I've got no time to argue with you. 又作"嚼舌头""嚼舌根"

【嚼烟】 jiáoyān chewing tobacco

【嚼子】 jiáozi bit (of a bridle)

## jiǎo

**角** jiǎo ① horn: 牛～ ox horn/ 鹿～ antler ② bugle; horn: 号～ bugle ③ sth. in the shape of a horn: 非洲之～ the Horn of Africa ④ corner: 墙～ corner (of a wall)/ 眼～ corner of the eye ⑤〈数〉 angle: 锐 (钝) ～ acute (obtuse) angle/ 直～ right angle/ 多面～ polyhedral angle ⑥ cape; promontory; headland: 好望～ the Cape of Good Hope ⑦ *jiao*, a fractional unit of money in China (= 1/10 of a *yuan* or 10 *fen*) ⑧〈量〉 quarter: 一～饼 a quarter of a pancake

另见 jué

【角尺】 jiǎochǐ angle square

【角动量】 jiǎodòngliàng 〈物〉 angular momentum

【角度】 jiǎodù ①〈数〉 angle: 撑条和横梁之间～太大。The brace is at too big an angle with the beam. ② point of view; angle: 从各个～来研究问题 examine the matter from various angles ◇ ～计 goniometer; angle gauge

【角钢】 jiǎogāng 〈冶〉 angle steel

【角弓反张】 jiǎogōng fǎnzhāng 〈医〉 opisthotonos

【角规】 jiǎoguī angle gauge

【角砾岩】 jiǎolìyán 〈地〉 breccia

【角楼】 jiǎolóu a watchtower at a corner of a city wall; corner tower; turret

【角落】 jiǎoluò corner; nook: 在院子的一个～里 in a corner of the courtyard/ 找遍每一个～ search every nook and cranny; search high and low/ 躲在阴暗的～里搞阴谋诡计 plot in a dark corner/ 喜讯传遍了祖国的各个～。The good news spread to every corner of the country.

【角马】 jiǎomǎ 〈动〉 gnu

【角膜】 jiǎomó 〈生理〉 cornea ◇ ～混浊 〈医〉 opacity of the cornea/ ～炎 keratitis

【角球】 jiǎoqiú 〈足球〉 corner (kick)

【角鲨】 jiǎoshā spiny dogfish

【角闪石】 jiǎoshǎnshí 〈矿〉 hornblende

【角速度】 jiǎosùdù 〈物〉 angular velocity

【角铁】 jiǎotiě 〈冶〉 angle iron

【角岩】 jiǎoyán 〈矿〉 hornstone

【角页岩】 jiǎoyèyán 〈矿〉 hornfels

【角质】 jiǎozhì 〈生〉 cutin ◇ ～层 〈植〉 cuticle

【角雉】 jiǎozhì 〈动〉 tragopan

【角柱体】 jiǎozhùtǐ prism

【角锥体】 jiǎozhuītǐ pyramid

**侥** jiǎo

【侥幸】 jiǎoxìng lucky; by luck; by a fluke: ～取胜 gain victory by sheer good luck; win by a fluke/ ～心理 the idea of leaving things to chance; trusting to luck

**佼** jiǎo 〈书〉 handsome; beautiful

【佼佼】 jiǎojiǎo 〈书〉 above average; outstanding

**狡** jiǎo crafty; foxy; cunning: ～计 crafty trick; ruse

【狡辩】 jiǎobiàn quibble; indulge in sophistry

【狡猾】 jiǎohuá sly; crafty; cunning; tricky

【狡赖】 jiǎolài deny (by resorting to sophistry): 证据确凿,

不容～。It's no use denying it, the evidence is conclusive.
【狡兔三窟】 jiǎotù sān kū a wily hare has three burrows — a crafty person has more than one hideout
【狡黠】 jiǎoxiá 〈书〉 sly; crafty; cunning
【狡诈】 jiǎozhà deceitful; crafty; cunning

**绞** jiǎo ① twist; wring; entangle: 把几股铁丝～在一起 twist several strands of wire together/ 把衣服～干 wring out wet clothes/ 心如刀～ feel as if a knife were being twisted in one's heart/ ～尽脑汁 rack one's brains/ 许多问题～在一起，闹不清楚。With so many things mixed up it's hard to make out what's what. ② wind: ～动辘轳 wind a windlass ③ hang by the neck ④〈机〉 reaming ⑤〈量〉 skein; hank: 一～毛线 a skein of woollen yarn
【绞肠痧】 jiǎochángshā 〈中医〉 dry cholera
【绞车】 jiǎochē winch; windlass
【绞架】 jiǎojià gallows
【绞盘】 jiǎopán capstan: 推杆～ bar capstan
【绞肉机】 jiǎoròujī meat mincer; mincing machine
【绞杀】 jiǎoshā strangle
【绞纱】 jiǎoshā 〈纺〉 skein ◇ ～染色 skein dyeing
【绞索】 jiǎosuǒ (the hangman's) noose
【绞痛】 jiǎotòng 〈医〉 angina: 肚子～ abdominal angina; colic/ 心～ angina pectoris
【绞刑】 jiǎoxíng death by hanging

**饺** jiǎo dumpling: 蒸～ steamed dumplings
【饺子】 jiǎozi dumpling (with meat and vegetable stuffing) ◇ ～皮 dumpling wrapper/ ～馅 filling for dumplings; stuffing

**皎** jiǎo clear and bright: ～月当空。A bright moon hung in the sky.
【皎皎】 jiǎojiǎo very clear and bright; glistening white: ～者易污。The immaculate stains easily. 或 The immaculate is easily sullied.
【皎洁】 jiǎojié (of moonlight) bright and clear

**铰** jiǎo 〈口〉 ① cut with scissors: ～一件男衬衣 cut out a shirt/ ～成两半 cut in two; cut into halves; cut in half ② bore with a reamer; ream: ～孔 ream a hole
【铰刀】 jiǎodāo 〈机〉 reamer
【铰接】 jiǎojiē 〈机〉 join with a hinge; articulate ◇ ～式大客车 articulated bus
【铰链】 jiǎoliàn hinge: ～接合 hinge joint

**脚** jiǎo ① foot: 赤～ barefoot ② base; foot: 墙～ the foot of a wall/ 山～ the foot of a hill ③〈方〉 dregs; residue: 茶～ leftover tea and tea leaves ④〈方〉 leg
【脚板】 jiǎobǎn 〈方〉 sole (of the foot): 练就一副铁～ train till one's feet are so toughened that one is capable of walking a long distance at a stretch; toughen one's feet till they're hard as leather
【脚背】 jiǎobèi instep
【脚本】 jiǎoběn script; scenario: 电影～ film script
【脚脖子】 jiǎobózi 〈方〉 ankle
【脚步】 jiǎobù step; pace: 加快～ quicken one's pace ◇ ～声 footfall; footsteps
【脚灯】 jiǎodēng 〈剧〉 footlights
【脚蹬子】 jiǎodēngzi pedal; treadle
【脚夫】 jiǎofū 〈旧〉 porter
【脚跟】 jiǎogēn heel: 站稳～ stand firm; gain a firm foothold
【脚尖】 jiǎojiān the tip of a toe; tiptoe: 踮着～走 walk on tiptoe
【脚力】 jiǎolì ① strength of one's legs: 他一天能走一百里，～真好。He's really got strong legs to be able to walk 100 *li* a day. ②〈旧〉 porter ③〈旧〉 payment to a porter
【脚镣】 jiǎoliào fetters; shackles
【脚炉】 jiǎolú foot warmer; foot stove
【脚面】 jiǎomiàn instep
【脚气】 jiǎoqì ①〈医〉 beriberi ②〈口〉 athlete's foot
【脚钱】 jiǎoqian 〈旧〉 payment to a porter
【脚手架】 jiǎoshǒujià 〈建〉 scaffold
【脚踏车】 jiǎotàchē 〈方〉 bicycle
【脚踏两只船】 jiǎo tà liǎng zhī chuán straddle two boats — have a foot in either camp
【脚踏实地】 jiǎo tà shídì have one's feet planted on solid ground — earnest and down-to-earth: 既要有远大的理想，又要～地干 have both an ambitious goal and a down-to-earth style of work
【脚踏脱粒机】 jiǎotà tuōlìjī pedal thresher
【脚腕子】 jiǎowànzi ankle 又作"脚腕儿"
【脚心】 jiǎoxīn the underside of the arch (of the foot); arch
【脚癣】 jiǎoxuǎn 〈医〉 ringworm of the foot; tinea pedis; athlete's foot
【脚丫子】 jiǎoyāzi 〈方〉 foot 又作"脚鸭子"
【脚印】 jiǎoyìn footprint; footmark; track: 侦察兵在雪地上发现了可疑的～。The scouts discovered suspicious footprints in the snow./ 踏着革命前辈的～前进 follow in the footsteps of the older generation of revolutionaries
【脚闸】 jiǎozhá 〈自行车〉 backpedalling brake; coaster brake
【脚掌】 jiǎozhǎng sole (of the foot)
【脚指甲】 jiǎozhījia toenail
【脚指头】 jiǎozhítou 〈口〉 toe
【脚趾】 jiǎozhǐ toe
【脚注】 jiǎozhù footnote

**矫** jiǎo ① rectify; straighten out; correct ② strong; brave: ～若游龙 as powerful as a flying dragon; as strong and brave as a lion ③ pretend; feign; dissemble: ～命 counterfeit an order; issue false orders
另见 jiáo
【矫健】 jiǎojiàn strong and vigorous: ～的步伐 vigorous strides
【矫捷】 jiǎojié vigorous and nimble; brisk
【矫情】 jiǎoqíng 〈书〉 be affectedly unconventional
另见 jiáoqing
【矫揉造作】 jiǎoróu zàozuò affected; artificial: ～的姿态 affected manners
【矫饰】 jiǎoshì feign in order to conceal sth.; dissemble: 这篇文章语言质朴，毫无～。This article is written in a simple style, free from any kind of affectation.
【矫枉过正】 jiǎo wǎng guò zhèng exceed the proper limits in righting a wrong; overcorrect
【矫形】 jiǎoxíng 〈医〉 orthopaedic
◇ ～术 orthopaedics/ ～外科 orthopaedic surgery/ ～医生 orthopaedist
【矫正】 jiǎozhèng correct; put right; rectify: ～发音 correct sb.'s pronunciation mistakes/ ～偏差 correct a deviation/ ～口吃 correct a stammer/ ～视力 correct defects of vision
【矫直机】 jiǎozhíjī 〈冶〉 straightening machine; straightener

**搅** jiǎo ① stir; mix: 把粥～一～ give the porridge a stir ② disturb; annoy: 她在工作，别～她。She's working. Don't disturb her.
【搅拌】 jiǎobàn stir; agitate; mix: 把农药和种子～在一起

mix insect powder with seed ◇ ～机 mixer/ ～器 stirrer; agitator
【搅动】 jiǎodòng mix; stir: 拿棍子～灰浆 stir the plaster with a stick
【搅混】 jiǎohun 〈口〉 mix; blend; mingle
【搅和】 jiǎohuo ① mix; blend; mingle: 这是两码事，别～在一起。They are two different matters. Don't mix them up. ② mess up; spoil: 事情都让他～糟了。He's messed everything up. 或 He's made a mess of everything.
【搅乱】 jiǎoluàn confuse; throw into disorder: 警惕敌人～我们的阵线 be on the alert and not let the enemy create confusion in our ranks
【搅扰】 jiǎorǎo disturb; annoy; cause trouble

## 湫

jiǎo 〈书〉 low-lying
另见 qiū
【湫隘】 jiǎo'ài narrow and low-lying

## 剿

jiǎo send armed forces to suppress; put down: ～匪 suppress bandits
另见 chāo
【剿灭】 jiǎomiè exterminate; wipe out

## 缴

jiǎo ① pay; hand over; hand in: ～税 pay taxes/ 上～ turn over (或 in) to the higher authorities ② capture: 他们～了三挺机枪。They captured three machine guns./ ～枪不杀! Lay down your arms and we'll spare your lives!
【缴获】 jiǎohuò capture; seize: ～很多战利品 seize a lot of booty/ 一切～要归公。Turn in everything captured.
【缴纳】 jiǎonà 见"交纳" jiāonà
【缴销】 jiǎoxiāo hand in for cancellation
【缴械】 jiǎoxiè ① disarm ② surrender one's weapons; lay down one's arms: ～投降 lay down one's arms and surrender

# jiào

## 叫

jiào ① cry; shout: 大～一声 give a loud cry; shout; cry out loudly/ 狗～ bark/ 羊～ bleat/ 汽笛在～。The steam whistle is blowing. ② call; greet: 外边有人～你。Somebody outside is calling you./ 你的电话～通了。Your call has been put through./ 这孩子腼腆，不爱～人。The child is shy and doesn't like to greet people. ③ hire; order: ～个出租汽车 hire (或 call) a taxi/ ～二百斤煤 order 200 *jin* of coal/ ～菜 order dishes (at a restaurant) ④ name; call: 人们～他小张。People call him Xiao Zhang./ 他～什么名儿? What's his name?/ 这棉花长得真～棒。That's what I call a really good crop of cotton./ 这能～虚心接受批评么? Can this be called readiness to accept criticism? ⑤ ask; order: ～他进来吗? Shall I ask him (to come) in?/ 医生～她卧床休息。The doctor ordered her to stay in bed. ⑥ 〈介〉〔用在被动式里引进主动者〕: ～你猜对了。You've guessed right./ 你～雨淋了吗? Did you get wet? ⑦ 〈方〉 male (animal): ～驴 jackass
【叫喊】 jiàohǎn shout; yell; howl
【叫好】 jiàohǎo applaud; shout "Bravo!"; shout "Well done!"
【叫花子】 jiàohuāzi 〈口〉 beggar
【叫唤】 jiàohuan cry out; call out: 疼得直～ cry out with pain/ 咬紧牙关，一声也不～ clench one's teeth and not utter a sound
【叫苦】 jiàokǔ complain of hardship or suffering; moan and groan: 她总是抢重活儿干，从来不～不叫累。She always grabs the heaviest jobs and never complains of hardship or fatigue./ 暗暗～ groan inwardly/ ～不迭 pour out endless grievances
【叫骂】 jiàomà shout curses
【叫卖】 jiàomài cry one's wares; peddle; hawk: 沿街～ hawk one's wares in the streets
【叫门】 jiàomén call at the door to be let in
【叫屈】 jiàoqū complain of being wronged; protest against an injustice
【叫嚷】 jiàorǎng shout; howl; clamour
【叫嚣】 jiàoxiāo clamour; raise a hue and cry: 发出战争～ clamour for war/ 大肆～ raise a terrific hue and cry; raise a hullabaloo
【叫醒】 jiàoxǐng wake up; awaken
【叫座】 jiàozuò draw a large audience; draw well; appeal to the audience
【叫做】 jiàozuò be called; be known as: 这种机器～起重机。This machine is called a crane./ 我们的工作方法～"从群众中来，到群众中去。" Our method of work may be described as "from the masses, to the masses." 又作"叫作"

## 觉

jiào sleep: 睡一～ have a sleep/ 午～ midday nap
另见 jué

## 校

jiào ① check; proofread; collate: ～长条样 read galley proofs/ 四～ the fourth proof; proofread for the fourth time ② compare
另见 xiào
【校场】 jiàochǎng 〈旧〉 drill ground
【校订】 jiàodìng check against the authoritative text
【校对】 jiàoduì ① proofread; proof ② proofreader ③ check against a standard; calibrate: 一切计量器都必须～合格才可以出厂。All measuring instruments must be calibrated before leaving the factory. ◇ ～符号 proofreader's mark
【校改】 jiàogǎi read and correct proofs
【校勘】 jiàokān collate ◇ ～学 textual criticism
【校样】 jiàoyàng proof sheet; proof: 已看完～ have read the proofs/ 付印～ final proof/ 长条～ galley proof
【校阅】 jiàoyuè read and revise
【校正】 jiàozhèng proofread and correct; rectify: ～错字 correct misprints ◇ ～补偿装置 〈机〉 correction and compensation device
【校准】 jiàozhǔn 〈机〉 calibration: 方位～ bearing calibration ◇ ～器 calibrator

## 较

jiào ① compare: 工作～前更为努力 work even harder than before/ ～一～劲儿 have a trial of strength ② comparatively; relatively; fairly; quite; rather: ～好 fairly good; quite good/ ～差 relatively poor/ 有～大的进步 have made considerable progress ③ clear; obvious; marked: 二者～然不同。There is a marked difference between the two. ④ dispute: 锱铢必～ quibble over every penny; dispute over every trifle
【较比】 jiàobǐ 〈方〉〈副〉 comparatively; relatively; fairly; quite
【较量】 jiàoliàng ① measure one's strength with; have a contest; have a trial (或 test) of strength: 经过反复的～ after repeated trials of strength ② haggle; argue; dispute

## 轿

jiào sedan (chair)
【轿车】 jiàochē ① 〈旧〉 (horse-drawn) carriage ② bus or car: 大～ bus; coach/ 小～ car; limousine; sedan
【轿子】 jiàozi sedan (chair)

## 教

jiào ① teach; instruct: 言传身～ teach by precept

and example/ ～子务农 encourage one's children to go in for farming/ 请～ ask for advice; consult ② religion: 信～ believe in a religion; be religious/ 基督～ Christianity ③ 见"叫" jiào ⑤⑥
另见 jiāo
【教案】 jiào'àn teaching plan; lesson plan
【教本】 jiàoběn textbook
【教鞭】 jiàobiān (teacher's) pointer
【教材】 jiàocái teaching material
【教程】 jiàochéng ① course of study ② (published) lectures: 《近代史～》 *A Course in Modern History*
【教导】 jiàodǎo ① instruct; teach; give guidance: 在党的～下 guided by the Party ② teaching; guidance: 革命领袖的～ teachings of revolutionary leaders/ 党的～记心间 bear in mind the Party's instructions ◇ ～队 training unit/ ～员 (battalion) political instructor
【教范】 jiàofàn 〈军〉 manual: 兵器～ a manual of arms; manual
【教改】 jiàogǎi 〈简〉(教学改革) educational reform
【教工】 jiàogōng teaching and administrative staff (of a school)
【教官】 jiàoguān 〈旧〉 drillmaster; instructor
【教规】 jiàoguī 〈宗〉 canon
【教皇】 jiàohuáng pope; pontiff ◇ ～通谕 Papal Encyclical
【教会】 jiàohuì (the Christian) church ◇ ～学校 missionary school
【教诲】 jiàohuì 〈书〉 teaching; instruction: 谆谆～ earnest teachings
【教具】 jiàojù teaching aid
【教科书】 jiàokēshū textbook
【教练】 jiàoliàn ① train; drill; coach: 持枪～ drill with weapons/ 徒手～ drill without weapons ② coach; instructor: 足球～ football coach/ ～兼队员 playing coach ◇ ～车 learner-driven vehicle/ ～船 training ship/ ～弹 practice projectile; dummy projectile; dummy/ ～机 trainer aircraft; trainer/ ～员 coach; instructor; trainer
【教派】 jiàopài 〈宗〉 religious sect; denomination
【教区】 jiàoqū parish
【教师】 jiàoshī teacher; schoolteacher
【教士】 jiàoshì 〈宗〉 priest; clergyman; Christian missionary
【教室】 jiàoshì classroom; schoolroom
【教授】 jiàoshòu ① professor: 副～ associate professor/ 客座～ visiting professor; guest professor ② instruct; teach: ～历史 teach history ◇～法 teaching methods; pedagogics
【教唆】 jiàosuō instigate; abet; put sb. up to sth.: 谁～他们这样做的呢? Who instigated them to do this? ◇ ～犯 abettor
【教堂】 jiàotáng church; cathedral
【教条】 jiàotiáo dogma; doctrine; creed; tenet: 马克思主义不是～而是行动的指南。Marxism is not a dogma, but a guide to action.
【教条主义】 jiàotiáozhǔyì dogmatism; doctrinairism ◇ ～者 dogmatist; doctrinaire
【教廷】 jiàotíng the Vatican; the Holy See ◇ ～大使 nuncio/ ～公使 internuncio
【教徒】 jiàotú believer (或 follower) of a religion
【教务】 jiàowù educational administration ◇ ～处 Dean's Office/ ～长 Dean of Studies
【教学】 jiàoxué ① teaching; education ② teaching and studying ③ teacher and student
◇ ～大纲 teaching programme; syllabus/ ～方法 teaching method/ ～方针 principles of teaching/ ～改革 transformation of education; reform in education/ ～内容 content of courses
【教学相长】 jiào-xué xiāng zhǎng teaching benefits teacher and student alike; teaching benefits teachers as well as students
【教训】 jiàoxun ① lesson; moral: 血的～ a lesson paid for with blood; lesson written in blood/ 吸取～ draw a lesson (或 moral) from sth.; take warning from sth./ 要牢记历史的～。We must keep these lessons of history firmly in mind. ② chide; teach sb. a lesson; give sb. a talking-to; lecture sb. (for wrongdoing, etc.)
【教研室】 jiàoyánshì teaching and research section
【教研组】 jiàoyánzǔ teaching and research group
【教养】 jiàoyǎng ① bring up; train; educate ② breeding; upbringing; education; culture
【教义】 jiàoyì 〈宗〉 religious doctrine; creed
【教益】 jiàoyì 〈书〉 benefit gained from sb.'s wisdom; enlightenment
【教友会】 Jiàoyǒuhuì 〈基督教〉 the Society of Friends; the Quakers
【教育】 jiàoyù ① education: ～必须为无产阶级政治服务，必须同生产劳动相结合。Education must serve proletarian politics and be combined with productive labour./ 起了巨大的～作用 have played a great educative role/ 用说服～的方法去解决思想问题 solve ideological problems by persuasion and education ② teach; educate; inculcate: ～每一个同志热爱人民群众 teach every comrade to love the people/ ～我们进一步认识基础理论的重要性 inculcate in us a better understanding of the importance of basic theory ◇ ～程度 level of education/ ～革命 revolution in education/ ～家 educationist; educator/ ～界 educational circles/ ～心理学 educational psychology/ ～学 pedagogy; pedagogics; education/ ～制度 system of education
【教育方针】 jiàoyù fāngzhēn policy for education; educational policy: 我们的～，应该使受教育者在德育、智育、体育几方面都得到发展，成为有社会主义觉悟的有文化的劳动者。Our educational policy must enable everyone who receives an education to develop morally, intellectually and physically and become a worker with both socialist consciousness and culture.
【教员】 jiàoyuán teacher; instructor: 汉语～ a teacher of Chinese ◇ ～休息室 staff room; common room
【教长】 jiàozhǎng 〈宗〉 imam; dean
【教长国】 jiàozhǎngguó 〈伊斯兰教〉 imamate
【教职员】 jiào-zhíyuán teaching and administrative staff
【教主】 jiàozhǔ the founder of a religion

**窖** jiào ① cellar or pit for storing things: 菜～ vegetable cellar ② store sth. in a cellar or pit

**酵** jiào ferment; leaven
【酵母】 jiàomǔ yeast ◇～菌 saccharomycete
【酵素】 jiàosù 〈化〉 ferment; enzyme

**藠** jiào
【藠头】 jiàotou 〈植〉 Chinese onion (*Allium chinense*)

**醮** jiào ① Taoist sacrificial ceremony: 打～ perform a Taoist ritual ② libation at an ancient wedding ceremony: 再～ (of a woman) remarry

## jiē

**节** jiē
另见 jié
【节骨眼】 jiēguyǎn 〈方〉 critical juncture; vital link: 就在这个～上，援军赶到了。At this critical moment reinforce-

ments rushed up./ 你回来得正是～上！ You've come back in the nick of time!/ 思想工作要做到～儿上。To help a person ideologically, you must put your finger on the right spot. 或 Ideological work must go straight to the point.

**阶** jiē ① steps; stairs: 台～ a flight of steps ② rank: 军～ military rank

【阶层】 jiēcéng (social) stratum: 社会～ social stratum/ 中间～ intermediate stratum

【阶地】 jiēdì 〈地〉 terrace

【阶段】 jiēduàn ① stage; phase: 过渡～ transitional stage/ 斗争的第一～ the first phase of the struggle/ 革命发展～论 the theory of the development of revolution by stages/ 社会主义社会是一个相当长的历史～。Socialist society covers a historical period of considerable length. ② 〈矿〉 level ◇ ～高度 level interval

【阶级】 jiējí (social) class ◇ ～报复 class vengeance/ ～本能 class instinct/ ～本质 class nature/ ～成分 class status/ ～斗争 class struggle/ ～队伍 class ranks/ ～分化 class polarization /～分析 class analysis/ ～观点 class viewpoint/ ～教育 class education/ ～觉悟 class consciousness/ ～立场 class stand/ ～路线 class line/ ～矛盾 class contradictions/ ～社会 class society/ ～性 class character; class nature/ ～异己分子 alien-class element; individual from an alien class/ ～阵线 class alignment

【阶级斗争熄灭论】 jiējí dòuzhēng xīmièlùn the theory of "the dying out of class struggle" — a revisionist fallacy which denies the existence of classes and class struggle in socialist society

【阶梯】 jiētī a flight of stairs; ladder: 进身的～ stepping stone ◇ ～教室 lecture theatre

【阶下囚】 jiēxiàqiú prisoner; captive

**疖** jiē

【疖子】 jiēzi ① 〈医〉 furuncle; boil ② 〈植〉 knot (in wood)

**皆** jiē 〈书〉 all; each and every: 人人～知 it is known to all; it is public knowledge

【皆大欢喜】 jiē dà huānxǐ everybody is happy; to the satisfaction of all

【皆伐】 jiēfá 〈林〉 clear felling

**结** jiē bear (fruit); form (seed): 开花～果 blossom and bear fruit/ 这些花～子儿了。These flowers have gone to seed.

另见 jié

【结巴】 jiēba ① stammer; stutter ② stammerer; stutterer

【结实】 jiēshí bear fruit; fructify

【结实】 jiēshi ① solid; sturdy; durable: 一双～的鞋子 a durable pair of shoes/ 这张桌子很～。This is a very solid table./ 拴～点儿。Tie it fast. ② strong; sturdy; tough: 个子不高但是长得很～ short but sturdy

**接** jiē ① come into contact with; come close to: 短兵相～ hand-to-hand fight; fighting at close quarters; close-range fighting ② connect; join; put together: ～电线 connect wires/ ～关系 establish contact (as in underground work)/ ～线头 tie broken threads; join two threads together/ 请～ 286 分机。Put me through to Extension 286, please./ 起来发言的人一个～一个。People got up to speak one after another. ③ catch; take hold of: ～球 catch a ball ④ receive: ～到一封信 receive a letter/ ～电话 answer the phone ⑤ meet; welcome: 到车站～人 go to the station to meet sb. ⑥ take over: ～工作 take over a job/ 把革命传统～过来，传下去 take over and carry forward revolutionary traditions

【接班】 jiēbān take one's turn on duty; take over from; succeed; carry on: 谁接你的班？Who comes on duty after you? 或 Who takes over from you?/ 接好革命的班 be worthy successors to the revolution

【接班人】 jiēbānrén successor: 培养千百万无产阶级革命事业的～ train millions of successors to the cause of proletarian revolution

【接触】 jiēchù ① come into contact with; get in touch with: 代表团～了各界人士。The delegation met with people from all walks of life. ② engage: 与敌人～ engage the enemy/ 小规模～ a minor (或 small-scale) engagement/ 双方武装力量已脱离～。The armed forces of the two sides have disengaged. ③ contact: ～不良 loose (或 poor) contact ◇ ～传染 contagion/ ～故障〈电〉 contact fault/ ～炉〈化〉 contact furnace

【接待】 jiēdài receive; admit: ～外宾 receive foreign guests/ 受到亲切～ be accorded a cordial reception/ 博物馆从上午九点到下午五点～观众。The museum is open from 9 a.m. to 5 p.m. ◇ ～单位 host organization/ ～人员 reception personnel/ ～室 reception room/ ～站 reception centre

【接敌】 jiēdí 〈军〉 close (或 contact) with the enemy ◇ ～队形 approach formation

【接地】 jiēdì ① 〈电〉 ground connection; grounding; earthing ② 〈航空〉 touchdown; ground contact ◇ ～线 〈电〉 ground wire; earth lead/ ～迎角 〈航空〉 landing angle

【接点】 jiēdiǎn 〈电〉 contact

【接二连三】 jiē'èr-liánsān one after another; in quick succession: 捷报～地传来。Reports of victory came in one after another.

【接防】 jiēfáng relieve a garrison; relieve ◇ ～部队 relieving unit

【接风】 jiēfēng give a dinner for a visitor from afar

【接羔】 jiēgāo 〈牧〉 deliver lambs ◇ ～房 lamb-delivery room/ ～季节 lambing season

【接骨】 jiēgǔ 〈医〉 set a (broken) bone; set a fracture

【接管】 jiēguǎn take over control; take over

【接合】 jiēhé 〈机〉 joint: 气密～ airtight joint/ 螺栓～ bolted joint ◇～点 〈军〉 junction point/ ～器 〈机〉 adapter

【接火】 jiēhuǒ 〈口〉 ① start to exchange fire: 先头部队跟敌人～了。The advanced detachment has started to exchange fire with the enemy. ② 〈电〉 energize: 电灯安好了，可还没～呢。The lights have been fixed, but not yet connected to the mains.

【接济】 jiējì give material assistance to; give financial help to

【接见】 jiējiàn receive sb.; grant an interview to: ～外宾 receive foreign guests

【接近】 jiējìn be close to; near; approach: ～国际水平 approach the international level/ 他们俩的意见很～。The two of them have almost identical views. 或 The two of them see pretty well eye to eye./ 该项工程～完成。The project is nearing completion./ 比分很～。It was a close game./ 这个人不容易～。That chap's rather standoffish./ 我舰飞速地～敌舰，开炮射击。Our warships quickly closed in on (或 closed with) the enemy vessel and opened fire.

【接力】 jiēlì relay: 四百米～ 400-metre relay ◇ ～棒 relay baton/ ～赛跑 relay race; relay

【接连】 jiēlián on end; in a row; in succession: ～好几天 for days on end/ ～三小时 for three hours at a stretch/ ～提出许多问题 raise one question after another/ 短期内～

打几仗 fight successive battles in a short time/ ～不断地传来好消息。Glad tidings came in rapid succession.

【接目镜】 jiēmùjìng eyepiece; ocular

【接纳】 jiēnà admit (into an organization): ～新会员 admit new members

【接片】 jiēpiàn 〈电影〉 splicing ◇ ～机 splicer

【接气】 jiēqì coherent: 这一段跟上一段不太～。This paragraph doesn't quite hang together with the preceding one.

【接洽】 jiēqià take up a matter with; arrange (business, etc.) with; consult with: 同有关部门～ take up a matter with the department concerned/ 他来～工作。He's here to talk business. 或 He's here on business./ 明天去参观展览会，我们正在～车辆。We are arranging transport for our visit to the exhibition tomorrow.

【接壤】 jiērǎng border on; be contiguous to; be bounded by ◇ ～地区 contiguous areas

【接任】 jiērèn take over a job; replace; succeed: 他的职务已由另一同志～。His job has been taken over by another comrade./ 她将～党委书记。She will replace the present secretary of the Party committee.

【接生】 jiēshēng deliver a child; practise midwifery ◇ ～员 midwife

【接收】 jiēshōu ① receive: ～无线电信号 receive radio signals ② take over (property, etc.); expropriate: ～敌军的武器装备 take over the enemy's arms and equipment ③ admit: ～新党员 recruit new Party members
◇ ～机 receiver/ ～天线 receiving antenna; receiving aerial/ ～仪式 take-over ceremony

【接手】 jiēshǒu ① take over (duties, etc.): 这项工作我刚～，还不熟悉。I'm new to the job; in fact, I've just taken over. ② 〈棒、垒球〉 catcher

【接受】 jiēshòu accept: ～邀请 accept an invitation/ ～任务 accept an assignment/ ～意见 take sb.'s advice/ ～马克思主义 embrace Marxism/ 容易～新思想 be readily receptive to new ideas/ ～教训 learn (或 draw) a lesson/ ～考验 face up to a test/ ～群众的监督 subject oneself to supervision by the masses ◇ ～书 〈外〉 instrument of acceptance

【接穗】 jiēsuì 〈植〉 scion

【接替】 jiētì take over; replace: 已经派人来～他的工作。A new person has been appointed to take over his work.

【接通】 jiētōng put through: 电话～了吗？ Have you got through?

【接头】 jiētóu ① connect; join; joint ②〈纺〉(纱条) piecing; (经纱) tying-in ③〈口〉 contact; get in touch with; meet: 我找谁～？ Who shall I get in touch with?/ ～地点 contact point; rendezvous ④ have knowledge of; know about: 这事我不～。I know nothing about it.

【接头儿】 jiētour connection; joint; junction: 四通～〈机〉 four-way connection/ 万向～〈机〉 universal joint

【接吻】 jiēwěn kiss

【接物镜】 jiēwùjìng objective lens; objective

【接线】 jiēxiàn 〈电〉 wiring
◇ ～图 wiring diagram; connection diagram/ ～箱 junction box/ ～柱 terminal; binding post

【接续】 jiēxù continue; follow: 此段应～前页末行。This paragraph should follow the last line of the previous page.

【接应】 jiēyìng ① come to sb.'s aid; coordinate with; reinforce: 一排冲上去了，二排随后～。Platoon One charged and was soon followed by Platoon Two. ② supply: 水泥一时～不上。Cement was in short supply at the time.

【接着】 jiēzhe ① catch: 给你一个苹果，～！ Here's an apple for you. Catch! ② follow; carry on: 一个～一个 one after another/ 你说完了，我～说几句。I'll add a few words when you finish./ ～干吧。Carry on with your work./ 土改以后～就搞合作化。The land reform was followed by agricultural cooperation./ ～我们又讨论了明年的计划。Next (或 Then, After that) we discussed plans for the following year.

【接踵】 jiēzhǒng 〈书〉 following on sb.'s heels: 来访者～而至。Visitors came one after another./ 摩肩～ jostle each other in a crowd

【接种】 jiēzhòng 〈医〉 have an inoculation; inoculate: ～防霍乱疫苗 inoculate sb. against cholera/ ～牛痘疫苗 be vaccinated

# 秸

jiē stalks left after threshing; straw: 秫～ sorghum stalks/ 麦～ wheat straw

【秸秆】 jiēgǎn straw ◇ ～肥 compost made of stalks

# 揭

jiē ① tear off; take off: 把墙上那幅画～下来。Take that picture off the wall. ② uncover; lift (the lid, etc.): ～盖子 take the lid off sth.; bring sth. into the open/ ～不开锅 have nothing in the pot; have nothing to eat; go hungry ③ expose; show up; bring to light: ～矛盾，找差距 expose contradictions and find out where one is lagging behind/ 把反党集团的罪行～深～透 thoroughly expose the crimes of the anti-Party clique/ ～人疮疤 pull the scab right off sb.'s sore; touch sb.'s sore spot; touch sb. on the raw ④〈书〉 raise; hoist: ～竿为旗 raise a bamboo pole to serve as a standard of revolt

【揭穿】 jiēchuān expose; lay bare; show up: ～谎言 expose a lie/ ～假面具 tear the mask off sb.'s face; unmask sb./ ～阴谋 lay bare an evil plot/ 他们的一切好话都已被他们自己的行为～。All their fine words have been belied by their own deeds.

【揭底】 jiēdǐ reveal the inside story

【揭短】 jiēduǎn rake up sb.'s faults

【揭发】 jiēfā expose; unmask; bring to light: ～检举反革命分子 expose and denounce counterrevolutionaries/ 根据已经～的材料 according to facts already revealed/ 我们～自己工作中的错误，目的是为了改正，把工作做得更好。We expose mistakes in our work in order to correct them and do our work better. ◇ ～批判会 exposure-criticism meeting

【揭竿而起】 jiē gān ér qǐ raise the standard of revolt; start an uprising; rise in rebellion: 公元前二〇九年，陈胜、吴广～，领导了中国历史上第一次农民大起义。In 209 B. C. Chen Sheng and Wu Guang raised the standard of revolt and led China's first great peasant uprising.

【揭开】 jiēkāi uncover; reveal; open: ～宇宙的奥秘 reveal the secrets of the universe/ ～两国关系史上的新篇章 open a new chapter in the annals of relations between the two countries/ ～新民主主义革命的序幕 raise the curtain on the New-Democratic Revolution

【揭露】 jiēlù expose; unmask; ferret out: ～敌人的阴谋 expose the enemy's plot/ ～其真面目 expose sb.'s true colours; show sb. up for what he is/ ～钻进党内的野心家、阴谋家 unmask the careerists and conspirators who have sneaked into the Party/ ～暗藏的敌特分子 ferret out hidden enemy agents/ ～矛盾，分析矛盾，正确处理矛盾 expose contradictions, analyse them and handle them correctly

【揭幕】 jiēmù unveil (a monument, etc.); inaugurate ◇ ～式 unveiling ceremony

【揭示】 jiēshì ① announce; promulgate ② reveal; bring to light: 马克思主义～了人类社会发展的客观规律。Marxism brought to light the objective laws governing the development of human society./ 小说作者深刻地～了人物的内心世界。The novelist subtly delineates the inner world of his characters. ◇ ～牌〈旧〉 notice board

【揭晓】 jiēxiǎo announce; make known; publish: 选举结果

已经～。The result of the election has been published.

**嗟** jiē 或 juē 〈书〉 sigh; lament: 悲～ sigh in sorrow/ ～悔无及 too late for regrets and lamentations

【嗟来之食】 jiē lái zhī shí food handed out in contempt; a handout

**街** jiē ① street ②〈方〉 country fair; market: 赶～ go to a fair; go to market

【街道】 jiēdào ① street ② residential district; neighbourhood ◇ ～办事处 subdistrict office/ ～服务站 neighbourhood service centre/ ～工厂 neighbourhood factory/ ～委员会 neighbourhood committee

【街坊】 jiēfang 〈口〉 neighbour

【街垒】 jiēlěi street barricade

【街面儿上】 jiēmiànrshang 〈口〉 ① (activities, etc.) in the street: 镇子不大,～倒挺热闹。Small as the town is, it has a busy street. 或 Though small, the town boasts a busy street. ② neighbourhood: ～都知道他会修收音机。Everybody in the neighbourhood knows he can repair radios.

【街市】 jiēshì downtown streets

【街谈巷议】 jiētán-xiàngyì street gossip

【街头】 jiētóu street corner; street: 十字～ (at the) crossroads/ 流落～ tramp the streets; be down and out in a city/ 涌上～ pour into the streets ◇ ～剧 street-corner skit; street performance

【街头巷尾】 jiētóu-xiàngwěi streets and lanes: ～,到处都是欢乐的人群。There are happy crowds in all the streets and lanes.

## jié

**孑** jié 〈书〉 lonely; all alone

【孑孓】 jiéjué wiggler; wriggler

【孑然】 jiérán 〈书〉 solitary; lonely; alone: ～一身 all alone in the world

**节** jié ① joint; node; knot: 竹～ bamboo joint/ 骨～ joint (of bones)/ ～材 nodal wood ② division; part: 音～ syllable ③〈量〉 section; length: 一～铁管 a length of iron pipe/ 两～课 two periods; two classes/ 八～车厢 eight railway coaches/ 第一章第二～ Chapter One, Section Two ④ festival; red-letter day; holiday: 过～ celebrate (或 observe) a festival/ 春～ the Spring Festival/ 国庆～ National Day ⑤ abridge: ～译 abridged translation ⑥ economize; save: ～煤 economize on coal; save coal ⑦ item: 细～ details/ 生活小～ trifling personal matters ⑧ moral integrity; chastity: 气～ moral integrity ⑨〈航海〉 knot: 现在船的速度是十八～。The ship is making 18 knots. 另见 jiē

【节哀】 jié'āi restrain one's grief

【节本】 jiéběn abridged edition; abbreviated version

【节操】 jiécāo 〈书〉 high moral principle; moral integrity

【节俭】 jiéjiǎn thrifty; frugal: 提倡～ encourage frugality

【节节】 jiéjié successively; steadily: ～胜利 win many victories in succession; go from victory to victory/ ～败退 retreat in defeat again and again; keep on retreating/ 产量～上升。Production rose steadily.

【节理】 jiélǐ 〈地〉 joint: 倾向(走向) ～ dip (strike) joint

【节令】 jiélìng climate and other natural phenomena of a season: ～不等人。Don't miss the right season in farming. 或 The seasons wait for no man./ 中秋节吃点月饼,应应～。Let's eat moon cakes at the Mid-Autumn Festival, as befits the occasion.

【节流】 jiéliú ① reduce expenditure: 开源～ broaden sources of income and reduce expenditure ②〈机〉 throttle: 全～ full throttle

【节录】 jiélù extract; excerpt

【节略】 jiélüè 〈外〉 memorandum; aide-mémoire

【节目】 jiémù programme; item (on a programme); number: 晚会的～ programme for the evening party/ 下一个～ the next item (或 number) ◇ ～单 programme; playbill

【节拍】 jiépāi 〈乐〉 metre ◇ ～器 metronome

【节气】 jiéqi a day marking one of the 24 divisions of the solar year in the traditional Chinese calendar; solar terms

【节日】 jiérì festival; red-letter day; holiday: ～气氛 festive air/ 致以～的祝贺 extend holiday greetings/ 穿上～的盛装 in one's holiday best; in gala dress/ 革命是被压迫者和被剥削者的盛大～。Revolutions are festivals of the oppressed and the exploited.

【节省】 jiéshěng economize; save; use sparingly; cut down on: ～时间 save time/ ～篇幅 save space/ ～人力物力 use manpower and material resources sparingly/ 财政的支出,应该根据～的方针。Thrift should be the guiding principle in our government expenditure.

【节外生枝】 jiéwài shēng zhī ① side issues or new problems crop up unexpectedly ② raise obstacles; deliberately complicate an issue: 快要达成协议时,对方又～。An agreement was about to be reached when the other side raised new issues.

【节温器】 jiéwēnqì 〈汽车〉 thermostat

【节衣缩食】 jiéyī-suōshí economize on food and clothing; live frugally

【节余】 jiéyú surplus (as a result of economizing)

【节育】 jiéyù birth control ◇ ～环 intrauterine device (IUD); the loop

【节约】 jiéyuē practise thrift; economize; save: ～粮食 save on food/ ～用电 economize on electricity/ ～开支 cut down expenses; retrench (expenditure)/ 厉行～ practise strict economy

【节肢动物】 jiézhī dòngwù arthropod

【节制】 jiézhì ① control; check; be moderate in: ～饮食 be moderate in eating and drinking ② temperance; abstinence ◇ ～闸〈水〉 check gate

【节奏】 jiézòu rhythm: ～明快 lively rhythm/ 有～地鼓掌 clap hands rhythmically

**讦** jié expose sb.'s past misdeeds: 攻～ rake up sb.'s past and attack him

**劫** jié 〈书〉 ① rob; plunder; raid: 打～ rob; loot ② coerce; compel ③ calamity; disaster; misfortune: 浩～ a great calamity/ ～后余生 be a survivor of a disaster

【劫持】 jiéchí kidnap; hold under duress; hijack: ～飞机 hijack an aeroplane ◇ ～者 hijacker

【劫夺】 jiéduó seize (a person or his property) by force

【劫掠】 jiélüè plunder; loot

【劫数】 jiéshù 〈佛教〉 inexorable doom; predestined fate

【劫狱】 jiéyù break into a jail and rescue a prisoner

**杰** jié ① outstanding; prominent ② outstanding person; hero

【杰出】 jiéchū outstanding; remarkable; prominent: ～贡献 a brilliant contribution/ 周恩来同志是中国人民伟大的无产阶级革命家、～的共产主义战士。Comrade Zhou Enlai was a great proletarian revolutionary of the Chinese people and an outstanding Communist fighter.

【杰作】 jiézuò masterpiece

诘 jié 〈书〉 closely question; interrogate

【诘问】 jiéwèn 〈书〉 closely question; interrogate; cross-examine

【诘责】 jiézé 〈书〉 censure; rebuke; denounce

洁 jié clean: 整～ clean and tidy; clean and neat

【洁白】 jiébái spotlessly white; pure white

【洁净】 jiéjìng clean; spotless

【洁身自好】 jié shēn zì hào ① refuse to be contaminated by evil influence; preserve one's purity ② mind one's own business in order to keep out of trouble

拮 jié

【拮据】 jiéjū in straitened circumstances; short of money; hard up

结 jié ① tie; knit; knot; weave: ～网 weave a net ② knot: 打～ tie a knot/ 活～ slipknot/ 死～ fast knot/ 蝴蝶～ bowknot ③ congeal; form; forge; cement: 牛奶上面～了一层皮。A skin has formed on the milk./ ～痂 form a scab; scab/ ～下深厚的革命友谊 forge a profound revolutionary friendship ④ settle; conclude: ～帐 settle accounts ⑤〈旧〉 written guarantee; affidavit: 具～ give a written guarantee ⑥〈电子〉 junction: p-n ～ p-n junction/ 生长～ grown junction ⑦〈生〉 node: 淋巴～ lymph node

另见 jiē

【结案】 jié'àn wind up a case

【结疤】 jiébā ①〈冶〉 scab ②〈医〉 become scarred

【结拜】 jiébài 〈旧〉 become sworn brothers or sisters

【结伴】 jiébàn go with: ～而行 go or travel in a group

【结冰】 jiébīng freeze; ice up; ice over

【结彩】 jiécǎi adorn (或 decorate) with festoons: 张灯～ decorate with lanterns and festoons

【结肠】 jiécháng 〈生理〉 colon

【结成】 jiéchéng form: ～同盟 form an alliance; become allies/ ～最广泛的统一战线 form the broadest united front/ ～一定的生产关系 enter into definite relations of production/ ～一伙 gang up; band together

【结仇】 jiéchóu start a feud; become enemies

【结存】 jiécún ① cash on hand; balance ② goods on hand; inventory

【结党营私】 jiédǎng-yíngsī form a clique to pursue selfish interests

【结缔组织】 jiédì zǔzhī 〈生理〉 connective tissue

【结构】 jiégòu ① structure; composition; construction: 经济～ economic structure/ 原子～ atomic structure/ 这篇文章～严密。This article is compact and well organized. ②〈建〉 structure; construction: 钢～ steel structure/ 钢筋混凝土～ reinforced concrete structure/ 铆合(焊接)～ riveted (welded) construction ③〈地〉 texture: 斑状～ porphyritic texture/ 致密～ compact texture

◇ ～钢 structural steel/ ～力学 structural mechanics/ ～式 〈化〉 structural formula/ ～图 structural drawing

【结关】 jiéguān customs clearance

【结果】 jiéguǒ ① result; outcome: 必然～ inevitable result/ 会谈的～ the outcome of the talks/ 这样瞎吵下去不会有什么～。Squabbling like this won't get you anywhere./ 经过一番争论，～他还是让步了。After a heated argument he finally gave in. ② kill; finish off

【结合】 jiéhé ① combine; unite; integrate; link: 把革命精神和科学态度～起来 combine revolutionary spirit with a scientific approach/ 理论与实践相～ combine theory with practice/ ～具体情况进行处理 deal with sth. in the light of specific conditions/ 知识分子必须与工农群众相～。Intellectuals must integrate with the masses of workers and peasants. ② be united in wedlock ◇ ～能〈物〉 binding energy

【结核】 jiéhé ①〈医〉 tuberculosis: 肺～ pulmonary tuberculosis/ 骨～ bone tuberculosis ②〈矿〉 nodule: 锰～ manganese nodule

◇ ～病 tuberculosis/ ～病院 tuberculosis hospital or sanatorium/ ～杆菌 tubercle bacillus/ ～菌素 tuberculin

【结喉】 jiéhóu 〈生理〉 Adam's apple

【结婚】 jiéhūn marry; get married ◇ ～登记 marriage registration/ ～证书 marriage certificate; marriage lines

【结集】 jiéjí ① concentrate; mass: ～兵力 concentrate troops ② collect articles, etc. into a volume: ～付印 compile a collection of writings and send it to the press

【结交】 jiéjiāo make friends with; associate with: 他～的朋友大多是青年工人。He associates mostly with young workers.

【结节】 jiéjié 〈生〉 tubercle; node

【结节虫】 jiéjiéchóng nodular worm

【结晶】 jiéjīng ① crystallize ② crystal: 盐～ salt crystals ③ crystallization: 集体智慧的～ a crystallization of collective wisdom/ 劳动的～ the fruit of labour

◇ ～断面〈化〉 crystalline fracture/ ～化学 crystal chemistry/ ～水 water of crystallization; crystal water/ ～学 crystallography/ ～岩石 crystalline rock

【结局】 jiéjú final result; outcome; ending: 小说的～ the ending of a novel/ 这是逆历史潮流而动的人的必然～。This is the inescapable fate of those who go against the current of history.

【结块】 jiékuài agglomerate; curdle

【结蜡】 jiélà 〈石油〉 paraffin (或 wax) precipitation ◇ ～事故 paraffin trouble

【结论】 jiélùn ①〈逻〉 conclusion (of a syllogism) ② conclusion; verdict: 得出～ draw (或 come to, reach) a conclusion/ 不要忙于下～。Don't jump to conclusions./ 对某人的历史作～ reach a conclusion on sb.'s personal history; pass (official) judgment on sb.'s history/ 这是否可行，还不能下～。Whether this is feasible is still an open question.

【结盟】 jiéméng form an alliance; ally; align

【结膜】 jiémó 〈生理〉 conjunctiva ◇ ～炎 conjunctivitis

【结欠】 jiéqiàn balance due

【结亲】 jiéqīn ①〈口〉 marry; get married ② (of two families) become related by marriage

【结清】 jiéqīng settle; square up: ～帐目 square accounts (with sb.)

【结球甘蓝】 jiéqiú gānlán cabbage

【结社】 jiéshè form an association ◇ ～自由 freedom of association

【结绳】 jiéshéng tie knots: ～记事 keep records by tying knots

【结石】 jiéshí 〈医〉 stone; calculus: 肾～ kidney stone

【结识】 jiéshí get acquainted with sb.; get to know sb.: ～了很多新朋友 have made a lot of new friends

【结束】 jiéshù end; finish; conclude; wind up; close: ～讲话 wind up a speech/ ～战争状态 terminate the state of war/ 代表团～了对我国的访问。The delegation has concluded its visit to China./ 主席宣布讨论～。The chairman declared the discussion closed./ 会议下午五时～。The meeting ended at 5 p.m./ 斗争远远没有～。The struggle is far from over. ◇ ～语 concluding remarks

【结算】 jiésuàn settle accounts; close (或 wind up) an account: 用人民币计价～ use Renminbi for quoting prices and settling accounts

【结尾】 jiéwěi ①ending; winding-up stage: ～工程 the winding-up work of a project/ 文章的～很有力量。The article has a forceful ending. ②〈乐〉coda
【结业】 jiéyè complete a course; wind up one's studies
【结余】 jiéyú cash surplus; surplus; balance
【结缘】 jiéyuán form ties (of affection, friendship, etc.); become attached to: 他从小就和音乐结了缘。He developed a liking for music even as a boy.
【结怨】 jiéyuàn contract enmity; incur hatred
【结扎】 jiézā 〈医〉ligation; ligature: ～血管 ligature (或 tie up) blood vessels/ 输卵管～术 ligation of oviduct/ 输精管～术 vasoligation
【结帐】 jiézhàng settle (或 square) accounts; balance the books

**桔** jié
另见 jú
【桔梗】 jiégěng 〈中药〉the root of balloonflower (*Platycodon grandiflorum*)

**桀** Jié the name of the last ruler of the Xia Dynasty (c. 21st — c. 16th century B.C.), traditionally considered a tyrant
【桀骜不驯】 jié'ào bù xún 〈书〉stubborn and intractable; obstinate and unruly
【桀犬吠尧】 Jié quǎn fèi Yáo the tyrant Jie's cur yapping at the sage-king Yao — utterly unscrupulous in its zeal to please its master

**捷** jié ①victory; triumph: 大～ a great victory/ 报～ announce a victory/ 首战告～ be victorious in the first battle; win the first battle ②prompt; nimble; quick: 敏～ quick; nimble; agile
【捷报】 jiébào news of victory; report of a success: ～频传。News of victory keeps pouring in.
【捷径】 jiéjìng shortcut: 走～ take a shortcut
【捷克斯洛伐克】 Jiékèsīluòfákè Czechoslovakia ◇ ～人 Czechoslovak; Czechoslovakian
【捷克语】 Jiékèyǔ Czech (language)
【捷足先登】 jiézú xiān dēng the swift-footed arrive first; the race is to the swiftest: 二班～，把最艰巨的任务抢走了。Squad Two grabbed the most difficult task before the others had a chance to.

**睫** jié eyelash; lash
【睫毛】 jiémáo eyelash; lash

**竭** jié exhaust; use up
【竭诚】 jiéchéng wholeheartedly; with all one's heart: ～拥护 give wholehearted support
【竭尽】 jiéjìn use up; exhaust: ～全力 spare no effort; do one's utmost; do all one can/ ～造谣诬蔑之能事 stop at nothing in spreading lies and slanders
【竭蹶】 jiéjué 〈书〉destitute; impoverished: 艰难～ hardship and destitution
【竭力】 jiélì do one's utmost; use every ounce of one's energy: ～支持 give all-out support/ ～反对 actively oppose/ ～鼓吹 boost with all one's might; energetically advocate/ ～抗拒 stubbornly resist
【竭泽而渔】 jié zé ér yú drain the pond to get all the fish; kill the goose that lays the golden eggs

**截** jié ①cut; sever: ～成两段 cut in two ②〈量〉section; chunk; length: 一～儿木头 a log/ 他话说了半～儿，又缩回去了。He broke off half way and said no more. ③stop; check; stem: 把惊马～住 stop a bolting horse/ ～流 dam a river/ ～球 intercept a pass ④by (a specified time); up to: ～至八月底 up to the end of August
【截长补短】 jié cháng bǔ duǎn take from the long to add to the short; draw on the strength of each to offset the weakness of the other
【截断】 jiéduàn ①cut off; block: ～敌人的退路 cut off the enemy's retreat/ ～河流 dam a river ②cut short; interrupt: 电话铃声～了他的话。He was interrupted by the telephone.
【截获】 jiéhuò intercept and capture: 游击队～了敌人一辆卡车。The guerrillas intercepted and captured an enemy truck.
【截击】 jiéjī intercept: ～敌增援部队 intercept the enemy's reinforcements ◇ ～导弹 interceptor (或 interception) missile/ ～机 interceptor
【截流井】 jiéliújǐng 〈建〉catch basin
【截煤机】 jiéméijī 〈矿〉coalcutter; cutter
【截面】 jiémiàn section: 横～ cross section/ 正～ normal section
【截然】 jiérán sharply; completely: ～对立 be diametrically opposed/ ～不同 poles apart; completely different; different as black and white/ 同他们以前的谈话～相反 completely contradict their previous statement/ 两者不能～分开。No hard and fast line can be drawn between the two.
【截瘫】 jiétān 〈医〉paraplegia
【截肢】 jiézhī 〈医〉amputation
【截止】 jiézhǐ ①end; close: 登记已经～了。Registration has closed./ 申请到本月二十日～。The 20th of this month is the closing day for applications. ②〈电〉cut-off: ～电平 cut-off level
【截至】 jiézhì by (a specified time); up to: ～本月底 by the end of this month/ ～目前为止 up to now

**碣** jié stone tablet: 墓～ tombstone

**羯** Jié Jie (Chieh), an ancient nationality in China
【羯羊】 jiéyáng wether

## jiě

**姐** jiě ①elder sister; sister ②a general term for young women
【姐夫】 jiěfu elder sister's husband; brother-in-law
【姐姐】 jiějie elder sister; sister
【姐妹】 jiěmèi ①sisters: 她没有～，只有一个哥哥。She has a brother but no sisters./ 她们～俩都是先进生产者。Both sisters are advanced workers. ②brothers and sisters: 你们～几个？How many brothers and sisters do you have?

**解** jiě ①separate; divide: ～剖 dissect/ 溶～ dissolve/ 瓦～ disintegrate ②untie; undo: ～缆 untie the mooring rope/ ～鞋带 undo shoelaces/ ～扣儿 unbutton ③allay; dispel; dismiss: ～热 allay a fever/ ～惑 dispel (或 remove) doubts/ ～油腻 cut the grease of a rich meal (as with a cup of tea, etc.) ④explain; interpret; solve: 注～ (explanatory) notes; annotation/ 新～ a new interpretation/ ～题 solve a (mathematical, etc.) problem ⑤understand; comprehend: 费～ hard to understand; obscure/ 令人不～ puzzling; incomprehensible ⑥relieve oneself: 小～ go to the lavatory (to urinate)/ 大～ go to the lavatory (to defecate) ⑦〈数〉solution: 求～ find the solution
另见 jiè; xiè

【解表】 jiěbiǎo 〈中医〉 induce sweat; diaphoresis ◇ ～药 diaphoretic
【解馋】 jiěchán satisfy a craving for good food
【解嘲】 jiěcháo try to explain things away when ridiculed: 自我～ find excuses to console oneself
【解除】 jiěchú remove; relieve; get rid of: ～职务 remove sb. from his post; relieve sb. of his office/ ～合同 terminate a contract/ ～武装 disarm/ ～禁令 lift a ban/ ～警报 sound the all clear/ ～婚约 renounce an engagement/ ～思想负担 have a load taken off one's mind; be relieved of a mental burden/ ～顾虑 free one's mind of apprehensions/ 旱象已经～。The dry spell is over.
【解答】 jiědá answer; explain: ～疑难问题 answer difficult questions
【解冻】 jiědòng ① thaw; unfreeze: ～季节 thawing season ② unfreeze (funds, assets, etc.)
【解毒】 jiědú ① 〈医〉 detoxify; detoxicate ② 〈中医〉 relieve internal heat or fever ◇ ～药 antidote
【解饿】 jiě'è satisfy one's hunger
【解乏】 jiěfá ① recover from fatigue: 他得好好睡一觉，才能～。He needs a good long sleep to get over his fatigue./ 烫烫脚～。Bathe your feet in hot water and you won't feel so tired. ② refreshing
【解法】 jiěfǎ 〈数〉 solution
【解放】 jiěfàng ① liberate; emancipate: ～思想 emancipate the mind; free oneself from old ideas/ 革命就是～生产力。Revolution means liberating the productive forces./ 无产阶级只有～全人类，才能最后～自己。Only by emancipating all mankind can the proletariat achieve its own final emancipation. ② liberation: ～前(后) before (after) liberation/ ～初期 the years just following liberation; the early post-liberation period ◇ ～区 liberated area
【解放军】 jiěfàngjūn ① liberation army ② 〈简〉(中国人民解放军) the Chinese People's Liberation Army; the PLA ③ PLA man
【解放战争】 jiěfàng zhànzhēng ① war of liberation ② China's War of Liberation (1945-1949)
【解雇】 jiěgù discharge; dismiss; fire
【解恨】 jiěhèn vent one's hatred; have one's hatred slaked: 这坏蛋打他一顿也不～。Thrashing this scoundrel wouldn't be enough to slake our hatred for him.
【解甲归田】 jiě jiǎ guī tián take off one's armour and return to one's native place; be demobilized
【解禁】 jiějìn lift a ban
【解痉】 jiějìng 〈中医〉 spasmolysis
【解救】 jiějiù save; rescue; deliver: 是毛主席和共产党把西藏农奴从苦难的深渊中～出来。It was Chairman Mao and the Communist Party that delivered the Tibetan serfs from the abyss of misery./ 通货膨胀政策～不了经济危机。Inflationary policies are no remedy for an economic crisis.
【解聚】 jiějù 〈化〉 depolymerization
【解决】 jiějué ① solve; resolve; settle: ～争端 settle a dispute/ ～困难 overcome a difficulty; find a way out of a difficulty/ ～问题 solve a problem; settle a question (或 an issue); work out a solution/ 很快地～战斗 bring a battle to a quick decision/ 不同质的矛盾，只有用不同质的方法才能～。Qualitatively different contradictions can only be resolved by qualitatively different methods. ② dispose of; finish off: 这一仗把敌人完全～了。In that battle we finished off all the enemy troops.
【解开】 jiěkāi untie; undo: ～头巾 untie a kerchief/ ～上衣 unbutton one's jacket/ ～这个谜 find a clue to the mystery/ ～疙瘩 get rid of a hang-up
【解渴】 jiěkě quench one's thirst: 这西瓜真～。This watermelon really quenches your thirst.
【解扣】 jiěkòu 〈电〉 trip: 自动～ automatic trip
【解理】 jiělǐ 〈地〉 cleavage
【解铃系铃】 jiělíng-xìlíng let him who tied the bell on the tiger take it off — whoever started the trouble should end it 又作"解铃还是系铃人"
【解码】 jiěmǎ decipher; decode
【解闷】 jiěmèn divert oneself (from boredom)
【解囊】 jiěnáng 〈书〉 open one's purse: ～相助 help sb. generously with money
【解聘】 jiěpìn dismiss an employee (usu. at the expiration of a contract)
【解剖】 jiěpōu dissect: 活体～ vivisection/ 尸体～ autopsy; postmortem examination/ 严于～自己 be strict in dissecting oneself ideologically; be strict in appraising oneself/ "～麻雀"的方法 the method of "dissecting a sparrow" — the method of analysing a typical case ◇ ～刀 scalpel/ ～学 anatomy
【解气】 jiěqì vent one's spleen; work off one's anger
【解卡】 jiěqiǎ 〈石油〉 free the stuck tools
【解劝】 jiěquàn soothe; mollify; comfort: 你去～几句，叫他别生气了。Say something to mollify his anger./ 经过同志们～，他们俩又和好了。Their comrades helped them patch up their quarrel.
【解散】 jiěsàn ① dismiss: 队伍～后，战士们都在操场上休息。After they were dismissed, the soldiers had a rest on the drill ground./ ～! (口令) Dismiss! ② dissolve; disband: ～组织 disband an organization
【解释】 jiěshì explain; expound; interpret: ～一个新词 explain a new word/ ～法律 interpret laws/ 用阶级斗争观点～历史 interpret history from the viewpoint of class struggle/ 对这件事你作何～? How do you account for this?/ 投票以前中国代表作了～性发言。Before casting his vote, the Chinese representative made an explanatory statement./ 这是误会，～一下就行了。This is a misunderstanding. A little explanation will clear it up./ 你应该虚心听取同志们的批评，不要老是～。You should listen carefully to the criticism of the comrades and not keep trying to explain things away. ◇ ～性备忘录 explanatory memorandum
【解手】 jiěshǒu relieve oneself; go to the toilet (或 lavatory)
【解数】 jiěshù skill; art: 使出浑身～ bring all one's skill into play
【解说】 jiěshuō explain orally; comment: 向观众～这种拖拉机的构造和性能 explain to the visitors the structure and performance of this type of tractor ◇ ～词 (口头) commentary; (文字) caption/ ～员 announcer; narrator; commentator
【解体】 jiětǐ disintegrate: 原始社会的～ the disintegration of primitive society
【解脱】 jiětuō free (或 extricate) oneself: 从困境中～出来 extricate oneself from a predicament/ 陷入不可～的危机 land oneself in an inextricable crisis
【解围】 jiěwéi ① force an enemy to raise a siege; rescue sb. from a siege ② help sb. out of a predicament; save sb. from embarrassment: 他们拿我开玩笑，你怎么不来给我～? Why didn't you come to my rescue when they were making fun of me?
【解析几何学】 jiěxī jǐhéxué analytic geometry
【解析数论】 jiěxī shùlùn 〈数〉 analytic theory of numbers
【解严】 jiěyán declare martial law ended; lift a curfew
【解约】 jiěyuē terminate an agreement; cancel (或 rescind) a contract
【解职】 jiězhí dismiss from office; discharge; relieve sb. of his post

## jiè

**介** jiè ① be situated between; interpose: 这座山～于两县之间。The mountain lies between two counties. ② take seriously; take to heart; mind: ～意 take offence; mind ③〈书〉upright: 耿～ honest and frank; upright ④ armour: ～胄之士 men in armour; ancient warriors ⑤ shell

【介词】jiècí 〈语〉preposition

【介电常数】jièdiàn chángshù dielectric constant

【介壳】jièqiào shell (of oysters, snails, etc.)

【介壳虫】jièqiàochóng scale insect

【介入】jièrù intervene; interpose; get involved: 不～无原则争论 not get involved in unprincipled disputes

【介绍】jièshào ① introduce; present: 让我～一下，这就是张同志。Allow me to introduce Comrade Zhang./ 作自我～ introduce oneself/ ～对象 introduce sb. to a potential marriage partner; find sb. a boy or girl friend/ 这种灭虫方法是去年才～到我们县来的。This method of pest control was introduced into our county only last year. ② recommend; suggest: 申请入党的人，必须有正式党员二人负责～。An applicant for Party membership must be recommended by two full Party members./ 我给你～一本书。I'll recommend you a book. ③ let know; brief: ～情况 brief sb. on the situation; put sb. in the picture; fill sb. in/ ～经验 pass on experience ◇ ～信 letter of introduction; reference

【介绍人】jièshàorén ① one who introduces or recommends sb.; sponsor: 他们二人是我的入党～。They are the two comrades who recommended me for Party membership. 或 The two of them were my sponsors when I applied for Party membership. ② matchmaker

【介形虫】jièxíngchóng mussel-shrimp

【介意】jièyì 〔多用于否定词后〕take offence; mind: 我是开玩笑，你可别～呀。I was only joking. I hope you won't take offence./ 即使有些批评过头了，他也不～。He didn't mind even when some criticisms were excessive.

【介音】jièyīn 〈语〉(in Chinese pronunciation) head vowel, any of the three vowels i, u, and ü in certain compound vowels, as i in iang

【介质】jièzhì 〈物〉medium: 工作～ actuating medium

【介子】jièzǐ 〈物〉meson; mesotron

**芥** jiè mustard
另见 gài

【芥菜】jiècài leaf mustard ◇ ～疙瘩 rutabaga
另见 gàicài

【芥蒂】jièdì 〈书〉ill feeling; unpleasantness; grudge: 心存～ bear a grudge

【芥末】jièmo mustard

【芥子】jièzǐ mustard seed

【芥子气】jièzǐqì 〈化〉mustard gas

**戒** jiè ① guard against: 力～浮夸 strictly avoid boasting and exaggeration ② exhort; admonish; warn: 引以为～ take warning from sth.; take sth. as an object lesson ③ give up; drop; stop: ～烟 give up smoking/ ～酒 stop drinking/ ～荤腥 go on a vegetarian diet ④〈宗〉Buddhist monastic discipline: 受～ attain the full status of a monk or nun ⑤ (finger) ring: 钻～ diamond ring

【戒备】jièbèi guard; take precautions; be on the alert: ～森严 be heavily guarded/ 处于～状态 be on the alert

【戒尺】jièchǐ 〈旧〉teacher's ruler for beating pupils

【戒除】jièchú give up; drop; stop: ～恶习 give up a bad habit

【戒刀】jièdāo Buddhist monk's knife

【戒骄戒躁】jièjiāo-jièzào guard against arrogance and rashness; be on guard against conceit and impetuosity

【戒律】jièlǜ 〈宗〉religious discipline; commandment 又作"戒条"

【戒心】jièxīn vigilance; wariness: 对某人怀有～ be on one's guard against someone; keep a wary eye on someone

【戒严】jièyán enforce martial law; impose a curfew; cordon off an area: 宣布～ proclaim martial law/ 敌人在车站～，搜捕游击队。The enemy cordoned off the railway station to search for the guerrillas.

【戒指】jièzhi (finger) ring

**届** jiè ① fall due: ～期 when the day comes; on the appointed date ②〈量〉〔用于定期会议、毕业的班级等〕: 第五～全国人民代表大会 the Fifth National People's Congress/ 本～联大 the present session of the U.N. General Assembly/ 本～毕业生 this year's graduates

【届满】jièmǎn at the expiration of one's term of office: 任期～。The term of office has expired.

【届时】jièshí when the time comes; at the appointed time; on the occasion: 大桥下月竣工，～将举行通车典礼。There will be an opening ceremony next month when the bridge is completed./ ～务请出席。Your presence is requested for the occasion.

**疥** jiè scabies

【疥虫】jièchóng 〈医〉sarcoptic mite

【疥疮】jièchuāng 〈医〉scabies

【疥蛤蟆】jièháma toad

【疥癣】jièxuǎn 〈牧〉mange: 羊～ sheep scab

**诫** jiè ① warn; admonish: 告～ give warning; admonish ②〈宗〉commandment: 十～ the Ten Commandments

**界** jiè ① boundary: 国～ the boundary of a country; national boundary/ 山西和陕西以黄河为～。The boundary between Shanxi and Shaanxi is the Huanghe River. ② scope; extent: 眼～ field of vision/ 外～ external world ③ circles: 新闻～ press circles/ 各～人民 all sections of the people; people of all walks of life ④ primary division; kingdom: 动(植，矿)物～ the animal (vegetable, mineral) kingdom ⑤〈地〉group: 古生～ the Palaeozoic group ⑥〈数〉bound: 上(下)～ upper (lower) bound

【界碑】jièbēi boundary tablet; boundary marker

【界尺】jièchǐ ungraduated ruler

【界河】jièhé boundary river

【界内球】jiènèiqiú 〈体〉in bounds; in

【界石】jièshí boundary stone or tablet

【界说】jièshuō 〈旧〉definition

【界外球】jièwàiqiú 〈体〉out-of-bounds; out

【界限】jièxiàn ① demarcation line; dividing line; limits; bounds: 划清马克思主义同修正主义的～ draw a clear line of demarcation between Marxism and revisionism/ 打破行业～，实行大协作 break the bounds of different trades and go in for extensive coordination/ 注意决定事物质量的数量～ pay attention to the quantitative limits that determine the qualities of things ② limit; end

【界线】jièxiàn ① boundary line ② 见"界限"①

【界桩】jièzhuāng boundary marker

**借** jiè ① borrow: 跟人～钱 borrow money from sb. ② lend: 把自行车～给我骑一下好吗？Could you lend me your bicycle? ③ make use of; take advantage of (an opportunity, etc.): 火～风势，越烧越旺。Fanned by the wind, the fire burned more and more furiously./ 部队～着月光急速前进。The troops marched swiftly forward by the light of the moon./ ～党代会的东风 make the most of the favourable situation brought about by the Party congress/ 我愿～此机会向大家表示感谢。I wish to take this opportunity to thank you all. ④ use as a pretext: ～"援助"之名,行掠夺之实 use "aid" as a pretext for plunder

【借词】 jiècí 〈语〉 loanword; loan

【借贷】 jièdài ① borrow or lend money ② debit and credit sides ◇ ～资本 loan capital

【借刀杀人】 jiè dāo shā rén murder with a borrowed knife — make use of another person to get rid of an adversary

【借调】 jièdiào temporarily transfer; loan: 他～到旅行社去工作了。He's on loan to the Travel Service.

【借读】 jièdú study at a school on a temporary basis

【借端】 jièduān use as a pretext: ～生事 find an excuse to make trouble; avail oneself of a pretext to stir up trouble

【借方】 jièfāng 〈簿记〉 debit; debit side

【借古讽今】 jiè gǔ fěng jīn use the past to disparage the present

【借故】 jiègù find an excuse: ～推托 find an excuse to refuse/ 他～走了。He found an excuse and left.

【借光】 jièguāng 〈套〉〔用于请别人给自己方便或向人询问〕excuse me: ～,～! Would you mind stepping to one side, please. 或 Out of the way, please./ ～,去百货大楼怎么走啊? Excuse me, but can you direct me to the Department Store?

【借花献佛】 jiè huā xiàn fó present Buddha with borrowed flowers — borrow sth. to make a gift of it

【借火】 jièhuǒ ask for a light: 劳驾,借个火儿。Excuse me. Would you mind giving me a light?

【借鉴】 jièjiàn use for reference; draw lessons from; draw on the experience of: 他们的做法有许多值得我们～的地方。There's much in their method that we can make use of./ ～外国的经验 use the experience of other countries for reference 又作"借镜"

【借据】 jièjù receipt for a loan (IOU)

【借口】 jièkǒu ① use as an excuse (或 pretext): 别拿忙做～而放松学习。Don't slacken your study on the excuse of being too busy. ② excuse; pretext: 找～ find an excuse (或 pretext)/ 制造～ invent an excuse; cook up a pretext

【借款】 jièkuǎn ① borrow or lend money; ask for or offer a loan ② loan

【借尸还魂】 jièshī-huánhún (of a dead person's soul) find reincarnation in another's corpse — (of sth. evil) revive in a new guise

【借书处】 jièshūchù loan desk (of a library)

【借书证】 jièshūzhèng library card

【借宿】 jièsù stay overnight at sb. else's place; put up for the night: 勘探队员在牧民家里～了一夜。Members of the prospecting team put up for one night in the homes of the herdsmen.

【借题发挥】 jiè tí fāhuī make use of the subject under discussion to put over one's own ideas; seize on an incident to exaggerate matters

【借条】 jiètiáo receipt for a loan (IOU)

【借问】 jièwèn 〈敬〉 may I ask

【借以】 jièyǐ so as to; for the purpose of; by way of: 试举数例,～说明问题的严重性。Let me give a few examples to show how serious the problem is.

【借用】 jièyòng ① borrow; have the loan of: ～一下你的铅笔。May I use your pencil? ② use sth. for another purpose: ～一句古诗表达自己的心情 quote a line from classical poetry to express one's feelings

【借债】 jièzhài borrow money; raise (或 contract) a loan: ～度日 live by borrowing

【借支】 jièzhī ask for an advance on one's pay

【借重】 jièzhòng rely on for support; enlist sb.'s help: 以后要～您的地方还多着呢。We'll need a lot more of your help in the future.

【借助】 jièzhù have the aid of; draw support from: ～望远镜观察天体 observe the celestial bodies with the aid of a telescope

## 解

jiè send under guard: 这个反革命分子已经～到县里去了。The counterrevolutionary has been sent to the county seat under guard.

另见 jiě; xiè

【解送】 jièsòng send under guard

## jie

## 价

jie ① 〈方〉〈助〉〔用在否定副词后加强语气〕: 不～。No! ②〔某些副词的后缀〕: 震天～响 make a thunderous noise/ 成天～忙 be busy all day long

另见 jià

## 家

jie 见"价" jie②

另见 jiā

## jīn

## 巾

jīn a piece of cloth (as used for a towel, scarf, kerchief, etc.): 手～ (face) towel/ 围～ scarf/ 餐～ napkin

【巾帼】 jīnguó ① ancient woman's headdress ② woman ◇ ～英雄 heroine

## 今

jīn ① modern; present-day: ～人 moderns; contemporaries; people of our era ② today: ～明两天 today and tomorrow/ ～晚 tonight; this evening ③ this (year); of this year: ～冬 this (coming) winter ④ now; the present: 至～ to date; until now; up to now/ 从～以后 from now on; henceforth/ ～胜于昔。The present is superior to the past.

【今后】 jīnhòu from now on; in the days to come; henceforth; hereafter; in future: ～的十年内 in the next decade; in the coming ten years/ ～的任务 the tasks ahead/ 希望～两国人民之间有更多的交往。We hope from now on there will be more exchanges between our two peoples.

【今年】 jīnnián this year

【今儿】 jīnr 〈方〉 today 又作"今儿个"

【今日】 jīnrì ① today ② present; now: ～中国 China now

【今生】 jīnshēng this life

【今世】 jīnshì ① this life ② this age; the contemporary age

【今天】 jīntiān ① today: 一年前的～ a year ago today ② the present; now

【今文】 jīnwén 见"隶书" lìshū

【今昔】 jīn-xī the present and the past; today and yesterday: 西安的～ Xi'an past and present; Xi'an yesterday and today/ ～对比,忆苦思甜 recall one's suffering in the old society and contrast it with one's happiness in the new

【今译】 jīnyì modern translation; modern-language version: 古诗～ ancient poems rendered into modern Chinese

【今音】 jīnyīn modern (as distinct from classical) pronunciation of Chinese characters

【今朝】 jīnzhāo 〈书〉 today; the present; now

## 斤

jīn *jin*, a unit of weight (=1/2 kilogram)

【斤斤计较】 jīnjīn jìjiào haggle over every ounce; be calculating: ～个人得失 be preoccupied with one's personal gains and losses

【斤两】 jīnliǎng weight: ～不足 short weight; underweight/ 他的话很有～。What he said should not be taken lightly. 或 What he said carried a lot of weight.

**金** jīn ① metals: 合～ alloy/ 五～店 hardware store ② money: 现～ cash; ready money ③ ancient metal percussion instruments: ～鼓齐鸣。All the gongs and drums are beating. ④ gold (Au): ～银财宝 gold, silver and other treasures/ 镀～ gild ⑤ golden: 红底～字 golden characters on a red background ⑥ (Jīn) the Jin Dynasty (1115-1234) ⑦ (Jīn) a surname

【金本位】 jīnběnwèi 〈经〉 gold standard

【金笔】 jīnbǐ (quality) fountain pen

【金币】 jīnbì gold coin

【金碧辉煌】 jīnbì-huīhuáng (of a building, etc.) looking splendid in green and gold; resplendent and magnificent

【金箔】 jīnbó goldleaf; gold foil

【金不换】 jīnbuhuàn not to be exchanged even for gold; invaluable; priceless: 浪子回头～。A prodigal who returns is more precious than gold.

【金蝉脱壳】 jīnchán tuō qiào slip out of a predicament like a cicada sloughing its skin; escape by cunning manoeuvring

【金城汤池】 jīnchéng-tāngchí ramparts of metal and a moat of boiling water — impregnable fortress

【金翅雀】 jīnchìquè greenfinch

【金疮】 jīnchuāng 〈中医〉 metal-inflicted wound; incised wound

【金额】 jīn'é 〈书〉 amount (或 sum) of money

【金刚】 Jīngāng Buddha's warrior attendant

【金刚努目】 Jīngāng nǔmù glare like a temple door god — be fierce of visage 又作"金刚怒目"

【金刚砂】 jīngāngshā 〈机〉 emery; corundum; carborundum ◇ ～磨床 emery grinder

【金刚石】 jīngāngshí diamond

【金刚钻】 jīngāngzuàn diamond ◇ ～钻头 diamond bit

【金戈铁马】 jīngē-tiěmǎ shining spears and armoured horses — a symbol of war in ancient China

【金工】 jīngōng metalworking; metal processing ◇ ～机械 metalworking machinery

【金箍棒】 jīngūbàng golden cudgel (a weapon used by the Monkey King in the novel *Pilgrimage to the West* 《西游记》)

【金光】 jīnguāng golden light (或 ray): 万道～ myriad golden rays/ ～闪闪 glittering; glistening/ 社会主义的～大道 the golden road of socialism

【金龟】 jīnguī tortoise

【金龟子】 jīnguīzǐ 〈动〉 scarab

【金合欢】 jīnhéhuān 〈植〉 sponge tree

【金衡】 jīnhéng troy (weight) ◇ ～制 troy weight; troy

【金红石】 jīnhóngshí 〈矿〉 rutile

【金花菜】 jīnhuācài (California) bur clover

【金黄】 jīnhuáng golden yellow; golden: 菜花一片～ a vast stretch of golden rape flowers

【金汇兑本位】 jīnhuìduì běnwèi 〈经〉 gold exchange standard

【金婚】 jīnhūn golden wedding

【金鸡】 jīnjī golden pheasant

【金鸡纳树】 jīnjīnàshù cinchona

【金鸡纳霜】 jīnjīnàshuāng 〈药〉 quinine

【金橘】 jīnjú 〈植〉 kumquat

【金科玉律】 jīnkē-yùlǜ golden rule and precious precept: 奉为～ accept as infallible law

【金库】 jīnkù national (或 state) treasury; exchequer

【金块】 jīnkuài gold bullion

【金缕玉衣】 jīnlǚ yùyī 〈考古〉 jade clothes sewn with gold thread

【金绿宝石】 jīnlǜ bǎoshí 〈矿〉 chrysoberyl

【金銮殿】 jīnluándiàn emperor's audience hall; throne room

【金霉素】 jīnméisù 〈药〉 aureomycin

【金门岛】 Jīnméndǎo Jinmen (Quemoy) Islands

【金牛座】 jīnniúzuò 〈天〉 Taurus

【金瓯无缺】 jīn'ōu wú quē unimpaired territorial integrity

【金漆】 jīnqī 〈工美〉 gold lacquer ◇ ～镶嵌制品 inlaid gold lacquerware

【金器】 jīnqì gold vessel

【金钱】 jīnqián money

【金钱豹】 jīnqiánbào leopard

【金枪鱼】 jīnqiāngyú tuna

【金融】 jīnróng finance; banking ◇ ～寡头 financial oligarch (或 magnate)/ ～机关 financial institution/ ～界 financial circles/ ～市场 money (或 financial) market/ ～中心 financial (或 banking) centre/ ～资本 financial capital

【金色】 jīnsè golden: ～的朝阳 golden rays of the morning sun; golden dawn

【金石】 jīnshí ① 〈书〉 metal and stone — a symbol of hardness and strength: 精诚所至，～为开。No difficulty is insurmountable if one sets one's mind on it. ② inscriptions on ancient bronzes and stone tablets ◇ ～学 the study of inscriptions on ancient bronzes and stone tablets; epigraphy

【金属】 jīnshǔ metal: 黑色～ ferrous metal/ 有色～ nonferrous metal ◇ ～加工 metal processing; metalworking/ ～结构 metal structure/ ～模 metal pattern/ ～切削机床 metal-cutting machine tool/ ～探伤器 flaw detector/ ～陶瓷 cermet/ ～性 metallicity

【金丝猴】 jīnsīhóu golden monkey; snub-nosed monkey

【金丝雀】 jīnsīquè canary

【金丝镶嵌】 jīnsī xiāngqiàn 〈工美〉 gold filigree

【金丝燕】 jīnsīyàn 〈动〉 esculent swift

【金条】 jīntiáo gold bar

【金文】 jīnwén inscriptions on ancient bronze objects

【金线鱼】 jīnxiànyú 〈动〉 red coat; golden thread

【金相学】 jīnxiàngxué metallography

【金小蜂】 jīnxiǎofēng tiny golden wasp; ptermalid

【金星】 jīnxīng Venus

【金银花】 jīnyínhuā honeysuckle ◇ ～露 〈中药〉 distilled liquid of honeysuckle

【金樱子】 jīnyīngzǐ 〈中药〉 the fruit of Cherokee rose (*Rosa laevigata*)

【金鱼】 jīnyú goldfish

【金玉】 jīnyù 〈书〉 gold and jade; precious stone and metals; treasures: ～良言 golden saying; invaluable advice/ ～其外，败絮其中 rubbish coated in gold and jade; fair without, foul within

【金元】 jīnyuán gold dollar; U.S. dollar

【金云母】 jīnyúnmǔ 〈矿〉 phlogopite

【金盏花】 jīnzhǎnhuā 〈植〉 pot marigold (*Calendula officinalis*)

【金针】 jīnzhēn ① 〈中医〉 acupuncture needle ② dried day lily flower

【金针菜】 jīnzhēncài 〈植〉 day lily

【金针虫】 jīnzhēnchóng wireworm

【金字塔】 jīnzìtǎ pyramid

【金字招牌】 jīnzì zhāopái ① gold-lettered signboard ② a vainglorious title

【金子】 jīnzi gold

# 津

jīn ① ferry crossing; ford: ～渡 a ferry crossing ② saliva: 生～止渴 help produce saliva and slake thirst ③ sweat: 遍体生～ perspire all over ④ moist; damp ⑤ (Jīn) short for Tianjin

【津巴布韦】 Jīnbābùwéi Zimbabwe

【津津乐道】 jīnjīn lè dào take delight in talking about; dwell upon with great relish

【津津有味】 jīnjīn yǒu wèi with relish; with gusto; with keen pleasure: 吃得～ eat with great relish/ 饲养员～地讲着每头牲口的习性。The stockman takes keen pleasure in talking about the habits of each of his draught animals./ 这个故事他们听得～。They listened to the story with great interest.

【津贴】 jīntiē subsidy; allowance

【津液】 jīnyè ①〈中医〉body fluid ② saliva

# 矜

jīn ① pity; sympathize with: ～恤 show sympathy and consideration for ② self-important; conceited: 骄～之气 arrogant airs ③ restrained; reserved: ～重 reserved and dignified

【矜持】 jīnchí restrained; reserved: 举止～ have a reserved manner

【矜夸】 jīnkuā conceited and boastful

# 筋

jīn ① muscle ②〈口〉tendon; sinew ③〈口〉veins that stand out under the skin: 她的手背上露着青～。The veins stand out on the back of her hands. ④ anything resembling a tendon or vein: 叶～ ribs of a leaf/ 钢～ reinforcing steel; steel reinforcement/ 这菜～多嚼不烂。The greens are full of fibres that you can't chew.

【筋斗】 jīndǒu ① somersault: 翻～ turn a somersault ② fall; tumble (over): 摔了个～ fall; have a fall; tumble over

【筋骨】 jīngǔ bones and muscles — physique: 武术可以锻炼～。Practising *wushu* strengthens the physique.

【筋节】 jīnjié muscles and joints — vital links in a speech or essay

【筋疲力尽】 jīnpí-lìjìn exhausted; played out; worn out; tired out

【筋肉】 jīnròu muscles

# 禁

jīn ① bear; stand; endure: 这布～洗吗? Will this cloth stand a lot of washing?/ 这鞋～穿。These shoes are durable. ② contain (或 restrain) oneself: 不～流下眼泪 cannot hold back one's tears

另见 jìn

【禁不起】 jīnbuqǐ be unable to stand (tests, trials, etc.): ～严峻考验 fail to stand rigorous tests

【禁不住】 jīnbuzhù ① be unable to bear or endure: 这种植物～冻。This plant can't stand frost./ 你怎么这样～批评? How is it that you can't stand a little bit of criticism? ② can't help (doing sth.); can't refrain from: ～笑了起来 can't help laughing; burst out laughing

【禁得起】 jīndeqǐ be able to stand (tests, trials, etc.): ～艰苦环境的考验 be able to stand the test of hardships

【禁得住】 jīndezhù be able to bear or endure: 河上的冰已经～人走了。The ice on the river is thick enough to walk on.

【禁受】 jīnshòu bear; stand; endure

# 襟

jīn ① front of a garment ② brothers-in-law whose wives are sisters: ～兄 husband of one's wife's elder sister; brother-in-law

【襟怀】 jīnhuái〈书〉bosom; (breadth of) mind: ～坦白 openhearted and above board; unselfish and magnanimous/ 共产主义者的伟大～ the breadth of vision of a communist

【襟翼】 jīnyì〈航空〉(wing) flap

## jǐn

# 仅

jǐn〈副〉only; merely; barely: ～次于 second only to/ 世所～见 have no parallel anywhere/ ～一人缺席。Only one is absent.

【仅仅】 jǐnjǐn〈副〉only; merely; barely: 这～是开始。This is only the beginning./ 这座桥～半年就完工了。This bridge was built in the short space of six months.

# 尽

jǐn ① to the greatest extent: ～早 as early as possible; at the earliest possible date ② within the limits of: ～着三天把事情办好。Get the job done in three days at the outside./ ～着一百块钱花。Don't spend more than 100 *yuan*. ③ give priority to: ～着年纪大的坐。Let the older people sit down first. ④〔用在表示方位的词前面，跟"最"相同〕at the furthest end of: ～北边 the northernmost end, etc./ ～底下 at the very bottom/ 他家住在村子～西头。He lives at the western end of the village. ⑤〈方〉keep on doing sth.: 他衣服都叫汗湿透了，还～着干呢。He was wet through with sweat, but he kept on working./ 这些日子～下雨。We're having an awful lot of rain these days.

另见 jìn

【尽管】 jǐnguǎn ①〈副〉feel free to; not hesitate to: 有什么问题～问。If you have any questions, don't hesitate to ask them./ 你～拿吧。You're welcome to it. 或 Take as much as you like./ 场院的活儿有我们，你～放心吧。Don't worry. We'll attend to all the work on the threshing ground. ②〈连〉though; even though; in spite of; despite: ～旱情严重，今年的小麦还是丰收了。Despite the serious drought, the wheat harvest this year was good./ ～斗争道路是曲折的，但是，最后胜利终将属于人民。The road of struggle is tortuous, but final victory will go to the people.

【尽可能】 jǐnkěnéng as far as possible; to the best of one's ability: ～早点儿来 come as early as possible/ 革命的政治内容和～完美的艺术形式的统一 the unity of revolutionary political content and the highest possible perfection of artistic form/ 我国的艰巨的社会主义建设事业，需要～多的知识分子为它服务。China needs the services of as many intellectuals as possible for the colossal task of building socialism.

【尽快】 jǐnkuài as quickly (或 soon, early) as possible: 请～答复。Please reply at your earliest convenience.

【尽量】 jǐnliàng to the best of one's ability; as far as possible: ～采用先进技术 make the widest possible use of advanced technology/ 请大家～发表意见。Please voice your opinions as fully as possible.

另见 jìnliàng

【尽先】 jǐnxiān〈副〉give first priority to: ～照顾孩子们 look after the children first/ ～生产这种农具 give first priority to producing this kind of farm tool

# 卺

jǐn〈书〉nuptial wine cup: 合～ drink the wedding cup; get married

# 紧

jǐn ① tight; taut; close: 把绳子拉～ pull the rope taut/ 把螺丝拧～ tighten the screw/ ～握手中枪 hold the gun tight in one's hands/ 这双鞋太～。These shoes are too tight. 或 These shoes pinch./ 他住在我的～隔壁。He lives right next door to me./ 日程安排得很～。The programme is packed./ 一个胜利～接着一个胜利。One victory followed another in quick succession./ 全国人民团结～。The whole nation is closely united. ② tighten: ～一～背包带 tighten the knapsack straps ③ urgent; pressing; tense: 任务～。The task is urgent./ 风声～。Things are tense./ 雨下得正～。It was raining hard./ 枪声越来越～。The firing got heavier and heavier./ 这篇报告厂里催得很～。The factory leadership are pressing us to hand in this report. ④ strict; stringent: 管得～ exercise strict control; be strict with ⑤ hard up; short of money: 手头～ be short of money; be hard up/ 银根～。Money is tight.

【紧逼】 jǐnbī press hard; close in on: 步步～ press on at every stage/ 全场～〈篮球〉 full-court (或 full) press

【紧凑】 jǐncòu compact; terse; well-knit: 这个工厂布局～。The factory is compactly laid out./ 影片情节～。The film has a well-knit plot./ 会议开得很～。It was a well-organized meeting./ 活动安排得很～ have a tight schedule

【紧跟】 jǐngēn follow closely; keep in step with: ～时代的步伐 keep in step with the times/ ～形势 keep abreast of the situation

【紧箍咒】 jǐngūzhòu the Incantation of the Golden Hoop, used by the Monk in the novel *Pilgrimage to the West* (《西游记》) to keep the Monkey King under control — inhibition

【紧急】 jǐnjí urgent; pressing; critical: 发出～呼吁 issue an urgent appeal/ 情况～。The situation is critical./ ～行动起来 act promptly; take immediate action
◇ ～措施 emergency measures/ ～法令 emergency act/ ～会议 emergency meeting/ ～集合 emergency muster/ ～空袭警报 emergency air-raid alarm/ ～起飞 scramble/ ～任务 urgent task/ ～信号 emergency (或 distress) signal/ ～状态 state of emergency/ ～着陆 emergency landing

【紧紧】 jǐnjǐn closely; firmly; tightly: ～相连 closely linked/ ～盯着 watch closely; stare fixedly; gaze steadfastly/ ～依靠群众 rely firmly on the masses/ ～抓住阶级斗争这个纲 firmly grasp class struggle as the key link/ 两人～握手。They clasped hands tightly./ 门关得～的。The door was shut tight.

【紧邻】 jǐnlín close neighbour

【紧锣密鼓】 jǐnluó-mìgǔ wildly beating gongs and drums — intense publicity campaign in preparation for some sinister undertaking, etc.

【紧密】 jǐnmì ① close together; inseparable: ～地团结在以华主席为首的党中央周围。Rally closely round the Party Central Committee headed by Chairman Hua./ 学习理论要～结合实际。Theoretical study must be closely integrated with practice. ② rapid and intense: 枪声～。There was rapid, intense firing.

【紧迫】 jǐnpò pressing; urgent; imminent: 时间～ be pressed for time/ 我有更～的事情要做。I have more pressing things to attend to.

【紧身儿】 jǐnshenr close-fitting undergarment

【紧缩】 jǐnsuō reduce; retrench; tighten: ～编制 reduce staff/ ～开支 cut down expenses; retrench; curtail outlay/ ～包围圈 tighten the ring of encirclement

【紧要】 jǐnyào critical; crucial; vital: ～关头 critical moment (或 juncture); crucial moment/ 无关～ of no consequence; of no importance/ 这一点十分～。That's an extremely important point. 或 That's a vital point.

【紧张】 jǐnzhāng ① nervous; keyed up: 神情～ look nervous/ 慢慢讲，别～。Speak slowly and don't be nervous./ 试验到了关键时刻，大家都～起来。Everybody was keyed up as the experiment reached a crucial point. ② tense; intense; strained: ～局势 a tense situation/ ～气氛 a tense atmosphere/ ～的战斗 intense fighting/ 两国关系～。Relations between the two countries are strained./ ～而有秩序的工作 intense but orderly work/ 团结～的集体生活 a collective life marked by solidarity and activity/ 这场比赛真～! What an exciting game!/ 工程正在～地进行。Construction was in full swing. ③ in short supply; tight: 这几天鸡蛋供应有点～。Eggs have been in rather short supply for the last few days. 或 There's been rather a shortage of eggs lately./ 这里只有一口井，用水比较～。There's only one well here and water is in great demand.

【紧着】 jǐnzhe 〈口〉 speed up; press on with; hurry: 时间不多了，咱们～干吧。There's not much time left. Let's hurry.

## 堇

jǐn

【堇菜】 jǐncài 〈植〉 violet

【堇青石】 jǐnqīngshí 〈矿〉 cordierite

【堇色】 jǐnsè violet

## 锦

jǐn ① brocade ② bright and beautiful: ～霞 rose-tinted clouds/ 前程似～ splendid prospects; glorious future

【锦标】 jǐnbiāo prize; trophy; title ◇ ～主义 cups and medals mania

【锦标赛】 jǐnbiāosài championship contest; championships: 世界乒乓球～ the World Table Tennis Championships

【锦缎】 jǐnduàn brocade

【锦鸡】 jǐnjī golden pheasant

【锦葵】 jǐnkuí 〈植〉 high mallow

【锦纶】 jǐnlún polyamide fibre

【锦囊妙计】 jǐnnáng miàojì instructions for dealing with an emergency; wise counsel

【锦旗】 jǐnqí silk banner (as an award or a gift)

【锦上添花】 jǐnshàng tiān huā add flowers to the brocade — make perfection still more perfect

【锦绣】 jǐnxiù as beautiful as brocade; beautiful; splendid: ～山河 a land of charm and beauty; a beautiful land/ ～前程 glorious future

## 谨

jǐn ① careful; cautious; circumspect: ～记在心 bear in mind/ ～守规则 strictly adhere to the rules ② solemnly; sincerely: ～致谢意。Please accept my sincere thanks./ 我～代表全体职工，向你们表示热烈的欢迎。On behalf of the staff and workers, I wish to extend to you our warmest welcome.

【谨防】 jǐnfáng guard against; beware of: ～扒手。Beware of pickpockets.

【谨上】 jǐnshàng 〈套〉〔用于书信具名后〕 sincerely yours

【谨慎】 jǐnshèn prudent; careful; cautious; circumspect: 谦虚～ modest and prudent/ 说话～ be guarded in one's speech/ ～从事 act with caution

【谨小慎微】 jǐnxiǎo-shènwēi overcautious

【谨严】 jǐnyán careful and precise: 治学～ careful and exact scholarship/ 文章结构～。The article is compact and carefully constructed.

【谨言慎行】 jǐnyán-shènxíng speak and act cautiously; be discreet in word and deed

## 馑

jǐn 见"饥馑" jījǐn

## 槿

jǐn 见"木槿" mùjǐn

# jìn

## 尽

jìn ① exhausted; finished: 取之不～ inexhaustible/

无穷无～ endless; inexhaustible/ 知无不言，言无不～。Say all you know and say it without reserve./ 千言万语表不～我们对党的热爱。Words cannot express our love for the Party. ② to the utmost; to the limit: 用～气力 exert oneself to the utmost ③ use up; exhaust: 一言难～。It can't be expressed in a few words. 或 It's a long story./ 一饮而～ empty a glass at one gulp; drain the cup with one gulp ④ try one's best; put to the best use: ～责任 do one's duty; discharge one's responsibility/ ～最大努力 do one's best; exert one's utmost effort/ 为建设社会主义～一分力量 do one's bit in building socialism/ 人～其才，物～其用 make the best possible use of men and material ⑤ all; exhaustive: 工具已～数交回。All the tools have been handed in./ 不可～信 not to be believed word for word; to be taken with a grain of salt/ ～收眼底 have a panoramic view
另见 jǐn

【尽力】 jìnlì do all one can; try one's best: ～而为 do one's best; do everything in one's power/ 我们一定～支援。We'll do our best to help.

【尽量】 jìnliàng (drink or eat) to the full
另见 jǐnliàng

【尽情】 jìnqíng to one's heart's content; as much as one likes: ～欢呼 cheer heartily/ ～歌唱 sing to one's heart's content

【尽人皆知】 jìn rén jiē zhī be known to all; be common knowledge

【尽人事】 jìn rénshì do what one can (to save a dying person, etc.); do all that is humanly possible (though with little hope of success)

【尽善尽美】 jìnshàn-jìnměi the acme of perfection; perfect

【尽是】 jìnshì full of; all; without exception: 这儿原来～石头。This place used to be full of boulders./ 这里展出的～新产品。All the exhibits here are new products./ 一路上～去参加庆祝活动的人群。There was a continuous stream of people going to the celebrations.

【尽头】 jìntóu end: 路的～ the end of the road

【尽心】 jìnxīn with all one's heart: ～竭力 (do sth.) with all one's heart and all one's might/ 医护人员～照看受伤的工人。The doctors and nurses did their utmost to tend the injured workers./ 这些年青人干活可～呢。These young people are really conscientious in their work.

【尽兴】 jìnxìng to one's heart's content; enjoy oneself to the full: ～而归 return after thoroughly enjoying oneself

【尽义务】 jìn yìwù ① do one's duty; fulfil one's obligation: 尽我们的国际主义义务 fulfil our internationalist duty ② work for no reward

【尽职】 jìnzhí fulfil one's duty: 他工作一向很～。He has always been a conscientious worker.

**进** jìn ① advance; move forward; move ahead: 不～则退。Move forward, or you'll fall behind. ② enter; come or go into; get into: ～屋 enter a house or room/ ～大学 enter college/ ～工厂当学徒 start work in a factory as an apprentice/ ～医院 be sent to hospital; be hospitalized/ 请～！Come in!/ 火车～站了。The train is pulling in. ③ receive: ～款 income/ 这家商店前几天刚～了一批货。This shop laid in a new stock of goods just a few days ago. ④ eat; drink; take: 共～晚餐 have supper together/ 滴水不～ not take even a drop of water — unable to eat or drink ⑤ submit; present: ～一言 give a word of advice ⑥〔用在动词后，表示到里面〕into; in: 走～车间 walk into the workshop/ 把子弹压～弹匣 press the cartridges into the magazine ⑦ any of the several rows of houses within an old-style residential compound ⑧〔用于足球等〕score a goal: ～了！It's in! 或 Goal!/ 这球没～。He's missed it.

【进逼】 jìnbī close in on; advance on; press on towards: 步步～ steadily close in

【进步】 jìnbù ① advance; progress; improve: 世界是在～的。The world is progressing. 或 The world moves ahead./ 今年我们农场各方面的工作都有了很大的～。Great advances have been made in every field of work on our farm this year./ 你的发音很有～。Your pronunciation has greatly improved. ② (politically) progressive: 思想～ have progressive ideas/ ～人士 progressive personages/ ～势力 progressive forces

【进场】 jìnchǎng ① march into the arena ②〈航空〉approach: ～失败 missed approach

【进城】 jìnchéng ① go into town; go to town ② enter the big cities (to live and work): ～以后他仍旧保持着艰苦朴素的作风。After he came into the city, he still kept up his style of hard work and plain living.

【进程】 jìnchéng course; process; progress: 历史～ the course of history

【进尺】 jìnchǐ 〈矿〉footage: 掘进（凿岩，开拓）～ drifting (drilling, tunnelling) footage

【进出】 jìnchū ① pass in and out: 这儿进进出出的人真多。What a lot of people are coming in and out of here./ 车辆由此～。Vehicles this way! ② (business) turnover: 这个商店每天有好几千元的～。This store has a daily turnover of several thousand *yuan*.

【进出口】 jìn-chūkǒu ① imports and exports ② exits and entrances; exit
◇ ～公司 import and export corporation/ ～贸易 import and export trade; foreign trade/ ～业务 imports and exports

【进刀】 jìndāo 〈机〉feed ◇ ～装置 feed arrangement; feed gear; feeder

【进度】 jìndù ① rate of progress (或 advance): 加快～ quicken the pace (或 *tempo*) ② planned speed; schedule: 我们已按照～完成了这道工序。We have finished this part of the process according to plan. ◇ ～报告 progress report/ ～表 progress chart

【进而】 jìn'ér proceed to the next step: 我们工厂准备首先实现半自动化，～实现完全自动化。Our factory plans first to achieve semiautomation and then proceed to complete automation.

【进发】 jìnfā set out; start: 列车向北京～。The train started for Beijing.

【进犯】 jìnfàn intrude into; invade: 打败～的敌人 beat back the invading enemy/ 全歼～之敌 wipe out all the invading enemy

【进风井】 jìnfēngjǐng 〈矿〉downcast (shaft)

【进攻】 jìngōng attack; assault; offensive: 做好～准备 get ready to take the offensive/ 发起全面～ launch an all-out offensive
◇ ～队形 attack formation/ ～命令 order to attack/ ～性武器 offensive weapon/ ～正面 frontage in attack; front of attack

【进贡】 jìngòng pay tribute (to a suzerain or emperor)

【进化】 jìnhuà evolution: 人是从类人猿～而来的。Man evolved from the anthropoid ape. ◇ ～论 the theory of evolution; evolutionism

【进货】 jìnhuò stock (a shop) with goods; lay in a stock of merchandise; replenish one's stock

【进击】 jìnjī advance on (the enemy)

【进见】 jìnjiàn call on (sb. holding high office); have an audience with

【进军】 jìnjūn march; advance: 向西北～ march into the Northwest/ 吹响～的号角 sound the bugle to advance; sound the advance/ 向科学技术现代化～ march towards the modernization of science and technology/ 县委发出了向沙漠～的号召。The county Party committee issued a call to conquer the desert.
【进口】 jìnkǒu ① enter port ② import ③ entrance ④〈机〉inlet: 鼓风～ blast inlet
◇ ～补贴 import subsidy/ ～港 port of entry/ ～货 imported goods; imports/ ～商 importer/ ～税 import duty/ ～限额 import quota/ ～许可证 import license
【进款】 jìnkuǎn income; receipts
【进来】 jìnlai come (或 get) in; enter: 让他～。Let him in.
【进来】 jinlai 〔用在动词后，表示到里面来〕: 她气喘吁吁地走～，浑身湿透了。She came in panting and soaked to the skin.
【进汽】 jìnqì 〈机〉admission: 高压～ high pressure admission
【进取】 jìnqǔ keep forging ahead; be eager to make progress; be enterprising: 永远保持谦虚和～的精神 always remain modest and keep forging ahead ◇ ～心 enterprising spirit; initiative; gumption; push
【进去】 jìnqu go in; get in; enter: 你～看看，我在门口等着。Go in and have a look, and I'll wait for you at the gate.
【进去】 jinqu 〔用在动词后，表示到里面去〕: 把桌子搬～ move the table in/ 冲～ rush in
【进入】 jìnrù enter; get into: ～阵地 get into position/ ～决赛阶段 enter the finals/ ～角色 enter into the spirit of a character; live one's part/ 现在我国社会主义革命和社会主义建设～了新的发展时期。China has now entered a new stage of development in socialist revolution and construction./ 运动已～高潮。The movement has reached a high tide.
【进身之阶】 jìnshēn zhī jiē stepping-stone (in one's official career)
【进食】 jìnshí take food; have one's meal
【进士】 jìnshì a successful candidate in the highest imperial examinations
【进水闸】 jìnshuǐzhá intake work; intake
【进退】 jìn-tuì ① advance and retreat: ～自如 free to advance or retreat (in a battle or game); have room for manoeuvre/ ～两难 difficult to advance or to retreat — in a dilemma/ ～维谷 caught in a dilemma ② sense of propriety: 不知～ have no sense of propriety
【进位】 jìnwèi 〈数〉carry (a number, as in adding)
【进项】 jìnxiang income; receipts
【进行】 jìnxíng ① be in progress; be underway; go on: 工作～得怎么样？How are you getting on with your work?/ 勘探工作已经在～。Prospecting is already in progress./ 手术～了六个小时。The operation lasted six hours./ 大会明天继续～。The conference continues tomorrow. ② carry on; carry out; conduct: ～社会主义革命 carry out socialist revolution/ 对党员～党的优良传统教育 educate Party members in the Party's fine tradition/ ～一场激烈的争论 carry on a spirited debate/ ～实地调查 make on-the-spot investigations/ ～科学实验 engage in scientific experiment/ ～核试验 conduct a nuclear test/ ～动员 mobilize; make a mobilization speech/ ～表决 put a question to the vote/ ～英勇斗争 wage a heroic struggle/ ～亲切的谈话 have a cordial conversation/ ～侵略 commit aggression/ ～抵抗 put up a resistance ③ be on the march; march; advance ◇ ～曲〈乐〉march
【进修】 jìnxiū engage in advanced studies; take a refresher course: 在职～ in-service training; on-the-job training/ 教师的业务～ teachers' vocational studies ◇ ～班 class for advanced studies/ ～生 graduate student
【进一步】 jìnyībù go a step further; further: ～发展我们两国之间的友好合作关系 further develop the friendly relations and cooperation between our two countries/ ～加强我军的革命化和现代化 take further steps to revolutionize and modernize our armed forces/ 对社会发展的规律性有了～的了解 have a better understanding of the laws of social development
【进展】 jìnzhǎn make progress; make headway: ～神速 advance at a miraculous pace/ 工程～很顺利。The project is making good progress. 或 Construction is proceeding smoothly./ 事情～如何？How are things going?/ 谈判毫无～。The talks have made no headway.
【进驻】 jìnzhù enter and be stationed in; enter and garrison: 部队已～该市。Troops have been garrisoned in that city.

**近** jìn ① near; close: 靠～些。Come closer./ ～在咫尺 be close at hand; be well within one's reach/ 歌声由远而～。The singing came closer and closer./ 他讲课总是由～及远，由浅入深。His lectures always proceed from the close to the distant and from the elementary to the profound./ 离国庆节很～了。National Day is drawing near. 或 It'll soon be National Day./ ～几年来 in recent years/ ～百年史 the history of the last hundred years/ ～在眼前 right before one's eyes; imminent ② approaching; approximately; close to: 年～六十 approaching sixty; getting on for sixty/ 观众～万人。There were nearly 10,000 spectators. ③ intimate; closely related: 两家走得挺～。The two families are on intimate terms. ④ easy to understand: 浅～ simple and easy to understand/ 言～旨远 simple in language but profound in meaning
【近便】 jìnbian close and convenient: 咱们找个～的饭馆吃点吧。Let's have a snack at the nearest restaurant./ 来回挺～的，不用搭车。It's no distance at all. There's no need to take a bus.
【近程】 jìnchéng short range: ～雷达 short-range radar
【近刺】 jìncì 〈军〉short thrust; short lunge
【近代】 jìndài modern times ◇～史 modern history
【近道】 jìndào shortcut
【近地点】 jìndìdiǎn 〈天〉perigee
【近东】 Jìndōng the Near East
【近海】 jìnhǎi coastal waters; inshore; offshore: 我国～有丰富的水产资源。Our country has rich offshore aquatic resources. ◇～渔业 inshore fishing
【近乎】 jìnhu ① close to; little short of: ～荒谬的论点 an argument little short of being ridiculous; an argument bordering on the absurd ②〈方〉intimate; friendly: 套～ try to be friendly with; try to chum (或 pal) up with; cotton up to
【近郊】 jìnjiāo outskirts of a city; suburbs; environs
【近景】 jìnjǐng 〈摄〉close shot
【近况】 jìnkuàng recent developments; how things stand: 中东～ recent developments in the Middle East/ 多日不见来信，不知～如何？I haven't heard from you for a long time. How are things with you?
【近来】 jìnlái recently; of late; lately
【近邻】 jìnlín near neighbour
【近路】 jìnlù shortcut: 走～ take a shortcut
【近旁】 jìnpáng nearby; near: 屋子～ near the house
【近迫作业】 jìnpò zuòyè 〈军〉construction under fire; sapping
【近期】 jìnqī in the near future: ～内无大雨。There won't be heavy rain in the coming few days. ◇ ～预报 short-

term forecast

【近亲】 jìnqīn close relative; near relation ◇ ～繁殖〈生〉inbreeding

【近日】 jìnrì ① recently; in the past few days ② within the next few days

【近日点】 jìnrìdiǎn 〈天〉 perihelion

【近世】 jìnshì modern times

【近视】 jìnshi myopia; nearsightedness; shortsightedness: 政治上的～ political myopia ◇ ～眼镜 spectacles for nearsighted persons

【近视眼】 jìnshiyǎn myopia; nearsightedness; shortsightedness: 他是～。He is shortsighted (或 nearsighted).

【近水楼台先得月】 jìn shuǐ lóutái xiān dé yuè a waterfront pavilion gets the moonlight first — the advantage of being in a favoured position

【近似】 jìnsì approximate; similar: 游击队采用～木马计的方法夺取了敌人的据点。The guerrillas captured the enemy stronghold by a method similar to the Trojan horse stratagem.

◇ ～读数 approximate reading/ ～计算 approximate calculation/ ～值〈数〉 approximate value

【近体诗】 jìntǐshī "modern style" poetry, referring to innovations in classical poetry during the Tang Dynasty (618-907), marked by strict tonal patterns and rhyme schemes

【近因】 jìnyīn immediate cause

【近于】 jìnyú bordering on; little short of: ～荒唐 little short of preposterous; bordering on the absurd

【近月点】 jìnyuèdiǎn 〈宇航〉 perilune

【近战】 jìnzhàn fighting at close quarters; close combat

【近朱者赤，近墨者黑】 jìn zhū zhě chì, jìn mò zhě hēi he who stays near vermilion gets stained red, and he who stays near ink gets stained black — one takes on the colour of one's company

# 妗

jìn

【妗子】 jìnzi 〈方〉 ① wife of one's mother's brother; aunt ② wife of one's wife's brother

# 劲

jìn ① strength; energy: 用～ put forth strength/ 加把～，不然你要落后了。Put on a spurt, or you'll fall behind./ 她仿佛有使不完的～。She seems to have inexhaustible energy. 或 She's a live wire./ 我烧是退了，可身上还是没～儿。My temperature is down, but I'm still feeling weak. ② vigour; spirit; drive; zeal: 保持革命战争时期的那么一股～ maintain the same vigour as in the years of revolutionary war/ 我就喜欢你们这股扎扎实实埋头苦干的～儿。I like your down-to-earth and hardworking spirit./ 要鼓实～，不要鼓虚～。We should encourage genuine enthusiasm, not sham enthusiasm./ 他跟我别着～哪！能听我的吗？How can you expect him to listen to me, when he's still in a huff with me? ③ air; manner; expression: 你这骄傲～儿得好好改改。You've got to get rid of your arrogant ways./ 瞧他那高兴～儿。See how happy he looks. ④ interest; relish; gusto: 打扑克没～，咱们去游泳吧。Playing cards is no fun; let's go swimming.

另见 jìng

【劲头】 jìntóu 〈口〉 ① strength; energy ② vigour; spirit; drive; zeal: 工作有～ be full of drive in one's work/ 一说参军，小伙子们～可足啦。The moment one talks of joining the army, the young fellows are all enthusiasm.

# 荩

jìn

【荩草】 jìncǎo 〈植〉 hispid arthraxon (*Arthraxon hispidus*)

# 浸

jìn soak; steep; immerse: 把衣服放在肥皂水里～一会儿再洗。Soak the clothes in soapy water for a while before you wash them.

【浸膏】 jìngāo 〈药〉 extract

【浸剂】 jìnjì 〈药〉 infusion

【浸礼】 jìnlǐ 〈基督教〉 baptism; immersion ◇ ～会 the Baptist Church; the Baptists

【浸泡】 jìnpào soak; immerse

【浸染】 jìnrǎn be contaminated; be gradually influenced

【浸软】 jìnruǎn macerate

【浸润】 jìnrùn ① soak; infiltrate: 春雨～着田野。The spring rain is soaking into the fields. ②〈医〉 infiltration

【浸透】 jìntòu soak; saturate; steep; infuse: 汗水～了他的衣裳。His clothes were soaked with sweat.

【浸种】 jìnzhǒng 〈农〉 seed soaking (in water): 温汤～ hot water treatment

【浸渍】 jìnzì soak; ret; macerate: 亚麻～ flax retting ◇ ～剂 soaker/ ～液 maceration extract

# 烬

jìn cinder: 灰～ ashes; cinders

# 晋

jìn ① enter; advance: ～见 have an audience with ② promote: 加官～爵 be promoted to a higher office and rank ③ (Jìn) the Jin Dynasty (265-420) ④ (Jìn) another name for Shanxi Province

【晋级】 jìnjí rise in rank; be promoted

【晋见】 jìnjiàn call on (sb. holding high office); have an audience with

【晋升】 jìnshēng promote to a higher office

【晋谒】 jìnyè 〈书〉 call on (sb. holding high office); have an audience with

# 靳

jìn ①〈书〉 be stingy; grudge ② (Jìn) a surname

# 禁

jìn ① prohibit; forbid; ban: 严～烟火。Smoking and lighting fires strictly forbidden (或 prohibited)./ ～赌 suppress gambling/ 解～ lift a ban; remove a ban ② imprison; detain: 监～ imprison ③ what is forbidden by law or custom; a taboo: 入国问～ on entering a country ask about its taboos/ 违～品 contraband (goods) ④ forbidden area: 宫～ the imperial palace

另见 jīn

【禁闭】 jìnbì confinement (as a punishment): 关～ be placed in confinement

【禁地】 jìndì forbidden area; restricted area; out-of-bounds area

【禁锢】 jìngù ① debar from holding office (in feudal times) ② keep in custody; imprison ③ confine: 历代封建统治阶级都力图用礼教把妇女～起来。All through the feudal ages the ruling class did their best to shackle women with Confucian ethics.

【禁忌】 jìnjì ① taboo ② avoid; abstain from: ～辛辣油腻 abstain from peppery or greasy food ③〈医〉 contraindication

【禁绝】 jìnjué totally prohibit; completely ban

【禁例】 jìnlì prohibitory regulations; prohibitions

【禁令】 jìnlìng prohibition; ban

【禁脔】 jìnluán a chunk of meat for one's exclusive consumption; one's exclusive domain: 视为～ regard as one's exclusive domain

【禁区】 jìnqū ① forbidden zone; restricted zone: 空中～〈军〉 restricted airspace/ 那里是～，不准过去。You can't go there. That place is out-of-bounds. ② (wildlife or plant) preserve; reserve; natural park ③〈足球〉 penalty area ④

〈篮球〉restricted area
【禁书】 jìnshū banned book
【禁烟】 jìnyān ban on opium-smoking and the opium trade
【禁欲主义】 jìnyùzhǔyì asceticism
【禁运】 jìnyùn embargo
【禁止】 jìnzhǐ prohibit; ban; forbid: 中国政府一贯主张全面～和彻底销毁核武器。The Chinese Government has consistently stood for the complete prohibition and thorough destruction of nuclear weapons./ ～砍伐树木。Felling trees is forbidden./ ～入内。No admittance./ ～停车。No parking./ ～通行。No thoroughfare. 或 Closed to traffic./ ～倒垃圾。No garbage here./ ～招贴。Post no bills.
【禁制品】 jìnzhìpǐn articles the manufacture of which is prohibited except by special permit; banned products

**觐** jìn ① present oneself before (a monarch) ② go on a pilgrimage
【觐见】 jìnjiàn present oneself before (a monarch); go to court; have an audience with

**噤** jìn ① keep silent ② shiver: 寒～ shiver with cold
【噤若寒蝉】 jìn ruò hánchán as silent as a cicada in cold weather — keep quiet out of fear

## jīng

**泾** Jīng short for the Jinghe River
【泾渭分明】 Jīng-Wèi fēnmíng as different as the waters of the Jinghe and the Weihe — entirely different

**京** jīng ① the capital of a country: 进～ go to the capital ② (Jīng) short for Beijing ③ ten million (an ancient numeral)
【京白】 jīngbái 〈剧〉parts in Beijing opera spoken in Beijing dialect
【京城】 jīngchéng 〈旧〉the capital of a country
【京都】 jīngdū 〈旧〉the capital of a country
【京胡】 jīnghú *jinghu*, a two-stringed bowed instrument with a high register; Beijing opera fiddle
【京畿】 jīngjī 〈书〉the capital city and its environs
【京剧】 jīngjù Beijing opera 又作"京戏"
【京韵大鼓】 jīngyùn dàgǔ story-telling in Beijing dialect with drum accompaniment
【京族】 Jīngzú the Jing (Ching) nationality, living in the Guangxi Zhuang Autonomous Region

**茎** jīng stem (of a plant); stalk

**经** jīng ①〈纺〉warp ②〈中医〉channels ③〈地〉longitude: 东(西)～ east (west) longitude ④ manage; deal in; engage in: ～商 engage in trade ⑤ constant; regular: ～常 regular; frequent/ 不～之谈 preposterous statement; cock-and-bull story ⑥ scripture; canon; classics: 佛～ Buddhist sutra; Buddhist scripture/ 圣～ the Holy Bible/ 各有一本难念的～。Each has his own hard nut to crack. 或 Each has his own trouble. ⑦ menses; menstruation ⑧ pass through; undergo: 途～上海 pass through Shanghai/ 身～百战 have fought many battles; be a veteran of many wars/ ～卡拉奇回国 return home via (或 by way of) Karachi ⑨ as a result of; after; through: ～商定 it has been decided through consultation that/ ～某人建议 upon sb.'s proposal/ ～检查，产品质量合格。Examination confirmed that the quality of the products was up to specification. ⑩ stand; bear; endure: ～得起时间的考验 can stand the test of time/ 革命意志薄弱的人～不起资产阶级糖衣炮弹的袭击。A weak-willed person in the revolutionary ranks cannot withstand the sugar-coated bullets of the bourgeoisie.
另见 jìng
【经闭】 jīngbì 〈中医〉amenorrhoea
【经编】 jīngbiān 〈纺〉warp knitting ◇ ～针织物 warp-knitted fabric
【经常】 jīngcháng ① day-to-day; everyday; daily: ～工作 day-to-day work/ ～开支 running expenses ② frequently; constantly; regularly; often: 领导干部一定要～关心群众疾苦。Leading cadres must always have the well-being of the masses at heart./ 这类问题是～发生的。This kind of problem frequently crops up. 或 This sort of thing is a common occurrence./ 他～上图书馆去。He goes to the library regularly. ◇ ～化 become a regular practice
【经典】 jīngdiǎn ① classics ② scriptures: 佛教～ Buddhist scriptures ③ classical: 马列主义～著作 Marxist-Leninist classics; classical works of Marxism-Leninism ◇ ～力学〈物〉classical mechanics/ ～作家 author of a classic; classic
【经度】 jīngdù longitude
【经断】 jīngduàn 〈中医〉menopause
【经费】 jīngfèi funds; outlay
【经风雨，见世面】 jīng fēngyǔ, jiàn shìmiàn face the world and brave the storm
【经管】 jīngguǎn be in charge of: ～财务 be in charge of financial affairs
【经过】 jīngguò ① pass; go through; undergo: 这汽车～动物园吗？Does this bus pass the Zoo?/ 世界观改造要～长期的甚至是痛苦的磨炼。To remould one's world outlook, one must undergo a long and even painful process of tempering. ② as a result of; after; through: ～充分讨论，大家取得了一致意见。After thorough discussion unanimity was achieved./ 工人阶级～自己的先锋队中国共产党实现对国家的领导。The working class exercises leadership over the state through its vanguard, the Chinese Communist Party. ③ process; course: 事件的全部～ the whole course of the incident; the whole process from beginning to end/ 事情的～是这样的。This is how it happened.
【经互会】 Jīnghùhuì 〈简〉(经济互助委员会) the Council of Mutual Economic Assistance (CMEA); Comecon
【经纪】 jīngjì ① manage (a business) ② manager; broker
【经纪人】 jīngjìrén broker; middleman; agent: 房地产～ estate agent/ 外汇～ foreign exchange broker
【经济】 jīngjì ① economy: 发展社会主义～ develop the socialist economy/ 国营～ the state sector of the economy/ 繁荣～ promote economic prosperity/ ～平衡 economic equilibrium/ ～失调 dislocation of the economy ② of industrial or economic value; economic: ～植物 economic plants ③ financial condition; income: ～宽裕 well-off; well-to-do/ ～拮据 be hard up ④ economical; thrifty: ～实惠 economical and practical/ ～地使用 use economically/ 不～ costing too much; uneconomical
◇ ～部门 branches of the economy; economic departments/ ～成分 sector of the economy; economic sector/ ～地理学 economic geography/ ～地位 economic status; economic position/ ～核算 economic accounting; business accounting/ ～核算单位 business accounting unit/ ～基础 economic base; economic basis/ ～林 economic forest/ ～命脉 economic lifeline; economic arteries; key branches of the economy/ ～危机 economic crisis/ ～学 economics/ ～学家 economist/ ～一体化 economic integration/ ～援助 economic aid/ ～杂交〈牧〉commercial crossbreeding/ ～制裁 economic sanctions/ ～作物 industrial crop; cash crop

【经济主义】 jīngjìzhǔyì economism

【经久】 jīngjiǔ ① prolonged: ～不息的掌声 prolonged applause ② durable: ～耐用 durable; able to stand wear and tear

【经理】 jīnglǐ ① handle; manage ② manager; director

【经历】 jīnglì ① go through; undergo; experience: 现代科学技术正在～着一场伟大的革命。Modern science and technology are undergoing a great revolution./ 我国石油工业的发展～了两条路线的激烈斗争。The development of China's oil industry has involved a fierce two-line struggle. ② experience: 我们两国人民过去都有遭受帝国主义压迫的共同～。Our two peoples share the same experience of having been oppressed by imperialism in the past./ 他这人～多,见识广。He's a man of wide knowledge and experience./ 老工人讲述的他在旧社会的苦难～深深教育了我。The old worker's account of how he had suffered in the old society taught me a lot.

【经纶】 jīnglún 〈书〉 ① comb and arrange silk threads — attend to state affairs ② statecraft; statesmanship: 大展～ put one's statecraft to full use; turn one's statesmanship to full account

【经络】 jīngluò 〈中医〉 main and collateral channels, regarded as a network of passages, through which vital energy circulates and along which the acupuncture points are distributed

【经脉】 jīngmài 〈中医〉 passages through which vital energy circulates, regulating bodily functions

【经密】 jīngmì 〈纺〉 warp density; ends per inch

【经年累月】 jīngnián-lěiyuè for years; year in year out

【经期】 jīngqī (menstrual) period

【经纱】 jīngshā 〈纺〉 ① warp ② end

【经商】 jīngshāng engage in trade; be in business

【经史子集】 jīng-shǐ-zǐ-jí Confucian classics, history, philosophy and *belles-lettres* — the four traditional categories of Chinese writings

【经始】 jīngshǐ 〈军〉 laying out the ground plan of a fortified work; tracing ◇ ～线 trace

【经手】 jīngshǒu handle; deal with: ～公款 handle public money/ 这件事是他～的。He's the one who handled this matter. ◇ ～人 person handling a transaction, particular job, etc.

【经受】 jīngshòu undergo; experience; withstand; stand; weather: ～了各种考验 experience all sorts of trials; stand up to all tests; withstand all trials and tribulations/ 在斗争中～锻炼 be tempered in the struggle

【经售】 jīngshòu sell on commission; deal in; distribute; sell

【经书】 jīngshū Confucian classics

【经外奇穴】 jīngwài qíxué 〈中医〉 extra nerve points, i.e. points not mentioned in the ancient medical classics

【经纬仪】 jīngwěiyí theodolite; transit ◇ ～测量 transit survey

【经线】 jīngxiàn ①〈纺〉 warp ②〈地〉 meridian (line)

【经销】 jīngxiāo sell on commission; deal in; distribute; sell ◇ ～处 agency

【经心】 jīngxīn careful; mindful; conscientious: ～搜集各种资料 take great care to collect all kinds of data/ 漫不～ careless; casual; negligent/ 干什么工作都要～。One should be conscientious in any kind of work.

【经学】 jīngxué study of Confucian classics

【经验】 jīngyàn ① experience: 交流～ exchange experience/ 介绍～ pass on one's experience/ ～丰富 have rich experience; be very experienced/ ～不足 lack experience; not be sufficiently experienced/ ～之谈 remark made by one who has had experience; the wise remark of an experienced person/ 直接(间接)～ direct (indirect) experience ② go through; experience ◇ ～批判主义 empirio-criticism

【经验主义】 jīngyànzhǔyì empiricism ◇ ～者 empiricist

【经意】 jīngyì careful; mindful: 他不～把茶杯碰倒了。He inadvertently knocked over a cup.

【经营】 jīngyíng manage; run; engage in: 统一(分散)～ unified (decentralized) management/ ～少量家庭副业 engage in limited household side-line production/ 发展多种～ promote a diversified economy/ 改善～管理 improve management and administration/ 苦心～ take great pains to build up (an enterprise, etc.)

【经由】 jīngyóu via; by way of: ～武汉去重庆 be bound for Chongqing via Wuhan

【经院哲学】 jīngyuàn zhéxué scholasticism

【经轴】 jīngzhóu 〈纺〉 warp beam

【经传】 jīngzhuàn ① Confucian classics and commentaries on them; Confucian canon ② classical works; classics: 名不见～ not well-known; a mere nobody

## 荆

jīng ① chaste tree; vitex ② (Jīng) a surname

【荆棘】 jīngjí thistles and thorns; brambles; thorny undergrowth

【荆棘载途】 jīngjí zài tú a path overgrown with brambles — a path beset with difficulties

【荆芥】 jīngjiè 〈中药〉 *jingjie* (*Schizonepeta tenuifolia*)

【荆条】 jīngtiáo twigs of the chaste tree (used for weaving baskets, etc.)

## 旌

jīng an ancient type of banner hoisted on a feather-decked mast

【旌旗】 jīngqí banners and flags

## 惊

jīng ① start; be frightened: 听到大坝出现险情,她心里一～。She started at the news that the dyke was in danger./ ～呆了 be stupefied ② surprise; shock; alarm: 一声～雷 a sudden clap of thunder ③ shy; stampede: 马～了。The horse shied./ 大雷雨～了牛群。The thunderstorm stampeded the cattle.

【惊诧】 jīngchà 〈书〉 surprised; amazed; astonished

【惊动】 jīngdòng alarm; alert; disturb: 枪声～了森林中的鸟兽。The report of a gun startled the birds and animals in the forest./ 注意隐蔽,不要～敌人。Take good cover and don't alert the enemy./ 别为这么点儿小事～他。Don't trouble him about such a trifling matter.

【惊愕】 jīng'è 〈书〉 stunned; stupefied

【惊风】 jīngfēng 〈中医〉 infantile convulsions: 急～ acute infantile convulsions

【惊弓之鸟】 jīng gōng zhī niǎo a bird startled by the mere twang of a bow-string; a badly frightened person

【惊骇】 jīnghài 〈书〉 frightened; panic-stricken

【惊呼】 jīnghū cry out in alarm

【惊慌】 jīnghuāng alarmed; scared; panic-stricken: ～不安 jittery; nervy/ ～失措 frightened out of one's wits; panic-stricken/ ～的神色 frightened looks/ 没有半点～ not in the least scared/ ～地叫了起来 cry out in alarm/ 不必～。Don't panic. 或 There's no cause for alarm. 又作"惊惶"

【惊魂未定】 jīnghún wèi dìng not yet recovered from a fright; still badly shaken

【惊悸】 jīngjì 〈书〉 palpitate with fear

【惊叫】 jīngjiào cry in fear; scream

【惊厥】 jīngjué ① faint from fear ② 〈医〉 convulsions

【惊恐】 jīngkǒng alarmed and panicky; terrified; panic-stricken; seized with terror: ～万状 in a great panic; convulsed with fear/ ～失色 pale with fear

【惊奇】 jīngqí wonder; be surprised; be amazed

【惊扰】 jīngrǎo alarm; agitate: 自相～ raise a false alarm
【惊人】 jīngrén astonishing; amazing; alarming: ～的成就 astonishing (或 amazing) achievements/ ～的毅力 amazing willpower/ 解放前矿上事故多得～。Before liberation there was a horrifying number of accidents in the mines.
【惊叹】 jīngtàn wonder at; marvel at; exclaim (with admiration): 这些精美的牙雕,使大家～不已。The exquisite ivory carvings won everybody's admiration. ◇ ～号 exclamation mark (!)
【惊涛骇浪】 jīngtāo-hàilàng ① terrifying waves; stormy sea ② a situation or life full of perils
【惊天动地】 jīngtiān-dòngdì shaking heaven and earth; earthshaking; world-shaking: ～的事业 earthshaking undertaking
【惊悉】 jīngxī be shocked to learn: ～某人不幸逝世 be distressed to learn of the passing away of sb.
【惊喜】 jīngxǐ pleasantly surprised: ～地叫了起来 call out in happy astonishment
【惊吓】 jīngxià frighten; scare: 这孩子受了～,睡得不安稳。The child has had a shock and isn't sleeping well.
【惊险】 jīngxiǎn alarmingly dangerous; breathtaking; thrilling: ～动作 astounding feat/ ～的表演 breathtaking performance/ ～的场面 thrilling scene ◇ ～小说 thriller
【惊心动魄】 jīngxīn-dòngpò soul-stirring; profoundly affecting: 一场～的路线斗争 a soul-stirring two-line struggle
【惊醒】 jīngxǐng ① wake up with a start ② rouse suddenly from sleep; awaken: 一声巨响把他从睡梦中～。He was awakened by a terrific bang.
【惊醒】 jīngxing sleep lightly; be a light sleeper: 他睡觉很～,有点响动都知道。He's a very light sleeper; any little noise disturbs him.
【惊讶】 jīngyà surprised; amazed; astonished; astounded
【惊疑】 jīngyí surprised and bewildered
【惊异】 jīngyì surprised; amazed; astonished; astounded
【惊蛰】 Jīngzhé the Waking of Insects (3rd solar term)

**猄** jīng 见"黄猄" huángjīng

**菁** jīng ① lush; luxuriant ② essence; cream
【菁华】 jīnghuá essence; cream; quintessence
【菁菁】 jīngjīng 〈书〉 lush; luxuriant

**晶** jīng ① brilliant; glittering: 亮～～ shining; glittering ② quartz; (rock) crystal ③ any crystalline substance
【晶格】 jīnggé 〈物〉 (crystal) lattice: 面心～ face-centred lattice/ 体心～ body-centred lattice
【晶粒】 jīnglì 〈物〉 crystalline grain; grain
【晶石】 jīngshí spar
【晶体】 jīngtǐ crystal: 多～ polycrystal ◇ ～点阵 crystal lattice/ ～发生学 crystallogeny/ ～学 crystallography
【晶体管】 jīngtǐguǎn transistor: 硅～ silicon transistor/ 锗～ germanium transistor ◇ ～收音机 transistor radio
【晶莹】 jīngyíng sparkling and crystal-clear; glittering and translucent: ～的露珠 sparkling dew
【晶状体】 jīngzhuàngtǐ 〈生理〉 crystalline lens

**腈** jīng 〈化〉 nitrile
【腈纶】 jīnglún acrylic fibres

**粳** jīng
【粳稻】 jīngdào round-grained nonglutinous rice; *japonica* rice
【粳米】 jīngmǐ polished round-grained nonglutinous rice

**睛** jīng eyeball: 定～一看 give sth. or sb. a good look/ 目不转～地看着 gaze fixedly

**精** jīng ① refined; picked; choice: ～盐 refined salt/ ～金 fine gold/ ～白米 polished white rice ② essence; extract: 去粗取～ discard the dross and select the essence/ ～讲多练 teach only the essential and ensure plenty of practice/ 鱼肝油～ cod-liver oil extract ③ perfect; excellent: ～良 excellent; superior; of the best quality ④ meticulous; fine; precise: ～收细打 careful reaping and threshing/ 这花瓶工艺很～。This vase is a piece of exquisite workmanship. ⑤ smart; sharp; clever; shrewd: 这小鬼真～。That's a really smart kid./ 小算盘打得～ be selfish and calculating ⑥ skilled; conversant; proficient: ～于绘画 skilled in painting ⑦ energy; spirit: 聚～会神 concentrate one's attention; be all attention ⑧ sperm; semen; seed: 受～ fertilization ⑨ 〈方〉 extremely; very: ～瘦 very lean; all skin and bone ⑩ goblin; spirit; demon: 白骨～ White Bone Demon/ 害人～ ogre; mischief-maker ⑪ 〈中医〉 the fundamental substance which maintains the functioning of the body; essence of life
【精兵】 jīngbīng picked troops; crack troops
【精兵简政】 jīngbīng-jiǎnzhèng better troops and simpler administration; better staff and simpler administration; streamlined administration
【精彩】 jīngcǎi brilliant; splendid; wonderful: ～的表演 a brilliant performance/ 发言中最～的地方 most interesting parts of a speech/ 这场球打得真～。This is an exciting game.
【精巢】 jīngcháo 〈生理〉 spermary; testis; testicle
【精诚】 jīngchéng 〈书〉 absolute sincerity; good faith
【精虫】 jīngchóng 〈生理〉 spermatozoon
【精萃】 jīngcuì cream; pick: 世界乒坛的～ the pick of the world's table-tennis players
【精粹】 jīngcuì succinct; pithy; terse
【精打细算】 jīngdǎ-xìsuàn careful calculation and strict budgeting
【精当】 jīngdàng precise and appropriate: 用词～ precise and appropriate wording; masterly choice of words
【精到】 jīngdào precise and penetrating
【精雕细刻】 jīngdiāo-xìkè work at sth. with the care and precision of a sculptor; work at sth. with great care
【精读】 jīngdú ① read carefully and thoroughly ② intensive reading
【精度】 jīngdù precision: 高～ high precision/ 机床的～达到国家标准。The precision of this lathe is up to state requirements.
【精干】 jīnggàn ① (of a body of troops, etc.) small in number but highly trained; crack: 一支～的小分队 a small detachment of picked troops ② keen-witted and capable: 队长虽然年轻,但很～。Young as he is, the team leader is very capable.
【精耕细作】 jīnggēng-xìzuò intensive and meticulous farming; intensive cultivation
【精光】 jīngguāng with nothing left: 刚插的秧苗被洪水冲得～。Every one of the newly planted seedlings was washed away by the flood.
【精悍】 jīnghàn ① capable and vigorous ② pithy and poignant
【精华】 jīnghuá cream; essence; quintessence: 我国民族文化的～ the cream of our national culture/ 去其糟粕,取其～ discard the dross and select the essence
【精加工】 jīngjiāgōng 〈机〉 finish machining; precision work

【精荚】 jīngjiá 〈动〉 spermatophore

【精简】 jīngjiǎn retrench; simplify; cut; reduce: ～节约 simplify administration and practise economy/ ～开支 cut expenses; retrench/ ～会议 cut (the number of) meetings to a minimum/ ～编制 reduce the staff/ ～机构 simplify (或 streamline) the administrative structure/ ～报表 reduce the number of forms; cut down paper work/ 国家机关都必须实行～的原则。Every organ of state must apply the principle of efficient and simple administration.

【精矿】 jīngkuàng concentrate

【精力】 jīnglì energy; vigour; vim: ～充沛 very energetic; full of vigour/ 把毕生～献给共产主义事业 devote the energies of a lifetime to the cause of communism/ 集中～解决主要矛盾 concentrate one's effort on solving the main contradiction

【精练】 jīngliàn concise; succinct; terse: 语言～ succinct language

【精炼】 jīngliàn ①〈冶〉 refine; purify: 火法～ fire refining/ 真空～ vacuum refining ② 见"精练" ◇ ～期 refining period

【精良】 jīngliáng excellent; superior; of the best quality: 制作～ of excellent workmanship/ 装备～ well-equipped

【精量播种】 jīngliàngbōzhǒng 〈农〉 precision drilling ◇ ～机 precision (seed) planter; precision (seed) drill

【精灵】 jīngling ① spirit; demon ②〈方〉 (of a child) clever; smart; intelligent

【精馏】 jīngliú 〈化〉 rectification ◇ ～酒精 rectified alcohol/ ～塔 rectifying (或 fractionating) tower

【精美】 jīngměi exquisite; elegant: ～的刺绣 elegant embroidery/ 包装～ beautifully packaged

【精密】 jīngmì precise; accurate: ～的观察 accurate (或 close) observation
◇ ～度 precision/ ～机床 precision machine tool/ ～仪器 precision instrument/ ～铸造 precision casting

【精明】 jīngmíng astute; shrewd; sagacious: ～的政治家 an astute statesman/ ～的小伙子 a bright young fellow

【精明强干】 jīngmíng qiánggàn intelligent and capable; able and efficient

【精囊】 jīngnáng 〈生理〉 seminal vesicle

【精疲力竭】 jīngpí-lìjié exhausted; worn out; tired out; spent

【精辟】 jīngpì penetrating; incisive: 进行～的分析 make a penetrating analysis/ ～的论述 a brilliant exposition

【精巧】 jīngqiǎo exquisite; ingenious: ～的牙雕 exquisite ivory carving/ 构造～ ingeniously constructed

【精确】 jīngquè accurate; exact; precise: ～的统计 accurate statistics/ 下一个～的定义 give a precise definition

【精锐】 jīngruì crack; picked: ～部队 crack troops; picked troops

【精深】 jīngshēn profound: 博大～ have both extensive knowledge and profound scholarship/ ～的理论 a comprehensive and profound theory

【精神】 jīngshén ① spirit; mind; consciousness: 国际主义～ the spirit of internationalism/ 崇高的～ noble spirit/ 作好～准备 be mentally prepared/ 给予～上的支持 give moral support/ ～上的负担 a load on one's mind/ ～空虚 be spiritually barren ② essence; gist; spirit: 传达文件的～ convey (或 pass on) the gist of a document/ 领会社论的～ try to understand the thrust of an editorial/ 贯彻代表大会的～ act in the spirit of the congress/ 译者没有体会原文的～。The translator failed to capture the spirit of the original.
◇ ～分裂症 schizophrenia/ ～鼓励 moral encouragement/ ～贵族 intellectual aristocrats/ ～枷锁 spiritual (或 mental) shackles/ ～面貌 mental attitude/ ～生活 cultural life/ ～食粮 nourishment for the mind/ ～世界 inner world; mental world/ ～支柱 spiritual (或 ideological) prop

【精神】 jīngshen ① vigour; vitality; drive: ～饱满 full of vigour (或 vitality); energetic/ 没有～ listless; languid/ 振作～ bestir oneself; summon up one's energy; get up steam ② lively; spirited; vigorous: 他穿上军装显得格外～。The army uniform made him look especially impressive./ 那孩子大大的眼睛，怪～的。That child with the big eyes is certainly full of life.

【精神病】 jīngshénbìng mental disease; mental disorder; psychosis
◇ ～人 mental patient/ ～学 psychiatry/ ～医生 psychiatrist/ ～院 psychiatric hospital; mental home (或 hospital, institution)

【精梳】 jīngshū 〈纺〉 combing
◇ ～机 comber/ ～毛纺 worsted spinning/ ～纱 combed yarn

【精饲料】 jīngsìliào concentrated feed; concentrate

【精髓】 jīngsuǐ marrow; pith; quintessence: 无产阶级专政的理论，是马克思主义的～。The theory of the dictatorship of the proletariat is the quintessence of Marxism.

【精通】 jīngtōng be proficient in; have a good command of; master: ～业务 be proficient in professional work/ ～英语 have a good command of English/ 各级领导干部要努力使自己成为～政治工作和业务工作的专家。Leading cadres at all levels must strive hard to become expert in both political and vocational work./ 对于马克思主义的理论，要能够～它、应用它，～的目的全在于应用。It is necessary to master Marxist theory and apply it, master it for the sole purpose of applying it.

【精卫填海】 jīngwèi tián hǎi the mythical bird *jingwei* trying to fill up the sea with pebbles — a symbol of dogged determination

【精细】 jīngxì meticulous; fine; careful: 手工十分～ show fine workmanship/ ～的计算 careful calculation/ 考虑问题很～ think matters over carefully; be circumspect/ 这件上衣做工～。This jacket is well-tailored.

【精心】 jīngxīn meticulously; painstakingly; elaborately: ～护理 nurse with the best of care/ ～设计，～施工 be meticulous in design and construction; painstakingly design and carefully construct/ ～策划的阴谋 a carefully calculated plot; an elaborately planned conspiracy/ ～炮制 elaborately cook up

【精选】 jīngxuǎn ①〈矿〉 concentration ② carefully chosen; choice: 用～的原料制成 made of choice material

【精盐】 jīngyán refined salt; table salt

【精液】 jīngyè 〈生理〉 seminal fluid; semen: 冻干～ 〈牧〉 freeze-dried semen

【精益求精】 jīng yì qiú jīng constantly improve sth.; keep improving: 对技术～ constantly improve one's skill/ 这首诗他还在反复推敲，～。He's still trying to polish and improve the poem.

【精轧】 jīngzhá 〈冶〉 finish rolling ◇ ～机 finishing mill; finisher

【精湛】 jīngzhàn consummate; exquisite: ～的技巧 consummate skill; superb technique/ 工艺～ exquisite workmanship; perfect craftsmanship

【精整】 jīngzhěng 〈冶〉 finishing

【精制】 jīngzhì make with extra care; refine ◇ ～品 highly finished products; superfines

【精致】 jīngzhì fine; exquisite; delicate: ～的丝织品 fine silks/ ～的烟盒 an exquisite cigarette case

【精装】 jīngzhuāng (of books) clothbound; hardback; hardcover ◇ ～本 *de luxe* edition

【精壮】 jīngzhuàng able-bodied; strong

【精子】 jīngzǐ 〈生理〉 sperm; spermatozoon

**兢** jīng

【兢兢业业】 jīngjīngyèyè cautious and conscientious: ～地为党工作一辈子 work conscientiously for the Party all one's life

**鲸** jīng whale

【鲸目动物】 jīngmù dòngwù cetacean
【鲸吞】 jīngtūn swallow like a whale; annex (territory)
【鲸须】 jīngxū baleen; whalebone
【鲸油】 jīngyóu whale oil; blubber: 割～ flench
【鲸鱼】 jīngyú whale
【鲸仔】 jīngzǎi whale calf

**鶄** jīng 见"䴖鶄" qújīng

## jǐng

**井** jǐng ① well: 打～ sink a well; drill a well ② sth. in the shape of a well: 矿～ pit; mine/ 油～ oil well ③ neat; orderly

【井壁】 jǐngbì wall of a well ◇ ～取心〈石油〉 side-wall coring/ ～坍塌 cave-in; caving
【井场】 jǐngchǎng 〈石油〉 well site
【井底】 jǐngdǐ ① the bottom of a well ②〈矿〉 shaft bottom; pit bottom ◇ ～车场 shaft station/ ～矿仓 shaft pocket
【井底之蛙】 jǐngdǐ zhī wā a frog in a well — a person with a very limited outlook
【井冈山】 Jǐnggāngshān the Jinggang Mountains
【井灌】 jǐngguàn 〈水〉 well irrigation
【井架】 jǐngjià ①〈石油〉 derrick: 轻便～ portable derrick (或 mast) ②〈矿〉 headframe; headgear; pitheadframe ③ wellhead
【井井有条】 jǐngjǐng yǒu tiáo in perfect order; shipshape; methodical: ～地工作 work methodically/ 各种仪器、工具摆得～。All the instruments and tools are kept in perfect order.
【井口】 jǐngkǒu ① the mouth of a well ②〈矿〉 pithead ③〈石油〉 wellhead ◇ ～气 wellhead gas; casinghead gas/ ～装置 wellhead assembly
【井喷】 jǐngpēn 〈石油〉 blowout
【井然】 jǐngrán 〈书〉 orderly; neat and tidy; shipshape; methodical: 秩序～ in good order
【井水不犯河水】 jǐngshuǐ bù fàn héshuǐ well water does not intrude into river water — I'll mind my own business, you mind yours
【井田制】 jǐngtiánzhì the "nine squares" system (of land ownership in China's slave society) with one large square divided into 9 small ones (like the Chinese character 井), the 8 outer ones being allocated to serfs who had to cultivate the central one for the serf owner
【井筒】 jǐngtǒng 〈矿〉 pit shaft ◇ ～隔间 shaft compartment/ ～掘进 shaft excavation
【井斜】 jǐngxié 〈石油〉 well deflection; well deviation: 第一口井～是1.7度。The first well had a deviation of 1.7 degrees from the vertical.
【井盐】 jǐngyán well salt

**阱** jǐng trap; pitfall; pit

**刭** jǐng 〈书〉 cut the throat: 自～ cut one's own throat

**肼** jǐng 〈化〉 hydrazine

**颈** jǐng neck
另见 gěng

【颈项】 jǐngxiàng neck
【颈椎】 jǐngzhuī 〈生理〉 cervical vertebra

**景** jǐng ① view; scenery; scene: 外～ exterior view/ 西湖美～ the enchanting scenery of the West Lake/ 雪～ a snow scene ② situation; condition: 好～不长。Good times do not last long. ③ scenery (of a play or film): 换～ change of scenery ④ scene (of a play): 第三幕第一～ Act III, scene 1 ⑤ admire; revere; respect: ～慕 esteem; revere ⑥ (Jǐng) a surname

【景德镇】 Jǐngdézhèn Jingdezhen
【景观】 jǐngguān 〈地〉 landscape: 自然～ natural landscape/ 岩溶～ karst landscape
【景教】 Jǐngjiào Nestorianism
【景况】 jǐngkuàng situation; circumstances: 她家的～越来越好了。Things are getting easier and easier for her family.
【景片】 jǐngpiàn a piece of (stage) scenery; flat
【景颇族】 Jǐngpōzú the Jingpo (Chingpo) nationality, living in Yunnan
【景气】 jǐngqì prosperity; boom: 不～ depression; slump
【景色】 jǐngsè scenery; view; scene; landscape: 深秋～ a late autumn scene/ 南方～ southern landscape/ 海上看日出，～特别美丽。At sea one can get a particularly beautiful view of the sunrise.
【景深】 jǐngshēn 〈摄〉 depth of field
【景泰蓝】 jǐngtàilán *cloisonné* enamel; *cloisonné*
【景天】 jǐngtiān 〈植〉 red-spotted stonecrop (*Sedum erythrostictum*)
【景物】 jǐngwù scenery: ～宜人 delightful scenery
【景象】 jǐngxiàng scene; sight; picture: 一派丰收～ one vast panorama of bumper crops/ 呈现出一片团结战斗的革命～ present a revolutionary scene of unity and militancy
【景仰】 jǐngyǎng respect and admire; hold in deep respect: 怀着无限～的心情 with boundless respect and admiration
【景遇】 jǐngyù 〈书〉 circumstances; one's lot
【景致】 jǐngzhì view; scenery; scene: 从塔顶可以看到全城的～。The tower commands a view of the whole town./ 一下雪，这里的～就更美了。This place looks even more beautiful after a fall of snow.

**儆** jǐng warn; admonish: 惩一～百 punish one to warn a hundred; make an example of sb.

**憬** jǐng

【憬悟】 jǐngwù wake up to reality; come to see the truth, one's error, etc.

**警** jǐng ① alert; vigilant: ～醒 be a light sleeper ② warn; alarm: ～告 warn ③ alarm: 火～ fire alarm ④〈简〉(警察) police: ～亭 police box

【警报】 jǐngbào alarm; warning; alert: 拉～ sound the alarm (或 siren)/ 解除空袭～ all clear/ 台风～ a typhoon warning/ 战斗～ combat alert ◇ ～器 siren; alarm/ ～系统 warning system
【警备】 jǐngbèi guard; garrison ◇ ～区 garrison command/ ～司令部 garrison headquarters
【警察】 jǐngchá police; policeman: 女～ policewoman/ 人民～ a people's policeman
【警笛】 jǐngdí ① police whistle ② siren
【警告】 jǐnggào ① warn; caution; admonish: 对敌人的军事

挑衅提出严重～ issue a serious warning to the enemy against their military provocations/ 我们一再～他不要跟那种人来往。We repeatedly admonished him not to associate with that sort of people. ② warning (as a disciplinary measure): 给予～处分 give sb. a disciplinary warning
◇ ～信号〈交〉warning signal

【警戒】 jǐngjiè ① warn; admonish ② be on the alert against; guard against; keep a close watch on: 采取～措施 take precautionary measures/ 沿公路放出～ post guards along the highway
◇ ～部队 outpost troops; security force (或 detachment)/ ～色〈动〉warning (或 aposematic) coloration/ ～水位 warning water level; warning stage/ ～艇 guard boat/ ～线 cordon; security line

【警句】 jǐngjù aphorism; epigram

【警觉】 jǐngjué vigilance; alertness: 引起～ arouse vigilance/ 政治～性 political alertness/ 海防战士～地注视着出现在海面上的黑点。The coastal guard kept a watchful eye on the black spot that had appeared out at sea.

【警犬】 jǐngquǎn police dog

【警惕】 jǐngtì be on guard against; watch out for; be vigilant: 保持高度～ maintain sharp vigilance /要特别～个人野心家和阴谋家。We must especially watch out for careerists and conspirators./ 提高～，保卫祖国 heighten our vigilance and defend our country/ ～地守卫着大桥 vigilantly guard the bridge ◇ ～性 vigilance

【警卫】 jǐngwèi (security) guard
◇ ～室 guardroom/ ～团 guards regiment/ ～员 bodyguard

【警钟】 jǐngzhōng alarm bell; tocsin: 指导员的话给我敲起了～。What the political instructor said sounded the alarm for me.

## jìng

**劲** jìng strong; powerful; sturdy: ～松 sturdy pines
另见 jìn

【劲敌】 jìngdí formidable adversary; strong opponent

【劲旅】 jìnglǚ strong contingent; crack force: 这个厂的篮球队可算是全市的一支～。This factory's basketball team is one of the strongest in the city.

**净** jìng ① clean: ～水 clean water/ 擦～ wipe sth. clean/ 这件褂子没洗～。This jacket hasn't been properly washed. ② completely: 用～ use up/ 这次夏收一定要做到地里～，场上～。In this summer harvest we must gather in every grain from the fields and from the threshing ground. ③ only; merely; nothing but: ～说不干 all talk, no action/ 这几天～刮大风。It's been very windy these last few days./ 别～打岔。Don't keep interrupting./ 桌上～是中草药的标本。There is nothing on the desk but specimens of medicinal herbs. ④ net: ～收入 net income/ ～出口 net export/ ～进口 net import ⑤ the "painted face", a character type in Beijng opera, etc.

【净高】 jìnggāo〈建〉clear height

【净荷载】 jìnghèzài net load

【净化】 jìnghuà purify: 水的～ purification of water ◇ ～塔 purifying column

【净尽】 jìngjìn completely; utterly: 消灭～ utterly annihilate

【净利】 jìnglì net profit

【净手】 jìngshǒu〈婉〉wash one's hands; relieve oneself

【净水厂】 jìngshuǐchǎng water treatment plant

【净余】 jìngyú remainder; surplus: 除去开支，～二百元。After deducting expenses, we have 200 *yuan* left.

【净值】 jìngzhí net worth; net value: 出口～ net export value/ 进口～ net import value

【净重】 jìngzhòng net weight

**径** jìng ① footpath; path; track: 曲～ a winding path ② way; means: 捷～ an easy way; shortcut ③〈副〉directly; straightaway: ～行办理 deal with the matter straightaway/ ～回广州 go straight back to Guangzhou ④ diameter: 半～ radius

【径迹】 jìngjì〈物〉track: 蜕变～ decay track ◇ ～起点 track origin

【径流】 jìngliú〈水〉runoff: 地表～ surface runoff/ 地下～ groundwater runoff

【径情直遂】 jìng qíng zhí suì as smoothly as one would wish: 战胜困难的过程往往不是～的。The process of overcoming a difficulty is usually not as direct and smooth as one would wish./ 事物是往返曲折的，不是～的。Events have their twists and turns and do not follow a straight line.

【径赛】 jìngsài〈体〉track ◇ ～项目 track events

【径庭】 jìngtíng〈书〉very unlike: 大相～ entirely different; poles apart

【径向】 jìngxiàng〈物〉radial ◇ ～间隙 radial clearance/ ～轴承 radial bearing

【径直】 jìngzhí〈副〉straight; directly; straightaway: 登山队员～向主峰进发。The mountaineers made straight for the summit./ 飞机将～飞往昆明。The plane will fly nonstop to Kunming./ ～写下去吧，等写完了再修改。Just go on writing and do the polishing when you've finished.

【径自】 jìngzì〈副〉without leave; without consulting anyone: 会没开完，他～走了。He left abruptly in the middle of the meeting.

**经** jìng〈纺〉warping
另见 jīng

**胫** jìng〈生理〉shin

【胫骨】 jìnggǔ shin bone; tibia

**痉** jìng

【痉挛】 jìngluán convulsion; spasm: 食管～ spasm of the esophagus; esophagospasm

【痉病】 jìngbìng〈中医〉febrile disease with symptoms such as convulsions, opisthotonos, trismus, etc.

**竞** jìng compete; contest; vie: 百里江面，千帆～发。A thousand boats set sail on a long stretch of the river.

【竞渡】 jìngdù ① boat race ② swimming race

【竞技】 jìngjì sports; athletics ◇ ～场 arena

【竞技状态】 jìngjì zhuàngtài form (of an athlete): ～好 in good form; in top form/ ～不好 not in good form; out of form; off one's game

【竞赛】 jìngsài contest; competition; emulation; race: 社会主义劳动～ socialist labour emulation drive/ 体育～ athletic contest (或 competition)/ 军备～ arms (或 armament) race ◇ ～规则 rules of a contest (或 competition)

【竞选】 jìngxuǎn enter into an election contest; campaign for (office); run for: ～总统 run for the presidency

【竞争】 jìngzhēng compete: 资本主义自由～ capitalist free competition ◇ ～价格 competitive price/ ～性 competitiveness

【竞走】 jìngzǒu heel-and-toe walking race

**竟** jìng ① finish; complete: 未～之业 unaccomplished

cause; unfinished task ② throughout; whole: ～夜 the whole night; throughout the night ③ in the end; eventually: 有志者事～成。Where there's a will there's a way. ④〈副〉〔表示有点出于意料之外〕unexpectedly; actually: 这么陡的峭壁，谁知他～爬上去了。Who would have expected that he could climb up that steep cliff? ⑤〈副〉go so far as to; go to the length of; have the impudence (或 effrontery) to

【竟敢】jìnggǎn have the audacity; have the impertinence; dare: 敌人～如此嚣张，我们不能不予以回击。When the enemy is on the rampage like this, we've got to hit back.

【竟然】jìngrán 〈副〉① unexpectedly; to one's surprise; actually: 这样宏伟的建筑，～只用十个月的时间就完成了。To think that such a magnificent building was completed in ten months!/ 想不到他们～把一座荒山变成了花果山。Who would have thought that they could turn a barren hill into an orchard? ② go so far as to; go to the length of; have the impudence (或 effrontery) to: ～不顾事实 go so far as to disregard the facts

## 敬

jìng ① respect: 尊～ respect; esteem; honour/ 致～ pay one's respects; salute ② respectfully: ～请光临 request the honour of your presence ③ offer politely: ～烟 offer a cigarette/ ～茶 serve tea/ ～你一杯! To your health!

【敬爱】jìng'ài respect and love: ～的领袖 esteemed (或 respected) and beloved leader; beloved leader

【敬辞】jìngcí term of respect; polite expression

【敬而远之】jìng ér yuǎn zhī stay at a respectful distance from sb.

【敬奉】jìngfèng ① piously worship ② offer respectfully; present politely

【敬酒】jìngjiǔ propose a toast; toast

【敬酒不吃吃罚酒】jìngjiǔ bù chī chī fájiǔ refuse a toast only to drink a forfeit — submit to sb.'s pressure after first turning down his request; be constrained to do what one at first declined

【敬老院】jìnglǎoyuàn home of respect for the aged; old folks' home

【敬礼】jìnglǐ ① salute; give a salute ② extend one's greetings: 向你们致以革命的～ extend to you our revolutionary greetings ③〈敬〉〔用于书信结尾〕: 此致～ with high respect; with best wishes

【敬佩】jìngpèi esteem; admire: 我们对第三世界人民的英勇斗争，深表～。We deeply esteem the people of the third world for their heroic struggle./ 大家以～的目光望着他。Everybody looked at him admiringly.

【敬挽】jìngwǎn 〔用于挽联、花圈等的落款〕with deep condolences from sb.

【敬畏】jìngwèi hold in awe and veneration; revere

【敬谢不敏】jìng xiè bù mǐn 〈套〉beg to be excused

【敬仰】jìngyǎng revere; venerate: 深受人民的爱戴和～ command deep love and reverence among the people

【敬意】jìngyì respect; tribute: 表示衷心的～ extend one's heartfelt respects; pay sincere tribute

【敬重】jìngzhòng deeply respect; revere; honour: 大家都十分～这位老红军战士。We all have great respect for the veteran Red Army man.

## 靖

jìng ① peace; tranquillity ② pacify: ～乱 put down a rebellion

## 境

jìng ① border; boundary: 国～ national boundary/ 在本省～内 within the boundaries of this province/ 越～ cross the border illegally ② place; area; territory: 敌～ enemy territory/ 如入无人之～ like entering an unpeopled land — meeting no resistance ③ condition; situation; circumstances: 困～ difficult position; predicament

【境地】jìngdì condition; circumstances: 处于狼狈的～ be in a sorry plight; be in a predicament/ 陷入完全孤立的～ land oneself in utter isolation

【境界】jìngjiè ① boundary ② extent reached; plane attained; state; realm: 达到崇高的思想～ attain a lofty realm of thought/ 理想～ ideal state; ideal

【境况】jìngkuàng condition; circumstances: ～不佳 in straitened circumstances

【境域】jìngyù ① condition; circumstances ② area; realm: 大同～ the realm of Great Harmony

【境遇】jìngyù circumstances; one's lot: 极困难的～ extremely adverse circumstances

## 静

jìng still; quiet; calm: 风平浪～ calm and tranquil/ 夜深人～ in the still of the night; at the dead of night/ 请～一～。Please be quiet.

【静电】jìngdiàn static electricity
◇ ～除尘器 electrostatic precipitator/ ～纺纱 electrostatic spinning/ ～感应 electrostatic induction/ ～荷 electrostatic charge/ ～计 electrometer/ ～学 electrostatics/ ～印刷〈印〉xerography

【静荷载】jìnghèzài 〈建〉dead load

【静力学】jìnglìxué 〈物〉statics: 气体～ aerostatics

【静脉】jìngmài 〈生理〉vein
◇ ～滴注法 intravenous drip/ ～曲张〈医〉varix; varicosity/ ～炎 phlebitis/ ～注射 intravenous injection

【静谧】jìngmì 〈书〉quiet; still; tranquil

【静默】jìngmò ① become silent: 会场上又是一阵～。Another spell of silence fell upon the meeting room. ② mourn in silence; observe silence: 为悼念革命先烈，全体起立，～致哀。All rose in silent tribute to the memory of the revolutionary martyrs.

【静穆】jìngmù solemn and quiet

【静悄悄】jìngqiāoqiāo very quiet: 屋子里～的。It was very quiet in the room.

【静态】jìngtài 〈物〉static state
◇ ～电阻 static resistance/～平衡 static equilibrium/ ～特性 static characteristic

【静物】jìngwù still life ◇～画 still life

【静养】jìngyǎng rest quietly to recuperate; convalesce: 希望你安心～。I hope you'll set aside your worries and have a good rest.

【静止】jìngzhǐ static; motionless; at a standstill: 相对～的状态 a state of relative rest/ 生活永远不是～的。Life is never at a standstill./ 形而上学宇宙观用孤立的、～的和片面的观点去看世界。The metaphysical world outlook sees things as isolated, static and one-sided.

【静坐】jìngzuò ① sit quietly ② sit still as a form of therapy
◇ ～罢工 sit-down (strike)/ ～示威 sit-in (demonstration); sit-down (protest)

## 镜

jìng ① looking glass; mirror: 铜～ bronze mirror/ 湖平如～。The lake is as smooth as a mirror. ② lens; glass: 放大～ magnifying glass; magnifier/ 墨～ sunglasses

【镜花水月】jìnghuā-shuǐyuè flowers in a mirror or the moon in the water — an illusion

【镜框】jìngkuàng ① picture frame ② spectacles frame

【镜片】jìngpiàn lens

【镜台】jìngtái dressing table

【镜头】jìngtóu ① camera lens: 远摄～ telephoto lens/ 可变焦距～ zoom lens/广角～ wide-angle lens ② shot; scene: 特技～ special effect shot; trick shot/ 特写～ close-up/ 伪装～ process shot

【镜匣】 jìngxiá a wooden case with a looking glass and other toilet articles; dressing case
【镜象】 jìngxiàng 〈物〉 mirror image
【镜子】 jìngzi ① mirror; looking glass ② 〈口〉 glasses; spectacles

## jiōng

**垧** jiōng 〈书〉 outermost suburbs
**扃** jiōng ① a bolt or hook for fastening a door from outside ② shut a door

## jiǒng

**迥** jiǒng 〈书〉 ① far away ② widely different: 他病前病后～若两人。He doesn't look like the same person after his illness.
【迥然】 jiǒngrán far apart; widely different: ～不同 utterly different; not in the least alike
**炯** jiǒng bright; shining
【炯炯】 jiǒngjiǒng 〈书〉 (of eyes) bright; shining: 他的一双眼睛～有神。He has a pair of bright piercing eyes.
**窘** jiǒng ① in straitened circumstances; hard up: 他一度生活很～。He was rather hard up for a time. ② awkward; embarrassed; ill at ease: 露出～态 show signs of embarrassment ③ embarrass; disconcert: 这个问题～得他无言可答。The question embarrassed him so much that he was quite at a loss for an answer.
【窘境】 jiǒngjìng awkward situation; predicament; plight
【窘迫】 jiǒngpò ① poverty-stricken; very poor: 生活～ live in poverty ② hard pressed; embarrassed; in a predicament: 处境～ find oneself in a predicament

## jiū

**纠** jiū ① entangle: ～缠 get entangled (或 bogged down) ② gather together: ～合一伙流氓 get together (或 round up) a bunch of hoodlums ③ correct; rectify: ～偏 rectify a deviation/ 有反必肃,有错必～。Counterrevolutionaries must be eliminated wherever found, mistakes must be corrected whenever discovered.
【纠察】 jiūchá ① maintain order at a public gathering ② picket ◇ ～队 pickets/ ～线 picket line
【纠缠】 jiūchán ① get entangled; be in a tangle: ～不清 too tangled up to unravel/ 防止在枝节问题上～不休 avoid endless quibbling over side issues/ 完成侦察任务要紧,不要与敌人～。Be sure to accomplish your scouting mission; don't get tied down by the enemy. ② nag; worry; pester: 他忙着呢,别～他了。He's busy. Stop pestering him.
【纠纷】 jiūfēn dispute; issue: 无原则～ an unprincipled dispute/ 国与国之间的～ disputes between countries/ 调解～ mediate an issue
【纠葛】 jiūgé entanglement; dispute: 他们之间发生了一点～。There's a dispute between them.
【纠集】 jiūjí 〈贬〉 get together; muster: ～一批打手 gather together a bunch of thugs/ ～残部 muster the remaining forces
【纠偏】 jiūpiān rectify a deviation; correct an error
【纠正】 jiūzhèng correct; put right; redress: ～错误 correct a mistake; redress an error/ ～姿势 correct sb.'s posture/ ～不正之风 check unhealthy tendencies/ 问题处理不当的,应予～。Cases which have not been handled properly should be put right.
**究** jiū ① study carefully; go into; investigate: 深～ go deeply into a matter; get to the bottom of a matter/ ～其根源 trace sth. to its source ② 〈书〉 actually; really; after all: ～应如何办理? How should this really be dealt with?/ ～系何因,尚待深查。The actual cause awaits further investigation.
【究办】 jiūbàn investigate and deal with: 依法～ investigate and deal with according to law
【究竟】 jiūjìng ① outcome; what actually happened: 大家都想知道个～。Everybody wants to know what actually happened./ 不管什么事,他总爱问个～。He always likes to get to the heart of a matter, whatever it may be. ② 〈副〉〔用于问句,表示追究〕 actually; exactly: 明天的会～谁去参加? Who is actually going to the meeting tomorrow?/ 你们～要什么? What exactly do you want?/ 这～是什么意思? Whatever does this mean?/ 他～上哪儿去了? Where on earth is he? ③ 〈副〉〔表示毕竟,到底〕 after all; in the end: 他～经验丰富,让他负责这项工作最合适。After all, he is very experienced, so it is only suitable to put him in charge of the job.
**鸠** jiū turtledove: 绿～ green pigeon
**赳** jiū
【赳赳】 jiūjiū valiant; gallant: 雄～ valiant; gallant
**阄** jiū lot: 抓～ draw lots/ 拈～决定 decide by lot
**揪** jiū ① hold tight; seize: ～住一个小偷 grab a thief/ 他承认了错误,就不要再～住不放。Now that he has admitted his mistake, we should not keep picking on him. ② pull; tug; drag: 别那么使劲～绳子。Don't pull so hard at the rope.
【揪辫子】 jiū biànzi seize sb.'s queue — seize upon sb.'s mistakes or shortcomings
【揪出】 jiūchū uncover; ferret out: ～暗藏的反革命分子 uncover (或 ferret out) hidden counterrevolutionaries
【揪痧】 jiūshā 〈中医〉 a popular treatment for sunstroke or other febrile diseases by repeatedly pinching the patient's neck, etc. to achieve congestion
【揪心】 jiūxīn 〈方〉 ① anxious; worried: 小杨到现在还没有回来,真叫人～。Xiao Yang's still not back. I'm really getting worried. ② heartrending; agonizing; gnawing: 伤口痛得～。There was a gnawing pain from the wound.
**啾** jiū
【啾啾】 jiūjiū 〈象〉〔形容许多小鸟一起叫的声音〕 chirps
**鬏** jiū bun; knot; chignon

## jiǔ

**九** jiǔ ① nine: ～车间 No. 9 Workshop/ ～连 the Ninth Company ② each of the nine nine-day periods beginning from the day after the Winter Solstice: 三～ the third nine-day period after the Winter Solstice; the coldest days of winter ③ many; numerous: 三弯～转 many twists and turns/ ～曲桥 a zigzag bridge

【九宫格儿】 jiǔgōnggér squared paper for practising Chinese calligraphy
【九归】 jiǔguī rules for doing division with a one-digit divisor on the abacus
【九级风】 jiǔjífēng 〈气〉 force 9 wind; strong gale
【九节狸】 jiǔjiélí 〈动〉 zibet; large Indian civet
【九九表】 jiǔjiǔbiǎo multiplication table
【九九归一】 jiǔ jiǔ guī yī when all is said and done; in the last analysis; after all: ～,还是他的话对。All things considered, what he says is right.
【九牛二虎之力】 jiǔ niú èr hǔ zhī lì the strength of nine bulls and two tigers — tremendous effort: 我们费了～才找到这种矿石。We found this ore only after great effort.
【九牛一毛】 jiǔ niú yī máo a single hair out of nine ox hides — a drop in the ocean
【九泉】 jiǔquán 〈书〉 grave; the nether world: ～之下 in the nether regions; after death
【九死一生】 jiǔ sǐ yī shēng a narrow escape from death
【九天】 jiǔtiān the Ninth Heaven; the highest of heavens
【九霄云外】 jiǔxiāo yúnwài beyond the highest heavens: 把个人安危抛到～ cast personal safety to the winds; totally disregard one's safety
【九一八事变】 Jiǔ Yībā Shìbiàn the September 18th Incident (the seizure of Shenyang in 1931 by the Japanese invaders, as a step towards their occupation of the entire Northeast)
【九月】 jiǔyuè ① September ② the ninth month of the lunar year; the ninth moon
【九州】 Jiǔzhōu ① a poetic name for China ② Kyushu

**久** jiǔ ① for a long time; long: 很～以前 long ago/ ～经考验的革命战士 a long-tested revolutionary fighter/ ～别重逢 meet after a long separation ② of a specified duration: 两个月之～ for as long as two months/ 来了有多～? How long have you been here?
【久病成医】 jiǔ bìng chéng yī 〈谚〉 prolonged illness makes a doctor of a patient
【久而久之】 jiǔ ér jiǔ zhī in the course of time; as time passes: 只要你注意搜集,～,资料就丰富了。If you keep on collecting, in time you'll have a wealth of data.
【久旱逢甘雨】 jiǔ hàn féng gānyǔ have a welcome rain after a long drought — have a long-felt need satisfied
【久航高度】 jiǔháng gāodù 〈航空〉 altitude for maximum endurance
【久航速度】 jiǔháng sùdù 〈航空〉 speed for maximum endurance
【久假不归】 jiǔ jiǎ bù guī put off indefinitely returning sth. one has borrowed; appropriate sth. borrowed for one's own use
【久久】 jiǔjiǔ for a long, long time: 社员们把医疗队送到村口,～不肯回去。The commune members stood for a long time at the edge of the village waving good-bye to the medical team./ 老支书的话～地回响在我的耳边。The old Party secretary's words were still ringing in my ears long after he said them.
【久违】 jiǔwéi 〈套〉 how long it is since we last met; I haven't seen you for ages
【久仰】 jiǔyǎng 〈套〉 I've long been looking forward to meeting you; I'm very pleased to meet you
【久远】 jiǔyuǎn far back; ages ago; remote: 年代～ of the remote past; age-old; time-honoured

**玖** jiǔ nine (used for the numeral 九 on cheques, etc., to avoid mistakes or alterations)

**灸** jiǔ 〈中医〉 moxibustion

**韭** jiǔ fragrant-flowered garlic; (Chinese) chives: 青～ young chives; chive seedlings
【韭菜】 jiǔcài fragrant-flowered garlic; (Chinese) chives
【韭黄】 jiǔhuáng hotbed chives

**酒** jiǔ alcoholic drink; wine; liquor; spirits
【酒吧间】 jiǔbājiān bar; barroom
【酒菜】 jiǔcài food and drink; food to go with wine or liquor
【酒厂】 jiǔchǎng brewery; winery; distillery
【酒店】 jiǔdiàn wineshop; public house
【酒馆】 jiǔguǎn public house
【酒鬼】 jiǔguǐ ① drunkard; sot ② toper; wine bibber
【酒壶】 jiǔhú wine pot; flagon
【酒花】 jiǔhuā 〈植〉 hops
【酒会】 jiǔhuì cocktail party
【酒家】 jiǔjiā wineshop; restaurant
【酒窖】 jiǔjiào wine cellar
【酒精】 jiǔjīng ethyl alcohol; alcohol ◇ ～比重计 spirit gauge/ ～灯 spirit lamp; alcohol burner
【酒量】 jiǔliàng capacity for liquor: 他～很大。He's a heavy drinker. 或 He can hold a lot of liquor.
【酒令】 jiǔlìng drinkers' wager game
【酒母】 jiǔmǔ distiller's yeast
【酒囊饭袋】 jiǔnáng-fàndài wine skin and rice bag — a good-for-nothing
【酒酿】 jiǔniáng fermented glutinous rice 又作"酒娘"
【酒器】 jiǔqì drinking vessel
【酒麴】 jiǔqū distiller's yeast
【酒肉朋友】 jiǔròu péngyou wine-and-meat friends; fair-weather friends
【酒石酸】 jiǔshísuān tartaric acid ◇ ～锑钾 〈药〉 antimony potassium tartrate
【酒食】 jiǔshí food and drink
【酒徒】 jiǔtú wine bibber
【酒窝】 jiǔwō dimple
【酒席】 jiǔxí feast
【酒药】 jiǔyào yeast for brewing rice wine or fermenting glutinous rice
【酒意】 jiǔyì a tipsy feeling: 已有几分～ be slightly tipsy; be mellow
【酒糟】 jiǔzāo distillers' grains
【酒糟鼻】 jiǔzāobí acne rosacea; brandy nose
【酒盅】 jiǔzhōng a small handleless wine cup 又作"酒钟"

## jiù

**旧** jiù ① past; bygone; old: ～社会 the old society/ ～思想 old way of thinking; timeworn ideas/ ～事重提 bring up a matter of the past/ ～的传统观念 outdated conventional ideas/ 破～俗,立新风 do away with old customs and introduce new ones/ ～貌变新颜 new scenes replacing the old ② used; worn; old: ～衣服 used (或 old) clothes/ 买～的 buy sth. secondhand ③ former; onetime: ～都 former capital ④ old friendship; old friend: 故～ old acquaintances
【旧案】 jiù'àn ① a court case of long standing ② old regulations; former practice
【旧病复发】 jiùbìng fù fā have a recurrence of an old illness; have a relapse
【旧地重游】 jiùdì chóng yóu revisit a once familiar place
【旧都】 jiùdū former capital
【旧恶】 jiù'è old grievance; old wrong: 不念～ forgive an

old wrong
【旧观】 jiùguān former appearance; old look: 迥非～ entirely different from what it used to be/ 那个养猪场由于实现了机械化自动化而一改～。With mechanization and automation, that pig farm has taken on a completely new look.
【旧恨新仇】 jiùhèn-xīnchóu new hatred piled on old: 看到这个地主分子搞破坏，我～一齐涌上心头。At the sight of the damage done by the landlord, I was filled with fresh hatred.
【旧货】 jiùhuò secondhand goods; junk: 我买的是～。I bought it secondhand. ◇ ～店 secondhand shop; junk shop/ ～市场 flea market
【旧交】 jiùjiāo old acquaintance
【旧金山】 Jiùjīnshān San Francisco
【旧居】 jiùjū former residence; old home
【旧历】 jiùlì the old Chinese calendar; the lunar calendar
【旧民主主义革命】 jiù-mínzhǔzhǔyì gémìng democratic revolution of the old type
【旧日】 jiùrì former days; old days
【旧诗】 jiùshī old-style poetry; classical poetry 参见"古体诗"gǔtǐshī;"近体诗"jìntǐshī
【旧石器时代】 jiùshíqì shídài the Old Stone Age; the Paleolithic Period
【旧时】 jiùshí old times; old days
【旧式】 jiùshì old type: ～文人 old-type scholars
【旧书】 jiùshū ① secondhand book; used (或 old) book ② books by ancient writers
【旧学】 jiùxué old Chinese learning (as distinct from the new or Western learning)
【旧约】 Jiùyuē 〈基督教〉 the Old Testament
【旧址】 jiùzhǐ site (of a former organization, building, etc.): 农会～ the site of the former peasant association/ 这是我们机关的～。Here's where our organization used to be.

**臼** jiù ① mortar: 石～ stone mortar ② any mortar-shaped thing ③ joint (of bones): 脱～ dislocation (of joints)
【臼齿】 jiùchǐ molar

**疚** jiù 〈书〉 remorse: 感到内～ have a guilty conscience

**咎** jiù ① fault; blame: 归～于人 lay the blame on sb. else ② censure; punish; blame: 既往不～ forgive sb.'s past misdeeds; let bygones be bygones
【咎由自取】 jiù yóu zì qǔ have only oneself to blame

**柩** jiù a coffin with a corpse in it
【柩车】 jiùchē hearse

**桕** jiù 〈植〉 Chinese tallow tree

**救** jiù ① rescue; save; salvage: 只有社会主义能够～中国。Only socialism can save China./ 他跳进急流，把孩子～了出来。He jumped into the torrent and rescued the child from drowning./ 病人得～了。The patient was saved./ 呼～ call out for help; send out SOS signals ② help; relieve; succour: 生产自～ tide over a disaster by production/ ～荒 send relief to a famine area; help to tide over a crop failure
【救兵】 jiùbīng relief troops; reinforcements
【救国】 jiùguó save the nation: 上中学时，他就参加了抗日～运动。As a middle-school student he joined in the movement to resist Japanese aggression and save the country.
【救护】 jiùhù relieve a sick or injured person; give first-aid; rescue: ～伤员 give first-aid to the wounded/ 奋勇～战友 valiantly go to the rescue of one's comrade-in-arms ◇ ～车 ambulance/ ～船 ambulance ship/ ～队 ambulance corps/ ～飞机 ambulance aircraft/ ～所 medical aid station (或 point)/ ～站 first-aid station
【救活】 jiùhuó bring sb. back to life
【救火】 jiùhuǒ fire fighting
◇ ～车 fire engine/ ～队 fire brigade/ ～队员 fireman; fire fighter
【救急】 jiùjí help sb. to cope with an emergency; help meet an urgent need: 你们支援我们这些材料，可真～了。You gave us this material just when we needed it most.
【救济】 jiùjì relieve; succour: ～灾区人民 provide relief to the people in a disaster area/ 社会～事业 social relief facilities ◇ ～费 relief fund/ ～粮 relief grain; relief food
【救苦救难】 jiùkǔ-jiùnàn help the needy and relieve the distressed
【救命】 jiùmìng save sb.'s life: ～！ Help! ◇ ～稻草 a straw to clutch at/ ～恩人 saviour
【救生】 jiùshēng lifesaving
◇ ～带 life belt/ ～筏 life raft/ ～圈 life buoy/ ～设备 lifesaving appliance; life preserver/ ～艇 lifeboat/ ～衣 life jacket/ ～员 lifeguard; lifesaver
【救世主】 jiùshìzhǔ 〈基督教〉 the Saviour; the Redeemer
【救死扶伤】 jiùsǐ-fúshāng heal the wounded and rescue the dying: ～，实行革命的人道主义。Heal the wounded, rescue the dying, practise revolutionary humanitarianism.
【救亡】 jiùwáng save the nation from extinction: ～图存 save the nation from subjugation and ensure its survival ◇ ～运动 national salvation movement
【救险车】 jiùxiǎnchē wrecking truck; wrecking car
【救星】 jiùxīng liberator; emancipator: 毛主席是全国各族人民的大～。Chairman Mao was the great liberator of the people of all our nationalities./ 来了～共产党，人民翻身得解放。With the coming of their emancipator the Communist Party, the people stood up and won liberation.
【救应】 jiùying aid and support; reinforce
【救援】 jiùyuán rescue; come to sb.'s help ◇ ～车 rescue car
【救灾】 jiùzāi provide disaster relief; send relief to a disaster area; help the people tide over a natural disaster
【救治】 jiùzhì bring a patient out of danger; treat and cure: 大批医务人员奔赴灾区～伤病员。Large numbers of medical workers hurried to the disaster area to give treatment to the sick and wounded.
【救助】 jiùzhù help sb. in danger or difficulty; succour

**厩** jiù stable; cattle-shed; pen
【厩肥】 jiùféi 〈农〉 barnyard manure

**就** jiù ① come near; move towards: 大家～拢来烤火取暖。They all moved towards the fire to get warm./ ～着路灯下棋 play chess by the light of a street lamp ② undertake; engage in; enter upon: ～学 go to school/ ～席 take one's seat; be seated at the table ③ accomplish; make: 功成业～ (of a person's career) be crowned with success/ 这个鼎是青铜铸～的。This tripod is made of bronze. ④ accomodate oneself to; suit; fit: 我反正有空，～你的时间吧。Make it anytime that suits you; I'm always free./ 只好～这块料子做了。We'll have to make do with the little material we've got. ⑤ go with: 炒鸡蛋～饭 have some scrambled eggs to go with the rice ⑥ with regard to; concerning; on: ～我所知 so far as I know/ 双方～共同关心的问题进行了会谈。The two sides held talks on questions of common interest./ 团长～冬训计划作了简要说明。The regiment commander gave a brief explanation of the plan for winter training. ⑦〈副〉at once; right away: 我这～去。I'll be going right away./ 一会儿～得。It'll be ready in a minute. ⑧〈副〉as early as; already: 他一九三六年～参加革命了。He joined the revolutionary ranks as early as 1936. ⑨〈副〉as soon as; right after: 他们放下行李卷儿，～奔工地去了。They started for the construction site as soon as they put their packs down. /说干～干 act without delay ⑩〈副〉as much as; as many as: 光回收废品一项，他们～给国家节约了二万元。Just by collecting scrap, they saved as much as 20,000 *yuan* for the state. ⑪〈副〉〔表示在某种条件或情况下自然会怎样〕: 没有革命的理论，～不会有革命的运动。Without revolutionary theory there can be no revolutionary movement./ 不经过艰苦奋斗，～不能胜利。We cannot be victorious without arduous struggle. ⑫〈副〉〔放在两个相同的成分之间，表示容忍〕: 丢了～丢了吧，以后小心点。If it's lost, it's lost. Just be more careful from now on. ⑬〈副〉〔表示原来或早已是这样〕: 我～料到他会等我们的。I knew he'd be waiting for us./ 我本来～不懂法语。I never said I knew any French. ⑭〈副〉only; merely; just: ～这一本了，看完请马上还。This is the only copy left. Please return it as soon as you finish reading it./ ～等你一个了。You're the only one we're waiting for./ 我～要几张纸。I just want a few sheets of paper. ⑮〈副〉〔表示坚决〕: 我～不信我们妇女干不了这一行。I just wouldn't believe that we women couldn't do this sort of work./ 他～不肯歇一歇。He simply refused to take a rest. ⑯〈副〉exactly; precisely: 我～要这只。This is the one I want./ 医务室～在这儿。This is where the clinic is. ⑰〈连〉even if: 你～不说，我也会知道。Even if you won't tell me, I'll know anyway.

【就伴】 jiùbàn accompany sb. (on a journey); travel together

【就便】 jiùbiàn at sb.'s convenience; while you're at it: ～也替我买一本。While you're about it, buy me a copy too.

【就此】 jiùcǐ at this point; here and now; thus: 讨论～结束。The discussion was thus brought to a close./ 工作虽然有了一点成绩，但不能～松懈下来。It's true that we have accomplished something, but this doesn't mean we can let up now.

【就地】 jiùdì on the spot: ～解决问题 settle the problem on the spot/ 将敌人～歼灭 wipe out the enemy on the spot ◇ ～视察〈军〉on-site-inspection

【就地取材】 jiùdì qǔcái use local materials; draw on local resources

【就范】 jiùfàn submit; give in: 迫使～ compel sb. to submit/ 不肯～ refuse to submit to control; refuse to give in

【就近】 jiùjìn (do or get sth.) nearby; in the neighbourhood; without having to go far: ～找个住处 find accommodation in the neighbourhood/ 现在村里有了中学，青年们都能～上学。Now that the village has its own middle school, the youngsters don't have to go far to attend classes.

【就寝】 jiùqǐn〈书〉retire for the night; go to bed

【就让】 jiùràng〈口〉even if: ～他来，也晚了。Even if he comes it will be too late.

【就任】 jiùrèn take up one's post; take office

【就势】 jiùshì making use of momentum: 对手扑过来，我～把他摔倒在地。As my opponent threw himself at me, I made use of his momentum to fling him to the ground.

【就事论事】 jiù shì lùn shì consider sth. as it stands: 我不清楚这件事的背景，只能～地谈谈。As I don't know the whole background, I can only judge the case as it stands.

【就是】 jiùshì ①〔用在句末表示肯定，多加"了"〕: 放心吧，我照办～了。Don't worry. I promise to do just as you say. ② quite right; exactly; precisely: ～嘛，我也是这么想的。Precisely. That's just what I had in mind. ③〈连〉〔下半句常用"也"呼应〕 even if; even: ～天塌下来我们也顶得住。Even if the sky falls, we'll be able to hold it up.

【就是说】 jiùshìshuō that is to say; in other words; namely

【就手】 jiùshǒu while you're at it: 你～把我的信件也带来吧。Please get my mail as well while you're at it./ ～把门关上。Close the door behind you.

【就算】 jiùsuàn〈口〉even if; granted that: ～你工作干得不错，也不应该骄傲吧。Granted you have not done badly, still there is no reason to be conceited.

【就位】 jiùwèi take one's place

【就绪】 jiùxù be in order; be ready: 一切都已～。Everything is ready (或 in order)./ 准备工作已经大致～。The preparations are more or less completed.

【就要】 jiùyào be about to; be going to; be on the point of: 火车～开了。The train is about to start. 或 The train is starting in a minute.

【就业】 jiùyè obtain employment; take up an occupation; get a job: 充分～ full employment/ ～不足 underemployment

【就医】 jiùyī seek medical advice; go to a doctor

【就义】 jiùyì be executed for championing a just cause; die a martyr: 英勇～ face execution bravely; die a hero's death

【就正】 jiùzhèng solicit comments (on one's writing): ～于读者 request (或 invite) the readers to offer their criticisms

【就职】 jiùzhí assume office: 宣誓～ take the oath of office; be sworn in ◇ ～典礼 inaugural ceremony; inauguration/ ～演说 inaugural speech

【就座】 jiùzuò take one's seat; be seated: 在主席台前列～的有… seated in the front row on the rostrum were…/ 贵宾们依次～。The honoured guests took their seats in due order.

**舅** jiù ① mother's brother; uncle ② wife's brother; brother-in-law ③〈书〉husband's father

【舅父】 jiùfù mother's brother; uncle

【舅舅】 jiùjiu〈口〉见"舅父"

【舅妈】 jiùmā〈口〉见"舅母"

【舅母】 jiùmǔ wife of mother's brother; aunt

【舅子】 jiùzi〈口〉wife's brother; brother-in-law

**鹫** jiù vulture

## jū

**车** jū chariot, one of the pieces in Chinese chess
另见 chē

**拘** jū ① arrest; detain ② restrain; restrict; limit; constrain: 无～无束 unconstrained; free and easy/ 长短不～ with no limit on the length ③ inflexible: ～泥 be a stickler for (form, etc.); rigidly adhere to (formalities, etc.)

【拘捕】 jūbǔ arrest

【拘谨】 jūjǐn overcautious; reserved: 初次见面时，他有些～，不大爱说话。At the first meeting he was rather reserved and withdrawn.

【拘禁】 jūjìn take into custody

【拘礼】 jūlǐ be punctilious; stand on ceremony: 熟不～ be too familiar with each other to stand on ceremony

【拘留】 jūliú detain; hold in custody; intern ◇ ～所 house of detention; lockup

【拘泥】 jūni be a stickler for (form, etc.); rigidly adhere to (formalities, etc.): ～于形式 rigidly adhere to form; be formalistic/ ～于细节 be very punctilious

【拘票】 jūpiào arrest warrant; warrant

【拘束】 jūshù ① restrain; restrict: 不要～孩子们的正当活动。Don't restrict the proper activities of children. ② constrained; awkward; ill at ease: 在生人面前显得～ look ill at ease in the presence of strangers/ 不要～。Make yourself at home.

【拘押】 jūyā take into custody

**狙** jū

【狙击】 jūjī snipe ◇ ～手 sniper/ ～战 sniping action

**居** jū ① reside; dwell; live: 侨～国外 reside abroad/ 穴～ live in caves ② residence; house: 故～ former residence/ 迁～ move house; change one's residence ③ be (in a certain position); occupy (a place): ～中 be in the middle/ ～世界首位 occupy first place in the world; rank first in the world/ 身～要职 hold an important post ④ claim; assert: 以专家自～ claim to be an expert; be a self-styled expert ⑤ store up; lay by: 囤积～奇 hoarding and profiteering ⑥ stay put; be at a standstill: 岁月不～。Time marches on. ⑦ (Jū) a surname

【居安思危】 jū ān sī wēi be prepared for danger in times of peace; be vigilant in peace time

【居多】 jūduō be in the majority: 我们球队里北方人～。Most of the players in our team are northerners.

【居高临下】 jū gāo lín xià occupy a commanding position (或 height)

【居功】 jūgōng claim credit for oneself: ～自傲 claim credit for oneself and become arrogant

【居间】 jūjiān (mediate) between two parties: ～调停 mediate between two parties; act as mediator ◇ ～人 intermediary; mediator

【居里】 jūlǐ 〈物〉 curie

【居留】 jūliú reside: 长期～ permanent residence ◇ ～权 right of residence/ ～证 residence permit

【居民】 jūmín resident; inhabitant ◇ ～点 residential area/ ～委员会 neighbourhood (或 residents') committee

【居然】 jūrán 〈副〉 ① unexpectedly; to one's surprise: 这么重的担子，他～挑着走了二十里。Who would have thought he could carry such a heavy load for 20 *li*? ② go so far as to; have the impudence (或 effrontery) to: ～当面撒谎 go so far as to tell a bare-faced lie/ 你怎么～相信这种谣言？How could you believe such a rumour?

【居士】 jūshì lay Buddhist

【居心】 jūxīn harbour (evil) intentions: ～不良 harbour evil intentions/ 他们～何在？What are they up to?

【居中】 jūzhōng ① (mediate) between two parties: ～斡旋 mediate between disputants ② be placed in the middle: 小标题一律～。Subheads should be placed in the middle of the column. 或 Centre the subheads.

【居住】 jūzhù live; reside; dwell: 他家一直～在乡下。His family have always lived in the country./ 苗族～地区 a region inhabited by the Miao nationality
◇ ～面积 living space; floor space/ ～期限 length of residence/ ～条件 housing conditions

**驹** jū ① colt ② foal: 怀～ be in (或 with) foal

【驹子】 jūzi foal

**疽** jū 〈中医〉 subcutaneous ulcer; deep-rooted ulcer

**掬** jū hold with both hands: 以手～水 scoop up some water with one's hands/ 笑容可～ radiant with smiles/ 憨态可～ charmingly naive

**据** jū 见"拮据" jiéjū
另见 jù

**锔** jū mend (crockery) with cramps
另见 jú

【锔子】 jūzi a cramp used in mending crockery

**趄** jū 见"趑趄" zījū
另见 qiè

**裾** jū 〈书〉 ① the full front of a Chinese gown ② the full front and back of a Chinese gown

【裾礁】 jūjiāo 〈地〉 fringing reef; shore reef

**鞠** jū ① rear; bring up: ～养 bring up ② (Jū) a surname

【鞠躬】 jūgōng ① bow: ～致谢 bow one's thanks/ 深深地鞠一个躬 make a deep bow; bow low ② 〈书〉 in a discreet and scrupulous manner

【鞠躬尽瘁】 jūgōng jìn cuì bend oneself to a task and exert oneself to the utmost; spare no effort in the performance of one's duty: ～，死而后已 bend one's back to the task until one's dying day; give one's all till one's heart stops beating

## jú

**局** jú ① chessboard ② game; set; innings: 第一～(乒乓球等) the first game; the first set; (板球、棒球、垒球) the first innings/ 下一～棋 play a game of chess ③ situation; state of affairs: 战～ the war situation/ 全～ the overall situation; the situation as a whole ④ largeness or smallness of mind; extent of one's tolerance of others: 有～度 be large-minded; be tolerant/ ～量不能容物 not tolerant of others ⑤ 〈旧〉 gathering: 饭～ a dinner party; a banquet ⑥ ruse; trap: 骗～ fraud; trap; swindle ⑦ limit; confine ⑧ part; portion ⑨ office; bureau: 邮～ post office/ 粮食～ grain bureau/ 电话～ telephone exchange ⑩ shop: 书～ publishing house

【局部】 júbù part: ～必须服从全局。The part must be subordinated to the whole./ 不能只顾～和眼前。One mustn't be concerned only with the partial and the immediate.
◇ ～地区 some areas; parts of an area/ ～利益 partial and local interests/ ～麻醉 local anaesthesia/ ～战争 local war; partial war

【局促】 júcù ① narrow; cramped: 这地方～，走动不便。This place is rather cramped; there's little room for free movement. ② 〈方〉 (of time) short: 三天太～，恐怕办不成。I'm afraid three days is not long enough for us to get it done. ③ feel or show constraint: ～不安 ill at ease

【局面】 júmiàn aspect; phase; situation: 出现了崭新的～。Things have taken on a new aspect./ 打开～ open up a new prospect; make a breakthrough

【局势】 júshì situation: 国际～ the international situation/ 紧张～ a tense situation; tension

【局外人】 júwàirén outsider

【局限】 júxiàn limit; confine: 颇有～ be rather limited (in outlook, etc.); have many limitations/ 由于时代和阶级地位的～ owing to the limitations of the times and one's class status/ 他的报告不～于教学法问题。His talk wasn't confined to teaching methods. ◇ ～性 limitations

**桔** jú 见"橘" jú

另见 jié

# 菊

jú chrysanthemum

【菊花】 júhuā chrysanthemum

【菊科】 júkē 〈植〉 the composite family

【菊石】 júshí 〈地〉 ammonite

【菊芋】 júyù 〈植〉 Jerusalem artichoke

# 锔

jú 〈化〉 curium (Cm)

另见 jū

# 橘

jú tangerine

【橘红】 júhóng ① tangerine (colour); reddish orange ② 〈中药〉 dried tangerine peel

【橘黄】 júhuáng orange (colour)

【橘络】 júluò 〈中药〉 tangerine pith

【橘汁】 júzhī orange juice

【橘子】 júzi tangerine

## jǔ

# 沮

jǔ ① 〈书〉 stop; prevent: ～其成行 stop sb. from going ② turn gloomy; turn glum

【沮丧】 jǔsàng dejected; depressed; dispirited; disheartened: 敌人士气～。The enemy's morale is low.

# 咀

jǔ chew

【咀嚼】 jǔjué ① masticate; chew ② mull over; ruminate; chew the cud

# 举

jǔ ① lift; raise; hold up: 高～马列主义大旗 hold high the great banner of Marxism-Leninism/ ～杯 raise one's glass (to propose a toast) ② act; deed; move: 壮～ a heroic undertaking/ 一～一动 every act and every move; every action ③ start: ～义 rise in revolt ④ elect; choose: 公～他当代表 choose him as representative ⑤ cite; enumerate: 我可以～出好几件事来说明。I can cite quite a few instances to illustrate./ ～不胜～ too numerous to mention ⑥ whole; entire: ～座 all those present

【举哀】 jǔ'āi ① 〈旧〉 wail in mourning ② go into mourning: 宣布全国～三天 declare three days national mourning

【举办】 jǔbàn conduct; hold; run: ～训练班 conduct a training course/ ～学习班 run a study class/ ～展览会 hold (或 put on) an exhibition/ ～音乐会 give a concert

【举措】 jǔcuò move; act: ～失当 make an ill-advised move

【举动】 jǔdòng movement; move; act; activity: ～缓慢 be slow in movement/ 轻率的～ a rash act

【举凡】 jǔfán 〈书〉 ranging from...to...; all...such as

【举国】 jǔguó the whole nation: ～欢腾。The whole nation is jubilant./ ～上下团结一致。There is solid unity throughout the nation./ 得到～一致的支持 enjoy nationwide support/ ～一致的愿望 the unanimous aspiration of the nation

【举火】 jǔhuǒ 〈书〉 ① light a fire: ～为号 light a beacon ② light a kitchen fire; light a stove

【举荐】 jǔjiàn recommend (a person)

【举例】 jǔlì give an example: ～说明 illustrate with examples

【举目】 jǔmù 〈书〉 raise the eyes; look: ～四望 look round/ ～远眺 look into the distance/ ～无亲 have no one to turn to (for help); be a stranger in a strange land

【举棋不定】 jǔ qí bù dìng hesitate about (或 over) what move to make; be unable to make up one's mind; vacillate; shilly-shally

【举人】 jǔrén a successful candidate in the imperial examinations at the provincial level in the Ming and Qing dynasties

【举世】 jǔshì throughout the world; universally: ～皆知 known to all/ ～公认 universally acknowledged/ ～瞩目 attract worldwide attention; become the focus of world attention/ ～闻名 of world renown; world-famous/ ～无双 unrivalled; matchless

【举事】 jǔshì 〈书〉 stage an uprising; rise in insurrection

【举手】 jǔshǒu raise (或 put up) one's hand or hands: 赞成的请～。Those in favour please put up their hands./ 举起手来! Hands up! ◇ ～表决 vote by a show of hands/ ～礼 hand salute

【举行】 jǔxíng hold (a meeting, ceremony, etc.): ～会谈 hold talks/ ～宴会 give (或 host) a banquet/ ～罢工 stage a strike/ 大会在人民大会堂～。The congress took place (或 was held) in the Great Hall of the People.

【举一反三】 jǔ yī fǎn sān draw inferences about other cases from one instance

【举止】 jǔzhǐ bearing; manner; mien: ～庄重 deport oneself in a dignified manner; carry oneself with dignity/ ～大方 have poise; have an easy manner; be gentle of mien

【举重】 jǔzhòng weight lifting ◇ ～运动员 weight lifter

【举足轻重】 jǔ zú qīng-zhòng hold the balance; prove decisive: 一支～的力量 a decisive force/ 处于～的地位 occupy a decisive position

# 枸

jǔ

另见 gǒu

【枸橼】 jǔyuán 〈植〉 citron ◇ ～酸 〈化〉 citric acid/ ～酸钠 〈药〉 sodium citrate

# 矩

jǔ ① carpenter's square; square ② rules; regulations ③ 〈物〉 moment: 力～ moment of force/ 动量～ moment of momentum

【矩臂】 jǔbì 〈物〉 moment arm

【矩形】 jǔxíng rectangle

【矩阵】 jǔzhèn 〈数〉 matrix

# 蒟

jǔ

【蒟酱】 jǔjiàng 〈植〉 betel pepper

# 龃

jǔ

【龃龉】 jǔyǔ 〈书〉 the upper and lower teeth not meeting properly — disagreement; discord

# 榉

jǔ 见"山毛榉" shānmáojǔ

# 踽

jǔ

【踽踽】 jǔjǔ 〈书〉 (walk) alone: ～独行 walk alone; walk in solitude

## jù

# 巨

jù huge; tremendous; gigantic: ～款 a huge sum of money/ 山村～变 tremendous changes in a mountain village/ ～幅标语 a huge poster/ ～型运输机 a giant transport plane

【巨擘】 jùbò ① thumb ② authority in a certain field

【巨大】 jùdà huge; tremendous; enormous; gigantic; immense: ～的胜利 a tremendous victory/ ～的力量 tremendous force; immense strength/ ～的工程 a giant project/ ～的规模 a massive scale/ 做出～的努力 make gigantic efforts

【巨额】 jù'é a huge sum: ～投资 huge investments/ ～利润 enormous profits/ ～赤字 huge financial deficits
【巨匠】 jùjiàng 〈书〉 great master; consummate craftsman
【巨流】 jùliú a mighty current: 汇成一股～ converge into a mighty current
【巨轮】 jùlún ① a large wheel: 历史的～ the wheel of history ② a large ship: 远洋～ a large oceangoing ship
【巨人】 jùrén giant; colossus ◇ ～症〈医〉 gigantism
【巨石文化】 jùshí wénhuà 〈考古〉 megalithic culture
【巨头】 jùtóu magnate; tycoon: 金融～ financial magnate
【巨细】 jù-xì big and small: 事无～ all matters, big and small
【巨星】 jùxīng 〈天〉 giant star; giant
【巨著】 jùzhù monumental work: 历史～ a magnum opus of historic significance

**句** jù ① sentence ②〈量〉: 两～诗 two lines of verse/ 我来说几～。Let me say a few words./ 一～话也没说 not utter a word
【句读】 jùdòu the period and the comma; sentences and phrases
【句法】 jùfǎ ① sentence structure ② 〈语〉 syntax
【句号】 jùhào full stop; full point; period (。) (.)
【句型】 jùxíng sentence pattern
【句子】 jùzi sentence ◇ ～成份 sentence element; member of a sentence

**讵** jù 〈书〉〔表示反问〕: ～料天气骤寒。We little expected that the weather would turn cold suddenly.

**拒** jù ① resist; repel: ～敌 resist the enemy; keep the enemy at bay ② refuse; reject: ～不接受 refuse to accept
【拒捕】 jùbǔ resist arrest
【拒付】 jùfù refuse payment; dishonour (a cheque)
【拒谏饰非】 jùjiàn-shìfēi reject representations and gloss over errors
【拒绝】 jùjué ① refuse: ～参加 refuse to participate/ ～发表意见 refuse to comment ② reject; turn down; decline: ～无理要求 turn down (或 reject) unreasonable demands/ ～别人的批评 reject other people's criticism

**苣** jù 见"莴苣" wōju
另见 qǔ

**具** jù ① utensil; tool; implement: 农～ farm tool (或 implement); agricultural implement ② 〈书〉〈量〉: 一～座钟 a desk clock/ 一～尸体 a corpse ③ possess; have: 初～规模 have begun to take shape ④ 〈书〉 provide; furnish: 谨～薄礼 allow me to present to you this trifling gift
【具备】 jùbèi possess; have; be provided with: ～党员条件 be qualified for Party membership
【具结】 jùjié 〈旧〉 sign an undertaking: ～领回失物 sign a receipt for restored lost property
【具名】 jùmíng put one's name to a document, etc.; affix one's signature
【具体】 jùtǐ concrete; specific; particular: 马克思列宁主义的普遍真理同革命的～实践相结合 the integration of the universal truth of Marxism-Leninism with the concrete practice of revolution/ 对于～情况作～的分析 make a concrete analysis of concrete conditions/ ～政策 specific policies/ 她谈得非常～。She spoke in very concrete terms./ ～日期未定。No exact date has been set./ 方案尚待～化。Details of the plan have yet to be worked out. ◇ ～劳动 concrete labour
【具体而微】 jù tǐ ér wēi small but complete; miniature
【具文】 jùwén mere formality; dead letter: 一纸～ a mere scrap of paper
【具有】 jùyǒu possess; have; be provided with: 这场运动～深远的历史意义。The present movement has profound historical significance./ 广州是一座～光荣革命传统的城市。Guangzhou is a city with a glorious revolutionary tradition./ 我们的军队～一往无前的精神。Our army is imbued with an indomitable spirit.

**炬** jù ① torch ② fire: 付之一～ be burnt down; be committed to the flames

**钜** jù 〈书〉 ① hard iron ② hook ③ great; huge

**俱** jù all; complete: 罪证～在。All the evidence of the crime is available.
【俱乐部】 jùlèbù club
【俱全】 jùquán complete in all varieties: 日用百货一应～。Goods for daily use are available in all varieties.

**剧** jù ① theatrical work; drama; play; opera: 独幕～ one-act play/ 粤～ Guangdong opera/ 广播～ radio play ② acute; severe; intense: ～痛 a severe pain/ ～变 a violent (或 drastic) change/ 产量～增 a sharp increase in output/ 病势加～。The patient's condition is getting worse.
【剧本】 jùběn ① drama; play ② script; (电影) scenario; (京剧、歌剧等) libretto: 分镜头～ shooting script ◇ ～创作 play writing; script writing
【剧场】 jùchǎng theatre
【剧烈】 jùliè violent; acute; severe; fierce: ～运动 strenuous exercise/ ～的斗争 a fierce struggle/ ～的对抗 acute antagonism/ ～的社会变动 radical social changes
【剧目】 jùmù a list of plays or operas: 保留～ repertoire
【剧评】 jùpíng a review of a play or opera; dramatic criticism
【剧情】 jùqíng the story (或 plot) of a play or opera: ～简介 synopsis
【剧团】 jùtuán theatrical company; opera troupe; troupe
【剧务】 jùwù ① stage management ② stage manager
【剧院】 jùyuàn theatre
【剧照】 jùzhào stage photo; still
【剧中人】 jùzhōngrén characters in a play or opera; *dramatis personae*
【剧终】 jùzhōng the end; curtain
【剧种】 jùzhǒng type (或 *genre*) of drama
【剧作家】 jùzuòjiā playwright; dramatist

**倨** jù 〈书〉 haughty; arrogant

**惧** jù fear; dread: 毫无所～ not cowed in the least; fearless/ 千难万险何所～? What is there to fear even if untold hardships lie ahead?
【惧内】 jùnèi 〈书〉 henpecked
【惧怕】 jùpà fear; dread
【惧色】 jùsè a look of fear: 面无～ look undaunted

**据** jù ① occupy; seize: ～为己有 take forcible possession of; appropriate ② rely on; depend on: ～险固守 take advantage of a natural barrier to put up a strong defence ③ according to; on the grounds of: ～报道 according to (press) reports; it is reported that/ ～我看 as I see it; in my opinion/ ～我所知 as far as I know/ ～实报告 report the facts; give a factual report/ ～理力争 argue strongly on just grounds/ 只有充分了解具体情况,才能～以

定出正确的政策。Correct policies can be formulated only on the basis of a thorough understanding of the actual situation. ④ evidence; certificate: 查无实～。Investigation reveals no evidence (against the suspect).
另见 jū

【据传】 jùchuán a story is going around that; rumour has it that
【据此】 jùcǐ on these grounds; in view of the above; accordingly
【据点】 jùdiǎn strongpoint; fortified point; stronghold
【据守】 jùshǒu guard; be entrenched in: ～交通要道 guard vital lines of communication; be entrenched in communication centres/ 掘壕～ dig in; entrench oneself
【据说】 jùshuō it is said; they say; allegedly: ～他在那里干得不错。They say he is doing quite well there./ 这场事故～是由于疏忽造成的。The accident was allegedly due to negligence.
【据悉】 jùxī it is reported

**距** jù ① distance: 行～ the distance between rows of plants ② be apart (或 away) from; be at a distance from: 两地相～十里。The two places are 10 *li* apart./ ～今已有十年。That was ten years ago. ③ spur (of a cock, etc.)

【距离】 jùlí ① distance: 保持一个～ keep one's distance; keep at a distance ② be apart (或 away) from; be at a distance from: ～车站十五里 15 *li* from the station/ 我们的工作～人民的要求还很远。What we have done falls far short of the expectations of the people.

**飓** jù

【飓风】 jùfēng hurricane

**锯** jù ① saw: 手～ handsaw/ 圆～ circular saw ② cut with a saw; saw: ～木头 saw wood

【锯齿】 jùchǐ sawtooth
【锯床】 jùchuáng 〈机〉 sawing machine: 圆盘～ circular sawing machine
【锯鳞鱼】 jùlínyú big-eyed soldierfish
【锯末】 jùmò sawdust
【锯木厂】 jùmùchǎng sawmill; lumber-mill
【锯条】 jùtiáo saw blade

**聚** jù assemble; gather; get together: 大家～在一起商量商量。Let's get together and talk it over.

【聚氨酯】 jù'ānzhǐ 〈化〉 polyurethane 又作"聚氨基甲酸酯"
【聚宝盆】 jùbǎopén treasure bowl — a place rich in natural resources; cornucopia
【聚苯乙烯】 jùběn yǐxī 〈化〉 polystyrene
【聚变】 jùbiàn 〈物〉 fusion: 核～ nuclear fusion/ 受控～ controlled fusion ◇ ～反应堆 fusion reactor
【聚丙烯】 jùbǐngxī 〈化〉 polypropylene
【聚丙烯腈】 jùbǐngxījīng 〈化〉 polyacrylonitrile
【聚餐】 jùcān dine together (usu. on festive occasions); have a dinner party
【聚光灯】 jùguāngdēng spotlight
【聚合】 jùhé ① get together ② 〈化〉 polymerization: 定向～ stereoregular (或 stereotactic) polymerization ◇ ～反应 polyreaction/ ～管 〈化纤〉 polymerizing pipe
【聚合物】 jùhéwù 〈化〉 polymer: 高分子～ high polymers/ 工程～ engineering polymers
【聚会】 jùhuì ① get together; meet: 老战友～在一起，格外亲热。The meeting of the old comrades-in-arms was extremely cordial. ② get-together
【聚积】 jùjī accumulate; collect; build up: ～革命力量 build up revolutionary forces
【聚集】 jùjí gather; assemble; collect: 机场上～着数千人，为代表团送行。Thousands of people gathered at the airport to see the delegation off.
【聚甲醛】 jùjiǎquán 〈化〉 polyformaldehyde
【聚歼】 jùjiān round up and annihilate; annihilate *en masse*
【聚焦】 jùjiāo 〈物〉 focusing: 指向～ directional focusing
【聚精会神】 jùjīng-huìshén concentrate one's attention; be all attention: ～地工作 concentrate on one's work; be intent on one's work/ ～地听 listen with rapt attention
【聚居】 jùjū inhabit a region (as an ethnic group); live in a compact community: 少数民族～的地区 regions where minority nationalities live in compact communities
【聚敛】 jùliǎn amass wealth by heavy taxation
【聚拢】 jùlǒng gather together
【聚氯乙烯】 jùlǜ yǐxī 〈化〉 polyvinyl chloride (PVC)
【聚醛树脂】 jùquán shùzhī 〈化〉 aldehyde resin
【聚伞花序】 jùsǎn huāxù 〈植〉 cyme
【聚沙成塔】 jù shā chéng tǎ many grains of sand piled up will make a pagoda — many a little makes a mickle
【聚首】 jùshǒu 〈书〉 gather; meet: ～一堂 gather together
【聚四氟乙烯】 jùsìfúyǐxī 〈化〉 polytetrafluoroethylene (PTFE)
【聚碳酸脂】 jùtànsuānzhī 〈化〉 polycarbonate
【聚酰胺】 jùxiān'àn 〈化〉 polyamide ◇ ～塑料 polyamide plastics
【聚星】 jùxīng 〈天〉 multiple star
【聚乙烯】 jùyǐxī 〈化〉 polyethylene; polythene
【聚乙烯醇】 jùyǐxīchún 〈化〉 polyvinyl alcohol
【聚酯】 jùzhǐ 〈化〉 polyester ◇ ～塑料 polyester plastics

**踞** jù ① crouch; squat ② sit

**遽** jù ① hurriedly; hastily: ～下结论 pass judgment hastily ② frightened; alarmed

【遽然】 jùrán 〈书〉 suddenly; abruptly: ～变色 suddenly change countenance

## juān

**涓** juān 〈书〉 a tiny stream

【涓埃】 juān'āi 〈书〉 insignificant; negligible: 尽～之力 make what little contribution one can; do one's bit
【涓滴】 juāndī 〈书〉 a tiny drop; dribble; driblet: ～归公 turn in every cent of public money
【涓涓】 juānjuān 〈书〉 trickling sluggishly

**捐** juān ① relinquish; abandon ② contribute; donate; subscribe: ～钱 contribute money/ 募～ solicit contributions; appeal for donations ③ tax: 上～ pay a tax

【捐款】 juānkuǎn ① contribute money ② contribution; donation; subscription
【捐弃】 juānqì 〈书〉 relinquish; abandon
【捐躯】 juānqū sacrifice one's life; lay down one's life: 为国～ lay down one's life for one's country
【捐税】 juānshuì taxes and levies
【捐献】 juānxiàn contribute (to an organization); donate; present: 他把全部藏书～给图书馆。He presented his whole collection of books to the library.
【捐赠】 juānzèng contribute (as a gift); donate; present: ～价值人民币二十万元的食品 contribute 200,000 *yuan* (RMB) worth of food
【捐助】 juānzhù offer (financial or material assistance); contribute; donate

**娟** juān 〈书〉 beautiful; graceful

【娟秀】 juānxiù 〈书〉 beautiful; graceful: 字迹～ beautiful handwriting; a graceful hand

**圈** juān ①shut in a pen; pen in: 把羊群～起来 herd the sheep into the pens ②〈口〉 lock up; put in jail
另见 juàn; quān

**鹃** juān 见"杜鹃" dùjuān

**镌** juān 〈书〉 engrave: ～碑 engrave a stone tablet
【镌刻】 juānkè 〈书〉 engrave

## juǎn

**卷** juǎn ①roll up: 把竹帘子～起来 roll up the bamboo screen/ ～起袖子就干 roll up one's sleeves and pitch in ②sweep off; carry along: 一个大浪把小船～走了。A huge wave swept the boat away./ 汽车飞驰而过，～起一阵尘土。A car sped past, raising a cloud of dust. ③cylindrical mass of sth.; roll: 花～儿 fancy-shaped (或 plaited, twisted) steamed roll/ 铺盖～儿 bedding roll ④〈量〉 roll; spool; reel: 一～手纸 a roll of toilet paper/ 一～软片 a roll of film
另见 juàn
【卷笔刀】 juǎnbǐdāo pencil sharpener
【卷层云】 juǎncéngyún 〈气〉 cirrostratus
【卷尺】 juǎnchǐ tape measure; band tape: 布～ cloth (或 linen) tape/ 钢～ steel tape
【卷发】 juǎnfà curly hair; wavy hair
【卷积云】 juǎnjīyún 〈气〉 cirrocumulus
【卷铺盖】 juǎn pūgai ①pack up and quit ②get the sack
【卷曲机】 juǎnqūjī 〈纺〉 crimping machine
【卷染机】 juǎnrǎnjī 〈纺〉 dye jigger
【卷绕】 juǎnrào 〈纺〉 winding ◇ ～机〈化纤〉 take-up machine
【卷刃】 juǎnrèn (of a knife blade) be turned
【卷入】 juǎnrù be drawn into; be involved in: ～漩涡 be drawn into a whirlpool/ ～一场纠纷 be involved in a dispute
【卷舌辅音】 juǎnshé fǔyīn 〈语〉 retroflex consonant
【卷舌元音】 juǎnshé yuányīn 〈语〉 retroflex vowel
【卷逃】 juǎntáo abscond with valuables
【卷筒】 juǎntǒng reel ◇ ～纸 web/ ～纸印刷机 web press
【卷土重来】 juǎn tǔ chóng lái stage a comeback
【卷尾猴】 juǎnwěihóu (weeping) capuchin; weeping monkey
【卷心菜】 juǎnxīncài 〈方〉 cabbage
【卷须】 juǎnxū 〈植〉 tendril
【卷烟】 juǎnyān ①cigarette ②cigar ◇ ～包装机 cigarette packer/ ～工业 cigarette industry/ ～机 cigarette (making) machine/ ～纸 cigarette paper
【卷扬机】 juǎnyángjī hoist; hoister
【卷叶蛾】 juǎnyè'é 〈动〉 leaf roller
【卷云】 juǎnyún 〈气〉 cirrus
【卷轴】 juǎnzhóu reel: 天线～ aerial reel
另见 juànzhóu
【卷子】 juǎnzi steamed roll
另见 juànzi

## juàn

**卷** juàn ①book: 手不释～ always have a book in one's hand; be a diligent reader ②volume: 第三～ Volume III/ 该图书馆藏书十万～。This library has 100,000 volumes. ③examination paper: 交～ hand in an examination paper ④file; dossier: 查～ look through the files
另见 juǎn
【卷轴】 juànzhóu 〈书〉 scroll
另见 juǎnzhóu
【卷子】 juànzi examination paper: 看～ mark examination papers
另见 juǎnzi
【卷宗】 juànzōng ①folder ②file; dossier

**倦** juàn weary; tired: 面有～容 look tired/ 毫无～意 not feel in the least tired

**绢** juàn thin, tough silk
【绢本】 juànběn silk scroll
【绢纺】 juànfǎng silk spinning
【绢花】 juànhuā 〈工美〉 silk flower
【绢画】 juànhuà classical Chinese painting on silk
【绢丝】 juànsī spun silk (yarn) ◇ ～纺绸 spun silk pongee/ ～织物 spun silk fabric
【绢网印花】 juànwǎng yìnhuā 〈纺〉 screen printing ◇ ～法 silk-screen process

**隽** juàn
【隽永】 juànyǒng 〈书〉 meaningful: 语颇～，耐人寻味。The remarks are meaningful and thought-provoking.

**眷** juàn ①family dependant: 女～ female members of a family ②〈书〉 have tender feeling for
【眷恋】 juànliàn 〈书〉 be sentimentally attached to (a person or place)
【眷念】 juànniàn 〈书〉 think fondly of; feel nostalgic about
【眷属】 juànshǔ family dependants

**圈** juàn pen; fold; sty: 羊～ sheepfold; sheep pen/ 猪～ pigsty
另见 juān; quān
【圈肥】 juànféi 〈农〉 barnyard manure

## juē

**撅** juē ①stick up: ～着尾巴 sticking up the tail/ ～嘴 pout (one's lips) ②〈口〉 break (sth. long and narrow); snap: 把树枝～成两段 break the twig in two

## jué

**孓** jué 见"孑孓" jiéjué

**决** jué ①decide; determine: 犹豫不～ hesitate; be unable to reach a decision; be in a state of indecision/ ～一胜负 fight it out ②〔用在否定词前面〕 definitely; certainly; under any circumstances: ～非恶意 be entirely without malice; bear no ill will whatsoever/ ～不退让 will under no circumstances give in/ 不达目的～不罢休。We'll never give up until the goal is reached. ③execute a person: 枪～ execute by shooting ④(of a dyke, etc.) be breached; burst
【决策】 juécè ①make policy; make a strategic decision ②policy decision; decision of strategic importance: 战略～ strategic decision ◇ ～机构 policy-making body/ ～人 policymaker
【决定】 juédìng ①decide; resolve; make up one's mind: 领导～派她去参加学习班。The leadership decided to send her

to a study class./ 理事会～下届友好邀请赛在北京举行。The Council resolved that the next friendship invitational tournament should be held in Beijing./ 一时～不了 cannot make up one's mind for the moment; be unable to come to a decision for the moment ②decision; resolution: 通过一项～ pass a resolution ③determine; decide: 思想上政治上的路线正确与否是～一切的。The correctness or incorrectness of the ideological and political line decides everything./ ～性胜利 a decisive victory ◇ ～论〈哲〉 determinism/ ～因素 decisive factor; determinant

【决定权】 juédìngquán power to make decisions: 有最后～ have the final say

【决斗】 juédòu ①duel ②decisive struggle

【决断】 juéduàn ①make a decision ②resolve; decisiveness; resolution

【决计】 juéjì ①have decided; have made up one's mind: 我～把工作搞完再走。I have decided to get the work done before I leave. ②definitely; certainly: 那样办～没错儿。We definitely can't go wrong if we do it that way. 或 There is absolutely nothing wrong with doing it that way.

【决口】 juékǒu (of a dyke, etc.) be breached; burst

【决裂】 juéliè break with; rupture: 与旧世界～ break with the old world

【决然】 juérán 〈书〉①resolutely; determinedly ②definitely; unquestionably; undoubtedly: 搞阴谋的人～没有好下场。Those who engage in conspiracies are bound to come to no good end.

【决赛】 juésài 〈体〉 finals: 半～ semifinals

【决胜】 juéshèng decide the issue of the battle; determine the victory ◇ ～局〈体〉 deciding game (或 set)

【决死】 juésǐ life-and-death: ～的斗争 a life-and-death struggle; a last-ditch fight

【决算】 juésuàn final accounts; final accounting of revenue and expenditure: 国家～ final state accounts

【决心】 juéxīn determination; resolution: 向党表～ pledge one's determination to the Party/ 下定～ make up one's mind; be resolute; be determined/ 有～,有信心 have both determination and confidence/ ～改正错误 be determined to correct one's mistake ◇ ～书 written pledge; statement of one's determination

【决一雌雄】 jué yī cí-xióng fight to see who is the stronger; fight it out

【决议】 juéyì resolution ◇ ～(草)案 draft resolution

【决意】 juéyì have one's mind made up; be determined: 他～要走。He's made up his mind to quit.

【决战】 juézhàn decisive battle; decisive engagement

**诀** jué ①rhymed formula: 十六字～ the sixteen-character formula ②knack; tricks of the trade: 秘～ secret of success; key to success ③bid farewell; part: 永～ part never to meet again; part for ever

【诀别】 juébié bid farewell; part

【诀窍】 juéqiào secret of success; tricks of the trade; knack: 你这么快就做得了,有什么～啊? You finished your job really fast. What's the secret of it?/ 你掌握了～就容易了。It's easy once you've got the knack of it. 或 It's simple if you know the trick.

**抉** jué 〈书〉 pick out; single out

【抉择】 juézé 〈书〉 choose: 作出～ make one's choice

**角** jué ①role; part; character: 主～ leading (或 principal) role; main character ②type of role (in traditional Chinese drama): 旦～ female role/ 丑～ clown ③actor or actress: 名～ a famous actor or actress ④contend; wrestle: ～斗 wrestle/ 口～ quarrel; bicker ⑤an ancient, three-legged wine cup ⑥〈乐〉 a note of the ancient Chinese five-tone scale, corresponding to 3 in numbered musical notation

另见 jiǎo

【角斗】 juédòu wrestle ◇ ～场 wrestling ring

【角力】 juélì have a trial of strength; wrestle

【角色】 juésè ①role; part: 她在这部电影里演哪个～? What part does she play in that film?/ 扮演了不光彩的～ play a contemptible role ②type of role (in traditional Chinese drama)

【角逐】 juézhú contend; tussle; enter into rivalry: 超级大国～的场所 an arena of fierce rivalry between the superpowers

**玦** jué penannular jade ring (worn as an ornament in ancient China)

**珏** jué two pieces of jade put together

**觉** jué ①sense; feel: 听～ sense of hearing/ 下过这场雪,就～出冷来了。After the snow it is really cold./ 身上～着不舒服 not feel well ②wake (up); awake: 如梦初～ as if waking from a dream ③become aware; become awakened

另见 jiào

【觉察】 juéchá detect; become aware of; perceive: 敌人没有～出我侦察排的行动。The enemy didn't detect our scouting platoon's movements./ 她～到这里面有问题。She sensed there was something wrong.

【觉得】 juéde ①feel: 一点儿也不～累 not feel tired at all ②think; feel: 我～应该先跟他商量一下。I think we should consult him first./ 我～他这几天情绪不好。I have a feeling that he's been in low spirits these last few days./ 你～这个计划怎么样? What do you think of the plan?

【觉悟】 juéwù ①consciousness; awareness; understanding: 政治～ political consciousness (或 understanding)/ 阶级～ class consciousness/ 提高无产阶级专政下继续革命的～ heighten one's awareness of the need to continue the revolution under the dictatorship of the proletariat ②come to understand; become aware of; become politically awakened: ～了的人民 an awakened people/ 经过这场斗争,他才～到改造世界观的重要性。It was only through this struggle that he came to see the importance of remoulding his world outlook.

【觉醒】 juéxǐng awaken: 第三世界的～ the awakening of the third world

**绝** jué ①cut off; sever: ～其后路 cut off his retreat/ 掌声不～ prolonged applause ②exhausted; used up; finished: 弹尽粮～ have run out of ammunition and provisions/ 法子都想～了。All possible ways have been tried. 或 All possibilities have been exhausted. ③desperate; hopeless: ～境 hopeless situation; impasse ④unique; superb; matchless: 她发的那球真～。Her serve was a beauty. ⑤extremely; most: ～大的错误 an egregious error; a grievous fault/ ～大多数 most; the overwhelming majority/ ～好的机会 an excellent opportunity/ ～早 extremely early ⑥〔用在否定词前〕absolutely; in the least; by any means; on any account: ～无此意 have absolutely no such intentions/ ～非偶然 by no means fortuitous/ ～不可脱离群众 must on no account divorce oneself from the masses ⑦leaving no leeway; making no allowance; uncompromising: 他尽管不同意,但是没把话说～。He disagreed, but he didn't say anything definitive. ⑧见"绝句"

【绝版】 juébǎn out of print
【绝笔】 juébǐ ①last words written before one's death ②the last work of an author or painter
【绝壁】 juébì precipice
【绝唱】 juéchàng the peak of poetic perfection: 堪称千古～ rank as a poetic masterpiece through the ages
【绝处逢生】 juéchù féng shēng be unexpectedly rescued from a desperate situation
【绝代】 juédài 〈书〉 unique among one's contemporaries; peerless: 才华～ unrivalled talent
【绝倒】 juédǎo 〈书〉 shake one's sides; roar with laughter: 令人～ sidesplitting
【绝顶】 juédǐng extremely; utterly: ～聪明 extremely intelligent/ ～愚蠢的行为 the height of folly
【绝对】 juéduì ①absolute: ～优势 absolute predominance; overwhelming superiority/ 保证党的～领导 ensure the absolute leadership of the Party/ 防止思想上的～化 avoid thinking in terms of absolutes ②absolutely; perfectly; definitely: ～可靠 absolutely reliable
◇ ～地租 absolute rent/ ～多数 absolute majority; overwhelming majority/ ～观念〈哲〉absolute idea/ ～量度〈物〉absolute measurement/ ～零度〈物〉absolute zero/ ～平均主义 absolute equalitarianism/ ～湿度〈气〉absolute humidity/ ～温度〈物〉absolute temperature/ ～音乐 absolute music/ ～真理〈哲〉absolute truth/ ～值〈数〉absolute value/ ～主义〈哲〉absolutism
【绝后】 juéhòu ①without offspring (或 issue) ②never to be seen again: 空前～ never known before and never to occur again; unique
【绝户】 juéhu ①without offspring (或 issue) ②a childless person
【绝迹】 juéjì disappear; vanish; be stamped out: 血吸虫病在我们县已经～。Schistosomiasis has been stamped out in our county.
【绝技】 juéjì unique skill; consummate skill
【绝交】 juéjiāo break off relations (as between friends or countries)
【绝经】 juéjīng 〈生理〉 menopause
【绝境】 juéjìng hopeless situation; impasse; blind alley; *cul-de-sac*: 濒于～ face an impasse
【绝句】 juéjù *jueju*, a poem of four lines, each containing five or seven characters, with a strict tonal pattern and rhyme scheme
【绝口】 juékǒu ①〔只用在"不"字后〕 stop talking: 赞不～ give unstinted praise; praise profusely/ 骂不～ heap endless abuse upon; pour out unceasing abuse ②keep one's mouth shut: ～不提 never say a single word about; avoid all mention of
【绝路】 juélù road to ruin; blind alley; impasse: 自寻～ court destruction; bring ruin upon oneself
【绝伦】 juélún unsurpassed; unequalled; peerless; matchless: 精美～ exquisite beyond compare; superb/ 荒谬～ utterly absurd; utterly preposterous
【绝密】 juémì top-secret; most confidential
【绝妙】 juémiào extremely clever; ingenious; excellent; perfect: ～的一招 a masterstroke/ ～的反面教材 excellent material for learning by negative example/ ～的讽刺 perfect irony
【绝命书】 juémìngshū ①suicide note ②note written on the eve of one's execution
【绝热】 juérè 〈物〉 heat insulation
◇ ～材料 heat-insulating material/ ～冷却 adiabatic cooling/ ～曲线 adiabatic curve; adiabatics/ ～压缩 adiabatic compression
【绝色】 juésè 〈书〉 (of a woman) exceedingly beautiful; of unrivalled beauty
【绝食】 juéshí fast; go on a hunger strike
【绝望】 juéwàng give up all hope; despair: ～情绪 feeling of despair/ ～的挣扎 desperate struggle
【绝无仅有】 juéwú-jǐnyǒu the only one of its kind; unique
【绝艺】 juéyì consummate art or skill
【绝育】 juéyù 〈医〉 sterilization
【绝缘】 juéyuán ①〈电〉 insulation ②be cut off from; be isolated from
◇ ～材料 insulating material; insulant/ ～套管 insulating sleeve; spaghetti (tubing)/ ～体 insulator/ ～子 insulator
【绝招】 juézhāo ①unique skill ②unexpected tricky move (as a last resort)
【绝症】 juézhèng incurable disease; fatal illness
【绝种】 juézhǒng (of a species) become extinct; die out

**倔** jué
另见 juè
【倔强】 juéjiàng stubborn; unbending

**掘** jué dig: ～井 dig a well/ 自～坟墓 dig one's own grave
【掘进】 juéjìn 〈矿〉 driving; tunnelling: 平巷～ drifting/ 快速～ quick tunnelling/ 全断面～ full-face tunnelling
【掘墓人】 juémùrén gravedigger
【掘土机】 juétǔjī excavator; power shovel

**崛** jué 〈书〉 rise abruptly
【崛起】 juéqǐ ①(of a mountain, etc.) rise abruptly; suddenly appear on the horizon ②rise (as a political force): 太平军～于广西金田村。The Taipings rose in revolt at Jintian Village, Guangxi.

**厥** jué ①faint; lose consciousness; fall into a coma: 昏～ fall to the ground in a faint ②〈书〉 his or her; its; their: ～后 thereafter/ ～父 his or her father

**谲** jué 〈书〉 cheat; swindle
【谲诈】 juézhà cunning; crafty

**蕨** jué 〈植〉 brake (fern)
【蕨类植物】 juélèi zhíwù pteridophyte

**獗** jué 见"猖獗" chāngjué

**橛** jué a short wooden stake; wooden pin; peg
【橛子】 juézi a short wooden stake; wooden pin; peg

**噱** jué 〈书〉 loud laughter: 可发一～ make one laugh out loud
另见 xué

**爵** jué ①the rank of nobility; peerage: 封～ confer a title (of nobility) upon ②an ancient wine vessel with three legs and a loop handle
【爵士】 juéshì ①knight ②Sir: 约翰·史密斯～ Sir John Smith
【爵士音乐】 juéshì yīnyuè jazz
【爵位】 juéwèi the rank (或 title) of nobility

**蹶** jué ①fall ②suffer a setback: 一～不振 collapse after one setback; never recover from a setback
另见 juě

**矍** jué

【矍铄】 juéshuò 〈书〉 hale and hearty

**嚼** jué masticate; chew
另见 jiáo

**攫** jué seize; grab: ～为己有 seize possession of; appropriate

【攫取】 juéqǔ seize; grab: ～别国的资源 grab the resources of other countries/ ～暴利 rake in exorbitant profits

**镢** jué 〈方〉 pick; pickaxe

【镢头】 juétou 〈方〉 pick; pickaxe

## juě

**蹶** juě
另见 jué

【蹶子】 juězi 〔用于〕: 尥～ (of horses, donkeys, etc.) kick

## juè

**倔** juè gruff; surly: 这老头儿脾气～。That old man is rather surly.
另见 jué

【倔头倔脑】 juètóu-juènǎo blunt of manner and gruff of speech

## jūn

**军** jūn ① armed forces; army; troops: 参～ join the army/ 学～ learn military affairs; learn from the PLA ② army: 全歼敌人一个～ wipe out an enemy army/ ～以上干部 cadres including and above the level of army commander; cadres of army level and above

【军备】 jūnbèi armament; arms: 扩充～ engage in arms expansion ◇ ～竞赛 armament (或 arms) race

【军部】 jūnbù army headquarters

【军操】 jūncāo military drill

【军车】 jūnchē military vehicle

【军刀】 jūndāo soldier's sword; sabre

【军队】 jūnduì armed forces; army; troops ◇ ～标号 military symbols

【军阀】 jūnfá warlord
◇ ～战争 war among warlords/ ～主义 warlordism/ ～作风 warlord ways; warlord style

【军法】 jūnfǎ military criminal code; military law: ～从事 punish by military law ◇ ～审判 court-martial

【军方】 jūnfāng the military

【军费】 jūnfèi military expenditure

【军分区】 jūnfēnqū military subarea

【军风纪】 jūnfēngjì soldier's bearing and discipline

【军服】 jūnfú military uniform; uniform ◇ ～呢 army coating

【军港】 jūngǎng naval port

【军工】 jūngōng ① war industry ② military project ◇ ～生产 war production

【军功】 jūngōng military exploit

【军官】 jūnguān officer

【军管】 jūnguǎn military control ◇ ～会〈简〉(军事管制委员会) military control commission

【军国主义】 jūnguózhǔyì militarism ◇ ～化 militarization/ ～者 militarist

【军号】 jūnhào bugle

【军徽】 jūnhuī army emblem

【军火】 jūnhuǒ munitions; arms and ammunition
◇ ～工业 munitions industry; armament industry/ ～舰 ammunition ship/ ～库 arsenal/ ～商 munitions merchant; arms dealer; merchant of death

【军机】 jūnjī ① military plan: 贻误～ delay or frustrate the fulfilment of a military plan ② military secret: 泄漏～ leak a military secret

【军籍】 jūnjí military status; one's name on the army roll: 保留～ retain one's military status/ 开除～ strike sb.'s name off the army roll; discharge sb. from the army

【军纪】 jūnjì military discipline

【军舰】 jūnjiàn warship; naval vessel

【军阶】 jūnjiē (military) rank; grade

【军界】 jūnjiè military circles; the military

【军垦】 jūnkěn reclamation of wasteland by an army unit
◇ ～农场 army reclamation farm; army farm

【军礼】 jūnlǐ military salute

【军力】 jūnlì military strength

【军粮】 jūnliáng army provisions; grain for the army ◇ ～库 military grain depot; army granary

【军龄】 jūnlíng length of military service: 他的～比我长。He has served in the army longer than I have.

【军令】 jūnlìng military orders: 颁布～ issue a military order

【军马】 jūnmǎ army horse ◇ ～场 army horse-breeding farm; army horse ranch

【军帽】 jūnmào army cap; service cap

【军民】 jūn-mín the army and the people; soldiers and civilians; military and civilian ◇ ～关系 the relations between the army and the people; army-people relations/ ～联防 army-civilian joint defence

【军旗】 jūnqí army flag; colours; ensign ◇ ～礼 colours salute

【军情】 jūnqíng military (或 war) situation: 刺探～ spy on the military movements; collect military information

【军区】 jūnqū military region; (military) area command: 各大～ the greater military areas ◇ ～司令部 the headquarters of a military area command

【军人】 jūnrén soldier; serviceman; armyman ◇ ～大会 soldiers' conference (of a company)/ ～家属 soldier's dependants; armyman's family members

【军容】 jūnróng soldier's discipline, appearance and bearing: 整饬～ strengthen army discipline and maintain required standards for appearance and bearing

【军师】 jūnshī military counsellor; army adviser

【军士】 jūnshì noncommissioned officer (NCO)

【军事】 jūnshì military affairs
◇ ～表演 display of military skills/ ～部署 military deployment; disposition of military forces/ ～法院 military tribunal (或 court)/ ～分界线 military demarcation line/ ～工业 war industry/ ～管制 military control/ ～管制委员会 military control commission/ ～基地 military base/ ～家 strategist/ ～科学 military science/ ～路线 military line/ ～民主 military democracy/ ～设施 military installations/ ～素质 military qualities; fighting capability/ ～体育 military sports/ ～条令 military manuals/ ～学 military science/ ～学家 military scientist/ ～学院 military academy (或 institute)/ ～训练 military training/ ～演习 military manoeuvre; war exercise/ ～野营 off-base military training; military training in the field/ ～优势 military superiority/ ～原则 principles of operation; military principles

【军事化】 jūnshìhuà militarize; place on a war footing: 经

济～ militarization of the economy/ 参加野营的学生过着～的生活。The students who went camping followed a military routine.

【军属】 jūnshǔ soldier's dependants; armyman's family

【军团】 jūntuán army group

【军委】 Jūnwěi 〈简〉(中国共产党中央军事委员会) the Military Commission of the Central Committee of the Communist Party of China

【军务】 jūnwù military affairs; military task

【军衔】 jūnxián military rank ◇ ～制度 system of military ranks

【军饷】 jūnxiǎng 〈旧〉 soldier's pay and provisions

【军校】 jūnxiào military school; military academy

【军械】 jūnxiè ordnance; armament
◇ ～处 ordnance department/ ～库 ordnance depot; arms depot; armoury/ ～员 armourer

【军心】 jūnxīn soldiers' morale: 动摇～ shake the army's morale/ ～大振。The morale of the troops has been greatly raised.

【军需】 jūnxū ① military supplies ② 〈旧〉 quartermaster
◇ ～船 storeship/ ～工厂 military supplies factory/ ～库 military supply depot/ ～品 military supplies; military stores

【军宣队】 jūnxuānduì 〈简〉(解放军毛泽东思想宣传队) Mao Zedong Thought propaganda team of the People's Liberation Army; PLA propaganda team

【军训】 jūnxùn military training

【军医】 jūnyī medical officer; military surgeon

【军营】 jūnyíng military camp; barracks

【军用】 jūnyòng for military use; military
◇ ～地图 military map/ ～飞机 warplane; military aircraft/ ～列车 military train/ ～物资 military supplies; *matériel*

【军邮】 jūnyóu army postal service; army post (或 mail)

【军援】 jūnyuán military aid

【军乐】 jūnyuè martial (或 military) music ◇ ～队 military band

【军长】 jūnzhǎng army commander

【军政】 jūn-zhèng army and government ◇ ～当局 civil and military authorities/ ～关系 the relations between the army and the government

【军政府】 jūnzhèngfǔ military government

【军职】 jūnzhí official post in the army; military appointment

【军种】 jūnzhǒng (armed) services

【军装】 jūnzhuāng military (或 army) uniform; uniform

**均** jūn ① equal; even: 劳逸不～ uneven allocation of work ② without exception; all: 各项准备工作～已就绪。All the preparatory work has been completed.

【均等】 jūnděng equal; impartial; fair

【均分】 jūnfēn divide equally; share out equally: 这批化肥由几个生产队～。This lot of fertilizer will be shared out equally among the different production teams.

【均衡】 jūnhéng balanced; proportionate; harmonious; even: 国民经济的～发展 the balanced (或 harmonious) development of the national economy/ 矛盾双方达到某种暂时的～。A certain temporary parity has been attained between the two sides of the contradiction. ◇ ～论〈哲〉 the theory of equilibrium

【均热】 jūnrè 〈冶〉 soaking ◇ ～炉 soaking pit

【均势】 jūnshì balance of power; equilibrium of forces; equilibrium; parity

【均摊】 jūntān share equally: ～费用 share the expenses equally

【均相】 jūnxiàng 〈化〉 homogeneous phase: ～催化剂 homogeneous catalyst

【均一】 jūnyī even; uniform; homogeneous ◇ ～性〈化〉 homogeneity

【均匀】 jūnyún even; well-distributed: ～的呼吸 even breathing/ ～撒播 even broadcasting of seeds/ 今年的雨水很～。Rainfall has been fairly well-distributed this year. ◇ ～混合物 〈化〉 homogeneous mixture

**君** jūn ① monarch; sovereign; supreme ruler ② gentleman; Mr.: 诸～ gentlemen/ 张刘二～ Messrs. Zhang and Liu

【君迁子】 jūnqiānzǐ 〈中药〉 the fruit of date plum (*Diospyros lotus*)

【君权】 jūnquán monarchical power

【君主】 jūnzhǔ monarch; sovereign
◇ ～国 monarchical state; monarchy/ ～立宪 constitutional monarchy/ ～制 monarchy/ ～专制 autocratic monarchy; absolute monarchy

【君子】 jūnzǐ a man of noble character; gentleman: 伪～ hypocrite/ 正人～ a man of moral integrity/ ～成人之美。A gentleman is always ready to help others attain their aims./ 以小人之心度～之腹 gauge the heart of a gentleman with one's own mean measure
◇ ～协定 gentlemen's agreement

**龟** jūn
另见 guī

【龟裂】 jūnliè ① (of parched earth) be full of cracks ② (of skin) chap

**钧** jūn ① an ancient unit of weight (equal to 30 *jin*) ② 〈敬〉 you; your: ～座 Your Excellency

**菌** jūn ① fungus ② bacterium
另见 jùn

【菌肥】 jūnféi 〈简〉(细菌肥料) bacterial manure

【菌苗】 jūnmiáo 〈医〉 vaccine

【菌丝】 jūnsī 〈植〉 hypha

【菌血症】 jūnxuèzhèng 〈医〉 bacteriemia

**皲** jūn

【皲裂】 jūnliè 〈书〉 (of skin) chap

## jùn

**俊** jùn ① handsome; pretty: 这小伙子长得挺～的。That lad is very handsome./ 这孩子长得多～哪！What a pretty little child! ② a person of outstanding talent

【俊杰】 jùnjié a person of outstanding talent; hero

【俊美】 jùnměi pretty

【俊俏】 jùnqiào pretty and charming

【俊秀】 jùnxiù pretty; of delicate beauty

**郡** jùn 〈史〉 prefecture

【郡县制】 jùnxiànzhì 〈史〉 the system of prefectures and counties (a system of local administration which took shape during the Spring and Autumn Period and the Qin Dynasty)

**浚** jùn dredge: ～渠 dredge a canal

【浚泥船】 jùnníchuán dredger

**峻** jùn ① (of mountains) high: 高山～岭 high mountains/ 险～ precipitous ② harsh; severe; stern: 严刑～法 harsh law and severe punishment

【峻峭】 jùnqiào high and steep

**骏** jùn fine horse; steed

【骏马】 jùnmǎ fine horse; steed

**菌** jùn mushroom

另见 jūn

**竣** jùn complete; finish: 告～ have been completed

【竣工】 jùngōng (of a project) be completed: 这座大楼已提前～。The building has been completed ahead of schedule.

# K

## kā

**咖** kā
另见 gā
【咖啡】 kāfēi coffee ◇～馆 café/ ～色 coffee (colour)
【咖啡因】 kāfēiyīn 〈药〉 caffeine 又作"咖啡硷"

**喀** kā 〈象〉 noise made in coughing or vomiting
【喀嚓】 kāchā 〈象〉 crack; snap: ～一声，树枝断了。The branch broke with a crack. 或 The branch snapped.
【喀尔巴阡山】 Kā'ěrbāqiānshān the Carpathians
【喀麦隆】 Kāmàilóng Cameroon ◇～人 Cameroonian
【喀斯特】 kāsītè 〈地〉 *karst* ◇～地形 *karst* topography

**揢** kā scrape with a knife

## kǎ

**卡** kǎ ① block; check: ～住通往海港的公路 block the road to the seaport/ 会计及时～住了这笔不必要的开支。The accountant checked this unnecessary spending in good time. ②〈简〉(卡路里) calorie
另见 qiǎ
【卡巴胂】 kǎbāshēn 〈药〉 carbarsone
【卡奔达】 Kǎbēndá Cabinda
【卡宾枪】 kǎbīnqiāng carbine
【卡车】 kǎchē lorry; truck
【卡尺】 kǎchǐ 〈机〉 (sliding) callipers: 游标～ vernier callipers
【卡介苗】 kǎjièmiáo 〈药〉 BCG vaccine (Bacille Calmette-Guérin)
【卡路里】 kǎlùlǐ 〈物〉 calorie
【卡那霉素】 kǎnàméisù 〈药〉 kanamycin
【卡片】 kǎpiàn card
◇ ～柜 card cabinet/ ～目录 card catalogue/ ～索引 card index
【卡其】 kǎqí 〈纺〉 khaki
【卡钳】 kǎqián 〈机〉 callipers: 内外～ combination callipers/ 内～ inside callipers/ 外～ outside callipers
【卡他】 kǎtā 〈医〉 catarrh
【卡塔尔】 Kǎtǎ'ěr Qatar ◇～人 Qatari
【卡特尔】 kǎtè'ěr 〈经〉 cartel

**咔** kǎ
【咔叽】 kǎjī 〈纺〉 khaki
【咔唑】 kǎzuò 〈化〉 carbazole

**咯** kǎ cough up: 把鱼刺～出来 cough up a fishbone
另见 gē; lo; luò
【咯痰】 kǎtán cough up phlegm
【咯血】 kǎxiě 〈医〉 spit blood; haemoptysis

**胩** kǎ 〈化〉 carbylamine; isocyanide

## kāi

**开** kāi ① open: ～锁 open a lock; unlock ② make an opening; open up; reclaim: 墙上～个窗口 make a window in the wall/ ～三千亩水稻田 open up 3,000 *mu* of paddy fields ③ open out; come loose: 花都～了。The flowers are all open./ 扣儿～了。The knot has come untied. ④ thaw; become navigable: 等河～了坐船走。Wait until the river is open and then go by boat. ⑤ lift (a ban, restriction, etc.): ～禁 lift a ban ⑥ start; operate: ～机器 operate a machine/ ～拖拉机 drive a tractor/ ～灯 turn on a light/ ～飞机 fly (或 pilot) an airplane/ 火车就要～了。The train is about to start. ⑦ (of troops, etc.) set out; move: 军队正～往前线。The troops are moving to the front. ⑧ set up; run: ～工厂 set up a factory/ ～茶馆 run a teahouse ⑨ begin; start: ～拍 start shooting (a film) ⑩ hold (a meeting, exhibition, etc.): ～运动会 hold an athletic meet ⑪ make a list of; write out: 把你需要领的工具～个单子。Make a list of the tools you need./ ～方子 write a prescription/ 我到党委去～介绍信。I'm going to get a letter of introduction from the Party Committee. ⑫ pay (wages, fares, etc.) ⑬ boil: 水～了。The water is boiling. ⑭ percentage: 大家认为他的功过是三七～。The general assessment of his work is 70% achievements and 30% mistakes. ⑮〈印〉 division of standard size printing paper: 四～ quarto/ 八～ octavo ⑯ carat: 十四～金 14-carat gold ⑰〔用在动词后，表示扩大或扩展〕: 消息传～了。The news has got about./ 这支歌儿流行～了。The song has become very popular. ⑱〔用在动词后，表示开始并继续下去〕: 冻得他哆嗦～了。He was shivering with cold.

**开** kai ①〔用在动词后，表示离开或分开〕: 躲～ get out of the way/ 把门开～。Open the door. ②〔用在动词后，表示容得下〕: 这间屋子大，五十个人也坐～了。This room is big enough to seat 50 people.

【开拔】 kāibá (of troops) move; set out
【开办】 kāibàn open; set up; start: ～训练班 start a training course
【开本】 kāiběn 〈印〉 format; book size: 八～ octavo/ 十六～ 16 mo/ 三十二～ 32 mo
【开标】 kāibiāo open sealed tenders
【开采】 kāicǎi mine; extract; exploit: ～煤炭 mine coal/ ～石油 recover petroleum/ ～天然气 tap (或 extract) natural gas
【开场】 kāichǎng begin: 他们到剧院时，戏已经～了。The play had already begun when they got to the theatre./ 支书简洁有力的发言，给会议做了个很好的～。The meeting got off to a good start with a short and forceful speech by the Party branch secretary.
【开场白】 kāichǎngbái ① prologue (of a play) ② opening (或 introductory) remarks
【开车】 kāichē ① drive or start a car, train, etc.: ～的时候精神要集中。You should concentrate your attention when driving. /快～了，大家上车吧。The bus is going to start. Hurry up, everybody. ② set a machine going
【开诚布公】 kāichéng-bùgōng speak frankly and sincerely
【开除】 kāichú expel; discharge: ～出党 expel from the Party/ ～学籍 expel from school/ ～公职 discharge sb. from public employment; take sb.'s name off the books
【开船】 kāichuán set sail; sail ◇～时间 sailing time; hour of sailing
【开创】 kāichuàng start; initiate: 十月革命～了人类历史的

新纪元。The October Revolution ushered in a new epoch in human history./ ～社会主义新风尚 initiate a new socialist custom/ 把毛主席～的无产阶级革命事业进行到底 carry through to the end our proletarian revolutionary cause pioneered by Chairman Mao

【开春】 kāichūn beginning of spring (usu. referring to the first month of the lunar year)

【开裆裤】 kāidāngkù open-seat (或 split) pants (for children)

【开刀】 kāidāo ①〈口〉perform or have an operation; operate or be operated on: 给病人～ operate on a patient/ 他得了阑尾炎，～了。He had an operation for appendicitis. ② behead; decapitate ③ make sb. the first target of attack: 拿某人～ make an example of sb.

【开导】 kāidǎo help sb. to see what is right or sensible; help sb. to straighten out his wrong or muddled thinking; enlighten: 他一时想不通，你～～他好吗？ He hasn't come round yet. Could you try and straighten him out?

【开倒车】 kāi dàochē turn the clock back; turn back the wheel of history

【开道】 kāidào ① clear the way: 鸣锣～ beat gongs to clear the way (for officials in feudal times); prepare the public for a coming event ②〈方〉make way: 喝令三山五岳～。Let the mountains make way.

【开动】 kāidòng ① start; set in motion: ～机器 start a machine/ ～宣传机器 set the propaganda machine in motion/ ～脑筋 use one's brains ② move; march: 队伍休息了一会儿又～了。The troops were on the move again after a short rest.

【开端】 kāiduān beginning; start: 良好的～ a good beginning /两国关系新的～ a new turn in the relations between the two countries

【开恩】 kāi'ēn show mercy; bestow favours

【开发】 kāifā develop; open up; exploit: ～山区 develop mountain areas/ ～油田 open up oilfields/ ～自然资源 exploit natural resources

【开饭】 kāifàn serve a meal: ～了。The meal's ready. 或 Time to eat!

【开方】 kāifāng 〈数〉extraction of a root; evolution

【开放】 kāifàng ① come into bloom ② lift a ban, restriction, etc. ③ open to traffic or public use: 新建的港口已向外轮～。The new port has been opened to foreign ships. ④ be open (to the public): 星期日图书馆照常～。The library is open on Sundays as well as on weekdays.

【开赴】 kāifù march to; be bound for: ～前线 march to the front/ 劳动大军即将～建设工地。A contingent of workers is leaving for the construction site.

【开工】 kāigōng ① (of a factory, etc.) go into operation: ～不足 be operating under capacity / 新厂～了。The new factory has gone into operation. ② (of work on a construction project, etc.) start: 水库工程～了。Construction of the reservoir has started. ◇ ～率 utilization of capacity

【开沟机】 kāigōujī ditching machine; trench digger

【开关】 kāiguān 〈电〉switch: 分档～ step switch/ 通断～ on-off switch ◇ ～厂 switchgear plant

【开锅】 kāiguō 〈口〉(of a pot) boil

【开国】 kāiguó found a state ◇ ～大典 founding ceremony (of a state)

【开航】 kāiháng ① become open for navigation: 又一条新航线～了。Another new air route has been opened up. / 运河～了。The canal is now open. ② set sail: 去武汉的船上午八点～。The boat for Wuhan sails at 8 a.m. ◇ ～日 sailing day

【开河】 kāihé ① construct a canal ② (of a river) thaw

【开合桥】 kāihéqiáo bascule bridge; folding bridge

【开户】 kāihù open (或 establish) an account

【开花】 kāihuā blossom; bloom; flower: 木兰要～了。The magnolias are beginning to blossom./ 心里乐开了花 burst with joy; feel elated/ 手榴弹在敌人头上开了花。The hand grenades exploded in the midst of the enemy. ◇ ～期〈植〉florescence

【开花结果】 kāihuā-jiēguǒ blossom and bear fruit — yield positive results

【开化】 kāihuà become civilized

【开怀】 kāihuái to one's heart's content: ～畅饮 drink (alcohol) to one's heart's content; go on a drinking spree

【开荒】 kāihuāng open up (或 reclaim) wasteland

【开会】 kāihuì hold or attend a meeting: 我要～去。I'm going to a meeting./ 他正在～。He's at a meeting./ 现在～。Let's start the meeting.

【开荤】 kāihūn begin or resume a meat diet; end a meatless diet

【开火】 kāihuǒ open fire: ～！（口令）Fire!

【开豁】 kāihuò ① open and clear: 雾气一散，四处都显得十分～。With the lifting of the mist, the view opened up. ② with one's mental outlook broadened: 听了报告，他的心里更～了。The report widened his horizons.

【开架】 kāijià open-shelf ◇ ～阅览室 open-shelf reading room

【开间】 kāijiān ①〈方〉the standard width of a room in an old-style house (about 10 *chi*, the length of a purlin): 单～ a house about 10 *chi* wide/ 双～ a one-room house about 20 *chi* wide ②〈方〉width of a room: 这间屋子～很大。The room is quite wide. ③〈建〉bay

【开讲】 kāijiǎng begin lecturing or story-telling

【开戒】 kāijiè break an abstinence (from smoking, drinking, etc.)

【开禁】 kāijìn lift a ban

【开卷】 kāijuàn open a book; read: ～有益。Reading is always profitable.

【开卷考试】 kāijuàn kǎoshì open-book examination

【开掘】 kāijué dig: ～运河 dig a canal

【开课】 kāikè ① school begins ② (chiefly in college) give a course; teach a subject: 开一门光合作用课 give a course in photosynthesis / 朱教授这学期给研究生～。Professor Zhu will give lectures to the research students this term.

【开垦】 kāikěn open up (或 reclaim) wasteland; bring under cultivation: ～荒山 bring barren hills under cultivation

【开口】 kāikǒu ① open one's mouth; start to talk: 难以～ find it difficult to bring the matter up/ 没等我～，他就抢先替我说了。Before I could open my mouth, he hastened to speak on my behalf. ② put the first edge on a knife

【开口闭口】 kāikǒu-bìkǒu every time one opens one's mouth; whenever one speaks

【开口销】 kāikǒuxiāo 〈机〉split pin

【开口子】 kāi kǒuzi ① (of a dyke) break; burst ② (of the skin) chap

【开快车】 kāi kuàichē ① step on the gas; open the throttle ② (of a machine) speed up ③ hurry through one's work; make short work of a job

【开矿】 kāikuàng open up a mine; exploit a mine

【开阔】 kāikuò ① open; wide: ～的广场 an open square ② tolerant: 心胸～ broad-minded; unprejudiced ③ widen: ～眼界 broaden one's outlook (或 horizons) ◇ ～地〈军〉open terrain; open ground; unenclosed ground

【开朗】 kāilǎng ① open and clear: 豁然～ suddenly see the light ② sanguine; optimistic: 性情～ of a sanguine disposition; always cheerful

【开犁】 kāilí ① start the year's ploughing ② plough the first furrow as a guideline

【开例】 kāilì create a precedent
【开镰】 kāilián start harvesting
【开列】 kāiliè draw up (a list); list: ～如下 as listed below/ ～清单 draw up (或 make out) a list; make an inventory
【开路】 kāilù ① open a way; blaze a trail: 逢山～,遇水搭桥 cut paths through the mountains and build bridges across the rivers ②〈电〉open circuit ◇ ～先锋 pathbreaker; trailblazer; pioneer
【开绿灯】 kāi lǜdēng give the green light: 我们绝不能给资产阶级思想～。We shall never give free rein to the spread of bourgeois ideas.
【开毛机】 kāimáojī 〈纺〉wool opener
【开门】 kāimén open the door: 有人敲门,快～去。 Somebody's knocking at the door. Quick, go and open it./在旧社会,大学不向工农子弟～。In the old society, universities were not open to the children of workers and peasants.
【开门办学】 kāimén bànxué open-door schooling
【开门红】 kāiménhóng make a good beginning; get off to a good start
【开门见山】 kāimén jiàn shān come straight to the point
【开门揖盗】 kāimén yī dào open the door to robbers; invite disaster by letting in evildoers
【开门整党】 kāimén zhěngdǎng open-door consolidation of the Party; a campaign to consolidate the Party with the help of the masses
【开门整风】 kāimén zhěngfēng open-door rectification of the work style; a campaign to rectify the style of work with the help of the masses
【开棉机】 kāimiánjī 〈纺〉opener: 棉箱～ hopper opener/ 豪猪～ porcupine opener
【开明】 kāimíng enlightened ◇ ～人士 enlightened persons
【开明绅士】 kāimíng shēnshì the enlightened gentry (individual landlords and rich peasants with democratic leanings who, influenced by the CCP's education and its policy of unity, favoured resistance against Japan, supported democracy and reduction of land rent and loan interest during the War of Resistance Against Japan, and, in the War of Liberation, opposed the reactionary U. S.-Chiang Kai-shek rule and approved of the land reform)
【开幕】 kāimù ① the curtain rises: 戏已经～了。The opera has begun. ② open; inaugurate: 展览会明天～。 The exhibition will open tomorrow./ 大会今天上午～了。The conference was inaugurated this morning. ◇ ～词 opening speech (或 address)/ ～式 opening ceremony
【开盘】 kāipán 〈经〉opening quotation (on the exchange) ◇ ～汇率 opening rate/ ～价格 opening price
【开炮】 kāipào ① open fire with artillery; fire ② fire criticism at sb.
【开坯】 kāipī 〈冶〉cogging; blooming ◇ ～机 cogging mill; bloomer
【开辟】 kāipì open up; start: ～航线 open an air or sea route/ ～专栏 start a special column/ ～财源 tap new financial resources/ ～革命根据地 set up a revolutionary base/ ～光辉灿烂的未来 open up the way to a bright future/ 中国共产党的诞生, ～了中国历史的新时代。 The birth of the Communist Party of China ushered in a new epoch in Chinese history.
【开篇】 kāipiān introductory song in *tanci* (弹词)
【开票】 kāipiào ① open the ballot box and count the ballots ② make out an invoice
【开屏】 kāipíng (of a peacock) spread its tail; display its fine tail feathers
【开启】 kāiqǐ open: 自动～ open automatically
【开枪】 kāiqiāng fire with a rifle, pistol, etc.; shoot: ～射击 open fire/ ～还击 return fire
【开腔】 kāiqiāng begin to speak; open one's mouth: 他半天不～。For a long time he didn't utter a word. 或 He kept silent for a long while.
【开窍】 kāiqiào have one's ideas straightened out: 他一听这么说,就～了。He straightened his ideas out as soon as the matter was explained to him.
【开球】 kāiqiú 〈足球〉kick off
【开山】 kāishān cut into a mountain (for quarrying,etc.)
【开山祖师】 kāishān zǔshī the founder of a religious sect or a school of thought
【开设】 kāishè ① open (a shop, factory, etc.) ② offer (a course in college, etc.)
【开始】 kāishǐ ① begin; start: 今天从第五课～。Today we'll begin with Lesson 5./ ～讨论实质性问题 come to substantive questions/ ～生效 take effect; come into effect (或 force) ② initial stage; beginning; outset: 革命的力量,～总是比较弱小的。Revolutionary forces are always weak at the outset.
【开士米】 kāishìmǐ 〈纺〉cashmere
【开市】 kāishì ① (of a shop) reopen after a cessation of business ② the first transaction of a day's business
【开释】 kāishì release (a prisoner)
【开水】 kāishuǐ ① boiling water ② boiled water
【开台】 kāitái begin a theatrical performance: ～锣鼓 a flourish of gongs and drums introducing a theatrical performance
【开天窗】 kāi tiānchuāng put in a skylight — leave a blank in a publication to show that sth. has been censored
【开天辟地】 kāitiān-pìdì ① when heaven was separated from earth — the creation of the world ② since the beginning of history: 贫下中农子女上大学,在咱们村还是～第一回。 This is the first time in the history of our village that sons and daughters of poor and lower-middle peasants have been sent to college.
【开庭】 kāitíng 〈法〉open a court session; call the court to order
【开通】 kāitōng remove obstacles from; dredge; clear: ～河道 dredge a river /坚冰已经打破,航道已经～。The ice has been broken; the road is open.
【开通】 kāitong open-minded; liberal; enlightened: 老大爷上夜校以后,脑筋更～了。After attending evening classes Grandpa became more open-minded.
【开头】 kāitóu begin; start: 我们的学习刚～。We've only just begun our study./ 请你先开个头儿。Would you make a start?/ 万事～难。The first step is always difficult./ 这篇文章～讲了我国当前的形势。The article begins with an account of the current situation in our country./ 你从一～就错了。You've been wrong from the start.
【开脱】 kāituō absolve; exonerate: ～罪责 absolve sb. from guilt or blame/ 替某人～ plead for sb.
【开拓】 kāituò ① open up: 在荒原上～出大片农田 open up large areas of wasteland and turn them into farmland/ 为发展石油工业～一条道路 open up a path for the development of the oil industry ②〈矿〉developing; opening ◇ ～巷道 development opening/ ～进尺 tunnelling footage
【开挖】 kāiwā excavate ◇ ～机械 excavating machinery
【开外】 kāiwài over; above: 他看起来有四十～。He looks over forty./ 东西相距六十里～ over sixty *li* from east to west
【开玩笑】 kāi wánxiào crack a joke; joke; make fun of: 他是跟你～呢,你别当真。He was only joking. Don't take it seriously./ 这可不是～的事情。This is no joke.
【开往】 kāiwǎng (of a train, ship, etc.) leave for; be bound for: ～广州的特快 the Guangzhou express
【开胃】 kāiwèi whet (或 stimulate) the appetite

【开小差】 kāi xiǎochāi ①(of a soldier) desert ②be absent-minded: 思想～ be woolgathering
【开销】 kāixiao ①pay expenses: 我带的钱够一路～的。I've brought enough money with me to cover the expenses of the trip. ②expense: 日常的～ daily expenses; running expenses/ 住在这儿～不大。Living is cheap here.
【开心】 kāixīn ①feel happy; rejoice: 他们去长城玩得很～。They went on a trip to the Great Wall and enjoyed it very much./ 人民大众～之日,就是反革命分子难受之时。The day of joy for the people is a day of woe for the counter-revolutionaries. ②amuse oneself at sb.'s expense; make fun of sb.: 别拿这老汉～了。Don't amuse yourself at the old man's expense.
【开学】 kāixué school opens; term begins
【开颜】 kāiyán smile; beam: 解放军进山寨,男女老少笑～。Men and women, old and young, beamed with joy when the PLA men entered the mountain village.
【开眼】 kāiyǎn open one's eyes; widen one's view (或 horizons); broaden one's mind: 这个展览会真叫人～。The exhibition is a real eye-opener.
【开演】 kāiyǎn (of a play, movie, etc.) begin: 今晚节目七点三十分～。The performance begins at 7:30 this evening.
【开业】 kāiyè ① (of a shop, etc.) start business ② (of a lawyer, doctor, etc.) open a private practice
【开夜车】 kāi yèchē work late into the night; put in extra time at night; burn the midnight oil
【开音节】 kāiyīnjié 〈语〉 open syllable
【开元音】 kāiyuányīn 〈语〉 open vowel
【开源节流】 kāiyuán jiéliú broaden sources of income and reduce expenditure; increase income and decrease expenditure
【开凿】 kāizáo cut (a canal, tunnel, etc.): 在山岩上～渠道 hew a channel through stony mountains
【开斋】 kāizhāi ①resume a meat diet ②〈伊斯兰教〉 come to the end of Ramadan ◇ ～节〈伊斯兰教〉 Lesser Bairam; the Festival of Fast-breaking
【开展】 kāizhǎn ①develop; launch; unfold: ～增产节约运动 launch a movement for increasing production and practising economy/ ～批评和自我批评 carry out criticism and self-criticism/ 我们现在思想战线上的一个重要任务,就是要～对于修正主义的批判。It is an important task for us to unfold criticism of revisionism on the ideological front now. ②open-minded; politically progressive: 政治上不～ lagging behind in political understanding; slow in political progress
【开战】 kāizhàn ①make war; open hostilities ②battle (against nature, conservative forces, etc.): 向穷山恶水～ battle against barren hills and untamed rivers ◇ ～理由 *casus belli*
【开绽】 kāizhàn come unsewn: 鞋后跟～了。The shoe has split at the heel.
【开张】 kāizhāng ①open a business; begin doing business: 重打锣鼓另～ reopen a business to the beating of gongs and drums; start all over again ②the first transaction of a day's business
【开仗】 kāizhàng make war; open hostilities
【开帐】 kāizhàng ①make out a bill ②pay the bill (at a restaurant, hotel, etc.)
【开支】 kāizhī ①pay (expenses): 这笔钱厂里不能～。The factory shouldn't foot this bill. ②expenses; expenditure; spending: 节省～ cut down expenses; retrench/ 军费～ military spending ③〈方〉 pay wages or salaries: 我们每月五号～。We get our pay on the 5th of every month.
【开宗明义】 kāizōng-míngyì make clear the purpose and main theme from the very beginning: ～第一章 in the first place
【开足马力】 kāizú mǎlì put into high gear; go full steam ahead; open the throttle
【开钻】 kāizuàn 〈石油〉 spud in

**揩** kāi wipe: 把桌子～干净 wipe the table clean
【揩油】 kāiyóu get petty advantages at the expense of other people or the state; scrounge

**锎** kāi 〈化〉 californium (Cf)

## kǎi

**凯** kǎi ①triumphant strains ②triumphant; victorious
【凯歌】 kǎigē a song of triumph; paean: ～阵阵,喜报频传。Songs of triumph are heard all round and good news keeps pouring in.
【凯旋】 kǎixuán triumphant return: 大军～归来。The army returned in triumph.

**剀** kǎi
【剀切】 kǎiqiè 〈书〉 ①true and pertinent: ～详明 true and clear in every detail ②earnest and sincere: ～教导 teach earnestly

**铠** kǎi
【铠甲】 kǎijiǎ (a suit of) armour
【铠装】 kǎizhuāng 〈电〉 armour ◇ ～电缆 armoured cable

**慨** kǎi ①indignant ②deeply touched: 感～ sigh with emotion ③generous: ～允 consent readily; kindly promise
【慨然】 kǎirán ①with deep feeling: ～长叹 heave a sigh of regret ②generously: ～相赠 give generously
【慨叹】 kǎitàn sigh with regret

**楷** kǎi ① model; pattern ② (in Chinese calligraphy) regular script: 小～ regular script in small characters/ 大～ regular script in big characters
【楷模】 kǎimó model; pattern
【楷书】 kǎishū (in Chinese calligraphy) regular script
【楷体】 kǎitǐ ①见"楷书" ②block letter

## kài

**忾** kài 见"敌忾" díkài

## kān

**刊** kān ①print; publish: 停～ suspend or stop publication (of a newspaper, etc.) ②periodical; publication: 报～ newspapers and magazines/ 周～ weekly (publication) ③delete or correct: ～误 correct errors in printing
【刊登】 kāndēng publish in a newspaper or magazine; carry: ～广告 print an advertisement; advertise
【刊物】 kānwù publication: 定期～ periodical (publication)
【刊行】 kānxíng print and publish
【刊载】 kānzǎi publish (in a newspaper or magazine); carry: 报纸上～了几篇有关激光技术的文章。The newspaper carried a few articles about laser technique.

**看** kān ①look after; take care of; tend: ～孩子 look after children/ ～瓜 keep watch in the melon fields/ ～牛

tend cattle/他病很重，得有人～着。He is seriously ill and needs someone to look after him./ 她一个人～两台机器。She minds two machines all by herself. ② keep under surveillance: ～住他，别让这坏家伙跑了！Keep an eye on that rascal. Don't let him run away.

另见 kàn

【看场】 kānchǎng guard the threshing floor (during the harvest season)

【看管】 kānguǎn ① look after; attend to: 留个人～行李。Someone will stay here to look after the luggage. ② guard; watch: ～犯人 guard prisoners

【看护】 kānhù ① nurse: ～病人 nurse the sick ② 〈旧〉 hospital nurse

【看家】 kānjiā ① look after the house; mind the house ② outstanding (ability); special (skill) ◇ ～本领 one's special skill

【看门】 kānmén ① guard the entrance; act as doorkeeper ② look after the house

【看青】 kānqīng keep watch over the ripening crops

【看守】 kānshǒu ① watch; guard: ～仓库 guard a storehouse/ ～犯人 guard prisoners ② turnkey; warder ◇ ～内阁 caretaker cabinet/ ～所 lockup for prisoners awaiting trial

【看押】 kānyā take into custody; detain

**勘** kān ① read and correct the text of; collate ② investigate; survey

【勘测】 kāncè survey

【勘察】 kānchá ① reconnaissance ② 〈地〉 prospecting

【勘探】 kāntàn exploration; prospecting: 磁法～ magnetic prospecting/ 地震～ seismic prospecting ◇ ～地震学 exploration seismology/ ～队 prospecting team

【勘误】 kānwù correct errors in printing ◇ ～表 errata; corrigenda

**龛** kān niche; shrine

**堪** kān ① may; can: ～称佳作 may be rated as a good piece of writing or a fine work of art/ ～当重任 be capable of shouldering important tasks; can fill a position of great responsibility ② bear; endure: 不～一击 cannot withstand a single blow; collapse at the first blow

**戡** kān suppress: ～平叛乱 suppress (或 put down) a rebellion

## kǎn

**坎** kǎn ① bank; ridge: 田～儿 a raised path through fields ② 〈书〉 pit; hole

【坎肩儿】 kǎnjiānr sleeveless jacket (usu. padded or lined)

【坎坷】 kǎnkě ① bumpy; rough: ～不平的道路 a rough and bumpy road ② 〈书〉 full of frustrations: ～一生 a lifetime of frustrations

【坎儿井】 kǎnrjǐng an irrigation system of wells connected by underground channels used in Xinjiang; karez

**侃** kǎn

【侃侃而谈】 kǎnkǎn ér tán speak with fervour and assurance

**砍** kǎn ① cut; chop; hack: 把树枝～下来 cut (或 lop) off a branch/ ～柴 cut firewood/ 把树～倒 fell a tree/ 这篇稿子太长，得～去一半。The article is too long and should be cut down by half. ② 〈方〉 throw sth. at: 拿砖头～狗 throw a brick at a dog

【砍刀】 kǎndāo chopper

【砍伐】 kǎnfá fell (trees)

【砍头】 kǎntóu chop off the head; behead

【砍土镘】 kǎntǔmàn a kind of mattock used by the Uygur nationality

【砍砸器】 kǎnzáqì 〈考古〉 chopper; chopping tool

**莰** kǎn 〈化〉 camphane; bornane

**槛** kǎn threshold

另见 jiàn

## kàn

**看** kàn ① see; look at; watch: ～电影 see a film; go to the movies/ ～戏 go to the theatre; see a play, an opera, etc./ ～电视 watch TV/ ～球赛 watch a ball game ② read: ～报 read a newspaper/ ～书 read (a book) ③ think; consider: 你～她这个人可靠吗？Do you think she's reliable?/ 你对这件事怎么～？What's your view on this matter?/ 比较全面地～问题 try and look at (或 approach) problems from all angles/ ～清形势 make a correct appraisal of the situation ④ look upon; regard: 把人民的利益～得高于一切 put the interests of the people above all else ⑤ treat (a patient or an illness): 李大夫把她的肺炎～好了。Dr. Li has cured her of pneumonia. ⑥ look after: ～顾 look after; take care of/ 她在幼儿园照～孩子。She looks after children in the kindergarten. ⑦ call on; visit; see: 我明天去～他。I'll go and see him tomorrow./ 有空我来～你。I'll drop in on you when I have time. ⑧ depend on: 明天是不是打场，得～天气。Whether we'll do the threshing tomorrow will depend on the weather. ⑨ mind; watch out: 别跑这么快！～摔着！Don't run so fast! Mind you don't fall. ⑩〔用在动词或动词结构后面，表示试一试〕: 试试～ have a try/ 等一等～wait and see/ 尝尝～。Just taste this.

另见 kān

【看病】 kànbìng ① (of a doctor) see a patient: 大夫出去～去了。The doctor's gone to see a patient./ 王大夫～很认真。Dr. Wang handles his cases with great care./ 哪位是给你～的大夫？Who is your doctor? ② (of a patient) see (或 consult) a doctor: 明天我要～去。I'm going to see a doctor tomorrow.

【看不惯】 kànbuguàn cannot bear the sight of; frown upon: 这种浪费现象我们～。We hate to see such waste.

【看不起】 kànbuqǐ look down upon; scorn; despise: 对于落后的人们，我们不应当～他们，而是要帮助他们。We shouldn't look down upon backward people, we should help them.

【看菜吃饭，量体裁衣】 kàn cài chīfàn, liàng tǐ cái yī fit the appetite to the dishes and the dress to the figure — adapt oneself to circumstances

【看成】 kànchéng look upon as; regard as: 你把我～什么人了？What do you take me for?

【看出】 kànchū make out; see: ～问题在那里 see where the trouble is/ 看不出真假 cannot tell whether it is genuine or fake

【看穿】 kànchuān see through: 群众立即～了他的诡计。The masses at once saw through his trick.

【看待】 kàndài look upon; regard; treat: 矛盾要分主次，不能一律～。We should distinguish between major and minor contradictions and not treat them all alike./ 奴隶主根本不把奴隶当人～。Slave owners never regarded (或

treated) their slaves as human beings.
【看到】 kàndào catch sight of; see: 拐个弯儿就可以~村子了。The village will come into view at the next turn./ 我们满意地~，两国的友好关系有了进一步的发展。We notice with gratification that the friendly relations between our two countries have further developed./ 我们的同志在困难的时候，要~成绩，要~光明，要提高我们的勇气。In times of difficulty we must not lose sight of our achievements, must see the bright future and must pluck up our courage.
【看得起】 kàndeqǐ have a good opinion of; think highly of: 在旧社会，有谁~我们清洁工人? In the old society who thought anything of us street cleaners?
【看跌】 kàndiē (of market prices) be expected to fall
【看法】 kànfa a way of looking at a thing; view: 对这个问题有两种不同的~。There are two different views on this question.
【看风使舵】 kàn fēng shǐ duò trim one's sails
【看见】 kànjian catch sight of; see: 你~老张了吗? Did you see Lao Zhang?/ 他们航行了二十天，才~陆地。They sighted land after being at sea for twenty days.
【看来】 kànlai it seems (或 appears); it looks as if: 这活儿~今天可以做完。It looks as if we'll be able to finish this job today./ ~他还没有拿定主意。Evidently he has not made up his mind yet.
【看破】 kànpò see through: ~那些卑劣勾当 see through those base tricks/ ~红尘 be disillusioned with the mortal world
【看齐】 kànqí ① dress: 向右(左)~! Dress right (left), dress! ② keep up with; emulate: 向先进工作者~ emulate the advanced workers
【看轻】 kànqīng underestimate; look down upon: 我们不应~自己的力量。We must not underestimate our own strength.
【看上】 kànshang take a fancy to; settle on: ~一位姑娘 take a fancy to a girl
【看台】 kàntái 〈体〉 bleachers; stand
【看透】 kàntòu ① understand thoroughly: 这一着棋我看不透。I don't quite understand this move./ ~修正主义的本质 clearly perceive the true nature of revisionism ② see through: 这个人我~了，没有什么真才实学。I've seen through him; he's not a man of real learning.
【看头】 kàntou 〈口〉 sth. worth seeing or reading: 这个展览会没什么~。There is nothing much to see in the exhibition. /这部小说很有~。This novel is well worth reading.
【看图识字】 kàn tú shí zì learn to read with the aid of pictures
【看望】 kànwang call on; visit; see: ~老战友 call on an old comrade-in-arms
【看样子】 kàn yàngzi 见"看来"
【看涨】 kànzhǎng (of market prices) be expected to rise
【看中】 kànzhòng take a fancy to; settle on: 这些布你~了哪块? Which piece of cloth have you settled on?
【看重】 kànzhòng regard as important; value; set store by: 不要只~书本知识，还要在实践中学习。We must not consider that book knowledge alone is important; we should also learn through practice./ ~友谊 set store by the ties of friendship
【看做】 kànzuò look upon as; regard as: 你把次要问题~主要问题了。You have taken a minor question for a major one./ 我们把世界各国人民的正义斗争~是自己的斗争。We look upon the just struggles of the people all over the world as our own. 又作"看作"

**瞰** kàn look down from a height; overlook: 鸟~ get a bird's-eye view

## kāng

**康** kāng ① well-being; health ② (Kāng) a surname
【康拜因】 kāngbàiyīn combine (harvester)
【康采恩】 kāngcǎi'ēn 〈经〉 concern
【康复】 kāngfù restored to health; recovered: 祝您早日~。Hope you'll soon be well again. 或 I wish you a speedy recovery.
【康健】 kāngjiàn healthy; in good health
【康乐】 kānglè peace and happiness
【康铜】 kāngtóng constantan
【康庄大道】 kāngzhuāng dàdào broad road; main road: 走社会主义~ take the broad road of socialism

**慷** kāng
【慷慨】 kāngkǎi ① vehement; fervent: ~陈词 present one's views vehemently ② generous; liberal: ~解囊 help sb. generously with money /慷他人之慨 be generous at other people's expense
【慷慨激昂】 kāngkǎi jī'áng impassioned; vehement: 他讲得~，非常感人。His impassioned speech was very moving.
【慷慨就义】 kāngkǎi jiùyì go to one's death like a hero; die a martyr's death

**槺** kāng 见"榔槺" lángkang

**糠** kāng ① chaff; bran; husk ② (usu. of a radish) spongy: 这萝卜~了。This radish has gone spongy.
【糠秕】 kāngbǐ ① chaff ② worthless stuff
【糠菜半年粮】 kāng-cài bànnián liáng have nothing to eat but chaff and wild herbs for half the year — lead a life of semistarvation
【糠醛】 kāngquán 〈化〉 furfural ◇ ~树脂 furfural resin

**鱇** kāng 见"鮟鱇" ānkāng

## káng

**扛** káng carry on the shoulder; shoulder: ~着锄头 carry a hoe on one's shoulder/ ~枪 shoulder a gun; bear arms 另见 gāng
【扛长活】 káng chánghuó work as a farm labourer on a yearly basis
【扛竿】 kánggān 〈杂技〉 acrobatics on a bamboo pole
【扛活】 kánghuó work as a farm labourer

## kàng

**亢** kàng ① high; haughty: 高~ loud and sonorous; resounding/ 不~不卑 neither supercilious nor obsequious ② excessive; extreme
【亢奋】 kàngfèn stimulated; excited
【亢旱】 kànghàn severe drought
【亢进】 kàngjìn 〈医〉 hyperfunction: 甲状腺机能~ hyperthyroidism

**伉** kàng
【伉俪】 kànglì 〈书〉 married couple; husband and wife

**抗** kàng ① resist; combat; fight: ~灾 fight natural calamities/ 美国黑人的~暴斗争 the Black Americans' struggle against violent repression/ ~癌药 anticancer drugs

② refuse; defy: ～捐～税 refuse to pay levies and taxes ③ contend with; be a match for: 分庭～礼 stand up to sb. as an equal
【抗爆】 kàngbào 〈化〉 antiknock ◇ ～剂 antiknock (agent); antidetonant/ ～汽油 antiknock gasoline
【抗辩】 kàngbiàn ① contradict ② 〈法〉 counterplea; demurrer
【抗病】 kàngbìng 〈农〉 disease-resistant ◇ ～性 disease resistance
【抗磁性】 kàngcíxìng 〈物〉 diamagnetism
【抗大】 Kàngdà the Chinese People's Anti-Japanese Military and Political College (set up in Yan'an during the War of Resistance Against Japan)
【抗倒伏】 kàng dǎofú 〈农〉 resistant to lodging; lodging-resistant
【抗毒素】 kàngdúsù 〈医〉 antitoxin ◇ ～血清 antitoxic serum
【抗旱】 kànghàn fight (或 combat) a drought: ～措施 drought-relief measures/ 这个新品种能～。This new variety is drought-resistant. ◇ ～性 drought resistance/ ～品种 〈农〉 drought-resistant variety
【抗衡】 kànghéng contend with; match
【抗洪】 kànghóng fight (或 combat) a flood
【抗坏血酸】 kànghuàixuèsuān 〈药〉 ascorbic acid; vitamin C
【抗击】 kàngjī resist; beat back: ～侵略者 resist the aggressors
【抗剪强度】 kàngjiǎn qiángdù 〈机〉 shearing strength
【抗拒】 kàngjù resist; defy
【抗菌素】 kàngjūnsù 〈药〉 antibiotic
【抗拉强度】 kànglā qiángdù 〈机〉 tensile strength
【抗老剂】 kànglǎojì 〈化〉 antiager
【抗美援朝战争】 Kàng Měi Yuán Cháo Zhànzhēng the War to Resist U.S. Aggression and Aid Korea (1950-1953)
【抗命】 kàngmìng defy orders; disobey
【抗日战争】 Kàng Rì Zhànzhēng the War of Resistance Against Japan (1937-1945)
【抗渗】 kàngshèn 〈水〉 impervious ◇ ～试验 impermeability test
【抗生菌肥】 kàngshēng jūnféi antibiotic fertilizer
【抗生素】 kàngshēngsù 〈药〉 antibiotic
【抗霜】 kàngshuāng 〈农〉 frost-resistant
【抗水性】 kàngshuǐxìng water-resistance; water-resisting property
【抗体】 kàngtǐ 〈医〉 antibody
【抗弯强度】 kàngwān qiángdù 〈机〉 bending strength
【抗压强度】 kàngyā qiángdù 〈机〉 compressive strength (或 resistance)
【抗药性】 kàngyàoxìng 〈医〉 resistance to the action of a drug: 产生～ become drug-fast
【抗议】 kàngyì protest: 提出～ lodge a protest ◇ ～集会 protest rally/ ～照会 note of protest
【抗原】 kàngyuán 〈医〉 antigen
【抗战】 kàngzhàn ① war of resistance against aggression ② 〈简〉(抗日战争) the War of Resistance Against Japan (1937-1945)
【抗张强度】 kàngzhāng qiángdù 见"抗拉强度"
【抗震】 kàngzhèn ① anti-seismic: ～结构 〈建〉 anti-seismic structure/ ～救灾工作 earthquake relief work ② 〈化〉 见"抗爆"
【抗争】 kàngzhēng make a stand against; resist

**炕** kàng ① *kang*; a heatable brick bed ② 〈方〉 bake or dry by the heat of a fire: 把湿麦子摊在炕上～干 spread the wet wheat on a heated *kang* to dry
【炕洞】 kàngdòng the flue of a *kang*
【炕头】 kàngtóu 〈口〉 ① the warmer end of a *kang* ② the edge of a *kang*
【炕席】 kàngxí *kang* mat
【炕沿】 kàngyán 〈口〉 the edge of a *kang*
【炕桌】 kàngzhuō a small, short-legged table for use on a *kang*; *kang* table

**钪** kàng 〈化〉 scandium (Sc)

## kāo

**尻** kāo 〔古书用语〕 buttocks; bottom

## kǎo

**考** kǎo ① give or take an examination, test or quiz: 我～～你。I'll give you a quiz. 或 Let me quiz you./ 你的数学～得怎么样? How did you do in the maths test (或 quiz)?/ 应～ sit for (或 take) an examination/ ～上大学 be admitted to a university ② check; inspect ③ study; investigate; verify: 待～ remain to be verified ④ 〈书〉 one's deceased father
【考查】 kǎochá examine; check: ～学生成绩 check students' work
【考察】 kǎochá ① inspect; make an on-the-spot investigation: ～水利工程 investigate water conservancy projects/ 出国～ go abroad on a tour of investigation ② observe and study: 应当在长期的群众斗争中,～和识别干部,挑选和培养接班人。It is essential to test and judge cadres and choose and train successors in the long course of mass struggle. ◇ ～团 observation (或 investigation) group/ ～组 study group
【考场】 kǎochǎng examination hall or room
【考订】 kǎodìng examine and correct; do textual research
【考古】 kǎogǔ ① engage in archaeological studies ② archaeology ◇ ～学 archaeology/ ～学家 archaeologist
【考核】 kǎohé examine; check; assess (sb.'s proficiency): 定期～ routine check/ ～干部 check on cadres/ 技术～制度业已建立。A system to assess technical proficiency has been established. ◇ ～飞行 check-out flight; check flight
【考究】 kǎojiu ① observe and study; investigate: 这问题很值得～。We need to go into the matter seriously. 或 This problem merits serious attention. ② fastidious; particular: 穿衣服不必过于～。One need not be too particular about dress. ③ exquisite; fine: 这本画册装订得很～。This album is beautifully bound.
【考据】 kǎojù textual criticism; textual research
【考卷】 kǎojuàn examination paper
【考虑】 kǎolǜ think over; consider: 让我～一下再答复你。Let me think it over before I give you an answer./ 这方面的情况你～了吗? Have you taken this aspect of the matter into account?/ 计划～不周。The plan has not been carefully thought out./ 不～个人得失 disregard personal gains and losses/ 给予同情的～ give sympathetic consideration to
【考勤】 kǎoqín check on work attendance ◇ ～簿 attendance record
【考取】 kǎoqǔ pass an entrance examination; be admitted to school or college (after an examination)
【考生】 kǎoshēng candidate for an entrance examination; examinee
【考试】 kǎoshì examination; test
【考题】 kǎotí examination questions; examination paper: 出～ set an examination paper; set examination questions
【考问】 kǎowèn examine orally; question

【考验】 kǎoyàn test; trial: 经受了严峻的～ have stood a severe test/ 久经～的革命战士 a tried revolutionary fighter/ 他经受了革命战争的严峻～。He went through the rigorous trials of revolutionary war.

【考证】 kǎozhèng textual criticism; textual research

**拷** kǎo flog; beat; torture

【拷贝】 kǎobèi 〈电影〉 copy ◇ ～纸 copy (或 copying) paper

【拷绸】 kǎochóu a rust-coloured variety of summer silk; gambiered Guangdong silk

【拷打】 kǎodǎ flog; beat; torture: 严刑～ subject sb. to severe torture

【拷花】 kǎohuā 〈纺〉 embossing ◇ ～布 embossed cloth

【拷问】 kǎowèn torture sb. during interrogation; interrogate with torture

**烤** kǎo ① bake; roast; toast: ～白薯 baked sweet potatoes/ ～馒头 toasted steamed bun/ 把湿衣裳～干 dry wet clothes by a fire ② scorching: 这炉子太～人。This stove is really scorching.

【烤电】 kǎodiàn 〈医〉 diathermy

【烤火】 kǎohuǒ warm oneself by a fire

【烤炉】 kǎolú oven

【烤面包】 kǎomiànbāo toast: 一片～ a slice of toast

【烤肉】 kǎoròu roast meat; roast ◇ ～叉 spit; skewer

【烤鸭】 kǎoyā roast duck: 北京～ roast Beijing duck

【烤烟】 kǎoyān flue-cured tobacco

**栲** kǎo 〈植〉 evergreen chinquapin

【栲胶】 kǎojiāo tannin extract

【栲栳】 kǎolǎo wicker basket

## kào

**铐** kào ① handcuffs ② put handcuffs on; handcuff: 把犯人～起来 handcuff the criminal

**犒** kào reward with food and drink

【犒劳】 kàolao reward with food and drink

【犒赏】 kàoshǎng reward a victorious army, etc. with bounties

**靠** kào ① lean against; lean on: 把梯子～在墙上 lean a ladder against a wall/ 背～背坐着 sit back to back ② keep to; get near; come up to: 车辆一律～右走。All vehicles should keep to the right./ 船已经～码头了。The ship has docked. ③ near; by: 疗养院～海。The sanatorium stands by the sea./ ～山吃山，～水吃水 those living on a mountain live off the mountain, those living near the water live off the water — make use of local resources ④ depend on; rely on: 他家里～他维持生活。His family depended on him for support. ⑤ trust: 可～ reliable; trustworthy

【靠岸】 kào'àn pull in to shore; draw alongside

【靠背】 kàobèi back (of a chair) ◇ ～椅 chair

【靠边】 kàobiān keep to the side: ～！～！Out of the way, please! 或 Mind your backs, please!/ 行人～走。Pedestrians keep to the side of the road./ ～儿站 stand aside; step aside; get out of the way

【靠不住】 kàobuzhù unreliable; undependable; untrustworthy: 这话～。This story cannot be relied upon.

【靠得住】 kàodezhù reliable; dependable; trustworthy: 这消息～吗？Is the information reliable?

【靠垫】 kàodiàn cushion (for leaning on)

【靠近】 kàojìn ① near; close to; by: ～咱们厂有一家百货公司。There's a department store near our factory. ② draw near; approach: 轮船慢慢地～码头。The ship is nearing the dock.

【靠拢】 kàolǒng draw close; close up: 向前～！Close ranks!

【靠模】 kàomú 〈机〉 profiling; modelling: ～铣床 profiling (或 copying) milling machine/ ～车床 copying lathe

【靠山】 kàoshan backer; patron; backing

【靠手】 kàoshǒu armrest

【靠枕】 kàozhěn back cushion

## kē

**坷** kē
另见 kě

【坷拉】 kēla 〈方〉 clod: 打～ break clods 又作"坷垃"

**苛** kē severe; exacting: ～待 treat harshly; be hard upon

【苛捐杂税】 kējuān-záshuì exorbitant taxes and levies

【苛刻】 kēkè harsh: ～的条件 harsh terms

【苛求】 kēqiú make excessive demands; be overcritical

【苛性】 kēxìng 〈化〉 causticity ◇ ～钾 caustic potash/ ～钠 caustic soda

【苛责】 kēzé criticize severely; excoriate

【苛政】 kēzhèng harsh (或 oppressive) government; tyranny: ～猛于虎。Tyranny is fiercer than a tiger.

**珂** kē 〈书〉 ① a jade-like stone ② an ornament on a bridle

【珂罗版】 kēluóbǎn collotype ◇ ～印刷 collotype printing

**柯** kē ① 〈书〉 stalk or branch ② 〈书〉 axe-handle; helve ③ (Kē) a surname

【柯尔克孜族】 Kē'ěrkèzīzú the Kirgiz (Khalkhas) nationality, living in the Xinjiang Uygur Autonomous Region

**科** kē ① a branch of academic or vocational study: 文～ the humanities; the liberal arts/ 理～ the sciences/ 眼～ department of ophthalmology ② a division or subdivision of an administrative unit; section: 财务～ finance section/ 卫生～ health section; clinic ③ 〈生〉 family: 猫～动物 animals of the cat family ④ pass a sentence: ～处徒刑 sentence sb. to imprisonment/ ～以罚金 impose a fine on sb.; fine ⑤ stage directions in classical Chinese drama

【科白】 kēbái actions and spoken parts in classical Chinese drama

【科班】 kēbān ① old-type opera school ② regular professional training: ～出身 be a professional by training

【科技】 kējì science and technology ◇ ～大学 university of science and technology/ ～界 scientific and technological circles/ ～术语 scientific and technical terminology

【科教片】 kējiàopiàn 〈简〉（科学教育影片） popular science film; science and educational film

【科举】 kējǔ imperial examinations ◇ ～制度 imperial examination system

【科摩罗】 Kēmóluó the Comoros

【科目】 kēmù ① subject (in a curriculum); course ② headings in an account book

【科室】 kēshì administrative or technical offices ◇ ～人员 office staff (或 personnel)

【科威特】 Kēwēitè Kuwait ◇ ～人 Kuwaiti

【科学】 kēxué science; scientific knowledge ◇ ～工作者 scientific worker; scientist/ ～幻想小说 science fiction/ ～家 scientist/ ～教育影片 popular science film/ ～普及读物 popular science books; popular science/ ～社会主义 scientific socialism/ ～实验 scientific experiment/ ～文献 scientific literature/ ～研究 scientific research/ ～仪器 scientific instruments (或 apparatus)/ ～种田 scientific farming

【科学技术】 kēxué-jìshù science and technology: ～是生产力。Science and technology are part of the productive forces.

【科学院】 kēxuéyuàn academy of sciences: 中国～ the Chinese Academy of Sciences; Academia Sinica

【科研】 kēyán scientific research ◇ ～机构 scientific research institution/ ～考察船 research ship/ ～人员 scientific research personnel

【科员】 kēyuán a member of an administrative section; section member

【科长】 kēzhǎng section chief

**疴** kē 〈书〉 illness: 沉～ severe and lingering illness

**砢** kē

【砢碜】 kēchen 〈方〉 见"寒伧" hánchen

**钶** kē 〈化〉 columbium (Cb)

**棵** kē 〈量〉: 一～树 a tree/ 一～大白菜 a (head of) Chinese cabbage

**颏** kē chin

**窠** kē nest; burrow

【窠臼】 kējiù 〈书〉 set pattern (usu. of writing or artistic creation): 不落～ show originality; be unconventional

**稞** kē

【稞麦】 kēmài 见"青稞" qīngkē

**颗** kē 〈量〉: 一～珠子 a pearl/ 一～黄豆 a soya bean

【颗粒】 kēlì ① anything small and roundish (as a bean, pearl, etc.); pellet ② grain: ～归仓 every grain to the granary ◇ ～肥料 granulated fertilizer/ ～物质 particulate matter/ ～细胞 granular cell

**榼** kē 〈考古〉 an ancient wine vessel

**磕** kē ① knock (against sth. hard): 摔了一跤，脸上～破了皮 fall and graze one's face/ 碗边儿～掉了一块 chip the edge of a bowl ② knock sth. out of a vessel, container, etc.: ～烟袋锅儿 knock the ashes out of a pipe; empty out a pipe

【磕巴】 kēba 〈口〉 stutter; stammer

【磕打】 kēda knock sth. out of a vessel, container, etc.; knock out: 把鞋～～ knock the dirt off one's shoes

【磕磕绊绊】 kēkebànbàn ① bumpy; rough ② limping

【磕磕撞撞】 kēkezhuàngzhuàng walk unsteadily; stumble or stagger along; reel

【磕碰】 kēpèng ① knock against; collide with; bump against: 这箱瓷器一路上磕磕碰碰的，碎了不少。This box of porcelain has been bumped about all the way here and quite a few pieces are broken. ② clash; squabble

【磕头】 kētóu kowtow

【磕头碰脑】 kētóu-pèngnǎo bump against things on every side (as in a room full of furniture); push and bump against one another (as in a crowd)

【磕膝盖】 kēxīgài 〈方〉 knee

**瞌** kē

【瞌睡】 kēshuì sleepy; drowsy: 打～ doze off; nod; have a nap/ 一宿没睡，白天～得很。I'm terribly sleepy today, I didn't sleep a wink last night.

**蝌** kē

【蝌蚪】 kēdǒu tadpole

**髁** kē 〈生理〉 condyle

## ké

**壳** ké ① shell: 鸡蛋～ egg shell/ 核桃～ walnut shell ② 〈机〉 housing; casing; case: 拼合～ 〈石油〉 split housing/ 涡轮～ turbine casing/ 护～ protecting case
另见 qiào

**咳** ké cough
另见 hāi

【咳嗽】 késou cough ◇ ～糖浆 cough syrup

**揢** ké 〈方〉 ① get stuck; wedge: 抽屉～住了，拉不开。The drawer's stuck. It won't open. ② create difficulties; make things difficult

## kě

**可** kě ① approve: 不置～否 decline to comment; be noncommittal ② can; may: 由此～见 thus it can be seen that; this proves/ 今秋～望丰收。We expect a good harvest this autumn. ③ need (doing); be worth (doing): 没有什么～担心的。There is nothing to worry about./ ～爱 lovable/ ～靠 reliable ④ fit; suit: 这回倒～了他的心了。It suited him perfectly this time. ⑤〈副〉 but; yet: 劳动很艰苦，～大家干劲十足。It was hard work, but everybody went at it with a will. ⑥〈副〉〔用于加强语气〕: ～别忘了。Mind you don't forget it. 或 Be sure to remember it./ 你～来了！So you're here at last!/ ～不是吗？That's just the way it is. 或 Exactly./ 有人这么说，～谁见过呢？So they say, but who has ever seen it? ⑦〈副〉〔表示疑问〕: 你～曾跟他谈过这个问题？ Did you ever talk it over with him? ⑧〈书〉 about: 重～千斤 weigh about 1,000 *jin*
另见 kè

【可爱】 kě'ài lovable; likable; lovely: ～的祖国 my beloved country/ 多么～的孩子！What lovely children!

【可悲】 kěbēi sad; lamentable

【可比价格】 kěbǐ jiàgé 〈经〉 fixed price; constant price

【可鄙】 kěbǐ contemptible; despicable; mean: 行为～ act contemptibly

【可变】 kěbiàn variable ◇ ～电容器 variable condenser (或 capacitor)/ ～资本 〈经〉 variable capital

【可采储量】 kěcǎi chǔliàng 〈石油〉 recoverable reserves

【可操左券】 kě cāo zuǒquàn be sure to succeed; be certain of success

【可拆】 kěchāi removable; detachable ◇ ～砂箱 〈机〉 snap flask/ ～装置〈机〉 detachable device

【可乘之机】 kě chéng zhī jī an opportunity that can be exploited to sb.'s advantage: 不给敌人以～ give the enemy no opportunity

【可耻】 kěchǐ shameful; disgraceful; ignominious: ～的失败 ignominious defeat/ 以爱学习为光荣，以不学习为～。It is praiseworthy to love study, and shameful to neglect it.

【可待因】 kědàiyīn 〈药〉 codeine
【可的松】 kědìsōng 〈药〉 cortisone
【可锻性】 kěduànxìng 〈冶〉 malleability; forgeability
【可锻铸铁】 kěduàn zhùtiě 〈冶〉 malleable (cast) iron
【可纺性】 kěfǎngxìng 〈纺〉 spinnability
【可歌可泣】 kěgē-kěqì move one to song and tears: ～的英雄事迹 heroic and moving deeds/ ～的斗争 an epic struggle
【可耕地】 kěgēngdì arable land; cultivable land
【可观】 kěguān considerable; impressive; sizable: 这个数目相当～。This is a considerable figure.
【可贵】 kěguì valuable; praiseworthy; commendable: ～的品质 fine qualities/ 这种积极性和热情是很～的。Such initiative and enthusiasm are highly commendable.
【可恨】 kěhèn hateful; detestable; abominable
【可加工性】 kějiāgōngxìng 〈机〉 machinability
【可见】 kějiàn it is thus clear (或 evident, obvious) that
【可见度】 kějiàndù visibility
【可见光】 kějiànguāng 〈物〉 visible light
【可惊】 kějīng surprising; startling
【可敬】 kějìng worthy of respect; respected
【可卡因】 kěkǎyīn 〈药〉 cocaine
【可靠】 kěkào reliable; dependable; trustworthy: ～消息 reliable information/ 这个人很～。This person is reliable (或 trustworthy)./ 贫下中农是工人阶级最～的同盟军。The poor and lower-middle peasants are the most dependable allies of the working class. ◇ ～性 reliability
【可可】 kěkě cocoa
【可控硅】 kěkòngguī 〈电子〉 silicon controlled rectifier (SCR); thyristor 又作"可控硅整流器"
【可口】 kěkǒu good to eat; nice; tasty; palatable: 这菜很～。This dish is very tasty.
【可怜】 kělián ① pitiful; pitiable; poor: 装出一付～相 put on a pitiable look ② have pity on; pity: 他这是自作自受，没人～他。Nobody feels sorry for him; he's got what he deserves. ③ meagre; wretched; miserable; pitiful: 这一带雨水少得～。There's terribly little rainfall in this area. 或 The rainfall is pitifully low in this area. ◇ ～虫 pitiful creature; wretch
【可裂变物质】 kělièbiàn wùzhì 〈物〉 fissile (或 fissionable) material
【可能】 kěnéng ① possible; probable: 提前一个月交工是完全～的。It's entirely possible to complete the project and hand it over one month ahead of time. /没有知识分子的参加，革命的胜利是不～的。Without the participation of the intellectuals victory in the revolution is impossible. ② probably; maybe: 他～不知道。 He probably doesn't know./ 她今天～会再来的。Maybe she'll pop in again today. ③ possibility: 事情发展有两种～。The matter may develop in two possible directions. ◇ ～性 possibility
【可逆】 kěnì reversible ◇ ～反应〈化〉 reversible reaction
【可怕】 kěpà fearful; frightful; terrible; terrifying: 真～！How dreadful!/ 困难再大也没什么～的。However great the difficulties, there's nothing to be afraid of.
【可欺】 kěqī ① gullible; easily duped ② easily cowed or bullied: 不要把我方的克制看做是软弱～。Do not take our restraint for a sign of weakness.
【可气】 kěqì annoying; exasperating: 这孩子刚换的衣服就弄脏了，真～！The child just changed his clothes and now he's got them dirty again. How annoying!
【可巧】 kěqiǎo as luck would have it; by a happy coincidence: 大家正念叨他，～他来了。We were just talking about him when he turned up.
【可取】 kěqǔ desirable: 双方认为增进两国人民之间的了解是～的。Both sides consider it desirable to further the understanding between the two peoples./ 这个方案有～之处。This plan has something to recommend it.
【可燃性】 kěránxìng 〈化〉 combustibility; flammability
【可溶性】 kěróngxìng 〈化〉 solubility
【可身】 kěshēn 〈方〉 be a good fit; fit nicely
【可视电话】 kěshì diànhuà picturephone
【可是】 kěshì 〈连〉 but; yet; however: 他们劳动了一天，虽然很累，～都很愉快。They were tired out after the day's work, but they all felt happy.
【可塑性】 kěsùxìng plasticity
【可望而不可即】 kě wàng ér bùkě jí within sight but beyond reach; unattainable; inaccessible
【可谓】 kěwèi one may well say; it may be said; it may be called: 党对他的教育挽救～仁至义尽。One may well say that the Party has done its very best to educate and save him.
【可恶】 kěwù hateful; abominable; detestable: 这些棉铃虫真～！What a curse those bollworms are!
【可惜】 kěxī it's a pity; it's too bad: ～我去晚了一步，最精彩的节目已经演过了。What a pity I was just too late for the best item on the programme./ 这手套还没破，扔了多～。The gloves aren't worn out yet. It would be a pity to throw them away.
【可喜】 kěxǐ gratifying; heartening: ～的成就 gratifying achievements/ 取得了～的进展 have made encouraging progress
【可笑】 kěxiào laughable; ridiculous; ludicrous; funny: 简直～！It's simply ridiculous!/ ～不自量 ridiculously overrate oneself; make oneself ridiculous by overestimating one's ability
【可心】 kěxīn satisfying; to the satisfaction (或 liking) of: 贫下中农的～人 a person the poor and lower-middle peasants really like
【可行】 kěxíng feasible: 是否～，请斟酌。Please consider if this is feasible.
【可疑】 kěyí suspicious; dubious; questionable: 形迹～ look suspicious ◇ ～分子 a suspect; a suspicious character
【可以】 kěyǐ ① can; may: 人类是～征服自然的。Man can conquer nature./ 问题一定会搞清楚的，你～放心。Don't worry. Things will be straightened out in the end./ 你～走了。You may go. ②〈口〉passable; pretty good; not bad: 这篇文章写得还～。This article is pretty good./ 她的英语还～。Her English is not at all bad. ③〈口〉awful: 他今天忙得真～。He's awfully busy today./ 你这张嘴真～！What a sharp tongue you've got!
【可意】 kěyì gratifying; satisfactory
【可有可无】 kěyǒu-kěwú not essential; not indispensable
【可着】 kězhe manage to make do: 你就～这块布裁吧。You'll have to make do with this piece of cloth.
【可知性】 kězhīxìng 〈哲〉 knowability: 世界～ knowability of the universe

**坷** kě 见"坎坷" kǎnkě
另见 kē

**渴** kě ① thirsty: 这里有开水，～了请随便喝。Here's some boiled water. Have a drink whenever you're thirsty. ② yearningly: ～念 yearn for
【渴望】 kěwàng thirst for; long for; yearn for: 许多青年～参加解放军。Many young people long to join the PLA.

## kè

**可** kè
另见 kě

【可汗】 kèhán 〈史〉khan

**克** kè ①can; be able to: 不~分身 be unable to leave what one is doing at the moment; can't get away ②restrain: ~制 exercise restraint ③overcome; subdue; capture (a city, etc.): 迭~名城 capture one important city after another/ 战无不胜，攻无不~ be invincible; carry all before one ④digest: ~食 help one's digestion ⑤set a time limit: ~期完工 set a date for completing the work ⑥gram (g.) ⑦a Tibetan unit of volume or dry measure (holding about 25 *jin* of barley) ⑧a Tibetan unit of land area equal to about 1 *mu*

【克当量】 kèdāngliàng 〈化〉gram equivalent

【克敌制胜】 kèdí-zhìshèng vanquish (或 conquer) the enemy

【克分子】 kèfēnzǐ 〈化〉gram molecule ◇ ~浓度 molarity

【克服】 kèfú ①surmount; overcome; conquer: ~困难 surmount a difficulty/ ~私心杂念 overcome selfish considerations/ ~官僚主义 get rid of bureaucracy/ ~片面性 eliminate one-sidedness ②〈口〉put up with (hardships, inconveniences, etc.): 这儿生活条件不太好，咱们先~点吧。The living conditions here are not very good, but let's put up with them for a while.

【克复】 kèfù retake; recapture; recover: ~失地 recover lost territory

【克格勃】 Kègébó KGB (the Soviet State Security Committee)

【克己奉公】 kèjǐ-fènggōng wholehearted devotion to public duty; work selflessly for the public interest

【克卡】 kèkǎ 〈物〉gram calorie

【克扣】 kèkòu embezzle part of what should be issued: ~军饷 pocket a portion of the soldiers' pay

【克拉】 kèlā carat

【克郎球】 kèlángqiú caroms

【克厘米】 kèlímǐ gram-centimetre

【克里奥尔语】 Kèlǐ'ào'ěryǔ Creole (language)

【克里姆林宫】 Kèlǐmǔlín Gōng the Kremlin

【克勤克俭】 kèqín-kèjiǎn be industrious and frugal

【克丘亚语】 Kèqiūyàyǔ Quechua (language)

【克山病】 kèshānbìng 〈医〉Keshan disease

【克什米尔】 Kèshímǐ'ěr Kashmir

【克丝钳】 kèsīqián combination pliers; cutting pliers

【克原子】 kèyuánzǐ 〈化〉gram atom

【克制】 kèzhì restrain; exercise restraint: ~自己的感情 restrain one's passion/ 表现很大的~ exercise great restraint

**刻** kè ①carve; engrave; cut: ~图章 engrave a seal/ ~蜡版 cut stencils/ 木~ woodcut ②a quarter (of an hour): 五点一~ a quarter past five ③moment: 此~ at the moment ④cutting; penetrating: 尖~ acrimonious; biting; sarcastic ⑤in the highest degree: 深~ penetrating; profound ⑥set a time limit

【刻板】 kèbǎn ①cut blocks for printing ②mechanical; stiff; inflexible: ~地照抄 copy mechanically

【刻版】 kèbǎn cut blocks for printing ◇ ~印刷 block printing

【刻本】 kèběn block-printed edition: 宋~ a Song Dynasty block-printed edition

【刻薄】 kèbó unkind; harsh; mean: 说~话 speak unkindly; make caustic remarks/ 待人~ treat people meanly

【刻不容缓】 kè bùróng huǎn brook no delay; demand immediate attention; be of great urgency: 大大加快我国国民经济发展的步伐，是~的。Greatly accelerating the development of our national economy is a task which brooks no delay.

【刻刀】 kèdāo burin; graver

【刻毒】 kèdú venomous; spiteful: ~的语言 venomed remarks

【刻度】 kèdù graduation (on a vessel or instrument) ◇ ~盘 graduated disc; dial/ ~瓶 graduated bottle

【刻骨】 kègǔ deeply ingrained; deep-rooted: ~仇恨 inveterate hatred; deep-seated hatred

【刻骨铭心】 kègǔ-míngxīn be engraved on one's bones and heart; remember with gratitude to the end of one's life

【刻花】 kèhuā engraved designs; carved designs

【刻画】 kèhuà depict; portray: ~英雄人物的形象 portray heroic characters

【刻苦】 kèkǔ ①assiduous; hardworking; painstaking: ~钻研 study assiduously ②simple and frugal: 生活~ lead a simple and frugal life

【刻下】 kèxià at present; at the moment

【刻意】 kèyì painstakingly; sedulously: ~求工 sedulously strive for perfection

【刻舟求剑】 kè zhōu qiú jiàn cut a mark on the side of one's boat to indicate the place where one's sword has dropped into the river— take measures without regard to changes in circumstances

【刻字】 kèzì carve (或 engrave) characters on a seal, etc. ◇ ~社 seal-engraving shop

**客** kè ①visitor; guest ②traveller; passenger: ~舱 passenger cabin ③travelling merchant ④customer: 房~ boarder; lodger ⑤settle or live in a strange place; be a stranger: 作~他乡 live in a strange land ⑥a person engaged in some particular pursuit: 政~ politician/ 刺~ assassin ⑦objective: ~观 objective

【客车】 kèchē ①passenger train ②bus

【客船】 kèchuán passenger ship (或 boat): 定期~ liner

【客串】 kèchuàn (of an amateur singer, actor, etc.) play a part in a professional performance; be a guest performer

【客店】 kèdiàn inn

【客队】 kèduì 〈体〉visiting team

【客饭】 kèfàn ①a meal specially prepared for visitors at a canteen ②set meal; table d'hôte

【客房】 kèfáng guest room

【客观】 kèguān objective
◇ ~规律 objective law/ ~实在 objective reality/ ~世界 objective world/ ~事物 objective things (或 reality)/ ~唯心主义 objective idealism/ ~真理 objective truth/ ~主义 objectivism

【客货船】 kè-huòchuán passenger-cargo vessel

【客机】 kèjī passenger plane; airliner

【客籍】 kèjí ①a settler from another province ②the province into which settlers move

【客家】 Kèjiā the Hakkas ◇ ~话 Hakka

【客满】 kèmǎn (of theatre tickets, etc.) sold out; full house

【客票】 kèpiào passenger ticket

【客气】 kèqi ①polite; courteous: 他对人很~。He is very polite to people./ 双方~了一番，就开始谈正事。After a few words of courtesy, they got down to business./ 别~。(对来客) Please don't stand on ceremony. 或 Make yourself at home. (对主人) Please don't bother. ②modest: 您太~了。You are being too modest.

【客卿】 kèqīng 〈书〉a person from one feudal state serving in the court of another

【客人】 kèrén ①visitor; guest ②guest (at a hotel, etc.)

【客商】 kèshāng travelling trader

【客套】 kètào polite formula; civilities: 我们是老朋友，用不着讲~。As old friends we don't need to stand on ceremony./ 他们~了几句，就坐下了。After an exchange of greetings, they took their seats.

【客体】 kètǐ 〈哲〉 object
【客厅】 kètīng drawing room; parlour
【客运】 kèyùn passenger transport; passenger traffic ◇ ～列车 passenger train
【客栈】 kèzhàn inn

**恪** kè scrupulously and respectfully
【恪守】 kèshǒu scrupulously abide by (a treaty, promise, etc.)

**课** kè ① subject; course: 主～ the main subject/ 必修～ required courses ② class: 上～ go to class/ 一节物理～ a class in physics/ 讲(听)～ give (attend) a lecture ③〈量〉 lesson: 第一～ Lesson One/ 这本教科书共有二十五～。This textbook contains 25 lessons. ④ tax ⑤ levy: ～以重税 levy heavy taxes
【课本】 kèběn textbook
【课表】 kèbiǎo school timetable
【课程】 kèchéng course; curriculum ◇ ～表 school timetable
【课间操】 kèjiāncāo setting-up exercises during the break
【课时】 kèshí class hour; period: 每周授课十六～ teach 16 periods a week
【课堂】 kètáng classroom; schoolroom
◇ ～教学 classroom instruction (或 teaching)/ ～讨论 classroom discussion/ ～作业 classwork
【课题】 kètí ① a question for study or discussion ② problem; task: 提出新的～ pose a new problem; set a new task
【课外】 kèwài extracurricular; outside class; after school
◇ ～辅导 instruction after class/ ～活动 extracurricular activities/ ～阅读 outside reading/ ～作业 homework
【课文】 kèwén text
【课业】 kèyè lessons; schoolwork
【课余】 kèyú after school; after class: 利用～时间进行义务劳动 do voluntary labour after school
【课桌】 kèzhuō (school) desk

**氪** kè 〈化〉 krypton (Kr)

**骒** kè
【骒马】 kèmǎ mare

**缂** kè
【缂丝】 kèsī 〈工美〉 a type of weaving done by the tapestry method in fine silks and gold thread

**锞** kè a small ingot of gold or silver
【锞子】 kèzi a small ingot of gold or silver: 银～ a silver ingot

**嗑** kè crack sth. between the teeth: ～瓜子儿 crack melon seeds

**溘** kè 〈书〉 suddenly: ～逝 pass away; die

## kēi

**剋** kēi 〈口〉 scold or beat: 挨～ get a scolding or take a beating

## kěn

**肯** kěn ① agree; consent: 我劝说了半天，他才～了。He did not agree until I had talked to him for a long time./ 首～ nod assent ② be willing to; be ready to: ～干 be willing to do hard work/ ～虚心接受意见 be ready to listen to criticism with an open mind/ 青年人最～学习。Young people are most eager to learn.
【肯定】 kěndìng ① affirm; confirm; approve; regard as positive: ～十月革命的伟大意义 affirm the great significance of the October Revolution/ ～成绩 affirm the achievements/ 对于我们的工作的看法，～一切或者否定一切，都是片面性的。In the appraisal of our work, it is one-sided to affirm everything or to negate everything. ② positive; affirmative: ～的判断 a positive assessment/ 他的回答是～的。His answer is in the affirmative. ③ definite; sure: 请给我一个～的答复。Please give me a definite answer./ 他今天来不来，我不能～。I'm not sure whether he will come today. ④ certainly; undoubtedly; definitely: 胜利～是属于人民的。Victory will undoubtedly go to the people./ ～按时送到 guarantee delivery on time
【肯尼亚】 Kěnníyà Kenya ◇ ～人 Kenyan

**垦** kěn cultivate (land); reclaim (wasteland): 军～农场 army reclamation farm
【垦荒】 kěnhuāng reclaim wasteland; bring wasteland under cultivation; open up virgin soil
【垦区】 kěnqū reclamation area
【垦殖】 kěnzhí reclaim and cultivate wasteland

**恳** kěn ① earnestly; sincerely: ～谈 talk earnestly ② request; beseech; entreat: 敬～ respectfully request
【恳切】 kěnqiè earnest; sincere: 言词～ speak in an earnest tone/ ～希望 earnestly (或 sincerely) hope
【恳请】 kěnqǐng earnestly request: ～协助。Your assistance is earnestly requested.
【恳求】 kěnqiú implore; entreat; beseech
【恳挚】 kěnzhì 〈书〉 earnest; sincere: 情意～ show sincere feeling/ 词意～ express oneself earnestly

**啃** kěn gnaw; nibble: ～骨头 gnaw a bone/ ～老玉米 nibble at an ear of corn/ ～书本 delve into books

## kēng

**坑** kēng ① hole; pit; hollow: 泥～ mud puddle/ 水～ puddle/ 粪～ manure pit/一个萝卜一个～ one radish, one hole — each has his own task, and there is nobody to spare ② tunnel; pit: 矿～ pit ③ bury alive ④ entrap; cheat: 奸商净～人。The profiteers cheated people right and left.
【坑道】 kēngdào ① 〈矿〉 gallery ② 〈军〉 tunnel ◇ ～工事 〈军〉 tunnel defences (或 fortifications)/ ～战 tunnel warfare
【坑害】 kēnghài lead into a trap; entrap
【坑坑洼洼】 kēngkengwāwā full of bumps and hollows; bumpy; rough
【坑木】 kēngmù 〈矿〉 pit prop; mine timber

**吭** kēng utter a sound or a word: 他坐在旁边一声不～。He sat there without saying a word.
另见 háng
【吭哧】 kēngchi ① puff and blow: 他背起麻包～～地走了。He heaved the sack on his back and staggered off, puffing and blowing from the strain. ② work hard; toil: 她～了半天才把文章写出来。She toiled a long time over her article. ③ hum and haw: 他～了好一会儿才说出来。He hummed and hawed for quite a while before he came out with it.
【吭气】 kēngqì 见"吭声"

【吭声】 kēngshēng utter a sound or a word: 你为什么不～？ Why do you keep silent?

**铿** kēng 〈象〉 clang; clatter: 拖拉机走在路上～～地响。Tractors clattered along the road.

【铿锵】 kēngqiāng ring; clang: 这首诗读起来～有力。This poem is sonorous and forceful.

【铿然】 kēngrán 〈书〉 loud and clear

## kōng

**空** kōng ① empty; hollow; void: ～箱子 an empty box/ 把抽屉腾～ empty out a drawer/ 这棵树被虫子蛀～了。This tree has been eaten hollow by worms./ 屋里～无一人。There isn't a single soul in the house. ② sky; air: 晴～ a clear sky ③ for nothing; in vain: ～跑一趟 make a journey for nothing/ ～忙 make fruitless efforts
另见 kòng

【空靶】 kōngbǎ air (或 aerial, airborne) target

【空包弹】 kōngbāodàn 〈军〉 blank cartridge

【空舱费】 kōngcāngfèi 〈交〉 dead freight

【空肠】 kōngcháng 〈生理〉 jejunum

【空城计】 kōngchéngjì empty-city stratagem (bluffing the enemy by opening the gates of a weakly defended city); presenting a bold front to conceal a weak defence

【空挡】 kōngdǎng 〈机〉 neutral (gear)

【空荡荡】 kōngdàngdàng empty; deserted: 农忙季节,人都下地了,村子里显得～的。In the busy season the village looked deserted when the peasants had gone to the fields.

【空洞】 kōngdòng ① cavity: 肺～ pulmonary cavity ② empty; hollow; devoid of content: ～的理论 empty theory/ ～的词句 empty phraseology/ ～无物 utter lack of substance; devoid of content

【空对地导弹】 kōng duì dì dǎodàn air-to-ground guided missile

【空对空导弹】 kōng duì kōng dǎodàn air-to-air guided missile

【空翻】 kōngfān 〈体〉 somersault; flip: 后～ backward somersault; backflip

【空泛】 kōngfàn vague and general; not specific: ～的议论 vague and general opinions; generalities

【空防】 kōngfáng air defence

【空腹】 kōngfù on an empty stomach: 此药需～服用。This medicine is to be taken on an empty stomach.

【空话】 kōnghuà empty talk; idle talk; hollow words: 说～ indulge in idle talk/ ～连篇 pages and pages of empty verbiage

【空怀】 kōnghuái 〈牧〉 nonpregnant; barren

【空欢喜】 kōnghuānxǐ rejoice too soon; be or feel let down

【空幻】 kōnghuàn visionary; illusory

【空际】 kōngjì in the sky; in the air

【空架子】 kōngjiàzi a mere skeleton; a bare outline

【空间】 kōngjiān space: 外层～ outer space
◇ ～点阵〈物〉 space lattice/ ～技术 space technology/ ～科学 space science/ ～站〈宇航〉 space station/ ～知觉 〈心〉 space perception

【空降】 kōngjiàng airborne ◇ ～兵 airborne force; parachute landing force/ ～地点 landing area

【空军】 kōngjūn air force
◇ ～部队 air (force) unit/ ～基地 air base/ ～司令部 general headquarters of the air force; air command/ ～司令员 commander of the air force/ ～武官 air *attaché*

【空空如也】 kōngkōng rú yě absolutely empty

【空口】 kōngkǒu eat dishes without rice or wine; eat rice or drink wine with nothing to go with it

【空口说白话】 kōngkǒu shuō báihuà make empty promises

【空口无凭】 kōngkǒu wú píng a mere verbal statement is no guarantee: ～,立字为证。Words of mouth being no guarantee, a written statement is hereby given.

【空旷】 kōngkuàng open; spacious: ～的原野 an expanse of open country; champaign

【空阔】 kōngkuò open; spacious: 水天～ a vast expanse of water and sky

【空廓】 kōngkuò open; spacious: 四望～ spacious and open on all sides

【空论】 kōnglùn empty talk

【空门】 kōngmén Buddhism: 遁入～ become a Buddhist monk or nun

【空濛】 kōngméng 〈书〉 hazy; misty: 山色～ hills shrouded in mist

【空气】 kōngqì ① air: 呼吸新鲜～ breathe fresh air/ 湿～ moist air ② atmosphere: ～紧张 a tense atmosphere
◇ ～弹道 aeroballistic (或 atmospheric) trajectory/ ～冷却 air-cooling/ ～力学 aeromechanics/ ～调节器 air conditioner/ ～污染 air pollution/ ～压缩机 air compressor

【空前】 kōngqián unprecedented: 我国石油工业正以～的速度向前发展。China's oil industry is developing at an unprecedented rate./ 我们的国家现在是～统一的。Never before has our country been as united as it is today./ 盛况～ an unprecedentedly grand occasion

【空前绝后】 kōngqián-juéhòu unprecedented and unrepeatable; unique

【空勤】 kōngqín air duty ◇ ～人员 aircrew; aircraft crew; flight crew

【空手】 kōngshǒu empty-handed

【空谈】 kōngtán ① indulge in empty talk ② empty talk; idle talk; prattle ◇ ～主义 phrase-mongering

【空头】 kōngtóu ① (on the stock exchange) bear; short-seller ② nominal; phony ◇ ～文学家 phony writer/ ～政治家 armchair politician

【空头支票】 kōngtóu zhīpiào ① dud (或 rubber) cheque; bad cheque ② empty promise; lip service

【空投】 kōngtóu air-drop; paradrop: ～救灾物资 air-drop relief supplies (to a stricken area)
◇ ～包 parapack/ ～场 dropping ground/ ～伞 aerial delivery parachute/ ～特务 air-dropped agent

【空文】 kōngwén ineffective law, rule, etc.: 一纸～ a mere scrap of paper

【空吸】 kōngxī 〈物〉 suction

【空袭】 kōngxí air raid; air attack ◇ ～警报 air raid alarm/ ～警报器 air raid siren

【空想】 kōngxiǎng idle dream; fantasy: 别～了,还是从实际出发吧。Stop daydreaming. Be realistic. ◇ ～家 dreamer; visionary

【空想社会主义】 kōngxiǎng shèhuìzhǔyì utopian socialism
◇ ～者 utopian socialist

【空心】 kōngxīn hollow ◇ ～长丝〈化纤〉 hollow filament/ ～砖 hollow brick
另见 kòngxīn

【空虚】 kōngxū hollow; void: 生活～ lead a life devoid of meaning/ 思想～ lack mental or spiritual ballast; be impractical in one's thinking/ 敌人后方～。The enemy rear is weakly defended.

【空穴】 kōngxué 〈电子〉 hole

【空穴来风】 kōngxué lái fēng an empty hole invites the wind — weakness lends wings to rumours

【空域】 kōngyù airspace: 战斗～ combat airspace

【空运】 kōngyùn air transport; airlift: ～救灾物资 airlift relief supplies (to a stricken area) ◇ ～货物 airfreight; air

cargo
【空战】 kōngzhàn air battle; aerial combat
【空中】 kōngzhōng in the sky; in the air; aerial; overhead ◇ ~补给 air-supply; air-resupply/ ~待战 air alert/ ~飞人〈杂技〉 flying trapeze/ ~加油 air refueling; inflight refueling/ ~禁区 restricted airspace/ ~警戒 air alert/ ~摄影 aerophotography/ ~掩护 air umbrella; air cover/ ~侦察 aerial reconnaissance/ ~走廊 air corridor; air lane
【空中楼阁】 kōngzhōng lóugé castles in the air
【空重】 kōngzhòng 〈交〉 empty weight
【空竹】 kōngzhú diabolo: 抖~ play diabolo
【空转】 kōngzhuàn ① (of a motor, etc.) idling; racing: 不要让马达~。Don't race your motor. ② (of a wheel) turn without moving forward; spin

**箜** kōng
【箜篌】 kōnghóu an ancient plucked stringed instrument

## kǒng

**孔** kǒng ① hole; opening; aperture: 钥匙~ keyhole/ 十七~桥 a seventeen-arched bridge ② 〈量〉: 一~土窑 a cave-dwelling ③ (Kǒng) a surname
【孔道】 kǒngdào a narrow passage providing the only means of access to a certain place; pass
【孔洞】 kǒngdòng opening or hole in a utensil, etc.
【孔径】 kǒngjìng ① 〈物〉 aperture ② 〈机〉 bore diameter
【孔孟之道】 Kǒng-Mèng zhī dào the doctrine of Confucius and Mencius
【孔庙】 Kǒngmiào Confucian temple
【孔雀】 kǒngque peacock ◇ ~绿 peacock green; malachite green/ ~石〈矿〉 malachite
【孔隙】 kǒngxì small opening; hole ◇ ~度〈地〉 porosity
【孔型】 kǒngxíng 〈冶〉 pass
【孔穴】 kǒngxué hole; cavity

**恐** kǒng ① fear; dread: 惊~ be alarmed ② terrify; intimidate: ~吓 threaten; intimidate ③ I'm afraid: 消息~不可靠。I'm afraid the information is not reliable./ ~另有原因。There may be some other reason for it.
【恐怖】 kǒngbù terror: 白色~ White terror ◇ ~分子 terrorist/ ~统治 reign of terror/ ~主义 terrorism
【恐吓】 kǒnghè threaten; intimidate ◇ ~信 blackmailing letter; threatening letter
【恐慌】 kǒnghuāng panic: ~万状 panic-stricken/ 使敌人感到~ throw the enemy into a panic; strike terror into the enemy
【恐惧】 kǒngjù fear; dread: ~不安 be frightened and restless
【恐龙】 kǒnglóng 〈古生物〉 dinosaur
【恐怕】 kǒngpà 〈副〉 ① I'm afraid: 这样做，~不行。I'm afraid this won't work. ② perhaps; I think: 他走了~有十天了。It's ten days now, I think, since he left./ ~要下雨。It looks like rain.
【恐水病】 kǒngshuǐbìng hydrophobia; rabies

**倥** kǒng
【倥偬】 kǒngzǒng 〈书〉 ① pressing; urgent: 戎马~ burdened with pressing military duties ② poverty-stricken; destitute

## kòng

**空** kòng ① leave empty or blank: 请把前面一排座位~出来。Please leave the front row of seats vacant./ 每段开头要~两格。 Leave two blank spaces at the beginning of each paragraph. ② unoccupied; vacant: ~房 a vacant room/ 车厢里~得很。 There are many vacant seats in the carriage. ③ empty space: 各行之间多留点~儿。Leave a little more space between the rows. ④ free time; spare time: 有~儿到我这儿来。Come over when you have time./ 今天没~，改日再谈吧。I'm busy today. Let's talk about it some other day.
另见 kōng
【空白】 kòngbái blank space: 版面上那块~可以补一篇短文。We can fill up that space with a short article./ 填补科学技术上的~ fill the gaps in science and technology ◇ ~表格 blank form/ ~支票 blank cheque
【空白点】 kòngbáidiǎn blank spot; gap; blank: 过去这个地区的煤炭工业是个~。Coal mining used to be nonexistent in this area.
【空当儿】 kòngdāngr 〈口〉 gap; break: 从一个~挤过去 squeeze through a gap/ 趁这~，我去把报纸拿来。 I'll go and fetch the newspapers during this break.
【空地】 kòngdì vacant lot; open ground; open space: 咱们把砖卸在那边~上吧。Let's leave the bricks on the open ground over there.
【空额】 kòng'é vacancy: ~已经补上。The vacancy has already been filled.
【空格】 kònggé blank space (on a form)
【空缺】 kòngquē vacant position; vacancy
【空隙】 kòngxì space; gap; interval: 铁轨接头的地方都有一定的~。There is a specified gap at every rail joint./ 战士们利用战斗~加固工事。The soldiers strengthened defensive works in the intervals of fighting.
【空暇】 kòngxiá free time; spare time; leisure
【空闲】 kòngxián ① idle; free: 我们车间里的机器没有一台是~的。None of the machines in our workshop are idle./ 等你~的时候，咱俩谈谈心。Let's have a heart-to-heart talk when you're free. ② free time; spare time; leisure: 战士们一有~时间就练习投弹。 The soldiers practise grenade-throwing whenever they have some spare time.
【空心】 kòngxīn on an empty stomach: 这剂药~吃。 This dose of medicine should be taken on an empty stomach.
另见 kōngxīn
【空子】 kòngzi ① gap; opening: 那孩子找了个~往里挤。The child found a gap and squeezed in. ② chance; opportunity: 严防坏人钻~ take strict precautions against giving bad people an opening

**控** kòng ① accuse; charge: 指~ accuse ② control; dominate: 遥~ remote control; telecontrol ③ turn (a container) upside down to let the liquid trickle out: 把瓶子先~一~再装油。Turn the bottle upside down to empty it before you fill it with oil.
【控告】 kònggào charge; accuse; complain: 向法院提出~ file charges in court/向国家机关提出~ lodge complaints with organs of state
【控诉】 kòngsù accuse; denounce: ~旧社会的罪恶 condemn the evils of the old society/ ~帝国主义的侵略罪行 denounce the imperialists' criminal act of aggression ◇ ~会 accusation meeting/ ~人 accuser
【控制】 kòngzhì control; dominate; command: ~局面 have the situation under control/ ~险要 command a strategic position/ 她~不住自己的感情。 She lost control of her feelings./ ~地面沉降 bring surface subsidence under control
◇ ~联想〈心理〉 controlled association/ ~论〈数〉 cybernetics/ ~数字〈经〉 control figure/ ~台〈自〉 console

## kōu

**扣** kōu

【扣脉】 kōumài 〈中医〉 hollow pulse

**抠** kōu ① dig or dig out with a finger or sth. pointed; scratch: 在地上～个洞 scratch a hole in the ground/ 把掉在缝里的豆粒～出来 dig out the beans from the crevices ② carve; cut: 在镜框边上～点花儿 carve a design on a picture frame ③ delve into; study meticulously: 这本书用不着一字一句地～。You needn't puzzle over every single word or phrase in the book. ④〈方〉stingy; miserly

【抠门儿】 kōuménr 〈方〉 stingy; miserly

【抠字眼儿】 kōu zìyǎnr pay too much attention to the shades of meaning of words; find fault with the choice of words

**眍** kōu (of the eyes) sink in; become sunken: 她病了一场，眼睛都～进去了。Her eyes were sunken after her illness.

## kǒu

**口** kǒu ① mouth ② opening; entrance; mouth: 胡同～儿 the entrance of an alley/ 河～ the mouth of a river; estuary/ 入～ entrance/ 出～ exit/ 瓶～ the mouth of a bottle/ 枪～ the muzzle of a gun/ 信箱的～儿 the slit of a letter box ③ a gateway of the Great Wall (often used in place names, e.g. 张家～ Zhangjiakou) ④ cut; hole: 伤～ wound; cut/ 衣服撕了个～儿 tear a hole in one's jacket/ 茶碗缺了个～儿。The rim of the teacup is chipped. ⑤ the edge of a knife: 刀卷～了。The edge of the knife is turned. ⑥ the age of a draft animal: 这匹马～还轻。This horse is still young. ⑦〈量〉: 一～井 a well/ 三～猪 three pigs/ 他家五～人。There are five people in his family.

【口岸】 kǒu'àn port: 通商～ trading port

【口碑】 kǒubēi public praise: ～载道 be praised everywhere

【口才】 kǒucái eloquence: 他很有～。He is an eloquent speaker.

【口吃】 kǒuchī stutter; stammer: 他说话有点～。He speaks with a slight stutter.

【口齿】 kǒuchǐ ① enunciation: ～清楚 have clear enunciation ② ability to speak: ～伶俐 be clever and fluent

【口臭】 kǒuchòu halitosis; bad breath

【口传】 kǒuchuán oral instruction

【口疮】 kǒuchuāng aphtha

【口袋】 kǒudài pocket

【口袋】 kǒudai bag; sack: 纸～儿 paper bag/ 面～ flour sack

【口风】 kǒufēng one's intention or view as revealed in what one says: 先探探他的～。Sound him out first.

【口服】 kǒufú ① profess to be convinced: ～心不服 pretend to be convinced/ 心服～ be sincerely convinced ② take orally: 不得～ not to be taken orally ◇ ～避孕药 oral contraceptive; the pill

【口福】 kǒufú gourmet's luck; the luck to get sth. very nice to eat

【口腹】 kǒufù food: ～之欲 the desire for good food/ 不贪～ not indulge one's appetite

【口供】 kǒugòng a statement made by the accused under examination

【口号】 kǒuhào slogan; watchword: 呼～ shout slogans

【口红】 kǒuhóng lipstick

【口惠】 kǒuhuì lip service; empty promise: ～而实不至 make a promise and not keep it; pay lip service

【口技】 kǒujì 〈杂技〉 vocal mimicry; vocal imitation

【口角】 kǒujiǎo corner of the mouth ◇ ～炎 perlèche
另见 kǒujué

【口紧】 kǒujǐn closemouthed; tight-lipped

【口径】 kǒujìng ① bore; calibre: 小～步枪 small-bore rifle/ 大～机枪 heavy-calibre machine gun/ ～155毫米的大炮 155mm. gun ② requirements; specifications; line of action: ～不合 not meet the requirements/ 对～ arrange to give the same story; give the same account by arrangement/ 咱俩说话～要一致。We two must speak along the same lines. 或 We two must have the same approach in speaking about this.

【口诀】 kǒujué a pithy formula (often in rhyme)

【口角】 kǒujué quarrel; bicker; wrangle
另见 kǒujiǎo

【口渴】 kǒukě thirsty

【口口声声】 kǒukoushēngshēng say again and again; keep on saying: 他～说不知道。He kept on pleading ignorance.

【口粮】 kǒuliáng grain ration

【口令】 kǒulìng ① word of command ② password; watchword; countersign: ～问答 challenge and reply

【口蜜腹剑】 kǒumì-fùjiàn honey-mouthed and dagger-hearted; honey on one's lips and murder in one's heart; hypocritical and malignant

【口蘑】 kǒumó a kind of dried mushroom (from Zhangjiakou 张家口)

【口气】 kǒuqì ① tone; note: 严肃的～ a serious tone/ 改变～ change one's tone/ 他说话有埋怨的～。There was a note of complaint in what he said./ ～强硬的声明 a strongly worded statement ② manner of speaking: 他的～真不小。He talked big. ③ what is actually meant; implication: 听他的～，好象感到为难。Judging by the way he spoke, he seemed to be in an awkward situation.

【口器】 kǒuqì mouthparts (of an insect)

【口腔】 kǒuqiāng 〈生理〉 oral cavity
◇ ～卫生 oral hygiene/ ～学 stomatology/ ～医院 stomatological hospital

【口琴】 kǒuqín mouth organ; harmonica

【口轻】 kǒuqīng ① not salty ② be fond of food that is not salty ③ (of a horse, donkey, etc.) young

【口若悬河】 kǒu ruò xuán hé let loose a flood of eloquence; be eloquent

【口哨儿】 kǒushàor whistling sound through rounded lips: 吹～ whistle (through rounded lips)

【口舌】 kǒushé ① quarrel; dispute ② talking round: 费了很大的～才把他说服。It took a lot of talking to convince him./ 不必费～了。You might as well save your breath.

【口实】 kǒushí a cause for gossip; handle: 贻人～ provide one's critics with a handle

【口试】 kǒushì oral examination; oral test

【口是心非】 kǒushì-xīnfēi say yes and mean no; say one thing and mean another

【口授】 kǒushòu ① oral instruction ② dictate: 他写的这封信是他父亲～的。The letter he wrote was dictated by his father.

【口述】 kǒushù oral account

【口水】 kǒushuǐ saliva: 流～ slobber

【口蹄疫】 kǒutíyì 〈牧〉 foot-and-mouth disease

【口条】 kǒutiáo pig's or ox's tongue (as food)

【口头】 kǒutóu oral: ～通知 notify orally/ ～革命派 a revolutionary in word/ ～上赞成，实际上反对 agree in words but oppose in deeds

◇ ~表决 voice vote; vote by "yes" and "no"/ ~汇报 oral report/ ~声明 oral statement/ ~文学 folk tales, ballads, etc. handed down orally

【口头禅】 kǒutóuchán pet phrase 又作"口头语"

【口腕】 kǒuwàn 〈动〉 oral arm

【口味】 kǒuwèi ① a person's taste: 合~ suit one's taste/ 不合~ not be to one's taste/ 各人~不同。Tastes differ. ② the flavour or taste of food: 这些菜都是湖南~。These are all Hunanese dishes.

【口吻】 kǒuwěn ① 〈动〉 muzzle; snout ② tone; note: 玩笑的~ jocular tone

【口香糖】 kǒuxiāngtáng chewing gum

【口信】 kǒuxìn oral message

【口形】 kǒuxíng 〈语〉 degree of lip-rounding

【口炎】 kǒuyán 〈医〉 stomatitis

【口眼㖞斜】 kǒu-yǎn wāixié 〈中医〉 facial paralysis

【口译】 kǒuyì oral interpretation

【口音】 kǒuyīn 〈语〉 oral speech sounds

【口音】 kǒuyin ① voice: 她一听是她儿子的~,就赶紧出来了。Recognizing her son's voice, she hurried out. ② accent: 说话带广东~ speak with a Guangdong accent

【口语】 kǒuyǔ spoken language

【口罩】 kǒuzhào gauze mask (worn over nose and mouth)

【口重】 kǒuzhòng ① salty ② be fond of salty food

【口诛笔伐】 kǒuzhū-bǐfá condemn both in speech and in writing: 开展革命大批判,人人都要~。Everybody should take part in the revolutionary mass criticism both in speech and in writing.

【口子】 kǒuzi opening; hole; cut; tear: 我手上拉的~快好了。The cut on my hand is nearly healed./ 袖子撕了个~。There is a tear in the sleeve./ 水渠开了~。The canal has burst its banks./ 可不能开这个~啊! Let's not set such a precedent!

## kòu

**叩** kòu ① knock: ~门 knock at a door ② kowtow

【叩头】 kòutóu kowtow

【叩头虫】 kòutóuchóng click beetle; snapping beetle

【叩问】 kòuwèn 〈书〉 make inquiries

【叩诊】 kòuzhěn 〈医〉 percussion ◇ ~锤 〈医〉 percussion hammer

**扣** kòu ① button up; buckle: 把衣服~上 button (up) one's coat/ 把皮带~上 buckle a belt/ 把门~上 latch the door/ ~扣子 do up the buttons ② place a cup, bowl, etc. upside down; cover with an inverted cup, bowl, etc.: 把缸~过来。Turn the vat upside down./ 用碗把菜~上,免得凉了。Cover the food with a bowl to keep it from getting cold. ③ detain; take into custody; arrest: 把反革命分子~起来 take the counterrevolutionary into custody/ 他违反交通规则,交通警~了他的自行车。The policeman took away his bike because he had violated traffic regulations. ④ deduct: ~工资 deduct a part of sb.'s pay ⑤ discount: 打九~ give a 10 per cent discount ⑥ knot; button; buckle: 系个~儿 tie (或make) a knot ⑦ smash (the ball)

【扣除】 kòuchú deduct: ~各种费用后,收入超过万元。After deducting costs, the income was more than 10,000 *yuan*./ 从工资里~房租 deduct rent from wages

【扣留】 kòuliú detain; arrest; hold in custody: 把走私犯~起来 detain the smuggler/ ~行车执照 suspend a driving licence

【扣帽子】 kòu màozi put a label on sb.: 批评要以理服人,不要乱~。When criticizing people, we must try to convince them through reasoning, not just put labels on them.

【扣人心弦】 kòu rén xīnxián exciting; thrilling: 一场~的比赛 an exciting match

【扣杀】 kòushā smash (the ball): 闪电般的~ swift killing smashes/ 大板~ overpowering smashes (in a table-tennis game)

【扣压】 kòuyā withhold; pigeonhole: ~稿件 withhold a manuscript from publication

【扣押】 kòuyā ① detain; hold in custody ② 〈法〉 distrain

【扣子】 kòuzi ① knot ② button ③ an abrupt break in a story to create suspense

**寇** kòu ① bandit; invader; enemy: 海~ pirate/ 敌~ the (invading) enemy ② invade: 入~ invade (a country) ③ (Kòu) a surname

【寇仇】 kòuchóu enemy; foe

**筘** kòu 〈纺〉 reed

**蔻** kòu 见"豆蔻" dòukòu

## kū

**刳** kū 〈书〉 hollow out: ~木为舟 hollow out a tree trunk and make it into a canoe; make a canoe out of a tree trunk

**枯** kū ① (of a plant, etc.) withered: ~草 withered grass/ ~叶 dead leaves ② (of a well, river, etc.) dried up: ~井 a dry well ③ dull; uninteresting: ~坐 sit in boredom

【枯草热】 kūcǎorè 〈医〉 hay fever

【枯肠】 kūcháng 〈书〉 impoverished mind: 搜索~ rack one's brains (for ideas or expressions)

【枯槁】 kūgǎo ① withered ② haggard: 形容~ look haggard

【枯黄】 kūhuáng withered and yellow: 树叶逐渐~了。The leaves are beginning to turn yellow.

【枯寂】 kūjì dull and lonely

【枯竭】 kūjié dried up; exhausted: 水源~。The source has dried up./ 财源~。Financial resources were exhausted.

【枯窘】 kūjiǒng dried up: 文思~ the source of one's inspiration has dried up; be devoid of inspiration; run out of ideas to write about

【枯木逢春】 kūmù féng chūn spring comes to the withered tree — get a new lease of life

【枯涩】 kūsè dull and heavy: 文字~ a dull and heavy style

【枯瘦】 kūshòu emaciated; skinny

【枯水】 kūshuǐ low water ◇ ~期 dry season

【枯萎】 kūwěi withered

【枯叶蛾】 kūyè'é lappet moth

【枯燥】 kūzào dull and dry; uninteresting: ~无味 dry as dust

【枯痔法】 kūzhìfǎ 〈中医〉 necrosis therapy of haemorrhoids

**哭** kū cry; weep: 放声大~ cry loudly; cry unrestrainedly/ ~了起来 burst into tears

【哭鼻子】 kūbízi 〈口〉 snivel

【哭哭啼啼】 kūkutítí endlessly weep and wail

【哭泣】 kūqì cry; weep; sob

【哭穷】 kūqióng go about telling people how hard up one is; complain of being hard up

【哭丧着脸】 kūsangzhe liǎn put on (或 wear) a long face; go around with a long face

【哭诉】 kūsù complain tearfully
【哭天抹泪】 kūtiān-mǒlèi wail and whine
【哭笑不得】 kū-xiào bude not know whether to laugh or to cry; find sth. both funny and annoying

**窟** kū ① hole; cave: 石～ cave; grotto ② den: 匪～ a robbers' den/ 赌～ a gambling-den
【窟窿】 kūlong ① hole; cavity: 耗子～ rat-hole/ 鞋底磨了个～ have worn a hole in the sole of one's shoe ② deficit; debt
【窟窿眼儿】 kūlongyǎnr small hole

**骷** kū
【骷髅】 kūlóu ① human skeleton ② human skull; death's-head

## kǔ

**苦** kǔ ① bitter: 这药～极了。This medicine tastes very bitter. ② hardship; suffering; pain: ～里生，甜里长 be born in misery but brought up in happiness/ 不忘阶级～ not forget the bitterness of class oppression/ 勘探队员以～为乐，以～为荣。The prospectors feel it a joy and an honour to work under hard conditions. ③ cause sb. suffering; give sb. a hard time: 这事可～了他了。This matter really gave him a hard time. ④ suffer from; be troubled by: ～旱 suffer from drought ⑤ painstakingly; doing one's utmost: 勤学～练 study and train hard/ ～劝 earnestly advise (或 exhort)/ ～～哀求 entreat piteously; implore urgently ⑥ 〈方〉 (cut off) too much: 指甲剪得太～ trim one's nails too short/ 树枝修得太～了。The trees are overpruned.
【苦差】 kǔchāi hard and unprofitable job
【苦楚】 kǔchǔ suffering; misery; distress
【苦处】 kǔchu suffering; hardship; difficulty: 你可不知道我当童养媳那时的～。You don't know how I suffered as a child bride.
【苦大仇深】 kǔdà-chóushēn suffer bitterly and nurse deep hatred
【苦胆】 kǔdǎn gall bladder
【苦恶鸟】 kǔ'èniǎo white-breasted water rail
【苦干】 kǔgàn work hard: ～精神 hard-working spirit/ ～加巧干 work hard and skilfully; work hard and use one's brain
【苦工】 kǔgōng hard (manual) work; hard labour
【苦功】 kǔgōng hard work; painstaking effort: 语言这东西，不是随便可以学好的，非下～不可。The mastery of language is not easy and requires painstaking effort./ 下～学习 study hard
【苦瓜】 kǔguā ① 〈植〉 balsam pear ② bitter gourd: 咱们俩是一根藤上的～。We are two bitter gourds on the same vine — we both suffered the same hard lot in the old society.
【苦海】 kǔhǎi sea of bitterness; abyss of misery: ～无边，回头是岸。The sea of bitterness has no bounds, repent and the shore is at hand./ 解放前的上海是冒险家的乐园，劳动人民的～。Preliberation Shanghai was paradise for the adventurers but hell for the working people./ 脱离～ get out of the abyss of misery
【苦寒】 kǔhán bitter cold
【苦尽甘来】 kǔjìn-gānlái when bitterness is finished, sweetness begins — after suffering comes happiness
【苦口】 kǔkǒu ① (admonish) in earnest: ～相劝 earnestly advise (或 exhort) ② bitter to the taste: 这些话都是～良药。The advice may be bitter medicine, but it will do good.
【苦口婆心】 kǔkǒu-póxīn urge sb. time and again with good intentions
【苦力】 kǔlì 〈旧〉 coolie
【苦楝子】 kǔliànzǐ 〈中药〉 chinaberry
【苦闷】 kǔmèn depressed; dejected; feeling low: 她生活在封建家庭里，精神上很～。She suffered greatly from the spiritual depression of life in a feudal family.
【苦难】 kǔnàn suffering; misery; distress: 帝国主义的战争使人民遭受了巨大的～。Wars launched by imperialism have caused the people untold suffering./ ～的深渊 the abyss of misery/ 老工人用自己的～家史来教育青年。The old worker taught the young people by telling the tragic history of his family.
【苦恼】 kǔnǎo vexed; worried: 受到一点挫折用不着～。You shouldn't feel vexed just because of a few setbacks.
【苦肉计】 kǔròujì the ruse of inflicting an injury on oneself to win the confidence of the enemy
【苦涩】 kǔsè ① bitter and astringent ② pained; agonized; anguished: ～的表情 a pained look
【苦水】 kǔshuǐ ① bitter water ② gastric secretion, etc. rising to the mouth ③ suffering (in the old society): 她是在～里泡大的。She grew up amidst suffering./ 吐～ pour out one's grievances
【苦思】 kǔsī think hard; cudgel one's brains
【苦思冥想】 kǔsī-míngxiǎng cudgel one's brains (to evolve an idea)
【苦痛】 kǔtòng pain; suffering
【苦头】 kǔtóu bitter taste: 这个井里的水带点～儿。Water from this well has a slightly bitter taste.
【苦头】 kǔtou suffering: 他在敌人的监狱里吃尽了～。He endured untold sufferings in the enemy prison./ 听不进群众意见，早晚要吃～的。If you turn a deaf ear to the masses' criticism, sooner or later you'll have to pay for it.
【苦味酸】 kǔwèisuān picric acid ◇ ～盐 picrate
【苦夏】 kǔxià loss of appetite and weight in summer
【苦笑】 kǔxiào forced smile; wry smile
【苦心】 kǔxīn trouble taken; pains: 煞费～ take great pains/ ～经营 painstakingly build up (an enterprise, etc.)
【苦心孤诣】 kǔxīn gūyì make extraordinarily painstaking efforts
【苦行】 kǔxíng 〈宗〉 ascetic practices ◇ ～主义 asceticism
【苦役】 kǔyì 〈法〉 hard labour; penal servitude
【苦于】 kǔyú suffer from (a disadvantage): ～不识字 handicapped by illiteracy/ ～时间紧 hard pressed for time
【苦战】 kǔzhàn wage an arduous struggle; struggle hard: 大家决心～二年，改变这个山区的面貌。We are determined to carry on a bitter struggle to transform the mountain area in two years.
【苦衷】 kǔzhōng difficulties that one is reluctant to discuss or mention: 应该体谅他的～。Allowance must be made for his difficulties./ 难言的～ feelings of pain or embarrassment which are hard to mention
【苦竹】 kǔzhú 〈植〉 bitter bamboo (*Pleioblastus amarus*)
【苦主】 kǔzhǔ the family of the victim in a murder case

## kù

**库** kù warehouse; storehouse: 粮食已经入～。The grain is already in the granary./ 汽车～ garage/ 军械～ armoury
【库藏】 kùcáng have in storage: ～图书三十万册。There are 300,000 books in the library.
【库存】 kùcún stock; reserve: 有大量～ have a large stock

of goods/ ～物资 goods kept in stock; reserve of materials
【库房】 kùfáng storehouse; storeroom
【库仑】 kùlún 〈电〉 coulomb ◇ ～定律 Coulomb's law
【库容】 kùróng 〈水〉 storage capacity

**裤** kù trousers; pants: 短～ shorts/ 棉～ cotton-padded trousers
【裤衩】 kùchǎ underpants; undershorts
【裤裆】 kùdāng crotch (of trousers)
【裤兜】 kùdōu trouser pocket
【裤缝】 kùfèng seams of a trouser leg
【裤脚】 kùjiǎo ① bottom of a trouser leg ② 〈方〉 trouser legs
【裤腿】 kùtuǐ trouser legs
【裤线】 kùxiàn creases (of trousers)
【裤腰】 kùyāo waist of trousers
【裤子】 kùzi trousers; pants

**酷** kù ① cruel; oppressive: ～吏 an oppressive (feudal) official ② very; extremely: ～寒 bitter cold/ ～似 be the very image of; be exactly like/ ～爱 ardently love
【酷烈】 kùliè cruel; fierce: ～的太阳 the scorching sun
【酷热】 kùrè extremely hot (weather): 天气～ a sweltering hot day
【酷暑】 kùshǔ the intense heat of summer
【酷刑】 kùxíng cruel (或 savage) torture

## kuā

**夸** kuā ① exaggerate; overstate; boast: ～口 boast; brag ② praise: 人人都～她爱劳动。 Everyone praised her for her love of labour./ 成绩不～跑不了，缺点不找不得了。 Merits uncited will not vanish; shortcomings undiscovered may prove disastrous.
【夸大】 kuādà exaggerate; overstate; magnify: ～困难 exaggerate the difficulties/ ～敌情 overestimate the enemy/ 原来的数字被～了。 The original figures were inflated.
【夸大其词】 kuādà qí cí make an overstatement; exaggerate
【夸奖】 kuājiǎng praise; commend: 工人师傅～他进步快。 The master worker praised him for his rapid progress.
【夸克】 kuākè 〈物〉 quark
【夸口】 kuākǒu boast; brag; talk big
【夸夸其谈】 kuākuā qí tán indulge in exaggerations
【夸脱】 kuātuō quart
【夸耀】 kuāyào brag about; show off; flaunt: 她从不～自己。 She never brags./ ～他的见识 show off his knowledge and experience
【夸赞】 kuāzàn speak highly of; commend; praise
【夸张】 kuāzhāng ① exaggerate; overstate: 你这样说未免太～了。 I'm afraid you've been exaggerating. 或 I'm afraid you've overstated the case./ ～的语言 inflated language; exaggerations/ 艺术～ artistic exaggeration ② 〈语〉 hyperbole

## kuǎ

**侉** kuǎ 〈方〉 ① (speak) with an accent ② big and clumsy; unwieldy
【侉子】 kuǎzi a person who speaks with an accent

**垮** kuǎ collapse; fall; break down: 这堵墙要～了。 The wall's going to collapse./ 我身体结实，累不～。 I'm very strong; no amount of hard work can wear me down./ 洪水冲～了堤坝。 The flood waters burst the dyke./ 打～敌人 put the enemy to rout
【垮台】 kuǎtái collapse; fall from power: 与人民为敌的人总是要～的。 Those who oppose the people will surely come to grief.

## kuà

**挎** kuà ① carry on the arm: ～着个篮子 with a basket on one's arm/ ～着胳膊 arm in arm ② carry sth. over one's shoulder or at one's side: ～着照相机 have a camera slung over one's shoulder
【挎包】 kuàbāo satchel

**胯** kuà hip
【胯骨】 kuàgǔ hipbone; innominate bone

**跨** kuà ① step; stride: ～进大门 step into a doorway/ 向前～一步 take a step forward/ ～过小沟 stride over a ditch/ 欢欣鼓舞地～入了新的一年 stride into the new year in high spirits ② bestride; straddle: ～上战马 mount (或 bestride) a war-horse/ 横～长江的大桥 a gigantic bridge spanning the Changjiang River. ③ cut across; go beyond: 亚洲地～寒、温、热三带。 Asia extends across the frigid, temperate and tropical zones./ 组织～地区的商品供应 organize transregional commodity supplies
【跨度】 kuàdù 〈建〉 span
【跨纲要】 kuà Gāngyào surpass the target set by the National Programme for Agricultural Development
【跨国公司】 kuàguó gōngsī transnational corporation
【跨栏赛跑】 kuàlán sàipǎo 〈体〉 hurdle race; the hurdles
【跨年度】 kuà niándù go beyond the year ◇ ～预算 a budget to be carried over to the next year
【跨线桥】 kuàxiànqiáo flyover; overpass
【跨越】 kuàyuè stride across; leap over; cut across: ～几个历史阶段 leap over several historical stages of development/ ～障碍 surmount an obstacle

## kuǎi

**㧟** kuǎi 〈方〉 ① scratch: ～痒痒 scratch an itch ② carry on the arm: ～着小竹篮 with a small bamboo basket on one's arm

**蒯** kuǎi ① wool grass ② (Kuǎi) a surname
【蒯草】 kuǎicǎo 〈植〉 wool grass

## kuài

**会** kuài
另见 huì
【会计】 kuàijì ① accounting ② bookkeeper; accountant ◇ ～年度 financial (或 fiscal) year

**快** kuài ① fast; quick; rapid: 请别说得那么～。 Please don't speak so fast./ 我的表～五分。 My watch is five minutes fast./ 他进步很～。 He has made rapid progress./ 大干～上 race against time and go all out ② speed: 这车能跑多～？ How fast can this car go? ③ hurry up; make haste: ～上车吧！ Hurry up and get on the bus!/ ～跟我走。 Quick, come with me. ④ soon; before long: 他～回来了。 He'll be back soon./ 我来了～两年了。 It is nearly two years since I came here./ 春节～到了。The Spring Festival is drawing near. ⑤ quick-witted; ingenious: 他脑子～。He's quick-witted. 或 He understands things quickly. ⑥ sharp: ～刀 a sharp knife ⑦ straightforward; forthright; plainspoken: 心直口～ straightforward and outspoken/ ～人～语 straightforward talk from a straightforward person ⑧ pleased; happy; gratified: 心中不～ feel unhappy/ 拍手称～ clap and cheer/ 大～人心 to the immense satisfaction of the people

【快板】 kuàibǎn 〈乐〉 *allegro*

【快板儿】 kuàibǎnr *kuaibanr*, rhythmic comic talk or monologue to the accompaniment of bamboo clappers; clapper talk ◇ ～书 story recited to the rhythm of bamboo clappers

【快报】 kuàibào wall bulletin; bulletin

【快步】 kuàibù 〈军〉 half step; trot

【快餐】 kuàicān quick meal; snack ◇ ～部 quick-lunch counter; snack counter

【快车】 kuàichē express train or bus: 特别～ special express

【快当】 kuàidang quick; prompt: 她做起事来又细心又～。She's quick and careful.

【快刀斩乱麻】 kuàidāo zhǎn luànmá cut a tangled skein of jute with a sharp knife; cut the Gordian knot

【快递】 kuàidì express delivery ◇ ～邮件 express mail

【快干】 kuàigān quick-drying ◇ ～漆 quick-drying paint

【快感】 kuàigǎn pleasant sensation; delight

【快攻】 kuàigōng quick attack (in ball games)

【快活】 kuàihuo happy; merry; cheerful: 孩子们～地打雪仗。The children were enjoying a snowball fight.

【快乐】 kuàilè happy; joyful; cheerful: ～的童年生活 a happy childhood/ 节日过得很～。The festival was spent joyfully.

【快马加鞭】 kuàimǎ jiā biān spur on the flying horse — at top speed; posthaste

【快慢】 kuài-màn speed: 这些按钮是管～的。These buttons control the speed. ◇ ～针 index (或 regulator) lever (in a clock or watch)

【快门】 kuàimén 〈摄〉 (camera) shutter ◇ ～开关 shutter release

【快事】 kuàishì a happening that gives great satisfaction or pleasure; delight: 引为～ recall (an event) with great satisfaction/ 生平一大～ one of the most delightful experiences in one's life

【快手】 kuàishǒu quick worker; deft hand

【快书】 kuàishū quick-patter (rhythmic storytelling accompanied by bamboo or copper clappers): 山东～ Shandong clapper ballad

【快速】 kuàisù fast; quick; high-speed ◇ ～部队 mobile force (或 troops, units)/ ～掘进 〈矿〉 high-speed drivage/ ～切削 〈机〉 high-speed cutting

【快艇】 kuàitǐng speedboat; motor boat; mosquito boat

【快慰】 kuàiwèi feel pleased with and derive comfort from sth.; be pleased: 我们都为她的进步感到～。We are all pleased with the progress she has made.

【快信】 kuàixìn express letter

【快硬水泥】 kuàiyìng shuǐní 〈建〉 quick-hardening cement

【快意】 kuàiyì pleased; satisfied; comfortable

【快鱼】 kuàiyú Chinese herring

【快照】 kuàizhào snapshot

【快中子】 kuàizhōngzǐ 〈物〉 fast (或 high-speed) neutron

【快嘴】 kuàizuǐ one who readily voices his thoughts; one who is quick to articulate his ideas

**块** kuài ① piece; lump; chunk: 糖～儿 fruit drops; lumps of sugar/ 把肉切成～儿 cut the meat into cubes ②〈量〉〔用于块状或某些片状的东西〕: 两～肥皂 two cakes of soap/ 一～面包 a piece of bread/ 一～手表 a wrist watch/ 一～试验田 an experimental plot ③〈口〉 *yuan*, the basic unit of money in China: 三～钱 three *yuan*

【块根】 kuàigēn 〈植〉 root tuber

【块规】 kuàiguī 〈机〉 slip gauge; gauge block

【块茎】 kuàijīng 〈植〉 stem tuber

【块垒】 kuàilěi 〈书〉 ① indignation ② gloom; depression

【块煤】 kuàiméi lump coal

【块儿】 kuàir 〈方〉 place: 我在这～工作好几年了。I've been working here for quite a few years now.

**侩** kuài middleman

**脍** kuài 〈书〉 meat chopped into small pieces; minced meat

【脍炙人口】 kuàizhì rénkǒu (of a piece of good writing, etc.) win universal praise; enjoy great popularity: 一首～的古诗 an oft-quoted and widely loved ancient poem

**筷** kuài chopsticks

【筷子】 kuàizi chopsticks: 火～ fire-tongs; tongs

**鲙** kuài

【鲙鱼】 kuàiyú Chinese herring

## kuān

**宽** kuān ① wide; broad: ～肩膀 broad-shouldered/ ～边草帽 broad-brimmed straw hat/ 眼界～ have a broad outlook ② width; breadth: 这条河有一里～。This river is one *li* wide. ③ relax; relieve: 听说他的病情并不严重，我们的心就～多了。We were greatly relieved to learn that his condition was not serious./ 把心放～一点。Don't worry. 或 Don't take it too hard. ④ extend: 限期能再～几天吗？Can the deadline be extended a few more days? ⑤ generous; lenient: 从～处理 treat with leniency/ 严以律己，～以待人 be strict with oneself and lenient with others ⑥ comfortably off; well-off: 他手头比过去～多了。He's much better off than before.

【宽畅】 kuānchàng free from worry; happy

【宽敞】 kuānchang spacious; roomy; commodious: ～的房子 a commodious house

【宽绰】 kuānchuo ① spacious; commodious: 这间屋子很～。The room is spacious. ② relax; relieve: 听了他的话，我心里～多了。I felt greatly relieved to hear what he said. 或 I felt a big load taken off my mind when I heard what he said. ③ comfortably off; well-off

【宽打窄用】 kuān dǎ zhǎi yòng budget liberally and spend sparingly

【宽大】 kuāndà ① spacious; roomy: ～的候车室 a spacious waiting room ② lenient; magnanimous: 受到～处理 be dealt with leniently; be accorded lenient treatment; receive clemency/ ～为怀 be magnanimous or lenient (with an offender)/ 实行镇压与～相结合的政策 adopt a policy of combining suppression with leniency (towards criminals)

【宽待】 kuāndài treat with leniency; be lenient in dealing with: ～俘虏 give lenient treatment to prisoners of war; treat prisoners of war leniently

【宽贷】 kuāndài pardon; forgive

【宽度】 kuāndù width; breadth: 领海～ the extent of the territorial sea

【宽广】 kuānguǎng broad; extensive; vast: ～的田野 a broad expanse of country/ 心胸～ broad-minded

【宽轨】 kuānguǐ broad gauge ◇ ～铁路 broad-gauge railway
【宽宏大量】 kuānhóng-dàliàng large-minded; magnanimous
【宽厚】 kuānhòu generous: 待人～ be generous to people
【宽解】 kuānjiě ease sb.'s anxiety; ease sb. of his trouble
【宽旷】 kuānkuàng extensive; vast: ～的草原 extensive grasslands
【宽阔】 kuānkuò broad; wide: ～的林荫道 a broad (或 wide) avenue/ ～的胸怀 broad-mindedness
【宽饶】 kuānráo forgive; show mercy; give quarter
【宽容】 kuānróng tolerant; lenient
【宽恕】 kuānshù forgive: 请求～ ask for forgiveness/ 立功赎罪，以求得人民～ perform meritorious service to atone for one's crimes and obtain clemency from the people
【宽慰】 kuānwèi comfort; console: ～她几句。Say something to comfort her./ 这样一想，我心里才～了些。 This thought brought me a little comfort.
【宽限】 kuānxiàn extend a time limit: ～一星期 give a week's grace/ 请～几天。Please extend the deadline a few days.
【宽心】 kuānxīn feel relieved: 说几句～话 say a few reassuring words
【宽衣】 kuānyī 〈敬〉 take off your coat: 请～。Do take off your coat.
【宽银幕】 kuānyínmù wide screen ◇ ～电影 wide-screen film
【宽裕】 kuānyù well-to-do; comfortably off; ample: 经济～ in easy circumstances; well-off/ 时间很～。 There's plenty of time yet.
【宽窄】 kuānzhǎi width; breadth; size: 这块布做窗帘，～正合适。This piece of cloth is just the right size for a curtain.
【宽纵】 kuānzòng indulge: 不要～自己。Don't be so self-indulgent.

**髋** kuān hip
【髋骨】 kuāngǔ 〈生理〉 hipbone; innominate bone

## kuǎn

**款** kuǎn ① sincere: ～曲 heartfelt feelings ② receive with hospitality; entertain ③ section of an article in a legal document, etc.; paragraph: 根据该条约的第六条第二～ according to Article 6, Section 2 of the Treaty ④ a sum of money; fund: 公～ public funds/ 筹～ raise funds/ 汇～ remit money ⑤ the name of sender or recipient inscribed on a painting or a piece of calligraphy presented as a gift ⑥ 〈书〉 leisurely; slow: ～步 with deliberate steps
【款待】 kuǎndài treat cordially; entertain: ～客人 entertain guests/ 感谢你对我们的盛情～。Thank you for the hospitality you have shown us.
【款冬】 kuǎndōng 〈植〉 coltsfoot
【款留】 kuǎnliú cordially urge (a guest) to stay
【款洽】 kuǎnqià 〈书〉 cordial and harmonious
【款曲】 kuǎnqū 〈书〉 heartfelt feelings: 互通～ express feelings of mutual affection or friendship
【款式】 kuǎnshì pattern; style; design
【款项】 kuǎnxiàng a sum of money; fund
【款识】 kuǎnzhì inscriptions (on bronzes, etc.)
【款子】 kuǎnzi a sum of money

## kuāng

**匡** kuāng ① rectify; correct: ～谬 correct mistakes ② 〈书〉 assist; save: ～我不逮 help me to overcome my shortcomings ③ (Kuāng) a surname
【匡正】 kuāngzhèng rectify; correct

**诓** kuāng deceive; hoax: 我哪能～你? How could I deceive you?
【诓骗】 kuāngpiàn deceive; hoax; dupe

**哐** kuāng 〈象〉 crash; bang: ～的一声，脸盆掉在地上了。The basin fell with a crash.
【哐啷】 kuānglāng 〈象〉 crash: ～一声把门关上 bang the door shut

**框** kuāng ① frame; circle ② 〈方〉 draw a frame round: 用红线把标题～起来 frame the heading in red/ 报上登载了～有黑边的烈士遗像。The newspaper carried the martyr's photo framed in black.
另见 kuàng
【框框】 kuāngkuang ① frame; circle ② restriction; convention; set pattern: 条条～ regulations and restrictions/ 突破旧～的限制 throw convention to the winds

**筐** kuāng basket
【筐子】 kuāngzi small basket

## kuáng

**狂** kuáng ① mad; crazy: 发～ go mad ② violent: 雨骤风～。The wind blew hard and the rain came down in sheets./ 股票价格～跌。 The stocks slumped. ③ wild; unrestrained: ～奔的马 a bolting horse/ 欣喜若～ be wild (或 beside oneself) with joy ④ arrogant; overbearing
【狂暴】 kuángbào violent; wild: ～的山洪 raging mountain torrents
【狂飙】 kuángbiāo hurricane
【狂放】 kuángfàng unruly or unrestrained
【狂吠】 kuángfèi bark furiously; howl
【狂风】 kuángfēng ① 〈气〉 whole gale ② fierce wind: ～呼啸。The wind howled./ ～暴雨 a violent storm
【狂轰滥炸】 kuánghōng-lànzhà wanton and indiscriminate bombing
【狂欢】 kuánghuān revelry; carnival
【狂澜】 kuánglán raging waves: 力挽～ do one's utmost to stem a raging tide or save a desperate situation
【狂犬病】 kuángquǎnbìng hydrophobia; rabies
【狂热】 kuángrè fanaticism: ～的军备竞赛 feverish armament race/ ～的信徒 a fanatical follower; fanatic; zealot ◇ ～性 fanaticism
【狂人】 kuángrén madman; maniac: ～呓语 ravings of a madman/ 帝国主义战争～ imperialist war maniacs
【狂妄】 kuángwàng wildly arrogant; presumptuous: ～自大 arrogant and conceited/ ～的野心 a wild ambition
【狂喜】 kuángxǐ wild with joy
【狂想曲】 kuángxiǎngqǔ 〈乐〉 rhapsody
【狂笑】 kuángxiào laugh wildly; laugh boisterously
【狂言】 kuángyán ravings; wild language: 口出～ talk wildly

**诳** kuáng
【诳语】 kuángyǔ lies; falsehood

**鵟** kuáng buzzard

## kuàng

**邝** Kuàng a surname

**况** kuàng ① condition; situation: 近~如何? How have you been recently? ② compare: 以古~今 draw parallels from history ③ 〈书〉 moreover; besides

【况且】 kuàngqiě 〈连〉 moreover; besides; in addition

**旷** kuàng ① vast; spacious: 地~人稀 a vast territory with a sparse population ② free from worries and petty ideas: 心~神怡 carefree and happy ③ neglect ④ loose-fitting: 这身衣服她穿着太~了。 The dress sits loosely on her.

【旷达】 kuàngdá broad-minded; bighearted

【旷废】 kuàngfèi neglect: ~学业 neglect one's studies

【旷费】 kuàngfèi waste: ~时间 waste one's time

【旷工】 kuànggōng stay away from work without leave or good reason

【旷古】 kuànggǔ from time immemorial: ~未闻 unheard-of; unprecedented

【旷课】 kuàngkè be absent from school without leave; cut school: 旷一堂课 cut a class

【旷日持久】 kuàngrì-chíjiǔ long-drawn-out; protracted; prolonged: ~的谈判 long-drawn-out negotiations

【旷野】 kuàngyě wilderness

【旷职】 kuàngzhí be absent from duty without leave or good reason

**矿** kuàng ① ore (或 mineral) deposit: 报~ report where deposits are found ② ore: 铁~ iron ore ③ mine: 煤~ coal mine; colliery/ 他在~上工作。He works at the mine.

【矿藏】 kuàngcáng mineral resources: 我国~丰富。 China is rich in mineral resources. ◇ ~量 (ore) reserves

【矿层】 kuàngcéng ore bed; ore horizon; seam

【矿产】 kuàngchǎn mineral products; minerals

【矿车】 kuàngchē mine car; tub; tram

【矿尘】 kuàngchén mine dust

【矿床】 kuàngchuáng mineral (或 ore) deposit; deposit: 金属~ metalliferous deposit/ 层状~ bedded deposit/ 海底~ submarine deposit

【矿灯】 kuàngdēng miner's lamp

【矿工】 kuànggōng miner

【矿浆】 kuàngjiāng ore pulp; pulp

【矿井】 kuàngjǐng mine; pit ◇ ~火灾 mine fire

【矿坑】 kuàngkēng pit

【矿脉】 kuàngmài mineral ore; mineral vein; lode

【矿棉】 kuàngmián mineral wool

【矿苗】 kuàngmiáo outcropping; outcrop; crop

【矿泥】 kuàngní sludge; slime; slurry

【矿区】 kuàngqū mining area ◇ ~铁路 mine railway

【矿泉】 kuàngquán mineral spring ◇ ~水 mineral water

【矿山】 kuàngshān mine
◇ ~地压 rock pressure/ ~工程图 mine map/ ~机械 mining machinery/ ~救护 mine rescue/ ~运输 mine haul (或 haulage); pit haulage

【矿石】 kuàngshí ore ◇ ~收音机 crystal receiver (或 set)

【矿体】 kuàngtǐ ore body

【矿田】 kuàngtián ore field

【矿物】 kuàngwù mineral: 伴生~ associated mineral ◇ ~界 mineral kingdom/ ~学 mineralogy

【矿样】 kuàngyàng sample ore

【矿业】 kuàngyè mining industry

【矿渣】 kuàngzhā slag ◇ ~水泥 slag cement/ ~砖 slag brick

【矿质肥料】 kuàngzhì féiliào 〈农〉 mineral fertilizer

【矿柱】 kuàngzhù (ore) pillar

**框** kuàng frame; case: 门~ door frame/ 窗~ window frame; window case/ 镜~儿 picture frame/ 眼镜~儿 rims (of spectacles)/ 无~眼镜 rimless spectacles
另见 kuāng

【框架】 kuàngjià 〈建〉 frame

【框子】 kuàngzi frame: 眼镜~ rims (of spectacles)

**眶** kuàng the socket of the eye: 热泪盈~ one's eyes filling with tears/ 眼泪夺~而出 tears starting from one's eyes

## kuī

**亏** kuī ① lose (money, etc.); have a deficit: ~了二百元 have a deficit of 200 *yuan*; have lost 200 *yuan*/ 盈~ profit and loss ② deficient; short: 理~ be in the wrong ③ treat unfairly: 你放心吧,~不了你。 Don't worry, we won't be unfair to you./ 人不~地,地不~人。The land won't fail people as long as people don't fail the land. ④ fortunately; luckily; thanks to: ~他提醒了我,要不我早忘了。Luckily he reminded me; otherwise I'd have forgotten all about it. ⑤〔反说,表示讥讽〕: ~他说得出口! And he had the nerve to say so! ⑥ (of the moon) wane

【亏本】 kuīběn lose money in business; lose one's capital: ~生意 a losing proposition

【亏仓】 kuīcāng 〈航海〉 broken stowage

【亏待】 kuīdài treat unfairly; treat shabbily

【亏得】 kuīde ① fortunately; luckily; thanks to: ~大家帮忙,我们才按时把这活干完。 Thanks to everybody's help, we finished the job on time. ②〔反说,表示讥讽〕: ~你长这么大,那么点事儿都不懂。 Fancy a big boy like you not understanding such a simple thing!

【亏负】 kuīfù let sb. suffer; let sb. down

【亏耗】 kuīhào loss by a natural process: 货物在运输中的~ losses incurred in the course of transportation

【亏空】 kuīkong ① be in debt ② debt; deficit: 拉~ get into debt/ 弥补~ meet (或 make up) a deficit; make up (for) a loss

【亏累】 kuīlěi show repeated deficits

【亏欠】 kuīqiàn have a deficit; be in arrears

【亏蚀】 kuīshí ① eclipse of the sun or moon ② lose (money) in business

【亏损】 kuīsǔn ① loss; deficit: 企业~ loss incurred in an enterprise ② general debility

【亏心】 kuīxīn have a guilty conscience ◇ ~事 a deed that troubles (或 weighs on) one's conscience

**岿** kuī

【岿然】 kuīrán towering; lofty: ~不动 steadfastly stand one's ground

**盔** kuī helmet

【盔甲】 kuījiǎ a suit of armour

**窥** kuī peep; spy

【窥测】 kuīcè spy out: ~方向,以求一逞 spy out the land in order to accomplish one's schemes; see which way the wind blows in order to achieve one's evil ends/ ~时机 bide one's time

【窥见】 kuījiàn get (或 catch) a glimpse of; detect: 从一个人的生活作风可以～他的思想意识。We can get a hint of a person's ideology from his life style.
【窥器】 kuīqì 〈医〉 speculum
【窥视】 kuīshì peep at; spy on: 民兵发现一个形迹可疑的人向屋内～。The militia spotted a suspicious character peeping into the house.
【窥伺】 kuīsì lie in wait for; be on watch for
【窥探】 kuītàn spy upon; pry about: ～军事秘密 pry into military secrets

## kuí

**奎** kuí
【奎宁】 kuíníng 〈药〉 quinine
**隗** Kuí a surname
**逵** kuí 〈书〉 thoroughfare
**馗** kuí 见"逵" kuí
**揆** kuí 〈书〉 ① conjecture; guess; estimate: ～其本意，或非如此。That presumably was not his original intention./ ～情度理 considering the circumstances and judging by common sense ② principle; standard
【揆度】 kuíduó 〈书〉 estimate; conjecture
**葵** kuí certain herbaceous plants with big flowers: 向日～ sunflower/ 蜀～ hollyhock/ 锦～ high mallow
【葵花】 kuíhuā sunflower: 朵朵～向太阳，革命人民心向党。Like sunflowers turning towards the sun, the hearts of the revolutionary people turn towards the Party. ◇ ～油 sunflower oil/ ～子 sunflower seeds
【葵扇】 kuíshàn palm-leaf fan
**喹** kuí
【喹啉】 kuílín 〈化〉 quinoline
**暌** kuí separate
【暌违】 kuíwéi 〈书〉 separate: ～数载。It's years since we parted.
**魁** kuí ① chief; head: 罪～ chief criminal; arch-criminal ② of stalwart build
【魁首】 kuíshǒu a person who is head and shoulders above others; the brightest and best: 文章～ outstanding writer of the day
【魁伟】 kuíwěi big and tall
【魁梧】 kuíwú big and tall; stalwart
【魁星】 kuíxīng the four stars in the bowl of the Big Dipper, or the one at the tip of the bowl
**睽** kuí
【睽睽】 kuíkuí stare; gaze: 众目～之下 in the public eye
**蝰** kuí
【蝰蛇】 kuíshé viper

## kuǐ

**傀** kuǐ
【傀儡】 kuǐlěi puppet: 殖民主义者及其～ colonialists and their stooges (或 puppets)
◇ ～戏 puppet show; puppet play/ ～政府 puppet government/ ～政权 puppet regime

## kuì

**匮** kuì 〈书〉 deficient
【匮乏】 kuìfá 〈书〉 short (of supplies); deficient
**溃** kuì ① (of a dyke or dam) burst: 千里之堤，～于蚁穴。One ant hole may cause the collapse of a thousand-*li* dyke. ② break through (an encirclement): ～围南奔 break through the encirclement and head south ③ be routed: 一触即～ be routed at the first encounter/ ～不成军 be utterly routed ④ fester; ulcerate
【溃败】 kuìbài be defeated; be routed
【溃决】 kuìjué (of a dyke or dam) burst
【溃烂】 kuìlàn 〈医〉 fester; ulcerate
【溃灭】 kuìmiè crumble and fall
【溃散】 kuìsàn be defeated and dispersed
【溃逃】 kuìtáo escape in disorder; fly pell-mell; flee helter-skelter
【溃退】 kuìtuì beat a precipitate retreat
【溃疡】 kuìyáng 〈医〉 ulcer: 胃～ gastric ulcer/ 十二指肠～ duodenal ulcer
**馈** kuì make a present of: ～送 present (a gift); make a present of sth.
【馈电】 kuìdiàn 〈电〉 feed: 交叉～ cross feed ◇ ～线 feed line; feeder
【馈赠】 kuìzèng present (a gift); make a present of sth.
**愦** kuì muddleheaded: 昏～ muddleheaded
**喟** kuì 〈书〉 sigh
【喟然长叹】 kuìrán chángtàn 〈书〉 sigh deeply; heave a deep sigh
【喟叹】 kuìtàn 〈书〉 sigh with deep feeling
**愧** kuì ashamed; conscience-stricken: 问心无～ have a clear conscience; have nothing on one's conscience/ 于心有～ have a guilty conscience; have something on one's conscience; feel ashamed
【愧恨】 kuìhèn ashamed and remorseful; remorseful: ～交集 overcome with shame and remorse/ 内心深自～ feel bitterly remorseful
【愧色】 kuìsè a look of shame: 面有～ look ashamed/ 毫无～ look unashamed (或 unabashed)
**聩** kuì 〈书〉 deaf; hard of hearing: 振聋发～ rouse the deaf and awaken the unhearing
**篑** kuì 〈书〉 basket for holding earth: 功亏一～ fail to build a mound for want of the last basket of earth — fall short of success for want of a final effort

## kūn

**坤** kūn female; feminine: ～表 woman's watch
【坤角儿】 kūnjuér 〈旧〉 actress
**昆** kūn ① elder brother ② 〈书〉 offspring: 后～ descendants; children

【昆布】 kūnbù 〈中药〉 kelp
【昆虫】 kūnchóng insect: 传病～ insect vector ◇ ～学 entomology; insectology/ ～学家 entomologist
【昆仑】 Kūnlún the Kunlun Mountains
【昆明】 Kūnmíng Kunming
【昆腔】 kūnqiāng melodies which originated in Kunshan (昆山), Jiangsu Province, in the Ming Dynasty; melodies for *Kunqu* opera
【昆曲】 kūnqǔ ① *Kunqu* opera ② melodies for *Kunqu* opera
【昆仲】 kūn-zhòng elder and younger brothers; brothers

**醌** kūn 〈化〉 quinone

**鲲** kūn enormous legendary fish, which could change into a roc
【鲲鹏】 kūnpéng roc (an enormous legendary bird transformed from a gigantic fish)

## kǔn

**捆** kǔn ① tie; bind; bundle up: ～行李 tie up one's baggage/ ～谷草 bundle up millet stalks/ 把他～起来 tie him up/ ～住手脚 bound hand and foot ② 〈量〉 bundle: 一～柴禾 a bundle of firewood
【捆绑】 kǔnbǎng truss up; bind; tie up
【捆扎】 kǔnzā tie up; bundle up

## kùn

**困** kùn ① be stranded; be hard pressed: 为病所～ be afflicted with illness ② surround; pin down: 把敌人～死在据点里 bottle up the enemy in his stronghold ③ tired: ～乏 tired; fatigued ④ sleepy: 你～了就睡吧。 Go to bed if you feel sleepy.
【困顿】 kùndùn ① tired out; exhausted ② in financial straits
【困厄】 kùn'è dire straits; distress
【困乏】 kùnfá tired; fatigued
【困惑】 kùnhuò perplexed; puzzled: ～不解 feel puzzled
【困境】 kùnjìng difficult position; predicament; straits: 陷于～ fall into dire straits; find oneself in a tight corner; land oneself in a fix/ 摆脱～ extricate oneself from a difficult position
【困窘】 kùnjiǒng in straitened circumstances; in a difficult position; embarrassed
【困倦】 kùnjuàn sleepy
【困苦】 kùnkǔ (live) in privation: 艰难～ difficulties and hardships
【困难】 kùnnan ① difficulty: 情况十分～。 Conditions are very difficult./ ～重重 be beset with difficulties ② financial difficulties; straitened circumstances: 生活～ live in straitened circumstances ◇ ～户 families with material difficulties
【困扰】 kùnrǎo perplex; puzzle: 为一个难题所～ be puzzled by a difficult question
【困守】 kùnshǒu defend against a siege; stand a siege: ～孤城 be entrenched in a beseiged city
【困兽犹斗】 kùnshòu yóu dòu cornered beasts will still fight; beasts at bay will put up a desperate fight

## kuò

**扩** kuò expand; enlarge; extend
【扩充】 kuòchōng expand; strengthen; augment: ～实力 expand (military or political) forces/ ～军备 arms (或 armaments) expansion/ ～设备 augment the equipment
【扩大】 kuòdà enlarge; expand; extend: ～战果 exploit the victory/ ～眼界 widen one's outlook; broaden one's horizons / ～政治影响 extend political influence/ ～集体福利事业 extend collective welfare undertakings; increase collective welfare facilities/ ～耕地面积 expand the area under cultivation/ 不断～人民公社的公共积累 steadily add to the accumulation fund of the people's commune ◇ ～会议 enlarged meeting (或 session, conference)/ ～再生产 expanded reproduction
【扩大化】 kuòdàhuà broaden the scope; magnify: 不把敌我矛盾～ not magnify the contradictions between ourselves and the enemy/ 使错误没有～ keep mistakes within bounds
【扩建】 kuòjiàn extend (a factory, mine, etc.) ◇ ～工程 extension (project)
【扩军】 kuòjūn arms expansion: ～备战 arms expansion and war preparations
【扩孔】 kuòkǒng 〈机〉 reaming ◇ ～钻头 reaming bit; reamer bit
【扩散】 kuòsàn spread; diffuse: 不让废气～ prevent the diffusion of waste gas/ 病菌～ proliferation of germs/ 癌～ proliferation of cancer; spread of cancer
【扩胸器】 kuòxiōngqì chest expander; chest developer
【扩音器】 kuòyīnqì ① megaphone ② audio amplifier
【扩展】 kuòzhǎn expand; spread; extend; develop: 我省水浇地已～到文化大革命前的三倍。 In our province the amount of land under irrigation is three times what it was before the Cultural Revolution.
【扩张】 kuòzhāng ① expand; enlarge; extend; spread: 对外～ expansionism; foreign aggrandizement/ ～野心 expansionist ambitions/ 领土～ territorial expansion (或 aggrandizement) ② 〈医〉 dilate: 血管～ blood vessel dilatation ◇ ～器 〈医〉 dilator/ ～战果〈军〉 exploitation of success/ ～主义 expansionism

**括** kuò ① draw together (muscles, etc.); contract ② include
【括号】 kuòhào brackets ([], (), 〈〉)
【括弧】 kuòhú parentheses
【括约肌】 kuòyuējī 〈生理〉 sphincter

**蛞** kuò
【蛞蝓】 kuòyú slug

**阔** kuò ① wide; broad; vast ② wealthy; rich
【阔别】 kuòbié long separated; long parted: ～多年的战友 long-separated comrades-in-arms
【阔步】 kuòbù take big strides: ～前进 advance with giant strides/ 昂首～ stride forward with one's chin up; stride proudly ahead
【阔绰】 kuòchuò ostentatious; liberal with money: ～的生活 an extravagant life
【阔幅平布】 kuòfú píngbù sheeting: 本色～ grey sheeting
【阔老】 kuòlǎo rich man 又作"阔佬"
【阔气】 kuòqi luxurious; extravagant; lavish: 花钱～ spend lavishly/ 摆～ display (或 parade) one's wealth
【阔叶树】 kuòyèshù broadleaf tree

**廓** kuò ① wide; extensive ② outline
【廓清】 kuòqīng sweep away; clean up

# L

## lā

**拉** lā ① pull; draw; tug; drag: ～弓 draw a bow/ ～风箱 work the bellows/ 把车～过来。Pull the cart over here./ 马～农具 horse-drawn farm implements/ 他把我～到一边。He drew me aside. ② transport by vehicle; haul: 套车去～肥料 get a cart ready to haul back the fertilizer ③ move (troops to a place): 把二班～到桥头 move Squad Two to the bridge ④ play (certain musical instruments): ～小提琴(手风琴) play the violin (accordion) ⑤ drag out; draw out; space out: ～长声音说话 drawl/ 成单行～开距离 form into single file and space out ⑥ give (或 lend) a helping hand; help: 他犯了错误，要～他一把。He's made mistakes and we must help him. ⑦ drag in; implicate: 这是你自己做的事，为什么要～上别人? It was all your own doing. Why drag in others? ⑧ draw in; win over; canvass: ～一派打一派的恶劣行径 the despicable act of drawing in one faction and hitting out at another/ ～选票 canvass votes; canvass/ ～买卖 tout; canvass orders; push sales ⑨ press; press-gang: 他父亲被国民党匪军～去当挑夫。His father was press-ganged to work as a carrier for the KMT bandits./ ～壮丁 grab sb. for military service; forcibly conscript; press-gang ⑩〈乒乓球〉lift ⑪ empty the bowels: 又吐又～ suffer from vomiting and diarrhoea ⑫ (Lā) short for Latin America

另见 lá; lǎ

【拉拔】 lābá 〈机〉 drawing

【拉扯】 lāche 〈口〉 ① drag; pull: 别～着我，让我走。Don't hold me back. Let me go. ② take great pains to bring up (a child): 别忘了是党把你～大的。Don't forget it's the Party that has brought you up. ③ implicate; drag in: 干吗把我～进去? Why drag me in? ④ chat: 他心里有事，无心跟我～。He had something on his mind and was in no mood to chat with me.

【拉出去】 lāchuqu pull out; drag out: ～、打进来是阶级敌人惯用的手段。It's a common practice of the class enemy to drag our people into their camp and to infiltrate our ranks.

【拉床】 lāchuáng 〈机〉 broaching machine

【拉大旗作虎皮】 lā dàqí zuò hǔpí use the great banner (of revolution, etc.) as a tiger-skin (to deck oneself out and intimidate people); drape oneself in the flag to impress people

【拉刀】 lādāo 〈机〉 broach

【拉倒】 lādǎo 〈口〉 forget about it; leave it at that; drop it: 你不同意，就～。Since you don't agree let's forget about it.

【拉丁美洲】 Lādīng Měizhōu Latin America

【拉丁文】 Lādīngwén Latin (language)

【拉丁字母】 Lādīng zìmǔ the Latin alphabet; the Roman alphabet

【拉肚子】 lā dùzi suffer from diarrhoea; have loose bowels

【拉队伍】 lā duìwǔ raise a force or contingent; form a band

【拉夫】 lāfū press-gang; press people into service

【拉幅机】 lāfújī 〈纺〉 stenter; tenter

【拉杆】 lāgān 〈机〉 pull rod; drag link; draw bar; tension link ◇ ～天线 telescopic antenna

【拉关系】 lā guānxi 〔多含贬义〕 try to establish a relationship with sb.; cotton up to: 拉亲戚关系 claim kinship

【拉后腿】 lā hòutuǐ hold sb. back; be a drag on sb.

【拉祜族】 Lāhùzú the Lahu nationality, living in Yunnan

【拉花】 lāhuā 〈工美〉 garland: 纸～ festoon; paper garland

【拉簧】 lāhuáng 〈机〉 extension spring

【拉火绳】 lāhuǒshéng 〈军〉 lanyard

【拉饥荒】 lā jīhuang 〈口〉 be in debt; run into debt

【拉架】 lājià try to stop people from fighting each other

【拉交情】 lā jiāoqing try to form ties with; cotton up to

【拉脚】 lājiǎo transport persons or goods by cart at a charge

【拉锯】 lājù ① work a two-handed saw ② be locked in a seesaw struggle ◇ ～地带 area which frequently changes hands in a war; scene of a seesaw battle/ ～战 seesaw battle

【拉开】 lākai ① pull open; draw back: ～抽屉 open the drawer/ ～窗帘 draw back the curtain/ ～枪栓 pull back the bolt (of a rifle)/ ～嗓门就唱 start singing when asked to without making a fuss ② increase the distance between; space out: 不要～距离! Close up!/ 比分逐渐～了。The gap between the scores gradually widened./ 把比分～到十六比八 pull away to 16—8; increase the lead to 16—8

【拉拉扯扯】 lālāchěchě ① pull (或 drag) sb. about ② exchange flattery and favours

【拉拉队】 lālāduì cheering squad; rooters

【拉力】 lālì 〈物〉 pulling force ◇ ～器〈体〉 chest-developer; chest-expander/ ～试验 〈机〉 pull (或 tension) test

【拉练】 lāliàn camp and field training

【拉链】 lāliàn zip fastener; zipper

【拉拢】 lālong draw sb. over to one's side; rope in: 宗派主义者总是～一些人，排挤一些人。Sectarians are always drawing some people in and pushing others out./ 不要受坏人～。Don't get roped in by bad people.

【拉马克学说】 Lāmǎkè xuéshuō 〈生〉 Lamarckism

【拉模】 lāmú 〈机〉 drawing die

【拉平】 lāpíng bring to the same level; even up: 双方比分渐渐～。The score gradually evened up.

【拉纤】 lāqiàn ① tow (a boat) ② act as go-between

【拉萨】 Lāsà Lhasa

【拉山头】 lā shāntóu form a faction

【拉伸】 lāshēn 〈纺〉 drawing; stretch ◇ ～加捻机 stretch twister/ ～络丝机 draw winder/ ～试验 tensile test/ ～应变〈机〉 tensile strain

【拉屎】 lāshǐ 〈口〉 empty the bowels; shit

【拉手】 lāshǒu 〈口〉 shake hands

【拉手】 lāshou handle (of a door, window, drawer, etc.)

【拉丝】 lāsī 〈冶〉 wiredrawing ◇ ～机 wiredrawing machine

【拉锁儿】 lāsuǒr zip fastener; zipper

【拉条】 lātiáo 〈机〉 brace; stay: 斜～ batter brace/ 链～ chain stay

【拉稀】 lāxī 〈口〉 have loose bowels; have diarrhoea

【拉下脸】 lāxia liǎn ① look displeased; pull a long face; put on a stern expression ② not spare sb.'s sensibilities

【拉下水】 lāxia shuǐ drag sb. into the mire; make an accomplice of sb.; corrupt sb.

【拉线开关】 lāxiàn kāiguān 〈电〉 pullswitch

【拉削】 lāxiāo 〈机〉 broaching
【拉秧】 lāyāng uproot plants after their edible portions have been harvested
【拉杂】 lāzá rambling; jumbled; ill-organized: 这篇文章写得太～。This article is very badly organized./ 我拉拉杂杂地就谈这些吧。I think I'll stop my rambling talk here.
【拉帐】 lāzhàng be in debt; run into debt

**垃** lā
【垃圾】 lājī rubbish; garbage; refuse: ～处理 garbage disposal/ 焚化～ refuse incineration/ 清除～ remove refuse ◇ ～箱 dustbin; ash can; garbage can
【垃圾堆】 lājīduī rubbish heap; refuse dump; garbage heap: 被扫进历史的～ be swept onto the rubbish heap of history

**啦** lā 见"哩哩啦啦" līlilālā
另见 la

**邋** lā
【邋遢】 lāta 〈口〉 slovenly; sloppy

## lá

**旯** lá 见"旮旯儿" gālár

**拉** lá ① slash; slit; cut; make a gash in: 把这块皮子～开 slit the leather/ 手上～了个口子 cut one's hand; get a cut in the hand ② chat: ～家常 have a chat
另见 lā; lǎ

**喇** lá 见"哈喇子" hālázi
另见 lǎ

## lǎ

**拉** lǎ 见"半拉" bànlǎ
另见 lā; lá

**喇** lǎ
另见 lá
【喇叭】 lǎba ① 〈乐〉 a popular name for *suona* (唢呐), a woodwind instrument ② 〈乐〉 brass-wind instruments in general or any of these instruments ③ loudspeaker ◇ ～花 (white-edged) morning glory/ ～口 bell (of a wind instrument)/ ～裤 flared trousers; bell-bottoms/ ～筒 megaphone
【喇嘛】 lǎma 〈宗〉 lama ◇ ～教 Lamaism/ ～庙 lamasery

## là

**剌** là 〈书〉 perverse; disagreeable: 乖～ perverse; contrary to reason

**落** là ① leave out; be missing: 这里～了两个字。Two words are missing here. ② leave behind; forget to bring: 我忙着出来，把票～在家里了。I was in a hurry and left my ticket at home. ③ lag (或 fall, drop) behind: ～下很远 fall (或 be left) far behind/ 谁也不愿意～在后面。No one likes to lag behind./ 他～了一个星期的课。He's a whole week behind with his lessons. 或 He missed a week's lessons.
另见 lào; luò

**腊** là ① the ancient practice of offering sacrifices to the gods in the twelfth month of the lunar year, hence the term "sacrificial" for the twelfth moon: ～尽冬残 towards the end of the (lunar) year ② cured (fish, meat, etc., generally done in the twelfth moon)
另见 xī
【腊八粥】 làbāzhōu rice porridge with nuts and dried fruit eaten on the eighth day of the twelfth lunar month
【腊肠】 làcháng sausage
【腊梅】 làméi 〈植〉 wintersweet
【腊肉】 làròu cured meat; bacon
【腊味】 làwèi cured meat, fish, etc.
【腊月】 làyuè the twelfth month of the lunar year; the twelfth moon

**辣** là ① peppery; hot ② (of smell or taste) burn; bite; sting: 切葱头～眼睛。When you slice an onion it makes your eyes sting./ ～得舌头发麻。The hot taste burns the tongue. ③ vicious; ruthless: 心毒手～ vicious and ruthless
【辣根】 làgēn 〈植〉 horseradish
【辣酱】 làjiàng thick chilli sauce
【辣酱油】 làjiàngyóu pungent sauce (similar to Worcestershire sauce)
【辣椒】 làjiāo hot pepper; chilli ◇ ～粉 chilli powder/ ～油 chilli oil
【辣手】 làshǒu ① ruthless method; vicious device ② 〈方〉 vicious; ruthless ③ 〈口〉 thorny; troublesome; knotty: 这件事真～。That's really a knotty problem. 或 That's a real hot potato.
【辣子】 làzi 〈口〉 hot pepper; cayenne pepper; chilli

**蜡** là ① wax ② candle: 点一支～ light a candle ③ polish: 地板～ floor wax; floor polish
【蜡版】 làbǎn mimeograph stencil (already cut) ◇ ～术 cerography
【蜡笔】 làbǐ wax crayon ◇ ～画 crayon drawing
【蜡虫】 làchóng wax insect
【蜡防印花法】 làfáng yìnhuāfǎ 〈纺〉 batik
【蜡光纸】 làguāngzhǐ glazed paper
【蜡果】 làguǒ 〈工美〉 wax fruit
【蜡黄】 làhuáng wax yellow; waxen; sallow: ～的脸 a sallow face
【蜡扦】 làqiān candlestick
【蜡染】 làrǎn 〈纺〉 wax printing
【蜡台】 làtái candlestick
【蜡纸】 làzhǐ ① wax paper ② stencil paper; stencil: 刻～ cut a stencil
【蜡烛】 làzhú (wax) candle
【蜡嘴雀】 làzuǐquè 〈动〉 hawfinch

**瘌** là
【瘌痢】 làlì 〈方〉 favus of the scalp
【瘌痢头】 làlitóu ① a person affected with favus on the head ② affected with favus on the head

**蝲** là
【蝲蛄】 làgǔ 〈动〉 crayfish
【蝲蝲蛄】 làlàgǔ 〈动〉 mole cricket

**鯻** là grunt; tigerfish

**镴** là solder

## la

**啦** la 〈助〉〔“了” le 和“啊” a 的合音，表示感叹、疑问等语气〕：他早来～！Why, he's been here a long time!/ 二组跟我们挑战～。Look! Group B has sent us a challenge./ 这回我可亲眼看见～！This time I've actually seen it for myself./ 她真来～？Has she really come?
另见 lā

**蓝** la 见“苤蓝” piěla
另见 lán

## lái

**来** lái ①come; arrive: 你～啦！Hello! 或 So you're here already./ 他什么时候～？When is he coming?/ 外宾还没有～。The foreign guests have not arrived yet./ 电～啦！The electricity is on!/ 我们都是～自五湖四海。We hail from all corners of the country./ ～函 incoming letter; your letter/ ～稿 a contribution received by an editor ②crop up; take place: 问题一～就设法解决 try to solve a problem as soon as it crops up/ 雷阵雨马上就要～了。A thunder shower is coming up. ③〔做某个动作，代替意义更具体的动词〕：你歇歇，让我～吧。You take a rest. Let me do it./（指请人吃东西）再～一点吧？Would you like a little more?/ 我自己～吧。（指吃东西）I'll help myself. 或（指做事）Let me do it myself./ ～一个动员。Let's get mobilized./ ～一个一百八十度的大转弯 make an about face; make a 180-degree turn/ 我们去打棒球，你～不～？We're going to play baseball. Do you want to join in?/（请演员表演）再～一个！Encore! ④〔跟“得”或“不”连用，表示可能或不可能〕：坡太陡，车子上不～。The car can't come up, the slope is so steep./ 他们俩很合得～。The two of them get along very well./ 你的稿子今天出得～吗？Will you be able to finish your article today? ⑤〔用在动词前面，表示要做某件事〕：请你～给大家读报。Will you please read the paper to us?/ 大家～想办法。Let's pool our ideas and see what to do. 或 Let's put our heads together and see how to do it. ⑥〔用在动词或动词结构后面，表示来做某件事〕：他回村看望乡亲们～了。He's come back to the village to see us folks./ 我们报喜～了。We've brought you good news. ⑦〔用在动词前面，表示后面部分是目的〕：你能用什么方法～帮助他呢？How are you going to help him? ⑧future; coming; next: ～年 the coming year; next year ⑨ever since: 别～无恙乎？How have you been since I saw you last?/ 十多天～ for the last ten days and more/ 两千年～ over the past 2,000 years ⑩〔用在“十”“百”“千”等数词或数量词后面，表示概数〕about; around: 二十～个 around twenty/ 两米～高 about two metres high/ 五十～岁 about fifty (years old) ⑪〔用在“一”“二”“三”等数词后面，列举理由〕：一～…，二～… in the first place..., in the second place.../ 我好久没去看他，一～路太远，二～没工夫。I haven't been to see him for a long time now. For one thing, he lives too far away; for another, I've been rather busy. ⑫〔诗歌中间用做衬字〕：正月里～是新春。Spring comes with the first moon of the new year.

**来** lai ①〔用在动词后面，表示动作朝着说话人所在的地方〕：过～！Come over here!/ 拿把锯～。Bring me a saw./ 象潮水般涌～ surge towards us like a rising tide/ 寄～许多宝贵意见 send in many valuable suggestions ②〔用在动词后面，表示动作的结果〕：一觉醒～ wake up after a sound sleep/ 信笔写～ write down one's ideas as they come to mind/ 说～话长。It's a long story.

【来宾】láibīn guest; visitor ◇ ～席 seats for guests

【来不得】láibude won't do; be impermissible: 这是一个科学问题，～半点虚伪。This is a matter of science, which permits no dishonesty.

【来不及】láibují there's not enough time (to do sth.); it's too late (to do sth.): 今天我们～去看他了。There's no time for us to go and see him today./ 写信已经～了，还是给他打个电报吧。It's too late to reach him by letter. Better send a telegram.

【来到】láidào arrive; come: 雨季～了。The rainy season has set in./ 你们终于～了。So here you are at last.

【来得】láide 〈口〉①competent; equal to: 样样农活她都～。She can cope with any kind of farmwork. ②emerge (from a comparison) as; come out as: 海水比淡水重，因此压力也～大。Sea water is heavier than freshwater, so its pressure is greater, too.

【来得及】láidejí there's still time; be able to do sth. in time; be able to make it: 赶快去，还～。Go at once while there's still time./ 春耕前把拖拉机修好，～吗？Can you get the tractor repaired in time for the spring ploughing?/ 我把车开快点还～。We can make it if I drive a bit faster.

【来电】láidiàn ①incoming telegram; your telegram; your message: 三月十七日～悉。Your message of March 17 received. ②send a telegram here: 请～告知。Please inform me by telegram.

【来而不往非礼也】lái ér bù wǎng fēi lǐ yě it is impolite not to reciprocate; one should return as good as one receives

【来犯】láifàn come to attack us; invade our territory: 坚决消灭敢于～之敌。Resolutely wipe out any enemy that dares to invade our territory.

【来访】láifǎng come to visit; come to call: 认真对待人民来信～ treat seriously the letters the people send in and the complaints they make when they call

【来复枪】láifùqiāng rifle

【来复线】láifùxiàn rifling

【来亨鸡】láihēngjī Leghorn

【来回】láihuí ①make a round trip; make a return journey; go to a place and come back: 从车间到我们宿舍～有一里地。It's one *li* from the workshop to our quarters and back./ ～有多远？How far is it there and back?/ 打个～儿 make a round trip ②back and forth; to and fro: 织布机上梭子～地飞动。The shuttle flies back and forth on the loom./ 在房间里～走动 pace up and down the room/ ～摇摆 oscillate; vacillate ◇ ～飞行 round-trip flight/ ～票 return ticket; round-trip ticket

【来回来去】láihuí-láiqù 〈方〉back and forth; over and over again: ～地跑了好多趟 run back and forth many times/ ～地说 say sth. over and over again; repeat again and again

【来件】láijiàn communication or parcel received

【来劲】láijìn 〈方〉①full of enthusiasm; in high spirits: 他越干越～儿。The longer he worked at it, the more enthusiastic he became. ②exhilarating; exciting; thrilling: 这样伟大的工程，可真～！What a magnificent project! How thrilling! ③jest with; annoy; offend: 你别跟我～。I won't stand any nonsense from you.

【来客】láikè guest; visitor

【来历】láilì origin; source; antecedents; background; past history: 查明～ trace to the source; ascertain a person's antecedents/ ～不明（指事物）of unknown origin;（指人）of dubious background or of questionable antecedents/ 提起这把手术刀可大有～。Talking of this scalpel, there is a long history to it.

【来临】 láilín arrive; come; approach: 每当春天～，这里是一片绿油油的庄稼。When spring comes, this place is an expanse of lush green crops.
【来龙去脉】 láilóng-qùmài origin and development; cause and effect: 弄清事情的～ find out the cause and effect of the incident/ 请你把事情的～跟我们讲一遍。Please tell us the whole story from beginning to end.
【来路】 láilù incoming road; approach: 六连挡住了敌人的～。Company Six blocked the enemy's path of approach.
【来路】 láilu origin; antecedents: ～不正（指物）of questionable origin;（指人）of dubious background/ ～不明的飞机 unidentified aircraft
【来路货】 láilùhuò 〈方〉 imported goods
【来年】 láinián the coming year; next year
【…来…去】 ...lái...qù 〔用在同一个动词或两个同义的动词后面，表示动作的不断反复〕 back and forth; over and over again: 飞来飞去 fly back and forth/ 挑来挑去 pick and choose/ 考虑来考虑去 turn sth. over and over again in one's mind/ 翻来复去睡不着 toss and turn in bed
【来人】 láirén bearer; messenger: 收条请交～带回。Please give the receipt to the bearer.
【来日方长】 láirì fāng cháng there will be ample time; there will be a time for that
【来生】 láishēng next life 又作"来世"
【来势】 láishì the force with which sth. breaks out; oncoming force: 这场雨～很猛。The rainstorm broke with tremendous force./ ～汹汹 bear down menacingly
【来苏】 láisū 〈药〉 lysol
【来头】 láitou ① connections; backing: ～不小 have powerful backing ② the motive behind (sb.'s words, etc.); cause: 他这些话是有～的，是冲着我们说的。He didn't say all that without cause; it was directed against us. ③ the force with which sth. breaks out ④〈口〉 interest; fun: 下棋没什么～儿，不如去打乒乓球。Playing chess is no fun. It'd be better to go and play table tennis.
【来往】 láiwǎng come and go: ～于津沪之间 travel between Tianjin and Shanghai/ 街上～的人很多。There are many people coming and going on the streets./ 翻修路面，禁止车辆～。Road under repair. No thoroughfare./ ～的信件 correspondence
【来往】 láiwang dealings; contact; intercourse: 我跟他从来没有任何～。I've never had any dealings with him./ 我们厂和附近公社经常～。Our factory has frequent contacts with the neighbouring communes.
【来文】 láiwén document received
【来信】 láixìn ① send a letter here: 到了那里就～。Write to us as soon as you get there./ 他好久没～了。I haven't heard from him for a long time. ② incoming letter: 十日～收到。I have received your letter of the 10th./ 人民～ letters from the people
【来意】 láiyì one's purpose in coming: 说明～ make clear what one has come for
【来由】 láiyóu reason; cause: 没～ without rhyme or reason/ 那个战士讲了他学针灸的～。The soldier explained how he came to study acupuncture.
【来源】 láiyuán ① source; origin: 经济～ source of income ② originate; stem from: 知识～于实践。Knowledge stems from practice.
【来者不拒】 láizhě bù jù refuse nobody; refuse nobody's request or offer
【来者不善，善者不来】 láizhě bù shàn, shànzhě bù lái ① he who has come is surely strong or he'd never have come along ② he who has come, comes with ill intent, certainly not on virtue bent
【来着】 láizhe 〈助〉〔表示曾经发生过什么事情〕: 你刚才说什么～？What were you saying just now?/ 他去年冬天还回家～。He was home only last winter./ 你忘了解放前咱们怎么受苦～？Don't you remember how we suffered before liberation?
【来之不易】 lái zhī bù yì it has not come easily; hard-earned: 我们的胜利～。Our victory was hard-won./ 每一粒粮食都～。Every single grain is the result of toil.
【来踪去迹】 láizōng-qùjī traces of sth.; traces of sb.'s whereabouts

**莱** lái

【莱菔】 láifú 〈植〉 radish ◇ ～子〈中药〉 radish seed
【莱诺铸排机】 láinuò zhùpáijī 〈印〉 linotype
【莱塞】 láisài 〈物〉 laser
【莱氏体】 láishìtǐ 〈机〉 ledeburite
【莱索托】 Láisuǒtuō Lesotho ◇ ～人（单数）Mosotho;（复数）Basotho

**徕** lái 见"招徕" zhāolái

**梾** lái

【梾木】 láimù 〈植〉 large-leaved dogwood (*Cornus macrophylla*)

**铼** lái 〈化〉 rhenium (Re)

## lài

**赉** lài 〈书〉 grant; bestow; confer: 赏～ give a reward; bestow a favour

**睐** lài 〈书〉 look at; glance; squint

**赖** lài ① rely; depend: 完成任务，还有～于大家的努力。Getting the job done depends on everyone's efforts./ ～以生存的条件 conditions on which persons or things rely (或 depend) for existence ② hang on in a place; drag out one's stay in a place; hold on to a place: 不容许侵略者～在别国的领土上。The aggressors must not be allowed to hold on to the territories of other countries./ ～着不走 hang on and refuse to clear out ③ deny one's error or responsibility; go back on one's word: ～是～不掉的。It's no good trying to deny it. 或 You simply can't deny it. ④ blame sb. wrongly; put the blame on sb. else: 自己错了还～别人，这就不对了。It's not right to blame others for one's own mistake. ⑤〈口〉 blame: 这事全～我。I'm entirely to blame for that. ⑥〈口〉 no good; poor: 庄稼长得真不～。The crops are not at all bad. ⑦ (Lài) a surname
【赖皮】 làipí 〈口〉 rascally; shameless; unreasonable: 耍～ act shamelessly
【赖债】 làizhài repudiate a debt
【赖帐】 làizhàng ① repudiate a debt ② go back on one's word

**癞** lài ①〈医〉 leprosy ②〈方〉 favus of the scalp

【癞蛤蟆】 làihámа toad: ～想吃天鹅肉 a toad lusting after a swan's flesh — aspiring after sth. one is not worthy of
【癞皮狗】 làipígǒu ① mangy dog ② loathsome creature
【癞子】 làizi a person affected with favus on the head

**籁** lài ① an ancient musical pipe ② sound; noise: 万～俱寂。Silence reigns supreme. 或 All is quiet and still.

## lán

**兰** lán orchid
【兰草】 láncǎo fragrant thoroughwort (*Eupatorium fortunei*)
【兰花】 lánhuā cymbidium; orchid
【兰州】 Lánzhōu Lanzhou

**岚** lán haze; vapour; mist

**拦** lán bar; block; hold back: ～住去路 block the way/他刚要说话，被他哥哥～住了。He was about to speak when he was stopped by his brother.
【拦挡】 lándǎng block; obstruct
【拦河坝】 lánhébà a dam across a river; dam
【拦击】 lánjī 〈乒乓球〉 volley
【拦截】 lánjié intercept: ～增援的敌人 intercept enemy reinforcements
【拦路】 lánlù block the way: ～抢劫 waylay; hold up
【拦路虎】 lánlùhǔ obstacle; stumbling block
【拦网】 lánwǎng 〈排球〉 block
【拦污栅】 lánwūzhà 〈水〉 trashrack
【拦蓄】 lánxù retain (floodwaters, etc.): ～山洪 retain the mountain flood
【拦腰】 lányāo by the waist; round the middle: ～抱住 seize round the middle; clasp sb. by the waist/ 大坝把河水～截断。The dam cut the river in the middle.
【拦鱼栅】 lányúzhà fish screen
【拦阻】 lánzǔ block; hold back; obstruct

**栏** lán ① fence; railing; balustrade; hurdle: 凭～ lean on a railing/ 跨～赛跑 hurdle race; the hurdles ② pen; shed: 牛～ cowshed ③ column: 备注～ remarks column/ 布告～ bulletin board; notice board
【栏杆】 lángān railing; banisters; balustrade

**婪** lán 见"贪婪" tānlán

**阑** lán ① late: 夜～人静 in the stillness of the night ② railing; balustrade
【阑干】 lángān ①〈书〉 crisscross; athwart ② railing; banisters; balustrade
【阑珊】 lánshān 〈书〉 coming to an end; waning: 春意～。Spring is waning.
【阑尾】 lánwěi 〈生理〉 appendix ◇ ～切除术 appendectomy/ ～炎 appendicitis

**蓝** lán ① blue ② indigo plant ③ (Lán) a surname
另见 la
【蓝宝石】 lánbǎoshí sapphire
【蓝本】 lánběn ① writing upon which later work is based; chief source ② original version (of a literary work)
【蓝靛】 lándiàn indigo
【蓝矾】 lánfán 〈化〉 blue vitriol; cupric sulphate
【蓝晶石】 lánjīngshí 〈矿〉 kyanite; disthene
【蓝皮书】 lánpíshū blue book
【蓝田人】 Lántiánrén 〈考古〉 Lantian Man (*Sinanthropus lantienensis*), primitive man of about 600,000 years ago whose fossil remains were found in Lantian, Shaanxi Province, in 1964
【蓝铜矿】 lántóngkuàng azurite; chessylite
【蓝图】 lántú blueprint
【蓝藻】 lánzǎo 〈植〉 blue green alga

**谰** lán calumniate; slander
【谰言】 lányán calumny; slander: 无耻～ a shameless slander

**澜** lán billows

**褴** lán
【褴褛】 lánlǚ ragged; shabby: 衣衫～ shabbily dressed; out at elbows; in rags

**篮** lán ① basket ② 〈篮球〉 goal; basket: 投～ shoot a basket; shoot
【篮板】 lánbǎn 〈篮球〉 backboard; bank
【篮板球】 lánbǎnqiú rebound: 控制～ control the rebounds/ 抓住～投篮入网 grab the rebound and sink a basket
【篮球】 lánqiú basketball
◇ ～场 basketball court/ ～队 basketball team/ ～架 basketball stands
【篮圈】 lánquān 〈篮球〉 ring; hoop
【篮子】 lánzi basket

**斓** lán 见"斑斓" bānlán

**镧** lán 〈化〉 lanthanum (La)

## lǎn

**览** lǎn ① look at; see; view: 游～ go sightseeing; tour/ 一～无余 take in everything at a glance ② read: 博～ read extensively/ 浏～ glance over; skim through (或 over)

**揽** lǎn ① pull sb. into one's arms; take into one's arms: 母亲把孩子～在怀里。The mother clasped the child to her bosom. ② fasten with a rope, etc.: 用绳子～上 put a rope around sth. ③ take on; take upon oneself; canvass: 他把责任都～到自己身上。He took all the responsibility on himself./ ～买卖 canvass business orders ④ grasp; monopolize: 包～ monopolize; undertake the whole thing/ ～权 arrogate power to oneself

**缆** lǎn ① hawser; mooring rope; cable: 解～ cast off; set sail/ 新船砍～下水。The new ship cut her cable and slipped into the water. ② thick rope; cable: 电～ power cable; cable
【缆车】 lǎnchē cable car ◇ ～铁道 cable railway
【缆道】 lǎndào cableway
【缆索】 lǎnsuǒ thick rope; cable ◇ ～铁道 funicular (railway)

**榄** lǎn 见"橄榄" gǎnlǎn

**罱** lǎn ① a kind of net used for fishing or for dredging up river sludge, etc. ② dredge up: ～河泥 dredge up sludge from a river
【罱泥船】 lǎnníchuán a boat used in collecting river sludge for fertilizer

**懒** lǎn ① lazy; indolent; slothful: 腿～ disinclined to move about; lazy about paying visits/ 人勤地不～。Where the tiller is tireless the land is fertile. ② sluggish; languid: 身上发～ feel sluggish
【懒得】 lǎnde not feel like (doing sth.); not be in the mood to; be disinclined to: 天太热，我～出去。It's too hot.

I don't feel like going out.
【懒惰】 lǎnduò lazy
【懒汉】 lǎnhàn sluggard; idler; lazybones: 懦夫～思想 the way of thinking of the coward and the sluggard
【懒猴】 lǎnhóu slender loris; loris
【懒散】 lǎnsǎn sluggish; negligent; indolent: 不要这样～，振作起来。Don't be so sluggish. Pull yourself together.
【懒洋洋】 lǎnyāngyāng languid; listless

## làn

**烂** làn ① sodden; mashed; pappy: 连下了三天雨，地上都是～泥。It's rained for three days on end and the ground is sodden./ 牛肉烧得很～。The beef is very tender. 或 The beef melts in your mouth./ 豆子煮～了。The beans are now soft enough to eat. ② rot; fester: 这样的阴雨天要防止～秧。In such wet weather we must prevent the seedlings from rotting./ 敌人一天天～下去，我们一天天好起来。The enemy rots with every passing day, while for us things are getting better and better./ 伤口～了。The wound is festering. ③ worn-out: 衣服穿～了。The clothes are worn-out./ ～纸片 scraps of paper ④ messy: 真是一本～帐。The accounts are all in a mess.
【烂糊】 lànhu (of food) mashed; pulpy
【烂漫】 lànmàn ① bright-coloured; brilliant: 山花～ bright mountain flowers in full bloom ② unaffected: 天真～ naive; innocent
【烂泥】 lànní mud; slush ◇ ～塘 a muddy pond
【烂熟】 lànshú ① thoroughly cooked ② know sth. thoroughly: 台词背得～ learn one's lines thoroughly
【烂摊子】 làntānzi a shambles; an awful mess
【烂醉】 lànzuì dead drunk: ～如泥 be dead drunk; be as drunk as a lord

**滥** làn ① overflow; flood ② excessive; indiscriminate: ～施轰炸 indiscriminate bombing; wanton bombing/ ～发钞票 reckless issuing of banknotes
【滥调】 làndiào hackneyed tune; worn-out theme: 陈词～ hackneyed and stereotyped expressions; *clichés*
【滥伐】 lànfá 〈林〉 denudation
【滥用】 lànyòng abuse; misuse; use indiscriminately: ～职权 abuse one's power/ ～经费 squander funds/ 不要～成语典故。We should not use proverbs and allusions indiscriminately.
【滥竽充数】 lànyú chōng shù pass oneself off as one of the players in an ensemble — be there just to make up the number (used of incompetent people or inferior goods)

## lāng

**啷** lāng 见"哐啷" kuānglāng

## láng

**郎** láng ① an ancient official title ②〔用于对男子的称呼〕: 令～ your son/ 新～ bridegroom/ 货～ street vendor ③〔女子称丈夫或情人〕 my darling ④ (Láng) a surname 另见 làng
【郎当】 lángdāng 见"锒铛" lángdāng
【郎舅】 láng-jiù a man and his wife's brother: 他们俩是～。Those two are brothers-in-law.
【郎猫】 lángmāo 〈口〉 tomcat
【郎中】 lángzhōng 〈方〉 a physician trained in herbal medicine; doctor

**狼** láng wolf
【狼把草】 lángbǎcǎo 〈植〉 bur beggar-ticks
【狼狈】 lángbèi in a difficult position; in a tight corner: ～不堪 in an extremely awkward position; in a sorry plight; in sore straits/ ～逃窜 flee in panic; flee helter-skelter/ 陷于～境地 find oneself in a fix; be caught in a dilemma (或 quandary)/ 显出一副～相 cut a sorry figure/ 傀儡政权的处境极为孤立和～。The puppet regime was extremely isolated and in dire straits./ 打得敌人十分～。The enemy was badly battered.
【狼狈为奸】 lángbèi wéi jiān act in collusion (或 cahoots) with each other
【狼奔豕突】 lángbēn-shǐtū run like a wolf and rush like a boar — tear about like wild beasts
【狼疮】 lángchuāng 〈医〉 lupus
【狼毒】 lángdú 〈中药〉 the root of *langdu* (*Euphorbia fisheriana*)
【狼狗】 lánggǒu wolfhound
【狼毫】 lángháo a writing brush made of weasel's hair
【狼獾】 lánghuān 〈动〉 glutton
【狼藉】 lángjí 〈书〉 in disorder; scattered about in a mess: 杯盘～ wine cups and dishes lying about in disorder after a feast/ 声名～ notorious; in disrepute; discredited
【狼吞虎咽】 lángtūn-hǔyàn gobble up; wolf down; devour ravenously
【狼尾草】 lángwěicǎo 〈植〉 Chinese pennisetum (*Pennisetum alopecuroides*)
【狼心狗肺】 lángxīn-gǒufèi ① rapacious as a wolf and savage as a cur; cruel and unscrupulous; brutal and cold-blooded ② ungrateful
【狼牙】 lángyá ① wolf's fang ② 〈植〉 cryptotaeneous cinquefoil (*Potentilla cryptotaeniae*)
【狼烟】 lángyān the smoke of wolves' dung burnt at border posts in ancient China to signal alarm: ～四起 with alarms raised at all border posts
【狼子野心】 lángzǐ yěxīn wolfish nature; wild ambition

**廊** láng porch; corridor; veranda: 回～ winding corridor/ 长～ the Long Corridor (in the Summer Palace, Beijing)/ 画～ picture gallery
【廊檐】 lángyán the eaves of a veranda
【廊子】 lángzi veranda; corridor

**琅** láng
【琅琅】 lángláng 〈象〉: ～的读书声 the sound of reading aloud

**榔** láng
【榔槺】 lángkang bulky; cumbersome
【榔头】 lángtou hammer

**锒** láng
【锒铛】 lángdāng ①〈书〉 iron chains: ～入狱 be chained and thrown into prison ② clank; clang

**鎯** láng
【鎯头】 lángtou hammer

**螂** láng 见"螳螂" tángláng; "蜣螂" qiāngláng; "蟑螂" zhāngláng

## lǎng

**朗** lǎng ① light; bright: 天～气清。The sky is clear and bright. ② loud and clear

【朗读】 lǎngdú read aloud; read loudly and clearly

【朗朗】 lǎnglǎng ①〈象〉 the sound of reading aloud ② bright; light

【朗诵】 lǎngsòng read aloud with expression; recite; declaim

## làng

**郎** làng 见"屎壳郎" shǐkelàng
另见 láng

**浪** làng ① wave; billow; breaker: 白～滔天 white breakers leaping skywards/ 麦～起伏 wheat rippling in the wind ② unrestrained; dissolute: 放～ dissolute; dissipated

【浪潮】 làngcháo tide; wave: 革命的～ the tide of revolution/ 罢工～ a wave of strikes

【浪船】 làngchuán swingboat

【浪荡】 làngdàng ① loiter about; loaf about ② dissolute; dissipated

【浪费】 làngfèi waste; squander; be extravagant: 反对～ combat waste/ ～时间 waste time; fritter away one's time

【浪花】 lànghuā spray; spindrift

【浪漫】 làngmàn romantic ◇ ～主义 romanticism

【浪头】 làngtou 〈口〉 ① wave ② trend: 赶～ follow the trend

【浪涌】 làngyǒng 〈电〉 surge ◇ ～放电器 surge arrester

【浪子】 làngzǐ prodigal; loafer; wastrel

【浪子回头】 làngzǐ huítóu 见"败子回头" bàizǐ huítóu

**莨** làng
另见 liáng

【莨菪】 làngdàng 〈植〉 (black) henbane

## lāo

**捞** lāo ① drag for; dredge up; fish for; scoop up from the water: 在河里～水草 dredge up water plants from the river/ ～鱼 net fish; catch fish ② get by improper means; gain: 他们能从这里～到什么好处呢? What good can they get from this?

【捞本】 lāoběn win back lost wagers; recover one's losses; recoup oneself

【捞稻草】 lāo dàocǎo ① (try to) take advantage of sth.: 休想在这件事上～。Don't imagine you can get anything out of it. ② clutch at a straw

【捞饭】 lāofàn rice boiled, strained and then steamed

【捞取】 lāoqǔ fish for; gain: ～政治资本 fish for political capital; seek political advantage

【捞一把】 lāo yī bǎ reap some profit; profiteer

【捞着】 lāozháo get the opportunity: 那天的电影,我没～看。I missed the film the other day.

## láo

**牢** láo ①〈书〉 pen; fold: 豕～ pigpen ② sacrifice: 太～ sacrificial ox ③ prison; jail: 坐～ be in prison ④ firm; fast; durable: 绳子没系～。The rope hasn't been tied fast.

【牢不可破】 láo bùkě pò unbreakable; indestructible: ～的友谊 unbreakable friendship

【牢固】 láogù firm; secure: 地基很～。The foundations are very firm.

【牢记】 láojì keep firmly in mind; remember well: ～党的基本路线 always bear in mind the Party's basic line

【牢靠】 láokao ① firm; strong; sturdy: 这堵墙不太～。This wall is not very strong. ② dependable; reliable: 办事～ dependable (或 reliable) in handling matters

【牢牢】 láoláo firmly; safely: ～掌握斗争大方向 hold fast to the general orientation of the struggle/ 政权～掌握在人民手里。Power rests firmly in the hands of the people.

【牢笼】 láolóng ① cage; bonds: 冲破旧思想的～ shake off the bonds of old ideas ② trap; snare: 陷入～ fall into a trap; be entrapped

【牢骚】 láosāo discontent; grievance; complaint: 满腹～ be querulous; be full of grievances/ 发～ grumble

【牢什子】 láoshízi 〈方〉 nuisance

【牢稳】 láowěn 〈口〉 stable; safe; secure: 梯子靠这儿比较～。The ladder will be more secure here.

【牢狱】 láoyù prison; jail

**劳** láo ① work; labour: 多～多得 more pay for more work ② put sb. to the trouble of: ～你帮个忙。Will you please do me a favour (或 give me a hand)? ③ fatigue; toil: 积～成疾 break down from constant overwork ④ meritorious deed; service: 汗马之～ distinctions won in battle; war exploits ⑤ express one's appreciation (to the performer of a task); reward: ～军 bring greetings and gifts to army units ⑥ (Láo) a surname

【劳保】 láobǎo 〈简〉(劳动保险) labour insurance

【劳瘁】 láocuì 〈书〉 exhausted from excessive work; wornout

【劳动】 láodòng ① work; labour: 不～者不得食。He who does not work, neither shall he eat./ ～创造世界。Labour creates the world./ 大家的～热情很高。Everyone worked with great enthusiasm. ② physical labour; manual labour: ～锻炼 temper oneself through manual labour
◇ ～保护 labour protection/ ～保护设施 labour safety devices/ ～保险 labour insurance/ ～保险条例 labour insurance regulations/ ～布 denim/ ～定额 work norm; production quota/ ～对象 subject of labour/ ～二重性 the twofold (或 dual) character of labour/ ～法 labour law/ ～改造 reform (of criminals) through labour/ ～号子 work song (sung to synchronize movements with one person leading)/ ～教养 reeducation (of juvenile delinquents, etc.) through labour/ ～节 International Labour Day (May 1)/ ～竞赛 labour emulation; emulation drive; emulation campaign/ ～量 amount of labour/ ～模范 model worker/ ～强度 labour intensity/ ～权 right to work/ ～群众 working people; labouring masses/ ～人民 labouring people; working people/ ～日 workday; working day/ ～生产率 labour productivity; productivity/ ～收入 income from work/ ～手段 means (或 instruments) of labour/ ～英雄 labour hero/ ～者 labourer; worker/ ～资料 means (或 instruments) of labour

【劳动观点】 láodòng guāndiǎn attitude to labour: 树立～ form a correct attitude towards labour/ 增强～ improve one's attitude to labour

【劳动化】 láodònghuà (of intellectuals) integrate oneself with the working people

【劳动力】 láodònglì ① labour (或 work) force; labour: 调剂～ adjust the use of the labour force/ ～调配 allocation of the labour force/ ～不足 short of manpower; shorthanded ② capacity for physical labour: 丧失～ lose one's ability to work; be rendered unfit for physical labour; be incapacitated; be disabled ③ able-bodied person: 全～和半～ able-bodied and semi-ablebodied (farm) workers/ 他年青力壮，是个强～。He's young and strong; he can do heavy work.

【劳顿】 láodùn 〈书〉 fatigued; wearied: 旅途～ fatigued by a journey; travel-worn

【劳而无功】 láo ér wú gōng work hard but to no avail; work fruitlessly

【劳方】 láofāng labour: ～与资方 labour and capital

【劳改】 láogǎi 〈简〉(劳动改造) reform (of criminals) through labour ◇ ～队 group sentenced to reform through labour/ ～农场 reform-through-labour farm

【劳工】 láogōng 〈旧〉 labourer; worker ◇ ～运动 labour movement

【劳绩】 láojì merits and accomplishments

【劳驾】 láojià 〈套〉(要求让路等) excuse me; (要求别人做事) may I trouble you: ～替我带个信儿。Would you mind taking a message for me?

【劳苦】 láokǔ toil; hard work: 不辞～ spare no pains/ ～大众 toiling masses; labouring people/ ～功高 have worked hard and performed a valuable service

【劳累】 láolèi tired; run-down; overworked

【劳力】 láolì labour; labour force: ～可能紧张一些，但我们一定努力完成任务。We may be a little short of labour, but we'll do our best to fulfil the task./ 合理安排～ rational allocation of labour

【劳碌】 láolù work hard; toil

【劳民伤财】 láomín-shāngcái tire the people and drain the treasury; waste money and manpower

【劳模】 láomó 〈简〉(劳动模范) model worker

【劳伤】 láoshāng 〈中医〉internal lesion caused by overexertion

【劳神】 láoshén be a tax on (one's mind); bother; trouble: 你现在身体不好，不要过于～。You're in poor health, so don't overtax yourself./ ～替我照顾一下孩子。Please keep an eye on my child.

【劳师】 láoshī 〈书〉 ① take greetings and gifts to army units ② tire troops: ～远征 tire the troops on a long expedition/ ～动众 mobilize too many troops; drag in lots of people

【劳什子】 láoshízi 〈方〉 nuisance

【劳损】 láosǔn 〈医〉 strain: 肌腱～ muscular strain

【劳武结合】 láo-wǔ jiéhé do both production and militia duties; engage in productive labour and perform militia duties

【劳心】 láoxīn work with one's mind or brains: ～者治人，劳力者治于人——这是儒家的反动观点。 Those who work with their brains rule and those who work with their brawn are ruled. That is a reactionary Confucianist view.

【劳燕分飞】 láo-yàn fēn fēi be like birds flying in different directions; part; separate

【劳役】 láoyì ① penal servitude; forced labour ② corvée ◇ ～地租 rent in the form of service; labour rent

【劳逸】 láo-yì work and rest: ～结合 strike a proper balance between work and rest; alternate work with rest and recreation/ ～不均 uneven allocation of work

【劳资】 láo-zī labour and capital ◇ ～关系 relations between labour and capital; labour-capital relations

## 唠

láo

【唠叨】 láodao chatter; be garrulous: 唠唠叨叨说个不停 chatter interminably

## 痨

láo consumptive disease; tuberculosis; consumption: 肺～ pulmonary tuberculosis

【痨病】 láobìng 〈中医〉 tuberculosis; TB

## 铹

láo 〈化〉 lawrencium (Lw)

## 醪

láo 〈书〉 ① wine with dregs; undecanted wine ② mellow wine

【醪糟】 láozāo fermented glutinous rice

### lǎo

## 老

lǎo ① old; aged: 人～心红 old but full of revolutionary spirit/ 活到～，学到～，改造到～。Learn, work and remould yourself as long as you live. ② old people: 扶～携幼 bringing along the old and the young/ 徐～ our revered Comrade Xu ③ of long standing; old: ～朋友 an old friend/ ～干部 a veteran cadre/ ～部下 a former subordinate/ 新～殖民主义者 neocolonialists and old-line colonialists; old and new colonialists ④ outdated: ～式 old-fashioned; outmoded; outdated ⑤ tough; overgrown: 肉太～。The meat is too tough./ 菠菜不收就～了。The spinach will be overgrown if we don't cut it now./ 青菜不要炒得太～。Don't overcook the greens. ⑥ (of colour) dark: 这件上衣颜色太～了。This jacket is too dark. ⑦ for a long time: ～没见你啊。I haven't seen you for ages. ⑧ always (doing sth.): 他住院期间～惦念着同志们。He was always thinking of his comrades when he was in hospital. ⑨ very: ～早 very early/ ～远 far away ⑩〈口〉 the youngest: ～闺女 the youngest daughter ⑪〔前缀，用于称人、排行次序、某些动、植物名〕: ～王 Lao Wang/ ～二 the second child or brother/ ～玉米 maize/ ～虎 tiger ⑫ (Lǎo) a surname

【老百姓】 lǎobǎixìng 〈口〉 common people; ordinary people; civilians: 这些活报剧～很欢迎。These skits are popular with the man in the street./ 既当"官"又当～ remain one of the common people while serving as an "official"

【老板】 lǎobǎn 〈旧〉 shopkeeper; proprietor; boss ◇ ～娘 shopkeeper's wife; proprietress

【老伴儿】 lǎobànr 〈口〉 (of an old married couple) husband or wife: 我的～ my old man or woman

【老鸨】 lǎobǎo a woman running a brothel; procuress; madam

【老辈】 lǎobèi one's elders; old folks

【老本】 lǎoběn principal; capital: 把～输光 lose one's last stakes

【老兵】 lǎobīng old soldier; veteran

【老伯】 lǎobó 〈尊〉 uncle

【老伯伯】 lǎobóbo 〈尊〉 granddad

【老财】 lǎocái 〈方〉 moneybags; landlord

【老巢】 lǎocháo nest; den; lair: 直捣土匪～ swoop down on the bandits' den

【老成】 lǎochéng experienced; steady: 少年～ young but steady; old head on young shoulders/ ～持重 experienced and prudent

【老处女】 lǎochǔnǚ old maid; spinster

【老粗】 lǎocū 〔多用作谦辞〕 uneducated person; rough and ready chap

【老搭档】 lǎodādàng old partner; old workmate

【老大】 lǎodà ① 〈书〉 old: 少壮不努力，～徒伤悲。If one does not exert oneself in youth, one will regret it in old age. 或 Laziness in youth means sorrow in old age. ② eldest child (in a family) ③ 〈方〉 master of a sailing vessel ④ greatly; very: 心里～不高兴 feel very annoyed

【老大哥】 lǎodàgē 〈尊〉 elder brother: 向工人～学习。Let's learn from our elder brothers, the workers.

【老大难】 lǎo-dà-nán long-standing, big and difficult (problem): ～单位 a unit with serious and long-standing problems/ ～的技术问题 a knotty technical problem of long standing

【老大娘】 lǎodàniáng 〈尊〉〔多用于不相识的〕 aunty; granny

【老大爷】 lǎodàye 〈尊〉〔多用于不相识的〕 uncle; grandpa

【老当益壮】 lǎo dāng yì zhuàng old but vigorous

【老道】 lǎodào 〈口〉 Taoist priest

【老弟】 lǎodì (a familiar form of address to a man much younger than oneself) young man; young fellow; my boy

【老吊】 lǎodiào 〈口〉 crane; hoisting machine

【老调】 lǎodiào hackneyed theme; platitude: ～重弹 harp on the same string; play the same old tune

【老掉牙】 lǎodiàoyá very old; out of date; obsolete; antediluvian: 这部机器已经～了。 This machine is completely obsolete.

【老底】 lǎodǐ sb.'s past; sb.'s unsavoury background: 揭～ dredge up some embarrassing facts about sb.'s past; dig up sb.'s unsavoury past; drag the skeleton out of sb.'s closet

【老夫】 lǎofū 〔用于自称〕 an old fellow like me

【老干部】 lǎogànbù veteran cadre

【老公】 lǎogōng 〈方〉 husband

【老公公】 lǎogōnggong 〈方〉 ① grandpa ② husband's father; father-in-law

【老古董】 lǎogǔdǒng ① old-fashioned article; antique ② old fogey

【老鸹】 lǎogua 〈口〉 crow

【老规矩】 lǎoguīju old rules and regulations; convention; established custom or practice: 新社会了，奶奶您那一套～不行了。We're in the new society now, grandma, your old way of doing things is no good any more./ 学生们按～办事，走以前先把老乡的院子打扫干净。Before they left, the students, as always, swept the villagers' courtyards clean.

【老汉】 lǎohàn ① old man ②〔用于自称〕 an old fellow like me

【老好人】 lǎohǎorén a benign and uncontentious person who is indifferent to matters of principle; one who tries never to offend anybody

【老狐狸】 lǎohúli ① old fox ② crafty scoundrel

【老虎】 lǎohǔ tiger

【老虎凳】 lǎohǔdèng rack (used as an instrument of torture)

【老虎屁股摸不得】 lǎohǔ pìgu mōbude like a tiger whose backside no one dares to touch

【老虎钳】 lǎohǔqián ① vice ② pincer pliers

【老花镜】 lǎohuājìng presbyopic glasses

【老花眼】 lǎohuāyǎn presbyopia

【老化】 lǎohuà 〈化〉 ageing

【老话】 lǎohuà ① old saying; saying; adage: 正如中国～说的 as the Chinese saying goes ② remarks about the old days: 我讲这些～，是让你们别忘了旧社会的苦。I'm telling you these things about the past so that you won't forget our sufferings in the old society.

【老皇历】 lǎohuángli last year's calendar; old history; obsolete practice: 你以为我们这儿还是一年一熟？～啦！ You think we still raise only one crop a year? That's old history.

【老黄牛】 lǎohuángniú ① willing ox ② a person who serves the people wholeheartedly

【老几】 lǎojǐ ① order of seniority among brothers or sisters: 你是～？ Where do you come in the family? 或 Are you the oldest, the second or what? ②〔用于反问，表示在某个范围内数不上〕: 你算～？ Who do you think you are?/ 我算～。I'm a nobody.

【老骥伏枥，志在千里】 lǎojì fú lì, zhì zài qiānlǐ an old steed in the stable still aspires to gallop a thousand *li* — old people may still cherish high aspirations

【老家】 lǎojiā native place; old home: 我～在山东。My old home is in Shandong.

【老奸巨猾】 lǎojiān-jùhuá a past master of machination and manoeuvre; a crafty old scoundrel; a wily old fox

【老茧】 lǎojiǎn callosity; callus

【老江湖】 lǎojiānghu 〈旧〉 a well-travelled, worldly-wise person; a person who has seen much of the world

【老将】 lǎojiàng veteran; old-timer: ～出马，一个顶俩。When a veteran goes into action, he can do the job of two.

【老交情】 lǎojiāoqing long-standing friendship; an old friend

【老街坊】 lǎojiēfang 〈口〉 old neighbour

【老境】 lǎojìng ① old age ② life and circumstances in old age

【老酒】 lǎojiǔ 〈方〉 wine (esp. Shaoxing rice wine)

【老老实实】 lǎolǎoshíshí honestly; conscientiously; in earnest: 向一切内行的人们～地学经济工作。 Learn conscientiously to do economic work from all who know the job.

【老脸皮】 lǎoliǎnpí thick-skinned 又作"老面皮"

【老练】 lǎoliàn seasoned; experienced: 他比起过去来已经～得多了。He's much more experienced and capable now than before./ 她办事很～。She is experienced and works with a sure hand.

【老林】 lǎolín 〈方〉 virgin forest

【老路】 lǎolù old road; beaten track: 走～ follow the beaten track; slip back into the old rut/ 咱们还是走那条～回家吧。Let's go home the usual way.

【老妈子】 lǎomāzi 〈旧〉 amah; maidservant

【老马识途】 lǎomǎ shí tú an old horse knows the way; an old hand is a good guide

【老迈】 lǎomài aged; senile

【老毛病】 lǎomáobìng old trouble; old weakness: 这是我的～，一到冬天就咳。My cough is an old trouble. I get it every winter./ 粗心大意是他的～。Carelessness is an old weakness of his.

【老谋深算】 lǎomóu-shēnsuàn circumspect and farseeing; experienced and astute

【老脑筋】 lǎonǎojīn old (或 outmoded) way of thinking: 你这～也该换换了。It's high time you got rid of your old way of thinking.

【老年】 lǎonián old age ◇ ～人 old people; the aged/ ～医学 gerontology

【老牛破车】 lǎoniú-pòchē an old ox pulling a rickety cart — making slow progress

【老农】 lǎonóng old farmer; experienced peasant

【老牌】 lǎopái old brand: ～帝国主义 old-line imperialism/ ～特务 an old hand at espionage

【老婆婆】 lǎopópo 〈方〉 ① granny ② husband's mother; mother-in-law

【老婆子】 lǎopózi 〈口〉 ① old biddy ②〔丈夫称妻子〕 my old woman

【老婆】 lǎopo 〈口〉 wife

【老圃】 lǎopǔ 〈书〉 expert vegetable grower

【老气】 lǎoqì 〈方〉 ① old mannish ② (of clothes) dark and old-fashioned

【老气横秋】 lǎoqì héngqiū ① arrogant on account of one's seniority ② lacking in youthful vigour

【老前辈】 lǎoqiánbèi one's senior; one's elder: 革命～ a veteran of the revolution

【老亲】 lǎoqīn ① old parents ② old relatives

【老区】 lǎoqū old liberated area

【老人】 lǎorén ① old man or woman; the aged; the old ② one's aged parents or grandparents
【老人星】 lǎorénxīng 〈天〉 Canopus
【老人家】 lǎorenjia ① a respectful form of address for an old person: 你～今年多大年纪了？How old are you, granddad (grandma)? ② parent: ～都好吗？How are your parents?
【老弱】 lǎo-ruò the old and weak
【老弱病残】 lǎo-ruò-bìng-cán the old, weak, sick and disabled
【老弱残兵】 lǎoruò-cánbīng remaining troops made up of the old and weak; those who on account of old age, illness, etc. are no longer active or efficient in work
【老生常谈】 lǎoshēng chángtán commonplace; platitude
【老师】 lǎoshī teacher
【老师傅】 lǎoshīfu 〈尊〉 master craftsman; experienced worker
【老实】 lǎoshi ① honest; frank: 做～人，说～话，办～事 be an honest person, honest in word and honest in deed/ ～说，我很不赞成这个意见。To be frank, I don't like the idea at all./ ～回答我的问题。Give me a straight answer./ ～交待 come clean; own up; make a clean breast of ② well-behaved; good: 放～点！Behave yourself! 或 None of your tricks!/ 这孩子可～了。The child is as good as gold./ 别以为这个地主分子现在已经～了。Don't imagine that the landlord is behaving himself now. ③〈婉〉 simpleminded; naive; easily taken in
【老手】 lǎoshǒu old hand; old stager; veteran: 干这一行他是～。He is an old hand at the trade./ 育种～ veteran breeder
【老鼠】 lǎoshǔ mouse; rat: ～过街，人人喊打。When a rat runs across the street, everybody cries, "Kill it!" (said of a person or thing hated by everyone)
【老死不相往来】 lǎo sǐ bù xiāng wǎnglái not visit each other all their lives; never be in contact with each other
【老太婆】 lǎotàipó old woman
【老太太】 lǎotàitai 〈尊〉 ① old lady ② your (my, his, etc.) mother
【老太爷】 lǎotàiyé 〈尊〉 ① elderly gentleman ② your (my, his, etc.) father
【老态龙钟】 lǎotài lóngzhōng senile; doddering
【老套】 lǎotào old stuff; old ways: 报纸要办得生动，切忌死板～。A newspaper should be lively and should avoid hackneyed stuff.
【老天爷】 lǎotiānyé God; Heavens: 我的～！My goodness! 或 Good Heavens! 或 Good Gracious!
【老头儿】 lǎotóur 〈口〉 old man; old chap
【老头子】 lǎotóuzi ① old fogey; old codger ② 〈口〉〔妻子称丈夫〕 my old man
【老顽固】 lǎowángu old stick-in-the-mud; old diehard; old fogey
【老王卖瓜，自卖自夸】 Lǎo Wáng mài guā, zì mài zì kuā Lao Wang selling melons praises his own goods — praise one's own work or wares
【老翁】 lǎowēng old man; greybeard
【老挝】 Lǎowō Laos ◇ ～人 Laotian; Lao/ ～语 Laotian (language); Lao
【老乡】 lǎoxiāng ① fellow-townsman; fellow-villager ② *Laoxiang*, a friendly form of address to a man in the countryside
【老小】 lǎo-xiǎo grown-ups and children; one's family: 一家～ the whole family
【老兄】 lǎoxiōng (a familiar form of address between male friends) brother; man; old chap
【老羞成怒】 lǎo xiū chéng nù fly into a rage out of shame; be shamed into anger
【老朽】 lǎoxiǔ decrepit and behind the times; old and useless
【老学究】 lǎoxuéjiū old pedant
【老眼光】 lǎoyǎnguāng old ways of looking at things; old views: 不能以～看新事物。One mustn't judge new things by old standards./ 你这是拿～看人，他跟以前不一样了。You are judging him by what he used to be. He's changed.
【老爷爷】 lǎoyéye ① great grandfather ② 〈尊〉 (often used by children) grandpa
【老爷】 lǎoye ① master; bureaucrat; lord: 做官当～ act as lords and masters/ 采取～式的态度 adopt a bureaucratic attitude ② 〈方〉 (maternal) grandfather; grandpa ◇ ～兵 pampered soldier
【老一辈】 lǎoyībèi older generation: ～无产阶级革命家 proletarian revolutionaries of the older generation; veteran proletarian revolutionaries
【老一套】 lǎoyītào the same old stuff; the same old story: 他们的所谓新建议无非是～。Their so-called new proposal is nothing but the same old stuff./ 改变～的做法 change outmoded methods
【老鹰】 lǎoyīng black-eared kite; hawk; eagle
【老油子】 lǎoyóuzi wily old bird; old campaigner
【老于世故】 lǎoyú shìgù versed in the ways of the world; worldly-wise
【老帐】 lǎozhàng old debts; long-standing debts: ～未清，又欠新帐。While old debts are still unpaid, new ones are incurred./ 翻～ bring up old scores
【老着脸皮】 lǎozhe liǎnpí unabashedly; unblushingly
【老中青三结合】 lǎo-zhōng-qīng sānjiéhé three-in-one combination of the old, the middle-aged and the young: 按照无产阶级革命事业接班人的条件和～的原则，建立各级领导班子 build up the leading bodies at all levels in accordance with the requirements for successors to the proletarian revolutionary cause and the principle of the three-in-one combination of the old, the middle-aged and the young
【老资格】 lǎozīge old-timer; veteran
【老子】 lǎozi ① 〈口〉 father ② 〔气忿或开玩笑的场合下的自称〕：～不吃你这一套！I'll have none of your nonsense!/ ～天下第一 regard oneself as No. 1 authority under heaven; think oneself the wisest person in the world
【老总】 lǎozǒng ① *Lao zong*, an old form of address to a soldier ② used with a surname as an affectionate form of address to a general or high-ranking commander of the PLA
【老祖宗】 lǎozǔzōng ancestor; forefather

**佬** lǎo 〈贬〉 man; guy; fellow: 阔～ a rich guy/ 美国～ Yankee

**姥** lǎo
【姥姥】 lǎolao 〈方〉 (maternal) grandmother; grandma

**栳** lǎo 见"栲栳" kǎolǎo

**铑** lǎo 〈化〉 rhodium (Rh)

## lào

**涝** lào waterlogging: 防～ prevent waterlogging/ 排～ drain waterlogged areas/ 庄稼～了。The crops suffered from waterlogging.
【涝洼地】 làowādì waterlogged lowland
【涝灾】 làozāi damage or crop failure caused by waterlogging

**烙** lào ①brand; iron: 给马～上印记 brand a horse/ ～衣服 iron clothes ②bake in a pan: ～两张饼 bake a couple of cakes
【烙饼】 làobǐng a kind of pancake
【烙铁】 làotie ①flatiron; iron ②soldering iron
【烙印】 làoyìn brand: 打上阶级的～ be stamped with the brand of a class

**落** lào
另见 là; luò
【落色】 làoshǎi discolour; fade
【落枕】 làozhěn 〈中医〉 stiff neck (caused by cold or an awkward sleeping posture)

**酪** lào ①junket ②thick fruit juice; fruit jelly: 红果～ haw jelly ③sweet paste made from crushed nuts; sweet nut paste: 核桃～ walnut cream
【酪氨酸】 lào'ānsuān 〈化〉 tyrosine
【酪素】 làosù 〈化〉 casein ◇ ～胶 casein glue 又作"酪朊"

## lè

**乐** lè ①happy; cheerful; joyful: 我心里～开了花。My heart swelled with happiness (或 was filled with joy)./ 助人为～ find pleasure in helping others ②be glad to; find pleasure in; enjoy: ～此不疲 always enjoy it; never be bored with it ③〈方〉 laugh; be amused: 他说的笑话把大家逗～了。His joke amused everyone./ 你～什么呀? What are you laughing at? 或 What's the joke?
另见 yuè
【乐不可支】 lè bùkě zhī overwhelmed with joy; overjoyed
【乐不思蜀】 lè bù sī Shǔ indulge in pleasure and forget home and duty
【乐得】 lèdé readily take the opportunity to; be only too glad to: 既然如此，我们～在这儿多呆几天。In that case, we'll be only too glad to spend a few more days here.
【乐观】 lèguān optimistic; hopeful; sanguine: ～的看法 an optimistic view/ ～的报道 a sanguine report/ 对前途很～ be optimistic about the future; be sanguine about the future/ 事情的发展是很可～的。The prospects are very bright. ◇ ～主义 optimism/ ～主义者 optimist
【乐果】 lèguǒ 〈农〉 Rogor
【乐呵呵】 lèhēhē buoyant; happy and gay: 他成天总是～的。He's always cheerful and gay.
【乐极生悲】 lè jí shēng bēi extreme joy begets sorrow
【乐趣】 lèqù delight; pleasure; joy: 工作中的～ delight in work/ 生活中的～ joys of life
【乐事】 lèshì pleasure; delight: 以助人为～ find pleasure in helping others
【乐陶陶】 lètáotáo 〈书〉 cheerful; happy; joyful
【乐天】 lètiān carefree; happy-go-lucky
【乐土】 lètǔ land of happiness; paradise
【乐意】 lèyì ①be willing to; be ready to: ～帮忙 be willing to help ②pleased; happy: 他听了这话有点不～。He seemed somewhat displeased with that remark.
【乐于】 lèyú be happy to; take delight in: ～为人民吃苦，勇于为革命牺牲 be ready to endure hardship for the people and die for the revolution
【乐园】 lèyuán paradise: 人间～ earthly paradise; paradise on earth/ 儿童～ children's playground
【乐滋滋】 lèzīzī 〈口〉 contented; pleased: 他听了这话心里～的。He was quite pleased to hear this.

**勒** lè ①rein in: ～马 rein in the horse ②force; coerce: ～交 force sb. to hand sth. over ③〈书〉 carve; engrave: ～碑 carve on a stone tablet ④〈物〉 lux; metre-candle
另见 lēi
【勒逼】 lèbī force; coerce: 地主～她父亲立即还债。The landlord forced her father to pay the debt at once.
【勒克司】 lèkèsī 〈物〉 lux; metre-candle
【勒令】 lèlìng compel (by legal authority); order
【勒派】 lèpài force sb. to pay levies or do corvée
【勒索】 lèsuǒ extort; blackmail: ～钱财 extort money from sb.

**鳓** lè Chinese herring

## le

**了** le 〈助〉 ①〔用在动词或形容词后面表示动作或变化已经完成〕: 去年我们公社打～几十眼井。Our commune sank dozens of wells last year./ 我等～半天他还没来。I've been waiting a long time, but he still hasn't turned up./ 水位已经低～两米。The water level has fallen by two metres./ 你先去，我下～班就去。You go ahead. I'll go right after work. ②〔用在句子的末尾或句中停顿的地方，表示肯定，表示出现新的情况，表示催促或劝止〕: 下雨～。It's started raining./ 是我错～。I was wrong./ 她开头不想来，后来还是来～。At first she didn't want to come, but she came in the end./ 你早来一天就见着他～。You would have seen him if you'd come a day sooner./ 走～，走～，不能再等～。Let's go. We can't wait any longer./ 别说话～! Stop talking!
另见 liǎo; liào

**饹** le 见"饸饹" héle

## lēi

**勒** lēi tie or strap sth. tight: 带子太松了，再～一～。The strap is too loose. Tighten it up a bit./ 背包带太紧，～得慌。The pack straps are too tight. They cut into the flesh./ ～紧裤带 tighten the belt
另见 lè
【勒脚】 lēijiǎo 〈建〉 plinth

**擂** lēi hit; beat: ～了一拳 give sb. a punch
另见 léi; lèi

## léi

**累** léi
另见 lěi, lèi
【累累】 léiléi ①clusters of; heaps of: 果实～ fruit hanging in clusters; fruit hanging heavy ②haggard; gaunt: ～若丧家之犬 wretched as a stray cur
另见 lěilěi
【累赘】 léizhui ①burdensome; cumbersome ②wordy; verbose: 这个句子太～。That's a clumsy, involved sentence. ③encumbrance; burden; nuisance: 行李带的多了，是个～。Too much luggage is a nuisance.

**雷** léi ①thunder ②mine: 布～ lay mines/ 扫～ sweep mines ③(Léi) a surname
【雷暴】 léibào 〈气〉 thunderstorm ◇ ～雨 thunderstorm rain

【雷达】 léidá radar: 全景～ panoramic radar ◇ ～测距 radar ranging/ ～干扰 radar jamming/ ～跟踪 radar tracking/ ～领航 radar navigation/ ～探测区 radar coverage/ ～信标 racon; radar beacon/ ～荧光屏 radar screen/ ～员(兵) radar operator; radarman/ ～制导导弹 radar-guided missile; radar homer

【雷打不动】 léi dǎ bù dòng ① unshakable; determined; unyielding ② (of an arrangement) not to be altered under any circumstances; final; inviolate

【雷电】 léidiàn thunder and lightning: ～交作 lightning accompanied by peals of thunder ◇ ～计 ceraunograph

【雷动】 léidòng thunderous: 欢声～ thunderous cheers

【雷公】 Léigōng Thunder God: ～打豆腐,拣软的欺。The God of Thunder strikes the beancurd — bullies pick on the soft and weak.

【雷汞】 léigǒng 〈化〉 mercury fulminate 又作"雷酸汞"

【雷管】 léiguǎn detonator; detonating cap; blasting cap; primer: 电～ electric detonator

【雷击】 léijī be struck by lightning

【雷厉风行】 léilì-fēngxíng (in carrying out policies, etc.) with the power of a thunderbolt and the speed of lightning; vigorously and speedily; resolutely

【雷米封】 léimǐfēng 〈药〉 rimifon

【雷鸣】 léimíng thunderous; thundery: ～般的掌声 thunderous applause

【雷鸟】 léiniǎo white partridge

【雷诺数】 léinuòshù 〈物〉 Reynolds number

【雷声】 léishēng thunderclap; thunder: ～隆隆 the rumble (或 roll) of thunder

【雷声大,雨点小】 léishēng dà, yǔdiǎn xiǎo loud thunder but small raindrops; much said but little done

【雷霆】 léitíng ① thunderclap; thunderbolt ② thunder-like power or rage; wrath: 大发～ fly into a rage

【雷霆万钧】 léitíng wàn jūn as powerful as a thunderbolt: 以～之力 with the force of a thunderbolt

【雷同】 léitóng ① echoing what others have said ② duplicate; identical

【雷丸】 léiwán 〈中药〉 stone-like omphalia (*Omphalia lapidescens*)

【雷雨云】 léiyǔyún 〈气〉 thundercloud

【雷阵雨】 léizhènyǔ thunder shower

**擂** léi pestle; pound
另见 lēi; lèi

**镭** léi 〈化〉 radium (Ra)

【镭疗】 léiliáo 〈医〉 radium therapy

【镭射气】 léishèqì 〈化〉 radium emanation

**羸** léi 〈书〉 thin; skinny

【羸弱】 léiruò 〈书〉 thin and weak; frail

**罍** léi 〈考古〉 an ancient urn-shaped wine-vessel

## lěi

**垒** lěi ① build by piling up bricks, stones, earth, etc.: ～一道墙 build a wall/ ～猪圈 build a pigsty ② rampart ③〈棒、垒球〉 base

【垒球】 lěiqiú softball ◇ ～棒 softball bat

**累** lěi ① pile up; accumulate: 日积月～ accumulate day by day and month by month/ 成千～万 thousands upon thousands ② continuous; repeated; running: 奋战～日 carry on the fight for several days running/ ～戒不改 refuse to mend one's ways despite repeated warnings ③ involve: 连～ involve; implicate; get sb. into trouble ④同"垒" lěi①
另见 léi; lèi

【累犯】 lěifàn ① recidivism ② recidivist

【累积】 lěijī accumulate: 头八个月完成的工程量～起来,已达到全年任务的百分之九十。The work done in the first eight months amounts to ninety per cent of the year's quota.

【累及】 lěijí implicate; involve; drag in: ～无辜 involve the innocent

【累计】 lěijì ① add up ② accumulative total; grand total

【累进】 lěijìn progression ◇ ～率 graduated rates/ ～税 progressive tax; progressive taxation

【累累】 lěilěi ① again and again; many times ② innumerable; countless: 罪行～ have a long criminal record; commit countless crimes/ 血债～的反革命分子 counter-revolutionaries who owe the masses many blood debts
另见 léiléi

【累卵】 lěiluǎn a stack of eggs — liable to collapse any moment; precarious: 危如～ as precarious as a stack of eggs; in an extremely precarious situation

【累年】 lěinián for years in succession; year after year

【累世】 lěishì for many generations; generation after generation

**磊** lěi

【磊落】 lěiluò open and upright: 胸怀～ openhearted and upright/ 光明～ open and aboveboard

**蕾** lěi flower bud; bud

【蕾铃】 lěilíng cotton buds and bolls

**儡** lěi 见"傀儡" kuǐlěi

## lèi

**肋** lèi ① rib ② costal region: 两～ both sides of the chest

【肋骨】 lèigǔ rib ◇ ～切除术 costectomy

【肋间肌】 lèijiānjī 〈生理〉 intercostal muscle

【肋膜】 lèimó 〈生理〉 pleura ◇ ～炎 pleurisy

【肋木】 lèimù 〈体〉 stall bars

【肋条】 lèitiao 〈方〉 ① rib ② pork ribs

**泪** lèi tear; teardrop: 她哭得～人儿一样。She was all tears.

【泪痕】 lèihén tear stains: 满脸～ a face bathed in tears/ ～斑斑 tear-stained

【泪花】 lèihuā tears in one's eyes: 她眼里闪烁着喜悦的～。Her eyes glistened with tears of joy.

【泪水】 lèishuǐ tear; teardrop

【泪汪汪】 lèiwāngwāng (eyes) brimming with tears

【泪腺】 lèixiàn 〈生理〉 lachrymal gland ◇ ～炎 dacryoadenitis

【泪眼】 lèiyǎn tearful eyes: ～模糊 eyes blurred by tears

【泪液】 lèiyè tear

【泪珠】 lèizhū teardrop

**类** lèi ① kind; type; class; category: 同～ be of a kind; belong to the same category/ 这是另一～问题。This is another kind of problem./ 诸如此～ things like that; and suchlike; and what not ② resemble; be similar to: 画虎不成反～犬 try to draw a tiger but end up with the likeness of a dog — attempt something too ambitious and end in failure/ ～乎神话 sound like a fairy tale

【类比】 lèibǐ 〈逻〉 analogy: 作历史的～ draw a historical analogy

【类别】 lèibié classification; category: 土壤的～ classification of soil/ 属于不同的～ belong to different categories

【类地行星】 lèidì xíngxīng 〈天〉 terrestrial planet

【类毒素】 lèidúsù 〈医〉 toxoid

【类木行星】 lèimù xíngxīng 〈天〉 Jovian planet

【类人猿】 lèirényuán anthropoid (ape)

【类书】 lèishū reference books with material taken from various sources and arranged according to subjects

【类似】 lèisì similar; analogous: 保证不再发生～事件 guarantee against the occurrence of similar incidents

【类推】 lèituī analogize; reason by analogy: 照此～ on the analogy of this

【类星体】 lèixīngtǐ 〈天〉 quasi-stellar object

【类型】 lèixíng type ◇～学 typology

**累** lèi ①tired; fatigued; weary: ～坏了 tired out; worn out; exhausted/ 不怕苦，不怕～ fear neither hardship nor fatigue ②tire; strain; wear out: ～活 tiring work; heavy work/ 看小字～眼睛。Reading small print strains the eyes. ③work hard; toil: 你～了一天，该休息了。You've been working hard all day. You need a rest./ 解放前他们～死～活地给资本家干活，还填不饱肚子。 Before liberation they worked themselves to the bone for the capitalists, but still could hardly keep body and soul together.
另见 léi; lěi

**酹** lèi 〈书〉 pour a libation

**擂** lèi ① beat (a drum) ② 见"擂台"
另见 lēi; léi

【擂台】 lèitái ring (for martial contests); arena: 摆～ give an open challenge / 打～ take up the challenge

## léng

**棱** léng ①arris; edge: 桌子～儿 edges of a table/ 见～见角 angular ②corrugation; ridge: 搓板的～儿 ridges of a washboard

【棱角】 léngjiǎo ①edges and corners ②edge; pointedness: 你对他的批评很有～。Your criticism of him was pointed./ 不要把～磨掉。Don't draw in your horns.

【棱镜】 léngjìng 〈物〉 prism: 三～ triangular prism ◇～分光 prismatic decomposition

【棱线】 léngxiàn 〈军〉 crest line

【棱柱体】 léngzhùtǐ 〈数〉 prism

【棱锥台】 léngzhuītái 〈数〉 frustrum of a pyramid

【棱锥体】 léngzhuītǐ 〈数〉 pyramid

**楞** léng 见"棱" léng

## lěng

**冷** lěng ①cold: ～天 the cold season; cold days/ 你～不～？Do you feel cold? ②cold in manner; frosty: ～若冰霜 frosty in manner ③〈方〉 cool: ～一下再吃。Let it cool off before you eat it. ④unfrequented; deserted; out-of-the-way: 屋里～清清的。The house looked deserted. ⑤strange; rare: ～字 a rarely used word; an unfamiliar word ⑥shot from hiding: ～枪 a sniper's shot ⑦(Lěng) a surname

【冷拔】 lěngbá 〈机〉 cold-drawing 又作"冷拉"

【冷板凳】 lěngbǎndèng cold bench — an indifferent post or a cold reception: 坐～ hold a title without any obligations of office; be kept waiting long for an assignment or an audience with a VIP

【冷冰冰】 lěngbīngbīng ice cold; icy; frosty: ～的脸色 cold expression; frosty looks/ ～的态度 icy manners

【冷布】 lěngbù (cotton) gauze

【冷不防】 lěngbufáng unawares; suddenly; by surprise: 打他一个～ take him unawares; catch him off guard

【冷餐】 lěngcān buffet ◇ ～招待会 buffet reception

【冷藏】 lěngcáng refrigeration; cold storage ◇（火车）～车 refrigerator car; refrigerator van/ ～工业 refrigeration industry/ ～库 cold storage; freezer/ ～汽车 cold storage truck/ ～箱 refrigerator; fridge

【冷场】 lěngchǎng ①awkward silence on the stage when an actor enters late or forgets his lines ②awkward silence at a meeting

【冷嘲热讽】 lěngcháo-rèfěng freezing irony and burning satire

【冷处理】 lěngchǔlǐ 〈机〉 cold treatment

【冷床】 lěngchuáng 〈农〉 cold bed; cold frame

【冷脆】 lěngcuì 〈冶〉 cold short

【冷淡】 lěngdàn ①cheerless; desolate ②cold; indifferent: 反映～ a cold response/ 对倡议表示～ show indifference towards a proposal/ ～的态度 a frigid manner ③treat coldly; cold-shoulder; slight

【冷调】 lěngdiào 〈美术〉 cool colour-tone; cool tone

【冷碟儿】 lěngdiér 〈方〉 cold dish; *hors d'oeuvres*

【冷冻】 lěngdòng freezing
◇ ～厂 cold storage plant/ ～干燥 freeze drying/ ～机 refrigerator; freezer/ ～剂 refrigerant/ ～精液 〈牧〉 frozen semen

【冷锻】 lěngduàn 〈机〉 cold forging; cold hammering

【冷锋】 lěngfēng 〈气〉 cold front

【冷敷】 lěngfū 〈医〉 cold compress

【冷宫】 lěnggōng cold palace — a place to which disfavoured queens and concubines were banished; limbo: 被打入～ be consigned to limbo

【冷光】 lěngguāng 〈物〉 cold light

【冷汗】 lěnghàn cold sweat: 出～ be in a cold sweat; break out in a cold sweat

【冷焊】 lěnghàn 〈机〉 cold welding

【冷荤】 lěnghūn cold meat; cold buffet

【冷货】 lěnghuò goods not much in demand; dull goods

【冷加工】 lěngjiāgōng 〈机〉 cold working

【冷箭】 lěngjiàn an arrow shot from hiding; sniper's shot: 放～ make a sneak attack

【冷静】 lěngjìng sober; calm: 头脑～ sober-minded; level-headed; cool-headed/ 保持～ keep calm/ 同志们的话使我～下来。The comrades' words sobered me.

【冷觉】 lěngjué 〈生理〉 sensation of cold; sense of cold

【冷酷】 lěngkù unfeeling; callous; grim: ～无情 unfeeling; cold-blooded/ 谎言掩盖不住～的现实。Lies cannot cover up grim reality.

【冷冷清清】 lěnglěngqīngqīng cold and cheerless; desolate: 对待同志要满腔热忱，不能～，漠不关心。We should be warm towards our comrades, not cold and indifferent./ 不要只靠少数人～地做工作。Do not rely entirely on a handful of people working in quiet isolation./ 会议开得～。The meeting was very dull.

【冷落】 lěngluò ①unfrequented; desolate: 狭窄～的胡同 an unfrequented narrow alley ②treat coldly; cold-shoulder; leave out in the cold: ～了客人 leave a guest out in the cold

【冷铆】 lěngmǎo 〈机〉 cold riveting
【冷门】 lěngmén ① a profession, trade or branch of learning that receives little attention ② an unexpected winner; dark horse: 那次比赛出了个～。The contest produced an unexpected winner. ◇ ～货 goods not much in demand; dull goods
【冷漠】 lěngmò cold and detached; unconcerned; indifferent
【冷凝】 lěngníng 〈物〉 condensation
◇ ～点 condensation point/ ～器 condenser/ ～物 condensate
【冷暖】 lěngnuǎn changes in temperature: 注意～ be careful about changes of temperature; take care of oneself/ 把群众的～时刻挂在心上 always be concerned with the well-being of the masses
【冷盘】 lěngpán cold dish; *hors d'oeuvres*
【冷僻】 lěngpì ① deserted; out-of-the-way ② rare; unfamiliar: ～的字眼 rarely used words/ ～的典故 unfamiliar allusions
【冷气】 lěngqì air conditioning: 这个剧院有～设备。The theatre is air-conditioned. ◇ ～机 air conditioner
【冷枪】 lěngqiāng sniper's shot
【冷清】 lěngqīng cold and cheerless; desolate; lonely; deserted
【冷却】 lěngquè cooling
◇ ～剂 coolant; cooler/ ～塔 cooling tower/ ～旋管 cooling worm; cooling coil
【冷热病】 lěngrèbìng ① 〈方〉 malaria ② capricious changes in mood; sudden waxing and waning of enthusiasm: 他的～又犯了。He's in one of his moods again.
【冷色】 lěngsè 〈美术〉 cool colour
【冷杉】 lěngshān 〈植〉 fir
【冷食】 lěngshí cold drinks and snacks ◇ ～部 cold drink and snack counter
【冷霜】 lěngshuāng cold cream
【冷水】 lěngshuǐ ① cold water: 泼～ throw cold water on; dampen sb.'s enthusiasm ② unboiled water ◇ ～浴 cold bath
【冷丝丝】 lěngsīsī a bit chilly
【冷飕飕】 lěngsōusōu (of wind) chilling; chilly
【冷笑】 lěngxiào sneer; laugh grimly; grin with dissatisfaction, helplessness, bitterness, etc.
【冷性肥料】 lěngxìng féiliào cold manure
【冷血动物】 lěngxuè dòngwù ① cold-blooded animal; poikilothermal animal ② an unfeeling person; a coldhearted person
【冷言冷语】 lěngyán-lěngyǔ sarcastic comments; ironical remarks
【冷眼】 lěngyǎn ① cool detachment ② cold shoulder
【冷眼旁观】 lěngyǎn pángguān ① look on coldly; stay aloof ② look on with a critical eye
【冷饮】 lěngyǐn cold drink
【冷遇】 lěngyù cold reception; cold shoulder: 遭到～ be given the cold shoulder; be left out in the cold
【冷錾】 lěngzàn 〈机〉 cold chisel
【冷轧】 lěngzhá 〈冶〉 cold rolling ◇ ～钢 cold-rolled steel/ ～机 cold-rolling mill
【冷战】 lěngzhàn cold war
【冷战】 lěngzhan 〈口〉 shiver: 打～ shiver with cold
【冷铸】 lěngzhù 〈冶〉 chill casting

## lèng

**愣** lèng ① distracted; stupefied; blank: 发～ stare blankly; look distracted/ 他～了半天没说话。For a long while he remained speechless./ 听到这消息他～住了。He was struck dumb by the news. ② 〈口〉 rash; reckless; foolhardy: ～小子 rash young fellow; young hothead
【愣干】 lènggàn 〈口〉 do things recklessly (或rashly); persist in going one's own way: 要遵守操作规程，不能～。You've got to observe the working regulations. You can't do things any way you like.
【愣劲儿】 lèngjìnr 〈方〉 dash; pep; vigour: 这些小伙子真有股子～。These boys are really full of pep.
【愣神儿】 lèngshénr stare blankly; be in a daze: 他站在一旁～，不知道想些什么。He stood by staring blankly, lost in thought.
【愣说】 lèngshuō 〈口〉 insist; allege; assert: 他～这里不能种水稻，现在不是种成了吗？He insisted that rice wouldn't grow here, but you see we've grown it.
【愣头愣脑】 lèngtóu-lèngnǎo rash; impetuous; reckless
【愣头儿青】 lèngtóurqīng 〈方〉 rash fellow; hothead

**睖** lèng
【睖睁】 lèngzheng stare blankly; be in a daze

## lī

**哩** lī
另见 li
【哩哩啦啦】 līlilālā 〈口〉 scattered; sporadic: ～下了一天雨。It rained off and on all day./ 跟上队伍，不要～的。Close up, don't straggle along.
【哩哩罗罗】 līliluōluō 〈口〉 verbose and unclear in speech; rambling and indistinct

## lí

**厘** lí ① *li*, a unit of length (=1/3 millimetre) ② *li*, a unit of weight (=0.05 grams) ③ *li*, a unit of area (=0.666 square metres) ④ *li*, one thousandth of a *yuan* ⑤ *li*, a unit of monthly interest rate (=0.1%): 月利率二～七 a monthly interest of 0.27% ⑥ *li*, a unit of annual interest rate (=1%): 年利率三～ an annual interest of 3% ⑦ a fraction; the least: 分～不差 without the slightest error; just right
【厘定】 lídìng collate and stipulate (rules and regulations, etc.)
【厘米】 límǐ centimetre ◇ ～波〈电〉 centimetre wave/ ～、克、秒单位 centimetre-gram-second unit (CGS unit)

**离** lí ① leave; part from; be away from: ～京赴穗 leave Beijing for Guangzhou/ 她～家已经三年了。She's been away from home for three years./ 身不～劳动，心不～群众 do manual labour regularly and always think of the masses ② off; away; from: 车站～这儿三里地。The railway station is three *li* from here./ ～国庆节只有十天了。National Day is only ten days away. ③ without; independent of: 发展工业～不了钢铁。Industry cannot develop without steel.
【离岸价格】 lí'àn jiàgé 〈经〉 free on board (FOB)
【离瓣】 líbàn 〈植〉 polypetalous; choripetalous ◇ ～花类 choripetalae
【离别】 líbié part (for a longish period); leave; bid farewell: 我～故乡已经两年了。It's two years since I left my hometown.
【离地间隙】 lídì jiànxì 〈汽车〉 road clearance; ground clearance
【离格儿】 lígér 〈口〉 go beyond what is proper; be out of place
【离合器】 líhéqì 〈机〉 clutch

【离婚】 líhūn divorce
【离间】 líjiàn sow discord; drive a wedge between; set one party against another
【离解】 líjiě 〈化〉 dissociation
【离经叛道】 líjīng-pàndào depart from the classics and rebel against orthodoxy
【离境】 líjìng leave a country or place ◇ ～签证 exit visa/ ～许可证 exit permit
【离开】 líkāi leave; depart from; deviate from: ～太原去大寨访问 leave Taiyuan to visit Dazhai/ ～本题 stray from the subject; digress/ 离不开手儿 be too busy with the job on hand; have one's hands full/ 我们一刻也不能～党的路线。We should never for a moment deviate from the Party's line.
【离奇】 líqí odd; fantastic; bizarre: ～的谎言 a fantastic lie/ 这事儿很～。This is a very odd business.
【离去角】 líqùjiǎo 〈汽车〉 angle of departure
【离群索居】 líqún-suǒjū live in solitude
【离任】 lírèn leave one's post: ～回国 leave one's post for home/ 即将～的大使 the outgoing ambassador
【离散】 lísàn dispersed; scattered about; separated from one another: 解放前～了的母女终于重新团聚了。Mother and daughter who were separated from each other before liberation have at long last been reunited.
【离题】 lítí digress from the subject; stray from the point: 发言不要～。Please keep to the subject.
【离乡背井】 líxiāng-bèijǐng 见"背井离乡" bèijǐng-líxiāng
【离心】 líxīn ① be at odds with the community or the leadership ② centrifugal
◇ ～泵 〈机〉 centrifugal pump/ ～机 centrifugal machine; centrifuge/ ～力 〈物〉 centrifugal force/ ～调节器 〈机〉 centrifugal governor
【离心离德】 líxīn-lídé dissension and discord; disunity
【离职】 lízhí ① leave one's job temporarily ② leave office
【离中趋势】 lízhōng qūshì 〈统计〉 dispersion
【离子】 lízǐ 〈物〉 ion: 阴～ anion/ 阳～ cation/ 氩～ argon ion
◇ ～泵 ionic pump/ ～束 ion beam/ ～淌度 ionic mobility/ ～雾 ion-atmosphere
【离子交换】 lízǐ jiāohuàn 〈化〉 ion exchange ◇ ～剂 ion exchanger/ ～树脂 ion exchange resin

**狸** lí racoon dog
【狸猫】 límāo leopard cat
【狸藻】 lízǎo 〈植〉 bladderwort (*Utricularia vulgaris*)

**骊** lí 〈书〉 black horse

**梨** lí pear
【梨膏】 lígāo 〈中药〉 pear syrup (for the relief of coughs)

**犁** lí ① plough ② work with a plough; plough: 地已经～了两遍。The fields have been ploughed twice.
【犁壁】 líbì 〈农〉 mouldboard 又作"犁镜"
【犁底层】 lídǐcéng 〈农〉 plough sole; plough pan
【犁铧】 líhuá ploughshare; share

**喱** lí 见"咖喱" gālí

**鹂** lí 见"黄鹂" huánglí

**蜊** lí 见"蛤蜊" géli

**漓** lí 见"淋漓" línlí

**璃** lí 见"玻璃" bōli; "琉璃" liúli

**犛** lí yak

**黎** lí ①〈书〉 multitude; host: ～庶 the multitude ② (Lí) a surname
【黎巴嫩】 Líbānèn Lebanon ◇ ～人 Lebanese
【黎民】 límín 〈书〉 the common people; the multitude
【黎明】 límíng dawn; daybreak
【黎族】 Lízú the Li nationality, living in Guangdong

**鲡** lí 见"鳗鲡" mánlí

**罹** lí 〈书〉 suffer from; meet with: ～病 suffer from a disease; fall ill
【罹难】 línàn 〈书〉 ① die in a disaster or an accident ② be murdered

**篱** lí hedge; fence: 竹～茅舍 thatched cottage with bamboo fence/ 树～ hedge; hedgerow
【篱笆】 líba bamboo or twig fence: ～墙 wattled wall

**藜** lí 〈植〉 lamb's-quarters
【藜芦】 lílú 〈植〉 black false hellebore

**黧** lí
【黧黑】 líhēi 〈书〉 (of complexion) dark

**蠡** lí 〈书〉 ① calabash shell serving as a dipper; dipper ② seashell
【蠡测】 lícè 〈书〉 measure the sea with an oyster shell—have a shallow understanding of a person or subject

## lǐ

**礼** lǐ ① ceremony; rite: 丧～ funeral ceremony; funeral/ 婚～ wedding ② courtesy; etiquette; manners: 行～ (give a) salute/ 彬彬有～ refined and courteous; urbane/ 失～行为 breach of etiquette; discourtesy ③ gift; present: 送～ give a present; send a gift
【礼拜】 lǐbài ①〈宗〉 religious service: 做～ go to church; be at church ②〈口〉 week: 下～ next week ③〈口〉 day of the week: 今天～几？What day is it today? ④〈口〉 Sunday: 今儿个～。Today is Sunday.
◇ ～寺 〈伊斯兰教〉 mosque/ ～堂 〈基督教〉 church/ ～天 〈口〉 Sunday
【礼宾司】 Lǐbīnsī the Department of Protocol; the Protocol Department ◇ ～司长 Director of the Protocol Department; Chief of Protocol
【礼部】 Lǐbù the Ministry of Rites in feudal China
【礼服】 lǐfú ceremonial robe or dress; full dress; formal attire
【礼花】 lǐhuā fireworks display
【礼记】 Lǐjì *The Book of Rites* 参见"五经" wǔjīng
【礼教】 lǐjiào the Confucian or feudal ethical code: 吃人的～ cannibalistic feudal ethics
【礼节】 lǐjié courtesy; etiquette; protocol; ceremony: ～性拜访 a courtesy call/ 这是～上所需要的。This is required by protocol. 或 This is demanded by etiquette./ 社交～ social etiquette
【礼帽】 lǐmào a hat that goes with formal dress: 大～ top hat
【礼貌】 lǐmào courtesy; politeness; manners: 有～ courteous; polite/ 没～ have no manners; be impolite
【礼炮】 lǐpào salvo; (gun) salute: 鸣～二十一响。A 21-gun

salute was fired.
【礼品】 lǐpǐn gift; present ◇（商店）～部 gift and souvenir department or counter
【礼器】 lǐqì 〈考古〉 sacrificial vessel
【礼轻人意重】 lǐ qīng rényì zhòng the gift is trifling but the feeling is profound; it's nothing much, but it's the thought that counts
【礼让】 lǐràng give precedence to sb. out of courtesy or thoughtfulness; comity: 国际～ the comity of nations/ 中速行驶，安全～。Drive at moderate speed; yield right of way for safety's sake.
【礼尚往来】 lǐ shàng wǎng-lái ① courtesy demands reciprocity ② deal with a man as he deals with you; pay a man back in his own coin
【礼数】 lǐshù 〈口〉 courtesy; etiquette
【礼俗】 lǐsú etiquette and custom
【礼堂】 lǐtáng assembly hall; auditorium
【礼物】 lǐwù gift; present
【礼仪】 lǐyí etiquette; rite; protocol
【礼遇】 lǐyù courteous reception: 受到～ be accorded courteous reception

**李** lǐ ① plum ② (Lǐ) a surname
【李代桃僵】 lǐ dài táo jiāng ① substitute one thing for another; substitute this for that ② sacrifice oneself for another person
【李子】 lǐzi plum

**里¹** lǐ ① lining; inside: 衣服～儿 the lining of a garment/ 这面是～儿，那面是面儿。This is the back, that is the front. ② inner: ～间 inner room ③ neighbourhood: 邻～ people of the neighbourhood ④〈书〉 hometown; native place: 返～ return to one's hometown ⑤ *li*, a Chinese unit of length (=1/2 kilometre)

**里²** li ① in; inside: 手～ in one's hands/ 小提箱～ in (或 inside) the suitcase ②〔附在"这""那""哪"等字后边表示地点〕: 这～ here/ 那～ there/ 县～发的通知 a circular issued by the county authorities
【里边】 lǐbian inside; in; within: 壁橱～ inside the cupboard/ 他一年～没有请过一次假。He has not once asked for leave during the whole year./ 这～有问题。There is something wrong here. 或 Something is wrong here.
【里程】 lǐchéng ① mileage ② course of development; course: 革命的～ the course of the revolution ◇ ～标 milepost/ ～表 odometer
【里程碑】 lǐchéngbēi milestone: 历史的～ a milestone in history
【里带】 lǐdài 〈口〉 inner tube (of a tyre)
【里海】 Lǐhǎi the Caspian Sea
【里急后重】 lǐjí-hòuzhòng 〈医〉 tenesmus
【里脊】 lǐji tenderloin
【里拉】 lǐlā lira
【里里外外】 lǐlǐwàiwài inside and outside: 屋子～都打扫得很干净。The house has been given a thorough cleaning inside and out./ ～一把手 competent in all one does, both inside and outside the house
【里弄】 lǐlòng 〈方〉 lanes and alleys; neighbourhood: 担任～工作 work on the neighbourhood committee
【里面】 lǐmiàn inside; interior: 宿舍～清洁豁亮。It's clean and bright inside the dormitory.
【里圈】 lǐquān 〈体〉 inner lane (of a running track)
【里手】 lǐshǒu ① the left-hand side (of a running vehicle or machine) ②〈方〉 expert; old hand
【里通外国】 lǐ tōng wàiguó have (或 maintain) illicit relations with a foreign country
【里头】 lǐtou inside; interior
【里屋】 lǐwū inner room
【里弦】 lǐxián the thicker inner string on the *huqin* (胡琴)
【里应外合】 lǐyìng-wàihé act from inside in coordination with forces attacking from outside; collaborate from within with forces from without
【里证】 lǐzhèng 〈中医〉 interior symptom-complex; diseases caused by the endogenous factors involving serious disorders in the internal organs
【里子】 lǐzi lining

**俚** lǐ vulgar
【俚俗】 lǐsú vulgar; unrefined; uncultured
【俚语】 lǐyǔ slang

**娌** lǐ 见"妯娌" zhóuli

**逦** lǐ 见"迤逦" yǐlǐ

**理** lǐ ① texture; grain (in wood, skin, etc.): 纹～ texture; grain/ 肌～ skin texture ② reason; logic; truth: 是他没～。He's the one who's been unreasonable./ 不可～喻 will not listen to reason; be impervious to reason/ 他讲的句句是～。There is truth in every word he says./ ～当如此。That's just as it should be. ③ natural science, esp. physics: ～工科 science and engineering/ 数～化 mathematics, physics and chemistry ④ manage; run: ～家 keep house; manage family affairs/ 有要事待～ have important business to attend to ⑤ put in order; tidy up: ～东西 put things in order ⑥〔多用于否定句〕 pay attention to; acknowledge: 置之不～ pay no attention to sth.; brush sth. aside/ 爱～不～ look cold and indifferent; be standoffish
【理财】 lǐcái manage money matters; conduct financial transactions
【理睬】 lǐcǎi 〔多用于否定句〕 pay attention to; show interest in: 没人～这事。Nobody pays any attention to this matter./ 不予～ ignore; turn a deaf ear to; pay no heed to
【理舱费】 lǐcāngfèi 〈航运〉 stowage charges
【理发】 lǐfà haircut; hairdressing: 我去～。I'm going to have a haircut. 或（指女子）I'm going to have my hair done. ◇ ～馆 barbershop; barber's; hairdresser's/ ～员 barber; hairdresser
【理工科大学】 lǐ-gōngkē dàxué college (或 university) of science and engineering
【理会】 lǐhuì ① understand; comprehend: 不难～ not difficult to understand ②〔多用于否定句〕 take notice of; pay attention to: 叫了他好几声，他都没～。We called him several times, but he took no notice of us.
【理货】 lǐhuò 〈航运〉 tally ◇ ～单 tally sheet/ ～员 tallyman; tally clerk
【理解】 lǐjiě understand; comprehend: 你的意思我完全～。I understand you completely. 或 I see perfectly well what you mean./ 加深～ deepen one's comprehension; acquire a better understanding/ 不可～ incomprehensible; beyond one's comprehension
【理解力】 lǐjiělì faculty of understanding; understanding; comprehension: ～强 have good understanding (或 comprehension)
【理科】 lǐkē ① science department in a college ② science (as a school subject)
【理亏】 lǐkuī be in the wrong: 自知～ know that one is in the wrong; realize that justice is not on one's side
【理亏心虚】 lǐkuī-xīnxū feel apprehensive because one is not

on solid ground
【理疗】 lǐliáo 〈医〉 physiotherapy ◇ ～科医生 physiotherapist
【理论】 lǐlùn theory: ～学习 study of Marxist theory/ 在～上 in terms of theory; on the theoretical plane; theoretically
◇ ～队伍 theoretical study and propaganda contingent/ ～化 theorize; raise to a theoretical plane/ ～家 theoretician; theorist/ ～水平 theoretical level
【理气】 lǐqì 〈中医〉 regulating the flow of vital energy and removing obstruction to it ◇ ～止痛药 medicines for regulating the flow of vital energy and assuaging the pain caused by functional disorder of various organs
【理屈词穷】 lǐqū-cíqióng fall silent on finding oneself bested in argument; be unable to advance any further arguments to justify oneself
【理事】 lǐshì member of a council; director: 常任～国 permanent member state of a council ◇ ～会 council; board of directors
【理所当然】 lǐ suǒ dāngrán of course; naturally: 他们的荒谬提案～地被否决了。Their absurd proposal was of course rejected.
【理想】 lǐxiǎng ideal: 共产主义的伟大～ the lofty ideal of communism/ 这天气出去郊游太～了。This is ideal weather for an outing.
◇ ～国 utopia/ ～气体 〈物〉 perfect gas; ideal gas/ ～主义 idealism
【理性】 lǐxìng reason: 失去～ lose one's reason/ 感性和～ the perceptual and the rational ◇ ～认识 〈哲〉 rational knowledge
【理学】 lǐxué 〈哲〉 a Confucian school of idealist philosophy of the Song and Ming Dynasties
【理血】 lǐxuè 〈中医〉 regulating blood condition, including its generation, circulation and removal of stasis
【理应】 lǐyīng ought to; should: ～归公 ought to be handed over to the state or collective
【理由】 lǐyóu reason; ground; argument: 有充分～相信 have every reason to believe/ 没有～抱怨 have no grounds for complaint/ 他提出的～不能成立。His argument is untenable./ 他想找～为自己的错误辩解。He tried to find an excuse for his error.
【理直气壮】 lǐzhí-qìzhuàng with justice on one's side, one is bold and assured: ～地回答 reply with perfect assurance/ ～地予以驳斥 justly and forcefully refute
【理智】 lǐzhì reason; intellect: 丧失～ lose one's reason; lose one's senses
【理中】 lǐzhōng 〈中医〉 regulating the functions of the stomach and spleen

**锂** lǐ 〈化〉 lithium (Li)
【锂云母】 lǐyúnmǔ 〈矿〉 lepidolite; lithia mica

**鲤** lǐ carp
【鲤鱼】 lǐyú carp
【鲤鱼钳】 lǐyúqián slip-joint pliers

**醴** lǐ 〈书〉 sweet wine

**鳢** lǐ murrel; snakehead

## lì

**力** lì ① power; strength; ability: 人～ manpower/ 物～ material resources/ 兵～ military strength; military capabilities/ 能～ ability; capability/ 视～ power of vision/ 魄～ drive and decisiveness; boldness ② 〈物〉 force: 磁～ magnetic force ③ physical strength: 大～士 a man of great strength/ ～不能支 unable to stand the strain any longer; too weak to stay on one's feet ④ do all one can; make every effort: ～谏 try all one can to remonstrate/ 办事不～ not do one's best in one's work; not pull one's weight
【力巴】 lìba 〈方〉 ① not adept; awkward; clumsy ② layman
【力臂】 lìbì 〈物〉 arm of force
【力不从心】 lì bù cóng xīn ability falling short of one's wishes; ability not equal to one's ambition
【力不胜任】 lì bù shèngrèn be unequal to one's task
【力场】 lìchǎng 〈物〉 field of force
【力畜】 lìchù draught animal; beast of burden
【力度】 lìdù 〈乐〉 dynamics
【力疾从公】 lì jí cóng gōng attend to one's duties in spite of illness
【力竭声嘶】 lìjié-shēngsī 见"声嘶力竭" shēngsī-lìjié
【力戒】 lìjiè strictly avoid; do everything possible to avoid; guard against: ～临战分散兵力 strictly avoid the dispersal of forces before an engagement/ ～浪费 do everything possible to avoid waste/ ～骄傲 guard against arrogance
【力矩】 lìjǔ 〈物〉 moment of force; moment: 合～ resultant moment/ 俯仰～ 〈机〉 pitching moment
【力量】 lìliang ① physical strength ② power; force; strength: 依靠群众的～ rely on the strength of the masses/ 国防～ defence capability/ 世界上没有任何～可以阻止历史车轮的前进。No force on earth can hold back the wheel of history.
【力偶】 lì'ǒu 〈物〉 couple
【力排众议】 lì pái zhòngyì prevail over all dissenting views
【力气】 lìqi physical strength; effort: 他很有～。He is a man of great strength./ 不费～是学不了大寨的。You can't learn from Dazhai without making an effort. / ～活儿 heavy work; strenuous work
【力求】 lìqiú make every effort to; do one's best to; strive to: 文字～精炼。Strive to be concise in writing./ 我们～取得一致意见。We'll do our best to reach an identity of views.
【力所能及】 lì suǒ néng jí in one's power: 在～的范围内 within one's power/ 退休老工人主动为集体做些～的工作。The retired workers volunteered to do what they could for the collective.
【力图】 lìtú try hard to; strive to: ～否认 try hard to deny/ ～摆脱困境 strive to get out of a predicament/ 敌军～挽回败局。The enemy made a desperate attempt to avert defeat.
【力挽狂澜】 lì wǎn kuánglán make vigorous efforts to turn the tide
【力线】 lìxiàn 〈物〉 line of force
【力学】 lìxué mechanics: 波动～ wave mechanics/ 断裂～ fracture mechanics/ 生物～ biomechanics
【力争】 lìzhēng ① work hard for; do all one can to: ～主动 do all one can to gain the initiative/ ～更大的丰收 work hard for a still bigger harvest/ ～少花钱，多办事 strive by every means to spend less and accomplish more ② argue strongly; contend vigorously: 据理～ argue strongly on just grounds

**历** lì ① go through; undergo; experience: ～尽艰辛 have gone through all kinds of hardships and difficulties ② all previous (occasions, sessions, etc.) ③ covering all; one by one: ～访各有关部门 have visited the departments concerned one by one ④ calendar: 阴(阳)～ lunar (solar) calendar

【历程】 lìchéng course: 回顾战斗的～ look back on the course of the struggle/ 我们党的光辉～ the glorious career of our Party
【历次】 lìcì all previous (occasions, etc.): 解放后～政治运动 the various political movements since liberation/ 中央的～指示 the successive directives of the Central Committee/ 在～比赛中她都取得了优异的成绩。She has done well in all past contests.
【历代】 lìdài successive dynasties; past dynasties: ～封建王朝 the feudal dynasties of past ages/ ～名画 famous paintings through the ages
【历法】 lìfǎ 〈天〉 calendar
【历届】 lìjiè all previous (sessions, governments, etc.): ～全国人民代表大会 all the previous National People's Congresses/ ～毕业生 graduates of all previous years
【历来】 lìlái always; constantly; all through the ages: ～如此。This has always been the case./ ～认为 have invariably insisted; have consistently held; have always maintained/ 这些岛屿～都是中国的领土。These islands have been Chinese territory from time immemorial.
【历历】 lìlì distinctly; clearly: ～在目 come clearly into view; leap up vividly before the eyes/ 往事～在心头。Past events remain fresh in my memory./ 湖水清澈，游鱼～可数。The water of the lake was so clear that every fish could be seen distinctly.
【历年】 lìnián ① over the years: ～的积蓄 savings over the years ② 〈天〉 calendar year
【历任】 lìrèn ① have successively held the posts of; have served successively as: 他～连长、营长、团长、师长等职。He successively held the posts of company, battalion, regiment and division commander. ② successive: 这个公社的～党委书记 the successive Party secretaries of this people's commune
【历时】 lìshí last (a period of time); take (a period of time): 手术～三小时。The operation lasted three hours./ ～八年的抗日战争 the eight-year-long War of Resistance Against Japan
【历史】 lìshǐ history; past records: 人民群众是～的创造者。The masses of the people are the makers of history./ ～清白 have a clean record/ 隐瞒自己的～ conceal one's past record/ ～上 in history; down the ages/ ～上犯过错误的人 those who formerly committed mistakes/ 用～观点看问题 look at the problem from a historical point of view/ 这场斗争具有重大的～意义。The struggle is of historic significance.
◇ ～博物馆 history (或 historical) museum/ ～潮流 the tide of history; historical trend/ ～地图 historical map or atlas/ ～反革命分子 historical counterrevolutionary; a person with counterrevolutionary antecedents/ ～观 conception of history/ ～剧 historical play/ ～人物 historical personage; historical figure/ ～问题 question of a political nature in sb.'s history/ ～小说 historical novel/ ～学家 historian/ ～循环论 historicism/ ～遗产 legacy of history; historical heritage
【历史唯物主义】 lìshǐ wéiwùzhǔyì historical materialism 又作"历史唯物论"
【历史唯心主义】 lìshǐ wéixīnzhǔyì historical idealism 又作"历史唯心论"
【历史性】 lìshǐxìng historic; of historic significance: ～胜利 a historic victory
【历书】 lìshū almanac
【历数】 lìshǔ count one by one; enumerate: ～侵略者的罪行 enumerate the crimes of the aggressors
【历元】 lìyuán 〈天〉 epoch
【历月】 lìyuè 〈天〉 calendar month

## 立

lì ① stand: 起～ stand up ② erect; set up: 把梯子～起来 set up the ladder/ ～界桩 erect boundary markers ③ upright; erect; vertical ④ found; establish; set up: ～国 found a state/ ～合同 sign a contract/ ～标兵 make sb. the pacesetter; set up a model ⑤ exist; live: 自～ be on one's feet/ 过去这块地不～苗。In the past nothing could grow on this tract of land. ⑥ immediate; instantaneous: ～见功效 produce immediate results; feel the effect immediately/ ～候回音。An immediate reply is requested. 或 Awaiting your prompt reply.
【立案】 lì'àn ① register; put on record ② 〈法〉 place a case on file for investigation and prosecution
【立场】 lìchǎng position; stand; standpoint: 阐明我们对这一问题的～ make clear our position on this question/ 马克思主义的～、观点和方法 the Marxist stand, viewpoint and method/ 站在党的～ keep to the stand of the Party/ 丧失～ depart from the correct stand/ ～坚定 be steadfast in one's stand; take a firm stand
【立春】 Lìchūn the Beginning of Spring (1st solar term)
【立党为公】 lì dǎng wèi gōng build a party serving the interests of the people: ～，还是立党为私？这是无产阶级政党和资产阶级政党的分水岭。To build a party serving the interests of the vast majority or one serving those of the minority? This is the watershed between proletarian and bourgeois political parties.
【立德粉】 lìdéfěn 〈化〉 lithopone
【立定】 lìdìng halt: ～！（口令）Halt!
【立定跳远】 lìdìng tiàoyuǎn 〈体〉 standing long jump
【立冬】 Lìdōng the Beginning of Winter (19th solar term)
【立法】 lìfǎ legislation ◇ ～机关 legislative body; legislature/ ～权 legislative power
【立方】 lìfāng ① 〈数〉 cube: 二的～ the cube of 2; $2^3$ ② 〈简〉（立方体） cube ③ 〈量〉 cubic metre; stere: 一～土 one cubic metre of earth
◇～根 〈数〉 cube root/ ～厘米 cubic centimetre/ ～米 cubic metre/ ～体 cube
【立竿见影】 lì gān jiàn yǐng set up a pole and see its shadow — get instant results
【立功】 lìgōng render meritorious service; do a deed of merit; win honour; make contributions: 立大功 render outstanding service/ 立新功 make new contributions/ 立一等功 win a first class merit citation/ 立集体三等功 be awarded a class three collective commendation/ ～者受奖。Those who render meritorious service receive awards./ ～赎罪 perform meritorious services to atone for one's crimes
◇ ～奖状 certificate for meritorious service; certificate of merit
【立柜】 lìguì clothes closet; wardrobe; hanging cupboard
【立户】 lìhù ① register for a household residence card; register for permanent residence ② open an account with the bank
【立即】 lìjí 〈副〉 immediately; at once; promptly: ～照办 carry out promptly/ 判处死刑，～执行 be sentenced to death and executed immediately
【立脚点】 lìjiǎodiǎn 见"立足点"
【立克次氏体】 lìkècìshìtǐ 〈医〉 rickettsia
【立刻】 lìkè 〈副〉 immediately; at once; right away: 我～就去。I'll go right away.
【立论】 lìlùn ① set forth one's views; present one's arguments ② argument; position; line of reasoning
【立面图】 lìmiàntú 〈建〉 elevation (drawing)
【立秋】 Lìqiū the Beginning of Autumn (13th solar term)
【立射】 lìshè 〈军〉 fire from a standing position
【立时】 lìshí 见"立刻"

【立式】 lìshì 〈机〉 vertical; upright: ～车床 vertical lathe/ ～钻床 upright drill; vertical drill
【立誓】 lìshì take an oath; vow
【立体】 lìtǐ ① three-dimensional; stereoscopic ② 〈数〉 solid ◇ ～电影 stereoscopic film; three-dimensional film/ ～化学 stereochemistry/ ～几何学 solid geometry/ ～交叉〈交〉 grade separation/ ～角 〈数〉 solid angle/ ～模型 space model/ ～派 cubism/ ～声 stereophony; stereo/ ～显微镜 stereoscopic microscope; stereomicroscope/ ～战争 three-dimensional warfare; triphibious warfare/ ～照相机 stereoscopic camera; stereo camera
【立夏】 Lìxià the Beginning of Summer (7th solar term)
【立宪】 lìxiàn constitutionalism: 君主～constitutional monarchy/ ～政体 constitutional government; constitutionalism
【立言】 lìyán expound one's ideas in writing; achieve glory by writing
【立意】 lìyì ① be determined; make up one's mind ② conception; approach: 这幅画～新颖。 This painting shows an interesting new approach.
【立于不败之地】 lì yú bù bài zhī dì establish oneself in an unassailable position; remain invincible; be in an impregnable position
【立正】 lìzhèng stand at attention: ～! (口令) Attention!
【立志】 lìzhì resolve; be determined: ～改革 be determined to carry out reforms; be resolved to institute reforms/ ～做无产阶级革命事业接班人 resolve to be a proletarian revolutionary successor
【立轴】 lìzhóu ① vertical scroll of painting or calligraphy ② 〈机〉 vertical shaft; upright shaft
【立锥之地】 lì zhuī zhī dì a place to stick an awl — a tiny bit of land: 无～ not possess a speck of land
【立姿】 lìzī 〈军〉 standing position
【立足】 lìzú ① have a foothold somewhere: 获得～之地 gain a foothold ② base oneself upon: ～于独立自主和自力更生 be based on independence and self-reliance/ ～基层，面向群众 have one's feet firmly planted at the grass roots and keep in view the broad masses of the people
【立足点】 lìzúdiǎn ① foothold; footing: 找不到～ be unable to find a foothold ② standpoint; stand: 把～移到工人阶级这方面来 change one's (class) stand to that of the working class; move one's feet over to the side of the working class

厉 lì ① strict; rigorous: ～禁 strictly forbid ② stern; severe: ～声 in a stern voice ③ (Lì) a surname
【厉兵秣马】 lìbīng-mòmǎ sharpen the weapons and feed the horses — get ready for battle
【厉害】 lìhai 见"利害" lìhai
【厉行】 lìxíng strictly enforce; rigorously enforce; make great efforts to carry out: ～节约 practise strict economy

吏 lì official; mandarin
【吏部】 Lìbù the Ministry of Official Personnel Affairs in feudal China

沥 lì ① drip; trickle: 滴～ patter ② drop: 余～ last drops
【沥涝】 lìlào waterlogging: ～成灾。Waterlogging has caused serious damage.
【沥青】 lìqīng pitch; asphalt; bitumen: 天然～ natural asphalt; natural bitumen
◇ ～混凝土 bituminous concrete; asphalt concrete/ ～基原油 asphalt-base crude oil/ ～路 bituminous road; asphalt road/ ～煤 pitch coal/ ～油毡 asphalt felt/ ～油纸 asphalt paper/ ～铀矿 uraninite
【沥水】 lìshuǐ waterlogging caused by excessive rainfall

丽 lì beautiful: ～人 a beauty/ 风和日～。The wind is gentle and the sun radiant. 或 The weather is glorious.

励 lì encourage
【励磁机】 lìcíjī 〈电〉 exciter
【励精图治】 lì jīng tú zhì (usu. of a feudal ruler) rouse oneself for vigorous efforts to make the country prosperous

利 lì ① sharp: ～刃 a sharp sword or blade/ ～爪 sharp claws ② favourable: 形势对他们不～。The situation is unfavourable to them. ③ advantage; benefit: 有～有弊。There are both advantages and disadvantages. ④ profit; interest: 连本带～ both principal and interest; profit as well as capital ⑤ do good to; benefit: ～己～人 benefit other people as well as oneself/ 毫不～己，专门～人 be utterly devoted to others without any thought of self
【利比里亚】 Lìbǐlǐyà Liberia ◇ ～人 Liberian
【利比亚】 Lìbǐyà Libya ◇ ～人 Libyan
【利弊】 lì-bì advantages and disadvantages; pros and cons: 权衡～ weigh the advantages and disadvantages
【利多卡因】 lìduōkǎyīn 〈药〉 lidocaine
【利福平】 lìfúpíng 〈药〉 rifampin (RFP)
【利害】 lì-hài advantages and disadvantages; gains and losses: 不计～ regardless of gains or losses/ ～冲突 conflict of interests/ 有共同的～关系 have common interests
【利害】 lìhai terrible; formidable: 这几天热得～。It's been terribly hot these few days./ 这着棋十分～。That's a devastating move./ 他这张嘴可～了。He has a sharp tongue./ 给敌人点～ teach the enemy a lesson
【利己主义】 lìjǐzhǔyì egoism
【利令智昏】 lì lìng zhì hūn be blinded by lust for gain
【利率】 lìlǜ 〈经〉 rate of interest; interest rate
【利落】 lìluo ① agile; nimble; dexterous: 动作～ agile movements/ 手脚～ dexterous; deft/ 说话不～ speak slowly and indistinctly ② neat; orderly: 他做事干净～。He is a neat worker. ③ settled; finished: 事情已经办～了。The matter is all settled.
【利眠宁】 lìmiánníng 〈药〉 librium
【利尿】 lìniào 〈医〉 diuresis ◇ ～剂 diuretic
【利器】 lìqì ① sharp weapon ② good tool; efficient instrument
【利钱】 lìqian interest
【利权】 lìquán ① economic rights ② financial power
【利润】 lìrùn profit ◇ ～率 profit margin; profit rate/ ～税 profits tax
【利索】 lìsuo 见"利落"
【利息】 lìxī interest ◇ ～回扣 interest rebate
【利血平】 lìxuèpíng 〈药〉 reserpine
【利益】 lìyì interest; benefit; profit: 为大多数人谋～ work for the interests of the vast majority of people/ 使人民群众得到～ benefit the masses of the people
【利用】 lìyòng ① use; utilize; make use of: ～废料 make use of scrap material; turn scrap material to good account/ 充分～最新科学技术成就 make full use of the latest achievements in science and technology/ 雷锋常～假日为周围群众做好事。On holidays Lei Feng often gave a helping hand to people in the neighbourhood. ② take advantage of; exploit: ～职权 take advantage of one's position and power; exploit one's office/ 受人～ be made use of; be a cat's-paw ◇ ～率 utilization ratio/ ～系数 utilization coefficient; utilization factor
【利诱】 lìyòu lure by promise of gain
【利欲熏心】 lìyù xūn xīn be blinded by greed; be obsessed with the desire for gain; be overcome by covetousness

**呖** lì

【呖呖】 lìlì 〈象〉〔形容鸟类清脆的叫声〕: 莺声～ warbling of the oriole

**戾** lì ① crime; sin ② perverse; unreasonable

**例** lì ① example; instance: 举～ give an example; cite an instance ② precedent: 破～ break all precedents; make an exception/ 援～ quote (或 follow) a precedent ③ case; instance: 患这种病的三十三～中,二十一～有显著好转。Out of the 33 cases of this disease, 21 showed marked progress. ④ rule; regulation: 旧～ an old rule/ 不在此～。That is an exception. ⑤ regular; routine

【例会】 lìhuì regular meeting

【例假】 lìjià ① official holiday; legal holiday ② 〈婉〉 menstrual period; period

【例句】 lìjù illustrative sentence; example sentence

【例如】 lìrú for instance; for example (e.g.); such as

【例题】 lìtí example

【例外】 lìwài exception: 毫无～ without exception

【例行公事】 lìxíng gōngshì ① routine; routine business ② mere formality

【例言】 lìyán introductory remarks; notes on the use of a book

【例语】 lìyǔ illustrative phrase; example word or phrase

【例证】 lìzhèng illustration; example; case in point

【例子】 lìzi example; case; instance

**隶** lì ① be subordinate to; be under ② a person in servitude: 奴～ slave ③ 见"隶书"

【隶书】 lìshū official script, an ancient style of calligraphy current in the Han Dynasty (206 B.C.—A.D. 220), simplified from *xiaozhuan* (小篆)

【隶属】 lìshǔ be subordinate to; be under the jurisdiction or command of: 局部～于全局。The part is subordinate to the whole./ 这支部队～市警备区。This unit is under the command of the municipal garrison.

**枥** lì 〈书〉 manger

**疠** lì pestilence; plague

**疬** lì 见"瘰疬" luǒlì

**栎** lì 〈植〉 oak

**荔** lì

【荔枝】 lìzhī litchi

**俐** lì 见"伶俐" línglì

**郦** Lì a surname

**俪** lì ① pair; couple ② husband and wife; married couple

**莉** lì 见"茉莉" mòlì

**莅** lì 〈书〉 arrive; be present: ～场 be present on the occasion/ ～会 be present at a meeting

【莅临】 lìlín 〈书〉 arrive; be present: 敬请～指导。Your presence and guidance are requested.

**砺** lì 〈书〉 ① whetstone ② whet; sharpen

**鬲** lì 〈考古〉 an ancient cooking tripod with hollow legs

**栗** lì ① 〈植〉 chestnut ② tremble; shudder: 不寒而～ tremble with fear ③ (Lì) a surname

【栗钙土】 lìgàitǔ chestnut soil

【栗色】 lìsè chestnut colour; maroon

【栗子】 lìzi chestnut

**猁** lì 见"猞猁" shēlì

**砾** lì gravel; shingle

【砾石】 lìshí gravel ◇ ～混凝土 gravel concrete/ ～路 gravel road

【砾岩】 lìyán 〈地〉 conglomerate

**粒** lì ① grain; granule; pellet: 砂～儿 grains of sand ② 〈量〉〔用于粒状物〕: 一～米 a grain of rice/ 三～子弹 three bullets/ 每服五～ dosage: 5 pills each time

【粒度】 lìdù 〈矿〉 size

【粒肥】 lìféi 〈简〉(颗粒肥料) granulated fertilizer

【粒选】 lìxuǎn 〈农〉 grain-by-grain seed selection

【粒雪】 lìxuě 〈地〉 firn; *névé*

【粒状】 lìzhuàng granular

【粒子】 lìzǐ 〈物〉 particle: 带电～ charged particle /高能～ energetic particle ◇ ～加速器 particle accelerator

**笠** lì a large bamboo or straw hat with a conical crown and broad brim

**唳** lì cry (of a crane)

**蛎** lì 见"牡蛎" mǔlì

**雳** lì 见"霹雳" pīlì

**痢** lì ① dysentery ② 见"瘌痢" làlì

【痢疾】 lìji dysentery: 阿米巴～ amoebic dysentery/ 细菌性～ bacillary dysentery

【痢特灵】 lìtèlíng 〈药〉 furazolidone

**僳** lì

【僳僳族】 Lìsùzú the Lisu nationality, living in Yunnan

## li

**哩** li 〈方〉〈助〉 ①〔跟"呢"相同,但只用于非疑问句〕: 天还早着～! It's still early. ②〔跟"啦"相同,用于列举事物〕: 历史～,地理～,哲学～,各种参考书都在书架上放着。History, geography, philosophy — you find all sorts of reference books on the shelves.

另见 lǐ

## liǎ

**俩** liǎ 〈口〉 ① two: 咱～ we two; both of us; the two of us/ 这种冰棍儿一毛～。You can get two of these ice-lollies for a *mao*. ② some; several: 给他～钱儿。Give him some money./ 那么多事情,这么～人干不了。There's so much to do that these few people can hardly cope. 或 There's too much work here for so few people.

另见 liǎng

## lián

**连** lián ① link; join; connect: 把零散的土地～成一片 join together scattered pieces of land/ 天～水，水～天。The sky and the water seem to merge./ 这两句话～不起来。The two sentences are disconnected. 或 The two sentences don't hang together. ② in succession; one after another; repeatedly: ～发三封电报 send three telegrams in succession/ ～挫强手 defeat strong opponents one after another/ ～战皆捷 win a series of victories; win battle after battle ③ including: ～你一共十个人。There'll be ten people, including you. ④ 〈军〉 company: ～指导员 company political instructor ⑤ even: ～小孩也参加了抗旱斗争。Even children joined in the battle against the drought. ⑥ (Lián) a surname

【连鬓胡子】 liánbìn húzi full beard

【连茬】 liánchá 〈农〉 continuous cropping

【连词】 liáncí 〈语〉 conjunction

【连带】 liándài related: 人的作风和思想是有～关系的。A person's work style is related to his ideology.

【连…带…】 lián...dài... ①〔表示前后两项包括在一起〕and; as well as: 连老带小一共二十三个人。There are altogether 23, including the old people and children. ②〔表示两种动作差不多同时发生〕and; while: 连说带比划 talking and gesticulating/ 连蹦带跳 hopping and skipping

【连带责任】 liándài zérèn 〈法〉 joint liability

【连裆裤】 liándāngkù ① child's pants with no slit in the seat ②〈方〉〔仅用于〕: 穿～ band together; collude; gang up

【连队】 liánduì 〈军〉 company

【连发】 liánfā 〈军〉 running fire ◇ ～枪 repeating rifle; magazine gun/ ～射击 burst (of fire)/ ～武器 repeating firearms

【连杆】 liángǎn 〈机〉 connecting rod

【连亘】 liángèn 〈书〉 continuous: 山岭～ a continuous stretch of mountains

【连拱坝】 liángǒngbà 〈水〉 multiple-arch dam; multi-arch dam

【连拱桥】 liángǒngqiáo multiple-arch bridge; multi-arch bridge

【连贯】 liánguàn ① link up; piece together; hang together: 长江大桥把南北交通～起来了。The Changjiang bridges link up the communication lines between north and south./ 把各种材料～起来考虑 piece together various kinds of data and ponder over them ② coherent; consistent: 文章写得很不～。This article is rather incoherent. ◇ ～性 coherence; continuity

【连锅端】 lián guō duān remove or destroy lock, stock and barrel: 伪军据点被游击队～了。The puppet troops' stronghold was completely destroyed by the guerrillas.

【连环】 liánhuán chain of rings ◇ ～画 a book (usu. for children) with a story told in pictures; picture-story book/ ～计 a set of interlocking stratagems; series of stratagems

【连击】 liánjī 〈体〉 double hit

【连枷】 liánjiā 〈农〉 flail

【连脚裤】 liánjiǎokù infant's pants with stockings attached

【连接】 liánjiē join; link: 把两条铁路线～起来 link up the two railway lines ◇ ～号 the mark "-", as in "1949-1979"/ ～线 〈乐〉 tie

【连襟】 liánjīn husbands of sisters: 他们是～。Their wives are sisters. 或 They are in-laws.

【连累】 liánlěi implicate; involve; get sb. into trouble

【连连】 liánlián 〈口〉 repeatedly; again and again: ～点头 nod again and again (to show agreement, etc.)

【连忙】 liánmáng promptly; at once: 他～道歉。He hastened to apologize.

【连绵】 liánmián continuous; unbroken; uninterrupted: 阴雨～。There was an unbroken spell of wet weather./ ～起伏的山峦 rolling hills

【连年】 liánnián in successive years; in consecutive years; for years running; for years on end: 战胜～干旱 conquer successive years of drought/ ～丰收 reap rich harvests for many years running/ 产量～上升。Output increases year after year.

【连皮】 liánpí (weight of goods) including the packing; gross (weight): ～三十斤。It weighs 30 *jin*, including the packing. 或 The gross weight is 30 *jin*.

【连篇】 liánpiān ① throughout a piece of writing; page after page: 空话～ pages and pages of empty verbiage ② one article after another; a multitude of articles

【连篇累牍】 liánpiān-lěidú lengthy and tedious; at great length: ～地发表文章 publish one article after another

【连谱号】 liánpǔhào 〈乐〉 accolade; brace

【连翘】 liánqiáo 〈中药〉 the capsule of weeping forsythia (*Forsythia suspensa*)

【连任】 liánrèn be reappointed or reelected consecutively; renew one's term of office: ～党支部书记 be reelected secretary of the Party branch/ ～部长 be reappointed minister

【连日】 liánrì for days on end; day after day: ～来 for the last few days/ ～刮大风。It blew hard for several days running.

【连射】 liánshè 〈军〉 running fire

【连史纸】 liánshǐzhǐ fine paper made from bamboo (produced in Jiangxi Province)

【连锁反应】 liánsuǒ fǎnyìng 〈物〉 chain reaction

【连天】 liántiān ① reaching (或 scraping) the sky: 高峰～ skyscraping peaks ② incessantly: 叫苦～ incessantly complain to high heaven ③ sky-rending: 杀声～ air-rending battle cries/ 炮火～。Gunfire licked the heavens.

【连同】 liántóng together with; along with: 图纸～清单一并送去。Send the blueprints along with the inventory.

【连谓式】 liánwèishì 〈语〉 sentence with consecutive predicates

【连写】 liánxiě joining of syllables in Chinese phonetic transcription, e.g. rénmín (人民), tuōlājī (拖拉机)

【连续】 liánxù continuous; successive; in a row; running: ～作战 continuous fighting; successive battles; consecutive operations/ ～爆破 continuous demolition/ ～十五年丰收 reap bumper harvests for fifteen years in succession/ ～工作八个小时 work eight hours at a stretch/ ～六年未出事故。There have been no accidents for six years running. ◇ ～航次 consecutive voyages/ ～谱〈物〉 continuous spectrum/ ～性 continuity; continuance/ ～铸锭机 continuous casting machine

【连夜】 liányè the same night; that very night: 他们～立起了井架。They got the derrick into place before the night was out.

【连衣裙】 liányīqún a woman's dress

【连阴天】 liányīntiān cloudy or rainy weather for several days running

【连用】 liányòng use consecutively; use together: 这两个词不能～。These two words do not go together.

【连载】 liánzǎi publish in instalments; serialize: 长篇～ serial (of a novel, etc.)

【连长】 liánzhǎng company commander

【连珠】 liánzhū like a chain of pearls or a string of beads —in rapid succession: ～似的机枪声 a continuous rattle of machine-gun fire

【连珠炮】 liánzhūpào continuous firing; drumfire: 说话象～

chatter away like a machine gun/ 象～似地向他提问 bombard him with questions; fire questions at him
【连缀】 liánzhuì ①join together; put together ②〈语〉cluster: 辅音～ consonant cluster
【连字号】 liánzìhào hyphen (-)
【连奏】 liánzòu 〈乐〉 *legato*
【连坐】 liánzuò 〈旧〉 be punished for being related to or friendly with sb. who has committed an offence
【连作】 liánzuò 〈农〉continuous cropping 又作"连种"

**奁** lián a toilet case used by women in ancient China

**帘** lián ① flag as shop sign: 酒～ wineshop sign ② curtain: 窗～ window curtain
【帘布】 liánbù cord fabric (in tyres) 又作"帘子布"
【帘栅管】 liánshānguǎn 〈电〉 screen-grid tube
【帘栅极】 liánshānjí 〈电〉 screen grid
【帘子】 liánzi 〈口〉 (hanging) screen; curtain

**怜** lián ① sympathize with; pity: 同病相～。Fellow sufferers sympathize with each other. ②见"怜爱"
【怜爱】 lián'ài love tenderly; have tender affection for
【怜悯】 liánmǐn pity; take pity on; have compassion for
【怜惜】 liánxī take pity on; have pity for: 决不～恶人。We should never take pity on evil people.
【怜恤】 liánxù 见"怜悯"

**涟** lián 〈书〉 ① ripples ② continual flow (of tears)
【涟漪】 liányī 〈书〉 ripples

**莲** lián 〈植〉 lotus
【莲花】 liánhuā lotus flower; lotus ◇ ～纹 lotus design
【莲蓬】 liánpeng seedpod of the lotus
【莲蓬头】 liánpengtóu shower nozzle
【莲台】 liántái a Buddha's seat in the form of a lotus flower; lotus throne 又作"莲座"
【莲子】 liánzǐ lotus seed

**联** lián ① ally oneself with; unite; join ② antithetical couplet: 春～ Spring Festival couplets
【联邦】 liánbāng federation; union; commonwealth: 英～ the British Commonwealth of Nations
◇ ～调查局 the (U.S.) Federal Bureau of Investigation (FBI)/ ～共和国 federal republic; federated republic/ ～制 federal system; federalism
【联苯胺】 liánběn'àn 〈化〉 benzidine
【联播】 liánbō radio hookup; broadcast over a radio network ◇ ～节目时间 network time
【联大】 Liándà 〈简〉 (联合国大会) the United Nations General Assembly
【联队】 liánduì 〈军〉 wing (of an air force)
【联防】 liánfáng joint defence; joint command of defence forces: 军民～ joint defence by army and militia; army-civilian defence
【联管节】 liánguǎnjié 〈机〉 pipe union; pipe coupling; union joint
【联管箱】 liánguǎnxiāng 〈机〉 header: 汽锅～ boiler header
【联合】 liánhé ① unite; ally: 全世界无产者，～起来! Workers of all countries, unite!/ ～一切可能～的力量 ally oneself with all forces that can be allied with ② alliance; union; coalition: 革命大～ grand revolutionary alliance ③ joint; combined: ～举办 jointly organize or sponsor/ ～进攻 combined attack; concerted attack ④〈生理〉 symphysis: 耻骨～ symphysis pubis
◇ ～兵种 combined arms/ ～采煤机 cutter-loader; combine/ ～词组 coordinative word group/ ～公报 joint *communiqué*/ ～企业 integrated complex/ ～声明 joint statement/ ～收割机 combine (harvester)/ ～行动 joint action; concerted action/ ～宣言 joint declaration/ ～演习 〈军〉 joint manoeuvre; joint exercise/ ～政府 coalition government/ ～作战 combined operation
【联合国】 Liánhéguó the United Nations (U.N.)
◇ ～安全理事会 the United Nations Security Council/ ～大会 the United Nations General Assembly/ ～秘书处 the United Nations Secretariat
【联合会】 liánhéhuì federation; union: 妇女～ women's federation/ 学生～ students' union
【联合王国】 Liánhé Wángguó the United Kingdom
【联欢】 liánhuān have a get-together: 节日～ gala celebrations/ 军民～ get-together of soldiers and civilians
◇ ～会 get-together/ ～节 festival/ ～晚会 (evening) party
【联接】 liánjiē ① 见"连接" liánjiē ②〈宇航〉 mate
【联结】 liánjié bind; tie; join: 共同的革命目标把我们紧紧～在一起。A common revolutionary goal has bound us closely together./ ～两国人民的友谊纽带 the ties of friendship that join the two peoples
【联军】 liánjūn allied forces; united army
【联立方程】 liánlì fāngchéng 〈数〉 simultaneous equations
【联络】 liánluò ① get in touch with; come into contact with: ～感情 make friendly contacts ② contact; liaison
◇ ～部 liaison department/ ～处 liaison office/ ～点 contact point/ ～官 liaison officer/ ～网 liaison net/ ～员 liaison man
【联盟】 liánméng alliance; coalition; league; union: 工农～ alliance of the workers and peasants; worker-peasant alliance/ 地主阶级和大资产阶级的反动～ reactionary coalition of the landlord class and the big bourgeoisie
【联绵词】 liánmiáncí 〈语〉 Chinese words consisting of two characters, often alliterated or rhymed (as 仿佛，逍遥，妯娌) 又作"联绵字"
【联名】 liánmíng jointly signed; jointly: ～发起 jointly initiate; jointly sponsor/ ～上书 submit a joint letter
【联翩】 liánpiān in close succession; together: 浮想～ thoughts thronging one's mind
【联赛】 liánsài 〈体〉 league matches: 足球～ league football matches
【联锁机构】 liánsuǒ jīgòu 〈机〉 interlocking mechanism
【联席会议】 liánxí huìyì joint conference; joint meeting
【联系】 liánxì ① contact; touch; connection; relation: 取得～ get in touch with; establish contact with/ 保持～ keep in contact (或 touch) with/ 有广泛的社会～ have wide social connections/ 巩固党和群众的～ strengthen the ties between the Party and the masses/ 事物的内(外)部～ the internal (external) relations of things ② integrate; relate; link; get in touch with: 理论～实际 integrate theory with practice; apply theory to reality/ 密切～群众 maintain close links with the masses/ 把两件事～起来看就清楚了。Relate the two problems to each other and you'll understand them clearly./ 看电影的问题，找俱乐部～。As for movies, please get in touch with the club.
【联想】 liánxiǎng associate; connect in the mind: 提起杭州，人们就～到西湖。People always associate Hangzhou with the West Lake.
【联运】 liányùn 〈交〉 through transport; through traffic: 国际铁路～ international railway through transport/ 火车汽车～ train-and-bus coordinated transport/ 水陆～ land-and-water coordinated transport; through transport by land and water ◇ ～票 through ticket/ ～提单 through bill of lading
【联轴节】 liánzhóujié 〈机〉 shaft coupling; coupling: 刚性～

rigid coupling/ 挠性～ flexible coupling/ 万向～ universal coupling

【联装炮】 liánzhuāngpào 〈军〉 multiple gun

**裢** lián 见"褡裢" dālian

**廉** lián ①honest and clean ②low-priced; inexpensive; cheap: 价～物美 good and cheap ③(Lián) a surname

【廉耻】 liánchǐ sense of honour; sense of shame

【廉价】 liánjià low-priced; cheap: ～书 a cheap book/ ～买进 buy cheap/ ～出售 sell at a low price; sell cheap ◇ ～部 bargain counter/ ～劳动力 cheap labour/ ～品 cheap goods; bargain

【廉洁】 liánjié honest: ～奉公 be honest in performing one's official duties

**鲢** lián silver carp

**臁** lián 〈生理〉 shank

【臁疮】 liánchuāng 〈中医〉 ulcer on the shank

**镰** lián sickle

【镰刀】 liándāo sickle

【镰鱼】 liányú 〈动〉 Moorish idol

**蠊** lián 见"蜚蠊" fěilián

## liǎn

**敛** liǎn ①hold back; restrain: ～足 hold back from going; check one's steps ②collect: 横征暴～ extort heavy taxes and levies

【敛财】 liǎncái accumulate wealth by unfair means

【敛迹】 liǎnjī temporarily desist from one's evil ways; lie low

【敛容】 liǎnróng 〈书〉 assume a serious expression

**脸** liǎn ① face; countenance: 笑～ a smiling face/ 丢～ lose face/ 不要～ shameless/ 没～见人 too ashamed to face anyone/ 撕破了～ put aside all considerations of face; not spare sb.'s sensibilities ②〈方〉 front: 门～儿 the vicinity of a city gate or the front of a shop

【脸蛋儿】 liǎndànr 〔多用来说年幼的人〕 cheeks; face

【脸红】 liǎnhóng ①blush with shame; blush ②flush with anger; get excited; get worked up

【脸红脖子粗】 liǎn hóng bózi cū get red in the face from anger or excitement; flush with agitation: 争得～ argue excitedly

【脸面】 liǎnmiàn face; self-respect; sb.'s feelings: 看我的～，不要生他的气了。For my sake, don't get angry with him.

【脸盘儿】 liǎnpánr the cast of one's face

【脸盆】 liǎnpén washbasin; washbowl ◇ ～架 washstand

【脸皮】 liǎnpí face; cheek: ～厚 thick-skinned; shameless/ ～薄 thin-skinned; shy; sensitive/ 居然有～说出这种话来 have the cheek (或 nerve) to say such things

【脸谱】 liǎnpǔ types of facial makeup in operas

【脸色】 liǎnsè ① complexion; look: ～红润 a ruddy complexion/ 他这几天～不好。He doesn't look well these days. ② facial expression: 一看他的～，我就知道有了好消息。 I could see from the expression on his face that there was good news./ 奴才看主子的～行事。 The flunkey adjusts his behaviour to his master's expression.

## liàn

**练** liàn ① white silk: 江平如～。The river lies as smooth as silk. ② boil and scour raw silk: ～漂〈纺〉 scouring and bleaching ③ practise; train; drill: ～跑 practise running/ ～字 practise calligraphy/ ～节目 rehearse/ ～单杠 train (或 practise) on the horizontal bar/ ～气功 do breathing exercises/ ～好本领 perfect one's skill/ ～好身体 do exercises to build up one's physique (或 health) ④experienced; skilled; seasoned: 老～ experienced and assured

【练兵】 liànbīng troop training; training ◇ ～场 drill ground; parade ground/ ～项目 training courses

【练操】 liàncāo (of troops, etc.) drill

【练达】 liàndá 〈书〉 experienced and worldly-wise

【练队】 liànduì drill in formation; drill for a parade

【练功】 liàngōng do exercises in gymnastics, *wushu*, acrobatics, etc.; practise one's skill

【练球】 liànqiú practise a ball game: 主队和客队在一起～。The home team and the visitors are practising together./ 赛前～ warm-up (before a match); knockup

【练鹊】 liànquè 〈动〉 long-tailed flycatcher

【练武】 liànwǔ do weapon practice; practise martial arts

【练习】 liànxí ① practise: ～射击 practise marksmanship/ ～写文章 practise writing ② exercise: 做～ do exercises/ 算术～ arithmetic exercises ◇ ～簿 exercise-book/ ～曲 〈乐〉 *étude*/ ～题 problems of an exercise; exercises

**炼** liàn ① smelt; refine: ～铅 smelt lead/ ～糖 refine sugar ② temper (a metal) with fire: 真金不怕火～。True gold does not fear the test of fire.

【炼丹】 liàndān (try to) make pills of immortality (as a Taoist practice)

【炼钢】 liàngāng steelmaking; steel-smelting ◇ ～厂 steel mill; steelworks/ ～工人 steelworker/ ～炉 steelmaking furnace; steel-smelting furnace

【炼焦】 liànjiāo coking ◇ ～厂 coking plant; cokery/ ～炉 coke oven/ ～炉煤气 coke-oven gas/ ～煤 coking coal

【炼金术】 liànjīnshù alchemy

【炼句】 liànjù try to find the best turn of phrase; polish and repolish a sentence

【炼乳】 liànrǔ condensed milk

【炼铁】 liàntiě iron-smelting ◇ ～厂 ironworks/ ～炉 iron-smelting furnace; blast furnace

【炼油】 liànyóu ① oil refining ② extract oil by heat ③ heat edible oil ◇ ～厂 〈石油〉 (oil) refinery

【炼狱】 liànyù 〈天主教〉 purgatory

【炼制】 liànzhì 〈化〉 refine: 石油～ petroleum refining

【炼字】 liànzì cudgel one's brains for the right word; try to find the exact word

**恋** liàn ① love: 初～ be in love for the first time; first love ② long for; feel attached to: ～家 reluctant to be away from home

【恋爱】 liàn'ài love: 谈～ be in love; have a love affair

【恋恋不舍】 liànliàn bù shě be reluctant to part with; hate to see sb. go: 解放军要走了，乡亲们～。The villagers couldn't bear to see the PLA men leave. 或 The villagers hated to see the PLA men go.

**殓** liàn put a body into a coffin; encoffin

**链** liàn ①chain: 铁～ iron chain/ 表～ watch chain ②cable length

【链扳手】 liànbānshǒu chain wrench

【链钩】 liàngōu 〈机〉 chain hook; sling

【链轨】 liànguǐ caterpillar track (of a tractor)

【链锯】 liànjù chain saw

【链轮】 liànlún 〈机〉 sprocket; chain wheel

【链霉素】 liànméisù 〈药〉 streptomycin

【链球】 liànqiú 〈体〉 hammer: 掷～ hammer throw

【链球菌】 liànqiújūn 〈微〉 streptococcus

【链上取代】 liànshàng qǔdài 〈化〉 chain substitution

【链式反应】 liànshì fǎnyìng 〈化〉 chain reaction

【链式磨木机】 liànshì mòmùjī 〈纸〉 caterpillar grinder; chain grinder

【链套】 liàntào 〈自行车〉 chain case

【链条】 liàntiáo ①chain ②〈自行车〉 roller chain; chain

【链烃】 liàntīng 〈化〉 chain hydrocarbon

【链罩】 liànzhào 〈自行车〉 chain guard; chain cover

【链子】 liànzi chain

**楝** liàn

【楝树】 liànshù 〈植〉 chinaberry

## liáng

**良** liáng ①good; fine: ～将 a good general; an able general/ ～工 a skilled worker/ ～马 a fine horse ②good people: 除暴安～ get rid of bullies and bring peace to good people ③〈书〉 very; very much: 获益～多 benefit a great deal

【良材】 liángcái ①good timber ②able person

【良策】 liángcè good plan; sound strategy

【良辰美景】 liángchén-měijǐng beautiful scene on a bright day

【良导体】 liángdǎotǐ 〈物〉 good conductor

【良方】 liángfāng ①effective prescription; good recipe ②good plan; sound strategy

【良好】 liánghǎo good; well: ～的愿望 good intentions/ 自我感觉～ feel fine/ ～的比赛风格 fine sportsmanship/ 为双方会谈创造～的气氛 create a favourable atmosphere for bilateral talks/ 打下～的基础 lay a sound foundation/ 水稻长势～。The rice is coming on splendidly./ 手术经过～。The operation came off well./ 财政贸易情况～。Finance and trade are in a good state.

【良机】 liángjī 〈书〉 good (或 golden) opportunity: 莫失～。Don't let this good opportunity slip.

【良久】 liángjiǔ 〈书〉 a good while; a long time

【良能】 liángnéng 〈哲〉 intuitive ability

【良师益友】 liángshī-yìyǒu good teacher and helpful friend

【良田】 liángtián good farmland; fertile farmland

【良心】 liángxīn conscience: ～上感到不安 have an uneasy conscience/ 说句～话 to be fair; in all fairness/ 有～的人 people with a conscience; good-hearted people/ 没～ conscienceless; ungrateful; heartless

【良药苦口】 liángyào kǔ kǒu good medicine tastes bitter: ～利于病，忠言逆耳利于行。Just as bitter medicine cures sickness, so unpalatable advice benefits conduct.

【良莠不齐】 liáng-yǒu bù qí the good and the bad are intermingled

【良知】 liángzhī 〈哲〉 intuitive knowledge

【良种】 liángzhǒng ①〈农〉 (fine) improved variety: 水稻～ improved varieties of rice ②〈牧〉 fine breed: ～马 a horse of fine breed ◇ ～场 seed multiplication farm

**凉** liáng ①cool; cold: ～风 cool breeze/ 饭～了。The food's got cold. ②discouraged; disappointed: 他一听这消息就～了半截。His heart sank at the news.

另见 liàng

【凉拌】 liángbàn (of food) cold and dressed with sauce ◇ ～生菜 tossed salad/ ～面 cold noodles in sauce

【凉菜】 liángcài cold dish

【凉粉】 liángfěn bean jelly

【凉快】 liángkuai ①nice and cool; pleasantly cool: 这里～，坐下来歇会儿。It's nice and cool here. Let's sit down and have a rest. ②cool oneself; cool off: 咱们到树荫下面去～一下吧！Let's sit in the shade and cool off a bit.

【凉棚】 liángpéng mat-awning; mat shelter

【凉伞】 liángsǎn sunshade; parasol

【凉薯】 liángshǔ 〈方〉 yam bean

【凉爽】 liángshuǎng nice and cool; pleasantly cool: ～的秋天 pleasantly cool autumn days

【凉水】 liángshuǐ ①cold water ②unboiled water

【凉丝丝】 liángsīsī coolish; rather cool; a bit cool

【凉飕飕】 liángsōusōu (of wind) chilly; chill

【凉台】 liángtái balcony; veranda

【凉亭】 liángtíng wayside pavilion; summer house; kiosk

【凉席】 liángxí summer sleeping mat (of woven split bamboo, etc.)

【凉鞋】 liángxié sandals

【凉药】 liángyào 〈中药〉 medicine of a cold nature (for reducing fever or inflammation); antipyretic

**莨** liáng

另见 làng

【莨绸】 liángchóu gambiered Guangdong silk

**梁** liáng ①roof beam: 架～ set a roof beam in place/ 横～ cross beam ②bridge: 桥～ bridge ③ridge: 山～ mountain ridge ④(Liáng) the Liang Dynasty (502-557), one of the Southern Dynasties ⑤(Liáng) a surname

【梁龙】 liánglóng 〈古生物〉 diplodocus

【梁桥】 liángqiáo beam bridge

【梁上君子】 liángshàng jūnzǐ gentleman on the beam—burglar; thief

**椋** liáng

【椋鸟】 liángniǎo starling

**量** liáng measure: ～地 measure land; measure a piece of ground/ 用斗～米 mete out rice with a *dou* measure/ ～身材 take sb.'s measurements/ ～尺寸 take sb.'s measurements/ ～体温 take sb.'s temperature

另见 liàng

【量杯】 liángbēi measuring glass; graduate

【量度】 liángdù measurement

【量规】 liángguī gauge

【量角器】 liángjiǎoqì protractor

【量具】 liángjù measuring tool ◇ ～刃具厂 measuring and cutting tools plant

【量瓶】 liángpíng measuring (或 graduated, volumetric) flask

【量热器】 liángrèqì calorimeter

【量日仪】 liángrìyí 〈天〉 heliometer

【量筒】 liángtǒng graduated (或 volumetric, measuring) cylinder; graduate

【量图仪】 liángtúyí map measurer

【量雪尺】 liángxuěchǐ 〈气〉 snow scale

【量雪器】 liángxuěqì 〈气〉 snow gauge

【量油尺】 liángyóuchǐ 〈机〉 oil dip rod; dipstick

【量雨筒】 liángyǔtǒng 〈气〉precipitation gauge

**粱** liáng 〈书〉①a fine strain of millet ②fine grain; choice food

**粮** liáng ①grain; food; provisions: ～棉双丰收 a bumper harvest of grain and cotton/ 要～有～,要人有人 have both provisions and manpower ready/ 弹尽～绝 run out of ammunition and food ②grain tax paid in kind: 交公～ pay grain tax to the state

【粮仓】 liángcāng granary; barn

【粮草】 liángcǎo army provisions; rations and forage (或 fodder)

【粮店】 liángdiàn grain shop

【粮库】 liángkù grain depot

【粮秣】 liángmò army provisions; rations and forage; grain and fodder: ～被服 grain, fodder, bedding and clothing ◇ ～库 ration depot

【粮票】 liángpiào food coupon; grain coupon

【粮食】 liángshi grain; cereals; food ◇ ～产量 grain yield/ ～储备 grain reserves; grain stock/ ～定量 monthly quota of food grain for an individual/ ～供应 staple food supply/ ～加工 grain processing/ ～局 grain bureau/ ～作物 cereal crops; grain crops

【粮饷】 liángxiǎng 〈旧〉provisions and funds for troops

【粮栈】 liángzhàn wholesale grain store; grain depot

【粮站】 liángzhàn grain distribution station; grain supply centre

## liǎng

**两** liǎng ①〔用于量词和"半"前面,也可用于"千""万""亿"前面〕two: ～匹马 two horses/ ～个半月 two and a half months/ ～千元 two thousand *yuan*/ ～亿二千万 two hundred and twenty million ②both (sides); either (side): ～鬓斑白 greying at the temples/ ～利 benefit both; be good for both sides/ 势不～立 irreconcilably hostile to each other; mutually exclusive/ 革命生产～不误。Carry on both revolution and production without neglecting either. ③a few; some: 我想讲～句。I'd like to say a few words./ 这事过～天再说。Let's leave it for a couple of days. ④*liang*, a unit of weight (＝50 grams) ⑤〈旧〉tael, a unit of weight for silver

【两败俱伤】 liǎng bài jù shāng both sides suffer (或 lose); neither side gains

【两半儿】 liǎngbànr two halves; in half; in two: 碟子摔成～了。The dish is broken in two./ 把苹果切成～ cut an apple in half

【两边】 liǎngbiān ①both sides; both directions; both places: 沟的～种着豆子。Beans were grown on both sides of the ditch./ 人群向～散开。The crowd dispersed in both directions./ 老大娘常常～走动,看望两个孙女儿。Grandma is always going back and forth, visiting her two granddaughters. ②both parties; both sides: ～讨好 try to please both sides/ ～都说好了,明儿下午赛球。The two teams have agreed to play the match tomorrow afternoon.

【两边倒】 liǎngbiāndǎo lean now to one side, now to the other; waver: 墙上一根草,风吹～。A single blade of grass atop the wall sways right and left in the wind.

【两便】 liǎngbiàn be convenient to both; make things easy for both: 您甭等我了,咱们～。Please don't wait for me. That might be more convenient for both of us.

【两参一改三结合】 liǎngcān yīgǎi sānjiéhé 〈简〉(干部参加劳动,工人参加管理,改革不合理的规章制度,工人、干部、技术人员三结合) two participations, one reform, three-way combination (cadre participation in productive labour and worker participation in management; reform of irrational and outmoded rules and regulations; close cooperation among workers, cadres and technicians) 参见"鞍钢宪法" Āngāng xiànfǎ

【两重】 liǎngchóng double; dual; twofold: ～任务 a twofold task/ 新旧社会～天。The old and new societies are two different worlds. ◇ ～性 〈哲〉dual nature; duality

【两次运球】 liǎngcì yùnqiú 〈篮球〉double dribble

【两党制】 liǎngdǎngzhì two-party system; bipartisan system

【两抵】 liǎngdǐ balance or cancel each other: 收支～。Income and expenditure balance each other. 或 The account balances.

【两点论】 liǎngdiǎnlùn 〈哲〉the doctrine that everything has two aspects (in accordance with the Marxist law that "one divides into two")

【两耳不闻窗外事】 liǎng ěr bù wén chuāngwài shì not care what is going on outside one's window—be oblivious of the outside world: ～,一心只读圣贤书 busy oneself in the classics and ignore what is going on beyond one's immediate surroundings

【两分法】 liǎngfēnfǎ application of the Marxist law that "one divides into two": 一个共产党人必须具备对于成绩与缺点、真理与错误这个～的马克思主义辩证思想。A Communist must acquire the Marxist dialectical concept of one dividing into two with regard to achievements and shortcomings, truth and falsehood.

【两回事】 liǎng huí shì two entirely different things; two different matters: 严格要求和求全责备是～。Being strict and being a nit-picker are two entirely different things.

【两极】 liǎngjí ①the two poles of the earth ②〈物〉the two poles (of a magnet or an electric battery)

【两极分化】 liǎngjí fēnhuà ①polarization; division (of a group, society, etc.) into two opposing extremes ②polarize; produce a polarization of

【两脚规】 liǎngjiǎoguī ①compasses ②dividers

【两可】 liǎngkě both will do; either will do: 我去不去～。It's all right with me whether I go or not./ ～之间 not knowing which to choose; maybe, maybe not

【两口子】 liǎngkǒuzi 〈口〉husband and wife; couple: 小～过得挺和美。The young couple get along quite happily. 又作"两口儿"

【两论起家】 liǎng lùn qǐjiā build up (an enterprise) by relying on Chairman Mao's two essays (i.e. *On Practice* and *On Contradiction*) for guidance: 学习大庆油田～的基本经验。Learn from Daqing oilfield's basic experience of relying on Chairman Mao's essays *On Practice* and *On Contradiction* for guidance.

【两码事】 liǎng mǎ shì 见"两回事"

【两面】 liǎngmiàn ①two sides; both sides; two aspects; both aspects: 这张纸～都写满了字。Both sides of the paper were covered with writing./ 问题的～我们都要看到。We should see both aspects of the problem. ②having a dual (或 double) character; dual; double: ～性 dual character/ ～手法 double-faced tactics; double-dealing; double game

【两面光】 liǎngmiànguāng (try to) please both parties

【两面夹攻】 liǎngmiàn jiāgōng make a pincer attack: 受到～ be caught in cross fire; be caught in a pincer attack

【两面派】 liǎngmiànpài double-dealer: ～的行为 double-faced behaviour; double-dealing; act of duplicity

【两面三刀】 liǎngmiàn-sāndāo double-dealing

【两难】 liǎngnán face a difficult choice; be in a dilemma: 进退～ can neither advance nor retreat; be in a dilemma

【两旁】 liǎngpáng both sides; either side: 大街～挤满了欢

迎的人群。The streets were lined with welcoming crowds.

【两栖】 liǎngqī 〈军〉 amphibious
◇ ～部队 amphibious forces; amphibious units/ ～动物 amphibious animal; amphibian/ ～植物 amphibious plant; amphibian/ ～作战 amphibious warfare; amphibious operations/ ～作战舰艇 amphibious (warfare) vessel

【两讫】 liǎngqì 〈商〉 the goods are delivered and the bill is cleared

【两全】 liǎngquán be satisfactory to both parties; have regard for both sides: ～的办法 measures satisfactory to both sides (或 in both respects)

【两全其美】 liǎngquán qí měi satisfy both sides; satisfy rival claims

【两审终审制】 liǎngshěn-zhōngshěnzhì 〈法〉 the system of the court of second instance being the court of last instance

【两世为人】 liǎng shì wéi rén barely escape with one's life; be lucky to have escaped death

【两手】 liǎngshǒu dual tactics: 用革命的～反对反革命的～ use revolutionary dual tactics to combat counterrevolutionary dual tactics/ 作～准备 prepare oneself for both eventualities

【两条道路】 liǎng tiáo dàolù two roads: 社会主义和资本主义～的斗争 struggle between the socialist road and the capitalist road

【两条路线】 liǎng tiáo lùxiàn two lines: ～的斗争 struggle between two lines; two-line struggle

【两条腿走路】 liǎng tiáo tuǐ zǒulù walking on two legs (referring to a series of policies for balancing the relations between industry and agriculture, heavy and light industry, enterprises run by the central government and those run by local authorities, etc.)

【两条心】 liǎng tiáo xīn in fundamental disagreement; not of one mind

【两跳】 liǎngtiào 〈乒乓球〉 double bounce

【两头】 liǎngtóu ① both ends; either end: ～尖 pointed at both ends/ ～儿跑 go back and forth between two places ② both parties; both sides: ～说情 intercede between two parties/ ～为难 find it hard to please either party; find it difficult to satisfy two conflicting demands/ ～落空 fall between two stools

【两头小,中间大】 liǎngtóu xiǎo, zhōngjiān dà small at both ends and big in the middle; a few at each extreme and many in between; a few advanced, a few backward, but the majority middling

【两下里】 liǎngxiàli both parties; both sides: 这办法对集体对个人～都有好处。This practice benefits both the collective and the individual./ ～都没意见。Neither of them has any objection. 又作"两下"

【两下子】 liǎngxiàzi a few tricks of the trade: 要做好工作,光靠这～是不够的。If we are to do good work, we can't rely on just these few tricks of the trade./ 你真有～! You really are smart!

【两相情愿】 liǎng xiāng qíngyuàn both parties are willing

【两厢】 liǎngxiāng ① wing-rooms on either side of a one-storey house ② both sides: 站立～ stand on either side

【两相】 liǎngxiàng 〈电〉 two-phase ◇ ～电动机 two-phase motor

【两小无猜】 liǎng xiǎo wú cāi (of a boy and a girl) be innocent playmates

【两性】 liǎngxìng ① both sexes ② 〈化〉 amphiprotic; amphoteric
◇ ～关系 sexual relations/ ～花 hermaphrodite flower/ ～胶体 〈化〉 amphoteric colloid; ampholytoid/ ～人 bisexual person; hermaphrodite

【两袖清风】 liǎng xiù qīngfēng 〈旧〉 (of an official) have clean hands; remain uncorrupted

【两样】 liǎngyàng different: ～做法,两种结果。Two different methods, two different results./ 有什么～? What's the difference?

【两翼】 liǎngyì 〈军〉 both wings; both flanks ◇ ～包抄 double envelopment

【两用】 liǎngyòng dual purpose ◇ ～炉子 dual-purpose stove/ ～雨衣 reversible raincoat

【两院制】 liǎngyuànzhì two-chamber system; bicameral system; bicameralism

【两造】 liǎngzào ① 〈法〉 both parties in a lawsuit; both plaintiff and defendant ② 〈方〉 two crops: 改一年～为一年三造 change from two crops a year to three

**俩** liǎng 见"伎俩" jìliǎng
另见 liǎ

**魉** liǎng 见"魍魉" wǎngliǎng

## liàng

**亮** liàng ① bright; light: 那个灯泡很～。That electric bulb is very bright./ 天～了。It's light already./ 地板擦得真～。The floor has been scrubbed clean and shiny. ② shine: 屋子里～着灯光。Lights were shining in the room./ 他把手电筒～了一下。He flashed the torch on for a second. ③ loud and clear: 她的嗓子真～。She has a resonant voice./ ～起嗓子 lift one's voice ④ enlightened: 你这一说,我心里头～了。I find what you say most enlightening. ⑤ show: 他把工作证～了一下就进去了。He showed his identity card and went in./ ～思想 lay bare one's innermost thoughts/ ～观点 declare one's position; air one's view

【亮底】 liàngdǐ put one's cards on the table; disclose one's plan, stand, views, etc.: 咱们还有多少储备金,你给大家亮亮底吧。Tell us frankly how much there is left of our reserve funds.

【亮度】 liàngdù 〈物〉 brightness; brilliance: 星的～ the brightness of a star/ 萤光屏～ screen brilliance

【亮光】 liàngguāng light: 一道～ a shaft of light ◇ ～漆 polish lacquer

【亮晶晶】 liàngjīngjīng glittering; sparkling; glistening: ～的星星 glittering stars/ ～的露珠 glistening dewdrops

【亮牌】 liàngpái lay one's cards on the table; have a showdown

【亮儿】 liàngr 〈口〉 light: 远处有一点～。A light gleamed in the distance./ 拿个～来。Bring a light.

【亮私】 liàngsī bare one's selfish thoughts (to have them analysed and criticized): ～不怕丑 unreservedly bare one's selfish thoughts (for analysis and criticism)

【亮堂堂】 liàngtāngtāng brightly lit; well lit; brilliant: 电灯把打麦场照得～的。Electric lights lit up the threshing ground.

【亮堂】 liàngtang ① light; bright: 这屋子又宽敞又～。The room is light and spacious. ② clear; enlightened: 经过反复讨论,大家心里更～了。After repeated discussions, we had a much better understanding of the whole thing.

【亮相】 liàngxiàng ① (of Beijing opera, dancing, etc.) strike a pose on the stage ② declare one's position; state one's views

**凉** liàng make or become cool: 把开水～一～再喝。Let the water cool before you drink it.
另见 liáng

**谅** liàng ① forgive; understand: 本着互～互让的精神 in

the spirit of mutual understanding and mutual accommodation/ 尚希见～。I hope you will excuse me. ② I think; I suppose; I expect: 前信～已收到。I expect you have received my last letter./ ～他也不会这样做。I don't think he'd do that./ ～必如此。I think it must be so. 或 Presumably it is so.

【谅解】 liàngjiě understand; make allowance for: 互相～ mutual understanding/ 达成～ reach an understanding/ 得到群众的～ gain the forgiveness of the masses

**辆** liàng 〈量〉〔用于车〕: 一～公共汽车 a bus/ 三～大车 three carts

**晾** liàng ① dry in the air; air: 草垫子该～一～了。The straw mattress needs to be aired. ② dry in the sun; sun: ～衣服 sun clothes; hang out the washing to dry/ 海滩上～着渔网。Fishnets are spread out on the beach to dry.

【晾干】 liànggān dry by airing: 草药已经～了。The medicinal herbs are dry now.

【晾烟】 liàngyān ① air-curing of tobacco leaves ② air-cured tobacco

【晾衣绳】 liàngyīshéng clothesline

**量** liàng ① capacity: 酒～ capacity for liquor/ 他饭～大。He's a big eater. ② quantity; amount; volume: 保质保～ guarantee both quantity and quality/ 工业产～ the volume of industrial output ③ estimate; measure: ～力 estimate one's own strength or ability (and act accordingly)

另见 liáng

【量变】 liàngbiàn 〈哲〉 quantitative change

【量才录用】 liàng cái lùyòng give sb. work suited to his abilities; assign jobs to people according to their abilities

【量词】 liàngcí 〈语〉 classifier (as 个，只，次，阵); measure word

【量纲】 liànggāng 〈物〉 dimension ◇ ～分析 dimensional analysis

【量力】 liànglì estimate one's own strength or ability (and act accordingly): 不自～ overrate one's ability; overreach oneself

【量力而行】 liànglì ér xíng do what one is capable of; act according to one's capability

【量入为出】 liàng rù wéi chū keep expenditures within the limits of income; live within one's mean

【量体裁衣】 liàng tǐ cái yī cut the garment according to the figure — act according to actual circumstances

【量刑】 liàngxíng 〈法〉 measurement of penalty

【量子】 liàngzǐ 〈物〉 quantum: 光～ light quantum ◇ ～化学 quantum chemistry/ ～力学 quantum mechanics/ ～论 quantum theory/ ～生物学 quantum biology

**踉** liàng

【踉跄】 liàngqiàng stagger: ～而行 stagger along

## liāo

**撩** liāo ① hold up (a curtain, skirt, etc. from the bottom) ② sprinkle (with one's hand): 先～些水再扫地。Sprinkle some water on the floor before sweeping it.

另见 liáo

## liáo

**辽** liáo ① distant; faraway ② (Liáo) the Liao Dynasty (916-1125) ③ (Liáo) short for Liaoning Province

【辽阔】 liáokuò vast; extensive: ～的土地 a vast expanse of land; vast territory/ 青藏高原面积～。The Qinghai-Xizang Plateau covers a vast area.

【辽宁】 Liáoníng Liaoning (Province)

【辽沈战役】 Liáo-Shěn Zhànyì the Liaoxi-Shenyang Campaign (Sept. 12—Nov. 2, 1948), the first of the three decisive campaigns of the War of Liberation

【辽远】 liáoyuǎn distant; faraway: ～的边疆 distant frontier regions

**疗** liáo treat; cure: 治～ treat (a patient); give medical care to/ 诊～ make a diagnosis and give treatment

【疗程】 liáochéng course (或 period) of treatment

【疗法】 liáofǎ therapy; treatment: 化学～ chemotherapy/ 新针～ new acupuncture therapy

【疗效】 liáoxiào curative effect

【疗养】 liáoyǎng recuperate; convalesce ◇ ～院 sanatorium; convalescent hospital (或 home)

**聊** liáo ① merely; just: ～表谢意 just a token of gratitude; just to show my appreciation ② a little; slightly: ～胜于无。It's better than nothing. ③ 〈口〉 chat: 晚饭后咱们～～。Let's have a chat after supper.

【聊备一格】 liáo bèi yī gé may serve as a specimen

【聊且】 liáoqiě tentatively; for the moment

【聊天儿】 liáotiānr 〈口〉 chat

【聊以自慰】 liáo yǐ zì wèi just to console oneself

【聊以卒岁】 liáo yǐ zú suì just to tide over the year

**寥** liáo ① few; scanty: ～～可数 just a sprinkling ② silent; deserted: 寂～ deserted and lonely

【寥廓】 liáokuò boundless; vast: ～的天空 the boundless sky

【寥寥无几】 liáoliáo wú jǐ very few

【寥落】 liáoluò few and far between; sparse; scattered: 疏星～ only a few solitary stars twinkling in the sky

【寥若晨星】 liáo ruò chénxīng as sparse as the morning stars; few and far between

**僚** liáo ① official: 官～ official; bureaucrat ② an associate in office: 同～ colleague

【僚机】 liáojī 〈军〉 ① wing plane; wingman ② wingman

【僚舰】 liáojiàn 〈军〉 consort

【僚属】 liáoshǔ 〈旧〉 officials under someone in authority; subordinates; staff

【僚佐】 liáozuǒ 〈旧〉 assistants in a government office

**寮** liáo small house; hut: 僧～ a monk's cell (或 hut)/ 茶～酒肆 teahouses and wineshops

【寮棚】 liáopéng shed; hut

**撩** liáo ① tease; tantalize ② provoke; stir up

另见 liāo

【撩拨】 liáobō ① tease; banter ② incite; provoke

【撩乱】 liáoluàn 见"缭乱" liáoluàn

**嘹** liáo

【嘹亮】 liáoliàng resonant; loud and clear: 歌声～。The singing is loud and clear./ ～的号角 a clarion call

**獠** liáo

【獠牙】 liáoyá long, sharp, protruding teeth: 青面～ be green-faced and long-toothed; have fiendish features

**缭** liáo ①entangled ②sew with slanting stitches: ～贴边 stitch a hem; hem

【缭乱】 liáoluàn confused; in a turmoil: 心绪～ in a confused state of mind/ 眼花～ be dazzled

【缭绕】 liáorǎo curl up; wind around: 炊烟～ smoke curling up from kitchen chimneys/ 歌声～。The song lingered in the air.

**燎** liáo burn
另见 liǎo

【燎泡】 liáopào blister raised by a burn or scald 又作"燎浆泡"

【燎原】 liáoyuán set the prairie ablaze: ～烈火 a blazing prairie fire/ 革命的烈火已成～之势。The flames of revolution are spreading far and wide.

**鹩** liáo

【鹩哥】 liáogē 〈动〉 hill myna

## liǎo

**了** liǎo ①know clearly; understand: 明～ understand ②end; finish; settle; dispose of: 没完没～ endless/ 未～之事 unfinished task; an unsettled matter/ 好吧！这事儿就这样～啦。All right, so that's that. ③〔放在动词之后，与"得""不"连用，表示可能〕: 办得～ can manage it / 受不～ cannot stand sth./ 你来得～来不～？Will you be able to come? ④〈书〉〔多用于否定〕 entirely: ～无惧色 not show a trace of fear; look completely undaunted
另见 le; liào

【了不得】 liǎobude ①terrific; extraordinary: 一下子歼灭敌人两个师，真～！It's really terrific to have wiped out two enemy divisions at one blow./ 一件～的大事 a matter of the utmost importance/ 高兴得～ extremely happy ②terrible; awful: 可～啦，他昏过去了！Good God! He's fainted./ 危险是有的，但并不是那么～。There was danger, but it wasn't so serious.

【了不起】 liǎobuqǐ amazing; terrific; extraordinary: ～的成就 an amazing achievement/ 反动派总以为自己～，其实不过是纸老虎。The reactionaries always think they are terrific, but in fact they are just paper tigers./ 有些人出了一点力就觉得～。There are people who swell with pride whenever they make some small contribution.

【了得】 liǎode 〔用于句尾，常跟在"还"字后面，表示情况严重〕: 哎呀！这还～！Oh! How outrageous (或 terrible, awful)!/ 过去要是遇到这样的大旱，那还～！How terrible such a drought would have been in the past!

【了结】 liǎojié finish; settle; wind up; bring to an end: ～一场纠纷 settle a dispute; end a conflict

【了解】 liǎojiě ①understand; comprehend: ～事物发展的规律 understand the laws of development of things/ ～会议的重要意义 grasp the significance of the conference/ 增进两国人民之间的～ promote understanding between the two peoples/ 部长对钻井队工人的思想和生活都很～。The minister has an intimate understanding of how the workers of the drilling teams live and work and what they think. ②find out; acquaint oneself with: 我们必须设法～全部情况。We must try to find out about the whole situation./ ～群众的思想动态 find out what the masses are thinking/ ～国内外技术发展状况 keep abreast of current developments in technology at home and abroad

【了局】 liǎojú ①end: 这就是故事的～。This is how the story ends. ②solution; settlement: 拖下去不是个～。Putting things off is no solution.

【了了】 liǎoliǎo 〈书〉 know clearly: 不甚～ not be too clear (about sth.); not know much (about sth.)/ 为仇为友，～分明。It is perfectly clear who are our friends and who are our foes.

【了却】 liǎoquè settle; solve: 这就～了我的一桩心事。That settled a matter which had been weighing on my mind.

【了然】 liǎorán understand; be clear: 一目～ be clear at a glance

【了如指掌】 liǎo rú zhǐ zhǎng know sth. like the palm of one's hand; have sth. at one's fingertips: 他对这一带的地形～。He knows the terrain of this locality like the back of his hand.

【了事】 liǎoshì dispose of a matter; get sth. over: 草草～ get through sth. in a careless or perfunctory way; rush through sth.

**钌** liǎo 〈化〉 ruthenium (Ru)
另见 liào

**蓼** liǎo 〈植〉 knotweed

【蓼蓝】 liǎolán 〈植〉 indigo plant

**潦** liǎo

【潦草】 liǎocǎo ①(of handwriting) hasty and careless; illegible ②sloppy; slovenly: 干活儿～ work in a slipshod way

【潦倒】 liǎodǎo be frustrated: 穷愁～ be penniless and frustrated; be down and out

**燎** liǎo singe
另见 liáo

## liào

**了** liào watch from a height or a distance
另见 le; liǎo

【了望】 liàowàng watch from a height or a distance; keep a lookout: 用望远镜～敌军阵地 look at the enemy's position through field glasses ◇ ～台 observation tower; lookout tower

**尥** liào

【尥蹶子】 liào juězi (of mules, horses, etc.) give a backward kick

**钌** liào
另见 liǎo

【钌铞儿】 liàodiàor hasp and staple

**料** liào ①expect; anticipate: 不出所～ as was expected/ ～定敌军会有行动 anticipate movements on the part of the enemy ②material; stuff: 原～ raw material/ 燃～ fuel/ ～备足了没有？Have we got enough material? ③(grain) feed: 多给牲口加点～。Put more grain in the fodder. ④〔多含贬意〕 makings; stuff: 我不是唱歌的～。I haven't got the makings of a singer./ 他这块～，干不了大事儿。A person like him can't do anything big.

【料车】 liàochē 〈冶〉 skip; skip car

【料到】 liàodào foresee; expect: 没～他会来。We didn't expect him to come./ 我们克服了许多没有～的困难。We overcame many unforeseen difficulties.

【料斗】 liàodǒu 〈冶〉 (charging) hopper

【料酒】 liàojiǔ cooking wine

【料理】 liàolǐ arrange; manage; attend to; take care of: ～家务 manage household affairs/ ～后事 make arrangements for a funeral/ 孩子们已能自己～生活。The children can take care of themselves now.

【料器】 liàoqì 〈工美〉 glassware

【料峭】 liàoqiào 〈书〉 chilly: 春寒～。There is a chill in the air in early spring.

【料事如神】 liào shì rú shén predict like a prophet; foretell with miraculous accuracy

【料想】 liàoxiǎng expect; think; presume: 真是～不到的事情! Who would have thought that would happen!/ 他～领导一定能批准他的请求。He fully expected that the leadership would grant his request.

【料子】 liàozi ① material for making clothes ②〈方〉 woollen fabric: ～裤 trousers made of woollen fabric

**撂** liào 〈口〉 ① put down; leave behind: 听说有急诊,医生～下筷子就走。Hearing that there was an emergency case, the doctor put down his chopsticks and left at once./ 咱们把她～下的活儿干完吧。Let's finish off the work she has left behind. ② throw down; knock down; shoot down: 一枪就～倒一个敌人 hit an enemy soldier with each shot

【撂挑子】 liào tiāozi throw up one's job: 挨了批评就～是不好的。It's bad to throw up one's job just because one's been criticized.

**廖** Liào a surname

**镣** liào fetters

【镣铐】 liàokào fetters and handcuffs; shackles; irons; chains: 戴上～ be shackled; be in chains

## liē

**咧** liē 见"大大咧咧" dàdaliēliē
另见 liě

## liě

**咧** liě
另见 liē

【咧嘴】 liězuǐ grin: 疼得直～ grin with pain/ 他咧着嘴笑。His face broadened into a grin.

## liè

**列** liè ① arrange; line up: 排～成行 arrange in a row or column/ ～队欢迎 line up to welcome sb./ ～出理由 set out one's reasons (for sth.)/ ～表 arrange (facts, figures, etc.) in tables or columns; tabulate/ ～为甲等 be classified as first-rate; be rated as class A ② list; enter in a list: 代表姓名～后。Listed below are the names of the delegates./ ～入议程 be placed on the agenda/ 名～前茅 be among the best of the successful candidates ③ row; file; rank: 站在斗争的最前～ stand in the forefront of the struggle ④〈量〉〔用于成行列的事物〕: 一～火车 a train ⑤ kind; sort: 不在讨论之～ not among the subjects to be discussed ⑥ various; each and every: ～国 various countries

【列兵】 lièbīng 〈军〉 private

【列车】 lièchē train: 直达～ through train/ 国际～ international train/ 上行(下行)～ up (down) train
◇ ～调度员 train dispatcher/ ～时刻表 train schedule; timetable/ ～员 attendant (on a train)/ ～长 head of a train crew

【列当】 lièdāng 〈植〉 broomrape

【列岛】 lièdǎo a chain of islands; archipelago: 澎湖～ the Penghu Islands

【列举】 lièjǔ enumerate; list: ～大量事实 cite numerous facts/ 计划中～了各种具体办法。Various concrete measures were enumerated in the plan.

【列宁主义】 Lièníngzhǔyì Leninism

【列强】 lièqiáng big powers

【列氏温度计】 lièshìwēndùjì 〈物〉 the Réaumur thermometer

【列席】 lièxí attend (a meeting) as a nonvoting delegate ◇ ～代表 delegate without the right to vote; nonvoting delegate

【列支敦士登】 Lièzhīdūnshìdēng Liechtenstein ◇ ～人 Liechtensteiner

【列传】 lièzhuàn biographies (in ancient Chinese history books)

**劣** liè bad; inferior; of low quality: 难分优～ very hard to tell which is better

【劣等】 lièděng of inferior quality; low-grade; poor

【劣根性】 liègēnxìng deep-rooted bad habits

【劣弧】 lièhú 〈数〉 minor arc

【劣迹】 lièjī misdeed; evil doing

【劣马】 lièmǎ ① inferior horse; nag ② vicious horse; fiery steed

【劣绅】 lièshēn evil gentry: 土豪～ local tyrants and evil gentry

【劣势】 lièshì inferior strength or position: 敌军已处于绝对～。The enemy forces were reduced to absolute inferiority.

【劣质】 lièzhì of poor (或 low) quality; inferior: ～煤 inferior coal; faulty coal

【劣种】 lièzhǒng inferior strain (或 breed, stock)

**冽** liè 〈书〉 cold: 凛～ piercingly cold

**洌** liè 〈书〉 (of water or wine) clear

**烈** liè ① strong; violent; intense: ～酒 a strong drink/ ～焰 a roaring blaze; raging flames/ 两霸之间的争夺愈演愈～。The rivalry between the two hegemonist powers is becoming increasingly acute. ② staunch; upright; stern: 刚～ fiery and forthright; upright and unyielding ③ sacrificing oneself for a just cause: 先～ martyr/ 壮～牺牲 die heroically; die a heroic death

【烈度】 lièdù intensity: 地震～ earthquake intensity

【烈风】 lièfēng 〈气〉 strong gale

【烈火】 lièhuǒ raging fire; raging flames: 革命斗争的～越烧越旺。The flames of revolutionary struggles are raging more and more fiercely.

【烈火见真金】 lièhuǒ jiàn zhēnjīn pure gold proves its worth in a blazing fire—people of worth show their mettle during trials and tribulations

【烈日】 lièrì burning sun; scorching sun: ～当空 with the scorching sun directly overhead

【烈士】 lièshì ① martyr: 革命～ revolutionary martyrs ② a person of high endeavour: ～暮年,壮心不已。The heart of a hero in his old age is as stout as ever. 或 A noble-hearted man retains his high aspirations even in old age. ◇ ～纪念碑 a monument to revolutionary martyrs/ ～墓 the grave of a revolutionary martyr

【烈属】 lièshǔ members of a revolutionary martyr's family

【烈性】 lièxìng ① spirited: ～汉子 a man of character ②

strong: ～酒 a strong (或 stiff) drink; hard liquor; spirits/ ～毒药 deadly poison/ ～炸药 high explosive
【烈性子】 lièxìngzi ① fiery disposition ② spitfire

**鴷** liè woodpecker

**捩** liè twist; turn: 转～点 turning point

**猎** liè hunt: ～虎 tiger hunting/ 从事渔～ engage in fishing and hunting
【猎豹】 lièbào 〈动〉 cheetah
【猎场】 lièchǎng hunting ground; hunting field
【猎刀】 lièdāo hunting knife
【猎狗】 liègǒu hunting dog; hound
【猎户】 lièhù hunter; huntsman
【猎户座】 lièhùzuò 〈天〉 Orion
【猎获】 lièhuò capture or kill in hunting; bag: ～两三只野兔 bag a couple of hares/ ～一头幼象 trap a young elephant ◇ ～物 bag
【猎奇】 lièqí hunt for novelty; seek novelty
【猎潜舰艇】 lièqián jiàntǐng 〈军〉 submarine chasers
【猎枪】 lièqiāng shotgun; fowling piece; hunting rifle
【猎取】 lièqǔ ① hunt: 原始社会的人用粗糙的石器～野兽。Primitive man hunted wild animals with crude stone implements. ② pursue; seek; hunt for: ～个人名利 pursue personal fame and gain/ ～廉价的声誉 make a bid for cheap popularity
【猎人】 lièrén hunter; huntsman
【猎手】 lièshǒu hunter
【猎鹰】 lièyīng falcon

**裂** liè split; crack; rend: 分～ split; break up/ ～成两半 be rent in two/ 杯子～了。The cup's cracked./ 他的手冻～了。His hands are chapped by the cold.
【裂变】 lièbiàn 〈原〉 fission: 核～ nuclear fission/ 自发～ spontaneous fission ◇ ～产物 fission product/ ～武器 the fission type of weapon
【裂齿】 lièchǐ 〈动〉 carnassial tooth
【裂缝】 lièfèng rift; crevice; crack; fissure: 墙上的～ crevices in a wall
【裂谷】 liègǔ 〈地〉 rift valley
【裂果】 lièguǒ 〈植〉 dehiscent fruit
【裂痕】 lièhén rift; crack; fissure: 这块玻璃有一道～。There is a crack in the glass./ 通过批评和自我批评,他们之间的～消除了。Through criticism and self-criticism the rift between them was healed.
【裂化】 lièhuà 〈石油〉 cracking: 催化～ catalytic cracking ◇ ～炉 cracking still (或 furnace, heater)/ ～气 cracked gas
【裂解】 lièjiě 〈化〉 splitting decomposition; splitting ◇ ～作用 splitting action
【裂开】 lièkāi split open; rend
【裂口】 lièkǒu ① breach; gap; split ② 〈地〉 vent ◇ ～火山锥 breached cone
【裂片】 lièpiàn 〈植〉 lobe (of a leaf)
【裂纹】 lièwén crackle (on pottery, porcelain, etc.) ◇ ～探测仪 〈冶〉 crack detector
【裂隙】 lièxì crack; crevice; fracture ◇ ～水 crevice water
【裂殖菌】 lièzhíjūn 〈微〉 schizomycete

**趔** liè
【趔趄】 lièqie stagger; reel: 他～着走进屋来。He staggered into the room.

**躐** liè 〈书〉 ① overstep; go beyond; skip over ② trample
【躐等】 lièděng skip over the normal steps: ～求进 try to advance by skipping necessary steps

**鬣** liè mane
【鬣狗】 liègǒu 〈动〉 hyena; striped hyena
【鬣羚】 lièlíng 〈动〉 serow

## lín

**邻** lín ① neighbour: 近～ a close neighbour ② neighbouring; near; adjacent: ～县 a neighbouring county/ ～座 an adjacent seat
【邻邦】 línbāng neighbouring country: 我们两国历来是友好的～。Our two countries have always been good neighbours.
【邻角】 línjiǎo 〈数〉 adjacent angles
【邻接】 línjiē border on; be next to; be contiguous to; adjoin: 西班牙～法国西南部。Spain borders on the southwest of France./ 化肥厂～农机厂。The chemical fertilizer plant adjoins the farm machinery plant.
【邻近】 línjìn near; close to; adjacent to: 我国东部跟朝鲜接壤,跟日本～。In the east, our country adjoins Korea and is close to Japan./ ～没有医院。There's no hospital in the neighbourhood.
【邻居】 línjū neighbour: 隔壁～ a next-door neighbour
【邻里】 línlǐ ① neighbourhood ② people of the neighbourhood; neighbours
【邻舍】 línshè 〈方〉 neighbour
【邻位】 línwèi 〈化〉 ortho-position ◇ ～化合物 ortho-compound

**林** lín ① forest; woods; grove: 松～ pine forest/ 竹～ bamboo grove ② circles: 艺～ art circles ③ forestry. ④ (Lín) a surname
【林产品】 línchǎnpǐn forest products
【林场】 línchǎng forestry centre (including tree nursery, lumber camp, etc.); tree farm
【林带】 líndài forest belt
【林地】 líndì forest land; woodland; timberland
【林分】 línfēn 〈林〉 standing forest; stand
【林冠】 línguān 〈林〉 crown canopy; crown cover
【林海】 línhǎi immense forest
【林垦】 línkěn forestry and land reclamation
【林立】 línlì stand in great numbers (like trees in a forest): 港口樯桅～。There is a forest of masts in the harbour.
【林龄】 línlíng 〈林〉 age of stand
【林木】 línmù ① forest; woods: ～葱郁 densely wooded ② 〈林〉 forest tree
【林檎】 línqín 〈植〉 Chinese pear-leaved crabapple
【林区】 línqū forest zone; forest region; forest
【林业】 línyè forestry ◇ ～工人 forest worker; forester
【林独】 línyì 〈动〉 lynx
【林荫道】 línyīndào boulevard; avenue
【林子】 línzi 〈口〉 woods; grove; forest

**临** lín ① face; overlook: ～街的窗子 a window overlooking the street/ 东～大海 border on the sea in the east/ 如～大敌 as if confronted with a formidable enemy ② arrive; be present: 亲～指导 come personally to give guidance/ 双喜～门。A double blessing has descended upon the house. ③ on the point of; just before; be about to: ～行 on the point of leaving; on the eve of departure/ ～睡 just before going to bed; at bedtime/ ～刑 just be-

fore execution ④ copy (a model of calligraphy or painting): ～画 copy a painting/ ～帖 practise calligraphy after a model
【临本】 línběn copy (of a painting, etc.)
【临别】 línbié at parting; just before parting: ～赠言 words of advice at parting; parting advice/ 作为～纪念 as a parting souvenir
【临产】 línchǎn about to give birth; parturient ◇ ～阵痛 labour pains; birth pangs
【临床】 línchuáng 〈医〉 clinical: 有丰富的～经验 have rich clinical experience
◇ ～表现 clinical manifestation/ ～检查 clinical examination/ ～学 clinical medicine/ ～医生 clinician/ ～应用 clinical practice
【临到】 líndào ① just before; on the point of: ～开会，她还在准备发言。She was still preparing her speech when the meeting began. ② befall; happen to: 这事如果～你的头上，你怎么办？What would you do if it happened to you?
【临机】 línjī 〈书〉 as the occasion requires: ～应变 adapt to changing circumstances; cope with any contingency
【临界】 línjiè 〈物〉 critical
◇ ～体积 critical size/ ～角 critical angle/ ～态 critical state/ ～温度 critical temperature
【临近】 línjìn close to; close on: ～黎明 close on daybreak/ ～太湖的一所疗养院 a sanatorium close by Taihu Lake
【临渴掘井】 lín kě jué jǐng not dig a well until one is thirsty — not make timely preparations
【临了】 línliǎo finally; in the end: 人人都想去，～只好由组长决定。Everyone wanted to go. In the end the group leader had to decide.
【临摹】 línmó copy (a model of calligraphy or painting)
【临盆】 línpén be giving birth to a child; be confined; be in labour
【临氢重整】 línqīngchóngzhěng 〈化〉 hydroforming ◇ ～汽油 hydroformer gasoline
【临时】 línshí ① at the time when sth. happens: 事先作好准备，免得～忙乱。Arrange everything in advance so that you won't be in a rush at the last moment. ② temporary; provisional; for a short time: ～工作人员 a temporary member of the staff/ ～凑合 make do for the moment/ ～办法 a temporary arrangement; makeshift measures
◇ ～代办〈外〉 *chargé d'affaires ad interim*/ ～动议 extempore motion/ ～法庭 provisional court/ ～费用 incidental expenses/ ～工 casual labourer; temporary worker/ ～户口 temporary residence permit/ ～停火 suspension of arms/ ～舞台 makeshift stage/ ～协议 interim agreement; provisional agreement/ ～议程 provisional agenda/ ～证书〈外〉 temporary credentials; temporary papers/ ～政府 provisional government; interim government/ ～主席 interim chairman
【临时抱佛脚】 línshí bào fójiǎo embrace Buddha's feet in one's hour of need; seek help at the last moment; make a frantic last-minute effort
【临死】 línsǐ on one's deathbed: 老队长在～前还惦记着队里的生产。Even on his deathbed, the old brigade leader was still thinking of the brigade's production problems.
【临头】 líntóu befall; happen: 大祸～。Disaster is imminent./ 事到～，我们要冷静。Now that the critical moment has come, we must keep cool.
【临危】 línwēi ① be dying (from illness) ② facing death or deadly peril; in the hour of danger: ～不惧 face danger fearlessly; betray no fear in an hour of danger
【临行】 línxíng before leaving; on departure: ～匆匆，不及告别。I left in such a hurry that I didn't have time to say goodbye.
【临渊羡鱼】 lín yuān xiàn yú stand on the edge of a pool and idly long for fish: ～，不如退而结网。It's better to go back and make a net than to stand by the pond and long for fish — one should take practical steps to achieve one's aims.
【临阵磨枪】 línzhèn mó qiāng sharpen one's spear only before going into battle — start to prepare only at the last moment
【临阵脱逃】 línzhèn tuōtáo desert on the eve of a battle; sneak away at a critical juncture
【临终】 línzhōng approaching one's end; immediately before one's death; on one's deathbed: ～遗言 deathbed testament; last words

**淋** lín pour; drench: 日晒雨～ sun-scorched and rain-drenched; exposed to the elements/ 浑身都～湿了 be drenched from head to foot
另见 lìn
【淋巴】 línbā 〈生理〉 lymph ◇ ～肉瘤 lymphosarcoma/ ～细胞 lymphocyte
【淋巴结】 línbājié 〈生理〉 lymph node (或 gland) ◇ ～炎 lymphnoditis/ ～肿 enlargement of lymph node
【淋漓】 línlí ① dripping wet: 大汗～ dripping with sweat/ 鲜血～ dripping with blood ② (of a piece of writing or a speech) free from inhibition: 痛快～ impassioned and forceful
【淋漓尽致】 línlí jìn zhì incisively and vividly; thoroughly: 刻画得～ portray most vividly/ 揭露得～ make a most telling exposure/ 他这番表演，真可谓～。He put on an act, which showed him up completely.
【淋淋】 línlín dripping: 湿～的衣服 dripping clothes
【淋洗】 línxǐ 〈化纤〉 drip washing
【淋浴】 línyù shower bath; shower

**啉** lín 见"喹啉" kuílín

**琳** lín 〈书〉 beautiful jade
【琳琅】 línláng beautiful jade; gem
【琳琅满目】 línláng mǎnmù a superb collection of beautiful things; a feast for the eyes: 展品～，美不胜收。One is dazzled by the endless array of beautiful exhibits. 或 The exhibition is a feast for the eyes.

**粼** lín
【粼粼】 línlín (of water, stone, etc.) clear; crystalline: ～碧波 clear, blue ripples

**遴** lín
【遴选】 línxuǎn 〈书〉 select sb. for a post; select; choose

**嶙** lín
【嶙峋】 línxún 〈书〉 ① (of mountain rocks, cliffs, etc.) jagged; rugged; craggy: 怪石～ jagged rocks of grotesque shapes ② (of a person) bony; thin

**霖** lín continuous heavy rain: 甘～ good soaking rain; timely rain
【霖雨】 línyǔ continuous heavy rain

**辚** lín
【辚辚】 línlín 〈象〉 rattle: 车～，马萧萧 chariots rattling and horses neighing

**磷** lín 〈化〉 phosphorus (P)
【磷肥】 línféi 〈农〉 phosphate fertilizer

【磷光】 línguāng 〈物〉 phosphorescence ◇ ～体 phosphor
【磷火】 línhuǒ will-o'-the wisp; phosphorescent light
【磷矿粉】 línkuàngfěn 〈农〉 ground phosphate rock
【磷燃烧弹】 línránshāodàn 〈军〉 phosphorous bomb
【磷酸】 línsuān 〈化〉 phosphoric acid ◇ ～铵 ammonium phosphate/ ～盐 phosphate
【磷细菌】 línxìjūn phosphobacteria
【磷脂】 línzhī 〈化〉 phosphatide ◇ ～酸 phosphatidic acid

**鳞** lín ① scale(of fish, etc.) ② like the scales of a fish: 遍体～伤 be covered with bruises or injuries; be a mass of bruises
【鳞次栉比】 líncì-zhìbǐ (of houses, etc.) row upon row of: 码头上新建的仓库～。Row upon row of newly built warehouses line the docks.
【鳞甲】 línjiǎ scale and shell (of reptiles and arthropods)
【鳞茎】 línjīng 〈植〉 bulb
【鳞片】 línpiàn ① scale (of fish, etc.) ② 〈植〉 bud scale
【鳞爪】 línzhǎo 〈书〉 ① scales and nails ② small bits; fragments; odd scraps

**麟** lín 见"麒麟" qílín

## lǐn

**凛** lǐn ① cold ② strict; stern; severe: ～遵 strictly abide by ③ afraid; apprehensive: ～于远行 be afraid of going on a long journey
【凛冽】 lǐnliè piercingly cold
【凛凛】 lǐnlǐn ① cold: 寒风～ a piercing wind ② stern; awe-inspiring: 威风～ majestic-looking; awe-inspiring
【凛然】 lǐnrán stern; awe-inspiring: 正气～ awe-inspiring righteousness/ 态度～ stern in manner

**廪** lǐn 〈书〉 granary: 仓～ granary

**檩** lǐn 〈建〉 purlin
【檩条】 lǐntiáo 〈建〉 purlin

## lìn

**吝** lìn stingy; mean; closefisted
【吝啬】 lìnsè stingy; niggardly; miserly; mean ◇ ～鬼 miser; niggard; skinflint
【吝惜】 lìnxī grudge; stint: 不～自己的力量 spare no effort; stint no effort

**赁** lìn rent; hire: 房屋出～ house to let/ ～费 rent; rental

**淋** lìn strain; filter: 用纱布把药～一下 strain the herbal medicine with a piece of gauze
另见 lín
【淋病】 lìnbìng 〈医〉 gonorrhoea
【淋溶】 lìnróng 〈地〉 leaching ◇ ～层 leached layer

**蔺** lìn ① 见"马蔺" mǎlìn ② (Lìn) a surname

**膦** lìn 〈化〉 phosphine

**躏** lìn 见"蹂躏" róulìn

## līng

**拎** līng 〈方〉 carry; lift: 他～着桶去打水。He was carrying a bucket to fetch water.

## líng

**〇** líng zero: 三～六号 No. 306 (number three-oh-six)/ 一九八～年 1980 (nineteen eighty)

**伶** líng 〈旧〉 actor or actress
【伶仃】 língdīng left alone without help; lonely: 孤苦～ alone and uncared for
【伶俐】 língli clever; bright; quick-witted: 这孩子真～! What a clever child!
【伶牙俐齿】 língyá-lìchǐ have the gift of the gab; have a glib tongue

**灵** líng ① quick; clever; sharp: 耳朵很～ have sharp ears/ 心～手巧 quick-witted and nimble-fingered; clever and deft ② efficacious; effective: ～药 an effective remedy/ 我们试了一下,果然很～。We tried it out and it really worked. ③ spirit; intelligence: 心～ the mind; the soul/ 英～ the spirit of the brave departed ④ fairy; sprite; elf: ～怪 elf; goblin ⑤ (remains) of the deceased; bier: 守～ stand as guards at the bier; keep vigil beside the bier/ ～前摆着花圈。Wreaths were laid in front of the coffin.
【灵便】 língbian ① nimble; agile: 他虽然上了年纪,手脚倒还～。Though getting on in years, he is still nimble./ 老大爷耳朵不～,请你说话大声点。Speak louder, please. Grandpa is hard of hearing. ② easy to handle; handy: 这把钳子使着真～。This pair of pincers is really handy.
【灵车】 língchē hearse
【灵床】 língchuáng bier
【灵丹妙药】 língdān-miàoyào miraculous cure; panacea
【灵感】 línggǎn inspiration
【灵魂】 línghún soul; spirit: ～深处 in one's innermost soul; in the depth of one's soul/ 出卖～ sell one's soul (to the enemy, etc.)
【灵活】 línghuó ① nimble; agile; quick: 手脚～ dexterous and quick in action/ 脑筋～ be quick-witted; have a supple mind ② flexible; elastic: ～机动的战略战术 flexible strategy and tactics ◇ ～性 flexibility; adaptability; mobility
【灵机】 língjī sudden inspiration; brainwave: 她～一动,想出了一个好办法。She had a brainwave and found a good solution.
【灵柩】 língjiù a coffin containing a corpse; bier
【灵猫】 língmāo 〈动〉 civet (cat): 大～ zibet
【灵敏】 língmǐn sensitive; keen; agile; acute: ～的嗅觉 an acute sense of smell/ 这架仪器很～。This instrument is highly sensitive. ◇ ～度 sensitivity
【灵巧】 língqiǎo dexterous; nimble; skilful; ingenious: 一双～的手 a pair of clever hands/ 做得真～。It's really ingeniously made./ 她的体操动作准确而～。Her movements in callisthenics were precise and nimble.
【灵堂】 língtáng mourning hall
【灵通】 língtōng having quick access to information; well-informed: 消息～人士 well-informed sources
【灵性】 língxìng intelligence (of animals): 这匹马很有～,能领会主人的意图。This horse is very intelligent. He can sense what the rider wants.

【灵验】 língyàn ① efficacious; effective: 这种药非常～。This medicine is highly efficacious. ② (of a prediction, etc.) accurate; right: 天气预报果然～。The weather forecast turned out to be accurate.
【灵长目动物】 língzhǎngmù dòngwù primate
【灵芝】 língzhī 〈中药〉 glossy ganoderma (*Ganoderma lucidum*)

**苓** líng 见"茯苓" fúlíng

**囹** líng
【囹圄】 língyǔ 〈书〉 jail; prison: 身人～ be behind prison bars; be thrown into prison

**玲** líng
【玲玲】 línglíng 〈书〉 tinkling of pieces of jade
【玲珑】 línglóng ① (of things) ingeniously and delicately wrought; exquisite: 小巧～ small and exquisite ② (of people) clever and nimble: 娇小～ petite and dainty
【玲珑剔透】 línglóng tītòu exquisitely carved; beautifully wrought: ～的玉石雕刻 exquisitely wrought jade carvings

**瓴** líng 〈书〉 water jar

**凌** líng ① insult: 盛气～人 arrogant and aggressive ② approach: ～晨 before dawn ③ rise high; tower aloft: ～霄 reach the clouds ④〈方〉 ice: 冰～ icicle ⑤ (Líng) a surname
【凌晨】 língchén in the small hours; before dawn: 七月三日～ in the small hours of July 3/ 火车将于明日～四时半到达。The train arrives at half past four tomorrow morning.
【凌迟】 língchí put to death by dismembering the body (a feudal form of capital punishment)
【凌驾】 língjià place oneself above; override: ～一切 overriding; predominant/ 决不能把个人～于党组织之上。One must never place oneself above the Party organization.
【凌空】 língkōng be high up in the air; soar or tower aloft: 铁路桥～飞架两山之间。High up in the air, a railway bridge spans the valley./ 飞机～而过。The plane streaked across the sky.
【凌厉】 línglì swift and fierce: 攻势～ a swift and fierce attack
【凌乱】 língluàn in disorder; in a mess: ～不堪 in a fearful mess; in a state of utter confusion
【凌虐】 língnüè 〈书〉 maltreat; tyrannize over
【凌日】 língrì 〈天〉 transit: 金星～ transit of Venus
【凌辱】 língrǔ insult; humiliate: 受到～ be humiliated; suffer humiliation
【凌霄花】 língxiāohuā 〈植〉 Chinese trumpet creeper (*Campsis grandiflora*)
【凌汛】 língxùn ice run
【凌云】 língyún 〈书〉 reach the clouds; soar to the skies: 壮志～ (cherish) high aspirations

**铃** líng ① bell: 门～ door bell ② anything in the shape of a bell: 哑～ dumbbell ③ boll; bud: 棉～ cotton boll
【铃铛】 língdang small bell
【铃鼓】 línggǔ 〈乐〉 tambourine
【铃兰】 línglán 〈植〉 lily of the valley

**鸰** líng 见"鹡鸰" jílíng

**陵** líng ① hill; mound: ～谷 hills and valleys ② imperial tomb; mausoleum: 中山～ the Sun Yat-sen Mausoleum/ 十三～ the tombs of 13 Ming emperors; the Ming Tombs
【陵墓】 língmù mausoleum; tomb
【陵寝】 língqǐn 〈书〉 emperor's or king's resting place; mausoleum
【陵替】 língtì 〈书〉 ① breakdown of law and order ② decline
【陵夷】 língyí 〈书〉 decline
【陵园】 língyuán tombs surrounded by a park; cemetery: 烈士～ cemetery (或 tombs) of revolutionary martyrs

**羚** líng antelope
【羚牛】 língniú takin
【羚羊】 língyáng antelope; gazelle: 大～ oryx ◇ ～角〈中药〉 antelope's horn

**聆** líng 〈书〉 listen; hear: ～教 hear your words of wisdom
【聆听】 língtīng listen (respectfully)

**菱** líng 〈植〉 ling; water chestnut; water caltrop
【菱角】 língjiao ling; water chestnut; water caltrop
【菱镁矿】 língměikuàng magnesite
【菱铁矿】 língtiěkuàng siderite
【菱锌矿】 língxīnkuàng smithsonite
【菱形】 língxíng rhombus; lozenge ◇ ～队形〈军〉 diamond formation/ ～六面体 rhombohedron

**棂** líng (window) lattice; latticework

**蛉** líng 见"白蛉" báilíng

**翎** líng plume; tail feather; quill: 孔雀～ peacock plumes; peacock feathers
【翎毛】 língmáo ① plume ② a type of classical Chinese painting featuring birds and animals
【翎子】 língzi ① peacock feathers worn at the back of a mandarin's hat ② long pheasant tail feathers worn on warriors' helmets in Chinese operas

**绫** líng a silk fabric resembling satin but thinner; damask silk: ～罗绸缎 silks and satins

**零** líng ① zero sign (0); nought: 五～六号 No. 506 (number five-oh-six)/ ～点～三 0.03 (point nought three) ②〔放在两个数量之间，表示较大的量之下附有较小的量〕: 一年～三天 a year and three days/ 三块～五分 three *yuan* and five *fen* ③ odd; with a little extra: 年纪六十有～ a little more than sixty years old/ 到会人数五百挂～儿。Five hundred odd were present at the meeting. ④ nought; zero; nil: 一减一等于～。One minus one leaves nought (或 zero)./ 我在这方面的知识几乎等于～。My knowledge of the subject is practically nil. ⑤ zero (on a thermometer): 摄氏～下十度 10 degrees below zero centigrade; minus ten degrees centigrade ⑥ fractional; part: 化整为～ break up the whole into parts ⑦ wither and fall: 凋～ withered, fallen and scattered about ⑧〈体〉 nil; love: ～比～ no score; love all/ 上半场的比分是二比～。The score at half-time was two-nil (或 two-nothing).
【零吃】 língchī 〈口〉 between-meal nibble
【零丁】 língdīng 见"伶仃" língdīng
【零度】 língdù zero: 气温降到～。The (atomospheric) temperature has fallen to zero./ ～以下 below zero; sub-zero
【零工】 línggōng ① odd job; short-term hired labour: 打～ do odd jobs ② odd-job man; casual labourer
【零花】 línghuā ① incidental expenses: 你留着这点钱在路上

～吧：Keep this money for incidental expenses on the way. ② pocket money
【零活儿】 línghuór odd jobs
【零件】 língjiàn spare parts; spares
【零乱】 língluàn 见"凌乱" língluàn
【零落】 língluò ① withered and fallen: 草木～ bare trees and withered grass ② decayed: 凄凉～的景象 a desolate scene ③ scattered; sporadic: ～的枪声 sporadic shooting; scattered reports of gunfire
【零卖】 língmài ① retail; sell retail ② sell by the piece or in small quantities: 这些茶具成套出售，不～。These tea things are sold by the set, not separately.
【零七八碎】 língqībāsuì ① scattered and disorderly: ～的东西放满了一屋子。The room is cluttered up with all kinds of things. ② miscellaneous and trifling things; odds and ends: 整天忙些个～儿 fuss over trifles all day long
【零钱】 língqián ① small change: 劳驾，把这十块钱换成～。Please give me small change for this ten-*yuan* note. ② pocket money
【零敲碎打】 língqiāo-suìdǎ do sth. bit by bit, off and on; adopt a piecemeal approach: 把这事一气儿解决了吧，别～了。Let's settle the matter at one stroke, not piecemeal. 或 Let's do this at one go, not bit by bit.
【零散】 língsan scattered: 桌子上～地放着几本书。Several books lie scattered on the desk./ 把～的情况凑到一块儿 piece together scraps of information
【零时】 língshí zero hour
【零食】 língshí between-meal nibbles; snacks: 吃～ nibble between meals
【零售】 língshòu retail; sell retail
◇ ～店 retail shop; retail store/ ～额 turnover (from retail trade)/ ～价格 retail price/ ～网 retail network/ ～总额 total volume of retail sales
【零数】 língshù remainder; fractional amount
【零碎】 língsuì ① scrappy; fragmentary; piecemeal: ～活儿 odd jobs/ ～东西 odds and ends/ 我们收集的材料还是～的。The material we have collected is still fragmentary./ 他每天有很多～事要办。Every day he has all sorts of things to attend to. ② odds and ends; oddments; bits and pieces: 她正在拾掇～儿。She is tidying up the odds and ends.
【零头】 língtóu ① odd: 这个袋子装一百斤，剩下四斤～怎么办？This bag holds 100 *jin*. What shall we do with the odd four *jin*?/ ～不算，我们花了二十元。We spent 20 *yuan*, not counting the small change. ② remnant (of cloth): 一块～布 a remnant
【零星】 língxīng ① fragmentary; odd; piecemeal: ～材料 fragmentary material/ ～土地 odd pieces of land/ 一些零零星星的消息 some odd scraps of news ② scattered; sporadic: ～小雨 occasional drizzles; scattered showers/ ～战斗 sporadic fighting
【零用】 língyòng ① small incidental expenses ② pocket money
◇ ～费 petty cash/ ～钱 pocket money/ ～帐 petty cash book; petty cash account
【零指数】 língzhǐshù 〈数〉 zero exponent
【零族】 língzú 〈化〉 zero group
【零嘴】 língzuǐ 〈方〉 见"零食"

**龄** líng ① age; years: 年～ age/ 高～ advanced in years/ 学～儿童 school-age children ② length of time; duration: 工～ length of service; number of years worked; years of service/ 党～ length of Party membership; Party standing/ 他是一位有二十五年工～的老工人。He is a veteran worker of twenty-five years' standing.

**鲮** líng
【鲮鲤】 línglǐ pangolin
【鲮鱼】 língyú dace

**櫺** líng 见"棂" líng

## lǐng

**令** lǐng 〈量〉 ream (of paper)
另见 lìng

**岭** lǐng ① mountain range: 大(小)兴安～ the Greater (Lesser) Xing'an Mountains ② mountain; ridge: 翻山越～ cross over mountain after mountain/ 崇山峻～ high mountain ridges ③ the Five Ridges
【岭南】 Lǐngnán south of the Five Ridges (the area covering Guangdong and Guangxi)

**领** lǐng ① neck: 引～而望 crane one's neck for a look; eagerly look forward to ② collar; neckband: 把大衣～儿翻起来 turn up one's coat collar/ 尖～儿 V-shaped collar ③ outline; main point: 要～ main points; essentials ④ 〈量〉: 一～席 a mat ⑤ lead; usher: ～兵打仗 lead troops into battle/ 把客人～到餐厅去 usher the guests into the dining hall/ ～我们参观学校 show us round the school ⑥ have jurisdiction over; be in possession of: ～土 territory ⑦ receive; draw; get: ～奖 receive a prize (或 an award)/ ～养老金 draw one's pension/ 学习材料已经～到了。We have already got our study material. ⑧ understand; comprehend; grasp: 心～神会 understand tacitly; readily take a hint
【领班】 lǐngbān 〈旧〉 gaffer; foreman
【领唱】 lǐngchàng ① lead a chorus ② leading singer (of a chorus)
【领带】 lǐngdài necktie; tie ◇ ～扣针 tiepin
【领导】 lǐngdǎo ① lead; exercise leadership: 担任～工作 shoulder the responsibility of leadership; hold a leading position/ 在我国，党是～一切的。In China the Communist Party exercises leadership in everything. ② leadership; leader: 社～ the commune leadership/ 他是我们厂的～。He's a leading cadre of our factory./ 这个错误由我们～上负责。We of the leadership must accept responsibility for this mistake.
◇ ～班子 leading group/ ～方法 method of leadership/ ～干部 leading cadre/ ～骨干 the backbone (或 mainstay, key members) of the leadership/ ～核心 leading nucleus; the core of leadership/ ～机关 leading body/ ～权 leadership; authority; overall control/ ～人 leader/ ～小组 leading group/ ～艺术 the art of leadership/ ～作风 the work style of the leadership
【领道】 lǐngdào 〈口〉 lead the way: 得找个人给我们～。We must find a guide to show us the way.
【领地】 lǐngdì ① manor (of a feudal lord) ② territory
【领队】 lǐngduì ① lead a group: 我们这次拉练谁～？Who's going to lead us on the route march? ② the leader of a group, sports team, etc. ◇ ～机〈军〉 lead aircraft
【领港】 lǐnggǎng ① pilot a ship into or out of a harbour; pilot ② (harbour) pilot
【领海】 lǐnghǎi territorial waters; territorial sea
◇ ～范围 extent of territorial waters/ ～宽度 breadth of the territorial sea/ ～线 boundary line of territorial waters
【领航】 lǐngháng ① navigate; pilot ② navigator; pilot

◇ ～飞机 pathfinder aircraft/ ～设备 navigation equipment/ ～员 navigator

【领会】 lǐnghuì understand; comprehend; grasp: ～文件的精神 grasp the essence of a document/ ～列宁国家学说的实质 master the essence of Lenin's teaching on the state/ 我还没有～你的意思。I still don't see your point.

【领江】 lǐngjiāng ① navigate a ship on a river ② river pilot

【领教】 lǐngjiào ①〈套〉〔用于接受人的教益或欣赏人的表演时〕thanks; much obliged: 你说得很对，～～！ You're quite right. Thanks for your advice. ② ask advice: 你有什么新的看法？我想～～。Have you some new ideas on the subject? If so, I'd very much like to hear them. ③〈讽〉experience; encounter: 他们的伎俩，我们早就～过了。We've had experience of their tricks.

【领结】 lǐngjié bow tie

【领巾】 lǐngjīn scarf; neckerchief: 红～ red scarf (as worn by a Young Pioneer)

【领空】 lǐngkōng territorial sky (或 air); territorial air space

【领口】 lǐngkǒu ① collarband; neckband: 这件毛衣～太小。The neckband of the sweater is too small. ② the place where the two ends of a collar meet

【领扣】 lǐngkòu collar button; collar stud

【领款】 lǐngkuǎn draw money ◇ ～人 payee

【领路】 lǐnglù lead the way

【领略】 lǐnglüè have a taste of; realize; appreciate: ～川菜风味 taste Sichuan dishes/ ～了今日塞外的大好风光 get some idea of how splendid are the sights north of the Great Wall today

【领情】 lǐngqíng feel grateful to sb.; appreciate the kindness: 同志们的好意，我十分～。I'm very grateful to you comrades for your kindness./ 你的心意我～，但是礼物不能收。I appreciate your kindness, but I can't accept your gift.

【领取】 lǐngqǔ draw; receive: ～工资 draw one's pay/ ～办公用品 get stationery for use in the office/ ～出入证 receive one's pass

【领事】 lǐngshì〈外〉 consul: 总～ consul general/ 副～ vice-consul/ 代理～ pro-consul
◇ ～裁判权 consular jurisdiction/ ～处 consular section/ ～馆 consulate/ ～条例 consular act/ ～团 consular corps (c.c.)/ ～委任书 certificate of appointment of consul; consular commission/ ～证书 exequatur

【领受】 lǐngshòu accept (kindness, etc.); receive: 她怀着激动的心情～了同志们的慰问。She was deeply moved by her comrades' comforting words.

【领水】 lǐngshuǐ ① inland waters ② territorial waters ◇ ～员 pilot; navigator

【领头】 lǐngtóu take the lead; be the first to do sth.: 我领个头，大家跟着一起唱吧。I'll lead off, if you comrades will join in./ 队伍由三个举红旗的青年～。At the head of the procession were three young men holding red flags./ ～的一架敌机被打下来了。The leading enemy plane was shot down.

【领土】 lǐngtǔ territory: 保卫国家的～完整 safeguard a country's territorial integrity
◇ ～不可侵犯性 territorial inviolability/ ～扩张 territorial expansion; territorial aggrandizement/ ～要求 territorial claim

【领悟】 lǐngwù comprehend; grasp

【领先】 lǐngxiān be in the lead; lead: 遥遥～ hold a safe lead/ 客队～五分。The visiting team led by five points./ 前半场球赛二比一，上海队～。The score at half-time stood at 2:1 in favour of the Shanghai Team./ 她～登上了山顶。She was the first to reach the top of the hill.

【领衔】 lǐngxián head the list of signers (of a document)

【领袖】 lǐngxiù leader

【领养】 lǐngyǎng adopt (a child)

【领有】 lǐngyǒu possess; own

【领域】 lǐngyù ① territory; domain; realm ② field; sphere; domain; realm: 上层建筑～ the realm of the superstructure/ 社会科学～ the domain of the social sciences/ 意识形态～ the ideological sphere

【领章】 lǐngzhāng collar badge; collar insignia

【领主】 lǐngzhǔ feudal lord; suzerain

【领子】 lǐngzi collar

## lìng

**另** lìng other; another; separate: ～想办法 try to find some other way/ ～有打算 have other plans/ ～搞一套 do what suits oneself; go one's own way/ ～立户头 open another (或 a separate) bank account/ 从一个极端跳到～一个极端 jump from one extreme to another/ ～行安排 make separate arrangements/ 全文～发。The full text will be dispatched separately./ 会议改期，时间～行通知。The meeting is postponed till further notice.

【另册】 lìngcè the other register (as distinct from the regular register 正册), a Qing Dynasty census book for listing disreputable people

【另寄】 lìngjì post separately; post under separate cover 又作"另邮"

【另起炉灶】 lìng qǐ lúzào set up a separate kitchen — make a fresh start; start all over again

【另请高明】 lìng qǐng gāomíng find someone better qualified (than myself)

【另外】 lìngwài in addition; moreover; besides: 咱们大队新买了两台拖拉机，～还买了一台脱粒机。Besides the two tractors, our brigade has bought a thresher./ 我还要跟你谈～一件事情。There's another thing I want to talk over with you.

【另眼相看】 lìng yǎn xiāng kàn ① regard (或 look up to) sb. with special respect ② view sb. in a new, more favourable light; see sb. in a new light

**令** lìng ① command; order; decree: 下～ issue an order/ 法～ laws and decrees ② make; cause: ～人满意 satisfactory; satisfying/ ～人鼓舞 heartening; inspiring; encouraging/ ～人深思 make one ponder; provide food for thought/ ～人作呕 make one sick; nauseating; revolting ③ season: 当～ in season/ 夏～时间 summer time ④ an ancient official title: 县～ county magistrate ⑤〈书〉good; excellent: ～名 good name; reputation ⑥〈敬〉your: ～尊 your father/ ～堂 your mother/ ～爱 your daughter/ ～郎 your son ⑦ drinking game: 行酒～ play a drinking game ⑧ song-poem; short lyric: 十六字～ a short poem set to the tune of *shiliuzi ling* (16-character poem)
另见 lǐng

【令箭】 lìngjiàn an arrow-shaped token of authority used in the army in ancient China

【令箭荷花】 lìngjiàn héhuā〈植〉 nopalxochia

【令行禁止】 lìng xíng jìn zhǐ strict enforcement of orders and prohibitions

**呤** lìng 见"嘌呤" piàolìng

## liū

**溜** liū ① slide; glide: 从山坡上～下来 slide down a

slope ②smooth: ～光 very smooth/ 滑～ slippery ③ sneak off; slip away: ～掉 sneak off; slip away/ 从后门～出去 slip out through the back door ④见"熘" liū
另见 liù

【溜边】 liūbiān 〈口〉 keep to the edge (of a road, river, etc.)

【溜冰】 liūbīng ①skating ②〈方〉 roller-skating ◇ ～场 skating rink

【溜槽】 liūcáo chute

【溜达】 liūda 〈口〉 stroll; saunter; go for a walk: 他在河边来回～。He sauntered up and down the river bank./ 吃完饭出去～～吧。Let's go for a stroll after the meal.

【溜光】 liūguāng 〈方〉 very smooth; sleek; glossy

【溜号】 liūhào 〈方〉 sneak away; slink off

【溜肩膀】 liūjiānbǎng ①sloping shoulders ②〈方〉 lacking a proper sense of responsibility; irresponsible

【溜须拍马】 liūxū-pāimǎ 〈口〉 fawn on; toady to; shamelessly flatter

【溜之大吉】 liū zhī dàjí make oneself scarce; sneak away; slink off

**熘** liū *sauté* (with thick gravy); quick-fry: ～肝尖 liver *sauté*/ ～鱼片 fish slices *sauté*

## liú

**刘** Liú a surname

【刘海儿】 liúhǎir bang; fringe: 她留着～。She wears her hair in bangs.

**浏** liú 〈书〉①(of water) clear; limpid ②(of wind) swift

【浏览】 liúlǎn glance over; skim through; browse: 这本书我只～过一遍。I've only skimmed through (或 glanced over) the book./ ～各种报章杂志 browse among newspapers and magazines

**流** liú ①flow: 江水东～。The river flows east./ 农村人口～入城市 flow of rural population into urban areas/ 伤口～脓。The wound is festering./ ～鼻涕 have a running nose/ ～涎 water at the mouth; slaver; slobber/ ～汗 perspire; sweat/ ～泪 shed tears ②moving from place to place; drifting; wandering: ～民 refugees ③spread; circulate: ～传甚广 spread far and wide ④change for the worse; degenerate: ～于形式 become a mere formality ⑤banish; send into exile ⑥stream of water: 中～ midstream/ 河～ river/ 逆～而上 sail against the current ⑦sth. resembling a stream of water; current: 气～ air current/ 电～ electric current ⑧class; rate; grade: 第一～作品 a first-rate (literary) work/ 考茨基之～ Kautsky and his like (或 ilk)

【流弊】 liúbì corrupt practices; abuses

【流产】 liúchǎn ①〈医〉 abortion; miscarriage: 人工～ induced abortion/ 习惯性～ habitual abortion ②miscarry; fall through: 他的计划～了。His project miscarried.

【流畅】 liúchàng easy and smooth: 文笔～ write with ease and grace/ 这篇文章读起来很～。The essay reads very smoothly.

【流程】 liúchéng ①technological process ②〈矿〉 circuit: 破碎～ crushing circuit/ 浮选～ flotation circuit ◇ ～图 flow chart; flow diagram

【流传】 liúchuán spread; circulate; hand down: 群众中广泛～着这位战斗英雄的事迹。Stories of the combat hero's exploits spread far and wide among the masses./ 古代～下来的寓言 fables handed down from ancient times

【流窜】 liúcuàn flee hither and thither: ～在山区的残匪不久都被消灭了。The remaining bandits who fled to the hills were soon wiped out.

【流弹】 liúdàn stray bullet

【流荡】 liúdàng roam about; rove

【流动】 liúdòng ①flow: 溪水缓缓地～。The brook flowed sluggishly. ②going from place to place; on the move; mobile: 放映队常年在农村～。Film projection teams are always on the move in the countryside.
◇ ～电影放映队 mobile film projection team; mobile cinema team/ ～红旗 mobile red banner (awarded to a team, workshop, etc. for outstanding performance and kept by it until another unit proves more deserving)/ ～货车 shop-on-wheels/ ～基金 circulating fund/ ～人口 floating population/ ～商店 mobile shop/ ～哨 person (或 soldier) on patrol duties; patrol/ ～售书站 mobile bookshop/ ～图书馆 travelling library/ ～性 mobility; fluidity/ ～资本 circulating capital; floating capital

【流毒】 liúdú ①exert a pernicious (或 baneful) influence: ～甚广 exert a widespread pernicious influence ②pernicious influence; baneful influence: 肃清修正主义路线的～ liquidate the pernicious influence of the revisionist line

【流芳百世】 liúfāng bǎishì leave a good name for a hundred generations; leave a reputation which will go down to posterity

【流放】 liúfàng ①banish; send into exile ②float (logs) downstream

【流感】 liúgǎn 〈简〉(流行性感冒) flu

【流光】 liúguāng 〈书〉 time: ～易逝。Time flies.

【流火】 liúhuǒ ①〈方〉 filariasis ②〈中医〉 erysipelas on the leg

【流浸膏】 liújìngāo 〈药〉 liquid extract

【流寇】 liúkòu ①roving bandits ②roving rebel bands

【流浪】 liúlàng roam about; lead a vagrant life: ～街头 roam the streets ◇ ～儿 waif; street urchin/ ～汉 tramp; vagrant

【流离失所】 liúlí shī suǒ become destitute and homeless; be forced to leave home and wander about: 解放前遇到荒年就有千千万万的农民～。Before liberation famine forced thousands upon thousands of peasants to wander about as refugees.

【流利】 liúlì fluent; smooth: 文章写得～。The article reads smoothly./ 她说一口～的英语。She speaks fluent English.

【流里流气】 liúliliúqì rascally

【流连忘返】 liúlián wàng fǎn enjoy oneself so much as to forget to go home; linger on, forgetting to return

【流量】 liúliàng rate of flow; flow; discharge: 管道～ flow of a pipe/ 河道～ discharge of a river/ 渡槽的～为十五至十八秒立方米。The aqueduct has a flow capacity of 15 to 18 cubic metres per second. ◇ ～计 flowmeter

【流露】 liúlù reveal; betray; show unintentionally: 真情的～ a revelation of one's true feelings/ 他的许多诗篇都～出对祖国的热爱。He shows ardent love for his country in many of his poems.

【流落】 liúluò wander about destitute: ～他乡 wander destitute far from home

【流氓】 liúmáng ①rogue; hoodlum; hooligan; gangster ②immoral (或 indecent) behaviour; hooliganism; indecency: 耍～ behave like a hoodlum; take liberties with women; act indecently
◇ ～集团 gang of hooligans (或 hoodlums); criminal gang/ ～无产者 *lumpen*-proletariat/ ～习气 hooliganism/ ～行为 indecent behaviour; hooliganism

【流明】 liúmíng 〈物〉 lumen

【流年】 liúnián 〈书〉 ①fleeting time: 似水～ time passing swiftly like flowing water ②(in fortune-telling) prediction

of a person's luck in a given year: ～不利 an unlucky year
【流派】 liúpài school; sect: 学术～ schools of thought
【流气】 liúqì hooliganism; rascally behaviour
【流沙】 liúshā drift sand; quicksand; shifting sand
【流失】 liúshī run off; be washed away: 水土～ loss of water and erosion of soil; soil erosion/ 黄金储备～ drain on gold reserves/ 堵住管道的漏洞,不让石油～ stop up the leaks in the pipe so that no oil will seep through
【流逝】 liúshì (of time) pass; elapse: 随着时间的～ with the passage of time
【流水】 liúshuǐ ① running water: ～不腐,户枢不蠹。Running water is never stale and a door-hinge never gets worm-eaten. ② turnover (in business)
◇ ～号 serial number/ ～线 assembly line/ ～账 day-to-day account; current account/ ～作业 flow process; assembly line method; conveyer system
【流苏】 liúsū tassels
【流俗】 liúsú 〈贬〉 prevalent custom; current fashion
【流速】 liúsù ①〈机〉 velocity of flow ②〈水〉 current velocity ◇ ～仪〈水〉 current meter
【流体】 liútǐ 〈物〉 fluid
◇ ～动力学 hydrokinetics; hydrodynamics/ ～静力学 hydrostatics/ ～力学 hydromechanics; fluid mechanics/ ～压力计 manometer
【流铁槽】 liútiěcáo 〈冶〉 iron runner
【流通】 liútōng circulate: 空气(货币、商品)～ circulation of air (money, commodities)
◇ ～费用 circulation costs/ ～管〈机〉 runner pipe/ ～货币 currency/ ～券〈旧〉 paper money issued by a provincial bank to be circulated in a given area/ ～手段 medium (或 means) of circulation
【流亡】 liúwáng be forced to leave one's native land; go into exile ◇ ～政府 government-in-exile
【流网】 liúwǎng 〈渔〉 drift net
【流纹岩】 liúwényán 〈地〉 rhyolite
【流线型】 liúxiànxíng streamline: ～汽车 streamlined car
【流星】 liúxīng ①〈天〉 meteor; shooting star ② an ancient weapon, composed of two iron balls fixed on a long iron chain ③〈杂技〉 meteors: 火～ fire-meteors/ 水～ water-meteors
◇ ～尘 meteoric dust/ ～防护〈宇航〉 meteoroid protection/ ～群 meteor stream; meteor swarm/ ～雨 meteor (或 meteoric) shower
【流行】 liúxíng prevalent; popular; fashionable; in vogue: 这是当时～的论调。This argument was prevalent at the time./ 这个民歌在陕北很～。This folk song is very popular in northern Shaanxi.
【流行病】 liúxíngbìng epidemic disease ◇ ～学 epidemiology
【流行性】 liúxíngxìng 〈医〉 epidemic
◇ ～感冒 influenza; flu/ ～脑脊髓膜炎 epidemic cerebrospinal meningitis/ ～腮腺炎 mumps
【流血】 liúxuè bleed; shed blood: 为革命流尽最后一滴血 shed the last drop of one's blood for the revolution/ ～斗争 a sanguinary struggle/ 政治是不～的战争,战争是～的政治。Politics is war without bloodshed while war is politics with bloodshed.
【流言】 liúyán rumour; gossip: 散布～ spread rumours/ ～飞语 rumours and slanders
【流域】 liúyù valley; river basin; drainage area: 黄河～ the Huanghe River valley (或 basin) ◇ ～面积 drainage area
【流渣槽】 liúzhācáo 〈冶〉 slag trough; slag (或 cinder) spout
【流质膳食】 liúzhì shànshí 〈医〉 liquid diet: 半～ semiliquid diet
【流转】 liúzhuǎn ① wander about; roam; be on the move: ～四方 wander up and down the country ② circulation (of goods or capital)

**留** liú ① remain; stay: 你～在原地。Stay where you are./ 会后支部书记～一下。Will Party branch secretaries please remain after the meeting. ② ask sb. to stay; keep sb. where he is: 他们一定要～我们吃午饭。They pressed us to stay for lunch./ 那我就不～你了。In that case I won't keep you any longer. ③ reserve; keep; save: ～座位 reserve a seat for sb./ ～饭 save food for sb./ ～作储备粮 set aside some grain for reserve/ 这本书是我给你～着的。I've kept this book for you. ④ let grow; grow; wear: ～胡子 grow a beard (或 moustache)/ ～小辫儿 wear plaits; wear one's hair in plaits/ ～短头发 wear one's hair short; have short hair; have bobbed hair ⑤ accept; take: 把礼物～下 accept a present ⑥ leave: 给她～个条 leave a note for her/ 这次参观给我们～下了深刻的印象。The visit made a deep impression on us.
【留班】 liúbān 〈口〉 (of pupils, etc.) fail to go up to the next grade; stay down
【留步】 liúbù 〈套〉 don't bother to see me out; don't bother to come any further
【留存】 liúcún ① preserve; keep: 此稿～ keep this copy on file ② remain; be extant
【留党察看】 liúdǎng chákàn be placed on probation within the Party (as an inner-Party disciplinary measure)
【留得青山在,不愁没柴烧】 liúdé qīngshān zài, bù chóu méi chái shāo as long as the green mountains are there, one need not worry about firewood
【留点】 liúdiǎn 〈天〉 stationary point
【留后路】 liú hòulù keep a way open for retreat; leave a way out: 给自己留条后路 leave oneself a way out; leave oneself an option
【留后手】 liú hòushǒu leave room for manoeuvre
【留话】 liúhuà leave a message; leave word
【留级】 liújí (of pupils, etc.) fail to go up to the next grade (或 year); repeat the year's work; stay down
【留局候领】 liújú hòulǐng 〈邮〉 *poste restante*; general delivery
【留空】 liúkòng leave a blank; leave a space in writing
【留兰香】 liúlánxiāng 〈植〉 spearmint
【留恋】 liúliàn ① be reluctant to leave (a place); can't bear to part (from sb. or with sth.): 临毕业时,同学们对学校都十分～。As their graduation day drew near, the students felt reluctant to leave their school. ② recall with nostalgia: ～过去 yearn for the past
【留量】 liúliàng 〈机〉 allowance: 机械加工～ stock allowance
【留门】 liúmén leave a door unlocked or unbolted
【留难】 liúnàn make things difficult for sb.; put obstacles in sb.'s way
【留尼汪】 Liúníwāng Réunion
【留念】 liúniàn accept or keep as a souvenir: 某某同志～ To Comrade so-and-so/ 照相～ have a photo taken as a memento
【留鸟】 liúniǎo 〈动〉 resident (bird)
【留情】 liúqíng show mercy or forgiveness: 对敌人毫不～ show the enemy no mercy; give the enemy no quarter
【留任】 liúrèn retain a post; remain (或 continue) in office
【留神】 liúshén be careful; take care: 过马路要～。Be careful when you cross the street./ ～,汽车来了! Mind the car!
【留声机】 liúshēngjī gramophone; phonograph
【留守】 liúshǒu stay behind to take care of things; stay behind for garrison or liaison duty (after the main force has left) ◇ ～处 rear office/ ～人员 rear personnel
【留宿】 liúsù ① put up a guest for the night ② stay over-

night; put up for the night
【留心】 liúxīn be careful; take care: ～别写错了。Mind you don't write it wrong./ ～听讲 listen attentively to a lecture
【留学】 liúxué study abroad ◇ ～生 student studying abroad; returned student
【留言】 liúyán leave one's comments; leave a message ◇～簿 visitors' book
【留一手】 liú yīshǒu hold back a trick or two (in teaching a trade or skill)
【留意】 liúyì be careful; look out; keep one's eyes open: 这是个细致活,稍不～就会出错。This is a delicate job. If you let your mind wander for a single moment, you'll do it wrong.
【留影】 liúyǐng take a photo as a memento; have a picture taken as a souvenir
【留用】 liúyòng continue to employ; keep on ◇ ～人员 personnel (of the old regime) who were kept on after liberation
【留余地】 liú yúdì allow for unforeseen circumstances; leave some leeway: 咱们订计划时要留有余地。When drawing up a plan, we should allow for unforeseen circumstances.
【留置权】 liúzhìquán 〈法〉 lien
【留种】 liúzhǒng 〈农〉 reserve seed for planting; have seed stock

## 琉 liú
【琉璃】 liúli coloured glaze ◇ ～塔 glazed pagoda/ ～瓦 glazed tile

## 硫 liú 〈化〉 sulphur (S)
【硫代硫酸钠】 liúdàiliúsuānnà 〈化〉 sodium thiosulphate
【硫分】 liúfèn 〈矿〉 sulphur content
【硫华】 liúhuá 〈化〉 sublimed sulphur
【硫化】 liúhuà 〈化〉 vulcanization
◇ ～汞 mercuric sulphide/ ～剂 vulcanized agent; curing agent/ ～染料 sulphur dyes/ ～物 sulphide/ ～橡胶 vulcanized rubber; vulcanizate
【硫磺】 liúhuáng 〈化〉 sulphur ◇ ～泉〈地〉 sulphur spring
又作"硫黄"
【硫苦】 liúkǔ 〈化〉 magnesium sulphate
【硫球群岛】 Liúqiú Qúndǎo the Ryukyu Islands
【硫塑料】 liúsùliào 〈化〉 thioplast
【硫酸】 liúsuān 〈化〉 sulphuric acid
【硫酸盐】 liúsuānyán 〈化〉 sulphate (e.g. 硫酸铜 cupric sulphate)

## 馏 liú 见"蒸馏" zhēngliú
另见 liù
【馏出油】 liúchūyóu 〈石油〉 distillate oil
【馏份】 liúfèn 〈石油〉 fraction; cut: 轻(重)～ light (heavy) fraction (或 cut)

## 榴 liú pomegranate
【榴弹】 liúdàn 〈军〉 high explosive shell ◇ ～炮 howitzer
【榴莲】 liúlián 〈植〉 durian
【榴霰弹】 liúxiàndàn shrapnel; canister (shot)

## 瘤 liú tumour: 毒～ malignant tumour
【瘤胃】 liúwèi 〈动〉 rumen ◇ ～臌胀〈牧〉 bloat
【瘤子】 liúzi 〈口〉 tumour

## 镏 liú
【镏金】 liújīn gold-plating: ～银器 gilded silverware

## 鹠 liú 见"鸺鹠" xiūliú

## 鎏 liú 〈书〉 ① fine gold ② 见"镏金"

# liǔ

## 柳 liǔ ① willow ② (Liǔ) a surname
【柳江人】 Liǔjiāngrén 〈考古〉 Liujiang man, a type of primitive man whose fossilized remains were found in 1958 at Liujiang, Guangxi
【柳琴】 liǔqín a plucked stringed instrument
【柳杉】 liǔshān 〈植〉 cryptomeria
【柳条】 liǔtiáo willow twig; osier; wicker
◇ ～筐 wicker basket/ ～箱 wicker suitcase (或 trunk)/ ～制品 wicker; wickerwork
【柳絮】 liǔxù (willow) catkin
【柳莺】 liǔyīng 〈动〉 willow warbler: 黄腰～ yellow-rumped willow warbler

## 绺 liǔ 〈量〉 tuft; lock; skein: 一～丝线 a skein of silk thread/ 一～头发 a lock (或 tuft, wisp) of hair

# liù

## 六 liù ① six: 棉纺～厂 No. 6 Cotton Textile Mill ② 〈乐〉 a note of the scale in *gongchepu* (工尺谱), corresponding to 5 in numbered musical notation
【六边形】 liùbiānxíng hexagon
【六部】 liùbù the six ministries in feudal China
【六朝】 Liù Cháo the Six Dynasties (222-589), namely, the Wu Dynasty (吴, 222-280), the Eastern Jin Dynasty (东晋, 317-420), the Song Dynasty (宋, 420-479), the Qi Dynasty (齐, 479-502), the Liang Dynasty (梁, 502-557) and the Chen Dynasty (陈, 557-589)
【六畜】 liùchù the six domestic animals (pig, ox, goat, horse, fowl and dog): ～兴旺。The domestic animals are all thriving.
【六分仪】 liùfēnyí 〈天〉 sextant
【六腑】 liùfǔ 〈中医〉 the six hollow organs (gallbladder, stomach, large intestine, small intestine, bladder and *sanjiao* 三焦)
【六级风】 liùjífēng 〈气〉 force 6 wind; strong breeze
【六角车床】 liùjiǎo chēchuáng 〈机〉 turret lathe
【六经辨证】 liùjīng biànzhèng 〈中医〉 analyzing and differentiating febrile diseases in accordance with the theory of six pairs of channels
【六六六】 liùliùliù 〈农〉 BHC (benzene hexachloride)
【六面体】 liùmiàntǐ hexahedron
【六气】 liùqì 〈中医〉 the six factors in nature (wind, cold, summer heat, humidity, dryness and fire)
【六亲】 liùqīn the six relations (father, mother, elder brothers, younger brothers, wife, children); one's kin: ～不认 refuse to have anything to do with all one's relatives and friends
【六神无主】 liù shén wú zhǔ all six vital organs failing to function — in a state of utter stupefaction
【六十四开】 liùshí sì kāi 〈印〉 sixty-fourmo; 64 mo
【六书】 liùshū 〈语〉 the six categories of Chinese characters
【六一国际儿童节】 Liù Yī Guójì Értóngjié International Children's Day (June 1)
【六淫】 liùyín 〈中医〉 the six external factors which cause

diseases; the excessive or untimely working of the six natural factors (wind, cold, summer heat, humidity, dryness and fire)

【六月】 liùyuè ① June ② the sixth month of the lunar year; the sixth moon

**陆** liù six (used for the numeral 六 on cheques, etc. to avoid mistakes or alterations)
另见 lù

**溜** liù ① swift current ② rainwater from the roof ③ roof gutter ④ row: 一～平房 a row of one-storeyed houses ⑤ surroundings; neighbourhood: 这～儿果木树很多。 There are plenty of fruit trees round our way.
另见 liū

【溜子】 liùzi 〈矿〉 scraper-trough conveyer

**碌** liù
另见 lù

【碌碡】 liùzhou 〈农〉 stone roller (for threshing grain, levelling a threshing floor, etc.)

**遛** liù ① saunter; stroll: 出去～～。 Let's go for a stroll. ② fill (a crevice, fissure, etc.)

【遛马】 liùmǎ walk a horse

【遛弯儿】 liùwānr 〈方〉 take a walk; go for a stroll

**馏** liù heat up in a steamer: 把凉馒头～一～ heat up the cold steamed bread
另见 liú

**鹨** liù 〈动〉 pipit: 树～ tree pipit/ 田～ paddy-field pipit

## lo

**咯** lo 〈助〉〔用于句末, 语气比"了" (le) 较重〕: 当然～ of course; needless to say
另见 gē; kǎ; luò

## lōng

**隆** lōng 见"黑咕隆咚" hēigulōngdōng
另见 lóng

## lóng

**龙** lóng ① dragon ② imperial: ～袍 imperial robe ③ a huge extinct reptile: 恐～ dinosaur ④ (Lóng) a surname

【龙船】 lóngchuán dragon boat

【龙胆】 lóngdǎn 〈植〉 rough gentian (*Gentiana scabra*) ◇ ～紫 〈药〉 gentian violet

【龙灯】 lóngdēng dragon lantern

【龙飞凤舞】 lóngfēi-fèngwǔ like dragons flying and phoenixes dancing — lively and vigorous flourishes in calligraphy

【龙骨】 lónggǔ ① a bird's sternum ② 〈中药〉 fossil fragments ③ keel

【龙骨车】 lónggǔchē dragon-bone water lift; square-pallet chain-pump

【龙睛鱼】 lóngjīngyú 〈动〉 dragon-eyes (a species of goldfish with prominent eyes and a large tail)

【龙井】 lóngjǐng *longjing*, a famous green tea produced in Hangzhou; Dragon Well tea

【龙卷】 lóngjuǎn 〈气〉 spout

【龙卷风】 lóngjuǎnfēng tornado

【龙口夺粮】 lóngkǒu duó liáng snatch food from the dragon's mouth — speed up the summer harvesting before the storm breaks

【龙葵】 lóngkuí 〈植〉 black nightshade

【龙门刨床】 lóngmén bàochuáng 〈机〉 double housing planer

【龙门起重机】 lóngmén qǐzhòngjī 〈机〉 gantry crane

【龙门石窟】 Lóngmén Shíkū the Longmen Grottoes (in Luoyang)

【龙门铣床】 lóngmén xǐchuáng 〈机〉 planer-type milling machine

【龙脑】 lóngnǎo 〈化〉 borneol; borneo camphor

【龙盘虎踞】 lóngpán-hǔjù like a coiling dragon and crouching tiger — a forbidding strategic point

【龙山文化】 Lóngshān wénhuà 〈考古〉 the Longshan Culture (of the Chalcolithic period 4,000 years ago, relics of which were first unearthed in Longshan, Shandong Province, in 1928)

【龙舌兰】 lóngshélán 〈植〉 century plant

【龙虱】 lóngshī 〈动〉 predacious diving beetle

【龙潭虎穴】 lóngtán-hǔxué dragon's pool and tiger's den — a danger spot

【龙套】 lóngtào actor playing a walk-on part in old-style opera; utility man: 跑～ be a utility man in a theatrical show; play a bit role

【龙腾虎跃】 lóngténg-hǔyuè dragons rising and tigers leaping — a scene of bustling activity: ～闹春耕 set about the spring ploughing with vigour and enthusiasm

【龙头】 lóngtóu ① tap; faucet; cock ② 〈方〉 handlebar (of a bicycle)

【龙头鱼】 lóngtóuyú 〈动〉 Bombay duck

【龙王】 Lóngwáng the Dragon King (the God of Rain in Chinese mythology)

【龙虾】 lóngxiā lobster

【龙涎香】 lóngxiánxiāng ambergris

【龙须草】 lóngxūcǎo 〈植〉 Chinese alpine rush (*Eulaliopsis binata*)

【龙牙草】 lóngyácǎo 〈植〉 hairyvein agrimony (*Agrimonia pilosa*)

【龙眼】 lóngyǎn 〈植〉 longan

【龙爪槐】 lóngzhǎohuái Chinese pagoda tree

【龙争虎斗】 lóngzhēng-hǔdòu a fierce struggle between two evenly-matched opponents

【龙钟】 lóngzhōng 〈书〉 decrepit; senile: 老态～ senile; doddering

【龙舟】 lóngzhōu dragon boat: ～竞渡 dragon-boat regatta; dragon-boat race

**茏** lóng

【茏葱】 lóngcōng verdant; luxuriantly green

**咙** lóng 见"喉咙" hóulóng

**珑** lóng 见"玲珑" línglóng

**昽** lóng 见"曚昽" ménglóng

**栊** lóng 〈书〉 ① window ② cage

**胧** lóng 见"朦胧" ménglóng

**眬** lóng 见"矇眬" ménglóng

**砻** lóng ① rice huller ② hull (rice)

【砻谷机】 lónggǔjī 〈农〉 rice huller

【砻糠】 lóngkāng rice chaff

**聋** lóng deaf; hard of hearing

【聋哑】 lóngyǎ deaf and dumb; deaf-mute ◇ ~人 deaf-mute/ ~学校 school for deaf-mutes/ ~症 deaf-mutism

【聋子】 lóngzi a deaf person

**笼** lóng ① cage; coop: 鸟~ birdcage/ 鸡~ chicken coop ② basket; container ③ (food) steamer: 刚出~的肉包子 meat-filled buns fresh from the food steamer ④ 〈方〉 put each hand in the opposite sleeve
另见 lǒng

【笼火】 lónghuǒ 〈方〉 light a coal fire with firewood; make a fire

【笼鸟】 lóngniǎo cage bird

【笼屉】 lóngtì bamboo or wooden utensil for steaming food; food steamer

【笼头】 lóngtou headstall; halter

【笼子】 lóngzi ① cage; coop ② basket; container
另见 lǒngzi

**隆** lóng ① grand ② prosperous; thriving ③ intense; deep: ~情厚谊 profound sentiments of friendship ④ swell; bulge: 他碰得前额~起一个大包。He got a bad bump on his forehead.
另见 lōng

【隆冬】 lóngdōng midwinter; the depth of winter

【隆隆】 lónglóng 〈象〉 rumble: 雷声(炮声)~ the rumble of thunder (gunfire)

【隆头鱼】 lóngtóuyú 〈动〉 wrasse

【隆重】 lóngzhòng grand; solemn; ceremonious: ~的典礼 a grand ceremony/ 受到~的接待 be accorded a grand reception; be given a red carpet reception/ 代表大会于昨日~开幕。The congress was solemnly opened yesterday.

**癃** lóng ① 〈书〉 infirmity ② bent with age; hunchbacked ③ 见"癃闭"

【癃闭】 lóngbì 〈中医〉 retention of urine; difficulty in urination

**窿** lóng 见"窟窿" kūlong

## lǒng

**陇** Lǒng another name for Gansu Province

**垄** lǒng ① ridge (in a field): 土改前我家房无一间,地无一~。Before the land reform my family hadn't a single room or a strip of land. ② raised path between fields

【垄断】 lǒngduàn monopolize: ~市场 monopolize (或 corner) the market/ 帝国主义最深厚的经济基础就是~。The deepest economic foundation of imperialism is monopoly. ◇ ~集团 monopoly group/ ~价格 monopoly price/ ~利润 monopolist profits/ ~资本 monopoly capital/ ~资本主义 monopoly capitalism/ ~资产阶级 monopoly capitalist class

【垄沟】 lǒnggōu field ditch; furrow

【垄作】 lǒngzuò 〈农〉 ridge culture

**拢** lǒng ① approach; reach: ~岸 come alongside the shore ② add up; sum up: 把帐~一~ sum up the accounts ③ hold (或 gather) together: 用绳子把柴火~住 tie the firewood in a bundle ④ comb (hair)

【拢共】 lǒnggòng altogether; all told; in all

【拢子】 lǒngzi a fine-toothed comb

**笼** lǒng ① envelop; cover: 烟~雾罩 be enveloped (或 hidden) in mist ② a large box or chest; trunk
另见 lóng

【笼络】 lǒngluò win sb. over by any means; draw over; rope in: ~人心 try to win people's support by hook or by crook

【笼统】 lǒngtǒng general; sweeping: 他的话说得很~。He spoke in very general terms./ 这么说未免太~了。That statement is rather too sweeping.

【笼罩】 lǒngzhào envelop; shroud: 晨雾~在湖面上。The lake is shrouded in morning mist.

【笼子】 lǒngzi a large box or chest; trunk
另见 lóngzi

## lòng

**弄** lòng 〈方〉 lane; alley; alleyway
另见 nòng

【弄堂】 lòngtáng 〈方〉 lane; alley; alleyway

## lōu

**搂** lōu ① gather up; rake together: ~柴火 rake up twigs, dead leaves, etc. (for fuel) ② hold up; tuck up: ~起袖子 tuck up one's sleeves ③ squeeze (money); extort: ~钱 extort money ④ 〈方〉 pull: ~扳机 pull a trigger
另见 lǒu

【搂草机】 lōucǎojī 〈农〉 rake

## lóu

**娄** Lóu a surname

【娄子】 lóuzi trouble; blunder: 捅~ make a blunder; get into trouble

**偻** lóu 见"佝偻病" gōulóubìng
另见 lǚ

【偻㑩】 lóuluo 见"喽罗" lóuluo

**喽** lóu
另见 lou

【喽罗】 lóuluo ① the rank and file of a band of outlaws ② underling; lackey

**楼** lóu ① a storied building: 办公~ office building ② storey; floor: 一~ (英) ground floor; (美) first floor/ 二~ (英) first floor; (美) second floor ③ superstructure: 城~ city-gate tower ④ (Lóu) a surname

【楼板】 lóubǎn floor; floorslab

【楼道】 lóudào corridor; passageway

【楼房】 lóufáng a building of two or more storeys

【楼面】 lóumiàn 〈建〉 floor ◇ ~面积 floor area

【楼上】 lóushàng upstairs: ~住的是一位退休老工人。A retired worker lives upstairs.

【楼台】 lóutái ① a high building; tower ② 〈方〉 balcony

【楼梯】 lóutī stairs; staircase ◇ ~平台 landing (of stairs)

【楼下】 lóuxià downstairs: ~的房间 a downstairs room; a room on the floor below

**蝼** lóu

【蝼蛄】 lóugū mole cricket
【蝼蚁】 lóuyǐ mole crickets and ants—nobodies; nonentities

**耧** lóu an animal-drawn seed plough; drill barrow; drill

**髅** lóu 见"髑髅" dúlóu; "骷髅" kūlóu

## lǒu

**搂** lǒu hold in one's arms; hug; embrace
另见 lōu
【搂抱】 lǒubào hug; embrace; cuddle

**篓** lǒu basket: 字纸～ wastepaper basket; wastebasket
【篓子】 lǒuzi basket

## lòu

**陋** lòu ①plain; ugly: 丑～ ugly ②humble; mean: ～室 a humble room/ ～巷 a mean alley ③vulgar; corrupt; undesirable: ～习 corrupt customs; bad habits ④(of knowledge) scanty; limited; shallow: 浅～ shallow; superficial
【陋规】 lòuguī objectionable practices
【陋俗】 lòusú undesirable customs
【陋习】 lòuxí corrupt customs; bad habits

**漏** lòu ①leak: 水壶～了。The kettle leaks./ ～雨了。The rain is leaking in./ 那个管子～煤气。That gas pipe leaks. ②water clock; hourglass: ～尽更残。The night is waning. ③divulge; leak: 走～消息 leak information ④be missing; leave out: ～了一行。A line is missing./ 这一项可千万不能～掉。Be sure not to leave out this item.
【漏报】 lòubào fail to report sth.; fail to declare (dutiable goods)
【漏疮】 lòuchuāng anal fistula
【漏电】 lòudiàn leakage of electricity
【漏洞】 lòudòng ①leak: 检查一下管道有没有～ check and see if there is any leak in the pipe ②flaw; hole; loophole: 他的话前后矛盾,～百出。What he says is inconsistent and full of holes./ 严格制度,堵塞～ tighten the rules and stop up all loopholes
【漏斗】 lòudǒu funnel
【漏风】 lòufēng ①air leak: 这个风箱～。This bellows is not airtight. ②speak indistinctly through having one or more front teeth missing ③(of information, secrets) leak out
【漏光】 lòuguāng light leak: 这个照相机～。The camera has a light leak.
【漏壶】 lòuhú water clock; clepsydra; hourglass
【漏划】 lòuhuà escape being classified as a landlord or rich peasant, etc.: ～地主 a landlord who escaped being classified as such
【漏勺】 lòusháo strainer; colander
【漏税】 lòushuì evade payment of a tax; evade taxation
【漏网】 lòuwǎng slip through the net; escape unpunished: 四面包围敌人,力求全歼,不使～。Encircle the enemy forces completely, strive to wipe them out thoroughly and do not let any escape from the net.
【漏子】 lòuzi ①〈口〉funnel ②flaw; hole; loophole

**瘘** lòu fistula
【瘘管】 lòuguǎn 〈医〉 fistula

**镂** lòu engrave; carve
【镂花】 lòuhuā 〈工美〉 ornamental engraving
【镂刻】 lòukè engrave; carve
【镂空】 lòukōng 〈工美〉 hollow out: ～的象牙球 hollowed-out ivory ball

**露** lòu 〈口〉 reveal; show
另见 lù
【露脸】 lòuliǎn look good as a result of receiving honour or praise
【露马脚】 lòu mǎjiao give oneself away; let the cat out of the bag
【露面】 lòumiàn show one's face; make (或 put in) an appearance; appear or reappear on public occasions
【露怯】 lòuqiè 〈方〉 display one's ignorance; make a fool of oneself
【露头】 lòutóu ①show one's head ②appear; emerge: 太阳刚～,我们就起来了。The sun had hardly appeared when we got up.
另见 lùtóu
【露馅儿】 lòuxiànr let the cat out of the bag; give the game away; spill the beans: 别再保密了,你的话已经～了。Don't try to keep it a secret any longer. You've already given the game away.
【露一手】 lòu yīshǒu make an exhibition of one's abilities or skills; show off

## lou

**喽** lou 〈助〉 ①〔用于预期的或假设的动作〕: 我吃～饭就走。I'll go as soon as I've eaten./ 他知道～一定很高兴。I'm sure he'll be glad to hear it. ②〔带有提醒注意的语气〕: 起床～。Look, it's time to get up.
另见 lóu

## lū

**噜** lū 见"咕噜" gūlū

## lú

**卢** Lú a surname
【卢比】 lúbǐ rupee
【卢布】 lúbù rouble
【卢森堡】 Lúsēnbǎo Luxembourg ◇～人 Luxembourger
【卢旺达】 Lúwàngdá Rwanda ◇～人 Rwandese

**庐** lú hut; cottage
【庐山真面目】 Lúshān zhēnmiànmù what Lushan Mountain really looks like—the truth about a person or a matter
【庐舍】 lúshè 〈书〉 house; farmhouse

**芦** lú 〈植〉 reed
另见 lǔ
【芦丁】 lúdīng 〈药〉 rutin
【芦根】 lúgēn 〈中药〉 reed rhizome
【芦沟桥事变】 Lúgōuqiáo Shìbiàn the Lugouqiao Incident, the incident staged at Lugouqiao near Beiping (now Beijing) on July 7, 1937 by the Japanese imperialists in their attempt to annex the whole of China, which marked the beginning of their all-out war of aggression against China
【芦花】 lúhuā reed catkins
【芦荟】 lúhuì 〈植〉 aloe
【芦笙】 lúshēng a reed-pipe wind instrument, used by the

Miao, Yao and Dong nationalities
【芦笋】 lúsǔn 〈植〉 asparagus
【芦苇】 lúwěi reed ◇ ～荡 reed marshes
【芦席】 lúxí reed mat

**炉** lú ① stove; furnace: 围～烤火 sit round a fire to get warm ② 〈量〉 heat: 一～钢 a heat of steel
【炉箅子】 lúbìzi grate
【炉衬】 lúchèn 〈冶〉 (furnace) lining ◇～寿命 lining durability
【炉顶】 lúdǐng 〈冶〉 furnace top; furnace roof
【炉甘石】 lúgānshí 〈中药〉 calamine
【炉火纯青】 lúhuǒ chúnqīng pure blue flame—high degree of technical or professional proficiency: 他的山水画达到了～的地步。He attained perfection in landscape painting.
【炉料】 lúliào 〈冶〉 furnace charge; furnace burden
【炉龄】 lúlíng 〈冶〉 furnace life
【炉盘】 lúpán stone or metal plate for standing a stove on as a precaution against fire
【炉前工】 lúqiángōng 〈冶〉 blast-furnace man; furnaceman
【炉身】 lúshēn 〈冶〉 (furnace) shaft; furnace stack
【炉膛】 lútáng the chamber of a stove or furnace
【炉条】 lútiáo fire bars; grate
【炉温】 lúwēn 〈冶〉 furnace temperature
【炉灶】 lúzào kitchen range; cooking range: 另起～ make a fresh start
【炉渣】 lúzhā slag; cinder
【炉子】 lúzi stove; oven; furnace

**胪** lú 〈书〉 set out; display; exhibit
【胪陈】 lúchén 〈书〉 narrate in detail; state
【胪列】 lúliè 〈书〉 enumerate; list

**栌** lú 见"黄栌" huánglú

**轳** lú 见"辘轳" lùlu

**鸬** lú
【鸬鹚】 lúcí cormorant

**铲** lú 〈化〉 rutherfordium (Rf)

**颅** lú cranium; skull
【颅骨】 lúgǔ 〈生理〉 skull
【颅腔】 lúqiāng 〈生理〉 cranial cavity

**舻** lú 见"舳舻" zhúlú

**鲈** lú 〈动〉 perch

## lǔ

**芦** lǔ 见"油葫芦" yóuhulǔ
另见 lú

**卤** lǔ ① bittern ② 〈化〉 halogen ③ stew (whole chickens or ducks, large cuts of meat, etc.) in soy sauce: ～鸡 pot-stewed chicken ④ thick gravy used as a sauce for noodles, etc.: 打～面 noodles served with thick gravy
【卤化】 lǔhuà 〈化〉 halogenate ◇～物 halogenide; halide
【卤水】 lǔshuǐ ① bittern ② brine
【卤素】 lǔsù 〈化〉 halogen
【卤味】 lǔwèi pot-stewed fowl, meat, etc. served cold
【卤族】 lǔzú 〈化〉 halogen family

**虏** lǔ ① take prisoner ② captive; prisoner of war
【虏获】 lǔhuò ① capture ② men and arms captured

**掳** lǔ carry off; capture
【掳掠】 lǔlüè pillage; loot: 奸淫～,无恶不作 rape and pillage and commit all kinds of atrocities

**鲁** lǔ ① stupid; dull ② rash; rough; rude ③ (Lǔ) another name for Shandong Province ④ (Lǔ) a surname
【鲁钝】 lǔdùn dull-witted; obtuse; stupid
【鲁莽】 lǔmǎng crude and rash; rash: ～行事 act rashly; act without thought/ 对待思想上的毛病决不能采取～的态度。In treating an ideological malady, one must never be crude.
【鲁莽灭裂】 lǔmǎng-mièliè rash and careless
【鲁米那】 lǔmǐnà 〈药〉 luminal

**橹** lǔ scull; sweep

**镥** lǔ 〈化〉 lutecium; lutetium (Lu)

## lù

**陆** lù ① land: 水～交通 land and water communications ② (Lù) a surname
另见 liù
【陆半球】 lùbànqiú 〈地〉 the continental hemisphere; the land hemisphere
【陆稻】 lùdào dryland rice; upland rice; dry rice
【陆地】 lùdì dry land; land ◇～棉 upland cotton
【陆风】 lùfēng 〈气〉 land breeze
【陆军】 lùjūn ground force; land force; army
【陆连岛】 lùliándǎo land-tied island; tombolo
【陆龙卷】 lùlóngjuǎn 〈气〉 tornado; landspout
【陆路】 lùlù land route: 走～ travel by land/ ～交通 overland communication; land communication
【陆生动物】 lùshēng dòngwù terrestrial animal
【陆台】 lùtái 〈地〉 table
【陆相】 lùxiàng 〈地〉 land facies ◇ ～沉积 continental deposit
【陆续】 lùxù one after another; in succession: 代表们～到达。The delegates arrived one after another.
【陆运】 lùyùn land transportation
【陆战队】 lùzhànduì 〈军〉 marine corps; marines

**录** lù ① record; write down; copy: 抄～ copy down/ 记～在案 put on record ② employ; hire: 收～ employ; take sb. on the staff ③ tape-record: 报告已经～下来了。The speech has been tape-recorded. ④ record; register; collection: 语～ quotation; a book of quotations/ 回忆～ memoirs; reminiscences
【录供】 lùgòng 〈法〉 take down a confession or testimony during an interrogation
【录井】 lùjǐng 〈石油〉 logging: 岩屑～ sieve residue logging
【录取】 lùqǔ enroll; recruit; admit: ～新学员五百名 enroll 500 students ◇ ～通知书 admission notice
【录像机】 lùxiàngjī videocorder: 磁带～ video tape recorder
【录音】 lùyīn sound recording: 实况～ on-the-spot recording; live-recording/ 磁带～ tape recording/ 放～ play back the recording
◇ ～报告 tape-recorded speech/ ～带 magnetic tape; tape/ ～机 (tape) recorder/ ～胶片 recording film/ ～摄影机 sound camera/ ～室 recording room

【录用】 lùyòng employ; take sb. on the staff: 量才～ give a person employment commensurate with his abilities

**赂** lù 见"贿赂" huìlù

**鹿** lù deer: 公～ stag; buck/ 母～ doe/ 小～ fawn

【鹿角】 lùjiǎo ① deerhorn; antler ② abatis ◇～胶〈中药〉 deerhorn glue

【鹿角菜】 lùjiǎocài 〈植〉 siliquose pelvetia (*Pelvetia siliquosa*)

【鹿圈】 lùjuàn deer enclosure; deer pen

【鹿皮】 lùpí deerskin

【鹿茸】 lùróng 〈中药〉 pilose antler (of a young stag)

【鹿肉】 lùròu venison

【鹿死谁手】 lù sǐ shuí shǒu at whose hand will the deer die —who will win the prize; who will gain supremacy: ～,尚难逆料。It's still hard to tell who will emerge victorious.

【鹿苑】 lùyuàn deer park

【鹿砦】 lùzhài 〈军〉 abatis 又作"鹿寨"

**绿** lù

另见 lǜ

【绿林好汉】 lùlín hǎohàn ① heroes of the greenwood; forest outlaws ② a band of bandits entrenched in a mountain stronghold; brigands

【绿林起义】 Lùlín Qǐyì the Lulin Uprising (A.D. 17)

**禄** lù official's salary in feudal China; emolument: 高官厚～ high position and handsome salary

**碌** lù ① commonplace; mediocre ② busy

另见 liù

【碌碌】 lùlù ① mediocre; commonplace: ～无能 incompetent; devoid of ability ② busy with miscellaneous work: 忙忙～ busy going about one's work; as busy as a bee

**路** lù ① road; path; way: 大～ broad road; highway/ 小～ path; trail ② journey; distance: 走很远的～ walk a long distance; make a long journey/ 一小时走十二里～ cover 12 *li* an hour ③ way; means: 生～ means of livelihood; a way out ④ sequence; line; logic: 理～ line of reasoning/ 思～ train of thought ⑤ region; district: 外～人 nonlocal people/ 南～货 southern products ⑥ route: 八～军 the Eighth Route Army/ 三～进军 advance along three routes/ 七～公共汽车 No. 7 bus ⑦ sort; grade; class: 头～货 top-notch goods/ 一～货 the same sort; birds of a feather ⑧ (Lù) a surname

【路拌】 lùbàn 〈交〉 road mix ◇ ～路面 road-mixed pavement

【路标】 lùbiāo ① road sign ② 〈军〉 route marking; route sign

【路不拾遗】 lù bù shí yí no one picks up and pockets anything lost on the road — descriptive of a high moral standard in society

【路程】 lùchéng distance travelled; journey: 三天～ a three days' journey/走了五百里的～ have covered a distance of 500 *li*

【路道】 lùdào 〈方〉 ① way; approach: 他人倒聪明,就是～没有走对。He's quite intelligent, but he doesn't have a correct approach to things. ② behaviour: 此人～不正。The person's behaviour is questionable.

【路德宗】 Lùdézōng 〈基督教〉 Lutheranism; the Lutheran Church

【路灯】 lùdēng street lamp; road lamp

【路堤】 lùdī 〈交〉 embankment

【路段】 lùduàn a section of a highway or railway

【路费】 lùfèi travelling expenses

【路轨】 lùguǐ ① rail ② track

【路过】 lùguò pass by or through (a place): 他每次～总要来看望他的老战友。Every time he passes by, he drops in to see his old comrades-in-arms./ 从天津到上海,～济南 pass through Jinan en route from Tianjin to Shanghai

【路基】 lùjī roadbed; bed

【路劫】 lùjié highway robbery; holdup; mugging

【路警】 lùjǐng railway police

【路径】 lùjìng ① route; way: ～不熟 not know one's way around ② method; ways and means

【路局】 lùjú railway administration; road bureau

【路口】 lùkǒu crossing; intersection: 三岔～ a fork in a road/ 十字～ crossroads

【路面】 lùmiàn road surface; pavement: 柔(刚)性～ flexible (rigid) pavement

【路牌】 lùpái street nameplate

【路签】 lùqiān 〈交〉 train-staff; staff

【路堑】 lùqiàn 〈交〉 cutting

【路人】 lùrén passerby; stranger: 视若～ treat sb. like a stranger

【路上】 lùshàng ① on the road ② on the way; en route: ～不要耽搁。Don't waste any time on the way./ 由于～的种种耽搁,我们比原计划迟到了两天。Owing to various delays en route, we arrived two days behind schedule./ ～要用的东西放在这个包里。Put the things you'll need for the journey in this bag.

【路数】 lùshù ① 见"路子" ② a movement in martial arts: 击剑的～ thrusts in fencing ③ exact details; inside story

【路条】 lùtiáo travel permit; pass

【路途】 lùtú ① road; path: 他熟悉这一带的～。He knows the roads in this district quite well. ② way; journey: ～遥远 a long way to go; far away

【路线】 lùxiàn ① route; itinerary: 旅行的～ the route of a journey/ 参观～图 visitors' itinerary ② line: 坚持毛主席的革命～ adhere to Chairman Mao's revolutionary line ◇～斗争 struggle between two lines; two-line struggle/ ～斗争觉悟 political awareness of two-line struggle/ ～教育 education in two-line struggle; education in the proletarian revolutionary line

【路遥知马力】 lù yáo zhī mǎlì distance tests a horse's stamina: ～,日久见人心。As distance tests a horse's strength, so time reveals a person's heart./ ～,事久见人心。As a long road tests a horse's strength, so a long task proves a person's heart.

【路障】 lùzhàng roadblock

【路子】 lùzi way; approach: ～不对等于白费劲儿。A wrong approach means a waste of effort.

**漉** lù seep through; filter

【漉网】 lùwǎng 〈纸〉 vat-net

**辘** lù

【辘轳】 lùlu windlass; winch

【辘辘】 lùlù 〈象〉 rumble: 车轮的～声 the rumbling of cart wheels/ 饥肠～ so hungry that one's stomach rumbles; one's stomach growling from hunger; famished

**戮** lù ① kill; slay: 杀～ slaughter ② 〈书〉 unite; join: ～力 join hands

【戮力同心】 lùlì tóngxīn 〈书〉 unite in a concerted effort; make concerted efforts

**璐** lù 〈书〉 jade

**鹭** lù egret; heron: 牛背～ cattle egret/ 池～ pond heron
【鹭鸶】 lùsī egret

**麓** lù 〈书〉 the foot of a hill or mountain: 华山北～ at the northern foot of Huashan Mountain

**露** lù ① dew ② beverage distilled from flowers, fruit or leaves; syrup: 果子～ fruit syrup ③ show; reveal; betray: 不～声色 not betray one's feelings or intentions/ ～出原形 reveal one's true colours; betray oneself
另见 lòu
【露点】 lùdiǎn 〈气〉 dew point: 温度～差 dew-point deficit ◇ ～湿度表 dew-point hygrometer
【露骨】 lùgǔ thinly veiled; undisguised; barefaced: 说得十分～ speak undisguisedly; speak in no equivocal terms/ ～地干涉别国内政 flagrantly interfere in the internal affairs of another country
【露光计】 lùguāngjì 〈摄〉 exposure meter
【露脊鲸】 lùjǐjīng 〈动〉 right whale
【露酒】 lùjiǔ alcoholic drink mixed with fruit juice
【露水】 lùshui dew
【露宿】 lùsù sleep in the open
【露天】 lùtiān in the open (air); outdoors: 今晚电影在～演。The film will be shown in the open air tonight.
◇～堆栈 open-air repository; open-air depot/～剧场 open-air theatre/ ～开采 opencast mining / ～矿 opencut; opencast; open-pit; strip mine/ ～煤矿 opencut coal mine
【露头】 lùtóu 〈矿〉 outcrop; outcropping
另见 lòutóu
【露头角】 lù tóujiǎo (of a young person) beginning to show ability or talent; budding: 参加会议的,有不少是初～的新作家。Present at the meeting were a number of budding writers.
【露营】 lùyíng camp (out); encamp; bivouac
【露珠】 lùzhū dewdrop

## lu

**氇** lu 见"氆氇" pǔlu

## lú

**驴** lú donkey; ass
【驴唇不对马嘴】 lúchún bù duì mǎzuǐ donkeys' lips don't match horses' jaws—incongruous; irrelevant: 这个比方有点～。The analogy is rather farfetched./ 他的回答～。His answer is irrelevant. 或 His answer is beside the point.
【驴打滚】 lúdǎgǔn a form of usury in the old society, the borrower having to pay interest on interest; snowballing usury
【驴骡】 lúluó hinny
【驴皮胶】 lúpíjiāo 〈中药〉 donkey-hide gelatin
【驴子】 lúzi 〈方〉 donkey; ass

**闾** lǘ ①〈书〉 the gate of (或 entrance to) an alley: 倚～而望 waiting at the entrance to the alley (for the return of one's son) ② alleys and lanes; neighbourhood
【闾里】 lǘlǐ 〈书〉 native village; home town
【闾巷】 lǘxiàng 〈书〉 alley; lane; alleyway

**榈** lǘ 见"棕榈" zōnglǘ

## lǚ

**吕** Lǚ a surname
【吕剧】 lǚjù Lü opera (of Shandong Province)
【吕宋】 Lǚsòng Luzon ◇～烟 Luzon cigar; cigar

**侣** lǚ companion; associate: 伴～ companion; partner/ 情～ lovers

**旅** lǚ ① travel; stay away from home ②〈军〉 brigade ③ troops; force: 军～之事 military affairs/ 劲～ a powerful army; a crack force
【旅伴】 lǚbàn travelling companion; fellow traveller
【旅程】 lǚchéng route; itinerary
【旅店】 lǚdiàn inn
【旅费】 lǚfèi travelling expenses
【旅馆】 lǚguǎn hotel
【旅进旅退】 lǚjìn-lǚtuì 〈书〉 always follow the steps of others, forward or backward—have no definite views of one's own
【旅居】 lǚjū reside abroad; sojourn: ～海外的侨胞 Chinese nationals residing abroad
【旅客】 lǚkè hotel guest; traveller; passenger: 过往～ travellers passing through; transients ◇～登记簿 hotel register
【旅社】 lǚshè hotel
【旅途】 lǚtú journey; trip: ～见闻 what one sees and hears during a trip; traveller's notes
【旅行】 lǚxíng travel; journey; tour: 作长途～ make a long journey/ 组织外国留学生到南方～ arrange a tour to the South for foreign students
◇～包 travelling bag/ ～车 station wagon/ ～闹钟 travelling clock/ ～社 travel service/ ～团 touring party/ ～支票 traveller's cheque/ ～证 travel certificate/ ～指南 guidebook
【旅游】 lǚyóu tour; tourism: ～事业 tourist trade; tourism
【旅长】 lǚzhǎng brigade commander

**捋** lǚ smooth out with the fingers; stroke: ～胡子 stroke one's beard/ 把纸～平 smooth out a piece of paper
另见 luō

**铝** lǚ 〈化〉 aluminium (Al)
【铝箔】 lǚbó aluminium foil
【铝胶】 lǚjiāo alumina gel
【铝热剂】 lǚrèjì 〈化〉 thermite ◇～燃烧弹 thermite bomb
【铝土矿】 lǚtǔkuàng bauxite

**偻** lǚ ① crooked (back): 伛～ humpback(ed); hunchback(ed) ②〈书〉 instantly; directly; at once: 不能～指 unable to point out straight away
另见 lóu

**屡** lǚ repeatedly; time and again: ～战～胜 have fought many battles and won every one of them; score one victory after another
【屡次】 lǚcì time and again; repeatedly: ～打破全国纪录 repeatedly break the national record
【屡次三番】 lǚcì-sānfān again and again; over and over again; many times: 我～提醒他要谨慎。I've reminded him over and over again that he should be cautious.
【屡见不鲜】 lǚ jiàn bù xiān common occurrence; nothing new
【屡教不改】 lǚ jiào bù gǎi refuse to mend one's ways des-

pite repeated admonition
【屡屡】 lǚlǚ 〈书〉 time and again; repeatedly
【屡试不爽】 lǚ shì bù shuǎng put to repeated tests and proved right; time-tested: 这种新农药杀虫效果良好，～。This new insecticide has proved effective every time it is used.

**缕** lǚ ①thread ②〈量〉 wisp; strand; lock: 一～烟 a wisp of smoke/ 一～麻 a strand of hemp ③detailed; in detail: ～陈 state in detail
【缕缕】 lǚlǚ continuously: 村中炊烟～上升。Wisps of smoke rose continuously from the village chimneys.
【缕述】 lǚshù state in detail; give all the details; go into particulars (或 detail)
【缕析】 lǚxī make a detailed analysis

**褛** lǚ 见"褴褛" lánlǚ

**膂** lǚ 〈书〉 backbone
【膂力】 lǚlì muscular strength; physical strength; brawn: ～过人 possessing extraordinary physical strength

**履** lǚ ①shoe: 革～ leather shoes ②tread on; walk on: 如～薄冰 as if walking on thin ice ③footstep: 步～艰难 walk with difficulty; hobble along ④carry out; honour; fulfil: ～约 honour an agreement; keep an appointment
【履带】 lǚdài 〈机〉 caterpillar tread; track: ～式拖拉机 caterpillar (或 crawler) tractor
【履历】 lǚlì personal details (of education and work experience); antecedents; *curriculum vitae*
【履险如夷】 lǚ xiǎn rú yí cross a dangerous pass as easily as walking on level ground — handle a crisis without difficulty
【履行】 lǚxíng perform; fulfil; carry out: ～职责 do one's duty/ ～诺言 keep one's word; fulfil (或 carry out) one's promise/ ～入党手续 go through the procedure for admission to the Party/ ～国际主义义务 fulfil internationalist obligations

## lǜ

**律** lǜ ①law; statute; rule ②〈书〉 restrain; keep under control: 严以～己 be strict with oneself; exercise strict self-discipline ③见"律诗"
【律吕】 lǜlǚ 〈乐〉 ①bamboo pitch-pipes used in ancient China ②temperament
【律师】 lǜshī lawyer; (英) barrister; (英) solicitor; (美) attorney
【律诗】 lǜshī *lüshi*, a poem of eight lines, each containing five or seven characters, with a strict tonal pattern and rhyme scheme

**虑** lǜ ①consider; ponder; think over: 深思熟～ careful consideration (或 deliberation) ②concern; anxiety; worry: 不足为～ give no cause for anxiety/ 过～ worry overmuch; be overanxious

**率** lǜ rate; proportion; ratio: 人口增长～ the rate of population increase/ 废品～ the rate (或 proportion) of rejects/ 回流～〈物〉 reflux ratio
另见 shuài

**绿** lǜ green: ～叶 green leaves/～油油的秧苗 green and lush seedlings
另见 lù

【绿宝石】 lǜbǎoshí emerald
【绿茶】 lǜchá green tea
【绿灯】 lǜdēng ①〈交〉 green light ②permission to go ahead with some project; green light: 开～ give the green light to
【绿豆】 lǜdòu mung bean; green gram ◇～芽 mung bean sprouts
【绿矾】 lǜfán 〈化〉 green vitriol
【绿肥】 lǜféi green manure ◇～作物 green manure crop
【绿化】 lǜhuà make (a place) green by planting trees, flowers, etc.; afforest: ～山区 afforest the mountain district/ ～城市 plant trees in and around the city/ 植树造林，～祖国。Plant trees everywhere and make the country green.
【绿蓝色】 lǜlánsè turquoise (blue)
【绿篱】 lǜlí 〈林〉 hedgerow; hedge
【绿帘石】 lǜliánshí 〈矿〉 epidote
【绿泥石】 lǜníshí 〈矿〉 chlorite
【绿松石】 lǜsōngshí 〈矿〉 turquoise
【绿头鸭】 lǜtóuyā 〈动〉 mallard
【绿藻】 lǜzǎo 〈植〉 green alga
【绿洲】 lǜzhōu oasis
【绿柱石】 lǜzhùshí 〈地〉 beryl

**氯** lǜ 〈化〉 chlorine (Cl)
【氯丙嗪】 lǜbǐngqín 〈药〉 chlorpromazine; wintermine
【氯丁橡胶】 lǜdīng xiàngjiāo 〈化〉 chloroprene rubber
【氯仿】 lǜfǎng 〈化〉 chloroform
【氯化物】 lǜhuàwù 〈化〉 chloride (e.g. 氯化钠 sodium chloride)
【氯喹】 lǜkuí 〈药〉 chloroquine
【氯磷定】 lǜlíndìng 〈药〉 pyraloxime methylchloride
【氯纶】 lǜlún 〈纺〉 polyvinyl chloride fibre
【氯霉素】 lǜméisù 〈药〉 chloromycetin; chloramphenicol
【氯气】 lǜqì 〈化〉 chlorine
【氯噻酮】 lǜsāitóng 〈药〉 chlorthalidone
【氯酸】 lǜsuān 〈化〉 chloric acid ◇～钾 potassium chlorate

**葎** lǜ
【葎草】 lǜcǎo 〈植〉 scandent hop (*Humulus scandens*)

**滤** lǜ strain; filter: 过～ filter
【滤波器】 lǜbōqì 〈电〉 wave filter: 带通～ band-pass filter/ 高通～ high-pass filter
【滤过性病毒】 lǜguòxìng bìngdú 〈医〉 filterable virus
【滤器】 lǜqì filter: 粗～ strainer
【滤色镜】 lǜsèjìng 〈摄〉 (colour) filter
【滤液】 lǜyè 〈化〉 filtrate
【滤纸】 lǜzhǐ 〈化〉 filter paper: 定量(定性)～ quantitative (qualitative) filter paper

## luán

**峦** luán 〈书〉 ①low but steep and pointed hill ②mountains in a range

**孪** luán twin
【孪生】 luánshēng twin: ～姐妹 twin sisters

**栾** luán ①〈植〉 goldenrain tree ②(Luán) a surname

**挛** luán contraction: 拘～ contraction/痉～ spasm; convulsions
【挛缩】 luánsuō contracture

**鸾** luán a mythical bird like the phoenix
【鸾凤】 luánfèng husband and wife: ～和鸣 be blessed with conjugal felicity; be a happy couple

**脔** luán 〈书〉 a small slice of meat
【脔割】 luángē 〈书〉 slice up; carve up

**銮** luán a small tinkling bell

## luǎn

**卵** luǎn ovum; egg; spawn
【卵白】 luǎnbái 〈动〉 white of an egg; albumen
【卵巢】 luǎncháo 〈生理〉 ovary
【卵黄】 luǎnhuáng 〈动〉 yolk
【卵磷脂】 luǎnlínzhī 〈生理〉 lecithin
【卵生】 luǎnshēng 〈动〉 oviparity ◇～动物 oviparous animal; ovipara
【卵石】 luǎnshí cobble; pebble; shingle
【卵胎生】 luǎntāishēng 〈动〉 ovoviviparity ◇～动物 ovoviviparous animal; ovovivipara
【卵细胞】 luǎnxìbāo egg cell; ovum
【卵翼】 luǎnyì cover with wings as in brooding; shield: 在帝国主义的～下 under the aegis of imperialism; shielded by imperialism
【卵子】 luǎnzǐ 〈生〉 ovum; egg

## luàn

**乱** luàn ① in disorder; in a mess; in confusion: 屋里很～,请你把它收拾一下。The room is in a mess; please tidy it up./ 这篇稿子太～,是不是给抄一下? The manuscript's too messy. How about copying it out?/ 这里太～,找个安静点的地方谈谈。It's too noisy here; let's find a quieter place to chat./ 敌军司令部里～作一团。There was great confusion in the enemy headquarters./ 敌人～了阵脚。The enemy was in disarray. ② disorder; upheaval; chaos; riot; unrest; turmoil: 内～ internal unrest/ 叛～ armed rebellion; mutiny ③ confuse; mix up; jumble: 扰～ create confusion; disturb; harass/ 各种木料～堆在一起。Logs and planks of all shapes and sizes were jumbled together. ④ confused (state of mind); in a turmoil: 我心里很～。My mind is in a turmoil. ⑤ indiscriminate; random; arbitrary: 给人～扣帽子 slap political labels on people right and left/ ～来 act recklessly/ ～作决定 make an arbitrary decision/ ～讲一气 speak indiscreetly; make irresponsible remarks/ ～花钱 spend money extravagantly/ ～说～动 be unruly in word or deed ⑥ promiscuous sexual behaviour; promiscuity
【乱兵】 luànbīng ① mutinous soldiers ② totally undisciplined troops
【乱纷纷】 luànfēnfēn disorderly; confused; chaotic: ～的人群 a tumultuous crowd
【乱坟岗】 luànféngǎng unmarked common graves; unmarked burial-mounds
【乱哄哄】 luànhōnghōng in noisy disorder; in a hubbub; tumultuous; in an uproar: 大家听到这个消息,～地议论起来。The news set them arguing heatedly among themselves.
【乱了营】 luànle yíng 〈方〉 be thrown into confusion; be in disarray
【乱离】 luànlí be separated by war; be rendered homeless by war
【乱伦】 luànlún commit incest
【乱蓬蓬】 luànpēngpēng dishevelled; tangled; jumbled: ～的头发 dishevelled hair; tangled hair/ ～的茅草 a jumbled mass of reeds
【乱七八糟】 luànqībāzāo at sixes and sevens; in a mess; in a muddle
【乱世】 luànshì troubled times; turbulent days
【乱说】 luànshuō speak carelessly; make irresponsible remarks; gossip: 当面不说,背后～ gossip behind people's backs but say nothing to their faces
【乱弹琴】 luàntánqín 〈口〉 act or talk like a fool; talk nonsense: 这简直是～。That's a lot of nonsense. 或 It's downright nonsense.
【乱套】 luàntào 〈方〉 muddle things up; turn things upside down: 要是各行其是,那就～了。If everyone acts as he pleases, everything will be in a muddle.
【乱腾腾】 luàntēngtēng confused; upset: 心里～的 feel all hot and bothered
【乱腾】 luànteng confusion; disorder; unrest
【乱葬岗子】 luànzàng gǎngzi unmarked common graves; unmarked burial-mounds
【乱糟糟】 luànzāozāo ① chaotic; in a mess: 屋子里～的。The room is in a mess. ② confused; perturbed: 心里～的 feel very perturbed
【乱真】 luànzhēn ① (of fakes) look genuine: 以假～ pass off a fake as genuine ② 〈物〉 spurious: ～放电 spurious discharge/ ～脉冲 spurious pulse
【乱子】 luànzi disturbance; trouble; disorder: 闹～ create a disturbance; cause trouble

## lüè

**掠** lüè ① plunder; pillage; sack: 我国许多珍贵文物被帝国主义～走了。Many of our cultural treasures have been plundered by imperialists. ② sweep past; brush past; graze; skim over: 凉风～面。A cool breeze brushed my face./ 探照灯～过夜空。The searchlights swept the night sky./ 燕子～水而过。The swallows skimmed over the water./ 她嘴角上～过一丝微笑。A faint smile flickered across her lips.
【掠地飞行】 lüèdì fēixíng minimum-altitude flight; treetop flight; hedgehopping
【掠夺】 lüèduó plunder; rob; pillage: 帝国主义～成性。Imperialism is predatory by nature.
【掠美】 lüèměi claim credit due to others: 这是她的高见,我不敢～。It was her idea. I can't claim credit for it. 又作"掠人之美"
【掠取】 lüèqǔ seize; grab; plunder: ～别国的资源 plunder the resources of other countries

**略** lüè ① brief; sketchy: 简～ sketchy; simple/ ～述大意 give a brief account ② slightly; a little; somewhat: ～加修改 make some slight changes; edit slightly/ ～有所闻 have heard a little about the matter/ ～有出入 vary slightly; there's a slight discrepancy ③ summary; brief account; outline: 史～ outline history; brief history/ 事～ a short biographical account ④ omit; delete; leave out: 从～ be omitted/ ～去不提 make no mention of; leave out altogether ⑤ strategy; plan; scheme: 方～ overall plan/ 策～ tactics/ 雄才大～ (a person of) great talent and bold vision; (a statesman or general of) rare gifts and bold strategy ⑥ capture; seize: 攻城～地 attack cities and seize territories
【略见一斑】 lüè jiàn yī bān catch a glimpse of; get a rough idea of

【略略】 lüèlüè slightly; briefly: 关于那个问题他只～说了几句。He touched only briefly on that question.
【略胜一筹】 lüè shèng yī chóu a notch (或 cut) above; slightly better
【略图】 lüètú sketch map; sketch
【略微】 lüèwēi slightly; a little; somewhat: ～有点感冒 have a slight cold; have a touch of flu
【略语】 lüèyǔ 〈语〉 abbreviation; shortening
【略知一二】 lüè zhī yī-èr have a smattering of; know something about

## lūn

**抡** lūn brandish; swing: ～刀 brandish a sword/ ～起大铁锤 swing a sledgehammer

## lún

**仑** lún 〈书〉 logical sequence; coherence

**伦** lún ① human relations, esp. as conceived by feudal ethics ② logic; order ③ peer; match: 绝～ peerless; matchless
【伦比】 lúnbǐ 〈书〉 rival; equal: 无与～ unrivalled; unequalled; peerless
【伦常】 lúncháng feudal order of importance or seniority in human relationships
【伦次】 lúncì coherence; logical sequence: 语无～ speak incoherently; babble like an idiot
【伦理】 lúnlǐ ethics; moral principles: 不同阶级有不同的～。Different classes have different ethics. ◇～学 ethics
【伦琴射线】 lúnqín shèxiàn 〈物〉 röntgen (或 roentgen) rays

**论** Lún *The Analects of Confucius*
另见 lùn
【论语】 Lúnyǔ *The Analects of Confucius; The Analects* 参见"四书" sìshū

**沦** lún ① sink: 沉～ sink into depravity, etc. ② fall; be reduced to: ～于敌手 fall into enemy hands/ ～为殖民地 be reduced to the status of a colony
【沦落】 lúnluò fall low; come down in the world; be reduced to poverty: ～街头 be driven onto the streets (to become a tramp, beggar or prostitute)
【沦亡】 lúnwáng (of a country) be annexed (或 subjugated)
【沦陷】 lúnxiàn (of territory, etc.) be occupied by the enemy; fall into enemy hands ◇～区 enemy-occupied area

**囵** lún 见"囫囵" húlún

**纶** lún ① black silk ribbon ② fishing line ③ synthetic fibre: 锦～ polyamide fibre/ 涤～ polyester fibre

**轮** lún ① wheel: 齿～ gear wheel/ 三～摩托 motor tricycle ② sth. resembling a wheel; disc; ring: 月～ the moon/ 光～ halo/ 年～〈植〉 annual ring ③ steamboat; steamer: 江～ river steamer ④ take turns: ～值 on duty by turns/ 下一个就～到你了。It will be your turn next. ⑤〈量〉: 一～红日 a red sun/ 一～明月 a bright moon ⑥〈量〉 round: 第一～比赛 the first round of the match/ 新的一～会谈 a new round of talks
【轮班】 lúnbān in shifts; in relays; in rotation
【轮唱】 lúnchàng 〈乐〉 round
【轮齿】 lúnchǐ 〈机〉 teeth of a cogwheel
【轮虫】 lúnchóng 〈动〉 wheel animalcule; rotifer
【轮船】 lúnchuán steamer; steamship; steamboat
【轮渡】 lúndù (steam) ferry: 火车～ train ferry
【轮番】 lúnfān take turns: 我们～给锅炉添煤。We took turns stoking the furnaces./ ～轰炸 bomb in waves
【轮辐】 lúnfú spoke
【轮箍】 lúngū tyre
【轮毂】 lúngǔ (wheel) hub; (wheel) boss; nave
【轮换】 lúnhuàn rotate; take turns
【轮回】 lúnhuí 〈佛教〉 samsara; transmigration
【轮机】 lúnjī ① turbine: 燃气～ combustion gas turbine/ 冲压空气～ ram-air turbine ② motorship engine; engine ◇～室 engine room/ ～员 engineer/ ～长 chief engineer
【轮距】 lúnjù track; tread
【轮空】 lúnkōng 〈体〉 bye: 他在第一轮比赛中～。He drew a bye in the first round of the tournament.
【轮廓】 lúnkuò outline; contour; rough sketch: 先画个～，再画细部。Draw an outline before you fill in the details./ 夜幕降临了，但厂房还能看见个～。Night fell, but the outline of the factory buildings was still discernible. 或 The factory buildings were silhouetted against the growing darkness./ 听了汇报后，新来的经理对这个公司的情况有了个～。After hearing the reports from below, the newly-appointed manager got a general picture of the situation in the company.
【轮流】 lúnliú take turns; do sth. in turn: 师徒俩～掌钎。The master-worker and the apprentice took turns holding the rock drill./ 他俩～值夜班。They work on night shifts in turn.
【轮牧】 lúnmù 〈牧〉 rotation grazing
【轮生】 lúnshēng 〈植〉 verticillate ◇～叶 verticillate leaves
【轮式拖拉机】 lúnshì tuōlājī 〈农〉 wheeled tractor
【轮胎】 lúntāi tyre: 防滑～ antiskid tyre; nonskid tyre/ 双层～ two ply tyre/ 翻制～ retreaded tyre ◇～帘子线 tyre cord/ ～压力计 tyre pressure gauge
【轮辋】 lúnwǎng rim (of a wheel)
【轮休】 lúnxiū have holidays by turns; rotate days off; stagger holidays
【轮训】 lúnxùn training in rotation
【轮椅】 lúnyǐ wheelchair
【轮轴】 lúnzhóu ①〈物〉 wheel and axle ② wheel axle
【轮转】 lúnzhuàn rotate ◇～印刷机 rotary press
【轮子】 lúnzi wheel
【轮作】 lúnzuò 〈农〉 crop rotation: 粮棉～ rotation of cereal crops and cotton

## lùn

**论** lùn ① discuss; talk about; discourse: 讨～ discuss/ 就事～事 talk about a matter in isolation; deal with a matter on its merits ② view; opinion; statement: 高～ your brilliant views; your wise counsel/ 舆～ public opinion/ 立～ argument; line of reasoning/ 持平之～ unbiased views ③ dissertation; essay: 《实践～》 *On Practice* ④ theory: 进化～ the theory of evolution/ 唯物～ materialism ⑤ mention; regard; consider: 相提并～ mention in the same breath/ 又当别～ should be regarded as a different matter ⑥ decide on; determine: 按质～价 determine the price according to the quality ⑦ by; in terms of: 鸡蛋～斤卖。Eggs are sold by the *jin*./ ～业务，她比组里其他同志要强些。So far as professional proficiency goes, she is better than the other members of the group.
另见 Lún

【论处】 lùnchǔ decide on sb.'s punishment; punish: 以违反纪律～ be punished for a breach of discipline
【论敌】 lùndí one's opponent in a debate
【论点】 lùndiǎn argument; thesis: 这篇文章～鲜明。The argument set forth in the article is clear-cut.
【论调】 lùndiào 〔常含贬义〕 view; argument: 这种～是错误的。Such views are erroneous.
【论断】 lùnduàn inference; judgment; thesis: 作出～ draw an inference/ "枪杆子里面出政权"是毛主席的著名～。"Political power grows out of the barrel of a gun" is a famous thesis of Chairman Mao's.
【论功行赏】 lùn gōng xíng shǎng dispense rewards or honours according to merit; award people according to their contributions
【论据】 lùnjù grounds of argument; argument: ～不足 insufficient grounds/ 有力的～ strong argument; valid reasons
【论理】 lùnlǐ ① normally; as things should be: ～她早可以退休了，可是她仍然为革命坚持工作。She really ought to have retired long ago, but she's still working hard for the revolution. ② logic: 合乎～ be logical; stand to reason ◇ ～学 logic
【论述】 lùnshù discuss; expound: ～人民战争的特点 discuss the characteristics of people's war/ 精辟的～ brilliant exposition
【论说】 lùnshuō ① exposition and argumentation: ～文 argumentation ② 〈口〉 见"论理"①
【论坛】 lùntán forum; tribune
【论题】 lùntí 〈逻〉 proposition
【论文】 lùnwén thesis; dissertation; treatise; paper: 学术～ an academic thesis (或 paper)/ 科学～ a scientific treatise
【论战】 lùnzhàn polemic; debate
【论争】 lùnzhēng argument; debate; controversy
【论证】 lùnzhèng ① demonstration; proof: 无可辩驳的～ irrefutable proof ② expound and prove: 文章～了无产阶级专政的必要性。The article proves the necessity of the proletarian dictatorship. ③ 见"论据"
【论著】 lùnzhù treatise; work; book
【论罪】 lùnzuì decide on the nature of the guilt: 按贪污～ be found guilty of corruption

## luō

**罗** luō
另见 luó
【罗嗦】 luōsuo ① long-winded; wordy: 他说话太～。He's far too long-winded./ 我再～几句。Let me say just another word or two. 或 Bear with me a little longer. ② overelaborate; troublesome: 这些手续真～。All these formalities are overelaborate. 又作"罗唆"

**捋** luō rub one's palm along (sth. long): ～起袖子 push up one's sleeve/ ～掉树枝上的叶子 strip a twig of its leaves
另见 lǚ
【捋虎须】 luō hǔxū stroke a tiger's whiskers — do sth. very daring; run great risks

## luó

**罗** luó ① a net for catching birds: ～网 net; trap ② catch birds with a net: 门可～雀 you can catch sparrows on the doorstep — visitors are few and far between ③ collect; gather together ④ display; spread out: 星～棋布 spread out like stars in the sky or chessmen on the chessboard ⑤ sieve; sift: ～面 sift flour ⑥ a kind of silk gauze: ～扇 silk gauze fan ⑦ 〈量〉 twelve dozen; a gross ⑧ (Luó) a surname
另见 luō
【罗布麻】 luóbùmá 〈植〉 bluish dogbane (*Apocynum venetum*)
【罗得西亚】 Luódéxīyà Rhodesia
【罗锅】 luóguō arched: ～桥 arch bridge
【罗锅儿】 luóguōr ① hunchbacked; humpbacked ② hunchback; humpback
【罗汉】 luóhàn 〈佛教〉 *arhat*
【罗汉松】 luóhànsōng 〈植〉 yew podocarpus
【罗经】 luójīng 〈航海〉 compass: 电～ gyrocompass/ 磁～ magnetic compass/ 航海～ mariner's compass
【罗口】 luókǒu 〈纺〉 rib cuff or rib collar; rib top (of socks)
【罗口灯泡】 luókǒu dēngpào screw socket bulb
【罗口灯头】 luókǒu dēngtóu screw socket
【罗拉】 luólā 〈机〉 roller
【罗勒】 luólè 〈植〉 sweet basil
【罗列】 luóliè ① spread out; set out: 厂房～在山坡上。Factory buildings spread out over the hillside. ② enumerate: 光～事实还不够，必须加以分析。It's not enough just to enumerate the facts. You've got to analyse them, too.
【罗马法】 Luómǎfǎ 〈法〉 Roman law
【罗马尼亚】 Luómǎníyà Romania ◇～人 Romanian/ ～语 Romanian (language)
【罗马数字】 Luómǎ shùzì Roman numerals
【罗马语族】 Luómǎ yǔzú 〈语〉 the Romance group of languages; Romance languages
【罗盘】 luópán compass
【罗圈腿】 luóquāntuǐ ① bowlegs; bandy legs ② bowlegged; bandy-legged
【罗网】 luówǎng net; trap: 自投～ walk right into the trap
【罗望子】 luówàngzǐ 〈植〉 tamarind
【罗纹机】 luówénjī rib knitting machine; ribber
【罗纹鸭】 luówényā falcated teal; falcated duck
【罗织】 luózhī 〈书〉 frame up: ～诬陷 frame sb. up/ ～罪名 cook up charges
【罗致】 luózhì enlist the services of; secure sb. in one's employment; collect; gather together: ～人材 enlist the services of able people

**㑩** luó 见"偻㑩" lóuluo

**萝** luó trailing plants: 藤～ Chinese wistaria/ 茑～ cypress vine
【萝卜】 luóbo radish
【萝芙木】 luófúmù 〈植〉 devilpepper

**猡** luó 见"猪猡" zhūluó

**逻** luó patrol: 巡～ patrol
【逻辑】 luóji logic: ～上的错误 an error in logic/ 数理～ mathematical logic/ 合乎～ logical/ 按照这种～ according to that kind of reasoning/ 这是什么～？ What sort of logic is that?
◇ ～电路 logical circuit/ ～思维 logical thinking/ ～学 logic/ ～学家 logician/ ～主语〈语〉 logical subject

**椤** luó 见"桫椤" suōluó

**锣** luó gong
【锣槌】 luóchuí (gong) hammer
【锣鼓】 luógǔ ① gong and drum: ～喧天 a deafening sound of gongs and drums ② traditional percussion instruments

③ ensemble of such instruments with gongs and drums playing the main part

**箩** luó a square-bottomed bamboo basket

【箩筐】 luókuāng a large bamboo or wicker basket

**骡** luó mule

【骡马店】 luómǎdiàn an inn with sheds for carts and animals

【骡子】 luózi mule

**螺** luó ① spiral shell; snail: 马蹄～ top shell/ 田～ field snail ② whorl (in fingerprint)

【螺钿】 luódiàn 〈工美〉 mother-of-pearl inlay: ～漆盘 lacquer tray inlaid with mother-of-pearl

【螺钉】 luódīng screw: 木～ wood screw; screwnail

【螺号】 luóhào conch; shell trumpet

【螺距】 luójù 〈机〉 (screw) pitch; thread pitch

【螺母】 luómǔ 〈机〉 (screw) nut 又作"螺帽" ◇ ～垫圈 nut collar

【螺栓】 luóshuān 〈机〉 (screw) bolt: 连接～ binder bolt; connecting bolt /地脚～ foundation bolt

【螺丝】 luósī 〈口〉 screw
◇ ～板牙 screw die; threading die/ ～刀 screwdriver/ ～钉 screw/ ～扣 thread (of a screw)/ ～母 (screw) nut/ ～起子 screwdriver

【螺蛳】 luósi spiral shell; snail

【螺纹】 luówén ① whorl (in fingerprint) ②〈机〉 thread (of a screw): 公制～ metric thread/ 惠氏～ Whitworth thread ◇ ～刀具 threading tool; screw tool

【螺旋】 luóxuán ① spiral; helix: ～式发展 spiral development; developing in spirals ②〈物〉 screw ◇ ～线 helix; helical line; spiral/ ～钻 spiral drill; (screw) auger

【螺旋桨】 luóxuánjiǎng 〈机〉 (screw) propeller; screw: 飞机～ airscrew; aircraft propeller ◇～调速器 propeller governor/ ～叶 propeller blade

【螺旋体】 luóxuántǐ 〈微〉 spirochaeta

## luǒ

**裸** luǒ bare; naked; exposed: 赤～～ stark-naked; undisguised

【裸鲤】 luǒlǐ naked carp

【裸露】 luǒlù uncovered; exposed: ～的煤层 exposed coal seam

【裸麦】 luǒmài 〈植〉 naked barley; highland barley

【裸体】 luǒtǐ naked; nude

【裸线】 luǒxiàn 〈电〉 bare wire

【裸装货】 luǒzhuānghuò nude cargo

【裸子植物】 luǒzǐ zhíwù 〈植〉 gymnosperm

**瘰** luǒ

【瘰疬】 luǒlì 〈医〉 scrofula

## luò

**荦** luò 〈书〉 prominent; outstanding: 卓～ extraordinary; outstanding; preeminent

【荦荦】 luòluò 〈书〉 conspicuous; apparent; obvious: ～大端 salient points

**洛** Luò the name of a river in Shaanxi and Henan provinces

【洛氏硬度】 Luòshì yìngdù 〈物〉 Rockwell hardness

**咯** luò 见"吡咯" bǐluò
另见 gē; kǎ; lo

**络** luò ① sth. resembling a net: 橘～ tangerine pith/ 丝瓜～ loofah ②〈中医〉 subsidiary channels in the human body through which vital energy, blood and nutriment circulate ③ hold sth. in place with a net: 她头上～着一个发网。She kept her hair in place with a net. ④ twine; wind: ～纱 winding yarn; spooling

【络合】 luòhé 〈化〉 complexing ◇ ～物 complex compound

【络离子】 luòlízǐ 〈化〉 complex ion

【络脉】 luòmài 〈中医〉 collaterals which connect channels; branches of channels

【络腮胡子】 luòsāihúzi whiskers; full beard

【络筒机】 luòtǒngjī 〈纺〉 (high speed) cone winder; winding machine; winder

【络盐】 luòyán 〈化〉 complex salt

【络绎不绝】 luòyì bù jué in an endless stream: 参观展览会的人～。A continuous stream of visitors came to the exhibition.

**骆** luò ① a white horse with a black mane, mentioned in ancient Chinese books ② (Luò) a surname

【骆驼】 luòtuo camel: 单峰～ dromedary; one-humped camel/ 双峰～ Bactrian camel; two-humped camel/ 无峰～ llama

【骆驼刺】 luòtuocì 〈植〉 camel thorn

【骆驼队】 luòtuoduì camel train; caravan

【骆驼绒】 luòtuoróng camel hair cloth

**珞** luò 见"赛璐珞" sàilùluò

【珞巴族】 Luòbāzú the Lhoba (Lopa) nationality, living in the Xizang Autonomous Region

**落** luò ① fall; drop: 有些棉桃～在地上了。Some cotton bolls have fallen on the ground. ② go down; set: 潮水～了。The tide is low (或 out)./ 太阳～山了。The sun has set. ③ lower: 把帘子～下来 lower the blinds ④ decline; come down; sink: 衰～ decline; go downhill/ 没～ be on the downgrade/ ～到这步田地 come to such a pass ⑤ lag behind; fall behind: 领导不应当～在群众运动的后头。The leadership should never lag behind the mass movement. ⑥ leave behind; stay behind: 不～痕迹 leave no trace ⑦ whereabouts: 下～ whereabouts ⑧ settlement: 村～ a small village; hamlet ⑨ fall onto; rest with: 突袭的任务～在二排肩上。The task of making a surprise attack fell to the Second Platoon. ⑩ get; have; receive: ～褒贬 be criticized; lay oneself open to censure/ 就这么办吧,我不怕～埋怨。Let's do it that way, then. I don't mind taking the blame.
另见 là; lào

【落笔】 luòbǐ start to write or draw; put pen to paper

【落膘】 luòbiāo (of livestock) become thin

【落泊(魄)】 luòbó be in dire straits; be down and out

【落草】 luòcǎo take to the greenwood; take to the heather; become an outlaw

【落差】 luòchā 〈水〉 ① drop ② head

【落潮】 luòcháo ebb tide

【落成】 luòchéng completion (of a building, etc.) ◇～典礼 inauguration ceremony (for a building, etc.)

【落锤】 luòchuí 〈机〉 drop hammer

【落得】 luòde get; end in: ～一场空 come to nothing; end up in smoke/ 搞阴谋诡计的人,必然要～可耻的下场。Plotters come to no good end.

【落地】 luòdì ①fall to the ground: 人头～ be killed or beheaded ②(of babies) be born: 呱呱～ come into the world with a cry; be born
◇～窗 French window/ ～灯 floor lamp; standard lamp/ ～式收音机 console (radio) set
【落地生根】 luòdìshēnggēn 〈植〉 air plant; life plant
【落第】 luòdì fail in an imperial examination
【落点】 luòdiǎn ①〈体〉 placement (of a ball): ～准 accuracy in placement ②〈军〉 point of fall
【落顶】 luòdǐng 〈矿〉 caving
【落发】 luòfà shave one's head — become a Buddhist monk or nun
【落果】 luòguǒ 〈农〉 premature drop
【落后】 luòhòu ①fall behind; lag behind: 思想～于现实的事是常有的。It often happens that thinking lags behind reality./ 上半场主队～一分。The home team trailed by one point at half time. ②backward: 改变山区～面貌 put an end to the backwardness of the mountainous areas ◇～地区 backward areas; less developed areas/ ～分子 backward element
【落户】 luòhù settle: 在农村～ settle in the countryside
【落花流水】 luòhuā-liúshuǐ like fallen flowers carried away by the flowing water; utterly routed: 敌人被打得～。The enemy was utterly routed.
【落花有意,流水无情】 luòhuā yǒu yì, liúshuǐ wú qíng shedding petals, the waterside flower pines for love, while the heartless brook babbles on — unrequited love
【落花生】 luòhuashēng 〈植〉 peanut; groundnut
【落荒而逃】 luòhuāng ér táo take to the wilds — be defeated and flee the battlefield; take to flight
【落价】 luòjià fall (或 drop) in price: 收音机～了。The price of radios has gone down.
【落角】 luòjiǎo 〈军〉 angle of fall
【落脚】 luòjiǎo stay (for a time); stop over; put up: 找个地方～ find a place to stay/ 在客店～ put up at an inn ◇～处 temporary lodging
【落井下石】 luò jǐng xià shí drop stones on someone who has fallen into a well — hit a person when he's down
【落空】 luòkōng come to nothing; fail; fall through: 两头～ fall between two stools/ 希望～ fail to attain one's hope/ 这事有～的危险。There is a danger that nothing will come of it.
【落款】 luòkuǎn write the names of the sender and the recipient on a painting, gift or letter; inscribe (a gift, etc.)
【落泪】 luòlèi shed tears; weep
【落铃】 luòlíng 〈农〉 shedding (或 premature dropping) of cotton bolls
【落落大方】 luòluò dàfāng natural and graceful
【落落寡合】 luòluò guǎ hé standoffish; unsociable; aloof
【落寞】 luòmò lonely; desolate 又作"落漠""落莫"
【落难】 luònàn meet with misfortune; be in distress
【落日】 luòrì setting sun
【落纱机】 luòshājī 〈纺〉 doffer
【落实】 luòshí ①practicable; workable: 生产计划要订得～。Production plans must be practicable. ②fix (或 decide) in advance; ascertain; make sure: 交货时间还没有最后～。The date of delivery hasn't been fixed yet./ 明天去收麦子的有多少人,要～一下。Make sure how many are going to bring in the wheat tomorrow. ③carry out; fulfil; implement; put into effect: ～党的政策 implement the policies of the Party/ 把巩固无产阶级专政的任务～到每个基层 fulfil the task of consolidating the dictatorship of the proletariat down to every grass-roots organization/ 民兵工作要做到组织～,政治～,军事～。Militia work must be carried through organizationally, politically and militarily. ④〈方〉 feel at ease: 心里总是不～ just can't set one's mind at ease
【落水狗】 luòshuǐgǒu dog in the water: 痛打～ flog the cur that's fallen into the water — be merciless with bad people even if they're down
【落汤鸡】 luòtāngjī like a drenched chicken; like a drowned rat; soaked through; drenched and bedraggled
【落体】 luòtǐ 〈物〉 falling body: 自由～ freely falling body
【落拓(魄)】 luòtuò ①〈书〉 in dire straits; down and out ②untrammelled by convention; casual; unconventional: ～不羁 unconventional and uninhibited
【落网】 luòwǎng (of a criminal) fall into the net — be caught; be captured: 主犯已经～。The chief criminal has been caught.
【落伍】 luòwǔ fall behind the ranks; straggle; drop behind; drop out: 在革命急速发展的时候,总不免有人要～的。When the revolution is developing rapidly, some people are bound to fall behind.
【落线】 luòxiàn 〈军〉 line of fall
【落选】 luòxuǎn fail to be chosen (或 elected); lose an election
【落叶】 luòyè ①fallen leaves ②〈植〉 deciduous leaf ◇～树 deciduous tree/ ～松 larch
【落照】 luòzhào the glow of the setting sun

## 摞

luò ①pile up; stack up: 把砖～起来 stack up the bricks ②〈量〉 pile; stack: 一～砖 a pile of bricks/ 一～书 a stack of books

# M

## ḿ

**呣** ḿ 〈叹〉〔表示疑问〕: ～,你说什么? Yes? What did you say? 或 Pardon?/ ～,是真的吗? Oh, really? 或 What? Is that true?
另见 m̀

## m̀

**呣** m̀ 〈叹〉〔表示应诺〕: ～,我知道了。Um-hum (或 Uh-huh, Yes), I see.
另见 ḿ

## mā

**妈** mā 〈口〉① ma; mum; mummy; mother ② a form of address for a married woman one generation one's senior: 姑～ (paternal) aunt/ 姨～ (maternal) aunt/ 大～ aunt (a form of address for one's father's elder brother's wife or for any elderly married woman)

【妈妈】 māma 〈口〉 ma; mum; mummy; mother

**抹** mā ① wipe: ～桌子 wipe a table clean/ ～一把脸 wipe one's face ② rub sth. down; slip sth. off: 把帽子～下来 slip one's cap off/ ～不下脸来 find it difficult to be strict with sb. (for fear of hurting his feelings)
另见 mǒ; mò

【抹布】 mābù rag (to wipe things with)

**麻** mā
另见 má

【麻麻黑】 māmahēi 〈方〉 (it is) dusk

【麻麻亮】 māmaliàng 〈方〉 (it is) just dawning; (day is) just beginning to break

**摩** mā
另见 mó

【摩挲】 māsa gently stroke
另见 mósuō

**嬷** mā

【嬷嬷】 māma 〈方〉 wet nurse

## má

**吗** má 〈方〉 what: 下午干～? What are we going to do this afternoon?
另见 mǎ; ma

**麻** má ① a general term for hemp, flax, etc. ② sesame: ～糖 sesame candy ③ rough; coarse: 这种纸一面光,一面～。This paper is smooth on one side and rough on the other. ④ pocked; pockmarked; pitted; spotty: ～脸 a pockmarked face/ 铸件上有～点。There are pits in the casting. ⑤ have pins and needles; tingle: 腿发～ have pins and needles in one's legs/ 针灸大夫问病人～不～。The acupuncturist asked the patient if he felt a tingling sensation. ⑥ anaesthesia: 针～ acupuncture anaesthesia/ 药～ drug anaesthesia ⑦ (Má) a surname
另见 mā

【麻包】 mábāo gunny-bag; gunnysack; sack

【麻痹】 mábì ①〈医〉 paralysis: 小儿～ infantile paralysis; poliomyelitis; polio/ 面部神经～ facial paralysis ② benumb; lull; blunt: ～人们的斗志 lull (或 blunt) people's fighting will ③ lower one's guard; slacken one's vigilance: ～大意 lower one's guard and become careless; be off one's guard

【麻布】 mábù ① gunny (cloth); sackcloth; burlap; hessian ② linen

【麻袋】 mádài gunny-bag; gunnysack; sack ◇ ～片 a piece of gunnysacking

【麻刀】 mádao 〈建〉 hemp; hair: ～灰泥 hemp-fibred plaster

【麻烦】 máfan ① troublesome; inconvenient: 这事要是太～,你就别管了。—一点也不～。Don't bother if it's too much trouble. — No trouble at all./ 这下可～了,我把钥匙锁在屋里了。What a nuisance. I've locked my key in the room./ 服务周到,不怕～ spare no pains to give good service/ 自找～ ask for trouble ② put sb. to trouble; trouble sb.; bother: 对不起,～你了。Sorry to have put you to so much trouble./ 这点小事不要去～他了。Don't bother him with such trifles.

【麻风】 máfēng 〈医〉 leprosy ◇ ～病人 leper

【麻花】 máhuā fried dough twist

【麻花钻】 máhuāzuàn 〈机〉 (fluted) twist drill

【麻黄】 máhuáng 〈植〉 Chinese ephedra (*Ephedra sinica*); *mahuang* ◇ ～硷〈药〉 ephedrine

【麻将】 májiàng mahjong ◇ ～牌 mahjong pieces; mahjong tiles

【麻酱】 májiàng sesame paste

【麻利】 máli quick and neat; dexterous; deft: 干活～ work dexterously; be a quick and neat worker

【麻木】 mámù ① numb ② apathetic; insensitive

【麻木不仁】 mámù bùrén apathetic; insensitive; unfeeling

【麻雀】 máquè (house) sparrow ◇ ～战 sparrow warfare (as a form of guerrilla warfare)

【麻雀虽小,五脏俱全】 máquè suī xiǎo, wǔzàng jù quán the sparrow may be small but it has all the vital organs — small but complete

【麻纱】 máshā ① yarn of ramie, flax, etc. ② cambric; haircords

【麻绳】 máshéng rope made of hemp, flax, jute, etc.

【麻线】 máxiàn flaxen thread; linen thread

【麻药】 máyào anaesthetic

【麻油】 máyóu sesame oil

【麻疹】 mázhěn 〈医〉 measles

【麻织品】 mázhīpǐn fabrics of flax, hemp, etc.; linen fabrics

【麻子】 mázi ① pockmarks ② a person with a pockmarked face

【麻醉】 mázuì ①〈医〉 anaesthesia; narcosis: 全身(局部、脊髓)～ general (local, spinal) anaesthesia/ 针刺～ acupuncture anaesthesia ② anaesthetize; poison: 用诲淫诲盗的电影～青年人 poison young people with films full of sex and violence
◇ ～剂 anaesthetic; narcotic/ ～品 narcotic; drug/ ～师

anaesthetist

## 麻 má

【麻痹】 mábì 见"麻痹" mábì
【麻风】 máfēng 见"麻风" máfēng
【麻疹】 mázhěn 见"麻疹" mázhěn

## 蟆 má 见"蛤蟆" háma

## mǎ

## 马 mǎ ① horse: 母～ mare/ 种～ stallion; stud/ 小～ pony ② horse, one of the pieces in Cinese chess ③ (Mǎ) a surname

【马鞍】 mǎ'ān saddle
【马鞍形】 mǎ'ānxíng the shape of a saddle — a falling-off between two peak periods: 由于修正主义路线的干扰，我厂生产一度出现了～。As a result of disruption by the revisionist line, there was a temporary falling-off in production at our factory.
【马帮】 mǎbāng a train of horses carrying goods; caravan
【马宝】 mǎbǎo 〈中药〉 bezoar of a horse
【马鼻疽】 mǎbíjū 〈牧〉 glanders
【马鞭】 mǎbiān horsewhip
【马弁】 mǎbiàn 〈旧〉 (officer's) bodyguard
【马表】 mǎbiǎo stopwatch
【马鳖】 mǎbiē leech
【马不停蹄】 mǎ bù tíng tí without a stop; nonstop: 部队～地赶到了目的地。The troops rushed to their destination without a single halt.
【马车】 mǎchē ① (horse-drawn) carriage ② cart
【马齿苋】 mǎchǐxiàn 〈植〉 purslane
【马达】 mǎdá motor
【马达加斯加】 Mǎdájiāsījiā Madagascar ◇ ～人 Madagascan
【马大哈】 mǎdàhā ① careless; forgetful ② a careless person; scatterbrain
【马刀】 mǎdāo sabre
【马到成功】 mǎ dào chénggōng win success immediately upon arrival; gain an immediate victory; win instant success
【马灯】 mǎdēng barn lantern; lantern
【马镫】 mǎdèng stirrup
【马兜铃】 mǎdōulíng 〈植〉 birthwort
【马队】 mǎduì ① a train of horses carrying goods; caravan ② a contingent of mounted troops; cavalry
【马尔代夫】 Mǎ'ěrdàifū Maldives ◇ ～人 Maldivian
【马尔加什语】 Mǎ'ěrjiāshíyǔ Malagasy (language)
【马尔萨斯主义】 Mǎ'ěrsàsīzhǔyì Malthusianism
【马尔维纳斯群岛】 Mǎ'ěrwéinàsī Qúndǎo Islas Malvinas
【马耳他】 Mǎ'ěrtā Malta ◇ ～人 Maltese/ ～语 Maltese (language)
【马粪纸】 mǎfènzhǐ strawboard
【马蜂】 mǎfēng hornet; wasp
【马蜂窝】 mǎfēngwō hornet's nest: 他这一说可捅了～。That remark of his stirred up a hornet's nest.
【马夫】 mǎfū 〈旧〉 groom
【马革裹尸】 mǎgé guǒ shī be wrapped in a horse's hide after death — die on the battlefield: 青山处处埋忠骨，何必～还？There are green hills everywhere to bury loyal bones; why wrap the corpse in horse hide and bring it back?
【马褂】 mǎguà mandarin jacket (worn over a gown)
【马赫数】 mǎhèshù 〈物〉 Mach number
【马赫主义】 Mǎhèzhǔyì 〈哲〉 Machism ◇ ～者 Machist
【马后炮】 mǎhòupào belated action or advice; belated effort: 我这个建议也许是～。My suggestion may already be too late./ 事情都做完了，你才说要帮忙，这不是～吗？You come and offer to help when the work's all done. Isn't that a bit late?
【马虎】 mǎhu careless; casual: ～了事 get it done in a slapdash manner/ 他这个人做事比较～。He's a rather careless fellow./ 这是个大事，不能～过去。This is a serious matter. It shouldn't be done just any old way.
【马鲛鱼】 mǎjiāoyú Spanish mackerel
【马脚】 mǎjiǎo sth. that gives the game away: 露出～ show the cloven hoof; give oneself away
【马厩】 mǎjiù stable
【马驹子】 mǎjūzi 〈口〉 colt; foal; pony
【马克】 mǎkè ① mark ② markka
【马克思列宁主义】 Mǎkèsī-Lièníngzhǔyì Marxism-Leninism ◇ ～者 Marxist-Leninist
【马克思主义】 Mǎkèsīzhǔyì Marxism ◇ ～哲学 Marxist philosophy/ ～者 Marxist/ ～政治经济学 Marxist political economy
【马口铁】 mǎkǒutiě tinplate; galvanized iron
【马裤】 mǎkù riding breeches ◇ ～呢 whipcord
【马拉犁】 mǎlālí 〈农〉 horse-drawn plough
【马拉松】 mǎlāsōng marathon ◇ ～赛跑 marathon race; marathon
【马拉维】 Mǎlāwéi Malawi ◇ ～人 Malawian
【马来半岛】 Mǎlái Bàndǎo the Malay Peninsula
【马来西亚】 Mǎláixīyà Malaysia ◇ ～人 Malaysian
【马来语】 Mǎláiyǔ Malay (language)
【马蓝】 mǎlán 〈植〉 acanthaceous indigo (*Strobilanthes cusia*)
【马里】 Mǎlǐ Mali ◇ ～人 Malian
【马力】 mǎlì 〈物〉 horsepower (h.p.): 开足～ at full speed; at full steam ◇ ～小时 horsepower-hour (hp-hr)
【马立克派】 Mǎlìkèpài 〈伊斯兰教〉 the Malikite school (或 sect)
【马列主义】 Mǎ-Lièzhǔyì 〈简〉（马克思列宁主义） Marxism-Leninism
【马蔺】 mǎlìn 〈植〉 Chinese small iris (*Iris pallasii* var. *chinensis*)
【马铃薯】 mǎlíngshǔ potato ◇ ～晚疫病 late blight of potato
【马六甲海峡】 Mǎliùjiǎ Hǎixiá the Strait of Malacca
【马鹿】 mǎlù 〈动〉 red deer
【马路】 mǎlù road; street; avenue
【马骡】 mǎluó 〈动〉 mule
【马马虎虎】 mǎmǎhūhū ① careless; casual: 他的信我只是～地看了一下。I merely glanced over his letter./ 产品出厂要严格检查，～可不行。Products must be strictly, not perfunctorily, inspected before they leave the factory. ② fair; not so bad: 这种牌子的香烟怎么样？——～，你来一支试试。How's this brand of cigarettes? — Not so bad. Try one. ③ not very good; just passable; so-so: 你的游泳技术怎么样？——～，游不远。Are you a good swimmer? — Just so-so. I can't swim far.
【马面鲀】 mǎmiàntún 〈动〉 black scraper
【马奶】 mǎnǎi mare's milk
【马趴】 mǎpā 〔多用于〕: 摔了个大～ fall flat on one's face
【马匹】 mǎpǐ horses
【马钱子】 mǎqiánzǐ 〈植〉 vomiting nut; nux vomica
【马前卒】 mǎqiánzú ① pawn ② cat's-paw
【马枪】 mǎqiāng carbine
【马球】 mǎqiú 〈体〉 polo
【马赛克】 mǎsàikè 〈建〉 mosaic ◇ ～铺面 mosaic pavement

【马上】 mǎshàng at once; immediately; straight away; right away: 我们～就动手。We'll start working straight away./ 你～就走吗？Are you leaving right away?/ 我～就回来。I won't be a minute. 或 I'll be back in a minute.
【马勺】 mǎsháo ladle
【马首是瞻】 mǎshǒu shì zhān take the head of the general's horse as guide — follow sb.'s lead
【马术】 mǎshù horsemanship
【马蹄】 mǎtí horse's hoof
◇ ～表 round or hoof-shaped desk clock; alarm clock/ ～声 hoofbeat; clatter of a horse's hoofs; clip-clop/ ～形 the shape of a hoof; U-shaped
【马蹄铁】 mǎtítiě ① horseshoe ② U-shaped magnet; horseshoe magnet
【马桶】 mǎtǒng nightstool; closestool; commode
【马头琴】 mǎtóuqín 〈乐〉 a bowed stringed instrument with a scroll carved like a horse's head, used by the Monggol nationality
【马尾松】 mǎwěisōng 〈植〉 masson pine
【马戏】 mǎxì circus ◇ ～团 circus troupe
【马熊】 mǎxióng brown bear
【马靴】 mǎxuē riding boots
【马缨丹】 mǎyīngdān 〈植〉 lantana
【马蝇】 mǎyíng horse botfly
【马扎】 mǎzhá campstool; folding stool
【马掌】 mǎzhǎng horseshoe
【马桩】 mǎzhuāng hitching post
【马鬃】 mǎzōng horse's mane
【马祖岛】 Mǎzǔdǎo Mazu Island

## 吗 mǎ
另见 má; ma
【吗啡】 mǎfēi 〈药〉 morphine

## 犸 mǎ
见"猛犸" měngmǎ

## 玛 mǎ
【玛瑙】 mǎnǎo agate
【玛雅人】 Mǎyǎrén Maya

## 码 mǎ
① a sign or thing indicating number: 页～ page number/ 价～ marked price/ 筹～ counter; chip ②〔指一件事或一类的事〕: 一～事 the same thing/ 两～事 two different things ③〈口〉pile up; stack: ～砖 stack bricks ④ yard (yd.)
【码头】 mǎtou ① wharf; dock; quay; pier ②〈方〉 port city; commercial and transportation centre: 跑～ travel from port to port as a trader; be a travelling merchant ◇ ～费 wharfage; dockage/ ～工人 docker; stevedore; longshoreman/ ～交货 ex wharf (或 pier, quay)
【码子】 mǎzi ① numeral: 苏州～ Suzhou numerals (traditionally used by shopkeepers to mark prices) ② counter; chip

## 蚂 mǎ
另见 mà
【蚂蟥】 mǎhuáng 〈动〉 leech
【蚂蚁】 mǎyǐ ant
【蚂蚁搬泰山】 mǎyǐ bān Tàishān ants can move Mount Taishan — the united efforts of the masses can accomplish mighty projects
【蚂蚁啃骨头】 mǎyǐ kěn gútou ants gnawing at a bone — a concentration of small machines on a big job; plod away at a big job bit by bit

# mà

## 骂 mà
① abuse; curse; swear; call names: ～人 swear (at people)/ ～不绝口 pour out a stream of abuse; curse unceasingly/ ～人话 abusive language; swearword; curse ② condemn; rebuke; reprove; scold: 这样铺张浪费，没有一个人不～。Such extravagance is an object of general condemnation./ 把孩子～了一顿 give one's child a scolding (或 dressing down)
【骂街】 màjiē shout abuses in the street; call people names in public: 泼妇～ like a shrew shouting abuses in the street
【骂骂咧咧】 màmaliēliē intersperse one's talk with curses; be foul-mouthed
【骂名】 màmíng bad name; infamy: 留下千古～ earn oneself eternal infamy

## 蚂 mà
另见 mǎ
【蚂蚱】 màzha 〈方〉 locust

# ma

## 吗 ma
〈助〉 ①〔用在句末，表示疑问〕: 下午有会～？ Is there a meeting this afternoon?/ 你找我有事～？ Is there something you want to see me about? ②〔用在句中停顿处，点出话题〕: 特殊情况～，还得特殊对待。Special cases, of course, need special consideration.
另见 má; mǎ

## 嘛 ma
〈助〉〔表示道理显而易见〕: 这也不能怪他，头一回做～。He's not to blame. After all, it was the first time he'd done it./ 这件事他是知道的～。He's well aware of it.

# mái

## 埋 mái
cover up (with earth, snow, etc.); bury: 雪把这口井～起来了。The well is buried in snow./ ～地雷 lay a mine
另见 mán
【埋藏】 máicáng lie hidden in the earth; bury: 这一带地下～着丰富的矿产。There are rich mineral deposits in this region./ 奴隶们～在心底的仇恨象火山一样爆发出来了。The slaves' hatred, which had lain buried deep in their hearts, erupted like a volcano.
【埋伏】 máifu ① ambush: 设下～ lay an ambush/ 中～ fall into an ambush/ 游击队～在青纱帐里。The guerrillas lay in ambush behind a green curtain of tall crops. ② hide; lie low
【埋没】 máimò ① bury; cover up (with earth, snow, etc.): 泥石流～了整个村庄。The mud-rock flow submerged the whole village. ② neglect; stifle: ～人材 stifle real talents/ 瞧，这儿有重要的资料，差点给～了。Look, here's some important source material we almost overlooked.
【埋头】 máitóu immerse oneself in; be engrossed in: ～苦干 quietly immerse oneself in hard work; quietly put one's shoulder to the wheel/ ～读书 bury oneself in books/ ～业务 engross oneself in vocational work
【埋头铆钉】 máitóu mǎodīng countersunk rivet
【埋线疗法】 máixiàn liáofǎ 〈中医〉 catgut embedding therapy (embedding a piece of catgut in a selected point to produce protracted stimulation)

【埋葬】 máizàng bury: ～旧世界,建设新世界 bury the old world and build a new one

**霾** mái 〈气〉 haze

## mǎi

**买** mǎi buy; purchase: 公社～了几台拖拉机。The commune has bought several tractors./ 这是人家送的,不是～的。It is a present, not a purchase./ ～东西 buy things; go shopping/ ～得起 can afford/ ～不起 cannot afford

【买办】 mǎibàn comprador ◇ ～资产阶级 comprador bourgeoisie

【买椟还珠】 mǎi dú huán zhū keep the glittering casket and give back the pearls to the seller — show lack of judgment

【买方】 mǎifāng the buying party (of a contract, etc.); buyer

【买好】 mǎihǎo try to win sb.'s favour; ingratiate oneself with; play up to

【买价】 mǎijià buying price

【买空卖空】 mǎikōng-màikōng speculate (in stocks, etc.)

【买麻藤】 mǎimáténg 〈植〉 sweetberry jointfir (*Gnetum montanum*)

【买卖】 mǎimai ① buying and selling; business; deal; transaction: 做成一笔～ make a deal/ ～兴隆。The business is brisk./ 今天～怎么样? How was business today? ② (private) shop ◇ ～婚姻 mercenary marriage/ ～人 businessman; trader; merchant

【买通】 mǎitōng bribe; buy over; buy off

【买帐】 mǎizhàng 〔多用于否定式〕 acknowledge the superiority or seniority of; show respect for: 他越是神气,我们越不买他的帐。The more airs he gives himself, the less respect we'll show him.

【买主】 mǎizhǔ buyer; customer

**荬** mǎi 见"苣荬菜" qǔmaicài

## mài

**迈** mài ① step; stride: ～过门槛 step over the threshold/ ～着矫健的步伐 walk with vigorous strides/ ～开双脚,到基层去。Get yourself moving and go down to the grass roots. ② advanced in years; old: 年～ aged

【迈步】 màibù take a step; make a step; step forward: ～走向讲台 step up to the platform/ 迈出第一步 make the first step

【迈进】 màijìn stride forward; forge ahead; advance with big strides: 向着共产主义伟大目标～ stride forward towards the great goal of communism

**麦** mài ① a general term for wheat, barley, etc. ② wheat ③ (Mài) a surname

【麦茬】 màichá 〈农〉 wheat stubble ◇ ～白薯 sweet potatoes grown after the wheat harvest/ ～地 a field from which wheat has been reaped

【麦地那】 Màidìnà Medina

【麦冬】 màidōng 〈中药〉 the tuber of dwarf lilyturf (*Ophiopogon japonicus*)

【麦蛾】 mài'é gelechiid (moth)

【麦尔登呢】 mài'ěrdēngní 〈纺〉 melton

【麦麸】 màifū wheat bran

【麦秆虫】 màigǎnchóng skeleton shrimp

【麦红吸浆虫】 màihóngxījiāngchóng wheat midge

【麦加】 Màijiā Mecca

【麦角】 màijiǎo 〈药〉 ergot

【麦秸】 màijiē wheat straw ◇ ～画 straw patchwork

【麦精】 màijīng malt extract ◇ ～鱼肝油 cod-liver oil with malt extract

【麦克风】 màikèfēng microphone; mike

【麦浪】 màilàng rippling wheat; billowing wheat fields

【麦粒肿】 màilìzhǒng 〈医〉 sty

【麦门冬】 màiméndōng 见"麦冬"

【麦片】 màipiàn oatmeal ◇ ～粥 oatmeal porridge; oatmeal

【麦秋】 màiqiū wheat harvest season ◇ ～假 wheat harvest vacation (for village schools)

【麦乳精】 màirǔjīng extract of malt and milk

【麦收】 màishōu wheat harvest

【麦穗】 màisuì ear of wheat; wheat head

【麦芒】 màiwáng awn of wheat

【麦芽】 màiyá malt ◇ ～糖 malt sugar; maltose

【麦蚜】 màiyá 〈动〉 wheat aphid 又作"麦蚜虫"

【麦子】 màizi wheat

**卖** mài ① sell: 把余粮～给国家 sell surplus grain to the state/ ～得快 sell well/ ～不出去 not sell well ② betray: ～友 betray one's friend ③ exert to the utmost; not spare: ～劲儿 exert all one's strength; spare no effort ④ show off: ～乖 show off one's cleverness

【卖唱】 màichàng sing for a living

【卖方】 màifāng the selling party (of a contract, etc.); seller

【卖狗皮膏药】 mài gǒupí gāoyào sell quack remedies; palm things off on people

【卖乖】 màiguāi show off one's cleverness

【卖关子】 mài guānzi stop a story at a climax to keep the listeners in suspense; keep people guessing: 结果怎么样呢?快说吧,别～了。How did it end? Come on! Don't keep us guessing.

【卖国】 màiguó betray one's country; turn traitor to one's country: ～求荣 seek power and wealth by betraying one's country; turn traitor for personal gain ◇ ～集团 traitorous clique/ ～条约 traitorous treaty/ ～行为 treasonable act/ ～贼 traitor (to one's country)/ ～主义 national betrayal

【卖好】 màihǎo curry favour with; ingratiate oneself with; play up to

【卖价】 màijià selling price

【卖劲儿】 màijìnr exert all one's strength; spare no effort: 姑娘们干活真～。The girls are really going all out in their work.

【卖力】 màilì exert all one's strength; spare no effort; do all one can

【卖力气】 mài lìqi ① exert all one's strength; exert oneself to the utmost; do one's very best ② live by the sweat of one's brow; make a living by manual labour

【卖命】 màimìng ① work oneself to the bone for sb.: 地主逼着长工们为他～。The landlord forced the farm labourers to work themselves to the bone. ② die (unworthily) for: 这些士兵没有一个愿意为帝国主义的侵略战争～。None of these soldiers wanted to die in the imperialists' war of aggression.

【卖弄】 màinong show off; parade: ～学问 show off one's learning; parade one's knowledge/ ～小聪明 show off one's smartness

【卖俏】 màiqiào play the coquette; coquette; flirt

【卖身】 màishēn ① sell oneself or a member of one's

family ②sell one's body; sell one's soul ◇ ～契 an indenture by which one sells oneself or a member of one's family

【卖身投靠】 màishēn tóukào barter away one's honour for sb.'s patronage; basely offer to serve some reactionary bigwig

【卖艺】 màiyì make a living as a performer: 在街头～ be a street-performer

【卖淫】 màiyín prostitution

【卖主】 màizhǔ seller

【卖座】 màizuò (of a theatre, etc.) draw large audiences; (of a restaurant, etc.) attract large numbers of customers: 那出戏可～啦。That play drew large audiences. 或 That play was a great draw.

**脉** mài ①〈生理〉arteries and veins ②〈简〉(脉搏) pulse: 号～ feel sb.'s pulse ③ vein: 叶～ veins in a leaf/ 矿～ ore vein; mineral vein

另见 mò

【脉搏】 màibó pulse: 他的～每分钟一百次。The beat of his pulse was a hundred./ 这部小说把握了我们时代的～。The novel throbs with the pulse of our times. ◇ ～计 sphygmometer

【脉冲】 màichōng 〈物〉 pulse ◇ ～发生器 pulser/ ～计数器 pulse counter/ ～雷达 pulse radar/ ～信号 pulse signal/ ～星〈天〉 pulsar

【脉动】 màidòng 〈物〉〈天〉 pulsation ◇ ～电流 pulsating current/ ～式喷气发动机 pulse-jet engine/ ～星 pulsating star

【脉管炎】 màiguǎnyán 〈医〉 vasculitis

【脉络】 màiluò ①〈中医〉 a general name for arteries and veins ② vein (of a leaf, etc.) ③ thread of thought; sequence of ideas: 这篇文章结构严谨，～分明。This article is closely knit and presents its ideas in a clear, logical way.

【脉石】 màishí 〈矿〉 gangue; veinstone ◇ ～矿物 gangue mineral

【脉息】 màixī pulse: ～微弱 have a weak pulse

【脉象】 màixiàng 〈中医〉 pulse condition; type of pulse

【脉泽】 màizé 〈物〉 maser

【脉诊】 màizhěn 〈中医〉 diagnosis by feeling the pulse

## mān

**颟** mān

【颟顸】 mānhan muddleheaded and careless

## mán

**埋** mán

另见 mái

【埋怨】 mányuàn blame; complain; grumble: 这场球打输了，大家找找原因，不要互相～。Instead of blaming one another for losing the game, let's find out what exactly went wrong./他的话里有～情绪。There was a note of complaint in what he said./ 他老爱～。He's always grumbling.

**蛮** mán ① rough; fierce; reckless; unreasoning: 野～ savage/ ～劲 sheer animal strength ② an ancient name for southern nationalities ③〈方〉 quite; pretty: 这电影～好。This is quite a good film. 或 This is a pretty good film.

【蛮不讲理】 mán bù jiǎnglǐ be impervious to reason; persist in being unreasonable

【蛮干】 mángàn act rashly; act recklessly; be foolhardy: 要苦干加巧干，不要～。We should work hard and intelligently, not blindly./ 那纯粹是～。That's downright foolhardy.

【蛮横】 mánhèng rude and unreasonable; arbitrary; peremptory: ～无理的要求 peremptory demands/ ～地拒绝合理建议 arbitrarily reject reasonable proposals

**谩** mán deceive; hoodwink

另见 màn

**蔓** mán

另见 màn; wàn

【蔓菁】 mánjing 〈植〉 turnip

**馒** mán

【馒头】 mántou steamed bun; steamed bread

**瞒** mán hide the truth from: 他把病情～着不跟同志们说。He didn't let his comrades know about his illness./ 不～你说 to tell you the truth

【瞒哄】 mánhǒng deceive; pull the wool over sb.'s eyes

【瞒上欺下】 mán shàng qī xià deceive those above and bully those below

【瞒天过海】 mán tiān guò hǎi cross the sea by a trick — practise deception

**鳗** mán eel

【鳗鲡】 mánlí eel

## mǎn

**满** mǎn ① full; filled; packed: 这两个抽屉都～了。Both drawers are full./ 屋里坐～了人。The room was packed with people./ 果树～山坡。The slope was covered with fruit trees./ 欢声笑语～山村。The mountain village rang with cheers and laughter./ ～～一卡车煤 a full truck-load of coal/ ～头大汗 one's face streaming with sweat ② fill: 再给你～上一杯。Let me fill your glass once more. ③ expire; reach the limit: 年～十八的青年 young people who have reached the age of 18/ 他的服役期还没～。His term of service hasn't expired yet./ 她到农村去还不～一年。It isn't a year yet since she went to live in the countryside./ 假期已～。The holidays are over. ④ completely; entirely; perfectly: ～不是那么回事。That wasn't the way it was at all./ 我～以为他会同意的。I had counted on him to agree with me. ⑤ satisfied: 不～ dissatisfied; discontented ⑥ complacent; conceited: 反骄破～ combat arrogance and complacence ⑦ (Mǎn) a surname ⑧ (Mǎn) the Man nationality 参见"满族"

【满不在乎】 mǎn bù zàihu not worry at all; not care in the least; give (或 take) no heed: 别人都替他着急，他却～。Everybody was anxious about him, but he wasn't worried at all.

【满城风雨】 mǎn chéng fēngyǔ (become) the talk of the town: 闹得～ create a sensation; create a scandal

【满打满算】 mǎndǎ-mǎnsuàn reckoning in every item (of income or expenditure); at the very most: 这项工程～有一百吨水泥就足够了。We need 100 tons of cement at most for this project.

【满额】 mǎn'é fulfil the (enrolment, etc.) quota: 我校今年招生已经～。Our school has already fulfilled its enrolment quota for this year.

【满分】 mǎnfēn full marks

【满腹】 mǎnfù have one's mind filled with: ～牢骚 full of

grievances; full of resentment/ ～狐疑 filled with suspicion; extremely suspicious

【满怀】 mǎnhuái ① have one's heart filled with; be imbued with: ～革命豪情 full of revolutionary pride and enthusiasm/ ～胜利的信心 fully confident of victory; with full confidence in victory/ ～着对战友的深情 imbued with ardent love for one's comrade-in-arms/ ～着对敌人的深仇大恨 burning with bitter hatred for the enemy ②〔多用于〕: 撞了个～ bump right into sb. ③ (of sheep, cattle, etc.) all with young

【满坑满谷】 mǎnkēng-mǎngǔ in large numbers; in great abundance; in plenty

【满口】 mǎnkǒu (speak) unreservedly; profusely; glibly: ～称赞 praise unreservedly (或 profusely)/ ～答应 readily promise/ ～谎言 spout lies

【满满当当】 mǎnmǎndāngdāng 〈口〉 full to the brim: 挑着～的两桶水 carry (或 tote) two brimming buckets of water/ 厩肥～地装了一大车。The cart was piled high with barnyard manure.

【满门】 mǎnmén the whole family

【满面】 mǎnmiàn have one's face covered with: 泪流～ tears streaming down one's cheeks/ ～笑容 grinning from ear to ear; be all smiles/ ～红光 glowing with health/ ～春风 beaming with satisfaction; radiant with happiness

【满目】 mǎnmù meet the eye on every side: ～荒凉。A scene of desolation met the eye on every side.

【满目疮痍】 mǎnmù chuāngyí 见"疮痍满目" chuāngyí mǎnmù

【满脑子】 mǎnnǎozi have one's mind stuffed with: ～资产阶级思想 be steeped in bourgeois ideology

【满腔】 mǎnqiāng have one's bosom filled with: ～仇恨 burning with hatred/ ～怒火 filled with rage/ ～热忱 filled with ardour and sincerity/ ～热情地接待顾客 attend to customers enthusiastically

【满身】 mǎnshēn have one's body covered with; be covered all over with: ～油泥 covered all over with grime/ ～是汗 sweat all over

【满师】 mǎnshī (of an apprentice) finish serving one's time; serve out one's apprenticeship

【满堂红】 mǎntánghóng all-round victory; success in every field: 今年我们厂是～，样样指标都提前完成了。Our factory has had all-round success this year. All our targets have been fulfilled ahead of schedule.

【满天】 mǎntiān all over the sky: ～星斗 a star-studded sky/ 乌云～。The sky is overcast with dark clouds./ 鹅毛大雪～飞。The snow is falling thick and heavy.

【满心】 mǎnxīn have one's heart filled with: ～欢喜 filled with joy

【满眼】 mǎnyǎn ① have one's eyes filled with: ～红丝 with bloodshot eyes ② meet the eye on every side: ～的山花 mountain flowers greeting the eye everywhere

【满意】 mǎnyì satisfied; pleased: 双方对会谈的结果表示～。Both sides expressed satisfaction with the results of the talks./ 大家对他的工作很～。Everyone was pleased with his work.

【满员】 mǎnyuán ①〈军〉 at full strength: 保证主力部队经常～ ensure that the main forces are always kept at full strength ② all seats taken: 二号车厢已经～。No. 2 carriage is full.

【满月】 mǎnyuè ① full moon ② a baby's completion of its first month of life: 孩子明天就～了。The baby will be a month old tomorrow.

【满载】 mǎnzài loaded to capacity; fully loaded; laden with: 一辆～木材的卡车 a truck fully loaded with timber/ 一艘～煤炭的货船 a freighter laden with coal/ 医疗队～着非洲人民的友谊回到北京。The medical team returned to Beijing, bringing with it the friendship of the African people. ◇ ～超轴运动〈交〉 movement for capacity loads and additional haulage

【满载而归】 mǎnzài ér guī come back with fruitful results; return from a rewarding journey

【满招损，谦受益】 mǎn zhāo sǔn, qiān shòu yì one loses by pride and gains by modesty

【满足】 mǎnzú ① satisfied; content; contented: ～于现状 be satisfied with the existing state of affairs; be content with things as they are/ 不～于已经取得的成绩 not rest content with one's achievements; not rest on one's laurels/ 学习的敌人是自己的～。Complacency is the enemy of study. ② satisfy; meet: ～人民的需要 satisfy (或 meet) the needs of the people/ 我们将尽可能地～你们的要求。We'll do our best to meet your demands.

【满族】 Mǎnzú the Man (Manchu) nationality, mainly distributed over the provinces of Liaoning, Heilongjiang, Jilin and Hebei, the municipality of Beijing and the Nei Monggol Autonomous Region

【满座】 mǎnzuò capacity audience; capacity house; full house: 这个剧演了一个月，场场～。The play ran for a month to capacity audiences.

**螨** mǎn 〈动〉 mite

## màn

**曼** màn ① graceful: 轻歌～舞 soft music and graceful dances ② prolonged; long-drawn-out: ～延 draw out (in length)

【曼丁哥语】 Màndīnggēyǔ Mande; Mandingo

【曼妙】 mànmiào 〈书〉 (of dancing) lithe and graceful

【曼声】 mànshēng (sing or recite in) lengthened sounds: ～吟诵 recite in slow, measured tones/ ～而歌 drawl out a song

【曼陀林】 màntuólín 〈乐〉 mandolin

【曼陀罗】 màntuóluó 〈植〉 datura

【曼延】 mànyán draw out (in length); stretch: ～曲折的羊肠小道 a winding footpath stretching into the distance

**谩** màn disrespectful; rude
另见 mán

【谩骂】 mànmà hurl invectives; fling abuses; rail: ～决不是战斗。To hurl abuse is no way to fight.

**漫** màn ① overflow; brim over; flood; inundate: 池塘的水～出来了。The pool overflowed its banks./ 水不深，只～过我脚面。The water wasn't deep. It only came up to my ankles. ② all over the place; everywhere: ～江碧透。The whole stream was emerald green. ③ free; unrestrained; casual: 红旗～卷。Red banners fluttered freely./ ～无目标 aimless; at random/ ～无止境 know no bounds; be without limit

【漫笔】 mànbǐ informal essay; literary notes

【漫不经心】 màn bù jīngxīn careless; casual; negligent

【漫步】 mànbù stroll; ramble; roam

【漫长】 màncháng very long; endless: ～的海岸线 a long coastline/ 在～的岁月中 during the long years; over the years/ 革命走过了～而曲折的道路。The revolution has followed a long and tortuous course.

【漫反射】 mànfǎnshè 〈物〉 diffuse reflection

【漫灌】 mànguàn flood irrigation

【漫画】 mànhuà caricature; cartoon

【漫漫】 mànmàn very long; boundless: ～长夜 endless

night/ 白雪～ a boundless expanse of snow

【漫山遍野】 mànshān-biànyě all over the mountains and plains; over hill and dale

【漫射】 mànshè 〈物〉 diffusion ◇ ～光 diffused light/ ～体 diffuser

【漫说】 mànshuō 见"慢说" mànshuō

【漫谈】 màntán (have an) informal discussion: 听完报告咱们～～一下吧。After we've heard the report, we'll talk about it.

【漫天】 màntiān ① filling the whole sky; all over the sky: ～大雾 a dense fog obscuring the sky/ ～大雪 whirling snow/ ～的革命烽火 flames of revolution raging across the horizon ② boundless; limitless: ～大谎 a monstrous lie/ ～要价 ask (或 demand) an exorbitant price

【漫无边际】 màn wú biānjì ① boundless ② straying far from the subject; rambling; discursive

【漫溢】 mànyì overflow; flood; brim over

【漫游】 mànyóu go on a pleasure trip; roam; wander: ～西湖 go boating on or roam around the West Lake

**蔓** màn
另见 mán; wàn

【蔓生植物】 mànshēng zhíwù trailing plant

【蔓延】 mànyán spread; extend: 火势～很快。The fire spread quickly.

**慢** màn ① slow: 反应～ be slow to react/ ～下来 slow down/ 我的表～一分钟。My watch is one minute slow./ 这钟一天～十秒。This clock loses ten seconds a day. ② postpone; defer: 且～! Hold on a moment. 或 Just a moment!/ 这事先～点儿告诉她。Don't tell her about this yet. ③ supercilious; rude: 傲～ arrogant; haughty/ 言词骄～ use arrogant language

【慢车】 mànchē slow train

【慢工出细活】 màngōng chū xìhuó slow work yields fine products

【慢镜头】 mànjìngtóu 〈电影〉 slow motion

【慢慢】 mànmàn slowly; gradually: 火车～地驶进了车站。Slowly the train pulled into the station./ ～来。Take your time. 或 Don't be in a rush./ 他～会想通的。He'll come round by and by.

【慢坡】 mànpō gentle slope

【慢说】 mànshuō let alone; to say nothing of: 他讲故事，～孩子，连大人都爱听。Even the adults like to listen to his stories, to say nothing of the children.

【慢腾腾】 màntēngtēng at a leisurely pace; unhurriedly; sluggishly: 你这么～的，什么时候能做完哪？When will you ever finish the job if you go on at this pace?

【慢条斯理】 màntiáo-sīlǐ leisurely; unhurriedly: 他说话做事总是～的。He always speaks slowly and acts unhurriedly.

【慢性】 mànxìng ① chronic: ～病 chronic disease ② slow (in taking effect): ～毒药 slow poison

【慢性子】 mànxìngzi ① phlegmatic temperament ② slowpoke; slow coach

【慢中子】 mànzhōngzǐ 〈物〉 slow neutron; low-speed neutron

【慢走】 mànzǒu ① don't go yet; stay; wait a minute ② 〈套〉〔用于送别时〕good-bye; take care

**幔** màn curtain; screen: 布～ cotton curtain

【幔帐】 mànzhàng curtain; screen; canopy

**嫚** màn 〈书〉 scorn; humiliate

**镘** màn trowel

## máng

**忙** máng ① busy; fully occupied: 你在～什么呢？What are you busy with (或 at)?/ 这两天～不～？Are you busy these days?/ 我一个人～不过来。I can't manage all this by myself./ 不要～于小事而忽略大事。Don't immerse yourself in minor matters to the neglect of major ones. ② hurry; hasten; make haste: ～从里屋出来 come hurrying out of the inner room; hasten out of the inner room/ ～着去开会 be in a hurry to go to a meeting/ 你～什么，再坐一会儿吧。What's the hurry? Stay a bit longer./ 别～于下结论。Don't jump to conclusions.

【忙合】 mánghe 〈口〉 be busy; bustle about: 他们俩已经～了一上午了。The two of them have been busy the whole morning.

【忙里偷闲】 mánglǐ tōuxián snatch a little leisure from a busy life

【忙碌】 mánglù be busy; bustle about: 为了全厂工人的生活，她成天～不停。She's busy all day looking after the daily life of the workers in the factory.

【忙乱】 mángluàn be in a rush and a muddle; tackle a job in a hasty and disorderly manner: 要克服～现象。Don't work in a rush and get into a muddle.

【忙人】 mángrén busy person

**芒** máng awn; beard; arista
另见 wáng

【芒刺在背】 mángcì zài bèi feel prickles down one's back—feel nervous and uneasy

【芒硝】 mángxiāo 〈化〉 mirabilite; Glauber's salt

【芒种】 Mángzhòng Grain in Ear (9th solar term)

**杧** máng

【杧果】 mángguǒ 〈植〉 mango

**盲** máng blind

【盲肠】 mángcháng 〈生理〉 caecum

【盲椿象】 mángchūnxiàng 〈动〉 plant bug

【盲从】 mángcóng follow blindly

【盲点】 mángdiǎn 〈生理〉 blind spot; scotoma

【盲动】 mángdòng act blindly; act rashly ◇ ～主义 putschism

【盲鳗】 mángmán hagfish

【盲目】 mángmù blind: ～崇拜 worship blindly/ ～乐观 be unrealistically optimistic/ 人口的～增长 unchecked growth of the population
◇ ～飞行 blind flight; instrument flying/ ～轰炸 blind bombing/ ～着陆 blind landing

【盲目性】 mángmùxìng blindness (in action): 去掉～，养成分析的习惯。Stop acting blindly and cultivate the habit of analysis.

【盲区】 mángqū 〈无〉 blind area

【盲人】 mángrén blind person

【盲人摸象】 mángrén mō xiàng like the blind men trying to size up the elephant — take a part for the whole

【盲人瞎马】 mángrén xiāmǎ a blind man on a blind horse — rushing headlong to disaster

【盲文】 mángwén braille

【盲哑教育】 máng-yǎ jiàoyù education for the blind and the deaf-mute

**氓** máng 见"流氓" liúmáng
另见 méng

**茫** máng ① boundless and indistinct ② ignorant; in the dark
【茫茫】 mángmáng boundless and indistinct; vast: ～大海 a vast sea/ ～草原 the boundless grasslands/ 在旧社会他感到前途～。In the old society, he felt that his prospects were bleak.
【茫然】 mángrán ignorant; in the dark; at a loss: ～无知 be utterly ignorant; be in the dark/ ～不知所措 be at a loss what to do; be at sea/ 显出～的神情 look blank
【茫无头绪】 máng wú tóuxù (of a thing) be confused like a tangle of flax; (of a person) not know where to begin

**硭** máng
【硭硝】 mángxiāo 〈化〉 mirabilite; Glauber's salt

## mǎng

**莽** mǎng ① rank grass ② rash
【莽苍】 mǎngcāng (of scenery) blurred; misty: 烟雨～ a vast blur of mist and rain
【莽汉】 mǎnghàn a boorish fellow; a boor
【莽莽】 mǎngmǎng ① luxuriant; rank ② (of fields, plains, etc.) vast; boundless
【莽原】 mǎngyuán wilderness overgrown with grass
【莽撞】 mǎngzhuàng crude and impetuous; rash: ～的小伙子 a young harum-scarum

**蟒** mǎng boa; python
【蟒蛇】 mǎngshé boa; python

## māo

**猫** māo cat: 雄～ tomcat/ 小～ kitten/ ～叫 mewing; purring
另见 máo
【猫哭老鼠】 māo kū lǎoshǔ the cat weeping over the dead mouse — shed crocodile tears
【猫头鹰】 māotóuyīng owl
【猫熊】 māoxióng panda; giant panda
【猫眼石】 māoyǎnshí 〈矿〉 cat's eye

## máo

**毛** máo ① hair; feather; down: 腋～ armpit hairs/ 羽～ feather/ 桃子上的～ the down of a peach ② wool: ～毯 woollen blanket/ ～袜 woollen stockings/ ～裤 long woollen underwear ③ mildew: 长～ become mildewed; be covered with mildew ④ semifinished: ～坯 semifinished product ⑤ gross: ～利 gross profit ⑥ little; small: ～孩子 a small child; a mere child ⑦ careless; crude; rash: ～头～脑 rash; impetuous ⑧ panicky; scared; flurried: 心里直发～ feel scared; be panic-stricken/ 吓～了 be in a flurry of alarm ⑨〈口〉 (of currency) be no longer worth its face value; depreciate ⑩〈口〉 *mao*, a fractional unit of money in China (=1/10 *yuan* or 10 *fen* 分) ⑪ (Máo) a surname
【毛白杨】 máobáiyáng 〈植〉 Chinese white poplar
【毛笔】 máobǐ writing brush
【毛边纸】 máobiānzhǐ writing paper made from bamboo
【毛病】 máobing ① trouble; mishap; breakdown: 发动机出了～。There's some trouble with the engine./ 这架收音机有点～。There's something wrong with the radio. ② defect; shortcoming; fault; mistake: 克服工作作风上的～ overcome defects in one's work style/ 犯了主观主义的～ make the mistake of being subjective; commit the error of subjectivism/ 他的～是性急。He's impetuous — that's the trouble with him. ③〈方〉 illness: 他胃有～。He has stomach trouble.
【毛玻璃】 máobōli frosted glass
【毛布】 máobù coarse cotton cloth; coarse calico
【毛糙】 máocao crude; coarse; careless: 这活做得太～。That's rather crude work./ 你做事怎么这么～？How could you be so careless?
【毛虫】 máochóng caterpillar 又作"毛毛虫"
【毛刺】 máocì 〈机〉 burr
【毛地黄】 máodìhuáng 〈药〉 digitalis
【毛豆】 máodòu young soya bean
【毛发】 máofà hair (on the human body and head)
【毛纺】 máofǎng wool spinning: 粗梳～ woollen spinning/ 精梳～ worsted spinning ◇ ～厂 woollen mill
【毛葛】 máogé 〈纺〉 poplin
【毛茛】 máogèn 〈植〉 buttercup
【毛骨悚然】 máogǔ sǒngrán with one's hair standing on end — absolutely terrified: 令人～ send cold shivers down one's spine; make sb.'s hair stand on end; be bloodcurdling
【毛巾】 máojīn towel ◇ ～被 towelling coverlet/ ～布 towelling/ ～架 towel rail or rack
【毛孔】 máokǒng 〈生理〉 pore
【毛口】 máokǒu 〈机〉 burr: 去～ burring
【毛拉】 máolā 〈伊斯兰教〉 *maula*; mullah
【毛梾】 máolái 〈植〉 long-petioled dogwood (*Cornus walteri*)
【毛蓝】 máolán darkish blue ◇ ～土布 dyed (或 blue) nankeen
【毛里求斯】 Máolǐqiúsī Mauritius ◇ ～人 Mauritian
【毛里塔尼亚】 Máolǐtǎníyà Mauritania ◇ ～人 Mauritanian
【毛利】 máolì gross profit
【毛料】 máoliào woollen cloth; woollens
【毛驴】 máolǘ donkey
【毛毛雨】 máomaoyǔ drizzle
【毛难族】 Máonánzú the Maonan nationality, living in the Guangxi Zhuang Autonomous Region
【毛坯】 máopī ① semifinished product ②〈机〉 blank
【毛皮】 máopí fur; pelt ◇ ～兽 fur-bearing animal
【毛票】 máopiào 〈口〉 banknotes of one, two or five *jiao* (角) denominations
【毛渠】 máoqú sublateral canal; sublateral
【毛茸茸】 máorōngrōng hairy; downy
【毛瑟枪】 máosèqiāng Mauser
【毛纱】 máoshā 〈纺〉 wool yarn: 粗纺～ woollen yarn/ 精纺～ worsted yarn
【毛石】 máoshí 〈建〉 rubble ◇ ～混凝土 rubble concrete
【毛手毛脚】 máoshǒu-máojiǎo careless (in handling things)
【毛丝】 máosī 〈纺〉 broken filament
【毛遂自荐】 Máo Suì zì jiàn offer one's services as Mao Sui (of the Warring States Period) did — volunteer one's services
【毛笋】 máosǔn the shoot of *mao* bamboo
【毛毯】 máotǎn woollen blanket
【毛桃】 máotáo wild peach
【毛细管】 máoxìguǎn capillary ◇ ～水〈农〉 capillary water
【毛细现象】 máoxì xiànxiàng 〈物〉 capillarity
【毛细血管】 máoxì xuèguǎn 〈生理〉 blood capillary
【毛虾】 máoxiā shrimp
【毛线】 máoxiàn knitting wool ◇ ～针 knitting needle
【毛象】 máoxiàng 〈古生物〉 mammoth
【毛样】 máoyàng 〈印〉 galley proof

【毛腰】 máoyāo 〈方〉arch one's back
【毛衣】 máoyī woollen sweater; sweater; woolly
【毛蚴】 máoyòu 〈动〉miracidium
【毛躁】 máozao ① short-tempered; irritable ② rash and careless
【毛泽东思想】 Máo Zédōng Sīxiǎng Mao Zedong Thought
【毛毡】 máozhān felt
【毛织品】 máozhīpǐn ① wool fabric; woollens ② woollen knitwear
【毛重】 máozhòng gross weight
【毛竹】 máozhú *mao* bamboo

**矛** máo lance; pike; spear
【矛盾】 máodùn ① contradictory: 自相～ self-contradictory/ ～百出 full of contradictions/ ～上交 pass on problems to a higher level instead of solving them oneself/ 这两种意见并不～。These two views are not contradictory (或 mutually exclusive). ②〈哲〉〈逻〉contradiction: ～的普遍性（特殊性） the universality (particularity) of contradiction/ 主要(非主要)～ principal (nonprincipal) contradiction/ ～的主要(次要)方面 the principal (secondary) aspect of a contradiction/ ～的同一性（斗争性） the identity (struggle) of opposites/ 对抗性(非对抗性)～ antagonistic (nonantagonistic) contradiction/ ～的转化 the transformation of a contradiction ◇ ～律〈逻〉the law of contradiction
【矛头】 máotóu spearhead: 批判的～指向修正主义路线。The spearhead of the criticism is directed at the revisionist line./ ～所向 the target of attack

**茅** máo ①〈植〉cogongrass ② (Máo) a surname
【茅草】 máocǎo 〈植〉cogongrass ◇ ～棚 thatched shed; thatched shack
【茅房】 máofáng 〈口〉latrine
【茅膏菜】 máogāocài 〈植〉sundew
【茅坑】 máokēng ①〈口〉latrine pit ②〈方〉latrine
【茅庐】 máolú thatched cottage
【茅塞顿开】 máo sè dùn kāi suddenly see the light
【茅舍】 máoshè 〈书〉thatched cottage
【茅厕】 máosi 〈口〉latrine
【茅台酒】 máotáijiǔ *Maotai* (spirit)
【茅屋】 máowū thatched cottage

**牦** máo
【牦牛】 máoniú yak

**猫** máo
另见 māo
【猫腰】 máoyāo 〈方〉arch one's back

**锚** máo anchor: 抛～ drop anchor; cast anchor/ 起～ weigh anchor
【锚地】 máodì anchorage
【锚雷】 máoléi 〈军〉mooring mine; moored buoyant mine
【锚爪】 máozhuǎ fluke (of an anchor)

**髦** máo 见"时髦" shímáo

**蝥** máo 见"斑蝥" bānmáo

**蟊** máo an insect destructive of the roots of seedlings
【蟊贼】 máozéi a person harmful to the country and people; pest

## mǎo

**卯** mǎo ① the fourth of the twelve Earthly Branches ② mortise
【卯劲儿】 mǎojìnr 〈口〉make a sudden all-out effort: 几个人一～，就把大石头撬下坡去了。With a sudden thrust, they sent the boulder rolling down the hillside.
【卯时】 mǎoshí the period of the day from 5 a.m. to 7 a.m.
【卯榫】 mǎosǔn mortise and tenon
【卯眼】 mǎoyǎn mortise

**铆** mǎo 〈机〉riveting: 风动～ pneumatic riveting/ 对接～ butt riveting/ 搭接～ lap riveting
【铆钉】 mǎodīng rivet ◇ ～距 rivet pitch/ ～枪 riveting gun
【铆工】 mǎogōng ① riveting ② riveter
【铆机】 mǎojī riveter: 风动～ pneumatic riveter/ 水力～ hydraulic riveter
【铆接】 mǎojiē riveting; rivet joint

## mào

**茂** mào ① luxuriant; exuberant; profuse: 根深叶～ deep roots and exuberant foliage ② rich and splendid: 图文并～。The picture and its accompanying essay are both excellent. ③〈化〉cyclopentadiene
【茂密】 màomì (of grass or trees) dense; thick: ～的森林 a dense forest
【茂盛】 màoshèng luxuriant; exuberant; flourishing: 庄稼长得很～。The crops are growing luxuriantly.

**冒** mào ① emit; send out (或 up, forth); give off: ～泡 send up bubbles; be bubbling/ ～气 give off steam; be steaming/ 泥浆从地下～出来。Mud oozed from underground./烟囱里～着白烟。White smoke rose from the chimneys./ 他脑门上直～汗。Sweat kept oozing out from his forehead./ 错误思想总是要～出来的。Wrong ideas are bound to manifest themselves. ② risk; brave: 小李～着生命危险抢救国家财产。Xiao Li risked his life to save state property./ 卡车～着敌机的轰炸扫射向前急驶。Braving the bombing and strafing of enemy planes, the truck sped ahead./ ～雨 braving the rain; in spite of the rain/ ～风险 run risks/ ～着风浪出海 put to sea in spite of wind and wave; venture out on a stormy sea ③ boldly; rashly: ～猜一下 make a bold guess; venture a guess ④ falsely (claim, etc.); fraudulently: 那人～称是连长的亲戚。The man falsely claimed to be a relative of the company commander. ⑤ (Mào) a surname
【冒充】 màochōng pretend to be (sb. or sth. else); pass sb. or sth. off as: ～内行 pretend to be an expert; pose as an expert/ 民兵识破了～解放军的敌特。The militiaman saw through the enemy agent who was trying to pass himself off as a PLA man.
【冒顶】 màodǐng 〈矿〉roof fall: 工作面～ face fall/ 大～ bulk caving
【冒渎】 màodú 〈书〉bother or annoy a superior
【冒犯】 màofàn offend; affront: 谁知道这一句话竟～了他？Who would have thought that the remark would offend him?/ ～禁令 violate a prohibition
【冒号】 màohào colon (:)
【冒火】 màohuǒ burn with anger; get angry; flare up
【冒尖儿】 màojiānr ① piled high above the brim: 筐里的土

豆装得～了。The basket is piled high with potatoes. ② a little over; a little more than: 十斤刚～ a little over ten *jin* ③ stand out; be conspicuous: 怕～ be afraid of becoming too conspicuous/ 她就爱～。She likes to be in the limelight. 或 She's too pushing. ④ begin to crop up: 问题一～,就及时采取了措施。Proper measures were taken as soon as the problem cropped up.

【冒进】 màojìn premature advance; rash advance

【冒口】 màokǒu 〈机〉 rising head; riser

【冒领】 màolǐng falsely claim as one's own: 虚报～ fraudulent applications and claims

【冒昧】 màomèi 〈谦〉 make bold; venture; take the liberty: ～陈辞 make bold to express my views; venture an opinion/ 不揣～ may I take the liberty to; I venture to

【冒名】 màomíng go under sb. else's name; assume another's name: ～顶替 take another's place by assuming his name

【冒牌】 màopái a counterfeit of a well-known trade mark; imitation; fake ◇ ～货 imitation; fake/ ～社会主义 bogus (或 sham) socialism

【冒失】 màoshi rash; abrupt: 说话～ speak without due consideration/ 这样冒冒失失去找他可不好。It's not appropriate to drop in on him so casually. ◇ ～鬼 harum-scarum

【冒天下之大不韪】 mào tiānxià zhī dà bùwěi defy world opinion; risk universal condemnation; fly in the face of the will of the people

【冒头】 màotóu begin to crop up: 不良倾向一～就要抓住它。Watch out for harmful tendencies and deal with them the moment they crop up.

【冒险】 màoxiǎn take a risk; take chances: 戴上安全帽再下去,不要～。Wear your safety helmet when you go down. Don't take any chances./ 小分队～穿过敌人的封锁线。The detachment ventured a thrust through the enemy blockade./ 军事～ military adventure ◇ ～家 adventurer/ ～政策 adventurist policy

【冒险主义】 màoxiǎnzhǔyì adventurism ◇ ～者 adventurist

**贸** mào trade: 外～ foreign trade

【贸然】 màorán rashly; hastily; without careful consideration: ～下结论 draw a hasty conclusion; jump to a conclusion

【贸易】 màoyì trade: 和别国进行～ trade with foreign countries; do business with other countries/ 对外～ foreign trade / 国内～ domestic trade/ 国际～ international trade ◇ ～差额 balance of trade/ ～额 volume of trade; turnover/ ～风〈气〉 trade wind/ ～逆差 unfavourable balance of trade/ ～顺差 favourable balance of trade/ ～协定 trade agreement/ ～议定书 trade protocol/ ～中心 trade centre

**耄** mào ① octogenarian ② advanced in years

**袤** mào 见"广袤" guǎngmào

**帽** mào ① headgear; hat; cap: 草～ straw hat/ 军～ service cap/ 安全～ safety helmet ② cap-like cover for sth.: 笔～儿 the cap of a pen/ 螺钉～ screw cap

【帽徽】 màohuī insignia (或 badge) on a cap: 红星～ red star insignia on a cap

【帽盔儿】 màokuīr skullcap

【帽舌】 màoshé peak (of a cap); visor

【帽檐】 màoyán the brim of a hat

【帽子】 màozi ① headgear; hat; cap ② label; tag; brand: 扣～ put a label on sb.; hurl an epithet at sb./ 批评要实事求是,不要乱扣～。Criticism should be based on facts; one shouldn't just stick labels on people./ 群众一致要求给这个坏家伙戴上反革命分子的～。The masses unanimously demanded that the villain be officially declared a counterrevolutionary./ 大庆油田的胜利建成使我国甩掉了"贫油"的～。The successful opening of the Daqing oilfield took the "oil-poor" label off China.

**瑁** mào 见"玳瑁" dàimào

**貌** mào looks; appearance: 美～ good looks/ 山村新～ the new look of a mountain village/ 人不可～相。Never judge people by their appearance.

【貌合神离】 màohé-shénlí (of two persons or parties) seemingly in harmony but actually at variance

【貌似】 màosì seemingly; in appearance: ～强大 seemingly powerful; outwardly strong/ ～公正 seemingly impartial

**懋** mào ①〈书〉 diligent ② luxuriant; profuse; lush

## me

**么** me ①〔后缀〕: 什～ what/ 多～ how/ 怎～ why; how/ 这～ such; so; in this way ②〔歌词中的衬字〕: 五月的花儿红呀～红似火。Red as fire are the flowers that bloom in May.

## méi

**没** méi 见"没有"

另见 mò

【没词儿】 méicír 〈口〉 ① can find nothing to say ② be at a loss for words; be stuck for an answer

【没错儿】 méicuòr ① I'm quite sure; you can rest assured: ～,准是小王告诉他的。I'm quite sure it was Xiao Wang who told him about it./ ～,就是他干的。There's no doubt about it. He's the one that did it. ② can't go wrong: 照说明书做,准保～。Just follow the directions. You can't go wrong.

【没法子】 méi fǎzi can do nothing about it; can't help it

【没关系】 méi guānxi it doesn't matter; it's nothing; that's all right; never mind

【没精打采】 méijīng-dǎcǎi listless; in low spirits; out of sorts; lackadaisical

【没…没…】 méi...méi... ①〔用在两个同义词前面,强调没有〕: 没完没了 endless; without end/ 没羞没臊 shameless; have no sense of shame ②〔用在两个反义词前面,表示应区别而未区别〕: 没轻没重 tactless/ 没大没小 impolite (to an elder); impertinent; impudent

【没门儿】 méiménr 〈方〉 ① have no access to sth.; have no means of doing sth.: 你能给我们弄几张戏票吗? ——我可～。Can you get us some tickets for the performance? — You're asking the wrong person. ② no go; nothing doing: 他想拉拢我? ～! He wants to rope me in? Not a chance!

【没命】 méimìng ① lose one's life; die: 要不是医生及时赶到,这小孩就～了。The child would have died if the doctor hadn't come in time. ② recklessly; desperately; like mad; for all one's worth: 敌兵～地逃跑。The enemy soldiers ran off as fast as their legs could carry them.

【没谱儿】 méipǔr 〈方〉 be unsure; have no idea: 这炉子一个月要烧多少煤,我可～。I have no idea how much coal this stove will consume each month./ 下一步该怎么走还～呢。We have no plan yet as to our next move.

【没趣】 méiqù feel put out; feel snubbed: 没有人理他,他觉得～,只好走了。Very much put out by their indifference, he slunk off./ 自讨～ ask for a snub

【没什么】 méi shénme it doesn't matter; it's nothing; that's all right; never mind: 你怎么了? ——～,有点头疼。What's the matter with you? — Just a bit of a headache; nothing serious.

【没事儿】 méishìr ① have nothing to do; be free; be at a loose end: 今晚～,我想去看电影。I've got nothing to do this evening. I think I'll go to the film. ② it doesn't matter; it's nothing; that's all right; never mind: 啃,踩了你的脚了。——～。Sorry to have stepped on your toe. — That's all right./ 外边乱哄哄的,出了什么事儿? ——～, 就几个孩子起哄。What's all that noise outside? — It's nothing. Only some kids making a row.

【没事找事】 méishì zhǎoshì ① ask for trouble; ask for it ② try hard to find fault; cavil

【没羞】 méixiū unabashed: 那么大的小子还哭,真～。 Tut, tut! Such a big boy crying.

【没有】 méiyǒu ① not have; there is not; be without: 屋里～人。There isn't anyone in the room./ 咱们生产队里～一家～余粮。Every family in our production team has grain to spare./ ～谁会赞成你的意见。Nobody will agree with you./ ～共产党就～新中国。Without the Communist Party there would be no New China./ ～矛盾, 就～世界。Without contradiction nothing would exist. ② not so... as: 这项试验～我们预料的那样顺利。The experiment didn't go as smoothly as we had expected. ③ less than: 他来了还～三天就走了。He was here less than three days. 或 He wasn't here even three days. ④ 〈副〉〔表示"已然""曾经"的否定〕: 他回来没有? —— 还～呢。Has he come back yet? — No, not yet./ 昨天我～见到他。I didn't see him yesterday./ ～改造好的富农分子 an unreformed rich peasant

【没有说的】 méiyou shuōde ① really good: 这小伙子思想好、劳动好,真是～。He's good in ideology and in work, a really fine young chap. ② there's no need to say any more about it; it goes without saying: ～,这是我们应尽的责任。It goes without saying that we should do it; it's our duty.

【没辙】 méizhé 〈方〉 can find no way out; be at the end of one's rope

## 玫 méi

【玫瑰】 méigui 〈植〉 rugosa rose; rose

## 枚 méi

〈量〉〔多用于形体小的东西〕: 三～纪念章 three badges/ 一～古币 an ancient coin

## 眉 méi

① eyebrow; brow ② the top margin of a page

【眉笔】 méibǐ eyebrow pencil

【眉飞色舞】 méifēi-sèwǔ with dancing eyebrows and radiant face—enraptured; exultant

【眉睫】 méijié (as close to the eye as) the eyebrows and eyelashes: 迫在～ urgent; imminent

【眉开眼笑】 méikāi-yǎnxiào be all smiles; beam with joy

【眉来眼去】 méilái-yǎnqù make eyes at each other; flirt with each other

【眉棱骨】 méiléngǔ superciliary ridge

【眉毛】 méimao eyebrow; brow

【眉毛胡子一把抓】 méimao húzi yībǎzhuā try to grasp the eyebrows and the beard all at once—try to attend to big and small matters all at once

【眉目】 méimù ① features; looks: ～清秀 have delicate features ② logic; sequence of ideas: 这篇文章～清楚。The article is clear and well-organized.

【眉目】 méimu prospect of a solution; sign of a positive outcome: 你托我办的事已经有点～了。About that job you asked me to do, I'm beginning to get somewhere with it. 或 I'm getting on with what you asked me to do./ 计划有了～。The plan is beginning to take shape.

【眉批】 méipī notes and commentary at the top of a page

【眉清目秀】 méiqīng-mùxiù have delicate features

【眉梢】 méishāo the tip of the brow: 喜上～ look very happy

【眉头】 méitóu brows: 皱～ knit the brows; frown/ ～一皱,计上心来。Knit the brows and a stratagem comes to mind.

【眉心】 méixīn between the eyebrows

【眉宇】 méiyǔ 〈书〉 forehead

## 莓 méi

certain kinds of berries: 草～ strawberry

## 梅 méi

① plum ② (Méi) a surname

【梅毒】 méidú 〈医〉 syphilis

【梅红色】 méihóngsè plum (colour)

【梅花】 méihuā ① plum blossom ② 〈方〉 wintersweet

【梅花鹿】 méihuālù sika (deer)

【梅童鱼】 méitóngyú baby croaker

【梅雨】 méiyǔ 〈气〉 plum rains 参见"黄梅雨" huángméiyǔ

【梅子】 méizi plum

## 猸 méi

【猸子】 méizi 〈动〉 crab-eating mongoose

## 媒 méi

① matchmaker; go-between: 做～ act as a matchmaker ② intermediary

【媒介】 méijiè intermediary; medium; vehicle: 空气是传播声音的～。Air is a medium of sound./ 传染疾病的～ vehicle of disease; vector

【媒婆】 méipó 〈旧〉 woman matchmaker

【媒染】 méirǎn mordant dyeing ◇ ～剂 〈化〉 mordant/ ～染料 mordant dye

【媒人】 méirén matchmaker; go-between

【媒质】 méizhì 〈物〉 medium: 吸收～ absorbing medium

## 煤 méi

coal: 粉～ fine coal/ 块～ lump coal/ 原～ raw coal

【煤仓】 méicāng coal bunker

【煤层】 méicéng coal seam; coal bed

【煤场】 méichǎng coal yard

【煤尘】 méichén coal dust ◇ ～爆炸 coal-dust explosion

【煤斗】 méidǒu coal scuttle; scuttle

【煤酚皂溶液】 méifēnzào róngyè 〈药〉 cresol and soap solution; saponated cresol solution; lysol

【煤矸石】 méigānshí gangue

【煤耗】 méihào coal consumption

【煤核儿】 méihúr partly-burnt briquet; coal cinder

【煤灰】 méihuī coal ash

【煤焦油】 méijiāoyóu coal tar

【煤精】 méijīng jet; black amber 又作"煤玉"

【煤矿】 méikuàng coal mine; colliery ◇ ～工人 coal miner

【煤气】 méiqì coal gas; gas: 你们家烧～吗? Do you use a gas stove at home?
◇ ～厂 gasworks; gashouse/ ～灯 gas lamp; gas light/ ～管 gas pipe/ ～机 gas engine/ ～炉 gas stove; gas furnace/ ～设备 gas fittings/ ～灶 gas range; gas cooker/ ～中毒 carbon monoxide poisoning; gas poisoning/ ～总管 gas main

【煤球】 méiqiú (egg-shaped) briquet

【煤炭】 méitàn coal ◇ ～工业 coal industry

【煤田】 méitián coalfield ◇ ～地质学 coal geology

【煤系】 méixì 〈地〉coal measures
【煤烟】 méiyān ① smoke from burning coal ② soot ◇ ～污染 smoke pollution
【煤窑】 méiyáo coalpit
【煤油】 méiyóu kerosene; paraffin ◇ ～灯 kerosene lamp/ ～炉 kerosene stove
【煤渣】 méizhā coal cinder ◇ ～路 cinder road/ ～跑道 cinder track
【煤砟子】 méizhǎzi small piece of coal
【煤砖】 méizhuān briquet

**楣** méi lintel (over a door)

**酶** méi 〈生化〉enzyme; ferment: 消化～ digestive ferment
【酶原】 méiyuán 〈生化〉zymogen; fermentogen

**鹛** méi babbler: 钩嘴～ scimitar babbler

**镅** méi 〈化〉americium (Am)

**霉** méi mould; mildew: 发～ go mouldy; mildew
【霉病】 méibìng 〈农〉mildew
【霉菌】 méijūn 〈微〉mould ◇ ～病 mycosis
【霉烂】 méilàn mildew and rot
【霉天】 méitiān early summer rains 参见"黄梅季" huángméijì

**糜** méi
另见 mí
【糜子】 méizi 〈植〉broom corn millet

## měi

**每** měi ① every; each; per: 节约～一分钱 save every penny/ ～星期五 every Friday/ ～四小时服一次 to be taken once every four hours/ ～人一把铁锨 a spade for each person/ 以～小时四十公里的速度行驶 drive at (a speed of) forty kilometres an hour/ ～时～刻 all the time; at all times/ ～年的平均产量 average yearly yield; average output *per annum* ② often: 春秋佳日，～作郊游。We often go for an outing in the country on fine days in spring and autumn.
【每当】 měidāng whenever; every time: ～我想起童年的悲惨遭遇，心情总是很不平静。Whenever I recall the misery of my childhood, my mind is in a turmoil.
【每逢佳节倍思亲】 měiféng jiājié bèi sī qīn on festive occasions more than ever we think of our dear ones far away
【每况愈下】 měi kuàng yù xià steadily deteriorate; go from bad to worse
【每每】 měiměi often: 他给青年讲村史，～一谈就是好几个钟头。When he talked to the young people about the history of the village, he would often go on for hours.

**美** měi ① beautiful; pretty: 风景多～啊! What beautiful scenery!/ 真、善、～ the true, the good and the beautiful ② very satisfactory; good: ～酒 good wine/ 价廉物～ good and inexpensive/ 日子过得挺～ live quite happily ③〈方〉be pleased with oneself: 瞧他这～劲儿。Look how pleased he is with himself. ④ (Měi) short for America
【美不胜收】 měi bùshèng shōu so many beautiful things that one simply can't take them all in
【美差】 měichāi cushy job
【美称】 měichēng laudatory title; good name: 四川向有天府之国的～。Sichuan has always enjoyed the reputation of being a "Heavenly Land of Plenty".
【美德】 měidé virtue; moral excellence
【美吨】 měidūn short ton
【美感】 měigǎn aesthetic feeling; aesthetic perception; sense of beauty
【美工】 měigōng 〈电影〉① art designing ② art designer
【美观】 měiguān pleasing to the eye; beautiful; artistic: 房间布置得很～。The room is artistically decorated.
【美国】 Měiguó the United States of America (U.S.A.) ◇ ～人 American
【美好】 měihǎo fine; happy; glorious: ～的日子 happy days; a happy life/ ～的将来 a glorious future/ ～的回忆 happy memories/ ～的远景 magnificent prospects
【美化】 měihuà beautify; prettify; embellish: ～环境 beautify the environment/ 竭力～自己 try hard to prettify oneself
【美景】 měijǐng beautiful scenery (或 landscape)
【美拉尼西亚】 Měilāníxīyà Melanesia
【美利奴羊】 měilìnúyáng Merino (sheep)
【美丽】 měilì beautiful: ～富饶的国家 a beautiful and richly-endowed country
【美满】 měimǎn happy; perfectly satisfactory: ～的生活 a happy life/ ～婚姻 a happy marriage; conjugal happiness
【美梦】 měimèng fond dream
【美妙】 měimiào beautiful; splendid; wonderful: ～的青春 the wonderful days of one's youth/ ～的诗句 beautiful verse/ 资本主义世界的经济情况很不～。The economic situation of the capitalist world is anything but splendid.
【美名】 měimíng good name; good reputation: 英雄～天下扬。A hero's good name spreads far and wide.
【美尼尔氏症】 měiní'ěrshìzhèng Ménière's syndrome (或 disease)
【美其名曰】 měi qí míng yuē call it by the fine-sounding name of
【美人】 měirén beautiful woman; beauty ◇ ～计 use of a woman to ensnare a man; sex-trap
【美人蕉】 měirénjiāo 〈植〉canna; Indian shot
【美容】 měiróng ① improve (a woman's) looks ② cosmetology ◇ ～院 beauty parlour; beauty shop
【美术】 měishù ① the fine arts; art: 工艺～ industrial arts; arts and crafts ② painting
◇ ～革 fancy leather/ ～工作者 art worker; artist/ ～馆 art gallery/ ～家 artist/ ～明信片 picture postcard/ ～片〈电影〉cartoons, puppet films, etc./ ～人型 artistic figurine/ ～字 artistic calligraphy; art lettering
【美术设计】 měishù shèjì artistic design: 舞台～ stage design
【美谈】 měitán a story passed on with approval: 传为～ be told from mouth to mouth with general approval
【美味】 měiwèi ① delicious food; delicacy ② delicious; dainty: ～小吃 dainty snacks
【美学】 měixué aesthetics
【美言】 měiyán put in a good word for sb.
【美育】 měiyù aesthetic education; art education
【美元】 měiyuán American dollar; U.S. dollar
【美中不足】 měi zhōng bù zú a blemish in an otherwise perfect thing; a fly in the ointment
【美洲】 Měizhōu America
【美洲虎】 měizhōuhǔ jaguar
【美洲狮】 měizhōushī cougar; puma
【美滋滋】 měizīzī very pleased with oneself

**镁** měi 〈化〉magnesium (Mg)
【镁光】 měiguāng magnesium light ◇ ～照明弹 magnesium

flare
【镁砂】 měishā 〈冶〉 magnesia; magnesite
【镁砖】 měizhuān 〈冶〉 magnesia brick

## mèi

**妹** mèi younger sister; sister
【妹夫】 mèifu younger sister's husband; brother-in-law
【妹妹】 mèimei younger sister; sister

**袂** mèi 〈书〉 sleeve

**昧** mèi ① have hazy notions about; be ignorant of: 素～平生 have never made sb.'s acquaintance ② hide; conceal: 拾金不～ not pocket the money one has picked up/ ～着良心 (do evil) against one's conscience
【昧心】 mèixīn (do evil) against one's conscience

**寐** mèi 〈书〉 sleep

**谜** mèi
另见 mí
【谜儿】 mèir 〈口〉 riddle: 猜～ guess a riddle

**媚** mèi ① fawn on; curry favour with; flatter; toady to: ～敌 curry favour with (或 toady to) the enemy ② charming; fascinating; enchanting: ～人的景色 enchanting scenery
【媚骨】 mèigǔ obsequiousness: 他在反动统治阶级面前没有丝毫的奴颜与～。He was free from all sycophancy or obsequiousness in the face of the reactionary ruling class.
【媚外】 mèiwài fawn on (或 toady to) foreign powers: 崇洋～ worship foreign things and fawn on foreign powers

**魅** mèi evil spirit; demon
【魅力】 mèilì glamour; charm; enchantment; fascination: 艺术～ artistic charm

## mēn

**闷** mēn ① stuffy; close: 开开窗吧，屋里太～了。Open the windows. The air here is too close. ② cover tightly: ～一会儿，茶味就出来了。Let the tea draw for a while and the flavour will come out./ 你有什么事就说吧，别～在心里。Speak out. Don't just brood over things. ③〈方〉 (of a sound) muffled: 说话～声～气的 speak in a muffled voice; won't come out with a clear statement ④ shut oneself or sb. indoors: 别老～在屋里。Don't shut yourself indoors all day.
另见 mèn
【闷气】 mēnqì stuffy; close
另见 mènqì
【闷热】 mēnrè hot and suffocating; sultry; muggy
【闷声不响】 mēnshēng bù xiǎng remain silent
【闷头儿】 mēntóur quietly; silently: ～干 work quietly; plod away silently

## mén

**门** mén ① entrance; door; gate: 请走南～。Please use the south entrance./ 前(后)～ front (back) door/ 校～ school gate/ 炉～ stove door ② valve; switch: 气～ air valve/ 电～ switch ③ way to do sth.; knack: 我到钢厂劳动了一段时间，对炼钢摸着点～儿了。After working in the steel mill for a while I got an inkling of how steel is made. ④ family: 豪～ wealthy and influential family ⑤ (religious) sect; school (of thought): 佛～ Buddhism ⑥ class; category: 分～别类 divide into different categories ⑦〈生〉 phylum: 亚～ subphylum/ 脊椎动物～ Vertebrata ⑧〈量〉: 一～大炮 a piece of artillery; a cannon; a gun/ 两～功课 two subjects; two courses ⑨〈计算机〉 gate: "与"～ AND gate/ "非"～ NOT gate ⑩ (Mén) a surname
【门巴族】 Ménbāzú the Moinba (Monba) nationality, living in the Xizang Autonomous Region
【门把】 ménbà door knob; door handle
【门板】 ménbǎn ① door plank ② shutter: 上～儿 put up the shutters
【门齿】 ménchǐ front tooth; incisor
【门当户对】 méndāng-hùduì be well-matched in social and economic status (for marriage)
【门道】 méndao 〈口〉 ① way to do sth.; knack: 治疗这种病，他们医院已经研究出～来了。Their hospital has found the way to cure this disease./ 技术革新的～很多。There are all sorts of possibilities for technical innovation. ② social connections; contacts
【门第】 méndì 〈旧〉 family status
【门吊】 méndiào 〈机〉 gantry crane
【门洞儿】 méndòngr gateway; doorway
【门阀】 ménfá a family of power and influence (in feudal China)
【门房】 ménfáng ① gate house; janitor's room; porter's lodge ② gatekeeper; doorman; janitor; porter
【门缝】 ménfèng a crack between a door and its frame
【门岗】 méngǎng gate sentry
【门户】 ménhù ① door: ～紧闭 with the doors tightly shut ② gateway; important passageway: 天津港是北京通往海洋的～。The port of Tianjin is Beijing's gateway to the sea. ③ faction; sect: ～之见 sectarian bias; sectarianism ④ family status
【门户开放政策】 ménhù kāifàng zhèngcè "Open Door" policy (which U.S. imperialism once foisted on China to secure the same privileges as the other imperialist powers)
【门环子】 ménhuánzi knocker
【门禁】 ménjìn entrance guard: ～森严 with the entrances heavily guarded
【门警】 ménjǐng police guard at an entrance
【门径】 ménjìng access; key; way: 经过反复实验，他终于找到了节省原料的～。Through repeated experiments he at last found the way to save raw materials.
【门静脉】 ménjìngmài 〈生理〉 portal vein
【门槛】 ménkǎn threshold
【门可罗雀】 mén kě luó què you can catch sparrows on the doorstep — where visitors are few and far between
【门客】 ménkè a hanger-on of an aristocrat
【门口】 ménkǒu entrance; doorway: 在～等候 wait at the door (或 gate)/ 走过学校～ walk past the school entrance/ 把客人送到～ see the guest to the door
【门框】 ménkuàng doorframe
【门廊】 ménláng 〈建〉 porch; portico
【门类】 ménlèi class; kind; category: 基础科学和技术科学这两大～ the two major departments of basic and technical sciences
【门帘】 ménlián door curtain; *portière*
【门联】 ménlián scrolls pasted on either side of the door forming a couplet; gatepost couplet
【门脸儿】 ménliǎnr 〈方〉 ① the vicinity of a city gate ② the façade of a shop; shop front
【门楼】 ménlóu an arch over a gateway

【门路】 ménlu ①knack; way: 摸到一些～ have learned the ropes; know one's way around/ 广开饲料～,发展养猪事业 tap new sources of feed to boost pig farming ②social connections (for securing jobs, etc.); pull: 找～ solicit help from potential backers
【门楣】 ménméi lintel (of a door)
【门面】 ménmian ①the façade of a shop; shop front: 三间～ a three-bay shop front ②appearance; façade: 装点～ keep up appearances; put up a facade; put on a front; do some window dressing ◇～话 formal and insincere remarks; lip service
【门牌】 ménpái ①(house) number plate ②house number: 你家～几号? What's the number of your house?
【门票】 ménpiào entrance ticket; admission ticket: 不收～ admission free
【门桥】 ménqiáo 〈军〉 raft of pontoons; boat raft
【门扇】 ménshàn door leaf
【门神】 ménshén door-god (whose pictures were often pasted on the front door of a house as a talisman in old China)
【门生】 ménshēng pupil; disciple
【门市】 ménshì retail sales ◇～部 retail department; sales department; salesroom
【门闩】 ménshuān (door) bolt; (door) bar
【门厅】 méntīng 〈建〉 entrance hall; vestibule
【门庭若市】 mén-tíng ruò shì the courtyard is as crowded as a marketplace — a much visited house
【门徒】 méntú disciple; follower; adherent
【门外汉】 ménwàihàn layman; the uninitiated
【门卫】 ménwèi entrance guard
【门牙】 ményá front tooth; incisor
【门诊】 ménzhěn outpatient service ◇～病人 outpatient; clinic patient/ ～部 clinic; outpatient department/ ～时间 consulting hours

**扪** mén 〈书〉 touch; stroke
【扪心自问】 ménxīn zìwèn examine one's conscience
【扪诊】 ménzhěn 〈医〉 palpation

**钔** mén 〈化〉 mendelevium (Md)

## mèn

**闷** mèn ①bored; depressed; in low spirits: 你一个人在这儿多～得慌,跟我们出去走走吧! Don't you feel bored staying here all alone? Why not come out with us for a walk? ②tightly closed; sealed
另见 mēn
【闷棍】 mèngùn staggering blow (with a cudgel)
【闷葫芦】 mènhúlu enigma; puzzle; riddle: 这几句没头没脑的话真把人装进～里了。These abrupt remarks were really a puzzle to everyone.
【闷倦】 mènjuàn bored and listless
【闷雷】 mènléi ①muffled thunder ②unpleasant surprise; shock
【闷闷不乐】 mènmèn bù lè depressed; in low spirits
【闷气】 mènqì the sulks: 生～ be sulky; be in the sulks
另见 mēnqì
【闷子车】 mènzichē boxcar

**焖** mèn boil in a covered pot over a slow fire; braise: ～饭 cook rice over a slow fire/ ～牛肉 braised beef

**懑** mèn 见"愤懑" fènmèn

## men

**们** men 〔用在代词或指人的名词后面,表示复数〕: 他～ they/ 人～ people/ 同志～ comrades

## mēng

**蒙** mēng ①cheat; deceive; dupe: 你～我! You're kidding me! ②make a wild guess: ～对了 make a lucky guess ③unconscious; senseless: 给打～了 be knocked senseless; be stunned by a blow/ 他觉得脑袋发～。He felt his head swimming.
另见 méng; Měng
【蒙蒙亮】 mēngmēngliàng first glimmer of dawn; daybreak: 天～他就起床了。He got up at daybreak.
【蒙骗】 mēngpiàn deceive; cheat; hoodwink; delude
【蒙头转向】 mēngtóu zhuànxiàng lose one's bearings; be utterly confused

## méng

**氓** méng the common people
另见 máng

**虻** méng horsefly; gadfly: 牛～ gadfly

**萌** méng sprout; shoot forth; bud; germinate
【萌发】 méngfā 〈植〉 sprout; germinate; shoot; bud: 茶树修剪后又～新枝。The tea plants sprouted new buds after the pruning.
【萌芽】 méngyá ①sprout; germinate; shoot; bud ②rudiment; shoot; seed; germ: 资本主义的～ the seeds of capitalism/ 处于～状态 in the embryonic stage; in the bud

**蒙** méng ①cover: ～上一层灰尘 be covered with a layer of dust/ ～住眼睛 be blindfolded/ ～头睡大觉 tuck oneself in and sleep like a log ②receive; meet with: ～大力协助,十分感谢。Thank you very much for your kind help. ③ignorant; illiterate: 启～ enlighten
另见 mēng; Měng
【蒙蔽】 méngbì hoodwink; deceive; hide the truth from; pull the wool over sb.'s eyes: ～一部分群众 hoodwink part of the masses/ 不要被花言巧语所～。Don't let yourself be fooled by honeyed words.
【蒙导法】 méngdǎofǎ 〈生〉 mentor method
【蒙汗药】 ménghànyào a narcotic believed to have been used by highwaymen, etc. to drug their victims; knockout drops
【蒙哄】 ménghǒng deceive; hoodwink; swindle; cheat
【蒙混】 ménghùn deceive or mislead people: ～过关 get by under false pretences
【蒙眬】 ménglóng 见"朦胧" ménglóng
【蒙昧】 méngmèi ①barbaric; uncivilized; uncultured: ～时代 age of barbarism ②ignorant; benighted; unenlightened: ～无知 unenlightened; childishly ignorant; illiterate ◇～主义 obscurantism
【蒙蒙】 méngméng drizzly; misty: ～细雨 a fine drizzle/ 烟雾～ misty
【蒙难】 méngnàn (of a revolutionary) be confronted by danger; fall into the clutches of the enemy
【蒙皮】 méngpí 〈航空〉 envelope; covering; skin
【蒙受】 méngshòu suffer; sustain: ～损失 sustain a loss/

～耻辱 be subjected to humiliation; be humiliated
【蒙太奇】 méngtàiqí 〈电影〉 montage
【蒙在鼓里】 méng zài gǔlǐ be kept inside a drum — be kept in the dark

**盟** méng ① alliance: 结～ form an alliance ② league (an administrative division of the Nei Monggol Autonomous Region, corresponding to a prefecture) ③ sworn (brothers)
另见 míng
【盟邦】 méngbāng allied country; ally
【盟国】 méngguó allied country; ally
【盟军】 méngjūn allied forces
【盟友】 méngyǒu ally
【盟员】 méngyuán a member of an alliance (或 league)
【盟约】 méngyuē oath of alliance; treaty of alliance
【盟主】 méngzhǔ the leader (或 chief) of an alliance

**濛** méng
【濛濛】 méngméng 见"蒙蒙" méngméng

**獴** méng 〈动〉 mongoose

**檬** méng 见"柠檬" níngméng

**曚** méng
【曚昽】 ménglóng 〈书〉 dim daylight

**朦** méng
【朦胧】 ménglóng ① dim moonlight; hazy moonlight ② obscure; dim; hazy: ～的景色 a hazy view

**矇** méng
【矇眬】 ménglóng half asleep; drowsy; somnolent: 睡眼～ eyes heavy with sleep; drowsy/ ～睡去 doze off/ ～中他仿佛听见有人敲门。While he was half asleep, he seemed to hear a knock on the door.

## měng

**猛** měng ① fierce; violent; energetic; vigorous: ～将 a valiant general/ ～虎 a fierce tiger/ 产量～增 a sharp increase in output/ 穷追～打 hotly pursue and fiercely attack/ 用力过～ use too much strength; overexert oneself/ 在背上击一～掌 give sb. a powerful shove in the back ② suddenly; abruptly: ～地往前一跳 suddenly jump forward/ ～吃一惊 be startled
【猛不防】 měngbufáng by surprise; unexpectedly; unawares: ～后面有人推了他一下。Suddenly someone gave him a push from behind.
【猛进】 měngjìn push ahead vigorously: 突飞～ advance by leaps and bounds
【猛劲儿】 měngjìnr ① a spurt of energy; dash: 她一个～，就超过了跑在前面的人。Putting on a spurt, she overtook all the other runners. ② great vigour: 这小伙子干活有股子～。This young chap works with vim and vigour.
【猛力】 měnglì vigorously; with sudden force: ～扣杀 smash with all one's strength/ 把手榴弹～一甩 throw a grenade with all one's might
【猛烈】 měngliè fierce; vigorous; violent: 发动～的进攻 wage a vigorous offensive/ ～的炮火 heavy shellfire/ 风势～。There was a fierce wind.
【猛犸】 měngmǎ 〈古生物〉 mammoth
【猛禽】 měngqín bird of prey
【猛然】 měngrán suddenly; abruptly: 我～想起来了。In a flash I remembered./ ～一拉 pull with a jerk
【猛士】 měngshì brave warrior
【猛兽】 měngshòu beast of prey
【猛醒】 měngxǐng suddenly wake up (to the truth) 又作"猛省"

**蒙** Měng the Monggol nationality 参见"蒙古族"①
另见 mēng; méng
【蒙古】 Měnggǔ Mongolia ◇～人 Mongolian/ ～语 Mongol (language)
【蒙古包】 měnggǔbāo yurt
【蒙古族】 Měnggǔzú ① the Monggol (Mongolian) nationality, distributed over the Nei Monggol Autonomous Region, Jilin, Liaoning, Heilongjiang, the Xinjiang Uygur Autonomous Region, Gansu, Qinghai, the Ningxia Hui Autonomous Region, Hebei and Henan ② the Mongols (of Mongolia)
【蒙栎】 měnglì 〈植〉 Mongolian oak (*Quercus mongolica*)

**锰** měng 〈化〉 manganese (Mn): ～结核 manganese nodule
【锰钢】 měnggāng manganese steel
【锰铁】 měngtiě ferromanganese

**蜢** měng 见"蚱蜢" zhàměng

**艋** měng 见"舴艋" zéměng

**蠓** měng midge; biting midge

**懵** měng muddled; ignorant
【懵懂】 měngdǒng muddled; ignorant

## mèng

**孟** mèng ① the first month (of a season) ② eldest (brother) ③ (Mèng) a surname
【孟德尔主义】 Mèngdé'ěrzhǔyì 〈生〉 Mendelism
【孟加拉】 Mèngjiālā Bengal
◇ ～人 Bengalese; Bengali/ ～湾 the Bay of Bengal/ ～语 Bengali (language)
【孟加拉国】 Mèngjiālāguó Bangladesh
【孟浪】 mènglàng rash; impetuous; impulsive: 不可～行事。Don't act rashly.
【孟什维克】 Mèngshíwéikè Menshevik
【孟什维主义】 Mèngshíwéizhǔyì Menshevism
【孟子】 Mèngzǐ *Mencius* 参见"四书" sìshū

**梦** mèng dream
【梦话】 mènghuà ① words uttered in one's sleep; somniloquy: 昨晚我听见你说～。I heard you talk in your sleep last night. ② daydream; nonsense
【梦幻】 mènghuàn illusion; dream; reverie: ～般的境界 a dreamlike world; dreamland
【梦幻泡影】 mènghuàn-pàoyǐng pipe dream; bubble; illusion
【梦见】 mèngjian see in a dream; dream about: 他～自己又回到了部队。He dreamt that he was back in the army.
【梦境】 mèngjìng dreamland; dreamworld; dream: 如入～ feel as if one were in a dream
【梦寐】 mèngmèi dream; sleep: ～难忘 be unable to forget sth. even in one's dreams

【梦寐以求】 mèngmèi yǐ qiú crave sth. so that one even dreams about it; long (或 yearn) for sth. day and night
【梦乡】 mèngxiāng dreamland: 进入～ go off to dreamland; fall asleep
【梦想】 mèngxiǎng ① dream of; vainly hope: 被推翻的剥削阶级～恢复他们失去的天堂。The overthrown exploiting classes vainly hope to regain their lost paradise. ② fond dream; earnest wish: 征服黄河的～,只有在社会主义制度下才能变成现实。Only under the socialist system can the long-cherished dream of conquering the Huanghe River become a reality.
【梦魇】 mèngyǎn 〈医〉 nightmare
【梦遗】 mèngyí 〈医〉 nocturnal emission; wet dream
【梦呓】 mèngyì ① somniloquy ② rigmarole
【梦游症】 mèngyóuzhèng somnambulism; sleepwalking 又作"梦行症"

## mī

**咪** mī
【咪咪】 mīmī ①〈象〉 mew; miaow ② smilingly: 笑～ be all smiles; be wreathed in smiles

**眯** mī ① narrow (one's eyes): ～着眼睛笑 narrow one's eyes into a smile/ ～着眼瞧 squint at ②〈方〉 take a nap: ～一会儿 take a short nap; have forty winks
另见 mí
【眯缝】 mīfeng narrow (one's eyes)

## mí

**弥** mí ① full; overflowing: ～漫 fill the air ② cover; fill: ～缝 plug up holes; gloss over faults ③ more: 欲盖～彰 try to cover sth. up only to make it more conspicuous
【弥补】 míbǔ make up; remedy; make good: ～损失 make up for (或 make good) a loss/ ～赤字 make up (或 meet) a deficit/ ～缺陷 remedy a defect/ 学习别人的优点,～自己的不足 learn from other people's strong points to counteract one's own weaknesses
【弥合】 míhé close; bridge: ～裂痕 close a rift
【弥勒】 Mílè 〈佛教〉 Maitreya
【弥留】 míliú 〈书〉 be dying: ～之际 on one's deathbed
【弥漫】 mímàn fill the air; spread all over the place: 烟雾～ heavy with smoke; smoke-laden; (of a place) be enveloped in mist
【弥撒】 mísa 〈天主教〉 Mass
【弥天大谎】 mítiān dàhuǎng monstrous (或 thundering, outrageous) lie
【弥天大罪】 mítiān dàzuì monstrous crime; heinous crime

**迷** mí ① be confused; be lost: ～了方向 lose one's bearings; get lost ② be fascinated by; be crazy about: 她对游泳着了～。She was crazy about swimming. ③ fan; enthusiast; fiend: 乒乓球～ a table tennis fan (或 enthusiast)/ 棋～ a chess fiend/ 官～ a person who craves office ④ confuse; perplex; fascinate; enchant: ～人的景色 scenery of enchanting beauty/ 财～心窍 be befuddled by a craving for wealth; be obsessed by lust for money
【迷宫】 mígōng labyrinth; maze
【迷航】 míháng (of a plane, ship, etc.) drift off course; lose one's course; get lost
【迷糊】 míhu ① misted; blurred; dimmed: 这么多花布我都看～了。I was simply dazzled by all these cotton prints. ② dazed; confused; muddled: 睡～了 dazed with sleep/ 他这个人有点～。He's somewhat muddleheaded.
【迷魂汤】 míhúntāng sth. intended to turn sb.'s head; magic potion: 灌～ try to ensnare sb. with honeyed words
【迷魂阵】 míhúnzhèn a scheme for confusing or bewildering sb.; maze; trap: 摆～ lay out a scheme to bewitch sb.; set a trap
【迷惑】 míhuo puzzle; confuse; perplex; baffle: 感到～不解 feel puzzled; feel perplexed/ ～敌人 confuse the enemy/ 不要被假象所～。Don't be misled by false appearances.
【迷离】 mílí blurred; misted: 睡眼～ eyes dim with sleep
【迷恋】 míliàn be infatuated with; madly cling to: ～资产阶级生活方式 be infatuated with (或 be addicted to) the bourgeois way of life
【迷路】 mílù ① lose one's way; get lost ②〈生理〉 inner ear; labyrinth
【迷茫】 mímáng ① vast and hazy: 大雪纷飞,原野一片～。The vast plain was obscured by the falling flakes of snow. ② confused; perplexed; dazed: 他脸上显出～的神情。There was a confused look on his face.
【迷梦】 mímèng pipe dream; fond illusion
【迷失】 míshī lose (one's way, etc.): ～方向 lose one's bearings; get lost
【迷途】 mítú ① lose one's way ② wrong path: 走入～ go astray
【迷途知返】 mítú zhī fǎn recover one's bearings and return to the fold; realize one's errors and mend one's ways
【迷惘】 míwǎng be perplexed; be at a loss
【迷雾】 míwù ① dense fog ② anything that misleads people: 妖风～ evil wind and miasma
【迷信】 míxìn ① superstition; superstitious belief; blind faith; blind worship ② have blind faith in; make a fetish of
【迷走神经】 mízǒu shénjīng 〈生理〉 vagus (nerve)

**谜** mí ① riddle; conundrum: 猜～ guess a riddle ② enigma; mystery; puzzle: 不解之～ unfathomable enigma; insoluble mystery (或 puzzle)/ 这件事到现在还是个～。The affair remains a mystery to this day.
另见 mèi
【谜底】 mídǐ ① answer (或 solution) to a riddle ② truth
【谜语】 míyǔ riddle; conundrum

**猕** mí
【猕猴】 míhóu macaque; rhesus monkey
【猕猴桃】 míhóutáo 〈植〉 yangtao (*Actinidia chinensis*)

**醚** mí 〈化〉 ether

**糜** mí ① gruel ② rotten ③ wasteful; extravagant ④ (Mí) a surname
另见 méi
【糜费】 mífèi waste: ～钱财 waste money
【糜烂】 mílàn ① rotten to the core; dissipated; debauched: 生活～ lead a fast life ②〈医〉 erosion ◇ ～性毒剂 〈军〉 vesicant agent; blister agent

**麋** mí elk
【麋羚】 mílíng hartebeest
【麋鹿】 mílù mi-lu; David's deer

**靡** mí waste: 奢～ wasteful; extravagant
另见 mǐ
【靡费】 mífèi waste; spend extravagantly

**麋** mí 见"茶麋" túmí

**醾** mí 见"酴醾" túmí

## mǐ

**米** mǐ ①rice ②shelled or husked seed: 花生～ peanut seed; peanut kernel/ 高粱～ grains of *kaoliang* ③metre ④(Mǐ) a surname

【米波】 mǐbō 〈无〉 metric wave

【米饭】 mǐfàn (cooked) rice

【米粉】 mǐfěn ①ground rice; rice flour: ～肉 pork steamed with ground glutinous rice ②rice-flour noodles

【米泔水】 mǐgānshuǐ water in which rice has been washed

【米黄】 mǐhuáng cream-coloured

【米酒】 mǐjiǔ rice wine

【米糠】 mǐkāng rice bran

【米粒】 mǐlì grain of rice

【米粮川】 mǐliángchuān rich rice-producing area: 昔日穷山沟,今日～。The barren gully of yesterday has become a granary.

【米色】 mǐsè cream-coloured

【米汤】 mǐtang ①water in which rice has been cooked ②thin rice or millet gruel; rice water

【米象】 mǐxiàng 〈动〉 rice weevil

【米制】 mǐzhì the metric system

【米珠薪桂】 mǐzhū-xīnguì rice is as precious as pearls and firewood as costly as cassia — exorbitantly high cost of living

【米烛光】 mǐzhúguāng 〈物〉 metre-candle; lux

**弭** mǐ 〈书〉 put down; get rid of; remove: ～患 remove the source of trouble

**脒** mǐ 〈化〉 amidine

**眯** mǐ (of dust, etc.) get into one's eye: 我～了眼了。Something has got into my eyes.

另见 mī

**靡** mǐ ①blown away by the wind: 所向披～ send the enemy fleeing helter-skelter; carry all before one ②〈书〉 no; not: ～日不思 not a day passes without one's thinking of sth. or sb.

另见 mí

【靡靡之音】 mǐmǐ zhī yīn decadent music

## mì

**泌** mì secrete

【泌尿科】 mìniàokē 〈医〉 urological department

【泌尿器官】 mìniào qìguān 〈生理〉 urinary organs

**宓** mì ①〈书〉 tranquil; quiet ②(Mì) a surname

**觅** mì look for; hunt for; seek: 鸟雀经常在这里～食。Birds often look for food here.

**秘** mì ①secret: ～事 a secret ②keep sth. secret; hold sth. back: ～而不宣 keep sth. secret; not let anyone into a secret ③〈简〉(使馆秘书) secretary: 一～ First Secretary

另见 bì

【秘本】 mìběn treasured private copy of a rare book

【秘方】 mìfāng secret recipe: 祖传～ a secret recipe handed down from generation to generation

【秘诀】 mìjué secret (of success): 成功的～ the secret of (或 key to) one's success

【秘密】 mìmì secret; clandestine; confidential: ～会议 secret meeting; closed-door session/ ～活动 clandestine activities/ ～文件 secret papers; confidential document/ 探索海底～ explore the secrets of the ocean bed

【秘史】 mìshǐ secret history (as of a feudal dynasty); inside story

【秘书】 mìshū secretary: 机要～ confidential secretary/ 私人～ private secretary ◇～处 secretariat/ ～长 secretary-general

**密** mì ①close; dense; thick: ～林 thick (或 dense) forest/ ～不透风 airtight/ 枪声很～。There was the sound of intensive gunfire./ 这两行苗栽得太～了。These two rows of seedlings are planted too close together. ②intimate; close: ～友 close friend; bosom friend ③fine; meticulous: 周～ carefully considered; meticulous ④secret: 绝～ top secret; strictly confidential/ ～通声息 secretly communicate with each other ⑤〈纺〉 density: 经～ warp density/ 纬～ weft density

【密闭】 mìbì airtight; hermetic

【密布】 mìbù densely covered: 阴云～。The sky is overcast. 或 Dark clouds are gathering./ 礁石～ thick with reefs

【密电】 mìdiàn ①cipher telegram ②secretly telegraph sb. ◇～码 cipher code

【密度】 mìdù ①density; thickness: 人口～ population density/ 兵力～ density of troops/ 火力～ density (或 volume) of fire ②〈物〉 density ◇ ～计 densimeter

【密封】 mìfēng ①seal up: ～的文件 sealed documents ②seal airtight; seal hermetically: ～的容器 hermetically-sealed chamber

◇ ～舱 sealed cabin; airtight cabin/ ～垫圈 〈机〉 sealing washer/ ～机身〈航空〉 closed fuselage/ ～压盖 〈机〉 sealing gland

【密集】 mìjí concentrated; crowded together: 人口～ densely populated; thickly populated/ 对敌人进行～包围 closely surround the enemy

◇ ～队形 close formation; tight formation/ ～轰炸 mass bombing/ ～炮火 intensive bombardment; concentrated fire; massed fire; drumfire

【密件】 mìjiàn a confidential paper or letter; classified matter; classified material

【密克罗尼西亚】 Mìkèluóníxīyà Micronesia

【密锣紧鼓】 mìluó-jǐngǔ 见"紧锣密鼓" jǐnluó-mìgǔ

【密码】 mìmǎ cipher; cipher code; secret code

◇～电报 cipher telegram/ ～机 cipher machine; cryptograph/ ～术 cryptography; cryptology/ ～员 cryptographer

【密码子】 mìmǎzi 〈生〉 codon

【密密层层】 mìmicéngcéng packed closely layer upon layer (或 ring upon ring); dense; thick: ～的人群 a dense crowd

【密密麻麻】 mìmimámá close and numerous; thickly dotted: 笔记本上写满了～的小字。The notebook was filled with small, closely-written characters.

【密密匝匝】 mìmizāzā thick; dense

【密谋】 mìmóu conspire; plot; scheme

【密切】 mìqiè ①close; intimate: ～配合 act in close coordination/ ～相关 be closely related/ ～联系群众 maintain close ties with the masses/ ～两国关系 build closer relations between the two countries ②carefully; intently; closely: ～注视 pay close attention to; watch closely

【密商】 mìshāng hold private counsel; hold secret talks
【密使】 mìshǐ secret emissary; secret envoy
【密室】 mìshì a room used for secret purposes: 策划于～ plot behind closed doors
【密实】 mìshi closely knit; dense; thick: 这件棉衣针脚做得真～。This padded jacket is sewn tightly with small stitches.
【密谈】 mìtán secret (或 confidential, private) talk; talk behind closed doors
【密探】 mìtàn secret agent; spy
【密陀僧】 mìtuósēng 〈化〉 litharge; yellow lead
【密位】 mìwèi 〈军〉 mil
【密纹唱片】 mìwén chàngpiàn long-playing record; microgroove record
【密西西比河】 Mìxīxībǐhé the Mississippi
【密写情报】 mìxiě qíngbào intelligence written in invisible ink, etc.
【密友】 mìyǒu close (或 fast) friend; bosom friend
【密语通信】 mìyǔ tōngxìn crypto-communication
【密约】 mìyuē secret agreement; secret treaty
【密云不雨】 mì yún bù yǔ dense clouds but no rain — trouble is brewing
【密植】 mìzhí 〈农〉 close planting: 合理～ rational close planting

**幂** mì ①〈数〉 power ②〈书〉 cloth cover
【幂级数】 mìjíshù 〈数〉 power series

**谧** mì 见"安谧" ānmì; "静谧" jìngmì

**蜜** mì ① honey ② honeyed; sweet
【蜜蜂】 mìfēng honeybee; bee
【蜜柑】 mìgān mandarin orange; tangerine orange
【蜜饯】 mìjiàn candied fruit; preserved fruit
【蜜橘】 mìjú tangerine
【蜜蜡】 mìlà beeswax
【蜜丸子】 mìwánzi 〈中药〉 a bolus made of powdered Chinese medicine and honey
【蜜腺】 mìxiàn 〈植〉 nectary
【蜜源】 mìyuán nectar source ◇～区 (bee) pasture/ ～植物 nectariferous (或 bee, honey) plant
【蜜月】 mìyuè honeymoon
【蜜枣】 mìzǎo candied date or jujube
【蜜渍】 mìzì candied; preserved in sugar

**嘧** mì
【嘧啶】 mìdìng 〈化〉 pyrimidine

## mián

**眠** mián ① sleep: 不～之夜 a sleepless night; a white night ② dormancy: 冬～ hibernate
【眠尔通】 mián'ěrtōng 〈药〉 miltown

**绵** mián ① silk floss ② continuous ③ soft
【绵薄】 miánbó 〈谦〉 (my) meagre strength; humble effort: 愿尽～。I'll do what little I can.
【绵绸】 miánchóu fabric made from waste silk
【绵亘】 miángèn (of mountains, etc.) stretch in an unbroken chain: 大别山～在河南、安徽和湖北三省的边界上。The Dabie Mountains stretch along the borders of Henan, Anhui and Hubei.
【绵里藏针】 miánlǐ cáng zhēn a needle hidden in silk floss — a ruthless character behind a gentle appearance; an iron hand in a velvet glove
【绵绵】 miánmián continuous; unbroken: 秋雨～。The autumn rain goes on and on.
【绵软】 miánruǎn ① soft: ～的羊毛 soft wool ② weak: 觉得浑身～ feel weak all over
【绵延】 miányán be continuous; stretch long and unbroken: ～千里的山脉 mountains extending (或 stretching) a thousand *li*/ 第二次世界大战后，局部战争一直～不断。Local wars have been going on continually ever since the end of World War II.
【绵羊】 miányáng sheep
【绵纸】 miánzhǐ tissue paper

**棉** mián ① a general term for cotton and kapok ② cotton: ～纺织品 cotton textiles ③ cotton-padded; quilted: ～大衣 cotton-padded overcoat/ ～衣 cotton-padded clothes
【棉袄】 mián'ǎo cotton-padded (或 quilted) jacket
【棉包】 miánbāo a bale of cotton
【棉被】 miánbèi a quilt with cotton wadding
【棉布】 miánbù cotton cloth; cotton
【棉纺】 miánfǎng cotton spinning ◇～厂 cotton mill
【棉凫】 miánfú 〈动〉 cotton teal
【棉红铃虫】 miánhónglíngchóng pink bollworm
【棉红蜘蛛】 miánhóngzhīzhū two-spotted spider mite
【棉猴儿】 miánhóur hooded cotton-padded coat; (knee-length) parka; anorak
【棉花】 miánhua cotton ◇ ～签 (cotton) swab
【棉卷】 miánjuǎn 〈纺〉 lap
【棉枯萎病】 miánkūwěibìng fusarium wilt of cotton
【棉裤】 miánkù cotton-padded trousers
【棉铃】 miánlíng cotton boll ◇～虫 bollworm/ ～象虫 boll weevil
【棉毛机】 miánmáojī interlock (knitting) machine
【棉毛裤】 miánmáokù cotton (interlock) trousers
【棉毛衫】 miánmáoshān cotton (interlock) jersey ◇～布 interlock (fabric)
【棉农】 miánnóng cotton grower
【棉绒】 miánróng cotton velvet
【棉纱】 miánshā cotton yarn ◇～头 (cotton) waste
【棉毯】 miántǎn cotton blanket
【棉桃】 miántáo cotton boll
【棉套】 miántào a cotton-padded covering for keeping sth. warm
【棉田】 miántián cotton field
【棉条】 miántiáo sliver ◇～桶 sliver can
【棉线】 miánxiàn cotton thread; cotton
【棉絮】 miánxù ① cotton fibre ② a cotton wadding (for a quilt)
【棉蚜虫】 miányáchóng cotton aphid
【棉衣】 miányī cotton-padded clothes
【棉织品】 miánzhīpǐn cotton goods; cotton textiles; cotton fabrics
【棉籽】 miánzǐ cottonseed
◇～饼 cottonseed cake/ ～绒 (cotton) linters/ ～油 cottonseed oil

## miǎn

**免** miǎn ① excuse sb. from sth.; exempt; dispense with: ～试 be excused from an examination/ ～服兵役 be exempt from military service/ 互相～办签证协议 mutual exemption of visas agreement/ 这些手续就～了。We'll dispense with the formalities. ② remove from office; dismiss;

relieve: 任～事项 appointments and removals/ 他工作太多,得给他～掉几项。He's got too much to do. He should be relieved of some of his jobs. ③ avoid; avert; escape: 事先做好准备,以～临时忙乱。Get prepared beforehand to avoid being rushed when the work starts./ ～于受灾 avert a disaster ④ not allowed: 闲人～进。No admittance except on business.

【免不了】 miǎnbuliǎo be unavoidable; be bound to be: 在前进的道路上,～会有困难。There are bound to be difficulties in the course of our advance.

【免除】 miǎnchú ① prevent; avoid: 兴修水利,～水旱灾害 build irrigation works to prevent droughts and floods/ 参加集体生产劳动,可以帮助干部～官僚主义。Participation in collective productive labour helps cadres to avoid bureaucracy. ② remit; excuse; exempt; relieve: ～债务 remit a debt/ ～一项任务 excuse sb. from a task; relieve sb. of a task

【免得】 miǎnde so as not to; so as to avoid: 多问几句,～走错路。Make some more inquiries so that you won't go the wrong way./ 我再说明一下,～引起误会。To avoid any misunderstanding, let me explain once again./ 你要是能去最好,～他跑一趟。It would be best if you could go. It would save him a trip.

【免费】 miǎnfèi free of charge; free; gratis: ～医疗 free medical care/ ～入场 admission free; be admitted gratis

【免冠】 miǎnguān ① take one's hat off (in salutation) ② without a hat on; bareheaded: 半身～正面相片 a half-length, bareheaded, full-faced photo

【免票】 miǎnpiào ① free pass; free ticket ② free of charge: 身高不满一米的儿童～。Children under a metre in height free of charge.

【免税】 miǎnshuì ① exempt from taxation ② tax-free; duty-free ◇ ～货物 duty-free goods

【免刑】 miǎnxíng 〈法〉 exempt from punishment

【免验】 miǎnyàn exempt from customs examination: ～放行 pass without examination (P.W.E.) ◇ ～证 *laissez-passer*

【免役】 miǎnyì exempt from service

【免疫】 miǎnyì 〈医〉 immunity (from disease): 获得性～ acquired immunity ◇ ～性 immunity

【免战牌】 miǎnzhànpái a sign used in ancient times to show refusal to fight: 挂～ refuse battle

【免职】 miǎnzhí remove sb. from office; relieve sb. of his post

【免罪】 miǎnzuì exempt from punishment

**勉** miǎn ① exert oneself; strive: ～力为之 exert oneself to the utmost; do one's best ② encourage; urge; exhort: 互～ encourage one another/ 自～ spur oneself on ③ strive to do what is beyond one's power: ～为其难 undertake to do a difficult job as best one can

【勉励】 miǎnlì encourage; urge: 同志们～她努力取得更大的成绩。Her comrades encouraged her to do still better./ 他～儿子要虚心向贫下中农学习。He urged his son to learn modestly from the poor and lower-middle peasants.

【勉强】 miǎnqiǎng ① manage with an effort; do with difficulty: 病人～喝了点粥。With an effort the patient ate some gruel. ② reluctantly; grudgingly: ～同意 reluctantly agree/ ～地笑了笑 force a smile/ 他接受了我们的建议,但是很～。He accepted our suggestion, but rather grudgingly. ③ force sb. to do sth.: 要是他不愿意去,就不要～他。If he doesn't want to go, don't force him to. ④ inadequate; unconvincing; strained; farfetched: 你的理由很～。The reason you give is rather unconvincing. ⑤ barely enough: 草料～够牲口吃一天。There's just enough cattle fodder for one day's feed./ 他的身高也许～能达到参军的标准。He might be tall enough to join the army./ ～的多数 a bare majority/ ～维持生活 eke out a bare living; scrape along

**娩** miǎn childbirth; delivery; parturition

**冕** miǎn crown: 加～礼 coronation

**湎** miǎn 见"沉湎" chénmiǎn

**缅** miǎn remote; far back

【缅甸】 Miǎndiàn Burma ◇～人 Burmese/ ～语 Burmese (language)

【缅怀】 miǎnhuái cherish the memory of; recall: ～革命先烈 cherish the memory of our revolutionary martyrs/ ～往事 recall past events

【缅茄】 miǎnqié 〈植〉 Shan pahudia (*Pahudia xylocarpa*)

【缅想】 miǎnxiǎng think of (past events); recall

**腼** miǎn

【腼腆】 miǎntian shy; bashful: 这孩子见了生人有点～。The child is shy with strangers.

**鮸** miǎn slate cod croaker

## miàn

**面** miàn ① face: ～带笑容 with a smile on one's face/ ～无惧色 not look at all afraid ② face (a certain direction): 这房子～南坐北。The house faces south. ③ surface; top; face: 桌～ the top of a table; tabletop/ 水～ the surface of the water/ 路～ road surface/ 钟～ clock face; dial ④ personally; directly: ～告 tell sb. personally/ ～交 deliver personally; hand-deliver ⑤ the right side; cover; outside: 书～儿破了。The cover of the book is torn./ 夹袄的～儿 the outside of a lined jacket/ 被～儿 the top covering of a quilt ⑥〈数〉 surface ⑦ an entire area (as opposed to particular points): 县委书记下去蹲点了,～上的工作他让我来抓。The county Party secretary has gone to work at a grass-roots unit and has left me in charge of the county. ⑧ side; aspect: 四～包围敌人 surround the enemy on all sides/ 这只是问题的一～。This is only one aspect of the question. ⑨ extent; range; scale; scope: 这次运动,群众发动的～很广。This movement has aroused the masses on a large scale./ 知识～广(窄) have a wide (narrow) range of knowledge ⑩〔方位词后缀〕: 前～ in front/ 左～ on the left/ 外～ outside ⑪〈量〉〔多用于扁平的物件〕: 一～镜子 a mirror/ 两～旗子 two flags ⑫ wheat flour; flour: 大米～ rice flour/ 玉米～ corn flour/ 白～ wheat flour ⑬ powder: 胡椒～ ground pepper/ 药～ medicinal powder ⑭ noodles ⑮〈方〉 soft and floury: 这块白薯真～。This sweet potato is soft and floury.

【面包】 miànbāo bread ◇～房 bakery/ ～干 rusk/ ～果 〈植〉 breadfruit/ ～渣儿 breadcrumbs; crumbs

【面不改色】 miàn bù gǎisè not change colour; remain calm; without turning a hair; without batting an eyelid

【面茶】 miànchá seasoned millet mush

【面辞】 miàncí go to say good-bye to sb.; take leave of sb.

【面对】 miànduì face; confront: ～现实 face reality; be realistic/ ～危险情况,镇定自若 remain calm in the face of danger/ ～这一派大好形势,怎能不欢欣鼓舞? Who wouldn't be happy to see such a good situation?

【面对面】 miàn duì miàn facing each other; face-to-face;

vis-à-vis: ～地坐着 sit face-to-face; sit vis-à-vis/ ～的斗争 a face-to-face struggle; direct confrontation

【面额】 miàn'é 〈经〉 denomination: 各种～的纸币 banknotes of different denominations/ ～为五元和十元的人民币 Renminbi in 5- and 10-*yuan* notes

【面肥】 miànféi leavening dough; leaven

【面粉】 miànfěn wheat flour; flour ◇～厂 flour mill

【面革】 miàngé 〈皮革〉 upper leather

【面红耳赤】 miànhóng-ěrchì be red in the face; be flushed: 争得～ argue until everyone is red in the face; have a heated argument/ 羞得～ flush with shame or shyness

【面糊】 miànhù paste

【面糊】 miànhu 〈方〉 soft and floury

【面黄肌瘦】 miànhuáng-jīshòu sallow and emaciated; lean and haggard

【面积】 miànji area: 我国～约为九百六十万平方公里。The area of China is about 9.6 million square kilometres./ 棉花种植～ the acreage under cotton/ 展览会～为三千平方米。The exhibition covers a floor space of 3,000 square metres.

【面颊】 miànjiá cheek

【面巾纸】 miànjīnzhǐ face tissues

【面筋】 miànjin gluten

【面具】 miànjù mask: 防毒～ gas mask

【面孔】 miànkǒng face: 严肃的～ a stern face/ 板起～ put on a stern expression/ 装出一副救世主的～ assume the guise of a saviour

【面临】 miànlín be faced with; be confronted with; be up against: ～一场严重的危机 be faced with a serious crisis/ 我们正～一场新的斗争。A new struggle lies ahead of us.

【面貌】 miànmào ① face; features: 他俩的～十分相似。The two of them look very much alike. ② appearance (of things); look; aspect: 精神～ mental outlook/ ～一新 take on a new look (或 aspect)/ 改变了中国的～ have changed the face of China/ 按照无产阶级的～改造世界 mould the world in the image of the proletariat

【面面俱到】 miànmiàn jù dào attend to each and every aspect of a matter

【面面相觑】 miànmiàn xiāng qù look at each other in blank dismay; gaze at each other in speechless despair

【面目】 miànmù ① face; features; visage: ～可憎 repulsive in appearance ② appearance (of things); look; aspect: ～全非 be changed or distorted beyond recognition/ 还其本来～ reveal sth. in its true colours/ 政治～不清 of dubious political background ③ self-respect; honour; sense of shame; face: 愧无～见人 feel too ashamed to face people

【面目一新】 miànmù yī xīn take on an entirely new look; present a completely new appearance; assume a new aspect

【面庞】 miànpáng contours of the face; face: 圆圆的～ a round face

【面洽】 miànqià discuss with sb. face to face; take up a matter with sb. personally: 有关事宜,请找张同志～。For particulars, please go and see Comrade Zhang.

【面前】 miànqián in (the) face of; in front of; before: 困难～不动摇 not waver in the face of difficulties/ 在凶恶的敌人～,他没有丝毫怯懦的表现。He did not show the slightest timidity before the ferocious enemy.

【面人儿】 miànrénr dough figurine

【面容】 miànróng facial features; face: ～消瘦 look emaciated

【面如土色】 miàn rú tǔsè look ashen; look pale: 吓得～ turn pale with fright

【面色】 miànsè ① complexion: ～苍白 look pale/ ～红润 have rosy cheeks; be ruddy-cheeked ② facial expression: ～忧郁 have a melancholy look; look worried

【面纱】 miànshā veil

【面善】 miànshàn look familiar

【面商】 miànshāng discuss with sb. face to face; consult personally

【面神经】 miànshénjīng 〈生理〉 facial nerve

【面生】 miànshēng look unfamiliar: 这个人～得很。I don't think I've seen this person before.

【面食】 miànshi cooked wheaten food

【面授机宜】 miàn shòu jīyí personally instruct sb. on the line of action to pursue; give confidential briefing

【面熟】 miànshú look familiar: 这人看着～,就是想不起来是谁。That person looks familiar but I simply can't place him.

【面塑】 miànsù 〈工美〉 dough modelling

【面谈】 miàntán speak to sb. face to face; take up a matter with sb. personally

【面汤】 miàntāng water in which noodles have been boiled

【面条】 miàntiáo noodles

【面团】 miàntuán dough

【面无人色】 miàn wú rénsè look ghastly pale

【面向】 miànxiàng ① turn one's face to; turn in the direction of; face: ～党旗庄严宣誓 stand facing the Party flag and make a solemn vow ② be geared to the needs of; cater to: ～工农兵 be geared to the needs of the workers, peasants and soldiers

【面谢】 miànxiè thank sb. in person

【面誉背毁】 miànyù-bèihuǐ praise sb. to his face and abuse him behind his back

【面罩】 miànzhào face guard

【面值】 miànzhí ① par value; face value; nominal value ② denomination

【面砖】 miànzhuān 〈建〉 face brick

【面子】 miànzi ① outer part; outside; face: 大衣的～ the outside of an overcoat ② reputation; prestige; face: 丢～ lose face/ 保全～ save face/ 爱～ be concerned about face-saving/ 撕破～ cast aside all considerations of face; not spare sb.'s sensibilities/ 有～ enjoy due respect/ 给～ show due respect for sb.'s feelings

## miāo

**喵** miāo 〈象〉 mew; miaow

## miáo

**苗** miáo ① young plant; seedling: 麦～儿 wheat seedling/ 工人阶级的好～～ a promising son of the working class ② the young of some animals: 鱼～ fry ③ vaccine: 牛痘～ (bovine) vaccine ④ sth. resembling a young plant: 火～儿 flame ⑤ (Miáo) a surname

【苗床】 miáochuáng seedbed

【苗木】 miáomù 〈林〉 nursery stock

【苗圃】 miáopǔ nursery (of young plants)

【苗期】 miáoqī 〈农〉 seedling stage

【苗条】 miáotiao (of a woman) slender; slim

【苗头】 miáotou symptom of a trend; suggestion of a new development: 要注意不良倾向的～。Watch out for symptoms of unhealthy tendencies./ 他一看～不对就溜了。He slipped off when he saw what was going to happen.

【苗裔】 miáoyì 〈书〉 progeny; descendants; offspring

【苗子】 miáozi ① 〈方〉 young plant; seedling ② young successor

【苗族】 Miáozú the Miao nationality, distributed over Guizhou, Hunan, Yunnan, the Guangxi Zhuang Autonomous Region, Sichuan and Guangdong

**描** miáo ①trace; copy: ～图样 trace designs; copy designs ②touch up; retouch: 练毛笔字，一笔是一笔，不要～。In practising Chinese calligraphy, write with a sure hand — don't retouch.

【描红】 miáohóng trace in black ink over characters printed in red (in learning to write with a brush)

【描画】 miáohuà draw; paint; depict; describe: ～出美好的前景 paint a bright future/ 漓江美景难以用语言来～。The beauty of the scenery along the Lijiang River defies description.

【描绘】 miáohuì depict; describe; portray: 这部小说生动地～了青年建设边疆的战斗生活。The novel vividly depicts the life and struggle of young people in reconstructing a frontier region.

【描金】 miáojīn 〈工美〉 trace a design in gold

【描摹】 miáomó depict; portray; delineate

【描述】 miáoshù describe: 详细～事情的经过 describe what happened in great detail

【描图】 miáotú tracing ◇～员 tracer/ ～纸 tracing paper

【描写】 miáoxiě describe; depict; portray: ～一位优秀画家的成长过程 describe how he grew up to be an outstanding painter

**瞄** miáo concentrate one's gaze on; take aim: ～得准，打得狠 take good aim and hit hard

【瞄准】 miáozhǔn take aim; aim; train on; lay; sight: 练习～ practise aiming/ ～靶心 aim at the bull's-eye/ 把高射炮～敌机 train the antiaircraft guns on the enemy planes ◇～环 ring sight/ ～具 sighting device; (gun) sight/ ～手 layer; pointer

**鹋** miáo 见"鸸鹋" érmiáo

## miǎo

**杪** miǎo ①the tip of a twig: 树～ tree top ②end (of a year, month or season): 岁～ the end of the year; year-end

**秒** miǎo second (=1/60 of a minute)

【秒表】 miǎobiǎo stopwatch; chronograph

【秒差距】 miǎochājù 〈天〉 parsec

【秒立方米】 miǎolìfāngmǐ 〈水〉 cubic metre per second

【秒针】 miǎozhēn second hand (of a clock or watch)

**渺** miǎo ①(of an expanse of water) vast ②distant and indistinct; vague: ～无人迹 remote and uninhabited/ ～若烟云 as vague as mist ③tiny; insignificant: ～不足道 insignificant; negligible; not worth mentioning

【渺茫】 miǎománg ①distant and indistinct; vague: 他走后音信～。We haven't heard from him since he left. ②uncertain: 前途～ have an uncertain future/ 希望～ have slim hopes (of success)

【渺小】 miǎoxiǎo tiny; negligible; insignificant; paltry: 个人的力量是～的。The strength of an individual is insignificant./ 我这种思想同铁人王进喜的思想境界相比是何等的～！How paltry my thoughts were when compared with the mental outlook of Iron Man Wang Jinxi.

**淼** miǎo 〈书〉 (of an expanse of water) vast

【淼茫】 miǎománg (of an expanse of water) stretch as far as the eye can see

**缈** miǎo 见"缥缈" piāomiǎo

**邈** miǎo 〈书〉 far away; remote

**藐** miǎo ①small; petty ②slight; despise: 言者谆谆，听者～～。The words were earnest but they fell on deaf ears.

【藐视】 miǎoshì despise; look down upon: 在战略上我们要～一切敌人，在战术上我们要重视一切敌人。Strategically we should despise all our enemies, but tactically we should take them all seriously.

【藐小】 miǎoxiǎo tiny; negligible; insignificant; paltry

## miào

**妙** miào ①wonderful; excellent; fine: 这主意真～。That's an excellent idea./ ～不可言 too wonderful for words; most intriguing/ 绝～的讽刺 a supreme irony ②ingenious; clever; subtle: 深得其中之～ have got the trick of it; fully appreciate its subtlety/ 他回答得很～。He made a clever answer.

【妙计】 miàojì excellent plan; brilliant scheme

【妙诀】 miàojué a clever way of doing sth.; knack

【妙品】 miàopǐn ①fine quality goods: 调味～ best-quality condiment ②fine work of art

【妙趣横生】 miàoqù héngshēng full of wit and humour; very witty

【妙手回春】 miàoshǒu huí chūn (of a doctor) effect a miraculous cure and bring the dying back to life

【妙用】 miàoyòng magical effect: 小小银针，大有～。A tiny acupuncture needle can work wonders.

【妙语】 miàoyǔ witty remark; witticism

**庙** miào ①temple; shrine ②temple fair: 赶～ go to the fair

【庙会】 miàohuì temple fair; fair

【庙宇】 miàoyǔ temple

**缪** Miào a surname

另见 miù; móu

## miē

**乜** miē

【乜斜】 miēxie ①squint: 他～着眼睛，眼角挂着讥诮的笑意。He squinted with a sneering look in the corner of his eye. ②(of eyes) half-closed: ～的睡眼 half-closed eyes heavy with sleep

**咩** miē 〈象〉 baa; bleat

## miè

**灭** miè ①(of a light, fire, etc.) go out: 火～了。The fire has gone out./ 灯突然～了。All of a sudden the lights went out. ②extinguish; put out; turn off: ～火 put out a fire; extinguish a fire/ 节约用电，人走灯～。Save electricity — turn off the lights when you leave. ③submerge; drown: ～顶 be drowned ④destroy; exterminate; wipe out: ～蝇 kill flies/ 长无产阶级的志气，～资产阶级的威风

enhance the morale of the proletariat and puncture the arrogance of the bourgeoisie

【灭茬机】 mièchájī 〈农〉 stubble cleaner

【灭虫宁】 mièchóngníng 〈药〉 bephenium

【灭此朝食】 miè cǐ zhāo shí will not have breakfast until the enemy is wiped out — be anxious to finish off the enemy immediately

【灭滴灵】 mièdīlíng 〈药〉 metronidazole; flagyl

【灭顶】 mièdǐng be drowned: 在人民战争的汪洋大海中，敌人遭到了～之灾。The enemy was swamped in the vast ocean of a people's war.

【灭火】 mièhuǒ ① put out a fire; extinguish a fire ② cut out an engine ◇ ～剂 fire-extinguishing chemical (或 agent)/ ～器 fire extinguisher

【灭迹】 mièjī destroy the evidence (of one's evildoing)

【灭绝】 mièjué become extinct: 现已～的动物 extinct animals

【灭绝人性】 mièjué rénxìng inhuman; savage; cannibalistic

【灭口】 mièkǒu (of a hidden criminal) do away with a witness or accomplice

【灭绦灵】 miètāolíng 〈药〉 niclosamide

【灭亡】 mièwáng be destroyed; become extinct; die out: 自取～ court destruction/ 帝国主义必然～。Imperialism is doomed.

【灭资兴无】 miè zī xīng wú eliminate bourgeois ideology, foster proletarian ideology; get rid of what is bourgeois and promote what is proletarian

【灭族】 mièzú extermination of an entire family (a punishment in ancient China)

**蔑** miè 〈书〉 ① slight; disdain: 轻～ disdain ② nothing; none: ～以复加 could not be surpassed; reach the limit ③ smear: 诬～ slander; vilify

【蔑视】 mièshì despise; show contempt for; scorn

**篾** miè ① thin bamboo strip ② the rind of reed or sorghum

【篾黄】 mièhuáng the inner skin of a bamboo stem

【篾匠】 mièjiàng a craftsman who makes articles from bamboo strips

【篾片】 mièpiàn ① thin bamboo strip ② 〈旧〉 hanger-on; sycophant

【篾青】 mièqīng the outer cuticle of a bamboo stem

【篾席】 mièxí a mat made of thin bamboo strips

## mín

**民** mín ① the people: 为～除害 rid the people of a scourge ② a member of a nationality: 回～ a Hui ③ a person of a certain occupation: 农～ peasant/ 渔～ fisherman/ 牧～ herdsman ④ of the people; folk: ～歌 folk song ⑤ civilian: 军～联防 joint defence by army and civilians/ ～船 a junk or small boat for civilian use

【民办】 mínbàn run by the local people: ～公助 run by the local people and subsidized by the state ◇～小学 a primary school run by the local people

【民变】 mínbiàn mass uprising; popular revolt

【民兵】 mínbīng ① people's militia; militia ② militiaman: 女～ militiawoman ◇ ～师 a contingent of the people's militia

【民不聊生】 mín bù liáo shēng the people have no means of livelihood; the masses live in dire poverty

【民法】 mínfǎ civil law

【民房】 mínfáng a house owned by a citizen

【民愤】 mínfèn popular indignation; the people's wrath: ～极大 have earned the bitter hatred of the people; have incurred the greatest popular indignation

【民歌】 míngē folk song

【民工】 míngōng a labourer working on a public project

【民国】 Mínguó the Republic of China (1912-1949)

【民航】 mínháng 〈简〉 (民用航空) civil aviation ◇ ～机 civil aircraft; civil airplane

【民间】 mínjiān ① among the people; popular; folk: 这个故事长久地在～流传。For generations the story has circulated among the people./ ～疾苦 hardships of the people ② nongovernmental; people-to-people: ～来往 nongovernmental contact; people-to-people exchange ◇～传说 popular legend; folk legend; folklore/ ～故事 folktale; folk story/ ～文学 folk literature/ ～舞蹈 folk dance/ ～协定 nongovernmental agreement/ ～验方 folk remedy; folk recipe/ ～艺术 folk art/ ～音乐 folk music

【民警】 mínjǐng people's police; people's policeman: 女～ people's policewoman

【民力】 mínlì financial resources of the people

【民气】 mínqì the people's morale; popular morale

【民情】 mínqíng ① condition of the people: 熟悉地理～ be familiar with the place and the people ② feelings of the people; public feeling

【民权】 mínquán civil rights; civil liberties; democratic rights

【民生】 mínshēng the people's livelihood: 国计～ the national economy and the people's livelihood/ ～凋敝。The people lived in destitution.

【民事】 mínshì 〈法〉 relating to civil law; civil ◇～案件 civil case/ ～管辖权 civil jurisdiction/ ～审判庭 the civil division of a people's court; civil court/ ～诉讼 civil action (或 process, lawsuit)

【民俗】 mínsú folk custom; folkways ◇～学 folklore

【民团】 míntuán 〈旧〉 civil corps (reactionary local armed forces organized by landlords)

【民校】 mínxiào ① sparetime school for adults ② school run by the local people

【民心】 mínxīn popular feelings; common aspiration of the people: ～所向 where the popular will inclines; (what conforms to) the common aspiration of the people/ 深得～ enjoy the ardent support of the people

【民谣】 mínyáo folk rhyme (esp. of the topical and political type)

【民意】 mínyì the will of the people; popular will ◇～测验 public opinion poll; poll

【民用】 mínyòng for civil use; civil ◇～航空 civil aviation/ ～机场 civil airport

【民怨沸腾】 mínyuàn fèiténg the people are boiling with resentment; seething popular discontent

【民乐】 mínyuè music, esp. folk music, for traditional instruments ◇ ～队 traditional instruments orchestra/ ～合奏 ensemble of traditional instruments

【民运】 mínyùn ① civil transport ② the army's propaganda and organizational work among the civilians during the revolutionary wars led by the Chinese Communist Party

【民贼】 mínzéi traitor to the people

【民政】 mínzhèng civil administration ◇～机关 civil administration organ

【民脂民膏】 mínzhī-míngāo flesh and blood of the people: 反动政府搜刮～。The reactionary government fed on the flesh and blood of the people.

【民众】 mínzhòng the masses of the people; the common people; the populace: 唤起～ arouse the masses ◇～团体 people's organization; mass organization

【民主】 mínzhǔ ① democracy; democratic rights: 党内～ inner-party democracy ② democratic: 他作风～。He has a democratic work-style.
◇（美国）～党 the Democratic Party/ ～改革 democratic reform/ ～革命 democratic revolution/ ～共和国 democratic republic/ ～人士 democratic personages/ ～协商 democratic consultation

【民主党派】 mínzhǔ dǎngpài democratic parties (those bourgeois and petty-bourgeois political parties that have accepted the leadership of the Chinese Communist Party and joined the revolutionary united front)

【民主集中制】 mínzhǔ-jízhōngzhì democratic centralism (the organizational principle of our Party and state, namely, centralism on the basis of democracy and democracy under centralized guidance)

【民主生活】 mínzhǔ shēnghuó democratic life: 坚持正常的～ maintain the normal practice of democracy

【民族】 mínzú nation; nationality: 中华～ the Chinese nation/ 被压迫～ oppressed nations/ 国内各～的团结 the unity of our various nationalities/ 少数～ minority nationality; national minority/ ～复兴 revival of nationhood; national rejuvenation
◇～败类 scum of a nation/ ～大家庭 the great family of nationalities/ ～独立 national independence/ ～革命 national revolution/ ～共同语 common national language/ ～解放运动 national liberation movement/ ～利己主义 national egoism/ ～民主革命 national-democratic revolution/ ～区域自治 regional autonomy of minority nationalities; regional national autonomy/ ～同化 national assimilation/ ～统一战线 national united front/ ～投降主义 national capitulationism/ ～文化宫 the Cultural Palace of the Nationalities/ ～形式 national style; national form/ ～虚无主义 national nihilism/ ～学 ethnology/ ～意识 national consciousness/ ～英雄 national hero/ ～杂居地区 multi-national area/ ～主义 nationalism/ ～政策 policy towards nationalities/ ～资产阶级 national bourgeoisie/ ～自决 national self-determination/ ～自信心 national confidence/ ～自尊心 national pride; national self-respect

## mǐn

**皿** mǐn 见"器皿" qìmǐn

**闵** Mǐn a surname

**泯** mǐn vanish; die out: 永存不～ be everlasting; be immortal

【泯灭】 mǐnmiè die out; disappear; vanish: 难以～的印象 an indelible impression

【泯没】 mǐnmò vanish; sink into oblivion; become lost: 烈士的功绩永远不会～。The contributions of the revolutionary martyrs will never be forgotten.

**抿** mǐn ① smooth (hair, etc.) with a wet brush ② close lightly; furl; tuck: ～着嘴笑 smile with closed lips; compress one's lips to smile/ 水鸟儿一～翅膀，钻入水中。The water bird tucked its wings and dived into the water. ③ sip: ～一口酒 take a sip of the wine

【抿子】 mǐnzi small hairbrush

**闽** Mǐn another name for Fujian Province

**悯** mǐn ① commiserate; pity: 其情可～。His case deserves sympathy. ② 〈书〉 sorrow

**敏** mǐn quick; nimble; agile

【敏感】 mǐngǎn sensitive; susceptible: 政治～ political sensitivity/ 他对机器里不正常的声音非常～。His ears are highly sensitive to any unusual sound in the machine. ◇ ～元件〈无〉sensitive element; sensor/ ～度 susceptibility

【敏化】 mǐnhuà 〈物〉 sensibilization; sensitization ◇ ～剂 sensitizer/ ～纸 sensitized paper

【敏捷】 mǐnjié quick; nimble; agile: 动作～ be quick in movement/ 守门员～地跃向右方，救出了险球。The goalkeeper leapt nimbly to the right and saved the goal.

【敏锐】 mǐnruì sharp; acute; keen: 目光～ have sharp eyes; be sharp-eyed/ 听觉～ have good (或 sharp) ears/ 嗅觉～ have a keen sense of smell/ ～的政治眼光 keen political insight

**鳘** mǐn slate cod croaker

## míng

**名** míng ① name: 地～ place name/ 一种～为九二〇的生长激素 a growth hormone known as 920/ 他～叫张南。His name is Zhang Nan. 或 He is called Zhang Nan. ② given name: 这位同志姓李～大刚。This comrade's surname is Li and his given name, Dagang. ③ fame; reputation; renown: 不为～，不为利 seek neither fame nor gain/ ～闻中外 well known both at home and abroad ④ famous; celebrated; well-known; noted: ～厨师 a famous cook/ ～诗人 a noted poet/ ～句 a well-known phrase; a much quoted line ⑤ express; describe: 不可～状 indescribable; nondescript ⑥〈量〉〔用于人〕: 十二～战士 twelve soldiers/ 得第一～ come in first; win first place

【名不副实】 míng bù fù shí the name falls short of the reality; be sth. more in name than in reality; be unworthy of the name or title: 一个～的军事学家 not a military expert in the real sense of the term 又作"名不符实"

【名不虚传】 míng bù xūchuán have a well-deserved reputation; deserve the reputation one enjoys; live up to one's reputation

【名册】 míngcè register; roll: 学生～ students' register; students' roll/ 部队～ muster roll/ 工作人员～ personnel roll

【名产】 míngchǎn famous product

【名称】 míngchēng name (of a thing or organization)

【名垂青史】 míng chuí qīngshǐ go down in history; be crowned with eternal glory

【名词】 míngcí ①〈语〉 noun; substantive ② term; phrase: 化学～ chemical term/ 新～儿 new expression; vogue word ③〈逻〉 name

【名次】 míngcì position in a name list; place in a competition: 我们参加这次运动会不是为了争～。We haven't come to this sports meet just to compete for places./ 按比赛成绩排列～ arrange the names of contestants in the order of their results

【名存实亡】 míngcún-shíwáng cease to exist except in name; exist in name only

【名单】 míngdān name list: 候选人～ list of candidates/ 入伍～ list of recruits

【名额】 míng'é the number of people assigned or allowed; quota of people: 代表～ the number of deputies to be elected or sent/ 招生～ the number of students to be enrolled; planned enrolment figure/ 今年的征兵～已满。This year's enlistment quota has already been filled./ 由于～有限，这次参观不能人人都去。Since the number of people allowed is limited, not everyone can go on this visit.

【名分】 míngfèn 〈旧〉 a person's status

【名副其实】 míng fù qí shí the name matches the reality; be sth. in reality as well as in name; be worthy of the name: 做一个～的共产党员 be a Communist worthy of the name/ 这真是～的奇迹。That's a veritable miracle. 又作"名符其实"

【名贵】 mínguì famous and precious; rare: ～药材 rare medicinal herbs/ ～的字画 priceless scrolls of calligraphy and painting

【名家】 míngjiā ① (Míngjiā) the School of Logicians (in the Spring and Autumn and Warring States Periods, 770-221 B.C.) ② a person of academic or artistic distinction; famous expert; master

【名将】 míngjiàng famous general; great soldier: 足球～ a football hero (或 star)

【名教】 míngjiào the Confucian ethical code

【名利】 mínglì fame and gain; fame and wealth ◇ ～思想 desire for personal fame and gain

【名列前茅】 míng liè qiánmáo be among the best of the successful candidates

【名流】 míngliú distinguished personages; celebrities

【名落孙山】 míng luò Sūn Shān fall behind Sun Shan (who was last on the list of successful candidates) — fail in a competitive examination

【名目】 míngmù names of things; items: ～繁多 a multitude of names (或 items); names of every description/ 巧立～ invent all kinds of names (as pretexts for exorbitant taxes or to pad an expense account)

【名牌】 míngpái ① famous brand: ～香烟 a famous brand of cigarettes ② nameplate; name tag

【名片】 míngpiàn visiting card; calling card: 留下～ leave one's card

【名气】 míngqi 〈口〉 reputation; fame; name: 有点～ enjoy some reputation; be quite well-known; have made a name for oneself

【名人】 míngrén famous person; eminent person; celebrity; notable

【名山大川】 míngshān-dàchuān famous mountains and great rivers

【名声】 míngshēng reputation; repute; renown: ～很坏 have an unsavoury reputation; be held in ill repute; be notorious/ 享有好～ enjoy a good reputation; be held in high repute

【名胜】 míngshèng a place famous for its scenery or historical relics; scenic spot ◇ ～古迹 places of historic interest and scenic beauty; scenic spots and historical sites

【名士】 míngshì 〈旧〉 ① a person with a literary reputation ② a celebrity with no official post ◇ ～派 an unconventional and self-indulgent old-style intellectual

【名手】 míngshǒu a famous artist, player, etc.

【名数】 míngshù 〈数〉 concrete number

【名堂】 míngtang ① variety; item: 别看他们只是个业余文工团,演出的～可多啦! It's true they're only an amateur troupe, but they have an amazingly large repertoire./ 这个坏家伙又在搞什么～? What's that villain up to now? ② result; achievement: 依靠集体力量,一定能搞出～来。As long as we rely on collective effort we can certainly achieve something./ 问了他半天也没问出个～。I questioned him for a long time but couldn't get anything out of him. ③ what lies behind sth.; reason: 敌军突然撤走了,这里面有什么～? What's behind the enemy's sudden retreat?/ 墙角上的砖这么砌是有～的。There's a reason for laying the corner bricks this way.

【名望】 míngwàng fame and prestige; good reputation; renown: 有～的大夫 a famous doctor

【名位】 míngwèi fame and position

【名物】 míngwù the name and description of a thing

【名下】 míngxià under sb.'s name; belonging or related to sb.: 这笔帐就记在我～吧。Charge these expenses to my account.

【名言】 míngyán well-known saying; celebrated dictum; famous remark

【名义】 míngyì ① name: 以革命的～ in the name of the revolution/ 以会议执行主席的～ in one's capacity as executive chairman of the conference/ 假借～ under false pretences ②〔后面多带"上"字〕nominal; titular; in name: ～上裁军,实际上扩军 disarmament in name, armament in reality ◇ ～工资〈经〉 nominal wages/ ～汇价〈经〉 nominal rate (of exchange)

【名誉】 míngyù ① fame; reputation: 闹～地位 be out for fame and position/ ～好 have a good reputation; be of high repute; be held in high esteem ② honorary ◇ ～会员 honorary member/ ～主席 honorary chairman; honorary president

【名噪一时】 míng zào yī shí gain considerable fame among one's contemporaries

【名正言顺】 míngzhèng-yánshùn come within one's jurisdiction; be perfectly justifiable

【名著】 míngzhù famous book; famous work: 文学～ a famous literary work; a literary masterpiece

【名字】 míngzi ① (given) name ② name: 这种花的～很特别。This flower has a peculiar name.

**明** míng ① bright; brilliant; light: ～月 a bright moon/ 灯火通～ be brightly lit; be brilliantly illuminated/ 天已微～。Day is breaking. ② clear; distinct: 是非愈辩愈～。As the debate progressed, it became clearer and clearer which side was right./ 情况不～。The situation is not clear./ 去向不～ whereabouts unknown/ 指～出路 point the way out ③ open; overt; explicit: ～一套暗一套 act one way in the open and another way in secret/ 我对你～说了吧。I'll be frank with you. ④ sharp-eyed; clear-sighted: 耳聪目～ have sharp ears and eyes/ 眼～手快 quick of eye and deft of hand ⑤ aboveboard; honest: ～人不做暗事。An honest man doesn't do anything underhand. ⑥ sight: 双目失～ go blind in both eyes/ 复～ regain one's sight ⑦ understand; know: 不～真相 not know the facts; be ignorant of the actual situation ⑧ immediately following in time: ～年 next year/ ～晚 tomorrow evening ⑨ (Míng) the Ming Dynasty (1368-1644) ⑩ (Míng) a surname

【明暗】 míng-àn light and shade ◇ ～对照法 〈美术〉 chiaroscuro

【明摆着】 míngbǎizhe obvious; clear; plain: 这不是～的事儿吗? Isn't this obvious? 或 Isn't it as clear as daylight?

【明白】 míngbai ① clear; obvious; plain: 他讲得～易懂。He spoke clearly and simply./ 这个问题很～。The matter is quite clear. ② frank; unequivocal; explicit: 你还是跟他讲～了好。It would be best to be frank with him./ 他～表示不赞成这个提议。He stated clearly that he didn't agree with the proposal. ③ sensible; reasonable: ～人 a sensible person ④ understand; realize; know: ～事理 know what's what; have good sense/ 我不～你的意思。I don't see what you mean./ 我忽然～了。The truth suddenly dawned on me.

【明辨是非】 míng biàn shì-fēi make a clear distinction between right and wrong

【明察暗访】 míngchá-ànfǎng observe publicly and investigate privately; conduct a thorough investigation

【明察秋毫】 míng chá qiūháo have eyes sharp enough to perceive an animal's autumn hair — be perceptive of the minutest detail: ～之末，而不见舆薪 be sharp-sighted enough to perceive the tip of an animal's autumn hair but unable to see a cartload of firewood — see the minute details but miss the major issue
【明畅】 míngchàng lucid and smooth
【明澈】 míngchè bright and limpid; transparent: ～的眼睛 bright and limpid eyes/ 湖水～如镜。The lake is like a mirror.
【明处】 míngchù ① where there is light: 你把相片拿到～来，让大家看个清楚。Bring the photo to the light so we can see it better. ② in the open; in public: 有话说在～。If you've got anything to say, say it openly./ 敌军在～，游击队在暗处。The guerrillas were acting under cover while the enemy troops were in the open.
【明灯】 míngdēng bright lamp; beacon: 指路～ a beacon lighting up one's way forward
【明断】 míngduàn 〈书〉 pass (fair) judgment
【明矾】 míngfán alum ◇ ～石 alumstone; alunite
【明沟】 mínggōu open drain
【明晃晃】 mínghuǎnghuǎng gleaming; shining: ～的刺刀 gleaming bayonets
【明火执仗】 mínghuǒ-zhízhàng carry torches and weapons in a robbery — conduct evil activities openly: ～的阶级敌人 class enemies operating in broad daylight
【明胶】 míngjiāo gelatin
【明净】 míngjìng bright and clean; clear and bright: ～的橱窗 a bright and clean shop window/ 北京秋天的天空分外～。In Beijing the autumn sky is especially clear and bright.
【明镜】 míngjìng bright mirror
【明快】 míngkuài ① lucid and lively; sprightly: ～的笔调 a lucid and lively style/ ～的节奏 sprightly rhythm ② straightforward; forthright: ～的性格 a forthright character
【明来暗往】 mínglái-ànwǎng have overt and covert contacts with sb.
【明朗】 mínglǎng ① bright and clear: ～的月色 bright moonlight/ ～的天空 a clear sky ② clear; obvious: 局势逐渐～。The situation is becoming clear./ 态度～ take a clear-cut position; adopt an unequivocal attitude ③ forthright; bright and cheerful: ～的性格 an open and forthright character/ 这幅画色调～。This picture is painted in bright, warm colours.
【明丽】 mínglì bright and beautiful: ～的秋色 a bright and beautiful autumn scene
【明亮】 míngliàng ① light; well-lit; bright: 宽敞而～的厂房 bright and spacious workshops/ 会议大厅里灯光～。The conference hall is brightly lit. ② bright; shining: ～的眼睛 bright eyes ③ become clear: 听了同志们这番解释，老张心里～了。The comrades' explanation helped Lao Zhang to straighten out his thinking.
【明了】 míngliǎo ① understand; be clear about: ～思想工作的重要性 understand the importance of ideological work/ 不～实际情况，就不能做出正确的判断。You can't form a correct judgment without a clear understanding of the actual situation. ② clear; plain: 简单～ simple and clear
【明令】 mínglìng explicit order; formal decree; public proclamation: ～取缔 proscribe by formal decree/ ～嘉奖 issue a commendation; mention in a citation
【明码】 míngmǎ ① plain code: ～电报 plain code telegram/ 用～发报 send a telegram in plain code ② 〈旧〉 with the price clearly marked: ～售货 put goods on sale with the prices clearly marked; sell at marked prices
【明媚】 míngmèi bright and beautiful; radiant and enchanting: 春光～ a radiant and enchanting spring scene
【明明】 míngmíng 〈副〉 obviously; plainly; undoubtedly: 这事～是他干的嘛！This is obviously his doing. 或 There can be no doubt that it was he who did it.
【明目张胆】 míngmù-zhāngdǎn brazenly; flagrantly: ～地进行武装干涉 brazenly commit an act of armed intervention
【明年】 míngnián next year
【明前】 míngqián a kind of green tea picked before Pure Brightness (清明, around April 5)
【明枪易躲，暗箭难防】 míngqiāng yì duǒ, ànjiàn nán fáng it is easy to dodge a spear in the open, but hard to guard against an arrow shot from hiding
【明确】 míngquè ① clear and definite; clear-cut; explicit; unequivocal: ～的目标 a clear aim/ ～的立场 a clear-cut stand/ ～的答复 a definite answer/ 用最～的语言警告敌人 warn the enemy in the most unequivocal terms/ 宪法～规定了我们国家的无产阶级性质。The Constitution clearly defines the proletarian nature of our state. ② make clear; make definite: 这篇社论进一步～了当前的中心任务。The editorial further defined the key task for the present period./ ～了学习的目的，我们的学习劲头就会更大。Once we're clear about the purpose of our study, we'll do it with ever greater enthusiasm.
【明儿】 míngr 〈口〉 ① tomorrow: ～见。See you tomorrow. ② one of these days; some day: ～你长大了，也开拖拉机好不好？What about you becoming a tractor driver too when you grow up?
【明日】 míngrì ① tomorrow ② the near future
【明日黄花】 míngrì huánghuā overblown blossoms — things that are stale and no longer of interest
【明太鱼】 míngtàiyú walleye pollack
【明天】 míngtiān ① tomorrow ② the near future: 光辉灿烂的～ a bright future
【明文】 míngwén (of laws, regulations, etc.) proclaimed in writing: ～规定 stipulate in explicit terms; expressly provide
【明晰】 míngxī distinct; clear: 雷达荧光屏上出现了～的图像。A distinct blip appeared on the radar screen.
【明虾】 míngxiā prawn
【明显】 míngxiǎn clear; obvious; evident; distinct: ～的优势 clear superiority/ ～的改进 distinct improvement/ ～的成效 tangible result/ 目标～。The target is quite clear./ 这很～是一个借口。This is evidently a pretext.
【明线】 míngxiàn 〈电子〉 open-wire line; open wire ◇ ～载波设备 open-wire carrier equipment
【明效大验】 míngxiào-dàyàn clinching proof of effectiveness; outstanding effect
【明信片】 míngxìnpiàn postcard: 美术～ picture postcard
【明星】 míngxīng 〈旧〉 star: 电影～ film star; movie star
【明修栈道，暗渡陈仓】 míng xiū zhàndào, àn dù Chéncāng pretend to prepare to advance along one path while secretly going along another; do one thing under cover of another
【明眼人】 míngyǎnrén a person with a discerning eye; a person of good sense
【明喻】 míngyù simile
【明哲保身】 míng zhé bǎo shēn be worldly wise and play safe
【明争暗斗】 míngzhēng-àndòu both open strife and veiled struggle
【明证】 míngzhèng clear proof: 西沙群岛自古即为我国领土，这些文物就是～。These cultural relics are clear proof that the Xisha Islands have been China's territory since ancient times.
【明知】 míngzhī know perfectly well; be fully aware: ～山

有虎，偏向虎山行 go deep into the mountains, knowing well that there are tigers there — go on undeterred by the dangers ahead

【明知故犯】 míngzhī-gùfàn knowingly violate (discipline, etc.); deliberately break (a rule, etc.); do sth. one knows is wrong

【明知故问】 míngzhī-gùwèn ask while knowing the answer

【明智】 míngzhì sensible; sagacious; wise: 表现出～的态度 show a sensible attitude/ 他这样决定是～的。It was wise of him to make that decision.

【明珠】 míngzhū bright pearl; jewel

【明珠暗投】 míngzhū àn tóu ① cast pearls before swine; find one's ability unrecognized ② a good person fallen among bad company

【明子】 míngzi pine torch

**鸣** míng ① the cry of birds, animals or insects: 鸡～ the crow of a cock/ 秋虫夜～ autumn insects chirping at night ② ring; sound: 耳～ ringing in the ears/ ～笛 blow a whistle/ ～鼓 beat a drum/ ～枪示警 fire a warning shot/ ～礼炮二十一响 fire a 21-gun salute/ 钟～三下。The clock struck three. ③ express; voice; air: ～谢 express one's thanks formally/ ～不平 complain of unfairness; cry out against an injustice/ 自～得意 be very pleased with oneself; preen oneself

【鸣镝】 míngdí whistling arrow (used in ancient times)

【鸣放】 míngfàng airing of views (through *dazibao*, meetings and other media)

【鸣锣开道】 míng luó kāi dào ① beat gongs to clear the way (for officials in feudal times) ② prepare the public for a coming event

【鸣禽】 míngqín songbird; singing bird

【鸣冤叫屈】 míngyuān-jiàoqū complain and call for redress; voice grievances

**茗** míng ① tender tea leaves ② tea: 品～ sip tea (to judge its quality); sample tea

**冥** míng ① dark; obscure: 幽～ dark hell; the nether world ② deep; profound: ～思 be deep in thought ③ dull; stupid: ～顽 thickheaded; stupid ④ underworld; the nether world: ～府 the nether world

【冥器】 míngqì funerary objects; burial objects

【冥思苦想】 míngsī-kǔxiǎng think long and hard; cudgel one's brains

【冥顽】 míngwán 〈书〉 thickheaded; stupid: ～不灵 impenetrably thickheaded

【冥王星】 míngwángxīng 〈天〉 Pluto

【冥想】 míngxiǎng deep thought; meditation: 苦思～ think long and hard; cudgel one's brains

**铭** míng ① inscription: 墓志～ inscription on the memorial tablet within a tomb/ 座右～ motto ② engrave: ～诸肺腑 engrave on one's mind (或 memory); bear firmly in mind

【铭感】 mínggǎn be deeply grateful: ～终身 remain deeply grateful for the rest of one's life

【铭记】 míngjì engrave on one's mind; always remember: 我国人民将世世代代～毛主席的恩情。Generation after generation of the Chinese people will recall with love and gratitude all they owe to Chairman Mao.

【铭刻】 míngkè ① inscription ② engrave on one's mind; always remember: 周总理的光辉形象永远～在人民的心中。The shining image of Premier Zhou Enlai is indelibly engraved on the memory of the people. ◇ ～学 epigraphy

【铭牌】 míngpái 〈机〉 data plate; nameplate

【铭文】 míngwén inscription; epigraph

**溟** míng 〈书〉 sea: 东～ the east sea

**盟** míng 另见 méng

【盟誓】 míngshì take an oath; make a pledge

**暝** míng 〈书〉 ① (of the sun) set; (of the sky) grow dark: 日将～。The sun is setting./ 天已～。Dusk has fallen. ② dusk; evening twilight

**瞑** míng

【瞑目】 míngmù close one's eyes in death — die content: 死不～ die discontent; die with everlasting regret

【瞑眩】 míngxuàn 〈中医〉 dizziness, nausea, etc. as a side effect of drugs

**螟** míng snout moth's larva

【螟虫】 míngchóng snout moth's larva

【螟蛾】 míng'é snout moth

【螟蛉】 mínglíng ① corn earworm ② adopted son

## mǐng

**酩** mǐng

【酩酊大醉】 mǐngdǐng dàzuì be dead drunk

## mìng

**命** mìng ① life: 逃～ run for one's life/ ～在旦夕 be on the verge of death; be dying ② lot; fate; destiny: 在旧社会，他认为自己受苦是～苦。In the old days he thought he had suffered because of his cruel fate. ③ order; command: 待～ await orders ④ assign (a name, title, etc.): ～题 assign a topic; set a question

【命案】 mìng'àn a case involving the killing of a person; homicide case

【命笔】 mìngbǐ 〈书〉 take up one's pen; set pen to paper: 欣然～ gladly set pen to paper; be happy to start writing

【命定】 mìngdìng determined by fate; predestined

【命根子】 mìnggēnzi one's very life; lifeblood: 无产阶级专政是我们劳动人民的～。The dictatorship of the proletariat is the lifeblood of us labouring people.

【命令】 mìnglìng order; command: 下～ issue an order/ 服从～ obey orders/ ～式的口气 a commanding tone/ 连长～一排担任警戒。The company commander ordered the first platoon to keep watch. ◇ ～句〈语〉 imperative sentence/ ～主义 commandism

【命脉】 mìngmài lifeblood; lifeline: 经济～ economic lifelines/ 水利是农业的～。Irrigation is the lifeblood of agriculture.

【命门】 mìngmén 〈中医〉 the gate of vitality, the area between the kidneys, generally regarded as the source of vitality, the function of which is to promote respiration, digestion, reproduction and the metabolism of body fluid

【命名】 mìngmíng name (sb. or sth.): 以白求恩医生～的医院 a hospital named after Dr. Norman Bethune/ 这条水渠被～为红旗渠。The canal was named the Red Flag Canal. ◇ ～大会 naming ceremony/ ～法 nomenclature

【命数法】 mìngshùfǎ 〈数〉 numeration

【命题】 mìngtí ① assign a topic; set a question: ～作文 assign a subject for composition ②〈数〉 proposition: ～演算 propositional calculus ③〈逻〉 proposition

【命途多舛】 mìngtú duō chuǎn suffer many a setback during one's life

【命运】 mìngyùn destiny; fate; lot: 悲惨的～ a tragic lot/ 这场斗争关系到党和国家的前途和～。On the outcome of the struggle hinges the future and destiny of our Party and state.

【命中】 mìngzhòng hit the target (或 mark); score a hit: 她第一枪就～靶心。Her first shot hit the bull's-eye. ◇ ～率 percentage of hits/ ～偏差 deviation of impact

## miù

**谬** miù wrong; false; erroneous; mistaken: ～见 a wrong view/ ～传 a false report/ 大～不然 be grossly mistaken

【谬奖】 miùjiǎng 〈谦〉 overpraise (me)

【谬论】 miùlùn fallacy; false (或 absurd) theory; falsehood: 驳斥现代修正主义的～ refute the fallacies of the modern revisionists

【谬误】 miùwù falsehood; error; mistake: 真理是在同～作斗争中间发展起来的。Truth develops through its struggle against falsehood.

【谬种】 miùzhǒng error; fallacy: ～流传，误人不浅。The dissemination of error does people great harm.

**缪** miù 见"纰缪" pīmiù
另见 Miào; móu

## mō

**摸** mō ① feel; stroke; touch: ～～刀口，看看快不快 feel the edge of a knife to see whether it is sharp/ 这衣料～着很软。This material feels soft./ 她轻轻地～了～孩子的头。She gently stroked the child's head. ② feel for; grope for; fumble: 在黑暗中～着下楼 grope one's way down the stairs in the dark/ 从床底下～出一双鞋来 fish out a pair of shoes from under the bed/ ～敌人岗哨 steal up to an enemy sentinel in the dark and get rid of him ③ try to find out; feel out; sound out: 你去～～他对这个问题的看法。Go and sound him out on this matter./ ～清敌情 find out about the enemy's situation/ ～透了这匹马的脾气 get to know the horse well/ ～不着头脑 be unable to make head or tail of sth./ ～出一套种植水稻的好经验 get a lot of good experience in growing rice

【摸底】 mōdǐ ① know the real situation: 这事我不～，你可以问问别人。I don't know much about this business. Please ask someone else. ② try to find out the real intention or situation; sound sb. out: 他是想摸我们的底。He was trying to feel us out.

【摸黑儿】 mōhēir 〈口〉 grope one's way on a dark night: ～赶路 press on with the journey at night/ 起早～地干 work from morning till night

【摸门儿】 mōménr 〈口〉 learn the ropes; get the hang of sth.

【摸索】 mōsuo ① grope; feel about; fumble: 在黑暗中～ grope (或 fumble) in the dark ② try to find out: ～种花生的规律 try to find out the laws (或 secret) of peanut growing

## mó

**谟** mó 〈书〉 plan: 宏～ a grand plan; a great project

**馍** mó 〈方〉 steamed bun; steamed bread

**麽** mó 见"幺麽" yāomó

**摹** mó copy; trace: 临～ copy a model of calligraphy or painting

【摹本】 móběn facsimile; copy

【摹仿】 mófǎng 见"模仿" mófǎng

【摹刻】 mókè ① carve a reproduction of an inscription or painting ② a carved reproduction of an inscription or painting

【摹拟】 mónǐ imitate; simulate

【摹写】 móxiě ① copy; imitate ② describe; depict: ～人物情状 depict characters in various situations

【摹印】 móyìn ① copy and print ② a style of characters or lettering on ancient imperial seals

**模** mó ① pattern; standard: 楷～ model; paragon ② imitate ③〈简〉(模范) model: 劳～ model worker
另见 mú

【模本】 móběn calligraphy or painting model

【模范】 mófàn an exemplary person or thing; model; fine example: 劳动～ model worker/ ～共青团员 model member of the Communist Youth League/ ～作用 exemplary role/ ～事迹 exemplary deeds/ ～地执行党的路线和政策 carry out the Party's line and policies in an exemplary way

【模仿】 mófǎng imitate; copy; model oneself on: ～动物的叫声 imitate the cries of animals/ 这部机器是～上海的一种新产品制造的。This machine is modelled on one recently made in Shanghai.

【模糊】 móhu ① blurred; indistinct; dim; vague: 字迹～了。The writing was blurred./ ～的景物 a hazy scene/ 只有～的印象 have only a vague idea of sth./ 她对这个问题还有一些～认识。She still has some confused ideas about that question. ② blur; obscure; confuse; mix up: 泪水～了他的双眼。Tears blurred his eyes. 或 His eyes were dim with tears./ 不能～阶级界限。Class distinctions must not be obscured. 又作"模胡"

【模棱两可】 móléng liǎngkě equivocal; ambiguous: 采取～的态度 take an equivocal attitude/ ～的提法 an ambiguous formulation

【模拟】 mónǐ imitate; simulate
◇ ～飞行〈军〉 simulated flight/ ～计算机 analogue computer/ ～人像 effigy/ ～试验 simulated test

【模数】 móshù 〈物〉 modulus: 弹性～ modulus of elasticity 又作"模量"

【模特儿】 mótèr 〈美术〉 model

【模型】 móxíng ① model: 船的～ a model of a ship; a model ship/ 原尺寸～ mock-up ② mould; matrix; pattern ◇ ～板 mould plate/ ～展品 scale model; replica

**膜** mó ① membrane: 细胞～ cell membrane/ 鼓～ tympanic membrane ② film; thin coating: 塑料薄～ plastic film/ 纸浆表面结了一层～。A thin film formed on the surface of the pulp.

【膜拜】 móbài prostrate oneself (before an idol or person); worship: 顶礼～ prostrate oneself in worship; pay homage to

【膜翅目】 móchìmù 〈动〉 Hymenoptera

【膜法】 mófǎ 〈环保〉 membrane method
【膜片】 mópiàn 〈仪表〉 diaphragm

**摩** mó ①rub; scrape; touch: 峻岭～天。The high mountains seem to scrape the sky. ②mull over; study: 揣～ try to fathom
另见 mā

【摩擦】 mócā ①rub: 轴颈在轴承面上～。The journal rubs against the bearing surface. ②〈物〉 friction: ～生热。Friction generates heat./ 滑动～ sliding friction/ 滚动～ rolling friction ③clash (between two parties); friction: 制造～ create friction/ 与某人发生～ have a brush with sb.
◇ ～力 〈物〉 frictional force; friction/ ～抛光 〈机〉 burnishing/ ～音 〈语〉 fricative/ ～桩 〈建〉 friction pile
【摩登】 módēng modern; fashionable
【摩电灯】 módiàndēng dynamo-powered lamp (on a bicycle, etc.)
【摩尔根主义】 Mó'ěrgēnzhǔyì 〈生〉 Morganism
【摩肩接踵】 mójiān-jiēzhǒng jostle each other in a crowd: 那天街上人特别多,真是～,川流不息。That day the street was jam-packed with people coming and going all the time.
【摩洛哥】 Móluògē Morocco ◇ ～人 Moroccan
【摩纳哥】 Mónàgē Monaco ◇ ～人 Monacan
【摩拳擦掌】 móquán-cāzhǎng rub one's fists and wipe one's palms — be eager for a fight; itch to have a go: 大家～,恨不得马上投入战斗。We all rolled up our sleeves, itching for the battle.
【摩挲】 mósuō stroke; caress
另见 māsa
【摩天】 mótiān skyscraping ◇ ～楼 skyscraper
【摩托】 mótuō motor
◇ ～车 motorcycle; motor bicycle; motorbike/ ～船 motorboat/ ～化部队 motorized troops

**磨** mó ①rub; wear: 他的脚上～了泡。His feet were blistered from the rubbing./ 没关系,就～破了一点皮。Nothing serious. Just a graze./ 袜子～破了。The socks are worn into holes./ 鞋跟～平了。The heels of the shoes are worn down./ 我劝了他半天,嘴皮都快～破了。I talked till my jaws ached, trying to bring him around. ②grind; polish: ～剪子 grind scissors; sharpen scissors/ ～大理石 polish marble/ ～墨 rub an ink stick against an inkstone; make ink for writing with a brush ③wear down; wear out: 他被这场病～得不成样子。The illness has worn him down to a mere shadow of his former self. ④trouble; pester; worry: 这孩子可真～人。What a little torment that child is./ 他不答应,你就跟他～。If he doesn't agree, just keep on at him until he does. ⑤obliterate; die out: 百世不～ will endure for centuries ⑥dawdle; waste time: 快走吧,别再～时间了。Stop dawdling and get going./ 这活最～工夫。This is a time-consuming job.
另见 mò

【磨版机】 mópǎnjī 〈印〉 graining machine
【磨擦】 mócā 见"摩擦" mócā
【磨蹭】 móceng move slowly; dawdle: 你这么磨磨蹭蹭的,什么时候才完得了啊? If you go on dawdling like this, when will you ever be able to finish?
【磨床】 móchuáng 〈机〉 grinding machine; grinder: 内圆～ internal grinder/ 外圆～ cylindrical grinder
【磨刀石】 módāoshí whetstone; grindstone
【磨革】 mógé 〈皮革〉 buffing ◇ ～机 buffing machine
【磨工】 mógōng 〈机〉 ①grinding work ②grinder ◇ ～车间 grindery
【磨光】 móguāng polish ◇ ～玻璃 polished glass/ ～机 polishing machine; glazing machine
【磨耗】 móhào wear and tear
【磨砺】 mólì go through the mill; steel oneself; harden oneself; discipline oneself
【磨练】 móliàn put oneself through the mill; temper oneself; steel oneself: 在艰苦斗争中～自己 temper (或 steel) oneself in hard struggle
【磨料】 móliào abrasive; abradant
【磨面革】 mómiàngé 〈皮革〉 buff (leather)
【磨灭】 mómiè wear away; efface; obliterate: 建立不可～的功勋 perform meritorious deeds never to be obliterated/ 留下不可～的印象 leave an indelible impression
【磨木机】 mómùjī 〈纸〉 (wood) grinder: 链式～ caterpillar grinder/ 袋式～ pocket grinder
【磨难】 mónàn tribulation; hardship; suffering
【磨砂玻璃】 móshā bōli ground glass; frosted glass
【磨蚀】 móshí 〈地〉 abrasion
【磨损】 mósǔn wear and tear: 这台机器基本上没有什么～。The machine shows scarcely any sign of wear and tear. ◇ ～留量 〈机〉 wear allowance
【磨削】 móxiāo 〈机〉 grinding ◇ ～裕量 grinding tolerance
【磨牙】 móyá ①grind one's teeth (in sleep) ②indulge in idle talk; argue pointlessly: 你别跟他～了。Don't waste your time arguing with him.
【磨洋工】 mó yánggōng loaf on the job; dawdle along
【磨嘴皮子】 mó zuǐpízi ①jabber; blah-blah: 成天～不干活,还能建设好社会主义? How can you build socialism if you just blah-blah and don't do a stroke of work? ②do a lot of talking: 这可是～的事。It'll take a hell of a lot of talking to settle this.

**蘑** mó mushroom

【蘑菇】 mógu ①mushroom ②worry; pester; keep on at: 你别跟她～了,她还有急事呢。Don't pester her. She's got something urgent to attend to. ③dawdle; dillydally: 你再这样～就赶不上火车了。If you go on dawdling like this, you'll miss the train. ◇ ～云 mushroom cloud/ ～战术 the tactics of "wear and tear" (wearing the enemy down and then wiping them out)

**魔** mó ①evil spirit; demon; devil; monster: 群～乱舞 a horde of demons dancing in riotous revelry/ 着了～似的 like one possessed ②magic; mystic: ～力 magic power

【魔怪】 móguài demons and monsters; fiends
【魔鬼】 móguǐ devil; demon; monster
【魔窟】 mókū den of monsters
【魔力】 mólì magic power; magic; charm
【魔难】 mónàn 见"磨难" mónàn
【魔术】 móshù magic; conjuring; sleight of hand ◇ ～演员 magician; conjurer
【魔王】 mówáng ①Prince of the Devils ②tyrant; despot; fiend
【魔掌】 mózhǎng devil's clutches; evil hands: 逃出敌人的～ escape from the clutches of the enemy
【魔杖】 mózhàng magic wand
【魔爪】 mózhǎo devil's talons; claws; tentacles: 斩断侵略者的～ cut off the tentacles of the aggressors

## mǒ

**抹** mǒ ①put on; apply; smear; plaster: ～点雪花膏 put on a little vanishing cream/ 面包上～点果酱 spread some jam on a piece of bread/ ～药膏 apply ointment/ 你～浆糊,我来贴大字报。You smear the wall with paste and

I'll stick the *dazibao* on it. ② wipe: ～眼泪 wipe one's eyes; be weeping/ ～把脸 wipe one's face ③ cross (或 strike, blot) out; erase: 把这一行字～了。Cross out this line./ ～掉磁带上的录音 erase the recording from a tape
另见 mā; mò
【抹脖子】 mǒ bózi cut one's own throat; commit suicide
【抹黑】 mǒhēi blacken sb.'s name; throw mud at; bring shame on; discredit: 这坏蛋是在往我们集体脸上～。That scoundrel is bringing shame on our collective.
【抹杀】 mǒshā blot out; obliterate; write off: 一笔～ write off at one stroke; deny completely/ 资产阶级企图～文艺作品的阶级性。The bourgeoisie tries to obliterate the class nature of literary works./ 历史事实是～不了的。The facts of history cannot be denied./ 修正主义者～社会主义和资本主义的区别，～无产阶级专政和资产阶级专政的区别。The revisionists deny the differences between socialism and capitalism, between the dictatorship of the proletariat and the dictatorship of the bourgeoisie. 又作"抹煞"
【抹香鲸】 mǒxiāngjīng sperm whale
【抹一鼻子灰】 mǒ yī bízi huī suffer a snub; meet with a rebuff
【抹子】 mǒzi 〈建〉 trowel

## mò

**万** mò
另见 wàn
【万俟】 Mòqí a surname

**末** mò ① tip; end: 秋毫之～ the tip of an animal's autumn hair ② nonessentials; minor details: 本～倒置 take the branch for the root; put the nonessentials before the essentials; put the cart before the horse ③ end; last stage: 周～ weekend/ 明～农民起义 the peasant uprisings towards the end of the Ming Dynasty/ 一学期的最～一天 the last day of a school term ④ powder; dust: 茶叶～儿 broken tea leaves; tea dust/ 锯～ sawdust/ 肉～儿 minced meat
【末班车】 mòbānchē last bus
【末代】 mòdài the last reign of a dynasty: ～皇帝 the last emperor of a dynasty
【末伏】 mòfú ① the last of the three ten-day periods of the hot season ② the first day of the last period of the hot season
【末后】 mòhòu finally
【末节】 mòjié minor details; nonessentials: 细枝～ minor details
【末了】 mòliǎo last; finally; in the end: 第五行～的那个字我不认识。I don't know the last word of the fifth line./ 他～还是同意了大家的意见。In the end he agreed with the others.
【末流】 mòliú the later and decadent stage of a school of thought, literature, etc.
【末路】 mòlù dead end; impasse
【末年】 mònián last years of a dynasty or reign
【末期】 mòqī last phase; final phase; last stage: 七十年代～ in the late seventies/ 第二次世界大战～ the last stage of the Second World War
【末日】 mòrì ①〈基督教〉 doomsday; Day of Judgment; Judgment Day: ～审判 Last Judgment ② end; doom: 封建王朝的～ the end of a feudal dynasty
【末梢】 mòshāo tip; end: 鞭子的～ the tip of a whip ◇ ～神经 nerve ending
【末世】 mòshì last phase (of an age): 封建～ the last years of feudalism
【末尾】 mòwěi ① end: 信的～ at the end of the letter/ 一切结论产生于调查情况的～，而不是在它的先头。Conclusions invariably come after investigation, and not before. ② 〈乐〉 *fine*; end
【末药】 mòyào 〈中药〉 myrrh
【末叶】 mòyè last years (of a century or dynasty): 十九世纪～ the end of the 19th century; the late 19th century
【末子】 mòzi powder; dust: 煤～ coal dust

**没** mò ① sink; submerge: 潜水艇很快就～入水中。It was not long before the submarine submerged./ 迅速沉～ sink fast ② overflow; rise beyond: 洪水几乎～过了大坝。The flood nearly overflowed the dam./ 水深～顶。The water goes above a man's head./ 雪深～膝。The snow was knee-deep. ③ disappear; hide: 出～ now appear, now disappear ④ confiscate; take possession of: ～收 confiscate ⑤ till the end: ～世 till the end of one's life ⑥ die
另见 méi
【没齿不忘】 mò chǐ bù wàng will never forget to the end of one's days; remember for the rest of one's life
【没落】 mòluò decline; wane: 反动～阶级 declining reactionary class/ 资本主义无可挽救地～下去，社会主义不可阻挡地兴盛起来。Capitalism is hopelessly on the decline while socialism is advancing with irresistible force.
【没奈何】 mònàihé be utterly helpless; have no way out; have no alternative: 等了他好久也没来，～我只好一个人去了。I waited for a long time, but he didn't show up, so I had to go alone.
【没收】 mòshōu confiscate; expropriate: ～官僚资本 confiscate bureaucrat capital
【没药】 mòyào 〈中药〉 myrrh

**沫** mò foam; froth: 啤酒～ froth on beer; the head on a glass of beer/ 肥皂～ soapsuds; lather/ 口吐白～ foam at the mouth
【沫子】 mòzi foam; froth

**茉** mò
【茉莉】 mòli 〈植〉 jasmine ◇ ～花茶 jasmine tea

**抹** mò ① daub; plaster: ～墙 plaster a wall; daub plaster on a wall ② skirt; bypass: ～过林子 skirt the edge of the forest
另见 mā; mǒ
【抹不开】 mòbukāi ① feel embarrassed; be put out: 本想说他两句，又怕他脸上～。I hesitated to criticize him for fear of making him uncomfortable. ② unable to act impartially for fear of offending sb.; afraid of impairing personal relations: 他有错误，就该批评，有什么～的？ If he's made mistakes, you should criticize him and not let personal considerations get in your way.
【抹灰】 mòhuī 〈建〉 plastering ◇ ～工 plasterer

**殁** mò 〈书〉 die: 病～ die of illness

**陌** mò ① a path between fields (running east and west): 阡～纵横。The paths crisscrossed in the fields. ② road: ～头杨柳 roadside willows
【陌路】 mòlù 〈书〉 stranger (whom one passes in the street): 视同～ treat like a stranger; cut sb. dead
【陌生】 mòshēng strange; unfamiliar: 对这些年青人来说，养鹿是一件～的事情。Breeding deer was something completely new for these young people./ 尽管我们初次见面，但并不感到～。Although this was only our first meeting,

we didn't feel like strangers./ 在会场上我看到许多～的面孔。I saw many unfamiliar faces at the meeting.
◇ ～人 stranger

脉 mò
另见 mài
【脉脉】 mòmò affectionately; lovingly; amorously: 她～地注视着远去的亲人。She followed with loving eyes her dear one's departing figure./ 温情～ full of tender affection; sentimental

莫 mò ①〈书〉no one; nothing; none: ～之能御。No one (或 Nothing) can resist it. ②no; not: ～知所措 not know what to do; be at a loss ③don't: 非公～入。No admittance except on business./ ～性急。Don't be impatient. 或 Take it easy. ④(Mò) a surname
【莫不】 mòbù there's no one who doesn't or isn't: 听到这胜利的消息，各族人民～为之欢欣鼓舞。People of all nationalities were jubilant on hearing the news of victory./ ～为之感动。There was no one who was unmoved.
【莫不是】 mòbùshì 见"莫非"
【莫测高深】 mò cè gāoshēn unfathomable; enigmatic
【莫大】 mòdà greatest; utmost: 感到～的光荣 feel greatly honoured/ ～的幸福 the greatest happiness/ ～的侮辱 a gross insult/ ～的愤慨 the utmost indignation
【莫非】 mòfēi 〈副〉can it be that; is it possible that: 老沈今天没有来，～又病了？Lao Shen is absent today. Can he be ill again?/ 听你的意思，～是我错了不成？Do you mean to say that I'm in the wrong?
【莫过于】 mòguòyú nothing is more... than: 最大的幸福～把一生献给共产主义事业。There's no greater happiness than that of dedicating one's life to communism.
【莫霍界面】 mòhuò jièmiàn 〈地〉Moho discontinuity; Moho
【莫名其妙】 mò míng qí miào ①be unable to make head or tail of sth.; be baffled: 他为什么讲这番话，真叫人～。It is quite baffling why he should have made such remarks. ②without rhyme or reason; inexplicable; odd: 她～地哭了起来。Quite unaccountably she burst out crying. 又作"莫明其妙"
【莫逆】 mònì very friendly; intimate: ～之交 bosom friends
【莫如】 mòrú would be better; might as well: 与其你去，～他来。It would be better for him to come than for you to go./ 她想既然来了，～跟着进去看看。Now that she'd come to the place, she thought she might as well go in with the others to have a look. 又作"莫若"
【莫桑比克】 Mòsāngbǐkè Mozambique ◇ ～人 Mozambican
【莫须有】 mòxūyǒu unwarranted; groundless; fabricated; trumped-up: ～的罪名 a fabricated charge; an unwarranted charge
【莫衷一是】 mò zhōng yī shì unable to agree or decide which is right: 众说纷纭，～。There are so many contradictory views that it is difficult to decide which is right. 或 As opinions vary, no decision can be reached.

秣 mò ①fodder ②feed animals
【秣马厉兵】 mòmǎ-lìbīng feed the horses and sharpen the weapons — make active preparations for war; prepare for battle

漠 mò ①desert ②indifferent; unconcerned: 冷～ cold and indifferent
【漠不关心】 mò bù guānxīn indifferent; unconcerned
【漠漠】 mòmò ①misty; foggy: 湖面升起一层～的烟雾。A thick mist rose over the lake. ②vast and lonely: 黄沙～ a vast stretch of yellow sand
【漠然】 mòrán indifferently; apathetically; with unconcern: ～置之 remain indifferent towards sth.; look on with unconcern
【漠视】 mòshì treat with indifference; ignore; overlook; pay no attention to: 不能～群众的意见。The masses' opinions must not be treated with indifference.

寞 mò lonely; deserted: 寂～ lonely

蓦 mò suddenly
【蓦地】 mòdì suddenly; unexpectedly; all of a sudden
【蓦然】 mòrán suddenly: ～想起 suddenly remember

墨 mò ①China (或 Chinese) ink; ink stick ②ink: 油～ printing ink ③handwriting or painting: 遗～ writing or painting left by the deceased ④learning: 胸无点～ without any learning; unlettered ⑤black; pitch-dark: 一个～黑的夜里 one pitch-dark night ⑥〈书〉corruption; graft; embezzlement: ～吏 corrupt officials ⑦tatooing the face (a punishment in ancient China) 参见"五刑" wǔxíng ⑧(Mò) Mohist School; Mohism ⑨(Mò) a surname
【墨宝】 mòbǎo ①treasured scrolls of calligraphy or painting ②〈敬〉your beautiful handwriting
【墨斗】 mòdǒu carpenter's ink marker
【墨斗鱼】 mòdǒuyú inkfish; cuttlefish
【墨盒】 mòhé ink box (for Chinese calligraphy or painting)
【墨迹】 mòjī ①ink marks: ～未干 before the ink is dry ②sb.'s writing or painting: 这是鲁迅的～。This is Lu Xun's calligraphy.
【墨家】 Mòjiā Mohist School (a school of thought in the Spring and Autumn and Warring States Periods, 770-221 B.C.) ◇ ～学说 Mohism
【墨晶】 mòjīng smoky quartz
【墨镜】 mòjìng sunglasses
【墨绿】 mòlǜ blackish green
【墨囊】 mònáng 〈动〉ink sac (of a cuttlefish)
【墨守成规】 mò shǒu chéngguī stick to conventions; stay in a rut
【墨水】 mòshuǐ ①prepared Chinese ink ②ink ③book learning: 他肚子里还有点～。He's a bit of a scholar.
◇ ～池 inkwell/ ～瓶 ink bottle/ ～台 inkstand
【墨西哥】 Mòxīgē Mexico
◇ ～人 Mexican/ ～湾 the Gulf of Mexico/ ～湾流 the Gulf Stream
【墨线】 mòxiàn ①the line in a carpenter's ink marker ②a line made by a carpenter's ink marker
【墨鱼】 mòyú inkfish; cuttlefish
【墨汁】 mòzhī prepared Chinese ink

默 mò ①silent; tacit: ～不作声 keep silent ②write from memory: ～生字 write the new words from memory
【默哀】 mò'āi stand in silent tribute: 全体起立～。All rose and stood in silent tribute./ ～三分钟 observe three minutes' silence
【默祷】 mòdǎo pray in silence; say a silent prayer
【默读】 mòdú read silently
【默默】 mòmò quietly; silently: ～无言 without saying a word; silently/ 他～地发誓要继承革命先烈的遗志。He vowed to himself that he would carry forward the cause left behind by the revolutionary martyrs.
【默默无闻】 mòmò wú wén unknown to the public; without attracting public attention: 一生～ remain obscure

all one's life
【默契】 mòqì ① tacit agreement; tacit understanding: 互相～ have a tacit mutual understanding; coordinate by tacit agreement ② secret agreement: 关于这个问题双方曾有～。The two sides had a secret agreement on this question.
【默然】 mòrán silent; speechless: ～无语 fall silent; be speechless
【默认】 mòrèn give tacit consent to; tacitly approve; acquiesce in: ～现状 give tacit consent to the *status quo*
【默写】 mòxiě write from memory
【默许】 mòxǔ tacitly consent to; acquiesce in

磨 mò ① mill; millstones: 电～ electric mill ② grind; mill: ～麦子 grind wheat/ ～面 mill flour/ ～豆腐 grind soya beans to make bean curd ③ turn round: 把大车～过来。Turn the cart round.
另见 mó
【磨不开】 mòbukāi 见"抹不开" mòbukāi
【磨坊】 mòfáng mill 又作"磨房"
【磨面机】 mòmiànjī flour-milling machine
【磨盘】 mòpán ① nether (或 lower) millstone ② 〈方〉 mill; millstones
【磨棚】 mòpéng grinding shed; mill shed

貘 mò 〈动〉 tapir

## mōu

哞 mōu 〈象〉〔形容牛叫的声音〕: moo; low; bellow

## móu

牟 móu ① try to gain; seek; obtain: ～利 seek profit ② (Móu) a surname
【牟取】 móuqǔ try to gain; seek; obtain: ～暴利 seek exorbitant profits

谋 móu ① stratagem; plan; scheme: 足智多～ wise and full of stratagems; resourceful/ 有勇无～ brave but not astute ② work for; seek; plot: 共产党员要为大多数人～利益。Communists should work for the interests of the vast majority./ ～独立,求解放 seek independence and liberation/ ～刺 plot to assassinate ③ consult: 不～而合 agree without previous consultation
【谋财害命】 móucái-hàimìng murder sb. for his money
【谋反】 móufǎn conspire against the state; plot a rebellion
【谋害】 móuhài ① plot to murder ② plot a frame-up against
【谋划】 móuhuà plan; scheme; try to find a solution
【谋略】 móulüè astuteness and resourcefulness; strategy: 此人颇有～。He is a man of resource and astuteness.
【谋求】 móuqiú seek; strive for; be in quest of: ～两国关系正常化 seek normalization of relations between the two countries/ ～解放 strive for liberation/ ～解决办法 try to find a solution
【谋取】 móuqǔ try to gain; seek; obtain: 不能为了～暂时的利益而牺牲原则。We mustn't seek temporary gain at the expense of principle.
【谋杀】 móushā murder
【谋生】 móushēng seek a livelihood; make a living: ～的手段 a means of life
【谋士】 móushì adviser; counsellor
【谋事】 móushì ① plan matters ② look for a job

眸 móu pupil (of the eye); eye: 凝～ fix (或 focus) one's eyes on/ 明～皓齿 have shining eyes and white teeth; be comely
【眸子】 móuzi pupil (of the eye); eye

蛑 móu 见"蝤蛑" yóumóu

缪 móu 见"绸缪" chóumóu; "未雨绸缪" wèi yǔ chóumóu
另见 Miào; miù

## mǒu

某 mǒu ① certain; some: ～日 at a certain date/ 张～ a certain person called Zhang/ 解放军～部 a certain unit of the PLA/ 在四川～地 somewhere in Sichuan Province/ ～些农产品 certain agricultural products/ 在～种程度上 to some (或 a certain) extent/ 在～种意义上 in a sense ② 〔用来代替自己的名字〕: 我李～不是干这种事的人。 Yours truly is not the sort of person to do a thing like that.
【某某】 mǒumǒu so-and-so: ～同志 Comrade so-and-so/ ～学校 a certain school
【某人】 mǒurén ① a certain person ② 〔用来代替自己的名字〕: 我王～从来不说假话。As for me, I've never told lies.

## mú

模 mú mould; matrix; pattern: 铜～ 〈印〉 matrix; (copper) mould
另见 mó
【模板】 múbǎn ① 〈建〉 shuttering; formwork ② 〈机〉 pattern plate
【模具】 mújù mould; matrix; pattern; die
【模压】 múyà mould pressing ◇ ～机 moulding press/ ～胶底皮鞋 leather shoes with moulded-on rubber soles
【模样】 múyàng ① appearance; look: 那人是什么～? What did that person look like?/ 这孩子的～象他妈妈。The child takes after his mother. ② approximately; about; around: 我等了有半小时～。I waited for about half an hour./ 那男的有三十岁～。The man was around thirty.
【模子】 múzi mould; matrix; pattern; die: 一个～里铸出来的 made out of the same mould; as like as two peas

## mǔ

母 mǔ ① mother ② one's female elders: 伯～ aunt/ 祖～ grandmother ③ female (animal): ～鸡 hen/ ～狗 bitch/ ～马 mare/ ～狼 she-wolf/ ～象 female elephant/ ～狮 lioness ④ nut (so called because of the female screw thread): 螺～ nut ⑤ origin; parent: 失败是成功之～。Failure is the mother of success.
【母爱】 mǔ'ài mother love; maternal love
【母本】 mǔběn 〈植〉 female parent: ～植株 maternal plant
【母畜】 mǔchù dam
【母蜂】 mǔfēng queen bee
【母机】 mǔjī ① machine tool ② mother aircraft; launching aircraft
【母老虎】 mǔlǎohǔ ① tigress ② vixen; shrew; termagant
【母亲】 mǔqin mother
【母权制】 mǔquánzhì matriarchy
【母体】 mǔtǐ 〈动〉 the mother's body; the (female) parent
【母系】 mǔxì ① maternal side ② matriarchal
◇ ～亲属 maternal relatives/ ～社会 matriarchal society/

～氏族公社 matrilineal commune/ ～氏族制 matriarchy
【母线】 mǔxiàn ①〈数〉generatrix; generator ②〈电〉bus; bus bar
【母校】 mǔxiào one's old school; Alma Mater
【母性】 mǔxìng maternal instinct
【母液】 mǔyè 〈化〉mother liquor; mother solution
【母音】 mǔyīn 〈语〉vowel
【母语】 mǔyǔ ① mother tongue ② parent language; linguistic parent
【母株】 mǔzhū 〈植〉maternal plant; mother plant

**亩** mǔ *mu*, a unit of area (=0.0667 hectares): ～产量 per *mu* yield

**牡** mǔ male: ～牛 bull
【牡丹】 mǔdan tree peony; peony
【牡蛎】 mǔlì 〈动〉oyster

**拇** mǔ
【拇指】 mǔzhǐ ① thumb ② big toe

**姆** mǔ 见"保姆" bǎomǔ
【姆夫蒂】 mǔfūdì 〈伊斯兰教〉mufti
【姆欧】 mǔ'ōu 〈电〉mho

## mù

**木** mù ① tree: 伐～ fell trees/ 果～ fruit tree/ 独～不成林。One tree does not make a forest. ② timber; wood: 松～ pinewood ③ made of wood; wooden: ～制家具 wooden furniture/ ～箱 wooden box/ ～桥 wooden bridge ④ coffin: 行将就～ have one foot in the grave ⑤ numb; wooden: 两脚都冻～了。Both feet were numb with cold./ 舌头～了，什么味儿也尝不出来。My tongue has lost all its sense of taste./ ～头～脑 wooden-headed; dull-witted
【木板】 mùbǎn plank; board ◇ ～床 plank bed
【木版】 mùbǎn 〈印〉block ◇ ～画 woodcut; wood engraving/ ～印花 〈纺〉block printing/ ～印刷 block printing
【木本植物】 mùběn zhíwù 〈植〉xylophyta; woody plant
【木菠萝】 mùbōluó 〈植〉jackfruit
【木材】 mùcái wood; timber; lumber ◇ ～厂 timber mill/ ～防腐 wood preservation
【木柴】 mùchái firewood
【木醋酸】 mùcùsuān 〈化〉pyroligneous acid
【木雕泥塑】 mùdiāo-nísù like an idol carved in wood or moulded in clay — as wooden as a dummy
【木牍】 mùdú 〈考古〉inscribed wooden tablet
【木蠹蛾】 mùdù'é 〈动〉wood moth; carpenter moth
【木耳】 mù'ěr an edible fungus (*Auricularia auricula-judae*)
【木筏】 mùfá raft
【木芙蓉】 mùfúróng 〈植〉cotton rose (*Hibiscus mutabilis*)
【木工】 mùgōng ① woodwork; carpentry ② woodworker; carpenter: 细～ cabinetmaker; joiner ◇ ～机械 woodworking machinery
【木瓜】 mùguā 〈植〉① Chinese flowering quince ②〈方〉papaya
【木管乐器】 mùguǎn yuèqì woodwind instrument; woodwind
【木化石】 mùhuàshí petrified wood; woodstone
【木屐】 mùjī clogs
【木简】 mùjiǎn 〈考古〉inscribed wooden slip
【木浆】 mùjiāng 〈纸〉wood pulp: 化学～ chemical wood pulp
【木匠】 mùjiang carpenter
【木焦油】 mùjiāoyóu 〈化〉wood tar
【木结构】 mùjiégòu 〈建〉timber structure; wood construction
【木槿】 mùjǐn 〈植〉rose of Sharon
【木精】 mùjīng 〈化〉wood spirit
【木刻】 mùkè woodcut; wood engraving ◇ ～术 xylography
【木兰】 mùlán 〈植〉lily magnolia
【木料】 mùliào timber; lumber
【木马】 mùmǎ ①〈体〉vaulting horse; pommelled horse ② (children's) hobbyhorse; rocking horse ◇ ～计 the stratagem of the Trojan horse; Trojan horse
【木棉】 mùmián silk cotton; kapok
【木乃伊】 mùnǎiyī mummy
【木偶】 mù'ǒu ① wooden image; carved figure: 象～似地站着 stand as still as a carved figure ② puppet; marionette ◇ ～剧 puppet show; puppet play/ ～片 puppet film
【木排】 mùpái raft
【木片】 mùpiàn wood chip
【木器】 mùqì wooden furniture; wooden articles
【木琴】 mùqín 〈乐〉xylophone
【木然】 mùrán stupefied
【木梳】 mùshū wooden comb
【木薯】 mùshǔ 〈植〉cassava
【木栓】 mùshuān 〈植〉phellem; cork
【木丝】 mùsī wood wool ◇ ～板〈建〉wood wool board
【木炭】 mùtàn charcoal ◇ ～画 charcoal drawing
【木通】 mùtōng 〈植〉akebi
【木头】 mùtou wood; log; timber
【木头人儿】 mùtourénr woodenhead; blockhead; slow coach
【木屋】 mùwū log cabin
【木犀】 mùxi ①〈植〉sweet-scented osmanthus ② egg beaten and then cooked ◇ ～饭 fried rice with scrambled eggs/ ～肉 pork fried with scrambled eggs/ ～汤 eggdrop soup
【木锨】 mùxiān wooden winnowing spade
【木星】 mùxīng 〈天〉Jupiter
【木已成舟】 mù yǐ chéng zhōu the wood is already made into a boat — what is done cannot be undone
【木俑】 mùyǒng 〈考古〉wooden figurine (used as a burial object)
【木鱼】 mùyú wooden fish (a percussion instrument made of a hollow wooden block, originally used by Buddhist priests to beat rhythm when chanting scriptures)
【木贼】 mùzéi 〈植〉scouring rush
【木质部】 mùzhìbù 〈植〉xylem

**目** mù ① eye: 双～失明 be blind in both eyes ②〈书〉look; regard: ～为奇迹 regard as a miracle ③ item: 细～ detailed items ④〈生〉order: 亚～ suborder ⑤ a list of things; catalogue; table of contents: 书～ book list
【目标】 mùbiāo ① objective; target: 命中～ hit the target (或 mark)/ 攻击～ target (或 objective) of attack/ 军事～ military objective; military target ② goal; aim; objective: 共产主义的伟大～ the great goal of communism/ 共同的革命～ a common revolutionary objective
【目不见睫】 mù bù jiàn jié the eye cannot see its lashes — lack self-knowledge
【目不交睫】 mù bù jiāo jié not sleep a wink
【目不识丁】 mù bù shí dīng not know one's ABC; be totally illiterate
【目不暇接】 mù bù xiá jiē the eye cannot take it all in; there are too many things for the eye to take in 又作"目不暇给"

【目不转睛】 mù bù zhuǎn jīng look with fixed eyes; watch with the utmost concentration
【目测】 mùcè <军> range estimation
【目次】 mùcì table of contents; contents
【目瞪口呆】 mùdèng-kǒudāi gaping; stupefied; dumbstruck: 吓得～ be struck dumb with fear
【目的】 mùdì purpose; aim; goal; objective; end: ～明确 have a definite purpose/ ～与手段 ends and means/ 怀着不可告人的～ harbour evil intentions; have ulterior motives/ 我们党的最终～,是实现共产主义。The ultimate aim of our Party is the realization of communism./ 我们的～一定能够达到。Our goal can certainly be attained. ◇ ～地 destination/ ～港 <航海> port of destination/ ～论 <哲> teleology
【目睹】 mùdǔ see with one's own eyes; witness
【目光】 mùguāng ① sight; vision; view: ～短浅 shortsighted/ ～锐利 sharp-eyed; sharp-sighted/ ～远大 farsighted; farseeing ② gaze; look: ～炯炯 flashing eyes/ 两人的～碰到一起。Their eyes met.
【目光如豆】 mùguāng rú dòu of narrow vision; shortsighted
【目光如炬】 mùguāng rú jù ① eyes blazing like torches — blazing with anger ② looking ahead with wisdom; farsighted
【目击】 mùjī see with one's own eyes; witness ◇ ～者 eyewitness; witness
【目见】 mùjiàn see for oneself: 耳闻不如～。Seeing a thing for oneself is better than hearing about it.
【目镜】 mùjìng <物> eyepiece; ocular
【目空一切】 mù kōng yīqiè consider everybody and everything beneath one's notice; be supercilious
【目力】 mùlì eyesight; vision: ～好(不好) have good (poor) eyesight
【目录】 mùlù ① catalogue; list: 图书～ library catalogue/ 出口商品～ a catalogue of export commodities; export list ② table of contents; contents ◇ ～学 bibliography
【目迷五色】 mù mí wǔsè ① dazzled by a riot of colour ② bewildered by a complicated situation
【目前】 mùqián at present; at the moment: ～形势 the present (或 current) situation/ ～的生产能力 existing production capacity/ 到～为止 up till the present moment; up till now; so far; to date/ ～我还不能给你肯定的答复。I can't give you a definite answer at the moment.
【目视飞行】 mùshì fēixíng <航空> visual flight
【目送】 mùsòng follow sb. with one's eyes; watch sb. go; gaze after: 李大妈站在村口～战士们远去。Aunt Li stood at the end of the village street gazing affectionately after the departing soldiers.
【目无法纪】 mù wú fǎjì disregard (或 flout) law and discipline
【目无全牛】 mù wú quánniú (of an experienced butcher) see an ox not as a whole (but only as parts to be cut) — be supremely skilled
【目无组织】 mù wú zǔzhī disregard organizational discipline; defy the leadership of one's organization
【目下】 mùxià at present; now
【目眩】 mùxuàn dizzy; dazzled: 灯光强烈,令人～。The light is too dazzling.
【目语】 mùyǔ communicate with the eyes
【目中无人】 mùzhōng wú rén consider everyone beneath one's notice; be supercilious; be overweening

## 仫 mù

【仫佬族】 Mùlǎozú the Mulam (Mulao) nationality, living in the Guangxi Zhuang Autonomous Region

## 沐 mù wash one's hair

【沐猴而冠】 mùhóu ér guàn a monkey with a hat on — a worthless person in imposing attire
【沐浴】 mùyù ① have (或 take) a bath ② bathe; immerse: 百里油田～着金色的朝晖。The vast oilfield was bathed in the golden rays of the morning sun.

## 苜 mù

【苜蓿】 mùxu <植> lucerne; alfalfa

## 牧 mù herd; tend: ～马 herd horses/ ～羊 tend sheep

【牧草】 mùcǎo herbage; forage grass
【牧场】 mùchǎng grazing land; pastureland; pasture 又作"牧地"
【牧放】 mùfàng herd; tend; put out to pasture
【牧歌】 mùgē ① pastoral song; pastoral ② <乐> madrigal
【牧工】 mùgōng hired herdsman
【牧民】 mùmín herdsman
【牧区】 mùqū pastoral area
【牧人】 mùrén herdsman
【牧师】 mùshi <基督教> pastor; minister; clergyman
【牧童】 mùtóng shepherd boy; buffalo boy
【牧畜】 mùxù livestock breeding; animal husbandry
【牧羊人】 mùyángrén shepherd
【牧业】 mùyè animal husbandry; stock raising ◇ ～公社 stock-raising commune
【牧主】 mùzhǔ herd owner (who owns livestock and pastures and hires herdsmen)

## 钼 mù <化> molybdenum (Mo)

【钼钢】 mùgāng molybdenum steel
【钼酸】 mùsuān molybdic acid ◇ ～铵 ammonium molybdate

## 募 mù raise; collect; enlist; recruit: ～款 raise money/ ～兵 recruit soldiers

【募兵制】 mùbīngzhì mercenary system
【募化】 mùhuà (of Buddhist monks or Taoist priests) collect alms
【募集】 mùjí raise; collect: ～资金 raise a fund
【募捐】 mùjuān solicit contributions; collect donations

## 墓 mù grave; tomb; mausoleum: 马克思～ Marx's grave/ 列宁～ the Lenin Mausoleum/ 烈士～ tombs of revolutionary martyrs

【墓碑】 mùbēi tombstone; gravestone
【墓道】 mùdào ① path leading to a grave; tomb passage ② aisle leading to the coffin chamber of an ancient tomb
【墓地】 mùdì graveyard; burial ground; cemetery
【墓室】 mùshì coffin chamber
【墓穴】 mùxué coffin pit; open grave
【墓葬】 mùzàng <考古> grave ◇ ～群 graves
【墓志】 mùzhì inscription on the memorial tablet within a tomb
【墓志铭】 mùzhìmíng inscription on the memorial tablet within a tomb; epitaph

## 幕 mù ① curtain; screen: ～启。The curtain rises./ ～落。The curtain falls. 或 Curtain./ 夜～ the veil of night ② act: 第一～ the first act; Act I/ 一出三～五场的话剧 a play in three acts and five scenes/ 长征时的情景一～一～地重现在我的眼前。Scene after scene of the Long March reappeared before my eyes.

【幕布】 mùbù ① (theatre) curtain ② (cinema) screen

【幕后】 mùhòu behind the scenes; backstage: 退居～ retire backstage/ ～操纵 pull strings (或 wires) behind the scenes/ ～活动 behind-the-scenes activities; backstage manoeuvring/ ～交易 behind-the-scenes deal; backstage deal/ ～人物 wirepuller; backstage manipulator

【幕间休息】 mùjiān xiūxi interval; intermission

【幕僚】 mùliáo ① aides and staff ② assistant to a ranking official or general in old China

**睦** mù peaceful; harmonious

【睦邻】 mùlín good-neighbourliness ◇ ～关系 good-neighbourly relations/ ～政策 good-neighbour policy

**慕** mù admire; yearn for: 爱～ love; adore/ 仰～ look up to with admiration/ ～名 out of admiration for a famous person

【慕尼黑】 Mùníhēi Munich ◇ ～协定 the Munich Agreement (1938)/ ～阴谋 the Munich conspiracy

【慕容】 Mùróng a surname

**暮** mù ① dusk; evening; sunset: 薄～ dusk ② towards the end; late: ～春 late spring/ 岁～ the end of the year

【暮霭】 mù'ǎi evening mist

【暮鼓晨钟】 mùgǔ-chénzhōng evening drum and morning bell in a monastery — timely exhortations to virtue and purity

【暮年】 mùnián declining years; old age; evening of one's life

【暮气】 mùqì lethargy; apathy: ～沉沉 lethargic; apathetic; lifeless

【暮色】 mùsè dusk; twilight; gloaming: ～苍茫 deepening dusk; spreading shades of dusk

**穆** mù ① solemn; reverent: 肃～ solemn ② (Mù) a surname

【穆罕默德】 Mùhǎnmòdé 〈伊斯兰教〉 Mohammed (c. 570-632), founder of Islam

【穆民】 mùmín believers in Islam

【穆斯林】 mùsīlín Moslem; Muslim

# N

## nā

**那** Nā a surname
另见 nà; nè; nèi

## ná

**拿** ná ① hold; take: ～去 take it away/ ～来 bring it here/ 他手里～的是什么？ What is he holding in his hand?/ 不～枪的敌人 enemies without guns ② seize; capture: ～下敌人的碉堡 capture the enemy's blockhouse ③ have a firm grasp of; be able to do; be sure of: 样样农活她都～得起来。She can do every kind of farm work./ ～不准 not be sure; feel uncertain/ 这事儿你～得稳吗？ Are you sure of it? ④ put sb. in a difficult position: 这件事你～不住人。Don't think that you can make things difficult by not doing the job. ⑤〈介〉〔引进所凭借的工具、材料、方法等〕: ～尺量 measure with a ruler/ ～事实证明 prove with facts; cite facts to prove/ 我们不能～原则作交易。We cannot barter away our principles./ ～几句话来概括 to sum up in a few words ⑥〈介〉〔引进所处置的对象〕: 别～他开玩笑。Don't make fun of him. 或 Don't crack jokes at his expense./ 我简直～他没有办法。I simply can't do anything with him.

【拿不出手】 nábuchū shǒu not be presentable: 我这笔字～。My handwriting is not presentable.

【拿大】 nádà〈方〉give oneself airs

【拿大顶】 ná dàdǐng〈体〉handstand 又作"拿顶"

【拿获】 náhuò apprehend (a criminal)

【拿架子】 ná jiàzi put on airs

【拿乔】 náqiáo strike a pose to impress people

【拿权】 náquán wield power; be in the saddle

【拿人】 nárén make things difficult for others; raise difficulties

【拿事】 náshì have the power to do sth. or to decide what to do: 父母都出门了，家里没有～的人。The parents are away; no one in the family can make a decision.

【拿手】 náshǒu adept; expert; good at: 剪纸她很～。She's good at making paper-cuts./ ～好戏 a game or trick one is good at

【拿主意】 ná zhǔyi make a decision; make up one's mind: 究竟去不去，你自己～吧。You'd better decide for yourself whether to go or not./ 我的主意拿定了。My mind is made up./ 她一直拿不定主意。She's been wavering all along.

**镎** ná〈化〉neptunium (Np)

## nǎ

**哪** nǎ ① which; what: 我们这里有两位姓张的，您要见的是～一位？ We've got two Zhangs here. Which one do you want to see?/ 你学的是～国语言？ What foreign language are you studying? ②〔表示反问〕: 没有革命前辈的流血牺牲，～有今天的幸福生活？ Without the sacrifices of the revolutionaries of the older generation, how could we have such a happy life today?/ ～有不剥削工人的资本家？ Is there a capitalist who does not exploit workers?
另见 na; něi

【哪个】 nǎge ① which: 你们是～班的？ Which class are you in? ②〈方〉who: ～在打电话？ Who's using the telephone?

【哪会儿】 nǎhuìr ① when: 你～才能脱稿？ When can you get the draft ready? ② whenever; any time: 你要～来就～来。Come any time you like.

【哪里】 nǎli ① where: 你到～去？ Where are you going? ② wherever; where: ～最艰苦就在～干 go and work where the work is hardest/ ～有压迫，～就有反抗。Where there is oppression, there is resistance. ③〔用于反问，表示否定〕: 我～知道他费了那么大的劲？ Little did I know what a great effort he'd made./ 你对我们帮助很大。—— ～，～。You gave us a lot of help. — It was nothing.

【哪门子】 nǎménzi〈方〉〔用于反问的语气，表示没有来由〕: 好好儿的，你哭～？ Everything is all right. What on earth are you crying for?/ 他说的是～事呀！ What the hell is he talking about?

【哪怕】 nǎpà〈连〉even; even if; even though; no matter how: ～是一粒米也不应该浪费。We should not waste even a single grain of rice./ ～是再大的困难我们也能克服。However great the difficulties may be, we can overcome them.

【哪儿】 nǎr〈口〉① where: 他上～去啦？ Where has he gone? ② wherever; anywhere: ～需要，我就上～去。I'll go wherever I'm needed./ ～都找不到他。He is nowhere to be found. ③〔用于反问，表示否定〕: 我～知道他不吃牛肉。How was I to know he didn't eat beef?

【哪些】 nǎxiē which; who; what: ～是你的？ Which ones are yours?/ ～人出席这次会议？ Who will attend the meeting?/ 你们讨论了～问题？ What problems did you discuss?

【哪样】 nǎyàng what kind of: 你要～颜色的？ What colour do you want?

## nà

**那** nà ① that: ～是我的过错。That was my fault./ ～是谁？ Who is that?/ ～是一九五八年的事。That was in 1958. ②〈连〉then; in that case: 你要是跟我们一块走，～就得快点。If you're coming with us, you must hurry./ ～我们就不再等了。In that case, we won't wait any longer.
另见 Nā; nè; nèi

【那达慕】 nàdámù Nadam Fair, a Mongolian traditional fair

【那个】 nàge ① that: ～孩子 that child/ ～根本谈不到。That's out of the question./ ～你甭担心。Don't you worry about that. ②〈口〉〔用在动词、形容词之前，表示夸张〕: 瞧他们干得～欢哪！ See how they're throwing themselves into their work! ③〈口〉〔代替不便直说的话，含有婉转或诙谐的意味〕: 你刚才的脾气也太～了。The way you lost your temper was a little too — you know what I mean.

【那会儿】 nàhuìr〈口〉at that time; then: 到～钢的产量将大大增加。By that time the steel output will have greatly increased./ ～我们还是新手。At that time we were greenhorns.

【那里】 nàli that place; there: 我刚从～回来。I've just come from there. 或 I've just been there./ ～气候怎么样？ What's the weather like there?

【那么】 nàme ① like that; in that way: 你不该～做。You shouldn't have done that. 或 You oughtn't to have acted the way you did./ 她不好意思～说。It embarrassed her to say that./ 问题没有他所想象的～复杂。The problem is not as complicated as he imagined. ②〔放在数量词前,表示估计〕about; or so: 再有～二三十个麻袋就够了。Another twenty or thirty sacks will probably be enough. ③〈连〉then; in that case; such being the case: 既然这样不行,～你打算怎么办呢？Since that's impossible, what are you going to do？又作"那末"

【那么点儿】 nàmediǎnr so little; so few: ～活儿,一天就可以干完了。We can finish that little bit of work in a day.

【那么些】 nàmexiē so much; so many: 她一个人照料～孩子,真不容易。She looks after all those kids by herself. That's not so easy.

【那么着】 nàmezhe do that; do so: 他～是为了集体。He did it for the collective./ 你再～,我就火了。If you do that again, I'll get angry.

【那儿】 nàr 〈口〉① 见"那里" ②〔用在"打""从""由"后面〕that time; then: 打～起,她就用心念书了。She's been studying hard since then.

【那时】 nàshí at that time; then; in those days: ～是旧社会,哪有咱穷人说话的地方？In the old society where could we poor people dare to open our mouths？/ 说时迟～快 in the twinkling of an eye; in an instant

【那些】 nàxiē those: ～水渠是一九五八年修成的。Those irrigation channels were built in 1958.

【那样】 nàyàng of that kind; like that; such; so: 他不象你～仔细。He's not so careful as you are./ ～儿也好,先试试再说。All right, let's try it out./ 这点小事你怎么就急得～儿了。Why let such trifles worry you so much?

**呐** nà

【呐喊】 nàhǎn shout loudly; cry out: ～助威 shout encouragement; cheer

**纳** nà ① receive; admit: 闭门不～ refuse to admit; shut sb. out ② accept: 采～ adopt ③ enjoy ④ pay; offer: 交～公粮 pay taxes in grain ⑤ sew close stitches (over a patch, etc.): ～鞋底子 stitch soles (of cloth shoes)

【纳粹】 Nàcuì Nazi ◇ ～分子 Nazi/ ～主义 Nazism

【纳福】 nàfú (usu. of elderly people) enjoy a life of ease and comfort

【纳罕】 nàhǎn be surprised; marvel

【纳贿】 nàhuì ① take bribes ② offer bribes

【纳凉】 nàliáng enjoy the cool (in the open air)

【纳闷儿】 nàmènr 〈口〉 feel puzzled; be perplexed; wonder: 他怎么还没给我回电呢？真叫人～。I wonder why he hasn't wired back yet./ 家里一个人也没有,他心里很～。He was surprised to find nobody at home.

【纳米比亚】 Nàmǐbǐyà Namibia

【纳入】 nàrù bring (或 channel) into: ～正轨 put sth. on the right course/ ～国家计划 bring sth. into line with the state plan/ 把整个国民经济～有计划、按比例、高速度发展的社会主义轨道 bring the country's entire economy into the orbit of planned, proportionate and high-speed socialist development

【纳纱制品】 nàshā zhìpǐn 〈工美〉 petit-point articles

【纳税】 nàshuì pay taxes ◇ ～人 taxpayer

【纳西族】 Nàxīzú the Naxi (Nahsi) nationality, living in Yunnan

【纳降】 nàxiáng accept the enemy's surrender

【纳新】 nàxīn take in the fresh — take in new Party members: ～对象 a candidate for Party membership; prospective Party member

**肭** nà 见"腽肭兽" wànàshòu

**衲** nà ① patch up ② patchwork vestment worn by a Buddhist monk

**钠** nà 〈化〉 sodium (Na)

【钠长石】 nàchángshí 〈矿〉 albite

【钠钙玻璃】 nàgài bōli soda-lime glass 又作"钠玻璃"

**捺** nà ① press down; restrain: ～着性子 control one's temper/ 勉强～住心头的怒火 barely manage to restrain one's anger ② right-falling stroke (in Chinese characters)

## na

**哪** na 〈助〉〔用在韵尾是 -n 的字后面,相当于"啊" a〕: 谢谢您～！Thank you!/ 我没留神～！I wasn't noticing./ 加油干～！Speed up! 或 Come on!
另见 nǎ; něi

## nǎi

**乃** nǎi 〈书〉① be: 失败～成功之母。Failure is the mother of success. ② so; therefore: 因山势高峻,～在山腰休息片时。It was a steep climb, so we rested for a while halfway up the hill. ③ only then: 惟虚心～能进步。You can make progress only if you are modest./ 今～知之。I didn't know it until now. ④ you; your: ～父 your father

【乃尔】 nǎi'ěr like this; to such an extent: 何其相似～！What a striking similarity!

【乃是】 nǎishì be: 人民群众～真正的英雄。The masses of the people are the true heroes.

【乃至】 nǎizhì and even: 中国革命的胜利对全中国～全世界都具有伟大的历史意义。The victory of the Chinese revolution had great historical significance for China and the world.

**艿** nǎi 见"芋艿" yùnǎi

**奶** nǎi ① breasts ② milk ③ suckle; breast-feed: ～孩子 suckle (或 breast-feed) a baby

【奶茶】 nǎichá tea with milk

【奶疮】 nǎichuāng mastitis

【奶粉】 nǎifěn milk powder; powdered milk; dried milk

【奶糕】 nǎigāo a baby food made of rice-flour, sugar, etc.

【奶酪】 nǎilào cheese

【奶妈】 nǎimā wet nurse

【奶名】 nǎimíng a child's pet name; infant name

【奶奶】 nǎinai 〈口〉① (paternal) grandmother; grandma ② a respecful form of address for an old woman

【奶牛】 nǎiniú milch cow; milk cow; cow

【奶皮】 nǎipí skin on boiled milk

【奶品】 nǎipǐn milk products; dairy products

【奶瓶】 nǎipíng feeding bottle; nursing bottle; baby's bottle

【奶水】 nǎishuǐ 〈口〉 milk: 她～足不足？Has she got enough milk to nurse her baby?

【奶糖】 nǎitáng toffee

【奶头】 nǎitóu 〈口〉① nipple; teat ② nipple (of a feeding bottle)

【奶牙】 nǎiyá milk tooth

【奶羊】 nǎiyáng milch goat

【奶油】 nǎiyóu cream ◇ ～分离器 cream separator

【奶罩】 nǎizhào brassiere; bra

【奶子】 nǎizi ①〈口〉 milk ②〈方〉 breasts

【奶嘴】 nǎizuǐ nipple (of a feeding bottle)

**氖** nǎi 〈化〉 neon (Ne)

【氖灯】 nǎidēng neon lamp; neon light; neon

【氖管】 nǎiguǎn neon tube

**迺** nǎi 见"乃" nǎi

## nài

**奈** nài

【奈何】 nàihé ①〔反问〕how; to no avail: 民不畏死，～以死惧之。The people fear not death, why threaten them with it? 徒唤～ utter bootless cries/ 无可～ be utterly helpless ② do sth. to a person: 其奈我何？What can they do to me?

**柰** nài a kind of apple

**耐** nài be able to bear or endure: 吃苦～劳 bear hardships and stand hard work/ ～穿 can stand wear and tear; be endurable/ 这种料子很～洗。This material washes well.

【耐波力】 nàibōlì seakeeping qualities (of a vessel)

【耐烦】 nàifán patient: 显出不～的样子 show signs of impatience

【耐寒】 nàihán cold-resistant: 耐严寒 resistant to low temperature ◇ ～性 cold resistance; winterhardiness

【耐旱植物】 nàihàn zhíwù drought-enduring plant

【耐火】 nàihuǒ fire-resistant; refractory ◇ ～材料 refractory (material); fireproof material/ ～衬砌 refractory lining/ ～水泥 refractory cement/ ～砖 refractory brick; firebrick

【耐久】 nàijiǔ lasting long; durable

【耐力】 nàilì endurance; staying power; stamina

【耐磨】 nàimó (of metals) wear-resisting; wearproof ◇～合金钢 wear-resisting alloy steel/ ～性 wearability; wear resistance/ ～硬度 abrasion hardness

【耐热】 nàirè heat-resisting; heatproof ◇ ～合金 heat-resisting alloy/ ～性 heat resistance

【耐人寻味】 nài rén xúnwèi afford food for thought: 他的话是很～的。What he said gives one much food for thought.

【耐蚀钢】 nàishígāng 〈冶〉 corrosion-resisting steel

【耐水作物】 nàishuǐ zuòwù water-tolerant crop

【耐酸】 nàisuān acidproof; acid-resisting ◇ ～缸器 acidproof stoneware/ ～混凝土 acid-resisting concrete

【耐心】 nàixīn patient: 用～说服的方法 adopt the method of patient persuasion/ 帮助同志解决思想问题要有～。We should exercise patience in helping comrades ideologically.

【耐性】 nàixìng patience; endurance

【耐印力】 nàiyìnlì 〈印〉 pressrun

【耐用】 nàiyòng durable: ～物品 durable goods; durables

**萘** nài 〈化〉 naphthalene

【萘酚】 nàifēn 〈化〉 naphthol

【萘乙酸】 nàiyǐsuān 〈农〉 methyl α-naphthyl acetate

**鼐** nài 〈书〉 a big tripod

## nān

**囡** nān 〈方〉 child: 男(女)小～ a little boy (girl)

【囡囡】 nānnān 〈方〉 little darling (used as a term of endearment for a child or a baby)

## nán

**男** nán ① man; male: ～病房 men's ward/ ～护士 male nurse/ ～主人公 hero/ ～学生 boy student/ ～佣人 manservant ② son; boy: 长～ one's eldest son ③ baron

【男厕所】 náncèsuǒ ① men's lavatory (或 toilet, room) ②〔用于公共厕所门上〕Gentlemen; Men; Gents

【男盗女娼】 nándào-nǚchāng behave like thieves and whores; be out-and-out scoundrels

【男低音】 nándīyīn 〈乐〉 bass

【男儿】 nán'ér man: 好～ a fine man

【男方】 nánfāng the bridegroom's or husband's side

【男高音】 nángāoyīn 〈乐〉 tenor

【男孩】 nánhái boy

【男家】 nánjiā the bridegroom's or husband's family

【男爵】 nánjué baron ◇ ～夫人 baroness

【男男女女】 nánnánnǚnǚ men and women: 全村～都投入了麦收战斗。The whole village, men and women alike, joined in harvesting the wheat.

【男女】 nán-nǚ men and women: ～青年 young men and women/ ～老少 men and women, old and young/ ～同工同酬。Men and women get equal pay for equal work.

【男女平等】 nán-nǚ píngděng equality of men and women; equality of the sexes

【男朋友】 nánpéngyou boyfriend

【男人】 nánrén ① man ② menfolk

【男人】 nánren 〈口〉 husband

【男生】 nánshēng man student; boy student; schoolboy

【男声】 nánshēng 〈乐〉 male voice ◇ ～合唱 men's chorus; male chorus

【男性】 nánxìng ① the male sex ② man

【男中音】 nánzhōngyīn 〈乐〉 baritone

【男装】 nánzhuāng men's clothing: 女扮～ a woman disguised as a man

【男子】 nánzǐ man; male ◇ ～单(双)打 men's singles (doubles)/ ～团体赛 men's team event

【男子汉】 nánzǐhàn man: 不象个～ not manly; not man enough

**南** nán ① south: ～风 a south wind/ 城～ south of the city/ 华～ south China/ ～屋 a room with a northern exposure/ 大军～下 large contingents of the army advancing south ② (Nán) a surname

【南半球】 nánbànqiú the Southern Hemisphere

【南北】 nán-běi ① north and south ② from north to south: 这个水库～足有五里。This reservoir extends a good five *li* from north to south./ 大江～一片丰收景象。Scenes of a bumper harvest greet the eye on both sides of the Changjiang River.

【南北朝】 Nán-Běi Cháo the Northern and Southern Dynasties (420-589)

【南部】 nánbù southern part; south: 广州位于广东省～。Guangzhou is in the south of Guangdong Province.

【南昌】 Nánchāng Nanchang

【南昌起义】 Nánchāng Qǐyì 见"八一南昌起义" Bā Yī Nánchāng Qǐyì

【南朝】 Nán Cháo the Southern Dynasties (420-589), namely, the Song Dynasty (宋, 420-479), the Qi Dynasty (齐, 479-502), the Liang Dynasty (梁, 502-557) and the Chen Dynasty (陈, 557-589)

【南方】 nánfāng ① south ② the southern part of the country, esp. the area south of the Changjiang River; the South: 住在～ live in the South/ ～风味 southern style;

southern flavour ◇ ～话 southern dialect/ ～人 southerner

【南风】 nánfēng south wind

【南瓜】 nánguā pumpkin; cushaw

【南国】 nánguó 〈书〉 the southern part of the country; the South: ～风光 southern scenery

【南海】 Nánhǎi the Nanhai Sea; the South China Sea

【南寒带】 nánhándài the south frigid zone

【南胡】 nánhú another name for *erhu* (二胡), a two-stringed bowed instrument

【南回归线】 nánhuíguīxiàn 〈地〉 the tropic of Capricorn

【南货】 nánhuò delicacies from south China (such as dried bamboo shoots, etc.)

【南极】 nánjí ① the South Pole; the Antarctic Pole ② the south magnetic pole
◇ ～光 〈天〉 southern lights; aurora australis/ ～圈 the Antarctic Circle/ ～洲 the Antarctic Continent; Antarctica

【南京】 Nánjīng Nanjing

【南柯一梦】 Nánkē yī mèng Nanke dream (from the story of a man who dreamed that he became governor of Nanke in the Kingdom of the Ants); illusory joy; fond dream

【南美洲】 Nán Měizhōu South America

【南泥湾精神】 Nánníwān jīngshén the spirit of Nanniwan (the spirit of arduous struggle shown by the Eighth Route Armymen who became self-sufficient in food and clothing by reclaiming barren land in Nanniwan, Shaanxi Province, during the War of Resistance Against Japan)

【南宁】 Nánníng Nanning

【南齐】 Nán Qí the Southern Qi Dynasty (479-502), one of the Southern Dynasties

【南腔北调】 nánqiāng-běidiào (speak with) a mixed accent

【南沙群岛】 Nánshā Qúndǎo the Nansha Islands

【南斯拉夫】 Nánsīlāfū Yugoslavia ◇ ～人 Yugoslav

【南宋】 Nán Sòng the Southern Song Dynasty (1127-1279)

【南天竹】 nántiānzhú 〈植〉 nandina

【南纬】 nánwěi south (或 southern) latitude

【南温带】 nánwēndài the south temperate zone

【南亚】 Nán Yà South Asia ◇ ～次大陆 the South Asian Subcontinent

【南洋】 Nányáng ① a general name used towards the end of the Qing Dynasty for the coastal provinces of Jiangsu, Zhejiang, Fujian and Guangdong ② an old name for the Malay Archipelago, the Malay Peninsula and Indonesia or for southeast Asia

【南辕北辙】 nányuán-běizhé try to go south by driving the chariot north — act in a way that defeats one's purpose

【南诏】 Nánzhào Nanzhao (Nanchao), a local regime in ancient China

【南针】 nánzhēn ① compass ② a guide (to action)

【南征北战】 nánzhēng-běizhàn fight north and south on many fronts: 这是一支解放战争中经过～的英雄连队。This is a renowned company of heroes which fought on many fronts in the Liberation War.

**难** nán ① difficult; hard; troublesome: 这道题～解。This problem is hard to solve./ 路～走。The road is bad. 或 The going is hard. ② put sb. into a difficult position: 这问题一下子把我～住了。The question put me on the spot. ③ hardly possible: ～说 it's hard to say; you never can tell/ ～忘 unforgettable ④ bad; unpleasant: ～吃 taste bad; be unpalatable/ ～听 unpleasant to the ear
另见 nàn

【难保】 nánbǎo one cannot say for sure: 今天～不下雨。You can't say for sure that it won't rain today.

【难产】 nánchǎn ① 〈医〉 difficult labour; dystocia ② (of a literary work, plan, etc.) be difficult of fulfilment; be slow in coming

【难处】 nánchǔ hard to get along (或 on) with: 他只是脾气暴躁些，并不～。He's a bit quick-tempered, but not difficult to get along with.

【难处】 nánchu difficulty; trouble: 他有他的～。He has his difficulties.

【难倒】 nándǎo daunt; baffle; beat: 这个问题可把我～了。This problem baffles (或 beats) me./ 什么事也难不倒共产党员。No difficulty can daunt a Communist.

【难道】 nándào 〈副〉〔用以加强反问语气〕: ～你忘了自己的诺言吗？Can yon have forgotten your promise?/ 这一点儿困难～我们还不能克服吗？Can't we overcome even such small difficulties?/ 这～还不明白吗？Isn't this perfectly clear?/ ～就罢了不成？How can we let the matter rest here?

【难得】 nándé ① hard to come by; rare: ～的好机会 a rare chance/ 这种草药很～。This medicinal herb is hard to come by./ 他在一年之内两次打破世界纪录，是十分～的。He's performed the rare feat of breaking a world record twice in one year. ② seldom; rarely: 我们～见面，你多待一会儿吧。Can't you stay a bit longer? We so seldom have a chance to get together.

【难点】 nándiǎn difficult point; difficulty

【难度】 nándù degree of difficulty; difficulty: 这个杂技动作～很大。This acrobatic feat is extremely difficult.

【难怪】 nánguài ① no wonder: ～找不到人，都开会去了。No wonder you can't find anybody here; they're all away at a meeting. ② understandable; pardonable: 他不大了解情况，搞错了也～。You can hardly blame him for the mistake he made; he didn't know much about the situation.

【难关】 nánguān difficulty; crisis: 渡过～ tide over a difficulty (或 crisis)/ 攻克技术～ break down a technical barrier; resolve key technical problems

【难过】 nánguò ① have a hard time: 解放前劳动人民的日子真～。In preliberation days, the working people led a miserable life. ② feel sorry; feel bad; be grieved: 他听到战友去世的消息，非常～。He was deeply grieved to learn that his comrade-in-arms had died.

【难乎为继】 nán hū wéi jì hard to keep up 又作"难以为继"

【难解难分】 nánjiě-nánfēn ① be inextricably involved (in a dispute); be locked together (in a struggle): 两军厮杀，～。The two opposing armies are locked in battle. ② be sentimentally attached to each other

【难堪】 nánkān ① intolerable; unbearable ② embarrassed: 感到～ feel very much embarrassed/ 处于～的境地 be in an extremely awkward (或 miserable) situation

【难看】 nánkàn ① ugly; unsightly: 这座楼房真～。This building is ugly./ 他听到这个消息，脸色变得很～。When he heard the news, his face took on a ghastly expression. ② shameful; embarrassing: 咱们在音乐会上要是演奏不好，那就太～了。It would be a shame if we put on a bad performance at the concert.

【难免】 nánmiǎn hard to avoid: 犯错误是～的，你认真改了就好了。Mistakes are hard to avoid, but if you correct them conscientiously, things will be all right./ 人们的看法有时～带片面性。Sometimes people can't help being one-sided in their views.

【难能可贵】 nán néng kě guì difficult of attainment, hence worthy of esteem; deserving praise for one's excellent performance or behaviour; estimable; commendable

【难人】 nánrén ① difficult; delicate; ticklish: 这种～的事，我办不了。I cannot handle such a ticklish question. ② a person handling a delicate matter

【难色】 nánsè appear to be reluctant or embarrassed: 面有～ show signs of reluctance or embarrassment

【难上难】 nánshàngnán extremely difficult 又作"难上加难"
【难舍难分】 nánshě-nánfēn loath to part from each other: 乡亲们送红军，真是～。The villagers could hardly tear themselves away from the departing Red Army men.
【难受】 nánshòu ① feel unwell; feel ill; suffer pain: 浑身疼得～ be aching all over ② feel unhappy; feel bad: 他知道事情做错了，心里很～。He felt bad when he realized his error.
【难说】 nánshuō it's hard to say; you never can tell: 他什么时候回来还很～。No one can tell when he will return.
【难题】 nántí difficult problem; a hard nut to crack; poser: 出～ set difficult questions/ 在这样干旱的地区种水稻可是一个～。How to grow rice in such a dry area is a difficult problem.
【难听】 nántīng ① unpleasant to hear: 这个曲子真～。This tune is not very pleasing to the ear. ② offensive; coarse: 你怎么骂人，多～！Why do you swear? It's really bad. ③ scandalous: 这事情说出去多～。The story will create a scandal once it gets out.
【难忘】 nánwàng unforgettable; memorable: ～的一课 an unforgettable lesson/ ～的岁月 memorable years
【难为情】 nánwéiqíng ① ashamed; embarrassed; shy: 试验不成功也别～。Don't feel ashamed if your experiment isn't a success./他听见别人这样夸他，感到很～。He was very embarrassed to hear people speak so highly of him. ② embarrassing; disconcerting: 答应吧，办不到；不答应吧，又有点～。It's not feasible to comply, but a bit embarrassing to refuse.
【难为】 nánwei ① embarrass; press: 她不会唱歌，就别～她了。She can't sing. So don't press her to. ② be a tough job to: 在战争年代，她一个人拉扯好几个孩子，真～她了。It was quite a job for her to bring up several children all by herself during the war. ③〈套〉〔用于感谢别人代自己做事〕：炕也给我们烧热了，大娘，真～你了。It was really very kind of you, grandma, to heat the *kang* for us.
【难闻】 nánwén smell unpleasant; smell bad
【难兄难弟】 nánxiōng-nándì〈讽〉two of a kind
另见 nànxiōng-nàndì
【难言之隐】 nán yán zhī yǐn sth. which it would be awkward to disclose; sth. embarrassing to mention; a painful topic
【难以】 nányǐ difficult to: ～捉摸 difficult to pin down; elusive; unintelligible/ ～想象 unimaginable/ ～形容 indescribable; beyond description/ ～逆料 hard to predict (或 forecast)/ ～置信 hard to believe

**喃** nán
【喃喃】 nánnán〈象〉mutter; murmur: ～自语 mutter to oneself

**楠** nán
【楠木】 nánmù〈植〉nanmu (*Phoebe nanmu*)

## nǎn

**赧** nǎn blushing
【赧然】 nǎnrán〈书〉blushing
【赧颜】 nǎnyán〈书〉blush; be shamefaced

**腩** nǎn 见"牛腩" niúnǎn

**蝻** nǎn the nymph of a locust
【蝻子】 nǎnzi the nymph of a locust

## nàn

**难** nàn ① calamity; disaster; adversity: 逃～ flee from danger; be a refugee ② take to task; blame: 非～ blame; reproach
另见 nán
【难民】 nànmín refugee ◇ ～营 refugee camp
【难兄难弟】 nànxiōng-nàndì fellow sufferers
另见 nánxiōng-nándì
【难友】 nànyǒu fellow sufferer

## nāng

**囔** nāng
【囔囔】 nāngnang speak in a low voice; murmur

## náng

**囊** náng ① bag; pocket: 药～ medicine bag/ 胶～ capsule ② anything shaped like a bag: 胆～ gallbladder
【囊虫】 nángchóng cysticercus ◇ ～病 cysticercosis
【囊空如洗】 náng kōng rú xǐ with empty pockets; penniless; broke
【囊括】 nángkuò include; embrace: ～四海 bring the whole country under imperial rule
【囊中物】 nángzhōngwù sth. which is in the bag — sth. certain of attainment
【囊肿】 nángzhǒng〈医〉cyst

**馕** náng a kind of crusty pancake (staple food of the Uygur and Kazak nationalities)
另见 nǎng

## nǎng

**曩** nǎng〈书〉former; past: ～时 in olden days; of yore

**攮** nǎng stab
【攮子】 nǎngzi dagger

**馕** nǎng cram food into one's mouth
另见 náng

## nàng

**齉** nàng snuffling: 受了凉，鼻子发～ snuffle with a cold
【齉鼻儿】 nàngbír ① snuffle; speak through the nose: 他感冒了，说话有点～。He had a cold and spoke with a slight snuffle. ② a person who speaks with a twang

## nāo

**孬** nāo〈方〉① bad ② cowardly
【孬种】 nāozhǒng coward

## náo

**呶** náo
【呶呶不休】 náonáo bù xiū〈书〉talk on and on foolishly or tediously

**挠** náo ① scratch: ～痒痒 scratch an itch ② hinder: 阻～ obstruct ③ yield; flinch: 不屈不～ indomitable; unyielding

【挠度】 náodù 〈建〉 deflection

【挠钩】 náogōu long-handled hook

【挠头】 náotóu ① scratch one's head ② difficult to tackle: 这可是～的事。This is a knotty problem.

【挠性】 náoxìng 〈物〉 flexibility

【挠秧】 náoyāng 〈农〉 weed rice fields and loosen the soil around the seedlings

**硇** náo

【硇砂】 náoshā 〈化〉〈矿〉 sal ammoniac

**铙** náo big cymbals

【铙钹】 náobó 〈乐〉 big cymbals

**蛲** náo

【蛲虫】 náochóng pinworm ◇ ～病 enterobiasis

**猱** náo a kind of monkey mentioned in ancient literature

【猱犬】 náoquǎn dhole; red dog

【猱升】 náoshēng 〈书〉 climb a tree as nimbly as a monkey

## nǎo

**恼** nǎo ① angry; irritated; annoyed: ～恨 resent ② unhappy; worried: 烦～ vexed; worried

【恼恨】 nǎohèn resent; hate: 他的批评是为你好，你可别～他。You shouldn't resent his criticism. He meant well.

【恼火】 nǎohuǒ annoyed; irritated; vexed: 对于他那种听不进批评的态度，我们感到～。We're annoyed at his not listening to criticism.

【恼怒】 nǎonù angry; indignant; furious

【恼人】 nǎorén irritating; annoying

【恼羞成怒】 nǎo-xiū chéng nù fly into a rage from shame; be shamed into anger

**脑** nǎo 〈生理〉 brain: 大～ cerebrum/ 小～ cerebellum/ ～动脉 cerebral artery/ 用～过度 overtax one's brain

【脑充血】 nǎochōngxuè 〈医〉 encephalemia

【脑袋】 nǎodai 〈口〉 head

【脑电波】 nǎodiànbō 〈生理〉 brain wave

【脑电图】 nǎodiàntú 〈医〉 electroencephalogram (EEG)

【脑海】 nǎohǎi brain; mind: 多年前的旧事又重现在他的～里。 Memories of things long past flashed across his mind.

【脑积水】 nǎojīshuǐ 〈医〉 hydrocephalus

【脑脊髓炎】 nǎojǐsuǐyán 〈医〉 encephalomyelitis

【脑脊液】 nǎojǐyè 〈生理〉 cerebrospinal fluid (CSF)

【脑浆】 nǎojiāng brains

【脑筋】 nǎojīn ① brains; mind; head: 动～ use one's brains (或 head)/ 你问老杨去。他～好，记得清。Ask Lao Yang, he has a good memory. ② way of thinking; ideas: 旧～ a person who clings to old-fashioned ideas; an old fogey

【脑壳】 nǎoké ① skull ② 〈方〉 head

【脑力劳动】 nǎolì láodòng mental work: 逐步消灭～和体力劳动的差别 gradually eliminate the distinction between mental and manual labour ◇ ～者 mental worker; brain worker

【脑满肠肥】 nǎomǎn-chángféi heavy-jowled and potbellied — the idle rich

【脑门子】 nǎoménzi 〈方〉 forehead; brow

【脑膜】 nǎomó 〈生理〉 meninx ◇ ～炎 meningitis

【脑桥】 nǎoqiáo 〈生理〉 pons

【脑上体】 nǎoshàngtǐ 〈生理〉 pineal body

【脑神经】 nǎoshénjīng 〈生理〉 cranial nerve

【脑室】 nǎoshì 〈生理〉 ventricles of the brain ◇ ～造影 〈医〉 ventriculography

【脑髓】 nǎosuǐ brains

【脑血管造影】 nǎoxuèguǎn zàoyǐng 〈医〉 cerebral angiography

【脑炎】 nǎoyán encephalitis; cerebritis: 流行性乙型～ epidemic encephalitis B

【脑溢血】 nǎoyìxuè 〈医〉 cerebral haemorrhage

【脑震荡】 nǎozhèndàng 〈医〉 cerebral concussion; concussion of the brain

【脑汁】 nǎozhī brains: 绞尽～ rack (或 cudgel) one's brains

【脑子】 nǎozi ① 〈口〉 brain ② brains; mind; head: 没～ have no brains/ 问题是复杂的，我们的～也要复杂一点。The problems are complicated, and our brains must be a little complicated, too.

**瑙** nǎo 见"玛瑙" mǎnǎo

【瑙鲁】 Nǎolǔ Nauru ◇ ～人 Nauruan

## nào

**闹** nào ① noisy: 这屋里太～。This room is too noisy. ② make a noise; stir up trouble: 叫孩子们别～了。Tell the children to stop making a noise (或 fooling around)./ ～着玩儿 do sth. for fun; be joking/ 又哭又～ make a tearful scene/ 游击队把这个敌占城镇～得天翻地覆。The guerrillas turned the enemy-occupied town upside down./ ～名誉地位 be out for fame and position ③ give vent (to one's anger, resentment, etc.): ～脾气 vent one's spleen; lose one's temper; be in a tantrum ④ suffer from; be troubled by: ～肚子 have diarrhoea/ ～眼睛 have eye trouble/ ～嗓子 have a sore throat/ ～虫灾 suffer from insect pests ⑤ go in for; do; make: ～生产 go in for production/ 把问题～清楚再发言。Don't speak until you've got the thing clear in your mind.

【闹别扭】 nào bièniu be difficult with sb.; be at odds with sb.

【闹病】 nàobìng fall ill; be ill

【闹独立性】 nào dúlìxìng assert one's independence — refuse to obey the leadership: 反对向党～ oppose the assertion of independence from the Party

【闹翻】 nàofān fall out with sb.

【闹翻身】 nào fānshēn fight for emancipation: 共产党领导咱穷人～。The Communist Party led us poor people in our struggle for emancipation.

【闹翻天】 nàofāntiān raise hell; raise a rumpus

【闹风潮】 nào fēngcháo carry on agitation; stage strikes, demonstrations, etc.

【闹革命】 nào gémìng carry out revolution; make revolution; rise in revolution

【闹鬼】 nàoguǐ ① be haunted ② play tricks behind sb.'s back; use underhand means

【闹哄哄】 nàohōnghōng clamorous; noisy

【闹饥荒】 nào jīhuang ① suffer from famine ② 〈方〉 be hard up

【闹剧】 nàojù farce

【闹乱子】 nào luànzi cause trouble

【闹情绪】 nào qíngxù be disgruntled; be in low spirits

【闹嚷嚷】 nàorāngrāng noisy: 外面～的，什么事呀？What's

all that noise about outside?

【闹市】 nàoshì busy streets; busy shopping centre; downtown area

【闹事】 nàoshì create a disturbance; make trouble

【闹笑话】 nào xiàohuà make a fool of oneself; make a stupid mistake: 不懂装懂就会～。If you pretend to know what you don't know, you'll only make a fool of yourself.

【闹意见】 nào yìjiàn be on bad terms because of a difference of opinion

【闹意气】 nào yìqì feel resentful because something is not to one's liking; sulk: 你有意见就提出来，不要～。If you have any complaint, don't just sulk; speak up.

【闹着玩儿】 nàozhe wánr joke: 他是跟你～的，你别当真。He was joking. Don't take it seriously./ 这可不是～的事。This is no joking matter (或 no joke).

【闹钟】 nàozhōng alarm clock

**淖** nào 〈书〉 mire

【淖尔】 nào'ěr 〔多用于地名〕nur (the Mongolian for "lake")

## nè

**讷** nè 〈书〉 slow (of speech): ～于言而敏于行 slow of speech but quick in action

**那** nè 〈口〉 that

另见 Nā; nà; nèi

## ne

**呢** ne 〈助〉 ①〔用在疑问句的末尾〕: 我错在哪儿～？What have I done wrong?/ 他们两人都有任务了，我～？They've both got something to do. What about me? ②〔用在陈述句的末尾，表示确认事实〕: 远得很，有好几千里地～。It's a long way off — thousands of *li* away. ③〔用在陈述句的末尾，表示动作或情况正在继续〕: 老张，有人找你～。Lao Zhang, somebody is looking for you. ④〔用在句中表示停顿〕: 如今～，可比以往任何时候都要强。As for the present, things are far better than at any time in the past.

另见 ní

## něi

**哪** něi 〈口〉 which; what

另见 nǎ; na

**馁** něi ① hungry; famished ② disheartened; dispirited: 气～ lose heart; be disheartened/ 胜不骄，败不～ not become dizzy with success, nor be discouraged by failure ③〈书〉 (of fish) putrid

## nèi

**内** nèi ① inner; within; inside: 房子～外都很干净。The house is clean inside and out./ 我们必须在三日～回到北京。We must return to Beijing within three days./ 党～的思想斗争 inner-Party ideological struggle ② one's wife or her relatives: ～弟 wife's younger brother; brother-in-law

【内白】 nèibái 〈剧〉 words spoken by an actor from offstage

【内部】 nèibù inside; internal; interior: ～联系 internal relations/ 事物的～规律性 inherent laws of a thing/ 人民～矛盾 contradictions among the people/ 在工人阶级～ within the working class/ 堡垒是最容易从～攻破的。The easiest way to capture a fortress is from within. ◇ ～刊物 restricted publication

【内场】 nèichǎng 〈棒、垒球〉 infield ◇ ～手 infielder

【内出血】 nèichūxuè 〈医〉 internal haemorrhage

【内地】 nèidì inland; interior; hinterland: ～城市 inland city/ 我国的～ the interior of our country

【内弟】 nèidì wife's younger brother; brother-in-law

【内电阻】 nèidiànzǔ 〈电〉 internal resistance

【内定】 nèidìng (of an official appointment) decided at the higher level but not officially announced

【内毒素】 nèidúsù 〈医〉 endotoxin

【内耳】 nèi'ěr 〈生理〉 inner ear ◇ ～眩晕综合症 Ménière's syndrome (或 disease)

【内分泌】 nèifēnmì 〈生理〉 endocrine; internal secretion ◇ ～失调 endocrinopathy/ ～系统 internal system/ ～腺 endocrine glands

【内锋】 nèifēng 〈足球〉 inside forward: 他踢左～。He plays inside left.

【内服】 nèifú 〈医〉 to be taken orally

【内阁】 nèigé cabinet: 影子～ shadow cabinet ◇ ～大臣 cabinet minister

【内功】 nèigōng exercises to benefit the internal organs

【内骨骼】 nèigǔgé 〈动〉 endoskeleton

【内果皮】 nèiguǒpí 〈植〉 endocarp

【内海】 nèihǎi ① inland sea ② continental sea

【内涵】 nèihán 〈逻〉 intension; connotation

【内行】 nèiháng expert; adept: 种稻子很～ know a lot about growing rice/ 充～ pose as an expert/ 要说木匠活呀，他可是～。When it comes to carpentry, he is quite a dab hand.

【内河】 nèihé inland river (或 waters, waterway) ◇ ～航行权 inland navigation rights/ ～运输 inland water transport

【内讧】 nèihòng internal conflict; internal strife; internal dissension

【内寄生物】 nèijìshēngwù 〈生〉 endoparasite

【内奸】 nèijiān a secret enemy agent within one's ranks; hidden traitor

【内角】 nèijiǎo 〈数〉 interior angle

【内接形】 nèijiēxíng 〈数〉 inscribed figure

【内景】 nèijǐng indoor setting; indoor scene; interior

【内径】 nèijìng 〈机〉 internal diameter; inside (或 inner) diameter (ID) ◇ ～规 internal gauge/ ～千分尺 inside micrometer

【内疚】 nèijiù compunction; guilty conscience: 感到～ feel compunction; have qualms of conscience

【内聚力】 nèijùlì 〈物〉 cohesive force; cohesion

【内卡钳】 nèikǎqián 〈机〉 inside callipers

【内科】 nèikē 〈医〉 (department of) internal medicine ◇～病房 medical ward/ ～医生 physician

【内窥镜】 nèikuījìng 〈医〉 endoscope ◇ ～检查 endoscopy

【内涝】 nèilào waterlogging

【内力】 nèilì 〈物〉 internal force

【内陆】 nèilù inland; interior; landlocked ◇ ～国 landlocked country/ ～河 continental river/ ～盆地 interior (或 inland) basin

【内乱】 nèiluàn civil strife; internal disorder

【内蒙古】 Nèi Měnggǔ Nei Monggol

【内蒙古自治区】 Nèi Měnggǔ Zìzhìqū the Nei Monggol (Inner Mongolia) Autonomous Region

【内幕】 nèimù what goes on behind the scenes; inside story

【内能】 nèinéng 〈物〉 internal energy; intrinsic energy

【内切圆】 nèiqiēyuán 〈数〉 inscribed circle

【内亲】 nèiqīn a relative on one's wife's side; in-law

【内勤】 nèiqín ① office staff ② internal or office work (as distinguished from work carried on mainly outside the office)

【内情】 nèiqíng inside information (或 story): 了解～ be an insider; be in the know

【内燃机】 nèiránjī 〈机〉 internal-combustion engine

【内燃机车】 nèirán jīchē diesel locomotive

【内人】 nèiren 〈旧〉 my wife

【内容】 nèiróng content; substance: ～和形式的统一 unity of content and form/ 他的演说,毫无～。His speech lacked substance (或 content)./ 这本书～丰富。This book has substantial content./ 这次谈话的～牵涉面很广。The talk covered a lot of ground. ◇ ～提要 synopsis; résumé

【内伤】 nèishāng ① 〈医〉 internal injury ② 〈中医〉 disorder of internal organs caused by improper diet, fatigue, emotional strains, sexual excess, etc.

【内胎】 nèitāi the inner tube of a tyre

【内廷】 nèitíng imperial palace

【内外】 nèi-wài ① inside and outside; domestic and foreign: 长城～ both sides of the Great Wall/ ～反动派 domestic and foreign reactionaries/ ～夹攻 attack from both within and without/ ～交困 beset with difficulties both at home and abroad ② around; about: 五十年～ in about fifty years

【内务】 nèiwù ① internal affairs ② 〈军〉 daily routine tasks to keep the barracks, etc. clean and tidy ◇ ～条令 〈军〉 interior service regulations

【内吸磷】 nèixīlín 〈农〉 demeton

【内线】 nèixiàn ① planted agent ② 〈军〉 interior lines: ～作战 fight (或 operate) on interior lines ③ inside (telephone) connections ◇ ～自动电话机 interphone

【内详】 nèixiáng name and address of sender enclosed

【内向】 nèixiàng 〈心〉 introversion

【内销】 nèixiāo sold inside the country; for the domestic market

【内斜视】 nèixiéshì 〈医〉 esotropia; cross-eye

【内心】 nèixīn heart; innermost being: ～深处 in one's heart of hearts/ 他～很矛盾。He is torn by conflicting thoughts./ 影片展示了一个坚强的革命战士的～世界。The film reveals the inner world of a staunch revolutionary fighter.

【内省】 nèixǐng 〈心〉 introspection ◇ ～心理学 introspective psychology

【内兄】 nèixiōng wife's elder brother; brother-in-law

【内秀】 nèixiù be intelligent without seeming so

【内焰】 nèiyàn 〈化〉 inner flame

【内衣】 nèiyī underwear; underclothes

【内因】 nèiyīn 〈哲〉 internal cause: 唯物辩证法认为,外因通过～而起作用。Materialist dialectics holds that external causes become operative through internal causes.

【内应】 nèiyìng a person operating from within in coordination with outside forces; a planted agent; a plant

【内应力】 nèiyìnglì 〈机〉 internal stress

【内忧外患】 nèiyōu-wàihuàn domestic trouble and foreign invasion

【内在】 nèizài inherent; intrinsic; internal ◇ ～规律 inherent law/ ～联系 inner link; internal relations/ ～论 〈哲〉 immanentism/ ～矛盾 inner (或 inherent) contradictions/ ～因素 internal factor

【内脏】 nèizàng internal organs; viscera

【内宅】 nèizhái 〈旧〉 inner chambers for womenfolk (in a rich man's residence)

【内债】 nèizhài internal debt

【内战】 nèizhàn civil war

【内政】 nèizhèng internal (或 domestic, home) affairs: 互不干涉～ noninterference in each other's internal affairs

【内侄】 nèizhí son of wife's brother; nephew

【内侄女】 nèizhínǚ daughter of wife's brother; niece

【内痔】 nèizhì 〈医〉 internal piles (或 haemorrhoids)

【内助】 nèizhù 〈书〉 wife

**那** nèi 〈口〉 that
另见 Nā; nà; nè

## nèn

**恁** nèn 〈方〉 ① such; so: ～大胆! How reckless! 或 What audacity! ② that: ～时 at that time

**嫩** nèn ① tender; delicate: ～叶 tender leaves/ 这肉炒得很～。This stir-fried meat is very tender./ 小孩子肉皮儿～。Young children have delicate skin./ 脸皮儿～ shy; bashful ② light: ～黄 light yellow/ ～绿 light green; soft green ③ inexperienced; unskilled: ～手 raw hand; new hand

【嫩色】 nènsè light colour; soft colour; pastel shade

## néng

**能** néng ① ability; capability; skill: 无～ lacking in ability; incompetent/ 一专多～ good at many things and expert in one ② 〈物〉 energy: 原子～ atomic energy/ 太阳～ solar energy/ 热～ thermal energy ③ able; capable: ～人 able person ④ can; be able to; be capable of: 她一分钟～打七十个字。She can type 70 words a minute./ 他好多了,～下床了。He's much better and can get up now./ 我干这个工作～行吗? Am I really fit for the job?

【能动】 néngdòng active; dynamic: 人的～作用 man's initiative (或 dynamic role)/ 从感性认识到理性认识之～的飞跃 the active leap from perceptual to rational knowledge/ ～地争取胜利 play a dynamic role in striving for victory

【能动性】 néngdòngxìng dynamic role; activity; initiative: 主观～ subjective activity/ 自觉的～ (man's) conscious dynamic role

【能干】 nénggàn able; capable; competent: 他是个很～的人。He is a man of great ability./ 这些女电工真～。These women electricians really know their job.

【能工巧匠】 nénggōng-qiǎojiàng skilful craftsman; dab hand

【能够】 nénggòu can; be able to; be capable of: ～独立工作 be able to work on one's own/ 他～说三种外国语。He can speak three foreign languages./ 这河的下游～行驶轮船。The lower reaches of the river are navigable for steamers.

【能级】 néngjí 〈物〉 energy level: 费密～ Fermi level/ 基态～ ground state level

【能见度】 néngjiàndù visibility: 地面～ ground visibility

【能力】 nénglì ability; capacity; capability: ～强 have great ability; be very capable/ 培养学生的推理～ develop the students' reasoning capacity/ 分析问题和解决问题的～ ability to analyse and solve problems/ 提高识别真假马克思主义的～ increase one's ability to distinguish true Marxism from false

【能量】 néngliàng ① 〈物〉 energy: ～转化 conversion of energy ② capabilities: 他们人数很少,～很大。Though few in number, they have enormous capacity for manoeuvre. ◇ ～交换 energy exchange/ ～守恒律 the law of conservation of energy

【能耐】 néngnai 〈口〉 ability; capability; skill: 她真有～,一

个人管这么多台机器。She shows great ability in minding so many machines all by herself.

【能…能…】 néng...néng... 〔表示"既能…又能"〕: 能攻能守 be good at offence and defence; be able to take the offensive or hold one's ground/ 能官能民 be ready to be an official or one of the common people/ 能文能武 be versed in both polite letters and martial arts; be able to wield both the pen and the gun/ 能上能下 be ready to work both at the top or at the grass roots; be ready to accept a higher or a lower post

【能人】 néngrén able person: ～背后有～。For every able person there is always one still abler.

【能事】 néngshì 〔常跟"尽"字配合〕 what one is particularly good at: 竭尽挑拨离间之～ stop at nothing to sow discord

【能手】 néngshǒu dab; expert; crackajack: 木刻～ a dab at wood engraving/ 技术革新～ a crackajack at technical innovation/ 她是插秧～。She is a good hand at transplanting rice.

【能说会道】 néngshuō-huìdào have the gift of the gab; have a glib tongue

【能源】 néngyuán the sources of energy; energy resources; energy: ～危机 energy crisis

【能愿动词】 néngyuàn dòngcí 〈语〉 modal verb

【能者多劳】 néngzhě duō láo able people should do more work (said as when asking sb. to perform a service or do extra work)

【能者为师】 néngzhě wéi shī let those who know teach

## ńg

**嗯** ńg 或 ń 〈叹〉〔表示疑问〕: ～，你说什么？What? What did you say?
另见 ňg; ǹg

## ňg

**嗯** ňg 或 ň 〈叹〉〔表示出乎意外或不以为然〕: ～，怎么又不见了？Hey! It's gone again./ ～！你怎么还没去？What! Haven't you started yet?
另见 ńg; ǹg

## ǹg

**嗯** ǹg 或 ǹ 〈叹〉〔表示答应〕: 他～了一声，就走了。He merely said, "H'm", and went away.
另见 ńg; ňg

## nī

**妮** nī

【妮子】 nīzi 〈方〉 girl; lass 又作"妮儿"

## ní

**尼** ní Buddhist nun

【尼庵】 ní'ān Buddhist nunnery

【尼泊尔】 Níbó'ěr Nepal ◇ ～人 Nepalese/ ～语 Nepali

【尼姑】 nígū Buddhist nun

【尼古丁】 nígǔdīng nicotine

【尼加拉瓜】 Níjiālāguā Nicaragua ◇ ～人 Nicaraguan

【尼龙】 nílóng 〈纺〉 nylon ◇ ～丝 nylon yarn/ ～袜 nylon socks

【尼罗河】 Níluóhé the Nile

【尼日尔】 Nírì'ěr the Niger ◇ ～人 Nigerois

【尼日利亚】 Nírìlìyà Nigeria ◇ ～人 Nigerian

【尼亚加拉瀑布】 Níyàjiālā Pùbù Niagara Falls

**泥** ní ① mud; mire ② mashed vegetable or fruit: 枣～ jujube paste/ 土豆～ mashed potato/ 苹果～ applesauce
另见 nì

【泥巴】 níbā 〈方〉 mud; mire

【泥肥】 níféi 〈农〉 sludge (used as manure)

【泥垢】 nígòu dirt; grime

【泥灰岩】 níhuīyán 〈地〉 marl

【泥浆】 níjiāng slurry; mud: 钻井～ drilling mud ◇ ～泵 slurry (或 mud, slush) pump/ ～工 mudman

【泥金】 níjīn coating material made of glue and powdered gold or other metals; golden paint

【泥坑】 níkēng mud pit; mire; morass: 陷在～里 get stuck in the mud/ 陷进机会主义的～ fall into the quagmire of opportunism

【泥疗】 níliáo 〈医〉 mud therapy

【泥煤】 níméi peat 又作"泥炭"

【泥淖】 nínào mire; bog; morass

【泥泞】 nínìng muddy; miry: ～的道路 a muddy road

【泥牛入海】 níniú rù hǎi like a clay ox entering the sea — never to be heard of again; gone forever

【泥盆纪】 Nípénjì 〈地〉 the Devonian Period

【泥菩萨】 nípúsà clay idol: ～过河，自身难保 like a clay idol fording a river — hardly able to save oneself (let alone anyone else)

【泥鳅】 níqiū loach

【泥人】 nírén 〈工美〉 clay figurine: 彩塑～ painted clay figurine

【泥沙】 níshā 〈地〉 silt

【泥沙俱下】 ní-shā jù xià mud and sand are carried along — there is a mingling of good and bad: 在革命高潮时期，各种人都来参加，未免～，鱼龙混杂。At the high tide of the revolution, people of all descriptions flocked to join in; so inevitably the waters were muddied and the bad became mixed with the good.

【泥石流】 níshíliú 〈地〉 mud-rock flow

【泥水匠】 níshuǐjiàng bricklayer; tiler; plasterer

【泥塑】 nísù clay sculpture

【泥塑木雕】 nísù-mùdiāo 见"木雕泥塑" mùdiāo-nísù

【泥胎】 nítāi ① unpainted clay idol ② unfired pottery

【泥潭】 nítán mire; morass; quagmire

【泥塘】 nítáng mire; bog; morass

【泥土】 nítǔ ① earth; soil: 春天的原野散发着～的芳香。In spring the fields give off the aroma of the earth. ② clay

【泥腿子】 nítuǐzi bumpkin; clodhopper

【泥瓦匠】 níwǎjiàng bricklayer; tiler; plasterer

【泥岩】 níyán 〈地〉 mudstone

【泥俑】 níyǒng 〈考古〉 clay figures buried with the dead; funerary clay figures; earthen figurines

【泥沼】 nízhǎo mire; swamp; morass; slough

**呢** ní (cloth made of) wool; woollen cloth (for heavy clothing); heavy woollen cloth; wool coating or suiting: 制服～ uniform coating/ 格子～ woollen check
另见 ne

【呢喃】 nínán twittering (of swallows)

【呢绒】 níróng woollen goods; wool fabric

【呢子】 nízi woollen cloth (for heavy clothing); heavy woollen cloth; wool coating or suiting

**怩** ní 见"忸怩" niǔní

**倪** ní ① 见"端倪" duānní ② (Ní) a surname

**铌** ní 〈化〉 niobium (Nb)

【铌铁矿】 nítiěkuàng columbite

**霓** ní 〈气〉 secondary rainbow

【霓虹灯】 níhóngdēng neon lamp; neon light; neon

**鲵** ní salamander

## nǐ

**拟** nǐ ① draw up; draft: ～稿 make a draft/ ～一个方案 draw up a plan ② intend; plan: ～于下月前往青岛 plan to go to Qingdao next month ③ imitate: 模～ imitate; copy

【拟订】 nǐdìng draw up; draft; work out: ～计划 draw up a plan; draft a plan/ ～具体办法 work out specific measures/ ～城市建设规划 map out a programme for municipal construction 又作"拟定"

【拟古】 nǐgǔ model one's literary or artistic style on that of the ancients: ～之作 a work modelled after the ancients

【拟人】 nǐrén 〈语〉 personification

【拟态】 nǐtài 〈生〉 mimicry; imitation

【拟议】 nǐyì ① proposal; recommendation: 事实证明他的～是正确的。Facts show that his recommendations were sound. ② draw up; draft: 小组一致通过了她所～的意见书。The group unanimously adopted the proposal she drew up.

【拟作】 nǐzuò a work done in the manner of a certain author

**你** nǐ ① you (second person singular): ～爸爸 your father ② you (second person plural): ～方 your side; you/ ～校 your school ③［泛指任何人］you; one; anyone: 碰到这么一个人，～有什么办法？What can you do with a person like that?/ 三个人～看看我，我看看～，谁也没说话。The three of them kept looking at one another without saying a word./ ～一言，我一语，谈得很热闹。A lively conversation went on with everybody joining in.

【你好】 nǐhǎo how do you do; how are you; hello

【你们】 nǐmen you (second person plural)

【你死我活】 nǐsǐ-wǒhuó life-and-death; mortal: ～的斗争 a life-and-death struggle/ 拼个～ fight to the bitter end

【你追我赶】 nǐzhuī-wǒgǎn try to overtake each other in friendly emulation

**旎** nǐ 见"旖旎" yǐnǐ

## nì

**泥** nì ① cover or daub with plaster, putty, etc.; putty; plaster: ～墙 cover the crevices in a wall with mud or plaster/ 把窗玻璃用油灰～上 fix a windowpane with putty ② stubborn, bigoted; obstinate: ～古 have bigoted belief in the ancients; obstinately follow ancient ways

另见 ní

【泥子】 nìzi 〈建〉 putty

**逆** nì ① contrary; counter: ～风 contrary wind; head wind ② go against; disobey; defy: ～时代潮流而动 go against the trend of the times ③ traitor: ～产 traitor's property ④ 〈数〉 inverse; converse: ～变换 inverse transformation/ ～定理 converse theorem

【逆差】 nìchā 〈商〉 adverse balance of trade; trade deficit: 国际收支～ an adverse (或 unfavourable) balance of international payments

【逆定理】 nìdìnglǐ 〈数〉 converse theorem

【逆耳】 nì'ěr grate on the ear; be unpleasant to the ear: ～的话 words or advice unpleasant to hear/ 忠言～。Good advice often jars on the ear.

【逆风】 nìfēng ① against the wind: ～行舟 sail against the wind ② contrary wind; head wind ◇ ～飞行 head-wind flight

【逆境】 nìjìng adverse circumstances; adversity

【逆来顺受】 nì lái shùn shòu meekly submit to oppression, maltreatment, etc.; resign oneself to adversity

【逆料】 nìliào anticipate; foresee: 事态的发展不难～。The course of events can be foreseen./ 月底能否成行尚难～。It's still hard to say whether we can leave before the end of the month.

【逆流】 nìliú adverse current; countercurrent: 一股反社会主义的～ an adverse current against socialism

【逆旅】 nìlǚ 〈书〉 inn; hotel

【逆水】 nìshuǐ against the current: ～行舟，不进则退。A boat sailing against the current must forge ahead or it will be driven back.

【逆温】 nìwēn 〈气〉 (temperature) inversion ◇ ～层 〈气〉〈地〉 inversion layer

【逆行】 nìxíng ① (of vehicles) go in a direction not allowed by traffic regulations; go in the wrong direction: 单行线，车辆不得～。One-way street (或 traffic). ② 〈天〉 retrograde motion

【逆证】 nìzhèng 〈中医〉 a severe case with unfavourable prognosis

【逆转】 nìzhuǎn take a turn for the worse; reverse; become worse; deteriorate

【逆子】 nìzǐ unfilial son

**昵** nì close; intimate: 亲～ very intimate

**匿** nì hide; conceal: 隐～ go into hiding; hide

【匿伏】 nìfú be in hiding; lurk

【匿迹】 nìjì go into hiding; stay in concealment: 销声～ be in hiding; disappear from the scene

【匿名】 nìmíng anonymous ◇ ～信 anonymous letter

【匿影藏形】 nìyǐng-cángxíng hide from public notice; conceal one's identity; lie low

**溺** nì ① drown: ～死 be drowned ② be addicted to: ～于酒色 given over to wine and woman

【溺爱】 nì'ài spoil (a child); dote on (a child)

【溺婴】 nìyīng drowning of infants; infanticide

【溺职】 nìzhí neglect of duty; dereliction

**睨** nì 〈书〉 look askance

**腻** nì ① greasy; oily: 这炖肉有点～。This stew is a bit greasy./ 汤太～了。The soup is too oily. ② be bored with; be tired of: 这些话我都听～了。I'm tired of listening to all this. ③ meticulous: 细～的描写 a minute description ④ dirt; grime: 尘～ dirt

【腻虫】 nìchóng aphid

【腻烦】 nìfan 〈口〉 ① be bored; be fed up: 这本书我看了多少遍都不觉得～。I never get bored reading and rereading this book. ② loathe; hate: 我最～说大话的人。I can't stand people who brag.

【腻味】 nìwei 〈方〉 get fed up

## niān

**拈** niān pick up (with the thumb and one or two fingers): 从罐子里～出一块糖 take a candy from the jar/ 信手～来 pick up at random

【拈阄儿】 niānjiūr draw lots

【拈轻怕重】 niānqīng-pàzhòng prefer the light to the heavy — pick easy jobs and shirk hard ones

**蔫** niān ① fade; wither; shrivel up; droop: 菠菜～了。The spinach is shrivelled up./ 花儿晒～了。The flowers drooped in the heat of the sun. ② listless; spiritless; droopy: 这孩子有点～，怕是病了。The child looks a bit listless. I'm afraid he's not well.

【蔫不唧儿】 niānbujīr 〈方〉 ① listless; droopy; sluggish ② quiet: 别看他平时～的，打起仗来可象个小老虎。Although he is usually rather quiet, he fights like a tiger in battle./ 我还想跟他说话，没想到他～地走了。When I turned to speak to him, he'd gone without my noticing.

## nián

**年** nián ① year: 去～ last year/ ～复一～ year after year; year in year out ② annual; yearly: ～产量 annual output; annual yield ③ age: ～过六十 over sixty (years old) ④ New Year: 拜～ pay a New Year visit ⑤ a period in one's life: 童～ childhood ⑥ a period in history: 近～来 in recent years/ 明朝末～ towards the end of the Ming Dynasty ⑦ harvest: 丰～ rich harvest ⑧ (Nián) a surname

【年报】 niánbào ① annual report; annual ② annals (of a learned society)

【年表】 niánbiǎo chronological table

【年成】 niáncheng the year's harvest: 好～ a good harvest/ ～不好 a lean year

【年初】 niánchū the beginning of the year: 去年～ at the beginning of last year

【年代】 niándài ① age; years; time: 战争～ during the war years/ ～久了，石碑上的字迹已经模糊了。The inscriptions on the stone tablet have become blurred with the passage of time./ 展出的古代文物都标明了～。The antiques on display are all marked with dates. ② a decade of a century: 八十～ the eighties/ 二十世纪七十～ the 1970s

【年底】 niándǐ the end of the year

【年度】 niándù year: 财政～ financial year; fiscal year/ ～计划 annual plan

【年份】 niánfen ① a particular year: 这两笔开支不在一个～。These two expenditures were not incurred in the same year. ② age; time: 这件瓷器的～比那件久。This piece of porcelain is older than that one.

【年富力强】 niánfù-lìqiáng in the prime of life; in one's prime

【年高德劭】 niángāo-déshào of venerable age and eminent virtue; venerable

【年糕】 niángāo New Year cake (made of glutinous rice flour)

【年庚】 niángēng the time (year, month, day and hour) of a person's birth; date of birth

【年关】 niánguān the end of the year (formerly time for settling accounts): 在旧社会，～是穷人的鬼门关。In the old society the end of the year was a terrible time for the poor.

【年号】 niánhào the title of an emperor's reign

【年华】 niánhuá time; years: 虚度～ idle away one's time; waste one's life

【年画】 niánhuà New Year (或 Spring Festival) pictures

【年会】 niánhuì annual meeting

【年货】 niánhuò special purchases for the Spring Festival: 办～ do Spring Festival shopping

【年级】 niánjí grade; year: 大学三～学生 third year university student/ 小学一～学生 first grade primary school pupil

【年纪】 niánjì age: 上了～ old; advanced in years/ ～轻 young/ 老大爷，您多大～了？ How old are you, Grandpa?

【年假】 niánjià ① New Year holidays ② winter vacation

【年鉴】 niánjiàn yearbook; almanac

【年景】 niánjǐng ① the year's harvest: 在正常的～下 in normal harvest years ② holiday atmosphere of the Spring Festival

【年历】 niánlì a calendar with the whole year printed on one sheet; single-page calendar

【年利】 niánlì annual interest ◇ ～率 annual interest rate

【年龄】 niánlíng age: 他参军还不够～。He is too young to join the army./ 从马的牙齿可以看出它的～。You can tell a horse's age from its teeth.

【年轮】 niánlún 〈植〉 annual ring; growth ring

【年迈】 niánmài old; aged: ～力衰 old and infirm; senile

【年年】 niánnián every year; year after year

【年谱】 niánpǔ a chronicle of sb.'s life

【年青】 niánqīng young

【年轻】 niánqīng young: ～人 young people/ ～力壮 young and vigorous/ ～一代 the younger (或 rising) generation

【年深日久】 niánshēn-rìjiǔ with the passage of time; as the years go by: 河里的泥沙淤积在这里，～便成了沙洲。The bar was formed by the mud and sand deposited here over a long period of time.

【年岁】 niánsuì ① age: 上了～的人 a person who is getting on in years ② years: 因为～久远，当时的具体情况已记不清了。As it happened so many years ago, I don't remember the details.

【年头】 niántóu ① year: 他到武汉已经三个～了。It's three years since he came to Wuhan. ② years; long time: 她干这一行有～了。She has been doing this sort of work for years./ 这些树不够～，还没成材呢。These trees need more time to grow into useful timber. ③ days; times: 那～ in those days ④ harvest: 今年～真好。This year's harvest is very good indeed.

【年息】 niánxī annual interest

【年限】 niánxiàn fixed number of years: 学习～ the number of years set for a course (of study)/ 工具使用～ the service life of a tool

【年夜】 niányè the eve of the lunar New Year

【年月】 niányue days; years

【年终】 niánzhōng the end of the year; year-end: ～结帐 year-end settlement of accounts/ ～评比 year-end appraisal of work

**粘** nián 见"黏" nián
另见 zhān

**鲇** nián catfish

【鲇鱼】 niányú catfish

**黏** nián sticky; glutinous: ～米 glutinous rice/ 这浆糊不～。This paste is not sticky enough.

【黏虫】 niánchóng armyworm

【黏度】 niándù 〈化〉 viscosity: 恩氏～ Engler viscosity ◇ ～计 viscosimeter

【黏附】 niánfù adhere ◇ ～力 adhesion/ ～体 adherend

【黏合】 niánhé 〈化〉 bind; bond; adhere ◇～剂 binder; adhesive; bonding agent
【黏糊】 niánhu ① sticky; glutinous ② languid; slow-moving
【黏胶】 niánjiāo 〈化〉 viscose ◇～长丝 viscose filament yarn/ ～短纤维 viscose staple fibre/ ～丝 viscose
【黏结】 niánjié cohere ◇～力 cohesion; cohesive force/ ～性 cohesiveness
【黏菌】 niánjūn 〈生〉 slime mould (或 fungus)
【黏膜】 niánmó 〈生理〉 mucous membrane; mucosa ◇～炎 mucositis
【黏土】 niántǔ clay: 耐火～ refractory clay ◇～矿物 clay mineral/ ～岩 clay rock
【黏性】 niánxìng stickiness; viscidity; viscosity ◇～油 viscous oil
【黏液】 niányè 〈生理〉 mucus
【黏着】 niánzhuó stick together; adhere
【黏着语】 niánzhuóyǔ 〈语〉 agglutinative language

## niǎn

**捻** niǎn ① twist with the fingers: ～线 twist thread/ 把油灯～大些 turn up the wick (of a lamp) ② sth. made by twisting: 纸～儿 a paper spill/ 灯～儿 lampwick
【捻度】 niǎndù 〈纺〉 number of turns (或 twists); twist
【捻军】 Niǎnjūn the Nian Army (the Torch Bearers, a peasant army that rose against the Qing Dynasty in the middle of the 19th century)
【捻线机】 niǎnxiànjī 〈纺〉 twisting frame
【捻针】 niǎnzhēn 〈中医〉 twirling or rotating of the acupuncture needle
【捻子】 niǎnzi ① spill ② wick

**辇** niǎn ① a man-drawn carriage used in ancient times ② imperial carriage

**碾** niǎn ① roller ② grind or husk with a roller: ～米 husk rice ③ crush: ～得粉碎 be crushed to powder; be crushed to pieces; be pulverized ④ flatten
【碾坊】 niǎnfáng grain mill 又作"碾房"
【碾米机】 niǎnmǐjī rice mill
【碾碎】 niǎnsuì pulverize
【碾子】 niǎnzi roller: 石～ stone roller

**撵** niǎn ① drive out; oust: 把人～走 drive sb. away/ ～下台 oust from a leading position ② 〈方〉 catch up: 我～不上他。I couldn't catch up with him.

## niàn

**廿** niàn twenty

**念** niàn ① think of; miss: 我们老～着你。We miss you very much. ② thought; idea: 杂～ distracting thoughts ③ read aloud: 她把党委的指示～给大家听。She read out the Party committee directive to everyone. ④ study; attend school: ～书 read; study/ 他～过中学。He has been to middle school.
【念白】 niànbái spoken parts of a Chinese opera
【念叨】 niàndao ① talk about again and again in recollection or anticipation; be always talking about: 他就是我们常常～的张大伯。This is the Uncle Zhang we're always talking about. ② talk over; discuss: 我有个事儿跟大家～～。I've got something to talk over with you.
【念佛】 niànfó chant the name of Buddha; pray to Buddha
【念经】 niànjīng recite or chant scriptures
【念旧】 niànjiù ① keep old friendships in mind ② for old time's sake
【念念不忘】 niànniàn bù wàng bear in mind constantly
【念念有词】 niànniàn yǒu cí ① mutter incantations ② mumble
【念头】 niàntou thought; idea; intention: 当时他心中只有一个～，就是为祖国增光。At that time he had only one thing in mind: to win credit for his country./ 你最好放弃这个～。You'd better give up the idea.
【念珠】 niànzhū beads; rosary

**埝** niàn a low bank between fields: 打～ build banks between fields

## niáng

**娘** niáng ① ma; mum; mother: 爹～ father and mother ② a form of address for an elderly married woman: 婶～ wife of one's father's younger brother; aunt/ 老大～ grandma ③ a young woman: 新～ bride
【娘家】 niángjia a married woman's parents' home
【娘舅】 niángjiù 〈方〉 brother of one's mother; uncle
【娘娘】 niángniang ① empress or imperial concubine of the first rank: 正宫～ emperor's wife; empress ② goddess: ～庙 a temple dedicated to the worship of a goddess
【娘胎】 niángtāi mother's womb: 出了～ be born
【娘姨】 niángyí 〈方〉 maidservant
【娘子】 niángzi ① 〈方〉 a form of address for one's wife ②〔多用于早期白话〕 a polite form of address for a young woman ◇～军 detachment of women; women soldiers

**酿** niáng 见"酒酿" jiǔniáng
另见 niàng

## niàng

**酿** niàng ① make (wine); brew (beer): ～酒 make wine ② make (honey): 蜜蜂～蜜。Bees make honey. ③ lead to; result in: ～祸 lead to disaster ④ wine: 佳～ good wine
另见 niáng
【酿成】 niàngchéng lead to; bring on; breed: 主观主义的批评往往～无原则的纠纷。Subjective criticism often breeds unprincipled disputes./ 小错不改往往～大错。Small mistakes left uncorrected will lead to big ones.
【酿酒】 niàngjiǔ make wine; brew beer ◇～厂 winery; brewery/ ～业 wine-making industry
【酿酶】 niàngméi 〈化〉 zymase
【酿热物】 niàngrèwù 〈农〉 ferment material
【酿造】 niàngzào make (wine, vinegar, etc.); brew (beer, etc.)

## niǎo

**鸟** niǎo bird
【鸟粪】 niǎofèn ① birds' droppings ② guano
【鸟尽弓藏】 niǎojìn-gōngcáng cast aside the bow once the birds are gone — cast sb. aside when he has served his purpose
【鸟瞰】 niǎokàn ① get a bird's-eye view: ～全城 get a bird's-eye view of the city ② general survey of a subject;

bird's-eye view ◇～图 bird's-eye view
【鸟类】 niǎolèi birds ◇～学 ornithology
【鸟笼】 niǎolóng birdcage
【鸟枪】 niǎoqiāng ① fowling piece ② air gun
【鸟兽】 niǎo-shòu birds and beasts; fur and feather: 作～散 scatter like birds and beasts; flee helter-skelter; stampede
【鸟语花香】 niǎoyǔ-huāxiāng birds sing and flowers give forth their fragrance — characterizing a fine spring day
【鸟篆】 niǎozhuàn bird script, an ancient form of Chinese written characters, resembling birds' footprints
【鸟嘴】 niǎozuǐ beak; bill

## 茑

niǎo
【茑萝】 niǎoluó 〈植〉 cypress vine

## 袅

niǎo slender and delicate
【袅袅】 niǎoniǎo ① curl upwards: 炊烟～。Smoke is curling upward from kitchen chimneys. ② wave in the wind: 垂杨～。Drooping willows are dancing in the wind. ③ linger: 余音～。The music lingered in the air long after the performance ended.
【袅娜】 niǎonuó slender and graceful; willowy

# niào

## 尿

niào ① urine ② urinate; make water; pass water 另见 suī
【尿崩症】 niàobēngzhèng 〈医〉 diabetes insipidus
【尿闭】 niàobì 〈医〉 anuria
【尿布】 niàobù diaper; napkin; nappy
【尿床】 niàochuáng wet the bed; bed-wetting
【尿胆素】 niàodǎnsù 〈医〉 urobilin ◇～原 urobilinogen
【尿道】 niàodào 〈生理〉 urethra ◇～炎 urethritis/ ～造影 urethrography
【尿毒症】 niàodúzhèng 〈医〉 uraemia
【尿肥】 niàoféi 〈农〉 urine (used as manure)
【尿盆】 niàopén chamber pot; urinal
【尿频】 niàopín 〈医〉 frequent micturition
【尿少症】 niàoshǎozhèng 〈医〉 oliguria
【尿失禁】 niàoshījìn 〈医〉 urinary incontinence; incontinence of urine
【尿素】 niàosù 〈化〉 urea; carbamide ◇～脱蜡 〈石油〉 urea dewaxing
【尿酸】 niàosuān 〈化〉 uric acid
【尿血】 niàoxiě 〈医〉 haematuria
【尿潴留】 niàozhūliú 〈医〉 retention of urine

## 脲

niào 〈化〉 urea; carbamide
【脲醛塑料】 niàoquán sùliào 〈化〉 urea-formaldehyde plastics

# niē

## 捏

niē ① hold between the fingers; pinch: 把米里的虫子～出来 pick the worms out of the rice ② knead with the fingers; mould: ～泥人儿 mould clay figurines ③ fabricate; make up: ～报 fake a report
【捏估】 niēgu ① give secret counsel; goad secretly ② act as a go-between
【捏合】 niēhé ① mediate; act as go-between ② engage in an illicit love affair with sb.; carry on with sb.
【捏合机】 niēhéjī 〈化纤〉 kneading machine
【捏积】 niējī 〈中医〉 a method of treating children's digestive disorders by kneading or massaging the muscles along the spine; chiropractic
【捏一把汗】 niē yī bǎ hàn be breathless with anxiety or tension: 看着他往悬崖上爬，大家都～。Watching him climb up the precipice, everybody was breathless with anxiety.
【捏造】 niēzào fabricate; concoct; fake; trump up: ～事实 invent a story; make up a story/ ～罪名 trump up charges/ ～数字 conjure up figures/ 纯属～。That's sheer fabrication.

# nié

## 苶

nié tired; listless; lethargic: 发～ look listless

# niè

## 聂

Niè a surname

## 涅

niè 〈书〉 ① alunite ② dye sth. black
【涅白】 nièbái opaque white
【涅槃】 nièpán 〈佛教〉 nirvana

## 臬

niè 〈书〉 ① target ② standard; criterion

## 啮

niè 〈书〉 gnaw
【啮齿动物】 nièchǐ dòngwù rodent
【啮合】 nièhé ① clench the teeth ② (of gears) mesh; engage: 这个小齿轮和另外两个齿轮相～。The pinion meshes with two other gear wheels./ 这两个齿轮～在一起。The two cogwheels are engaged.

## 嗫

niè
【嗫嚅】 nièrú 〈书〉 speak haltingly

## 镊

niè ① tweezers ② pick up sth. with tweezers
【镊子】 nièzi tweezers

## 镍

niè 〈化〉 nickel (Ni): ～币 nickel coin; nickel/ ～箔 nickel foil
【镍黄铁矿】 nièhuángtiěkuàng 〈矿〉 pentlandite; nicopyrite

## 颞

niè
【颞骨】 niègǔ 〈生理〉 temporal bone
【颞颥】 nièrú 〈生理〉 temple

## 蹑

niè ① lighten (one's step); walk on tiptoe: 他～着脚走出病房。He tiptoed out of the ward. ② 〈书〉 follow: ～踪 follow along behind sb.; track ③ tread; step on; walk with: ～足其间 join (a profession); follow (a trade); associate with (a certain type of people)
【蹑手蹑脚】 nièshǒu-nièjiǎo walk gingerly; walk on tiptoe

## 孽

niè evil; sin: 作～ do evil/ 妖～ evildoer; monster
【孽障】 nièzhàng (a term of abuse formerly used by the elders of a clan cursing their juniors) evil creature; vile spawn

## 蘖

niè 〈植〉 tiller: 麦子正在分～。The wheat is tillering.

# nín

## 您

nín 〈敬〉 you

# níng

## 宁

níng ① peaceful; tranquil ② short for the Ningxia

Hui Autonomous Region ③ another name for Nanjing: 沪～线 the Shanghai-Nanjing Railway
另见 nìng
【宁静】 níngjìng peaceful; tranquil; quiet: ～的夜晚 a tranquil night/ 心里渐渐～下来 calm down gradually
【宁夏】 Níngxià Ningxia
【宁夏回族自治区】 Níngxià Huízú Zìzhìqū the Ningxia Hui Autonomous Region

**拧** níng ① twist; wring: ～麻绳 twist hemp into rope/ 把衣服～干 wring out wet clothes/ 大家～成一股劲儿 pull together; make joint efforts ② pinch; tweak: ～了他一把 give him a pinch
另见 nǐng; nìng

**咛** níng 见"叮咛" dīngníng

**苎** níng 〈化〉 limonene

**狞** níng ferocious; hideous
【狞笑】 níngxiào grin hideously

**柠** níng
【柠檬】 níngméng lemon
◇～水 lemonade; lemon squash/ ～素〈化〉citrin; vitamin P/ ～酸〈化〉citric acid/ ～糖 lemon drops/ ～汁 lemon juice

**聍** níng 见"耵聍" dīngníng

**凝** níng ① congeal; curdle; coagulate: 用鲜血～成的战斗友谊 militant friendship cemented with blood ② with fixed attention: ～思 be lost in thought
【凝点】 níngdiǎn 〈物〉 condensation point
【凝固】 nínggù solidify
◇～点〈物〉 solidifying point/ ～汽油弹 〈军〉 napalm bomb/ ～浴 〈纺〉 coagulating bath
【凝华】 nínghuá 〈气〉 sublimate ◇ ～核 sublimation nucleus
【凝灰岩】 nínghuīyán 〈地〉 tuff
【凝集】 níngjí 〈化〉 agglutinate ◇ ～素 agglutinin
【凝结】 níngjié coagulate; congeal; condense: 湖面上～了一层薄冰。A thin layer of ice formed over the lake.
◇～剂〈化〉coagulant/ ～力 coagulability/ ～物 coagulum
【凝聚】 níngjù ① (of vapour) condense: 荷叶上～着晶莹的露珠。Glistening dewdrops have formed on the lotus leaves./ 南京长江大桥～着中国工人阶级的高度智慧。The Changjiang River Bridge at Nanjing is an embodiment of the superb wisdom of the Chinese working class. ②〈化〉coacervation
◇～层 coacervate
【凝练】 nínglìan concise; condensed; compact
【凝神】 níngshén with fixed (或 concentrated, rapt) attention: ～谛听 listen with rapt attention; listen attentively
【凝视】 níngshì gaze fixedly; stare
【凝析油】 níngxīyóu 〈石油〉 condensate
【凝血药】 níngxuèyào 〈医〉 coagulant
【凝滞】 níngzhì stagnate; move sluggishly: ～的目光 dull, staring eyes
【凝重】 níngzhòng dignified; imposing

## nǐng

**拧** nǐng ① twist; screw: ～开瓶盖 screw (或 twist) the cap off a bottle/ ～上盖子 screw a lid on/ ～紧螺丝 tighten up a screw ② wrong; mistaken: 他想说"小题大做", 说～了, 说成"大题小做"。He meant to say "make a mountain out of a molehill," but he got it the wrong way round and said "make a molehill out of a mountain". ③ differ; disagree; be at cross-purposes: 两个人越说越～。The more they talked, the more they disagreed.
另见 níng; nìng

## nìng

**宁** nìng ① rather; would rather; better ②〈书〉could there be: 山之险峻, ～有逾此? Could there be a mountain more precipitous than this? ③ (Nìng) a surname
另见 níng
【宁可】 nìngkě would rather; better: ～站着死, 绝不跪着生 would rather die on one's feet than live on one's knees/ 部队～绕道走, 也不踩庄稼。The troops would rather go by a roundabout way than tread on the crops./ ～小心一点。Better safe than sorry.
【宁肯】 nìngkěn would rather
【宁缺毋滥】 nìng quē wú làn rather go without than have something shoddy — put quality before quantity
【宁死不屈】 nìng sǐ bù qū rather die than submit (或 surrender)
【宁为玉碎, 不为瓦全】 nìng wéi yù suì, bù wéi wǎ quán rather be a shattered vessel of jade than an unbroken piece of pottery — better to die in glory than live in dishonour
【宁愿】 nìngyuàn 见"宁可"

**佞** nìng given to flattery: ～人 sycophant; toady

**泞** nìng 见"泥泞" nínìng

**拧** nìng 〈方〉 pigheaded; stubborn
另见 níng; nǐng

## niū

**妞** niū 〈口〉 girl

## niú

**牛** niú ① ox: 母～ cow/ 公～ bull ② (Niú) a surname
【牛蒡】 niúbàng 〈植〉great burdock ◇～子〈中药〉the achene of great burdock
【牛鼻子】 niúbízi the nose (或 muzzle) of an ox: 牵牛要牵～。We must lead an ox by the halter.
【牛车】 niúchē ox cart; bullock cart
【牛刀小试】 niúdāo xiǎo shì a master hand's first small display
【牛痘】 niúdòu ① cowpox ② smallpox pustule; vaccine pustule: 种～ give or get smallpox vaccination
【牛犊】 niúdú calf
【牛顿】 niúdùn 〈物〉 newton ◇～望远镜 Newtonian telescope
【牛耳】 niú'ěr 见"执牛耳" zhí niú'ěr
【牛肺疫】 niúfèiyì pleuropneumonia (of cattle)
【牛粪】 niúfèn cow dung
【牛鬼蛇神】 niúguǐ-shéshén monsters and demons — forces of evil; class enemies of all descriptions
【牛黄】 niúhuáng 〈中药〉 bezoar
【牛角】 niújiǎo ox horn ◇～画 horn mosaic/ ～制品 hornware
【牛角尖】 niújiǎojiān the tip of a horn — an insignificant or insoluble problem 参见"钻牛角尖" zuān niújiǎojiān

【牛劲】 niújìn ① great strength; tremendous effort ② stubbornness; obstinacy; tenacity: 这小伙子有股～，干一件事就非干到底不行。The lad is strong-willed; once he starts doing something, he won't leave off until he's finished it.
【牛栏】 niúlán cattle pen
【牛郎】 Niúláng the cowherd in the legend "the Cowherd and the Girl Weaver" ◇～星〈天〉Altair
【牛马】 niúmǎ oxen and horses — beasts of burden: 在旧社会，劳动人民过的是～不如的生活。In the old society the labouring people lived worse than beasts of burden.
【牛毛】 niúmáo ox hair: 多如～ as many as the hairs on an ox; countless; innumerable/ ～细雨 drizzle
【牛虻】 niúméng gadfly
【牛奶】 niúnǎi milk ◇～场 dairy/ ～糖 toffee
【牛腩】 niúnǎn 〈方〉 sirloin; tenderloin
【牛排】 niúpái beefsteak
【牛棚】 niúpéng cowshed
【牛皮】 niúpí ① cattlehide ②〔多用于〕: 吹～ talk big; brag/ ～大王 braggart
【牛皮糖】 niúpítáng a sticky candy
【牛皮癣】 niúpíxuǎn 〈医〉 psoriasis
【牛皮纸】 niúpízhǐ kraft paper
【牛脾气】 niúpíqi stubbornness; obstinacy; pigheadedness
【牛肉】 niúròu beef
【牛舌鱼】 niúshéyú tonguefish; tongue sole
【牛虱】 niúshī ox louse
【牛溲马勃】 niúsōu-mǎbó sth. cheap but useful
【牛头刨床】 niútóu bàochuáng 〈机〉 shaping machine; shaper
【牛头不对马嘴】 niútóu bù duì mǎzuǐ horses' jaws don't match cows' heads — incongruous; irrelevant
【牛蛙】 niúwā bullfrog
【牛尾】 niúwěi oxtail ◇ ～汤 oxtail soup
【牛尾鱼】 niúwěiyú flathead
【牛瘟】 niúwēn rinderpest; cattle plague
【牛膝】 niúxī 〈中药〉 the root of bidentate achyranthes (*Achyranthes bidentata*)
【牛仔裤】 niúzǎikù close-fitting pants; jeans

## niǔ

### 忸 niǔ
【忸怩】 niǔní blushing; bashful: ～作态 behave coyly; be affectedly shy

### 扭 niǔ ① turn round: 他～过头来看了一下。He looked over his shoulder. ② twist; wrench: 把树枝子～断 twist a twig and break it/ 用力把门～开 wrench the door open ③ sprain; wrench: ～了筋 wrench a tendon; sprain a muscle/ ～了腰 sprain one's back ④ roll; swing: 他走路一～一～的。He walks with a rolling gait. ⑤ seize; grapple with: ～送公安部门 seize sb. and hand him over to the public security authorities/ 两人～在一起。The two were grappling with each other.
【扭秤】 niǔchèng 〈物〉 torsion balance
【扭打】 niǔdǎ wrestle; grapple
【扭搭】 niǔda 〈口〉 walk with a swing; have a rolling gait
【扭角羚】 niǔjiǎolíng 〈动〉 takin
【扭结】 niǔjié twist together; tangle up
【扭亏增盈】 niǔ kuī zēng yíng make up deficits and increase surpluses
【扭力】 niǔlì 〈物〉 twisting (或 torsional, torque) force
【扭捏】 niǔnie be affectedly bashful: 有话快说，别扭扭捏捏的。Out with it. Don't be bashful.
【扭伤】 niǔshāng sprain; wrench: ～手腕 sprain one's wrist
【扭秧歌】 niǔ yāngge do the *yangko* dance
【扭转】 niǔzhuǎn ① turn round: 他～身子，向车间走去。He turned round and made for the workshop. ② turn back; reverse: ～局势 turn the tide; reverse a trend/ ～乾坤 bring about a radical change in the situation; reverse the course of events / ～被动局面 put an end to a passive state of affairs; regain the initiative/ 妄图～历史车轮 vainly attempt to turn back the wheel of history

### 纽 niǔ ① handle; knob: 秤～ the lifting cord of a steelyard/ 印～ the knob (或 handle) of a seal ② button: 衣～ button ③ bond; tie
【纽带】 niǔdài link; tie; bond: 友谊的～ ties of friendship/ 社会主义商业是工农业之间的重要～。Socialist trade is an important link between industry and agriculture.
【纽扣】 niǔkòu button
【纽襻】 niǔpàn button loop
【纽约】 Niǔyuē New York
【纽子】 niǔzi button

### 狃 niǔ be bound by; be constrained by: ～于习俗 be bound by custom

### 钮 niǔ ① 见"纽" niǔ ② 见"电钮" diànniǔ ③ (Niǔ) a surname

## niù

### 拗 niù stubborn; obstinate; difficult: 这老头子脾气很～。He is a difficult old fellow.
另见 ǎo; ào
【拗不过】 niùbuguò unable to dissuade; fail to talk sb. out of doing sth.: 他这个人脾气犟，你可～他。He is very obstinate; you won't be able to make him change his mind.

## nóng

### 农 nóng ①agriculture; farming: 务～ go in for agriculture ②peasant; farmer: 贫下中～ poor and lower-middle peasants/ 菜～ vegetable grower
【农产品】 nóngchǎnpǐn agricultural products; farm produce
【农场】 nóngchǎng farm: 国营～ state farm
【农村】 nóngcūn rural area; countryside; village ◇～电气化 electrification of the countryside/ ～集市 village fair; rural market/ ～人民公社 rural people's commune
【农贷】 nóngdài agricultural loans (或 credits)
【农夫】 nóngfū farmer
【农妇】 nóngfù 〈旧〉 peasant woman
【农户】 nónghù peasant household
【农会】 nónghuì peasant association (a mass organization led by the Chinese Communist Party) 又作"农协"
【农活】 nónghuó farm work
【农机】 nóngjī agricultural machinery; farm machinery
【农家】 nóngjiā peasant family ◇～肥 farm manure; farmyard manure
【农具】 nóngjù farm implements; farm tools
【农历】 nónglì the traditional Chinese calendar; the lunar calendar
【农林牧副渔】 nóng-lín-mù-fù-yú farming, forestry, animal husbandry, side-line production and fishery
【农忙】 nóngmáng busy season (in farming)
【农民】 nóngmín peasant; peasantry
◇～阶级 the peasantry/ ～起义 peasant uprising; peasant

revolt / ～协会 peasant association/ ～战争 peasant war

【农民运动讲习所】 Nóngmín Yùndòng Jiǎngxísuǒ the Peasant Movement Institute (directed by Comrade Mao Zedong in Guangzhou and later in Wuchang to train cadres for the peasant movement in the First Revolutionary Civil War, 1924-1927)

【农奴】 nóngnú serf ◇～制度 serf system; serfdom/ ～主 serf owner

【农渠】 nóngqú field ditch

【农时】 nóngshí farming season: 不违～ do farm work in the right season

【农事】 nóngshì farm work; farming

【农田】 nóngtián farmland; cropland; cultivated land ◇～基本建设 capital construction on farmland; farmland capital construction/ ～水利 irrigation and water conservancy/ ～水利建设 construction of water conservancy works

【农闲】 nóngxián slack season (in farming)

【农学】 nóngxué agronomy; agriculture ◇～家 agronomist

【农谚】 nóngyàn farmer's proverb; farmer's saying

【农药】 nóngyào agricultural chemical; farm chemical; pesticide ◇～污染 pesticide pollution

【农业】 nóngyè agriculture; farming ◇ ～地质学 agrogeology/ ～工程学 agricultural engineering/ ～工人 agricultural labourer; farm labourer; farm worker/ ～国 an agricultural country/ ～合作化 cooperative transformation of agriculture; agricultural cooperative (或 cooperation) movement/ ～化学 agricultural chemistry; agrochemistry/ ～机械 agricultural machinery; farm machinery/ ～集体化 the collectivization of agriculture/ ～气象学 agricultural meteorology; agrometeorology/ ～人口 agricultural population/ ～生产合作社 agricultural producers' cooperative/ ～生物学 agrobiology/ ～税 agricultural tax/ ～土壤学 agrology

【农业八字宪法】 nóngyè bā zì xiànfǎ the Eight-Point Charter for Agriculture (土 soil improvement, 肥 rational application of fertilizer, 水 water conservancy, 种 improved seed strains, 密 rational close planting, 保 plant protection, 管 field management and 工 improvement of farm implements)

【农业技术】 nóngyè jìshù agricultural technology; agrotechnique ◇～改造 the technical transformation of agriculture/ ～员 agrotechnician/ ～站 agrotechnical station

【农艺师】 nóngyìshī agronomist

【农艺学】 nóngyìxué agronomy

【农作物】 nóngzuòwù crops

**侬** nóng ①〈方〉 you ②〔用于旧诗文〕I

**浓** nóng ① dense; thick; concentrated: ～烟 dense smoke; thick smoke/ ～墨 thick, dark ink/ ～茶 strong tea/ ～硫酸 concentrated sulphuric acid ② (of degree or extent) great; strong: 兴趣很～ take a great interest in sth./ 玫瑰花香味很～。The rose has a heavy fragrance.

【浓度】 nóngdù consistency; concentration; density: 矿浆～ pulp density/ 当量～〈化〉 equivalent concentration

【浓厚】 nónghòu ① dense; thick: ～的云层 thick clouds ② strong; pronounced: ～的地方色彩 pronounced (或 marked) local colour/ ～的封建意识 a strong feudal mentality/ 孩子们对中国革命的历史兴趣很～。The children take a great interest in the history of the Chinese revolution.

【浓积云】 nóngjīyún 〈气〉 cumulus congestus

【浓眉】 nóngméi heavy (或 bushy, thick) eyebrows: ～大眼 heavy features

【浓密】 nóngmì dense; thick: ～的枝叶 thick foliage

【浓缩】 nóngsuō 〈化〉 concentrate; enrich ◇～物 concentrate/ ～铀 enriched uranium

【浓艳】 nóngyàn rich and gaudy: 色彩～ in gaudy colours

【浓郁】 nóngyù strong; rich: 桂花发出～的香味。Osmanthus blossoms give off (或 exhale) a rich perfume./ 这些作品具有～的农村生活气息。These works have a strong flavour of rural life.

【浓重】 nóngzhòng dense; thick; strong: 雾越发～了。The fog became thicker still./ 他画的花卉,设色十分～。His paintings of flowers are distinguished by their rich colours.

**哝** nóng

【哝哝】 nóngnong talk in undertones; murmur

**脓** nóng pus

【脓包】 nóngbāo ①〈医〉 pustule ② worthless fellow; good-for-nothing

【脓疮】 nóngchuāng running sore

【脓尿】 nóngniào 〈医〉 pyuria

【脓胸】 nóngxiōng 〈医〉 pyothorax

【脓肿】 nóngzhǒng 〈医〉 abscess: 肝～ liver abscess/ 阑尾～ appendicular abscess

**秾** nóng 〈书〉 luxuriant

## nòng

**弄** nòng ① play with; fool with: 小孩儿爱～沙土。Children like to play with sand./ 你别～闹钟了。Stop fooling with that alarm clock. ② do; manage; handle; get sb. or sth. into a specified condition: ～饭 prepare a meal; cook/ 你来不及了,我替你～吧。You haven't got enough time; let me do it for you./ 他这一说反把我～糊涂了。His explanation only made me feel more puzzled than ever./ 他把衣服～脏了。He got his clothes dirty./ 有些问题还需要～清楚。Certain questions have yet to be clarified./ ～得不好,就会前功尽弃。If we don't do a good job now, all the work we've done will be wasted. ③ get; fetch: 你去～点水来。Go and get some water. ④ play: ～手段 play tricks

另见 lòng

【弄错】 nòngcuò make a mistake; misunderstand: 你～了。You've got it wrong.

【弄好】 nònghǎo ① do well: 把事情～ do a good job ② finish doing sth.: 计划～了没有? Is the plan ready?

【弄坏】 nònghuài ruin; put out of order; make a mess of: 把事情～ make a mess of things

【弄假成真】 nòng jiǎ chéng zhēn what was make-believe has become reality

【弄僵】 nòngjiāng bring to a deadlock; deadlock

【弄巧成拙】 nòng qiǎo chéng zhuō try to be clever only to end up with a blunder; outsmart oneself

【弄清】 nòngqīng make clear; clarify; gain a clear idea of; understand fully: ～问题所在 get to the heart of the problem; clarify the point at issue/ ～情况 gain a clear idea of the situation; find out the real situation/ ～事实 set the facts straight/ ～是非 thrash out the rights and wrongs; distinguish right from wrong

【弄权】 nòngquán manipulate power for personal ends

【弄死】 nòngsǐ put to death; kill

【弄通】 nòngtōng get a good grasp of: 认真看书学习,～马克思主义。Read and study conscientiously and get a good grasp of Marxism.

【弄虚作假】 nòngxū-zuòjiǎ practise fraud; employ trickery; resort to deception
【弄糟】 nòngzāo make a mess of; mess up; bungle; spoil: 他一插手，就把事情全都～了。His meddling made a mess of everything.

## nòu

**耨** nòu 〈书〉 ① weeding hoe ② weeding

## nú

**奴** nú ① bondservant; slave ② enslave
【奴才】 núcai flunkey; lackey: 帝国主义的～ a lackey of imperialism ◇ ～相 servile behaviour; servility; shameless fawning
【奴化】 núhuà enslave ◇ ～政策 policy of enslavement
【奴隶】 núlì slave
◇～起义 slave uprising/ ～社会 slave society/ ～占有制度 slave-owning system/ ～主 slave owner; slaveholder/ ～主义 slavishness; slavish mentality
【奴仆】 núpú servant; lackey
【奴性】 núxìng servility; slavishness
【奴颜婢膝】 núyán-bìxī subservient; servile
【奴役】 núyì enslave; keep in bondage: 反抗帝国主义的～和压迫 resist enslavement and oppression by the imperialists/ 剥削阶级用种种手段来～劳动人民。The exploiting classes try every means to keep the toiling masses in slavery.

**孥** nú 〈书〉 ① sons and daughters; children ② wife and children

**驽** nú 〈书〉 ① inferior horse; jade ② (of a person) dull; incompetent
【驽钝】 núdùn 〈书〉 dull; stupid
【驽马】 númǎ 〈书〉 inferior horse; jade: ～千里，功在不舍。If a jade travels a thousand *li*, it's only through perseverance.

## nǔ

**努** nǔ ① put forth (strength); exert (effort): ～劲儿 put forth all one's strength ② protrude; bulge: ～着眼睛 with bulging eyes ③ injure oneself through overexertion: 箱子太沉，你别扛，看～着。Don't carry that heavy trunk, or you'll strain yourself.
【努力】 nǔlì make great efforts; try hard; exert oneself: ～工作 work hard/ ～发展生产 actively expand production/ 为实现科学技术现代化而～奋斗 exert oneself in the struggle for the modernization of science and technology/ 尽最大～ do one's utmost; do the best one can/ 大家再努一把力。Let's make still greater efforts./ 学好一门外语要作出极大的～。It takes great effort to master a foreign language./ ～办好广播，为全中国人民和全世界人民服务。Strive to do broadcasting work well and serve the people of China and the world.
【努嘴】 nǔzuǐ pout one's lips as a signal: 我向他努努嘴，让他先说。I pouted my lips at him, hinting that he should speak first.

**弩** nǔ crossbow
【弩弓】 nǔgōng crossbow

**胬** nǔ
【胬肉】 nǔròu a triangular mass of mucous membrane growing from the inner corner of the eye
【胬肉攀睛】 nǔròu pān jīng 〈中医〉 pterygium

## nù

**怒** nù anger; rage; fury: 发～ get angry; fly into a rage (或 passion)/ ～骂 curse furiously
【怒不可遏】 nù bùkě è be beside oneself with anger; boil with rage
【怒潮】 nùcháo ① angry tide; raging tide: 革命～汹涌澎湃。The raging tide of revolution surges forward. ② 〈地〉 (tidal) bore
【怒斥】 nùchì angrily rebuke; indignantly denounce
【怒冲冲】 nùchōngchōng in a rage; furiously
【怒发冲冠】 nùfà chōng guān bristle with anger; be in a towering rage (或 passion)
【怒放】 nùfàng in full bloom: 山花～。The mountain flowers are in full bloom./ 心花～ be wild with joy
【怒号】 nùháo howl; roar: 狂风～。A violent wind is howling.
【怒吼】 nùhǒu roar; howl: 狂风呼啸，大海～。The wind howled and the sea roared./ 示威群众的～震天动地。The angry shouts of the demonstrators rent the air.
【怒火】 nùhuǒ flames of fury; fury: 满腔～ be filled with fury/ ～中烧 be burning with anger (或 wrath)/ 压不住心头的～ be unable to restrain one's fury; be unable to control one's anger
【怒目】 nùmù glaring eyes; fierce stare: ～而视 stare angrily; look daggers at; glare at; glower at
【怒气】 nùqì anger; rage; fury: ～冲冲 in a great rage/ ～冲天 be in a towering rage (或 passion); give way to unbridled fury
【怒容】 nùróng an angry look: ～满面 a face contorted with anger; look very angry
【怒色】 nùsè an angry look: 面带～ wear an angry look
【怒视】 nùshì glare at; glower at; scowl at
【怒涛】 nùtāo furious (或 raging) billows: ～澎湃 billows raging with great fury
【怒形于色】 nù xíng yú sè betray one's anger; look angry
【怒族】 Nùzú the Nu nationality, living in Yunnan

## nǚ

**女** nǚ ① woman; female: ～教师 woman teacher/ ～大夫 woman doctor/ ～售货员 saleswoman/ ～运动员 sportswoman/ ～民兵 militiawoman/ ～演员 actress/ ～英雄 heroine/ ～飞行员 aviatrix/ ～职工 women staff members and women workers/ ～学生 girl student ② daughter; girl: 子～ sons and daughters; children
【女厕所】 nǚcèsuǒ ① women's lavatory (或 toilet); ladies' room ②〔用于公共厕所门上〕 Ladies; Women
【女车】 nǚchē woman's bicycle; lady's bicycle
【女低音】 nǚdīyīn 〈乐〉 alto
【女儿】 nǚ'ér daughter; girl
【女儿墙】 nǚ'érqiáng 〈建〉 parapet (wall)
【女方】 nǚfāng the bride's side; the wife's side
【女服务员】 nǚfúwùyuán ① air hostess; stewardess ② waitress
【女高音】 nǚgāoyīn 〈乐〉 soprano
【女工】 nǚgōng woman worker

【女红】 nǚgōng needlework
【女孩】 nǚhái girl
【女皇】 nǚhuáng empress
【女家】 nǚjiā the bride's side; the wife's family
【女眷】 nǚjuàn the womenfolk of a family
【女郎】 nǚláng young woman; maiden; girl
【女流】 nǚliú 〈贬〉 the weaker sex
【女朋友】 nǚpéngyou girl friend
【女人】 nǚrén woman; womenfolk
【女人】 nǚren 〈口〉 wife
【女色】 nǚsè woman's charms: 好～ be fond of women
【女神】 nǚshén goddess
【女生】 nǚshēng woman student; girl student; schoolgirl
【女声】 nǚshēng 〈乐〉 female voice ◇～合唱 women's chorus; female chorus
【女士】 nǚshì (a polite term for a woman, married or unmarried) lady; madam: ～们,先生们 ladies and gentlemen
【女王】 nǚwáng queen
【女巫】 nǚwū witch; sorceress
【女性】 nǚxìng ① the female sex ② woman: 新～ a modern woman; emancipated women
【女修道院】 nǚxiūdàoyuàn convent
【女婿】 nǚxu ① son-in-law ②〈口〉 husband
【女贞】 nǚzhēn 〈植〉 glossy privet (*Ligustrum lucidum*) ◇～子 〈中药〉 the fruit of glossy privet
【女真】 Nǚzhēn Nüzhen (Nuchen), an ancient nationality in China
【女中音】 nǚzhōngyīn 〈乐〉 *mezzo-soprano*
【女主角】 nǚzhǔjué feminine lead; leading lady
【女主人】 nǚzhǔren hostess
【女子】 nǚzǐ woman; female ◇～单(双)打 women's singles (doubles)/ ～团体赛 women's team event

**钕** nǚ 〈化〉 neodymium (Nd)

## nǜ

**衄** nǜ 〈书〉 ① nosebleed ② be defeated in battle

## nuǎn

**暖** nuǎn ① warm; genial: 天～了。It's getting warm. ② warm up: ～一～手 warm one's hands/ 阶级情谊～胸怀。Proletarian class feeling warms the heart.
【暖调】 nuǎndiào 〈美术〉 warm colour tone; warm tone
【暖房】 nuǎnfáng ①〈方〉 greenhouse; hothouse ② call on sb. who has moved into a new home to congratulate him
【暖锋】 nuǎnfēng 〈气〉 warm front
【暖烘烘】 nuǎnhōnghōng nice and warm
【暖壶】 nuǎnhú ① thermos flask; thermos bottle ② a teapot with a cosy ③ metal or earthen hotwater bottle
【暖和】 nuǎnhuo ① warm; nice and warm: 炉子一着,屋里就～了。The room became warm when the fire got going. ② warm up: 屋里有火,快进来～～吧! There is a fire in here; come in and warm yourself up.
【暖帘】 nuǎnlián quilted door curtain
【暖流】 nuǎnliú 〈地〉〈气〉 warm current
【暖瓶】 nuǎnpíng thermos flask; thermos bottle
【暖气】 nuǎnqì central heating ◇～片 (heating) radiator
【暖气团】 nuǎnqìtuán 〈气〉 warm air mass
【暖色】 nuǎnsè 〈美术〉 warm colour
【暖水瓶】 nuǎnshuǐpíng thermos flask; thermos bottle

## nüè

**疟** nüè malaria
另见 yào
【疟疾】 nüèji malaria; ague: 恶性～ pernicious malaria
【疟蚊】 nüèwén malarial (或 malaria) mosquito
【疟原虫】 nüèyuánchóng plasmodium; malarial parasite

**虐** nüè cruel; tyrannical
【虐待】 nüèdài maltreat; ill-treat; tyrannize
【虐杀】 nüèshā cause sb.'s death by maltreating him; kill sb. with maltreatment
【虐政】 nüèzhèng tyrannical government; tyranny

## nuó

**挪** nuó move; shift: 劳驾把桌子～到那边儿去。Move the table over there, please.
【挪动】 nuódòng move; shift: 往前～几步 move a few steps forward
【挪借】 nuójiè borrow money for a short time; get a short-term loan
【挪威】 Nuówēi Norway ◇～人 Norwegian/ ～语 Norwegian (language)
【挪窝儿】 nuówōr 〈方〉 ① move to another place ② move (house)
【挪用】 nuóyòng ① divert (funds): 不得～基本建设资金。The fund earmarked for capital construction is not to be diverted to any other purpose. ② misappropriate; embezzle: ～公款 misappropriation (或 embezzlement) of public funds

**娜** nuó 见"婀娜" ēnuó; "袅娜" niǎonuó

**傩** nuó exorcise
【傩神】 nuóshén a god which drives away pestilence

## nuò

**诺** nuò ① promise: 许～ promise ② yes: ～～连声 keep on saying "yes"
【诺言】 nuòyán promise: 履行～ fulfil one's promise; keep one's word

**喏** nuò 〈叹〉[表示让人注意自己所指示的事物]: ～,这不就是你的那把雨伞? There! Isn't that your umbrella?/ ～,～,要这样挖,才挖得快。Look, do it this way and you can dig faster.

**搦** nuò 〈书〉 hold in the hand: ～管 hold a pen; take up the pen

**锘** nuò 〈化〉 nobelium (No)

**懦** nuò cowardly; weak
【懦夫】 nuòfū coward; craven; weakling: ～懒汉思想 the coward's and sluggard's way of thinking
【懦弱】 nuòruò cowardly; weak

**糯** nuò glutinous (cereal)
【糯稻】 nuòdào glutinous rice
【糯米】 nuòmǐ polished glutinous rice

# O

## ō

**喔** ō 〈叹〉〔表示了解〕: ～,原来是你! Oh, so it's you!/ ～,原来你也这么想! Oh, so you feel the same way!
另见 wō

【喔唷】 ōyō 〈叹〉〔表示惊讶、痛苦〕: ～,这么大的西瓜! Oh, what a big watermelon!/ ～,好疼! Ouch, it hurts!

**噢** ō 见"喔" ō

## ó

**哦** ó 〈叹〉〔表示将信将疑〕: ～! 会有这样的事? What! How can that be? 或 Is that really so?
另见 é; ò

## ǒ

**嚄** ǒ 〈叹〉〔表示惊讶〕: ～! 亩产都超千斤了! What! The per-*mu* yield has topped 1,000 *jin*?
另见 huō

## ò

**哦** ò 〈叹〉〔表示领会、醒悟〕: ～,我懂了。Oh! I see. 或 Oh! Now I understand./ ～,我想起来了。Ah, I've got it./ ～! 你是老王。Ah, so you're Lao Wang.
另见 é; ó

## ōu

**区** Ōu a surname
另见 qū

**讴** ōu ① sing ② folk songs; ballads

【讴歌】 ōugē sing the praises of; celebrate in song; eulogize

**欧** Ōu ① short for Europe ② a surname

【欧化】 ōuhuà Europeanize; westernize

【欧椋鸟】 ōuliángniǎo starling

【欧姆】 ōumǔ 〈物〉 ohm ◇～表 ohmmeter/ ～定律 Ohm's law

【欧鸲】 ōuqú 〈动〉 robin; redbreast

【欧亚大陆】 Ōu-Yà dàlù Eurasia

【欧阳】 Ōuyáng a surname

【欧洲】 Ōuzhōu Europe ◇～经济共同体 the European Economic Community (E.E.C.)/ ～美元 Eurodollar

**瓯** ōu 〈方〉 bowl; cup

**殴** ōu beat up; hit: ～伤 beat and injure

【殴打】 ōudǎ beat up; hit: 互相～ come to blows; exchange blows

**鸥** ōu gull: 海～ sea gull

## ǒu

**呕** ǒu vomit; throw up

【呕吐】 ǒutù vomit; throw up; be sick: ～不止 keep vomiting

【呕心】 ǒuxīn exert one's utmost effort: ～之作 a work embodying one's utmost effort

【呕心沥血】 ǒuxīn-lìxuè shed one's heart's blood; take infinite pains; work one's heart out

【呕血】 ǒuxuè 〈医〉 haematemesis; spitting blood

**偶** ǒu ① image; idol: 木～ wooden image; puppet ② even (number); in pairs: 无独有～。It is not a unique instance, but has its counterpart. ③ mate; spouse: 配～ spouse ④ by chance; by accident; once in a while; occasionally: ～遇 meet by chance/ ～一为之 do sth. once in a while

【偶氮染料】 ǒudàn rǎnliào azo dyes

【偶尔】 ǒu'ěr once in a while; occasionally: 我们～见面。We see each other once in a long while.

【偶发】 ǒufā accidental; chance; fortuitous: ～事件 a chance occurrence

【偶犯】 ǒufàn ① casual offence ② casual offender

【偶合】 ǒuhé coincidence: 他们在这一点上见解一致完全是～。It is a mere coincidence that they see eye to eye on this point.

【偶然】 ǒurán accidental; fortuitous; chance: ～现象 accidental (或 fortuitous) phenomena/ ～遇见一个老朋友 run into an old acquaintance; meet an old friend by chance; come across an old friend ◇ ～误差 accidental error/ ～性〈哲〉 contingency; fortuity; chance

【偶数】 ǒushù 〈数〉 even number ◇～页〈印〉 even page

【偶蹄动物】 ǒutí dòngwù an artiodactyl

【偶像】 ǒuxiàng image; idol ◇～崇拜 idolatry/ ～化 idolize

**耦** ǒu 见"偶" ǒu②③

【耦合】 ǒuhé 〈物〉 coupling: 机械～ mechanical coupling ◇ ～电路 coupled (或 coupling) circuit/ ～系数 coupling coefficient

**藕** ǒu lotus root

【藕断丝连】 ǒuduàn-sīlián the lotus root snaps but its fibres stay joined — apparently severed, actually still connected

【藕粉】 ǒufěn lotus root starch

【藕荷】 ǒuhé pale pinkish purple 又作"藕合"

【藕节儿】 ǒujiér joints of a lotus root

【藕色】 ǒusè pale pinkish grey

## òu

**沤** òu soak; steep; macerate: ～麻 ret flax or hemp

【沤肥】 òuféi ① make compost ② wet compost; waterlogged compost

**怄** òu 〈方〉 ① irritate; annoy ② be irritated (或 annoyed)

【怄气】 òuqì be difficult and sulky: 怄了一肚子气 have a bellyful of repressed grievances/ 不要～。Don't sulk.

# P

## pā

**趴** pā ① lie on one's stomach; lie prone: ～在地上打靶 lie on the ground for target practice ② bend over; lean on: 他正～在桌子上画图。He was bending over the desk, drawing.

**啪** pā 〈象〉〔形容放枪、拍掌等声音〕: ～～两声枪响。Bang, bang, went the gun.

【啪嚓】 pāchā 〈象〉〔形容东西落地、撞击或碰碎等声音〕: ～一声，碗掉在地上碎了。The bowl dropped and broke with a crash.

【啪嗒】 pādā 〈象〉〔形容东西落地或撞击的声音〕: ～～的脚步声 pattering footsteps/ 打字机～～地响着。The typewriter was clattering away.

**葩** pā 〈书〉 flower: 一朵艺术上的奇～ a wonderful work of art

## pá

**扒** pá ① gather up; rake up: 把枯树叶～在一起 rake together the dead leaves ② stew; braise: ～羊肉 stewed mutton/ ～鸡 braised chicken
另见 bā

【扒犁】 páli 〈方〉 sledge; sleigh

【扒手】 páshǒu pickpocket

**杷** pá 见"枇杷" pípa

**爬** pá ① crawl; creep: 蛇正往洞里～。The snake is crawling into a hole. ② climb; clamber; scramble: ～树(绳，山) climb a tree (rope, mountain)/ 墙上～满了常春藤。The wall is covered all over with ivy.

【爬虫】 páchóng reptile

【爬竿】 págān 〈体〉 ① pole-climbing ② climbing pole

【爬犁】 páli 〈方〉 sledge; sleigh

【爬山虎】 páshānhǔ 〈植〉 Boston ivy

【爬行】 páxíng crawl; creep: 跟在别人后面一步一步地～ trail behind others at a snail's pace ◇～动物 reptile

【爬泳】 páyǒng 〈体〉 the crawl

**耙** pá ① rake: 木～ wooden rake ② make smooth with a rake; rake: 把地～平 rake the soil level
另见 bà

【耙子】 pázi rake

**琶** pá

【琶音】 páyīn 〈乐〉 *arpeggio*

**掱** pá

【掱手】 páshǒu pickpocket

**筢** pá bamboo rake

【筢子】 pázi bamboo rake

## pà

**怕** pà ① fear; dread; be afraid of: 一不～苦，二不～死 fear neither hardship nor death/ 不～疲劳 not be afraid of fatigue/ 不～任何困难 brave all difficulties ② I'm afraid; I suppose; perhaps: 事情～不这么简单。I'm afraid things are not so simple./ 这个瓜～有十几斤吧。This melon weighs more than ten *jin*, I should think.

【怕生】 pàshēng (of a child) be shy with strangers

【怕事】 pàshì be afraid of getting into trouble: 胆小～ timid and overcautious

【怕死】 pàsǐ fear (或 be afraid of) death: 革命不～，～不革命。Revolutionaries don't fear death; cowards don't make revolution. ◇～鬼 coward

【怕羞】 pàxiū coy; shy; bashful

**帕** pà handkerchief

【帕米尔高原】 Pàmǐ'ěr Gāoyuán the Pamirs

## pāi

**拍** pāi ① clap; pat; beat: ～巴掌 clap one's hands/ ～掉身上的土 pat one's clothes to get the dust off/ ～桌子大骂 strike the table and pour out a stream of abuse/ ～球 bounce a ball/ ～翅膀 flap wings; beat wings/ 惊涛～岸 mighty waves beating the shore ② bat; racket: 乒乓球～ ping-pong bat; table-tennis bat/ 苍蝇～儿 flyswatter ③ 〈乐〉 beat; time: 一小节四～ four beats in (或 to) a bar/ 这歌是几～的？—是 4/4 拍的。What time is the song in? — It's in four-four time. ④ take (a picture); shoot: ～照 take a picture/ ～电影 shoot (或 make) a film/ 这部小说已～成电影了。This novel has been made into a film. ⑤ send (a telegram, etc.): ～电报 send a telegram ⑥ 〈口〉 flatter; fawn on: ～马 lick sb.'s boots; flatter

【拍案】 pāi'àn strike the table (in anger, surprise, admiration, etc.): ～而起 smite the table and rise to one's feet

【拍案叫绝】 pāi àn jiào jué thump the table and shout "bravo!": 精彩的表演令人～。We were overwhelmed with admiration for the superb performance.

【拍板】 pāibǎn ① clappers ② beat time with clappers ③ rap the gavel: ～成交 strike a bargain; clinch a deal ④ have the final say; give the final verdict: 这事儿得由党委书记来～。The secretary of the Party Committee has the final say in this matter.

【拍打】 pāida pat; slap: ～身上的雪 pat (或 beat) the snow off one's clothes/ 波浪～着船舷 waves lapping against the sides of the boat

【拍发】 pāifā send (a telegram): ～消息 cable a dispatch or report

【拍号】 pāihào 〈乐〉 time signature

【拍节器】 pāijiéqì 〈乐〉 metronome

【拍马屁】 pāi mǎpì 〈口〉 lick sb.'s boots; flatter; soft-soap; fawn on

【拍卖】 pāimài ① auction ② selling off goods at reduced prices; sale

【拍摄】 pāishè take (a picture); shoot: ～一张照片 take a

photo/ ～特写镜头 shoot a close-up/ 把舞剧～成电影 film a dance drama/ 在～外景 be on location

【拍手】 pāishǒu clap one's hands; applaud: ～叫好 clap and shout "bravo!"/ ～称快 clap and cheer (usu. on being avenged)

【拍照】 pāizhào take a picture; photograph

【拍纸簿】 pāizhǐbù (writing) pad

【拍子】 pāizi ① bat; racket: 羽毛球(网球)～ badminton (tennis) racket ② 〈乐〉 beat; time: 打～ beat time/ 二(三,四)～ duple (triple, quadruple) time/ 单(复)～ simple (compound) time

## pái

**排** pái ① arrange; put in order: ～座位 arrange seats/ 把课桌～整齐 put the desks in order/ 节目单已～好。The programme has been arranged. ② row; line: 前(后)～ front (back) row ③ 〈量〉〔用于成行列的东西〕 row; line: 一～椅子 a row (或 line) of chairs ④ 〈军〉 platoon ⑤ rehearse: ～戏 rehearse a play ⑥ raft: 竹(木)～ bamboo (timber) raft ⑦ exclude; eject; discharge: ～脓 discharge pus/ 把水～出去 drain the water away ⑧ push: ～闼直入 push the door open and go straight in ⑨ pie: 苹果～ apple pie 另见 pǎi

【排版】 páibǎn 〈印〉 composing; typesetting: 机器～ machine composition/ 照相～ photocomposition

【排比】 páibǐ 〈语〉 parallelism

【排笔】 páibǐ broad brush comprising a row of pen-shaped brushes

【排场】 páichang ostentation and extravagance: 讲～ go in for ostentation and extravagance

【排斥】 páichì repel; exclude; reject: 同种电荷互相～。Two like electric charges repel one another./ ～异己 exclude outsiders; discriminate against those who hold different views

【排除】 páichú get rid of; remove; eliminate: ～障碍 remove (或 get over) an obstacle/ ～故障 fix a breakdown/ ～私心杂念 get rid of all selfish ideas/ 不能～这种可能性 cannot rule out this possibility/ 下定决心,不怕牺牲,～万难,去争取胜利。Be resolute, fear no sacrifice and surmount every difficulty to win victory.

【排挡】 páidǎng gear (of a car, tractor, etc.)

【排队】 páiduì form a line; line up; queue up: ～买票 line up for tickets/ ～上车 queue up for a bus/ ～前进 march in a column/ 把问题分类～ arrange the problems in order of importance and urgency

【排骨】 páigǔ spareribs: 糖醋～ spareribs in sweet-sour sauce

【排灌】 páiguàn irrigation and drainage ◇～设备 irrigation and drainage equipment/ ～网 irrigation and drainage network/ ～站 irrigation and drainage pumping station

【排行】 páiháng seniority among brothers and sisters: 他～第三。He's the third child of the family.

【排挤】 páijǐ push aside; push out; squeeze out; elbow out: 拉拢一些人,～一些人 draw some in, push others out/ 互相～ each trying to squeeze the other out

【排解】 páijiě ① mediate; reconcile: ～纠纷 mediate a dispute; reconcile a quarrel ② 见"排遣"

【排涝】 páilào drain flooded (或 waterlogged) fields

【排雷】 páiléi 〈军〉 removal of mines; mine clearance

【排练】 páiliàn rehearse: ～节目 have a rehearsal

【排列】 páiliè ① arrange; range; put in order: ～成行 arrange in a row (或 line, column)/ 按字母顺序～ arrange in alphabetical order ② 〈数〉 permutation

【排卵】 páiluǎn 〈生〉 ovulate ◇ ～期 period of ovulation

【排难解纷】 páinàn-jiěfēn mediate a dispute; pour oil on troubled waters

【排尿】 páiniào urinate; micturate ◇ ～困难〈医〉 dysuria

【排炮】 páipào (artillery) salvo; volley of guns

【排气】 páiqì 〈机〉 exhaust ◇ ～管 exhaust pipe

【排遣】 páiqiǎn divert oneself from loneliness or boredom

【排枪】 páiqiāng volley of rifle fire

【排球】 páiqiú volleyball

【排山倒海】 páishān-dǎohǎi topple the mountains and overturn the seas: 以～之势 with the momentum of an avalanche; with the force of a landslide and the power of a tidal wave

【排笙】 páishēng 〈乐〉 a reed pipe wind instrument with a keyboard

【排水】 páishuǐ drain off (或 away) water ◇～工程 drainage works/ ～沟渠 escape canal/ ～管 drain pipe/ ～管道 drainage pipeline

【排水量】 páishuǐliàng ① displacement: ～两万二千吨的远洋轮船 an ocean-going liner of 22,000 tons displacement ② discharge capacity (of a spillway, etc.)

【排他性】 páitāxìng exclusiveness ◇～集团 exclusive bloc

【排头】 páitóu the person at the head of a procession; file leader

【排外】 páiwài exclusive; antiforeign: 盲目～ blind opposition to everything foreign ◇～主义 exclusivism; exclusionism; xenophobia; antiforeignism

【排尾】 páiwěi the last person in a row; the person at the end of a row

【排泄】 páixiè ① drain: ～不畅 drainage difficulty ② excrete ◇～器官 excretory organ/ ～物 excreta; excrement

【排演】 páiyǎn rehearse

【排印】 páiyìn typesetting and printing

【排长】 páizhǎng platoon leader

【排中律】 páizhōnglǜ 〈逻〉 the law of excluded middle

【排钟】 páizhōng 〈乐〉 chimes

【排字】 páizì composing; typesetting ◇ ～车间 composing room/ ～工人 typesetter; compositor/ ～机 typesetter; composing machine/ ～架 composing frame/ ～手托 composing stick

**徘** pái

【徘徊】 páihuái ① pace up and down ② hesitate; waver: ～歧路 hesitate at the crossroads ③ 〈经〉 fluctuate

**牌** pái ① plate; tablet: 门～儿 doorplate/ 车～儿 number plate (on a vehicle)/ (衣帽间等的)号码～ check/ 招～ shop sign; signboard/ 路～ signpost ② brand: 名～儿货 goods of a well-known brand ③ cards, dominoes, etc.: 一副扑克～ a pack of playing cards

【牌匾】 páibiǎn board (fixed to a wall or the lintel of a door)

【牌坊】 páifāng memorial archway (或 gateway)

【牌号】 páihào ① the name of a shop; shop sign ② trademark

【牌价】 páijià ① list price ② market quotation

【牌楼】 páilou ① *pailou*, decorated archway ② temporary ceremonial gateway

【牌位】 páiwèi memorial tablet

【牌照】 páizhào license plate; license tag

【牌子】 páizi ① plate; sign: 存车～ tally (for parking a bicycle) ② brand; trademark: 老～ old brand; well-known brand

## pǎi

**迫** pǎi
另见 pò
【迫击炮】 pǎijīpào mortar ◇～弹 mortar projectile; mortar shell

**排** pǎi
另见 pái
【排子车】 pǎizichē large handcart

## pài

**派** pài ① group; school; faction; clique: 党～ political parties and groups/ 学～ school of thought/ 左～ leftists/ 各～政治力量 the different political forces ② style; manner and air: 气～ bearing ③〈量〉ⓐ〔用于派别〕: 三～学者 scholars of three different schools ⓑ〔用于景色、气象、声音、语言等，前面用"一"字〕: 好一～北国风光！What magnificent northern scenery!/ 一～胡言！A pack of nonsense! ④ send; dispatch; assign; appoint: ～代表团出席大会 send a delegation to the conference/ ～他担任车间主任 appoint him head of the workshop/ ～兵 dispatch troops/ ～工作 set sb. a task/ ～勤务 assign fatigue duties
【派别】 pàibié group; school; faction: ～斗争 factional strife
【派不是】 pài bùshi put the blame on sb.: 他自己不认错，还派别人的不是。Instead of admitting his mistakes, he shifted the blame onto others.
【派出机构】 pàichū jīgòu agency: 地区一级是省的～。The organ of state power at the prefectural level is an agency of the provincial authorities.
【派出所】 pàichūsuǒ local police station; police substation
【派饭】 pàifàn meals in peasant homes arranged for cadres, students, etc., temporarily staying at a village; arranged meals: 吃～ board with different peasant families by arrangement
【派款】 pàikuǎn impose levies of money
【派力斯呢】 pàilìsīní〈纺〉palace
【派遣】 pàiqiǎn send; dispatch: ～代表团 send a delegation/ ～驻外全权代表 dispatch a plenipotentiary (envoy) to a foreign country
【派生】 pàishēng derive: 由此～出来的问题 the questions derived therefrom ◇～词〈语〉derivative
【派头】 pàitóu style; manner: 他～真不小！He certainly puts on quite a show!
【派系】 pàixì factions (within a political party, etc.)
【派性】 pàixìng factionalism: 资产阶级～ bourgeois factionalism
【派驻】 pàizhù〈外〉accredit: ～联合国的代表 a representative accredited to the United Nations

**哌** pài
【哌嗪】 pàiqín〈化〉piperazine

**湃** pài 见"滂湃" pāngpài; "澎湃" pēngpài

## pān

**潘** Pān a surname

**攀** pān ① climb; clamber: ～着绳子往上爬 climb up a rope hand over hand ② seek connections in high places ③ involve; implicate: 乱咬乱～ make wild charges, while under interrogation, to implicate others
【攀扯】 pānchě implicate (sb. in a crime)
【攀登】 pāndēng climb; clamber; scale: ～峭壁 climb up a cliff/ ～科学技术新高峰 scale new heights in science and technology
【攀龙附凤】 pānlóng-fùfèng play up to people of power and influence; put oneself under the patronage of a bigwig
【攀亲】 pānqīn ① claim kinship: ～道故 claim ties of blood or friendship ②〈方〉arrange a match
【攀雀】 pānquè〈动〉penduline tit
【攀谈】 pāntán engage in small talk; chitchat
【攀缘】 pānyuán ① climb; clamber: ～而上 climb up ②〈旧〉climb the social ladder through pull ◇～植物 climber
【攀折】 pānzhé pull down and break off (twigs, etc.): 请勿～花木。Please don't pick the flowers.

## pán

**爿** pán〈方〉① slit bamboo or chopped wood ②〈量〉: 一～水果店 a fruit shop

**胖** pán〈书〉easy and comfortable: 心广体～ carefree and contented; fit and happy
另见 pàng

**盘** pán ① tray; plate; dish: 茶～儿 tea tray ② sth. shaped like or used as a tray, plate, etc.: 磨～ millstone/ 棋～ chessboard ③〈旧〉market quotation; current price ④ coil; wind; twist: 把绳子～起来 coil up the rope/ ～山小道 a winding mountain path/ 莫干山上下都是一十八～。There are eighteen hairpin bends on the way up Mogan Mountain. ⑤ build: ～炕 build a *kang*/ ～灶 build a brick cooking range ⑥ check; examine; interrogate: ～根究底 try to get to the heart of a matter ⑦〈旧〉transfer: ～店 transfer the ownership of a shop ⑧〈体〉game; set: 下一～棋 play a game of chess/ 以六比零胜了这一～ win the set in six straight games ⑨〈量〉: 一～香 a coil of incense/ 一～磨 a mill; a millstone/ 一～电线 a coil of wire/ 一～菜 a dish ⑩ (Pán) a surname
【盘剥】 pánbō practise usury; exploit: 重利～ lend money at usurious rates; exploit by lending money at exorbitant rates of interest
【盘查】 pánchá interrogate and examine: ～可疑的人 question a suspicious person
【盘缠】 pánchan〈口〉money for the journey; travelling expenses 又作"盘费"
【盘秤】 pánchèng a steelyard with a pan
【盘存】 páncún take inventory
【盘道】 pándào winding mountain paths; bends
【盘点】 pándiǎn check; make an inventory of: ～存货 take stock
【盘根错节】 pángēn-cuòjié ① with twisted roots and gnarled branches — complicated and difficult to deal with ② (of old social forces) deep-rooted
【盘古】 Pángǔ Pan Gu, creator of the universe in Chinese mythology: 自从～开天地 since Pan Gu separated heaven and earth; since the beginning of the world
【盘管】 pánguǎn〈机〉coil (pipe)
【盘桓】 pánhuán〈书〉stay; linger: ～终日 linger about all day long/ 我们在杭州～了几天，游览了各处名胜。We spent a few days sight-seeing in Hangzhou.
【盘簧】 pánhuáng〈机〉coil spring

【盘货】 pánhuò make an inventory of stock on hand; take stock: 今日～，停业半天。Closed for half a day for stocktaking.
【盘诘】 pánjié 〈书〉 cross-examine; question
【盘踞】 pánjù illegally or forcibly occupy; be entrenched: 我军一举歼灭了～海岛的敌人。At one stroke our troops wiped out the enemy who were entrenched on the island.
【盘库】 pánkù make an inventory of goods in a warehouse
【盘弄】 pánnòng play with; fiddle with; fondle
【盘儿菜】 pánrcài ready-to-cook dish of meat, vegetables, etc. (sold at the food market)
【盘绕】 pánrǎo twine; coil; wreathe: 长长的藤葛～在树身上。Long vines twine round the tree.
【盘算】 pánsuan calculate; figure; plan: 我们～了一下，产量将增加百分之五。We figured that the output would increase by five per cent.
【盘梯】 pántī winding staircase; spiral staircase
【盘条】 pántiáo 〈冶〉 wire rod
【盘腿】 pántuǐ cross one's legs: ～坐在炕上 sit cross-legged on a *kang*
【盘问】 pánwèn cross-examine; interrogate
【盘香】 pánxiāng incense coil
【盘旋】 pánxuán ① spiral; circle; wheel: 车队沿山路～而上。The motorcade spiralled up the mountain./ 飞机～侦察。The aircraft circled for reconnaissance./ 雄鹰在空中～。Eagles were wheeling in the air./ 这件事在我脑子里～了好久。I've been turning this over in my mind for a long while. ② linger; stay: 他在暖房里～了半天才离开。He lingered in the greenhouse for some time before he left.
【盘羊】 pányáng 〈动〉 argali
【盘帐】 pánzhàng check (或 audit, examine) accounts
【盘子】 pánzi tray; plate; dish

**槃** pán 见"涅槃" nièpán

**磐** pán
【磐石】 pánshí huge rock: 坚如～ as solid as a rock/ ～般的团结 rocklike unity; monolithic unity

**蹒** pán
【蹒跚】 pánshān walk haltingly; limp; hobble

**蟠** pán coil; curl
【蟠桃】 pántáo ① flat peach ② peach of immortality in Chinese mythology

## pàn

**判** pàn ① distinguish; discriminate ② obviously (different): 前后～若两人 be quite a different person; be no longer one's old self/ 两个世界～然不同。The two worlds are markedly different. ③ judge; decide: ～案 decide a case/ ～卷子 mark examination papers ④ sentence; condemn: ～五年徒刑 be sentenced to five years' imprisonment
【判别】 pànbié differentiate; distinguish: ～真假 distinguish the true from the false ◇～式 〈数〉 discriminant
【判处】 pànchǔ sentence; condemn: ～死刑 sentence sb. to death
【判词】 pàncí 〈法〉 court verdict
【判定】 pàndìng judge; decide; determine
【判断】 pànduàn ① judge; decide; determine: ～是非 judge (或 decide) what is right and what is wrong/ ～情况 assess (或 size up) the situation/ 你～得很正确。Your judgment is sound./ 正确的～来源于周密的调查研究。Correct judgments stem from thorough investigation and study. ② 〈逻〉 judgment ◇～词 〈语〉 a grammatical term for the character 是 used as a link word to form a compound predicate with a noun or pronoun/ ～力 judgment
【判据】 pànjù 〈物〉 criterion
【判决】 pànjué 〈法〉 court decision; judgment: ～有罪(无罪) pronounce sb. guilty (not guilty) ◇～书 court verdict; written judgment
【判例】 pànlì 〈法〉 legal precedent; judicial precedent: 国际法～ cases in international law
【判明】 pànmíng distinguish; ascertain: ～是非 distinguish between right and wrong/ ～真相 ascertain the facts/ ～责任 establish responsibility (for what has happened)
【判若云泥】 pàn ruò yún-ní as far removed as heaven is from earth; poles apart
【判罪】 pànzuì declare guilty; convict

**叛** pàn betray; rebel against: ～党 turn renegade from the Party; turn traitor to the Party; betray the Party/ ～国 betray one's country; commit treason
【叛变】 pànbiàn betray one's country, party, etc.; turn traitor; turn renegade; defect: ～投敌 turn traitor and go over to the enemy
【叛军】 pànjūn rebel army; rebel forces; insurgent troops
【叛离】 pànlí betray; desert
【叛乱】 pànluàn armed rebellion: 煽动～ incite people to rise in rebellion/ 镇压反革命～ suppress (或 put down) a counterrevolutionary rebellion
【叛卖】 pànmài betray; sell: ～祖国 betray one's country ◇～活动 traitorous activity; acts of treason
【叛逆】 pànnì ① rebel against; revolt against ② rebel: 封建礼教的～ a rebel against feudal ethics
【叛徒】 pàntú traitor; renegade; turncoat

**盼** pàn ① hope for; long for; expect: ～解放 long for liberation/ ～复。I await your reply. ② look: 左顾右～ glance right and left; look round
【盼头】 pàntou sth. hoped for and likely to happen; good prospects: 这事有～了。This business is looking hopeful now. 或 Things are looking up.
【盼望】 pànwàng hope for; long for; look forward to: ～着救星共产党 look forward to the coming of our liberator, the Communist Party/ 伤员们日夜～回前方。Day and night the wounded soldiers longed to return to the front.

**袢** pàn ① 见"襻" pàn ② 见"袷袢" qiāpàn

**畔** pàn ① side; bank: 河～ river bank; riverside/ 湖～ the shore of a lake ② the border of a field

**襻** pàn ① a loop for fastening a button: 纽～儿 button loop ② sth. shaped like a button loop or used for a similar purpose: 鞋～儿 shoe strap/ 篮子～儿 the handle of a basket ③ fasten with a rope, string, etc.; tie: 用绳子～上 fasten with a rope/ ～上几针 put in a few stitches

## pāng

**乓** pāng 〈象〉〔形容枪声、关门声、东西砸破声等〕 bang: 门～地一声关上了。The door banged shut.

**滂** pāng

【滂湃】 pāngpài (of water) roaring and rushing
【滂沱】 pāngtuó torrential: 大雨～。It's raining in torrents./ 涕泗～ let loose a flood of tears

**膀** pāng swell: ～肿 swollen; bloated
另见 bǎng; páng

## páng

**彷** páng
【彷徨】 pánghuáng walk back and forth, not knowing which way to go; hesitate: ～歧途 hesitate at the crossroads

**庞** páng ① huge ② innumerable and disordered ③ face: 面～ face ④ (Páng) a surname
【庞大】 pángdà huge; enormous; colossal; gigantic: 机构～ an unwieldy organization/ 开支～ an enormous expenditure/ ～的正规军 a massive regular army
【庞然大物】 pángrán dàwù huge monster; colossus; giant: 帝国主义看起来是个～，其实是纸老虎。Imperialism, which looks like a huge monster, is really a paper tiger.
【庞杂】 pángzá numerous and jumbled: 议论～ numerous and jumbled views/ 机构～ cumbersome administrative structure

**旁** páng ① side: 马路两～ both sides of the street/ 站在路～ stand by the roadside ② other; else: 还有～的建议吗? Any other suggestions?/ 他没说～的话。He didn't say anything else. ③ lateral radical of a Chinese character (e.g. 亻, 氵, etc.)
【旁白】 pángbái aside (in a play)
【旁边】 pángbiān side: 我坐在他～。I sat by his side./ ～有一棵树。There is a tree nearby.
【旁观】 pángguān look on; be an onlooker: 袖手～ look on with folded arms ◇～者 onlooker; bystander; spectator
【旁观者清】 pángguānzhě qīng the spectator sees most clearly; the onlooker sees the game best
【旁及】 pángjí take up (along with sth. more important): 他专攻历史,～考古。He is an historian, but also takes an interest in archaeology.
【旁路】 pánglù 〈电〉 bypass ◇～电容器 bypass capacitor
【旁门】 pángmén side door
【旁门左道】 pángmén-zuǒdào 见"左道旁门" zuǒdào-pángmén
【旁敲侧击】 pángqiāo-cèjī attack by innuendo; make oblique references
【旁人】 pángrén other people
【旁若无人】 páng ruò wú rén act as if there was no one else present — self-assured or supercilious
【旁听】 pángtīng be a visitor at a meeting, in a school class, etc. ◇～生 auditor/ ～席 visitors' seats; public gallery
【旁通管】 pángtōngguǎn 〈机〉 bypass pipe
【旁系亲属】 pángxì qīnshǔ collateral (relative)
【旁压力】 pángyālì 〈物〉 lateral pressure
【旁征博引】 pángzhēng-bóyǐn quote copiously from many sources
【旁证】 pángzhèng circumstantial evidence; collateral evidence
【旁支】 pángzhī collateral branch (of a family)

**膀** páng
另见 bǎng; pāng
【膀胱】 pángguāng (urinary) bladder ◇～炎 cystitis/ ～造影 cystography/ ～镜 cystoscope

**磅** páng
另见 bàng
【磅礴】 pángbó ① boundless; majestic: 五岭逶迤腾细浪，乌蒙～走泥丸。The Five Ridges wind like gentle ripples And the majestic Wumeng roll by, globules of clay. ② fill; permeate: 共产主义思想正～于全世界。Communist ideology is sweeping the world with tremendous momentum.

**螃** páng
【螃蟹】 pángxiè crab

**鳑** páng
【鳑鲏】 pángpí bitterling

## pǎng

**耪** pǎng loosen soil with a hoe: ～地 hoe the soil

**髈** pǎng 〈方〉 thigh

## pàng

**胖** pàng fat; stout; plump: 他～起来了。He's getting fat. 或 He's putting on weight.
另见 pán
【胖大海】 pàngdàhǎi 〈中药〉 the seed of boat-fruited sterculia (*Sterculia scaphigera*)
【胖乎乎】 pànghūhū plump; chubby; pudgy: 这个小孩的脸蛋～的。This child has plump (或 chubby) cheeks./ 婴儿的～的小手 an infant's pudgy fingers
【胖头鱼】 pàngtóuyú bighead; variegated carp
【胖子】 pàngzi fat person; fatty

## pāo

**抛** pāo ① throw; toss; fling: ～球 throw (或 toss) a ball/ ～出一项欺骗性的提案 dish out (或 trot out) a phoney proposal ② leave behind; cast aside: 跑到第三圈，他已经把别人远远地～在后面了。On the third lap he left the other runners far behind./ 被革命的潮流～在后面了 be tossed to the rear by the revolutionary current/ ～进历史的垃圾堆 be relegated to the garbage heap of history
【抛光】 pāoguāng 〈机〉 polishing; buffing: 摩擦～ burnishing ◇～剂 polishing compound; polish/ ～轮 polishing wheel; buff
【抛锚】 pāomáo ① drop anchor; cast anchor ② (of vehicles) break down: 汽车中途～了。The car broke down on the way.
【抛弃】 pāoqì abandon; forsake; cast aside: 被人民所～ be abandoned (或 spurned) by the people/ 我们决不会～真正的朋友。We shall never forsake (或 desert) our true friends.
【抛射体】 pāoshètǐ 〈物〉 projectile
【抛售】 pāoshòu sell (goods, shares, etc.) in big quantities, usu. in anticipation of or in order to bring about a fall in price
【抛头露面】 pāotóu-lùmiàn (of a woman in feudal society) show one's face in public
【抛物线】 pāowùxiàn 〈数〉 parabola
【抛掷】 pāozhì 〈书〉 throw; cast
【抛砖引玉】 pāozhuān-yǐnyù 〈谦〉 cast a brick to attract jade — offer a few commonplace remarks by way of introduc-

tion so that others may come up with valuable opinions

**泡** pāo ① sth. puffy and soft: 豆腐～儿 beancurd puff ② spongy: 这木料发～。This wood is spongy. ③〈量〉〔用于屎和尿〕: 撒一～尿 make water; urinate; piss/ 拉一～屎 have a shit

另见 pào

【泡桐】 pāotóng 〈植〉 paulownia

【泡子】 pāozi 〈方〉 a small lake

**脬** pāo 见"尿脬" suīpāo

## páo

**刨** páo ① dig; excavate: ～坑儿 dig a hole (或 pit)/ ～地 dig the ground/ ～白薯 dig (up) sweet potatoes ②〈口〉 excluding; not counting; minus: 十五天～去五天,只剩下十天了。Fifteen minus five — there are only ten days to go now./ 他家～去老人和孩子,有三个全劳力。There are three able-bodied workers in his family as well as some old folk and children.

另见 bào

【刨根儿】 páogēnr get to the root (或 bottom) of the matter: 他这人就爱～问底儿。He's never satisfied until he gets to the bottom of things.

【刨煤机】 páoméijī coal plough

**庖** páo 〈书〉 ① kitchen ② cook: 名～ famous *chef*

【庖厨】 páochú 〈书〉 kitchen

【庖代】 páodài 〈书〉 见"代庖" dàipáo

**咆** páo

【咆哮】 páoxiāo roar; thunder: 黄河～。The Huanghe River roars on./ ～如雷 be in a thundering rage; roar with rage

**狍** páo 〈动〉 roe deer

【狍子】 páozi 〈动〉 roe deer

**炮** páo 〈中医〉 prepare Chinese medicine by roasting it in a pan

另见 bāo; pào

【炮制】 páozhì ①〈中医〉 the process of preparing Chinese medicine, as by roasting, baking, simmering, etc. ②〈贬〉 concoct; cook up: ～反动纲领 concoct a reactionary programme/ 如法～ act after the same fashion; follow suit

**袍** páo robe; gown

【袍哥】 páogē 〈旧〉 (a member of) a reactionary gang in southwest China before liberation

【袍笏登场】 páohù dēngchǎng 〈讽〉 dress up and go on stage — said of a puppet upon his take-over

【袍泽】 páozé 〈书〉 fellow officers

【袍子】 páozi robe; gown: 皮～ fur robe

## pǎo

**跑** pǎo ① run: 他～得很快。He can run very fast./ ～百米 run the 100-metre dash/ 火车在飞～。The train is racing along. ② run away; escape; flee: 别让特务～了。See that the enemy agent doesn't escape./ 车带～气了。Air is escaping from the tyre./ 汽油都～了。The gas has all evaporated. ③〈方〉 walk: 我们～了五里路。We walked five *li*. ④ run about doing sth.; run errands: ～材料 run about collecting material or making inquiries/ ～买卖 be a commercial traveller/ 我～了好几家商店,才找到那种扳手。I had to run around to several shops to get that wrench./ 你这辆大车一天能～几个来回? How many round trips can your cart make in a day? ⑤ away; off: 吓～ frighten away/ 桌上的报纸叫风给刮～了。The newspaper blew off the table.

【跑表】 pǎobiǎo 〈体〉 stopwatch

【跑步】 pǎobù run; march at the double: ～走!(口令) At the double, quick march! / ～前进!(口令) Double time!

【跑车】 pǎochē racing bike

【跑单帮】 pǎo dānbāng travel around trading on one's own

【跑道】 pǎodào ①〈航空〉 runway ②〈体〉 track: 煤渣～ cinder track/ 塑料～ plastic track

【跑电】 pǎodiàn leakage of electricity

【跑江湖】 pǎo jiānghú wander about, making a living as an acrobat, fortuneteller, physiognomist, etc.

【跑警报】 pǎo jǐngbào run for shelter during an air raid

【跑垒】 pǎolěi 〈棒、垒球〉 baserunning ◇～员 base runner

【跑龙套】 pǎo lóngtào play a bit role; be a utility man

【跑马】 pǎomǎ ① have a ride on a horse ② horse race ◇～场 racecourse; the turf

【跑跑颠颠】 pǎopǎodiāndiān bustle about; be on the go: 老大娘在服务站成天～的,一心一意给大伙办事。The old lady is bustling about every day at the neighbourhood service centre, serving the people wholeheartedly.

【跑墒】 pǎoshāng 〈农〉 evaporation of water in soil

【跑堂儿的】 pǎotángrde 〈旧〉 waiter (in a restaurant)

【跑腿儿】 pǎotuǐr 〈口〉 run errands; do legwork: 我没干多少,就是跑跑腿儿。I didn't do much, just a bit of running around.

【跑鞋】 pǎoxié running shoes; track shoes

## pào

**泡** pào ① bubble: 肥皂～儿 soap bubbles/ 冒～儿 send up bubbles; rise in bubbles ② sth. shaped like a bubble: 手上起了～ get (或 raise) blisters on one's palm/ 电灯～ electric light bulb ③ steep; soak: 把种子放在温水里～一下 steep the seeds in lukewarm water/ 他是在苦水里～大的。He was brought up in bitter misery. ④ dawdle: 别瞎～了,快把工作做完! Stop dawdling and finish your work!

另见 pāo

【泡菜】 pàocài pickled vegetables; pickles

【泡茶】 pàochá make tea

【泡饭】 pàofàn ① soak cooked rice in soup or water ② cooked rice reheated in boiling water; thick gruel (from recooked rice)

【泡蘑菇】 pào mógu ① use delaying tactics; play for time; play a game of stalling ② importune; pester

【泡沫】 pàomò foam; froth: 啤酒～ the head on a glass of beer ◇～玻璃 cellular glass/ ～混凝土 foam concrete/ ～灭火器 foam extinguisher/ ～塑料 foamed plastics/ ～橡胶 foam rubber; froth rubber

【泡泡纱】 pàopàoshā 〈纺〉 seersucker

【泡影】 pàoyǐng visionary hope, plan, scheme, etc.; bubble: 化为～ vanish like soap bubbles; melt into thin air; go up in smoke; come to nothing

【泡罩塔】 pàozhàotǎ 〈化〉 bubble-cap tower (或 column)

**炮** pào ① big gun; cannon; artillery piece ② cannon, one of the pieces in Chinese chess

另见 bāo; páo
【炮兵】 pàobīng artillery; artillerymen ◇～部队 artillery (troops)/ ～连 battery/ ～阵地 artillery position; gun emplacement
【炮弹】 pàodàn (artillery) shell
【炮轰】 pàohōng bombard; shell
【炮灰】 pàohuī cannon fodder
【炮火】 pàohuǒ artillery fire; gunfire: 掩护～ (artillery) fire cover/ ～支援 artillery support/ ～准备 artillery preparation
【炮击】 pàojī bombard; shell
【炮架】 pàojià gun carriage; gun mount
【炮舰】 pàojiàn gunboat ◇～政策 gunboat policy/ ～外交 gunboat diplomacy
【炮口】 pàokǒu gun muzzle ◇～焰 muzzle flash
【炮楼】 pàolóu blockhouse
【炮声】 pàoshēng report (of a gun): ～隆隆 boom (或 roar) of guns
【炮手】 pàoshǒu gunner; artilleryman
【炮栓】 pàoshuān breechblock
【炮塔】 pàotǎ gun turret; turret
【炮台】 pàotái fort; battery
【炮膛】 pàotáng bore (of a gun)
【炮艇】 pàotǐng gunboat
【炮筒】 pàotǒng barrel (of a gun)
【炮筒子】 pàotǒngzi a person who shoots off his mouth
【炮尾】 pàowěi gun breech
【炮位】 pàowèi emplacement
【炮眼】 pàoyǎn ① porthole; embrasure ② blasthole; dynamite hole; borehole
【炮衣】 pàoyī gun cover
【炮战】 pàozhàn artillery action (或 engagement)
【炮仗】 pàozhang firecracker
【炮座】 pàozuò gun platform

**疱** pào blister; bleb
【疱疹】 pàozhěn ① bleb ② herpes: 带状～ herpes zoster; zoster ◇～净〈药〉 idoxuridine

## pēi

**呸** pēi 〈叹〉〔表示唾弃或斥责〕: pah; bah; pooh: ～! 胡说八道! Bah! That's nonsense!

**胚** pēi 〈生〉 embryo
【胚层】 pēicéng 〈生〉 germinal layer: 内～ entoderm/ 外～ ectoderm/ 中～ mesoderm
【胚根】 pēigēn 〈植〉 radicle
【胚盘】 pēipán 〈动〉 blastodisc; germinal disc
【胚乳】 pēirǔ 〈植〉 endosperm
【胚胎】 pēitāi 〈生〉 embryo ◇～学 embryology/ ～移植〈牧〉 embryo transfer; embryonic implantation
【胚芽】 pēiyá 〈植〉 plumule
【胚轴】 pēizhóu 〈植〉 plumular axis
【胚珠】 pēizhū 〈植〉 ovule

## péi

**陪** péi accompany; keep sb. company: 我～你到农场去。I'll accompany you to the farm./ ～外宾参观工厂 show foreign visitors round a factory/ ～病人 look after a patient
【陪伴】 péibàn accompany; keep sb. company
【陪绑】 péibǎng ① be taken to the execution ground together with those to be executed as a form of intimidation ② (of an innocent person) be criticized or punished together with the guilty
【陪衬】 péichèn ① serve as a contrast or foil; set off: 红旗在雪山的～下,显得分外鲜艳。The red flags stood out in sharp relief against the snow mountains. ② foil; setoff
【陪嫁】 péijià 〈方〉 dowry
【陪客】 péike a guest invited to a dinner party to help entertain the guest of honour
【陪审】 péishěn 〈法〉 ① act (或 serve) as an assessor (in a law case) ② serve on a jury ◇ ～团 jury/ ～员 juror; juryman/ ～制 jury system
【陪送】 péisong 〈口〉 ① give a dowry to a daughter; dower ② dowry
【陪同】 péitóng accompany: ～前往参观 accompany sb. on a visit/ 外宾们由革委会主任～,观看了演出。The foreign guests, accompanied by the chairman of the revolutionary committee, attended a performance.
【陪葬】 péizàng be buried with the dead

**培** péi ① bank up with earth; earth up: 在玉米根上～点土 earth up the roots of maize ② cultivate; foster; train: ～干 train cadres
【培土】 péitǔ 〈农〉 hill up; earth up
【培修】 péixiū repair (earthwork): ～堤坝 repair a dyke
【培训】 péixùn cultivate; train: ～赤脚医生 train barefoot doctors
【培养】 péiyǎng ① foster; train; develop: ～积极分子 foster activists/ 在党的～教育下 be nurtured and educated by the Party/ ～学生自学能力 foster the students' ability to study on their own/ ～和造就无产阶级革命事业的接班人 train and bring up successors for the cause of proletarian revolution ②〈生〉 culture: ～细菌 culture of bacteria ◇～基〈生〉culture medium/ ～瓶 culture bottle
【培育】 péiyù cultivate; foster; breed: ～小麦新品种 breed new varieties of wheat/ ～树苗 grow saplings
【培植】 péizhí cultivate; foster; train: ～中草药 cultivate medicinal herbs/ ～私人势力 build up one's personal influence

**赔** péi ① compensate; pay for: 玻璃是我打碎的,由我来～。I broke the glass, so I'll pay for it. ② stand a loss: ～钱 lose money in business transactions
【赔本】 péiběn sustain losses in business; run a business at a loss
【赔不是】 péi bùshi apologize
【赔偿】 péicháng compensate; pay for: ～损失 compensate (或 pay) for a loss; make good a loss/ 照价～ compensate according to the cost/ 保留要求～的权利 reserve the right to demand compensation for losses/ 战争～ war reparations ◇～费 damages/ ～协定 reparations agreement
【赔款】 péikuǎn ① pay an indemnity; pay reparations ② indemnity; reparations
【赔礼】 péilǐ offer (或 make) an apology; apologize
【赔笑】 péixiào smile obsequiously or apologetically
【赔帐】 péizhàng pay for the loss of cash or goods entrusted to one
【赔罪】 péizuì apologize

**锫** péi 〈化〉 berkelium (Bk)

**裴** Péi a surname

## pèi

**沛** pèi copious; abundant: ～然降雨。A copious rain began to fall./ 精力充～ be full of energy

**佩** pèi ① wear (at the waist, etc.): ～刀 wear a sword/ 腰～手枪 carry a pistol in one's belt ② an ornament worn as a pendant at the waist in ancient times: 玉～ jade pendant ③ admire: 他的国际主义精神十分可～。His internationalist spirit is altogether admirable.

【佩带】 pèidài wear: ～徽章 wear a badge

【佩服】 pèifu admire: 他机智勇敢,令人～。One must admire his resourcefulness and courage.

**帔** pèi short embroidered cape (worn over a woman's shoulders)

**配** pèi ① join in marriage: 婚～ marry ② mate (animals): ～马 mate horses ③ compound; mix: ～颜色 mix colours (on a palette)/ ～药 make up a prescription ④ distribute according to plan; apportion: ～售 ration ⑤ find sth. to fit or replace sth. else: ～钥匙 have a key made to fit a lock/ ～零件 replace parts ⑥ match: 颜色不～。The colours don't match./ 粉红～浅蓝。Pink and light blue go well together./ 这段唱腔要用笛子来～。This passage is to be sung to the accompaniment of a bamboo flute. ⑦ deserve; be worthy of; be qualified: 她不～当一名代表。She is not qualified to be a representative.

【配备】 pèibèi ① allocate; provide; fit out: ～拖拉机 allocate tractors/ ～助手 provide assistants/ 这些舰艇～有大口径炮。These ships are fitted with large-calibre guns. ② dispose (troops, etc.); deploy: 按地形～火力 dispose firepower according to terrain/ 从敌人～弱的地方插进去 thrust in where the enemy deployment is weak ③ outfit; equipment: 现代化的～ modern equipment

【配搭】 pèidā supplement; match; accompany: 这出戏,主角儿配角儿～得很整齐。Both the major and minor roles of the play are competently filled.

【配电】 pèidiàn 〈电〉 (power) distribution ◇ ～盘 distributor/ ～网 distribution network/ ～线路 distribution line

【配殿】 pèidiàn side hall in a palace or temple

【配对】 pèiduì ① pair: 这两只手套不～儿。These two gloves don't match (或 aren't a pair). ② 〈口〉 (of animals) mate

【配方】 pèifāng ① fill (或 make up) a prescription ② directions for producing chemicals or metallurgical products

【配合】 pèihé coordinate; cooperate; concert: ～作战 coordination of military operations/ ～行动 take concerted action/ 起～作用 play a supporting role/ 青年团要～党的中心工作。The Youth League must coordinate its activities with the central tasks of the Party./ 治疗过程中,病人和大夫～得很好。The patient cooperated very well with the doctors during the treatment. ◇ ～饲料〈牧〉 mixed feed; compound feed

【配给】 pèijǐ ration ◇～证 ration card (或 book)/ ～制 ration system

【配件】 pèijiàn ① fittings (of a machine, etc.): 窗～ window fittings/ 管子～ pipe fittings ② a replacement

【配角】 pèijué ① appear with another leading player; costar ② supporting role; minor role

【配料】 pèiliào 〈冶〉 burden: 高炉～ blast-furnace burden ◇～表 burden sheet/ ～计算 burden calculation

【配偶】 pèi'ǒu 〔多用于法令文件〕 spouse

【配色】 pèishǎi match colours; harmonize colours

【配属】 pèishǔ 〈军〉 attach (troops to a subordinate unit)

【配水闸】 pèishuǐzhá 〈水〉 distribution structure

【配糖物】 pèitángwù 〈化〉 glucoside

【配套】 pèitào form a complete set: 就地生产,就地～ manufacture complete sets of equipment locally ◇ ～工程〈水〉 conveyance system/ ～器材 necessary accessories

【配套成龙】 pèitào-chénglóng 见"成龙配套" chénglóng-pèitào

【配伍】 pèiwǔ 〈药〉 compatibility of medicines ◇～禁忌 incompatibility

【配戏】 pèixì support a leading actor; play a supporting role

【配烟】 pèiyān tobacco blending

【配药】 pèiyào make up a prescription

【配页】 pèiyè 〈印〉 gathering (leaves of a book)

【配音】 pèiyīn dub (a film, etc.): 给外国电影～ dub foreign films in Chinese ◇～机 dubbing machine

【配乐】 pèiyuè dub in background music

【配制】 pèizhì compound; make up: ～药剂 compound medicines

【配置】 pèizhì dispose (troops, etc.); deploy: ～兵力 dispose forces/ 纵深～ disposition in depth

【配种】 pèizhǒng 〈牧〉 breeding ◇ ～率 breeding rate/ ～站 breeding station

【配子】 pèizǐ 〈生〉 gamete ◇ ～体 gametophyte

**旆** pèi 〈书〉 flag

**辔** pèi bridle: 鞍～ saddle and bridle

【辔头】 pèitóu bridle

**霈** pèi 〈书〉 heavy rain

## pēn

**喷** pēn ① spurt; spout; gush: 喷泉向空中～水。The fountain spurted water into the air./ 石油从井口～了出来。Oil gushed from the well. ② spray; sprinkle: 给花～点水 sprinkle some water on the flowers/ 往果树上～农药 spray fruit trees with insecticide
另见 pèn

【喷薄】 pēnbó gush; spurt: ～欲出的一轮红日 the emerging sun with all its shimmering rays

【喷出岩】 pēnchūyán 〈地〉 extrusive rock

【喷灯】 pēndēng blowtorch; blowlamp

【喷饭】 pēnfàn laugh so hard as to spew one's food; split one's sides with laughter: 令人～ sidesplitting; screamingly funny

【喷粉器】 pēnfěnqì 〈农〉 duster

【喷灌】 pēnguàn sprinkling irrigation; spray irrigation ◇ ～器 sprinkler

【喷壶】 pēnhú watering can; sprinkling can

【喷火器】 pēnhuǒqì 〈军〉 flamethrower

【喷浆】 pēnjiāng 〈建〉 ① whitewashing ② guniting

【喷漆】 pēnqī spray paint; spray lacquer ◇～枪 paint (spraying) gun

【喷气发动机】 pēnqì fādòngjī jet engine

【喷气式】 pēnqìshì jet-propelled ◇ ～飞机 jet plane; jet aircraft; jet/ ～客机 jet airliner

【喷气织机】 pēnqì zhījī air-jet loom

【喷枪】 pēnqiāng spray gun

【喷泉】 pēnquán fountain

【喷洒】 pēnsǎ spray; sprinkle: ～农药 spray insecticide

【喷射】 pēnshè spray; spurt; jet: ～火焰 spurt flames
【喷水池】 pēnshuǐchí fountain
【喷丝头】 pēnsītóu 〈纺〉 spinning jet; spinning nozzle ◇～牵伸 spinneret draft/ ～组件 spinneret assembly
【喷嚏】 pēntì sneeze: 打～ sneeze
【喷头】 pēntóu ① shower nozzle ② sprinkler head
【喷雾】 pēnwù spraying ◇～器 sprayer; atomiser
【喷子】 pēnzi sprayer; spraying apparatus
【喷嘴】 pēnzuǐ spray nozzle; spray head

## pén

**盆** pén basin; tub; pot: 脸～ washbasin/ 澡～ bathtub/ 花～ flowerpot
【盆地】 péndì 〈地〉 basin: 柴达木～ the Qaidam Basin
【盆花】 pénhuā potted flower
【盆景】 pénjǐng 〈工美〉 potted landscape; miniature trees and rockery
【盆腔】 pénqiāng 〈生理〉 pelvic cavity ◇～炎 pelvic infection
【盆汤】 péntāng bathtub cubicle

## pèn

**喷** pèn ① in season: 西瓜正在～儿上。Watermelons are in season now. ②〈量〉crop: 头～儿棉花 the first crop of cotton
另见 pēn
【喷香】 pènxiāng fragrant; delicious: 饭菜～。The dishes smell delicious.

## pēng

**怦** pēng 〈象〉〔形容心跳〕: 他的心～～地跳。His heart thumped (或 went pit-a-pat).

**抨** pēng
【抨击】 pēngjī attack (in speech or writing); assail; lash out at

**砰** pēng 〈象〉〔形容撞击或重物落地的声音〕: ～的一声，门关上了。The door banged shut./ ～的一声，木板倒下来了。The plank fell on the ground with a thump.

**烹** pēng ① boil; cook: ～茶 brew tea; make tea ② fry quickly in hot oil and stir in sauce: ～对虾 quick-fried prawns in brown sauce
【烹饪】 pēngrèn cooking; culinary art: 擅长～ be good at cooking; be a good cook ◇～法 cookery; cuisine; recipe
【烹调】 pēngtiáo cook (dishes): 中国式～ Chinese cooking; Chinese cuisine

**澎** pēng splash; spatter
另见 péng
【澎湃】 pēngpài surge: 大海中波涛～。Waves surge in the sea./ 汹涌～的革命浪潮 the surging waves of revolution/ 心潮～ feel an upsurge of emotion

## péng

**朋** péng friend: 良～ good friend/ 宾～满座。There was a houseful of guests. 或 Visitors filled all the seats.

【朋比为奸】 péngbǐ wéi jiān act in collusion with; conspire; collude; gang up
【朋党】 péngdǎng clique; cabal
【朋友】 péngyou ① friend ② boy friend or girl friend

**棚** péng ① canopy or awning of reed mats, etc.: 凉～ awning ② shed; shack: 牲口～ livestock shed/ 自行车～ bicycle shed
【棚车】 péngchē ①〈铁道〉 box wagon; boxcar ② covered truck
【棚户】 pénghù 〈方〉 slum-dwellers; shack-dwellers
【棚子】 péngzi 〈口〉 shed; shack: 草～ straw mat shed

**彭** Péng a surname

**蓬** péng ①〈植〉 bitter fleabane (*Erigeron acris*) ② fluffy; dishevelled: ～着头 with dishevelled hair ③〈量〉〔用于枝叶茂盛的花草等〕: 一～竹子 a clump of bamboo
【蓬勃】 péngbó vigorous; flourishing; full of vitality: ～发展的社会主义建设事业 flourishing socialist construction/ 新生事物～兴起。Newborn things are springing up vigorously.
【蓬莱】 Pénglái a fabled abode of immortals
【蓬松】 péngsōng fluffy; puffy: ～的头发 fluffy hair
【蓬头垢面】 péngtóu-gòumiàn with dishevelled hair and a dirty face; unkempt

**硼** péng 〈化〉 boron (B)
【硼砂】 péngshā borax; sodium borate ◇～玻璃 borax glass
【硼酸】 péngsuān boric acid ◇～盐 borate

**鹏** péng roc
【鹏程万里】 péngchéng wànlǐ (make) a roc's flight of 10,000 *li* — have a bright future

**澎** péng
另见 pēng
【澎湖列岛】 Pénghú Lièdǎo the Penghu Islands; the Penghus

**篷** péng ① covering or awning on a car, boat, etc. ② sail (of a boat): 扯起～来 hoist the sails
【篷布】 péngbù tarpaulin: 用～把货物盖上 cover the goods with a tarpaulin
【篷车】 péngchē 见"棚车" péngchē

**膨** péng
【膨大】 péngdà expand; inflate
【膨大海】 péngdàhǎi 见"胖大海" pàngdàhǎi
【膨脝】 pénghēng ①〈书〉 potbellied ②〈方〉 bulky; unwieldy
【膨体纱】 péngtǐshā 〈纺〉 bulk yarn
【膨胀】 péngzhàng expand; swell; dilate; inflate: 金属受了热就会～。Metals expand when they are heated./ 通货～ inflation
◇ ～计 〈物〉 dilatometer/ ～系数 〈物〉 coefficient of expansion (或 dilatation)/ ～性 expansibility

**蟛** péng
【蟛蜞】 péngqí amphibious crab; brackish-water crab

## pěng

**捧** pěng ① hold or carry in both hands: ～着一个西瓜 hold a watermelon in both hands/ 她双手～着孩子的脸。She cupped the child's face in her hands./ 他～起水来喝了

一大口。He scooped up some water with his hands and took a big mouthful. ②〈量〉〔用于能捧的东西〕: 一～枣儿 a double handful of dates ③ boost; exalt; extol; flatter: 把某人～上天 praise sb. to the skies

【捧场】 pěngchǎng ① be a member of a *claque* ② boost; sing the praises of; flatter: 无原则的～ unprincipled praise/ 警惕资产阶级的～。 Beware of flattery from the bourgeoisie.

【捧腹】 pěngfù split (或 shake, burst) one's sides with laughter: 令人～ set people roaring with laughter; make one burst out laughing/ ～大笑 be convulsed with laughter

## pèng

**碰** pèng ① touch; bump: 这件精密仪器,你可别～。Mind you don't touch this precision instrument./ 把墨水瓶～翻了 knock the ink-bottle over/ 头～在门上 bump one's head against the door/ 在事实面前～得头破血流 butt one's head against a wall of hard facts ② meet; run into: 在街上～到一个熟人 run into an acquaintance in the street/ ～到困难 run up against difficulties/ 挖河没挖多深就～上了流沙。Before we'd got very far in digging the canal, we met with quicksand./ 我没～着他。I didn't see him. ③ take one's chance: ～～机会 take a chance

【碰杯】 pèngbēi clink glasses

【碰壁】 pèngbì run up against a stone wall; be rebuffed: 到处～ run into snags and be foiled everywhere/ 凭主观办事一定～。If you do things subjectively, you'll just run into a stone wall.

【碰钉子】 pèng dīngzi meet with a rebuff: 碰了个软钉子 be tactfully rebuked; be mildly rebuffed

【碰簧锁】 pènghuángsuǒ spring lock

【碰见】 pèngjiàn meet unexpectedly; run into: 你猜我昨晚在首都体育馆～谁了? Who do you think I ran into at the Capital Stadium last night?

【碰巧】 pèngqiǎo by chance; by coincidence: 我～也在那儿。I happened to be there too. 或 It just so happened that I was there too./ 正要送孩子上县医院,～医疗队到村里来了。We were going to send the child to the county hospital when a medical team arrived in the village.

【碰锁】 pèngsuǒ spring lock

【碰头】 pèngtóu meet and discuss; put (our, your, their) heads together: 决定下次～的时间 decide on the time of the next meeting/ 他们一～,很快就把问题解决了。They put their heads together and promptly solved the problem. ◇ ～会 brief meeting (mainly to exchange information)

【碰一鼻子灰】 pèng yī bízi huī be snubbed; meet with a rebuff

【碰运气】 pèng yùnqì try one's luck; take a chance

【碰撞】 pèngzhuàng ① collide; run into: 一辆卡车从后面～了我们的汽车。A lorry ran into our car from behind. ②〈物〉collision; impact: 核～ nuclear collision/ ～负载 impact load

## pī

**丕** pī 〈书〉big; great: ～绩 great achievements

**批** pī ① slap: ～颊 slap sb.'s face; box sb.'s ear ② criticize; refute: 大～修正主义,大～资本主义,大干社会主义 criticize revisionism and capitalism in a big way and go all out to build socialism/ ～深～透 criticize penetratingly and thoroughly ③ write instructions or comments on (a report from a subordinate, etc.): ～文件 write instructions on documents ④ wholesale: ～购 buy goods wholesale ⑤〈量〉batch; lot; group: 新到的一～化肥 a new lot of chemical fertilizer/ 分～下乡 go to the countryside in separate batches/ 一大～积极分子 large numbers of activists/ 出动多～飞机 dispatch wave after wave of planes ⑥〈口〉fibres of cotton, flax, etc. ready to be drawn and twisted

【批驳】 pībó ① veto an opinion or a request from a subordinate body ② refute; criticize; rebut: 逐点予以～ refute point by point

【批次】 pīcì batch (of aircraft, etc.)

【批斗】 pīdòu criticize and denounce sb. (at a public meeting)

【批发】 pīfā ① wholesale ② (of an official document) be authorized for dispatch: 那份电报是由副部长～的。That telegram was authorized for dispatch by the vice-minister. ◇ ～部 wholesale department/ ～价格 wholesale price

【批复】 pīfù give an official, written reply to a subordinate body

【批改】 pīgǎi correct: ～作业 correct students' papers

【批号】 pīhào lot number; batch number

【批量】 pīliàng batch; lot: ～生产 batch process

【批判】 pīpàn ① criticize: ～修正主义 criticize revisionism ② critique: «哥达纲领～» *Critique of the Gotha Programme* ◇ ～会 criticism meeting; criticism session/ ～文章 critical article/ ～现实主义 critical realism

【批判地】 pīpànde critically; discriminatingly: ～吸收 critically assimilate; assimilate with discrimination

【批评】 pīpíng ① criticize: ～缺点和错误 criticize shortcomings and mistakes ② criticism: ～与自我～ criticism and self-criticism/ 马克思主义是科学真理,不怕～,它是～不倒的。Marxism is scientific truth; it fears no criticism and cannot be overthrown by criticism./ 党内～是坚强党的组织,增加党的战斗力的武器。Inner-Party criticism is a weapon for strengthening the Party organization and increasing its fighting capacity.

【批示】 pīshì written instructions or comments on a report, memorandum, etc. submitted by a subordinate

【批语】 pīyǔ ① remarks on a piece of writing ② 见"批示"

【批阅】 pīyuè read over (official papers); read and amend or comment on (writings, texts, etc.)

【批注】 pīzhù ① annotate and comment on ② annotations and commentaries; marginalia

【批准】 pīzhǔn ratify; approve; sanction: ～条约 ratify a treaty/ 大会～了他的报告。The congress approved his report./ 党委～了他们的请求。The Party committee granted their request./ 计划须经～。The plan is subject to ratification (或 approval). ◇ ～书 instrument of ratification

**纰** pī (of cloth, thread, etc.) become unwoven or untwisted; be spoilt: 线～了。The thread came untwisted.

【纰漏】 pīlòu careless mistake; small accident; slip: 出了～ make a small error; make a slip

【纰缪】 pīmiù 〈书〉error; mistake

**坯** pī ① base; semifinished product; blank: 景泰蓝花瓶的铜～ copper base for a *cloisonné* flower vase ② unburnt brick; earthen brick; adobe

【坯布】 pībù 〈纺〉grey (cloth)

【坯革】 pīgé 〈皮革〉crust leather

【坯件】 pījiàn 〈机〉blank: 螺栓～ bolt blank

【坯子】 pīzi semifinished product; base; blank

**披** pī ① drape over one's shoulders; wrap around: ～

着棉大衣 have a padded overcoat draped over one's shoulders/ ～上衣服 throw on some clothing/ ～上节日的盛装 be colourfully decorated for the festival/ 一只～着羊皮的狼 a wolf in sheep's clothing/ ～着合法的外衣,干着非法的勾当 carry on illegal activities under the cloak of legality/ 一伙～着马列主义外衣的政治骗子 a bunch of political swindlers who deck themselves out as Marxist-Leninists ② open; unroll; spread out: ～卷 open a book ③ split open; crack: 这根竹竿～了。The bamboo stick has split.

【披风】 pīfēng cloak

【披肝沥胆】 pīgān-lìdǎn ① open up one's heart; speak without reserve; be open and sincere ② be loyal and faithful

【披挂】 pīguà ① put on a suit of armour: ～上阵 buckle on one's armour and go into battle ② a suit of armour

【披红】 pīhóng drape a band of red silk over sb.'s shoulders (on festive occasions, etc.): ～戴花 have red silk draped over one's shoulders and flowers pinned on one's breast (as a token of honour)

【披坚执锐】 pījiān-zhíruì wear armour and carry weapons — be a warrior

【披肩】 pījiān ① cape ② shawl

【披荆斩棘】 pījīng-zhǎnjí break through brambles and thorns — hack one's way through difficulties

【披览】 pīlǎn 〈书〉见"披阅"

【披露】 pīlù ① publish; announce: 这一消息已在报上～。The news has been published in the press. ② reveal; show; disclose: ～肝胆 open up one's heart; be openhearted

【披靡】 pīmǐ ① (of grass, etc.) be swept by the wind ② be routed; flee: 敌军望风～。The enemy troops fled pell-mell as soon as they heard our troops advancing./ 人民武装力量所向～。The people's armed forces carried all before them.

【披散】 pīsan (of hair, etc.) hang down loosely

【披沙拣金】 pī shā jiǎn jīn sort out the fine gold from the sand — get essentials from a large mass of material

【披头散发】 pītóu-sǎnfà with hair dishevelled; with hair in disarray

【披星戴月】 pīxīng-dàiyuè under the canopy of the moon and the stars — work or travel night and day

【披阅】 pīyuè open and read (a book); peruse: ～群书 peruse books of all sorts; read widely

## 砒 pī arsenic

【砒霜】 pīshuāng (white) arsenic

## 劈 pī

① split; chop; cleave: ～木柴 chop wood; split logs/ ～成两半 cleave sth. in two/ 这块木头好～。This log splits easily. ② right against (one's face, etc.): 大浪朝我们～面打来。Huge waves came crashing almost on top of us. ③ strike: 老树让雷～了。The old tree was struck by lightning. ④ 〈物〉 wedge

另见 pǐ

【劈波斩浪】 pībō-zhǎnlàng cleave through the waves

【劈刺】 pīcì 〈军〉 sabre or bayonet fighting ◇ ～训练 bayonet drill

【劈刀】 pīdāo ① chopper ② 〈军〉 sabre fighting

【劈里啪啦】 pīlipālā 〈象〉〔形容爆裂、拍打等的连续声音〕: 鞭炮～地响。The firecrackers were crackling and spluttering./ 敌人～乱打了一阵枪,就跑了。The enemy fired off a few random shots and fled.

【劈理】 pīlǐ 〈矿〉 cleavage

【劈脸】 pīliǎn right in the face: ～就是一巴掌 slap sb. on the face/ 一块石头～向他打来。A stone came hurtling towards his face.

【劈啪】 pīpā 〈象〉〔形容拍打或爆裂的声音〕: 把鞭子抽得～响 crack a whip/ 孩子们劈劈啪啪地鼓起掌来。The children began to clap their hands.

【劈山】 pīshān level off hilltops; blast cliffs: ～造田 level off hilltops and turn them into flat fields/ ～筑路 blast cliffs to build highways or railways/ ～引水 cleave hills and lead in water; cut through mountains to bring in water

【劈手】 pīshǒu make a sudden snatch: ～夺过枪来 snatch a gun away from sb.

【劈头】 pītóu ① straight on the head; right in the face: ～一拳 hit sb. right on the head/ 他走到门口～撞上了老王。As he reached the door, he bumped straight into Lao Wang. ② at the very start: 他一进门～就问:"准备好了吗?" The moment he entered the room he asked, "Is everything ready?"

【劈头盖脸】 pītóu-gàiliǎn right in the face: 倾盆大雨～地浇了下来。The rain came pelting down./ 记者们～向他提出许多问题。The reporters fired a volley of questions at him.

【劈胸】 pīxiōng right against the chest: ～一把抓住 grasp sb. by the front of his coat

## 噼 pī

【噼啪】 pīpā 见"劈啪" pīpā

## 霹 pī

【霹雷】 pīléi 〈口〉 thunderbolt; thunderclap

【霹雳】 pīlì thunderbolt; thunderclap: 晴天～ a bolt from the blue

# pí

## 皮 pí

① skin: 猪～ pigskin/ 香蕉～ banana skin/ 树～ bark/ 土豆～ potato peel/ 西瓜～ watermelon rind/ 擦破一块～ scrape a bit of skin off ② leather; hide: ～靴 leather boots/ ～大衣 fur coat ③ cover; wrapper: 书～儿 book cover; jacket/ 包袱～儿 cloth-wrapper ④ surface: 飘在水～儿上 float on the surface of the water ⑤ a broad, flat piece (of some thin material); sheet: 铁～ iron sheet/ 奶～儿 skin (on boiled milk) ⑥ become soft and soggy: 花生～了。The peanuts aren't crisp any more. ⑦ naughty: 这孩子真～! What a naughty child! ⑧ case-hardened: 他老挨剋,都～了。He gets scolded so often that he no longer cares. ⑨ rubber: ～筋儿 rubber band; elastic band ⑩ (Pí) a surname

【皮袄】 pí'ǎo fur-lined jacket

【皮包】 píbāo leather handbag; briefcase; portfolio

【皮包骨头】 pí bāo gútou skinny: 瘦得～ be only skin and bone

【皮鞭子】 píbiānzi leather-thonged whip

【皮层】 pícéng ① 〈生〉 cortex ② 〈生理〉 cerebral cortex

【皮尺】 píchǐ tape measure; tape

【皮带】 pídài ① leather belt ② 〈机〉 (driving) belt: 交叉～ cross belt/ 三角～ triangle belt
◇ ～车床 belt-driven lathe/ ～传动 belt transmission/ ～轮 (belt) pulley/ ～运输机 belt conveyer

【皮蛋】 pídàn preserved egg

【皮垫圈】 pídiànquān 〈机〉 leather washer; leather packing collar

【皮筏】 pífá skin raft

【皮肤】 pífū skin

【皮肤病】 pífūbìng skin disease; dermatosis ◇ ～学 dermatology

【皮肤科】 pífūkē 〈医〉 dermatological department; dermatology ◇ ～医生 dermatologist

【皮肤针】 pífūzhēn 〈中医〉 cutaneous acupuncture (performed with five or seven needles tied vertically to the end of a stick and tapped lightly at the skin surface of the affected area)

【皮肤真菌病】 pífū zhēnjūnbìng 〈医〉 dermatomycosis

【皮革】 pígé leather; hide

【皮辊花】 pígǔnhuā 〈纺〉 lap waste

【皮猴儿】 píhóur hooded fur overcoat; fur parka; fur anorak

【皮黄】 píhuáng ① short for *xipi* (西皮) and *erhuang* (二黄), two chief types of music in traditional Chinese operas ② Beijing opera

【皮货】 píhuò fur; pelt ◇ ～商 furrier; fur trader

【皮夹子】 píjiāzi wallet; pocketbook

【皮匠】 píjiang ① cobbler ② tanner

【皮胶】 píjiāo hide glue

【皮开肉绽】 píkāi-ròuzhàn the skin is torn and the flesh gapes open: 打得～ be bruised and lacerated (from flogging)

【皮毛】 pímáo ① fur ② smattering; superficial knowledge: 略知～ have only a superficial knowledge (of a subject)

【皮棉】 pímián ginned cotton; lint (cotton)

【皮内针】 pínèizhēn 〈中医〉 intradermal needling (acupuncture by embedding the needle subcutaneously for one or several days)

【皮钱儿】 píqiánr 见"皮垫圈"

【皮球】 píqiú rubber ball; ball

【皮实】 píshi ① sturdy: 这孩子真～，轻易不闹病。He's a sturdy child. He hardly ever gets ill. ② durable

【皮桶子】 pítǒngzi fur lining (for a jacket or an overcoat)

【皮下注射】 píxià zhùshè 〈医〉 subcutaneous (或 hypodermic) injection

【皮下组织】 píxià zǔzhī 〈生理〉 subcutaneous tissue

【皮线】 píxiàn 〈电〉 rubber-insulated wire; rubber-covered wire

【皮箱】 píxiāng leather suitcase; leather trunk

【皮相】 píxiàng skin-deep; superficial: ～之谈 superficial talk

【皮硝】 píxiāo 〈口〉 mirabilite; Glauber's salt

【皮笑肉不笑】 pí xiào ròu bù xiào put on a false smile

【皮鞋】 píxié leather shoes ◇ ～油 shoe polish

【皮炎】 píyán 〈医〉 dermatitis: 神经性～ neurodermatitis

【皮衣】 píyī ① fur clothing ② leather clothing

【皮影戏】 píyǐngxì leather-silhouette show; shadow play

【皮张】 pízhāng hide; pelt

【皮掌儿】 pízhǎngr outsole

【皮疹】 pízhěn 〈医〉 rash

【皮之不存，毛将焉附】 pí zhī bù cún, máo jiāng yān fù with the skin gone, what can the hair adhere to — a thing cannot exist without its basis

【皮脂腺】 pízhīxiàn 〈生理〉 sebaceous glands

【皮纸】 pízhǐ tough paper made from bast fibre of the paper mulberry, etc.

【皮质】 pízhì 〈生理〉 cortex: 大脑～ cerebral cortex

【皮重】 pízhòng tare

【皮子】 pízi ① leather; hide ② fur

## 枇 pí

【枇杷】 pípa loquat

## 毗 pí adjoin; be adjacent to

【毗连】 pílián adjoin; border on; be adjacent to: ～地区 contiguous zone/ 江苏北部同山东～。Northern Jiangsu borders on Shandong. 又作"毗邻"

## 铍 pí 〈化〉 beryllium (Be)

## 疲 pí tired; weary; exhausted: 精～力尽 completely exhausted; tired out

【疲惫】 píbèi tired out; exhausted: ～不堪 be in a state of utter exhaustion; be dog-tired

【疲敝】 píbì (of manpower, resources, etc.) be running low; become inadequate

【疲乏】 pífá weary; tired: 感到～ feel weary

【疲倦】 píjuàn tired; weary: 同错误思想作不～的斗争 wage tireless struggle against erroneous ideas

【疲劳】 píláo ① tired; fatigued; weary: 身心～ be weary in body and mind ② fatigue: 肌肉～ muscular fatigue/ 金属～ metal fatigue/ 弹性～ elastic fatigue ◇ ～强度 fatigue strength/ ～试验 fatigue test

【疲软】 píruǎn ① fatigued and weak: 两腿～ be weak in the legs ② 〈金融〉 weaken; slump: 那个国家的货币在外汇市场上～。The currency of that country is weakening on foreign exchanges.

【疲塌】 píta slack; negligent: 工作～ be slack at one's work

【疲于奔命】 píyú bēnmìng be kept constantly on the run; be tired out by too much running around; be weighed down with work: 使之～ tire sb. out by keeping him on the run

## 蚍 pí

【蚍蜉】 pífú ant

【蚍蜉撼大树】 pífú hàn dàshù an ant trying to topple a giant tree — ridiculously overrating one's own strength

## 啤 pí

【啤酒】 píjiǔ beer: 生～ draught beer/ 黑～ porter; brown ale; stout ◇ ～厂 brewery/ ～花 〈植〉 hops

## 琵 pí

【琵琶】 pípa *pipa*, a plucked string instrument with a fretted fingerboard

## 脾 pí spleen

【脾气】 píqi ① temperament; disposition: ～很好 have a good temper/ 摸熟机器的～ get to know the characteristics of a machine ② bad temper: ～大 hot-tempered/ 发～ lose one's temper; flare up

【脾切除】 píqiēchú 〈医〉 splenectomy

【脾胃】 píwèi taste: 不合～ not suit one's taste; not be to one's liking/ 两人～相投。The two have similar likes and dislikes.

【脾脏】 pízàng spleen

【脾肿大】 pízhǒngdà 〈医〉 splenomegaly

## 裨 pí 〈书〉 secondary; minor

另见 bì

【裨将】 píjiàng subordinate or lower-ranking general in ancient China

## 鲏 pí 见"鳑鲏" pángpí

## 蜱 pí 〈动〉 tick

## 罴 pí 〈动〉 brown bear

## 貔 pí 〈书〉 a mythical bearlike wild animal

【貔貅】 píxiū 〈书〉 ① a mythical wild animal ② brave troops

## 鼙 pí a drum used in the army in ancient China

## pǐ

**匹** pǐ ① be equal to; be a match for: 世无其～ matchless; peerless ② 〈量〉ⓐ〔用于马、骡等〕: 两～骡子 two mules/ 三～马 three horses ⓑ〔用于整卷的绸或布〕: 一～布 a bolt of cloth

【匹敌】 pǐdí be equal to; be well matched: 双方实力～。The two sides are well matched.

【匹夫】 pǐfū ① ordinary man: 国家兴亡，～有责。Every man has a share of responsibility for the fate of his country. ② an ignorant person: ～之勇 reckless courage; foolhardiness

【匹马单枪】 pǐmǎ-dānqiāng 见"单枪匹马" dānqiāng-pǐmǎ

【匹配】 pǐpèi ① 〈书〉 mate; marry ② 〈电〉 matching: 阻抗～ impedance matching ◇ ～变压器 matching transformer

【匹染】 pǐrǎn 〈纺〉 piece dyeing ◇ ～色布 piece-dyed cloth

**圮** pǐ 〈书〉 collapse; fall apart; be destroyed

**仳** pǐ

【仳离】 pǐlí 〈书〉 ① (of husband and wife) be separated ② divorce one's spouse, esp. forsake one's wife

**否** pǐ ① bad; wicked; evil ② censure: 臧～ pass judgment on (people)
另见 fǒu

【否极泰来】 pǐ jí tài lái out of the depth of misfortune comes bliss

**痞** pǐ ① a lump in the abdomen ② ruffian; riffraff: 地～ local ruffian

【痞块】 pǐkuài 〈中医〉 a lump in the abdomen 又作"痞积"

【痞子】 pǐzi ruffian; riffraff

**劈** pǐ ① divide; split: 把绳子～成三股 split the rope into three strands ② break off; strip off: ～白菜帮子 strip the outer leaves off cabbages ③ injure one's legs or fingers by opening them too wide
另见 pī

【劈叉】 pǐchà do the splits

【劈柴】 pǐchai kindling; firewood

**擗** pǐ break off: ～棒子 pick corn

**癖** pǐ addiction; weakness for: 嗜酒成～ be addicted to drinking

【癖好】 pǐhào favourite hobby; fondness for: 他有集邮的～。His favourite hobby is stamp collecting.

【癖性】 pǐxìng natural inclination; proclivity; propensity

## pì

**屁** pì wind (from bowels): 放～ break wind; fart

【屁股】 pìgu ① 〈口〉 buttocks; bottom; behind; backside: 拍拍～就走了 leave without a word of explanation; leave things in a mess ② 〈动〉 rump; haunch; hindquarters ③ end; butt: 香烟～ cigarette butt

【屁股蹲儿】 pìgudūnr 〈方〉〔多用于〕: 摔了个～ fall on one's behind (或 bottom)

【屁滚尿流】 pìgǔn-niàoliú 〔多用于〕: 吓得～ scare the shit out of sb.; wet one's pants in terror; be frightened out of one's wits

【屁话】 pìhuà shit; nonsense; rubbish

**辟** pì ① open up (territory, land, etc.); break (ground): 开～果园 lay out an orchard/ 另～专栏 start a new column (in a newspaper, etc.) ② penetrating; incisive: 精～ profound; incisive ③ refute; repudiate: ～谣 refute a rumour
另见 bì

【辟谣】 pìyáo refute a rumour

**媲** pì

【媲美】 pìměi compare favourably with; rival

**僻** pì ① out-of-the-way; secluded: ～巷 side lane/ ～处一隅 live in a remote corner ② eccentric: 怪～ eccentric ③ rare: ～字 rare word

【僻静】 pìjìng secluded; lonely: ～的地方 a secluded place

【僻壤】 pìrǎng an out-of-the-way place

**譬** pì example; analogy

【譬如】 pìrú for example; for instance; such as

【譬喻】 pìyù metaphor; simile; analogy; figure of speech

**䴙** pì

【䴙䴘】 pìtī 〈动〉 grebe

## piān

**片** piān
另见 piàn

【片盒】 piānhé 〈电影〉 film magazine

【片孔】 piānkǒng 〈电影〉 (film) perforation

【片盘】 piānpán 〈电影〉 film spool; bobbin

【片子】 piānzi ① a roll of film ② film; movie ③ gramophone record; disc
另见 piànzi

**扁** piān
另见 biǎn

【扁舟】 piānzhōu 〈书〉 small boat; skiff

**偏** piān ① inclined to one side; slanting; leaning: 正东～北 east by north/ 中间～右 (take a position) right of centre/ 太阳～西了。The sun is to the west./ 这一枪打～了。That shot missed./ 这个指标～低。The target is on the low side. ② partial; prejudiced: ～爱 have partiality for sth.; show favouritism to sb. ③ 〈套〉〔表示先用或已用过茶饭等〕: 谢谢，我已经先～了，您请自己吃吧。Thank you, I've eaten already. You go ahead. ④ 〈副〉〔相当于"偏偏"〕: 他为什么～要那样做？Why must he do it that way?/ 他～不听。He simply wouldn't listen./ 不该她去，她～要去。She was not supposed to go but she insisted on going.

【偏爱】 piān'ài have partiality for sth.; show favouritism to sb.

【偏安】 piān'ān (of a feudal regime) be content to retain sovereignty over a part of the country: ～一隅 content to exercise sovereignty over a part of the country

【偏差】 piānchā deviation; error: ～减为一毫米。The deviation is reduced to one millimetre./ 纠正执行政策中的～ correct any deviations made in implementing a policy

【偏方】 piānfāng 〈中医〉 folk prescription

【偏废】 piānfèi do one thing and neglect another; emphasize one thing at the expense of another: 二者不可～。Neither should be overemphasized at the expense of the other.

【偏航】 piānháng going off course; off-course; yaw
【偏护】 piānhù be partial to and side with: 不～任何一方 show no partiality to either side; be impartial; be unbiased
【偏激】 piānjī extreme: 意见～ hold extreme views/ 他这个人比较～。He tends to go to extremes.
【偏见】 piānjiàn prejudice; bias: 我对他没有～。I've no prejudice against him.
【偏口鱼】 piānkǒuyú flatfish
【偏枯】 piānkū ①〈中医〉hemiplegia ②lopsided (development, etc.)
【偏劳】 piānláo 〈套〉〔用于请人帮忙或谢人代自己做事〕: 谢谢你,多～了。Thanks for all your trouble./ 请你～吧。Can I trouble you to do it?
【偏离】 piānlí deviate; diverge: 船～了航线。The ship drifted off its course./ ～正确路线,革命就会受到挫折。A departure from the correct line will bring setbacks to the revolution.
【偏旁】 piānpáng character components, basic structural parts of Chinese characters (as 亻 in 住, 囗 in 固, 匚 in 匾, 令 in 拎, etc.)
【偏僻】 piānpì remote; out-of-the-way: ～的山区 a remote mountainous district/ 地点～。It is an out-of-the-way place.
【偏偏】 piānpiān 〈副〉①〔表示故意跟客观要求或客观情况相反〕: 我们劝他不要那样做,可他～不听。We tried to talk him out of it, but he just wouldn't listen. ②〔表示事实跟所希望或期待的恰恰相反〕: 他来找我,～我出差了。I happened to be away on business when he came to see me./ 事情的发展～同他的愿望相反。Things turned out just the opposite to what he wanted. ③〔表示范围,跟"单单"略同〕: 干吗～问他? Why ask him, of all people?/ 你为什么～不提这一点呢? Why did you choose to omit this point?
【偏颇】 piānpō 〈书〉biased; partial
【偏巧】 piānqiǎo it so happened that; as luck would have it: 我们正找她,～她来了。We were looking for her when she turned up./ 我找他两次,～都不在家。I called at his house twice, but he happened to be out each time.
【偏师】 piānshī ① wing or flank of an army ② auxiliary force
【偏食】 piānshí ①〈天〉partial eclipse: 日～ partial solar eclipse/ 月～ partial lunar eclipse ②〈医〉partiality for a particular kind of food
【偏瘫】 piāntān 〈医〉hemiplegia
【偏袒】 piāntǎn 见"偏护"
【偏题】 piāntí a catch (或 tricky) question (in an examination)
【偏听偏信】 piāntīng-piānxìn heed and trust only one side; listen only to one side; be biased
【偏头痛】 piāntóutòng 〈医〉migraine
【偏向】 piānxiàng ①erroneous tendency; deviation: 纠正～ correct a deviation/ 反对单纯追求数量的～ oppose the tendency to concentrate on quantity alone ②be partial to
【偏心】 piānxīn ①partiality; bias: 她对小儿子有点儿～。She makes rather a favourite of her youngest son./ 他丝毫不～。He is free from any bias. 或 He's absolutely impartial. ②〈机〉eccentric ◇ ～轮 eccentric (wheel)/ ～凸轮 eccentric cam
【偏压】 piānyā 〈电〉bias voltage; bias: 截止～ cut-off bias ◇ ～电池 bias battery
【偏远】 piānyuǎn remote; faraway: ～地区 remote districts
【偏振】 piānzhèn 〈物〉polarization: 光的～ polarization of light
【偏振光】 piānzhènguāng 〈物〉polarized light ◇ ～镜 polariscope/ ～显微镜 polarizing microscope
【偏正词组】 piān-zhèng cízǔ 〈语〉word group consisting of a modifier and the word it modifies
【偏重】 piānzhòng lay particular stress on: 学习只～记忆而忽视理解是不行的。In studying one shouldn't stress memorization at the expense of comprehension.
【偏转】 piānzhuǎn 〈物〉deflection ◇ ～系统 deflection system

## 犏 piān

【犏牛】 piānniú pien niu (offspring of a bull and a female yak)

## 翩 piān

【翩翩】 piānpiān ①lightly (dance, flutter, etc.): 蝴蝶在花丛中～飞舞。Butterflies are fluttering among the flowers. ②〈书〉elegant: ～少年 an elegant young man
【翩然】 piānrán 〈书〉lightly; trippingly: ～而至 come tripping down
【翩跹】 piānxiān 〈书〉lightly; trippingly: ～起舞 dance with quick, light steps; dance trippingly

## 篇 piān

①a piece of writing: 不朽的诗～ an immortal poem ②sheet (of paper, etc.): 歌～儿 song sheet/ 单～儿油印材料 mimeographed sheets ③〈量〉〔用于纸张、书页、文章等〕: 三～儿纸 three sheets (或 pieces) of paper/ 一～文章 a piece of writing; an article/ 这本书缺了一～儿。One leaf is missing from this book.
【篇幅】 piānfu ①length (of a piece of writing): 这篇文章～不太长。This article is not very long. ②space (on a printed page): ～有限 have limited space/ 报纸用大量～报道了这次会议的情况。The press gave the conference wide coverage.
【篇目】 piānmù table of contents; contents; list of articles
【篇章】 piānzhāng sections and chapters; writings: ～结构 structure of an article; composition/ 在民族解放斗争的史册上写下灿烂的～ add an illustrious chapter to the annals of national liberation struggles

# pián

## 便 pián

另见 biàn
【便便】 piánpián 见"大腹便便" dàfù piánpián
【便宜】 piányi ①cheap: ～货 goods sold at bargain prices/ 价钱相当～。It's a real bargain. 或 It's quite cheap. ②small advantages; petty gains: 贪小～ out for small advantages; on the fiddle ③let sb. off lightly: 这次～了他。This time we have let him off lightly.

## 骈 pián

parallel; antithetical: ～句 parallel sentences
【骈俪】 piánlì art of parallelism
【骈体】 piántǐ rhythmical prose style, marked by parallelism and ornateness
【骈文】 piánwén rhythmical prose characterized by parallelism and ornateness
【骈枝】 piánzhī 〈书〉①double toe or finger ②superfluous ◇ ～机构 superfluous structure

## 胼 pián

【胼胝】 piánzhī callosity; callus
【胼胝体】 piánzhītǐ 〈生理〉corpus callosum

## 蹁 pián

【蹁跹】 piánxiān 〈书〉whirling about (in dancing)

## piǎn

**谝** piǎn 〈方〉 show off: ～能 show off (one's abilities, skills, etc.)

## piàn

**片** piàn ① a flat, thin piece; slice; flake: 布～儿 small pieces of cloth/ 皂～ soap flakes/ 雪～ snowflakes/ 牛肉～ slices of beef/ 玻璃～儿 bits and pieces of glass/ 碎纸～儿 scraps of paper ② part of a place: 分～包干 divide up the work and assign a part to each individual or group ③ cut into slices: ～肉片儿 slice meat/ ～鱼片儿 flake a fish ④ incomplete; fragmentary; partial; brief: ～言 a few words ⑤〈量〉ⓐ〔用于成片的东西〕: 一～儿面包 a slice of bread/ 两～儿安眠药 two sleeping tablets ⓑ〔用于地面和水面等〕: 一～土地 a stretch of land/ 一～草地 a tract of meadow/ 一～汪洋 a vast sheet (或 expanse) of water ⓒ〔用于景色、气象、声音、心意等〕: 一～丰收景象 a vast countryside busy bringing in bumper crops/ 一～欢腾 a scene of great rejoicing/ 一～脚步声 a patter of footsteps/ 一～真心 in all sincerity

另见 piān

【片段】 piànduàn part; passage; extract; fragment: 谈话的～ parts (或 snatches) of a conversation/ 小说的一些～ certain passages of a novel/ 生活的～ an episode of sb.'s life; a slice of life/ ～的消息 bits of information/ ～的回忆 fragments of sb.'s reminiscences 又作"片断"

【片簧】 piànhuáng 〈机〉 leaf spring: 多～ multiple leaf spring

【片剂】 piànjì 〈药〉 tablet

【片甲不存】 piàn jiǎ bù cún not a single armoured warrior remains — the army is completely wiped out: 杀得敌人～ wipe out the enemy to a man 又作"片甲不留"

【片刻】 piànkè a short while; an instant; a moment

【片流】 piànliú 〈物〉 laminar flow

【片麻岩】 piànmáyán 〈地〉 gneiss

【片面】 piànmiàn ① unilateral: ～撕毁协议 unilaterally tear up an agreement/ ～之词 an account given by one party only; one party's version of an event, etc.; one person's word against another's ② one-sided: ～观点 a lopsided (或 one-sided) view/ ～地看问题 take a one-sided approach to problems/ ～强调 put undue emphasis on ◇ ～性 one-sidedness

【片时】 piànshí a short while; a moment

【片梭织机】 piànsuō zhījī 〈纺〉 gripper loom

【片瓦无存】 piàn wǎ wú cún not a single tile remains — be razed to the ground

【片言】 piànyán a few words; a phrase or two: ～可决 can be settled in a few words/ 挑出～只语 pick out a phrase or two

【片岩】 piànyán 〈地〉 schist

【片艳纸】 piànyànzhǐ a machine-glazed paper (glossy on one side)

【片纸只字】 piànzhǐ-zhīzì fragments of writing: 档案中并无～提及此事。There is no reference at all to this case in the files.

【片子】 piànzi ① flat, thin piece; slice; flake; scrap: 铁～ small pieces of sheetiron ② visiting card

另见 piānzi

**骗** piàn ① deceive; fool; hoodwink: 受～ be taken in; be deceived/ 这种花招～不了人。Nobody will be fooled by such tricks. ② cheat; swindle: ～钱 cheat sb. out of his money

【骗局】 piànjú fraud; hoax; swindle: 政治～ a political fraud/ 事实证明,这不过是个大～。Facts show that this is nothing but a swindle.

【骗取】 piànqǔ gain sth. by cheating; cheat (或 trick, swindle) sb. out of sth.; defraud: ～财物 defraud sb. of his money and belongings/ ～信任 worm one's way into sb.'s confidence/ ～支持 fool sb. into giving his support/ ～选票 wangle votes/ 弄虚作假,～荣誉 seek honour through fraud and deception

【骗人】 piànrén deceive people: ～的空话 deceitful empty talk/ ～的幌子 a camouflage; a smokescreen/ ～的勾当 a fraudulent practice (或 deal)/ 他们的一切花言巧语都是～的。All their fine words are nothing but humbug.

【骗术】 piànshù deceitful trick; ruse; hoax: 施行～ perpetrate a fraud

【骗子】 piànzi swindler; impostor; cheat; trickster: 政治～ a political swindler

## piāo

**剽** piāo ① rob: ～掠 plunder; loot ② nimble; swift

【剽悍】 piāohàn agile and brave; quick and fierce

【剽窃】 piāoqiè plagiarize; lift

**漂** piāo float; drift: 树叶在水上～着。Leaves were floating on the water./ 小船顺流～去。The boat drifted down the stream./ ～洋过海 travel far away across the sea

另见 piǎo; piào

【漂泊】 piāobó lead a wandering life; drift: ～异乡 wander aimlessly in a strange land

【漂浮】 piāofú ① float: 湖面上～着几只小船。A few boats are floating on the lake. ② (of style of work) superficial; showy

【漂砾】 piāolì 〈地〉 boulder

【漂流】 piāoliú ① be driven by the current; drift about ② 见"漂泊"

【漂移】 piāoyí 〈电子〉 drift ◇ ～晶体管 drift transistor

**缥** piāo

【缥缈】 piāomiǎo dimly discernible; misty: 虚无～ visionary; illusory

**飘** piāo wave to and fro; float (in the air); flutter: 红旗～～。Red flags are fluttering./ 稻花～香。The air was heavy with the aroma of the paddy fields./ 外面～着小雪。Outside it was snowing slightly./ 随风～来一阵阵花香。The scent of the flowers was wafted to us by the breeze.

【飘泊】 piāobó 见"漂泊" piāobó

【飘带】 piāodai streamer; ribbon

【飘荡】 piāodàng drift; wave; flutter: 小船随波～。The boat was drifting with the tide./ 彩旗在风中～。Coloured flags were flapping in the wind./ 小岛上～着军民的欢笑声。The tiny island rang with the joyous laughter of the local inhabitants and PLA men.

【飘浮】 piāofú 见"漂浮" piāofú

【飘忽】 piāohū ① (of clouds) move swiftly; fleet ② mobile; uncertain: ～不定 drift from place to place

【飘零】 piāolíng ① faded and fallen ② wandering; adrift; homeless; forsaken

【飘流】 piāoliú 见"漂流" piāoliú

【飘渺】 piāomiǎo 见"缥缈" piāomiǎo
【飘飘然】 piāopiāorán smug; self-satisfied; complacent
【飘然】 piāorán floating in the air: 浮云～而过。Fleecy clouds floated past.
【飘洒】 piāosǎ float; drift: 天空～着雪花。Snowflakes were swirling in the air.
【飘洒】 piāosa (of a person) suave; (of calligraphy) facile and graceful
【飘扬】 piāoyáng wave; flutter; fly: 五星红旗迎风～。The five-star red flag is fluttering in the wind.
【飘摇】 piāoyáo sway; shake; totter: 风雨～ buffeted by wind and rain; precarious; tottering
【飘逸】 piāoyì 〈书〉 possessing natural grace; elegant: 神采～ have an elegant bearing

**薸** piāo 〈方〉 duckweed

**螵** piāo
【螵蛸】 piāoxiāo the egg capsule of a mantis

## piáo

**朴** Piáo a surname
另见 pō; pò; pǔ

**嫖** piáo visit prostitutes; go whoring

**瓢** piáo gourd ladle; wooden dipper
【瓢虫】 piáochóng ladybug; ladybird
【瓢泼大雨】 piáopō dàyǔ heavy rain; torrential rain; downpour

## piǎo

**殍** piǎo 见"饿殍" èpiǎo

**漂** piǎo ① bleach ② rinse: 把衣服～干净 give the clothes a good rinse
另见 piāo; piào
【漂白】 piǎobái bleach: ～棉布 bleached cotton cloth ◇ ～粉 bleaching powder/ ～机 bleaching machine; bleacher/ ～率 bleachability
【漂洗槽】 piǎoxǐcáo 〈化〉 potcher

**瞟** piǎo look sidelong (或 askance) at; glance sideways at: ～了他一眼 cast a sidelong glance at him

## piào

**票** piào ① ticket: 火车～ train ticket/ 凭～入场。Admission by ticket only. ② ballot: 投～ cast a ballot; vote ③ bank note; bill: 零～儿 notes of small denominations; change ④ a person held for ransom by brigands; hostage: 绑～儿 kidnap (for ransom) ⑤ 〈旧〉 amateur performance (of Beijing opera, etc.): ～友儿 amateur performer (of Beijing opera, etc.)
【票额】 piào'é the sum stated on a cheque or bill; denomination; face value
【票房】 piàofáng ① 〈口〉(车站等) booking office; (戏院等) box office ② 〈旧〉 a club for amateur performers of Beijing opera ◇ ～价值 box-office value
【票根】 piàogēn counterfoil; stub
【票号】 piàohào 〈旧〉 a firm for exchange and transfer of money; exchange shop 又作"票庄"
【票价】 piàojià the price of a ticket; admission fee; entrance fee: ～一元。Admission one *yuan*.
【票据】 piàojù ① bill; note: 应收(应付)～ bills receivable (payable)/ 即期～ a demand note/ 流通～ negotiable instruments; negotiable papers/ 到期未付～ overdue bill ② voucher; receipt ◇ ～交换所 clearinghouse
【票面】 piàomiàn face (或 par, nominal) value: 各种～的邮票 stamps of various denominations ◇ ～价值 face value; par (value)
【票箱】 piàoxiāng ballot box
【票选】 piàoxuǎn elect (或 vote) by ballot; vote for sb.
【票子】 piàozi bank note; paper money; bill

**漂** piào
另见 piāo; piǎo
【漂亮】 piàoliang ① handsome; good-looking; pretty; beautiful: ～的小伙子 a handsome young man/ ～的小姑娘 a pretty little girl/ ～的衣服 pretty dress; fine clothes/ 打扮得漂漂亮亮的 be smartly dressed/ ～的色彩 beautiful colours ② remarkable; brilliant; splendid; beautiful: 打一个～仗 fight a fine battle; win a brilliant victory/ 普通话说得很～ speak beautiful standard Chinese/ 守门员这个球救得真～。The goalie made a beautiful save. ◇ ～话 fine words; high-sounding words

**骠** piào 〈书〉 ① (of horses) fast ② brave; valiant

**嘌** piào
【嘌呤】 piàolìng 〈化〉 purine

## piē

**氕** piē 〈化〉 protium ($H^1$)

**撇** piē ① cast aside; throw overboard; neglect: 不能只抓一头，把别的事都～在一旁。We should not just concentrate on one thing to the neglect of everything else./ 对犯错误的同志要帮助，不能一～下不管。We should help a comrade who has committed mistakes, and not ignore him. ② skim: ～油 skim off the grease/ ～沫儿 skim off the scum
另见 piě
【撇开】 piēkai leave aside; bypass: ～这个问题 bypass this issue/ 咱们把次要问题～不谈了吧。Let's leave aside questions of minor importance.
【撇弃】 piēqì cast away; abandon; desert

**瞥** piē shoot a glance at; dart a look at: 他刚要插嘴，妈妈～了他一眼。He was going to butt in when his mother darted a look of disapproval at him./ 《故宫一～》 *A Glimpse of the Imperial Palace*
【瞥见】 piējiàn get a glimpse of; catch sight of: 在大街上无意中～了一位多年不见的老友。In the street I caught sight of an old friend whom I had not seen for years.

## piě

**苤** piě
【苤蓝】 piělan 〈植〉 kohlrabi

**撇** piě ① throw; fling; cast: ～手榴弹 throw hand grenades ② left-falling stroke (in Chinese characters) ③

〈量〉: 两～浓眉,一双大眼 two bushy brows over a pair of big eyes

另见 piē

【撇嘴】 piězuǐ curl one's lip (in contempt, disbelief or disappointment); twitch one's mouth: 这女孩儿～要哭。The girl's mouth began to twitch; she was on the verge of tears.

## pīn

**拼** pīn ① put together; piece together: 把两块木板～起来 put two boards together side by side ② be ready to risk one's life (in fighting, work, etc.); go all out in work: ～到底 fight to the bitter end/ 不畏强手,敢打敢～ not fear a strong opponent but dare to stand up to him

【拼版】 pīnbǎn 〈印〉 makeup

【拼刺】 pīncì ① bayonet drill; bayonet practice ② bayonet charge: 和敌人～ fight it out with the enemy with bayonets

【拼凑】 pīncòu piece together; knock together; rig up: 她把零碎花布～起来,给小闺女做了一件褂子。She pieced together odds and ends of coloured cloth and made a jacket for her little girl./ ～一个反革命集团 knock together a counterrevolutionary clique

【拼命】 pīnmìng ① risk one's life; defy death; go all out regardless of danger to one's life: ～精神 the death-defying spirit/ 被围困的敌人摆出一副～的架势。The encircled enemy seemed to be getting ready for a last-ditch stand. ② exerting the utmost strength; for all one is worth; with all one's might; desperately: ～奔跑 run for all one is worth/ ～工作 work with all one's might/ 资本家～获取利润。The capitalists do their utmost to get as much profit as possible.

【拼盘】 pīnpán assorted cold dishes; *hors d'oeuvres*

【拼死】 pīnsǐ risk one's life; defy death; fight desperately: ～挣扎 wage a desperate struggle

【拼写】 pīnxiě spell; transliterate: 照汉语拼音方案～汉字 transliterate Chinese characters into the Chinese Phonetic Alphabet ◇ ～法 spelling; orthography

【拼音】 pīnyīn ① combine sounds into syllables ② spell; phoneticize ◇ ～文字 alphabetic (system of) writing/ ～字母 phonetic alphabet; phonetic letters

**姘** pīn have illicit relations with

【姘居】 pīnjū live illicitly as husband and wife; cohabit

【姘头】 pīntou paramour

## pín

**贫** pín ① poor; impoverished: ～无立锥之地 utterly destitute; in extreme poverty ② inadequate; deficient: ～油国 oil-poor country ③ garrulous; loquacious: 他的嘴真～。He is really too garrulous.

【贫病交迫】 pín-bìng jiāopò suffering from both poverty and sickness; sick as well as poor

【贫齿动物】 pínchǐ dòngwù edentate animal; edentate

【贫乏】 pínfá poor; short; lacking: 煤炭资源～的省份 provinces poor in coal deposits/ 经验～ lack experience/ 语言～ flat, monotonous language

【贫雇农】 pín-gùnóng poor peasants and farm labourers

【贫寒】 pínhán poor; poverty-stricken: ～人家 an impoverished family

【贫化】 pínhuà 〈矿〉 dilution: 矿石～ ore dilution

【贫瘠】 pínjí barren; infertile; poor: ～的土壤 poor soil; impoverished soil

【贫贱】 pínjiàn poor and lowly; in straitened and humble circumstances

【贫苦】 pínkǔ poor; poverty-stricken; badly off

【贫矿】 pínkuàng lean ore

【贫困】 pínkùn poor; impoverished; in straitened circumstances: 生活～ live in poverty ◇ ～化 pauperization

【贫民】 pínmín poor people; pauper: 城市～ the urban poor ◇ ～窟 slum/ ～区 slum area; slum district

【贫农】 pínnóng poor peasant ◇ ～团 the poor peasant league

【贫穷】 pínqióng poor; needy; impoverished

【贫弱】 pínruò (of a country) poor and weak

【贫下中农】 pín-xiàzhōngnóng poor and lower-middle peasants ◇ ～协会 poor and lower-middle peasants' association

【贫血】 pínxuè 〈医〉 anaemia: 脑～ cerebral anaemia/ 再生障碍性～ aplastic anaemia

【贫嘴】 pínzuǐ garrulous; loquacious

【贫嘴薄舌】 pínzuǐ-bóshé garrulous and sharp-tongued

**频** pín ① frequently; repeatedly: 捷报～传。Reports of new victories keep pouring in. ② 〈物〉 frequency: 音～ audio frequency

【频带】 píndài 〈物〉 frequency band

【频道】 píndào 〈电视〉 frequency channel

【频繁】 pínfán frequently; often: 两国人民之间交往～。There are frequent contacts between the people of the two countries.

【频率】 pínlǜ 〈物〉 frequency: ～范围 frequency range

【频频】 pínpín again and again; repeatedly: ～举杯 propose repeated toasts/ ～招手 wave one's hand again and again

【频仍】 pínréng 〈书〉 frequent: 外患～ be subject to repeated foreign aggression

**嫔** pín 〈书〉 ① a concubine of an emperor ② a woman attendant at court

**蘋** pín 〈植〉 clover fern

**顰** pín 〈书〉 knit the brows

## pǐn

**品** pǐn ① article; product: 商～ commodity; merchandise/ 农产～ farm produce/ 工业～ industrial products ② grade; class; rank: 上～ highest grade; top grade ③ character; quality: 人～ moral quality; character/ ～学兼优 (of a student) of good character and scholarship ④ taste sth. with discrimination; sample; savour: ～茶 sample tea/ ～～味儿 savour the flavour

【品尝】 pǐncháng taste; sample; savour

【品德】 pǐndé moral character

【品格】 pǐngé ① one's character and morals ② quality and style (of literary or artistic works)

【品红】 pǐnhóng ① pinkish red ② magenta; fuchsin

【品级】 pǐnjí ① official rank in feudal times ② grade (of products, commodities, etc.)

【品蓝】 pǐnlán reddish blue

【品类】 pǐnlèi category; class

【品绿】 pǐnlǜ light green; malachite green

【品貌】 pǐnmào ① looks; appearance ② character and looks

【品名】 pǐnmíng the name of an article; the name or description of a commodity
【品评】 pǐnpíng judge; comment on
【品题】 pǐntí 〈书〉 appraise (a person)
【品头论足】 pǐntóu-lùnzú ① make frivolous remarks about a woman's appearance ② find fault; be overcritical
【品脱】 pǐntuō pint
【品位】 pǐnwèi 〈矿〉 grade: 边际～ cut-off grade
【品味】 pǐnwèi taste; savour
【品系】 pǐnxì 〈生〉 strain
【品行】 pǐnxíng conduct; behaviour: ～端正 having good conduct; well-behaved/ ～不端 having bad conduct; ill-behaved
【品性】 pǐnxìng moral character
【品月】 pǐnyuè pale blue
【品质】 pǐnzhì ① character; quality: 道德～ moral character/ 工人阶级的优秀～ fine qualities of the working class ② quality (of commodities, etc.): ～优良 of the best quality ◇ ～因数 〈电〉 quality factor/ ～证明书 certificate of quality
【品种】 pǐnzhǒng ① 〈生〉 breed; variety: 羊的优良～ improved breeds of sheep ② variety; assortment: 货物～齐全 have a good assortment of goods/ 增加花色～ increase the variety of colours and designs

## pìn

**牝** pìn female (of some birds and animals): ～马 mare/ ～牛 cow/ ～鸡 hen

**聘** pìn ① engage: ～某人为顾问 engage sb. as a consultant/ 被～为名誉会长 be invited to be honorary chairman ② 〈旧〉 betroth ③ 〈口〉 (of a girl) get married or be married off
【聘礼】 pìnlǐ betrothal gifts (from the bridegroom's to the bride's family); bride-price
【聘请】 pìnqǐng engage; invite: ～一位工程师担任技校兼职教师 get an engineer to act as a part-time teacher in the technical school
【聘任】 pìnrèn engage; appoint to a position
【聘书】 pìnshū letter of appointment; contract

## pīng

**乒** pīng ① 〈象〉: ～的一声枪响 the crack of a rifle or pistol ② table tennis; ping-pong: ～坛 table tennis circles
【乒乓】 pīngpāng ① 〈象〉: 雹子打在屋顶上～乱响。 Hailstones were rattling on the roofs. ② table tennis; ping-pong
【乒乓球】 pīngpāngqiú ① table tennis; ping-pong ② table tennis ball; ping-pong ball
◇ ～拍 table tennis bat/ ～台 table tennis table/ ～网 table tennis net

**娉** pīng
【娉婷】 pīngtíng 〈书〉 (of a woman) have a graceful demeanour

## píng

**平** píng ① flat; level; even; smooth: 桌面不～。The table is not level./ 把纸铺～ smooth out the paper/ 让病人躺～ help the patient to lie stretched out/ 把地～一～ level the ground ② be on the same level; be on a par; equal: 水涨得～了河岸。The water rose until it was level with the banks./ ～世界纪录 equal a world record ③ 〈体〉 make the same score; tie; draw: 双方打成十五～。The two teams tied at 15-15./ 这场足球最后踢～了。The football game ended in a draw./ 场上比分是七～。The score is now seven all. ④ equal; fair; impartial: ～分 divide equally/ 持～之论 a fair argument; an unbiased view ⑤ calm; peaceful; quiet: 海上风～浪静。The sea was calm./ 经他一解释,老太太的气也就～了。 His explanation soothed the old woman's anger./ ～民愤 assuage popular indignation/ 为民～愤 redress the grievances of the people ⑥ put down; suppress: ～叛 put down a rebellion ⑦ average; common: ～日 on ordinary days ⑧ 〈语〉 见"平声" ⑨ (Píng) a surname
【平安】 píng'ān safe and sound; without mishap; well: ～到达目的地 arrive safe and sound; arrive without mishap/ ～无事。All is well./ 全家～。The whole family is well./ 一路～! Have a good trip! 或 Bon voyage! ◇ ～险 〈商〉 free of particular average (F.P.A.)
【平白】 píngbái for no reason; gratuitously: ～挨一顿骂 get a scolding for no reason at all
【平板】 píngbǎn dull and stereotyped; flat: 文章写得太～。The article is written in a flat style.
【平板玻璃】 píngbǎn bōli plate glass
【平板车】 píngbǎnchē flatbed tricycle; flatbed
【平版】 píngbǎn 〈印〉 lithographic plate ◇ ～印刷 lithographic printing; planographic printing
【平辈】 píngbèi of the same generation
【平布】 píngbù 〈纺〉 plain cloth
【平步青云】 píngbù qīngyún rapidly go up in the world; have a meteoric rise
【平舱费】 píngcāngfèi trimming charges
【平产】 píngchǎn be equal in output; have the same output
【平常】 píngcháng ① ordinary; common: 这种现象很～。This sort of thing is quite a common occurrence. ② generally; usually; ordinarily; as a rule: ～我很少进城。I don't go to town much as a rule./ 这个词儿～很少用。This word is seldom used on ordinary occasions.
【平车】 píngchē 〈铁道〉 flatcar; platform wagon; platform car
【平川】 píngchuān level land; flat, open country; plain: 一马～ a vast stretch of flat land
【平淡】 píngdàn flat; insipid; prosaic; pedestrian: ～无味的谈话 insipid (或 dull) conversation/ ～无奇的文章 pedestrian writing
【平等】 píngděng equality: ～待遇 equal treatment/ ～待人 treat others as equals/ 男女～ equality between the sexes/ ～互利 equality and mutual benefit/ ～协商 consultation on the basis of equality
【平底船】 píngdǐchuán flat-bottomed boat; flatboat; punt
【平地】 píngdì ① level the land (或 ground); rake the soil smooth ② level ground; flat ground
【平地风波】 píngdì fēngbō a sudden storm on a calm sea; a sudden, unexpected turn of events; unforeseen trouble
【平地机】 píngdìjī ① 〈农〉 land leveller; grader ② 〈交〉 road grader
【平地楼台】 píngdì lóutái high buildings rise from the ground — start from scratch
【平地一声雷】 píngdì yī shēng léi a sudden clap of thunder — a sudden big change, e.g. a sudden rise in fame and position; an unexpected happy event
【平调】 píng-diào 见"一平二调" yī píng èr diào
【平定】 píngdìng ① calm down: 他的情绪逐渐～下来。 He gradually calmed down. ② suppress; put down: ～叛乱 put down a rebellion
【平峒】 píngdòng 〈矿〉 adit; tunnel

【平凡】 píngfán ordinary; common: 在～的岗位上做出不～的成绩 achieve extraordinary successes at an ordinary post
【平反】 píngfǎn redress (a mishandled case); rehabilitate: 宣布给某人～ announce sb.'s rehabilitation
【平方】 píngfāng 〈数〉 square: 三的～是九。 The square of 3 is 9.
◇ ～根〈数〉square root/ ～公里 square kilometre/ ～米 square metre
【平房】 píngfáng single-storey house; one-storey house
【平分】 píngfēn divide equally; share and share alike; go halves; go fifty-fifty: ～土地 equal distribution of land/～兵力 divide one's forces evenly ◇ ～线〈数〉bisector
【平分秋色】 píngfēn qiūsè (of two parties) have equal shares (of honour, power, glory, etc.)
【平复】 píngfu ① calm down; subside; be pacified: 风浪渐渐地～了。The storm gradually subsided./ 事态～。The situation has quietened. ② be cured; be healed: 伤口～了。The wound is healed.
【平光】 píngguāng zero diopter; plain glass ◇ ～眼镜 plain glass spectacles
【平巷】 pínghàng 〈矿〉 drift; level
【平和】 pínghé gentle; mild; moderate; placid: 性情～ be of gentle (或 mild) disposition/ ～的语气 mild (或 placid) tone/ 这种药药性～。This medicine is quite mild.
【平衡】 pínghéng balance; equilibrium: 收支～ balance between income and expenditure/ 失去～ lose one's balance; be in a state of imbalance/ 保持～ maintain one's equilibrium; keep one's balance/ 逐渐在全国～工业布局 gradually distribute industry evenly all over the country/ 咱们组的计划还要跟别的组～一下。We'll have to fit in our plan with those of the other groups./ 政治经济发展的不～是资本主义的绝对规律。Uneven economic and political development is an absolute law of capitalism.
◇ ～常数〈化〉equilibrium constant/ ～价格 equilibrium price/ ～觉〈生理〉sense of equilibrium/ ～力 equilibrant/ ～木〈体〉balance beam/ ～器〈机〉balancer
【平滑】 pínghuá level and smooth; smooth ◇ ～肌〈生理〉smooth muscle
【平话】 pínghuà ① a style of storytelling popular in the Song Dynasty (960-1279) ② popular stories
【平缓】 pínghuǎn ① gently: 地势～。The terrain slopes gently./ 水流～。The water flows gently. ② mild; placid; gentle: ～的语调 a mild tone
【平毁】 pínghuǐ demolish; raze: ～壕沟 fill in trenches/ ～敌人留下的碉堡 raze the fortifications evacuated by the enemy
【平价】 píngjià par; parity: 汇兑～ par of exchange/ 铸币～ specie par/ 固定～ fixed parity
【平角】 píngjiǎo 〈数〉 straight angle
【平静】 píngjìng calm; quiet; tranquil: ～的夜晚 a quiet night/ ～的海面 a calm sea/ 他很激动,心情久久不能～。He was very excited, and it was long before he calmed down.
【平局】 píngjú draw; tie: 比赛最后打成～。The game ended in a draw./ 场上屡次出现～。The score was tied again and again./ 扳成～ equalize the score
【平均】 píngjūn ① average; mean: ～速度 average speed; mean velocity/ ～亩产量 per *mu* yield/ 按人口～计算收入 per capita income/ ～每年增长百分之五 increase by an average of 5% a year ② equally; share and share alike: ～分摊 share out equally
◇ ～利润〈经〉average profit/ ～寿命 average life span; life expectancy/ ～数 average; mean/ ～值 average value; mean value; mean/ ～主义 equalitarianism; egalitarianism
【平均律】 píngjūnlǜ 〈乐〉 equal temperament: 十二～ twelve-tone equal temperament
【平空】 píngkōng 见"凭空" píngkōng
【平口钳】 píngkǒuqián flat-nose pliers
【平列】 pínglié place side by side; place on a par with each other: 不能把客观原因与主观原因～起来分析。We should not put subjective reasons on a par with objective reasons in our analysis.
【平流】 píngliú 〈气〉 advection ◇ ～层 stratosphere
【平炉】 pínglú 〈冶〉 open-hearth furnace; open hearth
◇ ～钢 open-hearth steel/ ～利用系数 capacity factor of an open-hearth furnace/ ～炼钢法 open-hearth process
【平脉】 píngmài 〈中医〉 normal pulse
【平面】 píngmiàn 〈数〉 plane
◇～波〈物〉plane wave/ ～几何 plane geometry/ ～交叉〈交〉grade crossing; level crossing/ ～镜〈物〉plane mirror/ ～磨床 surface grinding machine
【平面图】 píngmiàntú ① plan ② plane figure
【平民】 píngmín the common people; the populace
【平年】 píngnián ①〈天〉non-leap year; common year ② average year (in crop yield)
【平平】 píngpíng average; mediocre; indifferent: 成绩～。The results are about up to the average.
【平铺直叙】 píngpū-zhíxù ① tell in a simple, straightforward way ② speak or write in a dull, flat style
【平起平坐】 píngqǐ-píngzuò sit as equals at the same table; be on an equal footing
【平权】 píngquán (enjoy) equal rights: 男女～ equal rights for men and women
【平绒】 píngróng 〈纺〉 velveteen
【平射】 píngshè 〈军〉 flat (trajectory) fire ◇ ～炮 flat fire gun; flat trajectory gun
【平生】 píngshēng all one's life; one's whole life: ～的志愿 one's lifelong aspiration (或 wish)/ ～艰苦朴素 live simply and work hard all one's life
【平声】 píngshēng 〈语〉 level tone, one of the four tones in classical Chinese, which has evolved into the high and level tone (阴平) and the rising tone (阳平) in modern standard pronunciation
【平时】 píngshí ① at ordinary times; in normal times: 他～住在厂里,星期六才回家。 Ordinarily he sleeps at the factory and goes home only on Saturdays. ② in peacetime: ～多流汗,战时少流血。Losing more sweat in peacetime (training, etc.) means shedding less blood in war. ◇ ～编制〈军〉peacetime establishment; peace organization (或 footing)/ ～兵力 peacetime strength
【平手】 píngshǒu draw: 两队打了个～。The two teams drew.
【平顺】 píngshùn smooth-going; plain sailing
【平素】 píngsù usually: 他～就不爱说话。He's usually very quiet. 或 He is a man of few words.
【平台】 píngtái terrace; platform
【平坦】 píngtǎn (of land, etc.) level; even; smooth: 地势～ smooth terrain/ 革命的道路决不是～的。The road of revolution is by no means smooth.
【平头】 píngtóu closely cropped hair; crop; crew cut: 留着～ have closely cropped hair
【平纹】 píngwén 〈纺〉 plain weave ◇ ～织物 plain cloth
【平稳】 píngwěn smooth and steady; smooth; stable: 我们的飞机飞得很～。We had a smooth flight./ 机器运转～。The machine runs smoothly./ 物价～。Prices are stable./ 病人的血压～。The patient's blood pressure is stable.
【平西】 píngxī (of the sun) be setting: 太阳已经～了,还这么热。It's almost sunset, but it's still so hot.
【平昔】 píngxī in the past: 我～对语法很少研究,现在开始感到一点兴趣了。I didn't go in for grammar seriously, but

now I'm beginning to take an interest in it.

【平息】 píngxī ① calm down; quiet down; subside: 一场风波～了。The tumult has subsided. 或 The trouble is over./ 他的怒气～了。His anger has cooled. ② put down (a rebellion, etc.); suppress

【平心而论】 píngxīn ér lùn in all fairness; to give sb. his due: ～，这出戏还算不错。In all fairness, it's not a bad play./ ～，他工作还是比较认真的。To give him his due, he is quite a conscientious worker.

【平心静气】 píngxīn-jìngqì calmly; dispassionately: ～地讨论 calmly discuss

【平信】 píngxìn ① ordinary mail ② surface mail

【平行】 píngxíng ① of equal rank; on an equal footing; parallel: ～机关 units (或 organizations) of equal rank; parallel organizations ② simultaneous; parallel: ～作业 parallel operations/ 就各种问题举行～的会谈 hold simultaneous talks on different subjects ③ 〈数〉 parallel ◇ ～六面体 〈数〉 parallelepiped/ ～脉〈植〉 parallel veins/ ～四边形〈数〉 parallelogram/ ～线 parallel lines

【平移】 píngyí 〈物〉 translation ◇ ～运动 translational motion

【平易】 píngyì ① unassuming; amiable: ～近人 amiable and easy of approach ② (of a piece of writing) easy; plain

【平庸】 píngyōng mediocre; indifferent; commonplace: ～的作家 a mediocre writer/ 才能～ of limited ability

【平鱼】 píngyú silvery pomfret; butterfish

【平原】 píngyuán plain; flatlands

【平月】 píngyuè February of a non-leap year

【平允】 píngyǔn 〈书〉 fair and just; equitable

【平仄】 píng-zè ① level and oblique tones ② tonal patterns in classical Chinese poetry

【平展】 píngzhǎn (of land, etc.) open and flat

【平整】 píngzhěng ① level: 他们～土地三万余亩。They levelled over 30,000 *mu* of land. ② neat; smooth

【平装】 píngzhuāng paperback; paper-cover; paperbound ◇ ～本 paperback (book); paperbound edition

【平装开关】 píngzhuāng kāiguān 〈电〉 flush switch

【平足】 píngzú 〈医〉 flatfoot

**评** píng ① comment; criticize; review: 博得好～ receive favourable comments; be well received/ 短～ brief commentary/ 书～ book review ② judge; appraise: 你来～～谁说得对。Now you be the judge and say which of us is right./ 被～为劳动模范 be elected a model worker

【评比】 píngbǐ appraise through comparison; compare and assess: ～产品质量 compare and appraise the quality of different products; make a public appraisal of the quality of different products

【评定】 píngdìng pass judgment on; evaluate; assess: ～训练成绩 evaluate the results of training

【评断】 píngduàn judge; arbitrate: ～是非 judge between right and wrong; arbitrate a dispute

【评分】 píngfēn ① give a mark; mark (students' papers, etc.) ② decide on workpoints (for a commune member)

【评工】 pínggōng evaluate (a commune member's) work: ～记分 evaluate work and allot workpoints; calculate workpoints on the basis of work done

【评功】 pínggōng appraise sb.'s merits: ～授奖大会 a meeting to announce commendations and issue awards/ ～摆好 enumerate sb.'s merits; speak of sb. in glowing terms

【评话】 pínghuà ① 见"平话" pínghuà ② professional storytelling in a local dialect: 苏州～ storytelling in Suzhou dialect

【评级】 píngjí ① grade (cadres, workers, etc.) ② grade (products according to quality)

【评价】 píngjià appraise; evaluate: 用马克思主义的观点～历史人物 appraise (或 evaluate) historical figures from a Marxist viewpoint/ 高度～ set a high value on; speak highly of; highly appraise

【评奖】 píngjiǎng decide on awards through discussion

【评介】 píngjiè review (a new book, etc.): 新书～ book review

【评剧】 píngjù *pingju*, a local opera of north and northeast China

【评理】 pínglǐ ① judge between right and wrong; decide which side is right: 谁是谁非，让大家来评个理。Let others judge who is right and who is wrong. ② reason things out; have it out: 咱们得找他评评理。Let's go and have it out with him.

【评论】 pínglùn ① comment on; discuss: 请党外群众参加～党员 ask non-Party people to join in the appraisal of Party members ② comment; commentary; review: 小～ short comments ◇ ～家 critic; reviewer/ ～员 commentator

【评判】 píngpàn pass judgment on; judge: ～胜负 decide who is the winner; judge between contestants/ ～优劣 judge which is superior ◇ ～员(体育、演讲等) judge; (音乐等) adjudicator

【评书】 píngshū storytelling (by a professional storyteller)

【评弹】 píngtán storytelling and ballad singing in Suzhou dialect

【评头论足】 píngtóu-lùnzú 见"品头论足" pǐntóu-lùnzú

【评薪】 píngxīn discuss and determine a person's wage-grade

【评选】 píngxuǎn choose through public appraisal: 被～为先进工作者 be chosen as an advanced worker

【评议】 píngyì appraise sth. through discussion: 给他多少补助，让群众～一下。Let the masses discuss the amount of financial help he should receive.

【评语】 píngyǔ comment; remark

【评阅】 píngyuè read and appraise (sb.'s writing, etc.)

【评注】 píngzhù ① make commentary and annotation ② notes and commentary

【评传】 píngzhuàn critical biography

**坪** píng level ground: 草～ lawn; grassplot/ 停机～ aircraft park; apron

**苹** píng

【苹果】 píngguǒ apple ◇ ～脯 preserved apple/ ～干 dried apple slices/ ～酱 apple jam/ ～酒 cider; applejack/ ～绿 apple green/ ～园 apple orchard

**凭** píng ① lean on; lean against: ～栏远眺 lean on a railing and gaze into the distance ② rely on; depend on: ～险抵抗 make use of a strategic vantage point to fight back ③ evidence; proof: 真～实据 ironclad evidence/ 口说无～。Verbal statements are no guarantee. ④ go by; base on; take as the basis: ～党性办事 act with Party spirit/ ～良心说 in all fairness/ ～票入场。Admission by ticket only./ ～票付款 payable to bearer/ 你～什么得出这个结论？What do you base this conclusion on?/ 你不能～他嘴上说的就算数。You can't take him at his word. ⑤ 〈连〉 no matter (what, how, etc.): ～你跑多快，我也赶得上。I'll catch up with you no matter how fast you run.

【凭单】 píngdān a certificate for drawing money, goods, etc.; voucher

【凭吊】 píngdiào visit (a historical site, etc.) and ponder on the past: ～古战场 pay a visit to an ancient battleground

【凭借】 píngjiè rely on; depend on: ～自己的力量 rely on one's own strength/ ～想象力 draw on one's imagination/ 人类的思维是～语言来进行的。Man thinks in words.

【凭据】 píngjù evidence; proof

【凭空】 píngkōng out of the void; out of thin air; without foundation; groundless: 这完全是～捏造。This is a sheer fabrication./ 他这种看法决不是～产生的。His view is by no means without foundation.

【凭眺】 píngtiào gaze from a high place into the distance; enjoy a distant view from a height

【凭信】 píngxìn trust; believe

【凭依】 píngyī base oneself on, rely on; have something to go by: 无所～ have nothing to go by

【凭仗】 píngzhàng rely on; depend on: 他们～着顽强不屈的精神克服了重重困难。They overcame all kinds of difficulties by dint of an indomitable spirit.

【凭照】 píngzhào certificate; permit; licence

【凭证】 píngzhèng proof; evidence; certificate; voucher: 完税～ tax payment receipt

## 屏

píng ① screen: 画～ painted screen ② a set of scrolls ③ shield sb. or sth.; screen
另见 bǐng

【屏蔽】 píngbì shield; screen: ～着这一带地方 provide a protective screen for this area ◇ ～电缆 shielded (或 screened) cable/ ～天线 screened (或 shielded) antenna

【屏风】 píngfēng screen

【屏极】 píngjí 〈电子〉 plate ◇ ～电路 plate circuit

【屏门】 píngmén screen door (between the outer and inner courtyards of an old-style Chinese residence)

【屏幕】 píngmù 〈电子〉 screen: 电视～ telescreen; screen

【屏条】 píngtiáo a set of hanging scrolls (usu. four in a row)

【屏障】 píngzhàng protective screen: 燕山是北京的天然～。The Yanshan Hills provide a natural defence for Beijing.

## 瓶

píng bottle; vase; jar; flask: 两～牛奶 two bottles of milk/ 热水～ thermos flask/ 花～ flower vase

【瓶胆】 píngdǎn glass liner (of a thermos flask)

【瓶装】 píngzhuāng bottled

【瓶子】 píngzi bottle

## 萍

píng duckweed

【萍水相逢】 píng-shuǐ xiāng féng (of strangers) meet by chance like patches of drifting duckweed

【萍踪】 píngzōng 〈书〉 tracks (或 whereabouts) of a wanderer

## 鲆

píng left-eyed flounder

# pō

## 朴

pō
另见 Piáo; pò; pǔ

【朴刀】 pōdāo a sword with a long blade and a short hilt wielded with both hands

## 钋

pō 〈化〉 polonium (Po)

## 泊

pō lake: 罗布～ Lop Nur/ 血～ pool of blood
另见 bó

## 坡

pō ① slope: 山～ a mountain slope; hillside/ 陡～ a steep slope/ 平～ a slight (或 gentle, gradual) slope ② sloping; slanting: 把板子～着放 put the board on a slant/ 坑边挖得太陡了，再～一点。The sides of the pit are too steep. Slope them a bit.

【坡地】 pōdì hillside fields; sloping fields; land on the slopes: ～梯田化 terracing of the land on the slopes

【坡度】 pōdù slope; gradient: 有六十度～的一段山路 a mountain path with a slope of 60 degrees

## 泼

pō ① sprinkle; splash; spill: 先～点儿水再扫。Sprinkle some water before you sweep. /互相～水 splash water on each other/ 这孩子把汤～了一地。The boy spilt the soup on the floor./ 别把脏水～到院子里。Don't throw the slops in the yard. ② rude and unreasonable; shrewish: 撒～ act hysterically and refuse to see reason

【泼妇】 pōfù shrew; vixen: ～骂街 like a shrew shouting abuse in the street

【泼辣】 pōla ① rude and unreasonable; shrewish ② pungent; forceful: 文章写得很～。The article is written in a pungent style. ③ bold and vigorous: 她工作很～。She is bold and vigorous in her work.

【泼冷水】 pō lěngshuǐ pour (或 throw) cold water on; dampen the enthusiasm (或 spirits) of

【泼墨】 pōmò 〈美术〉 splash-ink, a technique of Chinese ink-painting ◇ ～山水 splashed-ink landscape

【泼水节】 Pōshuǐjié the Water-Sprinkling Festival of the Dai (傣) and some other minority nationalities

## 颇

pō ① 〈书〉 inclined to one side; oblique: 偏～ biased; partial ② quite; rather; considerably: ～佳 quite good/ 影响～大 exert a considerable influence/ ～为费解 rather difficult to understand/ ～不以为然 highly disapprove of sth./ 他说的～有道理。There is a lot of sense in what he says.

# pó

## 婆

pó ① old woman ② a woman in a certain occupation: 媒～儿 woman matchmaker/ 收生～儿 midwife ③ husband's mother; mother-in-law

【婆家】 pójia husband's family

【婆罗门】 Póluómén Brahman ◇ ～教 Brahmanism

【婆娘】 póniáng 〈方〉 ① young married woman ② wife

【婆婆】 pópo ① husband's mother; mother-in-law ② 〈方〉 grandmother

【婆婆妈妈】 pópomāmā ① womanishly fussy ② sentimental; mawkish; maudlin

【婆娑】 pósuō whirling; dancing: ～起舞 start dancing/ 杨柳～。The willows dance in the breeze.

【婆姨】 póyí 〈方〉 ① young married woman ② wife

## 鄱

pó 〔用于地名〕: ～阳湖 Poyang Lake (Jiangxi Province)

## 皤

pó 〈书〉 white: 白发～然 white-haired

# pǒ

## 叵

pǒ 〈书〉 impossible

【叵测】 pǒcè 〈贬〉 unfathomable; unpredictable: 居心～ with hidden intent/ 心怀～ harbour dark designs; nurse evil intentions

**钷** pǒ 〈化〉 promethium (Pm)

**笸** pǒ

【笸箩】 pǒluo shallow basket

## pò

**朴** pò 〈植〉 Chinese hackberry (*Celtis sinensis*)

另见 Piáo; pō; pǔ

**迫** pò ① compel; force; press: 被～拿起武器 be compelled to take up arms/ ～敌投降 force the enemy to surrender/ ～于形势 under the stress of circumstances; under the pressure of events/ 为饥寒所～ be driven (to do sth.) by cold and hunger ② urgent; pressing: 从容不～ calm and unhurried ③ approach; go towards (或 near): ～近 get close to

另见 pǎi

【迫不得已】 pòbùdéyǐ have no alternative (but to); be forced (或 driven, compelled) to; (do sth.) against one's will

【迫不及待】 pò bùjí dài unable to hold oneself back; too impatient to wait: 他们错误估计形势，～地跳了出来。Miscalculating the situation, they rushed out into the open.

【迫害】 pòhài persecute: 政治～ political persecution/ 遭受～ suffer persecution; be subjected to persecution

【迫降】 pòjiàng 〈航空〉 forced landing; distress landing

【迫近】 pòjìn approach; get close to; draw near: ～敌人据点 close in on the enemy stronghold/ ～胜利 be nearing victory; come in sight of victory/ 行期～。The day of departure is drawing near.

【迫切】 pòqiè urgent; pressing; imperative: ～的需要 an urgent need; a crying need/ ～的心情 eager desire; eagerness ◇ ～性 urgency

【迫使】 pòshǐ force; compel: ～敌人缴械投降 force the enemy to hand over their weapons and surrender/ ～对方处于守势 force (或 drive) one's opponent into a defensive position/ 事态的发展～他重新考虑自己的决定。The march of events compelled him to reconsider his decision.

【迫在眉睫】 pò zài méijié ① extremely urgent ② imminent

**珀** pò 见"琥珀" hǔpò

**破** pò ① broken; damaged; torn; worn-out: ～碗 a broken bowl/ ～衣服 worn-out (或 ragged, tattered) clothes/ ～房子 a dilapidated (或 tumbledown) house/ 我的手～了。I've cut my hand. ② break; split; cleave; cut: 一～两半 break (或 split) into two/ ～浪前进 cleave (或 cut, plough) through the waves/ 把十元的票子～开 break a ten-*yuan* note ③ get rid of; destroy; break with: 大～天命观 eradicate the concept of the mandate of heaven/ ～旧俗，立新风 break with outmoded customs and establish new ones/ ～纪录 break a record ④ defeat; capture (a city, etc.): 大～敌军 inflict a crushing defeat on the enemy/ 城～之日 the day the city fell ⑤ expose the truth of; lay bare: 看～ see through/ 一语道～ get to the heart of the matter in a few words; puncture a fallacy with one remark ⑥ paltry; lousy: 这支～笔真气人！ This lousy pen really drives me mad!/ 这点～事两分钟就办完了。To settle a simple matter like this won't take more than two minutes.

【破案】 pò'àn solve (或 clear up) a case; crack a criminal case

【破败】 pòbài ruined; dilapidated; tumbledown: 那所房子已经～不堪。The house is dilapidated.

【破冰船】 pòbīngchuán icebreaker: 原子～ atomic icebreaker

【破擦音】 pòcāyīn 〈语〉 affricate

【破财】 pòcái suffer unexpected personal financial losses

【破产】 pòchǎn ① go bankrupt; become insolvent; become impoverished: ～地主 bankrupt landlords/ ～农民 impoverished peasants/ 银行～ bank failure ② come to naught; fall through; be bankrupt: 帝国主义的阴谋～了。The imperialist plot has fallen through./ 破了产的神话 an exploded myth

【破除】 pòchú do away with; get rid of; eradicate; break with: ～迷信 do away with superstitions or blind faith; topple old idols/ ～情面 not spare anybody's feelings

【破费】 pòfèi 〈套〉 spend money; go to some expense: 你何必这么～呢？Why must you go to this expense?/ 不要多～，随便吃点就行了。Don't go to any expense. I'll enjoy whatever there is to eat.

【破釜沉舟】 pòfǔ-chénzhōu break the cauldrons and sink the boats (after crossing) — cut off all means of retreat; burn one's boats

【破格】 pògé break a rule; make an exception: ～提升 break a rule to promote sb./ ～接待 break protocol to honour sb.

【破罐破摔】 pòguàn pò shuāi smash a pot to pieces just because it's cracked — write oneself off as hopeless and act recklessly

【破坏】 pòhuài ① destroy; wreck: ～桥梁 destroy a bridge ② do great damage to: ～生产 sabotage production/ ～团结 disrupt unity; undermine unity/ ～边界现状 disrupt the status quo along the boundary line/ ～名誉 damage sb.'s reputation/ 警惕敌人的～活动。Guard against enemy sabotage. ③ change (a social system, custom, etc.) completely or violently: ～旧世界，建设新世界。Destroy the old world and build a new one. ④ violate (an agreement, regulation, etc.); break: ～停战协定 violate an armistice agreement ⑤ decompose; destroy (the composition of a substance): 维生素 C 受热过度就会被～。Vitamin C is destroyed when overheated.

◇ ～分子 saboteur/ ～力 destructive power/ ～性 destructiveness

【破获】 pòhuò unearth; uncover: ～一个特务组织 unearth (或 uncover) a spy ring/ ～一起反革命案件 crack a counterrevolutionary case

【破击】 pòjī 〈军〉 attack and destroy; wreck; sabotage: ～敌人的交通线 wreck the enemy's communication lines

【破戒】 pòjiè ① break a religious precept ② break one's vow of abstinence

【破镜重圆】 pòjìng chóng yuán a broken mirror joined together — reunion of husband and wife after an enforced separation or rupture

【破旧】 pòjiù old and shabby; worn-out; dilapidated: 戴一顶～的草帽 wear a shabby straw hat/ ～的家具 old, disreputable furniture

【破旧立新】 pò jiù lì xīn destroy the old and establish the new

【破口大骂】 pòkǒu dàmà shout abuse; let loose a torrent of abuse

【破烂】 pòlàn ① tattered; ragged; worn-out: 一家～的小工厂 a small run-down factory ② 〈口〉 junk; scrap: 捡～ search a garbage heap for odds and ends ◇ ～货 worthless stuff; rubbish; trash

【破例】 pòlì break a rule; make an exception

【破脸】 pòliǎn turn against (an acquaintance or associate); fall out

【破裂】 pòliè burst; split; rupture; crack: 血管～ rupture (或 breaking) of a blood vessel/ 谈判～了。The negotia-

tions broke down./ 他们两口子感情～了。Their marriage has broken up.
【破落】 pòluò decline (in wealth and position); fall into reduced circumstances; be reduced to poverty: ～地主家庭 an impoverished landlord family ◇ ～户 a family that has gone down in the world
【破谜儿】 pòmèir ①〈口〉solve a riddle ②〈方〉ask a riddle
【破门】 pòmén ① burst (或 force) open the door: ～而入 force open a door ②〈宗〉excommunicate
【破灭】 pòmiè be shattered; fall through; evaporate: 他的幻想～了。He was disillusioned./ 他的希望～了。His hopes were shattered.
【破伤风】 pòshāngfēng 〈医〉tetanus
【破私立公】 pò sī lì gōng overcome selfishness and foster public spirit
【破碎】 pòsuì ① tattered; broken: ～的玻璃 broken glass/ 这张帛画已经～了。This painting on silk is in tatters. ② smash (或 break) sth. to pieces; crush: 这机器每小时可以～多少吨矿石？How many tons of ore can this machine crush in an hour? ◇ ～机 crusher; breaker/ ～险〈商〉risk of breakage
【破损】 pòsǔn damaged; worn; torn: 这本书有几页已经～。Some pages of the book are damaged.
【破题儿第一遭】 pò tír dìyī zāo the first time one ever does sth.; the first time ever: 登台演戏我还是～。This is the first time (that) I've acted on the stage.
【破涕为笑】 pò tì wéi xiào smile through tears
【破天荒】 pòtiānhuāng occur for the first time; be unprecedented
【破土】 pòtǔ ① break ground (in starting a building project, etc.) ② start spring ploughing ③ (of a seedling) break through the soil
【破袭战】 pòxízhàn 〈军〉sabotage operations
【破相】 pòxiàng (of facial features) be marred by a scar, etc.
【破晓】 pòxiǎo dawn; daybreak: 天将～。Day is breaking.
【破鞋】 pòxié 〈方〉loose woman
【破颜】 pòyán break into a smile
【破约】 pòyuē break one's promise
【破绽】 pòzhan ① a burst seam ② flaw; weak point: 看出～ spot sb.'s weak point/ 他的论证～百出。His argument is full of flaws.
【破折号】 pòzhéhào dash (—)

粕 pò 〈书〉dregs of rice

魄 pò ① soul: 魂飞～散 (be frightened) out of one's wits ② vigour; spirit: 气～ boldness of vision; spiritedness
另见 bó; tuò
【魄力】 pòli daring and resolution; boldness: 工作有～ be bold and resolute in one's work

## po

桲 po 见"榅桲" wēnpo

## pōu

剖 pōu ① cut open; rip open: 把鱼肚子～开 cut open the belly of a fish ② analyse; examine; dissect: ～明事理 analyse the whys and wherefores
【剖白】 pōubái explain oneself; vindicate oneself: ～心迹 lay one's heart bare
【剖腹产】 pōufùchǎn 〈医〉Caesarean birth ◇ ～术 Caesarean section (或 operation)
【剖腹自杀】 pōu fù zìshā (commit) *hara-kiri*
【剖解】 pōujiě analyse; dissect: ～细密 make a minute analysis
【剖里革】 pōulǐgé 〈皮革〉split
【剖面】 pōumiàn section: 横～ cross section/ 纵～ longitudinal section ◇ ～图 sectional drawing; section
【剖视图】 pōushìtú cutaway view
【剖析】 pōuxī analyse; dissect: ～问题的实质 analyse the essence of the problem

## póu

抔 póu 〈书〉hold sth. with cupped hands: 一～土 a handful of earth — a grave

## pǒu

掊 pǒu
【掊击】 pǒujī attack (in speech or writing); blast; lash out at

## pū

仆 pū fall forward; fall prostrate: 前～后继 one stepping into the breach as another falls
另见 pú

扑 pū ① throw oneself on; pounce on: 孩子一下子～到他妈的怀里去。The child threw himself into his mother's arms./ 老虎向山羊～去。The tiger sprang on the goat./ 一心～在集体事业上 devote oneself heart and soul to the cause of the collective ② rush at; attack: 直～匪徒的巢穴 swoop down on the bandits' lair/ ～蝴蝶 catch butterflies ③ flap; flutter: 鸭子～着翅膀。The duck flapped its wings. ④〈方〉bend over: ～在桌上看地图 bend over a map on the desk
【扑鼻】 pūbí assail the nostrils: 香气～。A sweet smell greeted us.
【扑哧】 pūchī 〈象〉〔形容笑声或水、气挤出的声音〕: ～一笑 titter; snigger/ ～一声，瓶子打开了。The bottle opened with a fizz.
【扑打】 pūdǎ ① swat: ～蝗虫 swat locusts ② beat; pat: ～身上的尘土 dust off one's clothes
【扑跌】 pūdiē ① wrestling ② fall forward
【扑尔敏】 pū'ěrmǐn 〈药〉chlorpheniramine
【扑粉】 pūfěn ① face powder ② talcum powder ③ apply powder
【扑救】 pūjiù put out a fire to save life and property
【扑克】 pūkè ① playing cards: 打～ play cards ② poker
【扑空】 pūkōng fail to get or achieve what one wants; come away empty-handed: 昨天我去找他，又～了。Yesterday I went to see him, but again he wasn't home./ 游击队已经转移，敌人扑了个空。The guerrillas had moved away and the enemy closed in on nothing.
【扑满】 pūmǎn earthenware money box; piggy bank
【扑面】 pūmiàn blow on (或 against) one's face: 春风～。The spring wind caressed our faces.
【扑灭】 pūmiè ① stamp out; put out; extinguish: ～火灾 put out a fire/ 妄图～革命的火焰 try in vain to stamp out (或 quench) the flames of revolution ② exterminate;

wipe out: ～蚊蝇 wipe out mosquitoes and flies
【扑热息痛】 pūrèxītòng 〈药〉 paracetamol
【扑朔迷离】 pūshuò mílí complicated and confusing
【扑簌】 pūsù (of tears) trickling down: 她眼泪扑簌簌地往下掉。Tears trickled down her cheeks.
【扑腾】 pūtēng 〈象〉 thump; thud: ～一声，包掉下来了。The bundle fell with a thud.
【扑腾】 pūteng move up and down; throb; palpitate: 他心里直～。His heart was throbbing./ 鱼在网里直～。The fish flopped about in the net.
【扑通】 pūtōng 〈象〉 flop; thump; splash; pit-a-pat: ～一声，跌倒在地上 fall with a flop on the ground/ ～一声，掉进水里 fall into the water with a splash/ 她的心～～地跳。Her heart went pit-a-pat.
【扑翼】 pūyì flapping wing ◇ ～飞机 flapping-wing aircraft; ornithopter

## 铺

pū ① spread; extend; unfold: ～桌布 spread a tablecloth/ 运动已经全面～开。The movement is fully under way. ② pave; lay: 一条～砖的小路 a path paved with bricks/ ～铁轨 lay a railway track/ ～路面 surface a road/ ～平道路 pave the way
另见 pù
【铺陈】 pūchén narrate in detail; describe at great length; elaborate
【铺衬】 pūchen small pieces of cloth used for patches
【铺床】 pūchuáng make the bed
【铺地砖】 pūdìzhuān floor tile; paving tile
【铺垫】 pūdiàn ① bedding ② foreshadowing: 这一段为故事的高潮作了～。This passage foreshadows the climax of the story.
【铺盖】 pūgai bedding; bedclothes ◇ ～卷儿 bedding roll; bedroll; luggage roll
【铺轨】 pūguǐ lay a railway track ◇ ～机 track-laying machine; tracklayer
【铺路机】 pūlùjī paver
【铺排】 pūpái ① put in order; arrange: 所有的事都～得停停当当。Everything was well arranged. ②〈方〉 be extravagant
【铺砌】 pūqì 〈建〉 pave
【铺设】 pūshè lay; build: ～双轨 lay a double-track/ ～友谊之路 open up a path of friendship
【铺天盖地】 pūtiān-gàidì blot out the sky and cover up the earth: 暴风雪～而来。The blizzard blotted out the sky and the land./ 大字报～。There were *dazibao* all over the place.
【铺叙】 pūxù narrate in detail; elaborate
【铺展】 pūzhǎn spread out; sprawl
【铺张】 pūzhāng extravagant: 反对～浪费 oppose extravagance and waste

## 噗

pū 〈象〉 puff: ～，一口气吹灭了蜡烛 blow out a candle with one puff/ 子弹把尘土打得～～直冒烟。Bullets whipped up the dust.
【噗嗤】 pūchī 见"扑哧" pūchī

# pú

## 仆

pú servant: 男～ manservant/ 女～ maidservant
另见 pū
【仆从】 púcóng footman; retainer; henchman ◇ ～国 vassal country
【仆仆风尘】 púpú fēngchén 见"风尘仆仆" fēngchén púpú
【仆人】 púrén (domestic) servant

## 匍

pú
【匍匐】 púfú ① crawl; creep: ～前进 crawl forward ② lie prostrate: ～在主子脚下 prostrate oneself before one's master ◇ ～茎〈植〉 stolon/ ～植物 creeper

## 菩

pú
【菩萨】 púsà ① Bodhisattva ② Buddha; Buddhist idol ③ a term applied to a kindhearted person: ～心肠 kindhearted and merciful
【菩提】 pútí 〈佛教〉 bodhi, supreme wisdom or enlightenment, necessary to the attainment of Buddhahood
【菩提树】 pútíshù pipal; bo tree; bodhi tree

## 脯

pú chest; breast
另见 fǔ
【脯子】 púzi breast meat (of chicken, duck, etc.): 鸡～ chicken breast

## 葡

pú
【葡萄牙】 Pútáoyá Portugal ◇ ～人 Portuguese/ ～语 Portuguese (language)
【葡萄】 pútao grape: 一串～ a bunch (或 cluster) of grapes ◇ ～弹〈军〉 grapeshot; grape/ ～干 raisin/ ～架 grape trellis/ ～酒 (grape) wine/ ～球菌〈微〉 staphylococcus/ ～胎〈医〉 hydatidiform mole; vesicular mole/ ～糖 glucose; grape sugar; dextrose/ ～藤 grapevine/ ～园 vineyard; grapery

## 蒲

pú ①〈植〉 cattail ②(Pú) a surname
【蒲包】 púbāo cattail bag; rush bag
【蒲草】 púcǎo the stem or leaf of cattail
【蒲公英】 púgōngyīng 〈植〉 dandelion
【蒲黄】 púhuáng 〈中药〉 cattail pollen
【蒲葵】 púkuí 〈植〉 Chinese fan palm
【蒲柳】 púliǔ 〈植〉 big catkin willow (*Salix gracilistyla*)
【蒲绒】 púróng cattail wool, used for stuffing pillows
【蒲扇】 púshàn cattail leaf fan
【蒲式耳】 púshì'ěr bushel
【蒲团】 pútuán cattail hassock; rush cushion
【蒲席】 púxí cattail mat; rush mat

## 璞

pú uncut jade
【璞玉浑金】 púyù-húnjīn uncut jade and unrefined gold — unadorned beauty

## 镤

pú 〈化〉 protactinium (Pa)

# pǔ

## 朴

pǔ simple; plain
另见 Piáo; pō; pò
【朴实】 pǔshí ① simple; plain: ～无华 simple and unadorned/ 文风～ simple style of writing ② sincere and honest; guileless: ～的工作作风 a down-to-earth style of work
【朴素】 pǔsù simple; plain: 衣著～ simply dressed/ ～的阶级感情 simple class feeling ◇ ～唯物主义 naive materialism
【朴直】 pǔzhí honest and straightforward: 文笔～ simple and straightforward writing
【朴质】 pǔzhì simple and unadorned; natural

## 浦

pǔ ①〔多用于地名〕 riverside; river mouth ②(Pǔ) a

surname

**埔** pǔ 〔用于地名〕: 黄～Huangpu (Guangdong Province)

**圃** pǔ garden: 菜～ vegetable plot/ 苗～ seed plot; (seedling) nursery

**普** pǔ general; universal: ～天下 all over the world; everywhere in the world

【普遍】 pǔbiàn universal; general; widespread; common: 有～意义 be of universal significance/ 进行一次～的马克思主义的教育运动 conduct a widespread (或 extensive) movement for Marxist education/ 我们市已经～用上了煤气灶。Gas stoves are now in common use in our city. ◇ ～规律 universal law/ ～性 universality/ ～优惠制 generalized preferential system/ ～真理 universal truth

【普查】 pǔchá ① general investigation (或 survey): 常见病～ general survey of common diseases/ 人口～ census ②〈地〉 reconnaissance survey

【普洱茶】 pǔ'ěrchá Pu'er tea (produced in southwestern Yunnan)

【普及】 pǔjí ① popularize; disseminate; spread: ～与提高相结合 combine popularization with the raising of standards/ ～文化科学知识 spread cultural and scientific knowledge among the people/ ～中等教育 make secondary education universal ② universal; popular ◇ ～本 popular edition/ ～教育 universal education

【普鲁本辛】 pǔlǔběnxīn 〈药〉 propantheline (bromide); probanthine

【普鲁卡因】 pǔlǔkǎyīn 〈药〉 procaine

【普米族】 Pǔmǐzú the Pumi nationality, living in Yunnan

【普什图语】 Pǔshítúyǔ Pushtu

【普特】 pǔtè pood

【普天同庆】 pǔtiān tóng qìng the whole world or nation joins in the jubilation

【普通】 pǔtōng ordinary; common; average: ～一兵 an ordinary soldier; a soldier in the ranks; a rank-and-filer/ ～人 the average person; the man in the street/ 这是两所～的房子。These are just two ordinary houses. ◇ ～法〈法〉 common law/ ～话 *putonghua*; common speech (of the Chinese language); standard Chinese pronunciation/ ～劳动者 ordinary labourer/ ～税则 general tariff / ～心理学 general psychology/ ～照会〈外〉 verbal note

【普选】 pǔxuǎn general election ◇ ～权 universal suffrage

【普照】 pǔzhào illuminate all things: 阳光～大地。The sun illuminates every corner of the land.

**溥** pǔ 〈书〉 ① broad ② common; universal

**谱** pǔ ① table; chart; register: 家～ family tree; genealogy/ 食～ cookbook; menu ② manual; guide: 棋～ chess manual ③ music score; music: 乐～ music score; music/ 歌～ music of a song ④ set to music; compose (music): 把毛主席的诗词～成歌曲 set Chairman Mao's poems to music/ 这首歌是谁～的曲? Who is the composer of the song? ⑤ sth. to count on; a fair amount of confidence: 心里没个～儿 have nothing definite in mind/ 做事有～儿 do things with confidence; know what one is doing

【谱斑】 pǔbān 〈天〉 flocculus

【谱表】 pǔbiǎo 〈乐〉 stave; staff: 大～ great stave

【谱号】 pǔhào 〈乐〉 clef: 高音～ treble clef; G clef/ 中音～ tenor clef; alto clef; C clef/ 低音～ bass clef; F clef

【谱系】 pǔxì 〈生〉 pedigree

【谱写】 pǔxiě compose (music): 这支曲子是在解放战争初期～的。The tune was composed at the beginning of the War of Liberation./ 在抗震救灾斗争中，英雄的唐山人民～了一曲毛泽东思想的凯歌。In their struggle to overcome the effects of the earthquake, the heroic people of Tangshan scored a victory for Mao Zedong Thought.

【谱子】 pǔzi 〈口〉 music score; music

**氆** pǔ

【氆氇】 pǔlu a woolen fabric made in Xizang

**镨** pǔ 〈化〉 praseodymium (Pr)

**蹼** pǔ web (of the feet of ducks, frogs, etc.)

【蹼趾】 pǔzhǐ webbed toe

【蹼足】 pǔzú webfoot; palmate foot

## pù

**铺** pù ① shop; store ② plank bed

另见 pū

【铺板】 pùbǎn bed board; bed plank

【铺保】 pùbǎo guarantee for a person, given by a shopkeeper

【铺面】 pùmiàn shop front

【铺位】 pùwèi bunk; berth

【铺子】 pùzi shop; store

**瀑** pù waterfall

【瀑布】 pùbù waterfall; falls; cataract

**曝** pù 〈书〉 expose to the sun

【曝光】 pùguāng 〈摄〉 exposure ◇ ～表 exposure meter/ ～宽容度 exposure latitude

【曝露】 pùlù 〈书〉 exposed to the open air

【曝气池】 pùqìchí 〈环保〉 aeration tank

# Q

## qī

**七** qī seven

注意 "七"字在第四声(去声)字前念第二声(阳平),如"七月"qíyuè;"七位"qíwèi。本词典为简便起见,条目中的"七"字,都注第一声(阴平)。

【七…八…】 qī...bā...〔嵌用动词或名词,表示多或多而杂乱〕: 七扭八歪 crooked; uneven; disorderly; irregular/ 七折八扣 various deductions/ 七颠八倒 at sixes and sevens; all upside down; topsy-turvy/ 大家七手八脚一会儿就把院子打扫干净了。With everybody lending a hand, the courtyard was soon swept clean.

【七边形】 qībiānxíng 〈数〉 heptagon

【"七·二一"大学】 Qī Èryī dàxué "July 21" college (set up in accordance with Chairman Mao's instructions of July 21, 1968)

【七级风】 qījífēng 〈气〉 force 7 wind; moderate gale

【七极管】 qījíguǎn 〈电〉 heptode

【七绝】 qījué a four-line poem with seven characters to a line and a strict tonal pattern and rhyme scheme 参见"绝句" juéjù

【七零八落】 qīlíng-bāluò scattered here and there; in disorder: ~的几间草房 a few ramshackle huts scattered here and there/ 敌人被打得~,四散奔逃。 Badly battered, the enemy fled in disorder.

【七律】 qīlǜ an eight-line poem with seven characters to a line and a strict tonal pattern and rhyme scheme 参见"律诗" lǜshī

【七拼八凑】 qīpīn-bācòu piece together; knock together; rig up: 用碎布~做成一个枕套 make a pillowcase from odd pieces of cloth/ 我们这个小工厂是自己动手~搞起来的。We rigged up this little factory with our own hands.

【七七事变】 Qī Qī Shìbiàn the July 7 Incident of 1937 参见"芦沟桥事变" Lúgōuqiáo Shìbiàn

【七巧板】 qīqiǎobǎn seven-piece puzzle; tangram

【七窍】 qīqiào the seven apertures in the human head, i.e. eyes, ears, nostrils and mouth

【七窍生烟】 qīqiào shēng yān fume with anger; foam with rage

【七情】 qīqíng ①the seven human emotions, namely, joy, anger, sorrow, fear, love, hate and desire ②〈中医〉 the seven emotional factors (joy, anger, melancholy, brooding, sorrow, fear and shock, considered to be the internal factors causing diseases)

【七鳃鳗】 qīsāimán lamprey

【七上八下】 qīshàng-bāxià be agitated; be perturbed: 他心里~的,不知怎么办才好。He was so agitated that he didn't know what to do.

【七十二变】 qīshí èr biàn seventy-two metamorphoses (said of the Monkey King, in the *Pilgrimage to the West* 《西游记》, who could change himself into seventy-two forms); countless changes of tactics

【七十二行】 qīshí èr háng all sorts of occupations; in every conceivable line of work

【七夕】 qīxī the seventh evening of the seventh moon (when according to legend the Cowherd 牛郎 and the Weaver Maid 织女 meet in Heaven)

【七言诗】 qīyánshī a poem with seven characters to a line 参见"古体诗" gǔtǐshī; "绝句" juéjù; "律诗" lǜshī

【七一】 Qī Yī July 1, anniversary of the founding of the Communist Party of China (1921)

【七月】 qīyuè ①July ②the seventh month of the lunar year; the seventh moon

【七政仪】 qīzhèngyí 〈天〉 orrery

【七嘴八舌】 qīzuǐ-bāshé lively discussion with everybody trying to get a word in; all talking at once: 方案一公布,大家就~地议论开了。Publication of the draft plan touched off a lively discussion, with everybody eager to put in a word.

**沏** qī infuse: ~茶 infuse tea; make tea

**妻** qī wife

【妻儿老小】 qī-ér lǎo-xiǎo a married man's entire family (parents, wife and children)

【妻离子散】 qīlí-zǐsàn breaking up or scattering of one's family

【妻孥】 qī-nú 〈书〉 wife and children

【妻子】 qī-zǐ wife and children

【妻子】 qīzi wife

**柒** qī seven (used for the numeral 七 on cheques, etc., to avoid mistakes or alterations)

**凄** qī ①chilly; cold: 风雨~~。Cold, cold are the wind and the rain. ②bleak and desolate: ~清 lonely and sad ③sad; wretched; miserable: ~楚 miserable

【凄惨】 qīcǎn wretched; miserable; tragic

【凄风苦雨】 qīfēng-kǔyǔ wailing wind and weeping rain — wretched circumstances

【凄厉】 qīlì sad and shrill: ~的叫声 sad, shrill cries/ 风声~。The wind was wailing.

【凄凉】 qīliáng dreary; desolate; miserable: 满目~ desolation all round/ 晚景~ lead a miserable and dreary life in old age

【凄切】 qīqiè plaintive; mournful

【凄然】 qīrán 〈书〉 sad; mournful: ~泪下 shed tears in sadness

**栖** qī ①(of birds) perch ②dwell; stay

【栖身】 qīshēn stay; sojourn: 无处~ have no place to stay

【栖息】 qīxī (of birds) perch; rest: 许多水鸟在岛上~。A great number of water fowls dwell on the island. ◇ ~地 habitat

**桤** qī

【桤木】 qīmù 〈植〉 alder

**萋** qī

【萋萋】 qīqī 〈书〉 luxuriant: 芳草~ a luxuriant growth of grass

**戚** qī ①relative: 皇亲国~ relatives of an emperor ②sorrow; woe: 休~相关 share joys and sorrows; share weal and woe ③(Qī) a surname

**期** qī ①a period of time; phase; stage: 假～ vacation/ 学～ school term/ 潜伏～ incubation period/ 第一～工程 the first phase of the project ②scheduled time: 到～ fall due/ 限～ set a time limit (或 deadline) ③〈量〉〔用于分期的事物〕: 最近一～的《中国画报》 the current issue of *China Pictorial*/ 短训班办了三～。The short-term training class has been run three times. ④make an appointment: 不～而遇 meet unexpectedly; meet by chance ⑤expect: ～待 expect; await
另见 jī

【期待】 qīdài expect; await; look forward to: 殷切地～你早日答复 eagerly await your early reply/ 我们一直～着这一天。We've been looking forward to this day for a long time.

【期货】 qīhuò 〈经〉 futures ◇ ～价格 forward price/ ～合同 forward contract; futures contract

【期间】 qījiān time; period; course: 就在这～ during this time; in this very period/ 会议～ in the course of the conference; during the conference

【期刊】 qīkān periodical ◇ ～阅览室 periodical reading room

【期考】 qīkǎo end-of-term examination; terminal examination

【期满】 qīmǎn expire; run out; come to an end: 合同～ when the contract expires; on the expiration of the contract/ 服役～ complete one's term of (military) service

【期票】 qīpiào promissory note

【期望】 qīwàng hope; expectation: 党对青年人寄予很大的～。The Party places high hopes on the young people./ 我们决不辜负人民的～。We will never disappoint the people's expectations.

【期限】 qīxiàn alloted time; time limit; deadline: 规定一个～ set a deadline; fix a target date/ 延长～ extend the time limit/ 必须在规定的～内完成这项工作。The work must be finished in the allotted time.

**欺** qī ①deceive: 自～～人 deceive oneself as well as others/ ～人之谈 deceitful words; deceptive talk ②bully; take advantage of: ～人太甚。That's going too far./ 不要把我们的克制当作软弱可～。Don't mistake our restraint for weakness or something you can take advantage of.

【欺负】 qīfu bully; treat sb. high-handedly: 大国不应当～小国。Big nations should not bully small ones.

【欺凌】 qīlíng bully and humiliate: 受尽了～ be subjected to endless bullying and humiliation/ 决不任人～ never allow oneself to be trodden upon

【欺瞒】 qīmán hoodwink; dupe; pull the wool over sb.'s eyes

【欺骗】 qīpiàn deceive; cheat; dupe: ～世界舆论 befuddle world opinion/ 这只能～那些不明真相的人。This can only deceive those who do not know the truth. 或 This can only mislead those who are not aware of the facts./ 戳穿资产阶级议会民主的～性 expose the fraudulent nature of bourgeois parliamentary democracy/ 揭露两面派的～性 expose the duplicity of the double-dealers

【欺软怕硬】 qīruǎn-pàyìng bully the weak and fear the strong

【欺上瞒下】 qīshàng-mánxià deceive one's superiors and delude one's subordinates

【欺生】 qīshēng ①bully or cheat strangers ②(of horses, mules, etc.) be ungovernable by strangers

【欺世盗名】 qīshì-dàomíng gain fame by deceiving the public; angle for undeserved fame

【欺侮】 qīwǔ bully; treat sb. high-handedly

【欺压】 qīyā bully and oppress; ride roughshod over

【欺诈】 qīzhà cheat; swindle

**漆** qī ①lacquer; paint: ～盘 lacquer tray ②coat with lacquer; paint: 把门～成深绿色 paint the door dark green/ 把桌子再～一遍 give the table another coat of paint ③(Qī) a surname

【漆包线】 qībāoxiàn 〈电〉 enamel-insulated wire

【漆布】 qībù varnished cloth

【漆革】 qīgé patent leather

【漆工】 qīgōng ①lacquering; painting ②lacquerer; lacquer man; painter

【漆黑】 qīhēi pitch-dark; pitch-black

【漆黑一团】 qīhēi yī tuán ①pitch-dark: 把形势描绘成～ paint a dark picture of the situation ②be entirely ignorant of; be in the dark: 这个问题在他心中还是～。He is still completely in the dark about the matter.

【漆画】 qīhuà 〈美术〉 lacquer painting

【漆匠】 qījiang ①lacquerware worker ②lacquerer; lacquer man; painter

【漆皮】 qīpí ①coat of paint ②shellac

【漆器】 qīqì lacquerware; lacquerwork: 脱胎～ bodiless lacquerware

【漆树】 qīshù lacquer tree

**噈** qī

【噈噈喳喳】 qīqīchāchā 〈象〉 chatter away; jabber

**槭** qī

【槭树】 qīshù maple

**蹊** qī
另见 xī

【蹊跷】 qīqiāo odd; queer; fishy

## qí

**齐** qí ①neat; even; uniform: 整～ neat and tidy/ 把桌子摆～ arrange the tables in an orderly way/ 剪得很～ be evenly trimmed/ 长短不～ not of uniform length ②on a level with: 水涨得～了岸。The water has risen until it's on a level with the river banks./ 在～腰深的水里筑坝 stand waist-deep in water to build the dam/ 把玉米秆～着根儿砍断 cut the cornstalks right down to the roots ③together; simultaneously: 男女老幼～动手。 Men and women, old and young, all pitched in./ 万炮～发。All the batteries fired at once. ④all ready; all present: 客人都来～了。 The guests are all present./ 一切准备～了。Everything is ready. ⑤alike; similar: 人心～，泰山移。When people work with one mind, they can even remove Mount Taishan. ⑥(Qí) the Southern Qi Dynasty (479-502), one of the Southern Dynasties ⑦(Qí) a surname

【齐备】 qíbèi all ready: 实验所需的东西都已～。The things necessary for the experiment are all ready.

【齐步走】 qíbùzǒu 〈军〉 ①quick march ②(口令) Quick time, march!

【齐唱】 qíchàng 〈乐〉 singing in unison; unison

【齐楚】 qíchǔ neat and smart: 衣冠～ be smartly dressed

【齐集】 qíjí assemble; gather; collect

【齐家文化】 Qíjiā wénhuà 〈考古〉 the Qijia culture, a culture of the Chalcolithic period, relics of which were first unearthed at Qijiaping, Gansu Province, in 1923

【齐名】 qímíng enjoy equal popularity; be equally famous

【齐明】 qímíng 〈物〉 aplanatic

◇ ～成象 aplanatic image formation/ ～点 aplanatic foci/ ～镜 aplanat

【齐全】 qíquán complete; all in readiness: 尺码～ have a complete range of sizes/ 登山队装备～。The mountaineers are fully equipped./新建的工人住宅设备～。The new workers' houses have all the necessary fittings./ 这商店虽然小，货物却很～。 The shop, though small, has a satisfactory variety of goods.

【齐射】 qíshè ‹军› salvo; volley

【齐声】 qíshēng in chorus; in unison: ～回答 answer in chorus/ ～欢呼 cheer in unison

【齐头并进】 qítóu bìngjìn advance side by side; do two or more things at once: 三路人马～。The three columns advanced simultaneously./ 这些工作要分轻重缓急，不要～。These jobs should be arranged in order of priority and not undertaken all at once.

【齐心】 qíxīn be of one mind (或 heart): 群众～了，一切事情就好办了。When the masses are of one heart, everything becomes easy./ ～协力 work as one; make concerted efforts

【齐整】 qízhěng neat; uniform: 运河两旁的柳树长得很～。The canal is flanked by neat rows of willows.

【齐奏】 qízòu ‹乐› playing (instruments) in unison; unison

## 祁

Qí a surname

【祁红】 qíhóng keemun (black tea)

## 芪

qí 见"黄芪" huángqí

## 祈

qí ① pray: ～年 pray for a good harvest ② entreat: 敬～指导。We respectfully request your guidance.

【祈祷】 qídǎo pray; say one's prayers

【祈求】 qíqiú earnestly hope; pray for

【祈使句】 qíshǐjù ‹语› imperative sentence

【祈望】 qíwàng hope; wish

## 其

qí ① his (her; its; their): ～父 his father/ 各得～所。Each is in his proper place. 或 Everyone is properly provided for. ② he (she, it, they): 不要任～自流。Don't let things slide./ 促～早日实现 help bring it about at an early date ③ that; such: 正当～时 just at that time; at the opportune moment/ 不乏～人。There is no lack of such people./ 如闻～声，如见～人 (so vividly described that) you seem to see and hear the person ④〔虚指〕: 大请～客 invite many guests to dinner; entertain lavishly ⑤ ‹书›‹助›〔表示揣测、反诘或命令〕: ～奈我何？What can they do to me?/ 子～勉之！Exert yourself to the utmost!

【其次】 qícì ① next; secondly; then: 先看生产车间，～再参观托儿所。Let's see the workshop first and then the nursery. ② secondary: 内容是主要的，形式还在～。 Content comes first, form second.

【其实】 qíshí ‹副› actually; in fact; as a matter of fact: ～情况不是那样。Actually, that is not the case./ 这台机器看起来复杂，～不难掌握。This machine looks complicated, but it's really not difficult to operate.

【其他】 qítā other; else: 除了整地，～活儿也需要人。We need people for other jobs besides levelling the land./ 还有什么～事情要我们做吗？Is there anything else you want us to do? 又作"其它"(用于事物)

【其余】 qíyú the others; the rest; the remainder: ～的人马上就来。The others will be here in a minute./ 这个突击队只有三名男的，～都是女同志。There are only three men in the shock team; the rest are women.

【其中】 qízhōng among (which, them, etc.); in (which, it, etc.): 乐在～ find pleasure in it/ 我们车间有五百人，～妇女占百分之六十。 There are five hundred workers in our shop, and 60 per cent of them are women.

## 奇

qí ① strange; queer; rare: ～事 a strange affair; an unusual phenomenon/ ～花异木 exotic flowers and rare trees ② surprise; wonder; astonish: 这是不足为～的。This is nothing to be surprised at.

另见 jī

【奇兵】 qíbīng an army suddenly appearing from nowhere; an ingenious military move

【奇耻大辱】 qíchǐ-dàrǔ galling shame and humiliation; deep disgrace: 这真是～。This is really galling and humiliating.

【奇功】 qígōng outstanding service: 屡建～ repeatedly perform outstanding service

【奇怪】 qíguài strange; surprising; odd: 陨石雨是一种自然现象，没有什么可～的。A meteorite shower is a natural phenomenon; there's nothing strange about it./ 真～，他们至今还一无所知。It's really surprising that they should still be in the dark.

【奇观】 qíguān marvellous spectacle; wonder: 自然界的～ a marvellous natural phenomenon

【奇货可居】 qíhuò kě jū hoard as a rare commodity

【奇迹】 qíjī miracle; wonder; marvel: 创造～ work wonders; accomplish wonders; perform miracles/ 医学上的～ a marvel of medical science/ 在共产党领导下，只要有了人，什么人间～也可以造出来。Under the leadership of the Communist Party, as long as there are people, every kind of miracle can be performed.

【奇景】 qíjǐng wonderful view; extraordinary sight: 冰峰～ a wonderful view of ice-capped peaks

【奇妙】 qímiào marvellous; wonderful; intriguing

【奇巧】 qíqiǎo (of art or handicraft) ingenious; exquisite

【奇谈】 qítán strange tale; absurd argument: 海外～ strange tales from over the seas

【奇特】 qítè peculiar; queer; singular

【奇文】 qíwén ① a remarkable piece of writing: ～共欣赏，疑义相与析。A remarkable work should be shared and its subtleties discussed. ② queer writing

【奇闻】 qíwén sth. unheard-of; a thrilling, fantastic story: 千古～ an unheard-of fantastic story

【奇袭】 qíxí surprise attack; raid

【奇形怪状】 qíxíng-guàizhuàng grotesque or fantastic in shape or appearance: ～的钟乳石 stalactites of grotesque shapes

【奇勋】 qíxūn ‹书› outstanding service; outstanding contribution

【奇异】 qíyì ① queer; strange; bizarre: ～的动物 rare animals ② curious: 他们都用～的眼光看着我。They all looked at me with curious eyes.

【奇遇】 qíyù ① happy encounter; fortuitous meeting ② adventure

【奇志】 qízhì high aspirations; lofty ideal

【奇装异服】 qízhuāng-yìfú exotic costume; bizarre dress; outlandish clothes

## 歧

qí ① fork; branch ② divergent; different

【歧管】 qíguǎn ‹机› manifold

【歧路】 qílù branch road; forked road

【歧视】 qíshì discriminate against: 种族～ racial discrimination

【歧途】 qítú wrong road: 误入～ take the wrong road by mistake; go astray/ 被引入～ be led astray

【歧义】 qíyì different meanings; various interpretations: 有～ be open to different interpretations; be equivocal

**荠** qí 见"荸荠" bíqi
另见 jì

**俟** qí 见"万俟" Mòqí
另见 sì

**耆** qí over sixty years of age; very old
【耆宿】 qísù venerated old people (of a community)

**脐** qí ①〈生理〉navel; umbilicus ② the abdomen of a crab
【脐带】 qídài 〈生理〉umbilical cord
【脐风】 qífēng 〈中医〉umbilical tetanus

**淇** qí 见"冰淇淋" bīngqílín

**萁** qí 〈方〉beanstalk

**畦** qí rectangular pieces of land in a field, separated by ridges, usu. for growing vegetables: 菜～ a vegetable bed
【畦灌】 qíguàn 〈农〉border method of irrigation

**崎** qí
【崎岖】 qíqū rugged: ～不平 rugged and rough/ ～的山路 a rugged mountain path

**骑** qí ① ride (an animal or bicycle); sit on the back of: ～马 ride a horse; be on horseback/ ～车回家 go home by bicycle/ 善～射 excel in horsemanship and marksmanship/ 我们党和国家的干部是普通劳动者，而不是～在人民头上的老爷。The cadres of our Party and state are ordinary workers and not overlords sitting on the backs of the people./ 帝国主义～在别国人民头上称王称霸的日子已一去不复返了。Gone for ever are the days when imperialism could ride roughshod over the people of other countries. ② cavalryman; cavalry: 铁～ cavalry
【骑兵】 qíbīng cavalryman; cavalry ◇ ～部队 mounted troops; cavalry unit
【骑缝】 qífèng a junction of the edges of two sheets of paper: 在单据的～上盖印 put a seal across the perforation between the two halves of a voucher
【骑虎难下】 qí hǔ nán xià ride a tiger and find it hard to get off — have no way to back down
【骑马订】 qímǎdìng 〈印〉saddle stitching
【骑马找马】 qí mǎ zhǎo mǎ look for a horse while sitting on one — hold on to one job while seeking a better one
【骑墙】 qíqiáng sit on the fence ◇ ～派 fence-sitter
【骑士】 qíshì knight; cavalier
【骑术】 qíshù horsemanship; equestrian skill

**骐** qí 〈书〉black horse

**琦** qí 〈书〉① fine jade ② outstanding; distinguished; admirable

**琪** qí fine jade

**棋** qí chess or any board game: 下一盘～ play a game of chess/ 象～ Chinese chess/ 国际象～ (international) chess
【棋逢对手】 qí féng duìshǒu meet one's match in a chess tournament; be well-matched in a contest 又作"棋逢敌手"
【棋迷】 qímí chess fan; chess enthusiast
【棋盘】 qípán chessboard; checkerboard
【棋谱】 qípǔ chess manual
【棋子】 qízǐ piece (in a board game); chessman

**蛴** qí
【蛴螬】 qícáo 〈动〉grub

**旗** qí ① flag; banner; standard: 国～ national flag/ 队～ team pennant/ 锦～ brocade banner ② of the "Eight Banners" (八旗): ～人 bannerman ③ banner, an administrative division of county level in the Nei Monggol Autonomous Region: 阿巴嘎～ the Abga Banner
【旗杆】 qígān flagpole; flag post
【旗鼓相当】 qí-gǔ xiāngdāng be well-matched: 这两个队～，打得十分激烈。The two teams were well-matched, and the game was hotly contested./ ～的对手 an opponent worthy of one's steel
【旗号】 qíhào 〔多用于贬义〕banner; flag: 打着社会主义的～，干着帝国主义的罪恶勾当 flaunt the banner of socialism while perpetrating the criminal acts of imperialism/ 打着马克思主义的～搞修正主义 practise revisionism under the signboard of Marxism
【旗舰】 qíjiàn flagship
【旗开得胜】 qí kāi déshèng win victory the moment one raises one's standard; win victory in the first battle; win speedy success
【旗袍】 qípáo a close-fitting woman's dress with high neck and slit skirt; cheongsam; a sheath with a slit skirt
【旗绳】 qíshéng halyard
【旗手】 qíshǒu standard-bearer
【旗鱼】 qíyú sailfish
【旗语】 qíyǔ semaphore; flag signal: 打～ signal by semaphore; semaphore
【旗帜】 qízhì ① banner; flag: 鲜红的～迎风飘扬。Bright red banners are fluttering in the breeze. ② stand; colours: ～鲜明 have a clear-cut stand
【旗子】 qízi flag; banner; pennant

**蜞** qí 见"蟛蜞" péngqí

**鲯** qí
【鲯鳅】 qíqiū 〈动〉dorado; dolphinfish

**鳍** qí 〈动〉fin: 背～ dorsal fin/ 腹～ ventral fin; pelvic fin/ 尾～ caudal fin
【鳍脚】 qíjiǎo 〈动〉clasper ◇ ～动物 Pinnipedia; pinniped

**麒** qí
【麒麟】 qílín *kylin*; (Chinese) unicorn
【麒麟座】 qílínzuò 〈天〉Monoceros

## qǐ

**乞** qǐ beg (for alms, etc.); supplicate: ～食 beg for food/ ～哀告怜 piteously beg for help
【乞丐】 qǐgài beggar
【乞力马扎罗山】 Qǐlìmǎzhāluóshān Kilimanjaro
【乞怜】 qǐlián beg for pity (或 mercy): 摇尾～ be like a dog wagging its tail pitifully; abjectly beg for mercy
【乞灵】 qǐlíng 〈书〉resort to; seek help from: ～于谣言和诡辩 resort to rumourmongering and sophistry
【乞求】 qǐqiú beg for; supplicate; implore: ～宽恕 beg for mercy (或 pardon)
【乞讨】 qǐtǎo beg; go begging: 沿街～ go begging from

door to door

【乞降】 qǐxiáng beg to surrender

【乞援】 qǐyuán ask for assistance; beg for aid

**岂** qǐ 〈书〉〈副〉〔表示反问〕: ～非白日做梦? Isn't that daydreaming?/ 这样做～不更实际些? Wouldn't that be more practical?

【岂但】 qǐdàn not only: ～青年人爱好运动,就连上了年纪的人也积极锻炼身体。Not only are the young keen on sports, even elderly people are enthusiastic about physical training.

【岂敢】 qǐgǎn 〈套〉 you flatter me; I don't deserve such praise or honour

【岂能】 qǐnéng how could; how is it possible: ～不辞而别? How could you leave without saying good-bye? 又作"岂可"

【岂有此理】 qǐ yǒu cǐ lǐ preposterous; outrageous: 真是～! This is really outrageous!

**企** qǐ ① stand on tiptoe ② anxiously expect sth.; look forward to

【企鹅】 qǐ'é penguin

【企口】 qǐkǒu 〈建〉 tongue-and-groove: ～接合 tongue-and-groove joint

【企求】 qǐqiú desire to gain; seek for; hanker after: 他一心只想把工作做好,从不～个人名利。All he wanted was to do his job well; he never sought personal gain.

【企图】 qǐtú 〔多含贬意〕attempt; try; seek: 敌军～突围,但未得逞。The enemy failed in his attempt to effect a breakthrough.

【企望】 qǐwàng hope for; look forward to: 这是我们多年所～的。This is what we have been looking forward to for years.

【企业】 qǐyè enterprise; business: 工矿～ factories, mines and other enterprises/ ～管理 business management ◇ ～家 entrepreneur; enterpriser

**启** qǐ ① open: ～门 open the door/ 幕～。The curtain rises. ② start; initiate: ～行 start on a journey ③ enlighten; awaken: ～发 arouse; inspire; enlighten ④〈书〉 state; inform: 敬～者 I beg to state; I wish to inform you ⑤〈书〉 letter; note: 谢～ a note of thanks

【启程】 qǐchéng set out; start on a journey

【启齿】 qǐchǐ open one's mouth; start to talk about sth.: 难以～ find it difficult to bring the matter up

【启碇】 qǐdìng weigh anchor

【启动】 qǐdòng start (a machine, etc.); switch on

【启发】 qǐfā arouse; inspire; enlighten: ～他们的阶级觉悟 arouse their class consciousness/ 老科学家的报告给了我们很多～。The old scientist's lecture greatly inspired us.

【启发式】 qǐfāshì elicitation method (of teaching); heuristic method

【启封】 qǐfēng ① unseal; break (或 remove) the seal ② open an envelop or wrapper

【启航】 qǐháng set sail; weigh anchor: 这艘货轮什么时候～? When does the freighter set sail?

【启蒙】 qǐméng ① impart rudimentary knowledge to beginners; initiate: ～老师 the teacher who introduces one to a certain field of study/ ～课本 children's primer ② enlighten; free sb. from prejudice or superstition

【启蒙运动】 Qǐméng Yùndòng the Enlightenment

【启明星】 qǐmíngxīng 〈天〉 Venus

【启示】 qǐshì enlightenment; inspiration; revelation: 从他的经验中得到很大～ gain a good deal of enlightenment from his experience; draw great inspiration from his experience

【启事】 qǐshì notice; announcement: 征稿～ a notice inviting contributions (to a magazine, newspaper, etc.)

【启衅】 qǐxìn start a quarrel; provoke discord; provoke dispute

【启用】 qǐyòng start using (an official seal, etc.)

【启运】 qǐyùn start shipment (of goods)

**杞** Qǐ a surname

【杞人忧天】 Qǐ rén yōu tiān like the man of Qi who was haunted by the fear that the sky might fall — entertain imaginary or groundless fears

**起** qǐ ① rise; get up; stand up: ～席 rise from the table/ 早睡早～ early to bed and early to rise ② remove; extract; pull: ～油 remove grease stains/ ～瓶塞 pull the cork from a bottle/ ～钉子 draw out a nail/ ～雷 clear mines/ 把画～下来 take down a picture ③ appear; raise: 脚上～水泡 get blisters on one's feet ④ rise; grow: ～风了。The wind is rising./ ～疑心 become suspicious/ ～作用 take effect ⑤ draft; work out: ～稿子 work out (或 make) a draft/ ～草 draft ⑥ build; set up: ～一堵墙 build a wall/ ～伙 set up a mess ⑦ start; begin: 从今天～ starting from today ⑧〈量〉 ⓐ case; instance: 两～大脑炎 two cases of cerebritis ⓑ batch; group: 分两～出发 set out in two groups (或 batches)

**起** qi ①〔用在动词后,表示动作的趋向〕: 拿～武器 take up arms/ 引～注意 draw one's attention ②〔用在动词后,常跟"不""得"连用,表示力量够得上或够不上〕: 买不～ can't afford to buy/ 经得～时间的考验 can stand the test of time

【起岸】 qǐ'àn bring (cargo, etc. from a ship) to land

【起爆】 qǐbào detonate ◇ ～帽 detonating cap/ ～剂 detonating agent; primer

【起笔】 qǐbǐ ① the first stroke of a Chinese character ② the start of each stroke in writing a Chinese character

【起草】 qǐcǎo draft; draw up: ～文件 draft (或 draw up) a document ◇ ～人 draftsman/ ～委员会 drafting committee

【起承转合】 qǐ-chéng-zhuǎn-hé introduction, elucidation of the theme, transition to another viewpoint and summing up — the four steps in the composition of an essay

【起程】 qǐchéng leave; set out; start on a journey: 日内～前往广州 leave for Guangzhou in a day or two

【起初】 qǐchū originally; at first; at the outset: 这个工厂～很小。The factory was originally very small./ ～他一个字也不认识,现在已经能够写信了。At first he couldn't read and write, but now he can even carry on a correspondence.

【起床】 qǐchuáng get up; get out of bed: 他们已经～了。They are already up. ◇ ～号 reveille

【起道机】 qǐdàojī 〈铁道〉 track jack

【起点】 qǐdiǎn starting point: 把成绩作为继续前进的新～ take achievements as starting points for further progress ◇ ～运费 minimum freight; minimum charge per bill of lading

【起电】 qǐdiàn 〈物〉 electrification; charge ◇ ～盘 electrophorus

【起碇】 qǐdìng weigh anchor

【起动】 qǐdòng start (a machine, etc.) ◇ ～电动机 starting motor/ ～机 starter

【起飞】 qǐfēi (of aircraft) take off ◇ ～全重 all-up weight

【起伏】 qǐfú rise and fall; undulate: 凝望远处山峦～ gaze at the mountain ranges rising and falling in the distance/ 微风中麦浪～ a field of wheat undulating in the breeze/ 阶级斗争时起时伏。Class struggle sometimes rises and sometimes falls.

【起稿】 qǐgǎo make a draft; draft
【起航】 qǐháng set sail
【起哄】 qǐhòng ① gather together to create a disturbance ② (of a crowd of people) jeer; boo and hoot
【起火】 qǐhuǒ ① fire breaking out ② cook meals: 在食堂吃饭比自己～方便多了。It's much more convenient to have meals in a mess hall than to do one's own cooking. ③ 〈方〉 get angry; flare up
【起火】 qǐhuo a kind of firecracker
【起家】 qǐjiā build up; grow and thrive; make one's fortune, name, etc.: 白手～ build up from nothing; start from scratch/ 大庆靠两论～。Daqing Oilfield has built itself up by relying on Chairman Mao's essays *On Practice* and *On Contradiction*.
【起见】 qǐjiàn 〔与"为"连用,表示目的〕 for the purpose of; in order to: 为醒目～ in order to make it stand out clearly
【起劲】 qǐjìn vigorously; energetically; enthusiastically: 干得很～ work very energetically
【起居】 qǐjū daily life: ～有恒 lead a regular life
【起圈】 qǐjuàn remove manure from a pigsty, sheepfold, etc.
【起开】 qǐkai 〈方〉 step aside; stand aside
【起来】 qǐlai ① stand up; sit up; rise to one's feet: 你～吃药吧。Sit up and take your medicine./ 有个小伙子～给老太太让了个座儿。A youngster stood up and offered his seat to the old lady. ② get up; get out of bed: 他们一～就下地了。They went to work in the fields as soon as they got up. ③ rise; arise; revolt: ～反抗压迫 rise against oppression/ ～,饥寒交迫的奴隶! Arise, ye prisoners of starvation!/ ～捍卫真理 come forward in defence of truth
【起来】 qilai ①〔用在动词后,表示向上〕: 把孩子抱～ take a child up in one's arms/ 中国人民站～了。The Chinese people have stood up. ②〔用在动词或形容词后,表示动作或情况开始并且继续〕: 唱～ start to sing/ 他这句话使我们大笑～。This remark of his set us roaring with laughter./ 天气暖和～了。It's getting warm. ③〔用在动词后,表示动作完成或达到目的〕:合唱队组织～了。The chorus has been organized./ 想～了,这是杜甫的诗句。I've got it. It's a line from Du Fu. ④〔用在动词后,表示印象或看法〕: 看～要下雨。It looks like rain./ 听～颇有道理。It sounds quite reasonable./ 说～容易,做～难。It's easier said than done.
【起立】 qǐlì stand up; rise to one's feet: ～欢迎 rise to welcome sb.
【起垄】 qǐlǒng 〈农〉 ridging: ～犁 ridging plough; ridger
【起落】 qǐ-luò rise and fall; up and down
【起落架】 qǐluòjià 〈航空〉 landing gear; alighting gear; undercarriage: ～放下 gear down; landing gear lowering/ ～收上 gear up; landing gear raising
【起码】 qǐmǎ ① minimum; rudimentary; elementary: ～的要求 minimum requirements/ ～的知识 rudimentary knowledge; elementary knowledge/ 国际关系中最～的准则 the most rudimentary principles governing international relations/ 最～的生活必需品 the bare necessities of life ② at least: 这是一个革命者～应该具备的条件。This is the very least one expects of a revolutionary./ 这项工程～要到五月才能完成。This project can't be completed until May at the earliest.
【起锚】 qǐmáo weigh anchor; set sail
【起名儿】 qǐmíngr give a name; name
【起跑】 qǐpǎo 〈体〉 start of a race: 在跑道上练～ practise starts on a running track ◇ ～线 starting line (for a race); scratch line (for a relay race)
【起讫】 qǐ-qì the beginning and the end
【起色】 qǐsè improvement; pickup: 她工作最近很有～。Recently there's been a great improvement in her work./ 水疗以后他的病有了～。He is beginning to pick up after a course of hydrotherapeutic treatment.
【起身】 qǐshēn ① get up; get out of bed ② leave; set out; get off
【起事】 qǐshì start armed struggle; rise in rebellion
【起誓】 qǐshì take an oath; swear
【起首】 qǐshǒu at first; in the beginning; originally
【起死回生】 qǐsǐ-huíshēng (of a doctor's skill) bring the dying back to life; snatch a patient from the jaws of death
【起诉】 qǐsù 〈法〉 bring a suit (或 an action) against sb.; sue; prosecute ◇ ～人 suitor; prosecutor/ ～书 indictment; bill of complaint
【起跳】 qǐtiào 〈体〉 take off ◇ ～板 take-off board/ ～线 take-off line (或 mark)
【起头】 qǐtóu ① start; originate: 这件事是谁起的头儿? Who started all this? ② at first; in the beginning: ～她答应来的,后来因为有别的事不能来了。At first she promised to come but then had another engagement and couldn't make it. ③ beginning: 万事～难。Everything is hard in the beginning.
【起网】 qǐwǎng 〈渔〉 (net) hauling ◇ ～机 net hauler
【起先】 qǐxiān at first; in the beginning
【起行】 qǐxíng start on a journey; set out
【起夜】 qǐyè get up in the night to urinate
【起义】 qǐyì uprising; insurrection; revolt: 农民～ a peasant uprising/ 敌军纷纷～投诚。Many enemy soldiers revolted and crossed over. ◇ ～军 insurrectionary army
【起意】 qǐyì 〔多含贬义〕 conceive a design
【起因】 qǐyīn cause; origin: 调查事故的～ investigate the cause of the accident
【起用】 qǐyòng reinstate (an official who has retired or been dismissed)
【起源】 qǐyuán ① origin: 生命的～ the origin of life ② originate; stem from: 一切知识均～于劳动。All knowledge originates from labour.
【起运】 qǐyùn start shipment: 货物业已～。The goods are on their way. ◇ ～地点 starting place for shipping; place of dispatch
【起赃】 qǐzāng track down and recover stolen goods
【起早贪黑】 qǐzǎo-tānhēi start work early and knock off late; work from dawn to dusk: 社员们～地往地里送粪。The commune members carted manure to the fields from dawn to dusk. 又作"起早搭黑"
【起重车】 qǐzhòngchē derrick car
【起重船】 qǐzhòngchuán crane ship
【起重机】 qǐzhòngjī hoist; crane; derrick: ～的起重能力 the lifting (或 hoisting) capacity of a crane/ 龙门～ gantry crane/ 塔式～ tower crane/ 门式～ portal crane
【起绉】 qǐzhòu wrinkle; crumple: 这料子～吗? Does this material wrinkle? ◇ ～工艺 〈纺〉 creping
【起子】 qǐzi ① bottle opener ② 〈方〉 baking powder ③ 〈方〉 screwdriver

**绮** qǐ ① figured woven silk material; damask ② beautiful; gorgeous
【绮丽】 qǐlì beautiful; gorgeous: 春天的西湖显得格外～。In spring the West Lake looks especially enchanting.

**稽** qǐ
另见 jī
【稽首】 qǐshǒu kotow

## qì

**气** qì ① gas: 沼～ marsh gas; methane/ 毒～ poisonous gas; poison gas ②air: 打开窗子透一透～open the window to let in some fresh air ③breath: 上～不接下～ be out of breath; gasp for breath/ 停下来歇口～ stop to catch one's breath ④smell; odour: 香～扑鼻。A sweet smell assailed the nostrils./ 臭～ bad odour; foul smell ⑤weather: 秋高～爽 fine autumn weather ⑥airs; manner: 官～ bureaucratic airs/ 书生～十足 bookish in the extreme/ 表面上～壮如牛,实际上胆小如鼠 outwardly fierce as a bull, but inwardly timid as a mouse ⑦spirit; morale: 打～ boost the morale; cheer on/ 朝～勃勃 vigorous; full of youthful vigour/ ～可鼓而不可泄。Morale should be boosted, not dampened. ⑧make angry; enrage: 我故意～他一下。I was deliberately trying to annoy him. 或 I got him angry on purpose. ⑨get angry; be enraged: ～得直哆嗦 tremble with rage/ 他说的是～话。He just said it to vent his anger. ⑩bully; insult: 挨打受～ be bullied and beaten ⑪〈中医〉vital energy; energy of life

【气昂昂】qì'áng'áng full of mettle; full of dash

【气泵】qìbèng 〈机〉air pump

【气藏】qìcáng 〈石油〉gas pool

【气冲冲】qìchōngchōng furious; beside oneself with rage

【气喘】qìchuǎn 〈医〉asthma: 阵发性～ spasmodic asthma

【气窗】qìchuāng transom (window); fanlight

【气锤】qìchuí 〈机〉pneumatic hammer; air hammer

【气垫】qìdiàn air cushion ◇ ～船 hovercraft

【气顶】qìdǐng 〈石油〉gas cap

【气动】qìdòng pneumatic ◇ ～工具 pneumatic tool

【气度】qìdù tolerance; bearing

【气短】qìduǎn ①breathe hard; be short of breath; pant: 快爬到山顶时,大家都感到～。By the time we got near the top of the hill, we were all out of breath. ②lose heart; be discouraged: 失败并没有使他～。He was not discouraged by failure.

【气氛】qìfēn atmosphere: 会谈是在亲切友好的～中进行的。The talks were held in a cordial and friendly atmosphere./ 讨论会的～始终很热烈。The atmosphere was lively throughout the discussion.

【气愤】qìfèn indignant; furious: 对于这种蛮横态度,大家无不感到～。Everybody was indignant at such an overbearing manner.

【气腹】qìfù 〈医〉①pneumoperitoneum ②(artificial) pneumoperitoneum

【气概】qìgài lofty quality; mettle; spirit: 不畏强暴敢于斗争的英雄～ the heroic spirit of daring to struggle against brute force

【气缸】qìgāng 〈机〉air cylinder; cylinder

【气割】qìgē 〈机〉gas cutting

【气根】qìgēn 〈植〉aerial root 又作"气生根"

【气功】qìgōng *qigong*, a system of deep breathing exercises

【气臌】qìgǔ 〈中医〉distension of the abdomen caused by accumulation of gas due to dysfunction of the spleen or to emotional factors

【气管】qìguǎn windpipe; trachea ◇ ～切开术 tracheotomy/ ～炎 tracheitis

【气贯长虹】qì guàn chánghóng imbued with a spirit as lofty as the rainbow spanning the sky; full of noble aspiration and daring

【气焊】qìhàn 〈机〉gas welding

【气候】qìhòu ①climate: 大陆性～ continental climate/ 海洋性～ oceanic climate ②climate; situation: 政治～ political climate/ 成不了～ will not get anywhere
◇ ～带 climatic zone/ ～图 climatic chart/ ～学 climatology/ ～志 climatography

【气呼呼】qìhūhū in a huff; panting with rage

【气化】qìhuà gasification

【气急败坏】qìjí bàihuài flustered and exasperated; utterly discomfited

【气节】qìjié integrity; moral courage: 革命者坚贞不屈的～ the unyielding integrity of a revolutionary

【气井】qìjǐng 〈石油〉gas well

【气孔】qìkǒng ①〈植〉stoma ②〈动〉spiracle ③〈冶〉gas hole ④〈建〉air hole

【气浪】qìlàng blast (of an explosion)

【气冷】qìlěng 〈机〉air cooling ◇ ～式发动机 air-cooled engine

【气力】qìlì effort; energy; strength: 我们得费很大～去完成这项工作。We'll have to exert great efforts to accomplish the task./ 这事需要花费～。This will take a lot of doing./ 他用出全身～向对手猛扑过去。He pounced on the adversary with all his strength.

【气量】qìliàng tolerance: ～大 large-minded; magnanimous/ ～小 narrow-minded/ ～大的人对这点小事是不会介意的。Broad-minded people won't bother about such trifles.

【气流】qìliú ①air current; airflow; airstream ②〈语〉breath
◇ ～纺纱 open-end spinning/ ～干扰 interference in airflow/ ～畸变 flow distortion

【气煤】qìméi gas coal

【气门】qìmén ①(air) valve of a tyre ②〈动〉spiracle; stigma

【气门心】qìménxīn 〈口〉valve inside

【气密】qìmì airtight; gastight; gasproof ◇ ～接合〈机〉airtight joint/ ～试验〈航空〉air seal test; leakage test

【气囊】qìnáng ①(of birds) air sac ②gasbag (of an aerostat)

【气恼】qìnǎo get angry; take offence; be ruffled

【气馁】qìněi become dejected; be discouraged; lose heart: 他多次遇到挫折,但从不～。He never lost heart despite repeated setbacks.

【气逆】qìnì 〈中医〉circulation of vital energy in the wrong direction

【气派】qìpài manner; style; air: 东方～的建筑物 architecture of oriental style

【气泡】qìpào air bubble; bubble

【气喷】qìpēn 〈石油〉gas blowout

【气魄】qìpò boldness of vision; breadth of spirit; daring: 以无产阶级革命家的～ with a proletarian revolutionary's boldness of vision/ 有改天换地的～ have the daring to reshape nature

【气枪】qìqiāng air gun; pneumatic gun: 玩具～ popgun

【气球】qìqiú balloon: 测风～ pilot balloon/ 定高～ constant-level balloon/ 彩色～ coloured balloon

【气圈】qìquān ①〈纺〉balloon ②〈气〉aerosphere

【气色】qìsè complexion; colour: ～很好 have a rosy complexion; have a good colour/ ～不好 look pale; be off colour

【气势】qìshì momentum; imposing manner: 民族解放运动的磅礴～the tremendous momentum of the national liberation movement/ ～雄伟的长城 the imposing Great Wall

【气势磅礴】qìshì pángbó of great momentum; powerful: 《黄河大合唱》～。*The Huanghe River Cantata* is full of power and grandeur./ 国家要独立,民族要解放,人民要革命的历史洪流～,奔腾向前。Countries want independence, nations want liberation, and the people want revolution — this historical tide is surging forward with great momentum.

【气势汹汹】qìshì xiōngxiōng fierce; truculent; overbearing: 看起来～,实际上十分虚弱 fierce in appearance but feeble in reality/ 革命人民决不会被反动派的～所吓倒。The revolutionary people will never be cowed by the bluster of the

reactionaries.
【气态】 qìtài 〈物〉 gaseous state
【气体】 qìtǐ gas
◇ ～动力学 aerodynamics/ ～发生器 gas generator/ ～分离器 gas separator/ ～力学 pneumatics/ ～燃料 gaseous fuel
【气田】 qìtián 〈石油〉 gas field
【气筒】 qìtǒng inflator; bicycle pump
【气头上】 qìtóushang in a fit of anger: 这是他～说的话，你不要在意。He said that in a fit of anger. Don't take it to heart.
【气团】 qìtuán 〈气〉 air mass: 冷～ cold air mass ◇ ～变性 air-mass modification
【气吞山河】 qì tūn shānhé imbued with a spirit that can conquer mountains and rivers; full of daring
【气味】 qìwèi ① smell; odour; flavour: ～难闻。The smell is awful. ②〔多含贬义〕smack; taste: 有沙文主义～ smack of chauvinism
【气味相投】 qìwèi xiāng tóu be birds of a feather; be two of a kind: 他们俩～。Both have lousy taste.
【气温】 qìwēn 〈气〉 air temperature; atmospheric temperature
【气息】 qìxī ① breath ② flavour; smell: 具有强烈的生活～ have the rich flavour of life
【气息奄奄】 qìxī yǎnyǎn at one's last gasp; at the point of death; like a person who is sinking fast
【气象】 qìxiàng ①〈气〉 meteorological phenomena ②〈气〉 meteorology ③ atmosphere; scene: 生气勃勃的新～ a new and dynamic atmosphere/ 一片欣欣向荣的社会主义农村新～ the exhilarating atmosphere of a flourishing socialist countryside
◇ ～工作者 a worker in meteorology/ ～观测 meteorological observation/ ～火箭 meteorological rocket/ ～台 meteorological observatory/ ～图 meteorological map/ ～卫星 meteorological satellite; weather satellite/ ～学 meteorology/ ～预报 weather forecast/ ～员 weatherman
【气象万千】 qìxiàng wànqiān spectacular; majestic: 天都峰上看群山，～。From the top of Tiandu, one can see range after range of mountains unfolding in all their majesty.
【气性】 qìxing temperament; disposition
【气胸】 qìxiōng 〈医〉 ① pneumothorax ② (artificial) pneumothorax
【气吁吁】 qìxūxū panting; gasping for breath
【气虚】 qìxū 〈中医〉 deficiency of vital energy
【气旋】 qìxuán 〈气〉 cyclone: 反～ anticyclone
【气血辨证】 qì-xuè biànzhèng 〈中医〉 analysing and differentiating the pathological condition according to the function of vital energy and the state of the blood
【气压】 qìyā 〈气〉 atmospheric pressure; barometric pressure: 高～ high pressure ◇ ～表 barometer/ ～沉箱〈建〉 pneumatic caisson
【气眼】 qìyǎn ①〈建〉 air hole ②〈冶〉 gas hole
【气焰】 qìyàn arrogance; bluster: ～嚣张 be swollen with arrogance
【气郁】 qìyù 〈中医〉 obstruction of the circulation of vital energy
【气质】 qìzhì ① temperament; disposition ② qualities; makings: 革命者的～ the makings of a revolutionary
【气滞】 qìzhì 〈中医〉 stagnation of the circulation of vital energy
【气肿疽】 qìzhǒngjū 〈牧〉 blackleg; black quarter
【气壮山河】 qì zhuàng shānhé full of power and grandeur; magnificent: 一篇～的宣言 a magnificent manifesto

**讫** qì ① settled; completed: 付～ paid/ 收～ received in full/ 验～ checked; examined ② end: 起～ the beginning and the end

**迄** qì ① up to; till: ～今 up to now; to this day; so far ②〔用于"未"或"无"前〕so far; all along: ～无音信。We have received no information so far.
【迄今】 qìjīn up to now; to this day; to date; so far: 人们～怀念着这些革命先烈。To this day people still cherish the memory of these revolutionary martyrs./ 他的态度～并无明显的转变。There has been no visible change in his attitude so far.

**汽** qì vapour; steam
【汽车】 qìchē automobile; motor vehicle; car
◇ ～吊 truck crane/ ～队 motor transport corps; fleet of cars (或 trucks)/ ～工业 auto industry/ ～库 garage/ ～修配厂 motor repair shop/ ～制造厂 automobile factory; motor works
【汽船】 qìchuán steamship; steamer
【汽锤】 qìchuí 〈机〉 steam hammer: 龙门～ arch type steam hammer
【汽灯】 qìdēng gas lamp
【汽笛】 qìdí steam whistle; siren; hooter: 鸣～ sound a siren
【汽缸】 qìgāng 〈机〉 cylinder ◇ ～组 cylinder block
【汽化】 qìhuà 〈物〉 vaporization ◇ ～热 heat of vaporization
【汽化器】 qìhuàqì ①〈机〉 carburettor ②〈化〉 vaporizer ◇ ～回火 backfiring in carburettor/ ～主射口 carburettor main jet
【汽酒】 qìjiǔ light sparkling wine
【汽轮发电机】 qìlún fādiànjī turbogenerator: 双水内冷～ turbogenerator with inner water-cooled stator and rotor
【汽轮机】 qìlúnjī steam turbine
【汽碾】 qìniǎn 〈机〉 steamroller
【汽水】 qìshuǐ aerated water; soft drink; soda water
【汽提】 qìtí 〈石油〉 strip ◇ ～油 stripped oil/ ～塔 stripping tower
【汽艇】 qìtǐng motorboat
【汽油】 qìyóu petrol; gasoline; gas: 航空～ aviation gasoline/ 凝固～ napalm

**弃** qì throw away; discard; abandon: ～之可惜 hesitate to discard sth.; be unwilling to throw away/ 敌军～城而逃。The enemy abandoned the city and fled.
【弃暗投明】 qì àn tóu míng forsake darkness for light — leave the reactionary side and cross over to the side of progress: 伪军官兵～的为数不少。Officers and men of the puppet army crossed over in large numbers to the side of the people.
【弃甲曳兵】 qìjiǎ-yèbīng (of troops) throw away their armour and trail their weapons behind them; be routed; flee pell-mell
【弃旧图新】 qì jiù tú xīn turn over a new leaf
【弃权】 qìquán ① abstain from voting: 两票～ two abstentions ②〈体〉 waive the right (to play); forfeit
【弃世】 qìshì pass away; die
【弃婴】 qìyīng ① abandon a baby ② foundling
【弃置】 qìzhì discard; throw aside: ～不用 be discarded; lie idle

**泣** qì ① weep; sob: ～诉 accuse while weeping; accuse amid tears/ ～不成声 choke with sobs ② tears: ～下如雨 shed tears like rain; weep copious tears

**亟** qì 〈书〉 repeatedly; again and again: ～来问讯 come repeatedly to ask for information
另见 jí

**契** qì ①〈书〉 engrave; carve ②contract; deed: 地～ title deed for land; land deed ③agree; get along well: 默～ tacit agreement (或 understanding)

【契丹】 Qìdān Qidan (Khitan), an ancient nationality in China

【契合】 qìhé agree with; tally with; correspond to: 与进化论相～ agree with the theory of evolution

【契机】 qìjī ①〈哲〉 moment ②turning point; juncture

【契据】 qìjù deed; contract; receipt

【契友】 qìyǒu close friend; bosom friend

【契约】 qìyuē contract; deed; charter: 租船～ contract of affreightment; charter party

**砌** qì ①build by laying bricks or stones: ～砖 lay bricks/ ～墙 build a wall (with bricks, stones, etc.)/ ～井壁 〈矿〉 build shaft lining ②step: 雕栏玉～ carved balustrades and marble steps

**跂** qì 〈书〉 stand on tiptoe

**葺** qì 〈书〉 ①cover a roof with straw; thatch ②repair; mend: 修～ repair (a house); make repairs

**碛** qì ①moraine ②desert

**器** qì ①implement; utensil; ware: 漆～ lacquerware/ 瓷～ chinaware; china; porcelain/ 玉～ jade article/ 乐～ musical instrument/ 拾音～ pickup; adapter ②organ: 生殖～ reproductive organs; generative organs; genitals ③capacity; talent: ～识 capability and judgment/ ～使 give sb. employment according to his ability

【器材】 qìcái equipment; material: 照相～ photographic equipment/ 线路～ line materials

【器官】 qìguān organ; apparatus: 发音～ organs of speech/ 消化～ digestive organs/ 呼吸～ respiratory apparatus

【器件】 qìjiàn parts of an apparatus or appliance: 电子～ electronic device

【器具】 qìjù utensil; implement; appliance: 日用～ household utensils; articles of daily use

【器量】 qìliàng tolerance: ～小 narrow-minded; petty

【器皿】 qìmǐn household utensils; containers esp. for use in the house

【器物】 qìwù implements; utensils

【器械】 qìxiè ①apparatus; appliance; instrument: 医疗～ medical appliances/ 体育～ sports apparatus/ 光学～ optical instrument ②weapon

【器械体操】 qìxiè tǐcāo gymnastics on or with apparatus

【器宇】 qìyǔ 〈书〉 bearing; deportment: ～轩昂 of dignified bearing

【器乐】 qìyuè 〈乐〉 instrumental music ◇ ～曲 composition for an instrument

【器重】 qìzhòng 〔上级对下级，长辈对晚辈〕 think highly of; regard highly

**憩** qì 〈书〉 rest

【憩息】 qìxī 〈书〉 rest; have a rest

## qiā

**掐** qiā ①pinch; nip: 把杈子～掉 pinch off the side shoots/ 不要～花。Don't nip off the flowers./ 把烟卷～了 stub out the cigarette ②clutch: ～脖子 seize sb. by the throat/ ～死 choke to death; throttle

【掐断】 qiāduàn nip off; cut off: ～电线 disconnect the wire/ ～水源 cut off the water supply

【掐尖儿】 qiājiānr pinch off young shoots, etc.

【掐丝】 qiāsī 〈工美〉 wire inlay; filigree: 景泰蓝花瓶上的～ wire inlay on a *cloisonné* vase

【掐算】 qiāsuàn count (或 reckon) sth. on one's fingers

【掐头去尾】 qiātóu-qùwěi break off both ends; leave out the beginning and the end: 这把芹菜～剩下不多了。With both ends gone, there's not much left of this bunch of celery./ 引用他这段话不能～。If you quote a passage from him, you should quote it in full.

**袷** qiā

【袷袢】 qiāpàn Uygur or Tajik robe buttoning down the front

**葜** qiā 见"菝葜" báqiā

## qiǎ

**卡** qiǎ ①wedge; get stuck: 鱼刺～在他的嗓子里。A fish bone sticks in his throat. ②clip; fastener: 发～ hairpin ③checkpost: 关～ checkpost
另见 kǎ

【卡具】 qiǎjù 〈机〉 clamping apparatus; fixture

【卡壳】 qiǎké ①〈军〉 jamming of cartridge or shell case ②get stuck; be held up; have a temporary stoppage

【卡口灯泡】 qiǎkǒu dēngpào bayonet-socket bulb

【卡口灯头】 qiǎkǒu dēngtóu bayonet socket

【卡盘】 qiǎpán 〈机〉 chuck

【卡子】 qiǎzi ①clip; fastener ②checkpost

【卡钻】 qiǎzuàn 〈石油〉 jamming of a drilling tool; sticking of tool

## qià

**洽** qià ①be in harmony; agree: 融～ be in harmony/ 意见不～ have different opinions; not see eye to eye ②consult; arrange with: ～商 make arrangements with; talk over with/ ～谈贸易事宜 hold trade talks

**恰** qià ①appropriate; proper ②just; exactly: ～到好处 just right/ ～似 exactly like

【恰当】 qiàdàng proper; suitable; fitting; appropriate: 用词～ use proper words/ 提出～的口号 propose a suitable slogan/ 采取～的措施 adopt appropriate measures

【恰好】 qiàhǎo just right; as luck would have it: 这块布～够做一件衬衣。This piece of cloth is just the right length for a shirt./ 民兵～这时赶到。The militiamen arrived in the nick of time.

【恰恰】 qiàqià just; exactly; precisely: 这～是我想说的话。That's exactly what I wanted to say./ ～相反 just the opposite; exactly the reverse

【恰巧】 qiàqiǎo by chance; fortunately; as chance would have it: 那天～我也在那里。I happened to be there that day, too.

【恰如其分】 qià rú qí fèn apt; appropriate; just right: ～的评价 an apt appraisal/ 给予～的批评 give a balanced criticism/ 对成绩和缺点作～的估计 make an appropriate estimate of the achievements and shortcomings

**髂** qià

【髂骨】 qiàgǔ 〈生理〉 ilium

## qiān

**千** qiān ① thousand: 成～上万 by the thousands and tens of thousands/ ～～万万 thousands upon thousands ② a great amount of; a great number of: ～百条建议 lots and lots of suggestions/ ～百年来的梦想 an age-old dream/ ～层饼 multi-layer steamed bread/ ～层底 strong cloth soles

【千变万化】 qiānbiàn-wànhuà ever changing: 国际阶级斗争的形势是错综复杂,～的。The situation with regard to international class struggle is intricate and volatile.

【千差万别】 qiānchā-wànbié differ in thousands of ways: 各地气候～。Climate varies from place to place./ 事物的～ the immense variety of things

【千锤百炼】 qiānchuí-bǎiliàn ① thoroughly tempered (或 steeled): 在三大革命运动中～ be repeatedly tempered in the three great revolutionary movements ② (of literary works) be polished again and again; be revised and rewritten many times; be highly finished

【千电子伏】 qiāndiànzǐfú 〈原〉 kiloelectron-volt (KeV)

【千儿八百】 qiān'erbābǎi 〈口〉 a thousand or slightly less

【千乏】 qiānfá 〈电〉 kilovar (KVAR)

【千方百计】 qiānfāng-bǎijì in a thousand and one ways; by every possible means; by hook or by crook: ～挖掘潜力 try in every possible way to tap the potential/ ～掩盖错误 use all one's ingenuity to cover up one's mistakes

【千分表】 qiānfēnbiǎo dial gauge; dial indicator

【千分尺】 qiānfēnchǐ micrometer: 外径～ outside micrometer/ 内径～ inside micrometer/ 游标～vernier micrometer

【千夫】 qiānfū 〈书〉 numerous people: ～所指 be universally condemned; face a thousand accusing fingers

【千伏】 qiānfú 〈电〉 kilovolt (Kv.) ◇ ～安 kilovolt-ampere (KVA)

【千古】 qiāngǔ ① through the ages; eternal; for all time: 成为～罪人 stand condemned through the ages/ ～奇闻 a fantastic story; a forever strange tale/ ～遗恨 eternal regret ②〔用于挽联、花圈的上款〕: 某某先生～! Eternal repose to Mr. So-and-so!

【千赫】 qiānhè kilohertz

【千斤】 qiānjīn a thousand *jin* — very heavy; weighty: ～重担 an exceptionally heavy load or responsibility

【千斤】 qiānjin ① 〈机〉 hoisting jack; jack ② 〈机〉 pawl

【千斤顶】 qiānjīndǐng 〈机〉 hoisting jack; jack: 油压～ hydraulic jack

【千金】 qiānjīn ① a thousand pieces of gold; a lot of money: ～难买 not to be had even for 1,000 pieces of gold; not to be bought with money/ 一掷～ spend money extravagantly; spend lavishly ② 〈敬〉 daughter (other than one's own)

【千钧一发】 qiān jūn yī fà 见"一发千钧" yī fà qiān jūn

【千卡】 qiānkǎ 〈物〉 kilocalorie (Kcal.)

【千克】 qiānkè kilogram (kg.)

【千里】 qiānlǐ a thousand *li* — a long distance: 沃野～ a vast expanse of fertile farmland

【千里光】 qiānlǐguāng 〈植〉 climbing groundsel (*Senecio scandens*)

【千里马】 qiānlǐmǎ a horse that covers a thousand *li* a day; a winged steed

【千里送鹅毛】 qiānlǐ sòng émáo a goose feather sent from a thousand *li* away: ～,礼轻情意重。The gift itself may be light as a goose feather; but sent from afar, it conveys deep feeling.

【千里迢迢】 qiānlǐ tiáotiáo thousands of *li* away; from afar; over a great distance

【千里眼】 qiānlǐyǎn ① farsighted person ② 〈旧〉 telescope; field glasses

【千里之堤,溃于蚁穴】 qiānlǐ zhī dī, kuì yú yǐxué one ant-hole may cause the collapse of a thousand *li* dyke — slight negligence may lead to great disaster

【千里之行,始于足下】 qiānlǐ zhī xíng, shǐ yú zú xià a thousand-*li* journey is started by taking the first step

【千虑一得】 qiān lǜ yī dé 见"愚者千虑,必有一得" yúzhě qiān lǜ, bì yǒu yī dé

【千虑一失】 qiān lǜ yī shī 见"智者千虑,必有一失" zhìzhě qiān lǜ, bì yǒu yī shī

【千枚岩】 qiānméiyán 〈地〉 phyllite

【千米】 qiānmǐ kilometre (Km.)

【千篇一律】 qiān piān yī lǜ stereotyped; following the same pattern: ～的论调 stereotyped views/ 那些文章～,没有什么新东西。Those articles repeat each other and contain nothing new.

【千奇百怪】 qiānqí-bǎiguài all kinds of strange things; an infinite variety of fantastic phenomena

【千秋】 qiānqiū ① a thousand years; centuries: ～万代 throughout the ages ② 〈敬〉 birthday (other than one's own)

【千日红】 qiānrìhóng 〈植〉 globe amaranth

【千丝万缕】 qiānsī-wànlǚ countless ties; a thousand and one links: 有着～的联系 have a thousand and one links; be tied in a hundred and one ways

【千头万绪】 qiāntóu-wànxù thousands of strands and loose ends; a multitude of things: 工作～,要抓主要矛盾。With many tasks to perform, we should first tackle what constitutes the main contradiction./ 心里～,不知从何说起。There are so many thoughts welling up in my mind that I really don't know where to start.

【千瓦】 qiānwǎ kilowatt (KW) ◇ ～小时 kilowatt-hour (KWh)

【千万】 qiānwàn ① ten million; millions upon millions ②〔表示恳切丁宁〕: 到达后～来信。Be sure to write us when you get there./ ～要小心啊! Do be careful!/ 这事儿～不可掉以轻心。We must under no circumstances take this lightly.

【千…万…】 qiān...wàn... 〔形容很多或表示强调〕: 千山万水 ten thousand crags and torrents; numerous mountains and rivers; a long and arduous journey/ 千难万险 numerous dangers and hazards/ 千军万马 thousands upon thousands of horses and soldiers — a powerful army; a mighty force/ 千刀万剐 hack sb. to pieces; give sb. a thousand cuts/ 千真万确 absolutely true/ 千丁宁万嘱咐 exhort sb. repeatedly

【千辛万苦】 qiānxīn-wànkǔ innumerable trials and tribulations; untold hardships: 地质勘探队历尽～,找到了不少新的矿藏。After innumerable hardships, the prospecting team discovered many new ores.

【千言万语】 qiānyán-wànyǔ thousands and thousands of words: ～说不尽党的恩情。No words can express our debt of gratitude to the Party.

【千载难逢】 qiān zǎi nán féng occurring only once in a thousand years; very rare: ～的机会 a golden opportunity; the chance of a lifetime

【千载一时】 qiān zǎi yī shí (of an opportunity) only once in a thousand years; golden

【千周】 qiānzhōu kilocycle (KC)

**仟** qiān thousand (used for the numeral 千 on cheques,

etc., to avoid mistakes or alterations)

**阡** qiān 〈书〉 a footpath between fields, running north and south

【阡陌】 qiānmò crisscross footpaths between fields

**扦** qiān a short slender pointed piece of metal, bamboo, etc.: 蜡～儿 candlestick/ 竹～ bamboo spike

【扦插】 qiānchā 〈农〉 cuttage

【扦子】 qiānzi ① a slender pointed piece of metal, bamboo, etc. ② a sharp-pointed metal tube used to extract samples of grains, etc. from sacks

**迁** qiān ① move: ～往他处 move to another place ② change: 事过境～。The matter is all over, and the situation has changed.

【迁都】 qiāndū move the capital to another place

【迁就】 qiānjiù accommodate oneself to; yield to: ～姑息 excessively accommodating; overlenient/ 无原则的～ unprincipled accommodation/ 在小事情上互相～着点儿 give in a little to each other over small matters/ 对资产阶级思想要斗争，不能～。We must combat bourgeois ideas, not yield to them. ◇ ～主义 excessive accommodation

【迁居】 qiānjū change one's dwelling place; move (house): ～外地 move away to another place

【迁怒】 qiānnù vent one's anger on sb. who's not to blame; take it out on sb.

【迁徙】 qiānxǐ move; migrate; change one's residence

【迁延】 qiānyán delay; defer; procrastinate: ～时日 cause a long delay; become long-drawn-out

【迁移】 qiānyí move; remove; migrate: 从城市～到农村 move from urban to rural areas

**钎** qiān drill rod; drill steel; borer

【钎子】 qiānzi hammer drill (for making holes in rock); rock drill

**牵** qiān ① lead along (by holding the hand, the halter, etc.); pull: ～牛下地 lead an ox to the fields/ 手～手 hand in hand/ ～着敌人的鼻子走 lead the enemy by the nose ② involve: 他不愿意～在这里头。He didn't want to get involved in it.

【牵肠挂肚】 qiāncháng-guàdù feel deep anxiety about; be very worried about

【牵扯】 qiānchě involve; implicate; drag in: 这事～很多人。A number of people have become involved in the matter.

【牵掣】 qiānchè ① hold up; impede: 互相～ hold each other up/ 抓主要问题，不要被枝节问题～住。Let's focus our attention on the main problem and not get bogged down in minor issues. ② pin down; check; contain

【牵动】 qiāndòng affect; influence: ～全局 affect the situation as a whole/ ～整个作战计划 affect the overall operational plan

【牵挂】 qiānguà worry; care: 没有～ free from care/ 好好工作，不要～家中老小。Do your work well and don't worry about us folks at home.

【牵累】 qiānlěi ① tie down: 受家务～ be tied down by household chores ② implicate; involve (in trouble)

【牵连】 qiānlián involve (in trouble); implicate; tie up with: 清查同这次破坏活动有～的人和事 investigate the individuals and incidents connected with the sabotage

【牵牛花】 qiānniúhuā (white-edged) morning glory

【牵牛星】 qiānniúxīng 〈天〉 Altair

【牵强】 qiānqiǎng forced (interpretation, etc.); farfetched: 这些理由都很～。These reasons are farfetched.

【牵强附会】 qiānqiǎng fùhuì draw a forced analogy; make a farfetched (或 irrelevant) comparison; give a strained interpretation

【牵切纺】 qiānqiēfǎng 〈纺〉 tow-to-yarn direct spinning

【牵涉】 qiānshè involve; drag in: 这项决定～很多部门。This decision involves many departments./ 他的发言既然～到我，我就想讲几句。Since he has dragged me into his speech, I'd like to say a few words.

【牵伸】 qiānshēn 〈纺〉 draft; drawing

【牵线】 qiānxiàn ① pull strings; pull wires; control from behind the scenes ② act as go-between ◇ ～人 wire-puller; go-between

【牵一发而动全身】 qiān yī fà ér dòng quánshēn pull one hair and the whole body is affected — a slight move in one part may affect the situation as a whole

【牵引】 qiānyǐn tow; draw: 这条线上的列车都由电力机车～。The trains on this line are all drawn by electric locomotives.

◇ ～车 tractor; tractor truck/ ～犁 trailed plough/ ～力 〈物〉 traction force; traction; pulling force/ ～能量〈交通〉 haulage capacity/ ～炮 towed artillery/ ～器〈医〉 tractor/ ～式滑翔机 towed glider

【牵制】 qiānzhì pin down; tie up; check; contain: ～敌人 pin down the enemy/ 这对敌人是一种～。This is a kind of check on the enemy. ◇ ～行动 containing action/ ～性攻击 diversionary attack

**悭** qiān

【悭吝】 qiānlìn stingy; miserly

**铅** qiān ① lead (Pb) ② lead (in a pencil); black lead

【铅白】 qiānbái 〈化〉 white lead

【铅版】 qiānbǎn 〈印〉 stereotype

【铅笔】 qiānbǐ pencil

◇ ～刀 small knife for sharpening pencils; pen-knife/ ～盒 pencil-case/ ～画 pencil drawing/ ～芯 lead (in a pencil); black lead

【铅玻璃】 qiānbōli 〈化〉 lead glass

【铅垂线】 qiānchuíxiàn 〈建〉 plumb line

【铅锤】 qiānchuí 〈建〉 plummet; plumb (bob)

【铅丹】 qiāndān 〈化〉 red lead; minium

【铅封】 qiānfēng lead sealing

【铅球】 qiānqiú 〈体〉 shot: 推～ shot put; putting the shot ◇ ～运动员 shot-putter

【铅丝】 qiānsī ① galvanized wire ② 〈电〉 lead wire

【铅条】 qiāntiáo ① 〈印〉 slug; lead ② lead (for a propelling pencil)

【铅印】 qiānyìn letterpress (或 relief, typographic) printing; stereotype

【铅直】 qiānzhí vertical; plumb

【铅中毒】 qiānzhòngdú 〈医〉 lead poisoning; saturnism

【铅字】 qiānzì 〈印〉 type; letter: 大号～ large type

◇ ～合金 type metal/ ～面 typeface/ ～盘 type case; letter board

**谦** qiān modest: ～和 modest and amiable

【谦卑】 qiānbēi humble; modest

【谦辞】 qiāncí self-depreciatory expression

【谦恭】 qiāngōng modest and courteous

【谦谦君子】 qiān qiān jūnzǐ ① 〈旧〉 a modest, self-disciplined gentleman ② a hypocritically modest person

【谦让】 qiānràng modestly decline: 你做这工作再合适不过，不要～了。You're just the person for the job. Don't decline out of modesty.

【谦虚】 qiānxū ① modest; self-effacing: ～谨慎 modest and prudent ② make modest remarks: 他～了一番，终于答应来做一次演讲。After making a few modest remarks he finally agreed to come and give a talk.

【谦逊】 qiānxùn modest; unassuming

**签** qiān ① sign; autograph: 请你～个字。Please sign your name here. ② make brief comments on a document ③ bamboo slips used for divination or drawing lots: 抽～ draw lots ④ label; sticker: 标～ label; sticker/ 航空邮～ air mail sticker/ 书～ bookmarker ⑤ a slender pointed piece of bamboo or wood: 牙～ tooth pick ⑥ tack: 把袖口～上 tack on a cuff

【签到】 qiāndào register one's attendance at a meeting or at an office; sign in ◇ ～簿 attendance book/ ～处 sign-in desk

【签订】 qiāndìng conclude and sign (a treaty, etc.): ～条约 sign a treaty/ ～合同 sign a contract/ ～协定的各方 the parties signatory to the agreement

【签发】 qiānfā sign and issue (a document, certificate, etc.)

【签名】 qiānmíng sign one's name; autograph: ～盖章 sign and affix one's seal; set one's hand and seal to/ 亲笔～的照片 an autographed picture/ 来宾～簿 visitors' book ◇ ～运动 signature drive

【签收】 qiānshōu sign after receiving sth.: 挂号信须由收件人～。A receipt for a registered letter is to be signed by the recipient. 或 A registered letter must be signed for by the recipient.

【签署】 qiānshǔ sign: ～联合公报 sign a joint *communiqué*/ ～意见 write comments and sign one's name (on a document)

【签证】 qiānzhèng visa; visé: 入(出)境～ entry (exit) visa/ 过境～ transit visa/ 一次有效出入境～ entry-exit visa valid for a single journey/ 互免～ mutual exemption of visas

【签注】 qiānzhù attach a slip of paper to a document with comments on it; write comments on a document (for a superior to consider)

【签字】 qiānzì sign; affix one's signature: ～后立即生效 come into force upon signature/ 中转～ sign a transfer (for a railway passenger) ◇ ～国 signatory state (或 power); signatory/ ～仪式 signing ceremony

**愆** qiān 〈书〉 fault; transgression: 前～ past faults

【愆期】 qiānqī 〈书〉 pass the appointed time; delay (payment, etc.)

## qián

**前** qián ① front: ～院 front courtyard/ 楼～ in front of the building ② forward; ahead: 勇往直～ go bravely forward; forge ahead dauntlessly/ 往～看 look forward ③ ago; before: 日～ a few days ago; the other day/ 晚饭～ before supper ④ preceding: ～一阶段 the preceding stage/ 战～ prewar/ 史～史 prehistory ⑤ former; formerly: ～校长 former principal of a school ⑥ first: 这次比赛的～六名 the first six places in this competition/ ～三排 the first three rows

【前半晌】 qiánbànshǎng 〈方〉 forenoon; morning

【前半天】 qiánbàntiān forenoon; morning

【前半夜】 qiánbànyè the first half of the night (from nightfall to midnight)

【前辈】 qiánbèi senior (person); elder; the older generation: 他们都是我的～。They are all my seniors./ 革命～ revolutionaries of the older generation

【前臂】 qiánbì forearm

【前边】 qiánbian ① in front; ahead ② above; preceding

【前叉】 qiánchā front fork (of a bicycle)

【前车之覆，后车之鉴】 qiánchē zhī fù, hòuchē zhī jiàn the overturned cart ahead is a warning to the carts behind

【前车之鉴】 qiánchē zhī jiàn warning taken from the overturned cart ahead; lessons drawn from others' mistakes: 这对我们是一个～。This is a warning for us.

【前尘】 qiánchén 〈书〉 the past: 回首～ look back upon the past

【前程】 qiánchéng ① future; prospect: 锦绣～ a bright (或 rosy) future/ ～远大 have brilliant prospects ② 〈旧〉 career

【前池】 qiánchí 〈水〉 forebay

【前导】 qiándǎo ① lead the way; march in front; precede ② a person who leads the way; guide: 以仪仗队为～ with the guard of honour marching at the head

【前敌】 qiándí front line: 身临～ come personally to the front ◇ ～委员会 front committee/ ～总指挥 frontline commander-in-chief

【前额】 qián'é forehead

【前方】 qiánfāng ① ahead: 注视着～ look (或 gaze) ahead ② the front: 开赴～ be dispatched to the front/ 支援～ support the front

【前锋】 qiánfēng ① vanguard: 部队～已到达目的地。The vanguard units have reached the destination. ② 〈体〉 forward

【前夫】 qiánfū former husband; ex-husband

【前赴后继】 qiánfù-hòujì advance wave upon wave

【前功尽弃】 qiángōng jìn qì all that has been achieved is spoiled; all one's previous efforts are wasted

【前滚翻】 qiángǔnfān 〈体〉 forward roll

【前汉】 Qián Hàn 见"西汉" Xī Hàn

【前后】 qián-hòu ① around (a certain time); about: 十点～ around 10 o'clock/ 在1949年～ round about 1949/ 春节～ around the Spring Festival ② from beginning to end; altogether: 这项工程，从动工到完成，～只用了十个月。The entire project, from beginning to end, took only ten months./ 她～来过四次。She has been here four times altogether. ③ in front and behind: 房子～都有树。There are trees both in front and at the back of the house./ ～受敌 be attacked by the enemy both front and back; be caught between two fires/ ～左右 on all sides; all around

【前…后…】 qián...hòu... ①〔表示两种事物或行为在空间或时间上一先一后〕: 前街后巷 front street and back lane/ 前思后想 think over again and again/ 前呼后拥 with many attendants crowding round/ 前倨后恭 be first supercilious and then deferential; change from arrogance to humility/ 前松后紧 be slack at the beginning and have to speed up towards the end ②〔表示动作的向前向后〕: 前俯后仰 bend forwards and backwards

【前胡】 qiánhú 〈中药〉 the root of purple-flowered peucedanum (*Peucedanum decursivum*)

【前记】 qiánjì 见"前言"

【前脚】 qiánjiǎo ① the forward foot in a step ②〔与"后脚"连用〕 no sooner... than; the moment (when): 你～走，他后脚就来了。He arrived the moment you had left.

【前襟】 qiánjīn the front part of a Chinese robe or jacket

【前进】 qiánjìn advance; go forward; forge ahead: 社会主义祖国在胜利～。Our socialist country is advancing triumphantly./ 同志们，～! Forward, comrades!/ 继续～ continue to make progress/ 大踏步～ make big strides forward

【前景】 qiánjǐng ① 〈摄〉 foreground ② prospect; vista; perspective: 美好的～ good prospects; a bright future/ 革命斗争的～ the prospects for the revolutionary struggle/ 开辟广阔的～ open vast vistas

【前臼齿】 qiánjiùchǐ 〈生理〉 premolar teeth
【前空翻】 qiánkōngfān 〈杂技〉 forward somersault in the air
【前例】 qiánlì precedent: 史无～ without precedent in history; unprecedented
【前列】 qiánliè front row (或 rank); forefront; van: 主席台～ the front row on the rostrum/ 站在斗争的～ stand in the forefront of the struggle
【前列腺】 qiánlièxiàn 〈生理〉 prostate (gland) ◇ ～素〈药〉 prostaglandin/ ～炎 prostatitis
【前掠翼】 qiánlüèyì 〈航空〉 buzzard-type wing
【前轮】 qiánlún (车辆) front wheel; (飞机) nosewheel
【前门】 qiánmén front door
【前门拒虎,后门进狼】 qiánmén jù hǔ, hòumén jìn láng drive the tiger away from the front door and let a wolf in at the back — fend off one danger only to fall prey to another
【前面】 qiánmian ① in front; at the head; ahead: 在房子～ in front of the house/ 走在队伍～ march at the head of the column/ ～就是宿营地。The campsite is right ahead./ 科学研究工作应当走在经济建设的～。Scientific research should anticipate economic construction. ② above; preceding: ～提到的原则 the above-mentioned principle/ ～的一章 the preceding chapter
【前脑】 qiánnǎo 〈生理〉 forebrain
【前年】 qiánnián the year before last
【前怕狼,后怕虎】 qián pà láng, hòu pà hǔ fear wolves ahead and tigers behind — be full of fears: 我们如果～,就什么事情也做不成。We'll never get anywhere if we are plagued by all sorts of fears.
【前排】 qiánpái front row: ～座位 front-row seats/ 在～就座 be seated in the front rows
【前炮】 qiánpào 〈军〉 forward gun (on a ship); bow-piece
【前仆后继】 qiánpū-hòujì no sooner has one fallen than another steps into the breach: 无数革命先烈为了共产主义事业～,英勇地献出了生命。Countless revolutionary martyrs, one stepping into the breach as another fell, have fought and laid down their lives for the cause of communism.
【前期】 qiánqī earlier stage; early days
【前愆】 qiánqiān 〈书〉 past faults
【前前后后】 qiánqiánhòuhòu the whole story; the ins and outs: 一件事情的～ the ins and outs of a matter
【前桥】 qiánqiáo 〈汽车〉 front axle ◇ ～壳 front axle housing
【前驱】 qiánqū forerunner; precursor; pioneer
【前驱期】 qiánqūqī 〈医〉 prodromal stage
【前人】 qiánrén forefathers; predecessors: ～总结的经验 experience summed up by our predecessors/ ～栽树,后人乘凉。One generation plants the trees under whose shade another generation rests — profiting by the labour of one's forefathers.
【前任】 qiánrèn predecessor: ～书记 former secretary/ 他的～ his predecessor/ ～总统 ex-president
【前日】 qiánrì the day before yesterday
【前晌】 qiánshǎng 〈方〉 forenoon; morning
【前哨】 qiánshào outpost; advance guard: 与敌～接触 skirmish with the enemy's advance guards
【前哨战】 qiánshàozhàn 〈军〉 skirmish
【前身】 qiánshēn predecessor: 八路军的～是工农红军。The Eighth Route Army grew out of the Workers' and Peasants' Red Army.
【前世】 qiánshì 〔迷信〕previous existence 又作"前生"
【前事不忘,后事之师】 qiánshì bù wàng, hòushì zhī shī past experience, if not forgotten, is a guide for the future
【前视图】 qiánshìtú 〈机〉 front view
【前束】 qiánshù 〈汽车〉 toe-in
【前所未闻】 qián suǒ wèi wén never heard of before: ～的奇迹 an unheard-of miracle
【前所未有】 qián suǒ wèi yǒu hitherto unknown; unprecedented: ～的盛况 an unprecedentedly grand occasion
【前台】 qiántái ① proscenium ② (on) the stage: 阶级敌人有的在～表演,有的在幕后指挥。Some class enemies appeared on the stage while others pulled strings behind the scenes.
【前提】 qiántí ①〈逻〉 premise: 大(小)～ major (minor) premise ② prerequisite; presupposition: 必要的～ essential prerequisite/ 矛盾的一方各以其另一方为自己存在的～。Each aspect of a contradiction presupposes the existence of the other aspect.
【前天】 qiántiān the day before yesterday: ～晚上 the night before last
【前厅】 qiántīng 〈建〉 antechamber; vestibule
【前庭】 qiántíng 〈生理〉 vestibule
【前头】 qiántou 见"前面"
【前途】 qiántú future; prospect: ～无量 have boundless prospects/ 你们的工作很有～。Your work has a great future.
【前往】 qiánwǎng go to; leave for; proceed to: 代表团已动身～日内瓦。The delegation has left for Geneva./ 他们将由西安～延安。From Xi'an they will proceed to Yan'an.
【前委】 qiánwěi 〈简〉(前敌委员会) the front committee
【前卫】 qiánwèi ①〈军〉 advance guard; vanguard ②〈体〉 halfback: 左～ left halfback; left half
【前无古人】 qián wú gǔrén without parallel in history; unprecedented
【前夕】 qiánxī eve: 解放～ on the eve of liberation; shortly before liberation
【前线】 qiánxiàn front; frontline: 上～ go to the front/ 远离～ far from the frontline
【前言】 qiányán preface; foreword; introduction
【前言不搭后语】 qiányán bù dā hòuyǔ utter words that do not hang together; talk incoherently
【前沿】 qiányán 〈军〉 forward position ◇ ～阵地 forward position/ ～指挥所 forward command post
【前仰后合】 qiányǎng-hòuhé rock (with laughter): 笑得～ rock (或 shake) with laughter
【前夜】 qiányè eve: 帝国主义是无产阶级社会革命的～。Imperialism is the eve of the social revolution of the proletariat.
【前因后果】 qiányīn-hòuguǒ cause and effect; the entire process: 这件事情的～已经调查得清清楚楚。The entire matter, its cause and effect, has been fully cleared up through investigation.
【前院】 qiányuàn front courtyard
【前站】 qiánzhàn 见"打前站" dǎ qiánzhàn
【前兆】 qiánzhào omen; forewarning; premonition: 地震的～ warning signs (或 indications) of an earthquake
【前者】 qiánzhě the former
【前肢】 qiánzhī 〈动〉 forelimb; foreleg
【前置词】 qiánzhìcí 〈语〉 preposition
【前装炮】 qiánzhuāngpào 〈军〉 muzzle-loading gun; muzzle-loader
【前缀】 qiánzhuì 〈语〉 prefix
【前奏】 qiánzòu prelude ◇ ～曲〈乐〉 prelude

## 钤

qián ① seal ② affix a seal to
【钤记】 qiánjì seal or stamp of a government organization in old China

## 荨

qián
【荨麻】 qiánmá 〈植〉 nettle
【荨麻疹】 qiánmázhěn 〈医〉 nettle rash; urticaria

## 钳

qián ① pincers; pliers; tongs: 老虎～ pincer pliers/ 克丝～ combination pliers/ 火～ fire (或 coal) tongs/ 手～ hand vice ② grip (with pincers); clamp ③ restrain: ～口不言 keep one's mouth shut; keep mum

【钳工】 qiángōng ① benchwork ② fitter

【钳形】 qiánxíng pincerlike: ～攻势 a pincer movement; a two-pronged offensive/ 形成～包围 form a pincerlike encirclement

【钳制】 qiánzhì clamp down on; suppress: ～舆论 muzzle (或 gag) public opinion

【钳爪】 qiánzhuǎ chela (of a crab, lobster, etc.)

【钳子】 qiánzi pliers; pincers; forceps

## 虔

qián pious; sincere

【虔诚】 qiánchéng pious; devout: ～的佛教徒 a pious adherent of Buddhism; devout Buddhist

【虔敬】 qiánjìng reverent

## 钱

qián ① copper coin; cash: 两个铜～ two coppers (或 cash) ② money: 挣～ make money/ 这个多少～? How much is this? ③ fund; sum: 这笔～是专为保健事业用的。The fund is earmarked for public health services./ 买拖拉机的～ the wherewithal to buy tractors ④ *qian*, a unit of weight (=5 grams) ⑤ (Qián) a surname

【钱包】 qiánbāo wallet; purse

【钱币】 qiánbì coin

【钱财】 qiáncái wealth; money: 浪费～ waste of money

【钱柜】 qiánguì money-locker; money-box; till

【钱粮】 qiánliáng 〈旧〉 ① land tax ② revenue: ～师爷 revenue clerk

【钱票】 qiánpiào 〈口〉 ① paper money ② vouchers used in canteens in place of cash

【钱塘潮】 Qiántángcháo the Qiantang bore

【钱庄】 qiánzhuāng old-style Chinese private bank

## 掮

qián 〈方〉 carry on the shoulder

【掮客】 qiánkè broker: 政治～ political broker

## 乾

qián 〈旧〉 male

【乾坤】 qiánkūn heaven and earth; the universe: 扭转～ bring about a radical change in the existing state of affairs; reverse the course of events

## 潜

qián ① latent; hidden: ～能 latent energy ② stealthily; secretly; on the sly

【潜藏】 qiáncáng hide; go into hiding

【潜伏】 qiánfú hide; conceal; lie low: ～特务 hidden enemy agent/ ～的疾病 an insidious disease/ ～着的危机 a latent crisis ◇ ～期〈医〉 incubation period

【潜航】 qiánháng (of a submarine) submerge ◇ ～深度 submerged depth/ ～速度 submerged speed

【潜力】 qiánlì latent capacity; potential; potentiality: 有很大～ have great potentialities/ 充分发挥～ fully bring out latent potentialities; bring the potential into full play/ 挖掘～ exploit potentialities; tap potentials

【潜流】 qiánliú 〈地〉 undercurrent; underflow

【潜热】 qiánrè 〈物〉 latent heat

【潜入】 qiánrù ① slip into; sneak into; steal in: ～敌占区 slip into the enemy-occupied area ② dive; submerge

【潜水】 qiánshuǐ ① go under water; dive ② 〈地〉 phreatic water
◇ ～器 scuba/ ～衣 diving suit/ ～钟 diving bell

【潜水艇】 qiánshuǐtǐng submarine

【潜水员】 qiánshuǐyuán diver; frogman ◇ ～病 caisson disease; decompression sickness

【潜台词】 qiántáicí 〈剧〉 unspoken words in a play left to the understanding of the audience or reader

【潜逃】 qiántáo abscond: 携公款～ abscond with public funds

【潜艇】 qiántǐng submarine ◇ ～探测器 submarine detector

【潜望镜】 qiánwàngjìng periscope

【潜心】 qiánxīn with great concentration: ～研究科学 apply oneself to scientific study with great concentration; devote oneself to the study of science

【潜行】 qiánxíng ① move under water ② move stealthily; slink

【潜血】 qiánxuè 〈医〉 occult blood ◇ ～试验 occult blood test

【潜移默化】 qiányí-mòhuà exert a subtle influence on sb.'s character, thinking, etc.; imperceptibly influence: 文艺对人们的思想起着～的作用。Literature and art exert an imperceptible influence on people's thinking.

【潜意识】 qiányìshí the subconscious; subconsciousness

【潜泳】 qiányǒng underwater swimming

【潜鱼】 qiányú pearlfish

【潜在】 qiánzài latent; potential: ～的力量 latent power

## 黔

qián ① 〈书〉 black ② (Qián) another name for Guizhou Province

【黔驴技穷】 Qián lǘ jì qióng the proverbial donkey in ancient Guizhou has exhausted its tricks

【黔驴之技】 Qián lǘ zhī jì tricks not to be feared; cheap tricks

【黔首】 qiánshǒu the common people (a term used in ancient China)

# qiǎn

## 浅

qiǎn ① shallow: ～水 shallow water; shoal water/ ～种 shallow sowing ② simple; easy: 这篇课文很～。This lesson is very easy. ③ superficial: 对问题的认识很～ just have a superficial understanding of the problem ④ not intimate; not close: 交情很～ not on familiar terms ⑤ (of colour) light: ～蓝 light blue/ ～黄 pale yellow ⑥ not long in time: 相处的日子还～ have not been together long

【浅薄】 qiǎnbó shallow; superficial; meagre: 他的历史知识很～。He has a very meagre knowledge of history.

【浅尝辄止】 qiǎn cháng zhé zhǐ stop after getting a little knowledge of a subject or about sth.; be satisfied with a smattering of a subject

【浅成岩】 qiǎnchéngyán 〈地〉 hypabyssal rock

【浅耕】 qiǎngēng shallow ploughing

【浅海】 qiǎnhǎi 〈地〉 shallow sea; epeiric sea; epicontinental sea ◇ ～水域 the shallow waters along the coast

【浅见】 qiǎnjiàn 〈谦〉 superficial view; humble opinion: 依我～ in my humble opinion

【浅近】 qiǎnjìn simple; plain; easy to understand: ～的文字 simple language

【浅口鞋】 qiǎnkǒuxié shoes with low-cut uppers

【浅陋】 qiǎnlòu meagre; mean: 学识～ have meagre knowledge

【浅色】 qiǎnsè light colour: ～的女衬衣 a light-coloured blouse

【浅释】 qiǎnshì simple explanation

【浅水池】 qiǎnshuǐchí the shallow end of a swimming pool; shallow pool

【浅说】 qiǎnshuō elementary introduction: 《无线电～》 *An*

*Elementary Introduction to Radio*
【浅滩】 qiǎntān shoal; shallows
【浅显】 qiǎnxiǎn plain; easy to read and understand: ～的道理 a plain truth/ ～通俗的科学读物 simple popular scientific literature
【浅易】 qiǎnyì simple and easy: ～读物 easy readings

遣 qiǎn ① send; dispatch: 派～ dispatch/ 调兵～将 dispatch officers and men; move troops; deploy forces ② dispel; expel: ～闷 dispel boredom/ 消～ diversion; pastime
【遣词造句】 qiǎncí-zàojù choice of words and building of sentences; wording and phrasing
【遣返】 qiǎnfǎn repatriate: ～战俘 repatriate prisoners of war
【遣散】 qiǎnsàn disband; dismiss; send away
【遣送】 qiǎnsòng send back; repatriate: ～回国 repatriate/ ～出境 deport

谴 qiǎn
【谴责】 qiǎnzé condemn; denounce; censure: 强烈～帝国主义掠夺他国自然资源 strongly condemn imperialism for plundering other countries' natural resources

缱 qiǎn
【缱绻】 qiǎnquǎn 〈书〉 (of love between man and woman) deeply attached to each other: ～之情 deep attachment; sentimental attachment

## qiàn

欠 qiàn ① owe; be behind with: ～债 owe a debt; run (或 get) into debt/ ～租 be behind with the rent/ ～情 owe sb. a debt of gratitude; be indebted to sb. ② not enough; lacking; wanting: ～佳 not good enough; not up to the mark/ 文字～通。The writing is not altogether grammatical./ 这一屉馒头～火。These buns haven't been steamed long enough./ ～三天就是一个月了。It's three days short of a month. ③ raise slightly (a part of the body): ～脚儿 slightly raise one's heels/ 他～了～身子又继续工作。He rose slightly and then sat down to work again. ④ yawn: 呵～ yawn
【欠产】 qiànchǎn shortfall in output
【欠户】 qiànhù debtor
【欠款】 qiànkuǎn money that is owing; arrears; balance due; debt
【欠缺】 qiànquē ① be deficient in; be short of: 我们的经验还很～。We are still lacking in experience. ② shortcoming; deficiency: 我们的工作还有很多～。There are still many shortcomings in our work.
【欠伸】 qiànshēn stretch oneself and yawn
【欠身】 qiànshēn raise oneself slightly; half rise from one's seat: 他～坐起，和客人打招呼。He raised himself to a half-sitting position to greet the visitors. 或 He made an attempt to sit up as he greeted the visitors.
【欠条】 qiàntiáo a bill signed in acknowledgement of debt; IOU
【欠妥】 qiàntuǒ not proper: 措词～ not properly worded
【欠息】 qiànxī debit interest
【欠帐】 qiànzhàng bills due; outstanding accounts
【欠资】 qiànzī 〈邮〉 postage due ◇ ～信 postage-due letter

纤 qiàn a rope for towing a boat; tow line: 拉～ track (a boat)
另见 xiān
【纤夫】 qiànfū boat tracker
【纤路】 qiànlù towpath; towing path; track road
【纤手】 qiànshǒu 〈旧〉 estate agent; real estate broker

芡 qiàn 〈植〉 Gorgon euryale (*Euryale ferox*)
【芡粉】 qiànfěn ① the seed powder of Gorgon euryale ② any starch used in cooking
【芡实】 qiànshí Gorgon fruit

茜 qiàn ① 见"茜草" ② alizarin red
【茜草】 qiàncǎo 〈植〉 madder
【茜素染料】 qiànsù rǎnliào 〈化〉 alizarin dyes

倩 qiàn 〈书〉 ① pretty; handsome ② ask sb. to do sth.: ～人执笔 ask sb. to write on one's behalf

堑 qiàn moat; chasm: 天～ natural chasm
【堑壕】 qiànháo 〈军〉 trench; entrenchment: ～工事 entrenchment works ◇ ～战 trench warfare

嵌 qiàn inlay; embed; set: 镶～螺钿的漆器 lacquerware inlaid with mother-of-pearl/ ～花的地面 a mosaic pavement

歉 qiàn ① apology: 道～ offer (或 make) an apology; apologize/ 抱～ be sorry ② crop failure: 以丰补～ make up for a crop failure with a bumper harvest
【歉年】 qiànnián lean year
【歉收】 qiànshōu crop failure; poor harvest: 因遭天灾而～ have a bad harvest due to natural disaster
【歉意】 qiànyì apology; regret: 表示～ offer an apology; express one's regret/ 谨致～。Please accept my apologies.

## qiāng

抢 qiāng 见"呼天抢地" hūtiān-qiāngdì
另见 qiǎng

呛 qiāng choke: 吃饭吃～了 choke over one's food/ 他喝得太猛，～着了。He took a big gulp and almost choked.
另见 qiàng

羌 qiāng
【羌活】 qiānghuó 〈植〉 notopterygium (*Notopterygium incisium*)
【羌族】 Qiāngzú ① the Qiang (Chiang) nationality, living in Sichuan ② Qiang, an ancient nationality in China

枪 qiāng ① rifle; gun; firearm: 机～ machine gun/ ～架 rifle rack; gun rack/ 持～致敬！(口令) Present arms! ② spear: 红缨～ a red-tasselled spear
【枪把】 qiāngbà the small of the stock; pistol grip
【枪毙】 qiāngbì execute by shooting
【枪刺】 qiāngcì bayonet
【枪带】 qiāngdài sling
【枪弹】 qiāngdàn ① cartridge ② bullet
【枪法】 qiāngfǎ marksmanship: 她～高明。She is a crack shot.
【枪放下】 qiāngfàngxià (口令) Order arms!
【枪杆子】 qiānggǎnzi the barrel of a gun; gun; arms: 拿起～上前线 take up arms and go to the front/ ～里面出政权。Political power grows out of the barrel of a gun. 又作"枪杆"

【枪管】 qiāngguǎn barrel (of a gun)
【枪机】 qiāngjī rifle bolt
【枪决】 qiāngjué 见"枪毙"
【枪口】 qiāngkǒu muzzle: 把~对准靶子 aim a gun at the target
【枪林弹雨】 qiānglín-dànyǔ a hail of bullets: 冒着~冲锋陷阵 charge under a hail of bullets; charge under heavy fire
【枪榴弹】 qiāngliúdàn rifle grenade
【枪炮】 qiāngpào firearms; arms; guns
【枪杀】 qiāngshā shoot dead
【枪伤】 qiāngshāng bullet wound
【枪上肩】 qiāngshàngjiān (口令) Shoulder arms!
【枪声】 qiāngshēng report of a gun; shot; crack: 听到远处的~ hear shots in the distance
【枪手】 qiāngshǒu ① marksman; gunner: 神~ an expert marksman; a crack shot ② 〈旧〉 spearman
【枪手】 qiāngshou one who sits for an examination in place of another person
【枪栓】 qiāngshuān rifle bolt
【枪膛】 qiāngtáng bore (of a gun)
【枪替】 qiāngtì sit for an examination in place of another person
【枪托】 qiāngtuō (rifle) butt; buttstock
【枪械】 qiāngxiè firearms
【枪眼】 qiāngyǎn ① embrasure; loophole ② bullet hole
【枪鱼】 qiāngyú marlin
【枪支】 qiāngzhī firearms ◇ ~弹药 firearms and ammunition
【枪子儿】 qiāngzǐr 〈口〉 ① cartridge ② bullet; shot

**戗** qiāng ① in an opposite direction: ~风行船 sail against the wind ② clash; be at loggerheads with: 他们说~了,吵起来啦。Their views clashed and this eventually led to a quarrel.
另见 qiàng

**戕** qiāng kill: 自~ kill oneself; commit suicide
【戕贼】 qiāngzéi injure; undermine: ~身体 undermine (或 ruin) one's health

**腔** qiāng ① cavity: 口(鼻)~ the oral (nasal) cavity/ 胸~ thoracic cavity/ 满~热情 full of enthusiasm ② tune; pitch: 高~ high pitched tune/ 唱走了~儿 sing out of tune/ 秦~ Shaanxi opera ③ accent: 他说话南~北调。He speaks with a mixture of accents./ 山东~ Shandong accent/ 学生~ schoolboy talk; classroom tone of a schoolboy ④ speech: 答~ answer/ 不开~ keep mum
【腔肠动物】 qiāngcháng dòngwù coelenterate
【腔调】 qiāngdiào ① tune: 京剧的~ tunes of Beijing opera/ 修正主义和帝国主义是一个~。The revisionists sing the same tune as the imperialists. ② accent; intonation: 听他说话的~象是河南人。Judging from his accent, he is probably from Henan.

**蜣** qiāng
【蜣螂】 qiāngláng 〈动〉 dung beetle

**锵** qiāng 〈象〉 clang; gong

**镪** qiāng
【镪水】 qiāngshuǐ strong acid: 硝~ nitric acid

## qiáng

**强** qiáng ① strong; powerful: 身~体壮 strong and healthy/ 能力很~ very capable/ 责任心~ have a strong sense of responsibility/ ~敌 formidable enemy ② by force: ~取 take by force/ ~令执行 arbitrarily give orders to carry out sth. ③ better: 我们的劳动条件一年比一年~。Our working conditions are getting better each year. ④ slightly more than; plus: 三分之一~ slightly more than one third
另见 jiàng; qiǎng
【强暴】 qiángbào ① violent; brutal: ~的行为 act of violence ② ferocious adversary: 不畏~ defy brute force
【强大】 qiángdà big and powerful; powerful; formidable: ~的人民解放军 the powerful People's Liberation Army/ 世界革命力量越来越~。The world revolutionary forces are getting stronger and stronger.
【强盗】 qiángdào robber; bandit: ~行为 banditry; robbery ◇ ~逻辑 gangster logic/ ~头子 gang boss; bandit chieftain
【强的松】 qiángdísōng 〈药〉 prednisone
【强调】 qiángdiào stress; emphasize; underline: 不适当地~情况特殊 lay undue stress on special circumstances/ 必须~产品质量。Emphasis must be placed on the quality of the products.
【强度】 qiángdù intensity; strength: 劳动~ the intensity of labour/ 钢的~ the strength of the steel/ 抗震~ shock strength/ 辐射~ radiation intensity
【强渡】 qiángdù 〈军〉 fight one's way across a river; force a river
【强风】 qiángfēng 〈气〉 strong breeze
【强攻】 qiánggōng take by storm; storm: ~敌人阵地 storm the enemy position
【强固】 qiánggù strong; solid: ~的工事 strong fortifications/ ~的基础 a solid foundation
【强国】 qiángguó powerful nation; power: 把我国建设成为社会主义的现代化~ build China into a modern, powerful socialist country
【强悍】 qiánghàn intrepid; doughty; valiant
【强横】 qiánghèng brutal and unreasonable; tyrannical
【强化】 qiánghuà strengthen; intensify; consolidate: ~人民的国家机器 strengthen the people's state apparatus
【强击机】 qiángjījī 〈军〉 attack plane
【强加】 qiángjiā impose; force: 不要~于人。Don't force your views on others.
【强奸】 qiángjiān rape; violate: ~民意 defile public opinion
【强碱】 qiángjiǎn 〈化〉 alkali; strong base
【强健】 qiángjiàn strong and healthy: 体魄~ be physically strong; have a strong constitution
【强将手下无弱兵】 qiángjiàng shǒuxià wú ruòbīng there are no poor soldiers under a good general
【强劲】 qiángjìng powerful; forceful: ~的海风 a strong wind blowing from the sea
【强劳动力】 qiángláodònglì able-bodied labourer
【强力霉素】 qiánglìméisù 〈药〉 doxycycline
【强烈】 qiángliè strong; intense; violent: ~的愿望 a strong desire/ ~的仇恨 intense hatred/ ~的对比 a striking contrast/ ~反对 strongly oppose/ ~谴责 vehemently condemn; vigorously denounce
【强弩之末】 qiángnǔ zhī mò an arrow at the end of its flight — a spent force
【强拍】 qiángpāi 〈乐〉 strong beat; accented beat: 次~ subsidiary strong beat
【强权】 qiángquán power; might: ~政治 power politics/ ~即公理 —— 这是帝国主义的逻辑。Might is right — that is the logic of imperialism.
【强溶剂】 qiángróngjì 〈化〉 strong solvent

【强盛】 qiángshèng (of a country) powerful and prosperous
【强似】 qiángsì be better than; be superior to: 今年的秋收～去年。The autumn harvest this year is better than that of last year.
【强酸】 qiángsuān strong acid
【强心剂】 qiángxīnjì 〈药〉 cardiac stimulant; cardiotonic
【强行】 qiángxíng force: ～闯入 force one's way in/ ～登陆 force a landing/ ～通过一项议案 force through a bill
【强行军】 qiángxíngjūn 〈军〉 forced march
【强硬】 qiángyìng strong; tough; unyielding: 措词～的声明 a strongly worded statement/ 提出～抗议 lodge a strong protest/ ～路线 tough line; hard line/ ～的态度 an uncompromising stand ◇ ～派 hardliner
【强有力】 qiángyǒulì strong; vigorous; forceful: 采取～的行动 take vigorous action
【强占】 qiángzhàn forcibly occupy; seize
【强震】 qiángzhèn 〈地〉 strong shock ◇ ～区 meizoseismal area
【强直】 qiángzhí 〈医〉 rigidity
【强制】 qiángzhì force; compel; coerce: ～劳动 forced labour/ ～手段 compulsory means; coercive measure/ ～执行 enforce/ ～机关 institutions of coercion/ ～性的命令 mandatory order/ 不能～人们接受一种艺术风格或一种学派。People cannot be compelled to accept one particular style of art or school of thought.
【强中自有强中手】 qiángzhōng zì yǒu qiángzhōng shǒu however strong you are, there's always someone stronger
【强壮】 qiángzhuàng strong; sturdy; robust ◇ ～剂〈药〉 roborant; tonic

**墙** qiáng wall
【墙报】 qiángbào wall newspaper
【墙壁】 qiángbì wall
【墙倒众人推】 qiáng dǎo zhòngrén tuī when a wall is about to collapse, everybody gives it a push — everybody hits a man who is down
【墙根】 qiánggēn the foot of a wall
【墙角】 qiángjiǎo a corner formed by two walls ◇ ～石 cornerstone
【墙脚】 qiángjiǎo ① the foot of a wall ② foundation: 挖～ cut the ground (from under sb.'s feet); undermine the foundation
【墙裙】 qiángqún 〈建〉 dado
【墙头】 qiángtóu the top of a wall ◇～草 grass on the top of a wall which sways with every wind — a person who bends with the wind
【墙纸】 qiángzhǐ 〈建〉 wall paper

**蔷** qiáng
【蔷薇】 qiángwēi 〈植〉 rose ◇ ～科 the rose family

**樯** qiáng 〈书〉 mast: 帆～如林 a forest of masts

## qiǎng

**抢** qiǎng ① rob; loot ② snatch; grab: 他把信～了过去。He snatched away the letter. ③ vie for; scramble for: ～球 scramble for the ball/ ～干重活 vie with each other for the hardest job ④ rush: ～收 rush in the harvest ⑤ scrape; scratch: 把锅底～一～ scrape the bottom of the pot/ 磨剪子～菜刀 sharpen scissors and kitchen knives
另见 qiāng
【抢白】 qiǎngbái reprove or satirize sb. to his face
【抢渡】 qiǎngdù speedily cross (a river)
【抢夺】 qiǎngduó snatch; wrest; seize: ～胜利果实 seize the fruits of victory
【抢购】 qiǎnggòu rush to purchase: ～风潮 panic purchasing
【抢劫】 qiǎngjié rob; loot; plunder
【抢救】 qiǎngjiù rescue; save; salvage: ～国家财产 save state property/ ～水淹了的庄稼 salvage flooded crops/ ～病人 give emergency treatment to a patient; rescue a patient/ ～无效。All rescue measures proved ineffectual. ◇ ～工作 rescue work/ ～组 rescue party
【抢掠】 qiǎnglüè loot; sack; plunder
【抢时间】 qiǎng shíjiān race against time: 农活有季节性，必须～。Farm work is seasonal, so we must race against time.
【抢收】 qiǎngshōu rush in the harvest; get the harvest in quickly
【抢先】 qiǎngxiān try to be the first to do sth.; anticipate; forestall: 他赶紧跑去堵堤上的决口，可是老队长已经～了。He hurried to help fill the breach in the dyke, but the old brigade leader had already got there before him.
【抢险】 qiǎngxiǎn rush to deal with an emergency (e.g. a breach in an embankment, a cave-in, etc.) ◇ ～队 emergency squad
【抢修】 qiǎngxiū rush to repair; do rush repairs: ～高炉 rush-repair a blast furnace
【抢占】 qiǎngzhàn race to control; seize; grab: ～制高点 race to control a commanding point
【抢种】 qiǎngzhòng rush-planting: ～晚稻 rush-plant the late rice

**羟** qiǎng
【羟基】 qiǎngjī 〈化〉 hydroxyl (group) ◇～化物 hydroxylate

**强** qiǎng make an effort; strive: ～作镇静 make an effort to appear composed; try hard to keep one's composure/ ～不知以为知 pretend to know what one does not know
另见 jiàng; qiáng
【强逼】 qiǎngbī compel; force
【强辩】 qiǎngbiàn defend oneself by sophistry
【强词夺理】 qiǎngcí-duólǐ use lame arguments; resort to sophistry; reason fallaciously
【强迫】 qiǎngpò force; compel; coerce: ～命令 resort to coercion and commandism/ ～敌机降落 compel the enemy plane to land
【强求】 qiǎngqiú insist on; impose: 各地情况不同，不能～一律。No uniformity should be imposed since conditions vary from place to place.
【强人所难】 qiǎng rén suǒ nán try to make sb. do sth. which he won't or can't
【强使】 qiǎngshǐ force; compel
【强颜欢笑】 qiǎng yán huānxiào put on an air of cheerfulness; try to look happy when one is sad

**襁** qiǎng
【襁褓】 qiǎngbǎo swaddling clothes: ～中 be in one's infancy

## qiàng

**呛** qiàng irritate (respiratory organs): 炸辣椒的味儿～鼻子。The smell of red pepper being fried irritates the nose./ 烟把我～着了。The smoke almost choked me.
另见 qiāng

**炝** qiàng ① boil (meat or vegetables) in water for a while, then dress with soy, vinegar, etc. ② fry sth. quickly in hot oil, then cook it with sauce and water

**戗** qiàng ①〈建〉prop ②〈方〉prop up; shore up: 用两根木头来～住这堵墙 prop up the wall with two logs
另见 qiāng

**跄** qiàng
【跄踉】 qiàngliàng stagger

## qiāo

**悄** qiāo
另见 qiǎo
【悄悄】 qiāoqiāo quietly; on the quiet: ～离开 leave quietly/ 他～儿地跟我全说了。He told me everything on the quiet.

**硗** qiāo
【硗薄】 qiāobó hard and infertile; barren

**跷** qiāo ① lift up (a leg); hold up (a finger): ～着腿坐着 sit with one's legs crossed ② on tiptoe: ～着脚走路 walk on tiptoe ③ stilts
【跷蹊】 qiāoqi fishy; dubious
【跷跷板】 qiāoqiāobǎn seesaw: 玩～ play on a seesaw

**蹻** qiāo 见"跷" qiāo

**敲** qiāo ① knock; beat; strike: ～门 knock at the door/ ～警钟 sound the alarm/ 钟刚～过四点。The clock has just struck four./ ～锣打鼓迎新年 usher in the new year with drums and gongs; beat drums and gongs to greet the new year ②〈口〉overcharge; fleece sb.: 给～去五块钱 be stung for five *yuan*
【敲边鼓】 qiāo biāngǔ speak or act to assist sb.; back sb. up
【敲打】 qiāoda ① beat; rap; tap: 锣鼓～得很热闹。Drums and gongs were beating boisterously. ②〈方〉say sth. to irritate sb.: 冷言冷语～人 irritate people with sarcastic remarks
【敲骨吸髓】 qiāogǔ-xīsuǐ break the bones and suck the marrow — cruel, bloodsucking exploitation; suck the lifeblood
【敲门砖】 qiāoménzhuān a brick picked up to knock on the door and thrown away when it has served its purpose — a stepping-stone to success
【敲诈】 qiāozhà extort; blackmail; racketeer: ～钱财 extort money
【敲竹杠】 qiāo zhúgàng take advantage of sb.'s being in a weak position to overcharge him; fleece

**劁** qiāo geld; castrate: ～猪 castrate a pig

**锹** qiāo spade: 挖一～深 dig a spade's depth; dig a spit deep/ 每一～煤 each shovelful of coal

**缲** qiāo hem with invisible stitches: 给手绢儿～边 hem a handkerchief

**橇** qiāo sledge; sled; sleigh

## qiáo

**乔** qiáo ① tall ② disguise ③ (Qiáo) a surname
【乔林】 qiáolín〈林〉high forest
【乔木】 qiáomù〈植〉arbor; tree
【乔其纱】 qiáoqíshā〈纺〉georgette
【乔迁】 qiáoqiān〔多用于祝贺〕move to a better place or have a promotion: ～之喜。Best wishes for your new home.
【乔装】 qiáozhuāng disguise: ～成商人 disguise oneself as a merchant

**侨** qiáo ① live abroad ② a person living abroad: 华～ overseas Chinese; Chinese nationals residing abroad/ 外～ foreign residents; aliens
【侨胞】 qiáobāo countrymen (或 nationals) residing abroad
【侨汇】 qiáohuì overseas remittance
【侨居】 qiáojū live abroad ◇ ～国 country of residence
【侨眷】 qiáojuàn relatives of nationals living abroad: 华侨及～ overseas Chinese and their relatives
【侨民】 qiáomín a national of a particular country residing abroad
【侨务】 qiáowù affairs concerning nationals living abroad

**荞** qiáo
【荞麦】 qiáomài buckwheat

**桥** qiáo bridge
【桥洞】 qiáodòng〈口〉bridge opening
【桥墩】 qiáodūn (bridge) pier
【桥拱】 qiáogǒng bridge arch
【桥孔】 qiáokǒng bridge opening
【桥梁】 qiáoliáng bridge: 起～作用 play the role of a bridge; serve as a link/ 商业是联结生产同消费的～。Commerce is a bridge that links production with consumption.
【桥楼室】 qiáolóushì〈造船〉bridge house
【桥牌】 qiáopái bridge (a card game): 打～ play bridge
【桥式起重机】 qiáoshì qǐzhòngjī bridge crane; overhead travelling crane
【桥塔】 qiáotǎ〈建〉bridge tower
【桥台】 qiáotái〈建〉abutment
【桥头】 qiáotóu either end of a bridge
【桥头堡】 qiáotóubǎo ①〈军〉bridgehead ②〈建〉bridge tower
【桥堍】 qiáotù either end of a bridge
【桥支座】 qiáozhīzuò bridge seat

**翘** qiáo ① raise (one's head) ② become warped: 木板～了。The board has warped.
另见 qiào
【翘楚】 qiáochǔ〈书〉an outstanding (或 talented) person: 医中～ an eminent physician
【翘企】 qiáoqǐ〈书〉raise one's head and stand on tiptoe — eagerly look forward to: 不胜～之至 look forward to sth. with eager anticipation
【翘首】 qiáoshǒu〈书〉raise one's head and look: ～星空 look up at the starry sky

**谯** qiáo
【谯楼】 qiáolóu〈书〉① watchtower ② drum tower

**憔** qiáo
【憔悴】 qiáocuì ① wan and sallow; thin and pallid ② (of plants) withered

**樵** qiáo ①〈书〉gather firewood ②〈方〉firewood
【樵夫】qiáofū woodcutter; woodman

**瞧** qiáo 〈口〉look; see: 等着~吧。Wait and see./ ~书 read a book/ 东~西~ look about/ 你~着办吧。You can do as you see fit.
【瞧病】qiáobìng 〈口〉①(of a patient) see (或 consult) a doctor ②(of a doctor) see a patient
【瞧不起】qiáobuqǐ 〈口〉look down upon; hold in contempt
【瞧不上眼】qiáobushàng yǎn 〈口〉consider beneath one's notice; turn one's nose up at
【瞧得起】qiáodeqǐ 〈口〉think much (或 highly) of sb.
【瞧见】qiáojian 〈口〉see; catch sight of

## qiǎo

**巧** qiǎo ①skilful; ingenious; clever: ~匠 a skilled (或 clever) workman/ 手~ clever with one's hands; dexterous ②cunning; deceitful; artful: ~言 cunning words; deceitful talk ③opportunely; coincidentally; as it happens; as luck would have it: 来得真~ arrive at a most opportune moment/ 无~不成书。There is no story without coincidences./ 他偏~那天不在。As luck would have it, he was away that day.
【巧夺天工】qiǎo duó tiāngōng wonderful workmanship (或 superb craftsmanship) excelling nature
【巧妇难为无米之炊】qiǎofù nán wéi wú mǐ zhī chuī the cleverest housewife can't cook a meal without rice — one can't make bricks without straw
【巧妇鸟】qiǎofùniǎo wren
【巧干】qiǎogàn work ingeniously; do sth. in a clever way
【巧合】qiǎohé coincidence
【巧计】qiǎojì clever device; artful scheme
【巧克力】qiǎokèlì chocolate
【巧立名目】qiǎo lì míngmù concoct various pretexts; invent all sorts of names: ~，搜刮民财 extort people's wealth under all sorts of pretexts
【巧妙】qiǎomiào ingenious; clever: ~的战术 ingenious tactics/ ~的手段 a clever move
【巧取豪夺】qiǎoqǔ-háoduó secure (sb.'s belongings, right, etc.) by force or trickery
【巧舌如簧】qiǎoshé rú huáng have a glib tongue
【巧事】qiǎoshì coincidence
【巧手】qiǎoshǒu a dab hand
【巧遇】qiǎoyù chance encounter

**悄** qiǎo ①quiet; silent ②〈书〉sad; worried; grieved
另见 qiāo
【悄然】qiǎorán ①sorrowfully; sadly: ~泪下 shed tears in sorrow; shed sad tears ②quietly; softly: ~离去 leave quietly
【悄声】qiǎoshēng quietly; in a low voice

**雀** qiǎo sparrow
另见 què
【雀盲眼】qiǎomangyǎn 〈方〉night blindness; nyctalopia

**愀** qiǎo
【愀然】qiǎorán 〈书〉①sorrowful-looking ②stern; grave-looking

## qiào

**壳** qiào shell; hard surface
另见 ké
【壳菜】qiàocài mussel

**俏** qiào ①pretty; smart; handsome: 打扮得真~ be smartly dressed ②sell well; be in great demand: ~货 goods in great demand
【俏丽】qiàolì handsome; pretty
【俏皮】qiàopi ①good-looking; smart ②lively and delightful; witty
【俏皮话】qiàopihuà ①witty remark; witticism; wisecrack ②sarcastic remark

**诮** qiào 〈书〉censure; blame

**窍** qiào ①aperture ②a key to sth.: 诀~ knack; trick of a trade
【窍门】qiàomén key (to a problem); knack: 找~ try to find the key to a problem; try to get the knack of doing sth.

**峭** qiào ①high and steep; precipitous ②severe; stern
【峭拔】qiàobá ①high and steep ②vigorous: 笔锋~ have a vigorous style of writing
【峭壁】qiàobì cliff; precipice; steep
【峭立】qiàolì rise steeply

**翘** qiào stick up; hold up; bend upwards; turn upwards
另见 qiáo
【翘辫子】qiào biànzi kick the bucket
【翘尾巴】qiào wěiba be cocky; get stuck-up: 别一有成绩就~。Don't get cocky when you've achieved something.

**撬** qiào prize; pry: 把箱子~开 prize (或 pry) open a box
【撬杠】qiàogàng crowbar

**鞘** qiào sheath; scabbard
另见 shāo
【鞘翅】qiàochì 〈动〉elytrum

## qiē

**切** qiē ①cut; slice: ~菜 cut up vegetables/ ~肉 slice meat ②〈数〉tangency
另见 qiè
【切变】qiēbiàn 〈物〉shear: 风~ 〈气〉wind shear
【切布机】qiēbùjī 〈纺〉rag cutter (或 chopper)
【切槽】qiēcáo 〈机〉grooving
【切齿机】qiēchǐjī 〈机〉gear cutting machine
【切除】qiēchú 〈医〉excision; resection: ~脂肪瘤 the resection (或 removal) of a lipoma/ 全(部分)~ total (partial) excision
【切磋】qiēcuō learn from each other by exchanging views; compare notes: 比赛后两国篮球运动员聚在一起，~球艺。The basketball players of the two countries got together and swopped pointers after the match.
【切点】qiēdiǎn 〈数〉point of tangency; point of contact
【切断】qiēduàn cut off: ~敌人后路 cut off the enemy's retreat/ ~电源 cut off the electricity supply

【切分音】 qiēfēnyīn 〈乐〉 syncopation
【切开】 qiēkāi 〈医〉 incision
【切块】 qiēkuài 〈食品〉 stripping and slicing
【切力】 qiēlì 〈物〉 shearing force; shear: 横～ transverse shear
【切面】 qiēmiàn ①〈数〉 tangent plane ② section ③ cut noodles; machine-made noodles
【切片】 qiēpiàn ① cut into slices ②〈医〉 section: ～检查 cut sections (of organic tissues) for microscopic examination
【切片机】 qiēpiànjī ① slicer ②〈纺〉 chipper ③〈医〉 microtome
【切线】 qiēxiàn 〈数〉 tangent (line)
【切削】 qiēxiāo 〈机〉 cutting: 金属～ metal cutting/ 高速～ high-speed cutting/ 粗～ rough cut
【切纸机】 qiēzhǐjī paper cutting machine; paper cutter

## qié

**茄** qié eggplant; aubergine
另见 jiā
【茄子】 qiézi eggplant; aubergine

## qiě

**且** qiě ①〈副〉 just; for the time being: 你～等一下。Just wait a little while./ 这事～放一下。Let the matter rest for the time being./ ～不说中文期刊,外文期刊也订了不少。Lots of periodicals in foreign languages have been subscribed to, not to mention those in Chinese. ②〈方〉〈副〉 for a long time: 这种钢笔～使呢。These fountain pens last a long time./ 他～来不了呢。He's a long time coming. ③〈书〉〈连〉 even: 死～不惧,况困难乎! Even death holds no fears for us, to say nothing of difficulties. ④〈书〉〈连〉 both... and...: 既高～大 both tall and heavy set; both high and wide
【且慢】 qiěmàn wait a moment; not go or do so soon: ～,听我把话说完。Wait a minute, let me finish what I have to say./ ～高兴! Don't rejoice too soon!
【且…且…】 qiě...qiě... while; as: 他们一路上且谈且走。All the way they talked as they walked.

## qiè

**切** qiè ① correspond to; be close to: 不～实际 not correspond to reality; unrealistic; impractical/ 译文不～原意。The translation does not quite correspond to the original. ② eager; anxious: 回国心～ be anxious to return to one's country ③ be sure to: ～勿迟延。Be sure not to delay./ ～不可自以为是。One should never be presumptuous and opinionated. ④ 见"反切" fǎnqiè
另见 qiē
【切齿】 qièchǐ gnash one's teeth: ～痛恨 gnash one's teeth in hatred
【切肤之痛】 qiè fū zhī tòng keenly felt pain
【切合】 qièhé suit; fit in with: 计划要～实际。Plans should be geared to actual circumstances./ ～人民的需要 fit in with the needs of the people
【切记】 qièjì be sure to keep in mind; must always remember
【切忌】 qièjì must guard against; avoid by all means: ～主观片面。Be careful to avoid being subjective and one-sided./ ～生冷 cold and raw food strictly forbidden
【切近】 qièjìn close to: 这样解释比较～作者原意。This interpretation seems to be closer to what is meant by the author.
【切脉】 qièmài 〈中医〉 feel the pulse
【切切】 qièqiè ① be sure to: ～不可骄傲。Be sure not to become conceited. 或 Guard against arrogance by every means. ②〔用于布告、条令等末尾〕: ～此布。This proclamation is hereby issued in all earnestness.
【切身】 qièshēn ① of immediate concern to oneself: ～利益 one's immediate or vital interests ② personal: ～体会 personal understanding; intimate knowledge
【切实】 qièshí ① feasible; practical; realistic: ～有效的办法 practical and effective measures/ ～可行的计划 a feasible (或 realistic) plan ② conscientiously; earnestly: ～改正错误 correct one's mistakes in real earnest/ 切切实实地工作 do one's job conscientiously
【切题】 qiètí keep to the point; be relevant to the subject: 写文章要～。When writing, keep to the subject.
【切诊】 qièzhěn 〈中医〉 pulse feeling and palpation, one of the four methods of diagnosis
【切中】 qièzhòng hit (the mark): 她的批评～要害。Her criticism struck home.

**妾** qiè concubine

**怯** qiè timid; cowardly; nervous
【怯场】 qièchǎng have stage fright
【怯懦】 qiènuò timid and overcautious
【怯弱】 qièruò timid and weak-willed
【怯生】 qièshēng 〈方〉 shy with strangers
【怯阵】 qièzhèn ① feel nervous when going into battle; be battle-shy ② have stage fright

**窃** qiè ① steal; pilfer: 行～ steal; practise theft/ ～案 larceny; burglary ② secretly; surreptitiously; furtively: ～笑 laugh secretly; laugh up one's sleeve/ ～～私议 exchange whispered comments ③〈谦〉〔指自己〕: ～以为 in my humble opinion; I presume
【窃国】 qièguó usurp state power ◇ ～大盗 arch usurper of state power
【窃据】 qièjù usurp; unjustly occupy: ～要职 usurp a high post; unjustly occupy a high post
【窃取】 qièqǔ usurp; steal; grab: ～机密情报 steal secret information/ ～别人的劳动果实 grab the fruits of other people's labour
【窃听】 qiètīng eavesdrop; wiretap; bug ◇ ～器 tapping device; listening-in device; bug
【窃贼】 qièzéi thief; burglar; pilferer

**挈** qiè ① take along: ～眷 take one's family along ② lift; raise; take up: 提纲～领 hold a net by the headrope or a coat by the collar — concentrate on the main points

**惬** qiè 〈书〉 be satisfied
【惬意】 qièyì be pleased; be satisfied

**趄** qiè slanting; inclined: ～坡 slope/ ～着身子 (of a person) leaning sideways
另见 jū

**箧** qiè 〈书〉 small suitcase: 藤～ wicker suitcase

**锲** qiè 〈书〉 carve; engrave
【锲而不舍】 qiè ér bù shě keep on carving unflaggingly — work with perseverance: 学习要有～的精神。Study requires

perseverance.

## qīn

**亲** qīn ① parent: 双～ parents ② blood relation; next of kin: ～兄弟 blood brother ③ relative: 近～ close relative; near kin/ 远～ distant relative ④ marriage; match: 说～ act as a matchmaker ⑤ bride: 迎～ (of the groom's family) send a party to escort the bride to the groom's home ⑥ close; intimate; dear: ～如一家 as dear to each other as members of one family ⑦ in person; oneself ⑧ kiss: 她～了～孩子的脸。She kissed the child on the cheek. 另见 qìng

【亲爱】 qīn'ài dear; beloved: ～的同志们 dear comrades/ ～的祖国 one's beloved country

【亲本】 qīnběn 〈生〉 parent: 轮回～ recurrent parent

【亲笔】 qīnbǐ ① in one's own handwriting: 这信是他～写的。This letter is in his own hand. ② one's own handwriting: 这是他的～。This is his handwriting. ◇ ～签名 one's own signature; autograph/ ～信 a personal, handwritten message; an autograph letter

【亲代】 qīndài 〈生〉 parental generation

【亲和力】 qīnhélì 〈化〉 affinity

【亲近】 qīnjìn be close to; be on intimate terms with: 这两人很～。Those two are on intimate terms./ 他对人热情诚恳，大家都愿意～他。As he is warmhearted and sincere, everyone wants to be friends with him.

【亲眷】 qīnjuàn 〈方〉 one's relatives

【亲口】 qīnkǒu (say sth.) personally: 这是他～告诉我的。He told me this himself.

【亲密】 qīnmì close; intimate: ～的战友 a close comrade-in-arms/ ～无间 be on very intimate terms with each other

【亲昵】 qīnnì very intimate: ～的称呼 an affectionate form of address

【亲戚】 qīnqi relative: 我在上海的～不多。I have very few relatives in Shanghai.

【亲切】 qīnqiè cordial; kind: ～的关怀 kind attention; loving care/ ～的教导 kind guidance/ ～的谈话 a cordial conversation/ 他的话我们感到很～。 What he said touched our hearts.

【亲热】 qīnrè affectionate; intimate; warmhearted: 我们都～地称她为大姐。We all affectionately refer to her as our elder sister./ ～地问长问短 make warmhearted inquiries (about sb.'s health, etc.)

【亲人】 qīnrén ① one's parents, spouse, children, etc.; one's family members: 他除母亲外，没有别的～。 His mother is the only other member of his family. ② dear ones; those dear to one: 感谢～解放军 thank our beloved Liberation Army

【亲善】 qīnshàn goodwill (between countries)

【亲身】 qīnshēn personal; firsthand: ～经历 personal experience; firsthand experience

【亲生】 qīnshēng one's own (children, parents): ～父母 one's own parents

【亲事】 qīnshì marriage

【亲手】 qīnshǒu with one's own hands; personally; oneself: 这些是他～种的树。 Those are the trees he planted with his own hands./ 你～做一做。Do it yourself.

【亲属】 qīnshǔ kinsfolk; relatives

【亲痛仇快】 qīn tòng chóu kuài sadden one's own people and gladden the enemy

【亲王】 qīnwáng prince

【亲信】 qīnxìn trusted follower

【亲眼】 qīnyǎn with one's own eyes; personally: 这是我～看见的。I saw it with my own eyes. /我们～看到了贵国人民对中国人民的友好情谊。We have seen for ourselves how friendly the people of your country are towards the people of China.

【亲友】 qīnyǒu relatives and friends; kith and kin

【亲鱼】 qīnyú parent fish

【亲政】 qīnzhèng (of a sovereign) take over the reins of government upon coming of age

【亲自】 qīnzì personally; in person; oneself: ～动手 personally take a hand in the work; do the job oneself/ ～拜访 make a personal call/ 你～去看看。 Go and see for yourself./ 他～带领我们参观博物馆。He showed us round the museum himself.

【亲族】 qīnzú members of the same clan

【亲嘴】 qīnzuǐ kiss

**侵** qīn ① invade; intrude into; infringe upon ② approaching: ～晓 approaching daybreak

【侵晨】 qīnchén towards dawn

【侵犯】 qīnfàn encroach on; infringe upon; violate: ～人权 infringe upon human rights/ ～领土和主权 violate a country's territorial integrity and sovereignty/ 决不允许～集体利益。No encroachment on the interests of the collective is allowed./ 社会主义的公共财产不可～。Socialist public property shall be inviolable.

【侵害】 qīnhài encroach on; make inroads on: 建造防护林，减少风沙的～ build shelterbelts to reduce encroachments by sandstorms/ 防止蝗虫～农作物 prevent the inroads of locusts on the crops/ 同～公民权利的行为作斗争 fight against any infringement of the rights of citizens

【侵略】 qīnlüè aggression; invasion: ～别国 commit aggression against another country/ 帝国主义～成性。Imperialism is aggressive by nature. ◇ ～国 aggressor (nation)/ ～军 aggressor troops; invading army/ ～行为 act of aggression/ ～战争 war of aggression/ ～者 aggressor; invader

【侵扰】 qīnrǎo invade and harass: ～边境 harass a country's frontiers; make border raids

【侵入】 qīnrù invade; intrude into; make incursions into: ～领海 intrude into a country's territorial waters/ 外国资本的～ the invasion of foreign capital/ 病菌已～肺部。Germs have invaded the lungs. ◇ ～岩〈地〉 intrusive rock; irruptive rock

【侵蚀】 qīnshí corrode; erode: 风雨的～ erosion by wind and rain/ 抵制资产阶级思想的～ resist the corrosive influence of bourgeois ideology ◇ ～土 eroded soil

【侵吞】 qīntūn ① embezzle; misappropriate: ～公款 embezzle public funds/ ～社会财富 appropriate social property ② swallow up; annex: ～别国领土 annex another country's territory

【侵袭】 qīnxí make inroads on; invade and attack; hit: 台风～沿海地区。The typhoon hit the coastal areas.

【侵占】 qīnzhàn invade and occupy; seize: ～别国领土 invade and occupy another country's territory/ ～公有土地 seize public land

**钦** qīn ① admire; respect ② by the emperor himself: ～定 (of a book, etc.) made by imperial order

【钦差】 qīnchāi imperial envoy; imperial commissioner 又作"钦差大臣"

【钦敬】 qīnjìng admire and respect

【钦佩】 qīnpèi admire; esteem: 表示～ express admiration for/ 他们坚持科学实验的精神令人～。Their persistence in scientific experiment commands admiration.

【钦仰】 qīnyǎng 〈书〉 revere; venerate; esteem

**衾** qīn 〈书〉 quilt

## qín

**芹** qín

【芹菜】 qíncài celery

**秦** Qín ① the Qin Dynasty (221-207 B.C.) ② another name for Shaanxi Province ③ a surname

【秦艽】 qínjiāo 〈植〉 large-leaved gentian (*Gentiana macrophylla*)

【秦皮】 qínpí 〈中药〉 the bark of ash (*Fraxinus bungeana*)

【秦腔】 qínqiāng Shaanxi opera, popular in the northwestern provinces

**琴** qín ① a general name for certain musical instruments: 小提～ violin/ 钢～ piano/ 口～ harmonica ② *qin*, a seven-stringed plucked instrument in some ways similar to the zither

【琴拨】 qínbō plectrum

【琴凳】 qíndèng music stool

【琴键】 qínjiàn key (on a musical instrument)

【琴马】 qínmǎ 〈乐〉 bridge (of a stringed instrument)

【琴鸟】 qínniǎo lyrebird

【琴书】 qínshū story-telling, mainly in song, with musical accompaniment

【琴弦】 qínxián string (of a musical instrument)

**覃** Qín a surname

另见 tán

**禽** qín birds: 鸣～ song birds/ 家～ (domestic) fowls; poultry

【禽龙】 qínlóng 〈古生物〉 iguanodon

【禽兽】 qínshòu birds and beasts: 衣冠～ a beast in human clothing/ ～行为 brutish acts; bestial acts

**勤** qín ① diligent; industrious; hardworking: ～学苦练 study diligently and train hard ② frequently; regularly: 衣服要～洗～换。Clothes should be changed and washed regularly./ 夏季雨水～。Rain is frequent in summer. ③ (office, school, etc.) attendance: 值～ be on duty/ 考～ check on work attendance

【勤奋】 qínfèn diligent; assiduous; industrious: 学习～ be diligent in one's studies

【勤工俭学】 qíngōng-jiǎnxué part-work and part-study system; work-study programme

【勤俭】 qínjiǎn hardworking and thrifty: ～建国 build up the country through thrift and hard work/ ～办社 run a people's commune industriously and thriftily/ ～持家 be industrious and thrifty in managing a household

【勤恳】 qínkěn diligent and conscientious: 勤勤恳恳地为人民服务 be diligent and conscientious in serving the people

【勤快】 qínkuai 〈口〉 diligent; hardworking: 她真～,一会儿也不闲着。She is diligent and keeps herself busy all the time.

【勤劳】 qínláo diligent; industrious; hardworking: ～勇敢的中国人民 the valiant and industrious Chinese people/ ～的双手 an untiring pair of hands

【勤勉】 qínmiǎn diligent; assiduous: ～好学 diligent and eager to learn

【勤务】 qínwù duty; service ◇ ～兵 orderly

【勤务员】 qínwùyuán ① odd-jobman (in an army unit or government office) ② servant: 我们一切工作干部,不论职位高低,都是人民的～。All our cadres, whatever their rank, are servants of the people.

【勤杂工】 qínzágōng odd-jobman; handyman

【勤杂人员】 qínzá rényuán personnel regularly doing certain odd jobs; odd-jobmen

**嗪** qín 见"哌嗪" pàiqín

**擒** qín capture; catch; seize: 生～ capture alive/ ～贼先～王。To catch bandits, first catch the ringleader.

【擒纵轮】 qínzònglún 〈机〉 escape wheel

**噙** qín hold in the mouth or the eyes: ～着烟袋 hold a pipe between one's lips/ ～着眼泪 eyes brimming with tears

**檎** qín 见"林檎" línqín

## qǐn

**锓** qǐn 〈书〉 carve; engrave

**寝** qǐn ① sleep: 废～忘食 (so absorbed or occupied as to) forget about eating and sleeping ② bedroom: 就～ go to bed ③ coffin chamber: 陵～ imperial burial place; mausoleum ④〈书〉 stop; end: 其事遂～。The matter was then allowed to rest. 或 No more was heard of the matter thereafter.

【寝具】 qǐnjù bedding

【寝食】 qǐn-shí sleeping and eating: ～不安 feel uneasy even when eating and sleeping; be worried waking or sleeping

【寝室】 qǐnshì bedroom; dormitory

## qìn

**沁** qìn ooze; seep; exude: 额上～出了汗珠。His forehead was oozing sweat.

【沁人心脾】 qìn rén xīn-pí gladdening the heart and refreshing the mind; mentally refreshing; refreshing

## qīng

**青** qīng ① blue or green: ～天 blue sky/ ～椒 green pepper ② black: ～布 black cloth ③ green grass; young crops: 踏～ walk on the green grass — go for an outing in early spring/ 看～ keep watch on the ripening crops ④ young (people): ～工 young workers ⑤ (Qīng) short for Qinghai Province

【青菜】 qīngcài ① green vegetables; greens ② Chinese cabbage

【青草】 qīngcǎo green grass

【青出于蓝】 qīng chūyú lán indigo blue is extracted from the indigo plant (but is bluer than the plant it comes from) — the pupil surpasses the master

【青春】 qīngchūn youth; youthfulness: 把～献给祖国 dedicate one's youth to one's country/ 充满着～的活力 be bursting with youthful vigour/ 焕发了革命～ regain one's revolutionary vigour ◇ ～期 puberty

【青瓷】 qīngcí celadon (ware)

【青葱】 qīngcōng verdant; fresh green: ～的竹林 a verdant grove of bamboo

【青翠】 qīngcuì verdant; fresh and green: 雨后，垂柳显得格外～。The weeping willows looked fresher and greener after the rain.
【青豆】 qīngdòu green soya bean
【青光眼】 qīngguāngyǎn 〈医〉 glaucoma
【青果】 qīngguǒ 〈方〉 Chinese olive
【青海】 Qīnghǎi Qinghai (Province)
【青花瓷】 qīnghuācí blue and white porcelain
【青黄不接】 qīng-huáng bù jiē when the new crop is still in the blade and the old one is all consumed — temporary shortage
【青筋】 qīngjīn blue veins: 他额角上暴起了～。Blue veins stood out on his temples.
【青稞】 qīngkē highland barley (grown in Xizang and Qinghai)
【青睐】 qīnglài 〈书〉 favour; good graces: 获得某人的～ find favour in sb.'s eyes; be in sb.'s good graces
【青莲色】 qīngliánsè pale purple; heliotrope
【青绿】 qīnglǜ dark green ◇ ～山水 traditional landscape painting characterized by the prominence of blue and green colours
【青梅】 qīngméi green plum
【青霉素】 qīngméisù 〈药〉 penicillin
【青面獠牙】 qīngmiàn-liáoyá green-faced and long-toothed — terrifying in appearance: 露出～的凶相 reveal the ferocious features of an ogre
【青苗】 qīngmiáo young crops; green shoots of (food) grains
【青年】 qīngnián youth; young people: ～时代 one's youth/ ～人 young people; youth/ ～学生 young students; student youth/ 毛泽东思想哺育下的一代 the younger generation nurtured by Mao Zedong Thought ◇ ～工作 youth work/ ～节 Youth Day (May 4)/ ～运动 youth movement
【青纱帐】 qīngshāzhàng the green curtain of tall crops: 游击队利用～作掩护。The guerrillas used the green curtain of tall crops as cover.
【青山】 qīngshān green hill: 留得～在，不愁没柴烧。As long as the green hills are there, one need not worry about firewood.
【青少年】 qīng-shàonián teen-agers; youngsters
【青史】 qīngshǐ annals of history: 永垂～ go down in the annals of history
【青丝】 qīngsī 〈书〉 black hair (of a woman or girl)
【青饲料】 qīngsìliào greenfeed; green fodder
【青松】 qīngsōng pine
【青苔】 qīngtái moss
【青檀】 qīngtán 〈植〉 wingceltis (*Pteroceltis tatarinowii*)
【青天】 qīngtiān ① blue sky ② 〈旧〉 a just judge; an upright magistrate
【青天霹雳】 qīngtiān pīlì 见"晴天霹雳" qíngtiān pīlì
【青铜】 qīngtóng bronze ◇ ～器 bronze ware/ ～时代 the Bronze Age
【青蛙】 qīngwā frog
【青虾】 qīngxiā freshwater shrimp
【青香薷】 qīngxiāngrú 〈中药〉 Chinese mosla (*Mosla chinensis*)
【青葙】 qīngxiāng 〈植〉 feather cockscomb (*Celosia argentea*) ◇ ～子 〈中药〉 the seed of feather cockscomb
【青眼】 qīngyǎn favour; good graces
【青杨】 qīngyáng Cathay poplar (*Populus cathayana*)
【青蝇】 qīngyíng greenbottle (fly)
【青鱼】 qīngyú black carp
【青云】 qīngyún high official position: ～直上 rapid advancement in one's career; meteoric rise
【青贮】 qīngzhù 〈农〉 ensiling ◇ ～饲料 ensilage; silage

**轻** qīng ① light: 油比水～。Oil is lighter than water./ ～武器 light arms; small arms ② small in number, degree, etc.: 年纪很～ be very young/ 他的病很～。His illness is not at all serious. ③ not important: 责任～ carry a light responsibility ④ gently; softly: ～拿～放。Handle gently./ 病人睡着了，～点儿！ Be quiet! The patient is asleep. ⑤ rashly: ～信 readily believe ⑥ belittle; make light of: 掉以～心 take sth. lightly/ 文人相～的恶习 the evil practice of scholars disparaging one another
【轻磅纸】 qīngbàngzhǐ lightweight paper
【轻便】 qīngbiàn light; portable: ～铁道 light railway/ ～桥 portable bridge/ ～镗床 portable boring machine
【轻薄】 qīngbó given to philandering; frivolous
【轻车熟路】 qīngchē-shúlù (drive in) a light carriage on a familiar road — (do) something one knows well and can manage with ease
【轻敌】 qīngdí take the enemy lightly; underestimate the enemy ◇ ～思想 tendency to take the enemy lightly
【轻而易举】 qīng ér yì jǔ easy to do: 这决不是～的事。It's certainly no easy job./ 不要以为～就可以把庄稼种好。Don't think you can do a good job in farming without making an effort.
【轻放】 qīngfàng put down gently: 易碎物品，小心～！ Fragile! Handle with care!
【轻风】 qīngfēng 〈气〉 light breeze
【轻浮】 qīngfú frivolous; flighty; light: 举止～ behave frivolously/ ～的行为 frivolous conduct
【轻歌曼舞】 qīnggē-mànwǔ sing merrily and dance gracefully
【轻工业】 qīnggōngyè light industry
【轻核】 qīnghé 〈物〉 light nucleus
【轻混凝土】 qīnghùnníngtǔ lightweight concrete
【轻活】 qīnghuó light work; soft job
【轻机枪】 qīngjīqiāng light machine gun
【轻贱】 qīngjiàn mean and worthless
【轻捷】 qīngjié spry and light; nimble: ～的脚步 brisk steps
【轻金属】 qīngjīnshǔ light metal
【轻举妄动】 qīngjǔ-wàngdòng act rashly; take reckless action: 不可～ make no move without careful thought
【轻快】 qīngkuài ① brisk; spry: 迈着～的步子 walk at a brisk pace ② lighthearted; lively: ～的曲调 lively tune
【轻狂】 qīngkuáng extremely frivolous
【轻量级】 qīngliàngjí 〈举重〉 lightweight
【轻慢】 qīngmàn treat sb. without proper respect; slight
【轻描淡写】 qīngmiáo-dànxiě touch on lightly; mention casually: 要认真检查自己的错误，不要～。You should criticize your own mistakes earnestly, and not just touch on them lightly.
【轻蔑】 qīngmiè scornful; disdainful; contemptuous: ～的眼光 a disdainful look
【轻诺寡信】 qīngnuò-guǎxìn make promises easily but seldom keep them
【轻泡货】 qīngpāohuò 〈交〉 light cargo
【轻炮兵】 qīngpàobīng light artillery
【轻飘飘】 qīngpiāopiāo light; buoyant: 垂柳～地摆动。The branches of the drooping willows were swaying lightly./ 她高兴地走着，脚底下～的。She tripped along joyfully as if treading on air.
【轻骑兵】 qīngqíbīng light cavalry
【轻巧】 qīngqiǎo ① light and handy: 一架～的录音机 a handy tape recorder/ 你说得倒～。You talk as if it were a simple matter. ② dexterous; deft: 他操纵机器动作非常～。He operates the machine dexterously.

【轻轻】 qīngqīng lightly; gently: 把孩子～地放在床上 put the baby on the bed gently/ ～地说 speak in a soft voice
【轻取】 qīngqǔ beat easily; win an easy victory; win hands down: ～第一局 win the first game easily (或 without effort)
【轻柔】 qīngróu soft; gentle: ～的枝条 pliable twigs/ ～的声音 a gentle voice
【轻纱】 qīngshā fine gauze
【轻伤】 qīngshāng slight (或 minor) wound; flesh wound: ～不下火线 not leave the frontline on account of minor wounds ◇ ～员 ambulant patient (或 case); walking wounded
【轻生】 qīngshēng make light of one's life — commit suicide
【轻声】 qīngshēng ① in a soft voice; softly: ～低语 speak softly; whisper ② 〈语〉 (in Chinese pronunciation) light tone, unstressed syllable pronounced without its original pitch
【轻视】 qīngshì despise; look down on; underestimate: ～反面教员的作用，就不是一个彻底的辩证唯物主义者。Whoever underestimates the role of teachers by negative example is not a thoroughgoing dialectical materialist.
【轻手轻脚】 qīngshǒu-qīngjiǎo gently; softly: 护士出来进去都～的，怕惊醒病人。The nurse moved around very softly so as not to wake the patient.
【轻率】 qīngshuài rash; hasty; indiscreet: ～的态度 reckless attitude/ ～从事 act rashly/ 这样处理太～了。It was indiscreet of you to handle it that way.
【轻松】 qīngsōng light; relaxed: ～的工作 light work; soft job; cushy job/ ～愉快 happy and relaxed/ ～地打败了对手 beat one's opponent with ease
【轻瘫】 qīngtān 〈医〉 paresis
【轻佻】 qīngtiāo frivolous; skittish; giddy: 举止～ skittish behaviour
【轻微】 qīngwēi light; slight; trifling; to a small extent: ～的伤亡 light casualties/ ～的头痛 a slight headache/ ～的损失 a trifling loss
【轻泻剂】 qīngxièjì 〈药〉 laxative
【轻信】 qīngxìn be credulous; readily place trust in; readily believe: 不要～谣言。Give no credence to rumours./ 重证据，不能～口供。Lay stress on evidence and do not readily believe confessions.
【轻型】 qīngxíng light-duty; light: ～机械 light-duty machinery/ ～载重汽车 light truck; light-duty truck/ ～飞机 light aircraft
【轻易】 qīngyì ① easily: 胜利成果不是～得来的。The fruits of victory were not easily won. ② lightly; rashly: 不要～地下结论。Don't draw hasty conclusions. 或 Don't jump to conclusions./ 他不～发表意见。He does not express an opinion rashly.
【轻音乐】 qīngyīnyuè light music
【轻盈】 qīngyíng slim and graceful; lithe; lissom: 她的自由体操动作～优美。 Her movements in free gymnastics are lithe and graceful./ 笑语～ talk and laugh merrily and lightheartedly.
【轻油】 qīngyóu light oil
【轻于鸿毛】 qīng yú hóngmáo lighter than a goose feather: 死有重于泰山，有～。One's death may be weightier than Taishan Mountain or lighter than a feather.
【轻重】 qīng-zhòng ① weight: 这两只箱子～不一样。The two boxes do not weigh the same. ② degree of seriousness; relative importance: 工作应分～缓急。 Work should be done in order of importance and urgency./ 此事无足～。It's a matter of no consequence./ 根据病情～决定病人是否住院。Whether a patient is to be hospitalized depends on how serious the case is. ③ propriety: 这个人说话不知～。That chap doesn't know the proper way to talk.
【轻重倒置】 qīng-zhòng dàozhì put the trivial above the important
【轻重量级】 qīngzhòngliàngjí 〈举重〉 light heavyweight
【轻装】 qīngzhuāng light; with light packs: ～就道 travel light/ ～前进 march with light packs
【轻装上阵】 qīngzhuāng shàngzhèn go into battle with a light pack — take part in a political movement with nothing on one's conscience
【轻罪】 qīngzuì 〈法〉 misdemeanour; minor offence; minor crime: ～重判不对，重罪轻判也不对。It is wrong to deal with a minor offence as if it were a major one and *vice versa*.

**氢** qīng 〈化〉 hydrogen (H)
【氢弹】 qīngdàn hydrogen bomb ◇ ～头 hydrogen warhead; H-warhead
【氢氟酸】 qīngfúsuān 〈化〉 hydrofluoric acid
【氢化】 qīnghuà 〈化〉 hydrogenation ◇ ～裂解 hydrocracking/ ～酶 hydrogenase/ ～物 hydride
【氢气】 qīngqì hydrogen ◇ ～球 hydrogen balloon
【氢氰酸】 qīngqíngsuān 〈化〉 hydrocyanic acid
【氢氧】 qīngyǎng 〈化〉 oxyhydrogen ◇ ～吹管 oxyhydrogen blowpipe/ ～焰 oxyhydrogen flame
【氢氧化物】 qīngyǎnghuàwù 〈化〉 hydroxide (e.g. 氢氧化铵 ammonium hydroxide)

**倾** qīng ① incline; lean; bend: 向左～ incline to the left/ 身子向前～ bend forward; lean forward ② deviation; tendency: 右～机会主义 Right opportunism/ "左"～盲动主义 "Left" putschism ③ collapse: 大厦将～ a great mansion on the point of collapse ④ overturn and pour out; empty: ～囊相助 empty one's purse to help; give generous financial support ⑤ do all one can; use up all one's resources: ～全力把工作做好 exert oneself to the utmost to do the work well
【倾巢】 qīngcháo (of the enemy or bandits) turn out in full force: 敌军～而出。The enemy turned out in full strength.
【倾城倾国】 qīngchéng-qīngguó (of a woman) lovely enough to cause the fall of a city or a state; exceedingly beautiful
【倾倒】 qīngdǎo ① topple and fall; topple over ② greatly admire: 为之～ be infatuated with sb.; be overwhelmed with admiration for sb.
【倾倒】 qīngdào tip; dump; empty; pour out: ～垃圾 dump rubbish/ 在忆苦会上～苦水 pour out one's grievances against the old social order at a meeting to recall past sufferings
【倾点】 qīngdiǎn 〈化〉 pour point; flow point
【倾覆】 qīngfù overturn; topple; capsize
【倾家荡产】 qīngjiā-dàngchǎn lose a family fortune
【倾角】 qīngjiǎo ① 〈物〉 dip ② 〈数〉 inclination ③ 〈地〉 dip angle ◇ ～测量仪 dipmeter
【倾慕】 qīngmù have a strong admiration for; adore
【倾盆大雨】 qīngpén dàyǔ heavy downpour; torrential rain; cloudburst: 赶上一场～ be caught in a downpour/ 下起了～。The rain was pelting down. 或 It was raining cats and dogs.
【倾诉】 qīngsù pour out (one's heart, troubles, etc.): ～衷肠 pour out one's heart; reveal one's innermost feelings
【倾谈】 qīngtán have a good, heart-to-heart talk
【倾听】 qīngtīng listen attentively to; lend an attentive ear to: ～群众的意见 listen attentively to the views of the masses
【倾吐】 qīngtǔ say what is on one's mind without reservation: ～衷情 unbosom oneself/ ～苦水 unburden oneself

of one's grievances

【倾箱倒箧】 qīngxiāng-dǎoqiè turn out all one's boxes and suitcases

【倾向】 qīngxiàng ① tendency; trend; inclination; deviation: 政治～ political inclination/ 要注意一种～掩盖另一种～。One must be alive to the possibility that one tendency may conceal another./ 反对右的和"左"的两种～ oppose Right and "Left" deviations ② be inclined to; prefer: 这两种方案我～于第一种。Of the two plans, I prefer the first.

【倾向性】 qīngxiàngxìng tendentiousness: 他的发言是有～的。His statement was frankly tendentious.

【倾销】 qīngxiāo dump: ～货物 dump goods

【倾斜】 qīngxié tilt; incline; slope; slant: 我国地势大致从西北向东南～。Generally speaking, the terrain of China slopes from northwest to southeast./ 地面微微向南～。The land inclines gently to the south./ 这墙有点～。The wall is a little out of the perpendicular.
◇ ～度 gradient/ ～角 angle of inclination; 〈航空〉 bank angle/ ～面 inclined plane

【倾泻】 qīngxiè come down in torrents: 山水～而下，汇成洪流。Streams rushed down the mountain and converged into a torrent.

【倾卸汽车】 qīngxiè qìchē dump truck; tipper

【倾心】 qīngxīn ① admire; fall in love with: 一见～ fall in love at first sight ② cordial; heart-to-heart: ～交谈 have a heart-to-heart talk

【倾轧】 qīngyà engage in internal strife; jostle against each other: 资产阶级政党内部，各派互相～。Different factions within bourgeois political parties are always trying to do each other down.

【倾注】 qīngzhù ① pour into: 几股山泉～到深潭里。Several mountain streams pour into the pool. ② throw (energy, etc.) into: 把全部心血～到工作中去 throw all one's energy into one's work

# 卿

qīng ① a minister or a high official in ancient times ② an emperor's form of address for a minister ③ a term of endearment formerly used between husband and wife or among close friends

# 清

qīng ① unmixed; clear: ～汤 clear soup/ ～水 clear water ② distinct; clarified: 分～ make a clear distinction/ 说不～ hard to explain/ 数不～ countless/ 问～底细 make sure of every detail; get to the bottom of the matter ③ quiet: ～静 quiet ④ completely; thoroughly: 把帐还～ pay up what one owes ⑤ settle; clear up; clean up: 帐～了吗? Has the account been settled (或 cleared up)?/ ～政治，～思想，～组织，～经济 clean things up in the fields of politics, ideology, organization and economy ⑥ count: ～一～行李的件数 count the pieces of luggage and see how many there are ⑦ (Qīng) the Qing Dynasty (1644-1911)

【清白】 qīngbái pure; clean; stainless: 历史～ have a clean personal record/ ～无辜 innocent

【清仓查库】 qīngcāng-chákù make an inventory (或 check-up) of warehouses

【清册】 qīngcè detailed list: 固定资产～ an inventory of fixed assets

【清茶】 qīngchá ① green tea ② tea served without refreshments

【清查】 qīngchá ① check: ～户口 check on residents; check residence cards ② uncover; comb out: ～反革命 ferret out counterrevolutionaries

【清偿】 qīngcháng pay off; clear off: ～债务 pay off (或 clear off) debts

【清唱】 qīngchàng sing opera arias (without makeup and acting) ◇ ～剧 〈乐〉 oratorio

【清澈】 qīngchè limpid; clear: ～的池塘 a limpid pool/ 湖水～见底。The lake water is so clear that you can see to the bottom.

【清晨】 qīngchén early morning

【清除】 qīngchú clear away; eliminate; get rid of: ～垃圾 clear away the rubbish/ ～障碍 remove obstacles/ 把叛徒～出党 clear the renegades out of the Party

【清楚】 qīngchu ① clear; distinct: 字迹～ written in a clear hand/ 发音～ a clear pronunciation/ 头脑～ a clear head/ 他的话说得不～。He didn't speak clearly. 或 What he said was ambiguous./ 把工作交代～ explain one's job clearly on handing it over/ 大是大非问题要彻底弄～。Major issues of principle must be thoroughly thrashed out. ② be clear about; understand: 这个问题你～不～? Do you understand this question or not?

【清创术】 qīngchuāngshù 〈医〉 *débridement*

【清脆】 qīngcuì clear and melodious: ～的歌声 clear and melodious singing

【清单】 qīngdān detailed list; detailed account: 货物～ a detailed list of goods; inventory

【清淡】 qīngdàn ① light; weak; delicate: ～的绿茶 weak green tea/ ～的花香 the delicate fragrance of flowers ② not greasy or strongly flavoured; light: ～的食物 light food ③ dull; slack: 生意～。Business is slack.

【清道夫】 qīngdàofū 〈旧〉 scavenger; street cleaner; street sweeper

【清点】 qīngdiǎn check; make an inventory; sort and count: ～物资 make an inventory of equipment and materials/ ～货物 take stock/ ～战利品 check and sort out spoils of war

【清队】 qīngduì 〈简〉(清理阶级队伍) purify the class ranks

【清炖】 qīngdùn boiled in clear soup (without soy sauce): ～鸡 stewed chicken without soy sauce

【清风】 qīngfēng cool breeze; refreshing breeze: ～徐来。A cool breeze blows gently.

【清高】 qīnggāo aloof from politics and material pursuits: 自鸣～ profess to be above politics and worldly considerations

【清稿】 qīnggǎo fair copy; clean copy

【清官】 qīngguān 〈旧〉 honest and upright official: ～难断家务事。Even an upright official finds it hard to settle a family quarrel.

【清规】 qīngguī 〈佛教〉 monastic rules for Buddhists

【清规戒律】 qīngguī jièlǜ ① regulations, taboos and commandments for Buddhists or Taoists ② restrictions and fetters: 过多的评头品足，数不尽的～ endless carping and countless taboos

【清寒】 qīnghán ① poor; in straitened circumstances: 家境～ come of an impoverished (或 poor) family ② cold and clear: 月色～ clear, cold moonlight

【清剿】 qīngjiǎo clean up; suppress; eliminate: ～土匪 clean up bandits; suppress bandits

【清教徒】 Qīngjiàotú Puritan

【清洁】 qīngjié clean: 整齐～ clean and tidy/ 人人要注意～卫生。Everybody should pay attention to sanitation and hygiene. ◇ ～队 cleaning squad/ ～工人 sanitation worker; street cleaner

【清洁提单】 qīngjié tídān clean bill of lading

【清劲风】 qīngjìngfēng 〈气〉 fresh breeze

【清净】 qīngjìng peace and quiet: 怕麻烦，图～ fear trouble and seek peace and quiet

【清静】 qīngjìng quiet: 咱们找个～的地方谈谈。Let's find a quiet place to chat.

【清君侧】 qīng jūncè rid the emperor of "evil" ministers (as part of a plot to stage a *coup d'état* or an armed rebellion)
【清蜡】 qīnglà 〈石油〉 paraffin removal
【清朗】 qīnglǎng ① cool and bright: ～的天气 clear and bright weather ② clear and resounding
【清冷】 qīnglěng ① chilly: 一个～的秋夜 a chilly autumn night ② deserted; desolate: 夜已深了，街上十分～。It was late at night and the streets were quite deserted.
【清理】 qīnglǐ put in order; check up; clear; sort out: 把房间～～ put the room in order; clean up the room/ ～物资 check up on equipment and materials/ ～债务 clear up debts/ ～仓库 take stock; make an inventory of warehouse stocks/ ～档案 put the archives in order; sort out documents/ ～阶级队伍 purify the class ranks
【清廉】 qīnglián honest and upright; free from corruption
【清凉】 qīngliáng cool and refreshing: ～饮料 cold drink; cooler/ 你的批评对我是一服很好的～剂。Your criticism had a sobering effect on me. ◇ ～油 cooling ointment; essential balm
【清亮】 qīngliang 〈口〉 crystal; clear; limpid
【清冽】 qīngliè 〈书〉 cool; chilly
【清棉】 qīngmián 〈纺〉 scutching ◇ ～机 scutcher/ ～间 blowing room
【清明】 qīngmíng ① (Qīngmíng) Pure Brightness (5th solar term) ② clear and bright: 月色～ clear and bright moonlight ③ sober and calm: 神志～ be in full possession of one's faculties
【清喷漆】 qīngpēnqī 〈化〉 clear lacquer
【清贫】 qīngpín (usu. of scholars in old days) be poor: 家境～ be a person of scanty means
【清漆】 qīngqī varnish: 透明～ clear varnish/ 皱纹～ shrivel varnish
【清热法】 qīngrèfǎ 〈中医〉 antipyretic method (using medicines of a cold nature to treat acute febrile diseases)
【清热药】 qīngrèyào antipyretic
【清瘦】 qīngshòu 〈婉〉 thin; lean; spare: 你病后略见～。You look rather thin after your illness.
【清爽】 qīngshuǎng ① fresh and cool: 晚风吹来，十分～。The evening breeze is cooling and refreshing. ② relieved; relaxed: 事情解决了，我心里也～了。Now that the matter is settled, I feel relieved.
【清水墙】 qīngshuǐqiáng 〈建〉 dry wall
【清算】 qīngsuàn ① clear (accounts); square ② settle accounts; expose and criticize: ～反党集团的滔天罪行 expose and criticize the towering crimes of the anti-Party clique ◇ ～协定 clearing agreement/ ～银行 clearing bank/ ～帐户 clearing account
【清谈】 qīngtán idle talk; empty talk: ～不能解决问题。Idle talk solves no problems.
【清汤】 qīngtāng clear soup; light soup
【清晰】 qīngxī distinct; clear: 她发音～。Her pronunciation is clear./ 远山的轮廓～可见。The outlines of the distant hills are clearly discernible. ◇ ～度 (电视) clarity; (传声) articulation
【清洗】 qīngxǐ ① rinse; wash; clean: ～炊具 clean cooking utensils ② purge; comb out: 把阶级异己分子～出去 comb out the alien class elements
【清闲】 qīngxián at leisure; idle: 他过不惯～的退休生活。He finds it difficult to get used to the idle life of retirement.
【清香】 qīngxiāng delicate fragrance; faint scent: 晨风吹来野花的～。The morning breeze carried with it the scent of wild flowers.
【清新】 qīngxīn pure and fresh; fresh: 雨后空气～。The air was pure and fresh after the rain./ 画报的版面～活泼。The layout of the pictorial is fresh and lively.
【清醒】 qīngxǐng ① clear-headed; sober: 保持～的头脑 keep a clear (或 cool) head; keep sober-minded/ 我们对形势要有～的估计。We should make a sober estimate of the situation./ 阶级斗争的现实使他～过来。The realities of class struggle have sobered him up. ② regain consciousness: 病人已经～过来。The patient has come to.
【清秀】 qīngxiù delicate and pretty: 面貌～ of fine, delicate features/ 山水～ beautiful landscape
【清选机】 qīngxuǎnjī 〈农〉 cleaner
【清雅】 qīngyǎ elegant; refined: 风格～ in an elegant style
【清样】 qīngyàng final proof; foundry proof
【清夜扪心】 qīngyè mén xīn examine one's conscience in the stillness of night
【清一色】 qīngyīsè ① all of one suit (in playing mahjong); flush ② all of the same colour; uniform; homogeneous: 运动员～地穿着红色运动服。The players were all dressed alike in red sports suits./ 宗派主义者爱搞所谓～。Sectarians are fond of so-called homogeneous bodies.
【清音】 qīngyīn ① a type of ballad-singing popular in Sichuan Province ② 〈语〉 voiceless sound
【清幽】 qīngyōu (of a landscape) quiet and beautiful
【清油】 qīngyóu 〈方〉 edible vegetable oil
【清早】 qīngzǎo 〈口〉 early in the morning; early morning
【清帐】 qīngzhàng square (或 clear) an account
【清真】 qīngzhēn Islamic; Muslim
◇ ～教 Islam; Islamism/ ～食堂 Muslims' canteen/ ～寺 mosque
【清蒸】 qīngzhēng steamed in clear soup (usu. without soy sauce): ～鱼 steamed fish

**蜻** qīng
【蜻蜓】 qīngtíng dragonfly
【蜻蜓点水】 qīngtíng diǎn shuǐ like a dragonfly skimming the surface of the water —touch on sth. without going into it deeply: 做调查工作不能～，要深入实际。To make an investigation, one should go into matters deeply, not just scratch the surface.

**鲭** qīng mackerel

## qíng

**情** qíng ① feeling; affection; sentiment: 热～ enthusiasm/ 温～ tender sentiments/ 阶级～，似海深。Class love is as deep as the ocean. ② love; passion: 谈～说爱 be courting; talk love/ ～欲 sexual passion ③ favour; kindness: 求～ ask for a favour; plead with sb. ④ situation; circumstances; condition: 军～ military situation/ 病～ patient's condition
【情报】 qíngbào intelligence; information: 科技～ scientific and technological information/ 搜集～ collect intelligence/ 刺探～ pry for information
◇ ～机关 intelligence agency/ ～人员 intelligence personnel; intelligence agent/ ～系统 intelligence channel
【情不自禁】 qíng bù zì jīn cannot refrain from; cannot help (doing sth.); be seized with a sudden impulse to: ～地流下泪来 cannot refrain from tears/ ～地笑起来 can't help laughing
【情操】 qíngcāo sentiment: 培养共产主义的～ foster communist values
【情敌】 qíngdí rival in love
【情调】 qíngdiào sentiment; emotional appeal: 不健康的小

资产阶级～ unhealthy sentimentalism of the petty bourgeoisie
【情窦初开】 qíngdòu chū kāi (of a young girl) first awakening (或 dawning) of love
【情分】 qíngfen mutual affection: 朋友～ friendship/ 兄弟～ fraternity; brotherhood
【情夫】 qíngfū lover
【情妇】 qíngfù mistress
【情感】 qínggǎn emotion; feeling
【情歌】 qínggē love song
【情话】 qínghuà lovers' prattle
【情怀】 qínghuái feelings: 抒发无产阶级的革命～ express the revolutionary thoughts and feelings of the proletariat
【情急智生】 qíngjí zhì shēng hit on a good idea in a moment of desperation
【情节】 qíngjié ① plot: 这个剧本～很复杂。The play has a very complicated plot./ ～紧凑 a tightknit plot ② circumstances: 根据～轻重,分别给予处理。Each will be dealt with according to the seriousness of his case.
【情景】 qíngjǐng scene; sight; circumstances: 兴奋热烈的～ an exhilarating scene/ 感人的～ a moving sight
【情境】 qíngjìng circumstances; situation
【情况】 qíngkuàng ① circumstances; situation; condition; state of affairs: 在这种～下 under these circumstances; such being the case/ 根据具体～ in accordance with specific conditions/ 在许多～下 in many cases/ 这种～必须改变。This state of affairs must change./ 现在～不同了。Now things are different./ 他们的～怎么样？How do matters stand with them?/ 那得看～而定。That depends. 或 It all depends. ② military situation: 前线有什么～？How is the situation at the front?/ 前面有～,做好战斗准备。There's enemy activity ahead. Prepare for combat.
【情理】 qínglǐ reason; sense: 合乎～ be reasonable; stand to reason/ 不近～ unreasonable; irrational/ ～难容 incompatible with the accepted code of human conduct
【情侣】 qínglǚ sweethearts; lovers
【情面】 qíngmian feelings; sensibilities: 留～ spare sb.'s feelings/ 不顾～ have no consideration for sb.'s feelings/ 对以前的错误一定要揭发，不讲～。The mistakes of the past must be exposed without sparing anyone's sensibilities.
【情趣】 qíngqù ① temperament and interest: 他们二人～相投。The two of them are temperamentally compatible (或 congenial). ② interest; appeal: 这首诗写得很有～。This poem is very charming.
【情人】 qíngrén sweetheart: ～眼里出西施。In the eye of the lover, his beloved is a beauty. 或 Beauty is in the eye of the beholder.
【情势】 qíngshì situation; circumstances; trend of events: ～危急。The situation is critical./ 对～作出估计 size up the situation ◇ ～不变 〈外〉 *rebus sic stantibus*
【情书】 qíngshū love letter
【情随事迁】 qíng suí shì qiān people's feelings change with the circumstances
【情态】 qíngtài spirit; mood: 生动地描绘了儿童的～ depict children's spirit vividly ◇ ～动词〈语〉 modal verb
【情同手足】 qíng tóng shǒuzú like brothers; with brotherly love for each other: 两国人民～。Our two peoples are bound together by ties of fraternal friendship.
【情投意合】 qíngtóu-yìhé find each other congenial; hit it off perfectly
【情形】 qíngxing circumstances; situation; condition; state of affairs: 两地～大不相同。Conditions in the two places differ greatly./ 大家看了这种～,非常气愤。People felt indignant at this state of affairs./ 这是一方面的～。This is one side of the picture.
【情绪】 qíngxù ① morale; feeling; mood; sentiments: ～高涨。Morale is high./ 防止急躁～ guard against rashness/ ～不高 be in low spirits/ 反帝～高涨。Anti-imperialist feeling ran high./ 全团战斗～高昂。The whole regiment is in fine fighting fettle. ② depression; moodiness; the sulks: 有点儿～ rather sulky/ 闹～ be in a fit of depression; be in low spirits; have a fit of the sulks
【情义】 qíngyì ties of friendship, comradeship, etc.: 阶级～重于泰山。Class love is weightier than Taishan Mountain.
【情谊】 qíngyì friendly feelings; friendly sentiments: 战斗～ militant bonds of friendship/ 兄弟～ brotherly affection
【情意】 qíngyì tender regards; affection; goodwill: 深厚的～ deep affection
【情由】 qíngyóu the hows and whys: 不问～ without asking about the circumstances or causes
【情有可原】 qíng yǒu kě yuán excusable; pardonable
【情欲】 qíngyù sexual passion; lust
【情愿】 qíngyuàn ① be willing to: 两相～ by mutual consent; both parties being willing ② would rather; prefer: 她～粉身碎骨,也不在敌人面前屈服。She would rather be cut to pieces than yield to the enemy.

**晴** qíng fine; clear: 天转～了。It's clearing up.
【晴和】 qínghé warm and fine: 天气～。It's a fine, warm day.
【晴空】 qíngkōng clear sky; cloudless sky: ～万里 a clear and boundless sky
【晴朗】 qínglǎng fine; sunny: 天气～。It's a sunny day.
【晴天】 qíngtiān fine day; sunny day
【晴天霹雳】 qíngtiān pīlì a bolt from the blue
【晴雨表】 qíngyǔbiǎo weatherglass; barometer: 阶级斗争的～ the barometer of class struggle

**氰** qíng 〈化〉 cyanogen; dicyanogen
【氰钴胺】 qínggǔ'àn 〈药〉 cyanocobalamin; vitamin $B_{12}$
【氰化】 qínghuà cyaniding ◇ ～法 cyanidation/ ～物 cyanide
【氰酸】 qíngsuān cyanic acid

**擎** qíng prop up; hold up; lift up: 众～易举。When there are many people it's easy to lift a load. 或 Many hands make light work.

## qǐng

**苘** qǐng
【苘麻】 qǐngmá 〈植〉 piemarker

**顷** qǐng ① *qing*, a unit of area (＝6.6667 hectares): 碧波万～ a boundless expanse of blue water ② 〈书〉 just; just now: ～接来信。I have just received your letter. ③ 〈书〉 a little while: 少～ after a while
【顷刻】 qǐngkè in a moment; in an instant; instantly: ～之间 in a twinkling; in no time/ ～瓦解 collapse instantly

**请** qǐng ① request; ask: ～他进来。Ask him in./ ～你多加指导。It is hoped you will give us guidance./ ～人来修机器 get someone to repair the machine; get the machine repaired ② invite; engage: ～医生 send for a doctor/ ～总工程师来讲课 invite the chief engineer to give a lecture ③ 〈敬〉 please: ～坐。Won't you sit down? 或 Please be seated./ ～安静。Be quiet, please./ ～速回信。Please reply as soon as possible.

【请安】 qǐng'ān pay respects to sb.; wish sb. good health
【请便】 qǐngbiàn do as you wish; please yourself: 你要是想现在去，那就～吧。Well, if you want to leave now, go ahead.
【请功】 qǐnggōng ask the higher level to record sb.'s meritorious deeds
【请假】 qǐngjià ask for leave: 请三天假 ask for three days' leave/ 她请病假回家了。She's gone home on sick leave. ◇ ～条 written request for leave (of absence)
【请柬】 qǐngjiǎn 〈书〉 invitation card
【请见】 qǐngjiàn 〈书〉 request an audience; ask for an interview
【请教】 qǐngjiào ask for advice; consult: 我们想～你几个问题。We wish to consult you on a few questions./ 向老工人～ consult a veteran worker/ 虚心向群众～ learn modestly from the masses
【请君入瓮】 qǐng jūn rù wèng kindly step into the vat — try what you have devised against others
【请客】 qǐngkè stand treat; invite sb. to dinner; entertain guests; give a dinner party
【请命】 qǐngmìng plead on sb.'s behalf
【请求】 qǐngqiú ask; request: ～宽恕 ask for forgiveness
【请示】 qǐngshì ask for (或 request) instructions: 向中央～ ask the Central Committee for instructions/ 事前～，事后报告 ask for instructions beforehand and submit reports afterwards
【请帖】 qǐngtiě invitation card; invitation: 发～ send out invitations
【请问】 qǐngwèn ①〈敬〉〔用于请对方回答问题〕: excuse me; please: ～，到火车站怎么走？Excuse me, but could you tell me how to get to the station? ② we should like to ask; it may be asked; one may ask: ～，要是不学大寨，咱们队能有今天吗？I'd like to ask, could our production brigade be what it is today without learning from Dazhai?
【请勿】 qǐngwù please don't: 本室书籍～携出室外。Please don't take the books out of this room./ ～吸烟。No smoking./ ～入内。No admittance./ ～践踏草地。Keep off the lawn.
【请降】 qǐngxiáng beg to surrender
【请缨】 qǐngyīng 〈书〉 request a cord from the emperor (to bind the enemy) — submit a request for a military assignment: ～杀敌 request to be sent to the front; volunteer for battle
【请愿】 qǐngyuàn present a petition; petition ◇ ～书 petition
【请战】 qǐngzhàn ask for a battle assignment ◇ ～书 written request for a battle assignment
【请罪】 qǐngzuì admit one's error and ask for punishment; apologize

## qìng

**庆** qìng ① celebrate; congratulate: ～丰收 celebrate a bumper harvest ② occasion for celebration: 国～ National Day ③ (Qìng) a surname
【庆大霉素】 qìngdàméisù 〈药〉 gentamicin
【庆典】 qìngdiǎn celebration; a ceremony to celebrate: 盛大～ grand celebrations
【庆父不死，鲁难未已】 Qìngfǔ bù sǐ, Lǔ nàn wèi yǐ until Qing Fu is done away with, the crisis in the state of Lu will not be over — there will always be trouble until he who stirs it up is removed
【庆功会】 qìnggōnghuì victory meeting
【庆贺】 qìnghè congratulate; celebrate
【庆幸】 qìngxìng rejoice: 值得～的事 a matter for rejoicing/ 可～的是，村子里人畜都安全转移了。Happily, both the villagers and their livestock have been safely evacuated.
【庆祝】 qìngzhù celebrate: ～国庆 celebrate National Day ◇ ～大会 celebration meeting

**亲** qìng
另见 qīn
【亲家】 qìngjia ① parents of one's daughter-in-law or son-in-law ② relatives by marriage

**磬** qìng ① chime stone ② inverted bell (a Buddhist percussion instrument)

**罄** qìng 〈书〉 use up; exhaust: 告～ be all used up; run out/ ～其所有 empty one's purse; offer all one has
【罄尽】 qìngjìn 〈书〉 with nothing left; all used up
【罄竹难书】 qìng zhú nán shū (of crimes, etc.) too numerous to record: 这个恶霸罪行累累，～。This local despot's crimes were too numerous to mention.

## qióng

**穷** qióng ① poor; poverty-stricken: ～山沟变成了米粮川。The once poor mountain village has become a granary. ② limit; end: 无～无尽 endless; inexhaustible/ 技～ exhaust one's whole bag of tricks; come to the end of one's rope ③ thoroughly: ～究 make a thorough (或 exhaustive) inquiry ④ extremely: ～奢极侈 extremely extravagant and luxurious
【穷棒子】 qióngbàngzi pauper
【穷棒子精神】 qióngbàngzi jīngshén the spirit of the paupers — the spirit of self-reliance, hard struggle and adherence to the socialist road under difficult conditions
【穷兵黩武】 qióngbīng-dúwǔ use all one's armed might to indulge in wars of aggression; wantonly engage in military aggression
【穷光蛋】 qióngguāngdàn 〈口〉 pauper; poor wretch
【穷极无聊】 qióngjí wúliáo ① be utterly bored ② absolutely senseless; disgusting
【穷尽】 qióngjìn limit; end: 群众的智慧是没有～的。The wisdom of the masses knows no bounds.
【穷寇】 qióngkòu hard-pressed enemy; tottering foe: 宜将剩勇追～。With power and to spare we must pursue the tottering foe.
【穷苦】 qióngkǔ poverty-stricken; impoverished
【穷困】 qióngkùn poverty-stricken; destitute; in straitened circumstances: 残酷的封建剥削使农民陷入～境地。The ruthless exploitation of feudalism reduced the peasantry to destitution.
【穷年累月】 qióngnián-lěiyuè for years on end; year after year
【穷期】 qióngqī termination; end: 战斗正未有～。The struggle will go on and on.
【穷人】 qióngrén poor people; the poor
【穷日子】 qióngrìzi days of poverty; straitened circumstances: 我们要把富日子当～过。We're well off now, but we should still live as if we were poor.
【穷山恶水】 qióngshān-èshuǐ barren mountains and unruly rivers
【穷奢极欲】 qióngshē-jíyù (indulge in) luxury and extravagance; (live a life of) wanton extravagance: 过着～的生活 wallow in luxury
【穷酸】 qióngsuān (of a scholar) poor and pedantic

【穷途末路】 qióngtú-mòlù *cul-de-sac*; dead end
【穷乡僻壤】 qióngxiāng-pìrǎng a remote, backward place
【穷凶极恶】 qióngxiōng-jí'è extremely vicious; utterly evil; atrocious; diabolical: ～的敌人 most vicious enemy/ 一副～的样子 with the look of a fiendish brute
【穷原竟委】 qióngyuán-jìngwěi get to the bottom of the matter; make a thorough inquiry into sth.
【穷则思变】 qióng zé sī biàn poverty gives rise to a desire for change
【穷追】 qióngzhuī go in hot pursuit: ～猛打 vigorously pursue and fiercely maul

**穹** qióng 〈书〉 ① vault; dome ② the sky
【穹苍】 qióngcāng 〈书〉 the vault of heaven; the firmament; the sky; the heavens
【穹顶】 qióngdǐng 〈建〉 dome
【穹隆】 qiónglóng 〈书〉 vault; arched roof ◇ ～构造 〈地〉 dome structure
【穹形】 qióngxíng vaulted; arched: ～的屋顶 a vaulted roof

**茕** qióng 〈书〉 ① solitary; alone ② dejected
【茕茕】 qióngqióng 〈书〉 all alone; lonely: ～孑立,形影相吊 standing all alone, body and shadow comforting each other

**琼** qióng 〈书〉 fine jade: ～楼玉宇 a richly decorated jade palace; a magnificent building/ ～阁 a jewelled palace
【琼脂】 qióngzhī agar-agar; agar ◇ ～培养基 agar medium/ ～酸 agaric acid/ ～糖 agarose

## qiū

**丘** qiū ① mound; hillock: 荒～ a barren hillock/ 沙～ a sand dune ② grave: 坟～ grave ③ (Qiū) a surname
【丘八】 qiūbā 〈旧〉 (a jocular term for) soldier
【丘陵】 qiūlíng hills: ～起伏 a chain of undulating hills ◇ ～地带 hilly country; hilly land
【丘鹬】 qiūyù 〈动〉 woodcock
【丘疹】 qiūzhěn 〈医〉 papule

**邱** Qiū a surname

**秋** qiū ① autumn: 深～ late autumn/ ～风 autumn wind ② harvest time: 麦～ time for the wheat harvest ③ year: 千～万代 for thousands of years / 一日不见,如隔三～。One day apart seems like three years — miss sb. very much. ④〔多指不好的〕a period of time: 多事之～ an eventful period; troubled times ⑤ (Qiū) a surname
【秋波】 qiūbō bright eyes of a beautiful woman: 送～ (of a woman) make eyes; ogle; cast amorous glances
【秋播】 qiūbō 〈农〉 autumn sowing
【秋分】 Qiūfēn the Autumnal Equinox (16th solar term)
【秋耕】 qiūgēng 〈农〉 autumn ploughing
【秋海棠】 qiūhǎitáng 〈植〉 begonia
【秋毫】 qiūháo autumn hair; newly-grown down; sth. so small as to be almost indiscernible
【秋毫无犯】 qiūháo wú fàn (of highly disciplined troops) not commit the slightest offence against the civilians; not encroach on the interests of the people to the slightest degree
【秋后】 qiūhòu after autumn; after the autumn harvest: 敌人象～的蚂蚱,蹦跶不了几天啦。 Like a grasshopper at the end of autumn, the enemy is on his last legs.
【秋后算帐】 qiūhòu suànzhàng square accounts after the autumn harvest — wait until after a political movement is over to settle accounts with the leadership or the masses ◇ ～派 people who bide their time to take revenge
【秋季】 qiūjì autumn ◇ ～作物 autumn crops
【秋老虎】 qiūlǎohǔ a spell of hot weather after the Beginning of Autumn (立秋)
【秋凉】 qiūliáng cool autumn days
【秋令】 qiūlìng ① autumn ② autumn weather
【秋千】 qiūqiān swing: 打～ have a swing
【秋色】 qiūsè autumn scenery: ～宜人 charming autumn scenery
【秋收】 qiūshōu autumn harvest
【秋收起义】 Qiūshōu Qǐyì the Autumn Harvest Uprising (an armed uprising led by Comrade Mao Zedong in 1927 in the Hunan-Jiangxi border region, which marked the Party's independent building of a revolutionary army)
【秋水】 qiūshuǐ autumn waters — limpid eyes (of a woman): 望穿～ gaze anxiously till one's eyes are worn out; eagerly look forward (to seeing a dear one)
【秋水仙】 qiūshuǐxiān 〈植〉 meadow saffron; autumn crocus ◇ ～素 〈药〉 colchicine
【秋天】 qiūtiān autumn
【秋征】 qiūzhēng collection of agricultural tax in kind after the autumn harvest
【秋庄稼】 qiūzhuāngjia autumn crops

**蚯** qiū
【蚯蚓】 qiūyǐn earthworm

**湫** qiū pond; pool
另见 jiǎo

**楸** qiū 〈植〉 Chinese catalpa

**鳅** qiū 见"泥鳅" níqiū;"鲯鳅" qíqiū

## qiú

**仇** Qiú a surname
另见 chóu

**囚** qiú ① imprison: 被～ be thrown into prison ② prisoner; convict: 死～ a convict sentenced to death
【囚车】 qiúchē prison van; prisoners' van
【囚犯】 qiúfàn prisoner; convict
【囚禁】 qiújìn imprison; put in jail; keep in captivity
【囚牢】 qiúláo prison; jail
【囚笼】 qiúlóng prisoner's cage
【囚室】 qiúshì prison cell
【囚首垢面】 qiúshǒu-gòumiàn with unkempt hair and dirty face
【囚徒】 qiútú convict; prisoner

**犰** qiú
【犰狳】 qiúyú 〈动〉 armadillo

**求** qiú ① beg; request; entreat; beseech: ～你帮忙,行吗? May I ask you a favour?/ 有～于人 have to look to others for help ② strive for; seek; try: ～进步 strive for further progress/ ～得一致 try to achieve a consensus ③ demand: 供不应～。Supply falls short of demand.
【求爱】 qiú'ài pay court to; woo
【求成】 qiúchéng hope for success: 急于～ be impatient

for success; hope to achieve quick results
【求告】 qiúgào implore; entreat; supplicate
【求根】 qiúgēn 〈数〉 extract a root
【求和】 qiúhé sue for peace
【求婚】 qiúhūn make an offer of marriage; propose
【求积仪】 qiújīyí 〈数〉 planimeter
【求见】 qiújiàn ask to see; request an interview; beg for an audience
【求教】 qiújiào ask for advice: 登门～ call on sb. for counsel; come to seek advice
【求救】 qiújiù ask sb. to come to the rescue; cry for help: 发出～的信号 signal an SOS; send an SOS
【求乞】 qiúqǐ beg: 沿门～ go begging from door to door
【求亲】 qiúqīn seek a marriage alliance
【求情】 qiúqíng plead; intercede; ask for a favour; beg for leniency: 向他～ plead with him/ 为某人～ intercede for sb.; beg (for mercy) on sb.'s behalf
【求全】 qiúquán ① demand perfection: 不要～责备。We shouldn't demand perfection. 或 Don't nitpick. ② try to round sth. off: 委曲～ make concessions to achieve one's purpose
【求饶】 qiúráo beg for mercy; ask for pardon
【求人】 qiúrén ask for help
【求胜】 qiúshèng strive for victory: ～心切 be anxious to gain victory
【求实精神】 qiúshí jīngshén matter-of-fact attitude; realistic approach: 把革命热情和～结合起来 combine revolutionary fervour with a realistic spirit
【求同存异】 qiú tóng cún yì seek common ground while reserving differences: 求大同存小异 seek common ground on major issues while reserving differences on minor ones
【求降】 qiúxiáng beg to surrender; hang out (或 hoist) the white flag
【求学】 qiúxué ① go to school; attend school ② pursue one's studies; seek knowledge
【求援】 qiúyuán ask for help; request reinforcements
【求战】 qiúzhàn seek battle: 战士们～心切。The men are itching to fight.
【求之不得】 qiú zhī bù dé all that one could wish for; most welcome: 这对他真是～的事情。This is just what he wants./ 这是～的好机会。This is a most welcome opportunity./ 给王师傅当徒弟，他真是～。He was only too glad to be an apprentice to Master Worker Wang.
【求知】 qiúzhī seek knowledge ◇ ～欲 thirst (或 craving) for knowledge
【求值】 qiúzhí 〈数〉 evaluation
【求助】 qiúzhù turn to sb. for help; seek help: 他理屈词穷，只好～于诡辩。As he had a weak case and could not defend himself, he had to resort to sophistry.

**泅** qiú swim
【泅渡】 qiúdù swim across: 武装～ swim across with one's weapons; swim across fully armed
【泅水】 qiúshuǐ swim

**酋** qiú ① chief of a tribe ② chieftain: 敌～ enemy chieftain/ 匪～ bandit chief
【酋长】 qiúzhǎng ① chief of a tribe ② sheik(h); emir
【酋长国】 qiúzhǎngguó sheikhdom; emirate

**球** qiú ① sphere; globe ② ball: 传～ pass the ball/ 网～ tennis ③ the globe; the earth: 全～战略 global strategy/ 东半～ the Eastern Hemisphere ④ anything shaped like a ball: 雪～ snowball
【球场】 qiúchǎng a ground where ball games are played; (volleyball, basketball, tennis, badminton, etc.) court; (football, baseball, softball, etc.) field
【球胆】 qiúdǎn bladder (of a ball)
【球队】 qiúduì (ball game) team
【球罐】 qiúguàn 〈石油〉 sphere
【球果】 qiúguǒ 〈植〉 cone
【球茎】 qiújīng 〈植〉 corm
【球茎甘蓝】 qiújīng gānlán 〈植〉 kohlrabi
【球菌】 qiújūn 〈微〉 coccus
【球类运动】 qiúlèi yùndòng ball games
【球门】 qiúmén 〈体〉 goal ◇ ～柱 goalpost
【球迷】 qiúmí (ball game) fan: 乒乓～ ping-pong fan
【球面】 qiúmiàn spherical surface
◇ ～车床 〈机〉 spherical turning lathe/ ～镜 〈物〉 spherical mirror/ ～天文学 spherical astronomy
【球磨床】 qiúmóchuáng 〈机〉 ball grinder
【球磨机】 qiúmójī 〈机〉 ball mill
【球墨铸铁】 qiúmò zhùtiě 〈冶〉 nodular cast iron
【球拍】 qiúpāi ① (tennis, badminton, etc.) racket ② (ping-pong) bat: 正(反)贴海绵～ outward (inward) pimpled rubber bat
【球赛】 qiúsài ball game; match
【球坛】 qiútán the ball-playing world; ball-playing circles; ball-players: ～盛会 a grand gathering of (table tennis, etc.) players/ ～新手 a new player; a newcomer to the tournament
【球体】 qiútǐ spheroid
【球团矿】 qiútuánkuàng 〈冶〉 pellet
【球网】 qiúwǎng net (for ball games)
【球窝节】 qiúwōjié 〈机〉 ball-and-socket joint
【球鞋】 qiúxié gym shoes; tennis shoes; sneakers
【球形】 qiúxíng spherical; globular; round
【球艺】 qiúyì skills in playing a ball game; ball game skills

**遒** qiú 〈书〉 powerful; forceful
【遒劲】 qiújìng 〈书〉 powerful; vigorous: 笔力～ vigorous strokes in calligraphy/ 苍老～的古松 a sturdy old pine tree

**裘** qiú ① 〈书〉 fur coat: 狐～ a fox fur coat ② (Qiú) a surname

## qū

**区** qū ① area; district; region: 山～ mountainous district/ 林～ forest/ 商业～ business section (of a city)/ 住宅～ residential quarters/ 风景～ scenic spot ② an administrative division: 天津市河东～ the Hedong District of Tianjin Municipality; Hedong District, Tianjin/ 自治～ autonomous region ③ distinguish; classify; subdivide
另见 Ōu
【区别】 qūbié ① distinguish; differentiate; make a distinction between: 把两者～开来 differentiate one from the other/ ～对待 deal with each case on its merits; deal with different things or people in different ways/ ～好坏 distinguish between good and bad ② difference: 这两个词在意义上没有～。There is no difference in meaning between the two words.
【区分】 qūfēn differentiate; distinguish: 严格～两类不同性质的矛盾 strictly distinguish between the two different types of contradictions/～两个历史时代 mark off two historical epochs
【区划】 qūhuà division into districts: 行政～ administrative divisions

【区间车】 qūjiānchē a train or bus travelling only part of its normal route
【区区】 qūqū trivial; trifling: ～小事,何足挂齿。Such a trifling thing is hardly worth mentioning.
【区时】 qūshí 〈天〉 zone time
【区域】 qūyù region; area; district: ～间合作 inter-regional cooperation ◇ ～会议 regional conference; local conference
【区域性】 qūyùxìng regional
◇ ～公约 regional convention/ ～同盟 regional alliance/ ～问题 a matter of regional significance/ ～战争 regional war

**曲** qū ① bent; crooked: 弯腰～背 with one's back bent/ ～径通幽 a winding path leading to a secluded spot ② bend (of a river, etc.) ③ wrong; unjustifiable: 是非～直 the rights and wrongs of a matter ④ (Qū) a surname
另见 qǔ
【曲笔】 qūbǐ ① a distortion of the facts (by an official historian) ② deliberate digression in writing
【曲别针】 qūbiézhēn paper clip
【曲柄】 qūbǐng 〈机〉 crank ◇ ～摇杆机构 crank and rocker mechanism/ ～钻 brace drill
【曲尺】 qūchǐ carpenter's square
【曲拱】 qūgǒng arched: ～石桥 arched stone bridge
【曲古霉素】 qūgǔméisù 〈药〉 trichomycin
【曲棍球】 qūgùnqiú ① field hockey ② hockey ball
【曲解】 qūjiě (deliberately) misinterpret; twist: 这话意思很明确,不可能～。These remarks are so clear that there can be no room for misinterpretation./ 你～了他的意思。You've misrepresented his meaning.
【曲颈甑】 qūjǐngzèng 〈化〉 retort
【曲里拐弯】 qūliguǎiwān 〈口〉 tortuous; zigzag: ～的胡同 a tortuous alley
【曲流】 qūliú 〈地〉 meander
【曲率】 qūlǜ 〈数〉 curvature ◇ ～计 flexometer
【曲面】 qūmiàn curved surface; camber: 内～ negative camber/ 外～ positive camber
【曲鳝】 qūshan 〈口〉 earthworm
【曲射】 qūshè 〈军〉 curved fire ◇ ～弹道 curved trajectory/ ～炮 curved-fire gun
【曲突徙薪】 qūtū-xǐxīn bend the chimney and remove the fuel (to prevent a possible fire) — take precautions against a possible danger
【曲线】 qūxiàn 〈数〉 curve
◇ ～球 〈棒、垒球〉 curve ball/ ～图 diagram (of curves)/ ～运动 〈物〉 curvilinear motion
【曲意逢迎】 qūyì féngyíng go out of one's way to curry favour
【曲折】 qūzhé ① tortuous; winding: 河道～。The river has a winding course./ 前途是光明的,道路是～的。The road is tortuous, but the prospects are bright. ② complications: 这件事情里面还有不少～。 There are many complications in this matter.
【曲直】 qū-zhí right and wrong: ～不分 not distinguish between right and wrong
【曲轴】 qūzhóu 〈机〉 crankshaft; bent axle ◇ ～磨床 crankshaft grinding machine/ ～箱 crankcase

**岖** qū 见"崎岖" qíqū

**驱** qū ① drive (a horse, car, etc.): ～车前往 drive (in a vehicle) to a place ② expel; disperse: ～云防雹 disperse clouds to prevent a hailstorm ③ run quickly: 驰～ gallop/ 并驾齐～ run neck and neck
【驱策】 qūcè ① drive; whip on ② order about: 任人～ allow oneself to be ordered about
【驱虫药】 qūchóngyào anthelmintic; vermifuge
【驱除】 qūchú drive out; get rid of
【驱动】 qūdòng 〈机〉 drive: 气顶～〈石油〉 gas-cap drive/ 溶解气～〈石油〉 dissolved-gas drive ◇ ～齿轮 driving gear
【驱蛔灵】 qūhuílíng 〈药〉 piperazine citrate
【驱遣】 qūqiǎn ① 〈书〉 drive away; banish; expel ② order about; drive
【驱散】 qūsàn disperse; dispel; break up: 阳光～了薄雾。The sun dispelled the mist.
【驱使】 qūshǐ ① order about: 供～ be ordered about; be at sb.'s beck and call/ 奴隶主把奴隶当作牛马任意～。 The slave owners drove their slaves as they drove their cattle. ② prompt; urge; spur on: 为好奇心所～ be prompted by curiosity
【驱逐】 qūzhú drive out; expel; banish: ～侵略者 drive out the aggressors/ ～出境 deport; expel ◇ ～机 pursuit plane/ ～舰 destroyer

**屈** qū ① bend; bow; crook: ～臂 crook one's arm ② subdue; submit: 宁死不～ would rather die than yield/ 不～不挠 indomitable; dauntless; unyielding ③ wrong; injustice: 受～ be wronged/ 叫～ complain about an injustice/ ～死 be wronged and driven to death; be persecuted to death ④ in the wrong: 理～ have a weak case ⑤ (Qū) a surname
【屈才】 qūcái do work unworthy of one's talents
【屈从】 qūcóng submit to; yield to
【屈打成招】 qū dǎ chéng zhāo confess to false charges under torture
【屈服】 qūfú surrender; yield; knuckle under: ～于外界的压力 yield to pressure from outside
【屈驾】 qūjià 〈旧〉〈敬〉 condescend (或 be kind enough) to make the journey: 明日请～来舍一叙。Would you be kind enough to come over to my place for a chat tomorrow?
【屈节】 qūjié forfeit one's honour
【屈就】 qūjiù 〈套〉 condescend to take a post offered
【屈辱】 qūrǔ humiliation; mortification
【屈氏体】 qūshìtǐ 〈冶〉 troostite
【屈膝】 qūxī go down on one's knees; bend one's knees: ～投降 go down on one's knees in surrender; knuckle under
【屈心】 qūxīn 〈口〉 have a guilty conscience: 你做出这样的事～不～哪? Has your action never given you a twinge of conscience?/ 这种～的事我不干。 I wouldn't do a mean thing like that.
【屈折语】 qūzhéyǔ 〈语〉 inflexional language
【屈肢葬】 qūzhīzàng 〈考古〉 flexed burial
【屈指】 qūzhǐ count on one's fingers: ～已经八年啦。Come to think of it, eight years have already passed.
【屈指可数】 qūzhǐ kě shǔ can be counted on one's fingers — very few
【屈尊】 qūzūn 〈套〉 condescend

**祛** qū dispel; remove; drive away: ～暑 drive away summer heat
【祛除】 qūchú dispel; get rid of; drive out: ～疑虑 dispel one's misgivings/ ～邪魔 drive out (或 exorcize) evil spirits
【祛风】 qūfēng 〈中医〉 dispel the wind; relieve rheumatic pains, colds, etc.
【祛风湿药】 qūfēngshīyào medicine for rheumatism
【祛痰】 qūtán make expectoration easy ◇ ～剂 expectorant
【祛疑】 qūyí 〈书〉 remove suspicion or doubts
【祛瘀活血】 qūyū huóxuè 〈中医〉 remove blood stasis and

promote blood circulation

蛆 qū maggot

蕖 qū 〈化〉 chrysene

躯 qū the human body: 血肉之～ mortal flesh and blood/ 为国捐～ lay down one's life for one's country

【躯干】 qūgàn 〈生理〉 trunk; torso

【躯壳】 qūqiào the body (as opposed to the soul); outer form

【躯体】 qūtǐ body

趋 qū ① hasten; hurry along: ～前 hasten forward/ 疾～而过 hurry past ② tend towards; tend to become: 大势所～ irresistible general trend/ 局势～于稳定。The situation is tending towards stability./ 他们的意见～于一致。They are reaching unanimity.

【趋奉】 qūfèng toady to; fawn on

【趋附】 qūfù ingratiate oneself with; curry favour with

【趋光性】 qūguāngxìng 〈生〉 phototaxis

【趋热性】 qūrèxìng 〈生〉 thermotaxis

【趋时】 qūshí 〈书〉 follow the fashion

【趋势】 qūshì trend; tendency: 世界是在进步的，前途是光明的，这个历史的总～任何人也改变不了。The world is progressing, the future is bright, and no one can change this general trend of history./ 他的病有进一步恶化的～。His condition is tending to deteriorate.

【趋向】 qūxiàng ① tend to; incline to: 日益～好转 tend to improve with each passing day/ 这个工厂的生产管理制度逐步～完善。This factory is gradually perfecting its system of production management. ② trend; direction ◇ ～动词 〈语〉 directional verb

【趋性】 qūxìng 〈生〉 taxis

【趋炎附势】 qūyán-fùshì curry favour with the powerful; play up to those in power

【趋药性】 qūyàoxìng 〈生〉 chemotaxis

【趋之若鹜】 qū zhī ruò wù go after sth. like a flock of ducks; scramble for sth.

蛐 qū

【蛐蛐儿】 qūqur 〈方〉 cricket

麹 qū leaven; yeast

【麹霉】 qūméi aspergillus

黢 qū black; dark: 黑～～ pitch-black; pitch-dark

【黢黑】 qūhēi pitch-black; pitch-dark

## qú

劬 qú ① fatigued ② diligent; hardworking

【劬劳】 qúláo 〈书〉 fatigued; overworked

鸲 qú

【鸲鹆】 qúyù 〈动〉 myna

渠 qú canal; ditch; channel: 灌溉～ irrigation canal/ 红旗～ the Red Flag Canal

【渠道】 qúdào ① irrigation ditch ② medium of communication; channel: 通过外交～ through diplomatic channels

【渠灌】 qúguàn 〈农〉 canal irrigation

【渠首工程】 qúshǒu gōngchéng 〈水〉 headwork

蕖 qú 见"芙蕖" fúqú

磲 qú 见"砗磲" chēqú

瞿 Qú a surname

【瞿麦】 qúmài 〈植〉 fringed pink

鼩 qú

【鼩鼱】 qújīng 〈动〉 shrew

癯 qú 〈书〉 thin; lean: 清～ thin

衢 qú 〈书〉 thoroughfare

蠼 qú

【蠼螋】 qúsōu 〈动〉 earwig

## qǔ

曲 qǔ ① *qu*, a type of verse for singing, which emerged in the Southern Song and Jin dynasties and became popular in the Yuan Dynasty ② song; tune; melody: 高歌一～ lustily sing a song/ 小～儿 ditty ③ music (of a song): 聂耳作～ music by Nie Er

另见 qū

【曲调】 qǔdiào 〈乐〉 tune (of a song); melody

【曲高和寡】 qǔ gāo hè guǎ highbrow songs find few singers; too highbrow to be popular

【曲剧】 qǔjù opera derived from ballad singing

【曲牌】 qǔpái the names of the tunes to which *qu* (曲) are composed 参见"曲"①

【曲谱】 qǔpǔ ① music score of Chinese operas ② a collection of tunes of *qu* (曲) 参见"曲"①

【曲式】 qǔshì 〈乐〉 musical form

【曲艺】 qǔyì *quyi*, folk art forms including ballad singing, story telling, comic dialogues, clapper talks, cross talks, etc.

【曲子】 qǔzi song; tune; melody

苣 qǔ

另见 jù

【苣荬菜】 qǔmaicài endive

取 qǔ ① take; get; fetch: 她回去～行李去了。She's gone back to fetch her luggage./ 我来～自行车。I came to collect my bike./ 上银行～钱 go and draw some money from the bank/ ～之于民，用之于民。What is taken from the people is used in the interests of the people. ② aim at; seek: ～乐 seek pleasure/ 自～灭亡 court destruction/ ～信于人 win confidence ③ adopt; assume; choose: ～慎重态度 adopt a cautious attitude/ 给孩子～个名儿 choose a name for a child; give a name to a child/ 不无可～之处 not without something to recommend it/ 不足～ inadvisable; undesirable

【取保】 qǔbǎo 〈法〉 get sb. to go bail for one: ～释放 be released on bail; be bailed out

【取材】 qǔcái draw materials: 就地～ make use of (或 draw on) local materials/ 这本小说～于炼钢工人的生活。This novel has drawn its material from the life of steel workers.

【取长补短】 qǔcháng-bǔduǎn learn from others' strong points to offset one's weaknesses: 新老干部互相学习，互相帮助，～。Veteran and new cadres learn from and help each other, to make up each other's deficiencies.

【取代】 qǔdài replace; substitute for; supersede; supplant: 社会主义必然～资本主义。Socialism is bound to replace capitalism. ◇ ～衍生物〈化〉substitution derivate
【取道】 qǔdào by way of; via: 代表团将～巴黎回国。The delegation will come back to China by way of Paris.
【取得】 qǔdé gain; acquire; obtain: 通过实践～经验 gain experience through practice/ ～有关方面同意 obtain the consent of those concerned/ ～完全一致的意见 reach complete identity of views/ ～群众支持 enlist popular support/ ～圆满成功 be crowned with success; achieve complete success/ ～相当大的进展 make considerable headway
【取缔】 qǔdì outlaw; ban; suppress: ～投机倒把 ban speculation and profiteering/ ～反动会道门 ban reactionary secret societies
【取而代之】 qǔ ér dài zhī replace sb.; supersede sb.
【取法】 qǔfǎ take as one's model; follow the example of: ～乎上,仅得乎中。Aim high or you'll fall below the average.
【取给】 qǔjǐ draw (supplies, etc.): 所需资金主要～于企业内部的积累。The funds needed will mainly be drawn from accumulation within the enterprise.
【取经】 qǔjīng ① go on a pilgrimage for Buddhist scriptures ② learn from sb. else's experience: 到兄弟厂去～ go to another factory to learn from its experience
【取景】 qǔjǐng find a view (to photograph, paint, etc.) ◇ ～器〈摄〉viewfinder
【取决】 qǔjué be decided by; depend on; hinge on: 我们明年能否夺得丰收，在很大程度上～于今冬的水利工程。Whether or not we'll have a good harvest next year depends to a large extent on the water conservancy works we'll build this winter.
【取乐】 qǔlè seek pleasure; find amusement; amuse oneself; make merry: 饮酒～ drink and make merry
【取力器】 qǔlìqì 〈汽车〉power takeoff
【取暖】 qǔnuǎn warm oneself (by a fire, etc.): 烤火～ warm oneself (或 keep warm) by the fire
【取齐】 qǔqí ① make even; even up: 先把两张纸～了再裁。Even up the edges of the two sheets of paper before you cut them./ 去年我们队的产量不如他们,今年已经～了。Last year our team's output was less than theirs, but this year we've caught up with them. ② assemble; meet each other: 下午三时我们在门口～。We'll assemble at the gate at 3 o'clock in the afternoon.
【取枪】 qǔqiāng 〈军〉take arms: ～！(口令) Take arms!
【取巧】 qǔqiǎo resort to trickery to serve oneself: 投机～ resort to dubious shifts to further one's interests; be opportunistic
【取舍】 qǔ-shě accept or reject; make one's choice: 对技术资料进行分析后决定～ analyse the technical data and then decide which to use
【取胜】 qǔshèng win victory; score a success: 以多～ win victory through numerical superiority/ 侥幸～ gain a victory by sheer luck
【取水口】 qǔshuǐkǒu 〈水〉water intake
【取消】 qǔxiāo cancel; call off; abolish: ～一次会议 cancel (或 call off) a meeting/ ～会员资格 deprive sb. of his membership/ ～决定 rescind a decision/ ～禁令 lift a ban ◇ ～主义 liquidationism
【取笑】 qǔxiào ridicule; make fun of; poke fun at
【取样】 qǔyàng sampling: 井壁～〈石油〉wall sampling/ ～检查 take a sample to check
【取悦】 qǔyuè try to please; ingratiate oneself with sb.
【取之不尽，用之不竭】 qǔ zhī bù jìn, yòng zhī bù jié inexhaustible

**娶** qǔ marry (a woman); take to wife
【娶亲】 qǔqīn (of a man) get married

**龋** qǔ
【龋齿】 qǔchǐ ① dental caries ② decayed tooth

## qù

**去** qù ① go; leave: 谁～都一样。It makes no difference who goes./ 他～多久了？How long has he been away?/ 你～过延安没有？Have you ever been to Yan'an?/ 从成都～重庆 leave Chengdu for Chongqing/ 给她～个电话。Give her a ring. 或 Call her up. ② remove; get rid of: ～皮 remove the peel or skin; peel/ ～掉官僚主义的工作作风 get rid of the bureaucratic style of work/ ～掉思想上的负担 get a load off one's mind ③ be apart from: 两地相～五十里。The two places are 50 *li* apart./ ～今五十余年 more than fifty years ago ④ of last year: ～冬 last winter ⑤〔用在另一动词前表示要作某事〕: 我们自己～想办法。We'll find a way out ourselves. ⑥〔用在动宾结构后表示去做某事〕: 他吃饭～了。He's gone to eat. ⑦〔用在动词结构(或介词结构)与动词(或动词结构)之间,表示后者是前者的目的〕: 到国营农场～看一位老战友 go to a state farm to see an old comrade-in-arms/ 用辩证唯物主义的观点～观察事物 look at things from a dialectical-materialist viewpoint ⑧〈方〉very; extremely: 那片林子可大了～了。That's really quite a forest./ 他到过的地方多了～了。He's been to a great many places. ⑨〈语〉见"去声" ⑩〈方〉play the part (或 role) of; act (the part of): 他在京剧《逼上梁山》里～林冲。He acted Lin Chong in the Beijing opera *Driven to Join the Liangshan Rebels*.

**去** qu ①〔用在动词后表示动作离开说话人所在地〕: 上～ go up/ 进～ go in/ 把这个给他捎～。Take this and give it to him. ②〔用在动词后表示动作的继续〕: 信步走～ stroll along/ 让他说～。Let him talk. 或 Let him say what he likes.
【去处】 qùchù ① place to go; whereabouts: 有谁知道他的～？Who knows his whereabouts? ② place; site: 这是一个风景优美的～。This is a beautiful place.
【去粗取精】 qùcū-qǔjīng discard the dross and select the essential
【去垢剂】 qùgòujì 〈化〉detergent
【去火】 qùhuǒ 〈中医〉reduce internal heat; relieve inflammation or fever
【去路】 qùlù the way along which one is going; outlet: 挡住敌人的～ block the enemy's way/ 给洪水找到～ find an outlet for the flood
【去敏灵】 qùmǐnlíng 〈药〉tripelennamine
【去年】 qùnián last year: ～十二月 last December/ ～此时 this time last year
【去声】 qùshēng 〈语〉falling tone, one of the four tones in classical Chinese and the fourth tone in modern standard Chinese pronunciation
【去世】 qùshì (of grown-up people) die; pass away
【去势】 qùshì 〈牧〉castrate; emasculate
【去痛定】 qùtòngdìng 〈药〉piminodine esylate
【去伪存真】 qùwěi-cúnzhēn eliminate the false and retain the true
【去污粉】 qùwūfěn household cleanser; cleanser
【去向】 qùxiàng the direction in which sb. or sth. has gone: 不知～ be nowhere to be found
【去雄】 qùxióng 〈植〉emasculate; castrate

【去杂去劣】 qùzá qùliè 〈农〉 roguing
【去职】 qùzhí no longer hold the post

**阒** qù quiet; still: ～无一人。All was quiet and not a soul was to be seen./ ～然无声 very quiet; absolutely still

**趣** qù ①interest; delight: 有～ interesting; delightful; amusing ②interesting: ～事 an interesting episode ③bent; purport: 志～ aspirations and interests; bent/ 本书旨～ the purport of the book

【趣剧】 qùjù farce
【趣味】 qùwèi ①interest; delight: ～无穷 be of infinite interest; afford the greatest delight; be fascinating ②taste; liking; preference: 迎合低级～ cater to vulgar tastes

**觑** qù ①look; gaze: 面面相～ gaze at each other in speechless despair/ 偷偷地～了他一眼 steal a glance at him ②〈口〉 narrow (one's eyes); squint: 他～着眼睛仔细地看一幅画。He was studying a painting with narrowed eyes.

## quān

**悛** quān 〈书〉 repent; make amends: 怙恶不～ be steeped in evil and refuse to repent

**圈** quān ①circle; ring: 画个～儿 draw a circle/ 包围～ ring of encirclement; encirclement/ 绕跑道跑两～ run around the track twice/ 这是他一千五百米赛跑的最后一～。This is his last lap in the 1,500-metre race./ 我到外面转了一～。I've been out for a walk./ 这话说得出～儿了。That's really going too far. ②circle; group: 他不是～里人。He doesn't belong to the inner circle. 或 He's not on the inside. ③enclose; encircle: 用篱笆把菜园～起来 enclose the vegetable garden with a fence ④mark with a circle: 把那个错字～了。Mark the wrong word with a circle.
另见 juān; juàn

【圈闭】 quānbì 〈石油〉 trap: 地层～ stratigraphic trap/ 背斜～ anticlinal trap
【圈点】 quāndiǎn ①punctuate (with periods or small circles) ②mark words and phrases for special attention with dots or small circles
【圈梁】 quānliáng 〈建〉 girth
【圈套】 quāntào snare; trap: 落入～ fall into a trap; play into sb.'s hands
【圈椅】 quānyǐ round-backed armchair
【圈阅】 quānyuè make a circle round one's name on a document submitted for approval to show that one has read it; tick off one's name listed on a circular, notice, etc. after reading it
【圈子】 quānzi circle; ring: 围成一个～站着 stand in a circle/ 说话不要绕～。Don't speak in a roundabout way. 或 Don't beat about the bush./ 走出家庭小～ come out of the narrow family circle/ 他的生活～很小。He moves in a very small circle./ 搞小～不好。A few banding together is no good.

## quán

**权** quán ①right: 选举～和被选举～ the right to vote and stand for election/ 在这个问题上没有发言～ not be entitled to speak on the matter; have no say in the matter ②power; authority: 当～ in power/ 越～ overstep one's authority/ 受～ be authorized (to do sth.) ③advantageous position: 主动～ initiative/ 霸～ hegemony/ 制空～ mastery of the air ④〈书〉 counterpoise; weight (of a steelyard) ⑤weigh: ～其轻重 weigh up one thing against another; weigh up the matter carefully ⑥tentatively; for the time being: ～充 act temporarily as; serve as a stopgap for ⑦expediency: 通～达变 adapt oneself to circumstances ⑧(Quán) a surname

【权变】 quánbiàn adaptability (或 flexibility) in tactics; tact
【权柄】 quánbǐng power; authority: 掌握～ be in power; be in the saddle
【权贵】 quánguì influential officials (in the old society); bigwigs
【权衡】 quánhéng weigh; balance: ～利弊 weigh the advantages and disadvantages; weigh the pros and cons
【权力】 quánlì power; authority: 国家～机关 organ of state power/ ～下放 delegate power to the lower levels/ 行使会议主席的～ exercise the functions of chairman of a conference; invoke the authority of chairman of a conference/ 中华人民共和国的一切～属于人民。All power in the People's Republic of China belongs to the people./ 这是他～范围以内的事。This matter comes within his jurisdiction.
【权利】 quánlì right: 劳动的～ the right to work/ 受教育的～ the right to education/ 政治～ political rights
【权谋】 quánmóu (political) tactics; trickery
【权能】 quánnéng powers and functions
【权且】 quánqiě for the time being; as a temporary measure: ～如此办理。This is to be carried out as an interim measure.
【权势】 quánshì power and influence
【权术】 quánshù political trickery; shifts in politics: 玩弄～ play politics
【权威】 quánwēi ①authority; authoritativeness: 革命无疑是天下最～的东西。A revolution is certainly the most authoritarian thing there is. ②a person of authority; authority ◇ ～人士 authoritative person; authoritative sources
【权限】 quánxiàn limits of authority; jurisdiction; competence: 在法律规定的～内 within the limits of one's authority as prescribed by law/ 确定委员会的～ define the competence (或 terms of reference) of the committee/ 属于自治区～以内的事务 matters that come within the jurisdiction of the autonomous region
【权宜】 quányí expedient: ～之计 an expedient measure; makeshift (device)
【权益】 quányì rights and interests: 维护民族经济～ safeguard national economic rights and interests
【权诈】 quánzhà trickery; craftiness

**全** quán ①complete: 不获～胜，决不收兵。We will never leave the field until complete victory is won./ 手稿已残缺不～。The manuscript is no longer complete./ 人都来～了吗？Is everybody here? ②whole; entire; full; total: ～中国 the whole of China; all over China/ ～称 full name/ ～书共三卷。The work is in three volumes. ③entirely; completely: ～错了 completely wrong; all wrong/ ～怪我。It's entirely my fault./ 我们一家～去了。My whole family went. ④make perfect or complete; keep intact: 两～其美 satisfy both sides ⑤(Quán) a surname

【全豹】 quánbào whole picture; overall situation: 未窥～ fail to see the whole picture; fail to grasp the overall situation 参见"管中窥豹" guǎnzhōng kuī bào
【全部】 quánbù whole; complete; total; all: ～情况就这样。That's all there is to it./ 公布这个月的～开支 make public the month's total expenditure/ 粮食～自给 be completely self-supporting in food grain/ 为革命贡献自己的～力量 contribute one's all to the revolution/ 要求赔偿～损失 de-

mand full compensation for the loss incurred/ ～歼灭入侵之敌 wipe out the invading enemy to the last man

【全才】 quáncái a versatile person; all-rounder: 文武～ be versed in both civil and military affairs

【全场】 quánchǎng ① the whole audience; all those present: ～欢声雷动。The audience broke out into thunderous cheers. ②〈体〉full-court; all-court: ～紧逼 all-court press; full-court press

【全程】 quánchéng whole journey; whole course: 自行车比赛～一百二十公里。The whole course of the bicycle race is 120 kilometres.

【全等】 quánděng 〈数〉 congruent ◇ ～形 〈数〉 congruent figures

【全动机翼】 quándòng jīyì all-moving wing (of an aircraft)

【全都】 quándōu all; without exception: 村里男女老少～出来欢迎贵宾。The whole village, men and women, old and young, turned out to welcome the distinguished visitors./ 去年栽的树～活了。All the trees planted last year have survived.

【全反射】 quánfǎnshè 〈物〉 total reflection

【全份】 quánfèn complete set: ～表册 a complete set of lists and forms

【全副】 quánfù complete: ～武装 fully armed; in full battle array

【全国】 quánguó the whole nation (或 country); nationwide; countrywide; throughout the country: ～人民 the people of the whole country; the people throughout the country; the whole nation/ ～上下 the whole nation from the leadership to the masses/ ～人口普查 a nationwide census/ ～运动会 the national games/ ～冠军 national champion

【全国农业发展纲要】 Quánguó Nóngyè Fāzhǎn Gāngyào *The National Programme for Agricultural Development* (1956-1967)

【全国性】 quánguóxìng nationwide; countrywide; national: ～报纸 a national newspaper; a newspaper with a nationwide circulation

【全国一盘棋】 quánguó yīpánqí coordinate all the activities of the nation like pieces in a chess game; take the whole country into account

【全会】 quánhuì plenary meeting; plenary session; plenum: 十届三中～ the Third Plenary Session of the Tenth Central Committee

【全集】 quánjí complete works; collected works: «鲁迅～» *The Complete Works of Lu Xun*/ «列宁～» *The Collected Works of Lenin*

【全家福】 quánjiāfú 〈方〉① a photograph of the whole family ② hotchpotch (as a dish)

【全景】 quánjǐng panorama; full view; whole scene: 西湖～ full view of the West Lake ◇ ～宽银幕电影 cinepanoramic/ ～摄影机 panoramic camera

【全局】 quánjú overall situation; situation as a whole: 影响～ affect the overall situation/ 胸有～ with the situation as a whole in mind/ 树立～观点 adopt an overall point of view/ ～利益 interests of the whole; general interests/ ～性问题 a matter of overall importance

【全军】 quánjūn the whole (或 entire) army: ～指战员 the officers and men of the whole army/ ～运动会 army-wide sports meet

【全开】 quánkāi 〈印〉 a standard-sized sheet: 一张～的宣传画 a full-size poster

【全劳动力】 quánláodònglì able-bodied farm worker

【全力】 quánlì with all one's strength; all-out; sparing no effort: ～支持 support with all one's strength; spare no effort to support; give all-out support/ 竭尽～ exert all one's strength; move heaven and earth; throw in one's whole might/ ～以赴 go all out; spare no effort ◇ ～爬升〈航空〉 full climb

【全貌】 quánmào complete picture; full view: 弄清问题的～ try to get a complete picture of the problem/ 从这里可以看到大桥的～。You can get a view of the whole bridge from here.

【全面】 quánmiàn overall; comprehensive; all-round: ～规划 overall planning/ ～总结 comprehensive summing-up/ ～崩溃 total collapse; *débâcle*/ ～进攻 an all-out attack/ ～战争 a full-scale war/ ～落实党的各项政策 implement the Party's policies in an all-round way/ ～地看问题 look at problems all-sidedly/ ～禁止和彻底销毁核武器 complete prohibition and thorough destruction of nuclear weapons/ 德智体～发展 develop in an all-round way — morally, intellectually and physically

【全苗】 quánmiáo 〈农〉 a full stand: 保证棉花～ ensure a full stand of cotton shoots

【全民】 quánmín the whole (或 entire) people; all the people: ～皆兵 an entire nation in arms; every citizen a soldier/ ～总动员 general mobilization of the nation/ "～国家""～党"是现代修正主义的谬论。The terms "a state of the whole people" and "a party of the entire people" are modern revisionist fallacies. ◇ ～所有制 ownership by the whole people

【全能】 quánnéng 〈体〉 all-round: ～运动员 all-round athlete; all-rounder/ ～冠军 all-round champion/ 获得女子～冠军 win the women's individual all-round title/ 五项～运动 pentathlon/ 十项～运动 decathlon

【全年】 quánnián annual; yearly: ～收入 annual income/ ～平均温度 mean annual temperature/ ～雨量 yearly rainfall

【全盘】 quánpán overall; comprehensive; wholesale: ～考虑 give overall consideration to/ ～接受 total and uncritical acceptance/ ～否定 total repudiation

【全球】 quánqiú the whole world: ～战略 global strategy/ 在～范围内 on a global scale

【全权】 quánquán full powers; plenary powers: ～证书 full powers/ 特命～公使 envoy extraordinary and minister plenipotentiary/ 特命～大使 ambassador plenipotentiary and extraordinary/ ～代表 plenipotentiary

【全然】 quánrán completely; entirely: ～不了解情况 be completely ignorant of the situation/ ～不计后果 in utter disregard of the consequences/ ～不顾个人安危 give no thought to one's own safety

【全日制】 quánrìzhì full-time ◇ ～教育 full-time schooling/ ～学校 full-time school

【全色】 quánsè 〈摄〉 panchromatic ◇ ～胶片 panchromatic film

【全身】 quánshēn the whole body; all over (the body): ～不适 general malaise/ ～发抖 shake all over/ ～湿透 be soaked to the skin/ ～是伤 be covered with cuts and bruises/ ～检查 a general physical checkup ◇ ～像 full-length picture

【全神贯注】 quánshén guànzhù be absorbed (或 engrossed) in; be preoccupied with: ～地学习毛主席著作 be absorbed in studying Chairman Mao's works/ ～地搞技术革新 be deeply engrossed in technical innovations/ ～地考虑问题 be preoccupied with a problem/ 她～地听着。She listened with rapt attention. 或 She was all ears.

【全盛】 quánshèng flourishing; in full bloom: ～时期 period of full bloom; prime; heyday

【全食】 quánshí 〈天〉 total eclipse ◇ ～带 path of total eclipse; belt (或 zone) of totality

【全始全终】 quánshǐ-quánzhōng see sth. through; stick to sth. to the very end

【全视图】 quánshìtú full view; general view
【全数】 quánshù total number; whole amount: 我们已～付讫。We have paid the whole amount.
【全速】 quánsù full (或 maximum, top) speed: ～前进 advance at full speed/ 这车～每小时一百二十公里。The car has a maximum speed of 120 kilometres an hour.
【全损】 quánsǔn total loss ◇ ～险 〈经〉 total loss only (T.L.O.)
【全套】 quántào complete set ◇ ～设备 a complete set of equipment
【全体】 quántǐ all; entire; whole: ～船员 the crew (of a ship); the ship's complement/ ～演员 the entire cast/ ～工作人员 the whole staff/ 开～会 meet in full session; hold a plenary session/ ～起立默哀。All rose to their feet in silent tribute./ ～起立，长时间鼓掌。There was a long standing ovation./ 内阁～辞职。The cabinet resigned *en bloc*.
【全天候】 quántiānhòu all-weather ◇ ～飞机 all-weather aircraft/ ～公路 all-weather road
【全托】 quántuō put one's child in a boarding nursery: 你的孩子是日托还是～？Does your child board at the nursery or go home in the evening? ◇ ～托儿所 boarding nursery
【全文】 quánwén full text: ～如下。The full text follows./ ～发表 publish in full/ ～记录 verbatim record
【全息电影】 quánxī diànyǐng holographic movie
【全息照相】 quánxī zhàoxiàng hologram: 激光～ laser hologram ◇ ～存储器 holographic memory/ ～术 holography
【全线】 quánxiàn all fronts; the whole line; the entire length: 边界～ the entire length of the boundary/ ～出击 launch an attack on all fronts/ 敌人已～崩溃。The enemy was put to rout all along the line./ 这条铁路已～通车。The whole railway line has been opened to traffic.
【全心全意】 quánxīn-quányì wholeheartedly; heart and soul: ～地为人民服务。Serve the people wholeheartedly.
【全休】 quánxiū complete rest: 大夫建议～一星期。The doctor prescribed a complete rest of one week.
【全音】 quányīn 〈乐〉 whole tone
【全音符】 quányīnfú 〈乐〉 whole note; semibreve
【全知全能】 quánzhī-quánnéng omniscient and omnipotent
【全脂奶粉】 quánzhī nǎifěn whole milk powder

**诠** quán
【诠释】 quánshì annotation; explanatory notes
【诠注】 quánzhù notes and commentary

**泉** quán ① spring: 温～ hot spring/ 矿～ mineral spring/ 喷～ fountain ② an ancient term for coin: ～币 ancient coin
【泉华】 quánhuá 〈地〉 sinter
【泉水】 quánshuǐ spring water; spring
【泉眼】 quányǎn the mouth of a spring; spring
【泉源】 quányuán ① fountainhead; springhead; wellspring ② source: 智慧(力量)的～ source of wisdom (strength)

**拳** quán ① fist: 挥～ shake one's fist ② 〈量〉: 打了一～ give a punch ③ boxing; pugilism: 练～ practise shadow boxing
【拳棒】 quánbàng 见"武术" wǔshù
【拳打脚踢】 quándǎ-jiǎotī cuff and kick; beat up
【拳击】 quánjī boxing; pugilism ◇ ～台 boxing ring/ ～运动员 boxer; pugilist
【拳曲】 quánqū curl; twist; bend: ～的头发 curly hair
【拳拳】 quánquán 〈书〉 sincere: ～之忱 sincere intention; sincerity/ ～服膺 have a sincere belief in
【拳师】 quánshī boxing coach; pugilist
【拳术】 quánshù Chinese boxing
【拳头】 quántou fist

**痊** quán recover from an illness
【痊愈】 quányù fully recover from an illness; be fully recovered: 她还没有～。She's not recovered yet./ 希望你早日～。I wish you a speedy recovery.

**筌** quán a bamboo fish trap

**蜷** quán curl up; huddle up
【蜷伏】 quánfú curl up; huddle up; lie with the knees drawn up: 他喜欢～着睡觉。He likes to sleep with his knees drawn up. 或 He likes to sleep curled up on his side.
【蜷曲】 quánqū curl; coil; twist: 一条蛇在草丛里～着。A snake lay coiled in the grass./ 他把两腿～起来做了个前滚翻。Drawing up his knees against his chest, he made a forward roll.
【蜷缩】 quánsuō roll up; huddle up; curl up: 刺猬一受到攻击就～成一团。A hedgehog rolls itself into a ball when attacked.

**醛** quán 〈化〉 aldehyde
【醛酸】 quánsuān aldehydic acid
【醛糖】 quántáng aldose
【醛酯】 quánzhǐ aldehydo-ester

**鬈** quán curly; wavy: ～发 curly hair
【鬈曲】 quánqū 〈纺〉 crimp; crinkle; curl: ～羊毛 crimpy wool; crinkled wool

**颧** quán cheekbone
【颧骨】 quángǔ cheekbone: ～突起 have prominent cheekbones

## quǎn

**犬** quǎn dog: 牧～ shepherd dog; sheep dog/ 猎～ hunting dog; hound/ 警～ police dog/ 鸡鸣～吠 the crowing of cocks and the barking of dogs — country sounds/ 丧家之～ a stray cur
【犬齿】 quǎnchǐ canine tooth
【犬马之劳】 quǎn-mǎ zhī láo serve like a dog or a horse: 效～ serve one's master faithfully; be at sb.'s beck and call
【犬儒】 quǎnrú cynic ◇ ～主义 cynicism
【犬牙】 quǎnyá ① canine tooth ② fang (of a dog)
【犬牙交错】 quǎnyá jiāocuò jigsaw-like; interlocking: 形成～的状态 form a jagged, interlocking pattern/ ～的战争 jigsaw pattern warfare

**绻** quǎn 见"缱绻" qiǎnquǎn

## quàn

**劝** quàn ① advise; urge; try to persuade: ～他戒烟 advise him to give up smoking/ ～他休息 urge him to take a rest/ 我～了他半天，他就是不听。I spent a long time trying to talk him round, but he just wouldn't listen. ② encourage: ～学 encourage learning
【劝导】 quàndǎo try to persuade; advise; induce: 耐心～ try patiently to talk sb. round/ 经过同志们～，他终于想通了。With the help of his comrades, he has finally straightened things out in his mind.

【劝告】 quàngào advise; urge; exhort: 医生～他注意休息。The doctor advised him to have a good rest./ 她不顾我们的一再～。She disregarded our repeated exhortations.
【劝架】 quànjià try to reconcile parties to a quarrel; try to stop people from fighting each other; mediate
【劝解】 quànjiě ① help sb. to get over his worries, etc.: 大家～了半天,她才消气了。It was some time before we succeeded in pacifying her. ② mediate; make peace between; bring people together: 他们吵架了,你去～一下。They've had a quarrel. You try and patch things up between them.
【劝戒】 quànjiè admonish; expostulate
【劝酒】 quànjiǔ urge sb. to drink (at a banquet)
【劝勉】 quànmiǎn advise and encourage: 互相～ help and encourage each other
【劝说】 quànshuō persuade; advise
【劝慰】 quànwèi console; soothe
【劝降】 quànxiáng induce to capitulate
【劝诱】 quànyòu induce; prevail upon
【劝止】 quànzhǐ 见"劝阻"
【劝阻】 quànzǔ dissuade sb. from; advise sb. not to: 你最好～他别那样干。You'd better dissuade him from doing that./ ～无效 try in vain to talk sb. out of doing sth.

**券** quàn certificate; ticket: 入场～ admission ticket/ 公债～ government bond
另见 xuàn

## quē

**炔** quē 〈化〉 alkyne: 乙～ acetylene
【炔雌醇】 quēcíchún 〈药〉 ethinyloestradiol

**缺** quē ① be short of; lack: ～人 be short of hands/ ～粮户 grain-deficient household/ 庄稼～肥～水就长不好。Lacking manure and water, crops won't grow well./ 这种原料较～。This kind of material is rather scarce./ 这本书～两页。Two pages are missing from this book./ 这些条件～一不可。Not a single one of these conditions can be dispensed with. ② incomplete; imperfect: 残～不全 incomplete; fragmentary/ 完美无～ flawless; perfect; impeccable ③ be absent: 人都到齐了,一个不～。No one is absent. Everybody's here. ④ vacancy; opening: 空～ vacancy; opening/ 补～ fill a vacancy
【缺德】 quēdé mean; wicked; villainous: 做～事 do sth. mean; play a mean trick/ 他这样做可真～。It's wicked of him to act like that.
【缺点】 quēdiǎn shortcoming; defect; weakness; drawback: 克服工作中的～ overcome shortcomings in one's work/ 这种药的主要～是败胃。The chief drawback of this medicine is that it spoils your appetite.
【缺额】 quē'é vacancy: 他们厂按编制还有五十名～。Their factory is still 50 people short of its quota of workers.
【缺乏】 quēfá be short of; lack; be wanting in: ～劳动力 be short of labour power/ ～经验 lack experience/ ～战斗力 have poor fighting capacity/ ～资源 be deficient in resources/ ～证据 want of proof
【缺货】 quēhuò be in short supply; be out of stock
【缺课】 quēkè be absent from school; miss a class: 缺了三课 miss three lessons/ 给一个因病～的学生补习功课 help a pupil who has missed some classes on account of illness
【缺口】 quēkǒu ① breach; gap: 篱笆上有个～。There is a gap in the fence./ 从敌人的侧翼打开一个～ make a breach in the enemy's flank ② 〈机〉 notch
【缺漏】 quēlòu gaps and omissions
【缺门】 quēmén gap (in a branch of learning, etc.): 填补工业中的一个～ fill a gap in industry
【缺勤】 quēqín absence from duty (或 work) ◇ ～率 absence rate
【缺少】 quēshǎo lack; be short of: ～零件 lack spare parts/ ～人手 be short of hands; be shorthanded/ 不可～的条件 indispensable conditions
【缺席】 quēxí absent (from a meeting, etc.): 因事～ be absent through being otherwise engaged/ 他这学期从没～过。He has never been absent from class this term. ◇ ～判决 〈法〉 judgment by default/ ～审判 〈法〉 trial by default
【缺陷】 quēxiàn defect; drawback; flaw; blemish: 生理～ physical defect/ 这个计划有些～。The plan has some shortcomings.
【缺嘴】 quēzuǐ 〈方〉 harelip

**阙** quē 〈书〉 ① fault; error ② 见"缺" quē
另见 què
【阙如】 quērú 〈书〉 be wanting
【阙疑】 quēyí leave the question open

## qué

**瘸** qué 〈口〉 be lame; limp: 左腿～了 be lame in the left leg/ 一步一～ walk with a limp
【瘸腿】 quétuǐ lame: ～的人 a lame person
【瘸子】 quézi 〈口〉 a lame person; cripple

## què

**却** què ① step back: 退～ go back; retreat ② drive back; repulse: ～敌 repulse the enemy ③ decline; refuse: 推～ decline; refuse ④ 〈副〉〔表示转折〕 but; yet; however; while: 她有许多话要说,一时～什么也说不出来。She had a lot to say, but at the time she was unable to utter a word. ⑤〔用在某些动词后,表示动作的完成〕: 冷～ cool off/ 了～一个心愿 fulfil a wish
【却病】 quèbìng 〈书〉 prevent or cure a disease: ～延年 prevent disease and prolong life
【却步】 quèbù step back (in fear or disgust); hang back: 望而～ shrink back at the sight (of sth. dangerous or disgusting)
【却之不恭】 què zhī bù gōng it would be impolite to decline: ～,受之有愧。To decline would be disrespectful but to accept is embarrassing.

**雀** què sparrow
另见 qiāo
【雀斑】 quèbān freckle
【雀鲷】 quèdiāo 〈动〉 damselfish
【雀麦】 quèmài 〈植〉 bromegrass; brome
【雀鹰】 quèyīng 〈动〉 sparrow hawk
【雀跃】 quèyuè jump for joy: 欢呼～ shout and jump for joy

**阕** què ①〈书〉 end: 乐～。The music ended. ②〈量〉〔用于歌曲或词〕: 一～词 a *ci* poem

**确** què ① true; reliable; authentic: ～有其事。It's a fact. 或 It really happened./ ～证 ironclad proof ② firmly: ～信 firmly believe
【确保】 quèbǎo ensure; guarantee: ～安全生产 ensure safe-

ty in production/ ～质量 guarantee quality/ ～适时播种。Be sure to do the sowing in good time.

【确定】 quèdìng ① define; fix; determine: 政治路线～之后，干部就是决定的因素。Once the political line is determined, cadres are a decisive factor./ ～会议宗旨 define the aims of the conference/ ～开会的日期和地点 determine (或 fix) the time and place for a meeting/ ～行军路线 decide the route of the march/ ～作战方案 decide on a battle plan/ ～任务 set the tasks/ ～地层的年代 ascertain the ages of the strata/ ～领海宽度 delimit the extent of territorial waters ② definite: ～的答复 a definite reply/ ～不移的结论 an incontestable conclusion

【确乎】 quèhū really; indeed: ～有效 really effective

【确立】 quèlì establish: ～无产阶级的领导 establish proletarian leadership/ ～共产主义世界观 form a communist world outlook

【确切】 quèqiè definite; exact; precise: ～的日期 an exact date/ ～的解释 a clear and unambiguous explanation/ 下个～的定义 give a precise definition

【确认】 quèrèn affirm; confirm; acknowledge: 与会各国～下述原则。The participating countries affirm the following principles.

【确实】 quèshí ① true; reliable: ～的消息 reliable information ② really; indeed: 这～是个很好的建议。This is really a very good suggestion./ 他～来过。Yes, he did come.

【确信】 quèxìn firmly believe; be convinced; be sure: 我们～正义的事业一定会胜利。 We firmly believe that a just cause is bound to triumph.

【确诊】 quèzhěn make a definite diagnosis; diagnose: 他的病尚未～。No diagnosis has been made of his disease.

【确凿】 quèzuò conclusive; authentic; irrefutable: ～的证据 conclusive evidence; absolute proof/ ～的事实 irrefutable facts

**阙** què ① watchtower on either side of a palace gate ② imperial palace: 宫～ imperial palace
另见 quē

**鹊** què magpie

【鹊巢鸠占】 què cháo jiū zhàn the turtledove occupies the magpie's nest — one person seizes another person's place, land, etc.

【鹊鸲】 quèqú magpie robin

**榷** què discuss: 商～ discuss; deliberate over

## qūn

**逡** qūn

【逡巡】 qūnxún 〈书〉 hesitate to move forward; hang back

## qún

**裙** qún skirt: 绸～ silk skirt/ 衬～ slip; petticoat/ 围～ apron

【裙带】 qúndài connected through one's female relatives: 通过～关系 with the help of one's female relatives; through petticoat influence

【裙子】 qúnzi skirt

**群** qún ① crowd; group: 人～ crowd/ 成～结队 in crowds; in flocks; in groups/ 鱼～ shoals of fish/ 建筑～ a building complex; a cluster of buildings/ ～山环抱 surrounded by hills/ ～起而攻之 rally together to attack sb. or sth.; rise up in struggle against sb. or sth. ② 〈量〉 group; herd; flock: 一～小孩 a group of children/ 一～人 a crowd of people/ 一～牛 a herd of cattle/ 一～羊 a flock of sheep/ 一～狼 a pack of wolves/ 一～蜜蜂 a swarm of bees

【群策群力】 qúncè-qúnlì pool the wisdom and efforts of everyone: 贫下中农～改造山河。The poor and lower-middle peasants pooled their wisdom and strength to transform the mountains and rivers.

【群岛】 qúndǎo archipelago

【群芳】 qúnfāng beautiful and fragrant flowers: ～竞艳 flowers vying with each other in beauty

【群婚】 qúnhūn group marriage; communal marriage

【群居】 qúnjū living in groups; gregarious; social ◇ ～动物 social animal/ ～昆虫 social insect

【群控制】 qúnkòngzhì group control

【群龙无首】 qún lóng wú shǒu a host of dragons without a head — a group without a leader

【群落】 qúnluò 〈生〉 community ◇ ～交错区 ecotone

【群氓】 qúnméng 〈书〉 the common herd

【群魔乱舞】 qún mó luàn wǔ a host of demons dancing in riotous revelry — rogues of all kinds running wild

【群青】 qúnqīng 〈化〉 ultramarine

【群情】 qúnqíng public sentiment; feelings of the masses: ～振奋。Everyone is exhilarated./ ～激昂。Popular feeling ran high.

【群体】 qúntǐ 〈生〉 colony

【群威群胆】 qúnwēi-qúndǎn mass heroism and daring

【群言堂】 qúnyántáng rule by the voice of the many: 我们提倡"～",反对"一言堂"。We advocate "letting everyone have his say" and oppose the practice of "what I say goes." 参见"一言堂" yīyántáng

【群英会】 qúnyīnghuì gathering of heroes; conference of outstanding workers

【群众】 qúnzhòng the masses: 遵守～纪律 maintain discipline in relations with the masses/ 坚定地相信～的大多数。Have firm faith in the majority of the people.
◇ ～大会 mass rally/ ～观点 the mass viewpoint/ ～工作 mass work/ ～团体 mass organization/ ～关系 one's relations (或 ties) with the masses/ ～监督 surveillance by the masses

【群众路线】 qúnzhòng lùxiàn the mass line: 搞什么工作都要走～。Whatever we do, we must follow the mass line.

【群众性】 qúnzhòngxìng of a mass character: ～体育活动 mass sports activities/ 中国气象工作的一个重要特点是它的～。Mass participation is a prominent feature of meteorological work in China.

【群众运动】 qúnzhòng yùndòng mass movement; mass campaign: 大搞～ unfold mass movements on a large scale

【群子弹】 qúnzǐdàn 〈军〉 case shot; canister (shot)

**麇** qún 〈书〉 flock together

【麇集】 qúnjí 〈书〉 swarm; flock together

# R

## rán

**然** rán ①right; correct: 大谬不～ entirely wrong; absurd/ 不以为～ object to; not approve ②so; like that: 知其～，不知其所以～ know the hows but not the whys/ 不尽～ not exactly so; not exactly the case ③〈书〉〈连〉 but; nevertheless; however: 此事虽小，～亦不可忽视。This is a minor point, but it must not be overlooked. ④〔副词或形容词后缀〕: 忽～ suddenly; all of a sudden/ 显～ obviously/ 巍～屹立 tower majestically

【然而】 rán'ér 〈连〉 yet; but; however: 试验失败了多次，～他们并不灰心。Time after time they failed in the experiment, but they did not lose heart.

【然后】 ránhòu 〈副〉 then; after that; afterwards: 贵宾们将在太原停留一天，～飞往上海。The distinguished guests will stay in Taiyuan for one day and then fly to Shanghai./ 我们先研究一下，～再决定。We'll consider the problem carefully before coming to any decision.

【然诺】 ránnuò 〈书〉 promise; pledge: 重～ be serious about making and keeping a promise

【然则】 ránzé 〈书〉〈连〉 in that case; then: ～如之何而可？Then, what is to be done?

**髯** rán whiskers; beard

**燃** rán burn; ignite; light: 易～物品 combustibles; inflammables/ ～起一堆篝火 light a bonfire/ ～起革命的烈火 spark off (或 kindle) the flames of revolution

【燃点】 rándiǎn ①ignite; kindle; set fire to; light ②〈化〉 ignition (或 burning, kindling) point

【燃放】 ránfàng set off (fireworks, etc.): ～爆竹 set off firecrackers

【燃料】 ránliào fuel: 标准～ ideal fuels/ 低热值～ low-calorie fuels
◇ ～比〈冶〉 fuel ratio/ ～电池 fuel cell/ ～库 fuel depot; fuel reservoir

【燃眉之急】 rán méi zhī jí as pressing as a fire singeing one's eyebrows — a matter of extreme urgency; a pressing need

【燃气轮机】 ránqìlúnjī gas turbine ◇ ～发电厂 gas turbine power station

【燃烧】 ránshāo ①burn; kindle: 干柴容易～。Dry wood burns easily./ 怒火～ burning with rage/ 革命的烈火在～。The flames of revolution are raging. ②〈化〉 combustion; inflammation
◇ ～弹 incendiary bomb/ ～剂 incendiary agent/ ～室〈机〉 combustion chamber; blast chamber; combustor/ ～性能 combustibility

【燃油泵】 rányóubèng fuel pump

## rǎn

**冉** rǎn 〈书〉 ①slowly ②(Rǎn) a surname

【冉冉】 rǎnrǎn 〈书〉 slowly; gradually: 一轮红日～升起。A red sun slowly rose.

**苒** rǎn 见"荏苒" rěnrǎn

**染** rǎn ①dye: 把一块布～成绿色 dye a piece of cloth green/ 我们的战旗是烈士的鲜血～红的。Our standard is dyed with the blood of our martyrs. ②catch (a disease); acquire (a bad habit, etc.); soil; contaminate: ～上了痢疾 have caught dysentery/ 污～ pollution/ 一尘不～ not soiled by a speck of dust; spotless/ 出污泥而不～ emerge unstained from the filth

【染病】 rǎnbìng catch (或 contract) an illness; be infected with a disease

【染毒】 rǎndú 〈军〉 contamination

【染坊】 rǎnfáng dyehouse; dye-works

【染缸】 rǎngāng dye vat; dyejigger

【染料】 rǎnliào dyestuff; dye: 活性～ reactive dye

【染色】 rǎnsè dyeing; colouring ◇ ～剂 colouring agent/ ～性 dyeability

【染色体】 rǎnsètǐ 〈生〉 chromosome

【染色质】 rǎnsèzhì 〈生化〉 chromatin

【染液】 rǎnyè dye liquor

【染印法】 rǎnyìnfǎ 〈电影〉 dye transfer process ◇ ～彩色电影 colour film made by the dye transfer process

【染指】 rǎnzhǐ take a share of sth. one is not entitled to; encroach on: 妄图～别国资源 attempt to encroach on the resources of other countries

## rāng

**嚷** rāng
另见 rǎng

【嚷嚷】 rāngrang 〈口〉 ①shout; yell; make an uproar: 谁在那儿～？Who is shouting there?/ 屋里一片乱～。The room was in an uproar. ②make widely known: 这件事，你可别～。Don't breathe a word about this.

## ráng

**禳** ráng 〈书〉 avert (a misfortune or disaster) by prayers

**瓤** ráng ①pulp; flesh; pith: 西瓜～ the pulp (或 flesh) of a watermelon ②the interior part of certain things: 信皮儿和信～儿 the envelope and the letter in it

【瓤子】 rángzi pulp; flesh; pith

## rǎng

**壤** rǎng ①soil: 沃～ fertile soil; rich soil ②earth: 天～之别 be as far removed as heaven from earth; be vastly different/ 有霄～之别。There is a world of difference. ③area: 穷乡僻～ a remote, backward place/ 接～ have a common border; be adjacent to each other

【壤土】 rǎngtǔ 〈农〉 loam

**攘** rǎng 〈书〉 ①reject; resist: ～外 resist foreign aggression ②seize; grab ③push up one's sleeves

【攘臂】 rǎngbì 〈书〉 push up one's sleeves and bare one's arms (in excitement or agitation): ～高呼 raise one's hands

and shout
【攘除】 rǎngchú 〈书〉 get rid of; weed out; reject: ～奸邪 get rid of the wicked
【攘夺】 rǎngduó 〈书〉 seize; grab

**嚷** rǎng shout; yell; make an uproar: 孩子们在～些什么？What are the children shouting about?/ 别～了！Stop yelling. 或 Don't make such a noise.
另见 rāng

## ràng

**让** ràng ① give way; give ground; yield; give up: 各不相～。Neither is willing to give ground./ 寸步不～ refuse to yield an inch; not budge an inch/ 见困难就上,见荣誉就～ dash towards difficulties and retreat from honours/ 你该～着弟弟一点。You ought to humour your younger brother a little./ 请～一～。Please step aside. 或 Excuse me./ 幸亏我～得快,要不早给那辆自行车撞倒了。Luckily I dodged in time, or I'd have been knocked down by the bike. ② invite; offer: ～茶 offer sb. tea/ 把客人～进里屋 invite guests into the inner room ③ let; allow; make: ～我想一想。Let me think it over./ 大夫不～她起来。The doctor told her to stay in bed./ 他～我把这个消息转告你。He told me to pass the message on to you./ 老板～学徒一天干十四小时的活。The boss made the apprentices work fourteen hours a day./ 对不起,～你久等了。Sorry to have kept you waiting. ④ let sb. have sth. at a fair price: 我们按原价把这辆大车～给你们队。We can let your production team have this cart at cost price. ⑤〈介〉〔在被动式里引进主动者〕:庄稼～大水冲跑了。The crops were washed away by the flood./ 行李～雨淋湿了。The luggage got wet in the rain.
【让步】 ràngbù make a concession; give in; give way; yield: 准备作出某些必要的～ be prepared to make some necessary concessions/ 不向无理要求～ not yield to any unreasonable demand
【让开】 ràngkai get out of the way; step aside; make way
【让路】 rànglù make way for sb. or sth.; give way; give sb. the right of way: 大家让让路。Please get out of the way, everybody./ 你们的工程得给重点工程～。Your project will have to make way for the main project.
【让球】 ràngqiú concede points: 教练员让了小李五个球。The coach conceded Xiao Li five points.
【让位】 ràngwèi ① resign sovereign authority; abdicate ② offer (或 give up) one's seat to sb. ③ yield to; give way to; change into: 经过大家的努力,困难的局面终于～于顺利的局面。As a result of collective effort, the difficult situation changed into a favourable one.
【让座】 ràngzuò ① offer (或 give up) one's seat to sb.: 他给一位抱孩子的妇女～。He offered his bus seat to a woman carrying a baby. ② invite guests to be seated

## ráo

**荛** ráo 〈书〉 firewood; faggot
【荛花】 ráohuā canescent wikstroemia (*Wikstroemia canescens*)

**饶** ráo ① rich; plentiful: ～有风趣 full of wit and humour ② have mercy on; let sb. off; forgive: 求～ beg for mercy /下回可不能轻～了你。We won't let you off so easily next time. ③ give sth. extra; let sb. have sth. into the bargain: 给你～上一个。I'll let you have one more./ 有两个人就够了,不要把他也～在里头。Two people will be enough; there is no need to drag him along, too. ④〈口〉〈连〉 although; in spite of the fact that: 这孩子,～怎么说他也不听。That child! Whatever you said, he simply wouldn't listen. ⑤ (Ráo) a surname
【饶命】 ráomìng spare sb.'s life
【饶舌】 ráoshé ① too talkative; garrulous ② say more than is proper; shoot off one's mouth
【饶恕】 ráoshù forgive; pardon
【饶沃】 ráowò (of soil) fertile; rich

**娆** ráo 见"妖娆" yāoráo

**桡** ráo oar
【桡动脉】 ráodòngmài 〈生理〉 radial artery
【桡骨】 ráogǔ 〈生理〉 radius

## rǎo

**扰** rǎo ① harass; trouble: 纷～ tumult; turmoil ②〈套〉 trespass on sb.'s hospitality: 叨～,叨～。Thank you for your hospitality./ 我～了他一顿饭。He kindly entertained me to dinner.
【扰乱】 rǎoluàn harass; disturb; create confusion: ～治安 disturb public order/ ～市场 disrupt the market/ ～军心 undermine the morale of an army/ ～视线 interfere with sb.'s view/ 谨防敌人～我们的阵线 guard against the enemy creating confusion within our ranks
【扰攘】 rǎorǎng hustle and bustle; noisy confusion; tumult: 干戈～ in the tumult of a raging war

**绕** rǎo 见"围绕" wéirǎo; "环绕" huánrǎo; "缠绕" chánrǎo; "缭绕" liáorǎo
另见 rào

## rào

**绕** rào ① wind; coil: ～线 wind thread/ 把铁丝～成圈 coil wire; wind wire into a coil ② move round; circle; revolve: 地球～着太阳转。The earth moves (或 revolves) round the sun./ 运动员～场一周。The athletes marched around the arena./ 飞机在机场上空～圈。The plane circled over the airfield. ③ make a detour; bypass; go round: 道路施工,车辆～行。Detour. Road under repair./ ～过暗礁 bypass hidden reefs; steer clear of submerged rocks/ 货轮～过好望角,驶入大西洋。The freighter rounded the Cape of Good Hope and sailed into the Atlantic./ 你必须明确回答这个问题,想～是～不过去的。You must give a definite answer to the question. There's no getting round it. ④ confuse; baffle; befuddle: 你的话把他～住了。What you said confused him.
另见 rǎo
【绕脖子】 rào bózi 〈方〉 ① beat about the bush; speak or act in a roundabout way ② involved; knotty; tricky: 这句话太～了。This sentence is too involved.
【绕道】 ràodào make a detour; go by a roundabout route: 前面有个水库,我们得～过去。There's a reservoir ahead. We'll have to make a detour./ 你不要一遇困难就～走。Don't always try to skirt round difficulties.
【绕口令】 ràokǒulìng tongue twister
【绕圈子】 rào quānzi ① circle; go round and round ② take a circuitous route; make a detour ③ 见"绕弯子"

【绕弯儿】 ràowānr ① go for a stroll (或 walk) ② 见"绕弯子"
【绕弯子】 rào wānzi talk in a roundabout way; beat about the bush: 有话直说，别～。If you have anything to say, say it. Don't beat about the bush.
【绕远儿】 ràoyuǎnr go the long way round: 那样走可就～了。If you take that route, you'll be going the long way round.
【绕组】 ràozǔ 〈电〉 winding: 双线～ bifilar winding
【绕嘴】 ràozuǐ (of a sentence, etc.) not be smooth; be difficult to articulate: 这句话很～。This sentence is a tongue twister

## rě

**惹** rě ① invite or ask for (sth. undesirable): ～麻烦 ask for trouble; invite trouble/ ～是非 provoke a dispute; stir up trouble ② offend; provoke; tease: 我～不起他。I cannot afford to offend him./ 我可没～他呀! I said nothing to provoke him. 或 I did nothing to provoke him./ 他这个人是不好～的。He's not a man to be trifled with. ③ attract; cause: ～人注意 attract attention/ ～人讨厌 make a nuisance of oneself/ 他的话把大家～得哈哈大笑。His words set everybody roaring with laughter.
【惹火烧身】 rě huǒ shāo shēn stir a fire only to burn oneself — court disaster; ask for trouble
【惹祸】 rěhuò court disaster; stir up trouble: 这都是我惹的祸。It was I who started all the trouble.
【惹气】 rěqì get angry: 不值得为这点小事～。It's senseless to get angry over such a trifle.
【惹事】 rěshì stir up trouble
【惹是生非】 rěshì-shēngfēi provoke a dispute; stir up trouble

## rè

**热** rè ① heat: 传～ conduct heat ② hot: ～水 hot water ③ heat up; warm up; warm: 把汤～一～ heat up the soup ④ fever; temperature: 发～ have a fever; run a fever/ 先给他退～再说。First bring down his temperature. ⑤ ardent; warmhearted: ～望 ardently wish; fervently hope/ ～心肠 warmheartedness; ardour/ 采取不冷不～的态度 be neither cold nor warm (towards sb.); take a lukewarm attitude ⑥ craze; fad: 乒乓～ intense popular interest in table tennis; ping-pong craze ⑦ envious; eager: 眼～ feel envious at the sight of sth. ⑧ in great demand; popular: ～货 goods in great demand; goods which sell well ⑨ thermal; thermo-: ～中子 thermal neutron/ ～磁 thermomagnetic
【热爱】 rè'ài ardently love; have deep love (或 affection) for: ～自己的工作 love one's work/ ～人民 have deep love for the people
【热补】 rèbǔ vulcanize (tyre, etc.)
【热潮】 rècháo great mass fervour; upsurge: 生产～ a great upsurge in production/ 掀起群众性体育锻炼的～ unfold a vigorous mass campaign for sports and physical training
【热忱】 rèchén zeal; warmheartedness; enthusiasm and devotion: 革命～ revolutionary zeal/ 对同志对人民极端的～ extreme warmheartedness towards one's comrades and the people
【热诚】 rèchéng warm and sincere; cordial: ～欢迎 cordially welcome/ ～地希望 sincerely hope
【热处理】 rèchǔlǐ 〈机〉 heat (或 thermal) treatment ◇ ～钢 heat-treated steel/ ～炉 heat-treatment furnace
【热脆性】 rècuìxìng 〈冶〉 hot-shortness; red-shortness
【热带】 rèdài the torrid zone; the tropics
◇ ～草原 savanna/ ～风暴 tropical storm/ ～鱼 tropical fish/ ～植物 tropical plants/ ～作物 tropical crops
【热导体】 rèdǎotǐ 〈物〉 heat conductor
【热电】 rèdiàn 〈物〉 pyroelectricity; thermoelectricity
◇ ～厂 heat and power plant/ ～偶 thermocouple/ ～体 pyroelectrics/ ～效应 pyroelectric effect/ ～学 pyroelectricity/ ～阻 thermal resistance
【热度】 rèdù ① degree of heat; heat ② fever; temperature: 你～降下去了吗? Has your temperature come down?
【热风炉】 rèfēnglú 〈冶〉 hot-blast stove
【热敷】 rèfū 〈医〉 hot compress
【热辐射】 rèfúshè 〈物〉 heat (或 thermal) radiation
【热功当量】 règōng dāngliàng 〈物〉 mechanical equivalent of heat
【热固塑料】 règù sùliào 〈化〉 thermosetting plastic
【热锅上的蚂蚁】 règuōshàngde mǎyǐ ants on a hot pan: 急得象～一样 as restless as ants on a hot pan
【热核】 rèhé thermonuclear
◇ ～爆炸 thermonuclear explosion/ ～弹头 thermonuclear warhead/ ～技术 thermonucleonics/ ～武器 thermonuclear weapon
【热核反应】 rèhé fǎnyìng 〈物〉 thermonuclear reaction: 受控～ controlled thermonuclear reaction ◇ ～堆 thermonuclear reactor
【热烘烘】 rèhōnghōng very warm: 炉火很旺，屋里～的。With the stove burning cheerfully, it's very warm in the room.
【热乎乎】 rèhūhū warm: 心里感到～的 feel it heartwarming
【热乎】 rèhu ① nice and warm; warm: 饭菜还～。The food is still warm./ 炕上真～。The *kang* is warm and cosy. ② warm and friendly; pally; chummy; thick: 他们一见面就很～。They chummed up with each other the moment they met.
【热火朝天】 rèhuǒ cháotiān buzzing (或 bustling) with activity; in full swing: 工地上一派～的景象。The construction site was bustling with activity./ 掀起～的农田基本建设高潮 bring about a vigorous upsurge in farmland capital construction
【热火】 rèhuo showing tremendous enthusiasm; exciting: 咱们厂的社会主义劳动竞赛搞得真～。The socialist emulation drive in our factory is really lively.
【热和】 rèhuo 〈口〉 见"热乎"
【热机】 rèjī 〈机〉 heat engine
【热寂】 rèjì 〈物〉 heat death
【热加工】 rèjiāgōng 〈冶〉 hot-working; hot work
【热扩散】 rèkuòsàn 〈物〉 thermal diffusion
【热辣辣】 rèlālā burning hot; scorching: 太阳晒得人～的。The sun feels scorching./ 他听了大家的批评，觉得脸上～的。After hearing everybody's criticism, he felt his cheeks burning.
【热浪】 rèlàng 〈气〉 heat wave; hot wave
【热力】 rèlì 〈机〉 heating power ◇ ～学 thermodynamics
【热恋】 rèliàn be passionately in love; be head over heels in love
【热量】 rèliàng 〈物〉 quantity of heat ◇ ～单位 thermal (或 heat) unit/ ～计 calorimeter
【热烈】 rèliè warm; enthusiastic; ardent: ～的祝贺 warm congratulations/ ～欢送 give sb. a warm send-off/ 进行～的讨论 have a lively discussion/ ～欢呼代表大会的胜利召开! Warmly hail the successful convening of the Congress!/ 大家对她的建议反应很～。Everybody responded enthusiastically to her proposal.
【热裂化】 rèlièhuà 〈石油〉 thermal cracking
【热流】 rèliú ① 〈气〉 thermal current ② warm current: 我

感到一股～传遍全身。I felt a warm current coursing through my body.

【热门】 rèmén in great demand; popular: ～货 goods in great demand; goods which sell well/ 赶～ follow a craze

【热敏电阻】 rèmǐn diànzǔ 〈电〉 thermal resistor; thermistor

【热闹】 rènao ① lively; bustling with noise and excitement: ～的菜市场 a food market bustling with activity; a busy food market/ 晚会很～。It was a very lively evening party. ② liven up; have a jolly time: 你说个笑话让大伙儿～～吧。Tell us a joke to liven things up./ 那天他们聚在一起～了一番。 That day they got together and had a jolly time. ③ a scene of bustle and excitement; a thrilling sight: 看～ watch the excitement; watch the fun

【热能】 rènéng 〈物〉 heat (或 thermal) energy

【热气】 rèqì steam; heat: 壶里开始冒～了。The kettle's just on the boil.

【热气腾腾】 rèqì téngténg ① steaming hot: ～的馒头 steaming hot buns ② seething with activity: 春耕生产搞得～。The spring ploughing is going full steam ahead.

【热切】 rèqiè fervent; earnest: ～的愿望 earnest wish; fervent hope/ ～希望各位提出宝贵意见。We earnestly hope that you will give us your valuable criticisms and suggestions.

【热情】 rèqíng ① enthusiasm; zeal; warmth: 以极大的革命～投入战斗 plunge into the battle with immense revolutionary zeal/ 一封～洋溢的感谢信 an ebullient letter of thanks ② warm; fervent; enthusiastic; warmhearted: ～接待 warmly receive; give sb. a warm reception/ ～支持这个倡仪 fervently (或 enthusiastically) support this proposal/ 对旅客非常～ be very warm towards the passengers

【热水袋】 rèshuǐdài hot-water bottle (或 bag)

【热水瓶】 rèshuǐpíng 〈口〉 thermos bottle (或 flask); thermos; vacuum bottle (或 flask)

【热塑塑料】 rèsù sùliào 〈化〉 thermoplastic

【热腾腾】 rètēngtēng steaming hot: ～的汤面 steaming hot noodles in soup

【热天】 rètiān hot weather; hot season; hot days

【热望】 rèwàng fervently hope; ardently wish

【热线】 rèxiàn ①〈物〉 heat ray ② hot line

【热象仪】 rèxiàngyí 〈电子〉 thermal imaging system

【热心】 rèxīn enthusiastic; ardent; earnest; warmhearted: ～集体福利事业 be enthusiastic in promoting public welfare/ ～为顾客服务 warmheartedly serve the customers/ ～科学 eager to promote science/ ～传授技术 make earnest efforts to pass on one's skill/ 张大妈待人真～。 Aunt Zhang has a warm heart.

【热心肠】 rèxīncháng 〈口〉warmheartedness

【热性肥料】 rèxìng féiliào 〈农〉 hot manure

【热学】 rèxué 〈物〉 heat (a branch of physics)

【热血】 rèxuè warm blood — righteous ardour: ～沸腾 burning with righteous indignation/ ～青年 ardent youth/ 甘洒～为人民 be ready to shed one's blood for the people

【热血动物】 rèxuè dòngwù warm-blooded animal; warm blood

【热压】 rèyā 〈化〉 hot pressing

【热药】 rèyào 〈中医〉 medicines of a hot or warm nature; tonics and stimulants

【热饮】 rèyǐn hot drinks

【热源】 rèyuán 〈物〉 heat source

【热轧】 rèzhá 〈冶〉 hot-rolling ◇ ～机 hot-rolling mill

【热战】 rèzhàn hot war; shooting war

【热障】 rèzhàng 〈物〉 heat barrier

【热证】 rèzhèng 〈中医〉 heat symptom-complex; febrile symptoms

【热值】 rèzhí 〈物〉 calorific value

【热中】 rèzhōng ① hanker after; crave: ～于个人名利 hanker after personal fame and gain ② be fond of; be keen on: ～于溜冰 be very fond of skating

【热中子】 rèzhōngzǐ 〈物〉 thermal neutron

## rén

**人** rén ① human being; man; person; people: 男～ man/ 女～ woman/ 黄种～ the yellow race; yellow/ 非洲～ African/ 外国～ foreigner; foreign national/ 四川～ a native of Sichuan; Sichuanese/ ～对自然界的认识 man's knowledge of nature/ 消灭～剥削～的制度 abolish the system of exploitation of man by man/ 一个高尚的～ a noble-minded person/ 表扬好～好事 praise good people and good deeds/ 团结得象一个～ be united as one/ 昨天有三个～来找你。Three people came to see you yesterday./ 他～在那儿,心可想着别的事。He was there all right, but his mind was elsewhere./ 你一个～行吗? Can you manage on your own?/ 这个座位有～吗? Is this seat occupied (或 taken)? ② adult; grown-up: 长大成～ become a grown-up ③ a person engaged in a particular activity: 工～ worker/ 军～soldier/ 主～ host ④ other people; people: 助～为乐 take pleasure in helping people/ 别小看～! Don't look down on people! ⑤ personality; character: 他～很好。He's a very nice man./ 为～公正 upright in character ⑥ state of one's health; how one feels: 这几天我～不大舒服。I haven't been feeling well for several days./ 送到医院,～已经昏迷过去了。When the patient was taken to hospital, he had already lost consciousness. ⑦ everybody; each; all: ～手一册。Everyone has a copy./ ～所共知 be known to all (或 everybody) ⑧ manpower; hand: 我们这里正缺～。We are shorthanded at the moment.

【人本主义】 rénběnzhǔyì 〈哲〉 humanism

【人不为己,天诛地灭】 rén bù wèi jǐ, tiānzhū-dìmiè unless a man looks out for himself, Heaven and Earth will destroy him; everyone for himself and the devil take the hindmost

【人才】 réncái ① a person of ability; a talented person; talent; qualified personnel: 难得的～ a person of extraordinary ability/ 科技～ qualified scientists and technicians/ ～辈出 people of talent coming forth in large numbers/ ～济济 a galaxy of talent ② 〈口〉 handsome appearance: 一表～ a man of striking appearance

【人称】 rénchēng 〈语〉 person: 第一～ the first person/ 不定～ indefinite person ◇ ～代词 personal pronoun

【人次】 réncì person-time: 参观展览会的总共约有二十万～。Admissions to the exhibition totalled about two hundred thousand.

【人大】 Réndà 〈简〉(全国人民代表大会) the National People's Congress ◇ ～常委会 the Standing Committee of the National People's Congress/ ～代表 deputy to the National People's Congress

【人道】 réndào ① humanity; human sympathy ② human; humane: 不～ inhuman ◇ ～主义 humanitarianism

【人地生疏】 rén-dì shēngshū be unfamiliar with the place and the people; be a complete stranger

【人丁】 réndīng population; number of people in a family: ～兴旺 have a growing family; have a flourishing population

【人定胜天】 rén dìng shèng tiān man can conquer nature; man will triumph over nature

【人堆儿】 rénduīr 〈口〉 crowd

【人贩子】 rénfànzi trader in human beings

【人防】 rénfáng 〈简〉(人民防空) people's air defence; civil air defence

【人粪尿】 rénfènniào 〈农〉 night soil; human wastes (或 excrement)

【人浮于事】 rén fú yú shì have more hands than needed; be overstaffed

【人格】 réngé ① personality; character; moral quality: ～高尚 have a noble character; have moral integrity ② human dignity ◇ ～化 personification

【人工】 réngōng ① man-made; artificial: ～湖 man-made lake/ ～降雨 artificial rainfall ② manual work; work done by hand: 抽水机坏了,只好用～车水。We had to move water by a chain pump because the electric pump had broken down. ③ manpower; man-day: 修建这条渠道不需要很多～。It won't take a lot of manpower to construct this irrigation canal./ 修这所房子用了多少～? How many man-days were put in on repairing the house?
◇ ～繁殖〈农〉 artificial propagation/ ～放顶〈矿〉 artificial caving/ ～孵化 artificial incubation/ ～更新〈林〉 artificial regeneration/ ～合成蛋白质 synthetic protein/ ～合成结晶胰岛素 synthetic crystalline insulin/ ～呼吸 artificial respiration/ ～降水 artificial precipitation/ ～降雨装置 artificial rain device; sprinkler/ ～流产 induced abortion/ ～肾 artificial kidney/ ～授粉〈农〉 artificial pollination/ ～授精〈牧〉 artificial insemination/ ～心肺机 heart-lung machine/ ～选择〈生〉 artificial selection

【人公里】 réngōnglǐ 〈交〉 passenger-kilometre

【人海】 rénhǎi a sea of faces; a huge crowd (of people)

【人和】 rénhé support of the people; unity and coordination within one's own ranks

【人欢马叫】 rénhuān-mǎjiào people bustling and horses neighing — a busy, prosperous country scene

【人寰】 rénhuán 〈书〉 man's world; the world

【人迹】 rénjì human footmarks (或 footprints); traces of human presence: ～罕至的地区 an untraversed region

【人家】 rénjiā ① household: 村子里有多少户～? How many households are there in the village? ② family: 勤俭～ an industrious and frugal family ③ *fiancé's* family: 她有了～儿了。She is engaged to be married.

【人家】 rénjia ①〔指自己或某人以外的人〕: ～能做到的,我们也能做到。If other people can do it, so can we. 或 What other people can do we can do, too./ ～都这么说。That's what everybody says. ②〔指某个人或某些人〕: 把信给～送去。Take the letter to him (her, them)./ ～解放军对咱们贫下中农多好啊! How kind the PLA men are to us poor and lower-middle peasants! ③〔指说话者本人〕: ～等你半天了。I've been waiting for you for quite a while./ 把～吓了一大跳。You gave me quite a fright.

【人间】 rénjiān man's world; the world: ～地狱 a hell on earth/ ～奇迹 a miracle

【人杰】 rénjié an outstanding personality

【人孔】 rénkǒng 〈建〉 manhole

【人口】 rénkǒu ① population: ～稠密的地区 densely populated area; thickly inhabited district/ ～众多(稀少) have a very large (a sparse) population ② number of people in a family: 他们家～不多。There aren't many people in their family.
◇ ～结构 population structure/ ～密度 density of population/ ～普查 census/ ～统计 vital statistics/ ～增长 population growth

【人困马乏】 rénkùn-mǎfá the men weary, their steeds spent — the entire force was exhausted

【人类】 rénlèi mankind; humanity: ～起源 the origin of mankind; the origin of the human species/ ～解放事业 the emancipation of mankind/ ～征服自然的斗争 man's struggle to conquer nature ◇ ～学 anthropology

【人力】 rénlì manpower; labour power: ～资源 human resources

【人力车】 rénlìchē ① a two-wheeled vehicle drawn by man ②〈旧〉 rickshaw

【人流】 rénliú stream of people

【人伦】 rénlún human relations (according to feudal ethics)

【人马】 rénmǎ forces; troops: 全部～已安全渡江。All the troops have crossed the river safely./ 大队～随后就到。The main force will arrive soon.

【人马座】 rénmǎzuò 〈天〉 Sagittarius

【人们】 rénmen people; men; the public: 草原上的～ people of the grasslands

【人面兽心】 rénmiàn-shòuxīn have the face of a man but the heart of a beast — a beast in human shape

【人民】 rénmín the people
◇ ～币 Renminbi (RMB)/ ～大会堂 the Great Hall of the People/ ～代表大会 people's congress/ ～法院 people's court/ ～法院院长 president of the people's court/ ～防空 people's air defence; civil air defence/ ～公社 people's commune/ ～检察院 people's procuratorate/ ～检察院检察长 chief procurator of the people's procuratorate/ ～警察 the people's police/ ～来信 letters from the masses/ ～民主专政 people's democratic dictatorship/ ～内部矛盾 contradictions among the people/ ～陪审员〈法〉 people's assessor/ ～勤务员 servant of the people/ ～群众 the masses/ ～团体 mass organization; people's organization/ ～武装部 people's armed forces department (of a commune, county, etc.)/ ～性 affinity to the people/ ～英雄纪念碑 the Monument to the People's Heroes/ ～战争 people's war/ ～政府 the People's Government

【人命】 rénmìng human life: ～案子 a case of homicide or manslaughter/ ～关天。A case involving human life is to be treated with the utmost care.

【人莫予毒】 rén mò yú dú no one dare harm me — an arrogant boast

【人怕出名猪怕壮】 rén pà chūmíng zhū pà zhuàng fame portends trouble for men just as fattening does for pigs

【人品】 rénpǐn ① moral standing; moral quality; character: ～很好 be a person of excellent character ②〈口〉 looks; bearing

【人情】 rénqíng ① human feelings; human sympathy; sensibilities: 不近～ not amenable to reason; unreasonable/ 不同的阶级有不同的～。Different classes have different feelings. ② human relationship: ～练达 experienced in the ways of the world/ ～之常 natural and normal ③ favour: 做个～ do sb. a favour ④ gift; present: 送～ send gifts; make a gift of sth. ◇ ～味 human touch; human interest

【人情世故】 rénqíng-shìgù worldly wisdom: 不懂～ not know the ways of the world

【人权】 rénquán human rights; rights of man

【人权宣言】 Rénquán Xuānyán ①(法国) Declaration of the Rights of Man and of the Citizen (1789) ②(联合国) Declaration of Human Rights

【人群】 rénqún crowd; throng; multitude

【人人】 rénrén everybody; everyone

【人山人海】 rénshān-rénhǎi huge crowds of people; a sea of people: 广场上～。The square was a sea of people.

【人身】 rénshēn living body of a human being; person
◇ ～安全 personal safety/ ～不可侵犯 inviolability of the person/ ～攻击 personal attack/ ～事故 personal injury caused by an accident/ ～自由 freedom of person; personal freedom

【人参】 rénshēn ginseng

【人生】 rénshēng life ◇ ～观 outlook on life/ ～哲学 philosophy of life

【人声】 rénshēng voice: 远处传来～。Voices came from afar. 或 Voices were heard in the distance./ ～嘈杂 a confusion of voices/ ～鼎沸 a hubbub of voices

【人士】 rénshì personage; public figure: 爱国～ patriotic personage/ 友好～ friendly personality/ 官方～ official quarters/ 体育界～ figures in the sports world / 文艺界～ people of literary and art circles/ 消息灵通～ informed sources/ 知名～ well-known figures; celebrities

【人世】 rénshì this world; the world: ～沧桑 tremendous changes in the world/ 不在～ be no longer living; be no longer in the land of the living

【人事】 rénshì ① human affairs; occurrences in human life ② personnel matters: ～调动 transfer of personnel/ ～更迭 change of personnel ③ ways of the world: 不懂～ not know the ways of the world ④ consciousness of the outside world: 不省～ lose consciousness ⑤ what is humanly possible: 尽～ do what is humanly possible; do one's best
◇ ～处 personnel division/ ～档案 personal file (或 dossier)/ ～关系 organizational affiliation/ ～制度 personnel system

【人手】 rénshǒu manpower; hand: ～太少 short of hands; shorthanded

【人寿年丰】 rénshòu-niánfēng the land yields good harvests and the people enjoy good health

【人丝斜纹绸】 rénsī xiéwénchóu 〈纺〉 rayon twill

【人体】 réntǐ human body ◇ ～模型 manikin

【人同此心,心同此理】 rén tóng cǐ xīn, xīn tóng cǐ lǐ everybody feels the same about this

【人头】 réntóu ① the number of people: 按～分 distribute according to the number of people ② relations with people: ～熟 know a lot of people ③ 〈方〉 moral quality; character: ～儿次 be not much of a person ◇ ～税〈旧〉 poll tax; capitation

【人望】 rénwàng 〈书〉 prestige; popularity

【人微言轻】 rénwēi-yánqīng the words of the lowly carry little weight

【人为】 rénwéi artificial; man-made: ～的障碍 an artificially imposed obstacle/ 这些困难完全是～的。These difficulties were purely man-made. ◇ ～地貌〈军〉 culture features/ ～嬗变〈物〉 artificial transmutation

【人为刀俎,我为鱼肉】 rén wéi dāo-zǔ, wǒ wéi yú-ròu be meat on sb.'s chopping block — be at sb.'s mercy

【人文科学】 rénwén kēxué the humanities; humane studies

【人文主义】 rénwénzhǔyì humanism

【人物】 rénwù ① figure; personage: 领袖～ a leading personage; a leading public figure/ 英雄～ a heroic figure; a hero or heroine/ 历史上的伟大～ great historic figures/ 大～ a big shot/ 小～ a nobody; a small potato/ 杰出的～ an outstanding personage ② person in literature; character: 典型～ typical character/ ～塑造 characterization
◇ ～表 characters (in a play or novel)/ ～画 figure painting

【人像】 rénxiàng portrait; image; figure ◇ ～靶 silhouette target

【人心】 rénxīn popular feeling; public feeling; the will of the people: 得～ have the support of the people; enjoy popular support/ 不得～ go against the will of the people; be unpopular/ ～丧尽 lose (或 forfeit) all popular sympathy/ 深入～ strike root in the hearts of the people/ 振奋～ boost popular morale/ 大快～ most gratifying to the people; to the great satisfaction of the people/ 收买～ curry favour with the public/ 这是～所向,大势所趋。This accords with the will of the people and the general trend of events.

【人行道】 rénxíngdào pavement; sidewalk

【人行横道】 rénxíng héngdào pedestrian crosswalk; pedestrian crossing

【人性】 rénxìng human nature; humanity: 具体的～ human nature in the concrete/ 灭绝～ most barbarous; utterly inhuman/ 在阶级社会里,没有什么超阶级的～。In class society there is no human nature above classes.

【人性】 rénxing normal human feelings; reason: 不通～ unfeeling and unreasonable

【人性论】 rénxìnglùn the theory of human nature — a fallacy put forward by the landlord class and the bourgeoisie, which denies the class character of human nature

【人选】 rénxuǎn person selected; choice of persons: 物色适当～ try to find a suitable person (for a job)/ 决定秘书长的～ decide who is to be secretary-general

【人烟】 rényān signs of human habitation: ～稀少(稠密) be sparsely (densely) populated/ 没有～ uninhabited; without a trace of human habitation

【人言可畏】 rényán kě wèi gossip is a fearful thing

【人仰马翻】 rényǎng-mǎfān men and horses thrown off their feet — utterly routed

【人影儿】 rényǐngr ① the shadow of a human figure ② the trace of a person's presence; figure: 她看见一个～在黑暗中消失了。She caught sight of a figure disappearing into the darkness./ 我等了半天,连个～也不见。I waited a long time but not a soul turned up.

【人员】 rényuán personnel; staff: 全体～ the entire personnel; the whole staff/ 党政工作～ Party and government personnel/ 机关工作～ office workers/ 技术～ technical personnel/ ～不足 understaffed; undermanned

【人缘儿】 rényuánr relations with people; popularity: ～好 be very popular; enjoy great popularity

【人云亦云】 rén yún yì yún echo the views of others; parrot

【人造】 rénzào man-made; artificial; imitation
◇ ～宝石 imitation jewel/ ～冰 artificial ice/ ～革 imitation (或 artificial) leather; leatherette/ ～棉 staple rayon/ ～丝 artificial silk; rayon/ ～卫星 man-made satellite/ ～纤维 man-made fibre/ ～橡胶 artificial rubber; synthetic rubber/ ～羊毛 artificial wool

【人证】 rénzhèng 〈法〉 testimony of a witness ◇ ～物证 human testimony and material evidence

【人之常情】 rén zhī chángqíng the way of the world; what is natural and normal (in human relationships)

【人质】 rénzhì hostage

【人中】 rénzhōng philtrum

【人种】 rénzhǒng ethnic group; race ◇ ～学 ethnology

【人字呢】 rénzìní 〈纺〉 herringbone

**壬** rén the ninth of the ten Heavenly Stems

**仁** rén ① benevolence; kindheartedness; humanity: ～政 policy of benevolence; benevolent government ② sensitive: 麻木不～ insensitive; apathetic ③ kernel: 核桃～ walnut kernel; walnut meat/ 花生～ shelled peanuts/ 虾～ shelled shrimps; shrimp meat

【仁爱】 rén'ài kindheartedness

【仁慈】 réncí benevolent; merciful; kind: 对敌人～就是对人民残忍。Mercy to the enemy means cruelty to the people.

【仁人志士】 rénrén-zhìshì people with lofty ideals

【仁兄】 rénxiōng 〔旧时敬词,多用于书信〕 my dear friend

【仁义道德】 rényì-dàodé humanity, justice and virtue; virtue and morality: 撕下剥削阶级～的假面具 tear off the exploiting classes' mask of humanity, justice and virtue

【仁者见仁,智者见智】 rénzhě jiàn rén, zhìzhě jiàn zhì the benevolent see benevolence and the wise see wisdom — different people have different views

【仁政】 rénzhèng policy of benevolence; benevolent government: 我们对反动派绝不施~。We definitely do not apply a policy of benevolence to the reactionaries.

【仁至义尽】 rénzhì-yìjìn do everything called for by humanity and duty; do what is humanly possible to help; show extreme forbearance: 我们对这些人,真可谓做到了~。We have really shown the utmost tolerance and patience towards these people.

**任** Rén a surname
另见 rèn

## rěn

**忍** rěn ① bear; endure; tolerate; put up with: 他~着剧痛,继续工作。He continued to work despite the intense pain./ ~饥挨饿 endure the torments of hunger/ ~着眼泪 hold back one's tears/ 是可~,孰不可~? If this can be tolerated, what cannot? ② be hardhearted enough to; have the heart to: 残~ cruel; ruthless/ 于心不~ not have the heart to

【忍不住】 rěnbuzhù unable to bear (或 endure); cannot help (doing sth.): 他痒得几乎~了。The itching was almost more than he could stand./ 她~掉下了眼泪。She couldn't hold back her tears.

【忍冬】 rěndōng 〈植〉 honeysuckle

【忍俊不禁】 rěnjùn bùjìn cannot help laughing

【忍耐】 rěnnài exercise patience; exercise restraint; restrain oneself

【忍气吞声】 rěnqì-tūnshēng swallow an insult; submit to humiliation

【忍让】 rěnràng exercise forbearance; be forbearing and conciliatory

【忍辱负重】 rěn rǔ fù zhòng endure humiliation in order to carry out an important mission

【忍受】 rěnshòu bear; endure; stand: ~艰难困苦 endure hardships/ 热得难以~ unbearably hot

【忍痛】 rěntòng very reluctantly: ~割爱 part reluctantly with what one treasures/ ~牺牲 reluctantly give up

【忍无可忍】 rěn wú kě rěn be driven beyond (the limits of) forbearance; come to the end of one's patience

【忍心】 rěnxīn have the heart to; be hardhearted enough to: 他不~拒绝他们的要求。He didn't have the heart to (或 couldn't bear to) turn down their request.

**荏** rěn ①〈书〉 weak; weak-kneed: 色厉内~ fierce of mien but faint of heart; threatening in manner but cowardly at heart ②〈植〉 common perilla (*Perilla frutescens*)

【荏苒】 rěnrǎn 〈书〉 (of time) elapse quickly or imperceptibly; slip by: 光阴~,转瞬又是一年。Time zipped by and the year was soon over.

**稔** rěn 〈书〉 ① harvest: 丰~ bumper harvest / 一年两~ two crops a year ② be familiar with sb.: ~知 know sb. quite well/ 素~have long been familiar with sb.

## rèn

**刃** rèn ① the edge of a knife, sword, etc.; blade: 刀~ knife blade ② sword; knife: 利~ sharp sword/ 白~战 bayonet fighting ③ kill with a sword or knife: 手~ stab sb. to death; kill with one's own hand

【刃具】 rènjù 〈机〉 cutting tool

**认** rèn ① recognize; know; make out; identify: ~出某人 identify a person; recognize a person/ ~敌为友 take a foe for a friend/ 自己的东西,自己来~。Come and pick out your own things./ 他的字真难~。His handwriting is barely legible. 或 His handwriting is hard to read. ② enter into a certain relationship with; adopt: ~师傅 apprentice oneself to sb./ ~她作闺女 adopt her as a daughter ③ admit; recognize; own: 公~ be generally acknowledged (或 recognized)/ ~个不是 offer an apology; apologize/ 承~ admit; recognize/ 否~ deny ④ undertake to do sth.: ~捐五十元 undertake to contribute 50 *yuan*; subscribe 50 *yuan* ⑤ accept as unavoidable; resign oneself to: 这东西一定得买,价钱贵一点我也~了。 I simply must buy it, even if I have to pay a little more for it.

【认错】 rèncuò acknowledge a mistake; admit a fault; make an apology

【认得】 rènde know; recognize: 这位同志你~吗? Do you know this comrade?/ 这地方我已经不~了。I can no longer recognize the place./ 你~回家的路吗? Can you find your way home?

【认定】 rèndìng ① firmly believe; maintain; hold: 马克思主义者~,矛盾存在于一切事物的发展过程中。Marxists maintain that contradiction exists in the process of development of all things. ② set one's mind on: 既然~了目标,就要坚持不懈地干下去。Now that you've set your mind on the goal, you must go through with the task.

【认购】 rèngòu offer to buy; subscribe: ~公债 subscribe for bonds

【认可】 rènkě approve: 得到领导的~ be approved by the leadership

【认领】 rènlǐng claim: 拾得钱包一个,希望失主前来~。Found a purse. Will the owner please come to claim it.

【认清】 rènqīng see clearly; recognize; get a clear understanding of: ~形势 get a clear understanding of the situation/ ~问题的性质 grasp the nature of the problem

【认生】 rènshēng (of a child) be shy with strangers

【认识】 rènshi ① know; understand; recognize: 你在哪儿~她的? Where did you get to know her?/ ~世界,改造世界 understand the world and change it/ ~自己的错误 see (或 realize) one's mistake/ 正确~当前的形势 have a correct understanding of the current situation ② understanding; knowledge; cognition: 感性(理性)~ perceptual (rational) knowledge/ 我们都谈了对这件事的~。We all said what we thought about the matter.
◇ ~过程 process of cognition/ ~论 theory of knowledge; epistemology/ ~能力 cognitive ability/ ~水平 level of understanding

【认输】 rènshū admit defeat; throw in (或 up) the sponge; give up

【认为】 rènwéi think; consider; hold; deem: 大家~这个建议是可行的。We all think (或 consider) this proposal feasible./ 你~怎样? What do you think of it?/ 这件事我们~有必要跟你们说清楚。We deem it neccessary to make this clear to you./ 你~这是真的吗? Do you believe it to be true?/ 我们~,国家不分大小,应该一律平等。We hold that all nations, big or small, should be equal./ 我们~民主是手段,而不是目的。We regard democracy as a means, not an end.

【认贼作父】 rèn zéi zuò fù take the foe for one's father; regard the enemy as kith and kin

【认帐】 rènzhàng acknowledge a debt (或 an account); admit what one has said or done: 错了就要～。If you're wrong, you should admit it./ 自己说的话，怎么不～? How can you go back upon your word?
【认真】 rènzhēn ① conscientious; earnest; serious: ～的自我批评 an earnest self-criticism/ ～执行党的政策 carry out the Party's policies conscientiously/ 进行～的研究 make a serious study ② take seriously; take to heart: 我说着玩儿的，他就～了。I was only joking, but he took it to heart.
【认证】 rènzhèng 〈法〉 attestation; authentication
【认字】 rènzì know or learn how to read: 我这个旧社会的文盲，今天也～了。I was an illiterate in the old society, but now I can read.
【认罪】 rènzuì admit one's guilt; plead guilty

**仞** rèn an ancient measure of length equal to seven or eight *chi* (尺)

**任** rèn ① appoint: 新～的厂长 the newly appointed director of the factory ② assume a post; take up a job: 他～教多年了。He has been a teacher for many years. ③ official post; office: 上～ take up an official post; assume office/ 离～ leave office/ 就～ assume office/ ～满 expiration of one's term of office/ ～内 during one's term (或 tenure) of office ④〈量〉〔用于担任官职的次数〕: 做过两～大使 have twice been ambassador ⑤ let; allow; give free rein to: ～其自流 let things run their course/ 资产阶级思想决不能～其泛滥。Bourgeois ideas must not be allowed to spread unchecked./ ～你挑选一个。Choose any one you like. ⑥ no matter (how, what, etc.): ～我们怎样劝说，他也不听。No matter how hard we tried to persuade him, he wouldn't listen./ ～谁也不能违反这些规定。No one is allowed to break the regulations, whoever he is.
另见 Rén
【任便】 rènbiàn as you like; as you see fit: 你来不来～。You may come or not as you see fit.
【任何】 rènhé any; whichever; whatever: 我们能战胜～困难。We can overcome any difficulty./ 没有～理由拒绝这个建议。There's no reason whatsoever to turn down this suggestion.
【任劳任怨】 rènláo-rènyuàn work hard and not be upset by criticism; willingly bear the burden of ffice
【任免】 rèn-miǎn appoint and remove (或 dismiss): 国务院依照法律的规定～行政人员。The State Council appoints and removes administrative personnel according to the provisions of the law. ◇ ～事项 appointments and removals
【任命】 rènmìng appoint: ～他为校长 appoint him president (of the university)
【任凭】 rènpíng ① at one's convenience; at one's discretion: 这事不能～他一人决定。This shouldn't be left entirely to his discretion. ② no matter (how, what, etc.): ～问题多复杂，我们也能搞清楚。We can solve the problem no matter how complicated it is./ ～你怎样说，事实总是事实。Whatever you say, facts are facts./ ～什么挫折都不能使他动摇。No setbacks can make him waver.
【任凭风浪起，稳坐钓鱼船】 rènpíng fēnglàng qǐ, wěn zuò diàoyúchuán sit tight in the fishing boat despite the rising wind and waves — hold one's ground despite pressure or opposition
【任期】 rènqī term of office; tenure of office: 全国人民代表大会每届～五年。The National People's Congress is elected for a term of five years.
【任情】 rènqíng let oneself go; to one's heart's content; as much as one likes
【任人唯亲】 rèn rén wéi qīn appoint people by favouritism
【任人唯贤】 rèn rén wéi xián appoint people on their merits; appoint people according to their political integrity and ability
【任务】 rènwu assignment; mission; task; job: 接受～ receive (或 accept) an assignment/ 我们保证完成～。We guarantee to fulfil (或 complete) our mission./ ～重，时间紧，The task is hard and we are pressed for time./ 这个～就交给我吧！Give this job to me./ 担负艰巨的～ shoulder heavy responsibilities ◇ ～观点 get-it-over-and-done-with attitude; perfunctory attitude
【任性】 rènxìng wilful; self-willed; wayward; headstrong
【任意】 rènyì wantonly; arbitrarily; wilfully: ～诬蔑 wantonly vilify/ ～捏造事实 indulge in pure fabrication/ ～歪曲历史 wilfully distort history/ ～掠夺别国资源 wantonly plunder other countries' resources/ ～欺负别人 bully people at will ◇ ～常数〈数〉 arbitrary constant/ ～球（足球）free kick; (手球) free throw
【任用】 rènyòng appoint; assign sb. to a post
【任职】 rènzhí hold a post; be in office: 在外交部～ work (或 hold a post) in the Ministry of Foreign Affairs/ 在～期间 during one's tenure of office
【任重道远】 rènzhòng-dàoyuǎn the burden is heavy and the road is long — shoulder heavy responsibilities

**妊** rèn be pregnant
【妊妇】 rènfù pregnant woman
【妊娠】 rènshēn gestation; pregnancy: 输卵管～ tubal pregnancy ◇ ～期 gestational period

**纫** rèn ① sew; stitch ② thread (a needle)

**韧** rèn pliable but strong; tenacious; tough
【韧带】 rèndài 〈生理〉 ligament
【韧皮部】 rènpíbù 〈植〉 bast; phloem
【韧皮纤维】 rènpí xiānwéi 〈植〉 bast fibre
【韧性】 rènxìng toughness; tenacity

**轫** rèn 见"发轫" fārèn

**饪** rèn 见"烹饪" pēngrèn

**葚** rèn 见"桑葚儿" sāngrènr
另见 shèn

## rēng

**扔** rēng ① throw; toss; cast: ～手榴弹 throw a hand grenade/ ～球 throw (或 toss) a ball/ 敌机～了几颗炸弹。The enemy plane dropped a few bombs. ② throw away; cast aside: 把它～了吧。Throw it away./ 被～进历史的垃圾堆 be relegated to (或 tossed on to) the rubbish heap of history/ 这事他早就～在脖子后边了。He'd clean forgotten about it.
【扔下】 rēngxia abandon; put aside; leave behind: 敌人～武器逃跑了。The enemy dropped their weapons and took to their heels./ 这工作我不能～不管。I can't leave the work half-finished.

## réng

**仍** réng ① remain: 一～其旧 remain the same; follow the beaten track ② 〈副〉 still; yet: ～有效力 be still effective; be still in force/ ～未痊愈 have not yet recovered/ ～须努力 must continue to make efforts

【仍旧】 réngjiù ① remain the same ②〈副〉still; yet: 他虽然遇到许多挫折，可是意志～那样坚强。His determination remains as strong as ever despite all the setbacks he has encountered./ 他～是十年前的老样子。After ten years, he still looked the same./ 有些问题～没有解决。Some problems remain to be solved.

【仍然】 réngrán 〈副〉still; yet

## rì

**日** rì ① sun: ～出 sunrise/ ～落 sunset ② daytime; day: ～～夜夜 day and night; night and day ③ day: 今～ today/ 多～不见了，你好吗？Haven't seen you for a long time. How are you?/ 我们改～再谈。Let's talk about it some other time. ④ daily; every day; with each passing day: 产量～增。Output is going up every day./ 天气～暖。It's getting warmer and warmer./ 第三世界国家在国际事务中的作用～趋重要。The third world countries are playing an increasingly important role in world affairs. ⑤ time: 春～ springtime; spring/ 来～ the days to come; the future

【日班】 rìbān day shift: 上～ be on the day shift

【日报】 rìbào daily paper; daily: 《人民日报》*Renmin Ribao* (the *People's Daily*)

【日本】 Rìběn Japan ◇ ～人 Japanese/ ～海 the Sea of Japan

【日薄西山】 rì bó xīshān the sun is setting beyond the western hills — declining rapidly; nearing one's end

【日不暇给】 rì bù xiá jǐ be fully occupied every day

【日常】 rìcháng day-to-day; everyday; daily: ～工作 day-to-day work; routine duties/ ～生活 everyday life; daily life/ ～用语 words and expressions for everyday use

【日场】 rìchǎng day show; daytime performance; matinée

【日程】 rìchéng programme; schedule: 访问～ itinerary of a visit/ 工作～ work schedule; programme of work/ 提到～上来 place (或 put) sth. on the order of the day ◇ ～表 schedule

【日戳】 rìchuō ① date stamp; dater ② datemark

【日耳曼人】 Rì'ěrmànrén Germanic people

【日珥】 rì'ěr 〈天〉prominence

【日工】 rìgōng ① daywork ② day labour ③ day labourer

【日光】 rìguāng sunlight; sunbeam ◇ ～浴 sunbath/ ～浴室 solarium/ ～疗法 heliotherapy

【日光灯】 rìguāngdēng fluorescent lamp; daylight lamp ◇ ～起动器 fluorescent lamp starter/ ～镇流器 fluorescent lamp ballast

【日晷】 rìguǐ sundial 又作"日规"

【日后】 rìhòu in the future; in days to come: 这东西～可能用得着。We may find it useful in future. 或 It may come in handy someday.

【日积月累】 rìjī-yuèlěi accumulate over a long period: 每天学一点，～也能学不少。Learn a little every day and in time you'll have learned a lot.

【日记】 rìjì diary: 记～ keep a diary/ 工作～ work diary; daily account of one's work ◇ ～本 diary

【日记帐】 rìjìzhàng journal; daybook

【日间】 rìjiān in the daytime; during the day

【日见】 rìjiàn with each passing day; day by day: ～好转 get better every day/ ～衰败 decline day by day

【日渐】 rìjiàn with each passing day; day by day: ～强壮 get stronger and stronger

【日界线】 rìjièxiàn 〈天〉date line

【日久】 rìjiǔ with the passing of time; in (the) course of time: ～天长 in (the) course of time; as the years go by

【日久见人心】 rìjiǔ jiàn rénxīn time reveals a person's heart; it takes time to know a person

【日来】 rìlái recently; of late; in the past few days

【日理万机】 rì lǐ wànjī attend to numerous affairs of state every day; be occupied with a myriad of state affairs

【日历】 rìlì calendar ◇ ～手表 calendar watch

【日冕】 rìmiǎn 〈天〉(solar) corona ◇ ～仪 coronagraph

【日暮途穷】 rìmù-túqióng the day is waning and the road is ending — approaching the end of one's days: 帝国主义已～。Imperialism is on its last legs (或 at the end of its rope).

【日内】 rìnèi in a few days; in a day or two; in a couple of days

【日内瓦】 Rìnèiwǎ Geneva

【日期】 rìqī date: 起程的～定了吗？Has the departure date been fixed?/ 信上的～是六月二日。The letter is dated June 2.

【日前】 rìqián a few days ago; the other day

【日趋】 rìqū with each passing day; gradually; day by day: 市场～繁荣。The market is becoming brisker day by day.

【日上三竿】 rì shàng sān gān the sun is three poles high — it's late in the morning (referring to getting up late)

【日射】 rìshè 〈气〉insolation ◇ ～病〈医〉sunstroke; insolation/ ～表 actinometer

【日食】 rìshí 〈天〉solar eclipse: 日环食 annular eclipse/ 日偏食 partial solar eclipse/ 日全食 total solar eclipse

【日头】 rìtou 〈方〉sun

【日托】 rìtuō day care: 这个托儿所只有～。This is only a day nursery. ◇ ～托儿所 day nursery

【日心说】 rìxīnshuō 〈天〉heliocentric theory

【日新月异】 rìxīn-yuèyì change with each passing day: 我国的社会主义建设正在～地向前发展。Our socialist construction is forging ahead and bringing about changes day after day.

【日夜】 rì-yè day and night; night and day; round the clock: ～警惕地守卫着边疆 vigilantly guard the borders day and night/ 我们厂～三班倒。Our factory operates round the clock on three shifts. ◇ ～商店 a shop open night and day; a round-the-clock shop; a day-and-night-service shop

【日以继夜】 rì yǐ jì yè night and day; round the clock

【日益】 rìyì increasingly; day by day: 矛盾～尖锐。The contradictions are becoming increasingly acute./ 我们的队伍～壮大。Our ranks are growing stronger day by day.

【日用】 rìyòng ① daily expenses ② of everyday use ◇ ～必需品 daily necessities; household necessities/ ～工业品 manufactured goods for daily use/ ～品 articles of everyday use

【日语】 Rìyǔ Japanese (language)

【日元】 rìyuán yen

【日月】 rìyuè life; livelihood: 解放前的～可真不好过啊！What a hard life we had before liberation!

【日月如梭】 rì-yuè rú suō the sun and the moon move back and forth like a shuttle — time flies

【日月星辰】 rì-yuè-xīngchén the sun, the moon and the stars; the heavenly bodies

【日晕】 rìyùn 〈气〉solar halo

【日照】 rìzhào sunshine: 长～植物 long-day plant/ 短～植物 short-day plant ◇ ～计 sunshine recorder/ ～时间 sunshine time

【日志】 rìzhì daily record; journal: 工作～ daily record of work/ 航海～ logbook; log

【日中】 rìzhōng 〈书〉noon; midday

【日子】 rìzi ① day; date: 这个～好不容易盼到了。The day we have been looking forward to has come at long last./ 定

一个～ fix a date ② time: 他走了有些～了。He's been away for some time./ 这些～我校师生在工厂实习。The teachers and students of our school have been doing field work at a factory recently. ③ life; livelihood: 今天我们的～多幸福啊！How happy is our life today!/ 勤俭过～ lead an industrious and frugal life/ 帝国主义者的～越来越不好过。The imperialists are finding the going tougher and tougher. 或 Things are getting harder and harder for the imperialists.

## róng

**戎** róng ①〈书〉army; military affairs: 投笔从～ cast aside the pen to join the army; give up intellectual pursuits for a military career ② (Róng) an ancient name for the peoples in the west ③ (Róng) a surname

【戎马】 róngmǎ〈书〉army horse: ～生涯 army life; military life

【戎装】 róngzhuāng〈书〉martial attire

**荣** róng ① grow luxuriantly; flourish: 欣欣向～ flourishing; thriving; growing luxuriantly/ 春～冬枯 grow in spring and wither in winter ② honour; glory: 引以为～ take it as an honour/ ～立一等功 be cited for meritorious service, first class/ 以艰苦为～ take pride in working under difficult conditions/ 为人民而死，虽死犹～！It is a glorious thing to die for the people. ③ (Róng) a surname

【荣归】 róngguī return in glory

【荣华富贵】 rónghuá-fùguì glory, splendour, wealth and rank; high position and great wealth

【荣获】 rónghuò have the honour to get or win: ～冠军 win the championship/ ～一枚奖章 be awarded a medal/ ～战斗英雄的称号 be awarded the honourable title of combat hero

【荣军】 róngjūn〈简〉(荣誉军人) disabled soldier (wounded in revolutionary war)

【荣辱】 róng-rǔ honour or disgrace

【荣幸】 róngxìng be honoured: 我们应邀访问贵国，感到非常～。We feel greatly honoured by your invitation to visit your country./ 如蒙光临，不胜～。We shall be greatly honoured by your gracious presence./ 今天很～能参加你们的晚会。It is a great honour to be with you at this evening party.

【荣耀】 róngyào honour; glory

【荣誉】 róngyù honour; credit; glory: 为祖国赢得～ win honour for one's country/ 爱护集体的～ cherish the good name of the collective ◇ ～感 sense of honour

【荣誉军人】 róngyù jūnrén disabled soldier (wounded in revolutionary war)

**茸** róng ① (of grass, etc.) fine and soft; downy ② young pilose antler

【茸茸】 róngróng (of grass, hair, etc.) fine, soft and thick; downy: 绿草～ a carpet of green grass

**绒** róng ① fine hair; down: 鸭～ eiderdown ② cloth with a soft nap or pile on one or either side: 丝～ velvet/ 灯芯～ corduroy/ 法兰～ flannel ③ fine floss for embroidery

【绒布】 róngbù flannelette; cotton flannel

【绒花】 rónghuā〈工美〉velvet flowers, birds, etc.

【绒裤】 róngkù sweat pants

【绒毛】 róngmáo ① fine hair; down; villus ②〈纺〉nap; pile

【绒毛膜上皮癌】 róngmáomó shàngpí'ái chorioepithelioma

【绒面革】 róngmiàngé suède (leather)

【绒头绳】 róngtóushéng ① wool (for tying pigtails) ②〈方〉knitting wool

【绒线】 róngxiàn ① floss for embroidery ②〈方〉knitting wool ◇ ～刺绣 crewelwork/ ～衫 woollen sweater

【绒绣】 róngxiù〈工美〉woollen needlepoint tapestry; woollen embroidery ◇ ～地毯 finished needlepoint carpet

【绒衣】 róngyī sweat shirt

**容** róng ① hold; contain: 这个礼堂能～一千人。The auditorium can hold a thousand people./ 可～水三万多立方米的蓄水池 a reservoir with a capacity of over 30,000 cubic metres/ 这座大桥可～四辆卡车并列通行。The bridge can take four lorries abreast. ② tolerate: 宽～ be tolerant ③ permit; allow: 详情～后再告。Permit me to give the details later./ 此事不～耽搁。The matter allows of no delay./ 不～歪曲 brook no distortion/ 不～怀疑 admit of no doubt ④ facial expression: 笑～ a smiling face/ 怒～ an angry look ⑤ appearance; looks: 市～ the appearance (或 look) of a city/ 阵～ lineup; battle array ⑥ (Róng) a surname

【容光焕发】 róngguāng huànfā one's face glowing with health

【容积】 róngjī volume ◇ ～吨 measurement ton

【容量】 róngliàng capacity

【容貌】 róngmào appearance; looks

【容纳】 róngnà hold; have a capacity of; accommodate: 首都体育馆能～一万八千观众。The Capital Stadium has a seating capacity of 18,000./ 他不能～不同意见。He can't tolerate dissenting views.

【容器】 róngqì container; vessel

【容情】 róngqíng〔多用于否定式〕show mercy: 我们对反革命分子决不～。We never show mercy to counterrevolutionaries.

【容人】 róngrén tolerant towards others; magnanimous; broad-minded

【容忍】 róngrěn tolerate; put up with; condone: 我们不能～这种浪费现象。We cannot tolerate such waste.

【容身】 róngshēn shelter oneself: 无～之地。There is no place for one in society.

【容限】 róngxiàn〈物〉tolerance; allowance: 光学～ optical tolerance

【容许】 róngxǔ ① tolerate; permit; allow: 情况不～我们再等待了。In such circumstances we can't afford to wait any longer./ 可以～你有三天的准备时间。You'll be allowed three days to prepare./ 我们不～任何外来干涉。We will brook no outside interference. ② possibly; perhaps: 此类事件，十年前～有之。Such things might possibly have happened ten years ago. ◇ ～负载〈电〉allowable load/ ～收缩量 shrinkage allowance

【容颜】 róngyán appearance; looks

【容易】 róngyì ① easy: 这台机床～操作。This lathe is easy to operate./ 说起来～做起来难。It's easier said than done./ 这种草药很～弄到。This medicinal herb is easy to come by. ② easily; likely; liable; apt: 他～生病。He often gets ill./ 这～引起误会。This is liable to cause misunderstanding./ 人们～把这两个问题混淆起来。People are apt to confuse the two issues.

【容重】 róngzhòng〈水〉unit weight

**嵘** róng 见"峥嵘" zhēngróng

**溶** róng dissolve: 樟脑～于酒精而不～于水。Camphor dissolves in alcohol, but not in water.

【溶化】 rónghuà ① dissolve: 盐在水里很快就～。Salt dissolves quickly in water. ② 见"融化" rónghuà

【溶剂】 róngjì〈化〉solvent

【溶胶】 róngjiāo〈化〉sol

【溶解】 róngjiě dissolve: 这种物质在水中不会～。This substance does not dissolve in water.
◇ ～度 solubility/ ～热 heat of solution/ ～物 dissolved matter
【溶菌素】 róngjūnsù 〈医〉 bacteriolysin
【溶溶】 róngróng 〈书〉 broad: 江水～。The river is broad and gentle.
【溶蚀】 róngshí 〈地〉 corrosion
【溶性油】 róngxìngyóu 〈化〉 soluble oil
【溶血】 róngxuè 〈医〉 haemolysis
【溶液】 róngyè 〈化〉 solution: 实在～ real solution/ 当量～ normal solution
【溶质】 róngzhì 〈化〉 solute

**蓉** róng ①见"芙蓉" fúróng ②(Róng) another name for Chengdu

**熔** róng melt; fuse; smelt
【熔池】 róngchí 〈冶〉 (molten) bath
【熔点】 róngdiǎn 〈物〉 melting (或 fusing, fusion) point
【熔断】 róngduàn 〈电〉 fusing ◇ ～器 fuse (box)
【熔化】 rónghuà melt: 纯铁加热到摄氏 1,535 度就～。Pure iron melts at 1,535°C.
◇ ～炉 melting furnace/ ～期 〈冶〉 melting stage/ ～速率 〈冶〉 melting rate
【熔剂】 róngjì 〈冶〉 flux
【熔解】 róngjiě 〈物〉 fuse; fusion ◇ ～热 heat of fusion
【熔炼】 róngliàn smelt: 闪速～ flash smelting ◇ ～炉 smelting furnace
【熔炉】 rónglú ① smelting furnace ② crucible; furnace: 革命～ the furnace of revolution
【熔融】 róngróng 〈化〉 melt ◇ ～纺丝 melting spinning/ ～挤压法 〈化纤〉 extrusion by melting
【熔岩】 róngyán 〈地〉 lava
【熔铸】 róngzhù founding; casting ◇ ～工 smelter

**榕** róng ①〈植〉 small-fruited fig tree; banyan ②(Róng) another name for Fuzhou

**蝾** róng
【蝾螈】 róngyuán 〈动〉 salamander; newt

**融** róng ① melt; thaw: 春雪易～。Spring snow soon melts. ② blend; fuse; be in harmony: 水乳交～ blend as well as milk and water; be in perfect harmony
【融合】 rónghé mix together; fuse; merge: 铜与锡的～ the fusion of copper and tin
【融化】 rónghuà melt; thaw: 湖上的冰已经～了。The ice on the lake has already melted./ 雪已开始～。The snow is beginning to thaw.
【融会贯通】 rónghuì guàntōng achieve mastery through a comprehensive study of the subject
【融解】 róngjiě melt; thaw
【融洽】 róngqià harmonious; on friendly terms: 干群关系很～。The relations between the cadres and the masses are harmonious.
【融融】 róngróng 〈书〉 ① happy and harmonious: 老战友欢聚一堂,其乐～。When old comrades-in-arms meet, their happiness knows no bounds. ② warm: 春光～。Spring fills the air with warmth.

## rǒng

**冗** rǒng ① superfluous; redundant: ～词 superfluous words ② full of trivial details ③ busyness: 拨～ find time in the midst of one's work
【冗长】 rǒngcháng tediously long; lengthy; long-winded; prolix: ～的讲演 a long and tedious speech
【冗员】 rǒngyuán redundant personnel
【冗杂】 rǒngzá ① (of writing) lengthy and jumbled ② (of affairs) miscellaneous
【冗赘】 rǒngzhuì verbose; diffuse

## róu

**柔** róu ① soft; supple; flexible: ～枝嫩叶 supple twigs and tender leaves ② soften: ～麻 soften jute, hemp, etc. ③ gentle; yielding; mild: 温～ gentle and soft/ ～中有刚 firm but gentle
【柔板】 róubǎn 〈乐〉 *adagio*
【柔道】 róudào *judo*
【柔和】 róuhe soft; gentle; mild: ～的光线 soft light/ ～的声音 a gentle (或 mild) voice; a soft sound/ 颜色～ a soft colour
【柔媚】 róumèi gentle and lovely
【柔嫩】 róunèn tender; delicate: ～的幼芽 tender sprouts
【柔情】 róuqíng tender feelings; tenderness
【柔韧】 róurèn pliable and tough
【柔软】 róuruǎn soft; lithe: ～的垫子 a soft cushion/ ～的动作 lithe movements ◇ ～体操 callisthenics
【柔弱】 róuruò weak; delicate: 身体～ in delicate health; weak; frail
【柔术】 róushù *jujitsu*
【柔顺】 róushùn gentle and agreeable; meek
【柔荑花序】 róuyí huāxù 〈植〉 catkin; ament
【柔鱼】 róuyú squid

**揉** róu rub; knead: 别～眼睛。Don't rub your eyes./ ～一～腿 rub one's legs/ ～面 knead dough/ 把信～成一团 crumple a letter into a ball
【揉搓】 róucuo rub; knead

**糅** róu mix; mingle
【糅合】 róuhé mix; form a mixture (usu. of things which don't blend well)

**蹂** róu
【蹂躏】 róulìn trample on; ravage; make havoc of; devastate: ～别国主权 trample upon the sovereignty of other countries/ 在帝国主义的～下 under the heel of imperialism/ 遭到～ suffer devastation, oppression, outrages, etc.

**鞣** róu tan: ～皮子 tan hides
【鞣料】 róuliào tanning material ◇ ～浸膏 tannin extract
【鞣酸】 róusuān 〈化〉 tannic acid

## ròu

**肉** ròu ① meat; flesh: 瘦～ lean meat/ 肥～ fat meat; fat/ ～制品 meat products/ 猪～ pork/ 牛～ beef/ 羊～ mutton ② pulp; flesh (of fruit): 果～ pulp of fruit/ 桂圆～ longan pulp
【肉饼】 ròubǐng meat pie
【肉搏】 ròubó fight hand-to-hand ◇ ～战 hand-to-nand fight (或 combat); bayonet fighting
【肉垂】 ròuchuí 〈动〉 wattle
【肉苁蓉】 ròucōngróng 〈中药〉 saline cistanche (*Cistanche salsa*)

【肉店】 ròudiàn butcher's (shop)
【肉丁】 ròudīng diced meat: 辣子～ diced pork with hot pepper
【肉冻】 ròudòng meat jelly; aspic: 鸡～ chicken in aspic
【肉豆蔻】 ròudòukòu 〈中药〉 nutmeg
【肉冠】 ròuguān 〈动〉 comb
【肉桂】 ròuguì 〈植〉 Chinese cassia tree
【肉瘤】 ròuliú 〈医〉 sarcoma
【肉麻】 ròumá nauseating; sickening; disgusting: ～的吹捧 fulsome praise
【肉末】 ròumò minced meat; ground meat
【肉排】 ròupái steak
【肉皮】 ròupí pork skin
【肉片】 ròupiàn sliced meat
【肉色】 ròusè yellowish pink
【肉食】 ròushí carnivorous ◇ ～动物 carnivorous animal; carnivore
【肉食】 ròushi meat
【肉丝】 ròusī shredded meat ◇ ～面 noodles with shredded meat
【肉松】 ròusōng dried meat floss
【肉穗花序】 ròusuì huāxù 〈植〉 spadix
【肉汤】 ròutāng broth
【肉体】 ròutǐ the human body; flesh: 消灭地主阶级不是～上消灭地主个人。To eliminate the landlords as a class does not mean to destroy them physically as individuals.
【肉丸子】 ròuwánzi meatball
【肉馅】 ròuxiàn meat stuffing; chopped (或 ground) meat
【肉刑】 ròuxíng corporal punishment
【肉芽】 ròuyá 〈医〉 granulation
【肉眼】 ròuyǎn naked eye: ～看不到 be invisible to the naked eye
【肉欲】 ròuyù carnal desire
【肉汁】 ròuzhī gravy; (meat) juice
【肉中刺】 ròuzhōngcì a thorn in one's flesh
【肉赘】 ròuzhuì wart

## rú

**如** rú ① in compliance with; according to: ～命 in compliance with your instructions ② like; as; as if: 我们革命意志坚～钢。Our revolutionary will is as strong as steel./ ～临大敌 as if faced with a formidable enemy/ ～你所说 as you've said ③〔用于否定〕can compare with; be as good as: 我不～他。I'm not as good as he is. 或 I can't compare with him. ④ for instance; such as; as: 唐朝有很多大诗人，～李白、杜甫、白居易等。The Tang Dynasty produced a host of great poets, such as Li Bai, Du Fu and Bai Juyi. ⑤〈连〉 if: ～处理得当，问题不难解决。The problem will not be difficult to solve, if properly handled. ⑥〈书〉 go to: ～厕 go to the toilet
【如常】 rúcháng as usual: 一切～。Things are as usual.
【如出一辙】 rú chū yī zhé be exactly the same as; be no different from; be cut from the same cloth
【如此】 rúcǐ so; such; in this way; like that: 似乎是～。So it appears./ 理当～。Rightly so./ ～重要的问题应呈报党委批准。Such an important problem should be submitted to the Party committee for approval./ 事已～，后悔也是枉然。Now it's done, regrets are of no avail. 或 It's no use crying over spilt milk./ 情况就是～。That's how things stand./ 农业战线形势大好，其它各条战线也是～。The situation is good on the agricultural front, as it is on the other fronts./ ～等等 and so on and so forth
【如此而已】 rúcǐ éryǐ that's what it all adds up to: ～，岂有他哉！That's all there is to it!
【如次】 rúcì as follows: 其理由～。The reasons are as follows.
【如堕五里雾中】 rú duò wǔlǐwù zhōng as if lost in a thick fog; utterly mystified
【如堕烟海】 rú duò yānhǎi as if lost on a misty sea; all at sea; completely at a loss: 他们不懂得辩证法，结果～，抓不住主要矛盾。They do not know dialectics and the result is that they are all at sea and unable to grasp the principal contradiction.
【如法炮制】 rú fǎ páozhì prepare herbal medicine by the prescribed method — follow a set pattern; follow suit
【如故】 rúgù ① as before: 依然～ remain the same as before; remain one's same old self ② like old friends: 一见～ feel like old friends at the first meeting; hit it off well right from the start
【如果】 rúguǒ 〈连〉 if; in case; in the event of: 你～要来，请事先告诉我。Let me know in advance if you're coming./ 我们～不加强学习，就会跟不上形势。We can't keep abreast of the developing situation unless we study harder./ ～不是他指引，我们就迷路了。If it weren't for him, we would have gone astray.
【如何】 rúhé how; what: 此事～办理？How are we to handle this matter?/ 他不知～是好。He didn't know what to do./ 这个电影你觉得～？How do you like the film? 或 What do you think of the film?
【如虎添翼】 rú hǔ tiān yì like a tiger that has grown wings — with might redoubled
【如火如荼】 rúhuǒ-rútú like a raging fire: 革命斗争～，迅猛发展。The revolutionary struggle is spreading like wildfire.
【如获至宝】 rú huò zhìbǎo as if one had found a treasure
【如饥似渴】 rújī-sìkě as if thirsting or hungering for sth.; eagerly: ～地学习马列主义 study Marxism-Leninism with great eagerness
【如胶似漆】 rújiāo-sìqī stick to each other like glue or lacquer; remain glued to each other; be deeply attached to each other
【如今】 rújīn nowadays; now: ～咱们山村也有了自己的大学生。Now our mountain village has its own college students.
【如来】 Rúlái 〈佛教〉 Tathagata; Buddha
【如狼似虎】 rúláng-sìhǔ as ferocious as wolves and tigers; like cruel beasts of prey
【如雷贯耳】 rú léi guàn ěr reverberate like thunder: 久闻大名，～。Your name has long resounded in my ears.
【如梦初醒】 rú mèng chū xǐng as if awakening from a dream
【如鸟兽散】 rú niǎo-shòu sàn flee helter-skelter; be utterly routed
【如期】 rúqī as scheduled; by the scheduled time; on schedule: 会议将～召开。The conference will be convened as scheduled./ 任务已～完成。The task has been accomplished according to schedule./ 货物已～运到。The goods arrived on schedule.
【如其】 rúqí 〈连〉 if
【如日中天】 rú rì zhōngtiān like the sun at high noon; at the apex (或 zenith) of one's power, career, etc.
【如入无人之境】 rú rù wú rén zhī jìng like entering an unpeopled land — breaking all resistance
【如若】 rúruò 〈连〉 if: ～不信，请拭目以待。If you don't believe it, wait and see./ ～不然 if not; otherwise
【如丧考妣】 rú sàng kǎo-bǐ look as if one had lost one's parents — look utterly wretched
【如上】 rúshàng as above: ～所述 as stated (或 mentioned) above

【如实】 rúshí strictly according to the facts; as things really are: ～地反映情况 report the situation accurately; reflect things as they really are
【如释重负】 rú shì zhòngfù as if relieved of a heavy load
【如数家珍】 rú shǔ jiāzhēn as if enumerating one's family valuables — very familiar with one's subject
【如数】 rúshù exactly the number or amount: ～偿还 pay back in full/ ～到齐 all present and correct
【如汤沃雪】 rú tāng wò xuě like melting snow with hot water — easily done
【如同】 rútóng like; as: 待我们～亲人一样 treat us like their kith and kin
【如下】 rúxià as follows: 这个计划的要点～。The main points of the plan are as follows./ 全文～。The full text follows./ 发表～声明 make the following statement
【如蚁附膻】 rú yǐ fù shān like ants seeking sth. rank-smelling — a swarm of people running after unwholesome things or leaning on influential people for support
【如意】 rúyì ① as one wishes: 很难万事～。You can't expect everything to turn out as you wish./ 称心～ after one's own heart ② *ruyi*, an S-shaped ornamental object, usu. made of jade, formerly a symbol of good luck
【如意算盘】 rúyì suànpan wishful thinking: 打～ indulge in wishful thinking /打乱了他的～ upset his smug calculations
【如影随形】 rú yǐng suí xíng like the shadow following the person — very closely associated with each other
【如鱼得水】 rú yú dé shuǐ feel just like fish in water; be in one's element
【如愿以偿】 rúyuàn yǐ cháng have one's wish fulfilled; achieve what one wishes
【如坐针毡】 rú zuò zhēnzhān feel as if sitting on a bed of nails; be on pins and needles; be on tenterhooks

**茹** rú ①〈书〉eat: ～素 be a vegetarian ② (Rú) a surname
【茹苦含辛】 rúkǔ-hánxīn 见"含辛茹苦" hánxīn-rúkǔ
【茹毛饮血】 rúmáo-yǐnxuè (of primitive man) eat birds and animals raw

**铷** rú 〈化〉rubidium (Rb)

**儒** rú ① (Rú) Confucianism; Confucianist ②〈旧〉scholar; learned man: 腐～ pedantic scholar
【儒艮】 rúgèn 〈动〉dugong
【儒家】 Rújiā the Confucianists (a school of thought in the Spring and Autumn and Warring States Periods 770-221 B.C.); the Confucian school
【儒生】 rúshēng 〈旧〉Confucian scholar

**濡** rú 〈书〉① immerse; moisten: ～笔 dip a writing brush in ink ② linger
【濡染】 rúrǎn immerse; imbue
【濡湿】 rúshī soak; make wet

**薷** rú 见"青香薷" qīngxiāngrú

**嚅** rú 见"嗫嚅" nièrú

**孺** rú child: 妇～ women and children
【孺子】 rúzǐ 〈书〉child

**蠕** rú wriggle; squirm
【蠕虫】 rúchóng worm; helminth ◇ ～学 helminthology
【蠕动】 rúdòng ① wriggle; squirm ②〈生理〉peristalsis
【蠕蠕】 rúrú wriggling; squirming
【蠕形动物】 rúxíng dòngwù Vermes

**颥** rú 见"颞颥" nièrú

## rǔ

**汝** rǔ 〈书〉you: ～辈 you people; you

**乳** rǔ ① breast ② milk: 炼～ condensed milk ③ any milk-like liquid: 豆～ bean milk ④ give birth to: 孳～〈书〉breed; multiply ⑤ newborn (animal); sucking: ～猪 sucking pig; suckling pig
【乳白】 rǔbái milky white; cream colour ◇ ～灯泡 opal bulb/ ～玻璃 opal glass; opalescent glass
【乳钵】 rǔbō mortar
【乳齿】 rǔchǐ milk tooth; deciduous tooth
【乳臭未干】 rǔchòu wèi gān still smell of one's mother's milk — be young and inexperienced; be wet behind the ears
【乳蛾】 rǔ'é 〈中医〉acute tonsillitis
【乳儿】 rǔ'ér nursing infant; suckling
【乳房】 rǔfáng ① breast; mamma ② (of a cow, goat, etc.) udder
【乳化】 rǔhuà 〈化〉emulsification ◇ ～剂 emulsifying agent; emulsifier/ ～原油 emulsified crude oil
【乳化液】 rǔhuàyè 〈化〉emulsion: 水包油～ oil-in-water emulsion/ 油包水～ water-in-oil emulsion
【乳剂】 rǔjì 〈化〉emulsion: 全色～〈摄影〉panchromatic emulsion
【乳胶】 rǔjiāo 〈化〉emulsion ◇ ～漆 emulsion paint; latex paint
【乳疽】 rǔjū 〈中医〉intramammary abscess
【乳酪】 rǔlào cheese
【乳糜】 rǔmí 〈生理〉chyle ◇ ～尿 chyluria
【乳名】 rǔmíng infant name; child's pet name
【乳母】 rǔmǔ wet nurse
【乳牛】 rǔniú dairy cattle; milch cow ◇ ～场 dairy farm
【乳酸】 rǔsuān lactic acid ◇ ～钙 calcium lactate
【乳糖】 rǔtáng milk sugar; lactose ◇ ～酶 lactase
【乳头】 rǔtóu ① nipple; teat; mammilla ② papilla: 视神经～ optic papilla ◇ ～状瘤 papilloma
【乳腺】 rǔxiàn 〈生理〉mammary gland ◇ ～癌 breast cancer/ ～炎 mastitis
【乳香】 rǔxiāng frankincense
【乳罩】 rǔzhào brassière; bra
【乳汁】 rǔzhī milk
【乳脂】 rǔzhī butterfat ◇ ～糖 toffee; taffy
【乳制品】 rǔzhìpǐn dairy products ◇ ～工业 dairy industry
【乳浊液】 rǔzhuóyè 〈化〉emulsion

**辱** rǔ ① disgrace; dishonour: 奇耻大～ galling shame and humiliation; terrible disgrace ② bring disgrace (或 humiliation) to; insult: 丧权～国 humiliate the nation and forfeit its sovereignty
【辱骂】 rǔmà abuse; call sb. names; hurl insults: ～和恐吓决不是战斗。Hurling insults and threats is no way to fight.
【辱命】 rǔmìng fail to accomplish a mission
【辱没】 rǔmò bring disgrace to; be unworthy of

## rù

**入** rù ① enter: ～境 enter a country/ 长江流～东海。The

Changjiang River empties into the Donghai Sea./ 投～更多人力 throw in more manpower/ 列～议程 put on the agenda ② join; be admitted into; become a member of: ～团 join the Chinese Communist Youth League ③ income: 岁～ annual income/ ～不敷出 income falling short of expenditure; unable to make ends meet ④ conform to; agree with: ～时 fashionable; *à la mode*/ ～情～理 fair and reasonable ⑤〈语〉见"入声"

【入仓】 rùcāng be stored in a barn; be put in storage: 粮食要晒干才能～。Grain must be aired in the sun before it can be stored.

【入场】 rùchǎng entrance; admission: 凭票～。Admission by ticket only./ 运动员在乐曲声中列队～。The athletes marched into the arena to the sound of music. ◇ ～券 (admission) ticket

【入超】 rùchāo unfavourable balance of trade

【入党】 rùdǎng join or be admitted to the (Chinese Communist) Party: 不但组织上～，而且思想上～ join the Party not only organizationally but ideologically

【入耳】 rù'ěr pleasant to the ear: 不～的话 unpleasant words/ 不堪～ (of language) offensive to the ear; obscene; vulgar

【入伏】 rùfú beginning of the hottest part of the summer: ～以来，常有阵雨。Since the dog days began, there have been frequent showers.

【入港】 rùgǎng ①〈交〉enter a port ② in full agreement; in perfect harmony: 二人谈得～。The two of them are deep in conversation and in perfect agreement with one another.

【入股】 rùgǔ buy a share; become a shareholder

【入骨】 rùgǔ to the marrow: 恨之～ bitterly hate; bear a bitter hatred for sb. or sth.

【入画】 rùhuà suitable for a painting; picturesque: 桂林山水，处处可以～。Every bit of Guilin scenery is worth painting.

【入伙】 rùhuǒ ① join a gang; join in partnership ② join a mess: 在我们食堂～ eat at our mess

【入境】 rùjìng enter a country ◇ ～登记 entrance registration/ ～签证 entry visa

【入境问俗】 rùjìng wèn sú on entering a country, inquire about its customs

【入口】 rùkǒu ① enter the mouth: 难于～ have a nasty taste/ 不可～！Not to be taken orally! ② entrance: 车站～处 entrance to the station

【入寇】 rùkòu invade

【入库】 rùkù be put in storage; be laid up

【入款】 rùkuǎn income; receipts

【入殓】 rùliàn put a corpse in a coffin; encoffin

【入列】 rùliè 〈军〉 take one's place in the ranks; fall in

【入门】 rùmén ① cross the threshold; learn the rudiments of a subject: 学英语～并不难，学好可不容易。Rudimentary English is easy to acquire, but mastery of the language is quite difficult./ 他是我的～师傅。He is the master who initiated me into the craft./ 我还没～呢。I don't even know the ABC of the subject yet. ② elementary course; ABC: 《英语语法～》 *Elementary English Grammar*/ 《摄影～》 *The ABC of Photography*

【入梦】 rùmèng ① fall asleep ② appear in one's dream

【入迷】 rùmí be fascinated; be enchanted: 他们的精采表演使观众看得入了迷。The audience was fascinated by their superb performance./ 看书看～了 be engrossed in a book

【入魔】 rùmó be infatuated; be spellbound

【入木三分】 rù mù sān fēn ① written in a forceful hand ② penetrating; profound; keen: 老队长的分析真是～。The old team leader's analysis was really penetrating.

【入侵】 rùqīn invade; intrude; make an incursion; make inroads: 消灭一切敢于～的敌人 wipe out all enemies who dare to invade our country/ 再次～ make another intrusion/ ～飞机 the intruding aircraft/ 军事～ military incursion

【入射角】 rùshèjiǎo 〈物〉 angle of incidence; incident angle

【入射线】 rùshèxiàn 〈物〉 incident ray

【入神】 rùshén ① be entranced; be enthralled: 他越说越起劲，大家越听越～。As he talked with more and more gusto, we came more and more under his spell. ② superb; marvellous: 这幅画画得真是～。This picture is really superb. 或 This is a marvellous picture.

【入声】 rùshēng 〈语〉 entering tone, one of the four tones in classical Chinese pronunciation, still retained in certain dialects

【入手】 rùshǒu start with; begin with; proceed from; take as the point of departure: 解决问题要从调查研究～。To solve a problem, one has to start with investigation./ 从改造世界观～ take the remoulding of one's world outlook as the point of departure

【入睡】 rùshuì go to sleep; fall asleep

【入土】 rùtǔ be buried; be interred: 快～了 have one foot in the grave

【入托】 rùtuō start going to a nursery: 办理小孩～手续 enrol a child in a nursery

【入微】 rùwēi in every possible way; in a subtle way: 体贴～ show every possible consideration; be extremely thoughtful/ 细腻～的表演 an exquisite performance

【入味】 rùwèi ① tasty: 菜做得很～。The dish is very tasty. ② interesting

【入伍】 rùwǔ enlist in the armed forces; join up

【入席】 rùxí take one's seat at a banquet, ceremony, etc.

【入选】 rùxuǎn be selected; be chosen

【入学】 rùxué ① start school: 我国儿童六、七岁～。In our country children start school at the age of six or seven. ② enter a school: 新生后天～。The new students will enter school the day after tomorrow./ 从～到毕业 from entrance to graduation ◇ ～考试 entrance examination/ ～年龄 school age

【入眼】 rùyǎn pleasing to the eye: 看不～ not to one's liking

【入药】 rùyào 〈中药〉 be used as medicine

【入夜】 rùyè at nightfall: ～，工地上灯火通明。When night fell the construction site was ablaze with light.

【入狱】 rùyù be put in prison; be sent to jail

【入院】 rùyuàn be admitted to hospital; be hospitalized

【入帐】 rùzhàng enter an item in an account; enter into the account book

【入赘】 rùzhuì marry into and live with one's bride's family

## 溽

rù 〈书〉 humid; damp

【溽暑】 rùshǔ sweltering summer weather

## 缛

rù elaborate; cumbersome: 繁文～节 unnecessary and overelaborate formalities; red tape

## 蓐

rù 〈书〉 straw mat or mattress

## 褥

rù cotton-padded mattress: 被～ bedding; bedclothes

【褥疮】 rùchuāng 〈医〉 bedsore

【褥单】 rùdān bed sheet

【褥套】 rùtào ① bedding sack ② mattress cover

【褥子】 rùzi cotton-padded mattress

## ruǎn

**阮** ruǎn ①见"阮咸" ②(Ruǎn) a surname

【阮咸】 ruǎnxián 〈乐〉 a plucked stringed instrument

**朊** ruǎn protein

**软** ruǎn ① soft; flexible; supple; pliable: ～椅 soft chair/ 柳条很～。Willow twigs are pliable. ② soft; mild; gentle: ～语 soft words/ 你对他～了些。You've been a bit soft with him./ 他的话太～了。What he said was too mild. ③ weak; feeble: 两腿发～。One's legs feel like jelly./ 欺～怕硬 bully the weak and fear the strong ④ poor in quality, ability, etc.: 货色～ poor-quality goods/ 工夫～ inadequate skill ⑤ easily moved or influenced: 心～ tender-hearted

【软刀子】 ruǎndāozi soft knife — a way of harming people imperceptibly

【软缎】 ruǎnduàn soft silk fabric in satin weave

【软腭】 ruǎn'è 〈生理〉 soft palate

【软风】 ruǎnfēng 〈气〉 light air

【软腐病】 ruǎnfǔbìng 〈农〉 soft rot

【软钢】 ruǎngāng mild steel; soft steel

【软膏】 ruǎngāo ointment; paste

【软骨头】 ruǎngǔtou a weak-kneed person; a spineless person; a coward

【软骨】 ruǎngǔ 〈生理〉 cartilage ◇ ～病 osteomalacia/ ～鱼 cartilaginous fish

【软管】 ruǎnguǎn flexible pipe or tube; hose: 铠装～ armoured hose

【软焊】 ruǎnhàn soft soldering; soldering

【软化】 ruǎnhuà ① soften: 使硬水～ soften hard water/ 态度～ become compliant ② win over by soft tactics: 敌人的高压和～政策都失败了。The enemy resorted to both tough and soft tactics, but succeeded in neither. ③ 〈皮革〉 bating

【软和】 ruǎnhuo 〈口〉 ① soft: ～的褥子 a soft mattress ② gentle; kind; soft: 给老太太说几句～话儿。Say some kind words (或 Say something nice) to please the old lady.

【软件】 ruǎnjiàn 〈计算机〉 software

【软禁】 ruǎnjìn put (或 place) sb. under house arrest

【软麻工艺】 ruǎnmá gōngyì 〈纺〉 (亚麻) bruising; (黄麻) batching

【软锰矿】 ruǎnměngkuàng pyrolusite

【软绵绵】 ruǎnmiánmián ① soft: ～的枕头 a soft pillow/ 这支歌～的。This song is too sentimental. ② weak: 她病好了,但身体仍然～的。She is well now, but she still feels weak.

【软磨】 ruǎnmó use soft tactics

【软木】 ruǎnmù cork ◇ ～塞 cork (as a stopper)

【软泥】 ruǎnní 〈地〉 ooze

【软片】 ruǎnpiàn (a roll of) film

【软弱】 ruǎnruò weak; feeble; flabby: 他病后身体～。His illness has left him weak./ ～无能 weak and incompetent/ ～可欺 be weak and easy to bully

【软食】 ruǎnshí soft diet; soft food; pap

【软水】 ruǎnshuǐ soft water

【软糖】 ruǎntáng soft sweets; jelly drops

【软梯】 ruǎntī 〈口〉 rope ladder

【软体动物】 ruǎntǐ dòngwù mollusc ◇ ～学 malacology

【软席】 ruǎnxí 〈交〉 soft seat or berth; cushioned seat or berth ◇ ～车厢 railway carriage with soft seats or berths

【软线】 ruǎnxiàn 〈电〉 flexible cord

【软硬兼施】 ruǎn-yìng jiān shī use both hard and soft tactics; couple threats with promises

【软玉】 ruǎnyù 〈矿〉 nephrite

【软脂】 ruǎnzhī palmitin ◇ ～酸 palmitic acid; palmic acid

## ruǐ

**蕊** ruǐ stamen or pistil: 雄～ stamen/ 雌～ pistil

## ruì

**芮** Ruì a surname

**枘** ruì tenon

【枘凿】 ruìzuò 〈书〉 incompatible

**蚋** ruì buffalo gnat; blackfly

**锐** ruì ① sharp; keen; acute: 尖～ pointed and sharp; sharp; acute ② vigour; fighting spirit: 养精蓄～ conserve strength and store up energy

【锐不可当】 ruì bùkě dāng can't be held back; be irresistible: 以～之势 with irresistible force/ 我军攻势迅猛,～。Our attack was so swift and violent that nothing could hold it back.

【锐角】 ruìjiǎo 〈数〉 acute angle

【锐利】 ruìlì sharp; keen: ～的匕首 a sharp dagger/ ～的武器 a sharp (或 powerful) weapon/ 目光～ sharp-eyed; sharp-sighted/ ～的攻势 a spirited attack/ ～的笔锋 a sharp pen; a vigorous style

【锐敏】 ruìmǐn sensitive; keen: ～的嗅觉 a keen sense of smell

【锐气】 ruìqì dash; drive: 表现了青年人的～ show the dashing spirit of young people/ 挫敌～ take the edge off the enemy's spirit

**瑞** ruì auspicious; lucky

【瑞典】 Ruìdiǎn Sweden ◇ ～人 Swede; the Swedish/ ～语 Swedish (language)

【瑞金】 Ruìjīn Ruijin

【瑞士】 Ruìshì Switzerland ◇ ～人 Swiss

【瑞香】 ruìxiāng 〈植〉 winter daphne (*Daphne odora*)

【瑞雪】 ruìxuě timely snow; auspicious snow: ～兆丰年。A timely snow promises a good harvest.

**睿** ruì 〈书〉 farsighted

【睿智】 ruìzhì 〈书〉 wise and farsighted

## rùn

**闰** rùn 〈天〉 intercalary

【闰年】 rùnnián leap (或 intercalary) year

【闰日】 rùnrì leap (或 intercalary) day

【闰月】 rùnyuè intercalary month in the lunar calendar; leap month

**润** rùn ① moist; smooth; sleek: 湿～ moist/ 墨色很～ in dark full-bodied ink ② moisten; lubricate: ～一～嗓子 moisten one's throat ③ embellish; touch up ④ profit; benefit: 分～ share in the benefit (或 profit)

【润笔】 rùnbǐ remuneration for a writer, painter or calligrapher

【润滑】 rùnhuá lubricate: 飞溅～法 splash lubrication ◇ ～系统 lubricating system; lubrication system/ ～油

lubricating oil; lubrication oil/ ～脂 (lubricating) grease

【润色】 rùnsè polish (a piece of writing, etc.); touch up: 这篇文章需要～一下。This article needs polishing.

【润饰】 rùnshì 见"润色"

【润燥】 rùnzào 〈中医〉 moisten the respiratory tract, skin, etc.

【润泽】 rùnzé ① moist; smooth; sleek: 这匹马全身～有光。The horse's coat was sleek and glossy./ 雨后荷花显得更加～了。After the rain the lotus flowers looked fuller. ② moisten; lubricate: 用油～轮轴 oil the axle

## ruò

**若** ruò ① like; seem; as if: ～有所失 feel as if something were missing; look distracted/ ～有所思 seem lost in thought; look pensive/ ～隐～现 appear indistinctly ② 〈书〉〈连〉 if: 人不犯我,我不犯人;人～犯我,我必犯人。We will not attack unless we are attacked; if we are attacked, we will certainly counterattack. ③ 〈书〉 you: ～辈 people like you

【若虫】 ruòchóng 〈动〉 nymph

【若非】 ruòfēi if not; were it not for: ～亲身经历,岂知其中甘苦。You cannot appreciate the difficulty except through personal experience.

【若干】 ruògān ① a certain number or amount: ～年 a number of years/ ～次 several times/ ～地区 certain areas ② how many; how much: 共得～? How many in all? 或 What is the sum total?

【若即若离】 ruòjí-ruòlí be neither friendly nor aloof; maintain a lukewarm relationship; keep sb. at arm's length

【若明若暗】 ruòmíng-ruò'àn have an indistinct (或 blurred) picture of; have a hazy (或 vague) notion about

【若是】 ruòshì 〈连〉 if

【若无其事】 ruò wú qí shì as if nothing had happened; calmly; casually: 发生这么大的事,你怎么还～? How can you remain indifferent when such an important thing has happened?

【若要人不知,除非己莫为】 ruò yào rén bù zhī, chúfēi jǐ mò wéi if you don't want others to know about it, don't do it

**偌** ruò such; so

【偌大】 ruòdà of such a size; so big: ～的地方 such a big place/ ～年纪 so old; so advanced in years

**弱** ruò ① weak; feeble: 他身体很～。He is very weak./ 由～变强 go from weakness to strength/ 他年纪虽老,干活并不～。Old as he is, he works energetically. ② young: 老～ old and young ③ inferior: 她的能力并不比别人～。She's no less capable than the others. ④ 〈书〉 lose (through death) ⑤〔接在分数或小数后面〕 a little less than: 三分之一～ a little less than one-third

【弱不禁风】 ruò bù jīn fēng too weak to stand a gust of wind; extremely delicate; fragile

【弱点】 ruòdiǎn weakness; weak point; failing

【弱碱】 ruòjiǎn 〈化〉 weak base

【弱脉】 ruòmài 〈中医〉 weak pulse

【弱拍】 ruòpāi 〈乐〉 weak beat; unaccented beat

【弱肉强食】 ruòròu-qiángshí the weak are the prey of the strong — the law of the jungle

【弱酸】 ruòsuān 〈化〉 weak acid

【弱小】 ruòxiǎo small and weak: ～民族 small and weak nations

【弱音器】 ruòyīnqì 〈乐〉 mute; sordine

**箬** ruò

【箬竹】 ruòzhú 〈植〉 indocalamus

# S

## sā

**仨** sā 〈口〉 three: 我们哥儿～ we three brothers/ 我来～。Give me three.

**挲** sā 见"摩挲" māsa
另见 suō

**撒** sā ① cast; let go; let out: ～网 cast a net; pay out a net/ 把手～开 let go one's hold ② throw off all restraint; let oneself go: ～酒疯 be drunk and act crazy; be roaring drunk
另见 sǎ

【撒旦】 sādàn 〈宗〉 Satan
【撒哈拉沙漠】 Sāhālā Shāmò the Sahara (Desert)
【撒欢儿】 sāhuānr 〈方〉 gambol; frisk
【撒谎】 sāhuǎng 〈口〉 tell a lie; lie: 当面～ tell a barefaced lie; lie in one's teeth
【撒娇】 sājiāo act like a spoiled child
【撒拉族】 Sālāzú the Salar (Sala) nationality, distributed over Qinghai and Gansu
【撒赖】 sālài make a scene; act shamelessly; raise hell
【撒尿】 sāniào 〈口〉 piss; pee
【撒泼】 sāpō be unreasonable and make a scene
【撒气】 sāqì ① (of a ball, tyre, etc.) leak; go soft; get a flat: 后带～了。The back tyre has got a puncture. 或 The back tyre is flat. ② vent one's anger or ill temper: 你别拿我～嘛。Don't take it out on me.
【撒手】 sāshǒu let go one's hold; let go: 你拿稳，我～了。Hold it tight. I'll let go./ ～不管 wash one's hands of the business; refuse to have anything more to do with the matter
【撒手锏】 sāshǒujiǎn an unexpected thrust with the mace — one's trump card
【撒腿】 sātuǐ start (running): ～就跑 make off at once; scamper
【撒野】 sāyě act wildly; behave atrociously

## sǎ

**洒** sǎ sprinkle; spray; spill; shed: ～滴滴畏 spray DDVP/ 别把汤～了。Don't spill the soup./ 甘～热血为人民 willingly shed one's blood for the people

【洒泪】 sǎlèi shed tears: ～告别 take a tearful leave
【洒扫】 sǎsǎo sprinkle water and sweep the floor; sweep: 黎明即起，～庭除。Rise at dawn and sweep the courtyard.
【洒水车】 sǎshuǐchē watering car; sprinkler
【洒脱】 sǎtuō free and easy

**撒** sǎ ① scatter; sprinkle; spread: ～农药 dust crops with an insecticide/ ～下革命的种子 sow seeds of revolution ② spill; drop: 她把～在路上的麦粒儿扫到一块儿。She swept up the grains of wheat that had spilled on the ground.
另见 sā

【撒播】 sǎbō broadcast sowing ◇ ～机 broadcast seeder; broadcaster
【撒肥机】 sǎféijī 〈农〉 fertilizer distributor; manure spreader
【撒粉】 sǎfěn 〈农〉 dusting ◇ ～器 duster
【撒施】 sǎshī 〈农〉 spread fertilizer over the fields; broadcast (fertilizer)

## sà

**卅** sà thirty

**飒** sà

【飒然】 sàrán 〈书〉 soughing
【飒飒】 sàsà 〈象〉 sough; rustle: 秋风～。The autumn wind is soughing in the trees.
【飒爽】 sàshuǎng 〈书〉 of martial bearing; valiant: ～英姿 of valiant and heroic bearing; bright and brave

**脎** sà 〈化〉 osazone

**萨** Sà a surname

【萨尔瓦多】 Sà'ěrwǎduō El Salvador ◇ ～人 Salvadoran
【萨克管】 sàkèguǎn 〈乐〉 saxophone
【萨克号】 sàkèhào 〈乐〉 saxhorn
【萨拉热窝】 Sàlārèwō Sarajevo
【萨摩亚】 Sàmóyà Samoa ◇ ～人 Samoan/ ～语 Samoan (language)
【萨其马】 sàqímǎ a kind of candied fritter

## sāi

**塞** sāi ① fill in; squeeze in; stuff: 箱子不太满，还可以再～点东西。There is still room in the suitcase to squeeze a few more things in./ 水管～住了。The waterpipe is clogged up. ② stopper: 软木～ cork
另见 sài; sè

【塞规】 sāiguī 〈机〉 plug gauge
【塞子】 sāizi stopper; cork; plug; spigot

**腮** sāi cheek

【腮帮子】 sāibāngzi 〈口〉 cheek
【腮托】 sāituō 〈乐〉 chin rest (of a violin or viola)
【腮腺】 sāixiàn 〈生理〉 parotid gland ◇ ～炎 parotitis; (流行性的) mumps

**噻** sāi

【噻吩】 sāifēn 〈化〉 thiophene
【噻唑】 sāizuò 〈化〉 thiazole

**鳃** sāi gill; branchia: ～盖 gill cover

## sài

**塞** sài a place of strategic importance: 边～ frontier fortress
另见 sāi; sè

【塞尔维亚-克罗地亚语】 Sài'ěrwéiyà-Kèluódìyàyǔ Serbo-Croatian

【塞拉利昂】 Sàilālì'áng Sierra Leone ◇ ～人 Sierra Leonian
【塞内加尔】 Sàinèijiā'ěr Senegal ◇ ～人 Senegalese
【塞浦路斯】 Sàipǔlùsī Cyprus ◇ ～人 Cypriot
【塞舌尔】 Sàishé'ěr Seychelles ◇ ～人 Seychellois
【塞外】 Sàiwài beyond (或 north of) the Great Wall: ～江南 lush southern-type fields north of the Great Wall
【塞翁失马,安知非福】 sàiwēng shī mǎ, ān zhī fēi fú when the old man on the frontier lost his mare, who could have guessed it was a blessing in disguise? —a loss may turn out to be a gain

**赛** sài ① match; game; competition; contest: 足球～ football match (或 game)/ 田径～ track and field events ② be comparable to; surpass: 我这萝卜～梨。These radishes of mine taste as good as pears.
【赛车】 sàichē 〈体〉 ① cycle racing; motorcycle race; automobile race ② racing bicycle
【赛过】 sàiguò overtake; be better than; surpass; exceed: 此处风光～江南。The scenery here surpasses that south of the lower reaches of the Changjiang River./ 战士们个个～小老虎。The soldiers were all as brave as young tigers.
【赛力散】 sàilìsǎn 〈农〉 phenylmercuric acetate
【赛璐珞】 sàilùluò celluloid
【赛马】 sàimǎ horse race
【赛跑】 sàipǎo race: 长距离～ long-distance race/ 一百米～ 100-metre dash/ 越野～ cross-country race
【赛艇】 sàitǐng 〈体〉 ① rowing ② racing boat; shell

## sān

**三** sān ① three ② more than two; several; many: ～弯九转 (full of) twists and turns/ ～思 think again and again; think twice (about doing sth.)
【三八妇女节】 Sān Bā Fùnǚjié International Working Women's Day (March 8)
【三宝】 sānbǎo 〈佛教〉 Triratna; the triad of the Buddha, the dharma, and the sangha
【三倍体】 sānbèitǐ 〈生〉 triploid
【三不管】 sānbùguǎn come within nobody's jurisdiction; be nobody's business
【三部曲】 sānbùqǔ trilogy
【三彩】 sāncǎi 〈考古〉 three-colour glazed pottery (esp. of the Tang Dynasty, 618-907)
【三槽出钢】 sāncáo chūgāng 〈冶〉 three-trough steel tapping technique
【三叉戟】 sānchājǐ trident
【三叉神经】 sānchā shénjīng 〈生理〉 trigeminal nerve
【三岔路口】 sānchà lùkǒu a fork in the road; a junction of three roads
【三长两短】 sāncháng-liǎngduǎn unexpected misfortune; sth. unfortunate, esp. death: 万一他有个～ if anything untoward should happen to him; in case he should die
【三重】 sānchóng triple; threefold: 遭受帝国主义、封建主义和官僚资本主义的～压迫 be subjected to a threefold oppression by imperialism, feudalism and bureaucrat-capitalism
【三重唱】 sānchóngchàng 〈乐〉 (vocal) trio
【三重奏】 sānchóngzòu 〈乐〉 (instrumental) trio
【三次方程】 sāncì fāngchéng 〈数〉 cubic equation
【三从四德】 sāncóng sìdé the three obediences (to father before marriage, to husband after marriage, and to son after the death of husband) and the four virtues (morality, proper speech, modest manner and diligent work) — spiritual fetters imposed on women in feudal society
【三大差别】 sān dà chābié the three major distinctions (between town and country, industry and agriculture. physical and mental labour): 逐步消灭～ gradually eliminate the distinctions between town and country, industry and agriculture, physical and mental labour
【三大法宝】 sān dà fǎbǎo the three magic weapons (of the Chinese Communist Party for defeating the enemy in the new-democratic revolution), namely, the united front, armed struggle and Party building
【三大革命运动】 sān dà gémìng yùndòng the three great revolutionary movements (of class struggle, the struggle for production and scientific experiment)
【三大纪律,八项注意】 sān dà jìlǜ, bā xiàng zhùyì the Three Main Rules of Discipline and the Eight Points for Attention of the Chinese People's Liberation Army (The Three Main Rules of Discipline are: 1. Obey orders in all your actions. 2. Don't take a single needle or piece of thread from the masses. 3. Turn in everything captured. The Eight Points for Attention are: 1. Speak politely. 2. Pay fairly for what you buy. 3. Return everything you borrow. 4. Pay for anything you damage. 5. Don't hit or swear at people. 6. Don't damage crops. 7. Don't take liberties with women. 8. Don't ill-treat captives.)
【三大民主】 sān dà mínzhǔ democracy in the three main fields (i.e. political, economic and military democracy at the company level in the People's Liberation Army)
【三大作风】 sān dà zuòfēng the Party's three important styles of work (integrating theory with practice, forging close links with the masses and practising self-criticism)
【三等秘书】 sānděng mìshū 〈外〉 third secretary
【三叠纪】 Sāndiéjì 〈地〉 the Triassic Period
【三定】 sāndìng the three fixed quotas (for production, purchase and marketing of grain)
【三度空间】 sāndù kōngjiān 〈哲〉 three-dimensional space
【三段论法】 sānduànlùnfǎ 〈逻〉 syllogism
【三法】 sānfǎ 〈中医〉 the three therapeutic methods of traditional Chinese medicine (diaphoresis, emetic measures, purgation and diuresis)
【三番五次】 sānfān-wǔcì again and again; time and again; over and over again; repeatedly
【三反运动】 Sānfǎn Yùndòng the movement against the three evils (corruption, waste and bureaucracy within the Party, government, army and mass organizations), 1951-1952
【三方】 sānfāng tripartite: ～会谈 tripartite talks
【三废】 sānfèi the three wastes (waste gas, waste water, and industrial residue): 从～中回收和提取大量有用物质 salvage large quantities of useful materials from the three wastes
【三伏】 sānfú ① the three ten-day periods of the hot season: ～天 dog days ② the last of the three periods of the hot season
【三副】 sānfù 〈航海〉 third mate; third officer
【三纲五常】 sāngāng wǔcháng the three cardinal guides (ruler guides subject, father guides son, and husband guides wife) and the five constant virtues (benevolence, righteousness, propriety, wisdom and fidelity) as specified in the feudal ethical code
【三个臭皮匠,合成一个诸葛亮】 sān ge chòupíjiang, héchéng yīge Zhūgě Liàng three cobblers with their wits combined equal Zhuge Liang the master mind — the wisdom of the masses exceeds that of the wisest individual 又作"三个臭皮匠,赛过诸葛亮"
【三个世界】 sān ge shìjiè the three worlds (the first world,

the second world and the third world): 毛主席关于～的理论是对马克思列宁主义的重大贡献。 Chairman Mao's theory of the three worlds is a major contribution to Marxism-Leninism.

【三顾茅庐】 sān gù máolú make three calls at the thatched cottage — repeatedly request sb. to take up a responsible post

【三光政策】 sānguāng zhèngcè the policy of "burn all, kill all, loot all" (once pursued by the Japanese invaders in China)

【三国】 Sān Guó the Three Kingdoms (220-265), namely, Wei (魏, 220-265), Shu Han (蜀汉, 221-263) and Wu (吴, 222-280)

【三合板】 sānhébǎn three-ply board; plywood

【三合星】 sānhéxīng 〈天〉 triple star

【三和两全】 sānhé liǎngquán the "three peacefuls and two entires" (peaceful transition, peaceful coexistence and peaceful competition; a state of the entire people and a party of the entire people) — peddled by the Soviet revisionist clique

【三核苷酸】 sānhégānsuān 〈生化〉 trinucleotide

【三化螟】 sānhuàmíng 〈农〉 yellow rice borer

【三级风】 sānjífēng 〈气〉 force 3 wind; gentle breeze

【三级所有,队为基础】 sān jí suǒyǒu, duì wéi jīchǔ three-level ownership by the commune, the production brigade and the production team, with the production team as the basic accounting unit

【三级跳远】 sān jí tiàoyuǎn 〈体〉 hop, step and jump; triple jump

【三极管】 sānjíguǎn 〈无〉 triode: 充气～ gas-filled triode/ 晶体～ transistor

【三季稻】 sānjìdào triple cropping of rice

【三尖瓣】 sānjiānbàn 〈生理〉 tricuspid valve ◇ ～狭窄〈医〉 tricuspid stenosis

【三焦】 sānjiāo 〈中医〉 the three visceral cavities housing the internal organs ◇ ～辨证 analysing and differentiating diseases according to the pathological changes in the three visceral cavities

【三角】 sānjiǎo ① triangle ② 〈数〉 trigonometry
◇ ～板 set square/ ～测量 triangulation; trigonometrical survey/ ～鲂〈动〉 triangular bream/ ～枫〈植〉 trident maple (*Acer buergerianum*)/ ～函数 trigonometric function/ ～肌〈生理〉 deltoid muscle/ ～裤 panties; briefs/ ～旗 pennant; pennon/ ～形〈数〉 triangle/ ～学〈数〉 trigonometry/ ～洲〈地〉 delta

【三角铁】 sānjiǎotiě ①〈乐〉 triangle ② angle iron; L-iron

【三脚架】 sānjiǎojià tripod

【三教九流】 sānjiào jiǔliú ① the three religions (Confucianism, Taoism and Buddhism) and the nine schools of thought (the Confucians, the Taoists, the *Yin-Yang*, the Legalists, the Logicians, the Mohists, the Political Strategists, the Eclectics and the Agriculturists) ② various religious sects and academic schools ③〈贬〉 people in various trades; people of all sorts

【三节棍】 sānjiégùn a cudgel of three linked sections; three-section cudgel

【三结合】 sānjiéhé three-in-one combination: ～设计小组 a three-in-one designing group (consisting of workers, technicians and cadres)/ 老、中、青～的领导班子 a leading body composed of the old, the middle-aged and the young

【三九天】 sānjiǔtiān the third nine-day period after the winter solstice — coldest days of winter

【三句话不离本行】 sān jù huà bù lí běnháng can hardly open one's mouth without talking shop; talk shop all the time

【三军】 sānjūn ① 〈旧〉 the army ② the three armed services

【三老四严】 sānlǎo sìyán the "three honests and four stricts" (be honest in thought, word and deed; set strict standards for work, organization, attitude and observance of discipline)

【三棱尺】 sānléngchǐ three-square rule; triangular scale

【三棱镜】 sānléngjìng 〈物〉 (triangular) prism

【三连音符】 sānlián yīnfú 〈乐〉 triplet

【三联单】 sānliándān triplicate form

【三磷酸腺甙】 sānlínsuānxiàndài 〈药〉 adenosine triphosphate (ATP)

【三令五申】 sānlìng-wǔshēn repeated injunctions

【三六九等】 sān-liù-jiǔděng various grades and ranks: 把工作分成～是错误的。 It is wrong to regard different kinds of work as indications of rank or grade.

【三轮车】 sānlúnchē tricycle; pedicab

【三轮摩托车】 sānlún mótuōchē motor tricycle

【三轮汽车】 sānlún qìchē three-wheeled automobile (或 motorcar)

【三氯杀螨砜】 sānlǜshāmǎnfēng 〈农〉 tetradiphon; tedion

【三昧】 sānmèi ①〈佛教〉 samadhi ② secret; knack: 深得其中～ master the secrets of an art

【三面红旗】 sān miàn hóngqí the Three Red Banners (the General Line for Socialist Construction, the Great Leap Forward and the People's Communes)

【三民主义】 sānmínzhǔyì the Three People's Principles (Nationalism, Democracy and the People's Livelihood), put forward by Dr. Sun Yat-sen

【三七】 sānqī 〈中药〉 pseudo-ginseng (*Panax pseudo-ginseng* var. *notoginseng*)

【三七开】 sān-qīkāi a seventy-thirty ratio: 对老李要～。 Lao Li's record should be assessed as 70 per cent achievements and 30 per cent mistakes.

【三秋】 sānqiū 〈农〉 the three autumn jobs (harvesting, ploughing and sowing)

【三三两两】 sānsānliǎngliǎng in twos and threes

【三色版】 sānsèbǎn 〈印〉 three-colour halftone; three-colour block

【三色堇】 sānsèjǐn 〈植〉 pansy

【三生有幸】 sānshēng yǒu xìng consider oneself most fortunate (to make sb.'s acquaintance, etc.)

【三十二分音符】 sānshí èr fēn yīnfú 〈乐〉 demisemiquaver; thirty-second note

【三十二开】 sānshí èr kāi thirty-twomo; 32mo

【三十六计,走为上计】 sānshí liù jì, zǒu wéi shàngjì of the thirty-six strategems, the best is running away — the best thing to do now is to quit 又作"三十六策,走为上策"

【三熟制】 sānshúzhì 〈农〉 triple-cropping system

【三水铝矿】 sānshuǐlǚkuàng gibbsite

【三思而行】 sān sī ér xíng think thrice before you act; look before you leap

【…三…四】 …sān…sì ①〔表示杂乱〕: 颠三倒四 incoherently; without order/ 丢三落四 always be forgetting things ②〔表示重复〕: 推三阻四 decline with all sorts of excuses

【三天打鱼,两天晒网】 sān tiān dǎ yú, liǎng tiān shài wǎng go fishing for three days and dry the nets for two — work by fits and starts; lack perseverance

【三天两头】 sāntiān-liǎngtóu 〈口〉 every other day; almost every day

【三通】 sāntōng 〈机〉 tee; tee joint ◇ ～管 three-way pipe

【三同】 sāntóng eat, live and work together (with the masses)

【三头六臂】 sāntóu-liùbì (with) three heads and six arms — superhuman

【三位一体】 sān wèi yī tǐ ①〈基督教〉 the Trinity ② trinity; three forming an organic whole; three in one
【三五成群】 sān-wǔ chéngqún in threes and fours; in knots
【三夏】 sānxià 〈农〉 the three summer jobs (planting, harvesting and field management)
【三弦】 sānxián 〈乐〉 *sanxian*, a three-stringed plucked instrument
【三项全能运动】 sān xiàng quánnéng yùndòng 〈体〉 triathlon
【三相】 sānxiàng 〈电〉 three-phase ◇ ～变压器 three-phase transformer
【三硝基甲苯】 sānxiāojījiǎběn 〈化〉 trinitrotoluene (TNT)
【三心二意】 sānxīn-èryì ① be of two minds; shilly-shally: 别～了,就这样办吧。Don't shilly-shally. Go right ahead. ② half-hearted: 为人民服务不能～。 We must not serve the people half-heartedly.
【三言两语】 sānyán-liǎngyǔ in a few words; in one or two words: 这事不是～能说清楚的。The matter can't be explained in a few words.
【三氧化物】 sānyǎnghuàwù 〈化〉 trioxide (e.g. "三氧化二砷" arsenic trioxide)
【三要三不要】 sānyào sānbùyào the three do's and the three don'ts (practise Marxism, and not revisionism; unite, and don't split; be open and aboveboard, and don't intrigue and conspire)
【三叶虫】 sānyèchóng 〈古生物〉 trilobite
【三月】 sānyuè ① March ② the third month of the lunar year; the third moon
【三灾八难】 sānzāi-bānàn numerous adversities and calamities
【三战两胜】 sān zhàn liǎng shèng 〈体〉 the best of three games
【三支两军】 sānzhī liǎngjūn three support's and two military's (support industry, support agriculture, and support the broad masses of the Left; military control and political and military training — tasks given to the PLA during the Great Proletarian Cultural Revolution)
【三只手】 sānzhīshǒu 〈方〉 pickpocket
【三趾鹑】 sānzhǐchún 〈动〉 button quail
【三自一包】 sānzì yībāo more plots for private use, more free markets, more enterprises with sole responsibility for their own profit or loss, and fixing output quotas on a household basis
【三座大山】 sān zuò dàshān the three big mountains (imperialism, feudalism and bureaucrat-capitalism, which weighed like mountains on the backs of the Chinese people before liberation)

**叁** sān three (used for the numeral 三 on cheques, etc. to avoid mistakes or alterations)

## sǎn

**伞** sǎn ① umbrella ② sth. shaped like an umbrella: 降落～ parachute
【伞兵】 sǎnbīng paratrooper; parachuter ◇ ～部队 parachute troops; paratroops
【伞齿轮】 sǎnchǐlún 〈机〉 bevel gear
【伞伐】 sǎnfá 〈林〉 shelterwood cutting
【伞房花序】 sǎnfáng huāxù 〈植〉 corymb
【伞投】 sǎntóu drop by parachute; parachute ◇ ～炸弹 parachute bomb; parabomb/ ～照明弹 parachute flare
【伞形花序】 sǎnxíng huāxù 〈植〉 umbel
【伞形科】 sǎnxíngkē 〈植〉 carrot family

**散** sǎn ① come loose; fall apart; not hold together: 背包～了。The blanket roll has come loose./ 木箱～了。The wooden box fell apart./ 麦包～了。The sack of wheat has spilled. ② scattered: 这个队的社员住得很～。The commune members in this team live rather far apart from one another. ③〈中药〉 medicine in powder form; medicinal powder
另见 sàn
【散兵】 sǎnbīng 〈军〉 skirmisher
◇ ～壕 fire trench/ ～坑 foxhole; pit/ ～线 skirmish line
【散兵游勇】 sǎnbīng-yóuyǒng stragglers and disbanded soldiers
【散光】 sǎnguāng astigmatism ◇ ～眼镜 astigmatic glasses
【散货】 sǎnhuò bulk cargo ◇ ～船 bulk freighter
【散记】 sǎnjì random notes; sidelights
【散剂】 sǎnjì 〈药〉 powder; pulvis
【散架】 sǎnjià ① fall apart; fall to pieces: 别再装了,大车快～了。Don't put any more on the cart, or it'll break. ② (feel as if) all one's limbs are out of joint
【散居】 sǎnjū live scattered: 游击队员～在老乡家里。The guerrillas lived scattered among the villagers.
【散漫】 sǎnmàn ① undisciplined; careless and sloppy: 克服小资产阶级的～性 overcome petty-bourgeois aversion to discipline ② unorganized; scattered: ～无组织的状态 a disorganized state of affairs
【散曲】 sǎnqǔ a type of verse popular in the Yuan, Ming and Qing dynasties, with tonal patterns modelled on tunes drawn from folk music
【散射】 sǎnshè 〈物〉 scattering
◇ ～粒子 scattering particles/ ～通信 scatter communication/ ～线 scattered rays
【散体】 sǎntǐ prose style free from parallelism; simple, direct prose style
【散文】 sǎnwén prose
【散文诗】 sǎnwénshī prose poem
【散装】 sǎnzhuāng bulk; in bulk
◇ ～饼干 loose cookies/ ～货物 bulk cargo; bulk freight/ ～汽油 petrol (或 gasoline) in bulk/ ～水泥 bulk cement/ ～运输 〈石油〉 bulk transportation

## sàn

**散** sàn ① break up; disperse: 会还没有～。The meeting is not over yet./ 大家别走～了。Let's not get separated./ 今天星期六,早点～吧。It's Saturday today. Let's stop a bit earlier./ 乌云～了。Dark clouds dispersed. ② distribute; disseminate; give out: ～传单 give out handbills; distribute leaflets ③ dispel; let out: 请打开门窗～～烟。Please open the door and windows to let the smoke out.
另见 sǎn
【散播】 sànbō disseminate; spread
【散布】 sànbù spread; disseminate; scatter; diffuse: ～流言蜚语 spread slanderous rumours/ 在一望无际的原野上～着一座座井架。Derricks are scattered here and there on the boundless plain.
【散步】 sànbù take a walk; go for a walk; go for a stroll
【散场】 sànchǎng (of a theatre, cinema, etc.) empty after the show
【散发】 sànfā ① send out; send forth; diffuse; emit: 花儿～着清香。The flowers sent forth a delicate fragrance./ ～着资产阶级思想的臭气 give off a foul smell of bourgeois ideology ② distribute; issue; give out: ～传单 distribute leaflets/ 作为正式文件～ be circulated as an official document

【散会】 sànhuì (of a meeting) be over; break up: 宣布～ declare the meeting over/ 一直到中午才～。The meeting didn't end until noon.
【散伙】 sànhuǒ (of a group, body or organization) dissolve; disband
【散开】 sànkai spread out or apart; disperse; scatter: 看热闹的群众～了。The crowd, which had gathered to watch the fun, dispersed.
【散热器】 sànrèqì radiator: 管式～ tubular radiator
【散失】 sànshī ① scatter and disappear; be lost; be missing: 防止图书～ prevent any loss of library books/ 有些古籍早已～。Some ancient works have long been lost./ ～的工具已经找到。The missing tools have been found. ② (of moisture, etc.) be lost; vaporize; dissipate
【散水】 sànshuǐ 〈建〉 apron
【散心】 sànxīn drive away one's cares; relieve boredom
【散逸】 sànyì 〈物〉 dissipation: 热～ heat dissipation

## sāng

**丧** sāng funeral; mourning
另见 sàng
【丧服】 sāngfú mourning apparel
【丧礼】 sānglǐ obsequies; funeral
【丧乱】 sāngluàn 〈书〉 disturbance; turmoil
【丧事】 sāngshì funeral arrangements
【丧葬】 sāngzàng burial; funeral ◇ ～费 funeral expenses
【丧钟】 sāngzhōng funeral bell; death knell; knell: 敲响殖民主义的～ sound the death knell of colonialism

**桑** sāng ① white mulberry; mulberry ② (Sāng) a surname
【桑白皮】 sāngbáipí 〈中药〉 the root bark of white mulberry
【桑蚕】 sāngcán silkworm ◇ ～丝 mulberry silk
【桑寄生】 sāngjìshēng 〈中药〉 parasitic loranthus (*Loranthus parasiticus*)
【桑皮纸】 sāngpízhǐ mulberry (bark) paper
【桑葚儿】 sāngrènr 〈口〉 mulberry
【桑葚】 sāngshèn mulberry
【桑树】 sāngshù white mulberry; mulberry
【桑榆暮景】 sāng-yú mùjǐng the evening of one's life
【桑园】 sāngyuán mulberry field
【桑梓】 sāngzǐ 〈书〉 one's native place

## sǎng

**搡** sǎng 〈方〉 push violently: 推推～～ pushing and shoving

**嗓** sǎng ① throat; larynx ② voice
【嗓门儿】 sǎngménr voice: 提高～ raise one's voice/ ～大 have a loud voice
【嗓音】 sǎngyīn voice: 他～洪亮。He has resonant voice. 或 His voice carries well.
【嗓子】 sǎngzi ① throat; larynx: ～疼 have a sore throat ② voice: ～好 have a good voice/ 他的～哑了。He's lost his voice.

**颡** sǎng 〈书〉 forehead

## sàng

**丧** sàng lose
另见 sāng
【丧胆】 sàngdǎn be terror-stricken; be smitten with fear: 我军向前推进，敌人闻风～。The enemy trembled with fear on hearing of our advance.
【丧魂落魄】 sànghún-luòpò be driven to distraction: 吓得～ be scared out of one's wits; be frightened out of one's life
【丧家之犬】 sàng jiā zhī quǎn stray cur: 惶惶如～ as frightened as a stray cur
【丧尽天良】 sàngjìn tiānliáng utterly devoid of conscience; conscienceless; heartless
【丧命】 sàngmìng meet one's death; get killed 又作"丧身"; "丧生"
【丧偶】 sàng'ǒu 〈书〉 bereft of one's spouse, esp. one's wife
【丧气】 sàngqì feel disheartened; lose heart; become crestfallen ◇ ～话 demoralizing words
【丧气】 sàngqi 〈口〉 be unlucky; be out of luck; have bad luck
【丧权辱国】 sàngquán-rǔguó humiliate the nation and forfeit its sovereignty; surrender a country's sovereign rights under humiliating terms: ～的条约 a treaty of national betrayal and humiliation
【丧失】 sàngshī lose; forfeit: ～信心 lose confidence/ ～时机 miss the opportunity/ ～立场 depart from the correct stand/ ～会员资格 forfeit one's membership/ 睡眠和休息～了时间，却取得了明天工作的精力。Sleep and rest involve loss of time, but they provide energy for next day's work.
【丧心病狂】 sàng xīn bìng kuáng frenzied; unscrupulous; perverse: ～地进行破坏活动 carry on frenzied wrecking activities

## sāo

**搔** sāo scratch: ～痒 scratch where it itches
【搔首】 sāoshǒu scratch one's head: ～踟蹰 scratch one's head in hesitation; hesitate
【搔头弄姿】 sāotóu-nòngzī 〈书〉 (of a woman) stroke one's hair in coquetry; be coquettish

**骚** sāo ① disturb; upset ② short for *Li Sao* (《离骚》), a poem by the 4th century B.C. poet and statesman Qu Yuan (屈原): ～体 poetry in the style of *Li Sao* ③ literary writings: ～人 poet ④ coquettish
【骚动】 sāodòng ① disturbance; commotion; ferment ② be in a tumult; become restless: 人群～起来。The crowd was in a tumult.
【骚客】 sāokè 〈书〉 poet
【骚乱】 sāoluàn disturbance; riot
【骚扰】 sāorǎo harass; molest: ～破坏活动 harassing and wrecking activities
【骚人墨客】 sāorén-mòkè 〈书〉 men of letters; *literati*

**缫** sāo reel silk from cocoons; reel
【缫丝】 sāosī silk reeling; filature ◇ ～厂 reeling mill; filature/ ～机 reeling machine; filature

**臊** sāo the smell of urine; foul smell
另见 sào

## sǎo

**扫** sǎo ① sweep; clear away: ～雪 sweep away the snow/ ～清道路 clear the path; pave the way ② pass

quickly along or over; sweep: 他向会场～了一眼。He swept his eyes over the meeting-place./ 探照灯光～过夜空。The searchlights swept across the night sky. ③ put all together: ～数归还 the whole amount returned
另见 sào
【扫除】 sǎochú ① cleaning; cleanup: 大～ general cleaning ② clear away; remove; wipe out: ～一切害人虫 sweep away all pests; away with all pests/ ～前进道路上的障碍 remove the obstacles on the road of advance/ ～文盲 eliminate (或 wipe out) illiteracy
【扫荡】 sǎodàng mop up: 粉碎敌人的～ smash the enemy's mopping-up operations
【扫地】 sǎodì ① sweep the floor ② (of honour, credibility, etc.) reach rock bottom; reach an all-time low; be dragged in the dust: 名誉～ be thoroughly discredited/ 威信～ be shorn of one's prestige/ 在农民运动的打击下,地主的威风～以尽。The peasant movement swept the landlords' prestige into the dust.
【扫雷】 sǎoléi mine sweeping (或 clearance) ◇ ～舰 minesweeper/ ～器 mine-sweeping apparatus; minesweeper
【扫盲】 sǎománg 〈简〉(扫除文盲) eliminate (或 wipe out) illiteracy ◇ ～班 literacy class/ ～运动 campaign to eliminate illiteracy; anti-illiteracy campaign
【扫描】 sǎomiáo 〈电〉 scanning: 行～ line scanning/ 飞点～ flying-spot scanning ◇ ～器 scanner
【扫墓】 sǎomù sweep a grave — pay respects to a dead person at his tomb
【扫平】 sǎopíng put down; crush; suppress: ～叛乱 put down a rebellion
【扫射】 sǎoshè strafe
【扫尾】 sǎowěi wind up; round off: ～工作 rounding-off work
【扫兴】 sǎoxìng have one's spirits dampened; feel disappointed: 真叫人～! How disappointing!

**嫂** sǎo ① elder brother's wife; sister-in-law ② sister (a form of address for a married woman about one's own age): 桂英～ Sister Guiying
【嫂嫂】 sǎosao 〈方〉 elder brother's wife; sister-in-law
【嫂子】 sǎozi 〈口〉 elder brother's wife; sister-in-law

## sào

**扫** sào
另见 sǎo
【扫帚】 sàozhou broom
【扫帚星】 sàozhouxīng 〈天〉 comet

**臊** sào shy; bashful: 害～ be bashful/ ～得脸通红 blush scarlet
另见 sāo

## sè

**色** sè ① colour: 红～ red/ 原～ primary colour ② look; countenance; expression: 满面喜～ beaming with joy ③ kind; description: 各～人等 people of every description; all kinds of people ④ scene; scenery: 湖光山～ a landscape of lakes and mountains ⑤ quality (of precious metals, goods, etc.): 成～好 of good quality ⑥ woman's looks: 姿～ good looks
另见 shǎi
【色彩】 sècǎi colour; hue; tint; shade: 地方～ local colour/ 文学～ literary flavour/ 感情～ emotional colouring
【色层分析】 sècéng fēnxī 〈物〉 chromatographic analysis ◇ ～法 chromatography
【色层谱】 sècéngpǔ 〈物〉 chromatogram
【色差】 sèchā ① 〈物〉 chromatism ② 〈纺〉 off colour; off shade
【色丹岛】 Sèdāndǎo Shikotan
【色淀】 sèdiàn 〈纺〉 (colour) lake: 绯红～ crimson lake
【色调】 sèdiào tone; hue: 暖～ warm tones
【色度计】 sèdùjì 〈物〉 colorimeter: 光电～ photoelectric colorimeter
【色基】 sèjī 〈化〉 colour base
【色厉内荏】 sè lì nèi rěn fierce of mien but faint of heart
【色盲】 sèmáng 〈医〉 achromatopsia; colour blindness
【色品】 sèpǐn 〈物〉 chroma; chromaticity
【色情】 sèqíng pornographic; sexy ◇ ～文学 pornography
【色球】 sèqiú 〈天〉 chromosphere
【色散】 sèsàn 〈物〉 chromatic dispersion
【色素】 sèsù 〈生〉 pigment ◇ ～沉着〈医〉 pigmentation
【色泽】 sèzé colour and lustre: ～鲜明 bright and lustrous
【色织厂】 sèzhīchǎng 〈纺〉 yarn-dyed fabric mill
【色纸】 sèzhǐ coloured paper

**涩** sè ① puckery; astringent: 这柿子～不～? Are these persimmons puckery? ② unsmooth; hard-going: 推子发～了,该上油了。This pair of hair-clippers doesn't work smoothly. It needs oiling. ③ obscure; difficult: 文句艰～ make difficult reading
【涩脉】 sèmài 〈中医〉 a weak, thready, uneven pulse

**啬** sè stingy; miserly

**铯** sè 〈化〉 cesium (Cs)

**塞** sè
另见 sāi; sài
【塞擦音】 sècāyīn 〈语〉 affricate
【塞音】 sèyīn 〈语〉 plosive
【塞责】 sèzé not do one's job conscientiously: 敷衍～ perform one's duty in a perfunctory manner

**瑟** sè 〈乐〉 *se*, a twenty-five-stringed plucked instrument, somewhat similar to the zither
【瑟瑟】 sèsè 〈象〉 (of the wind) rustle
【瑟缩】 sèsuō curl up with cold; cower

**穑** sè 见"稼穑" jiàsè

## sēn

**森** sēn ① full of trees ② 〈书〉 multitudinous; in multitudes: ～罗万象 myriads of things; everything under the sun ③ dark; gloomy: 阴～ gloomy; grim
【森林】 sēnlín forest
◇ ～调查 forest survey/ ～抚育 tending of woods/ ～覆被率 percentage of forest cover/ ～火灾 forest fire/ ～学 forestry/ ～资源 forest reserves
【森然】 sēnrán ① (of tall trees) dense; thick: 林木～ thickly wooded with tall trees ② awe-inspiring
【森森】 sēnsēn dense; thick; luxuriant: 松柏～ dense pine and cypress trees
【森严】 sēnyán stern; strict; forbidding: ～壁垒 strongly fortified/ 戒备～ heavily guarded/ 门禁～ with the entrance carefully guarded/ 等级～ be rigidly stratified; form

a strict hierarchy

## sēng

**僧** sēng Buddhist monk; monk
【僧多粥少】 sēng duō zhōu shǎo 见"粥少僧多" zhōu shǎo sēng duō
【僧伽罗语】 Sēngjiāluóyǔ Sinhalese
【僧侣】 sēnglǚ monks and priests; clergy ◇ ～主义 〈哲〉 fideism
【僧尼】 sēng-ní Buddhist monks and nuns
【僧俗】 sēng-sú monks and laymen
【僧徒】 sēngtú Buddhist monks
【僧院】 sēngyuàn Buddhist temple; Buddhist monastery

## shā

**杀** shā ① kill; slaughter: ～人放火，无恶不作 commit murder, arson and every crime imaginable ② fight; go into battle: ～出重围 fight one's way out of a heavy encirclement ③ weaken; reduce; abate: ～～敌人的威风 deflate the enemy's arrogance/ 风势稍～。The wind abated. ④ 〈方〉 smart: 碘酒涂在伤口上真～得慌。Iodine smarts when it is put on a cut. ⑤ take off; counteract: 白菜馅里放点盐～～水 put some salt in the chopped cabbage to draw out the water ⑥ in the extreme; exceedingly: 笑～人 absolutely ridiculous; terribly funny/ 闷～人 bored to death
【杀虫剂】 shāchóngjì 〈农〉 insecticide; pesticide
【杀敌】 shādí fight the enemy; engage in battle: 苦练～本领 practise hard to master combat skills/ 英勇～ be brave in battle; fight heroically
【杀风景】 shā fēngjǐng spoil the fun; be a wet blanket
【杀害】 shāhài murder; kill
【杀回马枪】 shā huímǎqiāng make a backward thrust at one's pursuer; wheel around and hit back
【杀鸡取卵】 shā jī qǔ luǎn kill the hen to get the eggs; kill the goose that lays the golden eggs
【杀鸡吓猴】 shā jī xià hóu kill the chicken to frighten the monkey — punish someone as a warning to others
【杀价】 shājià offer to buy sth. cheap, knowing the seller needs cash
【杀菌】 shājūn disinfect; sterilize ◇ ～剂 germicide; bactericide
【杀戮】 shālù massacre; slaughter: 惨遭～ be massacred in cold blood
【杀卵剂】 shāluǎnjì 〈农〉 ovicide
【杀螨剂】 shāmǎnjì 〈农〉 acaricide; miticide
【杀气】 shāqì ① murderous look: ～腾腾 with a murderous look on one's face; be out to kill ② vent one's ill feeling: 你有委屈就说出来，不该拿别人～。Get it off your chest if you feel you've been wronged. Don't take it out on others.
【杀人】 shārén kill a person; murder ◇ ～犯 murderer; manslayer; homicide
【杀人不见血】 shārén bù jiàn xiě kill without spilling blood; kill by subtle means
【杀人不眨眼】 shārén bù zhǎyǎn kill without batting an eyelid; kill without blinking an eye
【杀人如麻】 shārén rú má kill people like flies
【杀人越货】 shārén yuè huò kill a person and seize his goods
【杀伤】 shāshāng kill and wound; inflict casualties on: ～大批敌军 take a heavy toll of enemy troops/ 这种炮弹～力很强。This is a powerful antipersonnel shell. ◇ ～弹 fragmentation bomb; antipersonnel bomb
【杀身成仁】 shā shēn chéng rén die to achieve virtue — die for a just cause
【杀身之祸】 shā shēn zhī huò a fatal disaster
【杀鼠剂】 shāshǔjì rat poison; raticide
【杀头】 shātóu behead; decapitate
【杀一儆百】 shā yī jǐng bǎi execute one as a warning to a hundred

**沙** shā ① sand ② granulated; powdered: 豆～ bean paste ③ (of voice) hoarse; husky ④ (Shā) a surname
【沙蚕】 shācán clam worm
【沙场】 shāchǎng battlefield; battleground
【沙船】 shāchuán large junk
【沙袋】 shādài sandbag
【沙丁鱼】 shādīngyú sardine
【沙俄】 Shā É tsarist Russia
【沙发】 shāfā sofa; settee: 单人～ upholstered (或 padded) armchair
【沙岗】 shāgǎng sand hill
【沙锅】 shāguō earthenware pot; casserole
【沙果】 shāguǒ 〈植〉 Chinese pear-leaved crabapple
【沙狐】 shāhú corsac (fox)
【沙獾】 shāhuān sand badger
【沙荒】 shāhuāng sandy wasteland; sandy waste
【沙皇】 shāhuáng tsar: 新～ the New Tsars
【沙鸡】 shājī sandgrouse
【沙金】 shājīn alluvial gold; placer gold
【沙坑】 shākēng 〈体〉 jumping pit
【沙拉】 shālā salad
【沙梨】 shālí 〈植〉 sand pear
【沙里淘金】 shālǐ táo jīn wash grains of gold out of the sands — extract the essential from a large mass of material; get small returns for great effort
【沙砾】 shālì grit
【沙罗周期】 shāluó zhōuqī 〈天〉 saros
【沙漠】 shāmò desert: 塔克拉玛干～ the Taklamakan Desert
【沙盘】 shāpán 〈军〉 sand table ◇ ～作业 sand table exercise
【沙丘】 shāqiū (sand) dune: 流动～ moving dunes
【沙瓤】 shāráng mushy watermelon pulp
【沙沙】 shāshā 〈象〉 rustle: 风吹树叶～响。The leaves rustled in the wind.
【沙参】 shāshēn 〈中药〉 the root of straight ladybell (*Adenophora stricta*)
【沙滩】 shātān sandy beach
【沙特阿拉伯】 Shātè Ālābó Saudi Arabia ◇ ～人 Saudi Arabian
【沙文主义】 shāwénzhǔyì chauvinism
【沙哑】 shāyǎ hoarse; husky; raucous: 声音～ have a husky voice
【沙眼】 shāyǎn trachoma
【沙鱼】 shāyú shark
【沙枣】 shāzǎo 〈植〉 narrow-leaved oleaster (*Elaeagnus angustifolia*)
【沙蚤】 shāzǎo 〈动〉 sand hopper
【沙洲】 shāzhōu shoal; sandbar; sandbank
【沙蠋】 shāzhú 〈动〉 lugworm
【沙柱】 shāzhù dust devil; sand column
【沙锥】 shāzhuī 〈动〉 snipe
【沙子】 shāzi ① sand; grit ② small grains; pellets: 铁～ iron pellets; shot
【沙嘴】 shāzuǐ 〈地〉 sandspit

**纱** shā ① yarn: 棉～ cotton yarn/ ～厂 cotton mill ② gauze; sheer: 铁～ wire gauze

【纱包线】 shābāoxiàn cotton-covered wire
【纱布】 shābù gauze
【纱橱】 shāchú screen cupboard
【纱窗】 shāchuāng screen window
【纱灯】 shādēng gauze lantern
【纱锭】 shādìng 〈纺〉 spindle
【纱巾】 shājīn gauze kerchief
【纱笼】 shālóng sarong
【纱罗】 shāluó 〈纺〉 gauze
【纱线】 shāxiàn yarn
【纱罩】 shāzhào ① gauze or screen covering (over food) ② mantle (of a lamp)

**杉** shā 〈植〉 China fir
另见 shān

【杉篙】 shāgāo 〈建〉 fir pole
【杉木】 shāmù China fir

**刹** shā put on the brakes; stop; check: 把车～住 stop (或 brake) a car/ ～住歪风 check an unhealthy tendency
另见 chà

【刹把】 shābà 〈机〉 brake crank
【刹车】 shāchē ① stop a vehicle by applying the brakes; put on the brakes ② stop a machine by cutting off the power; turn off a machine ③ brake

**砂** shā sand; grit: 型～ 〈机〉 moulding sand; casting sand

【砂布】 shābù emery cloth; abrasive cloth: 刚玉～ corundum cloth
【砂浆】 shājiāng 〈建〉 mortar: 石灰～ lime mortar/ 水泥～ cement mortar
【砂矿】 shākuàng placer deposit; placer ◇ ～开采 placer mining; alluvial mining; placering
【砂砾】 shālì gravel; grit
【砂轮】 shālún 〈机〉 emery wheel; grinding wheel; abrasive wheel ◇ ～机 grinder
【砂囊】 shānáng 〈动〉 gizzard
【砂壤土】 shārǎngtǔ sandy loam
【砂糖】 shātáng granulated sugar
【砂田】 shātián sandy land
【砂土】 shātǔ sandy soil; sand
【砂箱】 shāxiāng 〈冶〉 sandbox; moulding box
【砂型】 shāxíng 〈冶〉 sand mould ◇ ～心 sand core
【砂岩】 shāyán 〈矿〉 sandstone
【砂眼】 shāyǎn 〈冶〉 sand holes; blowholes
【砂样】 shāyàng 〈石油〉 drilling mud cuttings
【砂纸】 shāzhǐ abrasive paper; sand paper: 玻璃～ glass paper/ 金刚～ emery paper
【砂质岩】 shāzhìyán 〈地〉 arenaceous rock

**痧** shā 〈中医〉 acute diseases such as cholera and sunstroke

【痧子】 shāzi 〈方〉 measles

**裟** shā 见"袈裟" jiāshā

**煞** shā ① stop; halt; check; bring to a close: ～住脚 stop short/ 文章写到这里还～不住。The article can't very well end here. ② tighten: ～一～腰带 tighten one's belt ③ 见"杀" shā ③⑤⑥
另见 shà

【煞笔】 shābǐ ① concluding lines of an article; ending of a piece of writing ② write the final line
【煞车】 shāchē ① 见"刹车" shāchē ② firmly fasten a load (on a vehicle); lash down
【煞尾】 shāwěi ① finish off; round off; wind up: 事情不多了，马上就可以～。There isn't much work left; we're winding up. ② final stage; end; ending: 这出戏的～很带劲。The play has a powerful ending.

**鲨** shā shark

【鲨鱼】 shāyú shark

## shǎ

**傻** shǎ ① stupid; muddleheaded: 你真～，他这点意思都听不出来。How stupid you were. You should have known what he was driving at./ 装～ act dumb; pretend not to know/ 吓～了 be dumbfounded; be stunned/ 你别～乎乎的，事情没有那么简单。Don't be naive. The matter is not so simple. ② think or act mechanically: 别一个劲儿～干，要讲究方法。Don't just keep slogging away. Pay attention to method.

【傻瓜】 shǎguā fool; blockhead; simpleton
【傻呵呵】 shǎhēhē simpleminded; not very clever: 别看他～的，心里可有数。Maybe he doesn't look very clever, but he knows what's what.
【傻劲儿】 shǎjìnr ① stupidity; foolishness ② sheer enthusiasm; doggedness: 不能光靠～，得找窍门。Enthusiasm alone won't do. You've got to work skilfully./ 这小伙子干活有股～。That youngster works with a will.
【傻头傻脑】 shǎtóu-shǎnǎo ① foolish-looking ② muddleheaded
【傻笑】 shǎxiào laugh foolishly; giggle; smirk
【傻眼】 shǎyǎn be dumbfounded; be stunned: 他一看考题就～了。When he saw the examination questions he got a nasty shock.
【傻子】 shǎzi fool; blockhead; simpleton

## shà

**啥** shà 〈方〉 what: 有～说～ say what one has to say; come out with what one thinks; speak one's mind/ 你不快走，还罗嗦个～？ It's time you went. Why do you keep on chattering away?/ 困难再大也没～了不起。Difficulties, no matter how great, are nothing to be afraid of.

**厦** shà a tall building; mansion: 高楼大～ tall buildings and great mansions
另见 xià

**歃** shà 〈书〉 suck

【歃血】 shàxuè smear the blood of a sacrifice on the mouth — an ancient form of swearing an oath

**煞** shà ① evil spirit; goblin ② very
另见 shā

【煞白】 shàbái ghastly pale; deathly pale; pallid
【煞费苦心】 shà fèi kǔxīn cudgel one's brains; take great pains: ～地寻找借口 cudgel one's brains to find an excuse/ 他们为了攻克技术难关，可真是～。They took great pains to solve the difficult technical problem.
【煞有介事】 shà yǒu jiè shì make a great show of being in earnest; pretend to be serious (about doing sth.)

**霎** shà a very short time; moment; instant: 一～ in a moment

【霎时间】 shàshíjiān in a twinkling; in a split second; in a jiffy

## shāi

**筛** shāi ① sieve; sifter; screen ② sift; sieve; screen; riddle: ～面 sieve flour; sift flour/ ～煤 screen coal/ ～砂砾 riddle gravel/ ～煤渣 sift cinders

【筛法】 shāifǎ 〈数〉 sieve method

【筛分】 shāifēn screening; sieving 又作“筛选” ◇ ～机 screening machine

【筛管】 shāiguǎn 〈植〉 sieve tube

【筛号】 shāihào screen size; screen mesh; mesh number

【筛糠】 shāikāng shiver: 吓得直～ shiver with fear; shake in one's shoes

【筛子】 shāizi sieve; sifter; screen: 粗～ riddle

## shǎi

**色** shǎi 〈口〉 colour: 这布掉～吗? Will this cloth fade? 另见 sè

【色子】 shǎizi dice: 掷～ play dice

## shài

**晒** shài ① (of the sun) shine upon: 日～雨淋 be exposed to the sun and rain/ 这里～得慌。There's too much sun here. ② dry in the sun; bask: ～粮食 dry grain in the sun/ ～被子 air a quilt/ 他的脸～黑了。His face is tanned./ 让孩子们尽量多～～太阳。Take the children out to get as much sun as possible.

【晒垡】 shàifá 〈农〉 sun the earth which has been ploughed up; sun the upturned soil

【晒坪】 shàipíng sunning ground

【晒台】 shàitái flat roof (for drying clothes, etc.)

【晒图】 shàitú make a blueprint; blueprint ◇ ～员 blueprinter/ ～纸 blueprint paper

【晒烟】 shàiyān sun-cured tobacco

【晒盐】 shàiyán evaporate brine in the sun to make salt

## shān

**山** shān ① hill; mountain ② anything resembling a mountain: 冰～ iceberg ③ bushes in which silkworms spin cocoons: 蚕上～了。The silkworms have gone into the bushes to spin their cocoons. ④ (Shān) a surname

【山坳】 shān'ào col

【山崩】 shānbēng landslide; landslip

【山苍子】 shāncāngzǐ 〈中药〉 the fruit of a cubeb litsea tree (*Litsea cubeba*)

【山茶】 shānchá 〈植〉 camellia

【山城】 shānchéng mountain city

【山川】 shānchuān mountains and rivers — land; landscape

【山慈姑】 shāncígu 〈植〉 edible tulip

【山村】 shāncūn mountain village

【山丹】 shāndān 〈植〉 morningstar lily (*Lilium concolor*)

【山道年】 shāndàonián 〈药〉 santonin

【山地】 shāndì ① mountainous region; hilly area; hilly country ② fields on a hill

【山顶】 shāndǐng the summit (或 top) of a mountain; hilltop

【山顶洞人】 Shāndǐngdòngrén 〈考古〉 Upper Cave Man, a type of primitive man who lived ten to twenty thousand years ago and whose fossil remains were found in 1933 at Zhoukoudian (周口店) near Beijing

【山东】 Shāndōng Shandong (Province)

【山东快书】 Shāndōng kuàishū Shandong clapper ballad

【山洞】 shāndòng cave; cavern

【山豆根】 shāndòugēn 〈植〉 subprostrate sophora (*Sophora subprostrata*)

【山风】 shānfēng 〈气〉 mountain breeze

【山峰】 shānfēng mountain peak

【山旮旯儿】 shāngālár 〈方〉 faraway hilly area; out-of-the-way place in the mountains; remote mountain area

【山冈】 shāngāng low hill; hillock

【山高水低】 shāngāo-shuǐdī unexpected misfortune; sth. unfortunate, esp. death

【山歌】 shāngē folk song (sung in the fields during or after work)

【山梗菜硷】 shāngěngcàijiǎn 〈药〉 lobeline

【山沟】 shāngōu gully; ravine; (mountain) valley

【山谷】 shāngǔ mountain valley

【山河】 shānhé mountains and rivers — the land of a country: 祖国的锦绣～ our beautiful land

【山核桃】 shānhétao 〈植〉 ① hickory ② hickory nut

【山洪】 shānhóng mountain torrents: ～暴发。Torrents of water rushed down the mountain.

【山货】 shānhuò ① mountain products (such as haws, chestnuts and walnuts) ② household utensils made of wood, bamboo, clay, etc.

【山鸡】 shānjī 〈方〉 pheasant

【山鸡椒】 shānjījiāo 〈植〉 cubeb litsea tree (*Litsea cubeba*)

【山积】 shānjī 〈书〉 pile mountain high

【山脊】 shānjǐ ridge (of a mountain or hill)

【山涧】 shānjiàn mountain stream

【山椒鸟】 shānjiāoniǎo 〈动〉 minivet

【山脚】 shānjiǎo the foot of a hill

【山口】 shānkǒu mountain pass; pass

【山岚】 shānlán 〈书〉 clouds and mists in the mountains

【山里红】 shānlihóng 〈植〉 large-fruited Chinese hawthorn (*Crataegus pinnatifida* var. *major*)

【山梁】 shānliáng ridge (of a mountain or hill)

【山林】 shānlín mountain forest; wooded mountain: ～地区 mountain and forest region; wooded and hilly lands

【山岭】 shānlǐng mountain ridge

【山麓】 shānlù the foot of a mountain ◇ ～丘陵 foothills

【山峦】 shānluán chain of mountains; multipeaked mountain: ～起伏 undulating hills

【山脉】 shānmài mountain range; mountain chain

【山猫】 shānmāo 〈动〉 leopard cat

【山毛榉】 shānmáojǔ 〈植〉 beech

【山盟海誓】 shānméng-hǎishì (make) a solemn pledge of love

【山明水秀】 shānmíng-shuǐxiù green hills and clear waters — picturesque scenery 又作“山清水秀”

【山南海北】 shānnán-hǎiběi south of the mountains and north of the seas — far and wide; all over the land: ～他那儿都到过。He has travelled far and wide./ ～,到处都有勘探人员的足迹。The prospectors have left their footprints all over the land.

【山炮】 shānpào mountain gun; mountain artillery

【山坡】 shānpō hillside; mountain slope

【山墙】 shānqiáng 〈建〉 gable

【山穷水尽】 shānqióng-shuǐjìn where the mountains and the rivers end — at the end of one's rope (或 tether, resources)

【山区】 shānqū mountain area
【山泉】 shānquán mountain spring
【山雀】 shānquè 〈动〉 tit
【山水】 shānshuǐ ① water from a mountain ② mountains and rivers; scenery with hills and waters: ～相连 be linked by common mountains and rivers/ 农业学大寨运动使我国的山山水水发生了巨大的变化。The movement to learn from Dazhai in agriculture has brought about great changes across the land. ③〈美术〉 traditional Chinese painting of mountains and waters; landscape ◇ ～画 mountains-and-waters painting; landscape painting
【山桃】 shāntáo 〈植〉 mountain peach
【山田】 shāntián hillside plot
【山桐子】 shāntóngzǐ 〈植〉 idesia
【山头】 shāntóu ① hilltop; the top of a mountain ② mountain stronghold; faction: 拉～ form a faction ◇ ～主义 mountain-stronghold mentality (a type of sectarianism)
【山窝】 shānwō out-of-the-way mountain area
【山西】 Shānxī Shanxi (Province)
【山系】 shānxì 〈地〉 mountain system
【山乡】 shānxiāng mountain area
【山响】 shānxiǎng deafening; thunderous: 鼓擂得～ drums beating thunderously/ 北风刮得门窗乒乒乓乓～。The doors and windows are rattling in the north wind.
【山魈】 shānxiāo 〈动〉 mandrill
【山鸦】 shānyā 〈动〉 chough
【山崖】 shānyá cliff
【山羊】 shānyáng ① goat ②〈体〉 buck ◇ ～胡子 goatee/ ～绒 cashmere
【山腰】 shānyāo half way up the mountain
【山药】 shānyao 〈植〉 Chinese yam
【山药蛋】 shānyaodàn 〈方〉 potato
【山雨欲来风满楼】 shānyǔ yù lái fēng mǎn lóu the wind sweeping through the tower heralds a rising storm in the mountains; the rising wind forebodes the coming storm
【山芋】 shānyù 〈方〉 sweet potato
【山鹬】 shānyù 〈动〉 woodcock
【山岳】 shānyuè lofty mountains ◇ ～冰川 mountain glacier; alpine glacier/ ～地区 mountainous region
【山楂】 shānzhā ① (Chinese) hawthorn ② haw ◇ ～糕 haw jelly 又作"山查"
【山寨】 shānzhài mountain fastness; fortified mountain village
【山珍海味】 shānzhēn-hǎiwèi delicacies from land and sea; dainties of every kind 又作"山珍海错"
【山茱萸】 shānzhūyú 〈中药〉 the fruit of medicinal cornel (*Cornus officinalis*)
【山庄】 shānzhuāng mountain villa
【山嘴】 shānzuǐ 〈地〉 spur

## 芟

shān ① mow (grass) ② weed out; eliminate
【芟除】 shānchú ① mow; cut down: ～杂草 weeding ② delete

## 杉

shān 〈植〉 China fir
另见 shā

## 删

shān delete; leave out: 这一段可以～去。This paragraph can be left out./ ～掉不必要的细节 cut out the unnecessary details
【删除】 shānchú delete; strike (或 cut, cross) out
【删繁就简】 shānfán-jiùjiǎn simplify sth. by cutting out the superfluous
【删改】 shāngǎi delete and change; revise: 稿子几经～才定下来。The draft was revised several times before it was finalized.
【删节】 shānjié abridge; abbreviate: 本报略有～ slightly abridged by our editorial staff ◇ ～本 abridged edition; abbreviated version/ ～号 ellipsis; suspension points; ellipsis dots (……) (...)

## 衫

shān unlined upper garment: 衬～ shirt/ 汗～ undershirt

## 苫

shān straw mat
另见 shàn
【苫布】 shānbù tarpaulin

## 姗

shān
【姗姗来迟】 shānshān lái chí be slow in coming; be late

## 钐

shān 〈化〉 samarium (Sm)

## 珊

shān
【珊瑚】 shānhú coral
◇ ～虫 coral polyp; coral insect/ ～岛 coral island/ ～礁 coral reef

## 栅

shān
另见 zhà
【栅极】 shānjí 〈电〉 grid: 抑制～ suppressor grid

## 舢

shān
【舢板】 shānbǎn sampan

## 扇

shān ① fan: ～火 fan a fire/ ～扇子 fan oneself; use a fan ② incite; instigate; fan up; stir up: ～阴风 fan up an evil wind; secretly stir up trouble
另见 shàn
【扇动】 shāndòng ① fan; flap: ～翅膀 flap the wings ② instigate; incite; stir up; whip up: ～无政府主义 incite anarchism/ ～资产阶级派性 whip up bourgeois factionalism/ 一小撮阶级敌人企图～群众闹事。A handful of class enemies tried to stir up trouble among the masses.
【扇风点火】 shānfēng-diǎnhuǒ fan the flames; inflame and agitate people; stir up trouble
【扇风机】 shānfēngjī ventilating fan
【扇惑】 shānhuò incite; agitate: ～人心 agitate people by demagogy

## 跚

shān 见"蹒跚" pánshān

## 煽

shān 见"扇" shān②

## 潸

shān 〈书〉 in tears; tearfully: ～然泪下 tears trickling down one's cheeks

## 膻

shān the smell of mutton: 这羊肉不～。This mutton hasn't got a strong smell.

# shǎn

## 闪

shǎn ① dodge; get out of the way: 往旁边一～ dodge swiftly to one side; jump out of the way ② twist; sprain: ～了腰 sprain one's back ③ lightning: 打～ flashes of lightning ④ flash; sparkle; shine: 远处灯光一～。There was a flash of light in the distance./ 一～而过 flash past; streak past/ 这时我脑子里～过一个念头。At this moment an idea flashed through my mind./ 毛主席著作～金光,照得咱

心里亮堂堂。Chairman Mao's works shine with golden light and illuminate our hearts and minds. ⑤ leave behind: 你去的时候叫我一声，可别把我～下。Please call for me when you go; don't leave me behind.
【闪避】 shǎnbì dodge; sidestep
【闪长岩】 shǎnchángyán diorite
【闪挫】 shǎncuò 〈中医〉 sudden strain or contusion of a muscle; sprain
【闪点】 shǎndiǎn 〈化〉 flash point
【闪电】 shǎndiàn lightning ◇ ～战 lightning war; blitzkrieg; blitz
【闪躲】 shǎnduǒ dodge; evade
【闪光】 shǎnguāng ① flash of light: 流星像一道～，划破黑夜的长空。 With a flash, the meteor shot across the night sky. ② gleam; glisten; glitter: 露珠在晨曦中～。Dewdrops glistened in the morning light. ◇ ～灯 〈摄〉 flash lamp; photoflash/ ～对头焊 flash-butt welding
【闪击战】 shǎnjīzhàn lightning war; blitzkrieg; blitz
【闪开】 shǎnkai get out of the way; jump aside; dodge: 车来了，快～！Look out! There's a bus coming.
【闪米特人】 Shǎnmǐtèrén Semite
【闪闪】 shǎnshǎn sparkle; glisten; glitter: ～的红星 a sparkling red star/ ～发光 sparkle; glitter/ 天空中电光～。Lightning flashed in the sky.
【闪身】 shǎnshēn ① dodge: 侦察兵一～机警地躲过了敌人的探照灯。The scout dodged nimbly and evaded the enemy's searchlight. ② sideways: ～进门 walk sideways through the door
【闪失】 shǎnshī mishap; accident: 要是有个～，怎么办呢? What if anything should go wrong?
【闪烁】 shǎnshuò ① twinkle; glimmer; glisten: 远处～着灯光。Lights glimmered in the distance./ 她的眼睛里～着喜悦的泪花。Her eyes glistened with tears of joy. ② evasive; vague; noncommittal: ～其词 speak evasively; hedge/ 他闪闪烁烁，不做肯定的答复。He hummed and hawed, giving no definite reply. 或 He was evasive and noncommittal. ③ 〈电〉 scintillation ◇ ～计数器 scintillation counter
【闪现】 shǎnxiàn flash before one: 英雄的形象～在我的眼前。The image of the hero flashed before my eyes.
【闪锌矿】 shǎnxīnkuàng 〈矿〉 (zinc) blende; sphalerite
【闪耀】 shǎnyào glitter; shine; radiate: 繁星～ glittering stars/ 他两眼～着刚毅的光芒。His eyes flashed with resolution./ 巴黎公社的原则～着不灭的光辉。The principles of the Paris Commune radiate with eternal light.
【闪蒸】 shǎnzhēng 〈石油〉 flash vaporization ◇ ～塔 flash tower

**陕** Shǎn short for Shaanxi Province
【陕西】 Shǎnxī Shaanxi (Province)

**映** shǎn blink; twinkle: 这孩子一～眼就不见了。The boy vanished in the twinkling of an eye.

## shàn

**讪** shàn ① mock; ridicule ② embarrassed; awkward; shamefaced: ～～地走开 walk away looking embarrassed
【讪笑】 shànxiào ridicule; mock; deride

**疝** shàn hernia: 腹股沟～ inguinal hernia/ 脐～ umbilical hernia
【疝气】 shànqì 〈医〉 hernia

**单** Shàn a surname
另见 chán; dān

**苫** shàn cover with a straw mat, tarpaulin, etc.: 要下雨了，快把麦子～上。Quick! It's going to rain, cover up the wheat.
另见 shān

**扇** shàn ① fan: 电～ electric fan ② leaf: 门～ door leaf/ 八～屏风 eight-leaf screen/ 隔～ partition ③ 〈量〉〔用于门窗等〕: 一～门 a door
另见 shān
【扇贝】 shànbèi 〈动〉 scallop; fan shell
【扇车】 shànchē winnowing machine; winnower
【扇骨子】 shàngǔzi the ribs (或 mount) of a fan
【扇面儿】 shànmiànr the covering of a fan
【扇形】 shànxíng ① fan-shaped ② 〈数〉 sector ◇ ～齿轮 〈机〉 sector (或 segment) gear
【扇子】 shànzi fan

**善** shàn ① good: 心怀不～ harbour ill intent/ 改恶从～ give up evil and return to good; mend one's ways ② satisfactory; good: ～策 a wise policy; the best policy ③ make a success of; perfect: 工欲～其事，必先利其器。A workman must sharpen his tools if he is to do his work well. ④ kind; friendly: 友～ be friendly; be kind and helpful ⑤ be good at; be expert (或 adept) in: 不～经管 not good at management/ ～破～立 be good at destroying the old and establishing the new/ 勇敢～战 be brave and skilful in battle/ ～观风色 quick to see which way the wind blows — very shrewd ⑥ properly: ～自保重 take good care of yourself/ ～为说辞 put in a good word for sb. ⑦ be apt to: ～变 be apt to change; be changeable/ ～忘 be forgetful; have a short memory
【善罢甘休】 shànbà-gānxiū 〔多用于否定〕 leave the matter at that; let it go at that: 敌人这一仗打败了，但决不会～的。The enemy will not take their defeat lying down.
【善本】 shànběn reliable text; good edition: ～书 rare book
【善处】 shànchǔ 〈书〉 deal discreetly with; conduct oneself well
【善后】 shànhòu deal with problems arising from an accident, etc.: 处理这次火灾的～ deal with the aftermath of the fire
【善举】 shànjǔ 〈书〉 philanthropic act or project
【善良】 shànliáng good and honest; kindhearted: ～的人们 good and honest people; people of goodwill/ ～愿望 the best of intentions/ 心地～ kindhearted
【善人】 shànrén philanthropist; charitable person; well-doer
【善始善终】 shànshǐ-shànzhōng start well and end well; do well from start to finish; see sth. through
【善心】 shànxīn mercy; benevolence: 反动派是不会对人民发～的。Reactionaries will never show kindness to the people.
【善意】 shànyì goodwill; good intentions: 出于～ out of goodwill; with the best intentions/ ～的批评 well-meaning criticism
【善有善报，恶有恶报】 shàn yǒu shànbào, è yǒu èbào good will be rewarded with good, and evil with evil
【善于】 shànyú be good at; be adept in: ～歌舞 be good at singing and dancing/ 我们不但～破坏一个旧世界，我们还将～建设一个新世界。We are not only good at destroying the old world, we are also good at building the new./ ～识别资产阶级野心家和阴谋家 be adept at spotting bourgeois careerists and conspirators/ 敢于斗争，～斗争 dare to struggle and know how to struggle

【善终】 shànzhōng die a natural death; die in one's bed

**禅** shàn
另见 chán

【禅让】 shànràng abdicate and hand over the crown to another person

**骟** shàn castrate or spay

**缮** shàn ① repair; mend: 房屋修～ house repairing ② copy; write out: ～清 make a fair copy

【缮写】 shànxiě write out; copy

**擅** shàn ① arrogate to oneself; do sth. on one's own authority: ～权 monopolize power; usurp power/ ～作主张 make a decision without authorization ② be good at; be expert in: 不～辞令 lack facility in polite or tactful speech

【擅长】 shàncháng be good at; be expert in; be skilled in: 他～侧泳。He has a good sidestroke.

【擅离职守】 shàn lí zhíshǒu be absent from one's post without leave; leave one's post without permission

【擅自】 shànzì do sth. without authorization: 不得～修改操作规程。No unauthorized changes may be made in the rules of operation./ ～行动 act presumptuously

**膳** shàn meals; board: 在食堂用～ have one's meals at the mess

【膳费】 shànfèi board expenses

【膳食】 shànshí meals; food: 流质～ liquid diet/ 半流质～ semiliquid diet

【膳宿】 shàn-sù board and lodging

**嬗** shàn

【嬗变】 shànbiàn ① evolution ②〈物〉transmutation: 自然～ natural transmutation/ 感生～ induced transmutation

**赡** shàn ① support; provide for: ～家养口 support a family ②〈书〉sufficient; abundant

【赡养】 shànyǎng support; provide for: ～父母 support one's parents ◇ (离婚后付给对方的)～费 alimony

**蟮** shàn 见"曲蟮" qūshan

**鳝** shàn eel; finless eel

## shāng

**伤** shāng ① wound; injury: 刀～ a knife wound/ 轻～ a slight injury/ 烫～ a scald/ 满身是～ be covered with cuts and bruises/ ～好了。The wound has healed. ② injure; hurt: 被汽车撞～ be knocked down and injured by a car/ 摔～ fall and hurt oneself/ ～感情 hurt sb.'s feelings ③ be distressed: 哀～ sad; sorrowful ④ get sick of sth.; develop an aversion to sth.: 这孩子吃糖吃～了。The child has got sick of eating sweets. ⑤ be harmful to; hinder: 无～大雅 involving no major principle; not matter much/ 有～国体 discredit one's country

【伤疤】 shāngbā scar

【伤兵】 shāngbīng wounded soldier

【伤病员】 shāng-bìngyuán the sick and wounded; noneffectives

【伤风】 shāngfēng catch cold; have a cold

【伤风败俗】 shāngfēng-bàisú offend public decency; corrupt public morals

【伤感】 shānggǎn sick at heart; sentimental

【伤害】 shānghài injure; harm; hurt: 不要～益鸟。Don't harm beneficial birds./ 饮酒过多会～身体。Excessive drinking is harmful to the health./ ～自尊心 injure (或 hurt) one's pride; hurt one's self-respect

【伤寒】 shānghán ①〈医〉typhoid fever; typhoid ②〈中医〉diseases caused by harmful cold factors; febrile diseases; fevers

【伤号】 shānghào the wounded

【伤耗】 shānghao damage: 这筐苹果刨去～还有四十斤。There are still forty *jin* of apples in this basket after taking out the damaged ones.

【伤痕】 shānghén scar; bruise

【伤筋动骨】 shāngjīn-dònggǔ be injured in the sinews or bones; have a fracture

【伤科】 shāngkē〈中医〉(department of) traumatology

【伤口】 shāngkǒu wound; cut: 洗～ bathe a wound

【伤脑筋】 shāng nǎojīn knotty; troublesome; bothersome: ～的问题 a knotty problem; headache/ 老下雨,真～。It's a nuisance the way it keeps on raining.

【伤神】 shāngshén overtax one's nerves; be nerve-racking

【伤食】 shāngshí〈中医〉dyspepsia caused by excessive eating or improper diet

【伤势】 shāngshì the condition of an injury (或 wound): ～很重 be seriously wounded (或 injured)

【伤亡】 shāng-wáng injuries and deaths; casualties: ～惨重 suffer heavy casualties ◇ ～报告〈军〉returns of losses

【伤心】 shāngxīn sad; grieved; broken-hearted: ～落泪 shed sad tears; weep in grief/ 别为这事～。Don't let it grieve you./ 丈夫有泪不轻弹,只因未到～处。A man does not easily shed tears until his heart is broken./ 这么好的庄稼给雹子打了真叫人～。It's really heartrending to see such fine crops damaged by the hailstorm. ◇ ～事 old sore; painful memory; grief

【伤心惨目】 shāngxīn-cǎnmù too ghastly to look at; tragic (scene)

【伤员】 shāngyuán wounded personnel; the wounded

**殇** shāng〈书〉die young

**商** shāng ① discuss; consult: 有要事相～。I have important matters to discuss with you. ② trade; commerce; business: 经～ engage in trade; be in business/ 通～ have trade relations ③ merchant; trader; businessman; dealer: 私～ businessman/ 盐～ salt dealer/ 奸～ profiteer ④〈数〉quotient ⑤〈乐〉a note of the ancient Chinese five-tone scale, corresponding to 2 in numbered musical notation ⑥ (Shāng) the Shang Dynasty (c. 16th—11th century B.C.) ⑦ (Shāng) a surname

【商标】 shāngbiāo trade mark ◇ ～注册 trade mark registration

【商埠】 shāngbù〈旧〉commercial (或 trading) port

【商场】 shāngchǎng market; bazaar

【商船】 shāngchuán merchant ship; merchantman

【商店】 shāngdiàn shop; store

【商定】 shāngdìng decide through consultation; agree: 经～ it has been decided through consultation that/ 已～的条款 the provisions already agreed upon/ 双方～建立大使级外交关系。The two sides have agreed to establish diplomatic relations at ambassadorial level.

【商队】 shāngduì a company of travelling merchants; trade caravan

【商法】 shāngfǎ〈法〉commercial law

【商贩】 shāngfàn small retailer; pedlar

【商港】 shānggǎng commercial port
【商贾】 shānggǔ 〈书〉 merchants
【商行】 shāngháng trading company; commercial firm
【商号】 shānghào shop; store; business establishment
【商会】 shānghuì chamber of commerce
【商界】 shāngjiè business circles; commercial circles
【商量】 shāngliang consult; discuss; talk over: 有事同群众～。Consult the masses when matters arise./ 全世界的事应由世界各国～着办。Matters that concern the whole world should be settled through consultation among all the nations./ 咱们得找支书～一下。We ought to talk it over with the Party branch secretary./ 这事好～。That can be settled through discussion.
【商路】 shānglù trade route
【商品】 shāngpǐn commodity; goods; merchandise ◇ ～拜物教 commodity fetishism/ ～交换 exchange of commodities/ ～经济 commodity economy/ ～粮 commodity grain; marketable grain/ ～流通 circulation of commodities; commodity circulation/ ～生产 commodity production/ ～输出 export of commodities/ ～税 commodity tax/ ～销售市场 outlet for goods/ ～制度 commodity system
【商洽】 shāngqià arrange with sb.; take up (a matter) with sb.
【商情】 shāngqíng market conditions ◇ ～预测 business forecasting
【商榷】 shāngquè discuss; deliberate: 这一点值得～。This point is open to question./ 提出几点意见，与诸位～。Here are a few points I wish to discuss with you.
【商人】 shāngrén businessman; merchant; trader
【商谈】 shāngtán exchange views; confer; discuss; negotiate: ～递交国书事宜 discuss matters relating to the presentation of credentials/ 望贵方即指派代表前来～。We hope that you will appoint representatives to come here for the negotiations.
【商讨】 shāngtǎo discuss; deliberate over: 就发展两国关系进行有益的～ hold useful discussions on developing relations between the two countries
【商务】 shāngwù commercial affairs; business affairs ◇ ～参赞 commercial counsellor/ ～处 commercial counsellor's office/ ～代表 commercial representative; trade representative/ ～代表处 trade representative's office; office of a trade delegation/ ～秘书 commercial secretary/ ～专员 commercial attaché
【商业】 shāngyè commerce; trade; business ◇ ～部门 commercial departments/ ～惯例 business practice/ ～机构 business organization; commercial undertaking/ ～区 business quarter; commercial district; business district/ ～网 commercial network; network of trading establishments/ ～信贷 commercial credit/ ～银行 commercial bank/ ～中心 commercial centre; trading centre; shopping centre/ ～资本 commercial capital; merchant capital
【商议】 shāngyì confer; discuss
【商约】 shāngyuē commercial treaty
【商酌】 shāngzhuó discuss and consider; deliberate over: 这个问题尚待～。This matter needs further discussion and consideration.

**觞** shāng 〈考古〉 wine cup; drinking vessel

**墒** shāng 〈农〉 moisture in the soil: 抢～ lose no time in sowing while there is sufficient moisture in the soil/ 保～ preserve the moisture of the soil
【墒情】 shāngqíng soil moisture content

**熵** shāng 〈物〉 entropy

## shǎng

**上** shǎng 〈语〉 见“上声” shàngshēng
另见 shàng; shang
【上声】 shǎngshēng 〈语〉 见“上声” shàngshēng

**垧** shǎng *shang*, a land measure equal to fifteen *mu* in most parts of the Northeast and three or five *mu* in the Northwest

**晌** shǎng ① part of the day: 前半～儿 morning/ 晚半～儿 dusk ② 〈方〉 noon: 歇～ take a midday nap or rest
【晌饭】 shǎngfàn 〈方〉 ① midday meal; lunch ② extra meal in the daytime during the busy farming season
【晌觉】 shǎngjiào 〈方〉 afternoon nap
【晌午】 shǎngwu 〈口〉 midday; noon: ～饭 midday meal; lunch

**赏** shǎng ① grant (或 bestow) a reward; award: 国王～给那个士兵一匹马。The king awarded the soldier a horse. ② reward; award: 有～有罚。Duly mete out rewards and punishments. ③ admire; enjoy; appreciate: ～月 admire the full moon; enjoy looking at the moon/ 奇文共～ share the pleasure of reading a rare piece of writing
【赏赐】 shǎngcì grant (或 bestow) a reward; award: 把奴隶～给贵族 award slaves to aristocrats/ 得到很多～ be given a handsome reward
【赏罚】 shǎng-fá rewards and punishments: ～严明 be strict and fair in meting out rewards and punishments
【赏格】 shǎnggé the size of a reward
【赏光】 shǎngguāng 〈套〉〔用于请对方接受邀请〕: 务请～ request the pleasure of your company
【赏鉴】 shǎngjiàn appreciate (a work of art)
【赏金】 shǎngjīn money reward; pecuniary reward
【赏识】 shǎngshí recognize the worth of; appreciate: 主编很～他这篇文章。The editor in chief thinks highly of this article of his./ 这个奴才深得其主子的～。That flunkey was in his master's good graces.
【赏玩】 shǎngwán admire the beauty of sth.; delight in; enjoy: ～山景 enjoy mountain scenery/ ～古董 delight in antiques
【赏心悦目】 shǎngxīn-yuèmù find the scenery pleasing to both the eye and the mind

## shàng

**上** shàng ① upper; up; upward: ～铺 upper berth/ 这头朝～ this side up/ 往～看 look up; look upward ② higher; superior; better: 报～一级党委 report to the Party committee immediately above/ 向～反映情况 report the situation to the higher organization/ 中～水平 above the average; better than the average/ 这个词是旧时下对～的称呼。This word was used in the old days to address one's superiors. ③ first (part); preceding; previous: ～册 the first volume; Volume One; Book One/ ～集 the first part; Part One; Volume One/ ～半夜 the first half of the night; before midnight/ 二十世纪～半叶 the first half of the twentieth century/ ～星期三 last Wednesday/ ～一季度 the previous quarter/ ～一段 the preceding (或 above, foregoing) paragraph ④ the emperor: ～谕 imperial decree ⑤ 〈乐〉 a note

of the scale in *gongchepu*（工尺谱）, corresponding to 1 in numbered musical notation ⑥ go up; mount; board; get on: ～坡 go up a slope/ ～山 go up a hill; go uphill/ ～公共汽车 get on a bus/ ～自行车 get on a bike/ ～飞机 board a plane/ ～船 go aboard a ship; go on board/ ～岸 go ashore; go on shore; land/ ～楼 go upstairs/ 逆流而～ go upstream; go against the current/ 干部要能～能下。A cadre should be ready to take a lower as well as a higher post./ 粮食亩产～《纲要》。The per-*mu* yield of grain has reached the target set in the National Programme for Agricultural Development. ⑦ go to; leave for: 你～哪儿去？ Where are you going?/ ～南京 leave for Nanjing/ 我～卫生室去一趟。I'm going to the clinic. ⑧ submit; send in; present: 李小红谨～ Yours respectfully, Li Xiaohong/ 随函附～八分邮票一张。Enclosed herewith is an eight-*fen* stamp. ⑨ forge ahead; go ahead: 快～，投篮！ Go ahead. Quick! Shoot!/ 有条件要～，没有条件创造条件也要～。When the conditions exist, go ahead; when they don't, create them and go ahead. ⑩〈剧〉appear on the stage; enter: 二战士左～。Enter left two soldiers. ⑪〈体〉enter the court or field: 换人：三号下，四号～。Substitution: Player No. 4 for No. 3./ 这一盘你～。You play this game. ⑫ fill; supply; serve: 给水箱～水 fill the tank with water/ 一连～了好几道菜。Several courses were served in succession. ⑬ place sth. in position; set; fix: ～刀具 fix a cutting tool/ ～梁 set the roof beams in place/ 行李还没～架。The luggage has not been put on the rack yet./ 麦秸正在～垛。The wheat stalks are being stacked./ 工件已经～了车床。The workpiece is already on the lathe. ⑭ apply; paint; smear: ～药膏 apply ointment/ ～肥 spread manure/ 给门～漆 paint the door/ 给机器～油 oil (或 grease) the machine ⑮ be put on record; be carried (in a publication): 我们厂的消息～了人民日报。*Renmin Ribao* carried a story about our factory./ 小王的先进事迹都～了电视了。Xiao Wang's model deeds have been publicized on TV. ⑯ wind; screw; tighten: 表该～了。The watch needs winding./ 螺丝没有～紧。The screw hasn't been tightened./ 门没～锁。The door isn't locked. ⑰ be engaged (in work, study, etc.) at a fixed time: 我今天～中班。I'm on the middle shift today./ 她的大女儿在～大学。Her eldest daughter is now in college. ⑱ up to; as many as: ～百人 up to a hundred people/～万 as many as ten thousand ⑲〈语〉见"上声"
另见 shǎng; shang

**上** shang ①〔用在动词后，表示由低处向高处〕: 爬～河堤 climb up to the top of the dyke/ 登～山顶 reach the summit/ 踏～非洲的土地 set foot on African soil/ 对敌人的新仇旧恨，一齐涌～心头。Hatred of the enemy, for old and new wrongs, welled up in his heart. ②〔用在动词后，表示达到目的〕: 锁～门 lock the door; lock up/ 穿～外衣 put on a coat/ 当～会计 become an accountant/ 没吃～饭 be too late for the meal/ 你跟他接～头了吗？ Have you got in touch with him? ③〔用在动词后，表示开始并继续〕: 她爱～了草原。 She's fallen in love with the grasslands./ 他拿起一把锨就干～了。He seized a shovel and set to. ④〔用在名词后，表示位置、范围或方面〕: 会～ at the meeting/ 报～说的 what is reported in the newspapers/ 事实～ in fact; in reality; actually/ 理论～ in theory; theoretically/ 由组织～决定 to be decided by the Party organization/ 这出戏政治～艺术～都很成功。The play is a success both politically and artistically./ 墙～有张地图。There's a map on the wall./ 把书放在桌～。Put the book on the table./ 咱们的赤脚医生，手～有老茧，脚～有泥巴，肩～有药箱，心～有贫下中农。Our barefoot doctors have got calluses on their hands, mud on their feet, medicine kits across their shoulders, and love for the poor and lower-middle peasants in their hearts.
另见 shǎng; shàng

【上班】 shàngbān go to work; start work; be on duty: 她～去了。She's gone to work./ 下午不～。We'll take the afternoon off. 或 No work this afternoon./ 我们每天早上八点钟～。We start work at 8 every morning. ◇ ～时间 work hours; office hours

【上半场】 shàngbànchǎng first half (of a game): ～比分多少？ What was the score at half time?

【上半晌】 shàngbànshǎng forenoon; morning

【上半身】 shàngbànshēn the upper part of the body; above the waist

【上半夜】 shàngbànyè before midnight

【上报】 shàngbào ① appear in the newspapers: 那位数学家刻苦钻研的事迹昨天～了。In yesterday's newspaper there was an article about how perseveringly that mathematician carried out his scientific research. ② report to a higher body; report to the leadership: 这件事应当立即～教育部，不容延误。This matter should be reported, without delay, to the Ministry of Education.

【上辈】 shàngbèi ① ancestors ② the elder generation of one's family; one's elders

【上臂】 shàngbì the upper arm

【上边】 shàngbian 见"上面"

【上膘】 shàngbiāo (of animals) become fat; fatten

【上宾】 shàngbīn distinguished guest; guest of honour

【上苍】 shàngcāng Heaven; God

【上操】 shàngcāo go out to drill; be drilling

【上策】 shàngcè the best plan; the best way out; the best thing to do

【上层】 shàngcéng upper strata; upper levels
◇ ～分子 members of the upper strata; upper-class elements/ ～人士 upper circles/ ～社会 upper classes of society; upper-class society/ ～小资产阶级 upper petty bourgeoisie

【上层建筑】 shàngcéng jiànzhù superstructure: ～领域 the realm of the superstructure

【上场】 shàngchǎng ①〈剧〉appear on the stage; enter: 战士甲～。Enter Soldier A. ②〈体〉enter the court or field; join in a contest: 双方运动员都已经～。Players of both teams have entered the court./ 今天该谁～？ Who's playing today? ◇ ～门 entrance (of a stage)

【上朝】 shàngcháo ① go to court ② hold court

【上床】 shàngchuáng go to bed

【上窜下跳】 shàngcuàn-xiàtiào run around on sinister errands

【上达】 shàngdá reach the higher authorities: 下情～ make the situation at the lower level known to the higher authorities

【上代】 shàngdài the previous generation; former generations

【上当】 shàngdàng be taken in; be fooled; be duped: 这回我可不～啦！ I won't be taken in this time./ 走这条路可～了，尽是水坑。We're fools to have chosen this path; it's full of puddles./ 不要上坏人的当。Don't let yourself be fooled by evil people./ 如果我们对阶级敌人丧失警惕性，那就会上大当。If we lower our guard against the class enemy, we'll really come to grief.

【上灯】 shàngdēng light the lamp; light up ◇ ～时分 lighting-up time

【上等】 shàngděng first-class; first-rate; superior: ～货 first-class goods/ ～料子 high-quality material

【上低音号】 shàngdīyīnhào〈乐〉baritone

【上帝】 Shàngdì God

【上吊】 shàngdiào hang oneself
【上冻】 shàngdòng freeze: 一定要在～以前把地基打好。We've got to finish the foundations before the ground freezes.
【上颚】 shàng'è maxilla (of a mammal); the upper jaw
【上方宝剑】 shàngfāng bǎojiàn the imperial sword (a symbol of high authority, investing the bearer with discretionary powers)
【上房】 shàngfáng main rooms (usu. facing south, within a courtyard)
【上访】 shàngfǎng apply for an audience with the higher authorities to appeal for help ◇ ～人员 visitors from the localities appealing to the higher authorities for help
【上坟】 shàngfén visit a grave to honour the memory of the dead
【上风】 shàngfēng ① windward: 咱们到烟的～头去吧。Let's get to windward of the smoke. 或 Let's go upwind of the smoke. ② advantage; superior position; upper hand: 占～ get the upper hand; win an advantage; prevail
【上纲】 shànggāng raise to the higher plane of principle: ～上线地进行批判 criticize from the higher plane of principle and two-line struggle/ 这个问题上不了纲。That's not a matter of principle.
【上告】 shànggào complain to the higher authorities or appeal to a higher court
【上工】 shànggōng go to work; start work: 夜班十点钟～。The night shift starts at 10.
【上供】 shànggòng offer up a sacrifice; lay offerings on the altar
【上钩】 shànggōu rise to the bait; swallow the bait; get hooked
【上古】 shànggǔ ancient times; remote ages ◇ ～史 ancient history
【上官】 Shàngguān a surname
【上光】 shàngguāng glazing; polishing ◇ ～机 glazing machine; glazer/ ～蜡 wax polish
【上轨道】 shàng guǐdào get on the right track; begin to work smoothly: 生产已～。Production is proceeding smoothly.
【上海】 Shànghǎi Shanghai
【上好】 shànghǎo first-class; best-quality; tip-top: ～烟叶 best-quality tobacco
【上颌】 shànghé 〈生理〉 the upper jaw; maxilla
【上呼吸道】 shànghūxīdào 〈生理〉 the upper respiratory tract ◇ ～感染 infection of the upper respiratory tract
【上火】 shànghuǒ ①〈方〉 get angry ②〈中医〉 suffer from excessive internal heat (with such symptoms as constipation, conjunctivitis and inflammation of the nasal and oral cavities)
【上级】 shàngjí higher level; higher authorities: ～党委 a Party committee of the higher level/ ～机关 higher authorities; a higher body/ ～领导 a leading body at a higher level/ 报告～ report to the higher authorities; report to one's superior/ 他是我的老～。He is my old chief.
【上江】 Shàngjiāng the upper Changjiang region
【上浆】 shàngjiāng 〈纺〉 sizing; (棉布) starching
【上将】 shàngjiàng (陆军, 美空军) general; (英空军) air chief marshal; (海军) admiral
【上交】 shàngjiāo turn over to the higher authorities; hand in: 多余器材应该～。Surplus equipment should be turned over to the higher authorities./ 不把矛盾～ not pass on difficulties to the leadership
【上胶机】 shàngjiāojī 〈纸〉 gluing machine
【上焦】 shàngjiāo 〈中医〉 the part of the body cavity above the diaphragm housing the heart and lungs
【上缴】 shàngjiǎo turn over (revenues, etc.) to the higher authorities ◇ ～利润 that part of the profits turned over to the state
【上街】 shàngjiē ① go into the street: ～示威 go on to (或 take to) the streets and demonstrate/ 大字报～ *dazibao* going up in the streets ② go shopping
【上届】 shàngjiè previous term or session; last: ～人大 the last People's Congress/ ～毕业生 last year's graduates
【上进】 shàngjìn go forward; make progress: 不求～ not strive to make progress ◇ ～心 the desire to do better; the urge for improvement
【上劲】 shàngjìn energetically; with gusto; with great vigour: 越干越～儿 work with increasing vigour (或 gusto)/ 越说越～儿 get more and more excited as one talks
【上课】 shàngkè ① attend class; go to class: 你昨天怎么没来～? Why didn't you come to class yesterday?/ 今天下午我们不～。We have no classes this afternoon. ② conduct a class; give a lesson (或 lecture): 学校八点开始～。Classes begin at 8./ 今天我们请了一位老红军战士给我们～。Today we invited a veteran Red Army man to give us a lecture.
【上空】 shàngkōng in the sky; overhead: 五星红旗在天安门广场～高高飘扬。The Five-Star Red Flag flies high above Tian'anmen Square.
【上口】 shàngkǒu ① be able to read aloud fluently: 孩子们把这首诗念了又念,现在都能琅琅～了。The children have read the poem several times, and can all recite it quite fluently now. ② be suitable for reading aloud; make smooth reading: 这段文字太艰深,不易～。The passage is too difficult and doesn't lend itself to reading aloud.
【上跨交叉】 shàngkuà jiāochā 〈交〉 overpass
【上款】 shàngkuǎn the name of the recipient (as inscribed on a painting or a calligraphic scroll presented as a gift)
【上蜡】 shànglà 〈纺〉 waxing ◇ ～机 waxing machine
【上来】 shànglai come up: 游了半天了,快～歇会儿吧。You've been swimming a long time now. Come out and have a rest.
【上来】 shanglai ①〔用在动词后,表示由低处到高处或由远处到近处来〕: 部队从两路增援～。Reinforcements arrived by two routes./ 外国朋友围～要他们签名留念。The foreign friends gathered around them and asked for their autographs. ②〔用在动词后,表示成功〕: 这个问题你答得～吗? Can you answer this question?/ 看他面熟,名字可叫不～。I know his face but I can't recall his name./ 等我爬到山顶的时候,气都快喘不～了。By the time I got to the top of the hill, I was quite out of breath. ③〈方〉〔用在形容词后,表示程度的增加〕: 天气热～了。The weather is getting hot.
【上联】 shànglián the first line of a couplet on a scroll
【上梁】 shàngliáng ① (of bicycles) cross bar; top tube ② (of buildings) upper beam: ～不正下梁歪。If the upper beam is not straight, the lower ones will go aslant — when those above behave unworthily, those below will do the same.
【上列】 shàngliè the above-listed; the above: ～各项 the items listed above; the above-listed items
【上流】 shàngliú ① upper reaches (of a river) ② belonging to the upper circles; upper-class: ～社会 high society; polite society
【上路】 shànglù set out on a journey; start off
【上马】 shàngmǎ ① mount (或 get on) a horse: ～!(口令) To horse! ② start (a project, etc.): 这项工程明年～。The project will start next year.
【上门】 shàngmén ① come or go to see sb.; call; drop in; visit: 他好久没～了。It's a long time since he last called./ 送货～ deliver goods to the doorstep ② shut the door (或 lock up) for the night; bolt the door

【上面】 shàngmian ① above; over; on top of; on the surface of: 飞机在云层～飞行。The plane flew above the clouds./ 粉墙～挂着大幅标语。Large streamers bearing slogans were hanging on the white wall./ 你的行李袋就在我的箱子～。Your bag is on top of my suitcase./ ～就是琉璃塔了。Further up is the glazed-tile pagoda./ 大桥～走汽车，下面走火车。The upper deck of the bridge is for motor vehicles, the lower deck for trains./ 运河～架了一座桥。A bridge has been built across the canal. ② above-mentioned; aforesaid; foregoing: ～所举的例子 the above-mentioned example/ ～这几条理由 the aforesaid reasons/ ～几个发言 the speeches you've just heard; the previous speeches ③ the higher authorities; the higher-ups: ～有指示。There are instructions from above. ④ aspect; respect; regard: 他在外文～下了很多功夫。He has put a lot of effort into his study of foreign languages.

【上年纪】 shàng niánji be getting on in years

【上盘】 shàngpán 〈矿〉 hanging wall

【上皮癌】 shàngpí'ái 〈医〉 epithelioma

【上皮组织】 shàngpí zǔzhī 〈生理〉 epithelial tissue

【上品】 shàngpǐn highest grade; top grade: 茅台是酒中～。*Maotai* is a top-grade spirit.

【上坡路】 shàngpōlù ① uphill road; upward slope ② upward trend; steady progress

【上铺】 shàngpù upper berth

【上气不接下气】 shàngqì bù jiē xiàqì gasp for breath; be out of breath

【上去】 shàngqu go up: 登着梯子～ go up (on) a ladder/ 车来了，咱们～吧。Here comes the bus. Let's get on./ 生产要～，干部要下去。If production is to go up, cadres must go down to the grass roots./ 过去由于规章制度不健全，这里的工作老是上不去。In the past, our work here could not move forward for lack of necessary rules and regulations.

【上去】 shangqu 〔用在动词后，表示由低到高，或由近及远，或由主体向对象〕: 爬～ climb up/ 把大车推～ push the cart up/ 看见排长回来了，大家赶忙迎～。Seeing the platoon leader returning, everybody rushed up to meet him./ 把国民经济搞～ push the national economy forward

【上染率】 shàngrǎnlǜ 〈纺〉 dye-uptake

【上任】 shàngrèn take up an official post; assume office

【上色】 shàngsè best-quality; top-grade: ～茶叶 top-grade tea

【上色】 shàngshǎi colour (a picture, map, etc.)

【上山下乡】 shàngshān-xiàxiāng (of educated urban youth) go and work in the countryside and mountain areas: ～知识青年 educated urban youth working in the countryside and mountain areas

【上上】 shàngshàng ① the very best: ～策 the best plan ② before last: ～星期 the week before last

【上身】 shàngshēn ① the upper part of the body: 光着～ be stripped to the waist/ 他～穿一件土布衬衫。He's wearing a shirt of handwoven cloth. ② upper outer garment; shirt; blouse; jacket: 姑娘们穿着白～，花裙子。The girls are wearing white blouses and bright-coloured skirts. ③ start wearing: 天冷了，棉袄该～了。It's getting cold. We'd better start wearing our padded jackets.

【上升】 shàngshēng rise; go up; ascend: 气温～。The temperature is going up./ 生产持续～。Production is rising steadily./ 一缕炊烟袅袅～。A wisp of smoke is curling up from the kitchen chimney./ 当时资本主义还处于～时期。At that time capitalism was still in the ascendant./ 使经验～为理论 raise experience to the level of theory/ 原来的次要矛盾现在已～为主要矛盾。What was formerly a secondary contradiction has now become the principal one. ◇ ～角 〈航空〉 angle of climb (或 ascent)/ ～气流 ascending air; up current/ ～失速 〈航空〉 advance stall/ ～转弯 〈航空〉 pull-up turn

【上声】 shàngshēng 或 shǎngshēng 〈语〉 falling-rising tone, one of the four tones in classical Chinese and the third tone in modern standard Chinese pronunciation

【上乘】 shàngshèng ①〈佛教〉 Mahayana; Great Vehicle ② a literary or artistic work of a high order

【上士】 shàngshì （美陆军）sergeant first class;（英陆军）staff sergeant;（美海军）petty officer first class;（英海军）chief petty officer;（美空军）technical sergeant;（英空军）flight sergeant

【上市】 shàngshì go (或 appear) on the market: 西红柿大量～。There are plenty of tomatoes on the market./ 这是刚～的苹果。These apples have just come in.

【上视图】 shàngshìtú 〈机〉 top view

【上手】 shàngshǒu ① left-hand seat; seat of honour ② start; begin: 今天的活一～就很顺利。Today's work went smoothly from the outset.

【上书】 shàngshū submit a written statement to a higher authority; send in a memorial

【上述】 shàngshù above-mentioned; aforementioned; aforesaid: 严格遵守～原则 strictly abide by the above-mentioned principles/ 达到～目标 achieve the aforementioned objectives

【上水】 shàngshuǐ ① sail upstream: ～船 upriver boat ② feed water to a steam engine, radiator (of an automobile), etc.

【上水道】 shàngshuǐdào 〈建〉 water-supply line

【上税】 shàngshuì pay taxes

【上司】 shàngsi superior; boss: 顶头～ one's immediate superior

【上诉】 shàngsù 〈法〉 appeal (to a higher court): 提出～ lodge an appeal
◇ ～法院 appellate court/ ～权 right of appeal/ ～人 appellant

【上算】 shàngsuàn paying; worthwhile: 烧煤气比烧煤～。It's more economical to use gas than coal.

【上岁数】 shàng suìshu 〈口〉 be getting on in years

【上台】 shàngtái ① go up onto the platform; appear on the stage: 她～演奏了两支钢琴曲子。She went up onto the platform and played two piano pieces. ② assume power; come (或 rise) to power

【上膛】 shàngtáng 〈军〉 (of a gun) be loaded: 子弹上了膛。The gun is loaded.

【上体】 shàngtǐ 〈书〉 the upper part of the body

【上天】 shàngtiān ① Heaven; Providence; God ② go up to the sky; fly sky-high: 我们又有一颗卫星～了。Another of our satellites has gone up.

【上天无路，入地无门】 shàng tiān wú lù, rù dì wú mén there is no road to heaven and no door into the earth — no way of escape; in desperate straits

【上头】 shàngtou 见"上面"①③④

【上尉】 shàngwèi （陆军、美空军）captain;（海军）lieutenant;（英空军）flight lieutenant

【上文】 shàngwén foregoing paragraphs or chapters; preceding part of the text: 见～ see above

【上沃尔特】 Shàng Wò'ěrtè the Upper Volta

【上午】 shàngwǔ forenoon; morning

【上下】 shàng-xià ① high and low; old and young: 全军～ the whole army, officers and men alike/ ～通气 full communication between the higher and lower levels/ ～一条心。The leadership and the rank and file are of one mind./ 举国～一片欢腾。The whole nation is jubilant./ 全家上上下下都很高兴。All members of the family, old and young, are very pleased. ② from top to bottom; up and down: ～打量 look sb. up and down; scrutinize sb. from head to foot/ 这个水塔～有五十米。The water tower is fifty metres high. ③ go up and down: 山上修了公路，汽车～很方便。With the completion of the highway up the mountain, cars can easily go up and down. ④ relative superiority or inferiority: 不相～ equally matched; about the same ⑤〔用在数量词后面〕about; or so; or thereabouts: 四十岁～ about forty years old; forty or so

【上下其手】 shàng-xià qí shǒu practise fraud; league together for some evil end

【上下文】 shàng-xiàwén context

【上弦】 shàngxián ①〈天〉first quarter (of the moon) ② wind up a clock or watch ◇ ～月 the moon at the first quarter

【上限】 shàngxiàn upper limit

【上相】 shàngxiàng come out well in a photograph; be photogenic

【上校】 shàngxiào (陆军、美空军) colonel; (海军) captain; (英空军) group captain

【上鞋】 shàngxié sole a shoe; stitch the sole to the upper

【上刑】 shàngxíng put sb. to torture; torture

【上行】 shàngxíng ①〈铁道〉up; upgoing: ～列车 up train ②〈航运〉upriver; upstream: ～船 upriver boat

【上行下效】 shàng xíng xià xiào those in subordinate positions will follow the example set by their superiors; if a leader sets a bad example, it will be followed by his subordinates; those below follow the (usu. bad) example of those above

【上旋】 shàngxuán 〈乒乓球〉top spin

【上学】 shàngxué go to school; attend school; be at school: 上过几年学 have been to school for a few years; have had a few years' schooling/ 解放前劳动人民根本没有～的机会。Before liberation the labouring people had simply no chance of going to school./ 这孩子～了没有? Is the child at school?

【上旬】 shàngxún the first ten-day period of a month

【上压力】 shàngyālì 〈物〉upward pressure

【上演】 shàngyǎn put on the stage; perform: 国庆节将～几个新戏。Several new plays will be performed on National Day./ 人民剧场今晚～什么节目? What's on at the People's Theatre this evening?

【上衣】 shàngyī upper outer garment; jacket

【上议院】 shàngyìyuàn upper house; the House of Lords (of Britain)

【上瘾】 shàngyǐn be addicted (to sth.); get into the habit (of doing sth.): 他抽烟抽上了瘾。He's got into the habit of smoking./ 这种药吃多了会～。This medicine is habit-forming.

【上映】 shàngyìng show (a film); screen: 近来有几部新片～。A number of new films have been shown recently.

【上游】 shàngyóu ① upper reaches (of a river) ② advanced position: 力争～ aim high; strive for the best/ ～无止境。One can always aim higher.

【上谕】 shàngyù imperial edict

【上涨】 shàngzhǎng rise; go up: 河水～。The river has risen./ 物价～。The prices are going up.

【上帐】 shàngzhàng make an entry in an account book; enter sth. in an account

【上阵】 shàngzhèn go into battle; pitch into the work: 男女老少齐～。Men and women, old and young, all pitched into the work./ 今晚比赛谁～? Who's going to play in tonight's match?

【上肢】 shàngzhī upper limbs

【上中农】 shàngzhōngnóng upper-middle peasant

【上装】 shàngzhuāng ① make up (for a theatrical performance) ②〈方〉upper outer garment; jacket

【上座】 shàngzuò seat of honour

**尚** shàng ①〈书〉〈副〉still; yet: 一息～存 as long as one lives; so long as there is still breath left in one/ ～待进一步讨论 pending further discussion/ 为时～早。It is still too early. 或 The time is not yet ripe./ 此事～未解决。The matter remains to be settled. 或 The problem is not resolved as yet. ② esteem; value; set great store by: 崇～ uphold; advocate/ ～武 set great store by martial qualities; emphasize military affairs ③ (Shàng) a surname

【尚方宝剑】 shàngfāng bǎojiàn 见"上方宝剑" shàngfāng bǎojiàn

【尚且】 shàngqiě 〈连〉〔提出程度更甚的事例作为衬托，下文常用"何况"等呼应，表示进一层的意思〕even: 大人～举不起来，何况小孩子。Even grown-ups can't lift it, to say nothing of children./ 你～不行，更不用说我了。If you can't do it, how can I?

【尚书】 shàngshū ① a high official in ancient China ② minister (in the Ming and Qing dynasties)

**绱** shàng stitch the sole to the upper

## shang

**裳** shang 见"衣裳" yīshang

另见 cháng

## shāo

**烧** shāo ① burn: 干柴好～。Wood burns better (或 more easily) when dry./ 咱们把这些废纸～掉吧。Let's burn up all this waste paper./ 侵略军到处～杀抢掠。The invaders burned, killed and looted wherever they went./ 把帽子～了一个洞 burn a hole in one's hat ② cook; bake; heat: ～饭 cook food; prepare a meal/ ～一点水 heat up some water/ 水～开了。The water is boiling./ ～炭 make charcoal/ ～砖 bake (或 fire) bricks ③ stew after frying or fry after stewing: ～茄子 stewed eggplant/ 红～肉 pork stewed in soy sauce ④ roast: ～鸡 roast chicken ⑤ run a fever; have a temperature: 病人～得厉害。The patient's running a high fever. 或 The patient has a high temperature. ⑥ fever: ～退了。The fever is down.

【烧杯】 shāobēi 〈化〉beaker

【烧饼】 shāobing sesame seed cake

【烧化】 shāohuà ① cremate ② burn (paper, etc. as an offering to the dead)

【烧荒】 shāohuāng burn the grass on waste land

【烧火】 shāohuǒ make a fire; light a fire; tend the kitchen fire

【烧碱】 shāojiǎn 〈化〉caustic soda

【烧结】 shāojié sintering; agglomeration; agglutination ◇ ～厂 sintering plant/ ～法〈冶〉sintering process/ ～剂〈化〉agglutinant

【烧酒】 shāojiǔ spirit usu. distilled from sorghum or maize; white spirit

【烧蓝】 shāolán 〈工美〉enameling

【烧卖】 shāomai 〈食品〉a steamed dumpling with the dough gathered at the top 又作"烧麦"

【烧毛】 shāomáo 〈纺〉singeing: 煤气～ gas singeing

【烧瓶】 shāopíng 〈化〉flask

【烧伤】 shāoshāng 〈医〉burn: 治疗大面积～ treat extensive burns/ 三度～ third-degree burns

【烧香】 shāoxiāng burn joss sticks (before an idol)
【烧心】 shāoxīn ①〈医〉 heartburn ②〈方〉 (of cabbages) turn yellow at the heart
【烧夷弹】 shāoyídàn incendiary bomb
【烧灼】 shāozhuó burn; scorch; singe

**捎** shāo take along sth. to or for sb.; bring to sb.: 请把这张报~给她。Take this paper to her, please./ 我给你孩子~来一点花生。I've brought your children some peanuts./ ~个口信 take a message to sb./ 替我给大家~个好。Please give my regards to everybody.
另见 shào
【捎带】 shāodài incidentally; in passing: 你上书店的话，~给我买张世界地图。If you happen to be going to the bookshop, please get me a map of the world.
【捎脚】 shāojiǎo pick up passengers or goods on the way; give sb. a lift

**梢** shāo tip; the thin end of a twig, etc.: 鞭~ whiplash/ 树~ the top of a tree/ 辫子~ the end of a plait
【梢头】 shāotóu ① the tip of a branch ②〈林〉 top log

**稍** shāo 〈副〉 a little; a bit; slightly; a trifle: ~加修改 make slight changes; make a few alterations/ ~胜一筹 just a little better/ 这大衣~长了一点。The coat is a bit too long./ 请~等一会儿。Please wait a moment. 或 Just a moment, please./ ~事休息后又继续开会。The meeting continued after a short interval.
【稍微】 shāowēi 〈副〉 a little; a bit; slightly; a trifle: ~搁点盐 put in a little salt/ 今天~有点冷。It's rather chilly today./ ~有点惊慌 be a trifle alarmed/ 这种颜色比那种~深一点。This colour is just a shade darker than that one.
【稍息】 shāoxī 〈军〉 stand at ease: ~!（口令）At ease!
【稍许】 shāoxǔ 见"稍微"
【稍纵即逝】 shāo zòng jí shì transient; fleeting: ~的机会 a fleeting opportunity

**筲** shāo pail (usu. made of bamboo strips or wood); bucket

**艄** shāo ① stern ② rudder; helm: 掌~ be at the helm
【艄公】 shāogōng ① helmsman ② boatman

**鞘** shāo whiplash
另见 qiào

## sháo

**勺** sháo ① spoon; ladle: 长柄~ ladle; dipper ② *shao*, an old unit of capacity (=1 centilitre)
【勺子】 sháozi ladle; scoop

**芍** sháo
【芍药】 sháoyao 〈植〉 Chinese herbaceous peony

**杓** sháo
【杓鹬】 sháoyù 〈动〉 curlew

**韶** sháo 〈书〉 splendid; beautiful
【韶光】 sháoguāng 〈书〉 ① beautiful springtime ② glorious youth 又作"韶华"
【韶山】 Sháoshān Shaoshan

## shǎo

**少** shǎo ① few; little; less: 以~胜多 defeat the many with the few/ ~花钱，多办事。Get more done on less money./ ~走弯路 avoid detours/ ~吃多餐 have many meals but little food at each/ 最近我们很~见到他。We've seen very little of him lately./ 现在我工作中困难~些了。Now I meet with fewer difficulties in my work./ 七比九~二。Seven is two less than nine. ② be short; lack: 我们还~两把椅子。We're still two chairs short./ 缺医~药 be short of doctors and medicine/ 咱们~一个好的守门员。We lack a good goalkeeper./ 帐算错了，~一块钱。This account is wrong; we're one *yuan* short. ③ lose; be missing: 看看~不~人。See if anyone is missing./ 这里肯定~了一个字。Surely, there's a word missing here./ 羊群里~了几只羊。A few sheep have been lost from the flock. ④ a little while; a moment: 请~候。Wait a moment, please. ⑤ stop; quit: ~废话! Stop talking rubbish!/ ~来这一套。Cut it out. 或 Quit that!/ ~给我装蒜! Stop pretending!
另见 shào
【少安毋躁】 shǎo ān wú zào don't be impatient, wait for a while
【少不得】 shǎobude cannot do without; cannot dispense with: 学科学，参考书是~的。Reference books are indispensable in scientific studies./ 这事~还要麻烦您。We may have to trouble you again about this.
【少不了】 shǎobuliǎo ① cannot do without; cannot dispense with: 这次比赛~你。We can't do without you for this match. ② be bound to; be unavoidable: 准备仓促，演出~会有缺点。The performance has been arranged at short notice, so it's bound to have shortcomings. ③ considerable: 困难看来~。It looks as if there are going to be a lot of difficulties.
【少而精】 shǎo ér jīng smaller quantity, better quality; fewer but better: 教学内容要~。Teaching content should be concise.
【少见多怪】 shǎojiàn-duōguài consider sth. remarkable simply because one has not seen it before; comment excitedly on a commonplace thing (out of ignorance or inexperience): 用不着~。There's nothing to be surprised at./ 也许是我~。Maybe it was all due to my own ignorance.
【少刻】 shǎokè after a little while; a moment later
【少量】 shǎoliàng a small amount; a little; a few
【少慢差费】 shǎo-màn-chā-fèi fewer, slower, poorer and more costly: 这种方法~。This method will get fewer and poorer results, and progress will be slower and costs higher. 或 That's an inefficient and expensive method.
【少陪】 shǎopéi 〈套〉 if you'll excuse me; I'm afraid I must be going now
【少顷】 shǎoqǐng 〈书〉 after a short while; after a few moments; presently
【少时】 shǎoshí after a little while; a moment later
【少数】 shǎoshù small number; few; minority: ~人 a small number of people; a few people; the minority/ 他们是~。They are in the minority./ ~服从多数。The minority is subordinate to the majority.
【少数民族】 shǎoshù mínzú minority nationality; national minority: 搞好汉族和~的关系 foster good relations between the Han nationality and the minority nationalities ◇~地区 areas inhabited by the minority nationalities; minority nationality regions/ ~干部 minority nationality cadres
【少许】 shǎoxǔ 〈书〉 a little; a few; a modicum

## shào

**少** shào ① young: 男女老～ men and women, old and young ② son of a rich family; young master: 阔～ a profligate son of the rich/ 恶～ young ruffian
另见 shǎo
【少白头】 shàobáitóu ① be prematurely grey ② a young person with greying hair
【少不更事】 shào bù gēng shì young and inexperienced; green: ～者 a greenhorn
【少妇】 shàofù young married woman
【少将】 shàojiàng (陆军、美空军) major general; (海军) rear admiral; (英空军) air vice marshal
【少奶奶】 shàonǎinai 〈旧〉 ① young mistress of the house ② your daughter-in-law
【少年】 shàonián ① early youth (from ten to sixteen) ② boy or girl of that age; juvenile
◇ ～单打 boys' and girls' singles/ ～读物 juvenile books; books for young people/ ～犯罪 juvenile delinquency/ ～宫 Children's Palace/ ～先锋队 Young Pioneers/ ～业余体校 children's sparetime sports school/ ～运动员 juvenile athlete/ ～之家 Children's Centre; Children's Club
【少年老成】 shàonián lǎochéng ① an old head on young shoulders ② a young person lacking in vigour and drive
【少女】 shàonǔ young girl
【少尉】 shàowèi (陆军、美空军) second lieutenant; (美海军) ensign; (英海军) acting sublieutenant; (英空军) pilot officer
【少先队】 shàoxiānduì 〈简〉(少年先锋队) Young Pioneers
◇ ～员 Young Pioneer
【少校】 shàoxiào (陆军、美空军) major; (海军) lieutenant commander; (英空军) squadron leader
【少爷】 shàoye 〈旧〉 ① young master of the house: ～脾气 behaviour of a spoilt boy ② your son
【少壮】 shàozhuàng young and vigorous: ～不努力，老大徒伤悲。If one does not exert oneself in youth, one will regret it in old age. 或 Laziness in youth spells regret in old age.

**邵** Shào a surname

**劭** shào 〈书〉 ① encourage; urge; exhort ② excellent; admirable: 年高德～ of venerable age and eminent virtue; venerable

**绍** shào carry on; continue
【绍兴酒】 shàoxīngjiǔ Shaoxing rice wine

**捎** shào drive (a cart) backwards; back (a cart)
另见 shāo
【捎马子】 shàomǎzi saddlebag
【捎色】 shàoshǎi fade (in colour)

**哨** shào ① sentry post; post: 岗～ sentry post/ 观察～ observation post/ 放～ be on sentry duty; stand guard; stand sentry ② (of birds) warble; chirp ③ whistle: 吹～ blow a whistle
【哨兵】 shàobīng sentry; guard
【哨所】 shàosuǒ sentry post; post: 前沿～ forward post; outpost
【哨子】 shàozi whistle

**潲** shào ① (of rain) slant in: 东边～雨。The rain is driving (或 slanting) in from the east. ② 〈方〉 sprinkle: 往菜上～水 sprinkle the vegetables with water ③ 〈方〉 hogwash; swill: 猪～ hogwash; swill

## shē

**奢** shē ① luxurious; extravagant: 穷～极欲 (indulge in) luxury and extravagance ② excessive; inordinate; extravagant: ～望 extravagant hopes
【奢侈】 shēchǐ luxurious; extravagant; wasteful: 生活～ live in luxury ◇ ～品 luxury goods; luxuries
【奢华】 shēhuá luxurious; sumptuous; extravagant: 陈设～ be luxuriously furnished
【奢靡】 shēmí extravagant; wasteful
【奢望】 shēwàng extravagant hopes; wild wishes

**猞** shē
【猞猁】 shēlì 〈动〉 lynx

**赊** shē buy or sell on credit
【赊购】 shēgòu buy on credit
【赊欠】 shēqiàn buy or sell on credit; give or get credit
【赊销】 shēxiāo sell on credit
【赊帐】 shēzhàng 见"赊欠"

**畲** Shē
【畲族】 Shēzú the She nationality, distributed over Fujian, Zhejiang, Jiangxi and Guangdong

## shé

**舌** shé ① tongue (of a human being or animal) ② sth. shaped like a tongue: 火～ tongues of flame/ 鞋～ the tongue of a shoe
【舌敝唇焦】 shébì-chúnjiāo talk till one's tongue and lips are parched; wear oneself out in pleading, expostulating, etc.
【舌根音】 shégēnyīn 〈语〉 velar
【舌尖】 shéjiān the tip of the tongue
◇ ～后音 〈语〉 blade-palatal/ ～前音 〈语〉 dental/ ～音 〈语〉 apical/ ～中音 〈语〉 blade-alveolar
【舌面后音】 shémiànhòuyīn 〈语〉 velar
【舌面前音】 shémiànqiányīn 〈语〉 dorsal
【舌鳎】 shétǎ 〈动〉 tonguefish; tongue sole
【舌苔】 shétāi 〈中医〉 coating on the tongue; fur
【舌头】 shétou ① tongue ② an enemy soldier captured for the purpose of extracting information: 侦察兵抓了个～。The scouts took a prisoner to get information.
【舌下神经】 shéxià shénjīng 〈生理〉 hypoglossal nerve
【舌炎】 shéyán 〈医〉 glossitis
【舌战】 shézhàn have a verbal battle with; argue heatedly: 一场～ a heated dispute; a battle royal
【舌状花】 shézhuànghuā 〈植〉 ligulate flower

**折** shé ① break; snap: 扁担～了。The shoulder pole broke./ 他们太使劲，把绳子拉～了。They pulled the rope so hard that it snapped. ② lose money in business
另见 zhē; zhé
【折本】 shéběn lose money in business: ～生意 a losing business; a bad bargain
【折耗】 shéhào damage (to goods during transit, storage, etc.); loss

**佘** Shé a surname

**蛇** shé snake; serpent
另见 yí

【蛇麻】 shémá 〈植〉 hop
【蛇莓】 shéméi 〈植〉 mock-strawberry
【蛇皮管】 shépíguǎn 〈电〉 flexible metal conduit
【蛇丘】 shéqiū 〈地〉 esker
【蛇蜕】 shétuì 〈中药〉 snake slough
【蛇纹石】 shéwénshí 〈矿〉 serpentine
【蛇蝎】 shéxiē snakes and scorpions — vicious people: 毒如～ as vicious as a viper
【蛇行】 shéxíng 〈书〉 move with the body on the ground; crawl
【蛇形】 shéxíng snakelike; S-shaped
【蛇足】 shézú fect added to a snake by an ignorant artist — sth. superfluous 参见"画蛇添足" huà shé tiān zú

## shě

**舍** shě ① give up; abandon: ～此别无他法。There is no other way than this. 或 This is the only way. ② give alms; dispense charity
另见 shè

【舍本逐末】 shěběn-zhúmò attend to trifles to the neglect of essentials
【舍不得】 shěbude hate to part with or use; grudge: 他是队里的好管家，～乱花一分钱。He is our team's good manager and hates to waste a single cent./ 他～穿那套新衣服。He begrudged wearing his new suit. 或 He was reluctant to wear his new suit.
【舍得】 shěde be willing to part with; not grudge: 练字必须～下功夫。To acquire good handwriting one mustn't begrudge time spent on practice./ ～一身剐，敢把皇帝拉下马。He who fears not being cut to pieces dares to unhorse the emperor.
【舍己为人】 shě jǐ wèi rén sacrifice one's own interests for the sake of others
【舍近求远】 shějìn-qiúyuǎn seek far and wide for what lies close at hand
【舍车保帅】 shějū-bǎoshuài give up a rook to save the king (in chess) — make minor sacrifices to safeguard major interests
【舍命】 shěmìng risk one's life; sacrifice oneself
【舍弃】 shěqì give up; abandon
【舍入】 shěrù 〈数〉 rounding off
【舍身】 shěshēn give one's life; sacrifice oneself: ～救人 give one's life to rescue sb.; sacrifice oneself to save others
【舍生取义】 shě shēng qǔ yì lay down one's life for a just cause
【舍死忘生】 shěsǐ-wàngshēng disregard one's own safety; risk one's life

## shè

**设** shè ① set up; establish; found: 指挥所～在前沿阵地上。The command post was set up in a forward position./ 部下面～六个司。Under the ministry there are six departments./ 我们这个市，下面～十个区。Our municipality is divided into ten districts. ② work out: ～计陷害 plot a frame-up; frame ③ 〈数〉 given; suppose; if: ～长方形的宽是 x 米。Suppose the width of a rectangle is x metres./ ～x=1 Given: x=1 ④ 〈书〉 if; in case: ～有困难，当助一臂之力。You can count on me to help in case of difficulty.
【设备】 shèbèi equipment; installation; facilities: 冶金～ metallurgical equipment/ 电气～ electrical installations/ 交通运输～ facilities for transport and communication/ 旅馆～齐全。The hotel is well appointed. ◇ ～利用率 utilization rate of equipment and installations
【设法】 shèfǎ think of a way; try; do what one can: 我们乐队正在～找个小提琴手。Our orchestra is trying to find a violinist.
【设防】 shèfáng set up defences; fortify; garrison: 层层～ set up defences in depth ◇ ～地带 fortified zone
【设计】 shèjì design; plan: 建筑～ architectural design/ 舞台～ stage design/ ～一座厂房 make designs for a factory building/ ～一种新机器 design a new machine/ ～一座水坝 project a dam/ ～版面 lay out a printed page ◇ ～洪水 〈水〉 design flood/ ～能力 designed capacity/ ～师 designer/ ～图 design drawing/ ～院 designing institute
【设立】 shèlì establish; set up; found: ～新的机构 set up a new organization
【设若】 shèruò if; suppose; provided
【设色】 shèsè fill in colours on a sketch; lay paint on (canvas); colour: ～柔和 painted in quiet colours
【设身处地】 shèshēn-chǔdì put oneself in sb. else's position; be considerate: 服务员事事～为旅客着想。The attendants look at everything from the passengers' angle and take care of their every need.
【设施】 shèshī installation; facilities: 防洪～ flood control installations/ 军事～ military installations/ 医疗～ medical facilities/ 集体福利～ collective welfare institutions
【设使】 shèshǐ if; suppose; in case
【设想】 shèxiǎng ① imagine; envisage; conceive; assume: 不堪～ too ghastly (或 dreadful) to contemplate/ 从最坏的可能来～ anticipate the worst; prepare for the worst/ 不能～反动派会自行退出历史舞台。It is inconceivable that the reactionaries should step down from the stage of history of their own accord./ 这样～是合乎逻辑的。It is logical to assume that. ② tentative plan; tentative idea: 这些只是我们的初步～。Those are just our tentative ideas. ③ have consideration for: 为群众～ take the interests of the masses into consideration/ 多为青少年～ give much thought to the needs of the younger generation
【设宴】 shèyàn give a banquet; fête: ～招待贵宾 give a banquet in honour of the distinguished visitors; fête the distinguished guests
【设营】 shèyíng 〈军〉 quartering; encampment ◇ ～地 camp site/ ～队 quartering party
【设置】 shèzhì set up; put up; install: ～专门机构 set up a special organization/ 给会议～重重障碍 place all sorts of obstacles before the conference/ 课程～ courses offered in a college or school; curriculum

**社** shè ① organized body; agency; society: 通讯～ news agency/ 合作～ cooperative/ 报～ newspaper office/ 出版～ publishing house ② people's commune: ～办企业 commune-run enterprise ③ the god of the land, sacrifices to him or altars for such sacrifices
【社会】 shèhuì society: 人类～ human society
◇ ～保险 social insurance/ ～必要劳动 socially necessary labour/ ～财富 wealth of society; public wealth/ ～党 Socialist Party/ ～地位 social position; social status/ ～帝国主义 social-imperialism/ ～调查 social investigation; social survey/ ～发展史 history of social development; history of development of society/ ～分工 division of labour in society/ ～福利 social welfare; public welfare/

～环境 social environment/ ～活动 social activities; public activities/ ～基础 social base; social basis/ ～科学 social sciences/ ～名流 noted public figures/ ～实践 social practice/ ～制度 social system

【社会工作】 shèhuì gōngzuò work, in addition to one's regular job, done for the collective: 他是党小组长,～相当多。As Party group leader, he has many duties outside his regular work.

【社会关系】 shèhuì guānxi ① human relations in society; social relations ② one's social connections

【社会学】 shèhuìxué sociology ◇ ～家 sociologist

【社会主义】 shèhuìzhǔyì socialism ◇ ～道路 socialist road/ ～改造 socialist transformation/ ～革命 socialist revolution/ ～建设 socialist construction/ ～觉悟 socialist consciousness/ ～劳动竞赛 socialist labour emulation/ ～制度 socialist system

【社会主义建设总路线】 shèhuìzhǔyì jiànshè zǒnglùxiàn the general line for socialist construction, namely, go all out, aim high and achieve greater, faster, better and more economical results in building socialism

【社会主义教育运动】 Shèhuìzhǔyì Jiàoyù Yùndòng the socialist education movement (a nationwide movement to clean things up in the fields of politics, economy, organization and ideology, 1963-1966)

【社稷】 shèjì the god of the land and the god of grain — the state; the country

【社交】 shèjiāo social intercourse; social contact

【社教】 Shèjiào 〈简〉(社会主义教育运动) the socialist education movement

【社论】 shèlùn editorial; leading article; leader

【社评】 shèpíng 〈旧〉 editorial

【社团】 shètuán mass organizations

【社戏】 shèxì village theatrical performance given on religious festivals in old times

【社员】 shèyuán ① a member of a society, etc.: 合作社～ cooperative member ② commune member ◇ ～大会 general meeting of commune members

## 舍

shè ① house; shed; hut: 牛～ cowshed/ 茅～ thatched hut/ 校～ school buildings ②〈谦〉〔用于对别人称比自己辈分低或年纪小的亲属〕: ～弟 my younger brother/ ～侄 my nephew ③ an ancient unit of distance equal to 30 *li*

另见 shě

【舍间】 shèjiān 〈谦〉 my humble abode; my house

【舍利】 shèlì 〈佛教〉 Buddhist relics ◇ ～塔 stupa; pagoda for Buddhist relics; Buddhist shrine

【舍亲】 shèqīn 〈谦〉 my relative

【舍下】 shèxià 〈谦〉 my humble abode; my house

【舍营】 shèyíng 〈军〉 billeting

## 涉

shè ① wade; ford: ～水过河 wade across a river; ford a stream/ 远～重洋 travel all the way from across the oceans ② go through; experience: ～险 go through dangers/ ～世不深 have scanty experience of life; have seen little of the world ③ involve

【涉及】 shèjí involve; relate to; touch upon: 双方的分歧～一些重大原则性问题。The differences between the two sides involve major matters of principle./ 遗传工程～的学科和技术面很广。Genetic engineering deals with a wide range of disciplines and technologies.

【涉猎】 shèliè do desultory reading; read cursorily: 有的书必须精读,有的只要稍加～即可。Some books are for intensive study and some are for cursory reading.

【涉禽】 shèqín 〈动〉 wading bird; wader

【涉讼】 shèsòng be involved in a lawsuit

【涉外】 shèwài concerning foreign affairs or foreign nationals

【涉嫌】 shèxián be suspected of being involved; be a suspect

【涉足】 shèzú 〈书〉 set foot in: ～其间 set foot there

## 射

shè ① shoot; fire: ～箭 shoot an arrow/ 速～ rapid fire/ 扫～ strafe/ 能骑善～ be a good horseman as well as a crack shot; be known for one's equestrian skill and marksmanship/ ～进一球 kick the ball into the goal; score a goal/ 炮弹～中了敌人坦克。The shell hit the enemy tank. ② discharge in a jet: 喷～ spout; spurt; jet/ 注～ inject ③ send out (light, heat, etc.): 反～ reflect/ 光芒四～ radiate brilliant light/ 探照灯～出一道道强光。The searchlights projected powerful beams of light. ④ allude to sth. or sb.; insinuate: 影～ insinuate

【射程】 shèchéng range (of fire): 有效～ effective range

【射弹】 shèdàn projectile

【射电天文学】 shèdiàn tiānwénxué radio astronomy

【射电望远镜】 shèdiàn wàngyuǎnjìng radio telescope

【射干】 shègān 〈植〉 blackberry lily

【射击】 shèjī ① shoot; fire: 向敌人～ fire at the enemy ②〈体〉 shooting ◇ ～场 shooting range/ ～地境 sector of fire/ ～孔 embrasure

【射箭】 shèjiàn ① shoot an arrow ②〈体〉 archery ◇ ～手 archer

【射角】 shèjiǎo angle of fire

【射界】 shèjiè area (或 field) of fire; firing area

【射孔】 shèkǒng 〈石油〉 perforation

【射猎】 shèliè hunting with bow and arrow or firearms

【射流】 shèliú 〈物〉 efflux ◇ ～技术 fluidics/ ～喷口 efflux nozzle

【射门】 shèmén 〈体〉 shoot (at the goal) ◇ ～手 goal getter

【射频】 shèpín 〈电〉 radio frequency ◇ ～放大器 radio frequency amplifier

【射手】 shèshǒu shooter; marksman: 机枪～ machine gunner

【射速】 shèsù firing rate

【射线】 shèxiàn 〈物〉 ray ◇ ～病 radiation sickness/ ～疗法 radiotherapy

## 赦

shè remit (a punishment); pardon: 大～ general pardon; amnesty/ 特～ special pardon

【赦免】 shèmiǎn remit (a punishment); pardon

【赦罪】 shèzuì absolve sb. from guilt; pardon sb.

## 摄

shè ① absorb; assimilate ② take a photograph of; shoot: ～下几个珍贵的镜头 take some superb shots ③ conserve (one's health) ④ act for: ～理 hold (an office) in an acting capacity

【摄动】 shèdòng 〈天〉 perturbation

【摄谱仪】 shèpǔyí 〈物〉 spectrograph

【摄取】 shèqǔ ① absorb; assimilate; take in: ～营养 absorb nourishment ② take a photograph of; shoot: ～镜头 shoot a scene

【摄生】 shèshēng 〈书〉 conserve one's health; keep fit

【摄氏温度计】 shèshìwēndùjì centigrade thermometer; Celsius thermometer

【摄象机】 shèxiàngjī pickup camera: 电视～ television camera

【摄影】 shèyǐng ① take a photograph: ～留念 have a souvenir photograph taken/ 航空～ aerial photography/ 红外～ infrared photography ② shoot a film; film: 全景 (内

景，外景）～ panoramic (interior, exterior) shooting ◇ ～记者 press photographer; cameraman/ ～棚 film studio/ ～师 photographer; cameraman/ ～室 photographic studio; photo studio/ ～展览 photographic exhibition; photo exhibition

【摄影机】 shèyǐngjī camera: 电影～ cinecamera; cinematograph/ 立体～ stereoscopic camera

【摄政】 shèzhèng act as regent ◇ ～王 prince regent

【摄制】 shèzhì 〈电影〉 produce: 北京电影制片厂～ produced by the Beijing Film Studio ◇ ～组 production unit

**慑** shè 〈书〉 fear; be awed: ～于无产阶级专政的强大威力 be awed by the power of the dictatorship of the proletariat

【慑服】 shèfú ① submit because of fear; succumb ② cow sb. into submission

**麝** shè ① musk deer ② musk

【麝牛】 shèniú musk-ox

【麝鼠】 shèshǔ muskrat

【麝香】 shèxiāng musk

## shéi

**谁** shéi 见"谁" shuí

## shēn

**申** shēn ① state; express; explain: 重～前令 reiterate the previous order ② the ninth of the twelve Earthly Branches ③ (Shēn) another name for Shanghai ④ (Shēn) a surname

【申报】 shēnbào ① report to a higher body ② declare sth. (to the Customs)

【申辩】 shēnbiàn defend oneself; explain oneself; argue (或 plead) one's case: 允许～ allow sb. to argue his case/ 被告有权～。The accused has the right to defend himself.

【申斥】 shēnchì rebuke (usu. one's subordinates); reprimand

【申明】 shēnmíng declare; state; avow: ～自己的立场 state one's position/ 辩证唯物论公开～自己是为无产阶级服务的。Dialectical materialism openly avows that it serves the proletariat.

【申请】 shēnqǐng apply for: ～入党 apply for Party membership/ ～入（出）境签证 apply for an entry (exit) visa/ ～调动工作 apply for a transfer; ask for a transfer; ask to be transferred to another job
◇ ～国 applicant country/ ～人 applicant/ ～书 (written) application

【申时】 shēnshí the period of the day from 3 p.m. to 5 p.m.

【申述】 shēnshù state; explain in detail: ～立场 state one's position/ ～来意 explain the purpose of one's visit/ ～自己的观点 expound one's views/ 谨～如下 have the honour to state the following/ 作进一步的～ make further observations

【申说】 shēnshuō state (reasons)

【申诉】 shēnsù appeal: 向上级提出～ appeal to the higher authorities/ 不服判决，提出～ appeal against a legal decision

【申讨】 shēntǎo openly condemn; denounce: ～反动派的罪行 denounce the crimes of the reactionaries

【申谢】 shēnxiè acknowledge one's indebtedness; express one's gratitude

【申冤】 shēnyuān ① redress an injustice; right a wrong ② appeal for redress of a wrong

**伸** shēn stretch; extend: ～胳臂 stretch one's arms/ ～大拇指 hold up one's thumb/ 两臂平～ extend (或 stretch, spread) one's arms horizontally/ 跳水时腿要～直。When you dive you must keep your legs straight./ 不要把头～出窗外。Don't put (或 stick) your head out of the window (of a bus, etc.)./ 早在十九世纪，帝国主义的魔爪就～进了中国。The imperialists stretched their claws into China as early as the nineteenth century.

【伸懒腰】 shēn lǎnyāo stretch oneself

【伸手】 shēnshǒu ① stretch (或 hold) out one's hand: 他～去拿碗。He reached for the bowl./ ～不见五指 so dark that you can't see your hand in front of you; pitch dark ② ask for help, etc.: ～派 a person who is in the habit of asking the higher level for help/ 尽管遭了水灾，他们却没有向国家～要一分钱。Although hit by the flood, they did not ask for a single copper from the state.

【伸缩】 shēnsuō ① stretch out and draw back; expand and contract; lengthen and shorten: 这架照像机的镜头可以前后～。The lens of this camera can be pulled back and forth. ② flexible; elastic; adjustable: 这些规定～性很大。These regulations are quite elastic (或 flexible)./ 没有～余地 leave one no latitude ◇ ～缝 〈建〉 expansion joint/ ～三角架 extension tripod

【伸腿】 shēntuǐ ① stretch one's legs ② step in (to gain an advantage) ③ 〈口〉 kick the bucket; turn up one's toes

【伸腰】 shēnyāo straighten one's back; straighten oneself up

【伸冤】 shēnyuān 见"申冤" shēnyuān

【伸展】 shēnzhǎn spread; extend; stretch: 草原一直～到遥远的天边。The prairie stretches to the distant horizon.

【伸张】 shēnzhāng uphold; promote: ～正气，打击歪风 promote healthy tendencies and combat unhealthy ones

**身** shēn ① body: ～心 body and mind/ 这套衣服挺合～。This suit fits perfectly./ 转过～去 turn round/ ～负重伤 be seriously injured (或 wounded)/ ～不离劳动，心不离群众 never give up manual labour and always have the masses at heart ② life: 欧阳海舍～救列车。Ouyang Hai gave his life to prevent a train from becoming derailed./ 以～殉职 die a martyr at one's post ③ oneself; personally: 以～作则 set a good example with one's own conduct/ 你～为组长，应当负起责任来。As group leader, you should take charge. ④ one's moral character and conduct: 修～ cultivate one's mind ⑤ the main part of a structure; body: 汽车车～ the body of a motor car/ 机～ fuselage/ 树～ trunk/ 船～ the body of a ship; hull ⑥ 〈量〉〔用于衣服〕 suit: 一～新衣服 a new suit

【身败名裂】 shēnbài-mínglìè lose all standing and reputation; bring disgrace and ruin upon oneself; be utterly discredited

【身板】 shēnbǎn 〈方〉 body; bodily health: ～儿挺结实 have a strong physique

【身边】 shēnbiān ① at (或 by) one's side: 老人把全家人叫到～。The old man summoned the whole family to his side./ 他在首长～工作，进步很快。Working at the side of the leading comrades, he has made rapid progress. ② (have sth.) on one; with one: ～没带钱 have no money on one/ 她～总是带着药箱。She never goes anywhere without her medical kit.

【身不由己】 shēn bù yóu jǐ involuntarily; in spite of oneself: 车子突然一停，他～地向前一扑。When the bus came to a sudden stop, he jerked forward involuntarily.

【身材】 shēncái stature; figure: ～矮小 short and slight of stature/ ～苗条 have a slender (或 slim) figure/ ～魁梧 of great height and powerful build; tall and sturdy

【身长】 shēncháng ① height (of a person) ② length (of a garment from shoulder to hemline)

【身段】 shēnduàn ① (woman's) figure ② (dancer's) posture

【身分】 shēnfen ① status; capacity; identity: 不合～ incompatible with one's status/ ～不明 of unknown identity; unidentified/ 暴露～ reveal one's identity/ 以官方（私人，个人）～发言 speak in an official (a private, a personal) capacity ② dignity: 有失～ be beneath one's dignity ◇ ～证 identity card; identification card 又作"身份"

【身高】 shēngāo height (of a person): 他～一米八。He is 180 centimetres in height.

【身故】 shēngù die: 因病～ die of an illness

【身后】 shēnhòu after one's death

【身价】 shēnjià ① social status: 突然～百倍 have a sudden rise in social status ② the selling price of a slave

【身教】 shēnjiào teach others by one's own example: ～胜于言教。Example is better than precept.

【身经百战】 shēn jīng bǎi zhàn have fought a hundred battles: ～的老战士 a veteran who has fought countless battles; a battle-tested veteran; a seasoned fighter

【身量】 shēnliang 〈口〉 height (of a person); stature: 她～不高。She's not tall.

【身临其境】 shēn lín qí jìng be personally on the scene: 这个场面写得很生动，使人有～之感。The scene is so vividly portrayed that the reader feels as if he is participating.

【身强力壮】 shēnqiáng-lìzhuàng (of a person) strong; tough; sturdy

【身躯】 shēnqū body; stature: 健壮的～ a sound body/ ～高大 tall of stature

【身上】 shēnshang ① on one's body: ～穿一件白衬衫 wear a white shirt/ 我～不舒服。I'm not feeling well./ 希望寄托在青年人～。Our hopes are placed on the young people. ② (have sth.) on one; with one: ～没带笔。I haven't got a pen with me./ ～有零钱吗？Have you got any change on you?

【身世】 shēnshì one's life experience; one's lot: ～凄凉 have had a sad life

【身手】 shēnshǒu skill; talent: 大显～ fully display one's talents; exhibit one's skill

【身受】 shēnshòu experience (personally): ～资本家的残酷剥削 suffer from cruel capitalist exploitation/ 感同～。I shall count it as a personal favour.

【身体】 shēntǐ ① body: 保持～平衡 keep one's balance ② health: 注意～ look after one's health/ ～非常健康 be in excellent health

【身体力行】 shēntǐ-lìxíng earnestly practise what one advocates

【身外之物】 shēn wài zhī wù external things; mere worldly possessions

【身先士卒】 shēn xiān shìzú lead one's men in a charge; charge at the head of one's men

【身心】 shēn-xīn body and mind: ～健康 sound in body and mind; physically and mentally healthy/ ～受到摧残 be physically injured and mentally affected

【身影】 shēnyǐng a person's silhouette; form; figure: 一个高大的～ a tall figure

【身孕】 shēnyùn pregnancy: 她有了三个月的～。She is three months pregnant.

【身在福中不知福】 shēn zài fú zhōng bù zhī fú growing up in happiness, one often fails to appreciate what happiness really means; not appreciate the happy life one enjoys

【身子】 shēnzi 〈口〉 ① body: 光着～ be naked/ ～不大舒服 not feel well ② pregnancy: 有了七个月的～ be seven months pregnant

【身子骨儿】 shēnzigǔr 〈方〉 one's health; physique: 爷爷的～还挺结实。Grandpa's enjoying good health. 或 Grandpa's still going strong.

**呻** shēn

【呻吟】 shēnyín groan; moan: 伤员的～ the moans of the wounded/ 无病～ moan and groan without being ill; make a fuss about an imaginary illness

**绅** shēn gentry: 土豪劣～ local tyrants and evil gentry

【绅士】 shēnshì gentleman; gentry

**参** shēn ginseng
另见 cān; cēn

**砷** shēn 〈化〉 arsenic (As)

**莘** shēn

【莘莘】 shēnshēn 〈书〉 numerous: ～学子 a great number of disciples; large numbers of students

**娠** shēn 见"妊娠" rènshēn

**深** shēn ① deep: 一口～井 a deep well/ 测量水～ sound the depth of the water / 雪～过膝 knee-deep snow/ 林～苔滑。The forest is thick and the moss is slippery. ② difficult; profound: 由浅入～ from the easy to the difficult/ 这本书给孩子看太～了。The book is too difficult for children. ③ thoroughgoing; penetrating; profound: 问题想得～ think deeply about a question/ 功夫～ have put in a great deal of effort/ 这个问题我没同他～谈。I didn't go deeply into the matter with him. ④ close; intimate: 交情～ be on intimate terms ⑤ dark; deep: ～蓝 dark blue/ ～红 deep red; crimson/ 颜色太～。The colour is too dark (或 deep). ⑥ late: ～秋 late autumn/ 夜～了。It was late at night. ⑦ very; greatly; deeply: ～恐 be very much afraid/ ～知 know very well; be fully (或 keenly) aware/ ～感 feel deeply; feel keenly/ ～信 be deeply convinced; firmly believe/ ～受感动 be deeply moved; be greatly touched/ ～表同情 show deep (或 profound) sympathy/ ～得人心 enjoy immense popular support

【深奥】 shēn'ào abstruse; profound; recondite: ～的哲理 abstruse philosophy; a profound truth

【深藏若虚】 shēn cáng ruò xū be modest about one's talent or learning; not be given to boasting or showing off

【深长】 shēncháng profound: 意味～ pregnant with meaning; significant

【深沉】 shēnchén ① dark; deep: 暮色～。The dusk is deepening. ② (of sound or voice) deep; heavy; dull: 大提琴～的音调 the deep notes of a cello/ ～的夯土声 the dull sound of earth being tamped ③ concealing one's real feelings: 这人很～。He's a deep one.

【深成岩】 shēnchéngyán 〈地〉 plutonic rock; plutonite

【深仇大恨】 shēnchóu-dàhèn bitter and deep-seated hatred; profound hatred

【深处】 shēnchù depths; recesses: 在密林～ in the depths (或 recesses) of the forest/ 在内心～ in the depth (或 innermost recesses) of one's heart/ 在灵魂～ in one's innermost soul/ 在思想～ in one's heart of hearts

【深度】 shēndù ① degree of depth; depth: 测量河水的～ sound the depth of the river ② profundity; depth: 他的发

言缺乏～。His speech lacks depth. ◇ ～计 depth gauge

【深更半夜】 shēngēng-bànyè at dead of night; in the depth (或 dead) of night; in the middle of the night

【深耕】 shēngēng 〈农〉 deep ploughing

【深沟高垒】 shēngōu-gāolěi deep trenches and high ramparts; strong defence

【深闺】 shēnguī boudoir

【深海】 shēnhǎi deep sea ◇ ～鱼 deep-sea fish/ ～资源 deep-sea resources

【深厚】 shēnhòu ① deep; profound: ～的无产阶级感情 deep (或 profound) proletarian feelings/ 结成～的战斗友谊 establish a profound and militant friendship ② solid; deep-seated: ～的基础 a solid foundation

【深呼吸】 shēnhūxī deep breathing

【深化】 shēnhuà deepen: 认识的～ deepening of cognition/ 矛盾的～ intensification of a contradiction

【深究】 shēnjiū go into (a matter) seriously; get to the bottom of (a matter): 对这些小事不必～。These are small matters and you don't have to go into them seriously.

【深居简出】 shēnjū-jiǎnchū live in the seclusion of one's own home; live a secluded life

【深刻】 shēnkè deep; profound; deepgoing: ～地阐明 expound profoundly/ 给某人留下～的印象 make a deep impression on sb./ 受到一次～的教育 learn a profound lesson/ ～的社会主义革命 a deepgoing socialist revolution

【深空】 shēnkōng 〈物〉 deep space

【深谋远虑】 shēnmóu-yuǎnlǜ think deeply and plan carefully; be circumspect and farsighted

【深浅】 shēnqiǎn ① depth: 你去打听一下这河的～，看能不能蹚水过去。Go and find out how deep the river is and whether we can wade across. ② proper limits (for speech or action); sense of propriety: 说话没～ speak without thought and often inappropriately ③ shade (of colour): 颜色～不同 of different shades

【深切】 shēnqiè heartfelt; deep; profound: ～的同情 deep sympathy/ ～关怀 be deeply concerned about; show profound concern for/ ～怀念 dearly cherish the memory of/ 表示～的哀悼 express one's heartfelt condolences (to the deceased's family); express one's profound grief (at sb.'s death)

【深情】 shēnqíng deep feeling; deep love: 战士们无限～地望着周总理的画像。The soldiers gazed with deep feeling at the portrait of Premier Zhou./ ～厚谊 profound sentiments of friendship

【深入】 shēnrù ① go deep into; penetrate into: ～实际 go deep into the realities of life/ ～敌后 penetrate far behind enemy lines/ ～基层 go down to the grass-roots units/ ～群众 immerse oneself (或 go deep) among the masses; go into the midst of the common people/ ～农业生产第一线 go right to the front line of agricultural production/ ～生活 plunge into the thick of life/ ～人心 strike root in the hearts of the people/ ～事物本质 probe deeply into the essence of things/ 诱敌～ lure the enemy in deep ② thorough; deepgoing: 做～细致的思想工作 conduct thoroughgoing and painstaking ideological work/ ～进行调查研究 make a thorough investigation and study/ 运动正在～发展。The movement is developing in depth.

【深入浅出】 shēnrù-qiǎnchū explain the profound in simple terms

【深山】 shēnshān remote mountains: ～老林 remote, thickly forested mountains

【深深】 shēnshēn profoundly; deeply; keenly: ～感到革命集体的温暖 feel the warmth of the revolutionary collective/ 在群众中～地扎下了根 strike deep root (或 take firm root) among the masses

【深水】 shēnshuǐ deepwater ◇ ～港 deepwater port/ ～码头 deepwater wharf/ ～炸弹 depth charge; depth bomb

【深思】 shēnsī think deeply about; ponder deeply over: 这难道不值得～吗？Is this not worth pondering? 或 Does this not call for deep thought?/ 这个问题值得我们～。This matter gives us much food for thought.

【深思熟虑】 shēnsī-shúlǜ careful consideration

【深邃】 shēnsuì ① deep: ～的山谷 a deep valley ② profound; abstruse; recondite: 寓意～ have a profound message

【深文周纳】 shēnwén-zhōunà (of feudal officials, judges, etc.) use every means to have an innocent person pronounced guilty; convict sb. by deliberately misinterpreting the law; frame up and punish severely

【深恶痛绝】 shēnwù-tòngjué hate bitterly; abhor; detest

【深夜】 shēnyè late at night; in the small hours of the morning: 工作到～ work late into the night

【深意】 shēnyì profound meaning

【深渊】 shēnyuān abyss: 苦难的～ the abyss of suffering (或 misery)

【深远】 shēnyuǎn profound and lasting; far-reaching: 具有～的历史意义 have profound historic significance

【深造】 shēnzào take a more advanced course of study or training; pursue advanced studies: 送到体育学院～ be sent to the Institute of Physical Culture for further training/ 上中央民族学院～ go to the Central Institute of Minority Nationalities for advanced studies

【深宅大院】 shēnzhái-dàyuàn a compound of connecting courtyards, each surrounded by dwelling quarters (usu. occupied by a single wealthy family in the old days); imposing dwellings and spacious courtyards

【深湛】 shēnzhàn profound and thorough: ～的著作 a profound work/ 功夫～ consummate skill

【深重】 shēnzhòng very grave; extremely serious: 危机～ be in the grip of a crisis/ 经过一百多年的反帝反封建斗争，灾难～的中华民族终于站起来了。After more than a hundred years of anti-imperialist, anti-feudal struggle, the calamity-ridden Chinese nation at last stood up.

**鲹** shēn scad

## shén

**什** shén

另见 shí

【什么】 shénme ①〔表示疑问〕 ⓐ〔单用，问事物〕: 他说～？What did he say?/ ～叫工作？工作就是斗争。What is work? Work is struggle. ⓑ〔用在名词前面，问人或事物〕: 他是～人？Who is he?/ 那是～颜色？What colour is it?/ 他～时候走？When will he leave? ②〔虚指，表示不肯定的事物〕: 我饿了，想吃点儿～。I'm hungry. I'd like to have a bite./ 好象出了～事儿。It seems something is amiss. ③〔任指〕 ⓐ〔用在"也"或"都"前面，表示所说的范围之内没有例外〕: 他～也不怕。He is afraid of nothing./ ～用处也没有 be quite worthless/ 只要认真学，～都能学会。If you study conscientiously, you can learn anything. ⓑ〔两个"什么"前后照应，表示由前者决定后者〕: 有～就说～。Just say what's on your mind./ ～藤结～瓜，～阶级说～话。Each plant yields its own fruit; each class speaks its own language. ④〔表示惊讶或不满〕: ～！没有水？What! (或 What's that?) No water?/ ～！九点了，车还没来！What's happened! 9 o'clock and the bus hasn't come yet! ⑤〔表示责难〕: 你笑～？What's so funny?/ 你说呀！装～哑巴？Speak! Stop playing dumb. ⑥〔表示不同意对方刚说的某一句话〕: ～不

懂！装糊涂就是了。What do you mean — not understand? You're just pretending./ ～自由企业！无非是自由剥削罢了。Free enterprise, indeed! Free exploitation — that's what it is! ⑦〔用在几个并列成分前面，表示列举不尽〕：～乒乓球啊，羽毛球啊，篮球啊，排球啊，他都会。He can play table tennis, badminton, basketball, volleyball, anything.

【什么的】 shénmede and so on; and what not: 她做了棉衣、棉鞋～，准备儿子下乡时穿。She made cotton-padded clothes and shoes and what not for her son to wear in the countryside./ 修个机器，换个零件～，他都能对付。Repairing a machine or replacing a part — he can cope with things like that all right.

## 甚 shén

另见 shèn

【甚么】 shénme 见"什么" shénme

## 神

shén ① god; deity; divinity ② supernatural; magical: ～效 magical effect; miraculous effect/ 用兵如～ direct military operations with miraculous skill ③ spirit; mind: 凝～ concentrate (或 focus) one's attention/ 走～ be absentminded/ 耗～ take up one's energy/ 闭目养～ close one's eyes and rest one's mind/ 他双目炯炯有～。He has a pair of bright piercing eyes. ④ expression; look: 眼～ expression in the eyes ⑤〈方〉smart; clever: 这孩子真～！What a smart child!/ 这家伙～了！This fellow is incredible!

【神不知，鬼不觉】 shén bù zhī, guǐ bù jué unknown to god or ghost — (do sth.) without anybody knowing it; in great secrecy

【神采】 shéncǎi expression; look: ～奕奕 glowing with health and radiating vigour

【神出鬼没】 shénchū-guǐmò come and go like a shadow; appear and disappear mysteriously

【神甫】 shénfu Catholic father; priest 又作"神父"

【神工鬼斧】 shéngōng-guǐfǔ 见"鬼斧神工" guǐfǔ-shéngōng

【神怪】 shén-guài gods and spirits

【神汉】 shénhàn sorcerer

【神乎其神】 shén hū qí shén fantastic; wonderful; miraculous: 吹得～ laud sth. or sb. to the skies

【神化】 shénhuà deify

【神话】 shénhuà mythology; myth; fairy tale: 揭穿现代修正主义者关于和平过渡的～ explode the modern revisionists' myth of peaceful transition

【神魂】 shénhún state of mind; mind: ～不定 be deeply perturbed/ ～颠倒 be infatuated

【神机妙算】 shénjī-miàosuàn wonderful foresight (in military operations, etc.)

【神经】 shénjīng nerve: 脑（感觉，交感）～ cranial (sensory, sympathetic) nerve/ ～紧张 be nervous
◇ ～毒气 nerve gas/ ～官能症 neurosis/ ～节 ganglion/ ～末梢 nerve ending/ ～衰弱 neurasthenia/ ～痛 neuralgia/ ～外科 neurosurgery/ ～系统 nervous system/ ～炎 neuritis/ ～原 neuron/ ～战 war of nerves/ ～质 nervousness/ ～中枢 nerve centre

【神经病】 shénjīngbìng ① neuropathy ② mental disorder: 这家伙有点～。That chap's not quite right in the head.

【神经过敏】 shénjīng guòmǐn ① neuroticism ② neurotic; oversensitive

【神龛】 shénkān a shrine for idols or ancestral tablets

【神力】 shénlì superhuman strength; extraordinary power

【神灵】 shénlíng gods; deities; divinities

【神秘】 shénmì mysterious; mystical: ～人物 a mysterious person; a person shrouded in mystery/ 哲学并不～。Philosophy is no mystery. ◇～化 make a mystery of/ ～主义 mysticism

【神妙】 shénmiào wonderful; marvellous; ingenious: ～的笔法 wonderful style of writing; ingenious brushwork

【神明】 shénmíng gods; deities; divinities: 奉若～ worship sb. or sth.; make a fetish of sth.

【神女】 shénnǚ ① goddess ②〈旧〉prostitute

【神炮手】 shénpàoshǒu crack gunner

【神品】 shénpǐn superb work (of art or literature); masterpiece

【神婆】 shénpó sorceress; witch

【神奇】 shénqí magical; mystical; miraculous: ～的效果 miraculous effect; magical effect/ 这些古代传说都被人们渲染上一层～的色彩。Through the ages, these legends have acquired an element of mystery and wonder.

【神气】 shénqi ① expression; air; manner: 他脸上显出得意的～。He had an air of complacency./ 他说话的～特别象他爸爸。He is very much like his father in the way he speaks. ② spirited; vigorous: 小明带上红领巾多～。Xiaoming looks quite impressive with his red scarf. ③ putting on airs; cocky; overweening: ～十足 putting on grand airs; very arrogant/ 呵！他倒～起来了。Humph! What airs he gives himself!/ 你～什么？What makes you think you're so wonderful? 或 You've got nothing to be cocky about.

【神气活现】 shénqi huóxiàn very cocky; as proud as a peacock

【神枪手】 shénqiāngshǒu crack shot; expert marksman; sharpshooter

【神情】 shénqíng expression; look: 露出愉快的～ look happy; wear a happy expression

【神麴】 shénqū〈中药〉medicated leaven

【神权】 shénquán ① religious authority; theocracy ② rule by divine right

【神色】 shénsè expression; look: ～不对 look queer/ ～慌张 look flustered/ ～自若 be perfectly calm and collected; show composure and presence of mind

【神圣】 shénshèng sacred; holy: ～职责 sacred duty/ ～权利 sacred right/ 我国领土～不可侵犯。Our territory is sacred and inviolable.

【神圣同盟】 Shénshèng Tóngméng〈史〉the Holy Alliance (1815-1830)

【神思】 shénsī state of mind; mental state: ～不定 be distracted

【神似】 shénsì be alike in spirit; be an excellent likeness: 不仅形似，而且～ be alike not only in appearance but also in spirit/ 他画的奔马，栩栩如生，极其～。The galloping horses he paints are extremely lifelike.

【神速】 shénsù marvellously quick; with amazing speed: 收效～ yield marvellously quick results/ ～地向前挺进 advance with lightning speed/ 兵贵～。Speed is precious in war.

【神算】 shénsuàn miraculous foresight; marvellous prediction

【神态】 shéntài expression; manner; bearing; mien: ～悠闲 look perfectly relaxed/ 看她的～象个舞蹈演员。From the way she carries herself she must be a dancer.

【神通】 shéntōng remarkable ability; magical power: ～广大 be infinitely resourceful/ 大显～ display one's prowess; give full play to one's ability

【神童】 shéntóng child prodigy

【神往】 shénwǎng be carried away; be rapt; be charmed: 令人～的西湖景色 the enchanting scenery of the West Lake

【神威】 shénwēi martial prowess; invincible might: 人民军队的～ the martial prowess of the people's army

【神物】 shénwù〈书〉① wonder; prodigy; phenomenon ② supernatural being; deity

【神仙】 shénxiɑn supernatural being; celestial being; immortal ◇ ～葫芦〈机〉chain block
【神像】 shénxiàng the picture or statue of a god or Buddha
【神学】 shénxué 〈宗〉theology
【神医】 shényī highly skilled doctor; miracle-working doctor
【神异】 shényì ① gods and spirits ② magical; mystical; miraculous
【神勇】 shényǒng extraordinarily brave
【神韵】 shényùn romantic charm (in literature and art)
【神职人员】 shénzhí rényuán clergy
【神志】 shénzhì consciousness; senses; mind: ～清醒 be in one's right mind; remain fully conscious/ ～昏迷 lose consciousness; be in a state of delirium
【神州】 Shénzhōu the Divine Land (a poetic name for China)

**钟** shén 〈化〉arsonium

## shěn

**沈** Shěn ① short for Shenyang ② a surname
【沈阳】 Shěnyáng Shenyang

**审** shěn ① careful: ～视 look closely at; gaze at; examine ② examine; go over: ～稿 go over a manuscript or draft ③ interrogate; try: ～案 try a case/ 公～ put sb. on public trial ④〈书〉know: 未～其详 not know the details ⑤〈书〉indeed; really: ～如其言。What he says is indeed true.
【审查】 shěnchá examine; investigate: ～属实。The fact was established after investigation./ ～经费 check up on the funds/ 报上级～批准 submit to the higher level for examination and approval/ ～证书〈外〉examination of credentials
【审处】 shěnchǔ ① try and punish: 交由人民法院～ hand over to the people's court for trial ② deliberate and decide
【审订】 shěndìng examine and revise: ～教材 revise teaching materials
【审定】 shěndìng examine and approve: 计划已由委员会～。The plan has been examined and approved by the committee.
【审干】 shěngàn 〈简〉(审查干部) examine the cadres' personal histories
【审核】 shěnhé examine and verify: ～预算 examine and approve a budget/ 这些数字必须加以～。These figures will have to be verified.
【审计】 shěnjì audit ◇ ～员 auditor
【审理】 shěnlǐ 〈法〉try; hear: ～案件 try a case; hear a case
【审美】 shěnměi appreciation of the beautiful: 不同阶级有不同的～观。Different classes have different aesthetic standards. ◇ ～能力 aesthetic judgment
【审判】 shěnpàn bring to trial; try: 受到人民的～ be tried by the people/ 由军事法庭～ be court-martialled ◇ ～程序 judicial procedure/ ～工作 administration of justice/ ～机关 judicial organ/ ～权 judicial authority; jurisdiction/ ～员 judge; judicial officer/ ～长 presiding judge
【审批】 shěnpī examine and approve: 报请上级～ submit to the higher level for examination and approval
【审慎】 shěnshèn cautious; careful; circumspect: ～从事 steer a cautious course/ ～地考虑问题 think over a problem carefully/ 处理这个问题必须～。The matter has to be handled with circumspection.
【审时度势】 shěnshí-duóshì judge the hour and size up the situation
【审问】 shěnwèn interrogate; question: 正在进行～。The interrogation is going on.
【审讯】 shěnxùn 〈法〉interrogate; try: ～俘虏 interrogate prisoners of war/ 送交军事法庭～ hand over to a military tribunal for interrogation
【审议】 shěnyì consideration; deliberation; discussion: 这个纲要草案已交给你们,请～。The draft outline (of the plan) is now submitted to you for consideration./ 提交全国人民代表大会～ submit sth. to the National People's Congress for examination and approval/ 这个计划在～中。The project is under discussion.
【审阅】 shěnyuè check and approve: 此讲话记录未经本人～。These notes of the speech have not been checked and approved by the speaker./ ～稿件 go over a manuscript

**哂** shěn 〈书〉smile
【哂纳】 shěnnà 〈套〉kindly accept (this small gift)

**谂** shěn 〈书〉know; be aware of

**婶** shěn ① wife of father's younger brother; aunt ② a form of address to a woman about one's mother's age; aunt; auntie: 张大～ Aunt Zhang
【婶母】 shěnmǔ wife of father's younger brother; aunt

## shèn

**肾** shèn 〈生理〉kidney
【肾结石】 shènjiéshí 〈医〉kidney stone; renal calculus
【肾上腺】 shènshàngxiàn 〈生理〉adrenal gland; adrenal ◇ ～素 adrenaline
【肾下垂】 shènxiàchuí 〈医〉nephroptosis
【肾炎】 shènyán nephritis
【肾盂】 shènyú 〈生理〉renal pelvis ◇ ～肾炎 pyelonephritis/ ～炎 pyelitis
【肾脏】 shènzàng kidney

**甚** shèn ① very; extremely: 知者～少。Very few people know about it./ ～为痛快 find it most satisfying ② more than: 他的病情恶化,日～一日。His condition got worse and worse. 或 His condition steadily deteriorated.
另见 shén
【甚而】 shèn'ér 〈连〉even; (go) so far as to
【甚或】 shènhuò 〈书〉〈连〉even; (go) so far as to; so much so that
【甚嚣尘上】 shèn xiāo chén shàng cause a temporary clamour
【甚至】 shènzhì 〈连〉even; (go) so far as to; so much so that: ～不惜承担最大的牺牲 not flinch from even the greatest sacrifices/ 他对同志们的批评置若罔闻,～反唇相讥。He not only ignored the criticism of his comrades but went so far as to be sarcastic.

**胂** shèn 〈化〉arsine

**渗** shèn ooze; seep: 包扎伤口的绷带上～出了血。Blood oozed out of the dressing.
【渗沟】 shèngōu sewer
【渗坑】 shènkēng seepage pit
【渗漏】 shènlòu seepage; leakage ◇ ～损失〈水〉seepage

loss
【渗滤】 shènlǜ 〈化〉 percolation filtration; percolation ◇ ～白土〈石油〉 percolation clay/ ～器 percolator
【渗入】 shènrù ① permeate; seep into: ～地下 permeate the ground; seep into the ground ② (of influence, etc.) penetrate; infiltrate
【渗色】 shènsè 〈纺〉 bleeding
【渗碳】 shèntàn 〈冶〉 carburization; cementation ◇ ～钢 carburizing steel/ ～体 cementite
【渗透】 shèntòu ①〈物〉 osmosis ② permeate; seep: 雨水～了泥土。The rain permeated the soil./ 每一件产品都～了工人同志的心血。Every product embodies the painstaking effort of the workers. ③ infiltrate: 经济～ economic infiltration
◇ ～性 permeability/ ～压力 osmotic pressure/ ～战术 infiltration tactics

**葚** shèn 见"桑葚" sāngshèn
另见 rèn

**慎** shèn careful; cautious: 谨小～微 overcautious/ 保守党和国家的机密，～之又～。One cannot be too careful in guarding Party and state secrets.
【慎重】 shènzhòng cautious; careful; prudent; discreet: 采取～的态度 adopt a prudent policy/ 处理这件事必须～。The matter has to be handled with great care./ 经过～考虑，我们决定延期开会。After careful consideration we decided to postpone the meeting.

**蜃** shèn 〈动〉 clam
【蜃景】 shènjǐng 〈气〉 mirage

**瘆** shèn horrify: ～人 making one's flesh creep; horrifying/ ～得慌 be horrified

## shēng

**升** shēng ① rise; hoist; go up; ascend: 东方红，太阳～。In the east the sky is red. The sun is rising. ② promote: 被提～到领导岗位 be promoted to positions of leadership ③ litre (l.): 一～啤酒 a litre of beer ④ *sheng*, a unit of dry measure for grain (=1 litre) ⑤ a *sheng* measure
【升班】 shēngbān go up (one grade in school)
【升船机】 shēngchuánjī ship lift
【升调】 shēngdiào 〈语〉 rising tune or tone
【升格】 shēnggé promote; upgrade: 将外交关系～为大使级 upgrade diplomatic relations to ambassadorial level/ 将各自外交代表由公使～为大使 promote the status of their respective diplomatic representatives from Minister to Ambassador
【升汞】 shēnggǒng 〈化〉 mercuric chloride
【升官发财】 shēngguān-fācái win promotion and get rich; (be out for) power and money
【升号】 shēnghào 〈乐〉 sharp
【升华】 shēnghuá ①〈物〉 sublimation ② raising of things to a higher level; distillation; sublimation: 艺术是现实生活的～。Art is the distillation of life. ◇ ～干燥 lyophilization
【升级】 shēngjí ① go up (one grade, etc.) ② escalate: 战争～ escalation (of a war)
【升降舵】 shēngjiàngduò 〈航空〉 elevator
【升降机】 shēngjiàngjī elevator; lift
【升力】 shēnglì 〈航空〉 lift ◇ ～特性 lift efficiency
【升幂】 shēngmì 〈数〉 ascending power ◇ ～级数 ascending power series
【升平】 shēngpíng peace: ～世界 peaceful world; peaceful life
【升旗】 shēngqí hoist (或 raise) a flag ◇ ～典礼 flag-raising ceremony
【升水】 shēngshuǐ 〈经〉 premium
【升堂入室】 shēngtáng-rùshì pass through the hall into the inner chamber — have profound scholarship; become highly proficient in one's profession
【升腾】 shēngténg leap up; rise: 火焰～。The flames leapt up.
【升限】 shēngxiàn 〈航空〉 ceiling ◇ ～高度 ceiling height
【升学】 shēngxué go to a school of a higher grade; enter a higher school ◇ ～率 proportion of students entering schools of a higher grade
【升压】 shēngyā 〈电〉 step up; boost ◇ ～变压器 step-up transformer/ ～器 booster
【升值】 shēngzhí 〈经〉 ① revalue ② appreciate

**生** shēng ① give birth to; bear: 新～儿 newborn baby/ ～孩子 give birth to a child ② grow: ～根 take root/ ～芽 sprout/ 新～力量 newly rising (或 emerging) forces ③ existence; life: 一～ all one's life; one's lifetime/ 起死回～ raise sb. from the dead; bring sb. back to life ④ livelihood: 谋～ earn one's livelihood; make a living ⑤ living: ～物 living things ⑥ get; have: ～冻疮 get chilblains ⑦ light (a fire): ～炉子 light a stove ⑧ unripe; green: ～的苹果 a green apple/ 这些桃子还是～的。The peaches are not ripe yet. ⑨ raw; uncooked: ～肉 raw meat/ 黄瓜可以～吃。Cucumbers can be eaten raw. ⑩ unprocessed; unrefined; crude: ～铁 pig iron/ ～皮 rawhide; (untanned) hide ⑪ unfamiliar; unacquainted; strange: ～词 new word/ 人～地不熟 a stranger in a strange place/ 刚到这里，工作很～。I've only just come here. I'm still not familiar with the work./ 这个小孩认～。The child is shy with strangers. ⑫ stiff; mechanical: ～凑 mechanically put together (disconnected words and phrases); arbitrarily dish up (unrelated facts) ⑬〔用在少数表示感情、感觉的词的前面〕very: ～恐 for fear that/ ～疼 very painful ⑭ pupil; student: 新型的师～关系 teacher-student relations of a new type ⑮ the male character type in Beijing opera, etc. ⑯〔某些指人的名词后缀〕: 医～ doctor
【生搬硬套】 shēngbān-yìngtào copy mechanically in disregard of specific conditions; apply or copy mechanically
【生病】 shēngbìng fall ill
【生菜】 shēngcài 〈植〉 romaine lettuce; cos lettuce
【生产】 shēngchǎn ① produce; manufacture: 很多工厂～农业机械。Many factories produce farm machinery./ 这个车间～螺丝钉。This shop manufactures screws./ 这个工厂已开始～。The plant has gone into operation./ 坚守～岗位 stick to one's post on the production front ② give birth to a child: 她快～了。She'll be having her baby soon. 或 She's expecting her baby soon.
◇ ～成本 cost of production/ ～大队 production brigade/ ～定额 production quota/ ～斗争 struggle for production/ ～队 production team/ ～方式 mode of production/ ～工具 tool of production/ ～关系 relations of production; production relations/ ～过剩 overproduction/ ～合作社 producers' cooperative/ ～建设兵团 production and construction corps/ ～劳动 productive labour/ ～力 productive forces/ ～率 productivity/ ～潜力 productive potentialities; latent productive capacity/ ～设备 production facilities/ ～手段 means of production/ ～指标 production quota/ ～资料 means of production/ ～总值 total output value
【生辰】 shēngchén birthday

【生成物】 shēngchéngwù 〈化〉 product; resultant
【生词】 shēngcí new word
【生存】 shēngcún subsist; exist; live: 鱼离开了水是不能~的。Fish cannot live without water. ◇ ~竞争 struggle for existence
【生地】 shēngdì ① 〈农〉 virgin soil; uncultivated land ② 〈中药〉 the dried rhizome of rehmannia (*Rehmannia glutinosa*)
【生动】 shēngdòng lively; vivid: ~的描写 lively description/ ~地反映了国内外大好形势 vividly reflect the good domestic and international situation/ 人民的生活是最~最丰富的文学艺术原料。The life of the people is the most vital and rich raw material for literature and art.
【生动活泼】 shēngdòng huópō lively; vivid and vigorous: ~的语言 vivid language/ 这次会开得~。It was a lively meeting.
【生发油】 shēngfàyóu hair oil
【生俘】 shēngfú capture (alive)
【生根】 shēnggēn take root; strike root: 在群众中~开花 take root and blossom among the masses
【生光】 shēngguāng 〈天〉 third contact (of a solar or lunar eclipse)
【生花妙笔】 shēnghuā miàobǐ (straight from) a gifted pen; (written with) a graphic pen
【生荒】 shēnghuāng 〈农〉 virgin soil; uncultivated land
【生活】 shēnghuó ① life: 日常~ daily life/ 政治~ political life/ 组织~ Party or League activities ② live: 一个人脱离了社会就不能~下去。One cannot live cut off from society. ③ livelihood: ~困难 be badly off/ 关心群众的~ be concerned with the well-being of the masses
◇ ~必需品 necessaries of life; daily necessities/ ~补助 extra allowance for living expenses/ ~方式 way of life; life style/ ~费用 living expenses; cost of living/ ~福利 welfare; welfare benefits/ ~环境 surroundings; environment/ ~经验 experience of life/ ~来源 source of income/ ~能力 〈生〉 viability/ ~水平 living standard/ ~条件 living conditions/ ~习惯 habits and customs/ ~细节 trifling matters of everyday life; domestic trivia/ ~用品 articles for daily use/ ~周期〈生〉life cycle/ ~资料 means of subsistence; means of livelihood/ ~作风 behaviour; conduct
【生活关】 shēnghuóguān the test of rigorous living conditions: 过好~ prove oneself able to lead a rigorous life; stand the test of a rigorous life
【生火】 shēnghuǒ make a fire; light a fire
【生机】 shēngjī ① lease of life: 一线~ a slim chance of survival; a gleam of hope ② life; vitality: 春天来了,田野里充满了~。Spring has come and the fields are full of life.
【生计】 shēngjì means of livelihood; livelihood: 另谋~ try to find some other means of livelihood
【生姜】 shēngjiāng 〈口〉 ginger
【生津】 shēngjīn 〈中医〉 promote the secretion of saliva or body fluid
【生境】 shēngjìng 〈生〉 habitat
【生就】 shēngjiù be born with; be gifted with: ~一张利嘴 have the gift of the gab
【生拉硬拽】 shēnglā-yìngzhuài ① drag sb. along kicking and screaming ② stretch the meaning
【生老病死】 shēng-lǎo-bìng-sǐ birth, age, illness and death: 在新中国,劳动人民~都有依靠。In New China, care during childbirth, old age and illness, as well as burial arrangements, are all guaranteed for the labouring people.
【生冷】 shēng-lěng raw or cold food: 忌食~。Avoid eating anything raw or cold.
【生离死别】 shēnglí-sǐbié part never to meet again; part for ever
【生理】 shēnglǐ physiology
◇ ~反应 physiological reaction/ ~缺陷 physiological defect; physiological deficiency/ ~学 physiology/ ~盐水 〈药〉 physiological saline; normal saline/ ~作用 physiological action
【生力军】 shēnglìjūn ① fresh troops ② fresh activists; new force: 文艺战线上的一支~ a vital new force on the art and literary front
【生灵】 shēnglíng 〈书〉 the people
【生灵涂炭】 shēnglíng tútàn the people are plunged into an abyss of misery
【生龙活虎】 shēnglóng-huóhǔ doughty as a dragon and lively as a tiger; brimming (或 bursting) with energy; full of vim and vigour: 小伙子干起活来真是~。When the lads work, they do it with furious energy.
【生路】 shēnglù means of livelihood; way out: 另谋~ try to find another job; look for a new means of livelihood/ 杀出一条~ fight one's way out (of an encirclement)
【生米煮成熟饭】 shēngmǐ zhǔchéng shúfàn the rice is cooked — what's done can't be undone
【生命】 shēngmìng life: ~不息,战斗不止 fight as long as one has a breath in one's body; go on fighting till one breathes one's last/ 政治~ political life/ 政策和策略是党的~。Policy and tactics are the life of the Party./ 学习古人语言中有~的东西 learn whatever is alive in the classical Chinese language
【生命力】 shēngmìnglì life-force; vitality: 具有强大的~ have great vitality
【生命线】 shēngmìngxiàn lifeline; lifeblood: 政治工作是一切经济工作的~。Political work is the lifeblood of all economic work.
【生命现象】 shēngmìng xiànxiàng biological phenomena: 用放射性同位素示踪技术探讨~ apply radioisotopic tracers to study biological phenomena
【生怕】 shēngpà for fear that; so as not to; lest: 她轻轻地走进卧室,~惊醒了孩子。She went into the bedroom softly so as not to wake her child.
【生僻】 shēngpì uncommon; rare: ~的字眼 rarely used words
【生平】 shēngpíng all one's life: ~事迹 one's life story/ 作者~简介 a brief account of the author's life; a biographical note on the author
【生漆】 shēngqī raw lacquer
【生气】 shēngqì ① take offence; get angry ② life; vitality: ~勃勃 dynamic; vigorous; full of vitality/ 青年是整个社会力量中的一部分最积极最有~的力量。Young people are the most active and dynamic force in society./ 解放前一些濒于绝境的工艺美术,现在充满了~。Certain arts and crafts which were on the verge of extinction before liberation are now flourishing.
【生前】 shēngqián before one's death; during one's lifetime: ~愿望 unrealized wish (of a person who has passed away)
【生擒】 shēngqín capture (alive)
【生趣】 shēngqù joy of life
【生人】 shēngrén stranger
【生日】 shēngri birthday
【生色】 shēngsè add colour to; add lustre to; give added significance to: 老师们的演出,为英语晚会~不少。The teachers' performance made the English evening more enjoyable.
【生涩】 shēngsè (of language) jerky; choppy; not smooth
【生杀予夺】 shēng-shā yǔ-duó hold power over sb.'s life and property; have sb. completely in one's power

【生身父母】 shēngshēn fù-mǔ one's own parents
【生事】 shēngshì make trouble; create a disturbance: 造谣～ spread rumours and make trouble
【生手】 shēngshǒu sb. new to a job
【生疏】 shēngshū ① not familiar: 人地～ be unfamiliar with the place and the people/ 我对这个地方并不算～。I'm no stranger here./ 我对这项工作很～。I don't know much about the job. ② out of practice; rusty: 他的英文有点～了。His English is getting rusty. ③ not as close as before: 多年不来往，我们的关系～了。We haven't been in touch with each other for years, so we're not as close as we used to be.
【生水】 shēngshuǐ unboiled water
【生丝】 shēngsī raw silk
【生死】 shēng-sǐ life and death: ～关头 a moment when one's fate hangs in the balance/ ～存亡的斗争 a life-and-death struggle/ ～攸关的问题 a matter of life and death; a matter of vital importance/ ～与共的战友 comrades-in-arms with a common destiny
【生态】 shēngtài organisms' habits, modes of life and relation to their environment; ecology
◇ ～变异 ecocline/ ～系统 ecosystem/ ～型 ecotype/ ～学 ecology
【生铁】 shēngtiě pig iron
【生土】 shēngtǔ 〈农〉 immature soil
【生吞活剥】 shēngtūn-huóbō swallow sth. raw and whole — accept sth. uncritically: 决不可～地搬用外国的经验。It's no good taking over the experience of foreign countries uncritically.
【生物】 shēngwù living things; living beings; organisms: 超显微镜～ ultramicroscopic organisms/ 浮游～ plankton/ 寄生～ parasites
◇ ～地理学 biogeography/ ～电流 〈生理〉 bioelectric current/ ～发生律 biogenetic law; recapitulation theory/ ～防治 〈农〉 biological control/ ～固氮 biological nitrogen fixation/ ～合成 biosynthesis/ ～化学 biochemistry/ ～碱 〈化〉 alkaloid/ ～膜 biomembrane/ ～气候学 bioclimatology/ ～圈 biosphere/ ～生态学 bioecology/ ～体 organism/ ～武器 〈军〉 biological weapon/ ～学 biology/ ～学家 biologist/ ～岩 biogenic rock; biolith/ ～遥测器 biopack/ ～战 〈军〉 biological warfare/ ～制品 biological product/ ～钟 biological clock; biochronometer; living clock
【生息】 shēngxī ① bear interest ② 〈书〉 live; grow; propagate: 休养～ recuperate and multiply; rest and build up one's strength/ 自古以来，我们的祖先就劳动、～、繁殖在这块土地上。From ancient times our forefathers have laboured, lived and multiplied on this land. ◇ ～资本 interest-bearing capital
【生橡胶】 shēngxiàngjiāo raw rubber; caoutchouc
【生肖】 shēngxiào any of the twelve animals, representing the twelve Earthly Branches, used to symbolize the year in which a person is born
【生效】 shēngxiào go into effect; become effective: 签字后立即～ become effective immediately upon signature/ 自签字之日起～ go into effect from the date of signature/ 在互换批准书以后立即～ come into force immediately on exchange of the instruments of ratification
【生性】 shēngxìng natural disposition
【生锈】 shēngxiù get rusty: 经常擦油，以免～。Oil it regularly to prevent rust./ 做一颗永不～的螺丝钉 be a screw that never rusts — be a rank-and-file revolutionary who serves the people heart and soul
【生涯】 shēngyá career; profession: 舞台～ a stage career/ 操笔墨～ write for a living
【生药】 shēngyào crude drug; dried medicinal herbs ◇ ～学 pharmacognosy
【生疑】 shēngyí be suspicious
【生意】 shēngyì tendency to grow; life and vitality: ～盎然 full of life/ 春天的大地一片蓬勃的～。Spring has filled the earth with life and vitality.
【生意】 shēngyi business; trade: 做～ do business/ 做成一笔～ make a deal; strike a bargain/ ～兴隆。Trade is brisk. 或 Business is booming. ◇ ～经 the knack of doing business; shrewd business sense
【生硬】 shēngyìng stiff; rigid; harsh: 态度～ be stiff in manner
【生油】 shēngyóu ① unboiled oil ② 〈方〉 peanut oil
【生油层】 shēngyóucéng 〈石油〉 source bed
【生育】 shēngyù give birth to; bear: ～子女 bear children/ 不能～ be unable to have children; be sterile/ 她已过了～年龄。She is past her child-bearing age.
【生源说】 shēngyuánshuō 〈生〉 biogenesis
【生造】 shēngzào coin (words and expressions): 不要～谁也不懂的词语。Do not coin words and expressions that nobody can understand. ◇ ～词 coinage
【生长】 shēngzhǎng ① grow: 小麦～良好。The wheat is growing well. 或 The wheat is doing fine. ② grow up; be brought up: 他～在武汉。He was born and brought up in Wuhan.
◇ ～点〈植〉 growing point/ ～率 growth rate/ ～期 growth period; growing period
【生殖】 shēngzhí reproduction: 无性～ asexual reproduction/ 有性～ sexual reproduction/ 营养体～ vegetative reproduction
◇ ～回游〈动〉 breeding migration/ ～孔 gonopore/ ～率 reproduction rate/ ～器 reproductive organs; genitals/ ～系统 reproductive system/ ～腺 gonad
【生猪】 shēngzhū 〈商〉 live pig; pig; hog; pork on the hoof
【生字】 shēngzì new word ◇ ～表 (a list of) new words

**声** shēng ① sound; voice: 脚步～ the sound of footsteps/ 小～说话 speak in a low voice ② make a sound: 不～不响 not utter a word; keep quiet ③ initial consonant (of a Chinese syllable): 双～ alliteration ④ tone: 四～ the four tones in classical and modern Chinese ⑤ 〈量〉: 我喊了他两～。I called him twice. ⑥ reputation: ～誉 reputation; fame; prestige
【声辩】 shēngbiàn argue; justify; explain away
【声波】 shēngbō 〈物〉 sound wave; acoustic wave
【声部】 shēngbù 〈乐〉 part (in concerted music)
【声称】 shēngchēng profess; claim; assert: ～已打破僵局 claim to have broken the deadlock
【声带】 shēngdài ① 〈生理〉 vocal cords ② 〈电影〉 sound track
【声调】 shēngdiào ① tone; note: ～激昂 in an impassioned tone/ ～低沉 in a low, sad voice ② 〈语〉 the tone of a Chinese character 参见"四声" sìshēng
【声东击西】 shēng dōng jī xī make a feint to the east and attack in the west
【声价】 shēngjià reputation: ～甚高 (of a person) be held in high repute; be held in high esteem
【声浪】 shēnglàng voice; clamour: 抗议的～ a wave of protest
【声泪俱下】 shēng-lèi jù xià shedding tears while speaking; in a tearful voice: 他～地诉说了自己的不幸遭遇。Tears streamed down his cheeks as he recounted his unhappy experience.
【声门】 shēngmén 〈生理〉 glottis
【声名】 shēngmíng reputation: ～狼藉 have a bad name; be notorious

【声明】 shēngmíng ① state; declare; announce: 庄严～ solemnly state ② statement; declaration: 联合～ joint statement
【声母】 shēngmǔ 〈语〉 initial consonant (of a Chinese syllable)
【声纳】 shēngnà 〈物〉 sonar (sound navigation and ranging)
【声囊】 shēngnáng 〈动〉 vocal sac
【声能学】 shēngnéngxué 〈物〉 sonics
【声频】 shēngpín 〈物〉 acoustic frequency
【声谱】 shēngpǔ 〈物〉 sound spectrum ◇ ～仪 sound spectrograph
【声气】 shēngqì ① information: 互通～ exchange information; keep in contact with each other ② 〈方〉 voice; tone: 小声小气地 in a low voice; in undertones
【声强】 shēngqiáng 〈物〉 sound intensity
【声色】 shēng-sè ① voice and countenance: 不动～ maintain one's composure; stay calm and collected ② 〈书〉 woman and song
【声色俱厉】 shēng-sè jù lì stern in voice and countenance
【声势】 shēngshì impetus; momentum: 虚张～ make a show of strength; bluff and bluster/ ～浩大 great in strength and impetus; mammoth (demonstration, etc.)/ 造成革命～ build up a revolutionary momentum
【声嘶力竭】 shēngsī-lìjié shout oneself hoarse; shout oneself blue in the face
【声速】 shēngsù 〈物〉 velocity of sound: 这种新型战斗机的巡航速度为～的二倍。The cruising speed of this new type of fighter is Mach two.
【声讨】 shēngtǎo denounce; condemn: 愤怒～反党集团的罪行 indignantly denounce the crimes of the anti-Party clique ◇ ～会 denunciation meeting
【声望】 shēngwàng popularity; prestige: 在群众中有很高的～ enjoy great prestige among the masses
【声威】 shēngwēi renown; prestige: ～大震 gain great fame and high prestige
【声息】 shēngxī ①〔多用于否定〕sound; noise: 没有一点～。Not a sound is heard. ② information: ～相闻 keep in touch with each other
【声响】 shēngxiǎng sound; noise: 这发动机～太大。This motor makes too much noise./ 瀑布奔泻，发出巨大的～。The waterfall came down with a rush and a roar.
【声学】 shēngxué acoustics: 建筑～ architectural acoustics/ 几何～ ray acoustics; geometrical acoustics/ 超～ ultrasonics
【声言】 shēngyán profess; claim; declare
【声音】 shēngyīn sound; voice
【声誉】 shēngyù reputation; fame; prestige: 维护国家的～ defend the honour of one's country/ 在国内外享有很高的～ enjoy great prestige both at home and abroad
【声援】 shēngyuán express support for; support: ～被压迫民族的正义斗争 support the oppressed nations in their just struggles
【声乐】 shēngyuè 〈乐〉 vocal music
【声韵学】 shēngyùnxué 〈语〉 phonology
【声张】 shēngzhāng make public; disclose: 不要～。Don't breathe a word of it to anyone.

**牲** shēng ① domestic animal ② animal sacrifice
【牲畜】 shēngchù livestock; domestic animals ◇ ～车〈铁道〉 livestock wagon; stock wagon; stock car
【牲粉】 shēngfěn 〈化〉 animal starch; glycogen
【牲口】 shēngkou draught animals; beasts of burden ◇ ～贩子 cattle dealer/ ～棚 stock barn; livestock shed

**笙** shēng 〈乐〉 *sheng*, a reed pipe wind instrument
【笙歌】 shēnggē 〈书〉 playing and singing

**甥** shēng sister's son; nephew
【甥女】 shēngnǚ sister's daughter; niece

## shéng

**绳** shéng ① rope; cord; string: 麻～ hemp rope/ 钢丝～ steel cable; wire rope ② restrict; restrain: ～以纪律 enforce discipline upon sb.
【绳鞭技】 shéngbiānjì 〈杂技〉 (doing) tricks with a whip; (performing) feats with a whip
【绳墨】 shéngmò ① carpenter's line marker ② 〈书〉 rules and regulations: 拘守～ stick to the rules
【绳索】 shéngsuǒ rope; cord: 砍断旧制度套在人民身上的～ cut the bonds forced on the people by the old system
【绳梯】 shéngtī rope ladder
【绳子】 shéngzi cord; rope; string

## shěng

**省** shěng ① economize; save: ～着点用 use sparingly/ ～时间 save time/ ～掉不少麻烦 save a lot of trouble/ 能～的就～ economize wherever possible ② omit; leave out: 这两个字不能～。These two words cannot be omitted./ ～一道工序 eliminate one step from the process ③ province: 江苏～ Jiangsu Province/ ～长 governor of a province/ ～人民代表大会 provincial people's congress
另见 xǐng
【省城】 shěngchéng provincial capital
【省吃俭用】 shěngchī-jiǎnyòng live frugally
【省得】 shěngde so as to save (或 avoid): 你就住在这儿吧，～天天来回跑。Better stay here to avoid having to go back and forth every day./ 到了就来信，～我挂念。Send me a letter as soon as you arrive so that I won't worry.
【省份】 shěngfèn province: 台湾是中国的一个～。Taiwan is one of China's provinces.
【省会】 shěnghuì provincial capital
【省界】 shěngjiè provincial boundaries
【省力】 shěnglì save effort; save labour: 这种耕作方法～不少。This method of farming saves a lot of labour.
【省略】 shěnglüè leave out; omit: 与主题关系不大的段落可以～。The irrelevant paragraphs can be omitted./ 这个句子的主语～了。The subject of the sentence is understood. ◇ ～号 ellipsis; suspension points; ellipsis dots (……) (...)/ ～句〈语〉 elliptical sentence
【省钱】 shěngqián save money; be economical: 每月省点钱 save some money each month
【省事】 shěngshì save trouble; simplify matters: 这样可以省很多事。We can make it much simpler this way./ 在食堂里吃饭～。It's more convenient to eat in the canteen.
【省委】 shěngwěi provincial Party committee ◇ ～书记 secretary of a provincial Party committee
【省心】 shěngxīn save worry: 孩子进了托儿所，我～多了。Having the child in kindergarten saves me a lot of worry.

## shèng

**圣** shèng ① sage; saint ② holy; sacred: 神～领土 sacred territory ③ emperor: ～上 His or Her Majesty
【圣餐】 shèngcān 〈宗〉 Holy Communion
【圣诞】 shèngdàn the birthday of Jesus Christ ◇ ～老人 Santa Claus/ ～树 Christmas tree

【圣诞节】 Shèngdànjié Christmas Day: ～前夜 Christmas Eve

【圣地】 shèngdì ①〈宗〉the Holy Land (或 City) ②sacred place; shrine: 延安是中国革命的～。Yan'an is a sacred place of the Chinese revolution.

【圣多美和普林西比】 Shèngduōměi hé Pǔlínxībǐ São Tomé and Príncipe

【圣公宗】 Shènggōngzōng 〈基督教〉Anglicanism; the Anglican Church

【圣赫勒拿岛】 Shènghèlènádǎo Saint Helena Island

【圣洁】 shèngjié holy and pure

【圣经】 Shèngjīng the Holy Bible; the Bible; Holy Writ

【圣灵节】 Shènglíngjié Whitsunday

【圣卢西亚】 Shènglúxīyà Saint Lucia

【圣马力诺】 Shèngmǎlìnuò San Marino ◇ ～人 San Marinese

【圣母】 shèngmǔ ①a female deity; goddess ②the (Blessed) Virgin Mary; Madonna

【圣人】 shèngrén sage; wise man

【圣贤】 shèngxián sages and men of virtue: 古语说:"人非～,孰能无过?" As the old saying goes, "Men are not saints, how can they be free from faults?"

【圣旨】 shèngzhǐ imperial edict

**胜** shèng ①victory; success: 得～ win (victory)/ 力争每战必～ try our best to ensure victory in every battle/ 战而～之 fight to win/ 我队以四～两负一平的成绩获得亚军。Our team finished second with four wins, two defeats and one tie./ ～不骄,败不馁 not dizzy with success, nor discouraged by failure ②surpass; be superior to; get the better of: 事实～于雄辩。Facts speak louder than words./ 聊～于无 better than nothing ③superb; wonderful; lovely: ～景 wonderful scenery ④be equal to; can bear: 力不能～ beyond one's ability/ 数不～数 too numerous to count; countless

【胜败】 shèng-bài victory or defeat; success or failure

【胜地】 shèngdì famous scenic spot: 避暑～ summer resort

【胜负】 shèng-fù victory or defeat; success or failure: 战争的～ the outcome of a war/ ～未定。Victory hangs in the balance./ 这场比赛～已定。The outcome of the game is a foregone conclusion./ 比赛的～是暂时的,友谊是永久的。To win or lose in a match is temporary while friendship between the contestants is lasting.

【胜迹】 shèngjì famous historical site

【胜利】 shènglì ①victory; triumph: 充满了～的信心 fully confident of victory/ ～果实 fruits of victory/ 敢于斗争,敢于～ dare to struggle and dare to win ②successfully; triumphantly: ～会师 triumphantly join forces/ ～完成任务 successfully carry out one's task/ 大会～闭幕。The conference has concluded successfully./ 沿着社会主义大道～前进 march triumphantly along the socialist road ◇ ～者 victor; winner

【胜券】 shèngquàn confidence in victory: 操～ be sure to win

【胜任】 shèngrèn competent; qualified; equal to: ～工作 be competent at a job; prove equal to the task/ ～愉快 be fully competent; be well qualified

【胜似】 shèngsì be better than; surpass

【胜诉】 shèngsù win a lawsuit (或 court case)

【胜算】 shèngsuàn 〈书〉a stratagem which ensures success: 操～ be sure of success

【胜仗】 shèngzhàng victorious battle; victory: 打～ win a battle; score a victory

**乘** shèng 〈史〉a war chariot drawn by four horses: 千～之国 a state with a thousand chariots

另见 chéng

**盛** shèng ①flourishing; prosperous: 桃花～开。The peach trees are in full bloom. 或 The peach blossoms are out./ 兴～ flourish ②vigorous, energetic: 火势很～。The fire is raging./ 年轻气～ young and aggressive ③magnificent; grand: ～举 a grand occasion (或 event) ④abundant; plentiful: ～意 great kindness ⑤popular; common; widespread: ～传 be widely known; be widely rumoured ⑥greatly; deeply: ～夸 praise highly ⑦(Shèng) a surname

另见 chéng

【盛产】 shèngchǎn abound in; teem with: ～煤铁 abound in coal and iron/ ～石油 be rich in oil/ ～鱼蟹 teem with fish and crabs

【盛大】 shèngdà grand; magnificent: ～欢迎 a rousing welcome/ ～招待会 a grand reception/ ～游行 a mammoth parade

【盛典】 shèngdiǎn grand ceremony

【盛服】 shèngfú 〈书〉splendid attire; rich dress

【盛会】 shènghuì distinguished gathering; grand meeting: 团结友谊的～ a grand gathering of unity and friendship/ 体育～ a magnificent sports meet

【盛极一时】 shèngjí yīshí be in fashion for a time; be all the rage at the moment

【盛况】 shèngkuàng grand occasion; spectacular event: ～空前 an exceptionally grand occasion

【盛名】 shèngmíng great reputation: ～之下,其实难副。It is hard to live up to a great reputation.

【盛气凌人】 shèngqì líng rén domineering; arrogant; overbearing: ～的样子 imperious bearing

【盛情】 shèngqíng great kindness; boundless hospitality: ～难却。It would be ungracious not to accept your invitation./ 受到～款待 be accorded lavish hospitality

【盛世】 shèngshì flourishing age; heyday: 太平～ times of peace and prosperity; piping times of peace

【盛事】 shèngshì grand occasion; great event

【盛暑】 shèngshǔ sweltering summer heat; very hot weather; the dog days

【盛衰】 shèng-shuāi prosperity and decline; rise and fall; ups and downs

【盛衰荣辱】 shèng-shuāi róng-rǔ prosperity and decline, glory and humiliation; rise and fall; ups and downs; vicissitudes of life

【盛夏】 shèngxià the height of summer; midsummer

【盛行】 shèngxíng be current (或 rife, rampant); be in vogue: ～一时 be in vogue for a time; prevail for a time

【盛宴】 shèngyàn grand banquet; sumptuous dinner 又作"盛筵"

【盛意】 shèngyì great kindness; generosity

【盛誉】 shèngyù great fame; high reputation: 中国丝绸在世界上素有～。Chinese silk has long been famous all over the world.

【盛赞】 shèngzàn highly praise; speak of sb. in glowing terms

【盛装】 shèngzhuāng splendid attire; rich dress: 穿着节日的～ be dressed in one's holiday best/ 天安门广场披上了节日的～。Tian'anmen Square is splendidly decorated for the festive occasion.

**剩** shèng surplus; remnant: ～货 surplus goods/ ～菜～饭 leftovers/ 所～无几。There is not much left.

【剩磁】 shèngcí 〈物〉residual magnetism

【剩下】 shèngxia be left (over); remain: ～多少? How much is left (over)?/ ～的敌军已经被我们消灭了。We have wiped out the remaining enemy troops./ 同志们都走了,就～我一个人了。The other comrades have all gone; I'm the only one left.

【剩余】 shèngyú surplus; remainder: 收支相抵,略有～。The reckoning up of revenue and expenditure shows a small surplus.
◇ ～产品 surplus products/ ～价值 surplus value/ ～劳动 surplus labour/ ～物资 surplus materials

## shī

**尸** shī corpse; dead body; remains: 死～ dead body; corpse/ 兽～ carcass

【尸骨】 shīgǔ skeleton 又作"尸骸"
【尸横遍野】 shī héng biànyě a field littered with corpses
【尸身】 shīshēn corpse; dead body; remains 又作"尸首"
【尸体】 shītǐ corpse; dead body; remains ◇ ～解剖 autopsy; postmortem (examination)
【尸位素餐】 shīwèi-sùcān hold down a job without doing a stroke of work

**失** shī ① lose: ～而复得 lost and found again/ 迷～方向 lose one's bearings ② miss; let slip: 坐～良机 let slip a good opportunity; lose a good chance ③ fail to achieve one's end: 大～所望 be greatly disappointed ④ mishap; defect; mistake: 唯恐有～ fear that there may be some mishap/ ～之于烦琐 have the defect of being too detailed ⑤ deviate from the normal: ～色 turn pale ⑥ break (a promise); go back on (one's word): ～信 break one's promise

【失败】 shībài ① be defeated; lose (a war, etc.): 遭到了可耻的～ meet with ignominious defeat ② fail: ～是成功之母。Failure is the mother of success. ◇ ～情绪 defeatist sentiments/ ～主义 defeatism
【失策】 shīcè unwise; inexpedient: 这样做非常～。It was a very unwise move.
【失察】 shīchá neglect one's supervisory duties
【失常】 shīcháng not normal; odd: 举止～ act oddly/ 精神～ be distraught; not be in one's right mind
【失宠】 shīchǒng fall into disfavour; be out of favour; be in disgrace
【失传】 shīchuán not be handed down from past generations; be lost: 一种～的艺术 a lost art/ 我国有些古代科学著作已经～。Some scientific books of ancient China have been lost.
【失措】 shīcuò lose one's presence of mind; lose one's head: 惊慌～ be panic-stricken
【失单】 shīdān a list of lost articles (或 property)
【失当】 shīdàng improper; inappropriate: 这个问题处理～。This problem was not properly handled.
【失道寡助】 shī dào guǎ zhù an unjust cause finds scant support
【失地】 shīdì lost territory: 收复～ recover lost territory
【失掉】 shīdiào ① lose: ～联系 lose contact with/ ～权力 be stripped of power/ ～民心 lose popular support ② miss: ～机会 miss a chance/ ～战机 fail to grasp a good opportunity to engage the enemy
【失和】 shīhé fail to keep on good terms; become estranged
【失魂落魄】 shīhún-luòpò driven to distraction: 吓得～ be scared out of one's wits; be frightened out of one's life
【失火】 shīhuǒ catch fire; be on fire
【失计】 shījì 见"失策"
【失脚】 shījiǎo lose one's footing; slip: ～跌倒 lose one's footing (或 balance) and fall
【失节】 shījié ① forfeit one's integrity; be disloyal ② (of a woman, according to feudal morality) lose one's chastity
【失禁】 shījìn 〈医〉 incontinence: 大小便～ incontinence of faeces and urine
【失敬】 shījìng 〈套〉 sorry I didn't recognize you; sorry
【失控】 shīkòng out of control; runaway
【失口】 shīkǒu a slip of the tongue
【失礼】 shīlǐ breach of etiquette; impoliteness; discourtesy
【失利】 shīlì suffer a setback (或 defeat): 军事上的～ military reverses/ 在这场乒乓球比赛中我方第一盘～。Our side lost the first game of the table-tennis match.
【失恋】 shīliàn be disappointed in a love affair
【失灵】 shīlíng (of a machine, instrument, etc.) not work or not work properly; be out of order: 开关～了。The switch is out of order.
【失落】 shīluò lose
【失密】 shīmì give away official secrets due to carelessness
【失眠】 shīmián (suffer from) insomnia: 病人昨夜～。The patient had a sleepless night last night.
【失明】 shīmíng lose one's sight; go blind: 双目～ lose the sight of both eyes
【失能性毒剂】 shīnéngxìng dújì 〈军〉 incapacitating agent
【失陪】 shīpéi 〈套〉 excuse me, but I must be leaving now
【失窃】 shīqiè have things stolen; suffer loss by theft
【失去】 shīqù lose: ～知觉 lose consciousness/ ～信心 lose confidence/ ～时效 be no longer effective; cease to be in force/ ～中国国籍 forfeit one's Chinese citizenship
【失散】 shīsàn be separated from and lose touch with each other; be scattered: 解放后,他找到了～多年的姐姐。After liberation he was reunited with his sister, whom he had had no news of for years.
【失色】 shīsè ① turn pale: 大惊～ turn pale with fright ② be eclipsed; be outshone: 黯然～ be cast into the shade; be eclipsed; pale into insignificance
【失闪】 shīshan mishap; unexpected danger
【失神】 shīshén ① inattentive; absent-minded ② out of sorts; in low spirits
【失慎】 shīshèn ① not cautious; careless ② 〈书〉 cause a fire through carelessness
【失声】 shīshēng ① cry out involuntarily ② lose one's voice: 痛哭～ be choked with tears
【失时】 shīshí miss the season; let slip the opportunity: 播种不能～。Don't miss the sowing season.
【失实】 shīshí inconsistent with the facts: 传闻～。The rumour was unfounded.
【失势】 shīshì lose power and influence; fall into disgrace
【失事】 shīshì (have an) accident: 飞机～ aviation accident; aeroplane crash
【失手】 shīshǒu accidentally drop: 他一～打碎了一个茶杯。He accidentally dropped a cup and broke it.
【失守】 shīshǒu fall: 城市～ the fall of a city
【失溲】 shīsōu 〈中医〉 incontinence of urine
【失速】 shīsù 〈航空〉 stall ◇ ～滑翔 stalled glide
【失算】 shīsuàn miscalculate; misjudge; be injudicious
【失态】 shītài forget oneself: 酒后～ forget oneself in one's cups
【失调】 shītiáo ① imbalance; dislocation: 供求～ imbalance of supply and demand/ 经济～ economic dislocation/ 雨水～ abnormal rainfall ② lack of proper care (after an illness, etc.): 产后～ lack of proper care after childbirth ③ 〈无〉 maladjustment; detuning
【失望】 shīwàng ① lose hope ② disappointed: 感到～ be disappointed/ 令人～ disappointing
【失物】 shīwù lost article; lost property ◇ ～招领处 Lost and Found Office; Lost Property Office

【失误】 shīwù 〔多指打球、下棋〕fault; muff: 接球～ muff a ball/ 由于发球～而丢了几分 lose several points through serving faults

【失陷】 shīxiàn (of cities, territory, etc.) fall; fall into enemy hands

【失效】 shīxiào ① lose efficacy; lose effectiveness; cease to be effective: 这药已～了。The medicine no longer has any effect./ 使水雷～ deactivate mines ② (of a treaty, an agreement, etc.) be no longer in force; become invalid: 自动～ automatically cease to be in force

【失笑】 shīxiào laugh in spite of oneself; cannot help laughing

【失谐】 shīxié 〈无〉 detuning; mismatching

【失信】 shīxìn break one's promise; go back on one's word

【失修】 shīxiū (of houses, etc.) be in bad repair; fall into disrepair: 年久～ have long been out of repair; have been neglected for years

【失学】 shīxué be deprived of education; be unable to go to school; be obliged to discontinue one's studies

【失血】 shīxuè lose blood: ～过多 excessive loss of blood

【失言】 shīyán make an indiscreet remark: 酒后～ make an indiscreet remark under the influence of alcohol

【失业】 shīyè lose one's job; be out of work; be unemployed ◇ ～率 rate of unemployment/ ～者 the unemployed; the jobless

【失宜】 shīyí 〈书〉 inappropriate: 处置～ handle improperly

【失意】 shīyì have one's aspirations, plans, etc. thwarted; be frustrated; be disappointed

【失音】 shīyīn 〈医〉 aphonia

【失迎】 shīyíng 〈套〉 fail to meet (a guest): ～！～！Excuse me for not meeting you at the gate./ 昨天～了,很抱歉。Sorry I was out when you called yesterday.

【失语症】 shīyǔzhèng 〈医〉 aphasia

【失约】 shīyuē fail to keep an appointment

【失着】 shīzhāo careless move; unwise move

【失真】 shīzhēn ① (of voice, images, etc.) lack fidelity; not be true to the original ② 〈无〉 distortion: 频率～ frequency distortion

【失之东隅,收之桑榆】 shī zhī dōngyú, shōu zhī sāngyú lose at sunrise and gain at sunset — make up on the roundabouts what you lose on the swings

【失之交臂】 shī zhī jiāo bì just miss the person or opportunity: 机会难得,幸勿～。Don't let slip such a golden opportunity.

【失职】 shīzhí neglect one's duty; dereliction of duty

【失重】 shīzhòng 〈物〉 weightlessness; zero gravity

【失主】 shīzhǔ owner of lost property

【失踪】 shīzōng be missing: 伤亡之外,尚有多人～。In addition to the killed and wounded, many were missing.

【失足】 shīzú ① lose one's footing; slip: ～落水 slip and fall into the water ② take a wrong step in life: 一～成千古恨。One false step brings everlasting grief.

## 师

shī ① teacher; master: 提倡尊～爱生 advocate students respecting teachers and teachers cherishing students ② model; example: 前事不忘，后事之～。Lessons learned from the past can guide one in the future. ③ a person skilled in a certain profession: 工程～ engineer/ 理发～ barber /技～ technician ④ of one's master or teacher: ～母 the wife of one's teacher or master ⑤ division: 步兵～ infantry division ⑥ troops; army: 正义之～ an army fighting for a just cause ⑦ (Shī) a surname

【师表】 shībiǎo 〈书〉 a person of exemplary virtue: 为人～ be worthy of the name of teacher; be a paragon of virtue and learning

【师部】 shībù 〈军〉 division headquarters

【师出无名】 shī chū wú míng dispatch troops without just cause

【师弟】 shīdì ① junior fellow apprentice ② the son of one's master (younger than oneself) ③ father's apprentice (younger than oneself)

【师法】 shīfǎ ① model oneself after (a great master); imitate ② knowledge or technique handed down by one's master

【师范】 shīfàn ① teacher-training; pedagogical: ～学院 teachers college; teachers training college ② normal school

【师父】 shīfu ① 见"师傅" ② a polite form of address to a monk or nun

【师傅】 shīfu master worker (a qualified worker as distinct from an apprentice)

【师娘】 shīniáng 〈口〉 the wife of one's teacher or master

【师团】 shītuán 〈军〉 division

【师兄】 shīxiōng ① senior fellow apprentice ② the son of one's master (older than oneself) ③ father's apprentice (older than oneself)

【师爷】 shīye a private assistant attending to legal, fiscal or secretarial duties in a local *yamen*; private adviser

【师长】 shīzhǎng ① 〈尊〉 teacher ② 〈军〉 division commander

【师直为壮】 shī zhí wéi zhuàng an army fighting for a just cause has high morale

【师资】 shīzī persons qualified to teach; teachers: ～不足 shortage of teachers/ 培训～ train teachers

## 虱

shī louse

【虱子】 shīzi louse

## 诗

shī poetry; verse; poem

【诗歌】 shīgē poems and songs; poetry: ～朗诵 recitation of poems; poetry readings

【诗话】 shīhuà notes on poets and poetry; notes on classical poetry

【诗集】 shījí collection of poems; poetry anthology

【诗经】 Shījīng *The Book of Songs* 参见"五经" wǔjīng

【诗句】 shījù verse; line

【诗剧】 shījù drama in verse; poetic drama

【诗篇】 shīpiān ① poem: 这些～抒发了作者的革命豪情。These poems express the revolutionary fervour of the poet. ② inspiring story: 我们时代的壮丽～ a magnificent epic of our era

【诗人】 shīrén poet

【诗兴】 shīxìng urge for poetic creation; poetic inspiration; poetic mood: ～大发 feel a strong urge to write poetry; be in an exalted, poetic mood

【诗意】 shīyì poetic quality or flavour: 饶有～ rich in poetic flavour; very poetic

【诗韵】 shīyùn ① rhyme (in poetry) ② rhyming dictionary

## 狮

shī lion

【狮身人面像】 shīshēn-rénmiànxiàng sphinx

【狮子】 shīzi lion

【狮子鼻】 shīzibí pug nose

【狮子搏兔】 shīzi bó tù not stint the strength of a lion in wrestling with a rabbit — go all out even when fighting a small enemy or tackling a minor problem

【狮子狗】 shīzigǒu pug-dog

【狮子头】 shīzitóu 〈食品〉 large meatball (usu. fried in deep oil first, before being braised with vegetables)

【狮子舞】 shīziwǔ lion dance

【狮子座】 shīzizuò 〈天〉 Leo

**鸸** shī 〈动〉 nuthatch

**施** shī ① execute; carry out: 无所～其技 no chance (for sb.) to play his tricks/ 他们一计不成,又～一计。Their first ruse having failed, they tried another. ② bestow; grant; hand out: ～恩 bestow favour ③ exert; impose: ～压力 exert pressure ④ use; apply: ～底肥 apply fertilizer to the subsoil ⑤ (Shī) a surname

【施放】 shīfàng discharge; fire: ～催泪弹 fire tear-gas shells/ ～烟幕 lay a smokescreen

【施肥】 shīféi spread manure; apply fertilizer

【施工】 shīgōng construction: 桥梁正在～。The bridge is under construction.
◇ ～单位 unit in charge of construction/ ～缝〈建〉construction joint/ ～人员 builder; constructor/ ～图 working drawing

【施加】 shījiā exert; bring to bear on: ～压力 bring pressure to bear on sb.; put pressure on sb./ ～影响 exert one's influence on sb.

【施礼】 shīlǐ salute

【施力点】 shīlìdiǎn 〈物〉 point of application

【施舍】 shīshě give alms; give in charity

【施事】 shīshì 〈语〉 the doer of the action in a sentence; agent

【施威】 shīwēi exhibit one's power; show severity

【施行】 shīxíng ① put in force; execute; apply: 本条例自公布之日起～。These regulations come into force upon promulgation. ② perform: ～手术 perform a surgical operation/ ～急救 administer first aid

【施用】 shīyòng use; employ

【施与】 shīyǔ grant; bestow

【施展】 shīzhǎn put to good use; give free play to: ～本领 put one's ability to good use; give full play to one's talent/ ～出种种威逼利诱的伎俩 resort to all kinds of threats and inducements/ ～阴谋诡计 carry out plots and schemes

【施政】 shīzhèng administration ◇ ～纲领 administrative programme

【施主】 shīzhǔ ① alms giver; benefactor ② 〈物〉 donor

**湿** shī wet; damp; humid: 小心点,别～了衣裳。Be careful! Don't get your clothes wet./ 别穿那双袜子,还～着呢。Don't wear those socks, they're still damp.

【湿痹】 shībì 〈中医〉 arthritis with fixed pain caused by dampness

【湿病】 shībìng 〈中医〉 diseases caused by dampness

【湿度】 shīdù humidity: 空气～ air humidity ◇ ～表 humidometer

【湿法冶金】 shīfǎ yějīn hydrometallurgy

【湿纺】 shīfǎng 〈纺〉 wet spinning

【湿淋淋】 shīlínlín dripping wet; drenched: 身上浇得～的 get dripping (或 soaking, sopping) wet; be soaked to the skin/ ～的衣服 sopping wet clothes

【湿漉漉】 shīlùlù wet; damp

【湿气】 shīqì ① moisture; dampness ② 〈中医〉 eczema; fungus infection of hand or foot

【湿热】 shīrè damp and hot

【湿润】 shīrùn moist: ～的土壤 damp soil/ 空气～ humid air/ 她眼睛～了。Her eyes were moist with tears.

【湿水货】 shīshuǐhuò water-damaged goods

【湿透】 shītòu wet through; drenched: 汗水～了他的衣服。His clothes are drenched with sweat.

【湿选】 shīxuǎn 〈矿〉 wet separation

【湿疹】 shīzhěn 〈医〉 eczema

**蓍** shī 〈植〉 alpine yarrow (*Achillea alpina*)

**嘘** shī 〈叹〉〔表示制止、驱逐等〕: ～,别作声! Sh (或 Hush)! Keep quiet!
另见 xū

**鲺** shī 〈动〉 yellowtail

**鲺** shī 〈动〉 carp louse; fish louse

## shí

**十** shí ① ten: ～倍 ten times; tenfold/ ～个指头有长短。Fingers are unequal in length — you can't expect everybody to be the same. ② topmost: ～成 100 per cent

【十八般武艺】 shíbā bān wǔyì skill in wielding the 18 kinds of weapons — skill in various types of combat: ～,样样精通 be skilful in using each and every one of the 18 weapons; be versatile

【十边地】 shíbiāndì small plots of land by the side of houses, roads, ponds, etc.

【十大功劳】 shídàgōngláo 〈中药〉 Chinese mahonia (*Mahonia fortunei*)

【十滴水】 shídīshuǐ 〈药〉 "10 drops", a popular medicine for summer ailments

【十冬腊月】 shídōng-làyuè the tenth, eleventh and twelfth months of the lunar year; the cold months of the year

【十恶不赦】 shí è bù shè guilty of unpardonable evil; unpardonably wicked

【十二分】 shí'èrfēn more than 100 per cent; extremely: 感到～的满意 be more than satisfied

【十二红】 shí'èrhóng 〈动〉 Japanese waxwing

【十二黄】 shí'èrhuáng 〈动〉 waxwing

【十二级风】 shí'èrjífēng 〈气〉 force 12 wind; hurricane

【十二平均律】 shí'èr píngjūnlǜ 〈乐〉 twelve-tone equal temperament

【十二月】 shí'èryuè ① December ② the twelfth month of the lunar year; the twelfth moon

【十二指肠】 shí'èrzhǐcháng 〈生理〉 duodenum ◇ ～溃疡 duodenal ulcer

【十分】 shífēn 〈副〉 very; fully; utterly; extremely: ～高兴 be very pleased; be elated/ ～难过 feel very sorry; feel very bad/ ～宝贵 most valuable/ ～有害 extremely harmful/ ～注意 pay close (或 the closest) attention to/ ～仇视 harbour intense hatred for/ ～猖狂 be on a rampage/ ～爱惜人力物力 use manpower and material resources most sparingly

【十级风】 shíjífēng 〈气〉 force 10 wind; whole gale

【十进制】 shíjìnzhì 〈数〉 the decimal system

【十六分音符】 shíliùfēn yīnfú 〈乐〉 semiquaver; sixteenth note

【十六开】 shíliù kāi 〈印〉 sixteenmo; 16mo

【十目所视,十手所指】 shí mù suǒ shì, shí shǒu suǒ zhǐ with many eyes watching and many fingers pointing — one cannot do wrong without being seen

【十拿九稳】 shíná-jiǔwěn 90 per cent sure; practically certain; in the bag: 这事情,我们是～了。We have the matter well in hand.

【十年九不遇】 shí nián jiǔ bù yù not occur once in ten years; be very rare: 这样大的洪水真是～。A flood of this sort is really unprecedented.

【十年树木,百年树人】 shí nián shù mù, bǎi nián shù rén 〈谚〉 it takes ten years to grow trees, but a hundred to rear

people
【十全十美】 shíquán-shíměi be perfect in every way; be the acme of perfection; leave nothing to be desired
【十三陵】 Shísānlíng the Ming Tombs (in Beijing)
【十室九空】 shí shì jiǔ kōng nine houses out of ten are deserted — a scene of desolation after a plague or war when the population is decimated
【十四行诗】 shísìhángshī sonnet
【十万八千里】 shíwàn bāqiān lǐ a distance of one hundred and eight thousand *li*; poles apart: 离题～ miles away from the subject; completely off the point
【十万火急】 shíwàn huǒjí ① posthaste ② Most Urgent (as a mark on dispatches)
【十项全能运动】 shí xiàng quánnéng yùndòng 〈体〉 decathlon
【十·一】 Shí Yī October 1, National Day of the People's Republic of China
【十一级风】 shíyījífēng 〈气〉 force 11 wind; storm
【十一月】 shíyīyuè ① November ② the eleventh month of the lunar year; the eleventh moon
【十月】 shíyuè ① October ② the tenth month of the lunar year; the tenth moon
【十月革命】 Shíyuè Gémìng the October Revolution (1917)
【十之八九】 shí zhī bā-jiǔ in eight or nine cases out of ten; most likely: ～他是误会了。Most likely there is some misunderstanding on his part. 又作"十有八九"
【十字镐】 shízìgǎo pick; pickaxe; mattock
【十字花科】 shízìhuākē 〈植〉 the mustard family
【十字架】 shízìjià cross
【十字街头】 shízì jiētóu crisscross streets; busy city streets
【十字军】 Shízìjūn ① 〈史〉 the Crusades ② crusade ③ crusader
【十字路口】 shízì lùkǒu crossroads: 徘徊在～ hesitate at the crossroads
【十足】 shízú 100 per cent; out-and-out; sheer; downright: 干劲～ full of energy/ ～的强权政治 100% (或 naked) power politics/ ～的唯心主义 sheer idealism/ ～的强盗逻辑 downright gangster logic

**什** shí ① assorted; varied; miscellaneous ② 〈书〉〔多用于分数或倍数〕ten: ～一 one tenth/ ～百 tenfold or hundredfold
另见 shén
【什件儿】 shíjiànr ① giblets: 炒～ fried giblets ② 〈方〉 metal decorations fixed on trunks, carriages, swords, etc.
【什锦】 shíjǐn 〈食品〉 assorted; mixed: ～饼干 assorted biscuits/ ～奶糖 assorted toffees
【什物】 shíwù articles for daily use; odds and ends; sundries

**石** shí ① stone; rock ② stone inscription: 金～ inscriptions on ancient bronzes and stone tablets ③ (Shí) a surname
另见 dàn
【石斑鱼】 shíbānyú grouper
【石板】 shíbǎn 〈建〉 slabstone; flagstone; flag
【石版】 shíbǎn 〈印〉 stone plate
【石碑】 shíbēi stone tablet; stele
【石笔】 shíbǐ slate pencil
【石壁】 shíbì cliff; precipice
【石菖蒲】 shíchāngpú 〈植〉 grass-leaved sweetflag (*Acorus gramineus*)
【石沉大海】 shí chén dàhǎi like a stone dropped into the sea — disappear for ever
【石担】 shídàn 〈体〉 stone barbell
【石刁柏】 shídiāobǎi 〈植〉 asparagus (*Asparagus officinalis*)
【石雕】 shídiāo ① stone carving ② carved stone
【石墩】 shídūn a block of stone used as a seat
【石方】 shífāng ① cubic metre of stone ② stonework: 一百万～ one million cubic metres of stonework
【石膏】 shígāo gypsum; plaster stone: 熟～ plaster; plaster of Paris/ 生～ plaster stone
◇ ～绷带 plaster bandage/ ～床 plaster bed/ ～夹板 plaster splint/ ～像 plaster statue; plaster figure
【石工】 shígōng ① masonry ② stonemason; mason
【石拱桥】 shígǒngqiáo stone arch bridge
【石鼓文】 shígǔwén 〈考古〉 inscriptions on drum-shaped stone blocks of the Warring States Period (475-221 B.C.)
【石斛】 shíhú 〈中医〉 the stem of noble dendrobium (*Dendrobium nobile*)
【石花菜】 shíhuācài 〈植〉 agar
【石化作用】 shíhuà zuòyòng 〈地〉 petrifaction
【石灰】 shíhuī lime: 生～ quick lime/ 熟～ slaked lime
◇ ～浆 lime white/ ～砂浆 lime mortar/ ～石 limestone/ ～水 limewash/ ～窑 limekiln/ ～质砂岩 calcareous sandstone
【石鸡】 shíjī 〈动〉 chukar
【石家庄】 Shíjiāzhuāng Shijiazhuang
【石匠】 shíjiang stonemason; mason
【石决明】 shíjuémíng 〈中药〉 the shell of abalone or sea-ear
【石刻】 shíkè ① carved stone ② stone inscription
【石窟】 shíkū rock cave; grotto: 龙门～ the Longmen Grottoes (in Luoyang)
【石窟寺】 shíkūsì 〈考古〉 the Cave Temple
【石块】 shíkuài stone; rock
【石蜡】 shílà paraffin wax ◇ ～油 paraffin oil
【石栗】 shílì 〈植〉 candlenut tree
【石硫合剂】 shí-liú héjì 〈农〉 lime sulfur
【石榴】 shíliu 〈植〉 pomegranate ◇ ～红 garnet (colour)/ ～石 〈矿〉 garnet
【石龙子】 shílóngzǐ 〈动〉 skink
【石绿】 shílǜ a green pigment made of malachite; mineral green
【石煤】 shíméi bone coal
【石棉】 shímián asbestos
◇ ～板 〈建〉 asbestos board/ ～衬里 〈机〉 asbestos lining/ ～瓦 〈建〉 asbestos shingle; asbestos tile
【石墨】 shímò graphite ◇ ～铀堆 graphite-uranium pile
【石磨】 shímò stone mill
【石楠】 shínán 〈植〉 Chinese photinia (*Photinia serrulata*)
【石脑油】 shínǎoyóu naphtha
【石女】 shínǚ a woman with a hypoplastic vagina
【石破天惊】 shípò-tiānjīng earth-shattering and heaven-battering; remarkably original and forceful (music, writing, etc.)
【石器】 shíqì ① stone implement; stone artifact ② stone vessel; stoneware ◇ ～时代 the Stone Age
【石青】 shíqīng 〈矿〉 azurite
【石蕊】 shíruǐ ① 〈植〉 reindeer moss ② 〈化〉 litmus ◇ ～试纸 litmus paper
【石蒜】 shísuàn 〈植〉 short-tube lycoris (*Lycoris radiata*)
【石笋】 shísǔn 〈地〉 stalagmite
【石锁】 shísuǒ 〈体〉 a stone dumbbell in the form of an old-fashioned padlock
【石炭纪】 Shítànjì 〈地〉 the Carboniferous Period
【石炭酸】 shítànsuān 〈化〉 carbolic acid
【石头】 shítou stone; rock: 心里好象一块～落了地 feel as though a load has been taken off one's mind
【石头子儿】 shítouzǐr 〈口〉 small stone; cobble; pebble
【石羊】 shíyáng 〈动〉 bharal; blue sheep

【石印】 shíyìn lithographic printing; lithography
◇ ～机 lithographic press/ ～石 lithographic stone/ ～油画 oleograph/ ～纸 lithographic paper
【石英】 shíyīng quartz
◇ ～玻璃 quartz glass/ ～卤钨灯〈摄〉 quartz tungsten halogen lamp/ ～岩 quartzite
【石油】 shíyóu petroleum; oil
◇ ～产品 petroleum products/ ～地质学 petroleum geology/ ～工业 oil industry; petroleum industry/ ～管路 petroleum pipeline/ ～化工厂 petrochemical works/ ～勘探 petroleum prospecting/ ～沥青 petroleum pitch/ ～运移 oil migration
【石油化学】 shíyóu huàxué petrochemistry ◇ ～产品 petroleum chemicals
【石油气】 shíyóuqì petroleum gas: 液化～ liquefied petroleum gas (LPG)
【石油输出国组织】 Shíyóu Shūchūguó Zǔzhí the Organization of Petroleum Exporting Countries (OPEC)
【石竹】 shízhú 〈植〉 China pink (*Dianthus chinensis*)
【石子】 shízǐ cobblestone; cobble; pebble: ～路 cobblestone street; cobbled road

**识** shí ① know: 一字不～ not know a single character — absolutely illiterate ② knowledge: 学～ learning; knowledge
另见 zhì
【识别】 shíbié distinguish; discern; spot: ～真假马克思主义 distinguish true Marxism from false; distinguish between genuine and sham Marxism/ ～力 discernment/ 善于～干部 know how to judge cadres/ 我们必须学会～伪装的敌人。We must learn how to see through enemies in disguise./ ～政治骗子 spot a political swindler
【识货】 shíhuò know all about the goods; be able to tell good from bad; know what's what: 不怕不～，就怕货比货。Don't worry about not knowing much about the goods; just compare and you will see which is better. 或 Don't fear it won't be appreciated; it stands up well to comparison.
【识见】 shíjiàn 〈书〉 knowledge and experience
【识荆】 shíjīng 〈书〉〈敬〉 have the honour of making your acquaintance
【识破】 shípò see through; penetrate: ～骗局 see through a fraud/ ～敌人的伪装 penetrate the disguise of the enemy
【识趣】 shíqù know how to behave in a delicate situation
【识时务者为俊杰】 shí shíwù zhě wéi jùnjié whosoever understands the times is a great man
【识途老马】 shí tú lǎomǎ an old horse which knows the way — a person of rich experience; a wise old bird
【识文断字】 shíwén-duànzì able to read; literate
【识相】 shíxiàng 〈方〉 be sensible; be tactful: 你还是～点，赶快走吧。You'd better be sensible and quit.
【识字】 shízì learn to read; become literate ◇ ～班 literacy class/ ～课本 reading primer; elementary reader

**时** shí ① time; times; days: 古～ ancient times/ 当～ at that time; in those days ② fixed time: 按～上班 get to work on time/ 准～到站 arrive at the station on time ③ hour: 报～ announce the hour; give the time signal/ 上午八～ at 8 o'clock in the morning; at 8 a.m. ④ season: 四～ the four seasons/ ～菜 delicacies of the season ⑤ current; present: ～下 at present ⑥ opportunity; chance: 失～ lose the opportunity; miss the chance/ 待～而动 bide one's time ⑦ now and then; occasionally; from time to time: ～有出现 occur now and then ⑧〔叠用〕 now...now ...; sometimes...sometimes...: ～断～续 on and off/ ～起～伏 now rise, now fall; have ups and downs/ 心情～喜～忧 have changing moods, now gay, now gloomy/ 镜头～远～近 sometimes long shots and sometimes close-ups ⑨〈语〉 tense: 过去～ the past tense ⑩ (Shí) a surname
【时差】 shíchā ① time difference ② 〈天〉 equation of time
【时常】 shícháng often; frequently
【时辰】 shíchen one of the 12 two-hour periods into which the day was traditionally divided, each being given the name of one of the 12 Earthly Branches
【时代】 shídài ① times; age; era; epoch: ～潮流 the tendency of the day; the trend of the times/ ～的需要 the needs of the times/ 开创一个新～ usher in a new era/ 反映我们～的面貌 reflect the features of our age/ 新～的凯歌 a paean of triumph to the new age/ 帝国主义和无产阶级革命的～ the epoch of imperialism and the proletarian revolution ② a period in one's life: 青年～ youth
【时而】 shí'ér ① from time to time; sometimes: 天上～飘过几片薄薄的白云。Every now and then fleecy clouds floated across the sky. ②〔叠用〕 now...now...; sometimes... sometimes...: 这天气变化无常，～晴天，～下雨！What changeable weather, fine one moment, raining the next!
【时分】 shífèn time: 黄昏～ at dusk; at twilight
【时光】 shíguāng ① time: ～不早了。It's getting late. ② times; years; days
【时号】 shíhào time signal
【时候】 shíhou ① (the duration of) time: 你写这篇文章用了多少～？How much time did you spend writing this article?/ 农忙的～ a busy farming season ② (a point in) time; moment: 现在是什么～了？What time is it?/ 就在这～ just at this moment
【时机】 shíjī opportunity; an opportune moment: 等待～ wait for an opportunity; bide one's time/ ～的选择 choice of the right moment; timing/ ～一到 when the opportunity arises; at the opportune moment/ ～不成熟。Conditions are not yet ripe. 或 The time is not yet ripe.
【时计】 shíjì 〈天〉 chronometer
【时价】 shíjià current price
【时间】 shíjiān ① (the concept of) time: ～与空间 time and space ② (the duration of) time: 这项工程需要多少～？How long will it take to finish this project?/ ～紧，任务重。Time is pressing and the task heavy./ ～到了。Time! 或 Time's up./ 办公～ office hours/ 不给敌人喘息的～ give the enemy no breathing space/ ～掌握得好 beautiful timing ③ (a point in) time: 现在的～是四点五分。The time now is five minutes past four./ 北京～十九点整 19 hours Beijing time
◇ ～表 timetable; schedule/ ～知觉〈心〉 time perception
【时间性】 shíjiānxìng timeliness: 新闻报导的～强。News reports must be timely./ 这项任务～强。This task must be fulfilled on time.
【时角】 shíjiǎo 〈天〉 hour angle
【时节】 shíjié ① season: 春耕～ the season for spring ploughing/ 清明～ at or around the Qing Ming festival ② time: 解放那～她才十二岁。She was only twelve at the time of liberation.
【时局】 shíjú the current political situation
【时刻】 shíkè ① time; hour; moment: 欢乐的～ a time of rejoicing/ 幸福的～ a happy moment/ 关键～ a critical moment ② constantly; always: ～准备保卫祖国 be ready to defend the country at any moment/ 时时刻刻为人民利益着想 always keep the people's interests in mind
【时刻表】 shíkèbiǎo timetable; schedule: 火车～ railway timetable; train schedule
【时令】 shílìng season: ～不正 unseasonable weather/ ～已交初秋。It is already early autumn. ◇ ～病 seasonal dis-

ease
【时髦】 shímáo fashionable; stylish; in vogue: ～的服装 fashionable clothes/ 赶～ follow the fashion
【时期】 shíqī period: 社会主义革命和社会主义建设～ the period of socialist revolution and socialist construction
【时区】 shíqū time zone
【时尚】 shíshàng fashion; fad
【时时】 shíshí often; constantly: ～想到 often recall or think about/ ～处处严格要求自己 be strict with oneself in all matters
【时式】 shíshì up-to-date style (of clothes, etc.)
【时势】 shíshì the current situation; the trend of the times; the way things are going: ～造英雄。The times produce their heroes.
【时事】 shíshì current events; current affairs
◇ ～报告 report on current events/ ～述评 current events survey/ ～学习 study of current affairs
【时速】 shísù speed per hour
【时态】 shítài 〈语〉 tense
【时务】 shíwù current affairs; the trend of the times: 不识～ show no understanding of the times
【时鲜】 shíxiān (of vegetables, fruits, etc.) in season: ～果品 fresh fruits
【时限】 shíxiàn time limit
【时效】 shíxiào ① effectiveness for a given period of time ② 〈法〉 prescription ③ ageing ◇ ～硬化 〈冶〉 age-hardening
【时新】 shíxīn stylish; trendy: ～的式样 up-to-date style
【时兴】 shíxīng fashionable; in vogue; popular 又作"时行"
【时样】 shíyàng the latest fashion
【时宜】 shíyí what is appropriate to the occasion: 不合～ be not appropriate to the occasion; be inappropriate; be out of keeping with the times
【时疫】 shíyì epidemic
【时运】 shíyùn luck; fortune: ～不济 have bad luck; down on one's luck
【时针】 shízhēn ① hands of a clock or watch ② hour hand
【时值】 shízhí 〈乐〉 duration; value
【时至今日】 shí zhì jīnrì at this late hour
【时钟】 shízhōng clock
【时装】 shízhuāng fashionable dress; the latest fashion

**实** shí ① solid: 里面是～的。It's solid. ② true; real; honest: ～心眼儿 honest and sincere/ ～有其事。It's a fact. ③ reality; fact: 名不副～。The name falls short of the reality. ④ fruit; seed: 开花结～ blossom and bear fruit
【实报实销】 shíbào-shíxiāo be reimbursed for what one spends
【实词】 shící 〈语〉 notional word
【实弹】 shídàn 〈军〉 live shell; live ammunition ◇ ～射击 firing practice; range practice/ ～演习 practice with live ammunition
【实地】 shídì on the spot: ～考察 on-the-spot investigation/ ～了解施工情况 learn on the spot how construction is proceeding
【实干】 shígàn get right on the job; do solid work ◇ ～家 man of action
【实话】 shíhuà truth: 说～ to tell the truth/ ～实说 not mince words; not beat about the bush
【实惠】 shíhuì ① material benefit: 从中得到～ really benefit from it ② substantial; solid: 让顾客吃到经济～的饭菜 serve the customers inexpensive but substantial meals
【实际】 shíjì ① reality; practice: 理论和～统一 the unity of theory and practice/ 客观～ objective reality/ 从～出发 proceed from actual conditions; be realistic/ ～上 in fact; in reality; actually/ 思想落后于～的事是常有的。It often happens that thinking lags behind reality. ② practical; realistic: ～经验 practical experience/ 你这种想法不～。This idea of yours is unrealistic./ 把革命气概和～精神结合起来 combine revolutionary sweep with practicality ③ real; actual; concrete: ～的例子 a concrete instance/ ～情况 the actual situation; reality/ ～生活水平 the real standard of living
◇ ～工资 real wages/ ～汇价 〈经〉 effective rate/ ～控制线 〈军〉 line of actual control/ ～收入 real income
【实价】 shíjià actual price
【实践】 shíjiàn ① practice: 中国革命的具体～ the concrete practice of the Chinese revolution/ ～出真知。Genuine knowledge comes from practice. ② put into practice; carry out; live up to: ～诺言 keep one's word; make good one's promise ◇ ～性 practicality; practicalness
【实据】 shíjù substantial evidence; substantial proof: 真凭～ ironclad evidence
【实况】 shíkuàng what is actually happening: 电视转播群众大会～ televise a mass rally; live telecast of a mass rally ◇ ～录音 on-the-spot recording; live recording/ ～转播 live broadcast; live telecast
【实力】 shílì actual strength; strength: 部队的～ the actual strength of the armed forces/ 军事～ military strength/ ～相当 match each other in strength; be well matched in strength ◇ ～地位 position of strength
【实例】 shílì living example; example
【实脉】 shímài 〈中医〉 forceful pulse
【实模铸造法】 shímú zhùzàofǎ 〈冶〉 cavityless casting
【实情】 shíqíng the true state of affairs; the actual situation; truth
【实权】 shíquán real power
【实生苗】 shíshēngmiáo 〈农〉 seedling
【实施】 shíshī put into effect; implement; carry out: 协定的条款正在付诸～。The provisions of the agreement are being put into effect./ 检查政策的～情况 check up on the implementation of the policy/ 监督宪法的～ supervise the enforcement of the constitution
【实事求是】 shíshì qiú shì seek truth from facts; be practical and realistic: ～的工作作风 a practical and realistic style of work/ ～的批评 criticism based on facts/ ～地拟定生产指标 set realistic production targets
【实数】 shíshù ① the actual amount or number ② 〈数〉 real number
【实体】 shítǐ ① 〈哲〉 substance ② 〈法〉 entity
【实物】 shíwù ① material object ② in kind
◇ ～地租 rent in kind/ ～工资 wages in kind/ ～幻灯机 epidiascope/ ～交易 barter/ ～税 tax paid in kind
【实习】 shíxí practice; fieldwork; field trip: 去煤矿～ go on a field trip to a coal mine/ 进行教学～ do practice teaching ◇ ～工厂 factory attached to a school/ ～生 trainee/ ～医生 intern
【实现】 shíxiàn realize; achieve; bring about: 为～我们的宏伟目标而奋斗 work hard to achieve our lofty goal; strive for the realization of our lofty goal/ ～优质高产 attain top quality and high output/ ～改革 bring about a reform/ ～粮食自给 become self-sufficient in grain/ ～农业、工业、国防和科学技术的现代化 accomplish the modernization of agriculture, industry, national defence, and science and technology/ 人民的夙愿～了。The people's long-cherished wish has come true.
【实像】 shíxiàng 〈物〉 real image
【实效】 shíxiào actual effect; substantial results: 注重～ emphasize practical results/ 如果这方法确有～，就应该推广。If the method proves to be really effective, it should be popularized.

【实心】 shíxīn ① sincere: ～实意 honest and sincere ② solid: 这种车胎是～的。These tyres are solid. ◇ ～球〈体〉 medicine ball

【实心眼儿】 shíxīnyǎnr ① having a one-track mind ② a person with a one-track mind

【实行】 shíxíng put into practice (或 effect); carry out; practise; implement: ～精兵简政的政策 put into effect the policy of better staff and simpler administration/ ～土地改革 carry out agrarian reform/ ～八小时工作制 institute an eight-hour (working) day/ ～科学种田 farm scientifically/ 对反动阶级～专政 exercise dictatorship over the reactionary classes/ 在人民内部～民主。Democracy is practised within the ranks of the people.

【实学】 shíxué real learning; sound scholarship

【实验】 shíyàn experiment; test: 做～ do (或 carry out) an experiment; make a test
◇ ～动物 animal used as a subject of experiment/ ～室 laboratory/ ～心理学 experimental psychology/ ～员 laboratory technician

【实业】 shíyè industry and commerce; industry ◇ ～家 industrialist

【实用】 shíyòng practical; pragmatic; functional: 既美观，又～ not only beautiful, but also practical/ ～美术 applied fine arts

【实用主义】 shíyòngzhǔyì 〈哲〉 pragmatism ◇ ～者 pragmatist

【实在】 shízài ① true; real; honest; dependable: ～的本事 real ability/ 心眼儿～ honest; trustworthy ② indeed; really; honestly: ～太好了 very good indeed/ 我～不知道。I really don't know. ③ in fact; as a matter of fact: 他装懂，～并没懂。He pretends to understand, but as a matter of fact he doesn't.

【实在】 shízai 〈方〉 (of work) well-done; done carefully: 工作做得很～。The work is well-done.

【实则】 shízé actually; in fact; in reality

【实战】 shízhàn actual combat: 从～需要出发 proceed from the needs of actual combat ◇ ～演习 combat exercise with live ammunition

【实证】 shízhèng 〈中医〉 a case of a physically strong patient running a high fever or suffering from such disorders as stasis of blood, constipation, etc.

【实证主义】 shízhèngzhǔyì 〈哲〉 positivism ◇ ～者 positivist

【实质】 shízhì substance; essence: 问题的～ the crux of the matter; the central point at issue/ ～性条款 substantive provision/ ～上 in substance; in essence; essentially; virtually

【实足】 shízú full; solid: 这袋麦子～一百斤。This sack of wheat is a full 100 *jin*./ 我～等了两个钟头。I waited for two solid hours. ◇ ～年龄 exact age

**拾** shí ① pick up (from the ground); collect: 孩子把～到的钱包交给了民警。The boy handed over to the people's police the purse he had picked up./ ～柴 collect firewood/ ～麦穗 glean (stray ears of) wheat ② ten (used for the numeral 十 on cheques, banknotes, etc. to avoid mistakes or alterations)

【拾掇】 shíduo ① tidy up; put in order: 我们把屋子～一下。Let's tidy up the room. ② repair; fix: 这机器有点毛病，你给～一下好吗？Something is wrong with the machine. Will you help me fix it? ③〈口〉 settle with; punish

【拾荒】 shíhuāng glean and collect scraps (to eke out an existence)

【拾金不昧】 shí jīn bù mèi not pocket the money one picks up

【拾零】 shílíng 〔多用于标题〕news in brief; titbits; sidelights

【拾取】 shíqǔ pick up; collect

【拾人牙慧】 shí rén yáhuì pick up phrases from sb. and pass them off as one's own

【拾遗】 shíyí ① appropriate lost property: 路不～。No one pockets anything found on the road. ② make good omissions: ～补阙 make good omissions and deficiencies

【拾音器】 shíyīnqì 〈电〉 pickup; adapter

**食** shí ① eat: 不劳动者不得～。He who does not work, neither shall he eat. ② meal; food: 废寝忘～ (be so engrossed as to) forget food and sleep/ 主～ staple food ③ feed: 猪～ pig feed ④ edible: ～油 edible oil; cooking oil ⑤ eclipse: 日～ solar eclipse/ 月～ lunar eclipse
另见 sì

【食变星】 shíbiànxīng 〈天〉 eclipsing variable

【食草动物】 shícǎo dòngwù herbivorous animal; herbivore

【食虫动物】 shíchóng dòngwù insectivorous animal; insectivore

【食道】 shídào 〈生理〉 esophagus

【食而不化】 shí ér bù huà eat without digesting — read without understanding

【食粪动物】 shífèn dòngwù coprophagous animal

【食腐动物】 shífǔ dòngwù saprophagous animal; scavenger; saprozoic

【食古不化】 shí gǔ bù huà swallow ancient learning without digesting it; be pedantic

【食管】 shíguǎn 〈生理〉 esophagus ◇ ～癌 cancer of the esophagus/ ～炎 esophagitis

【食火鸡】 shíhuǒjī 〈动〉 cassowary

【食积】 shíjī 〈中医〉 dyspepsia; indigestion

【食既】 shíjì 〈天〉 second contact (of an eclipse)

【食客】 shíkè a person sponging on an aristocrat; a hanger-on of an aristocrat

【食粮】 shíliáng grain; food: 精神～ spiritual food

【食量】 shíliàng capacity for eating; appetite

【食品】 shípǐn foodstuff; food; provisions: 罐头～ tinned (或 canned) food
◇ ～部 food department/ ～厂 bakery and confectionery; food products factory/ ～工业 food industry/ ～公司 food company/ ～加工 food processing/ ～商店 provisions shop

【食谱】 shípǔ recipes; cookbook

【食肉动物】 shíròu dòngwù carnivorous animal; carnivore

【食甚】 shíshèn 〈天〉 middle of an eclipse

【食宿】 shí-sù board and lodging

【食堂】 shítáng dining room; mess hall; canteen

【食糖】 shítáng sugar

【食物】 shíwù food; eatables; edibles ◇ ～摄入〈动〉 food intake/ ～污染 food pollution

【食相】 shíxiàng 〈天〉 phase of an eclipse

【食性】 shíxìng 〈动〉 feeding habits; eating patterns

【食血动物】 shíxuè dòngwù sanguivorous (或 haematophagous) animal

【食言】 shíyán go back on one's word; break one's promise: ～而肥 fail to make good one's promise; break faith with sb.

【食盐】 shíyán table salt; salt

【食蚁兽】 shíyǐshòu anteater

【食用】 shíyòng edible: ～植物油 edible vegetable oil

【食油】 shíyóu edible oil; cooking oil

【食欲】 shíyù appetite: ～不振 have a jaded appetite; have a poor appetite/ 促进～ stimulate (或 whet) the appetite; be appetizing

【食指】 shízhǐ index finger; forefinger

【食治】 shízhì 〈中医〉 food therapy; diet therapy

【食茱萸】 shízhūyú 〈植〉 ailanthus prickly ash (*Zanthoxylum*

*ailanthoides*)

**蚀** shí ① lose: 亏～ lose (money) in business ② erode; corrode: 风雨侵～ erosion by wind and rain/ 锈能～铁。Rust corrodes iron. ③ 见"食" shí ⑤

【蚀本】 shíběn lose one's capital: ～生意 a business running at a loss; a losing proposition; an unprofitable venture (或 undertaking)

【蚀刻】 shíkè etching

**鲥** shí

【鲥鱼】 shíyú hilsa herring; reeves shad

## shǐ

**史** shǐ ① history: 现代～ contemporary history/ 编年～ annals/ 断代～ dynastic history/ 国际关系～ history of international relations/ 有～以来 since the beginning of recorded history ② (Shǐ) a surname

【史册】 shǐcè history; annals: 载入～ go down in history/ 在民族解放斗争～上写下灿烂的篇章 add an illustrious page to the annals of national liberation struggles

【史抄】 shǐchāo extracts from history

【史官】 shǐguān official historian; historiographer

【史迹】 shǐjī historical site or relics

【史籍】 shǐjí 见"史书"

【史料】 shǐliào historical data; historical materials

【史前】 shǐqián prehistoric: ～时代 prehistoric age (或 times) ◇ ～学 〈考古〉 prehistory

【史乘】 shǐshèng history; annals

【史诗】 shǐshī epic

【史实】 shǐshí historical facts

【史书】 shǐshū history; historical records: 据～记载 according to historical records

【史无前例】 shǐ wú qiánlì without precedent in history; unprecedented

【史学】 shǐxué the science of history; historical science; historiography ◇ ～家 historian; historiographer

**矢** shǐ ① arrow: 飞～ flying arrow ② vow; swear: ～志不移 vow to adhere to one's chosen course

【矢车菊】 shǐchējú 〈植〉 cornflower (*Centaurea cyanus*)

【矢口否认】 shǐkǒu fǒurèn flatly deny

【矢量】 shǐliàng 〈数〉〈物〉 vector: 切变～ shear vector/ 风～ wind vector ◇ ～分析 vector analysis

**豕** shǐ 〈书〉 pig

**使** shǐ ① send; tell sb. to do sth.: ～人去打听消息 send sb. to make inquiries ② use; employ; apply: ～化肥 use chemical fertilizer/ 这支笔很好～。This pen writes well./ 心往一处想，劲往一处～ with everyone's thoughts and efforts directed towards one goal ③ make; cause; enable: 虚心～人进步，骄傲～人落后。Modesty helps one to go forward, conceit makes one lag behind./ ～革命遭到巨大损失 cause enormous losses to the revolution/ ～青少年在德、智、体几方面都得到发展 enable the youth to develop morally, intellectually and physically/ 修改原计划～之适合于新的情况 revise the original plan so as to gear it to the need of the new situation/ 帮助同志克服缺点，～他们能够大踏步前进 help comrades to overcome their shortcomings so that they can advance with great strides ④ envoy; messenger: 特～ special envoy/ 出～国外 be accredited to a certain country; be sent abroad as an envoy/ 信～ courier; messenger ⑤ if; supposing: 纵～ even if; even though

【使不得】 shǐbude ① cannot be used; useless; unserviceable: 这笔尖坏了，～了。This nib's broken — it can't be used. ② impermissible; undesirable: 你病刚好，干这种重活可～。You've just been ill, you mustn't do such heavy work.

【使出】 shǐchū use; exert: ～全副本领 use all one's resources/ ～浑身解数 use all one's skill/ ～最后一点力气 expend one's last bit of strength

【使得】 shǐde ① can be used; usable: 这个汽筒～使不得? Does this pump work all right? ② workable; feasible: 这个主意倒～。That's rather a good idea. ③ make; cause; render: ～家喻户晓 make known to everyone

【使馆】 shǐguǎn diplomatic mission; embassy ◇ ～工作人员 the staff of a diplomatic mission; embassy personnel/ ～馆长 head of a diplomatic mission

【使坏】 shǐhuài 〈口〉 be up to mischief; play a dirty trick

【使唤】 shǐhuan ① order about: 爱～人 be in the habit of ordering people about; be bossy ② 〈口〉 use; handle: 这些新式农具～起来很方便。These new farm implements are easy to use (或 handle)./ 这匹马不听生人～。This horse won't obey a stranger.

【使节】 shǐjié diplomatic envoy; envoy: 各国驻华～ diplomatic envoys to China; heads of diplomatic missions in China

【使劲】 shǐjìn exert all one's strength: ～干活 work hard/ ～蹬车 pedal (a bicycle) furiously/ ～划桨 strain at the oars/ 有使不完的劲 have inexhaustible energy/ 再使把劲 put in more effort; put on another spurt

【使君子】 shǐjūnzǐ 〈中药〉 the fruit of Rangoon creeper (*Quisqualis indica*)

【使领馆】 shǐ-lǐngguǎn diplomatic and consular missions; embassies and consulates

【使命】 shǐmìng mission: 无产阶级的历史～ the historical mission of the proletariat

【使女】 shǐnǚ maidservant; housemaid; chambermaid; maid

【使性子】 shǐ xìngzi get angry; lose one's temper

【使眼色】 shǐ yǎnsè tip sb. the wink; wink

【使用】 shǐyòng make use of; use; employ; apply: 我国各民族都有～自己的语言的自由。Every nationality in our country has the freedom to use its own language./ 灵活地～兵力 flexible employment of forces/ 新机器已开始～。The new machine has been put into operation./ ～种种手段 resort to every possible means/ ～方便 be easy to operate ◇ ～价值 〈经〉 use value/ ～率 rate of utilization/ ～面积 〈建〉 usable floor area/ ～权 〈法〉 right of use; right to use a thing/ ～寿命 service life (of machines)/ ～说明书 operation instructions

【使者】 shǐzhě emissary; envoy; messenger

**始** shǐ ① beginning; start: 自～至终 from beginning to end; from start to finish/ 不知～于何时 not know exactly when this came into being/ ～而不解，继而恍然。At first I didn't catch on; then I suddenly saw the light. ② 〈书〉〈副〉 only then; not ... until: 群众大会结束后，广场～能通行。Traffic cannot pass through the square until the mass meeting is over./ 坚持学习，～能不断进步。Steady progress can only be the result of persistent study. 或 Only persistent study yields steady progress.

【始末】 shǐ-mò beginning and end — the whole story: 事情的～ the whole story

【始新世】 Shǐxīnshì 〈地〉 the Eocene Epoch

【始业】 shǐyè the beginning of the school year: 秋季～。The school year begins in autumn.

【始终】 shǐzhōng from beginning to end; from start to finish; all along; throughout: 会谈～在友好的气氛中进行。The talks proceeded in a friendly atmosphere from beginning to end./ 手术过程中病人～是清醒的。The patient remained conscious throughout the operation.

【始终不渝】 shǐzhōng bù yú unswerving; steadfast: ～地支援各国人民的正义斗争 steadfastly support and aid the just struggles of the people of all countries/ 对党对人民忠心耿耿～ remain loyal and devoted to the Party and the people to the end of one's life

【始终如一】 shǐzhōng rú yī constant; consistent; persistent: ～地站在革命人民一边 consistently stand on the side of the revolutionary people

【始祖】 shǐzǔ first ancestor; earliest ancestor

【始祖鸟】 shǐzǔniǎo 〈古生物〉 archaeopteryx

**驶** shǐ ① sail; drive: ～入港口 sail into the harbour/ 火车～出车站。The train pulled out of the station. ② (of a vehicle, etc.) speed: 疾～而过 speed by; fly past

**屎** shǐ ① excrement; faeces; dung; droppings: 鸡～ chicken droppings/ 牛～ cow dung/ 拉～ empty the bowels; shit ② secretion (of the eye, ear, etc.): 耳～ earwax

【屎壳郎】 shǐkelàng 〈方〉 dung beetle

## shì

**士** shì ① bachelor (in ancient China) ② a social stratum in ancient China, between senior officials (大夫) and the common people (庶民) ③ scholar ④ noncommissioned officer: 上～(英) staff sergeant; (美) sergeant first class/ 中～ sergeant/ 下～ corporal ⑤ a person trained in a certain field: 护～ nurse ⑥ (commendable) person: 勇～ brave fighter; warrior/ 烈～ martyr ⑦ bodyguard, one of the pieces in Chinese chess

【士兵】 shìbīng rank-and-file soldiers; privates

【士大夫】 shìdàfū *literati* and officialdom (in feudal China)

【士女】 shìnǚ ① young men and women ② 见"仕女" shìnǚ

【士气】 shìqì morale: 鼓舞～ boost morale/ 我军～高昂。Our army's morale is high.

【士绅】 shìshēn gentry

【士卒】 shìzú soldiers; privates: 身先～ (of an officer) fight at the head of his men; lead the charge

**氏** shì ① family name; surname: 张～兄弟 the Zhang brothers ② *née*: 李王～ Mrs. Li, *née* Wang ③〔对名人专家的称呼〕: 陈～定理 Chen's theorem/ 摄～温度计 Celsius thermometer

【氏族】 shìzú clan

◇ ～公社 clan commune/ ～社会 clan society/ ～制度 clan system

**市** shì ① market: 米～ rice market/ 上～ be on the market; be in season ② city; municipality: 天津～ the City of Tianjin; Tianjin municipality/ ～革委会 municipal revolutionary committee/ ～中心 the heart of the city; city centre; downtown ③ pertaining to the Chinese system of weights and measures: ～尺 *chi*, a unit of length (=1/3 metre)

【市廛】 shìchán 〈书〉 stores in a market or street; market; business centre

【市场】 shìchǎng marketplace; market; bazaar: 国内外～ domestic and foreign markets/ ～供应充足。There is an ample supply of commodities. / ～繁荣。The market is brisk./ 这种错误理论在群众中的～越来越小。This erroneous theory finds less and less support among the people. ◇ ～价格 market price

【市秤】 shìchèng Chinese scale of weights

【市尺】 shìchǐ *chi*, a unit of length (=1/3 metre)

【市石】 shìdàn *dan*, a unit of dry measure for grain (=1 hectolitre)

【市担】 shìdàn *dan*, a unit of weight (=50 kilograms)

【市斗】 shìdǒu *dou*, a unit of dry measure for grain (=1 decalitre)

【市集】 shìjí ① fair ② small town

【市价】 shìjià market price

【市郊】 shìjiāo suburb; outskirts

【市斤】 shìjīn *jin*, a unit of weight (=1/2 kilogram)

【市井】 shìjǐng 〈书〉 marketplace; town: ～小人 philistine

【市侩】 shìkuài sordid merchant: ～习气 sordid merchants' ways; philistinism

【市面】 shìmiàn market conditions; business: ～繁荣。Trade is flourishing. 或 Business is brisk./ ～萧条。Business is slack.

【市民】 shìmín residents of a city; townspeople

【市亩】 shìmǔ *mu*, a unit of area (=0.0667 hectares)

【市区】 shìqū city proper; urban district

【市容】 shìróng the appearance of a city: 保持～整洁 keep the city clean and tidy/ 参观～ go sight-seeing in the city; have a look around the city

【市委】 shìwěi municipal Party committee

【市长】 shìzhǎng mayor

【市镇】 shìzhèn small towns; towns

【市政】 shìzhèng municipal administration ◇ ～工程〈建〉 municipal works; municipal engineering

【市制】 shìzhì the Chinese system of weights and measures 又作"市用制"

**示** shì show; notify; instruct: 出～证件 produce one's papers/ 暗～ hint; drop a hint/ 告～ notice/ 请～ ask for instructions/ ～悉。Your letter has been received. 或 Yours to hand.

【示波管】 shìbōguǎn 〈电〉 oscilloscope tube

【示波器】 shìbōqì 〈电〉 oscillograph; oscilloscope

【示范】 shìfàn set an example; demonstrate: 起～作用 play an exemplary role/ ～表演金属切削 put on a demonstration of metal-cutting technique ◇ ～飞行 demonstration flight

【示功器】 shìgōngqì 〈机〉 indicator

【示功图】 shìgōngtú 〈机〉 indicator card; indicator diagram

【示警】 shìjǐng give a warning; warn: 鸣锣～ give a warning by beating a gong

【示例】 shìlì give typical examples; give a demonstration

【示弱】 shìruò give the impression of weakness; take sth. lying down: 不甘～ not to be outdone

【示威】 shìwēi ① demonstrate; hold a demonstration ② put on a show of force; display one's strength ◇ ～游行 demonstration; parade; march

【示意】 shìyì signal; hint; motion: ～他出去 motion to him to go out/ 以目～ give a hint with the eyes; tip sb. the wink

【示意图】 shìyìtú ① sketch map: 边界东段～ a sketch map showing the eastern sector of the boundary/ 架设天线的～ illustrated instructions for installing antennae ②〈机〉 schematic diagram; schematic drawing

【示众】 shìzhòng publicly expose; put before the public: 游街～ parade sb. through the streets

【示踪物】 shìzōngwù 〈物〉 tracer

【示踪元素】 shìzōng yuánsù 〈物〉 tracer element

【示踪原子】 shìzōng yuánzǐ labelled atom; tagged atom; tracer

**世** shì ①lifetime; life: 今生今～ this present life ② generation: ～谊 friendship spanning many generations ③age; era: 当今之～ at present; nowadays ④world: 举～闻名 well known all over the world; world-famous ⑤〈地〉epoch: 古新～ the Palaeocene Epoch

【世仇】 shìchóu ①family feud ②bitter enemy (in a family feud)

【世传】 shìchuán be handed down through generations

【世代】 shìdài ①for generations; from generation to generation; generation after generation: ～相传 pass on from generation to generation/ 他家～务农。He comes from a long line of farmers. ②〈生〉generation ◇ ～交替〈生〉alternation of generations

【世道】 shìdào the manners and morals of the time: 唉！别提那吃人的旧～了！Hm! Let's not talk about that man-eat-man society.

【世故】 shìgù the ways of the world: 老于～ versed in the ways of the world; worldly-wise/ 人情～ worldly wisdom

【世故】 shìgu worldly-wise: 这人相当～。This chap is rather a smooth character.

【世纪】 shìjì century ◇ ～末 end of the century; *fin-de-siècle*

【世家】 shìjiā aristocratic family; old and well-known family

【世交】 shìjiāo ①friendship spanning two or more generations ②old family friends

【世界】 shìjiè world
◇ ～博览会 World's Fair/ ～大事 world events/ ～观 world outlook/ ～冠军 world champion/ ～纪录 world record/ ～时〈天〉universal time/ ～语 Esperanto/ ～主义 cosmopolitanism

【世界大战】 shìjiè dàzhàn world war: 第一次～ the First World War (1914-1918); World War I/ 第二次～ the Second World War (1939-1945); World War II

【世面】 shìmiàn various aspects of society; society; world; life: 见过～ have seen the world; have experienced life/ 经风雨,见～ face the world and brave the storm

【世人】 shìrén common people

【世上】 shìshang in the world; on earth: ～无难事,只怕有心人。Nothing in the world is difficult for one who sets his mind on it.

【世事】 shìshì affairs of human life

【世俗】 shìsú ①common customs: ～之见 common views ②secular; worldly

【世态】 shìtài the ways of the world: ～人情 the ways of the world/ ～炎凉 inconstancy of human relationships

【世外桃源】 shìwài táoyuán the Land of Peach Blossoms —a fictitious land of peace, away from the turmoil of the world; a haven of peace

【世袭】 shìxí hereditary: ～财产 hereditary property; patrimony/ ～制度 the hereditary system

【世系】 shìxì pedigree; genealogy

**仕** shì ①be an official; fill an office: 学而优则～。A good scholar will make an official — a Confucian doctrine. ②bodyguard, one of the pieces in Chinese chess

【仕女】 shìnǚ 〈美术〉traditional Chinese painting of beautiful women

【仕途】 shìtú 〈书〉official career

**式** shì ①type; style: 新～ new type; new style/ 雷锋～的人物 people of the Lei Feng type ②pattern; form: 程～ pattern; form to be copied ③ceremony; ritual: 开幕～ opening ceremony ④formula: 分子～ molecular formula ⑤〈语〉mood; mode: 叙述～ indicative mood

【式样】 shìyàng style; type; model: 各种～的服装 clothes in different styles/ 不同～的房屋 houses of different designs/ 各种～的车床 lathes of various models/ ～美观 graceful-looking; stylish

【式子】 shìzi ①posture ②formula

**似** shì
另见 sì

【似的】 shìde 〈助〉〔用在名词、代词或动词后面,表示跟某种事物或情况相似〕:象雪～那么白 as white as snow/ 他仿佛睡着了～。He seems to be asleep./ 这孩子乐得什么～。The child is as happy as a lark.

**试** shì ①try; test: ～一～ have a try/ ～穿 try on (a garment, shoes, etc.)/ ～跳(田径) trial jump; (跳水) trial dive/ ～～绳子结实不结实 test the strength of a rope/ ～产 trial production ②examination; test: 口～ oral examination

【试办】 shìbàn run an enterprise, etc. as an experiment; run a pilot scheme

【试表】 shìbiǎo 〈口〉take sb.'s temperature

【试场】 shìchǎng examination hall (或 room)

【试车】 shìchē 〈机〉test run; trial run

【试点】 shìdiǎn ①make experiments; conduct tests at selected points; launch a pilot project ②a place where an experiment is made; experimental unit

【试电笔】 shìdiànbǐ 〈电〉test pencil

【试飞】 shìfēi test flight; trial flight ◇ ～驾驶员 test pilot

【试管】 shìguǎn 〈化〉test tube ◇ ～架 test-tube stand (或 rack, support)

【试航】 shìháng ①trial trip; trial voyage or flight; shakedown cruise or flight ②shake down (a ship or an aeroplane)

【试剂】 shìjì 〈化〉reagent

【试金石】 shìjīnshí touchstone: 承认不承认无产阶级专政,是真假马克思主义的～。Recognition or nonrecognition of the dictatorship of the proletariat is the touchstone for distinguishing true Marxism from false.

【试卷】 shìjuàn examination paper; test paper

【试射】 shìshè 〈军〉fire for adjustment; trial fire

【试探】 shìtàn sound out; feel out; probe; explore: ～一下他对这个问题的看法 sound him out about the question

【试探性】 shìtànxìng trial; exploratory; probing: ～攻击 probing attack/ ～谈判 exploratory talks/ ～气球 trial balloon

【试题】 shìtí examination questions; test questions

【试图】 shìtú attempt; try

【试问】 shìwèn we should like to ask; it may well be asked; may we ask

【试想】 shìxiǎng 〔用于委婉的质问〕just think: ～你这样干下去会有好结果吗？Just think. Will it do you any good if you go on like this?

【试销】 shìxiāo ①place goods on trial sale ②trial sale ◇ ～专柜 trial sale counter

【试行】 shìxíng try out: 先～,再推广 first try out, then popularize/ 由上级批准～ be ratified by the higher authorities for trial implementation

【试选样品】 shìxuǎn yàngpǐn 〈机〉pilot model

【试演】 shìyǎn trial performance (of plays, operas, etc.)

【试验】 shìyàn trial; experiment; test: 水力～ hydraulic test/ 进行反坦克武器～ try out antitank weapons
◇ ～场 proving ground; testing ground/ ～农场 experimental farm/ ～田 experimental plot; experimental field/ ～性工厂 pilot plant

【试样】 shìyàng (test) sample
【试映】 shìyìng 〈电影〉 preview
【试用】 shìyòng ① try out ② on probation ◇ ～本 edition put out to solicit comments; trial edition/ ～品 trial products/ ～期 probation period/ ～人员 person on probation; probationer
【试运转】 shìyùnzhuǎn 〈机〉 test run; running-in
【试纸】 shìzhǐ 〈化〉 test paper: 石蕊～ litmus test paper/ 万用～ universal test paper/ 姜黄～ turmeric test paper
【试制】 shìzhì trial-produce; trial-manufacture: 一种新的播种机～成功了。A new seeding machine has been successfully trial-produced.
【试种】 shìzhòng plant experimentally: ～水稻 growing rice on a trial basis

**势** shì ① power; force; influence: 权～ (a person's) power and influence/ 仗～欺人 bully people on the strength of one's powerful connections ② momentum; tendency: 来～甚猛 come with tremendous force/ 以排山倒海之～ with the momentum of an avalanche ③ the outward appearance of a natural object: 地～ physical features of the land; terrain/ 山～ the lie of a mountain ④ situation; state of affairs; circumstances: ～难从命。Circumstances make it difficult for me to comply with your request./ ～所必然 inevitably; as a matter of course ⑤ sign; gesture: 作手～ make a sign with the hand/ 摆姿～ pose ⑥ male genitals: 去～ castration
【势必】 shìbì certainly will; be bound to: 饮酒过度，～影响健康。Excessive drinking will undoubtedly affect one's health.
【势不可当】 shì bùkě dāng irresistible: 革命的潮流汹涌澎湃，～。The revolution is surging forward irresistibly.
【势不两立】 shì bù liǎng lì mutually exclusive; extremely antagonistic; irreconcilable
【势均力敌】 shìjūn-lìdí match each other in strength: 双方～。The two sides are evenly matched./ 一场～的比赛 a close contest
【势力】 shìli force; power; influence: 壮大革命～ expand the revolutionary forces ◇ ～范围 sphere of influence
【势利】 shìli snobbish: ～小人 snob
【势利眼】 shìliyǎn ① snobbish attitude; snobbishness ② snob
【势能】 shìnéng 〈物〉 potential energy
【势如破竹】 shì rú pò zhú like splitting a bamboo; like a hot knife cutting through butter; with irresistible force: ～,所向披靡 smash all enemy resistance and advance victoriously everywhere
【势头】 shìtóu ① impetus; momentum: 风的～越来越大。It blew harder and harder. ②〈口〉 tendency; the look of things: 他见～不对,转身就走。Sensing that the odds were against him, he immediately turned back.
【势在必行】 shì zài bì xíng be imperative (under the circumstances)

**事** shì ① matter; affair; thing; business: 国家大～ affairs of state/ 把坏～变成好～ turn a bad thing into a good one/ ～非经过不知难。You never know how hard a task is until you have done it yourself./ 遇～和群众商量 consult the masses when problems arise ② trouble; accident: 出～ have an accident/ 平安无～。All is well./ 惹～ make trouble; stir up trouble/ 省了不少～ save a lot of trouble ③ job; work: 有～大家做。We should all share the work./ 找～ look for a job ④ responsibility; involvement: 这件案子里还有他的～呢。He was involved in the case too. ⑤ wait upon; serve: ～父母 wait upon one's parents ⑥ be engaged in: 不～生产 lead an idle life/ 无所～～ doing nothing; loafing
【事半功倍】 shì bàn gōng bèi get twice the result with half the effort
【事倍功半】 shì bèi gōng bàn get half the result with twice the effort
【事必躬亲】 shì bì gōng qīn see (或 attend) to everything oneself; take care of every single thing personally
【事变】 shìbiàn ① incident: 七七～ the July 7 Incident of 1937 ② emergency; exigency: 准备应付可能的突然～ be prepared against all possible emergencies ③ the course of events; events: 研究周围～的联系 look into the relations of events occurring around one
【事不宜迟】 shì bù yí chí one must lose no time in doing it; we must attend to the matter immediately; the matter brooks no delay
【事出有因】 shì chū yǒu yīn there is good reason for it; it is by no means accidental
【事到临头】 shì dào líntóu when things come to a head; when the situation becomes critical; at the last moment
【事端】 shìduān disturbance; incident: 挑起～ provoke incidents/ 制造～ create disturbances
【事故】 shìgù accident; mishap: 防止发生～ try to avert accidents/ 责任～ accident arising from sb.'s negligence
【事过境迁】 shìguò-jìngqiān the affair is over and the situation has changed; the incident is over and the circumstances are different
【事后】 shìhòu after the event; afterwards: 不要老是只作～的批评。Don't get into the habit of criticizing only after the event./ ～诸葛亮 be wise after the event
【事迹】 shìjī deed; achievement: 英雄～ heroic deeds
【事假】 shìjià leave of absence (to attend to private affairs); compassionate leave: 请两小时～ ask for two hours leave of absence
【事件】 shìjiàn incident; event: 流血～ bloody incident/ 二十世纪最伟大的～ the greatest event in the 20th century
【事理】 shìlǐ reason; logic: 明白～ be reasonable; be sensible
【事例】 shìlì example; instance: 典型～ a typical case
【事略】 shìlüè biographical sketch; short biographical account
【事前】 shìqián before the event; in advance; beforehand: ～跟群众商量 consult the masses in advance/ ～毫无准备 with no preparation at all/ ～请示，事后报告 ask for instructions in advance and submit reports afterwards; ask for instructions beforehand and report back afterwards
【事情】 shìqing affair; matter; thing; business: 急待解决的～ affairs to be settled right away/ 大家的～大家管。Public business is everybody's business./ ～的真相 the truth of the matter; the facts of the case/ ～也真巧 as luck would have it/ ～是这样的。It happened like this.
【事实】 shìshí fact: 与～不符 not tally with the facts/ ～俱在。The facts are all there./ ～恰恰相反。The facts are just the opposite. 或 The opposite is the case./ ～如此。This is how things are (或 stand).
【事实上】 shìshíshang in fact; in reality; as a matter of fact; actually: ～的承认 *de facto* recognition/ ～的停火 *de facto* cease-fire
【事事】 shìshì everything: ～都要从人民的利益出发。In whatever we do, our primary concern should be the interests of the people.
【事态】 shìtài state of affairs; situation: ～严重。The situation is serious./ ～在恶化。The situation is deteriorating./ ～的发展，证明了我们的看法是完全正确的。 The development of events entirely confirmed our view.

【事务】 shìwù ① work; routine: ～繁忙 have a lot (of work) to do ② general affairs
◇ ～性工作 routine work; daily routine/ ～员 office clerk/ ～主义 routinism/ ～主义者 a person bogged down in routine matters

【事物】 shìwù thing; object: ～的矛盾法则 the law of contradiction in things/ ～都是一分为二的。Everything divides into two.

【事先】 shìxiān in advance; beforehand; prior: ～做好准备 get everything ready beforehand/ ～跟他们打个招呼。Notify them in advance./ ～磋商 prior (或 preliminary) consultations/ ～酝酿 prior deliberation; exchange of views in advance/ ～策划的暗杀 a premeditated murder

【事项】 shìxiàng item; matter: 注意～ matters needing attention; points for attention

【事业】 shìyè ① cause; undertaking: 革命～ revolutionary cause/ 共产主义～ the cause of communism/ 文化教育～ cultural and educational undertakings ② enterprise; facilities: 集体福利～ collective welfare facilities or services/ 公用～ public utilities ◇ ～单位 institution/ ～费 operating expenses/ ～心 devotion to one's work; dedication

【事宜】 shìyí 〔多用于公文、法令〕matters concerned; arrangements: 商谈有关建馆～ discuss matters relating to the establishment of the embassy/ 讨论春耕～ discuss problems about the spring ploughing

【事由】 shìyóu ① the origin of an incident; particulars of a matter ②〔公文用语〕main content

【事与愿违】 shì yǔ yuàn wéi things go contrary to one's wishes

【事在人为】 shì zài rén wéi it all depends on human effort

【事主】 shìzhǔ the victim of a crime

**侍** shì wait upon; attend upon; serve: ～立一旁 stand at sb.'s side in attendance

【侍从】 shìcóng 〈旧〉 attendants; retinue ◇ ～副官 aide-de-camp (A.D.C.); aide

【侍奉】 shìfèng wait upon; attend upon; serve

【侍候】 shìhòu wait upon; look after; attend

【侍女】 shìnǚ maidservant; maid

【侍卫】 shìwèi imperial bodyguard

【侍者】 shìzhě 〈书〉 attendant; servant; waiter

**视** shì ① look at: 注～ look at closely ② regard; look upon: ～为莫大光荣 regard as a great honour/ ～如仇敌 look upon sb. as one's enemy ③ inspect; watch: 巡～ go on an inspection tour; go around and inspect

【视差】 shìchā 〈物〉 parallax

【视察】 shìchá inspect: ～边防部队 inspect a frontier guard unit

【视唱】 shìchàng sightsinging ◇ ～练耳 solfeggio

【视地平】 shìdìpíng 〈天〉 apparent horizon

【视而不见】 shì ér bù jiàn look but see not; turn a blind eye to: ～, 听而不闻 look but see not, listen but hear not/ 这是事实, 不能～。These are facts and you can't just ignore them.

【视轨道】 shìguǐdào 〈天〉 apparent orbit

【视角】 shìjiǎo angle of view; visual angle

【视界】 shìjiè field of vision; visual field

【视觉】 shìjué 〈生理〉 visual sense; vision; sense of sight
◇ ～象〈心〉 visual image/ ～印象〈心〉 eye (或 visual) impressions/ ～暂留 persistence of vision

【视力】 shìlì vision; sight: ～测验 eyesight test/ ～好(差) have good (poor) eyesight ◇ ～表 visual chart

【视亮度】 shìliàngdù 〈天〉 apparent brightness

【视频】 shìpín 〈物〉 video frequency

【视如敝屣】 shì rú bìxǐ regard as worn-out shoes; cast aside as worthless

【视若无睹】 shì ruò wú dǔ take no notice of what one sees; shut one's eyes to; turn a blind eye to; ignore

【视神经】 shìshénjīng 〈生理〉 optic nerve

【视事】 shìshì (of officials) attend to business after assuming office; assume office

【视死如归】 shì sǐ rú guī look upon death as going home; look death calmly in the face; face death unflinchingly

【视听】 shì-tīng seeing and hearing; what is seen and heard: 混淆～ throw dust in people's eyes; confuse the public/ 以正～ so that the public may know the facts; so as to clarify matters to the public

【视同儿戏】 shì tóng érxì treat (a serious matter) as a trifle; trifle with

【视同路人】 shì tóng lùrén regard as a stranger

【视图】 shìtú 〈机〉 view: 前～ front view/ 侧～ side view/ 上～ top view

【视网膜】 shìwǎngmó 〈生理〉 retina ◇ ～脱离 detachment of retina/ ～炎 retinitis

【视线】 shìxiàn line of vision; line of sight (in surveying)

【视星等】 shìxīngděng 〈天〉 apparent magnitude

【视野】 shìyě field of vision: 广阔的～ a wide field of vision

【视阈】 shìyù 〈生理〉 visual threshold

【视紫质】 shìzǐzhì 〈生理〉 visual purple

**饰** shì ① decorations; ornaments: 服～ clothes and ornaments/ 窗～ window decorations ② adorn; dress up; polish; cover up: 把文章修～一下 polish a piece of writing/ 文过～非 cover up one's mistakes/ 拒谏～非 reject representations and gloss over errors ③ play the role of; act the part of; impersonate: 她在《白毛女》里～喜儿。She played Xi'er in *The White-haired Girl*.

【饰词】 shìcí excuse; pretext

【饰物】 shìwù ① articles for personal adornment; jewelry ② ornaments; decorations

**室** shì room: 卧～ bedroom/ 会客～ reception room/ 办公～ office

【室内】 shìnèi indoor; interior: ～运动 indoor sport/ ～溜冰场 indoor skating rink/ ～游泳池 indoor swimming pool/ ～装饰 interior decoration

【室内乐】 shìnèiyuè 〈乐〉 chamber music

【室女座】 shìnǚzuò 〈天〉 Virgo

【室外】 shìwài outdoor; outside: ～活动 outdoor activities

**恃** shì rely on; depend on: 有～无恐 secure in the knowledge that one has strong backing

【恃才傲物】 shì cái ào wù be inordinately proud of one's ability; be conceited and contemptuous

【恃强凌弱】 shì qiáng líng ruò use one's strength to bully the weak

**拭** shì wipe away; wipe

【拭目以待】 shì mù yǐ dài wait and see

**柿** shì persimmon

【柿饼】 shìbǐng dried persimmon

【柿蒂】 shìdì 〈中药〉 the calyx and receptacle of a persimmon

【柿霜】 shìshuāng 〈中药〉 powder on the surface of a dried persimmon

【柿子】 shìzi persimmon

【柿子椒】 shìzijiāo sweetbell redpepper

**是** shì ①correct; right: 你说得～。What you said is right./ 似～而非 apparently right but actually wrong/ 实事求～ seek truth from facts ②yes; right: ～，我们一定完成任务。Right, we will fulfil the task. ③〈书〉this; that: ～日天气晴朗。It was fine that day./ ～可忍，孰不可忍? If this can be tolerated, what cannot? ④〔表示两种事物同一，或后者说明前者〕: 我～一个学生。I am a student. ⑤〔联系两种事物，表示陈述的对象属于"是"后面所说的情况〕: 院子里～冬天，屋子里～春天。It was winter outdoors, but spring indoors. ⑥〔与"的"字相应，有分类的作用〕: 这艘轮船～中国制造的。This ship was made in China./ 我～来看老王的。I came to see Lao Wang. ⑦〔表示存在〕: 前面～一片稻田。There is a stretch of rice fields ahead./ 满身～汗 sweating all over ⑧〔表示承认所说的，再转入正意〕: 这东西旧～旧，可还能用。Yes, it's old, but it can still be used./ 诗～好诗，就是长了点。It is a good poem all right, but it's a bit too long. ⑨〔"是"前后用相同的名词或动词(两次以上)，连用两个这样的格式，表示所说的几桩事物互不相干〕: 敌～敌，友～友，必须分清敌我的界限。A friend is a friend, a foe is a foe; one must be clearly distinguished from the other. ⑩〔表示适合〕: 这场雨下的～时候。This rain has come at just the right time./ 工具放的不～地方。The tools are not put in the right place. ⑪〔表示"凡是""任何"〕: ～集体的事大家都要关心。Whatever concerns the collective concerns all of us./ ～重活，他都抢着干。When there's a tough job, he always rushes to do it. ⑫〔重读，表示坚决肯定〕: 他～不知道。He certainly doesn't know./ 天气～冷。It's really cold. ⑬〔用于问句〕: 你～坐火车，还～坐汽车? Are you going by train or bus?/ 你～累了不～? You're tired, aren't you? ⑭〔用在句首，加重语气〕: ～谁告诉你的? Who told you?/ ～毛主席的革命路线指引我们从胜利走向胜利。It is Chairman Mao's revolutionary line that is guiding us from victory to victory. ⑮praise; justify: ～古非今 praise the past to condemn the present

【是的】 shìde ①yes; right; that's it ②见"似的" sìde

【是非】 shìfēi ①right and wrong: ～问题 a matter of right and wrong/ 明辨～ distinguish clearly between right and wrong/ ～自有公论。The public will judge the rights and wrongs of the case. ②quarrel; dispute: 搬弄～ tell tales; sow discord

【是非曲直】 shì-fēi qū-zhí rights and wrongs; truth and falsehood; merits and demerits: 不问～ not bother to look into the rights and wrongs of a case

【是否】 shìfǒu whether or not; whether; if: ～符合实际 whether or not it corresponds to reality/ 他～能来，还不一定。It's not certain whether he can come or not.

**适** shì ①fit; suitable; proper: ～于儿童阅读的书籍 books suitable for children ②right; opportune: ～量 just the right amount/ ～逢休假。It happened to be a holiday. ③comfortable; well: 舒～ comfortable/ 感到不～ not feel well ④go; follow; pursue: 无所～从 not know what course to pursue; be at a loss what to do

【适才】 shìcái 〈方〉just now

【适当】 shìdàng suitable; proper; appropriate: ～的工作 suitable work/ ～的安排 proper arrangement/ ～调整 appropriate readjustment/ ～时机 an opportune moment; the right moment/ 到～的时候 in due course

【适得其反】 shì dé qí fǎn run counter to one's desire; be just the opposite to what one wished: 多施肥能增产，但肥料过多会～。More fertilizer will raise the output, but too much will lead to just the opposite.

【适度】 shìdù appropriate measure; moderate degree: ～的体育活动有利于病人恢复健康。A moderate amount of physical exercise will help improve the patient's health.

【适逢其会】 shì féng qí huì happen to be present at the right moment

【适航性】 shìhángxìng (飞机) airworthiness; (船只) seaworthiness

【适合】 shìhé suit; fit: ～当地情况 be suited to local conditions/ ～他的口味 suit his taste; be to his taste/ 这类野生植物不～用作饲料。These wild plants are not fit for fodder.

【适可而止】 shìkě ér zhǐ stop before going too far; know when or where to stop; not overdo it

【适口】 shìkǒu agreeable to the taste; palatable

【适龄】 shìlíng of the right age: (入学) ～儿童 children of school age/ (入伍) ～青年 young people old enough to join the army

【适时】 shìshí at the right moment; in good time; timely: ～的号召 a timely call/ ～播种 begin sowing in good time/ ～召开经验交流会 call timely meetings to exchange experience

【适宜】 shìyí suitable; fit; appropriate: 他～做卫生工作。He's suitable for public health work./ 游泳对老年人也是～的。Swimming is good for old people too./ 这种土壤～种花生。This kind of soil is good for growing peanuts.

【适意】 shìyì agreeable; enjoyable; comfortable

【适应】 shìyìng suit; adapt; fit: ～革命斗争的需要 suit the needs of the revolutionary struggle/ ～时代的要求 keep abreast of the times/ ～环境 adapt oneself to circumstances/ 上层建筑要与经济基础相～。The superstructure should be suited to the economic base./ 人们的思想必须～已经变化了的情况。People must adapt their thinking to the changed conditions. ◇ ～性〈生〉adaptability/ ～症〈医〉indication

【适用】 shìyòng suit; be applicable: 这个新的种植法对我们这个地区很～。The new method of cultivation is suitable for our area./ 马克思列宁主义的基本原理是普遍～的。The fundamental tenets of Marxism-Leninism are universally applicable.

【适者生存】 shìzhě shēngcún 〈生〉survival of the fittest

【适值】 shìzhí just when: 昨日来访，～外出，憾甚。I called on you yesterday, but unfortunately you were out.

【适中】 shìzhōng ①moderate: 雨量～ moderate rainfall/ 大小～ moderate size ②well situated: 招待所地点～。The hostel is well situated.

**逝** shì ①pass: 时光易～。Time passes quickly. ②die; pass away: 病～ die of illness

【逝世】 shìshì pass away; die

**莳** shì ①〈方〉transplant: ～秧 transplant rice seedlings ②〈书〉plant; cultivate: ～花 grow flowers

**铈** shì 〈化〉cerium (Ce)

**弑** shì 〈书〉murder (one's sovereign or father)

**释** shì ①explain; elucidate: ～义 explain the meaning (of a word, etc.) ②clear up; dispel: ～疑 clear up (或 remove) doubts ③let go; be relieved of: ～手 loosen one's grip; let go/ 如～重负 (feel) as if relieved of a heavy load ④release; set free: ～俘 set prisoners free; release prisoners ⑤〈简〉(释迦牟尼) Sakyamuni ⑥Buddhism

【释放】 shìfàng ①release; set free: 刑满～ be released upon completion of a sentence ②〈物〉release: ～出能量 release energy

【释迦牟尼】 Shìjiāmóuní Sakyamuni, the founder of Buddhism
【释然】 shìrán 〈书〉 feel relieved; feel at ease

**嗜** shì have a liking for; be addicted to: ～酒 be addicted to drink
【嗜好】 shìhào ① hobby ② addiction; habit
【嗜血】 shìxuè bloodthirsty; bloodsucking: ～成性的法西斯匪徒 bloodthirsty fascists

**誓** shì ① swear; vow; pledge: ～为共产主义奋斗终身 pledge to dedicate one's life to the struggle for communism/～将革命进行到底 vow to carry the revolution through to the end ② oath; vow: 发～ take an oath; swear
【誓不罢休】 shì bù bàxiū swear not to stop; swear not to rest: 不达目的，～。We'll never give up until we reach our goal. 又作"誓不甘休"
【誓不两立】 shì bù liǎng lì swear not to coexist with one's enemy; resolve to destroy the enemy or die in the attempt; be irreconcilable
【誓词】 shìcí oath; pledge
【誓师】 shìshī ① a rally to pledge resolution before going to war ② take a mass pledge ◇ ～大会 a meeting to pledge mass effort; an oath-taking rally
【誓死】 shìsǐ pledge one's life; dare to die: ～保卫祖国 pledge to fight to the death in defending one's country/～保卫红色政权 be ready to die in defence of red political power
【誓言】 shìyán oath; pledge: 履行～ fulfil a pledge
【誓约】 shìyuē vow; pledge; solemn promise

**噬** shì bite: 吞～ swallow up/ 反～ make a false countercharge; hurl back an accusation
【噬菌体】 shìjūntǐ 〈生〉 bacteriophage; phage

**螫** shì sting
【螫针】 shìzhēn 〈动〉 sting; stinger

## shi

**匙** shi 见"钥匙" yàoshi
另见 chí

## shōu

**收** shōu ① receive; accept: ～发报 transmitting and receiving telegrams/ 请～下作为纪念。Please accept this as a souvenir./ 学校今年又～了一批研究生。The college has enrolled another group of research students this year./ 这本词典共～词六万余条。The dictionary contains over 60,000 entries. ② put away; take in: ～工具 put the tools away/ 洗的衣服～了没有？ Have you brought in the washing? ③ collect: ～水电费 collect water and electricity bills/ ～税 collect taxes/ ～废品 collect scrap ④ money received; receipts; income: 税～ tax revenue ⑤ harvest; gather in: ～庄稼 harvest (或 gather in) crops/ 秋～ autumn harvest ⑥ close: 伤～口了。The wound has healed. ⑦ bring to an end; stop: 时间不早了，今天就～了吧。 It's getting late. Let's call it a day. ⑧ restrain; control: 孩子玩得心都～不回来了。The boy can't get his mind off play.
【收报机】 shōubàojī telegraphic or radiotelegraphic receiver
【收编】 shōubiān incorporate into one's own forces
【收兵】 shōubīng withdraw (或 recall) troops; call off a battle: 不获全胜，决不～。We will not withdraw our forces till complete victory.
【收藏】 shōucáng collect; store up: ～古画 collect old paintings/ ～粮食 store up grain ◇ ～家 collector (of books, antiques, etc.)
【收操】 shōucāo bring drill to an end ◇ ～号 bugle call to dismiss; recall
【收场】 shōuchǎng ① wind up; end up; stop: 他的话匣子一打开，就不容易～。 Once he opens his trap, he just never stops./ 这件事不好～。 It's hard to wind this matter up./ 草草～ wind up a matter hastily or perfunctorily/ 看他怎样～。Let's wait and see how he's going to end it all. ② end; ending; denouement: 圆满的～ a happy ending
【收成】 shōucheng harvest; crop: 从来没有过的好～ a record harvest/ ～不好 poor harvests; crop failures/ 夺得秋季作物的好～ reap a good autumn harvest
【收存】 shōucún receive and keep
【收到】 shōudào receive; get; achieve; obtain: ～一封信 receive a letter/ ～良好效果 achieve good results
【收发】 shōufā ① receive and dispatch ② dispatcher ◇ ～室 office for incoming and outgoing mail
【收发报机】 shōu-fābàojī transmitter-receiver; transceiver
【收方】 shōufāng 〈簿记〉 debit; debit side
【收费】 shōufèi collect fees; charge
【收复】 shōufù recover; recapture: ～失地 recover lost territory/ ～城市 recapture a city
【收割】 shōugē reap; harvest; gather in: ～小麦 gather in the wheat ◇ ～机 harvester; reaper
【收工】 shōugōng stop work for the day; knock off; pack up: 该～了。It's time to knock off./ 我们今天下午五点半～。We stop work at 5:30 this afternoon.
【收购】 shōugòu purchase; buy: ～农副产品 purchase farm produce and sideline products ◇ ～价格 purchasing (或 procurement) price/ ～站 purchasing station (或 centre)
【收回】 shōuhuí ① take back; call in; regain; recall: ～发出的文件 recall the documents which have been issued/ ～借出的书籍 call in books lent/ ～主权 regain sovereignty/ ～贷款 recall loans/ ～投资 recoup capital outlay ② withdraw; countermand: ～建议 withdraw a proposal/ ～成命 countermand (或 retract) an order; revoke a command
【收货人】 shōuhuòrén consignee
【收获】 shōuhuò ① gather (或 bring) in the crops; harvest: 春天播种，秋天～ sow in spring and reap in autumn ② results; gains: 谈谈学习毛主席著作的～ talk about what one has learnt in studying Chairman Mao's works/ 一次很有～的访问 a most rewarding visit/ 你们的艰苦劳动，一定会有～。Your hard work will be duly rewarded. ◇ ～量 harvest yield; yield
【收集】 shōují collect; gather: ～民间验方 collect time-tested folk prescriptions/ ～废铁 collect scrap iron
【收监】 shōujiān take into custody; put in prison
【收件人】 shōujiànrén addressee; consignee
【收缴】 shōujiǎo take over; capture: ～敌人的武器 take over the enemy's arms
【收紧】 shōujǐn tighten up
【收据】 shōujù receipt ◇ ～簿 receipt book
【收口】 shōukǒu ① (of a wound) close up; heal ② (in knitting) binding off
【收款人】 shōukuǎnrén payee
【收敛】 shōuliǎn ① weaken or disappear: 她的笑容突然～了。Her smile suddenly disappeared. ② restrain oneself: 碰了钉子以后，他～些了。He has pulled in his horns since that setback. ③ 〈数〉 convergence ④ 〈医〉 astringent ◇ ～剂 astringent
【收殓】 shōuliàn lay a body in a coffin

【收留】 shōuliú take sb. in; have sb. in one's care
【收拢】 shōulǒng draw sth. in: 把网～ draw the net in
【收录】 shōulù ①〈旧〉employ; recruit; take on: ～几个职员 recruit some office workers ② include: 这篇文章已～在他的选集里。This essay is included in his selected works. ③ listen in and take down; take down; record: ～新闻广播 take down the news from the radio; make a recording of the news broadcast
【收罗】 shōuluó collect; gather; enlist: ～人才 recruit qualified personnel/ ～资料 collect data/ ～社会渣滓 gather together the dregs of society/ 这本小册子～了一些乌七八糟的东西。This pamphlet is a jumble of all sorts of rubbish.
【收买】 shōumǎi ① purchase; buy in: ～旧书 buy used books ② buy over; bribe: ～人心 buy popular support
【收盘】 shōupán 〈经〉closing quotation (on the exchange, etc.) ◇ ～汇率 closing rate/ ～价格 closing price
【收票员】 shōupiàoyuán ticket collector
【收起】 shōuqǐ pack up; cut out; stop: ～你们那一套高调吧! Cut out your high-sounding talk!/ ～你那套鬼把戏! None of your dirty tricks!/ 你这些空话还是～为好。You'd better stop this empty talk.
【收讫】 shōuqì ① payment received; paid ② (on a bill of lading, an invoice, etc.) all the above goods received; received in full
【收清】 shōuqīng received in full
【收容】 shōuróng take in; accept; house: ～伤员 take in wounded soldiers/ ～难民 house refugees ◇ ～所 collecting post
【收入】 shōurù ① income; revenue; receipts; earnings; proceeds: 集体(个人)～ collective (personal) income/ 副业～ income from sideline occupations/ 财政～ state revenue/ 总～ gross income/ 现金和粮食～ income in cash and grain/ ～和支出 receipts and expenditures; revenue and expenditure ② take in; include: 修订版～许多新词语。Many new words and phrases have been included in the revised edition.
【收生】 shōushēng midwifery ◇ ～婆 midwife
【收拾】 shōushi ① put in order; tidy; clear away: 把工具～一下。Put the tools in order./ ～屋子 tidy up the room/ ～床铺 make the bed/ ～碗筷 clear away the bowls and chopsticks; clear the table/ ～残局 clear up a messy situation ② get things ready; pack: ～药箱 get one's medical kit ready; pack one's medical kit/ ～行李 pack one's luggage; pack up one's things/ 咱们赶紧～～走吧。Let's get our things together at once and be off. ③ repair; mend: ～鞋子 mend shoes ④〈口〉settle with; punish: 早晚我们要～这个坏蛋。We'll settle with the scoundrel one of these days.
【收束】 shōushù ① bring together; collect: 把心思～一下 get into the frame of mind for work ② bring to a close: 写到这里,我的信也该～了。I think it is about time I wound up this letter. ③ pack (for a journey)
【收缩】 shōusuō ① contract; shrink: 金属遇冷就会～。Metals contract as they become cool./ 这种布下水后要～。This kind of cloth shrinks when it's washed. ② concentrate one's forces; draw back: 敌人～到几个据点里。The enemy drew back into a few fortified points. ③〈生理〉systole ◇ ～压 systolic pressure
【收摊儿】 shōutānr pack up the stall — wind up the day's business or the work on hand
【收条】 shōutiáo receipt
【收听】 shōutīng listen in: ～元旦社论 listen in to the New Year's Day editorial/ ～新闻广播 listen to the news broadcast/ 你的收音机能～多少电台? How many stations can you get on your radio set?
【收尾】 shōuwěi ① wind up: ～工作 winding up ② ending (of an article, etc.)
【收文】 shōuwén incoming dispatches ◇ ～簿 register of incoming dispatches
【收效】 shōuxiào yield results; produce effects; bear fruit: ～显著 bring notable results/ ～甚微 produce very little effect/ 这些轻工业项目具有投资少,～快的特点。These light industry projects are characterized by small investments and quick returns.
【收心】 shōuxīn ① get into the frame of mind for work; concentrate on more serious things ② have a change of heart
【收信人】 shōuxìnrén the recipient of a letter; addressee
【收押】 shōuyā take into custody; detain
【收养】 shōuyǎng take in and bring up; adopt: ～孤儿 adopt an orphan/ 爹妈死后,周伯伯就把我～下来了。After my parents died, Uncle Zhou took me in.
【收益】 shōuyì income; profit; earnings; gains
【收音】 shōuyīn ① (of radio) reception: ～情况良好。Reception is good. ② (of an auditorium, etc.) have good acoustics ◇ ～电唱两用机 radiogramophone
【收音机】 shōuyīnjī radio (set); wireless (set): 便携式～ portable radio/ 落地式～ console set
【收针】 shōuzhēn (in knitting) decreasing
【收支】 shōu-zhī revenue and expenditure; income and expenses: ～平衡。Revenue and expenditure are balanced./ 公布～帐目 publish a balance sheet ◇ ～逆差 balance of payments deficit
【收执】 shōuzhí ① (of a certificate, etc.) be issued to the person concerned for safekeeping ② receipt (issued by a government agency)

## shǒu

**手** shǒu ① hand: ～把～地教 take a person in hand and teach him how to do a job/ ～织的毛衣 a hand-knitted woollen sweater ② have in one's hand; hold: 人～一册。Everyone has a copy. ③ handy; convenient: ～册 handbook ④ personally: ～植 personally plant (a tree, etc.) ⑤ a person doing or good at a certain job: 拖拉机～ tractor driver/ 机枪～ machine gunner/ 助～ assistant/ 多面～ all-rounder/ 能～ a skilled (或 good) hand; crackerjack ⑥〈量〉〔用于技能、本领〕: 他有一～好手艺。He's a real craftsman. 或 He's a master of his craft./ 他真有两～。He really knows his stuff.
【手背】 shǒubèi the back of the hand
【手臂】 shǒubei arm
【手笔】 shǒubǐ ① sb.'s own handwriting or painting: 这一题词是鲁迅的～。This inscription is in Lu Xun's own handwriting. ② literary skill: 大～ a well-known writer; master
【手边】 shǒubiān on hand; at hand
【手表】 shǒubiǎo wrist watch
【手不释卷】 shǒu bù shì juàn always have a book in one's hand; be very studious
【手册】 shǒucè handbook; manual: 教师～ teacher's manual
【手抄本】 shǒuchāoběn hand-written copy
【手车】 shǒuchē handcart; wheelbarrow
【手戳】 shǒuchuō 〈口〉private seal; signet
【手倒立】 shǒudàolì 〈体〉handstand
【手电筒】 shǒudiàntǒng electric torch; flashlight
【手段】 shǒuduàn ① means; medium; measure; method: 达到目的的一种～ a means to an end/ 高压～ high-handed measures/ 强制～ coercive method; coercion/ 利用合法的斗争～ utilize the legal form of struggle/ 艺术～ artistic

medium/ 积累～ means of accumulation/ 支付～ means of payment/ 不择～ by fair means or foul; by hook or by crook; unscrupulously ② trick; artifice: 采用种种～ resort to all sorts of tricks; use every artifice

【手法】 shǒufǎ ① skill; technique: 国画的传统～ traditional technique of Chinese painting/ 艺术表现～ means of artistic expression ② trick; gimmick: 贼喊捉贼的拙劣～ the clumsy trick of thief crying "stop thief"/ 一种反动的宣传～ a reactionary propaganda gimmick/ 反革命两面派～ counterrevolutionary dual tactics/ 惯用～ habitual (或 customary) practice

【手风琴】 shǒufēngqín accordion: 六角～ concertina

【手扶拖拉机】 shǒufú tuōlājī walking tractor

【手感】 shǒugǎn 〈纺〉 feel; handle

【手稿】 shǒugǎo original (或 holograph) manuscript; manuscript

【手工】 shǒugōng ① handwork: 做～ do handwork/ ～费 payment for a piece of handwork ② by hand; manual: ～操作 done by hand; manual operations/ ～织的布 handwoven cloth/ ～制纸 handmade paper ③ 〈口〉 charge for a piece of handwork: 你这件上衣～多少? How much did you pay for the tailoring of this coat?

【手工业】 shǒugōngyè handicraft industry; handicraft ◇ ～生产合作社 handicraft producers' cooperative/ ～者 handicraftsman

【手工艺】 shǒugōngyì handicraft art; handicraft ◇ ～工人 craftsman; artisan/ ～品 articles of handicraft art; handicrafts

【手鼓】 shǒugǔ 〈乐〉 a small drum similar to the tambourine, used by the Uygur and other nationalities

【手迹】 shǒujì sb.'s original handwriting or painting

【手疾眼快】 shǒu jí yǎn kuài quick of eye and deft of hand

【手脚】 shǒujiǎo ① movement of hands or feet; motion: ～利落 nimble; agile/ ～不干净 sticky-fingered; questionable in money matters ② 〈方〉 underhand method; trick: 一定是有人从中弄～。Someone must have juggled things.

【手紧】 shǒujǐn closefisted; tightfisted

【手劲儿】 shǒujìnr muscular strength of the hand

【手巾】 shǒujin towel ◇ ～架 towel rack

【手锯】 shǒujù handsaw

【手卷】 shǒujuàn 〈美术〉 hand scroll

【手绢】 shǒujuàn handkerchief

【手铐】 shǒukào handcuffs: 带上～ be handcuffed

【手快】 shǒukuài deft of hand: 眼明～ quick of eye and deft of hand

【手拉葫芦】 shǒulā húlu 〈机〉 chain block

【手雷】 shǒuléi 〈军〉 antitank grenade

【手力千斤顶】 shǒulì qiānjīndǐng 〈机〉 hand jack

【手榴弹】 shǒuliúdàn hand grenade; grenade

【手炉】 shǒulú handwarmer

【手轮】 shǒulún 〈机〉 handwheel

【手忙脚乱】 shǒumáng-jiǎoluàn running around in circles; in a frantic rush; in a muddle

【手民】 shǒumín 〈书〉 typesetter: ～之误 misprint; typographical error

【手模】 shǒumó fingerprint

【手帕】 shǒupà 〈方〉 handkerchief

【手蹼】 shǒupǔ webbed gloves

【手旗】 shǒuqí 〈军〉 handflag; semaphore flag

【手气】 shǒuqì luck at gambling, card playing, etc.

【手钳】 shǒuqián hand vice; pliers

【手枪】 shǒuqiāng pistol
◇ ～慢加速比赛 〈体〉 centre-fire pistol/ ～速射 〈体〉 rapid-fire pistol/ ～套 holster

【手巧】 shǒuqiǎo skilful with one's hands; deft; dexterous: 心灵～ clever and deft

【手勤】 shǒuqín diligent; industrious; hardworking: 这徒弟～脚快。This apprentice is keen and quick in his work.

【手轻】 shǒuqīng not use too much force; handle gently

【手球】 shǒuqiú handball

【手软】 shǒuruǎn be irresolute when firmness is needed; be softhearted: 对阶级敌人不能～。One must not be soft on class enemies.

【手刹车】 shǒushāchē hand brake

【手生】 shǒushēng lack practice and skill; be out of practice

【手势】 shǒushì gesture; sign; signal: 打～ make a gesture; gesticulate ◇ ～语 sign language

【手书】 shǒushū ① write in one's own hand ② personal letter: 顷接～。I have just received your letter.

【手术】 shǒushù surgical operation; operation: 大(小)～ major (minor) operation/ 动～ perform or undergo an operation/ 高频电刀～ high frequency electrotomy
◇ ～刀 scalpel/ ～刀包 surgical kit/ ～室 operating room; operating theatre/ ～台 operating table

【手松】 shǒusōng freehanded; openhanded

【手套】 shǒutào ① gloves; mittens ② baseball gloves; mitts

【手提】 shǒutí portable
◇ ～包 handbag; bag/ ～打字机 portable typewriter/ ～箱 suitcase

【手头】 shǒutóu ① right beside one; on hand; at hand: 放在～待用 place right beside one in case of need/ ～工作挺多 have a lot of work on hand; have one's hands full/ 这本书我倒是有,可惜不在～。I have a copy of the book, but unfortunately not with me. ② one's financial condition at the moment: ～紧 be short of money; be hard up/ ～宽裕 be in easy circumstances; be quite well off at the moment

【手推车】 shǒutuīchē handcart; wheelbarrow

【手腕】 shǒuwàn artifice; finesse; stratagem: 耍～ play tricks; use artifices/ 政治～ political stratagem/ 外交～ diplomatic skill; diplomacy

【手腕子】 shǒuwànzi wrist

【手纹】 shǒuwén lines of the hand

【手无寸铁】 shǒu wú cùn tiě bare-handed; unarmed; defenceless

【手无缚鸡之力】 shǒu wú fù jī zhī lì lack the strength to truss up a chicken

【手舞足蹈】 shǒuwǔ-zúdǎo dance for joy

【手下】 shǒuxià ① under the leadership (或 guidance, direction) of; under: 在他～工作 work under him ② at hand: 东西不在～。I haven't got the thing with me. ③ at the hands of sb.: ～败将 one's vanquished foe; one's defeated opponent ④ one's financial condition at the moment

【手下留情】 shǒuxià liú qíng show mercy; be lenient

【手写体】 shǒuxiětǐ handwritten form; script

【手心】 shǒuxīn ① the palm of the hand ② control: 这事儿全捏在他～里。 He's got the matter in the palm of his hand.

【手续】 shǒuxù procedures; formalities: 办～ go through formalities/ 行政～ administrative formalities/ 法律～ legal formalities/ ～不完备 have not completed the formalities ◇ ～费 service charge; commission

【手癣】 shǒuxuǎn 〈医〉 tinea manuum; fungal infection of the hand

【手痒】 shǒuyǎng ① one's fingers itch ② have an itch to do sth.

【手摇泵】 shǒuyáobèng hand pump

【手摇发电机】 shǒuyáo fādiànjī 〈电〉 hand generator

【手艺】 shǒuyì ① craftsmanship; workmanship: ～高 be highly skilled ② handicraft; trade: 跟师傅学～ learn the trade from a master ◇ ～人 craftsman

【手淫】 shǒuyín masturbation

【手印】 shǒuyìn ① an impression of the hand ② thumb print; fingerprint

【手语】 shǒuyǔ sign language; dactylology

【手泽】 shǒuzé handwriting or articles left by one's forefathers

【手札】 shǒuzhá 〈书〉personal letter

【手掌】 shǒuzhǎng palm

【手杖】 shǒuzhàng walking stick; stick

【手指甲】 shǒuzhǐjia finger nail

【手指头】 shǒuzhítou 〈口〉 finger

【手纸】 shǒuzhǐ toilet paper

【手指】 shǒuzhǐ finger

【手重】 shǒuzhòng use too much force: 她上药时～了些。She pressed the wound a bit too hard when dressing it.

【手镯】 shǒuzhuó bracelet

【手足】 shǒuzú brothers: ～之情 brotherly affection

【手足无措】 shǒu-zú wúcuò all in a fluster; at a loss what to do

【手钻】 shǒuzuàn hand drill

**守** shǒu ① guard; defend: 把～关口 guard the pass/ ～城 defend a city/ ～球门 keep goal/ ～住阵地 hold the position ② keep watch: ～了一夜 keep watch for the whole night/ ～着伤员 look after the wounded ③ observe; abide by: ～纪律 observe discipline/ ～规矩 behave well/ ～信用 keep one's promise; be as good as one's word/ ～着老一套 stick to the old practice ④ close to; near: ～着水的地方要多养鱼。Where there is water nearby, make a special effort to breed fish.

【守备】 shǒubèi perform garrison duty; be on garrison duty; garrison ◇ ～部队 garrison force; (holding) garrison

【守财奴】 shǒucáinú miser

【守场员】 shǒuchǎngyuán 〈棒、垒球〉 fielder

【守车】 shǒuchē 〈铁道〉 guard's van; caboose

【守成】 shǒuchéng 〈书〉 maintain the achievements of one's predecessors

【守法】 shǒufǎ abide by (或 observe) the law; be law-abiding

【守寡】 shǒuguǎ remain a widow; live in widowhood

【守恒定律】 shǒuhéng dìnglǜ 〈物〉 conservation law: 能量～ the law of conservation of energy

【守候】 shǒuhòu ① wait for; expect: ～着前线的消息 wait for news from the front ② keep watch: ～在病人身旁 keep watch by the patient's bedside

【守护】 shǒuhù guard; defend ◇ ～神 〈宗〉 patron saint

【守节】 shǒujié (of a woman under feudalism) preserve chastity after the death of her husband; not remarry

【守旧】 shǒujiù adhere to past practices; stick to old ways; be conservative ◇ ～派 old liners

【守军】 shǒujūn defending troops; defenders

【守口如瓶】 shǒu kǒu rú píng keep one's mouth shut; breathe not a single word; be tight-mouthed

【守垒员】 shǒulěiyuán 〈棒、垒球〉 baseman

【守灵】 shǒulíng stand as guards at the bier; keep vigil beside the coffin

【守门】 shǒumén ① be on duty at the door or gate ② 〈体〉 keep goal ◇ ～员 goalkeeper

【守势】 shǒushì defensive: 采取～ be on the defensive

【守岁】 shǒusuì stay up late or all night on New Year's Eve

【守土】 shǒutǔ 〈书〉 defend the territory of one's country: ～有责 be duty-bound to defend the territory of one's country

【守望】 shǒuwàng keep watch ◇ ～台 watchtower

【守望相助】 shǒuwàng xiāng zhù (of neighbouring villages) keep watch and help defend each other; give mutual help and protection

【守卫】 shǒuwèi guard; defend: 海防战士警惕地～着祖国的海疆。The coastguardsmen vigilantly guard our territorial waters.

【守业】 shǒuyè maintain what has been achieved by one's forefathers or predecessors; safeguard one's heritage

【守夜】 shǒuyè keep watch at night; spend the night on watch

【守则】 shǒuzé rules; regulations: 工作～ work regulations

【守株待兔】 shǒu zhū dài tù stand by a stump waiting for more hares to come and dash themselves against it — trust to chance and windfalls

**首** shǒu ① head: 昂～ hold one's head high/ 搔～ scratch one's head ② first: ～批 the first batch ③ leader; head; chief: 祸～ chief culprit ④ bring charges against sb.: 出～ inform against sb. ⑤ 〈量〉〔用于诗歌〕: 一～歌 a song/ «唐诗三百～» *300 Tang Poems*

【首倡】 shǒuchàng initiate; start

【首车】 shǒuchē first bus

【首创】 shǒuchuàng initiate; originate; pioneer: ～精神 creative initiative; pioneering spirit/ ～月进尺一万米的纪录 set a record by drilling 10,000 metres a month

【首次】 shǒucì for the first time; first: ～航行 maiden (或 first) voyage/ ～公演 first (或 opening) performance; *première*

【首当其冲】 shǒu dāng qí chōng be the first to be affected (by a disaster, etc.); bear the brunt

【首都】 shǒudū capital (of a country)

【首恶】 shǒu'è chief criminal; principal culprit (或 offender)

【首府】 shǒufǔ ① 〈旧〉 the prefecture where the provincial capital is located ② the capital of an autonomous region or prefecture ③ the capital of a dependency or colony

【首级】 shǒují chopped-off head (in battle, etc.)

【首肯】 shǒukěn nod approval; nod assent; approve; consent

【首领】 shǒulǐng chieftain; leader; head

【首脑】 shǒunǎo head: 政府～ head of government ◇ ～会议 conference of heads of state or government; summit conference / ～人物 leading figure

【首屈一指】 shǒu qū yī zhǐ come first on the list; be second to none

【首任】 shǒurèn the first to be appointed to an office: ～驻中国大使 the first ambassador accredited to China

【首饰】 shǒushi (woman's personal) ornaments; jewelry ◇ ～盒 jewel case

【首鼠两端】 shǒushǔ liǎng duān be in two minds; shilly-shally

【首途】 shǒutú 〈书〉 set out on a journey; start a journey

【首陀罗】 Shǒutuóluó Sudra

【首尾】 shǒu-wěi ① the head and the tail; the beginning and the end: ～不能相顾。The vanguard is cut off from the rear. ② from beginning to end: 我对这个问题的看法是～一贯的。I have always been consistent in my views on this subject.

【首位】 shǒuwèi the first place: 放在～ put in the first place; place before everything else; give first priority to

【首席】 shǒuxí ① seat of honour: 坐～ be seated at the head of the table; be in the seat of honour ② chief ◇ ～代表 chief representative

【首先】 shǒuxiān ①first: ～发言 speak first/ ～到达工地 be the first to arrive at the construction site ②in the first place; first of all; above all: 我们的文学艺术都是为人民大众的，～是为工农兵的。All our literature and art are for the masses of the people, and in the first place for the workers, peasants and soldiers.

【首相】 shǒuxiàng prime minister

【首要】 shǒuyào of the first importance; first; chief: ～的事先办。First things first./ ～任务 the most important task/ ～分子 major culprit; ringleader/ 谁是我们的敌人？谁是我们的朋友？这个问题是革命的～问题。Who are our enemies? Who are our friends? This is a question of the first importance for the revolution.

【首义】 shǒuyì 〈书〉 be the first to rise in revolt

【首战告捷】 shǒuzhàn gào jié ①win the first battle ②〈体〉 score a victory in the first game

【首长】 shǒuzhǎng leading cadre; senior officer: 团～ senior officers of the regiment

## shòu

**寿** shòu ①longevity ②life; age: 长～ long life; longevity ③birthday: 祝～ congratulate sb. on his birthday ④〈婉〉 for burial: ～木 coffin (prepared before one's death) ⑤(Shòu) a surname

【寿材】 shòucái a coffin prepared before one's death; coffin

【寿辰】 shòuchén birthday (of an elderly person)

【寿礼】 shòulǐ birthday present (for an elderly person)

【寿面】 shòumiàn noodles eaten on one's birthday; birthday (或 longevity) noodles

【寿命】 shòumìng life-span; life: 平均～ average life-span (或 life expectancy)/ 机器～ service life of a machine/ 中子～ neutron lifetime

【寿桃】 shòutáo ①peaches offered as a birthday present ②(peach-shaped) birthday cake

【寿星】 shòuxing ①the god of longevity ②an elderly person whose birthday is being celebrated

【寿衣】 shòuyī graveclothes; shroud; cerements

【寿终正寝】 shòuzhōng-zhèngqǐn die in bed of old age; die a natural death

**受** shòu ①receive; accept: ～教育 receive an education/ ～礼 accept gifts ②suffer; be subjected to: ～损失 suffer losses/ ～压迫 suffer oppression/ ～监督 be subjected to supervision/ ～法律制裁 be dealt with according to law ③stand; endure; bear: ～不了 cannot bear; be unable to endure/ 真够～的。This is really hard to put up with. 或 It's really unbearable. ④〈方〉 be pleasant: ～听 be pleasant to hear/ ～看 be pleasant to look at

【受病】 shòubìng catch (或 contract) a disease; fall ill

【受潮】 shòucháo be affected with damp: 这屋子阴，东西容易～。The room gets no sun and things easily become damp.

【受宠若惊】 shòu chǒng ruò jīng be overwhelmed by an unexpected favour; feel extremely flattered

【受挫】 shòucuò be foiled; be baffled; be thwarted; suffer a setback

【受罚】 shòufá be punished

【受粉】 shòufěn 〈植〉 be pollinated

【受害】 shòuhài suffer injury; fall victim; be affected: ～不浅 suffer not a little; suffer a lot/ ～的一方 the aggrieved (或 injured) party/ 这次霜冻，～的庄稼不少。A lot of crops were damaged by the frost. ◇ ～国 the country that's been wronged; victimized country/ ～者 victim; sufferer

【受寒】 shòuhán catch a chill; catch cold

【受旱】 shòuhàn suffer from drought; be drought-stricken

【受话器】 shòuhuàqì (telephone) receiver

【受欢迎的人】 shòu huānyíng de rén 〈外〉 *persona grata*

【受贿】 shòuhuì accept (或 take) bribes

【受奖】 shòujiǎng be rewarded: 立功者～。Those who perform deeds of merit shall be rewarded.

【受戒】 shòujiè 〈佛教〉 be initiated into monkhood or nunhood

【受尽】 shòujìn suffer enough from; suffer all kinds of; have one's fill of: ～旧社会的苦 have one's fill of sufferings in the old society; have experienced untold sufferings in the old days/ ～帝国主义的压迫 have suffered enough from imperialist oppression/ ～反动派的折磨 suffer all kinds of tortures at the hands of the reactionaries

【受惊】 shòujīng be frightened; be startled

【受精】 shòujīng be fertilized: 体内(外)～ internal (external) fertilization/ 异体～ cross-fertilization/ 自体～ self-fertilization

【受精卵】 shòujīngluǎn 〈牧〉 zygote ◇ ～移植 zygote transplant

【受窘】 shòujiǒng be embarrassed; be in an awkward position

【受苦】 shòukǔ suffer (hardships); have a rough time: ～受难 live in misery; have one's fill of sufferings/ 咱们俩在旧社会都是受过苦的。Both of us suffered hardships in the old society.

【受累】 shòulěi get involved on account of sb. else

【受累】 shòulèi be put to much trouble; be inconvenienced: 他为了我们大家，可没少～。He's been put to no little trouble for our sake./ 让您～了。Sorry to have given you so much trouble.

【受理】 shòulǐ 〈法〉 accept and hear a case

【受凉】 shòuliáng catch cold

【受命】 shòumìng receive instructions

【受难】 shòunàn suffer calamities or disasters; be in distress: 战争～者 war victim

【受骗】 shòupiàn be deceived (或 fooled, cheated, taken in)

【受气】 shòuqì be bullied; suffer wrong ◇ ～包儿 a person whom anyone can vent his spite upon; one who always gets blamed (或 takes the rap)

【受权】 shòuquán be authorized: 新华社～发表如下声明。Xinhua News Agency is authorized to issue the following statement./ ～宣布 announce upon authorization

【受热】 shòurè ①be heated: 物体～则膨胀。When matter is heated, it expands. ②be affected by the heat; have heatstroke (或 sunstroke)

【受辱】 shòurǔ be insulted; be disgraced; be humiliated

【受伤】 shòushāng be injured; be wounded; sustain an injury: 头部受重伤 sustain a severe head injury

【受审】 shòushěn stand trial; be tried; be on trial

【受事】 shòushì 〈语〉 the object of the action in a sentence; object

【受暑】 shòushǔ suffer from heatstroke (或 sunstroke)

【受胎】 shòutāi become pregnant; be impregnated; conceive ◇ ～率〈牧〉 conception rate

【受托】 shòutuō be commissioned; be entrusted (with a task): 受朋友之托买一块手表 be asked to buy a watch for a friend/ ～照看房子 be entrusted with the care of a house

【受洗】 shòuxǐ 〈基督教〉 be baptized; receive baptism

【受降】 shòuxiáng accept a surrender

【受刑】 shòuxíng be tortured; be put to torture

【受训】 shòuxùn receive (或 undergo) training

【受益】 shòuyì profit by; benefit from; be benefited: 这本

书使我～不浅。This book has benefitted me a great deal./ ～面积达六万多亩。The area serviced exceeds 60,000 *mu*. ◇ ～人〈法〉 beneficiary

【受用】 shòuyòng benefit from; profit by; enjoy: ～不尽 benefit from sth. all one's life

【受用】 shòuyong 〈方〉〔多用于否定〕 feel comfortable: 今天身体有点不～。I feel a bit under the weather today.

【受援】 shòuyuán receive aid ◇ ～国 recipient country

【受孕】 shòuyùn become pregnant; be impregnated; conceive

【受灾】 shòuzāi be hit by a natural adversity (或 calamity) ◇ ～地区 disaster area; stricken (或 afflicted, affected) area

【受主】 shòuzhǔ 〈电子〉 acceptor

【受罪】 shòuzuì endure hardships, tortures, rough conditions, etc.; have a hard time: 大热天穿这么厚的衣服，真～！It's really awful to be wearing such heavy clothes on a hot day like this.

**狩** shòu 〈书〉 hunting (esp. in winter)

【狩猎】 shòuliè hunting ◇ ～专业队 professional hunting team

**兽** shòu ① beast; animal: 野～ wild animal ② beastly; bestial: 人面～心 a beast in human shape

【兽环】 shòuhuán door-knocker (often in the shape of an animal's head with a ring in its mouth)

【兽类】 shòulèi beasts; animals

【兽力车】 shòulìchē animal-drawn vehicle (或 cart)

【兽王】 shòuwáng the king of beasts — the lion

【兽行】 shòuxíng brutal act; brutality

【兽性】 shòuxìng brutish nature; barbarity

【兽医】 shòuyī veterinary surgeon; veterinarian; vet ◇ ～学 veterinary medicine; veterinary science/ ～站 veterinary station

【兽欲】 shòuyù animal (或 bestial) desire

**授** shòu ① award; vest; confer; give: ～旗 present (sb. with) a flag/ ～以全权 vest sb. with full authority ② teach; instruct: 函～ teach by correspondence; give a correspondence course

【授粉】 shòufěn 〈植〉 pollination: 人工～ artificial pollination

【授计】 shòujì confide a stratagem to sb.; tell sb. the plan of action

【授奖】 shòujiǎng award (或 give) a prize ◇ ～仪式 prize-giving ceremony

【授精】 shòujīng insemination: 人工～ artificial insemination

【授课】 shòukè give lessons; give instruction

【授命】 shòumìng ① give orders: ～组阁 authorize sb. to form a cabinet ② 〈书〉 give (或 lay down) one's life

【授权】 shòuquán empower; authorize: ～新华社发表声明 authorize Xinhua News Agency to make a statement

【授时】 shòushí ① 〈天〉 time service ② (in former times) issue the official calendar ◇ ～信号 time signal

【授受】 shòu-shòu grant and receive; give and accept: 私相～ give and accept in private; illegally pass things between individuals

【授勋】 shòuxūn confer orders or medals; award a decoration

【授意】 shòuyì incite (或 get) sb. to do sth.; inspire: 他这样干，是谁～的？Who got him to do that? 或 Who put him up to it?/ 我这封信是在老张～下写的。It was Lao Zhang who gave me the idea of writing the letter. 或 I drafted the letter at Lao Zhang's suggestion.

【授予】 shòuyǔ confer; award: ～"爱民模范连"的称号 confer the title "Model Company of Cherishing the People"

**售** shòu ① sell: 出～ put on sale/ ～完 be sold out ② 〈书〉 make (one's plan, trick, etc.) work; carry out (intrigues): 以～其奸 achieve one's treacherous purpose

【售货】 shòuhuò sell goods ◇ ～机 vending machine

【售货员】 shòuhuòyuán shop assistant; salesclerk: 女～ saleswoman; salesgirl; shopgirl

【售价】 shòujià selling price; price

【售卖】 shòumài sell

【售票处】 shòupiàochù ticket office; (火车站) booking office; (剧院等) box office

【售票口】 shòupiàokǒu wicket

【售票员】 shòupiàoyuán ticket seller; (公共汽车) conductor; (火车站) booking-office clerk; (剧院等) box-office clerk

**绶** shòu

【绶带】 shòudài ribbon (attached to an official seal or a medal)

【绶带鸟】 shòudàiniǎo paradise flycatcher

**瘦** shòu ① thin; emaciated: 脸～ be thin in the face/ 面黄肌～ be sallow and emaciated ② lean: ～肉 lean meat ③ tight: 这件上衣腰身～了点。The coat is a bit tight at the waist. ④ not fertile; poor: ～土薄田 poor soil and barren land

【瘦长】 shòucháng long and thin; tall and thin; lanky: 他是～个儿。He's a tall, lean chap.

【瘦果】 shòuguǒ 〈植〉 achene

【瘦煤】 shòuméi lean coal; meagre coal

【瘦弱】 shòuruò thin and weak; emaciated

【瘦小】 shòuxiǎo thin and small: 身材～ slight of figure (或 stature)

【瘦削】 shòuxuē very thin; gaunt: ～的面孔 a haggard face

【瘦子】 shòuzi a lean (或 thin) person

## shū

**书** shū ① write: 振笔直～ take up the pen and write vigorously ② style of calligraphy; script: 楷～ regular script ③ book: 一本关于中国历史的新～ a new work on Chinese history ④ letter: 家～ a letter to or from home ⑤ document: 证～ certificate/ 国～ letter of credence; credentials/ 批准～ instrument of ratification/ 议定～ protocol

【书包】 shūbāo satchel; schoolbag

【书报】 shū-bào books and newspapers

【书本】 shūběn book: ～知识 book learning; book knowledge

【书橱】 shūchú bookcase

【书呆子】 shūdāizi pedant; bookworm

【书挡】 shūdǎng bookend

【书店】 shūdiàn bookshop; bookstore; bookseller's

【书法】 shūfǎ penmanship; calligraphy ◇ ～家 calligrapher

【书房】 shūfáng study

【书后】 shūhòu postscript (by the author or sb. else)

【书画】 shū-huà painting and calligraphy

【书籍】 shūjí books; works; literature: 军事～ military literature

【书脊】 shūjǐ spine (of a book)

【书记】 shūji ① secretary: 党委～ secretary of the Party committee/ 总～ general secretary ② clerk ◇ ～处 secretariat/ ～员 〈法〉 clerk (of a court)

【书架】 shūjià bookshelf

【书简】 shūjiǎn letters; correspondence
【书经】 Shūjīng *The Book of History* 参见"五经" wǔjīng
【书局】 shūjú publishing house; press
【书刊】 shū-kān books and periodicals
【书库】 shūkù stack room
【书眉】 shūméi the top of a page; top margin
【书面】 shūmiàn written; in written form; in writing: ～材料 written material/ ～通知 written notice/ ～答复 written reply; answer in writing/ ～声明 written statement ◇ ～语 written language; literary language
【书名】 shūmíng the title of a book; title ◇ ～号 punctuation marks used to enclose the title of a book or an article (《》)/ ～页 title page
【书目】 shūmù booklist; title catalogue: 参考～ a list of reference books; bibliography
【书皮】 shūpí book cover; jacket; dust cover; cover: 塑料～ plastic cover ◇ ～纸 paper for covering books
【书评】 shūpíng book review
【书签】 shūqiān ① a title label pasted on the cover of a Chinese-style thread-bound book ② bookmark
【书生】 shūshēng intellectual; scholar: ～之见 a pedantic view
【书生气】 shūshēngqì bookishness: 切不可～十足，把复杂的阶级斗争看得太简单了。Never be so bookish and naive as to treat complex class struggle as a simple matter.
【书摊】 shūtān bookstall; bookstand
【书套】 shūtào slipcase
【书亭】 shūtíng book-kiosk; bookstall
【书写】 shūxiě write: ～标语 write slogans; letter posters ◇ ～规则 rules for writing/ ～纸 writing paper
【书信】 shūxìn letter; written message: 常有～往来 keep up a regular correspondence ◇ ～电 letter cable
【书信体】 shūxìntǐ epistolary style ◇ ～小说 epistolary novel
【书页】 shūyè page
【书院】 shūyuàn academy of classical learning
【书札】 shūzhá 〈书〉 letters; correspondence
【书斋】 shūzhāi study
【书桌】 shūzhuō desk; writing desk

**殳** shū an ancient weapon made of bamboo

**抒** shū express; give expression to; convey: 让大家各～己见。Let everybody freely express his views.
【抒发】 shūfā express; voice; give expression to: 这首诗～了战士的革命感情。The poem expresses the revolutionary fervour of the PLA men./ 这一唱段～了一个革命者的壮志豪情。This aria conveys the determination and lofty ideals of a revolutionary.
【抒情】 shūqíng express (或 convey) one's emotion ◇ ～散文 lyric prose/ ～诗 lyric poetry; lyrics
【抒写】 shūxiě express; describe: 这篇文章～了他在北京工作时的一些感受。The article describes how he felt while working in Beijing.

**枢** shū pivot; hub; centre: 神经中～ nerve centre
【枢纽】 shūniǔ pivot; hub; axis; key position: ～作用 a pivotal role/ 交通～ a hub of communications/ 水利～工程 a key water control (或 conservancy) project

**叔** shū ① father's younger brother; uncle ② a form of address for a man about one's father's age; uncle: 刘大～ Uncle Liu ③ husband's younger brother
【叔伯】 shūbai relationship between cousins of the same grandfather or great-grandfather: ～兄弟 first or second cousins on the paternal side; cousins
【叔父】 shūfù father's younger brother; uncle
【叔母】 shūmǔ wife of father's younger brother; aunt
【叔叔】 shūshu 〈口〉 ① father's younger brother; uncle ② uncle (a child's form of address for any young man one generation its senior)
【叔祖】 shūzǔ (paternal) grandfather's younger brother; granduncle
【叔祖母】 shūzǔmǔ wife of (paternal) grandfather's younger brother; grandaunt

**殊** shū ① different: 悬～ differ widely ② outstanding; special; remarkable: 待以～礼 receive sb. with unusual ceremony ③ very much; extremely; really: ～觉歉然 feel most regretful/ ～难相信 very difficult to believe; hardly credible/ ～深轸念 express deep solicitude; feel deeply concerned
【殊不知】 shūbùzhī little imagine; hardly realize: 我以为他还在北京，～他已经走了。I thought he was still in Beijing. I never dreamt that he had already left.
【殊死】 shūsǐ desperate; life-and-death: ～的搏斗 a life-and-death struggle/ 作～战 fight a last-ditch battle; put up a desperate fight
【殊途同归】 shū tú tóng guī reach the same goal by different routes
【殊勋】 shūxūn 〈书〉 outstanding merit; distinguished service

**倏** shū swiftly
【倏忽】 shūhū swiftly; in the twinkling of an eye: ～不见 quickly disappear

**淑** shū 〈书〉 kind and gentle; fair: ～女 a fair maiden

**菽** shū beans

**梳** shū ① comb: 木～ wooden comb ② comb one's hair, etc.
【梳理】 shūlǐ 〈纺〉 carding
【梳棉机】 shūmiánjī 〈纺〉 carding machine
【梳洗】 shūxǐ wash and dress ◇ ～用具 toilet articles
【梳妆】 shūzhuāng dress and make up: ～打扮 deck oneself out; dress smartly; be dressed up ◇ ～台 dressing table
【梳子】 shūzi comb

**舒** shū ① stretch; unfold ② easy; leisurely: ～徐 leisurely; in no hurry ③ (Shū) a surname
【舒畅】 shūchàng happy; entirely free from worry: 心情～ have ease of mind; feel happy
【舒服】 shūfu ① comfortable: 这把椅子坐着很～。This chair is very comfortable./ 舒舒服服是建设不了社会主义的。Socialism can't be built in ease and comfort. ② be well: 她今天不大～。She isn't well today.
【舒筋活络】 shūjīn-huóluò 〈中医〉 stimulate the circulation of the blood and cause the muscles and joints to relax
【舒卷】 shūjuǎn 〈书〉 roll back and forth: 白云～。The white clouds mass and scatter.
【舒适】 shūshì comfortable; cosy; snug: ～的生活 a comfortable life/ 房间不大，但很～。The rooms are not big but they're very cosy./ 孩子们都～地睡在小床上。All the children lay snug in their little beds.
【舒坦】 shūtan comfortable; at ease
【舒展】 shūzhan ① unfold; extend; smooth out: 荷叶～着，发出清香。The lotus leaves are unfolding, sending forth a delicate fragrance./ 问题解决了，老队长紧锁的眉头也～了。Once the problem was solved, the old team leader's knitted brows became smooth again. ② limber up; stretch:

～一下筋骨 limber up one's muscles and joints

【舒张】 shūzhāng 〈生理〉 diastole ◇ ～压 〈医〉 diastolic pressure

**疏** shū ① dredge (a river, etc.) ② thin; sparse; scattered: ～林 sparse woods/ ～～的几根胡子 a sparse beard/ 几点～星 a few scattered stars ③ (of family or social relations) distant: 不分亲～ regardless of relationship (family or social) ④ not familiar with: 人地生～ be unfamiliar with the place and the people; be a complete stranger ⑤ neglect: ～于职守 negligent of one's duties/ ～于防范 neglect to take precautions ⑥ scanty: 才～学浅 have little talent and less learning/ 志大才～ have great ambition but little talent ⑦ disperse; scatter: 仗义～财 be generous in aiding needy people

【疏导】 shūdǎo dredge

【疏果】 shūguǒ 〈农〉 fruit thinning

【疏忽】 shūhu carelessness; negligence; oversight: ～大意就可能造成事故。Carelessness is liable to cause accidents./ 我一时～,搞错了。I made the mistake through an oversight.

【疏花】 shūhuā 〈农〉 flower thinning

【疏浚】 shūjùn dredge: ～水道 dredge the waterways/ ～港口 dredge a harbour

【疏开】 shūkāi 〈军〉 extend; disperse; deploy: ～队形 dispersed formation; extended order; open order (或 formation)

【疏懒】 shūlǎn careless and lazy; indolent

【疏漏】 shūlòu careless omission; slip; oversight: 计划匆促拟成,难免有～之处。The plan was drawn up in haste, so there are bound to be oversights and omissions.

【疏落】 shūluò sparse; scattered: ～的村庄 scattered villages/ 河边疏疏落落有几棵柳树。The river was sparsely lined with willow trees.

【疏密】 shūmì density; spacing: ～不匀 of uneven density/ 花木栽得～有致。The flowers and trees are artistically spaced.

【疏散】 shūsàn ① sparse; scattered; dispersed: ～的村落 scattered villages ② evacuate: 我们要做好地震预报工作,以便及时～人口。We must do a good job of predicting earthquakes so that we can disperse the population in time.

【疏失】 shūshī careless mistake; remissness

【疏松】 shūsōng ① loose: 土质～。The soil is porous. ② loosen: ～土壤 loosen the soil

【疏通】 shūtōng ① dredge: ～田间的排水沟 dredge the irrigation ditches in the fields ② mediate between two parties

【疏远】 shūyuǎn drift apart; become estranged

**输** shū ① transport; convey: 油管把原油从油田直接～往港口。The pipeline carries crude oil direct from the oil field to the harbour. ② 〈书〉 contribute money; donate: 慷慨～将 make liberal contributions ③ lose; be beaten; be defeated: ～了一局 lose one game in the set

【输出】 shūchū ① export: 资本～ export of capital/ 革命不能～。Revolution cannot be exported. ② 〈电〉 output ◇ ～端数 fan-out/ ～功率 output power/ ～数据 data-out/ ～限额 〈经〉 export quota

【输电】 shūdiàn transmit electricity: 这个发电站已开始向山区～。The power station has begun to transmit electricity to the mountain area. ◇ ～网 power transmission network; grid system/ ～线路 transmission line

【输精管】 shūjīngguǎn 〈生理〉 spermatic duct; deferent duct ◇ ～结扎术 〈医〉 vasoligation/ ～炎 deferentitis

【输理】 shūlǐ be in the wrong: 你输了理,还有什么可辩的? You are in the wrong. Why argue?

【输卵管】 shūluǎnguǎn 〈生理〉 oviduct; Fallopian tube ◇ ～结扎术 〈医〉 tubal ligation/ ～炎 salpingitis

【输尿管】 shūniàoguǎn 〈生理〉 ureter ◇ ～炎 ureteritis

【输入】 shūrù ① import: ～新思想 the influx of new ideas ② 〈电〉 input ◇ ～端数 fan-in/ ～功率 input power/ ～数据 data-in/ ～限额 〈经〉 import quota

【输沙率】 shūshālǜ 〈水〉 silt discharge

【输送】 shūsòng carry; transport; convey: 卡车把货物～到边疆地区。Commodities are transported to border areas by truck./ ～新鲜血液 infuse new blood/ 大庆油田给其它油田～了大批工人、干部和技术人员。Daqing has provided other oilfields with large numbers of workers, cadres and technical personnel. ◇ ～带 conveyer belt/ ～机 conveyer

【输血】 shūxuè ① 〈医〉 blood transfusion ② give aid and support; bolster up; give sb. a shot in the arm: 这等于是给侵略者～打气。This is tantamount to giving the aggressor a shot in the arm. ◇ ～者 blood donor

【输氧】 shūyǎng 〈医〉 oxygen therapy

【输液】 shūyè 〈医〉 infusion

【输油管】 shūyóuguǎn petroleum pipeline

**蔬** shū vegetables: 布衣～食 coarse clothes and simple fare

【蔬菜】 shūcài vegetables; greens; greenstuff ◇ ～栽培 vegetable growing; vegetable farming

## shú

**秫** shú *kaoliang*; sorghum

【秫秸】 shújiē *kaoliang* stalk 又作"秫稭"

【秫米】 shúmǐ husked sorghum

**孰** shú 〈书〉 ① who; which: ～胜～负? Who wins and who loses?/ ～是～非? Which is right and which is wrong? ② what: 是可忍,～不可忍? If this can be tolerated, what cannot?

**赎** shú ① redeem; ransom: 把东西～回来 redeem a pledge ② atone for (a crime)

【赎当】 shúdàng redeem sth. pawned

【赎价】 shújià ransom price; ransom

【赎金】 shújīn ransom money; ransom

【赎买】 shúmǎi redeem; buy out ◇ ～政策 policy of redemption; buying-out policy

【赎身】 shúshēn (of slaves, prostitutes) redeem (或 ransom) oneself; buy back one's freedom

【赎罪】 shúzuì atone for one's crime: 立功～ perform meritorious services to atone for one's crime ◇ ～日 〈犹太教〉 Yom Kippur; Day of Atonement

**塾** shú private (或 family) school: ～师 tutor of a private (或 family) school

**熟** shú ① ripe: 西红柿～了。The tomatoes are ripe./ 一年两～ two crops a year ② cooked; done: ～肉 cooked meat/ 半生不～ half-cooked/ 饭已经～了。The rice is done. ③ processed: ～铜 wrought copper/ ～皮子 tanned leather ④ familiar: 这口音听起来很～。The voice sounds familiar. ⑤ skilled; experienced; practised: ～手 practised hand; old hand ⑥ deeply: ～睡 be in a deep sleep; be fast asleep

【熟谙】 shú'ān 〈书〉 be familiar with; be good at: ～水性 be an expert swimmer
【熟菜】 shúcài cooked food; prepared food
【熟成机】 shúchéngjī 〈化纤〉 ripening machine
【熟地】 shúdì ① cultivated land ② 〈中药〉 prepared rhizome of rehmannia (*Rehmannia glutinosa*)
【熟荒地】 shúhuāngdì 〈农〉 once cultivated land; abandoned land
【熟记】 shújì learn by heart; memorize; commit to memory
【熟客】 shúkè frequent visitor
【熟练】 shúliàn skilled; practised; proficient: ～工人 skilled worker/ ～地操纵机器 skilfully operate the machine/ 他枪法很～。He's a good shot.
【熟料】 shúliào ① 〈冶〉 grog; chamotte ② 〈建〉 clinker
【熟路】 shúlù familiar route; beaten track: 熟门～ a familiar road and a familiar door — things that one knows well 又作"熟道儿"
【熟能生巧】 shú néng shēng qiǎo skill comes from practice; practice makes perfect
【熟年】 shúnián a year of good harvests; bumper year
【熟人】 shúrén acquaintance; friend
【熟石膏】 shúshígāo plaster of Paris
【熟食】 shúshí prepared food; cooked food
【熟视无睹】 shú shì wú dǔ pay no attention to a familiar sight; turn a blind eye to; ignore: 对不良倾向决不能～。We must not turn a blind eye to unhealthy tendencies.
【熟识】 shúshi be well acquainted with; know well: 我们交往不多,不太～。We haven't met often and don't know each other very well./ ～敌我双方各方面的情况 familiarize ourselves with all aspects of the enemy's situation and our own
【熟睡】 shúshuì sleep soundly; be fast asleep
【熟丝】 shúsī 〈纺〉 boiled-off silk
【熟思】 shúsī ponder deeply; consider carefully; deliberate
【熟铁】 shútiě wrought iron
【熟土】 shútǔ 〈农〉 mellow soil
【熟悉】 shúxī know sth. or sb. well; be familiar with; have an intimate knowledge of: ～内情 know the ins and outs of the matter; know the inside story of; be in the know/ 用群众～的语言来写作 write in language familiar to the masses/ 你到了那里,要先～当地的情况。When you get there, first of all familiarize yourself with the situation./ 他对各项生产数字很～。He has the various production figures at his fingertips./ 他对这工作不～。He is new to the task.
【熟习】 shúxí be skilful at; have the knack of; be practised in: ～业务 be practised (或 well versed) in one's field of work/ ～蔬菜的栽培法 have the knack of growing vegetables
【熟语】 shúyǔ 〈语〉 idiom; idiomatic phrase
【熟知】 shúzhī know very well; know intimately
【熟字】 shúzì words already learned; familiar words

## shǔ

**黍** shǔ broomcorn millet (*Panicum miliaceum*)
【黍子】 shǔzi 见"黍"

**属** shǔ ① category: 金～ metals ② 〈生〉 genus: 亚～ subgenus/ 小麦和燕麦是同科的,但不同～。Wheat and oats are of the same family, but of different genera. ③ under; subordinate to: 这些厂～地方领导。These factories are run by the local authorities./ 所～单位和部门 subordinate units and departments ④ belong to: 我们两国同～第三世界。Both our countries belong to the Third World./ 西双版纳～亚热带气候。Xishuangbanna has a subtropical climate. ⑤ family members; dependents: 军～ families of armymen ⑥ be: 查明～实 prove to be true after investigation/ 实～无理 be really unreasonable ⑦ be born in the year of (one of the twelve animals): 她比我小一岁,是～牛的。She is one year younger than I am; she was born in the year of the ox. 参见"生肖" shēngxiào
另见 zhǔ
【属地】 shǔdì possession; dependency
【属国】 shǔguó vassal state; dependent state
【属相】 shǔxiang 〈口〉 见"生肖" shēngxiào
【属性】 shǔxìng 〈逻〉 attribute; property
【属于】 shǔyú belong to; be part of: 民主～上层建筑,～政治这个范畴。Democracy is part of the superstructure and belongs to the realm of politics./ 在现在世界上,一切文化或文学艺术都是～一定的阶级,～一定的政治路线的。In the world today all culture, all literature and art belong to definite classes and are geared to definite political lines.

**暑** shǔ heat; hot weather: 盛～ at the height of the summer; very hot weather/ 中～ get sunstroke; get heatstroke; suffer heat exhaustion/ 寒来～往 as summer goes and winter comes; as time passes
【暑假】 shǔjià summer vacation (或 holidays)
【暑期】 shǔqī summer vacation time ◇ ～训练班 summer course
【暑气】 shǔqì summer heat; heat
【暑热】 shǔrè hot summer weather
【暑天】 shǔtiān hot summer days; dog days
【暑瘟】 shǔwēn 〈中医〉 febrile diseases in summer, including encephalitis B, dysentry, malignant malaria, etc.

**署** shǔ ① a government office; office: 专员公～ prefectural commissioner's office ② make arrangements for; arrange: 部～春耕生产 make arrangements for the spring ploughing ③ handle by proxy; act as deputy: ～理部务 handle the ministry's affairs during the minister's absence ④ sign; put one's signature to: 签～协定 sign an agreement
【署名】 shǔmíng sign; put one's signature to: 全组同志都在信上署了名。The letter was jointly signed by all the comrades of the group./ 这条子没有～,不知是谁写的。I don't know who wrote this note. It's unsigned. ◇ ～人 the undersigned/ ～文章 a signed article

**数** shǔ ① count: 从一～到十 count from 1 to 10/ ～～看一行有多少棵苗。Count and see how many seedlings there are in a row. ② be reckoned as exceptionally (good, bad, etc.): 全班～他最高。He is the tallest in the class. ③ enumerate; list: 历～其罪 enumerate the crimes sb. has committed
另见 shù; shuò
【数不着】 shǔbuzháo not count as outstanding, important, etc.: 论游泳技术,在我们厂里可～我。I don't count as a good swimmer in our factory.
【数得着】 shǔdezháo be reckoned as outstanding, important, etc.: 在公社里,他是～的养猪能手。He is one of the outstanding pig-breeders of the commune.
【数典忘祖】 shǔ diǎn wàng zǔ give all the historical facts except those about one's own ancestors; forget one's own origins; be ignorant of the history of one's own country
【数九】 shǔjiǔ the nine periods (of nine days each) following the winter solstice: ～寒天 the coldest days of the year
【数来宝】 shǔláibǎo 〈曲艺〉 rhythmic storytelling to clap-

per accompaniment

【数落】 shǔluo 〈口〉 ① scold sb. by enumerating his wrongdoings; rebuke; reprove: 把他～一顿 give him a good scolding ② enumerate; cite one example after another

【数数儿】 shǔ shùr count; reckon: 孩子们在学～。The children are learning how to count.

【数说】 shǔshuō 见“数落”

【数一数二】 shǔyī-shǔ'èr count as one of the very best; ranking very high: 他在我们连里是～的射手。He is one of the best marksmen in our company.

**蜀** Shǔ another name for Sichuan Province

【蜀汉】 Shǔ Hàn the kingdom of Shu Han (221-263), one of the Three Kingdoms

【蜀葵】 shǔkuí 〈植〉 hollyhock (*Althaea rosea*)

【蜀犬吠日】 Shǔ quǎn fèi rì in Sichuan dogs bark at the sun (because it's a rare sight in that misty region) — an ignorant person makes a fuss about something which he alone finds strange

**鼠** shǔ mouse; rat

【鼠辈】 shǔbèi mean creatures; scoundrels

【鼠疮】 shǔchuāng 〈中医〉 scrofula

【鼠窜】 shǔcuàn scamper off like a rat; scurry away like frightened rats

【鼠笼式】 shǔlóngshì 〈电〉 squirrel-cage ◇ ～电动机 squirrel-cage motor

【鼠目寸光】 shǔmù cùn guāng a mouse can see only an inch; see only what is under one's nose; be shortsighted

【鼠窃狗偷】 shǔqiè-gǒutōu filch like rats and snatch like dogs — play petty tricks on the sly

【鼠麴草】 shǔqūcǎo 〈植〉 affine cudweed (*Gnaphalium affine*)

【鼠蹊】 shǔxī 〈生理〉 groin

【鼠咬热】 shǔyǎorè 〈医〉 rat-bite fever

【鼠疫】 shǔyì the plague

**薯** shǔ potato; yam: 白～ sweet potato/ 木～ cassava

【薯莨】 shǔliáng 〈植〉 dye yam (*Dioscorea cirrhosa*)

【薯蓣】 shǔyù 〈植〉 Chinese yam (*Dioscorea batatas*)

**曙** shǔ 〈书〉 daybreak; dawn

【曙光】 shǔguāng first light of morning; dawn: 胜利的～ the dawn of victory

【曙色】 shǔsè light of early dawn: 从窗口透进了灰白的～。The pale light of early dawn slanted in through the window.

## shù

**术** shù ① art; skill; technique: 医～ the art of healing; doctor's skill/ 美～ the fine arts/ 不学无～ have neither learning nor skill ② method; tactics: 战～ tactics/ 权～ political trickery
另见 zhú

【术语】 shùyǔ technical terms; terminology: 军事～ military terms/ 医学～ medical terminology

**戍** shù defend; garrison: ～边 garrison the frontiers

**束** shù ① bind; tie: 腰～皮带 wear a belt round one's waist ② 〈量〉 bundle; bunch; sheaf: 一～鲜花 a bunch of flowers/ 一～稻草 a sheaf of straw ③ control; restrain: 无拘无～ without any restraint ④ (Shù) a surname

【束缚】 shùfù tie; bind up; fetter: ～手脚 bind sb. hand and foot; tie sb.'s hands; hamper the initiative of/ ～生产力 fetter the productive forces/ 冲破旧思想的～ smash the trammels of old ideas/ 挣脱封建礼教的～ shake off the yoke of the feudal ethical code

【束射管】 shùshèguǎn 〈电子〉 beam tube

【束手】 shùshǒu have one's hands tied; be helpless: ～就擒 allow oneself to be seized without putting up a fight

【束手待毙】 shùshǒu dài bì fold one's hands and await destruction; helplessly wait for death; resign oneself to extinction

【束手无策】 shùshǒu wú cè be at a loss what to do; feel quite helpless; be at one's wit's end

【束脩】 shùxiū 〈旧〉 a private tutor's remuneration (或 emolument)

【束之高阁】 shù zhī gāogé bundle sth. up and place it on the top shelf; lay aside and neglect; shelve; pigeonhole: 如果有了正确的理论，只是把它空谈一阵，～，并不实行，那么，这种理论再好也是没有意义的。If we have a correct theory but merely prate about it, pigeonhole it and do not put it into practice, then that theory, however good, is of no significance.

**述** shù state; relate; narrate: 陈～意见 state one's views/ 略～其经过 relate briefly how it happened; give a brief account of the matter

【述评】 shùpíng review; commentary: 每周时事～ weekly review of current affairs/ 新华社记者～ commentary by a Xinhua correspondent

【述说】 shùshuō state; recount; narrate

【述职】 shùzhí report on one's work; report: 大使已回国～。The ambassador has gone back for consultations.

**树** shù ① tree: 苹果～ apple tree ② plant; cultivate: 十年～木，百年～人。It takes ten years to grow trees, but a hundred years to rear people. ③ set up; establish; uphold: 建～ achievement/ ～正气 uphold (或 foster) healthy tendencies/ ～雄心 have lofty ambitions; aim high

【树碑立传】 shùbēi-lìzhuàn 〈贬〉 glorify sb. by erecting a monument to him and writing his biography — build up sb.'s public image

【树杈】 shùchà crotch (of a tree)

【树丛】 shùcóng grove; thicket

【树大招风】 shù dà zhāofēng 〈谚〉 a tall tree catches the wind — a person in a high position is liable to be attacked

【树倒猢狲散】 shù dǎo húsūn sàn when the tree falls the monkeys scatter — when an influential person falls from power, his hangers-on disperse

【树敌】 shùdí make an enemy of sb.; set others against oneself; antagonize: ～太多 make too many enemies; antagonize too many people

【树墩】 shùdūn tree stump; stump

【树蜂】 shùfēng 〈动〉 wood wasp

【树干】 shùgàn tree trunk; trunk

【树高千丈，叶落归根】 shù gāo qiānzhàng, yè luò guī gēn a tree may grow a thousand *zhang* high, but its leaves fall back to the roots — a person residing away from home eventually returns to his native soil

【树冠】 shùguān crown (of a tree)

【树胶】 shùjiāo gum (of a tree)

【树懒】 shùlǎn 〈动〉 sloth

【树立】 shùlì set up; establish: ～榜样 set an example/ ～标兵 set sb. up as a pacemaker/ ～远大的革命理想 foster a lofty revolutionary ideal/ ～无产阶级世界观 acquire a proletarian world outlook/ ～共产主义劳动态度 cultivate the communist attitude towards labour

【树林】 shùlín woods; grove
【树苗】 shùmiáo sapling
【树木】 shùmù trees
【树皮】 shùpí bark ◇ ～画〈美术〉bark picture
【树鼩】 shùqú 〈动〉tree shrew
【树梢】 shùshāo the tip of a tree; treetop
【树蛙】 shùwā 〈动〉tree frog
【树阴】 shùyīn shade (of a tree) 又作"树荫"
【树欲静而风不止】 shù yù jìng ér fēng bù zhǐ the tree may prefer calm, but the wind will not subside — class struggle is inevitable in class society
【树枝】 shùzhī branch; twig
【树脂】 shùzhī resin: 离子交换～ ion exchange resin/ 中性～ resinene ◇ ～酸 resinic acid/ ～整理〈纺〉resin finishing

**竖** shù ① vertical; upright; perpendicular: 画一条～线 draw a vertical line ② set upright; erect; stand: ～旗杆 erect a flagstaff/ 这杆子我～不起来。I can't get the pole to stand up. ③ vertical stroke (in Chinese characters): "王"字的写法是三横一～。The character 王 is composed of one vertical and three horizontal strokes.
【竖井】 shùjǐng 〈矿〉(vertical) shaft
【竖立】 shùlì erect; set upright; stand: 天安门广场上～着马、恩、列、斯的巨幅画像。Huge portraits of Marx, Engels, Lenin and Stalin stand in Tian'anmen Square.
【竖起】 shùqi hold up; erect: ～大拇指 hold up one's thumb in approval; thumbs up/ ～一面大旗 hoist a huge banner/ ～耳朵听 prick up one's ears
【竖琴】 shùqín 〈乐〉harp
【竖蜻蜓】 shù qīngtíng 〈方〉handstand
【竖子】 shùzǐ 〈书〉① boy; lad ② mean fellow; fellow

**恕** shù ① forgive; pardon; excuse: 宽～ forgive/ ～罪 pardon an offence; forgive a sin ②〈套〉excuse me; beg your pardon: ～不奉陪。Excuse me (for not keeping you company)./ ～难从命。We regret that we cannot comply with your wishes. ③ forbearance (as advocated by Confucius)

**庶** shù ① multitudinous; numerous: 富～ rich and populous/ ～物 every kind of creature; all things ②〈旧〉of or by the concubine (as distinguished from the legal wife): ～出 be born of a concubine ③〈书〉so that; so as to: ～免误会 so as to avoid misunderstanding
【庶几乎】 shùjīhū 〈书〉〈连〉so that; so as to
【庶民】 shùmín 〈书〉the common people; the multitude
【庶母】 shùmǔ concubine of one's father
【庶务】 shùwù 〈旧〉① general affairs; business matters ② a person in charge of business matters

**数** shù ① number; figure: 代表人～ the number of delegates/ ～以万计 number tens of thousands/ 心中有～ have a good idea of how things stand; know what's what ②〈数〉number: 无理～ irrational number/ ～域 number field/ ～系 number system ③〈语〉number: 单(复)～ singular (plural) number ④ several; a few: ～百人 several hundred people/ ～分钟后 a few minutes later ⑤ fate; destiny
另见 shǔ; shuò
【数词】 shùcí 〈语〉numeral: 序～ ordinal number/ 基～ cardinal number
【数额】 shù'é number; amount: 超出～ exceed the number fixed/ 不足规定～ fall short of the amount required
【数据】 shùjù data: 科学～ scientific data ◇ ～处理 data processing/ ～存储系统 data-storage system/ ～库 data base
【数控】 shùkòng 〈机〉numerical control (Nc): 总体～ total numerical control
【数理逻辑】 shùlǐ luóji mathematical logic
【数理统计学】 shùlǐ tǒngjìxué mathematical statistics
【数量】 shùliàng quantity; amount: ～和质量并重 stress both quantity and quality/ ～上的差别 quantitative difference/ ～上的增减 increase or decrease in quantity/ 在～上占优势 be superior in numbers; have numerical superiority ◇ ～词〈语〉numeral-classifier compound (as 一次, 两个)
【数码】 shùmǎ ① numeral: 阿拉伯～ Arabic numerals/ 罗马～ Roman numerals ② number; amount
【数目】 shùmù number; amount
【数目字】 shùmùzì 见"数字"
【数学】 shùxué mathematics ◇ ～家 mathematician
【数值】 shùzhí 〈数〉numerical value ◇ ～天气预报 numerical weather forecast
【数轴】 shùzhóu 〈数〉number axis
【数珠】 shùzhū 〈佛教〉beads
【数字】 shùzì ① numeral; figure; digit: 阿拉伯～ Arabic numerals/ 天文～ astronomical figures ② quantity; amount: 不要单纯追求～。Don't just go after quantity. ◇ ～计算机 digital computer/ ～控制系统 numerical control system

**漱** shù gargle; rinse
【漱口】 shùkǒu rinse the mouth; gargle: 用盐水～ gargle with salt water ◇ ～杯 a glass or mug for mouth-rinsing or teeth-cleaning; tooth glass/ ～剂 gargle

**墅** shù villa

**澍** shù 〈书〉timely rain

## shuā

**刷** shuā ① brush: 牙～ toothbrush/ 油漆～ paintbrush/ 板～ scrub brush ② brush; scrub: ～鞋 brush shoes/ ～锅 clean (或 scour) a pot ③ daub; paste up: 用石灰浆～墙 whitewash a wall/ ～标语 paste up posters ④〈口〉eliminate; remove: 那个队直到半决赛才给～下来。That team was not eliminated until the semifinals. ⑤〈象〉〔形容迅速擦过去的声音〕swish; rustle: 玉米叶子被风吹得～～响。The corn leaves rustled in the wind.
另见 shuà
【刷洗】 shuāxǐ scrub: ～地板 scrub the floor
【刷新】 shuāxīn ① renovate; refurbish: ～门面 repaint the front (of a shop, etc.); put up a new shopfront ② break: ～纪录 break (或 better) a record/ 一再～生产纪录 shatter the production records again and again
【刷牙】 shuāyá brush (或 clean) one's teeth
【刷子】 shuāzi brush; scrub

## shuǎ

**耍** shuǎ ①〈方〉play: 叫孩子们到院子里～去。Tell the children to go and play in the courtyard./ 这可不是～的! It's no joke! ② play with; flourish: ～刀 flourish a sword; give a performance of swordplay/ ～猴儿 put on a monkey show ③ play (tricks): ～鬼把戏 play dirty tricks/ ～两面派 resort to double-dealing; be double-faced

【耍笔杆】 shuǎ bǐgǎn wield a pen; be skilled in literary tricks: 他光会～，碰到实际问题就束手无策。He knows only how to wield a pen and is helpless in the face of practical problems.
【耍花招】 shuǎ huāzhāo ① display showy movements in *wushu* (武术), etc. ② play (或 get up to) tricks: 别～了! None of your tricks!/ 你这是耍的什么花招? What are you up to? 或 What sort of game are you playing?/ 他又在～了。He is up to his tricks again.
【耍滑】 shuǎhuá try to shirk work or responsibility; act in a slick way 又作"耍滑头"
【耍赖】 shuǎlài act shamelessly; be perverse
【耍流氓】 shuǎ liúmáng behave like a hoodlum; take liberties with women; act indecently
【耍弄】 shuǎnòng make fun of; make a fool of; deceive
【耍盘子】 shuǎ pánzi 〈杂技〉 plate-spinning; disc-spinning
【耍脾气】 shuǎ píqi get into a huff; put on a show of bad temper
【耍贫嘴】 shuǎ pínzuǐ 〈方〉 be garrulous
【耍钱】 shuǎqián 〈方〉 gamble
【耍坛子】 shuǎ tánzi 〈杂技〉 juggling with jars; jar balancing act
【耍威风】 shuǎ wēifēng make a show of authority; throw one's weight about; be overbearing
【耍无赖】 shuǎ wúlài act shamelessly; be perverse
【耍笑】 shuǎxiào ① joke; have fun ② make fun of; play a joke on sb.
【耍心眼儿】 shuǎ xīnyǎnr exercise one's wits for personal gain; be calculating; pull a smart trick
【耍嘴皮子】 shuǎ zuǐpízi ① talk glibly; be a slick talker ② mere empty talk; lip service

## shuà

**刷** shuà
另见 shuā
【刷白】 shuàbái white; pale: 月亮把麦地照得～。The wheat fields turned white under the moon./ 听到这个不幸的消息，他的脸立刻变得～。He turned pale when he heard the bad news.

## shuāi

**衰** shuāi decline; wane: 兴～ rise and decline/ 体力渐～ get weaker physically/ 懒则～。Laziness leads to debility.
【衰败】 shuāibài decline; wane; be at a low ebb
【衰变】 shuāibiàn 〈物〉 decay: 核～ nuclear decay
【衰减】 shuāijiǎn 〈电〉 attenuation ◇ ～器 attenuator
【衰竭】 shuāijié 〈医〉 exhaustion; prostration: 心力～ heart failure
【衰老】 shuāilǎo old and feeble; decrepit; senile
【衰落】 shuāiluò decline; be on the wane; go downhill: 资本主义制度的～ the decline of the capitalist system
【衰弱】 shuāiruò weak; feeble: 久病之后身体～ be weak after a long illness/ 神经～ suffer from neurasthenia/ 攻势已经～。The offensive is losing momentum.
【衰颓】 shuāituí weak and degenerate
【衰退】 shuāituì fail; decline: 视力～ failing eyesight/ 记忆力～ be losing one's memory/ 经济～ economic recession/ 革命意志～的人，要经过整风重新振作起来。Those whose revolutionary will has been waning should regain their ardour through rectification.
【衰亡】 shuāiwáng become feeble and die; decline and fall; wither away
【衰微】 shuāiwēi 〈书〉 decline; wane
【衰朽】 shuāixiǔ 〈书〉 feeble and decaying; decrepit

**摔** shuāi ① fall; tumble; lose one's balance: 他～了好多次才学会骑自行车。He fell off many times before he learned to ride a bicycle. ② hurtle down; plunge: 飞机～下来了。The plane plunged to the ground. ③ cause to fall and break; break: 我不小心把玻璃杯～了。I accidentally broke a glass./ 他把腿～断了。He had a fall and broke his leg. ④ cast; throw; fling: 把帽子往床上一～ throw one's cap onto the bed
【摔打】 shuāida ① beat; knock: 把扫帚上的泥～～。Beat the dirt off the broom. ② rough it; temper oneself: 他从小就在渔船上，～出一副结实的身子。He built up a robust constitution roughing it on the fishing boats ever since he was small./ 在阶级斗争的风浪里～ temper oneself in the thick of class struggle
【摔跟头】 shuāi gēntou ① tumble; trip and fall ② trip up; come a cropper; make a blunder: 工作中听不进群众意见就容易～。One is likely to blunder in one's work if one refuses to listen to the masses.
【摔交】 shuāijiāo ① tumble; trip and fall ② trip up; come a cropper; blunder ③ 〈体〉 wrestling ◇ ～运动员 wrestler

## shuǎi

**甩** shuǎi ① move backward and forward; swing: ～胳膊 swing one's arms/ ～鞭子 crack a whip/ 小女孩一跑，辫子就来回～动。The girl's pigtails swing to and fro as she runs./ ～开膀子大干社会主义 go full steam ahead in building socialism ② throw; fling; toss: ～手榴弹 throw hand grenades ③ leave sb. behind; throw off: ～掉尾巴 throw off a pursuer (或 a tail)/ ～掉包袱 cast off a burden; get a load off one's back/ 他加快速度，一会儿就把别的运动员都～在后头了。Quickening his pace, he soon left all the other runners behind.
【甩车】 shuǎichē 〈铁道〉 uncouple a railway coach from the locomotive; uncouple
【甩卖】 shuǎimài disposal of goods at reduced prices; (markdown or reduction) sale
【甩手】 shuǎishǒu ① swing one's arms ② refuse to do; wash one's hands of: 这事该你负责，你可不能～不管。You can't wash your hands of this. It's your responsibility.

## shuài

**帅** shuài ① commander in chief: 统～ supreme commander/ 挂～ take command ② beautiful; graceful; smart: 他字写得真～。He writes a beautiful hand./ 他的双杠动作可～了! His movements on the parallel bars were very graceful. ③ commander in chief, the chief piece in Chinese chess ④ (Shuài) a surname

**率** shuài ① lead; command: ～师 command troops/ ～众前往 go (to a place) at the head of many people/ ～所部向我投诚 come over to our side with his troops ② rash; hasty: 草～ careless; cursory/ 轻～ hasty ③ frank; straightforward: 坦～ frank/ 直～ straightforward ④ generally; usually: 大～如此。This is usually the case.
另见 lǜ
【率尔】 shuài'ěr 〈书〉 rashly; hastily: 不可～应战。We

should not rashly accept battle.
【率领】 shuàilǐng lead; head; command: ～代表团 lead (或 head) a delegation/ 这支部队由他～。This unit is under his command./ 连长～全连战士冲锋。The company commander led his men in the charge.
【率先】 shuàixiān take the lead in doing sth.; be the first to do sth.
【率由旧章】 shuài yóu jiùzhāng follow the beaten track; act in accordance with established rules
【率真】 shuàizhēn forthright and sincere
【率直】 shuàizhí straightforward; unreserved; blunt

**蟀** shuài 见"蟋蟀" xīshuài

## shuān

**闩** shuān ① bolt; latch: 门～ door bolt ② fasten with a bolt or latch: 把门～好 bolt the door

**拴** shuān tie; fasten: 把马～在树上 tie (或 tether) a horse to a tree/ ～绳子晒衣服 put up a clothes line/ 把船～住。Make the boat fast.

**栓** shuān ① bolt; plug: 枪～ rifle bolt/ 消火～ fire hydrant; fireplug ② stopper; cork
【栓剂】 shuānjì 〈药〉 suppository
【栓皮】 shuānpí 〈林〉 cork
【栓皮栎】 shuānpílì 〈植〉 oriental oak (*Quercus variabilis*)
【栓塞】 shuānsè 〈医〉 embolism: 静脉～ venous embolism/ 肺(脑)～ pulmonary (cerebral) embolism
【栓子】 shuānzǐ 〈医〉 embolus

## shuàn

**涮** shuàn ① rinse: 把衣服～一～。Rinse the clothes./ 把这瓶子～一下。Give this bottle a rinse. ② scald thin slices of meat in boiling water; instant-boil: ～羊肉 instant-boiled mutton
【涮锅子】 shuànguōzi instant-boil slices of meat and vegetables in a chafing dish

## shuāng

**双** shuāng ① two; twin; both; dual: ～向交通 two-way traffic/ ～发动机飞机 twin-engined plane/ 思想劳动～丰收 do well both in ideological remoulding and in physical labour ② 〈量〉〔用于成对的东西〕 pair: 一～鞋 a pair of shoes ③ even: ～数 even numbers/ ～号座位 even-numbered seats ④ double; twofold: ～份 double the amount; twice as much
【双胞胎】 shuāngbāotāi twins
【双边】 shuāngbiān bilateral: ～会谈 bilateral talks/ ～贸易 bilateral trade; two-way trade/ ～条约 bilateral treaty
【双层】 shuāngcéng double-deck; having two layers; of two thicknesses: ～桥 double-decker bridge/ ～床 double-decker (bed, bunk)/ ～火车 double-decker/ ～玻璃窗 double window
【双重】 shuāngchóng double; dual; twofold: ～任务 double task; twofold task/ ～标准 double standard/ ～领导 dual leadership/ 起～作用 serve a dual purpose/ 帝国主义和封建主义的～压迫 the twofold oppression of imperialism and feudalism
◇ ～代表权 〈外〉 dual representation/ ～国籍 dual nationality/ ～人格 dual personality
【双唇音】 shuāngchúnyīn 〈语〉 bilabial (sound)
【双打】 shuāngdǎ 〈体〉 doubles: 男子(女子)～ men's (women's) doubles/ 男女混合～ mixed doubles
【双方】 shuāngfāng both sides; the two parties: 缔约国～ both signatory states; the contracting parties/ ～各执一词。Each side persisted in its own views./ ～同意 by mutual consent
【双峰驼】 shuāngfēngtuó 〈动〉 two-humped camel; Bactrian camel
【双幅】 shuāngfú double width: 这块料子是单幅的还是～的? Is this material single or double width?
【双杠】 shuānggàng 〈体〉 parallel bars
【双宫丝】 shuānggōngsī 〈纺〉 doupion silk
【双关】 shuāngguān having a double meaning: 一语～ a phrase with a double meaning ◇ ～语 pun
【双管】 shuāngguǎn double-barrelled: ～猎枪 double-barrelled shotgun
【双管齐下】 shuāng guǎn qí xià paint a picture with two brushes at the same time — work along both lines
【双轨】 shuāngguǐ 〈交〉 double track ◇ ～铁路 double-track railway
【双号】 shuānghào even numbers (of tickets, seats, etc.)
【双簧】 shuānghuáng 〈曲艺〉 a two-man act, with one speaking or singing while hiding behind the other who does the acting: 唱～ give a two-man comic show; collaborate
【双簧管】 shuānghuángguǎn 〈乐〉 oboe
【双季稻】 shuāngjìdào double cropping of rice; double-harvest rice
【双交】 shuāngjiāo 〈农〉 double cross
【双料】 shuāngliào of reinforced material; extra quality: ～脸盆 special quality basin; extra good quality basin
【双轮】 shuānglún 〈体〉 double round: 五十米～射箭 50-metre double round archery event
【双轮双铧犁】 shuānglún-shuānghuálí two-wheeled double-shared plough
【双面】 shuāngmiàn two-sided; double-edged; double-faced; reversible: ～刀片 a double-edged razor blade ◇ ～绣 double-faced embroidery/ ～摇纱机 double reeling frame/ ～印刷机 perfecting press; perfector/ ～织物 reversible cloth; reversibles
【双目显微镜】 shuāngmù xiǎnwēijìng binocular microscope
【双抢】 shuāngqiǎng rush-harvesting and rush-planting
【双亲】 shuāngqīn (both) parents; father and mother
【双球菌】 shuāngqiújūn 〈微〉 diplococcus
【双曲面】 shuāngqūmiàn 〈数〉 hyperboloid: 单叶～ hyperboloid of one sheet/ 双叶～ hyperboloid of two sheets
【双曲线】 shuāngqūxiàn 〈数〉 hyperbola
【双全】 shuāngquán complete in both respects; possessing both: 智勇～ possessing both wisdom and courage/ 文武～ be adept with both the pen and the sword
【双人床】 shuāngrénchuáng double bed
【双人舞】 shuāngrénwǔ dance for two people; *pas de deux*
【双日】 shuāngrì even-numbered days (of the month)
【双身子】 shuāngshēnzi 〈口〉 pregnant woman
【双生】 shuāngshēng twin: ～姐妹 twin sisters/ ～兄弟 twin brothers/ ～子 twins
【双声】 shuāngshēng 〈语〉 a phrase consisting of two or more characters with the same initial consonant (as 方法 fāngfǎ); alliteration
【双手】 shuāngshǒu both hands: 用我们的～建设社会主义新农村 build a new socialist countryside with our own hands/ 我举～赞成。I'm all for it.
【双数】 shuāngshù even numbers

【双双】 shuāngshuāng in pairs
【双糖】 shuāngtáng 〈化〉 disaccharide
【双体船】 shuāngtǐchuán catamaran
【双筒望远镜】 shuāngtǒng wàngyuǎnjìng binoculars; field glasses
【双喜】 shuāngxǐ double happiness: ～临门。A double blessing has descended upon the house.
【双下巴】 shuāngxiàba double chin
【双响】 shuāngxiǎng a firecracker which goes off twice; double-bang firecracker
【双向开关】 shuāngxiàng kāiguān two-way switch
【双星】 shuāngxīng 〈天〉 double star
【双眼皮】 shuāngyǎnpí double-fold eyelid
【双氧水】 shuāngyǎngshuǐ 〈药〉 hydrogen peroxide solution
【双翼机】 shuāngyìjī biplane
【双音节词】 shuāngyīnjiécí 〈语〉 disyllabic word; disyllable
【双鱼座】 shuāngyúzuò 〈天〉 Pisces
【双元音】 shuāngyuányīn 〈语〉 diphthong
【双月刊】 shuāngyuèkān bimonthly
【双职工】 shuāngzhígōng man and wife both at work; working couple
【双周刊】 shuāngzhōukān biweekly; fortnightly
【双绉】 shuāngzhòu 〈纺〉 *crêpe de Chine*
【双子叶植物】 shuāngzǐyè zhíwù dicotyledon
【双子座】 shuāngzǐzuò 〈天〉 Gemini
【双座】 shuāngzuò two-seater; double-seater: ～飞机 two-seater aircraft

**霜** shuāng ① frost ② frostlike powder: 糖～ frosting; icing/ 柿～ powder on the surface of a dried persimmon ③ white; hoar: ～鬓 grey (或 hoary) temples
【霜冻】 shuāngdòng frost
【霜害】 shuānghài frostbite; frost injury: 受～的农作物 frost-bitten crops
【霜花】 shuānghuā frostwork
【霜降】 Shuāngjiàng Frost's Descent (18th solar term)
【霜霉病】 shuāngméibìng 〈农〉 downy mildew
【霜期】 shuāngqī 〈气〉 frost season
【霜叶】 shuāngyè red leaves; autumn maple leaves

**孀** shuāng widow
【孀妇】 shuāngfù widow
【孀居】 shuāngjū be a widow; live in widowhood

**鹴** shuāng 见"鹔鹴" sùshuāng

## shuǎng

**爽** shuǎng ① bright; clear; crisp: 秋高气～。The autumn sky is clear and the air is crisp. ② frank; straightforward; openhearted: 豪～ straightforward; forthright ③ feel well: 身体不～ not feel well ④ deviate: 毫厘不～ not deviating a hair's breadth; without the slightest error
【爽口】 shuǎngkǒu tasty and refreshing
【爽快】 shuǎngkuai ① refreshed; comfortable: 洗完澡身上～多了 feel much refreshed after a bath ② frank; straightforward; outright: 为人～ be frank and straightforward/ 他～地说出了对我的看法。He told me frankly what he thought of me. ③ with alacrity; readily: ～地答应帮忙 readily agree to help/ 办事～ work readily and briskly
【爽朗】 shuǎnglǎng ① bright and clear: 深秋的天空异常～。In late autumn the sky is crystal clear. ② hearty; candid; frank and open; straightforward: ～的笑声 hearty laughter/ ～的性格 a frank and open personality
【爽利】 shuǎnglì brisk and neat; efficient and able: 办事～ be brisk and neat in one's work
【爽气】 shuǎngqì 〈方〉 见"爽快"
【爽然若失】 shuǎngrán ruò shī 〈书〉 not know what to do; be at a loss
【爽身粉】 shuǎngshēnfěn talcum powder
【爽性】 shuǎngxìng may just as well: 没多少活了，～干完了再休息。There isn't much work left. We might as well finish it before we have a rest.
【爽约】 shuǎngyuē 〈书〉 fail to keep an appointment; break an appointment
【爽直】 shuǎngzhí frank; straightforward; candid

## shuí

**谁** shuí 或 shéi ① who: 他是～？Who is he?/ 这是～的意见？Whose idea is it?/ ～不说他好。Who wouldn't speak well of him?/ 我是开玩笑，～知他竟当真了。I was only joking; who would have thought he would take it seriously. ② someone; anyone: 有～能帮助我就好了！If only someone could help me!/ 大家比着干，～都不甘落后。Everyone was competing, and nobody wanted to lag behind./ 他们俩～也说不服～。Neither of them could convince the other./ 大家看～合适就选～。You may select whoever you think is suitable.

## shuǐ

**水** shuǐ ① water: 淡～ fresh water/ 硬～ hard water ② river: 汉～ the Han River ③ a general term for rivers, lakes, seas, etc.; water: ～陆运输 land and water transportation/ ～上人家 boat dwellers/ ～平如镜。The surface of the water is as smooth as a mirror. ④ a liquid: 墨～ ink/ 桔子～ orangeade ⑤ (Shuǐ) a surname
【水坝】 shuǐbà dam
【水半球】 shuǐbànqiú 〈地〉 water hemisphere
【水泵】 shuǐbèng water pump
【水笔】 shuǐbǐ ① a stiff-haired writing brush ② watercolour paintbrush ③ 〈方〉 (fountain) pen
【水表】 shuǐbiǎo water meter
【水鳖】 shuǐbiē 〈植〉 frogbit (*Hydrocharis morsus-ranae*)
【水兵】 shuǐbīng seaman; sailor; bluejacket
【水玻璃】 shuǐbōli 〈化〉 water glass
【水彩】 shuǐcǎi watercolour ◇ ～画 watercolour (painting)/ ～颜料 watercolours
【水仓】 shuǐcāng 〈矿〉 sump
【水草】 shuǐcǎo ① water and grass: ～丰美 (a place) with plenty of water and lush grass/ 逐～而居 (of nomads) live where there is water and grass; rove about seeking water and grass ② waterweeds; water plants
【水虿】 shuǐchài 〈动〉 the nymph of the dragonfly, etc.
【水产】 shuǐchǎn aquatic product ◇ ～品 aquatic product/ ～业 aquatic products industry/ ～资源 aquatic resources
【水车】 shuǐchē ① waterwheel ② watercart; water wagon
【水成岩】 shuǐchéngyán 〈地〉 aqueous rock
【水程】 shuǐchéng journey by boat; voyage: 一百公里的～ a 100-kilometre journey by boat
【水池】 shuǐchí pond; pool; cistern
【水池子】 shuǐchízi ① 见"水池" ② sink
【水尺】 shuǐchǐ 〈水〉 water gauge
【水处理】 shuǐchǔlǐ 〈化〉 water treatment
【水到渠成】 shuǐ dào qú chéng where water flows, a channel

is formed — when conditions are ripe, success will come
【水道】 shuǐdào ① water course ② waterway; water route: 这次去上海，我想打～走。This time I'll go to Shanghai by water.
【水稻】 shuǐdào paddy (rice); rice ◇ ～插秧机 rice (或 paddy) transplanter/ ～土 rice (或 paddy) soil
【水滴石穿】 shuǐ dī shí chuān dripping water wears through rock — constant effort brings success
【水底电缆】 shuǐdǐ diànlǎn submarine cable; subaqueous cable
【水电】 shuǐ-diàn water and electricity: ～供应 water and electricity supply ◇ ～费 charges for water and electricity
【水电站】 shuǐdiànzhàn 〈简〉（水力发电站） hydroelectric (power) station; hydropower station
【水貂】 shuǐdiāo 〈动〉 mink
【水痘】 shuǐdòu 〈医〉 varicella; chicken pox
【水碓】 shuǐduì water-powered trip-hammer (for husking rice)
【水飞蓟】 shuǐfēijì 〈植〉 milk thistle (*Silybum marianum*)
【水粉】 shuǐfěn ① soaked noodles made from beans or sweet potatoes ② a cosmetic made from face powder and glycerine
【水粉画】 shuǐfěnhuà 〈美术〉 *gouache*
【水分】 shuǐfèn ① moisture content: 吸收～ absorb moisture ② exaggeration: 这个数字有～。This figure is inflated./ 这份报告有～。This report is somewhat exaggerated.
【水浮莲】 shuǐfúlián 〈植〉 water lettuce; water cabbage
【水工建筑物】 shuǐgōng jiànzhùwù hydraulic structure
【水沟】 shuǐgōu ditch; drain; gutter
【水垢】 shuǐgòu scale; incrustation: 除去锅炉里的～ scour out a boiler
【水臌】 shuǐgǔ 〈中医〉 ascites
【水管】 shuǐguǎn waterpipe
【水果】 shuǐguǒ fruit
◇ ～罐头 tinned (或 canned) fruit/ ～软糖 fruit jelly/ ～糖 fruit drops
【水合】 shuǐhé 〈化〉 hydration ◇ ～水 hydrate water/ ～物 hydrate 又作"水化"
【水红】 shuǐhóng bright pink; cerise
【水壶】 shuǐhú ① kettle ② canteen ③ watering can
【水葫芦】 shuǐhúlu 〈植〉 water hyacinth
【水花】 shuǐhuā spray
【水患】 shuǐhuàn flood; inundation
【水火】 shuǐ-huǒ ① fire and water — two things diametrically opposed to each other: ～不相容 be incompatible as fire and water ② extreme misery: 共产党拯救人民于～之中。The Communist Party saved the people from untold miseries.
【水火无情】 shuǐ-huǒ wúqíng floods and fires have no mercy for anybody
【水碱】 shuǐjiǎn scale; incrustation
【水浇地】 shuǐjiāodì 〈农〉 irrigated land
【水饺】 shuǐjiǎo boiled dumplings
【水解】 shuǐjiě 〈化〉 hydrolysis
◇ ～产物 hydrolysate/ ～蛋白〈药〉 protein hydrolysate/ ～质 hydrolyte
【水晶】 shuǐjīng crystal; rock crystal
◇ ～包〈食品〉 a steamed dumpling stuffed with lard and sugar/ ～玻璃 crystal (glass)/ ～宫 the Crystal Palace (of the Dragon King)/ ～棺 crystal sarcophagus/ ～体〈生理〉 crystalline lens
【水井】 shuǐjǐng well
【水酒】 shuǐjiǔ watery wine (said by a host of his own wine)
【水坑】 shuǐkēng puddle; pool; water hole: 臭～ cesspool; cesspit
【水库】 shuǐkù reservoir
【水牢】 shuǐláo water dungeon
【水老鸦】 shuǐlǎoyā 〈动〉 cormorant
【水涝】 shuǐlào waterlogging ◇ ～地 waterlogged land
【水雷】 shuǐléi 〈军〉 (submarine) mine: 敷设～ lay mines (in water)/ ～密布的河道 a heavily mined river
【水冷】 shuǐlěng water-cooling: ～式发动机 water-cooled engine/ ～系统 water-cooling system
【水力】 shuǐlì waterpower; hydraulic power
◇ ～发电 hydraulic electrogenerating/ ～发电站 hydroelectric (power) station; hydropower station/ ～开采〈矿〉 hydraulic mining; hydraulicking/ ～学 hydraulics/ ～资源 hydroelectric resources (或 potential); waterpower resources
【水利】 shuǐlì ① water conservancy: ～设施 water conservancy facilities ② irrigation works; water conservancy project: 兴修～ build irrigation works
◇ ～工程 irrigation works; water conservancy project (或 works)/ ～工程学 hydraulic engineering/ ～灌溉网 irrigation network/ ～化 bring all farmland under irrigation/ ～枢纽 key water control project/ ～资源 water resources
【水疗】 shuǐliáo 〈医〉 hydrotherapy
【水灵】 shuǐling 〈方〉 ① (of fruit, greens, etc.) fresh and juicy ② (of appearance) bright and beautiful; radiant and vivacious: 两只～的大眼睛 a pair of bright, beautiful eyes
【水流】 shuǐliú ① rivers; streams; waters: 在我国一切矿藏、～都属于全民所有。In China, all mineral resources and waters are the property of the whole people. ② current; flow: ～湍急(迟缓) rapid (sluggish) flow; rushing current
【水流星】 shuǐliúxīng 〈杂技〉 spinning bowls of water; water meteors
【水龙】 shuǐlóng fire hose; hose 又作"水龙带"
【水龙骨】 shuǐlónggǔ 〈植〉 wall fern; golden locks
【水龙卷】 shuǐlóngjuǎn 〈气〉 waterspout
【水龙头】 shuǐlóngtóu (water) tap; faucet; bibcock: 开(关)～ turn on (off) the tap/ 用后将～关紧。Don't leave the tap running after use.
【水陆】 shuǐ-lù land and water: ～并进 proceed by both land and water; conduct a combined operation by army and navy/ ～两用 amphibious
◇ ～交通线 land and water communication lines/ ～联运 water-land transshipment/ ～联运码头 a dock for joint land and water transport service/ ～坦克 amphibious tank/ ～运输 transportation by land and water
【水路】 shuǐlù waterway; water route: 由上海到武汉可以走～。One can travel from Shanghai to Wuhan by water.
【水铝矿】 shuǐlǚkuàng 〈矿〉 gibbsite
【水绿】 shuǐlǜ light green
【水轮泵】 shuǐlúnbèng (water) turbine pump ◇ ～站 (water) turbine-pump station
【水轮发电机】 shuǐlún fādiànjī water turbogenerator
【水轮机】 shuǐlúnjī hydraulic (或 water) turbine
【水落管】 shuǐluòguǎn 〈建〉 downspout; downpipe
【水落石出】 shuǐluò-shíchū when the water subsides the rocks emerge — the whole thing comes to light: 把事情辩个～ argue a matter out/ 我们一定要把这事弄个～。We must get to the bottom of this matter.
【水煤气】 shuǐméiqì 〈化〉 water gas
【水门】 shuǐmén water valve
【水门汀】 shuǐméntīng 〈方〉 cement
【水锰矿】 shuǐměngkuàng manganite
【水密】 shuǐmì 〈机〉 watertight
【水蜜桃】 shuǐmìtáo honey peach
【水磨】 shuǐmó polish with a waterstone
另见 shuǐmò

【水磨功夫】 shuǐmó gōngfu patient and precise work; painstaking work
【水磨石】 shuǐmóshí 〈建〉 terrazzo ◇ ～地面 terrazzo floor
【水墨画】 shuǐmòhuà 〈美术〉 ink and wash; wash painting: 中国～ Chinese ink and wash
【水磨】 shuǐmò ① water mill ② grind grain, etc. fine while adding water: ～年糕 New Year cake made from finely ground rice flour
另见 shuǐmó
【水母】 shuǐmǔ 〈动〉 jellyfish; medusa
【水泥】 shuǐní cement
◇ ～标号 strength of cement; cement grade/ ～厂 cement plant/ ～船 concrete boat; plastered boat/ ～瓦 cement tile
【水碾】 shuǐniǎn water-powered roller (for grinding grain)
【水鸟】 shuǐniǎo aquatic bird; water bird
【水牛】 shuǐniú (water) buffalo
【水暖工】 shuǐnuǎngōng plumber
【水泡】 shuǐpào ① bubble ② blister: 脚上打了～ get blisters on one's feet
【水疱】 shuǐpào blister
【水瓢】 shuǐpiáo (gourd) water ladle
【水平】 shuǐpíng ① horizontal; level: ～梯田 level terraced field; level terrace ② standard; level: 生活～ living standard/ 文化～ standard of education; cultural level/ 认识～ level of one's understanding/ 赶超世界先进～ attain and surpass advanced world levels/ 提高领导～ improve one's art of leadership
◇ ～飞行 horizontal (或 level) flight/ ～轰炸 〈军〉 horizontal (或 level) bombing/ ～贸易 〈经〉 horizontal trade/ ～面 horizontal plane; level (surface)/ ～线 horizontal line/ ～仪 level
【水泼不进，针插不进】 shuǐ pō bù jìn, zhēn chā bù jìn watertight and impenetrable
【水汽】 shuǐqì vapour; steam; moisture ◇ ～浓度 〈气〉 vapour concentration
【水枪】 shuǐqiāng 〈矿〉 giant; (hydraulic) monitor: 水采～ hydraulic giant
【水禽】 shuǐqín 〈动〉 waterfowl; water bird
【水情】 shuǐqíng 〈水〉 regimen
【水球】 shuǐqiú 〈体〉 water polo
【水曲柳】 shuǐqūliǔ 〈植〉 northeast China ash
【水渠】 shuǐqú ditch; canal
【水圈】 shuǐquān 〈地〉 hydrosphere
【水溶液】 shuǐróngyè 〈化〉 aqueous solution
【水乳交融】 shuǐ-rǔ jiāoróng as well blended as milk and water — in complete harmony: 干部和群众的关系亲密无间，～。The relationship between the cadres and the masses is one of perfect harmony./ 好的翻译可以使宾主谈得～。A fully qualified interpreter can help bring about a meeting of minds like milk mingling with water.
【水杉】 shuǐshān 〈植〉 metasequoia (*Metasequoia glyptostroboides*)
【水上飞机】 shuǐshàng fēijī seaplane; hydroplane
【水上飞行】 shuǐshàng fēixíng overwater flight
【水上居民】 shuǐshàng jūmín boat dwellers
【水上运动】 shuǐshàng yùndòng 〈体〉 aquatic sports; water sports ◇ ～会 aquatic sports meet
【水蛇】 shuǐshé 〈动〉 water snake
【水深火热】 shuǐshēn-huǒrè deep water and scorching fire — an abyss of suffering; extreme misery: 旧社会劳动人民生活在～之中。The working people lived in an abyss of misery in the old society. 或 Life was hell on earth for the working people in the old society.
【水生动物】 shuǐshēng dòngwù aquatic animal
【水生植物】 shuǐshēng zhíwù water (或 aquatic) plant; hydrophyte
【水声学】 shuǐshēngxué 〈物〉 marine acoustics
【水虱】 shuǐshī 〈动〉 beach louse
【水势】 shuǐshì the flow of water; rise and fall of floodwater: 密切注意～ keep a close eye on the flow of the water/ ～减退。The flood subsided (或 abated).
【水手】 shuǐshǒu seaman; sailor ◇ ～长 boatswain
【水刷石】 shuǐshuāshí 〈建〉 granitic plaster
【水松】 shuǐsōng 〈植〉 China cypress (*Glyptostrobus pensilis*)
【水塔】 shuǐtǎ water tower
【水獭】 shuǐtǎ 〈动〉 otter
【水潭】 shuǐtán puddle; pool
【水塘】 shuǐtáng pool; pond
【水田】 shuǐtián paddy field ◇ ～耙 paddy field harrow/ ～犁 paddy field plough
【水桶】 shuǐtǒng pail; bucket
【水头】 shuǐtóu ① 〈水〉 head ② flood peak; peak of flow
【水土】 shuǐtǔ ① water and soil: ～流失 soil erosion/ ～保持 water and soil conservation ② natural environment and climate: ～不服 unaccustomed to the climate of a new place; not acclimatized
【水汪汪】 shuǐwāngwāng (of children's or young women's eyes) bright and intelligent
【水网】 shuǐwǎng a network of rivers
【水位】 shuǐwèi water level: 高(低)～ high (low) water level/ 地下～ water table; groundwater level ◇ ～计 fluviograph
【水文】 shuǐwén hydrology
◇ ～测验 hydrologic survey/ ～地理学 hydrography/ ～地质学 hydrogeology/ ～队 hydrological team/ ～工作者 hydrologist/ ～年鉴 Water Year Book/ ～气象学 hydrometeorology/ ～设计 hydrologic design/ ～学 hydrology/ ～预报 hydrologic forecast/ ～站 hydrometric station; hydrologic station/ ～资料 hydrological data
【水污染】 shuǐwūrǎn water pollution
【水螅】 shuǐxī 〈动〉 hydra
【水系】 shuǐxì river system; hydrographic net
【水仙】 shuǐxiān 〈植〉 narcissus
【水险】 shuǐxiǎn marine insurance
【水线】 shuǐxiàn waterline
【水乡】 shuǐxiāng a region of rivers and lakes
【水箱】 shuǐxiāng water tank
【水泻】 shuǐxiè 〈医〉 watery diarrhoea
【水泄不通】 shuǐ xiè bù tōng not even a drop of water could trickle through; be watertight: 挤得～ be packed with people/ 围得～ be so closely besieged that not a drop of water could trickle through
【水榭】 shuǐxiè waterside pavilion
【水星】 shuǐxīng 〈天〉 Mercury
【水性】 shuǐxìng ① ability in swimming: 这姑娘的～很好。This girl is a good swimmer. ② the depth, currents and other characteristics of a river, lake, etc.
【水锈】 shuǐxiù ① scale; incrustation ② watermark (in water vessels)
【水压】 shuǐyā hydraulic (或 water) pressure ◇ ～机 hydraulic press
【水烟】 shuǐyān shredded tobacco for water pipes: 抽～ smoke a water pipe ◇ ～袋 water pipe
【水杨】 shuǐyáng 〈植〉 bigcatkin willow
【水杨酸】 shuǐyángsuān 〈化〉 salicylic acid ◇ ～钠 sodium salicylate
【水翼船】 shuǐyìchuán hydrofoil
【水银】 shuǐyín 〈化〉 mercury; quicksilver
◇ ～灯 mercury-vapour lamp/ ～气压表 〈气〉 mercury

(或 mercurial) barometer/ ～温度计〈气〉 mercury (或 mercurial) thermometer/ ～柱 mercury column

【水印】 shuǐyìn ①〈美术〉 watercolour block printing ② watermark

【水有源,树有根】 shuǐ yǒu yuán, shù yǒu gēn every river has its source and every tree its roots — everything has its origin

【水域】 shuǐyù waters; water area; body of water: 内陆～ inland waters/ 国际～ an international body of water; international waters

【水源】 shuǐyuán ① the source of a river; headwaters; waterhead: 黄河的～ the headwaters of the Huanghe River ② source of water: 寻找～ seek new sources of water

【水运】 shuǐyùn water transport ◇ ～码头 a port handling river cargo

【水灾】 shuǐzāi flood; inundation

【水葬】 shuǐzàng water burial

【水蚤】 shuǐzǎo water flea

【水藻】 shuǐzǎo algae

【水闸】 shuǐzhá sluice; water gate

【水涨船高】 shuǐ zhǎng chuán gāo when the river rises the boat goes up — particular things improve with the improvement of the general situation

【水针疗法】 shuǐzhēn liáofǎ 〈中医〉 acupuncture therapy with medicinal injection

【水蒸汽】 shuǐzhēngqì steam; water vapour

【水至清则无鱼】 shuǐ zhì qīng zé wú yú when the water is too clear there are no fish — one should not demand absolute purity

【水质】 shuǐzhì water quality ◇ ～保护〈环保〉 water quality protection/ ～污染 water pollution

【水蛭】 shuǐzhì leech

【水中捞月】 shuǐzhōng lāo yuè fish for the moon in the water — make impractical or vain efforts

【水肿】 shuǐzhǒng 〈医〉 oedema; dropsy

【水珠子】 shuǐzhūzi 〈口〉 drop of water

【水柱】 shuǐzhù water column

【水准】 shuǐzhǔn level; standard: 高（低）于一般～ above (below) average

◇ ～点 bench mark/ ～面 level surface; level plane/ ～器 spirit level/ ～仪 surveyor's level; levelling instrument

【水渍险】 shuǐzìxiǎn 〈经〉 with particular average (W.P.A.)

【水族】 Shuǐzú the Shui nationality, living mainly in Guizhou

【水族】 shuǐzú aquatic animals ◇ ～馆 aquarium

## shuì

**说** shuì try to persuade: 游～ go around urging rulers to adopt one's political views; peddle an idea; drum up support for a scheme or plan

另见 shuō

**税** shuì tax; duty: 营业～ business tax/ 进口（出口）～ import (export) duty

【税额】 shuì'é the amount of tax to be paid

【税款】 shuìkuǎn tax payment; taxation

【税率】 shuìlǜ tax rate; rate of taxation; tariff rate

【税目】 shuìmù tax items; taxable items

【税收】 shuìshōu tax revenue ◇ ～政策 tax policy

【税务局】 shuìwùjú tax bureau

【税务员】 shuìwùyuán tax collector

【税则】 shuìzé tax regulations

【税制】 shuìzhì tax system; taxation: 累进～ progressive taxation

【税种】 shuìzhǒng categories of taxes

**睡** shuì sleep: 他～着了。He's asleep./ 一～就～到大天亮 sleep like a log till broad daylight

【睡觉】 shuìjiào sleep: 该～了。It's time to go to bed./ 睡午觉 take a nap after lunch/ 睡懒觉 get up late; sleep in; sleep late/ 马上上床，好好地睡一觉。Get straight into bed and have a good sleep.

【睡莲】 shuìlián 〈植〉 water lily

【睡帽】 shuìmào nightcap

【睡梦】 shuìmèng sleep; slumber: 一阵敲门声把他从～中惊醒了。He was roused from sleep by a heavy pounding on the door.

【睡眠】 shuìmián sleep: ～不足 not have enough sleep ◇～疗法〈医〉 physiological sleep therapy

【睡醒】 shuìxǐng wake up

【睡衣】 shuìyī night clothes; pajamas

【睡意】 shuìyì sleepiness; drowsiness: 有几分～ feel somewhat sleepy; be drowsy

## shǔn

**吮** shǔn suck

【吮吸】 shǔnxī suck: 剥削阶级贪婪地～劳动人民的血汗。The exploiting classes greedily suck the blood of the labouring people.

## shùn

**顺** shùn ① in the same direction as; with: ～流而下 go downstream/ ～时针方向 clockwise ② along: ～着这条道儿走。Follow this road./ 水～着渠道流进地里。Water runs along the channel to the fields. ③ arrange; put in order: 这篇文章还得～一～。This essay needs polishing. ④ obey; yield to; act in submission to: 他不对嘛,怎么能～着他呢? How can we do as he wishes when he's obviously wrong? ⑤ suitable; agreeable: 不～他的意 not fall in with his wishes ⑥ take the opportunity to: ～致最崇高的敬意。I avail myself of this opportunity to renew to you the assurances of my highest consideration. ⑦ in sequence: 这些号码是一～的。These are serial numbers.

【顺坝】 shùnbà 〈水〉 longitudinal dike

【顺便】 shùnbiàn conveniently; in passing: 你～把这些学习材料带到车间去吧。Please take this study material with you to the workshop./ 这一点现在～提一下，以后还会讲到。I mention this point now in passing and shall refer to it again./ ～说一句 by the way; incidentally

【顺差】 shùnchā favourable balance; surplus: 贸易～ favourable balance of trade/ 国际收支～ favourable balance of payments; balance of payments surplus

【顺产】 shùnchǎn 〈医〉 natural labour

【顺畅】 shùnchàng smooth; unhindered: 病人的呼吸渐渐～了。The patient is beginning to breathe more easily.

【顺磁】 shùncí 〈物〉 paramagnetic: ～共振 paramagnetic resonance

【顺次】 shùncì in order; in succession; in proper sequence: 按问题的轻重缓急～解决 dispose of the problems one by one in order of importance and urgency

【顺从】 shùncóng be obedient to; submit to; yield to

【顺带】 shùndài 见"顺便"

【顺当】 shùndang smoothly; without a hitch

【顺导】 shùndǎo guide or steer (a movement, etc.) along its proper course

【顺道儿】 shùndàor 见"顺路"
【顺丁橡胶】 shùndīng xiàngjiāo 〈化〉 butadiene rubber
【顺耳】 shùn'ěr pleasing to the ear: 不要只爱听～的话。You shouldn't just listen to what pleases you.
【顺风】 shùnfēng ① have a favourable wind; have a tail wind: ～行船 sail with the wind/ 一路～ a pleasant journey; bon voyage ② favourable wind; tail wind
【顺风耳】 shùnfēng'ěr ① a person in traditional Chinese novels who can hear voices a long way off ② a well-informed person
【顺风转舵】 shùn fēng zhuǎn duò trim one's sails; take one's cue from changing conditions
【顺竿儿爬】 shùn gānr pá follow sb.'s cue and do everything to please him; readily fall in with other people's wishes
【顺口】 shùnkǒu ① read smoothly: 稿子经过这样一改，念起来就～多了。After being touched up, the essay reads more smoothly. ② say offhandedly: 他也不想想就～答应了。He agreed without thinking. ③〈方〉 suit one's taste: 这菜我吃着很～。I like the taste of this dish.
【顺口溜】 shùnkǒuliū doggerel; jingle
【顺理成章】 shùn lǐ chéng zhāng to write well, you must follow a logical train of thought; to do some work well, you must follow a rational line: 这显然是～的。This is undoubtedly logical.
【顺利】 shùnlì smoothly; successfully; without a hitch: 工作正在～进行。The work is going on smoothly./ 会议进行得很～。The meeting went off without a hitch./ 在～的情况下，要看到还会有困难。When circumstances are favourable, we must not forget that there will still be difficulties.
【顺路】 shùnlù ① on the way: 我昨天回家时～去看了看李大爷。I dropped in at Uncle Li's on my way home yesterday. ② direct route: 到王家庄这么走不～。This is not the most direct route to Wangjiazhuang Village.
【顺势】 shùnshì take advantage of an opportunity (as provided by an opponent's reckless move): 他向旁边一闪，～把敌人摔倒了。He dodged the enemy's assault and threw him to the ground.
【顺手】 shùnshǒu ① smoothly; without difficulty: 事情办得相当～。It was done without a hitch./ 开始试验有时不很～，也是很自然的。It is to be expected that an experiment will sometimes run into a snag at first. ② conveniently; without extra trouble: 出去时请～关上门。Would you close the door when you go out? ③ do sth. as a natural sequence or simultaneously: 我们扫完院子，～把房间也扫一扫。After sweeping the courtyard, we might as well clean the rooms. ④ handy; convenient and easy to use: 这把镰刀使起来挺～。This sickle is very handy.
【顺手牵羊】 shùnshǒu qiān yáng lead away a goat in passing — pick up sth. on the sly; walk off with sth.
【顺水】 shùnshuǐ downstream; with the stream
【顺水人情】 shùnshuǐ rénqíng a favour done at little cost to oneself
【顺水推舟】 shùnshuǐ tuī zhōu push the boat along with the current — make use of an opportunity to gain one's end
【顺遂】 shùnsuì go well; go smoothly
【顺藤摸瓜】 shùn téng mō guā follow the vine to get the melon — track down sb. or sth. by following clues
【顺我者昌，逆我者亡】 shùn wǒ zhě chāng, nì wǒ zhě wáng those who submit will prosper, those who resist shall perish (said of the arbitrary, brutal rule of a tyrant)
【顺心】 shùnxīn satisfactory: 诸事～。All is well./ 他父亲晚年过得挺～。His father spent the evening of his life in happiness.
【顺行】 shùnxíng 〈天〉 direct motion
【顺序】 shùnxù ① sequence; order: 文物按年代～展出。The cultural relics are displayed in chronological sequence./ 按字母～排列 in alphabetical order ② in proper order; in turn
【顺延】 shùnyán postpone: 运动会定于五月四日举行，遇雨～。The sports meet is scheduled for May 4th — subject to postponement in case of rain.
【顺眼】 shùnyǎn pleasing to the eye: 看着不～ be offensive to the eye; be an eyesore
【顺应】 shùnyìng comply with; conform to: ～历史发展的潮流 conform to the historical trend of the times; go with the tide of historical development
【顺证】 shùnzhèng 〈中医〉 a serious case which improves steadily
【顺嘴】 shùnzuǐ 见"顺口" ①②

**舜** Shùn Shun, the name of a legendary monarch in ancient China

**瞬** shùn wink; twinkling: 转～之间 in a twinkling
【瞬时】 shùnshí 〈物〉 instantaneous
◇ ～速度 instantaneous velocity/ ～性 instantaneity/ ～值 instantaneous value
【瞬息】 shùnxī twinkling: ～间 in the twinkling of an eye/ ～万变 undergoing a myriad changes in the twinkling of an eye; fast changing

## shuō

**说** shuō ① speak; talk; say: 请～慢一点儿。Please speak more slowly./ ～得多做得少 talk much but do little/ 你～得很对。What you say is quite true./ 那未免～得太轻了。That's putting it too mildly./ 俗话～，"吃一堑，长一智"。As the saying goes, "A fall into the pit, a gain in your wit." ② explain: 他～了又～，我还是不懂。He explained and explained, but I still couldn't understand./ 我一～他就明白了。I told him how and he caught on at once. ③ theory; teachings; doctrine: 著书立～ write books to expound a theory ④ scold: 他父亲～了他一顿。His father gave him a scolding (或 talking-to).
另见 shuì
【说白】 shuōbái spoken parts in an opera
【说不得】 shuōbude ① unspeakable; unmentionable ② scandalous
【说不定】 shuōbudìng perhaps; maybe: ～她已经走了。Maybe she's already left.
【说不过去】 shuō bu guòqù cannot be justified or explained away: 条件这样好，再不增产，可～。With such favourable conditions, we'll have no excuse if we fail to increase output.
【说不来】 shuōbulái cannot get along (with sb.): 我跟他～。I don't see eye to eye with him.
【说不上】 shuōbushàng ① cannot say; cannot tell: 他也～问题在哪儿。He can't put his finger on what's wrong./ 我～他来不来。I can't say whether he is coming or not. ② not worth mentioning: 这些材料～有什么史料价值。These materials can't be said to have much value as historical records.
【说唱】 shuōchàng a genre of popular entertainment consisting mainly of talking and singing, e.g. comic dialogue, *dagu* (大鼓), etc.

【说穿】 shuōchuān tell what sth. really is; reveal; disclose: ~了，无非是想推卸责任。To put it bluntly, this is shifting responsibility.
【说大话】 shuō dàhuà brag; boast; talk big
【说到底】 shuōdàodǐ in the final analysis; at bottom: 民族斗争，~，是一个阶级斗争问题。 In the final analysis, national struggle is a matter of class struggle.
【说到做到】 shuōdào zuòdào do what one says; match one's deeds to one's words; live up to one's word
【说道】 shuōdào say: 少先队员~:"我们要向雷锋叔叔学习。" "We must learn from Uncle Lei Feng," said the Young Pioneer.
【说…道…】 shuō...dào... 〔分别嵌用相对或相类的形容词或数词〕: 说长道短 make captious comments/ 说三道四 make irresponsible remarks/ 说东道西 chatter away on a variety of things
【说得过去】 shuōde guòqù justifiable; passable: 他的英语发音还~。His English pronunciation is passable.
【说得来】 shuōdelái can get along; be on good terms: 找一个跟他~的人去动员他。Get someone who is on good terms with him to try and persuade him.
【说定】 shuōdìng settle; agree on: 这件事基本上已经~了。The matter is as good as settled.
【说法】 shuōfa ① way of saying a thing; wording; formulation: 换一个~ say it in another way/ 这个意思可以有两种~。This idea can be formulated in two different ways. ② statement; version; argument: 那种~是不对的。That's a false statement./ 关于那件事，各人~不同。Different people have different versions of the incident./ 这种~是完全正确的。This argument is very sound./ 照他的~去做。Do as he says.
【说服】 shuōfú persuade; convince; prevail on; talk sb. over: 要耐心~他。Talk to him patiently to bring him round./她的话很有~力。What she says is very convincing./ 努力宣传，~群众 carry on energetic propaganda to convince the masses/ 用~教育的方法去解决属于思想性质的问题 settle questions of an ideological nature by the method of persuasion and education
【说好】 shuōhǎo come to an agreement or understanding: 我已经跟他~了，明天一块去看足球赛。I've arranged to go with him to tomorrow's football match.
【说合】 shuōhe ① bring two (or more) parties together: ~亲事 make a match ② talk over; discuss ③ 见"说和"
【说和】 shuōhe mediate a settlement; compose a quarrel: 你去给他们~~。Try to patch things up between them, will you?
【说话】 shuōhuà ① speak; talk; say: 他不爱~。He doesn't like to talk./ 感动得说不出话来 be too moved to say anything / 还是让事实来~吧。Let the facts speak for themselves./ ~不算话 go back on one's word/ ~要有证据，批评要注意政治。Statements should be based on facts and criticism should centre on politics./ 现在人民有了~的权利。Now the people have got the right to speak. ② chat; talk: 我找他~儿去。 I'd like to have a chat with him. ③ gossip; talk: 你这样干，别人当然要~。Considering what you've done, it's natural that people should be talking. ④ 〈口〉 in a minute; right away: ~就得。It'll be ready in a jiffy.
【说谎】 shuōhuǎng tell a lie; lie
【说教】 shuōjiào deliver a sermon; preach
【说客】 shuōkè a person often sent to win sb. over or enlist his support through persuasion; a persuasive talker
【说来话长】 shuōlái huà cháng it's a long story
【说理】 shuōlǐ argue; reason things out: 咱们找他~去。Let's go and reason things out with him./ 批判应该是充分~的。Criticism should be entirely reasonable./ 进行~斗争 wage a struggle by argument and reasoning
【说漏嘴】 shuōlòuzuǐ inadvertently blurt out
【说媒】 shuōméi act as matchmaker
【说明】 shuōmíng ① explain; illustrate; show: ~机器的用法 explain how a machine works/ 举例~ illustrate by examples/ ~理由 give reasons/ ~真相 give the facts/ 应用马克思列宁主义的观点~实际问题 apply the Marxist-Leninist viewpoint in elucidating practical problems/ 代表团认为有必要~自己的立场。The delegation deems it necessary to state its position./ 事实充分~这种做法是正确的。The results show clearly that this procedure is correct. ② explanation; directions; caption: 图片下边附有~。There is a caption under the picture. ◇ ~书 (a booklet of) directions; (technical) manual; synopsis (of a play or film)/ ~文 expository writing; exposition
【说破】 shuōpò 见"说穿"
【说亲】 shuōqīn act as matchmaker
【说情】 shuōqíng plead for mercy for sb.; intercede for sb.
【说书】 shuōshū storytelling
【说死】 shuōsǐ fix definitely; make it definite: 咱们~了，六点钟见面。Let's make it definite — we'll meet at 6 o'clock.
【说头儿】 shuōtour ① something to talk about: 问题已经解决了，没什么~了。Now that the problem is solved, nothing remains to be said. ② excuse: 你批评他，他总有~。Whenever you criticize him, he always has an excuse.
【说妥】 shuōtuǒ come to an agreement
【说项】 shuōxiàng put in a good word for sb.; intercede for sb.
【说笑】 shuōxiào chatting and laughing: 这时满屋子的人又说又笑，兴高采烈。The room was then full of people chatting animatedly and laughing.
【说一不二】 shuō yī bù èr mean what one says; stand by one's word: 老班长是~的，他答应的事一定能办到。The old squad leader is a man of his word; he never makes a promise he cannot keep.
【说嘴】 shuōzuǐ ① brag; boast: 咱们谁也别~。Let's not have any boasting. ② 〈方〉 argue; quarrel: 好和人~ like to quarrel with people

## shuò

**烁** shuò bright; shining: 闪~ twinkle; glimmer
【烁烁】 shuòshuò glitter; sparkle
**铄** shuò 〈书〉 ① melt (metal, etc.): ~石流金 sweltering ② waste away; weaken
**朔** shuò ① new moon ② the first day of the lunar month ③ north: ~风 north wind
【朔日】 shuòrì the first day of the lunar month
【朔望】 shuò-wàng the first and the fifteenth day of the lunar month; syzygy ◇ ~月 〈天〉 lunar month; lunation; synodic month
【朔月】 shuòyuè new moon
**硕** shuò large
【硕大无朋】 shuòdà wú péng of unparalleled size; gigantic: 整个地球可以想象为一块~的磁石。 The earth may be thought of as a gigantic magnet.
【硕果】 shuòguǒ rich fruits; great achievements
【硕果仅存】 shuòguǒ jǐn cún rare survival
【硕士】 shuòshì Master ◇ ~学位 Master's degree
**数** shuò frequently; repeatedly

另见 shǔ; shù

【数见不鲜】 shuò jiàn bù xiān common occurrence; nothing new

【数脉】 shuòmài 〈中医〉 rapid pulse (of more than 90 beats per minute)

## 蒴 shuò

【蒴果】 shuòguǒ 〈植〉 capsule

## sī

## 司 sī ① take charge of; attend to; manage: 各～其事。Each attends to his own duties. ② department (under a ministry): 外交部礼宾～ the Protocol Department of the Ministry of Foreign Affairs ③ (Sī) a surname

【司泵员】 sībèngyuán pump man; pumper

【司法】 sīfǎ administration of justice; judicature ◇ ～部门 judicial departments; judiciary/ ～机关 judicial organs/ ～鉴定 expert testimony (或 evidence)/ ～权 judicial powers

【司号员】 sīhàoyuán bugler; trumpeter

【司机】 sījī driver: 火车～ engine driver; locomotive engineer

【司空】 Sīkōng a surname

【司空见惯】 sīkōng jiàn guàn a common sight; a common occurrence: 在旧中国，穷人饿死街头是～的事情。People dying of hunger on the streets was a common sight in old China.

【司令】 sīlìng commander; commanding officer ◇ ～部 headquarters; command/ ～员 commander; commanding officer

【司炉】 sīlú stoker; fireman

【司马】 Sīmǎ a surname

【司马昭之心，路人皆知】 Sīmǎ Zhāo zhī xīn, lùrén jiē zhī Sima Zhao's ill intent is known to all — the villain's design is obvious

【司徒】 Sītú a surname

【司务长】 sīwùzhǎng ① mess officer ② company quartermaster

【司线员】 sīxiànyuán 〈体〉 linesman

【司药】 sīyào pharmacist; druggist; chemist

【司仪】 sīyí master of ceremonies

【司钻】 sīzuàn (head) driller: 副～ assistant driller

## 丝 sī ① silk ② a threadlike thing: 蜘蛛～ cobweb/ 铜～ copper wire/ 钨～ tungsten filament/ 肉～ meat cut into slivers; shredded meat/ 一～亮光 a thread of light ③ a tiny bit; trace: 一～不差 not a bit of difference/ 她脸上没有一～笑容。There isn't a trace of a smile on her face./ 一～风也没有。There isn't a breath of air. ④ *si*, a unit of weight (=0.0005 grams)

【丝虫】 sīchóng 〈动〉 filaria ◇ ～病 filariasis

【丝绸】 sīchóu silk cloth; silk ◇ ～之路 〈史〉 the Silk Road

【丝带】 sīdài silk ribbon; silk braid; silk sash

【丝杠】 sīgàng 〈机〉 guide screw; leading screw ◇ ～车床 leading screw lathe

【丝糕】 sīgāo steamed corn cake

【丝瓜】 sīguā towel gourd; dishcloth gourd ◇ ～络 loofah; vegetable sponge

【丝光】 sīguāng the silky lustre of mercerized cotton fabrics ◇ ～机 mercerizing range/ ～纱线 mercerized yarn

【丝毫】 sīháo 〔一般用于否定句〕 the slightest amount or degree; a bit; a particle; a shred; an iota: 我们～也不应当松懈自己的斗志。We must not, in the slightest degree, weaken our will to fight./ 拿不出～证据 cannot provide a shred of evidence/ ～不差 not err by a hair's breadth; tally in every detail; be just right

【丝极】 sījí 〈电〉 filament

【丝绵】 sīmián silk floss; silk wadding

【丝绒】 sīróng velvet; velour

【丝丝入扣】 sī-sī rù kòu (done) with meticulous care and flawless artistry

【丝网】 sīwǎng 〈印〉 silk screen ◇ ～印刷 screen printing/ ～印刷机 screen process press

【丝弦】 sīxián silk string (for a musical instrument)

【丝线】 sīxiàn silk thread (for sewing); silk yarn

【丝织品】 sīzhīpǐn ① silk fabrics ② silk knit goods

【丝竹】 sīzhú ① traditional stringed and woodwind instruments: ～乐 *ensemble* of such instruments ② music

【丝状】 sīzhuàng filiform

【丝锥】 sīzhuī 〈机〉 tap: 粗制～ taper tap/ 中～ second tap/ 精～ bottoming tap

## 私 sī ① personal; private: ～信 personal (或 private) letter ② selfish: 无～ unselfish; selfless ③ secret; private: ～话 confidential talk ④ illicit; illegal: ～设公堂 set up an illegal court; set up a kangaroo court

【私奔】 sībēn elopement

【私弊】 sībì corrupt practices

【私产】 sīchǎn private property

【私娼】 sīchāng unlicensed prostitute

【私仇】 sīchóu personal enmity (或 grudge)

【私德】 sīdé personal morals

【私邸】 sīdǐ 〈旧〉 private residence (of a high-ranking official)

【私法】 sīfǎ 〈法〉 private law

【私房】 sīfang ① private savings: ～钱 private savings of a family member ② confidential: 谈～话 exchange confidences

【私愤】 sīfèn personal spite: 泄～ vent personal spite

【私股】 sīgǔ private share (in a joint state-private enterprise)

【私货】 sīhuò smuggled goods; contraband goods

【私交】 sījiāo personal friendship

【私立】 sīlì 〈旧〉 privately run; private: ～学校 private school

【私利】 sīlì private (或 selfish) interests; personal gain: 图～ pursue private ends/ 不谋～ seek no personal gain

【私囊】 sīnáng private purse: 饱～ line one's pockets; feather one's nest

【私念】 sīniàn selfish motives (或 ideas)

【私情】 sīqíng personal relationships: 不徇～ not swayed by personal considerations

【私人】 sīrén ① private; personal: ～访问 private visit/ ～关系 personal relations ② one's own man: 任用～ fill a post with one's own man; practise nepotism ◇ ～代表 personal representative/ ～经济 private sector of the economy/ ～劳动 〈经〉 individual labour/ ～秘书 private secretary/ ～企业 private enterprise

【私商】 sīshāng businessman; merchant; trader

【私生活】 sīshēnghuó private life

【私生子】 sīshēngzǐ illegitimate child; bastard

【私事】 sīshì private (或 personal) affairs

【私塾】 sīshú old-style private school

【私逃】 sītáo abscond

【私通】 sītōng ① have secret communication with: ～敌人 have secret communication with the enemy ② illicit intercourse; adultery

【私下】 sīxià in private; in secret: ～商议 discuss a matter

in private

【私相授受】 sī xiāng shòu-shòu privately give and privately accept; make an illicit transfer: 不许拿公家的东西～。There must be no illicit transfer of public property.

【私心】 sīxīn selfish motives (或 ideas); selfishness: ～杂念 selfish ideas and personal considerations

【私刑】 sīxíng illegal punishment (meted out by a kangaroo court)

【私蓄】 sīxù private savings

【私营】 sīyíng privately owned; privately operated; private: ～工商业 privately owned industrial and commercial enterprises/ ～企业 private enterprise

【私有】 sīyǒu privately owned; private: 绝不能把公家财产占为～。One should never make public property one's private possession.
◇ ～财产 private property/ ～观念 private ownership mentality/ ～制 private ownership (of means of production)

【私语】 sīyǔ ① whisper: 窃窃～ talk in whispers ② confidence

【私欲】 sīyù selfish desire

【私章】 sīzhāng personal seal; signet

【私自】 sīzì privately; secretly; without permission: 本阅览室参考书不得～携出。No reference books are to be taken out of the reading room without permission.

**咝** sī 〈象〉〔形容炮弹、枪弹等飞过声〕whistle: 子弹～～～地从头顶上飞过。Bullets whistled overhead.

**思** sī ① think; consider; deliberate: 多～ think more/ 前～后想 think over again and again ② think of; long for: ～亲 think of one's parents with affection ③ thought; thinking: 文～ train of thought in writing/ 哀～ mourning

【思潮】 sīcháo ① trend of thought; ideological trend: 无政府主义～ the anarchist trend of thought/ 修正主义是一种国际性的资产阶级～。Revisionism is an international bourgeois ideological trend. ② thoughts: ～起伏 disquieting thoughts surging in one's mind

【思忖】 sīcǔn 〈书〉 ponder; consider

【思考】 sīkǎo think deeply; ponder over; reflect on: ～问题 ponder a problem/ 独立～ think things out for oneself; think independently

【思量】 sīliang consider; turn sth. over in one's mind

【思路】 sīlù train of thought; thinking: 打断～ interrupt one's train of thought/ 她的～很清楚。She thinks very clearly.

【思虑】 sīlǜ consider carefully; contemplate; deliberate

【思慕】 sīmù think of sb. with respect; admire

【思念】 sīniàn think of; long for; miss: ～战友 long for one's comrades-in-arms

【思索】 sīsuǒ think deeply; ponder: 用心～ do some hard thinking/ 周密地～ consider carefully/ 我一夜没睡着，反复～这个问题。I lay awake all night, turning the problem over and over in my mind.

【思维】 sīwéi 〈哲〉 thought; thinking ◇ ～方式 mode of thinking

【思想】 sīxiǎng thought; thinking; idea; ideology: 政治～ political thought/ 军事～ military thinking/ 无产阶级～ proletarian ideology/ 搞通～ straighten out one's thinking/ 同一切不正确的～作不疲倦的斗争 wage a tireless struggle against all incorrect ideas/ ～见面 have a frank exchange of ideas/ 有～准备 be mentally prepared/ ～内容好 have good ideological content/ 解除～顾虑 free one's mind of misgivings/ ～跟不上 lag behind in one's understanding
◇ ～包袱 sth. weighing on one's mind/ ～动向 ideological trend/ ～斗争 ideological struggle; mental struggle (或 conflict)/ ～方法 method (或 mode, way) of thinking/ ～改造 ideological remoulding/ ～革命化 revolutionization of one's ideology/ ～工作 ideological work/ ～家 thinker/ ～检查 check on one's thinking/ ～教育 ideological education/ ～境界 ideological level/ ～觉悟 political consciousness (或 awareness)/ ～体系 ideological system; ideology/ ～问题 problem arising from erroneous thinking; ideological problem/ ～性 ideological content (或 level)/ ～意识 ideology

【思绪】 sīxù ① train of thought; thinking: ～纷乱 a confused state of mind; a confused train of thought ② feeling: ～不宁 feel perturbed

**鸶** sī 见"鹭鸶" lùsī

**蛳** sī 见"螺蛳" luósī

**斯** sī ①〈书〉 this: ～时 at this moment/ ～人 this person/ 生于～，长于～ be born and brought up here ②〈书〉 then; thus ③ (Sī) a surname

【斯堪的纳维亚半岛】 Sīkāndìnàwéiyà Bàndǎo the Scandinavian Peninsula

【斯拉夫人】 Sīlāfūrén Slav

【斯里兰卡】 Sīlǐlánkǎ Sri Lanka ◇ ～人 Sri Lankan

【斯瓦希里语】 Sīwǎxīlǐyǔ Swahili (language)

【斯威士兰】 Sīwēishìlán Swaziland ◇ ～人 Swazi

【斯文】 sīwén refined; gentle: 他说话挺～的。He's a soft-spoken person.

**锶** sī 〈化〉 strontium (Sr)

**澌** sī ice floating on a river during the spring thaw

**厮** sī 〔多见于早期白话〕① male servant: 小～ page boy; page ② fellow; guy: 那～ that guy ③ with each other; together: ～混 fool (或 play) around together

【厮打】 sīdǎ come to blows; exchange blows; tussle

【厮杀】 sīshā fight at close quarters (with weapons)

**凘** sī

【凘灭】 sīmiè totally disappear

**撕** sī tear; rip: 把信～开 rip open a letter/ ～得粉碎 tear to shreds/ 从日历上～下一页 tear a page from the calendar/ ～下假面具 tear off the mask; unmask/ 上衣～了。The jacket is torn.

【撕毁】 sīhuǐ tear up; tear to shreds: ～协定 tear up an agreement; tear an agreement to shreds

**嘶** sī 〈书〉 ① neigh: 人喊马～ men shouting and horses neighing ② hoarse: 声～力竭 hoarse and exhausted

【嘶哑】 sīyǎ hoarse: 他讲话过多，嗓子都～了。He has talked himself hoarse.

## sǐ

**死** sǐ ① die: ～人 a dead person; the dead/ 打～ beat to death/ ～一般的寂静 a deathly stillness ② to the death: ～战 fight to the death ③ extremely; to death: 高兴～了 be extremely happy/ 累～了 be tired to death; be dog-tired/ 渴得要～ be parched with thirst; be dying for a drink/ 甜～了 much too sweet/ ～咸 terribly salty/ 我差点没笑～。I just about died laughing. ④ implacable; deadly: ～对头 sworn enemy ⑤ fixed; rigid; inflexible: ～规矩 a rigid rule/ ～教条 lifeless dogma/ 窗子钉～了。The window has been nailed fast. ⑥ impassable; closed: 把漏洞堵～ plug the holes; stop up loopholes

【死板】 sǐbǎn rigid; inflexible; stiff: 办事～ work in a mechanical way/ ～的公式 stereotyped formula

【死不】 sǐbù would rather die than; stubbornly refuse to: ～认错 stubbornly refuse to admit one's mistake/ ～放手 cling (或 hold on, hang on) to sth. like grim death/ ～改悔(回头) absolutely unrepentant; incorrigible/ ～要脸 be dead to all feelings of shame; be utterly shameless

【死不瞑目】 sǐ bù míngmù not close one's eyes when one dies — die with a grievance or everlasting regret

【死产】 sǐchǎn 〈医〉 stillbirth

【死党】 sǐdǎng sworn followers; diehard followers

【死得其所】 sǐ dé qí suǒ die a worthy death: 我们为人民而死，就是～。When we die for the people it is a worthy death.

【死敌】 sǐdí deadly enemy; mortal enemy; implacable foe

【死地】 sǐdì a fatal position; deathtrap: 置之～而后生 confront a person with the danger of death and he will fight to live/ 必欲置之～而后快 (hate sb. so much that one) cannot be happy with anything less than his death

【死读书】 sǐ dúshū study mechanically; be a bookworm

【死而后已】 sǐ érhòu yǐ until one's dying day; to the end of one's days: 他真是鞠躬尽瘁，～。Of him it can be said that he gave his best, gave his all, till his heart ceased to beat.

【死光】 sǐguāng death ray

【死鬼】 sǐguǐ 〔多用于骂人或开玩笑〕 devil: 你这个～，刚才跑到哪儿去了？You devil! Where have you been all this while?

【死海】 Sǐhǎi the Dead Sea

【死胡同】 sǐhútòng blind alley; dead end

【死缓】 sǐhuǎn 〈法〉 short for death sentence with a two-year reprieve and forced labour; stay of execution

【死灰复燃】 sǐhuī fù rán dying embers glowing again — resurgence; revival

【死活】 sǐhuó ① life or death; fate: 资本家只管赚钱，不顾工人～。The capitalist, bent upon profits, didn't care whether the workers lived or died. ② 〈口〉 anyway; simply: 他～不让我走。I wanted to go, but he simply wouldn't hear of it.

【死火山】 sǐhuǒshān extinct volcano

【死记硬背】 sǐjì-yìngbèi mechanical memorizing

【死寂】 sǐjì 〈书〉 deathly stillness: 夜深了，山谷里一片～。As night wore on, a deathly silence filled the valley.

【死角】 sǐjiǎo ① 〈军〉 dead angle; blind angle; dead space ② a spot as yet untouched by a political movement, etc.

【死结】 sǐjié fast knot

【死劲儿】 sǐjìnr 〈口〉 ① all one's strength; all one's might: 大家用～推，才把车子推出泥坑。Using all their strength, they pushed the cart out of the mud. ② with all one's strength (或 might); with might and main; for all one's worth: ～跑 run for all one's worth/ ～盯住他 watch him closely

【死扣儿】 sǐkòur 〈口〉 fast knot

【死里逃生】 sǐlǐ táoshēng escape by the skin of one's teeth; have a narrow escape; barely escape with one's life

【死力】 sǐlì ① all one's strength: 出～ exert one's utmost effort ② with all one's strength: ～抵抗 resist with might and main; fight tooth and nail

【死路】 sǐlù ① blind alley ② the road to ruin (或 destruction)

【死马当作活马医】 sǐmǎ dàngzuò huómǎ yī doctor a dead horse as if it were still alive — not give up for lost; make every possible effort

【死面】 sǐmiàn unleavened dough

【死命】 sǐmìng ① doom; death: 制敌于～ send the enemy to his doom ② desperately: ～挣扎 struggle desperately

【死难】 sǐnàn die in an accident or a political incident (esp. for a revolutionary cause): ～烈士 martyr

【死脑筋】 sǐnǎojīn one-track mind

【死皮赖脸】 sǐpí-làiliǎn thick-skinned and hard to shake off; brazen-faced and unreasonable

【死棋】 sǐqí a dead piece in a game of chess — a hopeless case; a stupid move

【死气沉沉】 sǐqì chénchén lifeless; spiritless; stagnant: 哪里不发动群众，哪里的工作就～。Where the masses are not roused, work will stagnate.

【死气白赖】 sǐqibáilài 〈方〉 pester people endlessly

【死契】 sǐqì irrevocable title deed

【死囚】 sǐqiú a convict sentenced to death; a convict awaiting execution

【死球】 sǐqiú 〈体〉 dead ball

【死去活来】 sǐqù-huólái half dead; half alive; hovering between life and death: 被打得～ be beaten half dead; be brutally beaten/ 哭得～ weep one's heart out

【死尸】 sǐshī corpse; dead body

【死守】 sǐshǒu ① defend to the death; defend to the last; make a last-ditch defence: ～阵地 defend the position to the last ② obstinately cling to; rigidly adhere to

【死水】 sǐshuǐ stagnant water

【死胎】 sǐtāi 〈医〉 stillborn foetus; stillbirth

【死土】 sǐtǔ 〈农〉 dead soil

【死亡】 sǐwáng death; doom: 挣扎在～线上 struggle for existence on the verge of death; struggle to stave off starvation/ 把病人从～边缘抢救过来 snatch the patient from the jaws of death/ 殖民主义正走向～。Colonialism is heading for its doom. ◇ ～率 death rate; mortality

【死无对证】 sǐ wú duìzhèng the dead cannot bear witness

【死心】 sǐxīn drop the idea forever; have no more illusions about the matter: 你还是死了这条心吧。You'd better give up the idea altogether.

【死心塌地】 sǐxīntādì be dead set; be hell-bent: ～跟反党集团走的只是一小撮。Only a handful of people were dead set on following the anti-Party clique./ ～的反革命分子 a die-hard (或 dyed-in-the-wool) counterrevolutionary

【死心眼儿】 sǐxīnyǎnr ① stubborn; as obstinate as a mule ② a person with a one-track mind

【死信】 sǐxìn ① dead letter ② news of sb.'s death

【死刑】 sǐxíng 〈法〉 death penalty; death sentence; capital punishment

【死讯】 sǐxùn news of sb.'s death

【死硬】 sǐyìng ① stiff; inflexible ② very obstinate; die-hard ◇ ～派 diehards

【死有余辜】 sǐ yǒu yú gū even death would be too good for him; even death would not expiate all his crimes

【死于非命】 sǐ yú fēimìng die an unnatural (或 a violent) death

【死者】 sǐzhě the dead; the deceased; the departed

【死罪】 sǐzuì capital offence (或 crime)

## sì

**巳** sì the sixth of the twelve Earthly Branches

【巳时】 sìshí the period of the day from 9 a.m to 11 a.m.

**四** sì ① four ② 〈乐〉 a note of the scale in *gongchepu* (工尺谱), corresponding to 6̣ in numbered musical notation

【四倍体】 sìbèitǐ 〈生〉 tetraploid
【四边】 sìbiān (on) four sides: ～儿围着篱笆 with a fence running all round
【四边形】 sìbiānxíng quadrilateral
【四不象】 sìbùxiàng ①〈动〉 David's deer; mi-lu ② nondescript; neither fish nor fowl
【四重唱】 sìchóngchàng 〈乐〉 (vocal) quartet
【四重奏】 sìchóngzòu 〈乐〉 (instrumental) quartet: 弦乐～ string quartet
【四处】 sìchù all around; in all directions; everywhere: ～逃窜 flee in all directions/ ～奔走 go hither and thither/ ～寻找 search high and low; look into every hole and corner
【四川】 Sìchuān Sichuan (Province)
【四大】 sìdà 〈简〉(大鸣、大放、大辩论、大字报) speaking out freely, airing views fully, holding great debates and writing big-character posters
【四叠体】 sìdiétǐ 〈生理〉 corpora quadrigemina
【四方】 sìfāng ① the four directions (north, south, east, west); all sides; all quarters: ～响应。Response came from every quarter. ② square; cubic: 一个～的盒子 a square box/ 一块四四方方的木头 a wooden cube
【四分五裂】 sìfēn-wǔliè fall apart; be rent by disunity; be all split up; disintegrate: 敌人内部～。The ranks of the enemy are all split up (或 disintegrating).
【四分音符】 sìfēn yīnfú 〈乐〉 crotchet, quarter note
【四国】 Sìguó Shikoku
【四海】 sìhǎi the four seas; the whole country; the whole world: 马克思列宁主义是放之～而皆准的。Marxism-Leninism is universally applicable./ ～为家 make one's home wherever one is
【四害】 sìhài the four pests (rats, bedbugs, flies and mosquitoes)
【四合院】 sìhéyuàn *siheyuan*, a compound with houses around a courtyard; quadrangle
【四环素】 sìhuánsù 〈药〉 tetracycline
【四级风】 sìjífēng 〈气〉 force 4 wind; moderate breeze
【四极管】 sìjíguǎn 〈无〉 tetrode
【四季】 sìjì the four seasons: 昆明～如春。In Kunming it's like spring all the year round.
【四季豆】 sìjìdòu kidney bean
【四郊】 sìjiāo suburbs; outskirts
【四脚蛇】 sìjiǎoshé lizard
【四旧】 sìjiù the "four olds" (old ideas, old culture, old customs and old habits)
【四开】 sìkāi 〈印〉 quarto ◇ ～本 quarto
【四类分子】 sìlèifènzǐ ① the four kinds of elements (landlords, rich peasants, counterrevolutionaries and bad elements) ② a person belonging to one of the above categories
【四邻】 sìlín one's near neighbours
【四六风】 sìliùfēng 〈医〉 umbilical tetanus of newborn babies
【四面】 sìmiàn (on) four sides; (on) all sides: ～受敌 be exposed to enemy attacks on all sides/ ～出击 hit out in all directions/ ～包围敌人 completely encircle the enemy forces
【四面八方】 sìmiàn-bāfāng all directions; all quarters; all around; far and near: 治河大军从～奔向工地。Hosts of river control workers rushed to the site from all directions.
【四面楚歌】 sìmiàn Chǔ gē be besieged on all sides; be utterly isolated
【四旁】 sìpáng ① back and front, left and right; all around ② the "four sides" (house side, village side, roadside and waterside) ◇ ～绿化 turning the "four sides" green (as part of an afforestation campaign)
【四平八稳】 sìpíng-bāwěn ① very steady; well organized: 办事～ be dependable in work/ 文章写得～。The essay is well argued. ② lacking in initiative and overcautious
【四起】 sìqǐ rise from all directions: 歌声～。Sounds of singing were heard from all around.
【四清运动】 Sìqīng Yùndòng the "four clean-ups" movement 参见"社会主义教育运动" Shèhuìzhǔyì Jiàoyù Yùndòng
【四散】 sìsàn scatter (或 disperse) in all directions
【四舍五入】 sìshě-wǔrù 〈数〉 rounding (off); to the nearest whole number
【四声】 sìshēng 〈语〉 ① the four tones of classical Chinese phonetics ② the four tones of modern standard Chinese pronunciation
【四时】 sìshí the four seasons
【四书】 sìshū The Four Books, namely, *The Great Learning* (《大学》), *The Doctrine of the Mean* (《中庸》), *The Analects of Confucius* (《论语》) and *Mencius* (《孟子》)
【四体不勤,五谷不分】 sìtǐ bù qín, wǔgǔ bù fēn can neither use one's four limbs nor tell the five grains apart (said of old-style intellectuals)
【四通八达】 sìtōng-bādá extend in all directions: 公路～。Highways radiate in all directions./ 全省交通运输～。Transport and communication lines link up all parts of the province.
【四围】 sìwéi all around: 这村子～都是菜地。All around the village are vegetable fields.
【四下里】 sìxiàli all around: ～都是伏兵。All around were troops lying in ambush./ ～一看,都是果树。Looking around, one can see a vast stretch of fruit trees.
【四新】 sìxīn the "four news" (new ideas, new culture, new customs and new habits): 破四旧,立～ do away with the "four olds" and cultivate the "four news"
【四言诗】 sìyánshī a type of classical poem with four characters to a line, popular before the Han Dynasty (206 B.C.-A.D. 220)
【四野】 sìyě the surrounding country; a vast expanse of open ground: ～茫茫,寂静无声。All is quiet on the vast expanse of open ground.
【四月】 sìyuè ① April ② the fourth month of the lunar year; the fourth moon
【四则】 sìzé 〈数〉 the four fundamental operations of arithmetic (addition, subtraction, multiplication and division)
【四诊】 sìzhěn 〈中医〉 the four methods of diagnosis (望 observation, 闻 auscultation and olfaction, 问 interrogation and 切 pulse feeling and palpation)
【四肢】 sìzhī the four limbs; arms and legs
【四至】 sìzhì the four boundaries of a piece of land or a construction site
【四周】 sìzhōu all around
【四足动物】 sìzú dòngwù quadruped; tetrapod

**寺** sì temple: 清真～ mosque
【寺院】 sìyuàn temple; monastery

**似** sì ① similar; like: 这两本书内容相～。These two books are similar in content./ 骄阳～火。The sun was scorching hot. ② seem; appear: ～曾相识 seem to have met before ③〔表示超过〕: 日子一年胜～一年。Life has been getting better year by year.
另见 shì
【似…非…】 sì...fēi... 〔嵌用同一个单音词,表示又像又不像的意思〕: 似懂非懂 have only a hazy notion; not quite understand/ 她似笑非笑。There's a faint smile on her face./ 这东西似绸非绸,不知是什么料子。This looks like silk but it isn't — I don't know what it is.

【似乎】 sìhu it seems; as if; seemingly: 他的意思～另有所指。It seems he was referring to something else./ ～明天要起风。It looks as if it'll be windy tomorrow.
【似是而非】 sì shì ér fēi apparently right but actually wrong; specious: ～的说法 a specious argument

**祀** sì 〈书〉 offer sacrifices to the gods or the spirits of the dead

**伺** sì watch; await
另见 cì
【伺服】 sìfú 〈电〉 servo
◇ ～传动 servo drive/ ～放大器 servo amplifier/ ～控制机构 servo-control mechanism
【伺机】 sìjī watch for one's chance: ～反扑 wait for an opportunity to stage a comeback/ ～而动 wait for the opportune moment to go into action

**饲** sì raise; rear
【饲槽】 sìcáo feeding trough
【饲草】 sìcǎo forage grass
【饲料】 sìliào forage; fodder; feed: 猪～ pig feed
◇ ～粉碎机 feed (或 fodder) grinder/ ～加工厂 feed-processing plant/ ～作物 forage (或 fodder, feed) crop
【饲养】 sìyǎng raise; rear: ～家禽 raise (或 rear) poultry/ ～牲畜 raise livestock ◇ ～场 feed lot; dry lot; farm/ ～员 stockman; poultry raiser; animal keeper (in a zoo)

**驷** sì
【驷马】 sìmǎ 〈书〉 a team of four horses: 一言既出，～难追。Even four horses cannot take back what one has said — what has been said cannot be unsaid.

**食** sì 〈书〉 bring food to; feed
另见 shí

**俟** sì 〈书〉 wait: ～机进攻 wait for an opportunity to attack/ 一～准备就绪，即行公开展出。The exhibition will be opened as soon as everything is in order.
另见 qí

**笥** sì bamboo-plaited basket or suitcase

**耜** sì a spade-shaped farm tool used in ancient China

**嗣** sì ① succeed; inherit: ～位 succeed to the throne ② heir; descendant: 后～ descendants
【嗣后】 sìhòu 〈书〉 hereafter; subsequently; afterwards; later on

**肆** sì ① wanton; unbridled: 大～攻击 wantonly vilify; launch an unbridled attack against ② four (used for the numeral 四 on cheques, etc. to avoid mistakes or alterations) ③ 〈书〉 shop: 茶楼酒～ teahouses and wineshops
【肆虐】 sìnüè indulge in wanton massacre or persecution; wreak havoc
【肆无忌惮】 sì wú jìdàn unbridled; brazen; unscrupulous: ～地攻击 make unbridled attacks
【肆意】 sìyì wantonly; recklessly; wilfully: ～歪曲事实 wantonly distort the facts/ ～践踏别国主权 wilfully trample upon other countries' sovereignty/ ～侮辱 resort to wanton insults

## si

**厕** si 见"茅厕" máosi
另见 cè

## sōng

**忪** sōng 见"惺忪" xīngsōng

**松** sōng ① pine ② loose; slack: 这里的土质很～。The soil here is very loose./ 套～了。The harness has come loose./ 绳子太～了。The rope is too slack./ 把绳子再放～点儿。Give the rope more play. ③ loosen; relax; slacken: ～～螺丝 loosen the screw a little bit/ 现在我们可以～一口气了。Now we can have a breathing spell. ④ not hard up: 现在手头～些 be better off ⑤ light and flaky; soft: 这点心～脆可口。The pastry is light and crisp./ 这种木料～，做家具不合适。The wood is too soft for making furniture. ⑥ dried meat floss; dried minced meat: 猪肉～ dried minced pork ⑦ (Sōng) a surname
【松绑】 sōngbǎng untie a person
【松弛】 sōngchí ① limp; flabby; slack: 肌肉～ flaccid muscles/ ～一下肌肉 relax the muscles ② lax: 纪律～ lax discipline
【松貂】 sōngdiāo pine marten
【松动】 sōngdong ① become less crowded ② not hard up ③ become flexible: 他的口气有点～。He has become a bit more flexible.
【松果体】 sōngguǒtǐ 〈生理〉 pineal body
【松花】 sōnghuā preserved egg
【松花江】 Sōnghuājiāng the Songhua River
【松鸡】 sōngjī capercaillie; grouse
【松焦油】 sōngjiāoyóu 〈化〉 pine tar
【松节油】 sōngjiéyóu 〈化〉 turpentine (oil)
【松紧】 sōngjǐn ① degree of tightness ② elasticity ◇ ～带 elastic cord; elastic
【松劲】 sōngjìn relax one's efforts; slacken (off): ～情绪 slack mood
【松口】 sōngkǒu ① relax one's bite and release what is held ② be less intransigent; soften; relent: 最后大夫～了，同意她出院。Finally the doctor relented and allowed her to leave the hospital.
【松快】 sōngkuai ① less crowded: 搬走一张桌子，屋里～多了。With a desk moved out, there's much more space in the room. ② relieved: 吃了药以后身上～多了。I feel much better after taking the medicine. ③ relax: 干了一天活，～～吧。After the day's work, let's relax a bit.
【松毛虫】 sōngmáochóng pine moth
【松明】 sōngmíng pine torches
【松气】 sōngqì relax one's efforts: 在节骨眼上决不能～。At this critical juncture we must not relax our efforts.
【松软】 sōngruǎn soft; spongy; loose: ～的表土 spongy topsoil
【松散】 sōngsǎn ① loose: 文章结构～。The article is loosely organized./ 掺点沙子使土质～一些。Add sand to make the soil more porous. ② inattentive
【松散】 sōngsan relax; take one's ease: 屋里太闷热，出去～～吧。It's too hot and stuffy in here. Let's go out for a breath of air.
【松手】 sōngshǒu loosen one's grip; let go
【松鼠】 sōngshǔ squirrel
【松树】 sōngshù pine tree; pine

【松松垮垮】 sōngsōngkuǎkuǎ behave in a lax, undisciplined way; be slack and perfunctory
【松塔】 sōngtǎ ①〈方〉 pinecone ②〈中药〉 the cone of lacebark pine
【松涛】 sōngtāo the soughing of the wind in the pines
【松土】 sōngtǔ 〈农〉 loosen the soil; scarify the soil ◇ ～机 loosener; scarifier
【松香】 sōngxiāng rosin; colophony ◇ ～油 retinol; rosin oil
【松懈】 sōngxiè relax; slacken; slack: ～斗志 relax one's will to fight/ 工作～ be slack in one's work
【松蕈】 sōngxùn pine mushroom
【松鸦】 sōngyā jay
【松烟墨】 sōngyānmò Chinese ink made from pine soot; pine-soot ink
【松针】 sōngzhēn pine needle
【松脂】 sōngzhī rosin; pine resin
【松子】 sōngzǐ pine nut

**凇** sōng 见"雾凇" wùsōng

**嵩** sōng (of mountains) high; lofty

## sǒng

**怂** sǒng
【怂恿】 sǒngyǒng instigate; incite; egg sb. on; abet

**悚** sǒng
【悚然】 sǒngrán terrified; horrified: 毛骨～ with one's hair standing on end

**耸** sǒng ① towering; lofty ② alarm; shock: 危言～听 exaggerate things just to frighten people
【耸动】 sǒngdòng ① shrug (one's shoulders) ② create a sensation: ～视听 create a sensation
【耸肩】 sǒngjiān shrug one's shoulders
【耸立】 sǒnglì tower aloft: 人民英雄纪念碑～在天安门广场上。The Monument to the People's Heroes towers aloft on Tian'anmen Square.
【耸人听闻】 sǒng rén tīngwén deliberately exaggerate so as to create a sensation: ～的谣言 a sensational rumour/ 这不是～,而是铁的事实。This is not alarmist talk, but a hard fact.
【耸入云霄】 sǒng rù yúnxiāo tower to the skies: ～的高山 a high mountain towering to the skies

## sòng

**讼** sòng ① bring a case to court ② dispute; argue
【讼棍】 sònggùn legal pettifogger; shyster
【讼事】 sòngshì lawsuit; litigation

**宋** Sòng ① the Song Dynasty (960-1279) ② the Song Dynasty (420-479), one of the Southern Dynasties ③ a surname
【宋体字】 sòngtǐzì Song typeface, a standard typeface first used in the Ming Dynasty (1368-1644) but popularly attributed to the Song Dynasty (960-1279)

**送** sòng ① deliver; carry: ～信 deliver a letter/ ～粪 carry manure to the fields/ ～公粮 deliver public grain/ ～医～药上门 deliver medical care right to the patient's home/ 十月革命一声炮响,给我们～来了马克思列宁主义。The salvoes of the October Revolution brought us Marxism-Leninism. ② give as a present; give: 姐姐～我一本书。My sister gave me a book. ③ see sb. off or out; accompany; escort: ～她回家 see her home/ 到车站～人 see sb. off at the station/ 把客人～到门口 see a guest to the door; walk a guest to the gate/ 我～你一段路。Let me walk with you part of the way./ ～孩子上学 take a child to school
【送别】 sòngbié 见"送行"
【送殡】 sòngbìn attend a funeral; take part in a funeral procession
【送风机】 sòngfēngjī 〈机〉 forced draught blower; blower
【送话器】 sònghuàqì 〈电〉 microphone
【送还】 sònghuán give back; return
【送货】 sònghuò deliver goods: ～上门 deliver goods to the door-step of a customer
【送交】 sòngjiāo deliver; hand over: 请把这封信～党委书记。Please take this letter to the Party Committee secretary./ 把犯罪分子～人民法院审判 hand the criminal over to the people's court for trial
【送旧迎新】 sòngjiù-yíngxīn see off the old and welcome the new; ring out the Old Year and ring in the New
【送客】 sòngkè see a visitor out
【送礼】 sònglǐ give sb. a present; present a gift to sb.: 请客～ give dinners or send gifts (in order to curry favour)
【送命】 sòngmìng lose one's life; get killed; go to one's doom
【送气】 sòngqì 〈语〉 aspirated ◇ ～音 aspirated sound
【送人情】 sòng rénqíng ① do favours at no great cost to oneself ② 〈方〉 make a gift of sth.
【送丧】 sòngsāng attend a funeral; take part in a funeral procession
【送死】 sòngsǐ 〈口〉 court death
【送往迎来】 sòngwǎng-yínglái see off those who depart and welcome those who arrive; speed the parting guests and welcome the new arrivals: 负责～事宜 be in charge of arrangements for receiving and seeing off guests
【送信儿】 sòngxìnr 〈口〉 send word; go and tell: 我已经给他～,让他马上来见你。I have sent him word to come and see you at once./ 你哥从东北回来了,去给你妈送个信儿。Go and tell your mother that your brother has come back from the Northeast.
【送行】 sòngxíng ① see sb. off; wish sb. bon voyage ② give a send-off party
【送葬】 sòngzàng take part in a funeral procession
【送终】 sòngzhōng attend upon a dying parent or other senior member of one's family; bury a parent

**诵** sòng ① read aloud; chant ② recite
【诵读】 sòngdú read aloud; chant

**颂** sòng ① praise; extol; eulogize; laud: 歌～ sing the praises of ② song; ode; paean; eulogy: 《延安～》 *Ode to Yan'an* ③ a section in *The Book of Songs* (《诗经》) consisting of sacrificial songs
【颂词】 sòngcí ① complimentary address; panegyric; eulogy ② a speech delivered by an ambassador on presentation of his credentials
【颂歌】 sònggē song; ode
【颂扬】 sòngyáng sing sb.'s praises; laud; extol; eulogize

## sōu

**溲** sōu 〈书〉 urinate

【溲血】 sōuxiě 〈中医〉 haematuria

搜 sōu search

【搜捕】 sōubǔ track down and arrest

【搜查】 sōuchá search; ransack; rummage ◇ ～证 search warrant

【搜刮】 sōuguā extort; plunder; expropriate; fleece: 反动统治阶级～人民大量钱财。The reactionary ruling class extorted large sums of money from the people.

【搜集】 sōují collect; gather: ～标本 collect specimens/ ～情报 gather information/ ～群众意见 solicit opinions from the masses

【搜罗】 sōuluó collect; gather; recruit: ～大量史料 collect a large amount of historical data/ ～人才 recruit qualified persons; scout for talent

【搜求】 sōuqiú seek

【搜身】 sōushēn search the person; make a body search

【搜索】 sōusuǒ search for; hunt for; scout around: ～失踪船只 search for missing boats/ 在山上～空投特务 comb the hills for air-dropped agents/ ～前进 advance and reconnoitre ◇ ～飞行 scouting flight

【搜索枯肠】 sōusuǒ kūcháng rack one's brains (for fresh ideas or apt expressions)

【搜寻】 sōuxún search for; look for; seek

【搜腰包】 sōu yāobāo search sb.'s pockets; search sb. for money and valuables

嗖 sōu 〈象〉 whiz: 汽车～的一声从他身边开过。The car whizzed by him.

馊 sōu sour; spoiled: 饭菜～了。The food has spoiled. 或 The food smells a bit off./ ～主意 rotten idea; lousy idea

飕 sōu 〈方〉 (of wind) make sth. dry or cool: 洗的衣服～干了。The washing has dried in the wind.

艘 sōu 〈量〉〔用于船只〕: 两～油船 two tankers

螋 sōu 见"蠼螋" qúsōu

## sǒu

叟 sǒu old man

嗾 sǒu

【嗾使】 sǒushǐ instigate; abet

薮 sǒu 〈书〉 ① a shallow lake overgrown with wild plants ② a gathering place of fish or beasts; den; haunt

擞 sǒu 见"抖擞" dǒusǒu

## sòu

嗽 sòu cough

## sū

苏 sū ① revive; come to: 死而复～ come back to life ② (Sū) short for Suzhou ③ (Sū) short for Jiangsu Province: ～南 southern Jiangsu ④ (Sū) 〈简〉(苏维埃) Soviet: ～区 (Chinese) Soviet Area (established during the Second Revolutionary Civil War period, 1927-1937) ⑤ (Sū) a surname

【苏白】 sūbái Suzhou dialect

【苏必利尔湖】 Sūbìlì'ěrhú Lake Superior

【苏打】 sūdá soda ◇ ～饼干 soda biscuit; soda cracker

【苏丹】 sūdān ① sultan ② (Sūdān) the Sudan ◇ ～人 Sudanese

【苏里南】 Sūlǐnán Surinam ◇ ～人 Surinamese

【苏联】 Sūlián the Soviet Union ◇ ～人 Soviet citizen

【苏门答腊】 Sūméndálà Sumatra

【苏门羚】 sūménlíng 〈动〉 serow

【苏维埃】 sūwéi'āi Soviet

【苏醒】 sūxǐng revive; regain consciousness; come to; come round: 他昏迷了一个多小时才～过来。He remained unconscious for more than an hour before he came to.

【苏绣】 sūxiù Suzhou embroidery

【苏伊士运河】 Sūyīshì Yùnhé the Suez Canal

【苏州码子】 Sūzhōu mǎzi Suzhou numerals, traditionally used by shopkeepers to mark prices

【苏子】 sūzǐ perillaseed

酥 sū ① crisp; short: ～糖 crunchy candy/ 香～鸡 savoury and crisp chicken ② shortbread: 杏仁～ almond shortbread ③ (of a person's limbs) limp; weak; soft

【酥脆】 sūcuì crisp: ～的饼干 crisp (或 short) biscuit

【酥麻】 sūmá limp and numb: 两腿～ one's legs feel weak and numb

【酥软】 sūruǎn limp; weak; soft

【酥油】 sūyóu butter ◇ ～茶 buttered tea

窣 sū 见"窸窣" xīsū

稣 sū revive; come to

## sú

俗 sú ① custom; convention: 移风易～ break with old customs; bring about a change in morals and mores ② popular; common: ～话 common saying/ 通～ popular (language, style, etc.) ③ vulgar: ～不可耐 unbearably vulgar ④ secular; lay: 僧～ monks and laymen; clergy and laity

【俗话】 súhuà common saying; proverb: ～说 as the saying goes

【俗名】 súmíng popular name; local name

【俗气】 súqi vulgar; in poor taste

【俗套】 sútào conventional pattern; convention: 不落～ conform to no conventional pattern

【俗语】 súyǔ common saying; folk adage

## sù

夙 sù 〈书〉 ① early in the morning ② long-standing; old: ～志 long-cherished ambition

【夙兴夜寐】 sùxīng-yèmèi rise early and retire late — hard at work night and day

【夙愿】 sùyuàn long-cherished wish

诉 sù ① tell; relate; inform: 告～ tell ② complain; accuse: 控～ accuse/ 倾～ pour out (one's feelings, troubles, etc.); unbosom oneself of; unburden oneself of ③ appeal to; resort to: 上～ appeal to a higher court/ ～诸武力 resort to force; appeal to arms

【诉苦】 sùkǔ vent one's grievances; pour out one's woes ◇ ～会 a meeting for pouring out grievances (against the old society and the reactionaries)

【诉说】 sùshuō tell; relate; recount: ～苦难家史 relate the family's sufferings in the old society/ ～苦衷 recount one's worries and difficulties; tell one's troubles

【诉讼】 sùsòng 〈法〉 lawsuit; litigation: 民刑～ civil and criminal lawsuits/ 对某人提出～ take (或 start) legal proceedings against sb./ 撤消～ withdraw an accusation; drop a lawsuit/ 提出离婚～ take (或 start) divorce proceedings
◇ ～代理人 agent *ad litem*; legal representative/ ～法 procedural law/ ～条例 rules of procedure

【诉状】 sùzhuàng 〈法〉 plaint; indictment: 向法院提出～ file a plaint at court

**肃** sù ① respectful ② solemn: 严～ solemn; serious; grave

【肃反】 sùfǎn 〈简〉(肃清反革命分子) elimination of counterrevolutionaries

【肃静】 sùjìng solemn silence: 全场～无声。A solemn silence reigned.

【肃立】 sùlì stand as a mark of respect: 奏国歌时全场～。All stood as the band struck up the national anthem. 或 Everyone stood when the national anthem was played./ ～默哀 stand in silent mourning

【肃穆】 sùmù solemn and respectful

【肃清】 sùqīng eliminate; clean up; mop up: ～反革命分子 root out (或 eliminate) counterrevolutionaries/ ～修正主义路线的流毒 eliminate the pernicious influence of the revisionist line/ ～敌军残部 mop up the remnants of the enemy

【肃然起敬】 sùrán qǐ jìng be filled with deep veneration: 使我～ call forth in me a feeling of profound respect

**素** sù ① white: ～服 white clothing (as a sign of mourning) ② plain; simple; quiet: ～色 plain colour ③ vegetable: 吃～ be a vegetarian/ 三荤一～ three meat dishes and one vegetable dish ④ native: ～性 one's disposition; one's temperament ⑤ basic element; element: 色～ pigment/ 毒～ poison/ 维生～ vitamin ⑥ usually; habitually; always: 我与他～不相识。I don't know him at all. 或 He's a perfect stranger to me.

【素材】 sùcái source material (of literature and art); material: 搜集小说～ gather material for a novel

【素菜】 sùcài vegetable dish

【素餐】 sùcān ① vegetarian meal ② be a vegetarian ③〈书〉 not work for one's living: 尸位～ hold down a job without doing a stroke of work

【素常】 sùcháng usually; habitually; ordinarily: ～他到十二点钟才睡觉。Ordinarily he doesn't go to bed until twelve o'clock at night.

【素淡】 sùdàn quiet (colour)

【素混凝土】 sùhùnníngtǔ plain concrete

【素净】 sùjing plain and neat; quiet (colour): 一套～的蓝衣服 a plain blue suit/ 花色～ a pattern in quiet colours

【素酒】 sùjiǔ ① wine served at a vegetarian feast ②〈方〉 vegetarian feast

【素来】 sùlái always; usually: 他～是严格遵守纪律的。He always strictly observes discipline.

【素昧平生】 sù mèi píngshēng have never met before: 一个～的人 a complete stranger/ 我同他～。I have never had the honour of making his acquaintance. 或 I know nothing about him.

【素描】 sùmiáo ① sketch ② literary sketch

【素朴】 sùpǔ simple and unadorned

【素日】 sùrì generally; usually: 他～不爱说话。He is usually very quiet.

【素食】 sùshí ① vegetarian diet ② be a vegetarian ◇ ～者 vegetarian

【素数】 sùshù 〈数〉 prime number

【素席】 sùxí vegetarian feast

【素馨】 sùxīn 〈植〉 jasmine

【素雅】 sùyǎ simple but elegant; unadorned and in good taste: 衣着～ be tastefully dressed in a simple style

【素养】 sùyǎng accomplishment; attainment: 艺术～ artistic accomplishment

【素因子】 sùyīnzǐ 〈数〉 prime factor

【素油】 sùyóu vegetable oil

【素质】 sùzhì ① quality: 提高部队的军政～ enhance the military and political quality of the troops ②〈心〉 diathesis

**速** sù ① fast; rapid; quick; speedy: 收效甚～ produce quick results; have a speedy effect ② speed; velocity: 音～ velocity of sound ③〈书〉 invite: 不～之客 uninvited guest; gate-crasher

【速成】 sùchéng speeded-up educational program ◇ ～班 accelerated course; crash course/ ～教学法 quick method of teaching/ ～识字法 quick method of achieving literacy

【速冻】 sùdòng quick-freeze: ～水果 (蔬菜) quick-frozen fresh fruits (vegetables)

【速度】 sùdù ①〈物〉 speed; velocity: 初～ initial velocity/ 匀～ uniform velocity/ 逃逸～〈宇航〉 escape velocity/ 轨道～ orbital velocity/ 巡航～ cruising speed ②〈乐〉 *tempo* ③ speed; rate; pace; tempo: 加快～ increase speed/ 生产～ the tempo of production/ 经济发展的～ the rate of economic development/ 工业化的～ the pace of industrialization ◇ ～计 speed indicator; speedometer/ ～滑冰〈体〉 speed skating

【速记】 sùjì shorthand; stenography ◇ ～员 stenographer

【速决】 sùjué quick decision: 速战～ fight a quick battle to force a quick decision ◇ ～战 war (或 battle) of quick decision

【速率】 sùlǜ speed; rate: 冷却～ rate of cooling

【速射】 sùshè 〈军〉 rapid fire ◇ ～炮 quick-firing gun; quick-firer

【速调管】 sùtiáoguǎn 〈无〉 klystron

【速效】 sùxiào quick results ◇ ～肥料 quick-acting fertilizer

【速写】 sùxiě ① sketch ② literary sketch

**宿** sù ① lodge for the night; stay overnight: 借～ ask for a night's lodging ②〈书〉 long-standing; old: ～志 long-cherished ambition ③〈书〉 veteran; old: ～将 veteran general ④ (Sù) a surname
另见 xiǔ; xiù

【宿根】 sùgēn 〈植〉 ① perennial root ② biennial root

【宿疾】 sùjí chronic complaint; old trouble

【宿命论】 sùmìnglùn 〈哲〉 fatalism ◇ ～者 fatalist

【宿舍】 sùshè hostel; living quarters; dormitory: 学生～ students' hostel (或 dormitory)/ 职工～ living quarters for staff and workers

【宿营】 sùyíng (of troops) take up quarters

【宿怨】 sùyuàn old grudge; old scores

【宿愿】 sùyuàn long-cherished wish

【宿主】 sùzhǔ 〈生〉 host: 中间～ intermediate host/ 终～ final host

**粟** sù ① millet ② (Sù) a surname

# 溯

sù ①go against the stream: ～流而上 go upstream ②trace back; recall: 回～往事 recall past events

【溯源】 sùyuán trace to the source: 追本～ track down the origin; trace to the source

# 塑

sù model; mould: ～像 mould a statue/ 泥～ clay sculpture

【塑炼】 sùliàn plasticate ◇ ～机 plasticator

【塑料】 sùliào plastics: 通用～ general-purpose plastics/ 工程～ engineering plastics/ 氟～ fluoroplastics/ 泡沫～ foam (或 foamed) plastics
◇ ～薄膜 plastic film/ ～胶布带〈电〉plastic adhesive tape/ ～热合机 plastic welder/ ～贴面板 plastic veneer/ ～印版〈印〉plastic (printing) plate/ ～炸弹 plastic bomb

【塑像】 sùxiàng statue

【塑造】 sùzào ① model; mould: ～石膏像 mould (或 model) a plaster figure ② portray: ～一个女民兵的英雄形象 portray a heroic militiawoman

# 嗉

sù

【嗉子】 sùzi crop (of a bird) 又作"嗉囊"

# 愫

sù 〈书〉sincere feeling; sincerity

# 鹔

sù

【鹔鹴】 sùshuāng a bird mentioned in ancient books

# 傈

sù 见"傈傈族" Lìsùzú

# 簌

sù

【簌簌】 sùsù ①〈象〉rustle: 风吹树叶～响。The leaves are rustling in the wind. ② (tears) streaming down

## suān

# 酸

suān ①〈化〉acid: 醋～ acetic acid ② sour; tart: ～梨 sour pear/ ～果 tart fruit/ 牛奶～了。The milk has turned sour. ③ sick at heart; grieved; distressed: 大娘鼻子一～，流下泪来。The old woman's nose twitched and she began to weep. ④ pedantic; impractical: ～秀才 impractical old scholar; priggish pedant ⑤ tingle; ache: 腰～背痛 have a pain in the back; have a backache

【酸菜】 suāncài pickled Chinese cabbage; Chinese sauerkraut

【酸处理】 suānchǔlǐ 〈石油〉acid treatment; acidation

【酸楚】 suānchǔ grieved; distressed

【酸度】 suāndù 〈化〉acidity

【酸酐】 suāngān 〈化〉acid anhydride

【酸解】 suānjiě 〈化〉acidolysis

【酸辣汤】 suānlàtāng vinegar-pepper soup

【酸溜溜】 suānliūliū ① sour ② tingle; ache: 走了一天路，我的腿肚子～的。My legs ached after I'd been walking all day. ③ sad; mournful

【酸马奶】 suānmǎnǎi koumiss

【酸梅】 suānméi smoked plum; dark plum ◇ ～汤 sweet-sour plum juice

【酸牛奶】 suānniúnǎi yoghurt; sour milk

【酸软】 suānruǎn aching and limp

【酸式盐】 suānshìyán 〈化〉acid salt

【酸甜苦辣】 suān-tián-kǔ-là sour, sweet, bitter, hot — joys and sorrows of life

【酸痛】 suāntòng ache: 浑身～ ache all over

【酸味】 suānwèi tart flavour; acidity

【酸洗】 suānxǐ 〈冶〉pickling; acid pickling ◇ ～试验〈化〉acid washing test

【酸性】 suānxìng 〈化〉acidity
◇ ～反应 acid reaction/ ～染料 acid dyes/ ～试验 acid test

【酸枣】 suānzǎo wild jujube

【酸值】 suānzhí 〈化〉acid value

## suàn

# 蒜

suàn garlic: 一辫～ a braid of garlic

【蒜瓣儿】 suànbànr garlic clove

【蒜黄】 suànhuáng blanched garlic leaves

【蒜苗】 suànmiáo garlic bolt

【蒜泥】 suànní mashed garlic

【蒜头】 suàntóu the head (或 bulb) of garlic

# 算

suàn ① calculate; reckon; compute; figure: ～～旅行的费用 calculate the cost of a journey/ 能写会～ good at writing and reckoning/ 请你～一～我该付多少钱？Please reckon up how much I must pay./ 他们～了一下，完成这项工程需要两年。They figured it would take two years to finish the project. ② include; count: ～上你，一共有十个人。There were ten people, including you./ 把我也～上。Count me in. ③ plan; calculate: 失～ miscalculate; make an unwise decision/ 暗～ plot against sb. ④ think; suppose: 我～他今天该动身了。I suppose he'll have started (或 be starting) today. ⑤ consider; regard as; count as: 他可以～一个车把势。He can be counted as a carter./解放前，我们这里的小麦亩产一百斤就～不错的了。Before liberation, we were lucky if we got 100 *jin* of wheat per *mu*./ 就～你对了，也不该那么说呀！Even if you are right, that's not the way to put it. ⑥ carry weight; count: 我一个人说的不～，还得大伙儿说。It's not just what I say, but what we all say, that counts./ 你怎么刚说了又不～了？You just made a promise and now you've gone back on it!/ 这点困难～不了什么。A little difficulty like this is nothing to us./ 世界上的事不应该由一两个国家说了～。One or two powers should not have the final say on world affairs. ⑦ at long last; in the end; finally: 现在～把情况弄清楚了。At long last we have got things clear. 或 We've finally sized up the situation./ 问题～解决了。The problem is finally solved. ⑧〔后面跟"了"〕let it be; let it pass: ～了，别说了。That's enough! Let it go at that. 或 Forget it./ 他不愿意去就～了吧，咱们反正去。If he doesn't want to go, he doesn't need to. We'll go anyway.

【算法】 suànfǎ 〈数〉algorithm

【算计】 suànji ① calculate; reckon ② consider; plan: 我正～着要上北京去。I am planning a trip to Beijing. ③ expect; figure: 我～他昨天回不来，果然没回来。I thought he wouldn't come back yesterday, and he didn't. ④ scheme; plot: 暗中～别人 secretly scheme against others

【算命】 suànmìng fortune-telling ◇ ～先生 fortune-teller

【算盘】 suànpan abacus: 打～ use an abacus/ 不要打个人小～。Don't be so calculating. ◇ ～子 beads (of an abacus)

【算是】 suànshì at last: 这一下你～猜着了。At last you've guessed right./ 我们的计划～实现了。At last our plan has materialized.

【算术】 suànshù arithmetic: 做～ do sums ◇ ～级数 arithmetic progression; arithmetic series/ ～平均值 arithmetic mean

【算数】 suànshù count; hold; stand: 个别情况不～。Isolated instances do not count./ 这条规定仍然～。This rule

still holds (或 stands)./ 我们说话是～的。We mean what we say.
【算学】 suànxué ① mathematics ② arithmetic
【算帐】 suànzhàng ① do (或 work out) accounts; balance the books; make out bills: ～算得快 be quick at accounts ② square (或 settle) accounts with sb.; get even with sb.: 以后再找这坏蛋～。We'll get even with the scoundrel later. 或 We'll make the scoundrel pay for this.
【算子】 suànzǐ 〈数〉 operator: 微分～ differential operator

## suī

**尿** suī urine
另见 niào
【尿脬】 suīpāo 〈方〉 bladder
**虽** suī 〈连〉 though; although; even if: 问题～小，但很典型。The question is small but typical./ ～死犹荣 honoured though dead; have died a glorious death
【虽然】 suīrán 〈连〉 though; although
【虽说】 suīshuō 〈口〉〈连〉 though; although
【虽则】 suīzé 〈连〉 though; although
**荽** suī 见"芫荽" yánsui
**睢** suī 见"暴戾恣睢" bàolì-zìsuī

## suí

**绥** suí 〈书〉 ① peaceful ② pacify
【绥靖】 suíjìng pacify; appease ◇ ～政策 policy of appeasement
**隋** Suí ① the Sui Dynasty (581-618) ② a surname
**随** suí ① follow: ～我来。Follow me. 或 Come along with me./ 派干部～军南下 send cadres south with the army ② comply with; adapt to: ～顺 yield and comply/ 只要你们做得对，我都～着。So long as what you do is right, I'll go along with you. ③ let (sb. do as he likes): ～你的便。Do as you please./ 去不去～你。Whether you go or not is up to you. ④ along with (some other action): 请你～手把门带上。Please close the door as you go out. 或 Please shut the door after you. ⑤〈方〉 look like; resemble: 她长得～她母亲。She looks like her mother. 或 She takes after her mother.
【随笔】 suíbǐ informal essay; jottings
【随便】 suíbiàn ① casual; random; informal: ～闲谈 chat; chitchat/ ～说了几句 make some casual remarks/ 你怎么能这样～答应呢？How could you agree so casually? ② do as one pleases: ～吃吧。Help yourselves./ (主人对客人)请～吧。Make yourself at home. ③ careless; slipshod: 说话～ not be careful about the way one talks ④ wanton; wilful; arbitrary: ～撕毁协议 wantonly tear up an agreement ⑤ anyhow; any: ～什么时候来都行。Come any time you like.
【随波逐流】 suíbō-zhúliú drift with the tide (或 current)
【随处】 suíchù everywhere; anywhere
【随从】 suícóng ① accompany (one's superior); attend ② retinue; suite; *entourage*
【随大溜】 suídàliù drift with the stream; follow (或 conform to) the general trend
【随带】 suídài ① going along with: 信外～书籍一包。Accompanying the letter is a parcel of books. ② have sth. taken along with one: ～行李两件 two pieces of luggage which a passenger takes along with him
【随地】 suídì anywhere; everywhere: 不要～扔东西。Don't litter.
【随动件】 suídòngjiàn 〈机〉 follower: 凸轮～ cam follower
【随风倒】 suífēngdǎo bend with the wind — be easily swayed (by whichever side has more power or influence)
【随风转舵】 suí fēng zhuǎn duò trim one's sails; take one's cue from changing conditions
【随和】 suíhe amiable; obliging: 脾气～ have an amiable disposition
【随后】 suíhòu 〈副〉 soon afterwards: 你先走，我～就去。You go first. I'll follow. 或 You go ahead. I'll be there right away.
【随机】 suíjī ①〈统计〉 random ②〈数〉 stochastic ◇ ～抽样 random sampling/ ～过程 stochastic process
【随机应变】 suíjī-yìngbiàn adapt oneself to changing conditions; act according to circumstances
【随即】 suíjí immediately; presently
【随口】 suíkǒu speak thoughtlessly or casually; blurt out whatever comes into one's head: ～答应 say "yes" absent-mindedly; agree without thinking
【随人俯仰】 suí rén fǔ-yǎng be at sb.'s beck and call; follow sb. servilely
【随身】 suíshēn (carry) on one's person; (take) with one: 他～没有带钱。He had no money on him./ 我～可以带几公斤行李？How many kilograms of luggage can I take with me? ◇ ～行李 personal luggage
【随声附和】 suí shēng fùhè echo what others say; chime in with others
【随时】 suíshí ① at any time; at all times: ～准备歼灭入侵之敌 be ready at all times to wipe out any invader/ ～掌握工作进程 constantly have a grip on the progress of the work; always know clearly how the work is progressing/ 有了问题～向我报告。Keep me informed of any problems that may arise. ② whenever necessary; as the occasion demands: ～纠正错误 correct mistakes as soon as they occur/ ～表扬好人好事 commend good people for their good deeds when the occasion arises
【随手】 suíshǒu conveniently; without extra trouble: 出门时～关灯。Turn the light off as you go out./ ～关门。Shut the door after you.
【随俗】 suísú comply with convention; do as everybody else does
【随…随…】 suí ... suí ... 〔分别用在两个动词或动词性词组前面，表示后一动作紧接前一动作〕: 随叫随到 be on call at any hour/ 雪随下随化。The snow melted as it fell.
【随同】 suítóng be in company with; be accompanying
【随乡入乡】 suí xiāng rù xiāng when in Rome do as the Romans do
【随想曲】 suíxiǎngqǔ 〈乐〉 caprice; *capriccio*
【随心所欲】 suí xīn suǒ yù follow one's inclinations; have one's own way; do as one pleases
【随行人员】 suíxíng rényuán *entourage*; suite; party: 总统及其～ the President and his *entourage*
【随意】 suíyì at will; as one pleases ◇ ～肌〈生理〉 voluntary muscle
【随遇而安】 suí yù ér ān feel at home wherever one is; be able to adapt oneself to different circumstances
【随遇平衡】 suíyù pínghéng 〈物〉 indifferent equilibrium
【随员】 suíyuán ① suite; retinue; *entourage* ②〈外〉 attaché
【随葬物】 suízàngwù funerary objects; burial articles
【随着】 suízhe along with; in the wake of; in pace with: ～运动的深入 with the deepening of the movement/ ～时间

的推移 as time goes on; with the lapse (或 passage) of time/ ～集体生产的稳步上升 alongside the steady growth of collective production/ ～我国工业的蓬勃发展，产业工人的队伍不断壮大。The ranks of industrial workers are steadily expanding along with the vigorous development of our country's industry./ ～经济建设的高潮的到来，不可避免地将要出现一个文化建设的高潮。An upsurge in economic construction is bound to be followed by an upsurge in the cultural field.

**遂** suí 见"半身不遂" bànshēn bùsuí
另见 suì

## suǐ

**髓** suǐ ①〈生理〉marrow: 脊～ spinal marrow (或 cord) ②〈植〉pith

## suì

**岁** suì ① year: ～末 the end of the year/ ～入 annual income/ ～出 annual expenditure/ 辞旧～，迎新年 ring out the Old Year and ring in the New ② year (of age): 三～女孩儿 a three-year-old girl; a little girl three years old/ 这匹马两～口。This horse is two years old. ③ year (for crops): 歉～ lean year

【岁差】 suìchā 〈天〉precession of the equinoxes

【岁暮】 suìmù 〈书〉the close of the year: ～天寒。Cold weather sets in as the year draws to its close.

【岁首】 suìshǒu 〈书〉the beginning of the year

【岁数】 suìshu 〈口〉age; years: 老大爷，您多大～了？How old are you, Grandpa?/ 妈是上了～的人了。Mother is getting on in years.

【岁星】 suìxīng an ancient name for the planet Jupiter

【岁修】 suìxiū annual repairs

【岁月】 suìyuè years: 艰苦斗争的～ years of arduous struggle/ ～不居。Time and tide wait for no man.

**祟** suì evil spirit; ghost: 作～ act like an evil spirit; haunt and plague

**遂** suì ① satisfy; fulfil: ～愿 have one's wish fulfilled ② succeed: 所谋不～ fail in an attempt ③〈书〉then; thereupon: 病人服药后腹痛～止。The patient's stomachache stopped after he took the medicine.
另见 suí

【遂心】 suìxīn after one's own heart; to one's liking: ～如意 perfectly satisfied

【遂意】 suìyì to one's liking

**碎** suì ① break to pieces; smash: 碗打～了。The bowl is smashed to pieces. ② broken; fragmentary: ～玻璃 bits of broken glass/ ～布 oddments of cloth ③ garrulous; gabby: 嘴太～ talk too much; be a regular chatterbox

【碎步儿】 suìbùr quick short steps

【碎石】 suìshí 〈建〉crushed stones; broken stones ◇ ～混凝土〈建〉crushed stone concrete/ ～机 stone crusher/ ～路 broken stone road; macadam road

【碎屑岩】 suìxièyán clastic rock

【碎音】 suìyīn 〈乐〉*acciaccatura*

【碎嘴子】 suìzuǐzi 〈方〉① chatter; jabber; prate: 两句话能说完的事就别犯～了。Don't talk on and on (或 jabber away) when you can say it in a few words. ② a garrulous person; a chatterbox

**隧** suì

【隧道】 suìdào tunnel ◇ ～效应〈电子〉tunnel effect/ ～管〈电子〉tunneltron

**燧** suì ① flint ② beacon fire

【燧石】 suìshí flint ◇ ～玻璃 flint glass

**邃** suì 〈书〉① remote (in time or space): ～古 remote antiquity ② deep; profound: 精～ profound

**穗** suì ① the ear of grain; spike: 麦～儿 the ear of wheat ② tassel; fringe ③ (Suì) another name for Guangzhou

【穗选】 suìxuǎn 〈农〉ear selection

【穗状花序】 suìzhuàng huāxù 〈植〉spike

【穗子】 suìzi tassel; fringe: 有～的旗 a banner fringed with tassels

## sūn

**孙** sūn ① grandson ② generations below that of the grandchild: 曾～ great-grandson/ 玄～ great-great-grandson ③ second growth of plants: ～竹 new shoots of bamboo from the old stump ④ (Sūn) a surname

【孙女】 sūnnǚ granddaughter ◇ ～婿 granddaughter's husband; grandson-in-law

【孙媳妇】 sūnxífu grandson's wife; granddaughter-in-law

【孙子】 sūnzi grandson

**狲** sūn 见"猢狲" húsūn

## sǔn

**笋** sǔn bamboo shoot

【笋干】 sǔngān dried bamboo shoots

【笋瓜】 sǔnguā 〈植〉winter squash

【笋鸡】 sǔnjī young chicken; broiler

【笋尖】 sǔnjiān tender tips of bamboo shoots

**损** sǔn ① decrease; lose: 增～ increase and decrease/ 亏～ loss ② harm; damage: 有益无～ can only do good, not harm/ ～公肥私 seek private gain at public expense; feather one's nest at public expense/ 以～人开始，以害己告终 begin with injuring others and end up ruining oneself/ 狂犬吠日，无～于太阳的光辉。A cur barking at the sun cannot detract from its glory. ③〈方〉sarcastic; caustic; cutting: 他爱～人。He delights in making caustic remarks./ 说话别太～。Don't be so sarcastic. ④〈方〉mean; shabby: 这法子真～。That's a mean trick.

【损害】 sǔnhài harm; damage; injure: ～庄稼 damage crops; be harmful to crops/ ～健康 impair one's health/ 光线不好，看书容易～视力。Reading in poor light is bad for one's eyes./ 决不能～群众的利益。On no account should the interests of the masses be infringed upon.

【损耗】 sǔnhào ① loss; wear and tear: 摩擦～ friction loss ②〈商〉wastage; spoilage ◇ ～费 cost of wear and tear/ ～率〈商〉proportion of goods damaged

【损坏】 sǔnhuài damage; injure: ～公物要赔。Pay for public property you damage.

【损人利己】 sǔn rén lì jǐ harm others to benefit oneself; benefit oneself at the expense of others

【损伤】 sǔnshāng ① harm; damage; injure: 不要～群众的积极性。Don't dampen the enthusiasm of the masses. ② loss:

敌军兵力~很大。The enemy forces suffered heavy losses.

【损失】 sǔnshī ① lose: ~坦克五辆 lose five tanks ② loss; damage: 遭受重大~ suffer (或 sustain) heavy losses

【损益】 sǔnyì ① increase and decrease: 斟酌~ consider making necessary adjustments ② profit and loss; gains and losses: ~相抵。The gains offset the losses. ◇ ~计算书 profit and loss statement

**隼** sǔn 〈动〉 falcon

**榫** sǔn tenon

【榫头】 sǔntou tenon 又作"榫子"

【榫眼】 sǔnyǎn mortise

## suō

**娑** suō

【娑罗双树】 suōluó shuāngshù 〈植〉 sal tree (*Shorea robusta*)

**莎** suō

【莎草】 suōcǎo 〈植〉 nutgrass flatsedge (*Cyperus rotundus*)

**唆** suō instigate; abet: 教~ instigate; abet

【唆使】 suōshǐ instigate; abet ◇ ~者 instigator; abettor

**挲** suō 见"摩挲" mósuō

另见 sā

**桫** suō

【桫椤】 suōluó 〈植〉 spinulose tree fern (*Cyathea spinulosa*)

**梭** suō shuttle: 无~织机 shuttleless loom

【梭标】 suōbiāo spear ◇ ~队 spear corps

【梭梭】 suōsuō 〈植〉 sacsaoul (*Holoxylon ammodendron*)

【梭巡】 suōxún 〈书〉 move around to watch and guard; patrol

【梭鱼】 suōyú (redeye) mullet

【梭子】 suōzi ① 〈纺〉shuttle ② cartridge clip ③ 〈量〉〔用于子弹〕clip: 打了一~子弹 fire a whole clip of ammunition

【梭子蟹】 suōzixiè swimming crab

【梭子鱼】 suōziyú barracuda

**睃** suō look askance at

**羧** suō 〈化〉 carboxyl

【羧基】 suōjī 〈化〉 carboxyl; carboxyl group

【羧酸】 suōsuān 〈化〉 carboxylic acid

**蓑** suō

【蓑衣】 suōyī straw or palm-bark rain cape

**缩** suō ① contract; shrink: 热胀冷~ expand with heat and contract with cold/ 这种布下水不~。This cloth won't shrink when it's washed. ② draw back; withdraw; recoil: 退~ flinch; shrink/ 他把身子一~。He shrank back (in shame, horror, etc.)./ 冷得~成一团 huddle oneself up with cold/ 敌人~回去了。The enemy has drawn back.

【缩尺】 suōchǐ reduced scale; scale ◇ ~图 scale drawing

【缩短】 suōduǎn shorten; curtail; cut down: ~学制 shorten the period of schooling/ ~距离 reduce the distance; narrow the gap/ ~战线 contract the front/ 把报告~一半 cut a report down to half its length/ 把停留时间~一天 cut short one's stay by one day

【缩放仪】 suōfàngyí pantograph

【缩合】 suōhé 〈化〉 condensation ◇ ~反应 condensation reaction/ ~物 condensation compound

【缩减】 suōjiǎn reduce; cut: ~开支 reduce (或 cut) spending/ ~军费 cut back military expenditure/ ~重叠的机构 trim overlapping organizations/ ~行政人员，增加科技人员 retrench administrative staff and expand scientific and technological staff

【缩聚】 suōjù 〈化〉 condensation polymerization ◇ ~物 condensation polymer

【缩手】 suōshǒu ① draw back one's hand ② shrink (from doing sth.)

【缩手缩脚】 suōshǒu-suōjiǎo ① shrink with cold ② be overcautious: 不要~。Don't be overcautious.

【缩水】 suōshuǐ (of cloth through wetting) shrink ◇ ~率 shrinkage

【缩头虫】 suōtóuchóng 〈动〉 bamboo worm

【缩头缩脑】 suōtóu-suōnǎo ① be timid; be fainthearted ② shrink from responsibility

【缩微胶片】 suōwēi jiāopiàn microfilm

【缩小】 suōxiǎo reduce; lessen; narrow; shrink: ~范围 reduce the scope; narrow the range/ 逐步~城乡差别 gradually reduce the distinction between town and country

【缩写】 suōxiě ① abbreviation ② abridge ◇ ~本 abridged edition (或 version)/ ~签字 initials

【缩印】 suōyìn reprint books in a reduced format

【缩影】 suōyǐng epitome; miniature

## suǒ

**所** suǒ ① place: 住~ dwelling place/ 各得其~ each in his proper place ②〔用作机关或其他办事地方的名称〕: 研究~ research institute/ 诊疗~ clinic/ 指挥~ command post ③ 〈量〉〔用于房屋等〕: 一~房子 a house/ 两~学校 two schools/ 这~医院 this hospital ④ 〈助〉 ⓐ〔跟"为"或"被"合用，表示被动〕: 为人~笑 be laughed at/ 被表面现象~迷惑 be misled by outward appearances/ 深为他的共产主义精神~感动 be deeply touched by his communist spirit ⓑ〔跟动词连用，代表接受动作的事物〕: 各尽~能 from each according to his ability/ 闻~未闻 unheard-of/ 无~不为 stop at nothing (in doing evil) ⓒ〔跟动词连用，动词后再用接受动作的事物的词〕: 我~认识的人 the people I know/ 大家~提的意见 the opinions various people put forward ⓓ〔跟动词连用，动词后再用"者"或"的"代表接受动作的事物〕: ~见者广 have wide experience/ 这是我们~拥护的。This is what we support.

【所部】 suǒbù troops under one's command

【所长】 suǒcháng what one is good at; one's strong point; one's forte

【所得】 suǒdé income; earnings; gains ◇ ~税 income tax

【所属】 suǒshǔ ① what is subordinate to one or under one's command: 命令~部队立即反攻 order the units under one's command to counterattack at once/ 教育部~单位 the organizations under the Ministry of Education ② what one belongs to or is affiliated with: 向~派出所填报户口 apply or register with the local police station for residence

【所谓】 suǒwèi ① what is called: ~民主，只是一种手段，不是目的。What is called democracy is only a means, not an end./ ~经济基础，就是生产关系，主要是所有制。By the economic base we mean the relations of production, chiefly ownership. ② so-called: ~"自由世界" the so-called "free world"

【所向披靡】 suǒ xiàng pīmí (of troops) carry all before one; sweep away all obstacles

【所向无前】 suǒ xiàng wú qián be invincible; be irresistible; break all enemy resistance 又作“所向无敌”
【所以】 suǒyǐ ①〈连〉〔表示因果关系〕so; therefore; as a result: 他有事，～没来。He hasn't come because he's got something else to do./ 我们之～一定会胜利，是因为我们的事业是正义的。The reason why we are bound to succeed is that our cause is just. ②〈口〉〔单独成句，表示“原因就在这里”〕: ～呀，要不然我怎么这么说呢？That's just the point, otherwise I wouldn't have said it. ③〔用于固定词组中作宾语，表示实在的情由或适宜的举动〕: 忘其～ forget oneself
【所以然】 suǒyǐrán the reason why; the whys and wherefores: 知其然而不知其～ know that sth. is so but not why it is so; know what is done but not why it is done/ 他说了半天还是没说出个～来。He talked a lot but made you none the wiser.
【所有】 suǒyǒu ① own; possess: 这些拖拉机归公社～。These tractors are owned by the commune. ② possessions: 尽其～ give everything one has; give one's all ③ all: 把～的劲儿都使出来 exert all one's strength ◇ ～格〈语〉possessive case/ ～权 proprietary rights; ownership; title
【所有制】 suǒyǒuzhì system of ownership; ownership: 全民～ ownership by the whole people/ 生产资料～的社会主义改造 socialist transformation of the system of ownership of the means of production
【所在】 suǒzài place; location: 风景优美的～ a picturesque place; a scenic spot/ 这是我们的力量～。That is where our strength lies. 或 Herein lies our strength./ ～多有 be found almost everywhere ◇ ～地 location; seat; site
【所致】 suǒzhì be caused by; be the result of: 这次事故是由于疏忽～。The accident was the result of (或 was due to) negligence.

## 索

suǒ ① large rope: 绳～ rope/ 麻～ hempen rope/ 船～ ship's rigging/ 绞～ (the hangman's) noose/ 铁～桥 chain bridge ② search: 遍～不得 search high and low for sth. in vain ③ demand; ask; exact: ～价 ask a price; charge/ ～债 demand payment of a debt/ ～赔 claim damages ④〈书〉all alone; all by oneself: 离群～居 live all alone ⑤〈书〉dull; insipid ⑥ (Suǒ) a surname
【索道】 suǒdào cableway; ropeway: 在河上架起～ throw a cableway across the river/ 高架～ telpher
【索马里】 Suǒmǎlǐ Somalia ◇ ～人 Somali/ ～语 Somali (language)
【索取】 suǒqǔ ask for; demand; exact; extort: ～样品 ask for a sample/ ～巨额赔款 extort a huge indemnity
【索然】 suǒrán dull; dry; insipid: ～寡味 flat and insipid
【索性】 suǒxìng〈副〉〔表示直截了当，干脆〕: 既然已经做了，～就把它做完。Since you have started the job, you might as well finish it./ 找了几个地方都没找着，～不再找了。It was nowhere to be found, so we simply gave it up for lost.
【索引】 suǒyǐn index: 卡片～ card index/ 书名～ title index/ 作者～ author index/ 标题～ subject index

## 唢

suǒ
【唢呐】 suǒnà *suona* horn, a woodwind instrument

## 琐

suǒ trivial; petty
【琐事】 suǒshì trifles; trivial matters: 家庭～ household affairs
【琐碎】 suǒsuì trifling; trivial
【琐闻】 suǒwén bits of news; scraps of information
【琐细】 suǒxì trifling; trivial
【琐屑】 suǒxiè〈书〉trifling; trivial

## 锁

suǒ ① lock: 挂～ padlock/ 弹簧～ spring lock ② lock up: ～门 lock a door/ ～在保险箱里 be locked up in a safe/ 双眉紧～ with knitted brows ③ lockstitch: ～眼 do a lockstitch on a buttonhole/ ～边 lockstitch a border
【锁骨】 suǒgǔ〈生理〉clavicle; collarbone
【锁簧】 suǒhuáng〈机〉locking spring
【锁匠】 suǒjiang locksmith
【锁紧】 suǒjǐn〈机〉locking: 自～ self-locking
【锁链】 suǒliàn ① chain ② shackles; fetters; chains
【锁阳】 suǒyáng〈中药〉Chinese cynomorium (*Cynomorium songaricum*)
【锁钥】 suǒyuè ① key: 解决问题的～ a key to the problem ② strategic gateway (to an important centre or a major city)

# suo

## 嗦

suo 见“哆嗦”duōsuo;“罗嗦”luōsuo

# T

## tā

**它** tā 〔称人以外的事物〕it: 这杯牛奶你喝了～。Drink this glass of milk.

【它们】 tāmen 〔称一个以上的事物〕they

**他** tā ① he: ～俩 the two of them/ ～家在农村。His home is in the countryside. ②〔泛指,不分男性和女性〕: 从远处看不出～是男的还是女的。You can't tell if it's a man or a woman from a distance./ 一个人要是离开了群众,～就将一事无成。Whoever divorces himself from the masses will accomplish nothing./ 每个孩子都讲了～学习雷锋的收获。Each child told what he or she had learnt from Lei Feng. ③〔虚指,用在动词和数量词之间〕: 好好睡～一觉 have a good sleep/ 再读～一遍 read it a second time ④ other; another; some other: 调往～处 be transferred to another place/留作～用 reserve for other uses/ 此人早已～去。He has long since left.

【他加禄语】 Tājiālùyǔ Tagalog (language)

【他妈的】 tāmāde 〈骂〉damn it; blast it; to hell with it

【他们】 tāmen 〔指人〕they: ～俩 the two of them/ ～公社丰收了。Their commune has reaped a bumper harvest.

【他人】 tārén another person; other people; others

【他日】 tārì 〈书〉some other time (或 day); some day; later on

【他杀】 tāshā 〈法〉homicide

【他山攻错】 tāshān gōng cuò stones from other hills may serve to polish the jade of this one — advice from others may help one overcome one's shortcomings

【他乡】 tāxiāng a place far away from home; an alien land: ～遇故知 run into an old friend in a distant land

**她** tā she

【她们】 tāmen 〔指女性〕they

**铊** tā 〈化〉thallium (Tl)

**趿** tā

【趿拉】 tāla wear cloth shoes with the backs turned in; shuffle about with the backs of one's shoes trodden down: 别～着鞋走路。Don't walk around with the backs of your shoes turned in.

【趿拉板儿】 tālabǎnr 〈方〉wooden slippers; clogs

【趿拉儿】 tālar 〈方〉slippers

**溻** tā 〈方〉(of clothes, etc.) become soaked with sweat

**塌** tā ① collapse; fall down; cave in: 墙～了。The wall collapsed./ 没什么好怕的,天不会～下来。There's nothing to be afraid of. The sky won't fall down. ② sink; droop: 他病了好久,两腮都～下去了。His cheeks were sunken after his long illness./ ～鼻梁 a flat nose/ 花儿晒～秧了。The flowers drooped in the hot sun. ③ calm down; settle down: ～下心去 set one's mind at ease; settle down to (work, etc.)

【塌方】 tāfāng ① cave in; collapse: 大坝出现～。A section of the dam has caved in. ② landslide; landslip

【塌实】 tāshi ① steady and sure; dependable: 工作～ be a steady worker; be steadfast in one's work ② free from anxiety; having peace of mind: 觉得～ have one's mind set at rest; feel secure about sth./ 睡得很～ enjoy a deep, quiet sleep; have a good, sound sleep/ 经过检查,发电机并没有毛病,我们心里就～了。We felt relieved when the generator was checked and found in order.

【塌台】 tātái collapse; fall from power

【塌陷】 tāxiàn subside; sink; cave in: 这座房子的地基～了。The foundations of this building have subsided.

**遢** tā 见"邋遢" lāta

**踏** tā

另见 tà

【踏实】 tāshi 见"塌实" tāshi

## tǎ

**溚** tǎ 〈化〉tar

**塔** tǎ ① Buddhist pagoda; pagoda ② tower: 水～ water tower/ 灯～ lighthouse; beacon ③〈化〉column; tower: 氧化～ oxidizing column (或 tower)/ 蒸馏～ distillation column (或 tower)

【塔吊】 tǎdiào tower crane

【塔夫绸】 tǎfūchóu taffeta

【塔吉克族】 Tǎjíkèzú the Tajik nationality, living in the Xinjiang Uygur Autonomous Region

【塔轮】 tǎlún 〈机〉cone pulley; stepped pulley

【塔塔尔族】 Tǎtǎ'ěrzú the Tatar (Tartar) nationality, living in the Xinjiang Uygur Autonomous Region

【塔台】 tǎtái 〈航空〉control tower

**獭** tǎ otter: 水～ (common) otter/ 海～ sea otter/ 旱～ marmot

**鳎** tǎ 〈动〉sole

## tà

**拓** tà make rubbings from inscriptions, pictures, etc. on stone tablets or bronze vessels

另见 tuò

【拓本】 tàběn a book of rubbings

【拓片】 tàpiàn rubbing (from a stone tablet or bronze vessel)

**沓** tà 〈书〉crowded; repeated: 杂～ numerous and disorderly/ 纷至～来 come thick and fast; keep pouring in

另见 dá

**闼** tà 〈书〉door; small door; wicket gate: 排～直入 push the door open and stride in (without knocking)

**挞** tà 〈书〉flog; whip: 鞭～ flog; lash

# 嗒 tà

另见 dā

【嗒然】 tàrán 〈书〉 dejected; despondent; depressed: ～若丧 deeply despondent

# 榻 tà

a long, narrow and low bed; couch: 竹～ bamboo couch/ 藤～ rattan (或 cane) couch/ 同～ sleep in the same bed; share a bed

# 踏 tà

①step on; tread; stamp: 把火～灭 tread out a fire/ ～平匪巢 smash the bandits' lair/ ～上贵国的土地 set foot on the soil of your country/ ～着先烈的血迹前进 march ahead along the path crimson with the blood of martyrs/ 勘探队～遍了祖国的山山水水。The prospecting team has traversed the length and breadth of the land. ② go to the spot (to make an investigation or survey)

另见 tā

【踏板】 tàbǎn ① treadle; footboard; footrest: 缝纫机～ the treadle of a sewing machine ②footstool (usu. placed beside a bed) ③〈乐〉 pedal (of a piano, etc.): 强音～ damper (或 loud) pedal/ 弱音～ soft pedal

【踏步】 tàbù mark time

【踏勘】 tàkān ①make an on-the-spot survey (of a railway line, construction site, etc.) ②〈旧〉 (of an official) make a personal investigation on the spot

【踏看】 tàkàn go to the spot to make an investigation

【踏破铁鞋无觅处，得来全不费工夫】 tàpò tiěxié wú mìchù, délai quán bù fèi gōngfu find sth. by chance after travelling far and wide in search of it

【踏青】 tàqīng go for a walk in the country in spring (when the grass has just turned green)

# 蹋 tà

见"糟蹋" zāota

## tāi

# 苔 tāi

见"舌苔" shétāi

另见 tái

# 胎 tāi

①foetus; embryo: ～形 the form of the foetus/ 怀～ become or be pregnant ②birth: 头～ first baby; firstborn/ 一～十五只小猪 fifteen piglets at a litter (或 at one farrow) ③padding; stuffing; wadding: 棉花～ the cotton padding of a quilt, etc. ④roughcast (in the making of china, *cloisonné*, etc.) ⑤tyre: 内～ inner tube (of a tyre)/ 外～ outer cover (of a tyre); tyre

【胎动不安】 tāidòng bù'ān 〈中医〉 a sign of approaching abortion characterized by movement of the foetus causing pain in the lower abdomen

【胎毒】 tāidú 〈中医〉 skin infections of newborn infants such as boils, blisters, eczema, etc. considered to be caused by febrile toxin inherited from the mother

【胎儿】 tāi'ér foetus; embryo

【胎发】 tāifà foetal hair; lanugo

【胎毛】 tāimáo foetal hair; lanugo

【胎膜】 tāimó 〈生理〉 foetal membrane

【胎盘】 tāipán 〈生理〉 placenta

【胎气】 tāiqi nausea, vomiting and oedema of legs during pregnancy

【胎生】 tāishēng 〈动〉 viviparity ◇ ～动物 viviparous animal; vivipara

【胎位】 tāiwèi 〈医〉 position of a foetus

【胎衣】 tāiyī (human) afterbirth

【胎座】 tāizuò 〈植〉 placenta

## tái

# 台 tái

①platform; stage; terrace: 讲～ platform; rostrum/ 了望～ watch tower; lookout/ 检阅～ reviewing stand/ 舞～ stage/ 下不了～ unable to extricate oneself from an awkward position; unable to get off the spot ②stand; support: 灯～ lampstand/ 蜡～ candlestick/ 导弹发射～ missile launching pad ③anything shaped like a platform, stage or terrace: 灶～ the top of a kitchen range/ 窗～ windowsill ④table; desk: 写字～ (writing) desk/ 梳妆～ dressing table/ 工作～ (work) bench ⑤broadcasting station: 中央人民广播电～ the Central People's Broadcasting Station/ 电视～ television broadcasting station ⑥ a special telephone service: 长途～ trunk call service; toll board; long distance/ 查号～ directory inquiries; information ⑦〈量〉: 一～戏 a theatrical performance/ 一～机车 a railway engine; a locomotive ⑧〔旧时称对方的敬辞〕: ～端 you/ ～命 your instructions ⑨(Tái) short for Taiwan Province

【台本】 táiběn a playscript with stage directions

【台布】 táibù tablecloth

【台步】 táibù the gait of an actor or actress in Beijing opera, etc.

【台秤】 táichèng platform scale; platform balance

【台词】 táicí actor's lines

【台灯】 táidēng desk lamp; table lamp; reading lamp

【台地】 táidì ①〈地〉 platform; tableland ②〈军〉 mesa

【台风】 táifēng 〈气〉 typhoon: 强～ violent typhoon ◇ ～动向 typhoon movement/ ～警戒线 typhoon detective line/ ～路径 typhoon track/ ～眼 typhoon eye

【台虎钳】 táihǔqián 〈机〉 bench vice

【台阶】 táijiē ①a flight of steps; steps leading up to a house, etc. ②chance to extricate oneself from an awkward position: 给他个～下吧。Give him an out. ③〈矿〉 bench: 上～ upper bench

【台历】 táilì desk calendar

【台面】 táimiàn 〈电子〉 mesa ◇ ～型晶体管 mesa transistor

【台钳】 táiqián 〈机〉 bench clamp

【台球】 táiqiú ①billiards ②billiard ball ③〈方〉 table tennis; ping-pong

【台田】 táitián 〈农〉 raised fields; platform fields

【台湾】 Táiwān Taiwan (Province)

【台柱子】 táizhùzi leading light; pillar; mainstay

【台子】 táizi ①〈口〉 platform; stage ②〈方〉 table; desk ③billiard table ④ ping-pong table

【台钻】 táizuàn 〈机〉 bench drill

# 邰 Tái

a surname

# 抬 tái

①lift; raise: ～手 raise one's hand/ 把桌子～起来 lift (up) the table/ 打击别人，～高自己 attack others so as to build up oneself ②(of two or more persons) carry: ～担架 carry a stretcher ③见"抬杠"①

【抬秤】 táichèng huge steelyard (usu. worked by three persons, with two lifting the steelyard on a shoulder pole and the third adjusting the weight)

【抬杠】 táigàng ①〈口〉 argue for the sake of arguing; bicker; wrangle: 他俩抬起杠来就没完。Those two can go on arguing for hours and hours. ②〈旧〉 carry a coffin on stout poles

【抬价】 táijià force up commodity prices

【抬肩】 táijian half the circumference of the sleeve where

it joins the shoulder
【抬举】 táiju praise or promote sb. to show favour; favour sb.: 不识～ not know how to appreciate favours
【抬头】 táitóu ① raise one's head: ～一看 look up ② gain ground; look up; rise: 防止资本主义自发势力～ prevent the spontaneous forces of capitalism from gaining ground ③ begin a new line, as a mark of respect, when mentioning the addressee in letters, official correspondence, etc. ④ 〈商〉 (on receipts, bills, etc.) name of the buyer or payee, or space for filling in such a name
【抬头纹】 táitóuwén wrinkles on one's forehead

**苔** tái 〈植〉 liver mosses
另见 tāi
【苔藓植物】 táixiǎn zhíwù bryophyte
【苔原】 táiyuán 〈地〉 tundra

**骀** tái 〈书〉 an inferior horse; a broken-down nag: 驽～ an inferior horse; a mediocre person

**炱** tái soot

**鲐** tái chub mackerel

**薹** tái 〈植〉 ① a kind of sedge ② the bolt of garlic, rape, etc.

## tài

**太** tài ① highest; greatest; remotest: ～空 the firmament; outer space ② more or most senior: ～老伯 granduncle/ ～老师 father of one's teacher or teacher of one's father ③ 〈副〉 excessively; too; over: ～晚 too late/ 水～烫,没法喝。The water is too hot to drink./ 那～过分了。That's going too far./ 这～不象话了! This is simply outrageous! 或 This is the height of absurdity!/ 他～客气了,使大家感到很拘束。He was so polite everybody felt ill at ease. ④ 〈副〉〔用于赞叹〕 extremely: 又见到您,～高兴了。I'm extremely glad to see you again./ ～感谢你了。Thanks a lot. 或 Thank you ever so much. ⑤ 〈副〉〔用于否定〕 very: 不～好 not very good; not good enough
【太白星】 tàibáixīng 〈天〉 Venus; Vesper
【太阿倒持】 Tài'ē dào chí hold the sword by the blade — surrender one's power to another at one's own peril
【太公】 tàigōng 〈方〉 great-grandfather
【太公钓鱼,愿者上钩】 Tàigōng diào yú, yuànzhě shàng gōu like the fish rising to Jiang Tai Gong's hookless and baitless line — a willing victim letting himself be caught
【太古】 tàigǔ remote antiquity ◇ ～代 〈地〉 the Archean (或 Archaeozoic) Era/ ～界 〈地〉 the Archean Group
【太后】 tàihòu mother of an emperor; empress dowager; queen mother
【太极拳】 tàijíquán *taijiquan*, a kind of traditional Chinese shadow boxing: 打～ do *taijiquan*
【太监】 tàijiàn (court) eunuch
【太空】 tàikōng the firmament; outer space
【太庙】 tàimiào the Imperial Ancestral Temple
【太平】 tàipíng peace and tranquility: ～盛世 piping times of peace/ ～无事。All is well. 或 Everything is all right./ 只有帝国主义被消灭了,才会有～。Only when imperialism is eliminated can peace prevail./ 提高警惕,不可存有～观念。Heighten vigilance and discard any false sense of security.
◇ ～龙头 fire hydrant; fire plug/ ～门 exit/ ～水缸 a vat filled with water for use in case of fire/ ～梯 fire escape
【太平花】 tàipínghuā Beijing mockorange (*Philadelphus pekinensis*)
【太平间】 tàipíngjiān mortuary
【太平鸟】 tàipíngniǎo waxwing
【太平天国】 Tàipíng Tiānguó the Taiping Heavenly Kingdom (1851-1864), established by Hong Xiuquan during the Taiping Revolution, the largest of peasant uprisings in China's history
【太平洋】 Tàipíngyáng the Pacific (Ocean)
【太婆】 tàipó 〈方〉 great-grandmother
【太上皇】 tàishànghuáng ① a title assumed by an emperor's father who abdicated in favour of his son ② overlord; supersovereign; backstage ruler
【太师椅】 tàishīyǐ an old-fashioned wooden armchair
【太岁】 tàisuì an ancient name for the planet Jupiter
【太岁头上动土】 tàisuì tóushang dòng tǔ provoke sb. far superior in power or strength
【太太】 tàitai 〈旧〉 ① Mrs.; madame: 王～ Mrs. Wang; Madame Wang ② the mistress of a household; madam; lady
【太息】 tàixī 〈书〉 heave a deep sigh
【太虚】 tàixū 〈书〉 the great void; the universe
【太学】 tàixué the Imperial College (in feudal China)
【太阳】 tàiyáng ① the sun: 青年人朝气蓬勃,好象早晨八九点钟的～。Young people, full of vigour and vitality, are like the sun at eight or nine in the morning. ② sunshine; sunlight: 晒～ bask in the sun/ ～地儿 a place where there is sunshine; sunny spot/ 今天～很好。It's a lovely sunny day.
◇ ～灯 〈医〉 sunlamp; sunlight lamp/ ～电池 solar cell/ ～辐射 〈气〉 solar radiation/ ～光 the sun's rays; sunlight; sunbeam; sunshine/ ～光谱 〈物〉 solar spectrum/ ～黑子 〈天〉 sunspot/ ～历 solar calendar/ ～炉 solar furnace/ ～帽 sun helmet; topee/ ～目视镜 〈天〉 helioscope/ ～能 solar energy/ ～年 〈天〉 solar year/ ～系 the solar system/ ～灶 solar energy stove; solar cooker
【太阳镜】 tàiyángjìng sunglasses
【太阳鸟】 tàiyángniǎo sunbird
【太阳穴】 tàiyángxué the temples
【太医】 tàiyī imperial physician
【太阴】 tàiyīn ① 〈方〉 the moon ② 〈天〉 lunar
◇ ～历 lunar calendar/ ～年 lunar year/ ～月 lunar month; lunation
【太原】 Tàiyuán Taiyuan
【太子】 tàizǐ crown prince

**汰** tài discard; eliminate

**态** tài ① form; appearance; condition: 形～ shape; morphology/ 姿～ posture; stance; gesture; attitude/ 事～的发展 the course of events; developments ② 〈物〉 state: 气～ gaseous state/ 液～ liquid state ③ 〈语〉 voice: 主动语～ the active voice
【态度】 tàidu ① manner; bearing; how one conducts oneself: ～和蔼 amiable; kindly/ 耍～ lose one's temper; get into a huff/ 你这是什么～? What sort of an attitude is that? 或 Is this the way to behave?/ 他今天～有些异常。He is not his usual self today. ② attitude; approach: 劳动～ attitude towards labour/ 改变自己的～ change one's attitude; shift one's position/ 把革命热情和科学～结合起来 combine revolutionary enthusiasm with a scientific approach/ 在原则问题上要表明我们的～。We must state our position on matters of principle./ 这家饭馆的服务～很好。The service is good at this restaurant.

【态势】 tàishì state; situation; posture: 战略～ strategic situation/ 军事～ military posture

**肽** tài 〈化〉 peptide

**钛** tài 〈化〉 titanium (Ti)

【钛白】 tàibái 〈化〉 titanium white; titanium dioxide 又作"钛白粉"

【钛铁矿】 tàitiěkuàng ilmenite

**泰** tài ① safe; peaceful: 康～ in good health/ 国～民安。The country is prosperous and the people live in peace. ② extreme; most: ～西 the West; the Occident

【泰国】 Tàiguó Thailand ◇ ～人 Thailander; Thai

【泰然】 tàirán calm; composed; self-possessed: ～处之 take sth. calmly; bear sth. with equanimity/ ～自若 behave with perfect composure; be self-possessed

【泰山】 Tàishān ① Mount Taishan; Taishan Mountain (a symbol of great weight or import): 人固有一死,或重于～,或轻于鸿毛。Though death befalls all men alike, it may be weightier than Mount Taishan or lighter than a feather./有眼不识～have eyes but fail to see Mount Taishan; entertain an angel unawares ② 〈旧〉 father-in-law

【泰山北斗】 tàishān běidǒu Mount Taishan and the Big Dipper (respectful epithet for a person of distinction)

【泰山压顶】 Tàishān yā dǐng bear down on one with the weight of Mount Taishan: ～不弯腰 not bend one's head even if Mount Taishan topples on one; not give in to any pressure or difficulty

【泰语】 Tàiyǔ Thai (language)

**酞** tài 〈化〉 phthalein

## tān

**坍** tān collapse; fall; tumble: 土墙～了。The earthern wall collapsed.

【坍方】 tānfāng ① cave in; collapse ② landslide; landslip

【坍塌】 tāntā cave in; collapse

【坍台】 tāntái 〈方〉 ① (of enterprises, etc.) collapse ② fall into disgrace; lose face

**贪** tān ① corrupt; venal: ～官污吏 corrupt officials; venal officials ② have an insatiable desire for: ～财 be greedy for money/ ～得无厌 be insatiably avaricious/ ～杯 be too fond of drink; be a winebibber/ ～玩 be too fond of play/ ～大求全 go in for grandiose projects/ ～多嚼不烂 bite off more than one can chew ③ covet; hanker after

【贪婪】 tānlán 〈书〉 avaricious; greedy; rapacious: ～的目光 greedy eyes/ ～地掠夺别国的资源 rapaciously plunder the resources of other countries

【贪恋】 tānliàn be reluctant to part with; hate to leave; cling to: ～西湖景色 hate to leave the beautiful West Lake/ ～舒适的生活 be reluctant to give up ease and comfort

【贪便宜】 tān piányi anxious to get things on the cheap; keen on gaining petty advantages

【贪生怕死】 tānshēng-pàsǐ cravenly cling to life instead of braving death; care for nothing but saving one's skin; be mortally afraid of death

【贪天之功】 tān tiān zhī gōng arrogate to oneself the merits of others; claim credit for other people's achievements

【贪图】 tāntú seek; hanker after; covet: ～安逸 seek ease and comfort/ ～小利 covet small advantages; hanker after petty gains/ 警惕～享乐的情绪 guard against the tendency to seek pleasure

【贪污】 tānwū corruption; graft: ～盗窃 graft and embezzlement/ ～腐化 corruption and degeneration; corruption/ ～和浪费是极大的犯罪。Corruption and waste are very great crimes. ◇ ～分子 a person guilty of corruption; grafter; embezzler

【贪心】 tānxīn ① greed; avarice; rapacity ② greedy; avaricious; insatiable; voracious: ～不足 insatiably greedy

【贪小失大】 tān xiǎo shī dà covet a little and lose a lot; seek small gains but incur big losses

【贪赃】 tānzāng take bribes; practise graft: ～枉法 take bribes and bend the law; pervert justice for a bribe

【贪嘴】 tānzuǐ greedy (for food); gluttonous

**滩** tān ① beach; sands: 海～ seabeach; beach/ 沙～ sand bank; sands ② shoal: 险～ dangerous shoals/ ～多水急 with many shoals and rapids

【滩头堡】 tāntóubǎo 〈军〉 beachhead

**摊** tān ① spread out: 把豆子～开晒一晒 spread the beans out to dry in the sun/ 把事情～到桌面上来谈 put the problems on the table and thrash them out ② take a share in: 每人～五毛钱。Each will contribute 5 *mao*. ③ vendor's stand; booth; stall: 水果～儿 fruit stand; fruit stall/ 报～ newsstand/ 收～儿 shut up shop; wind up the day's business ④ 〈量〉〔用于摊开的糊状物〕: 一～稀泥 a mud puddle/ 一～血 a pool of blood ⑤ fry batter in a thin layer: ～煎饼 make pancakes/ ～鸡蛋 make an omelet

【摊场】 tāncháng spread harvested grain on a threshing floor

【摊贩】 tānfàn street pedlar

【摊牌】 tānpái lay one's cards on the table; show one's hand (或 cards); have a showdown: 迫使对方～ force one's opponent to show his hand; force a showdown

【摊派】 tānpài apportion (expenses, work, etc.)

【摊晒机】 tānshàijī 〈农〉 tedder

【摊子】 tānzi ① vendor's stand; booth; stall: 菜～ vegetable stall (或 stand) ② the structure of an organization; setup: ～ 铺得太大 do sth. on too large a scale

**瘫** tān paralysis: 吓～了 be paralysed with fright

【瘫痪】 tānhuàn ① paralysis; palsy: ～病人 paralytic ② be paralysed; break down; be at a standstill: 交通运输陷于～。Transportation was at a standstill.

【瘫软】 tānruǎn (of arms, legs, etc.) weak and limp

【瘫子】 tānzi a person suffering from paralysis; paralytic

## tán

**坛** tán ① altar: 天～ the Temple of Heaven (in Beijing)/ 日～ the Altar to the Sun (in Beijing) ② a raised plot of land for planting flowers, etc.: 花～ (raised) flower bed ③ platform; forum: 讲～ speaker's platform ④ circles; world: 文～ the literary world; literary circles/ 棋～ chess circles ⑤earthen jar; jug:一～醋 a jar of vinegar/ 酒～ wine jug

【坛坛罐罐】 tántán-guànguàn pots and pans — personal possessions: 不怕打烂～ not be afraid of having one's pots and pans smashed — not fear loss of property or destruction of possessions (in time of war)

【坛子】 tánzi earthen jar

**昙** tán covered with clouds

【昙花】 tánhuā 〈植〉 broad-leaved epiphyllum (*Epiphyllum oxypetalum*)

【昙花一现】 tánhuā yī xiàn flower briefly as the broad-leaved epiphyllum; last briefly; be a flash in the pan: ～的人物 a transient figure

**谈** tán ① talk; chat; discuss: 我们好好～～。Let's have a good chat./ 我想同你们～一～文学创作问题。I would like to discuss with you the question of creative writing./ ～得来 get along well ② what is said or talked about: 奇～ strange talk; fantastic tale/ 无稽之～ fantastic talk; sheer nonsense ③ (Tán) a surname

【谈不到】 tánbudào out of the question: 没有政治上的独立，就～经济上的独立。Without political independence, you can't begin to talk about economic independence. 又作"谈不上"

【谈到】 tándào speak of; talk about; refer to: 他～我国工业发展的前景。He talked about the prospects for industrial development in our country.

【谈锋】 tánfēng volubility; eloquence: ～甚健 talk volubly; be a good talker; have the gift of the gab

【谈何容易】 tán hé róngyì easier said than done; by no means easy

【谈虎色变】 tán hǔ sè biàn turn pale at the mention of a tiger; turn pale at the mere mention of something terrible

【谈话】 tánhuà ① conversation; talk; chat: 亲切友好的～ a cordial and friendly conversation ② statement: 发表书面～ make a written statement

【谈家常】 tán jiācháng talk about everyday matters; engage in small talk; chitchat

【谈论】 tánlùn discuss; talk about

【谈判】 tánpàn negotiations; talks: 举行～ hold talks; hold negotiations/ 开始～ enter into (或 open) negotiations with/ 贸易～ trade negotiations; trade talks/ 重开～ resume the talks/ ～中断。The talks broke down. ◇ ～桌 conference table

【谈天】 tántiān chat; make conversation: ～说地 talk of everything under the sun

【谈吐】 tántǔ style of conversation

【谈笑风生】 tánxiào fēng shēng talk cheerfully and humorously

【谈笑自若】 tánxiào zìruò go on talking and laughing as if nothing had happened: 沉着镇静，～ go on talking and laughing without turning a hair

【谈心】 tánxīn heart-to-heart talk: 在同学间开展～活动 encourage heart-to-heart talks among fellow students

【谈言微中】 tán yán wēi zhòng speak tactfully but to the point; make one's point through hints

【谈助】 tánzhù topic of conversation: 足资～ serve as a good topic of conversation

**弹** tán ① shoot (as with a catapult, etc.); send forth: ～石子 shoot pebbles with a catapult ② spring; leap: 球从篮板上～回来。The ball rebounded from the backboard./ 从跳板上～起来 leap from the springboard ③ flick; flip: ～烟灰 flick the ash off a cigarette/ 把帽子上的灰尘～掉 flick the dust off a hat ④ fluff; tease: ～棉花 fluff (或 tease) cotton (with a bow) ⑤ play (a stringed musical instrument); pluck: ～钢琴 play the piano/ ～琵琶 pluck the *pipa*/ 老调重～ strike up a hackneyed tune; harp on the same old tune ⑥ elastic: ～性 elasticity ⑦ accuse; impeach: ～劾 impeach
另见 dàn

【弹词】 táncí 〈曲艺〉 storytelling (in various southern dialects) to the accompaniment of stringed instruments

【弹冠相庆】 tán guān xiāng qìng congratulate each other and dust off their old official's hats (in anticipation of fat jobs upon hearing of a mutual friend's appointment to a high post); congratulate each other on the prospect of getting good appointments

【弹劾】 tánhé impeach (a public official)

【弹花机】 tánhuājī cotton fluffer

【弹簧】 tánhuáng spring: 回动～ return spring/ 保险～ relief spring
◇ ～秤 spring balance/ ～床 spring bed/ ～钢 spring steel/ ～铰链 spring hinge/ ～门 swing door/ ～圈 spring coil/ ～锁 spring lock

【弹力】 tánlì elastic force; elasticity; resilience; spring: 失去～的橡皮圈 a perished rubber band
◇ ～尼龙 stretch nylon; elastic nylon/ ～纱 stretch yarn/ ～袜 stretch socks

【弹球】 tánqiú (play) marbles

【弹射】 tánshè 〈军〉 launch (as with a catapult); catapult; shoot off; eject
◇ ～器 catapult; ejector/ ～座舱 ejection capsule/ ～座椅 ejection (或 ejector) seat

【弹跳】 tántiào bounce; spring: ～力好 have a lot of spring ◇ ～板 〈体〉 springboard

【弹涂鱼】 tántúyú 〈动〉 mudskipper

【弹性】 tánxìng elasticity; resilience; spring: 又软又有～的地毯 soft and springy carpets/ 这种毛～大，拉力强。This wool possesses high resilience and tensile strength./ 球的～符合标准。The balls reach the specifications for bounce.
◇ ～极限 elastic limit/ ～计 elastometer/ ～抗 〈物〉 elastic reactance/ ～塑料 elastoplast/ ～体 elastomer

【弹压】 tányā suppress; quell

【弹指】 tánzhǐ a snap of the fingers: ～之间 in a flash; in the twinkling of an eye; in an instant

【弹奏】 tánzòu play (a stringed musical instrument); pluck

**覃** tán ① 〈书〉 deep: ～思 deep in thought ② (Tán) a surname
另见 Qín

**痰** tán phlegm; sputum

【痰喘】 tánchuǎn 〈中医〉 asthma due to excessive phlegm

【痰厥】 tánjué 〈中医〉 coma due to blocking of the respiratory system

【痰气】 tánqì 〈方〉 ① mental disorder ② apoplexy

【痰桶】 tántǒng 〈口〉 spittoon

【痰盂】 tányú spittoon; cuspidor

**谭** Tán a surname

**潭** tán ① deep pool; pond: 一～死水 a pond of stagnant water/ 龙～虎穴 dragon's pool and tiger's den — a danger spot ② 〈方〉 pit; depression

**檀** tán ① wingceltis ② (Tán) a surname

【檀板】 tánbǎn hardwood clappers

【檀香】 tánxiāng 〈植〉 white sandalwood; sandalwood
◇ ～木 sandalwood/ ～扇 sandalwood fan/ ～油 sandalwood oil/ ～皂 sandal soap

【檀香山】 Tánxiāngshān Honolulu

## tǎn

**忐** tǎn

【忐忑】 tǎntè perturbed; mentally disturbed: ～不安 uneasy;

fidgety

**坦** tǎn ① level; smooth: 平～ (of land, etc.) level; smooth ② calm; composed ③ open; candid

【坦白】 tǎnbái ① honest; frank; candid: ～对你说 to be frank with you; frankly speaking/ 襟怀～ honest and aboveboard ② confess; make a confession; own up (to): 彻底～交代 make a clean breast of (one's crimes)/ ～从宽,抗拒从严 leniency to those who confess their crimes and severity to those who refuse to

【坦荡】 tǎndàng ① (of a road, etc.) broad and level ② magnanimous; bighearted

【坦克】 tǎnkè tank
◇ ～兵 tank forces/ ～乘员 tank crew/ ～手 tankman

【坦然】 tǎnrán calm; unperturbed; having no misgivings: ～自若 calm and confident; completely at ease

【坦桑尼亚】 Tǎnsāngníyà Tanzania ◇ ～人 Tanzanian

【坦率】 tǎnshuài candid; frank; straightforward: 为人～ be frank and open/ ～地交换意见 have a frank exchange of views

【坦途】 tǎntú level road; highway: 攀登科学高峰,既无捷径,又无～。There are neither shortcuts nor easy paths to the heights of science.

**袒** tǎn ① leave (the upper part of the body) uncovered; be stripped to the waist or have one's shirt unbuttoned: ～胸露臂 (of a woman) exposing one's neck and shoulders; *décolleté* ② give unprincipled protection to; shield; shelter: 偏～ give unprincipled support to; be partial to

【袒护】 tǎnhù give unprincipled protection to; be partial to; shield: ～一方 be partial to one side/ 公然～ openly shield/ 你别～他。Don't make excuses for him.

**钽** tǎn 〈化〉 tantalum (Ta)

**毯** tǎn blanket; rug; carpet: 毛～ woollen blanket/ 绒～ flannelette blanket/ 地～ rug; carpet/ 挂～ tapestry

【毯子】 tǎnzi blanket

## tàn

**叹** tàn ① sigh: 长～一声 heave a deep sigh ② exclaim in admiration; acclaim; praise: 赞～ highly praise; sigh in admiration/ ～为奇迹 admire and praise sth. as a wonderful achievement

【叹词】 tàncí 〈语〉 interjection; exclamation

【叹服】 tànfú gasp in admiration: 令人～ compel (或 command) admiration

【叹气】 tànqì sigh; heave a sigh: 唉声～ sigh in despair

【叹赏】 tànshǎng admire; express admiration for

【叹为观止】 tàn wéi guān zhǐ acclaim (a work of art, etc.) as the acme of perfection

【叹息】 tànxī 〈书〉 heave a sigh; sigh

**炭** tàn charcoal: 木～ charcoal/ 烧～ make charcoal

【炭笔】 tànbǐ charcoal pencil

【炭画】 tànhuà 〈美术〉 charcoal drawing; charcoal

【炭火】 tànhuǒ charcoal fire

【炭疽】 tànjū 〈医〉 anthrax ◇ ～病 〈农〉 anthracnose

【炭盆】 tànpén charcoal brazier

【炭窑】 tànyáo charcoal kiln

**探** tàn ① try to find out; explore; sound: 试～ sound out; put out a feeler/ ～路 explore the way ② scout; spy; detective: 敌～ enemy scout/ 侦～ detective ③ visit; pay a call on: ～亲访友 visit one's relatives and friends ④ stretch forward: 有人从门口～进头来。Somebody popped his head in at the door./ 行车时不要～身窗外。Don't lean out of the window while the bus is in motion.

【探测】 tàncè survey; sound; probe: ～海底情况 survey the seabed/ ～水深 take soundings/ ～悬崖高度 gauge the height of a bluff ◇ ～器 sounder; probe; detector

【探访】 tànfǎng ① seek by inquiry or search: ～民间秘方 seek out secret medicinal recipes from among the people ② pay a visit to; visit

【探监】 tànjiān visit a prisoner

【探井】 tànjǐng ① 〈矿〉 prospect (或 test) pit; exploring (或 exploratory) shaft ② 〈石油〉 test well; exploratory well: 野猫～ wildcat

【探究】 tànjiū make a thorough inquiry; probe into: ～原因 look into the causes

【探空】 tànkōng 〈气〉 sounding ◇ ～气球 sounding balloon

【探口气】 tàn kǒuqi ascertain (或 find out) sb.'s opinions or feelings; sound sb. out

【探矿】 tànkuàng go prospecting; prospect

【探雷】 tànléi detect (或 locate) a mine ◇ ～器 mine detector

【探明】 tànmíng ascertain; verify: 已～的煤储量 proven (或 known) coal deposits/ 新油田的含油层结构已经～。The oil-bearing structure of the new oilfield has been verified.

【探囊取物】 tàn náng qǔ wù like taking something out of one's pocket — as easy as winking; as easy as falling off a log

【探亲】 tànqīn go home to visit one's family or go to visit one's relatives: 到故乡～访友 return to one's homeland to visit one's relatives and friends ◇ ～假 home leave

【探求】 tànqiú seek; pursue; search after (或 for): ～真理 seek truth

【探伤】 tànshāng 〈冶〉 flaw detection; crack detection ◇～仪 flaw detector

【探视】 tànshì visit: ～病人 visit a patient ◇ ～时间 visiting hours (in a hospital)

【探索】 tànsuǒ explore; probe: ～宇宙的秘密 probe (或 explore) the secrets of the universe/ 星际～ interplanetary exploration/ ～事物的本质 probe into the essence of things/ ～真理 seek truth/ 对一些具体政策问题,应当继续考察和～。We must further investigate and study certain specific policies.

【探讨】 tàntǎo inquire into; probe into: 从不同角度对问题进行～ approach a subject from different angles/ 对针麻原理作进一步的～ go further into the principles governing acupuncture anaesthesia/ ～性的访问 an exploratory visit

【探听】 tàntīng try to find out; make inquiries: ～下落 inquire about the whereabouts of sb. or sth./ ～消息 make inquiries about sb. or sth.; fish for information/ ～人家的私事 pry into other people's private affairs/ ～虚实 try to find out about an opponent, adversary, etc.; try to ascertain the strength of the enemy

【探头探脑】 tàntóu-tànnǎo pop one's head in and look about

【探望】 tànwàng ① look about: 她不时向窗外～。She looked out the window every now and then. ② visit: 回国～亲友 return to one's home country to visit relatives and friends

【探问】 tànwèn ① make cautious inquiries about: 他们一再～此事。They inquired about the matter time and again. ② inquire after

【探悉】 tànxī ascertain; learn; find out: 从有关方面～ learn from those concerned

【探险】 tànxiǎn explore; make explorations; venture into

the unknown: 到原始森林去～ explore a primeval forest ◇ ～队 exploring (或 exploration) party; expedition/ ～家 explorer
【探询】 tànxún 见"探问"
【探鱼仪】 tànyúyí 〈渔〉 fish detector; fish-finder
【探照灯】 tànzhàodēng searchlight: ～的灯光 searchlight beam
【探针】 tànzhēn 〈医〉 probe
【探子】 tànzi ① scout ② a thin tube used to extract samples of food grains, etc.

**碳** tàn 〈化〉 carbon (C)
【碳酐】 tàngān 〈化〉 carbonic anhydride
【碳黑】 tànhēi 〈化〉 carbon black
【碳化】 tànhuà 〈化〉 carbonization ◇ ～钙 calcium carbide/ ～硅 carborundum; silicon carbide/ ～物 carbide
【碳精】 tànjīng 〈电〉 carbon ◇ ～棒 carbon rod; carbon/ ～电极 carbon electrode
【碳氢化合物】 tànqīng huàhéwù 〈化〉 hydrocarbon
【碳刷】 tànshuā 〈电〉 carbon brush
【碳水化合物】 tànshuǐ huàhéwù 〈化〉 carbohydrate
【碳丝】 tànsī 〈电〉 carbon filament ◇ ～灯 carbon lamp
【碳素钢】 tànsùgāng 〈化〉 carbon steel
【碳酸】 tànsuān 〈化〉 carbonic acid ◇ ～钙 calcium carbonate/ ～钠 sodium carbonate; soda/ ～气 carbon dioxide; chokedamp/ ～氢钠 sodium bicarbonate; baking soda/ ～盐 carbonate

## tāng

**汤** tāng ① hot water; boiling water: 温～浸种 hot-water treatment of seeds ②〔多用于地名〕hot springs ③ soup; broth: 清～ clear soup; *consommé*/ 鸡～ chicken soup/ 肉～ broth/ 姜～ ginger tea/ 三菜一～ soup and three other courses ④ a liquid preparation of medicinal herbs; decoction: 柴胡～ a decoction of Chinese thorowax root (with other ingredients) ⑤ (Tāng) a surname
【汤包】 tāngbāo steamed dumplings filled with minced meat and gravy
【汤匙】 tāngchí tablespoon; soupspoon
【汤锅】 tāngguō 〈旧〉 slaughterhouse
【汤壶】 tānghú metal or earthenware hot-water bottle
【汤剂】 tāngjì 〈中医〉 decoction (of herbal medicine)
【汤加】 Tāngjiā Tonga ◇ ～人 Tongan
【汤面】 tāngmiàn noodles in soup
【汤婆子】 tāngpózi 〈方〉 见"汤壶"
【汤勺】 tāngsháo soup ladle
【汤头】 tāngtóu 〈中医〉 a prescription for a medical decoction ◇ ～歌诀 medical recipes in jingles; prescriptions in rhyme
【汤碗】 tāngwǎn soup bowl
【汤药】 tāngyào 〈中医〉 a decoction of medicinal ingredients
【汤圆】 tāngyuán stuffed dumplings made of glutinous rice flour served in soup

**铴** tāng
【铴锣】 tāngluó a small brass gong

**嘡** tāng 〈象〉 a loud ringing sound; clang

**羰** tāng 〈化〉 carbonyl (group)
【羰基】 tāngjī 〈化〉 carbonyl (group): ～键 carbonyl bond (或 link)

**蹚** tāng ① wade; ford: ～水过河 wade (across) a stream/ ～了一脚泥 get one's feet muddy through wading ② 〈农〉 turn the soil and dig up weeds (with a hoe, etc.)

## táng

**唐** Táng ① the Tang Dynasty (618-907): ～诗 Tang poetry ② a surname
【唐花】 tánghuā hothouse flower
【唐人街】 Tángrénjiē Chinatown
【唐三彩】 tángsāncǎi 〈考古〉 tri-coloured glazed pottery of the Tang Dynasty
【唐突】 tángtū brusque; rude; offensive: 出言～ make a blunt remark/ ～的行动 a presumptuous act

**堂** táng ① the main room of a house ② a hall (或 room) for a specific purpose: 人民大会～ the Great Hall of the People/ 讲～ lecture hall; lecture room/ 课～ classroom/ 食～ dining hall/ 澡～ bathhouse ③ court of law; a principal hall in a *yamen*: 过～ have a hearing; be tried ④ relationship between cousins, etc. of the same paternal grandfather or great-grandfather; of the same clan: ～兄弟 cousins on the paternal side; cousins ⑤ 〈量〉: 一～家具 a set (或 suite) of furniture/ 每天上四～课 have four classes every day
【堂奥】 táng'ào 〈书〉 ① the innermost recess of a hall ② the interior of a country ③ profundity of thought or knowledge; profundities
【堂房】 tángfáng 见"堂"④
【堂鼓】 tánggǔ a kind of drum used in Chinese operas
【堂倌】 tángguān 〈旧〉 waiter
【堂皇】 tánghuáng grand; stately; magnificent: 富丽～ beautiful and imposing; in majestic splendour; resplendent
【堂堂】 tángtáng ① dignified; impressive: 仪表～ dignified in appearance; impressive-looking ② (of a man) having high aspirations and boldness of vision ③ imposing; awe-inspiring; formidable: ～之阵 an imposing array of troops; awe-inspiring military strength
【堂堂正正】 tángtángzhèngzhèng ① impressive or dignified in personal appearance ② open and aboveboard
【堂屋】 tángwū central room (of a one-storey Chinese traditional house consisting of several rooms in a row)

**棠** táng 见"棠梨"
【棠棣】 tángdì 〈植〉 ① Chinese bush cherry ② a kind of white poplar
【棠梨】 tánglí 〈植〉 birchleaf pear (*Pyrus betulaefolia*)

**溏** táng half congealed; viscous
【溏便】 tángbiàn 〈中医〉 semiliquid (或 unformed) stool
【溏心】 tángxīn (of eggs) with a soft yolk: ～儿蛋 soft-boiled or soft-fried egg/ ～儿松花 preserved egg with a jelly-like yolk

**塘** táng ① dyke; embankment: 河～ river embankment/ 海～ seawall ② pool; pond: 鱼～ fish pond ③ hot-water bathing pool: 澡～ bathhouse; public baths
【塘肥】 tángféi pond sludge used as manure
【塘鳢】 tánglǐ 〈动〉 sleeper
【塘泥】 tángní pond sludge; pond silt
【塘堰】 tángyàn small reservoir (in a hilly area) 又作"塘坝"

**搪** táng ① ward off; keep out: ～风 keep out the wind/

～饥 allay one's hunger ② evade; do sth. perfunctorily: ～帐 put off a creditor ③ spread (clay, paint, etc.) over; daub: ～炉子 line a stove with clay ④ 见"镗" táng

【搪瓷】 tángcí enamel
◇ ～茶缸 enamel mug/ ～钢板 〈建〉 enamelled pressed steel/ ～器皿 enamelware

【搪塞】 tángsè stall sb. off; do sth. perfunctorily: ～他几句 stall him off with a vague answer/ ～差事 perform a duty perfunctorily

**樘** táng 〈建〉 door or window frame

**膛** táng ① thorax; chest: 胸～ chest/ 杀猪开～ slit a pig's throat and cut open its chest ② an enclosed space inside sth.; chamber: 炉～ stove chamber/ 枪～ bore (of a gun)/ 子弹上了～。The gun is loaded.

【膛线】 tángxiàn 〈军〉 rifling

**糖** táng ① sugar: 白～ refined sugar/ 砂～ granulated sugar/ 红～ brown sugar/ 冰～ crystal sugar; rock candy ② sugared; in syrup: ～姜 sugared ginger; ginger in syrup/ ～蒜 garlic in syrup; sweetened garlic ③ sweets; candy

【糖厂】 tángchǎng sugar refinery

【糖醋】 tángcù sugar and vinegar; sweet and sour ◇ ～排骨 sweet and sour spareribs/ ～鱼 fish in sweet and sour sauce

【糖甙】 tángdài 〈化〉 glucoside

【糖膏】 tánggāo massecuite; fillmass

【糖果】 tángguǒ sweets; candy; sweetmeats ◇ ～店 sweet shop; candy store; confectionery

【糖葫芦】 tánghúlu sugarcoated haws on a stick

【糖化】 tánghuà 〈化〉 saccharification ◇ ～饲料 saccharified pig feed; fermented feed

【糖浆】 tángjiāng syrup

【糖精】 tángjīng saccharin; gluside

【糖类】 tánglèi 〈化〉 carbohydrate

【糖量计】 tángliàngjì 〈化〉 saccharometer; saccharimeter

【糖料作物】 tángliào zuòwù 〈农〉 sugar crop

【糖萝卜】 tángluóbo ① 〈口〉 beet ② 〈方〉 preserved carrot

【糖酶】 tángméi 〈化〉 carbohydrase

【糖蜜】 tángmì molasses

【糖尿病】 tángniàobìng diabetes ◇ ～患者 diabetic

【糖水】 tángshuǐ syrup: ～桔子(荔枝) tangerines (lichees) in syrup

【糖衣】 tángyī sugarcoating: 这种药片有～。These pills are sugarcoated.

【糖衣炮弹】 tángyī pàodàn sugarcoated bullet: 要警惕资产阶级用～向我们进攻。We must be on guard against the bourgeoisie's attack with sugarcoated bullets.

【糖原】 tángyuán 〈化〉 glycogen 又作"糖元"

**镗** táng 〈机〉 boring

【镗床】 tángchuáng 〈机〉 boring machine; boring lathe; borer: 坐标～ jig boring machine

【镗刀】 tángdāo 〈机〉 boring cutter; boring tool

【镗孔】 tángkǒng 〈机〉 bore hole; boring

**螳** táng mantis

【螳臂当车】 táng bì dāng chē a mantis trying to stop a chariot — overrate oneself and try to hold back an overwhelmingly superior force

【螳螂】 tángláng 〈动〉 mantis

【螳螂捕蝉,黄雀在后】 tángláng bǔ chán, huángquè zài hòu the mantis stalks the cicada, unaware of the oriole behind — covet gains ahead without being aware of danger behind

## tǎng

**帑** tǎng 〈书〉 state treasury; funds in the state treasury: 公～ public funds

**傥** tǎng 〈连〉 if; supposing; in case: ～有不测 in case of accidents; if anything untoward should happen

【傥或】 tǎnghuò 见"傥若"

【傥来之物】 tǎng lái zhī wù an unexpected or undeserved gain; windfall

【傥然】 tǎngrán 见"傥若"

【傥若】 tǎngruò 〈连〉 if; supposing; in case: ～发现情况,立即报告。In case you find anything unusual, report immediately.

【傥使】 tǎngshǐ 见"傥若"

**淌** tǎng drip; shed; trickle: ～眼泪 shed tears/ ～口水 let saliva dribble from the mouth; slaver; slobber/ 伤口～血。Blood trickled from the wound./ 他脸上～着汗水。Sweat was dripping from his face./ 木桶漏水,～了一地。The pail leaked, so water ran all over the place.

**耥** tǎng weed and loosen the soil (in a paddy field)

【耥耙】 tǎngpá 〈农〉 paddy-field harrow

**躺** tǎng lie; recline: ～下歇歇 lie down and rest a while/ 不要～在过去的成绩上睡大觉。Don't rest content with past achievements. 或 Don't rest on your laurels.

【躺倒】 tǎngdǎo lie down: ～不干 stay in bed — refuse to shoulder responsibilities any longer

【躺柜】 tǎngguì a long low box with a lid on top; chest

【躺椅】 tǎngyǐ deck chair; sling chair

## tàng

**烫** tàng ① scald; burn: 让开水～着了 be scalded by boiling water/ ～了个泡 get a blister through being scalded (或 burnt)/ 热得～手 so hot that it burns (或 scalds) one's hand; scalding to the touch ② heat up in hot water; warm: ～酒 heat wine (by putting the container in hot water)/ ～澡 take a hot bath/ ～脚 bathe one's feet in hot water ③ very hot; scalding; boiling hot: 这汤真～! This soup is boiling hot! ④ iron; press: ～衣服 iron (或 press) clothes ⑤ perm; have one's hair permed: 冷～ cold wave/ 到理发店去～发 go to the hairdresser's for a perm

【烫发】 tàngfà give or have a permanent wave; perm

【烫金】 tàngjīn 〈印〉 gilding; bronzing: 布面～ cloth gilt ◇ ～机 〈印〉 gilding press; bronzing machine

【烫蜡】 tànglà polish with melted wax; wax (a floor, etc.)

【烫面】 tàngmiàn dough made with boiling water ◇ ～饺 steamed dumplings (made of dough prepared with boiling water)

【烫伤】 tàngshāng 〈医〉 scald

**趟**• tàng ① 〈量〉〔表示走动的次数〕: 到昆明去了一～ have been to Kunming once; have made a trip to Kunming/ 这辆卡车昨天往工地跑了三～。Yesterday the truck made three trips to the construction site./ 这～车是去广州的。This train goes to Guangzhou. 或 This is the Guangzhou train. ② 〈方〉 〈量〉〔用于成行的东西〕: 一～街 a street/ 两～桌子 two rows of tables

## tāo

**叨** tāo be favoured with; get the benefit of
另见 dāo
【叨光】 tāoguāng 〈套〉 much obliged to you
【叨教】 tāojiào 〈套〉 many thanks for your advice
【叨扰】 tāorǎo 〈套〉 thank you for your hospitality

**涛** tāo great waves; billows: 惊～骇浪 terrifying crashing waves/ 松～ the soughing of the wind in the pines

**绦** tāo silk ribbon; silk braid
【绦虫】 tāochóng 〈动〉 tapeworm; cestode ◇ ～病 〈医〉 taeniasis; cestodiasis
【绦子】 tāozi silk ribbon; silk braid

**掏** tāo ① draw out; pull out; fish out: 从口袋里～出笔记本 pull a notebook from one's pocket; take a notebook out of one's pocket/ ～手枪 draw a pistol/ ～炉灰 clear the ashes from a stove/ ～鸟窝 take young birds or eggs out of a nest; go bird's-nesting/ ～耳朵 pick one's ears/ ～尽红心为革命 devote oneself to the revolution heart and soul ② dig (a hole, etc.); hollow out; scoop out: 在墙上～一个洞 make a hole in the wall ③ steal from sb.'s pocket: 他的皮夹子被～了。He had his wallet stolen by a pickpocket.
【掏槽】 tāocáo 〈矿〉 cutting
【掏窟窿】 tāo kūlong 〈方〉 run (或 get, fall) into debt
【掏腰包】 tāo yāobāo 〈口〉 ① pay out of one's own pocket; foot a bill: 这顿饭我～。This meal is on me. ② pick sb.'s pocket

**滔** tāo inundate; flood
【滔滔】 tāotāo ① torrential; surging: 白浪～ whitecaps surging ② keeping up a constant flow of words: 口若悬河,～不绝 talk on and on in a flow of eloquence
【滔天】 tāotiān ① (of billows, etc.) dash to the skies: 波浪～ waves running high ② heinous; monstrous: ～罪行 monstrous crimes

**韬** tāo 〈书〉 ① sheath or bow case ② hide; conceal ③ the art of war
【韬光养晦】 tāoguāng-yǎnghuì hide one's capacities and bide one's time
【韬晦】 tāohuì conceal one's true features or intentions; lie low
【韬略】 tāolüè military strategy

**饕** tāo
【饕餮】 tāotiè ① *taotie*, a mythical ferocious animal ② a fierce and cruel person ③ voracious eater; glutton; gourmand ◇ ～纹 〈考古〉 *taotie* design

## táo

**逃** táo ① run away; escape; flee: ～出敌人监狱 escape from the enemy's prison/ 敌军望风而～。The enemy fled pell-mell before our army. ② evade; dodge; shirk; escape: ～债 dodge a creditor/ 罪责难～ cannot shirk responsibility for the crime/ 反革命再狡猾也～不过人民雪亮的眼睛。The counterrevolutionaries cannot escape the sharp eyes of the people, however cunning they may be.
【逃奔】 táobèn run away to (another place)
【逃避】 táobì escape; evade; shirk: ～现实 try to escape reality/ ～斗争 evade struggle/ ～责任 shirk responsibility/ ～困难 avoid (或 dodge) a difficulty
【逃兵】 táobīng army deserter; deserter
【逃窜】 táocuàn run away; flee in disorder: 敌军狼狈～。The enemy troops fled helter-skelter.
【逃遁】 táodùn flee; escape; evade: 仓皇～ flee in panic/ 在警觉的人民面前,阶级敌人无处～。Surrounded by an alert people, the class enemy can find no refuge.
【逃犯】 táofàn escaped criminal or convict
【逃荒】 táohuāng flee from famine; get away from a famine-stricken area
【逃命】 táomìng run (或 flee, fly) for one's life
【逃难】 táonàn flee from a calamity; be a refugee
【逃匿】 táonì escape and hide; go into hiding
【逃跑】 táopǎo run away; flee; take flight; take to one's heels ◇ ～主义 flightism (the advocacy or practice of running away from the battlefield or from difficulties in revolutionary struggle)
【逃散】 táosàn become separated in flight
【逃生】 táoshēng flee (或 run, fly) for one's life; escape with one's life: 死里～ barely escape with one's life; have a narrow escape; escape by the skin of one's teeth
【逃税】 táoshuì evade (或 dodge) a tax
【逃脱】 táotuō succeed in escaping; make good one's escape; get clear of: ～责任 succeed in evading responsibility/ 犯罪分子～不了人民的惩罚。The lawbreakers will never escape punishment by the people.
【逃亡】 táowáng become a fugitive; flee from home; go into exile ◇ ～地主 runaway (或 fugitive) landlord
【逃学】 táoxué play truant; cut class
【逃逸】 táoyì 〈书〉 escape; run away; abscond
【逃之夭夭】 táo zhī yāoyāo decamp; make one's getaway; show a clean pair of heels
【逃走】 táozǒu run away; flee; take flight; take to one's heels

**桃** táo ① peach ② a peach-shaped thing: 棉～ cotton boll
【桃符】 táofú ① peach wood charms against evil, hung on the gate on the lunar New Year's Eve in ancient times ② Spring Festival couplets
【桃脯】 táofǔ preserved peach
【桃红】 táohóng pink
【桃花】 táohuā peach blossom
【桃花心木】 táohuāxīnmù mahogany
【桃花汛】 táohuāxùn spring flood
【桃花鱼】 táohuāyú minnow
【桃李】 táolǐ peaches and plums — one's pupils or disciples: ～满天下 have pupils everywhere
【桃仁】 táorén ① 〈中药〉 peach kernel ② walnut meat; shelled walnut
【桃树】 táoshù peach (tree)
【桃源】 táoyuán 见"世外桃源" shìwài táoyuán
【桃子】 táozi peach

**陶** táo ① pottery; earthenware: ～俑 pottery figurine/ 彩～ painted pottery ② make pottery ③ cultivate; mould; educate: 熏～ exert a gradual, uplifting influence on; nurture ④ contented; happy: 乐～～ feel happy and contented ⑤ (Táo) a surname
【陶瓷】 táocí pottery and porcelain; ceramics ◇ ～工 potter/ ～片 〈考古〉 potsherd/ ～学 ceramics/ ～业 ceramics; ceramic industry

【陶管】 táoguǎn 〈建〉 earthenware pipe
【陶粒】 táolì 〈建〉 ceramsite ◇ ～混凝土 〈建〉 ceramsite concrete
【陶器】 táoqì pottery; earthenware
【陶然】 táorán happy and carefree
【陶土】 táotǔ 〈矿〉 potter's clay; pottery clay; kaolin
【陶文】 táowén 〈考古〉 inscription on pottery
【陶冶】 táoyě ① make pottery and smelt metal ② exert a favourable influence (on a person's character, etc.); mould: ～性情 mould a person's temperament
【陶醉】 táozuì be intoxicated (with success, etc.); revel in: 自我～ be intoxicated with self-satisfaction/ 我们不能～于已取得的成绩。We mustn't let success go to our heads.

**淘** táo ① wash in a pan or basket: ～米 wash rice ② clean out; dredge: ～阴沟 clean out a drain (或 sewer)/ ～茅房 remove night soil from a latrine/ ～井 dredge a well ③ tax (a person's energy): ～神 trying; bothersome ④〈方〉 naughty
【淘河】 táohé 〈动〉 pelican
【淘金】 táojīn 〈矿〉 panning
【淘箩】 táoluó a basket for washing rice in
【淘气】 táoqì naughty; mischievous ◇ ～鬼 mischievous imp; a regular little mischief
【淘神】 táoshén 〈口〉 trying; bothersome
【淘汰】 táotài ① eliminate through selection or competition: 他在第一轮比赛中就被～了。He was eliminated in the very first round. ② die out; fall into disuse: 这种机器已经～了。This kind of machine is already obsolete. ◇ ～赛 elimination series

**萄** táo grapes: ～酒 grape wine

**啕** táo 见"号啕" háotáo

## tǎo

**讨** tǎo ① send armed forces to suppress; send a punitive expedition against: ～平叛乱 put down a rebellion ② denounce; condemn: 声～ denounce ③ demand; ask for; beg for: ～帐 demand the payment of a debt; dun/ 去跟老张～点墨汁。Go and ask Lao Zhang for some Chinese ink. ④ marry (a woman): ～老婆 take a wife; get married ⑤ incur; invite: ～了个没趣儿 court a rebuff; ask for a snub/ 自～苦吃 bring trouble upon oneself; ask for trouble/ ～人喜欢 likable; cute ⑥ discuss; study: 商～ discuss
【讨伐】 tǎofá send armed forces to suppress; send a punitive expedition against
【讨饭】 tǎofàn beg for food; be a beggar
【讨好】 tǎohǎo ① ingratiate oneself with; fawn on; toady to; curry favour with ②〔多用于否定〕be rewarded with a fruitful result; have one's labour rewarded: 费力不～ put in much hard work, but get very little result; undertake a thankless task
【讨还】 tǎohuán get sth. back: 向恶霸地主～血债 make the despotic landlord pay his blood debt
【讨价】 tǎojià ask (或 name) a price
【讨价还价】 tǎojià-huánjià bargain; haggle
【讨教】 tǎojiào ask for advice
【讨论】 tǎolùn discuss; talk over: 参加～ join in the discussion
【讨论会】 tǎolùnhuì discussion; symposium: 科学～ science symposium
【讨便宜】 tǎo piányi seek undue advantage; try to gain sth. at the expense of others; look for a bargain
【讨乞】 tǎoqǐ beg alms; beg
【讨巧】 tǎoqiǎo act artfully to get what one wants; get the best for oneself at the least expense; choose the easy way out
【讨亲】 tǎoqīn 〈方〉 take a wife; get married
【讨情】 tǎoqíng 〈方〉 plead for sb.; beg sb. off: ～告饶 plead for leniency; beg for pardon
【讨饶】 tǎoráo beg for mercy; ask for forgiveness
【讨嫌】 tǎoxián disagreeable; annoying: 这孩子真讨人嫌。That child is a nuisance.
【讨厌】 tǎoyàn ① disagreeable; disgusting; repugnant: ～的天气 abominable weather ② hard to handle; troublesome; nasty: 气管炎是很～的病。Tracheitis is a nasty illness. ③ dislike; loathe; be disgusted with: 工人们很～他那官僚架子。The workers detest his bureaucratic airs.

## tào

**套** tào ① sheath; case; cover; sleeve: 枕～ pillowcase; pillowslip/ 毛笔～ cap of a writing brush/ 椅～ slipcover for a chair/ 轴～ axle sleeve/ 手枪～ holster ② cover with; slip over; encase in: ～上一件毛衣 slip on a sweater/ 把枕套～上 put the pillow in the pillowcase ③ that which covers (other garments, etc.): ～袖 oversleeve/ ～鞋 overshoes ④ overlap; interlink: 一环～一环 one ring linked with another — a closely linked succession ⑤ the bend of a river or curve in a mountain range: 河～ the Great Bend of the Huanghe River ⑥〈方〉 cotton padding (或 wadding); batting: 被～ cotton padding of a quilt; quilt padding ⑦ traces; harness: 牲口～ harness for a draught animal/ 雇～ hire a draught animal and a plough/ 拉～ pull a plough or cart ⑧ harness (an animal); hitch up (an animal to a cart): 我去～牲口。I'll go and harness the beast. ⑨ knot; loop; noose: 拴个～儿 tie a knot; make a loop/ 活～儿 slipknot; running knot ⑩ put a ring, etc. round; tie: ～上救生圈 put on a life ring/ ～马 lasso a horse ⑪ model on (或 after); copy: 生搬硬～ apply mechanically; copy indiscriminately/ ～公式 apply a formula/ 这一段是从现成文章上～下来的。This passage is modelled on one in another article. ⑫ convention; formula: 客～ polite remarks; civilities; pleasantries/ 老一～ the same old stuff; stereotype ⑬ coax a secret out of sb.; pump sb. about sth.: 拿话～他 coax the secret out of him; trick him into telling the truth ⑭ try to win (sb.'s friendship): ～交情 try to get in good with sb./ ～近乎 〈方〉 cotton up to ⑮〈量〉 set; suit; suite: 一～《列宁全集》a set of the *Collected Works of Lenin*/ 贯彻执行一整～两条腿走路的方针 implement a whole set of policies known as "walking on two legs"/ 两～衣服 two suits of clothes/ 一～房间 a flat
【套版】 tàobǎn 〈印〉 registering
【套包】 tàobāo collar for a horse
【套车】 tàochē harness an animal to a cart
【套购】 tàogòu fraudulently purchase (state-controlled commodities); illegally buy up: ～统购统销物资 illegally buy up goods for which there is a state monopoly of purchase and marketing
【套管】 tàoguǎn 〈石油〉 casing pipe; casing ◇ ～程序 casing programme
【套间】 tàojiān ① a small room opening off another; inner room ② apartment; flat
【套裤】 tàokù trouser legs worn over one's trousers; leggings

【套曲】 tàoqǔ 〈乐〉 divertimento ◇ ～形式 cyclical (或 cycle) form
【套色】 tàoshǎi 〈印〉 chromatography; colour process ◇ ～版 process plate; colourplate/ ～木刻 coloured woodcut
【套衫】 tàoshān pullover
【套数】 tàoshù ① a cycle of songs in a traditional opera ② a series of skills and tricks in *wushu* (武术), etc.
【套索】 tàosuǒ lasso; noose
【套筒】 tàotǒng 〈机〉 sleeve; muff: 气缸～ cylinder sleeve ◇ ～扳手 box spanner (或 wrench); socket wrench/ ～联轴节 muff coupling
【套问】 tàowèn find out by asking seemingly casual questions; tactfully sound sb. out
【套鞋】 tàoxié overshoes; rubbers; galoshes
【套袖】 tàoxiù oversleeve
【套印】 tàoyìn 〈印〉 chromatography: 彩色～ process printing ◇ ～本 chromatograph edition
【套用】 tàoyòng apply mechanically; use indiscriminately: 不能到处～这个公式。This formula cannot be applied indiscriminately.
【套语】 tàoyǔ polite formula
【套种】 tàozhòng 〈农〉 interplanting: 实行间作～ adopt intercropping and interplanting/ 小麦地里～棉花 interplant cotton with wheat 又作"套作"
【套子】 tàozi ① sheath; case; cover: 照相机～ camera case/ 沙发～ sofa cover/ 唱片～ (gramophone) record sleeve ② conventional (或 stereotyped) remark; conventionality ③〈方〉 cotton padding (或 wadding); batting

## tè

**忒** tè 〈书〉 error; mistake: 差～ error
另见 tēi; tuī

**忑** tè 见"忐忑" tǎntè

**特** tè ① special; particular; unusual; exceptional: ～使 special envoy/ 奇～ peculiar; quaint ② for a special purpose; specially: ～为此事而来 come specially for this purpose ③ secret agent; spy: 敌～ enemy agent/ 防～ guard against enemy agents ④ very; especially: 这个医生扎针～灵。That doctor is very good at giving needle treatment. ⑤〈书〉 but; only: 不～如此 not only that
【特别】 tèbié ① special; particular; out of the ordinary: 没什么～的地方 nothing out of the ordinary/ 他的口音很～。He has a peculiar accent. ② especially; particularly: 工作～努力 be especially hardworking/ 建设一支～能战斗的队伍 train a contingent of especially good fighters/ 质量～好 be of extra fine quality/ 老红军的报告～有教育意义。The veteran Red Army man's talk was particularly instructive./ 这里最需要医务人员,～是外科医生。We're very much in need of medical workers, especially surgeons. ③ going out of one's way to (do sth.); specially: 老大娘～为伤员燉了一只鸡。Granny cooked a chicken especially for the wounded soldier.
◇ ～会议 special meeting; special session/ ～开支 special expenses/ ～快车 express train; express/ ～提款权 special drawing rights (SDR)/ ～条款 special clause/ ～许可证 special license
【特产】 tèchǎn special local product; speciality; specialty: 东北～ specialities (或 special local products) of the Northeast/ 桐油是中国的～。Tung oil is a special product of China.
【特长】 tècháng what one is skilled in; strong point; speciality: 他有什么～? What is he skilled in?/ 绘画不是他的～。Painting is not his strong point./ 发挥每个人的～ give scope to everyone's special skill
【特出】 tèchū outstanding; prominent; extraordinary: ～的成绩 outstanding achievements/ ～的作用 a prominent role
【特此】 tècǐ 〔公文、书信用语〕: 定于明天上午八点在礼堂开会,～通知。It is hereby announced that there will be a meeting in the auditorium at 8 tomorrow morning.
【特大】 tèdà especially (或 exceptionally) big; the most: ～喜讯 excellent news; most welcome news/ ～丰收 an exceptional bumper harvest/ 战胜百年未遇的～干旱 overcome the worst drought in a century/ ～自然灾害 extraordinarily serious natural calamities/ ～洪水 a catastrophic flood/ ～号服装 outsize garments
【特等】 tèděng special grade (或 class); top grade ◇ ～舱 〈交〉 stateroom; *de luxe* cabin/ ～劳模 special-class model worker/ ～射手 crack shot; expert marksman
【特地】 tèdì 〈副〉 for a special purpose; specially: 我们是～来向您学习育秧的。We came specially to learn from you how to raise rice seedlings.
【特点】 tèdiǎn characteristic; distinguishing feature; peculiarity; trait: 生理～ physiological characteristics/ 照顾妇女的～ pay attention to the special needs of women/ 这个厂的产品具有工艺精湛,经久耐用的～。The products of this factory are noted for their fine workmanship and durability.
【特定】 tèdìng ① specially designated (或 appointed): ～的人选 a person specially designated for a post ② specific; specified; given: 在～的条件下 under given (或 specified) conditions/ 这种钢有～的用途。This kind of steel is used for specific purposes.
【特氟隆】 tèfúlóng 〈化〉 teflon
【特工】 tègōng secret service ◇ ～人员 special agent; secret service personnel
【特惠关税】 tèhuì guānshuì preferential tariff
【特混舰队】 tèhùn jiànduì (naval) task force
【特级】 tèjí special grade (或 class); superfine: ～茉莉花茶 superfine jasmine tea ◇ ～教师 teacher of a special classification/ ～战斗英雄 special-class combat hero; combat hero special grade
【特急】 tèjí extra urgent ◇ ～电 extra urgent telegram; flash message
【特辑】 tèjí ① special number (或 issue) of a periodical ② a special collection of short films
【特技】 tèjì ① stunt; trick ②〈电影〉 special effects ◇ ～飞行〈军〉 stunt flying; aerobatics/ ～镜头 trick shot/ ～摄影 trick photography/ ～跳伞 trick parachuting
【特价】 tèjià special offer; bargain price: ～出售 sell at a bargain price
【特刊】 tèkān special issue (或 number); special: 国庆～ special National Day issue
【特快】 tèkuài 〈交〉 express
【特立尼达和多巴哥】 Tèlìnídá hé Duōbāgē Trinidad and Tobago
【特例】 tèlì special case
【特洛伊木马】 Tèluòyī mùmǎ Trojan horse
【特命全权大使】 tèmìng quánquán dàshǐ ambassador extraordinary and plenipotentiary
【特命全权公使】 tèmìng quánquán gōngshǐ envoy extraordinary and minister plenipotentiary
【特派】 tèpài specially appointed ◇ ～记者 special correspondent; accredited journalist
【特遣部队】 tèqiǎn bùduì task force
【特屈儿】 tèqū'ér 〈化〉 tetryl

【特权】 tèquán privilege; prerogative: ～地位 privileged position/ 外交～ diplomatic privileges/ 不把职权变～ not use one's power to seek privileges ◇ ～阶层 privileged stratum/ ～思想 the idea that prerogatives and privileges go with position; the "special privilege" mentality
【特色】 tèsè characteristic; distinguishing feature (或 quality): 艺术～ artistic characteristics/ 富有民族～的歌舞节目 songs and dances with distinctive national features/ 象牙雕刻的传统～ the traditional features of ivory carving
【特设】 tèshè *ad hoc*: ～委员会 *ad hoc* committee
【特赦】 tèshè ① special pardon ② special amnesty: ～战犯 grant a special amnesty to war criminals ◇ ～令 decree (或 writ) of special pardon or amnesty
【特使】 tèshǐ special envoy
【特殊】 tèshū special; particular; peculiar; exceptional: ～条件下的～产物 a special product of special conditions/ ～情况 an exceptional case; special circumstances/ 革命战争的～规律 the specific laws of revolutionary war/ 由～到一般,又由一般到～ from the particular to the general and back again/ 这个病人的症状比较～。This patient has rather peculiar symptoms.
【特殊化】 tèshūhuà become privileged: 不搞～ seek no personal privileges/ 反对～ oppose privileges
【特殊性】 tèshūxìng particularity; peculiarity; specific characteristics: 矛盾的～ the particularity of contradiction/ 那个地区有它的～。That region has its specific characteristics.
【特为】 tèwèi for a special purpose; specially; going out of one's way to (do sth.): 我～来请你们去帮忙。I've come specially to ask you for help.
【特务】 tèwù special task (或 duties) ◇ ～营 special task battalion
【特务】 tèwu special (或 secret) agent; spy ◇ ～活动 espionage/ ～机关 secret service; espionage agency/ ～组织 secret service; spy organization
【特效】 tèxiào specially good effect; special efficacy ◇ ～药 specific drug; specific; effective cure
【特写】 tèxiě ① feature article or story; feature ② 〈电影〉 close-up ◇ ～镜头 close-up (shot)
【特性】 tèxìng specific property (或 characteristic)
【特许】 tèxǔ special permission ◇ ～证书 special permit; letters patent
【特压】 tèyā 〈化〉 extreme pressure ◇ ～添加剂 extreme pressure additive
【特邀】 tèyāo specially invite ◇ ～代表 specially invited representative
【特异】 tèyì ① exceptionally good; excellent; superfine: 成绩～ an excellent record (或 performance); extraordinary results ② peculiar; distinctive: ～的风格 distinctive style ◇ ～体质 〈医〉 idiosyncrasy
【特意】 tèyì 见"特地"
【特有】 tèyǒu peculiar; characteristic: 表现出青年～的热情 display the characteristic enthusiasm of youth/ 这是广东人～的一种说法。This is an expression peculiar to people from Guangdong.
【特约】 tèyuē engage by special arrangement ◇ ～稿 special contribution (to a publication)/ ～记者 special correspondent/ ～经售处 special sales agency/ ～评论员 special commentator/ ～维修店 special repair shop/ ～演员 guest actor/ ～撰稿人 special contributor
【特征】 tèzhēng characteristic; feature; trait: 面部～ facial characteristics/ 地理～ geographical features/ 民族～ national traits/ 计划经济是社会主义经济的一个基本～。Planned economy is a basic feature of the socialist economy.
【特指】 tèzhǐ refer in particular to: 我们所说的"小老虎"是～我们的副班长王发奋。The "Little Tiger" we're talking about is our deputy squad leader Wang Fafen.
【特种】 tèzhǒng special type; particular kind ◇ ～工艺 special arts and crafts; special handicraft products (of a particular place)/ ～技术部队 special technical units/ ～战争 special warfare

**铽** tè 〈化〉 terbium (Tb)

## tēi

**忒** tēi
另见 tè; tuī
【忒儿】 tēir 〈方〉〈象〉 flap: 麻雀～一声飞了。With a flap of its wings the sparrow flew off.

## tēng

**腾** tēng 〈象〉: 他～地一声跳到台上。He leaped on to the platform with a thump.
另见 téng

**熥** tēng heat up by steaming: 馒头凉了,～一～吧。The steamed buns are cold, let's heat them up.

**鼟** tēng 〈象〉: ～～的鼓声 the roll of drums

## téng

**疼** téng ① ache; pain; sore: 头～ have a headache/ 胃～ have a stomachache/ 嗓子～ have a sore throat/ 腿～ have a pain in the leg/ 浑身都～ be aching all over/ 你那个牙还～吗? Does your tooth still hurt? ② love dearly; be fond of; dote on: 奶奶最～小孙子。Granny dotes on her little grandson.
【疼爱】 téng'ài be very fond of; love dearly
【疼痛】 téngtòng pain; ache; soreness

**誊** téng transcribe; copy out: 照底稿～一份 make a clean copy of the draft
【誊录】 ténglù transcribe; copy out: ～文稿 copy out a manuscript
【誊清】 téngqīng make a fair copy of ◇ ～稿 fair copy
【誊写】 téngxiě transcribe; copy out ◇ ～版 〈印〉 stencil/ ～钢版 steel plate for cutting stencils/ ～蜡纸 stencil paper/ ～油墨 stencil ink
【誊印社】 téngyìnshè mimeograph service

**腾** téng ① gallop; jump; prance: ～跃 prance/ ～身而过 jump over sth. ② rise; soar: 升～ rise; ascend/ 飞～ soar ③ make room; clear out; vacate: ～出自己的房子给客人住 vacate one's own room to put up a visitor/ 给新来的同志～个地方 make room for a newcomer/ ～出更多的人来参加麦收 release more people to help with the wheat harvest ④〔用在某些动词后面,表示反复〕: 翻～ toss about; turn over and over/ 扑～ (of the heart) throb
另见 tēng
【腾贵】 ténggùi (of prices) shoot up; soar; skyrocket
【腾空】 téngkōng soar; rise high into the air; rise to the sky: 五彩缤纷的礼花～而起。Colourful fireworks shot into the sky.
【腾挪】 téngnuó ① transfer (funds, etc.) to other use: 专款专用,不得任意～。Funds earmarked for specific purposes

are not to be transfered at will. ② move sth. to make room: 把仓库里的东西～一下，好装水泥。Move the things in the storehouse to make room for the cement.

【腾腾】 téngténg steaming; seething: 热气～ steaming hot; seething with activity/ 烟雾～ hazy with smoke; smoke-laden/ 烈焰～ raging flames/ 杀气～ full of bellicosity; murderous-looking

【腾越】 téngyuè jump over: ～障碍 jump over obstacles

【腾云驾雾】 téngyún-jiàwù ① mount the clouds and ride the mist — speed across the sky ② feel giddy

## 滕

Téng a surname

## 藤

téng ① cane; rattan: ～制品 rattan work/ ～椅 cane chair; rattan chair/ ～盔 rattan helmet ② vine: 葡萄～ grape vine/ 西瓜～ watermelon vine

【藤本植物】 téngběn zhíwù 〈植〉 liana; vine

【藤黄】 ténghuáng 〈植〉 ① garcinia ② gamboge

【藤萝】 téngluó 〈植〉 Chinese wistaria (*Wisteria sinensis*)

【藤牌】 téngpái cane (或 rattan) shield; shield

【藤条】 téngtiáo rattan

【藤子】 téngzi 〈口〉 vine

## 螣

téng 〈动〉 stargazer

# tī

## 体

tī

另见 tǐ

【体己】 tīji ① intimate; confidential: ～话 things one says only to one's intimates ② 〈旧〉 private savings: ～钱 private savings of a family member

## 剔

tī ① clean with a pointed instrument; pick: ～骨头 pick a bone/ ～牙 pick one's teeth ② pick out and throw away; reject: 把烂梨～出去 pick out the rotten pears ③ rising stroke (in Chinese characters)

【剔除】 tīchú reject; get rid of: 吸取精华，～糟粕 absorb the essence and reject the dross

【剔红】 tīhóng carved lacquerware

## 梯

tī ① ladder; steps; stairs: 楼～ staircase/ 电～ lift; elevator ② shaped like a staircase; terraced: ～田 terraced fields

【梯次队形】 tīcì duìxíng 〈军〉 echelon formation

【梯队】 tīduì 〈军〉 echelon formation; echelon

【梯恩梯】 tī'ēntī 〈化〉 trinitrotoluene (TNT) ◇ ～当量 〈军〉 TNT equivalent

【梯级】 tījí stair; step

【梯己】 tīji 见"体己" tīji

【梯田】 tītián 〈农〉 terraced fields; terrace: 修～ build terraced fields; terrace mountain slopes

【梯形】 tīxíng ① ladder-shaped ② 〈数〉 (美) trapezoid; (英) trapezium ◇ ～翼 〈航空〉 trapezoidal wing; tapered airfoil

【梯子】 tīzi ladder; stepladder

## 锑

tī 〈化〉 antimony; stibium (Sb)

## 踢

tī ① kick: ～开绊脚石 kick away a stumbling block/ 一脚把门～开 open the door with a kick; kick the door open/ 把凳子～翻 kick over a stool/ 小心这马～人! Be careful! This horse kicks./ 资本家把张师傅～出了工厂大门。The boss kicked Master Worker Zhang out of the factory. ② play (football); kick: ～足球 play football/ ～进一个球 kick (或 score) a goal/ 他～中锋。He plays centre forward.

【踢蹬】 tīdeng kick at random: 这孩子坐在那儿还乱～。That child can't keep his legs still even when he's sitting down. 又作"踢腾"

【踢脚板】 tījiǎobǎn 〈建〉 skirting board; skirtboard

【踢皮球】 tī píqiú ① kick a ball; play children's football ② kick sth. back and forth like a ball; pass the buck

【踢踏舞】 tītàwǔ step dance; tap dance

## 鹈

tī 见"鹈鹕" pìtī

# tí

## 绨

tí a kind of thick silk

另见 tì

## 提

tí ① carry (in one's hand with the arm down): 手里～着篮子 carry a basket in one's hand ② lift; raise; promote: 这种自行车十分轻便，一只手就能～起来。This bicycle is very light. You can lift it with one hand./ 从井里～水 draw water from a well/ ～价 raise the price/ 把问题～到原则高度来分析 analyse a problem from the high plane of principle ③ shift to an earlier time; move up a date: 会议日期～前了。The date of the meeting has been moved up. ④ put forward; bring up; raise: ～问题 ask a question/ ～意见 make a criticism; make comments or suggestions/ ～抗议 lodge a protest/ ～条件 put forward conditions/ ～要求 make demands/ ～方案 suggest (或 propose) plans/ 把事情～到党委会去讨论 take (或 submit) the matter to the Party committee for discussion/ 把计划生育～到议事日程上来 put family planning on the agenda ⑤ draw (或 take) out; extract: ～款 draw money/ ～炼 extract and purify; refine ⑥ mention; refer to; bring up: 别再～那件事了。Don't bring that up again./ 报告中几次～到党中央的这项英明决定。The report included several references to the Party Central Committee's wise decision. ⑦ dipper: 油～ oil-dipper/ 酒～ wine dipper ⑧ rising stroke (in Chinese characters)

另见 dī

【提案】 tí'àn motion; proposal; draft resolution ◇ ～国 sponsor country (of a resolution); sponsor/ ～审查委员会 motions examination committee

【提拔】 tíba promote: ～某人担任领导工作 promote sb. to a position of leadership

【提包】 tíbāo handbag; shopping bag; bag; valise

【提倡】 tíchàng advocate; promote; encourage; recommend: ～晚婚和计划生育 advocate late marriage and family planning/ ～勤俭建国 spread the idea of building our country through diligence and thrift/ 要大力～共产主义劳动态度。The communist attitude towards labour should be energetically encouraged./ 这种做法值得～。This method deserves recommendation.

【提成】 tíchéng deduct a percentage (from a sum of money, etc.)

【提出】 tíchū put forward; advance; pose; raise: ～建议 put forward a proposal; make a suggestion/ ～一种新的理论 advance a new theory/ ～程序问题 raise a point of order/ ～警告 give (或 serve) a warning/ ～抗议 lodge a protest/ 向自己～更高的要求 set a still higher demand on oneself/ ～入党申请 hand in (或 submit) an application to join the Party; apply for Party membership/ ～修改和补充意见 propose amendments and addenda/ 五四运动～了"打倒孔家店"的响亮口号。The May 4th Movement raised the clarion call, "Down with the Confucian shop!"/ 新的形势向我们～了新的课题。The new situation has put new questions before us.

【提纯】 tíchún purify; refine ◇ ～复壮〈农〉purification and rejuvenation/ ～器 purifier

【提词】 tící 〈剧〉prompt: 我来～。I'll be the prompter.

【提单】 tídān bill of lading (B/L): 直达～ direct bill of lading/ 联运～ through bill of lading

【提法】 tífǎ the way sth. is put; formulation; wording: 他们不同意你对这个问题的～。They take exception to the way you put the question./ 这是个新的～。This is a new formulation./ 这只是个～问题。This is just a matter of wording.

【提纲】 tígāng outline: 写发言～ make an outline for a speech

【提纲挈领】 tígāng-qièlǐng take a net by the headrope or a coat by the collar — concentrate on the main points; bring out the essentials: 我来～地谈一谈。I'll just touch briefly on the essentials.

【提高】 tígāo raise; heighten; enhance; increase; improve: ～水位 raise the water level/ ～警惕 enhance (或 heighten) one's vigilance/ ～路线斗争觉悟 heighten one's awareness of the struggle between the two lines/ ～识别真假马克思主义的能力 sharpen one's ability to distinguish between genuine and sham Marxism/ ～认识 deepen one's understanding/ ～勇气 pluck up one's courage/ ～部队的战斗力 increase the combat effectiveness of the troops/ ～工作效率 raise working efficiency/ ～单位面积产量 raise the per unit yield/ ～产品质量 improve the quality of products/ 人民生活水平逐年～。The living standards of the people rise year by year.

【提供】 tígōng provide; supply; furnish; offer: 为轻工业～原料 supply light industry with raw materials/ ～援助 give aid; provide assistance/ ～贷款 offer a loan/ ～新的证据 furnish fresh evidence/ 历史给我们～了有益的经验教训。History affords us useful lessons.

【提行】 tíháng 〈印〉begin a new line

【提盒】 tíhé a tiered lunchbox with several round compartments one above the other and a handle

【提花】 tíhuā jacquard weave ◇ ～枕巾 jacquard pillow cover/ ～织机〈纺〉jacquard loom

【提货】 tíhuò pick up goods; take delivery of goods: 到火车站～ pick up goods at the railway station/ 请于三日内来车站～。Please take delivery of the goods at the station within three days. ◇ ～单 bill of lading (B/L)

【提交】 tíjiāo submit (a problem, etc.) to; refer to: 将决议草案～大会讨论 submit the draft resolution to the congress for discussion/ 把问题～革委会 refer the matter to the revolutionary committee

【提款】 tíkuǎn draw money (from a bank)

【提炼】 tíliàn extract and purify; abstract; refine: 从矿石中～金属 extract (或 abstract) metal from ore/ ～蔗糖 refine cane sugar/ 将生活素材～加工 refine the literary raw material gathered from life

【提梁】 tíliáng handle (of a basket, etc.); straps (of a handbag, etc.); hoop handle ◇ ～卣〈考古〉a ewer with a loop handle

【提名】 tímíng nominate: ～某人为代表 nominate sb. for representative

【提起】 tíqǐ ① mention; speak of: ～铁姑娘队没有一个不夸的。No one ever mentions the Iron Girls' team without praising it./ 昨天他还～你来着。He spoke of you only yesterday. ② raise; arouse; brace up: ～精神 raise one's spirits; brace oneself up/ ～人们的注意 call (或 arouse) people's attention

【提前】 tíqián ① shift to an earlier date; move up (a date); advance: 总攻的时间～了。The time for the general offensive has been moved up. ② in advance; ahead of time; beforehand: 明天要是割麦子，请～通知我们。If we are going to cut wheat tomorrow, please notify us in advance./ ～两个月完成全年生产指标 meet the year's production target two months ahead of time/ ～释放战犯 release war criminals before their sentences expire/ ～召开大会 convene the congress before the due date ◇ ～量〈军〉lead

【提挈】 tíqiè 〈书〉① lead; take with one; marshal: ～全军 marshal all one's forces ② guide and support; give guidance and help to

【提琴】 tíqín the violin family: 小～ violin/ 中～ viola/ 大～ violoncello; cello/ 低音～ double bass; contrabass

【提请】 tíqǐng submit sth. to: ～大会批准 submit to the congress for approval/ ～大家注意 call everybody's attention to sth.

【提取】 tíqǔ ① draw; pick up; collect: ～银行存款 draw money from a bank; withdraw bank deposits/ 到车站～行李 pick up (或 collect) one's luggage at the railway station ② extract; abstract; recover: 从油页岩中～石油 extract oil from shale/ 从废水中～有用物质 recover useful materials from waste water ◇ ～器 extractor/ ～塔 extraction column

【提神】 tíshén refresh oneself; give oneself a lift: 喝杯茶提提神 refresh oneself with a cup of tea

【提审】 tíshěn ① bring (a prisoner) before the court; bring (sb. in custody) to trial; fetch (a detainee) for interrogation ② review (a case tried by a lower court)

【提升】 tíshēng ① promote: ～他当排长 promote him to be platoon leader ② hoist; elevate ◇ ～机 hoist; elevator

【提示】 tíshì point out; prompt: 请把学习重点向大家～一下。Please brief us on the main points to be studied./ 如果她忘了台词，你就给她～一下。Prompt her if she forgets her lines.

【提味】 tíwèi render palatable (by adding condiments); season

【提问】 tíwèn put questions to; quiz: 回答老师的～ answer the teacher's questions

【提线木偶】 tíxiàn mù'ǒu marionette

【提箱】 tíxiāng suitcase

【提携】 tíxié ① lead (a child) by the hand ② guide and support; give guidance and help to

【提心吊胆】 tíxīn-diàodǎn have one's heart in one's mouth; be on tenterhooks: 资本主义国家有很多工人成天～，唯恐失业。Many workers in capitalist countries live in constant fear of unemployment.

【提醒】 tíxǐng remind; warn; call attention to: 如果我忘了，请你～我一下。Please remind me in case I should forget./ ～他早点儿来。Remind him to come early./ ～司机在这一带要低速行驶。Warn the driver to drive slowly in this area.

【提选】 tíxuǎn select; choose: ～耐旱品种 select drought-resistant varieties

【提讯】 tíxùn 见"提审"

【提要】 tíyào *précis;* summary; abstract; epitome; synopsis: 《哥达纲领批判》的～和注释 *précis* of and notes to *Critique of the Gotha Programme*/ 本书内容～ capsule summary (of the book)

【提议】 tíyì ① propose; suggest; move: 我～为两国人民的友谊干杯。I propose a toast to the friendship between the peoples of the two countries./ 我～现在休会。I move the meeting be adjourned. ② proposal; motion: 大会一致通过了他们的～。The meeting unanimously adopted their proposal./ 根据会议主席的～ on the motion of the chairman of the meeting

【提早】 tízǎo shift to an earlier time; be earlier than planned or expected: 汛期～了。The flood season is here earlier than expected./ ～出发 set out earlier than planned/ ～通知一声 notify in advance

【提制】 tízhì obtain through refining; distil; extract: 香草香精是从一种热带兰～出来的。Vanilla is extracted from a tropical orchid.

**啼** tí ①cry; weep aloud: 哭哭～～ weep and wail ② crow; caw: 鸡～。Cocks crow./ 月落乌～。The crows caw when the moon goes down.

【啼饥号寒】 tíjī-háohán cry from hunger and cold; cry out in hunger and cold

【啼哭】 tíkū cry; wail

【啼笑皆非】 tí-xiào jiē fēi not know whether to laugh or cry

**缇** tí 〈书〉 orange red

**鹈** tí

【鹈鹕】 tíhú pelican

**题** tí ①topic; subject; title; problem: 讨论～ topic for discussion/ 话～ subject of conversation/ 考～ examination questions/ 文不对～ wide of the mark; irrelevant; not to the point/ 离～ stray from the subject; digress ② inscribe: ～诗 inscribe a poem (on a painting, fan, wall, etc.)/ 某某～ an inscription by so-and-so

【题跋】 tíbá ①preface and postscript ②short comments, annotations, etc. on a scroll (of painting or calligraphy)

【题材】 tícái subject matter; theme: ～范围 range of subjects/ 这个剧本以土地革命为～。The theme of the play is the agrarian revolution./ 这是写小说的好～。This is good material for a novel.

【题词】 tící ①write a few words of encouragement, appreciation or commemoration ②inscription; dedication ③ foreword

【题花】 tíhuā title design

【题解】 tíjiě ①explanatory notes on the title or background of a book ②key to exercises or problems: «平面几何～» *Key to Exercises in Plane Geometry*

【题名】 tímíng inscribe one's name; autograph: 在照片上～ autograph a photograph/ ～留念 give one's autograph as a memento

【题目】 tímù ①title; subject; topic: 辩论的～ subject (或 topic) for a debate/ 这篇文章的～叫做«社会主义建设的伟大指针»。The article is entitled "A Great Guiding Principle for Socialist Construction". ②exercise problems; examination questions

【题签】 tíqiān ①write the title of a book on a label to be stuck on the cover ②a label with the title of a book on it

【题字】 tízì ①inscribe ② inscription; autograph: 书上有作者亲笔～。The book is autographed by the author.

**醍** tí

【醍醐】 tíhú finest cream

【醍醐灌顶】 tíhú guàn dǐng ①be filled with wisdom; be enlightened ②suddenly feel refreshed

**蹄** tí hoof: 马～ horse's hoofs/ 燉猪～ stewed pig's trotters

【蹄筋】 tíjīn tendons of beef, mutton or pork: 红烧～ tendons stewed in soy sauce

【蹄膀】 típǎng 〈方〉 the uppermost part of a leg of pork

【蹄子】 tízi ①〈口〉 hoof ②〈方〉 leg of pork

**鳀** tí 〈动〉 anchovy

## tǐ

**体** tǐ ①body; part of the body: 人～构造 the structure of the human body/ ～重 (body) weight/ 肢～ limbs ② substance; state of a substance: 固～ solid ③style; form: 文～ literary style; style of writing/ 旧～诗 old-style poems; classical poetry ④personally do or experience sth.; put oneself in another's position: 身～力行 earnestly practise what one advocates ⑤system: 政～ system of government/ 国～ state system ⑥〈语〉 aspect (of a verb)

另见 tī

【体壁】 tǐbì 〈动〉 body wall

【体裁】 tǐcái types or forms of literature

【体操】 tǐcāo gymnastics: 徒手～ freestanding exercise/器械～ gymnastics on or with apparatus/ 自由～ floor (或 free) exercise

◇ ～表演 gymnastic exhibition (或 display)/ ～服 gym outfit (或 clothes, suit)/ ～器械 gymnastic apparatus

【体察】 tǐchá experience and observe: 虚心～情况 be ready to look into matters with an open mind; not be prejudiced in sizing up situations

【体罚】 tǐfá corporal (或 physical) punishment

【体格】 tǐgé physique; build: ～强壮 of strong physique; of powerful build; of strong constitution ◇ ～检查 physical examination; health checkup

【体会】 tǐhuì know (或 learn) from experience; realize: 深有～ have an intimate knowledge of sth./ 谈谈我个人的～。I'll say a few words about my personal experience (或 understanding)./ 只有深入群众，才能真正～群众的思想感情。Only by going deep among the masses can we have a true understanding of their thoughts and feelings./ 你参加了这次科学讨论会，有什么～？ What have you learned from the symposium?

【体积】 tǐjī volume; bulk: ～大 bulky/ 容器的～ the volume of a container ◇ ～膨胀〈物〉 volume expansion

【体节】 tǐjié 〈动〉 body segment

【体力】 tǐlì physical (或 bodily) strength; physical power: 增强～ build up one's strength/ 消耗～ be a drain on one's (physical) strength; consume(或 sap) one's strength

【体力劳动】 tǐlì láodòng physical (或 manual) labour: 参加～ take part in (或 do) physical labour

【体例】 tǐlì stylistic rules and layout; style: 印刷～ style sheet; stylebook

【体谅】 tǐliang show understanding and sympathy for; make allowances for: 充分～人家的困难 make full allowances for their difficulties/ 她是很～人的。She is quite understanding.

【体面】 tǐmian ①dignity; face: 有失～ be a loss of face/ 他并不认为干这些事就会有失～。He did not consider it beneath his dignity to concern himself with these things./ 维持～ keep up appearances ②honourable; creditable: 不～的行为 disgraceful (或 disreputable) conduct ③good-looking: 长得～ be handsome

【体念】 tǐniàn give sympathetic consideration to

【体魄】 tǐpò physique: 强壮的～ strong (或 powerful) physique; vigorous health/ 锻炼～ go in for physical training

【体腔】 tǐqiāng 〈生理〉 body cavity

【体虱】 tǐshī 〈动〉 body louse

【体式】 tǐshì ①form of characters or letters: 汉语拼音字母

有手写体和印刷体两种～。There are two forms of the Chinese phonetic alphabet, the cursive and the printed. ② form of literary works: 词和律诗～不同。*Ci* poems are different in form from *lüshi* poems.

【体视】 tǐshì 〈物〉 stereo-: ～显微镜 stereomicroscope/ ～望远镜 stereotelescope

【体态】 tǐtài posture; carriage: ～轻盈 a graceful carriage

【体贴】 tǐtiē show consideration for; give every care to: ～病人 show a patient every consideration/ ～入微 look after with meticulous care; care for with great solicitude

【体统】 tǐtǒng decorum; propriety; decency: 不成～ most improper; downright outrageous/ 有失～ be disgraceful; be scandalous

【体外受精】 tǐwài shòujīng 〈动〉 external fertilization

【体味】 tǐwèi appreciate; savour: 仔细～这首诗的含义 savour the meaning of the poem

【体温】 tǐwēn (body) temperature: 给孩子量～。Take the child's temperature./ 她的～在上升。Her temperature is going up./ ～过低 hypothermia ◇ ～计 (clinical) thermometer

【体无完肤】 tǐ wú wán fū ① have cuts and bruises all over the body; be a mass of bruises: 被打得～ be beaten black and blue ② be thoroughly (或 scathingly) refuted: 这种修正主义论点早已被批得～。This revisionist fallacy has long been thoroughly refuted.

【体惜】 tǐxī understand and sympathize with

【体系】 tǐxì system; setup: 粉碎资产阶级的帮派～ smash the bourgeois factional setup/ 建成独立的、比较完整的工业～和国民经济～ complete an independent and fairly comprehensive industrial complex and economic system/ 完整地准确地掌握毛泽东思想～ have a broad and accurate grasp of Mao Zedong Thought as a system

【体现】 tǐxiàn embody; incarnate; reflect; give expression to: 《国际歌》～了巴黎公社的革命精神。The *Internationale* embodies the revolutionary spirit of the Paris Commune./ 这个提案～了发展中国家的利益和要求。This proposal reflects the interests and demands of the developing countries.

【体形】 tǐxíng bodily form; build

【体型】 tǐxíng type of build or figure

【体恤】 tǐxù understand and sympathize with; show solicitude for: ～烈士遗孤 show solicitude for the children of revolutionary martyrs

【体癣】 tǐxuǎn 〈医〉 ringworm of the body

【体循环】 tǐxúnhuán 〈生理〉 systematic circulation; greater circulation

【体验】 tǐyàn learn through practice; learn through one's personal experience: ～生活 observe and learn from real life

【体液】 tǐyè body fluid

【体育】 tǐyù physical culture; physical training; sports: 今天下午有一节～课。We'll have an hour of PE this afternoon.
◇ ～场 stadium/ ～道德 sportsmanship/ ～锻炼 physical training/ ～馆 gymnasium; gym/ ～活动 sports activities/ ～课 physical education (PE)/ ～疗法 physical exercise therapy/ ～用品 sports goods; sports requisites

【体制】 tǐzhì system of organization; system: 国家～ state system

【体质】 tǐzhì physique; constitution: 他们的～都很好。They all have good physique./ 各人的～不同，对疾病的抵抗力也不同。People's constitutions differ; so does their resistance to disease.

【体重】 tǐzhòng (body) weight: ～增加 put on weight; gain weight/ ～减轻 lose weight/ 她～六十公斤。She weighs 60 kilograms.

## tì

**屉** tì ① a food steamer with several trays; steamer tray: ～帽 the lid (或 cover) of a steamer/ 一～馒头 a trayful of steamed buns ② drawer: 三～桌 three-drawer desk

【屉子】 tìzi ① (one of) a set of removable trays (in furniture or a utensil) ② 〈方〉 drawer

**剃** tì shave: ～胡子 have a shave; shave oneself

【剃刀】 tìdāo razor

【剃度】 tìdù 〈佛教〉 tonsure

【剃头】 tìtóu ① have one's head shaved ② have one's hair cut; have a haircut

【剃枝虫】 tìzhīchóng 〈动〉 armyworm

**涕** tì ① tears: 痛哭流～ shed bitter tears; cry one's heart out/ 感激～零 be moved to tears of gratitude ② mucus of the nose; snivel

【涕泣】 tìqì 〈书〉 weep

**悌** tì 〈书〉 love and respect for one's elder brother

**绨** tì a silk and cotton fabric
另见 tí

**惕** tì cautious; watchful: 警～ be on the alert; watch out

**替** tì ① take the place of; replace; substitute for: 今天老王没来，谁～他？Lao Wang is absent today. Who'll take his place?/ 你歇会儿，我来～你。Have a rest. I'll take over. ② for; on behalf of: ～别人买火车票 buy a train ticket for someone/ ～顾客着想 think about the interests of the customers/ 别～我担心。Don't worry about me. ③ 〈书〉 decline: 兴～ rise and fall

【替代】 tìdài substitute for; replace; supersede: 用石油～煤 replace coal by petroleum; substitute petroleum for coal

【替工】 tìgōng ① work as a temporary substitute ② temporary substitute (worker): 找一个～ find a substitute; get a replacement

【替换】 tìhuan replace; substitute for; displace; take the place of: 教练决定让3号～8号。The coach decided to replace player No. 8 by No. 3./ 我们去～值夜班的同志。We are going to relieve the comrades on night duty./ 带上一套～的衣服。Take a change of clothes with you.

【替角儿】 tìjuér understudy

【替身】 tìshēn ① substitute; replacement; stand-in ② scapegoat

【替死鬼】 tìsǐguǐ 〈口〉 scapegoat; fall guy

【替罪羊】 tìzuìyáng scapegoat

**嚏** tì 〈书〉 sneeze

【嚏喷】 tìpen sneeze

## tiān

**天** tiān ① sky; heaven: 明朗的～ a clear sky/ 太阳一出满～红。The sky is aglow with the rising sun. ② overhead: ～桥 overline bridge; platform bridge ③ day: 每～ every day/ 前～ the day before yesterday/ 忙了一～ have had a busy day; have done a good day's work/ 夏天

～长夜短。In summer the days are long and the nights short. ④ a period of time in a day: 五更～ around four in the morning/ ～不早啦。It's getting late. ⑤ season: 春～ spring/ 三伏～ the hottest days of summer; dog days ⑥ weather: 下雨～ wet (或 rainy) weather/ ～越来越冷了。It's getting colder and colder./～大旱，人大干。The heavens may bring drought, but we can go all out. ⑦ nature: 人定胜～。Man will conquer nature./ 改～换地的革命精神 the revolutionary spirit of working hard to transform nature/ ～灾 natural calamity ⑧ God; Heaven: 归～ go to heaven; die/ ～知道！God knows!/ ～哪！Good Heavens!/ 谢～谢地！Thank Heaven!

【天安门】 Tiān'ānmén Tian An Men (the Gate of Heavenly Peace): ～广场 Tian'anmen Square/ ～城楼 the rostrum of Tian An Men

【天边】 tiānbiān horizon; the ends of the earth; remotest places: ～的渔帆 the sails of the fishing boats that appear on the horizon/ 远在～，近在眼前 seemingly far away, actually close at hand

【天兵】 tiānbīng troops from heaven — an invincible army

【天不怕，地不怕】 tiān bù pà, dì bù pà fear neither Heaven nor Earth; fear nothing at all; nothing daunted

【天才】 tiāncái genius; talent; gift; endowment: 世界上不存在什么生而知之的～。There is no such thing as a genius born with knowledge./ 这孩子有音乐～。The child has musical talent (或 a gift for music).

【天才论】 tiāncáilùn the theory of innate genius (according to which history is not made by the people but by heroes born with knowledge)

• 【天蚕】 tiāncán 〈动〉 giant silkworm; wild silkworm ◇ ～蛾 giant silkworm moth

【天长地久】 tiāncháng-dìjiǔ enduring as the universe; everlasting and unchanging

【天长日久】 tiāncháng-rìjiǔ after a considerable period of time: 由于水的侵蚀，～就形成了一个大溶洞。As a result of prolonged water erosion, a huge cave was formed.

【天车】 tiānchē 〈机〉 overhead travelling crane; shop traveller; (钻井机) crown block

【天秤座】 tiānchèngzuò 〈天〉 Libra

【天窗】 tiānchuāng 〈建〉 skylight

【天大】 tiāndà as large as the heavens; extremely big: ～的好事 an excellent thing

【天敌】 tiāndí 〈生〉 natural enemy

【天底】 tiāndǐ 〈天〉 nadir

【天底下】 tiāndǐxia 〈口〉 in the world; on earth: ～哪有这种道理！Nobody on earth would reason that way. 或 How preposterous!

【天地】 tiāndì ① heaven and earth; world; universe: 炮声震动～。The earth shook with the roar of guns. ② field of activity; scope of operation: 开辟科学研究的新～ open up a new field for scientific research/ 不要把自己关在办公室的小～里。Don't confine yourself within the four walls of an office.

【天地头】 tiān-dìtóu 〈印〉 top and bottom margins of a page; upper and lower margins of a page

【天电】 tiāndiàn 〈电〉 atmospherics; static ◇ ～干扰 statics; static disturbances

【天顶】 tiāndǐng 〈天〉 zenith

【天鹅】 tiān'é swan: 小～ cygnet ◇ ～绒毛 swansdown

【天鹅绒】 tiān'éróng velvet

【天鹅座】 tiān'ézuò 〈天〉 Cygnus

【天蛾】 tiān'é 〈动〉 hawkmoth; sphinx

【天翻地覆】 tiānfān-dìfù heaven and earth turning upside down: ～的变化 earthshaking (或 tremendous) changes

【天分】 tiānfèn special endowments; natural gift; talent: ～高 gifted; talented

【天府之国】 tiānfǔ zhī guó (usu. referring to Sichuan Province) the land of abundance; the land of plenty

【天赋】 tiānfù ① inborn; innate; endowed by nature ② natural gift; talent; endowments ◇ ～人权论 the theory of natural rights

【天干】 tiāngān the ten Heavenly Stems, used as serial numbers and also in combination with the twelve Earthly Branches to designate years, months, days and hours

【天罡星】 tiāngāngxīng 〈天〉 the Big Dipper

【天高地厚】 tiāngāo-dìhòu ① (of kindness) profound; deep ② how high the sky and how deep the earth — immensity of the universe; complexity of things: 不知～ have an exaggerated opinion of one's abilities; not understand things

【天各一方】 tiān gè yī fāng (of a family or friends) live far apart from each other

【天公】 tiāngōng the ruler of heaven; God: ～不作美。Unfortunately, the weather let us down.

【天公地道】 tiāngōng-dìdào absolutely fair: 在我看来，她这样处理真是～。In my opinion, the way she disposed of the matter was truly fair and reasonable.

【天宫】 tiāngōng heavenly palace

【天沟】 tiāngōu 〈建〉 gutter

【天光】 tiānguāng ① daylight; time of the day: ～不早了。It's getting late. ② 〈方〉 morning

【天国】 tiānguó the Kingdom of Heaven; paradise

【天河】 tiānhé 〈天〉 the Milky Way; the Galaxy

【天候】 tiānhòu weather: 全～公路 all-weather road/ 全～飞行 all-weather flight

【天花】 tiānhuā 〈医〉 smallpox

【天花板】 tiānhuābǎn ceiling

【天花粉】 tiānhuāfěn 〈中药〉 the root of Chinese trichosanthes (*Trichosanthes kirilowii*)

【天花乱坠】 tiānhuā luàn zhuì as if it were raining flowers — give an extravagantly colourful description: 吹得～ give an extravagant account of; make a wild boast about

【天皇】 tiānhuáng the emperor of Japan; Mikado

【天昏地暗】 tiānhūn-dì'àn ① a murky sky over a dark earth; dark all round: 呼啸的西北风夹着黄沙，刮得～。A howling northwest wind swept by, carrying yellow dust that darkened the sky and obscured everything else. ② in a state of chaos and darkness: 当时军阀混战，真是～哪！In those years, with the warlords fighting among themselves, the country was plunged into chaos and darkness.

【天机】 tiānjī ① nature's mystery; something inexplicable ② God's design; secret: 泄漏～ give away a secret

【天极】 tiānjí 〈天〉 celestial pole

【天际】 tiānjì 〈书〉 horizon

【天津】 Tiānjīn Tianjin

【天经地义】 tiānjīng-dìyì unalterable principle — right and proper; perfectly justified: 人民奋起造反动派的反，这是～的事。It is right and proper for the people to rise in rebellion against the reactionaries.

【天井】 tiānjǐng ① small yard; courtyard ② skylight ③ 〈矿〉 raise: 通风～ air raise

【天空】 tiānkōng the sky; the heavens

【天籁】 tiānlài 〈书〉 sounds of nature

【天蓝】 tiānlán sky blue; azure

【天狼星】 tiānlángxīng 〈天〉 Sirius

【天老儿】 tiānlaor albino

【天理】 tiānlǐ ① heavenly principles — feudal ethics as propounded by the Song Confucianists ② justice: 是无～。That would be a gross injustice.

【天良】 tiānliáng conscience: 丧尽～ conscienceless

【天亮】 tiānliàng daybreak; dawn: ～以前赶到 get there before daybreak

【天灵盖】 tiānlínggài top of the skull; crown (of the head)

【天龙座】 tiānlóngzuò 〈天〉 Draco

【天伦】 tiānlún 〈书〉 the natural bonds and ethical relationships between members of a family: ～之乐 family happiness

【天罗地网】 tiānluó-dìwǎng nets above and snares below; tight encirclement: 布下～,使罪犯无路可逃 spread a dragnet so the criminals have no way to escape

【天麻】 tiānmá 〈中药〉 the tuber of elevated gastrodia (*Gastrodia elata*)

【天马行空】 tiānmǎ xíng kōng a heavenly steed soaring across the skies — a powerful and unconstrained style

【天门冬】 tiānméndōng 〈中药〉 lucid asparagus (*Asparagus cochinchinensis*)

【天明】 tiānmíng daybreak; dawn

【天命】 tiānmìng God's will; the mandate of heaven; destiny; fate: 大寨人战胜自然的伟大成就有力地批判了～论。The Dazhai people's great victories over nature emphatically refute the idea of God's will.

【天幕】 tiānmù ① the canopy of the heavens ② backdrop (of a stage)

【天南地北】 tiānnán-dìběi ① far apart; poles apart: 他们哥儿俩～,见一次面不容易。 The two brothers live so far apart they don't often get a chance to see each other. ② from different places or areas: 他们来自～,参加石油会战。They came from all over the country to take part in the battle for oil.

【天南海北】 tiānnán-hǎiběi ① all over the country ② discursive; rambling: ～地谈起来 start chattering away about this and that; start a bull session

【天年】 tiānnián natural span of life; one's allotted span: 尽其～ die a natural death; live one's full span

【天牛】 tiānniú 〈动〉 longicorn; long-horned beetle

【天怒人怨】 tiānnù-rényuàn the wrath of God and the resentment of men; widespread indignation and discontent

【天疱疮】 tiānpàochuāng 〈医〉 pemphigus

【天棚】 tiānpéng ①〈建〉 ceiling ② awning or canopy, usu. made of reed matting and bamboo poles

【天平】 tiānpíng balance; scales: 分析～〈化〉 analytical balance

【天平动】 tiānpíngdòng 〈天〉 libration

【天气】 tiānqì weather: ～要变。The weather is changing./ ～转晴。It's clearing up./ 不管～如何,也要继续施工。Construction will go on in all weathers.

◇ ～图 weather map; synoptic chart/ ～形势预报 weather prognostics/ ～学 synoptic meteorology/ ～预报 weather forecast

【天堑】 tiānqiàn natural moat: 长江～ the natural moat of the Changjiang River

【天桥】 tiānqiáo overline bridge; platform bridge

【天琴座】 tiānqínzuò 〈天〉 Lyra

【天青】 tiānqīng reddish black

【天穹】 tiānqióng the vault of heaven

【天球】 tiānqiú 〈天〉 celestial sphere

◇ ～赤道 celestial equator/ ～仪 celestial globe/ ～子午圈 celestial meridian/ ～坐标 celestial coordinates

【天然】 tiānrán natural: ～财富 natural resources (或 wealth)/ ～景色 natural scenery/ ～障碍物 natural barrier; topographical barrier/ 中国无产阶级和广大的农民有一种～的联系。The Chinese proletariat has natural ties with the peasant masses.

◇ ～堤〈地〉 natural levee/ ～更新〈林〉 natural regeneration/ ～牧地 natural pasture

【天然气】 tiānránqì natural gas: 干～ dry gas; poor gas/ 湿～ wet gas; rich gas ◇ ～回注〈石油〉 gas injection

【天壤】 tiānrǎng 〈书〉 heaven and earth: ～之别 as far apart as heaven and earth; worlds (或 poles) apart; a world of difference

【天日】 tiānrì the sky and the sun; light: 重见～ once more see the light of day — be delivered from oppression or persecution

【天色】 tiānsè colour of the sky; time of the day as shown by the colour of the sky; weather: ～已晚。It is getting dark./ ～突变。The weather suddenly changed./ 看～要晴。It seems to be clearing up./ 看～怕要下雨。It looks like rain.

【天神】 tiānshén god; deity

【天生】 tiānshēng born; inborn; inherent; innate: 本事不是～的,是锻炼出来的。Ability is not innate, but comes through practice./ 他～聋哑。He was born a deaf-mute.

◇ ～桥〈地〉 natural bridge

【天时】 tiānshí ① weather; climate: ～不正 abnormal weather/ 庄稼活儿一定要趁～,早了晚了都不好。Farming should be done in season, neither too early nor too late. ② timeliness; opportunity

【天使】 tiānshǐ 〈宗〉 angel

【天书】 tiānshū a book from heaven; abstruse or illegible writing: 对我来说,这本书就跟～一样难懂。To me this book is as difficult as a book from heaven. 或 This book is all Greek to me./ 这封信字迹太潦草,象～似的。This letter is as illegible as hieroglyphics.

【天坛】 Tiāntán the Temple of Heaven (in Beijing)

【天堂】 tiāntáng paradise; heaven: 被推翻的剥削阶级时刻妄想恢复他们失去的～。Never for a moment do the overthrown exploiting classes give up their vain attempt to regain their lost paradise.

【天体】 tiāntǐ 〈天〉 celestial body

◇ ～光谱学 astrospectroscopy/ ～力学 celestial mechanics/ ～物理学 astrophysics/ ～演化学 cosmogony/ ～照相仪 astrograph

【天天】 tiāntiān every day; daily; day in, day out: ～锻炼身体 do physical training every day

【天庭】 tiāntíng the middle of the forehead

【天头】 tiāntóu the top (或 upper) margin of a page

【天王星】 tiānwángxīng 〈天〉 Uranus

【天网恢恢,疏而不漏】 tiānwǎng huīhuī, shū ér bù lòu the net of Heaven has large meshes, but it lets nothing through; the mills of God grind slowly, but they grind exceeding small; justice has a long arm

【天文】 tiānwén astronomy

◇ ～单位 astronomical unit/ ～导航 astronavigation; celestial navigation/ ～观测 astronomical observation/ ～馆 planetarium/ ～年历 astronomical yearbook; astronomical almanac/ ～时 astronomical time/ ～数字 astronomical figure; enormous figure/ ～台 (astronomical) observatory/ ～仪 astroscope/ ～照相术 astrophotography/ ～制导 celestial guidance/ ～钟 astronomical clock

【天文学】 tiānwénxué astronomy: 航海～ nautical astronomy/ 恒星～ stellar astronomy/ 空间～ space astronomy/ 球面～ spherical astronomy/ 射电～ radio astronomy

◇ ～家 astronomer

【天无绝人之路】 tiān wú jué rén zhī lù Heaven never seals off all the exits — there is always a way out

【天下】 tiānxià ① land under heaven — the world or China: ～大乱 great disorder under heaven; big upheaval throughout the world/ ～大治 great order across the land/ ～无敌 all-conquering; invincible/ 打～坐～ conquer and rule the country/ ～奇闻 unheard-of absurdity ② rule; domination: 新中国是劳动人民的～。The working people are masters of New China./ 那时是地主老财的～，哪有穷人说话的权利。In those days the landlords ruled the roost; the poor had no right to say a word.

【天下乌鸦一般黑】 tiānxià wūyā yībān hēi all crows are black — evil people are bad all over the world

【天仙】 tiānxiān ① goddess ② a beauty

【天仙子】 tiānxiānzǐ 〈中药〉 henbane seed (*Hyoscyamus niger*)

【天险】 tiānxiǎn natural barrier: 此山向有～之称。This mountain has long been known as a natural barrier.

【天线】 tiānxiàn 〈无〉 aerial; antenna: 架设～ put up an aerial/ 定向～ beam (或 directional) antenna/ 拉杆～ telescopic antenna

【天象】 tiānxiàng astronomical phenomena; celestial phenomena: 观测～ observe the heavenly bodies; astronomical observation ◇ ～仪〈天〉 planetarium

【天晓得】 tiānxiǎode 〈口〉 God (或 Heaven) knows: ～他在那儿待了多久。He stayed there God knows how long.

【天蝎座】 tiānxiēzuò 〈天〉 Scorpio; Scorpius

【天行赤目】 tiānxíngchìmù 〈中医〉 red and swollen eyes; conjunctivitis

【天性】 tiānxìng natural instincts; nature

【天幸】 tiānxìng a providential escape; a close shave

【天旋地转】 tiānxuán-dìzhuàn (feel as if) the sky and earth were spinning round; very dizzy: 昏沉沉，只觉得～ feel faint and dizzy as if the earth were spinning round

【天涯】 tiānyá the end of the world; the remotest corner of the earth: 浪迹～ rove all over the world

【天涯海角】 tiānyá-hǎijiǎo the ends of the earth; the remotest corners of the earth: 反革命分子就是跑到～，也逃不出人民的法网。The counterrevolutionaries cannot escape the people's net of justice even if they flee to the remotest parts.

【天衣无缝】 tiānyī wú fèng a seamless heavenly robe — flawless: 这篇文章，论证严密，～。The article is close-knit and its argument flawless.

【天意】 tiānyì God's will; the will of Heaven: 事在人为，不存在什么～。There is no such thing as the will of Heaven. It is man that decides everything.

【天鹰座】 tiānyīngzuò 〈天〉 Aquila

【天有不测风云】 tiān yǒu bù cè fēng-yún a storm may arise from a clear sky; something unexpected may happen any time: ～，人有旦夕祸福。〈谚〉 In nature there are unexpected storms and in life unpredictable vicissitudes.

【天渊】 tiānyuān 〈书〉 high heaven and deep sea; poles apart: 相去～ as far apart as the sky and the sea/ ～之别 a world of difference

【天灾】 tiānzāi natural disaster (或 calamity): 遭受～ suffer natural disasters

【天灾人祸】 tiānzāi-rénhuò natural and man-made calamities

【天葬】 tiānzàng celestial burial (by which bodies are exposed to birds of prey)

【天造地设】 tiānzào-dìshè created by nature; heavenly; ideal: 这里山水秀丽，真是个～的游览区。This beautiful place is a heavenly tourist resort.

【天真】 tiānzhēn innocent; simple and unaffected; artless; naive: ～烂漫的儿童 innocent and artless children/ ～的幻想 a naive delusion/ 你要相信这样的话，那就太～了。If you believe that sort of talk you're really naive.

【天之骄子】 tiān zhī jiāozǐ God's favoured one — an unusually lucky person

【天职】 tiānzhí bounden duty; vocation

【天轴】 tiānzhóu ① 〈机〉 line shaft ② 〈天〉 celestial axis

【天诛地灭】 tiānzhū-dìmiè 〔咒骂或发誓用语〕 stand condemned by God: 我要是说谎，～！ May heaven strike me down if I lie!

【天竺鲷】 tiānzhúdiāo 〈动〉 cardinal fish

【天竺葵】 tiānzhúkuí 〈植〉 fish pelargonium (*Pelargonium hortorum*)

【天竺鼠】 tiānzhúshǔ 〈动〉 guinea pig; cavy

【天主教】 Tiānzhǔjiào Catholicism ◇ ～会 the Roman Catholic Church/ ～徒 Catholic

【天资】 tiānzī natural gift; talent; natural endowments

【天子】 tiānzǐ the Son of Heaven — the emperor

【天字第一号】 tiān zì dìyī hào the greatest in the world; par excellence

**添** tiān ① add; increase: 增～光彩 add lustre to/ ～煤 put in more coal; stoke/ ～衣服 put on more clothes/ ～设早晚服务部 set up an additional department for after-hours service/ 为建设社会主义～砖加瓦 do one's little bit to help build socialism/ 社里～了两台拖拉机。The commune has acquired two more tractors./ 给你们～麻烦了。Sorry to have troubled you. ② 〈方〉 have a baby: 她最近～了个女孩儿。She recently had a daughter.

【添补】 tiānbu replenish; get more: 需要～机器零件 need a fresh supply of machine parts

【添丁】 tiāndīng have a baby (esp. a boy) born into the family

【添加剂】 tiānjiājì 〈化〉 additive

【添油加醋】 tiānyóu-jiācù add colour and emphasis to (a narration); add inflammatory details to (a story)

【添枝加叶】 tiānzhī-jiāyè embellish a story: 照我说的对他讲，可别～。Tell him exactly what I said and don't embroider./ 接着，他就～，甚至公开扯谎。Then he started to embellish and even lie outright.

【添置】 tiānzhì add to one's possessions; acquire: ～家俱 buy more furniture

**黇** tiān

【黇鹿】 tiānlù 〈动〉 fallow deer

## tián

**田** tián ① field; farmland; cropland: 犁～ plough a field/ 在～里劳动 work in the fields; work on the land/ 为革命种～ farming for the revolution/ 高产稳产～ stable and high yield cropland/ 耕者有其～ land to the tiller/ 油～ oilfield/ 煤～ coalfield ② (Tián) a surname

【田鳖】 tiánbiē 〈动〉 giant water bug; fish killer

【田畴】 tiánchóu 〈书〉 farmland; cultivated land; fields

【田地】 tiándì ① field; farmland; cropland ② wretched situation; plight: 真没想到事情会发展到这步～。I never dreamt things would come to such a pass./ 你怎么落到这步～！ How did you get into such a plight?

【田凫】 tiánfú 〈动〉 lapwing

【田赋】 tiánfù feudal land tax

【田埂】 tiángěng a low bank of earth between fields; ridge

【田鸡】 tiánjī frog

【田间】 tiánjiān field; farm
◇ ～持水量〈农〉 field capacity/ ～管理 field management/ ～劳动 field labour; farm work

【田径】 tiánjìng 〈体〉 track and field
◇ ～队 track and field team/ ～赛 track and field meet/ ～赛项目 track and field events/ ～运动 track and field sports; athletics/ ～运动员 athlete

【田菁】 tiánjing 〈植〉 sesbania

【田猎】 tiánliè 〈书〉 hunting

【田鹨】 tiánliù 〈动〉 paddy-field pipit
【田螺】 tiánluó 〈动〉 river snail
【田赛】 tiánsài 〈体〉 field events
【田鼠】 tiánshǔ vole: 普通～ field vole
【田野】 tiányě field; open country: 广阔的～ a vast field; a vast expanse of farmland
【田园】 tiányuán fields and gardens; countryside: ～生活 idyllic life/ ～风光 rural scenery ◇ ～诗 idyll; pastoral poetry/ ～诗人 pastoral poet
【田庄】 tiánzhuāng country estate

**恬** tián 〈书〉 ① quiet; tranquil; calm: ～适 quiet and comfortable ② not care at all; remain unperturbed
【恬不知耻】 tián bù zhī chǐ not feel ashamed; have no sense of shame; be shameless
【恬淡】 tiándàn indifferent to fame or gain
【恬静】 tiánjìng quiet; peaceful; tranquil
【恬然】 tiánrán 〈书〉 unperturbed; calm; nonchalant: 处之～ remain unruffled

**钿** tián 〈方〉 coin or money: 铜～ copper cash or money
另见 diàn

**甜** tián ① sweet; honeyed: 这西瓜好～哪! This watermelon is really sweet! ② sound: 睡得真～ have a sound (或 sweet) sleep; sleep soundly
【甜菜】 tiáncài ① beet: 糖～ sugar beet ② beetroot ◇ ～糖 beet sugar
【甜瓜】 tiánguā muskmelon
【甜美】 tiánměi ① sweet; luscious: 味道～ taste sweet; have a sweet taste/ ～多汁的桃儿 luscious and juicy peaches ② pleasant; refreshing: 睡了个～的午觉 have a refreshing nap after lunch
【甜蜜】 tiánmì sweet; happy: ～的回忆 happy (或 sweet) memories/ 孩子们笑得多么～! How merrily the children laughed!
【甜面酱】 tiánmiànjiàng a sweet sauce made of fermented flour
【甜品】 tiánpǐn sweetmeats
【甜食】 tiánshí sweet food; sweetmeats: 他爱吃～。He has a sweet tooth. 或 He likes sweet things.
【甜水】 tiánshuǐ ① fresh water: ～井 fresh water well ② sugar water — happiness; comfort: 这孩子是在～里长大的。The child's grown up in happy times.
【甜丝丝】 tiánsīsī ① pleasantly sweet: 这个菜～儿的。This dish is sweet and delicious. ② quite pleased; gratified; happy: 心里感到～的 feel quite pleased (或 happy)
【甜头】 tiántou ① sweet taste; pleasant flavour ② good; benefit (as an inducement): 尝到～ get something out of it; draw benefit from it
【甜味】 tiánwèi sweet taste: 有点～ taste sweet; have a sweet taste
【甜言蜜语】 tiányán-mìyǔ sweet words and honeyed phrases; fine-sounding words
【甜滋滋】 tiánzīzī 见"甜丝丝"②

**填** tián ① fill; stuff: 往坑里～土 fill a pit with earth/ ～枕芯 stuff a pillow/ 义愤～膺 be filled with righteous indignation ② write; fill in: ～表 fill in a form/ 别～错日期。Don't fill in the wrong date.
【填报】 tiánbào fill in a form and submit it to the leadership: 每周～工程进度 make a weekly progress report on a project
【填补】 tiánbǔ fill (a vacancy, gap, etc.): ～缺额 fill a vacancy/ ～亏空 make up a deficit/ ～科学技术领域的空白 fill in the gaps in the fields of science and technology
【填充】 tiánchōng ① fill up; stuff ② fill in the blanks (in a test paper) ◇ ～塔〈石油〉 packed column (或 tower)
【填词】 tiáncí compose a poem to a given tune of *ci* (词) 参见"词" cí③
【填方】 tiánfāng 〈建〉 fill
【填空】 tiánkòng ① fill a vacant position; fill a vacancy ② 见"填充"②
【填料】 tiánliào 〈机〉 packing; stuffing; filling; filler ◇ ～函 gland box; stuffing box
【填密】 tiánmì 〈机〉 packing: 液压～ hydraulic packing ◇ ～函 packing box
【填平】 tiánpíng fill and level up: ～弹坑 fill up craters/ 搬倒土山～沟,大搞人造小平原 flatten hills to fill up gullies and create man-made plains/ ～补齐 fill up the gaps
【填写】 tiánxiě fill in; write: ～表格 fill in a form/ ～入党志愿书 fill out an application form for Party membership/ 这里～你的姓名和住址。Please fill in the blanks here with your name and address.
【填鸭】 tiányā ① force-feed a duck ② force-fed duck ◇ ～式教学法 cramming (或 forced-feeding) method of teaching

## tiǎn

**忝** tiǎn 〈书〉〈谦〉 be unworthy of the honour: ～在相知之列 having the honour, though I'm unworthy of it, to be counted among your acquaintances

**殄** tiǎn extirpate; exterminate: 暴～天物 a reckless waste of grain, etc.

**腆** tiǎn ① sumptuous; rich ② 〈方〉 protrude; thrust out: ～着胸脯 stick out one's chest

**觍** tiǎn ① 〈书〉 ashamed: ～颜 shamefaced ② 〈口〉 brazen: ～着脸 brazen it out

**舔** tiǎn lick; lap: ～～嘴唇 moisten one's lips with the tongue

## tiāo

**佻** tiāo 见"轻～" qīngtiāo

**挑** tiāo ① choose; select; pick: ～最好的作种子 select the best for seeds/ ～毛病 pick faults; find fault/ 把那筐西红柿～一～ pick over that basket of tomatoes ② carry (或 tote) on the shoulder with a pole; shoulder: ～着一担菜 carry two baskets of vegetables on a shoulder pole/ ～水点种 carry (或 fetch) water for dibbling (seeds, young plants, etc.)/ ～起革命和生产的重担 shoulder heavy loads in both revolution and production ③ 〈量〉〔用于成挑儿的东西〕: 一～水 two buckets of water carried on a shoulder pole
另见 tiǎo
【挑刺儿】 tiāocìr 〈方〉 find fault; pick holes; be captious: 他就爱～。He's always finding fault with people.
【挑肥拣瘦】 tiāoféi-jiǎnshòu 〈贬〉 pick the fat or choose the lean — choose whichever is to one's personal advantage
【挑夫】 tiāofū 〈旧〉 porter
【挑拣】 tiāojiǎn pick; pick and choose: 挑挑拣拣 be

choosy/ 苹果都是好的，用不着～。 All the apples are good. There's no need to pick and choose.

【挑三拣四】 tiāosān-jiǎnsì pick and choose; be choosy

【挑剔】 tiāoti nitpick; be hypercritical; be fastidious: 总的来说，这个计划是好的，我们不应过于～。On the whole it's a good plan and we shouldn't nitpick.

【挑选】 tiāoxuǎn choose; select; pick out: ～和培养接班人 choose and train successors/ 百货商店有很多童装可供～。 The department store has a large choice of children's clothes.

【挑眼】 tiāoyǎn 〈方〉 be fastidious (about formalities, etc.)

【挑字眼儿】 tiāo zìyǎnr find fault with the choice of words

【挑子】 tiāozi carrying pole with its load; load carried on a shoulder pole

**祧** tiāo 〈书〉 be or become heir to: 承～ become heir to one's uncle who has no son

## tiáo

**条** tiáo ① twig: 柳～儿 willow twigs ② a long narrow piece; strip; slip: 布～ a strip of cloth/ ～石 a rectangular slab of stone/ 便～ a brief informal note/ 金～ gold bar ③ item; article: 逐～ item by item; point by point/ 这项条约的正文共八～。The main body of the treaty consists of eight articles. ④ order: 有～不紊 in perfect order; orderly ⑤〈量〉: 两～鱼 two fish/ 三～船 three ships/ 一～大街 an avenue/ 一～肥皂 a bar of soap/ 一～香烟 a carton of cigarettes/ 一～裤子 a pair of trousers/ 两～新闻 two pieces (或 items) of news/ 四～建议 four proposals/ 两～路线的斗争 struggle between the two lines; two-line struggle/ 跟工人一～心 be of one mind with the workers

【条案】 tiáo'àn a long narrow table 又作"条几"

【条播】 tiáobō 〈农〉 drilling ◇ ～机 seed drill; drill

【条分缕析】 tiáofēn-lǚxī make a careful and detailed analysis

【条幅】 tiáofú a vertically-hung scroll; scroll

【条钢】 tiáogāng bar iron

【条痕】 tiáohén 〈矿〉 streak

【条件】 tiáojiàn ① condition; term; factor: 自然～ natural conditions/ 贸易～ terms of trade/ 利用有利的～ make use of the favourable factors/ 在目前～下 given the present conditions; under present circumstances/ 在对等的～下给予优惠待遇 give preferential treatment on a reciprocal basis/ 为马克思主义政党的诞生准备～ prepare the ground for the founding of a Marxist party/ 有～要上，没有～，创造～也要上。When the conditions exist, go ahead; when they don't exist, then create them and go ahead. ② requirement; prerequisite; qualification: 提出～ list the prerequisites; put forward the requirements/ 革命接班人的五项～ the five requirements for successors to the revolution ◇ ～刺激〈生理〉conditioned stimulus/ ～反射〈生理〉conditioned reflex

【条款】 tiáokuǎn clause; article; provision: 最惠国～ most-favoured-nation clause/ 法律～ legal provision

【条理】 tiáolǐ proper arrangement or presentation; orderliness; method: 她工作很有～。She is a methodical worker./ 这篇文章～清楚。The article is well-organized.

【条例】 tiáolì regulations; rules; ordinances: 惩治反革命～ Regulations Regarding the Punishment of Counterrevolutionaries/ 组织～ organic rules

【条令】 tiáolìng 〈军〉 regulations: 内务～ routine service regulations

【条目】 tiáomù ① clauses and subclauses (in a formal document) ② entry (in a dictionary)

【条绒】 tiáoróng corduroy

【条鳎】 tiáotǎ 〈动〉 striped sole

【条条框框】 tiáotiáo kuāngkuang 〈贬〉 rules and regulations; conventions: 为～所束缚 be hedged in with rules and regulations/ 思想上的～ the trammels of conventional (或 outmoded) ideas

【条文】 tiáowén article; clause ◇ ～范例 standard clause

【条纹】 tiáowén stripe; streak ◇ ～布 striped cloth; stripe

【条锈病】 tiáoxiùbìng 〈农〉 stripe rust; yellow rust

【条约】 tiáoyuē treaty; pact: 互不侵犯～ mutual nonaggression treaty/ 多边～ multilateral pact

【条子】 tiáozi ① strip: 纸～ a narrow strip of paper; a slip of paper ② a brief informal note

**苕** tiáo 〈植〉 Chinese trumpet creeper

**迢** tiáo far; remote

【迢迢】 tiáotiáo far away; remote: 千里～ from a thousand *li* away; from afar

**调** tiáo ① mix; adjust: ～匀 mix well/ ～弦 tune a stringed instrument ② suit well; fit in perfectly: 风～雨顺 good weather for the crops; propitious weather/ 饮食失～ ailment caused by an unbalanced or irregular diet ③ mediate: ～人 mediator; peacemaker ④ tease; provoke 另见 diào

【调处】 tiáochǔ mediate; arbitrate: ～争端 arbitrate a dispute; act as mediator

【调挡】 tiáodǎng 〈机〉 gear shift

【调幅】 tiáofú 〈无〉 amplitude modulation

【调羹】 tiáogēng spoon

【调和】 tiáohe ① be in harmonious proportion: 雨水～。Rainfall is well distributed./ 这两种颜色配得很～。These two colours blend well. ② mediate; reconcile: 从中～ mediate; act as mediator ③ compromise; make concessions: 进行不～的斗争 wage uncompromising struggles/ 在路线问题上没有～的余地。There is no room for compromise on the question of the two lines.

【调护】 tiáohù care of a patient during convalescence; nursing: 病人需要特别～。The patient needs special care during his convalescence.

【调剂】 tiáojì ① make up (或 fill) a prescription ② adjust; regulate: ～劳动力 redistribute labour power/ ～生活 enliven one's life

【调浆】 tiáojiāng 〈纺〉 size mixing

【调焦】 tiáojiāo 〈摄〉 focusing ◇ ～镜头 focusing lens/ ～毛玻璃 focusing screen

【调节】 tiáojié regulate; adjust: ～室温 regulate the room temperature/ ～水流 regulate the flow of water/ 空气～ air conditioning/ 对货币的流通不断进行～ constantly readjust the amount of money in circulation

【调节器】 tiáojiéqì regulator; conditioner: 恒流～〈电〉 constant current regulator/ 空气～ air conditioner

【调解】 tiáojiě mediate; make peace: ～家庭纠纷 mediate in (或 patch up) a family quarrel

【调经】 tiáojīng 〈中医〉 regulate the menstrual function

【调理】 tiáoli ① nurse one's health; recuperate: 精心～ nurse with great care; careful nursing ② take care of; look after: ～牲口 look after livestock

【调料】 tiáoliào condiment; seasoning; flavouring

【调弄】 tiáonòng ① make fun of; tease ② arrange; adjust ③ instigate; stir up

【调配】 tiáopèi mix; blend: ～颜色 mix colours 另见 diàopèi

【调皮】 tiáopí ① naughty; mischievous: ～的孩子 a naughty

child/ ～捣蛋 mischievous ② unruly; tricky: ～的牲口 skittish beasts/ 科学是老老实实的学问,任何一点～都是不行的。Science means honest, solid knowledge; you can't just play around.

【调频】 tiáopín 〈电〉 frequency modulation

【调情】 tiáoqíng flirt

【调色板】 tiáosèbǎn 〈美术〉 palette

【调色刀】 tiáosèdāo 〈美术〉 palette knife; painting knife

【调色碟】 tiáosèdié 〈美术〉 colour mixing tray

【调色】 tiáoshǎi 〈美术〉 mix colours

【调试】 tiáoshì 〈计算机〉 debugging

【调速器】 tiáosùqì 〈机〉 governor

【调唆】 tiáosuo incite; instigate

【调停】 tiáoting mediate; intervene; act as an intermediary: 居间～ mediate (或 offer one's good offices) between two parties/ 对争端进行～ mediate (或 intervene in) a dispute

【调味】 tiáowèi flavour; season: 加点生姜～ flavour (或 season) food with some ginger ◇ ～品 flavouring; seasoning; condiment

【调戏】 tiáoxi take liberties with (a woman); assail (a woman) with obscenities

【调笑】 tiáoxiào make fun of; poke fun at; tease

【调谐】 tiáoxié ① harmonious ② 〈电〉 tuning ◇ ～范围 tuning range/ ～旋钮 tuning knob

【调压器】 tiáoyāqì 〈电〉 voltage regulator

【调养】 tiáoyǎng take good care of oneself (after an illness); build up one's health by rest and by taking nourishing food; be nursed back to health

【调音】 tiáoyīn 〈乐〉 tuning

【调整】 tiáozhěng adjust; regulate; revise: 工资～ adjustment of wages (usu. upwards)/ ～价格 readjust (或 modify) prices/ ～供求关系 regulate (或 readjust) supply and demand/ ～生产计划 revise production plans

【调整器】 tiáozhěngqì 〈机〉 adjuster: 自动松紧～ automatic slack adjuster

【调治】 tiáozhì recuperate under medical treatment

【调制】 tiáozhì 〈电〉 modulation: 音频～ voice modulation ◇ ～间隙 modulation gap

**笤** tiáo

【笤帚】 tiáozhou whisk broom

**髫** tiáo 〈书〉 a child's hanging hair

【髫龄】 tiáolíng 〈书〉 childhood

## tiǎo

**挑** tiǎo ① push sth. up with a pole or stick; raise: 把帘子～起来 raise the curtain/ ～灯夜战 fight by torchlight; continue working by lamplight ② poke; pick: ～火 poke a fire/ ～刺 pick out a splinter/ ～破水泡 prick a blister with a needle/ 把问题～开来说吧。Let's put all the cards on the table. ③ stir up; instigate: ～事 stir up trouble; sow discord ④ rising stroke (in Chinese characters) 另见 tiāo

【挑拨】 tiǎobō instigate; incite; sow discord: ～是非 foment discord/ ～民族关系 sow dissension among the various nationalities

【挑拨离间】 tiǎobō líjiàn sow dissension; foment discord; incite one against the other; drive a wedge between

【挑动】 tiǎodòng provoke; stir up; incite: ～内战 provoke civil war/ ～群众斗群众 incite the masses to struggle against each other

【挑逗】 tiǎodòu provoke; tease; tantalize

【挑花】 tiǎohuā cross-stitch work

【挑起】 tiǎoqǐ provoke; stir up; instigate: ～边境冲突 provoke a border conflict (或 clash)

【挑唆】 tiǎosuo incite; abet; instigate: 警惕有人在背后～。Beware of people stirring up trouble behind the scenes.

【挑衅】 tiǎoxìn provoke: 进行武装～ carry out armed provocation/ 故意～ deliberate provocation/ 提出～性的问题 raise provocative questions

【挑战】 tiǎozhàn ① throw down the gauntlet; challenge to battle: ～的口吻 a provocative tone/ 接受～ take up the gauntlet; accept a challenge ② challenge to a contest ◇ ～书 letter of challenge; challenge

**窕** tiǎo 见"窈窕" yǎotiǎo

## tiào

**眺** tiào look into the distance from a high place: 远～ look far into the distance

【眺望】 tiàowàng look into the distance from a high place

**粜** tiào sell (grain)

**跳** tiào ① jump; leap; spring; bounce: 高兴得～起来 jump for (或 with) joy/ ～下自行车 jump off a bicycle/ ～过一条沟 leap over a ditch/ 孩子们蹦蹦～～地进了教室。The children bounced into the classroom./ 他～过了二米的高度。He cleared two metres in the high jump./ ～出来向党进攻 come out into the open to attack the Party ② move up and down; beat: 他激动得心直～。His heart was throbbing with excitement./ 我眼皮老是～。My eyelids keep twitching all the time./ 她的心～正常。Her heartbeat is normal. ③ skip (over); make omissions: 从第一页～到第五页 jump from page one to page five/ ～过了三页 skip over three pages/ ～一针(编织) drop a stitch

【跳班】 tiàobān (of pupils) skip a grade

【跳板】 tiàobǎn ① gangplank ② springboard; diving board

【跳虫】 tiàochóng springtail; snowflea

【跳弹】 tiàodàn 〈军〉 ricochet ◇ ～轰炸 ricochet bombing; skip bombing

【跳动】 tiàodòng move up and down; beat; pulsate: 只要我的心脏还在～,我就要为人民工作。As long as my heart still beats, I will go on working for the people.

【跳房子】 tiào fángzi hopscotch 又作"跳间"

【跳高】 tiàogāo 〈体〉 high jump: 撑竿～ pole vault; pole jump ◇ ～运动员 high jumper

【跳行】 tiàoháng ① skip a line (in reading or transcribing) ② change to a new occupation

【跳级】 tiàojí (of pupils) skip a grade

【跳脚】 tiàojiǎo stamp one's foot: 气得～ stamp with rage

【跳栏】 tiàolán 〈体〉 hurdle race; the hurdles

【跳雷】 tiàoléi 〈军〉 bounding mine

【跳梁小丑】 tiàoliáng xiǎochǒu a buffoon who performs antics; contemptible scoundrel

【跳马】 tiàomǎ 〈体〉 ① vaulting horse ② horse-vaulting

【跳蝻】 tiàonǎn 〈动〉 the nymph of a locust

【跳皮筋】 tiào píjīn rubber band skipping; skipping and dancing over a chain of rubber bands 又作"跳猴皮筋"

【跳棋】 tiàoqí Chinese checkers; Chinese draughts

【跳球】 tiàoqiú 〈篮球〉 jump ball

【跳伞】 tiàosǎn ① parachute; bale out ② 〈体〉 parachute jumping ◇ ～区 parachute drop zone/ ～塔 parachute tower/ ～运动员 parachutist; parachuter

【跳神】 tiàoshén sorcerer's dance in a trance
【跳绳】 tiàoshéng rope skipping
【跳鼠】 tiàoshǔ 〈动〉 jerboa
【跳水】 tiàoshuǐ 〈体〉 dive: ～表演 diving exhibition/ 高(低)难度跳台～ variety (plain) high diving/ 跳板～ springboard diving/ 面对池反身～ reverse dive/ 向前(后)～ front (back) dive/ 面对板向内～ inward dive
【跳台】 tiàotái diving tower; diving platform
【跳汰选】 tiàotàixuǎn 〈矿〉 jigging: ～煤 coal jigging
【跳舞】 tiàowǔ dance
【跳箱】 tiàoxiāng 〈体〉 ① box horse; vaulting box ② jump over the box horse
【跳远】 tiàoyuǎn 〈体〉 long jump; broad jump: 三级～ hop, step and jump
【跳月】 tiàoyuè moon dance (a festive dance performed in the moonlight by young people of the Miao and Yi nationalities)
【跳跃】 tiàoyuè jump; leap; bound
【跳跃着陆】 tiàoyuè zhuólù 〈军〉 rebound landing
【跳蚤】 tiàozǎo flea

## tiē

**帖** tiē ① submissive; obedient: 服～ docile and obedient ② well-settled; well-placed: 办事妥～ manage things fittingly; handle matters well
另见 tiě; tiè

**贴** tiē ① paste; stick; glue: ～邮票 stick on a stamp/ ～大字报 put up *dazibao*/ ～上胶布 stick on a piece of adhesive tape ② keep close to; nestle closely to: ～墙站着 stand against the wall/ 这孩子紧紧～在妈妈身边。The child was nestling closely to its mother. ③ subsidies; allowance: 米～ food allowance/ 房～ housing allowance ④ 见"帖"② tiē ⑤ 〈量〉: 一～膏药 a piece of medicated plaster
【贴边】 tiēbiān hem (of a garment)
【贴饼子】 tiēbǐngzi ① bake corn or millet cakes on a pan ② corn or millet cakes so baked
【贴补】 tiēbu subsidize; help (out) financially: ～家用 help out with the family expenses
【贴花】 tiēhuā 〈纺〉 appliqué
【贴换】 tiēhuan trade sth. in; trade-in
【贴金】 tiējīn ① cover with gold leaf (或 gold foil); gild ② touch up; prettify: 别尽往自己脸上～了。Don't put feathers in your own cap. 或 Don't go blowing your own trumpet. ◇ ～漆 gold size
【贴近】 tiējìn press close to; nestle up against: 那孩子～他身边，轻声说了几句话。The child nestled up against him and murmured a few words.
【贴切】 tiēqiè (of words) apt; suitable; appropriate; proper: 这个比喻很～。This metaphor is very appropriate./ 我找不到～的词儿来表达我的意思。I can't find suitable words to express what I mean./ 这样说不～。That's not the right word for it./ 措词～ aptly worded; well-put
【贴身】 tiēshēn next to the skin: ～衣服 underclothes; underclothing
【贴水】 tiēshuǐ 〈商〉 agio
【贴题】 tiētí relevant; pertinent; to the point: 着墨不多，但是十分～ brief but very much to the point/ 你的话不～。What you say is irrelevant (或 beside the point).
【贴息】 tiēxī 〈商〉 ① pay interest in the form of a deduction when selling a bill of exchange, etc. ② interest so deducted; discount
【贴现】 tiēxiàn discount (on a promissory note) ◇ ～率 discount rate
【贴心】 tiēxīn intimate; close: ～朋友 a person one can confide in; bosom friend/ ～话 words spoken in confidence/ 老支书既是群众的引路人，又是群众的～人。The old Party secretary is both the leader and a close friend of the masses.

**萜** tiē 〈化〉 terpene

## tiě

**帖** tiě ① invitation: 请～ invitation/ 谢～ card of thanks; thank-you note (或 card) ② note; card: 字～儿 brief note ③ 〈方〉〈量〉: 一～药 a dose (或 draught) of herbal medicine
另见 tiē; tiè

**铁** tiě ① iron (Fe): 熟～ wrought iron/ 生～ pig iron; cast iron/ 废～ scrap iron/ ～工厂 ironworks/ 趁热打～。Strike while the iron is hot. ② arms; weapon: 手无寸～ completely unarmed; bare-handed ③ hard or strong as iron: ～拳 iron fist/ ～打的江山 unshakable state power ④ indisputable; unalterable: ～的事实 hard fact; ironclad evidence/ ～的纪律 iron discipline ⑤ resolve; determine: ～了心 be unshakable in one's determination ⑥ (Tiě) a surname
【铁案如山】 tiě'àn rú shān borne out by ironclad evidence
【铁板】 tiěbǎn iron plate; sheet iron
【铁板一块】 tiěbǎn yī kuài a monolithic bloc
【铁笔】 tiěbǐ ① a cutting tool used in carving seals, etc. ② stylus for cutting stencils; stencil pen
【铁箅子】 tiěbìzi ① grate (of a stove) ② gridiron; grill
【铁饼】 tiěbǐng 〈体〉 ① discus ② discus throw
【铁蚕豆】 tiěcándòu roasted broad bean
【铁杵磨成针】 tiěchǔ móchéng zhēn an iron pestle can be ground down to a needle — perseverance will prevail; little strokes fell great oaks
【铁窗】 tiěchuāng ① a window with iron grating ② prison bars; prison: ～风味 prison life; life behind bars
【铁磁共振】 tiěcí gòngzhèn 〈物〉 ferromagnetic resonance
【铁磁性】 tiěcíxìng ferromagnetism
【铁搭】 tiědā a rake with three to six teeth
【铁道】 tiědào railway; railroad: 地下～ underground (railway); tube; subway ◇ ～炮兵〈军〉 railway artillery
【铁道兵】 tiědàobīng 〈军〉 railway corps: 中国人民解放军～ the PLA railway engineering corps
【铁电现象】 tiědiàn xiànxiàng 〈物〉 ferroelectricity
【铁定】 tiědìng ironclad; fixed; unalterable: ～的事实 hard fact; ironclad evidence/ ～的局面 unalterable situation
【铁饭碗】 tiěfànwǎn iron rice bowl — a secure job
【铁杆儿】 tiěgǎnr ① stubborn; inveterate; dyed-in-the-wool: ～汉奸 out-and-out traitor ② of guaranteed high yield; surefire: ～庄稼 guaranteed high-yielding crop
【铁工】 tiěgōng ① ironwork ② ironworker; blacksmith
【铁公鸡】 tiěgōngjī iron cock — a stingy person; miser
【铁姑娘】 tiěgūniang iron girl ◇ ～队 Iron Girls Team
【铁箍】 tiěgū iron hoop
【铁观音】 tiěguānyīn a variety of oolong tea
【铁管】 tiěguǎn iron pipe; iron tube
【铁轨】 tiěguǐ rail
【铁汉】 tiěhàn man of iron (或 steel); man of iron will; a strong determined person
【铁合金】 tiěhéjīn 〈冶〉 ferroalloy
【铁黑】 tiěhēi 〈化〉 ① iron oxide black ② iron black

【铁红】 tiěhóng iron oxide red
【铁花】 tiěhuā 〈工美〉 ornamental work of iron; iron openwork
【铁画】 tiěhuà 〈工美〉 iron picture
【铁环】 tiěhuán iron hoop: 滚～ trundle a hoop; play with a hoop
【铁黄】 tiěhuáng iron oxide yellow
【铁活】 tiěhuó ironwork
【铁蒺藜】 tiějíli 〈军〉 caltrop
【铁甲】 tiějiǎ ① mail; armour ② 〈军〉 armour for vessels, vehicles, etc. ◇ ～车 armoured car; armoured vehicle
【铁匠】 tiějiang blacksmith; ironsmith ◇ ～铺 smithy; blacksmith's shop
【铁脚板】 tiějiǎobǎn iron soles — toughened feet
【铁军】 tiějūn iron army — invincible army
【铁矿】 tiěkuàng ① iron ore ② iron mine ◇ ～石 iron ore
【铁力木】 tiělìmù 〈植〉 ferreous mesua (*Mesua ferrea*)
【铁链】 tiěliàn iron chain; shackles
【铁路】 tiělù railway; railroad: ～运输 railway transportation; railway (或 rail) transport; shipping by rail/ 国际～联运 international railway through transport ◇ ～电气化 railway electrification/ ～干线 trunk railway/ ～公路两用桥 (railway and highway) combined bridge/ ～路基 railway bed/ ～网 railway network/ ～线 railway line/ ～油槽车 rail tank car; rail tanker
【铁马】 tiěmǎ ① cavalry: 金戈～ shining spears and armoured horses — a symbol of war in ancient China ② tinkling pieces of metal hanging from the eaves of pagodas, temples, etc.
【铁门】 tiěmén ① iron gate ② grille
【铁面无私】 tiěmiàn wú sī impartial and incorruptible
【铁牛】 tiěniú iron ox — tractor
【铁皮】 tiěpí iron sheet: 白～ tinplate; galvanized iron sheet/ 黑～ black sheet (iron)
【铁骑】 tiěqí 〈书〉 cavalry
【铁器】 tiěqì ironware ◇ ～时代 the Iron Age
【铁锹】 tiěqiāo spade; shovel
【铁青】 tiěqīng ashen; livid; ghastly pale: 气得脸色～ turn livid with rage
【铁人】 tiěrén iron man — a person of exceptional physical and moral strength: ～王进喜 Iron Man Wang Jinxi (outstanding oil worker of Daqing)/ 学习～精神 learn the Iron Man spirit
【铁纱】 tiěshā wire gauze; wire cloth
【铁砂】 tiěshā ① 〈矿〉 iron sand ② shot (in a shotgun cartridge); pellets
【铁杉】 tiěshān 〈植〉 Chinese hemlock (*Tsuga chinensis*)
【铁石心肠】 tiěshí xīncháng be ironhearted; have a heart of stone; be hardhearted
【铁树】 tiěshù 〈植〉 sago cycas (*Cycas revoluta*)
【铁树开花】 tiěshù kāi huā the iron tree in blossom — something seldom seen or hardly possible: 千年的铁树开了花，银针使得聋哑人说了话。 Miraculously, like the thousand-year-old iron tree bursting into blossom, many deaf-mutes have regained their power of speech after acupuncture treatment.
【铁水】 tiěshuǐ molten iron
【铁丝】 tiěsī iron wire
【铁丝网】 tiěsīwǎng ① wire netting; wire meshes ② wire entanglement: 有刺～ barbed wire entanglement
【铁素体】 tiěsùtǐ 〈冶〉 ferrite
【铁索】 tiěsuǒ cable; iron chain ◇ ～吊车 cable car/ ～桥 chain bridge
【铁塔】 tiětǎ ① iron tower; iron pagoda ② 〈电〉 pylon; transmission tower
【铁蹄】 tiětí iron heel — cruel oppression of the people
【铁桶】 tiětǒng metal pail (或 bucket); drum: 包围得～似的 be tightly encircled
【铁腕】 tiěwàn iron hand ◇ ～人物 an ironhanded (或 despotic, tyrannical) person; strong man
【铁锨】 tiěxiān shovel; spade
【铁线订书机】 tiěxiàn dìngshūjī wire stitcher; wire stitching machine
【铁线莲】 tiěxiànlián 〈植〉 cream clematis (*Clematis florida*)
【铁屑】 tiěxiè （锉后的）iron filings;（车削后的）iron chippings and shavings
【铁心】 tiěxīn 〈电〉 (iron) core
【铁锈】 tiěxiù rust
【铁盐】 tiěyán molysite
【铁陨石】 tiěyǔnshí iron meteorite
【铁砧】 tiězhēn anvil
【铁证】 tiězhèng ironclad proof; irrefutable evidence: ～如山 irrefutable, conclusive evidence

## tiè

**帖** tiè a book containing models of handwriting or painting for learners to copy: 习字～ a book of models of calligraphy for copying; calligraphy models/ 画～ a book of model paintings or drawings; painting models/ 碑～ a book of stone rubbings
另见 tiē; tiě

**餮** tiè greedy for food

## tīng

**厅** tīng ① hall: 餐～ dining hall; restaurant/（旅馆、剧场等的）休息～ lounge; *foyer*/ 会议～ conference hall/ 音乐～ concert hall/ 人民大会堂台湾～ Taiwan Room in the Great Hall of the People ② office: 办公～ general office ③ a government department at the provincial level: 湖南省教育～ the Education Department of Hunan Province

**汀** tīng 〈书〉 low, level land along a river; spit of land

**听** tīng ① listen; hear: ～广播 listen to the radio/ 兼～则明，偏信则暗。Listen to both sides and you will be enlightened, heed only one side and you will be benighted./ 请～我讲完。Please hear me out./ 我～了好一会儿，可什么也没～见。I listened for quite a while, but heard nothing./ 到群众中去走一走，～～他们的意见 go among the masses and hear what they have to say ② heed; obey: ～党的话。Do as the Party says./ 我劝他别去，他不～。I advised him not to go,but he wouldn't listen./ 对批评～不进去 turn a deaf ear to criticism ③ 〈书〉 administer; manage: ～讼 administer justice; hear a case (in a law court) ④ allow; let: ～任摆布 allow oneself to be ordered about ⑤ 〈方〉 tin; can: 三～猪肉罐头 three tins of pork
【听便】 tīngbiàn as one pleases; please yourself: 去留～。You may go or stay as you please.
【听差】 tīngchāi 〈旧〉 manservant; office attendant
【听从】 tīngcóng obey; heed; comply with: 时刻～党的召唤 be always ready to answer the call of the Party/ ～吩咐 be at sb.'s beck and call; do sb.'s bidding/ ～劝告 accept sb.'s advice
【听而不闻】 tīng ér bù wén hear but pay no attention;

turn a deaf ear to

【听骨】 tīnggǔ 〈生理〉 ear bones

【听候】 tīnghòu wait for (a decision, settlement, etc.); pending: ～分配 wait for one's assignment (to work)/ ～上级指示 pending further instructions from the higher authorities

【听话】 tīnghuà heed what an elder or superior says; be obedient

【听话儿】 tīnghuàr wait for a reply: 你的要求我们正在研究,过几天～。We're considering your request and will give you a reply in a few days.

【听见】 tīngjian hear: 我～有人敲门。I heard a knock at the door./ 她说的什么你～了吗? Did you catch what she said?/ 说话的声音小得几乎听不见 speak in a scarcely audible voice

【听讲】 tīngjiǎng listen to a talk; attend a lecture: 一面～,一面记笔记 take notes while listening to a lecture

【听觉】 tīngjué 〈生理〉 sense of hearing

【听课】 tīngkè ① visit (或 sit in on) a class ② attend a lecture

【听力】 tīnglì ① hearing: 经过针刺恢复了～ regain one's hearing after receiving acupuncture treatment ② aural comprehension (in language teaching)

【听命】 tīngmìng take orders from; be at sb.'s command: 俯首～ be at sb.'s beck and call

【听凭】 tīngpíng allow; let (sb. do as he pleases): ～别人的摆布 be at the mercy of others

【听其言观其行】 tīng qí yán guān qí xíng listen to what a person says and watch what he does; judge people by their deeds, not just by their words

【听其自然】 tīng qí zìrán let things take their own course; let matters slide

【听起来】 tīngqilai sound; ring: 她的建议～还不错。Her proposal sounds good./ 他的话～不诚恳。What he said seemed insincere. 或 His words rang hollow.

【听取】 tīngqǔ listen to: 经常～群众的意见 constantly heed the opinions of the masses/ ～工作报告 listen to a work report/ ～汇报 hear reports (from below); debrief

【听任】 tīngrèn allow; let (sb. do as he pleases): 不能～错误思想泛滥 never allow erroneous ideas to spread unchecked

【听神经】 tīngshénjīng 〈生理〉 auditory (或 acoustic) nerve

【听说】 tīngshuō be told; hear of: 我～她到南方去了。I hear she has gone to the south./ 我们从来没～过这种事。We've never heard of such a thing./ 这只不过是～而已。This is only hearsay. 或 It's nothing but hearsay.

【听天由命】 tīngtiān-yóumìng submit to the will of Heaven; resign oneself to one's fate; trust to luck

【听筒】 tīngtǒng ① (telephone) receiver ②〈电〉headphone; earphone ③〈医〉 stethoscope

【听闻】 tīngwén 〈书〉 ① hear: 骇人～ appalling; shocking ② what one hears

【听戏】 tīngxì go to the opera

【听写】 tīngxiě 〈教〉 dictation: 教师让学生～。The teacher gave the pupils (a piece of) dictation.

【听信】 tīngxìn ① wait for information: 今天开会就决定这件事儿,你～吧。The matter will be decided at today's meeting and we'll let you know the result. ② believe what one hears; believe: 不要～这种谣言。Don't believe such rumours.

【听诊】 tīngzhěn 〈医〉 auscultation ◇ ～器 stethoscope

【听政】 tīngzhèng (of a monarch or regent) hold court; administer affairs of state

【听之任之】 tīngzhī-rènzhī let sth. (undesirable, evil, etc.) go unchecked; take a laissez-faire attitude; let matters drift: 对于损害群众利益的事情,我们不能～。We cannot shut our eyes to things that harm the interests of the masses.

【听众】 tīngzhòng audience; listeners

【听装】 tīngzhuāng tinned; canned: ～奶粉 tinned milk powder

**烃** tīng 〈化〉 hydrocarbon: 开链～ open chain hydrocarbon/ 闭链～ closed chain hydrocarbon

【烃气】 tīngqì 〈化〉 hydrocarbon gas

**桯** tīng ① the shaft of an awl ② a small bedside table used in ancient China

【桯子】 tīngzi ① the shaft of an awl ② the floral axis of a vegetable

## tíng

**廷** tíng the court of a feudal ruler; the seat of a monarchical government: 清～ the Qing government

**亭** tíng ① pavilion; kiosk: 八角～ octagonal pavilion/ 茶～ tea stall/ 书～ bookstall/ 报～ newsstand/ 邮～ postal kiosk/ 凉～ wayside pavilion; kiosk ②〈书〉 well-balanced; in the middle; even: ～午 midday; noon

【亭亭】 tíngtíng 〈书〉 erect; upright: ～玉立 (of a woman) slim and graceful; (of a tree, etc.) tall and erect

【亭匀】 tíngyún 〈书〉 ① (of the human figure) well-proportioned; well-balanced ② (of the rhythm of a melody) regular; balanced

【亭子】 tíngzi pavilion; kiosk

【亭子间】 tíngzijiān 〈方〉 a small, dark back room over a kitchen; garret

**庭** tíng ① front courtyard; front yard ② law court: 民(刑)～ a civil (criminal) court

【庭园】 tíngyuán flower garden; grounds

【庭院】 tíngyuàn courtyard

【庭长】 tíngzhǎng 〈旧〉 the president of a law court; presiding judge

**莛** tíng the stem of a herb, etc.: 麦～儿 stalks of wheat

**停** tíng ① stop; cease; halt; pause: 雨～了。The rain has stopped./ 她～了一会儿,又接着讲下去。She paused a moment before going on with the story./ 咱们～下来休息休息,好吗? Let's stop and have a rest, shall we?/ 他不～地写着。He kept on writing. ② stop over; stay: 我在石家庄～了三天。I stopped over at Shijiazhuang for three days. ③ (of cars) be parked; (of ships) lie at anchor: 汽车～在哪儿? Where can we park the car?/ 船～在江心。The ship anchored in the middle of the river. ④〈口〉 part (of a total); portion: 十～儿有九～儿是好的。Nine out of ten are good.

【停摆】 tíngbǎi (of a pendulum) come to a standstill; stop: 钟～了。The clock's stopped.

【停办】 tíngbàn close down 又作"停闭"

【停泊】 tíngbó anchor; berth: 这个码头可以～五十多艘轮船。The docks can berth over fifty vessels./ 你们的货船～在五号码头。Your cargo boat is berthed at No.5 wharf./ 港口里～着我国新造的一艘远洋巨轮。One of our new ocean-going ships is lying at anchor in the harbour. ◇ ～处 berth; anchorage; roads; roadstead

【停产】 tíngchǎn stop production

【停车】 tíngchē ① stop; pull up: 下一站～十分钟。At the

next station we'll have a ten-minute stop. ② park: 此处不准～！No Parking! ③ (of a machine) stall; stop working: 机器～了，得加点油。The machine's stalled. It needs oiling./ 三号车间～修理。No. 3 Workshop has stopped working to undergo repairs. ◇ ～场 car park; parking lot; parking area

【停当】 tíngdang ready; settled: 一切准备～。Everything's ready. 或 All set.

【停电】 tíngdiàn power cut; power failure

【停顿】 tíngdùn ① stop; halt; pause; be at a standstill: 陷于～状态 be at a standstill; stagnate/ 继续革命不～ continue the revolution without slackening ② pause (in speaking): 念到这里要～一下。When you've read up to here, you pause.

【停放】 tíngfàng park; place: 人行道上不准～自行车。Don't park bicycles on the pavement.

【停飞】 tíngfēi 〈军〉 grounding of aircraft

【停工】 tínggōng stop work; shut down: ～待料 work being held up for lack of material

【停航】 tíngháng suspend air or shipping service: 班机因气候恶劣～。The regular flight is suspended on account of bad weather.

【停火】 tínghuǒ cease fire: ～协议 cease-fire agreement

【停机坪】 tíngjīpíng aircraft parking area; parking apron

【停刊】 tíngkān stop publication (of a newspaper, magazine, etc.)

【停靠】 tíngkào (of a train) stop; (of a ship) berth: 从上海开来的十四次列车～在二号站台，Train No. 14 from Shanghai stops at Platform No. 2./ 六艘万吨货轮可以同时在这个码头～。Six 10,000-ton freighters can berth at this dock. ◇ ～港 port of call

【停课】 tíngkè suspend classes: 那天学校～了。Classes were suspended that day.

【停灵】 tínglíng keep a coffin in a temporary shelter before burial

【停留】 tíngliú stay for a time; stop; remain: 代表团在延安～了一周。The delegation stayed in Yan'an for a week./ 在武汉～过夜 make an overnight stop at Wuhan/ 他在西安作短暂～。He had a brief stopover in Xi'an./ 人类对自然界的认识在不断发展，永远不会～在一个水平上。Man's understanding of nature is developing all the time; it never remains at the same level.

【停留时间】 tíngliú shíjiān 〈环保〉 retention period

【停食】 tíngshí 〈中医〉 gastric disorder; indigestion

【停水】 tíngshuǐ cut off the water supply; cut off the water: 明天上午八点至下午三点～。There will be no water tomorrow from 8 a.m. to 3 p.m.

【停妥】 tíngtuǒ be well arranged; be in order: 事情已商议～。The matter has been discussed and satisfactorily arranged.

【停息】 tíngxī stop; cease: 暴风雨～了。The storm has subsided.

【停歇】 tíngxiē ① stop doing business; close down ② stop; cease: 从上午八点工作到下午两点一直没有～ work from 8 a.m. until 2 p.m. without stopping (或 letup) ③ stop for a rest; rest: 队伍在小树林里～。The troops rested in a grove.

【停学】 tíngxué ① stop going to school; drop out of school ② suspend sb. from school

【停业】 tíngyè stop doing business; wind up a business; close down: 修理内部，暂时～。Closed temporarily for repairs.

【停匀】 tíngyún 见"亭匀" tíngyún

【停战】 tíngzhàn armistice; truce; cessation of hostilities ◇ ～谈判 armistice talks (或 negotiations)/ ～协定 armistice; truce agreement

【停职】 tíngzhí suspend sb. from his duties: ～反省 be temporarily relieved of one's post for self-examination

【停止】 tíngzhǐ stop; cease; halt; suspend; call off: ～工作 stop working/ ～营业 business suspended/ ～前进！Halt!/ ～敌对行动 cease hostilities/ ～供水 cut off the water supply; cut off the water/ ～广播 stop broadcasting; go off the air; close down/ ～罢工 call off a strike/ ～会籍 suspend sb.'s membership

【停滞】 tíngzhì stagnate; be at a standstill; bog down: 会谈～不前。The negotiations have bogged down (或 have reached a stalemate)./ 在国民党反动统治下，国民经济处于～状态。The national economy stagnated under KMT reactionary rule.

**蜓** tíng 见"蜻蜓" qīngtíng

**婷** tíng graceful

**霆** tíng thunderbolt

## tǐng

**挺** tǐng ① straight; erect; stiff: ～立 stand erect/ 直～～地躺着 lie stiff/ 笔～的衣服 well-pressed clothes ② stick out; straighten up (physically): ～胸 throw out one's chest; square one's shoulders/ ～起腰杆 straighten one's back; straighten up ③ endure; stand; hold out: 你～得住吗？Can you stand it?/ 他受了伤，还硬～着。Though wounded, he was still holding out. ④ very; rather; quite: ～好 very good/ 今天～冷。It's rather (或 pretty, quite) cold today. ⑤ 〈量〉〔用于机关枪〕: 轻重机枪六十余～ over sixty heavy and light machine guns

【挺拔】 tǐngbá ① tall and straight: ～的白杨 tall, straight poplars ② forceful: 笔力～ forceful strokes in handwriting or drawing

【挺杆】 tǐnggǎn 〈机〉 tappet: 阀门～ valve tappet ◇ ～间隙 tappet clearance

【挺进】 tǐngjìn (of troops) boldly drive on; press onward; push forward: ～敌后 boldly drive into the areas behind the enemy lines

【挺举】 tǐngjǔ 〈举重〉 clean and jerk

【挺立】 tǐnglì stand upright; stand firm: 几棵青松～在山坡上。Several pine trees stand erect on the hillside./ ～在反帝反霸斗争的前哨 stand firm in the forefront of the struggle against imperialism and hegemonism

【挺身】 tǐngshēn straighten one's back: ～反抗 stand up and fight; stand up to (an enemy, reactionaries, etc.)

【挺身而出】 tǐng shēn ér chū step forward bravely; come out boldly

【挺秀】 tǐngxiù tall and graceful

**铤** tǐng (run) quickly

【铤而走险】 tǐng ér zǒu xiǎn risk danger in desperation; make a reckless move

**艇** tǐng a light boat: 汽～ steamboat/ 炮～ gunboat/ 登陆～ landing craft

## tōng

**通** tōng ① open; through: 路～了。The road is now open./ 管子是～的。The pipe is not blocked./ 山洞打～了。The tunnel has been driven through./ 电话打～了。The call has been put through./ 这个主意行得～。This idea will work. ② open up or clear out by poking or jabbing: 用铅丝～烟嘴儿 poke a piece of wire through a cigarette holder to clean it/ ～炉子 poke the fire ③ lead to; go to: 四～八达 extend in all directions; be linked by rail and road to various parts of the country/ 这趟列车直～昆明。This train goes straight to Kunming. 或 This is a through train to Kunming. ④ connect; communicate: 两个房间是～着的。The two rooms are connected (或 open into each other)./ 互～情报 exchange information/ 互～有无 each supplies what the other needs; supply each other's needs ⑤ notify; tell: 互～姓名 each telling his name to the other/ ～个电话 give sb. a ring; call (或 phone) sb. up ⑥ understand; know: 他～三种语言。He knows three languages./ 弄～无产阶级专政理论 get a good grasp of the theory of the dictatorship of the proletariat/ 他思想～了。He's got his thinking straightened out. ⑦ authority; expert: 日本～ an expert on Japan/ 中国～ an old China hand; Sinologue ⑧ logical; coherent: 文理不～ ungrammatical and incoherent (writing) ⑨ general; common: ～称 a general term ⑩ all; whole: ～身 the whole body/ ～观全局 take an overall view of the situation ⑪ 〈书〉〈量〉〔用于文书电报〕: 一～电报 a telegram

另见 tòng

【通报】 tōngbào ① circulate a notice: ～表扬（批评）circulate a notice of commendation (criticism) ② circular: 关于情况的～ a circular on the situation ③ bulletin; journal: 《科学～》 *Science Bulletin*/ 《经济～》 *Economic Journal*

【通便剂】 tōngbiànjì 〈医〉 laxative; cathartic

【通病】 tōngbìng common failing

【通才】 tōngcái an all-round (或 versatile) person; a universal genius

【通草】 tōngcǎo 〈中药〉 the stem pith of the rice-paper plant (*Tetrapanax papyriferus*)

【通常】 tōngcháng general; usual; normal: ～情况下 under normal conditions/ 我～六点钟起床。I generally get up at six o'clock./ ～消息可靠人士 usually reliable sources

【通畅】 tōngchàng ① unobstructed; clear: 道路～。The road is clear./ 血液循环～ free circulation of the blood/ 大便～ free movement (of the bowels)/ 保持运输～ keep transportation going ② easy and smooth: 文字～ smooth writing

【通车】 tōngchē ① (of a railway or highway) be open to traffic ② have transport service: 从县城到每个公社都通了汽车。There's a bus service from the county town to every commune. 或 Buses run from the county town to every commune.

【通称】 tōngchēng ① be generally called; be generally known as: 汞～水银。Mercury is generally known as quicksilver. ② a general term

【通达】 tōngdá understand: ～人情 be understanding and considerate/ 见解～ hold sensible views; show good sense

【通道】 tōngdào thoroughfare; passageway; passage

【通敌】 tōngdí collude (或 collaborate) with the enemy; have illicit relations with the enemy

【通电】 tōngdiàn ① set up an electric circuit; electrify; energize: ～的铁丝网 electrified (或 live) wire entanglements ② circular (或 open) telegram: 大会～ the circular telegram of the conference/ ～全国 publish an open telegram to the nation

【通牒】 tōngdié diplomatic note: 最后～ ultimatum

【通都大邑】 tōngdū-dàyì large city; metropolis

【通读】 tōngdú read over (或 through): ～《毛泽东选集》第五卷 read the fifth volume of the *Selected Works of Mao Zedong* from cover to cover

【通分】 tōngfēn 〈数〉 reduction of fractions to a common denominator

【通风】 tōngfēng ① ventilate: 把窗子打开通通风。Open the windows to ventilate the room. 或 Open the windows to let in some fresh air./ ～降温 ventilation and cooling ② be well ventilated: 这屋里不～。This room is badly ventilated (或 is stuffy)./ 炉子不～。The stove doesn't draw well. ③ divulge information: ～报信 divulge secret information; tip sb. off
◇ ～管道 ventilating duct/ ～机 ventilator; fanner/ ～井 ventilation shaft; air shaft/ ～口 vent/ ～装置 ventilation installation

【通告】 tōnggào ① give public notice; announce ② public notice; announcement; circular

【通共】 tōnggòng in all; altogether; all told: 我们～十八个人。There are eighteen of us altogether.

【通过】 tōngguò ① pass through; get past; traverse: 电流～导线。Electricity passes through the wires./ 路太窄，汽车不能～。The road is too narrow for cars to get by./ 注意交通安全，一慢二看三～。Pay attention to traffic safety; slow down, look around and then go ahead./ 代表们～大厅进入会场。The delegates entered the assembly hall by way of the lobby./ 游击队～了敌人的封锁线。The guerrillas managed to run the enemy blockade./ 我们要打开局面就必须～这一关。We must overcome this obstacle to open a new phase in our work. ② adopt; pass; carry: 全国人民代表大会庄严地～了中华人民共和国宪法。The National People's Congress solemnly adopted the Constitution of the People's Republic of China./ 提案已一致～。The motion was carried unanimously./ 以压倒多数～ be passed by an overwhelming majority/ 议案没～。The bill did not get through. ③ by means of; by way of; by; through: ～协商取得一致 reach unanimity (或 a consensus) through consultation ④ ask the consent or approval of: 这个问题要～群众才能做出决定。No decision can be made on this matter until the masses have been consulted.

【通航】 tōngháng be open to navigation or air traffic: 北京与拉萨之间已～了。There is now air service between Beijing and Lhasa. ◇ ～水域 navigable waters

【通好】 tōnghǎo 〈书〉 (of nations) have friendly relations

【通红】 tōnghóng very red; red through and through: 她羞得满脸～。She blushed scarlet with shyness./ 高炉照得满天～。The sky was aglow with the fires of the blast furnaces.

【通话】 tōnghuà ① converse ② communicate by telephone
◇ ～计时器 peg count meter

【通婚】 tōnghūn be (或 become) related by marriage; intermarry

【通货】 tōnghuò 〈经〉 currency; current money ◇ ～膨胀 inflation/ ～收缩 deflation

【通缉】 tōngjī order the arrest of a criminal at large;l ist as wanted: 下～令 issue a wanted circular

【通奸】 tōngjiān commit adultery

【通经】 tōngjīng 〈中医〉 stimulate the menstrual flow (by emmenagogues or acupuncture)

【通栏标题】 tōnglán biāotí banner (或 streamer) headline; banner

【通力】 tōnglì concerted effort: ～合作 make a concerted (或 united) effort; give full cooperation to

【通例】 tōnglì general rule; usual practice: 星期天休息是学校的～。It is a general rule that schools close on Sundays.

【通连】 tōnglián be connected; lead to: 浴室和卧室是～的。The bathroom is off the bedroom.

【通联】 tōnglián communications and liaison ◇ ～工作

correspondence and liaison work
【通亮】 tōngliàng well-illuminated; brightly lit: 照明弹照得满天～。Star shells lit up the sky.
【通量】 tōngliàng 〈物〉 flux: 磁～ magnetic flux
【通令】 tōnglìng circular order; general order: ～各省 issue a general order to all provinces/ ～嘉奖 issue an order of commendation
【通路】 tōnglù thoroughfare; passageway; route: 将兵力集结于敌军必经的～两侧 concentrate forces on both sides of the route the enemy is sure to take
【通论】 tōnglùn ① a well-rounded argument ② a general survey: «地震学～» *General Seismology*
【通脉】 tōngmài 〈中医〉 ① promote blood circulation by invigorating vital energy ② promote lactation
【通明】 tōngmíng well-illuminated; brightly lit: 灯火～ be ablaze with lights; be brightly lit
【通年】 tōngnián throughout the year; all the year round
【通盘】 tōngpán overall; all-round; comprehensive: ～计划 overall planning/ ～估计 an all-round estimate/ ～安排 a comprehensive arrangement/ 把这个问题～研究一下 examine the question in its entirety
【通票】 tōngpiào through ticket
【通气】 tōngqì ① ventilate; aerate: 粘土结构紧，～性差。Clayey soils are tight and poorly aerated. ② be in touch (或 communication) with each other; keep each other informed: 各单位要经常～。The various units must keep in touch with each other./ 这件事你得跟他通个气。You should let him know of this matter. ◇ ～孔 air vent
【通窍】 tōngqiào understand things; be sensible or reasonable: 道理讲得很明白，可他就是不～。The reason was explained to him clearly, but he couldn't see it.
【通情达理】 tōngqíng-dálǐ showing good sense; reasonable: 群众是～的。The masses are reasonable./ ～地解决问题 solve a problem in a reasonable way
【通衢】 tōngqú thoroughfare
【通权达变】 tōngquán-dábiàn act as the occasion requires; adapt oneself to circumstances
【通人】 tōngrén a person of wide knowledge and sound scholarship
【通融】 tōngrong ① stretch rules, get around regulations, etc., to accommodate sb.; make an exception in sb.'s favour: 这事可以～。We can make an exception in this case. ② accommodate sb. with a short-term loan: 我想跟你～二十块钱。I wonder if you can lend me 20 *yuan*.
【通商】 tōngshāng (of nations) have trade relations: 订立～条约 conclude a trade treaty; sign a treaty of commerce ◇ ～口岸 trading port
【通身】 tōngshēn the whole body: ～是汗 sweat all over
【通史】 tōngshǐ comprehensive history; general history
【通式】 tōngshì 〈化〉 general formula
【通书】 tōngshū almanac
【通顺】 tōngshùn clear and coherent; smooth: 文理～ coherent writing/ 这个句子不～。This sentence doesn't read smoothly.
【通俗】 tōngsú popular; common: ～易懂 easy to understand/ 拿一句～的话来讲 to use a common expression/ 用～的语言说明深刻的道理 expound a profound truth in simple language ◇ ～读物 books for popular consumption; popular literature/ ～化 popularization
【通天】 tōngtiān ① exceedingly high or great: ～的本事 exceptional ability; superhuman skill ② direct access to the highest authorities
【通条】 tōngtiáo ① poker ② cleaning rod
【通通】 tōngtōng all; entirely; completely: ～拿去吧。Take away the lot. 或 Take them all./ ～卖完 completely sold out/ ～到了吗？Is everybody here? 或 Are we (you) all here?/ 一切魔鬼～都会被消灭。Monsters of all kinds shall be wiped out.
又作"通统"
【通同】 tōngtóng collude; gang up: ～作弊 act fraudulently in collusion with sb.; gang up to cheat
【通途】 tōngtú 〈书〉 thoroughfare: 天堑变～ a deep chasm turned into a thoroughfare
【通脱木】 tōngtuōmù 〈植〉 rice-paper plant (*Tetrapanax papyriferus*)
【通宵】 tōngxiāo all night; the whole night; throughout the night: ～达旦 all night long/ 干了个～ work all night/ ～值班 on duty all night ◇ ～服务部 a shop that is open all night; an all-night shop
【通晓】 tōngxiǎo thoroughly understand; be well versed in; be proficient in: ～几种文字 have a good command of several languages/ ～中国历史 have a good knowledge of Chinese history; be well versed in Chinese history
【通心粉】 tōngxīnfěn macaroni
【通信】 tōngxìn communicate by letter; correspond: 他经常跟我们～。He often writes to us./ 我们好久没有～了。We haven't corresponded for a long time.
◇ ～保密 〈军〉 communication (或 traffic) security/ ～兵 signal corps (或 unit, troops); signalman/ ～处 mailing address/ ～鸽 homing pigeon; carrier pigeon/ ～连 signal company/ ～联络 〈军〉 signal communication; communications and liaison/ ～犬 messenger dog/ ～枢纽 signal (或 communication) centre/ ～员 messenger; orderly
【通行】 tōngxíng ① pass (或 go) through: 自由～ can pass freely; have free passage/ 道路泥泞，卡车无法～。The road was too muddy for trucks./ 没有特别通行证，一律不准～。Nobody is allowed through without a special pass./ 停止～ closed to traffic ② current; general: 这是全国～的办法。This is the current practice throughout the country./ 这项规定在一些地区仍然～。This regulation is still in force in some districts.
◇ ～能力 〈交〉 traffic capacity/ ～权 right of way/ ～税 transit duty
【通行证】 tōngxíngzhèng pass; permit; safe-conduct; laissez-passer: 边境～ border pass/ 军事～ military pass/ 临时～ provisional pass
【通讯】 tōngxùn ① communication: 无线电～ radio(或 wireless) communication/ 红外线～ infrared ray communication/ 微波～ microwave communication/ 激光～ laser communication ② news report; news dispatch; correspondence; newsletter: 新华社～ Xinhua dispatches/ ～报导 news report; news dispatch; news story/ ～文学 reportage
◇ ～方法 means of communication/ ～设备 communication apparatus (或 equipment)/ ～卫星 communications satellite/ ～线路 communication line
【通讯录】 tōngxùnlù address book
【通讯社】 tōngxùnshè news agency; news (或 press) service: 新华～ Xinhua News Agency
【通讯员】 tōngxùnyuán reporter; (press) correspondent
【通夜】 tōngyè all night; the whole night; throughout the night: ～不眠 lie awake all night
【通用】 tōngyòng ① in common use; current; general: 国际会议～的语言 languages used at international conferences/ 全国～教材 national textbooks ② interchangeable: 这两个字可以～。These two words are interchangeable.
◇ ～货币 current money/ ～机械厂 universal machine works/ ～语种 commonly used languages/ ～月票 a monthly ticket for all urban and suburban lines
【通邮】 tōngyóu accessible by postal communication
【通则】 tōngzé general rule

【通知】 tōngzhī ① notify; inform; give notice: 请马上～他。Please notify him immediately. 或 Please let him know at once./ 把我们的决定～他 inform him of our decision/ 将集合地点～大家 notify everyone of the place of assembly/ 预先～ give advance notice ② notice; circular: 发出～ send out (或 dispatch) a notice/ 《中共中央～》 *Circular of the CPC Central Committee*

【通知书】 tōngzhīshū ① notice: 终止条约～ notice of termination of a treaty; notice of denunciation ② 〈商〉 advice note

## tóng

**同** tóng ① same; alike; similar: ～类（岁） the same kind (age)/ 异～ similarities and dissimilarities ② be the same as: "鐽"～"锤"。鐽 is the same as 锤. ③ together; in common: 和工人～吃，～住，～劳动 eat, live and work together with the workers; live with the workers, eat the same food and join them in physical labour/ ～甘苦，共患难 share weal and woe ④ 〈介〉〔引进动作的对象或比较的事物，跟"跟"相同〕: 有事～群众商量。Consult with the masses when problems arise./ 恶霸地主～豺狼一样凶恶。The despotic landlords were as ferocious as wolves. ⑤ 〈方〉〈介〉〔表示替人做事，跟"给"相同〕: 这封信我一直～你保存着。I've kept this letter for you all this time./ 别着急，我～你想个办法。Don't worry. I'll find a way out for you. ⑥ 〈连〉〔表示联合关系，跟"和"相同〕: 我～你一起去。I'll go with you.
另见 tòng

【同班】 tóngbān ① in the same class: ～同学 classmate ② classmate

【同伴】 tóngbàn companion

【同胞】 tóngbāo ① born of the same parents: ～兄弟（姐妹） full brothers (sisters) ② fellow countryman; compatriot: 台湾～ our compatriots in Taiwan

【同辈】 tóngbèi of the same generation

【同病相怜】 tóng bìng xiāng lián those who have the same illness sympathize with each other; fellow sufferers commiserate with each other

【同步】 tóngbù 〈物〉 synchronism: 载波～ carrier synchronization
◇ ～电动机 〈电〉 synchronous motor/ ～回旋加速器 〈物〉 synchrocyclotron/ ～加速器 〈物〉 synchrotron/ ～卫星 synchronous satellite

【同仇敌忾】 tóngchóu-díkài share a bitter hatred of the enemy

【同窗】 tóngchuāng ① study in the same school ② schoolmate

【同床异梦】 tóngchuáng-yìmèng share the same bed but dream different dreams — be strange bedfellows

【同等】 tóngděng of the same class, rank, or status; on an equal basis (或 footing): ～重要 of equal importance/ ～对待 put on an equal footing

【同等学力】 tóngděng xuélì (have) the same educational level (as graduates or a certain grade of students)

【同房】 tóngfáng ① of the same branch of a family ② 〈婉〉 (of husband and wife) sleep together; have sexual intercourse

【同分异构体】 tóngfēn-yìgòutǐ 〈化〉 isomer

【同甘共苦】 tónggān-gòngkǔ share weal and woe (或 comforts and hardships, joys and sorrows): ～的战友 comrades-in-arms sharing weal and woe; fellow fighters through thick and thin/ 与人民群众～ share the comforts and hardships of the masses

【同感】 tónggǎn the same feeling (或 impression): 老张认为这部小说的人物写得很成功，我也有～。Lao Zhang feels — and so do I — that the characters of this novel are very well drawn.

【同工同酬】 tónggōng-tóngchóu equal pay for equal work: 男女～。Men and women enjoy equal pay for equal work.

【同工异曲】 tónggōng-yìqǔ 见"异曲同工" yìqǔ-tónggōng

【同功酶】 tónggōngméi 〈生化〉 isoenzyme

【同归于尽】 tóng guīyú jìn perish together; end in common ruin

【同行】 tóngháng ① of the same trade or occupation ② a person of the same trade or occupation
另见 tóngxíng

【同化】 tónghuà ① assimilate (ethnic groups) ② 〈语〉 assimilation ◇ ～政策 the policy of national assimilation (as pursued by reactionary rulers)/ ～作用〈生〉 assimilation

【同伙】 tónghuǒ ① work in partnership; collude (in doing evil) ② partner; confederate

【同居】 tóngjū ① live together: 父母死后，他和叔父～。After his parents died, he lived with his uncle. ② cohabit

【同僚】 tóngliáo 〈旧〉 colleague; fellow official

【同流合污】 tóngliú-héwū wallow in the mire with sb.; associate with an evil person: 跟他们～ go along with them in their evil deeds

【同路】 tónglù go the same way: 咱俩～，一块儿走吧。Come along with me. I'm going that way too. ◇ ～人 fellow traveller

【同盟】 tóngméng alliance; league: 结成～ form (或 enter into) an alliance/ 没有～军的军队是打不胜敌人的。An army without allies cannot defeat the enemy.
◇ ～罢工 joint strike/ ～国 ally; allied nations;（第一次世界大战）the Central Powers;（第二次世界大战）the Allies/ ～军 allied forces; allies/ ～条约 treaty of alliance

【同名】 tóngmíng of the same name (或 title): 根据～小说摄制的电影 a film based on a novel of the same name/ 他与我～。He is my namesake.

【同谋】 tóngmóu ① conspire (with sb.) ② confederate; accomplice ◇ ～犯 accomplice

【同年】 tóngnián ① the same year: ～九月大桥竣工。The bridge was completed in September of the same year. ② 〈方〉 of the same age

【同期】 tóngqī ① the corresponding period: 他们第一季度的钢产量超过了历史～的最高水平。Their steel output in the first quarter of the year was higher than their previous record for the period. ② the same term (in school, etc.): 我和他～毕业。I graduated the same time as he.

【同情】 tóngqíng sympathize with; show sympathy for: 博得～ win sympathy/ 我很～你。I heartily sympathize with you. 或 I have every sympathy for you. ◇ ～罢工 sympathetic strike; strike in sympathy/ ～心 sympathy; fellow feeling

【同人】 tóngrén 〈旧〉 colleagues 又作"同仁"

【同上】 tóngshàng ditto; *idem*

【同声传译】 tóngshēng chuányì simultaneous interpretation: 有七种语言的～设备 be provided with facilities for simultaneous interpretation in seven languages

【同声相应，同气相求】 tóng shēng xiāng yìng, tóng qì xiāng qiú like attracts like

【同时】 tóngshí ① at the same time; simultaneously; meanwhile; in the meantime: ～发生 happen at the same time; coincide; concur/ ～存在 exist simultaneously; exist side by side; coexist/ 我们在加快工程进度的～，必须注意质量。While speeding up the work on the project, we must pay attention to ensuring its quality. ② moreover; besides; furthermore: 任务艰巨，～时间又很紧迫。The task is arduous; besides, there's not much time./ 造林可以保持水土，～也可以制止流沙。Afforestation conserves soil and water; it also checks drift sand.

【同事】 tóngshì ① work in the same place; work together: 我们～已经多年。We've worked together for years. ② colleague; fellow worker: 老～ an old colleague

【同室操戈】 tóng shì cāo gē family members drawing swords on each other — internal strife; internecine feud

【同素异形】 tóngsù yìxíng 〈化〉 allotropy ◇ ～体 allotrope; allotropic substance

【同岁】 tóngsuì of the same age: 我们两人～。We two are the same age.

【同位角】 tóngwèijiǎo 〈数〉 corresponding angles

【同位素】 tóngwèisù 〈化〉 isotope: 放射性～ radioisotope ◇ ～分离 isotope separation/ ～扫描器 radioisotope scanner/ ～探伤仪 isoscope

【同位语】 tóngwèiyǔ 〈语〉 appositive

【同温层】 tóngwēncéng 〈气〉 stratosphere

【同系物】 tóngxìwù 〈化〉 homologue

【同乡】 tóngxiāng a person from the same village, town or province; a fellow villager, townsman or provincial ◇ ～会 〈旧〉 an association of fellow provincials or townsmen

【同心】 tóngxīn ① concentric ② with one heart: ～干 work with one heart; fight as one man ◇ ～度〈机〉 concentricity/ ～圆〈数〉 concentric circles

【同心同德】 tóngxīn-tóngdé be of one heart and one mind; be dedicated heart and soul to the same cause: 广大军民～，坚决打败侵略者。The broad masses of people and armymen fought staunchly with one heart and one mind to defeat the aggressors.

【同心协力】 tóngxīn-xiélì work in full cooperation and with unity of purpose; work together with one heart; make concerted efforts

【同行】 tóngxíng travel together
另见 tóngháng

【同性】 tóngxìng ① of the same sex: ～恋爱 homosexuality ② of the same nature or character: ～的电互相排斥。Two like electric charges repel each other.

【同姓】 tóngxìng of the same surname: 他与我～。He is my namesake.

【同学】 tóngxué ① be in the same school; be a schoolmate of sb.: 我和他同过三年学。I studied in the same school with him for three years. ② fellow student; schoolmate ③ a form of address used in speaking to a student

【同样】 tóngyàng same; equal; similar: 用～的方法 use the same method/ ～情况下 under similar circumstances/ 他说英语和法语～流利。He speaks English and French with equal fluency.

【同业】 tóngyè ① the same trade or business ② a person of the same trade or business ◇ ～公会 trade council; trade association; guild

【同一】 tóngyī same; identical: 向～目标前进 advance towards the same goal/ 抱～观点的人 those who hold identical views ◇ ～律〈逻〉 the law of identity/ ～性〈哲〉 identity

【同义词】 tóngyìcí 〈语〉 synonym

【同意】 tóngyì agree; consent; approve: 我的意见你～吗？Do you agree with me?/ 他～这项建议。He consented to the proposal./ 这一改革需要得到上级党委～。This reform is subject to the approval of the next higher Party committee./ 征求对大使提名的～ request for agreement to the nomination of an ambassador/ 表示～前一位发言人的意见 express agreement with the previous speaker

【同音词】 tóngyīncí 〈语〉 homonym; homophone

【同余】 tóngyú 〈数〉 congruence ◇ ～数 congruent numbers

【同源多倍体】 tóngyuán-duōbèitǐ 〈生〉 autopolyploid

【同志】 tóngzhì comrade: 致以～的敬礼 with comradely greetings

【同舟共济】 tóng zhōu gòng jì cross a river in the same boat — people in the same boat help each other

【同轴】 tóngzhóu 〈电〉 coaxial ◇ ～电缆 coaxial cable

【同宗】 tóngzōng of the same clan; have common ancestry: 同姓不～ of the same surname, but not the same clan

**佟** Tóng a surname

**彤** tóng 〈书〉 red

【彤云】 tóngyún 〈书〉 ① red clouds ② dark clouds

**茼** tóng

【茼蒿】 tónghāo 〈植〉 crowndaisy chrysanthemum

**桐** tóng a general term for paulownia, phoenix tree and tung tree

【桐油】 tóngyóu tung oil ◇ ～树 tung tree

**铜** tóng copper (Cu): ～丝 copper wire/ ～像 bronze statue/ ～扣子 brass button

【铜氨液】 tóng'ānyè cuprammonia

【铜铵人造丝】 tóng'ǎn rénzàosī 〈纺〉 cuprammonium (或 copper) rayon

【铜板】 tóngbǎn 〈方〉 copper coin; copper

【铜版】 tóngbǎn 〈印〉 copperplate
◇ ～画〈美术〉 copperplate etching (或 engraving); copperplate/ ～印刷 copperplate printing/ ～印刷机 copperplate press; etching press/ ～纸 art (printing) paper

【铜臭】 tóngchòu the stink of money — profits-before-everything mentality: 满身～ stinking (或 filthy) with money; filthy rich

【铜鼓】 tónggǔ 〈考古〉 bronze drum

【铜管乐队】 tóngguǎn yuèduì brass band

【铜管乐器】 tóngguǎn yuèqì brass-wind instrument; brass wind

【铜壶滴漏】 tónghú dīlòu 〈考古〉 copper clepsydra

【铜活】 tónghuó ① brass or copper fittings, accessories, etc. ② work in copper; coppersmithing

【铜匠】 tóngjiang coppersmith

【铜镜】 tóngjìng 〈考古〉 bronze mirror

【铜蓝】 tónglán 〈矿〉 covellite; indigo copper

【铜绿】 tónglǜ 〈化〉 verdigris

【铜模】 tóngmú 〈印〉 matrix; (copper) mould ◇ ～雕刻机 matrix cutting machine

【铜器】 tóngqì bronze, brass or copper ware ◇ ～时代 the Bronze Age

【铜钱】 tóngqián copper cash

【铜墙铁壁】 tóngqiáng-tiěbì bastion of iron — impregnable fortress

【铜像】 tóngxiàng bronze statue

【铜元】 tóngyuán copper coin; copper

【铜子儿】 tóngzǐr 〈口〉 copper coin; copper

**童** tóng ① child: 顽～ naughty boy/ 牧～ cowherd; shepherd boy ② virgin: ～男 virgin boy/ ～女 maiden; virgin ③ bare; bald: ～山 bare hills ④ (Tóng) a surname

【童便】 tóngbiàn 〈中药〉 urine of boys under 12

【童工】 tónggōng ① child labourer ② child labour

【童话】 tónghuà children's stories; fairy tales

【童蒙】 tóngméng 〈书〉 childish ignorance
【童年】 tóngnián childhood
【童仆】 tóngpú 〈书〉 houseboys; menservants; servants
【童山】 tóngshān bare hills: ～秃岭 bare hills and mountains
【童声】 tóngshēng child's voice ◇ ～合唱 children's chorus
【童心】 tóngxīn (of an old man) childlike innocence; (of a young man) childishness; playfulness: ～未泯 still preserve traces of childishness or childlike innocence
【童养媳】 tóngyǎngxí a girl taken into the family as a daughter-in-law-to-be; child daughter-in-law; child bride: 解放前,～受的压迫比一般劳动妇女更深。Before liberation, child daughters-in-law had an even harder lot than most toiling women.
【童谣】 tóngyáo children's folk rhymes
【童贞】 tóngzhēn virginity; chastity
【童子】 tóngzǐ boy; lad
【童子鸡】 tóngzǐjī 〈方〉 young chicken; broiler
【童子军】 tóngzǐjūn boy scouts

**酮** tóng 〈化〉 ketone
【酮化】 tónghuà 〈化〉 ketonize

**瞳** tóng pupil (of the eye)
【瞳孔】 tóngkǒng 〈生理〉 pupil: 放大～ have one's pupils dilated ◇ ～开大 〈医〉 mydriasis/ ～缩小 〈医〉 myosis
【瞳人】 tóngrén pupil (of the eye) 又作"瞳仁"

## tǒng

**统** tǒng ① interconnected system: 传～ tradition/ 系～ system/ 血～ blood relationship ② gather into one; unite: 由老李～管 be under Lao Li's overall leadership ③ all; together: 这些东西～归你用。You have all these things at your disposal. ④ any tube-shaped part of an article of clothing, etc.: 皮～子 fur lining sewn up for a coat/ 长～皮靴 high boots
【统舱】 tǒngcāng steerage (passenger accommodation): ～旅客 steerage passenger/ 坐～ travel steerage
【统称】 tǒngchēng ① be called by a joint name: 武昌、汉口和汉阳常～为武汉。The cities of Wuchang, Hankou and Hanyang are often referred to as Wuhan. ② a general designation
【统筹】 tǒngchóu plan as a whole: ～全局 take the whole situation into account and plan accordingly/ ～规划 overall planning
【统筹兼顾】 tǒngchóu-jiāngù unified planning with due consideration for all concerned; making overall plans and taking all factors into consideration: ～、全面安排的方针 the policy of overall consideration and all-round arrangement/ 根据～的原则安排劳动就业 provide employment in accordance with the principle of overall consideration
【统共】 tǒnggòng altogether; in all: 我们小组～七个人。There are altogether seven people in our group.
【统购统销】 tǒnggòu tǒngxiāo state monopoly for purchase and marketing (of grain, cotton, etc.)
【统计】 tǒngjì ① statistics: 人口～ census; vital statistics/ 据不完全～ according to incomplete statistics (或 figures)/ 这些～数字很说明问题。These statistics throw a lot of light on the matter. 或 These statistics are very eloquent. ② add up; count: ～出席人数 count up the number of people present (at a meeting, etc.)/ 将图书分类整理并加以～ have the books classified, arranged in order and counted ◇ ～地图 statistical map/ ～力学 statistical mechanics/ ～数字 statistical figures; statistics/ ～推断 〈数〉 statistical inference/ ～图表 statistical graph (或 chart, table)/ ～学 statistics/ ～学家 statistician/ ～员 statistician/ ～资料 statistical data
【统铺】 tǒngpù a wide bed for a number of people (as in barracks, hostels, etc.)
【统属】 tǒngshǔ subordination: 彼此不相～。Neither is subordinate to the other.
【统帅】 tǒngshuài ① commander in chief; commander: 最高～ supreme commander/ 政治是～,是灵魂。Politics is the commander, the soul in everything. ② command: 政治～业务 put politics in command of professional work ◇ ～部 supreme command
【统率】 tǒngshuài command: 中国共产党中央委员会主席～全国武装力量。The Chairman of the Central Committee of the Communist Party of China commands the country's armed forces.
【统统】 tǒngtǒng 〈副〉 all; completely; entirely: 把杂草～除掉 get rid of all the weeds/ ～讲出来 make a clean breast of it
【统辖】 tǒngxiá have under one's command; exercise control over; govern
【统一】 tǒngyī ① unify; unite; integrate: ～思想 seek unity of thinking; reach a common understanding/ ～行动 seek unity of action; coordinate actions; act in unison/ 把理论同实践～起来 integrate theory with practice/ ～度量衡 standardize the system of weights and measures/ 完成解放台湾、～祖国的神圣事业 accomplish the sacred task of liberating Taiwan and unifying the country/ 革命的政治内容和尽可能完美的艺术形式的～ the unity of revolutionary political content and the highest possible perfection of artistic form/ 大家的意见逐渐～了。People gradually reached unanimity of opinion. 或 A consensus gradually emerged./ 秦始皇于公元前二二一年～中国。The First Emperor of Qin unified China in 221 B.C. ② unified; unitary; centralized: ～领导 unified leadership/ ～计划 unified planning/ ～分配 unified (或 centralized) distribution; centralized placement (of college graduates, etc.)/ ～的意见 consensus of opinion/ ～的多民族的国家 a unitary multi-national state ◇ ～体 〈哲〉 entity; unity/ ～性 〈哲〉 unity
【统一战线】 tǒngyī zhànxiàn united front: 国际反霸～ the international anti-hegemonist united front/ 进一步巩固和发展我国的革命～ further consolidate and develop the revolutionary united front in our country
【统治】 tǒngzhì rule; dominate: 推翻傀儡政权的反动～ overthrow the reactionary puppet rule/ 占～地位 occupy a dominant position/ 国家是阶级～的机关。The state is an organ of class domination. ◇ ～阶级 ruling class/ ～者 ruler
【统制】 tǒngzhì control: 严格～军用物资 exercise strict control over military supplies/ 经济～ economic control

**捅** tǒng ① poke; stab: 在硬纸盒上～个洞 poke a hole in the cardboard box/ 把炉子～～ give the fire a poke/ 用刺刀～ stab with a bayonet/ ～马蜂窝 stir up a hornets' nest; bring a hornets' nest about one's ears/ 他用胳膊肘～了我一下。He gave me a nudge. ② disclose; give away; let out: 谁把秘密给～出去了? Who gave away (或 let out) the secret?/ 他是个直性子,把看到的事儿都～出来了。He's a straightforward man, and told everything he'd seen.
【捅娄子】 tǒng lóuzi make a mess of sth.; make a blunder; get into trouble

**桶** tǒng ① tub; pail; bucket; keg; barrel: 水～ water

bucket/ 汽油～ petrol drum/ 一～牛奶 a pail of milk/ ～装啤酒 barrelled beer; draught beer ②〈石油〉barrel

**筒** tǒng ①a section of thick bamboo: 竹～ a thick bamboo tube ②a thick tube-shaped object: 笔～ brush pot/ 烟～ smokestack; chimney/ 邮～ pillar-box; mailbox ③ the tube-shaped part of an article of clothing: 袜～儿 the leg of a stocking/ 袖～儿 sleeve

【筒管】 tǒngguǎn 〈纺〉bobbin

【筒状花】 tǒngzhuànghuā 〈植〉tubular flower

【筒子】 tǒngzi tube or tube-shaped object: 竹～ bamboo tube/ 枪～ barrel of a gun

## tòng

**同** tòng 见"胡同儿" hútòngr
另见 tóng

**恸** tòng 〈书〉deep sorrow; grief: ～哭 wail; cry one's heart out

**通** tòng 〈量〉〔用于动作〕: 说了他一～ give him a talking-to/ 擂鼓三～ three rolls of the drums
另见 tōng

**痛** tòng ① ache; pain: 头～ (have a) headache/ 肚子～ (have a) stomachache/ 嗓子～ have a sore throat/ ～不～? Does it hurt? ②sadness; sorrow: 悲～ deep sorrow; grief ③ extremely; deeply; bitterly: ～饮 drink one's fill; drink to one's heart's content/ ～哭 cry bitterly/ ～骂 severely scold; roundly curse

【痛痹】 tòngbì 〈中医〉arthritis (aggravated by cold)

【痛斥】 tòngchì bitterly attack; scathingly denounce: ～谬论 sharply denounce a fallacy

【痛楚】 tòngchǔ pain; anguish; suffering

【痛处】 tòngchù sore spot; tender spot: 触及～ touch sb.'s sore spot; touch sb. on the raw

【痛定思痛】 tòng dìng sī tòng recall a painful experience; draw a lesson from a bitter experience

【痛风】 tòngfēng 〈医〉gout

【痛改前非】 tòng gǎi qiánfēi sincerely mend one's ways; thoroughly rectify one's errors

【痛感】 tònggǎn keenly feel: ～自己知识不足 keenly feel one's lack of knowledge

【痛恨】 tònghèn hate bitterly; utterly detest

【痛经】 tòngjīng 〈医〉dysmenorrhoea

【痛觉】 tòngjué 〈生理〉sense of pain

【痛哭】 tòngkū cry (或 weep) bitterly; wail: ～一场 have a good cry/ ～流涕 weep bitterly; cry one's heart out/ ～失声 be choked with tears

【痛苦】 tòngkǔ pain; suffering; agony: 关心病人的～ be concerned about the sufferings of the patient/ 精神上的～ mental agony/ 改造世界观，要经过长期的甚至是～的磨炼。To remould one's world outlook, one has to undergo a long and even painful process of tempering.

【痛快】 tòngkuai ① very happy; delighted; joyful: 看见麦子堆成了山，心里真～ be delighted at the sight of a mountain of wheat/ 感到从来没有过的～ be filled with joy as never before/ 图一时的～ seek momentary gratification ② to one's heart's content; to one's great satisfaction: 喝个～ drink one's fill/ 玩个～ have a wonderful time/ 这个澡洗得真～。I had a very refreshing bath. ③ simple and direct; forthright; straightforward: 说话很～ speak simply and directly; not mince matters/ 她这人～，心里有什么就说什么。She is frank and says what's on her mind./ 他～地答应了。He readily agreed.

【痛切】 tòngqiè with intense sorrow; most sorrowfully: ～反省 examine oneself with feelings of deep remorse

【痛恶】 tòngwù bitterly detest; abhor: 他的两面派行为令人～。His double-dealing was disgusting.

【痛惜】 tòngxī deeply regret; deplore: 我们都为失去一个好同志而感到～。We all deeply regretted the loss of such a good comrade.

【痛心】 tòngxīn pained; distressed; grieved: 这样浪费粮食令人～。It is distressing to see food being wasted like this./ 他对自己的错误感到很～。He keenly regretted his mistake.

【痛心疾首】 tòngxīn-jíshǒu with bitter hatred: 他～地说:"我上了这个坏家伙的当。""I was duped by that villain!" he said bitterly.

【痛痒】 tòngyǎng ① sufferings; difficulties: ～相关 share a common lot/ 关心群众的～ be concerned with the well-being of the masses ② importance; consequence: 无关～ a matter of no consequence

【痛阈】 tòngyù 〈医〉threshold of pain

## tōu

**偷** tōu ① steal; pilfer; make off with: 有人把我的雨衣～走了。Someone has made off with my raincoat. ② stealthily; secretly; on the sly: ～看 steal a glance; peek; peep/ ～听 eavesdropping; bugging; tapping/ ～越封锁线 run a blockade; slip through a cordon ③ find (time): ～空 take time off (from work)

【偷安】 tōu'ān seek temporary ease: 苟且～ seek only temporary ease and comfort

【偷盗】 tōudào steal; pilfer

【偷工减料】 tōugōng-jiǎnliào do shoddy work and use inferior material; scamp work and stint material; jerry-build

【偷鸡不着蚀把米】 tōu jī buzháo shí bǎ mǐ try to steal a chicken only to end up losing the rice; go for wool and come back shorn

【偷空】 tōukòng take time off (from work to do sth. else); snatch a moment

【偷懒】 tōulǎn loaf on the job; be lazy

【偷垒】 tōulěi 〈棒、垒球〉steal a base; steal

【偷梁换柱】 tōuliáng-huànzhù steal the beams and pillars and replace them with rotten timber — perpetrate a fraud

【偷漏】 tōulòu tax evasion

【偷窃】 tōuqiè steal; pilfer

【偷情】 tōuqíng carry on a clandestine love affair

【偷生】 tōushēng drag out an ignoble existence

【偷税】 tōushuì evade taxes

【偷天换日】 tōutiān-huànrì steal the sky and put up a sham sun — perpetrate a gigantic fraud

【偷偷】 tōutōu stealthily; secretly; covertly; on the sly (或 quiet): ～地溜走 sneak away/ ～地瞧了一眼 steal a glance at/ ～告诉他 tell him on the quiet

【偷偷摸摸】 tōutōumōmō furtively; surreptitiously; covertly

【偷袭】 tōuxí sneak attack; sneak raid; surprise attack

【偷闲】 tōuxián ① snatch a moment of leisure: 忙里～ snatch a little leisure from a busy life; allow oneself a bit of time ②〈方〉loaf on the job; be idle

【偷眼】 tōuyǎn steal a glance; take a furtive glance: 他～看了一下母亲的神色。He stole a glance at his mother's face.

【偷营】 tōuyíng make a surprise attack on an enemy camp; raid an enemy camp

【偷嘴】 tōuzuǐ take food on the sly

## tóu

**头** tóu ①head ②hair or hair style: 梳～ comb the hair/ 平～ crew cut/ 分～ parted hair ③top; end: 山～ the top of a hill; hilltop/ 桥西～ the west end of a bridge/ 中间粗，两～儿细 be thick in the middle and thin at both ends; taper off at both ends ④beginning or end: 从～儿讲起 tell the story from the very beginning/ 提个～儿 give sb. a lead/ 到～来 in the end; finally ⑤remnant; end: 蜡～儿 candle end/ 铅笔～儿 pencil stub (或 stump)/ 烟～ cigarette end (或 stub, stump) ⑥chief; head: 她是我们组的～儿。She is the head of our group. ⑦side; aspect: 他们是一～儿的。They are on the same side./ 事情不能只顾一～。We mustn't pay attention to only one aspect of the matter./ 两～落空 fall between two stools/ 既然决定了，就分～去办。Now that a decision has been taken, let each one do his job ⑧first: ～等 first-class/ ～胎 firstborn ⑨leading: ～马 lead horse ⑩〔用在数量词前面〕first: ～一遍 the first time/ ～半场比赛 the first half of a game/ ～三天 the first three days ⑪〈方〉〔用在"年"或"天"前面〕previous; last: ～年 last year; the previous year/ ～天 the day before; the previous day ⑫〈方〉before; prior to: ～五点就得动身 have to start before (或 by) five ⑬〈量〉ⓐ〔用于牛、驴、骡、羊等家畜〕: 三十～牛 thirty head of cattle/ 两～骡子 two mules ⓑ〔用于蒜〕: 一～蒜 a bulb of garlic

**头** tou ①〔名词后缀，接于名词、动词或形容词词根〕: 木～ wood/ 看～ sth. worth seeing/ 甜～儿 a foretaste of sweetness; benefit ②〔方位词后缀〕: 上～ above/ 下～ below

【头版】 tóubǎn front page (of a newspaper)

【头寸】 tóucùn 〈商〉①money market; money supply: ～紧(松)。Money is tight (easy). ②cash

【头灯】 tóudēng 〈矿〉head lamp

【头等】 tóuděng first-class; first-rate: ～大事 a matter of prime importance; a major event/ ～重要任务 a task of primary importance ◇ ～舱 first-class cabin/ ～品 first-rate (或 top quality) goods

【头顶】 tóudǐng the top (或 crown) of the head

【头发】 tóufa hair (on the human head) ◇ ～夹子 hairpin

【头伏】 tóufú 见"初伏" chūfú

【头骨】 tóugǔ 〈生理〉skull; cranium

【头号】 tóuhào ①number one; size one: ～字 size one type/ ～敌人 number one enemy; archenemy ②first-rate; top quality: ～大米 top-grade rice

【头花】 tóuhuā 〈工美〉headdress flower

【头昏】 tóuhūn dizzy; giddy: 我～。I feel dizzy. 或 My head is swimming.

【头角】 tóujiǎo brilliance (of a young person); talent: 初露～ begin to show ability or talent/ ～峥嵘 brilliant; very promising; outstanding

【头巾】 tóujīn scarf; kerchief

【头颈】 tóujǐng 〈方〉neck

【头里】 tóuli ①in front; ahead: 老张在～。Lao Zhang is in front./ 请～走，我马上就来。Please go ahead. I won't be a minute./ 她事事都走在～。She takes the lead in everything. ②in advance; beforehand: 咱们把话说在～。Let's make this clear in advance.

【头颅】 tóulú head: 抛～，洒热血 lay down one's life (for a just cause)

【头鲈鱼】 tóulúyú silver-spotted grunt

【头马】 tóumǎ lead horse

【头面人物】 tóumiàn rénwù prominent figure; bigwig; big shot

【头面】 tóumian woman's head-ornaments

【头目】 tóumù head of a gang; ringleader; chieftain: 小～ head of a small group in a gang

【头脑】 tóunǎo ①brains; mind: 她很有～。She has plenty of brains./ 不用～ not use one's head/ ～简单 simple-minded/ ～清醒 clearheaded; sober-minded/ 有政治～ be politically-minded/ 有冷静的～ have a cool head/ 把～里的资产阶级思想清除出去 rid one's mind of bourgeois ideas/ 胜利冲昏～ get dizzy with success; be carried away by success ②main threads; clue: 摸不着～ cannot make head or tail of sth.

【…头…脑】 …tóu…nǎo ①〔指脑筋〕: 昏头昏脑 muddleheaded; absentminded ②〔指首尾〕: 没头没脑 without rhyme or reason; abrupt ③〔指零头〕: 针头线脑儿 odds and ends needed for sewing

【头皮】 tóupí ①scalp: 搔～ scratch one's head/ 硬着～顶住 toughen one's scalp and butt back; resist firmly ②dandruff; scurf

【头人】 tóurén tribal chief; headman

【头生】 tóushēng firstborn

【头绳】 tóushéng ①string for binding a plait, bun, etc. ②〈方〉knitting wool

【头虱】 tóushī head louse

【头套】 tóutào actor's headgear

【头疼】 tóuténg (have a) headache

【头疼脑热】 tóuténg-nǎorè headache and slight fever; slight illness

【头痛】 tóutòng (have a) headache: ～得厉害 have a bad headache/ 这件事真让我～。This business is a headache for me.

【头痛医头，脚痛医脚】 tóutòng yī tóu, jiǎotòng yī jiǎo treat the head when the head aches, treat the foot when the foot hurts — treat symptoms but not the disease

【头头儿】 tóutóur 〈口〉head; chief; leader

【头头是道】 tóutóu shì dào clear and logical; closely reasoned and well argued: 战争的学问，有些人可以在书本上讲得～，但打起仗来却不一定能取胜。Some people may appear impressive when discoursing on military science in books, but when it comes to actual fighting, they may not win a battle.

【头陀】 tóutuó mendicant Buddhist monk

【头衔】 tóuxián title

【头像】 tóuxiàng head (portrait or sculpture)

【头胸部】 tóuxiōngbù 〈动〉cephalothorax

【头绪】 tóuxù main threads (of a complicated affair): ～太多 have too many things to attend to/ 茫无～ be in a hopeless tangle/ 理出个～来 get things into shape/ 事情渐渐有了～。Things are settling into shape.

【头癣】 tóuxuǎn 〈医〉favus of the scalp

【头羊】 tóuyáng bellwether

【头油】 tóuyóu hair oil; pomade

【头晕】 tóuyūn dizzy; giddy

【头针疗法】 tóuzhēn liáofǎ 〈中医〉head-acupuncture therapy

【头重脚轻】 tóuzhòng-jiǎoqīng top-heavy

【头状花序】 tóuzhuàng huāxù 〈植〉capitulum; head

【头子】 tóuzi chieftain; chief; boss: 机会主义路线的～ the arch-villain pushing an opportunist line/ 土匪～ bandit chief

【头足动物】 tóuzú dòngwù cephalopod

**投** tóu ①throw; fling; hurl: ～手榴弹 throw a hand grenade ②put in; drop: 把信～进邮筒 drop a letter into the pillar-box ③throw oneself into (a river, well, etc. to commit suicide): ～井(河) drown oneself in a well (river)

④ project; cast: 树影～在窗户上。The tree cast its shadow on the window./ 把眼光～到来访者身上 cast one's eyes on the visitor ⑤ send; deliver: ～书 deliver a letter ⑥ go to; join: ～军 join the army/ ～店 put up at an inn ⑦ fit in with; agree with; cater to: ～其所好 cater to sb.'s likes (或 tastes)/ 意气相～ find each other congenial

【投案】 tóu'àn give oneself up (或 surrender oneself) to the police

【投奔】 tóubèn go to (a friend or a place) for shelter: ～亲戚 seek refuge with relatives; go to one's relatives for help/ ～解放区参加革命 go to the liberated areas to join in the revolution

【投笔从戎】 tóu bǐ cóng róng throw aside the writing brush and join the army — renounce the pen for the sword

【投标】 tóubiāo submit a tender; enter a bid

【投产】 tóuchǎn go into operation; put into production: 这个农具厂是去年～的。This farm implement factory went into operation last year.

【投诚】 tóuchéng (of enemy troops, rebels, bandits, etc.) surrender; cross over: 向人民～ cross over to the side of the people

【投弹】 tóudàn ① drop a bomb ② throw a hand grenade ◇ ～高度 release altitude/ ～角 dropping angle/ ～器 bomb rack control; bomb release mechanism/ ～手 bombardier; grenadier

【投敌】 tóudí go over to the enemy; defect to the enemy

【投递】 tóudì deliver: ～信件 deliver letters/ 无法～,退回原处。Undeliverable, returned to sender./ 无法～的信 dead letter ◇ ～员 postman; letter (或 mail) carrier; mailman

【投放】 tóufàng ① throw in; put in: ～鱼饵 throw in the bait ② put (money) into circulation; put (goods) on the market

【投稿】 tóugǎo submit a piece of writing for publication; contribute (to a newspaper or magazine): 欢迎～。Contributions are welcome.

【投合】 tóuhé ① agree; get along: 他们俩脾气很～。The two of them are quite congenial. ② cater to: ～顾客的口味 cater to the tastes of the customers

【投机】 tóujī ① congenial; agreeable: 谈得很～ talk very congenially; have a most agreeable chat ② speculate: ～倒把 engage in speculation and profiteering ③ seize a chance to seek private gain; be opportunistic: ～取巧 seize every chance to gain advantage by trickery; be opportunistic

◇ ～倒把分子 profiteer; speculator/ ～分子 opportunist; political speculator/ ～商 speculator; profiteer

【投井下石】 tóu jǐng xià shí 见"落井下石" luò jǐng xià shí

【投考】 tóukǎo sign up for an examination: ～大学 sign up for a college entrance examination

【投靠】 tóukào go and seek refuge with sb.: ～亲友 go and seek refuge with one's relatives and friends/ ～反动派 throw in one's lot with the reactionaries/ 卖身～ barter away one's honour for sb.'s patronage

【投篮】 tóulán 〈篮球〉 shoot (a basket): 远(近)距离～ long (close-in) shot/ 跳起～ jump up and shoot/ ～不准 inaccurate shooting

【投票】 tóupiào vote; cast a vote: ～赞成 vote for; vote in favour of/ ～反对 vote against/ ～表决 decide by ballot/ 无记名～ secret ballot/ 去投票处～ go to the polls

◇ ～日 polling day/ ～箱 ballot box/ ～站 polling booth (或 station); the polls

【投契】 tóuqì 〈书〉 see eye to eye; get along well; be congenial

【投枪】 tóuqiāng javelin; (throwing) spear

【投亲】 tóuqīn go and live with relatives; seek refuge with relatives

【投入】 tóurù throw into; put into: ～战斗 throw (oneself, troops, etc.) into the battle/ ～生产 put into production; go into operation/ ～全部劳动力 throw in the whole labour force

【投射】 tóushè ① throw (a projectile, etc.); cast ② project (a ray of light); cast: 金色的阳光～到平静的海面上。The sun cast its golden rays on the calm sea./ 周围的人都对他～出惊异的眼光。All those around him looked at him with amazement.

【投身】 tóushēn throw oneself into: ～到火热的斗争中去 plunge into the fiery struggle/ ～革命 join the revolutionary ranks; join in the revolution

【投生】 tóushēng be reincarnated in a new body; be reborn

【投师】 tóushī seek instruction from a master: ～访友 learn from a master and call on friends to exchange knowledge or skills

【投手】 tóushǒu 〈棒、垒球〉 pitcher ◇ ～犯规 balk

【投鼠忌器】 tóu shǔ jì qì hesitate to pelt a rat for fear of smashing the dishes beside it; spare the rat to save the dishes — hold back from taking action against an evildoer for fear of involving good people

【投宿】 tóusù seek temporary lodging; put up for the night: ～客栈 put up at an inn for the night

【投胎】 tóutāi reincarnation

【投桃报李】 tóu táo bào lǐ give a plum in return for a peach — return present for present; exchange gifts

【投纬】 tóuwěi 〈纺〉 picking: 每分钟～数 picks per minute

【投降】 tóuxiáng surrender; capitulate ◇ ～派 capitulators; capitulationist clique/ ～主义 capitulationism

【投效】 tóuxiào 〈书〉 go and offer one's services

【投影】 tóuyǐng projection: 极～ polar projection/ 墨卡托地图～ Mercator (map) projection ◇ ～几何学 〈数〉 projective geometry/ ～图 〈机〉 projection drawing

【投掷】 tóuzhì throw; hurl: ～标枪(铁饼、手榴弹) throw a javelin (discus, hand grenade)

【投资】 tóuzī ① invest: ～工矿企业 invest in industrial and mining enterprises/ ～五万元 make an investment of 50,000 *yuan* ② money invested; investment: 国家～ state investment/ 发挥～效果 realize returns on an investment/ 收回本厂～ recoup the plant's capital outlay

◇ ～场所 outlet for investment/ ～基金 investment funds/ ～市场 investment market

## tòu

**透** tòu ① penetrate; pass through; seep through: 阳光～过窗户照进来。Sunlight came in through the windows./ 这双鞋不～水。These shoes are waterproof./ ～过现象看本质 see through the appearance to get at the essence ② tell secretly: ～消息 tell sb. news on the quiet/ ～个信儿 tip sb. off ③ fully; thoroughly; in a penetrating way: 桃熟～了。The peaches are quite ripe./ 他的衣服湿～了。His clothes are wet through./ 雨下～了。It was a real good soaker./ 把道理说～了 have thoroughly explained one's reasons; have driven the point home/ 对问题了解得很～ have an intimate knowledge of the subject; know the subject inside out/ 有意思～了 extremely interesting/ 他摸～了这台车床的脾气。He got to know this lathe very well. ④ appear; show: 他脸上～出幸福的微笑。A happy smile appeared on his face./ 白里～红 white touched with red

【透彻】 tòuchè penetrating; thorough: 她把问题分析得很～。

She made a penetrating analysis of the problem./ 有～的了解 have a thorough understanding/ 这一番话说得非常～。Those words really drove the point home.

【透翅蛾】 tòuchì'é 〈动〉 clearwing (moth)

【透顶】 tòudǐng 〈贬〉 thoroughly; downright; in the extreme; through and through: 反动～ downright reactionary; out-and-out reactionary/ 腐败～ thoroughly corrupt; rotten to the core; decadent in the extreme

【透风】 tòufēng ① let in air; ventilate: 打开窗户透透风 open the window and let in some air/ 这门关不严,有点～。This door doesn't fit very tightly and the wind blows through. ② divulge a secret; leak: 这个人嘴很紧,一点风也不透。The man was closemouthed and didn't drop a hint.

【透镜】 tòujìng 〈物〉 lens: 凹(凸)～ concave (convex) lens/ 分光～ beam-splitting lens/ 复合～ compound lens

【透亮儿】 tòuliàngr allow light to pass through: 这个暗室有点～。This darkroom lets in light.

【透亮】 tòuliang ① bright; transparent: 这间房子又向阳,又～。This room is sunny and bright. ② perfectly clear: 经你这么一说,我心里就～了。Thanks to your explanation, it's clear to me now.

【透漏】 tòulòu divulge; leak; reveal: 消息～出去了。The news has leaked out.

【透露】 tòulù divulge; leak; disclose; reveal: ～风声 leak (或 disclose) information/ 真相～出来了。The truth has come to light (或 has come out)./ 她跟她娘～过这个意思。She said to her mother something to that effect.

【透明】 tòumíng transparent: 不～ opaque/ 半～ translucent/ ～的纱巾 diaphanous veil
◇ ～度 transparency; diaphaneity/ ～计 diaphanometer/ ～漆 celluloid paint; clear lacquer/ ～体〈物〉transparent body/ ～纸 cellophane paper; cellophane

【透辟】 tòupì penetrating; incisive; thorough: ～的分析 penetrating analysis

【透平】 tòupíng 〈机〉 turbine 又作"透平机"

【透气】 tòuqì ① ventilate: 屋子太闷了,打开窗子透透气。The room is too stuffy. Open the windows and let some air in. ② breathe freely: 透不过气来 feel suffocated

【透热性】 tòurèxìng 〈物〉 diathermancy; diathermaneity

【透闪石】 tòushǎnshí 〈地〉 tremolite

【透射】 tòushè 〈物〉 transmission: 定向～ regular transmission ◇ ～比 transmittance/ ～率 transmissivity

【透视】 tòushì ① perspective ② 〈医〉 fluoroscopy; roentgenoscopy ◇ ～图 perspective drawing

【透水层】 tòushuǐcéng 〈地〉 pervious bed; permeable stratum

【透雨】 tòuyǔ saturating (或 soaking) rain; soaker

【透支】 tòuzhī ① 〈经〉 overdraw; make an overdraft: ～的帐户 overdrawn account ② draw one's salary in advance

## tū

**凸** tū protruding; raised: ～花银瓶〈工美〉a silver vase with a raised floral design/ ～面 convex

【凸岸】 tū'àn 〈地〉 convex bank

【凸版】 tūbǎn 〈印〉 relief printing plate ◇ ～轮转机 rotary letterpress machine/ ～印刷 letterpress; relief (或 typographic) printing

【凸窗】 tūchuāng bay window

【凸轮】 tūlún 〈机〉 cam: 推动～ actuating cam/ 急升～ quick lift cam ◇ ～轴 cam shaft

【凸面镜】 tūmiànjìng 〈物〉 convex mirror

【凸透镜】 tūtòujìng 〈物〉 convex lens

【凸缘】 tūyuán 〈机〉 flange: 环状～ collar flange/ 接头～ joint flange/ 管～ pipe flange

**秃** tū ① bald; bare: 他的头开始～了。He's getting bald./ ～山 bare (或 barren) hills/ ～树 bare trees; defoliated trees ② blunt; without a point: 铅笔～了。The pencil is blunt. ③ incomplete; unsatisfactory: 这篇文章的结尾显得有点～。This article seems to end rather lamely.

【秃笔】 tūbǐ bald writing brush — poor writing ability; low skill at composition: 我这支～不行,得找个笔杆子。I'm no good at writing; you'll have to find someone who is./ 非我这支～所能形容 beyond the power of my poor pen

【秃疮】 tūchuāng 〈口〉 favus of the scalp

【秃顶】 tūdǐng bald

【秃发病】 tūfàbìng alopecia

【秃鹫】 tūjiù cinereous vulture

【秃子】 tūzi baldhead

**突** tū ① dash forward; charge: ～入敌阵 charge into enemy positions/ 狼奔豕～ tear about like wild beasts ② sudden; abrupt: 气温～降。The temperature suddenly dropped. ③ projecting; sticking out ④ 〈书〉 chimney: 灶～ chimney

【突变】 tūbiàn ① sudden change: 认识过程中的～ a sudden change in the process of cognition ② 〈生〉 mutation: 自发～ spontaneous mutation ◇ ～体 〈生〉 mutant

【突出】 tūchū ① protruding; projecting; sticking out: 眼球～ bug-eyed/ ～的岩石 projecting rocks ② outstanding; prominent: ～的成就 outstanding achievements/ 这个例子～地说明了他的态度是错误的。This is a glaring example of his wrong attitude./ 他的优点和缺点都很～。His virtues are as conspicuous as his defects. ③ give prominence to; stress; highlight: 他的发言没有～重点。In his speech he failed to stress the main points./ 她老想～自己。She always tries to push herself forward. 或 She is very pushy. ◇ ～部 〈军〉 salient

【突飞猛进】 tūfēi-měngjìn advance by leaps and bounds; advance with seven-league strides; make giant strides: 我国社会主义建设事业～。Socialist construction is going ahead by leaps and bounds in our country.

【突击】 tūjī ① make a sudden and violent attack; assault ② make a concentrated effort to finish a job quickly; do a crash job: ～麦收 do a rush job of harvesting the wheat ◇ ～点 point of assault/ ～队 shock brigade/ ～任务 rush job; shock work/ ～手 shock worker/ ～战术 shock tactics

【突厥】 Tūjué Tujue (Turk), a nationality in ancient China

【突尼斯】 Tūnísī Tunisia ◇ ～人 Tunisian

【突破】 tūpò ① break through; make (或 effect) a breakthrough: ～防线 break through a defence line/ 医学上的～ a medical breakthrough ② surmount; break; top: ～难关 break the back of a tough job/ ～定额 overfulfil a quota/ 我们生产大队粮食亩产早已～千斤。Our production brigade topped 1,000 *jin* in its per *mu* grain yield long ago. ◇ ～地区〈军〉 area of penetration (或 breakthrough)/ ～点〈军〉 breakthrough point; point of penetration/ ～口〈军〉 breach; gap

【突起】 tūqǐ ① break out; suddenly appear: 战事～。Hostilities broke out. ② rise high; tower: 奇峰～。Peaks tower magnificently.

【突然】 tūrán suddenly; abruptly; unexpectedly: ～停止 suddenly stop; stop (或 pull up) short/ ～哭起来 burst into tears/ ～袭击 surprise attack/ 准备对付一切～事变 prepare for all eventualities (或 contingencies)

【突如其来】 tū rú qí lái arise suddenly; come all of a sudden

【突突】 tūtū 〈象〉: 她的心～地跳, Her heart went pit-a-pat./ 汽艇～地驶入港口。The motorboat chugged its way into the harbour.

【突围】 tūwéi break out of an encirclement

【突兀】 tūwù ①lofty; towering: ～的山石 towering crags/ 怪峰～。A grotesque peak thrusts itself towards the sky. ②sudden; abrupt; unexpected: 事情来得这么～, 使他简直不知所措。It all happened so suddenly he didn't know what to do.

【突袭】 tūxí surprise attack

**葖** tū 见"菁葖" gūtū

## tú

**图** tú ①picture; drawing; chart; map: 制～ make a drawing or chart/ 蓝～ blueprint/ 草～ (rough) sketch; draft/ 地形～ topographic map/ 天气～ weather map; synoptic chart/ 插～ illustration; plate ②scheme; plan; attempt: 宏～ great plan/ 另作他～ find another way out; work out a different scheme ③pursue; seek: ～私利 pursue private ends/ ～一时痛快 seek momentary satisfaction/ 不～名, 不～利, ～的是共产主义 strive for neither fame nor gain, but for communism/ ～一时之苟安, 贻百年之大患。One moment's false security can bring a century of calamities. ④intention; intent

【图案】 tú'àn pattern; design: 装饰～ decorative pattern; ornamental design/ 几何～ geometrical pattern ◇ ～操 callisthenic performance forming patterns

【图板】 túbǎn drawing board

【图版】 túbǎn plate (for printing photos, maps, illustrations, etc.)

【图表】 túbiǎo chart; diagram; graph: 统计～ statistical chart (或 table)

【图钉】 túdīng drawing pin; thumbtack

【图画】 túhuà drawing; picture; painting ◇ ～文字 〈语〉 picture writing/ ～纸 drawing paper

【图记】 tújì seal; stamp

【图鉴】 tújiàn illustrated (或 pictorial) handbook: «中草药～» *Pictorial Handbook of Chinese Medicinal Herbs*

【图解】 tújiě ①diagram; graph; figure: 用～说明 explain through diagrams ②〈数〉graphic solution ◇ ～法 graphic method

【图景】 tújǐng view; prospect: 展现出一幅壮丽的～ open up a magnificent prospect

【图例】 túlì legend (of a map, etc.); key

【图谋】 túmóu plot; scheme; conspire: ～不轨 hatch a sinister plot

【图片】 túpiàn picture; photograph: ～展览 photo (或 picture) exhibition/ ～说明 caption

【图谱】 túpǔ a collection of illustrative plates; atlas

【图穷匕首见】 tú qióng bǐshǒu xiàn when the map was unrolled, the dagger was revealed — the real intention is revealed in the end 又作"图穷匕见"

【图书】 túshū books: ～资料 books and reference materials ◇ ～馆 library/ ～馆管理员 librarian/ ～馆学 library science/ ～目录 catalogue of books; library catalogue

【图腾】 túténg totem

【图瓦卢】 Túwǎlú Tuvalu

【图像】 túxiàng picture; image: 立体～〈电子〉stereopicture ◇ ～识别 〈电子〉pattern recognition

【图形】 túxíng graph; figure: 几何～ geometric figure

【图样】 túyàng pattern; design; draft; drawing: 机器～ a draft for a machine

【图章】 túzhāng seal; stamp

【图纸】 túzhǐ blueprint; drawing: 建筑物的～ drawing of a building

**涂** tú ①spread on; apply; smear: ～漆 apply a coat of paint; paint/ ～点软膏 apply some ointment/ 给机器部件～油 smear machine parts with grease/ 木桩子上～了沥青。The wooden stakes are coated with pitch. ②scribble; scrawl: 别在墙上乱～。Don't scribble (或 scrawl) on the wall. ③blot out; cross out: ～掉几个字 cross out a few words ④(Tú) a surname

【涂层】 túcéng coat; coating: 减磨～ friction coat/ 反雷达～ antiradar coating

【涂改】 túgǎi alter: ～无效 invalid if altered

【涂料】 túliào coating; paint: 防腐～ anticorrosive paint/ 耐火～ refractory coating

【涂抹】 túmǒ ①daub; smear; paint ②scribble; scrawl: 信笔～ doodle

【涂片】 túpiàn 〈医〉smear: 血～ blood smear

【涂饰】 túshì ①cover with paint, lacquer, colour wash, etc. ②daub (plaster, etc.) on a wall; whitewash

【涂炭】 tútàn 〈书〉utter misery; great affliction; misery and suffering 参见"生灵涂炭" shēnglíng tútàn

【涂鸦】 túyā 〔多用作谦辞〕poor handwriting; scrawl; chicken tracks

【涂乙】 túyǐ 〈书〉prune (an essay, etc.); delete and change

【涂脂抹粉】 túzhī-mǒfěn apply powder and paint; prettify; whitewash: 为自己～ try to whitewash oneself

**荼** tú 〔见于古书〕①a bitter edible plant ②the white flower of reeds, etc.

【荼毒】 túdú 〈书〉afflict with great suffering; torment: ～生灵 plunge the people into the depths of suffering

【荼蘼】 túmí 〈植〉roseleaf raspberry (*Rubus rosaefolius* var. *Coronarius*)

**途** tú way; road; route: 沿～ along the way (或 road)/ ～中 on the way; *en route*/ 半～而废 give up halfway

【途程】 túchéng road; way; course: 革命的～ the course of the revolution

【途次】 túcì 〈书〉stopover; travellers' lodging

【途经】 tújīng by way of; *via*: ～太原前往大寨 go to Dazhai by way of Taiyuan

【途径】 tújìng way; channel: 寻找消除分歧的～ seek ways to eliminate differences/ 探索和平解决的～ explore avenues to a peaceful settlement/ 外交～ diplomatic channels

**徒** tú ①on foot: ～涉 wade through; ford ②empty; bare: ～手 bare-handed; unarmed ③merely; only: ～具形式 be a mere formality/ 不～无益,反而有害 not only useless, but harmful ④in vain; to no avail: ～费唇舌 waste one's breath/ ～自惊扰 frighten oneself without reason; become needlessly alarmed ⑤apprentice; pupil: 门～ pupil; disciple/ 学～ apprentice ⑥follower; believer: 佛教～ Buddhist ⑦〈贬〉person; fellow: 无耻之～ a shameless person/ 酒～ drunkard/ 赌～ gambler/ 歹～ rascal; evildoer; bandit/ 暴～ ruffian; thug ⑧(prison) sentence; imprisonment

【徒步】 túbù on foot: ～旅行 travel on foot

【徒弟】 túdi apprentice; disciple

【徒工】 túgōng apprentice

【徒劳】 túláo futile effort; fruitless labour: ～往返 make a futile journey; hurry back and forth for nothing

【徒劳无功】 túláo wú gōng make a futile effort; work to no avail

【徒然】 túrán in vain; for nothing; to no avail: ～耗费精力 waste one's energy (或 effort)
【徒手】 túshǒu bare-handed; unarmed ◇ ～操 free-standing exercises
【徒孙】 túsūn disciple's disciple
【徒刑】 túxíng 〈法〉 imprisonment; (prison) sentence: 有期～ specified (prison) sentence/ 无期～ life imprisonment (或 sentence)/ 判三年～ sentence sb. to three years' imprisonment
【徒长】 túzhǎng 〈农〉 excessive growth (of branches and leaves); spindling
【徒子徒孙】 túzǐ-túsūn 〈贬〉 disciples and followers; adherents; hangers-on and their spawn

**屠** tú ① slaughter (animals for food) ② massacre; slaughter: ～城 massacre the inhabitants of a captured city ③ (Tú) a surname
【屠刀】 túdāo butcher's knife
【屠夫】 túfū ① butcher ② a ruthless ruler
【屠户】 túhù butcher
【屠戮】 túlù 〈书〉 slaughter; massacre
【屠杀】 túshā massacre; butcher; slaughter: 军阀～罢工工人。The warlords butchered the strikers.
【屠宰】 túzǎi butcher; slaughter: ～牲畜 slaughter animals; butcher fat stock
◇ ～场 slaughterhouse/ ～率 dressing percentage/ ～税 tax on slaughtering animals

**酴** tú
【酴醾】 túmí ①〔见于古书〕a double-fermented wine ② 见"荼蘼" túmí

## tǔ

**土** tǔ ① soil; earth: ～坷拉 a lump of earth; clod/ 肥～ fertile (或 good) soil/ 瘠～ lean (或 poor) soil/ 用～把种子盖上 cover seeds with earth/ ～台 earthern platform/ ～路 dirt road/ 他鞋上都是～。There's dirt all over his shoes. ② land; ground: 国～ a country's territory; land/ 领～ territory; domain ③ local; native: ～音 local accent/ ～产 local product ④ homemade; indigenous: ～办法 indigenous methods/ ～杂肥 farmyard manure ⑤ unrefined; unenlightened: ～里～气 rustic; uncouth; countrified ⑥ opium: 烟～ opium
【土坝】 tǔbà 〈水〉 earth-filled dam; earth dam
【土包子】 tǔbāozi clodhopper; (country) bumpkin
【土豹】 tǔbào 〈动〉 buzzard
【土崩瓦解】 tǔbēng-wǎjiě disintegrate; crumble; fall apart; collapse like a house of cards
【土鳖】 tǔbiē 〈动〉 ground beetle
【土拨鼠】 tǔbōshǔ 〈动〉 marmot
【土布】 tǔbù handwoven (或 handloomed) cloth; homespun cloth
【土蚕】 tǔcán 〈方〉 ① the larva of a noctuid ② grub
【土产】 tǔchǎn local (或 native) product
【土地】 tǔdì ① land; soil: 肥沃的～ fertile land; good soil ② territory: 我国～辽阔,资源丰富。Our country has a vast territory and abundant resources.
◇ ～报酬递减律 the law of diminishing returns (a bourgeois economic theory)/ ～法 land law; agrarian law/ ～分红 dividend on land shares/ ～集中 concentration of landholdings/ ～税 land tax/ ～证 land certificate; land deed/ ～制度 land system
【土地】 tǔdi local god of the land; village god ◇ ～庙 a tiny temple housing the village god
【土地改革】 tǔdì gǎigé land reform; agrarian reform
【土地革命战争】 Tǔdì Gémìng Zhànzhēng the Agrarian Revolutionary War (1927-1937)
【土豆】 tǔdòu 〈口〉 potato
【土耳其】 Tǔ'ěrqí Turkey ◇ ～人 Turk/ ～语 Turkish (language)
【土法】 tǔfǎ indigenous method; local method ◇ ～上马 get on the job with local methods
【土方】 tǔfāng ① cubic metre of earth ② earthwork: ～工程 earthwork ③ 〈中医〉 folk recipe
【土匪】 tǔfěi bandit; brigand
【土改】 tǔgǎi 〈简〉(土地改革) land reform; agrarian reform
【土豪】 tǔháo local tyrant ◇ ～劣绅 local tyrants and evil gentry
【土话】 tǔhuà local, colloquial expressions; local dialect
【土皇帝】 tǔhuángdì local despot; local tyrant
【土黄】 tǔhuáng colour of loess; yellowish brown
【土货】 tǔhuò local product; native produce
【土家族】 Tǔjiāzú the Tujia (Tuchia) nationality, distributed over Hunan and Hubei
【土炕】 tǔkàng heatable adobe sleeping platform; adobe *kang*
【土牢】 tǔláo dungeon
【土霉素】 tǔméisù 〈药〉 terramycin; oxytetracycline
【土木】 tǔmù building; construction: 大兴～ go in for large-scale building (或 construction) ◇ ～工程 civil engineering/ ～工程师 civil engineer
【土坯】 tǔpī sun-dried mud brick; adobe
【土气】 tǔqi rustic; uncouth; countrified
【土壤】 tǔrǎng soil: 多腐植质的～ humus-rich soil/ 只要帝国主义还存在,就有发生侵略战争的～。As long as imperialism exists there will be soil for wars of aggression.
◇ ～改良 soil improvement; soil amelioration/ ～结构 soil structure/ ～湿度 soil moisture/ ～通气性 soil aeration/ ～渗透性 soil permeability/ ～学 soil science; pedology/ ～学家 pedologist/ ～质地 soil texture
【土人】 tǔrén natives; aborigines
【土色】 tǔsè ashen; pale: 面如～ turn deadly pale
【土生土长】 tǔshēng-tǔzhǎng locally born and bred; born and brought up on one's native soil
【土石方】 tǔshífāng cubic metre of earth and stone
【土司】 tǔsī ① system of appointing national minority hereditary headmen in the Yuan, Ming and Qing dynasties ② such a headman
【土豚】 tǔtún 〈动〉 earth pig
【土围子】 tǔwéizi fortified village
【土卫】 tǔwèi 〈天〉 satellite of Saturn; Saturnian satellite
【土温】 tǔwēn 〈农〉 soil temperature
【土星】 tǔxīng 〈天〉 Saturn ◇ ～光环 Saturn's rings
【土洋并举】 tǔ-yáng bìngjǔ use both indigenous and foreign methods; use both traditional and modern methods
【土洋结合】 tǔ-yáng jiéhé combine indigenous and foreign methods; combine traditional and modern methods
【土音】 tǔyīn local accent
【土语】 tǔyǔ local, colloquial expressions; local dialect
【土葬】 tǔzàng burial (of the dead) in the ground
【土纸】 tǔzhǐ handmade paper
【土冢】 tǔzhǒng grave mound
【土著】 tǔzhù original inhabitants; aboriginals; aborigines
【土专家】 tǔzhuānjiā self-taught expert; local expert
【土族】 Tǔzú the Tu nationality, living mainly in Qinghai

**吐** tǔ ① spit: ～核儿 spit out the pips, stone or pits/

～痰 spit; expectorate/ ～舌头 put (或 stick) out one's tongue/ 蚕～丝。Silkworms spin silk./ 机枪～着火舌。The machine gun was spitting fire. ② say; tell; pour out: ～实 tell the truth/ ～字清楚 enunciate clearly/ ～怨气 vent one's grievances/ 翻身农奴～出了千年的苦水。The emancipated serfs poured out the accumulated bitterness of hundreds of years.
另见 tù
【吐蕃】 Tǔfān Tibetan regime in ancient China
【吐根】 tǔgēn 〈植〉 ipecac (*Cephaelis ipecacuanha*) ◇ ～硷 〈药〉 emetine
【吐故纳新】 tǔ gù nà xīn get rid of the stale and take in the fresh
【吐露】 tǔlù reveal; tell: ～真情 unbosom oneself; tell the truth
【吐气】 tǔqì ① feel elated after unburdening oneself of resentment; feel elated and exultant: 扬眉～ blow off steam in rejoicing ② 〈语〉 aspirated ◇ ～音 aspirated sound
【吐弃】 tǔqì spurn; cast aside; reject
【吐绶鸡】 tǔshòujī turkey
【吐穗】 tǔsuì 〈农〉 earing (up); heading (of cereal plants)
【吐絮】 tǔxù 〈农〉 opening of bolls; boll opening

**钍** tǔ thorium (Th)

## tù

**吐** tù ① vomit; throw up: 恶心要～ feel sick; feel like vomiting (或 throwing up) ② give up unwillingly; disgorge: ～赃 disgorge ill-gotten gains
另见 tǔ
【吐酒石】 tùjiǔshí 〈药〉 tartar emetic
【吐沫】 tùmo saliva; spittle; spit
【吐血】 tùxiě spitting blood; haematemesis
【吐泻】 tù-xiè vomiting and diarrhoea

**兔** tù hare; rabbit: 家～ rabbit/ 野～ hare
【兔唇】 tùchún 〈医〉 harelip
【兔死狗烹】 tù sǐ gǒu pēng the hounds are killed for food once all the hares are bagged — trusted aides are eliminated when they have outlived their usefulness
【兔死狐悲】 tù sǐ hú bēi the fox mourns the death of the hare — like grieves for like
【兔狲】 tùsūn 〈动〉 steppe cat
【兔脱】 tùtuō 〈书〉 run away like a hare; escape; flee
【兔崽子】 tùzǎizi 〈骂〉 brat; bastard
【兔子】 tùzi hare; rabbit
【兔子不吃窝边草】 tùzi bù chī wōbian cǎo a rabbit doesn't eat the grass near its own hole (so that it will be protected) — a villain doesn't harm his nextdoor neighbours
【兔子尾巴长不了】 tùzi wěiba chángbuliǎo 〈贬〉 the tail of a rabbit can't be long — won't last long

**堍** tù the ramp of a bridge

**菟** tù
【菟丝子】 tùsīzǐ 〈中药〉 the seed of Chinese dodder (*Cuscuta chinensis*)

## tuān

**湍** tuān 〈书〉 ① (of a current) rapid; torrential ② rapids; rushing waters: 急～ a rushing current
【湍急】 tuānjí (of a current) rapid; torrential: 水流～。The current is swift.
【湍流】 tuānliú ① 〈书〉 swift current; rushing waters; torrent; rapids ② 〈物〉 turbulent flow; turbulence

## tuán

**团** tuán ① round; circular: ～扇 round fan ② sth. shaped like a ball: 缩成一～ curl up into a ball/ 汤～ boiled rice dumpling ③ roll sth. into a ball; roll: ～纸团儿 roll paper into a ball/ ～药丸 roll pills ④ unite; conglomerate ⑤ group; society; organization: 剧～ drama troupe/ 中央乐～ the Central Philharmonic Society/ 文工～ ensemble; art troupe/ 代表～ delegation; mission; deputation ⑥ 〈军〉 regiment ⑦ 〈简〉 (中国共产主义青年团) the Communist Youth League of China; the League: 入～ join the League; be admitted to the League/ ～籍 League membership ⑧ 〈量〉: 一～毛线 a ball of wool/ 一～面 a lump of dough
【团粉】 tuánfěn cooking starch
【团结】 tuánjié unite; rally: ～一致 unite as one/ ～对敌 unite to oppose the enemy; close ranks to fight the enemy/ ～一切可以～的力量 unite with all the forces that can be united/ ～在党中央的周围 rally around the Party's Central Committee/ 发扬～战斗的精神 carry forward the spirit of solidarity and militancy/ ～就是力量。Unity is strength./ ～、紧张、严肃、活泼。Be united, alert, earnest and lively.
【团聚】 tuánjù reunite: 被旧社会拆散的亲骨肉,解放不久就～了。Separated in the old society, the family was reunited soon after liberation./ 全家～ family reunion
【团矿】 tuánkuàng 〈冶〉 nodulizing; briquetting
【团粒】 tuánlì 〈农〉 granule ◇ ～结构 granular structure
【团脐】 tuánqí ① broad and rounded abdomen of a female crab ② female crab
【团体】 tuántǐ organization; group; team: 群众～ mass organization
◇ ～操 group callisthenics/ ～冠军 team title/ ～票 group ticket/ ～赛 team competition
【团团】 tuántuán round and round; all round: ～围住 surround completely; encircle/ 忙得～转 be up to one's ears in work; run round in circles
【团鱼】 tuányú soft-shelled turtle
【团员】 tuányuán ① member: 代表团～ a member of a delegation ② a member of the Communist Youth League of China; League member
【团圆】 tuányuán reunion: 全家～ family reunion ◇ ～饭 family reunion dinner
【团圆节】 Tuányuánjié the Mid-Autumn Festival (15th day of the 8th lunar month)
【团藻】 tuánzǎo 〈植〉 volvox
【团长】 tuánzhǎng ① 〈军〉 regimental commander ② head (或 chief, chairman) of a delegation, troupe, etc.
【团子】 tuánzi dumpling: 糯米～ dumpling made of glutinous rice/ 菜～ cornmeal dumpling with vegetable stuffing/ 饭～ rice ball

**抟** tuán 见"团" tuán③

## tuī

**忒** tuī 〈方〉 too; very: ～小 too small/ 路～滑。The road is very slippery.

另见 tè; tēi

**推** tuī ① push; shove: ～车 push a cart/ 把门～开 push (或 shove) the door open/ 把竹排～进河里 shove (或 push) the bamboo raft into the river/ ～铅球 shot put; put the shot (或 weight)/ 把子弹～上膛 ram a cartridge into the rifle chamber ② turn a mill or grindstone; grind: ～磨 turn a millstone/ ～点白面 grind some wheat into flour ③ cut; pare: ～头 have a haircut or cut sb.'s hair (with clippers)/ 用刨子～光 make smooth with a plane; plane ④ push forward; promote; advance: 把运动～向高潮 push the movement to a climax ⑤ infer; deduce: 类～ reason by analogy; analogize ⑥ push away; shirk; shift: 不要把重担子～给人家。Don't shift burdensome tasks onto others. ⑦ put off; postpone: 这项工作得抓紧,不能老是往后～。We have to get on with this job, we can't put it off day after day. ⑧ elect; choose: ～他担任小组长 elect him group leader; choose him to be group leader ⑨ hold in esteem; praise highly: ～许 esteem and commend

【推本溯源】 tuīběn-sùyuán trace the origin; ascertain the cause

【推波助澜】 tuībō-zhùlán make a stormy sea stormier; add fuel to the flames

【推测】 tuīcè infer; conjecture; guess: 根据～ by inference/ 不过是～而已 mere guesswork; nothing but conjecture/ 猿人化石可以帮助我们～猿人的生活情况。The fossil remains of ape-men can help us infer how they lived.

【推陈出新】 tuī chén chū xīn weed through the old to bring forth the new: 百花齐放,～。Let a hundred flowers blossom; weed through the old to bring forth the new.

【推诚相见】 tuīchéng xiāngjiàn deal with sb. in good faith; treat sb. with sincerity

【推迟】 tuīchí put off; postpone; defer: ～作出决定 defer making a decision/ 这个会议～几天开。The meeting will be postponed for a few days.

【推斥】 tuīchì 〈物〉 repulsion ◇ ～力 repulsive force

【推崇】 tuīchóng hold in esteem; praise highly: ～备至 have the greatest esteem for

【推辞】 tuīcí decline (an appointment, invitation, etc.)

【推戴】 tuīdài support sb. assuming leadership

【推挡】 tuīdǎng 〈乒乓球〉 half volley with push

【推倒】 tuīdǎo ① push over; overturn: 把他～在地 shove him to the ground ② repudiate; cancel; reverse: 这个计划不切实际,要～重来。The plan is not practical and has to be replaced with a new one./ 一切诬蔑不实之词,应予～。All slanders and libels should be repudiated.

【推动】 tuīdòng push forward; promote; give impetus to: ～工作 push the work forward; expedite the work/ ～社会向前发展 propel the society forward/ 在阶级社会里,阶级斗争是～历史发展的动力。Class struggle is the motive force of history in a class society. ◇ ～力 motive (或 driving) force

【推断】 tuīduàn infer; deduce: 经过周密的调查和分析才能作出正确的～。Correct inferences can be drawn only from careful investigation and analysis.

【推度】 tuīduó infer; conjecture; guess

【推翻】 tuīfān ① overthrow; overturn; topple: ～帝国主义、封建主义和官僚资本主义的统治 overthrow the rule of imperialism, feudalism and bureaucrat-capitalism ② repudiate; cancel; reverse: ～协议 repudiate an agreement/ ～原定计划 cancel the original plan

【推杆】 tuīgǎn 〈机〉 push rod

【推广】 tuīguǎng popularize; spread; extend: ～普通话 popularize the common spoken Chinese/ ～先进经验 spread advanced experience

【推己及人】 tuī jǐ jí rén put oneself in the place of another; treat other people as you would yourself; be considerate

【推荐】 tuījiàn recommend: ～她去当拖拉机手 recommend her for training as a tractor driver/ 向青年～优秀的文学作品 recommend outstanding literary works to the youth

【推进】 tuījìn ① push on; carry forward; advance; give impetus to: 把两国之间的友好关系～到一个新阶段 carry the friendly relations between the two countries to a new stage/ 对反帝反霸斗争起巨大的～作用 give great impetus to the struggle against imperialism and hegemonism ② 〈军〉 move forward; push; drive: 战线再次向前～。The battlefront has again moved forward./ 我团～到距离敌人只有几公里的地方。Our regiment drove to within a few kilometres of the enemy.

◇ ～剂 propellant/ ～力 propulsive force; driving power/ ～器 propeller

【推究】 tuījiū examine; study: ～事理 study the whys and wherefores of things

【推举】 tuījǔ ① elect; choose: 大家～他到大会发言。They chose him to speak on their behalf at the meeting. ② 〈举重〉 clean and press; press: ～一百三十七公斤 press 137 kilograms

【推理】 tuīlǐ 〈逻〉 inference; reasoning: 用～方法 by inference/ 类比～ reasoning from analogy

【推力】 tuīlì thrust: 螺旋桨～ propeller thrust/ 喷气发动机～ jet thrust

【推论】 tuīlùn inference; deduction; corollary

【推拿】 tuīná 〈中医〉 massage

【推敲】 tuīqiāo weigh; deliberate: ～词句 weigh one's words; seek the right word/ 这个提法是经过反复～的。This formulation was worked out after repeated deliberation./ 他写的东西经得起～。His writings can stand close scrutiny.

【推求】 tuīqiú inquire into; ascertain: ～地面沉降的原因 inquire into the causes of surface subsidence

【推却】 tuīquè refuse; decline: 他要请我吃饭,我～了。I declined his invitation to dinner.

【推让】 tuīràng decline (a position, favour, etc. out of modesty)

【推人犯规】 tuīrén fànguī 〈体〉 pushing

【推三阻四】 tuīsān-zǔsì decline with all sorts of excuses; give the runaround

【推事】 tuīshì 〈旧〉 judge

【推算】 tuīsuàn calculate; reckon: 日食发生的时间可以～出来。The time when a solar eclipse will occur can be calculated.

【推头】 tuītóu 〈口〉 ① have a haircut ② cut sb.'s hair (with clippers)

【推土机】 tuītǔjī bulldozer

【推推搡搡】 tuītuīsǎngsǎng push and shove: 大家慢慢走,别～的。Take it easy, don't push and shove.

【推托】 tuītuō offer as an excuse (for not doing sth.); plead: 她～嗓子疼,不肯唱。Pleading a sore throat, she refused to sing.

【推脱】 tuītuō evade; shirk: ～责任 evade (或 shirk) responsibility

【推挽】 tuīwǎn 〈电〉 push-pull ◇ ～电路 push-pull circuit

【推委】 tuīwěi shift responsibility onto others 又作"推诿"

【推想】 tuīxiǎng imagine; guess; reckon: 按现在的速度,可以～两年内我们县就能实现农业机械化了。At this speed, we expect our county's farming to be mechanized within two years.

【推销】 tuīxiāo promote sales; market; peddle: ～商品 promote the sale of goods/ ～修正主义黑货 peddle revisionist trash ◇ ～员 salesman

【推卸】 tuīxiè shirk (responsibility): ～责任,委过于人 shirk responsibility and shift the blame onto others

【推心置腹】 tuīxīn-zhìfù repose full confidence in sb.; confide in sb.: ～地交换意见 have a confidential exchange of views

【推行】 tuīxíng carry out; pursue; practise: ～新的政策 pursue a new policy/ 坚决反对超级大国～的强权政治和霸权主义 resolutely oppose the power politics and hegemonism practised by the superpowers

【推选】 tuīxuǎn elect; choose

【推延】 tuīyán put off; postpone: 把讨论～到明天 put off the discussion till tomorrow

【推移】 tuīyí ① (of time) elapse; pass: 随着时间的～ with the lapse (或 passage) of time; as time goes on (或 by) ② (of a situation, etc.) develop; evolve ◇ ～质〈水〉bed load

【推重】 tuīzhòng have a high regard for; hold in esteem: 《本草纲目》问世之后,深受人们的～。The *Compendium of Materia Medica* has been held in high esteem since it was first published.

【推子】 tuīzi hair-clippers; clippers

## tuí

**颓** tuí ① ruined; dilapidated: ～垣断壁 crumbling walls and dilapidated houses ② declining; decadent: 衰～ weak and degenerate; on the decline/ ～风败俗 decadent (或 depraved) customs ③ dejected; dispirited

【颓败】 tuíbài 〈书〉 declining; decadent

【颓废】 tuífèi dispirited; decadent: ～情绪 decadent sentiments ◇ ～派 the decadent school; the decadents

【颓靡】 tuímǐ downcast; dejected; crestfallen

【颓然】 tuírán 〈书〉 dejected; disappointed

【颓丧】 tuísàng dejected; dispirited; listless: 敌军士气～。The enemy is demoralized.

【颓势】 tuíshì declining tendency: 挽回～ turn the tide in one's favour

【颓唐】 tuítáng dejected; dispirited

## tuǐ

**腿** tuǐ ① leg: 大～ thigh/ 小～ shank/ 前～ foreleg/ 后～ hindleg/ ～快 quick-footed; swift-footed/ ～勤 tireless in running around/ 盘～而坐 sit cross-legged ② a leglike support: 桌子(椅子)～ legs of a table (chair) ③ ham: 云～ Yunnan ham

【腿肚子】 tuǐdùzi 〈口〉 calf (of the leg)

【腿脚】 tuǐjiǎo legs and feet — ability to walk: ～不灵便 have difficulty walking/ 这位老奶奶的～还很利落。This old lady still moves briskly.

【腿腕子】 tuǐwànzi ankle

【腿子】 tuǐzi 〈口〉 hired thug; lackey; henchman

## tuì

**退** tuì ① move back; retreat: 他往后～了几步。He stepped back a few paces. 或 He backed up several steps./ 敌人已经～了。The enemy has retreated./ ～一步说 even if that is so; even so ② cause to move back; withdraw; remove: ～敌 repulse the enemy/ 把子弹～出来 remove a cartridge from the breech of a gun; unload a gun ③ withdraw from; quit: ～党 withdraw from a political party ④ decline; recede; ebb: 潮水～了。The tide has receded. 或 The tide is on the ebb. ⑤ fade: ～色 fade ⑥ return; give back; refund: 把这份礼～掉。Return this gift./ 空瓶不～。Empty bottles are not refundable./ ～货 return merchandise/ ～钱 refund ⑦ cancel; break off: ～婚 break off an engagement/ ～掉订货 cancel an order

【退避】 tuìbì withdraw and keep off; keep out of the way

【退避三舍】 tuìbì sān shè retreat ninety *li* — give way to sb. to avoid a conflict

【退兵】 tuìbīng ① retreat; withdrawal: 传令～ order a retreat ② force the enemy to retreat: ～之计 a plan for repulsing the enemy

【退步】 tuìbù ① lag (或 fall) behind; retrogress: 这孩子功课～了。The boy's not doing so well in his studies as he used to./ 他思想上～了。He has slipped back ideologically. ② room for manoeuvre; leeway: 留个～ leave some room for manoeuvre; leave some leeway

【退潮】 tuìcháo ebb tide; ebb

【退出】 tuìchū withdraw from; secede; quit: ～战斗 withdraw from action; break contact/ ～会场 walk out of a meeting/ ～组织 withdraw (或 resign) from an organization/ ～比赛 withdraw from a competition; scratch/ ～历史舞台 step down from the stage of history

【退党】 tuìdǎng withdraw from (或 quit) a political party

【退佃】 tuìdiàn (of a landlord) cancel a tenancy

【退化】 tuìhuà ① 〈生〉 degeneration ② degenerate; deteriorate; retrograde

【退还】 tuìhuán return: ～公物 return public property/ ～抗议照会 reject a protest note

【退换】 tuìhuàn exchange (或 replace) a purchase: 产品不合规格,保证～。Replacement is guaranteed if the products are not up to standard. 或 We undertake to replace any product not up to specifications.

【退回】 tuìhuí ① return; send (或 give) back: 无法投递,～原处。Undeliverable, returned to sender./ 原稿已经～。The manuscript has been sent back. ② go (或 turn) back: 道路不通,我们只得～。Finding the road impassable, we had to turn back.

【退婚】 tuìhūn break off an engagement

【退火】 tuìhuǒ 〈冶〉 annealing

【退伙】 tuìhuǒ cancel an arrangement to eat at a mess; withdraw from a mess

【退路】 tuìlù ① route of retreat: 切断敌军～ cut off the enemy's retreat ② room for manoeuvre; leeway: 留个～ leave some leeway

【退赔】 tuìpéi return what one has unlawfully taken or pay compensation for it

【退票】 tuìpiào return a ticket; get a refund for a ticket

【退坡】 tuìpō fall off; backslide ◇ ～思想 falling off of revolutionary will or zeal

【退亲】 tuìqīn 见"退婚"

【退却】 tuìquè ① 〈军〉 retreat; withdraw: 战略～ strategic retreat ② hang back; shrink back; flinch

【退让】 tuìràng make a concession; yield; give in: 稍微～一点 give in a little/ 决不～一步 never yield an inch/ 在原则问题上从不～ never make concessions on matters of principle

【退热】 tuìrè 见"退烧"

【退色】 tuìshǎi fade: 这种布～吗? Will this cloth fade? 或 Is this cloth colourfast?

【退烧】 tuìshāo ① bring down (或 allay) a fever ② (of a person's temperature) come down: 他已经～了。His fever is gone. 或 His temperature has come down. ◇ ～药 antipyretic

【退税】 tuìshuì 〈经〉 drawback

【退缩】 tuìsuō shrink back; flinch; cower: 在困难面前从不

～ never flinch from difficulty
【退团】 tuìtuán withdraw from a youth league; give up league membership
【退位】 tuìwèi give up the throne; abdicate
【退伍】 tuìwǔ retire or be discharged from active military service; be demobilized; leave the army ◇～军人 demobilized soldier; ex-serviceman; veteran
【退席】 tuìxí ① leave a banquet or a meeting ② walk out: ～以示抗议 walk out in protest
【退休】 tuìxiū retire
◇ ～工人 retired worker/ ～金 retirement pay; pension/ ～年龄 retirement age
【退学】 tuìxué leave school; discontinue one's schooling: 因病～ leave school owing to bad health/ 勒令～ order to quit school
【退押】 tuìyā ① return a deposit ② (of a landlord) return deposits to tenants in the land reform
【退役】 tuìyì retire or be released from military service (on completing the term of reserve) ◇ ～军官 retired officer/ ～军人 ex-serviceman
【退隐】 tuìyǐn 〈旧〉 (of an official) retire from public life; go into retirement
【退赃】 tuìzāng give up (或 surrender, disgorge) ill-gotten gains
【退职】 tuìzhí resign or be discharged from office; quit working

**煺** tuì scald (a pig, chicken, etc.) in order to remove hairs or feathers: ～毛 remove the hairs or feathers (of a pig, chicken, etc.)

**蜕** tuì ① slough off; exuviate; moult ② exuviae: 蛇～ snake slough
【蜕变】 tuìbiàn ① change qualitatively; transform; transmute ② 〈物〉 decay: 感生～ induced decay/ 自发～ spontaneous decay
【蜕化】 tuìhuà ① slough off; exuviate ② degenerate ◇ ～变质分子 degenerate element; degenerate
【蜕皮】 tuìpí 〈动〉 cast off (或 shed) a skin; exuviate

**褪** tuì ① take off (clothes); shed (feathers): 小鸭～了黄毛。The ducklings have shed their yellow down. ② (of colour) fade
另见 tùn

## tūn

**吞** tūn ① swallow; gulp down: 把药丸～下去 swallow the pills/ 一口～掉 gobble up in one go; devour in one gulp ② take possession of; annex: 独～ take exclusive possession of
【吞并】 tūnbìng annex; gobble (或 swallow) up
【吞金】 tūnjīn swallow gold (to commit suicide)
【吞没】 tūnmò ① embezzle; misappropriate: ～巨款 misappropriate a huge sum ② swallow up; engulf: 小船被波浪～了。The little boat was engulfed in the waves.
【吞声】 tūnshēng 〈书〉 gulp down one's sobs; dare not cry out
【吞食】 tūnshí swallow; devour: 大鱼～小鱼。Big fish eat small fish.
【吞噬】 tūnshì swallow; gobble up; engulf: 白血球～细菌。White corpuscles engulf bacteria./ 洪水～了整个村庄。The flood waters engulfed the whole village. ◇ ～细胞 〈生理〉 phagocyte/ ～作用 〈生理〉 phagocytosis
【吞吐】 tūntǔ swallow and spit — take in and send out in large quantities: 这个港口一年可～三千万吨货物。This port can handle up to 30,000,000 tons of cargo a year. ◇ ～量 handling capacity (of a harbour); the volume of freight handled
【吞吞吐吐】 tūntūntǔtǔ hesitate in speech; hem and haw

**暾** tūn 〈书〉 newly-risen sun: 朝～ the early morning sun

## tún

**屯** tún ① collect; store up: ～粮 store up grain/ ～聚 assemble; collect ② station (troops); quarter (troops): ～兵 station troops ③ village (often used in village names): 皇姑～ Huanggu Village
【屯垦】 túnkěn station troops to open up wasteland
【屯田】 túntián have garrison troops or peasants open up wasteland and grow food grain (a policy pursued by feudal rulers since the Han Dynasty)
【屯扎】 túnzhā station (troops); quarter (troops)

**囤** tún store up; hoard: ～货 store goods
另见 dùn
【囤积】 túnjī hoard for speculation; corner (the market): ～小麦 corner the wheat market/ ～居奇 hoarding and cornering; hoarding and speculation

**饨** tún 见"馄饨" húntun

**豚** tún ① suckling pig ② pig
【豚鼠】 túnshǔ guinea pig; cavy

**鲀** tún globefish; balloonfish; puffer

**臀** tún buttocks
【臀部】 túnbù buttocks: 在～打一针 give or have an injection in the buttock
【臀鳍】 túnqí 〈动〉 anal fin
【臀疣】 túnyóu 〈动〉 monkey's ischial callosities; monkey's seat pads

## tǔn

**氽** tǔn 〈方〉 ① float; drift ② deep-fry: 油～花生米 fried peanuts

## tùn

**褪** tùn slip out of sth.: ～下一只袖子 slip one's arm out of one's sleeve
另见 tuì
【褪套儿】 tùntàor 〈方〉 ① break loose; free oneself; get oneself free ② shake off responsibility

## tuō

**托** tuō ① hold in the palm; support with the hand or palm: ～着盘子 hold a tray on one's palm/ 两手～腮 cup one's chin in one's hands ② sth. serving as a support: 枪～ the stock (或 butt) of a rifle, etc. ③ serve as a foil (或 contrast); set off: 衬～ make sth. stand out by contrast;

set off ④ ask; entrust: ～人买书 ask sb. to buy books for one/ ～人照看孩子 leave a child in sb.'s care/ 这事就～给她吧。Let's leave the matter to her. ⑤ plead; give as a pretext: ～病 plead illness ⑥ rely upon; owe to: ～庇 rely upon one's elder or an influential person for protection/ ～共产党的福，我们才能过上今天的好日子。We owe our happy life to the Communist Party.

【托词】 tuōcí ① find a pretext; make an excuse: ～谢绝 decline on some pretext ② pretext; excuse; subterfuge: 他说有事，不过是～。He said he was busy, but that was just an excuse.

【托儿所】 tuō'érsuǒ nursery; child-care centre; crèche

【托福】 tuōfú 〈套〉〔多用于回答别人的问候〕 thanks to you: 托您的福，我身体好多了。I'm much better now, thank you.

【托付】 tuōfù entrust; commit sth. to sb.'s care: 我们把这任务～给他了。We have entrusted him with the task.

【托故】 tuōgù give (或 find) a pretext; make an excuse: ～早退 leave early under some pretext

【托管】 tuōguǎn trusteeship ◇ ～国 trustee/ ～理事会 Trusteeship Council/ ～领土 trust territory/ ～制度 trusteeship

【托灰板】 tuōhuībǎn 〈建〉 hawk

【托架】 tuōjià 〈机〉 bracket: 发动机～ engine bracket ◇～臂 bracket arm

【托克劳群岛】 Tuōkèláo Qúndǎo the Tokelau Islands

【托拉斯】 tuōlāsī 〈经〉 trust

【托里拆利真空】 tuōlǐchāilì zhēnkōng 〈物〉 Torricellian vacuum

【托洛茨基主义】 Tuōluòcíjīzhǔyì Trotskyism

【托梦】 tuōmèng (of the ghost of one's kith and kin) appear in one's dream and make a request

【托名】 tuōmíng do sth. in sb. else's name

【托派】 Tuōpài Trotskyite; Trotskyist

【托盘】 tuōpán (serving) tray

【托人情】 tuō rénqíng ask an influential person to help arrange sth.; gain one's end through pull; seek the good offices of sb.

【托叶】 tuōyè 〈植〉 stipule

【托运】 tuōyùn consign for shipment; check: 你的行李～了吗？Have you checked your baggage? ◇ ～人 consignor/ ～物 consignment

【托子】 tuōzi base; support: 花瓶～ vase support (或 holder)

## 拖

**拖** tuō ① pull; drag; haul: 火车头～着十二个车皮。The locomotive was pulling (或 drawing) twelve carriages./ 拖轮～着几条小船。The tugboat was towing some small boats./ 把箱子从床底下～出来 drag (或 haul) a trunk out from under the bed/ ～着根竹竿 trail a bamboo pole along/ ～地板 mop the floor/ ～人下水 get sb. into hot water; get sb. into trouble/ ～住敌人 pin down the enemy/ 把身体～垮 wear oneself down/ 问题要彻底解决，不要～个尾巴。The problem must be solved once for all, without leaving any loose ends. ② delay; drag on; procrastinate: 再～就太晚了。Don't delay any more, or it'll be too late./ 这件工作～得太久了。This work has been dragging on far too long.

【拖把】 tuōbǎ mop

【拖车】 tuōchē trailer

【拖船】 tuōchuán tugboat; tug; towboat

【拖带】 tuōdài traction; pulling; towing

【拖后腿】 tuō hòutuǐ hinder (或 impede) sb.; hold sb. back; be a drag on sb.: 孩子要到西藏去工作，你可别～。The kid wants to go and work in Xizang; you shouldn't try to hold him back./ 一个车间完不成任务，就要拖全厂的后腿。One workshop failing to fulfil its quota will be a drag on the whole factory.

【拖拉】 tuōlā dilatory; slow; sluggish: 办事拖拖拉拉的 be dilatory in doing things/ ～作风 dilatory style of work/ 她工作从不～。She never puts off her work.

【拖拉机】 tuōlājī tractor: 手扶～ walking tractor ◇ ～厂 tractor plant/ ～手 tractor driver/ ～站 tractor station

【拖累】 tuōlěi ① encumber; be a burden on: 受家务～ be tied down by household chores/ 子女过多是个～。Too many children are a burden. ② implicate; involve

【拖轮】 tuōlún tugboat; tug; towboat

【拖泥带水】 tuōní-dàishuǐ messy; sloppy; slovenly: 这篇文章写得～。This article is sloppily written./ 办事要利落，不要～。Do things neatly, not sloppily.

【拖欠】 tuōqiàn be behind in payment; be in arrears; default: ～税款 be in arrears with tax payment

【拖沓】 tuōtà dilatory; sluggish; laggard

【拖网】 tuōwǎng trawlnet; trawl; dragnet ◇ ～渔船 trawler

【拖鞋】 tuōxié slippers

【拖延】 tuōyán delay; put off; procrastinate: 期限快到，不能再～了。The deadline is drawing near; we can't delay any more./ ～时间 play for time; stall (for time) ◇ ～战术 dilatory (或 delaying, stalling) tactics

## 脱

**脱** tuō ① (of hair, skin) shed; come off: 他脸晒～皮了。His face is peeling because of sunburn./ 头发～光了 lose all one's hair; become bald ② take off; cast off: ～鞋(衣服) take off one's shoes (clothes) ③ escape from; get out of: ～险 escape danger/ ～榫 be out of joint ④ miss out (words): 这一行里～了三个字。Three characters are missing in this line. ⑤ 〈书〉 neglect; slight ⑥ 〈书〉 if; in case

【脱靶】 tuōbǎ miss the target in shooting practice

【脱班】 tuōbān ① be late for work ② (of a bus, train, etc.) be behind schedule

【脱产】 tuōchǎn be released from production or one's regular work to take on other duties: ～学习一年 be released from work for one year's study/ 不～的理论队伍 a contingent of theoretical workers not withdrawn from production ◇ ～干部 a cadre (of a commune, factory, etc.) not engaged in production

【脱党】 tuōdǎng quit (或 leave) a political party; give up party membership

【脱发】 tuōfà 〈医〉 trichomadesis

【脱肛】 tuōgāng 〈医〉 prolapse of the anus

【脱稿】 tuōgǎo (of a manuscript) be completed: 这本书已～，即可付印。The book is completed and is ready for printing.

【脱轨】 tuōguǐ derail: 火车～了。The train was derailed.

【脱缰之马】 tuō jiāng zhī mǎ a runaway horse — uncontrollable; running wild: 通货膨胀如～ runaway inflation/ 物价飞腾，有如～。Prices were running wild.

【脱胶】 tuōjiāo ① (of parts joined with gum or glue) come unglued; come unstuck: 这件橡皮雨衣～了。The rubber of this raincoat has disintegrated. ② 〈化〉 degum: 生丝～ degumming of silk

【脱节】 tuōjié come apart; be disjointed; be out of line with: 管子焊得不好，容易～。Faultily welded piping is apt to come apart./ 理论与实践不能～。Theory must not be divorced from practice.

【脱臼】 tuōjiù 〈医〉 dislocation

【脱壳机】 tuōkéjī 〈农〉 huller; sheller

【脱口而出】 tuō kǒu ér chū say sth. unwittingly; blurt out; let slip

【脱蜡】 tuōlà 〈石油〉 dewaxing

【脱离】 tuōlí separate oneself from; break away from; be

divorced from: ～群众 cut oneself off from the masses; be divorced from the masses/ ～革命队伍 drop out of the revolutionary ranks/ ～实际 lose contact with reality; be divorced from reality/ 使双方武装力量～接触 disengage (或 separate) the armed forces of the two sides/ ～关系 break off relations; cut ties/ 病人～危险了。The patient is out of danger.

【脱粒】 tuōlì 〈农〉 ① threshing ② shelling ◇ ～机 thresher; sheller

【脱磷】 tuōlín 〈化〉 dephosphorization

【脱硫】 tuōliú 〈化〉 desulphurization; sweetening: ～原油 sweet crude

【脱漏】 tuōlòu be left out; be omitted; be missing: 这里～了一行。A line is missing here./ ～一针 drop a stitch (in knitting)

【脱落】 tuōluò drop; fall off (或 away); come off: 毛发～ lose (one's) hair/ 门的把手～了。The door handle has come off./ 墙上油漆已经～了。The paint on the wall has peeled off./ 蕾铃～ shedding of young bolls

【脱毛】 tuōmáo lose hair or feathers; moult; shed: 那只骆驼刚脱了毛。That camel has just shed.

【脱帽】 tuōmào take off (或 raise) one's hat (in respect): ～致敬 take off one's hat in salutation/ ～默哀 bare one's head and mourn in silence

【脱模】 tuōmú 〈冶〉 drawing of patterns

【脱泡】 tuōpào 〈纺〉 deaeration ◇ ～桶 deaerator

【脱坯】 tuōpī mould adobe blocks

【脱期】 tuōqī (of a periodical) fail to come out on time

【脱氢】 tuōqīng 〈化〉 dehydrogenation

【脱色】 tuōsè ① decolour; decolourize ② fade ◇ ～剂 decolourant; decolourizer

【脱身】 tuōshēn get away; get free; extricate oneself: 我事情太多,不能～。I have so much to do that I just can't get away.

【脱手】 tuōshǒu ① slip out of the hand: 他用力一扔,石块～飞了出去。With a powerful fling he sent the stone flying. ② get off one's hands; dispose of; sell: 这些货不好～。These goods are difficult to dispose of.

【脱水】 tuōshuǐ ① 〈医〉 deprivation (或 loss) of body fluids; dehydration ② 〈化〉 dehydration; dewatering ◇ ～机 hydroextractor; whizzer/ ～蔬菜 dehydrated vegetables

【脱俗】 tuōsú free from vulgarity; refined

【脱胎】 tuōtāi ① emerge from the womb of; be born out of: 社会主义社会是从资本主义社会～而来的。Socialist society emerges from the womb of capitalist society. ② 〈工美〉 a process of making bodiless lacquerware ◇ ～漆器 bodiless lacquerware

【脱胎换骨】 tuōtāi-huàngǔ be reborn; cast off one's old self; thoroughly remould oneself

【脱逃】 tuōtáo run away; escape; flee: 临阵～ flee from battle

【脱位】 tuōwèi 〈医〉 dislocation

【脱误】 tuōwù omissions and errors

【脱险】 tuōxiǎn escape (或 be out of) danger: 经过抢救,孩子～了。The child was out of danger after the emergency treatment.

【脱销】 tuōxiāo out of stock; sold out: 这本书～了。The book is out of stock. 或 The book is sold out.

【脱氧】 tuōyǎng 〈化〉 deoxidation; deoxidization ◇ ～剂 deoxidizer; deoxidant

【脱颖而出】 tuō yǐng ér chū the point of an awl sticking out through a bag — talent showing itself

【脱羽】 tuōyǔ (of birds) moult

【脱证】 tuōzhèng 〈中医〉 exhaustion of vital energy at the critical stage of an illness

【脱脂】 tuōzhī de-fat; degrease ◇ ～剂 〈皮革〉 degreasing agent/ ～棉 absorbent cotton/ ～奶粉 de-fatted milk powder; nonfat dried milk/ ～乳 skimmed milk/ ～纱布 absorbent gauze

## tuó

**驮** tuó carry (或 bear) on the back: 这头驴子能～三袋粮食。This donkey can carry three sacks of grain.
另见 duò

【驮畜】 tuóchù pack animal

【驮筐】 tuókuāng pannier

【驮马】 tuómǎ pack horse

**陀** tuó

【陀螺】 tuóluó top: 抽～ whip a top

【陀螺仪】 tuóluóyí 〈航空〉 gyroscope; gyro

**驼** tuó ① camel ② hunchbacked; humpbacked

【驼背】 tuóbèi ① hunchback; humpback ② hunchbacked; humpbacked

【驼峰】 tuófēng ① hump (of a camel) ② 〈交〉 hump ◇ ～调车场 hump yard/ ～调车法 hump switching

【驼鹿】 tuólù 〈动〉 elk; moose

【驼绒】 tuóróng ① camel's hair ② camel hair cloth

【驼色】 tuósè the colour of camel's hair; light tan

【驼子】 tuózi 〈口〉 hunchback; humpback

**沱** tuó 〈方〉 a small bay in a river (often used in place names)

【沱茶】 tuóchá a bowl-shaped compressed mass of tea leaves

**坨** tuó

【坨子】 tuózi ① lump: 泥～ a lump of mud; clod ② heap: 盐～ salt mound

**柁** tuó 〈建〉 girder

**砣** tuó ① the sliding weight of a steelyard ② stone roller ③ cut or polish jade with an emery wheel

【砣子】 tuózi an emery wheel for cutting or polishing jade

**鸵** tuó ostrich

【鸵鸟】 tuóniǎo ostrich ◇ ～政策 ostrich policy; ostrichism

**跎** tuó 见"蹉跎" cuōtuó

**酡** tuó 〈书〉 (of one's face) be flushed with drink

**橐** tuó ① 〈书〉 a kind of bag ② 〈象〉: ～～的脚步声 the tread of footsteps

**鼧** tuó

【鼧鼥】 tuóbá an ancient name for marmot

**鼍** tuó 〈动〉 Chinese alligator

## tuǒ

**妥** tuǒ ① appropriate; proper: 欠～ not proper; not

quite satisfactory/ 请～为保存。Please look after it carefully./ 以上意见～否，请指示。Please indicate whether you consider the above views sound or not. ②〔多用在动词后〕ready; settled; finished: 款已备～。The money is ready./ 事已办～。The matter has been settled.

【妥当】 tuǒdàng appropriate; proper: 办得很～ well handled; quite well done

【妥善】 tuǒshàn appropriate; proper; well arranged: ～安排 make appropriate arrangements/ 问题比较复杂，需要～处理。The problem is rather complicated and needs careful and skilful handling./ 互阅全权证书，认为～ examine each other's full powers and find them in good and due form

【妥帖】 tuǒtiē appropriate; fitting; proper: 看来这段译文不十分～。That doesn't seem to be an apt translation.

【妥协】 tuǒxié come to terms; compromise: 达成～ reach a compromise ◇ ～性 a tendency towards compromise (或 accommodation)

**庹** tuǒ 〈量〉arm spread; span

**椭** tuǒ

【椭率】 tuǒlǜ 〈数〉ellipticity

【椭面】 tuǒmiàn 〈数〉ellipsoid

【椭圆】 tuǒyuán 〈数〉ellipse ◇ ～截面 oval cross section/ ～星云〈天〉elliptical nebula/ ～柱面 elliptic cylinder/ ～锥面 elliptic cone

## tuò

**拓** tuò open up; develop: 开～边远地区 open up the border regions
另见 tà

【拓荒】 tuòhuāng open up virgin soil; reclaim wasteland ◇ ～者 pioneer; pathbreaker; trailblazer

【拓扑学】 tuòpūxué 〈数〉topology

**柝** tuò 〈书〉watchman's clapper (或 knocker)

**唾** tuò ① saliva; spittle ② spit

【唾骂】 tuòmà spit on and curse; revile

【唾沫】 tuòmo saliva; spittle

【唾弃】 tuòqì cast aside; spurn: 逆历史潮流而动的人终将被人民所～。Those who go against the trend of history will be cast aside by the people.

【唾手可得】 tuò shǒu kě dé extremely easy to obtain

【唾液】 tuòyè saliva ◇ ～腺 salivary gland

**萚** tuò 〈书〉fallen bark or leaves

**魄** tuò 见"落拓(魄)" luòtuò
另见 bó; pò

**箨** tuò 〈书〉sheaths of bamboo shoots

# W

## wā

**洼** wā ① hollow; low-lying: 这地太～，不适于种棉花。This is low-lying land and not suitable for cotton. ② low-lying area; depression: 水～儿 a waterlogged depression

【洼地】 wādì depression; low-lying land

【洼陷】 wāxiàn (of ground) be sunken; be low-lying

**挖** wā dig; excavate: ～井 dig (或 sink) a well/ ～隧道 excavate a tunnel/ ～防空洞 dig an air-raid shelter/ ～塘泥 scoop up sludge from a pond/ ～出隐藏的阶级敌人 ferret out hidden class enemies

【挖补】 wābǔ mend by replacing a damaged part

【挖槽机】 wācáojī 〈机〉 groover

【挖方】 wāfāng 〈建〉 ① excavation (of earth or stone) ② cubage of excavation

【挖根】 wāgēn dig sth. up by the roots; uproot: 检查错误要从自己思想上～。When examining one's mistakes, one should analyse their ideological roots.

【挖沟机】 wāgōujī ditcher; trencher; trench digger

【挖掘】 wājué excavate; unearth: ～古物 excavate ancient relics/ ～地下宝藏 unearth buried treasure/ ～企业潜力 tap the latent power (或 potentialities) of an enterprise

【挖掘机】 wājuéjī excavator; navvy: 迈步式～ walking excavator/ 履带式～ caterpillar excavator/ 索斗～ dragline excavator 又作"挖土机"

【挖空心思】 wākōng xīnsī 〔多含贬义〕 rack one's brains: ～为自己辩护 rack one's brains trying to justify oneself

【挖苦】 wāku speak sarcastically or ironically: 那话是～我的。That was a dig at me. ◇ ～话 ironical remarks; verbal thrusts

【挖泥船】 wāníchuán dredger; dredge

【挖墙脚】 wā qiángjiǎo 〈口〉 undermine the foundation; cut the ground from under sb.'s feet: 这就等于挖社会主义的墙脚。This is tantamount to undermining socialism.

【挖肉补疮】 wāròu-bǔchuāng 见"剜肉补疮" wānròu-bǔchuāng

**哇** wā 〈象〉〔形容呕吐声、哭声等〕: ～的一声哭了起来 burst out crying

另见 wa

【哇啦】 wālā 〈象〉 hullabaloo; uproar; din

**蛙** wā frog

【蛙人】 wārén frogman

【蛙式打夯机】 wāshì dǎhāngjī frog rammer

【蛙泳】 wāyǒng 〈体〉 breaststroke ◇ ～蹬腿 frog kick

## wá

**娃** wá ① baby; child ② 〈方〉 newborn animal: 鸡～ chick

【娃娃】 wáwa baby; child: 胖～ a chubby child ◇ ～床 crib; cot

【娃娃鱼】 wáwayú giant salamander

【娃子】 wázi ① 〈方〉 baby; child ② 〈方〉 newborn animal: 猪～ piglet ③ 〈旧〉 slave (among the minority nationalities in the Liangshan Mountains)

## wǎ

**瓦** wǎ ① tile: 无棱～ plain tile ② made of baked clay: ～器 earthenware ③ 〈电〉 watt

另见 wà

【瓦当】 wǎdāng 〈考古〉 eaves tile

【瓦房】 wǎfáng tile-roofed house

【瓦工】 wǎgōng ① bricklaying, tiling or plastering ② bricklayer; tiler; plasterer

【瓦匠】 wǎjiang bricklayer; tiler; plasterer

【瓦解】 wǎjiě disintegrate; collapse; crumble: ～敌军 disintegrate the enemy forces/ 傀儡政权已经土崩～了。The puppet regime has collapsed./ 经过三个月战斗，敌军全线～。After three months' fighting the whole enemy front crumbled.

【瓦楞】 wǎléng ① 〈建〉 rows of tiles on a roof ② corrugated ◇ ～铁皮 corrugated sheet iron/ ～纸 corrugated paper

【瓦砾】 wǎlì rubble; debris: 成了一片～ be reduced to rubble

【瓦垄】 wǎlǒng 见"瓦楞"①

【瓦垄子】 wǎlǒngzi 〈动〉 ark shell

【瓦圈】 wǎquān rim (of a bicycle wheel, cart wheel, etc.)

【瓦全】 wǎquán 见"宁为玉碎，不为瓦全" nìng wéi yù suì, bù wéi wǎ quán

【瓦时】 wǎshí 〈电〉 watt-hour

【瓦斯】 wǎsī gas ◇ ～爆炸 gas explosion/ ～筒 gas cylinder

【瓦特】 wǎtè 〈电〉 watt ◇ ～计 wattmeter

**佤** Wǎ

【佤族】 Wǎzú the Va (Wa) nationality, living in Yunnan

## wà

**瓦** wà cover (a roof) with tiles; tile

另见 wǎ

【瓦刀】 wàdāo (bricklayer's) cleaver

**袜** wà socks; stockings; hose

【袜带】 wàdài suspenders; garters

【袜套】 wàtào socks; ankle socks

【袜筒】 wàtǒng the leg of a stocking

【袜子】 wàzi socks; stockings; hose

**腽** wà

【腽肭脐】 wànàqí 〈中药〉 the penis and testes of an ursine seal

【腽肭兽】 wànàshòu 〈动〉 fur seal; ursine seal

## wa

**哇** wa 〈助〉〔"啊"受到前一个字收音 u 或 ao 的影响而发生的变音〕: 你怎么还不走～？Why haven't you gone yet, eh?/ 你好～？Well, how are you?

另见 wā

## wāi

**歪** wāi ① askew; crooked; inclined; slanting: ～戴帽子 have one's hat on crooked/ 这堵墙有点～。This wall is a little out of the perpendicular./ 小女孩儿～着头聚精会神地听故事。The little girl listened attentively to the story with her head tilted to one side. ② devious; underhand; crooked: ～主意 evil ideas; devil's advice/ ～道理 false reasoning

【歪打正着】 wāidǎ-zhèngzháo hit the mark by a fluke; score a lucky hit

【歪风】 wāifēng evil wind; unhealthy trend: ～邪气 evil winds and noxious influences; unhealthy trends and evil practices/ 打击～,发扬正气 combat evil trends and foster a spirit of uprightness

【歪门邪道】 wāimén-xiédào 见"邪门歪道" xiémén-wāidào

【歪曲】 wāiqū distort; misrepresent; twist: ～事实 distort the facts/ ～作者原意 misrepresent the author's meaning/ ～别人的话 twist people's words

【歪诗】 wāishī inelegant verses; doggerel

【歪歪扭扭】 wāiwāiniǔniǔ crooked; askew; shapeless and twisted: 字写得～ write a poor hand; scrawl

【歪斜】 wāixié crooked; askew; aslant

**㖞** wāi (of the mouth) awry

【㖞僻不遂】 wāipì bùsuí 〈中医〉 facial paralysis and hemiplegia after apoplexy

## wǎi

**崴** wǎi ① rugged (mountain path) ② sprain; twist: 把脚～了 sprain one's ankle

【崴子】 wǎizi 〈方〉 ① river bend ② mountain recess

## wài

**外** wài ① outer; outward; outside: ～屋 outer room/ 窗～ outside the window ② other: ～省 other provinces ③ foreign; external: ～商 foreign merchants/ 对～贸易 foreign trade; external trade ④ (relatives) of one's mother, sisters or daughters: ～孙 daughter's son; grandson ⑤ not of the same organization, class, etc.; not closely related: ～客 a guest who is not a relative/ 见～ regard sb. as an outsider/ 电话不～借。This telephone is not for public use. ⑥ besides; in addition; beyond: 此～ besides; into the bargain/ 预算～的开支 extra-budgetary expenditure ⑦ unofficial: ～传 unofficial biography

【外币】 wàibì foreign currency

【外边】 wàibian ① outside; out: 到～散步 go out for a walk/ 咱们上～去谈,好不好？Let's go outside to talk, shall we? ② a place other than where one lives or works: 她儿子在～工作。Her son works somewhere away from home. ③ exterior; outside: 行李卷儿～再裹一层塑料布。Wrap a plastic sheet round the bedroll.

【外表】 wàibiǎo outward appearance; exterior; surface: ～美观 have a fine exterior; look nice/ 事物的～ the outward appearance of things/ 从～看人 judge people by appearances

【外宾】 wàibīn foreign guest (或 visitor)

【外部】 wàibù ① outside; external: 事物的～联系 external relations of things/ ～世界 the external world ② exterior; surface

【外埠】 wàibù towns or cities other than where one is

【外层空间】 wàicéng kōngjiān outer space ◇ ～导弹 outer-space missile

【外层焰】 wàicéngyàn 〈化〉 outer flame

【外差】 wàichā 〈电〉 heterodyne: 超～ superheterodyne

【外场】 wàichǎng 〈棒、垒球〉 outfield ◇ ～手 outfielder

【外出血】 wàichūxuè 〈医〉 external haemorrhage

【外带】 wàidài ① tyre (cover): ～和里带都扎穿了。The tyre and the inner tube are both punctured. ② as well; besides; into the bargain: 这个厂生产农业机械,～修理各种农具。This factory, which produces agricultural machinery, repairs farm tools as a sideline.

【外敌】 wàidí foreign enemy

【外地】 wàidì parts of the country other than where one is: 代表团将在首都访问三天,然后再到～游览。The delegation will pay a three-day visit to the capital before leaving for other parts of the country.

【外电】 wàidiàn dispatches from foreign news agencies: 据～报导 according to reports from foreign news agencies

【外调】 wàidiào transfer (materials or personnel) to other localities: ～物资 materials allocated for transfer to other places

【外毒素】 wàidúsù 〈医〉 exotoxin

【外耳】 wài'ěr 〈生理〉 external ear

【外耳道】 wài'ěrdào 〈生理〉 external auditory meatus

【外分泌】 wàifēnmì 〈生理〉 exocrine; external secretion ◇ ～腺 exocrine gland

【外敷】 wàifū 〈医〉 apply (ointment, etc.) ◇ ～药 medicine for external application

【外感】 wàigǎn 〈中医〉 diseases caused by external factors

【外港】 wàigǎng outport

【外公】 wàigōng 〈方〉 (maternal) grandfather

【外功】 wàigōng exercises to benefit the muscles and bones

【外观】 wàiguān outward appearance; exterior: 这座大楼～很美。This is a fine-looking building.

【外国】 wàiguó foreign country: ～朋友 foreign friends/ 到～学习 go abroad to study ◇ ～人 foreigner/ ～语 foreign language

【外果皮】 wàiguǒpí 〈植〉 exocarp

【外行】 wàiháng ① layman; nonprofessional ② lay; unprofessional: 种庄稼他可不～。He's no amateur in farming. ◇ ～话 lay language; a mere dabbler's opinion

【外号】 wàihào nickname

【外患】 wàihuàn foreign aggression: 内忧～ internal disturbance and foreign aggression

【外汇】 wàihuì foreign exchange
◇ ～储备 foreign exchange reserve/ ～兑换率 rate of exchange/ ～官价 official exchange rate/ ～管理 (foreign) exchange control/ ～行情 exchange quotations/ ～交易 foreign exchange transaction/ ～平价 par of exchange; exchange parity/ ～收入 foreign exchange earnings (或 income)

【外货】 wàihuò foreign goods; imported goods

【外籍】 wàijí foreign nationality: ～工作人员 foreign personnel

【外寄生物】 wàijìshēngwù ectoparasite

【外加】 wàijiā more; additional; extra: 给你们十份报纸,～三本小册子。Here you are — ten copies of the newspaper, plus three pamphlets. ◇ ～电压 applied voltage

【外间】 wàijiān ① outer room ② 〈书〉 the external world; outside circles

【外交】 wàijiāo diplomacy; foreign affairs: 建立大使级的～关系 establish diplomatic relations at ambassadorial level/ 通过～途径解决 be settled through diplomatic channels/ 坚决贯彻毛主席的革命～路线 resolutely implement Chairman Mao's revolutionary line in foreign affairs

◇ ～部 the Ministry of Foreign Affairs; the Foreign Ministry/ ～部长 Minister of (或 for) Foreign Affairs; Foreign Minister/ ～辞令 diplomatic language (或 parlance)/ ～代表机构 diplomatic mission/ ～官 diplomat/ ～惯例 diplomatic practice/ ～护照 diplomatic passport/ ～豁免权 diplomatic immunities/～机关 diplomatic establishments/ ～家 diplomat/ ～礼节 diplomatic protocol/ ～签证 diplomatic visa/ ～人员 diplomatic personnel/ ～使节 diplomatic envoy/ ～使团 diplomatic corps/ ～使团团长 dean (或 doyen) of the diplomatic corps/ ～特权 diplomatic prerogatives (或 privileges)/ ～文书 diplomatic correspondence/ ～衔 diplomatic rank/ ～信袋 diplomatic pouch; diplomatic bag/ ～信使 diplomatic courier/ ～邮件 diplomatic mail/ ～政策 foreign policy

【外角】 wàijiǎo 〈数〉 exterior angle

【外接圆】 wàijiēyuán 〈数〉 circumscribed circle; circumcircle

【外界】 wàijiè ① the external (或 outside) world: 对～的认识 knowledge of the external world ② outside: 向～征求意见 solicit comments and suggestions from people outside one's organization/ 顶住～的种种压力 withstand all kinds of outside pressure

【外景】 wàijǐng outdoor scene; a scene shot on location; exterior: 拍摄～ film the exterior; shoot a scene on location

【外径】 wàijìng 〈机〉 external diameter; outside (或 outer) diameter

【外科】 wàikē 〈医〉 surgical department
◇ ～病房 surgical ward/ ～手术 surgical operation; surgery/ ～学 surgery/ ～医生 surgeon

【外壳】 wàiké outer covering (或 casing); shell; case: 热水瓶～ the outer casing of a thermos flask/ 电池～ battery case

【外快】 wàikuài extra income

【外来】 wàilái outside; external; foreign: ～干涉 outside interference; foreign (或 external) intervention/ ～干部 cadres not native to the locality ◇ ～人 a person from another place; nonnative/ ～语 word of foreign origin; foreign word; loanword

【外力】 wàilì ① outside force ②〈物〉 external force

【外流】 wàiliú outflow; drain: 美元～ dollar outflow/ 黄金～ gold bullion outflow

【外贸】 wàimào 〈简〉(对外贸易) foreign trade; external trade ◇ ～部 the Ministry of Foreign Trade

【外貌】 wàimào appearance; exterior; looks

【外面】 wàimiàn outward appearance; exterior; surface

【外面】 wàimian outside; out: 把椅子搬到～去 take the chair out/ 今天我们要在～吃饭。We'll eat (或dine) out today.

【外面儿光】 wàimiànrguāng deceptively smooth appearance; outward show: 做事要考虑实际效果，不能追求～。In handling matters, we must pay attention to actual results and not try to be flashy.

【外婆】 wàipó 〈方〉 (maternal) grandmother

【外戚】 wàiqī relatives of a king or emperor on the side of his mother or wife

【外强中干】 wàiqiáng-zhōnggān outwardly strong but inwardly weak; strong in appearance but weak in reality: 帝国主义是～的纸老虎。Imperialism is a paper tiger, outwardly strong but inwardly weak.

【外侨】 wàiqiáo foreign national; alien

【外切形】 wàiqiēxíng 〈数〉 circumscribed figure

【外勤】 wàiqín ① work done outside the office or in the field (as surveying, prospecting, news gathering, etc.) ② field personnel

【外倾】 wàiqīng 〈心〉 extroversion

【外圈】 wàiquān 〈体〉 outer lane; outside lane

【外人】 wàirén ① stranger; outsider: 别客气，我又不是～。Don't stand on ceremony. I'm no stranger./ 不足为～道 not to be mentioned to outsiders/ 你说吧，这里没～。Speak up. You're among friends. ② foreigner; alien

【外伤】 wàishāng an injury or wound; trauma ◇ ～性休克 traumatic shock/ ～学 traumatology

【外生殖器】 wàishēngzhíqì 〈生理〉 external genital organs

【外甥】 wàisheng sister's son; nephew

【外甥女】 wàishengnǚ sister's daughter; niece

【外事】 wàishì foreign affairs; external affairs: ～往来 dealings with foreign nationals or organizations

【外事组】 wàishìzǔ ① foreign affairs section ② a section dealing with foreign personnel and foreign visitors

【外手】 wàishǒu (when driving a vehicle or operating a machine) the right-hand side

【外孙】 wàisūn daughter's son; grandson

【外孙女】 wàisūnnǚ daughter's daughter; granddaughter

【外胎】 wàitāi tyre (cover)

【外逃】 wàitáo ① flee to some other place ② flee the country

【外套】 wàitào ① overcoat ② loose coat; outer garment

【外听道】 wàitīngdào 〈生理〉 external auditory meatus

【外头】 wàitou outside; out: 汽车在～。The car is outside./ 这事儿～全知道了。Even those on the outside know about it./ 夏天我常在～睡。In summer I often sleep outdoors.

【外围】 wàiwéi periphery: 首都～ the periphery of the capital ◇ ～防线 outer defence line/ ～组织 peripheral organization

【外文】 wàiwén foreign language

【外侮】 wàiwǔ foreign aggression; external aggression: 抵御～ resist foreign aggression

【外务】 wàiwù ① matters outside one's job ② foreign affairs; external affairs

【外线】 wàixiàn ①〈军〉 exterior lines: ～作战 fight on exterior lines; exterior-line operations ② outside (telephone) connections

【外乡】 wàixiāng another part of the country; some other place: ～口音 a nonlocal accent/ 他是～人。He is not from these parts.

【外向】 wàixiàng 〈心〉 extroversion

【外销】 wàixiāo for sale abroad or in another part of the country: ～产品 products for export; articles for sale in other areas

【外心】 wàixīn ① unfaithful intentions (of husband or wife) ②〈数〉 circumcentre

【外形】 wàixíng appearance; external form; contour

【外姓】 wàixìng (people) not of the same surname

【外延】 wàiyán 〈逻〉 extension

【外焰】 wàiyàn 〈化〉 outer flame

【外衣】 wàiyī ① coat; jacket; outer clothing; outer garment ② semblance; appearance; garb: 披着马列主义～的修正主义分子 revisionists in the garb of Marxism-Leninism

【外阴】 wàiyīn 〈生理〉 vulva ◇ ～炎 vulvitis

【外因】 wàiyīn 〈哲〉 external cause

【外用】 wàiyòng 〈药〉 external use; external application: ～药水 lotion/ 只能～ for external use only

【外语】 wàiyǔ foreign language ◇ ～教学 foreign language teaching/ ～学院 institute of foreign languages

【外域】 wàiyù 〈书〉 foreign lands

【外援】 wàiyuán foreign aid; outside help; external assistance

【外在】 wàizài external; extrinsic: ～因素 external factor ◇ ～性 externalism

【外债】 wàizhài external debt; foreign debt

【外长】 wàizhǎng 〈简〉(外交部长) Minister of (或 for) For-

eign affairs; Foreign Minister
【外罩】 wàizhào outer garment; dustcoat; overall
【外痔】 wàizhì external piles (或 haemorrhoids)
【外资】 wàizī foreign capital
【外族】 wàizú ①people not of the same clan ②foreigner; alien ③other nationalities
【外祖父】 wàizǔfù (maternal) grandfather
【外祖母】 wàizǔmǔ (maternal) grandmother

## wān

**弯** wān ①curved; tortuous; crooked: ～～的月牙儿 a crescent moon/ 累累的果实把树枝都压～了。Clusters of fruit weighed the branches down. ②bend; flex: ～弓 bend a bow/ ～着腰插秧 bend over to transplant rice ③turn; curve; bend: 拐～儿 go round curves; turn a corner
【弯路】 wānlù ①crooked road; tortuous path ②roundabout way; detour: 少走～ avoid detours/ 由于缺少经验，我们工作走了～。Owing to lack of experience we took a roundabout course in our work.
【弯曲】 wānqū winding; meandering; zigzag; crooked; curved: 一条～的山间小道 a winding mountain path/ 一根～的木棍 a crooked stick/ 小河弯弯曲曲地向东流去。The brook meanders eastwards.
【弯头】 wāntóu 〈机〉 elbow; bend: 回转～ return bend/ 接合～ joint elbow
【弯子】 wānzi bend; turn; curve

**剜** wān cut out; gouge out; scoop out: 把苹果烂的地方～掉。Scoop out the rotten part of the apple./ 凶残的奴隶主～掉了奴隶的双眼。The brutal slave owner gouged out the slave's eyes.
【剜肉补疮】 wānròu-bǔchuāng cut out a piece of one's flesh to cure a boil — resort to a remedy worse than the ailment; resort to a stopgap measure detrimental to long-term interests

**湾** wān ①a bend in a stream: 河～ river bend ②gulf; bay: 渤海～ Bohai Bay/ 墨西哥～ the Gulf of Mexico ③cast anchor; moor: 把船～在那边。Moor the boat over there.

**蜿** wān
【蜿蜒】 wānyán ①(of snakes, etc.) wriggle ②wind; zigzag; meander: 小溪～流过田野。The stream winds through the fields.

**豌** wān
【豌豆】 wāndòu pea ◇ ～黄 〈食品〉 pea flour cake/ ～象 〈动〉 pea weevil

## wán

**丸** wán ①ball; pellet: 泥～ mud ball ②pill; bolus: 每服两～ take two pills each time
【丸剂】 wánjì pill
【丸药】 wányào pill (或 bolus) of Chinese medicine
【丸子】 wánzi ①a round mass of food; ball: 肉～ meatball ②pill; bolus

**纨** wán 〈书〉 fine silk fabrics
【纨裤子弟】 wánkù zǐdì profligate son of the rich; fop; dandy; playboy 又作"纨袴子弟"
【纨扇】 wánshàn round silk fan

**完** wán ①intact; whole: ～好 in good condition; intact/ 覆巢之下无～卵。When a bird's nest is overturned no egg can remain intact. ②run out; use up: 我们的煤快烧～了。We're running out of coal./ 听～别人的话 hear sb. out/ 信纸用～了。The writing pad is used up. ③finish; complete; be over; be through: 我马上就～。I'll be through soon./ 会开～了。The meeting is over./ 下期续～ to be concluded in the next issue ④pay: ～税 pay taxes
【完备】 wánbèi complete; perfect: 一套～的工具 a complete set of tools/ 指出不～之处 point out the imperfections
【完毕】 wánbì finish; complete; end: 第一期工程已经～。The first phase of the project has been completed./ 一切准备～。Everything is ready.
【完璧归赵】 wánbì guī Zhào return the jade intact to the State of Zhao — return sth. to its owner in good condition
【完成】 wánchéng accomplish; complete; fulfil; bring to success (或 fruition): ～任务 complete one's mission; accomplish a task; discharge one's duty/ ～国家计划 fulfil the state plan/ ～生产指标 hit the production target; fulfil the production quota
【完蛋】 wándàn 〈口〉 be done for; be finished
【完稿】 wángǎo finish a piece of writing; complete the manuscript
【完工】 wángōng complete a project, etc.; finish doing sth.; get through: 这座桥一个月就～了。It took only one month to complete the bridge.
【完好】 wánhǎo intact; whole; in good condition: ～无缺 intact; undamaged/ 货物已到，～无损。The goods have arrived in good condition.
【完婚】 wánhūn 〈书〉 (of a man) get married; marry
【完结】 wánjié end; be over; finish: 事情并没有～。This is not the end of the matter.
【完竣】 wánjùn (of a project, etc.) be completed
【完粮】 wánliáng 〈旧〉 pay the grain tax
【完了】 wánliǎo come to an end; be over
【完满】 wánmǎn satisfactory; successful: 找个～的解决办法 seek a satisfactory solution/ 会议～结束。The meeting came to a satisfactory close.
【完美】 wánměi perfect; consummate: ～无疵 perfect; flawless
【完全】 wánquán ①complete; whole: 他话没说～。He didn't give a full picture./ 做一个～的革命派。Be a revolutionary in the full sense. 或 Be a true revolutionary. ②completely; fully; wholly; entirely; absolutely: ～错了 be completely wrong/ ～不同 be totally different; have nothing in common/ ～相反 be the exact opposite/ ～正确 perfectly right; absolutely correct/ ～彻底为人民服务 serve the people heart and soul/ 他～同意我们的意见。He fully agrees with us./ 她～不考虑个人得失。She gave no thought whatsoever to personal gain or loss.
◇ ～变态 〈生〉 complete metamorphosis/ ～燃烧 complete combustion/ ～叶 〈植〉 complete leaf
【完人】 wánrén perfect man: "金要足赤，人要～"的形而上学的思想 the metaphysical notion that "gold must be pure and man must be perfect"
【完善】 wánshàn perfect; consummate: 设备～ very well equipped/ 新生事物难免有不够～的地方。Imperfections are almost unavoidable in newborn things./ 我们厂的规章制度日趋～。The rules and regulations of our factory are being perfected.
【完事】 wánshì finish; get through; come to an end: 你～了没有？Have you finished (the job)?/ 他们校对到深夜才

～。They didn't finish their proofreading until late at night.

【完整】 wánzhěng complete; integrated; intact: ～的工业体系 an integrated (或 all-round, comprehensive) industrial system/ 维护领土～ safeguard territorial integrity/ 许多珍贵的历史文物～地保存下来了。Many precious historical relics have been preserved intact./ 没有经济上的独立,一个国家的独立是不～的。Without economic independence, no country can achieve complete independence.

**玩** wán ① play; have fun; amuse oneself: ～儿牌 play cards/ 咱们～儿盘棋好吗? Shall we have a game of chess?/ 孩子们都喜欢～儿。Children all love to play./ 我们在青岛～了几天。We spent a few days enjoying ourselves in Qingdao./ 真好～儿! That's great fun!/ 他是说着～儿的。He only said it for fun. 或 He was only joking. ② employ; resort to: ～儿邪的 employ underhand means; not play fair/ ～手段 resort to crafty manoeuvres; play tricks ③ trifle with; treat lightly: ～法 trifle with the law ④ enjoy; appreciate: ～月 enjoy looking at the moon/ ～儿邮票 make a hobby of collecting stamps ⑤ object for appreciation: 古～ curio; antique

【玩忽】 wánhū neglect; trifle with: ～职守 neglect (或 dereliction) of duty

【玩火】 wánhuǒ play with fire

【玩火自焚】 wánhuǒ zì fén he who plays with fire will get burnt; whoever plays with fire will perish by fire

【玩具】 wánjù toy; plaything: ～汽车 toy car ◇ ～店 toyshop

【玩弄】 wánnòng ① dally with: ～女性 philander; dally with women ② play with; juggle with: ～词句 juggle with words; go in for rhetoric ③ resort to; employ: ～种种阴谋诡计 resort to all sorts of schemes and intrigues/ ～新花招 employ some new tricks/ ～两面派手法 engage in double-dealing

【玩偶】 wán'ǒu doll; toy figurine

【玩儿命】 wánrmìng 〈口〉 gamble (或 play) with one's life; risk one's life needlessly: 在大街上撒把骑车简直是～。To ride a bicycle in the street without holding the handlebars is simply to play with one's own life.

【玩儿完】 wánrwán 〈口〉 the jig is up

【玩赏】 wánshǎng enjoy; take pleasure (或 delight) in: ～风景 enjoy (或 admire) the scenery

【玩世不恭】 wán shì bù gōng be cynical

【玩耍】 wánshuǎ play; have fun; amuse oneself

【玩味】 wánwèi ponder; ruminate: 他的话很值得～。His words are worth pondering.

【玩物】 wánwù plaything; toy

【玩物丧志】 wán wù sàng zhì riding a hobby saps one's will to make progress; excessive attention to trivia saps the will

【玩笑】 wánxiào joke; jest: 开～ play a joke (或 prank) on; make jests/ 他这是开～,你别认真。He's only joking; don't take him seriously.

【玩意儿】 wányìr 〈口〉 ① toy; plaything ② thing: 新鲜～ newfangled gadget/ 他手里拿的是什么～? What's that thing in his hand?/ 他是什么～! What kind of louse is he! 又作"玩艺儿"

**顽** wán ① stupid; dense; insensate: ～石 hard rock; insensate stone ② stubborn; obstinate: ～敌 stubborn enemy; inveterate foe ③ naughty; mischievous

【顽磁】 wáncí 〈物〉 magnetic retentivity

【顽钝】 wándùn dull and obtuse; stupid; thickheaded

【顽梗】 wángěng obstinate; perverse

【顽固】 wángù ① obstinate; stubborn; headstrong: ～不化 incorrigibly obstinate/ ～地坚持错误立场 stubbornly cling to one's wrong position ② bitterly opposed to change; die-hard ◇ ～分子 diehard; die-hard element/ ～派 the diehards

【顽抗】 wánkàng stubbornly resist: 敌人再～就消灭它。If the enemy continue to resist stubbornly, wipe them out.

【顽皮】 wánpí naughty; mischievous

【顽强】 wánqiáng indomitable; staunch; tenacious: ～的革命精神 indomitable revolutionary spirit/ 同疾病进行～的斗争 carry on a tenacious struggle against illness

【顽石点头】 wánshí diǎntóu (be so persuasive as to make) the insensate stones nod in agreement

【顽童】 wántóng naughty child; urchin

【顽癣】 wánxuǎn 〈中医〉 stubborn dermatitis (e.g. neurodermatitis)

【顽症】 wánzhèng chronic and stubborn disease; persistent ailment

**烷** wán alkane

【烷化】 wánhuà 〈化〉 alkanisation; alkylation ◇ ～汽油 alkylation gasoline

【烷基】 wánjī 〈化〉 alkyl ◇ ～胺 alkylamine

## wǎn

**宛** wǎn ① winding; tortuous ② 〈书〉 as if: 音容～在 as if the person were still alive

【宛然】 wǎnrán as if: 这里山清水秀,～江南风景。The scenery here has great charm, reminding one of the land south of the Changjiang River.

【宛如】 wǎnrú just like: 革命的群众运动,～大海的怒涛,汹涌澎湃。The revolutionary mass movement is surging like the waves of the sea.

【宛延】 wǎnyán 〈书〉 meander

【宛转】 wǎnzhuǎn ① 见"辗转" zhǎnzhuǎn ② 见"婉转" wǎnzhuǎn

**莞** wǎn

【莞尔】 wǎn'ěr 〈书〉 smile: 不觉～ cannot help smiling

**挽** wǎn ① draw; pull: ～弓 draw a bow/ 手～着手 arm in arm ② roll up: ～起袖子 roll up one's sleeves ③ lament sb.'s death: ～诗 elegy ④ coil up

【挽歌】 wǎngē dirge; elegy

【挽回】 wǎnhuí retrieve; redeem: ～败局 retrieve a defeat/ ～面子 save face/ ～劣势 retrieve oneself from an inferior position; improve one's position/ ～损失 retrieve a loss/ ～影响 redeem (或 retrieve) one's reputation/ 无可～ irredeemable; irretrievable

【挽救】 wǎnjiù save; remedy; rescue: ～病人的生命 save the patient's life/ 想出一个有效的～办法 think out an effective remedy/ 不顾党对他的教育和～ disregard the Party's efforts to educate and redeem him

【挽联】 wǎnlián elegiac couplet

【挽留】 wǎnliú urge (或 persuade) sb. to stay: 再三～ repeatedly urge sb. to stay; press sb. to stay

【挽马】 wǎnmǎ 〈牧〉 draught horse

**惋** wǎn sigh

【惋惜】 wǎnxī feel sorry for sb. or about sth.; sympathize with

**菀** wǎn 见"紫菀" zǐwǎn

**晚** wǎn ①evening; night: 今～ this evening; tonight ②far on in time; late: ～唐 the late Tang Dynasty/ 睡得～ go to bed late/ ～做总比不做好。Better late than never./ 现在去还不～。It's still not too late to go. ③younger; junior

【晚安】 wǎn'ān 〈套〉 good night

【晚班】 wǎnbān night shift: 上～ be on the night shift

【晚报】 wǎnbào evening paper

【晚辈】 wǎnbèi the younger generation; one's juniors: 我是他的～。I am his junior by one generation.

【晚餐】 wǎncān supper; dinner

【晚场】 wǎnchǎng evening show; evening performance

【晚车】 wǎnchē night train

【晚稻】 wǎndào late rice

【晚点】 wǎndiǎn (of a train, ship, etc.) late; behind schedule: 火车～了。The train is late.

【晚饭】 wǎnfàn supper; dinner

【晚会】 wǎnhuì an evening of entertainment; soirée; social evening; evening party: 除夕～ New Year's Eve entertainment

【晚婚】 wǎnhūn marry at a mature age

【晚间】 wǎnjiān (in the) evening; (at) night

【晚节】 wǎnjié integrity in one's later years: 保持革命～ maintain (或 uphold) one's revolutionary integrity in one's later years

【晚近】 wǎnjìn in recent years; during the past few years

【晚景】 wǎnjǐng ①evening scene ②one's circumstances in old age

【晚年】 wǎnnián old age; one's later (或 remaining) years: 过着幸福的～ spend one's remaining years in happiness

【晚娘】 wǎnniáng 〈方〉 stepmother

【晚期】 wǎnqī later period: ～作品 sb.'s later works; the works of sb.'s later period/ 十九世纪～ the late 19th century; the latter part of the 19th century/ 他的病已到～。His illness has reached an advanced stage.

【晚秋】 wǎnqiū late autumn; late in the autumn ◇ ～作物 late-autumn crops

【晚上】 wǎnshang (in the) evening; (at) night

【晚熟】 wǎnshú 〈农〉 late-maturing ◇ ～品种 late variety

【晚霜】 wǎnshuāng 〈农〉 late frost

【晚霞】 wǎnxiá sunset glow; sunset clouds

【晚香玉】 wǎnxiāngyù 〈植〉 tuberose

**脘** wǎn 见"胃脘" wèiwǎn

**婉** wǎn ①gentle; gracious; tactful: ～商 consult with sb. tactfully (或 politely)/ ～顺 complaisant; obliging ②beautiful; graceful; elegant: ～丽 beautiful; lovely

【婉辞】 wǎncí ①gentle words; euphemism ②graciously decline; politely refuse

【婉言】 wǎnyán gentle words; tactful expressions: ～相劝 gently persuade; plead tactfully/ ～谢绝 graciously decline; politely refuse

【婉约】 wǎnyuē 〈书〉 graceful and restrained

【婉转】 wǎnzhuǎn ①mild and indirect; tactful: 措词～ put it tactfully/ 他那话虽然说得～,意见却很尖锐。His remark, for all its mildness, is nevertheless a sharp criticism. ②sweet and agreeable: 歌喉～ a sweet voice; sweet singing

**輓** wǎn ①pull; draw: ～车 pull (或 draw) a cart or carriage ②lament sb.'s death

【輓歌】 wǎngē dirge; elegy

【輓联】 wǎnlián elegiac couplet

**绾** wǎn coil up: 把头发～起来 coil one's hair/ ～个扣儿 tie a knot

**皖** Wǎn another name for Anhui Province

**碗** wǎn bowl: 摆～筷 put out bowls and chopsticks for a meal; lay the table

## wàn

**万** wàn ①ten thousand ②a very great number; myriad: ～事～物 myriads of things; all nature/ ～里长空 vast clear skies ③absolutely; by all means: ～不得已 out of absolute necessity; as a last resort ④(Wàn) a surname 另见 mò

【万般】 wànbān ①all the different kinds ②utterly; extremely: ～无奈 have no alternative (but to)

【万变不离其宗】 wàn biàn bù lí qí zōng change ten thousand times without departing from the original aim or stand; remain essentially the same despite all apparent changes

【万次闪光灯】 wàncì shǎnguāngdēng 〈摄〉 multitime flash lamp

【万端】 wànduān multifarious: 变化～ multifarious changes; kaleidoscopic changes/ 感慨～ all sorts of feelings welling up in one's mind

【万恶】 wàn'è extremely evil; absolutely vicious: ～的旧社会 the vicious (或 evil) old society/ ～的殖民主义制度 the diabolical system of colonialism/ ～之源 the root of all evil

【万方】 wànfāng ①all places ②extremely; incomparably: 仪态～ incomparably graceful

【万分】 wànfēn very much; extremely: ～感谢 thank you very much indeed/ ～抱歉 be extremely sorry/ ～高兴 be very happy; be highly pleased

【万古】 wàngǔ through the ages; eternally; forever: ～长存 last forever; be everlasting

【万古长青】 wàngǔ chángqīng remain fresh forever; be everlasting: 祝两国人民的友谊～! May the friendship between our two peoples last forever!

【万花筒】 wànhuātǒng kaleidoscope

【万家灯火】 wànjiā dēnghuǒ a myriad twinkling lights (of a city)

【万劫不复】 wànjié bù fù beyond redemption

【万金油】 wànjīnyóu ①a balm for treating headaches, scalds and other minor ailments ②Jack of all trades and master of none

【万籁俱寂】 wànlài jù jì all is quiet; silence reigns supreme

【万里长城】 Wànlǐ Chángchéng the Great Wall

【万里长征】 wànlǐ chángzhéng a long march of ten thousand *li*: 夺取全国胜利,这只是～走完了第一步。To win countrywide victory is only the first step in a long march of ten thousand *li*.

【万隆】 Wànlóng Bandung ◇ ～会议 the Bandung Conference

【万马奔腾】 wànmǎ bēnténg ten thousand horses galloping ahead — going full steam ahead

【万马齐喑】 wànmǎ qí yīn ten thousand horses stand mute: 大字报打破了"～"的沉闷空气。The big-character posters dispelled the apathetic atmosphere in which "ten thousand horses were all muted."

【万难】 wànnán extremely difficult; utterly impossible: ～照办 impossible to do as requested/ ～同意 can by no means agree

【万难】 wànnàn all difficulties: 排除～ surmount all difficulties

【万能】 wànnéng ① omnipotent; all-powerful ② universal; all-purpose
◇ ～材料试验机 universal testing machine/ ～分度头 universal dividing head/ ～工具机 all-purpose machine/ ～胶 all-purpose adhesive/ ～润滑脂 multipurpose grease/ ～工作台 universal table/ ～拖拉机 multipurpose tractor

【万年】 wànnián ten thousand years; all ages; eternity: 遗臭～ leave a bad name for generations to come

【万年历】 wànniánlì perpetual calendar

【万年青】 wànniánqīng 〈植〉① evergreen ② Japanese rohdea (*Rohdea japonica*)

【万千】 wànqiān multifarious; myriad: 变化～ eternally changing; changing all the time/ 思绪～ myriads of thoughts welling up in one's mind

【万全】 wànquán perfectly sound; surefire: ～之计 a completely safe plan; a surefire plan

【万人坑】 wànrénkēng a large pit used as a common grave (for massacred people before liberation); mass grave; a pit of ten thousand corpses

【万人空巷】 wànrén kōng xiàng the whole town turns out (to welcome sb. or celebrate some event)

【万世】 wànshì all ages; generation after generation

【万事】 wànshì all things; everything: ～起头难。Everything's hard in the beginning.

【万事大吉】 wànshì dàjí everything is just fine; all's well with the world: 以为这次胜利了便～的思想是危险的。It is a dangerous illusion to think that after this victory everything will go off without a hitch.

【万事亨通】 wànshì hēngtōng everything goes well

【万事俱备，只欠东风】 wànshì jù bèi, zhǐ qiàn dōngfēng everything is ready, and all that we need is an east wind — all is ready except what is crucial

【万事通】 wànshìtōng 〈讽〉 know-all

【万寿无疆】 wànshòu-wújiāng (wish sb.) a long life

【万水千山】 wànshuǐ-qiānshān ten thousand crags and torrents — the trials of a long journey

【万死】 wànsǐ die ten thousand deaths: 罪该～ deserve to die ten thousand deaths/ ～不辞 willing to risk any danger to do one's duty

【万岁】 wànsuì ① long live: 全世界人民大团结～！Long live the great unity of the people of the world! ② the emperor; (直接称呼) Your Majesty; (间接称呼) His Majesty

【万万】 wànwàn ①〔用于否定〕absolutely; wholly: 我～没有想到。This idea never occurred to me./ 那是～不行的。That's absolutely out of the question. 或 That won't do at all. ② hundred million

【万无一失】 wàn wú yī shī no danger of anything going wrong; no risk at all; perfectly safe; surefire

【万物】 wànwù all things on earth

【万向】 wànxiàng 〈机〉 universal ◇ ～阀 universal valve/ ～联轴节 universal coupling

【万象】 wànxiàng every phenomenon on earth; all manifestations of nature: 春回大地，～更新。Spring comes round to the earth again and everything looks fresh and gay.

【万幸】 wànxìng very lucky (或 fortunate); by sheer luck

【万一】 wànyī ①〈连〉 just in case; if by any chance: ～有人找我，就请他留个条。If by any chance somebody comes to see me, ask him to leave a message. ② contingency; eventuality: 防备～ be ready for all eventualities; be prepared for the worst ③ one ten thousandth; a very small percentage: 笔墨不能形容其～。It simply beggars description.

【万应灵丹】 wànyìng língdān cure-all; panacea

【万用电表】 wànyòng diànbiǎo 〈电〉 avometer; multimeter

【万有引力】 wànyǒu yǐnlì 〈物〉 (universal) gravitation ◇ ～定律 the law of universal gravitation

【万丈】 wànzhàng lofty or bottomless: ～深渊 a bottomless chasm; abyss/ 怒火～ a towering rage; a fit of violent anger/ ～高楼平地起。Lofty towers are all built up from the ground. 或 Great oaks from little acorns grow.

【万众】 wànzhòng millions of people; the multitude: 喜讯传来，～欢腾。Millions of people rejoiced at the happy news.

【万众一心】 wànzhòng-yīxīn millions of people all of one mind: 我们～建设社会主义现代化强国。We are building a modern, powerful socialist country with one heart and one mind.

【万状】 wànzhuàng in the extreme; extremely: 危险～ extremely dangerous/ 惊恐～ be frightened out of one's senses

【万紫千红】 wànzǐ-qiānhóng a riot (或 blaze) of colour: 百花盛开，～。Flowers of all sorts are blooming in a riot of colour.

**萬** wàn ten thousand (used for the numeral 万 on cheques, etc. to avoid mistakes or alterations)

**腕** wàn wrist

【腕子】 wànzi wrist: 手～ wrist

【腕足动物】 wànzú dòngwù brachiopod

**蔓** wàn a tendrilled vine: 这棵黄瓜爬～了。This cucumber plant is climbing.
另见 mán; màn

## wāng

**汪** wāng ① (of liquid) collect; accumulate: 汤里～着油。There are blobs of fat in the soup. ②〈量〉〔用于液体〕: 一～雨水 a puddle of rainwater ③〈象〉 bark; bowwow ④ (Wāng) a surname

【汪汪】 wāngwāng ① tears welling up; tearful: 泪～的 with tearful eyes ②〈象〉 bark; yap; bowwow: 狗～地叫。A dog is barking.

【汪洋】 wāngyáng (of a body of water) vast; boundless: 一片～ a vast expanse (或 body) of water/ 陷敌于人民战争的～大海之中 engulf the enemy in the boundless ocean of people's war

## wáng

**亡** wáng ① flee; run away: 出～ flee; live in exile ② lose; be gone: 唇～齿寒。If the lips are gone, the teeth will feel cold. ③ die; perish: 阵～ die (或 fall) in battle ④ deceased: ～妻 deceased wife ⑤ conquer; subjugate: 苏修～我之心不死。The Soviet revisionists are bent on subjugating our country.

【亡故】 wánggù die; pass away; decease

【亡国】 wángguó ① subjugate a nation; let a state perish: ～灭种 national subjugation and genocide ② a conquered nation: ～之民 the people of a conquered nation ◇ ～奴 a slave of a foreign power; a slave without a country; a conquered people

【亡灵】 wánglíng the soul of a deceased person; ghost; spectre

【亡命】 wángmìng ①flee; seek refuge; go into exile ②desperate: ～之徒 desperado

【亡羊补牢】 wáng yáng bǔ láo mend the fold after a sheep is lost: ～，犹未为晚。It is not too late to mend the fold even after some of the sheep have been lost.

**王** wáng ①king; monarch: 国～ king ②〈书〉grand; great: ～父 grandfather ③(Wáng) a surname

【王八】 wángba ①tortoise ②〈骂〉cuckold ◇ ～蛋 bastard; son of a bitch

【王不留行】 wángbùliúxíng 〈中药〉the seed of cowherb (*Vaccaria segetalis*)

【王朝】 wángcháo ①imperial court; royal court ②dynasty: 封建～ feudal dynasties

【王储】 wángchǔ crown prince

【王道】 wángdào kingly way; benevolent government: 所谓～，跟霸道一样，也是封建统治者统治人民的一种手段。Like the way of might, the so-called kingly way was a means used by feudal rulers to rule the people.

【王法】 wángfǎ the law of the land; the law

【王公】 wánggōng princes and dukes; the nobility: ～大臣 princes, dukes and ministers/ ～贵族 the nobility

【王宫】 wánggōng (imperial) palace

【王冠】 wángguān imperial crown; royal crown

【王国】 wángguó ①kingdom ②realm; domain: 从必然～到自由～ from the realm of necessity to the realm of freedom/ 独立～ independent kingdom; private preserve

【王侯】 wánghóu princes and marquises; the nobility

【王后】 wánghòu queen consort; queen

【王浆】 wángjiāng royal jelly

【王牌】 wángpái trump card ◇ ～军 *elite* troops; crack units

【王室】 wángshì ①royal family ②imperial court; royal court

【王水】 wángshuǐ 〈化〉*aqua regia*

【王孙】 wángsūn prince's descendants; offspring of the nobility

【王位】 wángwèi throne: 继承～ succeed to the throne

【王子】 wángzǐ king's son; prince

【王族】 wángzú persons of royal lineage; imperial kinsmen

**芒** wáng 见"麦芒" màiwáng
另见 máng

**忘** wáng
另见 wàng

【忘八】 wángba 见"王八" wángba

## wǎng

**网** wǎng ①net: 鱼～ fishnet; fishing net/ 发～ hairnet/ 蜘蛛～ cobweb/ 电～ electrified barbed wire ②network: 铁路～ railway network/ 广播～ a network of broadcasting stations ③catch with a net; net: ～着了一条鱼 net a fish ④cover or enclose as with a net: 眼里～着红丝 have bloodshot eyes

【网兜】 wǎngdōu string bag

【网获量】 wǎnghuòliàng 〈渔〉haul

【网开一面】 wǎng kāi yī miàn leave one side of the net open — give the wrongdoer a way out

【网篮】 wǎnglán a basket with netting on top

【网罗】 wǎngluó ①a net for catching fish or birds; trap ②enlist the services of: ～人材 enlist able men/ ～一小撮反动分子 scrape together a handful of reactionaries

【网络】 wǎngluò 〈电〉network: 有源～ active network/ 无源～ passive network

【网屏】 wǎngpíng 〈印〉screen 又作"网版"

【网球】 wǎngqiú ①tennis ②tennis ball ◇ ～场 tennis court/ ～拍 tennis racket

【网眼】 wǎngyǎn mesh

【网状脉】 wǎngzhuàngmài 〈植〉netted (或 reticulated) veins: ～叶 net-veined (或 reticulate) leaf

【网子】 wǎngzi ①net ②hairnet

**枉** wǎng ①crooked: 矫～ straighten sth. crooked; right a wrong ②twist; pervert: ～法 pervert the law ③treat unjustly; wrong: 冤～ wrong sb. (with false charges, etc.)/ ～死 be wronged and driven to death ④in vain; to no avail: ～活了半辈子 have wasted half a lifetime

【枉法】 wǎngfǎ pervert the law: 贪脏～ take bribes and pervert the law

【枉费】 wǎngfèi waste; try in vain; be of no avail: ～唇舌 be a mere waste of breath/ ～心机 rack one's brains in vain; scheme without avail

【枉驾】 wǎngjià 〈敬〉I am honoured by your visit

【枉然】 wǎngrán futile; in vain; to no purpose

**罔** wǎng 〈书〉①deceive: 欺～ deceive; cheat ②no; not: 置若～闻 take no heed of; turn a deaf ear to

**往** wǎng ①go: 来来～～ coming and going ②in the direction of; toward: ～东走去 go in an eastward direction/ 这车开～福州。The train is bound for Fuzhou. ③past; previous: ～事 the past
另见 wàng

【往常】 wǎngcháng habitually in the past; as one used to do formerly: 他～不这样。He was not like that before./ 我们～都是天黑了才收工。We used to go on working until it got dark.

【往返】 wǎngfǎn go there and back; journey to and fro: ～于成都、重庆之间 travel to and fro between Chengdu and Chongqing/ ～要多少时间？How long does it take to go there and back?

【往复】 wǎngfù move back and forth; reciprocate: 循环～，以至无穷 repeat itself in endless cycles
◇ ～泵 reciprocating pump/ ～式发动机 reciprocating engine/ ～运动〈机〉reciprocating motion; alternating motion

【往还】 wǎnghuán contact; dealings; intercourse: 经常有书信～ write to each other regularly; keep in contact by correspondence

【往来】 wǎnglái ①come and go ②contact; dealings; intercourse: 贸易～ trade contacts; commercial intercourse/ 友好～ exchange of friendly visits; friendly intercourse/ 他们俩～密切。The two of them are in close contact. 或 They see a lot of each other. ◇ ～帐 current (或 open, running) account

【往年】 wǎngnián (in) former years

【往日】 wǎngrì (in) former days; (in) bygone days

【往事】 wǎngshì past events; the past: 回忆～ recollections of the past

【往往】 wǎngwǎng 〈副〉often; frequently; more often than not: 这里春天～刮大风。It often blows hard here in spring./ 有些人～只看到当前的、局部的、个人的利益。Some people are prone to see only immediate, partial and personal interests.

【往昔】 wǎngxī in the past; in former times

**惘** wǎng feel frustrated; feel disappointed

【惘然】 wǎngrán frustrated; disappointed: ～若失 feel lost

**辋** wǎng rim (of a wheel)

**魍** wǎng

【魍魉】 wǎngliǎng demons and monsters

## wàng

**妄** wàng ① absurd; preposterous: 狂～ wildly arrogant ② presumptuous; rash: ～作主张 make a presumptuous decision/ ～加评论 make improper comments

【妄动】 wàngdòng rash (或 reckless, ill-considered) action: 轻举～ take rash action

【妄念】 wàngniàn wild fancy; improper thought

【妄求】 wàngqiú inappropriate request; presumptuous demand

【妄人】 wàngrén 〈书〉an ignorant and presumptuous person

【妄图】 wàngtú try in vain; vainly attempt: ～打破一个缺口 vainly attempt to make a breach/ ～掩盖事实真相 try in vain to cover up the truth; vainly attempt to conceal the facts

【妄想】 wàngxiǎng vain hope; wishful thinking: 阶级敌人～变天。The class enemy indulges in vain hopes of staging a comeback.

【妄语】 wàngyǔ ① tell lies; talk nonsense ② wild talk; rant 又作"妄言"

【妄自菲薄】 wàng zì fěibó improperly belittle oneself; unduly humble oneself; underestimate one's own capabilities

【妄自尊大】 wàng zì zūndà have too high an opinion of oneself; be overweening; be self-important

**忘** wàng ① forget: 他把这事全～了。He forgot all about it. 或 He clean forgot about the whole thing./ 饮水不～掘井人。When you drink the water, think of those who dug the well./ 我永远也～不了入党的那一天。I'll always remember the day I joined the Party. ② overlook; neglect: 不要只看到事物的一面而～了另一面。Don't look at only one aspect of the thing and neglect the other./ 别～了给我打电话。Don't forget to phone me./ 我～了拿笔记本。I've left my notebook behind.
另见 wáng

【忘本】 wàngběn forget one's class origin; forget one's past suffering: 你们是工人的后代,可不能～哪! You're sons and daughters of workers. You mustn't forget your class origin./ 我们过上了幸福的生活,可不能～。We must not forget our old sufferings, now that we are living happy lives.

【忘掉】 wàngdiào forget; let slip from one's mind: 我当时忙于工作,把这件事给～了。I was so busy working it simply slipped my mind./ 咱们把这件不愉快的事～吧。Let's forget the unpleasantness.

【忘恩负义】 wàng'ēn-fùyì devoid of gratitude; ungrateful

【忘乎所以】 wàng hū suǒyǐ forget oneself: 心血来潮,～ be carried away by a sudden impulse; lose one's head in a moment of excitement/ 不要因为胜利而～。Don't get swollen-headed because of victory. 又作"忘其所以"

【忘怀】 wànghuái forget; dismiss from one's mind: 当时情景我久久不能～。For a long time afterwards I could not get the scene out of my mind./ ～得失 not worried about personal gains or losses

【忘记】 wàngjì ① forget: 我永不会～我们初次见面的那一天。I'll never forget the day we first met. ② overlook; neglect; forget: 不能～自己的责任。One mustn't neglect one's duties./ 他紧张地工作,～了去吃晚饭。He was working so hard that he forgot to go for supper.

【忘年交】 wàngniánjiāo ① friendship between generations ② good friends despite great difference in age

【忘情】 wàngqíng ①〔常用于否定〕be unruffled by emotion; be unmoved; be indifferent: 不能～ be still emotionally attached ② let oneself go: ～地歌唱 let oneself go and sing lustily

【忘却】 wàngquè forget

【忘我】 wàngwǒ oblivious of oneself; selfless: ～地工作 work selflessly; work untiringly/ ～的精神 spirit of selflessness

【忘形】 wàngxíng be beside oneself (with glee, etc.); have one's head turned: 得意～ get dizzy with success; have one's head turned by success

【忘性】 wàngxing forgetfulness: ～大 be forgetful; have a poor memory

**旺** wàng prosperous; flourishing; vigorous: 购销两～。Both purchasing and marketing are brisk./ 人畜两～。Both men and livestock are flourishing./ 屋中炉火烧得正～。There was a roaring fire in the room.

【旺季】 wàngjì peak period; busy season: 西红柿～ tomato season

【旺盛】 wàngshèng vigorous; exuberant: ～的革命精神 a vigorous revolutionary spirit/ 士气～ have high morale/ ～的生命力 exuberant vitality/ 麦子长势～。Wheat is growing luxuriantly.

【旺月】 wàngyuè busy month (in business)

**往** wàng 〈介〉to; toward: ～左拐 turn to the left/ ～南走 go southwards/ ～前看 look forward/ 劲～一处使 all directing their efforts toward the same goal/ 水～低处流。Water naturally flows downhill. 或 Water always finds its own level.
另见 wǎng

【往后】 wànghòu from now on; later on; in the future: ～我们要加倍努力。From now on we'll redouble our efforts./ ～的日子会更好。As time goes on we'll live an even better life.

**望** wàng ① gaze into the distance; look over: 登山远～ climb a mountain and gaze far afield/ 放眼～去 look ahead as far as the eye can reach/ ～了他一眼 shoot a glance at him ② call on; visit: 拜～ call to pay one's respects/ 看～ call on; visit ③ hope; expect: ～速归。Hoping you'll return as soon as possible./ ～回信。Awaiting your reply./ 丰收在～。A bumper harvest is in sight. ④ reputation; prestige: 德高～重 be of noble character and high prestige ⑤〈介〉〔表示"对着""朝着"〕: ～我点点头 nod at me/ ～他笑了笑 smile at him ⑥ full moon ⑦ the 15th day of a lunar month: 既～ the 16th day of a lunar month

【望板】 wàngbǎn 〈建〉roof boarding

【望尘莫及】 wàng chén mò jí so far behind that one can only see the dust of the rider ahead; too far behind to catch up; too inferior to bear comparison

【望穿秋水】 wàngchuān qiūshuǐ 见"望眼欲穿"

【望而却步】 wàng ér quèbù shrink back at the sight of (sth. dangerous or difficult); flinch

【望而生畏】 wàng ér shēng wèi be terrified (或 awed) by the sight of sb. or sth.: 令人～ awe-inspiring; forbidding

【望风】 wàngfēng be on the lookout (while conducting secret activities); keep watch

【望风而逃】 wàng fēng ér táo flee at the mere sight of the oncoming force

【望风披靡】 wàng fēng pīmǐ flee pell-mell (或 helter-skelter) at the mere sight of the oncoming force: 我军所到之处，敌人～。Wherever our troops went, the enemy fled pell-mell before them.
【望江南】 wàngjiāngnán 〈植〉 coffee senna (*Cassia occidentalis*)
【望楼】 wànglóu watchtower; lookout tower
【望梅止渴】 wàng méi zhǐkě quench one's thirst by thinking of plums — console oneself with false hopes; feed on fancies
【望日】 wàngrì the 15th day of a lunar month
【望文生义】 wàng wén shēng yì take the words too literally; interpret without real understanding
【望闻问切】 wàng-wén-wèn-qiè 见"四诊" sìzhěn
【望眼欲穿】 wàng yǎn yù chuān anxiously gaze till one's eyes are strained; have long been looking forward with eager expectancy
【望洋兴叹】 wàng yáng xīngtàn lament one's littleness before the vast ocean — bemoan one's inadequacy in the face of a great task
【望远镜】 wàngyuǎnjìng telescope: 色球～ chromospheric telescope/ 射电～ radio telescope/ 双筒～ binoculars; field glasses/ 天文～ astronomical telescope/ (剧场用)小～ opera glasses/ 反射～ reflecting telescope; reflector/ 折射～ refracting telescope; refractor/ 折反射～ catodioptric telescope ◇ ～瞄准器 telescopic sight
【望月】 wàngyuè full moon
【望诊】 wàngzhěn 〈中医〉 observation of the patient's complexion, tongue, expression, behaviour, etc., one of the four methods of diagnosis
【望族】 wàngzú 〈书〉 distinguished family; prominent family

## wēi

**危** wēi ① danger; peril: 居安思～ think of danger in times of peace ② endanger; imperil: ～及生命 endanger one's life ③ dying: 病～ be critically ill; be dying ④〈书〉 high; precipitous: ～楼 a high tower/ ～崖 a precipitous cliff ⑤〈书〉 proper: 正襟～坐 sit up properly ⑥ (Wēi) a surname
【危殆】 wēidài 〈书〉 in great danger; in jeopardy; in a critical condition: 病势～ be dangerously ill; be critically ill
【危地马拉】 Wēidìmǎlā Guatemala ◇ ～人 Guatemalan
【危笃】 wēidǔ 〈书〉 critically ill; on the point of death
【危害】 wēihài harm; endanger; jeopardize: ～革命 endanger the revolution/ ～农作物 harm the crops/ ～治安 jeopardize public security/ ～公共利益 harm the public interest ◇ ～性 harmfulness; perniciousness
【危机】 wēijī crisis: 经济～ economic crisis/ ～重重 bogged down in crises; crisis-ridden/ ～四伏 beset with crises; crisis-ridden
【危急】 wēijí critical; in imminent danger; in a desperate situation: ～关头 critical juncture (或 time, moment)/ 情况十分～。The situation is desperate./ 伤势～。The wound may be fatal.
【危局】 wēijú a dangerous (或 critical, desperate) situation
【危惧】 wēijù worry and fear; be apprehensive
【危难】 wēinàn danger and disaster; calamity: 处于～之中 be in dire peril
【危如累卵】 wēi rú lěi luǎn as precarious as a pile of eggs; in a precarious situation
【危亡】 wēiwáng in peril; at stake: 民族～的时刻 when the nation's existence is in peril; when the fate of the nation hangs in the balance
【危险】 wēixiǎn dangerous; perilous: 冒生命～ at the risk of one's life/ 脱离～ out of danger/ 有电，～！ Danger! Electricity!
◇ ～地带 danger zone/ ～品 dangerous articles; dangerous goods/ ～人物 a dangerous person; a danger/ ～信号 danger signal
【危言耸听】 wēiyán sǒngtīng say frightening things just to raise an alarm; exaggerate things just to scare people: 这不是～，而是历史多次证明了的真理。This is not alarmist talk; it is a truth repeatedly borne out by history.
【危在旦夕】 wēi zài dànxī on the verge of death or destruction: 生命～。Death is expected at any moment./ 该城～。The city may fall at any moment.

**委** wēi
另见 wěi
【委蛇】 wēiyí ① 见"逶迤" wēiyí ② 见"虚与委蛇" xū yǔ wēiyí

**威** wēi ① impressive strength; might; power: 军～ the might of an army; military prowess/ ～震四方 known far and wide for one's military prowess/ 示～ demonstrate one's strength ② by force
【威逼】 wēibī threaten by force; coerce; intimidate: ～利诱 alternate intimidation and bribery; combine threats with inducements
【威风】 wēifēng ① power and prestige: 农民一起来就把地主的～打下去了。As soon as the peasants were aroused, they smashed the power and prestige of the landlord class./ 灭敌人的～ puncture (或 deflate) the enemy's arrogance/ 游击队在敌占区大显～。The guerrillas impressively demonstrated their courage and power in the enemy-occupied area. ② imposing; impressive; awe-inspiring: 瞧！这些女民兵多么～！ Look at the militant bearing of these militia women!
【威风凛凛】 wēifēng lǐnlǐn majestic-looking; awe-inspiring
【威风扫地】 wēifēng sǎodì with every shred of one's prestige swept away — completely discredited
【威吓】 wēihè intimidate; threaten; bully: 不顾敌人～ in defiance of the enemy's intimidation
【威力】 wēilì power; might: 群众运动的～ the power of the mass movement/ 人民战争～无穷。The might of people's war knows no bounds. 或 People's war is an invincible force.
【威灵仙】 wēilíngxiān 〈中药〉 the root of Chinese clematis (*Clematis chinensis*)
【威名】 wēimíng fame based on great strength or military exploits; prestige; renown: 人民子弟兵，～天下扬。The fame of the people's soldiers has spread far and wide.
【威尼斯】 Wēinísī Venice
【威权】 wēiquán authority; power
【威慑】 wēishè terrorize with military force; deter ◇ ～力量 deterrent force; deterrent
【威士忌】 wēishìjì whisky
【威势】 wēishì power and influence
【威望】 wēiwàng prestige: 崇高的～ high prestige
【威武】 wēiwǔ ① might; force; power: ～不能屈 not to be subdued by force ② powerful; mighty: ～雄壮 full of power and grandeur
【威胁】 wēixié threaten; menace; imperil: ～邻国的安全 threaten (或 menace) the security of a neighbouring country/ 超级大国的军备竞赛严重～着世界和平。The arms race between the superpowers is seriously imperilling world peace.

【威信】 wēixìn prestige; popular trust: 这个县委书记在群众中有很高的～。The country Party secretary has high prestige among the masses.
【威严】 wēiyán ① dignified; stately; majestic; awe-inspiring ② prestige; dignity: 保持～ keep up one's prestige
【威仪】 wēiyí impressive and dignified manner

**逶** wēi
【逶迤】 wēiyí winding; meandering: ～的山路 a winding mountain path/ 这条铁路～在群山之中。The railway winds its way through the mountains.

**萎** wēi decline: 火～了。The fire is going out.
另见 wěi

**偎** wēi snuggle up to; lean close to
【偎抱】 wēibào hug; cuddle
【偎依】 wēiyī snuggle up to; lean close to: 孩子～在母亲的怀里。The child snuggled up in its mother's arms.

**隈** wēi 〈书〉 ① river bend ② mountain recess

**煨** wēi ① cook over a slow fire; stew; simmer: ～牛肉 stewed beef ② roast (sweet potatoes, etc.) in fresh cinders

**微** wēi ① minute; tiny: 细～ minute; tiny/ 相差甚～。The difference is slight (或 negligible)./ ～火 slow fire/ ～云 thin clouds/ ～雨 drizzle ② profound; abstruse: 精～ subtle ③ decline: 衰～ on the decline ④ one millionth part of; micro-: ～米 micron (μ)
【微安】 wēi'ān 〈电〉 microampere ◇ ～计 microammeter
【微波】 wēibō 〈电子〉 microwave
◇ ～管 microwave tube/ ～理疗机 microwave therapeutic apparatus/ ～区 microwave region/ ～遥感 microwave remote sensing/ ～遥感器 microwave remote sensor
【微薄】 wēibó meagre; scanty: 收入～ have a meagre income/ 尽我们～的力量。We'll exert what little strength we have. 或 We'll do what little we can.
【微不足道】 wēi bùzú dào not worth mentioning; insignificant; inconsiderable; negligible
【微词】 wēicí 〈书〉 veiled criticism
【微法拉】 wēifǎlā 〈电〉 microfarad
【微分】 wēifēn 〈数〉 differential: 二项式～ binomial differential
◇ ～法 differentiation/ ～分析 differential analysis/ ～学 differential calculus
【微风】 wēifēng 〈气〉 gentle breeze
【微观】 wēiguān microcosmic
◇ ～世界 microcosmos; microcosm/ ～物理学 microphysics/ ～现象 〈物〉 microphenomenon
【微乎其微】 wēi hū qí wēi very little; next to nothing: 我一个人的力量是～的。On my own I can do very little.
【微积分学】 wēijīfēnxué 〈数〉 infinitesimal calculus; calculus
【微贱】 wēijiàn humble; lowly
【微粒】 wēilì ① particle: ～回降 〈物〉 fallout ② 〈物〉 corpuscle ◇ (光的)～说 corpuscular theory
【微粒体】 wēilìtǐ 〈植〉 microsome
【微量】 wēiliàng trace; micro-
◇ ～元素 trace element/ ～分析 microanalysis/ ～化学 microchemistry/ ～天平 microbalance
【微脉】 wēimài 〈中医〉 scarcely perceptible pulse
【微茫】 wēimáng 〈书〉 blurred; hazy
【微米】 wēimǐ micron (μ)
【微妙】 wēimiào delicate; subtle: 关系～ subtle relations/ 谈判进入～阶段。The negotiations have entered a delicate stage.
【微末】 wēimò trifling; insignificant: ～的贡献 an insignificant contribution/ ～的成就 an achievement of minor importance
【微气象计】 wēiqìxiàngjì micrometeorograph
【微热】 wēirè 〈医〉 low-grade fever
【微弱】 wēiruò faint; feeble; weak: 呼吸～ faint breath/ 光线～ faint light; glimmer/ 脉搏～ feeble pulse/ ～的声音 a thin voice/ ～的多数 a slender majority
【微生物】 wēishēngwù microorganism; microbe ◇ ～农药 microbial pesticide/ ～学 microbiology
【微调】 wēitiáo 〈电〉 fine tuning; trimming ◇ ～电容器 trimmer (condenser); padder
【微微】 wēiwēi ① slight; faint: ～一笑 smile faintly ② micromicro-; pico-: ～法拉 〈物〉 micromicrofarad; picofarad/ ～秒 picosecond
【微细】 wēixì very small; tiny: ～的血管 very small blood vessels
【微小】 wēixiǎo small; little: 极其～ infinitely small; infinitesimal/ ～的希望 slender hopes/ ～的进步 meagre progress
【微笑】 wēixiào smile
【微行】 wēixíng travel incognito
【微型】 wēixíng miniature; mini-
◇ ～化 microminiaturization/ ～汽车 minicar; mini/ ～照相机 miniature camera; minicam/ ～组件 〈电〉 micromodule
【微血管】 wēixuèguǎn (blood) capillary
【微言大义】 wēiyán-dàyì sublime words with deep meaning
【微恙】 wēiyàng slight illness; indisposition
【微震】 wēizhèn ① slight shock ② 〈地〉 〈物〉 microseism

**薇** wēi 见"蔷薇" qiángwēi

**巍** wēi towering; lofty
【巍峨】 wēi'é towering; lofty: ～的群山 lofty mountains
【巍然】 wēirán towering; lofty; majestic; imposing: ～屹立 stand lofty and firm; stand rock-firm/ 大桥～横跨在江上。The bridge stands majestic astride the river.
【巍巍】 wēiwēi towering; lofty: ～井岗山 the towering Jinggang Mountains

## wéi

**为** wéi ① do; act: 敢作敢～ decisive and bold in action; act with daring/ 事在人～。Human effort is the decisive factor. ② act as; serve as: 选她～人民代表 elect her a people's deputy/ 以此～凭。This will serve as a proof./ 有诗～证。A poem testifies to that. ③ become: 变沙漠～良田 turn the desert into arable land/ 一分～二。One divides into two. ④ be; mean: 一公里～二华里。One kilometer is equivalent to two *li*. ⑤ 〈介〉〔跟"所"字合用,表示被动〕: ～人民所爱戴 be loved and respected by the people/ 不～表面现象所迷惑 not be confused by superficial phenomena ⑥ 〈书〉〈助〉〔常跟"何"相应,表示疑问〕: 何以家～? What need have I of a home?
另见 wèi
【为非作歹】 wéifēi-zuòdǎi do evil; commit crimes; perpetrate outrages
【为富不仁】 wéi fù bù rén be rich and cruel; be one of the heartless rich
【为难】 wéinán ① feel embarrassed; feel awkward: ～的事 an awkward matter/ 使人～ embarrass sb.; put sb. in an awkward situation ② make things difficult for: 故意～ deliberately make things difficult for sb.

【为期】 wéiqī (to be completed) by a definite date: 以两周～ not to exceed two weeks/ 举办～一个月的摄影展览 hold a photo exhibition lasting a month/ 会议～三天。The meeting is scheduled to last three days./ ～不远。The day is not far off.
【为人】 wéirén behave; conduct oneself: ～正直 be upright
【为生】 wéishēng make a living: 以狩猎～ make a living as a hunter
【为时过早】 wéi shí guò zǎo premature; too early; too soon: 现在下结论～。It's still too early to reach a conclusion.
【为首】 wéishǒu with sb. as the leader; headed (或 led) by: 以某某～的代表团 a delegation headed (或 led) by so-and-so
【为数】 wéishù amount to; number: ～不少 come up to a large number; amount to quite a lot/ ～不多 have only a small number
【为所欲为】 wéi suǒ yù wéi 〈贬〉 do as one pleases; do whatever one likes; have one's own way
【为伍】 wéiwǔ associate with: 羞与～ think it beneath one to associate with sb.
【为限】 wéixiàn be within the limit of; not exceed: 费用以一百元～。The expenses shall not exceed 100 *yuan*.
【为止】 wéizhǐ up to; till: 迄今～ up to now; so far/ 到去年年底～ up to the end of last year/ 一直等到他回来～ wait till he returns/ 今天的讨论到此～。That's all for today's discussion.
【为重】 wéizhòng attach most importance to: 以大局～ put the general interest first/ 以人民的利益～ value the interests of the people above everything else
【为主】 wéizhǔ give first place to; give priority to: 以自力更生～,外援为辅 rely mainly on one's own efforts while making external assistance subsidiary/ 精神鼓励和物质鼓励相结合、而以精神鼓励～的方针 the policy of combining moral encouragement with material reward, with stress on the former

## 韦

wéi ① leather ② (Wéi) a surname
【韦伯】 wéibó 〈物〉 weber (Wb)

## 圩

wéi dyke; embankment: 筑～ build dykes
另见 xū
【圩田】 wéitián low-lying paddy fields surrounded with dykes
【圩垸】 wéiyuàn protective embankments in lakeside areas
【圩子】 wéizi ① protective embankments surrounding low-lying fields ② 见"围子" wéizi①

## 违

wéi ① disobey; violate: ～令 disobey orders/ ～警 violation of police regulations ② be separated: 久～了。I haven't seen you for ages.
【违碍】 wéi'ài taboo; prohibition
【违拗】 wéi'ào disobey; defy
【违背】 wéibèi violate; go against; run counter to: ～原则 violate a principle/ ～人民的意志 go against the will of the people/ ～马克思主义 run counter to Marxism/ ～自己的诺言 go back on one's word/ ～历史事实 be contrary to the historical facts
【违法】 wéifǎ break the law; be illegal: ～乱纪 violate the law and discipline/ ～行为 illegal activities; unlawful practice/ ～失职 transgression of the law and neglect of duty
【违反】 wéifǎn violate; run counter to; transgress; infringe: ～党的政策 run counter to the policy of the Party/ ～劳动纪律 violate labour discipline/ ～交通规则 violate traffic regulations/ ～刑法 commit a criminal offence/ ～事实 fly in the face of facts/ ～历史潮流 run counter to the trend of history/ ～决议的精神 be contrary to the spirit of the resolution/ ～社会发展规律 go against the laws of social development
【违犯】 wéifàn violate; infringe; act contrary to: ～纪律 violation of discipline; breach of discipline
【违禁】 wéijìn violate a ban ◇ ～品 contraband (goods)
【违抗】 wéikàng disobey; defy: ～命令 disobey orders; act in defiance of orders/ ～上级 defy the higher leading body; defy one's superiors; be insubordinate
【违例】 wéilì 〈体〉 breach of rules
【违误】 wéiwù 〔公文用语〕 disobey orders and cause delay: 迅速办理,不得～。This is to be acted upon without delay.
【违宪】 wéixiàn violation of the constitution: ～行为 unconstitutional act
【违心】 wéixīn against one's will; contrary to one's convictions: ～之论 words uttered against one's conscience; obviously insincere talk
【违约】 wéiyuē ① break a contract; violate a treaty ② break one's promise; break off an engagement
【违章】 wéizhāng break rules and regulations: ～行驶 drive against traffic regulations

## 围

wéi ① enclose; surround: 用篱笆把菜园子～上 enclose the vegetable patch with a fence/ 团团～住 completely surround; encircle; besiege/ ～着炉子坐 sit around a fire/ ～着他问长问短 gather round him, asking all sorts of questions/ ～湖造田 (build dykes to) reclaim land from a lake; reclaim lake bottom land and plant it to crops ② all round; around: 四～都是山。There are mountains all round. ③ 〈量〉〔两手拇指和食指或两只胳膊合拢的长度〕: 树大十～ a tree trunk ten arm spans around
【围脖儿】 wéibór 〈方〉 muffler; scarf
【围城】 wéichéng ① encircle (或 besiege) a city ② besieged city
【围城打援】 wéi chéng dǎ yuán besiege a city to annihilate the enemy relief force
【围攻】 wéigōng ① besiege; lay siege to: 停止～ abandon a siege ② jointly speak or write against sb.; jointly attack sb.: 遭到～ come under attack from all sides; be caught in a cross fire
【围击】 wéijī besiege; lay siege to
【围歼】 wéijiān surround and annihilate
【围剿】 wéijiǎo encircle and suppress
【围巾】 wéijīn muffler; scarf
【围垦】 wéikěn (build dykes to) reclaim land from marshes; enclose tideland for cultivation
【围困】 wéikùn besiege; hem in; pin down: 把敌人～在少数据点中 pin down the enemy in a few strongholds
【围拢】 wéilǒng crowd around
【围屏】 wéipíng 〈工美〉 (folding) screen
【围棋】 wéiqí *weiqi*, a game played with black and white pieces on a board of 361 crosses; *go*
【围墙】 wéiqiáng enclosure; enclosing wall
【围裙】 wéiqún apron
【围绕】 wéirào ① round; around: 月亮～着地球旋转。The moon revolves round the earth. ② centre on; revolve round: 这场斗争始终是～着走什么道路这个根本问题进行的。The struggle has always centred on the fundamental question of which road to take./ ～中心任务安排其他工作 arrange other work around the central task
【围网】 wéiwǎng 〈渔〉 purse seine; purse net ◇ ～渔船 purse seiner; purse boat
【围魏救赵】 wéi Wèi jiù Zhào besiege Wei to rescue Zhao — relieve the besieged by besieging the base of the besiegers

【围岩】 wéiyán 〈矿〉 country rock; surrounding rock
【围堰】 wéiyàn cofferdam; coffer
【围子】 wéizi ① defensive wall or stockade surrounding a village: 土～ fortified village ② curtain
【围嘴儿】 wéizuǐr bib

**闱** wéi ① a side gate of an imperial palace ② imperial examination hall (in feudal China)
【闱墨】 wéimò selections from papers of successful candidates at imperial examinations

**桅** wéi mast: 船～ mast/ ～顶 masthead
【桅灯】 wéidēng ①〈航海〉 mast head light; range light ② barn lantern
【桅杆】 wéigān mast
【桅樯】 wéiqiáng mast

**惟** wéi ① only; alone: ～你是问。You'll be held personally responsible. ②〈书〉 but: 母已痊愈,～体力尚未恢复。Mother's well now, but she hasn't fully recovered her strength yet. ③ thinking; thought: 思～ thinking ④〈书〉〈助〉〔用在年、月、日之前〕: ～二月既望 on the 16th of the second moon
【惟独】 wéidú only; alone: 人家都回家了,～她还在工作。She kept on working when all the others had gone home./ 他心里总是装着别人,～没有他自己。 His thoughts always turn to other people; hardly ever does he think of himself.
【惟恐】 wéikǒng for fear that; lest: ～落后 for fear that one should lag behind/ ～天下不乱 desire to see the world plunged into chaos; crave nothing short of nationwide chaos; desire to stir up trouble/ 我几次提醒他,～他忘了。I reminded him several times lest he should forget.
【惟利是图】 wéi lì shì tú be bent solely on profit; be intent on nothing but profit; put profit-making first: ～的思想 profit-before-everything mentality
【惟妙惟肖】 wéimiào-wéixiào 见"维妙维肖" wéimiào-wéixiào
【惟命是听】 wéi mìng shì tīng always do as one is told; be absolutely obedient 又作"惟命是从"
【惟我独尊】 wéi wǒ dú zūn overweening; extremely conceited
【惟一】 wéiyī only; sole: ～可行的办法 the only feasible way/ ～合法的政府 the sole legitimate government/ ～出路 the only way out
【惟有】 wéiyǒu only; alone: ～充分发动群众,才能取得胜利。Only when the masses are fully mobilized can victory be won./ ～通过暴力革命,才能打碎资产阶级国家机器。The bourgeois state machinery cannot be smashed except by a violent revolution.

**唯** wéi only; alone
另见 wěi
【唯成分论】 wéichéngfènlùn the theory of the unique importance of class origin
【唯恐】 wéikǒng 见"惟恐" wéikǒng
【唯理论】 wéilǐlùn 〈哲〉 rationalism
【唯利是图】 wéi lì shì tú 见"惟利是图" wéi lì shì tú
【唯美主义】 wéiměizhǔyì aestheticism
【唯名论】 wéimínglùn 〈哲〉 nominalism
【唯命是听】 wéi mìng shì tīng 见 "惟命是听" wéi mìng shì tīng
【唯能说】 wéinéngshuō 〈物〉 energetics
【唯我独尊】 wéi wǒ dú zūn 见"惟我独尊" wéi wǒ dú zūn
【唯我主义】 wéiwǒzhǔyì 〈哲〉 solipsism
【唯武器论】 wéiwǔqìlùn the theory that weapons alone decide the outcome of war
【唯物辩证法】 wéiwù biànzhèngfǎ 〈哲〉 materialist dialectics
【唯物论】 wéiwùlùn 〈哲〉 materialism
【唯物史观】 wéiwù shǐguān 〈哲〉 materialist conception of history; historical materialism
【唯物主义】 wéiwùzhǔyì 〈哲〉 materialism
【唯心论】 wéixīnlùn 〈哲〉 idealism
【唯心史观】 wéixīn shǐguān 〈哲〉 idealist conception of history; historical idealism
【唯心主义】 wéixīnzhǔyì 〈哲〉 idealism
【唯一】 wéiyī 见"惟一" wéiyī

**维** wéi ① tie up; hold together: ～系 hold together; maintain ② maintain; safeguard; preserve: ～护 safeguard; defend; uphold ③ thinking; thought ④〈数〉 dimension: 三～空间 three-dimensional space
【维持】 wéichí keep; maintain; preserve: ～秩序 keep order; maintain order/ ～现状 maintain the *status quo*; let things go on as they are/ ～生活 support oneself or one's family ◇ ～会 peace preservation association (a local puppet organization during the War of Resistance Against Japan, 1937-1945)
【维多利亚湖】 Wéiduōlìyàhú Lake Victoria
【维尔京群岛】 Wéi'ěrjīng Qúndǎo the Virgin Islands
【维管束】 wéiguǎnshù 〈植〉 vascular bundle
【维护】 wéihù safeguard; defend; uphold: ～团结 uphold unity/ ～人民的利益 safeguard the people's interests/ ～国家主权 defend state sovereignty/ ～民族尊严 vindicate (或 defend) national honour
【维纶】 wéilún 〈纺〉 polyvinyl alcohol fibre
【维棉】 wéimián 〈纺〉 vinylon and cotton blend
【维妙维肖】 wéimiào-wéixiào remarkably true to life; absolutely lifelike: 这幅画把儿童天真活泼的神态画得～。This picture catches the innocent vivacity of children.
【维尼纶】 wéinílún 〈纺〉 vinylon
【维生素】 wéishēngsù vitamin: 丁种～ vitamin D ◇ ～缺乏症 vitamin-deficiency; avitaminosis
【维数】 wéishù 〈数〉 dimension; dimensionality ◇ ～论 dimension theory
【维他命】 wéitāmìng vitamin
【维吾尔族】 Wéiwú'ěrzú the Uygur (Uighur) nationality, living in the Xinjiang Uygur Autonomous Region
【维系】 wéixì hold together; maintain: ～人心 maintain popular morale
【维新】 wéixīn reform; modernization: 变法～ Constitutional Reform and Modernization (1898)/ 日本明治～ the Meiji Reformation of Japan (1868)
【维修】 wéixiū keep in (good) repair; service; maintain: ～房屋 maintain houses and buildings/ ～汽车 service a car/ 设备～ maintenance (或 upkeep) of equipment/ ～得很好 be in good repair ◇ ～费 maintenance cost; upkeep/ ～工 maintenance worker

**帷** wéi curtain
【帷幕】 wéimù heavy curtain 又作"帷幔"
【帷幄】 wéiwò 〈书〉 army tent: 运筹～ devise strategies within a command tent
【帷子】 wéizi curtain: 床～ bed-curtain

**嵬** wéi 〈书〉 lofty; towering

## wěi

**伪** wěi ① false; fake; bogus: ～证 false witness/ ～钞

counterfeit (或 forged) bank note/ ～科学 pseudoscience/ 去～存真 eliminate the false and retain the true ② puppet; collaborationist: ～政权 puppet regime

【伪币】 wěibì ① counterfeit money; counterfeit (或 forged) bank note; spurious coin ② money issued by a puppet government

【伪顶】 wěidǐng 〈矿〉 false roof

【伪军】 wěijūn puppet army or soldier

【伪君子】 wěijūnzǐ hypocrite

【伪善】 wěishàn hypocritical: ～的言词 hypocritical words ◇ ～者 hypocrite

【伪书】 wěishū ancient books found to have been incorrectly dated, forged, or attributed to a wrong author; ancient books of dubious authenticity

【伪托】 wěituō forge ancient literary or art works, or pass off modern works as ancient ones

【伪造】 wěizào forge; falsify; fabricate; counterfeit: ～签名 forge a signature/ ～证件 forge a certificate/ ～帐目 falsify accounts/ ～历史 fabricate history; falsify history/ ～货币 counterfeit money; forge money/ ～的文件 spurious (或 fake, forged) document; pseudograph ◇ ～品 counterfeit; forgery/ ～罪 forgery

【伪装】 wěizhuāng ① pretend; feign: ～进步 pretend to be progressive/ ～中立 feign neutrality ② disguise; guise; mask: 以～出现的反革命分子 counterrevolutionaries in disguise/ 假的就是假的,～应当剥去。Sham is sham, and the mask must be stripped off. ③〈军〉 camouflage: 高射炮已经用树枝～起来。 The antiaircraft guns have been camouflaged with boughs of trees.
◇ ～工事 camouflage works/ ～猎潜舰 Q-boat/ ～网 camouflage net; garnished net

【伪足】 wěizú 〈动〉 pseudopodium

## 伟

wěi big; great: 身体魁～ tall and broad-shouldered; gigantic in stature; stalwart/ 雄～ magnificent/ ～力 mighty force

【伟大】 wěidà great; mighty: 生的～,死的光荣。A great life! A glorious death!/ 我们～的祖国 our great country/ ～的事业 a great undertaking/ ～的政治力量 a mighty political force/ ～的胜利 a signal victory

【伟绩】 wěijī great feats; great exploits; brilliant achievements

【伟晶岩】 wěijīngyán 〈地〉 pegmatite

【伟人】 wěirén a great man; a great personage: 当代的～ a great man of our time

【伟业】 wěiyè 〈书〉 great cause; exploit

## 苇

wěi reed

【苇箔】 wěibó reed matting

【苇塘】 wěitáng reed pond

【苇席】 wěixí reed mat

【苇子】 wěizi reed

## 纬

wěi ① weft; woof ②〈地〉 latitude: 北～四十度 forty degrees north latitude

【纬编】 wěibiān 〈纺〉 weft knitting ◇ ～针织物 weft-knitted fabric

【纬度】 wěidù 〈地〉 latitude: 高(低)～ high (low) latitudes

【纬纱】 wěishā 〈纺〉 ① weft (yarn); woof; filling ② pick

【纬线】 wěixiàn ①〈地〉 parallel ②〈纺〉 weft

## 尾

wěi ① tail: 牛～ ox-tail ② end: 排～ a person standing at the end of a line ③ remaining part; remnant: 扫～工程 the final phase of a project ④〈量〉〔用于鱼〕: 两～鱼 two fish

另见 yǐ

【尾巴】 wěiba ① tail: 夹起～逃跑 run away with one's tail between one's legs/ 夹着～做人 behave oneself tuck one's tail between one's legs; pull one's head in/ ～翘上了天 be very cocky ② tail-like part: 飞机～ the tail of a plane/ 彗星～ the tail of a comet ③ servile adherent; appendage: 不要做落后分子的～。Don't tail behind backward elements. ④ a person shadowing sb.: 甩掉～ throw off one's tail

【尾巴主义】 wěibazhǔyì tailism

【尾大不掉】 wěi dà bù diào ① leadership rendered ineffectual by recalcitrant subordinates ② (of an organization) too cumbersome to be effective

【尾灯】 wěidēng tail light; tail lamp

【尾骨】 wěigǔ 〈生理〉 coccyx

【尾矿】 wěikuàng 〈矿〉 tailings

【尾鳍】 wěiqí tail fin; caudal fin

【尾气】 wěiqì 〈化〉 tail gas

【尾欠】 wěiqiàn ① owe a small balance ② balance due

【尾声】 wěishēng ①〈乐〉 coda ② epilogue: 序幕和～ prologue and epilogue ③ end: 会谈已接近～。The talks are drawing to an end.

【尾数】 wěishù odd amount in addition to the round number (usually of a credit balance)

【尾水】 wěishuǐ 〈水〉 tail water

【尾随】 wěisuí tail behind; tag along after; follow at sb.'s heels: 孩子们～着巡回演出队走了好远。The kids followed the mobile cultural troupe for quite a distance.

【尾须】 wěixū 〈动〉 cercus

【尾翼】 wěiyì 〈航空〉 tail surface; empennage

【尾蚴】 wěiyòu 〈动〉 cercaria

【尾追】 wěizhuī in hot pursuit; hot on the trail of

【尾子】 wěizi 〈方〉 odd amount in addition to the round number (usually of a credit balance): 伙食～ mess savings

【尾座】 wěizuò 〈机〉 tailstock

## 炜

wěi 〈书〉 bright

## 玮

wěi 〈书〉 valuable; precious: ～宝 rare treasure

## 委

wěi ① entrust; appoint: ～以重任 entrust sb. with an important task ② throw away; cast aside: ～弃 discard/ ～之于地 cast sth. upon the ground ③ shift: ～过于人 put the blame on sb. else ④ indirect; roundabout: ～婉 mild and roundabout; tactful ⑤〈书〉 end: 原～ the beginning and the end ⑥ listless; dejected: ～靡 listless; dispirited ⑦〈书〉 actually; certainly: ～系实情。This is the true story. ⑧〈简〉(委员) committee member: 常～ member of a standing committee ⑨〈简〉(委员会) committee; commission; council: 党～ Party committee

另见 wēi

【委顿】 wěidùn tired; exhausted; weary

【委靡】 wěimǐ listless; dispirited; dejected: 精神～ listless; dispirited and inert/ ～不振 dispirited; in low spirits; dejected and apathetic

【委内瑞拉】 Wěinèiruìlā Venezuela ◇ ～人 Venezuelan

【委派】 wěipài appoint; delegate; designate

【委曲】 wěiqū (of roads, rivers, etc.) winding; tortuous

【委曲求全】 wěiqū qiú quán compromise out of consideration for the general interest; stoop to compromise

【委屈】 wěiqu ① feel wronged; nurse a grievance: 诉～ pour out one's grievances (或 troubles) ② put sb. to great inconvenience: 你只好～一点。You'll have to put up with it./ 对不起,～你了。Sorry to have made you go through all this. 或 Sorry to have put you to such inconvenience.

【委任】 wěirèn appoint: ～某人为首席顾问 appoint sb. chief adviser
◇ ～书 certificate of appointment/ ～统治 mandate/ ～统治地 mandated territory/ ～状 certificate of appointment
【委实】 wěishí really; indeed: 我～不知道。I really don't know./ ～不容易 by no means easy
【委琐】 wěisuǒ ①〈书〉 petty; trifling ② of wretched appearance
【委托】 wěituō entrust; trust: ～他负责这项工作 entrust him with responsibility for the work/ 队长～我主持今天的会议。The team leader asked me to chair the meeting on his behalf./ 这事就～你了。I leave this matter in your hands./ 代表们带着人民的～,聚集一堂,共商国家大事。Mandated by the people, the delegates assembled to discuss state affairs.
◇ ～商店 commission shop; commission house
【委婉】 wěiwǎn mild and roundabout; tactful: ～的语气 a mild tone/ 他批评得很～。He made his criticism very tactfully. ◇ ～语 euphemism
【委员】 wěiyuán committee member ◇ ～会 committee; commission; council
【委罪】 wěizuì put the blame on sb. else

**娓** wěi
【娓娓】 wěiwěi (talk) tirelessly: ～不倦 talk tirelessly/ ～动听 speak with absorbing interest/ ～而谈 talk volubly

**诿** wěi 见"委" wěi③

**萎** wěi wither; wilt; fade
另见 wēi
【萎靡】 wěimǐ 见"委靡" wěimǐ
【萎蔫】 wěiniān 〈植〉 wilting
【萎缩】 wěisuō ① wither; shrivel ② (of a market, economy, etc.) shrink; sag ③〈医〉 atrophy: 肝～ hepatatrophy; atrophy of the liver/ 肌肉～ amyotrophy; muscular atrophy
【萎陷疗法】 wěixiàn liáofǎ 〈医〉 collapse therapy
【萎谢】 wěixiè wither; fade

**唯** wěi 〈书〉 yea
另见 wéi
【唯唯诺诺】 wěiwěinuònuò be a yes-man; be obsequious

**猥** wěi ① numerous; multifarious: ～杂 miscellaneous ② base; obscene; salacious; indecent
【猥鄙】 wěibǐ 〈书〉 base; mean; despicable
【猥贱】 wěijiàn lowly; humble
【猥劣】 wěiliè 〈书〉 abject; base; mean
【猥陋】 wěilòu 〈书〉 base; mean; despicable
【猥琐】 wěisuǒ of wretched appearance
【猥亵】 wěixiè ① obscene; salacious ② act indecently towards (a woman)

**痿** wěi
【痿症】 wěizhèng 〈中医〉 flaccid paralysis; motor impairment as shown by weakness and numbness of the limbs, etc.

**韪** wěi 见"冒天下之大不韪" mào tiānxià zhī dà bùwěi

**鲔** wěi ①〔见于古书〕 sturgeon ② yaito tuna

## wèi

**卫** wèi ① defend; guard; protect: 保家～国 protect our homes and defend our country/ 自～ self-defence ② (Wèi) a surname
【卫兵】 wèibīng guard; bodyguard
【卫道】 wèidào defend traditional moral principles ◇ ～士〈贬〉 apologist
【卫队】 wèiduì squad of bodyguards; armed escort ◇ ～长 captain of the guard
【卫护】 wèihù protect; guard
【卫矛】 wèimáo 〈植〉 winged euonymus (*Euonymus alatus*)
【卫气营血辨证】 wèiqì-yíngxuè biànzhèng 〈中医〉 analysing, differentiating and judging the development of a (usually febrile) disease by studying the four conditions of the human body: superficial resistance, nutrition, vital function and blood
【卫生】 wèishēng hygiene; health; sanitation: 讲～ pay attention to hygiene/ 个人～ personal hygiene/ 工业～ industrial hygiene/ 公共～ public health/ 环境～ environmental sanitation/ 劳动～ labour hygiene/ 喝生水,不～。Drinking unboiled water is bad for the health.
◇ ～带 sanitary towel; sanitary napkin/ ～队 medical unit; medical team/ ～防疫站 sanitation and antiepidemic station/ ～间 toilet/ ～局 public health bureau/ ～科 health section/ ～裤 sweat pants/ ～球 camphor ball; mothball/ ～设备 sanitary equipment/ ～室 clinic/ ～学 hygiene; hygienics/ ～衣 sweat shirt/ ～员 health worker; medical orderly; medic/ ～院 commune hospital; hospital/ ～知识 hygienic knowledge/ ～纸 toilet paper
【卫士】 wèishì bodyguard
【卫戍】 wèishù garrison: 北京～区 the Beijing Garrison Command ◇ ～部队 garrison force
【卫星】 wèixīng ① satellite; moon: 木星有几个～? How many moons has the planet Jupiter? ② artificial satellite; man-made satellite: 气象～ weather satellite; meteorological satellite/ 通讯～ communications satellite ◇ ～城 satellite town/ ～国 satellite state; satellite country

**为** wèi ①〈介〉〔表示行为的对象〕: ～什么人的问题,是一个根本的问题,原则的问题。The question of "for whom?" is fundamental; it is a question of principle./ ～大多数人谋利益 work in the interests of the vast majority of people ②〈介〉〔表示原因〕: ～胜利而欢呼 hail a victory/ 我们～生活在伟大的社会主义祖国而自豪。We are proud to be living in our great socialist country. ③〈介〉〔表示目的〕: ～方便起见 for the sake of convenience/ 不～名,不～利 seek no personal fame or gain/ ～革命种田 till the land for the revolution/ 让我们～实现这一宏伟目标而共同努力。Let us strive together to attain this splendid goal. ④〈介〉〔表示"对""向"〕: 且～诸君言之。Now I'll inform you about it. ⑤〈书〉 stand for; support
另见 wéi
【为此】 wèicǐ to this end; for this reason (或 purpose); in this connection: ～而作出种种努力 make every effort to that end/ ～,大会作出一项重要决定。The conference made a very important decision in this connection./ 我们都～感到欢欣鼓舞。We all feel delighted and encouraged by this./ ～,我们不能投票。For this reason we must abstain from voting.
【为何】 wèihé why; for what reason
【为虎傅翼】 wèi hǔ fù yì give wings to a tiger — assist an evildoer 又作"为虎添翼"
【为虎作伥】 wèi hǔ zuò chāng help a villain do evil
【为了】 wèile for; for the sake of; in order to: ～巩固无产阶级专政 for the sake of consolidating the dictatorship of the proletariat/ ～保证我们的党和国家不改变颜色 in order to guarantee that our Party and country do not change

their colour

【为民请命】 wèi mín qǐngmìng plead in the name of the people; plead for the people: 打着～的幌子 pose as a spokesman of the people

【为人作嫁】 wèi rén zuò jià sewing sb. else's trousseau — doing work for others with no benefit to oneself

【为什么】 wèishénme why; why (或 how) is it that: ～犹豫不决呢？Why hesitate?/ ～不和群众商量呢？Why not consult the masses?

【为我之物】 wèi wǒ zhī wù 〈哲〉 thing-for-us

【为渊驱鱼】 wèi yuān qū yú drive the fish into deep waters — drive one's friends to the side of the enemy: ～，为丛驱雀 drive the fish into deep waters and the sparrows into the thickets

## 未

wèi ① have not; did not: 意犹～尽 have not given full expression to one's views/ 走访～遇。I called but you were out./ 尚～恢复健康 not yet recovered (from illness); not yet restored to health ② not: ～知可否 not know whether sth. can be done ③ the eighth of the twelve Earthly Branches

【未爆弹】 wèibàodàn 〈军〉 dud

【未必】 wèibì may not; not necessarily: 他～知道。He doesn't necessarily know./ 事情～会如此。Things may not necessarily turn out that way.

【未便】 wèibiàn not be in a position to; find it hard to: ～擅自处理 cannot do it without authorization/ ～立即答复 find it difficult to give an immediate reply

【未卜先知】 wèi bǔ xiān zhī foresee; have foresight

【未曾】 wèicéng have not; did not: ～听说过 never heard of it/ 历史上～有过的奇迹 a miracle unprecedented in history

【未尝】 wèicháng ① have not; did not: 她一夜～合眼。She didn't get a wink of sleep the whole night. ②〔用在否定词前面，表示委婉的肯定〕: 这～不是好主意。That might not be a bad idea./ 那样也～不可。That should be all right./ ～没有可取之处 not without its merits

【未成年】 wèichéngnián not yet of age; under age

【未定】 wèidìng uncertain; undecided; undefined: 行期～。The date of departure is not yet fixed. ◇ ～稿 draft/ ～界 undefined boundary; undemarcated boundary

【未敢苟同】 wèi gǎn gǒutóng 〈书〉 beg to differ; cannot agree: 你的意见，我～。I beg to differ. 或 Let's agree to differ.

【未婚】 wèihūn unmarried; single ◇ ～夫 *fiancé*/ ～妻 *fiancée*

【未决】 wèijué unsettled; outstanding: 悬而～的问题 an outstanding issue; an open (或 a pending) question/ 胜负～。The outcome (of the battle or contest) is not yet decided. ◇ ～犯 prisoner awaiting trial; culprit

【未可】 wèikě cannot: ～乐观 give no cause for optimism; nothing to be optimistic about/ 前途～限量 have a brilliant future

【未可厚非】 wèi kě hòu fēi be not altogether inexcusable; give no cause for much criticism

【未来】 wèilái ① coming; approaching; next; future: ～的一年 the coming year; next year/ 在～的斗争中 in the struggle to come/ ～二十四小时内将有暴雨。There will be a rainstorm within 24 hours. ② future; tomorrow: 美好的～ a glorious future/ ～是属于人民的。Tomorrow belongs to the people. ◇ ～派 futurism

【未老先衰】 wèi lǎo xiān shuāi prematurely senile; old before one's time

【未了】 wèiliǎo unfinished; outstanding: ～事宜 unfinished business/ ～的手续 formalities still to be complied with/ ～的债务 outstanding debts/ ～的心愿 an unfulfilled wish

【未免】 wèimiǎn rather; a bit too; truly: 这～太过份。This is really going too far./ 他的话～太多。He's rather talkative./ 你这样作～操之过急。You were a bit too impetuous in doing that.

【未能】 wèinéng fail to; cannot: ～实现 fail to materialize/ 阴谋～得逞 be frustrated in one's plot/ 他们～取得预期的结果。They have failed to achieve the expected result.

【未能免俗】 wèinéng miǎn sú be unable to rise above the conventions; cannot but follow conventional practice

【未然】 wèirán 见"防患未然" fáng huàn wèi rán

【未时】 wèishí the period of the day from 1 p.m. to 3 p.m.

【未始】 wèishǐ 见"未尝"②

【未遂】 wèisuì not accomplished; abortive: 政变～。The coup d'état aborted./ 自杀～ an attempted suicide ◇ ～罪 〈法〉 attempted crime; attempt

【未完】 wèiwán unfinished: ～待续 to be continued

【未详】 wèixiáng unknown: 本书作者～。The author of the book is unknown./ 病因～。What brought on the illness is not clear.

【未央】 wèiyāng 〈书〉 not ended: 夜～。The night is yet young.

【未雨绸缪】 wèi yǔ chóumóu repair the house before it rains; provide for a rainy day; take precautions

【未知量】 wèizhīliàng 〈数〉 unknown quantity

【未知数】 wèizhīshù ① 〈数〉 unknown number ② unknown; uncertain: 这事能不能办成还是个～。It's still uncertain whether this can be arranged.

## 位

wèi ① place; location: 座～ seat ② position: 名～ fame and position ③ throne: 即～ come to the throne/ 篡～ usurp the throne ④ 〈数〉 place; figure; digit: 个～ unit's place/ 十～ ten's place/ 小数～ decimal place/ 计算到小数点后五～ calculate to five decimal places/ 四～数 four-figure number; four-digit number ⑤ 〈量〉〔用于人，含敬意〕: 各～代表！Fellow Delegates!/ 今天我们家要来几～朋友。We have some friends coming to see us today.

【位次】 wèicì precedence; seating arrangement ◇ ～卡 place card

【位能】 wèinéng 〈物〉 potential energy

【位势米】 wèishìmǐ 〈气〉 geopotential metre

【位移】 wèiyí 〈物〉 displacement

【位于】 wèiyú 〈书〉 be located; be situated; lie: ～亚洲东部 be situated in the eastern part of Asia

【位置】 wèizhi ① seat; place: 请按指定的～坐。Will everybody please take his proper seat. ② place; position: 《红楼梦》在我国文学史上占有重要～。*A Dream of the Red Mansions* occupies an important place in the history of Chinese literature.

【位子】 wèizi seat; place

## 味

wèi ① taste; flavour: 甜～儿 a sweet taste ② smell; odour: 香～儿 a sweet smell; fragrance; aroma/ 臭～儿 an offensive (或 foul) smell; stench; stink ③ interest: 语言无～ insipid language; colourless language ④ distinguish the flavour of: 细～其言 ponder his words/ 玩～ ponder; ruminate ⑤ 〈量〉 ingredient (of a Chinese medicine prescription): 这个方子共有七～药。The prescription specifies seven medicinal herbs. 或 Seven medicinal herbs are prescribed.

【味道】 wèidao taste; flavour: 这个菜～很好。This dish is delicious./ 你们年轻人没尝过当童工是什么～。You young people don't know what it was like to slave away as a child labourer./ 心里有一股说不出的～ have an indescribable feeling/ 他的话里有点讽刺的～。There's a touch of irony in his remarks.

【味精】 wèijīng monosodium glutamate; gourmet powder

【味觉】 wèijué sense of taste

【味蕾】 wèilěi 〈生理〉 taste bud

【味同嚼蜡】 wèi tóng jiáo là it is like chewing wax — insipid

**畏** wèi ① fear: 大无～ fearless; dauntless/ 不～强敌 stand in no fear of a formidable enemy ② respect: 后生可～。Youth are to be regarded with respect.

【畏避】 wèibì avoid sth. out of fear; recoil from; flinch from

【畏光】 wèiguāng 〈医〉 photophobia

【畏忌】 wèijì have scruples; fear; dread

【畏惧】 wèijù fear; dread: 彻底的唯物主义者是无所～的。Thoroughgoing materialists are fearless.

【畏难】 wèinán be afraid of difficulty: ～情绪 fear of difficulty

【畏怯】 wèiqiè cowardly; timid; chickenhearted

【畏首畏尾】 wèishǒu-wèiwěi be full of misgivings; be overcautious

【畏缩】 wèisuō recoil; shrink; flinch: 在困难面前从不～ never shrink (或 flinch) from difficulty/ ～不前 recoil in fear; hesitate to press forward; hang back

【畏途】 wèitú 〈书〉 a dangerous road — a perilous undertaking: 视为～ regard it as a dangerous road to take; be afraid to undertake it

【畏葸】 wèixǐ 〈书〉 timid; afraid: ～不前 be afraid to advance

【畏友】 wèiyǒu esteemed friend

【畏罪】 wèizuì dread punishment for one's crime: ～潜逃 abscond to avoid punishment/ ～自杀 commit suicide to escape punishment

**胃** wèi stomach

【胃癌】 wèi'ái cancer of the stomach; gastric carcinoma

【胃病】 wèibìng stomach trouble; gastric disease

【胃肠炎】 wèichángyán gastroenteritis

【胃蛋白酶】 wèidànbáiméi 〈生理〉 pepsin

【胃毒剂】 wèidújì 〈农〉 stomach poison

【胃镜】 wèijìng gastroscope ◇ ～检查 gastrocopy

【胃口】 wèikǒu ① appetite: ～好 have a good appetite/ 没有～ have no appetite ② liking: 对～ to one's liking

【胃溃疡】 wèikuìyáng gastric ulcer

【胃扩张】 wèikuòzhāng dilatation of the stomach; gastrectasis

【胃切除术】 wèiqiēchúshù gastrectomy

【胃酸】 wèisuān hydrochloric acid in gastric juice: ～过多 hyperchlorhydria; hyperacidity/ ～过少 hypochlorhydria; hypoacidity

【胃痛】 wèitòng stomachache; gastralgia

【胃脘】 wèiwǎn 〈中医〉 gastral cavity

【胃下垂】 wèixiàchuí ptosis of the stomach; gastroptosis

【胃腺】 wèixiàn 〈生理〉 gastric gland

【胃炎】 wèiyán gastritis

【胃液】 wèiyè 〈生理〉 gastric juice

**谓** wèi ① say: 或～ someone says/ 可～神速 may well be termed lightning speed ② call; name: 所～ so-called/ 此之～形式主义。This is what is called formalism./ 何～平衡？What is meant by equilibrium? ③ meaning; sense: 无～的话 senseless talk; twaddle

【谓语】 wèiyǔ 〈语〉 predicate

**尉** wèi ① 见"尉官" ② (Wèi) a surname

另见 yù

【尉官】 wèiguān a military officer above the rank of warrant officer and below that of major; a junior officer

**遗** wèi 〈书〉 offer as a gift; make a present of sth.: ～之千金 present sb. with a generous gift of money

另见 yí

**喂** wèi ① 〈叹〉[招呼的声音] hello; hey: ～,请接三一三号分机。Hello, extension 313, please!/ ～,你的围巾快掉了。Hey, your scarf is slipping off. ② feed: ～猪 feed pigs/ 给病人～饭 feed a patient

【喂奶】 wèinǎi breast-feed; suckle; nurse

【喂养】 wèiyǎng feed; raise; keep: ～家禽 keep fowls

**渭** Wèi short for the Weihe River

**猬** wèi 〈动〉 hedgehog

【猬集】 wèijí 〈书〉 (of matters) as numerous as the spines of a hedgehog: 诸事～ have too many things to attend to; have too many irons in the fire

**蔚** wèi 〈书〉 ① luxuriant; grand ② colourful: 云蒸霞～。The rosy clouds are slowly rising.

【蔚蓝】 wèilán azure; sky blue: ～的天空 a bright blue sky/ ～的海洋 the blue sea

【蔚然成风】 wèirán chéng fēng become common practice; become the order of the day: 干部参加集体生产劳动已～。Cadres taking part in collective productive labour has become the order of the day.

【蔚为大观】 wèi wéi dàguān present a splendid sight; afford a magnificent view: 展出的美术作品,～。There's a splendid array of works of art on display.

**慰** wèi ① console; comfort: ～勉 comfort and encourage ② be relieved: 知你平安到达,甚～。I am greatly relieved to learn that you have arrived safely.

【慰劳】 wèiláo bring gifts to, or send one's best wishes to, in recognition of services rendered

【慰问】 wèiwèn express sympathy and solicitude for; extend one's regards to; convey greetings to; salute: 对灾区人民表示～ express sympathy and solicitude for the people of disaster areas/ 同志们辛苦了,我们特来～你们。Comrades, you've been working hard. We've come to salute you./ 请向他们转达我们亲切的～。Please convey to them our sincere solicitude.

◇ ～袋 gift bag/ ～团 a group sent to convey greetings and appreciation/ ～信 a letter expressing one's appreciation or sympathy/ ～演出 a special performance as an expression of gratitude or appreciation

【慰唁】 wèiyàn condole with sb.

**魏** Wèi ① the Kingdom of Wei (220-265), one of the Three Kingdoms ② a surname

【魏碑】 Wèibēi ① tablet inscriptions of the Northern Dynasties (386-581) ② model calligraphy represented by the aforesaid inscriptions

**鳚** wèi 〈动〉 blenny

## wēn

**温** wēn ① warm; lukewarm: ～水 lukewarm water ②

temperature: 体～ temperature (of the body) ③ warm up: 把酒～一下 warm up the wine ④ review; revise: ～课 review (或 revise) one's lessons ⑤ (Wēn) a surname

【温饱】 wēnbǎo dress warmly and eat one's fill: 终年劳累,不得～ toil all the year round without enough to eat and wear

【温标】 wēnbiāo 〈物〉 thermometric scale: 华氏～ Fahrenheit's thermometric scale/ 摄氏～ Celsius' thermometric scale/ 开氏～ Kelvin's thermometric scale

【温差】 wēnchā difference in temperature; range of temperature: 这里白天和夜晚的～很大。The temperature here varies greatly between day and night.

【温差电】 wēnchādiàn 〈物〉 thermoelectricity ◇ ～检波器 thermodetector/ ～偶 thermoelectric couple; thermocouple

【温床】 wēnchuáng ①〈农〉 hotbed ② breeding ground; hotbed: 小生产是产生资本主义的～。Small-scale production is a hotbed of capitalism.

【温存】 wēncún ① attentive (usu. to a person of the opposite sex) ② gentle; kind

【温带】 wēndài temperate zone

【温度】 wēndù temperature: 室内(外)～ indoor (outdoor) temperature ◇ ～计〈气〉 thermograph

【温度表】 wēndùbiǎo thermometer: 摄氏～ centigrade (或 Celsius) thermometer/ 华氏～ Fahrenheit thermometer

【温故知新】 wēngù-zhīxīn ① gain new insights through restudying old material ② reviewing the past helps one to understand the present

【温和】 wēnhé ① temperate; mild; moderate: 气候～ a temperate climate ② gentle; mild: 性情～ a gentle disposition/ 语气～ a mild tone ◇ ～派 moderates
另见 wēnhuo

【温厚】 wēnhòu gentle and kind; good-natured

【温和】 wēnhuo lukewarm; warm: 汤还～呢。The soup is still warm.
另见 wēnhé

【温觉】 wēnjué 〈生理〉 sense of heat

【温暖】 wēnnuǎn warm: 天气～ warm weather/ 感到革命大家庭的～ feel the warmth of living in the big revolutionary family/ 对同志象春天般的～ be as mild as spring towards one's comrades

【温情】 wēnqíng ① tender feeling: ～脉脉 full of tender feeling ② too softhearted: 你对他太～了。You're too lenient with him. ◇ ～主义 excessive tenderheartedness; undue leniency

【温泉】 wēnquán hot spring

【温柔】 wēnróu gentle and soft

【温湿计】 wēnshījì hygrothermograph; thermohygrograph

【温室】 wēnshì hothouse; greenhouse; glasshouse; conservatory: ～育苗 nurse young plants in hothouses

【温顺】 wēnshùn docile; meek: 象小羊一般～ as meek as a lamb

【温汤浸种】 wēntāng jìnzhǒng 〈农〉 hot water treatment of seeds

【温暾】 wēntūn 〈方〉 lukewarm; tepid: ～水 lukewarm water 又作"温吞"

【温文尔雅】 wēnwén-ěryǎ gentle and cultivated

【温习】 wēnxí review; revise: ～功课 review one's lessons

【温煦】 wēnxù warm

【温血动物】 wēnxuè dòngwù warm-blooded animal

【温驯】 wēnxún (of animals) docile; meek; tame

**榅** wēn

【榅桲】 wēnpo 〈植〉 quince (*Cydonia oblonga*)

**瘟** wēn 〈中医〉 acute communicable diseases

【瘟病】 wēnbìng 〈中医〉 seasonal febrile diseases

【瘟神】 wēnshén god of plague

【瘟疫】 wēnyì pestilence

**鳁** wēn sardine

【鳁鲸】 wēnjīng 〈动〉 sei whale; rorqual

## wén

**文** wén ① character; script; writing: 钟鼎～ inscriptions on ancient bronze objects/ 《说～解字》 *Analytical Dictionary of Characters* ② language: 英～ the English language ③ literary composition; writing: ～如其人。The writing mirrors the writer./ 情～并茂 excellent in both content and language ④ literary language: 半～半白 half literary and half vernacular ⑤ culture: ～物 cultural relic ⑥ formal ritual: 虚～ a mere formality ⑦ civilian; civil: ～职 civilian post ⑧ gentle; refined: ～野之分 the difference between crudeness and refinement ⑨ certain natural phenomena: 天～ astronomy/ 水～ hydrology ⑩ cover up; paint over: ～过饰非 conceal faults and gloss over wrongs ⑪ 〈量〉[用于旧时的铜钱]: 一～钱 a cash/ 一～不值 not worth a farthing ⑫ (Wén) a surname

【文本】 wénběn text; version: 本合同两种～同等有效。Both texts of the contract are equally valid.

【文笔】 wénbǐ style of writing: ～流利 write in an easy and fluent style

【文不对题】 wén bù duì tí irrelevant to the subject; beside the point; wide of the mark

【文不加点】 wén bù jiā diǎn never blot a line in writing — have a facile pen

【文才】 wéncái literary talent; aptitude for writing

【文采】 wéncǎi ① rich and bright colours ② literary grace; literary talent: 这个人很有～。This is a man of unusual literary talent.

【文昌鱼】 wénchāngyú 〈动〉 lancelet

【文抄公】 wénchāogōng plagiarist

【文辞】 wéncí diction; language: ～优美 exquisite diction; elegant language

【文从字顺】 wéncóng-zìshùn readable and fluent

【文旦】 wéndàn 〈方〉 pomelo

【文斗】 wéndòu verbal struggle

【文牍】 wéndú official documents and correspondence ◇ ～主义 red tape

【文法】 wénfǎ grammar

【文房四宝】 wénfáng sìbǎo the four treasures of the study (writing brush, ink stick, ink slab and paper)

【文风】 wénfēng style of writing: 整顿～ rectify the style of writing

【文风不动】 wénfēng bù dòng absolutely still

【文稿】 wéngǎo manuscript; draft

【文告】 wéngào proclamation; statement; message

【文革】 Wéngé 〈简〉(文化大革命) the Cultural Revolution

【文蛤】 wéngé 〈动〉 clam

【文工团】 wéngōngtuán song and dance ensemble; art troupe; cultural troupe

【文官】 wénguān civil official

【文冠果】 wénguānguǒ 〈植〉 shiny-leaved yellowhorn (*Xanthoceras sorbifolia*)

【文过饰非】 wénguò-shìfēi conceal faults and gloss over wrongs; gloss over one's faults; cover up (或 explain away) one's errors

【文豪】 wénháo literary giant; great writer; eminent writer

【文化】 wénhuà ① civilization; culture: 中国～ Chinese

civilization (或 culture)/ 仰韶～ the Yangshao Culture/ ～和思想阵地 positions on the cultural and ideological fronts ② education; culture; schooling; literacy: 学～ acquire an elementary education; acquire literacy; learn to read and write/ 有社会主义觉悟有～的劳动者 a worker with both socialist consciousness and culture; a socialist-minded cultured (或 educated) worker/ 她的～程度比我高。She's better educated than I.

◇ ～参赞 cultural counsellor; cultural attaché/ ～宫 palace of culture; cultural palace/ ～馆(站) cultural centre/ ～机关 cultural institution/ ～交流 cultural exchange/ ～界 cultural circles/ ～课 literacy class; general knowledge course/ ～侵略 cultural aggression; cultural penetration/ ～人 cultural worker; intellectual/ ～渗透 cultural infiltration/ ～事业 cultural establishments; cultural undertakings/ ～水平 cultural level; educational level/ ～遗产 cultural heritage; cultural legacy/ ～遗址 a site of ancient cultural remains; remains of an ancient culture/ ～用品 stationery/ ～专制主义 cultural tyranny

【文化大革命】 Wénhuà Dàgémìng 〈简〉(无产阶级文化大革命) the Great Proletarian Cultural Revolution; the Great Cultural Revolution

【文火】 wénhuǒ slow fire; gentle heat: ～焖四十分钟 simmer gently for forty minutes

【文集】 wénjí collected works

【文件】 wénjiàn documents; papers; instruments
◇ ～编号 the reference or serial number of a document/ ～袋 documents pouch; dispatch case/ ～柜 filing cabinet

【文教】 wénjiào 〈简〉(文化教育) culture and education
◇ ～界 cultural and educational circles/ ～事业 cultural and educational work; culture and education

【文静】 wénjìng gentle and quiet

【文具】 wénjù writing materials; stationery ◇ ～店 stationer's; stationery shop

【文科】 wénkē liberal arts ◇ ～学校 liberal arts school/ ～院校 colleges of arts

【文库】 wénkù a series of books issued in a single format by a publisher; library

【文莱】 Wénlái Brunei

【文理】 wénlǐ unity and coherence in writing: ～通顺 have unity and coherence; make smooth reading/ ～不通 be illogical and ungrammatical

【文盲】 wénmáng an illiterate person: 扫除～ wipe out illiteracy

【文明】 wénmíng ① civilization; culture: 物质～ material civilization/ ～古国 a country with an ancient civilization ② civilized

【文墨】 wénmò writing: 粗通～ barely know the rudiments of writing

【文鸟】 wénniǎo 〈动〉 mannikin

【文痞】 wénpǐ literary prostitute

【文凭】 wénpíng diploma

【文人】 wénrén man of letters; scholar; *literati*: ～相轻。Scholars tend to scorn each other.

【文弱】 wénruò gentle and frail-looking: ～书生 a frail scholar

【文身】 wénshēn 〈书〉 tattoo

【文史】 wénshǐ literature and history ◇ ～馆 Research Institute of Culture and History/ ～资料 historical accounts of past events

【文书】 wénshū ① document; official dispatch ② copy clerk

【文思】 wénsī the thread of ideas in writing; the train of thought in writing: ～敏捷 have a ready pen

【文坛】 wéntán the literary world (或 arena, circles); the world of letters

【文体】 wéntǐ ① type of writing; literary form; style ② 〈简〉(文娱体育) recreation and sports ◇ ～活动 recreational and sports activities

【文恬武嬉】 wén tián wǔ xī (of a corrupt regime) the civil officials are indolent and the military officers frivolous

【文武】 wén-wǔ civil and military: ～官员 civil and military officials/ ～双全 be well versed in both polite letters and martial arts

【文物】 wénwù cultural relic; historical relic: ～保护 preservation of cultural relics; protection of historical relics

【文献】 wénxiàn document; literature: 历史～ historical documents/ 马列主义～ Marxist-Leninist literature ◇ ～记录片 documentary (film)

【文选】 wénxuǎn selected works; literary selections: 《列宁～》 *Selections from Lenin*/ 活叶～ loose-leaf literary selections

【文学】 wénxué literature
◇ ～家 writer; man of letters; *literati*/ ～流派 schools of literature/ ～批评 literary criticism/ ～作品 literary works

【文学语言】 wénxué yǔyán ① 〈语〉 standard speech ② literary language

【文雅】 wényǎ elegant; refined; cultured; polished: 举止～ refined in manner

【文言】 wényán classical Chinese ◇ ～文 writings in classical Chinese; classical style of writing

【文艺】 wényì literature and art
◇ ～创作 literary and artistic creation/ ～队伍 ranks of writers and artists/ ～复兴 the Renaissance/ ～工作 work in the literary and artistic fields/ ～工作者 literary and art workers; writers and artists/ ～会演 theatrical festival/ ～节目 programme of entertainment; theatrical items; theatrical performance/ ～界 literary and art circles; the world of literature and art/ ～理论 theory of literature and art/ ～路线 line in literature and art/ ～批评 literary or art criticism/ ～批评家 literary or art critic/ ～思潮 trend of thought in literature and art/ ～团体 literature and art organization; theatre company; theatre troupe/ ～作品 literary and artistic works/ ～座谈会 forum on literature and art

【文娱】 wényú cultural recreation; entertainment ◇ ～活动 recreational activities

【文责】 wénzé the responsibility an author should assume for his own writings; author's responsibility: ～自负。The author takes sole responsibility for his views.

【文摘】 wénzhāi abstract; digest

【文章】 wénzhāng ① essay; article ② literary works; writings ③ hidden meaning; implied meaning: 话里有～。There is an insinuation in that remark. 或 That's an insinuating remark./ 其中大有～。There is a lot behind all this.

【文职】 wénzhí civilian post ◇ ～人员 nonmilitary personnel

【文质彬彬】 wénzhì bīnbīn gentle; suave

【文绉绉】 wénzhōuzhōu genteel: 说话～的 speak in an elegant manner

【文竹】 wénzhú 〈植〉 asparagus fern (*Asparagus plumosus*)

【文字】 wénzì ① characters; script; writing: 楔形～ cuneiform characters/ 拼音～ alphabetic writing ② written language: ～宣传 written propaganda/ ～游戏 play with words; juggle with terms/ 有～可考的历史 recorded history ③ writing (as regards form or style): ～清通 lucid writing
◇ ～方程〈数〉 literal equation/ ～改革 reform of a writing system/ ～学 philology/ ～狱〈史〉 imprisonment or execution of an author for writing sth. considered offensive by the imperial court; literary inquisition

**纹** wén lines; veins; grain: 脸上的皱～ lines on one's

face; furrows/ 细～木 fine-grained wood
【纹理】 wénlǐ veins; grain: 有～的大理石 veined marble/ 这木头的～很好看。This wood has a beautiful grain.
【纹路儿】 wénlur lines; grain
【纹丝不动】 wénsī bù dòng absolutely still: 没有一点风，柳条儿～。There wasn't a breath of wind and the willow twigs were absolutely still.
【纹银】 wényín fine silver

**闻** wén ① hear: ～讯 hear the news/ 听而不～ listen but not hear; turn a deaf ear to ② news; story: 要～ important news ③ well-known; famous: ～人 well-known figure ④ reputation: 秽～ ill repute ⑤ smell: 你～～这是什么味儿？ Smell this and see what it is. ⑥ (Wén) a surname
【闻风而动】 wén fēng ér dòng immediately respond to a call; go into action without delay
【闻风丧胆】 wén fēng sàng dǎn become terror-stricken (或 panic-stricken, terrified) at the news
【闻过则喜】 wén guò zé xǐ feel happy when told of one's errors; be glad to have one's errors pointed out
【闻名】 wénmíng ① well-known; famous; renowned: ～全国 well-known throughout the country/ 世界～ world-famous; world-renowned ② be familiar with sb.'s name; know sb. by repute: ～不如见面。Knowing a person by repute is not as good as seeing him in the flesh.
【闻人】 wénrén well-known figure; famous man; celebrity
【闻所未闻】 wén suǒ wèi wén unheard-of: 他们给我讲了很多～的事情。They told me a lot of things I had never heard before.
【闻诊】 wénzhěn 〈中医〉 auscultation and smelling, one of the four methods of diagnosis

**蚊** wén mosquito
【蚊香】 wénxiāng mosquito-repellent incense
【蚊帐】 wénzhàng mosquito net ◇ ～纱 mosquito netting
【蚊子】 wénzi mosquito

## wěn

**刎** wěn cut one's throat: 自～ cut one's own throat

**抆** wěn 〈书〉 wipe: ～泪 wipe one's tears

**吻** wěn ① lips ② kiss ③ an animal's mouth
【吻合】 wěnhé be identical; coincide; tally: 意见～ have identical views/ 他讲的情况和我听到的～。 His account tallies with what I heard. ◇ ～术〈医〉 anastomosis

**紊** wěn disorderly; confused
【紊流】 wěnliú 〈物〉 turbulence; turbulent flow
【紊乱】 wěnluàn disorder; chaos; confusion: 秩序～ in a state of chaos/ 新陈代谢功能～ metabolic disorder

**稳** wěn ① steady; firm: 把桌子放～ make the table steady/ 站～ stand steadily; stand firm/ 坐～ sit tight/ 站～无产阶级立场 stick firmly to a proletarian stand/ 她做事很～。She is steady and reliable in doing things./ 企图～住阵脚 try to maintain one's position; attempt to hold one's ground ② sure; certain: 这事你拿得～吗？ Are you quite sure of it?/ 这场比赛他～赢。He is certain to win the game.
【稳步】 wěnbù with steady steps; steadily: ～前进 advance steadily; make steady progress/ 生产～上升。Production is going up steadily.
【稳操左券】 wěn cāo zuǒquàn have full assurance of success 又作"稳操胜券"
【稳产高产】 wěnchǎn gāochǎn high and stable yields: ～田 land (或 fields) with high, stable yields
【稳当】 wěndang reliable; secure; safe: ～的办法 a reliable method
【稳定】 wěndìng ① stable; steady: 物价～。Prices remain stable./ 情绪～ be in a calm, unruffled mood/ ～的多数 a stable majority/ 不～的国际金融市场 a shaky international monetary market ② stabilize; steady: ～物价 stabilize commodity prices/ ～情绪 set sb.'s mind at rest; reassure sb.
◇ ～剂〈化〉 stabilizer/ ～平衡〈物〉 stable equilibrium/ ～装置〈化〉 stabilization plant
【稳固】 wěngù firm; stable: ～的基础 a firm (或 solid) foundation/ ～的政权 a stable government
【稳健】 wěnjiàn firm; steady: 迈着～的步子 walk with firm steps/ 办事～ go about things steadily/ 他这个人很～。He's a steady person. ◇ ～派 moderates
【稳流】 wěnliú 〈物〉 steady flow
【稳如泰山】 wěn rú Tàishān as stable as Mount Taishan
【稳妥】 wěntuǒ safe; reliable: ～的计划 a safe plan/ 我看这样办更～。I think it's safer to do it this way.
【稳扎稳打】 wěnzhā-wěndǎ ① go ahead steadily and strike sure blows ② go about things steadily and surely
【稳重】 wěnzhòng steady; staid; sedate
【稳准狠】 wěn-zhǔn-hěn sure, accurate and relentless: ～地打击一小撮阶级敌人 strike surely, accurately and relentlessly at the handful of class enemies

## wèn

**问** wèn ① ask; inquire: ～路 ask the way/ 不懂就～。Ask when you don't know./ 我～他为什么要那样做。I asked him why he did it./ 他在食堂～了一下开饭的时间。He inquired about the meal times at the canteen. ② ask after; inquire after: 他信里～起你。He asks after you in his letter. ③ interrogate; examine: 审～ interrogate ④ hold responsible: 出了事唯你是～。You'll be held responsible if anything goes wrong.
【问安】 wèn'ān pay one's respects (usu. to elders); wish sb. good health
【问案】 wèn'àn try (或 hear) a case
【问长问短】 wèncháng-wènduǎn take the trouble to make detailed inquiries
【问答】 wèn-dá questions and answers ◇ ～练习 question-and-answer drills
【问道于盲】 wèn dào yú máng ask the way from a blind person — seek advice from one who can offer none
【问寒问暖】 wènhán-wènnuǎn ask after sb.'s health with deep concern; be solicitous for sb.'s welfare
【问好】 wènhǎo send one's regards to; say hello to: 请代我向你父亲～。Please give my regards to your father. 或 Remember me to your father./ 他向您～。He wished to be remembered to you.
【问号】 wènhào ① question mark; interrogation mark (或 point) (？) ② unknown factor; unsolved problem: 致癌的真正原因还是个～。The exact cause of cancer is still unknown.
【问候】 wènhòu send one's respects (或 regards) to; extend greetings to: 致以亲切的～ extend cordial greetings
【问津】 wènjīn 〈书〉〔多用于否定句〕 make inquiries (as about prices or the situation): 不敢～ not dare to make

inquiries (as about prohibitively priced goods)/ 无人～ nobody cares to ask about sth.

【问荆】 wènjīng 〈植〉 meadow pine (*Equisetum arvense*)

【问世】 wènshì be published; come out: 本书作者的一部新小说即将～。A new novel by the same author will soon come out.

【问题】 wèntí ① question; problem; issue: 我提个～。May I ask a question?/ 悬而未决的～ an outstanding issue/ 原则～ a question (或 matter) of principle/ 思想～ an ideological problem/ 关键～ a key problem/ ～的关键 the heart (或 crux) of the matter ② trouble; mishap: 那台车床出～了。Something has gone wrong with that lathe./ 一路上没出～。The trip went off without mishap. ◇ ～单 *questionnaire*

【问心无愧】 wèn xīn wú kuì have a clear conscience; feel no qualms upon self-examination

【问心有愧】 wèn xīn yǒu kuì feel a twinge of conscience; have a guilty conscience

【问讯】 wènxùn inquire; ask ◇ ～处 inquiry office; information desk

【问诊】 wènzhěn 〈中医〉 interrogation, one of the four methods of diagnosis

【问罪】 wènzuì denounce; condemn: 兴师～ send a punitive force against; denounce sb. publicly for his crimes or serious errors

**汶** Wèn short for the Wenshui River

**璺** wèn crack (on glassware or earthenware): 碗上有一道～。The bowl has a crack.

## wēng

**翁** wēng ① old man: 渔～ an old fisherman ② father ③ father-in-law: ～姑 a woman's parents-in-law/ ～婿 father-in-law and son-in-law ④ (Wēng) a surname

**嗡** wēng 〈象〉 drone; buzz; hum: 蜜蜂～～地飞。Bees are buzzing all around.

**鹟** wēng 〈动〉 flycatcher

## wěng

**蓊** wěng

【蓊郁】 wěngyù 〈书〉 lush; luxuriant

## wèng

**瓮** wèng urn; earthen jar: 水～ water jar/ 菜～ a jar for pickling vegetables

【瓮声瓮气】 wèngshēng-wèngqì in a low, muffled voice

【瓮中之鳖】 wèngzhōng zhī biē a turtle in a jar — bottled up; trapped

【瓮中捉鳖】 wèngzhōng zhuō biē catch a turtle in a jar — go after an easy prey

**蕹** wèng

【蕹菜】 wèngcài water spinach

**齆** wèng

【齆鼻儿】 wèngbír ① speak with a nasal twang due to a stuffy nose ② a person who speaks with a nasal twang

## wō

**挝** wō 见"老挝" Lǎowō

**涡** wō whirlpool; eddy: 水～ eddies of water

【涡虫】 wōchóng 〈动〉 turbellarian worm; turbellarian

【涡流】 wōliú ① the circular movement of a fluid; whirling fluid; eddy ② 〈物〉 eddy current; vortex flow

【涡轮】 wōlún turbine

◇ ～发电机 turbogenerator/ ～机 turbine/ ～螺旋桨发动机 turboprop (engine)/ ～喷气发动机 turbojet (engine)

【涡旋】 wōxuán 〈气〉 vortex: 大气～ atmospheric vortex

**倭** Wō an old name for Japan

【倭瓜】 wōguā 〈方〉 pumpkin; cushaw

【倭寇】 Wōkòu 〈史〉 Japanese pirates (operating in Chinese coastal waters from the fourteenth to the sixteenth century)

**莴** wō

【莴苣】 wōju lettuce

【莴笋】 wōsǔn asparagus lettuce

**窝** wō ① nest: 鸟～ bird's nest/ 鸡～ hencoop; roost/ 蜂～ beehive ② lair; den: 贼～ thieves' den/ 土匪～ bandits' lair; bandits' nest ③ a hollow part of the human body; pit: 夹肢～ armpit/ 心～ the pit of the stomach ④ 〈方〉 place: 这炉子真碍事，给它挪个～儿。The stove's in the way; let's move it to some other place./ 他就是不动～儿。He refused to budge. ⑤ harbour; shelter: ～赃 harbour stolen goods ⑥ hold in; check: ～着一肚子火 be simmering with rage; be forced to bottle up one's anger ⑦ bend: 把铁丝～个圆圈 bend the wire into a circle/ 别把画片～了。Be careful not to bend (或 crease) the picture. ⑧ 〈量〉〔用于动物〕 litter; brood: 一～十只小猪 ten piglets at a litter/ 一～小鸡 a brood of chickens

【窝藏】 wōcáng harbour; shelter: ～罪犯 give shelter to (或 harbour) a criminal

【窝工】 wōgōng enforced idleness due to poor organization of work; holdup in the work through poor organization

【窝囊】 wōnang ① feel vexed; be annoyed: 受～气 be subjected to petty annoyances/ 这事办得真～。That's really botched it up. ② good-for-nothing; hopelessly stupid

【窝囊废】 wōnangfèi 〈方〉 good-for-nothing; worthless wretch

【窝棚】 wōpeng shack; shed; shanty

【窝窝头】 wōwotóu steamed bread of corn, sorghum, etc. 又作"窝头"

【窝主】 wōzhǔ a person who harbours criminals, loot or contraband goods

**喔** wō 〈象〉 cock's crow: ～～～! Cock-a-doodle-doo! 另见 ō

**蜗** wō snail

【蜗杆】 wōgǎn 〈机〉 worm ◇ ～轴 worm shaft

【蜗居】 wōjū 〈书〉 humble abode

【蜗轮】 wōlún 〈机〉 worm gear; worm wheel

【蜗牛】 wōniú snail

**踒** wō sprain (one's ankle or wrist); strain

## wǒ

**我** wǒ ① I ② we: ～方 our side; we/ ～军 our army/ 敌～矛盾 contradictions between ourselves and the enemy ③〔"你""我"对举，表示泛指〕: 大家你帮～，～帮你，很快就把活儿干完了。With each one giving the other a hand, they soon got the job done. ④ self: 自～牺牲 self-sacrifice/ 忘～的献身精神 selfless devotion

【我们】 wǒmen we

【我行我素】 wǒ xíng wǒ sù persist in one's old ways (no matter what others say); stick to one's old way of doing things

## wò

**沃** wò ① fertile; rich: ～土 fertile soil; rich soil/ ～野千里 a vast expanse of fertile land ② irrigate: ～田 irrigate farmland

**肟** wò 〈化〉 oxime

**卧** wò ① lie: 仰～ lie on one's back ② (of animals or birds) crouch; sit ③ for sleeping in: ～室 bedroom/ ～铺 sleeping berth ④〈方〉 poach (eggs)

【卧病】 wòbìng be confined to bed; be laid up

【卧车】 wòchē ① sleeping car; sleeping carriage; sleeper ② automobile; car; limousine; sedan

【卧床】 wòchuáng lie in bed: 大夫叫她～休息两天。The doctor told her to stay in bed for a couple of days.

【卧倒】 wòdǎo drop to the ground; take a prone (或 lying-down) position: ～！(口令) Lie down! 或 Hit the ground!

【卧房】 wòfáng bedroom

【卧果儿】 wòguǒr 〈方〉 poached egg

【卧具】 wòjù bedding (provided on a train or ship)

【卧铺】 wòpù sleeping berth; sleeper

【卧射】 wòshè 〈军〉 prone fire

【卧式】 wòshì 〈机〉 horizontal: ～镗床 horizontal boring machine/ ～发动机 horizontal engine

【卧室】 wòshì bedroom

【卧榻】 wòtà 〈书〉 bed

【卧薪尝胆】 wò xīn cháng dǎn sleep on brushwood and taste gall — undergo self-imposed hardships so as to strengthen one's resolve to wipe out a national humiliation

【卧姿】 wòzī 〈体〉 prone position

**渥** wò 〈书〉 wet; moisten

**握** wò hold; grasp: 紧～手中枪 hold one's gun with a firm grip

【握别】 wòbié shake hands at parting; part: ～以来，已逾三月。It is more than three months since we parted.

【握力】 wòlì the power of gripping; grip ◇ ～器〈体〉 spring-grip dumb-bells

【握拳】 wòquán make a fist; clench one's fist

【握手】 wòshǒu shake hands; clasp hands

**硪** wò a flat stone or iron rammer with ropes attached at the sides: 打～ operate a rammer

**幄** wò 〈书〉 tent

**斡** wò

【斡旋】 wòxuán ① mediate: 由于他从中～，双方的争端得到了解决。Through his mediation the dispute between the two parties was settled. ②〈法〉 good offices

**龌** wò

【龌龊】 wòchuò dirty; filthy: 卑鄙～ sordid; foul

## wū

**乌** wū ① crow ② black; dark: ～云 black clouds; dark clouds ③〈书〉〔用于反问〕: ～足道哉？What's there worth mentioning about it? ④ (Wū) a surname

另见 wù

【乌鲳】 wūchāng 〈动〉 black pomfret

【乌尔都语】 Wū'ěrdūyǔ Urdu

【乌饭树】 wūfànshù oriental blueberry (*Vaccinium bracteatum*)

【乌干达】 Wūgāndá Uganda ◇ ～人 Ugandan

【乌龟】 wūguī ① tortoise ② cuckold ◇ ～壳 tortoiseshell

【乌合之众】 wūhé zhī zhòng a disorderly band; a motley crowd; rabble; mob

【乌黑】 wūhēi pitch-black; jet-black

【乌呼】 wūhū 见"呜呼" wūhū

【乌桕】 wūjiù 〈植〉 Chinese tallow tree

【乌拉】 wūlā ① *wula*, corvée labour formerly imposed on Xizang serfs ② *wula* labourer

另见 wùla

【乌拉尔】 Wūlā'ěr Ural ◇ ～山 the Ural Mountains; the Urals

【乌拉圭】 Wūlāguī Uruguay ◇ ～人 Uruguayan

【乌兰牧骑】 wūlánmùqí a Nei Monggol revolutionary cultural troupe mounted on horseback

【乌鳢】 wūlǐ 〈动〉 snakehead; snakeheaded fish

【乌亮】 wūliàng glossy black; jet-black: ～的头发 dark, glossy hair; raven locks

【乌溜溜】 wūliūliū (of eyes) dark and liquid: 一双～的眼睛 sparkling, black eyes

【乌龙茶】 wūlóngchá oolong (tea)

【乌鲁木齐】 Wūlǔmùqí Ürümqi

【乌梅】 wūméi smoked plum; dark plum

【乌木】 wūmù 〈植〉 ebony

【乌七八糟】 wūqībāzāo ① in a horrible mess; in great disorder ② obscene; dirty; filthy

【乌纱帽】 wūshāmào ① black gauze cap (worn by feudal officials) ② official post: 丢～ be dismissed from office

【乌苏里江】 Wūsūlǐjiāng the Wusuli River

【乌头】 wūtóu 〈中药〉 the rhizome of Chinese monkshood (*Aconitum carmichaeli*)

【乌托邦】 wūtuōbāng Utopia

【乌鸦】 wūyā crow

【乌烟瘴气】 wūyān-zhàngqì foul atmosphere; pestilential atmosphere: 搞得～ foul up/ 旧中国的官场简直是～。Officialdom was simply foul in old China.

【乌药】 wūyào 〈中药〉 the root of three-nerved spicebush (*Lindera strychnifolia*)

【乌有】 wūyǒu 〈书〉 nothing; naught: 化为～ come to nothing (或 naught)

【乌鱼】 wūyú 〈动〉 snakehead; snakeheaded fish

【乌云】 wūyún black clouds; dark clouds: ～遮天。Black clouds blotted out the sky. 或 The sky was covered with dark clouds.

【乌枣】 wūzǎo smoked jujube; black jujube

【乌贼】 wūzéi 〈动〉 cuttlefish; inkfish

【乌孜别克族】 Wūzībiékèzú the Ozbek (Uzbek) nationality,

living in the Xinjiang Uygur Autonomous Region

**污** wū ① dirt; filth: 血～ blood stains ② dirty; filthy; foul: ～泥 mud; mire ③ corrupt: 贪官～吏 corrupt officials ④ defile; smear: 玷～ stain; sully; tarnish

【污点】 wūdiǎn stain; spot; blemish; smirch

【污垢】 wūgòu dirt; filth

【污秽】 wūhuì 〈书〉 filthy; foul

【污迹】 wūjì stain; smear; smudge

【污蔑】 wūmiè ① 见"诬蔑" wūmiè ② defile; sully; tarnish

【污泥】 wūní mud; mire; sludge
◇ ～浓缩〈环保〉 sludge thickening/ ～膨胀 sludge bulking/ ～脱水 sludge dewatering/ ～消化 sludge digestion

【污泥浊水】 wūní-zhuóshuǐ filth and mire: 荡涤旧社会遗留下来的～ clean up the filth left by the old society

【污七八糟】 wūqībāzāo 见"乌七八糟" wūqībāzāo

【污染】 wūrǎn pollute; contaminate: 大气层～ atmosphere pollution/ 放射性～ radioactive contamination/ 环境～ environmental pollution/ 空气～ air pollution/ 水～ water contamination/ 飘尘～ floating (或 airborne) dust pollution/ 工业粉尘～ industrial dust pollution/ 噪音～ noise pollution
◇ ～地带 contaminated zone/ ～计数管 contamination counter/ ～物 pollutant; contaminant/ ～指示生物 pollution indicating organism

【污辱】 wūrǔ ① humiliate; insult ② defile; sully; tarnish

【污水】 wūshuǐ foul (或 polluted, waste) water; sewage; slops: 生活～ domestic sewage
◇ ～处理 sewage disposal; sewage treatment/ ～处理厂 sewage treatment plant/ ～管 sewage pipe; sewer (pipe)/ ～管道 sewage conduit; sewer line/ ～灌溉 sewage irrigation/ ～净化 sewage purification

【污浊】 wūzhuó (of air, water, etc.) dirty; muddy; foul; filthy

**邬** Wū a surname

**巫** wū ① shaman; witch; wizard ② (Wū) a surname

【巫婆】 wūpó witch; sorceress

【巫师】 wūshī wizard; sorcerer

【巫术】 wūshù witchcraft; sorcery

【巫医】 wūyī witch doctor

**呜** wū 〈象〉 toot; hoot; zoom: 轮船上的汽笛～～叫。The ship's whistle kept hooting./ 汽车～的一声飞驰而过。The car zoomed past.

【呜呼】 wūhū ① 〈书〉 alas; alack ② die: 一命～ give up the ghost

【呜呼哀哉】 wūhū-āizāi ① alas ② dead and gone ③ all is lost

【呜咽】 wūyè sob; whimper

**诬** wū accuse falsely

【诬告】 wūgào lodge a false accusation against; bring a false charge against; trump up a charge against ◇ ～案件 frame-up; trumped-up case

【诬害】 wūhài injure by spreading false reports about; calumniate; malign

【诬赖】 wūlài falsely incriminate: ～好人 incriminate innocent people

【诬蔑】 wūmiè slander; vilify; calumniate; smear: 造谣～ rumourmongering and mudslinging; calumny and slander/ ～不实之词 slander and libel

【诬陷】 wūxiàn frame a case against; frame sb.

**屋** wū ① house ② room: 里～ inner room

【屋顶】 wūdǐng roof; housetop ◇ ～花园 roof garden

【屋脊】 wūjǐ ridge (of a roof): 世界～ the roof of the world

【屋架】 wūjià roof truss

【屋面】 wūmiàn 〈建〉 roofing: 瓦～ tile roofing ◇ ～板 roof boarding

【屋檐】 wūyán eaves

【屋宇】 wūyǔ house

【屋子】 wūzi room: 三间～ three rooms

**钨** wū tungsten; wolfram (W)

【钨钢】 wūgāng wolfram steel; tungsten steel

【钨砂】 wūshā tungsten ore

【钨丝】 wūsī tungsten filament ◇ ～灯 tungsten lamp

## wú

**无** wú ① nothing; nil: 从～到有 grow out of nothing; start from scratch ② not have; there is not; without: ～一定计划 without a definite plan ③ not: ～碍大局 not affect the situation as a whole/ ～须乎着急。There's no need to get excited. ④ regardless of; no matter whether, what, etc.: 事～大小，都有人负责。Everything, big and small, is properly taken care of.

【无伴奏合唱】 wúbànzòu héchàng *a cappella*

【无被选权】 wúbèixuǎnquán ineligible

【无比】 wúbǐ incomparable; unparalleled; matchless: ～的优越性 incomparable (或 unparalleled) superiority/ ～的毅力 tremendous determination/ ～英勇 unrivalled in bravery/ ～愤怒 furiously indignant

【无边无际】 wúbiān-wújì boundless; limitless; vast: ～的大海 a boundless ocean/ ～的沙漠 a vast expanse of desert

【无柄叶】 wúbǐngyè 〈植〉 sessile leaf

【无病呻吟】 wú bìng shēnyín ① moan and groan without being ill; make a fuss about an imaginary illness ② adopt a sentimental pose

【无补】 wúbǔ of no help; of no avail: 这样恐怕～于事。That would be of no avail./ 空谈～于实际。Mere words won't help matters.

【无不】 wúbù all without exception; invariably: 同志们对这种英勇行为～表示钦佩。All the comrades, without exception, expressed great admiration for this heroic act./ 大家～为之感动。None were unmoved.

【无产阶级】 wúchǎnjiējí the proletariat: ～革命路线 a proletarian revolutionary line/ ～化 acquire proletarian qualities

【无产阶级文化大革命】 Wúchǎnjiējí Wénhuà Dàgémìng the Great Proletarian Cultural Revolution (1966-1977)

【无产阶级专政】 wúchǎnjiējí zhuānzhèng dictatorship of the proletariat; proletarian dictatorship: 巩固和加强～ consolidate and strengthen the dictatorship of the proletariat

【无产者】 wúchǎnzhě proletarian

【无常】 wúcháng ① variable; changeable: 反复～ capricious; uncertain ② 〈佛教〉 impermanence

【无偿】 wúcháng free; gratis; gratuitous: ～援助 aid given gratis (或 gratuitously)/ 提供～经济援助 render economic assistance gratis; give free economic aid

【无耻】 wúchǐ shameless; brazen; impudent: ～谰言 shameless slander/ ～之尤 brazen in the extreme; the height of shamelessness/ ～之徒 a person who has lost all sense of shame; a shameless person

【无酬劳动】 wúchóu láodòng 〈经〉 unpaid labour

【无出其右】 wú chū qí yòu second to none; matchless; unequalled

【无从】 wúcóng have no way (of doing sth.); not be in a position (to do sth.): 我们不了解情况，～答复这类问题。As we do not know the facts, we are in no position to answer such questions./ 心中千言万语，一时～说起 have a thousand things to say but not know where to begin

【无党派人士】 wúdǎngpài rénshì a public figure without party affiliation; nonparty personage

【无敌】 wúdí unmatched; invincible; unconquerable: ～于天下 unmatched anywhere in the world; invincible

【无底洞】 wúdǐdòng a bottomless pit (that can never be filled)

【无地自容】 wú dì zì róng can find no place to hide oneself for shame; feel too ashamed to show one's face; look for a hole to crawl into

【无的放矢】 wú dì fàng shǐ shoot an arrow without a target; shoot at random: 批评要有针对性，不要～。Criticism shouldn't be random shooting; it should be to the point.

【无动于衷】 wú dòng yú zhōng aloof and indifferent; unmoved; untouched; unconcerned: 对这种情况，我们不能～。We cannot remain indifferent in such a situation./ 他对我的忠告～。He turned a deaf ear to my advice.

【无独有偶】 wúdú-yǒu'ǒu 〔多含贬义〕 it is not unique, but has its counterpart; not come singly but in pairs

【无毒蛇】 wúdúshé nonpoisonous snake

【无度】 wúdù immoderate; excessive: 饮食～ excessive (或 immoderate) eating and drinking/ 挥霍～ squander wantonly

【无端】 wúduān for no reason: ～侮辱 a gratuitous insult

【无恶不作】 wú è bù zuò stop at nothing in doing evil; stop at no evil; commit all manner of crimes

【无法】 wúfǎ unable; incapable: ～应付 unable to cope with; at the end of one's resources/ ～形容 beyond description/ ～解脱的困境 an inextricable dilemma/ ～投递，退回原处。Undeliverable, returned to sender.

【无法无天】 wúfǎ-wútiān defy laws human and divine; become absolutely lawless; run wild

【无方】 wúfāng not in the proper way; in the wrong way; not knowing how: 经营～ mismanagement

【无妨】 wúfāng there's no harm; may (或 might) as well: 你～试一试。There's no harm in having a try.

【无纺织物】 wúfǎng zhīwù 〈纺〉 adhesive-bonded fabric

【无非】 wúfēi nothing but; no more than; simply; only: 我想说的～是那么几句话。What I want to say is no more than (或 nothing but) this./ ～是好坏两种可能。There are only two possibilities, a good one and a bad one.

【无风】 wúfēng 〈气〉 calm

【无风不起浪】 wú fēng bù qǐ làng there are no waves without wind; there's no smoke without fire

【无风带】 wúfēngdài 〈气〉 calm belt; calm zone

【无缝钢管】 wúfèng gāngguǎn seamless steel tube (或 pipe) ◇ ～厂 seamless (steel) tubing mill

【无干】 wúgān have nothing to do with: 这事与你～。It has nothing to do with you. 或 It's none of your business./ 这全是我的过错，跟别人～。It was entirely my fault; nobody else had anything to do with it.

【无功受禄】 wú gōng shòu lù get a reward without deserving it

【无辜】 wúgū ① innocent ② an innocent person

【无故】 wúgù without cause or reason: 不得～缺席。Nobody may be absent without reason.

【无怪】 wúguài no wonder; not to be wondered at: 厂里正在大搞技术革新，～他们这么忙。With the technical innovation movement in full swing in their factory, no wonder they're so busy.

【无关】 wúguān have nothing to do with: 此事与他～。It has nothing to do with him./ 那也～大局。That does not matter very much./ ～紧要 of no importance; immaterial/ ～痛痒的自我批评 irrelevant or superficial self-criticism/ ～痛痒的话 comment without any bite; irrelevant or pointless remarks

【无规】 wúguī 〈物〉 random ◇ ～介质 random media/ ～取向 random orientation

【无轨电车】 wúguǐ diànchē trackless trolley; trolleybus

【无国籍】 wúguójí 〈外〉 stateless ◇～者 a stateless person

【无害通过】 wúhài tōngguò 〈法〉 innocent passage

【无核化】 wúhéhuà denuclearize

【无核区】 wúhéqū nuclear-free zone

【无核武器国家】 wú-héwǔqì guójiā nonnuclear country 又作"无核国家"

【无核武器区】 wú-héwǔqìqū nuclear-weapon-free zone

【无花果】 wúhuāguǒ 〈植〉 fig

【无话不谈】 wú huà bù tán keep no secrets from each other; be in each other's confidence

【无机】 wújī 〈化〉 inorganic
◇ ～肥料 inorganic fertilizer; mineral fertilizer/ ～化合物 inorganic compound/ ～化学 inorganic chemistry/ ～界 the inorganic world/ ～物 inorganic substance; inorganic matter/ ～盐 inorganic salts

【无稽】 wújī unfounded; fantastic; absurd: ～之谈 fantastic talk; sheer nonsense

【无级】 wújí 〈机〉 stepless ◇ ～调速 stepless speed regulation/ ～变速装置 stepless speed change device

【无几】 wújǐ very few; very little; hardly any: 所剩～。There's very little left./ 两人的年岁相差～。The two are almost the same age.

【无脊椎动物】 wújǐzhuī dòngwù invertebrate

【无计可施】 wú jì kě shī at one's wits' end; at the end of one's tether

【无记名投票】 wújìmíng tóupiào secret ballot

【无济于事】 wú jì yú shì of no avail; to no effect

【无家可归】 wú jiā kě guī wander about without a home to go to; be homeless

【无价之宝】 wú jià zhī bǎo priceless treasure; invaluable asset

【无坚不摧】 wú jiān bù cuī overrun all fortifications; carry all before one; be all-conquering

【无间】 wújiàn 〈书〉 ① not keeping anything from each other; very close to each other: 亲密～的朋友 close friends; bosom friends ② continuously; without interruption: 坚持户外锻炼，寒暑～ keep on doing outdoor exercise all the year round

【无精打采】 wújīng-dǎcǎi listless; lackadaisical; in low spirits; out of sorts

【无拘束】 wújūshù unrestrained; unconstrained: 在～的气氛中 in an unconstrained atmosphere/ 大家～地发表意见。Everyone freely expressed his views. 又作"无拘无束"

【无可比拟】 wúkě bǐnǐ incomparable; unparalleled

【无可非议】 wúkě fēiyì blameless; beyond reproach; above criticism

【无可厚非】 wúkě hòufēi give no cause for much criticism

【无可讳言】 wúkě huìyán there is no hiding the fact: 这些都是～的事实。All these are indisputable facts.

【无可救药】 wúkě jiùyào incorrigible; incurable

【无可奈何】 wúkě nàihé have no way out; have no alternative: 敌人～，只好又回到谈判桌上来。The enemy had no alternative but to return to the conference table./ ～花落去。Flowers will die, do what one may.

【无可无不可】 wúkě-wúbùkě not care one way or another:

我去也行,不去也行,~。I don't care whether I go or not.
【无可争辩】 wúkě zhēngbiàn indisputable; irrefutable
【无可置疑】 wúkě zhìyí indubitable; unquestionable
【无孔不入】 wú kǒng bù rù ① (of odours, ideas, etc.) be all-pervasive ② (of persons) seize every opportunity (to do evil)
【无愧】 wúkuì feel no qualms; have a clear conscience: 问心~ feel no qualms upon self-examination/ ~于共产党员的称号 be worthy of the name of a communist
【无赖】 wúlài ① rascally; scoundrelly; blackguardly: 耍~ act shamelessly ② rascal
【无理】 wúlǐ unreasonable; unjustifiable: ~要求 unreasonable demands/ ~阻挠 unjustifiable obstruction/ ~指责 unwarranted accusations; groundless charges
【无理取闹】 wúlǐ qǔnào wilfully make trouble; be deliberately provocative
【无理数】 wúlǐshù 〈数〉 irrational number
【无力】 wúlì ① lack strength; feel weak: 四肢~ feel weak in one's limbs ② unable; incapable; powerless: 一个人是~完成这项任务的。One person alone can't accomplish this task. 或 No one can do this job single-handed.
【无量】 wúliàng measureless; immeasurable; boundless: 前途~ a boundless future
【无聊】 wúliáo ① bored ② senseless; silly; stupid: 不要讲这种~的话。Don't make such silly remarks.
【无论】 wúlùn 〈连〉 no matter what, how, etc.; regardless of: ~是谁都不能违反劳动纪律。Nobody is supposed to break labour discipline, no matter who he is./ ~发生什么情况,你都要保持冷静。Keep calm, whatever happens.
【无论如何】 wúlùn rúhé in any case; at any rate; whatever happens; at all events: 你~得来一趟。You've got to come, whatever happens. /我们~得把丢失的文件找到。At all costs, we have to find the missing document./ ~,现在已经来不及了。Anyhow, it's too late now./ 我们~不能急躁。On no account must we be impetuous.
【无米之炊】 wú mǐ zhī chuī cook a meal without rice; make bricks without straw 参见"巧妇难为无米之炊" qiǎo fù nán wéi wú mǐ zhī chuī
【无名】 wúmíng ① nameless; unknown ② indefinable; indescribable: ~的恐惧 an indefinable feeling of terror
◇ ~高地〈军〉 an unnamed hill/ ~氏 an anonymous person/ ~小卒 a nobody/ ~英雄 an unknown hero/ ~指 the third finger; ring finger/ ~肿毒〈中医〉 nameless sores or boils
【无奈】 wúnài ① cannot help but; have no alternative; have no choice: 他出于~,只得表示同意。He had no choice but to agree. ② but; however: 他本想来的,~临时有会,来不了。He had meant to come, but was prevented by an unexpected meeting.
【无能】 wúnéng incompetent; incapable: 软弱~ weak and incompetent
【无能为力】 wú néng wéi lì powerless; helpless; incapable of action: 人类对于自然界不是~的。Man is not powerless before nature.
【无宁】 wúnìng 见"毋宁" wúnìng
【无期徒刑】 wúqī túxíng life imprisonment: 判处~ be sentenced to imprisonment for life; be given a life sentence
【无情】 wúqíng merciless; ruthless; heartless: ~的打击 a merciless blow/ ~的事实 harsh reality; hard facts/ 水火~。Fire and water have no mercy./ 历史的辩证法是~的。The dialectics of history is inexorable.
【无穷】 wúqióng infinite; endless; boundless; inexhaustible: ~的烦恼和忧虑 endless troubles and worries/ ~无尽的智慧和力量 inexhaustible wisdom and power/ 言有尽而意~。There's an end to the words, but not to their message.
◇ ~大〈数〉 infinitely great; infinity/ ~小〈数〉 infinitely small; infinitesimal
【无权】 wúquán have no right: ~干预 have no right to interfere/ ~追索〈法〉 without recourse
【无人】 wúrén ① unmanned: ~火箭 unmanned rocket/ ~驾驶飞机 unmanned plane; pilotless plane; robot plane ② depopulated: ~区 a depopulated zone; no man's land ③ self-service: ~售书处 self-service bookstall
【无任】 wúrèn 〈书〉 extremely; immensely: ~感激 be deeply grateful
【无任所大使】 wúrènsuǒ dàshǐ ambassador-at-large
【无如】 wúrú 见"无奈"②
【无伤大雅】 wú shāng dàyǎ not affect the whole; not matter much
【无上】 wúshàng supreme; paramount; highest: ~权力 supreme power/ ~光荣 the highest honour
【无神论】 wúshénlùn atheism ◇ ~者 atheist
【无生代】 Wúshēngdài 〈地〉 the Azoic Era
【无生物】 wúshēngwù inanimate object; nonliving matter
【无声】 wúshēng noiseless; silent
◇ ~打字机 noiseless typewriter/ ~片 silent film/ ~手枪 pistol with a silencer
【无声无臭】 wúshēng-wúxiù unknown; obscure
【无时无刻】 wúshí-wúkè all the time; incessantly: 我们~不在想念你。You are constantly in our thoughts.
【无事不登三宝殿】 wú shì bù dēng sānbǎodiàn never go to the temple for nothing; would not go to sb.'s place except on business, for help, etc.; I wouldn't come to you if I hadn't something to ask of you
【无事生非】 wú shì shēng fēi make trouble out of nothing; be deliberately provocative
【无视】 wúshì ignore; disregard; defy: ~别国主权 disregard the sovereignty of other countries/ ~人民的意志 defy the will of the people
【无熟料水泥】 wúshúliào shuǐní 〈建〉 clinker-free cement
【无数】 wúshù ① innumerable; countless: ~的事实 innumerable facts ② not know for certain; be uncertain: 这计划是否可行,我心中~。I'm not too sure whether the plan will work.
【无双】 wúshuāng unparalleled; unrivalled; matchless: 举世~ absolutely unrivalled
【无霜期】 wúshuāngqī frost-free period
【无水】 wúshuǐ 〈化〉 anhydrous: ~溶剂 anhydrous solvent/ ~酸 anhydrous acid
【无私】 wúsī selfless; disinterested; unselfish: 给予~的援助 give (或 render) disinterested assistance/ ~才能无畏。Only the selfless can be fearless.
【无梭织机】 wúsuō zhījī 〈纺〉 shuttleless loom
【无所不包】 wú suǒ bù bāo all-embracing; all-encompassing
【无所不能】 wú suǒ bù néng omnipotent
【无所不为】 wú suǒ bù wéi stop at nothing; do all manner of evil: 匪军烧杀掳掠,~。The bandit troops massacred, burned and looted, stopping at nothing.
【无所不用其极】 wú suǒ bù yòng qí jí resort to every conceivable means; stop at nothing; go to any length: 这个家伙造谣诽谤、挑拨离间,~。That scoundrel went all the way in rumourmongering, mudslinging and sowing dissension.
【无所不在】 wú suǒ bù zài omnipresent; ubiquitous: 矛盾的斗争~。The struggle between opposites is ubiquitous.
【无所不知】 wú suǒ bù zhī omniscient
【无所不至】 wú suǒ bù zhì ① penetrate everywhere: 细菌活动的范围很广,~。Bacteria are active practically everywhere. ② spare no pains (to do evil); be capable of anything;

stop at nothing: 威胁利诱,～ use intimidation, bribery and every other means/ 反动派对少数民族压迫剥削,～。The reactionaries oppressed and exploited minority nationalities in every possible way.
【无所措手足】 wú suǒ cuò shǒu-zú be at a loss as to what to do
【无所事事】 wú suǒ shì shì be occupied with nothing; have nothing to do; idle away one's time
【无所适从】 wú suǒ shì cóng not know what course to take; be at a loss as to what to do
【无所畏惧】 wú suǒ wèijù fearless; dauntless; undaunted
【无所谓】 wúsuǒwèi ① cannot be designated as; not deserve the name of: 这是随便说的,～什么批评。It was a passing remark; I didn't mean to criticize anybody. ② be indifferent; not matter: 采取～的态度 adopt an indifferent attitude/ 你替他着急,他自己却好象～似的。You are worried about him, but he himself doesn't seem to care./ 他去不去～。It makes no difference whether he goes or not.
【无所用心】 wú suǒ yòngxīn not give serious thought to anything: 饱食终日,～ be sated with food and remain idle
【无所作为】 wú suǒ zuòwéi attempt nothing and accomplish nothing; be in a state of inertia: ～和骄傲自满的论点都是错误的。Ideas of inertia and complacency are both wrong.
【无题】 wútí no title (used as a title for writings for which the author cannot find, or chooses not to give, a title)
◇ ～诗 a poem without a title; titleless poem
【无条件】 wútiáojiàn unconditional; without preconditions: 建议～地立即举行谈判 propose that negotiations be held at once without preconditions/ ～地、全心全意地到群众中去 go among the masses unreservedly and wholeheartedly
◇ ～反射〈生理〉 unconditioned reflex/ ～投降 unconditional surrender
【无头案】 wútóu'àn a case without any clues; unsolved mystery
【无往不利】 wú wǎng bù lì go smoothly everywhere; be ever successful: 依靠党,依靠群众,工作就～。Rely on the Party and the masses and you will succeed wherever you go.
【无往不胜】 wú wǎng bù shèng ever-victorious; invincible
【无往不在】 wú wǎng bù zài present everywhere; omnipresent
【无妄之灾】 wú wàng zhī zāi unexpected calamity; undeserved ill turn
【无微不至】 wú wēi bù zhì meticulously; in every possible way: 党对青年的关怀～。Our Party takes every care of the youth.
【无为】 wúwéi letting things take their own course (a Taoist concept of human conduct); inaction; inactivity: ～而治 govern by doing nothing that goes against nature
【无味】 wúwèi ① tasteless; unpalatable: 食之～,弃之可惜 unappetizing and yet not bad enough to throw away ② dull; insipid; uninteresting: 枯燥～ dry as dust
【无畏】 wúwèi fearless; dauntless
【无谓】 wúwèi meaningless; pointless; senseless: ～的争吵 a pointless quarrel/ ～的牺牲 a meaningless (或 senseless) sacrifice
【无…无…】 wú…wú… 〔分别用在两个意义相同或相近的词或词素前面,强调没有〕: 无尽无休 incessant; endless/ 无穷无尽 inexhaustible; endless/ 无牵无挂 have no cares/ 无忧无虑 free from care; carefree/ 无依无靠 have no one to depend on; helpless/ 无影无踪 disappear completely; vanish without a trace
【无息贷款】 wúxī dàikuǎn interest-free loan
【无隙可乘】 wú xì kě chéng no crack to get in by; no loophole to exploit; no weakness to take advantage of; no chink in sb.'s armour: 他们时刻保持警惕,坏人～。They were always on the alert so that no opening was left for the enemy to exploit.
【无暇】 wúxiá have no time; be too busy: ～他顾 have no time to attend to other things
【无限】 wúxiàn infinite; limitless; boundless; immeasurable: 对华主席～热爱 have boundless love for Chairman Hua/ ～光明的未来 a future of incomparable brightness/ 对共产主义事业～忠诚 absolute devotion to the cause of communism/ 人的生命是有限的,可是为人民服务是～的。A man's life is limited, but there is no limit to serving the people./ 人民群众有～的创造力。The masses have unlimited creative power./ 批评要实事求是,不要～上纲。Criticism should be fair and not exaggerated.
◇ ～大〈数〉 infinitely great; infinity/ ～公司 unlimited company/ ～花序 indefinite inflorescence/ ～小〈数〉 infinitely small; infinitesimal
【无限期】 wúxiànqī indefinite duration: ～罢工 a strike of indefinite duration/ ～搁置动议 shelve a motion *sine die*/ ～休会 adjourn indefinitely; adjourn *sine die*
【无限制】 wúxiànzhì unrestricted; unbridled; unlimited
【无线】 wúxiàn wireless: ～电话 radiotelephone; radiophone/ ～电报 wireless telegram; radiotelegram
【无线电】 wúxiàndiàn radio
◇ ～测向器 radio direction finder; radio goniometer/ ～传真 radiofacsimile/ ～导航设备 radio navigation aid/ ～发射机 radio transmitter/ ～干扰 radio jamming/ ～收发两用机 transceiver/ ～收音机 radio receiver/ ～探空仪 radiosonde/ ～天文学 radio astronomy/ ～通信 radio communication; wireless communication
【无效】 wúxiào of (或 to) no avail; invalid; null and void: 医治～ fail to respond to medical treatment/ 宣布合同～ declare a contract invalid (或 null and void); invalidate (或 nullify) a contract/ 宣布选举～ nullify an election
◇ ～分蘖〈农〉 ineffective tillering
【无懈可击】 wú xiè kě jī with no chink in one's armour; unassailable; invulnerable: 这篇文章论证周密,～。The article is closely reasoned and the arguments are unassailable.
【无心】 wúxīn ① not be in the mood for: 他工作还没做完,～去看电影。He was in no mood to go to the film, as he hadn't finished his work. ② not intentionally; unwittingly; inadvertently: 他说这话是～的,你可别见怪。Don't take offence. He didn't say it intentionally./ 言者～,听者有意。A casual remark sounds deliberate to a suspicious listener. 或 A careless word may be important information to an attentive listener.
【无形】 wúxíng invisible: ～的枷锁 invisible shackles/ ～的战线 invisible fronts/ ～贸易 invisible trade/ ～进(出)口 invisible import (export)
【无形中】 wúxíngzhōng imperceptibly; virtually: 这～成了风气。This has imperceptibly become a common practice./ 他～成了我的助手。He's virtually become my assistant.
【无性】 wúxìng 〈生〉 asexual: ～世代 asexual generation/ ～生殖 asexual reproduction/ ～杂交 asexual hybridization
【无休止】 wúxiūzhǐ ceaseless; endless: ～地争论 argue on and on
【无须】 wúxū need not; not have to: ～顾虑 need not worry/ ～细说。It's unnecessary to go into details. 又作"无须乎"
【无烟火药】 wúyān huǒyào smokeless powder; ballistite
【无烟煤】 wúyānméi anthracite
【无恙】 wúyàng 〈书〉 in good health; well; safe: 安然～

safe and sound/ 别来～？I trust you've been in good health since we last met?
【无业游民】 wúyè yóumín vagrant
【无疑】 wúyí beyond doubt; undoubtedly: 这种行为～是错误的。Such conduct is undoubtedly wrong.
【无以复加】 wú yǐ fù jiā in the extreme: 荒谬到了～的地步 be absurd in the extreme
【无异】 wúyì not different from; the same as; as good as: 这件复制品几乎与原作～。The reproduction is almost as good as the original.
【无益】 wúyì unprofitable; useless; no good
【无意】 wúyì ① have no intention (of doing sth.); not be inclined to: ～参加 have no intention of joining/ ～于此 not interested in that; not keen on it ② inadvertently; unwittingly; accidentally: 他们在挖井时，～中发现了一些古代文物。While digging a well they accidentally unearthed some ancient relics.
【无意识】 wúyìshí unconscious: ～的动作 an unconscious act (或 movement)
【无翼鸟】 wúyìniǎo kiwi
【无垠】 wúyín boundless; vast: 一望～的草原 a boundless prairie
【无影灯】 wúyǐngdēng 〈医〉 shadowless lamp
【无庸】 wúyōng 见"毋庸" wúyōng
【无用】 wúyòng useless; of no use ◇ ～能 〈机〉unavailable energy
【无由】 wúyóu 〈书〉 not be in a position (to do sth.); have no way (of doing sth.)
【无与伦比】 wú yǔ lúnbǐ incomparable; unparalleled; unique; without equal: 他在地质学方面的贡献是～的。His contribution in the field of geology was unparalleled.
【无原则】 wúyuánzé unprincipled: ～纠纷 an unprincipled dispute
【无缘无故】 wúyuán-wúgù without cause or reason; for no reason at all: 世上决没有～的爱，也没有～的恨。There is absolutely no such thing in the world as love or hatred without reason or cause.
【无源】 wúyuán 〈无〉 passive ◇ ～天线 passive antenna
【无源之水】 wú yuán zhī shuǐ water without a source: 理论脱离实践，就成了～，无本之木。Theory divorced from practice would be like water without a source, or a tree without roots.
【无韵诗】 wúyùnshī blank verse
【无政府主义】 wúzhèngfǔzhǔyì anarchism
【无知】 wúzhī ignorant: ～妄说 ignorant nonsense/ 出于～ out of ignorance
【无止境】 wúzhǐjìng have no limits; know no end: 科学的发展是～的。The development of science has no limits.
【无中生有】 wú zhōng shēng yǒu purely fictitious; fabricated
【无重力】 wúzhònglì 〈宇航〉 agravic ◇ ～状态 null-gravity state
【无足轻重】 wú zú qīng-zhòng of little importance (或 consequence); insignificant: ～的人物 a nobody; a nonentity
【无罪】 wúzuì innocent; not guilty: ～释放 set a person free with a verdict of "not guilty"/ 宣判～ acquit sb. of a crime
【无坐力炮】 wúzuòlìpào recoilless gun

**毋** wú 〈书〉〈副〉〔表示禁止或劝阻〕no; not: ～临渴而掘井。Don't wait till you are thirsty to dig a well./ ～令逃逸。You must not let him escape.
【毋宁】 wúnìng 〈副〉 rather... (than); (not so much...) as: 与其固守，～出击。Better to strike out than to entrench oneself in defence./ 这与其说是奇迹，～说是历史发展的必然。It is the necessary outcome of historical development rather than a miracle.
【毋庸】 wúyōng need not: ～讳言 no need for reticence

**吾** wú 〈书〉I or we: ～辈 we/ ～国 my or our country
【吾侪】 wúchái 〈书〉 we
【吾人】 wúrén 〈书〉 we

**芜** wú 〈书〉 ① overgrown with weeds: 荒～ lie waste ② grassland: 平～ open grassland ③ mixed and disorderly; miscellaneous: ～词 superfluous words
【芜菁】 wújīng 〈植〉 turnip
【芜杂】 wúzá mixed and disorderly; miscellaneous

**吴** Wú ① the Kingdom of Wu (222-280), one of the Three Kingdoms ② a surname

**梧** wú
【梧桐】 wútóng 〈植〉 Chinese parasol (tree)

**鹀** wú 〈动〉 bunting

**蜈** wú
【蜈蚣】 wúgong 〈动〉 centipede
【蜈蚣草】 wúgongcǎo 〈植〉 ciliate desert-grass (*Eremochloa ciliaris*)

**鼯** wú
【鼯鼠】 wúshǔ 〈动〉 flying squirrel

## wǔ

**五** wǔ ① five: ～十 fifty/ ～倍 fivefold; quintuple/ ～分之一 one fifth/ ～十年代 the fifties ② 〈乐〉 a note of the scale in *gongchepu* (工尺谱), corresponding to 6 in numbered musical notation
【五保户】 wǔbǎohù a household enjoying the five guarantees (childless and infirm old persons who are guaranteed food, clothing, medical care, housing and burial expenses by the people's commune)
【五倍子】 wǔbèizǐ 〈中药〉 Chinese gall; gallnut ◇ ～虫 gall makers
【五边形】 wǔbiānxíng pentagon
【五步蛇】 wǔbùshé 〈动〉 long-noded pit viper
【五彩】 wǔcǎi ① the five colours (blue, yellow, red, white and black) ② multicoloured: ～缤纷 colourful; blazing with colour
【五重唱】 wǔchóngchàng 〈乐〉 (vocal) quintet
【五重奏】 wǔchóngzòu 〈乐〉 (instrumental) quintet
【五代】 Wǔ Dài the Five Dynasties (907-960), namely, the Later Liang Dynasty (后梁, 907-923), the Later Tang Dynasty (后唐, 923-936), the Later Jin Dynasty (后晋, 936-946), the Later Han Dynasty (后汉, 947-950), and the Later Zhou Dynasty (后周, 951-960)
【五斗柜】 wǔdǒuguì chest of drawers
【五毒】 wǔdú ① the five poisonous creatures (scorpion, viper, centipede, house lizard and toad) ② the "five evils" 参见"五反运动"
【五反运动】 Wǔfǎn Yùndòng the movement, begun in 1952, against the "five evils" (bribery, tax evasion, theft of state property, cheating on government contracts and stealing of economic information, as practised by owners of private industrial and commercial enterprises)
【五分制】 wǔfēnzhì 〈教〉 the five-grade marking system

【五更】 wǔgēng ① the five watches (或 periods) of the night ② the fifth watch of the night; just before dawn: 起～，睡半夜 retire at midnight and rise before dawn
【五谷】 wǔgǔ ① the five cereals (rice, two kinds of millet, wheat and beans) ② food crops: ～丰登 an abundant harvest of all food crops
【五官】 wǔguān ①〈中医〉 the five sense organs (ears, eyes, lips, nose and tongue) ② facial features: ～端正 have regular features
【五光十色】 wǔguāng-shísè ① multicoloured; bright with many colours ② of great variety; of all kinds; multifarious
【五湖四海】 wǔhú-sìhǎi all corners of the land: 我们都是来自～，为了一个共同的革命目标走到一起来了。We hail from all corners of the country and have joined together for a common revolutionary objective.
【五花八门】 wǔhuā-bāmén multifarious; of a wide (或 rich) variety
【五花肉】 wǔhuāròu streaky pork
【五级风】 wǔjífēng 〈气〉 force 5 wind; fresh breeze
【五极管】 wǔjíguǎn 〈电子〉 pentode
【五加】 wǔjiā 〈植〉 slender acanthopanax (*Acanthopanax gracilistylus*)
【五角大楼】 Wǔjiǎo Dàlóu the Pentagon
【五角星】 wǔjiǎoxīng five-pointed star
【五金】 wǔjīn ① the five metals (gold, silver, copper, iron and tin) ② metals; hardware
◇ ～厂 hardware factory/ ～店 hardware store/ ～商 dealer in hardware; ironmonger
【五经】 wǔjīng the Five Classics, namely, *The Book of Songs* (《诗经》), *The Book of History* (《书经》), *The Book of Changes* (《易经》), *The Book of Rites* (《礼记》) and *The Spring and Autumn Annals* (《春秋》)
【五绝】 wǔjué a four-line poem with five characters to a line and a strict tonal pattern and rhyme scheme 参见"绝句" juéjù
【五劳】 wǔláo 〈中医〉 exhaustion or lesion of the five internal organs (heart, liver, spleen, lungs and kidneys)
【五里雾】 wǔlǐwù thick fog: 如堕～中 as if lost in a thick fog; utterly mystified
【五敛子】 wǔliǎnzǐ 〈中药〉 the fruit of carambola (*Averrhoa carambola*)
【五岭】 wǔlǐng the Five Ridges (across the borders between Hunan and Jiangxi on the one hand and Guangdong and Guangxi on the other)
【五律】 wǔlǜ an eight-line poem with five characters to a line and a strict tonal pattern and rhyme scheme 参见"律诗" lǜshī
【五氯硝基苯】 wǔlǜxiāojīběn 〈农〉 pentachloronitrobenzene; PCNB
【五内】 wǔnèi 〈书〉 viscera: ～俱焚 be rent with grief
【五年计划】 wǔnián jìhuà Five-Year Plan
【五七干校】 Wǔ Qī gànxiào May 7 cadre school (named after Chairman Mao's May 7 Directive of 1966)
【五七指示】 Wǔ Qī Zhǐshì Chairman Mao's May 7 Directive of 1966
【五日京兆】 wǔ rì jīngzhào an official who doesn't expect to remain long in office
【五卅运动】 Wǔ Sà Yùndòng the May 30th Movement (1925)
【五色】 wǔsè 见"五彩"
【五声音阶】 wǔshēng yīnjiē 〈乐〉 five-tone scale; pentatonic scale
【五十步笑百步】 wǔshí bù xiào bǎi bù one who retreats fifty paces mocks one who retreats a hundred — the pot calls the kettle black
【五四运动】 Wǔ Sì Yùndòng the May 4th Movement of 1919 (an anti-imperialist, anti-feudal, political and cultural movement influenced by the October Revolution and led by intellectuals having the rudiments of Communist ideology)
【五体投地】 wǔ tǐ tóu dì prostrate oneself before sb. in admiration: 佩服得～ admire sb. from the bottom of one's heart; worship sb.
【五味】 wǔwèi ① the five flavours (sweet, sour, bitter, pungent and salty) ② all sorts of flavours
【五味子】 wǔwèizǐ 〈中药〉 the fruit of Chinese magnoliavine (*Schisandra chinensis*)
【五线谱】 wǔxiànpǔ 〈乐〉 staff; stave
【五香】 wǔxiāng ① the five spices (prickly ash, star aniseed, cinnamon, clove and fennel) ② spices ◇ ～豆 spiced beans
【五项全能运动】 wǔ xiàng quánnéng yùndòng 〈体〉 pentathlon
【五小工业】 wǔxiǎo gōngyè the five small industrial enterprises (producing iron and steel, coal, chemical fertilizer, cement and machinery)
【五星红旗】 Wǔxīng Hóngqí the Five-Starred Red Flag (the national flag of the People's Republic of China)
【五星上将】 wǔxīng shàngjiàng five-star general
【五刑】 wǔxíng the five chief forms of punishment in ancient China (tattooing the face 墨, cutting off the nose 劓, cutting off the feet 剕, castration 宫 and decapitation 大辟)
【五行】 wǔxíng the five elements (metal, wood, water, fire and earth, held by the ancients to compose the physical universe and later used in traditional Chinese medicine to explain various physiological and pathological phenomena)
【五言诗】 wǔyánshī a poem with five characters to a line 参见"古体诗" gǔtǐshī; "绝句" juéjù; "律诗" lǜshī
【五颜六色】 wǔyán-liùsè of various colours; multicoloured; colourful
【五一国际劳动节】 Wǔ Yī Guójì Láodòngjié May 1, International Labour Day; May Day
【五音】 wǔyīn 〈乐〉 the five notes of the ancient Chinese five-tone scale
【五月】 wǔyuè ① May ② the fifth month of the lunar year; the fifth moon ◇ ～节 the Dragon Boat Festival (the 5th day of the 5th lunar month)
【五岳】 wǔyuè the Five Mountains, namely, Taishan Mountain (泰山) in Shandong, Hengshan Mountain (衡山) in Hunan, Huashan Mountain (华山) in Shaanxi, Hengshan Mountain (恒山) in Shanxi and Songshan Mountain (嵩山) in Henan
【五脏】 wǔzàng 〈中医〉 the five internal organs (heart, liver, spleen, lungs and kidneys) ◇ ～六腑 the vital organs of the human body
【五指】 wǔzhǐ the five fingers (thumb, index finger, middle finger, third finger and little finger)
【五子棋】 wǔzǐqí gobang

**午** wǔ ① noon; midday ② the seventh of the twelve Earthly Branches
【午饭】 wǔfàn midday meal; lunch
【午后】 wǔhòu afternoon
【午前】 wǔqián forenoon; before noon; morning
【午时】 wǔshí the period of the day from 11 a.m. to 1 p.m.
【午睡】 wǔshuì ① afternoon nap; noontime snooze ② take (或 have) a nap after lunch

【午休】 wǔxiū noon break; midday rest; noontime rest; lunch hour
【午夜】 wǔyè midnight

**伍** wǔ ① five (used for the numeral 五 on cheques, banknotes, etc. to avoid mistakes or alterations) ② the basic five-man unit of the army in ancient China; army: 入～ join the army/ 革命队～ battalions (或 ranks) of the revolution ③ company: 羞与为～ be ashamed of sb.'s company ④ (Wǔ) a surname

**妩** wǔ
【妩媚】 wǔmèi lovely; charming

**忤** wǔ ① disobedient: ～逆 disobedient (to parents) ② uncongenial: 与人无～ bear no ill will against anybody

**武** wǔ ① military: ～官 military officer ② connected with boxing skill, swordplay, etc. ③ valiant; fierce: 威～ martial-looking ④ (Wǔ) a surname
【武备】 wǔbèi 〈书〉 defence preparations, specifically the condition of the armed forces and armaments
【武昌鱼】 wǔchāngyú 〈动〉 blunt-snout bream (*Megalobrama amblycephala*)
【武打】 wǔdǎ acrobatic fighting in Chinese opera or dance
【武斗】 wǔdòu resort to violence (in a debate, dispute, etc.)
【武断】 wǔduàn arbitrary decision; subjective assertion
【武工】 wǔgōng skill in acrobatics in Chinese opera
【武工队】 wǔgōngduì 〈简〉(武装工作队) armed working team (operating under the leadership of the Chinese Communist Party in enemy-occupied areas during the War of Resistance Against Japan, 1937-1945)
【武功】 wǔgōng ①〈书〉 military accomplishments ② 见"武工"
【武官】 wǔguān ① military officer ②〈外〉 military attaché: 海(空)军～ naval (air) attaché ◇ ～处 military attaché's office
【武汉】 Wǔhàn Wuhan
【武火】 wǔhuǒ high heat (in cooking)
【武库】 wǔkù armoury; arsenal
【武力】 wǔlì ① force ② military force; armed might; armed strength; force of arms: ～镇压 armed suppression/ 诉诸～ resort to force
【武器】 wǔqì weapon; arms: 常规～ conventional weapons/ 轻～ small arms/ 核～ nuclear weapons/ 放下～ lay down one's arms/ 拿起～ take up arms ◇ ～装备 weaponry
【武士】 wǔshì ① palace guards in ancient times ② man of prowess; warrior; knight ◇ ～俑 warrior figure
【武士道】 wǔshìdào *bushido*
【武术】 wǔshù *wushu*, martial arts such as shadowboxing, swordplay, etc., formerly cultivated for self-defence, now a form of physical culture
【武艺】 wǔyì skill in *wushu* 参见"武术"
【武装】 wǔzhuāng ① arms; military equipment; battle outfit: 全副～ (in) full battle gear ② armed forces: 人民～ the armed forces of the people/ ～夺取政权 seizure of power by armed force ③ equip (或 supply) with arms; arm: ～到牙齿 be armed to the teeth/ 用马列主义、毛泽东思想～头脑 arm one's mind with Marxism-Leninism-Mao Zedong Thought
◇ ～部队 armed forces/ ～冲突 armed clash/ ～带 Sam Browne belt/ ～斗争 armed struggle/ ～干涉 armed intervention/ ～力量 armed power; armed forces/ ～起义 armed uprising (或 insurrection)/ ～泅渡 swim with one's weapons; swim in battle gear/ ～人员 armed personnel

**侮** wǔ insult; bully: 不可～ not to be bullied/ 外～ foreign aggression
【侮慢】 wǔmàn slight; treat disrespectfully
【侮辱】 wǔrǔ insult; humiliate; subject sb. to indignities

**捂** wǔ seal; cover; muffle: ～鼻子 cover one's nose with one's hand/ ～着耳朵 stop one's ears/ ～盖子 keep the lid on; cover up the truth

**鹉** wǔ 见"鹦鹉" yīngwǔ

**舞** wǔ ① dance: 集体～ group dance/ 秧歌～ *yangko* dance/ 腰鼓～ drum dance/ 红绸～ red silk dance ② move about as in a dance: 手～足蹈 dance for joy/ 雪花飞～ snowflakes dancing in the air ③ dance with sth. in one's hands: ～剑 perform a sword-dance ④ flourish; wield; brandish: 挥～大棒 brandish the big stick/ 挥～指挥棒 wield the baton
【舞伴】 wǔbàn dancing partner
【舞弊】 wǔbì fraudulent practices; malpractices; irregularities; embezzlement: 我们在清查帐目时发现了他的～行为。We discovered his irregularities while checking the accounts.
【舞场】 wǔchǎng dance hall; ballroom
【舞蹈】 wǔdǎo dance
◇ ～病〈医〉 chorea/ ～动作 dance movement/ ～家 dancer/ ～设计 choreography
【舞动】 wǔdòng wave; brandish
【舞会】 wǔhuì dance; ball: 举行～ hold a dance
【舞剧】 wǔjù dance drama; ballet
【舞弄】 wǔnòng wave; wield; brandish: ～刀枪 brandish swords and spears
【舞女】 wǔnǚ dancing girl; dance-hostess; taxi dancer
【舞曲】 wǔqǔ dance music; dance
【舞台】 wǔtái stage; arena: 政治～ political arena (或 scene, stage)/ 在国际～上 in the international arena
◇ ～布景 (stage) scenery; *décor*/ ～工作人员 stagehand/ ～记录片 stage documentary/ ～监督 stage director/ ～设计 stage design/ ～效果 stage effect/ ～艺术 stagecraft
【舞厅】 wǔtīng ballroom; dance hall
【舞文弄墨】 wǔwén-nòngmò ① pervert the law by playing with legal phraseology ② engage in phrase-mongering

## wù

**兀** wù 〈书〉 ① rising to a height; towering ② bald
【兀鹫】 wùjiù 〈动〉 griffon vulture
【兀立】 wùlì stand upright
【兀自】 wùzì still

**乌** wù
另见 wū
【乌拉】 wùla leather boots lined with *wula* sedge
另见 wūlā
【乌拉草】 wùlacǎo 〈植〉 *wula* sedge

**勿** wù 〈副〉〔表示禁止或劝阻〕: 请～吸烟 No Smoking/ ～谓言之不预也。Do not say that you have not been forewarned. 或 Do not blame us for not having forewarned you.

**戊** wù the fifth of the ten Heavenly Stems

【戊戌变法】 Wùxū Biànfǎ the Reform Movement of 1898 (whose leading spirits, Kang Youwei, Liang Qichao and Tan Sitong, represented the interests of the liberal bourgeoisie and the enlightened landlords)

**务** wù ① affair; business: 公～ official business/ 任～ task; job/ 不急之～ business requiring no immediate attention; a matter of no great urgency ② be engaged in; devote one's efforts to: ～农 be engaged in agriculture; be a farmer/ 不～正业 not engage in honest work; not attend to one's proper duties ③ must; be sure to: ～使大家明了这一点。Be sure to make this point clear to everyone./ ～请光临指导。You are cordially invited to come and give guidance.

【务必】 wùbì must; be sure to: 你～在本周内去看望他一次。Be sure to go and see him before the week is out.

【务实】 wùshí deal with concrete matters relating to work

【务使】 wùshǐ make sure; ensure

【务须】 wùxū 见"务必"

【务虚】 wùxū discuss principles or ideological guidelines

**芴** wù 〈化〉 fluorene

**坞** wù ① a depressed place: 船～ dock/ 花～ sunken flower-bed ② 〈书〉 a fortified building; castle

**物** wù ① thing; matter: 废～ waste matter/ 矿～ minerals/ 公～ public property/ 以～易～ barter/ 地大～博 vast territory and rich resources ② the outside world as distinct from oneself; other people: 待人接～ the way one gets along with people ③ content; substance: 言之无～ talk or writing devoid of substance

【物产】 wùchǎn products; produce

【物故】 wùgù 〈书〉 pass away; die

【物归原主】 wù guī yuánzhǔ return sth. to its rightful owner

【物候学】 wùhòuxué phenology

【物换星移】 wùhuàn-xīngyí change of the seasons

【物极必反】 wù jí bì fǎn things will develop in the opposite direction when they become extreme

【物价】 wùjià (commodity) prices: ～稳定。Prices remain stable./ ～波动 price fluctuation/ ～飞涨。Prices skyrocketed. ◇ ～政策 pricing policy/ ～指数 price index

【物件】 wùjiàn 〈方〉 thing; article

【物尽其用】 wù jìn qí yòng make the best use of everything; let all things serve their proper purpose

【物镜】 wùjìng 〈物〉 objective (lens)

【物理】 wùlǐ ① innate laws of things ② physics
◇ ～变化 physical change/ ～化学 physical chemistry/ ～疗法 physical therapy; physiotherapy

【物理学】 wùlǐxué physics: 理论～ theoretical physics/ 应用～ applied physics/ 原子核～ nuclear physics ◇ ～家 physicist

【物力】 wùlì material resources; *matériel*: 节约人力～ use manpower and material resources sparingly/ 我军人力～的来源 our army's sources of manpower and *matériel*

【物品】 wùpǐn article; goods: 贵重～ valuables/ 零星～ sundries; odds and ends

【物色】 wùsè look for; seek out; choose: ～这方面的人才 look for qualified persons in this field

【物体】 wùtǐ body; substance; object: 运动～ a body in motion/ 透明～ a transparent substance (或 object)

【物以类聚】 wù yǐ lèi jù things of one kind come together; like attracts like; birds of a feather flock together

【物议】 wùyì criticism from the people: 免遭～ so as to avoid public censure; so as not to incur criticism by the masses

【物证】 wùzhèng material evidence

【物质】 wùzhì matter; substance; material
◇ ～不灭律 the law of conservation of matter/ ～财富 material wealth/ ～储备 reserve supply; stockpile/ ～刺激 material incentive/ ～鼓励 material reward/ ～基础 material base/ ～力量 material strength; material force/ ～利益 material benefits; material gains/ ～生活 material life/ ～世界 the material (或 physical) world/ ～条件 material conditions or prerequisites/ ～性〈哲〉 materiality/ ～运动 the motion of matter/ ～资料 material goods

【物种】 wùzhǒng 〈生〉 species

【物资】 wùzī goods and materials
◇ ～调度 distribution of materials/ ～管理 handling of goods and materials/ ～交流 interflow of commodities

**误** wù ① mistake; error: 失～ error/ 笔～ a slip of the pen/ 经验主义把局部经验～认为普遍真理。Empiricism mistakes fragmentary experience for universal truth. ② miss: ～了火车 miss a train ③ harm: ～人子弟 harm the younger generation; lead young people astray/ 生产学习两不～。Neither production nor political study is to suffer. ④ by mistake; by accident: ～伤 accidentally injure

【误差】 wùchā error: 平均～ mean error; average error/ 仪器～ instrumental error/ 概然～ probable error/ ～极微的精密零件 precision parts with very close tolerances/ ～不超过千分之三毫米 with a tolerance of less than three-thousandths of a millimetre ◇ ～函数 error function/ ～率 error rate

【误点】 wùdiǎn late; overdue; behind schedule: 飞机～了。The plane is overdue (或 late)./ 火车～十分钟。The train was ten minutes late (或 behind schedule).

【误工】 wùgōng ① delay one's work ② loss of working time

【误会】 wùhuì ① misunderstand; mistake; misconstrue: 你～了我的意思。You've mistaken my meaning./ 你一定是搞～了。You must have misunderstood. 或 You must be mistaken. ② misunderstanding: 消除～ dispel (或 remove) misunderstanding

【误解】 wùjiě ① misread; misunderstand: 你～了我的话。You misunderstood what I said. ② misunderstanding: 你亲自去和他谈谈，以免引起～。Go and talk to him yourself so that there will be no misunderstanding.

【误入歧途】 wù rù qítú go astray; be misled

【误杀】 wùshā 〈法〉 manslaughter

【误伤】 wùshāng ① accidentally injure ② accidental injury

【误事】 wùshì ① cause delay in work or business; hold things up ② bungle matters

**悟** wù realize; awaken: ～出其中的道理 realize why it should be so

【悟性】 wùxing power of understanding; comprehension

**恶** wù loathe; dislike; hate: 好～ likes and dislikes/ 可～ loathsome; hateful
另见 ě; è

【恶寒】 wùhán 〈中医〉 aversion to cold

**晤** wù meet; interview; see

【晤面】 wùmiàn meet; see

【晤谈】 wùtán meet and talk; have a talk; interview

**焐** wù warm up: 把被窝～热 warm up the bedding/ 用热水袋～一～手 warm one's hands with a hot-water bottle

# 寤 wù

【寤子】 wùzi 〈医〉 naevus; mole

# 骛 wù go after; seek for: 好高～远 reach for what is beyond one's grasp; aim too high

# 雾 wù ① fog: 薄～ mist ② fine spray: 喷～器 sprayer

【雾标】 wùbiāo 〈交〉 fog buoy

【雾滴】 wùdī 〈环保〉 droplet

【雾号】 wùhào 〈交〉 fog signal

【雾化器】 wùhuàqì atomizer

【雾气】 wùqì fog; mist; vapour

【雾凇】 wùsōng 〈气〉 (soft) rime ◇ ～雾 rime fog

# 寤 wù 〈书〉 awake

# 鹜 wù 〈书〉 duck

# X

## xī

**夕** xī ① sunset: 朝发～至 start at daybreak and arrive at sunset ② evening; night: 除～ New Year's Eve/ 旦～ this morning or evening — in a short time/ 这些问题不是一朝一～能够解决的。These problems cannot be solved overnight.

【夕烟】 xīyān evening mist

【夕阳】 xīyáng the setting sun

【夕照】 xīzhào the glow of the setting sun; evening glow: 满目青山～明。On all sides, verdant sunset-bathed hills greet the eye.

**兮** xī 〈书〉〈助〉〔跟现代的"啊"相似〕: 大风起～云飞扬。A gale has risen and is sweeping the clouds across the sky.

**汐** xī tide during the night; nighttide

**西** xī ① west: ～屋 west room/ 太原以～ to the west of Taiyuan/ 往～去 head west ② (Xī) Occidental; Western: ～乐 Western music

【西安】 Xī'ān Xi'an

【西安事变】 Xī'ān Shìbiàn the Xi'an Incident (which occurred in Xi'an on December 12, 1936, when Zhang Xueliang and Yang Hucheng, Kuomintang generals influenced by the Chinese Communist Party's policy of an anti-Japanese national united front, imprisoned Chiang Kai-shek and demanded that he cease the civil war and unite with the Communist Party)

【西班牙】 Xībānyá Spain ◇ ～人 Spaniard/ ～语 Spanish (language)

【西半球】 xībànqiú the Western Hemisphere

【西北】 xīběi ① northwest ② (Xīběi) northwest China; the Northwest ◇ ～风 northwest (或 northwesterly) wind

【西伯利亚】 Xībólìyà Siberia

【西餐】 xīcān Western-style food

【西番莲】 xīfānlián 〈植〉 ① passionflower ② dahlia

【西方】 xīfāng ① the west ② (Xīfāng) the West; the Occident: ～国家 the Western countries

【西风】 xīfēng west (或 westerly) wind ◇ ～带〈气〉 westerlies

【西服】 xīfú Western-style clothes ◇ ～料 suiting

【西府海棠】 xīfǔ hǎitáng 〈植〉 midget crabapple

【西瓜】 xīguā watermelon ◇ ～子 watermelon seed

【西汉】 Xī Hàn the Western Han Dynasty (206 B.C.—A.D. 24)

【西红柿】 xīhóngshì tomato

【西葫芦】 xīhúlu 〈植〉 pumpkin; summer squash

【西晋】 Xī Jìn the Western Jin Dynasty (265-316)

【西经】 xījīng 〈地〉 west longitude: ～一百六十五度 longitude 165°W

【西力生】 xīlìshēng 〈农〉 ceresan

【西门】 Xīmén a surname

【西南】 xīnán ① southwest ② (Xīnán) southwest China; the Southwest ◇ ～风 southwest (或 southwesterly) wind

【西南非洲】 Xīnán Fēizhōu South West Africa

【西宁】 Xīníng Xining

【西欧】 Xī Ōu Western Europe

【西皮】 xīpí 〈剧〉 *xipi*, one of the two chief types of music in traditional Chinese operas

【西沙群岛】 Xīshā Qúndǎo the Xisha Islands

【西晒】 xīshài (of a room) with a western exposure; facing west, and hot on summer afternoons

【西式】 xīshì Western style: ～点心 Western-style pastry

【西天】 xītiān 〈佛教〉 Western Paradise

【西维因】 xīwéiyīn 〈农〉 sevin; carbaryl

【西魏】 Xī Wèi the Western Wei Dynasty (535-556), one of the Northern Dynasties

【西西】 xīxī cc; c.c. (cubic centimetre)

【西夏】 Xī Xià the Western Xia regime (1038-1227)

【西学】 xīxué Western learning (a late Qing Dynasty term for Western natural and social sciences)

【西洋】 Xīyáng the West; the Western world ◇ ～人 Westerner/ ～文学 Western literature

【西洋景】 xīyángjǐng ① peep show ② hanky-panky; trickery: 拆穿～ expose sb.'s tricks; strip off the camouflage 又作"西洋镜"

【西洋参】 xīyángshēn 〈中药〉 American ginseng (*Panax quinquefolium*)

【西药】 xīyào Western medicine

【西医】 xīyī ① Western medicine (as distinguished from traditional Chinese medicine) ② a doctor trained in Western medicine

【西印度群岛】 Xīyìndù Qúndǎo the West Indies

【西域】 Xīyù the Western Regions (a Han Dynasty term for the area west of Yumenguan 玉门关, including what is now Xinjiang and parts of Central Asia)

【西乐】 xīyuè Western music

【西藏】 Xīzàng Xizang (Tibet)

【西藏自治区】 Xīzàng Zìzhìqū the Xizang (Tibet) Autonomous Region

【西周】 Xī Zhōu the Western Zhou Dynasty (c. 11th century — 771 B.C.)

【西装】 xīzhuāng Western-style clothes

**吸** xī ① inhale; breathe in; draw: ～进新鲜空气 inhale fresh air/ 深深～一口气 draw a deep breath ② absorb; suck up: 用粉笔把墨水～干 blot ink with a piece of chalk/ 海绵～水。A sponge absorbs water. ③ attract; draw to oneself: 磁石～铁。A magnet attracts iron.

【吸尘器】 xīchénqì dust catcher; dust collector: 真空～ vacuum cleaner

【吸虫】 xīchóng fluke: 肺～ lung fluke/ 肝～ liver fluke/ 血～ blood fluke

【吸毒】 xīdú drug taking ◇ ～者 drug addict

【吸附】 xīfù 〈化〉 adsorption ◇ ～剂 adsorbent/ ～器 adsorber/ ～水 adsorbed water/ ～作用 adsorption

【吸力】 xīlì suction; attraction: 相互～ mutual attraction/ 地心～ force of gravity ◇ ～计 suction gauge

【吸墨纸】 xīmòzhǐ blotting paper

【吸奶器】 xīnǎiqì 〈医〉 breast pump

【吸泥泵】 xīníbèng dredge pump

【吸盘】 xīpán 〈动〉 sucking disc; sucker

【吸取】 xīqǔ absorb; draw; assimilate: ～水分 absorb

water/ ～精华 absorb the quintessence/ ～教训 draw a lesson/ 从群众斗争中～政治营养 derive political nourishment from mass struggles
【吸热】 xīrè absorption of heat ◇ ～反应〈化〉 endothermic reaction
【吸声】 xīshēng 〈建〉 sound absorption ◇ ～材料 sound-absorbing material; acoustic absorbent
【吸湿】 xīshī moisture absorption ◇ ～剂 hygroscopic agent/ ～性 hygroscopicity
【吸食】 xīshí suck; take in
【吸收】 xīshōu ① absorb; suck up; assimilate; imbibe; draw: ～养分 assimilate nutriment/ ～水分 suck up moisture/ ～知识 absorb (或 imbibe) knowledge/ 批判地～古代文化遗产 critically assimilate ancient cultural heritage/ 这个设计～了老工人的先进经验。The design incorporates the advanced experience of veteran workers. ② recruit; enrol; admit: ～入党 admit into the Party/ 要～更多的同志参加这项工作。We should recruit more comrades for the work. 或 We should draw more comrades into the work.
◇ ～光谱〈物〉 absorption spectrum/ ～剂 absorbent/ ～率 absorptivity/ ～塔〈化〉 absorption tower/ ～作用〈物〉 absorption
【吸吮】 xīshǔn suck; absorb: 资本家～工人的血汗。The capitalists suck the blood of the workers.
【吸铁石】 xītiěshí magnet; lodestone
【吸血鬼】 xīxuèguǐ bloodsucker; vampire
【吸烟】 xīyān smoke ◇ ～室 smoking room
【吸引】 xīyǐn attract; draw; fascinate: ～注意力 attract attention/ 把敌人火力～过来 draw enemy fire on oneself/ 被工地热火朝天的场面～住了 be fascinated by the hustle and bustle of the construction site/ 这部电影对观众很有～力。This film has a strong appeal to the audience. ◇ ～器〈医〉 aspirator

**希** xī ① hope: 敬～读者指正。It is hoped that the readers will kindly point out our errors./ ～准时到会。Please get to the meeting on time. ② rare; scarce; uncommon
【希伯来语】 Xībóláiyǔ Hebrew (language)
【希罕】 xīhan ① rare; scarce; uncommon: 骆驼在南方是～的东西。Camels are a rare sight in the south. ② value as a rarity; cherish: 你不～,我还～呢。You may not cherish it, but I do./ 谁～你的臭钱? Who cares about your lousy money? ③ rare thing; rarity: 看～儿 enjoy the rare sight of sth./ 这么大的人参可是个～儿。Such a big ginseng root is certainly a rarity.
【希冀】 xījì 〈书〉 hope for; wish for; aspire after
【希腊】 Xīlà Greece
◇ ～人 Greek/ ～语 Greek (language)/ ～正教 the Greek Orthodox Church/ ～字母 the Greek alphabet
【希奇】 xīqí rare; strange; curious: 十月下雪在这儿不是什么～的事。Snow in October is nothing strange in this place.
【希少】 xīshǎo 见"稀少" xīshǎo
【希图】 xītú harbour the intention of; try to; attempt to: ～蒙混过关 try to wangle; try to get by under false pretences/ ～牟取暴利 go after quick profits
【希望】 xīwàng hope; wish; expect: 把～变成现实 turn hopes into reality/ 大有成功的～ promise high hopes of success; stand a very good chance of success/ 这就是同志们对你的～。This is what the comrades expect of you./ 那时候我们是多么～把水引到这儿来啊! How we wished then that the water over there could be diverted to our area!/ ～寄托在你们青年人身上。Our hope is placed on you young people./ 我们的党,我们的国家是大有～的。Our Party and our country are both full of promise.
【希有】 xīyǒu 见"稀有" xīyǒu

**夕** xī 见"窀夕" zhūnxī

**昔** xī former times; the past: 今～对比 contrast the past with the present/ 今胜于～。The present is superior to the past.
【昔年】 xīnián 〈书〉 in former years
【昔日】 xīrì in former days (或 times): ～荒坡,今日良田。The once barren hillsides are now good farmland.

**析** xī ① divide; separate: 分崩离～ fall to pieces; come apart ② analyse; dissect; resolve: ～义 analyse the meaning (of a word, etc.)
【析出】 xīchū 〈化〉 separate out
【析象管】 xīxiàngguǎn 〈电子〉 image dissector
【析疑】 xīyí 〈书〉 resolve a doubt; clear up a doubtful point

**矽** xī 〈化〉 silicon (Si)
【矽肺】 xīfèi 〈医〉 silicosis
【矽钢】 xīgāng 〈冶〉 silicon steel

**郗** Xī a surname

**唏** xī 〈书〉 sob
【唏嘘】 xīxū 〈书〉 sob; sigh

**奚** xī ①〈书〉 why; how; where; what ② (Xī) a surname
【奚落】 xīluò scoff at; taunt; gibe

**牺** xī 〈书〉 a beast of a uniform colour for sacrifice; sacrifice: ～牛 sacrificial ox
【牺牲】 xīshēng ① a beast slaughtered for sacrifice; sacrifice ② sacrifice oneself; die a martyr's death; lay down one's life: 英勇～ die a heroic death/ 这是他～前留下的党费。These are the Party dues that he left behind before he met his death. ③ sacrifice; give up; do sth. at the expense of: ～个人利益 sacrifice one's personal interests/ ～质量而去追求数量是错误的。It is wrong to sacrifice quality to quantity./ 老张～休息时间为生产大队赶修脱粒机。Lao Zhang gave up his spare time to repair the brigade's thresher. ◇ ～品 victim; prey

**息** xī ① breath: 屏～ hold one's breath/ 一～尚存 so long as there is breath left in one/ 战斗到最后一～ fight to one's last breath ② news: 信～ news; message ③ cease; stop: 风止雨～。The wind has subsided and the rain stopped./ 经久不～的掌声 prolonged applause ④ rest: 按时作～ work and rest according to the timetable ⑤ grow; multiply: 蕃～ multiply greatly ⑥ interest: 年～ annual interest/ 无～贷款 interest-free loan ⑦〈书〉 one's children
【息怒】 xīnù cease to be angry; calm one's anger
【息票】 xīpiào interest coupon
【息肉】 xīròu 〈医〉 polyp; polypus
【息事宁人】 xīshì-níngrén ① patch up a quarrel and reconcile the parties concerned ② make concessions to avoid trouble; gloss things over to stay on good terms
【息息相关】 xīxī xiāng guān be closely linked; be closely bound up: 中国人民的革命事业是和世界人民的革命事业～的。The revolutionary cause of the Chinese people is closely bound up with that of the other peoples of the world.

**淅** xī 〈书〉wash rice

【淅沥】 xīlì 〈象〉[形容轻微的雨声等]: 雨声～ the patter of rain

**惜** xī ① cherish; value highly; care for tenderly: 爱～ cherish; treasure/ ～寸阴 value every bit of time; make good use of every moment ② spare; grudge; stint: ～指失掌 stint a finger only to lose the whole hand — try to save a little only to lose a lot/ 不～工本 spare neither labour nor money; spare no expense ③ have pity on sb.; feel sorry for sb.: 惋～ feel sorry for

【惜别】 xībié be reluctant to part; hate to see sb. go: 我们怀着～的心情,送走了老战友。We reluctantly parted with our old comrades-in-arms.

【惜力】 xīlì be sparing of one's energy; not do one's best: 小张干活从不～。Xiao Zhang never spares himself in his work.

**烯** xī

【烯烃】 xītīng 〈化〉alkene

**硒** xī 〈化〉selenium (Se)

**晞** xī 〈书〉① dry: 晨露未～ before the dew is dry ② the first light of day; daybreak: 东方未～ before daybreak

**欷** xī

【欷歔】 xīxū 〈书〉sob; sigh

**悉** xī ① all; entirely: ～力 go all out; spare no effort ② know; learn; be informed of: 熟～ know very well/ 惊～ be shocked to learn/ 来函敬～。Your letter has come to hand.

【悉数】 xīshǔ enumerate in full detail: 不可～ too many to enumerate

【悉数】 xīshù 〈书〉all; every single one: ～奉还 return all that has been borrowed or taken away

【悉心】 xīxīn devote all one's attention; take the utmost care: ～研究 devote oneself to the study of sth./ ～照料病人 take the utmost care of the patient

**晰** xī clear; distinct: 明～ clear; lucid/ 清～ distinct

**翕** xī 〈书〉① amiable and compliant ② furl; fold; shut: ～张 furl and unfurl; close and open

**稀** xī ① rare; scarce; uncommon: 物以～为贵。When a thing is scarce, it is precious. ② sparse; scattered: 地广人～ a vast, sparsely populated area/ 月明星～。The moon is bright and the stars are few. ③ watery; thin: 粥太～了。This gruel is too thin./ 我想吃点儿～的。I'd like to have some liquid food.

【稀薄】 xībó thin; rare: 山顶空气～。The air is thin on the top of the mountain.

【稀饭】 xīfàn rice or millet gruel; porridge

【稀罕】 xīhan 见"希罕" xīhan

【稀客】 xīkè rare visitor

【稀烂】 xīlàn ① completely mashed; pulpy: 肉煮得～。The meat was cooked to a pulp. ② smashed to pieces (或 smithereens); broken to bits: 敌人碉堡被打得～。The enemy pillbox was smashed to smithereens.

【稀里糊涂】 xīlihútu not knowing what one is about; muddleheaded

【稀奇】 xīqí 见"希奇" xīqí

【稀少】 xīshǎo few; rare; scarce: 人口～ a sparse population/ 街上行人～。There were few people in the street.

【稀释】 xīshì 〈化〉dilute ◇ ～剂 diluent; thinner/ ～测定 dilution metering

【稀疏】 xīshū few and scattered; few and far between; thin; sparse: ～的晨星 a few scattered morning stars/ ～的头发 thin hair; sparse hair/ ～的枪声 scattered shots; sporadic firing/ 林木～。The woods are sparse.

【稀松】 xīsōng ① poor; sloppy: 这活儿干得～。This is sloppy work. ② unimportant; trivial: 别把这些～的事放在心里。Don't take such trivial matters to heart.

【稀土金属】 xītǔ jīnshǔ 〈化〉rare-earth metal

【稀土元素】 xītǔ yuánsù 〈化〉rare-earth element

【稀稀拉拉】 xīxilālā sparse; thinly scattered: 这块地的庄稼怎么长得～的？How is it that the crops on this plot are so sparse? 又作"稀稀落落"

【稀有】 xīyǒu rare; unusual

【稀有金属】 xīyǒu jīnshǔ 〈化〉rare metal

【稀有元素】 xīyǒu yuánsù 〈化〉rare element

**腊** xī 〈书〉dried meat
另见 là

**犀** xī rhinoceros

【犀角】 xījiǎo rhinoceros horn

【犀利】 xīlì sharp; incisive; trenchant: ～的目光 sharp eyes/ 谈锋～ incisive in conversation/ 文笔～ a trenchant pen

【犀鸟】 xīniǎo hornbill

【犀牛】 xīniú rhinoceros

**溪** xī small stream; brook; rivulet

【溪涧】 xījiàn mountain stream

【溪流】 xīliú brook; rivulet

**锡** xī 〈化〉tin (Sn)

【锡伯族】 Xībózú the Xibe (Sibo) nationality, distributed over the Xinjiang Uygur Autonomous Region and Liaoning

【锡箔】 xībó tinfoil paper (formerly used as funeral offerings)

【锡匠】 xījiang tinsmith

【锡金】 Xījīn Sikkim

【锡剧】 xījù Wuxi opera, a local opera popular in southern Jiangsu and Shanghai

【锡矿】 xīkuàng tin ore

【锡镴】 xīla 〈方〉① solder ② tin

【锡石】 xīshí 〈矿〉cassiterite; tinstone

【锡纸】 xīzhǐ silver paper; tinfoil

**裼** xī 〈书〉unbutton or divest one's upper garment

**皙** xī 〈书〉fair-skinned; light-complexioned

**徯** xī 〈书〉① wait ② 见"蹊" xī

**熄** xī extinguish; put out: ～灯 put out the light/ 火～了。The fire has gone out.

【熄灯号】 xīdēnghào lights-out; taps

【熄风】 xīfēng 〈中医〉relieve dizziness, high fever, infantile convulsions, epilepsy, etc.

【熄灭】 xīmiè go out; die out: 只要还有阶级存在,阶级斗争就不会～。So long as there are classes, class struggle will not die out.

**豨** xī 〈书〉pig; hog

【豨莶】 xīxiān 〈中药〉common St. Paulswort (*Siegesbeckia*

*orientalis*)

**熙** xī ① bright; sunny ② prosperous ③ gay; merry

【熙来攘往】 xīlái-rǎngwǎng 见"熙熙攘攘"

【熙熙攘攘】 xīxīrǎngrǎng bustling with activity; with people bustling about

**蜥** xī

【蜥蜴】 xīyì lizard

**嘻** xī ①〈书〉〈叹〉〔表示惊叹〕: ～，技至此乎！How wonderful! What superb skill! ②〈象〉〔形容笑声〕: ～～地笑 giggle

【嘻嘻哈哈】 xīxīhāhā laughing and joking; laughing merrily; mirthful

**膝** xī knee

【膝盖】 xīgài knee ◇ ～骨 kneecap; patella

【膝关节】 xīguānjié knee joint

【膝腱反射】 xījiàn fǎnshè 〈医〉 knee jerk

**嬉** xī 〈方〉 play; sport

【嬉皮士】 xīpíshì hippy; hippie

【嬉皮笑脸】 xīpí-xiàoliǎn grinning cheekily; smiling and grimacing

【嬉戏】 xīxì 〈书〉 play; sport: 湖面上鸭群在～。Ducks are sporting on the lake.

【嬉笑】 xīxiào be laughing and playing: 孩子们的～声 the happy laughter of children at play

**窸** xī

【窸窣】 xīsū 〈象〉 rustle

**熹** xī 〈书〉 dawn; brightness

【熹微】 xīwēi 〈书〉 (of morning sunlight) dim; pale: 晨光～ the dim light (或 first faint rays) of dawn

**螅** xī 见"水螅" shuǐxī

**歙** xī 〈书〉 inhale

**蹊** xī 〈书〉 footpath

另见 qī

【蹊径】 xījìng 〈书〉 path; way

**蟋** xī

【蟋蟀】 xīshuài 〈动〉 cricket

【蟋蟀草】 xīshuàicǎo 〈植〉 yard grass

**谿** xī 〈书〉 ① 见"溪" xī ② 见"勃谿" bóxī

**曦** xī 〈书〉 sunlight (usu. in early morning): 晨～ early morning sunlight

**鼷** xī

【鼷鼠】 xīshǔ house mouse

## xí

**习** xí ① practise; exercise; review: 自～ study by oneself/ 复～ review (one's lessons) ② get accustomed to; be used to; become familiar with: ～闻 often hear/ 不～水性 be not good at swimming ③ habit; custom; usual practice: 积～ old habit; longstanding practice/ 陋～ bad custom ④ (Xí) a surname

【习非成是】 xí fēi chéng shì accept what is wrong as right as one grows accustomed to it

【习惯】 xíguàn ① be accustomed to; be used to; be inured to: ～于过部队生活 be accustomed (或 inured) to army life/ 这样潮湿的天气我实在不～。I just can't get used to this damp weather. ② habit; custom; usual practice: 从小培养劳动～ cultivate the habit of doing manual labour from childhood/ 破除旧～，树立新风尚 break down outmoded customs and establish new ones/ ～成自然。Once you form a habit, it comes natural to you. ◇ ～法 common law; customary law/ ～势力 force of habit

【习见】 xíjiàn (of things) commonly seen: ～的现象 a common sight

【习气】 xíqì bad habit; bad practice: 官僚～ habitual practice of bureaucracy; bad bureaucratic habits

【习染】 xírǎn 〈书〉 ① contract (a bad habit); fall into a bad habit of ② bad habit

【习尚】 xíshàng common practice; custom

【习俗】 xísú custom; convention

【习题】 xítí exercises (in school work)

【习习】 xíxí (of the wind) blow gently: 微风～。A gentle breeze is blowing.

【习性】 xíxìng habits and characteristics: 熊猫的～ the habits and characteristics of the giant panda

【习焉不察】 xí yān bù chá too accustomed to sth. to call it in question

【习以为常】 xí yǐ wéi cháng be used (或 accustomed) to sth.

【习用】 xíyòng habitually use

【习与性成】 xí yǔ xìng chéng habits become one's second nature

【习语】 xíyǔ idiom

【习字】 xízì practise penmanship; do exercises in calligraphy ◇ ～帖 copybook; calligraphy model

【习作】 xízuò ① do exercises in composition ② an exercise in composition, drawing, etc.

**席** xí ① mat: 草～ straw mat ② seat; place: 入～ take one's seat/ 来宾～ seats for visitors/ 该党在议会选举中失去了十五～。That party lost 15 seats in the parliamentary election. ③ feast; banquet; dinner: ～间宾主频频举杯。Host and guests frequently raised their glasses during the feast. ④〈量〉: 一～酒 a banquet/ 一～话 a talk (with sb.); a conversation ⑤ (Xí) a surname

【席不暇暖】 xí bù xiá nuǎn not sit long enough to warm the seat; be in a tearing hurry; be constantly on the go

【席次】 xícì the order of seats; seating arrangement; one's place among the seats arranged: 按指定～入座 take one's assigned seat; sit down in one's place

【席地】 xídì on the ground: ～而坐 sit on the ground

【席卷】 xíjuǎn ① roll up like a mat; carry everything with one; take away everything: ～而去 make off with everything that one can lay hands on ② sweep across; engulf: 暴风雪～大草原。A blizzard swept across the vast grasslands./ 一九二九年一场空前的经济危机～了整个资本主义世界。In 1929, an economic crisis of unprecedented dimensions engulfed the entire capitalist world.

【席棚】 xípéng ① mat shed ② mat hoarding: 大字报～ a mat hoarding for big-character posters

【席位】 xíwèi seat (at a conference, in a legislative assembly, etc.)

**袭** xí ① make a surprise attack on; raid: 夜～ night raid/ 偷～ surprise attack; sneak raid/ 花气～人。The fragrance of flowers assails one's nose. ② follow the pattern of; carry on as before: 因～ carry on (an old tradition, etc.)/ 抄～ plagiarize ③〈书〉〈量〉〔用于成套的衣服〕: 衣一～ a suit of clothes

【袭击】 xíjī make a surprise attack on; surprise; raid: ～敌军阵地 make a surprise attack on the enemy positions/ 沿海一带受到台风的～。The coastal areas were hit by a typhoon.

【袭取】 xíqǔ ① take by surprise ② 见"袭用"

【袭扰】 xírǎo 〈军〉 harassing attack

【袭用】 xíyòng take over (something that has long been used in the past): ～古方 take over an age-old recipe/ ～老谱 follow old practice

**媳** xí daughter-in-law

【媳妇】 xífù ① son's wife; daughter-in-law ② the wife of a relative of the younger generation: 侄～ nephew's wife/ 孙～ grandson's wife

【媳妇儿】 xífur 〈方〉 ① wife ② a young married woman

**檄** xí 〈书〉 ① a call to arms (in ancient times) ② announce or denounce in such a call

【檄文】 xíwén ① an official call to arms ② an official denunciation of the enemy

## xǐ

**洗** xǐ ① wash; bathe: ～衣服 wash clothes/ ～干净 wash sth. clean/ ～伤口 bathe a wound/ 碧空如～ a cloudless blue sky ②〈宗〉 baptize: 受～ receive baptism; be baptized ③ redress; right: ～冤 right a wrong; redress a grievance ④ kill and loot; sack: ～城 massacre the inhabitants of a captured city/ 血～ plunge (the inhabitants) in a bloodbath; massacre ⑤ develop (a film) ⑥ shuffle (cards, etc.)

【洗尘】 xǐchén give a dinner of welcome (to a visitor from afar)

【洗涤】 xǐdí wash; cleanse
◇ ～槽〈化〉 washing tank/ ～剂 detergent/ ～器〈化〉 scrubber/ ～塔〈化〉 washing tower

【洗耳恭听】 xǐ ěr gōng tīng listen with respectful attention

【洗发剂】 xǐfàjì shampoo

【洗剂】 xǐjì 〈药〉 lotion

【洗劫】 xǐjié loot; sack

【洗井】 xǐjǐng 〈石油〉 flushing

【洗礼】 xǐlǐ ①〈宗〉 baptism ② severe test: 炮火的～ the baptism of fire/ 受过战斗的～ have gone through (the test of) battle

【洗脸盆】 xǐliǎnpén washbasin; washbowl

【洗煤】 xǐméi 〈矿〉 coal washing ◇ ～厂 coal washery; coal cleaning plant

【洗片】 xǐpiàn 〈摄〉 develop (a film) ◇ ～机 developing machine

【洗染店】 xǐrǎndiàn cleaners and dyers; laundering and dyeing shop

【洗手】 xǐshǒu ① (of a thief, bandit, etc.) stop doing evil and reform oneself ② wash one's hands of sth.

【洗刷】 xǐshuā ① wash and brush; scrub: ～地板 scrub the floor ② wash off; clear oneself of (opprobrium, stigma, guilt, etc.): 加强调查研究，～唯心精神 strengthen investigation and study and wipe out idealism

【洗头】 xǐtóu wash one's hair; shampoo

【洗胃】 xǐwèi 〈医〉 gastric lavage

【洗心革面】 xǐxīn-gémiàn turn over a new leaf; thoroughly reform oneself

【洗选】 xǐxuǎn 〈矿〉 washing

【洗雪】 xǐxuě wipe out (a disgrace); redress (a wrong)

【洗眼杯】 xǐyǎnbēi eyecup

【洗衣】 xǐyī wash clothes; do one's washing
◇ ～板 washboard/ ～店 laundry/ ～粉 washing powder/ ～机 washing machine; washer/ ～刷 wash brush

【洗印】 xǐyìn 〈摄〉 developing and printing; processing
◇ ～机 (film) processor

【洗澡】 xǐzǎo have (或 take) a bath; bathe

【洗濯】 xǐzhuó wash; cleanse

**玺** xǐ imperial or royal seal

**徙** xǐ move (from one place to another)

【徙居】 xǐjū move house: ～内地 move up-country

**铣** xǐ mill
另见 xiǎn

【铣床】 xǐchuáng 〈机〉 milling machine; miller

【铣刀】 xǐdāo 〈机〉 milling cutter

【铣工】 xǐgōng ① milling (work) ② miller; milling machine operator

**喜** xǐ ① happy; delighted; pleased: 心中暗～ secretly feel pleased/ ～不自胜 be delighted beyond measure; be beside oneself with joy/ 笑在脸上，～在心里 with a smile on one's face and joy in one's heart/ ～获丰收 reap a bumper harvest/ 华北地区～降瑞雪。There was a welcome fall of seasonable snow in north China. ② happy event (esp. wedding); occasion for celebration: 报～ report good news/ 大～的日子 a day of great happiness; a joyful occasion; an occasion for celebration ③〈口〉 pregnancy: 有～ be expecting; be in the family way ④ be fond of; like; have an inclination for: ～读书 be fond of reading/ 猴子性～攀缘。Monkeys have a natural inclination for climbing.

【喜爱】 xǐ'ài like; love; be fond of; be keen on: ～户外活动 be keen on outdoor activities/ 我们最～这首歌曲。We like this song best.

【喜报】 xǐbào a bulletin of glad tidings: 大红～ a report of happy tidings written on crimson paper/ 立功～ a bulletin announcing meritorious service

【喜冲冲】 xǐchōngchōng look exhilarated; be in a joyful mood

【喜出望外】 xǐ chū wàng wài be overjoyed (at an unexpected gain, good news, etc.); be pleasantly surprised

【喜好】 xǐhào like; love; be fond of; be keen on: 她从小就～音乐。She's been a music lover since childhood.

【喜欢】 xǐhuan ① like; love; be fond of; be keen on: ～看电视 like watching TV/ 这孩子真讨人～。This is a lovable child./ 她最不～吹吹拍拍。She loathes boasting and flattery. ② happy; elated; filled with joy: 听到胜利的消息好不～ become elated at the news of victory

【喜酒】 xǐjiǔ ① wine drunk at a wedding feast ② wedding feast

【喜剧】 xǐjù comedy ◇ ～演员 comedian

【喜马拉雅山】 Xǐmǎlāyǎshān the Himalayas

【喜怒无常】 xǐ-nù wú cháng subject to changing moods

【喜气洋洋】 xǐqì yángyáng full of joy; jubilant: 社员们～地交公粮。The commune members are jubilantly sending in their tax grain to the state.

【喜庆】 xǐqìng ① joyous; jubilant: 在这～的日子里 on this day of jubilation; on this happy occasion ② happy event

【喜鹊】 xǐque 〈动〉 magpie

【喜人】 xǐrén gratifying; satisfactory: 取得～的成果 achieve satisfactory results/ 形势～。The situation is gratifying./ 好一派～的丰收景象! What a fine sight this good harvest is!/ 麦苗长势～。The wheat is coming on beautifully.
【喜色】 xǐsè happy expression; joyful look: 面有～ wear a happy expression
【喜事】 xǐshì ① happy event; joyous occasion ② wedding
【喜闻乐见】 xǐwén-lèjiàn love to see and hear; love: 为劳动人民所～的作品 literary and artistic works loved by the labouring people
【喜笑颜开】 xǐxiào-yánkāi light up with pleasure; be wreathed in smiles
【喜新厌旧】 xǐxīn-yànjiù love the new and loathe the old — be fickle in affection
【喜形于色】 xǐ xíng yú sè be visibly pleased; light up with pleasure
【喜讯】 xǐxùn happy news; good news; glad tidings
【喜洋洋】 xǐyángyáng beaming with joy; radiant
【喜雨】 xǐyǔ seasonable rain; a welcome fall of rain: 普降～ a widespread fall of seasonable rain; a seasonable fall of rain over a wide area
【喜悦】 xǐyuè happy; joyous: 怀着万分～的心情 with a feeling of immeasurable joy
【喜滋滋】 xǐzīzī feeling pleased; filled with joy

**葸** xǐ 〈书〉 fear; dread; be afraid: 畏～不前 be too timid to go ahead; hang back

**屣** xǐ 〈书〉 shoe: 敝～ worn-out shoes

**禧** xǐ auspiciousness; happiness; jubilation: 恭贺新～。Happy New Year!

**蟢** xǐ 〈动〉 sand borer

## xì

**戏** xì ① play; sport: 嬉～ sport; have fun/ 二龙～珠 two dragons playing with a pearl ② make fun of; joke: ～言 say something for fun; joke ③ drama; play; show: 京～ Beijing opera/ 马～ circus show (或 performance)/ 去看～ go to the theatre/ 这场～演得很精彩。It was a wonderful performance./ 好～还在后头呢。The really interesting part of the show is yet to come.
【戏班】 xìbān theatrical troupe (或 company)
【戏词】 xìcí actor's part (或 lines)
【戏法】 xìfǎ conjuring; juggling; tricks; magic: 变～ juggle; conjure; perform tricks/ ～人人会变,各有巧妙不同。Many are the magicians, but each has his own tricks.
【戏剧】 xìjù drama; play; theatre: 现代～ modern drama; the modern theatre/ 一个富有～性的事件 a dramatic event ◇ ～家 dramatist/ ～界 theatrical circles/ ～评论 dramatic criticism
【戏迷】 xìmí theatre fan
【戏目】 xìmù theatrical programme
【戏弄】 xìnòng make fun of; play tricks on; tease; kid
【戏曲】 xìqǔ ① traditional opera: 地方～ local operas ② singing parts in *chuanqi* (传奇) and *zaju* (杂剧)
【戏台】 xìtái 〈口〉 stage
【戏谑】 xìxuè banter; crack jokes
【戏院】 xìyuàn theatre
【戏照】 xìzhào a photo of a person in stage costume
【戏装】 xìzhuāng theatrical (或 stage) costume

**系** xì ① system; series: 太阳～ the solar system/ 镧～〈化〉 lanthanide series/ 语～ (language) family/ 派～ faction ② department (in a college); faculty: 哲学～ the department of philosophy ③ tie; fasten: ～马 tether a horse ④ relate to; bear on: 名誉所～ have a direct bearing on one's reputation/ 成败～于此举 stand or fall by this ⑤ feel anxious; be concerned: ～念 feel concerned about ⑥〈书〉 be: 纯～试验性质 be purely experimental in character/ 其母～山东人。His mother is a native of Shandong.
另见 jì
【系词】 xìcí ①〈逻〉 copula ②〈语〉 copulative verb; linking verb
【系列】 xìliè series; set: 一～的问题 a series of problems/ 一～政策 a whole set of policies/ 运载～ vehicle series ◇ ～化 seriation
【系念】 xìniàn 〈书〉 be anxious about; worry about; feel concerned about
【系数】 xìshù 〈数〉 coefficient: 光学～ optical coefficient
【系统】 xìtǒng ① system: 灌溉～ irrigation system/ 财贸～ departments of trade and finance and affiliated organizations/ 通过组织～ through organizational channels ② systematic: 作～的研究 make a systematic study/ ～地说明 explain in a systematic way ◇ ～化 systematize/ ～性 systematicness

**细** xì ① thin; slender: ～铁丝 thin wire ② in small particles; fine: ～沙 fine sand/ 玉米面磨得很～。The corn flour has been ground very fine. ③ thin and soft: ～嗓子 a thready voice ④ fine; exquisite; delicate: ～瓷 fine porcelain (或 china)/ 这几件象牙雕刻做得真～! What exquisite (或 delicate) ivory carvings these are!/ 粗粮～作 make delicacies out of coarse food grain ⑤ careful; meticulous; detailed: ～看 examine carefully; scrutinize/ ～问 make detailed inquiries; ask about details/ 工作做得～ be meticulous in one's work ⑥ minute; trifling: ～节 minute detail/ 事无巨～ all matters, big and small/ 分工很～ have an elaborate division of labour
【细胞】 xìbāo cell
◇ ～壁 cell wall/ ～分裂 cell division/ ～核 cell nucleus/ ～膜 cell membrane/ ～学 cytology/ ～质 cytoplasm
【细布】 xìbù fine cloth
【细部】 xìbù detail (of a drawing)
【细长】 xìcháng long and thin; tall and slender: ～的身材 a tall and slender figure
【细齿】 xìchǐ 〈机〉 serration ◇ ～拉刀 serration broach/ ～螺母 serrated nut
【细纺】 xìfǎng finespun
【细高挑儿】 xìgāotiǎor 〈方〉 ① a tall and slender figure ② a tall, slender person
【细工】 xìgōng fine workmanship
【细故】 xìgù trivial matter; trifle
【细活】 xìhuó a job requiring fine workmanship or meticulous care; skilled work
【细节】 xìjié details; particulars: 讨论计划的～ discuss the details of a plan; go into the particulars of a plan/ 通过～描写来表现人物性格 portray a character through the description of detail
【细颈现象】 xìjǐng xiànxiàng 〈化纤〉 necking phenomena
【细菌】 xìjūn germ; bacterium
◇ ～肥料 bacterial fertilizer/ ～农药 bacterial pesticide/ ～武器 bacteriological (或 germ) weapon/ ～学 bacteriology/ ～学家 bacteriologist/ ～战 bacteriological (或 germ) warfare

【细粮】 xìliáng flour and rice
【细脉】 xìmài 〈中医〉 thready pulse
【细毛】 xìmáo fine, soft fur
【细毛羊】 xìmáoyáng fine-wool sheep
【细密】 xìmì ① fine and closely woven; close: 质地～ of close texture/ 针脚～ in fine close stitches/ ～的纹理 a close grain ② meticulous; detailed: ～的分析 a detailed analysis
【细木工】 xìmùgōng ① joinery ② joiner; cabinetmaker
【细目】 xìmù ① detailed catalogue ② specific item; detail
【细嫩】 xìnèn delicate; tender: ～的皮肤 delicate skin
【细腻】 xìnì ① fine and smooth ② exquisite; minute: ～的描写 a minute description/ ～的表演 an exquisite performance
【细巧】 xìqiǎo exquisite; dainty; delicate: ～的图案 an exquisite design
【细绒线】 xìróngxiàn fingering yarn
【细软】 xìruǎn jewelry, expensive clothing and other valuables
【细润】 xìrùn fine and glossy: 瓷质～。The porcelain is fine and glossy.
【细弱】 xìruò thin and delicate; slim and fragile: ～的身子 of slim and delicate build/ 声音～ a feeble voice
【细纱】 xìshā 〈纺〉 spun yarn ◇ ～机 spinning frame
【细声细气】 xìshēng-xìqì in a soft voice; soft-spoken
【细石器】 xìshíqì 〈考古〉 microlith ◇ ～文化 microlithic culture
【细水长流】 xìshuǐ cháng liú ① economize to avoid running short ② go about sth. little by little without a letup
【细碎】 xìsuì in small, broken bits: ～的脚步声 the sound of light and hurried footsteps
【细微】 xìwēi slight; fine; subtle: ～的变化 slight (或 subtle) changes/ ～差别 a fine distinction; a subtle difference
【细小】 xìxiǎo very small; tiny; fine; trivial: ～的零件 small parts (of a machine)/ ～的雨点 tiny raindrops/ ～的事情 trivial matters
【细心】 xìxīn careful; attentive: ～观察 carefully observe/ ～护理伤员 nurse the wounded with care/ ～地倾听群众的意见 listen attentively to the views of the masses
【细辛】 xìxīn 〈中药〉 the root of Chinese wild ginger (*Asarum Sieboldii*)
【细雨】 xìyǔ drizzle; fine rain
【细则】 xìzé detailed rules and regulations
【细帐】 xìzhàng itemized account
【细针密缕】 xìzhēn-mìlǚ ① in fine, close stitches ② (work) in a meticulous way
【细枝末节】 xìzhī-mòjié minor details; nonessentials
【细支纱】 xìzhīshā 〈纺〉 fine yarn
【细致】 xìzhì careful; meticulous; painstaking: 做～的思想工作 do painstaking ideological work/ 她想得很～。She thought it out in detail./ 这活做得很～。This is a careful piece of work.
【细作】 xìzuò spy; secret agent

**阋** xì 〈书〉 quarrel; strife: 兄弟～于墙。Brothers quarrel at home.

**隙** xì ① crack; chink; crevice: 墙～ a crack in the wall/ 云～ a rift in the clouds ② gap; interval: 农～ interval between busy seasons in farming ③ loophole; opportunity: 无～可乘 no loophole to take advantage of/ 乘～突围 seize an opportunity to break through the encirclement ④ discord; rift: 并无嫌～ bear no ill will (或 grudge)
【隙地】 xìdì unoccupied place; open space

## xiā

**呷** xiā 〈方〉 sip: ～一口茶 take a sip of tea

**虾** xiā shrimp: ～群 a shoal of shrimps/ 对～ prawn/ 龙～ lobster
【虾兵蟹将】 xiābīng-xièjiàng shrimp soldiers and crab generals — ineffective troops
【虾干】 xiāgān dried shrimps
【虾蛄】 xiāgū mantis shrimp
【虾酱】 xiājiàng shrimp paste
【虾米】 xiāmi ① dried, shelled shrimps ② 〈方〉 small shrimps
【虾皮】 xiāpí dried small shrimps
【虾仁】 xiārén shelled fresh shrimps; shrimp meat
【虾油】 xiāyóu shrimp sauce
【虾子】 xiāzǐ shrimp roe (或 eggs) ◇ ～酱油 shrimp-roe soy sauce

**瞎** xiā ① blind: ～了一只眼 blind in one eye ② groundlessly; foolishly; to no purpose: ～讲 speak groundlessly/ ～花钱 spend money foolishly/ ～干 go it blind/ ～猜 make a wild guess/ ～费劲儿 make a vain effort ③ 〈方〉 (of thread, etc.) become tangled
【瞎扯】 xiāchě ① talk irresponsibly; talk rubbish ② talk at random about anything under the sun; waffle; natter
【瞎话】 xiāhuà untruth; lie: 说～ tell a lie; lie
【瞎闹】 xiānào ① act senselessly; mess about ② fool around; be mischievous: 赶快做作业，别～。Do your homework quickly and don't fool around.
【瞎说】 xiāshuō talk irresponsibly; talk rubbish
【瞎指挥】 xiāzhǐhuī issue confused orders; give arbitrary and impracticable directions; mess things up by giving wrong orders
【瞎抓】 xiāzhuā do things without a plan; go about sth. in a haphazard way
【瞎子】 xiāzi a blind person: ～摸鱼 a blind person groping for fish — act blindly/ ～点灯白费蜡 like lighting a candle for a blind person — a sheer waste

## xiá

**匣** xiá a small box (或 case); casket
【匣子】 xiázi a small box (或 case); casket

**狎** xiá be improperly familiar with
【狎昵】 xiánì be improperly familiar with

**侠** xiá
【侠客】 xiákè a person adept in martial arts and given to chivalrous conduct (in olden times)
【侠义】 xiáyì having a strong sense of justice and ready to help the weak; chivalrous

**峡** xiá gorge: 三门～ the Sanmen Gorge/ 海～ strait
【峡谷】 xiágǔ gorge; canyon
【峡湾】 xiáwān 〈地〉 fiord

**狭** xiá narrow: 坡陡路～。The slope is steep and the path narrow.
【狭隘】 xiá'ài ① narrow: ～的山道 a narrow mountain path ② narrow and limited; parochial: ～的看法 a narrow view/ 心胸～ be narrow-minded ◇ ～民族主义 narrow (或

parochial) nationalism/ ～性 narrow-mindedness; parochialism

【狭长】 xiácháng long and narrow

【狭路相逢】 xiálù xiāng féng (of adversaries) meet face to face on a narrow path — come into unavoidable confrontation

【狭小】 xiáxiǎo narrow and small; narrow: ～的阁楼 a poky attic/ 气量～ be intolerant; be narrow-minded/ 走出～的圈子 step out of one's narrow circle

【狭义】 xiáyì narrow sense

【狭窄】 xiázhǎi ① narrow; cramped: ～的胡同 a narrow lane (或 alley) ② narrow and limited; narrow: 心地～ be narrow-minded/ 见识～ be limited in knowledge and narrow in experience ③〈医〉stricture

**遐** xiá〈书〉① far; distant ② lasting; long: ～龄 advanced age

【遐迩】 xiá'ěr〈书〉far and near: ～闻名 be well-known far and near; enjoy widespread renown

【遐想】 xiáxiǎng reverie; daydream

**瑕** xiá ① flaw in a piece of jade ② flaw; defect; shortcoming

【瑕不掩瑜】 xiá bù yǎn yú one flaw cannot obscure the splendour of the jade — the defects cannot obscure the virtues

【瑕疵】 xiácī flaw; blemish

【瑕瑜互见】 xiá-yú hù jiàn have defects as well as merits; have both strong and weak points

**暇** xiá free time; leisure: 无～兼顾 be too busy to attend to other things/ 自顾不～ be unable even to fend for oneself (much less look after others); be busy enough with one's own affairs

**辖** xiá ① linchpin ② have jurisdiction over; administer; govern: 省～市 a municipality (或 city) under the jurisdiction of the provincial government/ 下～四个兵团 have four army corps under its command

【辖区】 xiáqū area under one's jurisdiction

**霞** xiá rosy clouds; morning or evening glow: 晚～ the glow of sunset; sunset clouds/ 彩～ (the many hues of) rosy clouds

【霞光】 xiáguāng rays of morning or evening sunlight: ～万道 a myriad of sun rays/ 彩云万朵,～四射。Rays of sunlight shine through multihued clouds.

【霞石】 xiáshí〈矿〉nepheline

**黠** xiá〈书〉crafty; cunning

## xià

**下** xià ① below; down; under; underneath: 零～五度 five degrees below zero/ 上至司令员,～至普通战士 from the commander down to the rank and file/ 树～ under the tree/ 山～ at the foot of the hill ② lower; inferior: 分为上、中、～三等 divided into three grades: the upper, the middle and the lower ③ next; latter; second: ～一班车 the next bus/ ～半月 the latter (或 second) half of the month/ ～半辈子 the latter half of one's life; the rest of one's life/ ～册 the last of two or three volumes ④ downward; down: 防止圆木～滑 prevent the logs from rolling down/ 物价～跌。Prices dropped./ 俘虏敌师长以～六千人 capture 6,000 enemy troops from the division commander downward ⑤〔表示属于一定范围、情况、条件等〕: 在党的领导～ under the leadership of the Party/ 在这种情况～ in such circumstances/ 在同志们的帮助～ with the help of the comrades ⑥〔表示当某个时间或时节〕: 眼～ at the moment; at present/ 年～ during the lunar New Year ⑦〔用在数字后,表示方面或方位〕: 往四～一看 look all around/ 两～里都同意。Both sides have agreed. ⑧ descend; alight; get off: ～山 descend the mountain/ ～飞机 alight from a plane/ ～车 get off a car or bus/ ～床 get out of bed/ ～楼 descend the stairs; go or come downstairs/ 顺流而～ sail downstream ⑨ (of rain, snow, etc.) fall: 雪～得很大。The snow is falling heavily. 或 It's snowing hard./ ～雹子了。It's hailing. ⑩ issue; deliver; send: ～命令 issue (或 give) orders/ ～请帖 send an invitation ⑪ go to: ～车间 go to the workshop/ ～馆子 go and eat in a restaurant; eat out ⑫ exit; leave: 从左边门儿～ exit from the left door/ 换人,四号～,三号上。Substitution, No.3 for No.4. ⑬ put in; cast: ～作料 put in the condiments/ ～网打鱼 cast a net to catch fish/ ～面条 cook noodles ⑭ take away (或 off); dismantle; unload: 把纱窗～下来 take the screen window off/ ～了俘虏的枪 disarm the captured soldier/ 船上的货还没～完。The cargo hasn't all been unloaded yet. ⑮ form (an opinion, idea, etc.): ～结论 draw a conclusion/ ～决心 make a resolution; be determined/ ～定义 give a definition; define ⑯ apply; use: ～力气 put forth strength; make an effort; exert oneself/ 对症～药 prescribe the right remedy for an illness ⑰ (of animals) give birth to; lay: ～了一窝小猪 give birth to a litter of piglets/ ～蛋 lay eggs ⑱ capture; take: 连～数城 capture several cities in succession ⑲ give in: 双方相持不～。Neither side would give in (或 yield). ⑳ finish (work, etc.); leave off: ～夜班 come off night duty ㉑〔用于否定式〕 be less than: 不～一万人 no less than ten thousand people ㉒〈量〉〔用于动作的次数〕: 敲了三～门 give three knocks on the door/ 摇了几～旗子 wave the flag several times

**下** xia ①〔用在动词后,表示由高处到低处〕: 坐～ sit down/ 躺～ lie down/ 跑～山 run down a hill ②〔用在动词后,表示有空间,能容纳〕: 这房间能坐～五十人。The room can hold (或 seat) fifty people./ 这么多菜我吃不～。I can't eat all this food. ③〔用在动词后,表示动作的完成或结果〕: 打～扎实的基础 lay a solid foundation/ 准备～必需的材料 prepare necessary material

【下巴】 xiàba ① the lower jaw ② chin

【下摆】 xiàbǎi ① the lower hem of a gown, jacket or skirt ② width of such a hem

【下班】 xiàbān come or go off work; knock off

【下半场】 xiàbànchǎng second half (of a game)

【下半旗】 xià bànqí fly a flag at half-mast

【下半晌】 xiàbànshǎng〈口〉afternoon

【下半夜】 xiàbànyè the time after midnight; the latter half of the night

【下辈】 xiàbèi ① future generations; offspring ② the younger generation of a family

【下笔】 xiàbǐ put pen to paper; begin to write or paint: 不知如何～ be at a loss as to how to begin writing or painting/ ～千言,离题万里。A thousand words from the pen in a stream, but ten thousand *li* away from the theme. — write quickly but stray from the theme

【下边】 xiàbian 见"下面"

【下不来】 xiàbulái ① refuse to come down: 她的体温～。Her temperature won't come down. ② cannot be accomplished: 这道墙没有五千块砖～。You can't build that wall with less than 5,000 bricks. ③ feel embarrassed: 几句话说

得他脸上～。He was visibly embarrassed at the remarks.

【下不为例】 xià bù wéi lì not to be taken as a precedent; not to be repeated: 就这一回,～。Just this once.

【下操】 xiàcāo ① have drills: 我们上午～,下午听课。We have drills in the morning and lectures in the afternoon. ② finish drilling: 他刚～回来。He's just back from drill.

【下策】 xiàcè a bad plan; an unwise decision; the worst thing to do; a stupid move

【下层】 xiàcéng ① lower levels: 深入～ go to lower-level units; go down to the grass-roots level ② lower strata

【下场】 xiàchǎng ① 〈剧〉 go off stage; exit ② 〈体〉 leave the playing field ◇ ～门 exit (of a stage)

【下场】 xiàchang end; fate: 遭到可耻～ come to a disgraceful end; meet with an ignominious fate/ 搞阴谋诡计的人绝不会有好～。Those who plot and conspire will certainly come to no good end.

【下车伊始】 xià chē yī shǐ the moment one alights from the official carriage — the moment one takes up one's official post

【下沉】 xiàchén sink; subside; submerge: 敌舰起火～。The enemy warship caught fire and sank./ 潜水艇逐渐～。The submarine gradually submerged./ 地基～。The foundations have subsided.

【下处】 xiàchu one's temporary lodging during a trip

【下穿交叉】 xiàchuān jiāochā 〈交〉 underpass; undercrossing

【下船】 xiàchuán go ashore; disembark

【下垂】 xiàchuí ① hang down; droop ② 〈医〉 prolapse: 子宫～ prolapse of the uterus; metroptosis/ 胃～ gastroptosis

【下存】 xiàcún (of a sum) remain after deduction: 这笔款子提了二十元,～八十元。Twenty *yuan* has been drawn from the account and there is still 80 *yuan* left.

【下达】 xiàdá make known (或 transmit) to lower levels: ～作战命令 issue orders of operation/任务已经～。The task has been assigned.

【下等】 xiàděng low-grade; inferior

【下地】 xiàdì ① go to the fields: ～劳动 go to work in the fields ② leave a sickbed: 他病好多了,现在能～了。He is getting much better now and is up and about again.

【下碇】 xiàdìng cast anchor: 船在九江～。The ship anchored at Jiujiang.

【下毒手】 xià dúshǒu strike a vicious blow; lay murderous hands on sb.: 背后～ stab sb. in the back

【下颚】 xià'è the lower jaw; mandible

【下法】 xiàfǎ 〈中医〉 laxative (或 purgative) remedy

【下凡】 xiàfán (of gods or immortals) descend to the world

【下饭】 xiàfàn ① go with rice: 你这两个菜都不喜欢,拿什么～呀? If you don't like either of the two dishes, what are you going to have with your rice? ② go well with rice: 这个菜下酒不～。This dish goes well with wine, but not with rice.

【下放】 xiàfàng ① transfer to a lower level: 权力～ transfer power to a lower level/ 企业～ put an enterprise under a lower administrative level ② transfer (cadres, etc.) to work at the grass-roots level or to do manual labour in the countryside or in a factory ◇ ～干部 a cadre transferred to a lower level or to do manual labour in the countryside or in a factory

【下风】 xiàfēng ① leeward: 工业区一般都设在城市的～。Industrial districts are generally situated to the leeward of the cities. ② disadvantageous position: 占～ be at a disadvantage

【下岗】 xiàgǎng come or go off sentry duty

【下工】 xiàgōng come or go off work; stop work; knock off

【下工夫】 xià gōngfu put in time and energy; concentrate one's efforts: 在技术革新上狠～ devote a lot of time and energy to technical innovation/ 你要学好一门外语就要舍得～。If you want to master a foreign language, you must put in a lot of effort./ 改造世界观要在理论联系实际上～。In remoulding one's world outlook, one must concentrate one's efforts on integrating theory with practice.

【下跪】 xiàguì kneel down; go down on one's knees

【下海】 xiàhǎi go to sea; put out to sea: ～捕鱼 go fishing on the sea

【下颌】 xiàhé 〈生理〉 the lower jaw; mandible ◇ ～骨 lower jawbone; mandible

【下怀】 xiàhuái one's heart's desire: 正中～ be exactly what one wants

【下级】 xiàjí ① lower level: ～服从上级。The lower level is subordinate to the higher level. ② subordinate: 帮助～解决工作中的问题 help one's subordinates to solve the problems they encounter in their work

◇ ～干部 junior cadre/ ～机关 government office at a lower level/ ～军官 low-ranking (或 junior) officer/ ～组织 subordinate organization

【下贱】 xiàjiàn low; mean; degrading: 只有剥削阶级才把劳动看作～的事情。Only the exploiting classes look upon labour as something degrading.

【下江】 Xiàjiāng lower reaches of the Changjiang River ◇ ～人 a native of one of the provinces on the lower reaches of the Changjiang River

【下降】 xiàjiàng descend; go or come down; drop; fall; decline: 飞机开始～。The plane began to descend./ 气温显著～。There was a marked drop in the temperature./ 药品价格平均～百分之三十七。The prices of medicines dropped 37% on an average./ 生产成本逐年～。Production costs come down every year./ 出生率～ a decline in the birth rate

【下焦】 xiàjiāo 〈中医〉 the part of the body cavity below the umbilicus, housing the bladder, kidneys and bowels

【下脚】 xiàjiǎo ① get a foothold; plant one's foot: 没有～的地方 be unable to gain a footing (或 foothold); have nowhere to plant one's foot ② leftover bits and pieces ◇ ～料 leftover bits and pieces (of industrial material, etc.)/ ～棉 cotton waste

【下界】 xiàjiè the world of mortals; the world of man

【下酒】 xiàjiǔ ① go with wine: 买点花生米～ buy some peanuts to go with the wine ② go well with wine: 这菜不～。This dish doesn't go very well with wine. ◇ ～菜 a dish that goes with wine

【下课】 xiàkè get out of class; finish class: ～后再去。Go there after class./ 现在～。The class is dismissed. 或 The class is over.

【下款】 xiàkuǎn ① name of the donor (as inscribed on a painting or a calligraphic scroll presented as a gift) ② signature at the end of a letter

【下来】 xiàlai come down: 梯子不牢,快～! Come down at once! The ladder isn't steady./ 昨天省里～两位领导干部。Two leading cadres came down from the provincial capital yesterday.

【下来】 xialai ①〔用在动词后,表示由高处向低处或由远处向近处来〕: 把树上的苹果都摘～。Pick all the apples off the tree./ 溪水从山上流～。The stream flows down from the mountain. ②〔用在动词后,表示从过去继续到现在或过去从开始继续到最后〕: 古代流传～的寓言 fables handed down from ancient times/ 所有上夜校的人都坚持～了。All those who joined the evening classes went on with them to the end. ③〔用在动词后,表示动作的完成或结果〕: 风突然停

了～。The wind dropped all of a sudden./ 剩～的就这么些了。This is all that's left. ④〔用在形容词后面,表示程度继续增加〕:他的声音慢慢低了～。His voice trailed off./ 天色渐渐黑～。It was getting darker and darker.

【下里巴人】 xiàlǐ Bārén ① Song of the Rustic Poor (a folk song of the state of Chu) ② popular literature or art

【下连当兵】 xiàlián dāngbīng (of officers) go down to the companies to serve in the ranks (to gain experience and improve leadership)

【下联】 xiàlián the second line of a couplet

【下列】 xiàliè listed below; following: 应注意～几点。Attention should be paid to the following points.

【下令】 xiàlìng give orders; order: 团长～紧急集合。The regiment commander ordered (或 gave orders for) an emergency muster.

【下流】 xiàliú ① lower reaches (of a river): 黄河～ the lower reaches of the Huanghe River ② low-down; mean; obscene; dirty: ～的谩骂 scurrilous attacks; coarse invectives/ ～的勾当 base acts/ ～的玩笑 dirty (或 obscene) jests; coarse jokes ◇ ～话 obscene (或 dirty, foul) language; obscenities

【下落】 xiàluò ① whereabouts: 打听某人的～ inquire about sb.'s whereabouts/ 有一件古物现在～不明。The whereabouts of one of the antiques is unknown. ② drop; fall: 气球～的地点 the place where the balloon has fallen

【下马】 xiàmǎ ① get down (或 dismount) from a horse ② discontinue (a project, etc.): 这项工程不能～。This project should not be abandoned.

【下马威】 xiàmǎwēi severity shown by an official on assuming office: 给他个～ deal him a head-on blow at the first encounter

【下面】 xiàmian ① below; under; underneath: 大桥～ under the bridge/ 图表～的说明 the caption below the chart/ 褥子～铺着一领席。There is a mat underneath the mattress. ② next; following: ～该谁了? Who's next?/ 必须记住～几点。The following points should be borne in mind./ ～请老李谈谈。Now we'll ask Lao Li to say something. ③ lower level; subordinate: 细心倾听～的意见 listen carefully to the views of one's subordinates/ 了解～的情况 find out about how things are at the lower levels

【下品】 xiàpǐn low-grade; inferior

【下坡路】 xiàpōlù downhill path; downhill journey; decline: 走～ go downhill; be on the decline

【下铺】 xiàpù lower berth

【下棋】 xiàqí play chess; have a game of chess

【下欠】 xiàqiàn ① still owing: ～八元 with 8 *yuan* still owing ② a sum still owing: 全数还清,并无～。The debt has been fully paid up.

【下情】 xiàqíng conditions at the lower levels; feelings or wishes of the masses: ～上达 make the situation at the lower levels known to the higher levels/ 不了解～ not know what is going on at the lower levels

【下去】 xiàqu ① go down; descend: ～看看是谁在楼下敲门。Go downstairs and see who's knocking at the door./ 到站了,快～。Here we are, let's get off at once. ② go on; continue: 你这样～要累垮的。If you go on like this you'll crack up.

【下去】 xiaqu ①〔用在动词后,表示由高处到低处或由近处向远处去〕:洪水退～了。The flood has receded./ 把犯人带～ take the prisoner away/ 把敌人的火力压～ silence the enemy's fire ②〔用在动词后,表示从现在继续到将来〕:坚持～ stick it out/ 她激动得说不～。She was so overcome with emotion that she couldn't go on./ 希望两国人民世世代代友好～。We hope the people of the two countries will remain friendly from generation to generation. ③〔用在形容词后,表示程度继续增加〕:看来天气还会冷～。It seems it will get even colder.

【下身】 xiàshēn ① the lower part of the body ② private parts ③ trousers

【下乘】 xiàshèng ①〈佛教〉Hinayana; Little Vehicle ② literary or artistic work of low order; inferior work

【下剩】 xiàshèng 〈口〉be left: ～的种子不多了。There aren't many seeds left.

【下士】 xiàshì (陆军或英空军) corporal; (英海军) petty officer second class; (美海军) petty officer third class

【下手】 xiàshǒu ① put one's hand to; start; set about; set to: 不知从何～ not know where to start; not know how to set about a job ② right-hand seat: 坐在主宾的～ sit on the right hand of the chief guest ③〈口〉assistant; helper: 打～ act as assistant

【下首】 xiàshǒu right-hand seat

【下书】 xiàshū 〈书〉deliver a letter

【下属】 xiàshǔ subordinate

【下水】 xiàshuǐ ① enter the water; be launched: 又一艘新船～了。Another new ship was launched. ② take to evildoing; fall into evil ways: 拖人～ involve sb. in evildoing; entice (或 inveigle) sb. into evildoing ③ downriver; downstream: ～船 downriver boat ◇ ～典礼 launching ceremony

【下水】 xiàshui offal: 猪～ pig's offal

【下水道】 xiàshuǐdào sewer

【下榻】 xiàtà 〈书〉stay (at a place during a trip): ～于新侨饭店 stay at the Xinqiao Hotel

【下台】 xiàtái ① step down from the stage or platform ② fall out of power; leave office: 被赶～ be driven out of office; be thrown out ③〔多用于否定式〕get out of a predicament or an embarrassing situation: 没法～ be unable to back down with good grace/ 叫他下不了台 put him on the spot

【下体】 xiàtǐ 〈书〉① the lower part of the body ② private parts

【下同】 xiàtóng 〔多用于附注〕 similarly hereinafter; the same below

【下头】 xiàtou 见"下面"①③

【下文】 xiàwén ① what follows in the passage, paragraph, article, etc.: ～再作阐述 be explained in the ensuing chapters or paragraphs ② later development; outcome; sequel: 申请书交上去两个星期了,还没有～。The application was handed in a couple of weeks ago, but so far there's been no reply./ 事情并没有就此结束,还有～哩。The matter didn't end there; there was a sequel to it.

【下午】 xiàwǔ afternoon

【下弦】 xiàxián 〈天〉last (或 third) quarter ◇ ～月 the moon at the last (或 third) quarter

【下限】 xiàxiàn lower limit; prescribed minimum; floor level; floor: 溶液比重不能低于～。The specific gravity of the solution should be kept above the prescribed minimum.

【下乡】 xiàxiāng go to the countryside: ～知识青年 educated urban youth working in the countryside

【下行】 xiàxíng ①〈铁道〉down: ～列车 down train ②〈航运〉downriver; downstream ③ (of a document) to be issued to the lower levels

【下旋】 xiàxuán 〈乒乓〉underspin; backspin

【下旬】 xiàxún the last ten-day period of a month

【下药】 xiàyào ① prescribe medicine: 对症～ prescribe the right remedy for an illness ② put in poison

【下野】 xiàyě (of a ruler) retire from the political arena; be forced to relinquish power

【下议院】 xiàyìyuàn ① lower house; lower chamber ② the

House of Commons
【下意识】 xiàyìshí subconsciousness
【下游】 xiàyóu ① lower reaches (of a river) ② backward position: 甘居～ be resigned to being backward
【下狱】 xiàyù throw into prison; imprison
【下葬】 xiàzàng bury; inter
【下肢】 xiàzhī 〈生理〉 lower limbs; legs
【下中农】 xiàzhōngnóng lower-middle peasant
【下种】 xiàzhǒng sow (seeds)
【下装】 xiàzhuāng remove theatrical makeup and costume
【下坠】 xiàzhuì 〈医〉 straining (at stool); tenesmus
【下钻】 xiàzuàn 〈石油〉 run the drilling tool into the well ◇ ～速度 running speed
【下作】 xiàzuo ① low-down; mean; obscene; dirty ② 〈方〉 greedy; gluttonous

## 吓

xià frighten; scare; intimidate: ～坏了 be terribly frightened; be overcome with fear/ ～破了胆 be scared out of one's wits/ 把我～一跳 give me a start (或 scare)/ 这种困难～不倒我们。Difficulties like this don't scare us.
另见 hè
【吓唬】 xiàhu 〈口〉 frighten; scare; intimidate

## 夏

xià ① summer ② (Xià) an ancient name for China: 华～ China ③ the Xia Dynasty (c. 21st—c. 16th century B.C.) ④ (Xià) a surname
【夏布】 xiàbù grass cloth; grass linen
【夏侯】 Xiàhóu a surname
【夏候鸟】 xiàhòuniǎo summer resident (或 bird)
【夏季】 xiàjì summer
【夏枯草】 xiàkūcǎo 〈中药〉 selfheal (*Prunella vulgaris*)
【夏历】 xiàlì the traditional Chinese calendar; the lunar calendar
【夏粮】 xiàliáng summer grain crops
【夏令】 xiàlìng ① summer; summertime ② summer weather: 春行～ summer weather in spring; exceptionally warm days in spring ◇ ～商品 commodities for summer use/ ～营 summer camp
【夏眠】 xiàmián 〈动〉 aestivation
【夏收】 xiàshōu summer harvest ◇ ～作物 summer crops
【夏天】 xiàtiān summer
【夏衣】 xiàyī summer clothing; summer wear
【夏至】 Xiàzhì the Summer Solstice (10th solar term)
【夏装】 xiàzhuāng 见"夏衣"

## 厦

xià
另见 shà
【厦门】 Xiàmén Xiamen (Amoy)

## 罅

xià 〈书〉 crack; rift; chink: 云～ a rift in the clouds/ 石～ a crack in a rock
【罅漏】 xiàlòu 〈书〉 omission; shortcoming; deficiency: ～之处，有待订补。Shortcomings will be remedied in future editions.
【罅隙】 xiàxì 〈书〉 crack; rift; chink

# xiān

## 仙

xiān celestial being; immortal
【仙丹】 xiāndān elixir of life
【仙姑】 xiāngū ① female immortal (或 celestial) ② sorceress
【仙鹤】 xiānhè red-crowned crane
【仙鹤草】 xiānhècǎo 〈中药〉 hairyvein agrimony (*Agrimonia pilosa*)
【仙后座】 xiānhòuzuò 〈天〉 Cassiopeia
【仙境】 xiānjìng fairyland; wonderland; paradise
【仙客来】 xiānkèlái 〈植〉 cyclamen
【仙女】 xiānnǚ female celestial; fairy maiden
【仙女座】 xiānnǚzuò 〈天〉 Andromeda
【仙人】 xiānrén celestial being; immortal
【仙人掌】 xiānrénzhǎng 〈植〉 cactus
【仙山琼阁】 xiānshān qiónggé a jewelled palace in elfland's hills
【仙逝】 xiānshì 〈婉〉 pass away
【仙王座】 xiānwángzuò 〈天〉 Cepheus
【仙子】 xiānzǐ 见"仙女"

## 先

xiān ① earlier; before; first; in advance: ～人后己 put others before oneself; put other people's interest ahead of one's own/ 他比我～到。He arrived earlier than I did./ 我～说几句。Let me say a few words first./ 你～拟个提纲再写。Make an outline before you start writing./ 没有什么～于经验的知识。There is no knowledge prior to experience./你不必～付款。You don't have to pay in advance./ 同志们～别走。Don't go yet, comrades. ② elder generation; ancestor: 祖～ ancestor; forefather ③ deceased; late: ～父 my late father ④ 〈口〉 earlier on; before: 你～怎么不告诉我? Why didn't you tell me before?
【先辈】 xiānbèi elder generation; ancestors: 继承革命～的事业 carry forward the cause of the older generation of revolutionaries
【先导】 xiāndǎo guide; forerunner; precursor: 错误常常是正确的～。Error is often the precursor of what is correct.
【先睹为快】 xiān dǔ wéi kuài consider it a pleasure to be among the first to read (a poem, article, etc.)
【先端】 xiānduān 〈植〉 tip (of a leaf, flower, fruit, etc.)
【先发制人】 xiān fā zhì rén gain the initiative by striking first; forestall the enemy: 采取～的手段 take preemptive measures
【先锋】 xiānfēng vanguard; van: 打～ fight in the van; be a pioneer/ 共产党员的～作用和模范作用是十分重要的。The exemplary vanguard role of the Communists is of vital importance.
【先锋队】 xiānfēngduì vanguard: 共产党是工人阶级的～。The Communist Party is the vanguard of the working class.
【先后】 xiān-hòu ① early or late; priority; order: 革命不分～。Whether one makes revolution early or late, one is equally welcome./ 这些事都该办，可也得有个～。All these matters should be tackled, but they should be taken up in order of priority. ② successively; one after another: 代表团～在北京、上海等地参观访问。The delegation first went to Beijing and afterwards to Shanghai and other places.
【先见之明】 xiān jiàn zhī míng prophetic vision; foresight
【先进】 xiānjìn advanced
◇ ～单位 advanced unit/ ～分子 advanced element/ ～个人 advanced individual/ ～工作者 advanced worker/ ～集体 advanced group (或 collective)/ ～经验 advanced experience/ ～事迹 meritorious (或 exemplary) deeds
【先决】 xiānjué prerequisite: ～条件 prerequisite; precondition
【先来后到】 xiānlái-hòudào in the order of arrival; first come, first served
【先礼后兵】 xiān lǐ hòu bīng take strong measures only after courteous ones fail; try peaceful means before resorting to force
【先例】 xiānlì precedent: 开～ set (或 create) a precedent/ 有～可援 have a precedent to go by
【先烈】 xiānliè martyr: 革命～ revolutionary martyr

【先令】 xiānlìng ① shilling ② schilling
【先期】 xiānqī earlier on; in advance: 代表团的部分团员已~到达。Some members of the delegation had arrived at an earlier date.
【先前】 xiānqián before; previously: 这孩子比~高多了。The child is much taller than before./ ~咱们村压根儿就没诊疗所。Previously there was no clinic in our village at all.
【先遣】 xiānqiǎn sent in advance ◇ ~部队 advance troops (或 force)/ ~队 advance party
【先驱】 xiānqū pioneer; forerunner; harbinger: 聂耳、冼星海是中国革命音乐的~。Nie Er and Xian Xinghai were pioneers of China's revolutionary music.
【先人】 xiānrén ① ancestor; forefather ② my late father
【先入为主】 xiān rù wéi zhǔ first impressions are strongest; preconceived ideas keep a strong hold; be prejudiced
【先入之见】 xiān rù zhī jiàn preconception; preconceived idea; prejudice
【先声】 xiānshēng first signs; herald; harbinger: 一七八九年的法国革命是十九世纪各国资产阶级革命的~。The French Revolution of 1789 heralded other bourgeois revolutions in the 19th century.
【先声夺人】 xiānshēng duó rén forestall one's opponent by a show of strength; overawe others by displaying one's strength
【先生】 xiānsheng ① teacher: 要做人民的~,先做人民的学生。To be a teacher of the people, one must first be their pupil. ② mister (Mr.); gentleman; sir: 总统~ Mr. President/ 女士们,~们 ladies and gentlemen ③〈方〉doctor ④〈旧〉[多用于]: 帐房~ bookkeeper/ 算命~ fortune-teller
【先世】 xiānshì forefathers; ancestors
【先手】 xiānshǒu on the offensive (in chess): ~棋 an offensive move
【先天】 xiāntiān ① congenital; inborn: ~畸形 congenital malformation/ ~性心脏病 congenital heart disease/ ~不足 be congenitally deficient; suffer from an inherent shortage ②〈哲〉*a priori*; innate: 人的知识不是~就有的,而是从社会实践中来的。Man's knowledge is not innate but comes from social practice.
【先头】 xiāntóu ① ahead; in front; in advance: ~部队 an advance party of soldiers; vanguard/ 走在最~ walk ahead of all other people ② before; formerly; in the past: 你~没说过这事。You didn't mention this before./ 她~已来过两次。She's been here twice already./ 一切结论产生于调查情况的末尾,而不是在它的~。Conclusions invariably come after investigation, and not before.
【先下手为强】 xiān xiàshǒu wéi qiáng he who strikes first gains the advantage; to take the initiative is to gain the upper hand: ~,后下手遭殃。〈谚〉He who strikes first prevails, he who strikes late fails.
【先行】 xiānxíng ① go ahead of the rest; start off before the others: 兵马未动,粮草~。Food and fodder should go ahead of troops and horses. ② beforehand; in advance: ~通知 notify in advance/ 新产品将在本市~试销。The new products will first be put on trial sale in this city.
【先行官】 xiānxíngguān commander of an advance unit or vanguard: 铁路运输是国民经济的~。Railway transportation is the vanguard of the national economy.
【先行者】 xiānxíngzhě forerunner: 纪念伟大的革命~孙中山先生! Let us pay tribute to our great revolutionary forerunner, Dr. Sun Yat-sen!
【先验】 xiānyàn 〈哲〉*a priori*: ~知识 *a priori* knowledge ◇ ~论 apriorism
【先斩后奏】 xiān zhǎn hòu zòu execute the criminal first and report to the emperor afterwards — act first and report afterwards
【先兆】 xiānzhào omen; portent; sign; indication: 地震的~ indications of an impending earthquake/ 不祥的~ ill omen ◇ ~流产 threatened abortion
【先哲】 xiānzhé a great thinker of the past; sage
【先知】 xiānzhī ① a person of foresight ②〈宗〉prophet
【先知先觉】 xiānzhī-xiānjué ① a person of foresight ② having foresight

**纤** xiān fine; minute: ~尘 fine dust
另见 qiàn
【纤度】 xiāndù 〈纺〉fibre number; size
【纤毛】 xiānmáo 〈生〉cilium ◇ ~运动 ciliary movement
【纤毛虫】 xiānmáochóng 〈动〉infusorian
【纤巧】 xiānqiǎo dainty; delicate
【纤弱】 xiānruò slim and fragile; delicate
【纤维】 xiānwéi fibre; staple: 天然(合成、人造)~ natural (synthetic, man-made) fibre/ ~长度 fibre length; staple ◇ ~板 fibreboard/ ~蛋白〈生化〉fibrin/ ~蛋白原〈生化〉fibrinogen/ ~集束〈化纤〉collection of filaments/ ~瘤〈医〉fibroma/ ~束〈化纤〉tow/ ~植物 fibre plant
【纤维素】 xiānwéisù 〈化〉cellulose ◇ ~分解菌 cellulose-decomposing bacterium; cellvibrio
【纤细】 xiānxì very thin; slender; fine; tenuous: ~的头发 fine hair/ ~的游丝 tenuous gossamer
【纤小】 xiānxiǎo fine; tenuous

**氙** xiān 〈化〉xenon (Xe)
【氙气灯】 xiānqìdēng xenon lamp

**籼** xiān
【籼稻】 xiāndào long-grained nonglutinous rice; *indica* rice
【籼米】 xiānmǐ polished long-grained nonglutinous rice

**莶** xiān 见"豨莶" xīxiān

**掀** xiān lift (a cover, etc.): ~门帘 lift the door curtain/ ~掉盖子 take the lid off/ 把对手~翻在地 throw the opponent off his balance/ 在两国关系史上~开了新的一页 open a new chapter in the annals of relations between the two countries
【掀动】 xiāndòng lift; start; set in motion: 春风~了她的衣襟。The spring breeze lifted the edge of her blouse.
【掀起】 xiānqǐ ① lift; raise ② surge; cause to surge: 大海~了巨浪。Big waves surged on the sea. ③ set off (a movement, etc.); start: ~社会主义劳动竞赛的新高潮 set off (或 start) a new upsurge of socialist labour emulation

**锨** xiān shovel

**跹** xiān 见"翩跹" piānxiān

**酰** xiān 〈化〉acyl

**鲜** xiān ① fresh: ~奶 fresh milk/ ~蘑 fresh mushrooms ② bright-coloured; bright: 这块布颜色太~。This cloth is too bright. ③ delicious; tasty ④ delicacy: 时~ delicacies of the season ⑤ aquatic foods: 海~ seafood
另见 xiǎn
【鲜卑】 Xiānbēi Xianbei (Sienpi), an ancient nationality in China
【鲜红】 xiānhóng bright red; scarlet: ~的党旗 the bright red flag of the Party
【鲜花】 xiānhuā fresh flowers; flowers
【鲜货】 xiānhuò ① fresh fruit or vegetables ② fresh aquatic

foods ③ fresh medicinal herbs

【鲜美】 xiānměi delicious; tasty

【鲜明】 xiānmíng ① (of colour) bright: 色彩～ in bright colours; bright-coloured ② clear-cut; distinct; distinctive: ～的对照 a striking (或 sharp) contrast/ ～的节奏 strongly accented rhythms/ 主题～ have a distinct theme/ 富有～的地方特色 be characterized by a distinctive local style or flavour/ 我们必须坚持真理，而真理必须旗帜～。We must firmly uphold the truth, and truth requires a clear-cut stand.

【鲜嫩】 xiānnèn fresh and tender

【鲜皮】 xiānpí 〈皮革〉 fresh hide; greenhide

【鲜血】 xiānxuè blood: ～凝成的战斗友谊 militant friendship cemented (或 sealed) with blood

【鲜艳】 xiānyàn bright-coloured; gaily-coloured: 颜色～ in gay colours/ ～夺目 dazzlingly beautiful; resplendent/ 穿着～的民族服装 wearing bright national costume

【鲜于】 Xiānyú a surname

## xián

**闲** xián ① not busy; idle; unoccupied: ～不住 refuse to stay idle; always keep oneself busy/ 不吃～饭 won't be an idler ② not in use; unoccupied; lying idle: ～房 unoccupied (或 vacant) room or house/ 别让机器～着！Don't let the machine stand idle./ 没有一辆车～着。There's not a single free vehicle. 或 All the vehicles are in use. ③ spare (或 free) time; leisure: 今天她不得～。She has no time to spare today.

【闲扯】 xiánchě chat; engage in chitchat

【闲荡】 xiándàng saunter; stroll; loaf

【闲工夫】 xiángōngfu spare time; leisure

【闲逛】 xiánguàng saunter; stroll

【闲话】 xiánhuà ① digression: ～少说，书归正传。Enough of this digression; let's return to our story. 或 However, to continue the story. ② complaint; gossip: 别让人说咱们的～。We mustn't give anyone cause for complaint./ 她可不爱说人～。She's not fond of gossip. ③〈书〉talk casually about; chat about: ～当年 chat about bygone days

【闲居】 xiánjū stay at home idle

【闲空】 xiánkòng free time; spare time; leisure

【闲聊】 xiánliáo chat

【闲气】 xiánqì anger about trifles: 我可没功夫生这份儿～。I'm too busy to lose my temper over such a little thing. 或 I've no time to get angry about such a trivial matter.

【闲钱】 xiánqián 〈口〉 spare cash

【闲情逸致】 xiánqíng-yìzhì leisurely and carefree mood; leisure and mood for enjoyments

【闲人】 xiánrén ① an unoccupied person; idler: 现在正是农忙季节，村里一个～也没有。It's the busy season and nobody in the village is idle. ② persons not concerned: ～免进。No admittance except on business. 或 Admittance to staff only.

【闲散】 xiánsǎn ① free and at leisure; at a loose end ② unused; idle: ～资金 idle capital/ ～土地 scattered plots of unutilized land

【闲事】 xiánshì ① a matter that does not concern one; other people's business: 爱管～ like to poke one's nose into other people's business/ 别管～！Mind your own business. 或 None of your business. ② unimportant matter

【闲适】 xiánshì leisurely and comfortable

【闲书】 xiánshū light reading

【闲谈】 xiántán chat; engage in chitchat

【闲暇】 xiánxiá leisure

【闲心】 xiánxīn leisurely mood: 没有～管这种事 be too busy to think about such matters; not be in the mood to bother about such matters

【闲杂】 xiánzá without fixed duties: ～人员 people without fixed duties; miscellaneous personnel

【闲置】 xiánzhì leave unused; let sth. lie idle; set aside: ～的机器 idle machines

**贤** xián ① virtuous; worthy; able: 任人唯～ appoint people on their merits ② a worthy person; an able and virtuous person: 让～ relinquish one's post in favour of sb. better qualified ③〈敬〉〔旧时用于平辈或晚辈〕: ～弟 my worthy brother; your good self

【贤达】 xiándá prominent personage; worthy

【贤惠】 xiánhuì (of a woman) virtuous

【贤良】 xiánliáng (of a man) able and virtuous

【贤明】 xiánmíng wise and able; sagacious

【贤人】 xiánrén a person of virtue; worthy

**弦** xián ① bowstring; string ② the string of a musical instrument ③〈方〉 spring (of a watch, etc.) ④〈数〉 chord ⑤〈数〉 hypotenuse

【弦脉】 xiánmài 〈中医〉 taut pulse

【弦外之音】 xián wài zhī yīn overtones; implication

【弦乐队】 xiányuèduì string orchestra (或 band)

【弦乐器】 xiányuèqì stringed instrument

【弦子】 xiánzi 〈乐〉 a three-stringed plucked instrument

**涎** xián saliva

【涎皮赖脸】 xiánpí-làiliǎn brazenfaced; shameless and loathsome; cheeky

【涎水】 xiánshuǐ 〈方〉 saliva

**咸** xián ① salted; salty: ～鱼 salt fish/ ～蛋 salted egg/ 菜太～了。The dish is too salty. ②〈书〉 all: ～受其益。All benefited from it.

【咸菜】 xiáncài salted vegetables; pickles

【咸肉】 xiánròu salt meat; bacon

【咸水】 xiánshuǐ salt water ◇ ～湖 saltwater lake/ ～鱼 saltwater fish

**娴** xián 〈书〉 ① refined ② adept; skilled: ～于辞令 be gifted with a silver tongue

【娴静】 xiánjìng gentle and refined

【娴熟】 xiánshú adept; skilled: 弓马～ adept in archery and horsemanship/ ～的技巧 consummate skill/ 她在平衡木上动作～。She showed great skill in her exercises on the balance beam.

【娴雅】 xiányǎ (of a woman) refined; elegant

**舷** xián the side of a ship; board: 左～ port/ 右～ starboard

【舷边】 xiánbiān gunwale; gunnel

【舷窗】 xiánchuāng porthole

【舷梯】 xiántī ① gangway ladder; accommodation ladder ② ramp

**衔** xián ① hold in the mouth: ～着烟斗 have a pipe between one's teeth/ 燕子～泥筑窠。Swallows carry bits of earth in their bills to build nests. ② harbour; bear: ～恨 harbour resentment; bear a grudge ③ rank; title: 大使～常驻代表 permanent representative with the rank of ambassador

【衔接】 xiánjiē link up; join: 大桥把两条公路～起来。The bridge links up the two highways./ 使计划互相～ make

the plans dovetail
【衔铁】 xiántiě 〈电〉 armature
【衔冤】 xiányuān nurse a bitter sense of wrong; have a simmering sense of injustice

**鹇** xián 见"白鹇" báixián

**痫** xián 〈医〉 epilepsy

**嫌** xián ①suspicion: 避～ avoid suspicion/ 特～ a suspected enemy agent ②ill will; resentment; enmity; grudge: 前～尽释。All previous ill will has been removed. 或 We have agreed to bury the hatchet. ③dislike; mind; complain of: ～麻烦 not want to take the trouble; think it troublesome/ 大家都～他脾气太急。Everybody disliked him because of his hot temper./ 你不～我们在这里抽烟吧? You don't mind us smoking here, do you?/ 只要是革命工作,他从不～多。So long as it's revolutionary work, he never complains of having too much to do./ 这文章内容不错,只是文字略～罗唆。The article is good in content, only it's a bit wordy.
【嫌气细菌】 xiánqì xìjūn anaerobic bacteria; anaerobes
【嫌弃】 xiánqì dislike and avoid; cold-shoulder: 不要～犯过错误的同志。Don't cold-shoulder comrades who have made mistakes.
【嫌恶】 xiánwù detest; loathe
【嫌隙】 xiánxì feeling of animosity; enmity; ill will; grudge
【嫌疑】 xiányí suspicion: 有间谍～ be suspected of being a spy ◇ ～犯 suspect/ ～分子 suspected person; marked man
【嫌怨】 xiányuàn grudge; resentment; enmity

## xiǎn

**冼** Xiǎn a surname

**险** xiǎn ①a place difficult of access; narrow pass; defile: 天～ natural barrier/ 无～可守 have no tenable defence position; be strategically indefensible ②danger; peril; risk: 遇～ meet with danger/ 脱～ be out of danger/ 冒～ run a risk ③sinister; vicious; venomous: 阴～ sinister ④by a hair's breadth; by inches; nearly: ～遭不幸 come within an ace of death/ 好～哪! That was a near thing!
【险隘】 xiǎn'ài strategic pass; defile
【险恶】 xiǎn'è ①dangerous; perilous; ominous: 处境～ be in a perilous position/ 病情～ be dangerously ill ②sinister; vicious; malicious; treacherous: ～的用心 sinister (或 vicious) intentions; evil motives
【险峰】 xiǎnfēng perilous peak
【险工】 xiǎngōng dangerous section (of a dyke or embankment)
【险境】 xiǎnjìng dangerous situation: 脱离～ be out of danger
【险峻】 xiǎnjùn dangerously steep; precipitous
【险区】 xiǎnqū danger zone
【险胜】 xiǎnshèng win by a narrow margin: 以二十一比十九～ win the game by the close score of 21-19
【险滩】 xiǎntān dangerous shoal; rapids
【险些】 xiǎnxiē narrowly (escape from sth. untoward); nearly: ～掉到水里 nearly fall into the water
【险要】 xiǎnyào strategically located and difficult of access
【险诈】 xiǎnzhà sinister and crafty
【险症】 xiǎnzhèng dangerous illness
【险阻】 xiǎnzǔ (of roads) dangerous and difficult: 崎岖～的山路 a dangerous and difficult mountain path/ 不畏艰难～ not be afraid of dangers and difficulties

**显** xiǎn ①apparent; obvious; noticeable: 药的效果还不～。The effect of the medicine is not yet noticeable. ②show; display; manifest: 深色衣服不～脏。Dark clothes do not show the dirt. ③illustrious and influential
【显摆】 xiǎnbai 〈方〉 show off 又作"显白"
【显达】 xiǎndá illustrious and influential
【显得】 xiǎnde look; seem; appear: 他～有点紧张。He seems a bit nervous./ 屋子这么一布置,～宽敞多了。Arranged the way it is, the room looks much more spacious.
【显而易见】 xiǎn ér yì jiàn obviously; evidently; clearly
【显赫】 xiǎnhè illustrious; celebrated: ～的战功 illustrious war exploits/ 声势～ have a powerful influence/ ～的名声 great renown/ ～一时的殖民帝国 the once mighty colonial empire
【显花植物】 xiǎnhuā zhíwù phanerogam
【显见】 xiǎnjiàn obvious; self-evident; apparent: ～的理由 an obvious (或 apparent) reason
【显灵】 xiǎnlíng (of a ghost or spirit) make its presence or power felt
【显露】 xiǎnlù become visible; appear; manifest itself: 他脸上～出亲切的笑容。A genial smile appeared on his face./ 这次运动的深刻影响正在各个方面～出来。The profound influence of the movement is manifesting itself in every field.
【显明】 xiǎnmíng obvious; manifest; distinct; marked: ～的道理 an obvious truth/ ～的对照 a sharp contrast/ ～的特点 a distinct (或 marked) characteristic
【显然】 xiǎnran obvious; evident; clear: 这～是另一码事。That's obviously quite another matter./ 很～,这么大的工程只有靠人民公社的集体力量才能完成。It is quite evident that a project of such magnitude can be accomplished only through the collective effort of the people's commune.
【显色染料】 xiǎnsè rǎnliào 〈化〉 developing dye
【显身手】 xiǎn shēnshǒu display one's talent or skill
【显圣】 xiǎnshèng (of the ghost of a saintly person) make its presence or power felt
【显示】 xiǎnshì ①show; display; demonstrate; manifest: ～力量 make a show of force; display one's strength/ 这些文物～出中国古代劳动人民的高度智慧。These cultural relics demonstrate the great intelligence of the labouring people of ancient China./ 人民公社在战胜自然灾害中～了巨大威力。The people's communes have manifested their tremendous strength in conquering natural calamities. ②〈石油〉 show; indication: 石油(天然气)～ oil (gas) shows/ 地面～ surface indications
【显微胶片】 xiǎnwēi jiāopiàn microfilm; microfiche; (书页摄影用) bibliofilm
【显微镜】 xiǎnwēijìng microscope
【显微术】 xiǎnwēishù 〈物〉 microscopy
【显微阅读机】 xiǎnwēi yuèdújī microfilm viewer (或 reader)
【显微照片】 xiǎnwēi zhàopiàn micrograph
【显微照相术】 xiǎnwēi zhàoxiàngshù ①microphotography ②micrography
【显现】 xiǎnxiàn manifest (或 reveal) oneself; appear; show: 雾气逐渐消失,重叠的山峦一层一层地～出来。As the mist lifted, the mountains revealed themselves one behind the other.
【显象管】 xiǎnxiàngguǎn 〈电子〉 kinescope
【显形】 xiǎnxíng show one's (true) colours; betray oneself
【显性】 xiǎnxìng 〈生〉 dominance ◇ ～性状 dominant character

【显眼】 xiǎnyǎn conspicuous; showy: 把大字报贴在～的地方 put up a big-character poster in a conspicuous place/ 穿得太～ be loudly (或 showily) dressed
【显要】 xiǎnyào ① powerful and influential: ～人物 an influential figure ② influential figure; important personage; VIP
【显影】 xiǎnyǐng 〈摄〉 develop
◇ ～机 developing machine/ ～剂 developer/ ～盘 developing dish/ ～纸 developing-out paper
【显著】 xiǎnzhù notable; marked; striking; remarkable; outstanding: 收效～ yield notable results/ 有～的进步 make marked progress/ 取得～的成就 achieve remarkable success/ ～的特征 outstanding characteristics/ 各报均以～地位刊载了这条消息。This news was prominently featured in all the papers.
【显字管】 xiǎnzìguǎn 〈电子〉 charactron

**铣** xiǎn
另见 xǐ
【铣铁】 xiǎntiě cast iron

**跣** xiǎn 〈书〉 barefooted: ～足 barefooted

**鲜** xiǎn little; rare: ～见 rarely seen; seldom met with
另见 xiān

**藓** xiǎn 〈植〉 moss

## xiàn

**见** xiàn appear; become visible 参见"图穷匕首见" tú qióng bǐshǒu xiàn
另见 jiàn

**苋** xiàn amaranth
【苋菜】 xiàncài three-coloured amaranth (*Amaranthus tricolor*)

**县** xiàn county
【县城】 xiànchéng county seat; county town
【县份】 xiànfèn 〔不和专名连用〕 county: 我们那儿是个小～。Ours is a small county.
【县委】 xiànwěi county Party committee
【县长】 xiànzhǎng the head of a county; county magistrate
【县志】 xiànzhì general records of a county; county annals

**现** xiàn ① present; current; existing: ～阶段 the present stage/ ～况 the existing (或 present) situation/ ～派张同志前往你处接洽。We are now sending Comrade Chang along to get in touch with you. ② (do sth.) in time of need; extempore: ～打的烧饼 sesame cakes just out of the oven/ 这点技术也是工作中～学的。What skill I have has been picked up on the job./ 他在晚会上～编了一首诗。He improvised a poem at the evening party. ③ (of money) on hand: ～钱 ready money; cash ④ cash; ready money: 付～ pay cash ⑤ show; appear: 她脸上～出一丝笑容。A faint smile appeared on (或 crept over) her face.
【现场】 xiànchǎng ① scene (of an incident): 作案～ the scene of a crime/ 保护～ keep the scene (of a crime or accident) intact ② site; spot: 工作～ worksite/ 试验～ testing ground
◇ ～表演 on-the-spot (或 live) demonstration/ ～采访 spot coverage/ ～会议 on-the-spot meeting/ ～勘验 inspection of the scene of a crime or accident/ ～指导 on-the-spot guidance
【现成】 xiànchéng ready-made: 买～衣服 buy ready-made clothes; buy clothes off the peg/ 吃～的 eat whatever is ready or prepared by others
【现成饭】 xiànchéngfàn food ready for the table; unearned gain
【现成话】 xiànchénghuà an onlooker's unsolicited comments; a kibitzer's comments
【现存】 xiàncún extant; in stock: ～的手稿 extant manuscripts/ ～物资 goods and materials in stock
【现代】 xiàndài ① modern times; the contemporary age ② modern; contemporary: ～交通工具 modern means of communication/ ～作家 modern (或 contemporary) writer/ ～题材 contemporary theme
◇ ～派 modernist school/ ～史 contemporary history/ ～修正主义 modern revisionism
【现代化】 xiàndàihuà modernize: ～企业 modernized enterprise/ ～设备 sophisticated equipment/ 实现四个～ achieve the four modernizations (of agriculture, industry, national defence, and science and technology)/ 对于我们来说，社会主义和四个～是不可分割的。As to us, socialism and the four modernizations are indivisible.
【现地作业】 xiàndì zuòyè 〈军〉 terrain exercise
【现货】 xiànhuò 〈商〉 merchandise on hand; spots
◇ ～价格 spot price/ ～交易 spot transaction; over-the-counter trading/ ～市场 spot market
【现浇】 xiànjiāo 〈建〉 cast-in-place; cast-in-situ ◇ ～混凝土 cast-in-place (或 cast-in-situ) concrete
【现今】 xiànjīn nowadays; these days
【现金】 xiànjīn ① ready money; cash ② cash reserve in a bank
◇ ～付款 cash payment; payment in cash/ ～交易 cash transaction/ ～帐 cash account; cash book/ ～支出 out-of-pocket expenses
【现款】 xiànkuǎn ready money; cash
【现蕾】 xiànlěi 〈农〉 (of cotton flowers) squaring ◇ ～期 squaring period (或 stage)
【现钱】 xiànqián 〈口〉 ready money; cash
【现任】 xiànrèn ① at present hold the office of: 她～公社党委书记。At present she holds the position of commune Party secretary. ② currently in office; incumbent: ～邮局局长过去是邮递员。The present postmaster used to be a postman.
【现身说法】 xiàn shēn shuō fǎ advise sb. or explain sth. by using one's own experience as an example
【现时】 xiànshí now; at present
【现实】 xiànshí ① reality; actuality: 脱离～ be divorced from reality; be unrealistic/ 面对～ face the facts/ 理想变成了～。A dream has come true. ② real; actual: ～的阶级斗争 actual (或 current) class struggle/ ～生活 real (或 actual) life/ ～意义 practical or immediate significance/ 采取～的态度 adopt a realistic attitude
【现实主义】 xiànshízhǔyì realism ◇ ～文学 realistic literature/ ～者 realist
【现世】 xiànshì ① this life ② lose face; be disgraced; bring shame on oneself
【现下】 xiànxià 〈口〉 now; at present
【现…现…】 xiàn...xiàn... 〔嵌用两个动词，表示为某个目的而临时采取某种行动〕: 现吃现做 cook for immediate consumption/ 现编现唱 make up a song as one sings/ 现学现教 learn while one teaches/ 现用现买 buy for immediate use
【现象】 xiànxiàng appearance (of things); phenomenon: 社会～ social phenomenon/ 向不良～作斗争 combat unhealthy phenomena/ 看事情不要只看～，要看本质。We should not judge things simply by their appearance; we

must grasp their essence.

【现行】 xiànxíng ①currently in effect; in force; in operation: ～法令 decrees in effect/ ～规章制度 rules and regulations in force/ ～政策 present policies ②(of a criminal) active ◇ ～反革命分子 active counterrevolutionary/ ～犯〈法〉 criminal caught in, before or immediately after the act

【现形】 xiànxíng reveal one's true features; betray oneself

【现眼】 xiànyǎn 〈方〉 make a spectacle (或 fool) of oneself; lose face: 丢人～ make a fool of oneself; be a disgrace

【现洋】 xiànyáng silver dollar 又作"现大洋"

【现役】 xiànyì ①active service; active duty: 服～ be on active service ②on active service; on active duty; active ◇ ～兵员 personnel on active service/ ～军队 active military unit/ ～军官 officer on the active list/ ～军人 serviceman/ ～年限 term of active service

【现有】 xiànyǒu now available; existing: ～材料 materials now available (或 on hand); available information

【现在】 xiànzài now; at present; today: ～劳动人民是国家的主人。Today the working people are the masters of our country.

【现状】 xiànzhuàng present (或 current) situation; *status quo*; existing state of affairs: 研究这个国家的历史和～ study the history and present condition of this country/ 改变(维持)～ change (maintain) the *status quo*/ 安于～ be content with things as they are

**限** xiàn ①limit; bounds: 期～ time limit/ 以年底为～ set the end of the year as the deadline ②set a limit; limit; restrict: ～一个月完成 allow one month to finish sth./ 每人～购四张票。Each customer is limited to four tickets./ 人数不～。There is no restriction (或 limit) on the number of people./ 不要～得太死,要有点灵活性。Don't make rigid restrictions, allow a certain latitude.

【限定】 xiàndìng prescribe (或 set) a limit to; limit; restrict: ～时间完成 prescribe a time limit for fulfilment/ 参加这次讨论会的人数～为一百四十人。 Participation in the discussion will be limited to 140.

【限度】 xiàndù limit; limitation: 超过～ go beyond (或 exceed) the limit/ 最大～地发挥人的主观能动性 bring people's subjective initiative into full play/ 把非生产性的开支减少到最低～ reduce nonproductive expenditures to a minimum/ 我们的忍耐是有～的。There is a limit to our patience.

【限额】 xiàn'é norm; limit; quota: ～以上(以下)的工业企业 above-norm (below-norm) industrial enterprises

【限幅器】 xiànfúqì 〈无〉 limiter: 接收机～ receiver limiter

【限量】 xiànliàng limit the quantity of; set bounds to: 前途不可～ have boundless prospects

【限令】 xiànlìng order sb. to do sth. within a certain time: ～某人于四十八小时内离境 order sb. to leave the country within 48 hours; give sb. 48 hours' notice to leave the country

【限期】 xiànqī ①within a definite (或 set) time: ～报到 report for duty by the prescribed time/ ～撤退 withdraw within a stated time/ 这项工程～完成。This project must be completed within the specified time. ②time limit; deadline: ～已满。The time limit has been reached./ 给他三天～ give him three days (to do sth.)

【限位】 xiànwèi 〈机〉 spacing ◇ ～套筒 spacing collar

【限于】 xiànyú be confined to; be limited to: 学习雷锋的群众运动不～部队和青年。The mass movement to learn from Lei Feng is not confined to the army and young people./ ～篇幅,来电不能一一登载。As space is limited, it is impossible to publish all the messages we have received./ ～个人的思想水平 due to one's limited ideological level

【限制】 xiànzhì place (或 impose) restrictions on; restrict; limit; confine: 年龄～ age limit/ ～数量 limit to a number or amount/ ～资产阶级权利 restrict bourgeois right/ ～发言时间 restrict (或 limit) the time allowed for a speaker/ ～在必要的范围内 confine sth. within necessary limits/ 受健康状况的～ be handicapped by one's poor health/ 解放后我们对资本主义工商业采取了利用、～、改造的政策。After liberation we adopted a policy of utilization, restriction and transformation towards capitalist industry and commerce. ◇ ～器〈电〉 limiter

【限制性】 xiànzhìxìng restricted; restrictive: ～会议 restricted meeting ◇ ～定语〈语〉 restrictive attribute/ ～内切酶〈生化〉 restriction enzyme

**线** xiàn ①thread; string; wire: 丝～ silk thread/ ～团 a ball of string; a reel of thread/ 铜～ copper wire ②made of cotton thread: ～衣 ～裤 cotton knitwear ③〈数〉 line: 直～ straight line ④sth. shaped like a line, thread, etc.: 光～ ray ⑤route; line: 供应～ supply route (或 line)/ 航～ airline or shipping line/ 铁道～ railway line/ 沪宁～ the Shanghai-Nanjing Railway (line) ⑥demarcation line; boundary: 边界～ boundary line/ 军事分界～ military demarcation line/ 海岸～ coastline ⑦(political) line ⑧brink; verge: 在死亡～上 on the verge of death/ 在饥饿～上 on the brink of starvation ⑨clue; thread: 案子的～儿断了。The clue could not be followed up. ⑩〈量〉[用于抽象事物,数词限用"一"]: 一～希望 a ray (或 gleam) of hope/ 一～光明 a gleam of light/ 一～生机 a slim chance of life

【线材】 xiàncái 〈冶〉 wire rod

【线虫】 xiànchóng nematode ◇ ～病 nematodiasis

【线春】 xiànchūn a silk fabric with a geometric design (for spring wear)

【线电压】 xiàndiànyā 〈电〉 line voltage

【线段】 xiànduàn 〈数〉 line segment

【线规】 xiànguī 〈机〉 wire gauge

【线间】 xiànjiān 〈乐〉 space

【线路】 xiànlù ①〈电〉 circuit; line: 电话～ telephone line ②〈交〉 line; route: 公共汽车～ bus line/ 航空～ airline ◇ ～工人 wireman; lineman/ ～图〈电〉 circuit diagram

【线描】 xiànmiáo line drawing

【线呢】 xiànní cotton suitings

【线膨胀】 xiànpéngzhàng 〈物〉 linear expansion

【线圈】 xiànquān 〈电〉 coil: 初级(次级)～ primary (secondary) coil

【线绳】 xiànshéng cotton rope

【线速度】 xiànsùdù 〈物〉 linear velocity

【线索】 xiànsuǒ clue; thread: 破案的～ clues for solving a case/ 故事的～ threads of a story/ 为深入研究提供～ provide leads for further study

【线毯】 xiàntǎn cotton (thread) blanket

【线条】 xiàntiáo ①〈美术〉 line: 粗犷、雄浑的～ bold and vigorous lines ②lines: 这个陶俑～非常优美。The lines of this pottery figurine are very graceful.

【线头】 xiàntóu ①the end of a thread ②an odd piece of thread

【线香】 xiànxiāng a slender stick of incense

【线形动物】 xiànxíng dòngwù round worm

【线形叶】 xiànxíngyè 〈植〉 linear leaf

【线性】 xiànxìng 〈数〉 linear: ～方程 linear equation/ ～规划 linear programming/ ～函数 linear function

【线轴儿】 xiànzhóur ①a reel for thread; bobbin ②a reel (或 spool) of thread

【线装】 xiànzhuāng traditional thread binding (of Chinese books) ◇ ～本 thread-bound edition/ ～书 thread-bound Chinese book

**宪** xiàn ① statute ② constitution: 制～ draw up a constitution

【宪兵】 xiànbīng military police; military policeman; *gendarme* ◇ ～队 *gendarmerie*; military police corps

【宪法】 xiànfǎ constitution; charter: ～草案 draft constitution/ 中华人民共和国～ the Constitution of the People's Republic of China/ 鞍钢～ the Charter of the Anshan Iron and Steel Company

【宪章】 xiànzhāng charter: 联合国～ the United Nations Charter

【宪政】 xiànzhèng constitutional government; constitutionalism

**陷** xiàn ① pitfall; trap ② get stuck or bogged down: ～进泥里 get stuck in the mud/ ～在日常事务堆里 get bogged down in everyday routine/ 在错误的泥坑里越～越深 sink deeper and deeper into the quagmire of error/ ～于孤立 find oneself isolated ③sink; cave in: 深～的两颊 sunken cheeks/ 地基下～。The foundations have sunk (或 caved in). ④ frame (up): ～人于罪 frame sb. (up); incriminate sb. ⑤ (of a town, etc.) be captured; fall: 城～之日 the day the city fell ⑥ defect; deficiency: 缺～ defect; flaw

【陷害】 xiànhài frame (up); make a false charge against: ～好人 frame up an innocent person/ 政治～ political frame-up

【陷阱】 xiànjǐng pitfall; pit; trap: 布设～ lay a trap

【陷坑】 xiànkēng pitfall; pit

【陷落】 xiànluò ① subside; sink in; cave in: 许多盆地都是因地壳～而形成的。Many basins were formed by the subsidence of the earth's crust. ② (of territory) fall into enemy hands ◇ ～地震 depression earthquake

【陷入】 xiànrù ① sink (或 fall) into; land oneself in; be caught in; get bogged down in: ～被动地位 fall into a passive position/ ～重围 find oneself tightly encircled/ ～困境 land in a predicament; be put in a tight spot; be cornered/ ～无休止的争论 be bogged down in endless debates/ ～唯心论和形而上学 degenerate into idealism and metaphysics/ 谈判～僵局。The negotiations came to a deadlock. ② be lost in; be immersed in; be deep in: ～沉思 be lost in thought; be deep in meditation

【陷型模】 xiànxíngmú 〈机〉 swage

**馅** xiàn filling; stuffing: 肉～儿 meat filling/ 饺子～儿 stuffing for dumplings

【馅儿饼】 xiànrbǐng meat pie

**羡** xiàn admire; envy: 人人称～ be the admiration of everyone

【羡慕】 xiànmù admire; envy: 她很～我有这样一个好老师。She envies me my good teacher.

**献** xiàn ① offer; present; dedicate; donate: ～哈达 present a *hada* (a ceremonial silk scarf)/ 敬～花圈 lay a wreath/ ～给我的老战友杨根思 Dedicated to Yang Gensi, my old comrade-in-arms/ 医生护士纷纷为伤员们～血。The doctors and nurses all donated blood for the wounded./ 刘胡兰为中国人民的解放事业～出了她年轻的生命。Liu Hulan gave her young life for the cause of the liberation of the Chinese people. ② show; put on; display: ～殷勤 show sb. excessive attentions; pay one's addresses

【献宝】 xiànbǎo ① present a treasure ② offer a valuable piece of advice or one's valuable experience ③ show off what one treasures

【献策】 xiàncè offer advice; make suggestions

【献丑】 xiànchǒu 〈谦〉〔用于表演或写作时〕show oneself up; show one's incompetence (或 inadequacy): 一定要我唱，就只好～了。Since you insist, I'll make a fool of myself and sing.

【献词】 xiàncí congratulatory message: 新年～ New Year message

【献计】 xiànjì offer advice; make suggestions: 在技术革新中人人～献策。Everyone suggested ways and means for technical innovation.

【献技】 xiànjì show one's skill

【献礼】 xiànlǐ present a gift: 以优异成绩向党的生日～ greet the Party's birthday with new and outstanding successes

【献媚】 xiànmèi try to ingratiate oneself with; make up to

【献旗】 xiànqí present a banner

【献身】 xiànshēn devote (或 dedicate) oneself to; give one's life for: ～于无产阶级革命事业 devote oneself to the cause of proletarian revolution/ 愿为共产主义事业～ be ready to give one's life for the cause of communism

**腺** xiàn gland: 汗(泪、唾液)～ sweat (lachrymal, salivary) gland

【腺瘤】 xiànliú 〈医〉 adenoma

**霰** xiàn 〈气〉 graupel

【霰弹】 xiàndàn 〈军〉 case shot; canister (shot)

## xiāng

**乡** xiāng ① country; countryside; village; rural area: 城～物资交流 flow of goods between town and country (或 urban and rural areas); exchange of goods between the city and the countryside ② native place; home village or town: 回～ return to one's native place/ 丝绸之～ the home of silk ③ township (a former rural administrative unit under the county)

【乡巴佬】 xiāngbalǎo 〈贬〉 (country) bumpkin

【乡村】 xiāngcūn village; countryside; rural area

【乡间】 xiāngjiān village; country: ～小贩 village pedlar/ ～别墅 country villa

【乡里】 xiānglǐ ① home village or town ② fellow villager or townsman

【乡僻】 xiāngpì far from town; out-of-the-way

【乡亲】 xiāngqīn ① a person from the same village or town; fellow villager or townsman ② local people; villagers; folks: 把粮食分给～们 distribute the grain among the villagers/ ～们，八路军回来啦！Folks, the Eighth Route Army is back with you again!

【乡绅】 xiāngshēn country gentleman; squire

【乡思】 xiāngsī homesickness; nostalgia

【乡土】 xiāngtǔ ① native soil; home village ② of one's native land; local: ～风味 local flavour
◇ ～观念 provincialism/ ～教材 teaching material reflecting local conditions and suited to local needs/ ～志 local records or annals

【乡下】 xiāngxia 〈口〉 village; country; countryside: 他刚从～来。He's just come from the countryside. ◇ ～人 country folk; country cousin

【乡音】 xiāngyīn accent of one's native place; local accent

【乡邮】 xiāngyóu rural postal service ◇ ～员 rural postman

【乡愿】 xiāngyuàn 〈书〉 hypocrite

【乡镇】 xiāngzhèn ① villages and towns ② small towns

# 相

xiāng ① each other; one another; mutually: 素不～识 not know each other/ ～距太远 too far apart ②〔表示一方对另一方的动作〕: 实不～瞒 to tell you the truth/ 另眼～看 look upon sb. with special respect or concern; view sb. in a new, more favourable light ③ see for oneself (whether sb. or sth. is to one's liking): ～女婿 take a look at one's prospective son-in-law ④ (Xiāng) a surname
另见 xiàng

【相安无事】 xiāng'ān wú shì live in peace with each other

【相帮】 xiāngbāng 〈方〉 help; aid

【相比】 xiāngbǐ compare: 二者不能～。There's no comparison between the two (of them)./ 跟先进单位～,我们还有很大差距。We still have a long way to go to catch up with the advanced units. 或 We are far behind the advanced units.

【相差】 xiāngchà differ: 两者～无几。There's hardly any difference between the two./ 我们的工作跟党的要求～还很远。Our work still falls far short of what the Party requires of us.

【相称】 xiāngchèn match; suit: 这两种颜色配在一起很～。The two colours match very well./ 这头巾跟你的年龄不～。This kerchief doesn't suit a person of your age./ 你这种工作作风与党员的称号很不～。Your work style is not worthy of a Party member.

【相持】 xiāngchí be locked in a stalemate: 双方～不下。Neither side was ready to yield./ 战争处于～阶段。The war was at a stalemate.

【相处】 xiāngchǔ get along (with one another): 不好～ difficult to get along with/ ～得很好 get on well with each other/ 我们～时间不长，但已经结下了深厚的友谊。We've not been together long, but we've become close friends.

【相传】 xiāngchuán ① tradition has it that...; according to legend ② hand down or pass on from one to another: 世代～ hand down from generation to generation

【相当】 xiāngdāng ① match; balance; correspond to; be equal to; be commensurate with: 得失～。The gains balance the losses./ 他们俩年龄～。They are well-matched in age. 或 They're about the same age./ ～于省一级的自治区 autonomous regions analogous to provinces/ 水坝高达七十八米，～于二十层的大楼。The dam rises to a height of 78 metres, or the height of a 20-storey building. ② suitable; fit; appropriate: 他一时想不出～的字眼来。At the time he couldn't think of a suitable word for it./ 这个工作还没有找到～的人。We haven't found a fit person for the job yet. ③ quite; fairly; considerably: ～好 fairly good/ 演出～成功。The performance was quite a success./ 社会主义社会是一个～长的历史阶段。Socialist society covers a historical period of considerable length.

【相得益彰】 xiāng dé yì zhāng each shining more brilliantly in the other's company; bring out the best in each other; complement each other

【相等】 xiāngděng be equal: 数量～ be equal in amount (或 quantity, number); be numerically equal/ 这两间房子的面积～。The two rooms have the same amount of floor space.

【相抵】 xiāngdǐ offset; balance; counterbalance: 收支～，尚余一百五十元。The accounts show a favourable balance of 150 *yuan*.

【相对】 xiāngduì ① opposite; face to face: ～而坐 sit opposite (或 facing) each other; sit face to face/ 两山遥遥～。The two hills stand opposite each other at a distance./ 美是与丑～的。Beauty is the opposite of ugliness. ② relative: 平衡是～的，不平衡是绝对的。Balance is relative, imbalance is absolute. ③ relatively; comparatively: ～稳定 relatively stable/ ～地说 comparatively speaking
◇ ～高度〈测〉 relative altitude (或 height)/ ～湿度〈气〉 relative humidity/ ～速度〈物〉 relative velocity/ ～误差〈数〉 relative error/ ～性 relativity/ ～运动〈物〉 relative motion/ ～真理〈哲〉 relative truth/ ～值 relative value/ ～主义〈哲〉 relativism

【相对论】 xiāngduìlùn 〈物〉 the theory of relativity; relativity: 广(狭)义～ the general (special) theory of relativity

【相对论性】 xiāngduìlùnxìng 〈物〉 relativistic ◇ ～量子理论 relativistic quantum theory/ ～物理学 relativistic physics

【相反】 xiāngfǎn opposite; contrary: 朝～方向驶去 drive off in the opposite direction/ 结果与我们的愿望恰好～。The result turned out contrary to our expectations.

【相反相成】 xiāngfǎn-xiāngchéng (of two things) be both opposite and complementary to each other; oppose each other and yet also complement each other

【相仿】 xiāngfǎng similar; more or less the same: 内容～ be similar in content/ 年纪～ be about the same age

【相逢】 xiāngféng meet (by chance); come across

【相符】 xiāngfú conform to; tally (或 agree) with; correspond to (或 with): 报告与事实～。The report tallies with the facts.

【相辅而行】 xiāng fǔ ér xíng coordinate; go together

【相辅相成】 xiāngfǔ-xiāngchéng supplement each other; complement each other

【相干】 xiānggān ①〔多用于否定句或疑问句〕 have to do with; be concerned with: 这件事与她有什么～? What has this to do with her?/ 这事与你不～。This has nothing to do with you. ②〈物〉 coherent ◇ ～散射 coherent scattering/ ～性 coherence; coherency

【相隔】 xiānggé be separated by; be apart; be at a distance of: ～万里 be thousands of *li* apart; be a long way away from each other/ ～多年 after an interval of many years/ ～千山万水 be separated by numerous rivers and mountains/ 从我上次来到现在～不过两三个月，情况已经发生了很大的变化。It's only two or three months since my last visit here, but the situation has greatly changed.

【相关】 xiāngguān be interrelated: 体育事业和人民健康密切～。Physical culture has a direct bearing on the people's health.

【相好】 xiānghǎo ① be on intimate terms ② intimate friend ③ have an affair with ④ lover or mistress

【相互】 xiānghù mutual; reciprocal; each other: 增进～了解 promote mutual understanding/ ～影响 influence each other; interact/ ～关系 mutual relation; interrelation/ ～作用 interaction; interplay

【相继】 xiāngjì in succession; one after another: 代表们～发言。The delegates spoke in succession (或 one after another).

【相间】 xiāngjiàn alternate with: 黑白～ black alternating with white; in black and white check

【相交】 xiāngjiāo ① intersect: 直线 *AB* 与直线 *CD* ～于 *E* 点上。Line *AB* intersects line *CD* at *E*. ② make friends with: ～有年 have been friends for years

【相近】 xiāngjìn ① close; near: 地点～的两个学校 two neighbouring schools/ 比分～。The score was very close. ② be similar (或 close) to: 两人性格～。The two of them are similar in character.

【相距】 xiāngjù apart; at a distance of; away from: 两地～不到二里。The two places are less than two *li* apart./ 这两个桥墩之间～二十米。The distance between the two piers of the bridge is 20 metres.

【相连】 xiānglián be linked together; be joined: 两地有铁路～。The two places are linked by rail./ 两国山水～。The two countries are joined by common mountains and rivers.

【相劝】 xiāngquàn persuade; offer advice: 好意～ offer well-meaning advice
【相商】 xiāngshāng consult: 有要事～。I have something important to consult you about.
【相生相克】 xiāngshēng-xiāngkè mutual promotion and restraint between the five elements (a concept held by the ancients to explain natural phenomena and later used in traditional Chinese medicine, etc.)
【相识】 xiāngshí ① be acquainted with each other: 素不～ have never met; not be acquainted with each other ② acquaintance: 老～ an old acquaintance
【相思】 xiāngsī yearning between lovers; lovesickness: 单～ one-sided love; unrequited love ◇ ～病 lovesickness
【相思鸟】 xiāngsīniǎo red-billed leiothrix
【相思子】 xiāngsīzǐ 〈植〉 ① jequirity; jequirity bean; love pea ② ormosia seed
【相似】 xiāngsì resemble; be similar; be alike: 面貌～ look alike/ 何其～乃尔！ What a striking similarity! ◇ ～形〈数〉 similar figures
【相提并论】 xiāngtí-bìnglùn 〔多用于否定式〕 mention in the same breath; place on a par: 两者不能～。The two cannot be mentioned in the same breath.
【相通】 xiāngtōng communicate with each other; be interlinked: 这是两间～的屋子。These are two communicating rooms./ 这两个院子有门～。The two courtyards open onto (或 into) each other./ 我们的心是～的。Our hearts beat in harmony.
【相同】 xiāngtóng identical; the same; alike: 我们在这个问题上观点～。We have identical (或 the same) views on this question./ 两者毫无～之处。The two have nothing in common./ 不同性质的矛盾不能用～的方法去处理。Contradictions different in nature must not be treated alike (或 in the same way).
【相投】 xiāngtóu be congenial; agree with each other: 兴趣～ have similar tastes and interests; find each other congenial
【相象】 xiāngxiàng resemble; be similar; be alike: 这两种花很～。These two flowers are very much alike.
【相信】 xiāngxìn believe in; be convinced of; have faith in: ～真理 believe in truth/ ～自己的事业是正义的 be convinced of the justice of one's cause/ 我们应当～群众，我们应当～党，这是两条根本的原理。We must have faith in the masses and we must have faith in the Party. These are two cardinal principles.
【相形见绌】 xiāng xíng jiàn chù prove definitely inferior; pale by comparison; be outshone
【相沿成习】 xiāng yán chéng xí become a custom through long usage
【相依】 xiāngyī depend on each other; be interdependent: ～为命 depend on each other for survival/ 唇齿～ be as close as lips and teeth; be closely related and mutually dependent
【相宜】 xiāngyí suitable; fitting; appropriate: 在那个场合你说这样的话是不～的。What you said on that occasion was not appropriate./ 秋分种麦最～。The Autumnal Equinox is the best time for wheat-sowing.
【相应】 xiāngyìng corresponding; relevant: 随着工业的发展，对环境保护也采取了～的措施。With the development of industry, appropriate measures have been taken to protect the environment./ 大会一致谴责这种侵略行为，并通过了～的决议。The conference unanimously condemned this act of aggression and passed relevant resolutions.
【相映】 xiāngyìng set each other off; form a contrast: ～成趣 form a delightful contrast; contrast finely with each other
【相与】 xiāngyǔ ① get along with sb.; deal with sb.: 极难～ extremely difficult to get along with (或 deal with) ② with each other; together: ～大笑 have a good laugh together
【相约】 xiāngyuē agree (on meeting place, date, etc.); reach agreement; make an appointment
【相知】 xiāngzhī ① be well acquainted with each other; know each other well: ～有素 have known each other long ② bosom friend; great friend
【相左】 xiāngzuǒ 〈书〉 ① fail to meet each other ② conflict with each other; fail to agree; be at odds with

**香** xiāng ① fragrant; sweet-smelling; aromatic; scented: 稻～千里 the fragrance of ripening rice spreading a thousand *li*/ 茉莉花～ the sweet scent of jasmines ② savoury; appetizing: 这饭真～！ This rice is really appetizing./ 炒什么菜啊？好～呀！ Mmm! What's cooking? It smells delicious. ③ with relish; with good appetite: 吃得很～ eat with relish; enjoy the food/ 昨晚没睡好，吃饭不～。I have no appetite because I didn't sleep well last night. ④ (sleep) soundly ⑤ popular; welcome: 这种自行车在农村很～。This type of bicycle is most popular in the countryside./ 在修正主义路线控制的地方，坏人不臭，好人不～。Where the revisionist line prevailed, bad people were not looked down on and good people were not looked up to. ⑥ perfume or spice: 麝～ musk/ 檀～ sandalwood ⑦ incense; joss stick: 盘～ incense coil/ 蚊～ mosquito-repellent incense
【香案】 xiāng'àn a long altar on which incense burners are placed; incense burner table
【香槟酒】 xiāngbīnjiǔ champagne
【香菜】 xiāngcài coriander
【香草】 xiāngcǎo 〈植〉 sweetgrass
【香肠】 xiāngcháng sausage
【香椿】 xiāngchūn 〈植〉 Chinese toon (*Toona sinensis*)
【香榧】 xiāngfěi 〈植〉 Chinese torreya (*Torreya grandis*) ◇ ～子 Chinese torreya nut
【香粉】 xiāngfěn face powder
【香馥馥】 xiāngfūfū strongly scented; richly fragrant
【香附子】 xiāngfùzǐ 〈中药〉 the rhizome of nutgrass flatsedge (*Cyperus rotundus*)
【香干】 xiānggān smoked bean curd
【香菇】 xiānggū *Xianggu* mushroom
【香瓜】 xiāngguā muskmelon
【香花】 xiānghuā ① fragrant flower ② writings, artistic works, etc. that help consolidate the dictatorship of the proletariat and advance the cause of socialism
【香火】 xiānghuǒ ① joss sticks and candles burning at a temple: ～甚盛 (of a temple) have many worshippers; attract a large number of pilgrims ② burning joss stick; burning incense: 用～点爆竹 light a firecracker with a burning joss stick
【香蕉】 xiāngjiāo banana
【香蕉水】 xiāngjiāoshuǐ 〈化〉 banana oil
【香精】 xiāngjīng essence: 食用～ flavouring essence/ 合成～ compound essence ◇ ～油 essential oil
【香客】 xiāngkè pilgrim
【香料】 xiāngliào ① perfume ② spice ◇ ～厂 perfumery
【香炉】 xiānglú incense burner
【香茅】 xiāngmáo 〈植〉 lemongrass ◇ ～醛〈化〉 citronellal/ ～油 citronella oil
【香喷喷】 xiāngpēnpēn ① sweet-smelling ② savoury; appetizing: 一碗～的炖肉 a bowl of savoury (pork) stew
【香片】 xiāngpiàn scented tea
【香蒲】 xiāngpú 〈植〉 cattail
【香气】 xiāngqì sweet smell; fragrance; aroma
【香水】 xiāngshuǐ perfume; scent

【香酥鸡】 xiāngsūjī crisp fried chicken
【香梭鱼】 xiāngsuōyú red barracuda
【香甜】 xiāngtián ① fragrant and sweet: ～的瓜果 sweet melons and fruits ② (sleep) soundly: 小伙子们劳动了一天,晚上睡得格外～。The boys slept soundly after a day's work.
【香味】 xiāngwèi sweet smell; fragrance; scent; perfume
【香烟】 xiāngyān ① cigarette ② incense smoke: ～缭绕 coiling incense smoke ◇ ～盒 cigarette case/ ～头 cigarette butt (或 end)
【香油】 xiāngyóu sesame oil
【香鼬】 xiāngyòu alpine weasel
【香鱼】 xiāngyú sweetfish; ayu
【香橼】 xiāngyuán 〈植〉 citron
【香云纱】 xiāngyúnshā 〈纺〉 gambiered Guangdong gauze
【香皂】 xiāngzào perfumed (或 scented) soap; toilet soap
【香獐】 xiāngzhāng musk deer
【香脂】 xiāngzhī ① face cream ② balm; balsam
【香烛】 xiāngzhú joss sticks and candles (burned when offering sacrifices to gods or ancestors)

**厢** xiāng ① wing (usu. of a one-storeyed house); wing-room: 一正两～ a central room with two wing-rooms ② railway carriage or compartment; (theatre) box: 车～ carriage/ 包～ box ③ the vicinity outside of a city gate: 城～ the city proper and areas just outside its gates ④ side: 一～情愿 one-sided wish; one's own wishful thinking/ 让开大路,占领两～ leave the high road alone and seize the land on both sides (as in mobile warfare)
【厢房】 xiāngfáng wing (usu. of a one-storeyed house); wing-room

**湘** Xiāng ① short for the *Xiangjiang* River (in Hunan Province) ② another name for Hunan Province
【湘妃竹】 xiāngfēizhú mottled bamboo
【湘剧】 xiāngjù Hunan opera
【湘绣】 xiāngxiù Hunan embroidery

**葙** xiāng 见"青葙" qīngxiāng

**箱** xiāng ① chest; box; case; trunk: 大木～ wooden trunk; chest/ 货～ packing box/ 书～ a box for books/ 皮～ leather suitcase/ 垃圾～ dustbin; garbage can; ash can ② anything in the shape of a box: 风～ bellows
【箱底】 xiāngdǐ ① the bottom of a chest ② valuables stowed away at the bottom of the chest; one's store of valuables
【箱笼】 xiānglǒng (a traveller's) boxes and baskets; luggage; baggage
【箱型照相机】 xiāngxíng zhàoxiàngjī box camera
【箱子】 xiāngzi chest; box; case; trunk

**襄** xiāng 〈书〉 assist; help: 共～义举 let everybody help to promote this worthy undertaking
【襄理】 xiānglǐ 〔旧时银行、企业用语〕assistant manager
【襄助】 xiāngzhù assist

**镶** xiāng ① inlay; set; mount: 金～玉嵌 inlaid with gold and jade/ ～宝石 set gems; mount precious stones/ 给窗子～玻璃 glaze a window ② rim; edge; border: 给裙子～花边 edge a skirt with lace
【镶板】 xiāngbǎn 〈建〉 panel
【镶嵌】 xiāngqiàn inlay; set; mount: ～银丝漆器 silver-inlaid lacquerware/ ～细工 inlaid work; marquetry; mosaic
【镶牙】 xiāngyá put in a false tooth; insert an artificial tooth

## xiáng

**详** xiáng ① detailed; minute: ～谈 speak in detail (或 at length); go into details ② details; particulars: ～见附录。For details, see the appendix./ ～述自己的论点 elaborate one's thesis ③ know clearly: 作者生卒年月不～。The author's dates are unknown.
【详尽】 xiángjìn detailed; exhaustive; thorough: ～的记载 a detailed record/ ～的调查 a thorough investigation/ 对问题进行～的研究 make an exhaustive study of a subject
【详密】 xiángmì elaborate; meticulous: ～的计划 a meticulous plan
【详明】 xiángmíng full and clear: ～的注解 full and clear annotations
【详情】 xiángqíng detailed information; details; particulars: ～后报。Details to follow./ ～请问办事处。Please apply to the office for particulars.
【详实】 xiángshí full and accurate: ～的材料 full and accurate data (或 material)
【详图】 xiángtú detail (drawing): 发动机～ engine detail
【详细】 xiángxì detailed; minute: ～的报告 a detailed report/ ～了解情况 acquire detailed knowledge of the situation/ ～占有材料 collect all the available material; have all the relevant data at one's fingertips/ ～地描述 give a minute description/ 请说～点。Please explain in greater detail.

**降** xiáng ① surrender; capitulate: 宁死不～ rather die than surrender ② subdue; vanquish; tame: ～妖伏魔 vanquish demons and monsters
另见 jiàng
【降伏】 xiángfú subdue; vanquish; tame: ～劣马 break in a wild horse
【降服】 xiángfú yield; surrender
【降龙伏虎】 xiánglóng-fúhǔ subdue the dragon and tame the tiger — overcome powerful adversaries
【降顺】 xiángshùn 〈书〉 yield and pledge allegiance to

**祥** xiáng auspicious; propitious; lucky
【祥瑞】 xiángruì auspicious sign; propitious omen

**翔** xiáng circle in the air: 翱～ soar; hover
【翔实】 xiángshí full and accurate

## xiǎng

**享** xiǎng enjoy: 共～胜利的欢乐 share the joy of victory
【享福】 xiǎngfú enjoy a happy life; live in ease and comfort
【享乐】 xiǎnglè lead a life of pleasure; indulge in creature comforts ◇ ～思想 preoccupation with pleasure-seeking/ ～主义 hedonism; pleasure-seeking
【享年】 xiǎngnián 〈敬〉 die at the age of
【享受】 xiǎngshòu ① enjoy: ～公费医疗 enjoy public health services ② enjoyment; treat: 贪图～ seek ease and comfort/ 看这样的好戏,既是一次生动的政治教育,也是一种艺术～。A good play like this is a vivid political lesson as well as an artistic treat.
【享用】 xiǎngyòng enjoy the use of; enjoy

【享有】 xiǎngyǒu enjoy (rights, prestige, etc.): ～崇高的威望 enjoy high prestige; be held in esteem/ 在我国,妇女～同男子平等的权利。Women in our country enjoy equal rights with men.

**响** xiǎng ① sound; noise: 听不见～儿了。No more sound was heard./ 一声炮～ the report of a cannon/ 两～的爆竹 double-bang firecrackers ② make a sound; sound; ring: ～锣 sound a gong/ 电话铃～了。The telephone rang./ 全场～起暴风雨般的掌声。A stormy applause broke out in the hall. 或 The hall resounded with stormy applause./ 扩音器不～了。The loudspeaker's stopped working./ 他一声不～地走了。He left without a word. ③ noisy; loud: 收音机开得太～了。The radio's too loud (或 noisy). ④ echo: ～应 respond; answer

【响板】 xiǎngbǎn 〈乐〉 castanets

【响鼻】 xiǎngbí (of a horse, mule, etc.) snort

【响彻】 xiǎngchè resound (或 reverberate) through: 一曲～云霄的凯歌 a song of triumph that resounds through the skies/ 炮声～山谷。The roar of guns reverberated in the valley.

【响动】 xiǎngdòng sound of sth. astir: 夜很静,一点～也没有。The night was quiet, and there was no sound of anything astir.

【响度】 xiǎngdù 〈物〉 loudness; volume

【响遏行云】 xiǎng è xíngyún (of singing) be so sonorous it stops the passing clouds

【响亮】 xiǎngliàng loud and clear; resounding; resonant; sonorous: ～的回答 a loud and clear reply; an unequivocal reply/ ～的声音 a resounding voice/ 一记～的耳光 a heavy slap in the face; a smart box on the ear

【响器】 xiǎngqì 〈乐〉 Chinese percussion instruments

【响声】 xiǎngshēng sound; noise: 沙沙的～ rustling sound

【响尾蛇】 xiǎngwěishé rattlesnake

【响音】 xiǎngyīn 〈语〉 resonant

【响应】 xiǎngyìng respond; answer: ～党的号召 respond to (或 answer) the Party's call

**饷** xiǎng ① 〈书〉 entertain (with food and drink) ② 〈旧〉 pay (for soldiers, policemen, etc.): 月～ monthly pay

**飨** xiǎng 〈书〉 provide dinner for; entertain: ～客 entertain a guest/ 以～读者 offer to the readers

**想** xiǎng ① think: ～问题 think over a problem/ ～得真周到 have really thought of everything/ ～办法 think of a way; try to find a solution (或 way out)/ 让我～一～。Let me think it over. 或 Let me see./ 也要～～困难。We must also anticipate difficulties. ② suppose; reckon; consider; think: 我～他今天不会来。I don't think he'll be coming today./ 我～我该走了。I'm afraid I must be going now. ③ want to; would like to; feel like (doing sth.): 你～看足球赛吗? Do you want to see (或 feel like seeing) a football match?/ 我也～试试。I'd also like to have a try. ④ remember with longing; miss: 你走了以后,我们都很～你。After you left, we all missed you.

【想必】 xiǎngbì presumably; most probably (或 likely): 这事～你知道。You most probably know this./ 他没有答复,～没有收到我的信。No word from him yet; presumably he hasn't received my letter.

【想不到】 xiǎngbudào unexpected: 这真是～的事! This is something quite unexpected!/ ～家乡变化这么大。I never expected my village would have changed so much./ 真～会在这儿见到你。Fancy seeing you here!

【想不开】 xiǎngbukāi take things too hard; take a matter to heart: 别为这些小事～。Don't take such small things to heart.

【想当然】 xiǎngdāngrán assume sth. as a matter of course; take for granted: 我们不能凭～办事。We must not act on assumptions.

【想到】 xiǎngdào think of; call to mind: 忽然～一件重要的事情 suddenly think of something important/ 经常～人民的利益 always have the interests of the people at heart/ 在这紧急关头,工人们首先～的是抢救国家财产。At this critical moment, the workers' first thought was to save state property./ 我们没～你会来。We didn't expect you (to come).

【想得到】 xiǎngdedào 〔多用于反问〕 think; imagine; expect: 谁～会出事故? Who would have thought there'd be an accident?

【想得开】 xiǎngdekāi not take to heart; take philosophically; try to look on the bright side of things: 这老太太最～了。This old lady always looks at the bright side of things.

【想法】 xiǎngfǎ think of a way; do what one can; try: ～给大伙儿弄点水喝喝。Try and get some drinking water for everyone.

【想法】 xiǎngfa idea; opinion; what one has in mind: 这个～不错。This is a good idea./ 按我的～ in my opinion; to my mind/ 把你的～给大家说说。Tell us what you have in mind.

【想方设法】 xiǎngfāng-shèfǎ do everything possible; try every means; try by hook or by crook

【想见】 xiǎngjiàn infer; gather: 从这些事情上,你可以～他的为人。From these instances you can gather what kind of person he is.

【想来】 xiǎnglái it may be assumed that; presumably: 他的话～不是没有根据的。I suppose what he says is not groundless.

【想念】 xiǎngniàn remember with longing; long to see again; miss: 我们都很～老大娘。We all miss grandma very much./ 侨胞～祖国。Overseas Chinese cherish the memory of their home land.

【想起】 xiǎngqǐ remember; recall; think of; call to mind: ～解放前的苦难生活 recall (或 remember) the miserable life before liberation/ 他看起来面熟,可我一下子想不起来他是谁。He looked familiar to me but I couldn't immediately place him./ 我忽然～忘了锁门了。It suddenly occurred to me that I had left the door unlocked.

【想入非非】 xiǎngrù fēifēi indulge in fantasy; allow one's fancy to run wild

【想通】 xiǎngtōng straighten out one's thinking; become convinced; come round: 我～了。I've come round to the idea now./ 只要～了,他就会积极地去干。Once he's straightened out his thinking, he'll go all out on the job./ 你要是一时想不通,还可以再想想。Think the matter over again if you're still not convinced.

【想头】 xiǎngtou 〈口〉 ① idea: 老李有个～。Lao Li's got an idea. ② hope: 没什么～了。There's no hope now.

【想望】 xiǎngwàng desire; long for: 他从小就～着当一名拖拉机手。He's longed to be a tractor driver ever since he was a child.

【想象】 xiǎngxiàng ① imagine; fancy; visualize: 难以～ hard to imagine (或 visualize)/ ～不到的困难 unimaginable difficulties ② 〈心〉 imagination ◇ ～力 imaginative power (或 faculty); imagination

**鲞** xiǎng dried fish: 鳗～ dried eel

## xiàng

**向** xiàng ① direction: 风～ wind direction/ 人心所～ (the trend of) popular sentiment ② face; turn towards: 这间屋子～东。This room faces east./ 葵花朵朵～太阳。Sunflowers turn towards the sun. ③ take sb.'s part; side with; be partial to: ～理不～人 stand by what is right, not by a particular person; side with whoever is right ④〈介〉〔表示动作的方向〕:～上级汇报工作 report to one's superior on one's work/ ～人民宣传 carry on propaganda among the people/ ～自然开战 wage a battle against nature/ ～纵深发展 develop in depth/ ～王杰同志学习。Learn from Comrade Wang Jie. ⑤ always; all along: ～无此例。There's no precedent for this. ⑥ (Xiàng) a surname

【向背】 xiàng-bèi support or oppose: 人心～ whether the people are for or against; the will of the people

【向壁虚构】 xiàng bì xūgòu make up out of one's head; fabricate

【向导】 xiàngdǎo guide: 革命党是群众的～。A revolutionary party is the guide of the masses.

【向光性】 xiàngguāngxìng 〈生〉 phototropism

【向后】 xiànghòu towards the back; backward: ～看 look back/ ～撤 withdraw/ ～转!(口令) About face! 或 About turn!/ ～转走!(口令) To the rear, march!

【向来】 xiànglái always; all along: ～如此。It has always been so./ 我～不抽烟。I have never smoked.

【向量】 xiàngliàng 〈数〉 vector ◇ ～分析 vector analysis

【向前】 xiàngqián forward; onward; ahead: 奋勇～ forge ahead/ 使革命～发展 carry the revolution forward/ 采取～看的态度 adopt a forward-looking attitude/ ～看!(口令) Eyes front! 或 Ready, front!

【向日葵】 xiàngrìkuí sunflower

【向日性】 xiàngrìxìng 〈植〉 heliotropism

【向上】 xiàngshàng upward; up: 卡车沿着盘山公路～爬去。The trucks climbed the twisting mountain road./ 好好学习,天天～。Study well and make progress every day.

【向上爬】 xiàngshàngpá be intent on personal advancement: 有～的思想 have the mentality of a careerist (或 social climber)

【向水性】 xiàngshuǐxìng 〈生〉 hydrotropism

【向往】 xiàngwǎng yearn for; look forward to: ～着北京 yearn for Beijing/ ～幸福的新生活 look forward to a happy new life/ ～共产主义 cherish the ideal of communism

【向下】 xiàngxià downward; down: 滑雪运动员飞快地～滑去。The skiers sped down the slope./ 领导干部要善于～作调查。Leading cadres should be good at investigating conditions at the lower levels.

【向斜】 xiàngxié 〈地〉 syncline ◇ ～谷 synclinal valley

【向心力】 xiàngxīnlì 〈物〉 centripetal force

【向性】 xiàngxìng 〈生〉 tropism

【向阳】 xiàngyáng ① exposed to the sun; sunny ② with a sunny usu. southern, exposure: 这间屋～。The room has a southern exposure.

【向右】 xiàngyòu towards the right: ～转!(口令) Right face! 或 Right turn!/～转走!(口令) By the right flank, march!

【向隅】 xiàngyú 〈书〉 stand in a corner — be disappointed for lack of opportunity; feel left out

【向隅而泣】 xiàngyú ér qì weep all alone in a corner; be left to grieve in the cold

【向着】 xiàngzhe ① turn towards; face: ～光明的未来前进 advance towards a bright future ②〈口〉 take sb.'s part; side with; be partial to: 她说话在理,我就～她。I take her part because she's right./ 老奶奶～小孙女。Grandma favours her little granddaughter.

【向左】 xiàngzuǒ towards the left: ～转!(口令) Left face! 或 Left turn!/ ～转走!(口令) By the left flank, march!

**巷** xiàng lane; alley
另见 hàng

【巷战】 xiàngzhàn street fighting

**项** xiàng ① nape (of the neck) ②〈量〉〔用于分项目的事物〕: 八～原则 eight principles/ 一～一～地进行解释 explain item by item/ 第五条第二款第三～ article 5, clause 2, item 3/ 还有一～工作要做。There is another job to do. ③ sum (of money): 进～ income/ 欠～ liabilities ④〈数〉 term ⑤ (Xiàng) a surname

【项背】 xiàngbèi a person's back: ～相望 (walk) one after another in close succession/ 不可望其～ cannot hold a candle to sb.

【项链】 xiàngliàn necklace

【项目】 xiàngmù item: 出口～ goods for export; export items/ 基本建设～ capital construction project/ 援助～ aid project/ 训练～ training courses/ 田径～ track and field events

【项圈】 xiàngquān necklet; necklace

【项庄舞剑,意在沛公】 Xiàng Zhuāng wǔ jiàn, yì zài Pèigōng Xiang Zhuang performed the sword dance as a cover for his attempt on Liu Bang's life — act with a hidden motive

**相** xiàng ① looks; appearance: 长～儿 a person's appearance/ 一副可怜～ a pitiful appearance; a sorry figure/ 一脸凶～ a fierce look on one's face ② bearing; posture: 站没站～,坐没坐～ not know how to stand or sit properly/ 这孩子睡～不好。The child sleeps sprawled all over the bed. ③ look at and appraise: ～马 look at a horse to judge its worth/ 人不可以貌～。Never judge a person by his appearance. ④〈书〉 assist ⑤〈书〉 prime minister ⑥ ministers in Japanese government ⑦ photograph: 照个～ take a photo; have a photo taken ⑧〈地〉 facies: 海～ marine facies/ 浅海～ neritic facies/ 煤～ coaly facies ⑨〈物〉 phase: 调～ phase modulation ⑩ elephant, one of the pieces in Chinese chess
另见 xiāng

【相册】 xiàngcè photo album

【相机】 xiàngjī ① watch for an opportunity: ～行事 act as the occasion demands; do as one sees fit/ ～而动 wait for an opportunity to act; bide one's time ② camera

【相角】 xiàngjiǎo photo corner

【相控阵雷达】 xiàngkòngzhèn léidá 〈军〉 phased-array radar

【相貌】 xiàngmào facial features; looks; appearance: ～端正 have regular features

【相面】 xiàngmiàn tell sb.'s fortune by reading his face; practise physiognomy

【相片】 xiàngpiàn photograph; photo

【相声】 xiàngsheng 〈曲艺〉 comic dialogue; cross talk: 说～ perform a comic dialogue

【相纸】 xiàngzhǐ (photographic) printing paper; photographic paper

**象** xiàng ① elephant ② appearance; shape; image: 万～更新。All things take on a new aspect. 或 Everything looks new and fresh. ③ imitate: ～声 onomatopoeia ④ be like; resemble; take after: 姐妹俩长得很～。The two sisters are very much alike./ 这孩子～他父亲。The child takes after its father./ ～猛虎下山一样向敌人扑去 charge at the enemy like tigers dashing down a mountain/ ～雷锋一样全心全意为人民服务 serve the people wholeheartedly as Lei Feng did ⑤ look as if; seem: ～要下雨了。It looks like rain./ ～是有人在敲门。It sounds like somebody's knocking on the door. ⑥ such as; like: ～黄继光这样的英雄人物,将永远活在人民的心里。Heroes such as Huang Jiguang will always live in the hearts of the people. ⑦ elephant, one of the pieces in Chinese chess

【象鼻】 xiàngbí trunk; proboscis

【象鼻虫】 xiàngbíchóng weevil; snout beetle

【象差】 xiàngchā 〈物〉 aberration

【象话】 xiànghuà [多用于否定或反问] reasonable; proper; right: 大家都忙,就我在家休息,～吗？How can I take it easy at home when everybody else is so busy?/ 你发这么大脾气～吗？Aren't you ashamed to fly into such a rage?/ 真不～！That's really the limit. 或 It's simply outrageous.

【象脚鼓】 xiàngjiǎogǔ 〈乐〉 a drum on a pedestal, shaped like an elephant's leg, used by several minority nationalities in Yunnan

【象皮病】 xiàngpíbìng 〈医〉 elephantiasis

【象棋】 xiàngqí (Chinese) chess

【象散】 xiàngsàn 〈物〉 astigmatism ◇ ～镜 astigmatoscope/ ～透镜 astigmatic lens

【象声】 xiàngshēng 〈语〉 onomatopoeia ◇ ～词 onomatope

【象限】 xiàngxiàn 〈数〉 quadrant ◇ ～仪〈天〉 quadrant

【象形】 xiàngxíng 〈语〉 pictographic characters or pictographs, e.g. 日 (sun) and 月 (moon) — one of the six categories of Chinese characters (六书) ◇ ～文字 pictograph; hieroglyph/ ～字 pictographic character

【象牙】 xiàngyá elephant's tusk; ivory: ～雕刻 ivory carving (或 sculpture)/ ～制品 ivories/ ～之塔 ivory tower

【象牙海岸】 Xiàngyá Hǎi'àn the Ivory Coast

【象牙质】 xiàngyázhì ① (made of) ivory: ～刀把 the ivory handle of a knife ② 〈生理〉 dentine

【象样】 xiàngyàng up to the mark; presentable; decent; sound: 他的针线活还挺～的。His needlework is quite presentable./ 这屋里连张～的桌子也没有。There isn't even a decent table in this room./ 他提不出～的理由来解释他的行动。He couldn't give any sound reason for his action.

【象征】 xiàngzhēng ① symbolize; signify; stand for: 斧头镰刀～工人农民。The hammer and sickle symbolize (或 stand for) the workers and peasants. ② symbol; emblem; token: 友谊的～ emblem (或 symbol) of friendship

【象征性】 xiàngzhēngxìng symbolic; emblematic; token: 韶山——北京～长跑 a symbolic "Shaoshan—Beijing" long-distance run

## 像

xiàng ① likeness (of sb.); portrait; picture: 画～ portrait/ 铜～ bronze statue ② 〈物〉 image: 虚(实)～ virtual (real) image ③ 见"象" xiàng ④⑤⑥

【像话】 xiànghuà 见"象话" xiànghuà

【像样】 xiàngyàng 见"象样" xiàngyàng

【像章】 xiàngzhāng badge (或 button) with sb.'s likeness on it: 毛主席～ a Chairman Mao badge

## 橡

xiàng ① oak ② rubber tree

【橡浆】 xiàngjiāng rubber latex

【橡胶】 xiàngjiāo rubber: 天然～ natural rubber/ 合成～ synthetic rubber/ 生～〈化〉 raw rubber; caoutchouc/ 海绵～ foam rubber

◇ ～草〈植〉 Russian dandelion; kok-saghyz/ ～厂 rubber plant/ ～轮胎 rubber tyre/ ～树 rubber tree/ ～种植园 rubber plantation

【橡皮】 xiàngpí ① rubber ② eraser; rubber

◇ ～版〈印〉 rubber plate/ ～船 rubber boat/ ～膏〈医〉 adhesive plaster/ ～胶水 rubber cement/ ～筋 rubber band/ ～泥 plasticine/ ～手套 rubber (operating) gloves/ ～艇 pneumatic boat; rubber dinghy/ ～图章 rubber-stamp/ ～外包线〈电〉 rubber-sheathed wire

【橡实】 xiàngshí acorn ◇ ～管〈电子〉 acorn tube

# xiāo

## 肖

Xiāo a surname

另见 xiào

【肖氏回跳硬度】 xiāoshì huítiào yìngdù 〈物〉 Shore hardness

## 枭

xiāo ① owlet ② 〈书〉 fierce and ambitious: ～雄 a fierce and ambitious person; a formidable man

【枭首示众】 xiāoshǒu shìzhòng cut off a person's head and hang it up as a warning to all

## 枵

xiāo 〈书〉 empty; hollow

【枵腹从公】 xiāo fù cóng gōng attend to official duties on an empty stomach

## 削

xiāo ① pare (或 peel) with a knife: ～苹果 pare (或 peel) an apple/ ～铅笔 sharpen a pencil/ ～木头 whittle a piece of wood ② 〈乒乓球〉 cut; chop: ～球 cut; chop

另见 xuē

## 哓

xiāo

【哓哓不休】 xiāoxiāo bù xiū argue endlessly

## 骁

xiāo valiant; brave

【骁将】 xiāojiàng 〈书〉 valiant general

【骁勇】 xiāoyǒng 〈书〉 brave; valiant

## 哮

xiāo ① heavy breathing; wheeze ② roar; howl: 咆～ roar; thunder

【哮喘】 xiāochuǎn 〈医〉 asthma

## 消

xiāo ① disappear; vanish: 云～雾散。The clouds dispersed and the fog lifted./ 红肿已～。The swelling has gone down./ 他的气～了。He has cooled down. ② eliminate; dispel; remove: ～烟除尘 eliminate smoke and dust/ ～痰 reduce phlegm/ ～愁解闷 divert oneself from boredom; dispel depression or melancholy ③ pass the time in a leisurely way; while away (the time): ～夏 pass the summer in a leisurely way ④ 〈方〉[前面常有"不""只""何"等] need; take: 来回只～一个星期。It takes only a week to get there and back./ 不～说 needless to say; it goes without saying

【消沉】 xiāochén downhearted; low-spirited; dejected; depressed: 意志～ demoralized; despondent

【消除】 xiāochú eliminate; dispel; remove; clear up: ～分歧 eliminate (或 iron out) differences/ ～顾虑 dispel misgivings/ ～隐患 remove a hidden danger/ ～误会 clear up a misunderstanding

【消导】 xiāodǎo 〈中医〉 cure indigestion

【消毒】 xiāodú disinfect; sterilize: 用酒精～ sterilize in (或 with) alcohol/ 用漂白粉～ disinfect with bleaching powder ◇ ～剂 disinfectant/ ～牛奶 sterilized (或 pasteurized) milk

【消防】 xiāofáng fire control; fire fighting; fire protection ◇ ～车 fire engine (或 truck)/ ～队 fire brigade/ ～人员 fire fighter/ ～设备 fire-fighting equipment/ ～水龙 fire hose/ ～演习 fire drill/ ～站 fire station

【消费】 xiāofèi consume

◇ ～城市 consumer-city/ ～合作社 consumers' cooperative/ ～品 consumer goods/ ～者 consumer/ ～资料 means of subsistence
【消光剂】 xiāoguāngjì 〈化纤〉 dulling agent
【消耗】 xiāohào consume; use up; deplete; expend: ～精力 consume one's energy/ ～大量武器弹药 expend large amounts of arms and ammunition/ ～敌人的有生力量 wear down the enemy's effective strength/ 人力物力的～ a drain on manpower and material resources ◇ ～热〈医〉 hectic fever/ ～战 war of attrition
【消化】 xiāohuà digest: 好～ digestible; easy to digest/ 帮助学生～所学的东西 help the students digest what they have learnt
◇ ～不良 indigestion; dyspepsia/ ～道 alimentary canal; digestive tract/ ～酶 digestive ferment/ ～系统 digestive system/ ～液 digestive juice
【消火栓】 xiāohuǒshuān fire hydrant
【消极】 xiāojí ① negative: ～因素 negative factor/ ～影响 negative influence ② passive; inactive: ～抵抗(防御) passive resistance (defence)/ 态度～ take a passive attitude; remain inactive/ 情绪～ be dispirited/ ～怠工 be slack in work
【消解】 xiāojiě clear up; dispel
【消渴病】 xiāokěbìng 〈中医〉 ① diabetes ② any disease with the symptom of frequent drinking and urination
【消弭】 xiāomǐ put an end to; prevent: ～水患 prevent floods
【消灭】 xiāomiè ① perish; die out; pass away: 自行～ perish (或 die out) of itself/ 发生、发展和～的过程 the process of coming into being, developing and passing away ② eliminate; abolish; exterminate; wipe out: ～剥削制度 eliminate the system of exploitation/ 阶级的～ the abolition of classes/ ～病虫害 wipe out insect pests and plant diseases/ ～敌人一个师 wipe out an enemy division
【消磨】 xiāomó ① wear down; fritter away: ～志气 sap one's will/ ～精力 fritter away one's energy ② while (或 idle) away: ～岁月 while away the time/ ～时间 kill time; pass the time
【消气】 xiāoqì cool down; be mollified
【消遣】 xiāoqiǎn ① divert oneself; while away the time: 在火车上下棋～ beguile the train journey by playing chess ② pastime; diversion
【消融】 xiāoróng melt: 冰雪～ melting of ice and snow
【消散】 xiāosàn scatter and disappear; dissipate: 雾～了。The mist has lifted./ 他脸上的愁容～了。The worried expression has disappeared from his face.
【消色差】 xiāosèchā 〈物〉 achromatism ◇ ～透镜 achromatic lens; achromat
【消声】 xiāoshēng 〈建〉 noise elimination ◇ ～器 silencer; muffler
【消失】 xiāoshī disappear; vanish; dissolve; die (或 fade) away: ～在浓雾中 disappear in the dense fog/ ～在人群中 be lost in a crowd
【消逝】 xiāoshì die (或 fade) away; vanish; elapse: 火车的隆隆声慢慢～了。The rumbling of the train slowly died away./ 随着时间的～ with the lapse of time
【消释】 xiāoshì clear up; dispel: ～疑虑 dispel misgivings/ 误会～了。The misunderstanding has been cleared up.
【消受】 xiāoshòu ①〔多用于否定〕enjoy: 无福～ not have the luck to enjoy; be unable to enjoy ② endure; bear
【消瘦】 xiāoshòu become thin (或 emaciated): 身体一天天～下去 be getting thinner every day/ 显得有点～ look a bit emaciated
【消损】 xiāosǔn wear and tear
【消亡】 xiāowáng wither away; die out: 到了共产主义，国家就自行～了。With the coming of communism the state will wither away.
【消息】 xiāoxi ① news; information: 本地～ local news/ 头版～ a front-page story/ 据新华社～ according to a Xinhua dispatch/ ～灵通人士 a well-informed source ② tidings; news: 杳无～ have not heard from sb. since; have had no news of sb. or sth.
【消炎】 xiāoyán 〈医〉 diminish (或 counteract, allay) inflammation; dephlogisticate ◇ ～剂 antiphlogistic
【消夜】 xiāoyè 〈方〉 ① midnight snack ② have a midnight snack
【消长】 xiāo-zhǎng growth and decline: 双方力量的～ growth and decline of the relative strength of the two sides
【消肿】 xiāozhǒng 〈医〉 subsidence of a swelling; detumescence

**宵** xiāo night: 通～ all night; throughout the night
【宵禁】 xiāojìn curfew: 实行～ impose a curfew/ 解除～ lift a curfew

**逍** xiāo
【逍遥】 xiāoyáo free and unfettered: ～自在 be leisurely and carefree
【逍遥法外】 xiāoyáo fǎ wài go scot-free; be (或 remain) at large

**鸮** xiāo owl
【鸮卣】 xiāoyǒu 〈考古〉 an owl-shaped bronze wine jar

**萧** xiāo ① desolate; dreary ② (Xiāo) a surname
【萧规曹随】 Xiāo guī Cáo suí Cao (a Han Dynasty prime minister) followed the rules set by Xiao (his predecessor) — follow established rules
【萧墙】 xiāoqiáng 〈书〉 screen wall facing the gate of a Chinese house: ～之祸 trouble arising at home; trouble from within; internal strife
【萧瑟】 xiāosè ① rustle in the air: 秋风～。The autumn wind is soughing. ② bleak; desolate
【萧森】 xiāosēn 〈书〉 dreary and desolate
【萧疏】 xiāoshū ① desolate ② (of trees, leaves, etc.) sparse but graceful; thinly scattered
【萧索】 xiāosuǒ bleak and chilly; desolate
【萧条】 xiāotiáo ① desolate; bleak: 一片～的景象 a desolate scene on all sides ② 〈经〉 depression: 经济～ economic depression; slump/ 生意～。Business is bad (或 slack).
【萧萧】 xiāoxiāo 〈书〉〈象〉: 车辚辚，马～。Chariots rumble and roll; horses whinny and neigh./ 风～。The wind soughs and sighs.

**硝** xiāo ① nitre; saltpetre ② 〈皮革〉 tawing
【硝化】 xiāohuà 〈化〉 nitrify
◇ ～甘油 nitroglycerine/ ～棉 nitrocotton/ ～纤维素 nitrocellulose
【硝基】 xiāojī nitro- ◇ ～苯 nitrobenzene/ ～烷 nitroalkane
【硝镪水】 xiāoqiāngshuǐ 〈化〉 nitric acid
【硝石】 xiāoshí nitre; saltpetre: 智利～ Chile nitre (或 saltpetre); sodium nitre
【硝酸】 xiāosuān 〈化〉 nitric acid ◇ ～盐 nitrate (e.g. ～钾 potassium nitrate)
【硝烟】 xiāoyān smoke of gunpowder

**销** xiāo ① melt (metal) ② cancel; annul: 注～ write off; cancel ③ sell; market: 畅～ sell well/ 滞～ sell

poorly/ 产～平衡 balance between production and marketing ④ expend; spend: 开～ expenditure ⑤ pin: 开尾～〈机〉 cotter (或 split) pin/ 锁～ locking pin
【销案】 xiāo'àn close a case
【销毁】 xiāohuǐ destroy by melting or burning: ～罪证 destroy incriminating evidence/ ～核武器 the destruction of nuclear weapons
【销魂】 xiāohún be overwhelmed with sorrow or joy; feel transported
【销假】 xiāojià report back after leave of absence
【销路】 xiāolù sale; market: ～很好 have a good sale; find a good market/ 没有～ find no sale (或 market)
【销声匿迹】 xiāoshēng-nìjī keep silent and lie low; disappear from the scene
【销售】 xiāoshòu sell; market
◇ ～价格 selling price/ ～量 sales volume/ ～税 sales tax/ ～总额 total (或 aggregate) sales
【销行】 xiāoxíng sell; be on sale: ～各地 be on sale everywhere/ ～百万册 have sold a million copies
【销赃】 xiāozāng 〈法〉 disposal of stolen goods
【销帐】 xiāozhàng cancel or remove from an account; write off
【销子】 xiāozi pin; peg; dowel

**蛸** xiāo 见"螵蛸" piāoxiāo

**潇** xiāo 〈书〉 (of water) deep and clear
【潇洒】 xiāosǎ natural and unrestrained
【潇潇】 xiāoxiāo ① whistling and pattering: 风雨～ the whistling of wind and pattering of rain ② drizzly

**箫** xiāo *xiao*, a vertical bamboo flute

**霄** xiāo ① clouds: 高入云～ towering into the clouds ② sky; heaven
【霄汉】 xiāohàn 〈书〉 the sky; the firmament
【霄壤】 xiāorǎng heaven and earth: 有～之别 be as far apart (或 as different) as heaven and earth

**魈** xiāo 见"山魈" shānxiāo

**嚣** xiāo clamour; hubbub; din: 叫～ clamour
【嚣张】 xiāozhāng rampant; arrogant; aggressive: ～一时 run rampant (或 wild) for a time/ 气焰～ swollen with arrogance

## xiáo

**淆** xiáo confuse; mix: 混～ mix up; confuse; obscure/ ～惑 confuse; bewilder
【淆乱】 xiáoluàn confuse; befuddle: ～视听 befuddle the minds of the public

## xiǎo

**小** xiǎo ① small; little; petty; minor: ～姑娘 a little girl/ ～国 a small country/ ～问题 a minor question/ ～声说话 speak in a low voice/ 风～些了。The wind has dropped a little./ 鞋～了点儿。These shoes are a bit too tight. ② for a while; for a short time: ～坐 sit for a while/ ～住 stay for a few days ③ young: 一家老～ the whole family, old and young/ ～儿子 the youngest son/ 她比我～。She is younger than I am./ ～鸡 chick; chicken/ ～牛 calf/ ～狗 puppy/ ～猫 kitten ④〈谦〉〔称自己或与自己有关的人或事物〕: ～女 my daughter ⑤〔用于姓、名、排行等之前〕: ～王 Little Wang; Xiao Wang
【小八路】 xiǎo Bālù little 8th Route Army man
【小白菜】 xiǎobáicài a variety of Chinese cabbage; pakchoi
【小百货】 xiǎobǎihuò small articles of daily use
【小班】 xiǎobān the bottom class in a kindergarten
【小半】 xiǎobàn less than half; lesser (或 smaller) part
【小报】 xiǎobào small-sized newspaper; tabloid
【小辈】 xiǎobèi younger member of a family; junior
【小本经营】 xiǎoběn jīngyíng ① business with a small capital ② do business in a small way
【小便】 xiǎobiàn ① urinate; pass (或 make) water; empty one's bladder ② urine ◇ ～处(池) urinal
【小辫儿】 xiǎobiànr short braid; pigtail
【小辫子】 xiǎobiànzi a mistake or shortcoming that may be exploited by others; vulnerable point; handle: 有～给人抓 have vulnerable points that others may capitalize on/ 抓住～不放 get a handle on sb. to make things hard for him
【小标题】 xiǎobiāotí subheading; subhead
【小步】 xiǎobù 〈军〉 half step
【小步舞曲】 xiǎobùwǔqǔ 〈乐〉 minuet
【小不点儿】 xiǎobudiǎnr 〈方〉 ① very small; tiny ② tiny tot
【小菜】 xiǎocài ① pickled vegetables; pickles ② 〈方〉 meat, fish and vegetable dishes; common dishes
【小册子】 xiǎocèzi booklet; pamphlet
【小产】 xiǎochǎn miscarriage; abortion
【小肠】 xiǎocháng 〈生理〉 small intestine
【小潮】 xiǎocháo 〈地〉 neap (tide)
【小车】 xiǎochē ① wheelbarrow; handbarrow; handcart; pushcart ② sedan (car)
【小吃】 xiǎochī ① snack; refreshments ② cold dish; made dish ◇ ～部 snack counter; refreshment room/ ～店 snack bar; lunchroom
【小丑】 xiǎochǒu clown; buffoon: 扮演～角色 play the buffoon
【小丑跳梁】 xiǎochǒu tiàoliáng a contemptible wretch making trouble
【小春】 xiǎochūn 〈方〉 the tenth lunar month; late autumn: ～作物 crops sown in late autumn
【小词】 xiǎocí 〈逻〉 minor term
【小葱】 xiǎocōng shallot; spring onion
【小聪明】 xiǎocōngming cleverness in trivial matters; petty trick: 耍～ play petty tricks
【小刀】 xiǎodāo ① small sword ② pocket knife
【小道理】 xiǎodàoli minor principle
【小道消息】 xiǎodào xiāoxi hearsay; grapevine
【小调】 xiǎodiào ① ditty ② 〈乐〉 minor: A ～协奏曲 concerto in A minor
【小动作】 xiǎodòngzuò petty action; little trick (或 manoeuvre): 搞～ get up to little tricks
【小豆】 xiǎodòu red bean
【小队】 xiǎoduì team; squad
【小恩小惠】 xiǎo'ēn-xiǎohuì petty (或 small) favours; economic sops (或 bait)
【小儿】 xiǎo'ér ① children ② 〈谦〉 my son
【小儿科】 xiǎo'érkē 〈医〉 (department of) paediatrics ◇ ～医生 paediatrician
【小儿麻痹症】 xiǎo'ér mábìzhèng 〈医〉 infantile paralysis; poliomyelitis; polio
【小贩】 xiǎofàn pedlar; vendor; hawker
【小费】 xiǎofèi tip; gratuity
【小斧】 xiǎofǔ hatchet: 单刃～ half hatchet

【小腹】 xiǎofù underbelly; lower abdomen
【小个子】 xiǎogèzi little chap; small fellow
【小工】 xiǎogōng unskilled labourer
【小姑】 xiǎogū husband's younger sister; sister-in-law
【小鼓】 xiǎogǔ 〈乐〉 side drum; snare drum
【小褂】 xiǎoguà (Chinese-style) shirt
【小广播】 xiǎoguǎngbō spreading of hearsay information; grapevine
【小鬼】 xiǎoguǐ ① imp; goblin ② little devil (a term of endearment in addressing a child)
【小孩儿】 xiǎoháir 〈口〉 child 又作"小孩子"
【小寒】 Xiǎohán Slight Cold (23rd solar term)
【小号】 xiǎohào 〈乐〉 trumpet
【小黑麦】 xiǎohēimài triticale: 异源八倍体～ allooctoploid triticale
【小户】 xiǎohù ① small family ② family of limited means and without powerful connections
【小黄鱼】 xiǎohuángyú little yellow croaker
【小伙子】 xiǎohuǒzi 〈口〉 lad; young fellow (或 chap); youngster
【小集团】 xiǎojítuán clique; faction
【小蓟】 xiǎojì 〈中药〉 field thistle (*Cephalanoplos segetum*)
【小建】 xiǎojiàn a lunar month of 29 days 又作"小尽"
【小将】 xiǎojiàng ① young general ② young militant; young pathbreaker
【小脚】 xiǎojiǎo bound feet
【小轿车】 xiǎojiàochē sedan (car); limousine
【小节】 xiǎojié ① small matter; trifle: 生活～ matters concerning personal life/ 不拘～ not bother about small matters; not be punctilious ② 〈乐〉 bar; measure ◇ ～线〈乐〉 bar line; bar
【小结】 xiǎojié ① brief (或 preliminary) summary; brief sum-up; interim summary ② summarize briefly: ～一下前阶段的工作 summarize briefly the work done in the previous stage
【小解】 xiǎojiě urinate; pass (或 make) water
【小姐】 xiǎojie ① Miss ② young lady
【小襟】 xiǎojīn the smaller or inner piece on the right side of a Chinese garment which buttons on the right
【小舅子】 xiǎojiùzi 〈口〉 wife's younger brother; brother-in-law
【小楷】 xiǎokǎi ① regular script in small characters, as used in Chinese calligraphy exercises ② 〈印〉 lowercase (letter)
【小看】 xiǎokàn 〈口〉 look down upon; belittle
【小康】 xiǎokāng comparatively well-off; comfortably off: ～之家 a comfortable family
【小考】 xiǎokǎo mid-term examination; quiz
【小口径】 xiǎokǒujìng small-bore ◇ ～步枪 small-bore rifle
【小老婆】 xiǎolǎopo concubine
【小两口】 xiǎoliǎngkǒu 〈口〉 young couple
【小萝卜】 xiǎoluóbo radish
【小麦】 xiǎomài wheat
◇ ～赤霉病 wheat scab/ ～吸浆虫 wheat midge/ ～线虫病 nematode disease of wheat/ ～腥黑穗病 bunt of wheat
【小卖部】 xiǎomàibù ① a small shop attached to a school, factory, theatre, etc. (selling cigarettes, confectionery, etc.) ② buffet; snack counter
【小满】 Xiǎomǎn Grain Full (8th solar term)
【小猫熊】 xiǎomāoxióng lesser panda
【小毛】 xiǎomáo short-haired pelt
【小米】 xiǎomǐ millet: ～粥 millet gruel
【小名】 xiǎomíng pet name for a child; childhood name
【小拇指】 xiǎomuzhǐ 〈口〉 little finger
【小脑】 xiǎonǎo 〈生理〉 cerebellum
【小年】 xiǎonián ① a lunar year in which the last month has 29 days ② 〈农〉 off year
【小农】 xiǎonóng small farmer ◇ ～经济 small-scale peasant economy; small-scale farming by individual owners
【小跑】 xiǎopǎo 〈口〉 trot; jog
【小朋友】 xiǎopéngyǒu ① children ② (form of address by an adult to a child) little boy or girl; child
【小便宜】 xiǎopiányi small gain; petty advantage: 贪～ go after petty advantages
【小品】 xiǎopǐn a short, simple literary or artistic creation; essay; sketch: 历史～ short historical essay/ 广播～ short piece for broadcasting ◇ ～文 familiar essay; essay
【小评论】 xiǎopínglùn (short) comment
【小气候】 xiǎoqìhòu 〈气〉 microclimate
【小气】 xiǎoqi ① stingy; niggardly; mean ② 〈方〉 narrow-minded; petty
【小前提】 xiǎoqiántí 〈逻〉 minor premise
【小巧玲珑】 xiǎoqiǎo línglóng small and exquisite
【小球藻】 xiǎoqiúzǎo 〈植〉 chlorella
【小曲儿】 xiǎoqǔr ditty; popular tune
【小圈子】 xiǎoquānzi small circle (或 set) of people; small coterie: 搞～ form a small coterie ◇ ～主义 "small circle" mentality
【小犬座】 xiǎoquǎnzuò 〈天〉 Canis Minor
【小人】 xiǎorén ① 〈旧〉 a person of low position ② a base (或 mean) person; villain; vile character: ～得志 villains holding sway
【小人儿书】 xiǎorénrshū 〈口〉 picture-story book
【小人物】 xiǎorénwù an unimportant person; a nobody; cipher; nonentity
【小日子】 xiǎorìzi easy life of a small family
【小商品】 xiǎoshāngpǐn small commodities ◇ ～经济 small commodity economy/ ～生产者 small commodity producer
【小舌】 xiǎoshé 〈生理〉 uvula
【小生产】 xiǎoshēngchǎn small (或 small-scale) production ◇ ～者 small producer
【小乘】 xiǎoshèng 〈佛教〉 Hinayana; Little Vehicle
【小狮座】 xiǎoshīzuò 〈天〉 Leo Minor
【小时】 xiǎoshí hour
【小时候】 xiǎoshíhou 〈口〉 in one's childhood; when one was young: 这是他～的照片。These are his childhood photos.
【小市民】 xiǎoshìmín urban petty bourgeois
【小事】 xiǎoshì trifle; petty thing; minor matter: 大事做不来,～又不做 disdain minor assignments while being unequal to major ones
【小试锋芒】 xiǎo shì fēngmáng display only a small part of one's talent
【小手工业者】 xiǎoshǒugōngyèzhě small handicraftsman
【小手小脚】 xiǎoshǒu-xiǎojiǎo ① stingy; mean ② lacking boldness; timid; niggling
【小叔子】 xiǎoshūzi 〈口〉 husband's younger brother; brother-in-law
【小暑】 Xiǎoshǔ Slight Heat (11th solar term)
【小数】 xiǎoshù 〈数〉 decimal ◇ ～点 decimal point
【小水】 xiǎoshuǐ 〈中医〉 urine
【小说】 xiǎoshuō novel; fiction: 长篇～ novel/ 中篇～ medium-length novel; novelette/ 短篇～ short story ◇ ～家 novelist; writer of fiction
【小苏打】 xiǎosūdá 〈化〉 sodium bicarbonate
【小算盘】 xiǎosuànpan selfish calculations: ～打得精 be very calculating
【小提琴】 xiǎotíqín violin
【小提琴手】 xiǎotíqínshǒu violinist: 首席～ concertmaster

【小题大作】 xiǎo tí dà zuò make a fuss over a trifling matter; make a mountain out of a molehill
【小天地】 xiǎotiāndì one's own little world
【小艇】 xiǎotǐng small boat; skiff
【小偷】 xiǎotōu petty (或 sneak) thief; pilferer: ～小摸 pilfering
【小土地出租者】 xiǎo tǔdì chūzūzhě lessor of small plots
【小团体主义】 xiǎotuántǐzhǔyì cliquism; small-group mentality
【小腿】 xiǎotuǐ shank
【小巫见大巫】 xiǎowū jiàn dàwū like a small sorcerer in the presence of a great one — feel dwarfed; pale into insignificance by comparison
【小五金】 xiǎowǔjīn metal fittings (e.g. nails, wires, hinges, bolts, locks, etc.); hardware
【小先生】 xiǎoxiānsheng little teacher (said of a student who sometimes plays the role of an assistant)
【小写】 xiǎoxiě ① the ordinary form of a Chinese numeral (e.g. 一，二，三，as against 壹，贰，叁) ② small letter
【小心】 xiǎoxīn take care; be careful; be cautious: ～火烛！Guard against fire!/ ～轻放！Handle with care!/ 过马路要～。Be careful when crossing the street./ ～油漆！Mind the wet paint!
【小心眼儿】 xiǎoxīnyǎnr narrow-minded; petty
【小心翼翼】 xiǎoxīn yìyì with great care; cautiously
【小行星】 xiǎoxíngxīng 〈天〉 minor planet
【小型】 xiǎoxíng small-sized; small-scale; miniature: ～企业 small enterprise/ ～运动会 a small-scale athletic meet/ ～拖拉机 baby (或 small) tractor/ ～照相机 miniature camera
【小熊猫】 xiǎoxióngmāo lesser panda
【小熊座】 xiǎoxióngzuò 〈天〉 Ursa Minor
【小学】 xiǎoxué primary (或 elementary) school
【小学生】 xiǎoxuéshēng (primary school) pupil; schoolchild; schoolboy or schoolgirl: 甘当群众的～ willing to be a pupil of the masses
【小雪】 Xiǎoxuě Slight Snow (20th solar term)
【小循环】 xiǎoxúnhuán 〈生理〉 pulmonary circulation
【小阳春】 xiǎoyángchūn balmy weather in the tenth lunar month: 十月～ fine warm weather in the tenth lunar month
【小样】 xiǎoyàng 〈印〉 galley proof
【小业主】 xiǎoyèzhǔ small (或 petty) proprietor
【小夜曲】 xiǎoyèqǔ 〈乐〉 serenade
【小衣】 xiǎoyī 〈方〉 underpants; drawers
【小姨子】 xiǎoyízi 〈口〉 wife's younger sister; sister-in-law
【小意思】 xiǎoyìsi small token of kindly feelings; mere trifle: 这是我的一点儿～，送给你做个纪念。This is just a little keepsake for you.
【小音阶】 xiǎoyīnjiē 〈乐〉 minor scale
【小引】 xiǎoyǐn introductory note; foreword
【小雨】 xiǎoyǔ light rain
【小月】 xiǎoyuè ① a solar month of 30 days ② a lunar month of 29 days
【小月】 xiǎoyue miscarriage; abortion
【小灶】 xiǎozào special mess
【小帐】 xiǎozhàng tip; gratuity
【小照】 xiǎozhào small-sized photograph
【小指】 xiǎozhǐ little finger or toe
【小传】 xiǎozhuàn brief biography; biographical sketch; profile
【小篆】 xiǎozhuàn an ancient style of calligraphy, adopted in the Qin Dynasty (221-207 B.C.) for the purpose of standardizing the script
【小资产阶级】 xiǎozīchǎnjiējí petty bourgeoisie
【小字】 xiǎozì small character ◇ ～报 small-character poster
【小子】 xiǎozi 〈口〉 ① boy: 他有两个孩子，一个闺女，一个～。He has two children, one girl and one boy. ②〔含轻蔑意〕 bloke; fellow; chap
【小组】 xiǎozǔ group: 党～ group under a Party branch; Party group/ ～讨论 group discussion ◇ ～委员会 subcommittee

**晓** xiǎo ① dawn; daybreak: 拂～ foredawn/ ～行夜宿 (of a person on a journey) start at dawn and stop at dusk ② know: 谁个不知，哪个不～？There's not a person who doesn't know. ③ let sb. know; tell: ～以利害 warn sb. of the consequences
【晓得】 xiǎode know: 天～！God knows!
【晓示】 xiǎoshì tell explicitly; notify
【晓谕】 xiǎoyù 〈书〉 give explicit instructions (或 directions)

**筱** xiǎo ①〈书〉 thin bamboo ② a substitute for 小 in a person's name

## xiào

**孝** xiào ① filial piety ② mourning: 带～ in mourning
【孝服】 xiàofú mourning (dress)
【孝敬】 xiàojìng give presents (to one's elders or superiors)
【孝顺】 xiàoshùn show filial obedience
【孝悌】 xiàotì filial piety and fraternal duty
【孝子】 xiàozǐ ① dutiful son ② son in mourning
【孝子贤孙】 xiàozǐ-xiánsūn worthy progeny; true son: 地主阶级的～ worthy progeny of the landlord class

**肖** xiào resemble; be like: 维妙维～ absolutely lifelike
另见 Xiāo
【肖像】 xiàoxiàng portrait; portraiture ◇ ～画 portrait-painting

**效** xiào ① effect: 见～ produce an effect; prove effective ② imitate; follow the example of: 上行下～。Those in subordinate positions will follow the example set by their superiors. ③ devote (one's energy or life) to; render (a service): ～死 ready to give one's life for a cause
【效法】 xiàofǎ follow the example of; model oneself on; learn from: 他治学严谨，值得～。His meticulous scholarship is worthy of emulation.
【效果】 xiàoguǒ ① effect; result: ～不大 not be very effective; produce little effect/ 试验治虫药的～ test the effectiveness of the insecticide/ 取得良好的～ achieve good results ②〈剧〉 sound effects
【效劳】 xiàoláo work in the service of; work for: 乐于～ be glad to offer one's services
【效力】 xiàolì ① render a service to; serve: 为国～ serve one's country ② effect: 这药很有～。The medicine is efficacious./ 两种文本具有同等～。Both texts (in two different languages) are equally authentic. ◇ ～射〈军〉 fire for effect
【效率】 xiàolǜ efficiency: ～高 efficient/ ～低 inefficient/ 这项革新使工作～提高五倍。The innovation raised efficiency fivefold.
【效命】 xiàomìng go all out to serve sb. regardless of the consequences: ～疆场 ready to lay down one's life on the battlefield
【效能】 xiàonéng efficacy; usefulness: 充分发挥水、肥的～ make the best possible use of irrigation and fertilizer
【效颦】 xiàopín 见"东施效颦" Dōngshī xiào pín

【效验】 xiàoyàn intended effect; desired result: 没有～ prove ineffective; fall flat/ 这种方法具有明显的～。This method produces tangible results.
【效益】 xiàoyì beneficial result; benefit: 灌溉～ irrigation benefit
【效应】 xiàoyìng 〈物〉effect: 陀螺～ gyroscopic effect/ 微观～ microeffect ◇ ～器〈生理〉effector
【效用】 xiàoyòng effectiveness; usefulness: 充分发挥水库的～ make full use of the reservoir
【效尤】 xiàoyóu knowingly follow the example of a wrongdoer: 以儆～ to warn others against following a bad example
【效忠】 xiàozhōng pledge loyalty to; devote oneself heart and soul to: ～于社会主义祖国 pledge one's loyalty to one's socialist motherland; devote oneself heart and soul to one's socialist motherland ◇ ～信 letter pledging allegiance; letter of fealty

**校** xiào ① school: 夜～ night school/ ～办工厂 school-run (或 campus) workshop ② field officer
另见 jiào
【校车】 xiàochē school bus
【校风】 xiàofēng school spirit: 学习延安抗大的优良～ learn from the spirit of the Chinese People's Anti-Japanese Military and Political College in Yan'an
【校官】 xiàoguān field officer; field grade officer
【校规】 xiàoguī school regulations
【校徽】 xiàohuī school badge
【校刊】 xiàokān school magazine; college journal
【校历】 xiàolì school calendar
【校庆】 xiàoqìng anniversary of the founding of a school or college
【校舍】 xiàoshè schoolhouse; school building
【校外】 xiàowài outside school; after school ◇ ～辅导员 after-school activities counsellor/ ～活动站 after-school activities club
【校务】 xiàowù administrative affairs of a school or college
【校医】 xiàoyī school doctor
【校友】 xiàoyǒu alumnus or alumna
【校园】 xiàoyuán campus; school yard
【校长】 xiàozhǎng ①（中小学）headmaster; principal ②（大专院校）president; chancellor
【校址】 xiàozhǐ the location of a school or college

**笑** xiào ① smile; laugh: 微～ smile/ 真～死人 be terribly funny/ 小伙子被批准入伍，～得合不上嘴。The young man grinned from ear to ear when his application to join the army was approved. ② ridicule; laugh at: 叫人～掉大牙 ridiculous enough to make people laugh their heads off/ 他刚学，别～他。He's just started learning. Don't laugh at him.
【笑柄】 xiàobǐng laughingstock; butt; joke: 这句话已成为～。That remark has become a standing joke.
【笑哈哈】 xiàohāhā laughingly; with a laugh
【笑话】 xiàohua ① joke; jest: 说～ crack a joke/ 闹～ make a fool of oneself; make a funny mistake ② laugh at; ridicule: 他们一直等着看我们的～，可到头来让人～的是他们自己。They had been waiting to have a good laugh at us, but in the end, the joke was on them.
【笑剧】 xiàojù farce
【笑里藏刀】 xiàolǐ cáng dāo hide a dagger in a smile — with murderous intent behind one's smiles
【笑脸】 xiàoliǎn smiling face: ～相迎 greet sb. with a smile/ 陪～ meet rudeness with a flattering smile
【笑料】 xiàoliào laughingstock; joke
【笑骂】 xiàomà deride and taunt
【笑眯眯】 xiàomīmī smilingly; with a smile on one's face: 他老是～的。He's always smiling.
【笑面虎】 xiàomiànhǔ smiling tiger — an outwardly kind but inwardly cruel person
【笑纳】 xiàonà 〈套〉kindly accept (this small gift of mine)
【笑气】 xiàoqì 〈化〉laughing gas; nitrous oxide
【笑容】 xiàoróng smiling expression; smile: 慈祥的～ a kindly smile/ ～可掬 be radiant with smiles/ ～满面 be all smiles; have a broad smile on one's face/ 她脸上露出一丝～。A faint smile crept over her face.
【笑谈】 xiàotán laughingstock; object of ridicule: 传为～ become a standing joke
【笑窝】 xiàowō dimple
【笑嘻嘻】 xiàoxīxī grinning; smiling broadly
【笑颜】 xiàoyán smiling face
【笑靥】 xiàoyè 〈书〉① dimple ② smiling face
【笑逐颜开】 xiào zhú yán kāi beam with smiles; be wreathed in smiles

**啸** xiào ① whistle ② howl; roar: 虎～ the roar of a tiger
【啸聚】 xiàojù 〈书〉band together; gang up: ～山林 go to the greenwood

## xiē

**些** xiē 〔表示不定的数量〕: 这～ these/ 那么～ that much; that many/ 前～日子 a few days ago; sometime ago/ 买～东西 do some shopping/ 好～人 a lot of people/ 稍大～ a little bigger/ 好～了吗? Are you better?
【些微】 xiēwēi slightly; a little; a bit: ～有点儿疼 hurt slightly; be a bit painful/ 这颜色～深了一点。The colour is a trifle too dark.

**揳** xiē 〈方〉drive (a wedge, nail, etc.): 在墙上～个钉子 drive (或 knock) a nail into the wall

**楔** xiē
【楔规】 xiēguī 〈机〉wedge gauge
【楔形文字】 xiēxíng wénzì cuneiform (characters); sphenogram
【楔子】 xiēzi ① wedge ② peg ③ prologue or interlude in Yuan Dynasty drama ④ prologue in some modern novels

**歇** xiē ① have a rest: ～一会儿 have a short rest/ ～口气儿 stop for a breather; take (或 have) a breather ② stop (work, etc.); knock off: ～伏 stop work during the dog days/ ～会儿，喝杯茶。Let's knock off for a cup of tea. ③〈方〉go to bed: 你～了吗? Are you in bed?
【歇班】 xiēbān be off duty; have time off: 今天小王～。Xiao Wang is off duty today.
【歇顶】 xiēdǐng get a bit thin on top; be balding
【歇工】 xiēgōng stop work; knock off
【歇后语】 xiēhòuyǔ a two-part allegorical saying, of which the first part, always stated, is descriptive, while the second part, sometimes unstated, carries the message, e.g. 泥菩萨过河——自身难保 a clay idol fording a river — hardly able to save oneself (let alone assist anyone else)
【歇肩】 xiējiān take the load off one's shoulder for a rest
【歇脚】 xiējiǎo stop on the way for a rest: 咱们到那边荫凉地歇歇脚吧。Let's stop for a rest in the shade over there.
【歇凉】 xiēliáng 〈方〉enjoy the cool in some shade; relax

in a cool place
【歇晌】 xiēshǎng take a midday nap or rest
【歇手】 xiēshǒu stop doing sth.
【歇斯底里】 xiēsīdǐlǐ hysteria: ～大发作 go into hysterics; become hysterical
【歇宿】 xiēsù put up (somewhere) for the night; make an overnight stop
【歇息】 xiēxi ① have a rest ② go to bed; put up for the night
【歇业】 xiēyè close a business; go out of business

**蝎** xiē scorpion
【蝎虎】 xiēhǔ gecko; house lizard
【蝎子】 xiēzi scorpion

## xié

**协** xié ① joint; common: ～办 do sth. jointly ② assist
【协定】 xiédìng ① agreement; accord: 贸易～ trade agreement ② reach an agreement on sth.
【协会】 xiéhuì association; society: 中国人民对外友好～ the Chinese People's Association for Friendship with Foreign Countries
【协理】 xiélǐ ① assist in the management (of an enterprise, etc.) ②〔旧时银行、企业用语〕 assistant manager ◇ ～员〈军〉 political assistant (of the PLA)
【协力】 xiélì unite efforts; join in a common effort: ～进攻 launch a joint assault
【协商】 xiéshāng consult; talk things over: 民主～ democratic consultation/ ～一致的原则 the principle of reaching unanimity through consultation/ 需要和有关部门～。It's necessary to consult with the departments concerned. ◇ ～会议 consultative conference
【协调】 xiétiáo coordinate; concert; harmonize; bring into line: 使我们的行动～起来 coordinate our activities/ 国民经济各部门的发展必须互相～。Development of the different branches of the national economy should be well coordinated./ 他的意见好象和大家不～。His opinions don't seem to be in tune with those of the others./ 体操运动员的动作～优美。The gymnast's movements are harmonious and graceful. ◇ ～委员会 coordination committee
【协同】 xiétóng work in coordination with; cooperate with: ～作战 fight in coordination/ 民兵～解放军守卫海岛。The militia cooperate with the PLA men in guarding the island./ 此事请～办理。Your cooperation is requested in handling this matter. ◇ ～动作〈军〉 coordinated action
【协议】 xiéyì ① agree on: 一致～的文件 a document unanimously agreed upon ② agreement: 达成～ reach an agreement/ 口头～ verbal agreement
【协约国】 Xiéyuēguó the *Entente* countries (during World War I)
【协助】 xiézhù assist; help; give assistance; provide help: 副总理～总理工作。The Vice-Premiers assist the Premier in his work.
【协奏曲】 xiézòuqǔ 〈乐〉 concerto: 钢琴(小提琴)～ piano (violin) concerto
【协作】 xiézuò cooperation; coordination; combined (或 joint) efforts: 发扬共产主义的～精神 bring into play the communist spirit of cooperation/ 实行几个行业间的大～ organize extensive cooperation (或 coordination) between different trades/ 经济～区 economically coordinated regions/ 双方～得很好。The two sides cooperated harmoniously./ 这是几个厂～的产物。This is a product of the combined efforts of several factories.

**邪** xié ① evil; heretical; irregular: 不信～ not believe in heresy; refuse to be taken in by fallacies/ 改～归正 give up one's evil ways and return to the right path; turn over a new leaf/ 咱们按原则办事,决不搞～的歪的。We'll stick to principles and never engage in irregularities. ② 〈中医〉 unhealthy environmental influences that cause disease
【邪财】 xiécái 〈方〉 ill-gotten gains
【邪道】 xiédào evil ways; depraved life; vice: 走～ lead a depraved life; abandon oneself to evil ways
【邪恶】 xié'è evil; wicked; vicious: ～的念头 wicked thoughts
【邪乎】 xiéhu 〈口〉 ① extraordinary: 天旱得～。This drought is abnormal./ 他说得～。His story sounds incredible. ② severe: 疼得～。The pain is terrible.
【邪路】 xiélù evil ways; vice: 他受资产阶级思想的腐蚀走上了～。Corrupted by bourgeois ideology, he took to evil ways./ 个别人企图把运动引向～。Certain individuals tried to lead the movement astray.
【邪门儿】 xiéménr 〈方〉 strange; odd; abnormal: 这天气真～,这时候还下雪。What strange weather — snowing at this time of the year!/ 真～,钥匙刚才还在这儿呢! That's strange! The key was here just a minute ago.
【邪门歪道】 xiémén-wāidào crooked ways (或 means); dishonest practices (或 methods)
【邪魔】 xiémó evil spirit; demon
【邪念】 xiéniàn evil thought; wicked idea: 他起了～。A wicked idea came into his head.
【邪气】 xiéqì perverse trend; evil influence: 打击资本主义的歪风～ hit at the evil influence of capitalism/ 使正气上升,～下降 encourage healthy trends and check unhealthy ones
【邪说】 xiéshuō heresy; heretical ideas; fallacy
【邪心】 xiéxīn 见"邪念"
【邪行】 xiéxíng evil deeds

**胁** xié ① the upper part of the side of the human body ② coerce; force: 裹～ force to take part; coerce/ 威～ threaten
【胁变】 xiébiàn 〈物〉 strain: 局部～ local strain/ 过度～ overstrain ◇ ～硬化 strain hardening/ ～张量 strain tensor
【胁持】 xiéchí 见"挟持" xiéchí
【胁从】 xiécóng be an accomplice under duress ◇ ～分子 reluctant (或 unwilling) follower; accomplice under duress
【胁肩谄笑】 xiéjiān chǎnxiào cringe and smile obsequiously
【胁迫】 xiépò coerce; force
【胁强】 xiéqiáng 〈物〉 stress: 外施～ applied stress/ 张～ tensile stress

**挟** xié ① hold sth. under the arm: ～泰山以超北海 carry Taishan Mountain under one's arm and leap over the north sea — an impossibility ② coerce; force sb. to submit to one's will: 要～ coerce/ ～天子以令诸侯 have the emperor in one's power and order the dukes about in his name ③ harbour (resentment, etc.)
【挟持】 xiéchí ① seize sb. on both sides by the arms ② hold sb. under duress
【挟嫌】 xiéxián 〈书〉 harbour resentment; bear a grudge: ～报复 bear resentment against sb. and retaliate
【挟制】 xiézhì take advantage of sb.'s weakness to enforce obedience; force sb. to do one's bidding

**谐** xié ① in harmony; in accord: 和～ harmonious ② 〈书〉 come to an agreement; settle: 事～之后,即可动身。We shall set out immediately once the matter is settled. ③ humorous: 诙～ humorous; jocular
【谐和】 xiéhé harmonious; concordant
【谐声】 xiéshēng 见"形声" xíngshēng
【谐谑】 xiéxuè banter: 语带～ speak somewhat jokingly
【谐谑曲】 xiéxuèqǔ 〈乐〉 *scherzo*
【谐音】 xiéyīn ① homophonic; homonymic ② 〈乐〉 partials
【谐振】 xiézhèn 〈物〉 resonance: 空腔～ cavity resonance ◇ ～腔 resonant cavity

**偕** xié together with; in the company of: ～行 travel together
【偕老】 xiélǎo husband and wife grow old together
【偕同】 xiétóng in the company of; accompanied by; along with

**斜** xié oblique; slanting; inclined; tilted: ～圆锥〈数〉 oblique cone/ 这根线～了。The line is slanting./ 柱子有点～。The pillar is a little tilted./ ～躺在沙发上 recline on a sofa/ 把桌子～过来 turn the table sideways/ ～着眼看人 cast sidelong glances at sb.; look sideways at sb.
【斜边】 xiébiān ①〈数〉 hypotenuse ②〈机〉 bevel edge
【斜长石】 xiéchángshí 〈矿〉 plagioclase
【斜高】 xiégāo 〈数〉 slant height
【斜角】 xiéjiǎo ①〈数〉 oblique angle ②〈机〉 bevel angle ◇ ～规〈机〉 bevel square
【斜井】 xiéjǐng ①〈矿〉 inclined shaft; slope ②〈石油〉 inclined well; slant hole
【斜路】 xiélù wrong path: 正路不走走～ turn from the right road and take the wrong one — give up an honest life for a dishonest one/ 忘记我党的基本路线,就会走到～上去。We shall go astray if we forget the basic line of our Party.
【斜率】 xiélǜ 〈数〉 slope
【斜面】 xiémiàn ①〈数〉 inclined plane ②〈机〉 oblique plane; bevel (face)
【斜坡】 xiépō slope
【斜射】 xiéshè 〈军〉 oblique fire
【斜视】 xiéshì ①〈医〉 strabismus ② look sideways; cast a sidelong glance: 目不～ not look sideways; refuse to be distracted
【斜视图】 xiéshìtú 〈机〉 oblique drawing
【斜体字】 xiétǐzì 〈印〉 italics
【斜纹】 xiéwén 〈纺〉 twill (weave) ◇ ～布 twill; drill
【斜线】 xiéxiàn oblique line ◇ ～号 slant (/)
【斜眼】 xiéyǎn ①〈医〉 strabismus ② wall-eye or cross-eye ③ a wall-eyed or cross-eyed person
【斜阳】 xiéyáng setting sun
【斜轴线】 xiézhóuxiàn 〈数〉 oblique axis

**携** xié ① carry; take along: ～眷 bring one's wife and children along/ ～款潜逃 abscond with funds/ ～械投诚 come over from the enemy's side bringing weapons ② take (或 hold) sb. by the hand: 让我们～起手来,共同前进。Let us join hands and advance together.
【携带】 xiédài carry; take along: ～方便 be easy to carry about/ 随身～的物品 things carried on one's person/ 旅客每人可～行李二十公斤。Each passenger can take up to twenty kilograms of luggage.
【携手】 xiéshǒu hand in hand: ～并进 go forward hand in hand

**鞋** xié shoes
【鞋拔子】 xiébázi shoehorn
【鞋帮】 xiébāng upper (of a shoe)
【鞋带】 xiédài shoelace; shoestring
【鞋底】 xiédǐ sole (of a shoe)
【鞋垫】 xiédiàn shoe-pad; insole
【鞋粉】 xiéfěn shoe powder
【鞋跟】 xiégēn heel (of a shoe)
【鞋匠】 xiéjiang shoemaker; cobbler
【鞋扣】 xiékòu shoe buckle
【鞋里】 xiélǐ shoe lining
【鞋面】 xiémiàn instep; vamp
【鞋刷】 xiéshuā shoe brush
【鞋楦】 xiéxuàn last for shaping a shoe; shoe tree
【鞋样】 xiéyàng shoe pattern; outline of sole
【鞋油】 xiéyóu shoe polish (或 cream)

**撷** xié 〈书〉 pick; pluck

## xiě

**写** xiě ① write: ～得一手好字 have good handwriting; write a good hand/ 这支笔不好～。This pen doesn't write well./ 标语牌上～着"抓革命,促生产"。The placard reads "Grasp revolution and promote production". ② compose; write: ～诗 compose a poem/ ～日记 make an entry in one's diary; keep a diary/ ～科学论文 write scientific papers; write theses on scientific subjects ③ describe; depict: ～景 describe the scenery/ ～一个英雄的成长过程 depict the growth of a hero ④ paint; draw: ～生 paint from life
另见 xiè
【写稿】 xiěgǎo write for (或 contribute to) a magazine, etc.: 你给我们的黑板报写篇稿好吗? Will you write an article for our blackboard newspaper?/ 他经常为儿童刊物～。He is a regular contributor to children's magazines.
【写生】 xiěshēng 〈美术〉 paint from life; draw, paint or sketch from nature: 人物～ portrait from life ◇ ～画 sketch
【写实】 xiěshí write or paint realistically
【写意】 xiěyì 〈美术〉 freehand brushwork in traditional Chinese painting (characterized by vivid expression and bold outline)
另见 xièyì
【写照】 xiězhào portrayal; portraiture: 百花盛开春满园是今日文坛的～。The world of letters can be portrayed today as a garden with a hundred flowers in bloom.
【写真】 xiězhēn ① portray a person; draw a portrait ② portrait ③ describe sth. as it is
【写字台】 xiězìtái writing desk; desk
【写作】 xiězuò writing: 从事～ take up writing as one's career ◇ ～班子 writing group/ ～技巧 writing technique

**血** xiě 〈口〉 blood: ～的教训 a lesson paid for (或 written) in blood/ 流了一点～,不要紧。There was just a little bleeding. Nothing serious.
另见 xuè
【血晕】 xiěyùn bruise

## xiè

**写** xiè
另见 xiě
【写意】 xièyì 〈方〉 comfortable; enjoyable
另见 xiěyì

**泻** xiè ① flow swiftly; rush down; pour out: 大江奔腾,一～千里。The (Changjiang) River rolls and roars on and on for a thousand *li*. ② have loose bowels; have diarrhoea: 上吐下～ suffer from vomiting and diarrhoea
【泻肚】 xièdù have loose bowels; have diarrhoea
【泻湖】 xièhú 〈地〉 lagoon
【泻盐】 xièyán Epsom salts; salts
【泻药】 xièyào laxative; cathartic; purgative

**泄** xiè ① let out; discharge; release: 开闸～洪 open a sluice to release floodwater/ 象个～了气的皮球 like a deflated rubber ball — dejected ② let out (a secret); leak (news, secrets, etc.) ③ give vent to; vent: ～私愤 give vent to personal spite
【泄底】 xièdǐ reveal or expose what is at the bottom of sth.
【泄洪】 xièhóng 〈水〉 flood discharge ◇ ～道 flood-relief channel; floodway/ ～隧洞 flood-discharge tunnel
【泄劲】 xièjìn lose heart; feel discouraged; be disheartened; slacken one's efforts: 他近来有点～。He has been a bit disheartened lately./ 继续努力,不要～! Keep at it, don't relax!
【泄漏】 xièlòu leak; let out; divulge; give away: ～秘密 let out (或 divulge. give away) a secret/ 消息已～出去了。The news has leaked out.
【泄露】 xièlù let out; reveal: 敌人无意中～了行动计划。The enemy unwittingly revealed their plan of action.
【泄密】 xièmì divulge a secret; betray confidential matters: ～事件 (case of) leakage of a state or Party secret
【泄气】 xièqì ① lose heart; feel discouraged; be disheartened: 困难面前不～ keep one's end up in the face of difficulties/ 我不该说那些～话。I shouldn't have made those discouraging (或 pessimistic) remarks. ② disappointing; frustrating; pathetic: 这么矮他都跳不过去,真～! He can't even jump that high. How pathetic!
【泄水】 xièshuǐ 〈水〉 sluicing
◇ ～道 sluiceway/ ～工程 outlet work/ ～孔 outlet/ ～闸 sluice gate; sluice
【泄泻】 xièxiè 〈中医〉 have loose bowels; have diarrhoea
【泄殖腔】 xièzhíqiāng 〈动〉 cloacal chamber; cloaca

**卸** xiè ① unload; discharge; lay down: ～车 unload a vehicle/ ～担子 lay down a burden/ ～牲口 unhitch a draught animal ② remove; strip: ～零件 remove parts from a machine; strip a machine/ 把门～下来 lift a door off its hinges ③ get rid of; shirk: ～责 shirk the responsibility
【卸车】 xièchē unload (goods, etc.) from a vehicle; unload
【卸货】 xièhuò unload (或 discharge) cargo; unload: 从船上～ unload a ship; land goods from a ship ◇ ～港〈交〉 port of discharge; unloading port
【卸磨杀驴】 xiè mò shā lú kill the donkey the moment it leaves the millstone — get rid of sb. as soon as he has done his job
【卸任】 xièrèn be relieved of one's office
【卸装】 xièzhuāng remove stage makeup and costume

**屑** xiè ① bits; scraps; crumbs: 纸～ scraps of paper/ 煤～ (coal) slack/ 金属～ metal filings/ 面包～ crumbs (of bread) ② trifling: 琐～ trifling; trivial ③〔多用于〕: 不～ disdain to do sth.

**械** xiè ① tool; instrument: 机～ machine; mechanism ② weapon: 军～ weapons; arms; ordnance ③ 〈书〉 fetters, shackles, etc.

【械斗】 xièdòu fight with weapons between groups of people

**谢** xiè ① thank: ～了又～ thank again and again/ 多～。Thanks a lot. ② 〈书〉 make an apology; excuse oneself: ～过 apologize for having done sth. wrong/ ～病 excuse oneself on grounds of illness ③ decline: 敬～不敏 beg to be excused ④ (of flowers, leaves) wither ⑤ (Xiè) a surname
【谢忱】 xièchén gratitude; thankfulness: 承蒙协助,谨致～。Allow us to express our thanks for your kindly help.
【谢词】 xiècí thank-you speech
【谢绝】 xièjué 〈婉〉 refuse; decline: 婉言～ politely decline; politely refuse/ ～参观。Not open to visitors.
【谢幕】 xièmù answer (或 respond to) a curtain call
【谢世】 xièshì 〈书〉 pass away; die
【谢天谢地】 xiètiān-xièdì thank goodness; thank heaven: ～,你总算回来了! Thank goodness, you're back at last!
【谢帖】 xiètiě a note of thanks; a thank-you note
【谢谢】 xièxie thanks; thank you
【谢意】 xièyì gratitude; thankfulness: 预致～ thank you in anticipation/ 谨致薄礼,聊表～。Please accept this gift and my gratitude.
【谢罪】 xièzuì apologize for an offence; offer an apology

**亵** xiè ① treat with irreverence; be disrespectful ② obscene; indecent
【亵渎】 xièdú blaspheme; profane; pollute

**解** xiè ①〈口〉 understand; see: ～不开这个道理 can't see the point ② (Xiè) a surname
另见 jiě; jiè

**榭** xiè a pavilion or house on a terrace: 水～ waterside pavilion/ 歌台舞～ halls for the performance of songs and dances

**懈** xiè slack; lax: 松～ slacken; relax; let up/ 作不～的努力 make unremitting efforts
【懈怠】 xièdài slack; sluggish: 学习上不可～。Don't slack off in your studies.

**邂** xiè
【邂逅】 xièhòu 〈书〉 meet (a relative, friend, etc.) unexpectedly; run into sb.; meet by chance

**蟹** xiè crab: 寄居～ hermit crab/ 沙～ ghost crab/ 梭子～ swimming crab
【蟹粉】 xièfěn 〈方〉 crab meat
【蟹黄】 xièhuáng the ovary and digestive glands of a crab
【蟹獴】 xièméng 〈动〉 crab-eating mongoose
【蟹青】 xièqīng greenish-grey (colour)

**瀣** xiè 见"沆瀣" hàngxiè

## xīn

**心** xīn ① the heart ② heart; mind; feeling; intention: 爱国～ patriotic feeling; patriotism/ 羞耻之～ sense of shame/ 伤人的～ wound (或 hurt) sb.'s feelings/ ～往一处想,劲往一处使 think and work with one heart and one mind/ 你的～是好的,但是事情办得不好。You meant well but you didn't handle the job well./ 他人在这儿,～不在。He himself is here, but his thoughts are elsewhere. ③ centre; core: 手～ the hollow of the palm/ 核～ core; nucleus/ 白菜～ the heart of a Chinese cabbage

【心爱】 xīn'ài love; treasure: ～的人 one's beloved; loved one/ ～的东西 treasured (或 prized) possession

【心安理得】 xīn'ān-lǐdé feel at ease and justified; have an easy conscience

【心包】 xīnbāo 〈生理〉 pericardium ◇ ～炎 pericarditis

【心病】 xīnbìng ① worry; anxiety: 这事老悬着，一直是他的～。Not having this matter settled has always worried him. ② sore point; secret trouble

【心搏】 xīnbó 〈生理〉 heartbeat

【心不在焉】 xīn bù zài yān absent-minded; inattentive; preoccupied (with sth. else): ～地听着 listen absent-mindedly

【心裁】 xīncái idea; conception; mental plan: 独出～ show originality; be original

【心肠】 xīncháng ① heart; intention: ～软 have a soft heart; be softhearted/ 好～ kindhearted/ 他真是个热～！He's a really warmhearted person! ② state of mind; mood

【心潮】 xīncháo a tidal surge of emotion; surging thoughts and emotions: ～澎湃 feel an upsurge of emotion/ ～翻滚 one's mind being in a tumult

【心慈手软】 xīncí-shǒuruǎn softhearted: 对阶级敌人不能～。We should not be softhearted towards class enemies.

【心胆俱裂】 xīn-dǎn jù liè be frightened out of one's wits; be terror-stricken: 吓得敌人～ strike terror into the enemy's hearts

【心得】 xīndé what one has learned from work, study, etc.: 谈谈学习毛主席著作的～ talk about what one has gained from studying Chairman Mao's works

【心地】 xīndì a person's mind, character, moral nature, etc.: ～坦白 candid; open/ ～单纯 simpleminded/ ～善良 good-natured; kindhearted

【心电描记器】 xīndiàn miáojìqì 〈医〉 electrocardiograph

【心电图】 xīndiàntú 〈医〉 electrocardiogram

【心动过速】 xīndòng guòsù 〈医〉 tachycardia: 阵发性～ paroxysmal tachycardia

【心动徐缓】 xīndòng xúhuǎn 〈医〉 bradycardia

【心动周期】 xīndòng zhōuqī 〈生理〉 cardiac cycle

【心耳】 xīn'ěr 〈生理〉 auricle

【心烦】 xīnfán be vexed; be perturbed: ～意乱 be terribly upset

【心房】 xīnfáng 〈生理〉 atrium (of the heart)

【心浮】 xīnfú flighty and impatient; unstable

【心服】 xīnfú be genuinely convinced; acknowledge (one's defeat, mistake, etc.) sincerely: ～口服 be sincerely convinced

【心腹】 xīnfù ① trusted subordinate; henchman; reliable agent ② confidential: 说～话 tell sb. sth. in strict confidence; confide in sb.; exchange confidences/ ～事 a secret in the depth of one's heart

【心腹之患】 xīnfù zhī huàn disease in one's vital organs — serious hidden trouble or danger

【心甘情愿】 xīngān-qíngyuàn be most willing to; be perfectly happy to: 为了革命，就是牺牲生命也～。If need be, I will willingly give my life for the revolution./ ～当人民的勤务员 be a willing servant of the people

【心肝】 xīngān ① conscience: 没～ heartless ② darling; deary

【心广体胖】 xīnguǎng-tǐpán carefree and contented; fit and happy

【心寒】 xīnhán 〈方〉 be bitterly disappointed: 令人～ chill the heart; be bitterly disappointing

【心狠】 xīnhěn cruel; merciless: ～手辣 cruel and evil; wicked and merciless

【心花怒放】 xīnhuā nùfàng burst with joy; be wild with joy; be elated

【心怀】 xīnhuái ① harbour; entertain; cherish: ～叵测 harbour dark designs; have evil intentions/ ～不满 feel discontented; nurse a grievance/ ～鬼胎 entertain dark schemes; have ulterior motives ② intention; purpose ③ state of mind; mood

【心慌】 xīnhuāng ① be flustered; be nervous; get alarmed: ～意乱 be alarmed and nervous ② 〈方〉 (of the heart) palpitate

【心灰意懒】 xīnhuī-yìlǎn be disheartened; be downhearted

【心火】 xīnhuǒ ① 〈中医〉 internal heat, symptoms of which include mental uneasiness, thirst, rapid pulse, etc. ② hidden anger; pent-up fury

【心肌】 xīnjī 〈生理〉 cardiac muscle; myocardium ◇ ～梗塞 myocardial infarction/ ～炎 myocarditis

【心机】 xīnjī thinking; scheming: 枉费～ rack one's brains in vain; make futile efforts/ 费尽～ leave no stone unturned; try all ingenious ways; take great pains; cudgel one's brains

【心迹】 xīnjì the true state of one's mind; true motives or feelings: 表明～ lay bare one's true feelings

【心急】 xīnjí impatient; short-tempered: ～火燎 burning with impatience

【心计】 xīnjì calculation; scheming; planning: 工于～ adept at scheming; very calculating/ 这个年轻人做事很有～。This young chap does things intelligently.

【心悸】 xīnjì 〈医〉 palpitation

【心焦】 xīnjiāo anxious; worried: 真叫人～啊！This is really worrying!/ 我们等得好～！How anxiously we waited!

【心绞痛】 xīnjiǎotòng 〈医〉 angina pectoris

【心惊胆战】 xīnjīng-dǎnzhàn tremble with fear; shake with fright

【心惊肉跳】 xīnjīng-ròutiào palpitate with anxiety and fear; be filled with apprehension

【心境】 xīnjìng state (或 frame) of mind; mental state; mood: ～不好 be in a bad mood/ ～非常愉快 be in a very happy mood

【心静】 xīnjìng calm: ～自然凉。So long as one keeps calm, one doesn't feel the heat too much.

【心坎】 xīnkǎn the bottom of one's heart: 我从～里感谢您。I thank you from the bottom of my heart./ 字字句句都说到我～上。Each word struck a chord in my heart.

【心口】 xīnkǒu the pit of the stomach

【心口如一】 xīn-kǒu rú yī say what one thinks; be frank and unreserved

【心旷神怡】 xīnkuàng-shényí relaxed and happy; carefree and joyous

【心劳日拙】 xīn láo rì zhuō fare worse and worse for all one's scheming

【心理】 xīnlǐ psychology; mentality: 这位保育员很懂得孩子们的～。That kindergarten teacher understands the children's psychology very well./ 不要养成依赖别人的～。Don't get into the habit of depending on others./ 这是一般人的～。This is how ordinary people feel about it./ 他老说有心脏病，其实是～作用。He's always complaining of heart trouble; but it's only his imagination.
◇ ～病态 morbid state of mind/ ～测验学 psychometry/ ～分析 psychoanalysis/ ～疗法 psychotherapy/ ～学 psychology/ ～学家 psychologist/ ～因素 psychological factor/ ～战 psychological warfare

【心力】 xīnlì mental and physical efforts: 费尽～ make strenuous efforts/ ～交瘁 be mentally and physically exhausted ◇ ～衰竭〈医〉 heart failure

【心里】 xīnli in the heart; at heart; in (the) mind: ～发闷

feel constriction in the area of the heart/ ～不痛快 feel bad about sth./ 记在～ keep (或 bear) in mind/ ～有事 have sth. on one's mind/ ～装着亿万人民 have at heart the well-being of hundreds of millions/ 毛主席永远活在我们～。Chairman Mao will live forever in our hearts.

【心里话】 xīnlihuà one's innermost thoughts and feelings: 说出工人的～ give voice to the workers' innermost feelings/ 我看他没有说～。I don't think he has come out with what's on his mind./ 说～,我真不想去。To be honest, I just don't want to go.

【心连心】 xīn lián xīn heart linked to heart: 我国各族人民～。The hearts of the people of all our nationalities are linked to each other./ 华主席和我们～。Chairman Hua's heart and ours beat as one.

【心灵】 xīnlíng ① clever; intelligent; quick-witted: ～手巧 clever and deft ② heart; soul; spirit: ～深处 deep in one's heart/ 在她幼小的～里 in her childish heart

【心领】 xīnlǐng 〈套〉〔表示辞谢〕: 雅意～。I appreciate your kindness but must decline the offer.

【心领神会】 xīnlǐng-shénhuì understand tacitly; readily take a hint: 这个奴才对主子的意图～。The lackey understood tacitly what his master wanted.

【心律】 xīnlǜ 〈医〉 rhythm of the heart ◇ ～不齐 arrhythmia

【心乱如麻】 xīn luàn rú má have one's mind as confused as a tangled skein; be utterly confused and disconcerted; be terribly upset

【心满意足】 xīnmǎn-yìzú be perfectly content (或 satisfied)

【心明眼亮】 xīnmíng-yǎnliàng see and think clearly; be sharp-eyed and clearheaded

【心目】 xīnmù ① mood; frame of mind: 以娱～ to amuse oneself ② memory: 动人情景犹在～。The moving scene remains (或 is still) fresh in our memories. ③ mind; mental view: 在某些人的～中 in some people's eyes/ 在我的～中,他是个好同志。In my view (或 To my mind), he is a good comrade.

【心皮】 xīnpí 〈植〉 carpel

【心平气和】 xīnpíng-qìhé even-tempered and good-humoured; calm: ～地交换意见 exchange views calmly

【心窍】 xīnqiào capacity for clear thinking: 权迷～ be obsessed by a lust for power/ 被资产阶级派性迷住了～ be maddened by bourgeois factionalism/ 他的话打开了我的～,知道该怎么办了。What he said cleared up my thinking and then I knew what to do next.

【心情】 xīnqíng frame (或 state) of mind; mood: ～愉快 be in a cheerful frame (或 state) of mind; be in a good (或 happy) mood; have a light heart/ ～激动 be excited; be thrilled/ ～沉重 with a heavy heart/ ～舒畅 have ease of mind/ ～不一样,感受也不同。People in different frames of mind feel differently about things.

【心曲】 xīnqǔ 〈书〉 ① innermost being; mind: 乱我～ disturb my peace of mind ② sth. weighing on one's mind: 倾诉～ pour out one's secret concern (或 pent-up feelings); lay one's heart bare

【心如刀割】 xīn rú dāo gē feel as if a knife were piercing one's heart: 她听到这不幸的消息～。The sad news stabbed her to the heart.

【心软】 xīnruǎn be softhearted; be tenderhearted

【心神】 xīnshén mind; state of mind: ～不定 have no peace of mind; be distracted

【心声】 xīnshēng heartfelt wishes; aspirations; thinking: 表达人民的～ voice the aspirations of the people/ 言为～。One's words reflect one's thinking. 或 What the heart thinks the tongue says.

【心室】 xīnshì 〈生理〉 ventricle

【心事】 xīnshi sth. weighing on one's mind; a load on one's mind; worry: ～重重 be laden with anxiety; be weighed down with care/ 了结一桩～ take a load off one's mind/ 她好象有什么～似的。She seems to have something on her mind.

【心输出量】 xīnshūchūliàng 〈生理〉 cardiac output

【心术】 xīnshù intention; design: ～不正 harbour evil intentions (或 designs)

【心思】 xīnsi ① thought; idea: 坏～ a wicked idea/ 想～ ponder; contemplate/ 我猜不透他的～。I can't read his mind. 或 I can't figure out what's on his mind. ② thinking: 用～ do a lot of thinking; think hard/ 白费～ rack one's brains in vain; make futile efforts ③ state of mind; mood: 没有～去看戏 not be in the mood to see a play

【心酸】 xīnsuān be grieved; feel sad

【心算】 xīnsuàn mental arithmetic; doing sums in one's head

【心疼】 xīnténg ① love dearly: 这样惯孩子不是～他。Pampering a child like this is not loving him. ② feel sorry; be distressed: 这么浪费,叫人看了～。It makes one's heart ache to see such waste.

【心田】 xīntián ① heart ② intention

【心跳】 xīntiào palpitation

【心头】 xīntóu mind; heart: 记在～ bear (或 keep) in mind/ ～恨 rankling hatred/ 抑制不住～的喜悦 be unable to conceal one's delight

【心土】 xīntǔ 〈农〉 subsoil

【心窝儿】 xīnwōr 〈口〉 the pit of the stomach

【心无二用】 xīn wú èr yòng one cannot keep one's mind on two things at the same time; one should concentrate on one's work

【心细】 xīnxì careful; scrupulous: 胆大～ bold but cautious

【心弦】 xīnxián heartstrings: 动人～ tug at one's heartstrings

【心心相印】 xīn-xīn xiāng yìn have mutual affinity; be kindred spirits

【心胸】 xīnxiōng breadth of mind: ～开阔 broad-minded; unprejudiced/ ～狭窄 narrow-minded; intolerant

【心虚】 xīnxū ① afraid of being found out; with a guilty conscience: 做贼～ have a guilty conscience ② lacking in self-confidence; diffident

【心绪】 xīnxù state of mind: ～不宁 in a disturbed state of mind; in a flutter/ ～烦乱 emotionally upset; in an emotional turmoil

【心血】 xīnxuè painstaking care (或 effort): 费尽～ expend all one's energies/ 多年～的结晶 the fruit of many years' painstaking labour

【心血来潮】 xīnxuè lái cháo be prompted by a sudden impulse; be seized by a whim: ～,忘乎所以 forget oneself in an impulsive moment; be carried away by one's whims and act recklessly

【心眼儿】 xīnyǎnr ① heart; mind: ～小 oversensitive; petty/ 打～里热爱新社会 love the new society with all one's heart/ 一个～为集体 devote oneself heart and soul to the collective; work for the collective wholeheartedly/ 看到孩子们这么幸福，大家从～里感到高兴。It warms the cockles of the heart to see the children so happy. ② intention: 没安好～ have bad intentions; be up to no good/ ～好 good-natured; kindhearted ③ intelligence; cleverness: 他有～,什么事都想得周到。He is alert and thoughtful./ 长点～,别受人家的骗。Smarten up and don't be taken in. ④ unfounded doubts; unnecessary misgivings: ～多 full of unnecessary misgivings; oversensitive

【心意】 xīnyì ① regard; kindly feelings: 这点礼物是我们大

家的一点～。This little gift is a token of our regard. ② intention; purpose: 你们不了解他的～。You don't understand his intention.

【心音】 xīnyīn 〈生理〉 heart sounds; cardiac sounds: 第一(第二)～ the first (second) heart sound

【心硬】 xīnyìng hardhearted; stonyhearted; callous; unfeeling

【心有余而力不足】 xīn yǒuyú ér lì bùzú the spirit is willing, but the flesh is weak; unable to do what one wants very much to do

【心有余悸】 xīn yǒu yújì one's heart still fluttering with fear; have a lingering fear

【心猿意马】 xīnyuán-yìmǎ restless and whimsical; fanciful and fickle; capricious

【心愿】 xīnyuàn cherished desire; aspiration; wish; dream

【心悦诚服】 xīn yuè chéng fú feel a heartfelt admiration; be completely convinced: 支部书记的一番话说得她～。She was completely convinced by the Party secretary's arguments./ 他对你们的批评～。He fully accepted your criticism.

【心杂音】 xīnzáyīn 〈医〉 heart murmur

【心脏】 xīnzàng the heart
◇ ～病 heart disease/ ～导管 cardiac catheter/ ～地带 heartland/ ～起搏器 (cardiac) pacemaker

【心照】 xīnzhào understand without being told; have an understanding: ～不宣 have a tacit understanding

【心直口快】 xīnzhí-kǒukuài frank and outspoken

【心中有数】 xīnzhōng yǒu shù have a pretty good idea of; know fairly well; know what's what: 对计划执行情况～ have a pretty clear idea of how the plan is being carried out/ 只有深入群众,调查研究,才能真正做到～。Only by going deep among the masses to make investigations can you really get to know how things stand.

【心轴】 xīnzhóu 〈机〉 mandrel: 花键～ splined mandrel

【心子】 xīnzi ① (of things) centre; heart; core ② 〈方〉 the heart of a pig, sheep, etc. as food

【心醉】 xīnzuì be charmed; be enchanted; be fascinated

**芯** xīn rush pith
另见 xìn

**辛** xīn ① hot (in taste, flavour, etc.); pungent ② hard; laborious: 艰～ hardships ③ suffering: ～酸 sad; bitter ④ the eighth of the ten Heavenly Stems ⑤ (Xīn) a surname

【辛迪加】 xīndíjiā 〈经〉 syndicate

【辛亥革命】 Xīnhài Gémìng the Revolution of 1911 (the Chinese bourgeois democratic revolution led by Dr. Sun Yat-sen which overthrew the Qing Dynasty)

【辛苦】 xīnkǔ ① hard; toilsome; laborious: 犁地这活儿很～。Ploughing is hard work. ② work hard; go to great trouble; go through hardships: 这事恐怕还得你～一趟。I'm afraid you'll have to take the trouble of going there to see about it./ 同志们～了。You comrades have been working hard./ 路上～了。You must have had a tiring journey. 或 Did you have a good trip?

【辛辣】 xīnlà pungent; hot; bitter: ～的味道 a sharp (或 pungent) flavour/ ～的讽刺 bitter irony; biting sarcasm

【辛劳】 xīnláo pains; toil: 日夜～ toil day and night/ 不辞～ spare no pains

【辛勤】 xīnqín industrious; hardworking: ～劳动 work hard; labour assiduously

【辛酸】 xīnsuān sad; bitter; miserable: ～泪 hot and bitter tears/ ～的往事 sad (或 poignant) memories/ 饱尝旧社会的～ taste to the full the bitterness of life in the old society

【辛烷值】 xīnwánzhí 〈化〉 octane number (或 value)

【辛辛苦苦】 xīnxīnkǔkǔ take a lot of trouble; take great pains; work laboriously: ～地收集技术革新的资料 take great pains in collecting data for technical innovation/ ～的官僚主义 a painstaking but bureaucratic style of work

【辛夷】 xīnyí 〈中药〉 the flower bud of lily magnolia (*Magnolia liliflora*)

**欣** xīn glad; happy; joyful: 欢～ happy; joyful/ ～逢佳节 on the happy occasion of the festival

【欣然】 xīnrán 〈书〉 joyfully; with pleasure: ～接受 accept with pleasure/ ～同意 gladly consent; readily agree

【欣赏】 xīnshǎng appreciate; enjoy; admire: 音乐～ music appreciation/ ～风景 enjoy (或 admire) the scenery/ 我很～这个花园的格局。I admire the layout of this garden. 或 I like the way the garden is laid out.

【欣慰】 xīnwèi be gratified: 我们对实验的成功感到～。We were gratified at the success of the experiment./ 获悉你身体康复,至感～。I am relieved to learn that you have recovered from your illness.

【欣悉】 xīnxī be glad (或 happy) to learn

【欣喜】 xīnxǐ glad; joyful; happy: ～若狂 be wild with joy; go into raptures

【欣羡】 xīnxiàn 〈书〉 admire

【欣欣向荣】 xīnxīn xiàng róng thriving; flourishing; prosperous: 一派～的景象 a picture of prosperity/ 我国国民经济～。Our national economy is thriving.

【欣幸】 xīnxìng be glad and thankful

**锌** xīn 〈化〉 zinc (Zn)

【锌白】 xīnbái 〈化〉 zinc white

【锌版】 xīnbǎn 〈印〉 zinc plate; zincograph ◇ ～印刷术 zincography

【锌钡白】 xīnbèibái 〈化〉 lithopone

【锌粉】 xīnfěn 〈化〉 zinc powder

**新** xīn ① new; fresh; up-to-date: ～社会 the new society/ ～技术 new (或 up-to-date) technique/ 最～消息 the latest news/ ～殖民主义 neocolonialism ② newly; freshly; recently: ～建的工厂 a newly built factory/ ～上油漆的门 a freshly-painted door/ 他是～来的。He's a new arrival. ③ recently married: ～人 newlywed ④ (Xīn) short for the Xinjiang Uygur Autonomous Region

【新兵】 xīnbīng new recruit; recruit ◇ ～报到站 reception centre (或 station); recruiting depot

【新陈代谢】 xīn-chén dàixiè ① 〈生〉 metabolism: 生物都有～,有生长、繁殖和死亡。All living matter undergoes a process of metabolism: it grows, reproduces and perishes. ② the new superseding the old: ～是宇宙间普遍的永远不可抵抗的规律。The supersession of the old by the new is a general, eternal and inviolable law of the universe.

【新仇旧恨】 xīnchóu-jiùhèn new hatred piled on old; old scores and new

【新春】 xīnchūn the 10 or 20 days following Lunar New Year's Day

【新村】 xīncūn new residential quarter; new housing development (或 estate): 工人～ new workers' housing estate

【新大陆】 Xīn Dàlù the New World — the Americas

【新房】 xīnfáng bridal chamber

【新妇】 xīnfù bride

【新官上任三把火】 xīnguān shàngrèn sān bǎ huǒ a new official applies strict measures; a new broom sweeps clean

【新赫布里底】 Xīn Hèbùlǐdǐ New Hebrides

【新婚】 xīnhūn newly-married: ～夫妇 newly-married

couple; newlyweds
【新纪元】 xīnjìyuán new era; new epoch: 开创～ usher in a new epoch; open a new era
【新加坡】 Xīnjiāpō Singapore
【新疆】 Xīnjiāng Xinjiang
【新疆维吾尔自治区】 Xīnjiāng Wéiwú'ěr Zìzhìqū the Xinjiang Uygur (Uighur) Autonomous Region
【新交】 xīnjiāo new acquaintance; new friend: 他与老王是～。He and Lao Wang have become acquainted only recently.
【新教】 Xīnjiào 〈宗〉 Protestantism ◇ ～徒 Protestant
【新近】 xīnjìn recently; lately; in recent times
【新居】 xīnjū new home; new residence
【新喀里多尼亚】 Xīn Kālǐduōníyà New Caledonia
【新来乍到】 xīnlái-zhàdào newly arrived: 我～，请多帮助。I'm a newcomer here and would be glad to have your help.
【新郎】 xīnláng bridegroom
【新霉素】 xīnméisù 〈药〉 neomycin
【新民主主义】 xīn-mínzhǔzhǔyì new democracy ◇ ～革命 new-democratic revolution
【新名词】 xīnmíngcí new term; new expression; vogue word; newfangled phrase: 满口～ mouthing newfangled phrases
【新年】 xīnnián New Year: ～好！Happy New Year!/ ～献词 New Year message
【新娘】 xīnniáng bride
【新篇章】 xīnpiānzhāng new page: 两国关系史上的～ a new page in the history of relations between the two countries
【新瓶装旧酒】 xīnpíng zhuāng jiùjiǔ old wine in a new bottle — the same old stuff with a new label
【新奇】 xīnqí strange; novel; new: ～的想法 a novel idea/ 他初到矿山时，处处觉得～。When he first got to the mine, everything struck him as new.
【新区】 xīnqū ① newly developed area; newly added district ② newly liberated area (during the Third Revolutionary Civil War, 1945-1949)
【新人】 xīnrén ① people of a new type: ～新事 new people and new things/ 培养共产主义的～ foster the new communist man ② new personality; new talent: 科学界涌现出了一批～。A new batch of gifted people has emerged in the world of science. ③ newlywed, esp. the bride
【新生】 xīnshēng ① newborn; newly born: ～婴儿 newborn (baby) ② new life; rebirth; regeneration: 一九四九年一月三十一日北京解放了，这个古城从此获得了～。With its liberation on January 31, 1949, the centuries-old city of Beijing was reborn./ 解放后这种古老的民间艺术获得了～。Liberation gave this age-old folk art a new life. ③ new student ◇ ～资产阶级分子 newborn bourgeois element
【新生代】 Xīnshēngdài 〈地〉 the Cenozoic Era
【新生力量】 xīnshēng lìliàng newly emerging force; new rising force; new force
【新生事物】 xīnshēng shìwù newly emerging things; new things
【新诗】 xīnshī free verse written in the vernacular
【新石器时代】 Xīnshíqì Shídài the Neolithic Age; the New Stone Age
【新时期的总任务】 xīnshíqī de zǒngrènwù the general task for the new period — the task is firmly to carry out the line of the Eleventh Party Congress, steadfastly continue the revolution under the dictatorship of the proletariat, deepen the three great revolutionary movements of class struggle, the struggle for production and scientific experiment, and transform China into a great and powerful socialist country with modern agriculture, industry, national defence and science and technology by the end of the century
【新式】 xīnshì new type; latest type; new-style: ～农具 new types of farm implements; improved farm implements/ ～武器 modern weapons
【新手】 xīnshǒu new hand; raw recruit
【新斯的明】 xīnsīdímíng 〈药〉 neostigmine
【新四军】 Xīnsìjūn the New Fourth Army (led by the Chinese Communist Party during the War of Resistance Against Japan)
【新文化运动】 xīnwénhuà yùndòng the New Culture Movement (around the time of the May 4th Movement in 1919)
【新文学】 xīnwénxué new-vernacular literature (promoted by the May 4th Movement in 1919)
【新闻】 xīnwén news: 头版～ front-page news (或 story)/ 简明～ news in brief
◇ ～处 office of information; information service/ ～稿 press (或 news) release/ ～工作者 journalist/ ～公报 press *communiqué*/ ～广播 newscast/ ～记者 newsman; newspaperman; reporter; journalist/ ～简报 news summary/ ～界 press circles; the press/ ～片 newsreel; news film/ ～司 department of information/ ～图片橱窗 newsphoto display case/～纸 newsprint
【新西兰】 Xīnxīlán New Zealand ◇ ～人 New Zealander
【新鲜】 xīnxiān ① fresh: ～空气 fresh air/ ～牛奶 fresh milk/ 鱼有点不～了。The fish is slightly off./ 尝个～ have a taste of what is just in season ② new; novel; strange: ～经验 new (或 fresh) experience/ 这话真～。That's a strange thing to say.
【新兴】 xīnxīng new and developing; rising; burgeoning: ～工业城市 a developing industrial city/ ～的独立国家 newly independent countries/ ～势力 the rising forces; the forces in the ascendant
【新星】 xīnxīng 〈天〉 nova: 超～ supernova
【新型】 xīnxíng new type; new pattern
【新学】 xīnxué new learning 参见"西学" xīxué
【新医】 xīnyī ① new Chinese medicine (Chinese medicine integrated with Western medicine) ② Western medicine
【新颖】 xīnyǐng new and original; novel: 题材～ original in choice of subject (或 theme)/ 式样～ in a novel style
【新约】 Xīnyuē 〈基督教〉 the New Testament
【新月】 xīnyuè ① crescent ② 〈天〉 new moon ◇ ～形沙丘 〈地〉 crescent dune; barchan
【新殖民主义】 xīn-zhímínzhǔyì neocolonialism; new colonialism ◇ ～者 neocolonialist
【新装】 xīnzhuāng new clothes: 山村换～。The mountain village takes on a new look.

**薪** xīn ① firewood; faggot; fuel ② salary: 发～ pay out the salary
【薪俸】 xīnfèng salary; pay
【薪金】 xīnjīn salary; pay
【薪尽火传】 xīn jìn huǒ chuán as one piece of fuel is consumed, the flame passes to another — the torch of learning is passed on from teacher to student and from generation to generation
【薪水】 xīnshui salary; pay; wages
【薪炭林】 xīntànlín 〈林〉 fuel forest

**馨** xīn 〈书〉 strong and pervasive fragrance
【馨香】 xīnxiāng 〈书〉 ① fragrance ② smell of burning incense
【馨香祷祝】 xīnxiāng dǎozhù ① burn incense and pray to the gods ② earnestly pray for sth.; sincerely wish

## xín

**寻** xín
另见 xún

【寻短见】 xín duǎnjiàn commit suicide; take one's own life

【寻死】 xínsǐ ① try to commit suicide; attempt suicide ② commit suicide

【寻死觅活】 xínsǐ-mìhuó repeatedly attempt suicide (in order to threaten)

【寻思】 xínsi think sth. over; consider: 你～～这事该怎么办。Think over what to do about it.

## xìn

**芯** xìn core: 岩～ core
另见 xīn

【芯子】 xìnzi ① fuse; wick: 蜡烛～ candle wick ② the forked tongue of a snake

**信** xìn ① true: ～而有征 borne out by evidence ② confidence; trust; faith: 取～于民 win the people's confidence (或 trust)/ 失～ break faith (或 one's promise)/ ～得过 trustworthy ③ believe: ～不～由你 believe it or not/ ～以为真 accept sth. as true ④ profess faith in; believe in: ～佛 profess Buddhism ⑤ at will; at random; without plan: ～步 walk aimlessly ⑥ sign; evidence: ～号 signal/ 印～ official seal ⑦ letter; mail: 公开～ an open letter/ 证明～ certificate; certification ⑧ message; word; information: 口～ a verbal message; an oral message/ 还没有～儿呢。No news yet./ 你到达后给我来个～儿。Please send me word of your arrival. ⑨ fuse: 炸药～管 fuse in a blasting charge

【信标灯】 xìnbiāodēng beacon light

【信步】 xìnbù take a leisurely walk; stroll; walk aimlessly

【信贷】 xìndài credit: 长期～ long-term credit ◇ ～额度 line of credit/ ～资金 credit funds; funds for extending credit

【信风】 xìnfēng 〈气〉 trade (wind): 反～ antitrade wind; antitrades ◇ ～带 trade-wind zone

【信封】 xìnfēng envelope

【信奉】 xìnfèng believe in: ～基督教 be a Christian

【信服】 xìnfú completely accept; be convinced: 令人～的论据 convincing argument; argument that carries conviction

【信鸽】 xìngē carrier pigeon; homing pigeon; homer

【信管】 xìnguǎn fuse: 触发～ contact fuse/ 延期～ delay-action fuse/ 近炸～ proximity fuse

【信号】 xìnhào signal: 灯光～ light signal/ 识别～ identification signal/ 杂乱～〈无〉 hash/ (船只)遇难～ distress signal; SOS/ (铁路)臂板～ semaphore
◇ ～兵 signalman/ ～刺激〈心理〉 signal stimulus/ ～弹 signal flare/ ～灯 signal lamp/ ～枪〈军〉 flare (或 signal, pyrotechnic) pistol

【信汇】 xìnhuì mail transfer (M/T)

【信笺】 xìnjiān letter paper; writing paper

【信件】 xìnjiàn letters; mail

【信教】 xìnjiào profess a religion; be religious

【信口雌黄】 xìnkǒu címhuáng make irresponsible remarks; wag one's tongue too freely

【信口开河】 xìnkǒu kāihé talk irresponsibly; wag one's tongue too freely; talk nonsense

【信赖】 xìnlài trust; count on; have faith in: 她是群众～的好干部。She's a good cadre trusted by the masses.

【信念】 xìnniàn faith; belief; conviction

【信任】 xìnrèn trust; have confidence in: 得到人民的～ enjoy the trust (或 confidence) of the people ◇ ～投票 vote of confidence

【信赏必罚】 xìnshǎng-bìfá due rewards and punishments will be meted out without fail

【信实】 xìnshí trustworthy; honest; reliable

【信史】 xìnshǐ true (或 authentic) history; faithful historical account

【信使】 xìnshǐ courier; messenger: 外交～ diplomatic messenger ◇ ～证明书 courier's credentials

【信誓旦旦】 xìnshì dàndàn pledge in all sincerity and seriousness; vow solemnly

【信手拈来】 xìnshǒu niānlái have words, material, etc. at one's fingertips and write with facility

【信守】 xìnshǒu abide by; stand by: ～协议 abide (或 stand) by an agreement/ ～诺言 keep a promise; be as good as one's word/ ～不渝 be unswervingly faithful (to one's promise, etc.)

【信天翁】 xìntiānwēng 〈动〉 albatross

【信条】 xìntiáo article of creed (或 faith); creed; precept; tenet

【信筒】 xìntǒng pillar-box; mailbox

【信徒】 xìntú believer; disciple; follower; adherent; devotee: 佛教～ Buddhist

【信托】 xìntuō trust; entrust
◇ ～公司 trust company/ ～基金 trust fund/ ～商店 commission shop (或 house, agent)

【信物】 xìnwù authenticating object; token; keepsake

【信息】 xìnxī ① information; news; message ② 〈数〉 information
◇ ～编码〈计算机〉 information encoding/ ～传递 information transmission/ ～存储器〈计算机〉 information-storing device/ ～论〈数〉 information theory/ ～体〈生化〉 informosome/ ～载体 information carrier/ ～子〈生化〉 informofer

【信箱】 xìnxiāng ① letter box; mailbox ② post-office box (P.O.B.)

【信心】 xìnxīn confidence; faith: 满怀～ full of confidence/ 有～提前完成任务 be confident of fulfilling a task ahead of schedule/ 我对这药～不大。I haven't much faith in this medicine.

【信仰】 xìnyǎng faith; belief; conviction: 政治～ political conviction/ 宗教～ religious belief ◇ ～主义〈哲〉 fideism

【信义】 xìnyì good faith; faith: 有～ act in good faith/ 无～ be perfidious

【信用】 xìnyòng ① trustworthiness; credit: 讲～ keep one's word/ 失去～ lose one's credit ② 〈经〉 credit
◇ ～放款 unsecured loan; loan on credit/ ～合作社 credit cooperative/ ～证 letter of credit (L/C)

【信誉】 xìnyù prestige; credit; reputation: 享有很高的国际～ enjoy high international prestige

【信札】 xìnzhá letters

【信纸】 xìnzhǐ letter paper; writing paper

**衅** xìn quarrel; dispute: 寻～ pick a quarrel with sb./ 挑～ provoke

【衅端】 xìnduān 〈书〉 a cause for a quarrel or dispute

## xīng

**兴** xīng ① prosper; rise; prevail; become popular: ～衰 rise and decline; ups and downs/ 新社会不～这一套了。We don't go in for that sort of thing in the new society.

② start; begin: ～工 start construction/ ～兵 send an army ③ encourage; promote: 大～调查研究之风 energetically encourage the practice of investigation and study ④〈书〉get up; rise: 夙～夜寐 rise early and retire late — work hard ⑤〈方〉〔通常用于否定〕permit; allow: 不～胡说! None of your nonsense! ⑥〈方〉maybe; perhaps: 明天他也～来，也～不来。He may or may not come tomorrow.

另见 xìng

【兴办】 xīngbàn initiate; set up: ～集体福利事业 initiate collective welfare work

【兴奋】 xīngfèn ① be excited: 他～得睡不着觉。He was too excited to fall asleep. ②〈生理〉excitation ◇ ～剂 excitant; stimulant/ ～性 excitability

【兴风作浪】 xīngfēng-zuòlàng stir up (或 make) trouble; fan the flames of disorder

【兴革】 xīnggé 〈书〉initiation (of the new) and abolition (of the old); reforms

【兴建】 xīngjiàn build; construct: 正在～一座大坝。A dam is now under construction./ 又～了一个化肥厂。Another fertilizer plant has been built.

【兴利除弊】 xīnglì-chúbì promote what is beneficial and abolish what is harmful

【兴隆】 xīnglóng prosperous; thriving; flourishing; brisk: 生意～。Business is brisk.

【兴起】 xīngqǐ rise; spring up; be on the upgrade: 激光是六十年代初期～的一门新科学。Laser is a new branch of science which rose in the early 1960s./ 一个社会主义建设的新高潮正在～。A new upsurge in socialist construction is in the making.

【兴盛】 xīngshèng prosperous; flourishing; thriving; in the ascendant: 国家～ prosperity of the nation

【兴师】 xīngshī 〈书〉send an army; dispatch troops

【兴师动众】 xīngshī-dòngzhòng move troops about and stir up the people — drag in many people (to do sth.): 这点小事，用不着～。It's only a small matter; you needn't make a fuss about it and drag in a lot of people.

【兴师问罪】 xīngshī wèn zuì send a punitive expedition against

【兴亡】 xīng-wáng rise and fall (of a nation)

【兴旺】 xīngwàng prosperous; flourishing; thriving: 集体经济越办越～。The collective economy is growing more and more prosperous./ 青年人朝气蓬勃，正在～时期。Young people, full of vitality, are in the heyday of life./ 我们的队伍必定会～起来。Our ranks will surely swell./ 我国的科学技术一定会～发达起来。China's science and technology will certainly grow and flourish.

【兴无灭资】 xīng wú miè zī foster proletarian ideology and eliminate bourgeois ideology: 思想文化战线的根本任务就是～。The basic task on the ideological and cultural fronts is to promote what is proletarian and liquidate what is bourgeois.

【兴修】 xīngxiū start construction (on a large project); build: ～水利 build water conservancy projects/ ～居民楼 construct apartment buildings

【兴许】 xīngxǔ 〈方〉perhaps; maybe

【兴妖作怪】 xīngyāo-zuòguài conjure up a host of demons to make trouble; stir up trouble

## 星

xīng ① star: ～空 starlit sky; starry sky ② heavenly body: 彗～ comet/ 卫～ satellite ③ bit; particle: 一～半点 a tiny bit/ 火～儿 spark ④ small marks on the arm of a steelyard indicating *jin* and its fractions

【星表】 xīngbiǎo 〈天〉star catalogue

【星辰】 xīngchén stars

【星虫】 xīngchóng 〈动〉siphon-worm

【星等】 xīngděng 〈天〉(stellar) magnitude

【星斗】 xīngdǒu stars: 满天～ a star-studded sky

【星号】 xīnghào asterisk (*)

【星河】 xīnghé 〈天〉the Milky Way

【星火】 xīnghuǒ ① spark: ～燎原。A single spark can start a prairie fire. ② shooting star; meteor: 急如～ most urgent

【星际】 xīngjì interplanetary; interstellar: ～飞行 interplanetary (或 space) flight

【星罗棋布】 xīngluó-qíbù scattered all over like stars in the sky or men on a chessboard; spread all over the place: 全国中小型水利工程～。Small and medium-sized irrigation works spread all over the country.

【星期】 xīngqī ① week: 今天～几? What day (of the week) is it today?/ 本～ this week/ 上～ last week/ 下～ next week ② Sunday: ～休息。Sunday is a holiday. 或 Sunday is our day off.

◇ ～日(天) Sunday (Sun.)/ ～一 Monday (Mon.)/ ～二 Tuesday (Tues.)/ ～三 Wednesday (Wed.)/ ～四 Thursday (Thur.)/ ～五 Friday (Fri.)/ ～六 Saturday (Sat.)

【星球】 xīngqiú celestial (或 heavenly) body

【星散】 xīngsàn 〈书〉(of one's family, friends, etc.) scattered about like the stars; scattered far and wide

【星鲨】 xīngshā 〈动〉gummy shark

【星体】 xīngtǐ 〈天〉celestial (或 heavenly) body

【星图】 xīngtú 〈天〉star chart; star map; star atlas

【星团】 xīngtuán 〈天〉(star) cluster

【星系】 xīngxì 〈天〉galaxy: 总～ metagalaxy ◇ ～天文学 extragalactic astronomy/ ～团 cluster of galaxies

【星星】 xīngxīng tiny spot: 天空晴朗，一～云彩也没有。The sky is clear and bright without a speck of cloud./ ～之火，可以燎原。A single spark can start a prairie fire.

【星星】 xīngxing 〈口〉star

【星星点点】 xīngxīngdiǎndiǎn tiny spots; bits and pieces: 对于科学的最新成就我只是～知道一些。I have only fragmentary knowledge of the latest scientific achievements.

【星宿】 xīngxiù constellation

【星夜】 xīngyè on a starlit (或 starry) night; by night: ～启程 set out by starlight; set out in great haste

【星移斗转】 xīngyí-dǒuzhuǎn change in the positions of the stars — change of the seasons; passage of time

【星云】 xīngyún 〈天〉nebula: 旋涡～ spiral nebula/ 银河～ galactic nebula/ 蟹状～ Crab Nebula/ 网状～ network nebula ◇ ～团 nebulous cluster

【星占】 xīngzhān divine by astrology; cast a horoscope ◇ ～术 astrology

【星震】 xīngzhèn 〈天〉starquake

【星座】 xīngzuò 〈天〉constellation

## 惺

xīng

【惺忪】 xīngsōng (of eyes) not yet fully open on waking up: 睡眼～ eyes still heavy with sleep; sleepy eyes

【惺惺】 xīngxīng ① clearheaded; awake ② wise; intelligent: ～惜～。The wise appreciate one another. ③ 见"假惺惺" jiǎxīngxing

【惺惺作态】 xīngxīng zuò tài be affected; simulate (friendship, innocence, etc.)

## 猩

xīng orangutan

【猩红】 xīnghóng scarlet; bloodred

【猩红热】 xīnghóngrè 〈医〉scarlet fever

【猩猩】 xīngxing 〈动〉orangutan: 大～ gorilla/ 黑～ chimpanzee

【猩猩草】 xīngxingcǎo 〈植〉painted euphorbia (*Euphorbia heterophylla*)

**腥** xīng ①raw meat or fish: 荤～ dishes of meat or fish ②having the smell of fish, seafood, etc.

【腥臭】 xīngchòu stinking smell as of rotten fish; stench

【腥黑穗病】 xīnghēisuìbìng 〈农〉 bunt

【腥气】 xīngqì ①the smell of fish, seafood, etc. ②stinking; fishy

【腥膻】 xīngshān smelling of fish or mutton

【腥味儿】 xīngwèir smelling of fish; fishy

## xíng

**刑** xíng ①punishment: 死～ capital punishment; the death penalty/ ～满释放 be released after serving a sentence ②torture; corporal punishment: 用～ put sb. to torture; torture

【刑部】 Xíngbù the Ministry of Punishments in feudal China

【刑场】 xíngchǎng execution ground

【刑罚】 xíngfá 〈法〉 penalty; punishment

【刑法】 xíngfǎ 〈法〉 penal code; criminal law

【刑法】 xíngfa corporal punishment; torture: 动了～ administer corporal punishment/ 受了～ suffer corporal punishment

【刑具】 xíngjù instruments of torture; implements of punishment

【刑律】 xínglǜ 〈法〉 criminal law: 触犯～ violate the criminal law

【刑期】 xíngqī 〈法〉 term of imprisonment; prison term

【刑事】 xíngshì 〈法〉 criminal; penal
◇ ～案件 criminal case/ ～处分 criminal sanction/ ～法庭 criminal court/ ～犯 criminal offender; criminal/ ～犯罪 criminal offence; crime/ ～管辖权 criminal jurisdiction/ ～诉讼 criminal suit/ ～责任 responsibility for a crime

【刑讯】 xíngxùn 〈法〉 inquisition by torture: ～逼供 extort a confession by torture; subject sb. to the third degree

**邢** Xíng a surname

**行** xíng ①go: 步～ go on foot; walk/ 日～百里 cover a hundred *li* a day ②travel: ～程 route or distance of travel/ 非洲之～ a trip to Africa ③temporary; makeshift: ～灶makeshift cooking stove④be current; prevail; circulate: 风～一时 be popular (或 in fashion) for a time; be all the rage/ 货币发～ monetary issue; issue of bank notes ⑤do; perform; carry out; engage in: 实～ carry out; put into effect/ 简便易～ simple and easy to do/ ～窃 commit theft/ ～骗 practise deception; cheat ⑥〔用于双音动词前，表示进行某项活动〕: 另～安排 make other (或 separate) arrangements ⑦behaviour; conduct: 品～ character; conduct/ 言～ words and deeds ⑧all right; O. K.: 在快车道上骑车不～。 Cycling along the motorway is not allowed./ 你替我到邮局跑一趟，～吗？—— ～! Would you run over to the post office for me? — O. K.! ⑨capable; competent: 老王，你真～！Lao Wang, you are really terrific (或 something great)!/ 你看他干这工作～吗？Do you think he is up to it?/ 不要认为只有自己才～。Don't think that you're the only capable one. ⑩〈书〉 soon: ～将完毕 soon to be completed
另见 háng

【行百里者半九十】 xíngbǎilǐzhě bàn jiǔshí ninety *li* is only half of a hundred-*li* journey — the going is toughest towards the end of a journey; one must sustain one's effort when a task is nearing completion

【行板】 xíngbǎn 〈乐〉 *andante*

【行波】 xíngbō 〈无〉 travelling wave ◇ ～管 travelling wave tube

【行不通】 xíngbutōng won't do (或 work); get nowhere: 这个计划～。This plan won't work./ 这样的作法是绝对～的。This course of action will get us absolutely nowhere.

【行车】 xíngchē drive a vehicle
◇ ～里程 distance travelled by a vehicle; mileage/ ～速率 driving speed/ ～执照 driver's (或 driving) license

【行成于思】 xíng chéng yú sī a deed is accomplished through taking thought; success depends on forethought

【行程】 xíngchéng ①route or distance of travel: ～一万多公里 travel over 10,000 kilometres ②〈机〉 stroke; throw; travel: 活塞～ piston travel/ 滑枕～ ram stroke/ 偏心轮～ throw of eccentric

【行船】 xíngchuán sail a boat; navigate

【行刺】 xíngcì assassinate

【行动】 xíngdòng ①move (或 get) about: ～不便 have difficulty getting about/ ～缓慢 move slowly; be slow-moving ②act; take action: ～起来 go into action/ 按计划～。Proceed according to plan. ③action; operation: 军事～ military operations ◇ ～纲领 programme of action

【行方便】 xíng fāngbian make things convenient for sb.; be accommodating

【行宫】 xínggōng imperial palace for short stays away from the capital; temporary dwelling place of an emperor when away from the capital

【行好】 xínghǎo act charitably; be merciful (或 charitable)

【行贿】 xínghuì bribe; offer a bribe; resort to bribery

【行将】 xíngjiāng 〈书〉 about to; on the verge of: ～就道 about to set out on a journey/ ～灭亡的反动势力 reactionary forces on the verge of extinction

【行将就木】 xíngjiāng jiù mù be getting nearer and nearer the coffin — be fast approaching death; have one foot in the grave

【行脚】 xíngjiǎo (of a monk) travel far and wide ◇ ～僧 itinerant monk

【行劫】 xíngjié commit robbery; rob

【行进】 xíngjìn march forward; advance

【行经】 xíngjīng ①go (或 pass) by: 火车～天津的时候，已是半夜了。It was midnight when the train passed through Tianjin. ②〈生理〉 menstruate

【行径】 xíngjìng act; action; move: 侵略～ act of aggression/ 野蛮～ barbarous act/ 一切扩张主义的～是注定要失败的。All expansionist moves are doomed to failure.

【行军】 xíngjūn (of troops) march: 夜～ night march; march by night/ 急～ rapid march
◇ ～床 camp bed; camp cot/ ～锅 field cauldron/ ～壶 canteen/ ～警戒 protection while on the move; security on the march/ ～灶 field kitchen

【行乐】 xínglè 〈书〉 indulge in pleasures; seek amusement; make merry

【行礼】 xínglǐ salute

【行李】 xíngli luggage; baggage: 超重～ excess luggage/ 手提～ hand-luggage
◇ ～车〈铁道〉 luggage van; baggage car/ ～寄存处 check-room/ ～架 luggage (或 baggage) rack/ ～票 luggage (或 baggage) check

【行李卷儿】 xínglijuǎnr bedroll; bedding roll; bedding pack

【行猎】 xíngliè 〈书〉 hunt; go hunting

【行旅】 xínglǚ traveller; wayfarer: ～称便 travellers find it convenient

【行囊】 xíngnáng 〈书〉 travelling bag

【行期】 xíngqī date of departure: ～已近。The date of departure is drawing near.

【行乞】 xíngqǐ beg one's bread; beg alms; beg

【行人】 xíngrén pedestrian: ～走便道。Pedestrians, keep to the sidewalk (或 footpath)!

【行若无事】 xíng ruò wú shì behave as if nothing had happened

【行色】 xíngsè circumstances or style of departure: ～匆匆 in a hurry to go on a trip/ 以壮～ (give a grand send-off, etc.) to enable sb. to depart in style

【行善】 xíngshàn do good works

【行商】 xíngshāng itinerant trader; pedlar

【行尸走肉】 xíngshī-zǒuròu a walking corpse — one who vegetates; an utterly worthless person

【行时】 xíngshí ① (of a thing) be in vogue; be all the rage ② (of a person) be in the ascendent

【行使】 xíngshǐ exercise; perform: ～检察权 exercise procuratorial authority

【行驶】 xíngshǐ (of a vehicle, ship, etc.) go; ply; travel: 列车向南～。The train is going south./ 长江下游可以～万吨轮船。The lower reaches of the Changjiang River are navigable by 10,000-ton steamers./ 汽车正以每小时八十公里的速度～着。The car was doing eighty kilometres an hour.

【行事】 xíngshì ① act; handle matters: 按计划～ act according to plan ② behaviour; conduct

【行书】 xíngshū running hand (in Chinese calligraphy)

【行署】 xíngshǔ 〈简〉(行政公署) administrative office (within a province)

【行述】 xíngshù a brief biography of a deceased person (usu. accompanying an obituary notice) 又作"行状"

【行头】 xíngtou actor's costumes and paraphernalia

【行为】 xíngwéi action; behaviour; conduct: 正义的～ righteous action/ 不法～ illegal act ◇ ～主义 〈心〉 behaviourism

【行文】 xíngwén ① style or manner of writing: ～流畅 read smoothly ② (of a government office) send an official communication to other organizations

【行销】 xíngxiāo be on sale; sell: ～全国 be on sale throughout the country

【行星】 xíngxīng 〈天〉 planet

【行刑】 xíngxíng carry out a death sentence; execute

【行凶】 xíngxiōng commit physical assault or murder; do violence

【行医】 xíngyī practise medicine (usu. on one's own)

【行营】 xíngyíng field headquarters

【行辕】 xíngyuán field headquarters

【行云流水】 xíngyún-liúshuǐ (of style of writing) like floating clouds and flowing water — natural and smooth: 他的文章如～，流畅自然。He writes with natural grace.

【行政】 xíngzhèng administration
◇ ～部门 administrative department (或 unit); executive branch; administration/ ～处分 disciplinary sanction/ ～管理 administration/ ～命令 administrative decree (或 order)/ ～区 administrative area/ ～区域 administrative division/ ～人员 administrative personnel (或 staff)/ ～委员会 administrative council

【行政村】 xíngzhèngcūn administrative village (a grass-roots administrative unit in some old liberated areas during the War of Resistance Against Japan and the early days of liberation)

【行政公署】 xíngzhèng gōngshǔ administrative office (within a province): 省革命委员会可以按地区设立～，作为自己的派出机构。Revolutionary committees at the provincial level may establish administrative offices as their agencies in prefectures.

【行之有效】 xíng zhī yǒuxiào effective (in practice); effectual: ～的办法 effective measures

【行止】 xíngzhǐ 〈书〉 ① whereabouts: ～不明 whereabouts unknown/ ～无定 there's no telling where sb. is ② behaviour; conduct: ～有亏。His conduct has some shortcomings.

【行装】 xíngzhuāng outfit for a journey; luggage: 整理～ pack (for a journey)

【行踪】 xíngzōng whereabouts; track: ～不定 be of uncertain whereabouts/ 特务企图隐匿～。The spy tried to cover his tracks.

【行走】 xíngzǒu walk: 起重机下，禁止～或停留。Walking or standing under the crane is prohibited./ 在崎岖的山路上～ walk on a rugged mountain path

## 形

**形** xíng ① form; shape: 不成～ shapeless; formless/ 方～ square ② body; entity: 有～ tangible/ 无～ intangible ③ appear; look: 喜～于色 look very pleased; beam with undisguised happiness ④ compare; contrast: 相～之下 by comparison; by contrast

【形变】 xíngbiàn 〈物〉 deformation: 弹性～ elastic deformation

【形成】 xíngchéng take shape; form: ～鲜明的对比 form a sharp contrast/ ～巩固的工农联盟 form a solid worker-peasant alliance/ 在几十年生活中～的思想意识 ideology which has been shaped over decades of life/ ～风气 become a common practice/ 我国国民经济新跃进的局面正在～。A new leap forward is taking shape in our national economy./ 近代自然科学是从有了实验科学之后才～的。Modern natural science came into being only after the emergence of experimental science./ 这个艺术团已经～了独特的风格。This performing arts troupe has evolved a style of its own./ 谈判～僵局。The negotiations have come to a deadlock. ◇ ～层 〈植〉 cambium

【形单影只】 xíngdān-yǐngzhī a solitary form, a single shadow — extremely lonely; solitary

【形而上学】 xíng'érshàngxué 〈哲〉 metaphysics

【形骸】 xínghái 〈书〉 the human skeleton; the human body

【形迹】 xíngjì ① a person's movements and expression: 不露～ betray nothing in one's expression and movements/ ～可疑 of suspicious appearance; suspicious-looking ② formality: 不拘～ without formality; not standing on ceremony

【形容】 xíngróng ① 〈书〉 appearance; countenance: ～憔悴 looking wan; thin and pallid ② describe: 难以～ difficult to describe; beyond description

【形容词】 xíngróngcí 〈语〉 adjective

【形声】 xíngshēng 〈语〉 pictophonetic characters, with one element indicating meaning and the other sound, e.g. 江 (river) — one of the six categories of Chinese characters (六书)

【形式】 xíngshì form; shape: 从思想内容到艺术～ both in ideological content and in artistic form/ 以大字报的～提出建议 put forward suggestions in the form of *dazibao*/ ～地看问题 consider a question in a mechanical way ◇ ～主义 formalism

【形式逻辑】 xíngshì luóji 〈逻〉 formal logic

【形式上】 xíngshìshang in form; formal: ～的一致 formal unity/ ～的独立 nominal independence/ 在～保持外交关系 maintain formal diplomatic relations

【形势】 xíngshì ① terrain; topographical features: ～险要 strategically important terrain ② situation; circumstances: ～越来越好。The situation is getting better and better./ ～逼人。The situation is pressing. 或 The situation demands action./ ～发展的必然结果 the inevitable result of developing circumstances

【形似】 xíngsì be similar in form or appearance

【形态】 xíngtài ① form; shape; pattern: 社会经济～ social-economic formation; economic formation of society ② 〈语〉 morphology ◇ ～学 morphology
【形体】 xíngtǐ ① shape (of a person's body); physique; body ② form and structure: 文字的～ form of the written character
【形象】 xíngxiàng image; form; figure: 塑造革命英雄～ create images of revolutionary heroes/ ～地表现了大庆人的革命精神 vividly depict the revolutionary spirit of the people of Daqing
【形象思维】 xíngxiàng sīwéi thinking in (terms of) images: 诗是用～的。Poetry conveys ideas by means of images.
【形形色色】 xíngxíngsèsè of every hue; of all shades; of all forms; of every description: ～的反动派 reactionaries of every hue/ ～的错误思想 erroneous ideas of every description/ 马克思主义、列宁主义、毛泽东思想是在同～的机会主义的斗争中发展起来的。Marxism-Leninism-Mao Zedong Thought has developed through struggle against all brands of opportunism.
【形影不离】 xíng-yǐng bù lí inseparable as body and shadow; always together
【形影相吊】 xíng-yǐng xiāng diào body and shadow comforting each other — extremely lonely; sad and solitary: 茕茕孑立，～ standing all alone, body and shadow comforting each other
【形状】 xíngzhuàng form; appearance; shape
【形"左"实右】 xíng "zuǒ" shí yòu "Left" in form but Right in essence

**型** xíng ① mould: 砂～ sand mould ② model; type; pattern: 新～ new model/ 血～ blood group
【型板】 xíngbǎn 〈机〉 template; templet
【型锻】 xíngduàn 〈机〉 swaged forging; swaging
【型钢】 xínggāng 〈冶〉 section (steel); shape ◇ ～轧机 shape (rolling) mill
【型号】 xínghào model; type
【型砂】 xíngshā 〈机〉 moulding sand
【型心】 xíngxīn 〈冶〉 core: 干砂～ baked core/ 粘土～ loam core

## xǐng

**省** xǐng ① examine oneself critically: 反～ make a self-examination; introspect ② visit (esp. one's parents or elders) ③ become conscious; be aware: 不～人事 lose consciousness
另见 shěng
【省察】 xǐngchá examine oneself critically; examine one's thoughts and conduct
【省亲】 xǐngqīn pay a visit to one's parents or elders (living at another place)
【省视】 xǐngshì ① call upon; pay a visit to ② examine carefully; inspect
【省悟】 xǐngwù 见"醒悟" xǐngwù

**醒** xǐng ① regain consciousness; sober up; come to: 酒醉未～ be drunk and not sobered up yet/ 他～过来了。He's come to. ② wake up; be awake: 如梦初～ like awakening from a dream/ 他还～着呢。He is still awake. ③ be clear in mind: 头脑清～ keep a cool head ④ be striking to the eye: ～眼 catch the eye
【醒盹儿】 xǐngdǔnr 〈方〉 wake up from a nap; shake off drowsiness
【醒豁】 xǐnghuò clear; explicit: 道理说得～。The argument is clearly presented.
【醒酒】 xǐngjiǔ dispel the effects of alcohol; sober up
【醒目】 xǐngmù (of written words or pictures) catch the eye; attract attention; be striking: ～的标语 eye-catching slogans/ ～的标题 bold headlines
【醒悟】 xǐngwù come to realize (或 see) the truth, one's error, etc.; wake up to reality

**擤** xǐng blow (one's nose): ～鼻涕 blow one's nose

## xìng

**兴** xìng mood or desire to do sth.; interest; excitement: 游～ the mood for sight-seeing/ 酒～ excitement due to drinking/ 诗～ an exalted, poetic mood
另见 xīng
【兴冲冲】 xìngchōngchōng (do sth.) with joy and expedition; excitedly: 他～地跑进来，告诉我这个好消息。He rushed into the room excitedly and told me the good news.
【兴高采烈】 xìnggāo-cǎiliè in high spirits; in great delight; jubilant: 人们～地参加祝捷大会。People were jubilant at the victory celebration.
【兴会】 xìnghuì a sudden flash of inspiration; brain wave: 这首诗是乘一时的～写成的。This poem was improvised on the spur of the moment.
【兴趣】 xìngqù interest: 怀着极大的～观看农民画家的作品 look at the paintings by peasant artists with great interest/ 我对下棋不感～。I'm not interested in chess.
【兴头】 xìngtóu enthusiasm; keen interest: 我们厂的工人对体育活动～很大。The workers of our factory are very keen on sport.
【兴头上】 xìngtóushang at the height of one's enthusiasm: 小伙子们干活儿正在～，忘记了休息。The young people were so carried away with their work that they forgot to stop for a rest.
【兴味】 xìngwèi interest: ～索然 uninterested; bored stiff/ 青少年们～盎然地阅读各种新出版的小说。Teen-agers read the newly-published novels with keen interest.
【兴致】 xìngzhì interest; mood to enjoy: ～勃勃 full of zest

**杏** xìng apricot
【杏红】 xìnghóng apricot pink
【杏黄】 xìnghuáng apricot yellow; apricot (colour)
【杏仁】 xìngrén apricot kernel; almond

**性** xìng ① nature; character; disposition: 本～ inherent character; nature ② property; quality: 药～ medicinal properties/ 酒～ alcoholic strength ③〔后缀，表示性质、范围或方式〕: 正确～ correctness/ 可能～ possibility/ 灵活～ flexibility/ 阶级～ class nature (或 character) ④ sex: 男(女)～ the male (female) sex/ ～行为 the sex act ⑤ 〈语〉 gender: 阳～ the masculine gender/ 阴～ the feminine gender/ 中～ the neuter gender
【性别】 xìngbié sexual distinction; sex
【性病】 xìngbìng venereal disease; V. D.
【性格】 xìnggé nature; disposition; temperament: ～开朗 have a bright and cheerful disposition
【性激素】 xìngjīsù 〈生理〉 sex hormone
【性急】 xìngjí impatient; short-tempered
【性交】 xìngjiāo sexual intercourse
【性命】 xìngmìng life
【性命交关】 xìngmìng jiāoguān (a matter) of life and death; of vital importance 又作"性命攸关"

【性能】 xìngnéng function (of a machine, etc.); performance; property: ～试验 performance test/ 反应堆～ reactor behaviour/ 阻冻～ antifreezing property/ 这种插秧机～良好。This kind of rice transplanter performs satisfactorily.
【性器官】 xìngqìguān 〈生理〉 sexual organs; genitals
【性情】 xìngqíng disposition; temperament; temper: ～温柔 have a gentle disposition/ ～暴躁 have an irascible temperament; be short-tempered
【性腺】 xìngxiàn 〈生理〉 sexual (或 sex) gland
【性欲】 xìngyù sexual desire (或 urge)
【性质】 xìngzhì quality; nature; character: 硫酸的化学～ the chemical properties of sulphuric acid/ 弄清问题的～ ascertain the nature of the problem/ 中国革命的～ the character of the Chinese revolution
【性状】 xìngzhuàng shape and properties; properties; character: 土壤的理化～ the physicochemical properties of soil/ 显性～ 〈生〉 dominant character ◇ ～分歧 〈生〉 character divergence
【性子】 xìngzi ① temper: 使～ get into a temper/ 这匹马的～很野。This is a vicious horse. ② strength; potency: 这药～平和。This is a mild drug./ 这酒的～很烈。This liquor is very strong.

**幸** xìng ① good fortune: 有～ be lucky; have good fortune/ ～甚 very fortunate indeed ② rejoice: 庆～ congratulate oneself; rejoice ③〈书〉 I hope; I trust: ～勿推却。I hope that you will not refuse. 或 Pray do not refuse. ④ fortunately; luckily: ～未成灾。Fortunately it didn't cause a disaster. ⑤〈书〉 favour: 得～ gain favour/ ～臣 a favourite at court ⑥ (of a monarch) come; arrive: 巡～ imperial tour of inspection
【幸而】 xìng'ér luckily; fortunately
【幸福】 xìngfú ① happiness; well-being: 为人民谋～ work for the well-being of the people/ 祝你～。I wish you happiness. ② happy: ～的回忆 happy memories/ 老人在敬老院里过着～的晚年。In the Home of Respect for the Aged, the old people are leading a happy life in their remaining years.
【幸好】 xìnghǎo 见"幸亏"
【幸亏】 xìngkuī 〈副〉 fortunately; luckily: 我～走得早,才没叫雨淋了。Luckily I left early and wasn't caught in the rain.
【幸免】 xìngmiǎn escape by sheer luck; have a narrow escape: ～于难 escape death by sheer luck; escape death by a hair's breadth/ 侵略者在村里大肆屠杀,连小孩也难～。The invaders massacred the villagers, not even sparing little children.
【幸事】 xìngshì good fortune; blessing
【幸喜】 xìngxǐ 见"幸亏"
【幸运】 xìngyùn ① good fortune; good luck ② fortunate; lucky ◇ ～儿 fortune's favourite; lucky fellow
【幸灾乐祸】 xìngzāi-lèhuò take pleasure in (或 gloat over) others' misfortune

**姓** xìng surname; family (或 clan) name: 他～王。He is surnamed Wang. 或 His surname is Wang.
【姓名】 xìngmíng surname and personal name; full name
【姓氏】 xìngshì surname

**悻** xìng
【悻悻】 xìngxìng angry; resentful: ～而去 go away angry; leave in a huff

## xiōng

**凶** xiōng ① inauspicious; ominous: ～兆 ill omen ② crop failure: ～年 a year of crop failure or famine; a bad year ③ fierce; ferocious: 这个人样子真～。This chap looks really fierce. ④ terrible; fearful: 病势很～ terribly ill/ 闹得太～了！What a terrific row! /这场雨来势很～。The rain came down with a vengeance. ⑤ act of violence; murder: 行～ commit physical assault or murder
【凶暴】 xiōngbào fierce and brutal
【凶残】 xiōngcán fierce and cruel; savage and cruel
【凶多吉少】 xiōngduō-jíshǎo bode ill rather than well; be fraught with grim possibilities
【凶恶】 xiōng'è fierce; ferocious; fiendish
【凶犯】 xiōngfàn one who has committed homicide or mayhem; murderer
【凶悍】 xiōnghàn fierce and tough
【凶耗】 xiōnghào news of sb.'s death
【凶狠】 xiōnghěn fierce and malicious
【凶横】 xiōnghèng fierce and arrogant
【凶猛】 xiōngměng violent; ferocious: 山洪来势～。The mountain torrents rushed down with a terrifying force.
【凶器】 xiōngqì tool or weapon for criminal purposes; lethal weapon
【凶杀】 xiōngshā homicide; murder: 这是一起～案。This is a case of murder.
【凶神】 xiōngshén demon; fiend
【凶神恶煞】 xiōngshén-èshà devils; fiends
【凶事】 xiōngshì ① unlucky matters — death, burial, etc. ② violence that involves casualties
【凶手】 xiōngshǒu murderer; assassin; assailant (who has caused injury to sb.)
【凶死】 xiōngsǐ die by violence; meet a violent end
【凶险】 xiōngxiǎn in a very dangerous state; critical: 病情～ dangerously ill; critically ill; in a critical condition
【凶相】 xiōngxiàng ferocious features; fierce look: ～毕露 look thoroughly ferocious; unleash all one's ferocity
【凶信】 xiōngxìn news of sb.'s death
【凶焰】 xiōngyàn ferocity; aggressive arrogance: ～万丈 extremely ferocious
【凶宅】 xiōngzhái haunted house; unlucky abode
【凶兆】 xiōngzhào ill omen; boding of evil

**兄** xiōng ① elder brother: 胞～ elder brother of the same parents ② a courteous form of address between men
【兄弟】 xiōngdì ① brothers: 我们～三人 we three brothers/ 阶级～ class brothers ② fraternal; brotherly: ～党 fraternal parties/ ～般的团结 fraternal solidarity; brotherly unity
【兄弟】 xiōngdi 〈口〉 ① younger brother ② a familiar form of address for a man younger than oneself: 大～,这件事就托你了。And so, brother, I'll leave the matter in your hands. ③ your humble servant; I
【兄弟阋墙】 xiōngdì xì qiáng quarrel between brothers; internal dispute: 兄弟阋于墙,外御其侮。Brothers quarrelling at home join forces against attacks from without. 或 Internal disunity dissolves at the threat of external invasion.
【兄长】 xiōngzhǎng a respectful form of address for an elder brother or a man friend

**芎** xiōng 见"川芎" chuānxiōng

**匈** xiōng 〈书〉 见"胸" xiōng
【匈奴】 Xiōngnú Xiongnu (Hun), an ancient nationality in China
【匈牙利】 Xiōngyálì Hungary ◇ ～人 Hungarian/ ～语

Hungarian (language)

汹 xiōng

【汹汹】 xiōngxiōng 〈书〉① the sound of roaring waves ② violent; truculent: 气势～ blustering and truculent ③ tumultuous; agitated: 议论～ tumultuous debate; heated discussion/ 群情～。Public feeling ran high. 或 Public opinion was deeply stirred.

【汹涌】 xiōngyǒng tempestuous; turbulent: 波涛～ turbulent waves/ 革命洪流～向前。The raging tide of revolution surges forward.

【汹涌澎湃】 xiōngyǒng pēngpài surging; turbulent; tempestuous: ～的历史潮流 a tempestuous historical trend

胸 xiōng ① chest; bosom; thorax: 挺～ throw out one's chest/ 孩子把脸贴在母亲的～前。The child buried its face in its mother's bosom. ② mind; heart: ～怀祖国, 放眼世界 have the whole country in mind and the whole world in view; keep at heart the interests of both one's own country and the whole world

【胸靶】 xiōngbǎ 〈军〉 chest silhouette

【胸部】 xiōngbù chest; thorax ◇ ～手术 thoracic operation

【胸骨】 xiōnggǔ 〈生理〉 breastbone; sternum

【胸怀】 xiōnghuái mind; heart: ～坦白 openhearted; frank/ 共产主义者的伟大～ a communist's breadth of vision/ 暖人～的同志情谊 heartwarming comradeship

【胸甲】 xiōngjiǎ cuirass; breastplate

【胸襟】 xiōngjīn mind; breadth of mind: ～开阔 broad-minded; large-minded/ ～狭窄 narrow-minded; small-minded

【胸口】 xiōngkǒu the pit of the stomach

【胸膜】 xiōngmó 〈生理〉 pleura ◇ ～炎 pleurisy

【胸脯】 xiōngpú chest: 挺起～ throw out one's chest/ 拍～保证 strike one's chest as a gesture of guarantee or reassurance

【胸鳍】 xiōngqí 〈动〉 pectoral fin

【胸腔】 xiōngqiāng thoracic cavity

【胸墙】 xiōngqiáng 〈军〉 breastwork; parapet

【胸膛】 xiōngtáng chest: 挺起～ throw out one's chest

【胸围】 xiōngwéi chest measurement; bust

【胸无点墨】 xiōng wú diǎn mò unlearned; unlettered

【胸像】 xiōngxiàng (sculptured) bust

【胸有成竹】 xiōng yǒu chéngzhú have a well-thought-out plan, strategem, etc.: 明年的生产计划, 队长已～。The team leader has a well-thought-out plan for next year's production.

【胸中有数】 xiōngzhōng yǒu shù have a good idea of how things stand: 只有深入群众, 调查研究, 才能做到对情况～。Only by making careful investigations among the masses can we come to know the true state of affairs.

【胸椎】 xiōngzhuī 〈生理〉 thoracic vertebra

## xióng

雄 xióng ① male: ～猫 male cat; tomcat ② grand; imposing: ～伟 imposing; magnificent ③ powerful; mighty: ～兵 a powerful army ④ a person or state having great power and influence: 英～ hero/ 战国七～ the seven powerful states of the Warring States Period (475-221 B.C.)

【雄辩】 xióngbiàn convincing argument; eloquence: ～地证明 prove incontrovertibly; be eloquent proof of/ 事实胜于～。Facts speak louder than words.

【雄才大略】 xióngcái-dàlüè (a man of) great talent and bold vision; (a statesman or general of) rare gifts and bold strategy

【雄蜂】 xióngfēng 〈动〉 drone

【雄关】 xióngguān impregnable pass

【雄厚】 xiónghòu rich; solid; abundant: ～的人力物力 rich human and material resources/ 资金～ abundant funds

【雄花】 xiónghuā 〈植〉 male flower; staminate flower

【雄黄】 xiónghuáng 〈矿〉 realgar; red orpiment

【雄浑】 xiónghún vigorous and firm; forceful: ～的诗篇 powerful poetry/ 笔力～ vigour of strokes in calligraphy or drawing/ ～高亢的乐曲 resounding music

【雄鸡】 xióngjī cock; rooster

【雄健】 xióngjiàn robust; vigorous; powerful: ～的步伐 vigorous strides

【雄赳赳】 xióngjiūjiū valiantly; gallantly: ～, 气昂昂 valiantly and spiritedly

【雄蕊】 xióngruǐ 〈植〉 stamen

【雄师】 xióngshī powerful army: 百万～ a million bold warriors; a mighty army one million strong

【雄图】 xióngtú great ambition; grandiose plan: ～大业 a grandiose and noble enterprise; a great cause

【雄伟】 xióngwěi grand; imposing; magnificent: ～壮丽 grand; sublime/ ～的天安门 the magnificent Tian An Men

【雄文】 xióngwén profound and powerful writing; great works

【雄心】 xióngxīn great ambition; lofty aspiration: 树～, 立壮志, 向科学技术现代化进军。Foster lofty ideals, set high goals and march forward for the modernization of science and technology.

【雄心壮志】 xióngxīn-zhuàngzhì lofty aspirations and great ideals: 无产阶级的～ the lofty aspirations of the proletariat; high proletarian ideals/ 树立～ set up high aims and lofty aspirations; set one's sights high

【雄性不育】 xióngxìng bùyù 〈生〉 male sterility: ～系 male-sterile line; A-line/ ～保持系 maintain line; B-line/ ～恢复系 restorer line; R-line

【雄蚁】 xióngyǐ 〈动〉 aner

【雄壮】 xióngzhuàng full of power and grandeur; magnificent; majestic: ～的军乐 majestic martial music

【雄姿】 xióngzī majestic appearance; heroic posture: 我国喷气式战斗机编队飞行的～ the imposing sight of our jet fighters flying in formation/ 南京长江大桥的～ a magnificent view of the Changjiang Bridge at Nanjing

熊 xióng ① bear: 白～ polar bear/ 狗～ Asiatic black bear ② 〈方〉 rebuke; upbraid; scold ③ (Xióng) a surname

【熊蜂】 xióngfēng bumblebee

【熊猴】 xiónghóu 〈动〉 Assamese macaque

【熊猫】 xióngmāo 〈动〉 panda: 大～ giant panda/ 小～ (lesser) panda

【熊熊】 xióngxióng flaming; ablaze; raging: 革命斗争的～烈火 raging flames of revolutionary struggle

【熊掌】 xióngzhǎng bear's paw (as a rare delicacy)

## xiū

休 xiū ① stop; cease: 争论不～ argue ceaselessly ② rest: ～大礼拜 have a day off every two weeks ③ 〈旧〉 cast off one's wife and send her home ④ 〈副〉〔多见于早期白话〕 don't: ～要胡言乱语。Don't talk nonsense. ⑤ 〈书〉 good fortune: ～咎 good and bad fortune; weal and woe

【休会】 xiūhuì adjourn: 无限期～ adjourn indefinitely (或 *sine die*)/ 会议～一周。The meeting was adjourned for a week./ ～期间 between sessions; when the meeting stands adjourned/ 会议主席宣布～十分钟。The chairman of the

meeting announced a ten-minute recess.
【休假】 xiūjià (of workers, students, etc.) have (或 take, go on) a holiday or vacation; (of soldiers, personnel working abroad, etc.) be on leave or furlough: ～一周 have a week's holiday/ 回国～ go home on furlough
【休克】 xiūkè 〈医〉 shock: 电～ electric shock/ 病人～了。The patient is suffering from shock.
【休眠】 xiūmián 〈生〉 dormancy
◇ ～火山 dormant volcano/ ～期 〈生〉 rest period/ ～芽 〈植〉 resting (或 dormant) bud
【休戚】 xiū-qī weal and woe; joys and sorrows: ～与共 share weal and woe; stand together through thick and thin/ ～相关,患难与共 be bound by a common cause and go through thick and thin together
【休憩】 xiūqì have (或 take) a rest; rest
【休息】 xiūxi have (或 take) a rest; rest: ～一会儿 rest for a while; have a rest/ 幕间～ intermission; interval/ 课间～ break (between classes)/ ～一天 have (或 take) a day off/ 百货公司元旦不～。The department store is open as usual on New Year's Day. ◇ ～室 lounge; lobby; vestibule; *foyer*
【休闲】 xiūxián 〈农〉 lie fallow ◇ ～地 fallow (land)
【休想】 xiūxiǎng don't imagine that it's possible: 你～逃脱。Don't imagine you can get away.
【休学】 xiūxué suspend one's schooling without losing one's status as a student
【休养】 xiūyǎng recuperate; convalesce: 逐步扩充劳动者休息和～的物质条件 gradually expand material facilities for the working people to rest and recuperate ◇ ～所 sanatorium; rest home
【休养生息】 xiūyǎng shēngxī (of a nation) recuperate and multiply; rest and build up strength; rehabilitate
【休业】 xiūyè ① suspend business; be closed down: 今天～。Closed today. ② (of a short-term course, etc.) come to an end; wind up
【休战】 xiūzhàn truce; cease-fire; armistice: ～状态 (state of) cease-fire
【休整】 xiūzhěng (of troops) rest and reorganization
【休止】 xiūzhǐ stop; cease: 无～地争论 argue ceaselessly/ 这座火山已进入～状态。The volcano is inactive. ◇ ～符 〈乐〉 rest

**咻** xiū 〈书〉 make a din
【咻咻】 xiūxiū 〈象〉〔喘气声或某些动物的叫声〕: ～地喘气 pant noisily/ 小鸭～地叫着。The ducklings are cheeping.

**修** xiū ① embellish; decorate: 装～铺面 paint and decorate the front of a shop ② repair; mend; overhaul: ～收音机 repair a radio/ ～鞋 mend shoes/ 农机修理做到了大～不出县,小～不出社队。It is now possible to have major overhauls of farm machines done within the county and minor ones in communes or brigades./ 一定要把淮河～好。The Huaihe River must be harnessed. ③ write; compile: ～史 write history/ ～县志 compile the historical and other records of a county ④ study; cultivate: 自～ study by oneself ⑤ build; construct: ～铁路 build a railway/ ～水库 construct a reservoir/ ～渠 dig irrigation ditches ⑥ trim; prune: ～指甲 trim (或 manicure) one's fingernails ⑦ 〈书〉 long; tall and slender: 茂林～竹 dense forests and tall bamboos ⑧ 〈简〉(修正主义) revisionism: 反～防～ combat and prevent revisionism
【修补】 xiūbǔ ① mend; patch up; repair; revamp: ～渔网 mend fishing nets/ ～衣服 patch clothes/ ～篱笆 mend a fence ② 〈医〉 repair
【修长】 xiūcháng tall and thin; slender: ～的身材 a slender figure
【修船厂】 xiūchuánchǎng shipyard; dockyard
【修辞】 xiūcí rhetoric
【修辞格】 xiūcígé 〈语〉 figures of speech
【修辞学】 xiūcíxué 〈语〉 rhetoric
【修道】 xiūdào cultivate oneself according to a religious doctrine
【修道院】 xiūdàoyuàn 〈宗〉(男) monastery; (女) convent
【修订】 xiūdìng revise: ～条约 revise a treaty/ ～教学计划 revise a teaching plan ◇ ～本 revised edition
【修复】 xiūfù ① repair; restore; renovate: 这段铁路已～通车。This section of the railway has been repaired and reopened to traffic./ ～有历史意义的建筑物 renovate historic buildings ② 〈医〉 repair
【修改】 xiūgǎi revise; modify; amend; alter: ～计划 revise a plan/ ～宪法 amend (或 revise) a constitution/ 对宣言草案提出建设性的～意见 submit constructive amendments to the draft declaration
【修函】 xiūhán 〈书〉 write a letter
【修好】 xiūhǎo ① 〈书〉 foster cordial relations between states ② 〈方〉 do good works
【修剪】 xiūjiǎn prune; trim; clip: ～果枝 prune fruit trees/ ～指甲 trim one's fingernails
【修建】 xiūjiàn build; construct; erect: ～机场 build an airport/ ～纪念碑 erect a monument/ ～桥梁 construct a bridge
【修脚】 xiūjiǎo pedicure ◇ ～师 pedicurist
【修旧利废】 xiū jiù lì fèi repair and utilize old or discarded things
【修浚】 xiūjùn dredge: ～河道 dredge a river
【修理】 xiūlǐ repair; mend; overhaul; fix: ～机器 repair (或 fix) a machine/ 正在～ be under repair/ 当场～,立等可取。Repairs done while you wait. ◇ ～店 fix-it shop; repair shop/ ～行业 repairing trades
【修面】 xiūmiàn 〈方〉 shave; have a shave ◇ ～膏 shaving cream/ ～刷 shaving brush
【修明】 xiūmíng 〈书〉 (of a government) honest and enlightened
【修女】 xiūnǚ 〈宗〉 nun (of the Roman Catholic and Greek Orthodox churches); sister: 当～ become a nun; enter a convent
【修配】 xiūpèi make repairs and supply replacements ◇ ～车间 repair and spare parts workshop
【修葺】 xiūqì repair; renovate: ～一新 take on a new look after renovation; be completely renovated
【修缮】 xiūshàn repair; renovate: ～房屋 repair houses
【修身】 xiūshēn cultivate one's moral character
【修士】 xiūshì 〈宗〉 brother (of the Roman Catholic and Greek Orthodox churches); friar
【修饰】 xiūshì ① decorate; adorn; embellish: ～公园,准备迎接五一。The parks are decorated for the May Day celebrations. ② make up and dress up ③ polish (a piece of writing) ④ 〈语〉 qualify; modify ◇ ～剂 〈皮革〉 dressing agent/ ～语 〈语〉 modifier
【修书】 xiūshū 〈旧〉 ① compile a book ② write a letter
【修行】 xiūxing practise Buddhism or Taoism: 出家～ become a Buddhist or Taoist monk or nun
【修修补补】 xiūxiūbǔbǔ patch up; tinker
【修养】 xiūyǎng ① accomplishment; training; mastery: 马列主义～ one's understanding of Marxism-Leninism/ 有艺术～ be artistically accomplished ② self-cultivation: 革命者要到斗争中去锻炼,而不能闭门～。Revolutionaries should temper themselves in struggle, not go in for self-cultivation behind closed doors.
【修业】 xiūyè study at school: ～年限 length of schooling/

～证书 certificate showing courses attended

【修造】 xiūzào build as well as repair: ～轮船 build or repair ships

【修整】 xiūzhěng ① repair and maintain: ～农具 repair and maintain farm implements ② prune; trim: ～果树 prune fruit trees

【修正】 xiūzhèng ① revise; amend; correct: 坚持真理，～错误 uphold the truth and correct one's mistakes/ ～草案 a revised draft/ ～后的决议草案 the draft resolution as amended/ 提出对建议的～意见 put forward amendments to the proposal ② mutilate (Marxism-Leninism); revise ◇ ～案 amendment/ ～角〈航空〉correction angle

【修正主义】 xiūzhèngzhǔyì revisionism: 否定马克思主义的基本原则，否定马克思主义的普遍真理，这就是～。 It is revisionism to negate the basic principles of Marxism and to negate its universal truth.
◇ ～分子 revisionist (element)/ ～思潮 revisionist trend/ ～者 revisionist

【修枝】 xiūzhī 〈农〉 pruning ◇ ～剪 pruning scissors; pruning shears

【修筑】 xiūzhù build; construct; put up: ～公路 build highways/ ～工事 construct defences; build fortifications (或 defence works)/ ～堤坝 put up dykes

**脩** xiū ① 见"束脩" shùxiū ② 见"修" xiū

**羞** xiū ① shy; bashful: 害～ feel bashful/ ～红了脸 blush ② shame; disgrace: 遮～ conceal (或 hide) one's shame/ 恼～成怒 get angry from shame ③ feel ashamed: ～与为伍 consider it beneath one (或 feel ashamed) to associate with sb. ④ 见"馐" xiū

【羞惭】 xiūcán be ashamed: 满面～ be shamefaced

【羞耻】 xiūchǐ sense of shame; shame: ～之心 sense of shame/ 真不知天下有～事 lose all sense of shame

【羞答答】 xiūdādā coy; shy; bashful 又作"羞羞答答"

【羞愤】 xiūfèn ashamed and resentful

【羞愧】 xiūkuì ashamed; abashed: ～难言 be ashamed beyond words/ ～地低着头 hang one's head for shame

【羞明】 xiūmíng 〈医〉 photophobia

【羞怯】 xiūqiè shy; timid; sheepish: ～得说不出话来 be too shy to utter a word

【羞人】 xiūrén feel embarrassed or ashamed: 羞死人 simply die of shame; feel terribly embarrassed

【羞辱】 xiūrǔ ① shame; dishonour; humiliation ② humiliate; put sb. to shame

【羞涩】 xiūsè shy; bashful; embarrassed

**鸺** xiū

【鸺鹠】 xiūliú 〈动〉 owlet

**馐** xiū 〈书〉 delicacy; dainty: 珍～ a rare delicacy

**貅** xiū 见"貔貅" píxiū

## xiǔ

**朽** xiǔ ① rotten; decayed: 枯木～株 withered trees and rotten stumps ② senile: 老～ old and useless

【朽迈】 xiǔmài 〈书〉 old and weak; senile; decrepit

【朽木】 xiǔmù ① rotten wood or tree ② a hopeless case; a good-for-nothing

【朽木粪土】 xiǔmù-fèntǔ rotten wood and dirt; a worthless person; useless stuff

**宿** xiǔ 〈量〉〔用于计算夜〕: 住一～ stay for one night/ 谈了半～ chat till midnight
另见 sù; xiù

## xiù

**秀** xiù ① (of grain crops) put forth flowers or ears: ～穗 put forth ears ② elegant; beautiful: 眉清目～ having well-chiselled features; handsome/ 山清水～ beautiful hills and waters; lovely scenery ③ excellent: 优～ excellent; first-rate

【秀才】 xiùcai ① *xiucai*, one who passed the imperial examination at the county level in the Ming and Qing dynasties ② scholar; skilful writer: 他是我们生产队里的～。 He is the scholar in our production team.

【秀丽】 xiùlì beautiful; handsome; pretty: 这个小姑娘长得很～。 This little girl is very pretty.

【秀美】 xiùměi graceful; elegant: 书法～ beautiful handwriting

【秀气】 xiùqi ① delicate; elegant; fine: 眉眼生得～ have beautiful eyes ② (of manners) refined; urbane ③ delicate and well-made

**岫** xiù 〈书〉 ① cave ② hill: 远～ a distant hill

**袖** xiù ① sleeve: 长(短)～ long (short) sleeves ② tuck inside the sleeve: 他～着手，踱来踱去。He paced the floor, his hands tucked deep in his sleeves.

【袖标】 xiùbiāo armband

【袖口】 xiùkǒu cuff (of a sleeve): 衬衫～ wristband

【袖手旁观】 xiùshǒu pángguān look on (或 stand by) with folded arms; look on unconcerned: 看到损害国家财产的现象，不能～。 We must not stand by with folded arms when people damage state property.

【袖章】 xiùzhāng armband

【袖珍】 xiùzhēn pocket-size; pocket: ～式半导体收音机 pocket-size transistor radio/ ～字典 pocket dictionary/ ～照相机 vest-pocket camera/ ～潜艇 midget submarine ◇ ～本 pocket edition

【袖子】 xiùzi sleeve

**绣** xiù ① embroider: 在桌布上～花 embroider flowers on a tablecloth/ 挎包上～着"为人民服务"五个大字。 On the satchel are embroidered the words: "Serve the People." ② embroidery: 苏～ Suzhou embroidery

【绣墩】 xiùdūn 〈工美〉 garden stool

【绣花】 xiùhuā embroider; do embroidery
◇ ～被面 embroidered quilt cover/ ～丝线 floss silk/ ～鞋 embroidered shoes/ ～针 embroidery needle

【绣花枕头】 xiùhuā zhěntou ① a pillow with an embroidered case ② an outwardly attractive but worthless person

【绣球】 xiùqiú ① a ball made of strips of silk ② 〈植〉 bigleaf hydrangea

【绣像】 xiùxiàng ① tapestry (或 embroidered) portrait ② exquisitely drawn portrait

【绣眼鸟】 xiùyǎnniǎo 〈动〉 silvereye; white-eye

**臭** xiù ① odour; smell: 纯空气是无色无～的。Pure air is colourless and odourless. ② 见"嗅" xiù
另见 chòu

【臭腺】 xiùxiàn 〈动〉 scent gland

【臭味相投】 xiùwèi xiāngtóu share the same rotten tastes, habits, etc.; be two of a kind

**宿** xiù 〈天〉an ancient term for constellation
另见 sù; xiǔ

**锈** xiù ① rust ② become rusty: 门上的锁～住了。The lock on the door is rusty and won't open.

【锈病】 xiùbìng 〈农〉rust: 小麦秆～ wheat stem rust

**溴** xiù 〈化〉bromine (Br)

【溴化物】 xiùhuàwù 〈化〉bromide

【溴水】 xiùshuǐ 〈化〉bromine water

【溴酸】 xiùsuān 〈化〉bromic acid

**嗅** xiù smell; scent; sniff: 警犬～来～去，终于找到了踪迹。The police dog scented about till he found the trail./ 我们对任何东西都要用鼻子～一～，鉴别其好坏。We should take a sniff at everything and distinguish the good from the bad.

【嗅觉】 xiùjué (sense of) smell; scent: ～很灵 have a keen sense of smell/ 政治～灵敏 be politically sharp

【嗅神经】 xiùshénjīng 〈生理〉olfactory nerve

## xū

**圩** xū 〈方〉country fair: 赶～ go to a fair
另见 wéi

【圩场】 xūchǎng 〈方〉country fair; market

**戌** xū the eleventh of the twelve Earthly Branches

【戌时】 xūshí the period of the day from 7 p. m. to 9 p. m.

**吁** xū 〈书〉① sigh: 长～短叹 sighs and groans; moan and groan ② 〈叹〉〔表示惊异〕: why; oh
另见 yù

【吁吁】 xūxū 〈象〉: 气喘～ pant; puff hard

**胥** xū 〈书〉① petty official ② all; each and every: 万事～备。Everything is ready. ③ (Xū) a surname

【胥吏】 xūlì 〈书〉petty official

**须** xū ① must; have to: 务～注意下列各项。Attention must be paid to the following./ ～作出很大努力 have to make a great effort ② 〈书〉await: ～我片刻 wait a moment for me ③ beard; mustache: 留～ grow a beard ④ (动物) palpus; feeler; (植物) tassel

【须发】 xūfà beard and hair: ～皆白 white hair and beard

【须根】 xūgēn 〈植〉fibrous root

【须眉】 xūméi 〈书〉beard and eyebrows — a man

【须要】 xūyào must; have to: 做这项工作～细心。This work needs to be done carefully.

【须臾】 xūyú 〈书〉moment; instant: ～之间，雨过天晴。In an instant the rain stopped and the sky cleared up./ ～不可离 cannot do without even for a moment

【须知】 xūzhī ① one should know that; it must be understood (或 borne in mind) that: ～胜利来之不易。It must be borne in mind that the victory is hard-won. ② points for attention; notice: 游览～ tourist guide; information for tourists/ 旅客～ notice to travellers, passengers, etc.

【须子】 xūzi (动物) palpus: (植物) tassel: 虾～ feelers of a shrimp/ 玉米～ tassels of maize

**虚** xū ① void; emptiness: 太～ the great void; the universe/ 乘～而入 infiltrate by taking advantage of the other side's unpreparedness; exploit a weak point ② empty; void; unoccupied: 座无～席。There was no empty seat. 或 All seats were occupied. ③ diffident; timid: 胆～ timid; milk-livered/ 心里有点～ feel rather diffident ④ in vain: 不～此行 have not made the trip in vain/ 箭不～发。Not a single arrow missed its target. ⑤ false; nominal: ～名 false reputation/ 耳闻为～，眼见为实。What you hear about may be false; what you see is true. ⑥ humble; modest: 谦～ modest ⑦ weak; in poor health: 气～ lacking in vital energy; sapless/ 身体很～ be very weak physically ⑧ guiding principles; theory: 务～ discuss principles or ideological guidelines/ 以～带实。Let correct ideology guide practical work. ⑨ 〈物〉virtual: ～阴极 virtual cathode

【虚报】 xūbào make a false report: ～账目 cook accounts/ ～冒领 make a fraudulent application and claim

【虚词】 xūcí 〈语〉function word; form word

【虚度】 xūdù spend time in vain; waste: ～光阴 fritter away one's time/ 我们不能让青春～。We must not let our youth slip idly by.

【虚浮】 xūfú impractical; superficial: ～的计划 an impractical plan/ 作风～ have a superficial style of work

【虚根】 xūgēn 〈数〉imaginary root

【虚构】 xūgòu fabricate; make up: ～的情节 a made-up story/ ～的人物 a fictitious character/ 纯属～ an out-and-out fabrication; a sheer fabrication

【虚汗】 xūhàn abnormal sweating due to general debility

【虚怀若谷】 xūhuái ruò gǔ have a mind as open as a valley; be very modest; be extremely open-minded

【虚幻】 xūhuàn unreal; illusory: ～的情景 a mere illusion

【虚假】 xūjiǎ false; sham: 资本主义社会的～繁荣 false prosperity in capitalist society/ ～的安全感 a false sense of security/ ～的可能性 spurious possibility/ ～的友谊 hypocritical friendship/ 我感到他对人有点～。I don't think he is quite honest with people.

【虚价】 xūjià 〈经〉nominal price

【虚焦点】 xūjiāodiǎn 〈物〉virtual focus

【虚惊】 xūjīng false alarm: 受了一场～ be the victim of a false alarm

【虚夸】 xūkuā exaggerative; bombastic; boastful

【虚痨】 xūláo 〈中医〉consumptive disease; consumption

【虚脉】 xūmài 〈中医〉feeble pulse

【虚名】 xūmíng undeserved reputation

【虚拟】 xūnǐ ① invented; fictitious: 这个故事是～的。This is a fictitious story. ② suppositional ◇ ～语气 〈语〉the subjunctive mood

【虚胖】 xūpàng 〈医〉puffiness

【虚情假意】 xūqíng-jiǎyì false display of affection; hypocritical show of friendship

【虚荣】 xūróng vanity: 不慕～ not affected by vanity; not vain ◇ ～心 vanity

【虚弱】 xūruò ① in poor health; weak; debilitated: 病后身体很～ suffer from general debility after an illness; be very weak after an illness ② weak; feeble: 兵力～ weak in military strength/ ～的本质 inherent (或 intrinsic) weakness/ 一切反动派在本质上都是～的。All reactionaries are in essence feeble.

【虚设】 xūshè nominal; existing in name only: 这个机构形同～。That organization is but an empty shell.

【虚实】 xū-shí false or true — the actual situation (as of the opposing side): 探听～ try to find out about an opponent, etc.; try to ascertain the strength (of the enemy)/ 以虚虚实实的战术使敌人疲于奔命 tire out the enemy by feints and ambushes

【虚数】 xūshù ① unreliable figure ② 〈数〉imaginary number

【虚岁】 xūsuì nominal age (reckoned by the traditional method, i.e. considering a person one year old at birth and adding a year each lunar new year)

【虚套子】 xūtàozi mere formalities; conventionalities

【虚脱】 xūtuō 〈医〉 collapse; prostration

【虚妄】 xūwàng unfounded; fabricated; invented: ～的故事 a fabricated story

【虚伪】 xūwěi sham; false; hypocritical: ～的资产阶级民主 sham democracy of the bourgeoisie / 知识的问题是一个科学问题，来不得半点～和骄傲。Knowledge is a matter of science, and no dishonesty or conceit whatsoever is permissible.

【虚位以待】 xū wèi yǐ dài leave a seat vacant (或 save a seat) for sb. 又作"虚席以待"

【虚温】 xūwēn 〈气〉 virtual temperature

【虚文】 xūwén ① rules and regulations that have become a dead letter; dead letter ② empty forms: ～浮礼 mere formalities; conventionalities

【虚无】 xūwú nihility; nothingness ◇ ～主义 nihilism/ ～主义者 nihilist

【虚无缥缈】 xūwú-piāomiǎo purely imaginary; entirely unreal; visionary; illusory

【虚线】 xūxiàn ① dotted line or line of dashes ② 〈数〉 imaginary line

【虚象】 xūxiàng 〈物〉 virtual image

【虚心】 xūxīn open-minded; modest: ～听取别人的意见 listen to people's criticisms with an open mind/ ～使人进步，骄傲使人落后。Modesty helps one to go forward, whereas conceit makes one lag behind.

【虚掩】 xūyǎn with the door left unlocked or unlatched

【虚应故事】 xū yìng gùshì do sth. perfunctorily as a mere matter of form or as a routine practice

【虚有其表】 xū yǒu qí biǎo look impressive but lack real worth; appear better than it is

【虚与委蛇】 xū yǔ wēiyí deal with sb. courteously but without sincerity; pretend politeness and compliance

【虚张声势】 xū zhāng shēngshì make an empty show of strength; bluff and bluster; be swashbuckling

【虚证】 xūzhèng 〈中医〉 chronic diseases marked by deficiency of vital energy and lowering of body resistance

【虚字】 xūzì empty word; function word; form word

**需** xū ① need; want; require: 急～ need badly/ ～款甚巨 require a big sum of money ② necessaries; needs: 必～品 necessaries/ 军～ military supplies (或 requirements)

【需求】 xūqiú requirement; demand

【需要】 xūyào ① need; want; require; demand: 到党和人民最～的地方去 go wherever the Party and the people need us most/ 这所房子～修理。The house wants repairing./ 这种情况～立即采取措施。This situation requires (或 demands) immediate action./ 世界观的彻底改变～一个很长的时间。A thorough change in world outlook takes a very long time. ② needs: 从群众的～出发 make the needs of the masses our starting point/ 保证人民吃穿的基本～ ensure the people their basic needs in food and clothing ◇ ～功率 〈电〉 required power

**嘘** xū ① breathe out slowly ② utter a sigh ③ (of cooking fire, steam, etc.) come into contact with sth.; scald; burn: 掀笼屉时小心热气～着手。Don't scald your hands when you open the steamer. 把馒头在火上～一～。Put the steamed bread over the fire for a while. ④ 〈叹〉 sh; hush ⑤ 〈方〉 hiss; boo: 把他～下台去 hiss (或 boo) him off the platform

另见 shī

【嘘寒问暖】 xūhán-wènnuǎn inquire after sb.'s well-being; be solicitous about sb.'s health

【嘘唏】 xūxī 〈书〉 sob

**墟** xū ① ruins: 废～ ruins ② 见"圩" xū

**歔** xū

【歔欷】 xūxī 〈书〉 sob: 暗自～ sob in secret

## xú

**徐** xú ① slowly; gently: 清风～来。A refreshing breeze is blowing gently. ② (Xú) a surname

【徐步】 xúbù walk slowly (或 leisurely); stroll

【徐徐】 xúxú 〈书〉 slowly; gently: 鲜艳的五星红旗～升起。The bright Five-Star Red Flag slowly went up the pole.

## xǔ

**许** xǔ ① praise: 赞～ praise; commend ② promise: 他～过我一张票。He promised me a ticket. ③ allow; permit: 这项任务限三天完成，不～拖延。The task must be accomplished within three days and permits of no delay. ④ maybe; perhaps: 他今天没来，～是生病了。He didn't come today; perhaps he's ill. ⑤〔表示约略的估计〕: 少～ somewhat; a little/ 年四十～ about forty years old ⑥〈书〉 place: 何～人？Where does the person come from? ⑦ (Xǔ) a surname

【许多】 xǔduō many; much; a great deal of; a lot of: ～人 many people/ 积累了～经验 have accumulated much experience/ 我们有～工作要做。We have a lot of work to do.

【许久】 xǔjiǔ for a long time; for ages: 大家商量了～。We talked things over for a long time./ 我们～没有通信了。We have not corresponded for ages.

【许可】 xǔkě permit; allow: 凡是条件～的地方 wherever conditions permit

【许可证】 xǔkězhèng licence; permit: 出口～ an export licence

【许诺】 xǔnuò make a promise; promise

【许配】 xǔpèi (said of an arranged marriage) betroth a girl

【许愿】 xǔyuàn ① make a vow (to a god) ② promise sb. a reward

**诩** xǔ 〈书〉 brag; boast: 自～为… style oneself…; boast that one is…

**栩** xǔ

【栩栩】 xǔxǔ vivid; lively: ～如生 lifelike; to the life

**醑** xǔ 〈药〉 spirit: 樟脑～ camphor spirit

【醑剂】 xǔjì 〈药〉 spirit

## xù

**旭** xù 〈书〉 brilliance of the rising sun

【旭日】 xùrì the rising sun: ～东升 the sun rising in the eastern sky

**序** xù ① order; sequence: 顺～ sequence/ 程～ procedure/ 井然有～ in perfect order ② arrange in order: ～齿 〈书〉 arrange (seats, etc.) in order of age ③ introductory; initial: ～战 initial battle ④ preface: ～文 preface;

foreword ⑤ a type of local school in ancient times
【序跋】 xùbá preface and postscript
【序列】 xùliè alignment; array: 战斗～ battle array; battle order
【序幕】 xùmù prologue; prelude: 五四运动是我国新民主主义革命的～。The May 4th Movement was the prelude to China's new-democratic revolution.
【序曲】 xùqǔ 〈乐〉 overture
【序时帐】 xùshízhàng 〈会计〉 journal
【序数】 xùshù ordinal number; ordinal
【序文】 xùwén preface; foreword
【序言】 xùyán preface; foreword
【序战】 xùzhàn 〈军〉 initial battle

**恤** xù ① pity; sympathize: 体～ understand and sympathize with ② give relief; compensate: 抚～ comfort and compensate a disabled person or a bereaved family
【恤金】 xùjīn pension for a disabled person or the family of the deceased

**叙** xù ① talk; chat: ～家常 chitchat ② narrate; recount; relate ③ assess; appraise: ～功 assess service and give credit for it ④ 见"序"②④
【叙别】 xùbié have a farewell talk
【叙旧】 xùjiù talk about the old days
【叙利亚】 Xùlìyà Syria ◇ ～人 Syrian
【叙事】 xùshì narrate; recount ◇ ～曲〈乐〉 ballade/ ～诗 narrative poem/ ～文 narrative; narrative prose
【叙述】 xùshù narrate; recount; relate
【叙说】 xùshuō tell; narrate
【叙谈】 xùtán chat; chitchat
【叙文】 xùwén 见"序文" xùwén
【叙言】 xùyán 见"序言" xùyán
【叙用】 xùyòng appoint (an official); employ

**畜** xù raise (domestic animals)
另见 chù
【畜产】 xùchǎn livestock (或 animal) products
【畜牧】 xùmù raise (或 rear) livestock or poultry: 从事～ go in for animal husbandry ◇ ～场 animal farm; livestock (或 stock) farm/ ～业 animal (或 livestock) husbandry; livestock farming
【畜养】 xùyǎng raise (domestic animals)

**酗** xù
【酗酒】 xùjiǔ excessive drinking: ～滋事 get drunk and create a disturbance

**绪** xù ① thread; order in sequence or arrangement: 头～ main threads (of a complicated affair); main lines/ 准备就～ be all set ② mental or emotional state: 心～不宁 be in a state of agitation ③ task; cause; undertaking: 续未竟之～ carry on an unfinished task; take up where another has left off
【绪论】 xùlùn introduction
【绪言】 xùyán introduction

**续** xù ① continuous; successive ② continue; extend; join: 待～ to be continued/ ～会 extended session; follow-up meeting/ 这条绳子太短，再～上一截儿吧。This piece of string is too short. Join another piece on to it. ③ add; supply more: 壶要烧干了，赶快～水。The kettle (on the fire) is nearly dry. Put some more water in it, quick./ 炉子该～煤了。The fire needs more coal.
【续编】 xùbiān continuation (of a book); sequel
【续订】 xùdìng renew one's subscription (to a newspaper or magazine)
【续断】 xùduàn 〈中药〉 teasel root
【续航力】 xùhánglì (飞机) endurance; (轮船) cruising radius
【续集】 xùjí continuation (of a book); sequel
【续假】 xùjià extend one's leave of absence; extend leave: ～一星期 have one's leave extended for another week
【续借】 xùjiè renew (a library book)
【续命汤】 xùmìngtāng a decoction to stimulate a dying person; lifesaver
【续弦】 xùxián 〈旧〉 remarry after the death of one's wife

**絮** xù ① (cotton) wadding ② sth. resembling cotton: 柳～ (willow) catkin ③ wad with cotton: ～被子 wad a quilt with cotton/ ～棉衣 line (或 wad) one's clothes with cotton ④ long-winded; garrulous
【絮叨】 xùdao long-winded; garrulous; wordy
【絮棉】 xùmián cotton for wadding

**婿** xù ① son-in-law ② husband: 夫～ husband/ 妹～ younger sister's husband

**蓄** xù ① store up; save up: 这个水库能～多少水？How much water can this reservoir hold? ② grow: ～须 grow a beard/ ～发 wear one's hair long ③ entertain (ideas); harbour: ～念已久 have long entertained such ideas
【蓄电池】 xùdiànchí storage battery; accumulator ◇ ～车 battery car
【蓄洪】 xùhóng 〈水〉 store floodwater: ～防旱 store floodwater for use against a drought ◇ ～工程 flood storage project
【蓄积】 xùjī store up; save up: ～粮食 store up grain
【蓄谋】 xùmóu premeditate: ～已久 long premeditated/ ～迫害 harbour a design of persecuting sb.
【蓄水】 xùshuǐ retain (或 store) water: 在山坡上建池～ dig ponds on the slopes to store water/ 这水库能～二千万立方米。This reservoir has a storage capacity of 20 million cubic metres. ◇ ～池 cistern; reservoir/ ～工程 (water) storage project
【蓄意】 xùyì premeditated; deliberate: ～挑衅 premeditated provocation/ ～进行破坏 deliberately sabotage/ ～干涉别国内政 be bent on interfering in other countries' internal affairs

**煦** xù 〈书〉 warm; balmy: 春风和～ a balmy spring breeze

## xu

**蓿** xu 见"苜蓿" mùxu

## xuān

**轩** xuān ① 〈书〉 high; lofty ② a small room or veranda with windows ③ a high-fronted, curtained carriage used in ancient times ④ 〈书〉 window or door
【轩昂】 xuān'áng dignified; imposing: 气宇～ have an imposing appearance; have an impressive presence
【轩敞】 xuānchǎng spacious and bright
【轩然大波】 xuānrán dàbō a great disturbance; a mighty uproar

【轩轾】 xuān-zhì high or low; good or bad: 不分～ be equal; be on a par

**宣** xuān ①declare; proclaim; announce: ～示 declare; make known publicly/ ～赦 proclaim a general amnesty/ ～旨 announce an imperial decree ②lead off (liquids); drain: ～泄洪水 drain off floodwater ③(Xuān) a surname

【宣布】 xuānbù declare; proclaim; announce: ～独立 declare (或 proclaim) independence/ ～会议开始 declare a meeting open; call a meeting to order/ ～无效 declare sth. invalid (或 null and void)/ ～戒严 declare (或 proclaim) martial law/ ～一件事 make an announcement

【宣称】 xuānchēng assert; declare; profess

【宣传】 xuānchuán conduct propaganda; propagate; disseminate; give publicity to: ～马克思主义、列宁主义、毛泽东思想 propagate Marxism-Leninism-Mao Zedong Thought/ ～共产主义思想 disseminate communist ideas/ ～党的方针政策 publicize the Party's general and specific policies/ ～群众 spread propaganda among the masses/ 做～要看对象。In doing propaganda we must consider our audience.

◇ ～车 propaganda car/ ～工具 instrument (或 means) of propaganda or publicity; mass media/ ～工作者 propagandist/ ～画 picture poster/ ～机构 propaganda organ/ ～机器 propaganda machine/ ～品 propaganda (或 publicity) material/ ～员 propagandist

【宣传队】 xuānchuánduì propaganda team: 文艺～ performing arts propaganda team

【宣读】 xuāndú read out (in public): ～中央文件 read out a Central Committee document

【宣告】 xuāngào declare; proclaim: ～成立 proclaim the founding of (a state, organization, etc.)/ ～无效 declare sth. null and void/ ～破产 declare bankruptcy; go bankrupt

【宣讲】 xuānjiǎng explain and publicise

【宣教】 xuānjiào propaganda and education

【宣判】 xuānpàn 〈法〉 pronounce judgment: ～有罪(无罪) pronounce sb. guilty (not guilty)

【宣誓】 xuānshì take (或 swear) an oath; make a vow; make a pledge: 庄严～ make a solemn vow/ 入党～ take the oath on being admitted to the Party/ ～就职 take an oath of office; be sworn in

【宣泄】 xuānxiè ①lead off (liquids); drain ②get sth. off one's chest; unbosom oneself

【宣叙调】 xuānxùdiào 〈乐〉 recitative

【宣言】 xuānyán declaration; manifesto: 《共产党～》 *Manifesto of the Communist Party*

【宣扬】 xuānyáng publicise; propagate; advocate; advertise: ～好人好事 give publicity to good people and their good deeds/ 反对～资产阶级生活方式 oppose all attempts to propagate the bourgeois way of life

【宣战】 xuānzhàn declare (或 proclaim) war

【宣纸】 xuānzhǐ *Xuan* paper, a high quality paper made in Xuancheng (宣城), Anhui Province, esp. good for traditional Chinese painting and calligraphy

**萱** xuān

【萱草】 xuāncǎo tawny daylily

**喧** xuān noisy: 锣鼓～天 a deafening sound of gongs and drums

【喧宾夺主】 xuān bīn duó zhǔ a presumptuous guest usurps the host's role; the secondary supersedes the primary

【喧哗】 xuānhuá confused noise; hubbub; uproar: 请勿～。Quiet, please!/ 笑语～ uproarious talk and laughter/ 门外一阵～。There was a hubbub outside the door.

【喧闹】 xuānnào noise and excitement; bustle; racket

【喧嚷】 xuānrǎng clamour; hubbub; din; racket: 人声～ a hubbub of voices; loud confused voices

【喧扰】 xuānrǎo noise and disturbance; tumult

【喧腾】 xuānténg noise and excitement; hubbub: 广场上一片～。A hubbub filled the square.

【喧嚣】 xuānxiāo ①noisy: ～的车马声 the noise of dense traffic ②clamour; hullabaloo; din: ～鼓噪 make a clamour; stir up a commotion/ 诸如此类的论调～一时。This sort of talk created quite a stir.

**暄** xuān ①〈书〉 warmth (of the sun): 负～ bask in the sunshine ②〈方〉 fluffy; soft: 馒头很～。The steamed bread is very fluffy./ 沙土地～,不好走。It's hard to walk on the soft sand.

【暄腾】 xuānteng 〈方〉 fluffy; soft

**煊** xuān 见"暄" xuān ①

## xuán

**玄** xuán ①black; dark: ～狐 a black fox ②profound; abstruse: ～理 a profound theory ③〈口〉 unreliable; incredible: 这话太～了。That's a pretty tall story.

【玄妙】 xuánmiào mysterious; abstruse

【玄明粉】 xuánmíngfěn 〈中药〉 compound of glauber-salt and liquorice

【玄青】 xuánqīng deep black

【玄参】 xuánshēn 〈中药〉 the root of Zhejiang figwort

【玄孙】 xuánsūn great-great-grandson

【玄武岩】 xuánwǔyán 〈地〉 basalt

【玄虚】 xuánxū deceitful trick; mystery: 故弄～ purposely turn simple things into mysteries; be deliberately mystifying

【玄学】 xuánxué ① a philosophical sect in the Wei (220–265) and Jin (265–420) dynasties ②〈哲〉 metaphysics

【玄之又玄】 xuán zhī yòu xuán mystery of mysteries — extremely mysterious and abstruse

**旋** xuán ①revolve; circle; spin: 觉得天～地转 feel as if heaven and earth were spinning round and round; feel one's head swim/ 一架飞机在空中盘～。An airplane is circling in the sky. ②return; come back: 凯～ return in triumph/ ～里 return home ③part of the scalp where the hair is whorled ④〈书〉 soon: 入场券～即发完。All the tickets were soon distributed.

另见 xuàn

【旋耕】 xuángēng rotary tillage ◇ ～机 rotary cultivator; rotocultivator

【旋管】 xuánguǎn 〈化〉 coil; coiled pipe; coiler

【旋光性】 xuánguāngxìng 〈物〉 optical rotation

【旋回】 xuánhuí 〈地〉 cycle: 造山～ orogenic cycle/ 构造～ tectonic cycle

【旋律】 xuánlǜ 〈乐〉 melody

【旋毛虫】 xuánmáochóng trichina

【旋钮】 xuánniǔ 〈机〉 knob

【旋桥】 xuánqiáo 〈建〉 swing bridge

【旋绕】 xuánrǎo curl up; wind around: 炊烟～。Smoke is curling up from the kitchen chimneys./ 他们的歌声在山谷中～。Their songs reverberated throughout the valley.

【旋塞】 xuánsāi 〈机〉 cock: 放水～ drain cock /三通～ three-way cock

【旋涡】 xuánwō whirlpool; vortex; eddy

【旋涡星云】 xuánwō xīngyún 〈天〉 spiral nebula
【旋翼机】 xuányìjī 〈航空〉 rotary-wing aircraft; rotorcraft
【旋踵】 xuánzhǒng 〈书〉 in the brief time it takes to turn round on one's heel — in an instant: ～即逝 vanish before one has time to turn round; disappear in the twinkling of an eye
【旋转】 xuánzhuǎn revolve; gyrate; rotate; spin: 陀螺在～。The top is spinning./ 地球绕地轴～,同时也围绕太阳～。The earth revolves round the sun on its own axis./ 顺时针方向～ clockwise rotation/ 逆时针方向～ counterclockwise rotation ◇ ～球 〈体〉 spinning ball/ ～钻井 〈石油〉 rotary drilling
【旋转乾坤】 xuánzhuǎn qiánkūn effect a drastic change in nature or the established order of a country; be earth-shaking

**悬** xuán ① hang; suspend: ～灯结彩 hang up lanterns and festoons; adorn with lanterns and festoons ② outstanding; unresolved: ～而未决的问题 an outstanding question/ 这笔账～了好久了。This account has remained unsettled for a long time. ③ feel anxious; be solicitous: ～念 be anxious about (sb. who is elsewhere) ④ imagine: ～拟 imagine; conjecture ⑤ far apart: ～隔 be separated by a great distance ⑥ 〈方〉 dangerous: 在快车道上骑自行车,可真～。Cycling in the fast traffic lane is really dangerous.
【悬案】 xuán'àn ① unsettled law case ② outstanding issue; unsettled question
【悬臂】 xuánbì 〈机〉 cantilever
◇ ～梁 〈建〉 cantilever beam/ ～起重机 cantilever crane/ ～桥 cantilever bridge
【悬浮】 xuánfú 〈化〉 suspension: ～体 suspended substance; suspension/ ～染色 suspension dyeing/ ～固体 〈环保〉 suspended solid
【悬谷】 xuángǔ 〈地〉 hanging valley
【悬挂】 xuánguà ① hang; fly: ～中国国旗的远洋轮船 ocean liners flying the Chinese flag/ 墙上～着毛主席和华主席的画像。The portraits of Chairman Mao and Chairman Hua hang on the wall./ 高大的建筑物上～着巨幅标语。Huge streamers trailed from tall buildings. ② 〈汽车〉 suspension ◇ ～犁 〈农〉 mounted plough
【悬乎】 xuánhu 〈方〉 dangerous; unsafe: 真～! 她差点让汽车给撞了。Whew, that was dangerous! She nearly got run over by the car./ 这件事让他去办,有点～。It's not safe to leave the matter in his hands.
【悬胶】 xuánjiāo 〈化〉 suspensoid ◇ ～态 suspensoid state
【悬空】 xuánkōng ① hang in the air; suspend in midair: 这件事不能老～,要抓紧解决。Let's deal with the matter now; it's hung in the air too long. ② be divorced from reality
【悬梁】 xuánliáng hang oneself from a beam: ～自尽 commit suicide by hanging oneself from a beam; hang oneself
【悬料】 xuánliào 〈冶〉 hanging
【悬铃木】 xuánlíngmù 〈植〉 plane tree
【悬念】 xuánniàn ① 〈书〉 be concerned about (sb. who is elsewhere) ② audience involvement in a film or play; reader involvement in a piece of literature
【悬赏】 xuánshǎng offer (或 post) a reward: ～缉拿逃犯 offer a reward for the capture of a runaway criminal; set a price on a runaway criminal's head
【悬殊】 xuánshū great disparity; wide gap: 力量～ a great disparity in strength/ 资本主义国家贫富～。There is a wide gap between the rich and the poor in capitalist countries.
【悬索结构】 xuánsuǒ jiégòu 〈建〉 suspended-cable structure
【悬索桥】 xuánsuǒqiáo suspension bridge
【悬梯】 xuántī hanging ladder
【悬腕】 xuánwàn (write big characters) with the wrist raised, i.e. not touching the desk
【悬想】 xuánxiǎng imagine; fancy
【悬心吊胆】 xuánxīn-diàodǎn on tenterhooks; filled with anxiety or fear
【悬崖】 xuányá overhanging (或 steep) cliff; precipice: ～绝壁 sheer precipice and overhanging rocks
【悬崖勒马】 xuányá lè mǎ rein in at the brink of the precipice — wake up to and escape disaster at the last moment
【悬雍垂】 xuányōngchuí 〈生理〉 uvula

## xuǎn

**选** xuǎn ① select; choose; pick: 挑～ pick and choose/ 比赛前～场地 choose sides before a contest ② elect: 普～ general election/ 我们～她当生产队长。We elected her leader of our production team./ 入～ be chosen (或 selected); be elected ③ selections; anthology: 文～ an anthology of prose/ 诗～ selected poems/ 民歌～ selections of folk songs
【选拔】 xuǎnbá select; choose: ～运动员 select athletes ◇ ～赛 (selective) trials/ ～委员会 selection committee
【选本】 xuǎnběn anthology; selected works
【选材】 xuǎncái select (suitable) material
【选场】 xuǎnchǎng selected scenes (from an opera, etc.)
【选读】 xuǎndú selected readings: 文学～ selected readings in literature
【选购】 xuǎngòu pick out and buy; choose: 新到各种花布,欢迎～。A new variety of cotton prints awaits your choice.
【选集】 xuǎnjí selected works (或 writings); selections; anthology: «毛泽东选集» *Selected Works of Mao Zedong*
【选举】 xuǎnjǔ elect: 直接(间接)～ direct (indirect) election/ 无记名投票～ elect by secret ballot
◇ ～程序 electoral procedure (或 proceedings)/ ～单位 electoral unit/ ～法 electoral law/ ～结果 election results (或 returns)
【选举权】 xuǎnjǔquán the right to vote; franchise: 有～和被～ have the right to vote and to stand for election
【选矿】 xuǎnkuàng 〈矿〉 ore dressing; mineral separation; beneficiation ◇ ～厂 ore dressing plant; concentration plant
【选民】 xuǎnmín (个人) voter; elector; (全体) constituency; electorate
◇ ～榜 list of eligible voters/ ～登记 registration of voters/ ～名册 voting register/ ～证 elector's certificate; voter registration card
【选派】 xuǎnpài select; detail: ～五名民兵守卫仓库 detail five militiamen to guard the warehouse/ ～代表参加会议 depute sb. to attend a conference; select sb. as representative to a conference
【选票】 xuǎnpiào vote; ballot
【选区】 xuǎnqū electoral (或 election) district; electoral ward; constituency
【选曲】 xuǎnqǔ selected songs (或 tunes): «白毛女»～ selected tunes from *The White-haired Girl*
【选取】 xuǎnqǔ select; choose
【选手】 xuǎnshǒu an athlete selected for a sports meet; (selected) contestant; player: 参加体操比赛的～有几百名。There were hundreds of contestants in the gymnastics competition.
【选修】 xuǎnxiū take as an elective course: 我们班大部分同学～英语。Most of the students of our class take English as an elective course. ◇ ～课 elective course
【选样】 xuǎnyàng sampling; sample

【选育】 xuǎnyù 〈农〉 seed selection; breeding: ～良种小麦 wheat variety development by selection
【选择】 xuǎnzé select; choose; opt: ～日期 choose a date/ 自然～ natural selection/ 没有～的余地 have no choice at all ◇ ～场地 〈体〉 choice of ends
【选种】 xuǎnzhǒng 〈农〉 seed selection

**烜** xuǎn ① ablaze ② bright
【烜赫】 xuǎnhè of great renown and influence

**癣** xuǎn tinea; ringworm
【癣疥之疾】 xuǎnjiè zhī jí only a skin complaint — some slight ailment

## xuàn

**泫** xuàn drip; trickle
【泫然】 xuànrán (usu. of tears) fall; trickle

**券** xuàn 见"拱券" gǒngxuàn
另见 quàn

**炫** xuàn 〈书〉 ① dazzle: 光彩～目 blindingly bright; dazzling splendour ② show off; display: 自～其能 show off one's ability
【炫示】 xuànshì show off; display
【炫耀】 xuànyào make a display of; show off; flaunt: ～力量 flaunt one's strength/ ～武力 make a show of force/ ～自己的学问 parade one's learning

**绚** xuàn gorgeous
【绚烂】 xuànlàn splendid; gorgeous: ～的朝霞 gorgeous morning clouds/ ～的杜鹃花 splendid azaleas
【绚丽】 xuànlì gorgeous; magnificent: ～多彩 bright and colourful; gorgeous/ ～的景色 magnificent scenery

**昡** xuàn sunshine; sunlight

**眩** xuàn 〈书〉 ① dizzy; giddy: 头晕目～ feel dizzy ② dazzled; bewildered: ～于名利 dazzled by the prospect of fame and wealth; obsessed with a desire for fame and wealth
【眩晕】 xuànyùn 〈医〉 ① dizziness: 一阵～ a fit of dizziness ② vertigo

**旋** xuàn ① whirl: ～风 whirlwind ② turn sth. on a lathe; lathe; pare: 把一根圆钢～成车轴 shape a round piece of steel into an axle/ 给孩子～一个苹果吃。Peel an apple for the child. ③〈副〉 at the time; at the last moment: ～用～买 buy sth. when you need it; buy for immediate use/ 客人到了～做，就来不及了。It'll be too late to start preparing dinner when the guests have arrived.
另见 xuán
【旋床】 xuànchuáng 〈机〉 (turning) lathe
【旋风】 xuànfēng whirlwind
【旋子】 xuànzi ① copper plate (for making sheets of bean-starch jelly) ② hot water container for warming wine

**渲** xuàn 〈书〉 wash (a piece of drawing paper) with watercolours
【渲染】 xuànrǎn ① apply colours to a drawing ② play up; exaggerate; pile it on: ～战争恐怖 play up the horrors of war/ 轻快的舞蹈给这场戏～了欢乐气氛。The lively dance heightened the joyous atmosphere of the scene.

**楦** xuàn ① shoe last ② hat block ③ shape with a last or block: ～鞋 last a shoe
【楦子】 xuànzi ① shoe last; shoe tree ② hat block

## xuē

**削** xuē 〔专用于合成词〕 pare; whittle; cut: 剥～ exploit
另见 xiāo
【削壁】 xuēbì precipice; cliff
【削价】 xuējià cut prices; lower the price
【削减】 xuējiǎn cut (down); reduce; slash; whittle down: ～非生产性开支 cut down nonproductive expenditures; cut back on nonproductive spending/ 抗议资本家～工资 protest against wage-cuts by capitalists
【削弱】 xuēruò weaken; cripple: 人民的武装只能加强，不能～。The people's armed forces must be strengthened, not weakened./ ～敌人的力量 cripple (或 weaken) the enemy
【削足适履】 xuē zú shì lǚ cut the feet to fit the shoes; act in a Procrustean manner

**靴** xuē boots: 马～ riding boots/ 雨～ rubber boots
【靴子】 xuēzi boots

**薛** Xuē a surname

## xué

**穴** xué ① cave; den; hole: 洞～ cave/ 蚁～ ant hole/ 虎～ tiger's lair/ 匪～ bandits' den ② grave ③〈中医〉 acupuncture point; acupoint
【穴播】 xuébō 〈农〉 bunch planting
【穴居】 xuéjū live in caves ◇ ～人 cave dweller; troglodyte
【穴位】 xuéwèi 〈中医〉 acupuncture point; acupoint ◇ ～注射疗法 therapy of point injection

**学** xué ① study; learn: 为革命而～ study for the revolution/ ～文化 acquire an elementary education; learn to read and write/ ～外语 learn (或 study) a foreign language/ ～先进 emulate the advanced/ 跟人～绘画 take lessons in painting/ 把新技术～到手 master a new skill/ 你的功课～会了吗？Have you learned your lessons?/ 活到老，～到老。Keep on learning as long as you live. ② imitate; mimic: 这孩子～他爸爸走路的样子。The boy imitates his father's way of walking./ ～鸡叫 mimic the crowing of a cock ③ learning; knowledge: 才疏～浅 have little talent and less learning ④ subject of study; branch of learning: 数～ mathematics/ 文～ literature/ 政治经济～ political economy ⑤ school; college: 小～ primary school/ 中～ middle school/ 大～ college; university/ 上～ go to school
【学报】 xuébào learned journal; journal
【学潮】 xuécháo student strike; campus upheaval
【学而不厌】 xué ér bù yàn have an insatiable desire to learn
【学阀】 xuéfá scholar-tyrant
【学费】 xuéfèi tuition fee; tuition
【学分】 xuéfēn 〈教〉 credit ◇ ～制 the credit system
【学风】 xuéfēng style of study: 发扬理论联系实际的好～ carry forward the good style of study of integrating theory with practice
【学府】 xuéfǔ seat of learning; institution of higher learning
【学好】 xuéhǎo learn from good examples; emulate good

【学会】 xuéhuì ① learn; master: 她～了游泳。She's learned to swim./ ～各种斗争方式 master all forms of struggle ② learned society; institute: 中国人民外交～ the Chinese People's Institute of Foreign Affairs
【学籍】 xuéjí one's status as a student; one's name on the school roll: 保留～ retain one's status as a student/ 取消～ be struck off the school roll
【学究】 xuéjiū pedant ◇ ～气 pedantry
【学科】 xuékē branch of learning; course; subject; discipline
【学力】 xuélì knowledge; educational level; academic attainments: 具有同等～ have the same educational level (as school graduates)
【学历】 xuélì record of formal schooling
【学龄】 xuélíng school age: ～儿童 children of school age; school-age children/ ～前儿童 preschool children; preschoolers
【学名】 xuémíng ① scientific name (e.g. Latin name for plants, etc.) ② formal name used at school (as distinguished from pet name at home)
【学年】 xuénián school (或 academic) year ◇ ～考试 year-end examination
【学派】 xuépài school of thought; school
【学期】 xuéqī school term; term; semester
【学前教育】 xuéqián jiàoyù preschool education; infant school education
【学舌】 xuéshé ① mechanically repeat other people's words; parrot: 鹦鹉～ imitate mechanically; parrot ② 〈口〉 loose-tongued; gossipy
【学生】 xuésheng ① student; pupil: 医科～ a medical student/ ～运动 student movement/ ～时代 school days/ 一派～腔 all in student jargon ② disciple; follower ◇ ～会 student union; student association/ ～证 student's identity card
【学时】 xuéshí class hour; period
【学识】 xuéshí learning; knowledge; scholarly attainments: ～渊博 have great learning; be learned/ ～浅薄 have little learning
【学士】 xuéshì ① scholar: 文人～ scholars; men of letters ② bachelor: 文～ Bachelor of Arts (B.A.)
【学术】 xuéshù learning; science: ～领域 sphere of learning/ 国际～交流活动 international academic exchanges
◇ ～报告 learned report; academic report /～界 academic circles/ ～论文 research paper; scientific paper; thesis/ ～讨论会 academic discussion; scientific conference; symposium/ ～团体 learned society/ ～研究 academic research
【学说】 xuéshuō theory; doctrine: 阶级斗争～ the theory of class struggle/ 达尔文的进化论～ Darwin's theory of evolution
【学堂】 xuétáng 〈旧〉 school
【学徒】 xuétú apprentice; trainee: 在机床厂～ be an apprentice in a machine tool plant/ ～期满 have served one's apprenticeship ◇ ～工 apprentice
【学位】 xuéwèi academic degree; degree: 博士～ doctor's degree; doctorate/ 名誉～ honorary degree
【学问】 xuéwen learning; knowledge; scholarship: 做～ engage in scholarship; do research/ ～高深的人 a man of great learning; an erudite scholar/ 别看种菜好象没啥，其实大有～。Growing vegetables looks easy, but actually it takes a lot of learning.
【学无止境】 xué wú zhǐjìng knowledge is infinite; there is no limit to knowledge
【学习】 xuéxí study; learn; emulate: 马克思列宁主义是一切革命者都应该～的科学。The science of Marxism-Leninism must be studied by all revolutionaries./ ～别人的长处，克服自己的弱点 emulate others' strong points and overcome one's own weaknesses/ 以王铁人为～的榜样 model oneself on Iron Man Wang; follow the example of Iron Man Wang
◇ ～班 study class/ ～成绩 academic record; school record/ ～年限 period of schooling
【学衔】 xuéxián academic rank (或 title)
【学校】 xuéxiào school; educational institution: 师范～ teachers' school; normal school/ 专业～ specialized school/ 高等～ institution of higher learning
【学业】 xuéyè one's studies; school work
【学以致用】 xué yǐ zhì yòng study for the purpose of application; study sth. in order to apply it
【学员】 xuéyuán student (usu. of a college or a training course)
【学院】 xuéyuàn college; academy; institute: 师范～ teachers training college/ 军事～ military institute/ 建筑工程～ institute of civil engineering/ 美术～ school of art/ 音乐～ conservatory (或 academy) of music
【学者】 xuézhě scholar; learned man; man of learning
【学制】 xuézhì ① educational (或 school) system: ～改革 reform in the school system ② length of schooling: 缩短～ shorten the period of schooling

**噱** xué 〈方〉 laugh: 发～ make one laugh; excite laughter
另见 jué
【噱头】 xuétóu 〈方〉 ① words or act meant to amuse or to excite laughter: 这个丑角～真多。That clown is full of amusing tricks./ 卖弄～ play to the gallery ② tricks meant to deceive: 不要摆～! Don't try any tricks! 或 None of your tricks!

## xuě

**雪** xuě ① snow: 一场大～ a heavy fall of snow/ 路上积～很深。The roads are deep in snow. ② wipe out (a humiliation); avenge (a wrong): ～耻 avenge an insult; wipe out a humiliation/ 昭～ right a wrong; clear sb. of an unjust or unfounded charge; rehabilitate
【雪白】 xuěbái snow-white; snowy white
【雪板】 xuěbǎn 〈体〉 ski
【雪豹】 xuěbào 〈动〉 snow leopard
【雪暴】 xuěbào snowstorm; blizzard
【雪崩】 xuěbēng snowslide; avalanche
【雪堆】 xuěduī snow drift
【雪纺绸】 xuěfǎngchóu 〈纺〉 chiffon
【雪糕】 xuěgāo 〈方〉 ice cream
【雪恨】 xuěhèn wreak vengeance; avenge: 报仇～ avenge oneself; take revenge
【雪花】 xuěhuā snowflake
【雪花膏】 xuěhuāgāo vanishing cream
【雪鸡】 xuějī 〈动〉 snow cock
【雪茄】 xuějiā cigar
【雪晶】 xuějīng 〈气〉 snow crystals
【雪犁】 xuělí 〈农〉 snow plough
【雪里红】 xuělǐhóng 〈植〉 potherb mustard
【雪亮】 xuěliàng bright as snow; shiny: 把自行车擦得～ polish the bike till it has a good shine/ 灯光～ dazzling lamplight/ 阶级敌人尽管狡猾，但人民的眼睛是～的。The class enemy may be cunning but the people's eyes are discerning.
【雪柳】 xuěliǔ 〈植〉 fontanesia (*Fontanesia fortunei*)
【雪盲】 xuěmáng 〈医〉 snow blindness

【雪片】 xuěpiàn snowflake: 贺电如～飞来。Messages of congratulation poured in./ 请战书象～似地飞向指挥部。Headquarters was swamped by an avalanche of applications for battle assignments.
【雪橇】 xuěqiāo sled; sledge; sleigh
【雪青】 xuěqīng lilac (colour)
【雪雀】 xuěquè 〈动〉 snow finch
【雪人】 xuěrén snowman
【雪上加霜】 xuě shàng jiā shuāng snow plus frost — one disaster after another
【雪条】 xuětiáo 〈方〉 ice-lolly; frozen sucker; popsicle
【雪线】 xuěxiàn 〈地〉 snow line
【雪冤】 xuěyuān clear sb. of a false charge; redress a wrong
【雪原】 xuěyuán snowfield
【雪杖】 xuězhàng 〈体〉 (ski) pole; (ski) stick
【雪中送炭】 xuě zhōng sòng tàn send charcoal in snowy weather — provide timely help

**鳕** xuě cod

## xuè

**血** xuè ① blood: 流～ shed blood/ 出～ bleed/ ～的教训 a lesson paid for with blood; a lesson written in blood ② related by blood: ～亲 blood relation
另见 xiě
【血案】 xuè'àn murder case
【血本】 xuèběn principal; original capital
【血崩症】 xuèbēngzhèng 〈医〉 metrorrhagia
【血沉】 xuèchén 〈医〉 erythrocyte sedimentation rate (ESR)
【血管】 xuèguǎn 〈生理〉 blood vessel ◇ ～瘤 haemangioma; angioma/ ～造影 angiography
【血海】 xuèhǎi a sea of blood: ～深仇 a huge debt of blood; intense and deep-seated hatred
【血汗】 xuèhàn blood and sweat; sweat and toil: ～钱 money earned by hard toil/ 资本家吮吸工人的～。Capitalists fatten themselves on the workers' sweat and toil.
【血红】 xuèhóng blood red
【血红蛋白】 xuèhóng dànbái 〈生化〉 haemoglobin
【血迹】 xuèjì bloodstain: ～斑斑 bloodstained/ 踏着烈士的～前进 march along the path crimson with the martyrs' blood
【血浆】 xuèjiāng 〈生理〉 (blood) plasma
【血竭】 xuèjié 〈中药〉 dragon's blood (*Daemonorops draco*)
【血口喷人】 xuèkǒu pēn rén make unfounded and malicious attacks upon sb.; venomously slander
【血库】 xuèkù 〈医〉 blood bank
【血亏】 xuèkuī 〈中医〉 anaemia
【血泪】 xuèlèi tears of blood: ～帐 debts of blood and tears/ ～斑斑的家史 family history of blood and tears/ 旧社会劳苦大众家家都有一部～史。In the old society all working people had a family history written in blood and tears.
【血淋淋】 xuèlínlín dripping with blood; bloody
【血尿】 xuèniào 〈医〉 blood in the urine; haematuria
【血泊】 xuèpō pool of blood
【血气】 xuèqì ① animal spirits; sap; vigour: ～方刚 full of sap ② courage and uprightness: 有～的青年 a courageous and upright youth
【血清】 xuèqīng 〈生理〉 (blood) serum ◇ ～病 serum sickness (或 disease)
【血球】 xuèqiú 〈生理〉 blood cell; blood corpuscle
【血肉】 xuèròu flesh and blood: ～之躯 the human body; flesh and blood
【血肉相连】 xuèròu xiānglián as close as flesh and blood: ～的阶级兄弟 class brothers as close to each other as flesh and blood/ 和人民群众～ maintain flesh-and-blood ties with the masses of the people
【血色】 xuèsè redness of the skin; colour: 脸上几乎没有～ have little colour in the cheeks; look pale
【血色素】 xuèsèsù 〈生理〉 haemochrome
【血书】 xuèshū a letter (expressing one's determination, last wish, etc.) written in one's own blood
【血栓】 xuèshuān 〈医〉 thrombus ◇ ～形成 thrombosis
【血糖】 xuètáng 〈医〉 blood sugar
【血统】 xuètǒng blood relationship; blood lineage; extraction: 中国～的外国人 foreign nationals of Chinese descent/ 德国～的美国人 Americans of German extraction/ ～工人 (industrial) worker of working-class parentage
【血吸虫】 xuèxīchóng blood fluke ◇ ～病 snail fever; schistosomiasis
【血象】 xuèxiàng 〈医〉 blood picture; hemogram
【血小板】 xuèxiǎobǎn 〈生理〉 (blood) platelet
【血腥】 xuèxīng reeking of blood; bloody; sanguinary: ～的白色恐怖 bloody white terror/ ～味 smell of blood/ ～统治 sanguinary (或 bloodstained) rule/ 反动统治者～地镇压人民。The reactionary rulers carried out a bloody suppression of the people.
【血型】 xuèxíng 〈生理〉 blood group; blood type ◇ ～分类 typing of blood
【血性】 xuèxìng courage and uprightness
【血胸】 xuèxiōng 〈医〉 haemothorax
【血虚】 xuèxū 〈中医〉 deficiency of blood and pathological changes caused by it
【血循环】 xuèxúnhuán 〈生理〉 blood circulation
【血压】 xuèyā 〈生理〉 blood pressure: 高～ high blood pressure; hypertension/ 低～ low blood pressure; hypotension ◇ ～计 sphygmomanometer
【血液】 xuèyè blood: 新鲜～ fresh blood/ 石油是工业的～。Petroleum is the lifeblood of industry. ◇ ～体外循环 〈医〉 extracorporeal circulation
【血衣】 xuèyī bloodstained garment; clothes covered with gore
【血印】 xuèyìn bloodstain
【血友病】 xuèyǒubìng haemophilia
【血雨腥风】 xuèyǔ-xīngfēng a foul wind and a rain of blood — reactionary reign of terror
【血缘】 xuèyuán ties of blood; consanguinity; blood relationship
【血债】 xuèzhài a debt of blood: ～累累 have heavy blood debts/ ～要用血来还。Debts of blood must be paid in blood. 或 Blood must atone for blood.
【血战】 xuèzhàn bloody (或 sanguinary) battle: ～到底 fight to the last drop of one's blood; fight to the bitter end
【血肿】 xuèzhǒng 〈医〉 haematoma

**谑** xuè 〈书〉 crack a joke; banter; tease: 戏～ banter; tease/ ～而不虐 tease without embarrassing

## xūn

**勋** xūn merit; meritorious service; achievement: 功～ meritorious service; contribution
【勋绩】 xūnjī meritorious service; outstanding contribution
【勋爵】 xūnjué ① a feudal title of nobility conferred for meritorious service ② (英国) Lord
【勋劳】 xūnláo meritorious service: 卓著～ noted for mer-

itorious service
【勋业】 xūnyè 〈书〉 meritorious service and great achievement
【勋章】 xūnzhāng medal; decoration

**埙** xūn an ancient egg-shaped, holed wind instrument

**熏** xūn ① smoke; fumigate: 烟把厨房的墙壁～黑了。The kitchen walls were blackened by smoke./ 我被烟～得直流眼泪。The smoke brought tears to my eyes./ ～蚊子 smoke out mosquitoes/ ～房间 fumigate a room ② treat (meat, fish, etc.) with smoke; smoke: ～鱼 smoked fish
另见 xùn
【熏风】 xūnfēng 〈书〉 a warm southerly breeze
【熏染】 xūnrǎn exert a gradual, corrupting influence on: 受资产阶级思想的～ be gradually influenced by bourgeois ideas
【熏陶】 xūntáo exert a gradual, uplifting influence on; nurture; edify: 起～作用 exert an edifying influence on/ 在集体主义精神的～下,孩子们互相关心,互相帮助。Nurtured in the spirit of collectivism, the children care for each other and help each other.
【熏蒸】 xūnzhēng ① stifling; suffocating: 暑气～ stifling summer heat ② 〈中医〉 fuming or steaming — treating diseases with fumes as in moxibustion or with steam generated by boiling medicinal herbs ③ fumigate ◇ ～剂 〈农〉 fumigant
【熏制】 xūnzhì smoke; fumigate (sth. with jasmine, etc.); cure (meat, etc.) by smoke

**薰** xūn 〈书〉 ① a kind of sweet grass ② fragrance (of flowers, etc.) ③ 见"熏" xūn

**曛** xūn ① dim glow of the setting sun ② dusk; nightfall

**醺** xūn drunk: 醉～～的 dead drunk; tight/ 微～ tipsy

## xún

**旬** xún ① a period of ten days: ～日 ten days/ 兼～ twenty days/ 上(中、下)～ the first (second, last) ten days of a month/ 按～计算 calculate in ten-day periods ② a period of ten years in a person's age (applied only to old persons): 八～老母 80-year-old mother
【旬刊】 xúnkān a publication appearing once every ten days

**驯** xún ① tame and docile: ～象 a tame elephant ② tame; domesticate: 善于～虎 good at taming tigers/ ～马 break in a horse
【驯服】 xúnfú ① docile; tame; tractable ② tame; break; domesticate: 这匹野马终于被～了。The wild horse was finally broken in./ ～洪水 bring a flood under control
【驯化】 xúnhuà domestication; taming: 鹿群经过～,可以放牧。Deer can be tamed and trained to go out to pasture.
【驯良】 xúnliáng tractable; docile; tame and gentle
【驯鹿】 xúnlù 〈动〉 reindeer
【驯顺】 xúnshùn tame and docile
【驯养】 xúnyǎng raise and train (animals); domesticate

**寻** xún ① look for; search; seek: ～物 look for sth. lost/ ～欢作乐 seek pleasure ② an ancient measure of length, equal to about eight *chi* (尺)
另见 xín
【寻常】 xúncháng ordinary; usual; common: 不～ unusual; out of the ordinary/ 异乎～的冷 extraordinarily cold/ 在我国,妇女开拖拉机是很～的事。In our country it's a common thing for women to drive tractors.
【寻的】 xúndì 〈军〉 target-seeking; homing ◇ ～导弹 homing missile
【寻访】 xúnfǎng look for (sb. whose whereabouts is unknown); try to locate; make inquiries about
【寻根究底】 xúngēn-jiūdǐ get to the bottom of things; inquire deeply into
【寻机】 xúnjī look for an opportunity
【寻开心】 xún kāixīn 〈方〉 make fun of; joke
【寻觅】 xúnmì seek; look for
【寻求】 xúnqiú seek; explore; go in quest of: ～真理 seek truth/ ～打开僵局的途径 explore possible paths for ending the stalemate
【寻事生非】 xúnshì-shēngfēi seek a quarrel; make trouble
【寻味】 xúnwèi chew sth. over; ruminate; think over: 他这番话耐人～。What he has said affords much food for thought.
【寻衅】 xúnxìn pick a quarrel; provoke
【寻章摘句】 xúnzhāng-zhāijù cull phrases but not meaning; write in *clichés* without originality
【寻找】 xúnzhǎo seek; look for

**巡** xún ① patrol; make one's rounds: ～夜 go on night patrol/ 矿上的医生每天～诊。The doctors at the mine make their rounds of visits every day. ② 〈量〉〔用于给全座斟酒〕 round of drinks: 酒过三～。The wine has gone round three times.
【巡边员】 xúnbiānyuán 〈足球〉 linesman
【巡捕】 xúnbǔ police or policeman (in former foreign concessions) ◇ ～房 police station (in former foreign concessions)
【巡查】 xúnchá go on a tour of inspection; make one's rounds
【巡风】 xúnfēng keep watch
【巡航】 xúnháng cruise
◇ ～半径 〈军〉 cruising radius/ ～导弹 cruise missile/ ～速度 cruising speed
【巡回】 xúnhuí go the rounds; tour; make a circuit of: 剧团正在全国各地～演出。The theatrical troupe is touring the country./ 教师到放牧点上进行～教学。The teachers make a circuit of the herding centres to give lessons.
◇ ～大使 roving ambassador/ ～放映队 mobile film projection unit/ ～剧团 itinerant theatrical troupe/ ～医疗队 mobile medical team
【巡警】 xúnjǐng 〈旧〉 policeman
【巡礼】 xúnlǐ ① visit a sacred land; go on a pilgrimage ② tour; sight-seeing
【巡逻】 xúnluó go on patrol; patrol: 执行～任务 be on patrol duty; be on one's beat
◇ ～队 patrol party; patrol/ ～护卫舰 patrol escort/ ～艇 patrol boat/ ～线 patrol route
【巡视】 xúnshì make (或 be on) an inspection tour; tour: ～各地 make an inspection tour of various places
【巡幸】 xúnxìng 〈旧〉 (of a monarch) go on an inspection tour
【巡洋舰】 xúnyángjiàn cruiser
【巡弋】 xúnyì (of warships) cruise

**询** xún ask; inquire: 查～ make inquiries (about)
【询问】 xúnwèn ask about; inquire: ～我们学习情况 ask us about our studies/ ～病状 inquire about sb.'s illness

**洵** xún 〈书〉 truly; indeed

**峋** xún 见"嶙峋" línxún

**浔** xún ①〈书〉 waterside ②(Xún) another name for Jiujiang (九江)

**荀** Xún a surname

**循** xún follow; abide by: ～此前进 proceed along this line/ ～例 follow the usual practice; follow a precedent

【循规蹈矩】 xúnguī-dǎojǔ follow rules, orders, etc. docilely; conform to convention; toe the line

【循环】 xúnhuán circulate; cycle: ～不息 move in endless cycles/ 四季的～ the cycle of the seasons/ 血液～ blood circulation/ 恶性～ vicious circle/ 四程～ 〈机〉 four stroke cycle
◇ ～论证 〈逻〉 argue in a circle/ ～赛 〈体〉 round robin/ ～系统 〈生理〉 the circulatory system/ ～小数 〈数〉 recurring decimal/ ～信用证 revolving letter of credit

【循名责实】 xún míng zé shí expect the reality to correspond to the name

【循序】 xúnxù in proper order or sequence: ～渐进 follow in order and advance step by step; proceed in an orderly way and step by step

【循循善诱】 xúnxún shàn yòu be good at giving systematic guidance; teach with skill and patience

**鲟** xún 〈动〉 sturgeon

## xùn

**讯** xùn ①interrogate; question: 审～犯人 interrogate a prisoner ②message; dispatch: 电～ a telegraphic report; dispatch/ 据新华社～ according to a Xinhua dispatch/ 消防队闻～赶到。On hearing the alarm the fire brigade rushed to the scene.

【讯问】 xùnwèn ①interrogate; question: ～被告人 interrogate the defendant ②ask about; inquire

**训** xùn ①lecture; teach; train: ～他一顿 give him a lecture (或 a dressing down)/ 受～ undergo training ②standard; model; example: 不足为～ not fit to serve as a model

【训斥】 xùnchì reprimand; rebuke; dress down

【训词】 xùncí admonition; instructions

【训诂】 xùngǔ explanations of words in ancient books; gloss ◇ ～学 critical interpretation of ancient texts

【训话】 xùnhuà 〈旧〉 (give) an admonitory talk to subordinates

【训诲】 xùnhuì 〈书〉 instruct; teach

【训诫】 xùnjiè ①admonish; advise ②rebuke; reprimand

【训练】 xùnliàn train; drill: ～部队 train troops/ 实战～ exercises under battle conditions/ ～有素的运动员 a well-trained athlete

【训练班】 xùnliànbān training class; training course: 养猪～ a training course in pig-farming/ 短期～ short course

【训令】 xùnlìng 〈旧〉 instructions; order; directive

**汛** xùn flood; high water: 秋～ autumn floods/ 防～ flood control/ ～情严重。The flood (situation) is serious.

【汛期】 xùnqī 〈水〉 flood (或 high-water) season

**迅** xùn fast; swift

【迅即】 xùnjí immediately; at once: 此事望～处理。It is hoped that immediate action will be taken on this matter.

【迅疾】 xùnjí swift; rapid

【迅捷】 xùnjié fast; agile; quick

【迅雷不及掩耳】 xùnléi bùjí yǎn ěr a sudden peal of thunder leaves no time for covering the ears; as sudden as lightning: 以～之势袭击敌人 fall on the enemy with the suddenness of a thunderbolt

【迅猛】 xùnměng swift and violent: 水势～异常。The flood roared on, swift and violent.

【迅速】 xùnsù rapid; swift; speedy; prompt: 动作～ swift in action; quick-moving/ 工农业的～发展 rapid development of industry and agriculture/ ～取得成效 produce speedy results/ ～作出决定 come to a prompt decision/ ～召开现场会 lose no time in calling an on-the-spot meeting/ 我国石油工业发展～。Our oil industry is expanding by leaps and bounds.

**逊** xùn ①abdicate ②modest: 谦～ modest/ 出言不～ speak insolently ③〈书〉 inferior: 稍～一筹 be slightly inferior

【逊色】 xùnsè be inferior: 毫无～ be by no means inferior/ 其他玉雕跟这件相比大为～。Other jade carvings pale beside this.

【逊位】 xùnwèi abdicate

**徇** xùn ①〈书〉 give in to; submit to; comply with ②见"殉" xùn②

【徇情】 xùnqíng 〈书〉 act wrongly out of personal considerations; practise favouritism: ～枉法 bend the law for the benefit of relatives or friends

【徇私】 xùnsī 见"徇情"

**殉** xùn ①be buried alive with the dead ②sacrifice one's life for

【殉国】 xùnguó die (或 give one's life) for one's country

【殉难】 xùnnàn die (for a just cause or for one's country)

【殉葬】 xùnzàng be buried alive with the dead: ～的奴隶 slaves buried alive with their deceased masters ◇ ～品 funerary object; sacrificial object/ ～制度 institution of burying the living with the dead

【殉职】 xùnzhí die at one's post; die in the course of performing one's duty; die in line of duty

**熏** xùn 〈方〉 be poisoned or suffocated by coal gas
另见 xūn

**蕈** xùn 〈植〉 gill fungus

# Y

## yā

**丫** yā bifurcation; fork
【丫杈】 yāchà ① fork (of a tree); crotch ② crotched; forked
【丫鬟】 yāhuan 〈旧〉 slave girl; servant girl
【丫头】 yātou ① 〈方〉 girl ② 〈旧〉 slave girl

**压** yā ① press; push down; hold down; weigh down: ～扁 press flat; flatten/ ～碎 crush (to pieces)/ 用石头～住地图的四角 put a stone on each corner of the map to hold it down/ 果子把树枝～弯了。The fruit weighed the branches down./ 这盒子怕～。This box won't stand much weight./ 中国人民推翻了～在头上的三座大山。The Chinese people overthrew the three big mountains (imperialism, feudalism and bureaucrat capitalism) that had lain like a dead weight on their backs. ② keep under control; control; keep under; quell: 喝点热水把咳嗽～一～ drink some hot water to ease a cough/ ～住阵脚 keep the troops in battle array; hold the line/ ～低嗓门 lower one's voice; speak under one's breath/ 强～住心头怒火 try hard to control one's anger; hold back one's rage/ 我们的重机枪～住了敌人的火力。Our heavy machine guns stilled the enemy's fire. ③ bring pressure to bear on; suppress; daunt; intimidate: 不受捧,不怕～ withstand both flattery and pressure/ 别拿大帽子～人。Don't you try to intimidate people by pinning labels on them./ 再大的自然灾害也～不垮我们。 Even a greater natural calamity cannot daunt us./ 资本家妄图～工人复工。The capitalists vainly tried to force the workers to end the strike. ④ approach; be getting near: 太阳～山了。The setting sun was touching the hilltop. ⑤ pigeonhole; shelve: 这份公文～了不少时间。This document was pigeonholed for quite some time. ⑥ risk (money, etc.) on sth.; stake ⑦ pressure: 血～ blood pressure
另见 yà
【压宝】 yābǎo a gambling game, played with dice under a bowl; stake
【压仓物】 yācāngwù 〈航海〉 ballast
【压秤】 yāchèng be relatively heavy per unit volume: 干稻草不～。Dry straw doesn't weigh much.
【压床】 yāchuáng 〈机〉 press (machine): 手板～ arbor press
【压倒】 yādǎo overwhelm; overpower; prevail over: ～一切的任务 an overriding task/ 以～多数通过一项决议 pass a resolution by an overwhelming majority/ 困难压不倒我们。No difficulty can overwhelm us./ 东风～西风。The East Wind prevails over the West Wind./ 任何敌人也不能～我们,而只会被我们所～。No enemy can crush us while we can crush every enemy.
【压电】 yādiàn 〈物〉 piezoelectricity ◇ ～晶体 piezocrystal; piezoelectric crystal/ ～拾音器 piezoelectric pickup
【压锻】 yāduàn 〈冶〉 press forging
【压队】 yāduì bring up the rear
【压服】 yāfú force (或 compel) sb. to submit: ～手段 coercive measure/ 解决思想问题只能靠说服,不能～。Ideological problems can be solved only through persuasion, not by coercion.
【压盖】 yāgài 〈机〉 gland ◇ ～填料 gland packing
【压挤】 yājǐ 〈机〉 extrusion ◇ ～成形 extrusion moulding
【压价】 yājià force prices down; demand a lower price: ～出售 undersell/ ～百分之二十五 force the price down by 25 per cent
【压惊】 yājīng help sb. get over a shock (by entertaining him, etc.)
【压井】 yājǐng 〈石油〉 kill the well
【压境】 yājìng (of enemy troops) press on to the border: 大军～。A large enemy force is bearing down upon the border.
【压力】 yālì ① 〈物〉 pressure: 大气～ atmospheric (或 barometric) pressure/ 外界～ ambient pressure ② overwhelming force; pressure: 对某人施加～ bring pressure to bear on sb.
◇ ～锅 pressure cooker/ ～机 press/ ～计 pressure gauge; manometer
【压裂】 yāliè 〈石油〉 fracture: 水力～ hydraulic fracturing ◇ ～车 fracturing unit truck
【压路机】 yālùjī road roller; roller
【压迫】 yāpò ① oppress; repress: ～其他民族的民族不可能是自由的。No nation can be free if it oppresses other nations./ 国家是一个阶级～另一个阶级的机关。The state is a machine with which one class represses another. ② constrict: 肿瘤～神经,引起疼痛。The tumour constricts the nerves and causes pain./ 病人胸部有～感。The patient feels a constriction in the chest. ◇ ～阶级 oppressor class/ ～者 oppressor
【压气】 yāqì calm sb.'s anger: 说几句好话给他压压气。Say a few agreeable words to calm him down.
【压强】 yāqiáng 〈物〉 intensity of pressure; pressure ◇ ～计 pressure gauge
【压青】 yāqīng 〈农〉 green manuring (或 dressing)
【压热效应】 yārè xiàoyìng 〈物〉 piezocaloric effect
【压舌板】 yāshébǎn 〈医〉 (tongue) depressor
【压岁钱】 yāsuìqián money given to children as a lunar New Year gift (in the old days)
【压缩】 yāsuō compress; condense; reduce; cut down: ～开支 cut down (或 reduce) expenses; retrench/ 这篇文章可以～一下。The article can be cut down. ◇ ～饼干 ship biscuit; pilot bread; hardtack/ ～空气 compressed air
【压缩机】 yāsuōjī compressor: 空气～ air compressor
【压条】 yātiáo 〈农〉 layering 又作"压枝"
【压痛】 yātòng 〈医〉 tenderness
【压头】 yātóu 〈水〉 pressure head: 有效～ effective head
【压线】 yāxiàn 〈体〉 line ball
【压延机】 yāyánjī 〈机〉 calender; mangler
【压抑】 yāyì ① constrain; inhibit; depress; hold back: 心情～ feel constrained/ 这部影片气氛比较～。The film is rather depressing. ② oppressive; stifling: 胸口感到～ feel tight in the chest
【压韵】 yāyùn rhyme: 这两句不～。These two lines don't rhyme.
【压载舱】 yāzàicāng 〈航海〉 ballast tank
【压榨】 yāzhà ① press; squeeze: ～甘蔗 press sugar cane ② oppress and exploit; bleed: 垄断资本家加紧对劳动人民的～。The monopoly capitalists are intensifying their exploitation of the working people. ◇ ～机 squeezer; mangle
【压纸型机】 yāzhǐxíngjī 〈印〉 stereotype press
【压制】 yāzhì ① suppress; stifle; inhibit: ～批评 suppress

(或 muzzle) criticism/ ～不同意见 stifle differing opinions/ ～群众的首创精神 inhibit the initiative of the masses/ 采用～手段 adopt repressive measures ②〈机〉pressing ◇～板 pressboard/ ～射击〈军〉neutralizing (或 neutralization) fire
【压轴子】 yāzhòuzi ① the last item but one on a theatrical programme ② present a theatrical performance as the last but one item on a programme: 明儿晚上拿《空城计》来～。Let's have *The Empty City Ruse* as the second major item for tomorrow evening's performance.
【压铸】 yāzhù 〈冶〉die-casting

**呀** yā ①〈叹〉〔表示惊异〕ah; oh: ～,下雪了! Oh, it's snowing! ②〈象〉creak: 门～的一声开了。The door opened with a creak.
另见 ya

**押** yā ① give as security; mortgage; pawn; pledge: 以手表作～ leave one's watch as security ② detain; take into custody: 在～犯 criminal in custody ③ escort: ～车 escort goods on a train, truck, etc./ ～行李 escort luggage/ 把小偷～到派出所去 escort the thief to the police station/ ～下去! Take him away. ④ signature; mark in lieu of signature: 画～ mark (a document) in lieu of signature; sign
【押宝】 yābǎo 见"压宝" yābǎo
【押当】 yādàng ① pawn sth. ② a small pawnshop
【押解】 yājiè send (a criminal or captive) under escort; escort: ～出境 deport under escort
【押金】 yājīn cash pledge; deposit
【押款】 yākuǎn 〈商〉① borrow money on security ② a loan on security
【押送】 yāsòng send under escort; escort
【押尾】 yāwěi sign or mark in lieu of signature at the end of a document
【押运】 yāyùn escort (goods) in transportation
【押韵】 yāyùn 见"压韵" yāyùn
【押帐】 yāzhàng leave (或 offer) sth. as security for a loan
【押租】 yāzū rent deposit

**哑** yā 见"呀" yā
另见 yǎ

**鸦** yā crow
【鸦胆子】 yādǎnzǐ 〈中药〉Java brucea (*Brucea javanica*)
【鸦片】 yāpiàn opium
【鸦片战争】 Yāpiàn Zhànzhēng the Opium War (Britain's invasion of China, 1840-1842)
【鸦雀】 yāquè 〈动〉crow tit
【鸦雀无声】 yā-què wú shēng not even a crow or sparrow can be heard — silence reigns

**桠** yā fork (of a tree)
【桠杈】 yāchà ① fork (of a tree); crotch ② crotched; forked

**鸭** yā duck: 母～ duck/ 公～ drake/ 小～ duckling
【鸭蛋】 yādàn duck's egg ◇ ～青 pale blue/ ～圆 oval
【鸭梨】 yālí a kind of pear grown in Hebei Province
【鸭绒】 yāróng duck's down; eiderdown: ～被 eiderdown quilt; duck's down quilt/ ～背心 duck's down waistcoat
【鸭舌帽】 yāshémào peaked cap
【鸭胗儿】 yāzhēnr duck's gizzard
【鸭跖草】 yāzhícǎo 〈中药〉dayflower (*Commelina communis*)
【鸭子儿】 yāzǐr 〈口〉duck's egg
【鸭子】 yāzi 〈口〉duck
【鸭嘴笔】 yāzuǐbǐ drawing pen; ruling pen
【鸭嘴兽】 yāzuǐshòu platypus; duckbill; duckmole

## yá

**牙** yá ① tooth ② tooth-like thing: 轮～ cog ③ ivory: ～筷 ivory chopsticks/ ～章 ivory seal
【牙碜】 yáchen ① (of food) gritty ② (of language) jarring; coarse
【牙齿】 yáchǐ tooth
【牙床】 yáchuáng ①〈生理〉gum ② ivory-inlaid bed
【牙雕】 yádiāo ivory carving
【牙粉】 yáfěn tooth powder
【牙疳】 yágān 〈医〉noma; cancrum oris
【牙膏】 yágāo toothpaste
【牙垢】 yágòu tartar; dental calculus
【牙关】 yáguān mandibular joint: 咬紧～ clench (或 grit) one's teeth ◇ ～紧闭〈医〉lockjaw
【牙行】 yáháng 〈旧〉① middleman ② broker house
【牙科】 yákē 〈医〉(department of) dentistry ◇ ～医生 dentist; dental surgeon/ ～诊疗所 dental clinic
【牙口】 yákou ① the age of a draught animal as shown by the number of its teeth: 看一看～ look at a draught animal's teeth to determine its age ② the condition of an old person's teeth: 您这么大年纪,～可不错呀! You've certainly got good teeth for your age.
【牙轮】 yálún gear wheel; gear
【牙买加】 Yámǎijiā Jamaica ◇ ～人 Jamaican
【牙鲆】 yápíng 〈动〉lefteye flounder (*Paralichthys*)
【牙签】 yáqiān toothpick
【牙刷】 yáshuā toothbrush
【牙髓】 yásuǐ 〈生理〉dental pulp ◇ ～炎 pulpitis
【牙痛】 yátòng toothache
【牙牙】 yáyá 〈象〉babble: ～学语 babble out one's first speech sounds; learn to speak
【牙医】 yáyī dentist
【牙龈】 yáyín 〈生理〉gum ◇ ～炎 gingivitis
【牙质】 yázhì ① made of ivory: ～的刀把 ivory knife handle ②〈生理〉dentine
【牙周病】 yázhōubìng 〈医〉periodontosis
【牙周炎】 yázhōuyán 〈医〉periodontitis
【牙子】 yázi ①〈口〉serrated edge ②〈旧〉middleman

**伢** yá 〈方〉child; kid
【伢子】 yázi 〈方〉child; kid

**芽** yá bud; sprout; shoot
【芽孢】 yábāo 〈生〉gemma (of a fungus)
【芽变】 yábiàn 〈植〉bud mutation
【芽茶】 yáchá young tea leaves; bud-tea
【芽豆】 yádòu sprouted broad bean
【芽接】 yájiē 〈植〉bud grafting; budding
【芽眼】 yáyǎn 〈植〉eye

**蚜** yá
【蚜虫】 yáchóng aphid; aphis: 苹果～ apple aphid/ 棉～ cotton aphid

**涯** yá margin; limit: 一望无～ stretching beyond the horizon; boundless

**崖** yá precipice; cliff
【崖壁】 yábì precipice

**睚** yá 〈书〉the corner of the eye

【睚眦】 yázì 〈书〉 ① angry stare ② small grievance: ～必报 seek revenge for the smallest grievance

## 衙 yá

【衙门】 yámen *yamen*, government office in feudal China: ～八字开,有理无钱莫进来。The *yamen* gate is open wide; with right but no money, don't go inside.

【衙役】 yáyi *yamen* runner

# yǎ

## 哑 yǎ

① mute; dumb ② hoarse; husky: ～嗓子 husky (或 hoarse) voice/ 嗓子喊～了 shout oneself hoarse

另见 yā

【哑巴】 yǎba a dumb person; mute: ～吃黄连,有苦说不出 be unable to express one's discomfort, like a dumb person tasting bitter herbs; be compelled to suffer in silence/ 今儿个怎么～了? Why are you so silent today? 或 Have you lost your tongue?

【哑巴亏】 yǎbakuī 〔用于〕: 吃～ be unable to speak out about one's grievances; be forced to keep one's grievances to oneself

【哑剧】 yǎjù dumb show; pantomime

【哑口无言】 yǎkǒu wúyán be left without an argument; be rendered speechless

【哑铃】 yǎlíng 〈体〉 dumbbell

【哑谜】 yǎmí puzzling remark; enigma; riddle: 别给我们打～啦! Don't keep us guessing.

【哑然】 yǎrán 〈书〉 ①〔多用于〕: ～无声。Silence reigns. ②〔多用于〕: ～失笑 unable to stifle a laugh; can't help laughing

【哑子】 yǎzi 〈方〉 a dumb person; mute

## 雅 yǎ

① standard; proper; correct ② refined; elegant: 古～ of classic elegance ③〈敬〉〔用于对方的情意、举动〕: ～教 your esteemed opinion ④ a section in *The Book of Songs* (《诗经》) consisting of dynastic hymns ⑤〈书〉 acquaintance; friendship: 无一日之～ not have the pleasure of knowing sb.

【雅尔塔】 Yǎ'ěrtǎ Yalta

【雅观】 yǎguān 〔多用于否定〕 refined (in manner, etc.); in good taste: 很不～ most unseemly; rather unsightly

【雅量】 yǎliàng ① magnanimity; generosity ② great capacity for liquor

【雅鲁藏布江】 Yǎlǔzàngbùjiāng the Yarlung Zangbo (Yalu Tsangpo) River

【雅俗共赏】 yǎ-sú gòng shǎng (of a work of art or literature) appeal to both the more and the less cultured; suit both refined and popular tastes

【雅兴】 yǎxìng aesthetic mood: ～不浅 be really in an aesthetic mood; have a really keen interest in sth./ 无此～ not be in such a poetic mood; be in no mood for such things

【雅意】 yǎyì 〈敬〉 your kindness; your kind offer

【雅正】 yǎzhèng ①〈书〉 standard; correct ② upright; righteous ③〈套〉〔用于把自己的诗文书画送人时,表示请对方指教〕 would you kindly point out my inadequacies

【雅致】 yǎzhì refined; tasteful: 陈设～ tastefully furnished

【雅座】 yǎzuò private room (in a restaurant, etc.)

# yà

## 轧 yà

①roll; run over: 把路面～平 roll a road surface/ 被车～伤 get run over and injured by a car/ ～碎 crush to pieces/ ～棉花 gin cotton ② oust; squeeze out; push out: 倾～ engage in internal strife; jostle against each other ③〈象〉〔形容机器开动时发出的声音〕: 机声～～。The machine is clicking away.

另见 gá; zhá

【轧板机】 yàbǎnjī 〈冶〉 mangle

【轧光】 yàguāng 〈纺〉 calendering ◇ ～机 calender

【轧花】 yàhuā 〈纺〉 cotton ginning ◇ ～厂 cotton ginning mill/ ～机 cotton gin

## 亚 yà

① inferior; second: 不～于人 second to none; not inferior to anyone ② (Yà) short for Asia

【亚得里亚海】 Yàdélǐyàhǎi the Adriatic (Sea)

【亚非会议】 Yà-Fēi Huìyì the Asian-African Conference

【亚砜】 yàfēng 〈化〉 sulphoxide

【亚急性】 yàjíxìng 〈医〉 subacute ◇ ～病 subacute disease

【亚军】 yàjūn second place (in a sports contest); runner-up: 他在百米赛跑中得了～。He came second in the 100-metre dash. 或 He was runner-up in the 100-metre dash./ 上海队获～。The Shanghai team won second place.

【亚硫酸】 yàliúsuān 〈化〉 sulphurous acid

【亚麻】 yàmá 〈植〉 flax

◇ ～布 linen (cloth)/ ～精纺机 〈纺〉 flax spinning frame/ ～子 linseed/ ～子油 linseed oil

【亚马孙河】 Yàmǎsūnhé the Amazon

【亚平宁山脉】 Yàpíngníng Shānmài the Apennines

【亚热带】 yàrèdài subtropical zone; subtropics; semitropics

【亚速尔群岛】 Yàsù'ěr Qúndǎo the Azores

【亚铁】 yàtiě 〈化〉 ferrous: 氯化～ ferrous chloride

【亚音速】 yàyīnsù 〈物〉 subsonic speed ◇ ～飞机 subsonic aircraft

【亚油酸】 yàyóusuān 〈化〉 linoleic acid

【亚洲】 Yàzhōu Asia

## 压 yà

另见 yā

【压根儿】 yàgēnr 〈口〉〔多用于否定句〕 from the start; in the first place; altogether: ～就不知道 have had no idea from the start; not know anything about it/ 他全忘了,好象～就没有这回事。He's clean forgotten about it, as if it had never happened.

## 讶 yà

〈书〉 be surprised; be astonished; wonder

## 迓 yà

〈书〉 welcome; meet

## 砑 yà

press and smooth (leather, cloth, etc.); calender

【砑光】 yàguāng calendering ◇ ～机 〈印〉 calender; 〈纺〉 mangle

## 垭 yà

〈方〉〔多用于地名〕 strip of land between hills

## 娅 yà

见"姻娅" yīnyà

## 氩 yà

〈化〉 argon (Ar)

## 揠 yà

〈书〉 pull up; tug upward

【揠苗助长】 yà miáo zhù zhǎng try to help the shoots grow by pulling them upward — spoil things by excessive enthusiasm

# ya

## 呀 ya

〈助〉〔"啊"受前一字韵母 a, e, i, o, ü 的影响而发生的变音〕：她是谁～？Who is she?/ 快来～！Come here, quick!
另见 yā

## yān

**咽** yān 〈生理〉 pharynx
另见 yàn; yè

【咽喉】 yānhóu ①〈生理〉 pharynx and larynx; throat ② strategic (或 vital) passage; key link: ～要地 key junction/ 直布罗陀海峡是地中海通向大西洋的～。The Straits of Gibraltar are the strategic passage between the Mediterranean and the Atlantic.
【咽头】 yāntóu 〈生理〉 pharynx
【咽峡炎】 yānxiáyán angina
【咽炎】 yānyán pharyngitis

**恹** yān
【恹恹】 yānyān 〈书〉 weak and weary through illness

**烟** yān ① smoke ② mist; vapour: 云～ clouds and mist ③ (of eyes) be irritated by smoke: 谁在这里生火啊？都～得睁不开眼了。Who's lighting the stove here? I can't even open my eyes for the smoke. ④ tobacco or cigarette: 烤～ flue-cured tobacco/ 抽支～ have a cigarette; have a smoke/ 一袋～的功夫 time enough to smoke a pipeful of tobacco ⑤ opium: 禁～ ban opium
【烟霭】 yān'ǎi 〈书〉 mist and clouds
【烟波】 yānbō mist-covered waters: ～浩渺的太湖 the wide expanse of misty Taihu Lake
【烟草】 yāncǎo tobacco
【烟囱】 yāncōng chimney; funnel; stovepipe
【烟袋】 yāndài small-bowled long-stemmed (tobacco) pipe ◇ ～锅 the bowl of a (long-stemmed) pipe
【烟道】 yāndào 〈建〉 flue (pipe) ◇ ～尘 flue dust/ ～气 flue gas
【烟斗】 yāndǒu (tobacco) pipe ◇ ～架 pipe rack/ ～丝 pipe tobacco
【烟鬼】 yānguǐ ① opium addict ② heavy smoker
【烟锅】 yānguō 〈方〉 pipe bowl
【烟海】 yānhǎi a vast sea of fog — huge and voluminous: 浩如～ a tremendous amount (of data, etc.); voluminous/ 如堕～ be lost in a fog
【烟盒】 yānhé cigarette case
【烟灰】 yānhuī tobacco or cigarette ash ◇ ～缸 ashtray
【烟火】 yānhuǒ ① smoke and fire: 动～ light a fire and cook/ 严禁～！Smoking or lighting fires strictly forbidden. ② cooked food ◇ ～食 cooked food
【烟火】 yānhuo fireworks: 放～ let off fireworks; put on a display of fireworks
【烟碱】 yānjiǎn 〈化〉 nicotine ◇ ～中毒 nicotinism
【烟晶】 yānjīng 〈地〉 smoky quartz; smoky topaz
【烟具】 yānjù smoking paraphernalia; smoking set
【烟卷儿】 yānjuǎnr 〈口〉 cigarette
【烟煤】 yānméi bituminous coal; soft coal
【烟幕】 yānmù smoke screen ◇ ～弹 smoke shell; smoke bomb
【烟农】 yānnóng tobacco grower
【烟丝】 yānsī cut tobacco; pipe tobacco
【烟酸】 yānsuān 〈化〉 nicotinic acid; niacin ◇ ～缺乏症 〈医〉 pellagra
【烟筒】 yāntong chimney; funnel; stovepipe
【烟头】 yāntóu cigarette end (或 stub, butt, stump)
【烟土】 yāntǔ crude opium
【烟雾】 yānwù smoke; mist; vapour; smog: ～弥漫 full of smoke/ ～笼罩着大地。The land is draped in a veil of mist./ 厨房里～腾腾。The kitchen is filled with steam and smoke.
【烟霞】 yānxiá 〈书〉 mist and clouds in the twilight
【烟消云散】 yānxiāo-yúnsàn vanish like mist and smoke; completely vanish
【烟叶】 yānyè tobacco leaf; leaf tobacco
【烟瘾】 yānyǐn a craving for tobacco: 他～可大了。He's a heavy smoker. 或 He smokes like a chimney.
【烟油】 yānyóu tobacco tar
【烟雨】 yānyǔ misty rain
【烟柱】 yānzhù column of smoke
【烟子】 yānzi soot
【烟嘴儿】 yānzuǐr cigarette holder

**殷** yān 〈书〉 blackish red
另见 yīn
【殷红】 yānhóng blackish red; dark red

**胭** yān
【胭脂】 yānzhi rouge ◇ ～红 carmine

**淹** yān ① flood; submerge; inundate: 修好河堤，庄稼就不怕～了。When the river dike is completed, the crops will be safe against floods. ② be tingling from sweat ③〈书〉 wide: 学识～博 have a wide knowledge; be well-read; be learned
【淹灌】 yānguàn 〈农〉 basin irrigation
【淹没】 yānmò submerge; flood; inundate; drown: 被～的田地 inundated fields/ 企图阻挡历史潮流的人终将被历史潮流所～。Those who try to hold back the tide of history will eventually be drowned by it./ 他的讲话被欢呼声～了。His speech was drowned out by cheers.
【淹死】 yānsǐ drown

**阉** yān castrate or spay: ～鸡 capon/ ～牛 bullock/ ～羊 wether/ ～猪 hog
【阉割】 yāngē ① castrate or spay ② deprive a theory, etc. of its essence; emasculate: 新老修正主义者总是企图～马克思主义的革命灵魂。Revisionists old and new have always tried to strip Marxism of its revolutionary essence.

**焉** yān 〈书〉 ① here; herein: 她心不在～。Her mind is elsewhere. 或 She is absent-minded./ 罪莫大～。There is no greater crime than this. ②〔多用于反问〕 how; why: ～能不去？How could I possibly not go?/ 不入虎穴，～得虎子？How can you catch tiger cubs without entering the tiger's lair? 或 Nothing venture, nothing have. ③〔表示只有在某种条件下才能怎样〕：必知乱之所自起，～能治之。You have to know how the trouble arose before you can deal with it. ④〈助〉：有厚望～ cherish high hopes for/ 少～，月出于东山之上。After a little while, the moon lifted itself above the eastern hills.

**湮** yān 〈书〉 ① fall into oblivion; bury in oblivion ② clog up; stop
【湮灭】 yānmiè bury in oblivion; annihilate
【湮没】 yānmò ① fall into oblivion; be neglected; be forgotten: ～无闻 sink into oblivion; drift into obscurity/ 在封建社会劳动人民有许多发明创造都被～了。In feudal society many of the inventions of the working people were neglected. ②〈物〉 annihilation: ～光子 annihilation photon

**腌** yān preserve in salt; salt; pickle; cure: ～菜 pickled

vegetables; pickles/ ～鱼 salted fish/ ～肉 salted meat; bacon
另见 ā

**鄢** Yān a surname

**嫣** yān 〈书〉 handsome; beautiful
【嫣红】 yānhóng bright red
【嫣然】 yānrán 〈书〉 beautiful; sweet: ～一笑 give a winsome smile

**燕** Yān ① northern Hebei Province ② a surname
另见 yàn

## yán

**延** yán ① prolong; extend; protract: 蔓～ spread/ 苟～残喘 be on one's last legs; linger on in a steadily worsening condition ② postpone; delay: 大会遇雨顺～。In case of rain the mass meeting will be postponed till the first fine day. ③ engage; send for: ～医 send for a doctor
【延安】 Yán'ān Yan'an
【延安精神】 Yán'ān jīngshén the Yan'an Spirit — the spirit of self-reliance and hard struggle developed by the people of Yan'an and the Shaanxi-Gansu-Ningxia Border Region during 1936-1948
【延长】 yáncháng lengthen; prolong; extend: 输油管～了二百公里。The oil pipeline has been extended another 200 kilometres./ 会议～了三天。The conference was prolonged for three more days. ◇ ～号〈乐〉 pause/ ～线 extension (或 extended) line
【延迟】 yánchí delay; defer; postpone: 展览会开幕的日期～了。The opening of the exhibition has been postponed.
【延宕】 yándàng procrastinate; delay; keep putting off
【延发】 yánfā 〈军〉 delayed action ◇ ～引信 delayed-action (或 delay) fuse
【延搁】 yángē procrastinate; delay
【延胡索】 yánhúsuǒ 〈中药〉 *yanhusuo* (*Corydalis yanhusuo*)
【延缓】 yánhuǎn delay; postpone; put off: ～工作进度 retard the progress of work/ 这个手术可以～几天再做。The operation can be put off for a few days.
【延年益寿】 yánnián-yìshòu (of tonics, etc.) prolong life; promise longevity
【延聘】 yánpìn 〈书〉 engage; employ
【延期】 yánqī postpone; defer; put off: ～付款 defer payment/ 比赛因雨～。The game was put off on account of rain./ 要求～十年偿还债务 demand a ten-year moratorium/ 办理签证～手续 have one's visa extended; extend a visa ◇ ～炸弹 delayed-action bomb
【延请】 yánqǐng engage; employ; send for
【延烧】 yánshāo (of fire) spread
【延伸】 yánshēn extend; stretch; elongate: 铁路一直～到海边。The railway line stretches right to the coast. ◇ ～火力〈军〉 creeping (或 lift) fire/ ～率〈冶〉 percentage elongation
【延绳钓】 yánshéngdiào 〈渔〉 longline fishing; long-lining
【延髓】 yánsuǐ 〈生理〉 medulla oblongata
【延误】 yánwù incur loss through delay: ～时机 miss an opportunity because of a delay/ ～时日 lose time
【延性】 yánxìng 〈物〉 ductility
【延续】 yánxù continue; go on; last: 不能让这种状况～下去。This state of affairs must not be allowed to continue./ 旱象～了半年之久。The drought lasted for as long as six months. ◇ ～性 continuity
【延音】 yányīn 〈乐〉 *tenuto*

**言** yán ① speech; word: 发～ make a speech; take the floor/ 无～以对 have nothing to say in reply/ 有～在先 let it be clearly understood beforehand/ 一～不发 not utter a word ② say; talk; speak: 自～自语 talk to oneself/ ～明 state explicitly; clearly stipulate/ 妙在不～中。The best part lies in what is left unsaid./ 不幸而～中。The prophecy has unfortunately come true. ③ character; word: 全书近二十万～。It is a book of nearly 200,000 words. ④ (Yán) a surname
【言必信,行必果】 yán bì xìn, xíng bì guǒ promises must be kept and action must be resolute; always be true in word and resolute in deed
【言必有中】 yán bì yǒu zhòng whenever one speaks, one speaks to the point; whenever one says something one hits the nail on the head
【言不及义】 yán bù jí yì never talk about anything serious; talk frivolously
【言不由衷】 yán bù yóuzhōng speak insincerely; speak with one's tongue in one's cheek
【言出法随】 yán chū fǎ suí 〔旧时布告用语〕 upon its promulgation the law shall be enforced to the letter
【言传】 yánchuán explain in words: 只可意会,不可～ only to be sensed, not explained
【言传身教】 yánchuán-shēnjiào teach by personal example as well as verbal instruction
【言辞】 yáncí one's words; what one says: ～恳切 be sincere in what one says 又作"言词"
【言而无信】 yán ér wú xìn fail to keep faith; go back on one's word
【言归于好】 yán guī yú hǎo make it up with sb.; become reconciled
【言归正传】 yán guī zhèngzhuàn to come back to our story; to return to the subject
【言过其实】 yán guò qí shí exaggerate; overstate
【言和】 yánhé make peace; become reconciled; bury the hatchet: 握手～ shake hands and make it up
【言简意赅】 yánjiǎn-yìgāi concise and comprehensive; compendious
【言教】 yánjiào teach by word of mouth; give verbal directions: ～不如身教。Example is better than precept.
【言路】 yánlù channels through which criticisms and suggestions may be communicated to the leadership: 广开～ provide wide opportunities for airing views; encourage the free airing of views/ 堵塞～ stifle criticisms and suggestions
【言论】 yánlùn opinion on public affairs; expression of one's political views; speech: 我们的一切～和行动都应符合人民的利益。Everything we say and do must be in the interests of the people./ 我们看一个人,不仅要听他的～,还要看他的行动。We must judge a person not only by his words, but also by his deeds. ◇ ～自由 freedom of speech
【言人人殊】 yán rén rén shū different people give different views; each person offers a different version
【言谈】 yántán the way one speaks or what he says: ～举止 speech and deportment/ ～之间可以看出他很懂行。It's clear from the way he talks that he knows the subject well.
【言听计从】 yántīng-jìcóng always follow sb.'s advice; act upon whatever sb. says; have implicit faith in sb.
【言外之意】 yán wài zhī yì implication; what is actually meant: 体会到文章的～ read between the lines 文作"言下之意"
【言为心声】 yán wéi xīnshēng words are the voice of the

mind; what the heart thinks the tongue speaks
【言行】 yánxíng words and deeds; statements and actions: ～不一 one's deeds do not match (或 square with) one's words; one's actions are not in keeping with one's promises/ ～一致 be as good as one's word
【言犹在耳】 yán yóu zài ěr the words are still ringing (或 reverberating) in one's ears
【言语】 yányǔ spoken language; speech: ～和文字 spoken and written language/ ～粗鲁 speak rudely
【言语】 yányu 〈方〉 speak; talk; answer: 他这个人不爱～。 He is a man of few words./ 人家问你这事儿，你怎么不～? Why didn't you say something when people asked you about it?/ 你走的时候～一声儿。Let me know when you leave.
【言者无罪，闻者足戒】 yánzhě wú zuì, wénzhě zú jiè blame not the speaker but be warned by his words
【言之成理】 yán zhī chéng lǐ sound reasonable; speak in a rational and convincing way
【言之无物】 yán zhī wú wù (of speech or writing) be devoid of substance; be just empty verbiage
【言之有据】 yán zhī yǒu jù speak on good grounds

**严** yán ① tight: 把窗户关～了。Shut the window tight./ 他的嘴很～。He is tight-mouthed. ② strict; severe; stern; rigorous: ～以律己，宽以待人 be strict with oneself and broad-minded towards others/ ～加批驳 sternly refute/ ～是爱，松是害。Strictness helps, indulgence spoils. ③〈旧〉 father: 家～ my father ④ (Yán) a surname
【严办】 yánbàn deal with severely; punish with severity
【严惩】 yánchéng punish severely: ～不贷 punish severely without mercy; punish mercilessly/ ～入侵之敌 deal the invaders a crushing blow
【严词】 yáncí in strong terms; in stern words: ～谴责 denounce in strong terms; sternly condemn/ ～拒绝 give a stern rebuff; sternly refuse
【严冬】 yándōng severe winter
【严防】 yánfáng be strictly on guard against; take strict precautions against: ～阶级敌人破坏 take strict precautions against sabotage by the class enemy
【严格】 yángé strict; rigorous; rigid; stringent: ～履行协定条款 strictly implement the terms of the agreement/ ～训练，～要求 go in for rigorous training and set strict demands; train hard and strictly/ 作出～的规定 set rigid (或 stringent) rules/ ～规章制度 rigorously enforce rules and regulations/ ～说来 strictly speaking
【严寒】 yánhán severe cold; bitter cold
【严谨】 yánjǐn ① rigorous; strict: ～的科学态度 a rigorous scientific approach ② compact; well-knit: 文章结构～。The essay is well-knit.
【严禁】 yánjìn strictly forbid (或 prohibit): ～体罚 strictly forbid corporal punishment
【严紧】 yánjin tight; close: 防守～ guard carefully
【严峻】 yánjùn stern; severe; rigorous; grim: ～的考验 a severe test; a rigorous test/ ～的态度 a stern (或 an uncompromising) attitude/ ～的局势 a grim situation
【严酷】 yánkù ① harsh; bitter; grim: ～的现实 harsh reality/ ～的教训 a bitter lesson/ ～的斗争 a grim struggle ② cruel; ruthless: ～的剥削 cruel exploitation
【严厉】 yánlì stern; severe: ～制裁 apply stern (或 severe) sanctions/ ～的批评 severe criticism/ ～声讨 sternly (或 strongly) denounce
【严密】 yánmì tight; close: ～封锁 impose a tight blockade/ ～监视 put under close surveillance; keep close watch over/ ～防范 take strict precautions against/ ～注视国际局势的发展 closely follow the development of world events/ 组织～ be well-organized
【严明】 yánmíng strict and impartial: 赏罚～ be strict and impartial in meting out rewards and punishments; give rewards and punishments impartially/ 纪律～ observe strict discipline; be highly disciplined
【严实】 yánshi 〈方〉 ① tight; close: 门关得挺～。The door is shut tight. ② (hide) safely: 游击队把粮食藏～了才转移。The guerrillas carefully hid their food grain before they moved on.
【严丝合缝】 yánsī héfèng fit together perfectly; join tightly; dovetail
【严肃】 yánsù serious; solemn; earnest: ～地指出 point out in all earnestness/ ～的态度 a serious attitude/ ～的气氛 a solemn atmosphere/ 进行～的斗争 conduct a serious struggle/ 为了～党纪 to enforce Party discipline
【严刑】 yánxíng cruel torture: ～拷打 cruelly torture; cruelly beat up
【严刑峻法】 yánxíng-jùnfǎ severe law; draconian law
【严阵以待】 yán zhèn yǐ dài be ready in full battle array; stand in combat readiness
【严整】 yánzhěng in neat formation: 军容～。The troops are in gallant array.
【严正】 yánzhèng solemn and just; serious and principled; stern: ～立场 solemn and just stand/ 发表～声明 issue a solemn statement; solemnly declare/ ～警告 serve a stern warning
【严重】 yánzhòng serious; grave; critical: ～后果 serious (或 grave) consequences/ ～关头 critical juncture/ 病情～ be seriously ill/ 事态～。The situation is grave./ 感到～不安 feel grave concern; feel deeply disturbed/ 有～问题的人 a person guilty of a serious misdeed or a person with a dubious background/ 资本主义思想～的人 those imbued with capitalist thinking/ 问题的～性在于 the gravity of the question lies in the fact that ◇ ～警告 serious warning

**芫** yán
另见 yuán
【芫荽】 yánsui 〈植〉 coriander

**妍** yán 〈书〉 beautiful: 百花争～。A hundred flowers contend in beauty.

**沿** yán ① along: ～着海岸航行 sail along the coast/ ～着毛主席的革命路线前进 advance along Chairman Mao's revolutionary line ② follow (a tradition, pattern, etc.): 世代相～ be handed down from generation to generation ③ trim (with tape, ribbon, etc.): 在衣领上～一道边 trim the collar of a garment ④ edge; border: 炕～儿 the edge of a *kang*
另见 yàn
【沿岸】 yán'àn along the bank or coast; littoral or riparian: 长江～ along (the banks of) the Changjiang River/ 地中海～国家 the littoral countries of the Mediterranean/ 尼日尔河～国家 riparian states along the Niger
【沿边儿】 yánbiānr trim (with tape, ribbon, etc.)
【沿革】 yángé the course of change and development; evolution: 社会风俗的～ the evolution of social customs
【沿海】 yánhǎi along the coast; coastal; littoral ◇ ～城市 coastal city/ ～岛屿 offshore islands/ ～地区 coastal areas; coastland/ ～国家 coastal state (或 country); littoral state (或 country)/ ～航船 coaster/ ～航行 coastal navigation; cabotage/ ～贸易 coasting trade; cabotage/ ～渔业 inshore fishing/ ～自然资源 the natural resources of coastal waters
【沿阶草】 yánjiēcǎo 〈植〉 dwarf lilyturf

【沿路】 yánlù along the road; on the way: ～看到庄稼长势良好 see thriving crops along the way

【沿途】 yántú on the way; throughout a journey: 参观团～受到热情的接待。The visiting group was warmly received throughout its journey. ◇ ～贸易 way-port trade

【沿袭】 yánxí carry on as before; follow: ～陈规 follow convention

【沿线】 yánxiàn along the line: 铁路～的村镇 villages and towns along the railway line

【沿用】 yányòng continue to use (an old method, etc.): ～原来的名称 continue to use the old name

**炎** yán ① scorching; burning hot: ～夏 hot summer ② inflammation: 嗓子发～ suffer from an inflammation of the throat/ 阑尾～ appendicitis

【炎热】 yánrè scorching; blazing; burning hot: 冒着～ braving the sweltering heat

【炎暑】 yánshǔ hot summer; sweltering summer days; dog days

【炎炎】 yányán scorching; sweltering; blazing: 赤日～ the scorching sun

【炎症】 yánzhèng inflammation

**岩** yán ① rock ② cliff; crag

【岩岸】 yán'àn 〈地〉 rocky coast

【岩层】 yáncéng rock stratum; rock formation

【岩洞】 yándòng grotto

【岩浆】 yánjiāng 〈地〉 magma ◇ ～分异作用 magmatic differentiation/ ～岩 magmatic rock/ ～作用 magmatism

【岩羚】 yánlíng 〈动〉 chamois

【岩溶】 yánróng 〈地〉 karst ◇ ～地形 karst topography

【岩石】 yánshí rock ◇ ～力学 rock mechanics/ ～圈 lithosphere/ ～突出 〈矿〉 rock burst/ ～学 petrology

【岩相】 yánxiàng 〈地〉 lithofacies ◇ ～图 lithofacies map

【岩心】 yánxīn 〈地〉 (drill) core ◇ ～回收率 core recovery/ ～筒 core barrel/ ～样品 core sample

【岩性学】 yánxìngxué 〈地〉 lithology

【岩盐】 yányán rock salt; halite

【岩羊】 yányáng blue sheep; bharal

【岩样】 yányàng ①〈地〉 rock specimen ②〈矿〉 core sample

**研** yán ① grind; pestle: ～成粉末 grind into fine powder/ ～墨 rub an ink stick on an inkslab (to prepare ink for brush writing) ② study: 钻～ study intensively

【研钵】 yánbō mortar

【研杵】 yánchǔ pestle; pounder

【研究】 yánjiū ① study; research: ～自然规律 study the laws of nature/ 科学～ scientific research ② consider; discuss; deliberate: 这些问题党委正在～。These matters are under review (或 consideration) by the Party committee. ◇ ～工作者 research worker/ ～生 postgraduate (student); graduate student/ ～所 research institute/ ～员 research fellow/ ～院 research institute; graduate school

【研磨】 yánmó ① grind; pestle ② abrade; polish ◇ ～粉 abrasive powder/ ～料 abrasive

【研讨】 yántǎo deliberate; discuss

【研制】 yánzhì ① prepare; manufacture; develop: ～新式武器 develop new weapons ②〈中药〉 prepare medicinal powder by pestling

**盐** yán salt: 精～ refined salt/ 正～ normal salt

【盐巴】 yánbā 〈方〉 salt; common (或 table) salt

【盐层】 yáncéng salt deposit; salt bed

【盐场】 yánchǎng saltern; saltworks

【盐池】 yánchí salt pond

【盐肤木】 yánfūmù 〈植〉 Chinese sumac ◇ ～根皮 〈中药〉 the root bark of Chinese sumac

【盐湖】 yánhú salt lake

【盐花】 yánhuā a little salt; a pinch of salt: 汤里搁点儿～儿。Put just a little salt in the soup.

【盐碱化】 yánjiǎnhuà salinization (of soil)

【盐碱土】 yánjiǎntǔ saline-alkali soil

【盐井】 yánjǐng salt well; brine pit

【盐矿】 yánkuàng salt mine

【盐卤】 yánlǔ bittern

【盐瓶】 yánpíng saltcellar; saltshaker

【盐汽水】 yánqìshuǐ salt soda water

【盐泉】 yánquán brine (或 salt) spring

【盐霜】 yánshuāng salt efflorescence

【盐水】 yánshuǐ salt solution; brine ◇ ～选种 seed sorting by salt water

【盐酸】 yánsuān 〈化〉 hydrochloric acid

【盐田】 yántián salt pan; salina

【盐土】 yántǔ 〈农〉 solonchak; saline soil

【盐业】 yányè salt industry

【盐沼】 yánzhǎo salt marsh

【盐渍土】 yánzìtǔ 〈农〉 salinized soil

**阎** yán ①〈书〉 the gate of a lane ② (Yán) a surname

【阎罗】 Yánluó 〈宗〉 Yama

【阎王】 Yánwang ① Yama; King of Hell: 活～ living King of Hell; devil incarnate/ 见～ die ② an extremely cruel and violent person ◇ ～殿 the Palace of Hell/ ～账 usurious loan; shark's loan

**筵** yán ①〈书〉 formerly, a bamboo mat spread on the floor for people to sit ② feast; banquet: 喜～ a wedding feast

【筵席】 yánxí ① seats arranged at a banquet ② feast; banquet

**蜒** yán 见"蚰蜒" yóuyán; "蜿蜒" wānyán

**颜** yán ① face; countenance: 和～悦色 with a kind and pleasant countenance ② prestige; face: 无～见人 not have the face to appear in public ③ colour: 五～六色 of all colours; multicoloured; colourful ④ (Yán) a surname

【颜料】 yánliào pigment; colour; dyestuff

【颜面】 yánmiàn ① face: ～神经 facial nerve ② prestige; face: 顾全～ save face/ ～扫地 lose face altogether; be thoroughly discredited

【颜色】 yánsè ① colour ② countenance; facial expression: 给他一点～看看 make it hot for him; teach him a lesson

【颜色】 yánshai 〈口〉 pigment; dyestuff

**檐** yán ① eaves ② ledge; brim: 帽～儿 the visor of a cap; the brim of a hat

【檐沟】 yángōu 〈建〉 eaves gutter

【檐子】 yánzi eaves

## yǎn

**奄** yǎn 〈书〉 ① cover; overspread ② all of a sudden; suddenly

【奄忽】 yǎnhū 〈书〉 suddenly; quickly

【奄奄】 yǎnyǎn feeble breathing: 气息～ breathe feebly; be

sinking fast; be dying/ ～一息 at one's last gasp; on the verge of death

**俨** yǎn 〈书〉 majestic; solemn; dignified

【俨然】 yǎnrán 〈书〉 ① solemn; dignified: 望之～ look dignified ② neatly arranged: 屋舍～ houses set out in neat order ③ just like: 这孩子说起话来～是个大人。This child speaks just like a grown-up./ ～以恩人自居 assume the airs of a benefactor

【俨如】 yǎnrú just like: ～白昼 as bright as day

**衍** yǎn 〈书〉 ① spread out; develop; amplify ② redundant; superfluous

【衍变】 yǎnbiàn develop; evolve

【衍射】 yǎnshè 〈物〉 diffraction ◇ ～角 diffraction angle/ ～线 diffracted ray

【衍生物】 yǎnshēngwù 〈化〉 derivative: 纤维素～ 〈纺〉 cellulose derivatives

【衍文】 yǎnwén redundancy due to misprinting or miscopying

**掩** yǎn ① cover; hide: ～口而笑 hide one's smile/ ～鼻而过 pass by (sth. nauseating) holding one's nose ② shut; close: ～卷 close a book/ 虚～着门 with the door left unlocked or unlatched ③ 〈方〉 get squeezed (或 pinched) while shutting a door, lid, etc.: 小心门～了手。Don't get your fingers caught in the door. ④ attack by surprise: ～袭 launch a surprise attack

【掩蔽】 yǎnbì screen; shelter; cover ◇ ～部 〈军〉 shelter/ ～物 〈军〉 screen/ ～阵地 covered position

【掩藏】 yǎncáng hide; conceal

【掩耳盗铃】 yǎn ěr dào líng plug one's ears while stealing a bell; deceive oneself; bury one's head in the sand

【掩盖】 yǎngài cover; conceal: 一个倾向～着另一个倾向。One tendency conceals another./ 谎言～不了事实。Lies cannot cover up (或 conceal) the facts.

【掩护】 yǎnhù screen; shield; cover: ～进攻 screen an advance/ 用身体～战友 shield one's comrade-in-arms with one's body/ 游击队～村里的群众转移。The guerrillas covered the villagers' evacuation. ◇ ～部队 covering force/ ～火力 covering fire

【掩埋】 yǎnmái bury

【掩人耳目】 yǎn rén ěr-mù deceive the public; hoodwink people

【掩杀】 yǎnshā 〈书〉 make a surprise attack; pounce on (the enemy)

【掩饰】 yǎnshì cover up; gloss over; conceal: ～错误 gloss over (或 cover up) one's mistakes/ ～真实的意图 conceal one's true intentions/ ～不住内心的恐慌 be unable to hide (或 conceal) one's fears/ 毫不～自己的感情 make no secret of one's feelings

【掩体】 yǎntǐ 〈军〉 blindage; bunker: 炮兵～ emplacement

【掩星】 yǎnxīng 〈天〉 occultation: 月～ lunar occultation

【掩映】 yǎnyìng set off (one another): 红楼翠竹互相～。The red building and green bamboos set each other off.

**眼** yǎn ① eye: 亲～看见 see with one's own eyes ② look; glance: 瞪了他一～ give him a hard look/ 瞥了他一～ shoot a glance at him/ 一～就认出是她 recognize her at first glance ③ small hole; aperture: 针～ the eye of a needle/ 打个～ bore a hole/ 网～ mesh (of a net) ④ key point: 节骨～儿 critical juncture ⑤ 〈围棋〉 trap ⑥ an unaccented beat in traditional Chinese music: 一板三～ one accented beat and three unaccented beats in a bar ⑦ 〈量〉: 两～井 two wells

【眼巴巴】 yǎnbābā ① (expecting) eagerly; anxiously: 大家～地盼着他回来。We were eagerly looking forward to his return. ② helplessly (watching sth. unpleasant happen)

【眼白】 yǎnbái 〈方〉 the white of the eye

【眼岔】 yǎnchà mistake one for another: 刚才看见的不是他，是我～了。He's not the person I saw just now. I mistook someone else for him.

【眼馋】 yǎnchán 〈方〉 covet; be envious

【眼眵】 yǎnchī gum (in the eyes)

【眼底下】 yǎndǐxia ① right before one's eyes ② at the moment: 先处理～的事。Let's settle the business on hand first.

【眼点】 yǎndiǎn 〈动〉 eyespot; stigma

【眼福】 yǎnfú the good fortune of seeing sth. rare or beautiful: ～不浅 be lucky enough to see sth./ 一饱～ feast one's eyes on sth.

【眼干症】 yǎngānzhèng 〈医〉 xerophthalmia

【眼高手低】 yǎngāo-shǒudī have grandiose aims but puny abilities; be fastidious but imcompetent

【眼观六路，耳听八方】 yǎn guān liùlù, ěr tīng bāfāng have sharp eyes and keen ears — be observant and alert

【眼光】 yǎnguāng ① eye: 锐利的～ sharp eyes/ 大家的～都集中到他身上。Everyone turned their eyes on him. ② sight; foresight; insight; vision: ～远大 farsighted/ ～短浅 shortsighted/ 政治～ political foresight/ 历史～ historical perspective/ 有～的政治家 a farsighted statesman/ 他开始用新的～来观察周围事物。He began to view everything around him in a different light./ 不能用老～来看新事物。One mustn't judge new things by old standards.

【眼红】 yǎnhóng ① covet; be envious; be jealous ② furious

【眼花】 yǎnhuā have dim eyesight; have blurred vision: 使人头昏～ make one's head swim; be dazzling/ 耳不聋眼不花 (of an old person) be neither hard of hearing nor dim-sighted

【眼花缭乱】 yǎnhuā liáoluàn be dazzled: 使人～的杂技表演 a dazzling display of acrobatics

【眼尖】 yǎnjiān be sharp-eyed; have sharp eyes

【眼睑】 yǎnjiǎn 〈生理〉 eyelid

【眼见得】 yǎnjiànde 〈方〉 (of sth. unpleasant) be evident: 病人～不行了。It's clear that the patient won't pull through.

【眼角】 yǎnjiǎo the corner of the eye; canthus

【眼睫毛】 yǎnjiémáo 〈口〉 eyelash

【眼界】 yǎnjiè field of vision (或 view); outlook: 扩大～ widen one's field of vision; broaden one's horizon/ 这次去大寨参观，真是大开～。The visit to Dazhai was a real eye-opener./ 形而上学限制了他的～。Metaphysics limited his outlook.

【眼镜】 yǎnjìng glasses; spectacles: 戴～ wear glasses

【眼镜猴】 yǎnjìnghóu tarsier

【眼镜蛇】 yǎnjìngshé cobra

【眼睛】 yǎnjing eye: 群众的～是雪亮的。The masses are sharp-sighted. 或 The masses have sharp eyes.

【眼看】 yǎnkàn ① soon; in a moment: 暴风雨～就要来了。The storm will start any moment./ ～天就要亮了。It'll be daylight soon. ② watch helplessly; look on passively: 咱们哪能～着他走邪道不管呢？ How can we sit idly by and watch him go astray?

【眼科】 yǎnkē 〈医〉 (department of) ophthalmology ◇ ～学 ophthalmology/ ～医生 oculist; ophthalmologist; eye doctor

【眼眶】 yǎnkuàng ① eye socket; orbit: 他～里含着热泪。His eyes were filled with tears. ② rim of the eye

【眼泪】 yǎnlèi tears: ～汪汪 eyes brimming with tears

【眼力】 yǎnlì ① eyesight; vision: ～好(差) have good (poor)

eyesight ②judgment; discrimination: 老支书看人很有～。The old Party branch secretary is good at sizing people up.

【眼里】 yǎnli within one's vision; in one's eyes: ～没有群众 not take the masses into account/ 看在～,记在心里 bear in mind what one sees; see and heed/ ～有活 see where there's work to be done; know where one can be of use/ 在他～,我还是个孩子。In his eyes, I'm only a child./ 这点困难她根本不放在～。She thinks nothing of a difficulty like that.

【眼帘】 yǎnlián eye: 映入～ come into view; greet (或 meet) the eye

【眼明手快】 yǎnmíng-shǒukuài quick of eye and deft of hand; sharp-eyed and quick-moving

【眼内压】 yǎnnèiyā 〈生理〉 intraocular pressure

【眼泡】 yǎnpāo upper eyelid

【眼皮】 yǎnpí eyelid: 侦察兵就在敌人～底下活动。The scouts are active under the enemy's very noses.

【眼前】 yǎnqián ① before one's eyes: ～是一片碧绿的稻田。Before our eyes was a stretch of green paddy fields. ② at the moment; at present; now: ～利益服从长远利益 subordinate immediate interests to long-term interests/ 不能只顾～,不管将来。One must not think only of the present and neglect the future./ 胜利就在～。Victory is at hand.

【眼球】 yǎnqiú eyeball

【眼圈】 yǎnquān ①eye socket; orbit: ～红了 be on the verge of tears ② rim of the eye

【眼热】 yǎnrè covet; be envious

【眼色】 yǎnsè hint given with the eyes; meaningful glance; wink: 使～ tip sb. the wink; wink at sb./ 看某人的～行事 take one's cue from sb.

【眼神】 yǎnshén ① expression in one's eyes ②〈方〉 eyesight: ～不济 have poor eyesight

【眼生】 yǎnshēng look unfamiliar: 来客很～。I haven't seen the visitor before.

【眼屎】 yǎnshǐ 〈方〉 gum (in the eyes)

【眼熟】 yǎnshú look familiar: 这人看着很～。That person looks familiar.

【眼跳】 yǎntiào twitching of the eyelid

【眼窝】 yǎnwō eye socket

【眼下】 yǎnxià at the moment; at present; now: ～正是秋收大忙季节。We're right in the middle of the autumn harvest rush.

【眼弦赤烂】 yǎnxián chìlàn 〈中医〉 blepharitis

【眼药】 yǎnyào medicament for the eyes; eye ointment or eyedrops

【眼晕】 yǎnyùn feel dizzy (owing to faulty vision)

【眼罩】 yǎnzhào ① eyeshade ② blinkers (for a horse)

【眼睁睁】 yǎnzhēngzhēng (looking on) helplessly or unfeelingly: 咱不能～地看着庄稼被水淹了。We can't just sit here and watch the crops being flooded.

【眼中钉】 yǎnzhōngdīng thorn in one's flesh (或 side)

【眼珠子】 yǎnzhūzi 〈口〉 eyeball

**偃** yǎn 〈书〉 ① fall on one's back: ～卧 lie supine; lie on one's back ② lay down ③ desist; cease: ～武修文 desist from military activities and encourage culture and education

【偃旗息鼓】 yǎnqí-xīgǔ lower the banners and muffle the drums — cease all activities

**演** yǎn ① develop; evolve: 愈～愈烈 grow in intensity ② deduce; elaborate: 推～ deduce ③ drill; practise: ～算 perform mathematical calculations ④ perform; play; act; put on: 她在《洪湖赤卫队》里～韩英。She plays the part of Han Ying in the opera *Red Guards of Honghu Lake.*/ ～电影 show a film/ ～五场 give (或 put on) five performances

【演变】 yǎnbiàn develop; evolve: 从猿到人的～过程 evolution from ape to man

【演唱】 yǎnchàng sing (in a performance)

【演出】 yǎnchū perform; show; put on a show: 为工农兵～ perform (或 put on a performance) for the workers, peasants and soldiers/ 登台～ appear on the stage/ 首次～ first performance or show; *première* (of a play, film, etc.); *début* (of an actor or actress)/ ～结束后,领导同志登台祝贺～成功。After the final curtain, the leading comrades went up onto the stage to congratulate the actors and actresses on their fine performances. ◇ ～本 acting version; script/ ～单位 producer/ ～节目 items on the programme; programme

【演化】 yǎnhuà evolution

【演技】 yǎnjì acting

【演讲】 yǎnjiǎng give a lecture; make a speech; lecture

【演进】 yǎnjìn gradual progress; evolution

【演练】 yǎnliàn drill: 地面～ 〈航空〉 ground drill

【演示】 yǎnshì demonstrate

【演说】 yǎnshuō ① deliver a speech; make an address ② speech

【演算】 yǎnsuàn perform mathematical calculations

【演替】 yǎntì 〈生〉 succession

【演武】 yǎnwǔ practise traditional martial arts

【演习】 yǎnxí manoeuvre; exercise; drill; practice: 军事～ military manoeuvre; war exercise/ 民兵～ militia drill/ 实弹～ live ammunition manoeuvres

【演戏】 yǎnxì ① put on a play; act in a play ② playact; pretend: 别再～了。Stop playacting.

【演义】 yǎnyì historical novel; historical romance: 《三国～》 *The Romance of the Three Kingdoms*

【演绎】 yǎnyì 〈逻〉 deduction ◇ ～法 the deductive method

【演员】 yǎnyuán actor or actress; performer ◇ ～表 cast

【演奏】 yǎnzòu give an instrumental performance; play a musical instrument (in a performance): ～琵琶 play the *pipa* ◇ ～能手 virtuoso

**魇** yǎn have a nightmare

**鼹** yǎn mole

【鼹鼠】 yǎnshǔ mole

## yàn

**厌** yàn ① be disgusted with; detest: ～弃 detest and reject ② be fed up with; be bored with; be tired of: 看～了 have seen more than enough of sth. /吃～了 be sick of eating sth./ 不～其烦 not mind taking all the trouble ③ be satisfied: 贪得无～ be insatiably greedy

【厌烦】 yànfán be sick of; be fed up with

【厌倦】 yànjuàn be weary of; be tired of

【厌弃】 yànqì detest and reject

【厌世】 yànshì be world-weary; be pessimistic

【厌恶】 yànwù detest; abhor; abominate; be disgusted with

【厌氧微生物】 yànyǎng wēishēngwù anaerobe

【厌战】 yànzhàn be weary of war; be war-weary ◇ ～情绪 war-weariness

**沿** yàn water's edge; bank: 河～ riverside/ 沟～儿 edge of a ditch

另见 yán

**砚** yàn inkstone; inkslab
【砚池】 yànchí inkstone; inkslab
【砚台】 yàntái inkstone; inkslab

**咽** yàn swallow: 细嚼慢～ chew carefully and swallow slowly/ 他话到嘴边又～了回去。He was on the point of saying something when he checked himself./ ～不下这口气 unable to stomach (或 take) an insult, etc., like that
另见 yān; yè
【咽气】 yànqì breathe one's last; die

**彦** yàn 〈书〉 a man of virtue and ability

**宴** yàn ① entertain at a banquet; fête: ～客 entertain guests at a banquet ② feast; banquet: 盛～ grand banquet; magnificent feast ③ ease and comfort
【宴安鸩毒】 yàn'ān zhèndú seeking pleasure is like drinking poisoned wine
【宴会】 yànhuì banquet; feast; dinner party ◇ ～厅 banquet hall
【宴请】 yànqǐng entertain (to dinner); fête: ～贵宾 entertain the distinguished guests
【宴席】 yànxí banquet; feast

**晏** yàn ① late: ～起 get up late ② ease and comfort ③ (Yàn) a surname

**艳** yàn ① gorgeous; colourful; gaudy: 百花争～。Flowers blossom in a riot of colour./ 这布的花色太～了。The cloth is too gaudy. ② amorous: ～诗 love poem in a flowery style ③ 〈书〉 admire; envy: ～羡 admire; envy
【艳丽】 yànlì bright-coloured and beautiful; gorgeous: ～夺目 of dazzling beauty/ 词藻～ flowery diction/ 打扮得非常～ be gorgeously dressed
【艳阳天】 yànyángtiān bright spring day; bright sunny skies

**唁** yàn extend condolences
【唁电】 yàndiàn telegram (或 cable) of condolence; message of condolence
【唁函】 yànhán letter (或 message) of condolence

**验** yàn ① examine; check; test: ～护照 examine (或 check) a passport ② prove effective; produce the expected result: 应～ come true/ 屡试屡～ prove successful in every test
【验潮器】 yàncháoqì 〈气〉 tide gauge
【验电器】 yàndiànqì electroscope
【验方】 yànfāng 〈中医〉 proved recipe
【验关】 yànguān customs examination
【验光】 yànguāng optometry
【验枪】 yànqiāng 〈军〉 inspect arms
【验尸】 yànshī 〈法〉 postmortem; autopsy
【验收】 yànshōu check and accept; check before acceptance; check upon delivery: 逐项～ check item by item before acceptance/ 工程已由国家～。The completed project has been checked and accepted by the government. ◇ ～单 receipt (issued after examination and acceptance of goods)/ ～试验 acceptance test
【验算】 yànsuàn 〈数〉 checking computations ◇ ～公式 check formula
【验血】 yànxiě blood test
【验证】 yànzhèng test and verify

**谚** yàn proverb; saying; adage; saw: 农～ peasants' proverb; farmers' saying/ 古～ old saw
【谚语】 yànyǔ proverb; saying; adage; saw

**焰** yàn flame; blaze: 烈～ blazing (或 raging) flames
【焰火】 yànhuǒ 〈方〉 fireworks

**雁** yàn wild goose
【雁来红】 yànláihóng 〈植〉 tricolour amaranth (*Amaranthus tricolor*)

**堰** yàn weir
【堰塞湖】 yànsèhú 〈地〉 barrier lake

**酽** yàn (of tea, etc.) thick; strong: 茶太～。The tea's too strong.

**餍** yàn 〈书〉 ① have enough (food); be satiated ② satisfy

**燕** yàn ① swallow: 家～ house swallow ② 见"宴" yàn
另见 Yān
【燕鸻】 yànhéng 〈动〉 pratincole
【燕麦】 yànmài oats
【燕鸥】 yàn'ōu 〈动〉 tern
【燕雀】 yànquè 〈动〉 brambling; bramble finch
【燕雀处堂】 yàn-què chǔ táng swallows and sparrows nesting in the hall, unmindful of the spreading blaze — oblivious of imminent danger
【燕隼】 yànsǔn 〈动〉 hobby
【燕尾服】 yànwěifú swallowtail; swallow-tailed coat; tailcoat; tails
【燕窝】 yànwō edible bird's nest
【燕鱼】 yànyú 〈动〉 Spanish mackerel
【燕子】 yànzi swallow

**赝** yàn 〈书〉 counterfeit; spurious; fake
【赝本】 yànběn spurious edition or copy
【赝币】 yànbì 〈书〉 counterfeit coin
【赝晶体】 yànjīngtǐ 〈物〉 pseudocrystal
【赝品】 yànpǐn counterfeit; fake; sham

## yāng

**央** yāng ① entreat ② centre ③ 〈书〉 end; finish: 夜未～。The night is not yet spent.
【央告】 yānggào beg; ask earnestly
【央求】 yāngqiú beg; plead; implore: ～宽恕 beg for mercy/ 他再三～红军把他收下。He pleaded with the Red Army men again and again to take him into their ranks.

**泱** yāng
【泱泱】 yāngyāng 〈书〉 ① (of waters) vast ② magnificent: ～大国 a great and proud country

**殃** yāng ① calamity; disaster; misfortune: 遭～ meet with (或 suffer) disaster ② bring disaster to: 祸国～民 bring calamity to the country and the people

**秧** yāng ① seedling; sprout: 黄瓜～儿 cucumber sprout ② rice seedling: 插～ transplant rice seedlings ③ vine: 白薯～ sweet potato vine ④ young; fry: 鱼～ young fish; fry/ 猪～ piglets
【秧歌】 yānggē *yangko* (dance), a popular rural folk dance: 扭～ do the *yangko* ◇ ～剧 *yangko* opera

【秧鸡】 yāngjī 〈动〉water rail
【秧苗】 yāngmiáo rice shoot; rice seedling
【秧田】 yāngtián rice seedling bed
【秧子】 yāngzi 见"秧"①③④

**鸯** yāng 见"鸳鸯" yuānyang

## yáng

**羊** yáng ① sheep: 绵～ sheep/ 山～ goat/ 母～ ewe/ 公～ ram/ 小～ lamb/ ～叫 baa; bleat ② (Yáng) a surname
【羊肠线】 yángchángxiàn 〈医〉catgut (suture)
【羊肠小道】 yángcháng xiǎodào narrow winding trail; meandering footpath
【羊齿】 yángchǐ 〈植〉bracken; fern
【羊痘】 yángdòu 〈牧〉sheep pox
【羊肚蕈】 yángdǔxùn 〈植〉morel
【羊羔】 yánggāo lamb
【羊倌】 yángguān shepherd
【羊毫】 yángháo writing brush made of goat's hair
【羊角锤】 yángjiǎochuí claw hammer
【羊角风】 yángjiǎofēng epilepsy
【羊脚碾】 yángjiǎoniǎn 〈建〉sheepfoot roller
【羊圈】 yángjuàn sheepfold; sheep pen
【羊毛】 yángmáo sheep's wool; fleece ◇ ～衫 woollen sweater; cardigan/ ～袜 woollen socks or stockings
【羊毛出在羊身上】 yángmáo chū zài yáng shēnshang after all, the wool still comes from the sheep's back — in the long run, whatever you're given, you pay for
【羊膜】 yángmó 〈生理〉amnion
【羊排】 yángpái mutton chop; lamb chop
【羊皮】 yángpí sheepskin: 披着～的狼 a wolf in sheep's clothing
【羊皮纸】 yángpízhǐ parchment
【羊群里头出骆驼】 yángqún lǐtou chū luòtuo stand out like a camel in a flock of sheep
【羊绒衫】 yángróngshān cashmere sweater
【羊肉】 yángròu mutton: 烤～串 mutton cubes roasted on a skewer; kebab
【羊水】 yángshuǐ 〈生理〉amniotic fluid
【羊桃】 yángtáo 〈植〉carambola
【羊痫风】 yángxiánfēng epilepsy
【羊踯躅】 yángzhízhú 〈植〉Chinese azalea
【羊质虎皮】 yángzhì-hǔpí a sheep in a tiger's skin — outwardly strong, inwardly weak

**阳** yáng ① (in Chinese philosophy, medicine, etc.) *yang*, the masculine or positive principle in nature ② the sun ③ south of a hill or north of a river: 衡～ Hengyang (a city situated on the south side of Hengshan Mountain)/ 洛～ Luoyang (a city situated on the north side of the Luohe River) ④ in relief: ～文 characters cut in relief ⑤ open; overt: 阴一套,～一套 act one way in public and another in private; be engaged in double-dealing ⑥ belonging to this world; concerned with living beings ⑦ 〈物〉positive: ～离子 positive ion; cation ⑧ male genitals
【阳春】 yángchūn spring (season)
【阳春白雪】 yángchūn báixuě ① the Spring Snow (a melody of the *élite* in the State of Chu) ② highbrow art and literature
【阳春面】 yángchūnmiàn 〈方〉noodles in a simple sauce
【阳地植物】 yángdì zhíwù sun plant
【阳电】 yángdiàn positive electricity
【阳奉阴违】 yángfèng-yīnwéi overtly agree but covertly oppose; comply in public but oppose in private; feign compliance
【阳沟】 yánggōu open drain; ditch
【阳关道】 yángguāndào broad road; thoroughfare: 你走你的～,我过我的独木桥。You take the open road, I'll cross the log bridge — you go your way, I'll go mine.
【阳光】 yángguāng sunlight; sunshine: ～充足 full of sunlight; with plenty of sunshine (或 sun); sunny/ ～普照大地。Sunlight floods the earth. 或 The sun illuminates every corner of the land.
【阳极】 yángjí 〈物〉positive pole; positive electrode; anode ◇ ～板 〈电〉positive plate/ ～栅 anode grid/ ～射线 positive ray
【阳间】 yángjiān this world
【阳历】 yánglì solar calendar
【阳平】 yángpíng 〈语〉rising tone, the second of the four tones in modern standard Chinese pronunciation
【阳畦】 yángqí 〈农〉seed bed with windbreaks; cold bed
【阳起石】 yángqǐshí 〈矿〉actinolite
【阳伞】 yángsǎn parasol; sunshade
【阳台】 yángtái balcony
【阳痿】 yángwěi 〈医〉impotence
【阳文】 yángwén characters cut in relief
【阳性】 yángxìng ① 〈医〉positive: ～反应 positive reaction ② 〈语〉masculine gender
【阳虚】 yángxū 〈中医〉deficiency of *yang*; lack of vital energy

**扬** yáng ① raise: ～手 raise one's hand (and beckon)/ ～起灰尘 raise (或 kick up) a dust/ ～鞭催马 flourish the whip to urge on the horse; whip one's horse on ② throw up and scatter; winnow: ～谷去糠 winnow the chaff from the grain ③ spread; make known: 宣～ propagate; publicize
【扬长而去】 yángcháng ér qù stalk off; swagger off
【扬场】 yángcháng 〈农〉winnowing ◇ ～机 winnowing machine; winnower
【扬程】 yángchéng 〈水〉lift: 高～水泵 high-lift pump/ 高～抽水站 high-lift pumping station
【扬帆】 yángfān 〈书〉hoist the sails; set sail
【扬花】 yánghuā 〈农〉flowering (of cereal crops)
【扬眉吐气】 yángméi-tǔqì feel proud and elated
【扬名】 yángmíng make a name for oneself; become famous: ～天下 become world-famous; become known throughout the country
【扬旗】 yángqí 〈铁道〉semaphore
【扬弃】 yángqì ① develop what is useful or healthy and discard what is not ② 〈哲〉sublate
【扬琴】 yángqín dulcimer
【扬声器】 yángshēngqì loudspeaker: 高频～ tweeter/ 低频～ woofer
【扬水】 yángshuǐ pump up water ◇ ～泵 lift pump/ ～站 pumping station
【扬汤止沸】 yáng tāng zhǐ fèi try to stop water from boiling by scooping it up and pouring it back — an ineffectual remedy
【扬言】 yángyán threaten (that one is going to take action): ～要进行报复 threaten to retaliate
【扬扬】 yángyáng triumphantly; complacently: 得意～ be immensely proud; look triumphant/ ～自得 be very pleased with oneself; be complacent
【扬州】 Yángzhōu Yangzhou
【扬子鳄】 yángzǐ'è 〈动〉Chinese alligator

杨 yáng ① poplar ② (Yáng) a surname
【杨柳】 yángliǔ ① poplar and willow ② willow
【杨梅】 yángméi 〈植〉 red bayberry (*Myrica rubra*)
【杨树】 yángshù poplar
【杨桃】 yángtáo 〈植〉 carambola
【杨枝鱼】 yángzhīyú pipefish

佯 yáng pretend; feign; sham: ~作不知 feign ignorance; pretend not to know/ ~死 feign death; play dead
【佯攻】 yánggōng 〈军〉 feign (或 simulate) attack; make a feint
【佯言】 yángyán 〈书〉 tell lies; lie

疡 yáng 〈医〉 sore: 溃~ ulcer

洋 yáng ① vast; multitudinous ② ocean: 太平~ the Pacific Ocean ③ foreign: ~房 Western-style house ④ modern: ~办法 modern methods ⑤ 〈旧〉 silver coin
【洋八股】 yángbāgǔ foreign stereotyped writing; foreign stereotypes
【洋白菜】 yángbáicài cabbage
【洋菜】 yángcài agar 又作"洋粉"
【洋场】 yángchǎng metropolis infested with foreign adventurers (usu. referring to preliberation Shanghai): ~恶少 rich young bully in a metropolis (in old China)
【洋车】 yángchē 〈口〉 rickshaw
【洋葱】 yángcōng onion
【洋地黄】 yángdìhuáng 〈药〉 digitalis
【洋服】 yángfú Western-style clothes
【洋镐】 yánggǎo pickax
【洋鬼子】 yángguǐzi foreign devil (a term used in preliberation China for foreign invaders): 假~ imitation foreign devil — comprador, etc.
【洋行】 yángháng foreign firm (in preliberation China)
【洋灰】 yánghuī cement
【洋火】 yánghuǒ 〈口〉 matches
【洋金花】 yángjīnhuā 〈中药〉 datura flower (*Datura metel*)
【洋泾浜】 yángjīngbāng pidgin (English)
【洋里洋气】 yángliyángqì in an ostentatiously foreign style
【洋流】 yángliú 〈地〉 ocean current
【洋奴】 yángnú slave of a foreign master; flunkey of imperialism; worshipper of everything foreign: ~买办 lackeys and compradors in the service of foreign bosses ◇~思想 slavish mentality towards all things foreign/ ~哲学 slavish comprador philosophy; blind worship of everything foreign
【洋气】 yángqì ① foreign flavour; Western style ② outlandish ways
【洋琴】 yángqín dulcimer
【洋人】 yángrén foreigner
【洋嗓子】 yángsǎngzi a voice trained in the Western style of singing
【洋为中用】 yáng wéi Zhōng yòng make foreign things serve China
【洋务运动】 Yángwù Yùndòng Westernization Movement (to introduce techniques of capitalist production, initiated by comprador bureaucrats in the latter half of the 19th century in order to preserve the feudal rule of the Qing government)
【洋相】 yángxiàng 〔多用于〕: 出~ make an exhibition of oneself
【洋洋】 yángyáng ① numerous; copious: ~万言 run to ten thousand words — be very lengthy ② 见"扬扬" yángyáng
【洋洋大观】 yángyáng dàguān spectacular; grandiose; imposing
【洋洋洒洒】 yángyángsǎsǎ voluminous; at great length: ~一大篇 a magnificent piece of writing
【洋溢】 yángyì be permeated with; brim with: 热情~的讲话 a speech brimming with warm feeling/ 宴会上~着团结友好的热烈气氛。The banquet was permeated with a warm atmosphere of unity and friendship.
【洋油】 yángyóu 〈方〉 imported oil; kerosene: 中国人民依靠~的日子已经一去不复返了。The days when the Chinese people had to rely on imported oil are gone forever.
【洋芋】 yángyù 〈方〉 potato

徉 yáng 见"徜徉" chángyáng

烊 yáng 〈方〉 ① melt ② dissolve

## yǎng

仰 yǎng ① face upward; ~着睡 sleep on one's back/ ~天大笑 laugh sardonically ② admire; respect; look up to: 瞻~ look at with reverence; pay one's respects to ③ rely on: ~给于人 rely on others for support
【仰八叉】 yǎngbachā 〈口〉〔多用于〕: 摔了个~ fall flat on one's back
【仰角】 yǎngjiǎo 〈数〉 angle of elevation
【仰慕】 yǎngmù admire; look up to
【仰人鼻息】 yǎng rén bíxī be dependent on the pleasure of others; be slavishly dependent
【仰韶文化】 Yǎngsháo wénhuà 〈考古〉 Yangshao culture, a culture of the Neolithic period, relics of which were first unearthed in Yangshao Village, Mianchi County, Henan Province, in 1921
【仰望】 yǎngwàng ① look up at: ~天安门城楼 look up at the gate tower of Tian An Men ② 〈书〉 respectfully seek guidance or help from; look up to
【仰卧】 yǎngwò lie on one's back; lie supine ◇ ~起坐 〈体〉 (do) sit-ups
【仰泳】 yǎngyǒng 〈体〉 backstroke
【仰仗】 yǎngzhàng rely on; look to sb. for backing (或 support)

养 yǎng ① support; provide for: ~家 support a family ② raise; keep; grow: ~鸭 raise ducks/ ~鸟 keep pet birds/ ~花 grow flowers ③ give birth to: 她~了个儿子。She gave birth to a boy. ④ foster; adoptive: ~父(母) foster father (mother)/ ~子(女) adopted son (daughter) ⑤ form; acquire; cultivate: ~成良好的习惯 cultivate good habits ⑥ rest; convalesce; recuperate one's health; heal: ~身体 recuperate/ ~好伤 heal one's wounds ⑦ maintain; keep in good repair: ~路 maintain a road or railway
【养兵】 yǎngbīng 〈旧〉 maintain an army
【养兵千日,用兵一时】 yǎng bīng qiānrì, yòng bīng yīshí maintain an army for a thousand days to use it for an hour
【养病】 yǎngbìng take rest and nourishment to regain one's health; recuperate: 他在家~呢。He's recuperating at home.
【养蚕业】 yǎngcányè sericulture
【养分】 yǎngfèn nutrient: 土壤~ soil nutrient
【养蜂场】 yǎngfēngchǎng apiary; bee yard
【养蜂业】 yǎngfēngyè apiculture; beekeeping
【养虎遗患】 yǎng hǔ yí huàn to rear a tiger is to court calamity — appeasement brings disaster

【养护】 yǎnghù ①maintain; conserve: 道路～ road maintenance/ 生物资源～ conservation of living resources ② curing: 混凝土～ concrete curing
【养活】 yǎnghuo 〈口〉①support; feed: ～一家子 support (或 feed) a family/ 农民的血汗～了地主老财。The landlords lived off the sweat and blood of the peasants. ② raise (animals): 大队～了上千头猪。Our brigade raises nearly a thousand pigs. ③ give birth to: ～孩子 have a baby
【养鸡场】 yǎngjīchǎng chicken run; chicken farm
【养精蓄锐】 yǎngjīng-xùruì conserve strength and store up energy
【养老】 yǎnglǎo ① provide for the aged (usu. one's parents) ② live out one's life in retirement ◇ ～金 old-age pension
【养料】 yǎngliào nutriment; nourishment: 革命的作家应该从工农兵的斗争生活中吸收～。Revolutionary writers should draw nourishment from the struggles of the workers, peasants and soldiers.
【养路】 yǎnglù maintain a road or railway ◇ ～费 road toll/ ～道班 road maintenance crew
【养马场】 yǎngmǎchǎng (horse) ranch
【养神】 yǎngshén rest to attain mental tranquility; repose: 闭目～ sit in repose with one's eyes closed
【养生】 yǎngshēng preserve one's health; keep in good health: ～之道 the way to keep in good health
【养兔场】 yǎngtùchǎng rabbit warren
【养痈成患】 yǎng yōng chéng huàn a carbuncle neglected becomes the bane of your life — leaving evil unchecked spells ruin 又作"养痈遗患"
【养鱼池】 yǎngyúchí fishpond
【养育】 yǎngyù bring up; rear: ～子女 bring up children
【养殖】 yǎngzhí breed (aquatics): ～海带 cultivate kelp
【养猪场】 yǎngzhūchǎng pig farm; piggery
【养尊处优】 yǎngzūn-chǔyōu enjoy high position and live in ease and comfort; live in clover

**氧** yǎng 〈化〉 oxygen (O)
【氧合作用】 yǎnghé zuòyòng 〈生理〉 oxygenation
【氧化】 yǎnghuà 〈化〉 oxidize; oxidate
◇ ～剂 oxidizer; oxidant/ ～铁 ferric oxide/ ～物 oxide/ ～焰 oxidizing flame/ ～抑制剂 oxidation retarder (或 inhibitor)/ ～作用 oxidation
【氧气】 yǎngqì oxygen
◇ ～顶吹转炉 oxygen top-blown convertor/ ～炼钢 oxygen steelmaking/ ～面具 oxygen mask/ ～瓶 oxygen cylinder/ ～枪 〈冶〉 oxygen lance/ ～帐 〈医〉 oxygen tent
【氧乙炔吹管】 yǎngyǐquē chuīguǎn 〈机〉 oxyacetylene blowpipe

**痒** yǎng itch; tickle: 浑身发～ itch all over/ 搔到～处 scratch where it itches — hit the nail on the head/ 怕～ ticklish
【痒痒】 yǎngyang 〈口〉 itch; tickle: 蚊子咬得腿上直～。The mosquito bites on my leg itch terribly.

## yàng

**怏** yàng
【怏怏】 yàngyàng disgruntled; sullen: ～不乐 unhappy about sth.; morose

**恙** yàng 〈书〉 ailment; illness: 无～ in good health/ 偶染微～ feel slightly indisposed
【恙虫】 yàngchóng 〈动〉 tsutsugamushi mite ◇ ～热 tsutsugamushi disease; scrub typhus

**样** yàng ① appearance; shape: 这两支笔～儿差不多,色儿不一样。These two pens are alike except that they're different colours./ 几年没见,他还是那个～儿。It's years since I last saw him, but he still looks the same. ② sample; model; pattern: 鞋～ outline of a shoe; shoe pattern/ 校～ proof sheet ③〈量〉 kind; type: 三～儿菜 three kinds of vegetables; three dishes/ 商店虽小,各～货物俱全。Small as it is, the shop stocks all kinds of wares.
【样板】 yàngbǎn ① sample plate ② templet ③ model; prototype; example ◇ ～田 demonstration field (或 plot); model plot
【样本】 yàngběn ① sample book ②〈印〉 sample; specimen: 字体～ type specimen book
【样机】 yàngjī 〈航空〉 prototype (aeroplane)
【样品】 yàngpǐn sample (product); specimen
【样式】 yàngshì pattern; type; style; form: 各种～的羊毛衫 woollen sweaters in all styles
【样样】 yàngyàng every kind; each and every; all: 地里的活她～都会。She knows how to do every kind of farm work./ 这孩子德、智、体～都好。The child is developing in every way, morally, intellectually and physically.
【样张】 yàngzhāng 〈印〉 specimen page
【样子】 yàngzi ① appearance; shape: 这件大衣的～很好看。This coat is well cut./ 这活做得不象～。This job has been done too crudely. ② manner; air: 看他那高兴的～。How happy he looks!/ 装出一副公正的～ assume a righteous posture (或 manner, air) ③ sample; model; pattern: 衣服～ clothes pattern/ 做出～来 set an example ④〈口〉 tendency; likelihood: 天象是要下雨的～。It looks like rain./ 看～这星期他来不了。It seems (或 looks as if) he won't be able to come this week.

**漾** yàng ① ripple: 荡～ ripple; undulate ② brim over; overflow: 碗里的汤快～出来了。The soup in the bowl is brimming over./ 他脸上～出了笑容。His face broadened into a smile.
【漾奶】 yàngnǎi (of a baby) throw up milk

## yāo

**幺** yāo ① one (used for the numeral 一 orally) ②〈方〉 youngest: ～妹 youngest sister
【幺麽】 yāomó 〈书〉 petty; insignificant; paltry: ～小丑 despicable wretch

**夭** yāo ① die young ②〈书〉 tender; young: ～桃秾李 beautiful peach and plum blossoms — a beautiful young lady
【夭亡】 yāowáng die young
【夭折】 yāozhé ① die young ② come to a premature end: 谈判中途～。The negotiations came to a premature end.

**吆** yāo
【吆喝】 yāohe ① cry out; call: 走的时候～一声。Give us a shout when it's time to leave. ② cry one's wares: 她头一次上街卖菜,不好意思～。The first time she went out selling vegetables, she was too shy to cry out for customers. ③ loudly urge on (an animal): 牲口不听～。The animal wouldn't obey its driver.

**约** yāo 〈口〉 weigh: 给我～二斤肉。Weigh me out two *jin* of meat./ ～～多重。See how much it weighs.
另见 yuē

【约克夏猪】 yāokèxiàzhū Yorkshire (hog)

**妖** yāo ① goblin; demon; evil spirit ② evil and fraudulent: ～术 sorcery; witchcraft; black art ③ bewitching; coquettish: 打扮得～里～气 (of a woman) be seductively dressed

【妖风】 yāofēng evil wind; noxious trend: 刮起一股修正主义～ stir up an evil revisionist trend

【妖怪】 yāoguài monster; bogy; goblin; demon

【妖精】 yāojing ① evil spirit; demon ② alluring woman

【妖媚】 yāomèi seductively charming; bewitching

【妖魔】 yāomó evil spirit; demon

【妖魔鬼怪】 yāomó-guǐguài demons and ghosts; monsters of every description

【妖孽】 yāoniè ① person or event associated with evil or misfortune ② evildoer

【妖娆】 yāoráo 〈书〉 enchanting; fascinating

【妖人】 yāorén sorcerer; enchanter

【妖物】 yāowù evil spirit; monster

【妖言】 yāoyán heresy; fallacy: ～惑众 spread fallacies to deceive people

【妖艳】 yāoyàn pretty and coquettish

【妖冶】 yāoyě pretty and coquettish

**要** yāo ① demand; ask ② force; coerce
另见 yào

【要求】 yāoqiú ask; demand; require; claim: ～入党 ask to join the Party; apply for admission to the Party/ ～发言 ask to be heard; ask for the floor/ 严格～自己 set strict demands on oneself; be strict with oneself/ 达到质量～ fulfil quality requirements/ 提出领土～ make territorial claims/ ～赔偿 claim compensation/ 这项工作～精神高度集中。This job calls for intense concentration.

【要挟】 yāoxié coerce; put pressure on; threaten: 对小国进行～ use coercion against small nations/ ～对方 put pressure on the other party

**腰** yāo ① waist; small of the back: 齐～深 waist-deep; up to the waist/ 弯～ bend down; stoop/ ～酸腿疼 aching back and legs/ 扭了～ sprain one's back muscles/ 两手叉～ with one's hands on one's hips; akimbo/ 拦～抱住 seize sb. round the middle ② waist (of a garment): 裤～ waist of trousers ③ pocket: 我～里还有些钱。I've still got some money in my pocket. ④ middle: 半山～ halfway up a mountain; on a hillside

【腰板儿】 yāobǎnr back: 直起～ straighten one's back/ 他八十多了，～还挺硬朗。He is well over eighty, but he's still quite strong.

【腰包】 yāobāo purse; pocket: 肥了资本家的～ line the pockets of the capitalists/ 把钱装进自己的～ pocket the money

【腰部】 yāobù waist; small of the back

【腰带】 yāodài waistband; belt; girdle

【腰杆子】 yāogǎnzi ① back: 挺起～ straighten one's back — be confident and unafraid ② backing; support: ～硬 have strong backing

【腰鼓】 yāogǔ waist drum

【腰果树】 yāoguǒshù 〈植〉 cashew

【腰花】 yāohuā scalloped pork or lamb kidneys: 炒～ stir-fried kidneys

【腰肌劳损】 yāojī láosǔn strain of lumbar muscles; psoatic strain

【腰身】 yāoshēn waistline; waist; waist measurement; girth: 她的～很细。She has a slender waist./ 这条裤子～太大。These trousers are too big in the waist.

【腰痛】 yāotòng lumbago

【腰眼】 yāoyǎn either side of the small of the back

【腰斩】 yāozhǎn ① cutting sb. in two at the waist (a punishment in ancient China) ② cut sth. in half

【腰椎】 yāozhuī 〈生理〉 lumbar vertebra

【腰子】 yāozi 〈口〉 kidney

**邀** yāo ① invite; request: 应～出席 be present by invitation ② solicit; seek: ～准 seek approval; ask permission ③ intercept: ～击 intercept (the enemy); waylay

【邀功】 yāogōng 〈书〉 take credit for someone else's achievements: ～请赏 take credit and seek rewards for someone else's achievements

【邀击】 yāojī intercept (the enemy); waylay

【邀集】 yāojí invite to meet together; call together: 今天～大家来开个座谈会。You have been invited here today to hold a forum.

【邀请】 yāoqǐng invite: ～代表团来中国访问 invite the delegation to visit China/ 应中国政府的～ at the invitation of the Chinese Government/ 发出～ send (或 extend) an invitation ◇ ～国 host country/ ～赛 〈体〉 invitational tournament

## yáo

**尧** Yáo Yao, a legendary monarch in ancient China

【尧舜】 Yáo-Shùn Yao and Shun, legendary monarchs in ancient China — ancient sages

**肴** yáo meat and fish dishes

【肴馔】 yáozhuàn sumptuous courses at a meal

**姚** Yáo a surname

**珧** yáo 见"江珧" jiāngyáo

**窑** yáo ① kiln: 砖～ brickkiln ② (coal) pit: 小煤～ small coal pit ③ cave dwelling

【窑洞】 yáodòng cave dwelling

【窑灰钾肥】 yáohuī jiǎféi flue ash potash

**谣** yáo ① ballad; rhyme: 民～ popular verse; ballad/ 童～ children's rhyme ② rumour: 造～ cook up a story and spread it around; start a rumour/ 辟～ refute a rumour

【谣传】 yáochuán ① rumour; hearsay ② it is rumoured that; rumour has it that

【谣言】 yáoyán rumour; groundless allegation: 散布～ spread (或 circulate) rumours/ 戳穿～ give the lie to a rumour ◇ ～攻势 rumourmongering campaign

**遥** yáo 〈书〉 distant; remote; far: 千里之～ at a distance of a thousand *li*; a thousand *li* away

【遥测】 yáocè telemetering: 空间～ space telemetry ◇ ～计 telemeter/ ～术 telemetry/ ～温度计 telethermometer

【遥感】 yáogǎn 〈电子〉 remote sensing: 红外～ infrared remote sensing

【遥控】 yáokòng remote control; telecontrol ◇ ～飞机 remote control aircraft; telecontrolled airplane/ ～开关 teleswitch/ ～力学 telemechanics/ ～无人驾驶飞机 drone (aircraft)

【遥望】 yáowàng look into the distance

【遥相呼应】 yáo xiāng hūyìng echo each other at a dis-

tance; coordinate with each other from afar
【遥遥】 yáoyáo far away; a long way off: ～领先 be far ahead; get a good lead/ ～相对 stand far apart facing each other/ ～无期 not (realizable, etc.) within the foreseeable future
【遥远】 yáoyuǎn distant; remote; faraway: ～的将来 the distant (或 remote) future/ ～的山村 a remote mountain village/ ～的边疆 remote frontiers/ 路途～ a long journey; a long way to go

## 摇

yáo shake; wave; rock; turn: ～铃 ring a bell/ ～扇子 wave a fan/ ～辘轳 turn a windlass/ ～船 row a boat/ ～橹 scull/ 小狗～着尾巴跑了。The little dog ran off wagging its tail.
【摇摆】 yáobǎi sway; swing; rock; vacillate: 柳枝迎风～。The branches of the willow trees swayed in the breeze./ 船身～。The ship rocked./ 左右～ vacillate now to the left, now to the right ◇ ～舞 rock and roll
【摇臂】 yáobì 〈机〉 rocker (或 rock, rocking) arm ◇ ～轴 rocker shaft/ ～钻床 radial drilling machine
【摇床】 yáochuáng 〈矿〉 table: 选矿～ cleaning table/ 粗选～ roughing table
【摇唇鼓舌】 yáochún-gǔshé flap one's lips and beat one's tongue — wag one's tongue; engage in loose talk (to stir up trouble)
【摇荡】 yáodàng rock; sway
【摇动】 yáodòng ① wave; shake: 欢迎的群众～着花束。The welcoming crowd waved their bouquets. ② sway; rock: 大树在狂风中～。The big tree rocked in the strong wind.
【摇撼】 yáohàn give a violent shake to; shake to the root or foundation; rock
【摇晃】 yáohuang rock; sway; shake: 地震时大楼都～了。The tall buildings shook during the earthquake./ 这椅子有点～。The chair is a bit rickety (或 shaky)./ 他病了很久,走起路来摇摇晃晃的。He walked with faltering steps after a long illness.
【摇篮】 yáolán cradle: 革命～ the cradle of the revolution/ 我国古代文化的～ the cradle of ancient Chinese culture ◇ ～曲 〈乐〉 lullaby; cradlesong; *berceuse*
【摇耧】 yáolóu rock a drill barrow in planting; plant with a drill barrow
【摇蜜】 yáomì 〈农〉 extract honey ◇ ～机 honey extractor
【摇旗呐喊】 yáo qí nàhǎn wave flags and shout battle cries — bang the drum for sb.
【摇钱树】 yáoqiánshù a legendary tree that sheds coins when shaken — a ready source of money
【摇纱机】 yáoshājī 〈纺〉 reeling frame
【摇身一变】 yáo shēn yī biàn 〈贬〉 give oneself a shake and change into another form — suddenly change one's identity: 解放初期,这个特务～,钻进了革命队伍。At the time of liberation this special agent changed his identity and sneaked into the revolutionary ranks.
【摇手】 yáoshǒu shake one's hand in admonition or disapproval
【摇头】 yáotóu shake one's head
【摇头摆尾】 yáotóu-bǎiwěi shake the head and wag the tail — assume an air of complacency or levity
【摇头晃脑】 yáotóu-huàngnǎo wag one's head — look pleased with oneself; assume an air of self-approbation or self-conceit
【摇尾乞怜】 yáo wěi qǐ lián wag the tail ingratiatingly — fawn
【摇蚊】 yáowén 〈动〉 midge; chironomid
【摇摇欲坠】 yáoyáo yù zhuì tottering; crumbling; on the verge of collapse: ～的殖民统治 the tottering colonial rule/ ～的反动政权 a crumbling reactionary regime
【摇曳】 yáoyè flicker; sway: ～的灯光 flickering light/ 垂柳在微风中轻轻～。The willow branches swayed gently in the breeze.
【摇椅】 yáoyǐ rocking chair

## 徭

yáo
【徭役】 yáoyì corvée

## 瑶

yáo 〈书〉 precious jade
【瑶族】 Yáozú the Yao nationality, distributed over the Guangxi Zhuang Autonomous Region, Hunan, Yunnan, Guangdong and Guizhou

## 鳐

yáo 〈动〉 ray; skate

# yǎo

## 杳

yǎo 〈书〉 distant and out of sight: ～无踪迹 disappear without a trace; vanish
【杳如黄鹤】 yǎo rú huánghè disappear like the yellow crane — nowhere to be found
【杳无音信】 yǎo wú yīnxìn there has been no news whatsoever about sb.; have never been heard of since

## 咬

yǎo ① bite; snap at: ～不动 too tough to bite (或 chew)/ ～了一口 take a bite/ ～紧牙关 grit (或 clench) one's teeth; endure with dogged will/ 一口～定 assert emphatically; insist ② grip; bite: 这个旧螺母～不住扣儿了。This old nut won't bite (或 grip). ③ (of a dog) bark: 鸡叫狗～ cocks crow and dogs bark ④ incriminate another person (usu. innocent) when blamed or interrogated: 反～一口 trump up a countercharge against one's accuser; make a false countercharge ⑤ pronounce; articulate: 这个字他～不准。He can't pronounce this word correctly./ ～字清楚 clear articulation (或 enunciation) ⑥ be nitpicking (about the use of words): ～字眼儿 be nitpicking on words
【咬耳朵】 yǎo ěrduo 〈口〉 whisper in sb.'s ear; whisper
【咬群】 yǎoqún 〈口〉 ① (of a domestic animal) be prone to fight within the herd ② (of a person) be apt to pick a quarrel within a group
【咬舌儿】 yǎoshér ① lisp ② lisper
【咬文嚼字】 yǎowén-jiáozì pay excessive attention to wording
【咬牙】 yǎoyá ① grit (或 set, clench, gnash) one's teeth: 恨得直～ gnash one's teeth in hatred ② grind one's teeth (in sleep)
【咬牙切齿】 yǎoyá-qièchǐ gnash one's teeth: ～地咒骂 curse between one's teeth
【咬住】 yǎozhù ① bite into; grip with one's teeth ② grip; take firm hold of; refuse to let go of: 别老～我那句话不放。Don't keep nagging me about that remark of mine./ 追击部队紧紧～敌人。The pursuing troops were close on the heels of the enemy./ 他掉转机头,～了敌机。He swung his fighter around and got on the tail of the enemy plane.

## 窈

yǎo
【窈窕】 yǎotiǎo 〈书〉 ① (of a woman) gentle and graceful ② (of a palace, landscape, etc.) secluded

## 舀

yǎo ladle out; spoon up (或 out); scoop up: ～汤 ladle out soup
【舀子】 yǎozi dipper; ladle; scoop

# yào

**疟** yào
另见 nüè
【疟子】 yàozi 〈口〉 malaria

**药** yào ① medicine; drug; remedy: 服～ take medicine/ 良～ good medicine; a good remedy/ 煎～ decoct herbal medicine ② certain chemicals: 火～ gunpowder/ 杀虫～ insecticide/ 耗子～ rat poison; ratsbane ③〈书〉 cure with medicine: 不可救～ incurable; incorrigible ④ kill with poison: ～老鼠 poison rats
【药材】 yàocái medicinal materials; crude drugs
【药草】 yàocǎo medicinal herbs
【药厂】 yàochǎng pharmaceutical factory
【药典】 yàodiǎn pharmacopoeia
【药店】 yàodiàn drugstore; chemist's shop; pharmacy
【药方】 yàofāng prescription: 开～ write out a prescription
【药房】 yàofáng ① drugstore; chemist's shop; pharmacy ② hospital pharmacy; dispensary
【药费】 yàofèi expenses for medicine; charges for medicine
【药粉】 yàofěn (medicinal) powder
【药膏】 yàogāo ointment; salve
【药罐子】 yàoguànzi ① a pot for decocting herbal medicine ② chronic invalid
【药衡】 yàohéng apothecaries' measure or weight
【药剂】 yàojì medicament; drug ◇ ～师 pharmacist; druggist/ ～学 pharmaceutics; pharmacy
【药酒】 yàojiǔ medicinal liquor
【药理】 yàolǐ ① pharmacodynamics ② pharmacology ◇ ～学 pharmacology
【药力】 yàolì efficacy of a drug (或 medicine): ～发作。The drug is taking effect./ ～达不到。The medicine was not potent enough to produce the desired effect.
【药棉】 yàomián absorbent cotton
【药面】 yàomiàn (medicinal) powder
【药捻子】 yàoniǎnzi 〈中医〉 a slender roll of medicated paper or gauze (to be inserted into wounds, boils, etc.)
【药农】 yàonóng a peasant who cultivates or collects medicinal herbs; medicinal herb grower or collector; herbalist
【药片】 yàopiàn (medicinal) tablet
【药品】 yàopǐn medicines and chemical reagents
【药瓶】 yàopíng medicine bottle
【药铺】 yàopù herbal medicine shop
【药签】 yàoqiān swab
【药石】 yàoshí medicines and stone needles for acupuncture — remedies: ～罔效。All medical treatment has failed./ ～之言 exhortations
【药水】 yàoshuǐ ① liquid medicine; medicinal liquid ② lotion
【药丸】 yàowán pill: 大～ bolus
【药味】 yàowèi ① herbal medicines in a prescription ② flavour of a drug
【药物】 yàowù medicines; pharmaceuticals; medicaments ◇ ～过敏 drug allergy/ ～化学 pharmaceutical chemistry/ ～学 materia medica/ ～中毒 drug poisoning
【药箱】 yàoxiāng medical kit; medicine-chest: 急救～ first-aid kit
【药性】 yàoxìng property of a medicine
【药引子】 yàoyǐnzi 〈中医〉 an ingredient added to enhance the efficacy of a dose of medicine
【药用炭】 yàoyòngtàn medical charcoal
【药浴】 yàoyù 〈牧〉 dipping: 羊～ sheep dipping ◇ ～池 dipping vat
【药皂】 yàozào medicated soap
【药渣】 yàozhā dregs of a decoction
【药疹】 yàozhěn 〈医〉 drug rash; drug eruption

**要** yào ① important; essential: ～事 an important matter (或 affair)/ 择～记录 note down the essential points/ 上述规定希严格执行为～。It is imperative that the above rules be strictly observed. ② want; ask for; wish; desire: 国家～独立，民族～解放，人民～革命，已成为不可抗拒的历史潮流。Countries want independence, nations want liberation and the people want revolution — this has become an irresistible historical trend./ 这双鞋我还～呢。I want to keep these shoes./ 谁没有票，问她～。Anyone without a ticket can ask her for one./ ～炮兵指挥所。Artillery command post, please. ③ ask (或 want) sb. to do sth.: 老大爷～我替他写封信。The old man asked me to write a letter for him./ 班长～我们五点以前归队。The squad leader told us to get back before five o'clock. ④ want to; wish to: 这位同志～见司令员。This comrade wishes to see the commander./ 我还有几句话～说。I'd like to say a few more words. ⑤ must; should; it is necessary (或 imperative, essential): ～相信群众。We must have faith in the masses. ⑥ shall; will; be going to: ～下雨了。It's going to rain. ⑦ need; take: 这项任务～十天才能完成。It will take ten days to get the work done./ 这活儿～不了这么多人。You don't need so many people for this job. ⑧〔表示估计，用于比较〕: 你们～比我们辛苦得多。You must have had a much tougher time than we did. ⑨〈连〉 if; suppose; in case: 明天～下雨，我们就不去了。If it rains tomorrow, we won't go./ 他～来不了呢？Suppose he can't come?/ 我～赶不回来，你替我说一声。In case I can't get back in time, please apologize for me.
另见 yāo
【要隘】 yào'ài strategic pass
【要不】 yàobù 〈连〉 otherwise; or else; or: 我得马上走，～就赶不上火车了。I have to leave at once or I'll miss the train. 又作"要不然"
【要不得】 yàobude no good; intolerable: 这种自私行为～。Such selfish acts are not to be tolerated.
【要不是】 yàobushi if it were not for; but for: ～他们勇敢地抢救国家财产，那损失可就大了。If it weren't for their courage in rescuing the state property, the loss would have been enormous.
【要冲】 yàochōng communications centre (或 hub): 军事～ strategic point/ 兰州是西北交通的～。Lanzhou is the communications hub of the Northwest.
【要道】 yàodào thoroughfare: 交通～ important line of communications; vital communications line
【要得】 yàodé 〈方〉 good; fine; desirable: 这个办法～！That's a good idea!
【要地】 yàodì important place; strategic point
【要点】 yàodiǎn ① main points; essentials; gist: 抓住～ grasp the main points/ 讲话的～ the gist of a speech ② key strongpoint: 战略～ strategic point
【要犯】 yàofàn important criminal
【要饭】 yàofàn beg (for food or money) ◇ ～的 beggar
【要害】 yàohài ① vital part; crucial point: ～部位 vital part/ ～部门 key department/ 回避～问题 evade the crucial question (或 issue)/ 击中～ hit home/ 这篇文章的～是反对党的领导。The crucial point of this article is opposition to Party leadership. ② strategic point
【要好】 yàohǎo ① be on good terms; be close friends: 他们

俩从小就很～。The two of them have been close friends since childhood. ② eager to improve oneself; try hard to make progress: 这孩子很～。The kid is eager to make progress.
【要价】 yàojià ask a price; charge: ～过高 demand an exorbitant price; ask too much/ 对方在谈判中～越来越高。The other party demanded more and more in the negotiations.
【要件】 yàojiàn ① important document ② important condition
【要津】 yàojīn 〈书〉 key post: 位居～ hold a key post
【要紧】 yàojǐn ① important; essential: 随便做什么工作，最～的是实事求是。In whatever we do, the most important thing is to be realistic and down-to-earth./ 我有点～的事儿跟他商量。I have something urgent to discuss with him. ② be critical; be serious; matter: 衣服淋湿了不～，场上的麦子一定得苫好。We must cover the wheat on the threshing ground even if we get wet ourselves./ 不～，你明天去也可以。You can go tomorrow. It doesn't matter. ③ 〈方〉 be in a hurry to; be anxious to: ～去上班 be in a hurry to go to work
【要领】 yàolǐng ① main points; essentials; gist: 不得～ fail to grasp the main points; not see what sb. is driving at; miss the point ② essentials (of an exercise in military or athletic training): 掌握～ grasp the essentials
【要略】 yàolüè outline; summary
【要么】 yàome 〈连〉 or; either...or...: 赶快给他发个电报，～挂个长途也行。Send him a telegram at once, or call him long-distance./ ～他来，～我去，我们总得碰个头。Either he comes here or I go there; in any case we've got to see each other.
【要面子】 yào miànzi be keen on face-saving; be anxious to keep up appearances
【要命】 yàomìng ① drive sb. to his death; kill: 这样短的期限，要了我的命，也完成不了定额。I cannot fulfil the quota in such a short time even if I kill myself. ② confoundedly; extremely; awfully; terribly: 热得～ awfully hot ③ a nuisance: 真～，车胎又没气了。What an awful nuisance. The tyre's flat again.
【要强】 yàoqiáng be eager to excel; be anxious to outdo others
【要人】 yàorén very important person (V.I.P.); important personage
【要塞】 yàosài fort; fortress; fortification
【要是】 yàoshi if; suppose; in case: ～下雨怎么办？ What if it rains? 或 Suppose it rains?
【要素】 yàosù essential factor; key element
【要闻】 yàowén important news; front-page story
【要言不烦】 yào yán bù fán terse; succinct
【要员】 yàoyuán 〈旧〉 important official
【要帐】 yàozhàng demand payment of a debt; press for repayment of a loan; dun
【要职】 yàozhí important post: 身居～ hold an important post
【要旨】 yàozhǐ main idea; gist

**钥** yào
另见 yuè
【钥匙】 yàoshi key: 一把～开一把锁 open different locks with different keys — use different methods to deal with different people or problems

**鹞** yào ① harrier ② sparrow hawk
【鹞鹰】 yàoyīng sparrow hawk
【鹞子】 yàozi ① sparrow hawk ② 〈方〉 kite

**曜** yào 〈书〉 ① sunlight ② shine; illuminate

**耀** yào ① shine; illuminate; dazzle: 照～ shine upon; illuminate ② boast of; laud: 夸～ boast about ③ honour; credit
【耀斑】 yàobān 〈天〉 solar flare
【耀武扬威】 yàowǔ-yángwēi make a show of one's strength; swagger around
【耀眼】 yàoyǎn dazzling: 车灯～。The headlights are dazzling./ ～的红旗 bright red flags

## yē

**耶** yē
另见 yé
【耶和华】 Yēhéhuá 〈宗〉 Jehovah
【耶路撒冷】 Yēlùsālěng Jerusalem
【耶稣】 Yēsū 〈宗〉 Jesus
◇ ～会 the Society of Jesus; the Jesuits/ ～基督 Jesus Christ/ ～教 Protestantism

**倻** yē 见"伽倻琴" jiāyēqín

**掖** yē tuck in; thrust in between: 把被角～好 tuck in the corner of the quilt/ 把纸条从门缝里～进去 slip a note under the door/ 腰里～着枪 with a pistol in one's belt
另见 yè

**椰** yē 〈植〉 coconut palm; coconut tree; coco
【椰雕】 yēdiāo 〈工美〉 coconut carving
【椰干】 yēgān copra
【椰蓉】 yēróng 〈食品〉 shredded coconut stuffing
【椰油】 yēyóu coconut oil (或 butter)
【椰枣】 yēzǎo 〈植〉 ① date palm ② date
【椰子】 yēzi ① coconut palm; coconut tree; coco ② coconut
◇ ～肉 coconut meat/ ～糖 coconut candy/ ～汁 coconut milk

**噎** yē ① choke: 慢点吃，留神别～着。Eat slowly. Be careful not to choke. ② 〈方〉 render sb. speechless by saying sth. blunt or rude; choke off: 他一句话就把她给～回去了。She was just going to say something when that one remark of his choked her off.
【噎膈】 yēgé 〈中医〉 cancer of the esophagus

## yé

**爷** yé ① 〈方〉 father: ～娘 father and mother ② 〈方〉 grandfather ③ uncle (a respectful form of address for an elderly man) ④〈旧〉 a form of address for an official or rich man: 老～ sir; master; lord/ 少～ young master (of the house) ⑤ god: 老天～ God; Heaven
【爷们】 yémen 〈方〉 ① man; menfolk ② husband
【爷儿】 yér 〈口〉〔长辈和晚辈男子合称，后面常带数量词〕 men of two or more generations: ～俩并肩战斗。Father and son fought side by side.
【爷儿们】 yérmen 〈口〉〔长辈和晚辈男子合称〕 men of two or more generations
【爷爷】 yéye 〈口〉 ① (paternal) grandfather ② grandpa (a respectful form of address for an old man)

**耶** yé 〈书〉〈助〉〔表示疑问的语气〕: 是～非～？ Is it

or isn't it? 或 Yes or no?
另见 yē

揶 yé

【揶揄】 yéyú 〈书〉 ridicule; deride

yě

也 yě ①〈副〉 also; too; as well; either: 我妹妹～是售货员。My sister is a shop assistant too./ 你不去,我～不去。If you're not going, I'm not going either./ 中国是一个社会主义国家,～是一个发展中国家。China is a socialist country, and a developing country as well./ 什么工作都要走群众路线,卫生工作～是一样。It is necessary to follow the mass line in all work, including health work. ②〈副〉〔表示强调,常跟"再""一点""连"等字连用〕:他病得一点～不想吃。He is so ill that he doesn't feel like eating anything./ 现在连偏僻的山区～用上了拖拉机。Nowadays tractors are used even in remote mountainous regions./ 旧社会的苦,我永远～不会忘记。I shall never forget my sufferings in the old society. ③〈副〉〔表示转折或让步,常跟上文的"虽然""即使"等呼应〕:我即使干不了重活,～可以干点轻活嘛。 If I can't do heavy work, I can still do some light work./ 你不说我～知道。You don't have to tell me. I know already. ④〈副〉〔表示委婉等语气〕: ～只好这样了。We'll have to leave it at that./ 这袋土豆～就一百斤。 This sack of potatoes weighs a hundred *jin* at most. ⑤〈书〉〈助〉 ⓐ〔表示判断、解释等语气〕:陈胜者,阳城人～。Chen Sheng was a native of Yangcheng. ⓑ〔表示嘱咐〕:不可不慎～。You must be very careful. ⓒ〔表示感叹〕:何其毒～! How pernicious! ⓓ〔表示疑问或反诘〕:何～? How is that? 或 Why so? ⓔ〔用于句中,表示停顿〕:地之相去～,千有余里。The place is over a thousand *li* away.

【也罢】 yěbà ①〔表示容忍或只得如此〕:这次不去～,下次可一定要让我去。All right, I won't go this time but next time you must let me go. ②〈助〉〔叠用,表示不以某种情况为条件〕 whether...or...; no matter whether: 刮风～,下雪～,他都坚持长跑。He keeps up his long-distance running whether it's windy or snowy.

【也好】 yěhǎo ① it may not be a bad idea; may as well: 说明一下～。Better give an explanation./ 让他们自己干一干～,实践出真知嘛。 We might as well let them do it themselves, since real knowledge comes from practice. ②〔叠用,表示不以某种情况为条件〕whether ... or ...; no matter whether: 学习～,劳动～,他都很积极。He is enthusiastic about both study and physical labour.

【也门】 Yěmén Yemen ◇ ～人 Yemeni; Yemenite

【也许】 yěxǔ 〈副〉 perhaps; probably; maybe: 他～病了。Perhaps he's ill./ 我～来,～不来。I may or may not come.

【也…也…】 yě...yě... ①〔表示并列〕:操场上也有打球的,也有跑步的。Some of the people on the sports ground are playing ball games, some are running./ 他也不抽烟,也不喝酒。He neither smokes nor drinks. ②〔表示不以某种情况为条件〕:天好我们也干,天不好我们也干。We never stop working, rain or shine./ 你去也得去,不去也得去。You've got to go, whether you want to or not./ 他左想也不是,右想也不是。He just couldn't make up his mind either way.

冶 yě ① smelt (metal) ②〈书〉 seductively dressed or made up

【冶金】 yějīn metallurgy ◇ ～工业 metallurgical industry/ ～学 metallurgy

【冶炼】 yěliàn smelt ◇ ～操作 smelting operation/ ～厂 smeltery/ ～炉 smelting furnace/ ～时间 duration of heat

【冶容】 yěróng ① seductively made up ② seductive looks

野 yě ① open country; the open: 田～ open fields ② limit; boundary: 分～ line of demarcation/ 视～ field of vision ③ not in power; out of office: 在～党 a party not in power/ 下～ be forced to relinquish power ④ wild; uncultivated; undomesticated; untamed: ～花 wild flower/ ～鸭 wild duck ⑤ rude; rough: 说话太～ use coarse language; speak rudely/ 动作太～ rough play ⑥ unrestrained; abandoned; unruly: 放了几天假, 这孩子的心都玩～了。After the fun he's had during the holidays, the boy can't concentrate on his school work.

【野菜】 yěcài edible wild herbs

【野餐】 yěcān picnic

【野草】 yěcǎo weeds: ～丛生 be overgrown (或 choked) with weeds

【野传】 yěchuán 〈棒、垒球〉 wild throw ◇ ～球 passed ball

【野地】 yědì wild country; wilderness

【野果】 yěguǒ wild fruit

【野火】 yěhuǒ prairie fire; bush fire: ～烧不尽,春风吹又生。Not even a prairie fire can destroy the grass; it grows again when the spring breeze blows.

【野鸡】 yějī (ring-necked) pheasant

【野菊花】 yějúhuā mother chrysanthemum

【野驴】 yělǘ Asiatic wild ass; kiang

【野蛮】 yěmán ① uncivilized; savage ② barbarous; cruel; brutal: ～的种族主义 barbarous racism/ ～的屠杀 brutal massacre

【野猫】 yěmāo ① wildcat ② stray cat ③〈方〉 hare

【野牛】 yěniú wild ox

【野炮】 yěpào field gun; field artillery

【野蔷薇】 yěqiángwēi 〈植〉 multiflora rose

【野禽】 yěqín wild fowl

【野人】 yěrén savage

【野生】 yěshēng wild; uncultivated; feral ◇ ～动物 wild animal; wildlife/ ～植物 wild plant

【野史】 yěshǐ unofficial history

【野兽】 yěshòu wild beast; wild animal

【野兔】 yětù hare

【野外】 yěwài open country; field: 在～工作 do fieldwork ◇ ～生活 outdoor life/ ～演习 〈军〉 field exercise/ ～作业 fieldwork; field operation

【野豌豆】 yěwāndòu 〈植〉 vetch (*Vicia sativa*)

【野味】 yěwèi game (as food)

【野心】 yěxīn wild ambition; careerism: 侵略～ aggressive ambitions/ ～不死 cling to one's ambitious designs/ ～勃勃 be overweeningly ambitious; be obsessed with ambition ◇ ～家 careerist/ ～狼 a vicious wolf — a person of wicked ambition

【野性】 yěxìng wild nature; unruliness

【野营】 yěyíng camp; bivouac: 出外～ go camping ◇ ～训练 camp and field training

【野战】 yězhàn 〈军〉 field operations ◇ ～仓库 field depot/ ～工事 fieldwork/ ～军 field army/ ～炮 fieldpiece; field gun/ ～医院 field hospital

【野猪】 yězhū wild boar

yè

业 yè ① line of business; trade; industry: 各行各～ all trades and professions; different trades and callings; all walks of life/ 矿～ mining industry ② occupation; profession; employment; job: 失～ be out of a job; be unemployed ③ course of study: 结～ complete a course of study; graduate ④ cause; enterprise: 创～ start an enterprise; do pioneering work ⑤ estate; property: 家～ family property ⑥ engage in: ～农 engage in farming ⑦ already: ～已核实 have already been verified

【业绩】 yèjī outstanding achievement: 老一代无产阶级革命家的光辉～ the glorious achievements of proletarian revolutionaries of the older generation

【业经】 yèjīng already: ～批准 have been approved

【业务】 yèwù vocational work; professional work; business: 正确处理政治与～的关系 correctly handle the relations between politics and vocational work/ 钻研～ diligently study one's profession/ 恢复正常～ resume normal business ◇ ～范围 scope of business/ ～能力 professional ability/ ～水平 professional skill; vocational level/ ～协定 business agreement/ ～学习 vocational study/ ～知识 professional knowledge

【业余】 yèyú sparetime; after-hours; amateur: 他利用～时间给同志们修收音机。He repaired radios for his comrades during his spare time.
◇ ～爱好 hobby/ ～爱好者 amateur/ ～教育 sparetime education/ ～理论学习 theoretical study after workhours/ ～文艺工作者 amateur literary and art workers/ ～学校 sparetime school

【业障】 yèzhàng 见"孽障" nièzhàng

【业主】 yèzhǔ owner (of an enterprise or estate); proprietor

**叶** yè ① leaf; foliage: 落～ fallen leaves ② leaf-like thing: 百～窗 shutter; blind/ 一～扁舟 a small boat ③ page; leaf ④ part of a historical period: 清朝末～ the closing period of the Qing Dynasty/ 二十世纪中～ the middle of the twentieth century; mid-20th century ⑤ (Yè) a surname

【叶斑病】 yèbānbìng 〈农〉 leaf spot

【叶柄】 yèbǐng 〈植〉 petiole; leafstalk

【叶蝉】 yèchán 〈动〉 leafhopper

【叶蜂】 yèfēng 〈动〉 sawfly

【叶公好龙】 Yègōng hào lóng Lord Ye's love of dragons — professed love of what one really fears

【叶红素】 yèhóngsù 〈生化〉 phylloerythrin

【叶猴】 yèhóu 〈动〉 leaf monkey

【叶黄素】 yèhuángsù 〈化〉 xanthophyll

【叶蜡石】 yèlàshí 〈矿〉 pyrophyllite

【叶绿素】 yèlǜsù 〈生化〉 chlorophyll

【叶绿体】 yèlǜtǐ 〈生化〉 chloroplast

【叶轮】 yèlún 〈机〉 impeller; vane wheel ◇ ～泵 vane pump

【叶落归根】 yè luò guī gēn falling leaves settle on their roots — a person residing elsewhere finally returns to his ancestral home

【叶脉】 yèmài 〈植〉 (leaf) vein

【叶片】 yèpiàn ① 〈植〉 (leaf) blade ② 〈机〉 vane ◇ ～式压缩机 vane compressor

【叶鞘】 yèqiào 〈植〉 leaf sheath

【叶酸】 yèsuān 〈药〉 folic acid

【叶锈病】 yèxiùbìng 〈农〉 leaf rust

【叶序】 yèxù 〈植〉 phyllotaxy; leaf arrangement

【叶子】 yèzi leaf

**页** yè page; leaf: 活～ loose leaf/ 一本三百～的书 a book of three hundred pages/ 打开新的一～ open up a new chapter

【页边】 yèbiān margin

【页码】 yèmǎ page number

【页心】 yèxīn 〈印〉 type page

【页岩】 yèyán 〈地〉 shale ◇ ～油 shale oil

**曳** yè drag; haul; tug; tow

【曳光弹】 yèguāngdàn 〈军〉 tracer bullet or shell; tracer

【曳力】 yèlì 〈物〉 drag force

【曳绳钓】 yèshéngdiào 〈渔〉 trolling

**夜** yè night; evening: 冬天昼短～长。In winter the days are short and the nights long./ 三天三～讲不完。It would take days to tell it all.

【夜班】 yèbān night shift

【夜半】 yèbàn midnight

【夜叉】 yèchā ① 〈佛教〉 yaksha (a malevolent spirit) ② a hideous, ferocious person

【夜长梦多】 yècháng-mèngduō a long night is fraught with dreams — a long delay means many hitches

【夜场】 yèchǎng evening show

【夜车】 yèchē ① night train ②〔多用于〕: 开～ work deep into the night; burn the midnight oil

【夜出动物】 yèchū dòngwù nocturnal animal

【夜大学】 yèdàxué evening university

【夜蛾】 yè'é 〈动〉 noctuid

【夜分】 yèfēn 〈书〉 midnight

【夜工】 yègōng night work; night job: 打～ work at night; do a night job 又作"夜作"

【夜光表】 yèguāngbiǎo luminous watch

【夜光虫】 yèguāngchóng noctiluca

【夜光螺】 yèguāngluó green snail

【夜航】 yèháng night flight or navigation

【夜壶】 yèhú chamber pot

【夜间】 yèjiān at night: ～行军 march by night; night march/ ～施工 carry on construction work at night ◇ ～演习 night exercise/ ～战斗机 night fighter

【夜交藤】 yèjiāoténg 〈中药〉 the vine of multiflower knotweed (*Polygonum multiflorum*)

【夜景】 yèjǐng night scene (或 view): 一幅壮丽的长江大桥～ the magnificent view of the Changjiang bridge at night

【夜来香】 yèláixiāng 〈植〉 cordate telosma

【夜阑人静】 yèlán-rénjìng in the dead of night; in the still (或 quiet) of the night

【夜郎自大】 Yèláng zìdà ludicrous conceit of the king of Yelang — parochial arrogance

【夜里】 yèli at night

【夜盲】 yèmáng 〈医〉 nyctalopia; night blindness

【夜猫子】 yèmāozi 〈方〉 ① owl ② a person who goes to bed late; night owl

【夜明珠】 yèmíngzhū a legendary luminous pearl

【夜幕】 yèmù curtain of night; gathering darkness: ～笼罩着大地。The land is enveloped in a curtain of darkness./ ～降临。Night has fallen.

【夜尿症】 yèniàozhèng enuresis; bed-wetting

【夜勤】 yèqín night duty

【夜曲】 yèqǔ 〈乐〉 nocturne

【夜色】 yèsè the dim light of night: 趁着～ by starlight or moonlight

【夜视仪】 yèshìyí 〈军〉 night vision device (或 instrument)

【夜啼】 yètí 〈中医〉 morbid night crying of babies

【夜晚】 yèwǎn night

【夜望镜】 yèwàngjìng 〈军〉 snooperscope

【夜袭】 yèxí night attack (或 raid)

【夜宵】 yèxiāo food (或 refreshments) taken late at night; midnight snack

【夜校】 yèxiào night (或 evening) school

【夜行军】 yèxíngjūn night march

【夜以继日】 yè yǐ jì rì day and night; round the clock: 工程正在～地进行。Work is going on day and night at the

construction site.
【夜莺】 yèyīng nightingale
【夜鹰】 yèyīng goatsucker; nightjar
【夜游神】 yèyóushén the legendary god on patrol at night — a person who is up and about at night; night owl
【夜战】 yèzhàn 〈军〉 night fighting
【夜总会】 yèzǒnghuì nightclub

**咽** yè 见"哽咽" gěngyè; "呜咽" wūyè
另见 yān; yàn

**烨** yè 〈书〉 ① firelight or sunlight ② (of light) bright

**晔** yè 〈书〉 (of light) bright

**液** yè liquid; fluid; juice: 体～ body fluid/ 胃～ gastric juice
【液化】 yèhuà 〈化〉 liquefaction
◇ ～器 liquefier/ ～天然气 liquefied natural gas (LNG)/ ～石油气 liquefied petroleum gas (LPG)
【液晶】 yèjīng 〈物〉 liquid crystal
【液冷】 yèlěng 〈机〉 liquid cooling (或 cooled) ◇ ～式内燃机 liquid cooled engine
【液力】 yèlì 〈机〉 hydraulic ◇ ～变速箱 hydraulic transmission box/ ～制动器 hydraulic brake
【液泡】 yèpào 〈生〉 vacuole
【液态】 yètài 〈物〉 liquid state ◇ ～空气 liquid air
【液体】 yètǐ liquid
◇ ～比重计 hydrometer/ ～燃料 liquid fuel/ ～燃料火箭发动机〈军〉 liquid-fuel rocket engine
【液压】 yèyā hydraulic pressure
◇ ～泵 hydraulic pump/ ～表 hydraulic pressure gauge/ ～成形 hydroform/ ～传动 hydraulic transmission (或 drive)/ ～联轴节 hydraulic coupling

**掖** yè ① support sb. by the arm ② help; assist; promote: 奖～ 〈书〉 encourage by rewarding and promoting
另见 yē

**谒** yè 〈书〉 call on (a superior or an elder person); pay one's respects to: ～陵 pay homage at sb.'s mausoleum
【谒见】 yèjiàn call on (a superior or a senior in the clan hierarchy); have an audience with

**腋** yè ① 〈生理〉 axilla; armpit ② 〈植〉 axil
【腋臭】 yèchòu underarm odour
【腋毛】 yèmáo armpit hair
【腋窝】 yèwō armpit
【腋芽】 yèyá 〈植〉 axillary bud

**靥** yè dimple

## yī

**一** yī ① one: ～万～ eleven thousand/ 三千～ three thousand one hundred/ ～营～连 the First Company of the First Battalion/ 棉纺～厂 No. 1 Cotton Mill ② single; alone; only one: ～枪就打中了目标 hit the target with a single shot/ 你～个人行吗？Can you manage all by yourself? ③ same: 意见不～。Opinions differ./ ～根藤上的苦瓜 bitter gourds from the same vine — people with a similar bitter past/ 军民～家。The army and the people are of one family. ④ whole; all; throughout: ～冬 the whole winter; all winter; throughout the winter/ ～脸的土 one's face covered with dust/ ～屋子的人都欢腾起来。Everybody in the room was overjoyed. ⑤ each; per; every time: 四个小组，～组五人 four groups with five people in each/ ～小时六十公里 at 60 kilometres per hour/ 大家～提起那艰苦创业的日子，总有说不完的话。Every time we talk about the hard pioneering days, we have so much to say that we can't get it all out. ⑥ also; otherwise: 汞溴红～名红汞。Merbromin is also known as mercurochrome. ⑦ concentrated; wholehearted: ～心～意 heart and soul; wholeheartedly ⑧〔表示动作是一次或短暂的〕: 笑～笑 give a smile/ 歇～歇 have a rest/ 等～等 wait a bit/ 瞧～眼 take a look/ 咳～声 give a cough ⑨〔用在动词或动量词之前，表示先做某个动作，下文说明动作结果〕: ～跳跳了过去 get over in one jump/ 他～脚把球踢进了球门。He kicked the ball into the goal. 或 He kicked a goal./ 经他这么～说，大家又都有信心了。This explanation of his restored our confidence. ⑩〔与"就""即"等字相呼应，表示两事时间紧接〕 once; as soon as: ～做好准备，就破土动工。Construction will begin as soon as preparations are completed./ 天～亮社员们就下地干活。At dawn the commune members started off to work in the fields. ⑪ 〈书〉〈助〉〔用于某些词前加强语气〕: 事态之严重～至于此！To think that things should have come to such a pass!/ ～似瓮中捉鳖 be as easy as catching a turtle in a jar ⑫ 〈乐〉 a note of the scale in *gongchepu* (工尺谱), corresponding to 7 in numbered musical notation

注意 在第四声(去声)字前念第二声(阳平)，如"一半" yíbàn; "一共" yígòng。在第一、二、三声(阴平、阳平、上声)字前念第四声(去声)，如"一天" yìtiān; "一年" yìnián; "一点" yìdiǎn。本词典为简便起见，条目中的"一"字，都注第一声(阴平)。

【一把手】 yībǎshǒu ① a party to an undertaking; a member; a hand: 我们准备搭伙干，你也算上～吧。We're going to pool our efforts. Shall we count you in? ② a good hand: 她干农活可真是～。She is really good at farm work.
【一把抓】 yībǎzhuā ① take everything into one's own hands ② try to tackle all problems at once regardless of their relative importance
【一败涂地】 yī bài tú dì suffer a crushing defeat
【一班人】 yībānrén members of a squad — a small body of people working together: 党委～ the members of the Party committee
【一般】 yībān ① same as; just like: 他们俩～高。The two of them are the same height./ 火车飞～地驰去。The train flashed past like lightning. ② general; ordinary; common: ～号召和个别指导相结合 combine general calls (for action) with specific guidance/ ～工作人员 ordinary personnel; an ordinary member of the staff/ ～的做法 common practice/ ～说来 generally speaking/ 我～早上六点起床。I usually get up at 6 in the morning./ 他只是～地说了说，没有详谈。He just spoke in general terms and didn't elaborate./ 这部小说写得～。This novel is only mediocre. 或 There's nothing striking about this novel.
◇ ～等价物 universal equivalent/ ～规律 universal law; general rule/ ～性辩论 general debate
【一般化】 yībānhuà vague generalization: 防止领导～ avoid giving only vague, general directions
【一般见识】 yībān jiànshi lower oneself to the same level as sb.: 别跟他～！You don't want to bother yourself arguing with a person like him.
【一板一眼】 yībǎn-yīyǎn following a prescribed pattern in speech or action; scrupulous and methodical
【一半】 yībàn one half; half; in part: ～以上 more than half/ 歉收～由于干旱，～由于虫灾。The crop failure was due in part to drought and in part to insect pests.

【一…半…】 yī… bàn… 〔分别用在同义词或近义词前，表示不多或不久〕：这活儿一时半会儿完不了。This job can't be finished in a short while./ 我只听到一句半句的。What I heard was very fragmentary.

【一半天】 yībàntiān in a day or two

【一辈子】 yībèizi all one's life; throughout one's life; as long as one lives; a lifetime: ～也忘不了。I won't forget as long as I live./ 改造世界观是～的事。Remoulding one's world outlook is a lifelong task./ ～不干，～不会。If you never do a thing yourself, you'll never know how to do it./ 一个人做点好事并不难，难的是～做好事。It is not hard for one to do a bit of good. What is hard is to do good all one's life.

【一本万利】 yī běn wàn lì a small investment brings a ten thousand-fold profit; make big profits with a small capital

【一本正经】 yī běn zhèngjīng in all seriousness; in dead earnest: 装得～的样子 be sanctimonious

【一鼻孔出气】 yī bíkǒng chūqì breathe through the same nostrils — sing the same tune

【一笔勾销】 yī bǐ gōuxiāo write off at one stroke; cancel: 前帐～ cancel all debts

【一笔抹杀】 yī bǐ mǒshā blot out at one stroke; condemn out of hand; totally negate: 这些成绩是不能～的。These achievements cannot be gainsaid.

【一臂之力】 yī bì zhī lì a helping hand: 助我～ lend me a hand

【一边】 yībiān ① one side: 这块木料只有～光滑。Only one side of this piece of wood is smooth./ 站在人民群众～ side with the masses of the people ②〔表示一个动作跟另一个动作同时进行〕at the same time; simultaneously: 他～往前走，～唱着歌儿。He sang as he strolled along./ ～喝茶，～聊天 chat over a cup of tea

【一边倒】 yībiāndǎo ① lean to one side; side with sb. without reservation ② predominate; enjoy overwhelming superiority

【一并】 yībìng 〈副〉 along with all the others; in the lump: 连同类似情况～考虑 to be considered together with all similar cases

【一病不起】 yī bìng bù qǐ take to one's bed and never leave it again; fall ill and die

【一波未平，一波又起】 yī bō wèi píng, yī bō yòu qǐ hardly has one wave subsided when another rises — one trouble follows another

【一…不…】 yī… bù… ①〔分别用在两个动词前面，表示动作或情况一经发生就不改变〕：一去不返 gone never to return/ 一定不易 unalterable ②〔分别用在一个名词和一个动词前面，表示强调或夸张〕：一字不漏 without missing a single word/ 一动不动 not move an inch; not stir; be perfectly still

【一不怕苦，二不怕死】 yī bù pà kǔ, èr bù pà sǐ fear neither hardship nor death

【一不做，二不休】 yī bù zuò, èr bù xiū carry the thing through, whatever the consequences; in for a penny, in for a pound

【一步登天】 yī bù dēng tiān reach the sky in a single bound — attain the highest level in one step; have a meteoric rise

【一步一个脚印儿】 yī bù yīge jiǎoyìnr every step leaves its print — work steadily and make solid progress

【一差二错】 yīchā-èrcuò possible mistake or mishap: 万一有个～ just in case there is a slip somewhere; just in case of accidents

【一场空】 yīchángkōng all in vain; futile: 竹篮打水～ as futile as drawing water with a bamboo basket

【一唱百和】 yī chàng bǎi hè when one starts singing, all the others join in — (of a suggestion, etc.) meet with general approval

【一唱一和】 yīchàng-yīhè sing a duet with sb.; sing the same tune; echo each other

【一朝天子一朝臣】 yī cháo tiānzǐ yī cháo chén every new sovereign brings his own courtiers — a new chief brings in new aides

【一尘不染】 yī chén bù rǎn not soiled by a speck of dust; spotless: 仪器上～。The apparatus is spotlessly clean./ 警卫战士身居闹市，～。The garrison troops remain uncontaminated amidst the temptations of a big city.

【一成不变】 yī chéng bù biàn immutable and frozen; invariable; unalterable: ～的东西是没有的。Nothing is immutable./ 没有～的规则。There is no hard and fast rule.

【一筹莫展】 yī chóu mò zhǎn can find no way out; be at one's wits' end; be at the end of one's tether

【一触即发】 yī chù jí fā may be triggered at any moment; be on the verge of breaking out: 武装冲突有～之势。Armed conflict may break out at any moment./ 形势～。It's an explosive situation.

【一触即溃】 yī chù jí kuì collapse at the first encounter

【一锤定音】 yī chuí dìng yīn set the tune with one beat of the gong — give the final word

【一次】 yīcì once: 我只跟他见过～面。I've met him only once./ 机器～试运成功。The machine worked successfully on its first test run. ◇ ～方程〈数〉linear equation/ ～函数〈数〉linear function

【一蹴而就】 yī cù ér jiù accomplish in one move

【一大二公】 yī dà èr gōng (of people's communes) large in size and collective in nature; larger in size and having a higher degree of public ownership (than the cooperatives)

【一旦】 yīdàn ① in a single day; in a very short time: 毁于～ be destroyed in one day ② once; in case; now that: 代表先进阶级的正确思想，～被群众掌握，就会变成改造社会、改造世界的物质力量。Once the correct ideas characteristic of the advanced class are grasped by the masses, these ideas turn into a material force which changes society and changes the world./ 他们多年相处，～分别，不免依依不舍。After being together for years, they can't bear to part from each other.

【一刀两断】 yī dāo liǎng duàn sever at one blow — make a clean break

【一道】 yīdào together; side by side; alongside: 我们～走吧。Let's go together./ 干部应当和工人～参加生产劳动。Cadres should take part in productive labour alongside the workers./ 学校、家长和社会～担负起教育下一代的责任。School, parents and society share the responsibility of educating the younger generation.

【一得之功】 yī dé zhī gōng just an occasional, minor success: 不要沾沾自喜于～。Don't feel self-satisfied over just a minor success.

【一得之愚】 yī dé zhī yú 〈谦〉 my humble opinion

【一等】 yīděng first-class; first-rate; top-grade ◇ ～功 Merit Citation, First Class/ ～秘书 First Secretary/ ～品 first-rate (或 top-quality) product

【一点论】 yīdiǎnlùn the doctrine that everything has only one aspect; the doctrine affirming only one aspect

【一点儿】 yīdiǎnr a bit; a little: ～也不累 not feel the least bit tired/ ～都不知道 have not the faintest idea/ ～用处也没有 utterly useless/ 这事我知道～。I know a little about it./ 壶里水只剩下这么～了。This is all the water that's left in the kettle./ 还有～希望。There is still a gleam of hope./ 这是我们的～心意。This is just a small token of our appreciation./ 桌上没有～灰尘。There isn't a speck of dust on the desk.

【一点一滴】 yīdiǎn-yīdī every little bit: ～地积累资料 gather material bit by bit

【一丁点儿】 yīdīngdiǎnr 〈方〉 a wee bit

【一定】 yīdìng ① fixed; specified; definite; regular: 工人们每个月都有～的生产指标。The workers have fixed monthly production quotas./ 按照～的规格进行生产 work according to specifications/ 勘探队员成天在野外作业,没有～的住处。The prospectors are always out in the field and never settle down in a fixed place./ 她一忙起来,吃饭睡觉都没有～的时间了。When she gets really busy, she doesn't keep regular hours for eating or sleeping. ② certainly; surely; necessarily: 我们的目的～要达到。我们的目的～能够达到。Our goal must be attained. Our goal can unquestionably be attained./ ～要搞好同志间的团结。It is imperative to achieve unity among comrades./ 全世界人民的革命斗争～胜利。The revolutionary struggle of the people throughout the world is bound to triumph./ 帝国主义～要灭亡。Imperialism is doomed to extinction./ 我们～要解放台湾! We are determined to liberate Taiwan!/ 他～是被什么要紧事拖住了。He must have been held up by some urgent business./ 星期天～来啊! Be sure to come on Sunday. ③ given; particular; certain: 在～意义上 in a certain sense/ 在～程度上 to a certain degree/ 在～条件下 under given conditions/ 在阶级社会里,报纸都是为～阶级服务的。In a class society, newspapers all serve a particular class. ④ proper; fair; due: 具有～规模的工厂 a fair-sized factory/ 作出了～的贡献 have made some contributions/ 达到～水平 reach a fairly high level/ 给以～的重视 attach due importance to

【一定之规】 yīdìng zhī guī ① fixed pattern ② one's own way

【一动】 yīdòng easily; frequently; at every turn: 他～就生气。He takes offence easily.

【一度】 yīdù once; on one occasion; for a time: 一年～ once a year; yearly; annually/ 他因病～休学。He stopped going to school for a time on account of illness.

【一端】 yīduān one aspect (或 side) of the matter: 此其～。This is one aspect of the matter./ 各执～ each sticking to his own argument

【一…而…】 yī... ér... 〔分别用在两个动词前面,表示前一个动作很快产生了结果〕: 一怒而去 go away in a temper; leave in anger/ 一饮而尽 empty the glass at one gulp/ 一拥而上 rush up in a crowd/ 一掠而过 skim over

【一而再,再而三】 yī ér zài, zài ér sān again and again; time and again; repeatedly

【一二】 yī-èr one or two; just a few; just a little: 略知～ know a little about; have some idea about/ 邀请～知己 invite a few close friends

【一…二…】 yī...èr... 〔分别加在某些双音节形容词的两个词素前面,表示强调〕: 一清二白 perfectly clean; unimpeachable; spotless/ 一清二楚 perfectly clear; as clear as daylight; crystal clear

【一二报数】 yī'èr bàoshù 〈军〉 By twos, number!

【一二·九运动】 Yī'èr Jiǔ Yùndòng the December 9th Movement (a demonstration staged on December 9, 1935 by Beijing students under the leadership of the Chinese Communist Party, calling for resistance to Japanese aggression and national salvation)

【一发千钧】 yī fà qiān jūn a hundredweight hanging by a hair — in imminent peril: 在这～的时刻 at this critical moment

【一帆风顺】 yī fān fēng shùn plain (或 smooth) sailing: 革命从来就不是～的。Revolution is never plain sailing.

【一反常态】 yī fǎn chángtài depart from one's normal behaviour; act out of character

【一方面】 yī fāngmiàn ① one side: 这只是事情的～。This is only one side of the matter. ②〔常叠用〕 on the one hand..., on the other hand...; for one thing..., for another...: 他们～很想去医院看望班长,～又怕影响他休息。On the one hand they wanted very much to visit their squad leader in hospital; on the other hand, they didn't want to disturb his rest./ 这场球打输了,～是由于对方实力较强,另～也是因为我们没有配合好。We lost the game because, for one thing, our opponents were quite strong and, for another, our teamwork was poor.

【一分为二】 yī fēn wéi èr 〈哲〉 one divides into two: 事物都是～的。Everything divides into two.

【一风吹】 yīfēngchuī scatter to the winds; dismiss (charges, etc.) altogether; cancel the whole thing

【一夫多妻制】 yīfū-duōqīzhì polygyny; polygamy

【一夫一妻制】 yīfū-yīqīzhì monogyny; monogamy

【一概】 yīgài 〈副〉 one and all; without exception; totally; categorically: ～拒绝 reject without exception/ ～排斥 totally exclude

【一概而论】 yīgài ér lùn 〔多用于否定〕 treat (different matters) as the same: 不能～ not to be lumped together

【一干二净】 yīgān-èrjìng thoroughly; completely: 忘得～ clean (或 completely) forget/ 把自己洗刷得～ try to absolve oneself from all blame

【一个劲儿】 yīgejìnr continuously; persistently: 雨～地下。It kept on raining./ 她～地要求到边疆去。She persistently asked for permission to go to work in a frontier region.

【一个心眼儿】 yīge xīnyǎnr ① have one's heart set on sth.; devotedly; stubbornly: ～跟党走 devotedly follow the Party ② be of one mind: 我们大家都是～。We are all of one mind.

【一共】 yīgòng altogether; in all; all told: ～二十个。There are twenty in all (或 all told)./ ～多少人? How many are there altogether?

【一股脑儿】 yīgǔnǎor 〈方〉 completely; lock, stock and barrel; root and branch 又作"一古脑儿"

【一鼓作气】 yī gǔ zuò qì press on to the finish without letup; get sth. done in one vigorous effort: 他们～爬上山顶。They pressed on without letup until they got to the top of the hill.

【一贯】 yīguàn consistent; persistent; all along: ～政策 consistent policy/ ～为群众做好事 have persistently (或 all along) been doing good for the people

【一贯道】 Yīguàndào a reactionary secret society which, under the cover of religious activities, served the Japanese invaders and Kuomintang reactionaries

【一棍子打死】 yī gùnzi dǎsǐ knock sb. down at one stroke; finish off with one blow; completely negate: 对待犯错误的同志,要批评帮助,不能～。Instead of bludgeoning our erring comrades, we should help them with criticism.

【一锅粥】 yīguōzhōu a pot of porridge — a complete mess; all in a muddle: 乱成～ be all muddled up

【一国三公】 yī guó sān gōng a state with three rulers — divided leadership

【一哄而起】 yī hōng ér qǐ (of a group of people) be aroused to precipitate action; rush headlong into mass action

【一哄而散】 yī hòng ér sàn break up (或 disperse) in a hubbub

【一呼百诺】 yī hū bǎi nuò have hundreds at one's beck and call

【一呼百应】 yī hū bǎi yìng hundreds respond to a single call

【一环扣一环】 yī huán kòu yī huán (of steps in a process) closely linked

【一晃】 yīhuǎng flash: 窗外有个人影,～就不见了。A figure flashed past the window.

【一晃】 yīhuàng (of time) pass in a flash: ～几年又过去了。

Several years passed in a flash.

【一挥而就】 yī huī ér jiù a flourish of the pen and it's done; finish a piece of writing or a painting at one go

【一回生,二回熟】 yī huí shēng, èr huí shú ① first time strangers, second time friends; soon get to know each other ② first time awkward (或 clumsy), second time skilful; difficult at first, easy later on

【一回事】 yī huí shì ① one and the same (thing): 他们所说的是～。They were talking about the same thing. ② one thing: 主观愿望是～,实际情况又是～。Subjective wishes are one thing, objective reality is another.

【一会儿】 yīhuìr ① a little while: 咱们歇～。Let's rest for a while. ② in a moment; presently: 我～就来。I'll be coming in a moment. 或 I won't be a minute./ ～地上就积起了一层雪。Soon the ground was covered with a layer of snow. ③〔叠用在两个反义词前面,表示情况的交替〕now ... now...; one moment... the next...: 天气～晴～阴。The weather is now clear, now cloudy./ 他～这么说,～那么说。He says one thing one moment and another thing the next.

【一级风】 yījífēng 〈气〉 force 1 wind; light air

【一己】 yījǐ oneself: ～之私 one's own selfish interests

【一技之长】 yī jì zhī cháng proficiency in a particular line (或 field); professional skill; speciality

【一见如故】 yī jiàn rú gù feel like old friends at the first meeting

【一见钟情】 yī jiàn zhōngqíng fall in love at first sight

【一箭双雕】 yī jiàn shuāng diāo shoot two hawks with one arrow; kill two birds with one stone

【一经】 yījīng 〈副〉〔表示只要经过某种步骤或行为〕as soon as; once: 错误～发现,就应立即纠正。Mistakes should be corrected as soon as detected.

【一…就…】 yī... jiù... 〔表示两事时间上前后紧接〕no sooner ...than...; the moment...; as soon as; once: 这情况她一看就明白了。She took in the situation at a glance./ 他一接到通知就动身了。He started off as soon as he got the message.

【一举】 yījǔ with one action; at one stroke; at one fell swoop: ～粉碎反党集团 smash the anti-Party clique at one blow/ ～歼灭来犯之敌 wipe out the invaders at one fell swoop/ ～成名 become famous overnight; achieve instant fame

【一举两得】 yī jǔ liǎng dé kill two birds with one stone

【一句话】 yī jù huà in a word; in short

【一蹶不振】 yī jué bù zhèn collapse after one setback; never be able to recover after a setback

【一看二帮】 yī kàn èr bāng observe and help: 对犯错误的同志要～。With comrades who have made mistakes, we should not only see how they behave but give them help.

【一刻千金】 yīkè qiānjīn every minute is precious

【一孔之见】 yī kǒng zhī jiàn a peephole view; a narrow view; a limited view

【一口】 yī kǒu ① a mouthful; a bite: 吸～气 draw a breath/ ～吃不成个胖子。You can't build up your constitution on one mouthful. ② with certainty; readily; flatly: ～断定 arbitrarily assert; allege/ ～答应 readily agree; readily promise/ ～回绝 flatly refuse

【一口气】 yīkǒuqì ① one breath: 只要我还有～,就要为党和人民工作。As long as there's a breath left in me, I'll work for the Party and the people. ② in one breath; without a break; at one go; at a stretch: ～干完 finish the work at one go/ ～跑了五千米 run 5,000 metres at a stretch

【一块儿】 yīkuàir ① at the same place: 在～工作 work at the same place ② together: ～去 go together

【一来二去】 yīlái-èrqù in the course of contacts: 他们常在地里一块儿干活,～地也就熟了。As they often work together in the fields, they have got to know each other quite well.

【一览】 yīlǎn general survey; bird's-eye view: 《北京名胜古迹～》 *A Guide to the Historical Relics and Scenic Spots of Beijing*

【一览表】 yīlǎnbiǎo table; schedule: 火车行车时间～ railway timetable

【一览无余】 yī lǎn wú yú take in everything at a glance

【一揽子】 yīlǎnzi wholesale; package ◇ ～计划 package plan/ ～交易 package deal

【一劳永逸】 yī láo yǒng yì get sth. done once and for all: ～的解决办法 a solution that holds good for all time; a permanent solution

【一力】 yīlì do one's best; do all one can: ～成全 do one's best to help (sb. to achieve his aim)

【一连】 yīlián 〈副〉 in a row; in succession; running: ～三年获得丰收 reap good harvests for three years in a row/ ～下了三天雨。It rained for three days running.

【一连串】 yīliánchuàn a succession of; a series of; a string of; a chain of: ～的事件 a succession of events/ ～问题 a series of questions

【一了百了】 yī liǎo bǎi liǎo ① all troubles end when the main trouble ends ② death ends all one's troubles

【一鳞半爪】 yīlín-bànzhǎo odd bits; fragments: ～的情况 odd bits of information/ ～的知识 fragmentary knowledge

【一溜儿】 yīliùr 〈方〉 ① row: ～平房 a row of one-storey houses ② neighbourhood; vicinity: 他就住在那～。He lives somewhere around there.

【一溜歪斜】 yīliù wāixié 〈方〉 (walk, etc.) unsteadily in a zigzag

【一溜烟】 yīliùyān (run away) swiftly: 小汽车～开走了。The car sped off./ 他～就没影儿了。He disappeared in an instant (或 a flash).

【一路】 yīlù ① all the way; throughout the journey: ～上说说笑笑 chat cheerfully all the way/ ～多保重。Take care of yourself on the journey./ ～平安! Have a pleasant journey. 或 Have a good trip. 或 *Bon voyage*./ 客队～领先。The visiting team led from the beginning. ② of the same kind: ～货 one of a kind; birds of a feather ③ go the same way; take the same route: 咱们是～吗? Are we going the same way? ④ single file: 成～纵队齐步走 march (in) single file/ ～纵队 single column

【一律】 yīlǜ ① same; alike; uniform: ～对待 treat in the same way (或 equally)/ 不宜强求～。No rigid uniformity should be sought. ② all; without exception: 国家不分大小,应该～平等。All countries, big or small, should be equal (或 on an equal footing).

【一落千丈】 yī luò qiānzhàng drop a thousand *zhang* in one fall — suffer a disastrous decline

【一马当先】 yī mǎ dāngxiān take the lead; be in the forefront

【一马平川】 yī mǎ píngchuān a wide expanse of flat land; flat country

【一脉相承】 yī mài xiāng chéng come down in one continuous line; can be traced to the same origin

【一毛不拔】 yī máo bù bá unwilling to give up even a hair — very stingy

【一面】 yīmiàn ① one side; one aspect: 这座房子朝南的～有两个窗户。The house has two windows on the south side./ 这里的条件既有有利的～,也有不利的～。The situation here has both favourable and unfavourable aspects. ②〔表示一个动作跟另一个动作同时进行〕at the same time; simultaneously: ～教,～学 learn while teaching/ 他～说着,～

朝门口走去。So saying, he made for the door.

【一面之词】 yīmiàn zhī cí the statement of only one of the parties

【一面之交】 yī miàn zhī jiāo have met only once; be casually acquainted

【一鸣惊人】 yī míng jīng rén (of an obscure person) amaze the world with a single brilliant feat; set the world on fire

【一命呜呼】 yī mìng wūhū die; kick the bucket

【一模一样】 yīmú-yīyàng exactly alike; as like as two peas: 她长得跟她母亲～。She's the image of her mother.

【一目了然】 yī mù liǎorán be clear at a glance

【一目十行】 yī mù shí háng take in ten lines at a glance — read rapidly

【一年半载】 yīnián-bànzǎi a year or so; in about a year

【一年到头】 yī nián dào tóu throughout the year; all (the) year round

【一年生】 yīniánshēng 〈植〉 annual ◇ ～植物 annual plant; annual

【一年四季】 yīnián-sìjì throughout (the four seasons of) the year; all the year round

【一年之计在于春】 yī nián zhī jì zàiyú chūn the whole year's work depends on a good start in spring

【一念之差】 yī niàn zhī chā a wrong decision made in a moment of weakness (with serious consequences); a momentary slip

【一诺千金】 yī nuò qiānjīn a promise that will be kept; that's a solemn promise

【一拍即合】 yī pāi jí hé fit in readily; chime in easily: 他的资产阶级思想同修正主义路线～。His bourgeois ideas fit in easily with the revisionist line.

【一盘散沙】 yī pán sǎnshā (like) a sheet of loose sand — in a state of disunity

【一偏】 yīpiān one-sided: ～之见 one-sided view

【一瞥】 yīpiē ① a quick glance: 就在这～之间，我看出了她非常激动。In a quick glance I noticed her agitation. ② a glimpse; a brief survey: «长城～» *A Glimpse of the Great Wall*

【一贫如洗】 yī pín rú xǐ penniless; in utter destitution

【一品红】 yīpǐnhóng 〈植〉 poinsettia

【一平二调】 yī píng èr diào equalitarianism and indiscriminate transfer of resources

【一抔黄土】 yī póu huángtǔ ①〈书〉 a handful of yellow earth — a grave ② sth. utterly insignificant

【一暴十寒】 yī pù shí hán work hard for one day and do nothing for ten — work by fits and starts

【一妻多夫制】 yīqī-duōfūzhì polyandry

【一齐】 yīqí 〈副〉 at the same time; simultaneously; in unison: ～鼓掌 clap hands in unison/ ～努力 make a concerted effort/ ～出动 go into action simultaneously/ 人和行李～到了。The luggage arrived at the same time as the passengers.

【一起】 yīqǐ ① in the same place: 住在～ live in the same place ② together; in company: 奶奶和孙女儿～进城。Grandma went downtown with her granddaughter./ 三大革命运动～抓 keep a tight hold on all the three great revolutionary movements at once/ 让我们团结在～，战斗在～，胜利在～。Let us stand together, fight together and win together. ③〈方〉 altogether; in all: 这几件东西～多少钱？How much is that altogether?

【一气】 yīqì ① at one go; without a break; at a stretch: ～游了三千米 swim three thousand metres at a stretch ② of the same gang; hand in glove: 串通～ work hand in glove; collude ③ a spell; a fit: 瞎闹～ raise hell; kick up a row/ 胡吹～ tell tall stories

【一气呵成】 yīqì hē chéng ① (of an essay) form a coherent whole; make smooth reading ② get sth. done at one go; accomplish sth. without any interruption or letup

【一钱不值】 yī qián bù zhí not worth a penny; utterly worthless; mere trash

【一窍不通】 yī qiào bù tōng know nothing about (a subject); lack the slightest knowledge of; be utterly ignorant of

【一切】 yīqiè all; every; everything: 抓住～机会 seize every opportunity/ 把～献给祖国 give one's all to one's country/ ～为了前线的胜利 everything for victory at the front/ ～行动听指挥。Obey orders in all your actions.

【一清早】 yīqīngzǎo early in the morning

【一穷二白】 yī qióng èr bái poor and blank: 改变我国"～"的面貌 lift our country from the state of "poverty and blankness"

【一丘之貉】 yī qiū zhī hé jackals from the same lair; birds of a feather

【一去不复返】 yī qù bù fù fǎn gone for ever; gone never to return

【一人得道，鸡犬升天】 yī rén dé dào, jī-quǎn shēng tiān when a man attains the Tao (enlightenment and immortality), even his pets ascend to heaven — when a man gets to the top, all his friends and relations get there with him

【一任】 yīrèn 〈书〉 allow: 岂能～他胡作非为？How can we let him run amuck?

【一仍旧贯】 yī réng jiù guàn stick to the old practice; follow the old routine

【一日千里】 yīrì qiānlǐ a thousand *li* a day — at a tremendous pace; with giant strides: 我国的社会主义建设在～地向前发展。The socialist construction of our country is forging ahead at a tremendous pace.

【一日三秋】 yīrì sānqiū one day (away from a dear one) seems like three years

【一如既往】 yī rú jìwǎng just as in the past; as before; as always: 我们将～坚决支持你们的正义斗争。We will, as always, firmly support your just struggle.

【一扫而光】 yī sǎo ér guāng make a clean sweep of; clear off; finish off; get rid of sth. lock, stock and barrel: 忧郁的心情～ rid oneself of all shadows of anxiety

【一色】 yīsè ① of the same colour: 水天～。The water and the sky are of one hue. ② of the same type; uniform: ～的瓦房 tiled houses of a uniform style

【一闪念】 yīshǎnniàn a fleeting thought

【一身】 yīshēn ① the whole body; all over the body: ～是泥 covered all over with mud/ ～是汗 be sweating all over ② a suit: ～新衣服 a new suit of clothes ③ a single person: 孑然～ solitary; all alone

【一身两役】 yī shēn liǎng yì hold two jobs at the same time; serve in a dual capacity

【一身是胆】 yī shēn shì dǎn know no fear; be absolutely fearless

【一神教】 yīshénjiào monotheism

【一生】 yīshēng all one's life; throughout one's life: 鲁迅的～是战斗的～，革命的～。Lu Xun's was a fighting life, a revolutionary life.

【一声不响】 yī shēng bù xiǎng not say a word; not utter a sound

【一失足成千古恨】 yī shīzú chéng qiāngǔ hèn a single slip may cause lasting sorrow; the error of a moment becomes the regret of a lifetime

【一时】 yīshí ① a period of time: 此～彼～。Times have changed. ② for a short while; temporary; momentary: 风行～ be popular for a while; be all the rage/ ～的多数 a temporary majority/ 为～的表面现象所迷惑 be misled by transient phenomena; be taken in by appearances/ 不凭

～的热情 not rely on a moment's enthusiasm/ ～想不起来 can't recall offhand (或 for the moment)/ 看一个人不要光看他的～一事。Don't judge a person by a single act or a short period of his life. ③〔叠用〕now..., now...; one moment..., the next: 他的病～好,～坏。He'd be better for a while and then have a relapse.

【一时半刻】 yīshí-bànkè a short time; a little while: 他～还回不来。He won't be back for a little while yet.

【一时一刻】 yīshí-yīkè 〔多用于否定〕for a single moment: ～也不要脱离群众。Never for a single moment cut yourself off from the masses.

【一事】 yīshì 〈方〉 be related (organizationally or professionally); belong to the same organization: 你们都是～吗? Are you all together?/ 这两家公司实际是～。The two firms are actually one and the same outfit.

【一事无成】 yī shì wú chéng accomplish nothing; get nowhere: 知识分子如果不和工农民众相结合,则将～。The intellectuals will accomplish nothing if they fail to integrate themselves with the workers and peasants.

【一视同仁】 yī shì tóng rén treat equally without discrimination

【一手】 yīshǒu ① proficiency; skill: 露～ show off one's skill/ 业务上有～ be proficient in one's own line; know one's stuff/ 这个篮球队在防守上很有～。This basketball team has a very strong defence. ② trick; move: 他这～可真毒辣! What a vicious trick he played! ③ single-handed; all by oneself; all alone: 这场争端是他们～挑起的。The dispute was all started by them./ 小王是他叔叔～拉扯大的。Xiao Wang was brought up all along by his uncle./ ～包办 keep everything in one's own hands; take everything on oneself

【一手遮天】 yī shǒu zhē tiān shut out the heavens with one hand — hide the truth from the masses; hoodwink the public

【一瞬】 yīshùn an instant; a flash; the twinkling of an eye: ～即逝 vanish in a flash

【一丝不苟】 yī sī bù gǒu not be the least bit negligent; be scrupulous about every detail; be conscientious and meticulous

【一丝不挂】 yī sī bù guà not have a stitch on; be stark-naked

【一丝一毫】 yīsī-yīháo a tiny bit; an iota; a trace: 没有～的差别 without the least difference

【一塌糊涂】 yītāhútú in a complete mess; in an awful (或 terrible) state: 他把事情弄得～。He has made a mess of the job./ 屋子乱得～。The room was a complete mess./ 为了一件小事争得～ make a fearful row over a mere trifle

【一体】 yītǐ ① an organic (或 integral) whole: 融成～ merge into an organic whole ② all people concerned; to a man: 上述各项望～遵照。It is expected that the above stipulations will be observed by all.

【一天】 yī tiān ① a day: ～二十四小时都有人值班。There are people on duty round the clock. ② one day (in the past): ～,老李谈起他参加红军的经过。One day, Lao Li talked about how he had joined the Red Army. ③〈方〉 the whole day; all (the) day; from morning till night: 忙碌了～ have been busy all day

【一天到晚】 yī tiān dào wǎn from morning till night; from dawn to dusk; all day long

【一条龙】 yītiáolóng ① one continuous line: 十几辆卡车排成～,向前开动。A dozen trucks moved ahead one after another in a long line. ② a connected sequence; a coordinated process: 实行产、运、销～ make production, transportation and marketing a coordinated process

【一条心】 yī tiáo xīn be of one mind; be at one: 跟党～ be at one with the Party/ 众人～,黄土变成金。If we're all of one heart and one mind, we can change clay into gold.

【一通百通】 yī tōng bǎi tōng grasp this one thing and you'll grasp everything; sort this one thing out and you'll sort out all the rest

【一同】 yītóng 〈副〉 together; at the same time and place: ～出发 set out together

【一统】 yītǒng unify (a country): ～天下 unify the whole country/ 大～ a unified domain

【一头】 yītóu ① directly; headlong: ～扎进水里 plunge headlong into the water ② a head: 他比我高～。He is a head taller than I am./ 白马领先～获胜。The white horse won by a head.

【一头儿沉】 yītóurchén 〈方〉 ① heavy-at-one-end, a desk with a cupboard or drawers at one end ② be partial (in mediation)

【一团和气】 yī tuán héqì keep on good terms with everyone at the expense of principle; keep on the right side of everyone

【一团漆黑】 yī tuán qīhēi pitch-dark — utterly hopeless: 把我们的工作描绘成～是完全错误的。It is completely wrong to describe our work as an utter failure.

【一团糟】 yītuánzāo a complete mess; chaos

【一退六二五】 yī tuì liù èr wǔ evade (或 deny) all responsibility

【一网打尽】 yī wǎng dǎjìn catch the whole lot in a dragnet; round up the whole gang at one fell swoop

【一往情深】 yīwǎng qíngshēn be passionately devoted; be head over heels in love

【一往无前】 yīwǎng wúqián press forward with indomitable will: ～的精神 indomitable spirit

【一望无际】 yī wàng wú jì stretch as far as the eye can see; stretch to the horizon: ～的大草原 a boundless stretch of grassland

【一位论派】 Yīwèilùnpài 〈基督教〉 Unitarianism

【一味】 yīwèi 〈副〉 blindly: ～蛮干 persist in acting blindly/ ～地固执成见 stubbornly stick to one's own view/ ～迁就 make endless concessions; make one concession after another

【一文不名】 yī wén bù míng penniless

【一问三不知】 yī wèn sān bù zhī say "I don't know" to every question — not know a thing; be entirely ignorant

【一窝蜂】 yīwōfēng like a swarm of bees: 孩子们～似地奔向海滩。The children swarmed towards the beach.

【一无是处】 yī wú shìchù without a single redeeming feature; devoid of any merit: 不要把他说得～。Don't talk as if he had no saving graces.

【一无所长】 yī wú suǒcháng have no special skill; be Jack of all trades

【一无所有】 yī wú suǒyǒu not own a thing in the world; not have a thing to one's name

【一无所知】 yī wú suǒzhī know nothing about; not have the least inkling of; be absolutely ignorant of

【一五一十】 yīwǔ-yīshí (narrate) systematically and in full detail: 他把事情～地都给同志们讲了。He told his comrades the whole story exactly as it had happened.

【一物降一物】 yī wù xiáng yī wù there is always one thing to conquer another; everything has its vanquisher

【一误再误】 yī wù zài wù ① make one error after another; keep on making mistakes ② make things worse by repeated delays: 你这病要抓紧治,可不能～了。You should go and see a doctor at once. You mustn't put it off any more.

【一息尚存】 yī xī shàng cún so long as one still has a breath left; till one's last gasp: 我只要～,就要努力为党工作。I'll work hard for the Party as long as I live.

【一席话】 yī xí huà what one says during a conversation: 他的～打动了我的心。What he said touched my heart./ 听君～，胜读十年书。I profit more from one consultation with you than from ten years of reading.

【一系列】 yīxìliè a series of: ～措施 a series of measures/ ～问题 a whole series of questions/ ～的事件 a whole train of events

【一下】 yīxià ①〔用在动词前后，表示做一次或试着做〕one time; once: 亲～孩子的脸 give the baby a kiss on the cheek/ 拍～他的肩膀 give him a pat on the shoulder/ ～打死两个苍蝇 kill two flies with one swat/ 让我想～。Let me think a bit. 或 Let me see./ 打听～再说。Better make some inquiries first./ 请等～。Wait a minute, please./ 老鹰～就把小鸡叼走了。The hawk snatched away the chick at one swoop. ② in a short while; all at once; all of a sudden: 灯～又亮了。After a little while the lights went on again./ 这天气，～冷，～热。Look at this weather. It's cold one moment and hot the next./ 天～阴了下来。It became overcast all of a sudden./ 不能希望人们把旧观念～都清除掉。One cannot expect people to get rid of their old ideas overnight.

【一线】 yīxiàn a ray of; a gleam of: ～希望 a gleam of hope/ ～光明 a ray of light

【一相情愿】 yī xiāng qíngyuàn one's own wishful thinking 又作"一厢情愿"

【一向】 yīxiàng ① earlier on; lately: 前～雨水多。There was quite a lot of rain earlier on./ 这～进步不小吧？You must have made a lot of progress lately. ②〈副〉consistently; all along: 我国～支持世界各国人民的正义斗争。China has consistently supported the just struggles of the peoples of the world.

【一小撮】 yī xiǎocuō a handful: ～阶级敌人 a handful of class enemies

【一笑置之】 yī xiào zhì zhī dismiss with a laugh (或 smile); laugh off

【一些】 yīxiē 〈量〉a number of; certain; some; a few; a little: 有～国家 some (或 a number of) countries/ 作～适当的调整 make certain appropriate readjustments/ 有～事情我还不明白。There are a few things that still puzzle me./ 只剩这～了，够吗？There's only this much left. Is it enough?/ 我想说的就这～。That's all I wanted to say.

【一泻千里】 yī xiè qiānlǐ ① (of a river) rush down a thousand *li* — flow down vigorously ② (of a writer's style) bold and flowing

【一蟹不如一蟹】 yī xiè bùrú yī xiè each crab is smaller than the one before — each one is worse than the last

【一心】 yīxīn ① wholeheartedly; heart and soul: ～为革命 devote oneself wholeheartedly to the revolution/ 她～想着队里的工作。She always has the work of her production team at heart./ 共产党～为人民。The Communist Party serves the people heart and soul./ 贫下中农～奔社会主义。The poor and lower-middle peasants are determined to march along the socialist road. ② of one mind; at one: 万众～。Millions of people are all of one mind.

【一心一德】 yīxīn-yīdé be of one heart and one mind

【一心一意】 yīxīn-yīyì heart and soul; wholeheartedly

【一星半点】 yīxīng-bàndiǎn a tiny bit; a very small amount: 这可是细活，不能有～差错。This is a high precision job. There mustn't be the slightest slip.

【一行】 yīxíng a group travelling together; party: 代表团～十三人于昨天下午抵京。The thirteen-person delegation arrived in Beijing yesterday afternoon./ 副总理及其～ the Vice-Premier and his party

【一言不发】 yī yán bù fā not say a word; keep one's mouth shut

【一言既出，驷马难追】 yī yán jì chū, sìmǎ nán zhuī a word once spoken cannot be overtaken even by a team of four horses — what is said cannot be unsaid

【一言难尽】 yī yán nán jìn it is hard to explain in a few words; it's a long story

【一言堂】 yīyántáng what I say goes; one person alone has the say; one person lays down the law: 要搞"群言堂"，不搞"～"。Let all have a say, not just one.

【一言为定】 yī yán wéi dìng that's settled then

【一言以蔽之】 yī yán yǐ bì zhī to sum up in a word

【一氧化物】 yīyǎnghuàwù 〈化〉monoxide (e.g. 一氧化碳 carbon monoxide)

【一样】 yīyàng the same; equally; alike; as...as...: ～耐用 equally durable/ 他跟他哥哥跑得～快。He runs as fast as his brother./ 我买的伞和你的～。The umbrella I've bought is the same as yours.

【一叶障目，不见泰山】 yī yè zhàng mù, bù jiàn Tàishān a leaf before the eye shuts out Mount Taishan — have one's view of the important overshadowed by the trivial

【一叶知秋】 yī yè zhī qiū the falling of one leaf heralds the autumn; it is a straw in the wind; a small sign can indicate a great trend

【一一】 yīyī one by one; one after another: ～检查 examine one by one/ 没时间～介绍 have no time to go into details or cover everything/ ～告别 say goodbye to everyone; bid farewell to all, one after another

【一…一…】 yī...yī... ①〔分别用在两个名词前面〕ⓐ〔表示整个〕: 一生一世 one's whole life; all one's life ⓑ〔表示数量极少〕: 一言一行 every word and deed/ 一举一动 every act/ 一点一滴 every drop; every bit/ 不拿群众一针一线 not take a single needle or piece of thread from the masses ②〔分别用在同类的动词前面，表示动作的连续〕: 一瘸一拐 limping along/ 一蹦一跳 skipping and hopping ③〔分别用在相对的动词前面，表示动作协调配合或交替进行〕: 一问一答 one asking and the other answering/ 一打一拉 strike and stroke alternately; hit and cajole by turns; alternate hard and soft tactics ④〔分别用在相反的方位词、形容词等前面，表示相反的方位或情况〕: 一东一西 one east, one west; poles apart/ 一长一短 one short, one long

【一衣带水】 yī yī dài shuǐ a narrow strip of water: ～的邻邦 close neighbours separated only by a strip of water

【一意孤行】 yī yì gū xíng cling obstinately to one's course; act wilfully; be bent on having one's own way

【一应】 yīyīng all; everything: ～俱全。Everything needed is there./ ～工具均已备齐。All the tools are ready.

【一语道破】 yī yǔ dàopò lay bare the truth with one penetrating remark; hit the nail on the head

【一语破的】 yī yǔ pò dì hit the mark with a single comment

【一元化】 yīyuánhuà centralized; unified: 加强党的～领导 strengthen centralized Party leadership/ 实行～的领导 exercise unified leadership

【一元论】 yīyuánlùn 〈哲〉monism

【一元酸】 yīyuánsuān 〈化〉monoacid; monoatomic acid

【一院制】 yīyuànzhì unicameral (或 one chamber) legislature

【一月】 yīyuè January

【一再】 yīzài time and again; again and again; repeatedly: ～宣称 declare time and again/ ～表示感谢 express one's gratitude again and again/ 一让再让 make one concession after another/ 一拖再拖 postpone again and again

【一早】 yīzǎo 〈口〉early in the morning: 我明天～就告诉他。I'll let him know first thing tomorrow morning.

【一长制】 yīzhǎngzhì system of one-man leadership

【一着不慎，满盘皆输】 yī zhāo bù shèn, mǎn pán jiē shū one careless move and the whole game is lost

【一朝】 yīzhāo ① in one day: ～覆亡 collapse (或 be toppled) in one short day ② once: ～被蛇咬，十年怕井绳。Once bitten by a snake, one shies at a coiled rope for the next ten years — once bitten, twice shy.

【一朝一夕】 yīzhāo-yīxī in one morning or evening; overnight; in one day: 非～之功 not the work of a single day/ 不是～所能完成的 cannot be accomplished overnight

【一针见血】 yī zhēn jiàn xiě pierce to the truth with a single pertinent remark; hit the nail on the head: ～地指出 point out sharply

【一枕黄粱】 yī zhěn huángliáng Golden Millet Dream — a brief dream of grandeur

【一阵】 yīzhèn a burst; a fit; a peal: ～掌声 a burst of applause/ ～咳嗽 a fit (或 spasm) of coughing/ ～阵笑声 peals of laughter/ ～狂风 a violent gust of wind; a blast (of wind)/ ～枪声 a burst of gunfire/ 脸上红～,白～ one's face turning now red, now pale

【一阵子】 yīzhènzi a period of time; a spell: 这～尽下雨。We've had a spell of rainy weather.

【一知半解】 yīzhī-bànjiě have a smattering of knowledge; have scanty (或 half-baked) knowledge

【一直】 yīzhí ①straight: ～走 go straight ahead; keep straight on ②〈副〉continuously; always; all along; all the way: 雪～下了两天两夜。It snowed for two days and nights on end./ 我们～是同事。We've been colleagues all along./ 从年初起～到现在 from the beginning of the year right up to now; ever since the beginning of the year

【一纸空文】 yī zhǐ kōngwén a mere scrap of paper

【一致】 yīzhì showing no difference; identical; unanimous; consistent: 观点～ hold identical views; be of the same view/ 步调～ march in step; act in unison/ 官兵～ unity between officers and men/ 取得完全～的意见 reach unanimity; reach a consensus/ 提案～通过了。The resolution was adopted (或 carried) unanimously./ 举国上下,～努力。The whole nation is working together with one mind./ 一切被压迫民族的根本利益是～的。The fundamental interests of all oppressed nations coincide./ 我们的作法和党委的要求是～的。Our approach is in keeping with what the Party committee requires of us./ 体例前后不～。The style is inconsistent.

【一掷千金】 yī zhì qiānjīn ① stake a thousand pieces of gold on one throw ② throw away money like dirt; spend money like water

【一专多能】 yī zhuān duō néng expert in one thing and good at many

【一准】 yīzhǔn 〈副〉sure; surely; certainly: 他～来吗？Is he sure to come?/ 今年的收成～比去年强。This year's harvest will surely top last year's.

【一字长蛇阵】 yīzì chángshézhèn single-line battle array: 摆开～ string out in a long line

【一字儿】 yīzìr in a row; in a line: 靶场上～站着十名射手。Ten marksmen stood in a row on the range.

【一字一板】 yīzì-yībǎn (speak) unhurriedly and clearly

【一总】 yīzǒng ① altogether; all told; in all: ～二十个人。There are twenty people altogether./ 我们～花了三十块钱。We spent thirty *yuan* in all. ② all: 那～是你的错儿。It was all your fault.

**衣** yī ① clothing; clothes; garment: 丰～足食 have ample food and clothing/ 和～而睡 sleep in one's clothes/ 上～ jacket/ 毛～毛裤 woolen sweater and pants/ ～不蔽体 be dressed in rags ② coating; covering: 糖～ sugar coating/ 炮～ gun cover ③〈中医〉afterbirth: 胞～(human) afterbirth

【衣胞】 yībao (human) afterbirth

【衣钵】 yībō a Buddhist monk's mantle and alms bowl which he hands down to his favourite disciple; legacy: 继承老沙皇的～ inherit the mantle of the old Tsars

【衣橱】 yīchú wardrobe

【衣蛾】 yī'é casemaking clothes moth

【衣分】 yīfēn 〈农〉ginning outturn; gin turnout

【衣服】 yīfu clothing; clothes: 外边冷,多穿些～。It's cold outside. Put on more clothes.

【衣钩】 yīgōu clothes hook

【衣冠】 yīguān hat and clothes; dress: ～不整 be sloppily dressed

【衣冠楚楚】 yīguān chǔchǔ be immaculately dressed

【衣冠禽兽】 yīguān qínshòu a beast in human attire; brute

【衣冠冢】 yīguānzhǒng a tomb containing personal effects of the deceased, whose remains are either missing or buried elsewhere

【衣柜】 yīguì wardrobe

【衣架】 yījià ① coat hanger; clothes-rack ② clothes tree; clothes stand

【衣襟】 yījīn the one or two pieces making up the front of a Chinese jacket

【衣锦还乡】 yī jǐn huán xiāng return to one's hometown in silken robes — return home after making good

【衣料】 yīliào material for clothing; dress material

【衣帽间】 yīmàojiān cloakroom

【衣裳】 yīshang 〈口〉clothing; clothes

【衣食住行】 yī-shí-zhù-xíng food, clothing, shelter and transportation — basic necessities of life

【衣物】 yīwù clothing and other articles of daily use

【衣箱】 yīxiāng suitcase; trunk

【衣鱼】 yīyú silverfish; fish moth; bookworm

【衣着】 yīzhuó clothing, headgear and footwear: ～整洁 be neatly dressed

**伊** yī ① he or she ②〈书〉〈助〉: ～于胡底？Where will it all end? ③ (Yī) a surname

【伊甸园】 yīdiànyuán 〈基督教〉the Garden of Eden; paradise

【伊拉克】 Yīlākè Iraq ◇ ～人 Iraqi

【伊朗】 Yīlǎng Iran ◇ ～人 Iranian

【伊始】 yīshǐ beginning: 就职～ upon assuming office/ 下车～ as soon as one alights from the official carriage — on arrival at a new post

【伊斯兰教】 Yīsīlánjiào Islam; Islamism ◇ ～国家 Islamic country/ ～历 the Moslem Calendar/ ～徒 Moslem

【伊蚊】 yīwén 〈动〉yellow-fever mosquito

**医** yī ① doctor (of medicine): 军～ medical officer; surgeon/ 解放前农村缺～少药。Before liberation there were few doctors and little medicine in the countryside. ② medical science; medical service; medicine: 行～ practise medicine/ ～用温度计 clinical thermometer/ 送～送药到山寨 take medicine and medical service to mountain villages ③ cure; treat: 给牧民～病 give medical treatment to herdsmen/ 把他的病～好 cure him of his illness

【医道】 yīdào 〔多指中医〕art of healing; medical knowledge; physician's skill

【医经】 yījīng 〈中医〉ancient Chinese medical classics

【医科】 yīkē medical courses in general; medicine ◇ ～大学 medical university

【医理】 yīlǐ principles of medical science; medical knowledge

【医疗】 yīliáo medical treatment: 公费～ public health services/ ～卫生工作 medical and health work ◇ ～队 medical team/ ～辐射学 atomic (或 radiological) medicine/ ～机构 medical establishment (或 institution)/ ～器械 medical apparatus and instruments/ ～事故 unskilful and faulty medical or surgical treatment; malpractice/ ～体育 medico-athletics/ ～站 medical station; health centre

【医生】 yīshēng doctor; medical man: 内科～ physician/ 外科～ surgeon/ 实习～ intern/ 主治～ doctor in charge/ 住院～ resident doctor

【医师】 yīshī (qualified) doctor

【医士】 yīshì practitioner with secondary medical school education

【医书】 yīshū 〔多指中医〕medical book

【医术】 yīshù medical skill; art of healing

【医务】 yīwù medical matters ◇ ～工作者 medical worker/ ～人员 medical personnel (或 staff, workers); public health worker/ ～所 clinic

【医学】 yīxué medical science; medicine ◇ ～科学院 academy of medical sciences/ ～文献 medical literature/ ～遗产 medical heritage

【医药】 yīyào medicine ◇ ～常识 general medical knowledge/ ～费 medical expenses (或 costs)

【医院】 yīyuàn hospital: 儿童～ children's hospital/ 综合性～ general hospital

【医治】 yīzhì cure; treat; heal: ～无效 fail to respond to any medical treatment/ ～战争创伤 heal war wounds

【医嘱】 yīzhǔ doctor's advice (或 orders)

【医助】 yīzhù assistant doctor (in the army)

**依** yī ① depend on: 相～为命 depend on each other for existence; be bound by a common destiny ② comply with; listen to; yield to: 不能因为孩子小,就什么都～着他。You shouldn't comply with every wish of his just because he is a child./ 当初要是～了他们的主张,今天就不可能有这个水电站。If we had listened to them, this hydropower station would never have been built./ 你要是把这些资料弄丢了,我可不～你。If you lose these data, I'll never forgive you. ③ according to; in the light of; judging by: ～法惩办 punish according to law; deal with in accordance with the law; bring to justice/ ～我看 in my view; as I see it/ ～当时情况来说 in the light of the situation at the time; as matters then stood

【依此类推】 yī cǐ lèituī the rest may be deduced by analogy; and so on and so forth

【依次】 yīcì in proper order; successively: 他们～入座。They take their seats in proper order./ ～递补 fill vacancies in order of precedence/ ～说明下列问题 illustrate the following points in their given order

【依从】 yīcóng comply with; yield to: 她坚持要单独去,我只好～她了。Since she insisted on going alone, I had to comply.

【依存】 yīcún depend on sb. or sth. for existence: 相互～ be interdependent

【依附】 yīfù depend on; attach oneself to; become an appendage to: ～权贵 attach oneself to bigwigs

【依旧】 yījiù as before; still: 书房的陈设～未变。The study is furnished as it was before./ 他～是那个老样子。He still looks his old self./ 山河～。The landscape remains unchanged.

【依据】 yījù ① according to; in the light of; on the basis of; judging by: ～上述意见 in accordance with the above views/ ～马列主义的理论 on the basis of Marxist-Leninist theory ② basis; foundation: 提供科学～ provide scientific basis for sth./ 这些遗址是我们研究殷代文化的重要～。These sites form an important basis for our study of the culture of the Yin Dynasty./ 当时我们没有什么蓝图可以作～。We didn't have any blueprints to go by at that time.

【依靠】 yīkào ① rely on; depend on: ～自己的力量 depend on one's own strength/ 垄断资本家～战争发财。The monopolists look to war for profits. 或 Monopoly capital battens on war. ② something to fall back on; support; backing: 寻找～ seek support/ 生活有～ have one's livelihood assured

【依赖】 yīlài rely on; be dependent on: ～别人 be dependent on others ◇ ～思想 the dependent mentality/ ～性 dependence

【依恋】 yīliàn be reluctant to leave; feel regret at parting from

【依凭】 yīpíng rely on; depend on

【依然】 yīrán still; as before: ～有效 still hold good; remain valid

【依然故我】 yīrán gù wǒ ① one's circumstances haven't changed much ② one is still one's same old self

【依然如故】 yīrán rú gù remain as before; remain unchanged (或 the same)

【依顺】 yīshùn be obedient: 百依百顺 be all obedience

【依托】 yītuō ① rely on; depend on ② support; prop; backing

【依稀】 yīxī vaguely; dimly: ～记得 vaguely remember/ ～可见 faintly (或 dimly) visible

【依样画葫芦】 yī yàng huà húlu copy mechanically

【依依】 yīyī reluctant to part: ～不舍 be reluctant to part; cannot bear to part

【依仗】 yīzhàng count on; rely on: ～权势 rely on one's power and position; count on one's powerful connections

【依照】 yīzhào according to; in the light of: ～党中央指示办事 act in accordance with the directives of the Party Central Committee/ ～情况而定 decide as circumstances require/ ～法律规定的条件 under conditions prescribed by law

**咿** yī

【咿呀】 yīyā ① 〈象〉 squeak; creak: ～的桨声 the squeak of oars in oarlocks/ 咿咿呀呀的提琴声 squeaky notes of a violin ② prattle; babble

**铱** yī 〈化〉 iridium (Ir)

【铱金笔】 yījīnbǐ iridium-point pen

**猗** yī 〈书〉 ① 〈助〉〔多用于句末,相当于"啊"〕: 河水清且涟～。The clear river ripples on. ② 〈叹〉〔表示赞美〕: ～欤盛哉! Magnificent! 或 Superb!

**揖** yī (make a) bow with hands clasped

**壹** yī one (used as the numeral 一 on cheques, banknotes, etc. to avoid mistakes or alterations)

**漪** yī 〈书〉 ripples

**噫** yī 〈叹〉 alas

**繄** yī ① only; alone ② be tantamount to

**黟** yī 〔用于地名〕: ～县 Yixian

## yí

**匜** yí 〈考古〉 ladle (shaped like a gourd); gourd-shaped ladle

**仪** yí ① appearance; bearing: 威～ dignified bearing ② ceremony; rite: 司～ master of ceremonies ③ present; gift: 贺～ present for wedding, birthday, etc. ④ apparatus; instrument: 地震～ seismograph

【仪表】 yíbiǎo ① appearance; bearing: ～堂堂 noble and dignified/ ～大方 poised and graceful ② meter ◇ ～板 instrument panel; (汽车、飞机) dashboard/ ～厂 instrument and meter plant

【仪器】 yíqì instrument; apparatus: 精密～ precision instrument/ 自记～ recording instrument ◇ ～厂 instrument plant/ ～制造工业 instrument-making industry

【仪容】 yíróng looks; appearance

【仪式】 yíshì ceremony; rite; function: 协定签字～ a ceremony for signing an agreement/ 宗教～ religious rites

【仪态】 yítài 〈书〉 bearing; deportment: ～万方 (of a beauty) appear in all her glory

【仪仗】 yízhàng flags, weapons, etc. carried by a guard of honour

【仪仗队】 yízhàngduì guard of honour; honour guard: 陆海空三军～ a guard of honour of the three services

**圯** yí 〈书〉 bridge

**夷** yí 〈书〉 ① smooth; safe: 化险为～ turn danger into safety; head off a disaster ② raze: ～为平地 level to the ground; raze ③ exterminate; wipe out: ～族 extermination of an entire family (a punishment in ancient times) ④ a name for ancient tribes in the east ⑤ 〈旧〉 foreign country; foreigner

**沂** Yí short for the Yihe River

**诒** yí 见"贻" yí

**宜** yí ① suitable; appropriate; fitting: 适～ appropriate; fitting and proper/ 老幼咸～ suitable (或 good) for both young and old ② should; ought to: 不～操之过急。 You should not act in haste.

【宜人】 yírén pleasant; delightful: 气候～ pleasant (或 delightful) weather/ 景物～ attractive (或 charming) scenery

**怡** yí 〈书〉 happy; joyful; cheerful: 心旷神～ feel relaxed and happy

【怡然】 yírán happy; contented: ～自得 happy and pleased with oneself

**迤** yí 见"逶迤" wēiyí
另见 yǐ

**饴** yí maltose: 甘之如～ enjoy sth. bitter as if it were sweet as malt sugar — gladly endure hardships

【饴糖】 yítáng maltose; malt sugar

**迻** yí 见"移" yí

【迻录】 yílù 〈书〉 write down; transcribe

【迻译】 yíyì 〈书〉 translate

**贻** yí 〈书〉 ① make a gift of sth.; present ② bequeath; leave behind: ～患 sow seeds of disaster

【贻贝】 yíbèi 〈动〉 mussel

【贻害】 yíhài leave a legacy of trouble: ～无穷 entail untold troubles

【贻人口实】 yí rén kǒushí give occasion for talk; give people grounds for ridicule; be a source of ridicule

【贻误】 yíwù affect adversely; bungle: ～工作 affect the work adversely/ ～战机 bungle the chance of winning a battle; forfeit a chance for combat/ ～青年 mislead young people

【贻笑大方】 yíxiào dàfāng make a laughingstock of oneself before experts; incur the ridicule of experts

**荑** yí 〈书〉 clear the fields of weeds; weed

**咦** yí 〈叹〉〔表示惊异〕 well; why: ～，你怎么又来了？ Why, you're here again!/ ～，这是怎么回事？ Hey, what's all this about?

**姨** yí ① one's mother's sister; aunt ② one's wife's sister; sister-in-law: 大～子 one's wife's elder sister/ 小～子 one's wife's younger sister

【姨表】 yíbiǎo maternal cousin: ～兄弟 male maternal cousins/ ～姐妹 female maternal cousins

【姨夫】 yífu the husband of one's maternal aunt; uncle 又作"姨父"

【姨妈】 yímā 〈口〉 (married) maternal aunt; aunt

【姨母】 yímǔ maternal aunt; aunt

【姨儿】 yír 〈口〉 maternal aunt; aunt

【姨太太】 yítàitai 〈口〉 concubine

**胰** yí 〈生理〉 pancreas

【胰蛋白酶】 yídànbáiméi 〈生化〉 trypsin

【胰岛】 yídǎo 〈生理〉 pancreas islet

【胰岛素】 yídǎosù 〈药〉 insulin: 完全人工合成结晶牛～ total synthetic crystalline bovine insulin

【胰淀粉酶】 yídiànfěnméi 〈生化〉 amylopsin

【胰酶】 yíméi 〈药〉 pancreatin

【胰腺】 yíxiàn 〈生理〉 pancreas ◇ ～炎 pancreatitis

【胰液】 yíyè 〈生理〉 pancreatic juice

【胰脂酶】 yízhīméi 〈生化〉 pancreatic lipase; steapsin

【胰子】 yízi ① 〈口〉 pancreas (of pigs, sheep, etc.) ② 〈方〉 soap

**痍** yí 〈书〉 wound; trauma: 满目疮～。 Everywhere a scene of desolation meets the eye.

**移** yí ① move; remove; shift: ～走 move away/ ～沙造田 create farmland by removing sand drifts/ 把立足点～到工农方面来 move over to the side of the workers and peasants; shift one's stand to that of the workers and peasants ② change; alter: 献身革命志不～ dedicate oneself to the revolution with unshakeable will

【移调】 yídiào 〈乐〉 transposition ◇ ～乐器 transposing instrument

【移动】 yídòng move; shift: 冷气团正向南～。 A cold air mass is moving southward./ 把靶位向左～两米。 Shift the target two metres to the left.

【移防】 yífáng be shifted elsewhere for garrison duty

【移风易俗】 yífēng-yìsú change prevailing habits and customs; transform social traditions

【移行】 yíháng divide (a word) with a hyphen at the end of a line

【移花接木】 yíhuā-jiēmù ① graft one twig on another; graft ② stealthily substitute one thing for another

【移交】 yíjiāo ① turn over; transfer; deliver into sb.'s custody: 这批仪器已经～给研究所了。These instruments have been turned over to the research institute. ② hand over one's job to a successor: 他临走前把工作～给我了。Before he left he handed over his job to me.
【移居】 yíjū move one's residence; migrate
【移苗】 yímiáo transplant seedlings
【移民】 yímín ① migrate; (移出) emigrate; (移入) immigrate ② (移出) emigrant; (移入) immigrant ◇ ～点 settlement/ ～法 immigration laws
【移山倒海】 yíshān-dǎohǎi remove mountains and drain seas — transform nature
【移栽】 yízāi transplant
【移植】 yízhí ① transplant: ～秧苗 transplant seedlings ② 〈医〉 transplanting; grafting
【移樽就教】 yí zūn jiùjiào take one's wine cup to another person's table to seek his advice — go to sb. for advice

**蛇** yí 见"委蛇" wēiyí
另见 shé

**遗** yí ① lose: ～失 lose ② something lost: 路不拾～。No one pockets anything found on the road. ③ omit: ～忘 forget/ 补～ addendum ④ leave behind; keep back; not give: 不～余力 spare no efforts ⑤ leave behind at one's death; bequeath; hand down: ～风 customs handed down from past generations/ ～作 posthumous work (of an author, etc.)/ ～骨 remains (of the dead) ⑥ involuntary discharge of urine, etc.: 梦～ nocturnal emission; wet dream
另见 wèi

【遗产】 yíchǎn legacy; inheritance; heritage: 留下(继承)～ bequeath (inherit) a legacy/ 历史～ a legacy of history/ 文化～ cultural heritage ◇ ～承受人 legatee/ ～税 inheritance tax; succession duty
【遗臭万年】 yí chòu wànnián leave a stink for ten thousand years — go down in history as a byword of infamy
【遗传】 yíchuán 〈生〉 heredity; inheritance: 交叉～ criss-cross inheritance/ 这种病不会～。The disease is not hereditary.
◇ ～病 hereditary disease/ ～密码 genetic code/ ～特征 hereditary feature; heredity/ ～信息 hereditary (或 genetic) information/ ～学 genetics/ ～学家 geneticist/ ～因子 genetic factor
【遗传工程学】 yíchuán gōngchéngxué 〈生〉 genetic engineering
【遗毒】 yídú evil legacy; harmful tradition; pernicious influence
【遗腹子】 yífùzǐ posthumous child
【遗稿】 yígǎo a manuscript left unpublished by the author at his death; posthumous manuscript
【遗孤】 yígū orphan
【遗骸】 yíhái remains (of the dead)
【遗憾】 yíhàn regret; pity: 对此表示～ express regret over the matter/ 一点不感到～ have no regrets/ 非常～,我不能接受你的邀请。I am very sorry I will not be able to accept your invitation./ 今晚的音乐会你不能来,实在～。It's really a pity that you can't come to the concert this evening.
【遗恨】 yíhèn eternal regret
【遗迹】 yíjī historical remains; vestige; traces: 古代人类的～ traces of ancient man/ 古代村落的～ sites of ancient villages/ 封建～ vestiges of feudalism
【遗精】 yíjīng 〈医〉 (seminal) emission
【遗老】 yílǎo ① surviving adherent of a former dynasty; old fogy; old diehard ② 〈书〉 old people who have witnessed big social changes
【遗留】 yíliú leave over; hand down: 历史上～下来的边界问题 boundary questions left over by history/ 帝国主义统治～下来的问题 a legacy of imperialist rule/ 草案中仍然～几个问题。There are still a few points to clear up in the draft.
【遗漏】 yílòu omit; leave out: 重要～ an important omission/ 名单上有～。There are some names missing from the list.
【遗民】 yímín ① adherents of a former dynasty ② survivors of a great upheaval
【遗墨】 yímò letters, manuscripts, scrolls of painting or calligraphy, etc. left behind by the deceased
【遗尿】 yíniào 〈医〉 enuresis; bed-wetting
【遗弃】 yíqì abandon; forsake; cast off: ～妻儿 forsake one's wife and children/ 敌军～大批辎重。The enemy abandoned (或 left behind) large quantities of supplies.
【遗缺】 yíquē vacancy
【遗容】 yíróng ① remains (of the deceased): 瞻仰～ pay one's respects to the remains of sb. ② a portrait of the deceased
【遗少】 yíshào young man with the mentality of an old fogy; young diehard
【遗失】 yíshī lose: 他的借书证～了。He has lost his library card./ ～声明 lost property notice
【遗矢】 yíshǐ 〈书〉 empty one's bowels; defecate
【遗事】 yíshì ① incidents of past ages ② deeds of those now dead
【遗书】 yíshū ①〔多用做书名〕 posthumous papers; writings of an author now dead ② a letter or note left by one immediately before death
【遗孀】 yíshuāng widow; relict
【遗体】 yítǐ remains (of the dead): 向～告别 pay one's last respects to the remains
【遗忘】 yíwàng forget
【遗物】 yíwù things left behind by the deceased
【遗像】 yíxiàng a portrait of the deceased
【遗训】 yíxùn teachings of the deceased
【遗言】 yíyán words of the deceased; (a person's) last words
【遗愿】 yíyuàn unfulfilled wish of the deceased; last wish; behest: 为实现毛主席、周总理的～而努力奋斗 strive to carry out the behests of Chairman Mao and Premier Zhou
【遗址】 yízhǐ ruins; relics: 古城～ the ruins of an ancient city
【遗志】 yízhì unfulfilled wish; behest; work bequeathed by the deceased: 继承先烈～ carry out the behest of the martyrs; continue the work left by the martyrs
【遗嘱】 yízhǔ testament; will; dying words
【遗著】 yízhù posthumous work (of an author)

**颐** yí 〈书〉 ① cheek: 支～ cheek in palm ② keep fit; take care of oneself
【颐和园】 Yíhéyuán the Summer Palace (in Beijing)
【颐养】 yíyǎng 〈书〉 keep fit; take care of oneself
【颐指气使】 yízhǐ-qìshǐ order people about by gesture; be insufferably arrogant

**疑** yí ① doubt; disbelieve; suspect: 坚信不～ firmly believe; not have the slightest doubt/ 无可置～ beyond doubt; undoubtedly/ 释～ remove doubts; dispel suspicion ② doubtful; uncertain: ～点 doubtful (或 questionable) point/ 存～ leave the question open
【疑案】 yí'àn doubtful (或 disputed) case; open question; mystery

【疑兵】 yíbīng troops deployed to mislead the enemy; deceptive deployment
【疑病】 yíbìng 〈医〉 hypochondriasis
【疑点】 yídiǎn doubtful (或questionable) point: 这个案件还有几个～。There are still a few questionable points in the case.
【疑窦】 yídòu cause for suspicion; suspicion: 顿生～ suddenly feel suspicious/ 启人～ arouse (或 awaken, raise) sb.'s suspicion
【疑惑】 yíhuò feel uncertain; not be convinced: ～不解 feel puzzled; have doubts
【疑惧】 yíjù apprehensions; misgivings
【疑虑】 yílǜ misgivings; doubt: 消除心中的～ clear one's mind of doubt; free sb. from doubts and misgivings
【疑难】 yínàn difficult; knotty: ～问题 a knotty problem/ ～病症 difficult and complicated cases (of illness)
【疑神疑鬼】 yíshén-yíguǐ be terribly suspicious; be even afraid of one's own shadow
【疑团】 yítuán doubts and suspicions: 满腹～ be full of doubts and suspicions/ ～顿释。The suspicions were cleared up at once.
【疑问】 yíwèn query; question; doubt: 毫无～ doubtless; without a doubt; without question ◇ ～句 interrogative sentence
【疑心】 yíxīn suspicion: 起～ become suspicious/ ～生暗鬼。Suspicions create imaginary fears./ 一看村里整个儿变了样,我真～自己走错了路。Finding the village completely changed, I really began to wonder whether I had come to the right place.
【疑心病】 yíxīnbìng a suspicious frame of mind: 犯～ be oversuspicious (或 paranoiac)
【疑义】 yíyì doubt; doubtful point: 毫无～ no doubt/ 对这一点难道还有～吗? Can there be any doubt about it?
【疑云】 yíyún misgivings or suspicion clouding one's mind: ～消散。The misgivings were dispelled.
【疑阵】 yízhèn deceptive battle array to mislead the enemy; stratagem

**嶷** yí 〔用于地名〕: 九～ Mount Jiuyi

**彝** yí 〈考古〉 wine vessel: ～器 sacrificial vessel
【彝族】 Yízú the Yi nationality, distributed over Yunnan, Sichuan and Guizhou

## yǐ

**乙** yǐ ① the second of the ten Heavenly Stems ② second: ～等 the second grade; grade B ③〈乐〉 a note of the scale in *gongchepu* (工尺谱), corresponding to 7 in numbered musical notation
【乙胺】 yǐ'àn 〈化〉 ethylamine; aminoethane
【乙苯】 yǐběn ethylbenzene; phenylethane
【乙醇】 yǐchún ethanol; alcohol
【乙醚】 yǐmí ether
【乙醛】 yǐquán acetic aldehyde; acetaldehyde
【乙炔】 yǐquē acetylene; ethyne ◇ ～焊 acetylene welding
【乙烷】 yǐwán ethane
【乙烯】 yǐxī ethylene: 聚～ polyethylene; polythene ◇ ～基 vinyl
【乙酰】 yǐxiān acetyl ◇ ～胆硷 acetylcholine/ ～唑胺〈药〉 acetazolamide; diamox 又作"乙酰基"
【乙种粒子】 yǐzhǒng lìzǐ 〈物〉 beta particle
【乙种射线】 yǐzhǒng shèxiàn 〈物〉 beta ray

**已** yǐ ① stop; cease; end: 争论不～ argue endlessly; be bogged down in endless argument ② already: 问题～解决。The problem has already been solved./ 雨季～过。The rainy season is over./ 为时～晚。It's too late./ ～成定局 be a foregone conclusion ③〈书〉 thereafter; afterwards: ～而 later on; shortly afterwards ④〈书〉 too: 不为～甚 refrain from going to extremes in meting out punishment, etc.
【已故】 yǐgù deceased; late: ～地质学家李四光 the late geologist Li Siguang
【已经】 yǐjīng already: 天～黑了。It's already dark./ 这样～不错了。It's good enough as it is./ 这点前面～说过了。This has been dealt with above.
【已决犯】 yǐjuéfàn 〈法〉 convicted prisoner; convict
【已然】 yǐrán be already so; have already become a fact: 与其补救于～,不如防患于未然。To forestall is better than to amend. 或 Prevention is better than cure.
【已往】 yǐwǎng before; previously; in the past
【已知数】 yǐzhīshù 〈数〉 known number

**以** yǐ ① use; take: ～粮为纲，全面发展 take grain as the key link and ensure an all-round development/ ～我之长，攻敌之短 utilize our strong points to attack the enemy's weak points/ ～共同对敌的大局为重 set the general interest of fighting against the common enemy above everything else/ ～丰补歉 store up in fat years to make up for lean ones; have high yield areas help low yield areas/ 赠～鲜花 present sb. with a bouquet/ ～其人之道，还治其人之身。Deal with a man as he deals with you. 或 Pay somebody back in his own coin. ② according to: ～时启闭 open and close according to schedule/ ～到达先后为序 in order of arrival ③ because of: 不～人废言 not reject a saying because the speaker is what or who he is/ 不～失败自馁,不～成功自满 not lose heart because of failure nor feel conceited because of success/ 何～知之? How do you know? ④ in order to; so as to: ～示区别 so as to distinguish this from other cases/ ～应急需 in order to answer an urgent need ⑤〈书〉 at (a certain time); on (a fixed date): 余～三月一日返。I returned on March the first. ⑥〈书〉〈连〉〔跟"而"用法相同〕 and; as well as: 淅沥～潇飒 raindrops pattering and wind rustling/ 城高～厚。The city wall is high and thick. ⑦〔放在方位词前表明时间、地位、方向或数量的界限〕: 十年～前 ten years ago or earlier/ 五千～内 less than five thousand/ 县团～上 of county or regiment level and higher/ 黄河～北 (to the) north of the Huanghe River
【以暴易暴】 yǐ bào yì bào replace one tyranny by another
【以便】 yǐbiàn so that; in order to; so as to; with the aim of; for the purpose of: 集中兵力包围敌人,～聚而歼之 encircle the enemy with a concentrated force with the aim of annihilating him/ 今晚作好准备,～明天一早动身 make preparations today for an early start tomorrow
【以次】 yǐcì ① in proper order: 主人～给来宾斟酒。The host filled the guests' glasses in turn. ② the following: ～各章 the following chapters
【以德报怨】 yǐ dé bào yuàn return good for evil; requite ingratitude with kindness
【以点带面】 yǐ diǎn dài miàn fan out from point to area; use the experience of selected units to promote work in the entire area
【以毒攻毒】 yǐ dú gōng dú combat poison with poison; use poison as an antidote for poison
【以讹传讹】 yǐ é chuán é incorrectly relay an erroneous message (so that it becomes increasingly distorted)

【以耳代目】 yǐ ěr dài mù rely upon hearsay instead of seeing for oneself
【以攻为守】 yǐ gōng wéi shǒu use attack as a means of defence; attack in order to defend
【以古非今】 yǐ gǔ fēi jīn disparage the present by extolling the past
【以寡敌众】 yǐ guǎ dí zhòng pit the few against the many; fight against heavy odds
【以观后效】 yǐ guān hòu xiào (lighten a punishment and) see how the offender behaves
【以后】 yǐhòu after; afterwards; later; hereafter: 全国解放～ after (或 following) the liberation of the whole country/ 从今(那)～ from now (then) on/ 至于～怎么样，我就不知道了。I don't know what happened later on./ 会议今天开始，大概一星期～结束。The conference begins today and will probably close in a week's time./ 别着急，～你会有机会去的。Don't worry. You'll have a chance to go.
【以及】 yǐjí as well as; along with; and: 党和国家领导人～各有关方面负责人 Party and government leaders as well as responsible cadres of departments concerned
【以己度人】 yǐ jǐ duó rén judge others by oneself; measure others' corn by one's own bushel
【以假乱真】 yǐ jiǎ luàn zhēn mix the spurious with the genuine
【以近】 yǐjìn 〈交〉 up to: 济南～的火车票 train tickets up to Jinan
【以儆效尤】 yǐ jǐng xiàoyóu to warn others against following a bad example; as a warning to others
【以来】 yǐlái since: 一九五八年大跃进～ since the Great Leap Forward of 1958/ 长期～ for a long time past/ 三年～ in the past three years
【以礼相待】 yǐ lǐ xiāng dài treat sb. with due respect
【以理服人】 yǐ lǐ fú rén convince people by reasoning
【以邻为壑】 yǐ lín wéi hè use one's neighbour's field as a drain — shift one's troubles onto others
【以卵投石】 yǐ luǎn tóu shí throw an egg against a rock — court defeat by fighting against overwhelming odds 又作"以卵击石"
【以貌取人】 yǐ mào qǔ rén judge people solely by their appearance
【以免】 yǐmiǎn in order to avoid; so as not to; lest: 仔细检查～出错 check carefully to avoid mistakes/ 自行车要放在存车处，～影响交通。Bicycles should be left at parking lots so as not to block the traffic.
【以内】 yǐnèi within; less than: 本年度～ within this year/ 五十人～ less than fifty people
【以前】 yǐqián before; formerly; previously: 我～的同事 a former colleague of mine/ ～各版 all the preceding (或 previous) editions/ 在明朝～ prior to the Ming Dynasty/ 我～没看过这个戏。I've never seen this opera before./ ～他当理发员。He used to be a barber.
【以求】 yǐqiú in order to; in an attempt to: ～一逞 in the hope of realizing one's ambition; in a bid for success/ ～全胜 so as to achieve complete victory
【以色列】 Yǐsèliè Israel ◇ ～人 Israeli; Israelite
【以上】 yǐshàng ① more than; over; above: 五十人～ over (或 more than) fifty people/ 县和县～的人民代表大会 people's congresses at county level and above/ 十岁～的孩子 children of ten and over ② the above; the foregoing; the above-mentioned: ～各位同志会后请留下。The above-mentioned comrades will please remain after the meeting./ ～是我的几点建议。Those are a few of my suggestions./ 我完全同意～几位代表的发言。I fully agree with the delegates who have already spoken.
【以身试法】 yǐ shēn shì fǎ defy the law
【以身殉职】 yǐ shēn xùnzhí die at one's post
【以身作则】 yǐ shēn zuò zé set an example
【以太】 yǐtài 〈物〉 ether
【以退为进】 yǐ tuì wéi jìn retreat in order to advance; make concessions in order to gain advantages
【以外】 yǐwài beyond; outside; other than; except: 长城～ beyond the Great Wall/ 营房～ outside the barracks/ 汉族～的各兄弟民族代表 delegates of fraternal nationalities other than the Han nationality/ 雾太大，五米～就看不见了。There was such a heavy fog that one could not see further than five metres./ 除了这间～，所有的屋子都打扫了。All the rooms have been cleaned except this one./ 除此～，还有一件事要麻烦你。There's another thing I have to trouble you about.
【以往】 yǐwǎng before; formerly; in the past: 今年的收成比～哪年都好。This year's harvest is better than any previous year's./ 这里～是一片荒野。This place used to be a vast expanse of wasteland.
【以为】 yǐwéi think; believe; consider: 我还～是她呢。I thought it was her./ 党委～那样作比较好。The Party Committee considers it better to do it that way./ 我们不要～自己不了解的东西，广大群众也不了解。We must not assume that things we ourselves cannot understand are not understood by the masses.
【以…为…】 yǐ…wéi… take… as…; regard… as…: 工业以钢为纲。Steel must be taken as the key link in industry./ 以我为主 take ourselves (或 our side, our way, etc.) as the dominant factor; keep the initiative in our own hands
【以下】 yǐxià ① below; under: 零度～ sub-zero/ 三岁～儿童 children under three/ 俘获敌师长～三千人。3,000 of the enemy, from their divisional commander down, were taken prisoner. ② the following: ～是代表名单。The following is a list of the delegates./ ～就来谈谈具体办法。Now I'm coming to the concrete measures.
【以眼还眼，以牙还牙】 yǐ yǎn huán yǎn, yǐ yá huán yá an eye for an eye and a tooth for a tooth
【以一当十】 yǐ yī dāng shí pit one against ten
【以逸待劳】 yǐ yì dài láo wait at one's ease for an exhausted enemy or opponent
【以远】 yǐyuǎn 〈交〉 beyond: 只售济南～的车票。Only tickets for Jinan and beyond are available. ◇ ～权 the right to extend a flying route
【以怨报德】 yǐ yuàn bào dé return evil for good; requite kindness with ingratitude
【以正视听】 yǐ zhèng shì-tīng in order to ensure a correct understanding of the facts
【以至】 yǐzhì ① down to; up to: 这个县每个公社、大队、小队～一家一户都有储备粮。Grain is stored in every household, team, brigade and commune of this county./ 团长、师长～军长都到这个连队来帮助总结经验。Commanders of the regiment, the division and even the army came to this company to help sum up its experience. ② to such an extent as to…; so…that…: 他工作非常专心，～连饭都忘了吃了。He was so absorbed in his work that he even forgot his meals. 又作"以至于"
【以致】 yǐzhì 〔多用来指不好的结果〕 so that; with the result that; consequently; as a result: 小王平时训练不刻苦，～射击考核没有及格。Xiao Wang didn't practise hard, so he failed the marksmanship test./ 有些人不认真学习，～思想落后于形势。Some people don't study hard, with the result that their thinking lags behind events.
【以资】 yǐzī as a means of: ～证明 in testimony thereof; this is to certify that/ ～弥补 to make up the deficit; to make up a shortage/ ～鼓励 as an encouragement
【以子之矛，攻子之盾】 yǐ zǐ zhī máo, gōng zǐ zhī dùn set

your own spear against your own shield — refute sb. with his own argument

**钇** yǐ 〈化〉 yttrium (Y)

**矣** yǐ 〔古汉语助词〕 ①〔用在句末，跟"了"相同〕：悔之晚～。It's too late for regrets. ②〔表示感叹〕：毒～哉！Diabolical! 或 How ruthless!

**尾** yǐ ① hairs on a horse's tail ② spikelets on a cricket's tail
另见 wěi

**苡** yǐ 见"薏苡" yìyǐ

**迤** yǐ go (或 extend) towards：天安门～西是中山公园。To the west of Tian An Men is Zhongshan Park.
另见 yí

【迤逦】 yǐlǐ winding; tortuous; meandering

**蚁** yǐ ant：兵～ soldier ant; dinergate/ 工～ ergate; worker ant/ 雄～ aner/ 雌～ gyne
【蚁蚕】 yǐcán 〈动〉 newly-hatched silkworm
【蚁巢】 yǐcháo ant nest
【蚁鴷】 yǐliè 〈动〉 wryneck
【蚁丘】 yǐqiū ant hill

**酏** yǐ
【酏剂】 yǐjì 〈药〉 elixir

**倚** yǐ ① lean on or against; rest on or against：～栏远眺 lean on the parapet and gaze into the distance ② rely on; count on：～势欺人 take advantage of one's position to bully people ③〈书〉 biased; partial：不偏不～ unbiased; impartial
【倚靠】 yǐkào ① lean on or against; rest on or against ② 见"依靠" yīkào
【倚赖】 yǐlài 见"依赖" yīlài
【倚老卖老】 yǐ lǎo mài lǎo take advantage of one's seniority or old age (to ignore manners, regulations, etc.); flaunt one's seniority
【倚音】 yǐyīn 〈乐〉 *appoggiatura*
【倚仗】 yǐzhàng rely on; count on：～权势 rely on one's power and position; count on one's powerful connections
【倚重】 yǐzhòng rely heavily on sb.'s service

**椅** yǐ chair
【椅子】 yǐzi chair
【椅子顶】 yǐzidǐng 〈杂技〉 balancing on a pyramid of chairs

**旖** yǐ
【旖旎】 yǐnǐ 〈书〉 charming and gentle

## yì

**弋** yì 〈书〉 a retrievable arrow with a string attached to it

**义** yì ① justice; righteousness：见～勇为 be ready to take up the cudgels for a just cause/ 大～灭亲 sacrifice ties of blood to righteousness ② righteous; equitable; just：～战 just war/ ～行 righteous deed ③ human ties; relationship：情～ ties of friendship, comradeship, etc. ④ meaning; significance：词～ the meaning of a word/ 一词多～ polysemy ⑤ adopted; adoptive：～女 adopted daughter/ ～母 adoptive mother ⑥ artificial; false：～发 false hair
【义不容辞】 yì bùróng cí be duty-bound; have an unshirkable duty：～的国际主义义务 an unshirkable (或 bounden) internationalist duty
【义齿】 yìchǐ 〈医〉 false tooth
【义愤】 yìfèn righteous indignation; moral indignation：激于～ be roused to righteous indignation/ 革命～ revolutionary indignation
【义愤填膺】 yìfèn tián yīng be filled with (righteous) indignation
【义和团运动】 Yìhétuán Yùndòng the Yihetuan Movement (an anti-imperialist armed struggle waged by north China peasants and handicraftsmen in 1900)
【义举】 yìjǔ a magnanimous act undertaken for the public good
【义理】 yìlǐ argumentation (of a speech or essay)
【义卖】 yìmài a sale of goods (usu. at high prices) for charity or other worthy causes; charity bazaar
【义旗】 yìqí the banner of an army fighting a just war; banner of righteousness：举～ raise the banner of righteousness; rise against injustice
【义气】 yìqi code of brotherhood; personal loyalty：讲～ be loyal (to one's friends)
【义师】 yìshī an army fighting a just war; righteous army
【义士】 yìshì a high-minded or chivalrous person; a person who upholds justice; righteous man
【义无反顾】 yì wú fǎngù honour permits no turning back; be duty-bound not to turn back
【义务】 yìwù ① duty; obligation：公民的基本权利与～ the fundamental rights and duties of citizens/ 条约规定的～ treaty obligations/ 履行所承担的～ carry out commitments ② volunteer; voluntary：我是来尽～的。I've come to do voluntary service.
◇ ～兵 compulsory serviceman/ ～兵役制 compulsory military service; conscription/ ～教育 compulsory education/ ～劳动 voluntary labour
【义形于色】 yì xíng yú sè with indignation written on one's face
【义学】 yìxué 〈旧〉 private or community-run schools charging no tuition; free school
【义演】 yìyǎn benefit performance
【义勇军】 yìyǒngjūn army of volunteers; volunteers ◇ ～进行曲 March of the Volunteers
【义正词严】 yìzhèng-cíyán speak sternly out of a sense of justice; speak with the force of justice
【义肢】 yìzhī 〈医〉 artificial limb
【义冢】 yìzhǒng burial ground for the destitute

**亿** yì a hundred million
【亿万】 yìwàn hundreds of millions; millions upon millions：～人民 hundreds of millions of people; the people in their hundreds of millions ◇ ～富翁 billionaire
【亿万斯年】 yìwàn sī nián (for) billions of years; (for) aeons; time without end; eternity

**忆** yì recall; recollect
【忆苦】 yìkǔ recall one's suffering in the old society ◇ ～饭 a poor meal specially prepared to recall past suffering (of the working people)/ ～会 a meeting to recall past suffering
【忆苦思甜】 yì kǔ sī tián recall past suffering and think over the source of present happiness; tell of one's suffer-

ings in the old society and one's happiness in the new; contrast past misery with present happiness

**艺** yì ① skill: 球～ skill in a ball game/ ～高人胆大。Boldness of execution stems from superb skill. ② art: 文～ literature and art

【艺龄】 yìlíng length of sb.'s artistic career: 他有三十多年～。He's been on the stage for over thirty years.

【艺名】 yìmíng stage name (of an actor or actress)

【艺人】 yìrén ① actor or artist (in local drama, storytelling, acrobatics, etc.) ② artisan; handicraftsman

【艺术】 yìshù ① art: 为～而～，超阶级的～，实际上是不存在的。There is in reality no such thing as art for art's sake or art that stands above classes. ② skill; art; craft: 领导～ art of leadership ③ conforming to good taste: 这个房间布置得很～。The room is tastefully furnished.
◇ ～标准 artistic criterion/ ～风格 artistic style/ ～技巧 artistry; craftsmanship/ ～家 artist/ ～界 art circles/ ～品 work of art/ ～团 art ensemble; troupe of musicians and artists/ ～形式 artistic form; forms of art/ ～性 artistic quality; artistry/ ～造诣 artistic attainments/ ～指导 art director

【艺苑】 yìyuàn the realm of art and literature; art and literary circles: ～奇葩 exquisite works of art

**刈** yì mow; cut down

【刈草机】 yìcǎojī mowing machine; mower

**艾** yì 见"怨艾" yuànyì
另见 ài

**议** yì ① opinion; view: 异～ disagreement; dissident view/ 提～ propose; move ② discuss; exchange views on; talk over: ～而不决 discuss sth. without reaching a decision/ 我们对各种方案都～了～。We exchanged views on each of the different proposals.

【议案】 yì'àn proposal; motion

【议程】 yìchéng agenda: 列入～ place on the agenda; include in the agenda/ 第二项～ the second item on the agenda

【议定书】 yìdìngshū protocol: 贸易～ trade protocol/ 附加～ additional protocol

【议和】 yìhé negotiate peace

【议会】 yìhuì parliament; legislative assembly: 召开(解散)～ convene (dissolve) parliament/ 修正主义的"～道路" the revisionist "parliamentary road"
◇ ～党团 parliamentary groups/ ～斗争 parliamentary struggle/ ～迷 parliamentary cretinism/ ～制度 parliamentarism

【议价】 yìjià ① negotiate a price ② negotiated price

【议决】 yìjué resolve after deliberation; pass a resolution

【议论】 yìlùn comment; talk; discuss: 大发～ speak at great length/ ～不休 carry on endless discussions/ 人们对这件事～纷纷。Everybody is talking about the matter.

【议事】 yìshì discuss official business ◇ ～规则 rules of procedure; rules of debate/ ～日程 agenda; order of the day

【议题】 yìtí subject under discussion; topic for discussion

【议席】 yìxí seat in a legislative assembly

【议员】 yìyuán member of a legislative assembly; (英) Member of Parliament (MP); (美) Congressman or Congresswoman

【议院】 yìyuàn legislative assembly; parliament; congress

【议长】 yìzhǎng speaker (of a legislative body); president

**亦** yì 〈书〉 also; too: 反之～然 and the reverse is also true; and *vice versa*/ ～工～农 be both worker and peasant

【亦步亦趋】 yìbù-yìqū ape sb. at every step; imitate sb.'s every move; blindly follow suit

【亦即】 yìjí that is; i.e.; namely; viz.

**屹** yì 〈书〉 towering like a mountain peak

【屹立】 yìlì stand towering like a giant; stand erect: 人民英雄纪念碑～在天安门广场上。The Monument to the People's Heroes stands like a giant on Tiananmen Square.

【屹然】 yìrán towering; majestic: ～不动 stand firm and erect

**异** yì ① different: 大同小～ identical on major issues though with minor differences; essentially the same though differing on minor points/ ～父(母)兄弟 half brothers/ ～词 dissenting words; disagreement ② strange; unusual; extraordinary: ～兆 strange omen/ ～香 extraordinary fragrance/ 奇才～能 extraordinary talents and abilities ③ surprise: 深以为～ it strikes one as very strange ④ other; another: ～日 some other day/ ～地 a strange land ⑤ separate: 离～ divorce

【异步】 yìbù 〈物〉 asynchronous ◇ ～发电机 asynchronous generator/ ～计算机 asynchronous computer

【异彩】 yìcǎi extraordinary (或 radiant) splendour: 革命文艺大放～ revolutionary art and literature blossoming in radiant splendour

【异常】 yìcháng ① unusual; abnormal: ～现象 abnormal phenomena/ 神色～ not be one's usual self ② extremely; exceedingly; particularly: ～危险 extremely dangerous/ ～丰富 exceedingly rich/ ～需要 particularly necessary

【异读】 yìdú variant pronunciation

【异端】 yìduān heterodoxy; heresy: ～邪说 heretical beliefs; unorthodox opinions

【异构化】 yìgòuhuà 〈化〉 isomerization

【异国】 yìguó foreign country (或 land): ～情调 an exotic atmosphere

【异乎寻常】 yì hū xúncháng unusual; extraordinary: ～地热心 unusually enthusiastic

【异花传粉】 yìhuā chuánfěn 〈植〉 cross pollination

【异花受精】 yìhuā shòujīng 〈植〉 allogamy; cross fertilization

【异化】 yìhuà ① 〈哲〉 alienation ② 〈语〉 dissimilation
◇ ～作用〈生〉 dissimilation

【异己】 yìjǐ dissident; alien: 排除～ discriminate against those who hold different views; get rid of dissidents/ 阶级～分子 alien-class element

【异教】 yìjiào paganism; heathenism ◇ ～徒 pagan; heathen

【异军突起】 yìjūn tūqǐ a new force suddenly coming to the fore

【异口同声】 yìkǒu-tóngshēng with one voice; in unison: 大家～地称赞她献身教育事业的精神。Everybody spoke in praise of her devotion to the cause of education.

【异曲同工】 yìqǔ-tónggōng different tunes rendered with equal skill — different in approach but equally satisfactory in result

【异体受精】 yìtǐ shòujīng 〈动〉 allogamy; cross-fertilization

【异体字】 yìtǐzì a variant form of a Chinese character

【异同】 yì-tóng similarities and differences

【异味】 yìwèi ① rare delicacy ② peculiar smell

【异物】 yìwù ① foreign matter; foreign body: 食管～ a foreign body in the esophagus ② 〈书〉 a dead person; ghost

【异乡】 yìxiāng foreign land; strange land
【异想天开】 yì xiǎng tiān kāi indulge in the wildest fantasy; have a very fantastic idea
【异心】 yìxīn infidelity; disloyalty
【异形钢材】 yìxíng gāngcái special-shaped steel
【异形管】 yìxíngguǎn 〈机〉 special pipe
【异性】 yìxìng ① the opposite sex ② different in nature: ～的电互相吸引。Unlike electric charges attract each other.
【异烟肼】 yìyānjǐng 〈药〉 isoniazid; rimifon
【异言】 yìyán 〈书〉 dissenting words: 并无～ raise no objection
【异样】 yìyàng ① difference: 多年没见了,看不出他有什么～。We haven't seen each other for many years, but he doesn't look any different. ② unusual; peculiar: ～服装 peculiar dress/ 人们都用～的眼光打量他。Everyone sized him up with curious eyes.
【异议】 yìyì objection; dissent: 提出～ raise an objection; take exception to; challenge/ 独持～ be the only one to dissent/ 如果没有～,提案就算通过了。If there are no objections, we shall consider the resolution adopted.
【异源多倍体】 yìyuán-duōbèitǐ 〈生〉 allopolyploid
【异重流】 yìzhòngliú 〈水〉 density current
【异族】 yìzú different race or nation: ～通婚 mixed marriages

**译** yì translate; interpret: 笔～ written translation/ 口～ oral interpretation/ ～成英语 translate into English/ ～码 decode/ ～成电码 coding/ ～成密码 enciphering
【译本】 yìběn translation: «石头记»的英～ an English translation of *The Story of the Stone*
【译笔】 yìbǐ the quality or style of a translation: ～流畅。The translation reads smoothly.
【译电】 yìdiàn ① encode; encipher ② decode; decipher ◇ ～费 coding fee/ ～员 decoder; code clerk; cryptographer/ ～组 code and cipher section
【译码】 yìmǎ decode; decipher ◇ ～器 decoder; decipherer
【译名】 yìmíng translated term or name
【译述】 yìshù translate (或 render) freely
【译文】 yìwén translated text; translation
【译意风】 yìyìfēng simultaneous interpretation installation
【译音】 yìyīn transliteration
【译员】 yìyuán interpreter
【译者】 yìzhě translator
【译制】 yìzhì dub ◇ ～片 dubbed film

**抑** yì ① restrain; repress; curb: ～价 keep down the price/ ～强扶弱 curb the violent and assist the weak ② 〈书〉〈连〉 or
【抑或】 yìhuò 〈书〉〈连〉 or
【抑菌作用】 yìjūn zuòyòng 〈医〉 bacteriostasis
【抑扬】 yìyáng (of sound) rise and fall; modulate: ～顿挫 cadence; modulation in tone
【抑郁】 yìyù depressed; despondent; gloomy: ～不平 feel disgruntled ◇ ～症〈医〉 depression
【抑止】 yìzhǐ restrain; check
【抑制】 yìzhì ① restrain; control; check: ～自己的愤怒 restrain one's anger/ ～自己的感情 control one's emotion/ 眼泪～不住直往下流 can't hold back one's tears/ 利用辐射～洋葱发芽 check the sprouting of onions by radiation ② 〈生理〉 inhibition ◇ ～剂〈化〉 inhibitor/ ～神经 inhibitory nerve

**呓** yì talk in one's sleep
【呓语】 yìyǔ ① talk in one's sleep ② crazy talk; ravings: 狂人～ ravings of a madman

**邑** yì ① city: 通都大～ big city; metropolis ② county

**佚** yì 见"逸" yì

**役** yì ① labour; service: 劳～ corvée; forced labour/ 兵～ military service ② use as a servant: 奴～ enslave ③ servant: 仆～ servant; flunkey/ 衙～ *yamen* runner ④ battle; campaign: 乌林之～ the battle of Wulin
【役畜】 yìchù draught animal; beast of burden
【役龄】 yìlíng enlistment age
【役使】 yìshǐ work (an animal); use: 地主把长工当牛马一样～。The landlord made the farmhands toil like beasts of burden.

**诣** yì ① call on (sb. one respects); visit ② (academic or technical) attainments: 学术造～ scholarly attainments

**易** yì ① easy: 不～解决 not easy to solve/ ～患感冒 catch cold easily; be susceptible to colds/ ～涝地区 areas liable to waterlogging ② amiable: 平～近人 amiable and easy of access ③ change: ～手 change hands ④ exchange: 以物～物 barter/ ～货协定 an agreement on the exchange of commodities ⑤ (Yì) a surname
【易感者】 yìgǎnzhě 〈医〉 susceptible person; susceptible
【易经】 Yìjīng *The Book of Changes* 参见"五经" wǔjīng
【易洛魁人】 Yìluòkuírén Iroquois
【易燃物】 yìránwù combustibles; inflammables
【易熔点】 yìróngdiǎn 〈物〉 eutectic point
【易熔合金】 yìróng héjīn 〈冶〉 fusible alloy
【易如反掌】 yì rú fǎnzhǎng as easy as turning one's hand over; as easy as falling off a log

**驿** yì post
【驿道】 yìdào post road
【驿站】 yìzhàn post (where formerly couriers changed horses or rested)

**绎** yì 〈书〉 unravel; sort out: 演～ deduction

**狭** yì 见"林狭" línyì

**奕** yì
【奕奕】 yìyì radiating power and vitality: 神采～ glowing with health and radiating vitality

**弈** yì 〈书〉 ① *weiqi*, a game played with black and white pieces on a board of 361 crosses; *go* ② play chess

**疫** yì epidemic disease; pestilence: 鼠～ the plague/ 时～ epidemic disease/ 防～ epidemic prevention
【疫病】 yìbìng epidemic disease
【疫疠】 yìlì epidemic disease; pestilence
【疫苗】 yìmiáo 〈医〉 vaccine
【疫情】 yìqíng information about and appraisal of an epidemic; epidemic situation ◇ ～报告站 station for reporting epidemic diseases

**轶** yì 见"逸" yì ③④
【轶事】 yìshì anecdote

**益** yì ① benefit; profit; advantage: 受～良多 derive (或 receive) much benefit ② beneficial ③ increase: 延年～寿 prolong life ④ all the more; increasingly: ～发困难 increasingly difficult/ 多多～善 the more the better

【益虫】 yìchóng beneficial insect
【益处】 yìchu benefit; profit; good
【益母草】 yìmǔcǎo 〈中药〉 motherwort (*Leonurus heterophyllus*)
【益鸟】 yìniǎo beneficial bird
【益友】 yìyǒu friend and mentor: 良师～ good teacher and helpful friend

**谊** yì friendship: 深情厚～ profound friendship

**挹** yì 〈书〉 ① scoop up; ladle out ② pull

**悒** yì 〈书〉 sad; worried: ～～不乐 feel depressed; mope

**逸** yì ① ease; leisure: 有劳有～ alternate work with rest ② escape; flee: 逃～ escape ③ be lost: ～书 ancient works no longer extant ④ excel: ～群 excel all others
【逸乐】 yìlè comfort and pleasure
【逸民】 yìmín hermit (in ancient times); recluse
【逸事】 yìshì anecdote (esp. about a famous person)
【逸闻】 yìwén anecdote

**翌** yì 〈书〉 immediately following in time; next: ～日 next day/ ～年 next year

**翊** yì 〈书〉 assist (a ruler): ～戴 assist and support (a ruler)

**勚** yì ①〈书〉 toil; hard work ② (of an edge, point, etc.) become worn; become dull or blunt: 螺丝扣～了。The threads of the screw are worn.

**溢** yì ① overflow; spill: 河水四～。The river overflowed. ② excessive: ～美 undeserved praise; compliment
【溢出】 yìchū spill over; overflow
【溢洪道】 yìhóngdào 〈水〉 spillway
【溢流坝】 yìliúbà 〈水〉 overfall dam; spillway dam

**意** yì ① meaning; idea: 词不达～。The words fail to convey the meaning. ② wish; desire; intention: 好～ a good intention ③ anticipate; expect: 不～ contrary to expectation; unexpectedly ④ suggestion; hint; trace: 颇有秋～ make one feel that autumn has set in
【意表】 yìbiǎo what one does not expect: 出人～ beyond one's expectation; unexpectedly
【意大利】 Yìdàlì Italy ◇ ～人 Italian/ ～语 Italian (language)
【意会】 yìhuì sense: 只可～,不可言传 can be sensed, but not explained in words
【意见】 yìjiàn ① idea; view; opinion; suggestion: 交换～ exchange ideas (或 views); compare notes/ 倾听群众的～ listen carefully to the views (或 opinions) of the masses/ 提出修改～ make suggestions for revision/ ～一致 have identical views; be of one mind/ ～分歧 have a difference (或 divergence) of opinion; disagree ② objection; differing opinion; complaint: 我对这种办法很有～。I strongly object to this method. 或 I take vigorous exception to this approach./ 大家对你～很大。People have a lot of complaints about you./ 有～要拿到桌面上来。Those who differ should air their views openly. ◇ ～簿 visitors' book; customers' book/ ～箱 suggestion box
【意匠】 yìjiàng artistic conception (of a poem, painting, etc.)
【意境】 yìjìng artistic conception: 这幅油画～深远。This painting is magnificently conceived.
【意料】 yìliào anticipate; expect: 这是～中的事。That's to be expected./ 出乎～ unexpected; unforeseen; surprising
【意念】 yìniàn idea; thought: 这时每人脑子里都只有一个～: "胜利!" At that moment victory was the one idea that occupied everyone's mind. 或 Then, everybody had only one thought in mind: victory.
【意气】 yìqì ① will and spirit: ～高昂 high-spirited ② temperament: ～相投 be alike in temperament; be congenial with each other ③ personal feelings (或 prejudice): ～用事 be swayed by personal feelings/ ～之争 a dispute caused by personal feelings
【意气风发】 yìqì fēngfā high-spirited and vigorous; daring and energetic
【意趣】 yìqù interest and charm
【意识】 yìshí ① 〈哲〉 consciousness ②〔常与"到"字连用〕be conscious (或 aware) of; awake to; realize: ～到自己的责任 be conscious of one's responsibilities ◇ ～流〈心〉 stream of consciousness/ ～域 〈心〉 sphere of consciousness
【意识形态】 yìshí xíngtài 〈哲〉 ideology: 社会～ social ideology/ ～方面的阶级斗争 class struggle in the ideological field
【意思】 yìsi ① meaning; idea: 我不明白你的～。I don't understand what you mean./ 你这是什么～?What do you mean by that?/ 文章的中心～ the central idea of an article ② opinion; wish; desire: 我的～是走着去。In my opinion, (或 I think) we should walk./ 你是不是有～跟她见见面? Do you wish to meet her? ③ a token of affection, appreciation, gratitude, etc.: 这不过是我的一点儿～,请收下吧。Please accept this little gift as a token of my appreciation. ④ suggestion; hint; trace: 天有点要下雨的～。It looks like rain. ⑤ interest; fun: 他觉得年画展览很有～。He found the exhibition of New Year pictures very interesting./ 打乒乓球很有～。Ping-pong is a lot of fun.
【意图】 yìtú intention; intent: 领会上级～ understand the intentions of the higher organization
【意外】 yìwài ① unexpected; unforeseen: 感到～ be surprised; be taken by surprise ② accident; mishap: 以免发生～ so as to avoid accidents
【意味】 yìwèi ① meaning; significance; implication: ～深长的一笑 a meaning smile/ 他的话～深长，值得玩味。What he said is significant and worth pondering. ② interest; overtone; flavour: 这首诗～无穷。This is a poem of unlimited interest./ 带有文学～的新闻报道 a news report with a literary flavour
【意味着】 yìwèizhe signify; mean; imply: 这一数字～生产提高了两倍。This figure means a twofold increase in production.
【意想】 yìxiǎng imagine; expect: ～不到的效果 unexpected results
【意向】 yìxiàng intention; purpose: 敌军～不明。The enemy's intentions are not clear.
【意象】 yìxiàng image; imagery
【意兴】 yìxìng interest; enthusiasm: ～索然 have not the least interest/ ～勃勃 be highly enthusiastic
【意义】 yìyì meaning; sense; significance: 在某种～上 in a sense/ 具有重大历史～的事件 an event of historic significance/ 一部富有教育～的影片 a very instructive film/ 这样做没有～。There's no point in doing that./ 这个词有三个～。This word has three distinct meanings.
【意译】 yìyì free translation
【意愿】 yìyuàn wish; desire; aspiration: 表达了人民的～ express the wishes of the people
【意在言外】 yì zài yán wài the meaning is implied

【意旨】 yìzhǐ intention; wish; will: 秉承某人的～ in compliance with sb.'s wish
【意志】 yìzhì will: 钢铁～ iron will; iron determination/ ～坚强 strong-willed/ ～消沉 demoralized; despondent/ 锻炼～ temper one's willpower
【意中人】 yìzhōngrén the person one is in love with; person of one's heart

**裔** yì 〈书〉① descendants; posterity: 华～美国人 an American of Chinese descent ② borderland; distant land

**肄** yì study
【肄业】 yìyè study in school or at college: 他曾在大学～二年。He was in college for two years.

**缢** yì 〈书〉hang: 自～ hang oneself

**蜴** yì 见"蜥蜴" xīyì

**瘗** yì 〈书〉bury

**镒** yì an ancient unit of weight (=20 or 24 *liang*)

**毅** yì firm; resolute: 刚～ fortitude
【毅力】 yìlì willpower; will; stamina: 惊人的～ amazing willpower/ 百折不回的～ indomitable will/ 以无比的～跟疾病作斗争 battle against illness with matchless stamina/ 完成这项工作需要坚强的～。It'll require great willpower to accomplish the task.
【毅然】 yìrán resolutely; firmly; determinedly

**薏** yì
【薏米】 yìmǐ 〈中药〉the seed of Job's tears 又作"薏仁米"
【薏苡】 yìyǐ 〈植〉Job's tears

**劓** yì cutting off the nose (a punishment in ancient China)

**臆** yì ① chest ② subjectively
【臆测】 yìcè conjecture; surmise; guess
【臆断】 yìduàn assume; suppose
【臆说】 yìshuō assumption; supposition
【臆造】 yìzào fabricate (a story, reason, etc.); concoct

**翼** yì ① the wing of a bird, aeroplane, etc.: 从左右两～夹攻敌人 attack the enemy on both flanks/ 主楼的两～ the two wings of the main building ② 〈书〉assist (a ruler); aid: ～助 render assistance (to a ruler)
【翼侧】 yìcè 〈军〉flank ◇ ～攻击 flank attack/ ～迂回 outflank
【翼手动物】 yìshǒu dòngwù 〈动〉bat; chiropter
【翼手龙】 yìshǒulóng 〈古生物〉pterodactyl
【翼型】 yìxíng 〈航空〉wing section; aerofoil
【翼翼】 yìyì cautiously: 小心～ with exceptional caution; very carefully
【翼状胬肉】 yìzhuàng nǔròu 〈医〉pterygium

**翳** yì 〈中医〉slight corneal opacity; nebula

**癔** yì
【癔病】 yìbìng 〈医〉hysteria ◇ ～患者 hysteriac

**镱** yì 〈化〉ytterbium (Yb)

**懿** yì 〈书〉exemplary: ～行 exemplary conduct

## yīn

**因** yīn ① 〈书〉follow; carry on: 陈陈相～ follow a set routine; stay in the same old groove ② 〈书〉on the basis of; in accordance with; in the light of: 疗效～人而异。The curative effect varies from person to person. ③ cause; reason: 外～ external cause/ 近～ immediate cause/ 事出有～。There is good reason for it. 或 It is by no means accidental. ④ because of; as a result of: ～病请假 ask for sick leave/ ～公牺牲 die while on duty; die at one's post/ 会议～故改期。The meeting has been postponed for some reason.
【因材施教】 yīn cái shī jiào teach students in accordance with their aptitude
【因此】 yīncǐ therefore; for this reason; consequently: 这个干部办事公道，～社员们都拥护他。He is a fair-minded cadre, so all the commune members support him.
【因次】 yīncì 〈物〉dimension ◇ ～分析 dimensional analysis
【因地制宜】 yīn dì zhì yí suit measures to local conditions: ～地进行密植 carry out close planting in line with local conditions
【因而】 yīn'ér thus; as a result; with the result that: 他们农业机械化搞得好，～大大提高了生产率。Their success in mechanizing farm work greatly raised their productivity.
【因果】 yīnguǒ ① cause and effect ② 〈佛教〉karma; preordained fate
◇ ～关系 causality/ ～律 law of causation; law of causality/ ～性 causality
【因陋就简】 yīn lòu jiù jiǎn make do with whatever is available; do things simply and thriftily
【因人成事】 yīn rén chéng shì rely on others for success in work
【因人设事】 yīn rén shè shì create a job to accommodate a person
【因势利导】 yīn shì lì dǎo adroitly guide action according to circumstances: ～，夺取胜利 make the best use of the situation and guide the struggle to victory
【因素】 yīnsù factor; element: 积极～ positive factors/ 人的～ the human factor/ 生产力的基本～是生产资料和劳动力。The basic factors in the productive forces are the means of production and manpower. ◇ ～论〈哲〉theory of factors
【因为】 yīnwei because; for; on account of
【因袭】 yīnxí follow (old customs, methods, rules, etc.); copy: ～陈规 follow outmoded rules/ ～前人 follow in the footsteps of one's predecessors
【因小失大】 yīn xiǎo shī dà try to save a little only to lose a lot
【因循】 yīnxún ① follow (old customs, etc.); continue in the same old rut: ～守旧 stick to old ways; follow the beaten path ② procrastinate: ～坐误 sit back and allow the situation to deteriorate; procrastinate until it is too late
【因噎废食】 yīn yē fèi shí give up eating for fear of choking — refrain from doing sth. necessary for fear of a slight risk
【因由】 yīnyóu reason; cause; origin
【因缘】 yīnyuán ① 〈佛教〉principal and subsidiary causes; cause ② predestined relationship
【因子】 yīnzǐ 〈数〉factor ◇ ～分解 factorization

**阴** yīn ① (in Chinese philosophy, medicine, etc.) *yin*, the feminine or negative principle in nature ② the moon: ～历 lunar calendar ③〈气〉overcast: 天～了。The sky is overcast. ④ shade: 树～ the shade of a tree ⑤ north of a hill or south of a river: 华～ Huayin (a county situated on the north side of Huashan Mountain)/ 江～ Jiangyin (a county situated on the south side of the Changjiang River) ⑥ back: 碑～ the back of a stone tablet ⑦ in intaglio: ～文 characters cut in intaglio ⑧ hidden; secret; sinister: ～一套，阳一套 act one way in public and another in private; be engaged in double-dealing/ ～谋 sinister plot ⑨ of the nether world ⑩〈物〉negative: ～离子 negative ion; anion ⑪ private parts (esp. of the female) ⑫ (Yīn) a surname

【阴暗】 yīn'àn dark; gloomy: ～的角落 a dark corner (where plots are hatched)/ ～的脸色 a glum face/ ～的心理 mentality marked by antipathy and gloom/ ～面 the dark (或 seamy) side of things

【阴部】 yīnbù〈生理〉private parts; pudenda

【阴沉】 yīnchén cloudy; overcast; gloomy; sombre: 一早上天都是～的。The sky was cloudy (或 grey) all morning./ 脸色～ have a sombre countenance; look glum

【阴错阳差】 yīncuò-yángchā (a mistake or error due to) a strange combination of circumstances 又作"阴差阳错"

【阴丹士林】 yīndānshìlín〈化〉indanthrene

【阴道】 yīndào〈生理〉vagina ◇ ～炎 vaginitis

【阴德】 yīndé a good deed to the doer's credit in the next world

【阴地植物】 yīndì zhíwù shade plant

【阴电】 yīndiàn negative electricity

【阴毒】 yīndú insidious; sinister

【阴风】 yīnfēng ill (或 evil) wind: 扇～，点鬼火 fan the winds of evil and spread the fires of turmoil; foment trouble

【阴干】 yīngān be placed in the shade to dry; dry in the shade

【阴沟】 yīngōu sewer

【阴魂】 yīnhún soul; spirit: ～不散。The soul (或 spirit) refuses to leave.

【阴极】 yīnjí〈物〉negative pole; negative electrode; cathode: 冷～ cold cathode ◇ ～激励 cathode drive

【阴极射线】 yīnjí shèxiàn〈物〉cathode ray ◇ ～管 cathode-ray tube

【阴间】 yīnjiān the nether world

【阴茎】 yīnjīng〈生理〉penis

【阴冷】 yīnlěng ① (of weather) gloomy and cold; raw ② (of a person's look) sombre; glum

【阴历】 yīnlì lunar calendar: ～正月 the first month of the lunar year

【阴凉】 yīnliáng ① shady and cool: 此药宜置于～处。The medicine should be kept in a cool, dark place. ② cool place; shade: 找个～儿歇歇。Let's have a rest in the shade.

【阴霾】 yīnmái haze

【阴毛】 yīnmáo〈生理〉pubes

【阴门】 yīnmén〈生理〉vaginal orifice 又作"阴户"

【阴谋】 yīnmóu plot; scheme; conspiracy: ～诡计 schemes and intrigues/ ～破坏 plot sabotage/ ～复辟 plot to restore the old order/ ～篡权 scheme to usurp power/ ～手段 conspiratorial means ◇ ～集团 conspiratorial clique (或 group)/ ～家 schemer; intriguer; conspirator

【阴囊】 yīnnáng〈生理〉scrotum

【阴平】 yīnpíng high and level tone, the first of the four tones in modern standard Chinese pronunciation

【阴森】 yīnsēn gloomy; gruesome; ghastly: ～的树林 a deep, dark forest/ ～可怕 ghastly and bloodcurdling

【阴山】 Yīnshān the Yinshan Mountains

【阴虱】 yīnshī〈动〉crab louse

【阴私】 yīnsī shameful secret

【阴天】 yīntiān overcast sky; cloudy day

【阴文】 yīnwén characters cut in intaglio

【阴险】 yīnxiǎn sinister; insidious; treacherous: ～毒辣 sinister and ruthless

【阴性】 yīnxìng ①〈医〉negative: ～反应 negative reaction ②〈语〉feminine gender

【阴虚】 yīnxū〈中医〉deficiency of *yin* (insufficiency of body fluid), with irritability, thirst, constipation, etc. as symptoms

【阴阳】 yīn-yáng (in Chinese philosophy, medicine, etc.) *yin* and *yang*, the two opposing principles in nature, the former feminine and negative, the latter masculine and positive

【阴阳怪气】 yīnyáng guàiqì ① (of one's manner of speaking) mystifying; enigmatic; deliberately ambiguous ② eccentric; queer; cynical: 他这个人～的。He's a queer chap.

【阴阳家】 Yīnyángjiā the *Yin-Yang* School; the School of Positive and Negative Forces (in the Period of the Warring States, 475-221 B.C.)

【阴阳历】 yīnyánglì lunisolar calendar

【阴阳先生】 yīnyáng xiānsheng geomancer (usu. employed as a funeral adviser)

【阴影】 yīnyǐng shadow: 树木的～ shadows of trees/ 肺部有～ have a shadow on one's lungs

【阴雨】 yīnyǔ overcast and rainy: ～连绵 cloudy and drizzly for days on end; an unbroken spell of wet weather

【阴郁】 yīnyù gloomy; dismal; depressed: 天色～。The weather is gloomy./ 心情～ feel gloomy (或 depressed)

【阴云】 yīnyún dark clouds: ～密布。The sky is overcast. 或 The sky is covered with dark clouds.

**音** yīn ① sound: 乐～ musical sound/ 噪～ noise/ 说话的口～很重 speak with a strong accent ② news; tidings: 佳～ welcome news; glad tidings ③〈物〉tone: 复～ complex tone/ 纯～ pure tone; simple tone

【音爆】 yīnbào〈航空〉sonic boom

【音标】 yīnbiāo〈语〉phonetic symbol; phonetic transcription

【音波】 yīnbō〈物〉sound wave

【音叉】 yīnchā tuning fork

【音程】 yīnchéng〈乐〉interval

【音调】 yīndiào tone

【音符】 yīnfú〈乐〉note

【音高】 yīngāo〈乐〉pitch

【音阶】 yīnjiē〈乐〉scale

【音节】 yīnjié〈语〉syllable ◇ ～文字 syllabic language 又作"音缀"

【音量】 yīnliàng volume (of sound) ◇ ～控制 volume control

【音律】 yīnlǜ〈乐〉temperament

【音名】 yīnmíng〈乐〉musical alphabet

【音频】 yīnpín〈物〉audio frequency ◇ ～振荡器〈电〉audio-frequency oscillator

【音品】 yīnpǐn 见"音色"

【音儿】 yīnr〈方〉① voice ② implication: 听话听～ listen for the meaning behind sb.'s words

【音容】 yīnróng〈书〉the likeness of the deceased: ～宛在 as if the person were in the flesh

【音色】 yīnsè tone colour; timbre

【音诗】 yīnshī〈乐〉tone poem

【音势】 yīnshì〈语〉intensity of sound

【音素】 yīnsù〈语〉phoneme ◇ ～文字 phonemic language

【音速】 yīnsù〈物〉velocity (或 speed) of sound: 超～ su-

personic/ 高超～ hypersonic
【音位】 yīnwèi 〈语〉 phoneme
【音响】 yīnxiǎng sound; acoustics ◇ ～水雷〈军〉sonic (或 sound, acoustic) mine/ ～效果 sound effects; acoustics
【音信】 yīnxìn mail; message; news: 互通～ communicate with each other; be in correspondence with each other/ 他走后杳无～。We have not heard from him since he left. 又作"音讯"
【音型】 yīnxíng 〈乐〉 figure
【音译】 yīnyì transliteration
【音域】 yīnyù 〈乐〉 range; compass; register
【音乐】 yīnyuè music
◇ ～会 concert/ ～家 musician/ ～片 musical (film)/ ～厅 concert hall/ ～形象 musical image/ ～学院 conservatory of music
【音韵学】 yīnyùnxué 〈语〉 phonology ◇ ～家 phonologist
【音障】 yīnzhàng 〈物〉 sound (或 sonic) barrier
【音值】 yīnzhí 〈语〉 value
【音质】 yīnzhì ① tone quality ② acoustic fidelity

## 茵

yīn mattress: 绿草如～ a carpet of green grass
【茵陈】 yīnchén 〈中药〉 capillary artemisia (*Artemisia capillaris*)

## 洇

yīn (of ink) spread and sink in: 这种纸写字容易～。Ink blots on this paper.
【洇色】 yīnsè diffusion or running of colouring matter; bleeding

## 姻

yīn ① marriage: 联～ connect by marriage ② relation by marriage: ～兄弟 brothers-in-law
【姻亲】 yīnqīn relation by marriage: ～关系 relationship by marriage; affinity
【姻娅】 yīnyà relatives by marriage; in-laws
【姻缘】 yīnyuán the happy fate which brings lovers together: 美满～ a happy marriage; conjugal felicity

## 荫

yīn shade
另见 yìn
【荫蔽】 yīnbì ① be shaded or hidden by foliage: 野战医院～在树林中。The field hospital lies hidden among the trees. ② cover; conceal: ～集结 concentrate under cover/ ～的斗争 covert struggle

## 氤

yīn
【氤氲】 yīnyūn 〈书〉 (of smoke or mist) dense; thick; enshrouding: 云烟～ enshrouding mist

## 殷

yīn 〈书〉 ① abundant; rich ② eager; ardent: 期望甚～ cherish high hopes ③ hospitable: 招待甚～ offer cordial hospitality ④ (Yīn) the Yin Dynasty, the later period of the Shang (商) Dynasty ⑤ (Yīn) a surname
另见 yān
【殷钢】 yīngāng 〈冶〉 invar
【殷鉴】 yīnjiàn 〈书〉 setback which serves as a warning to others: ～不远。One need not look far for a lesson.
【殷切】 yīnqiè ardent; eager: ～的期望 ardent expectations
【殷勤】 yīnqín eagerly attentive; solicitous: 受到～接待 be accorded solicitous hospitality/ 献～ do everything to please; pay one's addresses to
【殷实】 yīnshí well-off; substantial: ～人家 well-off families/ ～的商号 a substantial firm
【殷墟】 Yīnxū 〈考古〉 Yin Dynasty ruins

## 铟

yīn 〈化〉 indium (In)

## 堙

yīn 〈书〉 ① mound ② block up

## 喑

yīn 〈书〉 silent; mute: ～哑 mute; dumb

# yín

## 吟

yín ① chant; recite: ～诗 recite or compose poetry ② song (as a type of classical poetry): «秦妇～» *Song of a Qin Lady* ③ the cry of certain animals: 龙～虎啸 the roar of dragons and tigers
【吟风弄月】 yínfēng-nòngyuè sing of the moon and the wind — write sentimental verse
【吟诵】 yínsòng chant; recite
【吟味】 yínwèi recite with relish; recite with appreciation: 反复～ recite again and again in appreciation
【吟咏】 yínyǒng recite (poetry) with a cadence; chant

## 垠

yín 〈书〉 boundary; limit: 一望无～ stretch as far as the eye can see; stretch beyond the horizon

## 狺

yín
【狺狺】 yínyín 〈书〉 yap; yelp: ～狂吠 bark frenziedly

## 淫

yín ① excessive: ～雨 excessive rains ② loose; wanton: 骄奢～逸 lordly, luxurious, loose and idle; wallowing in luxury and pleasure ③ licentious; lewd; lascivious ④ obscene; pornographic: ～书 pornographic book/ ～画 obscene picture
【淫荡】 yíndàng loose in morals; lascivious; licentious; lewd
【淫秽】 yínhuì obscene; salacious; bawdy
【淫乱】 yínluàn (sexually) promiscuous; licentious
【淫威】 yínwēi abuse of power; despotic power
【淫猥】 yínwěi obscene
【淫羊藿】 yínyánghuò 〈中药〉 longspur epimedium (*Epimedium macranthum*)

## 寅

yín the third of the twelve Earthly Branches
【寅吃卯粮】 yín chī mǎo liáng eat next year's food; eat one's corn in the blade; anticipate one's income
【寅时】 yínshí the period of the day from 3 a.m. to 5 a.m.

## 银

yín ① silver (Ag) ② relating to currency or money: ～行 bank ③ silver-coloured: ～发 silver hair/ ～色 silvery
【银白】 yínbái silvery white
【银白杨】 yínbáiyáng white poplar
【银杯】 yínbēi silver cup
【银本位】 yínběnwèi 〈经〉 silver standard
【银币】 yínbì silver coin
【银鲳】 yínchāng 〈动〉 silvery pomfret
【银川】 Yínchuān Yinchuan
【银锭】 yíndìng silver ingot
【银耳】 yín'ěr 〈中药〉 tremella
【银根】 yíngēn 〈经〉 money market; money: ～紧 tight/ ～松 easy
【银汉】 yínhàn 〈书〉 the Milky Way
【银汉鱼】 yínhànyú 〈动〉 silverside
【银行】 yínháng bank: ～存款 bank deposit/ 外汇指定～ authorized bank (for dealing in foreign exchange)
◇ ～存折 bankbook; passbook/ ～家 banker/ ～信贷 bank credit
【银河】 yínhé 〈天〉 the Milky Way ◇ ～系 the Milky Way system; the Galaxy

【银狐】 yínhú silver fox
【银灰】 yínhuī silver grey
【银婚】 yínhūn silver wedding
【银匠】 yínjiàng silversmith
【银两】 yínliǎng silver (used as currency)
【银楼】 yínlóu silverware shop
【银幕】 yínmù (motion-picture) screen
【银鸥】 yín'ōu 〈动〉 herring gull
【银牌】 yínpái silver medal
【银器】 yínqì silverware
【银钱】 yínqián money
【银鼠】 yínshǔ 〈动〉 snow weasel
【银条】 yíntiáo silver bar
【银屑病】 yínxièbìng 〈医〉 psoriasis
【银杏】 yínxìng 〈植〉 ginkgo
【银样镴枪头】 yín yàng làqiāngtóu a pewter spearhead that shines like silver — an impressive-looking but useless person
【银鱼】 yínyú 〈动〉 whitebait; salangid
【银圆】 yínyuán silver dollar 又作"银元""银洋"
【银质奖】 yínzhìjiǎng silver medal
【银朱】 yínzhū vermilion ◇ ～涂料 vermilion paint
【银子】 yínzi silver

**龈** yín gum

**夤** yín 〈书〉 ① hold sb. in respectful awe ② deep: ～夜 in the depth of the night; at the dead of night
【夤缘】 yínyuán 〈书〉 make use of one's connections to climb up; try to advance one's career by currying favour with important people

## yǐn

**尹** yǐn ① an ancient official title: 府～ prefect ② (Yǐn) a surname

**引** yǐn ① draw; stretch: ～弓 draw a bow ② lead; guide: ～路 lead the way/ 把长江水～到黄河 divert water from the Changjiang River to the Huanghe River ③ leave: ～避 keep (或 stay, steer) clear of; make way for ④ lure; attract: ～入圈套 lure into a trap; ensnare/ 抛砖～玉 cast a brick to attract jade/ ～火 kindle a fire ⑤ cause; make: 他这一句话～得大家笑起来。His remark set everybody laughing. ⑥ quote; cite: ～某人的话 quote sb./ ～以为荣 cite sth. as an honour; take it as an honour/ ～文 quoted passage; quotation ⑦ a unit of length (=$33^1/_3$ metres)
【引爆】 yǐnbào ignite; detonate ◇ ～装置 igniter
【引柴】 yǐnchái kindling 又作"引火柴"
【引出】 yǐnchū draw forth; lead to: ～正确的结论 draw correct conclusions/ 在一定的条件下,坏的东西可以～好的结果,好的东西也可以～坏的结果。In given conditions, a bad thing can lead to good results and a good thing to bad results.
【引导】 yǐndǎo guide; lead: 毛泽东思想～中国人民从胜利走向胜利。Mao Zedong Thought guides the Chinese people from victory to victory./ 主人～贵宾们参观了车间。The hosts showed the distinguished guests around the workshops.
【引逗】 yǐndòu ① tantalize; tease ② lure; entice
【引渡】 yǐndù 〈法〉 extradite
【引而不发】 yǐn ér bù fā draw the bow but not discharge the arrow: ～,跃如也。Draw the bow without shooting, just indicate the motions.
【引发】 yǐnfā 〈化〉 initiation ◇ ～剂 initiator
【引吭高歌】 yǐn háng gāo gē sing joyfully in a loud voice; sing heartily
【引航】 yǐnháng 〈航海〉 pilotage
【引号】 yǐnhào quotation marks (""): 双～ double quotation marks ("")/ 单～ single quotation marks (' ')
【引河】 yǐnhé ① irrigation channel ② diversion canal
【引火烧身】 yǐn huǒ shāo shēn draw fire against oneself — make self-criticism to encourage criticism from others
【引见】 yǐnjiàn introduce; present
【引荐】 yǐnjiàn recommend
【引进】 yǐnjìn ① recommend ② introduce from elsewhere: ～新的小麦品种 introduce new varieties of wheat/ ～技术装备 import technology and equipment
【引经据典】 yǐnjīng-jùdiǎn quote the classics; copiously quote authoritative works
【引咎】 yǐnjiù 〈书〉 hold oneself responsible for a serious mistake; take the blame: ～辞职 take the blame and resign
【引狼入室】 yǐn láng rù shì invite a wolf into the house — open the door to a dangerous foe
【引理】 yǐnlǐ 〈数〉 lemma
【引力】 yǐnlì 〈物〉 gravitation; gravitational force; attraction: 核～ nuclear attraction/ 万有～ universal gravitation ◇ ～场 gravitational field
【引领】 yǐnlǐng 〈书〉 crane one's neck to look into the distance — eagerly look forward to sth.
【引流】 yǐnliú 〈医〉 drainage: 十二指肠～ duodenal drainage ◇ ～管 drainage tube
【引起】 yǐnqǐ give rise to; lead to; set off; touch off; cause; arouse: ～严重后果 lead to grave consequences/ ～连锁反应 set off a chain reaction/ ～公愤 arouse (或 touch off) public indignation/ ～强烈的反响 cause strong repercussions/ ～怀疑 arouse suspicion/ ～注意 bring to sb.'s attention/ ～一场热烈的讨论 evoke a heated discussion
【引桥】 yǐnqiáo 〈交〉 bridge approach
【引擎】 yǐnqíng 〈机〉 engine ◇ ～盖 bonnet; hood
【引人入胜】 yǐn rén rù shèng (of scenery, literary works, etc.) fascinating; enchanting; bewitching: 把报纸办得～ make the newspaper interesting and absorbing
【引人注目】 yǐn rén zhùmù noticeable; conspicuous; spectacular: ～的横幅标语 an eye-catching slogan on a banner/ ～的特点 conspicuous features/ ～的变化 spectacular changes
【引入】 yǐnrù lead into; draw into: ～歧途 lead sb. onto a wrong path; lead sb. astray ◇ ～品种 〈农〉 introduced variety
【引申】 yǐnshēn extend (the meaning of a word, etc.) ◇ ～义 extended meaning
【引水】 yǐnshuǐ ① pilot a ship into harbour ② draw or channel water: ～灌田 channel water into the fields/ ～上山 draw water up a hill ③ 〈水〉 diversion: ～工程 diversion works ◇ ～员 pilot
【引退】 yǐntuì retire from office; resign
【引文】 yǐnwén quoted passage; quotation
【引线】 yǐnxiàn ① 〈电〉 lead (wire) ② go-between ③ catalyst
【引信】 yǐnxìn detonator; fuse: 触发～ contact fuse/ 延期～ delay fuse
【引言】 yǐnyán foreword; introduction
【引以为戒】 yǐn yǐ wéi jiè learn a lesson (from a previous error, etc.); take warning 又作"引为鉴戒"
【引用】 yǐnyòng ① quote; cite: 他在文章中～了毛主席的话。In his article he quoted Chairman Mao. ② recommend; appoint
【引诱】 yǐnyòu lure; seduce: ～敌人进入伏击圈 lure the enemy into a trap/ 企图用金钱和美女来～意志薄弱的人 try

to lure the weak-willed with money and women
【引证】 yǐnzhèng quote or cite as proof or evidence
【引种】 yǐnzhòng <农> introduce a fine variety
【引子】 yǐnzi ① <剧> an actor's opening words ② <乐> introductory music ③ introductory remarks; introduction ④ <中药> an added ingredient (to enhance the efficacy of medicines)

**饮** yǐn ① drink: ～茶 drink tea/ 冷～ cold drinks ② keep in the heart; nurse: ～恨 nurse a grievance ③ <中药> a decoction of Chinese medicine to be taken cold
另见 yìn
【饮弹】 yǐndàn <书> be hit by a bullet: ～身亡 be killed by a bullet
【饮恨】 yǐnhèn <书> nurse a grievance: ～而终 die with a grievance in one's heart
【饮料】 yǐnliào drink; beverage
【饮片】 yǐnpiàn <中药> prepared herbal medicine in small pieces ready for decoction
【饮泣】 yǐnqì <书> weep in silence: ～吞声 swallow one's tears; weep silent tears
【饮食】 yǐnshí food and drink; diet: 给病人规定～ put a patient on a diet
◇ ～店 eating house/ ～疗法 <医> dietotherapy; dietetic treatment/ ～卫生 dietetic hygiene/ ～业 catering trade
【饮水器】 yǐnshuǐqì <牧> drinking bowl; drinker
【饮水思源】 yǐn shuǐ sī yuán when you drink water, think of its source — never forget where one's happiness comes from
【饮用水】 yǐnyòngshuǐ drinking water; potable water
【饮鸩止渴】 yǐn zhèn zhǐ kě drink poison to quench thirst — seek temporary relief regardless of the consequences

**蚓** yǐn 见"蚯蚓" qiūyǐn

**隐** yǐn ① hidden from view; concealed: ～瞒 conceal; hide ② latent; dormant; lurking: ～患 hidden danger
【隐蔽】 yǐnbì conceal; take cover: 公开的和～的活动 overt and covert activities/ 游击队～在高粱地里。The guerrillas took cover in the sorghum fields./ ～! (口令) Take cover!
◇ ～运动 <军> concealed movement/ ～阵地 covered position
【隐藏】 yǐncáng hide; conceal; remain under cover: ～在革命队伍里的资产阶级野心家 a bourgeois careerist hidden in the revolutionary ranks/ ～得很深的反革命分子 a counterrevolutionary who has long succeeded in staying hidden
【隐恶扬善】 yǐn'è yáng shàn cover up sb.'s faults and publicize his merits; hide sb.'s wrongdoing and praise his good deeds
【隐伏】 yǐnfú lie concealed (或 hidden); lie low
【隐睾症】 yǐngāozhèng <医> cryptorchidism
【隐函数】 yǐnhánshù <数> implicit function
【隐花植物】 yǐnhuā zhíwù <植> cryptogam
【隐患】 yǐnhuàn hidden trouble; hidden danger; snake in the grass: 消除～ remove a hidden peril
【隐讳】 yǐnhuì avoid mentioning; cover up: 不要～自己的缺点。One should not gloss over one's shortcomings.
【隐晦】 yǐnhuì obscure; veiled: 文字写得很～ be couched in ambiguous terms
【隐疾】 yǐnjí unmentionable disease (e.g. V.D.)
【隐居】 yǐnjū live in seclusion; withdraw from society and live in solitude; be a hermit
【隐瞒】 yǐnmán conceal; hide; hold back: ～错误 conceal one's mistakes/ ～事实 withhold the truth; hide (或 hold back) the facts
【隐秘】 yǐnmì ① conceal; hide: ～不说 not disclose a secret/ 地道的出口开在～的地方。The exit of the tunnel is concealed. ② secret: 刺探～ pry into sb.'s secrets
【隐匿】 yǐnnì <书> hide; go into hiding; lie low
【隐情】 yǐnqíng facts one wishes to hide
【隐忍】 yǐnrěn bear patiently; forbear: ～不言 forbear from speaking
【隐射】 yǐnshè insinuate; hint; throw out innuendoes
【隐士】 yǐnshì recluse; hermit
【隐私】 yǐnsī one's secrets; private matters one wants to hide
【隐痛】 yǐntòng secret anguish
【隐头花序】 yǐntóu huāxù <植> hypanthodium
【隐退】 yǐntuì go and live in seclusion; retire from political life
【隐显墨水】 yǐnxiǎn mòshuǐ invisible ink
【隐性】 yǐnxìng <生> recessiveness ◇ ～性状 recessive character
【隐姓埋名】 yǐnxìng-máimíng conceal one's identity; keep one's identity hidden; live incognito
【隐隐】 yǐnyǐn indistinct; faint: ～的雷声 a distant roll of thunder/ ～可见 faintly visible/ 感到～作痛 feel a dull pain
【隐忧】 yǐnyōu secret worry
【隐语】 yǐnyǔ enigmatic language; insinuating language
【隐喻】 yǐnyù <语> metaphor
【隐约】 yǐnyuē indistinct; faint: ～可以听到远处传来的歌声。We could faintly hear singing in the distance./ 晨雾中一座座井架～可见。Derricks could be seen dimly in the morning mist./ ～其词 use ambiguous language; speak in equivocal terms
【隐衷】 yǐnzhōng feelings or troubles one wishes to keep to oneself

**瘾** yǐn ① addiction; habitual craving: 吸毒上～ be addicted to drugs; be a drug addict/ 发烟～ have an urge to smoke; crave a cigarette/ 过～ satisfy a craving ② strong interest (in a sport or pastime): 有球～ have a passion for ball games/ 他看小说看上～了。He's crazy about novels.
【瘾头】 yǐntóu addiction; strong interest: 你们游泳的～儿可真不小。You people are certainly keen on swimming.

## yìn

**印** yìn ① seal; stamp; chop: 盖～ affix one's seal; stamp a seal ② print; mark: 脚～ footprint/ 手～ fingerprint ③ print; engrave: ～书 print books/ 这照片～得不清楚。This photo is not well printed./ 深深～在脑子里 be engraved on one's mind ④ tally; conform: ～证 verify ⑤ (Yìn) a surname
【印把子】 yìnbàzi seal of authority; official seal: 在新中国, ～掌握在劳动人民手里。In New China, the labouring people hold the seal of authority (或 wield political power).
【印版】 yìnbǎn <印> (printing) plate
【印次】 yìncì <印> impression
【印地语】 Yìndìyǔ Hindi
【印第安人】 Yìndì'ānrén American Indian; Red Indian; Indian
【印度】 Yìndù India ◇ ～教 <宗> Hinduism/ ～人 Indian
【印度尼西亚】 Yìndùníxīyà Indonesia ◇ ～人 Indonesian/ ～语 Indonesian (language)
【印度洋】 Yìndùyáng the Indian Ocean
【印度支那】 Yìndù-Zhīnà Indo-China

【印发】 yìnfā print and distribute
【印盒】 yìnhé seal box
【印花】 yìnhuā ①〈纺〉printing：～丝绸 printed silk ② revenue stamp; stamp
◇ ～布 prints; printed calico/ ～厂 printworks/ ～机〈纺〉printing machine/ ～棉布 cotton print/ ～税 stamp duty; stamp tax
【印加人】 Yìnjiārén Inca
【印鉴】 yìnjiàn a specimen seal impression for checking when making payments
【印泥】 yìnní red ink paste used for seals
【印谱】 yìnpǔ a collection of impressions of seals by famous seal-engravers; a book of ancient seals
【印染】 yìnrǎn printing and dyeing (of textiles) ◇ ～厂 printing and dyeing mill
【印数】 yìnshù 〈印〉printing; impression：～八万册 an impression of 80,000 copies
【印刷】 yìnshuā printing：这本书正在～中。The book is in the press./ 第一次～ first impression (或 printing)/ 立体～ stereoscopic printing; three-dimensional printing/ 三色版～ three-colour halftone
◇ ～厂 printing house; press/ ～错误 misprint; typographic error/ ～电路 printed circuit/ ～工人 printing worker; printer/ ～合金 type metal/ ～品 printed matter/ ～术 art of printing; printing/ ～体 block letter; print hand/ ～纸 printing paper
【印刷机】 yìnshuājī 〈印〉printing machine; press：滚筒～ cylinder press/ 轮转～ rotary press/ 双面～ perfecting press; perfector
【印台】 yìntái ink pad; stamp pad
【印纹陶文化】 yìnwéntáo wénhuà 〈考古〉Stamped Pottery Culture
【印相纸】 yìnxiàngzhǐ 〈摄〉photographic paper
【印象】 yìnxiàng impression：我对他～很好。I have a good impression of him./ 这个城市给外宾们留下了深刻的～。The city left a deep impression on foreign visitors.
◇ ～派 impressionist school; impressionist/ ～主义 impressionism
【印信】 yìnxìn official seal
【印行】 yìnxíng print and distribute; publish
【印油】 yìnyóu stamp-pad ink
【印章】 yìnzhāng seal; signet; stamp ◇ ～学 sigillography
【印证】 yìnzhèng confirm; corroborate; verify：有待～ yet to be confirmed
【印子】 yìnzi ① mark; trace; print：脚～ footprint ② 见"印子钱"
【印子钱】 yìnziqián 〈旧〉usury：放～ practise usury/ 借～ borrow from a usurer

**饮** yìn give (animals) water to drink; water：～马 water a horse
另见 yǐn

**茚** yìn 〈化〉indene

**荫** yìn ① shady; damp and chilly ② (of a feudal ruler) confer privileges on sb.'s descendants in consideration of his distinguished service ③ 见"荫庇"
另见 yīn
【荫庇】 yìnbì 〈旧〉protection by one's elders or ancestors
【荫凉】 yìnliáng shady and cool

**胤** yìn 〈书〉offspring; posterity

**鮣** yìn remora; shark sucker

**窨** yìn basement
【窨井】 yìnjǐng 〈建〉inspection shaft; inspection well

## yīng

**应** yīng ① answer; respond：喊他他不～。I called him, but he didn't answer. ② agree (to do sth.); promise; accept：这事是我～下来的，由我负责吧。I'm the one who took on the job, so let me take care of it. ③ should; ought to：～享受的权利 a right to which one is entitled/ ～尽的义务 one's bounden duty/ ～予考虑 merit consideration/ 发现错误～立即纠正。When a mistake is discovered, it should be corrected at once. ④ (Yīng) a surname
另见 yìng
【应当】 yīngdāng should; ought to：咱们是同志，～互相帮助。As comrades we ought to help each other.
【应得】 yīngdé (well) deserved; due：罪有～。One deserves one's punishment. 或 The punishment fits the crime./ ～的一份 a due share
【应分】 yīngfèn part of one's job：帮助顾客选购商品是我们售货员～的事。It's part of our job as shop assistants to help customers choose what they want to buy.
【应该】 yīnggāi should; ought to; must：干部～参加集体生产劳动。Cadres must take part in collective productive labour./ 甭谢，这是我们～做的事。Don't mention it. We've only done our duty.
【应届毕业生】 yīngjiè bìyèshēng graduating students or pupils; this year's graduates
【应名儿】 yīngmíngr only in name; nominally：他们～是近亲，实际上不大来往。Nominally they're close relatives, but they don't see much of each other.
【应有】 yīngyǒu due; proper; deserved：发挥它～的作用 play its proper role/ 做出～的贡献 make a due contribution/ 遭到～的回击 receive a deserved rebuff
【应有尽有】 yīngyǒu-jìnyǒu have everything that one expects to find：这家商店日用品～。This general store has just about everything you'd expect to find.
【应允】 yīngyǔn assent; consent：点头～ nod assent (或 approval)

**英** yīng ①〈书〉flower：落～缤纷 petals falling in riotous profusion ② hero; outstanding person：群～会 a gathering of heroes; a conference of outstanding workers ③ (Yīng) a surname
【英镑】 yīngbàng pound sterling：～结存 sterling balance ◇ ～区 the sterling area
【英才】 yīngcái person of outstanding ability
【英尺】 yīngchǐ foot
【英寸】 yīngcùn inch
【英吨】 yīngdūn long ton; gross ton
【英国】 Yīngguó Britain; England：～护照 British passport/ ～文学 English literature ◇ ～管〈乐〉English horn/ ～人 the British; Englishman or Englishwoman
【英豪】 yīngháo heroes; outstanding figures 又作"英杰"
【英吉利海峡】 Yīngjílì Hǎixiá the English Channel
【英俊】 yīngjùn ① eminently talented; brilliant ② handsome and spirited; smart：一个～的小伙子 a handsome young chap
【英里】 yīnglǐ mile
【英联邦】 Yīngliánbāng the British Commonwealth (of Nations)
【英两】 yīngliǎng ounce
【英灵】 yīnglíng spirit of the brave departed; spirit of a

martyr 又作"英魂"
【英名】 yīngmíng illustrious name
【英明】 yīngmíng wise; brilliant: ～领袖 wise leader/ ～的论断 brilliant thesis/ ～远见 wisdom and foresight; sagacity (或 acumen) and farsightedness
【英亩】 yīngmǔ acre
【英气】 yīngqì heroic spirit
【英文】 Yīngwén English (language)
【英武】 yīngwǔ of soldierly (或 martial) bearing
【英仙座】 yīngxiānzuò 〈天〉 Perseus
【英雄】 yīngxióng hero: 女～ heroine/ ～本色 the true quality of a hero/ ～气概 heroic spirit; mettle/ 革命～主义 revolutionary heroism/ ～所见略同。Great minds think alike.
【英雄无用武之地】 yīngxióng wú yòngwǔ zhī dì a hero with no place to display his prowess — no scope to exercise one's abilities
【英勇】 yīngyǒng heroic; valiant; brave; gallant: ～奋斗 fight heroically/ ～善战 brave and skilful in battle/ ～就义 die a heroic death (on the enemy's execution ground)/ ～不屈 show unyielding heroism
【英语】 Yīngyǔ English (language)
【英姿】 yīngzī heroic bearing: 飒爽～ valiant and heroic in bearing; bright and brave

**莺** yīng warbler; oriole
【莺歌燕舞】 yīnggē-yànwǔ orioles sing and swallows dart — the joy of spring; a scene of prosperity

**婴** yīng baby; infant
【婴儿】 yīng'ér baby; infant ◇ ～车 perambulator; baby carriage 又作"婴孩"

**罂** yīng 〈书〉 small-mouthed jar
【罂粟】 yīngsù 〈植〉 opium poppy ◇ ～花 poppy flower

**嘤** yīng 〈象〉 chirp: ～其鸣矣,求其友声。A bird sings to call forth a friend's response.

**缨** yīng ① tassel: 红～枪 red-tasselled spear ② sth. shaped like a tassel: 萝卜～子 radish leaves ③ ribbon

**樱** yīng ① cherry ② oriental cherry
【樱花】 yīnghuā oriental cherry: 日本～ Japanese flowering cherry
【樱桃】 yīngtáo cherry

**鹦** yīng
【鹦哥】 yīnggē parrot
【鹦哥绿】 yīnggēlǜ parrot green
【鹦鹉】 yīngwǔ parrot: 长尾～ parakeet/ 虎皮～ budgerigar
【鹦鹉螺】 yīngwǔluó nautilus
【鹦鹉热】 yīngwǔrè 〈医〉 psittacosis; parrot fever
【鹦鹉学舌】 yīngwǔ xuéshé repeat the words of others like a parrot; parrot
【鹦嘴鱼】 yīngzuǐyú parrot fish

**膺** yīng 〈书〉 ① breast: 义愤填～ be filled with righteous indignation ② bear; receive: 荣～勋章 receive a decoration/ ～此重任 hold a post of great responsibility
【膺选】 yīngxuǎn 〈书〉 be elected

**鹰** yīng hawk; eagle
【鹰鼻鹞眼】 yīngbí-yàoyǎn hawk-nosed and vulture-eyed — sinister and fierce-looking
【鹰钩鼻子】 yīnggōubízi aquiline nose
【鹰犬】 yīngquǎn falcons and hounds — lackeys; hired thugs
【鹰隼】 yīngsǔn 〈书〉 hawks and falcons — brutal or fierce people

## yíng

**迎** yíng ① go to meet; greet; welcome; receive: ～上前去同客人握手 step forward to greet the guest and shake hands with him/ 喜～新春 joyously see in the lunar New Year ② move towards; meet face to face: ～着困难上 meet difficulties head-on
【迎春】 yíngchūn 〈植〉 winter jasmine
【迎风】 yíngfēng ① facing (或 against) the wind: ～飞翔 fly against the wind ② down the wind; with the wind: 彩旗～招展。Coloured flags fluttered in the breeze. ◇ ～面 windward side
【迎合】 yínghé cater to; pander to: ～对方心理 go along with the other side/ ～低级趣味 pander to low tastes
【迎候】 yínghòu await the arrival of: 在宾馆门口～贵宾 await the arrival of the distinguished guest at the entrance of the guest house
【迎击】 yíngjī meet (an approaching enemy) head-on
【迎接】 yíngjiē meet; welcome; greet: 到火车站～贵宾 meet a distinguished guest at the railway station/ 工人们决心以新的成绩来～五一节。The workers are determined to greet May Day with new achievements.
【迎面】 yíngmiàn head-on; in one's face: ～走上去同他们打招呼 step forward to greet them/ 微风～吹来 a breeze blowing in one's face
【迎刃而解】 yíng rèn ér jiě (of a bamboo) split all the way down once it's been chopped open — (of a problem) be readily solved: 捉住了主要矛盾,一切问题就～了。Once the principal contradiction is grasped, all problems can be readily solved.
【迎头】 yíngtóu head-on; directly: 给侵略者以～痛击 deal head-on blows to the invaders
【迎头赶上】 yíngtóu gǎnshàng try hard to catch up
【迎新】 yíngxīn ① see the New Year in: 送旧～ ring out the Old Year and ring in the New ② welcome new arrivals: ～晚会 an evening party to welcome newcomers
【迎迓】 yíngyà 〈书〉 meet; welcome
【迎战】 yíngzhàn meet (an approaching enemy) head-on

**茔** yíng 〈书〉 grave: 祖～ ancestral graves

**盈** yíng ① be full of; be filled with: 热泪～眶 one's eyes brimming with tears ② have a surplus of
【盈亏】 yíng-kuī ① profit and loss: 自负～ (of an enterprise) assume sole responsibility for its own profits or losses ② the waxing and waning of the moon
【盈利】 yínglì profit; gain: ～五百万元 net a profit of five million *yuan*
【盈余】 yíngyú surplus; profit: ～两千元 have a surplus of 2,000 *yuan*

**荧** yíng 〈书〉 ① glimmering: 一灯～然。A light is glimmering. ② dazzled; perplexed: ～惑 bewilder
【荧光】 yíngguāng 〈物〉 fluorescence; fluorescent light ◇～灯 fluorescent lamp/ ～屏 fluorescent screen

**莹** yíng 〈书〉 ① jade-like stone ② lustrous and transparent

**营** yíng ① seek: ～利 seek profits ② operate; run: 国～ state-operated; state-run ③ camp; barracks: 安～ pitch a camp ④ battalion: ～部 battalion headquarters/ ～教导员 battalion political instructor

【营地】 yíngdì campsite; camping ground

【营房】 yíngfáng barracks

【营火】 yínghuǒ campfire ◇ ～会 campfire party

【营建】 yíngjiàn construct; build

【营救】 yíngjiù succour; rescue: 设法～被捕的同志 try to rescue the arrested comrades

【营垒】 yínglěi ① barracks and the enclosing walls ② camp: 革命～ revolutionary camp

【营生】 yíngshēng earn (或 make) a living: 靠打铁～ earn a living as a blacksmith

【营生】 yíngsheng 〈方〉 job: 找个～ look for a job

【营私】 yíngsī seek private gain; feather one's nest: ～舞弊 engage in malpractices for selfish ends; practise graft/ 结党～ form a clique (或 band together) for selfish purposes

【营养】 yíngyǎng nutrition; nourishment: 富于～ nourishing; nutritious ◇ ～不良 malnutrition; undernourishment/ ～价值 nutritive value/ ～品 nutriment/ ～素 nutrient/ ～学 nutriology

【营业】 yíngyè do business: 暂停～ business temporarily suspended/ 照常～ business as usual/ 商店上午九时开始～。The shops open at nine in the morning. ◇ ～报告 business report/ ～额 turnover; volume of business/ ～时间 business hours; (银行) banking hours/ ～收入 business income (或 earnings, receipts)/ ～税 business tax; transactions tax; turnover tax/ ～员 shop employees (including buyers, travelling salespersons and shop assistants)

【营造】 yíngzào construct; build: ～防风林 plant windbreak forests

【营长】 yíngzhǎng battalion commander

【营帐】 yíngzhàng tent

**萤** yíng firefly; glowworm

【萤火虫】 yínghuǒchóng firefly; glowworm

【萤石】 yíngshí 〈矿〉 fluorite; fluorspar

**萦** yíng 〈书〉 entangle; encompass: 琐事～身 be preoccupied with trivialities; get bogged down in petty matters

【萦怀】 yínghuái occupy one's mind

【萦回】 yínghuí hover; linger: ～脑际 linger in one's mind

【萦绕】 yíngrǎo hover; linger

**滢** yíng 〈书〉 crystal clear

**楹** yíng principal columns of a hall

【楹联】 yínglián couplet written on scrolls and hung on the pillars of a hall

**潆** yíng

【潆洄】 yínghuí swirl

**蝇** yíng fly

【蝇拍】 yíngpāi flyswatter; flyflap

【蝇头】 yíngtóu small as the head of a fly; tiny: ～小楷 very small (hand-written) characters/ ～小利 petty profits

【蝇营狗苟】 yíngyíng-gǒugǒu shamelessly seek personal gain

**嬴** Yíng a surname

**赢** yíng ① win; beat: 这场比赛谁～了? Who won the game?/ 我象棋下不～他。I can't beat him at Chinese chess. ② gain (profit)

【赢得】 yíngdé win; gain: ～独立 win (或 attain) independence/ ～长时间的掌声 draw prolonged applause/ ～群众的赞扬 win praise from the masses

【赢利】 yínglì profit; gain

【赢余】 yíngyú surplus; profit: 略有～ with a small favourable balance

**瀛** yíng 〈书〉 sea; ocean

## yǐng

**郢** Yǐng capital of the State of Chu (楚): ～爰 gold coin of Chu

**颖** yǐng 〈书〉 ① glume; grain husk ② tip (as of a writing brush); point ③ clever

【颖果】 yǐngguǒ 〈植〉 caryopsis

【颖慧】 yǐnghuì 〈书〉 (of a teen-ager) clever; bright; intelligent

【颖悟】 yǐngwù 〈书〉 (of a teen-ager) clever; bright

**影** yǐng ① shadow; reflection; image: 树～ shadow of a tree/ 湖光塔～ a lake with the reflection of a pagoda in it/ 倒～ inverted image ② trace; vague impression: 他早就忘得没～儿了。He's clean forgotten it. ③ photograph; picture: 合～ group photo (或 picture) ④ motion picture; film; movie: ～迷 film (或 movie) fan

【影壁】 yǐngbì ① screen wall (facing the gate inside or outside a traditional Chinese courtyard) ② wall with carved murals

【影集】 yǐngjí photograph (或 picture, photo) album

【影片】 yǐngpiàn film; movie

【影评】 yǐngpíng film review

【影射】 yǐngshè allude to; hint obliquely at; insinuate: ～攻击 attack by innuendo

【影条】 yǐngtiáo 〈纺〉 shadow stripes: ～巴里纱 shadow-stripe voile

【影响】 yǐngxiǎng ① influence; effect: 产生巨大～ exert a tremendous influence; produce a great impact/ 消除天灾的～ fight off the effects of natural calamities/ 这样做～不好。This would create a bad impression. ② affect; influence: 不受气候或温度～ not affected by weather or temperature changes/ ～质量 impair the quality/ ～威信 lower one's prestige/ ～工程进度 hold up the project/ ～群众的积极性 chill (或 dampen) the enthusiasm of the masses/ ～工作 interfere with one's work

【影印】 yǐngyìn 〈印〉 photomechanical printing; photo-offset process: ～珍本书籍 photolithograph rare books ◇ ～版 process plate/ ～本 photo-offset copy; facsimile/ ～照相机 process camera/ ～制版 photomechanical process

【影影绰绰】 yǐngyǐngchuòchuò vaguely; dimly; indistinctly: 远处～地有一些小山。A few hills loomed in the distance.

【影院】 yǐngyuàn cinema; movie theatre

【影子】 yǐngzi ① shadow; reflection ② trace; sign; vague impression: 找了他半天,连个～也没见。I looked for him a long time but never even caught a glimpse of him./ 事情已经过了好多年,我脑子里连点～都没有了。It happened so long ago that I haven't the vaguest recollection of it. ◇ ～内阁 shadow cabinet

**瘿** yǐng ①〈中医〉 goitre ② gall

【瘿虫】 yǐngchóng 〈动〉 gall insect

## yìng

**应** yìng ① answer; respond; echo: 山鸣谷～。The valleys echo the sounds of the mountains. ② comply with; grant: 有求必～ grant whatever is requested/ 以～急需 in order to fill an urgent need/ 为～广大读者需要 to meet the needs of the broad reading public/ ～中国政府的邀请 at the invitation of the Chinese government ③ suit; respond to: ～景 do sth. for the occasion ④ deal with; cope with: 从容～敌 meet the enemy calmly

另见 yīng

【应变】 yìngbiàn ① meet an emergency (或 contingency) ② 〈物〉 strain: ～硬化 strain hardening ◇ ～措施 emergency measure/ ～计 strainometer

【应承】 yìngchéng agree (to do sth.); promise; consent: 这件事他一口～下来了。He agreed to do it without hesitation.

【应酬】 yìngchou ① have social intercourse with; treat with courtesy: 不善～ socially inept/ ～几句 exchange a few polite words ② 〈旧〉 dinner party: 今天晚上有个～。I've been invited to dinner this evening. ◇ ～信件 courtesy letter

【应答】 yìngdá reply; answer: ～如流 reply readily and fluently

【应对】 yìngduì reply; answer: 善于～ good at repartee

【应付】 yìngfu ① deal with; cope with; handle: ～复杂局面 deal with complicated situations/ 准备～可能的突然事变 be prepared against possible emergencies/ ～自如 handle a situation with ease; be equal to the occasion ② do sth. perfunctorily; do sth. after a fashion: ～事儿 go through the motions/ 采取～的态度 take a perfunctory attitude ③ make do: 我这双凉鞋今年夏天还可以～过去。I'll make do with these sandals for this summer.

【应急】 yìngjí meet an urgent need; meet an emergency (或 contingency) ◇ ～措施 emergency measure/ ～计划 contingency plan; crash programme

【应接不暇】 yìngjiē bù xiá have more visitors or business than one can attend to: 顾客很多,售货员～。There were so many customers that the shop assistants couldn't attend to them all.

【应景】 yìngjǐng do sth. for the occasion ◇ ～诗 occasional verses

【应考】 yìngkǎo take (或 sit for) an examination: ～的人很多。Many sat for the examination.

【应力】 yìnglì 〈物〉 stress: 正～ direct stress/ 内～ internal stress/ 预～ prestress

【应募】 yìngmù respond to a call for recruits; enlist; join up

【应诺】 yìngnuò agree (to do sth.); promise; undertake

【应声】 yìngshēng happen right at the sound of sth.: 鸟枪一响,野鸭～而落。The wild duck fell at the report of the shotgun.

【应声虫】 yìngshēngchóng yesman; echo

【应时】 yìngshí ① seasonable; in season: ～货品 seasonable goods/ ～瓜果 fruits of the season/ 西红柿正～。Tomatoes are in season. ② at once; immediately: 敌人一推门,地雷～就炸了。No sooner had the enemy soldier pushed the door open than the mine exploded.

【应验】 yìngyàn come true; be confirmed; be fulfilled: 他的话～了。What he said has come true.

【应邀】 yìngyāo at sb.'s invitation; on invitation: ～出席大会的有在京的外国友人。Among those invited to attend the meeting were some of the foreign friends in Beijing./ ～派代表团参加庆祝活动 send a delegation to attend the celebrations at sb.'s invitation

【应用】 yìngyòng apply; use: 把理论～于实践 apply theory to practice/ 防御和进攻的交替～ the alternate use of defence and attack ◇ ～化学 applied chemistry/ ～科学 applied science

【应用文】 yìngyòngwén practical writing (as in official documents, notices, receipts, etc.)

【应运而生】 yìngyùn ér shēng arise at the historic moment; emerge as the times require

【应战】 yìngzhàn ① meet an enemy attack: 沉着～ meet the attack calmly ② accept (或 take up) a challenge ◇ ～书 letter accepting a challenge

【应诊】 yìngzhěn (of a doctor) see patients

【应征】 yìngzhēng ① be recruited: ～入伍 be recruited into the army ② respond to a call for contributions (to a publication): ～的稿件 contributions to a periodical, etc. at the editor's public invitation

**映** yìng reflect; mirror; shine: 朝霞～在湖面上。The glory of the dawn is mirrored on the lake./ 他的脸被炉火～得通红。His cheeks shone red before the glowing oven.

【映衬】 yìngchèn set off: 红墙碧瓦,互相～。The red walls and green tiles set each other off beautifully.

【映山红】 yìngshānhóng 〈植〉 azalea

【映射】 yìngshè shine upon; cast light upon: 阳光～在江面上。The sun shines upon the river.

【映象】 yìngxiàng image

【映照】 yìngzhào shine upon; cast light upon

**硬** yìng ① hard; stiff; tough: ～铅笔 hard pencil/ ～领 stiff collar/ ～刷子 stiff brush ② strong; firm; tough; obstinate: 心肠～ hardhearted/ 话说得很～ express oneself in strong terms/ ～不承认错误 obstinately refuse to admit one's error/ ～的不行来软的。When hard tactics failed, soft methods were used. ③ manage to do sth. with difficulty: ～充好汉 act the hero/ ～撑着干 force oneself to work hard/ ～压住心头怒火 choke down one's anger/ ～搬别人的经验 copy other people's experience mechanically ④ good (quality); able (person): 货色～ goods of high quality/ ～手 a good hand

【硬邦邦】 yìngbāngbāng very hard; very stiff

【硬棒】 yìngbang 〈方〉 strong; hale and hearty; sturdy: 老人的身体还挺～。The old man is still hale and hearty.

【硬币】 yìngbì coin; specie: 一个五分的～ a five-*fen* piece (或 coin)/ 用～支付 payment in specie

【硬度】 yìngdù 〈物〉 hardness: 维氏～ Vickers hardness ◇ ～计 sclerometer

【硬腭】 yìng'è 〈生理〉 hard palate

【硬功夫】 yìnggōngfu great proficiency; masterly skill: 练就一身～ acquire masterly skill through intensive training

【硬骨头】 yìnggǔtou hard bone — a dauntless, unyielding person: ～六连 the Hard-Boned Sixth Company/ 革命的～ revolutionary backbone

【硬骨鱼】 yìnggǔyú bony fish

【硬汉】 yìnghàn a dauntless, unyielding man; a man of iron 又作"硬汉子"

【硬化】 yìnghuà ① harden: 经久～ 〈机〉 age hardening ② 〈医〉 sclerosis: 动脉～ arteriosclerosis/ 血管～ vascular sclerosis

【硬件】 yìngjiàn 〈计算机〉 hardware

【硬结】 yìngjié ① indurate; harden ② 〈医〉 scleroma

【硬朗】 yìnglang 〈口〉 hale and hearty: 他七十多了,身骨子还挺～。He's over seventy but still going strong.

【硬煤】 yìngméi hard coal; anthracite
【硬锰矿】 yìngměngkuàng psilomelane
【硬面】 yìngmiàn 〈食品〉 stiff dough
【硬模】 yìngmú 〈机〉 die ◇ ～铸造 diecasting
【硬木】 yìngmù hardwood ◇ ～家具 hardwood furniture
【硬磐】 yìngpán 〈地〉 hardpan
【硬碰硬】 yìng pèng yìng ① confront the tough with toughness ② (of a job) demanding solid, painstaking work or real skill: 改山造田可是～的事。To transform hills into fields is an extremely tough job.
【硬拼】 yìngpīn fight recklessly
【硬砂岩】 yìngshāyán 〈地〉 greywacke
【硬石膏】 yìngshígāo anhydrite
【硬是】 yìngshì 〈方〉 ① actually (accomplish sth. extremely difficult): 民工们～打通了这座大山，修成了隧道。The peasant labourers literally (或 actually) hewed a tunnel through that rocky mountain. ② just; simply: 医生嘱咐他卧床休息，可他～不听。The doctor advised him to stay in bed, but he just wouldn't listen.
【硬水】 yìngshuǐ hard water
【硬说】 yìngshuō stubbornly insist; assert; allege: 他～他做得对。He obstinately asserted that he had done the right thing./ 她～她不累。She insisted that she wasn't tired.
【硬挺】 yìngtǐng endure with all one's will; hold out with all one's might: 你牙疼别～着，快去治治吧。Don't just try to put up with your toothache. Go and see the dentist./ 那小伙子受了伤，还～着把活干完。In spite of his injuries, the young man stuck it out.
【硬通货】 yìngtōnghuò hard currency
【硬席】 yìngxí 〈交〉 hard seats (on a train) ◇ ～卧铺 hard sleeper; sleeping carriage with hard berths
【硬橡胶】 yìngxiàngjiāo 〈化〉 hard rubber; ebonite; vulcanite
【硬性】 yìngxìng rigid; stiff; inflexible: 至于具体做法，不作～规定。As for the details of the procedure, we won't lay down any hard and fast (或 rigid) rules.
【硬玉】 yìngyù jadeite
【硬仗】 yìngzhàng tough (或 hard-fought) battle; formidable task: 一支能打～的石油钻井队 a drilling crew equal to the most formidable tasks
【硬着头皮】 yìngzhe tóupí toughen one's scalp — brace oneself; force oneself to do sth. against one's will: ～顶住 brace oneself and bear with it; hold out tenaciously/ 我～把这碗苦药喝了下去。I forced myself to gulp down the bowl of bitter medicine.
【硬脂】 yìngzhī 〈化〉 tristearin; stearin ◇ ～酸 〈化〉 stearic acid/ ～酸盐 stearate/ ～油 stearine oil
【硬纸板】 yìngzhǐbǎn hardboard; cardboard
【硬质合金】 yìngzhì héjīn 〈冶〉 hard alloy; hard metal ◇～刀具 〈机〉 hard alloy cutter; hard metal tool
【硬质塑料】 yìngzhì sùliào 〈化〉 rigid plastics: 半～ semi-rigid plastics

**媵** yìng 〈书〉 ① maid accompanying a bride to her new home ② concubine

## yō

**育** yō 见"杭育" hángyō
另见 yù

**哟** yō 〈叹〉〔表示轻微的惊异〕: ～，你踩我的脚了。Oh! You've stepped on my foot.
另见 yo

**唷** yō 见"喔唷" ōyō

## yo

**哟** yo 〈助〉〔用在句尾表示祈使语气〕: 用力拉～! Heave ho!
另见 yō

## yōng

**佣** yōng ① hire (a labourer) ② servant: 女～ woman servant; maid
另见 yòng
【佣工】 yōnggōng 〈旧〉 hired labourer; servant

**拥** yōng ① hold in one's arms; embrace; hug: 把孩子紧紧～在怀里 hug the child tightly ② gather around: 一群青年～着一个老教师走出来。An old teacher came out, surrounded by a group of young people./ 病人～被而坐。The patient sat wrapped in a quilt. ③ crowd; throng; swarm: 一～而入 swarm in/ 欢乐的人群～向天安门。Jubilant crowds surged towards Tian An Men. ④ support: 军爱民，民～军。The army cherishes the people and the people support the army. ⑤ have; possess: ～兵十万 have an army of 100,000
【拥抱】 yōngbào embrace; hug; hold in one's arms: 两国选手热烈～，互致问候。The players of the two countries warmly embraced and greeted each other.
【拥戴】 yōngdài support (sb. as leader): 受到全国人民的～ enjoy the support of the whole nation
【拥护】 yōnghù support; uphold; endorse: ～中国共产党的领导 support the leadership of the Chinese Communist Party/ 我们～这个决定。We endorse this decision.
【拥挤】 yōngjǐ crowd; push and squeeze: 上下班时间，公共汽车特别～。The buses are especially crowded during the rush hours./ 不要～! Don't push!
【拥军优属】 yōngjūn-yōushǔ (of civilians) support the army and give preferential treatment to families of revolutionary armymen and martyrs
【拥塞】 yōngsè jam; congest: 街道～ streets jammed with traffic
【拥有】 yōngyǒu possess; have; own: ～核武器 possess nuclear weapons/ ～丰富的矿藏 have rich mineral resources/ ～广大的人力资源 command vast reserves of manpower/ 一个～十万人口的新城市 a new town of 100,000 people
【拥政爱民】 yōngzhèng-àimín (of the army) support the government and cherish the people

**痈** yōng 〈医〉 carbuncle: 养～遗患 neglecting a carbuncle will cause trouble — failure to deal sternly with evil-doers will lead to serious trouble
【痈疽】 yōngjū ulcer

**邕** Yōng another name for Nanning

**庸** yōng ① commonplace; mediocre: ～言～行 commonplace words and deeds ② inferior; second-rate ③〈书〉〔用于否定式〕 need: 无～细述，This needn't be related in detail. 或 There is no need to go into details. ④〈书〉〔表示反问〕: ～可弃乎? How could this possibly be relinquished?
【庸才】 yōngcái 〈书〉 mediocre person; mediocrity
【庸碌】 yōnglù mediocre and unambitious: ～无能 mediocre and incompetent

【庸人】 yōngrén mediocre person
【庸人自扰】 yōngrén zì rǎo worry about troubles of one's own imagining
【庸俗】 yōngsú vulgar; philistine; low: 相互吹捧的～作风 the vulgar ways of logrolling
◇ ～化 vulgarize; debase/ ～进化论 〈哲〉 vulgar evolutionism/ ～唯物主义 〈哲〉 vulgar materialism
【庸医】 yōngyī quack; charlatan
【庸中佼佼】 yōng zhōng jiǎojiǎo a giant among dwarfs

**雍** yōng ①〈书〉harmony ②(Yōng) a surname
【雍容】 yōngróng natural, graceful and poised: ～华贵 elegant and poised; *distingué*/ 态度～ have a dignified bearing

**慵** yōng 〈书〉 weary; lethargic; languid: ～困 tired and sleepy

**墉** yōng 〈书〉 city wall; high wall

**壅** yōng ①stop up; obstruct ②heap soil or fertilizer over and around the roots (of plants and trees): ～土 hilling/ ～肥 heap fertilizer around the roots
【壅塞】 yōngsè clogged up; jammed; congested: 水道～。The waterway is blocked up.

**臃** yōng
【臃肿】 yōngzhǒng ① too fat to move: 穿得太～ be cumbersomely dressed; be encumbered by too much clothing ② overstaffed: ～的机构 overstaffed organizations

**鳙** yōng
【鳙鱼】 yōngyú variegated carp; bighead

## yóng

**喁** yóng 〈书〉a fish sticking its mouth out of the water 另见 yú
【喁喁】 yóngyóng 〈书〉〈喻〉 everyone looking up to sb.

## yǒng

**永** yǒng perpetually; forever; always: 毛泽东思想～放光芒。Mao Zedong Thought will shine forever./ ～葆革命青春 always keep one's revolutionary spirit young/ ～不变心 remain loyal till one's dying day
【永别】 yǒngbié part never to meet again; part forever; be parted by death
【永垂不朽】 yǒng chuí bù xiǔ be immortal: 革命烈士～! Eternal glory to the revolutionary martyrs!
【永磁】 yǒngcí 〈物〉 permanent magnetism ◇ ～发电机 permanent-magnet generator/ ～体 permanent magnet
【永冻层】 yǒngdòngcéng 〈地〉 permafrost horizon
【永恒】 yǒnghéng eternal; perpetual: ～的友谊 eternal friendship/ ～的真理 eternal truth ◇ ～运动〈物〉perpetual motion
【永久】 yǒngjiǔ permanent; perpetual; everlasting; forever; for good (and all)
◇ ～冻土 permafrost/ ～积雪 firn (snow)/ ～雪线 firn line/ ～主权 permanent sovereignty/ ～中立 permanent neutrality
【永诀】 yǒngjué 〈书〉 part forever; be separated by death
【永生】 yǒngshēng ①〈宗〉 eternal life ② immortal: ～的战士 immortal fighter/ ～永世 for ever and ever
【永世】 yǒngshì forever: ～难忘 will never forget it for the rest of one's life/ ～长存 live for ever and ever
【永远】 yǒngyuǎn 〈副〉always; forever; ever: ～高举和坚决捍卫毛主席的伟大旗帜 always hold high and staunchly defend the great banner of Chairman Mao/ 中国现在不做超级大国，将来也～不做超级大国。China is not a superpower, nor will she ever become one.
【永志不忘】 yǒng zhì bù wàng will always bear in mind; will always cherish the memory of sb. or sth.

**甬** Yǒng another name for Ningbo
【甬道】 yǒngdào ① paved path leading to a main hall or a tomb ② corridor

**泳** yǒng swim: 仰～ backstroke/ 蛙～ breaststroke

**咏** yǒng ①chant; intone: 吟～ recite (a poem) ② express or narrate in poetic form: «～梅» *Ode to the Plum Blossom*
【咏叹】 yǒngtàn intone; chant; sing
【咏叹调】 yǒngtàndiào 〈乐〉 aria
【咏赞】 yǒngzàn sing the praises of; praise

**俑** yǒng wooden or earthen human figure buried with the dead in ancient times; tomb figure; figurine: 陶～ pottery figurine/ 武士～ warrior figure

**勇** yǒng brave; valiant; courageous: ～冠三军 distinguish oneself by peerless valour in battle/ 越战越～ one's courage mounts as the battle progresses/ 智～双全 have both wisdom and courage
【勇敢】 yǒnggǎn brave; courageous: 勤劳～的人民 a brave and industrious people/ ～善战 courageous and skilful in battle
【勇猛】 yǒngměng bold and powerful; full of valour and vigour: ～前进 march boldly forward
【勇气】 yǒngqì courage; nerve: 鼓起～ pluck up (或 muster up) one's courage
【勇士】 yǒngshì a brave and strong man; warrior
【勇往直前】 yǒng wǎng zhí qián march forward courageously; advance bravely
【勇武】 yǒngwǔ valiant: ～过人 surpass others in valour; be surpassingly valorous
【勇于】 yǒngyú be brave in; be bold in; have the courage to: ～负责 be brave in shouldering responsibilities/ ～承认错误 have the courage to admit one's mistakes/ ～创新 be bold in making innovations

**涌** yǒng ① gush; well; pour; surge: 泪如泉～ tears well up in one's eyes/ 石油喷～而出。Oil gushed out./ 大家都向外～。The crowd was pouring out. ② rise; surge; emerge: 风啸浪～。The wind howls; the waves rise./ 一排排巨浪向石滩～来。Huge waves surged over the rocks./ 多少往事～上心头。Memories of the past welled up in my mind./ 东方～出一轮红日。A red sun rose in the east.
【涌现】 yǒngxiàn emerge in large numbers; spring up; come to the fore: 新人新事不断～。New people and new things are constantly emerging.

**恿** yǒng 见"怂恿" sǒngyǒng

**蛹** yǒng pupa: 蝶～ chrysalis/ 蚕～ silkworm chrysalis

**踊** yǒng leap up; jump up
【踊跃】 yǒngyuè ① leap; jump: ～欢呼 leap and cheer ② vying with one another; eagerly; enthusiastically: ～响应号

召 respond to a call enthusiastically/ ～参军 vie with one another to join the army/ 会上发言～。People took the floor one after another./ 今晚的晚会大家肯定会～参加的。I'm sure everybody will be eager to come to this evening's party.

**鲬** yǒng flathead; sand gurnard

## yòng

**用** yòng ① use; employ; apply: ～手掰 break with one's hands/ ～火烤 bake over the fire/ ～水煮 boil in water/ ～针刺麻醉做外科手术 employ acupuncture anaesthesia in surgery/ ～马克思主义观点研究历史 study history from a Marxist viewpoint/ ～严格的科学态度从事研究工作 do research with a strictly scientific attitude/ ～共产党员的标准来衡量自己 measure oneself by the standards of a Communist/ ～我们自己的双手来建设社会主义 build socialism with our own hands/ ～五十八秒钟跑完全程 run the course in 58 seconds ② expenses; outlay: 家～ family expenses/ 零～钱 pocket money; spending money ③ usefulness; use: 有～ useful/ 没～ useless; worthless/ 有点～ be of some use ④〔多用于否定〕need: 不～开灯。There's no need to turn on the light./ 不～担心。Don't worry. ⑤〈敬〉eat; drink: 请～茶。Won't you have some tea, please. ⑥〈书〉hence; therefore: ～特函达。Hence this letter.

【用兵】 yòngbīng use military forces; resort to arms: 不得已而～ have no alternative but to resort to arms/ 善于～ well versed in the art of war/ ～如神 direct military operations with miraculous skill; work miracles in manoeuvring troops; be a superb military commander

【用不了】 yòngbuliǎo ① have more than is needed: 把～的钱存在银行里 put the spare money in the bank ② less than: ～三天，他们就可以把地全部耕完。They will finish ploughing the fields in less than three days.

【用不着】 yòngbuzháo ① not need; have no use for: 把～的书放回书架。Put back the books you are not using on the shelves. ② there is no need to; it is not worth while to: ～为这些小事争论不休。There's no need to keep arguing about such triflings.

【用材林】 yòngcáilín commercial forest; timber forest

【用场】 yòngchǎng use: 有～ be useful/ 派大～ be turned to good account/ 派新～ be put to new uses

【用处】 yòngchu use; good: 这两件东西，各有各的～。Each of the two things has its own use./ 抱怨有什么～？What's the use (或 good) of complaining?/ 不要扔掉，将来会有～。Don't throw it away; it may come in handy.

【用得着】 yòngdezháo ① find sth. useful; need: 别看这台机器旧，我们目前正～。Although the machine is old, it serves our purpose at present./ 这里可能～古代希腊的一段寓言。Here it might be useful to quote an ancient Greek fable./ 没多少活儿了，还～那么多人吗？There isn't much work left. Do we still need so many people? ② there is need to; it is necessary to; it is worth while to: ～派车去接他们吗？Is it necessary to send a car for them?

【用度】 yòngdù expenditure; expense; outlay: 他家人口多，～大。He has a big family and many expenses.

【用法】 yòngfǎ use; usage: ～说明 directions (for use)/《英语～词典》*A Dictionary of English Usage*

【用费】 yòngfèi expense; cost

【用功】 yònggōng hardworking; diligent; studious: ～读书 be studious; study diligently; be diligent in one's studies

【用户】 yònghù consumer; user: 征求～意见 ask for consumers' opinions/ 电话～ telephone subscriber ◇ ～电报 telex

【用劲】 yòngjìn exert oneself (physically); put forth one's strength: 大家一齐～，把大石头搬开了。We all heaved together and removed the boulder.

【用具】 yòngjù utensil; apparatus; appliance: 炊事～ kitchen (或 cooking) utensils/ 消防～ fire-fighting apparatus/ 救生～ lifesaving equipment/ 打猎～ hunting gear

【用力】 yònglì exert oneself (physically); put forth one's strength: ～把门推了一下 give the door a hard push

【用品】 yòngpǐn articles for use: 生活～ articles for daily use; daily necessities/ 办公～ things for office use; stationery

【用人】 yòngrén ① choose a person for a job; make use of personnel: 善于～ know how to choose the right person for the right job; know how to make proper use of personnel/ ～不当 not choose the right person for the job ② need hands: 现在正是～的时候。Now's the time when we are in need of personnel.

【用人】 yòngren 〈旧〉servant: 女～ maidservant

【用事】 yòngshì ① act: 意气～ be swayed by one's feelings and act rashly/ 感情～ act impetuously ②〈书〉be in power

【用途】 yòngtú use: 橡胶的～很广。Rubber has many uses.

【用武】 yòngwǔ use force; display one's abilities or talents: 大有～之地。There's ample scope for one's abilities.

【用项】 yòngxiàng items of expenditure; expenditures

【用心】 yòngxīn ① diligently; attentively; with concentrated attention: ～学习 concentrate on one's studies; study diligently/ ～听讲 listen attentively to a lecture/ ～思索 think hard ② motive; intention: 别有～ have ulterior motives/ ～何其毒也！How vicious his intentions are!/ ～良苦 have really given much thought to the matter

【用以】 yòng yǐ in order to; so as to: 略举数例，～说明这一原理。Here are a few examples to illustrate this principle.

【用意】 yòngyì intention; purpose: ～很好 with good intentions/ 你这是什么～？Just what are you up to? 或 What's your game?

【用印】 yòngyìn affix an official seal (to a document); seal (a document)

【用语】 yòngyǔ ① choice of words; wording: ～不当 inappropriate choice of words; incorrect wording ② phraseology; term: 商业～ commercial phraseology

**佣** yòng commission
另见 yōng

【佣金】 yòngjīn commission; brokerage; middleman's fee

## yōu

**优** yōu ① excellent: 品学兼～ be a good student of good character ②〈旧〉actor or actress: 名～ a famous actor or actress

【优待】 yōudài give preferential (或 special) treatment: ～军属 give favoured treatment to servicemen's families/ ～外宾 give special consideration to foreign guests ◇ ～券 complimentary ticket

【优等】 yōuděng high-class; first-rate; excellent ◇ ～品 high-class (或 first-rate) product/ ～生 top student

【优点】 yōudiǎn merit; strong (或 good) point; advantage; virtue: ～和缺点 merits and demerits; virtues and defects; strong and weak points/ 这个办法有很多～。This method has many advantages.

【优抚】 yōufǔ give special care to disabled servicemen, and to family members of revolutionary martyrs and servicemen:

烈属～金 allowance to the family members of revolutionary martyrs
【优厚】 yōuhòu munificent; liberal; favourable: 待遇～ excellent pay and conditions; liberal wages and benefits
【优弧】 yōuhú 〈数〉 major arc
【优惠】 yōuhuì 〈经〉 preferential; favourable: 按～条件提供的经济援助 economic assistance given on liberal (或 favourable) terms
◇ ～贷款 loan on favourable terms/ ～待遇 preferential treatment/ ～关税协定 preferential tariff agreements/ ～价格 preferential prices/ ～权 preferential rights
【优良】 yōuliáng fine; good: 成绩～ get good marks; make a good showing/ 艰苦朴素的～作风 fine style of hard work and plain living/ 推广水稻～品种 popularize fine (或 good) varieties of rice
【优伶】 yōulíng 〈旧〉 actor or actress
【优美】 yōuměi graceful; fine; exquisite: 风景～ fine scenery/ ～的舞蹈动作 graceful dance movements/ ～的民间艺术 exquisite folk arts
【优容】 yōuróng 〈书〉 treat with leniency
【优柔寡断】 yōuróu guǎduàn irresolute and hesitant; indecisive: 他是个～的人。He's indecisive.
【优生学】 yōushēngxué 〈生〉 eugenics
【优胜】 yōushèng winning; superior
◇ ～红旗 championship red banner/ ～奖 winning prize/ ～者 winner; champion
【优势】 yōushì superiority; preponderance; dominant position: 军事～ military superiority/ ～兵力 superior force/ 占～ occupy a dominant position; gain the upper hand
【优渥】 yōuwò 〈书〉 liberal; munificent; favourable
【优先】 yōuxiān have priority; take precedence: ～发展基础工业 give priority to the development of the basic industries/ 必须～考虑的一个问题 a question which claims precedence over all others; a first (或 top) priority ◇ ～权 priority; preference
【优秀】 yōuxiù outstanding; excellent; splendid; fine: ～作品 (literary or artistic) works of excellence/ ～电影 highly rated films/ ～的共产党员 an exemplary Communist/ 中华民族的～儿女 worthy sons and daughters of the Chinese nation/ 今天打靶，他得了个～。He got an "excellent" in today's target practice.
【优选法】 yōuxuǎnfǎ optimum seeking method; optimization
【优异】 yōuyì excellent; outstanding; exceedingly good: 考试成绩～ do exceedingly well in an examination/ 他们在修建新铁路的工作中作出了～的成绩。They have performed brilliant exploits in building the new railway.
【优游】 yōuyóu 〈书〉 leisurely and carefree: ～自在 leisurely and carefree/ ～岁月 pass one's days in carefree leisure
【优遇】 yōuyù give special treatment: 格外～ exceptionally good treatment
【优裕】 yōuyù affluent; abundant: 生活～ be well-off; be well-to-do; live in affluence
【优越】 yōuyuè superior; advantageous: 处于～的地位 be in an advantageous position/ ～条件 favourable conditions
◇ ～感 sense of superiority; superiority complex
【优越性】 yōuyuèxìng superiority; advantage: 社会主义制度的～ the superiority of the socialist system/ 充分发挥人民公社的～ give full play to the advantages of the people's commune
【优哉游哉】 yōuzāi-yóuzāi 〈书〉 living a life of ease and leisure; leisurely and carefree; leisurely and unhurried
【优质】 yōuzhì high (或 top) quality; high grade: 开展～高产运动 launch a campaign for good quality and high output ◇ ～钢 high-quality steel/ ～混凝土 quality concrete

**忧** yōu ① worry; be worried: ～国～民 be concerned about one's country and one's people ② sorrow; anxiety; concern; care: 无～无虑 carefree; free from all anxieties
【忧愁】 yōuchóu sad; worried; depressed: 面容～ look worried
【忧愤】 yōufèn worried and indignant
【忧患】 yōuhuàn suffering; misery; hardship: 饱经～ have gone through a good deal
【忧惧】 yōujù worried and apprehensive
【忧虑】 yōulǜ worried; anxious; concerned: 深感～ feel extremely anxious; be very worried/ 他的～不是没有根据的。His anxiety is not uncalled-for.
【忧闷】 yōumèn depressed; feeling low; weighed down with cares
【忧伤】 yōushāng distressed; weighed down with sorrow; laden with grief
【忧心】 yōuxīn 〈书〉 worry; anxiety: ～忡忡 heavyhearted; care-laden; laden with anxieties/ ～如焚 burning with anxiety; extremely worried
【忧郁】 yōuyù melancholy; heavyhearted; dejected

**攸** yōu 〈书〉〔常用于〕: 性命～关 a matter of life and death/ 责有～归。The responsibility should lie where it belongs.

**呦** yōu 〈叹〉〔表示惊异〕: ～！你怎么也来了？Hey! Fancy seeing you here.

**幽** yōu ① deep and remote; secluded; dim: ～林 a secluded wood ② secret; hidden: ～怨 bitterness hidden in one's heart/ ～居 live in seclusion ③ quiet; tranquil; serene: ～深 deep and quiet ④ imprison: ～囚 imprison; place in confinement ⑤ of the nether world: ～魂 ghost
【幽暗】 yōu'àn dim; gloomy
【幽闭】 yōubì 〈书〉 ① put under house arrest ② confine oneself indoors
【幽愤】 yōufèn hidden resentment
【幽谷】 yōugǔ a deep and secluded valley
【幽会】 yōuhuì a secret meeting of lovers; a lovers' rendezvous; tryst
【幽魂】 yōuhún ghost
【幽寂】 yōujì secluded and lonely
【幽禁】 yōujìn put under house arrest; imprison
【幽静】 yōujìng quiet and secluded; peaceful: 这里环境很～。It's rather peaceful and secluded around here.
【幽灵】 yōulíng ghost; spectre; spirit
【幽门】 yōumén 〈生理〉 pylorus ◇ ～梗阻 〈医〉 pyloric stenosis
【幽冥】 yōumíng the nether world
【幽默】 yōumò humorous ◇ ～感 sense of humour
【幽情】 yōuqíng exquisite feelings: 发思古之～ muse over things of the remote past
【幽趣】 yōuqù the delightful serenity of seclusion
【幽深】 yōushēn (of forests, palaces, etc.) deep and serene; deep and quiet: ～的峡谷 a deep gorge
【幽思】 yōusī ① ponder; meditate ② thoughts on things remote
【幽邃】 yōusuì 〈书〉 deep and quiet
【幽微】 yōuwēi (of sound, smell, etc.) faint; weak
【幽闲】 yōuxián ① (of a woman) gentle and serene ② 见"悠闲" yōuxián 又作"幽娴"
【幽香】 yōuxiāng a delicate (或 faint) fragrance
【幽雅】 yōuyǎ (of a place) quiet and tastefully laid out
【幽咽】 yōuyè 〈书〉 ① whimpering: ～的哭泣 low sobs;

whimpers ② murmuring: 泉水～ a murmuring spring

【幽幽】 yōuyōu ① (of light or sound) faint: ～啜泣 sob quietly/ ～的路灯 dim street lamps ② 〈书〉 looming in the distance

【幽怨】 yōuyuàn hidden bitterness (of a young woman thwarted in love)

**悠** yōu ① long-drawn-out; remote in time or space ② leisurely ③ 〈口〉 swing: 他抓住绳子～了过去。He held on to the rope and swung across.

【悠长】 yōucháng long; long-drawn-out: ～的岁月 long years/ ～的汽笛声 the drawn-out sound of a siren

【悠荡】 yōudàng swing (to and fro); sway (back and forth)

【悠忽】 yōuhū 〈书〉 lazy and idle

【悠久】 yōujiǔ long; long-standing; age-old: 历史～ have a long history/ ～的文化 a civilization (或 culture) of long standing/ ～的传统 an age-old tradition

【悠然】 yōurán ① carefree and leisurely: ～自得 be carefree and content ② long; distant; far away: ～神往 one's thoughts turn to things distant

【悠闲】 yōuxián leisurely and carefree: ～自在 leisurely and carefree

【悠扬】 yōuyáng (of music, etc.) rising and falling; melodious: ～的歌声 melodious singing

【悠悠】 yōuyōu ① long; long-drawn-out; remote: ～长夜。The night seemed to drag. ② leisurely; unhurried: ～自得 carefree and content

【悠悠荡荡】 yōuyōudàngdàng floating about

【悠悠忽忽】 yōuyōuhūhū ① loiter ② be in a trance

【悠远】 yōuyuǎn ① a long time ago; long ago; distant: ～的往事 events of the distant past ② far off (或 away); remote; distant: 山川～ mountains and rivers far, far away

【悠着】 yōuzhe 〈方〉 take things easy: ～点劲，别太猛了。Take it easy (或 Easy)! Don't go at it so hard.

## yóu

**尤** yóu ① outstanding: 择～ pick out the best/ 无耻之～ have absolutely no sense of shame; brazen in the extreme ② particularly; especially: 这一点～为重要。This is even more important./ 此地盛产水果，～以梨桃著称。The place abounds with fruit, especially pears and peaches. ③ fault; wrongdoing: 效～ knowingly follow the example of a wrongdoer ④ have a grudge against; blame: 怨天～人 blame god and man — blame everyone and everything but oneself ⑤ (Yóu) a surname

【尤其】 yóuqí 〈副〉 especially; particularly: 大家干得都很猛，～是小王。Everyone was working energetically, especially Xiao Wang./ 讲话的第一部分～重要。The first part of the speech is particularly important.

**由** yóu ① cause; reason: 原～ cause/ 理～ reason ② because of; due to: ～粗心大意造成的错误 mistakes due to carelessness/ 咎～自取 have only oneself to blame ③ by; through: ～边门出去。Exit by the side door./ ～此入内。This way in. 或 Entrance./ ～群众推荐 be recommended by the masses/ ～民主协商选举产生 be elected after democratic consultation ④ follow; obey: 事不～己。Things are beyond one's control. 或 Things are getting out of hand./ ～她去吧。Let her do as she pleases. ⑤ 〈介〉〔表示某事归某人去做〕: 这件事～他处理。Leave it to him./ 须～支部大会通过 be subject to acceptance by a general meeting of the Party branch ⑥ 〈介〉〔表示凭借〕: 水～氢与氧化合而成。Water is composed of hydrogen and oxygen. ⑦ 〈介〉〔表示起点〕 from: ～银川出发 set off from Yinchuan/ ～点到面 spread over a whole area from one point/ ～浅入深 proceed from the easy to the difficult/ ～下而上 from bottom to top; from the lower level upward; from below

【由不得】 yóubude ① not be up to sb. to decide; be beyond the control of: 这件事～我。It's not up to me./ 事到如今就～你了。You have no choice in the matter at this late hour. ② cannot help: ～笑了起来 can't help laughing

【由此】 yóucǐ from this; therefrom; thus: ～前进 go forward from here/ ～看来 judging from this; in view of this/ ～产生的一切后果 all consequences arising therefrom/ ～弄出许多错误 make many mistakes as a consequence

【由此可见】 yóu cǐ kě jiàn thus it can be seen; this shows; that proves: ～，多数人是赞成这个计划的。Thus it can be seen that the majority are in favour of the plan.

【由来】 yóulái origin: 分歧的～ origin of differences

【由来已久】 yóulái yǐ jiǔ long-standing; time-honoured: 争论～。The dispute is of long-standing./ 这种风俗～。This is a time-honoured custom.

【由头】 yóutou pretext: 找～ find a pretext

【由于】 yóuyú 〈介〉 owing to; thanks to; as a result of; due to; in virtue of: ～健康关系 on health grounds/ ～同志们的共同努力，工作进行得很顺利。Owing to the concerted efforts of the comrades, work is going on smoothly.

【由衷】 yóuzhōng from the bottom of one's heart; sincere; heartfelt: ～之言 words which come from the bottom of one's heart; sincere words/ 表示～的感激 extend one's heartfelt thanks/ 对于你的进步，我感到～的高兴。I heartily rejoice at the progress you've made.

**邮** yóu ① post; mail: 信～了吗？Has the letter been posted (或 mailed)? ② postal; mail: ～路 postal (或 mail) route

【邮包】 yóubāo postal parcel; parcel ◇ ～保险 parcel post insurance

【邮差】 yóuchāi 〈旧〉 postman

【邮车】 yóuchē postal (或 mail) car

【邮船】 yóuchuán ocean liner; liner; packet ship

【邮戳】 yóuchuō postmark

【邮袋】 yóudài mailbag; postbag; (mail) pouch

【邮递】 yóudì ① send by post (或 mail) ② postal (或 mail) delivery ◇ ～员 postman; mailman

【邮电】 yóudiàn post and telecommunications ◇ ～部 Ministry of Posts and Telecommunications/ ～局 post and telecommunications office/ ～业务 postal and telecommunications service

【邮费】 yóufèi postage: ～免收 post-free

【邮购】 yóugòu mail-order ◇ ～部 mail-order department

【邮汇】 yóuhuì remit by post

【邮寄】 yóujì send by post; post

【邮件】 yóujiàn postal matter; post; mail: 挂号～ registered post/ 航空～ air mail/ 小包～ a postal packet

【邮局】 yóujú post office

【邮路】 yóulù postal (或 mail) route: ～遍及全国。A postal network now covers the whole country.

【邮票】 yóupiào postage stamp; stamp: 一套纪念～ a set of commemorative stamps

【邮亭】 yóutíng postal kiosk

【邮筒】 yóutǒng pillar-box; postbox; mailbox

【邮箱】 yóuxiāng postbox; mailbox

【邮政】 yóuzhèng postal service ◇ ～编码 postcode; zip code/ ～代办所 postal agency/ ～汇票 postal money order; postal order/ ～局 post office/ ～局长 postmaster/ ～网 postal network/ ～信箱 post-office

box (P. O. B.)
【邮资】 yóuzī postage: 国内～ postage paid for inland mail/ 国外～ postage paid for overseas mail/ ～已付 postage paid; postpaid

**犹** yóu 〈书〉①just as; like: 虽死～生 live on in spirit ②still: 记忆～新 be still fresh in one's memory
【犹大】 Yóudà Judas
【犹如】 yóurú just as; like; as if: 灯火辉煌,～白昼。The place was lit up as bright as day.
【犹太复国主义】 Yóutài fùguózhǔyì Zionism
【犹太教】 Yóutàijiào Judaism ◇ ～教士 rabbi/ ～堂 synagogue
【犹太人】 Yóutàirén (男) Jew; (女) Jewess
【犹疑】 yóuyi hesitate
【犹豫】 yóuyù hesitate; be irresolute: ～不决 hesitate; remain undecided/ 毫不～ without the least hesitation/ 犹犹豫豫 shilly-shally

**油** yóu ①oil; fat; grease: 植物～ vegetable oil/ 猪～ pork fat; lard ②apply tung oil or paint: ～门窗 paint the doors and windows/ ～饰一新 freshly varnished (或 painted) ③be stained with oil or grease: 衣服～了。The coat has got oil stains on it. ④oily; glib: 这家伙嘴～得很。The fellow has a very glib tongue.
【油泵】 yóubèng 〈机〉 oil pump
【油饼】 yóubǐng ①deep-fried dough cake ②〈农〉 oil cake
【油布】 yóubù oilcloth; oilskin; tarpaulin
【油彩】 yóucǎi greasepaint; paint
【油菜】 yóucài rape ◇ ～籽 rapeseed
【油藏】 yóucáng 〈石油〉 oil deposit; oil pool: 地层～ stratigraphic oil pool/ 构造～ structural oil pool/ 岩性～ lithological oil pool
【油层】 yóucéng 〈石油〉 oil reservoir; oil layer; oil horizon ◇ ～压力 reservoir pressure/ ～动态 reservoir behaviour (或 performance)
【油茶】 yóuchá ①〈植〉 tea-oil tree; oil-tea camellia ②a gruel of sweetened, fried flour ◇ ～面儿 flour fried in beef fat with sugar and sesame
【油船】 yóuchuán (oil) tanker; oil carrier
【油淬火】 yóucuìhuǒ 〈机〉 oil hardening (或 quenching)
【油灯】 yóudēng oil lamp
【油坊】 yóufáng oil mill
【油封】 yóufēng 〈机〉 oil seal
【油橄榄】 yóugǎnlǎn 〈植〉 olive
【油膏】 yóugāo 〈药〉 ointment
【油瓜】 yóuguā 〈植〉 large-fruited hodgsonia (*Hodgsonia macrocarpa*) 又作"油渣果"
【油管】 yóuguǎn 〈石油〉 ①oil pipe: 铺设～ lay oil pipes ②oil tube: 未下～的井 untubed well/ ～深度 tubing depth
【油罐】 yóuguàn oil tank; storage tank ◇ ～汽车 oil car (或 truck)
【油光】 yóuguāng glossy; shiny; varnished: 把车子擦得～锃亮 put a good shine on the car
【油壶】 yóuhú oilcan; oiler
【油葫芦】 yóuhulǔ 〈动〉 a kind of field cricket (*Gryllus testaceus*)
【油花儿】 yóuhuār drops of oil on the surface of soup; blobs of fat
【油滑】 yóuhuá slippery; foxy
【油画】 yóuhuà oil painting: 画～ paint in oils
【油灰】 yóuhuī 〈建〉 putty
【油迹】 yóujī oil stains; grease spots: ～斑斑 covered with grease spots
【油井】 yóujǐng oil well: 钻一口～ drill (或 bore) a well
【油锯】 yóujù 〈林〉 chain saw ◇ ～手 chain-saw operator
【油库】 yóukù oil depot; tank farm: 转运～ oil terminal
【油矿】 yóukuàng ①oil deposit ②oil field
【油料作物】 yóuliào zuòwù oil-bearing crops; oil crops
【油绿】 yóulǜ glossy dark green
【油轮】 yóulún (oil) tanker
【油码头】 yóumǎtou oil jetty; oil wharf; tanker (loading) terminal
【油麦】 yóumài 〈植〉 naked oats
【油毛毡】 yóumáozhān 〈建〉 asphalt felt
【油门】 yóumén 〈机〉 ①throttle ②〈口〉 accelerator: 踩～ step on the accelerator
【油苗】 yóumiáo 〈石油〉 oil seepage
【油墨】 yóumò printing ink: 快干～ quicksetting ink
【油母页岩】 yóumǔ-yèyán oil shale
【油泥】 yóuní greasy filth; grease: 这表需要擦～。The watch needs cleaning and oiling.
【油腻】 yóunì ①greasy; oily: 不爱吃～的东西 not care for greasy (或 oily) food ②greasy food; oily food
【油皮】 yóupí 〈方〉 outermost layer of skin: 只是擦破了点～儿。It's only a scratch.
【油漆】 yóuqī ①paint: 一层～ a coat of paint/ ～未干! Wet paint! 或 Fresh paint! ②cover with paint; paint: 把大门～一下 have the gate painted ◇ ～工人 painter
【油气界面】 yóuqì jièmiàn 〈石油〉 oil gas interface
【油枪】 yóuqiāng 〈机〉 oil gun
【油腔滑调】 yóuqiāng-huádiào glib; unctuous: 说起话来～ speak glibly; have a glib tongue
【油泉】 yóuquán oil spring
【油然】 yóurán ①spontaneously; involuntarily: 敬慕之心,～而生。Admiration wells up in one's heart. ②densely; profusely: ～作云 clouds beginning to gather
【油溶性染料】 yóuróngxìng rǎnliào oil-soluble dyes
【油鞣】 yóuróu 〈皮革〉 oil tanning
【油砂】 yóushā 〈石油〉 oil sand: 稠～ heavy oil sand ◇ ～层 pay sand
【油石】 yóushí 〈机〉 oilstone
【油柿】 yóushì 〈植〉 wild kaki persimmon (*Diospyros kaki* var. *silvestris*)
【油水】 yóushuǐ ①grease: 这个菜～太大。This dish is too greasy. ②profit: ～不大 not very profitable/ 捞到一点～ pick up a few crumbs; make a profit
【油松】 yóusōng 〈植〉 Chinese pine
【油酥】 yóusū short; crisp; flaky: ～点心 short pastry
【油酸】 yóusuān 〈化〉 oleic acid
【油田】 yóutián oil field: ～开发 oil field development (或 exploitation)/ 多层～ multi-pay oil field
【油条】 yóutiáo deep-fried twisted dough sticks
【油桐】 yóutóng 〈植〉 tung oil tree; tung tree
【油桶】 yóutǒng oil drum
【油头粉面】 yóutóu-fěnmiàn sleek-haired and creamy-faced — coquettish or dandified in appearance
【油头滑脑】 yóutóu-huánǎo slick; flippant
【油汪汪】 yóuwāngwāng ①dripping with oil; full of grease ②glossy; shiny
【油位】 yóuwèi 〈机〉 oil level ◇ ～表 oil (level) gauge
【油污】 yóuwū greasy dirt
【油箱】 yóuxiāng fuel tank: 副～ auxiliary fuel tank; auxiliary tank
【油压】 yóuyā 〈机〉 oil pressure
◇ ～泵 oil pressure pump/ ～表 oil pressure gauge/ ～机 hydraulic (或 oil) press/ ～千斤顶 hydraulic (或 oil) jack/ ～传动 hydraulic transmission
【油烟】 yóuyān lampblack
【油页岩】 yóuyèyán oil shale

【油印】 yóuyìn mimeograph: ～一百份 mimeograph a hundred copies ◇ ～机 mimeograph/ ～蜡纸 stencil; stencil paper
【油浴】 yóuyù 〈化〉 oil bath
【油渣】 yóuzhā ① dregs of fat ② 〈石油〉 oil residue
【油毡】 yóuzhān 〈建〉 asphalt felt 又作"油毛毡"
【油脂】 yóuzhī oil; fat: 植物～ vegetable fat or oil/ 动物～ animal fat or oil; tallow; grease
【油纸】 yóuzhǐ oilpaper
【油子】 yóuzi ① black sticky substance: 烟袋～ tar inside a tobacco pipe ② 〈方〉 foxy old hand
【油棕】 yóuzōng 〈植〉 oil palm
【油嘴】 yóuzuǐ ① glib ② glib talker
【油嘴滑舌】 yóuzuǐ-huáshé glib-tongued

## 疣

yóu 〈医〉 wart

## 柚

yóu
另见 yòu
【柚木】 yóumù 〈植〉 teak

## 莜

yóu
【莜麦】 yóumài 〈植〉 naked oats

## 铀

yóu 〈化〉 uranium (U): 浓缩～ enriched uranium
【铀后元素】 yóuhòu yuánsù 〈化〉 transuranium element; transuranium

## 蚰

yóu
【蚰蜒】 yóuyán 〈动〉 common house centipede
【蚰蜒草】 yóuyáncǎo alpine yarrow (*Achillea alpina*)

## 游

yóu ① swim ② rove around; wander; travel; tour: 周～世界 travel round the world; go on a world tour/ ～山玩水 travel from place to place enjoying the beauties of nature; go on trips to different scenic spots ③ roving; itinerant: ～民 vagrant ④ 〈书〉 associate with: 交～甚广 have a wide circle of acquaintances ⑤ part of a river; reach: 上～ the upper reaches (of a river) ⑥ (Yóu) a surname
【游伴】 yóubàn travel companion
【游标】 yóubiāo 〈机〉 vernier: ～卡尺 vernier caliper/ ～千分尺 vernier micrometer
【游船】 yóuchuán pleasure-boat
【游荡】 yóudàng loaf about; loiter; wander
【游动】 yóudòng move about; go from place to place ◇ ～哨 a roving sentry; a patrol
【游逛】 yóuguàng go sight-seeing; stroll about
【游击】 yóujī guerrilla warfare: 打～ fight as a guerrilla; conduct guerrilla warfare
◇ ～队 guerrilla forces; a guerrilla detachment/ ～队员 guerrilla; partisan/ ～区 guerrilla area/ ～战 guerrilla war (或 warfare)
【游记】 yóujì travel notes; travels
【游街】 yóujiē parade sb. through the streets: ～示众 parade sb. through the streets to expose him before the public
【游客】 yóukè visitor (to a park, etc.); tourist; excursionist; sightseer
【游览】 yóulǎn go sight-seeing; tour; visit: ～西湖 go sight-seeing on the West Lake/ ～长城 visit the Great Wall
◇ ～车 tourist coach/ ～地 place for sight-seeing; excursion centre/ ～图 tourist map
【游廊】 yóuláng covered corridor (linking two or more buildings); veranda
【游离】 yóulí ① dissociate; drift away: ～分子 one who quits the collective ② 〈化〉 free ◇ ～酸 〈化〉 free acid/ ～状态 〈化〉 free state
【游历】 yóulì travel for pleasure; travel; tour: ～过很多地方 have travelled extensively
【游民】 yóumín vagrant; vagabond: 无业～ vagrant
【游牧】 yóumù move about in search of pasture; rove around as a nomad
◇ ～部落 nomadic tribe/ ～生活 nomadic life; nomadism
【游憩】 yóuqì stroll about or have a rest
【游禽】 yóuqín natatorial bird
【游人】 yóurén visitor (to a park, etc.); sightseer; tourist
【游刃有余】 yóu rèn yǒu yú handle a butcher's cleaver skilfully — do a job with skill and ease; be more than equal to a task
【游手好闲】 yóushǒu-hàoxián idle about; loaf: ～,不务正业 idle about and do no decent work
【游水】 yóushuǐ swim
【游说】 yóushuì go about selling an idea; go about drumming up support for an idea; go canvassing
【游丝】 yóusī ① gossamer ② 〈机〉 hairspring
【游艇】 yóutǐng yacht; pleasure-boat
【游玩】 yóuwán ① amuse oneself; play: 孩子们经常去海滨～。The children often go to the beach to play. ② go sight-seeing; stroll about
【游戏】 yóuxì ① recreation; game: 做～ play games ② play: 孩子们在公园里～。The children are playing in the park.
【游侠】 yóuxiá 见"侠客" xiákè
【游仙诗】 yóuxiānshī poetry about immortals
【游行】 yóuxíng parade; march; demonstration: 节日～ gala parade/ 抗议～ protest march/ 饥饿～ hunger march/ 举行～示威 hold a demonstration ◇ ～队伍 contingents of paraders or marchers; procession
【游兴】 yóuxìng interest in going on an excursion or sight-seeing
【游移】 yóuyí (of attitude, policy, etc.) waver; vacillate; wobble: ～不定 keep on vacillating/ ～于两者之间 waver between the two/ 一点～的余地也没有了。There is no wavering.
【游弋】 yóuyì cruise: 在海上～ cruise on the sea
【游艺】 yóuyì entertainment; recreation ◇ ～节目 programme (of musical and other performances)/ ～室 recreation room
【游泳】 yóuyǒng swim: 去～ go for a swim; go swimming/ 在～中学习～ learn to swim by swimming
◇ ～比赛 swimming contest/ ～池 swimming pool/ ～馆 natatorium/ ～裤 bathing (或 swimming) trunks/ ～帽 bathing (或 swimming) cap/ ～衣 swimsuit; swimming suit (或 costume); bathing suit (或 costume)
【游园】 yóuyuán ① visit a garden or park: 陪外宾～ accompany a foreign guest on a visit to a park ② mass celebrations in parks: 党和国家领导人和群众一道参加五一节～联欢。Party and state leaders joined the masses in the parks for the May Day celebrations.
【游资】 yóuzī idle fund; idle money; floating capital
【游子】 yóuzǐ 〈书〉 man travelling or residing in a place far away from home
【游子】 yóuzi decoy

## 鱿

yóu
【鱿鱼】 yóuyú squid

## 鲉

yóu scorpionfish

## 蝣

yóu 见"蜉蝣" fúyóu

**蝤** yóu

【蝤蛑】 yóumóu 〈动〉 swimming crab

**鼬** yóu

【鼬子】 yóuzi decoy

## yǒu

**友** yǒu ① friend: 好～ close friend/ 战～ comrade-in-arms ② friendly

【友爱】 yǒu'ài friendly affection; fraternal love: 团结～ fraternal unity/ 阶级～ class brotherhood

【友邦】 yǒubāng friendly nation (或 country)

【友好】 yǒuhǎo ① close friend; friend: 生前～ friends of the deceased ② friendly; amicable: ～访问 friendly visit/ 会谈在～的气氛中进行。The talks proceeded in a friendly atmosphere./ 发表热情～的讲话 make a warm and friendly speech

◇～代表团 goodwill mission/ ～人士 friendly personage; friend/ ～使者 envoy of friendship/ ～条约 treaty of friendship/ ～协会 friendship association/ ～邀请赛 friendship invitational tournament

【友军】 yǒujūn friendly forces

【友情】 yǒuqíng friendly sentiments; friendship

【友人】 yǒurén friend: 国际～ foreign friend

【友善】 yǒushàn 〈书〉 friendly; amicable

【友谊】 yǒuyì friendship: 深厚的～ profound friendship/ 建立～ build (或 forge) ties of friendship/ ～第一,比赛第二。Friendship first, competition second. ◇ ～赛 friendly match

**有** yǒu ①have; possess: 我～一个弟弟。I have a younger brother./ 她～热情,～朝气。She is full of vigour and enthusiasm./ 属于全民所～ belong to the whole people/ ～百利而无一弊 have every advantage and no drawback ② there is; exist: 屋里～人吗？Is there anyone in the room?/ 这座位～人吗？ Is this seat taken?/ 还～许多工作要做。Much still remains to be done. ③〔表示估量或比较〕: 水～三米多深。The water is more than 3 metres deep./ 他～你这么高。He is as tall as you./ 问题～那么严重吗？Is the problem that serious? ④〔表示发生或出现〕: 一～问题就去解决 deal with a problem as soon as it crops up/ 在同志们的帮助下,他～了很大进步。With the help of his comrades, he has made great progress. ⑤〔表示多，大〕: ～经验 be experienced/ ～了年纪 be getting on in years ⑥〔用于泛指,跟"某"的作用相近〕: ～一天我在街上碰见他了。One day I ran into him in the street./ ～些事还需要商量。Certain things are still open to discussion. ⑦〔用在"人""时候""地方"前面,表示一部分〕: ～人说可以,～人说不可以。Some say yes, some say no./ 这里～时候也能热到三十九度。The temperature here sometimes goes up to thirty-nine degrees centigrade./ 这个措施～地方适用, ～地方不适用。This measure is suited to some localities, but not to others. ⑧〔用在某些动词的前面组成套语,表示客气〕: ～劳远迎。I deeply appreciate your kindness in coming so far to meet me.

另见 yòu

【有碍】 yǒu'ài be a hindrance to; get in the way of; obstruct: ～交通 hinder traffic/ ～观瞻 be repugnant to the eye; be an eyesore

【有案可稽】 yǒu àn kě jī be a matter of record; be on record; be documented 又作"有案可查"

【有板有眼】 yǒubǎn-yǒuyǎn rhythmical; measured; orderly: 他说话～。Whatever he says is well presented.

【有备无患】 yǒubèi-wúhuàn where there is precaution, there is no danger; preparedness averts peril

【有鼻子有眼儿】 yǒubízi-yǒuyǎnr with every detail vividly described: 她说得～,就象真有那么一回事。She described the whole thing in such vivid detail that it sounded quite real.

【有产阶级】 yǒuchǎnjiējí propertied class

【有酬劳动】 yǒuchóu láodòng 〈经〉 paid labour

【有待】 yǒudài remain (to be done); await: ～解决 remain to be solved/ ～证明 have yet to be proved/ ～上级作出最后决定 await final decision by the higher level/ ～进一步讨论 pending further discussion

【有的】 yǒude some: ～这样说,～那样说。Some say one thing, some say another.

【有的是】 yǒudeshì have plenty of; there's no lack of: 她～时间。She has all the time in the world./ 这种草药山上～。There are plenty of these herbs in the hills.

【有底】 yǒudǐ know how things stand and feel confident of handling them; be fully prepared for what is coming: 他心里～,一点不慌。He was not at all nervous, for he knew what to expect.

【有的放矢】 yǒu dì fàng shǐ shoot the arrow at the target — have a definite object in view

【有点儿】 yǒudiǎnr ① some; a little: 水壶里还～水。There's still some water in the kettle./ 看来～希望 look a bit hopeful ② 〈副〉 somewhat; rather; a bit: ～反感 feel a bit resentful; have a touch of resentment/ ～不好意思 be somewhat embarrassed

【有方】 yǒufāng with the proper method; in the right way: 领导～ exercise able leadership

【有福同享,有祸同当】 yǒu fú tóng xiǎng, yǒu huò tóng dāng share joys and sorrows; share weal and woe; stick together through thick and thin

【有功】 yǒugōng have rendered great service; have performed meritorious service: ～部队 troops with a fine record of service; meritorious army unit/ 对革命～ have rendered service to the revolution; have made contributions to the revolution

【有关】 yǒuguān have something to do with; have a bearing on; relate to; concern: 这件事与他～。He has something to do with the matter./ 这些问题都跟哲学～。All these questions relate to philosophy./ ～全局 have a bearing on the situation as a whole/ ～世界革命的问题 a question concerning the world revolution/ 阅读～的文件 read the relevant documents/ 保证～国家的合法权利 safeguard the legitimate rights of such countries as may be affected

◇～部门 the department concerned/ ～当局 the authorities concerned; the proper authorities/ ～方面 the parties concerned/ ～组织 related organization

【有光】 yǒuguāng ① glazed ② 〈纺〉 bright ◇ ～人造丝 bright rayon/ ～纸 (machine glazed) cap paper; glazed paper

【有轨电车】 yǒuguǐ diànchē tramcar; streetcar

【有鬼】 yǒuguǐ there's something fishy: 这里面～。There's something fishy about it. 或 One smells a rat here./ 他心里～。He's got a guilty conscience.

【有过之无不及】 yǒu guò zhī wú bùjí 〔多用于坏的方面〕 go even farther than; outdo

【有害】 yǒuhài harmful; pernicious; detrimental: 对健康～ harmful (或 detrimental) to one's health/ ～的影响 pernicious effects/ 无政府主义对革命集体是十分～的。Anarchism is extremely harmful to a revolutionary collective.

【有恒】 yǒuhéng persevering

【有会子】 yǒuhuìzi 〈口〉 quite a long while; quite some time: 他出去可～啦！He's been out for quite a while.

【有机】 yǒujī ①〈化〉organic ② organic: ～的整体 an organic whole/ ～的组成部分 an organic part; a component part
◇ ～玻璃 polymethyl methacrylate; plexiglass; perspex/ ～肥料 organic fertilizer or manure/ ～合成 organic synthesis/ ～化合物 organic compound/ ～化学 organic chemistry/ ～体 organism/ ～物质 organic matter (或 substance)
【有机可乘】 yǒu jī kě chéng there's an opportunity to take advantage of; there's a loophole that can be used
【有计划】 yǒu jìhuà in a planned way; according to plan: ～、按比例、高速度地发展我国的国民经济 develop our national economy proportionately, in a planned way and at a high speed
【有价证券】 yǒujià zhèngquàn negotiable securities; securities
【有救】 yǒujiù can be saved (或 cured, remedied): 好了,这病～了! Thank goodness, we've found a cure for the disease.
【有孔虫】 yǒukǒngchóng foraminifer
【有口皆碑】 yǒu kǒu jiē bēi win universal praise; be universally acclaimed
【有口难分】 yǒu kǒu nán fēn find it hard to vindicate oneself 又作"有口难辩"
【有口难言】 yǒu kǒu nán yán cannot bring oneself to mention sth.; find it hard or embarrassing to bring up a matter
【有口无心】 yǒukǒu-wúxīn be sharp-tongued but not malicious: 他是～,你别见怪。He didn't really mean what he said, so don't take it to heart.
【有赖】 yǒulài depend on; rest on: 要实现这项改革～于大家共同努力。The success of the innovation depends on our concerted efforts.
【有理】 yǒulǐ ① reasonable; justified; in the right: 你讲的～。What you say is quite reasonable./ ～走遍天下,无理寸步难行。With justice on your side, you can go anywhere; without it, you can't take a step. ②〈数〉rational
◇ ～分式 rational fraction/ ～函数 rational function/ ～数 rational number
【有力】 yǒulì strong; powerful; forceful; energetic; vigorous: ～的思想武器 powerful ideological weapon/ 进行～的斗争 conduct a vigorous struggle; wage an energetic struggle/ 给以～的支援 give strong (或 effective) support/ 提供～的证据 provide strong evidence; furnish convincing proof/ 作出～的回答 give a forceful answer/ ～地打击了歪风邪气 hit hard at evil trends
【有利】 yǒulì advantageous; beneficial; favourable: ～于巩固无产阶级专政 be advantageous to the consolidation of the dictatorship of the proletariat/ 向～于人民的方向发展 develop in a direction favourable to the people/ ～于改进领导作风 help improve the style of leadership/ ～于打败侵略者 contribute to the defeat of the aggressors/ 形势对我们～。The situation is to our advantage.
◇ ～地形〈军〉favourable terrain/ ～时机 opportune time/ ～条件 favourable condition
【有利可图】 yǒu lì kě tú have good prospects of gain; stand to gain; be profitable
【有两下子】 yǒu liǎng xiàzi〈口〉have real skill; know one's stuff: 他干活又快又好,真～。He works fast and well; he obviously knows his stuff.
【有零】 yǒulíng odd: 三十～ thirty odd/ 一千～ just over a thousand
【有门儿】 yǒuménr〈口〉① find the beginning of a solution; be hopeful (of success): 听他的口气,这事看来～了。Judging by the way he spoke, he might get the matter off the ground now. ② get the hang: 这活儿他干了几次,现在有点门儿了。After several trials, he began to get the hang of the work.
【有名】 yǒumíng well-known; famous; celebrated: ～的乒乓球运动员 a famous (或 well-known) table tennis player/ ～的科学家 a celebrated scientist
【有名无实】 yǒumíng-wúshí in name but not in reality; merely nominal; titular
【有目共睹】 yǒu mù gòng dǔ be there for all to see; be obvious to all
【有目共赏】 yǒu mù gòng shǎng have a universal appeal
【有奶便是娘】 yǒu nǎi biàn shì niáng whoever suckles me is my mother; submit oneself to anyone who feeds one; lick the hand of anyone who throws a few crumbs
【有年】 yǒunián〈书〉for years
【有盼儿】 yǒupànr〈方〉become hopeful
【有期徒刑】 yǒuqī túxíng〈法〉set term of imprisonment: 判～七年 be sentenced to seven years' imprisonment
【有其父,必有其子】 yǒu qí fù, bì yǒu qí zǐ like father, like son
【有钱】 yǒuqián rich; wealthy: ～能使鬼推磨。With money you can make the devil turn the millstone. 或 Money makes the mare to go. ◇ ～人 the rich; the wealthy
【有求必应】 yǒu qiú bì yìng respond to every plea; grant whatever is requested
【有趣】 yǒuqù interesting; fascinating; amusing: ～的故事 an interesting story/ ～的游戏 a fascinating game; an exciting game
【有日子】 yǒu rìzi ① for quite a few days; for days: 咱们～没见面了。We haven't seen each other for quite a few days. ② have fixed a date: 你们结婚～了没有? Have you fixed the date for the wedding?
【有色】 yǒusè coloured: 戴着～眼镜看事情 look at things through coloured spectacles — take a distorted view ◇ ～金属 nonferrous metal/ ～人种 coloured race (或 people)
【有神论】 yǒushénlùn theism ◇ ～者 theist
【有生力量】 yǒushēng lìliàng effective strength; effectives: 歼灭敌人～ wipe out the enemy's effective strength; annihilate the enemy effectives
【有生以来】 yǒu shēng yǐlái ever since one's birth: ～第一次 the first time in one's life (或 in all one's born days)
【有声片】 yǒushēngpiàn sound film; talkie
【有声有色】 yǒushēng-yǒusè full of sound and colour — vivid and dramatic: 故事讲得～ tell a story dramatically
【有识之士】 yǒu shí zhī shì a person with breadth of vision; a man of insight
【有时】 yǒushí sometimes; at times; now and then: 他～也写几句诗。Sometimes he writes a few lines of poetry./ 阶级斗争是长期的、曲折的,～甚至是很激烈的。The class struggle is long and tortuous and at times even very acute.
【有史以来】 yǒu shǐ yǐlái since the beginning (或 dawn) of history; throughout history: ～最大的陨石雨 the biggest meteorite shower in history
【有始无终】 yǒushǐ-wúzhōng start sth. but fail to carry it through
【有始有终】 yǒushǐ-yǒuzhōng carry sth. through to the end
【有事】 yǒushì ① when problems crop up; if sth. happens: ～同群众商量 consult with the masses when problems crop up/ 做好准备,一旦～,马上出动。Get prepared so that you can set off immediately if something happens. ② occupied; busy: 你今晚～吗? Have you anything on this evening?/ 我现在～。I'm busy now.
【有恃无恐】 yǒushì-wúkǒng secure in the knowledge that one has strong backing
【有数】 yǒushù ① know exactly how things stand; have a definite idea of what one's doing: 进行调查研究,做到心中～ make investigations so as to be sure how things stand/ 这样一摸底,大家心里就～了。With this stocktaking, we

know where we are./ 你放心，怎么做我心里～。 Don't worry. I know what I'm doing. ② not many; only a few: 只剩下～的几天了，得加把劲儿。 There are only a few days left. We must get a move on.

【有丝分裂】 yǒusī fēnliè 〈生〉 mitosis

【有所】 yǒusuǒ to some extent; somewhat: 两国关系～改善。 The relations between the two countries have improved to some extent./ 销售价格～降低。There's been some reduction in the selling prices./ 我对这一决议，～保留。 I have my reservations about this resolution./ 人类总得不断地总结经验，～发现，～发明，～创造，～前进。Man has constantly to sum up his experience and go on discovering, inventing, creating and advancing.

【有蹄动物】 yǒutí dòngwù ungulate

【有条不紊】 yǒutiáo-bùwěn in an orderly way; methodically; systematically: 他做起事来～。He works methodically./ ～地进行生产 carry on production in a systematic fashion

【有望】 yǒuwàng hopeful: 丰收～。There's hope of a bumper harvest.

【有为】 yǒuwéi promising: ～的青年 a promising young person/ 年轻～ young and promising

【有…无…】 yǒu…wú… ①〔表示只有前者而没有后者〕: 有职无权 hold the post but not the power; be a figurehead/ 有眼无珠 have eyes but see not/ 有气无力 feeble ②〔表示强调有前者而没有后者〕: 有害无益 not helpful but harmful/ 有增无减 increase steadily/ 有去无还 gone never to return ③〔表示有了前者就可以没有后者〕: 有备无患。Preparedness averts peril. ④〔表示似有似无〕: 有意无意 wittingly or unwittingly; consciously or unconsciously; by accident or design

【有喜】 yǒuxǐ 〈口〉 be pregnant; be expecting

【有隙可乘】 yǒu xì kě chéng there is a crack to squeeze through -- there is a loophole to exploit

【有限】 yǒuxiàn limited; finite: 为数～ limited in number; not many/ 文化水平～ have had little schooling/ 对情况了解～ have a limited knowledge of the situation/ 人的生命是～的，但为人民服务是无限的。There is a limit to one's life, but no limit to serving the people.

◇ ～公司 limited company; limited-liability company/ ～花序 〈植〉 definite inflorescence/ ～级数 〈数〉 finite progression; finite series/ ～主权论 (social-imperialist) theory of limited sovereignty

【有线】 yǒuxiàn wired

◇ ～传真 wirephoto/ ～电报学 wire telegraphy/ ～广播 wire (或 wired) broadcasting; rediffusion on wire/ ～广播网 wire-broadcasting network; wired broadcast network/ ～广播站 wired broadcast station; rediffusion station/ ～通讯 wire communication

【有效】 yǒuxiào efficacious; effective; valid: 采取～步骤 take effective steps/ 这药治哮喘病很～。 This is an efficacious (或 effective) drug for asthma./ 这张车票三日内～。This train ticket is good (或 valid) for three days./ 这个指示仍然～。The directive still holds good./ 两种文本同样～。Both texts are equally authentic.

◇ ～分蘖 〈农〉 effective tillering/ ～功率 〈电〉 effective power; useful power/ ～荷载 useful load/ ～库容 〈水〉 effective storage/ ～票 valid ballot paper/ ～数字 significant digits

【有效期】 yǒuxiàoqī term (或 period) of validity; time of efficacy: 延长合同的～ prolong the contract's period of validity/ 本条约～为三十年。The present treaty shall be valid for 30 years./ 这个胶卷已过了～。 This film has passed its expiry date.

【有些】 yǒuxiē ① some: ～人在看书，～人在谈天。 Some people were reading, some were talking./ ～旧机器还能用。Some of the old machines are still serviceable. ② somewhat; rather: ～不满意 be somewhat dissatisfied/ ～失望 be rather disappointed

【有心】 yǒuxīn ① have a mind to; set one's mind on: 我～去看看他，又怕打扰他。I'd like to go and see him, but I don't want to disturb him. ② intentionally; purposely: 他是～说给你听的。What he said was intended for you.

【有心人】 yǒuxīnrén ① a person who sets his mind on doing sth. useful; a person with high aspirations and determination: 世上无难事，只怕～。Nothing in the world is difficult for one who sets his mind on it. ② an observant and conscientious person

【有形】 yǒuxíng tangible; visible

◇ ～贸易 visible trade/ ～损耗 material loss/ ～资产 tangible assets; tangibles

【有性】 yǒuxìng 〈生〉 sexual

◇ ～生殖 zoogamy; sexual reproduction/ ～世代 sexual generation/ ～杂交 sexual hybridization

【有血有肉】 yǒuxuè-yǒuròu (of descriptions in literary works, etc.) true to life; vivid: 这个人物写得～。The portrayal of the character is lifelike./ 这篇报道～。This news report is full of vivid details.

【有言在先】 yǒu yán zài xiān make clear beforehand; forewarn: 不是～，过时不候吗？ Wasn't it clearly understood that we wouldn't wait for anyone who was late?

【有眼不识泰山】 yǒu yǎn bù shí Tàishān have eyes but fail to see Taishan Mountain; entertain an angel unawares

【有益】 yǒuyì profitable; beneficial; useful: ～的格言 good popular maxims/ 作出～的贡献 make valuable contributions/ ～于健康 good for one's health/ 做一个～于人民的人 be a person who is of value to the people/ 世界上所有国家的～的东西，我们都要学。We should learn what is useful from every country in the world.

【有意】 yǒuyì ① have a mind to; be inclined (或 disposed) to: ～帮忙 be disposed to help ② intentionally; deliberately; purposely: ～歪曲 deliberately distort/ ～刁难 make things difficult for sb. on purpose/ 这书是他～留给我们看的。He has left this book here especially for us to read.

【有意识】 yǒuyìshí consciously: ～地克服自己的缺点 make conscious efforts to overcome one's weaknesses

【有意思】 yǒu yìsi ① significant; meaningful: 他说的话很～。What he said was significant. ② interesting; enjoyable: 今天的晚会很～。The performance this evening was most enjoyable.

【有勇无谋】 yǒuyǒng-wúmóu have valour but lack strategy; be brave but not resourceful; be foolhardy

【有…有…】 yǒu…yǒu… ①〔分别用在意思相反或相对的两个词前，表示兼而有之〕: 有利有弊 have both advantages and disadvantages/ 有来有往 give-and-take; reciprocal/ 有赏有罚 mete out punishments or rewards as the case demands ②〔分别用在意思相同或相近的两个词前，表示强调〕: 有职有权 hold both the post and the power; have authority commensurate with one's post; exercise the power that goes with one's post/ 有条有理 methodical; systematic; orderly/ 有说有笑 talking and laughing/ 有凭有据 fully substantiated; well-documented/ 有名有姓 identifiable by both given name and surname — of verifiable identity

【有余】 yǒuyú ① have a surplus; have enough and to spare: 粮食自给～ have grain enough and to spare/ 绰绰～ more than enough; enough and to spare ② odd: 二十～ twenty odd

【有源】 yǒuyuán 〈电〉 active ◇ ～电路 active circuit/ ～器件 active device; active parts

【有则改之,无则加勉】 yǒu zé gǎi zhī, wú zé jiā miǎn correct mistakes if you have made any and guard against them if you have not
【有朝一日】 yǒuzhāo-yīrì some day; one day
【有志者事竟成】 yǒuzhìzhě shì jìng chéng where there's a will there's a way
【有志之士】 yǒu zhì zhī shì a person of noble aspirations; a person with lofty ideals
【有助于】 yǒuzhùyú contribute to; be conducive to; conduce to: 这次访问～增进我们两国人民的相互了解。This visit has contributed to a better understanding between the peoples of our two countries./ 体育锻炼～增强体质。Exercise is conducive to good health.

**卣** yǒu 〈考古〉 an ancient small-mouthed wine vessel

**酉** yǒu the tenth of the twelve Earthly Branches
【酉时】 yǒushí the period of the day from 5 p.m. to 7 p.m.

**莠** yǒu ① green bristlegrass ② bad people: 良～不齐。The good and the bad are intermingled.

**铕** yǒu 〈化〉 europium (Eu)

**牖** yǒu 〈书〉 window

**黝** yǒu black; dark
【黝黑】 yǒuhēi dark; swarthy: 胳膊晒得～ with sunburnt arms

## yòu

**又** yòu 〈副〉 ①〔表示重复或继续〕: 读了～读 read again and again/ 一年～一年 year after year ②〔表示几种情况或性质同时存在〕 ⓐ〔单用〕: 五四运动是反对帝国主义的运动,～是反对封建主义的运动。The May 4th Movement was at once anti-imperialist and anti-feudal. ⓑ〔连用〕: ～打～拉 strike and stroke alternately/ ～惊～喜 be pleasantly surprised/ ～便宜～好 cheap but good/ 她～想去,～不想去,拿不定主意。She couldn't make up her mind whether to go or not./ 你不能～要马儿跑得好,～要马儿不吃草。You can't expect the horse to run fast when you don't let it graze. ③〔表示意思上更进一层或在某个范围之外有所补充〕: 天很黑,～下着雨,路更难走了。On top of it being dark it rained, which made the going even tougher./ 除了拖拉机,我们～添了一台插秧机。In addition to the tractor, we have acquired a new rice transplanter. ④〔表示整数之外再加零数〕: 一～二分之一 one and a half ⑤〔表示转折〕: 我想去,～怕没时间。I'd like to go, but I'm not sure if I can find the time. ⑥〔用在否定句或反问句里,加强语气〕: 这活儿～不重,我一个人顶得下来。That's not a hard job. I'm sure I can manage it myself.
【又红又专】 yòuhóng-yòuzhuān both red and expert; both socialist-minded and vocationally proficient
【又及】 yòují postscript (PS)

**右** yòu ① the right side; the right: 靠～走 keep to the right ② west: 山～ areas west of the Taihang Mountains, specifically Shanxi Province ③ the right side as the side of precedence: 无出其～ second to none ④ the Right: ～倾观点 views of a Rightist tendency/ 思想太～ too far to the Right in thinking
【右边锋】 yòubiānfēng 〈足球〉 outside right; right wing
【右边】 yòubian the right (或 right-hand) side; the right
【右舵】 yòuduò right standard rudder; right rudder
【右锋】 yòufēng 〈篮球〉 right forward
【右后卫】 yòuhòuwèi 〈足球〉 right back
【右面】 yòumiàn the right (或 right-hand) side
【右内锋】 yòunèifēng 〈足球〉 inside right
【右派】 yòupài ① the Right; the right wing: 国民党～ the right wing of the Kuomintang; the Kuomintang right-wingers ②〈简〉(资产阶级右派) bourgeois Rightist; Rightist
【右前轮】 yòuqiánlún 〈汽车〉 off-front wheel
【右前卫】 yòuqiánwèi 〈足球〉 right halfback; right half
【右倾】 yòuqīng Right deviation: ～保守 Right-deviationist conservatism/ ～思想 Right-deviationist thinking ◇ ～机会主义 Right opportunism
【右手】 yòushǒu ① the right hand ② 见"右首"
【右首】 yòushǒu the right-hand side; the right: 他～坐着一位老大娘。An old woman was seated on his right.
【右舷】 yòuxián starboard
【右旋】 yòuxuán 〈化〉 dextrorotation ◇ ～糖酐〈药〉 dextran/ ～物质 dextrorotatory substance
【右翼】 yòuyì ①〈军〉 right wing; right flank ② the Right; the right wing ◇ ～分子 right-winger; member of the Right

**幼** yòu ① young; under age: 年～无知 young and ignorant/ ～畜 young animal; young stock ② children; the young: 扶老携～ bringing along the old and the young
【幼虫】 yòuchóng 〈动〉 larva
【幼儿】 yòu'ér child; infant ◇ ～教育 preschool education/ ～园 kindergarten; nursery school; infant school
【幼龄林】 yòulínglín 〈林〉 young growth
【幼苗】 yòumiáo seedling
【幼年】 yòunián childhood; infancy
【幼体】 yòutǐ 〈生〉 the young; larva
【幼小】 yòuxiǎo immature
【幼芽】 yòuyá young shoot; bud
【幼稚】 yòuzhì ① young ② childish; puerile; naive: ～可笑 ridiculously childish/ ～的想法 naive ideas
【幼稚病】 yòuzhìbìng ①〈心〉 infantilism ② infantile disorder: «共产主义运动中的"左派"～» *"Left-Wing" Communism, an Infantile Disorder*
【幼子】 yòuzǐ the youngest son

**有** yòu 〈书〉〔表示整数之外再加零数〕: 三十～八年 thirty-eight years
另见 yǒu

**佑** yòu help; protect; bless

**侑** yòu 〈书〉 press (sb. to eat or drink); urge

**宥** yòu 〈书〉 excuse; forgive: 尚希见～。Please accept my apologies.

**柚** yòu 〈植〉 shaddock; pomelo
另见 yóu
【柚子】 yòuzi shaddock; pomelo

**囿** yòu 〈书〉 ① animal farm; enclosure; park: 鹿～ deer farm; deer park ② limited; hampered: ～于成见 blinded by prejudice/ ～于习俗 constrained by custom/ ～于见闻 handicapped by lack of knowledge and experience

**诱** yòu ① guide; lead; induce: 循循善～ be good at giving systematic guidance; teach with patience and skill

② lure; seduce; entice: ～敌深入 lure the enemy in deep/ ～人的景色 captivating scenery
【诱虫灯】 yòuchóngdēng moth-killing lamp 又作"诱蛾灯"
【诱导】 yòudǎo guide; lead; induce: 这些问题可以～大家去思考。These are thought-provoking questions. ◇ ～反应〈化〉 induced reaction
【诱饵】 yòu'ěr bait
【诱发】 yòufā bring out (sth. potential or latent); induce; cause to happen: 把麻疹～出来 bring out the rash of measles (by administering medicine)
【诱供】 yòugòng trap a person into a confession; induce a person to make a confession: 既不～也不逼供。Neither trickery nor coercion is used to secure confessions.
【诱拐】 yòuguǎi abduct; carry off (a woman) by fraud; kidnap (a child)
【诱惑】 yòuhuò ① entice; tempt; seduce; lure: 用资产阶级生活方式～青年 tempt the young with the bourgeois way of life ② attract; allure: 窗外是一片～人的景色。The window commands a charming view.
【诱奸】 yòujiān entice into unlawful sexual intercourse; seduce
【诱骗】 yòupiàn inveigle; cajole; trap; trick
【诱杀】 yòushā trap and kill; lure to destruction: 用灯光～棉铃虫 lure bollworms to their death with lamps
【诱降】 yòuxiáng lure into surrender
【诱致】 yòuzhì lead to; cause: ～堕落 lead to one's degeneration

**蚴** yòu 〈动〉 the larva of a tapeworm or the cercaria of a schistosome: 毛～ miracidium/ 尾～ cercaria

**釉** yòu glaze: 青～瓷器 blue glazed porcelain/ ～里红 underglaze red
【釉工】 yòugōng glazer
【釉面砖】 yòumiànzhuān 〈建〉 glazed tile
【釉陶】 yòutáo glazed pottery
【釉质】 yòuzhì 〈生理〉 enamel
【釉子】 yòuzi glaze

**鼬** yòu 〈动〉 weasel: 白～ stoat
【鼬獾】 yòuhuān ferret badger

## yū

**迂** yū ① circuitous; winding; roundabout: ～道访问 make a detour to call on sb. ② clinging to outworn rules and ideas; pedantic: ～论 pedantic talk/ 这人有点～。He's a bit of a pedant.
【迂夫子】 yūfūzǐ pedant
【迂腐】 yūfǔ stubborn adherence to outworn rules and ideas; pedantry: ～的见解 pedantic ideas
【迂缓】 yūhuǎn slow in movement; dilatory
【迂回】 yūhuí ① circuitous; tortuous; roundabout: 历史的发展是曲折的，～的。History moves in zigzags and by roundabout ways./ ～曲折 full of twists and turns; circuitous; tortuous/ ～前进 advance by a roundabout route ②〈军〉 outflank: 向敌人左侧～ outflank the enemy on the left ◇ ～战术 outflanking tactics
【迂阔】 yūkuò high-sounding and impracticable: ～之论 impractical views
【迂曲】 yūqū tortuous; circuitous: ～的山路 a tortuous mountain path
【迂拙】 yūzhuō impractical and foolish

**淤** yū ① become silted up: 水渠里～了很多泥沙。The channel is almost choked with silt. ② silt: 引～肥田 fertilize the soil with silt/ 河～ sludge from a riverbed ③ stasis (of blood)
【淤斑】 yūbān 〈医〉 ecchymosis
【淤地坝】 yūdìbà 〈水〉 silt arrester
【淤点】 yūdiǎn 〈医〉 petechiae
【淤灌】 yūguàn 〈农〉 warping
【淤积】 yūjī silt up; deposit: 洪水过后，地里～了一层泥浆。When the flood subsided, it left a layer of mud in the fields.
【淤泥】 yūní silt; sludge; ooze
【淤塞】 yūsè silt up; be choked with silt: 航道～。The waterway is silted up.
【淤血】 yūxuè extravasated blood
【淤滞】 yūzhì (of the flow of a river, etc.) be retarded by silt; silt up

**瘀** yū 见"淤" yū ③

## yú

**与** yú 见"欤" yú
另见 yǔ; yù

**于** yú 〈介〉 ①〔表示时间、处所、范围等〕: 第一次世界大战爆发～一九一四年。The First World War broke out in 1914./ 运动正处～高潮。The movement is at its high tide./ 闻名～世界 famous all over the world; of world renown ②〔表示动作的方向〕: 求助～人 ask people for help ③〔用在动词后面，表示交与，付出等〕: 光荣归～中国共产党。The credit goes to the Communist Party of China. ④〔引进对象或事物的关系者〕: 忠～祖国 be loyal to one's country/ 有利～提高产量 be conducive to higher yields/ 这样～你自己不利。It won't do you any good. ⑤〔表示起点或出发点〕: 出～自愿 of one's own free will; of one's own accord/ 出～无知 out of ignorance ⑥〔表示比较〕: 人固有一死，或重～泰山，或轻～鸿毛。Though death befalls all men alike, it may be weightier than Mount Tai or lighter than a feather. ⑦〔表示被动〕: 见笑～人 be laughed at ⑧ (Yú) a surname
【于今】 yújīn ① up to the present; since: 延安一别，～十年。It is ten years since we parted in Yan'an. ② nowadays; today; now: 这城市建设得真快，～已看不出它原来的面貌了。The city has been built up really fast; it's changed beyond recognition.
【于是】 yúshì 〈连〉 thereupon; hence; consequently; as a result

**予** yú 〈书〉 I
另见 yǔ
【予取予求】 yúqǔ-yúqiú 〈书〉 take from me as sb. pleases — make unlimited demands

**余** yú ① surplus; spare; remaining: ～钱 spare money (或 cash)/ 下～部分 the remaining part; the remainder; the rest/ 落日～辉 afterglow/ 收支相抵，尚～五十元。After paying all the expenses, there is a balance of fifty *yuan*. ② more than; odd; over: 五十～年 fifty odd years/ 二百～斤 over 200 *jin* ③ beyond; after: 工作之～ after working hours; after work ④〈书〉 I ⑤ (Yú) a surname
【余波】 yúbō repercussions: 这场纠纷～未平。The trouble hasn't ended; there are still repercussions.

【余存】 yúcún balance; remainder: 核对销售数量和～数量 check the amount of sales and stock/ 取出一百元,～五十元。The balance is 50 *yuan* after the withdrawal of 100.
【余党】 yúdǎng remnants of an overthrown clique (或 gang); remaining confederates
【余地】 yúdì leeway; margin; room; latitude: 有足够的回旋～。There is plenty of room for manoeuvre./ 还有改进的～。There is still room for improvement./ 订计划要留有～。When drawing up a plan, one should leave some margin.
【余毒】 yúdú residual poison; pernicious vestige; pernicious influence: 肃清修正主义路线的～ eliminate the pernicious influence of the revisionist line
【余额】 yú'é ① vacancies yet to be filled ② remaining sum
【余割】 yúgē 〈数〉 cosecant
【余函数】 yúhánshù 〈数〉 complementary function
【余悸】 yújì lingering fear: 心有～ have a lingering fear
【余烬】 yújìn ashes; embers: 劫后～ a devastated waste of smouldering embers
【余可类推】 yú kě lèituī the rest may be inferred by analogy
【余沥】 yúlì 〈书〉 heeltap — a small share of benefit
【余粮】 yúliáng surplus grain: 把～卖给国家 sell surplus grain to the state ◇ ～户 household with grain to spare; grain-surplus household
【余年】 yúnián one's remaining years
【余孽】 yúniè remaining evil element; leftover evil; surviving supporter of an evil cause: 封建～ dregs of feudalism
【余切】 yúqiē 〈数〉 cotangent
【余缺】 yúquē surplus and deficiency: 互通有无,调剂～ each making up the other's deficiency from his own surplus
【余生】 yúshēng ① the remainder of one's life; one's remaining years ② survival (after a disaster): 虎口～ a person snatched from the jaws of death
【余剩】 yúshèng surplus; remainder
【余矢】 yúshǐ 〈数〉 coversed sine
【余数】 yúshù 〈数〉 remainder: 八减五,～为三。Take 5 from 8 and the remainder is 3.
【余威】 yúwēi remaining prestige or influence
【余味】 yúwèi agreeable aftertaste; pleasant impression: ～无穷 leave a lasting and pleasant impression or aftertaste
【余隙】 yúxì 〈机〉 clearance: 切屑～ chip clearance
【余暇】 yúxiá spare time; leisure time; leisure 又作"余闲"
【余下】 yúxià remaining: ～的同志 the other comrades
【余弦】 yúxián 〈数〉 cosine ◇ ～定律 the cosine law
【余兴】 yúxìng ① lingering interest; a wish to prolong a pleasant diversion ② entertainment after a meeting or a dinner party
【余因子】 yúyīnzi 〈数〉 complementary divisor
【余音】 yúyīn lingering sound: ～缭绕。The music lingered in the air.
【余勇可贾】 yúyǒng kě gǔ still having plenty of fight left in one; with strength yet to spare
【余裕】 yúyù enough and to spare; ample: ～的时间 time to spare
【余震】 yúzhèn 〈地〉 aftershock

**欤** yú 〈书〉〈助〉〔表示疑问、感叹〕: 可不慎～! How could one fail to exercise caution?

**盂** yú a broad-mouthed receptacle for holding liquid; jar: 痰～ spittoon

**臾** yú 见"须臾" xūyú

**鱼** yú ① fish: 两条～ two fish ② (Yú) a surname
【鱼白】 yúbái ① fish sperm; milt ② 见"鱼肚白"
【鱼鳔】 yúbiào air bladder (of fish)
【鱼叉】 yúchā fish spear; fishgig; fish fork
【鱼翅】 yúchì shark's fin
【鱼虫】 yúchóng water flea (used as fish feed)
【鱼唇】 yúchún shark's lip
【鱼刺】 yúcì fishbone: 剔掉～ bone a fish
【鱼道】 yúdào 〈水〉 fishway; fishpass
【鱼肚】 yúdǔ fish maw (as food)
【鱼肚白】 yúdùbái the whitish colour of a fish's belly — grey dawn: 东方已露出～。The sky is turning bright in the east. 或 Day is breaking.
【鱼饵】 yú'ěr (fish) bait
【鱼粉】 yúfěn fish meal
【鱼肝油】 yúgānyóu cod-liver oil
【鱼竿】 yúgān fishing rod
【鱼钩】 yúgōu fishhook
【鱼狗】 yúgǒu 〈动〉 kingfisher
【鱼贯】 yúguàn one following the other; in single file: ～而入 enter in single file; file in
【鱼胶】 yújiāo fish glue; isinglass
【鱼雷】 yúléi 〈军〉 torpedo ◇ ～发射管 torpedo tube/ ～快艇 torpedo boat
【鱼类学】 yúlèixué ichthyology
【鱼鳞】 yúlín fish scale; scale: 刮去～ scrape the scales off a fish; scale a fish
【鱼鳞坑】 yúlínkēng pits arranged like fish scales, dug on mountain slopes for holding water or planting trees; fish-scale pits
【鱼龙】 yúlóng 〈古生物〉 ichthyosaur
【鱼龙混杂】 yú-lóng hùnzá dragons and fish jumbled together — good and bad people mixed up
【鱼露】 yúlù 〈食品〉 fish sauce
【鱼卵】 yúluǎn (fish) roe
【鱼米之乡】 yú-mǐ zhī xiāng a land of fish and rice — a land of plenty
【鱼苗】 yúmiáo fry 又作"鱼花"
【鱼目混珠】 yúmù hùn zhū pass off fish eyes as pearls — pass off the sham as the genuine
【鱼漂】 yúpiāo cork on a fishing line; float
【鱼群】 yúqún shoal of fish
【鱼肉】 yúròu ① the flesh of fish ② fish and meat: 人为刀俎,我为～ be meat on sb.'s chopping block — be at sb.'s mercy ③ cut up like fish and meat — cruelly oppress: 反动官吏～百姓。The reactionary officials savagely oppressed the people.
【鱼石脂】 yúshízhī 〈药〉 ichthammol; ichthyol
【鱼水】 yú-shuǐ fish and water: ～情深 be close as fish and water/ 军民关系亲如～。The army and the people are as inseparable as fish and water.
【鱼松】 yúsōng 〈食品〉 dried fish floss
【鱼藤】 yúténg 〈植〉 trifoliate jewelvine (*Derris trifoliata*) ◇ ～精 〈农〉 derris extract/ ～酮 〈农〉 rotenone
【鱼梯】 yútī 〈水〉 fish ladder
【鱼网】 yúwǎng fishnet; fishing net
【鱼尾号】 yúwěihào boldface square brackets (【 】)
【鱼鲜】 yúxiān fish and shellfish as food; seafood
【鱼腥草】 yúxīngcǎo 〈植〉 cordate houttuynia (*Houttuynia cordata*)
【鱼汛】 yúxùn fishing season
【鱼秧】 yúyāng fingerling
【鱼鹰】 yúyīng ① osprey; fish hawk; sea eagle ② cormorant

【鱼油】 yúyóu fish oil
【鱼游釜中】 yú yóu fǔzhōng like fish swimming in a cooking pot — in imminent peril
【鱼跃】 yúyuè 〈排球〉fish dive: ～救球 diving save; diving retrieve
【鱼闸】 yúzhá 〈水〉fish lock
【鱼种】 yúzhǒng fingerling
【鱼子】 yúzǐ 〈食品〉roe ◇ ～酱 caviare

**俞** Yú a surname

**竽** yú 〈乐〉an ancient wind instrument

**谀** yú 〈书〉flatter: 阿～ flatter and toady/ ～辞 flattering words; flattery

**娱** yú ① give pleasure to; amuse: 聊以自～ just to amuse oneself ② joy; pleasure; amusement: 耳目之～ pleasures of the senses
【娱乐】 yúlè amusement; entertainment; recreation ◇ ～场所 public place of entertainment/ ～活动 recreational activities; recreation/ ～室 recreation room

**馀** yú 见"犰馀" qiúyú

**隅** yú ① corner; nook: 城～ the corner of a city wall ② outlying place; border: 海～ seaboard

**喁** yú
另见 yóng
【喁喁】 yúyú 〈书〉whisper: ～私语 talk in whispers

**萸** yú 见"茱萸" zhūyú

**渔** yú ① fishing: ～船 fishing boat/ ～村 fishing village ② take sth. one is not entitled to: ～利 reap unfair gains
【渔产】 yúchǎn aquatic products
【渔场】 yúchǎng fishing ground; fishery
【渔港】 yúgǎng fishing port (或 harbour)
【渔歌】 yúgē fisherman's song
【渔鼓】 yúgǔ ① a percussion instrument made of bamboo, used to accompany the chanting of folk tales ② chanting of folk tales to the accompaniment of such an instrument
【渔火】 yúhuǒ lights on fishing boats
【渔获量】 yúhuòliàng catch
【渔具】 yújù fishing tackle (或 gear)
【渔利】 yúlì ① reap unfair gains; profit at others' expense: 从中～ take advantage of a situation to benefit oneself; cash in on other people's efforts ② easy gains; spoils: 坐收～ effortlessly reap the spoils of a contest fought by others; profit from others' conflict
【渔猎】 yúliè fishing and hunting
【渔轮】 yúlún fishing vessel
【渔民】 yúmín fisherman; fisherfolk
【渔业】 yúyè fishery ◇ ～区 fishing zone/ ～协定 fisheries agreement/ ～资源 fishery resources

**渝** yú ① (of one's attitude or feeling) change: 始终不～ unswerving; consistent ② (Yú) another name for Chongqing

**腴** yú ① fat; plump: 丰～ plump; well rounded out ② fertile: 膏～ fertile

**愉** yú pleased; happy; joyful; cheerful: 面有不～之色 wear an annoyed expression; look displeased
【愉快】 yúkuài happy; joyful; cheerful: ～的微笑 a happy smile/ ～的事 something pleasant; a joyful event/ 心情～ be in a cheerful frame of mind/ 祝你在中国逗留期间过得～。I hope you'll have a pleasant stay in China.
【愉悦】 yúyuè joyful; cheerful; delighted

**逾** yú ① exceed; go beyond: ～额 exceed the allowed amount/ 情～骨肉 dearer than one's own flesh and blood/ ～常 out of the ordinary; unusual/ 这位老人已年～七十。The old man is over seventy. ② 〈书〉even more: 痛乃～甚。Then the pain became even more acute.
【逾期】 yúqī exceed the time limit; be overdue
【逾越】 yúyuè exceed; go beyond: ～权限 overstep one's authority/ ～界限 go beyond the limits; go out of bounds/ ～常规 depart from the usual practice/ 不可～的鸿沟 an impassable gulf; an insurmountable barrier

**揄** yú 〈书〉① draw ② raise
【揄扬】 yúyáng praise

**愚** yú ① foolish; stupid: ～不可及 couldn't be more foolish; be hopelessly stupid ② make a fool of; fool: 为人所～ be fooled (或 duped) by sb. ③ 〈谦〉I: ～见 my humble opinion
【愚笨】 yúbèn foolish; stupid; clumsy
【愚蠢】 yúchǔn stupid; foolish; silly
【愚钝】 yúdùn slow-witted; stupid
【愚公移山】 Yúgōng yí shān the Foolish Old Man removed the mountains: ～,改造中国。Transform China in the spirit of the Foolish Old Man who removed the mountains.
【愚昧】 yúmèi ignorant; benighted: ～落后 ignorant and backward/ ～无知 benighted
【愚民政策】 yúmín zhèngcè policy of keeping the people in ignorance; obscurantist policy; obscurantism
【愚弄】 yúnòng deceive; hoodwink; make a fool of; dupe
【愚顽】 yúwán ignorant and stubborn
【愚妄】 yúwàng ignorant but self-important; stupid but conceited
【愚者千虑,必有一得】 yúzhě qiān lǜ, bì yǒu yī dé even a fool occasionally hits on a good idea
【愚拙】 yúzhuō stupid and clumsy

**瑜** yú ① fine jade; gem ② lustre of gems — virtues; good points: 瑕不掩～。The defects do not obscure the virtues.

**榆** yú
【榆树】 yúshù elm
【榆叶梅】 yúyèméi flowering plum

**觎** yú 见"觊觎" jìyú

**虞** yú 〈书〉① supposition; prediction: 以备不～ be prepared for any contingency ② anxiety; worry: 兴修水利,水旱无～ build irrigation works so as to have no worries about drought or flood/ 无冻馁之～ be secure against hunger and cold ③ deceive; cheat; fool: 尔～我诈 each trying to cheat the other ④ (Yú) a surname
【虞美人】 yúměirén 〈植〉corn poppy

**舆** yú ① 〈书〉carriage; chariot: 舍～登舟 change from

a carriage to a boat ②〈书〉sedan chair: 彩～ decorated sedan chair ③ area; territory: ～地 territory ④ public; popular: ～论 public opinion

【舆论】 yúlùn public opinion: 作～准备 prepare public opinion/ 大造反革命～ whip up counterrevolutionary opinion/ 国际～ world opinion ◇ ～工具 mass media; the media/ ～界 the media; press circles

【舆情】 yúqíng public sentiment; popular feelings: 洞察～ know public sentiment well

【舆图】 yútú 〈书〉map

**畬** yú 〈书〉climb over a wall

**蝓** yú 见"蛞蝓" kuòyú

## yǔ

**与** yǔ ① give; offer; grant: ～人方便 give help to others; make things easy for others/ 信件已交～本人。The letter has been given to the person concerned. ② get along with; be on good terms with: 此人易～。He is easy to get along with. 或 He is not difficult to approach./ ～国 friendly country; allied state ③ help; support: ～人为善的批评 criticism aimed at helping those criticized ④〈介〉〔引进动作的对象〕: ～困难作斗争 strive to overcome difficulties/ ～人民为敌 be hostile to the people; set oneself against the people ⑤〈连〉and; together with: 工业～农业 industry and agriculture/ ～友人同往 go together with a friend
另见 yú; yù

【与虎谋皮】 yǔ hǔ móu pí ask a tiger for its skin — request sb. (usu. an evil person) to act against his own interests

【与其】 yǔqí 〈连〉〔比较两件事的利害得失而决定取舍的时候，用在放弃的一面，后常用"不如"或"毋宁"呼应〕: 你～坐车，不如坐船。It's better for you to go by boat than by train./ ～说是粗心大意，不如说是不负责任。It's not so much carelessness as irresponsibility.

【与日俱增】 yǔ rì jù zēng grow with each passing day; be steadily on the increase

【与世长辞】 yǔ shì chángcí depart from the world for ever; pass away

【与世无争】 yǔ shì wú zhēng hold oneself aloof from the world; stand aloof from worldly success

【与众不同】 yǔ zhòng bù tóng out of the ordinary

**予** yǔ give; grant; bestow: 授～奖状 award sb. a citation of merit/ 免～处分 exempt sb. from punishment/ ～以表扬 commend sb./ ～人口实 give people a handle
另见 yú

**宇** yǔ ① eaves ② house: 庙～ temple ③ space; universe; world: ～内 in the world

【宇称】 yǔchēng 〈物〉parity ◇ ～不守恒 parity nonconservation/ ～守恒 parity conservation

【宇航】 yǔháng 〈简〉(宇宙航行) astronavigation; space navigation

【宇宙】 yǔzhòu universe; cosmos
◇ ～尘 〈天〉cosmic dust/ ～飞船 spaceship; spacecraft/ ～飞行 space flight/ ～飞行员 astronaut; spaceman; cosmonaut/ ～观 world view; world outlook/ ～航行学 astronautics/ ～火箭 space rocket/ ～空间 cosmic (或 outer) space/ ～线 〈物〉cosmic ray/ ～站 space station

【宇宙航行】 yǔzhòu hángxíng astronavigation; space navigation ◇ ～员 astronaut; spaceman; cosmonaut

【宇宙速度】 yǔzhòu sùdù 〈宇航〉cosmic (或 astronautical) velocity: 第一～ first cosmic velocity; circular (或 orbital) velocity/ 第二～ second cosmic velocity

**屿** yǔ small island; islet: 岛～ islands and islets; islands

**羽** yǔ ① feather; plume ②〈乐〉a note of the ancient Chinese five-tone scale, corresponding to 6 in numbered musical notation

【羽冠】 yǔguān crest (of a bird)

【羽化】 yǔhuà ① ascend to heaven and become immortal ②〈婉〉(of a Taoist) die ③〈动〉emergence; eclosion

【羽毛】 yǔmáo feather; plume: 美丽的～ beautiful plumage/ ～丰满 become full-fledged ◇ ～画 feather patchwork; feather picture

【羽毛球】 yǔmáoqiú ① badminton ② shuttlecock

【羽毛扇】 yǔmáoshàn feather fan: 摇～的 the man with a feather fan — the mastermind behind an intrigue

【羽毛未丰】 yǔmáo wèi fēng unfledged; young and immature

【羽纱】 yǔshā camlet

【羽翼】 yǔyì ① wing ② assistant

**伛** yǔ

【伛偻】 yǔlǚ 〈书〉with one's back bent

**雨** yǔ rain: 大～ a heavy rain/ 毛毛～ drizzle/ 大～倾盆。The rain is pelting down.

【雨暴】 yǔbào 〈气〉rainstorm

【雨布】 yǔbù waterproof cloth; waterproof

【雨层云】 yǔcéngyún 〈气〉nimbostratus

【雨点】 yǔdiǎn raindrop

【雨过天晴】 yǔ guò tiān qíng the sun shines again after the rain

【雨后春笋】 yǔ hòu chūnsǔn (spring up like) bamboo shoots after a spring rain: 社办工业象～一样蓬勃发展起来。Commune-run industries have sprung up like mushrooms.

【雨季】 yǔjì rainy season

【雨具】 yǔjù rain gear (i.e. umbrella, raincoat, etc.)

【雨量】 yǔliàng 〈气〉rainfall
◇ ～计 rain gauge/ ～强度 rainfall density/ ～站 precipitation station; rainfall station

【雨露】 yǔlù ① rain and dew ② favour; grace; bounty

【雨帽】 yǔmào ① rain cap ② hood

【雨棚】 yǔpéng 〈建〉canopy

【雨前】 yǔqián a kind of green tea, picked before Grain Rain (about mid-April)

【雨情】 yǔqíng rainfall (in a given area)

【雨区】 yǔqū rain area; rain field

【雨伞】 yǔsǎn umbrella

【雨水】 yǔshuǐ ① rainwater; rainfall; rain: ～足 adequate rainfall/ ～调和。The rainfall is just right. ② (Yǔshuǐ) Rain Water (2nd solar term) ◇ ～管 〈建〉downspout; downpipe; rain pipe

【雨蛙】 yǔwā 〈动〉tree toad

【雨鞋】 yǔxié rubber boots; galoshes; rubbers

【雨燕】 yǔyàn 〈动〉swift

【雨衣】 yǔyī raincoat; waterproof

【雨意】 yǔyì signs of approaching rain: 颇有～。It looks like rain.

【雨云】 yǔyún 〈气〉nimbus

**语** yǔ ① language; tongue; words: 汉～ the Chinese language/ 本族～ mother tongue/ 甜言蜜～ honeyed words

② speak; say: 低～ speak in a low voice; whisper/ 不言不～ not say a word; keep silent ③ set phrase; proverb; saying: ～云,"将欲取之，必先与之。" As the saying goes, "Give in order to take." ④ nonlinguistic means of communicating ideas; sign; signal: 旗～ flagsignal; semaphore/ 手～ dactylology; sign language
另见 yù

【语病】 yǔbìng faulty wording or formulation
【语词】 yǔcí words and phrases
【语调】 yǔdiào 〈语〉 intonation
【语法】 yǔfǎ grammar
【语汇】 yǔhuì vocabulary
【语句】 yǔjù sentence
【语录】 yǔlù recorded utterance; quotation: 毛主席～ quotations from Chairman Mao ◇ ～板 board on which a quotation is written or painted/ ～牌 placard bearing a quotation
【语气】 yǔqì ① tone; manner of speaking: ～友好 a friendly tone/ 用婉转的～说 speak in a tactful manner/ 听他的～，这事大概有点不妙。From the way he spoke about the matter, I gathered something had gone wrong. ② 〈语〉 mood: 祈使～ imperative mood
【语态】 yǔtài 〈语〉 voice: 主动(被动)～ active (passive) voice
【语体】 yǔtǐ 〈语〉 type of writing; style: 口语～ colloquialism/ 科学～ scientific style of writing
【语体文】 yǔtǐwén prose written in the vernacular
【语文】 yǔwén ① Chinese (as a subject of study or a means of communication): 他的～程度怎么样？How good is his Chinese? ② 〈简〉(语言和文学) language and literature
【语无伦次】 yǔ wú lúncì speak incoherently
【语系】 yǔxì 〈语〉 family of languages; language family
【语序】 yǔxù 〈语〉 word order
【语焉不详】 yǔ yān bù xiáng not speak in detail; not elaborate
【语言】 yǔyán language: ～隔阂 language barrier/ ～与文字 spoken and written language
◇ ～规范化 standardization of speech/ ～科学 linguistic science/ ～学 linguistics; philology/ ～学家 linguist; philologist
【语义学】 yǔyìxué semantics
【语音】 yǔyīn ① speech sounds ② pronunciation: 她的～好。She has good pronunciation.
◇ ～课 phonetics class/ ～学 phonetics/ ～学家 phonetician
【语源学】 yǔyuánxué etymology
【语重心长】 yǔzhòng-xīncháng sincere words and earnest wishes: ～的劝告 earnest advice
【语助词】 yǔzhùcí 〈语〉 an auxiliary word that indicates mood 参见"助词" zhùcí 又作"语气助词"
【语族】 yǔzú branch: 印欧语系日耳曼～ the Germanic branch of the Indo-European language family

**禹** Yǔ ① the reputed founder of the Xia Dynasty (c. 21st — 16th century B.C.) ② a surname

**圄** yǔ 见"囹圄" língyǔ

**圉** yǔ 〈书〉 horse stable

**庾** yǔ 〈书〉 an enclosure for storing grain

**瘐** yǔ

【瘐死】 yǔsǐ 〈书〉 (of a prisoner) die of hunger or disease

**龉** yǔ 见"龃龉" jǔyǔ

**窳** yǔ 〈书〉 corrupt; bad: ～败 corrupt/ ～劣 of inferior quality

## yù

**与** yù take part in; participate in
另见 yú; yǔ

【与会】 yùhuì participate in a conference ◇ ～国 countries attending a conference; participating countries/ ～者 conferee; participant
【与闻】 yùwén have a participant's knowledge of; be let into (a secret, etc.): ～其事 have a participant's knowledge of a matter; be in the know/ 不能让这样的人～国家机密。We mustn't allow such a person access to confidential matters of the state.

**玉** yù ① jade ② 〈书〉 (of a person, esp. a woman) pure; fair; handsome; beautiful: 亭亭～立 fair, slim and graceful ③ 〈敬〉 your: ～照 your photograph

【玉版宣】 yùbǎnxuān 〈纸〉 strong white *Xuan* paper
【玉帛】 yùbó 〈书〉 jade objects and silk fabrics, used as state gifts in ancient China: 化干戈为～ turn hostility into friendship
【玉成】 yùchéng 〈敬〉 kindly help secure the success of sth.: 深望～此事。It is earnestly hoped that you will accomplish the matter.
【玉带】 yùdài jade belt
【玉雕】 yùdiāo jade carving; jade sculpture ◇ ～工人 jade carver
【玉皇大帝】 Yùhuáng Dàdì the Jade Emperor (the Supreme Deity of Taoism)
【玉茭】 yùjiāo 〈方〉 maize; corn
【玉洁冰清】 yùjié-bīngqīng as pure as jade and as clean as ice; pure and noble
【玉筋鱼】 yùjīnyú sand lance
【玉兰】 yùlán 〈植〉 yulan magnolia (*Magnolia denudata*)
【玉兰片】 yùlánpiàn 〈食品〉 dried slices of tender bamboo shoots
【玉米】 yùmǐ ① maize; Indian corn; corn ② ear of maize (或 corn)
◇ ～大斑病 〈农〉 leaf blight of corn/ ～黑粉病 〈农〉 corn smut/ ～花 popcorn/ ～粒 kernel of corn; grain of corn/ ～面 maize flour; cornmeal/ ～螟 corn borer/ ～脱粒机 maize sheller/ ～芯 corncob; cob/ ～粥 maize gruel
【玉器】 yùqì jade article; jade object; jadeware ◇ ～工厂 jade workshop
【玉色】 yùsè jade green; light bluish green
【玉石】 yùshí jade
【玉石俱焚】 yù-shí jù fén jade and stone burned together — destruction of good and bad alike
【玉蜀黍】 yùshǔshǔ maize; corn
【玉碎】 yùsuì 见"宁为～，不为瓦全" nìng wéi yù suì, bù wéi wǎ quán
【玉兔】 yùtù 〈书〉 the Jade Hare — the moon
【玉玺】 yùxǐ imperial jade seal
【玉音】 yùyīn 〔旧时书信用语〕 your letter
【玉宇】 yùyǔ ① residence of the immortals ② the universe
【玉簪】 yùzān ① jade hairpin ② 〈植〉 fragrant plantain lily (*Hosta plantaginea*)

**驭** yù drive (a carriage)

【驭手】 yùshǒu soldier in charge of pack animals; driver of a military pack train: 炮车～ gun-carriage driver

**芋** yù ①〈植〉taro ②〈植〉tuber crops: 洋～ potato/ 山～ sweet potato

【芋艿】 yùnǎi 〈植〉 taro

【芋头】 yùtou 〈植〉 ① taro ②〈方〉 sweet potato

**吁** yù appeal; plead: 呼～ appeal/ ～请 implore; plead; petition

另见 xū

**妪** yù 〈书〉 old woman

**育** yù ① give birth to: 生儿～女 give birth to children; have children ② rear; raise; bring up: ～秧 raise rice seedlings ③ educate: 德～ moral education

另见 yō

【育成品种】 yùchéng pǐnzhǒng 〈农〉 improved variety

【育雏】 yùchú 〈牧〉 brood ◇ ～器 brooder

【育儿袋】 yù'érdài 〈动〉 brood pouch; marsupium

【育肥】 yùféi 〈牧〉 fatten

【育苗】 yùmiáo 〈农〉 grow (或 raise) seedlings ◇ ～区 nursery garden

【育性】 yùxìng 〈农〉 fertility

【育秧】 yùyāng raise rice seedlings

【育婴堂】 yùyīngtáng 〈旧〉 foundling hospital

【育种】 yùzhǒng 〈农〉 breeding: 杂交～ crossbreeding/ 作物～ crop breeding ◇ ～家 breeder

**郁** yù ① strongly fragrant: 馥～ full of fragrance ② luxuriant; lush ③ gloomy; depressed: 忧～ sad and depressed ④ (Yù) a surname

【郁闭】 yùbì 〈林〉 closing: 林冠～ canopy closure ◇ ～度 canopy density

【郁积】 yùjī pent-up: ～的愤怒 pent-up fury/ 仇恨～在心头 hatred smouldering in one's bosom

【郁结】 yùjié 见"郁积"

【郁金】 yùjīn 〈中药〉 the root-tuber of aromatic turmeric (*Curcuma aromatica*)

【郁金香】 yùjīnxiāng 〈植〉 tulip

【郁闷】 yùmèn gloomy; depressed: ～之感 a feeling of oppression

【郁血】 yùxuè 〈医〉 stagnation of the blood; venous stasis

【郁郁】 yùyù 〈书〉 ① lush; luxuriant: 苍松翠柏～葱葱。Green and luxuriant are the pines and cypresses. ② gloomy; melancholy; depressed: ～不乐 depressed; melancholy; joyless ③ strongly fragrant ④ elegant; refined: 文采～ displaying literary elegance

**语** yù 〈书〉 tell; inform: 不以～人 not to be divulged

另见 yǔ

**昱** yù 〈书〉 ① sunlight; sunshine ② shine; illuminate

**狱** yù ① prison; jail: 入～ be imprisoned; be put in prison/ 越～ escape from prison ② lawsuit; case: 断～ hear and pass judgment on a case

【狱吏】 yùlì 〈旧〉 warder; prison officer; jailer

【狱卒】 yùzú 〈旧〉 prison guard; turnkey

**浴** yù bath; bathe: 淋～ shower bath/ 日光～ sunbath/ 海水～ sea bathing

【浴场】 yùchǎng outdoor bathing place: 海滨～ bathing beach

【浴池】 yùchí ① common bathing pool (in a public bathhouse) ② public bathhouse; public baths

【浴巾】 yùjīn bath towel

【浴盆】 yùpén bathtub

【浴室】 yùshì bathroom; shower room

【浴血】 yùxuè bathed in blood; bloody: ～奋战 fight a bloody battle

【浴衣】 yùyī bathrobe

**峪** yù valley; ravine

**预** yù in advance; beforehand: ～付 pay in advance/ ～祝成功 wish sb. success/ 勿谓言之不～。Do not say that we haven't warned you.

【预报】 yùbào forecast: 天气～ weather forecast/ 地震～ earthquake forecast; earthquake prediction

【预备】 yùbèi prepare; get ready: ～功课 prepare lessons/ 你们～好了吗？Are you all ready?/ 各就位，～，跑！Ready! Set! Go! 或 On your mark! Get set! Go!

◇ ～党员 probationary Party member/ ～队 reserve force; reserves/ ～金 reserve fund/ ～期 probationary period/ ～役 〈军〉 reserve duty (或 service)

【预卜】 yùbǔ augur; foretell: ～吉凶 try to predict good or bad fortune/ 结果如何尚难～。The result is hard to foretell.

【预测】 yùcè calculate; forecast: ～日蚀 calculate an eclipse of the sun/ ～台风 detect a typhoon

【预产期】 yùchǎnqī 〈医〉 expected date of childbirth

【预处理】 yùchǔlǐ pretreatment

【预订】 yùdìng subscribe; book; place an order: ～杂志 subscribe to a magazine/ ～火车票 book a train ticket/ ～一本书 place an order for a book/ 座位已经～一空。All seats are booked.

【预定】 yùdìng fix in advance; predetermine; schedule: 在～时间 at the fixed time/ 在～地点着陆 make a landing in a predetermined area/ 这项工程～在明年完成。The project is scheduled for completion next year.

【预断】 yùduàn prejudge

【预防】 yùfáng prevent; take precautions against; guard against: 贯彻以～为主的医疗方针 carry out the policy of putting prevention first in medical work/ 采取～措施 take preventive measures/ ～火灾 take precautions against fire ◇ ～注射 preventive (或 prophylactic) inoculation

【预感】 yùgǎn ① premonition; presentiment: 不祥的～ an ominous presentiment ② have a premonition

【预告】 yùgào ① announce in advance; herald ② advance notice: 新书～ notice on forthcoming books; books in preparation

【预购】 yùgòu purchase in advance ◇ ～合同 forward purchasing contract

【预后】 yùhòu 〈医〉 prognosis: ～良好 favourable prognosis

【预计】 yùjì calculate in advance; estimate: 大楼～十个月可以完工。It is estimated that the building will be completed in ten months.

◇ ～产量 estimated output/ ～到达时间 〈航海〉 estimated time of arrival (E.T.A.)/ ～数据 predicted data; scheduled data

【预见】 yùjiàn ① foresee; predict: ～不到的困难 unforeseen difficulties/ 这是可以～到的。This can be predicted. ② foresight; prevision: 英明的～ brilliant foresight ◇ ～性 foresight; farsightedness

【预科】 yùkē preparatory course (in a college)

【预料】 yùliào expect; predict; anticipate: 和我们的～相反 contrary to our expectations/ 今年的收成比人们～的要好得多。This year's harvest was much better than expected

(或 anticipated).

【预谋】 yùmóu premeditate; plan beforehand ◇ ～杀人 premeditated murder; murder with malice prepense

【预期】 yùqī expect; anticipate: 达到～的效果 achieve the desired (或 hoped-for) results/ 结果和～的相反。The results are contrary to expectations.

【预热】 yùrè 〈机〉 preheat

【预赛】 yùsài 〈体〉 preliminary contest; preliminary heats; preliminary; trial match

【预示】 yùshì betoken; indicate; presage; forebode: 灿烂的晚霞～明天又是好天气。The splendid evening glow in the sky means another fine day tomorrow.

【预算】 yùsuàn budget
◇ ～赤字 budget deficit/ ～结余 budget surplus/ ～年度 budget year/ ～收入 budgetary receipts/ ～项目 budget items

【预习】 yùxí (of students) prepare lessons before class

【预先】 yùxiān in advance; beforehand: ～通知 notify in advance/ ～声明 state explicitly beforehand/ ～警告 forewarn/ ～感谢 thank sb. in anticipation

【预想】 yùxiǎng anticipate; expect: 得到～的结果 obtain the anticipated results

【预言】 yùyán ① prophesy; predict; foretell ② prophecy; prediction ◇ ～家 prophet

【预演】 yùyǎn preview (of a performance or motion picture)

【预应力】 yùyìnglì 〈物〉 prestressing force
◇ ～构件 prestressed component/ ～混凝土 prestressed concrete

【预约】 yùyuē make an appointment: ～挂号 have an appointment with a doctor

【预展】 yùzhǎn preview (of an exhibition)

【预兆】 yùzhào omen; presage; sign; harbinger: 吉祥的～ an auspicious omen/ 胜利的～ a harbinger of victory/ 下雨的～ a sign of coming rain

【预制】 yùzhì prefabricate ◇ ～构件 〈建〉 prefabricated components/ ～装配式房屋 prefabricated house; prefab

**欲** yù ① desire; longing; wish: 食～ a desire for food; appetite/ 求知～ thirst for knowledge ② wish; want; desire: 畅所～言 pour out all that one wishes to say; speak one's mind freely/ 为所～为 do whatever one likes; act wilfully ③ about to; just going to; on the point of: 摇摇～坠 on the verge of collapse; crumbling; tottering

【欲罢不能】 yù bà bùnéng be unable to stop even though one wants to; cannot help carrying on

【欲盖弥彰】 yù gài mí zhāng the more one tries to hide, the more one is exposed; try to hide a mistake, only to make it more conspicuous

【欲壑难填】 yùhè nán tián greed is like a valley that can never be filled; avarice knows no bounds

【欲加之罪,何患无词】 yù jiā zhī zuì, hé huàn wú cí if you are out to condemn sb., you can always trump up a charge

【欲擒故纵】 yù qín gù zòng leave sb. at large the better to apprehend him; allow sb. more latitude first to keep a tighter rein on him afterwards

【欲取姑与】 yù qǔ gū yǔ give in order to take; make concessions for the sake of future gains

【欲速则不达】 yù sù zé bù dá more haste, less speed; haste makes waste

【欲望】 yùwàng desire; wish; lust

**域** yù land within certain boundaries; territory; region: 领～ territory; domain; field; realm/ 异～ foreign lands/ 绝～ inaccessible remote areas

**谕** yù 〈书〉〔旧时用于上级对下级或长辈对晚辈〕instruct; tell: 面～ tell sb. in person/ 上～ imperial edict/ 顷奉手～。I have just received your instructions.

**尉** yù
另见 wèi

【尉迟】 Yùchí a surname

**阈** yù ①〈书〉 threshold; doorsill ②〈生理〉 threshold: 痛～ pain threshold/ 视～ visual threshold

**寓** yù ① reside; live: 暂～友人处 be staying with a friend ② residence; abode: 公～ apartment house; block of flats ③ imply; contain: 这个故事～有深意。This story contains a profound lesson. 或 The moral of the story is profound./ 矛盾的普遍性即～于矛盾的特殊性之中。 It is precisely in the particularity of contradiction that the universality of contradiction resides.

【寓公】 yùgōng ① formerly, a government official residing away from home (usu. in a big city) ② bureaucrats or rich people in exile

【寓居】 yùjū make one's home in (a place other than one's native place): 他晚年～上海。He made Shanghai his home in his old age.

【寓目】 yùmù 〈书〉 look over

【寓所】 yùsuǒ residence; abode; dwelling place

【寓言】 yùyán fable; allegory; parable

【寓意】 yùyì implied meaning; moral; message; import: ～深刻 be pregnant with meaning

**裕** yù ① abundant; plentiful: 富～ abundant; affluent; well-to-do; well-off ②〈书〉 make (a country or people) rich

【裕固族】 Yùgùzú the Yugur (Yuku) nationality, living in Gansu

【裕如】 yùrú effortlessly; with ease: 应付～ handle with ease

**遇** yù ① meet: 不期而～ meet by chance; chance encounter/ ～雨 be caught in a rain ② treat; receive: 优～ treat sb. with special consideration ③ chance; opportunity: 机～ favourable circumstances; opportunity

【遇刺】 yùcì be attacked by an assassin: ～身死 be assassinated

【遇到】 yùdào run into; encounter; come across: 在路上～一个老同学 run into an old schoolmate on the way/ ～意外的问题 come across unforeseen problems/ ～埋伏 run into an ambush

【遇害】 yùhài be murdered

【遇见】 yùjiàn meet; come across: ～一位朋友 meet a friend

【遇救】 yùjiù be rescued; be saved

【遇难】 yùnàn ① die (或 be killed) in an accident ② be murdered

【遇事】 yùshì when anything crops (或 comes) up: ～不慌 be unruffled whatever happens/ ～和群众商量 consult with the masses when matters arise

【遇事生风】 yù shì shēng fēng sow discord whenever possible

【遇险】 yùxiǎn meet with a mishap; be in danger; be in distress: ～船只 ship in distress ◇ ～信号 distress signal; SOS

**喻** yù ① explain; make clear; inform: 晓～ give explicit instructions; explain clearly; tell explicitly/ ～之以理 reason with sb.; try to make sb. see reason ② understand;

know: 家～户晓 known to every household; widely known ③ analogy: 比～ analogy; metaphor ④ (Yù) a surname

**御** yù ① drive (a carriage): ～者 carriage driver ② of an emperor; imperial: ～花园 imperial garden/ 告～状 bring an accusation against sb. before the emperor/ ～林军 palace guards ③ resist; keep out; ward off: ～敌 resist the enemy/ ～寒 keep out the cold

【御夫座】 yùfūzuò 〈天〉 Auriga

【御侮】 yùwǔ resist foreign aggression

【御用】 yùyòng ① for the use of an emperor ② serve as a tool; be in the pay of: 资产阶级的～政党 a political party in the pay of the bourgeoisie ◇ ～报刊 hired (或 controlled, paid) press/ ～文人 hired scribbler; hack writer

**鸲** yù 见"鸲鹆" qúyù

**誉** yù ① reputation; fame: ～满全球 of world renown; famed the world over ② praise; eulogize: 毁～参半 be as much censured as praised; get both praise and censure

**蓣** yù 见"薯蓣" shǔyù

**煜** yù 〈书〉 illuminate; shine

**愈** yù ① heal; recover; become well: 病～ recover from an illness/ 伤口尚未痊～。The wound is not yet healed. ② better: 彼～于此。That one is better than this one. ③〔叠用,表示程度随着条件的发展而发展〕: ～多～好 the more the better/ 山路～走～陡。The mountain path becomes steeper and steeper as you go up./ 真理～辩～明。Truth becomes clearer through debate./ 人民武装力量～战～强。The people's armed forces grow stronger and stronger through fighting./ 毛主席的书我们～读心里～亮堂。The more we read Chairman Mao's works, the clearer our minds become.

【愈合】 yùhé 〈医〉 heal: 伤口很快～了。The wound healed quickly.

【愈加】 yùjiā all the more; even more; further: 变得～模糊 become even more indistinct

**蜮** yù 见"鬼蜮" guǐyù

**豫** yù 〈书〉 ① pleased: 面有不～之色 look displeased ② comfort: 逸～亡身。Overindulgence leads to ruin. ③ (Yù) another name for Henan Province: ～剧 Henan opera

**鹬** yù sandpiper; snipe

【鹬蚌相争,渔人得利】 yù bàng xiāng zhēng, yúrén dé lì when the snipe and the clam grapple, the fisherman profits — it's the third party that benefits from the tussle

【鹬鸵】 yùtuó 〈动〉 kiwi

**鬻** yù 〈书〉 sell; vend: ～文为生 make a living with one's pen/ 卖官～爵 sell official posts and titles/ 卖儿～女 sell one's children

## yuān

**鸢** yuān 〈动〉 kite

【鸢尾】 yuānwěi 〈植〉 iris

**冤** yuān ① wrong; injustice: 不白之～ unrighted wrong; unredressed injustice/ ～有头,债有主。Every injustice has its perpetrator, every debt has its debtor. ② feeling of bitterness; hatred; enmity: ～仇 rancour; enmity ③ 〈方〉 kid; fool; pull sb.'s leg: 我不～你。I'm not kidding. ④ bad luck; loss; disadvantage: 白跑一趟,真～! What bad luck, nothing came of my trip.

【冤仇】 yuānchóu rancour; enmity

【冤家】 yuānjiā ① enemy; foe: ～对头 opponent and foe ②〔多用于旧时戏曲民歌中〕one's destined love; sweetheart; lover: 不是～不聚头。Enemies and lovers are destined to meet.

【冤家路窄】 yuānjiā lù zhǎi enemies are bound to meet on a narrow road — one can't avoid one's enemy (much as one wants to)

【冤屈】 yuānqū ① wrong; treat unjustly ② wrongful treatment; injustice: 受～ be wronged; suffer an injustice

【冤头】 yuāntou 〈方〉 enemy; foe: 老百姓的直接～ the mortal and immediate enemies of the people

【冤枉】 yuānwang ① wrong; treat unjustly: ～好人 wrong an innocent person ② not worthwhile; not repaying the effort: 在这件小事上,花那么多时间,真～。It wasn't worthwhile to spend so much time on such a trifle./ 花～钱 waste money; not get one's money's worth/ 走～路 go the long way

【冤狱】 yuānyù an unjust charge or verdict; a miscarriage of justice; frame-up: 平反～ reverse an unjust verdict

**鸳** yuān

【鸳鸯】 yuānyang ① mandarin duck ② an affectionate couple

**渊** yuān ① deep pool: 深～ a deep pool; abyss ② deep: ～泉 a deep spring

【渊博】 yuānbó broad and profound; erudite: 学识～ erudite; learned

【渊深】 yuānshēn profound; deep; erudite

【渊薮】 yuānsǒu a gathering place of fish or beasts; den; haunt: 盗贼的～ a den (或 haunt) of bandits and thieves/ 罪恶的～ a hotbed (或 breeding ground) of crime; a sink of iniquity

【渊源】 yuānyuán origin; source: 历史～ historical origins

## yuán

**元** yuán ① first; primary: ～月 the first month of the year; January ② chief; principal: ～戎 〈书〉 supreme commander ③ basic; fundamental: ～素 element ④ unit; component: 第一单～ unit one/ 一～化领导 unified (或 centralized) leadership ⑤ 见"圆" yuán⑤⑥ ⑥ (Yuán) the Yuan Dynasty (1271-1368) ⑦ (Yuán) a surname

【元宝】 yuánbǎo a shoe-shaped gold or silver ingot used as money in feudal China ◇ ～铁 〈机〉 V-block

【元旦】 Yuándàn New Year's Day

【元古代】 Yuángǔdài 〈地〉 the Proterozoic Era

【元件】 yuánjiàn element; component; cell: 传输～ transfer element/ 电光～ electrooptic cell/ 电路～ circuit component/ 敏感～ sensor

【元老】 yuánlǎo senior statesman; founding member (of a political organization, etc.)

【元谋人】 Yuánmóurén Yuanmou Man, whose fossil remains, about 1,700,000 years old, were found in Yuanmou, Yunnan Province, in 1965

【元年】 yuánnián the first year of an era or the reign of an emperor

【元配】 yuánpèi 〈旧〉first wife
【元气】 yuánqì vitality; vigour: ～旺盛 full of vitality/ 大伤～ undermine one's constitution; sap one's vitality/ 恢复～ regain one's strength (或 health, vigour)
【元青】 yuánqīng black: ～布 black cloth
【元曲】 yuánqǔ a type of verse popular in the Yuan Dynasty (1271—1368), including *zaju* (杂剧) and *sanqu* (散曲), sometimes referring to *zaju* only 参见"杂剧" zájù; "散曲" sǎnqǔ
【元戎】 yuánróng 〈书〉 supreme commander
【元首】 yuánshǒu head of state
【元帅】 yuánshuài ① marshal; (英陆军) Field Marshal; (英空军) Marshal of the Royal Air Force; (英海军) Admiral of the Fleet ② supreme commander (in ancient times)
【元素】 yuánsù ① element ②〈数〉〈化〉element: 稀有～ rare element ◇ ～分析〈化〉ultimate analysis/ ～周期表 periodic table of elements
【元宵】 yuánxiāo ① the night of the 15th of the 1st lunar month ② sweet dumplings made of glutinous rice flour (for the Lantern Festival) ◇ ～节 the Lantern Festival (15th of the 1st lunar month)
【元凶】 yuánxiōng prime culprit; arch-criminal
【元勋】 yuánxūn a man of great merit; founding father: 革命～ a veteran revolutionary of great distinction/ 开国～ founders of a state
【元夜】 yuányè 〈书〉见"元宵"①
【元音】 yuányīn 〈语〉vowel
【元鱼】 yuányú soft-shelled turtle

## 芫 yuán
另见 yán
【芫花】 yuánhuā lilac daphne

## 园 yuán
① an area of land for growing plants: 果～ orchard/ 葡萄～ vineyard ② a place for public recreation: 动物～ zoological garden; zoo/ 植物～ botanical garden
【园地】 yuándì ① garden plot ② field; scope: 扩大文学创作的～ broaden the scope of literary creation/ 为科学家开辟广阔的～ open up vast fields of activity for scientists
【园丁】 yuándīng gardener
【园林】 yuánlín gardens; park
【园圃】 yuánpǔ garden; ground used for growing vegetables, flowers or fruit
【园田】 yuántián vegetable garden: 耕作～化 garden-style cultivation of farmland
【园艺】 yuányì horticulture; gardening ◇ ～家 horticulturist/ ～学 horticulture; gardening

## 员 yuán
① a person engaged in some field of activity: 人～ personnel/ 炊事～ cook/ 售货～ shop assistant/ 指挥～ commander ② member: 党～ Party member/ 工会会～ member of a trade union/ 人民公社社～ commune member ③〈量〉〔用于武将〕: 一～大将 an able general
【员额】 yuán'é specified number of personnel
【员工】 yuángōng staff; personnel: 师生～ teachers, students, administrative personnel and workers

## 垣 yuán
〈书〉wall: 城～ city wall

## 爰 yuán
〈书〉① whence; from what place ② hence; thereupon; consequently

## 原 yuán
① primary; original; former: ～计划 original plan/ ～义 original (或 primary) meaning/ ～单位 the organization (或 unit) one formerly belonged to/ ～职 former post/ ～班人马 the old cast; the former staff ② unprocessed; raw: ～矿石 raw ore/ ～油 crude oil ③ excuse; pardon: 情有可～ excusable; pardonable ④ level, open country; plain: 华北平～ the North China Plain ⑤ (Yuán) a surname
【原版】 yuánbǎn original edition (of a book, etc.)
【原本】 yuánběn ① original manuscript; master copy ② the original (from which a translation is made) ③ originally; formerly: 他～住在山东。Originally he lived in Shandong Province.
【原材料】 yuán-cáiliào raw and processed materials: ～消耗下降 a drop in consumption of raw and other materials ◇ ～工业 raw and semifinished materials industries
【原肠】 yuáncháng 〈动〉primitive gut; archenteron
【原虫】 yuánchóng 〈动〉protozoon
【原动力】 yuándònglì motive power (或 force); motivity
【原封】 yuánfēng with the seal unbroken; intact: ～退回 return to the sender a parcel or letter unopened/ ～不动 be left intact
【原稿】 yuángǎo original manuscript; master copy
【原告】 yuángào 〈法〉(民事) plaintiff; (刑事) prosecutor
【原级】 yuánjí 〈语〉positive degree
【原籍】 yuánjí ancestral home: 他～广东。His ancestral home is in Guangdong Province.
【原来】 yuánlái ① original; former: ～的想法 original idea/ 他还住在～的地方。He still lives in the same place. ②〔表示发现真实情况〕: ～如此! So that's how it is! 或 Oh, I see./ ～是你呀! So it's you./ 这～是个骗局。It turned out to be a fraud.
【原理】 yuánlǐ principle; tenet: 根本的～ a cardinal principle/ 数学的基本～ fundamentals of mathematics/ 马克思主义的基本～是永远不会过时的。The fundamental tenets of Marxism-Leninism will never become outdated.
【原粮】 yuánliáng unprocessed food grains
【原谅】 yuánliàng excuse; forgive; pardon: 我来晚了,请～。Please excuse me for being late.
【原料】 yuánliào raw material
【原煤】 yuánméi raw coal
【原棉】 yuánmián 〈纺〉raw cotton ◇ ～等级 grades of raw cotton
【原木】 yuánmù log
【原配】 yuánpèi 〈旧〉first wife
【原色】 yuánsè 〈物〉primary colours
【原审】 yuánshěn 〈法〉first trial
【原生动物】 yuánshēng dòngwù protozoon ◇ ～学 protozoology
【原生矿物】 yuánshēng kuàngwù primary mineral
【原生生物】 yuánshēng shēngwù protist
【原生植物】 yuánshēng zhíwù protophyte
【原生质】 yuánshēngzhì 〈生〉protoplasm
【原始】 yuánshǐ ① original; firsthand: ～记录 original record/ ～资料 firsthand information (或 data); source material ② primeval; primitive
◇ ～公社 primitive commune/ ～积累 primitive accumulation/ ～群 primitive horde/ ～人 primitive man/ ～森林 primeval forest; virgin forest/ ～社会 primitive society
【原索动物】 yuánsuǒ dòngwù protochordate; prochordate
【原委】 yuánwěi how a thing happened from beginning to end; the whole story; all the details: 不明～,妄加评论 make presumptuous comments out of ignorance
【原文】 yuánwén original text; the original: 我没看过这本

书的～。I have not read the book in the original./ 引用～要加引号。Put quoted passages in quotation marks./ ～如此 *sic*/ 把抄件跟～核对一下 check the copy against the original

【原先】 yuánxiān former; original: 照～的计划做 act according to the original plan/ 他～是个海员，现在已经成了一位作家。He used to be a sailor, but now he's become a writer./ 我～以为他不会同意，没想到他居然答应了。I thought that he would not agree, but to my surprise he said "Yes".

【原形】 yuánxíng original shape; the true shape under the disguise: ～毕露 be revealed for what one is; show one's true colours

【原型】 yuánxíng 〈机〉 prototype

【原盐】 yuányán crude salt

【原野】 yuányě open country; champaign

【原意】 yuányì meaning; original intention: 曲解～ distort the meaning/ 这不是我们的～。This was not our original intention. 或 This is not what we meant.

【原因】 yuányīn cause; reason: ～和结果 cause and effect/ 成功的～ reasons for the success/ 产生这种现象有两方面的～。Two things account for the occurrence.

【原油】 yuányóu crude oil; crude: 含硫～ sour crude/ 低硫～ sweet crude/ 多蜡～ waxy crude/ 无蜡～ wax-free crude ◇ ～分馏塔 crude fractionating tower/ ～裂化设备 crude cracker

【原宥】 yuányòu pardon; forgive

【原原本本】 yuányuánběnběn from beginning to end: 我把这件事～讲给他们听了。I told them the whole story exactly as it happened./ 把上级的指示～地向群众传达 make known to the masses the directives of the higher authorities exactly as they are

【原则】 yuánzé principle: ～问题 a matter of principle/ ～分歧 differences in principle/ ～上同意 agree in principle/ 具有高度的～性 be highly principled; have a strong sense of principle/ 坚持马克思列宁主义的～立场 adhere to the principled stand of Marxism-Leninism

【原址】 yuánzhǐ former address

【原主】 yuánzhǔ original owner (或 proprietor): 物归～ return sth. to its (rightful) owner

【原著】 yuánzhù original work; original: 学习马克思的～ study Marx's works/ 我不懂俄文，没有读过高尔基的～。As I don't know Russian, I've never read Gorky in the original.

【原状】 yuánzhuàng original state; previous condition; *status quo ante*: 恢复～ restore the *status quo ante*; restore to the former state

【原子】 yuánzǐ atom: 标记～ labelled atom
◇ ～尘 fallout/ ～弹 atom bomb; atomic bomb; A-bomb/ ～动力船 atomic-powered ship/ ～反应堆 atomic reactor; atomic pile/ ～核 atomic nucleus/ ～价 valence; atomicity/ ～键 atomic bond/ ～量 atomic weight/ ～论 atomic theory; atomism/ ～能 atomic energy/ ～炮 atomic gun/ ～团 atomic group/ ～武器 atomic weapon/ ～物理学 atomic physics/ ～序数 atomic number/ ～战争 atomic war (或 warfare)

【原作】 yuánzuò original work; original: 译文保持了～的风格。The translation reproduces the style of the original.

**袁** Yuán a surname

**圆** yuán ① round; circular; spherical: ～孔 a round hole/ ～锉 round file/ 月～了。The moon is full. ②〈数〉 circle ③ tactful; satisfactory: 他这话说得不～。What he said was not very tactful. ④ make plausible; justify: 自～其说 make one's statement consistent; justify oneself/ ～谎 patch up a lie ⑤ *yuan*, the monetary unit of China, equal to 10 *jiao* or 100 *fen* ⑥ a coin of fixed value and weight: 银～ silver dollar/ 铜～ copper coin

【圆材】 yuáncái 〈林〉 roundwood; log

【圆场】 yuánchǎng mediate; help to effect a compromise: 打～ mediate a dispute; smooth things over

【圆成】 yuánchéng help sb. to attain his aim

【圆唇元音】 yuánchúnyuányīn 〈语〉 round vowel

【圆顶】 yuándǐng 〈天〉 dome

【圆规】 yuánguī compasses: 一个～ a pair of compasses/ 制图～ drawing compasses/ 长杆～ beam compasses

【圆号】 yuánhào 〈乐〉 French horn; horn

【圆滑】 yuánhuá smooth and evasive; slick and sly

【圆滑线】 yuánhuáxiàn 〈乐〉 slur

【圆锯】 yuánjù 〈机〉 circular saw

【圆括号】 yuánkuòhào parentheses; curves (( ))

【圆满】 yuánmǎn satisfactory: ～成功 complete success/ ～的答案 a satisfactory answer/ 问题～地解决了。The problem has been solved satisfactorily./ 邀请赛在友好团结的气氛中～结束。The invitational tournament was rounded off in an atmosphere of friendship and solidarity.

【圆盘】 yuánpán disc ◇ ～耙 disc harrow/ ～犁 disc plough

【圆圈】 yuánquān circle; ring

【圆润】 yuánrùn mellow and full: ～的嗓音 a sweet, mellow voice

【圆鲹】 yuánshēn 〈动〉 round scad

【圆熟】 yuánshú skilful; proficient; dexterous

【圆通】 yuántōng flexible; accommodating

【圆舞曲】 yuánwǔqǔ 〈乐〉 waltz

【圆心】 yuánxīn the centre of a circle ◇ ～角 〈数〉 central angle

【圆形】 yuánxíng circular; round ◇ ～建筑 round building; rotunda

【圆周】 yuánzhōu circumference
◇ ～接缝 〈机〉 circumferential seam/ ～率 ratio of the circumference of a circle to its diameter ($\pi$)/ ～运动 〈物〉 circular motion

【圆珠笔】 yuánzhūbǐ ball-point pen; ball-pen

【圆柱】 yuánzhù 〈数〉 cylinder

【圆锥】 yuánzhuī circular cone; taper
◇ ～根 〈植〉 conical root/ ～花序 〈植〉 panicle/ ～台 〈数〉 frustum of a cone

【圆桌】 yuánzhuō round table ◇ ～会议 round-table conference

【圆子】 yuánzi ① dumpling (made of glutinous rice flour) ② 〈方〉 (meat, fish, etc.) ball

【圆凿方枘】 yuánzuò-fāngruì like a square tenon for a round mortise — at variance with each other

**湲** yuán 见"潺湲" chányuán

**援** yuán ① pull by hand; hold: 攀～ climb up by holding on to sth./ ～笔疾书 take up a pen and write quickly ② quote; cite: 有例可～。There's a precedent to quote. ③ help; aid; rescue: 求～ ask for help; appeal for aid; request reinforcements/ 围点打～ encircle an enemy post in order to attack reinforcements coming to its aid

【援救】 yuánjiù rescue; save; deliver from danger

【援军】 yuánjūn reinforcements; relief troops

【援例】 yuánlì cite (或 quote) a precedent

【援手】 yuánshǒu 〈书〉 aid; save; rescue

【援外】 yuánwài foreign aid: ～物资 materials in aid of a foreign country

【援引】 yuányǐn ① quote; cite: ～例证 cite an example/ ～法律条文 invoke a legal provision ② recommend or appoint one's friends or favourites
【援用】 yuányòng quote; cite; invoke: ～成例 cite a precedent/ ～条约 invoke a treaty
【援助】 yuánzhù help; support; aid: 已经获得革命胜利的人民，应该～正在争取解放的人民的斗争。The people who have triumphed in their own revolution should help those still struggling for liberation./ 国际～ international support/ 给他们一切可能的～ give them every possible help/ 不附带条件的～ aid with no strings attached/ 技术～ technical assistance

**鼋** yuán 〈动〉 soft-shelled turtle
【鼋鱼】 yuányú soft-shelled turtle

**源** yuán ① source (of a river); fountainhead: 饮水思～ when drinking water think of its source — remember where one's happiness comes from/ 木有本，水有～。Every tree has its roots and every river has its source. ② source; cause: 财～ source of income/ 病～ cause of a disease
【源流】 yuánliú source and course (of a river, etc.); origin and development
【源泉】 yuánquán source; fountainhead: 生活是文艺创作的～。Life is the source of literary and artistic creation.
【源头】 yuántóu fountainhead; source
【源源】 yuányuán in a steady stream; continuously: 大庆石油通过这条输油管～不断地流往北京。Through this pipeline, crude oil flows from Daqing to Beijing in a steady stream./ 运往市场的蔬菜～不绝。There is a steady flow of vegetables to the market.
【源源本本】 yuányuánběnběn 见"原原本本" yuányuánběnběn
【源远流长】 yuán yuǎn liú cháng a distant source and a long stream — of long standing and well established: 我们两国人民的友谊～。The friendship between our two peoples goes back to ancient times.

**猿** yuán ape: 类人～ anthropoid ape/ 从～到人 from ape to man
【猿猴】 yuánhóu apes and monkeys
【猿人】 yuánrén ape-man: 北京～ Peking man (*Sinanthropus pekinensis*)

**缘** yuán ① reason: 无～无故 without rhyme or reason; for no reason at all/ ～何到此？What's your reason for coming here? ② edge; fringe; brink: 外～ outer fringe (或 edge)/ 这个城市处于沙漠南～。This city is located on the southern fringe of the desert. ③ along: ～溪行 walk along the stream ④ predestined relationship: 姻～ predestined marriage/ 有一面之～ happen to have met once
【缘分】 yuánfèn lot or luck by which people are brought together: 咱俩又在一起了，真是有～。So we're together again. It must be fate./ 烟、酒跟我没有～。Smoking and drinking don't appeal to me.
【缘故】 yuángù cause; reason
【缘木求鱼】 yuán mù qiú yú climb a tree to catch fish — a fruitless approach
【缘起】 yuánqǐ ① genesis; origin ② an account of the founding of an institution or the beginning of a project
【缘由】 yuányóu reason; cause

**辕** yuán ① shafts of a cart or carriage ② the outer gate of a government office in ancient times ③ a government office in ancient times
【辕马】 yuánmǎ horse in the shafts; shaft-horse
【辕门】 yuánmén 见"辕"②

**䝼** yuán 〈动〉 ibex
【䝼羊】 yuányáng ibex

**螈** yuán 见"蝾螈" róngyuán

**橼** yuán 见"枸橼" jǔyuán; "香橼" xiāngyuán

## yuǎn

**远** yuǎn far; distant; remote: ～不及 far inferior to/ ～～超过 far exceed/ 敬而～之 stay at a respectful distance from sb./ ～隔重洋 be separated by vast oceans/ 十三陵水库离这里多～？How far is the Ming Tombs Reservoir from here?/ ～在公元十一世纪，中国已使用火药。Gunpowder was used in China as far back as the 11th century.
【远程】 yuǎnchéng long-range; long-distance: ～火箭 long-range rocket/ ～航行 long voyage
【远大】 yuǎndà long-range; broad; ambitious: 眼光～ be farsighted; have a broad vision/ 前途～ (of a person) have a bright future/ ～的计划 a long-range plan; an ambitious plan/ ～的理想 lofty ideals
【远道】 yuǎndào a long way: ～而来 come a long way; come from afar
【远地点】 yuǎndìdiǎn 〈天〉 apogee
【远东】 Yuǎndōng the Far East
【远方】 yuǎnfāng distant place: ～的来客 a guest from afar
【远房】 yuǎnfáng distantly related: ～亲戚 a distant relative; remote kinsfolk
【远古】 yuǎngǔ remote antiquity: 在～时代 in remote antiquity/ 从～流传下来的故事 a legend from ancient times
【远见】 yuǎnjiàn foresight; vision: ～卓识 foresight and sagacity
【远交近攻】 yuǎnjiāo-jìngōng befriend distant states while attacking those nearby
【远郊】 yuǎnjiāo outer suburbs
【远近】 yuǎnjìn ① far and near: ～闻名 be known far and wide ② distance: 不论～我都去。I'll go no matter how far it is./ 这两条路～差不多。The distance is about the same by either road.
【远景】 yuǎnjǐng ① distant view; long-range perspective; prospect: ～规划 a long-range plan/ 共产主义的壮丽～ the splendid prospects of communism ② 〈电影〉 long shot
【远距离操纵】 yuǎnjùlí cāozòng remote control; telecontrol
【远虑】 yuǎnlǜ foresight; long view: 深谋～ think deeply and plan carefully; be circumspect and farsighted
【远期】 yuǎnqī at a specified future date; forward: ～汇价 forward rate/ ～外汇 forward exchange
【远亲】 yuǎnqīn distant relative (或 relation); remote kinsfolk: 常言说，～不如近邻。As the saying goes, neighbours are dearer than distant relatives.
【远日点】 yuǎnrìdiǎn 〈天〉 aphelion
【远射程炮】 yuǎnshèchéngpào long-range gun
【远摄镜头】 yuǎnshè jìngtóu ① 〈电影〉 long shot ② 〈摄影〉 telephoto lens
【远视】 yuǎnshì 〈医〉 long sight; farsightedness; hyperopia; hypermetropia ◇ ～眼镜 spectacles for long sight; spectacles for the farsighted
【远水不解近渴】 yuǎnshuǐ bù jiě jìnkě distant water cannot

quench present thirst — the aid is too slow in coming to be of any help

【远水救不了近火】 yuǎnshuǐ jiùbuliǎo jìnhuǒ distant water won't put out a fire close at hand — a slow remedy cannot meet an urgency

【远台】 yuǎntái 〈乒乓球〉 far from the table ◇ ～防守 long defence; far-from-table defence/ ～削球 off-table chop

【远行】 yuǎnxíng go on a long journey

【远洋】 yuǎnyáng ① ocean ② of the open sea beyond the littoral zone; oceanic ◇ ～航行 oceangoing voyage/ ～货轮 oceangoing freighter/ ～渔业 deep-sea (或 pelagic) fishing

【远因】 yuǎnyīn remote cause

【远缘杂交】 yuǎnyuán zájiāo 〈农〉 distant hybridization

【远月点】 yuǎnyuèdiǎn 〈天〉 apocynthion

【远征】 yuǎnzhēng expedition ◇ ～军 expeditionary army (或 force)

【远志】 yuǎnzhì ① great and far-reaching ambition; high aspiration ② 〈中药〉 the root of the narrow-leaved polygala (*Polygala tenuifolia*)

【远走高飞】 yuǎnzǒu-gāofēi fly far and high; be off to distant parts

【远足】 yuǎnzú pleasure trip on foot; hike; walking tour

【远祖】 yuǎnzǔ remote ancestor

## yuàn

**苑** yuàn 〈书〉 ① enclosed ground for growing trees, keeping animals, etc.; gardens: 御～ imperial gardens/ 鹿～ deer park ② centre (of art and literature, etc.): 艺～ a centre of the arts; the art world ③ (Yuàn) a surname

**怨** yuàn ① resentment; enmity: 结～ arouse sb.'s enmity; incur ill will/ ～色 a resentful (或 discontented) look/ 不计较个人恩～ give no thought to personal grievances ② blame; complain: 不要老是抱～。Don't always complain./ 这件事～我。I am to blame for this.

【怨不得】 yuànbude ① cannot blame: 这件事～老李，都怪我。Lao Li is not to blame for this. It's all my fault. ② no wonder: 班车坏了，～他们迟到了。The bus broke down. No wonder they were late.

【怨毒】 yuàndú 〈书〉 enmity; hatred

【怨怼】 yuànduì 〈书〉 resentment; enmity

【怨愤】 yuànfèn discontent and indignation

【怨府】 yuànfǔ 〈书〉 object of general indignation

【怨恨】 yuànhèn ① have a grudge against sb.; hate ② resentment; grudge; enmity

【怨偶】 yuàn'ǒu 〈书〉 an unhappy couple

【怨气】 yuànqì grievance; complaint; resentment: 出～ air one's grievances; vent one's resentment/ 一肚子～ be full of complaints (或 grievances)

【怨声载道】 yuànshēng zài dào cries of discontent rise all round; complaints are heard everywhere

【怨天尤人】 yuàntiān-yóurén blame god and man — blame everyone and everything but oneself

【怨言】 yuànyán complaint; grumble: 从未发过一句～ never utter a word of complaint

【怨艾】 yuànyì 〈书〉 resentment; grudge

**院** yuàn ① courtyard; yard; compound: 前～ front yard/ 场～ threshing ground/ 居民大～ neighbourhood compound/ ～里种了几棵枣树。There are some jujube trees in the courtyard. ② a designation for certain government offices and public places: 法～ law court/ 科学～ the academy of sciences/ 疗养～ sanatorium/ 电影～ cinema

【院落】 yuànluò courtyard; yard; compound

【院士】 yuànshì academician

【院子】 yuànzi courtyard; yard; compound: ～里练不出千里马，温室里长不出万年松。A fiery steed is not trained in a courtyard, nor does a pine grow sturdy in a greenhouse.

**垸** yuàn 见"圩垸" wéiyuàn

**愿** yuàn ① hope; wish; desire: 如～以偿 have one's wishes fulfilled; obtain what one desires/ 平生之～ a lifelong wish ② be willing; be ready: 我～为共产主义奋斗终生。I will devote my entire life to the cause of communism. ③ vow (made before Buddha or a god): 还～ redeem a vow ④ 〈书〉 honest and cautious

【愿望】 yuànwàng desire; wish; aspiration: 从团结的～出发 start from the desire for unity/ 全世界人民的共同～ the common aspirations of the world's people/ 他参军的～终于实现了。His wish to join the army has at last come true.

【愿意】 yuànyì ① be willing; be ready: ～作出任何牺牲 be willing to make any sacrifice ② wish; like; want: 他们～你留在这里。They want you to remain here.

## yuē

**曰** yuē 〈书〉 ① say: 孙子～:"知彼知己，百战不殆。" Sun Wu Zi said, "Know the enemy and know yourself, and you can fight a hundred battles with no danger of defeat." ② call; name: 美其名～ describe sth. euphemistically as; give sth. the fine-sounding name of

**约** yuē ① make an appointment; arrange: 我想跟王经理～个时间谈谈。I'd like to make an appointment with Mr. Wang, the manager./ 我们～好下星期一碰头。We agreed to meet next Monday. ② ask or invite in advance: 请～他来。Please ask him to come./ 我已～了王同志。I've invited Comrade Wang. ③ pact; agreement; appointment: 立～ make a pact; come to an agreement/ 商～ commercial treaty/ 践～ keep an appointment ④ restrict; restrain: ～束 restrain; bind ⑤ economical; frugal: 节～ economize/ 自奉甚～ live economically; lead a frugal life ⑥ simple; brief: ～言之 in brief; in a word ⑦ about; around; approximately: ～五十人 about fifty people ⑧ 〈数〉 reduction of a fraction: 十分之五可以～成二分之一。Five over ten can be reduced to one over two.

另见 yāo

【约旦】 Yuēdàn Jordan ◇ ～人 Jordanian

【约定】 yuēdìng agree on; appoint; arrange: ～会晤地点 agree on a meeting place/ 在～的时间 at the appointed time

【约定俗成】 yuēdìng súchéng established by usage; accepted through common practice

【约法】 yuēfǎ provisional constitution

【约法三章】 yuē fǎ sān zhāng agree on a three-point law — make a few simple rules to be observed by all concerned

【约分】 yuēfēn 〈数〉 reduction of a fraction

【约会】 yuēhuì appointment; engagement; date: 订个～ make an appointment/ 我今天晚上有个～。I have an engagement this evening.

【约集】 yuējí meet by appointment; gather

【约计】 yuējì count roughly; come roughly to

【约略】 yuēlüè rough; approximate: ～的估计 a rough (或 approximate) estimate/ 这件事我～知道一些。I know something about the matter.

【约莫】 yuēmo about; roughly: 现在～有十点钟。It is about ten now./ 我们等了～有一个小时的光景。We waited for an hour or so./ 离这儿～有三里路。It's about three *li* from here.

【约期】 yuēqī fix a date; appoint a time: ～会谈 fix a date to hold talks/ 误了～ fail to keep the appointment

【约请】 yuēqǐng invite; ask

【约束】 yuēshù keep within bounds; restrain; bind: 用革命的纪律～自己 keep oneself within the bounds of revolutionary discipline ◇ ～力 binding force

【约数】 yuēshù ① approximate number ② 〈数〉 divisor: 公～ common divisor

【约言】 yuēyán promise; word; pledge: 遵守～ keep one's promise (或 word)/ 违背～ break one's promise; go back on one's word/ 实行～ redeem one's pledge

## yuè

**月** yuè ① the moon: 新～ a new moon; crescent ② month: ～底 the end of the month/ ～工 a labourer hired by the month/ ～产量 monthly output ③ full-moon shaped; round

【月白】 yuèbái bluish white; very pale blue

【月半】 yuèbàn the 15th day of a month

【月报】 yuèbào ① monthly magazine; monthly ② monthly report

【月饼】 yuèbǐng moon cake (esp. for the Mid-Autumn Festival)

【月长石】 yuèchángshí 〈矿〉 moonstone

【月度】 yuèdù monthly: ～计划 a monthly plan

【月份】 yuèfèn month: 上～ last month/ 八～的产量比七～提高了百分之五。In August output was 5% higher than in July.

【月份牌】 yuèfènpái 〈口〉 calendar

【月宫】 yuègōng the palace of the moon — the moon

【月光】 yuèguāng moonlight; moonbeam

【月光花】 yuèguānghuā large moonflower

【月桂树】 yuèguìshù laurel; bay tree

【月华】 yuèhuá ① moonlight: ～如水 watery moonbeams; a flood of translucent moonlight ② 〈气〉 lunar corona

【月季】 yuèjì 〈植〉 Chinese rose

【月经】 yuèjīng menses; menstruation; period ◇ ～不调 menoxenia; abnormal menstruation/ ～带 sanitary belt (或 napkin)/ ～过多 menorrhagia; excessive menstruation/ ～周期 menstrual cycle

【月刊】 yuèkān monthly magazine; monthly

【月历】 yuèlì monthly calendar

【月利】 yuèlì monthly interest

【月亮】 yuèliang the moon ◇ ～门儿 moon gate

【月杪】 yuèmiǎo 〈书〉 the end of the month

【月票】 yuèpiào monthly ticket

【月琴】 yuèqín a four-stringed plucked instrument with a full-moon-shaped sound box

【月球】 yuèqiú 〈天〉 the moon ◇ ～火箭 〈宇航〉 moon rocket

【月色】 yuèsè moonlight

【月石】 yuèshí 〈化〉 borax

【月食】 yuèshí 〈天〉 lunar eclipse: 月全食 total lunar eclipse/ 月偏食 partial lunar eclipse 又作"月蚀"

【月台】 yuètái railway platform ◇ ～票 platform ticket

【月头儿】 yuètóur 〈口〉 ① the beginning of the month ② time for monthly payment: 到～了，该付房租了。It's time to pay the month's rent.

【月息】 yuèxī monthly interest

【月下老人】 yuèxià lǎorén the old man under the moon — the god who unites persons in marriage; matchmaker

【月相】 yuèxiàng 〈天〉 phase of the moon

【月薪】 yuèxīn monthly pay

【月牙】 yuèyá 〈口〉 crescent moon

【月夜】 yuèyè moonlit (或 moonlight) night

【月晕】 yuèyùn lunar halo

【月震】 yuèzhèn moonquake

【月中】 yuèzhōng the middle of a month

【月子】 yuèzi ① month of confinement after giving birth to a child: 坐～ be in confinement ② time of childbirth; confinement: 她的～是二月初。She's expecting her baby at the beginning of February. ◇ ～病 puerperal fever

**乐** yuè ① music: 奏～ play music/ 器～ instrumental music/ 声～ vocal music ② (Yuè) a surname
另见 lè

【乐池】 yuèchí orchestra pit; orchestra

【乐段】 yuèduàn 〈乐〉 period

【乐队】 yuèduì orchestra; band: 交响～ symphony (或 philharmonic) orchestra/ 军～ military band ◇ ～指挥 conductor; bandmaster

【乐府】 yuèfǔ ① an official conservatory in the Han Dynasty (206 B.C.–A.D. 220) for collecting and composing folk songs and ballads ② (poetic *genre* of) folk songs and ballads in the Han style

【乐句】 yuèjù 〈乐〉 phrase

【乐理】 yuèlǐ 〈乐〉 music theory

【乐律】 yuèlǜ 〈乐〉 temperament

【乐谱】 yuèpǔ music score; music ◇ ～架 music stand

【乐器】 yuèqì musical instrument; instrument: 管～ wind instrument/ 弦～ stringed instrument/ 打击～ percussion instrument

【乐曲】 yuèqǔ musical composition; composition; music

【乐团】 yuètuán ① philharmonic society ② philharmonic orchestra

【乐音】 yuèyīn musical sound; tone

【乐章】 yuèzhāng 〈乐〉 movement

**刖** yuè cutting off the feet (a form of punishment in ancient China)

**岳** yuè ① high mountain: 五～ the Five Mountains ② wife's parents: ～家 family of one's wife's parents ③ (Yuè) a surname

【岳父】 yuèfù wife's father; father-in-law 又作"岳丈"

【岳母】 yuèmǔ wife's mother; mother-in-law

**钥** yuè key
另见 yào

**悦** yuè ① happy; pleased; delighted: 不～ displeased/ 和颜～色 a kindly countenance; a genial look ② please; delight: 取～于人 try to please sb.

【悦耳】 yuè'ěr pleasing to the ear; sweet-sounding: ～的音乐 sweet (或 melodious) music/ 歌声～。The singing is pleasant.

【悦服】 yuèfú heartily admire

【悦目】 yuèmù pleasing to the eye; good-looking

**阅** yuè ① read; go over: ～报 read newspapers/ ～卷 go over examination papers ② review; inspect: ～兵 review troops ③ experience; pass through: 试行已～三月。

Three months have passed since we started to try this out.

【阅兵】 yuèbīng review troops ◇ ～场 parade ground/ ～典礼 dress parade/ ～式 military review; parade

【阅读】 yuèdú read: ～杂志 read magazines

【阅览】 yuèlǎn read ◇ ～室 reading room

【阅历】 yuèlì ① see, hear or do for oneself: ～过很多事 have seen much of the world ② experience: ～浅 having little experience; inexperienced

【阅世】 yuèshì 〈书〉 see the world: ～渐深 gain more and more experience of life

**钺** yuè a battle-axe used in ancient China

**跃** yuè leap; jump: ～上马背 leap onto a horse/ 一～而起 get up with a jump; jump up all of a sudden/ ～居世界首位 leap to first place in the world

【跃进】 yuèjìn make (或 take) a leap; leap forward: 整个工业出现了～的局面。The whole industrial front is developing by leaps and bounds./ 我们大队小麦亩产由二百斤～到五百斤。Our brigade's output of wheat has jumped from 200 *jin* to 500 *jin* per *mu*.

【跃迁】 yuèqiān 〈物〉 transition: 自发～ spontaneous transition/ 俘获～ capture transition ◇ ～概率 transition probability

【跃然】 yuèrán appear vividly: 义愤之情～纸上。The author shows his righteous indignation in his writing.

【跃跃欲试】 yuèyuè yù shì be eager to have a try; itch to have a go

**越** yuè ① get over; jump over: ～墙而逃 escape by climbing over the wall/ 翻山～岭 cross over mountain after mountain ② exceed; overstep: ～出范围 overstep the bounds; exceed the limits/ ～出政策界限 go beyond the bounds of policy ③ (of one's voice or emotion) be at a high pitch: 歌声清～ sing in a clarion voice/ 激～ intense; vehement; loud and strong

【越冬】 yuèdōng live through (或 survive) the winter ◇ ～作物 winter crop; overwintering crop

【越发】 yuèfā ① all the more; even more: 自从学大寨以后，我们干得～起劲了。Ever since we started learning from Dazhai, we have been working even harder. ②〔跟上文"越"或"越是"呼应，作用跟"越…越…" the more...the more 相同〕: 越是性急，～容易出差错。The more impatient you are, the more mistakes you'll make.

【越轨】 yuèguǐ exceed the bounds; transgress: ～行为 impermissible behaviour; transgression

【越过】 yuèguò cross; surmount; negotiate: ～戈壁沙漠 cross the Gobi Desert/ ～障碍 surmount obstacles/ ～激流险滩 negotiate turbulent rivers and treacherous shoals

【越级】 yuèjí ① bypass the immediate leadership: ～提出申诉 bypass the immediate leadership and present one's appeals and complaints to higher levels ② (of personnel promotion) skip a grade or rank: ～提升 promote sb. more than one grade at a time

【越界】 yuèjiè overstep the boundary; cross the border

【越境】 yuèjìng cross the boundary illegally; sneak in or out of a country

【越橘】 yuèjú 〈植〉 cowberry

【越剧】 yuèjù Shaoxing opera

【越来越…】 yuèlái yuè...〔表示程度随着时间发展〕 more and more: 越来越好 get better and better/ 发挥越来越大的作用 play an increasingly important role

【越南】 Yuènán Viet Nam ◇ ～人 Vietnamese/ ～语 Vietnamese (language)

【越权】 yuèquán exceed (或 overstep) one's power or authority; *ultra vires*

【越位】 yuèwèi 〈体〉 offside

【越野】 yuèyě cross-country ◇ ～汽车 cross-country (motor) vehicle/ ～赛跑 cross-country race

【越铀元素】 yuèyóu yuánsù 〈化〉 transuranic element

【越狱】 yuèyù escape from prison; break prison ◇ ～犯 prison breaker

【越…越…】 yuè... yuè...〔表示程度随着条件的发展而发展〕 the more...the more...: 越多越好 the more the better/ 越战越强 grow stronger with the fighting/ 犯了错误则要求改正，改正得越迅速，越彻底，越好。Once a mistake is made, we should correct it, and the more quickly and thoroughly the better.

【越俎代庖】 yuè zǔ dài páo exceed one's functions and meddle in others' affairs; take sb. else's job into one's own hands

**粤** Yuè another name for Guangdong Province

【粤剧】 yuèjù Guangdong opera

## yūn

**晕** yūn ① dizzy; giddy: 有点头～ feel a bit dizzy (或 giddy) ② swoon; faint: ～了过去 lose consciousness; faint; swoon

另见 yùn

【晕倒】 yūndǎo fall in a faint; pass out

【晕厥】 yūnjué 〈医〉 syncope; faint

【晕头转向】 yūntóu zhuànxiàng confused and disoriented: 把敌人打得～ hit the enemy so hard that he's thrown into confusion/ 这道算题真难，把我搞得～。This mathematics problem is really difficult; it's got me confused.

【晕晕忽忽】 yūnyunhūhū ① dizzy; giddy ② muddleheaded

**氲** yūn 见"氤氲" yīnyūn

## yún

**云** yún ①〈书〉 say: 人～亦～ repeat what others say; parrot ② cloud ③ (Yún) short for Yunnan Province ④ (Yún) a surname

【云彩】 yúncai 〈口〉 cloud

【云层】 yúncéng cloud layer: 在～上面飞行 fly above the clouds

【云顶】 yúndǐng 〈气〉 cloud top

【云端】 yúnduān high in the clouds

【云贵高原】 Yún-Guì Gāoyuán the Yunnan-Guizhou Plateau

【云海】 yúnhǎi a sea of clouds

【云汉】 yúnhàn 〈书〉 the Milky Way

【云集】 yúnjí come together in crowds; gather; converge: 各地代表～首都。Representatives from all over the country gathered in the capital.

【云量】 yúnliàng 〈气〉 cloudiness

【云锣】 yúnluó 〈乐〉 Chinese gong chimes

【云幂】 yúnmì 〈气〉 ceiling ◇ ～高度 ceiling height/ ～气球 ceiling balloon

【云母】 yúnmǔ 〈矿〉 mica ◇ ～板岩 mica-slate/ ～电容器 mica condenser/ ～片 mica sheet; sheet mica/ ～片岩〈地〉 mica schist; micacite

【云南】 Yúnnán Yunnan (Province)

【云气】 yúnqì thin, floating clouds

【云雀】 yúnquè 〈动〉 skylark

【云杉】 yúnshān 〈植〉 dragon spruce (*Picea asperata*)
【云室】 yúnshì 〈物〉 cloud chamber: 威耳孙～ Wilson (cloud) chamber
【云梯】 yúntī scaling ladder
【云图】 yúntú 〈气〉 cloud atlas; cloud chart
【云团】 yúntuán 〈气〉 cloud cluster
【云雾】 yúnwù cloud and mist; mist: 拨开～见青天 scatter the clouds and see the blue sky ◇ ～天 soupy weather
【云霞】 yúnxiá rosy clouds
【云消雾散】 yúnxiāo-wùsàn the clouds melt and the mists disperse — vanish into thin air
【云霄】 yúnxiāo the skies: 锣鼓声响彻～。The beating of gongs and drums resounded to the skies.
【云烟】 yúnyān cloud and mist: 过眼～ as transient as a fleeting cloud
【云游】 yúnyóu (of a Buddhist monk or a Taoist priest) roam; wander
【云雨】 yúnyǔ 〈书〉 sexual intercourse; making love
【云云】 yúnyún 〈书〉〔引用文句或谈话时,表示结束或有所省略〕: 他来信说读了不少新书,颇有心得～。He wrote to say that he had read several new books and profited greatly from them.

## 匀

yún ① even: 颜色涂得不～。The colour is not evenly spread./ 麦苗出得很～。The wheat sprouts are growing very evenly. ② even up; divide evenly: 这两份多少不均,再～一～吧。These two shares are not equal. Please even them up. ③ spare: 我们种子比较多,可以～给你们一些。We've got more seeds than we need. We can spare you some.
【匀称】 yúnchèn well-proportioned; well-balanced; symmetrical: 身材～ of proportional build
【匀净】 yúnjìng uniform; even: 这块布染得很～。This cloth is evenly dyed.
【匀脸】 yúnliǎn rub powder and paint evenly on one's face
【匀溜】 yúnliu ① even and smooth (in texture) ② of the right consistency
【匀染】 yúnrǎn 〈纺〉 level dyeing ◇ ～剂 levelling agent
【匀实】 yúnshi 〈口〉 even; neat; uniform
【匀速运动】 yúnsù yùndòng 〈物〉 uniform motion
【匀整】 yúnzhěng neat and well spaced; even and orderly: 他的字写得很～。His handwriting is very neat.

## 芸

yún
【芸豆】 yúndòu kidney bean
【芸薹】 yúntái 〈植〉 rape
【芸香】 yúnxiāng 〈植〉 rue
【芸芸众生】 yúnyún zhòngshēng 〈佛教〉 all living things; all mortal beings

## 纭

yún
【纭纭】 yúnyún numerous and disorderly; diverse and confused

## 昀

yún sunlight; sunshine

## 耘

yún weed: ～田 weed the fields/ 春耕夏～ spring ploughing and summer weeding
【耘锄】 yúnchú 〈农〉 hoe

# yǔn

## 允

yǔn ① permit; allow; consent: 应～ consent/ ～从 comply ② fair; just: 公～ fair; equitable
【允当】 yǔndàng proper; suitable
【允诺】 yǔnnuò promise; consent; undertake: 欣然～ readily consent
【允许】 yǔnxǔ permit; allow: 不～任何破坏纪律的现象存在 permit no breach of discipline/ 请～我代表全厂职工向你们致谢。Allow me to thank you on behalf of our factory. ◇ ～误差 〈机〉 allowable error; permissible error/ ～载荷 allowable load

## 陨

yǔn fall from the sky or outer space
【陨落】 yǔnluò (of a meteorite, etc.) fall from the sky or outer space
【陨灭】 yǔnmiè ① fall from outer space and burn up ② 〈书〉 meet one's death; perish
【陨石】 yǔnshí 〈天〉 aerolite; stony meteorite ◇ ～雨 meteorite shower
【陨铁】 yǔntiě 〈天〉 meteoric iron; iron meteorite; siderite
【陨星】 yǔnxīng 〈天〉 meteorite: 石～ aerolite; stony meteorite/ 铁～ siderite; iron meteorite/ 石铁～ siderolite; stony iron meteorite ◇ ～学 meteoritics

## 殒

yǔn perish; die
【殒灭】 yǔnmiè 〈书〉 meet one's death; perish
【殒命】 yǔnmìng 〈书〉 meet one's death; perish

# yùn

## 孕

yùn pregnant: 怀～ be pregnant; be conceived/ 避～ contraception
【孕畜】 yùnchù pregnant domestic animal
【孕妇】 yùnfù pregnant woman
【孕期】 yùnqī 〈医〉 pregnancy; gestation
【孕穗】 yùnsuì 〈农〉 booting ◇ ～期 boot stage
【孕吐】 yùntù 〈医〉 vomiting during pregnancy; morning sickness
【孕育】 yùnyù be pregnant with; breed: ～着危险 be fraught with danger/ ～着共产主义的萌芽 carry within itself the seeds of communism

## 运

yùn ① motion; movement ② carry; transport: ～往河边 carry to the riverside/ 货～ freight transport/ 空～ air transport; airlift ③ use; wield; utilize: ～笔 wield the pen/ ～思 exercise one's mind ④ fortune; luck; fate: 好～ good luck/ 不走～ be out of luck; have no luck
【运程】 yùnchéng 〈交〉 haul
【运筹帷幄】 yùnchóu wéiwò devise strategies within a command tent: ～之中,决胜千里之外 sit within a command tent and devise strategies that will assure victory a thousand *li* away
【运筹学】 yùnchóuxué operational research; operations research
【运动】 yùndòng ① motion; movement: 直线～ rectilinear motion/ 行星的～ the movement of a planet/ ～是物质的存在方式。Motion is the mode of existence of matter./ 乘敌～之际,打击敌人。Attack the enemy while he is on the move. ② sports; athletics; exercise: 室外～ outdoor sports/ 游泳是我喜爱的～。Swimming is my favourite sport./ 散步也是一种～。Walking is also a form of exercise. ③ (political) movement; campaign; drive: 群众～ mass movement/ 整风～ rectification movement/ 爱国卫生～ patriotic public health campaign
◇ ～场 sports (或 athletic) ground; playground/ ～服装 sportswear/ ～学 〈物〉 kinematics/ ～员 sportsman or

sportswoman; athlete; player/ ～战 mobile war (或 warfare)/ ～知觉 <心> consciousness of motion
【运动】 yùndong <旧> arrange things through pull
【运动会】 yùndònghuì sports meet; athletic meeting; games: 全国～ national games
【运费】 yùnfèi transportation expenses; freight; carriage: 到付～ freight payable at destination
◇ ～表 freight list/ ～单 freight note/ ～吨 freight ton/ ～率 freight rate/ ～免付 carriage free/ ～条款 freight clause/ ～已付 freight (或 carriage) paid/ ～预付 freight prepaid; advanced freight
【运河】 yùnhé canal: 大～ the Grand Canal ◇ ～税 canal dues
【运脚】 yùnjiǎo <方> transport charge; freight; carriage
【运煤船】 yùnméichuán coal carrier; collier
【运气】 yùnqì (the art of) directing one's strength, through concentration, to a part of the body
【运气】 yùnqi fortune; luck: 碰～ try one's luck; take one's chance/ 唉，～老是不好。Just my luck!/ 这回可来了～了。This time my luck's in.
【运球】 yùnqiú <体> dribble
【运输】 yùnshū transport; carriage; conveyance: 陆上(水路)～ land (water) transport; transport by land (water)
◇ ～部队 <军> transportation troops/ ～船 cargo ship; transport ship/ ～队 transport corps (或 team)/ ～方式 modes of transport/ ～工具 means of transport; conveyance/ ～公司 transport company/ ～里程 transport mileage/ ～量 freight volume/ ～能力 transport capacity; carrying capacity/ ～网 transport network/ ～业 transport service; carrying trade; transportation
【运输机】 yùnshūjī ①<航空> transport plane; airfreighter ②<矿> conveyor
【运送】 yùnsòng transport; ship; convey: ～物资 ship (或 transport) goods and materials
【运算】 yùnsuàn <数> operation: 四则～ the four fundamental operations of arithmetic/ 每秒钟～二百万次 capable of 2,000,000 calculations per second
◇ ～分析 operational analysis/ ～微积分 operational calculus/ ～误差 arithmetic error
【运算器】 yùnsuànqì <计算机> arithmetic unit
【运销】 yùnxiāo (commodity) transportation and sale
【运行】 yùnxíng move; be in motion: 在轨道上～ move in orbit/ 地球绕太阳～。The earth revolves round the sun./ 列车～时，请勿打开车门。Don't open the door while the train is in motion.
【运用】 yùnyòng utilize; wield; apply; put to use: ～国家机器 wield the state machinery/ ～自如 handle very skilfully; have a perfect command of/ ～马列主义分析问题，解决问题 apply Marxism-Leninism to the analysis and solution of problems
【运载工具】 yùnzài gōngjù means of delivery: 战略～ strategic vehicles
【运载火箭】 yùnzài huǒjiàn carrier rocket
【运载技术】 yùnzài jìshù delivery technology
【运转】 yùnzhuǎn ① revolve; turn round: 行星绕着太阳～。The planets revolve round the sun. ② work; operate: 机器～正常。The machine is running well.

## 郓
Yùn a surname

## 恽
Yùn a surname

## 晕
yùn ① dizzy; giddy; faint: 头～目眩 have a dizzy spell; be afflicted with vertigo ② <气> halo: 日～ solar halo/ 月～ lunar halo
另见 yūn
【晕车】 yùnchē carsickness: 好～ be liable to carsickness
【晕船】 yùnchuán seasickness
【晕高儿】 yùngāor <方> feel giddy when on a height
【晕机】 yùnjī airsickness
【晕针】 yùnzhēn <中医> a fainting spell during acupuncture treatment

## 酝
yùn
【酝酿】 yùnniàng ① brew; ferment: 这场大辩论～已久。This great debate has been brewing for a long time. ② have a preliminary informal discussion; deliberate on: ～候选人名单 consider and talk over the list of candidates/ 大家先～一下。Let's have an exchange of views first./ 经过反复～协商，选举了出席大会的代表。Delegates to the congress were elected after repeated deliberations and consultations.

## 愠
yùn <书> angry; irritated: 面有～色 look irritated
【愠怒】 yùnnù be inwardly angry

## 韵
yùn ① musical (或 agreeable) sound: 琴～悠扬。Sweet music was being played on the lute. ② rhyme: 押～ be in rhyme/ ～书 rhyming dictionary ③ charm: 风～ personal charm; graceful bearing
【韵白】 yùnbái parts in Beijing opera where the traditional pronunciation of certain words is slightly different from that in current Beijing dialect
【韵腹】 yùnfù <语> the essential vowel in a compound vowel, as a in iang
【韵脚】 yùnjiǎo the rhyming word that ends a line of verse; rhyme
【韵律】 yùnlǜ ① metre (in verse) ② rules of rhyming; rhyme scheme ◇ ～学 prosody
【韵母】 yùnmǔ <语> simple or compound vowel (of a Chinese syllable), sometimes with a terminal n or ng
【韵事】 yùnshì ① literary or artistic pursuits, often with pretence to good taste and refinement ② romantic affair
【韵头】 yùntóu head vowel, any of the three vowels i, u and ü in certain compound vowels, as i in iang
【韵尾】 yùnwěi tail vowel, the terminal sound (vowel or nasal consonant) of certain compound vowels, as o in ao, ng in iang
【韵味】 yùnwèi lingering charm; lasting appeal: 她的唱腔很有～。Her singing has a special pleasing quality about it.
【韵文】 yùnwén literary composition in rhyme; verse

## 熨
yùn iron; press: ～衣服 iron (或 press) clothes
【熨斗】 yùndǒu flatiron; iron: 电～ electric iron

## 蕴
yùn <书> accumulate; hold in store; contain
【蕴藏】 yùncáng hold in store; contain: 我国地下～着丰富的矿物资源。Our country is rich in mineral resources./ 群众中～了极大的社会主义的积极性。The masses have a vast reservoir of enthusiasm for socialism. ◇ ～量 reserves; deposits
【蕴涵】 yùnhán ①<书> contain ②<逻> implication
【蕴藉】 yùnjiè <书> temperate and refined; cultured and restrained: 风流～ graceful but not showy; urbanely charming
【蕴蓄】 yùnxù lie hidden and undeveloped; be latent

# Z

## zā

**扎** zā tie; bind: ～小辫儿 tie up one's plaits; plait one's hair; wear one's hair in plaits/ ～一根红头绳 tie one's plait with a piece of red yarn/ ～彩 hang up festoons
另见 zhā; zhá

**匝** zā ‹书› ① circle; circumference: 绕树三～ circle a tree three times ② dense; full: 密密～～ dense; thick

【匝地】 zādì ‹书› all over the ground; everywhere: 柳荫～。The willow trees cast their shadows all around.

【匝月】 zāyuè ‹书› a full month

**咂** zā ① sip; suck: ～一口酒 take a sip of wine ② make clicks (of admiration, praise, etc.) ③ taste (或 savour) carefully

【咂嘴】 zāzuǐ make clicks (of admiration, praise, etc.)

**拶** zā ‹书› force; compel; coerce
另见 zǎn

**臜** zā 见"腌臜" āza

## zá

**杂** zá ① miscellaneous; sundry; mixed: ～事儿 miscellaneous affairs/ ～而不乱 mixed but not confused/ ～七～八的东西 odds and ends; a medley ② mix; mingle: 夹～ be mixed up with; be mingled with/ 这片苹果树中～有几棵梨树。There are a few pear trees scattered among these apple trees.

【杂拌儿】 zábànr ① assorted preserved fruits; mixed sweetmeats ② mixture; miscellany; medley; hotchpotch

【杂草】 zácǎo weeds; rank grass: ～丛生 be overgrown with weeds

【杂凑】 zácòu knock together: 由流氓、土匪等～成的一支反动武装 a reactionary force knocked together of hooligans, bandits, and the like

【杂费】 záfèi ① incidental (或 miscellaneous) expenses; incidentals ② sundry fees (或 charges); extras

【杂感】 zágǎn ① random (或 stray) thoughts ② a type of literature recording such thoughts

【杂环】 záhuán ‹化› heterocycle; heterocyclic ring ◇ ～化合物 heterocyclic compound

【杂烩】 záhuì ① a stew of various ingredients; mixed stew; hotchpotch ② mixture; miscellany; medley; hotchpotch

【杂货】 záhuò sundry goods; groceries: 日用～ various household supplies ◇ ～店 grocery

【杂和菜】 záhuocài mixed stew (of leftovers)

【杂和面儿】 záhuomiànr maize flour mixed with a little soya bean flour

【杂记】 zájì ① jottings; notes ② miscellanies (as a type of literature)

【杂技】 zájì acrobatics ◇ ～团 acrobatic troupe/ ～演员 acrobat

【杂家】 zájiā the Eclectics, a school of thought flourishing at the end of the Warring States Period and the beginning of the Han Dynasty

【杂交】 zájiāo ‹生› hybridize; cross: 无性～ vegetative (或 asexual) hybridization/ 有性～ sexual hybridization/ 苹果与梨～ cross the apple with the pear/ 通过～改良水稻品种 improve paddy varieties through hybridization ◇ ～水稻 hybrid rice/ ～玉米 hybrid (或 crossbred) maize/ ～育种 crossbreeding

【杂居】 zájū (of two or more nationalities) live together: 少数民族～地区 an area inhabited by several minority nationalities

【杂剧】 zájù *zaju*, poetic drama set to music, flourishing in the Yuan Dynasty (1271-1368), usu. consisting of four acts called *zhe* (折), with one character having the singing role in each *zhe*

【杂粮】 záliáng food grains other than wheat and rice

【杂乱】 záluàn mixed and disorderly; in a jumble; in a muddle: 抽屉里的东西很～。The things in the drawer were all in a jumble.

【杂乱无章】 záluàn wú zhāng disorderly and unsystematic; disorganized

【杂面】 zámiàn ① flour made from various kinds of beans ② noodles made from such flour

【杂念】 zániàn distracting thoughts

【杂牌】 zápái a less known and inferior brand ◇ ～货 goods of an inferior brand

【杂品】 zápǐn sundry goods; groceries

【杂糅】 záróu mix; mingle; blend: 古今～ a blending of the ancient and the modern

【杂散】 zásǎn ‹物› stray ◇ ～磁场 stray magnetic field/ ～辐射 stray radiation

【杂色】 zásè variegated; parti-coloured; motley

【杂食动物】 záshí dòngwù omnivorous animal

【杂耍】 záshuǎ variety show; vaudeville

【杂税】 záshuì miscellaneous levies

【杂碎】 zásui chopped cooked entrails of sheep or oxen

【杂沓】 zátà numerous and disorderly: ～的脚步声 the clatter of footsteps

【杂文】 záwén essay

【杂务】 záwù odd jobs; sundry duties

【杂音】 záyīn ① noise ② ‹电› static ③ ‹医› murmur: 心脏～ heart murmur

【杂院儿】 záyuànr a compound occupied by many households

【杂志】 zázhì ① magazine ② 〔多用作书名〕 records; notes ◇ ～架 magazine rack

【杂质】 zázhì ① impurity ② ‹化› foreign matter (或 substance)

【杂种】 zázhǒng ① ‹生› hybrid; crossbreed ② ‹骂› bastard; son of a bitch ◇ ～不育性 hybrid sterility/ ～优势 ‹生› hybrid vigour; heterosis/ ～猪 cross-bred pig

**砸** zá ① pound; tamp: 把地基～实 tamp the foundations solid/ ～了脚 have one's foot squashed ② break; smash: 碗～了。The bowl is broken./ ～核桃 crack walnuts/ ～碎锁链 smash the shackles/ 把门～开 smash (或 ram) the door open ③ ‹方› fail; fall through; be bungled: 事儿办～了。The job was bungled.

【砸锅】 záguō ‹方› fail; fall through; be bungled

## zǎ

**咋** zǎ 〈方〉 how; why: 情况～样? How are things?/ 你看该～办? What do you think we should do?/ 你～不去? Why don't you go?
另见 zhā; zhà

## zāi

**灾** zāi ① calamity; disaster: 天～ natural disaster/ 水～ flood/ 旱～ drought/ 虫～ plague of insects ② personal misfortune; adversity: 没病没～ good health and good luck; with one's health all right and luck not bad/ 三～八难,五痨七伤 numerous adversities and calamities, infirmities and diseases

【灾变说】 zāibiànshuō 〈地〉 catastrophism

【灾害】 zāihài calamity; disaster: 自然～ natural calamity

【灾患】 zāihuàn 〈书〉 calamity; disaster: 屡经～ suffer calamity after calamity

【灾荒】 zāihuāng famine due to crop failures

【灾祸】 zāihuò disaster; calamity; catastrophe: ～临头。A great disaster is befalling (或 imminent).

【灾民】 zāimín victims of a natural calamity

【灾难】 zāinàn suffering; calamity; disaster; catastrophe: ～深重 disaster-ridden/ ～性的后果 disastrous consequences/ 避免一场大～ avert a catastrophe/ 给殖民地人民带来巨大的～ bring great suffering to the colonial people

【灾情】 zāiqíng the condition of a disaster: ～严重。The losses caused by the disaster were serious./ 这场雨减轻了～。The rain reduced the effects of the drought.

【灾区】 zāiqū disaster area: 地震～ earthquake-stricken area/ 旱～ drought-stricken area/ 水～ flooded area/ 重～ severely afflicted area

【灾殃】 zāiyāng suffering; calamity; disaster

**甾** zāi 〈化〉 steroid

**哉** zāi 〈书〉〈助〉 ①〔表示感叹〕: 呜呼!哀～! Alas!/ 诚～斯言! How true that is! ②〔与疑问词合用表示疑问或反诘〕: 胡为乎来～? Why has it come?/ 何～? Why? 或 Wherefore?/ 有何难～? What's so difficult about it?

**栽** zāi ① plant; grow: ～树 plant trees/ ～花 grow flowers/ ～秧 transplant seedlings (as of tomatoes or eggplants) ② stick in; insert; plant: ～电线杆子 erect a wire pole ③ force sth. on sb.; impose: ～上罪名 frame sb.; fabricate a charge against sb. ④ tumble; fall: ～倒 fall down

【栽跟头】 zāi gēntou ① tumble; fall ② suffer a setback; come a cropper

【栽培】 zāipéi ① cultivate; grow: 先进的～技术 advanced cultivation techniques/ 棉花～ the culture of cotton/ ～野生植物 domesticate wild plants ② foster; train; educate ③ 〈旧〉 help advance sb.'s career; patronize ◇ ～品种 cultivar/ ～植物 cultivated plant

【栽赃】 zāizāng ① plant stolen or banned goods on sb. ② frame sb.; fabricate a charge against sb.

【栽植】 zāizhí plant; transplant

【栽种】 zāizhòng plant; grow

【栽子】 zāizi young plant; seedling: 柳树～ willow slips/ 桃树～ peach seedlings

## zǎi

**仔** zǎi 〈方〉 ① son ② young animal; whelp
另见 zī; zǐ

**宰** zǎi ① slaughter; butcher: ～猪 butcher pigs ② govern; rule: 主～ dominate; dictate ③ government official (in ancient China)

【宰割】 zǎigē invade, oppress and exploit: 任人～ allow oneself to be trampled upon

【宰杀】 zǎishā slaughter; butcher

【宰相】 zǎixiàng prime minister (in feudal China); chancellor: ～肚里能撑船。A prime minister's heart is big enough to pole a boat in — a great person should be largehearted or magnanimous.

【宰制】 zǎizhì rule; dominate

**载** zǎi ① year: 一年半～ six to twelve months; six months to a year ② put down in writing; record: ～入记录 record in the minutes; place on record/ ～入史册 go down in history/ 刊～ publish (in a newspaper or magazine); carry/ 据报～ according to press reports/ 条约中～明 be clearly stated in the treaty
另见 zài

**崽** zǎi 〈方〉 ① son ② young animal; whelp

【崽子】 zǎizi 〔多用作骂人的话〕 whelp; bastard: 兔～ brat/ 狗～ son of a bitch

## zài

**再** zài 〈副〉 ① another time; again; once more: ～试一次 try again; have another try/ 一而～,～而三 again and again; repeatedly/ ～创新纪录 set another record/ 我不能～喝了。I can't drink any more./ ～来一个! Encore! ② 〔表示更加〕: 还有～大点儿的吗? Have you got a bigger one?/ ～好不过了。It couldn't be better./ 声音～大一点。Still louder, please./ ～冷的天我也不怕。I can stand colder weather than this. ③〔表示如果继续怎样〕: ～过几年,山村就要整个变样了。A few more years and there will be a complete change in the mountain village./ ～不走我们就赶不上火车了。We'll miss the train if we delay any longer. ④ 〔表示一个动作发生在另一个动作结束之后〕: 先到张家,～到李家。First go to the Zhangs', and then to the Lis'./ 你做完了功课～出去。Finish your homework before you go out./ 咱们跟群众商量后～决定。Let's consult with the masses before making a decision. ⑤〔表示另外有所补充〕: ～则 moreover; furthermore; besides/ ～不然 if not; or else; otherwise/ 到会的有社队干部,～就是贫下中农代表。Present at the meeting were commune cadres of different levels and also representatives of the poor and lower-middle peasants. ⑥ come back; return: 青春不～。One's youth never returns./ 良机难～。Opportunity knocks but once.

【再版】 zàibǎn ① second edition ② 〈旧〉 reprint; second impression

【再不】 zàibu 〈口〉 or else; or: 派老王去,～小李也行。Send Lao Wang, or else Xiao Li.

【再出口】 zàichūkǒu 〈商〉 reexport

【再次】 zàicì once more; a second time; once again: ～感谢你们的帮助。Thank you once again for your help./ 防止类似事件～发生 prevent the occurrence of similar incidents

【再度】 zàidù once more; a second time; once again: ～访问贵国 visit your country a second time/ ～当选 be reelected
【再会】 zàihuì 〈套〉 good-bye; see you again
【再婚】 zàihūn remarry; marry again
【再加】 zàijiā in addition; besides; on top of that: 下着大雨,～道儿不熟,所以他迟到了。What with the heavy rain and his not knowing the way, he was late.
【再嫁】 zàijià (of a woman) remarry
【再见】 zàijiàn 〈套〉 good-bye; see you again
【再教育】 zàijiàoyù reeducation: 接受～ receive reeducation; be reeducated
【再接再励】 zàijiē-zàilì make persistent efforts; continue to exert oneself; work ceaselessly and unremittingly
【再进口】 zàijìnkǒu 〈商〉 reimport
【再起】 zàiqǐ recurrence; resurgence; revival: 防止边境冲突～ prevent the recurrence of border clashes
【再三】 zàisān over and over again; time and again; again and again; repeatedly: ～考虑 consider over and over again/ ～嘱咐 bid or tell again and again
【再审】 zàishěn ① review ② 〈法〉 retrial
【再生】 zàishēng ① be a second so-and-so (a well-known figure already dead): 他手艺真巧,简直是鲁班～。His carpentry is really exquisite. He's another Lu Ban. ② 〈生〉 regeneration ③ reprocess; regenerate ◇ ～稻 ratooning rice/ ～检波器 〈无〉 regenerative detector/ ～纤维素 regenerated cellulose/ ～橡胶 reclaimed (或 regenerated) rubber
【再生产】 zàishēngchǎn 〈经〉 reproduction: 简单～ simple reproduction/ 扩大～ reproduction on an extended scale; extended (或 expanded) reproduction
【再生父母】 zàishēng fùmǔ one's great benefactor (usu. one's saviour)
【再衰三竭】 zài shuāi sān jié be nearing exhaustion; be weakened and demoralized
【再说】 zàishuō ① put off until some time later: 这事先搁两天～。Let's put the matter aside for a couple of days. ② 〈连〉 what's more; besides: 现在去找他太晚了,～我路也不熟。It's too late to go and see him now; besides, I don't quite know the way.
【再贴现】 zàitiēxiàn 〈经〉 rediscount
【再现】 zàixiàn (of a past event) reappear; be reproduced: ～在眼前 reappear before one's eyes/ 使红军过雪山的场面在银幕上～ reproduce on the screen scenes of the Red Army crossing snowcapped mountains
【再造】 zàizào give sb. a new lease on life: 恩同～ a favour tantamount to giving sb. a new lease on life
【再者】 zàizhě 〈书〉 moreover; furthermore; besides

**在** zài ① exist; be living: 这问题还～,并没有解决。The problem still exists. It's not solved yet./ 被推翻的剥削阶级人还～,心不死。People of the overthrown exploiting classes are still around and remain unreconciled to their defeat. ②〔表示人或物的位置〕: 我父母～农村。My parents are in the countryside./ 你的钢笔～桌子上呢。Your pen is on the table. ③ join or belong to an organization; be a member of an organization ④ 〈介〉〔表示时间、地点、情形、范围等〕: 事情发生～去年。It happened last year./ ～研究所工作 work in a research institute/ ～会上发言 speak at a meeting/ ～我看来 in my opinion; as I see it/ «～中国共产党第十一次全国代表大会上的政治报告» *Political Report to the Eleventh National Congress of the Communist Party of China*/ ～理论上 in theory; theoretically/ ～和平共处五项原则基础上 on the basis of the Five Principles of Peaceful Coexistence/ ～无产阶级领导之下 under the leadership of the proletariat/ ～这种情况下 under these circumstances/ ～农业学大寨群众运动的推动下 spurred by the mass movement to learn from Dazhai in agriculture/ ～国际事务中 in international affairs/ ～党内 within (或 inside) the Party/ ～全国范围内 throughout the country/ ～此期间 during this period/ ～革命的重要关头 at important junctures of the revolution/ ～这方面 in this respect ⑤〈副〉〔表示动作正在进行〕: 她～游泳。She is swimming./ 革命～发展,人民～前进。Revolution is in the ascendant and the people are on the march. ⑥ rest with; depend on: 学习好,主要～自己努力。Getting good results in one's studies depends mainly on one's own efforts./ 事～人为。Human effort is the decisive factor.
【在案】 zài'àn be on record: 记录～ be put on record; be a matter of record
【在编人员】 zàibiān rényuán permanent staff; those on the regular payroll
【在场】 zàichǎng be on the scene; be on the spot; be present: 当时我没～。I wasn't there at the time.
【在朝】 zàicháo hold office at court
【在行】 zàiháng be expert at sth.; know a job, trade, etc. well: 这方面我不～。I'm no expert at that./ 他打草鞋很～。He's good at weaving straw sandals./ 她对收音机很～。She knows a lot about radio sets.
【在乎】 zàihu ①〔多用于否定式〕care about; mind; take to heart: 满不～ not care a bit/ 只要能学会,少睡点觉倒不～。As long as I can learn it, I don't mind if I have to cut down on my sleep./ 战士们一天走一百里路毫不～。The soldiers think nothing of marching a hundred *li* a day. ② 见"在于"
【在即】 zàijí near at hand; shortly; soon: 完工～ will soon be completed; be nearing completion
【在家】 zàijiā ① be at home; be in: 你爸～吗? Is your father in?/ 我们让她～好好休息。We told her to stay home and have a good rest. ② 〈宗〉 remain a layman ◇ ～人 layman
【在教】 zàijiào be a believer (in a religion, esp. Islam)
【在劫难逃】 zài jié nán táo if you're doomed, you're doomed; there's no escape
【在理】 zàilǐ reasonable; sensible; right: 这话说得～。That's a perfectly reasonable statement./ 她说得～,我当然听她的。She's right, so of course I'll do what she says.
【在世】 zàishì be living: 他～的时候 in his lifetime/ 他妈要是还～,看到这样的好光景,该有多高兴啊! If his mother were alive, how happy she would be to see such good times.
【在所不辞】 zài suǒ bù cí will not refuse under any circumstances; will not hesitate to: 为革命赴汤蹈火～。I wouldn't hesitate to go through fire and water for the revolution.
【在所不惜】 zài suǒ bù xī will not grudge; will never balk at: 为了共产主义事业,即使牺牲生命也～。To advance the cause of communism, we will never balk at any sacrifice, even that of our lives.
【在所难免】 zài suǒ nánmiǎn can hardly be avoided; be unavoidable: 工作没有经验,出点差错～。Slips are unavoidable when you are new to your work.
【在逃】 zàitáo 〈法〉 has escaped; be at large ◇ ～犯 escaped criminal; criminal at large
【在望】 zàiwàng ① be visible; be in sight; be in view: 山头隐隐～。The mountain top was dimly visible. ② will soon materialize; be in sight; be in the offing: 胜利～。Victory is in sight./ 小麦丰收～。The wheatfields promise a good harvest.
【在位】 zàiwèi 〈旧〉 be on the throne; reign

【在握】 zàiwò be in one's hands; be within one's grasp; be under one's control: 大权～ with power in one's hands/ 胜利～。Victory is within grasp.
【在下】 zàixià 〈旧〉〈谦〉 I
【在先】 zàixiān formerly; in the past; before
【在心】 zàixīn feel concerned; mind; be attentive: 别看他大大咧咧的，什么事他都很～。He appears unconcerned, but nothing escapes his attention./ 这事儿请您在点儿心。Please keep an eye on the matter.
【在押】 zàiyā 〈法〉 be under detention; be in custody; be in prison ◇ ～犯 criminal in custody; prisoner
【在野】 zàiyě not be in office; be out of office ◇ ～党 a party not in office
【在意】 zàiyì 〔多用于否定式〕 take notice of; care about; mind; take to heart: 他只顾看信，别人对他说的话，他都没～。He was poring over the letter and didn't take any notice of what people were saying to him./ 这些小事他是不会～的。He won't take such trifles to heart.
【在于】 zàiyú ① lie in; rest with: 我们的力量～人民。Our strength lies in the people. ② be determined by; depend on: 有收无收～水，多收少收～肥。Water determines whether or not we have a harvest, and fertilizer determines whether the harvest is big or small.
【在在】 zàizài 〈书〉 everywhere; in all aspects: ～皆是 can be seen everywhere
【在职】 zàizhí be on the job; be at one's post: ～训练 in-service training/ ～期间 during one's tenure of office ◇ ～干部 cadres at their posts
【在座】 zàizuò be present (at a meeting, banquet, etc.): ～的还有几位归国华侨。Among those present were a few returned overseas Chinese./ 有客人～，她没好意思说。She was too embarrassed to bring it up in front of the guest./ 请～的同志们多提意见。We hope you comrades here will not hesitate to give your opinions and criticisms.

**载** zài ① carry; hold; be loaded with: ～客 carry passengers/ 卡车上满～着化肥。The truck was fully loaded with chemical fertilizer./ 代表团满～着中国人民的友谊回国。The delegation returned home bearing the friendship of the Chinese people. ② all over the road; everywhere along the way: 风雪～途。Whirling snow swept over the road. ③〈书〉 and; as well as; at the same time: ～笑～言 talking and laughing at the same time
另见 zǎi
【载波】 zàibō carrier wave; carrier: 三路～ three-channel carrier
◇ ～电报 carrier telegraphy/ ～电话机 carrier telephone/ ～电流 carrier current/ ～抑制 carrier suppression
【载歌载舞】 zàigē-zàiwǔ festively singing and dancing: 人们～热烈欢迎贵宾。Singing and dancing, people gave the distinguished guests a warm welcome.
【载荷】 zàihè load
【载货】 zàihuò carry cargo (或 freight)
◇ ～吨位 cargo tonnage/ ～甲板 cargo deck/ ～容积 cargo carrying capacity
【载频】 zàipín 〈无〉 carrier frequency ◇ ～放大器 carrier amplifier/ ～振荡器 carrier oscillator
【载人飞行器】 zàirén fēixíngqì manned vehicle
【载体】 zàitǐ 〈化〉 carrier: 催化剂～ catalyst carrier
【载运】 zàiyùn convey by vehicles, ships, etc.; transport; carry: 本市公共汽车每天～乘客十万左右。The city buses carry about 100,000 passengers a day.
【载重】 zàizhòng load; carrying capacity: 这辆卡车～多少？What's the carrying capacity of this truck?
◇ ～表尺 deadweight scale/ ～吨位 deadweight tonnage/ ～量 loading capacity; deadweight capacity (of a ship, etc.)/ ～汽车 truck; lorry/ ～线 load line; load waterline/ ～线标志 load line mark; freeboard mark; Plimsoll mark

## zān

**糌** zān
【糌粑】 zānba *zanba*, roasted *qingke* barley (青稞) flour, a staple food of the Zang nationality

**簪** zān ① hairpin: 碧玉～ emerald hairpin ② wear in one's hair: ～花 wear flowers in one's hair
【簪子】 zānzi hair clasp

## zán

**咱** zán ① we (including both the speaker and the person or persons spoken to): ～工人是国家的主人。We workers are masters of our country. ②〈方〉 I
另见 zan
【咱们】 zánmen ① we (including both the speaker and the person or persons spoken to): ～军民是一家。We, the army and the people, are all one family./ ～商量一下。Let's talk it over. ②〈方〉 I ③〈方〉 you: ～别哭，妈出去一会儿就回来。Don't cry, Mom will be back in a little while.

## zǎn

**拶** zǎn press or squeeze hard
另见 zā
【拶指】 zǎnzhǐ squeezing a person's fingers between sticks (a torture in old China)
【拶子】 zǎnzi sticks for squeezing a person's fingers (as a torture in old China)

**噆** zǎn 〈书〉 ① hold in the mouth ② sting; bite

**攒** zǎn accumulate; hoard; save: ～钱 save (或 scrape) up money/ 他把～的钱都买了书。He spent all his savings on books.
另见 cuán

**趱** zǎn ①〔多见于早期白话〕 hurry (或 rush) through: 紧～了一程 rush through one part of the journey ② urge; hasten: ～马向前 urge on a horse

## zàn

**暂** zàn ① of short duration: 短～ of short duration; brief ② temporary; for the time being; for the moment: ～别 temporary separation/ ～不答复 put off replying/ ～代 act for sb./ ～住 stay temporarily (at a place) /～停营业 business suspended
【暂定】 zàndìng arranged for the time being; tentative; provisional: ～议程 tentative agenda/ ～办法 provisional measures/ 学习期限～两年。The term of study is tentatively fixed at two years.
【暂缓】 zànhuǎn postpone; put off; defer: ～作出决定 put off (或 defer) making a decision
【暂记帐】 zànjìzhàng suspense account
【暂且】 zànqiě for the time being; for the moment: 讨论～告一段落吧。Let's stop the discussion for the time being./

这是后话，～不提。But I'm anticipating.

【暂缺】 zànquē ①(of a post) be left vacant for the time being ②(of a commodity) be out of stock at the moment

【暂时】 zànshí temporary; transient: ～的需要 temporary needs/ ～现象 transient phenomenon/ 比赛的胜负是～的，而友谊是长久的。The results of contests are transient, but friendship is lasting./ 这事～就这样定了吧。Let's make it a tentative decision./ 他～来不了。He can't come right away./ ～停刊 (of a periodical, etc.) temporarily suspend publication

【暂停】 zàntíng ①suspend: ～付款 suspend payment/ 会议～，明天继续举行。The meeting is adjourned till tomorrow. ②〈体〉time-out: 要求～ ask for time-out

【暂行】 zànxíng provisional; temporary: ～条例 provisional regulations/ ～规定 temporary provisions

**錾** zàn ①engrave on gold or silver; carve; chisel: ～字 engrave characters/ ～花 carve flowers or patterns ②engraving tool; chisel

【錾刀】 zàndāo (engraver's) burin; graver

【錾子】 zànzi chisel (for cutting stone)

**赞** zàn ①support; favour; assist: ～助 support; assistance ②praise; commend: 盛～ highly praise ③eulogy: 像～ an inscription eulogizing the subject of a portrait/ 《天安门～》 *Ode to Tian An Men*

【赞比亚】 Zànbǐyà Zambia ◇ ～人 Zambian

【赞不绝口】 zàn bù jué kǒu be profuse in praise; be full of praise

【赞成】 zànchéng approve of; favour; agree with; endorse: 咱们明天去郊游，你～吗？ How about going on an outing tomorrow?/ 我完全～。I'm all for it./ 他最不～你们这样搞。He doesn't like the way you do it at all./ 六票～，三票反对 six votes for and three against/ ～意见 assenting views/ ～的请举手。Those in favour please raise their hands. ◇ ～票 affirmative vote

【赞歌】 zàngē song of praise; paean: 一曲民族团结的～ a paean of national solidarity

【赞美】 zànměi praise; eulogize: ～社会主义制度的优越性 praise the superiority of the socialist system ◇ ～诗〈基督教〉hymn

【赞佩】 zànpèi esteem; admire

【赞赏】 zànshǎng appreciate; admire: 对这一友好行动表示～ express appreciation for this friendly act/ 他们非常～这些精美的工艺品。They greatly admired the exquisite handicrafts.

【赞颂】 zànsòng extol; eulogize; sing the praises of

【赞叹】 zàntàn gasp in admiration; highly praise: 演员们的高超演技令人～。People gasped with admiration at the superb skill of the performers.

【赞同】 zàntóng approve of; agree with; endorse: 这一主张得到普遍的～。This proposition met with general approval (或 acceptance)./ 我们～这项决议。We subscribe to the resolution./ 全车间一致～这项改革。The whole workshop unanimously agreed to this reform.

【赞许】 zànxǔ speak favourably of; praise; commend: 得到很多人的～ win the approval of many/ 值得～ deserve commendation; be commendable; be worthy of praise

【赞扬】 zànyáng speak highly of; praise; commend: ～声中找差距 seek out one's shortcomings amidst a shower of praise/ 这种一心为公的精神值得～。This spirit of selflessness deserves commendation./ 热烈～两国人民之间的友谊 pay warm tribute to the friendship between the two peoples/ 他们的良好体育作风博得广泛的～。Their fine sportsmanship won widespread acclaim.

【赞语】 zànyǔ words of praise; praise

【赞助】 zànzhù support; assistance: 这个展览会得到当地华侨的～。The exhibition had the help and support of the overseas Chinese there.

## zan

**咱** zan 〈方〉〔用在"这咱""那咱""多咱"里，是"早晚"二字的合音〕：你多～来的？When did you come?
另见 zán

## zāng

**赃** zāng ①stolen goods; booty; spoils: 分～ share the booty; divide the spoils ②bribes: 贪～ take bribes; practise graft

【赃官】 zāngguān corrupt official

【赃款】 zāngkuǎn money stolen, embezzled or received in bribes; illicit money

【赃物】 zāngwù ①stolen goods; booty; spoils ②bribes

**脏** zāng dirty; filthy: ～衣服 dirty (或 soiled) clothes; dirty linen/ ～水 filthy water; slops; sewage/ 别把桌布弄～了。Don't dirty the tablecloth./ 去掉脑子里资产阶级的～东西 rid one's mind of bourgeois muck (或 garbage)
另见 zàng

【脏字】 zāngzì obscene word; swearword; dirty word: 说话别带～。Don't swear.

**臧** zāng ①〈书〉good; right ②(Zāng) a surname

【臧否】 zāngpǐ 〈书〉pass judgment (on people): ～人物 pass judgment on people

## zǎng

**驵** zǎng 〈书〉fine horse; steed

## zàng

**脏** zàng internal organs of the body, usu. referring to the heart, liver, spleen, lungs and kidneys; viscera: 心～ heart/ 肾～ kidneys
另见 zāng

【脏腑】 zàngfǔ 〈中医〉internal organs including the heart, liver, spleen, lungs, kidneys, stomach, gall, intestines and bladder; viscera

【脏器】 zàngqì internal organs of the body; viscera

【脏象】 zàngxiàng 〈中医〉state of internal organs (visceral manifestations indicating physiological function as well as pathological changes of the internal organs)

**葬** zàng bury; inter: 海～ sea-burial/ 火～ cremation

【葬礼】 zànglǐ funeral (或 burial) rites; funeral

【葬身】 zàngshēn be buried: ～鱼腹 become fish food; be swept to a watery grave; be drowned/ 死无～之地 die without a burial place — come to a bad end/ ～在人民战争的汪洋大海之中 get drowned in the vast ocean of people's war

【葬送】 zàngsòng ruin; spell an end to: 右倾机会主义路线～了一九二四——一九二七年的大革命。The Right opportunist line was the ruin of the Great Revolution of 1924-1927.

**藏** zàng ①storing place; depository: 宝～ precious (mineral) deposits ②Buddhist or Taoist scriptures: 道～ Taoist scriptures ③(Zàng) short for the Xizang Autonomous Region ④(Zàng) the Zang nationality 参见"藏族"
另见 cáng
【藏红花】 zànghónghuā ①〈植〉 saffron crocus ②〈中药〉 saffron
【藏剧】 zàngjù Zang opera
【藏蓝】 zànglán purplish blue
【藏历】 Zànglì lunar calendar used by the Zang nationality
【藏青】 zàngqīng dark blue
【藏族】 Zàngzú the Zang (Tibetan) nationality, distributed over the Xizang Autonomous Region, Qinghai, Sichuan, Gansu and Yunnan

## zāo

**遭** zāo ①meet with (disaster, misfortune, etc.); suffer: ～难 meet with misfortune; suffer disaster/ 几～挫折 suffer repeated setbacks/ ～灾 be hit by a natural calamity/ 险～不测 have a near (或 narrow) escape ②〈量〉 round: 用绳子绕两～ wind the string around twice/ 走一～ make a trip ③〈量〉 time; turn: 在这么多人面前讲话,我还是头一～。This is the first time I have ever spoken to such a big audience./ 一～生,两～熟。Strangers at first meeting become familiar at the next.
【遭到】 zāodào suffer; meet with; encounter: ～失败 suffer (或 meet with) defeat/ ～拒绝 meet with refusal; be turned down/ ～困难 encounter (或 run up against) difficulties/ 这个工厂在地震中～严重破坏。This factory was seriously damaged during the earthquake.
【遭逢】 zāoféng meet with; come across; encounter: ～盛世 live in prosperous times/ ～不幸 suffer misfortune
【遭际】 zāojì circumstances; lot
【遭劫】 zāojié meet with catastrophe
【遭受】 zāoshòu suffer; be subjected to; sustain: ～资本家的剥削 suffer exploitation by capitalists/ ～帝国主义的压迫 suffer (或 be subjected to) imperialist oppression/ ～损失 sustain losses/ ～水灾 be hit by floods
【遭殃】 zāoyāng suffer disaster; suffer: 资本主义复辟,人民就要～。If capitalism were restored, it would be a disaster for the people.
【遭遇】 zāoyù ①meet with; encounter; run up against: ～不幸 meet with misfortune; have hard luck/ 先头部队与敌人～了。The advance unit encountered (或 ran into) the enemy. ②(bitter) experience; (hard) lot: 咱们有着共同的历史～。We have shared the same historical experiences. 或 We have had a common lot./ 他后来的～我就不知道了。I don't know what became of him later. ◇ ～战 meeting engagement; encounter (action); contact battle

**糟** zāo ①distillers' grains; grains ②be pickled with grains or in wine: ～鱼 fish pickled with grains or in wine; pickled fish ③rotten; poor: 这案板～了。The chopping board is rotten./ 他身体很～。He is in very poor health. ④in a wretched (或 terrible) state; in a mess: 把事情搞～了 make a mess of sth./ ～了,饭糊啦! Damn it! The rice is burning!
【糟糕】 zāogāo 〈口〉 how terrible; what bad luck; too bad: ～,我把钥匙锁在屋里了。Oh, no, I've locked the key in the room!/ 真～,误了火车啦。What bad luck! We've missed the train./ 更～的是,他把介绍信丢了。To make things worse, he lost the letter of introduction.
【糟害】 zāohài 〈方〉 (of birds or beasts) damage; make havoc of: 野兔～庄稼。Hares damage crops.
【糟行】 zāoháng distiller 又作"糟坊"
【糟践】 zāojian 〈方〉见"糟蹋"
【糟糠】 zāokāng distillers' grains, husks, chaff, etc. — foodstuffs for the poor ◇ ～之妻 wife who has shared her husband's hard lot
【糟粕】 zāopò waste matter; dross; dregs: 剔除～,吸取精华 reject the dross and assimilate the essence
【糟蹋】 zāota ①waste; ruin; spoil: ～粮食 waste grain/ 剪裁时要小心,别把料子～了。Cut the material carefully, don't spoil it. ②insult; trample on; ravage: 侵略军把这个村子～得不成样子。The invading troops left the village in a terrible state./ 说话可不要这样～人。You shouldn't talk about anyone like that. ③violate (a woman) 又作"糟踏"
【糟心】 zāoxīn vexed; annoyed; dejected: 事情搞得这样,真～。I'm really vexed (或 It's a damned nuisance) things have turned out this way.

## záo

**凿** záo ①chisel ②cut a hole; chisel or dig: ～一个窟窿 bore a hole/ ～山劈岭 tunnel through mountains and cut across ridges/ ～冰 make a hole in the ice/ 把船～沉 scuttle the ship
另见 zuò
【凿井】 záojǐng ①dig (或 sink, bore) a well ②〈矿〉 shaft sinking; pit sinking: 冻结法～ freeze sinking
【凿密】 záomì 〈机〉 caulking
【凿死理儿】 záo sǐlǐr 〈方〉 obstinate; stubborn; dogged
【凿岩】 záoyán 〈矿〉 (rock) drilling ◇ ～机 rock drill
【凿子】 záozi chisel

## zǎo

**早** zǎo ①(early) morning: 从～到晚 from morning till night/ 清～ early in the morning ②long ago; as early as; for a long time: 我～知道了。I knew that long ago. 或 That's no news to me./ 我～就想来看你了。I've been wanting to see you for a long time./ ～在二十世纪初 as early as the beginning of the twentieth century ③early; in advance; beforehand: 你～点儿来。Come early./ ～作准备 get prepared in advance; make timely preparations/ ～知如此,我就不回去了。If I'd known this beforehand I would not have gone back./ 电影离开演还～哩。It's still quite a while before the film starts. ④〈套〉 good morning
【早安】 zǎo'ān good morning
【早班】 zǎobān morning shift
【早餐】 zǎocān breakfast
【早操】 zǎocāo morning (setting-up) exercises
【早产】 zǎochǎn 〈医〉 premature delivery
【早场】 zǎochǎng morning show (at a cinema, theatre, etc.)
【早车】 zǎochē morning train or coach
【早晨】 zǎochén (early) morning
【早春】 zǎochūn early spring
【早稻】 zǎodào early (season) rice
【早点】 zǎodiǎn (light) breakfast
【早饭】 zǎofàn breakfast
【早花】 zǎohuā 〈农〉 early blossoming
【早婚】 zǎohūn marrying too early: ～妨碍工作和学习。Marrying too early hinders one's work and study.
【早年】 zǎonián one's early years: 他～参加革命。He took

part in the revolution in his early years.

【早期】 zǎoqī early stage; early phase: ～作品 sb.'s early works; the works of sb.'s earlier period/ ～食道癌 early stage carcinoma of the esophagus

【早起】 zǎoqi 〈方〉 (early) morning

【早日】 zǎorì at an early date; early; soon: 请～答复。Your early reply is requested. 或 Please reply at your earliest convenience./ 祝你～恢复健康。I hope you'll get well soon. 或 I wish you a speedy recovery./ ～完工 complete the project as soon as possible

【早上】 zǎoshang (early) morning

【早熟】 zǎoshú ① 〈生理〉 precocity: ～的孩子 a precocious child ② early-maturing; early-ripe ◇ ～品种 early-maturing variety; early variety/ ～作物 early-maturing crop; early crop

【早衰】 zǎoshuāi 〈医〉 premature senility (或 decrepitude); early ageing

【早霜】 zǎoshuāng early frost

【早退】 zǎotuì leave earlier than one should; leave early

【早晚】 zǎowǎn ① morning and evening: ～各服一丸 take one pill in the morning and one in the evening ② sooner or later: 他～得去。He'll have to go there sooner or later. ③ time: 他一清早就走了，这～多半已经到家了。He left early in the morning and should be home by now. ④ 〈方〉 some time in the future; some day: 你～上城里来，到我们这里坐坐。Drop in on us when you come to town. ◇ ～服务部 before-and-after-hours shop

【早先】 zǎoxiān previously; in the past: 这儿～是臭水塘，现在成了工人新村了。There used to be a stagnant pond here; now there are workers' flats.

【早泄】 zǎoxiè 〈医〉 premature ejaculation

【早已】 zǎoyǐ long ago; for a long time: 他～打定主意了。He made up his mind long ago.

【早早儿】 zǎozǎor as early as possible; well in advance: 要来，明天～来。If you want to come, come early tomorrow./ 既然要办，就～办。Since we've decided to do it, let's do it as soon as possible.

**枣** zǎo jujube; (Chinese) date; *tsao*

【枣红】 zǎohóng purplish red; claret

【枣泥】 zǎoní jujube paste

【枣树】 zǎoshù jujube tree

【枣椰】 zǎoyē date palm

**蚤** zǎo flea: 沙～ beach flea/ 水～ water flea

**澡** zǎo bath: 洗～ take a bath; bathe

【澡盆】 zǎopén bathtub

【澡堂】 zǎotáng public baths; bathhouse

【澡塘】 zǎotáng ① common bathing pool (in a bathhouse) ② 见"澡堂"

**藻** zǎo ① algae ② aquatic plants ③ literary embellishment: 辞～ ornate diction

【藻井】 zǎojǐng 〈建〉 sunk panel; caisson ceiling

【藻类学家】 zǎolèixuéjiā algologist

【藻类植物】 zǎolèi zhíwù algae

【藻煤】 zǎoméi boghead coal

【藻饰】 zǎoshì 〈书〉 embellishments in writing

## zào

**灶** zào ① kitchen range; cooking stove ② kitchen; mess; canteen: 学生～ students' dining room (或 canteen)

【灶神】 Zàoshén kitchen god 又作"灶君"；"灶王爷"

【灶台】 zàotái the top of a kitchen range

**皂** zào ① black ② *yamen* runner ③ soap: 香～ toilet soap/ 药～ medicated soap

【皂白】 zào-bái black and white — right and wrong: ～不分 make no distinction between right and wrong

【皂化】 zàohuà 〈化〉 saponification ◇ ～剂 saponifier

【皂荚】 zàojiá 〈植〉 Chinese honey locust 又作"皂角"

【皂隶】 zàolì *yamen* runner

【皂洗机】 zàoxǐjī 〈纺〉 soaper: 平幅～ open soaper

**造** zào ① make; build; create: ～一台铣床 make (或 manufacture) a milling machine/ ～房子 build a house/ ～舆论 create (或 prepare) public opinion/ ～预算 make (或 draw up) a budget/ ～表 draw up a form or list/ ～册 compile a register ② invent; cook up; concoct: 捏～ fabricate; concoct/ ～假帐 cook accounts ③ train; educate: 深～ pursue advanced studies/ 可～之才 a person suitable for training; a promising (或 hopeful) young person ④ 〈书〉 go to; arrive at: ～府 call at your house ⑤ one of the two parties in a legal agreement or a lawsuit: 两～ both parties ⑥ 〈方〉 crop: 早～ early crops/ 一年三～ three crops a year

【造币厂】 zàobìchǎng a mint

【造成】 zàochéng create; cause; give rise to; bring about: ～生动活泼的政治局面 create a lively political situation/ ～革命声势 build up revolutionary momentum/ ～既成事实 bring about a *fait accompli*/ ～巨大损失 cause enormous losses/ ～假象 put up a facade; create a false impression

【造船】 zàochuán shipbuilding ◇ ～厂 shipyard; dockyard/ ～工业 shipbuilding industry

【造次】 zàocì 〈书〉 ① hurried; hasty: ～之间 in one's hurry; in a moment of haste ② rash; impetuous: ～行事 act rashly

【造端】 zàoduān 〈书〉 begin; originate

【造反】 zàofǎn rise in rebellion; rebel; revolt: 对反动派～有理。It is right to rebel against reactionaries.

【造访】 zàofǎng 〈书〉 pay a visit (或 call); call on: 登门～ call at sb.'s house; pay sb. a visit

【造福】 zàofú bring benefit to; benefit: ～于人类 bring benefit to mankind/ 为后代～ benefit future generations

【造化】 zàohuà 〈书〉 the Creator; Nature

【造化】 zàohua good fortune; good luck: 有～ be born under a lucky star; be lucky

【造价】 zàojià cost (of building or manufacture): 这种桥～比较低。It costs less to build this kind of bridge.

【造就】 zàojiù ① bring up; train: ～一代新人 bring up a new generation/ 无产阶级必须～自己的知识分子队伍。The proletariat must build up its own army of intellectuals./ 伟大的革命斗争会～伟大的人物。A great revolutionary struggle creates great figures. ② achievements; attainments (usu. of young people)

【造句】 zàojù sentence-making

【造块】 zàokuài 〈冶〉 agglomeration

【造林】 zàolín afforestation ◇ ～面积 afforestation (或 afforested) area/ ～学 silviculture

【造陆运动】 zàolù yùndòng 〈地〉 epeirogenic (或 epeirogenetic) movement; epeirogeny; epeirogenesis

【造孽】 zàoniè 〈佛教〉 do evil; commit a sin

【造山带】 zàoshāndài 〈地〉 orogenic zone

【造山运动】 zàoshān yùndòng orogenic movement; orogeny; orogenesis

【造物】 zàowù the divine force that created the universe;

Nature ◇ ～主〈基督教〉 God; the Creator
【造像】 zàoxiàng 〈美术〉 statue
【造型】 zàoxíng ① modelling; mould-making: 这些古代工艺品～优美。These ancient art objects are beautifully shaped. ② model; mould ③〈机〉 moulding: 干砂～ dry sand moulding/ 潮砂～ green sand moulding/ 开砂～ open sand moulding ◇ ～板〈机〉 mould board/ ～艺术 plastic arts
【造谣】 zàoyáo cook up a story and spread it around; start a rumour: ～生事 start a rumour to create trouble; stir up trouble by rumourmongering
【造诣】 zàoyì (academic or artistic) attainments: ～很高 of great attainments
【造影】 zàoyǐng 〈医〉 radiography: 支气管～ bronchography
【造渣】 zàozhā 〈冶〉 slag making; slag formation
【造纸】 zàozhǐ papermaking ◇ ～厂 paper mill/ ～机 paper machine
【造作】 zàozuò make; manufacture
【造作】 zàozuo affected; artificial

**慥** zào 〈书〉 hurriedly; hastily
【慥慥】 zàozào 〈书〉 honest and sincere

**簉** zào 〈书〉 secondary; subsidiary: ～室 concubine

**噪** zào ① (of birds, insects, etc.) chirp: 蝉～ the chirping of cicadas ② a confusion of voices: 鼓～ make an uproar; clamour/ 名～一时 be a celebrity for a time
【噪鹃】 zàojuān Chinese koel
【噪鹛】 zàoméi laughing thrush
【噪音】 zàoyīn noise: 低～马达 low-noise motor ◇ ～污染 noise pollution/ ～抑制〈无〉 noise suppression

**燥** zào dry: ～热 hot and dry

**躁** zào rash; impetuous; restless: 戒骄戒～ guard against arrogance and rashness (或 impetuosity)/ 性子～ quick-tempered; hot-tempered/ ～动 move restlessly
【躁急】 zàojí restless; uneasy
【躁狂】 zàokuáng 〈医〉 mania ◇ ～者 maniac

## zé

**则** zé ① standard; norm; criterion: 准～ criterion; standard/ 以身作～ set an example by one's own conduct ② rule; regulation: 章～ rules and regulations/ 法～ law; rule ③〈书〉 imitate; follow: ～先烈之言行 follow the example of the martyrs in word and deed ④〈量〉〔用于分项或自成段落的文字的条数〕: 新闻一～ an item of news/ 寓言四～ four fables ⑤〈书〉〈连〉ⓐ〔表示因果、条件等〕: 物体热～涨,冷～缩。Objects expand when heated and contract when cooled./ 有～改之,无～加勉。Correct mistakes if you have made any and guard against them if you have not./ 不战～已,战～必胜。Fight no battle unless victory is sure./ 少～几年,多～几十年 several years at least and several decades at most; between several years and several decades ⓑ〔表示转折、对比等〕: 好～好,只是太贵。It's good but too expensive./ 今～不然。However, things are quite different today./ 资本主义已是日薄西山,社会主义～如旭日东升。Capitalism is already on the decline whereas socialism is rising like the morning sun. ⑥〈书〉〔用于"一、二(再)、三"等后面,列举原因或理由〕: 这篇课文不合适,一～太长,二～太难。This text is unsuitable. For one thing it's too long, for another it's too difficult. ⑦〈书〉〔表示肯定判断〕: 心之官～思。The office of the mind is to think.
【则甚】 zéshèn 〔多用于早期白话〕 what for: 问他～? Why ask him?
【则声】 zéshēng make a sound; utter a word: 不～ keep silent

**责** zé ① duty; responsibility: 爱护公物,人人有～。It is everybody's duty to take good care of public property. ② demand; require: 严以～己,宽以待人 be strict with oneself and broad-minded towards others/ 求全～备 demand perfection; nitpick ③ question closely; call sb. to account ④ reproach; blame; reprove: 自～ reprove oneself/ 斥～ reprimand; rebuke; denounce/ 痛～ rebuke severely; castigate ⑤ punish: 笞～ punish by flogging
【责备】 zébèi reproach; blame; reprove; take sb. to task: ～的眼光 a look of reproach/ 受到良心的～ feel a prick of conscience
【责成】 zéchéng instruct (sb. to fulfil a task); charge (sb. with a task); enjoin (sb. to do sth.): ～小组委员会提出报告 instruct the subcommittee to submit a report
【责罚】 zéfá punish
【责怪】 zéguài blame: 这事不应该～他。He should not be blamed for this.
【责令】 zélìng order; instruct; charge: ～主管部门采取有力措施 instruct the department in charge to take effective measures
【责骂】 zémà scold; rebuke; dress down
【责难】 zénàn censure; blame: 受到各方面的～ incur censure from various quarters
【责任】 zérèn ① duty; responsibility: ～重大 have a grave responsibility/ 先进的有～帮助后进的。The advanced are duty-bound to help those lagging behind./ 我不过是尽了自己的～罢了。I've done no more than my duty./ 负起～来。Shoulder your responsibility. ② responsibility for a fault or wrong; blame: 追究～ ascertain where the responsibility lies/ 你不应该把～推到别人身上。You shouldn't shift the blame onto others./ 这事如果搞不好,你要负～。If anything goes wrong, you'll have to answer for it.
◇ ～感 sense of responsibility (或 duty)/ ～事故 accident due to negligence; accident involving criminal or civil liability/ ～心 sense of responsibility (或 duty)/ ～制 system of job responsibility
【责问】 zéwèn call (或 bring) sb. to account
【责无旁贷】 zé wú páng dài there is no shirking the responsibility; be duty-bound
【责有攸归】 zé yǒu yōu guī responsibility rests where it belongs

**泽** zé ① pool; pond: 沼～ marsh; swamp/ 湖～ lakes ② damp; moist: 润～ moist; wet ③ lustre (of metals, pearls, etc.): 光～ lustre; gloss; sheen/ 色～ colour and lustre ④〈书〉 favour; beneficence
【泽国】 zéguó 〈书〉 ① a land that abounds in rivers and lakes ② inundated area: 尽成～ a whole area became submerged
【泽泻】 zéxiè 〈中药〉 the rhizome of oriental water plantain (*Alisma plantago-aquatica* var. *orientale*)

**择** zé select; choose; pick: ～友 choose friends/ 二者任～其一 choose either of the two/ ～日起程 fix a departure date/ 不～手段 by hook or by crook; unscrupulously 另见 zhái
【择伐】 zéfá 〈林〉 selective cutting (或 felling)
【择吉】 zéjí 〈旧〉 pick an auspicious day (for a marriage, funeral, etc.)

【择交】 zéjiāo choose friends: 慎重～ choose friends with care
【择善而从】 zé shàn ér cóng choose and follow what is good
【择捉】 Zézhuō Etorofu

**啧** zé ① compete for a chance to speak; dispute ② click of the tongue
【啧有烦言】 zé yǒu fán yán there are a lot of complaints
【啧啧】 zézé ① click of the tongue: ～称羡 click the tongue in admiration/ ～叹赏 be profuse in one's praise ② 〔形容说话声〕: 人言～。There is a good deal of unfavourable comment.

**帻** zé man's headdress used in ancient China

**舴** zé
【舴艋】 zéměng 〈书〉 boat

**箦** zé bed mat made of woven strips of bamboo

**赜** zé 〈书〉 subtle; abstruse

## zè

**仄** zè ① narrow: 逼～ narrow; cramped ② 〈语〉见"仄声"
【仄声】 zèshēng 〈语〉oblique tones, i.e., the falling-rising tone (上声), the falling tone (去声) and the entering tone (入声), as distinct from the level tone (平声) in classical Chinese pronunciation

## zéi

**贼** zéi ① thief ② traitor; enemy: 卖国～ traitor (to one's country)/ 工～ scab; blackleg ③ crooked; wicked; evil; furtive: ～眼 shifty eyes; furtive glance ④ crafty; sly; cunning; deceitful: 老鼠真～。Rats are really cunning. ⑤〈书〉 injure; harm; murder: ～害 murder ⑥ 〈方〉〈副〉〔多用于令人不满意的或不正常的情况〕extremely; disagreeably: ～冷 terribly cold/ ～亮 disagreeably glossy or dazzling
【贼船】 zéichuán pirate ship: 上～ board the pirate ship—join a reactionary faction
【贼喊捉贼】 zéi hǎn zhuō zéi a thief crying "Stop thief"
【贼眉鼠眼】 zéiméi-shǔyǎn shifty-eyed; thievish-looking
【贼去关门】 zéi qù guānmén lock the door after the thief has gone 又作"贼走关门"
【贼头贼脑】 zéitóu-zéinǎo behaving stealthily like a thief; stealthy; furtive
【贼心】 zéixīn wicked heart; evil designs; evil intentions: ～不死 refuse to give up one's evil designs
【贼星】 zéixīng (a popular name for) meteor
【贼赃】 zéizāng stolen goods; booty; spoils

**鲗** zéi cuttlefish

## zěn

**怎** zěn 〈方〉 why; how: 这样的好收成,社员～能不高兴呢？How can the commune members help rejoicing over such a good harvest?/ 你～不早说呀？Why didn't you say so earlier?
【怎的】 zěndi 〈方〉 what; why; how: 他就是不去,我能～？He just won't go. What can I do about it? 又作"怎地"
【怎么】 zěnme ①〔询问性质、状况、方式、原因等〕: 这是～回事？What's all this about?/ ～办？What's to be done?/ 你～啦？What's the matter with you? 或 Why, is anything the matter?/ 你～没去看电影？Why didn't you go to the film?/ 我～没听说过这事儿？How come I never heard of it?/ 你～搞的！See what you've done!/ 这个词～拼？How do you spell the word? ②〔泛指性质、状况或方式〕: 该～办就～办 do what must be done/ 你～说,我就～做。I'll do as you say./ ～强调也不过分 cannot be emphasized too strongly; cannot be overemphasized ③〔用于否定式,表示程度不够〕: 这地方我不～熟悉。I don't know much about the place./ 这首歌我还没～学会。I haven't quite learnt the song yet.
【怎么得了】 zěnme déliǎo where will it all end; what a terrible thing it would be; this is one hell of a mess
【怎么样】 zěnmeyàng ①〔询问性质、状况、方式等〕: 骑车去～？What (或 How) about going by bike?/ 后来这孩子～了？What became of the child?/ 演出的情况～？How was the performance? ②〔委婉说法,用于否定式〕: 这把扳子不～。This spanner isn't up to much./ 她唱歌不～。She's not much of a singer./ 他一时不小心,我们也不好把他～。We couldn't be too hard on him, he was just being careless.
【怎么着】 zěnmezhe ①〔询问动作或情况〕: 看完戏我就回家,你打算～？I'm going straight home after the play. What about you?/ 下午干什么？是小组讨论还是～？What's on this afternoon, group discussion or what? ②〔泛指动作或情况〕: ～也得把试验进行下去。The experiment must be carried on whatever happens./ 革命纪律人人要遵守,不能想～就～。Revolutionary discipline must be observed by all. No one can just do as he pleases.
【怎奈】 zěnnài 〔多见于早期白话〕 but; however
【怎样】 zěnyàng ①〔询问性质、状况、方式等〕: 这件事你～解释？How do you explain it?/ 步兵和炮兵～配合作战？How do the infantry and the artillery coordinate with each other? ②〔泛指性质、状况或方式〕: 想想从前～,再看看现在～ think of the past and look at the present

## zèn

**谮** zèn 〈书〉 falsely charge; slander; calumniate: ～言 slander; calumny

## zēng

**曾** zēng ① relationship between great-grandchildren and great-grandparents ② (Zēng) a surname
另见 céng
【曾母暗沙】 Zēngmǔ Ànshā Zengmu Reef
【曾孙】 zēngsūn great-grandson
【曾孙女】 zēngsūnnǚ great-granddaughter
【曾祖】 zēngzǔ (paternal) great-grandfather
【曾祖母】 zēngzǔmǔ (paternal) great-grandmother

**憎** zēng hate; detest; abhor: 爱～分明 be clear about what to love and what to hate/ 面目可～ repulsive in appearance
【憎称】 zēngchēng derogatory name for sb. one hates or loathes
【憎恨】 zēnghèn hate; detest
【憎恶】 zēngwù abhor; loathe; abominate

**增** zēng increase; gain; add: 产量猛～。Output in-

creased sharply./ 与日俱～ grow with each passing day; be on the increase/ ～高温室的温度 raise the temperature of a hothouse/ ～拨资金 allocate more funds/ ～兵 throw in more troops; augment one's forces; reinforce
【增白剂】 zēngbáijì 〈化〉 brightening agent; brightener
【增补】 zēngbǔ augment; supplement: 人员略有～。The staff has been slightly augmented./ 该书内容有所～。The book has been supplemented with new material. ◇ ～本 enlarged edition
【增产】 zēngchǎn increase production: ～节约 increase production and practise economy/ ～不增人 increase production without increasing the work force
【增充剂】 zēngchōngjì 〈化〉 extender
【增订】 zēngdìng revise and enlarge (a book) ◇ ～本 revised and enlarged edition
【增多】 zēngduō grow in number or quantity; increase: 来华参观访问的外国朋友日益～。More and more foreign friends come to visit China.
【增光】 zēngguāng add lustre to; do credit to; add to the prestige of: 为国～ do credit to one's country
【增加】 zēngjiā increase; raise; add: ～积累 increase accumulation/ ～收入 increase income/ ～工资 get a raise in pay/ ～困难 add to the difficulties; multiply the difficulties/ ～复种面积 extend the area of double or triple cropping; enlarge the multiple-cropping area/ ～体重 put on weight/ ～抵抗力 build up one's resistance to disease/ 产量比去年～一倍。Output is double that of last year./ 报名人数由三千～到五千。The number of applicants has gone up from 3,000 to 5,000.
【增进】 zēngjìn enhance; promote; further: ～各国人民的相互了解和友谊 promote (或 further) mutual understanding and friendship between the peoples of all countries/ ～健康 improve one's health/ ～食欲 whet one's appetite
【增刊】 zēngkān supplement (to a newspaper or periodical); supplementary issue
【增量】 zēngliàng 〈数〉 increment
【增强】 zēngqiáng strengthen; heighten; enhance: ～战斗力 strengthen fighting capacity; increase combat effectiveness/ ～信心 heighten one's confidence/ ～斗志 raise (或 heighten, boost) one's morale/ ～党性 enhance Party spirit/ ～防御力量 strengthen defence/ 发展体育运动，～人民体质。Promote physical culture and build up the people's health./ 夜间风力将～到六级。The wind will rise to force 6 at night. ◇ ～塑料 reinforced plastics
【增删】 zēng-shān additions and deletions
【增生】 zēngshēng 〈医〉 hyperplasia; proliferation; multiplication
【增塑剂】 zēngsùjì 〈化〉 plasticizer; plastifier
【增添】 zēngtiān add; increase: ～设备 get additional equipment/ ～力量和信心 gain strength and confidence/ 新出土的文物为研究古代史～了资料。The new archaeological finds provide fresh material for the study of ancient history./ 为社会主义大厦～一砖一瓦 add a brick and a tile to the edifice of socialism; do one's bit towards building socialism
【增效剂】 zēngxiàojì 〈化〉 synergist
【增益】 zēngyì 〈电〉 gain: 高～ high gain/ 分贝～ decibel gain ◇ ～控制 gain control
【增音机】 zēngyīnjī 〈讯〉 repeater
【增援】 zēngyuán 〈军〉 reinforce ◇ ～部队 reinforcements; reinforcing units
【增长】 zēngzhǎng increase; rise; grow: 平均～百分之四十 register an average increase of 40%/ 有计划地控制人口的～ control population growth in a planned way/ ～才干 enhance (或 develop) one's abilities/ ～知识 broaden (或 enrich) one's knowledge/ 产量比解放前～了七倍半。Output is 8.5 times what it was before liberation. ◇ ～率 rate of increase; growth rate
【增值】 zēngzhí 〈经〉 rise (或 increase) in value; appreciation; increment
【增殖】 zēngzhí ① 〈医〉 hyperplasia; proliferation; multiplication: 细胞～ proliferation of cells ② breed; reproduce; multiply; propagate ◇ ～率〈牧〉 rate of increase

**缯** zēng an ancient term for silk fabrics

**罾** zēng a square-shaped fishing net with poles as supports

## zèng

**综** zèng 〈纺〉 heddle; heald: ～框 heald frame
另见 zōng

**锃** zèng 〈方〉 (of utensils, etc.) polished: ～亮 shiny

**甑** zèng ① an ancient earthen utensil for steaming rice ② rice steamer ③ a utensil for distilling water, etc.: 曲颈～ retort
【甑子】 zèngzi rice steamer

**赠** zèng give as a present; present as a gift: ～书 present sb. with a book/ 某某敬～ with the compliments of so-and-so
【赠答】 zèngdá present each other with gifts, poems, etc.
【赠品】 zèngpǐn (complimentary) gift; giveaway
【赠送】 zèngsòng give as a present; present as a gift: 向演员～花篮 present a basket of flowers to the performers ◇ ～仪式 presentation ceremony
【赠言】 zèngyán words of advice or encouragement given to a friend at parting: 临别～ parting words of advice or encouragement
【赠阅】 zèngyuè (of a book, periodical, etc.) given free by the publisher ◇ ～本 complimentary copy

## zhā

**扎** zhā ① prick; run or stick (a needle, etc.) into: 手指上～了一根刺 prick one's finger on a thorn; have a splinter in one's finger/ ～一刀 stab with a knife ② 〈方〉 plunge into; get into: ～到人群里 dash into the crowd/ 扑通一声，他～进水里去了。He dived into the water with a splash./ 一头～进书堆里 bury oneself in books
另见 zā; zhá
【扎耳朵】 zhā ěrduo 〈口〉 grate (或 jar) on the ear; be ear-piercing
【扎根】 zhāgēn take root: ～于群众之中 take root among the masses/ ～农村干革命 strike root in the countryside and work for the revolution
【扎花】 zhāhuā 〈口〉 embroider
【扎猛子】 zhā měngzi 〈方〉 dive
【扎煞】 zhāsha 〈方〉 ① (of hands, branches, etc.) spread; stretch out: 他～着两只手，不知道干什么好。He spread out his arms, not knowing what to do. ② (of hair, etc.) stand on end
【扎实】 zhāshi ① sturdy; strong ② solid; sound; down-to-earth: 工作很～ do a solid job/ 扎扎实实地开展技术革新的群众运动 develop the mass movement for technical innova-

tion in a down-to-earth manner/ 这门基础课她学得很～。She has a good grasp of this basic course.
【扎手】 zhāshǒu ① prick the hand: 树上有刺,留神～。The tree is thorny. Mind you don't prick your hands. ② difficult to handle; thorny: 这事真～。This is really a hard nut to crack.
【扎眼】 zhāyǎn ① dazzling; offending to the eye; loud; garish: 这块布的颜色太～。This cloth is too dazzling./ 她穿得很～。She's loudly dressed. ② offensively conspicuous
【扎伊尔】 Zhāyī'ěr Zaïre ◇ ～人 Zaïrian
【扎针】 zhāzhēn 〈中医〉 give or have an acupuncture treatment: 上医务室～ go to the clinic for acupuncture treatment

**咋** zhā
另见 zǎ; zhà
【咋呼】 zhāhu 〈方〉 ① shout blusteringly ② show off 又作"咋唬"

**查** zhā ① 见"楂" zhā ② (Zhā) a surname
另见 chá

**哳** zhā 见"啁哳" zhāozhā

**渣** zhā ① dregs; sediment; residue: 豆腐～ soya-bean residue (after making bean curd)/ 蔗～ bagasse/ 猪油～儿 cracklings/ 炉～ slag; cinder ② broken bits: 面包～儿 (bread) crumbs
【渣油】 zhāyóu 〈石油〉 residuum; residual oil ◇ ～路 residual-oil road
【渣滓】 zhāzǐ dregs; sediment; residue: 溶液的～ dregs of a solution/ 社会～ dregs of society

**喳** zhā 〈象〉: 喜鹊的～～声 the chatter of magpies
另见 chā

**揸** zhā 〈方〉 ① pick up sth. with the fingers ② spread one's fingers

**猹** zhā badger-like wild animal

**楂** zhā 见"山楂" shānzhā
另见 chá

## zhá

**扎** zhá pitch (a tent, etc.)
另见 zā; zhā
【扎营】 zháyíng pitch a tent or camp; encamp
【扎挣】 zházheng 〈方〉 move with difficulty (because of physical weakness)

**札** zhá ① thin pieces of wood used for writing on in ancient China ② 〈书〉 letter: 适奉大～。I have just received your esteemed letter.
【札记】 zhájì reading notes

**轧** zhá roll (steel)
另见 gá; yà
【轧钢】 zhágāng steel rolling ◇ ～机 rolling mill
【轧钢厂】 zhágāngchǎng steel rolling mill: 大型～ heavy rolling mill
【轧辊】 zhágǔn 〈冶〉 roll; roller ◇ ～调整装置 roll adjusting device
【轧机】 zhájī 〈冶〉 rolling mill: 二辊式～ two-high mill/ 可逆式～ reversing mill/ 连续式～ continuous mill
【轧制】 zházhì 〈冶〉 rolling ◇ ～钢 rolled steel/ ～公差 rolling tolerance

**闸** zhá ① floodgate; sluice gate ② dam up water ③ brake: 气～ air (或 pneumatic) brake/ 踩～ step on the brake/ 捏～ apply the hand brake/ 紧急～ emergency brake/ 制动～ damper brake ④ 〈口〉 switch: 扳～ operate a switch; switch on or off
【闸流管】 zháliúguǎn 〈电子〉 thyratron
【闸门】 zhámén ① (水闸) sluice gate; gate; (船闸) lock gate ② 〈机〉 throttle valve
【闸瓦】 zháwǎ 〈机〉 brake shoe

**炸** zhá fry in deep fat or oil; deep-fry: ～豆腐 deep-fried bean curd/ ～糕 fried cake
另见 zhà
【炸酱】 zhájiàng fried bean sauce (usu. with minced meat) ◇ ～面 noodles served with such sauce

**铡** zhá ① hand hay cutter; fodder chopper ② cut up with a hay cutter: ～猪草 chop fodder for pigs
【铡草机】 zhácǎojī hay cutter; chaffcutter
【铡刀】 zhádāo hand hay (或 straw) cutter; fodder chopper

## zhǎ

**拃** zhǎ ① measure by handspans; span ② 〈量〉 span: 这块布有三～宽。This cloth is three spans wide.

**眨** zhǎ blink; wink: 眼睛一～ blink (one's eyes)/ 他向我～了～眼。He winked at me.
【眨巴】 zhǎba 〈方〉 blink: 这孩子的眼睛直～,想是困了。The child is blinking his eyes. He must be sleepy.
【眨眼】 zhǎyǎn very short time; wink; twinkle: 一～的工夫 in the twinkling of an eye

**砟** zhǎ tiny fragments of stone, coal, etc.: 炉灰～儿 cinder

**鲊** zhǎ 〈书〉 salted fish

## zhà

**乍** zhà ① first; for the first time: ～一听 at first hearing/ ～看起来 at first glance/ 新来～到 be a newcomer; be a new arrival ② suddenly; abruptly: ～暖还寒。After suddenly getting warmer, the weather has turned cold again./ 天气～冷～热。The temperature changes abruptly. ③ spread; extend: ～翅 spread wings
【乍得】 Zhàdé Chad ◇ ～人 Chadian

**诈** zhà ① cheat; swindle: 尔虞我～ each trying to cheat or outwit the other/ ～人钱财 swindle people out of their money; get money by fraud ② pretend; feign: ～死 feign (或 fake) death; play dead/ ～败 feign defeat ③ bluff sb. into giving information: 他是拿话～我。He was trying to draw me out.
【诈唬】 zhàhu bluff; bluster
【诈骗】 zhàpiàn defraud; swindle ◇ ～犯 swindler

【诈降】 zhàxiáng pretend to surrender; feign surrender
【诈语】 zhàyu lie; falsehood; fabrication

**咋** zhà 〈书〉 bite
另见 zǎ; zhā
【咋舌】 zhàshé be left speechless or breathless (with wonder or fear): 杂技演员的惊险动作使观众为之～。The acrobat's feat took the audience's breath away.

**咤** zhà 见"叱咤风云" chìzhà fēngyún

**炸** zhà ① explode; burst: 暖瓶～了。The thermos flask has burst. ② blow up; blast; bomb: ～桥 blow up a bridge/ ～毁 blow up; blast to pieces; demolish/ 把障碍物～掉 blast away the barriers/ ～平 bomb flat/ ～沉 bomb and sink/ 把敌人的工事～开一个口子 blow a hole in the enemy fortifications ③〈口〉 fly into a rage; flare up: 肺都气～了 flare up; explode with rage ④〈方〉 scamper; flee in terror: 鸡～了窝了。The chickens have all fled from their coop.
另见 zhá
【炸弹】 zhàdàn bomb: 爆破～ demolition bomb/ 杀伤～ antipersonnel bomb/ 定时～ time bomb ◇ ～坑 bomb-crater; crater
【炸胶】 zhàjiāo 〈化〉 blasting gelatine
【炸雷】 zhàléi 〈方〉 a clap of thunder
【炸药】 zhàyào explosive (charges); dynamite: 烈性～ high explosive/ 甘油～ dynamite/ 可塑性～ plastic explosive ◇ ～包 pack (或 satchel) of dynamite; explosive package; satchel charges

**栅** zhà railings; paling; bars: 木～ paling; palisade/ 铁～ iron railings; metal rails; iron bars/ 炉～ grate
另见 shān
【栅栏】 zhàlan ① railings; paling; bars ②〈军〉 boom: ～网 boom nets

**痄** zhà
【痄腮】 zhàsai 〈医〉 mumps

**蚱** zhà
【蚱蜢】 zhàměng grasshopper

**榨** zhà ① press; extract: ～甘蔗 press sugar cane/ ～油 extract oil/ ～干血汗 wring every ounce of sweat and blood out of sb. ② a press for extracting juice, oil, etc.
【榨菜】 zhàcài hot pickled mustard tuber
【榨取】 zhàqǔ squeeze; extort
【榨油机】 zhàyóujī oil press

## zhāi

**斋** zhāi ① 见"斋戒" ② vegetarian diet adopted for religious reasons: 吃～ practise abstinence from meat (as a religious exercise); be a vegetarian for religious reasons ③ give alms (to a monk) ④ room or building: 书～ study/ 学生宿舍第三～ Student Hostel No. 3
【斋戒】 zhāijiè abstain from meat, wine, etc. (when offering sacrifices to gods or ancestors); fast
【斋期】 zhāiqī fast days; fast
【斋月】 zhāiyuè 〈伊斯兰教〉 Ramadan; the month of fast

**摘** zhāi ① pick; pluck; take off: ～棉花(苹果) pick cotton (apples)/ ～花 pluck flowers/ 把眼镜～下来 take off one's glasses/ ～帽子 take off one's hat or cap/ 把灯泡～下来 remove the bulb/ ～白菜帮子 strip a cabbage of its outer leaves/ ～掉落后帽子 cast off (或 remove) the label of "backwardness"; catch up with the others ② select; make extracts from: ～译 translation of selected passages ③ borrow money when in urgent need
【摘抄】 zhāichāo ① take passages; make extracts; extract; excerpt ② extracts; excerpts: 雷锋日记～ pages (或 excerpts) from Lei Feng's diary
【摘除】 zhāichú 〈医〉 excise: ～腹部肿瘤 excise an abdominal tumour
【摘记】 zhāijì ① take notes: 报告很长,我只～了要点。The report was rather long. I just jotted down the main points. ② extracts; excerpts
【摘借】 zhāijiè borrow money when in urgent need
【摘录】 zhāilù ① take passages; make extracts; extract; excerpt ② extracts; excerpts: 文件～ extracts from a document
【摘棉铃机】 zhāimiánlíngjī 〈农〉 cotton stripper
【摘要】 zhāiyào ① make a summary: ～发表 publish excerpts (或 extracts) of sth. ② summary; abstract; *précis*: 社论～ the summary of an editorial
【摘引】 zhāiyǐn quote
【摘由】 zhāiyóu key extracts (of a document); *résumé*

## zhái

**宅** zhái residence; house: 赵～ the Zhaos' residence
【宅门】 zháimén ① gate of an old-style big house ② family living in such a house
【宅院】 zháiyuàn a house with a courtyard; house
【宅子】 zháizi 〈口〉 residence; house

**择** zhái select; choose; pick
另见 zé
【择不开】 zháibukāi ① unable to disentangle (或 undo): 线乱成了一团,怎么也～了。The thread is all in a tangle. I simply can't undo it. ② cannot get away from: 一点儿工夫也～ not have a moment to spare
【择菜】 zháicài trim vegetables for cooking
【择席】 zháixí be unable to sleep well in a new place: 我从来不～。I never have trouble sleeping in a strange place.

**翟** Zhái a surname

## zhǎi

**窄** zhǎi ① narrow: ～道 narrow path ② petty; narrow: 心眼儿～ petty; oversensitive ③ hard up; badly off
【窄轨铁路】 zhǎiguǐ tiělù narrow-gauge railway

## zhài

**债** zhài debt: 欠～ get (或 go) into debt; be in debt/ 还～ pay (或 repay, pay back) one's debt/ 借～ borrow money
【债户】 zhàihù debtor
【债款】 zhàikuǎn loan
【债权】 zhàiquán 〈法〉 creditor's rights ◇ ～国 creditor nation/ ～人 creditor
【债券】 zhàiquàn bond; debenture ◇ ～持有者 bondholder
【债台高筑】 zhàitái gāo zhù be heavily in debt; be up to one's ears in debt; be debt-ridden

【债务】 zhàiwù debt; liabilities ◇ ～国 debtor nation/ ～人 debtor
【债主】 zhàizhǔ creditor

**砦** zhài 见"鹿砦" lùzhài; "桩砦" zhuāngzhài

**寨** zhài ① stockade ② stockaded village ③ camp: 营～ military camp/ 安营扎～ pitch a camp; encamp ④ mountain stronghold
【寨子】 zhàizi stockaded village

## zhān

**占** zhān practise divination
另见 zhàn
【占卜】 zhānbǔ practise divination; divine
【占卦】 zhānguà divine by means of the Eight Diagrams (八卦)
【占课】 zhānkè divine by tossing coins
【占梦】 zhānmèng divine by interpreting dreams
【占星】 zhānxīng divine by astrology; cast a horoscope ◇ ～术 astrology

**沾** zhān ① moisten; wet; soak: 泪～襟 tears wet the front of one's jacket ② be stained with: ～水 get wet/ ～上了泥 be stained with mud/ 双手～满人民鲜血的刽子手 a butcher stained with the blood of the people ③ touch: 他跑得真快，脚不～地似的。He ran so fast that his feet seemed hardly to touch the ground./ 一～枕头就着 fall asleep as soon as one's head hits the pillow/ 烟酒不～ touch neither tobacco nor alcohol ④ get sth. out of association with sb. or sth.: ～点便宜 get a bargain
【沾边】 zhānbiān ① touch on (或 upon) only lightly: 检讨多少遍,思想不～ make self-criticism again and again but never touch on one's real thinking/ 这事他也沾了点边儿。He was involved in the affair to a certain extent. ② be close to what it should be; be relevant: 他唱得不怎么样，就是这几句还沾点边。He didn't sing well and those were the only lines that sounded anything like the way they should./ 你讲的一点也不～。What you say is completely irrelevant.
【沾光】 zhānguāng benefit from association with sb. or sth.: 我们工厂每周放电影,附近小孩儿都～。Kids in the neighbourhood enjoy the chance of seeing our factory's weekly film.
【沾亲带故】 zhānqīn-dàigù have ties of kinship or friendship
【沾染】 zhānrǎn be infected with; be contaminated by; be tainted with: 伤口～了细菌。The wound was infected with germs./ ～资产阶级生活作风 be contaminated by the bourgeois style of life/ ～坏习气 be tainted with bad habits/ ～官僚主义的灰尘 be tainted with the dust of bureaucracy ◇ ～剂〈军〉 contaminant/ ～区〈军〉 contaminated area
【沾手】 zhānshǒu ① touch with one's hand: 雪花一～就化。Snowflakes melt as they fall on one's hand. ② have a hand in: 看来这事他沾了手。It seems that he has a hand in the matter./ 这活儿她一～就会了。She got the hang of the job the moment she started it.
【沾沾自喜】 zhānzhān zì xǐ feel complacent; be pleased with oneself: 不要～于一得之功。Don't be complacent over occasional success.

**毡** zhān felt: ～帽 felt hat
【毡房】 zhānfáng yurt
【毡子】 zhānzi felt; felt rug; felt blanket

**粘** zhān glue; stick; paste: 把两块木片～在一起 glue the two chips of wood together/ 把信封～上 seal (up) an envelope/ 这糖不～牙。This candy doesn't stick to your teeth.
另见 nián
【粘连】 zhānlián 〈医〉 adhesion: 瘢痕性～ cicatricial adhesion
【粘贴】 zhāntiē paste; stick: 在墙上～标语 paste slogans on the wall

**詹** Zhān a surname

**谵** zhān rave; be delirious
【谵妄】 zhānwàng 〈医〉 delirium
【谵语】 zhānyǔ 〈书〉 delirious speech; wild talk; ravings

**瞻** zhān look up or forward
【瞻顾】 zhāngù 〈书〉 look ahead and behind
【瞻念】 zhānniàn look to; think of: ～前途 think of the future
【瞻前顾后】 zhānqián-gùhòu look ahead and behind — be overcautious and indecisive
【瞻望】 zhānwàng look forward; look far ahead: ～未来 look to the future
【瞻仰】 zhānyǎng look at with reverence: ～毛主席遗容 pay one's respects to the remains of Chairman Mao/ ～烈士陵园 pay a visit to the martyrs' mausoleum

## zhǎn

**斩** zhǎn ① chop; cut: ～断侵略者的魔爪 chop off the claws of the invaders/ 快刀～乱麻 cut the Gordian knot ② behead; decapitate: ～尽杀绝 kill all; wipe out the whole lot
【斩草除根】 zhǎncǎo-chúgēn cut the weeds and dig up the roots — destroy root and branch; stamp out the source of trouble
【斩钉截铁】 zhǎndīng-jiétiě resolute and decisive; categorical: ～地拒绝 give a categorical rebuff/ 他说得～。He spoke with curt finality.
【斩假石】 zhǎnjiǎshí 〈建〉 artificial stone; imitation stone
【斩首】 zhǎnshǒu behead; decapitate

**展** zhǎn ① open up; spread out; unfold; unfurl: ～卷 open a book/ 风～红旗。The red flags are fluttering in the wind./ 舒眉～眼 beam with joy ② put to good use; give free play to: ～技 give full play to one's skill/ 立大志，～宏图 cherish high aspirations and carry out a great plan ③ postpone; extend; prolong: ～限 extend a time limit ④ exhibition: 画～ painting exhibition/ 预～ preview ⑤ (Zhǎn) a surname
【展翅】 zhǎnchì spread the wings; get ready for flight: ～高飞 soar to great heights
【展出】 zhǎnchū put on display; be on show (或 view); exhibit: 展览会上～了各种各样的机床。A good variety of machine tools are on display at the exhibition.
【展缓】 zhǎnhuǎn postpone; extend; prolong: 行期一再～。The date for departure was postponed again and again./ 限期不得～。The time limit is not to be extended.
【展开】 zhǎnkāi ① spread out; unfold; open up: 把地图～ unfold the map/ 把队伍～ deploy the forces ② launch; unfold; develop; carry out: ～社会主义劳动竞赛 launch a socialist emulation drive/ ～攻势 unfold an offensive/ ～思想斗争 wage an ideological struggle/ ～热烈的讨论 set off

an animated discussion/ 运动会的各项比赛已全面～。The sports meet is now in full swing.

【展览】 zhǎnlǎn put on display; exhibit; show: 工业～ industrial exhibition/ 菊花～ chrysanthemum show/ 故宫博物院里有瓷器～。There is an exhibit of porcelain in the Palace Museum./ 部分新出土的文物正在国外～。Some of the ancient relics recently unearthed are on display abroad. ◇ ～馆 exhibition centre (或 hall)/ ～会 exhibition/ ～品 exhibit; item on display/ ～室 exhibition room; showroom

【展品】 zhǎnpǐn exhibit; item on display: 请勿抚摸～。Please do not touch the exhibits.

【展期】 zhǎnqī ① extend a time limit; postpone: 会议～举行。The meeting has been postponed./ 交易会～两天结束。The fair will be extended for another two days. ② duration of an exhibition; exhibition period

【展示】 zhǎnshì open up before one's eyes; reveal; show; lay bare: ～人物的内心世界 reveal a character's inner world/ 这场辩论～了问题的实质。The debate laid bare the essence of the issue.

【展望】 zhǎnwàng ① look into the distance: 登上山顶向四周～ climb to the top of the mountain and get a view of the surrounding country ② look into the future; look ahead: ～未来 look forward to the future/ ～前程,信心百倍。Looking ahead, we are filled with boundless confidence. ③ forecast; prospect: 八十年代～ prospects for the 1980's; 1980's in prospect

【展现】 zhǎnxiàn unfold before one's eyes; emerge; develop: 到了工地,一派繁忙的景象～在我们眼前。As we reached the construction site, a scene of bustling activity presented itself before our eyes.

【展性】 zhǎnxìng 〈物〉 malleability

【展转】 zhǎnzhuǎn 见"辗转" zhǎnzhuǎn

**盏** zhǎn ① small cup: 酒～ small wine cup ② 〈量〉〔用于灯〕: 一～电灯 an electric lamp

**崭** zhǎn ① 〈书〉 towering (over) ② 〈方〉 fine; swell

【崭新】 zhǎnxīn brand-new; completely new: 穿一身～的制服 wear a brand-new tunic suit/ ～的阶段 a completely new stage/ 文艺界呈现出一派～的气象。An entirely new atmosphere prevails in artistic and literary circles.

**搌** zhǎn wipe or dab (with a soft dry object) to sop up liquid: 纸上落了一滴墨水,快拿吸墨纸～一～吧。A drop of ink has fallen on the paper; blot it up quickly.

【搌布】 zhǎnbu dishcloth; dish towel

**辗** zhǎn

【辗转】 zhǎnzhuǎn ① pass through many hands or places: ～流传 spread from place to place; pass through many places/ 他从上海～到达陕北。He left Shanghai and reached northern Shaanxi after passing through many different places. ② toss about (in bed): ～不能成眠 toss and turn (in bed); unable to go to sleep ◇ ～相除法〈数〉 division algorithm

【辗转反侧】 zhǎnzhuǎn fǎncè toss about (in bed); toss and turn restlessly

**黵** zhǎn 〈方〉 make dirty; dirty; soil: 深色布禁 (jīn)～。Dark cloth doesn't show the dirt.

## zhàn

**占** zhàn ① occupy; seize; take: 霸～ forcibly occupy; seize/ 多吃多～ take more than one is entitled to; grab more than one's share/ ～用不少时间 take up much time ② constitute; hold; make up; account for: ～多(少)数 constitute the majority (minority)/ ～统治地位 hold (或 occupy) a dominant position/ ～世界第一位 rank first in the world/ ～总产值的百分之四十 make up (或 account for, amount to) 40 per cent of the total output value/ 光明面～优势,黑暗面～劣势。The bright side predominates over the dark./ 海洋几乎～地球表面四分之三。The sea covers nearly three-fourths of the earth's surface.

另见 zhān

【占据】 zhànjù occupy; hold: ～重要的战略地位 occupy a position of strategic importance

【占领】 zhànlǐng capture; occupy; seize: ～要塞 capture a fort/ 对于农村的阵地,社会主义如果不去～,资本主义就必然会去～。If socialism does not occupy the rural positions, capitalism inevitably will. ◇ ～军 occupation army/ ～区 occupied area

【占便宜】 zhàn piányi ① gain extra advantage by unfair means; profit at other people's expense: 占小便宜 gain petty advantages ② advantageous; favourable: 你个子高,打篮球～。A tall fellow like you has an advantage in playing basketball.

【占先】 zhànxiān take precedence; take the lead; get ahead of: 上个月劳动竞赛,第一组～了。The first team led all the others in last month's emulation drive.

【占线】 zhànxiàn 〈电话〉 the line's busy (或 engaged) ◇ ～通道〈电〉 active channel

【占有】 zhànyǒu ① own; possess; have: ～生产资料 own the means of production/ ～第一手资料 have firsthand data ② occupy; hold: 商业在国民经济中～重要地位。Commerce occupies an important place in the national economy.

【占着茅坑不拉屎】 zhànzhe máokēng bù lāshǐ neither shit nor get off the pot — hold on to a post without doing any work and not let anyone else take over; be a dog in the manger

**战** zhàn ① war; warfare; battle; fight: 持久～ protracted war/ 运动～ mobile warfare/ 夜～ night fighting ② fight: ～而胜之 fight and defeat the enemy/ 为保卫祖国而～ fight to defend one's motherland ③ shiver; tremble; shudder: 冷得打～ shiver with cold ④ (Zhàn) a surname

【战败】 zhànbài ① be defeated; be vanquished; suffer a defeat; lose (a battle or war) ② defeat; vanquish; beat ◇ ～国 vanquished (或 defeated) nation

【战报】 zhànbào war *communiqué*; battlefield report

【战备】 zhànbèi war preparedness; combat readiness: 加强～ step up combat readiness/ ～观念强 be prepared against war/ 一级～ first-degree combat readiness ◇ ～等级 degree of combat readiness/ ～工作 preparations against war/ ～粮 grain stockpiled in case of war/ ～行军 tactical march; tactical movement/ ～状态 combat readiness

【战场】 zhànchǎng battlefield; battleground; battlefront: 开辟新～ open another front/ 西北～ the Northwest theatre/ 奔赴～ go to the front

【战车】 zhànchē (war) chariot

【战刀】 zhàndāo sabre

【战地】 zhàndì battlefield; battleground; combat zone ◇ ～记者 war correspondent/ ～指挥部 field headquarters

【战抖】 zhàndǒu tremble; shiver; shudder

【战斗】 zhàndòu ① fight; battle; combat; action: 英勇～ put up a heroic fight/ 进行了数十次～ have fought scores of battles/ 作好～准备 get ready for action; be combat ready/

投入～ go into battle/ 在～中牺牲 be killed in action/ 每一次胜利都是经过激烈～赢得的。Each victory was won through fierce struggle. ② militant; fighting: ～的友谊 militant friendship/ ～的诗篇 militant poem/ ～岗位 fighting post/ 致以～的敬礼 with militant greetings/ 满怀～豪情 be filled with militant pride/ 充分发挥支部的～堡垒作用 give full play to the role of the Party branch as a fighting bastion
◇ ～部队 combat forces/ ～部署 tactical disposition/ ～队 fighting force/ ～队形 battle formation/ ～轰炸机 fighter-bomber/ ～机 fighter plane; fighter/ ～舰艇 combat vessels/ ～命令 combat orders/ ～任务 combat mission; fighting task/ ～性 militancy/ ～序列 order of battle; battle array/ ～意志 will to fight/ ～英雄 combat hero/ ～员 fighter

【战斗力】 zhàndòulì combat effectiveness (或 strength, capability); fighting capacity: ～强(弱) high (low) combat effectiveness/ 有～ combat-worthy/ 党组织的～ the fighting power (或 capacity) of a Party organization

【战端】 zhànduān the beginning of a war: 重启～。War broke out again.

【战犯】 zhànfàn war criminal

【战费】 zhànfèi war expenses

【战俘】 zhànfú prisoner of war (P.O.W.) ◇ ～营 prisoner-of-war camp/ ～收容所 prisoner-of-war collecting post

【战歌】 zhàngē battle song; fighting song: 大跃进～ battle song of the Great Leap Forward

【战功】 zhàngōng meritorious military service; outstanding military exploit; battle achievement: 立～ distinguish oneself in action/ 赫赫～ brilliant achievements in war

【战鼓】 zhàngǔ war drum; battle drum

【战国】 Zhànguó the Warring States (475-221 B.C.)

【战果】 zhànguǒ results of battle; combat success; victory: 取得辉煌～ achieve splendid results on the battlefield/ 扩大～ exploit the victory (或 success)

【战壕】 zhànháo trench; entrenchment

【战后】 zhànhòu postwar: ～时期 postwar period

【战火】 zhànhuǒ flames of war: 在那～纷飞的岁月里 in those war-ridden years

【战祸】 zhànhuò disaster of war

【战机】 zhànjī opportunity for combat: 抓住～消灭敌人有生力量 seize the opportunity for wiping out enemy effectives/ 丧失～ miss the opportunity to win a battle

【战绩】 zhànjì military successes (或 exploits, feats); combat gains

【战舰】 zhànjiàn warship

【战局】 zhànjú war situation

【战况】 zhànkuàng situation on the battlefield; progress of a battle

【战利品】 zhànlìpǐn spoils of war; captured equipment; war trophies (或 booty)

【战例】 zhànlì a specific example of a battle (in military science): 有名的～ a famous battle

【战栗】 zhànlì tremble; shiver; shudder: 吓得全身～ tremble all over with fear

【战列舰】 zhànlièjiàn battleship

【战列巡洋舰】 zhànliè xúnyángjiàn battle cruiser

【战乱】 zhànluàn chaos caused by war

【战略】 zhànlüè strategy: 全球～ global strategy
◇ ～部署 strategic plan (或 deployment, disposition)/ ～储备 strategic reserves (或 stockpiles)/ ～反攻 strategic counteroffensive/ ～核武器 strategic nuclear weapons/ ～家 strategist/ ～决战 decisive strategic engagement; strategically decisive battle/ ～思想 strategic thinking/ ～物资 strategic materials/ ～学 science of strategy/ ～要地 strategic area (或 place); important strategic point

【战马】 zhànmǎ battle steed; war-horse

【战前】 zhànqián prewar: ～时期 prewar period/ ～动员 mobilization before a battle

【战勤】 zhànqín civilian war service

【战区】 zhànqū war zone; theatre of operations

【战胜】 zhànshèng defeat; triumph over; vanquish; overcome: ～敌人 defeat (或 vanquish) the enemy/ ～困难 overcome (或 surmount) difficulties/ ～自然灾害 conquer natural disasters/ 社会主义必然要～资本主义。Socialism is bound to triumph over capitalism./ 增强无产阶级～资产阶级的力量 enhance the power of the proletariat for victory over the bourgeoisie ◇ ～国 victorious nation

【战时】 zhànshí wartime ◇ ～编制 wartime establishment; war footing/ ～内阁 wartime cabinet

【战士】 zhànshì ① soldier; man: 人民解放军～ PLA soldier (或 man) ② champion; warrior; fighter: 国际主义～ champion of internationalism/ 杰出的共产主义～ an outstanding fighter for communism

【战事】 zhànshì war; hostilities: ～结束 conclusion of the war; termination of hostilities

【战书】 zhànshū written challenge to war; letter of challenge

【战术】 zhànshù (military) tactics
◇ ～核武器 tactical nuclear weapons/ ～学 science of tactics/ ～训练 tactical training/ ～演习 tactical manoeuvre/ ～指挥员 commander of a tactical operation

【战天斗地】 zhàntiān-dòudì fight against heaven and earth; combat nature; brave the elements

【战无不胜】 zhàn wú bù shèng invincible; ever-victorious; all-conquering: ～的毛泽东思想万岁! Long live invincible Mao Zedong Thought!

【战线】 zhànxiàn battle line; battlefront; front: ～太长 overextended battle line; far-flung battlefront/ 思想～ the ideological front/ 在各条～上 on every front of endeavour; on all fronts

【战役】 zhànyì campaign; battle: 淮海～ the Huai-Hai Campaign/ ～性的进攻 offensive campaign ◇ ～学 science of campaigns/ ～指挥员 commander of a campaign

【战鹰】 zhànyīng fighting eagle (an affectionate term for a fighter plane)

【战友】 zhànyǒu comrade-in-arms; battle companion: ～的情谊 comradeship-in-arms/ 亲密～ close comrades-in-arms

【战云】 zhànyún war cloud: ～密布 gathering war clouds

【战战兢兢】 zhànzhànjīngjīng ① trembling with fear; with fear and trepidation: 敌军怕遭埋伏，～地向前移动。Fearing an ambush, the enemy troops advanced with trepidation. ② with caution; gingerly

【战争】 zhànzhēng war; warfare: ～的双方 the two sides in a war; both belligerents/ 从～中学习～。Learn warfare through fighting in war./ ～是政治的继续。War is the continuation of politics.
◇ ～边缘政策 brink of war policy; brinkmanship/ ～贩子 warmonger/ ～机器 war machine; war apparatus/ ～狂 war mania; war hysteria/ ～狂人 war maniac/ ～冒险 war venture; war gamble/ ～升级 war escalation/ ～温床 hotbed of war/ ～政策 policy of war; bellicose policy/ ～状态 state of war

## 栈

**栈** zhàn ① warehouse: 货～ warehouse; storehouse ② inn: 客～ inn ③ shed; pen: 羊～ sheep pen ④ 见"栈道"

【栈道】 zhàndào a plank road built along the face of a cliff

【栈房】 zhànfáng ① warehouse; storehouse ② 〈方〉 inn

【栈桥】 zhànqiáo (港口) landing stage; (火车站) loading bridge

**站** zhàn ① stand; be on one's feet; take a stand: ～起来 stand up; rise to one's feet/ 往后～～! Stand back!/ 别拿椅子了,就～着看吧。Don't bother to get chairs. Let's just stand and watch./ 我都～了一天了。I've been on my feet all day./ ～得高,看得远 stand on a high plane and see far ahead; have vision; be farsighted/ ～在党的立场上 uphold the stand of the Party/ ～到马克思列宁主义方面来 come over to the side of Marxism-Leninism ② stop; halt: 这车中途不～。This bus makes no stops along the way./ 不怕慢,只怕～。It's better to go slowly than just to mark time. ③ station; stop: 火车～ railway station/ 公共汽车～ bus stop/ 长途汽车～ bus station/ 终点～ terminal; terminus ④ station or centre for rendering certain services: 服务～ service station (或 centre)/ 校外活动～ after-school activities centre/ 粮～ grain supply centre/ 拖拉机～ tractor station

【站队】 zhànduì line up; fall in; stand in line: 我们站好了队准备出发。We lined up and got ready to start.

【站岗】 zhàngǎng stand (或 mount) guard; be on sentry duty; stand sentry: 今天晚上我～。I'm on sentry duty tonight./ 站好最后一班岗 (of one who is about to leave his job) continue working hard till the last minute

【站柜台】 zhàn guìtái serve as a shop assistant: 商业局干部经常到商店～。Cadres of the Commerce Bureau often go to shops to serve behind the counter.

【站票】 zhànpiào ticket for standing room ◇ ～观众 standee

【站台】 zhàntái platform (in a railway station) ◇ ～票 platform ticket

【站稳】 zhànwěn ① come to a stop: 等车～了再下。Don't get out until the car stops. ② stand firm; take a firm stand: ～脚跟 get a firm foothold; stand firm/ ～无产阶级立场 take a firm proletarian stand

【站长】 zhànzhǎng head of a station, centre, etc.: 火车站～ stationmaster

【站住】 zhànzhù ① stop; halt: 他听到有人叫他～。He heard someone calling to him to stop./ ～,要不就开枪了! Halt, or I fire!/ 谁?～! Who's that? Don't move! ② stand firmly on one's feet; keep one's feet: 风刮得人都站不住了。The wind was so strong that one could hardly keep one's feet. ③ stand (或 hold) one's ground; consolidate one's position ④ hold water; be tenable: 他的说法站不住。His opinion doesn't hold water.

【站住脚】 zhànzhùjiǎo ① stop; halt: 他跑得太快,一下子站不住脚。He was running too fast to stop suddenly. ② stand (或 hold) one's ground; consolidate one's position: 我们向敌人猛烈攻击,打得他们站不住脚。We attacked the enemy so fiercely that they couldn't hold their ground./ 游击队不依靠群众就站不住脚。The guerrillas would be unable to hold their ground if they failed to rely on the masses. ③ stay put: 忙得站不住脚 be so busy one can't stand still ④ hold water; be tenable: 这些论点没有一个是站得住脚的。None of these arguments are tenable.

**绽** zhàn split; burst: 衣裳～线了。The seam has split (或 burst)./ 鞋开～了。The shoe has split open.

**湛** zhàn ① profound; deep: 精～ consummate; exquisite ② crystal clear ③ (Zhàn) a surname

【湛蓝】 zhànlán azure blue; azure

**颤** zhàn tremble; shiver; shudder: 她打了一个寒～。A cold shiver ran down her spine.

另见 chàn

【颤栗】 zhànlì tremble; shiver; shudder

**蘸** zhàn dip in (ink, sauce, etc.): ～墨水 dip in ink/ 大葱～酱 scallions dipped in thick sauce

【蘸火】 zhànhuǒ 〈口〉 quenching

【蘸水钢笔】 zhànshuǐ gāngbǐ pen (with a nib fixed into a penholder)

## zhāng

**张** zhāng ① open; spread; stretch: ～开手 open one's hand/ ～翅膀 spread the wings/ ～网 spread a net/ ～开双臂 stretch out both arms/ ～弓 draw a bow/ ～帆 make sail; hoist sail ② set out; display: 大～筵席 lay on a feast ③ magnify; exaggerate: 夸～ exaggerate; overstate ④ look: 东～西望 gaze (或 peer) around ⑤ opening of a new shop: 开～ open a business; begin doing business ⑥ 〈量〉: 一～桌子 a table/ 两～床 two beds/ 一～纸 a piece (或 sheet) of paper/ 一～弓 a bow/ 你这～嘴啊! What a tongue you've got! ⑦ (Zhāng) a surname

【张本】 zhāngběn ① an anticipatory action ② a hint foreshadowing later developments in a story; an anticipatory remark

【张大】 zhāngdà magnify; exaggerate; publicize widely: ～其词 exaggerate/ ～其事 publicize the matter widely

【张灯结彩】 zhāngdēng-jiécǎi be decorated with lanterns and coloured streamers

【张挂】 zhāngguà hang up (a picture, curtain, etc.)

【张冠李戴】 Zhāng guān Lǐ dài put Zhang's hat on Li's head — attribute sth. to the wrong person or confuse one thing with another

【张皇】 zhānghuáng 〈书〉 ① alarmed; scared; flurried; flustered: ～失措 be in a flurry of alarm; lose one's head; get into a panic ② magnify; exaggerate

【张家长,李家短】 Zhāng jiā cháng, Lǐ jiā duǎn the virtues of the Zhangs and the defects of the Lis — gossip

【张口结舌】 zhāngkǒu-jiéshé be agape and tongue-tied; be at a loss for words: 他被问得～,半天说不出话来。He was stumped by the questions and remained tongue-tied for a good while.

【张狂】 zhāngkuáng flippant and impudent; insolent

【张力】 zhānglì 〈物〉 ① tension: 表面～ surface tension ② pulling force ◇ ～计 tensiometer

【张量】 zhāngliàng 〈数〉 tensor

【张罗】 zhāngluo ① take care of; get busy about: 场院的活让王大爷～。Uncle Wang will take care of the work on the threshing floor./ 要带的东西早点儿收拾好,不要临时～。Get your things ready in good time to avoid a last-minute rush./ 他还没有对象,您给～～。He hasn't got a girl to marry yet. Can't you do something about it? ② raise (funds); get together (money, etc.): ～一笔钱 raise a sum of money ③ greet and entertain (guests); attend to (customers, etc.): 她正忙着～客人。She's busy looking after the guests./ 我们坐一会儿就走,您别～。We'll only stay for a few minutes. Please don't bother (about serving tea, etc.)./ 顾客很多,一个售货员～不过来。There were too many customers for one shop assistant to attend to.

【张目】 zhāngmù ① open one's eyes wide ②〔多用于〕:为某人～ boost sb.'s arrogance; build up another

【张三李四】 Zhāng Sān Lǐ Sì Zhang, Li or anybody; any Tom, Dick or Harry

【张贴】 zhāngtiē put up (a notice, poster, etc.): ～海报 put up posters/ ～通告 post a notice/ 禁止～。Post no bills.

【张望】 zhāngwàng ① peep (through a crack, etc.) ② look

around: 探头～ crane one's neck and look around
【张牙舞爪】 zhāngyá-wǔzhǎo bare fangs and brandish claws — make threatening gestures; engage in sabre rattling
【张扬】 zhāngyáng make widely known; make public; publicize: 四处～ publicize everywhere; spread (a story) all over the place/ 这事还没定下来，先别～出去。The final decision hasn't been made yet, so don't spread this around.
【张应力】 zhāngyìnglì 〈物〉 tensile stress
【张嘴】 zhāngzuǐ ① open one's mouth (to say sth.): 他正要～，一个年轻妇女抢先说了。He was on the point of saying something when a young woman started to speak. ② ask for a loan or a favour: 我想找他帮忙，又不好意思～。I would have liked him to give me a hand, but found it embarrassing to ask.

**章** zhāng ① chapter; section: 全书共二十～。The book has twenty chapters./ 乐～ movement (of a symphony, etc.) ② order: 杂乱无～ disorderly and unsystematic ③ rules; regulations; constitution: 规～ rules and regulations/ 党～ the Party Constitution ④ seal; stamp: 盖～ affix one's seal; seal; stamp/ 公～ official seal ⑤ badge; medal: 领～ collar badge (或 insignia)/ 奖～ medal; decoration/ 袖～ armband ⑥ (Zhāng) a surname
【章程】 zhāngchéng rules; regulations; constitution
【章程】 zhāngcheng 〈方〉 solution; way: 我心里还没个准～。I'm not sure yet what's the best way.
【章动】 zhāngdòng 〈天〉 nutation: 黄经～ nutation in longitude/ 倾角～ nutation in obliquity
【章法】 zhāngfǎ ① presentation of ideas in a piece of writing; art of composition: 文章结构严谨，很有～。The article is well organized and the ideas are skilfully presented. ② orderly ways; methodicalness: 他办事很有～。He is quite methodical in his work./ 碰到这样意外的事，他乱了～。He was thrown off balance by such an unexpected turn of events.
【章回小说】 zhānghuí xiǎoshuō a type of traditional Chinese novel with each chapter headed by a couplet giving the gist of its content
【章节】 zhāngjié chapters and sections
【章句】 zhāngjù ① chapters, sections, sentences and phrases in ancient writings ② syntactic and semantic analysis of ancient writings
【章鱼】 zhāngyú octopus
【章则】 zhāngzé rules and regulations

**彰** zhāng clear; evident; conspicuous: ～～若是 as clear (或 obvious) as that/ ～～在人耳目 be clear for all to see
【彰明较著】 zhāngmíng jiào zhù very obvious; easily seen

**嫜** zhāng 〈书〉 husband's father; father-in-law: 姑～ husband's parents; parents-in-law

**獐** zhāng river deer
【獐头鼠目】 zhāngtóu-shǔmù with the head of a buck and the eyes of a rat — repulsively ugly and sly-looking
【獐子】 zhāngzi river deer

**璋** zhāng a jade tablet

**樟** zhāng camphor tree
【樟木】 zhāngmù camphorwood
【樟脑】 zhāngnǎo camphor ◇ ～丸 camphor ball; mothball/ ～油 camphor oil
【樟树】 zhāngshù camphor tree

**蟑** zhāng
【蟑螂】 zhāngláng cockroach; roach

## zhǎng

**长** zhǎng ① older; elder; senior: 比他年～ older than him/ 他比我～一辈。He belongs to my father's generation. ② eldest; oldest: ～兄 eldest brother/ ～女 eldest daughter ③ chief; head: 科～ section chief/ 代表团团～ head of a delegation ④ grow; develop: 青年时期是～身体的时期。Youth is the time of physical growth./ 庄稼～得很旺。The crops are growing very well./ 这孩子光～个儿，不～肉。The child keeps growing taller but doesn't fill out. ⑤ come into being; begin to grow; form: ～疮 have a boil/ ～癌 get cancer/ ～锈 get rusty/ 孩子～牙了。The baby is teething./ ～叶子了。The leaves are coming out./ 桃树～虫了。The peach tree is wormy. ⑥ acquire; enhance; increase: ～见识 increase one's knowledge; gain experience/ 此风不可～。Such a tendency is not to be encouraged./ ～自己的志气，灭敌人的威风 boost our morale and dampen the enemy's spirit
另见 cháng
【长辈】 zhǎngbèi elder member of a family; elder; senior
【长大】 zhǎngdà grow up; be brought up: 在红旗下～ be brought up (或 grow up) under the red flag
【长官】 zhǎngguān 〈旧〉 senior officer or official; commanding officer
【长机】 zhǎngjī 〈军〉 lead aircraft; leader
【长进】 zhǎngjìn progress: 在学习上很有～ make good progress in one's studies
【长老】 zhǎnglǎo ① elder ② elder of a Buddhist monastery
【长势】 zhǎngshì the way a crop is growing: 作物～良好。The crops are doing well./ 棉花～喜人。The cotton is coming along fine.
【长孙】 zhǎngsūn ① son's eldest son; eldest grandson ② (Zhǎngsūn) a surname
【长相】 zhǎngxiàng 〈口〉 looks; features; appearance: ～好 be good-looking/ 看她们的～好象是姐儿俩。They look like sisters.
【长者】 zhǎngzhě ① elder; senior ② venerable elder
【长子】 zhǎngzǐ eldest son ◇ ～继承权 (right of) primogeniture; birthright

**涨** zhǎng (of water, prices, etc.) rise; go up: 河水暴～。The river suddenly rose. 或 The river was in spate.
另见 zhàng
【涨潮】 zhǎngcháo rising tide; flood tide: 正在～。The tide is at the flood.
【涨风】 zhǎngfēng upward trend of prices
【涨价】 zhǎngjià rise in price
【涨落】 zhǎng-luò (of water, prices, etc.) rise and fall; fluctuate: 潮水的～ ebb and flow of the tide/ 价格的～ fluctuations of prices

**掌** zhǎng ① palm: 击～为号 signal by clapping hands ② strike with the palm of the hand; slap: ～嘴 slap sb. on the face ③ hold in one's hand; be in charge of; control; wield: ～兵权 wield military power; have command of the armed forces ④ the bottom of certain animals' feet; pad; sole: 脚～ sole (of a human foot)/ 鸭～ duck's foot/ 熊～ bear's paw ⑤ shoe sole or heel: 鞋子打前

后～ have a shoe soled and heeled ⑥ horseshoe: 这匹马该钉～了。It's time for the horse to be shod.

【掌鞭】 zhǎngbiān 〈方〉 cart driver; carter

【掌灯】 zhǎngdēng ① hold a lamp in one's hand ② light an oil lamp

【掌舵】 zhǎngduò be at the helm; operate the rudder; take the tiller; steer a boat: 我们有华主席～,革命事业就能继续胜利前进。With Chairman Hua at the helm, our revolutionary cause will continue to advance victoriously. ◇ ～人 helmsman; steersman

【掌骨】 zhǎnggǔ 〈生理〉 metacarpal bone

【掌故】 zhǎnggù anecdotes: 文坛～ literary anecdotes/ 他熟悉这座城市的～。He knows a lot of historical anecdotes about this city.

【掌管】 zhǎngguǎn be in charge of; administer: ～财政 administer finances/ ～一个部门 be in charge of a department/ 各项事务都有专人～。Everything is taken care of by specially assigned people.

【掌柜】 zhǎngguì shopkeeper; manager (of a shop)

【掌权】 zhǎngquán be in power; wield power; exercise control

【掌上明珠】 zhǎngshàng míngzhū a pearl in the palm — a beloved daughter

【掌勺儿】 zhǎngsháor be the *chef* ◇ ～的 *chef*

【掌声】 zhǎngshēng clapping; applause: 经久不息的～ prolonged applause/ 全场～雷动。The audience burst into thunderous applause.

【掌握】 zhǎngwò ① grasp; master; know well: ～马列主义 grasp Marxism-Leninism/ ～党的政策 have a good grasp of the Party's policies/ ～新情况 keep abreast of new developments/ ～工作进程 keep informed on how the work is progressing/ ～一门外国语 have a good command of a foreign language/ ～现代生产技能和科学知识 master modern techniques of production and scientific knowledge/ ～思想教育,是团结全党进行伟大政治斗争的中心环节。Ideological education is the key link to be grasped in uniting the whole Party for great political struggles. ② have in hand; take into one's hands; control: ～办公室的钥匙 keep the key to the office/ ～局势 have the situation well in hand; have the situation under control/ ～主动权 have the initiative in one's hands/ ～自己的命运 take one's destiny into one's own hands; be master of one's own destiny/ ～国家的经济命脉 control the economic lifelines of the country/ ～斗争大方向 keep to the general orientation of the struggle/ ～会议 preside over a meeting/ ～分寸 exercise sound judgment; act or speak properly

【掌心】 zhǎngxīn the centre (或 hollow) of the palm: 孙悟空跳不出如来佛的～。The Monkey King cannot jump out of Buddha's palm — be unable to escape.

【掌印】 zhǎngyìn keep the seal — be in power

【掌子】 zhǎngzi 〈矿〉 face; work area ◇ ～面 face

## 礃

zhǎng

【礃子】 zhǎngzi 见"掌子" zhǎngzi

## zhàng

## 丈

zhàng ① *zhang*, a unit of length (=3 1/3 metres) ② measure (land): 清～ make an exact measurement of the land ③ a form of address for certain male relatives by marriage: 岳～ wife's father; father-in-law/ 姐～ elder sister's husband; brother-in-law/ 姑～ the husband of one's father's sister; uncle

【丈夫】 zhàngfū man: ～气概 manliness

【丈夫】 zhàngfu husband

【丈量】 zhàngliáng measure (land): ～土地 measure land; take the dimensions of a field

【丈母娘】 zhàngmuniáng wife's mother; mother-in-law 又作"丈母"

【丈人】 zhàngren wife's father; father-in-law

## 仗

zhàng ① 〈书〉 weaponry; weapons: 仪～ flags, weapons, etc. carried by a guard of honour/ 明火执～ carry torches and weapons in a robbery — conduct evil activities openly ② hold (a weapon): ～剑 hold a sword ③ rely on; depend on: 这事我一人干不了,全～大家帮忙。I can't manage it on my own. I must rely on all of you for help. ④ battle; war: 打～ go to war; be at war/ 硬～ hard-fought battle; tough fight/ 打了一个漂亮～ won a brilliant victory/ 打好春耕这一～ make a success of this spring ploughing

【仗势欺人】 zhàng shì qī rén take advantage of one's or sb. else's power to bully people; bully others on the strength of one's powerful connections or position

【仗恃】 zhàngshì rely on (an advantage)

【仗义疏财】 zhàng yì shū cái be generous in aiding needy people

【仗义执言】 zhàng yì zhí yán speak out from a sense of justice

## 杖

zhàng ① cane; stick: 扶～而行 walk with a cane/ 手～ (walking) stick ② rod or staff used for a specific purpose: 擀面～ rolling pin ③ flogging with a stick (a punishment in ancient China)

## 帐

zhàng ① curtain; canopy: 营～ tent/ 蚊～ mosquito net ② account: 记～ keep accounts/ 结～ settle (或 square) accounts ③ account book ④ debt; credit: 还～ repay a debt/ 赊～ buy or sell on credit

【帐簿】 zhàngbù account book 又作"帐本"

【帐单】 zhàngdān bill; check

【帐房】 zhàngfáng 〈旧〉 ① accountant's office ② accountant

【帐钩】 zhànggōu bed-curtain or mosquito net hook

【帐户】 zhànghù account: 非贸易～ noncommercial account/ 在银行开立(结束)～ open (close) an account with a bank

【帐款】 zhàngkuǎn funds on account; credit

【帐面价值】 zhàngmiàn jiàzhí book value

【帐目】 zhàngmù items of an account; accounts: 清理～ square accounts/ 定期公布～ publish the accounts regularly/ ～公开 accounts open to public inspection/ ～不清。The accounts (或 books) are not in order.

【帐幕】 zhàngmù tent

【帐篷】 zhàngpeng tent: 搭(拆)～ pitch (strike) a tent

【帐子】 zhàngzi ① bed-curtain ② mosquito net

## 胀

zhàng ① expand; distend: 热～冷缩 expand when heated and contract when cooled ② swell; be bloated: 肿～ swollen/ 吃多了,感到肚子有点发～ feel bloated after overeating

## 涨

zhàng ① swell after absorbing water, etc.: 豆子泡～了。The beans swelled up after being soaked. ② (of the head) be swelled by a rush of blood: 气得～红了脸 redden (或 flush) with anger/ 头昏脑～ feel one's head swimming ③〔用于度量衡或货币的数目〕 be more, larger, etc. than expected: 上个月他钱花～了。Last month he couldn't make ends meet./ 把布一量,～出了半尺。When the cloth was measured, it was found to be half a *chi* longer than expected.

另见 zhǎng

**障** zhàng ①hinder; obstruct ②barrier; block: 路～ roadblock; barricade

【障碍】 zhàng'ài ①hinder; obstruct ②obstacle; obstruction; barrier; impediment: 扫清～ clear away obstacles/ 制造～ erect barriers; create obstacles
◇ ～船〈军〉 blockship/ ～赛跑 steeplechase; obstacle race/ ～物 obstacle; barrier; entanglement

【障蔽】 zhàngbì block; obstruct; shut out: ～视线 obstruct one's view

【障眼法】 zhàngyǎnfǎ cover-up; camouflage: 玩弄～ throw dust into people's eyes

【障子】 zhàngzi a barrier made of reeds, sorghum stalks or closely planted shrubs; hedge

**幛** zhàng a large, oblong sheet of silk with an appropriate message attached, presented at a wedding, birthday or funeral

【幛子】 zhàngzi 见"幛"

**嶂** zhàng a screen-like mountain peak: 层峦叠～ peaks rising one higher than another

**瘴** zhàng miasma

【瘴疠】 zhànglì communicable subtropical diseases, such as pernicious malaria, etc.

【瘴气】 zhàngqì miasma

## zhāo

**钊** zhāo 〈书〉 encourage; spur; exhort

**招** zhāo ①beckon: 他把手一～,要我跟上。He beckoned me to follow. ②recruit; enlist; enrol: ～工 recruit workers ③attract; incur; court: ～苍蝇 attract flies/ ～灾 court disaster; invite calamity/ ～人嫌 incur odium/ ～人喜欢的孩子 a charming (或 lovable) child ④provoke; tease: 别～这孩子。Don't tease the child. ⑤confess; own up: 不打自～ confess without being pressed ⑥〈方〉 infect; be contagious: 这病～人。This disease is catching. ⑦trick; device; move: 你这一～可真高。That was really a brilliant stroke (或 move, idea) of yours.

【招安】 zhāo'ān (of feudal rulers) offer amnesty and enlistment to rebels: 受～ (of former rebels) accept amnesty and serve the ruler

【招标】 zhāobiāo invite tenders (或 bids, public bidding)

【招兵】 zhāobīng recruit soldiers; raise troops

【招兵买马】 zhāobīng-mǎimǎ recruit men and buy horses — raise or enlarge an army; recruit followers

【招待】 zhāodài receive (guests); entertain; serve (customers): 设宴～外宾 give a dinner for (或 in honour of) foreign guests/ ～客人 entertain guests/ 谢谢你们的热情～。Thank you for your kind hospitality.
◇ ～费 entertainment allowance or expenses/ ～券 complimentary ticket/ ～所 guest house; hostel

【招待会】 zhāodàihuì reception: 冷餐～ buffet reception/ 记者～ press conference/ 举行～ give (或 hold) a reception

【招风】 zhāofēng catch the wind — attract too much attention and invite trouble

【招风耳】 zhāofēng'ěr protruding ears

【招抚】 zhāofǔ 见"招安"

【招供】 zhāogòng make a confession of one's crime; confess

【招股】 zhāogǔ raise capital by floating shares

【招呼】 zhāohu ①call: 那边有人～你。Someone over there is calling you. ②hail; greet; say hello to: 热情地打～ greet warmly ③notify; tell: ～他赶快来开会。Tell him to come to the meeting at once./ 你要是不去,事先打个～。Let me know beforehand if you won't be going. ④take care of: ～老人 take care of old people ⑤〈方〉 mind; take care: 路上有冰,～滑倒了。The road is icy. Mind you don't slip.

【招魂】 zhāohún call back the spirit of the dead

【招架】 zhāojià ward off blows; hold one's own: ～不住 unable to hold one's own; unable to withstand/ 只有～之功,没有还手之力 can only parry sb.'s blows without being able to hit back

【招考】 zhāokǎo give public notice of entrance examination; admit (students, applicants, etc.) by examination

【招徕】 zhāolái solicit (customers or business); canvass: ～顾客 solicit customers/ 以广～ so as to have more customers

【招揽】 zhāolǎn solicit (customers or business); canvass: ～主顾 solicit customers/ ～生意 canvass business orders; drum up trade

【招领】 zhāolǐng announce the finding of lost property: 失物～(布告标题) Found/ 拾物～处 Lost and Found

【招募】 zhāomù recruit; enlist

【招女婿】 zhāo nǔxu have the groom move into one's house after the marriage

【招牌】 zhāopai shop sign; signboard: 据说这～是一位名书法家写的。This signboard is said to have been written by a famous calligrapher./ 打着社会主义的～,干资本主义的勾当 practise capitalism under the signboard of socialism

【招盘】 zhāopán put a business up for sale

【招聘】 zhāopìn give public notice of a vacancy to be filled; invite applications for a job: ～技术工人 advertise for skilled workers

【招亲】 zhāoqīn ①见"招女婿" ②marry into and live with one's bride's family

【招惹】 zhāore ①provoke; incur; court: ～是非 bring trouble on oneself ②〈方〉〔多用于否定式〕 tease; provoke: 这人～不得。You'd better not provoke that fellow.

【招认】 zhāorèn confess one's crime; plead guilty

【招生】 zhāoshēng enrol new students; recruit students
◇ ～制度 enrolment system; admissions system

【招事】 zhāoshì bring trouble on oneself; invite trouble

【招收】 zhāoshōu recruit; take in: ～工人 recruit workers/ ～大学生 enrol new students in universities and colleges

【招手】 zhāoshǒu beckon; wave: 他～要我进去。He beckoned me in./ ～致意 wave one's greetings; wave back in acknowledgement

【招数】 zhāoshù 见"着数" zhāoshù

【招贴】 zhāotiē poster; placard; bill ◇ ～画 pictorial poster (或 placard)

【招降】 zhāoxiáng summon sb. to surrender

【招降纳叛】 zhāoxiáng-nàpàn recruit deserters and traitors

【招笑儿】 zhāoxiàor 〈方〉 laughable; funny

【招摇】 zhāoyáo act ostentatiously

【招摇过市】 zhāoyáo guò shì swagger through the streets — blatantly seek publicity

【招摇撞骗】 zhāoyáo-zhuàngpiàn swindle and bluff

【招引】 zhāoyǐn attract; induce: 灯光～蛾子。Lights attract moths.

【招灾惹祸】 zhāozāi-rěhuò court disaster; invite trouble: 这孩子老给大人～。This child is always making trouble for his parents.

【招展】 zhāozhǎn flutter; wave: 工地上红旗～。Red flags

fluttered over the construction site.

【招致】 zhāozhì ① recruit (followers); scout about for (talents, etc.) ② incur; bring about; lead to: ～意外的损失 incur unexpected losses/ ～失败 cause defeat/ ～无穷后患 lead to endless trouble

【招赘】 zhāozhuì 见"招女婿"

**昭** zhāo clear; obvious

【昭然若揭】 zhāorán ruò jiē abundantly clear; all too clear

【昭示】 zhāoshì make clear to all; declare publicly: ～全国 declare to the whole nation

【昭雪】 zhāoxuě exonerate; rehabilitate: 冤案得到了～。The wrong has been righted. 或 The person wronged has been rehabilitated.

【昭彰】 zhāozhāng clear; manifest; evident: 罪恶～ have committed flagrant crimes

【昭著】 zhāozhù clear; evident; obvious: 成绩～ have achieved signal successes

**着** zhāo ① a move in chess: 高～儿 a clever move/ 走错一～ make a false move; take a wrong step ② trick; device; move: 这一～厉害。That's a shrewd move./ 他没～儿了。He's at the end of his tether. ③〈方〉 all right; O.K.: ～,咱们就这么办。O.K., we'll do it that way.

另见 zháo; zhe; zhuó

【着数】 zhāoshù ① a move in chess or a movement in *wushu* (武术) ② trick; device

**啁** zhāo

另见 zhōu

【啁哳】 zhāozhā 〈书〉 twitter

**朝** zhāo ① early morning; morning: ～阳 morning sun ② day: 一～有事 should anything happen some day/ 今～ today; the present

另见 cháo

【朝不保夕】 zhāo bù bǎo xī not know in the morning what may happen in the evening; be in a precarious state

【朝不谋夕】 zhāo bù móu xī be unable to plan out one's day; be preoccupied with the current crisis 又作"朝不虑夕"

【朝发夕至】 zhāo fā xī zhì start at dawn and arrive at dusk — a short journey

【朝晖】 zhāohuī morning sunlight: 祖国大地尽～。This vast land of ours is glowing in the morning sun.

【朝令夕改】 zhāo lìng xī gǎi issue an order in the morning and rescind it in the evening; make unpredictable changes in policy

【朝露】 zhāolù 〈书〉 morning dew — ephemeral; transitory

【朝气】 zhāoqì youthful spirit; vigour; vitality: 革命～ revolutionary vigour/ 有～ be full of vigour

【朝气蓬勃】 zhāoqì péngbó full of youthful spirit; full of vigour and vitality; imbued with vitality: ～的青年 spirited young people/ ～的先锋队组织 a vigorous vanguard organization

【朝秦暮楚】 zhāo Qín mù Chǔ serve the State of Qin in the morning and the State of Chu in the evening — quick to switch sides; fickle; inconstant

【朝三暮四】 zhāosān-mùsì blow hot and cold; play fast and loose; chop and change

【朝思暮想】 zhāosī-mùxiǎng yearn day and night

【朝夕】 zhāoxī ① morning and evening; from morning to night; day and night; daily: ～相处 be together from morning to night; be closely associated ② a very short time: 只争～ seize the day, seize the hour; seize every minute

【朝霞】 zhāoxiá rosy clouds of dawn; rosy dawn

【朝阳】 zhāoyáng the rising sun; the morning sun

另见 cháoyáng

## zháo

**着** zháo ① touch: 上不～天,下不～地 touch neither the sky nor the ground; be suspended in midair/ 说话不～边际 not speak to the point ② feel; be affected by (cold, etc.): ～风 become unwell through being in a draught ③ burn: 炉子～得很旺。The fire is burning briskly in the stove./ 灯都～了。The lights are all on. ④〔用在动词后,表示已经达到目的或有了结果〕: 猜～了 have guessed right/ 打～了 have hit the mark/ 你见～他了吗? Did you get to see him? ⑤〈方〉 fall asleep: 他躺下就～了。He fell asleep as soon as he lay down.

另见 zhāo; zhe; zhuó

【着慌】 zháohuāng get alarmed; become flustered (或 jittery); be thrown into a panic: 这下子他可～了。At that point he panicked.

【着火】 zháohuǒ catch fire; be on fire: ～啦! Fire!/一见麦垛～,社员们赶紧上去把火扑灭了。Seeing the wheat stack on fire, the commune members rushed up and put it out.

【着急】 zháojí worry; feel anxious: 别～,安心养病。Just take care of yourself and don't worry./ 着什么急。There's nothing to worry about./ 等得～了 become impatient with waiting/ 冷静点,别～。Keep calm. Don't get excited.

【着凉】 zháoliáng catch cold; catch a chill: 外面有点冷,当心～。It's chilly outside; be careful not to catch cold.

【着忙】 zháománg be in a hurry (或 rush)

【着迷】 zháomí be fascinated; be captivated: 观众越看越～。The audience watched the performance with growing fascination./ 孩子们听故事都听得着了迷。The children were spellbound by the story.

【着魔】 zháomó be bewitched; be possessed: 他这几天练乒乓球象着了魔似的。He's been practising ping-pong like crazy these few days.

【着三不着两】 zháo sān bù zháo liǎng ill-considered; thoughtless: 说话～ speak thoughtlessly

## zhǎo

**爪** zhǎo claw; talon

另见 zhuǎ

【爪哇】 Zhǎowā Java

【爪牙】 zhǎoyá talons and fangs — lackeys; underlings: 帝国主义的～ a lackey of imperialism

**找** zhǎo ① look for; try to find; seek: 他到处在～你。He's been looking for you all over the place./ ～矿 look for mineral deposits/ ～到油田 discover an oil field/ ～出地震的规律 discover the laws of earthquakes/ ～工作 look (或 hunt) for a job/ ～机会 look for (或 seek) an opportunity/ ～出路 seek a way out/ 从世界观上～原因 seek the cause (of an error) in a person's world outlook/ ～答案 try to find the answer ② want to see; call on; approach; ask for: 有人～你。Someone wants to see you./ 有人来～过我吗? Did anyone ask for me?/ 明天再来～你。I'll call on you again tomorrow./ 干吗不去～老杨帮忙? Why not go and ask Lao Yang for help?/ ～我有什么事? What can I do for you? 或 What do you want to see me about?/ 出了问题可得～你。If anything goes wrong, we'll hold you responsible. ③ give change: 他～我两块钱。He gave me two *yuan* change./ 这是～给你的钱。Here's your change./ 两不～。That's just right.

【找补】 zhǎobu make up a deficiency: 请点一下,不够再～。Count it, please. We'll make it up if there's any shortage./ 这儿没焊好,再～两下。The welding is faulty here. Let's touch it up.

【找碴儿】 zhǎochár find fault; pick holes; pick a quarrel

【找对象】 zhǎo duìxiàng 〈方〉 look for a partner in marriage

【找麻烦】 zhǎo máfan ① look for trouble: 自～ ask for trouble; ask for it ② cause sb. trouble: 对不起,给你们～了。I'm sorry to have caused you so much trouble.

【找平】 zhǎopíng make level; level up or down: 右手边儿还差两层砖,～了再下班。The right side needs two more layers of bricks. Let's lay them before knocking off for the day.

【找齐】 zhǎoqí ① make uniform; even up: 打埂得～。The tops of ridges should be made even. ② make up a deficiency: 先付一部分,差多少交货时～。We'll pay you part of the sum now. The balance will be paid on delivery of the goods.

【找钱】 zhǎoqián give change

【找事】 zhǎoshì ① look (或 hunt) for a job ② pick a quarrel

【找死】 zhǎosǐ court death

【找头】 zhǎotou change (from money paid): 这是给你的～。Here is your change.

【找寻】 zhǎoxún look for; seek

**沼** zhǎo natural pond

【沼气】 zhǎoqì marsh gas; firedamp; methane ◇ ～池 methane-generating pit

【沼泽】 zhǎozé marsh; swamp; bog ◇ ～地 marshland/ ～土 bog soil

## zhào

**召** zhào call together; convene; summon

【召唤】 zhàohuàn call; summon: 共产党员时刻听从党～。A communist always heeds the Party's call.

【召回】 zhàohuí recall: ～大使 recall an ambassador ◇ ～国书 letter of recall

【召祸】 zhàohuò 〈书〉 court disaster

【召集】 zhàojí call together; convene: 把干部～在一起 call the cadres together/ ～会议 call (或 convene) a conference ◇ ～人 convener

【召见】 zhàojiàn ① call in (a subordinate) ② 〈外〉 summon (an envoy) to an interview

【召开】 zhàokāi convene; convoke: 庆祝全国人民代表大会的～ celebrate the convening (或 opening) of the National People's Congress/ ～一次国际会议 convene an international conference

【召之即来】 zhào zhī jí lái come as soon as called: ～,来之能战,战之能胜。Be ready to assemble at the first call and be capable of fighting and winning.

**兆** zhào ① sign; omen; portent: 不祥之～ an ill (或 evil) omen ② portend; foretell: 瑞雪～丰年。A timely snow promises a good harvest. ③ million; mega- ④ a million millions; billion

【兆赫】 zhàohè 〈电子〉 megahertz; megacycle per second

【兆头】 zhàotou sign; omen; portent

【兆周】 zhàozhōu 〈无〉 megacycle

**诏** zhào 〈书〉 ① instruct ② imperial edict

【诏书】 zhàoshū imperial edict

**赵** Zhào a surname

【赵公元帅】 Zhàogōng yuánshuài Marshal Zhao, or Zhao Gongming, God of Wealth in Chinese folklore

**笊** zhào

【笊篱】 zhàoli a bamboo, wicker or wire strainer

**棹** zhào 〈方〉 ① oar ② row (a boat)

**照** zhào ① shine; illuminate; light up: 金色的太阳～在天安门城楼上。The golden sun shines upon the gate tower of Tian An Men./ 毛泽东思想的阳光把我们的心儿～亮。The rays of Mao Zedong Thought illuminate our hearts./ 车灯把大路～得通亮。The headlights lit up the road./ 拿手电～路 light the way with a torch ② reflect; mirror: ～镜子 look in the mirror ③ take a picture (或 photograph); photograph; film; shoot: 我想～一张相。I want to have a picture taken./ 这镜头可不容易～。This scene is by no means easy to shoot. ④ photograph; picture: 剧～ stage photo; still ⑤ license; permit: 禁止无～行车。It is forbidden to drive without a license. ⑥ take care of; look after: ～看 look after; attend to; keep an eye on ⑦ notify: 知～ notify; inform ⑧ contrast: 对～ contrast; check against ⑨ understand: 心～不宣 have a tacit understanding ⑩ in the direction of; towards: ～这个方向走。Go in this direction. ⑪ according to; in accordance with: ～他们的说法 according to what they say/ ～规章办事 act in accordance with the regulations/ ～我看,线路有毛病。It seems to me there's something wrong with the circuit.

【照搬】 zhàobān indiscriminately imitate; copy: 全盘～人家的经验 copy indiscriminately the experience of others

【照办】 zhàobàn act accordingly; act in accordance with; act upon; comply with; follow: 你说得对,我们就照你的办。If what you propose is right, we will act upon it./ 你们提出的要求我们尽量～。We'll try our best to comply with your request.

【照本宣科】 zhào běn xuān kē read item by item from the text; repeat what the book says

【照壁】 zhàobì a screen wall facing the gate of a house 又作"照墙"

【照常】 zhàocháng as usual: ～营业 business as usual

【照抄】 zhàochāo ① copy word for word: 这个材料请你～一份。Please make a copy of this material. ② 见"照搬"

【照度】 zhàodù 〈物〉 intensity of illumination; illuminance

【照发】 zhàofā ① issue as before: 女工产假期间工资～。Women workers are entitled to maternity leave with full pay. 或 Women workers receive full pay during maternity leave. ②〔文件批语〕approved for distribution

【照拂】 zhàofú 〈书〉 look after; care for; attend to: 请惠予～。Please be so kind as to take good care of him.

【照顾】 zhàogu ① give consideration to; show consideration for; make allowance(s) for: ～到两国的友好关系 out of consideration for the friendship of the two countries/ ～全局 take the whole into account; consider the situation as a whole/ ～多数 make allowance for the majority; think in terms of the majority/ ～实际需要 consider actual needs/ ～他的困难 take his difficulties into account/ 给予适当～ give appropriate preferential treatment/ 青年团的工作要～青年的特点。The Youth League in its work must take the characteristics of youth into consideration. ② look after; care for; attend to: ～伤员 look after the wounded/ 烈军属受到政府的特别～。Families of martyrs and servicemen receive special care from the government. ③ 〈旧〉

(of a customer) patronize
【照管】 zhàoguǎn look after; tend; be in charge of: ～孩子 look after a child; mind a child/ ～机器 tend a machine/ ～仓库 be in charge of a storehouse
【照葫芦画瓢】 zhào húlu huà piáo draw a dipper with a gourd as a model — copy; imitate
【照护】 zhàohù look after (patients, the wounded, etc.)
【照会】 zhàohuì ① present (或 deliver, address) a note to (a government) ② note: 提出～ present (或 deliver, address) a note/ 交换～ exchange notes/ 普通～ note verbale/ 正式～ personal note
【照价】 zhàojià according to the set (或 arranged) price: ～付款 pay according to the arranged price/ 如有损坏,～赔偿 pay the full price for anything damaged
【照旧】 zhàojiù as before; as usual; as of old: 程序～。The procedure remains unchanged./ 参观改期,入场券～有效。Visit postponed. Tickets remain valid.
【照看】 zhàokàn look after; attend to; keep an eye on: ～病人 attend to a patient/ 劳驾帮我～一下行李。Will you please keep an eye on my luggage.
【照例】 zhàolì as a rule; as usual; usually: 我们～是在星期六下午开团小组会。As a rule, we have our League group meeting on Saturday afternoon./ 那天早上,他～起得很早。That morning he got up very early, as usual.
【照料】 zhàoliào take care of; attend to: ～烈士子女 care for the children of revolutionary martyrs/ 她把小女儿托给一位老大娘～。She left her baby daughter in the care of an old woman./ 你放心走吧,队里的事有我们～。Don't you worry. We'll take care of things in the team while you're away.
【照临】 zhàolín shine on; illuminate; light up: 曙光～大地。The early sun bathes the land in light.
【照猫画虎】 zhào māo huà hǔ draw a tiger with a cat as a model — copy; imitate
【照面儿】 zhàomiànr ① put in an appearance; show up; turn up: 他始终不～。He never showed up./ 互不～ avoid each other ② encounter; come across: 打个～ come face to face with sb.; run into sb.
【照明】 zhàomíng illumination; lighting: 舞台～ stage illumination
◇ ～弹 flare; star shell/ ～电路 lighting circuit/ ～炮弹 illuminating shell/ ～装置 lighting installation
【照片】 zhàopiàn photograph; picture: 彩色～ colour photograph/ 加印～ print off copies from a negative; make copies of a print
【照射】 zhàoshè shine; illuminate; light up; irradiate: 用紫外线～ irradiate with ultraviolet rays
【照说】 zhàoshuō ordinarily; as a rule: ～这时候该热了。As a rule, it should be warm by now./ ～我们早就应当通知你的。We ought to have told you much earlier.
【照相】 zhàoxiàng take a picture (或 photograph); photograph: 我们星期天～去。Let's go and take photographs this Sunday./ 宾主在一起照了相。Guests and host were photographed together./ 缩微～ microphotograph
◇ ～版 process plate/ ～簿 photo album/ ～弹〈军〉 photoflash bomb; flash bomb/ ～复制 photocopy/ ～馆 photo studio/ ～胶版印刷 photo-offset process/ ～平版印刷 photolithography/ ～凸版术 photoengraving/ ～枪〈军〉 gun camera/ ～纸 photographic paper/ ～制版 photomechanical process/ ～制图 photomap 又作"照像"
【照相机】 zhàoxiàngjī camera: 反射式～ reflex camera/ 立体～ stereoscopic (或 stereo) camera/ 全景～ panoramic camera/ 小型～ miniature camera; minicamera; minicam/ 折叠式～ folding camera/ 制版～〈印〉 process camera
【照样】 zhàoyàng ① after a pattern or model: 照着样儿画 draw after a model/ 照这个样儿做 do it this way ② in the same old way; all the same; as before: ～办理 act in the same way; follow suit/ 他们在不利条件下～完成了任务。Despite adverse circumstances, they fulfilled their task just the same.
【照妖镜】 zhàoyāojìng monster-revealing mirror; demon-detector
【照耀】 zhàoyào shine; illuminate: 灿烂的阳光～着祖国大地。A bright sun is shining over our country.
【照应】 zhàoyìng coordinate; correlate: 文章要前后～。A composition must be well organized.
【照应】 zhàoying look after; take care of: 火车上乘务员对旅客～得很好。The attendants on the train take good care of the passengers.
【照准】 zhàozhǔn 〔旧时公文用语〕 request granted
【照准仪】 zhàozhǔnyí 〈机〉 alidade

**罩** zhào ① cover; overspread; wrap: 工人们下班时都细心地把仪器～好。The workers carefully covered all the instruments before they went off work./ 山坡上～着一层薄雾。The mountain slope was wrapped in a thin mist./ 棉袄外面～着一件蓝布褂儿 wear a blue dustcoat over one's cotton-padded jacket ② cover; shade; hood; casing: 玻璃～ glass cover/ 灯～ lampshade/ 发动机～ (engine) hood/ 保险～〈机〉 protecting casing ③ a bamboo fish trap
【罩袍】 zhàopáo dust-robe; dust-gown; overall
【罩棚】 zhàopéng an awning over a gateway or a courtyard
【罩衫】 zhàoshān overall; dustcoat
【罩袖】 zhàoxiù 〈方〉 oversleeve; sleevelet
【罩衣】 zhàoyī dustcoat; overall
【罩子】 zhàozi cover; shade; hood; casing

**肇** zhào 〈书〉 ① start; commence; initiate ② cause (trouble, etc.)
【肇端】 zhàoduān 〈书〉 beginning
【肇祸】 zhàohuò cause trouble; cause an accident
【肇始】 zhàoshǐ 〈书〉 start; commence; initiate
【肇事】 zhàoshì cause trouble; create a disturbance ◇ ～者 a person who has created a disturbance; troublemaker

## zhē

**折** zhē 〈口〉 ① roll over; turn over: ～个跟斗 turn a somersault ② pour back and forth between two containers: 开水太烫,拿两个杯子～一～就凉了。The water's boiling hot. Pour it from one cup to another to cool it.
另见 shé; zhé
【折腾】 zhēteng 〈口〉 ① turn from side to side; toss about: 他～了好几个钟头才睡着。He tossed about in bed for hours before he got to sleep. ② do sth. over and over again: 徒工把旧机器拆了又安，安了又拆，～了好多回。The young apprentice again and again took the old machine apart and then put it together. ③ cause physical or mental suffering; get sb. down: 牙疼真～人。A toothache can get you down.

**蜇** zhē sting: 当心别给马蜂～了。Mind the wasps don't sting you.
另见 zhé
【蜇针】 zhēzhēn 〈动〉 sting; stinger

**遮** zhē ① hide from view; cover; screen: 月亮给云彩～住了。The moon was hidden by clouds./ 拿塑料布把脱粒机～起来 spread a plastic sheet over the thresher/ 乌鸦

的翅膀～不住太阳的光辉。A crow's wings can never shut out the sunlight. ② block; obstruct; impede: ～道 block the way ③ keep out: ～风挡雨 keep out wind and rain
【遮蔽】 zhēbì ① hide from view; cover; screen ② obstruct; block: ～视线 obstruct the view ③〈军〉defilade ◇ ～物〈军〉defilade/ ～阵地 defiladed position
【遮藏】 zhēcáng hide; conceal; cover up
【遮丑】 zhēchǒu gloss over one's blemishes; hide one's shame; cover up one's defect
【遮挡】 zhēdǎng shelter from; keep out: ～寒风 keep out the cold wind/ 用帘子把窗户～起来 cover the window with a curtain
【遮断】 zhēduàn〈军〉interdict ◇ ～射击 interdiction fire
【遮盖】 zhēgài ① cover; overspread: 山路全给大雪～住了。The mountain paths were all covered by snow. ② hide; conceal; cover up: 错误总是～不住的。Mistakes can never be hidden.
【遮光罩】 zhēguāngzhào〈摄〉lens hood
【遮拦】 zhēlán block; obstruct; impede
【遮羞】 zhēxiū hush up a scandal; cover up one's embarrassment ◇ ～布 fig leaf
【遮掩】 zhēyǎn ① cover; overspread; envelop: 远山被云雾～着。The distant hills were enveloped in clouds and mist. ② cover up; hide; conceal: 大胆承认错误，不要遮遮掩掩。Admit your mistakes courageously. Don't try to cover them up.
【遮眼法】 zhēyǎnfǎ cover-up; camouflage
【遮阳】 zhēyáng sunshade ◇ ～板〈建〉sunshading board

## zhé

**折** zhé ① break; snap: ～断一根树枝 break off a branch/ ～断腿 fracture (或 break) one's leg ② suffer the loss of; lose: 损兵～将 suffer heavy casualties ③ bend; twist: 曲～ twists and turns ④ turn back; change direction: 边界由此～向西南。From here the boundary turns southwestward./ 他刚走出不远又～了回来。He hadn't gone very far when he turned back. ⑤ be convinced; be filled with admiration: 心～ be deeply convinced; be filled with heartfelt admiration ⑥ convert into; amount to: 把市斤～成公斤 convert (或 change) *jin* into kilograms/ 这笔外币～成人民币是多少？How much does this sum of foreign money amount to in Renminbi? ⑦ discount; rebate: 打八～ give 20% discount; charge 80% of the original price ⑧ an act of *zaju*(杂剧) 参见"杂剧" zájù ⑨ fold: 把信～好 fold the letter/ 把纸对～起来 fold the sheet of paper in two ⑩ booklet in accordion form with a slipcase, used for keeping accounts, etc.; folder: 存～ deposit book; bankbook ⑪ turning stroke (in Chinese characters)
另见 shé; zhē
【折板结构】 zhébǎn jiégòu〈建〉folded plate structure
【折半】 zhébàn reduce (a price) by half; give 50% discount: 按原价～出售 sell at 50% discount; sell at half price
【折布机】 zhébùjī〈纺〉folding machine
【折尺】 zhéchǐ folding rule
【折冲】 zhéchōng〈书〉repulse or subdue the enemy: ～御侮 repel foreign aggression
【折冲樽俎】 zhéchōng zūnzǔ outmanoeuvre the enemy over glasses of wine; win by diplomacy; engage in diplomatic negotiations
【折叠】 zhédié fold: 把报纸～好 fold up the newspaper ◇ ～床(椅) folding bed (chair)/ ～翼飞机 folding-wing aircraft
【折兑】 zhéduì exchange (gold or silver) for money; convert
【折服】 zhéfú ① subdue; bring into submission: 艰难困苦～不了为正义事业而奋斗的人。No hardship can subdue people fighting for a just cause. ② be convinced; be filled with admiration: 令人～ compel admiration
【折光度】 zhéguāngdù〈物〉dioptre
【折合】 zhéhé convert into; amount to: 把美元～成瑞士法郎 convert dollars into Swiss francs/ 一英镑～成人民币是多少？How much is a pound in terms of Renminbi? 或 How many Renminbi *yuan* to the pound?/ 水泥每包五十公斤，～一百市斤。Each bag of cement weighs 50 kilogrammes, that is, 100 *jin*.
【折回】 zhéhuí turn back (halfway)
【折价】 zhéjià convert into money; evaluate in terms of money: ～退赔 pay compensation at the market price
【折旧】 zhéjiù〈经〉depreciation
◇ ～费 depreciation charge/ ～基金 depreciation fund/ ～率 rate of depreciation
【折扣】 zhékou discount; rebate: 这价钱已经打了～了。This is the discounted price./ 执行上级指示不打～ carry out instructions to the letter
【折门】 zhémén〈建〉folding door; accordion door
【折磨】 zhémo cause physical or mental suffering; torment: 受疾病的～ suffer severely from a lingering illness/ 受尽～ suffer a lot
【折辱】 zhérǔ〈书〉humiliate
【折扇】 zhéshàn folding fan
【折射】 zhéshè〈物〉refraction
◇ ～本领 refractivity; refringence/ ～波 refracted wave/ ～计 refractometer/ ～角 angle of refraction; refraction angle/ ～率 index of refraction; refracting power/ ～望远镜 refracting telescope
【折实】 zhéshí ① reckon the actual amount after a discount ② adjust payment in accordance with the price index of certain commodities
【折算】 zhésuàn convert ◇ ～率 conversion rate
【折头】 zhétou〈方〉discount; rebate
【折线】 zhéxiàn〈数〉broken line ◇ ～图 broken-line graph
【折腰】 zhéyāo〈书〉bow: 江山如此多娇，引无数英雄竞～。This land so rich in beauty Has made countless heroes bow in homage.
【折页】 zhéyè〈印〉folding ◇ ～机 folding machine
【折帐】 zhézhàng pay a debt in kind
【折纸】 zhézhǐ paper folding
【折中】 zhézhōng compromise: ～方案 a compromise proposal ◇ ～主义 eclecticism 又作"折衷"
【折子】 zhézi booklet in accordion form with a slipcase, used for keeping accounts, etc.
【折子戏】 zhézixì highlights from operas

**哲** zhé ① wise; sagacious ② wise man; sage: 先～ the sages of old
【哲理】 zhélǐ philosophic theory; philosophy
【哲人】 zhérén〈书〉sage; philosopher
【哲学】 zhéxué philosophy ◇ ～家 philosopher

**辄** zhé〈书〉① always; often: 所言～听 always heed sb.'s advice/ 动～得咎 be frequently taken to task; be blamed for whatever one does ② then: 饮少～醉 get drunk after a few sips

**蛰** zhé〈书〉hibernate
【蛰伏】 zhéfú ①〈动〉dormancy; hibernation ② 见"蛰居"
【蛰居】 zhéjū live in seclusion: ～书斋 cloister oneself in one's study

**奢** zhé 〈书〉fear; dread

**蜇** zhé 见"海蜇" hǎizhé
另见 zhē

**谪** zhé 〈书〉① relegate a high official to a minor post in an outlying district (as a form of punishment in feudal times); banish; exile ② (of fairies, etc.) be banished from Heaven ③ censure; blame: 众口交～ be censured by everybody

**磔** zhé ① dismemberment of the body (as a form of punishment in ancient China) ② 〈书〉 right-falling stroke (in Chinese characters)

**辙** zhé ① the track of a wheel; rut ② rhyme (of a song, poetic drama, etc.): 合～ in rhyme ③〈方〉〔多用在"有""没"后面〕 way; idea: 没～ can find no way out; be at the end of one's rope

【辙叉】 zhéchā 〈铁道〉frog

【辙乱旗靡】 zhéluàn-qímǐ crisscross chariot tracks and drooping banners — signs of an army in headlong flight

## zhě

**者** zhě ①〈助〉〔用在形容词或动词后面，或带有形容词或动词的词组后面，代替人或事物〕: 老～ old man/ 大～ the big one/ 前(后)～ the former (latter)/ 贫(富)～ the poor (rich)/ 读～ reader/ 出版～ publisher/ 胜利～ victor/ 符合标准～ those which are up to standard ②〈助〉〔用在"工作"和"主义"后面，表示从事某项工作或信仰某个主义的人〕: 医务工作～ medical worker/ 马克思主义～ Marxist ③〈书〉〈助〉〔用在"二""三""数"等词后面，指上文所说的几件事物〕: 二～必居其一。It must be one or the other./ 两～缺一不可。Neither is dispensable. ④〈书〉〈助〉〔用在词、词组、分句后面表示停顿〕: 风～，空气流动而成。Wind is air in motion. ⑤〔多用在古诗词和早期白话中〕 this: ～边 this side; here

**锗** zhě 〈化〉germanium (Ge)

**赭** zhě reddish brown; burnt ochre

【赭石】 zhěshí 〈矿〉ochre

**褶** zhě pleat; crease: 百～裙 pleated skirt; accordion-pleated skirt/ 把衬衫上的～儿熨平 iron the wrinkles out of the shirt

【褶皱】 zhězhòu ①〈地〉fold ② wrinkle (in the skin) ◇ ～山 folded mountain/ ～作用 folding

【褶子】 zhězi ① pleat ② crease; fold; wrinkle ③ wrinkle (on the face)

## zhè

**这** zhè ① this: ～地方 this place/ ～一回 this time/ ～究竟是怎么回事? What's all this about?/ ～都是我们厂的新产品。These are new products from our plant./ ～才是好孩子! That's a good boy (girl)! 或 That's a dear!/ ～消息我知道了。I've heard that news already. 或 Yes, so I've heard./ ～就对了。Now, you're on the right track. 或 Now, that's better. ② now: 他～才知道锻炼身体的好处。Only now does he see the good of taking exercise./ 我～就走。I'm leaving right now.
另见 zhèi

【这般】 zhèbān such; so; like this: ～仔细 so careful/ ～大小 this size; this big/ 如此～ thus and thus; thus and so

【这边】 zhèbiān this side; here: 风景～独好。The landscape here is beyond compare./ 正义在我们～。Justice is on our side./ 到～来。Come over here.

【这次】 zhècì this time; present; current: ～会议 the present session/ ～运动 the current movement (或 campaign)/ ～我们提前三天完成了任务。This time we fulfilled our task three days ahead of schedule.

【这个】 zhège ① this one; this: ～比那个沉。This one is heavier than that one./ 他为了～忙了好几天。He's been busy with this for quite a few days. ②〈口〉〔用在动词、形容词之前，表示夸张〕so; such: 看见大象吹口琴，孩子们～乐啊! When they saw the elephant blowing the mouth organ, the children roared with laughter.

【这会儿】 zhèhuìr 〈口〉now; at the moment; at present: 你～又上哪儿去呀? Where are you going now?/ ～电话占线。The line's busy at the moment. 又作"这会子"

【这里】 zhèlǐ here: 我们～一年种两季稻子。We grow two crops of rice a year here.

【这么】 zhème so; such; this way; like this: 他就是～个人。That's just like him./ 那个句子应该～译。The sentence should be translated this way./ 大家都～说。So they say./ 往～挪一挪。Move over this way a little bit. 又作"这末"

【这么点儿】 zhèmediǎnr such a little bit: ～水，怕不够喝。I'm afraid so little water won't be enough to drink.

【这么些】 zhèmexiē so much; so many: ～活儿，得有个人帮帮你吧? Surely you need some help with so much work?/ ～人，坐得开吗? Is there seating for that many people?

【这么着】 zhèmezhe like this; so: ～才能瞄准。You should take aim like this./ ～好。It's better this way./ 要是～，那我就去吧。In that case, I'll go.

【这儿】 zhèr 〈口〉① here ②〔只用在"打""从""由"后面〕 now; then: 打～起我就要天天学英语了。From now on I'm going to study English every day./ 从～以后我再也没见着他。Since then I haven't seen him again.

【这山望着那山高】 zhè shān wàngzhe nà shān gāo it's always the other mountain that looks higher; always think the grass is greener on the other side; never happy where one is

【这些】 zhèxiē these: ～日子我们特别忙。We've been particularly busy these days. 又作"这些个"

【这样】 zhèyàng so; such; like this; this way: 别走～快。Don't walk so fast./ ～的文学作品很受群众欢迎。Literary works of this kind are well received by the masses./ 他怎么病成～了? How did he get so ill?/ 如果你们觉得可以～办，就～办。If you people feel this is the right thing to do, then do it./ ～那样的问题 various problems; one question or another; all sorts of problems/ 一会儿～，一会儿那样 now one way, now another/ 情况就是～。That's how it is.

**柘** zhè 〈植〉three-bristle cudrania (*Cudrania tricuspidata*)

**浙** Zhè short for Zhejiang Province

【浙江】 Zhèjiāng Zhejiang (Province)

**蔗** zhè sugarcane

【蔗螟】 zhèmíng sugarcane borer

【蔗农】 zhènóng sugarcane grower

【蔗糖】 zhètáng ①〈化〉sucrose ② cane sugar ◇ ～酶 sucrase/ ～蜜 cane molasses

【蔗渣】 zhèzhā bagasse

## 鹧

zhè

【鹧鸪】 zhègū 〈动〉 Chinese francolin; partridge

【鹧鸪菜】 zhègūcài 〈中药〉 *zhegucai* (*Caloglossa leprieurii*)

## zhe

**着** zhe 〈助〉 ①〔表示动作或状态的持续〕: 他们正谈～话呢。They are having a talk./ 别站～,坐下吧。Don't just stand there; sit down./ 大门敞～。The gate is wide open./ 山顶覆盖～积雪。The mountaintop is covered with snow./ 茶几上放～一瓶花。A vase of flowers stands on the tea table. ②〔加强命令或嘱咐的语气〕: 你听～。You just listen./ 快～点儿。Be quick./ 脚步轻～点儿。Walk more quietly. ③〔加在某些动词后面,使变成介词〕: 沿～ along/ 挨～ next to/ 朝～ towards

另见 zhāo; zháo; zhuó

【着呢】 zhene 〔表示程度深〕: 她农活干得好～。She's really good at farm work. 或 She's a dab hand at farm work./ 天还早～。It's still quite early./ 街上热闹～。The street is bustling with noise and excitement.

## zhèi

**这** zhèi 〔常用在量词或数量词前〕 this: ～本词典 this dictionary/ ～三架飞机 these three planes

另见 zhè

## zhēn

**贞** zhēn ① loyal; faithful: 坚～ staunch and faithful ② (of women) chastity or virginity ③ divination (in ancient times)

【贞操】 zhēncāo ① chastity or virginity ② loyalty; moral integrity

【贞节】 zhēnjié chastity or virginity, i.e. remaining chaste and faithful to one's husband or betrothed, even after his death, as demanded by the Confucian moral code

【贞洁】 zhēnjié chaste and undefiled

【贞烈】 zhēnliè ready to die to preserve one's chastity

**针** zhēn ① needle: 绣花～ embroidery needle/ 毛线～ knitting needle ② stitch: 在袜子上缝两～ sew (或 put) a couple of stitches in a sock/ 织漏一～ drop a stitch/ 伤口缝了四～。The wound was closed with four stitches. ③ anything like a needle: 松～ pine needle/ 大头～ pin/ 时(分)～ hour (minute) hand ④ injection; shot: 打～ give or have an injection ⑤ acupuncture

【针鼻儿】 zhēnbír the eye of a needle

【针砭】 zhēnbiān ① an ancient form of acupuncture ② point out sb.'s errors and offer salutary advice

【针布】 zhēnbù 〈纺〉 card clothing

【针插不进,水泼不进】 zhēn chā bù jìn, shuǐ pō bù jìn impenetrable and watertight — (of a political organization or an administrative unit) not allowing even a leading body to look into its affairs

【针刺疗法】 zhēncì liáofǎ acupuncture treatment

【针刺麻醉】 zhēncì mázuì acupuncture anaesthesia: ～心脏手术 heart surgery with acupuncture anaesthesia

【针对】 zhēnduì ① be directed against; be aimed at; counter: 这个条约不～任何第三国。The treaty is not directed against any third country./ 这个讲话～性很强。There was no mistaking what the talk was aimed at./ ～这种倾向,我们需要加强自然科学的基础理论的研究。To counter this tendency, we must strengthen research in the basic theories of natural science. ② in the light of; in accordance with; in connection with: ～儿童的特点进行教育 educate children in accordance with their special characteristics/ ～这种情况 in view of this situation

【针锋相对】 zhēnfēng xiāng duì give tit for tat; be diametrically opposed to: 进行～的斗争 wage a tit-for-tat (或 blow-for-blow) struggle against/ 对于反动派,我们的方针是～。Towards the reactionaries our policy is to give tit for tat.

【针箍】 zhēngū 〈方〉 thimble

【针剂】 zhēnjì 〈药〉 injection

【针尖】 zhēnjiān the point of a needle; pinpoint: ～儿对麦芒儿 a pin against an awn — diamond cut diamond/ ～大的窟窿,斗大的风。A big wind can blow through a small hole — a little leak will sink a great ship.

【针脚】 zhēnjiao stitch: ～很匀。The stitches are neat./ 顺着线头找～ pick up clues

【针灸】 zhēnjiǔ acupuncture and moxibustion ◇ ～铜人 a bronze figure marked with acupuncture points

【针梳机】 zhēnshūjī 〈纺〉 gill box

【针头】 zhēntóu 〈医〉 syringe needle

【针头线脑】 zhēntóu-xiànnǎo 〈口〉 odds and ends needed for sewing; needle and thread, etc.

【针尾鸭】 zhēnwěiyā 〈动〉 pintail

【针线】 zhēnxian needlework ◇ ～包 sewing kit/ ～活 needlework; stitching; sewing

【针眼】 zhēnyǎn ① the eye of a needle ② pinprick

【针眼】 zhēnyan 〈医〉 sty

【针鼹】 zhēnyǎn 〈动〉 echidna; spiny anteater

【针叶树】 zhēnyèshù coniferous tree; conifer

【针织】 zhēnzhī knitting: ～外衣 knitted (或 knit) coat ◇ ～厂 knitting mill; knit goods mill/ ～机 knitting machine/ ～品 knit goods; knitwear; hosiery

【针黹】 zhēnzhǐ 〈书〉 needlework

**侦** zhēn detect; scout; investigate

【侦查】 zhēnchá 〈法〉 investigate (a crime)

【侦察】 zhēnchá 〈军〉 reconnoitre; scout: 敌后～ reconnoitre the enemy rear/ 进行～活动 conduct reconnaissance/ 火力～ reconnaissance by fire/ ～敌情 gather intelligence about the enemy

◇ ～兵 scout/ ～部队 reconnaissance troops (或 unit); scouting force/ ～飞行 reconnaissance flight/ ～机 reconnaissance plane; scout/ ～卫星 reconnaissance (或 spy) satellite/ ～员 scout

【侦缉】 zhēnjī track down and arrest

【侦探】 zhēntàn ① do detective work ② detective; spy ◇ ～小说 detective story

【侦听】 zhēntīng 〈军〉 intercept (enemy radio communications); monitor ◇ ～器 detectaphone/ ～台 intercept station

**珍** zhēn ① treasure: 奇～异宝 rare treasures ② precious; valuable; rare: ～禽异兽 rare birds and animals ③ value highly; treasure: ～赏 treasure and delight in (curios, etc.); highly value and appreciate

【珍爱】 zhēn'ài treasure; love dearly; be very fond of: 他非常～老战士送给自己的针线包。He treasures the sewing kit the old soldier gave him.

【珍宝】 zhēnbǎo jewellery; treasure

【珍宝岛】 Zhēnbǎodǎo Zhenbao Island

【珍本】 zhēnběn rare edition; rare book

【珍藏】 zhēncáng collect (rare books, art treasures, etc.)

【珍贵】 zhēnguì valuable; precious: ～药材 valuable ingredients of traditional Chinese medicine/ ～的历史文物 precious historical relics/ ～的纪念品 precious mementos
【珍品】 zhēnpǐn treasure: 艺术～ art treasure
【珍奇】 zhēnqí rare: ～的动物 rare animals
【珍视】 zhēnshì value; prize; cherish; treasure: 教育青年人～今天的美好生活 teach young people to prize the happy life they lead today/ ～我们两国人民之间的友谊 treasure the friendship between the peoples of our two countries
【珍玩】 zhēnwán rare curios
【珍闻】 zhēnwén news titbits; fillers: 世界～ world briefs (或 miscellany)
【珍惜】 zhēnxī treasure; value; cherish: ～革命的成果 treasure the fruits of the revolution/ ～时间 value one's time/ ～劳动人民创造出来的财富 cherish the wealth created by the labouring people
【珍馐】 zhēnxiū delicacies; dainties 又作"珍羞"
【珍异】 zhēnyì rare
【珍重】 zhēnzhòng ① highly value; treasure; set great store by: ～我们两党之间的团结 highly value the solidarity between our two parties ② take good care of yourself: 两人紧紧握手，互道～。They clasped hands, each asking the other to take good care of himself.
【珍珠】 zhēnzhū pearl ◇ ～贝 pearl shell; pearl oyster
【珍珠港】 Zhēnzhūgǎng Pearl Harbour
【珍珠鸡】 zhēnzhūjī 〈动〉 guinea fowl
【珍珠梅】 zhēnzhūméi 〈植〉 false spiraea
【珍珠米】 zhēnzhūmǐ 〈方〉 maize; (Indian) corn
【珍珠岩】 zhēnzhūyán pearlite

## 胗

zhēn gizzard
【胗肝儿】 zhēngānr gizzard and liver (esp. chicken's or duck's)

## 祯

zhēn 〈书〉 auspicious; propitious

## 桢

zhēn ① hardwood ② terminal posts used in building a wall in ancient times
【桢干】 zhēngàn 〈书〉 core member; backbone (element)

## 真

zhēn ① true; real; genuine: 去伪存～ eliminate the false and retain the true/ ～丝 real silk/ 这幅宋人的画是～的。This is a genuine Song painting. ② really; truly; indeed: 我～不知道。I really don't know./ 他～信了。He actually believed it./ ～感激 be truly grateful/ ～有你的！You're a smart fellow, you are!/ 演出～精采。The performance was just splendid./ 时间过得～快！How time flies! ③ clearly; unmistakably: 你看得～么？Can you see clearly?/ 字音咬得～ pronounce words distinctly ④ 见"真书"
【真北】 zhēnběi true north
【真才实学】 zhēncái-shíxué real ability and learning; genuine talent: 有～的科技人员 well-trained scientific and technical workers
【真诚】 zhēnchéng sincere; genuine; true: ～的愿望 a sincere wish (或 desire)/ ～的友谊 true friendship/ ～悔过 sincerely (或 genuinely) repent/ ～合作 sincerely cooperate
【真刀真枪】 zhēndāo-zhēnqiāng real swords and spears — the real thing: ～地干起来 start a shooting war; start in real earnest
【真地平】 zhēndìpíng 〈天〉 true horizon
【真谛】 zhēndì true essence; true meaning: 人生的～ the true meaning of life
【真鲷】 zhēndiāo genuine porgy; red porgy
【真分数】 zhēnfēnshù 〈数〉 proper fraction
【真格的】 zhēngéde 〈方〉 real; true: 你别再装着玩儿啦，说～吧。Stop joking and tell me the truth./ ～，你到底去不去？Seriously, are you going or not?
【真个】 zhēngè 〈方〉 really; truly; indeed: ～了不起 really wonderful
【真果】 zhēnguǒ 〈植〉 true fruit
【真迹】 zhēnjì authentic work (of painting or calligraphy)
【真假】 zhēn-jiǎ true and false; genuine and sham: 辨别～ tell the true from the false/ 识别～马克思主义 distinguish genuine from sham Marxism/ 真真假假 the true mingled with the false; a mixture of truth and falsehood
【真金不怕火炼】 zhēnjīn bù pà huǒ liàn true gold fears no fire — a person of integrity can stand severe tests
【真菌】 zhēnjūn fungus
【真空】 zhēnkōng 〈物〉 vacuum: 未尽～ partial vacuum ◇ ～泵 vacuum pump/ ～处理 〈冶〉 vacuum treatment/ ～弹道 vacuum trajectory; vacuum flight path/ ～地带 〈军〉 no-man's-land/ ～电弧炉 vacuum arc furnace/ ～镀膜 vacuum coating/ ～管 〈电子〉 vacuum valve (或 tube)/ ～过滤 vacuum filtration/ ～技术 vacuum technique/ ～吸尘器 vacuum cleaner/ ～压铸 vacuum die casting
【真理】 zhēnlǐ truth: 马克思列宁主义的普遍～ the universal truth of Marxism-Leninism/ 坚持～，修正错误 uphold the truth and correct mistakes
【真面目】 zhēnmiànmù true features; true colours: 不识庐山～，只缘身在此山中。I see not the true face of Lushan because I am in the mountains./ 认清其～ see sb. in his true colours; know sb. for what he is
【真名实姓】 zhēnmíng-shíxìng real name
【真皮】 zhēnpí 〈生理〉 derma
【真凭实据】 zhēnpíng-shíjù conclusive evidence; hard evidence
【真漆】 zhēnqī lacquer
【真枪实弹】 zhēnqiāng-shídàn real guns and bullets; live ammunition: 进行～的演习 conduct exercises (或 manoeuvres) with live ammunition
【真切】 zhēnqiè vivid; clear; distinct: 这篇通讯写得～感人。The report is vividly written and very moving./ 看得～ see clearly
【真情】 zhēnqíng ① the real (或 true) situation; the facts; the actual state of affairs; truth ② true feelings; real sentiments: ～的流露 a revelation of one's true feelings
【真确】 zhēnquè ① true; real; authentic: ～的消息 authentic (或 reliable) news ② clear; distinct
【真人真事】 zhēnrén-zhēnshì real people and real events; actual persons and events
【真善美】 zhēn-shàn-měi the true, the good and the beautiful
【真实】 zhēnshí true; real; authentic: ～的感情 true feelings; real sentiments/ ～情况 the real (或 true) situation; how things actually stand/ ～记录 authentic records ◇ ～感 sense of reality/ ～性 truthfulness; authenticity
【真是】 zhēnshi 〔表示不满意的情绪〕: 他把一支新笔丢了，～。It's too bad he's lost his new pen./ 下点雨就不让我们去，～。Just because of a bit of rain we're not allowed to go. The idea!/ 你也～，连灯也不关，就走了。Look at this! You didn't even turn off the light when you left.
【真书】 zhēnshū (in Chinese calligraphy) regular script
【真率】 zhēnshuài sincere; unaffected; straightforward
【真髓】 zhēnsuǐ essence
【真相】 zhēnxiàng the real (或 true) situation; the real (或 actual) facts; the actual state of affairs; truth: 掩盖～ cover up the facts/ 弄清事情的～ clarify the truth of the matter/ ～大白。The whole truth has come out./ 给人以

假象，而将～荫蔽着 conceal one's true features and give a false impression/ 这就是事情的～。This is the actual state of affairs. 又作"真象"

【真心】 zhēnxīn wholehearted; heartfelt; sincere: ～拥护 give wholehearted support to/ ～话 sincere words/ 说～话 speak from the bottom of one's heart/ ～悔改 sincerely repent and earnestly reform oneself

【真心实意】 zhēnxīn-shíyì genuinely and sincerely; truly and wholeheartedly; wholeheartedly; sincerely: ～地为人民谋福利 sincerely and wholeheartedly work for the well-being of the people/ ～地支持 wholeheartedly support

【真正】 zhēnzhèng genuine; true; real: ～的吉林人参 genuine Jilin ginseng/ ～的朋友 a true friend/ ～的革命者 a true (或 genuine) revolutionary/ ～领会文件的精神实质 have a real grasp of the essence of the document/ ～的马列主义政党 genuine Marxist-Leninist parties/ ～负起责任来 shoulder the responsibilities in earnest/ ～有力量的是人民。It's the people who are really powerful.

【真知】 zhēnzhī genuine (或 real) knowledge: 实践出～。Real knowledge comes from practice.

【真知灼见】 zhēnzhī-zhuójiàn real knowledge and deep insight; penetrating judgment

【真值表】 zhēnzhíbiǎo 〈物〉 truth table

【真挚】 zhēnzhì sincere; cordial: ～的友谊 sincere friendship

【真珠】 zhēnzhū pearl ◇ ～层 〈动〉 pearly (或 nacreous) layer

【真主】 Zhēnzhǔ 〈伊斯兰教〉 Allah

## 砧

zhēn hammering block; anvil: 台～ 〈机〉 bench anvil/ 锻～〈机〉 smith anvil

【砧板】 zhēnbǎn chopping block

【砧骨】 zhēngǔ 〈生理〉 incus; anvil

【砧木】 zhēnmù 〈农〉 stock

【砧子】 zhēnzi 〈口〉 hammering block; anvil

## 斟

zhēn pour (tea or wine): 给她～一杯酒。Pour her a glass of wine.

【斟酌】 zhēnzhuó consider; deliberate: 再三～ consider carefully again and again/ ～词句 weigh one's words/ ～办理 act at one's discretion; act as one sees fit/ ～情况作适当调整 make appropriate adjustments according to circumstances

## 甄

zhēn ①〈书〉 discriminate; distinguish; examine: ～选 select ② (Zhēn) a surname

【甄拔】 zhēnbá select: ～人才 select people of talent

【甄别】 zhēnbié ① examine and distinguish; screen; discriminate ② reexamine a case

## 榛

zhēn 〈植〉 hazel

【榛鸡】 zhēnjī hazel grouse

【榛莽】 zhēnmǎng 〈书〉 luxuriant vegetation

【榛实】 zhēnshí hazelnut

【榛子】 zhēnzi ① hazel ② hazelnut

## 箴

zhēn 〈书〉 ① admonish; exhort ② a type of didactic literary composition

【箴言】 zhēnyán admonition; exhortation; maxim

## 臻

zhēn 〈书〉 attain (a high level): 交通日～便利。Transportation and communications are becoming easier day by day./ 方法日～完善。The methods are being perfected.

## 鱵

zhēn 〈动〉 halfbeak

# zhěn

## 诊

zhěn examine (a patient)

【诊病】 zhěnbìng diagnose a disease

【诊察】 zhěnchá examine (a patient)

【诊断】 zhěnduàn diagnose: 物理～ physical diagnosis/ 医生～这病是胸膜炎。The doctor diagnosed the illness (或 case) as pleurisy. ◇ ～书 medical certificate

【诊疗】 zhěnliáo make a diagnosis and give treatment ◇ ～器械 medical instruments/ ～室 consulting room/ ～所 clinic; dispensary

【诊脉】 zhěnmài feel the pulse

【诊视】 zhěnshì examine (a patient)

【诊室】 zhěnshì consulting room

【诊所】 zhěnsuǒ clinic

【诊治】 zhěnzhì make a diagnosis and give treatment

## 枕

zhěn ① pillow ② rest the head on: ～着胳臂睡觉 sleep with one's head resting on one's arm ③ 〈机〉 block: 靠～ backing block/ 转～ swivel block

【枕戈待旦】 zhěn gē dài dàn lie with one's head pillowed on a spear, waiting for day to break; be ready for battle; maintain combat readiness

【枕骨】 zhěngǔ 〈生理〉 occipital bone

【枕巾】 zhěnjīn a towel used to cover a pillow

【枕木】 zhěnmù 〈铁道〉 sleeper; tie

【枕套】 zhěntào pillowcase; pillowslip

【枕头】 zhěntou pillow

【枕席】 zhěnxí ① a mat used to cover a pillow; pillow mat ② bed

【枕心】 zhěnxīn pillow (without the pillowcase)

## 轸

zhěn 〈书〉 ① the cross board at the rear of an ancient carriage ② carriage ③ sorrowful; distressed

【轸念】 zhěnniàn 〈书〉 sorrowfully cherish the memory of sb.; think anxiously about: 殊深～ express great solicitude for sb.

## 疹

zhěn rash: 荨麻～ nettle rash

【疹子】 zhěnzi 〈口〉 measles

## 畛

zhěn 〈书〉 raised paths between fields

【畛域】 zhěnyù 〈书〉 boundary: 不分～ make no distinctions

## 缜

zhěn

【缜密】 zhěnmì careful; meticulous; deliberate: ～的计划 a deliberate (或 carefully thought-out) plan/ ～的分析 a careful (或 minute) analysis/ ～的研究 a meticulous study

# zhèn

## 阵

zhèn ① battle array (或 formation): 长蛇～ single-line battle formation ② position; front: 上～杀敌 go to the front to fight the enemy ③ a period of time: 病了一～儿 be ill for some time/ 那～儿 in those days; then/ 这～儿 these days; recently ④〈量〉〔表示事情或动作经过的段落〕: 一～雨 a spatter of rain/ 一～风 a gust (或 blast) of wind/ 一～寒潮 a cold spell/ 一～咳嗽 a fit (或 spasm) of coughing/ 一～热烈的掌声 a burst of warm applause

【阵地】 zhèndì position; front: 进入～ get into position/ 人在～在 fight to the death in defence of one's position;

hold one's position at all costs/ ～攻击(防御) positional attack (defence)/前沿～ a forward position/ 思想～ ideological front ◇ ～战 positional warfare

【阵脚】 zhènjiǎo ① front line ② position; situation; circumstances: 稳住～ secure one's position/ 乱了～ be thrown into confusion

【阵容】 zhènróng ① battle array (或 formation) ② lineup: ～强大 have a strong lineup/ 演员～整齐 a well-balanced cast

【阵势】 zhènshì ① battle array (或 formation); a disposition of combat forces: 摆开～ deploy the ranks in battle array/ 敌人的～全给打乱了。The enemy formations were completely broken up. ② situation; condition; circumstances

【阵痛】 zhèntòng 〈医〉 labour pains; throes (of childbirth)

【阵亡】 zhènwáng be killed in action; fall in battle

【阵线】 zhènxiàn front; ranks; alignment: 反帝～ the anti-imperialist front/ 革命～ an alignment of revolutionary forces/ 阶级～ class alignment

【阵雪】 zhènxuě snow shower

【阵营】 zhènyíng a group of people who pursue a common interest; camp: 革命～ a revolutionary camp

【阵雨】 zhènyǔ shower

【阵子】 zhènzi 见"阵"③④

**鸩** zhèn ① a legendary bird with poisonous feathers ② 〈书〉 poisoned wine ③〈书〉 kill sb. with poisoned wine

【鸩毒】 zhèndú poisoned wine

**振** zhèn ① shake; flap: ～翅 flap the wings; flutter/ ～笔直书 wield the pen furiously ② rise with force and spirit; brace up: 食欲不～ lose one's appetite; have a jaded appetite/ 精神为之一～ feel one's spirits buoyed up/ 我军士气大～。The morale of our troops was greatly boosted.

【振拔】 zhènbá 〈书〉 extricate oneself from a predicament and brace oneself up to action

【振臂】 zhènbì raise one's arm: 他～高呼"共产党万岁!" He raised his arm and shouted: "Long live the Communist Party!"

【振荡】 zhèndàng ①〈物〉 vibration ②〈电〉 oscillation: 本机～ local oscillation/ 寄生～ parasitic oscillation ◇ ～电路 oscillating circuit/ ～管 oscillator valve/ ～器 oscillator

【振捣器】 zhèndǎoqì 〈建〉 vibrator

【振动】 zhèndòng 〈物〉 vibration: 简谐～ simple harmonic vibration/ 等时～ isochronous vibration ◇ ～计 vibrometer; vibration meter/ ～频率 vibration frequency

【振奋】 zhènfèn ① rouse oneself; rise with force and spirit; be inspired with enthusiasm: 人人～，个个当先 everyone full of vigour, each one forging ahead ② inspire; stimulate: ～人心 inspire people; fill people with enthusiasm/ ～士气 boost (或 raise) the morale (of the troops)/ ～革命精神 inspire revolutionary enthusiasm; enhance revolutionary vigour; encourage a revolutionary spirit/ 令人～的消息 heartening news

【振幅】 zhènfú 〈物〉 amplitude (of vibration): 脉冲～ pulse amplitude ◇ ～畸变 amplitude distortion

【振聋发聩】 zhènlóng-fākuì rouse the deaf and awaken the unhearing; awaken the deaf; enlighten the benighted

【振兴】 zhènxīng develop vigorously; promote: ～教育事业 vitalize education/ ～工业 vigorously develop industry

【振振有辞】 zhènzhèn yǒu cí speak plausibly and at length

【振作】 zhènzuò bestir (或 exert) oneself; display vigour: ～精神 bestir oneself; brace (或 cheer) up/ ～起来! Brace up! 或 Pull yourself together!

**朕** zhèn ① I, the sovereign; we (used by a royal person in proclamations instead of I) ② 〈书〉 sign; omen

【朕兆】 zhènzhào sign; omen; portent: 有～可寻。There are signs for us to read.

**赈** zhèn relieve; aid: 以工代～ provide work as a form of relief

【赈济】 zhènjì relieve; aid: ～灾民 relieve the people in stricken areas; aid the victims of natural calamities

【赈款】 zhènkuǎn relief fund

【赈灾】 zhènzāi relieve the people in stricken areas

**震** zhèn ① shake; shock; vibrate; quake: 地～ earthquake/ 他捶了一下桌子，杯子被～得跳起来。He gave the table a thump which shook the cups. ② greatly excited; deeply astonished; shocked: ～骇 shocked; stunned; astounded

【震波】 zhènbō 〈地〉 seismic wave; earthquake wave ◇ ～图 seismogram

【震颤】 zhènchàn tremble; quiver ◇ ～性麻痹 paralysis agitans

【震旦纪】 Zhèndànjì 〈地〉 the Sinian Period

【震荡】 zhèndàng shake; shock; vibrate; quake: 五洲～风雷激。The Five Continents are rocking, wind and thunder roaring.

【震动】 zhèndòng shake; shock; vibrate; quake: 春雷～山谷。Spring thunder shook the valley./ 火车～了一下，开走了。The train pulled out with a jerk./ 十月革命～了全世界。The October Revolution shook the world./ ～全国 reverberate through the whole country/ 引起了广泛的～ produce wide repercussions/ 这番话对他的思想～很大。The talk made a great impaction him.

【震耳欲聋】 zhèn ěr yù lóng deafening: ～的鞭炮声 the deafening noise of firecrackers

【震古烁今】 zhèngǔ-shuòjīn surpassing the ancients and amazing the contemporaries — earthshaking

【震撼】 zhènhàn shake; shock; vibrate: ～天地的英雄气概 earthshaking heroism

【震惊】 zhènjīng shock; amaze; astonish: ～中外 shock the country and the whole world

【震怒】 zhènnù be enraged; be furious

【震慑】 zhènshè awe; frighten

【震音】 zhènyīn 〈乐〉 *tremolo*

【震源】 zhènyuán 〈地〉 focus (of an earthquake)

【震中】 zhènzhōng 〈地〉 epicentre ◇ ～区 epicentral area

**镇** zhèn ① press down; keep down; ease: ～痛 ease pain ② calm; tranquil; at ease: ～静 calm ③ guard; garrison: 坐～ assume personal command (of a garrison, etc.) ④ garrison post: 军事重～ strategic post ⑤ town ⑥ cool with cold water or ice: 冰～啤酒 iced beer/ 把西瓜放在冷水里～一～ put the watermelon in cold water for a while to chill it

【镇定】 zhèndìng calm; cool; composed; unruffled: 神色～ be calm and collected; show composure and presence of mind/ 保持～ keep cool; remain calm; keep one's head

【镇反运动】 Zhènfǎn Yùndòng 见"镇压反革命运动"

【镇静】 zhènjìng calm; cool; composed; unruffled: 遇到紧急情况要～。Keep calm in an emergency./ 努力～下来 compose oneself with an effort ◇ ～钢 〈冶〉 killed steel/ ～剂 sedative; tranquillizer

【镇流管】 zhènliúguǎn 〈电〉 ballast tube

【镇流器】 zhènliúqì 〈电〉 ballast

【镇守】 zhènshǒu guard (a strategically important place); garrison

【镇痛】 zhèntòng ① ease pain ②〈医〉analgesia: 针刺～ acupuncture analgesia ◇ ～效果 analgesic effect

【镇压】 zhènyā ① suppress; repress; put down: ～叛乱 put down a rebellion/ 不～剥削者的反抗，革命的胜利就不能巩固。The victory of the revolution can't be consolidated unless the resistance of the exploiters is crushed. ②〈口〉execute (a counterrevolutionary): 那个杀人犯已经依法～了。The murderer was executed according to law. ③〈农〉rolling; compacting; tamping ◇ ～器〈农〉(land) roller

【镇压反革命运动】 Zhènyā Fǎngémìng Yùndòng the Movement to Suppress Counterrevolutionaries (1950-1952)

【镇纸】 zhènzhǐ paperweight

## zhēng

**丁** zhēng
另见 dīng

【丁丁】 zhēngzhēng〈书〉〈象〉: 伐木～。Clang, clang goes the woodman's axe.

**正** zhēng the first month of the lunar year; the first moon
另见 zhèng

【正月】 zhēngyuè the first month of the lunar year; the first moon: ～初一 the lunar New Year's Day

**争** zhēng ① contend; vie; strive: ～领导权 contend for leadership/ 不～一日之短长 not strive for only temporary superiority/ 不～一城一地的得失 not contend for a city or a piece of ground (in mobile warfare)/ ～名～利 strive (或 scramble) for fame and gain/ ～挑重担 rush to carry the heaviest load; vie with each other for the hardest job/ ～分夺秒 race (或 work) against time; make every minute and second count/ ～着发言 try to have the floor before others/ 春～日，夏～时。〈农谚〉In spring every day counts, in summer every hour. ② argue; dispute: 你们在～什么？What are you arguing about?/ ～长论短 squabble; argue ③〈方〉short of; wanting: 总数还～多少？How many more are needed to make up the total? ④〔多用于诗、词、曲中〕how; why: ～知 how does one know/ ～奈 nevertheless; unfortunately

【争霸】 zhēngbà contend (或 struggle) for hegemony; scramble (或 strive) for supremacy

【争辩】 zhēngbiàn argue; debate; contend: 无休止的～ an endless debate/ 无可～ indisputable; incontestable/ 真理不怕～。Truth does not fear contention.

【争吵】 zhēngchǎo quarrel; wrangle; squabble: 无谓的～ a pointless quarrel/ 激烈的～ fierce (或 bitter) wrangling/ ～不休 bicker (或 squabble) endlessly

【争持】 zhēngchí refuse to give in; stick to one's guns

【争斗】 zhēngdòu fight; struggle; strife

【争端】 zhēngduān controversial issue; dispute; conflict: 国际～ an international dispute/ 边界～ a border dispute/ ～当事国 parties to a dispute (between nations)/ 调解两国～ act as mediator in a conflict between two countries

【争夺】 zhēngduó fight (或 contend, scramble) for; enter into rivalry with sb. over sth.; vie with sb. for sth.: ～制高点 fight (或 contend) for possession of a commanding height/ 两霸～的重点 the focus of contention between the two hegemonist powers/ ～市场 scramble for markets/ ～势力范围 scramble for spheres of influence/ ～核优势 vie for nuclear superiority/ 资产阶级同我们～青年一代。The bourgeoisie tries to win the younger generation away from us.

【争光】 zhēngguāng win honour (或 glory) for: 为社会主义祖国～ win honour for our socialist homeland; bring credit to (或 be a credit to) our socialist country

【争衡】 zhēnghéng scramble for supremacy; strive for mastery; be in rivalry with

【争论】 zhēnglùn controversy; dispute; debate; contention: 不同意见的～ controversies over differing opinions/ 激烈的～ a heated dispute/ ～不休 an endless debate/ ～的双方 the two contending sides/ ～之点 the point at issue/ 科学上不同学派的自由～ free contention among different schools in science

【争鸣】 zhēngmíng contend: 百家～。A hundred schools of thought contend.

【争气】 zhēngqì try to make a good showing; try to win credit for; try to bring credit to: 为中国工人阶级～ bring credit to the Chinese working class/ 有人说这活儿妇女干不了，我们得争这口气。Some people say women can't do this job, but we'll show them.

【争取】 zhēngqǔ strive for; fight for; win over: ～民族解放 strive for national liberation/ ～群众 win over the masses/ ～入党 strive to qualify for Party membership/ ～时间 race (或 work) against time/ ～主动 take the initiative/ 要～一切可以～的人，团结一切可以团结的人。We must win over all people who can be won over, unite with all people who can be united.

【争权夺利】 zhēngquán-duólì scramble for power and profit

【争先】 zhēngxiān try to be the first to do sth.: 大家～发言。Everyone tried to get the floor./ 人人跃进，个个～。All took part in the leap forward, each trying to outdo the others.

【争先恐后】 zhēngxiān-kǒnghòu strive to be the first and fear to lag behind; vie with each other in doing sth.: ～地报名参军 vie with each other in signing up for military service

【争雄】 zhēngxióng 见"争霸"

【争议】 zhēngyì dispute; controversy: 有～的地区 a disputed area/ 有～的条款 a contentious clause

【争执】 zhēngzhí disagree; dispute; stick to one's position (或 guns): ～不下。Each sticks to his own stand (或 to his guns).

**怔** zhēng seized with terror; terrified; panic-stricken

【怔忡】 zhēngchōng〈中医〉palpitation

**征** zhēng ① go on a journey: ～帆 a ship on a long journey ② go on an expedition (或 a campaign): 出～ go on an expedition/ 南～北战 fighting north and south; campaigning up and down the country/ ～马 battle steed ③ levy (troops); call up; draft: 应～入伍 be drafted ④ levy (taxes); collect; impose: ～粮 impose grain levies; collect grain taxes ⑤ ask for; solicit: ～稿 solicit contributions (to a journal, etc.) ⑥ evidence; proof: 有实物可～。There is solid evidence./ 无～之言 an unfounded assertion ⑦ sign; portent

【征兵】 zhēngbīng conscription; draft; call-up ◇ ～法 conscription (或 draft) law/ ～年龄 conscription age; age for enlistment/ ～站 drafting centre/ ～制 universal military service; conscription system

【征尘】 zhēngchén dust which settles on one during a journey

【征调】 zhēngdiào requisition; call up: ～物资和人员 requisition supplies and draft personnel

【征伐】 zhēngfá go on a punitive expedition

【征服】 zhēngfú conquer; subjugate: 用武力～ conquer by force of arms/ ～自然 conquer nature/ ～黄河 tame the Huanghe River
【征购】 zhēnggòu requisition by purchase: 粮食～ grain purchases by the state/ ～任务 state purchase quotas
【征候】 zhēnghòu sign: 病人已有好转的～。The patient shows signs of a turn for the better.
【征集】 zhēngjí ① collect: ～签名 collect signatures (for an appeal)/ ～军粮 collect grain for the army/ ～物资 the acquisition of supplies ② draft; call up; recruit: ～新兵 recruitment/ 战时～ wartime draft/ ～补充兵员 call up new recruits to replenish the ranks/ 定期～和退役 periodic call-up and demobilization
【征募】 zhēngmù enlist; recruit
【征聘】 zhēngpìn give public notice of vacancies to be filled; invite applications for jobs; advertise for (a secretary, teacher, etc.)
【征求】 zhēngqiú solicit; seek; ask for: ～意见 solicit (或 seek) opinions; ask for criticisms/ 广泛～群众意见 consult the broad masses; solicit opinions from the general public/ ～学生对教学的意见 gather students' opinions on teaching/ ～订户 solicit (或 canvass for) subscriptions ◇ ～意见本 an edition for soliciting comments; trial edition
【征实】 zhēngshí levies in kind; grain levies (或 tax)
【征收】 zhēngshōu levy; collect; impose: ～赋税 levy (或 collect) taxes/ ～进口税 impose import duties/ ～烟草税 put a tax on tobacco
【征税】 zhēngshuì levy (或 collect) taxes; taxation ◇ ～货物 dutiable goods
【征讨】 zhēngtǎo go on a punitive expedition
【征途】 zhēngtú journey: 艰险的～ a perilous journey/ 踏上革命的～ embark on the road of revolution
【征文】 zhēngwén solicit articles or essays ◇ ～启事 a notice soliciting contributions for a special issue, etc.
【征象】 zhēngxiàng sign; symptom
【征询】 zhēngxún seek the opinion of; consult
【征引】 zhēngyǐn quote; cite
【征用】 zhēngyòng take over for use; commandeer; requisition: ～人力、物力、财力 requisition manpower, material or funds/ 国家可以对城乡土地实行～。The state may take over for use urban and rural land.
【征战】 zhēngzhàn go on an expedition (或 a campaign)
【征召】 zhēngzhào ① call up; enlist; draft; conscript: ～入伍 enlist in the army ② 〈书〉 appoint to an official position
【征兆】 zhēngzhào sign; omen; portent

## 挣

zhēng
另见 zhèng
【挣扎】 zhēngzhá struggle: ～着坐起来 struggle to a sitting position/ 进行垂死的～ put up a last-ditch struggle/ ～在死亡线上 struggle for existence on the brink of death; struggle for a bare subsistence

## 峥

zhēng
【峥嵘】 zhēngróng ① lofty and steep; towering ② outstanding; extraordinary: 头角～ (of youth) outstanding; very promising; brilliant/ ～岁月 eventful years

## 狰

zhēng
【狰狞】 zhēngníng ferocious; savage; hideous: ～面目 ferocious features; a vile visage

## 症

zhēng
另见 zhèng
【症瘕积聚】 zhēngjiǎ jījù 〈中医〉 a lump in the abdomen causing distension and pain
【症结】 zhēngjié crux; crucial reason: 这就是问题的～所在。Therein lies the crux of the problem.

## 钲

zhēng a bell-shaped percussion instrument, used in ancient times by troops on march

## 睁

zhēng open (the eyes): ～一只眼，闭一只眼 turn a blind eye to sth.; wink at sth./ ～着眼睛说瞎话 tell a barefaced (或 out-and-out) lie
【睁眼瞎子】 zhēngyǎn xiāzi illiterate person

## 铮

zhēng
【铮鏦】 zhēngcōng 〈象〉 clank; clang
【铮铮】 zhēngzhēng 〈象〉 clank; clang

## 筝

zhēng ① *zheng*, a 21- or 25-stringed plucked instrument in some ways similar to the zither ② 见"风筝" fēngzheng

## 蒸

zhēng ① evaporate ② steam: ～饭 steam rice/ 菜凉了，～一～。The food is cold. Let's warm it up in the steamer.
【蒸饼】 zhēngbǐng steamed cake
【蒸发】 zhēngfā evaporate ◇ ～计 evaporimeter/ ～蒸腾 evapotranspiration
【蒸锅】 zhēngguō a pot for steaming food; steamer
【蒸饺】 zhēngjiǎo steamed dumpling (with meat and vegetable stuffing)
【蒸馏】 zhēngliú 〈物〉 distillation: 拔顶～〈化〉 topping distillation/ 常压～〈化〉 atmospheric distillation/ 真空～〈化〉 vacuum distillation
◇ ～器 distiller; retort/ ～水 distilled water/ ～塔 distilling tower
【蒸笼】 zhēnglóng food steamer (usu. made of bamboo)
【蒸呢】 zhēngní 〈纺〉 decatizing; decating
【蒸气】 zhēngqì vapour
【蒸汽】 zhēngqì steam
◇ ～发生器 steam generator/ ～供暖 steam heating/ ～锅炉 steam boiler/ ～机 steam engine/ ～机车 steam locomotive/ ～绞车 steam winch/ ～浴 steam bath
【蒸球】 zhēngqiú 〈纸〉 rotary spherical digester
【蒸食】 zhēngshi steamed wheaten foods
【蒸腾】 zhēngténg (of steam) rising: 热气～ steaming ◇ ～作用〈植〉 transpiration
【蒸蒸日上】 zhēngzhēng rì shàng becoming more prosperous every day; flourishing; thriving: 一派～、欣欣向荣的景象 a scene of prosperity/ 我国的社会主义建设～。Our socialist construction is advancing full steam ahead./ 随着机械化的发展，农业生产～。With the development of mechanization, agriculture is becoming more and more flourishing.

# zhěng

## 拯

zhěng save; rescue; deliver
【拯救】 zhěngjiù save; rescue; deliver: 党把我从火坑中～出来。The Party rescued (或 delivered) me from a hell on earth.

## 整

zhěng ① whole; complete; full; entire: ～砖 a whole (或 an unbroken) brick/ ～夜 the whole night; all night long/ 敌人～团～团地投降。Whole regiments of the enemy surrendered./ 一～页 a full page/ 十二点～ twelve o'clock sharp/ 恰好～一年。It's a year to the day. ② in good order; neat; tidy: 仪容不～ untidy in one's appearance/ 衣冠不～ slovenly in one's dress; not properly dressed ③ put in order; rectify: ～改 rectify and reform/ ～社 check up on and consolidate people's communes ④ repair; mend; renovate: ～修 renovate/ ～旧如新 repair sth. old and make it as good as new ⑤ make sb. suffer; punish; fix: 挨～ be the target of criticism or attack ⑥〈方〉do; make; work: 这东西我看见人～过，并不难。I once saw someone do it. It's not very difficult./ 绳子给～断了。The rope was broken.

【整备】 zhěngbèi reorganize and outfit (troops)

【整编】 zhěngbiān reorganize (troops)

【整饬】 zhěngchì ①put in order; strengthen: ～纪律 strengthen discipline ② in good order; neat; tidy: 服装～ neatly dressed

【整除】 zhěngchú 〈数〉 be divided with no remainder; divide exactly

【整党】 zhěngdǎng consolidate the Party organization: ～建党 Party consolidation and Party building

【整地】 zhěngdì 〈农〉 soil preparation (i.e. preparation of land for sowing or planting by ploughing, harrowing, levelling, etc.)

【整点】 zhěngdiǎn 〈数〉 integral point

【整队】 zhěngduì dress the ranks; get (或 bring) the ranks into orderly alignment; line up: ～出发 get the ranks in good order and set out; set out in orderly formation/ ～入场 file into the arena, auditorium, etc.

【整顿】 zhěngdùn rectify; consolidate; reorganize: ～文风 rectify the style of writing/ ～纪律 strengthen discipline/ ～组织 overhaul and consolidate an organization/ ～领导班子 consolidate or reorganize a leading body/ ～规章制度 reestablish rules and regulations/ ～好各方面的工作 straighten things out in every field of work/ 我们的足球队要好好～一下。Our football team needs a good shake-up.

【整风】 zhěngfēng rectification of incorrect styles of work: ～就是全党通过批评和自我批评来学习马克思主义。Rectification means the whole Party studying Marxism through criticism and self-criticism. ◇ ～运动 rectification movement

【整个】 zhěnggè whole; entire: ～上午 the whole morning/ ～会场响起热烈的掌声。The whole hall resounded with applause./ ～国民经济 the whole national economy/ ～社会 the whole of society/ ～国际形势 the entire international situation/ ～革命事业 the entire revolutionary cause/ 在～社会主义阶段 throughout the stage of socialism/ 他把这件事～儿给忘了。He clean forgot about that./ ～说来 (taken) as a whole; on the whole; by and large

【整合】 zhěnghé 〈地〉 conformity

【整洁】 zhěngjié clean and tidy; neat; trim: 房间收拾得很～。The room is kept clean and tidy (或 spick-and-span)./ 衣着～ neatly dressed

【整经】 zhěngjīng 〈纺〉 warping: 分段～ sectional warping ◇ ～机 warping machine

【整理】 zhěnglǐ put in order; straighten out; arrange; sort out: ～房间 put a room in order; tidy a room/ ～桌上的东西 straighten out the things on the table/ ～书架上的书 rearrange the books on the shelves/ ～资料 sort out the data/ ～中国医药学 systematize Chinese medicine and pharmacology/ 搜集～民歌 collect and collate folk songs/ ～财政 regulate finances/ ～行装 pack one's things for a journey/ ～文化遗产 sift our cultural heritage/ ～化石 dress fossils

【整料】 zhěngliào material all in one piece for a given job

【整流】 zhěngliú 〈电〉 rectification ◇ ～管 rectifier tube/ ～子 commutator

【整流器】 zhěngliúqì 〈电〉 rectifier: 硅～ silicon rectifier/ 硅可控～ silicon-controlled rectifier; thyristor

【整齐】 zhěngqí ① in good order; neat; tidy: 保持队伍～ keep the ranks in good order/ 字写得清楚～ clear and neat handwriting/ 服装～ neatly dressed/ ～划一 uniform/ 被子叠得整整齐齐的。The quilts were rolled up tidily. ② even; regular: 出苗～ an even emergence of seedlings/ ～的牙齿 regular teeth/ 一排排～的工人住宅 well-laid-out blocks of workers' quarters/ 迈着～的步伐 march in step/ 这个篮球队阵容～。This basketball team has a well-balanced lineup.

【整容】 zhěngróng ① tidy oneself up (i.e. have a haircut, a shave, etc.) ② face-lifting

【整数】 zhěngshù ①〈数〉 integer; whole number ② round number (或 figure)

【整套】 zhěngtào a complete (或 whole) set of: ～设备 a complete set of equipment/ 这就是他们的一～观点。This is the sum total of their views./ 对这个问题他有一～看法。He has a lot of views of his own on this matter.

【整体】 zhěngtǐ whole; entirety: 从～上看形势 view the situation as a whole/ ～的一个组成部分 an integral part of the whole/ 为了～的利益牺牲局部的利益 give up individual or local interests for the sake of the whole/ 以党和人民的～利益为出发点 starting out from the overall interests of the Party and the people ◇ ～吊装〈建〉 integral hoisting

【整体观念】 zhěngtǐ guānniàn ① the concept of viewing the situation as a whole ②〈中医〉 an organic conception of the human body, viewing its various parts as forming an organic whole

【整天】 zhěngtiān the whole day; all day; all day long: 干了三～ work for three whole days/ 他拆洗被褥忙了一～。He's been busy all day (或 the whole day) unstitching and washing his bedding.

【整形】 zhěngxíng 〈医〉 plastic ◇ ～手术 plastic operation/ ～外科 plastic surgery; plastics

【整修】 zhěngxiū rebuild; renovate; recondition: ～水利工程 rebuild water conservancy projects/ ～梯田 reinforce terraced fields/ ～房子 renovate a house

【整训】 zhěngxùn train and consolidate (troops)

【整整】 zhěngzhěng whole; full: ～半小时 a whole half hour/ ～两天 two whole days/ ～一小时 a full (或 good) hour/ ～六公里 a good six kilometres/ ～五十年 fully fifty years/ ～一个月 a solid month/ ～三百万元 a good three million *yuan*

【整枝】 zhěngzhī 〈农〉 training; pruning: 棉花～ pruning of cotton plants/ 葡萄～ training of vines

【整治】 zhěngzhì ① renovate; repair; dredge (a river, etc.): ～房屋 renovate a house/ ～机器 repair a machine/ ～航道 dredge waterways/ ～河道 the realignment of a river ② punish; fix: 这坏蛋得～一下。That scoundrel needs to be punished. ③ do; work at: ～饭菜 prepare food/ ～庄稼 field management

【整装】 zhěngzhuāng get one's things ready (for a journey, etc.): ～待发 ready and waiting/ ～待命 be ready for orders

## zhèng

**正** zhèng ① straight; upright: 这画挂得不～。This picture is not straight./ 把柱子扶～ set the post upright/ ～北(南、西、东) due north (south, west, east) ② situated in the middle; main: ～门 main entrance/ ～厅 main hall ③ (of time) punctually; sharp: 九点～ at nine o'clock sharp ④ obverse; right: 布的～面 the right side of the cloth ⑤ honest; upright: 方～ upright; righteous ⑥ correct; right: ～路 the correct path; the right way/ ～论 a correct and sensible view ⑦ (of colour or flavour) pure; right: ～黄 pure yellow/ 味儿不～ not the right flavour ⑧ principal; chief: ～副班长 squad leader and deputy squad leader/ ～驾驶员 first pilot/ ～税和附加税 regular tax and surtax ⑨ (of figures, designs, etc.) regular: ～八边形 regular octagon/ ～多面体 regular polyhedron ⑩ 〈物〉 positive; plus: ～晶体 positive crystal/ ～离子 positive ion; cation ⑪ 〈数〉 positive: ～号 positive sign; plus sign ⑫ rectify; correct; set right: ～一～帽子 put one's cap straight/ ～音 correct one's pronunciation ⑬ just; right; precisely; exactly: ～如你所说的 just as you say/ 大小～合适 just the right size/ ～中奸计 fall right into the villain's trap/ ～因为如此 precisely because of this/ 我～要谈这个问题。I'm just coming to that point./ 这～是我们需要的东西。This is exactly what we need. 或 This is just the thing we need./ 那人～是张同志。It was none other than Comrade Zhang./ ～是这些人创造了这样伟大的奇迹。They are the very people who worked such wonders. ⑭〔表示动作的进行、状态的持续〕: ～下着雨呢。It's raining./ 时钟～打十二点。The clock was striking twelve.

另见 zhēng

【正本】 zhèngběn ① original (of a document): 将～送存档案库 deposit the original in the archives ② reserved copy (of a library book)

【正本清源】 zhèngběn-qīngyuán radically reform; thoroughly overhaul: 采取～的措施 take measures for thoroughgoing reform

【正比】 zhèngbǐ 〈数〉 direct ratio

【正比例】 zhèngbǐlì 〈数〉 direct proportion

【正步】 zhèngbù 〈军〉 parade step; goose step: ～走!(口令) Parade step, march!

【正册】 zhèngcè regular register (used in the Qing Dynasty for listing honest people)

【正长石】 zhèngchángshí orthoclase

【正长岩】 zhèngchángyán syenite

【正常】 zhèngcháng normal; regular: 在～情况下 under normal conditions/ 发动机运转～。The engine is functioning normally./ 恢复～ return to normal/ ～的党内民主生活 normal practice of democracy in the Party/ 脉搏～ have a normal pulse/ 两国关系～化 normalization of the relations between the two countries

【正大】 zhèngdà upright; honest; aboveboard: ～光明 open and aboveboard; just and honourable

【正当】 zhèngdāng just when; just the time for: ～春耕之时 just the time for spring ploughing/ ～人手少的时候，他们来了。They came to help just when we were short of hands.

【正当年】 zhèngdāngnián in the prime of life; in one's prime

【正当时】 zhèngdāngshí the right season or time: 秋分种麦～。The Autumnal Equinox is the right time for sowing wheat.

【正当中】 zhèngdāngzhōng right in the middle (或 centre)

【正当】 zhèngdàng proper; appropriate; legitimate: 通过～途径 in proper ways; by appropriate means; through proper channels/ 他们的要求是完全～的。Their demand is entirely justified./ 国家保护华侨和侨眷的～的权利和利益。The state protects the just rights and interests of overseas Chinese and their relatives.

【正道】 zhèngdào the right way (或 course); the correct path: 走～ follow the correct path/ 这才是～。That's the correct thing to do.

【正点】 zhèngdiǎn (of ships, trains, etc.) on schedule; on time; punctually: ～运行 running on schedule/ 火车～到达。The train arrived on time (或 punctually).

【正电】 zhèngdiàn positive electricity

【正电荷】 zhèngdiànhè positive charge

【正电子】 zhèngdiànzǐ positive electron; positron

【正殿】 zhèngdiàn main hall (in a palace or temple)

【正定霉素】 zhèngdìngméisù 〈药〉 daunomycin

【正多边形】 zhèngduōbiānxíng 〈数〉 regular polygon 又作"正多角形"

【正法】 zhèngfǎ execute (a criminal): 就地～ execute (a criminal) on the spot

【正反】 zhèng-fǎn positive and negative: 总结～两方面的经验 sum up both positive and negative experience/ ～两方面的看法 the pros and cons

【正方】 zhèngfāng square: ～盒子 a square box ◇ ～形 square

【正房】 zhèngfáng ① principal rooms (in a courtyard, usu. facing south) ② legal wife (as contrasted with concubine)

【正告】 zhènggào earnestly admonish; warn sternly

【正割】 zhènggē 〈数〉 secant

【正骨】 zhènggǔ 〈中医〉 bonesetting

【正规】 zhèngguī regular; standard

◇ ～部队 regular troops; regulars/ ～化 regularize; standardize; be put on a regular basis/ ～军 regular army/ ～学校 regular school/ ～战争 regular warfare

【正轨】 zhèngguǐ the right (或 correct) path: 纳入～ lead onto the correct path; put on the right track

【正好】 zhènghǎo ① just in time; just right; just enough: 你来得～。You've come just in time./ 这双鞋我穿～。This pair of shoes fits me nicely./ 这笔钱～买台抽水机。This is just enough money for a pump./ 这～证明我们的作法是对的。That only goes to prove that our approach is correct. ② happen to; chance to; as it happens: 小王～从那儿路过。Xiao Wang happened (或 chanced) to be passing by./ 我身边～有五块钱。As it happens, I have five *yuan* with me.

【正号】 zhènghào positive sign; plus sign

【正火】 zhènghuǒ 〈冶〉 normalizing

【正极】 zhèngjí 〈电〉 positive electrode; positive pole; anode ◇ ～板 〈电〉 positive plate

【正教】 Zhèngjiào the Orthodox Church

【正襟危坐】 zhèngjīn-wēizuò 〈书〉 straighten one's clothes and sit properly; be all seriousness

【正经八百】 zhèngjīng-bābǎi 〈方〉 serious; earnest: 这是～的事。This is a serious matter. 或 This is no joke.

【正经】 zhèngjing ① decent; respectable; honest: ～人 a decent person ② serious: 钱必须用在～地方。Money must be put to right uses./ ～事儿 serious affairs/ 谈～事 talk business ③ standard: ～货 standard goods ④〈方〉 really; truly; indeed: 这黄瓜长得还～不错呢! The cucumbers are really doing fine.

【正楷】 zhèngkǎi (in Chinese calligraphy) regular script 又作"正书"

【正理】 zhènglǐ correct principle; valid reason (或 argument); the right thing to do

【正梁】 zhèngliáng 〈建〉 ridge purlin

【正六面体】 zhèngliùmiàntǐ 〈数〉 regular hexahedron

【正路】 zhènglù 见"正道"

【正门】 zhèngmén front door (或 gate); main entrance

【正面】 zhèngmiàn ① front; frontage; facade: 房屋的～ the front (或 facade) of a house/ ～进攻 frontal attack/ ～冲突 head-on confrontation (或 clash) ② the obverse side; the right side: 牛皮纸的～ the right side of kraft paper/ 硬币的～ the obverse side of a coin/ 皮革的～ the grain side of leather/ ～和反面 the obverse and the reverse sides of a thing; both sides ③ positive: ～教育 educate by positive measures or examples; positive education/ ～阐明自己的观点 state one's views in a positive way/ ～和反面的历史经验 positive and negative historical lessons ④ directly; openly: 有问题请～提出来。Please ask your question directly. ◇ ～人物 positive character/ ～图 front view

【正派】 zhèngpài upright; honest; decent: ～人 a decent person/ 作风～ honest and upright in one's ways

【正片】 zhèngpiàn ①〈摄〉positive ②〈电影〉copy ③〈电影〉feature (film)

【正品】 zhèngpǐn certified products (或 goods); quality products (或 goods)

【正气】 zhèngqì ① healthy atmosphere (或 tendency): 发扬～ encourage healthy trends; encourage standing up for what is right/ ～上升。A healthy atmosphere prevails. ②〈中医〉vital energy

【正巧】 zhèngqiǎo ① happen to; chance to; as it happens: 他们～带有仪器。They happened (或 chanced) to have their instruments with them./ ～两位民兵到那儿巡逻,及时发现了火情。As it happened, two militiamen were there on patrol and spotted the fire as soon as it started. ② just in time; in the nick of time; just at the right time: 你来得～,我们马上就要出发了。You've come just in time. We're leaving immediately.

【正切】 zhèngqiē 〈数〉tangent

【正确】 zhèngquè correct; right; proper: ～的立场 a correct stand/ 你这样做是～的。What you are doing is right./ ～处理国家、集体、个人三者之间的关系 maintain a proper balance in the relationship between the state, the collective and the individual/ ～对待自己,～对待群众 adopt a correct attitude towards oneself and the masses/ ～估计客观形势 accurately appraise the objective situation/ ～的批评 well-founded criticism ◇ ～性 correctness; soundness; validity

【正人君子】 zhèngrén-jūnzǐ 〈旧〉a man of honour; gentleman: 打扮成～ masquerade as a gentleman

【正色】 zhèngsè ①〈书〉pure colours ② adopt a stern countenance: ～拒绝 refuse sternly

【正史】 zhèngshǐ history books written in biographical style 参见"纪传体" jìzhuàntǐ

【正式】 zhèngshì formal; official; regular: ～列入记录 be officially placed on record/ 代表团的～成员 a regular (或 full) member of the delegation/ 大会于八月二十四日～开幕。The conference formally opened on August 24. ◇ ～党员 full member of the Party; full Party member/ ～访问 official (或 formal) visit/ ～会谈 formal talks/ ～记录 official records/ ～声明 official statement/ ～文本 official text

【正视】 zhèngshì face squarely; face up to; look squarely at: ～困难 face difficulties squarely; face up to difficulties/ ～现实 look reality in the face/ ～缺点 acknowledge one's shortcomings/ 不～事实 shut one's eyes to facts ◇ ～图〈机〉front view; elevation

【正事】 zhèngshì one's proper business: 现在咱们谈～。Now let's talk business.

【正手】 zhèngshǒu 〈体〉forehand: ～抽球 forehand drive

【正数】 zhèngshù 〈数〉positive number

【正态分布】 zhèngtài fēnbù 〈统计〉normal distribution

【正题】 zhèngtí ① subject (或 topic) of a talk or essay: 转入～ come to the subject/ 离开～ wander (或 digress) from the subject/ 不离～ stick to one's text ②〈哲〉thesis

【正体】 zhèngtǐ ① standardized form of Chinese characters ② 见"正楷" ③ block letter

【正厅】 zhèngtīng ① main hall (in the middle) ② stalls (in a theatre)

【正统】 zhèngtǒng ① legitimism ② orthodox: ～观念 orthodox ideas ◇ ～派 orthodox party or school

【正文】 zhèngwén main body (of a book, etc.); text: 书的～ the text of a book/ 词典～ the main body of a dictionary; the dictionary proper

【正午】 zhèngwǔ high noon

【正误】 zhèngwù correct (typographical) errors ◇ ～表 errata; corrigenda

【正弦】 zhèngxián 〈数〉sine ◇ ～波〈电〉sine wave

【正凶】 zhèngxiōng 〈法〉principal murderer

【正盐】 zhèngyán 〈化〉normal salt

【正颜厉色】 zhèngyán-lìsè look serious and severe; put on a stern countenance

【正业】 zhèngyè regular occupation; proper duties: 不务～ not attend to one's proper duties; not engage in honest work

【正义】 zhèngyì ① justice: 主持～ uphold justice/ 为～而战 fight for justice/ ～之师 an army dedicated to a just cause ② just; righteous: ～立场 a just stand/ ～的事业 a just cause/ 一切进步的战争都是～的,一切阻碍进步的战争都是非～的。All wars that are progressive are just, and all wars that impede progress are unjust. ◇ ～感 sense of justice (或 righteousness); sense of what is right

【正音】 zhèngyīn ① correct one's pronunciation ② standard pronunciation ◇ ～法〈语〉orthoepy

【正在】 zhèngzài 〈副〉〔表示动作在进行中〕in process of; in course of: 他们～聊天。They're having a chat./ 许多问题～讨论。Many questions are under discussion./ ～修建一条新铁路。A new railway is under construction./ ～进行磋商。Consultations are under way.

【正直】 zhèngzhí honest; upright; fair-minded: ～的人 an honest person; a person of integrity

【正治】 zhèngzhì 〈中医〉normal treatment, i.e. administering medicines of a cold nature to treat a febrile disease

【正中】 zhèngzhōng middle; centre: 把茶具放在桌子～。Put the tea-things right in the middle (或 centre) of the table.

【正中下怀】 zhèng zhòng xiàhuái be just what one hopes for; fit in exactly with one's wishes

【正字】 zhèngzì ① correct a wrongly written character or a misspelt word ② 见"正楷" ③ 见"正体"① ◇ ～法〈语〉orthography

【正宗】 zhèngzōng orthodox school

**证** zhèng ① prove; demonstrate: 求～ seek to prove/ ～几何定理 demonstrate (或 prove) a geometric theorem ② evidence; proof; testimony: 作～ give evidence; bear testimony/ 确～ proof positive; conclusive evidence/ 物～ material evidence ③ certificate; card: 出生～ birth certificate/ 工作～ employee's I.D. card/ 许可～ permit ④ disease; illness

【证词】 zhèngcí testimony

【证婚人】 zhènghūnrén chief witness at a wedding ceremony

【证件】 zhèngjiàn credentials; papers; certificate: 请出示～。Please show your credentials (或 papers).

【证据】 zhèngjù evidence; proof; testimony: 搜集～ collect evidence/ 提出～ offer testimony/ ～确凿的叛徒 a proven renegade/ 直接～〈法〉direct evidence

【证明】 zhèngmíng ① prove; testify; bear out: 充分～ fully prove/ 雄辩地～ give (或 be) eloquent proof of/ 无数事实已～了这一点。Countless facts have proved this point./ 这个英明论断早已为中国革命的胜利所～。This brilliant thesis has long since been borne out by the victory of the Chinese revolution. ② certificate; identification; testimonial: 医生～ medical certificate ◇ ～文件 certificate; testimonial; papers

【证明书】 zhèngmíngshū certificate; testimonial: 质量～ certificate of quality/ 产地～ certificate of origin/ 健康～ health certificate

【证券】 zhèngquàn negotiable securities ◇ ～交易所 stock exchange

【证人】 zhèngren witness ◇ ～席 witness-box; witness stand

【证实】 zhèngshí confirm; verify: 有待～ remain to be confirmed/ ～一个科学上的假设 verify a scientific hypothesis

【证书】 zhèngshū certificate; credentials: 结婚～ marriage certificate; marriage lines/ 毕业～ diploma ◇ ～审查委员会 credentials committee

【证物】 zhèngwù 〈法〉 exhibit (produced in court as evidence)

【证验】 zhèngyàn ① verify ② real results; efficacy

【证章】 zhèngzhāng badge

**诤** zhèng 〈书〉 criticize sb.'s faults frankly; admonish; expostulate

【诤言】 zhèngyán 〈书〉 forthright admonition

【诤友】 zhèngyǒu 〈书〉 a friend who will give forthright admonition

**郑** Zhèng a surname

【郑重】 zhèngzhòng serious; solemn; earnest: 态度～ be serious in one's attitude/ ～表示 earnestly declare; solemnly state/ ～声明 solemnly declare/ ～其事 seriously; in earnest

【郑州】 Zhèngzhōu Zhengzhou

**政** zhèng ① politics; political affairs: 议～ discuss political affairs ② certain administrative aspects of government: 民～ civil administration/ 邮～ postal service/ 财～ (public) finance ③〈旧〉 affairs of a family or an organization: 家～ household management/ 校～ school administration

【政变】 zhèngbiàn coup d'état; coup: 发动～ stage a coup d'état/ 粉碎反革命～阴谋 smash a counterrevolutionary coup plot

【政策】 zhèngcè policy: ～教育 education in policy/ 提高～水平 enhance the understanding of policy/ 划清～界限 draw clear lines of demarcation in applying a policy

【政党】 zhèngdǎng political party

【政敌】 zhèngdí political opponent

【政法】 zhèngfǎ politics and law ◇ ～学院 institute of political science and law

【政府】 zhèngfǔ government
◇ ～部门 government departments/ ～机构 government apparatus/ ～机关 government bodies (或 organizations)/ ～人士 government circles/ ～首脑 head of government

【政纲】 zhènggāng political programme; platform

【政工组】 zhènggōngzǔ political work section (或 office)

【政绩】 zhèngjī achievements in one's official career

【政见】 zhèngjiàn political view

【政教分离】 zhèng-jiào fēnlí separation of religion from politics; separation of the church from the state

【政界】 zhèngjiè political circles; government circles: 退出～ withdraw from political life

【政局】 zhèngjú political situation; political scene

【政客】 zhèngkè politician

【政令】 zhènglìng government decree (或 order)

【政论】 zhènglùn political comment ◇ ～家 political commentator; political writer/ ～文 political essay

【政权】 zhèngquán political (或 state) power; regime: 夺取～和巩固～ seize and consolidate political power/ 国家～ state power/ 革命～ a revolutionary regime/ 革命的根本问题是～问题。 The fundamental question of revolution is political power. ◇ ～机关 organs of state (或 political) power

【政社合一】 zhèng-shè héyī integrate (或 merge) government administration with commune management: 农村人民公社是～的组织。The rural people's commune is an organization which integrates government administration and economic management.

【政事】 zhèngshì government affairs

【政体】 zhèngtǐ system (或 form) of government

【政委】 zhèngwěi 〈简〉(政治委员) political commissar (of a PLA regiment and above); commissar

【政务】 zhèngwù government affairs; government administration ◇ ～院 the Government Administration Council (of the Central People's Government of the People's Republic of China, replaced in 1954 by the State Council)

【政协】 zhèngxié 〈简〉(中国人民政治协商会议) the Chinese People's Political Consultative Conference (C.P.P.C.C.): ～是中国共产党领导下的革命统一战线组织。The C.P.P.C.C. is a revolutionary united front organization led by the Communist Party of China.

【政治】 zhèngzhì politics; political affairs: ～挂帅 put politics in command/ ～历史清白(清楚) have a clean (clear) political record/ ～上可靠 politically reliable
◇ ～避难 (political) asylum/ ～表现 political behaviour or record/ ～部 political department/ ～待遇 political treatment/ ～犯 political offender; political prisoner/ ～纲领 political programme; platform/ ～基础 political basis/ ～家 statesman/ ～教导员 political instructor (of a PLA battalion)/ ～经济学 political economy/ ～觉悟 political consciousness (或 awareness, understanding)/ ～空气 political atmosphere/ ～立场 political stand/ ～路线 political line/ ～面目 political affiliation or background/ ～派别 political grouping or faction/ ～骗子 political swindler/ ～权利 political rights/ ～生命 political life/ ～态度 political attitude/ ～委员 political commissar (of a PLA regiment and above); commissar/ ～舞台 political arena (或 stage, scene)/ ～信仰 political conviction (或 belief)/ ～性 political nature/ ～嗅觉 political sense of smell; political acumen (或 sensitiveness)/ ～学 political science; government/ ～指导员 political instructor (of a PLA company)

【政治局】 zhèngzhìjú the Political Bureau ◇ ～常务委员 member of the Standing Committee of the Political Bureau/ ～委员 member of the Political Bureau

【政治协商会议】 zhèngzhì xiéshāng huìyì 见"政协"

**挣** zhèng ① struggle to get free; try to throw off: ～脱枷锁 throw off the shackles ② earn; make: ～饭吃 earn a living/ 一个月～七十块钱 earn (或 make) seventy *yuan* a month
另见 zhēng

【挣揣】 zhèngchuài 〈书〉 struggle; strive hard

【挣命】 zhèngmìng struggle to save one's life

【挣钱】 zhèngqián earn (或 make) money: ～养家 earn money to support one's family

**帧** zhèng 〈量〉〔用于字画〕: 一～油画 an oil painting

【帧频】 zhèngpín 〈电视〉 frame frequency; picture frequency

**阐** zhèng struggle; contend

**症** zhèng disease; illness: 不治之～ incurable disease/ 急～ acute disease
另见 zhēng
【症候】 zhènghou ① disease ② symptom
【症状】 zhèngzhuàng symptom: 前驱～ premonitory (或 signal) symptoms/ 早期～ early (或 incipient) symptoms

## zhī

**之** zhī 〈书〉①〔代替人或事物，限于做宾语〕: 取而代～ replace (或 supersede) someone/ 偶一为～ do something once in a while/ 将如～何？ What is to be done? ②〔虚用，无所指〕: 总～ to sum up; in short; in a word/ 久而久～ with the lapse of time; as time passes/ 手之舞～，足之蹈～ dance with joy ③ this: ～子于归。The maiden goes to her future home. ④〈助〉〔用在定语和中心词之间，表示领属关系或一般的修饰关系〕: 钟鼓～声 the sound of drums and bells/ 原因～一 one of the reasons/ 无价～宝 a priceless treasure/ 一水～隔 be separated only by a river/ 以我～长，攻敌～短 utilize our strong points to attack the enemy at his weak points ⑤〈助〉〔用在主谓结构之间，取消它的独立性，使变成偏正结构〕: 皮～不存，毛将焉附？ With the skin gone, to what can the hair attach itself?/ 如因势利导，则如水～就下，极为自然。 If we guide the matter along its course of development, it will proceed as naturally as water flows downwards. ⑥ go; leave: 由京～渝 leave Beijing for Chongqing/ 君将何～？ Where are you bound for?
【之后】 zhīhòu later; after; afterwards: 三天～ three days later/ 这次大会～ following this conference/ 从那～她没来过。She hasn't been here since then./ ～他又给我写了两封信。Afterwards he wrote to me twice.
【之乎者也】 zhī-hū-zhě-yě pedantic terms; literary jargon; archaisms: 老学究满口～，教人半懂不懂。The old pedant used so many archaisms that half of what he said was unintelligible.
【之前】 zhīqián before; prior to; ago: 在她动身～ prior to her departure/ 这药在睡觉～吃。Take the medicine before bedtime./ 两星期～他还在这儿。He was here until two weeks ago.
【之字路】 zhīzìlù zigzag course; S curve in a road

**支** zhī ① prop up; put up: ～帐篷 put up a tent/ 用两张凳子把木板～起来 prop up the board with two stools/ 两手～着头 rest one's head in both hands ② protrude; raise: ～着耳朵听 prick up one's ears ③ support; sustain; bear: ～前 support the front/ 乐不可～ overwhelmed with joy; overjoyed/ 孩子疼得～不住了。The child couldn't bear the pain. ④ send away; put sb. off: 把他们～开 put them off with excuses; send them away upon some pretext/ 这事甭～别人了，你自个儿去吧。Don't send anyone else; better go yourself. ⑤ pay or draw (money): ～拨 pay a sum of money or transfer a sum of money in payment/ 上银行～款 go to the bank to draw money/ 收～ income and expenses; revenue and expenditure/ 预～一百块钱 get an advance of 100 *yuan* ⑥ branch; offshoot: ～店 branch store/ 邮政～局 branch post office/ 党总～ general Party branch ⑦〈量〉〔用于队伍、歌曲、电灯光度等〕: 三～队伍 three contingents of troops/ 一～新歌 a new song/ 一～钢笔 a pen/ 一个六十～光的灯泡 a 60-watt bulb ⑧〈纺〉 count: 六十～纱 60-count yarn/ 细(中)～棉纱 fine (medium) count yarn ⑨ the twelve Earthly Branches ⑩ (Zhī) a surname
【支部】 zhībù branch (esp. of the Chinese Communist Party or the Chinese Communist Youth League): 党(团)～ Party (League) branch
◇ ～大会 general membership meeting of the branch/ ～书记 branch secretary/ ～委员 member of the branch committee
【支承】 zhīchéng 〈机〉 supporting; bearing
◇ ～点 bearing point/ ～力 supporting force/ ～圈 backup ring; support ring
【支撑】 zhīcheng ① prop up; sustain; support: 坑道顶儿用柱子～着。The pillars sustain the roof of the pit./ 病人～着坐了起来。The patient propped himself up into a sitting position. ②〈建〉 strut; brace ◇ ～点〈军〉 strong point; centre of resistance
【支持】 zhīchí ① sustain; hold out; bear: 他冻得～不住了。He was so cold he couldn't hold out any longer. ② support; back; stand by: 在国际上得到越来越广泛的～ enjoy wider and wider international support/ ～被压迫人民的斗争 support the struggle of the oppressed peoples/ 给予坚决的～ give strong backing to/ 全世界各国人民的正义斗争，都是互相～的。The just struggles of the people of all countries support each other./ 我完全～这个建议。I am all for this proposal.
【支出】 zhīchū ① pay (money); expend; disburse ② expenses; expenditure; outlay; disbursement: 追加～ supplementary expenditure/ 国防～ expenditure on national defence/ 收入与～相抵。The income balances the expenditure.
【支绌】 zhīchù (of funds) not enough; insufficient: 由于经费～ due to insufficient funds
【支点】 zhīdiǎn 〈物〉 fulcrum
【支队】 zhīduì detachment: 游击～ a guerrilla detachment
【支墩坝】 zhīdūnbà 〈水〉 buttress dam
【支付】 zhīfù pay (money); defray: ～水电费 pay for electricity and water/ 立即～ immediate payment ◇ ～手段 means of payment/ ～协定 payments agreement
【支工】 zhīgōng support industry
【支行】 zhīháng subbranch (of a bank)
【支架】 zhījià support; stand; trestle: 自行车～ prop stand of a bicycle
【支解】 zhījiě dismemberment
【支离】 zhīlí ① fragmented; broken; disorganized ② (of writing) trivial and jumbled; incoherent
【支离破碎】 zhīlí-pòsuì torn to pieces; broken up; fragmented
【支流】 zhīliú ① tributary; affluent: 珠江的一条～ a tributary of the Zhujiang River ② minor aspects; nonessentials: 看问题时，不要把～当作主流。In considering a problem, one mustn't mistake the nonessentials for the essentials.
【支脉】 zhīmài offshoot (of a mountain range); branch range: 天山的～ a branch range of the Tianshan Mountains/ 伏牛山是秦岭的～。The Funiu Mountains are an offshoot of the Qinling Mountain Range.
【支农】 zhīnóng support agriculture; supply the needs of agriculture
◇ ～产品 goods produced to support agriculture; products serving the needs of agriculture/ ～大军 aid-agriculture contingent/ ～工业 aid-agriculture industries
【支派】 zhīpài branch; sect; offshoot
【支派】 zhīpai order; send; dispatch
【支配】 zhīpèi ① arrange; allocate; budget: 合理～劳动力 make a proper allocation of the labour force/ 善于～自己的时间 be good at budgeting one's time ② control; dominate; govern: 受人～ be controlled by others/ 受自

然规律的～ be subject to the laws of nature/ 思想～行动。People's actions are governed by their ideology.

【支票】 zhīpiào cheque; check: 开～ write a cheque/ 划线～ crossed cheque/ 空白～ blank cheque/ 空头～ rubber cheque/ 来人～ bearer cheque/ 保付～ certified cheque/ 旅行～ traveller's cheque ◇ ～簿 chequebook/ ～票根 stub of a cheque; counterfoil

【支气管】 zhīqìguǎn bronchus ◇ ～扩张 bronchiectasis/ ～性气喘 bronchial asthma/ ～炎 bronchitis

【支渠】 zhīqú branch (irrigation) canal

【支取】 zhīqǔ draw (money): ～存款 draw one's deposit (from a bank)

【支使】 zhīshi ① order about: 不听老板的～ refuse to be ordered about by the boss ② send away; put sb. off

【支书】 zhīshū secretary of a Party or League branch; branch secretary

【支枢】 zhīshū 〈机〉 pivot

【支数】 zhīshù 〈纺〉 number (of yarn); count: 纱线～ yarn number; yarn size

【支吾】 zhīwu prevaricate; equivocate; hum and haw: ～其词 speak evasively; hum and haw

【支线】 zhīxiàn branch line; feeder (line): 铁路～ feeder railway/ 公路～ feeder highway

【支应】 zhīyìng ① cope with; deal with ② prevaricate; equivocate ③ wait on; attend to: ～门户 attend to the door

【支援】 zhīyuán support; assist; help: 各行各业都要大力～农业。All trades and professions must do their best to support agriculture./ 大家踊跃储蓄，～社会主义建设。Let's all deposit our savings in the bank to help socialist construction. ◇ ～部队 support unit; supporting troops

【支柱】 zhīzhù pillar; prop; mainstay: 矿用～ pit prop/ 无产阶级专政的～ pillar (或 mainstay) of the dictatorship of the proletariat

【支柱根】 zhīzhùgēn 〈植〉 prop root

【支子】 zhīzi ① stand; support: 自行车～ kickstand of a bicycle/ 火～ trivet ② gridiron (as a cooking utensil)

【支左】 zhīzuǒ help the Left; support the broad masses of the Left

**汁** zhī juice: 橘子～ orange juice/ 牛肉～ beef extract/ 乳～ milk/ 椰子～ coconut milk/ 墨～ prepared Chinese ink

【汁水】 zhīshui 〈方〉 juice: 这种果子～很多。This fruit is juicy.

【汁液】 zhīyè juice

**只** zhī ① single; one only: ～字不提 not say a single word (about sth.) ②〈量〉: 两～手 two hands/ 一～鸡 a chicken/ 三～箱子 three suitcases/ 一～小船 a boat 另见 zhǐ

【只身】 zhīshēn alone; by oneself: ～独往 go there alone/ ～在外 be away from home all by oneself

【只言片语】 zhīyán-piànyǔ a word or two; a few isolated words and phrases: 只听见～ catch (或 overhear) only a word or two/ 未留下～ leave behind not even a single word

**卮** zhī ancient wine vessel

**芝** zhī

【芝加哥】 Zhījiāgē Chicago

【芝兰】 zhīlán irises and orchids (symbolic of noble character, true friendship, or beautiful surroundings): 如入～之室 like going into a room full of fragrant orchids — benefit from associating with people of a noble character

【芝麻】 zhīma ① sesame: ～开花节节高。A sesame stalk puts forth blossoms notch by notch, higher and higher. ② sesame seed: 拣了～,丢了西瓜 pick up the sesame seeds but overlook the watermelons — concentrate on minor matters to the neglect of major ones ◇ ～酱 sesame paste/ ～油 sesame-seed oil; sesame oil

**吱** zhī 〈象〉: 门～地一声开了。The door creaked open. 另见 zī

**枝** zhī ① branch; twig: 柳～ willow branches ②〈量〉: 一～步枪 a rifle/ 一～蜡烛 a candle/ 一～梅花 a spray of plum blossoms

【枝杈】 zhīchà branch; twig

【枝接】 zhījiē 〈农〉 scion grafting

【枝节】 zhījié ① branches and knots — minor matters: ～问题 a minor problem; a side issue/ 不要过多地注意那些枝枝节节。Don't pay too much attention to the minor issues. ② complication; unexpected difficulty: 横生～ raise unexpected difficulties; deliberately complicate an issue; create side issues

【枝解】 zhījiě dismemberment

【枝蔓】 zhīmàn branches and tendrils — complicated and confused: 文字～,不得要领。The writing is confused and the main points are not clear.

【枝条】 zhītiáo branch; twig

【枝桠】 zhīyā branch; twig 又作"枝丫"

【枝叶】 zhīyè ① branches and leaves: 那棵大樟树～茂盛。That big camphor tree is a mass of branches and leaves. ② nonessentials; minor details

【枝子】 zhīzi branch; twig

**知** zhī ① know; realize; be aware of: 强不～以为～ pretend to know what one doesn't know/ ～过必改 always correct an error when one becomes aware of it/ ～其然并力求～其所以然 know the how and endeavour to know the why ② inform; notify; tell: 通～ inform; notify ③ knowledge: 求～欲 thirst for knowledge/ 经过努力学习,可以由无～转化为有～,由～之不多转化为～之甚多。By assiduous study, ignorance can be transformed into knowledge and scanty knowledge into substantial knowledge. ④ administer; be in charge of: ～县 official administering a county; county magistrate

【知彼知己,百战不殆】 zhī bǐ zhī jǐ, bǎi zhàn bù dài know the enemy and know yourself, and you can fight a hundred battles with no danger of defeat

【知道】 zhīdao know; realize; be aware of: 我不～这事儿。I know nothing about it./ 你的意思我～。I know what you mean. 或 I see your point./ 他们～问题的严重性。They realize how serious the problem is./ 我们～在前进的路上还会有困难。We are aware that on our way forward there will still be difficulties.

【知底】 zhīdǐ know the inside story; be in the know

【知法犯法】 zhī fǎ fàn fǎ knowingly violate the law; deliberately break the law

【知更鸟】 zhīgēngniǎo robin; redbreast

【知己】 zhījǐ ① intimate; understanding: ～的朋友 bosom (或 intimate) friend/ 和他很～ be on intimate terms with him/ ～话 intimate words; heart-to-heart talk ② bosom (或 intimate) friend

【知交】 zhījiāo bosom (或 intimate) friend: 他和我父亲是～。He is an intimate friend of my father's.

【知觉】 zhījué ① consciousness: 失去～ lose consciousness;

pass out/ 恢复～ recover consciousness; come to ②〈心〉 perception ◇ ～常性 perceptual constancies

【知客】 zhīkè ①〈旧〉person in charge of reception at ceremonies ② monk in charge of monastery reception

【知了】 zhīliǎo 〈动〉cicada

【知名】 zhīmíng well-known; noted; celebrated; famous: ～人士 well-known (或 noted) personage; public figure; celebrity/ 海内～ be known throughout the country

【知母】 zhīmǔ 〈中药〉 rhizome of wind-weed (*Anemarrhena asphodeloides*)

【知难而进】 zhī nán ér jìn press forward in the face of difficulties; advance despite difficulties

【知难而退】 zhī nán ér tuì beat a retreat in the face of difficulties; shrink back from difficulties

【知其一,不知其二】 zhī qí yī, bù zhī qí èr know only one aspect of a thing; have only a one-sided view: 总之,事物都有两点而不是一点。说只有一点,叫～。In short, there are two aspects to everything, not just one. To say there is only one is to be aware of one aspect and be ignorant of the other.

【知情】 zhīqíng know the facts of a case or the details of an incident; be in the know: ～不报 conceal what one knows of a case ◇ ～人 person in the know; insider

【知情达理】 zhīqíng-dálǐ reasonable; sensible

【知趣】 zhīqù know how to behave in a delicate situation; be sensible; be tactful

【知人善任】 zhī rén shàn rèn (of a leader) know one's subordinates well enough to assign them jobs commensurate with their abilities

【知人之明】 zhī rén zhī míng ability to appreciate a person's character and capability; a keen insight into a person's character

【知人知面不知心】 zhī rén zhī miàn bù zhī xīn you may know a person's face but not his heart; one may know a person for a long time without understanding his true nature

【知识】 zhīshi ① knowledge: ～渊博 have a wide range of knowledge; be erudite; be learned/ 技术～ technical know-how/ 书本～ book learning/ 获得生产斗争～ acquire a knowledge of the struggle for production ② pertaining to learning or culture; intellectual ◇ ～界 intellectual circles; the intelligentsia

【知识分子】 zhīshifènzǐ intellectual; the intelligentsia: 党的～政策 the Party's policy towards intellectuals/ 劳动人民要知识化,～要劳动化。Working people should master intellectual work and intellectuals should integrate themselves with the working people.

【知识青年】 zhīshi qīngnián school leavers; school graduates

【知无不言,言无不尽】 zhī wú bù yán, yán wú bù jìn say all you know and say it without reserve

【知悉】 zhīxī know; learn; be informed of: 业已～ have already learned of the matter

【知晓】 zhīxiǎo know; be aware of; understand

【知心】 zhīxīn intimate; understanding: ～朋友 intimate (或 bosom) friend/ ～话 intimate words; heart-to-heart talk

【知行】 zhī-xíng 〈哲〉 knowing and doing ◇ ～统一观 the theory of the unity of knowing and doing

【知音】 zhīyīn a friend keenly appreciative of one's talents; bosom friend: 革命文艺～多,一人唱歌众人和。Everyone loves revolutionary art; when one starts singing all take part.

【知遇】 zhīyù have found a patron or superior appreciative of one's ability

【知照】 zhīzhào inform; notify; tell: 你去～他一声,说我已经回来了。Please go and tell him I've come back.

【知足】 zhīzú be content with one's lot

**肢** zhī limb: 四～ the four limbs (of the human body)

【肢解】 zhījiě dismemberment

【肢势】 zhīshì 〈牧〉 standing (或 erect) posture (of domestic animals)

【肢体】 zhītǐ ① limbs ② limbs and trunk

**织** zhī ① weave: 纺～ spinning and weaving/ ～席 weave (或 make) a mat ② knit: ～毛衣 knit a sweater

【织补】 zhībǔ darning; invisible mending

【织布】 zhībù weaving cotton cloth; weaving ◇ ～工 weaver

【织布鸟】 zhībùniǎo weaverbird

【织机】 zhījī loom: 多梭箱～ multiple box loom

【织锦】 zhījǐn ① brocade ② picture-weaving in silk: 风景～ landscape woven in silk ◇ ～厂 brocade mill

【织锦缎】 zhījǐnduàn tapestry satin

【织女】 zhīnǚ ① woman weaver ② (Zhīnǚ) the Girl Weaver in the legend "The Cowherd and the Girl Weaver" ③〈天〉 Vega (α Lyrae) ◇ ～星〈天〉 Vega (α Lyrae)

【织袜机】 zhīwàjī hosiery machine

【织物】 zhīwù fabric: 机织～ woven fabric ◇ ～经纬密度 thread count/ ～耐磨试验 wear testing

【织造】 zhīzào weaving ◇ ～厂 weaving mill

【织针】 zhīzhēn knitting needle

【织轴】 zhīzhóu 〈纺〉 beam (of a loom)

**指** zhī

另见 zhí; zhǐ

【指甲】 zhījia nail: 手～ fingernail/ 脚～ toenail ◇ ～刀 nail clippers/ ～油 nail polish

【指甲花】 zhījiahuā garden balsam

**祗** zhī 〈书〉 venerate; respect

**胝** zhī 见"胼胝" piánzhī

**栀** zhī

【栀子】 zhīzi 〈植〉 Cape jasmine

**脂** zhī ① fat; grease; tallow: 油～ fat; grease/ 含～羊毛 wool in the grease ② rouge: 胭～ rouge

【脂肪】 zhīfáng fat: 动物～ animal fat /植物～ vegetable fat ◇ ～肝〈医〉 fatty liver/ ～酶〈生化〉 lipase/ ～酸 fatty acid/ ～组织〈生理〉 adipose tissue

【脂粉】 zhīfěn rouge and powder; cosmetics

【脂膏】 zhīgāo ① fat; grease ② fruits of the people's labour; wealth of the people

【脂瘤】 zhīliú 〈医〉 lipoma

【脂麻】 zhīma ① sesame ② sesame seed

【脂眼鲱】 zhīyǎnfēi Pacific round herring

【脂油】 zhīyóu 〈方〉 leaf fat

**掷** zhī throw; cast: ～色子 throw dice; play dice

另见 zhì

**蜘** zhī

【蜘蛛】 zhīzhū spider: 海～ sea spider ◇ ～丝 the thread of a spider web; cobweb/ ～网 spider (或 spider's) web; cobweb

【蜘蛛抱蛋】 zhīzhūbàodàn 〈植〉 (common) aspidistra (*Aspidistra elatior*)

## zhí

**执** zhí ① hold; grasp: 手～红旗 hold (或 carry) a red banner ② take charge of; direct; manage: ～教 be a teacher; teach/ ～炊 cook; prepare meals ③ stick to (one's views, etc.); persist: 各～己见。Each sticks to his own view. ④ carry out; observe: ～礼甚恭 punctiliously observe etiquette; treat sb. with great respect ⑤ catch; capture: 战败被～ be captured after being defeated in battle ⑥ written acknowledgement: 回～ receipt

【执笔】 zhíbǐ write; do the actual writing: 这张大字报是集体讨论，由老王～的。The *dazibao* was discussed by us all, but Lao Wang did the actual writing.

【执法】 zhífǎ enforce (或 execute) the law: ～如山 enforce the law strictly

【执绋】 zhífú take part in a funeral procession

【执迷不悟】 zhí mí bù wù obstinately stick to a wrong course; be perverse; refuse to come to one's senses

【执牛耳】 zhí niú'ěr (of an ancient prince presiding over a ceremony marking the conclusion of an alliance) hold the plate on which the ears of a sacrificial bull lie — be the acknowledged leader; occupy a leading position; rule the roost

【执拗】 zhíniù stubborn; pigheaded; wilful

【执行】 zhíxíng carry out; execute; implement: ～任务 carry out a task; perform a mission/ ～命令 execute an order/ ～党的纪律 enforce Party discipline/ ～政策 implement a policy

◇ ～机构 executive body/ ～机关 executive organ/ ～秘书 executive secretary/ ～委员会 executive committee/ ～员〈法〉 marshal (responsible for executing all civil case decisions and criminal case decisions concerning questions of property)/ ～主席 executive (或 presiding) chairman

【执意】 zhíyì insist on; be determined to; be bent on: 他～要走。He insisted on leaving./ 她～不收彩礼。She firmly refused to accept betrothal presents from her *fiancé's* family.

【执掌】 zhízhǎng wield; be in control of: ～兵权 wield military power

【执照】 zhízhào license; permit: 驾驶～ driver's license

【执政】 zhízhèng be in power; be in office; be at the helm of the state ◇ ～党 the party in power (或 in office); the ruling (或 governing) party

【执著】 zhízhuó inflexible; rigid; punctilious

**直** zhí ① straight: 街道又宽又～。The streets are wide and straight./ 把铁丝拉～ straighten a piece of wire ② straighten: ～起腰来 straighten one's back; stand up straight ③ vertical; perpendicular: ～行的文字 characters written from top to bottom/ ～上云霄 soar straight up into the sky/ 这屋子～里有六米，横里有三米。The room is 6 metres in length and 3 in width. ④ just; upright: 正～ upright; fair-minded/ 是非曲～ rights and wrongs; truth and falsehood ⑤ frank; straightforward: 心～口快 plain-spoken and straightforward; frank and outspoken/ ～认不讳 admit frankly; own up readily/ 我就～说了。I'll speak very frankly. ⑥ stiff; numb: 天太冷，手指都冻～了。It was so cold that my fingers were frozen stiff. ⑦ vertical stroke (in Chinese characters) ⑧ directly; straight: 一～走 go straight ahead/ ～奔火车站 head direct for the railway station/ ～通港口 lead directly to the harbour/ ～飞北京 fly nonstop to Beijing ⑨ continuously: 新井～往外喷油。Oil gushed continuously from the new well./ 他冻得～哆嗦。He was so cold that he kept shivering./ 这个故事逗得她～乐。The story tickled her fancy. ⑩ just; simply: 待他～如兄弟 treat him just like a brother/ 疼得～像针扎一样 feel a piercing pain

【直播】 zhíbō 〈农〉 direct seeding

【直布罗陀海峡】 Zhíbùluótuó Hǎixiá the Strait(s) of Gibraltar

【直肠】 zhícháng 〈生理〉 rectum

◇ ～癌 carcinoma of the rectum/ ～镜〈医〉 proctoscope/ ～炎 proctitis; rectitis

【直尺】 zhíchǐ straightedge

【直齿轮】 zhíchǐlún 〈机〉 straight gear

【直翅目昆虫】 zhíchìmù kūnchóng orthopteran

【直刺】 zhícì ①〈击剑〉 straight thrust ②〈中医〉 perpendicular inserting (in acupuncture)

【直达】 zhídá through; nonstop: ～福州的火车 a through train to Fuzhou

◇ ～车 through train or through bus/ ～车票 through ticket/ ～路线 through route

【直到】 zhídào ① until: 我们～昨晚才接到通知。We didn't get the notice until last night. ② up to: ～现在我们还没有接到正式通知。We've received no official information about it up to now.

【直根】 zhígēn 〈植〉 taproot

【直贡呢】 zhígòngní 〈纺〉 venetian

【直观】 zhíguān directly perceived through the senses; audio-visual

◇ ～教具 aids to object teaching; audio-visual aids/ ～教学 object teaching/ ～教学课 object lesson

【直角】 zhíjiǎo 〈数〉 right angle ◇ ～尺 square/ ～三角形 right (或 right-angled) triangle

【直接】 zhíjiē direct; immediate: ～原因 immediate cause; direct cause/ ～会晤 meet sb. in person/ 由公社～经营 be run directly by the commune/ ～交涉 negotiate directly with sb.; talk things over face to face with sb.

◇ ～宾语〈语〉 direct object/ ～经验〈哲〉 direct experience/ ～起飞 rolling (或 follow-through) takeoff; rolling start/ ～染料 direct dyes/ ～税 direct tax/ ～选举 direct election/ ～着陆 straight-in landing

【直截了当】 zhíjié-liǎodàng straightforward; blunt; point-blank: ～的回答 a point-blank answer/ ～地说吧。Let's put it bluntly. 或 Come straight to the point./ ～地拒绝对方的无理要求 flatly reject the other side's unreasonable demands

【直径】 zhíjìng 〈数〉 diameter: 大～〈机〉 major diameter/ 小～〈机〉 minor diameter

【直觉】 zhíjué 〈心〉intuition ◇ ～主义 intuitionism

【直立茎】 zhílìjīng 〈植〉 erect stem

【直流电】 zhíliúdiàn direct current (D.C.)

【直眉瞪眼】 zhíméi-dèngyǎn ① stare in anger; fume ② stare blankly; be in a daze; be stupefied: 他～地站在那里，也不说话。He stood there staring blankly, saying nothing.

【直射距离】 zhíshè jùlí 〈军〉 battle-sight range; point-blank range

【直升飞机】 zhíshēng fēijī helicopter; copter

◇ ～机场 heliport/ ～母舰 helicopter carrier/ ～运载 helilift

【直抒己见】 zhí shū jǐ jiàn state one's views frankly; be plainspoken

【直属】 zhíshǔ directly under; directly subordinate (或 affiliated) to: 国务院～机关 departments directly under the State Council

【直率】 zhíshuài frank; candid; straightforward: 你～地告诉我吧。Now tell me frankly./ 她说话很～。She is very straightforward in what she says.

【直爽】 zhíshuǎng frank; candid; straightforward; forthright: 性格～ forthright in character
【直挺挺】 zhítǐngtǐng straight; stiff; bolt upright: ～地站着 stand ramrod straight/ ～地坐着 sit bolt upright
【直系亲属】 zhíxì qīnshǔ directly-related members of one's family — parents, spouse and children
【直辖】 zhíxiá directly under the jurisdiction of: 文化部～机构 organizations directly under the Ministry of Culture ◇ ～市 municipality directly under the Central Government
【直线】 zhíxiàn ① straight line: ～距离二十里 twenty *li* as the crow flies ② steep; sharp (rise or fall): 捕鱼量～上升。The total catch of fish has shot up./ 废品率～下降。The rate of rejects fell sharply. ◇ ～飞行 rectilinear (或 straight) flight/ ～加速器〈物〉 linear accelerator/ ～爬高 rectilinear (或 straight) climb/ ～运动〈物〉 rectilinear motion
【直心眼儿】 zhíxīnyǎnr 〈口〉 open; frank; straightforward
【直性子】 zhíxìngzi ① straightforward; downright; forthright ② straightforward person: 他是个～，有什么说什么。He's a straightforward chap, always ready to say what's on his mind.
【直言】 zhíyán speak bluntly; state outright: 恕我～。Excuse me for speaking bluntly.
【直言不讳】 zhíyán bù huì speak without reservation; not mince words; call a spade a spade: 他～地指出我们工作中的缺点。He pointed out the shortcomings in our work without mincing words.
【直译】 zhíyì literal translation; word-for-word translation
【直音】 zhíyīn 〈语〉 traditional method of indicating the pronunciation of a Chinese character by citing another character with the same pronunciation
【直展云】 zhízhǎnyún 〈气〉 cloud with vertical development
【直至】 zhízhì ① till; until: 继续战斗，～胜利。Keep on fighting till victory is assured. ② up to: ～此时 up to this moment

## 侄 zhí brother's son; nephew

【侄女婿】 zhínǚxu husband of brother's daughter; niece's husband
【侄女】 zhínü brother's daughter; niece
【侄孙】 zhísūn brother's grandson; grandnephew
【侄孙女】 zhísūnnü brother's granddaughter; grandniece
【侄媳妇】 zhíxífu wife of brother's son; nephew's wife
【侄子】 zhízi brother's son; nephew 又作"侄儿"

## 指 zhí

另见 zhī; zhǐ
【指头】 zhítou ① finger ② toe

## 值 zhí ① value: 币～ currency value ② be worth: 这～多少钱？How much (或 What) is this worth?/ 不～一提 not worth mentioning/ 跑这一趟不～。The trip is not worthwhile. ③ happen to: 你上次来访，正～我外出。I happened to be out when you called./ ～此贵国三十周年国庆之际 on the occasion of the 30th anniversary of your National Day ④ be on duty; take one's turn at sth.: ～夜 be on night duty; be on the night shift/ 轮～ work in shifts ⑤ 〈数〉 value

【值班】 zhíbān be on duty: 今天谁～？Who's on duty today?/ 他值夜班。He's on night duty. 或 He's on the night shift. ◇ ～员 person on duty
【值当】 zhídàng 〈方〉 be worthwhile; be to one's advantage
【值得】 zhíde be worth; merit; deserve: ～买 be worth buying/ ～赞许 deserve commendation; be praiseworthy/ ～怀疑 be open to doubt/ ～仔细考虑 warrant careful consideration/ 历史的经验～注意。Historical experience merits attention./ 李贺的诗很～一读。Li He's poems are well worth reading.
【值分布理论】 zhífēnbù lǐlùn 〈数〉 value distribution theory
【值钱】 zhíqián costly; valuable
【值勤】 zhíqín (of armymen, policemen, etc.) be on duty; be on point duty: 晚上有民兵～巡逻。There are night patrols by the militia. ◇ ～交通警 policeman on point duty/ ～人员 personnel on duty
【值日】 zhírì be on duty for the day; be one's turn to be on duty: 今天谁～打扫教室？Whose turn is it to clean the classroom today? ◇ ～表 rota; duty roster/ ～生 student on duty
【值星】 zhíxīng (of army officers) be on duty for the week: 本周是王连长～。Company commander Wang is the officer of the week.

## 职 zhí ① duty; job: 尽～ fulfil one's duty/ 本～工作 one's own job ② post; office: 调～ be transferred to another post/ 在～干部 cadres at their posts/ 撤～ be removed (或 dismissed) from office/ 就～ take office; assume office

【职别】 zhíbié official rank
【职称】 zhíchēng the title of a technical or professional post (such as engineer, professor, lecturer, academician, etc.)
【职分】 zhífèn ① duty ② official post; position
【职工】 zhígōng ① staff and workers; workers and staff members ② 〈旧〉 workers; labour ◇ ～运动 labour movement; trade union movement
【职能】 zhínéng function: 货币的～ the functions of money
【职权】 zhíquán powers or authority of office: 行使～ exercise one's functions and powers/ 超越～ overstep one's authority; exceed one's powers
【职权范围】 zhíquán fànwéi limits (或 scope) of one's functions and powers; terms of reference: 在自己的～内 within one's functions and powers
【职守】 zhíshǒu post; duty: 擅离～ leave one's post without permission/ 忠于～ be faithful in the discharge of one's duties
【职位】 zhíwèi position; post
【职务】 zhíwù post; duties; job: 履行～ do (或 perform) one's duties/ 我们～不同，但都是为人民服务。Our jobs may be different but we all serve the people.
【职衔】 zhíxián post and rank
【职业】 zhíyè occupation; profession; vocation: 从事各种～的人 people of all occupations/ 这里填上你的姓名、～等等。Put down your name, occupation, etc. here./ 他的～是医生。He is a doctor by profession./ 我们的～有保障。Our jobs are secure. ◇ ～病 occupational disease/ ～团体 professional organization/ ～外交官 career diplomat/ ～学校 vocational school/ ～运动员 professional athlete; professional
【职员】 zhíyuán office worker; staff member; functionary
【职责】 zhízé duty; obligation; responsibility: 应尽的～ bounden duty/ 神圣～ sacred duty/ 分清～ define the duties incumbent on each person or post
【职掌】 zhízhǎng 〈书〉 ① be in charge of: ～财务 be in charge of financial affairs ② duty; charge
【职志】 zhízhì 〈书〉 lifework; mission: 以教育为～ take education as one's lifework

## 植 zhí ① plant; grow: ～树 plant trees/ 移～ transplant ② set up; establish: ～党营私 set up a clique for one's own selfish interests

【植保】 zhíbǎo 〈简〉(植物保护) plant protection; crop protection ◇ ～机械 equipment for plant protection/ ～员 plant protector

【植被】 zhíbèi 〈植〉 vegetation

【植皮术】 zhípíshù 〈医〉 skin grafting

【植绒】 zhíróng 〈纺〉 flocking

【植树】 zhíshù 〈林〉 tree planting: ～造林 afforestation ◇ ～机 tree-planting machine; tree planter

【植物】 zhíwù plant; flora ◇ ～保护 plant (或 crop) protection/ ～病害 plant disease/ ～检疫 plant quarantine/ ～胶 vegetable gum or glue/ ～界 plant kingdom; vegetable kingdom/ ～净化〈环保〉 plant purification/ ～区系 flora/ ～群落 plant community/ ～生长调节剂〈农〉 plant growth regulator/ ～性神经〈生理〉 autonomic nerve/ ～学 botany/ ～学家 botanist/ ～油 vegetable oil/ ～育种 plant breeding/ ～园 botanical garden/ ～志 flora

【植株】 zhízhū 〈农〉 plant

**殖** zhí breed; multiply: 生～ breed; reproduce/ 繁～ multiply; propagate

【殖民】 zhímín establish a colony; colonize: 非～化 decolonize; decolonization ◇ ～国家 colonialist power/ ～扩张 colonial expansion/ ～战争 colonialist war

【殖民地】 zhímíndì colony: 沦为～ be reduced to a colony ◇ ～国家 colonial country/ ～人民 people under colonial rule; colonial people

【殖民主义】 zhímínzhǔyì colonialism: ～祸害 the scourge of colonialism/ 新～ new colonialism; neocolonialism/ 坚决反对新老～ resolutely combat old and new colonialism ◇～者 colonialist

**跖** zhí 见"蹠" zhí

**摭** zhí 〈书〉 pick up

【摭拾】 zhíshí 〈书〉 pick; gather; collect: ～群言 collect views from various sources

**踯** zhí

【踯躅】 zhízhú 〈书〉 walk to and fro; loiter around: ～街头 tramp the streets

**蹠** zhí ①〈生理〉 metatarsus ②〈书〉 sole of the foot ③〈书〉 tread

【蹠骨】 zhígǔ 〈生理〉 metatarsal bones

## zhǐ

**止** zhǐ ①stop: 中～ stop halfway; discontinue; suspend/ 不达目的不～ refuse to give up without attaining one's aim/ ～痒 stop the itching/ ～渴 quench one's thirst ②to; till: 到目前为～ to date; till now/ 从本月十号起到十六号～ from the 10th to the 16th of this month ③only; 不～一次 not just once; more than once

【止步】 zhǐbù halt; stop; go no further: ～不前 halt; stand still/ 如果就此～,就会前功尽弃。 If we stop where we are, all our previous efforts will be wasted./ 游人～ no visitors 或 out of bounds

【止动机构】 zhǐdòng jīgòu 〈机〉 stop motion (mechanism)

【止付】 zhǐfù 〈经〉 stop payment ◇ ～通知书 stop-payment notice

【止境】 zhǐjìng end; limit: 学无～。 There is no end to learning./ 科学的发展是没有～的。 There is no limit to the development of science.

【止咳】 zhǐké relieve a cough ◇ ～糖浆 cough syrup

【止痛】 zhǐtòng relieve pain; stop pain ◇ ～药 anodyne; analgesic; pain-killer

【止息】 zhǐxī cease; stop: 就是阶级消灭了,先进同落后的斗争也不会～。 Even after classes have disappeared, the struggle between the advanced and the backward will not cease.

【止泻药】 zhǐxièyào antidiarrheal

【止血】 zhǐxuè stop bleeding; stanch bleeding ◇ ～带 tourniquet/ ～器 haemostat/ ～药 haemostatic

**只** zhǐ 〈副〉 only; merely: ～剩一个了。 There is only one left./ 我～想问一个问题。 I have just one question. 另见 zhī

【只不过】 zhǐ bùguò only; just; merely: 这～是一种猜测。 It's just (或 nothing but) a guess./ 别害怕,他～是吓唬你。 Don't be afraid. He was only trying to frighten you.

【只得】 zhǐdé have no alternative but to; be obliged to; have to: 他们～把会议延期。 They had no alternative but to put the meeting off./ 没有桥,我们～涉水过去。 As there was no bridge, we were obliged to wade across.

【只顾】 zhǐgù ① be absorbed in: 他～干他的事。 He was entirely absorbed in his work. ②〈副〉 merely; simply

【只管】 zhǐguǎn 〈副〉 ①by all means: 有意见～提出来。 Don't hesitate to put forward your suggestions if you have any./ 你～干下去。 Go ahead by all means. ②merely; simply

【只好】 zhǐhǎo have to; be forced to: ～作罢 be forced to give up/ ～另想办法 cannot but seek other means/ 末班车过去了,我们～走回家。 As the last bus had gone, we had to walk home.

【只是】 zhǐshì ① merely; only; just: 我今天进城,～去看看朋友,没有什么要紧的事儿。 Today I'm going to town just to see friends, not on business./ 这～个时间问题。 It is merely a question of time. ②simply: 大家问他是什么事,他～笑,不回答。 When people asked him what had happened, he simply laughed without replying. ③however; but then: 这架电视机不错,～小了点。 This TV set is quite good, only it's a bit too small.

【只消】 zhǐxiāo 〈方〉 all one has to do is; you only need to: ～来个电话,货物马上送到。 Just give us a ring and the goods will be delivered without delay.

【只许州官放火,不许百姓点灯】 zhǐ xǔ zhōuguān fànghuǒ, bù xǔ bǎixìng diǎndēng the magistrates are free to burn down houses, while the common people are forbidden even to light lamps; one may steal a horse while another may not look over the hedge

【只要】 zhǐyào 〈连〉 so long as; provided: ～阶级存在,阶级斗争就不可避免。 So long as classes exist, class struggle is inevitable./ ～虚心,就会进步。 Provided you are modest, you'll surely make progress.

【只要功夫深,铁杵磨成针】 zhǐyào gōngfu shēn, tiěchǔ mó-chéng zhēn constant grinding can turn an iron rod into a needle — perseverance spells success

【只有】 zhǐyǒu 〈连〉 only; alone: ～依靠群众,才能做好工作。 Only by relying on the masses can you do your work well./ ～他知道这事的内情。 He alone knows the inside story./ 这样～好处,没有坏处。 This is all to the good and no harm can come of it.

【只争朝夕】 zhǐ zhēng zhāo-xī seize the day, seize the hour; seize every minute; race against time

**旨** zhǐ ① purport; purpose; aim: 主～ purport; main purpose/ 宗～ purpose; aim/ ～在唤起民众 for the purpose of arousing the masses/ ～在加快工程进度的措施 measures aimed at speeding up the project ② decree: 圣～ imperial decree ③〈书〉tasty; delicious: ～酒 excellent wine

【旨趣】 zhǐqù 〈书〉 purport; objective

【旨意】 zhǐyì decree; order: 你这样做是奉谁的～？On whose orders did you do this?

**址** zhǐ location; site: 厂～ factory site/ 地～ address

**芷** zhǐ 见"白芷" báizhǐ

**纸** zhǐ ① paper: 一张白～ a blank sheet of paper ②〈量〉[书信、文件的张数]: 一～空文 a mere scrap of paper

【纸板】 zhǐbǎn paperboard; cardboard: 波纹～ corrugated cardboard ◇ ～盒(箱) cardboard case or box; carton

【纸版】 zhǐbǎn 〈印〉 paper mould; paper matrix

【纸包不住火】 zhǐ bāobuzhù huǒ you can't wrap fire in paper — there is no concealing the truth; truth will out

【纸币】 zhǐbì paper money; paper currency; note: 发行～ issue (bank) notes/ 不兑现～ fiat money

【纸花】 zhǐhuā paper flower

【纸浆】 zhǐjiāng paper pulp; pulp ◇ ～板 pulp board/ ～厂 pulp mill/ ～筛滤器 pulp strainer/ ～原材 pulpwood/ ～制造机 macerator

【纸老虎】 zhǐlǎohǔ paper tiger: 一切反动派都是～。All reactionaries are paper tigers.

【纸捻】 zhǐniǎn spill of rolled paper used to light a pipe, etc.; (paper) spill

【纸牌】 zhǐpái playing cards

【纸钱】 zhǐqián paper made to resemble money and burned as an offering to the dead

【纸上谈兵】 zhǐshàng tán bīng fight only on paper; be an armchair strategist; engage in idle theorizing

【纸绳】 zhǐshéng paper string

【纸型】 zhǐxíng 〈印〉 paper mould; paper matrix ◇ ～干燥机 scorcher

【纸烟】 zhǐyān cigarette

【纸鱼】 zhǐyú silverfish; fish moth

【纸鸢】 zhǐyuān kite

【纸张】 zhǐzhāng paper

【纸醉金迷】 zhǐzuì-jīnmí (a life of) luxury and dissipation

**祉** zhǐ 〈书〉 happiness; blessedness

**指** zhǐ ① finger: 屈～可数 can be counted on one's fingers — very few/ 天黑得伸手不见五～。It was so dark that you couldn't see your own fingers (或 couldn't see your hand in front of your face). ② fingerbreadth; digit: 两～宽的纸条 a strip of paper two fingerbreadths wide/ 下了四～雨。We had about three inches of rain. ③ point at; point to: 时针～向十二点。The hour hand points to twelve./ 千人所～,无病而死。When a thousand people point accusing fingers at a man he will die even though not ill — it is dangerous to incur public wrath. ④ indicate; point out; refer to: 党中央给我们～航向。The Party's Central Committee charts our course./ ～出正确方向 point out the correct way/ ～出缺点 point out sb.'s shortcomings/ 他的话不是～你说的。His remarks were not directed at you. ⑤ depend on; count on: 他们就～着你帮忙哩。They're counting on your help.
另见 zhī; zhí

【指北针】 zhǐběizhēn compass

【指标】 zhǐbiāo target; quota; norm; index: 完成国家计划规定的～ attain the targets (或 fulfil the norms) set in the state plan/ 生产～ production target/ 质量～ quality index

【指不胜屈】 zhǐ bù shèng qū too numerous to be counted on the fingers; a great many

【指斥】 zhǐchì reprove; reprimand; denounce

【指导】 zhǐdǎo guide; direct: ～我们思想的理论基础是马克思列宁主义。The theoretical basis guiding our thinking is Marxism-Leninism./ 正确的～路线 correct line of guidance/ ～战争的规律 laws for directing war/ 老农～青年干农活。The old peasants instructed (或 directed) the youths in farm work. ◇ ～思想 guiding ideology

【指导员】 zhǐdǎoyuán 〈军〉 political instructor (of a PLA company)

【指点】 zhǐdiǎn give directions (或 pointers, advice); show how (to do sth.): 教练耐心地～他们。The coach patiently instructs them./ 请给我们～～。Please show us how to do it./ 经他一～,我就全明白了。A few pointers from him made it all clear to me.

【指定】 zhǐdìng appoint; assign: ～谈判代表 appoint representatives to the negotiations/ 在～地点见面 meet at the designated place/ ～一位党委副书记主持这项工作 assign a deputy secretary of the Party committee to direct the work

【指法】 zhǐfǎ 〈乐〉 fingering

【指骨】 zhǐgǔ 〈生理〉 phalanx

【指画】 zhǐhuà point at; point to

【指环】 zhǐhuán (finger) ring

【指挥】 zhǐhuī ① command; direct; conduct: ～一个连 command a company; be in command of a company/ ～交通 direct traffic/ ～乐队 conduct an orchestra/ ～若定 direct (work, etc.) with perfect ease; give highly competent leadership/ 继承毛主席遗志,听从华主席～。Carry out Chairman Mao's behests and obey Chairman Hua's orders./ 我们的原则是党～枪,而决不容许枪～党。Our principle is that the Party commands the gun, and the gun must never be allowed to command the Party. ② commander; director ③〈乐〉 conductor
◇ ～棒〈乐〉 baton/ ～舱〈宇航〉 command module/ ～车 command car/ ～刀 officer's sword/ ～官 commanding officer; commander/ ～所 command post/ ～塔台〈航空〉 control tower/ ～系统 command system/ ～员 commander

【指挥部】 zhǐhuībù command post; headquarters: 防空～ air defence command/ 前沿～ forward command post/ 会战～ campaign headquarters

【指教】 zhǐjiào 〈套〉 give advice or comments: 请多多～。Kindly give us your advice./ 望不吝～。I hope you won't spare your comments.

【指靠】 zhǐkào depend on (for one's livelihood); look to (for help); count on: 这件事我们就～你了。We'll count on you for this.

【指控】 zhǐkòng accuse; charge: 有人～他纳贿。He's been accused of taking bribes.

【指令】 zhǐlìng ① instruct; order; direct ② instructions; order; directive ③〈计算机〉 instruction ◇ 遥控～ remote control command

【指鹿为马】 zhǐ lù wéi mǎ call a stag a horse — deliberately misrepresent

【指路明灯】 zhǐlù míngdēng beacon light; beacon: 毛泽东思想是我们前进的～。Mao Zedong Thought is the beacon lighting our advance.

【指路牌】 zhǐlùpái signpost; fingerpost; guidepost

【指名】 zhǐmíng mention by name; name: ～攻击 assail sb. by name/ ～道姓 name names/ 领导上～要小赵参加会议。The leadership named Xiao Zhao as the one to attend the meeting.

【指明】 zhǐmíng show clearly; demonstrate; point out: ～两者之间的差别 show clearly the difference between the two/ ～出路 point the way out

【指南】 zhǐnán guide; guidebook

【指南车】 zhǐnánchē an ancient Chinese vehicle with a wooden figure always pointing to the south

【指南针】 zhǐnánzhēn compass: 十二世纪初我国航海已普遍使用～。By the early twelfth century the compass was already in general use among Chinese navigators.

【指派】 zhǐpài appoint; name; designate: ～她当车间主任 appoint her (to be) workshop director /～代表出席会议 name delegates to the conference

【指日可待】 zhǐ rì kě dài can be expected soon; be just round the corner: 胜利～。Victory is just round the corner.

【指桑骂槐】 zhǐ sāng mà huái point at the mulberry and abuse the locust — point at one but abuse another; make oblique accusations

【指使】 zhǐshǐ instigate; incite; put sb. up to sth.: ～少数坏人进行破坏 incite a handful of bad elements to engage in sabotage/ 受别人～ act on sb.'s instigation/ 揭露幕后～者 expose the person behind the scenes; unmask the hidden instigator

【指示】 zhǐshì ① indicate; point out: ～前进的方向 indicate the direction of advance ② instruct: ～部队立即出发 instruct the troops to set out at once ③ directive; instructions: 下达～ give instructions ◇ ～板〈仪表〉indicator board/ ～代词〈语〉demonstrative pronoun/ ～灯 pilot lamp (或 light); indicator lamp/ ～功率〈机〉indicated power/ ～剂〈化〉indicator

【指示器】 zhǐshìqì indicator: 刻度盘～ dial indicator/ 液面～ level indicator

【指事】 zhǐshì 〈语〉 self-explanatory characters, e.g. 上 (above) and 下 (below) — one of the six categories of Chinese characters (六书)

【指手划脚】 zhǐshǒu-huàjiǎo ① make gestures; gesticulate: ～地高谈阔论 talk volubly with animated gestures ② make indiscreet remarks or criticisms

【指数】 zhǐshù index number; index: 综合～ composite index/ 物价～ price index/ 生活费～ cost of living index ◇ ～函数〈数〉exponential function/ ～化 indexation/ ～律〈数〉index law

【指望】 zhǐwang ① look to; count on: ～有一天能实现这个计划 look forward to the day when this plan will be put in practice/ ～他长大了好好为人民服务。We hope that he'll grow up to serve the people heart and soul./ ～你帮助 count on you for help ② prospect; hope: 解放了,我们才有了～。It was liberation which brought us hope./ 他这病还有～吗? Is there still hope of his recovery?

【指纹】 zhǐwén ① loops and whorls on a finger ② fingerprint ◇ ～学 dactylography

【指向】 zhǐxiàng directional ◇ ～天线 directional antenna/ ～植物 compass plant

【指引】 zhǐyǐn point (the way); guide; show: 沿着毛主席～的方向前进 advance along the course charted by Chairman Mao/ 在无产阶级革命路线～下 under the guidance of the proletarian revolutionary line

【指印】 zhǐyìn fingerprint; finger mark: 按～ make a fingerprint

【指责】 zhǐzé censure; criticize; find fault with: 横加～ make unwarranted charges/ 受到舆论的～ be subjected to the censure of public opinion/ 用事实回击他们的～ answer their attacks with facts/ 我们怎能～这种实事求是的态度呢? How can we find fault with this realistic approach?

【指摘】 zhǐzhāi pick faults and criticize; censure

【指战员】 zhǐzhànyuán officers and men (of the PLA)

【指针】 zhǐzhēn ① indicator; pointer; needle ② guiding principle; guide: 作为今后工作的～ as a guide for future work ③〈中医〉pressing with a finger (on an acupuncture point); finger-pressing

【指正】 zhǐzhèng ① point out mistakes so that they can be corrected ②〈套〉make a comment or criticism: 请惠予～。Please oblige me with your valuable comments. 或 Be kind enough to give me your opinion.

【指重表】 zhǐzhòngbiǎo 〈石油〉 weight indicator

**枳** zhǐ 〈植〉 trifoliate orange

【枳壳】 zhǐqiào 〈中药〉 fruit of citron or trifoliate orange

**咫** zhǐ an ancient measure of length, equal to 8 *cun* (寸)

【咫尺】 zhǐchǐ 〈书〉 very close: 近在～ close at hand

【咫尺天涯】 zhǐchǐ-tiānyá a short distance away, and yet poles apart — see little of each other though living nearby

**趾** zhǐ ① toe ② foot

【趾高气扬】 zhǐgāo-qìyáng strut about and give oneself airs; be swollen with arrogance

【趾甲】 zhǐjiǎ toenail

**黹** zhǐ 〈书〉 needlework; embroidery: 针～ needlework

**酯** zhǐ 〈化〉 ester: ～化 esterification/ ～酶 esterase

**徵** zhǐ 〈乐〉 a note of the ancient Chinese five-tone scale, corresponding to 5 in numbered musical notation

## zhì

**至** zhì ① to; until: 从左～右 from left to right/ 继续斗争,直～取得彻底胜利 continue the struggle until complete victory is won/ 截～上月底为止 up to the end of last month ②〈书〉extremely; most: 感人～深 deeply moving; extremely moving/ 是为～盼。That is our sincerest hope./ ～嘱。See that you act accordingly.

【至宝】 zhìbǎo most valuable treasure: 如获～ feel as if one had found a priceless treasure

【至诚】 zhìchéng complete sincerity: 出于～ in all sincerity; from the bottom of one's heart

【至诚】 zhìcheng sincere; straightforward: ～的朋友 a sincere friend

【至迟】 zhìchí at (the) latest: 这条铁路～五月通车。This railway will be opened to traffic in May at the latest.

【至多】 zhìduō 〈副〉 at (the) most: 这张画～两个星期就能画好。It'll take two weeks at most to finish the painting.

【至高无上】 zhìgāo-wúshàng most lofty; paramount; supreme: ～的事业 most lofty undertaking/ ～的权力 absolute power

【至交】 zhìjiāo most intimate friend; best friend

【至今】 zhìjīn up to now; to this day; so far: ～没有人提出过反对意见。Up to now no one has raised any objections./ 我～未得到他的答复。So far I've had no reply from him.

【至理名言】 zhìlǐ-míngyán famous dictum; maxim; axiom; golden saying

【至亲】 zhìqīn very close relative; close kin: ～好友 close relatives and good friends

【至上】 zhìshàng supreme; the highest

【至少】 zhìshǎo 〈副〉 at (the) least: ～有一万人参加了大会。At least ten thousand people attended the rally./ 他并不了解我，～是了解得不全面。He doesn't understand me, or at any rate not fully./ ～可以说，这样处理不妥。This is not the proper way to handle the matter, to say the least.

【至死】 zhìsǐ unto death; till death: ～不屈 not yield even unto death/ ～不悟 incorrigibly stubborn

【至于】 zhìyú ① as for; as to: ～其他问题，以后再说。As for other matters, we'll take them up later. ② go so far as to: 他不～不来开会吧？He wouldn't go so far as to refuse to come to the meeting, would he?

**忮** zhì 〈书〉 jealousy

**识** zhì 〈书〉 ① remember; commit to memory: 博闻强～ have wide learning and a retentive memory; have encyclopaedic knowledge ② mark; sign: 款～ inscriptions (on bronzes, etc.)

另见 shí

**志** zhì ① will; aspiration; ideal: ～坚如钢 have an iron will; have a will of steel/ 胸怀大～ cherish high ideals; have lofty aspirations/ 立～当优秀的科学家 be determined to become a first-rate scientist ② keep in mind: 永～不忘 forever bear in mind ③ records; annals: 县～ annals of a county/ 《三国～》 *History of the Three Kingdoms* ④ mark; sign: 标～ mark

【志哀】 zhì'āi indicate mourning: 下半旗～ fly a flag at half-mast as a sign of mourning

【志大才疏】 zhì dà cái shū have great ambition but little talent; have high aspirations but little ability

【志气】 zhìqi aspiration; ambition: 有～ have high aspirations

【志趣】 zhìqù aspiration and interest; inclination; bent

【志士】 zhìshì person of ideals and integrity: ～仁人 people with lofty ideals/ 爱国～ noble-minded patriot

【志同道合】 zhìtóng-dàohé cherish the same ideals and follow the same path; have a common goal

【志向】 zhìxiàng aspiration; ideal; ambition: 青年人应有远大的～。Young people should have lofty aspirations.

【志愿】 zhìyuàn ① aspiration; wish; ideal ② do sth. of one's own free will; volunteer ◇ ～兵 volunteer (soldier)

【志愿军】 zhìyuànjūn people who volunteer to fight in another country; volunteers

【志愿书】 zhìyuànshū application form: 入党～ application for Party membership

**豸** zhì 〈书〉 insect without feet or legs (mentioned in ancient books): 虫～ insects

**治** zhì ① rule; govern; administer; manage: ～国 administer a country/ ～家 manage a household/ 自～ self-government; autonomy ② order; peace: 达到天下大～ achieve great order across the land ③ 〈旧〉 seat of a local government: 县～ county seat/ 省～ provincial capital ④ treat (a disease); cure: ～好战争创伤 heal the wounds of war/ 他的病不久就～好了。He was soon cured of his illness. ⑤ control; harness (a river); wipe out: ～沙 sand-control/ ～山～水 transform mountains and tame rivers/ ～淮 harness the Huai River/ ～碱 combat alkalinity/ ～蝗 eliminate locusts ⑥ punish: 惩～ punish ⑦ study; research: 专～宋史 specialize in the history of the Song Dynasty

【治安】 zhì'ān public order; public security: 维持～ maintain public order ◇ ～保卫委员会 public security committee

【治本】 zhìběn effect a permanent cure; get at the root (of a problem, etc.); take radical measures: 河流的～工程 project for the permanent control of a river

【治标】 zhìbiāo merely alleviate the symptoms of an illness; bring about a temporary solution (of a problem, etc.); take stopgap measures

【治病救人】 zhìbìng-jiùrén cure the sickness to save the patient: 要以"～"的态度帮助犯错误的同志。To help comrades who have made mistakes, we should adopt the approach of "curing the sickness to save the patient".

【治国】 zhìguó administer (或 run) a country; manage state affairs: ～安民 run the country well and give the people peace and security/ 抓纲～ grasp the key link of class struggle and bring about great order across the land

【治理】 zhìlǐ ① administer; govern: ～国家 administer a country; run a state ② harness; bring under control; put in order: ～河流 harness a river; bring a river under control/ 实行山、水、田、林、路综合～。The problems concerning mountains, rivers, farmland, forests and roads should be tackled in a comprehensive way.

【治疗】 zhìliáo treat; cure: 住院～ be hospitalized/ ～效果 therapeutic effect/ 她还在医院～。She is still under treatment in hospital. ◇ ～学 therapeutics

【治丧】 zhìsāng make funeral arrangements ◇ ～委员会 funeral committee

【治世】 zhìshì times of peace and prosperity

【治水】 zhìshuǐ regulate rivers and watercourses; prevent floods by water control

【治丝益棼】 zhì sī yì fén sort out silk threads improperly only to tangle them further — do sth. which only makes matters worse; make confusion worse confounded

【治外法权】 zhìwài fǎquán extraterritoriality; exterritoriality; extrality

【治学】 zhìxué pursue one's studies; do scholarly research: 他以～严谨著称。He is noted for his meticulous scholarship.

【治愈率】 zhìyùlǜ 〈医〉 cure rate

【治装】 zhìzhuāng 〈书〉 purchase things necessary (esp. clothes) for a long journey

【治罪】 zhìzuì punish sb. (for a crime)

**帜** zhì 〈书〉 flag; banner: 独树一～ fly one's own colours — develop a school of one's own

**炙** zhì ① broil; roast ② 〈书〉 roast meat

【炙手可热】 zhì shǒu kě rè if you stretch out your hand you feel the heat — the supreme arrogance of a person with great power

**帙** zhì 〈书〉 cloth slip-case for a book

**郅** zhì 〈书〉 most; extreme

**质** zhì ① nature; character: 性～ nature; character/ 本～ innate character; essence ② quality: 按～分等 grade according to quality/ ～的飞跃 a qualitative leap/ 优～钢 high-quality (或 high-grade) steel ③ matter; substance: 流～食物 liquid food/ 木～纤维 wood fibre ④ simple; plain: ～直 upright; straightforward/ ～言之 to put it bluntly ⑤ question: ～疑 call in question ⑥ 〈书〉 pawn: 典～ pawn; mortgage ⑦ 〈书〉 pledge: 以此为～ with this as a pledge/ 人～ hostage

【质变】 zhìbiàn 〈哲〉 qualitative change: 部分～ partial qualitative change

【质地】 zhìdì ① quality of a material; texture; grain: ～细密 of close texture; fine-grained ② character; disposition

【质点】 zhìdiǎn 〈物〉 particle

【质粒】 zhìlì 〈生〉 plasmid

【质量】 zhìliàng ① quality: ～好 of high quality/ ～不高 of low quality; inferior/ 提高～ improve the quality ② 〈物〉 mass: 相对论～ relativistic mass
◇ ～比〈物〉 mass ratio/ ～检查制度 rules for testing quality/ ～守恒〈物〉 conservation of mass/ ～作用定律〈物〉 law of mass action

【质料】 zhìliào material: 这套衣服的～很好。This suit is made of very good material.

【质能关系式】 zhì-néng guānxìshì 〈物〉 mass-energy relation

【质朴】 zhìpǔ simple and unadorned; unaffected; plain: 文字～ written in a simple style/ 为人忠厚～ be simple and honest; be unsophisticated

【质谱】 zhìpǔ 〈物〉 mass spectra ◇ ～分析 mass spectrographic analysis/ ～仪 mass spectrometer; mass spectrograph

【质数】 zhìshù 〈数〉 prime number

【质问】 zhìwèn question; interrogate; call to account: 提出～ bring sb. to account

【质询】 zhìxún address inquiries to; ask for an explanation: 人民代表大会代表有权向国家机关提出～。Deputies to the People's Congresses have the right to address inquiries to state organs.

【质疑】 zhìyí call in question; query: 对他的说法提出～ query (或 question) the validity of his statement

【质疑问难】 zhìyí-wènnàn raise doubts and difficult questions for discussion

【质子】 zhìzǐ proton ◇ ～轰击 proton bombardment/ ～加速器 proton accelerator

## 制

zhì ① make; manufacture: 中国～ made in China/ 机～ machine-made/ 精～糖 refined sugar ② work out; formulate: 因地～宜 work out measures to suit local conditions ③ restrict; control: 限～ restrict/ 控～ control/ ～敌于死命 have the enemy by the throat; spell death to the enemy ④ system: 公～ the metric system/ 八级工资～ the eight-grade wage scale

【制版】 zhìbǎn 〈印〉 plate making: 平版～ lithographic plate making

【制备】 zhìbèi 〈化〉 preparation: 氧的～ preparation of oxygen

【制币】 zhìbì standard national currency ◇ ～厂 mint

【制表】 zhìbiǎo 〈统计〉 tabulation

【制裁】 zhìcái sanction; punish: 实行～ apply sanctions (against); impose sanctions (upon)/ 受到法律～ be punished according to law/ 给以严厉～ mete out severe punishment to sb.

【制成品】 zhìchéngpǐn finished products; manufactured goods; manufactures

【制导】 zhìdǎo control and guide (a missile, etc.) ◇ ～系统 guidance system/ ～炸弹 guided bomb

【制订】 zhìdìng work (或 map) out; formulate: ～《汉语拼音方案》 work out *The Scheme for the Chinese Phonetic Alphabet*

【制定】 zhìdìng lay down; draw up; formulate; draft: ～操作规程 lay down operating rules/ ～宪法 draw up a constitution/ ～政策 formulate a policy/ ～计划 work out a plan/ ～法律 make laws/ ～法令 enact decrees

【制动】 zhìdòng apply the brake; brake
◇ ～火箭 retro-rocket/ ～距离〈交〉 braking (或 stopping) distance/ ～器 brake

【制度】 zhìdù system; institution: 规章～ rules and regulations/ 党委制是保证集体领导的重要～。The Party committee system is an important Party institution for ensuring collective leadership.

【制伏】 zhìfú check; subdue; bring under control: ～风沙 check wind and sand/ ～敌人 subdue the enemy/ 这条河给～了。The river was brought under control.

【制服】 zhìfú ① uniform ② 见"制伏" ◇ ～呢 uniform cloth

【制高点】 zhìgāodiǎn 〈军〉 commanding elevation (或 point, ground, height)

【制革】 zhìgé process hides; tan ◇ ～厂 tannery/ ～工人 tanner

【制海权】 zhìhǎiquán 〈军〉 mastery of the seas; command of the sea

【制剂】 zhìjì 〈药〉 preparation: 标准～ standard preparation

【制空权】 zhìkōngquán 〈军〉 control of the air; air domination

【制冷】 zhìlěng 见"致冷" zhìlěng

【制粒机】 zhìlìjī granulator

【制片人】 zhìpiànrén 〈电影〉 producer

【制品】 zhìpǐn products; goods: 奶～ dairy products/ 黄麻～ jute goods/ 竹～ articles made of bamboo; bamboo articles

【制胜】 zhìshèng get the upper hand of; subdue: ～敌人 subdue the enemy/ 出奇～ defeat one's opponent by a surprise move

【制糖】 zhìtáng refine sugar ◇ ～厂 sugar refinery

【制图】 zhìtú ①〈地〉 charting; map-making ②〈机〉〈建〉 drafting
◇ ～学 cartography/ ～仪器 drawing (或 drafting) instrument/ ～员〈地〉 cartographer; 〈机〉〈建〉 draftsman

【制销】 zhìxiāo 〈机〉 cotter

【制药】 zhìyào pharmacy ◇ ～厂 pharmaceutical factory/ ～学 pharmaceutics

【制音器】 zhìyīnqì 〈乐〉 damper

【制约】 zhìyuē restrict; condition: 受历史条件的～ be restricted by historical conditions/ 互相～ condition each other; interact

【制造】 zhìzào ① make; manufacture: 中国～的飞机 China-made aircraft/ 这设备是我们自己～的。The equipment is of our own manufacture. ② engineer; create; fabricate: ～纠纷 create trouble; sow dissension/ ～紧张局势 create tension/ ～分裂 foment splits/ ～谣言 fabricate rumours (或 lies)/ ～假象 put up a false front/ ～重重障碍 raise one obstacle after another/ ～烟幕 spread a smoke screen/ ～内乱 stir up internal strife/ ～舆论 mould public opinion
◇ ～商 manufacturer/ ～业 manufacturing industry

【制止】 zhìzhǐ check; curb; prevent; stop: ～流沙 curb shifting sand/ ～通货膨胀 check (或 halt) inflation/ ～派别活动 put an end to factional activities/ 我做了一个手势，～他再说下去。I made a gesture to stop him from saying any more.

【制作】 zhìzuò make; manufacture: ～家具 make furniture/ 精心～的银器 elaborately wrought silverware

## 栉

zhì 〈书〉 comb

【栉比】 zhìbǐ 〈书〉 placed closely side by side (like the teeth of a comb)

【栉风沐雨】 zhìfēng-mùyǔ be combed by the wind and washed by the rain — travel or work despite wind and rain

## 峙

zhì 〈书〉 stand erect; tower: 对～ stand up against each other; confront each other/ ～立 stand towering

**桎** zhì 〈书〉 fetters

【桎梏】 zhìgù 〈书〉 fetters and handcuffs; shackles: 打碎精神上的～ smash spiritual shackles

**轾** zhì 见"轩轾" xuān-zhì

**致** zhì ① send; extend; deliver: ～电 send a telegram/ ～贺 extend one's congratulations/ 向革命烈士～哀 pay one's respects to revolutionary martyrs ② devote (one's efforts, etc.): 专心～志 be wholeheartedly devoted to; be wholly absorbed in ③ incur; result in; cause: 招～失败 cause defeat/ 学以～用 learn sth. in order to use it; gear one's study to practical use ④ manner or style that engages attention or arouses interest: 别～ original in style; unique ⑤ fine; delicate: 工作细～ be meticulous in one's work/ 精～ exquisite

【致癌物质】 zhì'ái wùzhì 〈医〉 carcinogen; carcinogenic substance

【致病菌】 zhìbìngjūn 〈医〉 pathogenic bacteria

【致辞】 zhìcí make (或 deliver) a speech: 请来宾向大会～ call upon a guest to address the conference/ 新年～ New Year message 又作"致词"

【致敬】 zhìjìng salute; pay one's respects to; pay tribute to: 鸣礼炮二十一响～ fire a 21-gun salute/ 向劳动模范～! Salute the model workers! ◇ ～电 message of greeting

【致冷】 zhìlěng refrigeration ◇ ～剂 refrigerant/ ～循环 refrigeration cycle

【致力】 zhìlì devote oneself to; work for: ～于中医学的研究 devote (或 dedicate) oneself to the study of traditional Chinese medical science

【致密】 zhìmì fine and close; compact: ～的观察 careful (或 close) observation/ 结构～ fine and close in texture ◇ ～结构〈地〉 compact texture

【致命】 zhìmìng causing death; fatal; mortal; deadly: ～的打击 a deadly blow/ ～伤 a mortal (或 vital) wound/ ～的弱点 fatal weakness

【致使】 zhìshǐ cause; result in: 由于地址字迹不清,～信件无法投递。It is impossible to deliver this letter because the address is illegible.

【致死】 zhìsǐ causing death; lethal; deadly: ～原因 cause of death ◇ ～剂量 lethal dose/ ～性毒气 lethal gas

【致谢】 zhìxiè express one's thanks (或 gratitude); extend thanks to: 谨此～。We hereby express our thanks.

【致意】 zhìyì give one's regards (或 best wishes); present one's compliments; send one's greetings: 请向边防战士们～。Please give our best wishes to the frontier guards./ 点头(挥手)～ nod (wave) a greeting/ 向欢呼群众挥手～ wave to the cheering crowd in acknowledgement

**秩** zhì 〈书〉 ① order: ～然不紊 orderly; shipshape ② 〈书〉 decade: 七～寿辰 seventieth birthday

【秩序】 zhìxù order; sequence: 工作～ sequence of work/ 维持社会～ maintain public order/ 紧张而有～的工作 intense but orderly work

**挚** zhì 〈书〉 sincere; earnest: 诚～ sincere/ 真～的友谊 true friendship

【挚友】 zhìyǒu intimate friend; bosom friend

**贽** zhì 〈书〉 gift presented to a senior at one's first visit as a mark of esteem

**掷** zhì throw; cast: 投～ throw; fling/ 弃～ cast aside; throw away/ 孤注一～ risk everything on a single throw; stake all one has

另见 zhī

【掷标枪】 zhì biāoqiāng 〈体〉 javelin throw

【掷弹兵】 zhìdànbīng 〈军〉 grenadier

【掷弹筒】 zhìdàntǒng grenade discharger; grenade launcher

【掷还】 zhìhuán 〈书〉 please return (to the writer, etc.): 前请审阅之件,请早日～为荷。Please return at your earliest convenience the manuscript (或 draft, material) submitted to you for approval.

【掷界外球】 zhì jièwàiqiú 〈足球〉 throw-in

【掷铁饼】 zhì tiěbǐng 〈体〉 discus throw

**窒** zhì 〈书〉 stop up; obstruct: ～塞 stop up; block

【窒碍】 zhì'ài 〈书〉 have obstacles; be obstructed

【窒闷】 zhìmèn close; stuffy

【窒息】 zhìxī stifle; suffocate: 浓烟几乎使他～。The dense smoke almost suffocated him. ◇ ～弹 stifling bomb/ ～性毒气 asphyxiating (或 choking) gas

**鸷** zhì 〈书〉 ferocious; violent: ～鸟 birds of prey

**痔** zhì haemorrhoids; piles

【痔疮】 zhìchuāng haemorrhoids; piles

【痔漏】 zhìlòu 〈医〉 anal fistula

**滞** zhì stagnant; sluggish

【滞碍】 zhì'ài block (up); obstruct

【滞洪】 zhìhóng 〈水〉 flood detention ◇ ～区 detention basin; retarding basin

【滞留】 zhìliú be detained; be held up

【滞纳金】 zhìnàjīn fine for delaying payment; fine for paying late; overdue fine

【滞销】 zhìxiāo unsalable; unmarketable ◇ ～货 unsalable (或 slow-selling) goods; a drug on the market

**痣** zhì nevus; mole: 色～ pigmented mole (或 nevus)/ 胎～ birthmark

**蛭** zhì leech

【蛭石】 zhìshí 〈矿〉 vermiculite

**智** zhì wisdom; resourcefulness; wit: 足～多谋 wise and resourceful/ ～穷才尽 at the end of one's wits (或 resources)/ 斗～ a battle of wits

【智齿】 zhìchǐ 〈生理〉 wisdom tooth

【智多星】 zhìduōxīng nickname for Wu Yong, the resourceful strategist of the peasant army in the *Water Margin* (《水浒传》); resourceful person; mastermind

【智慧】 zhìhuì wisdom; intelligence: 吸取群众的～ draw on the wisdom of the masses/ 勤劳～的人民 the industrious and ingenious people/ 这些壮丽的古代建筑显示了劳动人民的高度～。These magnificent ancient buildings demonstrate the great intelligence of the labouring people.

【智力】 zhìlì intelligence; intellect ◇ ～测验 intelligence test

【智利】 Zhìlì Chile ◇ ～人 Chilean

【智略】 zhìlüè wisdom and resourcefulness

【智谋】 zhìmóu resourcefulness: 靠勇敢也靠～ rely on both courage and resourcefulness/ 人多～高。More people mean more ideas.

【智囊】 zhìnáng brain truster ◇ ～团 brain trust

【智取】 zhìqǔ take (a fort, town, etc.) by strategy: 只可～,不可强攻。The only way to take the enemy position is by

strategy, not by forceful attack.
【智术】 zhìshù trickery; stratagem
【智勇双全】 zhì-yǒng shuāng quán both intelligent and courageous; both brave and resourceful
【智育】 zhìyù intellectual education; intellectual development: 使学生在德育、~、体育几方面都得到发展 enable the students to develop morally, intellectually and physically
【智者千虑,必有一失】 zhìzhě qiān lǜ, bì yǒu yī shī even the wise are not always free from error

**彘** zhì 〈书〉 pig; swine

**锧** zhì 〈书〉 ① chopping block ② (ancient) executioner's block: 斧~ (executioner's) axe and block

**置** zhì ① place; put: 安~ find a place for; help sb. to settle down/ 搁~ put aside; shelve; pigeonhole ② set up; establish; install: 设~新课程 establish new courses/ 装~配电盘 install a switchboard/ ~酒款待 give a feast to entertain sb. ③ buy: ~一身衣服 buy a suit or have one made to order/ 添~一些家具 buy some furniture
【置办】 zhìbàn buy (durables); purchase: ~家具 buy furniture/ ~图书仪器 procure books and instruments
【置备】 zhìbèi purchase (equipment, furniture, etc.)
【置辩】 zhìbiàn 〈书〉〔多用于否定〕argue (in self-defence): 不屑~ disdain to argue/ 不容~ indisputable
【置换】 zhìhuàn 〈化〉 displacement; replacement
【置若罔闻】 zhì ruò wǎng wén turn a deaf ear to; pay no heed to: 我多次劝告,他都~。I cautioned him many times but he paid no heed.
【置身】 zhìshēn place oneself; stay: ~事外 stay aloof from the affair; keep out of the business; refuse to be drawn into the matter/ ~于群众之中 place oneself in the midst of the masses
【置信】 zhìxìn 〔多用于否定〕believe: 难以~ hard to believe; unbelievable; incredible
【置疑】 zhìyí 〔多用于否定〕 doubt: 不容~ allow of no doubt; not be open to doubt
【置之不理】 zhì zhī bù lǐ ignore; brush aside; pay no attention to: 对于这种挑衅,我们不能~。 We cannot ignore such provocations.
【置之度外】 zhì zhī dù wài give no thought to; have no regard for: 他为了抢救落水儿童,把个人安危~。 He went to the rescue of a drowning child regardless of his personal safety. 或 He ventured his life to save a child from drowning.
【置之脑后】 zhì zhī nǎo hòu banish from one's mind; ignore and forget
【置之死地而后快】 zhì zhī sǐdì érhòu kuài will be content with nothing less than sb.'s destruction

**雉** zhì pheasant
【雉堞】 zhìdié crenelation
【雉鸠】 zhìjiū turtledove

**稚** zhì young; childish: 幼~ childish
【稚虫】 zhìchóng 〈动〉 naiad
【稚气】 zhìqì childishness
【稚子】 zhìzǐ (innocent) child

**觯** zhì an ancient drinking vessel

**踬** zhì 〈书〉 ① trip; stumble: 颠~ trip over sth. ② suffer a setback: 屡试屡~ fail at each trial

## zhōng

**中** zhōng ① centre; middle: 居~ in the centre/ 冀~ central Hebei ② (Zhōng) China: 洋为~用 make foreign things serve China ③ in; among; amidst: 记在心~ keep in mind/ 跳入水~ jump into the water ④ middle; mid: 月~ in the middle of a month/ ~年 middle age ⑤ medium; intermediate: ~号 medium-sized ⑥ mean; halfway between two extremes: 适~ moderate ⑦ intermediary: 作~ act as an intermediary; be a middleman ⑧ in the process of: 在修建~ being built; under construction/ 发展~国家 developing country/ 历史在斗争~发展,世界在动荡~前进。History develops in struggle and the world advances amidst turbulence. ⑨ fit for; good for: 不~用 good for nothing ⑩ 〈方〉 all right; O.K.: ~不~? Is it all right?/ 这办法~! This way works!
另见 zhòng
【中班】 zhōngbān ① middle shift; swing shift: 上~ be on the middle shift; work the swing shift ② the middle class in a kindergarten
【中板】 zhōngbǎn 〈冶〉 medium plate
【中饱】 zhōngbǎo batten on money entrusted to one's care; line one's pockets with public funds or other people's money; embezzle
【中保】 zhōng-bǎo middleman and guarantor
【中波】 zhōngbō 〈无〉 medium wave
【中不溜儿】 zhōngbùliūr 〈口〉 fair to middling; middling
【中部】 zhōngbù central section; middle part: 根据地~ the central section of the base area/ 在高原~ in the middle part of the plateau
【中餐】 zhōngcān Chinese meal; Chinese food
【中草药】 zhōngcǎoyào Chinese herbal medicine
【中策】 zhōngcè the second best plan
【中层】 zhōngcéng middle-level ◇ ~干部 middle-level cadres
【中产阶级】 zhōngchǎnjiējí middle class; middle bourgeoisie
【中常】 zhōngcháng middling; average: ~年景 average harvest/ 这孩子学习成绩~。The child's work at school is about average.
【中程】 zhōngchéng intermediate range; medium range ◇ ~导弹 intermediate-range missile; medium-range missile/ ~轰炸机 medium bomber
【中垂线】 zhōngchuíxiàn 〈数〉 perpendicular bisector
【中辍】 zhōngchuò stop (doing sth.) halfway; give up halfway
【中词】 zhōngcí 〈逻〉 middle term
【中稻】 zhōngdào semilate rice; middle-season rice
【中等】 zhōngděng ① medium; moderate; middling: ~个儿 of medium height/ ~城市 medium-sized city ② secondary: ~教育 secondary school education/ ~专科学校 technical secondary school; polytechnic school
【中点】 zhōngdiǎn 〈数〉 midpoint
【中东】 Zhōngdōng the Middle East
【中断】 zhōngduàn suspend; break off; discontinue: ~谈判 break off the negotiations (或 talks)/ 两国关系~了好多年。Relations between the two countries were suspended for many years./ 交通~了几小时。Traffic was held up for a few hours.
【中队】 zhōngduì ① 〈军〉 military unit corresponding to a company; squadron: 战斗机~ fighter squadron ② a unit composed of several groups: 交通~ a detachment of traffic police

【中耳】 zhōng'ěr 〈生理〉 auris media; middle ear ◇ ～炎 otitis media
【中饭】 zhōngfàn midday meal; lunch
【中锋】 zhōngfēng ①〈足球〉〈水球〉 centre forward ②〈篮球〉 centre
【中伏】 zhōngfú ① the second of the three ten-day periods of the hot season (sometimes lasting twenty days instead of ten) ② the first day of the second period of the hot season
【中服】 zhōngfú 见"中装"
【中耕】 zhōnggēng 〈农〉 intertill ◇ ～机 cultivator/ ～作物 intertilled crop
【中共】 Zhōng Gòng 〈简〉(中国共产党) the Communist Party of China (CPC)
【中共中央】 Zhōng Gòng Zhōngyāng 〈简〉(中国共产党中央委员会) the Central Committee of the Communist Party of China
◇ ～军事委员会 the Military Commission of the Central Committee of the Chinese Communist Party/ ～全会 Plenary Session of the Central Committee of the CPC/ ～政治局 the Political Bureau of the Central Committee of the Chinese Communist Party
【中古】 zhōnggǔ ① the middle ancient times (in Chinese history, from the 3rd to the 9th century) ② medieval times; Middle Ages ◇ ～史 medieval history
【中国】 Zhōngguó China
◇ ～话 the Chinese language; Chinese/ ～画 traditional Chinese painting/ ～人 Chinese/ ～字 Chinese characters; the Chinese written language
【中国工农红军】 Zhōngguó Gōng-Nóng Hóngjūn the Chinese Workers' and Peasants' Red Army (1928-1937)
【中国工农民主政府】 Zhōngguó Gōng-Nóng Mínzhǔ Zhèngfǔ the Chinese Workers' and Peasants' Democratic Government (of the revolutionary base areas during the Second Revolutionary Civil War, 1927-1937)
【中国共产党】 Zhōngguó Gòngchǎndǎng the Communist Party of China; the Chinese Communist Party
【中国共产主义青年团】 Zhōngguó Gòngchǎnzhǔyì Qīngniántuán the Communist Youth League of China
【中国科学院】 Zhōngguó Kēxuéyuàn the Chinese Academy of Sciences
【中国人民解放军】 Zhōngguó Rénmín Jiěfàngjūn the Chinese People's Liberation Army
【中国人民政治协商会议】 Zhōngguó Rénmín Zhèngzhì Xiéshāng Huìyì the Chinese People's Political Consultative Conference
【中国人民志愿军】 Zhōngguó Rénmín Zhìyuànjūn the Chinese People's Volunteers
【中国社会科学院】 Zhōngguó Shèhuì Kēxuéyuàn the Chinese Academy of Social Sciences
【中国猿人】 Zhōngguó yuánrén 见"北京人" Běijīngrén
【中果皮】 zhōngguǒpí 〈植〉 mesocarp
【中和】 zhōnghé 〈化〉 neutralization ◇ ～剂 neutralizer
【中华】 Zhōnghuá China
【中华民族】 Zhōnghuá Mínzú the Chinese nation
【中华人民共和国】 Zhōnghuá Rénmín Gònghéguó the People's Republic of China ◇ ～国务院 the State Council of the People's Republic of China
【中级】 zhōngjí middle rank; intermediate ◇ ～人民法院 intermediate people's court
【中继】 zhōngjì 〈电〉 relay
◇ ～器 repeater/ ～线 trunk line/ ～站 relay station
【中坚】 zhōngjiān nucleus; hard core; backbone: ～分子 backbone elements/ 干部的～力量 nucleus (或 hard core) of cadres/ 贫农是农民协会的～。The poor peasants were the backbone of the peasant associations.
【中间】 zhōngjiān ① among; between: 生活在人民群众～ live among the masses of the people/ 坐在他们两人～ sit between the two of them/ 她是我们三人～最年轻的。She is the youngest of us three. ② centre; middle: ～突破 make a breakthrough at the centre (或 in the middle)/ 从我家到工厂,～要换车。I have to change buses on the way from home to the factory.
◇ ～剥削 middleman's exploitation/ ～道路 middle road/ ～地带 intermediate zone/ ～分子 middle (或 intermediate) element/ ～阶层 intermediate strata/ ～力量 middle-of-the-road forces; intermediate forces/ ～路线 middle-of-the-road line; middle road/ ～派 middle-of-the-roaders; middle elements; intermediate sections (或 forces)/ ～体〈化〉 intermediate/ ～线 〈机〉 medium line/ ～状态 intermediate state
【中将】 zhōngjiàng 〈军〉(英美陆军,美空军) lieutenant general; (英空军) air marshal; (英美海军) vice admiral
【中焦】 zhōngjiāo 〈中医〉 the part of the body cavity between the diaphragm and the umbilicus housing the spleen, stomach, etc.
【中介】 zhōngjiè intermediary; medium
【中介子】 zhōngjièzǐ 〈物〉 neutretto
【中景】 zhōngjǐng 〈电影〉 medium shot
【中距离】 zhōngjùlí 〈体〉 middle distance ◇ ～赛跑 middle-distance race
【中看】 zhōngkàn be pleasant to the eye: ～不中吃 look nice but not taste nice; be pleasant to the eye but not agreeable to the palate
【中栏】 zhōnglán 〈体〉 intermediate hurdles
【中立】 zhōnglì neutrality: 守～ observe neutrality/ 保持～ remain neutral/ 永久～ permanent neutrality
◇ ～地带 neutral zone/ ～法 law of neutrality; neutrality law/ ～国 neutral state/ ～政策 policy of neutrality/ ～主义 neutralism
【中量级】 zhōngliàngjí 〈举重〉 middleweight
【中林】 zhōnglín 〈林〉 middle forest
【中流】 zhōngliú midstream
【中流砥柱】 zhōngliú dǐzhù firm rock in midstream; mainstay: 共产党领导的武装和民众是抗日战争的～。The armed forces and the people led by the Communist Party were the mainstay in the War of Resistance Against Japan.
【中落】 zhōngluò (of family fortunes) decline; ebb
【中美洲】 Zhōng Měizhōu Central America
【中脑】 zhōngnǎo 〈生理〉 mesencephalon; midbrain
【中年】 zhōngnián middle age ◇ ～人 a middle-aged person
【中农】 zhōngnóng middle peasant
【中篇小说】 zhōngpiān xiǎoshuō medium-length novel; novelette
【中频】 zhōngpín 〈无〉 intermediate frequency
【中气候】 zhōngqìhòu mesoclimate
【中秋节】 Zhōngqiūjié the Mid-autumn Festival (15th day of the 8th lunar month)
【中人】 zhōngrén middleman; go-between; mediator; intermediary
【中沙群岛】 Zhōngshā Qúndǎo the Zhongsha Islands
【中山狼】 zhōngshānláng the Zhongshan wolf in the fable — a person who repays good with evil
【中山装】 zhōngshānzhuāng Chinese tunic suit: 穿着一身灰色～ in gray tunic and trousers
【中生代】 Zhōngshēngdài 〈地〉 Mesozoic Era; Mesozoic
【中石器时代】 zhōng-shíqì shídài Mesolithic Period; Middle Stone Age
【中士】 zhōngshì 〈军〉(英美陆军、英空军) sergeant; (美海军) petty officer second class; (英海军) petty officer first class;

(美空军) staff sergeant
【中世纪】 zhōngshìjì Middle Ages
【中式】 zhōngshì Chinese style: ～服装 Chinese-style clothing
【中式盐】 zhōngshìyán 〈化〉 neutral salt 又作"中性盐"
【中枢】 zhōngshū centre: 领导～ leading centre/ 电讯～ telecommunications centre/ 神经～ nerve centre ◇ ～神经系统 〈生理〉 central nervous system
【中碳钢】 zhōngtàngāng 〈冶〉 medium carbon steel
【中堂】 zhōngtáng ① central scroll (hung in the middle of the wall of the main room) ② a form of address for a Grand Secretary in the Ming and Qing dynasties
【中提琴】 zhōngtíqín viola
【中天】 zhōngtiān 〈天〉 culmination; meridian passage (或 transit)
【中听】 zhōngtīng pleasant to the ear; agreeable to the hearer
【中途】 zhōngtú halfway; midway: ～停留 stop halfway; stop over/ ～下汽车 get off the car midway/ 这趟公共汽车～不停。 This is a nonstop bus./ 他原是学建筑的，～改行搞地质了。 At first he studied architecture, but later he switched to geology./ 开会不要～退场。 Don't leave before the meeting is over. 或 Don't leave when the meeting is in progress.
【中外】 Zhōng-wài China and foreign countries: 驰名～ well known both in China and abroad/ 古今～ both ancient and modern, Chinese and foreign; at all times and in all countries
【中微子】 zhōngwēizǐ 〈物〉 neutrino
【中卫】 zhōngwèi 〈足球〉 centre halfback
【中位数】 zhōngwèishù 〈统计〉 median
【中尉】 zhōngwèi 〈军〉(美陆、空军) first lieutenant; (美海军) lieutenant junior grade; (英陆军) lieutenant; (英海军) sublieutenant; (英空军) flying officer
【中文】 Zhōngwén the Chinese language; Chinese: ～书刊 books and magazines in Chinese
【中午】 zhōngwǔ noon; midday
【中西】 Zhōng-Xī Chinese and Western: ～医结合 combine traditional Chinese and Western medicine
【中线】 zhōngxiàn ① 〈篮球〉〈排球〉 centre line ② 〈足球〉 halfway line ③ 〈数〉 central line
【中校】 zhōngxiào (英美陆军, 美空军) lieutenant colonel; (英美海军) commander; (英空军) wing commander
【中心】 zhōngxīn centre; heart; core; hub: 在广场～ at the centre of the square/ 抓住问题的～ get to the heart of the matter/ 商业(贸易)～ business (trade) centre/ 陆路交通的～ hub of overland communications ◇ ～城市 key city/ ～工作 central task/ ～规 〈机〉 centre gauge/ ～环节 key link; central link/ ～思想 central idea; gist/ ～问题 central issue; crucial question/ ～线 〈机〉 centre line/ ～项 〈哲〉 central term
【中兴】 zhōngxīng resurgence (usu. of a nation)
【中星仪】 zhōngxīngyí 〈天〉 meridian instrument; transit instrument
【中型】 zhōngxíng medium-sized; middle-sized: ～词典 a medium-sized dictionary
【中性】 zhōngxìng ① 〈化〉 neutral: ～反应 neutral reaction/ ～树脂 neutral resin/ ～土〈农〉 neutral soil ② 〈语〉 neuter: ～名词 neuter noun
【中学】 zhōngxué ① middle school: 初(高)级～ junior (senior) middle school ② a late Qing Dynasty term for Chinese traditional learning; Chinese learning ◇ ～生 middle school student
【中旬】 zhōngxún the middle ten days of a month: 四月～ the middle ten days of April
【中央】 zhōngyāng ① centre; middle: 湖的～有一座亭子。 At the centre of the lake, there is a pavilion. ② central authorities (of a state, party, etc.): 党～ the Central Committee of the Party; the Party Central Committee/ 发挥～和地方两个积极性。 Both central and local initiative should be brought into play./ ～和地方企业并举 simultaneous development of national and local enterprises ◇ ～各部门 departments under the Party's Central Committee and the State Council/ ～工作会议 the Central Working Conference/ ～机构 central organs (或 institutions)/ ～领导同志 leading comrades of the central authorities/ ～全会 plenary session of the Central Committee/ ～银行 central bank/ ～直属机关 departments under the Party Central Committee
【中央集权】 zhōngyāng jíquán centralization (of authority): ～的国家 centralized state power/ ～的封建君主制 centralized feudal monarchy
【中央情报局】 Zhōngyāng Qíngbàojú the Central Intelligence Agency (CIA)
【中央条约组织】 Zhōngyāng Tiáoyuē Zǔzhī the Central Treaty Organization (CENTO)
【中药】 zhōngyào traditional Chinese medicine ◇ ～铺 shop (或 store) of traditional Chinese medicines; Chinese pharmacy/ ～学 traditional Chinese pharmacology
【中叶】 zhōngyè middle period: 十九世纪～ the mid-1800s; the middle of the 19th century
【中医】 zhōngyī ① traditional Chinese medical science ② doctor of traditional Chinese medicine; practitioner of Chinese medicine ◇ ～学 traditional Chinese medicine/ ～学院 college of traditional Chinese medicine/ ～研究院 academy of traditional Chinese medicine
【中音号】 zhōngyīnhào 〈乐〉 althorn; alto horn
【中庸】 zhōngyōng ① the golden mean (of the Confucian school): ～之道 the doctrine of the mean ② (Zhōngyōng) *The Doctrine of the Mean* 参见"四书" sìshū
【中用】 zhōngyòng 〔多用于否定〕 of use; useful: 不～ be of no use
【中游】 zhōngyóu ① middle reaches (of a river) ② the state of being middling: 甘居～ be resigned to the middling state; be content to stay middling
【中雨】 zhōngyǔ 〈气〉 moderate rain
【中原】 Zhōngyuán Central Plains (comprising the middle and lower reaches of the Huanghe River)
【中云】 zhōngyún 〈气〉 medium cloud
【中支】 zhōngzhī 〈纺〉 medium-counts ◇ ～纱 medium-count yarn
【中止】 zhōngzhǐ discontinue; suspend; break off: ～谈判 suspend (或 break off) negotiations
【中指】 zhōngzhǐ middle finger
【中注管】 zhōngzhùguǎn 〈冶〉 running-gate
【中专】 zhōngzhuān 〈简〉(中等专科学校) special or technical secondary school; polytechnic school
【中转】 zhōngzhuǎn 〈交〉 change trains ◇ ～站 transfer station
【中装】 zhōngzhuāng traditional Chinese clothing
【中子】 zhōngzǐ 〈物〉 neutron: 快～ fast neutron/ 热～ thermal neutron/ 瞬发～ prompt neutron ◇ ～弹 neutron bomb/ ～物理学 neutronics/ ～源 neutron source

## 忠

zhōng loyal; devoted; honest
【忠臣】 zhōngchén official loyal to his sovereign
【忠诚】 zhōngchéng loyal; faithful; staunch: 对革命无限～

be boundlessly loyal to the revolution/ ～党的教育事业。Be devoted to the Party's educational task./ 我们对人民必须～老实。We must be honest and faithful to the people.
【忠告】 zhōnggào ① sincerely advise; admonish ② sincere advice; advice
【忠厚】 zhōnghòu honest and tolerant; sincere and kindly
【忠实】 zhōngshí true; faithful: ～于无产阶级国际主义 be true to proletarian internationalism/ ～执行毛主席的革命路线 faithfully follow Chairman Mao's revolutionary line/ ～于原文 true (或 faithful) to the original/ ～的信徒 faithful disciple/ ～的走狗 faithful running dog; faithful lackey
【忠顺】 zhōngshùn loyal and obedient: ～的奴仆 willing servant
【忠心】 zhōngxīn loyalty; devotion: 赤胆～ ardent loyalty; wholehearted devotion; utter devotion
【忠心耿耿】 zhōngxīn gěnggěng loyal and devoted; most faithful and true: ～为革命 be loyal and devoted to the revolution; work most faithfully for the revolution
【忠言】 zhōngyán sincere advice; earnest advice
【忠言逆耳】 zhōngyán nì ěr good advice jars on the ear: ～利于行。Honest advice, though unpleasant to the ear, induces good conduct.
【忠于】 zhōngyú true to; loyal to; faithful to; devoted to: ～祖国，～人民 be loyal to one's country and people/ ～职守 be devoted to one's duty
【忠贞】 zhōngzhēn loyal and steadfast: ～不渝 unswerving in one's loyalty/ ～不屈 staunch and indomitable

**终** zhōng ① end; finish: 年～ end of the year/ 自始至～ from beginning to end; from start to finish/ 善始善～ start well and end well; see sth. through ② death; end: 临～ on one's deathbed; just before one dies ③ eventually; after all; in the end: ～非良策。It's not a good plan after all./ 共产主义～将实现。Communism will ultimately be realized. ④ whole; entire; all: ～岁 the whole year; throughout the year/ ～日 all day long; all day
【终场】 zhōngchǎng ① end of a performance or show ② 〈旧〉 final session in an examination
【终点】 zhōngdiǎn ① terminal point; destination: 旅行的～ destination of a journey ② 〈体〉 finish ◇ ～线 〈体〉 finishing line; finishing tape/ ～站 terminus
【终端】 zhōngduān 〈电〉 terminal ◇ ～电缆 terminal cable/ ～局 〈邮〉 terminal station
【终伏】 zhōngfú 见"末伏" mòfú
【终古】 zhōnggǔ 〈书〉 forever
【终归】 zhōngguī eventually; in the end; after all: 要两面派～不会有好下场。Double-dealers will come to no good end./ 他～还是个新手。After all he is still a new hand./ 孩子～是孩子。Children will be children.
【终极】 zhōngjí ultimate: ～目标 ultimate aim
【终结】 zhōngjié end; final stage: 这不是斗争的～，而只是开始。This is just the beginning, not the end, of the struggle.
【终究】 zhōngjiū eventually; in the end; after all: 一个人的力量～有限。The strength of the individual is limited after all./ 你～会明白的。In the end you'll understand.
【终久】 zhōngjiǔ 见"终究"
【终局】 zhōngjú end; outcome: 战争的～ the outcome of a war
【终了】 zhōngliǎo end (of a period): 学期～ the end of the (school) term
【终南捷径】 Zhōngnán jiéjìng ① shortcut to high office; royal road to fame ② shortcut to success
【终年】 zhōngnián ① (all) the year round; throughout the year: ～积雪的高山 mountains perennially covered with snow ② the age at which one dies: 他～七十八岁。He died at the age of seventy-eight.
【终曲】 zhōngqǔ 〈乐〉 finale
【终身】 zhōngshēn lifelong; all one's life: ～伴侣 lifelong companion (referring to one's husband or wife)/ ～事业 one's lifework/ ～大事 an important event in one's life (usu. marriage)
【终审】 zhōngshěn 〈法〉 last instance; final judgment ◇ ～法院 court of last instance
【终生】 zhōngshēng all one's life: 为共产主义奋斗～ struggle for communism all one's life/ ～难忘的教训 a lesson for life
【终霜】 zhōngshuāng 〈气〉 latest frost
【终天】 zhōngtiān all one's life: ～之恨 lifelong regret; eternal regret
【终于】 zhōngyú at (long) last; in the end; finally: 他们～赢得了独立。At long last they won their independence./ 中国登山队～胜利地登上了珠峰。The Chinese mountaineering expedition finally succeeded in scaling Mount Qomolangma.
【终止】 zhōngzhǐ ① stop; end: 要求～这种不正常状态 demand an end to this abnormal state of affairs/ ～日期 closing date ② termination; annulment; abrogation: ～条约通知书 notice of termination of a treaty; notice of denunciation ③ 〈乐〉 cadence

**盅** zhōng handleless cup: 茶～ teacup/ 酒～ winecup

**钟** zhōng ① bell: 撞～ toll (或 ring) a bell ② clock: 电～ electric clock ③ time as measured in hours and minutes: 六点～ six o'clock/ 十分～ ten minutes ④ concentrate (one's affections, etc.) ⑤ handleless cup ⑥ (Zhōng) a surname
【钟爱】 zhōng'ài dote on (a child); cherish
【钟摆】 zhōngbǎi pendulum
【钟表】 zhōngbiǎo clocks and watches; timepiece ◇ ～店 watchmaker's shop/ ～油 watchmaker's oil
【钟点】 zhōngdiǎn 〈口〉 ① a time for sth. to be done or to happen: 到～儿了，我们快走吧！It's time; let's be off. ② hour
【钟鼎文】 zhōngdǐngwén 见"金文" jīnwén
【钟楼】 zhōnglóu ① bell tower; belfry ② clock tower
【钟琴】 zhōngqín 〈乐〉 carillon
【钟情】 zhōngqíng be deeply in love: 一见～ fall in love at first sight
【钟乳石】 zhōngrǔshí 〈地〉 stalactite
【钟头】 zhōngtóu 〈口〉 hour

**衷** zhōng inner feelings; heart: 由～之言 words spoken from the bottom of one's heart
【衷肠】 zhōngcháng 〈书〉 words right from one's heart: 畅叙～ pour out one's heart
【衷情】 zhōngqíng 〈书〉 heartfelt emotion; inner feelings: 久别重逢，互诉～。Meeting again after a long separation, they opened their hearts to each other.
【衷曲】 zhōngqū 〈书〉 heartfelt emotion; inner feelings
【衷心】 zhōngxīn heartfelt; wholehearted; cordial: 表示～的感激 express one's heartfelt gratitude/ ～拥护 give wholehearted support/ 表示～的祝贺 extend cordial greetings/ ～感谢你的帮助。I thank you for your help from the bottom of my heart.

**螽** zhōng

【螽斯】 zhōngsī 〈动〉 katydid; long-horned grasshopper

## zhǒng

**肿** zhǒng swelling; swollen: 我的腿～了。My legs are swollen./ ～消了一点。The swelling has gone down a little.

【肿骨鹿】 zhǒnggǔlù 〈古生物〉 thick-jawed deer

【肿瘤】 zhǒngliú 〈医〉 tumour: 良(恶)性～ benign (malignant) tumour ◇ ～医院 tumour hospital

【肿胀】 zhǒngzhàng ① swelling ②〈中医〉 oedema and abdominal distension

**种** zhǒng ①〈生〉 species: 本地～ endemic species/ 亚～ subspecies/ 外地～ exotic species ② race: 黄～人 the yellow race ③ seed; strain; breed: 麦～ wheat seeds/ 良～牛 good breed of cattle ④ guts; grit: 有～的站出来! Let anyone who has guts step forward! ⑤ kind; sort; type: 各～仪器 all kinds of instruments/ 这～论调 this sort of argument/ 四十～钢材 forty types of rolled steel
另见 zhòng

【种畜】 zhǒngchù 〈牧〉 breeding stock; stud stock

【种肥】 zhǒngféi 〈农〉 seed manure

【种间杂交】 zhǒngjiān zájiāo 〈农〉 interspecific hybridization (或 cross)

【种类】 zhǒnglèi kind; type; variety: 不同～的刀具 cutters of different kinds/ ～繁多 a great variety

【种马】 zhǒngmǎ stud ◇ ～场 stud farm; stud

【种内杂交】 zhǒngnèi zájiāo 〈农〉 intraspecific hybridization (或 cross)

【种牛】 zhǒngniú bull kept for covering

【种姓】 zhǒngxìng caste (of India) ◇ ～制度 caste system

【种种】 zhǒngzhǒng all sorts (或 kinds) of; a variety of: 设置了～障碍 put up all sorts of obstacles/ 由于～原因 for a variety of reasons/ 用～手段 by hook or by crook; resort to every means (或 trick)/ 凡此～,不一而足。Such instances are legion.

【种子】 zhǒngzǐ seed
◇ ～处理 seed treatment/ ～清选机 seed cleaner/ ～田 seed-breeding field/ ～选手〈体〉 seeded player; seed/ ～植物 seed plant

【种族】 zhǒngzú race: ～平等 racial equality/ ～问题实质上是阶级问题。The racial question is in essence a class question.
◇ ～隔离 racial segregation; (南非) apartheid/ ～灭绝 genocide/ ～歧视 racial discrimination/ ～主义 racism; racialism/ ～主义者 racist

**冢** zhǒng tomb; grave: 古～ ancient tomb

**踵** zhǒng 〈书〉 ① heel: 接～ follow on sb.'s heels ② call in person: ～门道谢 call in person to express one's thanks ③ follow close behind

【踵事增华】 zhǒng shì zēng huá 〈书〉 carry on a predecessor's task and make a greater success of it; take over and carry forward

【踵武】 zhǒngwǔ 〈书〉 follow in sb.'s footsteps; imitate; follow suit

## zhòng

**中** zhòng ① hit; fit exactly: 射～靶心 hit the bull's eye/ 击～要害 hit the most vulnerable point; hit home/ 猜～ guess right/ 你说～了。You've hit it. 或 That's right. ② be hit by; fall into; be affected by; suffer: 腿上～了一枪 be shot in the leg/ ～计 be taken in; fall into a trap/ ～埋伏 fall into an ambush/ ～煤气 be gassed
另见 zhōng

【中的】 zhòngdì hit the mark; hit the nail on the head: 批驳有力,语语～。The refutation is forceful and every word hits home.

【中毒】 zhòngdú poisoning; toxicosis: 食物～ food poisoning/ 酒精～ alcoholism/ 煤气～ gas poisoning

【中风】 zhòngfēng apoplexy

【中奖】 zhòngjiǎng draw a prizewinning ticket (或 win a prize) in a lottery; get the winning number in a bond

【中肯】 zhòngkěn ① apropos; pertinent; to the point: ～的评语 pertinent remarks/ 回答简短而～。The reply was brief and to the point./ 作出～的分析 make a sound analysis ②〈物〉 critical ◇ ～质量 critical mass

【中签】 zhòngqiān be the lucky number (in drawing lots, etc.)

【中伤】 zhòngshāng slander; malign; vilify: 造谣～ spread slanderous rumours/ 恶语～ malign sb. viciously

【中暑】 zhòngshǔ ① suffer heatstroke (或 sunstroke); be affected by the heat ② heatstroke; sunstroke

【中选】 zhòngxuǎn be chosen; be selected

【中意】 zhòngyì be to one's liking; catch the fancy of: 这些暖瓶,我一个都不～。None of these thermosflasks is to my liking.

**众** zhòng ① many; numerous: 寡不敌～ be hopelessly outnumbered; fight against hopeless odds ② crowd; multitude: 大～ the multitude; the masses/ 观～ spectators; audience/ 听～ audience; listeners

【众多】 zhòngduō multitudinous; numerous: 我国人口～,地大物博。Our country has a large population, vast territory and abundant resources.

【众寡悬殊】 zhòng-guǎ xuánshū a great disparity in numerical strength

【众口难调】 zhòng kǒu nán tiáo it is difficult to cater for all tastes

【众口铄金】 zhòng kǒu shuò jīn public clamour can confound right and wrong

【众口一词】 zhòng kǒu yī cí with one voice; unanimously

【众目睽睽】 zhòng mù kuíkuí the eyes of the masses are fixed on sb. or sth.: ～之下 in the public eye; in the public gaze

【众目昭彰】 zhòng mù zhāozhāng the masses are sharp-eyed

【众怒难犯】 zhòng nù nán fàn you cannot afford to incur public wrath; it is dangerous to incur the anger of the masses

【众叛亲离】 zhòngpàn-qīnlí the masses are in rebellion and one's friends are deserting; be opposed by the masses and deserted by one's followers; be utterly isolated

【众擎易举】 zhòng qíng yì jǔ many hands make light work

【众人】 zhòngrén everybody: ～拾柴火焰高。When everybody adds fuel the flames rise high.

【众生】 zhòngshēng 〈佛教〉 all living creatures

【众矢之的】 zhòng shǐ zhī dì target of public criticism (或 censure)

【众数】 zhòngshù 〈统计〉 mode

【众说纷纭】 zhòng shuō fēnyún opinions vary: ～,莫衷一是。As opinions vary, no unanimous conclusion can be drawn.

【众所周知】 zhòng suǒ zhōu zhī as everyone knows; as is known to all; it is common knowledge that

【众望】 zhòngwàng people's expectations; popular confidence: 不孚～ fall short of people's expectations/ ～所归 enjoy popular confidence

【众议院】 zhòngyìyuàn (美、澳、日等) House of Representatives; (意、墨、智等) Chamber of Deputies

【众志成城】 zhòng zhì chéng chéng unity of will is an impregnable stronghold; unity is strength

**仲** zhòng ① (of the three months in a season) second: ～春 second month of spring ② (of brothers) second in order of birth: ～兄 the second eldest brother ③ middle; intermediate ④ (Zhòng) a surname

【仲裁】 zhòngcái arbitrate: 对争端进行～ arbitrate a dispute

◇ ～法庭 arbitration tribunal; court of arbitration/ ～人 arbitrator/ ～书 (arbitration) award/ ～协定 arbitration agreement

【仲春】 zhòngchūn second month of spring; the middle of spring

【仲冬】 zhòngdōng second month of winter; midwinter

【仲秋】 zhòngqiū second month of autumn; midautumn

【仲夏】 zhòngxià second month of summer; midsummer

**种** zhòng grow; plant; cultivate: ～水稻 grow rice/ ～庄稼 plant crops/ ～玉米的那六亩地 the six *mu* of land sown to maize/ ～一块试验田 cultivate an experimental plot/ 过去这里的水田多数只～一季，现在全部～两季。Most paddy fields here used to yield only one crop a year, but now they all yield two crops.

另见 zhǒng

【种地】 zhòngdì till (或 cultivate) land; go in for farming

【种痘】 zhòngdòu vaccination (against smallpox): 这孩子～了吗？Has the baby been vaccinated? 又作"种牛痘"

【种瓜得瓜，种豆得豆】 zhòng guā dé guā, zhòng dòu dé dòu plant melons and you get melons, sow beans and you get beans — as you sow, so will you reap

【种花】 zhònghuā ① cultivate (或 grow) flowers ② 〈方〉 vaccination (against smallpox)

【种田】 zhòngtián till the land; farm

【种植】 zhòngzhí plant; grow: 油菜～面积 rape-growing areas; areas sown to rape ◇ ～园 plantation/ ～园主 plantation owner; planter

**重** zhòng ① weight: 举～ weight lifting/ 毛(净)～ gross (net) weight/ 这条鱼有三斤～。This fish weighs three *jin*. ② heavy; weighty; important: 工作很～ have a heavy work load/ ～税 heavy (或 oppressive) taxation/ 以友谊为～ set store by friendship/ 分别轻～ distinguish the trivial from the important/ 话说得太～了。That's putting it too strongly./ 为人民利益而死，就比泰山还～。To die for the people is weightier than Mount Tai. ③ considerable in amount or value: ～赏 a handsome reward/ ～金购买 pay a high price for ④ deep; heavy; serious: 情意～ deep affection/ 私心很～ extremely selfish/ 山东口音很～ have a marked (或 heavy) Shandong accent/ 病～ be seriously ill/ 受了～伤 be severely injured ⑤ lay stress on; attach importance to: ～调查研究 lay stress on investigation and study/ ～男轻女的封建思想 the feudal idea of regarding men as superior to women ⑥ discreet: 自～ self-respect/ 慎～ careful; cautious

另见 chóng

【重办】 zhòngbàn severely punish (a criminal)

【重兵】 zhòngbīng a large number of troops; massive forces: 派驻～ station massive forces/ 有～把守 be heavily guarded

【重创】 zhòngchuāng inflict heavy losses (或 casualties) on; maul (heavily)

【重大】 zhòngdà great; weighty; major; significant: 具有～的现实意义 be of great immediate significance/ ～的原则分歧 a major difference of principle/ ～成就 significant (或 tremendous) achievements/ ～胜利 a signal victory/ ～问题 vital problem; major issue/ ～损失 heavy losses

【重担】 zhòngdàn heavy burden; difficult task: 为革命敢挑～ dare to shoulder heavy burdens for the revolution/ 把～子留给自己 take the difficult tasks for oneself/ 抢挑～rush to shoulder heavy responsibilities

【重地】 zhòngdì important place (usually not open to the public): 施工～，闲人免进。Construction Site. No Admittance.

【重点】 zhòngdiǎn focal point; stress; emphasis: 突出～ make the focal (或 key) points stand out/ ～工程 major (或 priority) project/ ～高等院校 key institutes of higher learning/ ～单位和企业 key units and enterprises/ ～进攻 attacks against key sectors/ 工作～ focal point of the work/ 把医疗卫生工作的～放到农村去。In medical and health work, put the stress on the rural areas./ 今天～讨论技术革新问题。Our discussion today will centre on technical innovation. 或 We'll focus our discussion today on technical innovation./ 两霸争夺遍及世界，～在欧洲。The contention between the two hegemonist powers reaches every corner of the globe, but the cockpit is Europe.

【重读】 zhòngdú 〈语〉 stress: ～音节 stressed syllable/ 非～音节 unstressed syllable

【重负】 zhòngfù heavy burden; heavy load: 如释～ feel as if relieved of a heavy load

【重工业】 zhònggōngyè heavy industry

【重过磷酸钙】 zhòngguòlínsuāngài 〈农〉 double superphosphate

【重轰炸机】 zhònghōngzhàjī heavy bomber

【重活】 zhònghuó heavy work

【重机关枪】 zhòngjīguānqiāng heavy machine gun

【重价】 zhòngjià high price: ～收购古物 offer high prices for antiques

【重金属】 zhòngjīnshǔ 〈化〉 heavy metal

【重晶石】 zhòngjīngshí 〈矿〉 barite; heavy spar

【重力】 zhònglì 〈物〉 gravity; gravitational force

◇ ～坝 〈水〉 gravity dam/ ～场 gravitational field/ ～秤 gravity balance/ ～加速度 acceleration of gravity/ ～水 〈水〉 gravitational water; free water/ ～选矿 〈矿〉 gravity separation (或 concentration)/ ～仪 gravity meter; gravimeter/ ～异常 gravity anomaly

【重利】 zhònglì ① high interest: ～盘剥 practise usury ② huge profit

【重量】 zhòngliàng weight ◇ ～单 weight list (或 memo)/ ～证明书 weight certificate; surveyor's report on weight

【重量级】 zhòngliàngjí 〈举重〉 heavyweight

【重炮】 zhòngpào heavy artillery; heavy artillery piece; heavy gun

【重切削】 zhòngqiēxiāo 〈机〉 heavy cut

【重氢】 zhòngqīng 〈化〉 heavy hydrogen; deuterium

【重任】 zhòngrèn important task; heavy responsibility: 身负～ be charged with important tasks

【重商主义】 zhòngshāngzhǔyì mercantilism

【重视】 zhòngshì attach importance to; pay attention to; think highly of; take sth. seriously; value: ～对妇女干部的培养 devote much attention to the training of women cadres/ ～这件事 take the matter seriously/ ～群众的发明创造 set great store by the creative efforts of the masses/ ～基础理论的研究工作 pay great attention to basic theoretical research/ 全党一定要～农业。The whole Party should attach great importance to agriculture.

【重水】 zhòngshuǐ 〈化〉 heavy water
【重听】 zhòngtīng hard of hearing
【重托】 zhòngtuō great trust: 不辜负贫下中农对我们的～ justify the great trust placed in us by the poor and lower-middle peasants
【重武器】 zhòngwǔqì heavy weapons
【重心】 zhòngxīn ①〈物〉 centre of gravity ② heart; core; focus: 问题的～ the heart of a matter
【重型】 zhòngxíng heavy-duty; heavy ◇ ～机床 heavy-duty machine tool/ ～卡车 heavy-duty truck; heavy truck
【重要】 zhòngyào important; significant; major: ～人物 important figure; prominent personage; VIP/ ～关头 critical juncture/ ～任务 vital task; important mission/ ～原则 cardinal principle/ ～政策 major policy/ ～因素 key factor ◇ ～性 importance; significance
【重音】 zhòngyīn ①〈语〉 stress; accent: 句子～ sentence stress/ 单词～ word stress ②〈乐〉 accent ◇ ～符号 stress mark; accent
【重用】 zhòngyòng put sb. in an important position
【重油】 zhòngyóu heavy oil
【重元素】 zhòngyuánsù 〈化〉 heavy element
【重镇】 zhòngzhèn place of strategic importance

## zhōu

**州** zhōu ①〈旧〉 an administrative division ② (autonomous) prefecture

**舟** zhōu 〈书〉 boat: 轻～ a light boat/ 泛～ go boating
【舟车】 zhōuchē 〈书〉 ① vessel and vehicle ② journey: ～劳顿 fatigued by a long journey; travel-worn
【舟楫】 zhōují 〈书〉 vessels: 江河湖泽给我们以～和灌溉之利。Rivers and lakes provide us with water transport and irrigation.
【舟子】 zhōuzǐ 〈书〉 boatman

**诌** zhōu fabricate (tales, etc.); make up: 别胡～了。Stop making up wild stories.

**周** zhōu ① circumference; periphery; circuit: 圆～ circumference (of a circle)/ 运动员绕场一～。The athletes made a circuit of the arena./ 在村子四～植树 plant trees round the village ② make a circuit; move in a circular course ③ all; whole; all over; all around: 众所～知 as is known to all/ ～身 the whole body ④ thoughtful; attentive: 丁宁～至 give thoughtful advice/ 计划不～ not well planned; not planned carefully enough/ 招待不～ not be attentive enough to guests ⑤ week: 上～ last week ⑥〈电〉 cycle: 千～ kilocycle/ 兆～ megacycle ⑦ help out (the needy); relieve ⑧ (Zhōu) the Zhou Dynasty (c. 11th century — 256 B.C.) ⑨ (Zhōu) a surname
【周报】 zhōubào weekly publication; weekly
【周边】 zhōubiān 〈机〉 periphery
【周遍】 zhōubiàn all round; all over
【周波】 zhōubō 〈电〉 cycle
【周长】 zhōucháng girth; circumference; perimeter: ～五米的烟筒 a funnel five metres in girth/ 水库的～ the perimeter of a reservoir/ 湖的～十二公里。The lake is 12 kilometres in circumference.
【周到】 zhōudao attentive and satisfactory; thoughtful; considerate: 服务～ offer good service/ 想得很～ be very thoughtful (或 considerate)/ 安排得很～ be satisfactorily arranged; be carefully worked out
【周而复始】 zhōu ér fù shǐ go round and begin again; go round and round; move in cycles
【周济】 zhōujì help out (the needy); relieve
【周刊】 zhōukān weekly publication (或 magazine); weekly
【周密】 zhōumì careful; thorough: ～思考 think over carefully/ 进行～的调查 carry out a thorough investigation/ ～的分析 a detailed analysis/ ～的计划 a well-conceived plan
【周末】 zhōumò weekend
【周年】 zhōunián anniversary: 建厂十五～ the 15th anniversary of the founding of the factory/ 一百～ centenary
【周期】 zhōuqī period; cycle: 工作～〈机〉 action cycle ◇ ～表〈化〉 periodic table/ ～律〈化〉 periodic law
【周期性】 zhōuqīxìng periodicity; cyclicity: ～循环 periodic return/ ～经济危机 periodic (或 cyclical) economic crises/ 疟疾～发作 periodic attacks of malaria
【周全】 zhōuquán ① thorough; comprehensive ②〈旧〉 help sb. attain his aim
【周身】 zhōushēn the whole body; all over the body: ～疼痛 ache all over
【周岁】 zhōusuì one full year of life: 今天孩子满～。Today is the child's first birthday./ 他三十二～。He is thirty-two years old.
【周围】 zhōuwéi around; round; about: 关心～的群众 have concern for the people around one/ 团结在党的～ rally round the Party/ 环顾～ look about; look around/ ～环境 surroundings; environment ◇ ～神经系统〈生理〉 peripheral nervous system/ ～温度〈机〉 environment (或 ambient) temperature
【周详】 zhōuxiáng comprehensive; complete; careful: 考虑～ give careful consideration to
【周旋】 zhōuxuán ① mix with other people; socialize: ～于达官贵人之间 move in high society ② deal with; contend with: 游击队长期在山区和侵略者～。For a long time, the guerrillas fought the invaders in hilly country.
【周延】 zhōuyán 〈逻〉 distribution
【周游】 zhōuyóu travel round; journey round: ～世界 travel round the world/ ～各国 travel to many countries; travel far and wide
【周章】 zhōuzhāng 〈书〉 ① be scared: 狼狈～ be scared out of one's wits; be panic-stricken ② trouble; effort: 煞费～ take great pains; spare no effort
【周折】 zhōuzhé twists and turns; setbacks: 这事恐怕要费一番～。I'm afraid this business will cause us a good deal of bother./ 几经～，才告成功。Only after many setbacks was success achieved.
【周转】 zhōuzhuǎn ①〈经〉 turnover: 加速资本～ speed up capital turnover ② have enough to meet the need: 义务劳动的学生很多，土筐～不开。We have many students here to do volunteer labour, but there aren't enough carrying baskets to go round. ◇ ～率 turnover rate/ ～资金 working fund; revolving fund; circulating fund

**洲** zhōu ① continent ② islet in a river; sand bar
【洲际】 zhōujì intercontinental ◇ ～弹道导弹 intercontinental ballistic missile/ ～导弹 intercontinental missile

**啁** zhōu
另见 zhāo
【啁啾】 zhōujiū 〈书〉〈象〉 (of birds) twitter; chirp; warble

**粥** zhōu gruel (made of rice, millet, etc.); porridge; congee: 小米～ millet gruel
【粥少僧多】 zhōu shǎo sēng duō the gruel is meagre and the monks are many — not enough to go round

## zhóu

**妯** zhóu
【妯娌】 zhóuli wives of brothers; sisters-in-law

**轴** zhóu ① axle; shaft: 车～ car axle; axle/ 曲～ crank shaft/ 心～ spindle ② axis: 地～ the earth's axis/ 椭圆的长(短)～ the major (minor) axis of an ellipse ③ spool; rod: 线～儿 spool (for thread)/ 画～ roller for a scroll of Chinese painting ④〈量〉: 一～线 a spool of thread/ 一～山水画 a scroll painting of scenery
另见 zhòu
【轴衬】 zhóuchèn 〈机〉axle bush
【轴承】 zhóuchéng 〈机〉bearing: 滚珠～ ball bearing ◇～衬 bearing bush/ ～钢 bearing steel
【轴对称】 zhóuduìchèn 〈数〉axial symmetry
【轴距】 zhóujù wheelbase (of a vehicle)
【轴流泵】 zhóuliúbèng axial-flow pump; axial pump
【轴套】 zhóutào 〈机〉axle sleeve
【轴线】 zhóuxiàn ①〈机〉axis: 垂直～ normal axis ② spool thread; spool cotton
【轴向】 zhóuxiàng 〈机〉axial ◇～剖面 axial section/ ～运动 axial motion
【轴心】 zhóuxīn ①〈机〉axle centre ② axis ◇～国 Axis powers; the Axis

**碡** zhóu 见"碌碡" liùzhou

## zhǒu

**肘** zhǒu elbow
【肘接】 zhǒujiē 〈机〉toggle (或 elbow) joint
【肘节】 zhǒujié 〈机〉toggle: 制动～ brake toggle
【肘子】 zhǒuzi ① upper part of a leg of pork ② elbow

**帚** zhǒu broom

## zhòu

**纣** Zhòu name of the last ruler of the Shang Dynasty (c. 16th — 11th century B.C.), reputedly a tyrant

**宙** zhòu time (conceived as past, present and future)
参见"宇宙" yǔzhòu

**绉** zhòu crape; crepe: 派力斯～ palace crepe
【绉布】 zhòubù cotton crepe; crepe
【绉纱】 zhòushā crape

**咒** zhòu ① incantation: 念～ chant incantations ② curse; damn: 诅～ curse
【咒骂】 zhòumà curse; swear; abuse; revile
【咒语】 zhòuyǔ incantation

**胄** zhòu ① helmet: 甲～ armour and helmet ② descendants; offspring: 贵～ descendants of feudal rulers or aristocrats

**昼** zhòu daytime; daylight; day: ～伏夜出 hide by day and come out at night
【昼出动物】 zhòuchū dòngwù diurnal animal
【昼夜】 zhòu-yè day and night; round the clock: ～看守 keep watch round the clock/ ～警戒 be on a round-the-clock alert/ 他们英勇地战斗了七～。They battled heroically for seven days and nights.

**轴** zhòu 见"压轴子" yāzhòuzi
另见 zhóu

**皱** zhòu wrinkle; crease: 这种料子不起～。This material won't crease./ 注意别把地图弄～了。Mind you don't crumple the map.
【皱眉头】 zhòu méitóu knit (或 contract) one's brows; frown
【皱胃】 zhòuwèi 〈动〉abomasum
【皱纹】 zhòuwén wrinkles; lines: 满脸～ have a wrinkly face/ 眼角的～ crow's-feet
◇～法兰绒 crepe flannel/ ～革 shrink leather/ ～纸 crepe paper
【皱褶】 zhòuzhě fold

**骤** zhòu ① (of a horse) trot: 驰～ gallop ② sudden; abrupt: 一阵～雨 a passing heavy shower/ 天气～变。There was a sudden change of weather./ 狂风～起。A sudden gale struck.
【骤然】 zhòurán suddenly; abruptly: ～离去 leave abruptly/ ～响起雷鸣般的掌声。Stormy applause broke forth suddenly.

**籀** zhòu 〈书〉① read aloud; recite ② 见"籀文"
【籀文】 zhòuwén a style of calligraphy, current in the Zhou Dynasty (c. 11th century — 256 B.C.)

## zhū

**朱** zhū ① vermilion; bright red ② cinnabar ③ (Zhū) a surname
【朱笔】 zhūbǐ writing brush dipped in red ink (formerly used in marking students' papers or writing comments on official documents)
【朱顶雀】 zhūdǐngquè redpoll (linnet)
【朱红】 zhūhóng vermilion; bright red
【朱鹭】 zhūlù (crested) ibis
【朱门】 zhūmén vermilion gates — red-lacquered doors of wealthy homes: ～酒肉臭,路有冻死骨。Behind the vermilion gates meat and wine go to waste while out on the road lie the bones of those frozen to death.
【朱墨】 zhūmò ① red and black: ～套印 printed in red and black ② ink made of cinnabar
【朱批】 zhūpī comments or remarks written in red with a brush
【朱漆】 zhūqī red paint; red lacquer: ～大门 vermilion gates/ ～木箱 red-lacquered chest
【朱雀】 zhūquè rosefinch
【朱砂】 zhūshā cinnabar
【朱文】 zhūwén characters on a seal carved in relief

**诛** zhū 〈书〉① put (a criminal) to death: 伏～ be executed/ ～锄异己 wipe out dissenters ② punish: 卖国贼人人得而～之。Everybody has the right to punish traitors.
【诛戮】 zhūlù 〈书〉kill; put to death
【诛求无已】 zhūqiú wú yǐ make endless exorbitant demands
【诛心之论】 zhūxīn zhī lùn penetrating criticism; exposure of sb.'s ulterior motives

**侏** zhū 〈书〉dwarf

【侏罗纪】 Zhūluójì 〈地〉 Jurassic Period
【侏儒】 zhūrú dwarf; midget; pygmy

**茱** zhū

【茱萸】 zhūyú 见"山茱萸" shānzhūyú; "食茱萸" shízhūyú

**珠** zhū ① pearl: 明～ bright pearl; jewel ② bead: 露～ beads of dew; dewdrops/ 算盘～ beads on an abacus/ 泪～儿 teardrop
【珠宝】 zhūbǎo pearls and jewels; jewelry ◇ ～店 a jeweller's (shop)/ ～商 jeweller
【珠翠】 zhūcuì pearls and jade; ornaments made with pearls and jade
【珠光体】 zhūguāngtǐ 〈冶〉 pearlite
【珠玑】 zhūjī 〈书〉 pearl; gem: 字字～ each word a gem
【珠江】 Zhūjiāng the Zhujiang River; the Pearl River
【珠兰】 zhūlán *zhulan* tree
【珠联璧合】 zhūlián-bìhé strings of pearls and girdles of jade — a perfect pair; a happy combination
【珠穆朗玛峰】 Zhūmùlǎngmǎfēng Mount Qomolangma
【珠算】 zhūsuàn reckoning by the abacus; calculation with an abacus
【珠圆玉润】 zhūyuán-yùrùn round as pearls and smooth as jade — excellent singing or polished writing
【珠子】 zhūzi ① pearl ② bead

**株** zhū ① trunk of a tree; stem of a plant ② individual plant; plant: 幼～ young plant; sapling ③〈量〉: 两～梨树 two pear trees
【株距】 zhūjù 〈农〉 spacing in the rows
【株连】 zhūlián involve (others) in a criminal case; implicate
【株守】 zhūshǒu hold on stubbornly to (a silly idea, etc.) 参见"守株待兔" shǒu zhū dài tù

**诸** zhū ① all; various: 编辑部～同志 all the comrades of the editorial department/ 自然科学～部门 the various branches of natural science ②〈书〉〔"之于"或"之乎"的合音〕: 付～实施 put into practice; bring into effect/ 有～? Is there (such a thing)? ③ (Zhū) a surname
【诸多】 zhūduō 〈书〉〔用于抽象事物〕a good deal; a lot of: ～不便 a lot of trouble; great inconvenience
【诸葛】 Zhūgé a surname
【诸葛亮】 Zhūgé Liàng ① Zhuge Liang, a statesman and strategist in the period of the Three Kingdoms (220-265), who became a symbol of resourcefulness and wisdom in Chinese folklore ② a person of great wisdom and resourcefulness; mastermind
【诸葛亮会】 zhūgéliànghuì a meeting of Zhuge Liangs — a meeting to pool the wisdom of the collective
【诸侯】 zhūhóu dukes or princes under an emperor
【诸如】 zhūrú such as
【诸如此类】 zhūrú cǐ lèi things like that; such; and so on and so forth: ～, 不胜枚举。Such instances are too numerous to mention./ ～的科学发明，都大大提高了劳动生产率。Scientific inventions such as these have raised labour productivity by a big margin.
【诸位】 zhūwèi 〈敬〉〔总称所指的若干人〕: ～有什么意见，欢迎提出来。You are welcome to put forward your views./ ～女士，～先生! Ladies and Gentlemen!
【诸子百家】 zhūzǐ bǎijiā the various schools of thought and their exponents during the period from pre-Qin times to the early years of the Han Dynasty

**猪** zhū pig; hog; swine: 小～ pigling; piglet/ 母～ sow/ 公～ boar
【猪草】 zhūcǎo greenfeed for pigs
【猪场】 zhūchǎng pig farm; piggery
【猪丹毒】 zhūdāndú swine erysipelas; diamond-skin disease
【猪肝】 zhūgān pork liver
【猪倌】 zhūguān swineherd
【猪獾】 zhūhuān sand badger
【猪圈】 zhūjuàn pigsty; pigpen; hogpen
【猪苓】 zhūlíng 〈中药〉 umbellate pore fungus (*Polyporus umbellata*)
【猪笼草】 zhūlóngcǎo 〈植〉 common nepenthes (*Nepenthes mirabilis*)
【猪猡】 zhūluó 〈方〉 pig; swine
【猪苗】 zhūmiáo piglet; pigling
【猪囊虫病】 zhūnángchóngbìng pork measles
【猪排】 zhūpái pork chop
【猪皮】 zhūpí pigskin; hogskin
【猪气喘病】 zhūqìchuǎnbìng swine enzootic pneumonia
【猪肉】 zhūròu pork
【猪舍】 zhūshè pig (或 hog) house
【猪食】 zhūshí pig feed; pigwash; swill ◇ ～缸 (pig) trough
【猪瘟】 zhūwēn swine fever; hog cholera
【猪油】 zhūyóu lard
【猪鬃】 zhūzōng (hog) bristles

**铢** zhū an ancient unit of weight, equal to 1/24 *liang* (两)
【铢积寸累】 zhūjī-cùnlěi accumulate little by little; build up bit by bit
【铢两悉称】 zhū-liǎng xī chèn exactly equal in weight; have the same weight

**蛛** zhū spider
【蛛丝马迹】 zhūsī-mǎjī thread of a spider and trail of a horse — clues; traces
【蛛网】 zhūwǎng spider web; cobweb
【蛛形动物】 zhūxíng dòngwù arachnid
【蛛蛛】 zhūzhu spider

**潴** zhū 〈书〉 ① (of water) collect; accumulate; store ② puddle; pool
【潴留】 zhūliú 〈医〉 retention: 尿～ retention of urine

## zhú

**术** zhú 见"白术" báizhú; "苍术" cāngzhú
另见 shù

**竹** zhú bamboo: ～篓 bamboo crate (或 basket)/ ～林 bamboo forest; groves of bamboo
【竹板】 zhúbǎn bamboo clappers
【竹帛】 zhúbó bamboo slips and silk (used for writing on during ancient times); ancient books
【竹筴鱼】 zhúcèyú saurel; horse mackerel
【竹蛏】 zhúchēng 〈动〉 razor clam; razor shell
【竹竿】 zhúgān bamboo pole; bamboo
【竹黄】 zhúhuáng handicraft articles made from bamboo with its green covering removed ◇ ～菌〈中药〉 bamboo parasitic fungus
【竹鸡】 zhújī bamboo partridge
【竹简】 zhújiǎn bamboo slip (used for writing on during ancient times)
【竹节虫】 zhújiéchóng stick insect; walkingstick
【竹节钢筋】 zhújié gāngjīn corrugated bar

【竹刻】 zhúkè bamboo carving; bamboo engraving
【竹篮打水一场空】 zhúlán dǎshuǐ yīchángkōng draw water with a bamboo basket — all in vain
【竹帘画】 zhúliánhuà 〈工美〉 painting on a bamboo curtain
【竹马】 zhúmǎ a bamboo stick used as a toy horse
【竹排】 zhúpái bamboo raft
【竹器】 zhúqì articles made of bamboo
【竹鼠】 zhúshǔ bamboo rat
【竹笋】 zhúsǔn bamboo shoots
【竹叶青】 zhúyèqīng ① green bamboo snake ② bamboo-leaf-green liqueur, a pale green *Fen* (汾) liquor or a light yellow *Shaoxing* (绍兴) wine
【竹芋】 zhúyù 〈植〉 arrowroot
【竹枝词】 zhúzhīcí ① ancient folk songs with love as their main theme ② occasional poems in the classical style devoted to local topics
【竹纸】 zhúzhǐ paper made from young bamboo
【竹子】 zhúzi bamboo

**竺** Zhú a surname

**烛** zhú ① candle: 蜡～ (wax) candle/ ～心 candlewick ② 〈书〉 illuminate; light up: 火光～天。Leaping flames lit up the sky. ③ watt: 二十五～灯泡 a 25-watt bulb
【烛光】 zhúguāng 〈物〉 candlepower; candle
【烛花】 zhúhuā snuff: 剪～ trim off the snuff (of a candle); snuff
【烛台】 zhútái candlestick
【烛照】 zhúzhào 〈书〉 illuminate; light up

**逐** zhú ① pursue; chase: 追～ pursue; chase/ ～水草而居 move from place to place in search of water and grass ② drive out; expel: ～出门外 drive out of the door ③ one by one: ～项 item by item/ ～月 month by month/ ～条加以说明 explain point by point
【逐步】 zhúbù step by step; progressively: ～加以解决 settle sth. step by step/ ～降低生产成本 progressively reduce the production cost
【逐个】 zhúgè one by one: 我们得～研究这些问题。We must look into these matters one by one.
【逐渐】 zhújiàn gradually; by degrees: 他对情况～熟悉起来了。He's gradually getting better acquainted with the situation./ 天～暗下来了。It's getting darker and darker.
【逐客令】 zhúkèlìng order for guests to leave: 下～ show sb. the door
【逐鹿】 zhúlù 〈书〉 chase the deer — fight for the throne; bid for state power: ～中原 fight among rivals for the throne/ 群雄～ feudal lords vying for the throne; powerful politicians fighting for supremacy
【逐年】 zhúnián year by year; year after year: 产量～增加。Production has been increasing year after year.
【逐日】 zhúrì day by day; every day: 病情～好转。The patient's condition is improving day by day.
【逐水】 zhúshuǐ 〈中医〉 relieve oedema or abdominal distension through diuresis or purgation
【逐一】 zhúyī one by one: 对这些规定～加以说明 explain all these provisions one by one
【逐字】 zhúzì word for word; verbatim: ～记录 verbatim record
【逐字逐句】 zhú zì zhú jù word by word and sentence by sentence; word for word: ～地宣读文件 read the document word by word and sentence by sentence/ ～的翻译 word-for-word (或 literal) translation

**筑** Zhú another name for Guiyang
另见 zhù

**舳** zhú stern (of a ship, etc.)
【舳舻】 zhúlú 〈书〉 a convoy of ships, stem touching stern

**蠋** zhú larva of a butterfly or moth

**躅** zhú 〈书〉 footprint; footmark

## zhǔ

**主** zhǔ ① host: 宾～ host and guest ② owner; master: 奴隶～ slave owner/ 企业～ proprietor of an enterprise/ 当家作～ be master in one's own house ③ person or party concerned: 买～ buyer/ 卖～ seller ④ 〈基督教〉 God; Lord ⑤ 〈伊斯兰教〉 Allah ⑥ main; primary: ～航道 main (或 principal) channel/ 预防为～ put prevention first ⑦ manage; direct; be in charge of: ～其事 be in charge of the business; manage the affairs ⑧ indicate; signify: 早霞～雨,晚霞～晴。Rosy morning clouds indicate rain, and a rosy sunset means fine weather. ⑨ hold a definite view about sth.; advocate: ～和 advocate peace; be for a peaceful settlement/ 我一时心里没～。For a moment I just didn't know what to do.
【主办】 zhǔbàn direct; sponsor: 展览会将由外贸部～。The exhibition will be sponsored by (或 held under the auspices of) the Ministry of Foreign Trade.
【主笔】 zhǔbǐ 〈旧〉 ① editor in chief ② chief commentator
【主编】 zhǔbiān ① chief editor (或 compiler); editor in chief ② supervise the publication of (a newspaper, magazine, etc.); edit
【主宾席】 zhǔbīnxí head table (at a banquet, etc.); seat for the guest of honour
【主持】 zhǔchí ① take charge (或 care) of; manage; direct: ～日常事务 take care of routine matters/ ～县委工作 be in charge of the county Party committee ② preside over; chair: ～讨论 chair a discussion/ ～今晚的宴会 host this evening's banquet/ 会议由汪书记～。Secretary Wang presided over the meeting. ③ uphold; stand for: ～正义 uphold justice
【主词】 zhǔcí 〈逻〉 subject term; subject
【主次】 zhǔ-cì primary and secondary: 我们干工作要分清～。In our work we must differentiate what is primary from what is secondary.
【主从】 zhǔ-cóng principal and subordinate: ～关系 the relationship between the principal and the subordinate
【主导】 zhǔdǎo leading; dominant; guiding: 起～作用 play a leading role/ 工业是国民经济的～。Industry is the leading factor in the national economy./ 新中国建立以来,毛主席的革命路线在各条战线上始终占～地位。Chairman Mao's revolutionary line has held sway on all fronts since the founding of New China.
◇ ～风 〈建〉 prevailing wind/ ～思想 dominant ideas; guiding ideology/ ～主题 〈乐〉 *leitmotiv*
【主调音乐】 zhǔdiào yīnyuè homophony
【主动】 zhǔdòng ① initiative: 争取～ try to gain the initiative; contend for the initiative/ ～帮助人 help others of one's own accord/ 我们应～派人去支援。We ought to send people to help on our own initiative. ② 〈机〉 driving
◇ ～齿轮 driving gear/ ～轴 driving shaft; driving spindle
【主动脉】 zhǔdòngmài 〈生理〉 aorta ◇ ～弓 arch of aorta/ ～炎 aortitis
【主队】 zhǔduì 〈体〉 home team; host team

【主发动机】 zhǔfādòngjī 〈宇航〉 sustainer
【主伐】 zhǔfá 〈林〉 final felling (或 cutting)
【主犯】 zhǔfàn 〈法〉 prime culprit; principal criminal (或 offender); principal: ～和从犯 principal and accessories in a crime
【主峰】 zhǔfēng the highest peak in a mountain range
【主妇】 zhǔfù housewife; hostess
【主干】 zhǔgàn ①〈植〉 trunk ② main force; mainstay
【主根】 zhǔgēn 〈植〉 main root; taproot
【主攻】 zhǔgōng 〈军〉 main attack
◇ ～部队 main attack force/ ～方面 main phase of attack/ ～方向 main direction of attack
【主顾】 zhǔgù customer; client
【主观】 zhǔguān subjective: ～努力 subjective efforts/ ～愿望 subjective desire; wishful thinking/ ～地对待问题 a subjective approach to problems/ 在改造客观世界的同时改造～世界 transform one's subjective world while transforming the objective world
◇ ～能动性 〈哲〉 subjective initiative; conscious activity/ ～唯心主义 〈哲〉 subjective idealism/ ～主义 subjectivism
【主管】 zhǔguǎn ① be responsible for; be in charge of: 谁～这项工作？ Who is in charge of this job? ② person in charge ◇ ～部门 department responsible for the work/ ～机关 competent authorities; responsible institution
【主婚】 zhǔhūn (usu. of the parents of the bride and the bridegroom) preside over a wedding ceremony
【主机】 zhǔjī ①〈机〉 main engine ②〈军〉 lead plane; leader
【主祭】 zhǔjì officiate at funeral or sacrificial rites
【主见】 zhǔjiàn ideas or thoughts of one's own; one's own judgment; definite view: 没有～ have no definite views of one's own/ 她这人很有～。She knows her own mind.
【主讲】 zhǔjiǎng be the speaker; give a lecture
【主将】 zhǔjiàng chief commander; commanding general
【主教】 zhǔjiào 〈宗〉 bishop: 大～ archbishop/ 红衣～ cardinal
【主井】 zhǔjǐng 〈矿〉 main shaft
【主句】 zhǔjù 〈语〉 main (或 principal) clause
【主角】 zhǔjué leading role; lead; protagonist: 在该片中演～ play the lead in the film/ 女～ a leading lady
【主考】 zhǔkǎo ① be in charge of an examination ② chief examiner (in a school, etc.)
【主课】 zhǔkè main subject; major course
【主力】 zhǔlì main force; main strength of an army
◇ ～兵团 main formations/ ～队员 〈体〉 top players of a team/ ～舰 capital ship
【主力军】 zhǔlìjūn main (或 principal) force
【主梁】 zhǔliáng 〈建〉 girder
【主粮】 zhǔliáng staple food grain
【主流】 zhǔliú ① main stream; main current; mother current ② essential or main aspect; main trend: ～和支流 principal and secondary aspects
【主麻】 zhǔmá 〈伊斯兰教〉 Djumah (Friday)
【主谋】 zhǔmóu ① head a conspiracy; be the chief plotter ②〈法〉 chief instigator
【主脑】 zhǔnǎo ① control centre; centre of operation ② leader; chief
【主权】 zhǔquán sovereign rights; sovereignty: 领土～ territorial sovereignty ◇ ～国家 a sovereign state
【主人】 zhǔrén ① master: 在我国社会主义制度下，人民是国家的～。Under our socialist system, the people are the masters of the country. ② host: 女～ hostess ③ owner: 房子的～ owner of the house
【主人公】 zhǔréngōng leading character in a novel, etc.; hero or heroine; protagonist
【主人翁】 zhǔrénwēng ① master: 新社会的～ masters of the new society/ 有一种～感 have a sense of being the master of one's own affairs ② 见"主人公"
【主任】 zhǔrèn director; head; chairman: 总政治部～ Director of the General Political Department/ 居民委员会～ head of the neighbourhood committee/ 革委会～ chairman of the revolutionary committee/ 国家计划委员会～ Minister in charge of the State Planning Commission
【主食】 zhǔshí staple food; principal food
【主使】 zhǔshǐ instigate; incite; abet
【主题】 zhǔtí theme; subject; motif; *leitmotiv*: 诗的～ the subject of a poem/ 作品的～思想 the theme of a literary work ◇ ～歌 〈电影〉 theme song
【主体】 zhǔtǐ ① main body; main part; principal part: 以贫农为～的农会 peasant associations with the poor peasants as their main body/ 一支以青年为～的突击队 a shock force composed mainly of young people ②〈哲〉 subject: ～和客体 subject and object; the perceiver and the world
◇ ～工程 principal part of a project
【主谓词组】 zhǔ-wèi cízǔ 〈语〉 subject-predicate word group
【主谓句】 zhǔ-wèijù 〈语〉 subject-predicate sentence
【主文】 zhǔwén 〈法〉 main body of a court verdict
【主席】 zhǔxí ① chairman (of a meeting): 当～ be in the chair; preside over a meeting② chairman or president (of an organization or a state) ◇ ～台 rostrum; platform/ ～团 presidium
【主心骨】 zhǔxīngǔ ① backbone; mainstay; pillar: 他是我们队里的～。He is the mainstay of our team. ② definite view; one's own judgment: 他这个人没有～。 He has no judgment of his own.
【主星】 zhǔxīng 〈天〉 primary (component) ◇ ～序 main sequence
【主刑】 zhǔxíng 〈法〉 principal penalty
【主修】 zhǔxiū ① specialize (in a subject); major: 她～原子物理。She majors in atomic physics. ② be responsible for the repair or overhaul (of a machine): 王师傅～这台磨床。Master Worker Wang is responsible for the overhaul of this grinder. ◇ ～科目 major subjects
【主演】 zhǔyǎn act the leading role (in a play or film)
【主要】 zhǔyào main; chief; principal; major: ～敌人 chief enemy/ ～矛盾 principal contradiction/ ～目的 major objective/ ～因素 primary factor/ ～农作物 staple crops/ 会议～讨论了两个问题。The conference dealt mainly with two questions.
【主义】 zhǔyì doctrine; -ism: 唯物～ materialism/ 达尔文～ Darwinism/ 个人～ individualism/ 资本～ capitalism
【主意】 zhǔyì ① idea; plan: 好～ a good idea ② decision; definite view: 打定～ make a decision; make up one's mind/ 改变～ change one's mind/ 拿不定～ be in two minds (about sth.)/ 我一时没了～。I was quite at a loss, then.
【主音】 zhǔyīn 〈乐〉 keynote; tonic
【主语】 zhǔyǔ 〈语〉 subject
【主宰】 zhǔzǎi dominate; dictate; decide: ～自己的命运 decide one's own destiny; be master of one's own fate/ 帝国主义～世界的时代已经一去不复返了。Gone forever are the days when imperialism could dominate the world.
【主张】 zhǔzhāng ① advocate; stand for; maintain; hold: ～自力更生 advocate self-reliance/ ～改革 favour reforms/ 我们～文艺为工农兵服务。We maintain that literature and art should serve the workers, peasants and soldiers. ② view; position; stand; proposition: 这是我们一贯的～。That has been our consistent stand./ 听起来两种～都有理由。Both propositions sound reasonable.
【主旨】 zhǔzhǐ purport; substance; gist: 文章的～ the gist

of the article
【主治医生】 zhǔzhì yīshēng physician-in-charge; doctor in charge of a case
【主轴】 zhǔzhóu 〈机〉 main shaft; spindle ◇ ～箱 spindle box
【主子】 zhǔzi master; boss: ～和奴才 the boss and his flunkey; master and servant

**拄** zhǔ lean on (a stick, etc.): ～着拐棍走 walk with a stick

**渚** zhǔ 〈书〉 small piece of land surrounded by water; islet: 江～ islet in a river

**属** zhǔ 〈书〉 ① join; combine: ～文 compose a piece of prose writing/ 前后相～ (of two parts) join together ② fix (one's mind) on; centre (one's attention, etc.) upon: ～望 centre one's hope on; look forward to
另见 shǔ
【属意】 zhǔyì 〈书〉 fix one's mind on sb. (as one's choice, favourite, etc.)
【属垣有耳】 zhǔ yuán yǒu ěr walls have ears; someone has his ear to the wall

**煮** zhǔ boil; cook: ～鸡蛋 boil eggs/ ～饭 cook rice
【煮豆燃萁】 zhǔ dòu rán qí burn beanstalks to cook beans — fratricidal strife
【煮呢】 zhǔní 〈纺〉 potting

**嘱** zhǔ enjoin; advise; urge
【嘱咐】 zhǔfu enjoin; tell; exhort: 再三～ exhort again and again; din sth. into sb./ ～他保守秘密 enjoin him to secrecy/ 临终～ death-bed injunction/ 大夫～他好好休息。The doctor told him to take a good rest.
【嘱托】 zhǔtuō entrust: 她～我办这件事。She entrusted me with the task.

**瞩** zhǔ gaze; look steadily: 高瞻远～ stand high and see far; take a broad and long-term view; show great foresight
【瞩目】 zhǔmù 〈书〉 fix one's eyes upon; focus one's attention upon: 举世～ be the focus of world attention
【瞩望】 zhǔwàng 〈书〉 ① look forward to: ～已久 have been eagerly looking forward to it for a long time ② gaze at; look long and steadily upon

## zhù

**伫** zhù 〈书〉 stand for a long while
【伫候】 zhùhòu 〈书〉 stand waiting: ～佳音 look forward to hearing good news from you
【伫立】 zhùlì 〈书〉 stand still for a long while

**苎** zhù
【苎麻】 zhùmá 〈植〉 ramie

**助** zhù help; assist; aid: 互～ help each other/ ～消化 aid digestion/ ～一臂之力 lend sb. a helping hand/ ～人为乐 find it a pleasure to help others
【助爆药】 zhùbàoyào 〈军〉 booster charge; booster
【助产士】 zhùchǎnshì 〈医〉 midwife
【助词】 zhùcí 〈语〉 auxiliary word, an unstressed form word which performs the grammatical functions of structure (as 的,地,得,所), of tense (as 了,着,过) or of mood (as 呢,吗,吧,啊)
【助动词】 zhùdòngcí 〈语〉 auxiliary verb
【助攻】 zhùgōng 〈军〉 holding (或 secondary) attack ◇ ～部队 holding element
【助剂】 zhùjì 〈纺〉 auxiliary
【助教】 zhùjiào assistant (of a college faculty)
【助桀为虐】 zhù Jié wéi nüè aid King Jie in his tyrannical rule; help a tyrant to do evil
【助理】 zhùlǐ assistant: 部长～ assistant minister
【助跑】 zhùpǎo 〈体〉 run-up; approach
【助燃】 zhùrán 〈化〉 combustion-supporting ◇ ～气体 combustion-supporting gas
【助熔剂】 zhùróngjì flux
【助色团】 zhùsètuán 〈化〉 auxochrome
【助手】 zhùshǒu assistant; helper; aide
【助听器】 zhùtīngqì audiphone; hearing aid; deaf-aid
【助推级】 zhùtuījí 〈宇航〉 booster
【助威】 zhùwēi boost the morale of; cheer (for): 给我们的篮球队～ cheer for our basketball team
【助兴】 zhùxìng liven things up; add to the fun
【助学金】 zhùxuéjīn stipend; grant-in-aid: 领～的学生 a grant-aided student
【助战】 zhùzhàn ① assist in fighting ② bolster sb.'s morale
【助长】 zhùzhǎng 〈贬〉 encourage; abet; foster; foment: ～侵略者的野心 whet the ambitions of the aggressors/ ～歪风邪气 encourage the evil trends
【助纣为虐】 zhù Zhòu wéi nüè aid King Zhou in his tyrannical rule; help a tyrant to do evil

**住** zhù ① live; reside; stay: ～城外 live outside the city/ ～旅馆 stay at a hotel/ ～上新房 move into a new house ② stop; cease: 雨～了。The rain has stopped. ③〔做动词的补语,表示牢固、稳当、停顿、静止等〕: 站～! Halt!/ 愣～了 be struck dumb; be left speechless/ 支持不～ cannot withstand/ 扣～一封信 stop a letter/ 记～ bear in mind; remember
【住持】 zhùchí 〈宗〉 (Buddhist or Taoist) abbot
【住处】 zhùchù residence; dwelling (place); lodging; quarters: 找到～没有? Have you found accommodation?/ 我不知道他的～。I don't know where he lives.
【住房】 zhùfáng housing; lodgings: ～问题 the housing problem; accommodation
【住户】 zhùhù household; resident: 院内有三家～。There are three households in the compound./ 这儿有姓马的～吗? Is there anyone named Ma living here?
【住家】 zhùjiā (of one's family) live; reside in: 他在郊区～。He lives with his family in the suburbs.
【住口】 zhùkǒu shut up; stop talking: 你给我～! Hold your tongue!
【住手】 zhùshǒu stay one's hand; stop: 他不做完不肯～。He won't stop until he finishes the job.
【住宿】 zhùsù stay; put up; get accommodation: 他今晚在旅店～。He will put up at an inn for the night./ 给客人安排～ find lodgings (或 arrange accommodation) for the visitors/ 大学生大部分在校～。Most college students are boarders.
【住所】 zhùsuǒ dwelling place; residence; domicile: 固定～ permanent dwelling place; domicile
【住院】 zhùyuàn be in hospital; be hospitalized: ～期间 during one's hospitalization; while in hospital ◇ ～病人 inpatient/ ～部 inpatient department/ ～处 admission office/ ～费 hospitalization expenses/ ～医生 resident (physician)
【住宅】 zhùzhái residence; dwelling ◇ ～区 residential quarters (或 district)

【住址】 zhùzhǐ address

**注** zhù ① pour: 大雨如～。The rain poured down. ② concentrate; fix: 全神贯～ concentrate on; be engrossed in; be preoccupied with ③ stakes (in gambling): 孤～一掷 stake everything on a single throw ④ annotate; explain with notes: 批～ provide critical and explanatory notes for; annotate ⑤ notes: 附～ annotations/ 脚～ footnote ⑥ record; register

【注册】 zhùcè register ◇ ～处 registration office; registrar's office/ ～商标 registered trademark

【注带】 zhùdài 〈纺〉 casting

【注定】 zhùdìng be doomed; be destined: ～要失败 be doomed to failure/ 命中～ decreed by fate; predestined

【注脚】 zhùjiǎo footnote

【注解】 zhùjiě ① annotate; explain with notes ② (explanatory) note; annotation

【注明】 zhùmíng give clear indication of: ～出处 give sources (of quotations, etc.)/ 该表未～日期。That form is undated.

【注目】 zhùmù gaze at; fix one's eyes on: 引人～ spectacular/ 行～礼 salute with eyes

【注入】 zhùrù pour into; empty into: 长江～东海。The Changjiang River empties into the East China Sea./ ～式教学法 the spoon-feeding way of teaching; cramming ◇ ～井〈石油〉 injection well

【注射】 zhùshè 〈医〉 inject: 肌肉(皮下，静脉)～ intramuscular (hypodermic, intravenous) injection/ 往静脉里～葡萄糖 inject glucose into the veins/ 给病人～青霉素 give the patient an injection of penicillin ◇ ～器 injector; (医用) syringe/ ～针头 syringe needle

【注视】 zhùshì look attentively at; gaze at: 久久～着陌生人的脸 look fixedly at the stranger's face for a long time/ 密切～会议的进展 closely follow the progress of the conference/ 雷达兵目不转睛地～着荧光屏。The radarman's eyes were glued to the screen.

【注释】 zhùshì explanatory note; annotation ◇ ～读物 annotated readings

【注疏】 zhùshū 〈书〉 notes and commentaries

【注水】 zhùshuǐ 〈石油〉 water flooding: 边缘～ edgewater flooding/ ～动态 flood performance

【注销】 zhùxiāo cancel; write off: 把借条～ cancel a written acknowledgment of a loan; cancel an I.O.U./ 账已～。The account has been written off.

【注意】 zhùyì pay attention to; take note (或 notice) of: ～工作方法 pay attention to methods of work/ 必须～团结一切可以团结的人。Care must be taken to unite with all those that can be united with./ 我没～他什么时候走的。I didn't notice when he left./ ～,马上就要点炮啦！Look out! We're ready to blast./ ～别摔倒。Mind you don't fall. ◇ ～广度 〈心〉 attention span; range of attention/ ～力 attention/ ～事项 matters needing attention; points for attention

【注音】 zhùyīn 〈语〉 phonetic notation: 课文有～吗？Is the text marked with phonetic symbols?

【注音字母】 zhùyīn zìmǔ the national phonetic alphabet (in use before the publication of the Scheme for the Chinese Phonetic Alphabet) 又作"注音符号"

【注油】 zhùyóu (润滑油) oiling; (润滑脂) greasing; (燃油) fuel-injection ◇ ～枪 grease gun; oil gun

【注重】 zhùzhòng lay stress on; pay attention to; attach importance to: ～基本功的训练 lay stress on basic training

**杼** zhu ① 〈纺〉 reed ② shuttle

**贮** zhù store; save; lay aside: ～蓄 save up/ ～粮备荒 store grain against a lean year

【贮备】 zhùbèi store up; have in reserve; lay aside

【贮藏】 zhùcáng store up; lay in: ～过冬的大白菜 lay in cabbages for the winter/ 这一带地下～着丰富的矿产。This place is rich in mineral deposits.

【贮存】 zhùcún store; keep in storage ◇ ～期 storage time

【贮木场】 zhùmùchǎng timber depot; timber yard; lumber yard

**驻** zhù ① halt; stay: ～足 make a temporary stay/ 敌～我扰。When the enemy halts, we harass him. ② be stationed: 一连～在黄村。The First Company is stationed at Huangcun Village./ 我国～英大使 our ambassador to Britain/ 中国～埃及大使馆 Chinese Embassy in Egypt/ ～京记者 resident correspondent in Beijing

【驻跸】 zhùbì 〈书〉 (of a monarch on a tour) stay temporarily; stop over; put up

【驻地】 zhùdì ① place where troops, etc. are stationed: 边防军～ frontier guard station/ 地质勘探队的～ encampment of a geological prospecting team ② seat (of a local administrative organ)

【驻防】 zhùfáng be on garrison duty; garrison: ～福州 garrison Fuzhou ◇ ～部队 garrison (troops)

【驻节公使】 zhùjié gōngshǐ 〈外〉 minister resident

【驻守】 zhùshǒu garrison; defend: ～山海关 garrison the Shanhaiguan Pass

【驻屯】 zhùtún (of troops) be stationed; be quartered

【驻在国】 zhùzàiguó 〈外〉 state to which a diplomatic envoy is accredited

【驻扎】 zhùzhá (of troops) be stationed; be quartered: ～重兵 station a huge force

**炷** zhù 〈书〉 ① wick (of an oil lamp) ② burn: ～香 burn a joss stick ③ 〈量〉: 一～香 a burning joss stick

**祝** zhù ① express good wishes; wish: ～你健康。I wish you the best of health./ ～你旅途愉快。Have a pleasant journey. 或 *Bon voyage*!/ ～我们两国人民的友谊万古长青！May the friendship between our two peoples be everlasting! ② (Zhù) a surname

【祝词】 zhùcí ① congratulatory speech (at a ceremony, etc.); congratulations ② prayers at sacrificial rites in ancient times

【祝福】 zhùfú ① blessing; benediction ② new year's sacrifice (an old custom in certain parts of Zhejiang Province)

【祝贺】 zhùhè congratulate: ～演出成功 congratulate the artists on their successful performance/ 向你～！Congratulations!/ ～两国建交 acclaim the establishment of diplomatic relations between the two countries/ 致以兄弟般的～ extend fraternal greetings

【祝捷】 zhùjié celebrate a victory ◇ ～大会 victory celebration (meeting)

【祝酒】 zhùjiǔ drink a toast; toast: 向来宾们～ toast the guests/ 致～辞 propose a toast/ 答谢～ respond (或 reply) to a toast

【祝寿】 zhùshòu congratulate (an elderly person) on his or her birthday

【祝颂】 zhùsòng express good wishes

【祝愿】 zhùyuàn wish: 致以良好的～ with best wishes/ ～贵国日益繁荣昌盛。We wish your country ever growing prosperity.

**柱** zhù ① post; upright; pillar; column: 门～ doorposts/ 房～ pillars of a house; upright/ 圆～ column ② sth.

shaped like a column:水～ water column/ 水银～ mercury column ③〈数〉cylinder
【柱顶】 zhùdǐng 〈建〉capital
【柱廊】 zhùláng 〈建〉colonnade
【柱面】 zhùmiàn 〈数〉cylinder: 椭圆～ elliptic cylinder
【柱身】 zhùshēn 〈建〉shaft
【柱石】 zhùshí pillar; mainstay: 中国人民解放军是无产阶级专政的～。The Chinese People's Liberation Army is the pillar of the dictatorship of the proletariat.
【柱头】 zhùtóu ①〈植〉stigma ②〈建〉column cap; column head ③〈方〉post; pillar
【柱状剖面】 zhùzhuàng pōumiàn 〈地〉columnar section; geologic column
【柱子】 zhùzi post; pillar
【柱座】 zhùzuò 〈建〉column base

## 疰 zhù

【疰夏】 zhùxià 〈中医〉a summer disease, usu. contracted by children with symptoms of fever, loss of appetite, lassitude, etc.

## 著

zhù ① marked; outstanding: 卓～ outstanding; distinguished/ 臭名昭～ notorious ② show; prove: 颇～成效 prove rather effective ③ write: ～书 write books/ ～录 put down in writing; record ④ book; work: 名～ a celebrated piece of writing; a famous work/ 新～ sb.'s latest work/ 译～ a translation
【著称】 zhùchēng 〈书〉celebrated; famous: 以风景优美～ be celebrated for its scenic beauty
【著名】 zhùmíng famous; celebrated; well-known: ～论断 a celebrated (或 well-known) thesis/ 李时珍是明代～的药物学家。Li Shizhen was a famous pharmacologist of the Ming Dynasty.
【著述】 zhùshù ① write; compile: 从事～ be engaged in writing or compiling scholarly works ② book
【著者】 zhùzhě author; writer
【著作】 zhùzuò ① work; book; writings: 古代医学～ ancient books on medicine; ancient medical literature ② write: 他一生～甚多。He wrote many books during his lifetime. 或 He was a prolific author. ◇ ～权 copyright

## 蛀

zhù ① moth or any other insect that eats books, clothes, wood, etc. ② (of moths, etc.) eat; bore through: 这件呢大衣给虫子～了。This woollen coat is moth-eaten.
【蛀齿】 zhùchǐ decayed tooth; dental caries
【蛀虫】 zhùchóng insect that eats books, clothes or wood; moth; borer
【蛀心虫】 zhùxīnchóng borer

## 筑

zhù build; construct: ～路 construct a road/ ～堤 build a dyke
另见 Zhú
【筑埂机】 zhùgěngjī 〈农〉ridger
【筑室道谋】 zhù shì dào móu ask every passerby how to build one's house — have no idea or plan of one's own and accomplish nothing

## 铸

zhù casting; founding: ～钟 cast a bell/ ～钱 coin (或 mint) money/ ～成大错 make a gross error
【铸币】 zhùbì coin; specie ◇ ～权 mintage
【铸锭】 zhùdìng 〈冶〉ingot casting
【铸钢】 zhùgāng 〈冶〉cast steel
【铸工】 zhùgōng 〈冶〉① foundry work ② foundry worker; founder ◇ ～车间 foundry (shop)/ ～鼓风机 foundry fan
【铸件】 zhùjiàn 〈冶〉cast; casting: 干砂～ dry sand casting/ 压～ die casting/ 冷硬～ chill (或 chilled) casting
【铸铁】 zhùtiě ① iron casting ② cast iron: 球墨～ nodular cast iron
【铸型】 zhùxíng casting mould
【铸造】 zhùzào casting; founding: 无砂～ sandless casting/ 蜡模～ investment casting; lost wax casting ◇ ～车间 foundry; casting shop
【铸字】 zhùzì 〈印〉typefounding; typecasting ◇ ～工场 typefoundry/ ～工人 typefounder/ ～机 typecasting machine

## 翥 zhù 〈书〉(of birds) fly; soar

## 箸 zhù chopsticks

# zhuā

## 抓

zhuā ① grab; seize; clutch: ～权 grab power/ ～机会 seize an opportunity/ 他～起帽子就往外走。He snatched up his cap and made for the door. ② scratch: ～痒痒 scratch an itch/ 猫把孩子的手～了。The cat scratched the child's hand. ③ arrest; catch; press-gang: ～特务 catch an enemy agent/ ～壮丁 press-gang able-bodied men ④ stress; pay special attention to: ～重点 stress the essentials/ ～思想问题 pay special attention to ideological problems/ ～苗头 watch out for the first signs ⑤ take charge of; be responsible for: 他是～工会工作的。He is in charge of trade union work.
【抓辫子】 zhuā biànzi seize on sb.'s mistake or shortcoming; capitalize on sb.'s vulnerable point
【抓膘】 zhuābiāo fatten (pigs, cattle, etc.)
【抓差】 zhuāchāi draft sb. for a particular task; press sb. into service
【抓点】 zhuādiǎn concentrate on work at selected units: ～带面 draw experience from selected units to promote overall work
【抓斗】 zhuādǒu grab bucket; grab: 双瓣式～ two-jaw grab
【抓耳挠腮】 zhuā'ěr-náosāi tweak one's ears and scratch one's cheeks (as a sign of anxiety or delight); scratch one's head
【抓纲治国】 zhuā gāng zhì guó grasp the key link of class struggle and bring about great order across the land; grasp the key link in running the country
【抓革命,促生产】 zhuā gémìng, cù shēngchǎn grasp revolution, promote production
【抓工夫】 zhuā gōngfu make good use of one's time; find time (to do sth.)
【抓紧】 zhuājǐn firmly grasp; pay close attention to: ～学习 attend to one's studies in earnest; study hard/ ～时机 seize the opportunity/ ～时间 make the best use of one's time/ 抓而不紧,等于不抓。Not to grasp firmly is not to grasp at all./ 必须把粮食～,必须把棉花～,必须把布匹～。We must pay close attention to grain, cotton and cotton cloth.
【抓阄儿】 zhuājiūr draw lots
【抓举】 zhuājǔ 〈举重〉snatch
【抓两头,带中间】 zhuā liǎngtóu, dài zhōngjiān grasp the two ends to bring along the middle — sustain the advanced and help the backward so as to encourage the vast majority to move along
【抓瞎】 zhuāxiā 〈口〉find oneself at a loss; be in a rush and muddle; be thrown off balance
【抓岩机】 zhuāyánjī 〈矿〉grab loader; grab
【抓药】 zhuāyào ① make up (或 fill) a prescription of Chinese

herbal medicine ② have a prescription of Chinese herbal medicine made up (或 filled)

【抓住】 zhuāzhù ① catch (或 seize) hold of; grip: ～她的胳膊 catch hold of her arm/ ～一点小事做文章 seize on a trifle and make an issue of it; make a fuss about something trivial ② catch; capture: ～个小偷 catch a thief ③ grip sb.'s attention: 这出戏一开场就～了观众。The play gripped the attention of the audience from the moment the curtain rose.

## zhuǎ

**爪** zhuǎ claw; talon
另见 zhǎo

【爪尖儿】 zhuǎjiānr pig's trotters; pettitoes

【爪儿】 zhuǎr 〈口〉 ① paw of a small animal ② foot of a utensil: 三～锅 a pan standing on three feet

【爪子】 zhuǎzi 〈口〉 claw; paw; talon: 猫～ a cat's paws/ 鹰～ an eagle's talons

## zhuāi

**拽** zhuāi 〈方〉 fling; throw; hurl: 把皮球～出去 fling the ball out
另见 zhuài

## zhuǎi

**踹** zhuǎi 〈方〉 waddle

## zhuài

**拽** zhuài 〈方〉 pull; drag; haul: 生拉硬～ drag sb. along against his will/ 一把～住不放 catch hold of sb. or sth. and not let go
另见 zhuāi

## zhuān

**专** zhuān ① for a particular person, occasion, purpose, etc.; focussed on one thing; special: 心不～ not concentrate (on any one thing)/ ～车 special train or car/ 奎宁～治疟疾。Quinine is a specific for malaria./ 他～找重活干。He made a point of picking the heaviest jobs for himself. ② expert: 又红又～ be both red and expert; be both politically conscious and professionally competent ③ monopolize: ～权 monopolize power

【专案】 zhuān'àn special case for investigation; case: 这件事应成立～。This should be made a special case for investigation.
◇ ～材料 material connected with a case; dossier/ ～人员 those engaged in the examination of a case/ ～组 special group for the examination of a case

【专差】 zhuānchāi special mission (或errand): 他～去北京。He went to Beijing on a special mission.

【专长】 zhuāncháng speciality; special skill or knowledge: 学有～ have specialized knowledge of a subject; be expert in a special field of study/ 制图是她的～。Cartography is her speciality.

【专场】 zhuānchǎng special performance; show intended for a limited audience

【专诚】 zhuānchéng for a particular purpose; specially: ～拜访 pay a special visit to sb.

【专程】 zhuānchéng special trip: ～赴广州迎接贵宾 make a special trip to Guangzhou to welcome the honoured guests

【专电】 zhuāndiàn special dispatch (或 telegram)

【专断】 zhuānduàn make an arbitrary decision; act arbitrarily

【专攻】 zhuāngōng specialize in: 他～空间技术。He specializes in space technology.

【专号】 zhuānhào special issue (of a periodical)

【专横】 zhuānhèng imperious; peremptory; domineering: ～跋扈 imperious and despotic

【专机】 zhuānjī ① special plane ② private plane

【专家】 zhuānjiā expert; specialist: 水稻～ expert in rice-growing/ 眼科～ ophthalmologist; eye specialist

【专刊】 zhuānkān ① special issue or column ② monograph

【专科学校】 zhuānkē xuéxiào college for professional training; training school

【专款】 zhuānkuǎn special fund: ～专用 earmark a fund for its specified purpose only

【专栏】 zhuānlán special column: 书评～ book review column ◇ ～作家 columnist

【专利】 zhuānlì patent ◇ ～品 patent; patented article/ ～权 patent right; patent

【专卖】 zhuānmài monopoly; exclusive possession of the trade in some commodity

【专门】 zhuānmén special; specialized: ～研究化学 specialize in chemistry/ ～为儿童写的故事 stories specially written for children/ 今后你就～搞会计工作好了。From now on you'll concentrate on accounting alone.
◇ ～机构 special agency; special organ/ ～人材 people with professional skill/ ～人民法院 special people's court/ ～术语 technical terms; nomenclature/ ～知识 specialized knowledge; expertise; technical know-how

【专名】 zhuānmíng 〈语〉 proper noun

【专区】 zhuānqū prefecture; subprovincial administrative region

【专人】 zhuānrén person specially assigned for a task or job: 这项工作一定要有～负责。Someone must be put in charge of the work./ 这个文件是～送来的。The document was brought by a special messenger.

【专任】 zhuānrèn full-time; regular: ～教员 full-time teacher

【专擅】 zhuānshàn 〈书〉 usurp authority; act without authorization from one's superior

【专使】 zhuānshǐ special envoy

【专属经济区】 zhuānshǔ jīngjìqū exclusive economic zone

【专属渔区】 zhuānshǔ yúqū exclusive fishing zone

【专署】 zhuānshǔ prefectural commissioner's office

【专题】 zhuāntí special subject; special topic
◇ ～报告 report (或 lecture) on a special topic/ ～调查 investigation of a special subject/ ～讨论 seminar/ ～研究 monographic study/ ～著作 monograph

【专线】 zhuānxiàn ① special railway line ② special telephone line; line for special use

【专心】 zhuānxīn concentrate one's attention; be absorbed: ～致志 wholly absorbed; with single-hearted devotion/ 学习必须～。Study requires undivided attention.

【专修】 zhuānxiū specialize in: ～数学 specialize in mathematics ◇ ～科 special (training) course

【专业】 zhuānyè ① special field of study; specialized subject; speciality; discipline: 这个系有八个～。This department offers eight specialities. ② specialized trade or profession; special line: ～生产会议 a conference on specialized trades
◇ ～队伍 professional contingent/ ～课 specialized course/ ～人员 personnel in a specific field/ ～学校 vocational

school/ ～知识 professional knowledge
【专业化】 zhuānyèhuà specialization: 广泛实行～协作 carry out extensive coordination among specialized departments
【专一】 zhuānyī single-minded; concentrated: 心思～ with concentrated attention/ 爱情～ be constant in love
【专用】 zhuānyòng for a special purpose: ～车床 special-purpose lathe/ ～电话 telephone for special use
【专员】 zhuānyuán ① assistant director; (administrative) commissioner: 礼宾司～ an assistant director of the Protocol Department/ 商务～ commercial attaché ② person specially assigned for a job
【专责】 zhuānzé specific responsibility: 分工明确,各有～。The division of labour is clear-cut, each one being charged with specific responsibilities.
【专政】 zhuānzhèng dictatorship
◇ ～对象 object (或 target) of dictatorship/ ～工具 instrument of dictatorship/ ～机关 organ of dictatorship
【专职】 zhuānzhí ① sole duty; specific duty ② full-time: 他是工会的～干部。He is a full-time cadre of the trade union.
【专制】 zhuānzhì ① autocracy ② autocratic; despotic: ～帝王 autocratic monarch; despotic emperor/ 君主～ autocratic (或 absolute) monarchy
◇ ～君主 autocrat/ ～政府 autocratic government/ ～政体 autocracy
【专注】 zhuānzhù concentrate one's attention on; be absorbed in; devote one's mind to
【专著】 zhuānzhù monograph; treatise

**砖** zhuān brick: 砌～ lay bricks/ ～房 brick house/ ～墙 brick wall
【砖茶】 zhuānchá brick tea
【砖厂】 zhuānchǎng brickfield; brickyard
【砖红壤】 zhuānhóngrǎng laterite
【砖红壤性土】 zhuānhóngrǎngxìngtǔ lateritic soil
【砖坯】 zhuānpī unfired brick
【砖头】 zhuāntóu fragment of a brick
【砖头】 zhuāntou 〈方〉 brick
【砖窑】 zhuānyáo brickkiln

## zhuǎn

**转** zhuǎn ① turn; shift; change: 好～ take a turn for the better/ ～败为胜 turn defeat into victory/ ～弱为强 transform (或 grow) from weak to strong/ 晴～多云 change from fine to cloudy/ 她～过头来和我说话。She spoke to me over her shoulder. ② pass on; transfer: 这封信请你～给他。Please pass the letter on to him./ 把她的邮件～寄到她的新地址 forward her mail to her new address/ ～党的组织关系 transfer the registration of one's Party membership from one unit to another
另见 zhuàn
【转变】 zhuǎnbiàn change; transform: ～立场 change one's stand; shift one's ground/ 世界观的～ change in one's world outlook/ 把一种能～为另一种能 transform one form of energy into another/ 经过尖锐的思想斗争,他～了。Intense mental struggle has brought about a change in him.
【转播】 zhuǎnbō relay (a radio or TV broadcast) ◇ ～台 relay station
【转车】 zhuǎnchē change trains or buses; transfer to another train or bus
【转船】 zhuǎnchuán change to another ship; transship
【转达】 zhuǎndá pass on; convey; communicate: 请向他～我的问候。Please give him my regards.
【转道】 zhuǎndào make a detour; go by way of
【转调】 zhuǎndiào 〈乐〉 modulation
【转动】 zhuǎndòng turn; move; turn round: ～手腕子 flex one's wrist/ ～门把手 turn the door knob/ 水龙头转不动。The tap's stuck.
另见 zhuàndòng
【转发】 zhuǎnfā transmit: 此件～全国。This document is to be transmitted throughout the country.
【转法】 zhuǎnfǎ 〈军〉 facing
【转告】 zhuǎngào pass on (word); communicate; transmit: 他把这消息～了他的姐姐。He passed on the news to his sister.
【转化】 zhuǎnhuà 〈哲〉 change; transform: 向反面～ transform oneself into one's opposite; change into the reverse
【转圜】 zhuǎnhuán ① save (a situation) ② mediate
【转换】 zhuǎnhuàn change; transform: ～方向 change direction/ ～话题 change the subject of conversation; switch the conversation to another subject ◇ ～开关 change-over switch
【转机】 zhuǎnjī a favourable turn; a turn for the better: 他的病有了～。The patient has taken a turn for the better. 或 His condition is improving.
【转嫁】 zhuǎnjià ① (of women) marry again; remarry ② shift; transfer: 把责任～给他人 shift off one's responsibility; put the blame on someone else/ 向别国～金融危机 shift a financial crisis on to other countries
【转交】 zhuǎnjiāo pass on; transmit: 请把这个包裹～给王同志。Please pass this parcel on to Comrade Wang./ 来信请由中国大使馆～。Address my mail care of (或 c/o) the Chinese Embassy.
【转角】 zhuǎnjiǎo street corner; corner
【转口】 zhuǎnkǒu transit ◇～货物 transit goods/ ～贸易 *entrepôt* trade
【转脸】 zhuǎnliǎn ① turn one's face ② in no time; in the twinkling of an eye: 他刚才还在这儿,怎么～就不见了？He was here just now. How come he disappeared in a wink?
【转捩点】 zhuǎnlièdiǎn turning point
【转卖】 zhuǎnmài resell
【转年】 zhuǎnnián ① the coming year; next year ② 〈方〉 the following year
【转念】 zhuǎnniàn reconsider and give up an idea; think better of: 他刚想开口,但一～,又不说了。He was just going to speak when he thought better of it.
【转让】 zhuǎnràng transfer the possession of; make over
【转入】 zhuǎnrù change over to; shift to; switch to: ～敌后 go into the enemy's rear/ ～地下 go underground/ ～正常 return to normal/ ～下一个项目 move on to the next item/ 由进攻～防御 switch (或 shift) from the offensive to the defensive
【转身】 zhuǎnshēn (of a person) turn round; face about
【转生】 zhuǎnshēng 〈佛教〉 reincarnation; transmigration
【转手】 zhuǎnshǒu ① pass on: 你就直接交给他,不必要我～了。Give it directly to him; there is no need to do it through me. ② sell what one has bought
【转述】 zhuǎnshù report; relate sth. as told by another: 我只是～他的话。I am merely reporting what he said.
【转瞬】 zhuǎnshùn in a twinkle; in a flash
【转送】 zhuǎnsòng ① pass on; transmit on ② make a present of what one has been given
【转体】 zhuǎntǐ 〈体〉 turn; twist ◇ ～跳 turning leap/ ～跳水 twist dive
【转托】 zhuǎntuō ask someone else to do what is asked of one: 你让我办的事,我已～老张了。I've asked Lao Zhang to take care of the matter you spoke to me about.
【转弯】 zhuǎnwān turn a corner; make a turn: 邮局一～儿就是。The post office is just round (或 right around) the

corner./ 来一个一百八十度的大～ make a 180-degree turn; do an about-face/ 他是个直性子,说话从来不会～儿。He's straightforward; he never minces his words./ 右～走!(横队) Right wheel! (纵队) Right turn march! 或 Column right march!/ 给他们一个～的余地 give them some leeway

【转弯抹角】 zhuǎnwān-mòjiǎo ① full of twists and turns: 我们～地走了好一会才找到那个地方。We had to take a tortuous route before we got to the place./ 这条路～的,可难走了。This road is full of twists and turns, which makes the going hard. ② beat about the bush; speak in a roundabout way

【转危为安】 zhuǎn wēi wéi ān take a turn for the better and be out of danger; pull through

【转文】 zhuǎnwén lard one's speech with literary allusions

【转向】 zhuǎnxiàng ① change direction ② change one's political stand ◇ ～架〈铁道〉 bogie/ ～装置 steering gear
另见 zhuànxiàng

【转学】 zhuǎnxué (of a student) transfer to another school

【转眼】 zhuǎnyǎn in the twinkling of an eye; in an instant; in a flash: 这孩子一～就不见了。The child disappeared in the twinkling of an eye./ ～间,一个月就过去了。A month passed before we knew it.

【转业】 zhuǎnyè (of an armyman) be transferred to civilian work ◇ ～军人 armyman transferred to civilian work

【转移】 zhuǎnyí ① shift; transfer; divert: ～兵力 shift forces; transfer troops/ ～视线 divert sb.'s attention/ ～目标 distract people's attention from sth. or sb./ ～斗争大方向 divert (或 deflect) the general orientation of the struggle/ 游击队～了。The guerrillas have moved away. ② change; transform: ～社会风气 change prevalent social customs/ 阶级斗争是客观存在,不依人的意志为～的。Class struggle is an objective reality independent of man's will. ③〈医〉 metastasis: 癌～ the metastasis of a carcinoma

【转义】 zhuǎnyì 〈语〉 transferred meaning; figurative sense

【转引】 zhuǎnyǐn quote from a secondary source: ～自《政府工作报告》 quoted in the *Report on the Work of the Government*

【转运】 zhuǎnyùn ① transport; transfer; transship ② have a change of luck; luck turns in one's favour ◇ ～公司 transport company; forwarding agency/ ～站 transfer post

【转载】 zhuǎnzǎi reprint sth. that has been published elsewhere; reprint: 各报都～了这篇报道。The report was reprinted in all the newspapers.

【转赠】 zhuǎnzèng make a present of sth. given to one

【转战】 zhuǎnzhàn fight in one place after another: ～大江南北 fight successively in different parts north and south of the Changjiang River

【转帐】 zhuǎnzhàng transfer accounts

【转折】 zhuǎnzhé ① a turn in the course of events: 世界历史上的急剧～ an abrupt turn in world history ② transition (of an essay) ◇ ～点 turning point

【转辙器】 zhuǎnzhéqì 〈铁道〉 switch

【转正】 zhuǎnzhèng ① (of a probationary member of the Communist Party of China) become a full member after completion of the probationary period ② (of a temporary worker) become a regular worker

【转注】 zhuǎnzhù 〈语〉 mutually explanatory or synonymous characters, e.g. 老 (old age) and 考 (long life, aged) — one of the six categories of Chinese characters (六书)

【转租】 zhuǎnzū sublet; sublease

## zhuàn

**传** zhuàn ① commentaries on classics: 经～ Confucian classics and commentaries on them ② biography: 外～ unauthorized biography/ 别～ supplementary biography/ 小～ biographical sketch; profile ③ a novel or story written in historical style: 《水浒～》 *Water Margin*
另见 chuán

【传记】 zhuànjì biography

【传略】 zhuànlüè brief biography; biographical sketch

**转** zhuàn ① turn; revolve; rotate: 砂轮～得很快。The grinding wheel turns very quickly./ 地球绕着太阳～。The earth revolves round the sun./ 你在这儿～来～去干什么? What are you hanging around here for? ②〈量〉 revolution: 每分钟二千～ 2,000 revolutions per minute; 2,000 r.p.m.
另见 zhuǎn

【转碟】 zhuàndié 〈杂技〉 plate-spinning

【转动】 zhuàndòng turn; revolve; rotate: ～辘轳把 turn the crank of a windlass/ 这个电厂的涡轮全是用核动力～的。All the turbines of this power plant are driven by nuclear energy./ 经过修理,机器又～起来了。The machine started working again after being put right.
另见 zhuǎndòng

【转炉】 zhuànlú 〈冶〉 converter ◇ ～钢 converter steel/ ～炼钢法 converting process

【转轮手枪】 zhuànlún shǒuqiāng revolver

【转门】 zhuànmén 〈建〉 revolving door

【转盘】 zhuànpán ①〈机〉 turntable ②〈体〉 giant stride ③〈杂技〉 disc-spinning ④〈石油〉 rotary table: ～速度 rotary speed

【转数】 zhuànshù 〈机〉 revolution: 每分钟～ revolutions per minute (r.p.m.)/ 额定～ rated revolution

【转速】 zhuànsù rotational speed ◇ ～计 tachometer

【转台】 zhuàntái revolving stage

【转向】 zhuànxiàng lose one's bearings; get lost: 晕头～ get confused and lose one's bearings; feel one's head reeling
另见 zhuǎnxiàng

【转椅】 zhuànyǐ swivel chair; revolving chair

【转悠】 zhuànyou 〈口〉 ① turn; move from side to side: 他眼珠一～就想出个主意。He rolled his eyes and hit upon an idea. ② stroll; saunter; take a leisurely walk

【转子】 zhuànzǐ 〈机〉 rotor ◇ ～发动机 〈汽车〉 Wankel engine

**啭** zhuàn 〈书〉 (of birds) twitter; sing

**赚** zhuàn ① make a profit; gain: ～钱 make money; make a profit/ ～钱生意 a profitable business; a paying proposition (或 concern) ②〈方〉 profit ③〈方〉 earn
另见 zuàn

【赚头】 zhuàntou 〈口〉 profit

**馔** zhuàn 〈书〉 food: 盛～ sumptuous dinner

**撰** zhuàn write; compose: 为报纸～稿 write articles for a newspaper

【撰著】 zhuànzhù write; compose

**篆** zhuàn ① 见"篆书" ② seal

【篆刻】 zhuànkè seal cutting

【篆书】 zhuànshū seal character (a style of Chinese calligraphy, often used on seals)

## zhuāng

**妆** zhuāng ① apply makeup; make up: 梳～ dress one's hair and apply makeup ② woman's personal adornments

③ trousseau
【妆奁】 zhuānglián trousseau
【妆饰】 zhuāngshì adorn; dress up; deck out

**庄** zhuāng ① village: 王家～ Wangjiazhuang Village ② manor ③ a place of business: 钱～ old-fashioned Chinese private bank/ 饭～ restaurant ④ banker (in a gambling game) ⑤ serious; grave: 亦～亦谐 serious and facetious at the same time; seriocomic ⑥ (Zhuāng) a surname
【庄户】 zhuānghù peasant household ◇ ～人 peasant/ ～人家 peasant family
【庄家】 zhuāngjia banker (in a gambling game)
【庄稼】 zhuāngjia crops: 种～ grow crops/ 晚～ late crops ◇ ～地 cropland; fields/ ～汉 farmer; peasant/ ～活儿 farm work/ ～人 peasant; farmer
【庄严】 zhuāngyán solemn; dignified; stately: ～地声明 solemnly declare/ 态度～ dignified in manner/ 追悼会会场～肃穆。The mourning hall was filled with a solemn silence.
【庄园】 zhuāngyuán manor
【庄重】 zhuāngzhòng serious; grave; solemn
【庄子】 zhuāngzi 〈口〉 village; hamlet

**桩** zhuāng ① stake; pile: 打～ drive piles ②〈量〉: 一～大事 an important matter / 一～买卖 a business transaction
【桩砦】 zhuāngzhài 〈军〉 post obstacles
【桩子】 zhuāngzi stake; pile

**装** zhuāng ① dress up; attire; deck; play the part (或 role) of; act: 她～老大娘真像。She acted an old woman and really looked the part. ② outfit; clothing: 春～ a spring outfit/ 学生～ students' uniform/ 童～ children's wear (或 clothing) ③ stage makeup and costume: 上～ dress and put on makeup (for a theatrical performance)/ 卸～ remove stage makeup and costume ④ pretend; feign; make believe: ～病 pretend sickness; malinger/ ～死 feign death; sham dead/ ～傻 pretend to be naive or stupid/ ～出一副可怜相 assume a pitiable look/ 不要不懂～懂。Don't pretend to know what you don't know. ⑤ load; pack; hold: ～车 load a truck (或 cart)/ ～箱 pack a box; put sth. in a crate; crate/ ～料 feed (a machine)/ ～烟袋 fill one's pipe/ 这书包～不下这么多东西。This satchel won't hold so many things. ⑥ install; fit; assemble: 给门～上锁 fit a lock on the door/ ～个无线电 assemble a radio set/ 我们村家家户户都～上了电灯。Electric lights have been installed in every house in our village.
【装扮】 zhuāngbàn ① dress up; attire; deck out ② disguise; masquerade: ～成朋友的敌人是最危险的。The most dangerous enemy is one who disguises himself as a friend.
【装备】 zhuāngbèi ① equip; fit out: ～新式武器 be equipped with modern weapons ② equipment; outfit: 军事～ military equipment/ 配置全套国产～ be fitted out with complete sets of Chinese-made equipment/ 登山运动员的～ a mountaineer's outfit
【装裱】 zhuāngbiǎo mount (a picture, etc.)
【装船】 zhuāngchuán shipment: 分批～ partial shipment
【装点】 zhuāngdiǎn decorate; dress; deck: 大厅里～着花彩。The hall was decorated with festoons.
【装订】 zhuāngdìng binding; bookbinding: 布面～ clothbound/ 皮面～ bound in leather / 硬面～ hardbound ◇ ～车间 bookbindery; bindery/ ～工人 bookbinder/ ～机 bookbinding machine; binding machinery
【装疯卖傻】 zhuāngfēng-màishǎ feign madness and act like an idiot; play the fool
【装裹】 zhuāngguo ① dress a corpse; wrap (a corpse) in a shroud ② shroud; burial suit
【装糊涂】 zhuāng hútu pretend not to know; feign ignorance
【装潢】 zhuānghuáng ① mount (a picture, etc.); decorate; dress ② decoration; mounting; packaging: ～讲究的茅台酒 tastefully packaged bottles of *maotai* 又作"装璜"
【装货】 zhuānghuò loading (cargo) ◇ ～单 shipping order/ ～港 port of shipment; port of loading
【装机容量】 zhuāngjī róngliàng 〈电〉 installed capacity
【装甲】 zhuāngjiǎ ① plate armour ② armoured ◇ ～兵 armoured force (或 troops)/ ～车 armoured car/ ～列车 armoured train/ ～师 armoured division/ ～输送车 armoured carrier
【装假】 zhuāngjiǎ pretend; feign; make believe
【装殓】 zhuāngliàn dress and lay a corpse in a coffin
【装料】 zhuāngliào ① feed (a machine) ②〈冶〉 loading; charging
【装聋作哑】 zhuānglóng-zuòyǎ pretend to be deaf and dumb; pretend to be ignorant of sth.
【装门面】 zhuāng ménmiàn put up a front; maintain an outward show; keep up appearances
【装模作样】 zhuāngmú-zuòyàng be affected; attitudinize; put on an act
【装配】 zhuāngpèi assemble; fit together: ～机器 assemble a machine ◇ ～车间 assembly shop; fitting shop/ ～工 assembler; fitter/ ～件 assembly parts/ ～线 assembly line
【装腔】 zhuāngqiāng behave affectedly; be artificial: ～作势 be affected or pretentious; strike a pose
【装饰】 zhuāngshì decorate; adorn; ornament; deck: 彩旗和鲜花把公园～得十分绚丽。The park was gaily decorated with bunting and flowers. ◇ ～品 ornament/ ～图案 decorative pattern/ ～音〈乐〉 grace note; grace; ornament
【装束】 zhuāngshù dress; attire: 看他的～，可能是藏族。Judging from his dress, he's probably a Tibetan.
【装蒜】 zhuāngsuàn 〈口〉 pretend not to know; feign ignorance: 你比谁都明白，别～了！Don't pretend; you know better than anybody else.
【装填】 zhuāngtián 〈军〉 load; ram
【装卸】 zhuāngxiè ① load and unload: ～货物 load and unload a truck, ship, etc.; load and unload goods ② assemble and disassemble: 他会～自行车。He can take a bicycle apart and put it back again. ◇ ～工 loader; (码头) stevedore/ ～时间 〈航运〉 lay days
【装修】 zhuāngxiū fit up (a house, etc.): ～门面 fit up the front of a shop
【装样子】 zhuāng yàngzi put on an act; do sth. for appearance sake
【装药】 zhuāngyào 〈军〉 powder charge; filling
【装运】 zhuāngyùn load and transport; ship
【装载】 zhuāngzài loading ◇ ～量 loading capacity
【装帧】 zhuāngzhèng binding and layout (of a book, magazine, etc.): 一本～精美的书 a beautifully designed and bound book
【装置】 zhuāngzhì ① install; fit: 仪器已经～好了。The instrument has been installed. ② installation; unit; device; plant: 雷达～ radar installation/ 自停～ automatic stop arrangement/ 磨煤～ coal-pulverizing plant/ 配电～ power distribution unit/ 减震～ damping device/ 防护～ protective equipment

## zhuǎng

**奘** zhuǎng 〈方〉 big and thick; stout; robust

## zhuàng

**壮** zhuàng ① strong; robust: ～苗 strong sprout/ 他身体很～。He is sturdy. 或 He has a strong physique. ② magnificent; grand: 雄～ magnificent; full of grandeur ③ strengthen; make better: ～声势 to lend impetus and strength; to make it appear more vigorous and impressive/ 以～观瞻 (deck out a place) to make it more sightly

【壮大】 zhuàngdà grow in strength; expand; strengthen: 第三世界的～ the growing strength of the Third World/ ～集体经济 strengthen the collective economy/ ～革命力量 expand the revolutionary forces/ 科技工作人员的队伍不断～。The ranks of the scientists and technological workers are growing steadily.

【壮胆】 zhuàngdǎn embolden; boost sb.'s courage

【壮丁】 zhuàngdīng ‹旧› able-bodied man (subject to conscription)

【壮工】 zhuànggōng unskilled labourer

【壮观】 zhuàngguān grand (或 magnificent) sight: 节日的广场到处红旗飘扬,显得格外～。With red flags fluttering everywhere in celebration of the festival, the square looked most magnificent.

【壮锦】 zhuàngjǐn Zhuang brocade

【壮举】 zhuàngjǔ magnificent feat; heroic undertaking: 史无前例的～ an unparalleled feat

【壮阔】 zhuàngkuò vast; grand; magnificent; grandiose: 波澜～ surging forward with great momentum; unfolding on a magnificent scale

【壮丽】 zhuànglì majestic; magnificent; glorious: ～的景色 magnificent scenery; majestic view/ 一篇～的史诗 a magnificent (或 glorious) epic/ 一曲毛泽东思想的～凯歌 a stirring song of victory for Mao Zedong Thought

【壮烈】 zhuàngliè heroic; brave: ～牺牲 heroically give one's life; die a hero's death

【壮年】 zhuàngnián the more robust years of a person's life (between thirty and fifty); prime of life

【壮士】 zhuàngshì heroic man; hero; warrior

【壮实】 zhuàngshi sturdy; robust: 一个～的小伙子 a sturdy young chap

【壮志】 zhuàngzhì great aspiration; lofty ideal: ～凌云 with soaring aspirations/ ～未酬 with one's lofty aspirations unrealized

【壮族】 Zhuàngzú the Zhuang (Chuang) nationality, distributed over the Guangxi Zhuang Autonomous Region, Yunnan and Guangdong

**状** zhuàng ① form; shape: 其～不一 of different forms/ 奇形怪～ of grotesque shapes ② state; condition: 现～ present state of affairs; *status quo* ③ describe: 不可名～ indescribable; nondescript; beyond description ④ account; record: 功～ an account of sb.'s meritorious service ⑤ written complaint; plaint: 告～ lodge a complaint (或 an accusation); file a suit (against sb.) ⑥ certificate: 奖～ certificate of commendation/ 委任～ certificate of appointment; commission

【状况】 zhuàngkuàng condition; state; state of affairs: 健康～ state of health; health/ 改善这种～ remedy this state of affairs/ 经济～ (a person's) financial situation; (a country's) economic situation

【状貌】 zhuàngmào appearance; form

【状态】 zhuàngtài state; condition; state of affairs: 心理～ psychology; state of mind/ 无组织～ disorganized state of affairs/ 战争～ state of war ◇ ～图‹治› state diagram

【状语】 zhuàngyǔ ‹语› adverbial modifier; adverbial

【状元】 zhuàngyuan ① Number One Scholar, title conferred on the one who came first in the highest imperial examination ② the very best (in any field): 行行出～。Every profession produces its own leading authority.

【状子】 zhuàngzi ‹口› written complaint; plaint

**撞** zhuàng ① bump against; run into; strike; collide: ～车 collision of vehicles/ ～墙 bump against a wall/ ～了个满怀 bump into sb./ ～钟 toll (或 strike) a bell/ 一辆卡车～坏了我们的汽车。A lorry ran into our car and damaged it./ 被卡车～倒了 be knocked down by a truck/ 两船在雾中相～。Two ships collided in the fog. ② meet by chance; bump into; run into: 我不想见他,偏～上他了。I tried to avoid him, but it was just my luck to bump into him. ③ rush; dash; barge: 横冲直～ barge around; dash about madly

【撞击】 zhuàngjī ram; dash against; strike: 波浪～着岩石。The breakers dashed on the rocks.

【撞见】 zhuàngjiàn meet or discover by chance; run across; catch sb. in the act

【撞骗】 zhuàngpiàn look about for a chance to swindle; swindle

【撞锁】 zhuàngsuǒ ① spring lock ② ‹口› find that sb. is not home: 我昨儿晚上去你家串门,没想到～了。I went to your place last night and found the door locked.

【撞针】 zhuàngzhēn ‹军› firing pin

**幢** zhuàng ‹方› ‹量›: 一～三层楼房 a three-storeyed building

另见 chuáng

**戆** zhuàng

【戆直】 zhuàngzhí ‹书› blunt and tactless; simple and honest

## zhuī

**追** zhuī ① chase (或 run) after; pursue: ～兵 pursuing troops/ ～上他 catch up with him/ 紧～不舍 be in hot pursuit; be hot on sb.'s trail/ 把比分～到十比十一 close the margin to 10-11; catch up and bring the score to 10-11 ② trace; look into; get to the bottom of: ～穷根 trace the root cause of one's poverty ③ seek; go after: ～名逐利 seek fame and wealth ④ recall; reminisce: ～念往事 reminisce about the past; recall early days/ 抚今～昔 recall the past and compare it with the present ⑤ retroactively; posthumously: ～授一级战斗英雄称号 be posthumously awarded the title of Combat Hero Class 1

【追本溯源】 zhuīběn-sùyuán trace to its source; get at the root of the matter

【追逼】 zhuībī ① pursue closely (a fleeing enemy) ② press for (repayment); extort (a confession)

【追捕】 zhuībǔ pursue and capture

【追查】 zhuīchá investigate; trace; find out: ～事故原因 investigate the causes of an accident/ ～谣言 trace a rumour to its source

【追悼】 zhuīdào mourn over a person's death ◇ ～会 memorial meeting

【追肥】 zhuīféi ‹农› top application; topdressing

【追赶】 zhuīgǎn quicken one's pace to catch up; run after; pursue: 他已走远,你～不上了。You won't be able to catch him now — he's too far away.

【追根】 zhuīgēn get to the bottom of sth.: 这件事一定得～

究底。We must get to the root of the matter.
【追回】 zhuīhuí recover: ～赃物 recover stolen property
【追悔】 zhuīhuǐ repent; regret: ～莫及 too late to repent
【追击】 zhuījī pursue and attack; follow up: ～敌人 pursue and attack the enemy/ 战略～ strategic pursuit ◇ ～部队 pursuit troops/ ～战 warfare of pursuit and attack
【追记】 zhuījì ① write down afterwards or from memory ② cite (或 award) posthumously: ～特等功 be posthumously awarded a Special-Class Merit citation
【追加】 zhuījiā add to (the original amount): ～支出 make an additional expenditure/ ～预算 supplement a budget; make a supplementary budget
【追剿】 zhuījiǎo pursue and wipe out ◇ ～队 pursuit detachment
【追究】 zhuījiū look into; find out; investigate: ～事故的责任 investigate and affix the responsibility for an accident; find out who is to blame for an accident
【追求】 zhuīqiú ① seek; pursue: ～真理 seek truth; be in pursuit of truth/ ～名誉地位 be after fame and position/ 单纯～数量的偏向 the tendency to concentrate on quantity alone ② woo; court; chase; run after
【追认】 zhuīrèn ① subsequently confirm or endorse; recognize retroactively: ～一项法令 subsequently endorse a decree ② admit or confer posthumously: ～为共产党员 be posthumously admitted as a member of the Communist Party
【追溯】 zhuīsù trace back to; date from: 这个传说可以～到遥远的过去。The legend goes (或 can be traced) back to remote antiquity./ 我们两国人民之间的友谊可以～到第五世纪。The friendship between our two peoples dates from the 5th century.
【追随】 zhuīsuí follow: ～不舍 follow sb. closely/ ～错误路线 follow an erroneous line ◇ ～者 follower; adherent; following
【追问】 zhuīwèn question closely; make a detailed inquiry; examine minutely: ～事实真相 make detailed inquiries about the facts/ 我们～他渔船失踪的原因。We questioned him trying to find out how the fishing boat got lost.
【追想】 zhuīxiǎng recall; reminisce
【追叙】 zhuīxù ① tell about the past; relate; recount ② narration of earlier episodes; flashback
【追寻】 zhuīxún pursue; search; track down
【追忆】 zhuīyì recollect; recall; look back: ～往事,历历在目。As I look back, scenes of the past leap before my eyes./ 年代太久,难以～。It happened ages ago and I can't call it to mind.
【追赃】 zhuīzāng order the return of stolen money or goods; recover stolen money or goods; make sb. disgorge the spoils
【追赠】 zhuīzèng confer posthumously (a title)
【追逐】 zhuīzhú ① pursue; chase ② seek; quest: ～高额利润 seek exorbitant profits
【追踪】 zhuīzōng follow the trail of; track; trace

**椎** zhuī vertebra: 颈～ cervical vertebra/ 胸～ thoracic vertebra
【椎骨】 zhuīgǔ 〈生理〉 vertebra
【椎间盘突出症】 zhuījiānpán tūchūzhèng 〈医〉 protrusion of the intervertebral disc

**锥** zhuī ① awl ② anything shaped like an awl ③ bore; drill: ～孔 make a hole with an awl ④〈数〉 cone
【锥度】 zhuīdù 〈机〉 taper ◇ ～规 taper gauge
【锥栗】 zhuīlì 〈植〉 chinquapin
【锥面】 zhuīmiàn 〈数〉 cone
【锥形】 zhuīxíng 〈机〉 taper; cone
【锥子】 zhuīzi awl

## zhuì

**坠** zhuì ① fall; drop: ～马 fall off a horse/ 飞机～入海中。The plane crashed into the sea. ② weigh down: 苹果把树枝～得弯弯的。The branches were bending down with the weight of the apples. 或 The apples weighed the branches down. ③ weight; a hanging object: 铅～ plummet/ 扇～儿 pendant of a fan
【坠地】 zhuìdì 〈书〉 (of a child) be born
【坠毁】 zhuìhuǐ (of a plane, etc.) fall and break; crash
【坠落】 zhuìluò fall; drop
【坠子】 zhuìzi ① 〈方〉 weight; plummet; pendant ② ear pendant ③ ballad singing to the accompaniment of the *zhuiqin* (坠琴), popular in Henan Province

**缀** zhuì ① sew; stitch: 补～ mend; patch/ 你的袖子扯破了,我给你～上两针。Your sleeve's torn. I'll put in a few stitches for you. ② put words together correctly; compose: ～文 compose an essay; write a composition ③ embellish; decorate: 点～ embellish; adorn/ 天上～满了星星。The sky was studded with twinkling stars.

**惴** zhuì
【惴惴不安】 zhuìzhuì bù ān 〈书〉 be anxious and fearful; be alarmed and on tenterhooks

**缒** zhuì let down (with a rope): ～城而出 let oneself or sb. down a city wall by a rope

**赘** zhuì ① superfluous; redundant: 不待～言。It would be superfluous to dwell on the matter any more. ② (of a man) go to live in the household of one's in-laws on getting married; (of the bride's parents) gain a son-in-law in such a manner ③ 〈方〉 be burdensome; be cumbersome: 孩子多了真～人。It's really burdensome to have many children.
【赘瘤】 zhuìliú anything superfluous or useless
【赘述】 zhuìshù give unnecessary details; say more than is needed: 不必一一～。It is unnecessary to go into details.
【赘婿】 zhuìxù a son-in-law who lives in the home of his wife's parents
【赘疣】 zhuìyóu ① wart ② anything superfluous or useless

## zhūn

**肫** zhūn ① gizzard (of a fowl): 鸭～ duck gizzard ② 〈书〉 sincere; genuine

**窀** zhūn
【窀穸】 zhūnxī 〈书〉 grave; tomb

**谆** zhūn
【谆谆】 zhūnzhūn earnestly and tirelessly: ～教导 earnestly instruct/ ～告诫 repeatedly admonish

## zhǔn

**准** zhǔn ① allow; grant; permit: 获～ obtain permission/ ～假两周 grant sb. two weeks' leave/ 不～吸烟。No smoking. ② in accordance with; follow: ～前例处理 to be settled by following precedent ③ standard; norm; criterion: 以此为～ take this as the standard (或 criterion)/ 标～ standard; criterion/ ～则 norm; standard; criterion ④ accurate; exact: 投篮不～ inaccurate shooting (in basketball)/ 这表走得～。The watch keeps good time. ⑤ definitely; certainly: 我明天～去。I'll certainly be there tomorrow. ⑥ quasi-; para-: ～军事组织 paramilitary organization/ ～单色光〈物〉quasi-monochromatic light

【准保】 zhǔnbǎo 〈副〉certainly; for sure: 你现在给他打电话，他～会来。He will certainly come if you ring him up now./ 我检查了两遍，～没错儿。I've checked twice. You can be sure there's no mistake.

【准备】 zhǔnbèi ① prepare; get ready: 为会议～文件 prepare documents for a meeting./ 作最坏的～ prepare for the worst/ 随时～歼灭入侵之敌 be prepared at all times to wipe out any invader/ 你～好了吗？Are you ready?/ 新的世界大战的危险依然存在，各国人民必须有所～。The danger of a new world war still exists, and the people of all countries must get prepared. ② intend; plan: 今年暑假我～回老家看看。I intend to visit my native place this summer vacation./ 我们～下星期一开始试验。We plan to start the experiment next Monday. ◇ ～活动〈体〉warming-up exercise; limbering-up exercise/ ～阶段 preparatory stage

【准将】 zhǔnjiàng (英陆军) brigadier; (英空军) air commodore; (海军) commodore; (美陆、空军) brigadier general

【准确】 zhǔnquè accurate; exact; precise: ～而有力地打击敌人 deal accurate and powerful blows at the enemy/ ～地说明 explain in precise terms ◇ ～度 degree of accuracy; accuracy/ ～性 accuracy

【准儿】 zhǔnr 〈口〉certain; sure: 心里有～ feel sure; know what one is doing/ 成不成没～。The chances of success are uncertain./ 这种天气可没～。You can never be certain about this kind of weather.

【准绳】 zhǔnshéng criterion; yardstick

【准时】 zhǔnshí punctual; on time; on schedule: ～起飞 take off at the scheduled time/ 请～出席。Please be punctual. 或 You are requested to come on time.

【准头】 zhǔntou 〈口〉accuracy (in speech, marksmanship, etc.): 枪法挺有～ shoot well; be a good shot/ 他说话没有～。You can't depend on what he says.

【准尉】 zhǔnwèi warrant officer: 一级～(英) warrant officer (class I); (美陆、空军) chief warrant officer; (美海军) commissioned warrant officer/ 二级～(英) warrant officer (class II); (美陆、空军) warrant officer, junior grade; (美海军) warrant officer

【准星】 zhǔnxīng front sight (of a gun)

【准许】 zhǔnxǔ permit; allow

【准予】 zhǔnyǔ grant; approve; permit: ～入境 allow sb. to enter the country/ ～休假 grant a leave

【准则】 zhǔnzé norm; standard; criterion: 行为～ code of conduct/ 外交～ diplomatic norms/ 国际法的起码～ elementary requirements of international law/ 热力学～ thermodynamic criterion

【准直】 zhǔnzhí 〈物〉collimation ◇ ～透镜 collimating lens/ ～仪 collimator

## zhuō

**拙** zhuō ① clumsy; awkward; dull: 手～ be all thumbs/ ～于言词 be inarticulate; be clumsy in expressing oneself ② 〈谦〉my: ～著 my writing

【拙笨】 zhuōbèn clumsy; dull; unskilful

【拙见】 zhuōjiàn 〈谦〉my humble opinion

【拙荆】 zhuōjīng 〈旧〉my wife

【拙劣】 zhuōliè clumsy; inferior: ～表演 a clumsy performance; a bad show/ ～手法 inferior tactics; clumsy trick

**卓** zhuō ① tall and erect: ～立 stand upright ② eminent; outstanding: 成绩～然 achieve outstanding results ③ (Zhuō) a surname

【卓见】 zhuōjiàn excellent opinion; brilliant idea

【卓绝】 zhuōjué unsurpassed; extreme; of the highest degree: 英勇～ extremely brave/ 艰苦～ extreme hardships and difficulties

【卓识】 zhuōshí judicious judgment; sagacity: 远见～ foresight and sagacity

【卓有成效】 zhuō yǒu chéngxiào fruitful; highly effective: 进行～的努力 have made fruitful efforts/ 几年来绿化荒山已～。In the past few years good results have been attained in afforesting the barren hills.

【卓越】 zhuōyuè outstanding; brilliant; remarkable: ～的成就 remarkable achievements/ ～的科学家 a brilliant scientist/ 作出～的贡献 make outstanding contributions

【卓著】 zhuōzhù distinguished; outstanding; eminent: 该省农业机械化的工作成效～。That province has achieved outstanding results in farm mechanization.

**捉** zhuō ① clutch; hold; grasp: ～笔 hold a pen/ ～住不放 seize hold of sb. or sth. and not let go ② catch; capture: 活～ capture sb. alive/ 贼喊～贼 a thief crying "stop thief"

【捉刀】 zhuōdāo write (an article, etc.) for someone else; ghostwrite ◇ ～人 ghostwriter

【捉襟见肘】 zhuōjīn-jiànzhǒu pull down one's jacket to conceal the raggedness, only to expose one's elbows — have too many difficulties to cope with; have too many problems to tackle

【捉迷藏】 zhuō mícáng ① hide-and-seek; blindman's buff ② be tricky and evasive; play hide-and-seek: 你就直说吧，不要跟我～了。Get straight to the point. Don't beat about the bush.

【捉摸】 zhuōmō 〔多用于否定〕fathom; ascertain: ～不定 difficult to ascertain; unpredictable; elusive

【捉拿】 zhuōná arrest; catch: ～逃犯 arrest an escaped prisoner/ ～归案 bring sb. to justice

【捉弄】 zhuōnòng tease; make fun of; embarrass

**桌** zhuō ① table; desk: 餐～ dining table/ 书～ writing desk/ ～椅板凳 tables, chairs and benches — ordinary household furniture ② 〈量〉: 三～客人 three tables of guests (at a dinner party)

【桌布】 zhuōbù tablecloth

【桌灯】 zhuōdēng desk lamp

【桌面】 zhuōmiàn top of a table; tabletop

【桌面儿上】 zhuōmiànrshang on the table; aboveboard; in public: ～的话 polite and unimpeachable remarks/ 把问题摆到～来 place problems on the table; bring problems out into the open

【桌子】 zhuōzi table; desk

## zhuó

**灼** zhuó ① burn; scorch: ～伤 burn ② bright; luminous

【灼见】 zhuójiàn profound view; penetrating view: 真知～ profound knowledge and penetrating insight

【灼热】 zhuórè scorching hot

【灼灼】 zhuózhuó 〈书〉shining; brilliant: 目光～ with keen,

sparkling eyes

## 茁 zhuó

【茁壮】 zhuózhuàng healthy and strong; sturdy: 小麦长得很～。The wheat has grown sturdy./ 无产阶级革命事业的接班人正在～成长。Successors to the revolutionary cause of the proletariat are reaching maturity.

## 浊 zhuó

① turbid; muddy: ～水 turbid water/ ～流 muddy stream/ 污～ dirty; filthy ② deep and thick: ～声～气 in a deep, raucous voice ③ chaotic; confused; corrupted

【浊点】 zhuódiǎn 〈化〉 cloud point

【浊世】 zhuóshì ①〈书〉 the corrupted world; chaotic times ②〈佛教〉 the mortal world

【浊音】 zhuóyīn 〈语〉 voiced sound

## 斫 zhuó

hack (with an axe or sword)

## 酌 zhuó

① pour out (wine); drink: 对～ (two people) have a drink together/ 独～ drink alone ② a meal with wine: 便～ informal dinner ③ consider; think over; use one's discretion: ～办 act according to one's judgment; do as one thinks fit/ 请～加修改。Make any alterations as you may think fit./ 以上几点意见是否可行,请～定。Please weigh the above points and see if they are practicable.

【酌量】 zhuóliàng consider; deliberate; use one's judgment

【酌情】 zhuóqíng take into consideration the circumstances; use one's discretion: ～处理 settle a matter as one sees fit; act at one's discretion

## 诼 zhuó

〈书〉 calumny; slander

## 着 zhuó

① wear (clothes): 穿～整齐 be neatly dressed/ 吃～不尽 have as much food and clothing as one wants ② touch; come into contact with: 附～ adhere to ③ apply; use: 再～一把力 make one more effort/ ～墨不多 sketchily painted or described ④ whereabouts: 寻找无～ whereabouts unknown; nowhere to be found/ 经费无～ no funds available ⑤ send: 请～人前来领取。Please send someone here for it. ⑥〔旧时公文用语,表示命令的口气〕: 以上规定,～即施行。The above regulations are to be enforced immediately.

另见 zhāo; zháo; zhe

【着笔】 zhuóbǐ put (或 set) pen to paper; begin to write or paint: 不知如何～ not know how to begin the writing or the painting

【着力】 zhuólì put forth effort; exert oneself: ～描写 concentrate one's efforts on depicting sb. or sth.; take great pains to describe/ 无从～ fail to see where to direct one's efforts

【着陆】 zhuólù land; touch down: 飞机就要～了。The plane is about to land. 或 The plane is going to touch down. ◇ ～舱 landing module/ ～场 landing field; landing ground/ ～接地 touchdown

【着落】 zhuóluò ① whereabouts: 遗失的行李已经有～了。The missing luggage has been found. ② assured source: 这笔经费还没有～。We still don't know where to get the funds from.

【着棋】 zhuóqí 〈方〉 play chess

【着色】 zhuósè put colour on; colour ◇ ～法 colouring/ ～剂 colouring agent; colouring material

【着实】 zhuóshí ① really; indeed: 这台播种机～不错。This seeder is very good indeed./ 为了改装这台机器,他们～花了些功夫。They really put in a good deal of time refitting the machine. ② severely: ～说了他一顿 give him a good talking-to; lecture him severely

【着手】 zhuóshǒu put one's hand to; set about: ～一项工作 set about a job/ ～编制计划 start drawing up plans/ 从调查研究～ start with investigation and study

【着想】 zhuóxiǎng consider (the interests of sb. or sth.): 为人民的利益～ think about the interests of the people/ 他是为你～才劝你不要去的。It was for your good that he advised you not to go.

【着眼】 zhuóyǎn have sth. in mind; see (或 view) from the angle of: ～于人民 have the people in mind/ ～于未来 have one's eyes on the future/ 这些措施都～于建立宏大的又红又专的科技队伍。All these measures are aimed at building a huge contingent of scientists and technicians who are both red and expert. ◇ ～点 starting point; focus of attention; object in mind

【着意】 zhuóyì act with care and effort; take pains: ～经营 manage with diligent care

【着重】 zhuózhòng stress; emphasize: ～指出 emphatically point out/ ～说明问题的重要性 stress the importance of the matter/ 这里我想～地讲一个问题。Here I would like to go into one question in particular. ◇ ～号 mark of emphasis (as in "正是他本人")

## 啄 zhuó

peck: 小鸡～米。The chicks are pecking at the rice.

【啄花鸟】 zhuóhuāniǎo flowerpecker

【啄木鸟】 zhuómùniǎo woodpecker

## 琢 zhuó

chisel; carve: 翡翠～成的小茶壶 a small carved jadeite teapot

另见 zuó

【琢磨】 zhuómó ① carve and polish (jade) ② improve (literary works); polish; refine

另见 zuómo

## 斵 zhuó

〈书〉 chop; hack

【斵轮老手】 zhuó lún lǎoshǒu expert wheelwright; old hand

## 濯 zhuó

〈书〉 wash: ～足 wash one's feet

【濯濯】 zhuózhuó 〈书〉 (of mountains) bare; bald: 童山～ treeless hills

## 擢 zhuó

〈书〉 ① pull out; extract ② raise (in rank); promote

【擢发难数】 zhuó fà nán shǔ (of crimes) be as countless as the hairs on a head; be too numerous to count

【擢升】 zhuóshēng 〈书〉promote; advance (to a higher position or rank)

【擢用】 zhuóyòng 〈书〉 promote to a post

## 镯 zhuó

bracelet: 玉～ jade bracelet

# zī

## 仔 zī

另见 zǎi; zǐ

【仔肩】 zījiān 〈书〉 official burdens or responsibilities

## 吱 zī

〈象〉 ① (of mice) squeak ② (of small birds) chirp; peep

另见 zhī

【吱声】 zīshēng 〈方〉 utter sth.; make a sound: 我们问他几遍,他都没～。We asked him several times, but couldn't get a peep out of him.

## 孜 zī

【孜孜】 zīzī diligent; industrious; hardworking: ～以求 diligently strive after; assiduously seek

【孜孜不倦】 zīzī bù juàn diligently; assiduously; indefatigably

## 咨 zī consult; take counsel

【咨文】 zīwén ① <旧> official communication (between government offices of equal rank) ② report delivered by the head of a government on affairs of state: 国情～ (美) State of the Union Message

【咨询】 zīxún seek advice from; hold counsel with; consult ◇ ～机关 advisory body/ ～委员会 consultative (或 advisory) committee

## 姿 zī ① looks; appearance: ～色 (of a woman) good looks ② gesture; carriage; posture: 舞～ a dancer's posture and movements

【姿容】 zīróng looks; appearance: ～秀美 good-looking; pretty

【姿色】 zīsè (of a woman) good looks: 略有几分～ be rather good-looking

【姿势】 zīshì posture; gesture: 直立的～ an erect posture/ ～优美 have a graceful carriage

【姿态】 zītài ① posture; carriage: 各种不同～的泥塑 clay figures in various postures ② attitude; pose: 以一个普通劳动者的～出现 (of a senior cadre) appear among the masses as an ordinary worker/ 装出一副反帝的～ adopt a pose of fighting against imperialism/ 采取高～ show magnanimity; exercise forbearance; be tolerant

## 兹 zī <书> ① this: ～事体大。This is indeed a serious matter. ② now; at present: ～将新到书籍开列如下。Below is a list of books recently received. ③ year: 今～ this year/ 来～ the coming year

## 资 zī ① money; expenses: 投～ put money in; invest/ 川～ travelling expenses/ 劳～双方 labour and capital ② subsidize; support: ～敌 give supplies to the enemy; support the enemy ③ provide; supply: 可～对比 provide a contrast/ 广泛报道,以～鼓励 give wide publicity by way of encouragement/ 以～补救 to serve as a remedy ④ endowment; natural ability: 天～ natural endowments; aptitude ⑤ qualifications; record of service: 年～ years of service; seniority

【资本】 zīběn ① capital: 不变(可变)～ constant (variable) capital/ 垄断～ monopoly capital/ ～的周转 turnover of capital/ ～原始积累 primitive accumulation of capital ② what is capitalized on; sth. used to one's own advantage: 你怎么能把集体取得的成绩看作个人的～? How could you capitalize on what the group has achieved?
◇ ～帝国主义 capitalist-imperialism/ ～货物 capital goods/ ～市场 capital market/ ～输出 export of capital

【资本家】 zīběnjiā capitalist: 不法～ lawbreaking capitalist

【资本主义】 zīběnzhǔyì capitalism: 国家垄断～ state monopoly capitalism/ 自由～ *laissez-faire* (或 non-monopoly) capitalism/ ～工商业的社会主义改造 the socialist transformation of capitalist industry and commerce
◇ ～道路 the capitalist road/ ～复辟 the restoration of capitalism/ ～经济成份 capitalist sector of the economy/ ～倾向 tendencies towards capitalism/ ～社会 capitalist society/ ～生产方式 capitalist mode of production/ ～制度 capitalist system/ ～自发势力 spontaneous capitalist forces/ ～总危机 general crisis of capitalism

【资财】 zīcái capital and goods; assets: 清点～ make an inventory of the assets (of a factory, etc.)

【资产】 zīchǎn ① property ② capital fund; capital ③ <经> assets: 固定(流动)～ fixed (liquid) assets/ ～冻结 freezing of assets ◇ ～负债表 <经> statement of assets and liabilities; balance sheet

【资产阶级】 zīchǎnjiējí the capitalist class; the bourgeoisie: 民族～ the national bourgeoisie/ 官僚～ the bureaucrat-capitalist class
◇ ～分子 bourgeois element/ ～革命 bourgeois revolution/ ～个人主义 bourgeois individualism/ ～化 become bourgeoisified/ ～民主 bourgeois democracy/ ～民主革命 bourgeois-democratic revolution/ ～权利 bourgeois right/ ～世界观 bourgeois world outlook/ ～思想 bourgeois ideas; bourgeois ideology/ ～专政 the dictatorship of the bourgeoisie

【资方】 zīfāng those representing capital; capital ◇ ～人员 capitalists and their representatives/ ～代理人 agent of the owner of a private enterprise; agent of a capitalist

【资格】 zīge ① qualifications: 具备必要的～ have the requisite qualifications; be qualified/ 取消比赛～ be disqualified from the contest/ 取消预备党员～ annul the status of sb. as a probationary Party member/ 你们有什么～向别的国家发号施令? What right have you to dictate to other countries? ② seniority: 摆老～ flaunt one's seniority ◇ ～审查委员会 credentials committee/ ～证书 credentials

【资金】 zījīn fund: 建设～ funds for construction/ 发展工业的～ funds for developing industry

【资力】 zīlì financial strength: ～雄厚 have a large capital; be financially powerful

【资历】 zīlì qualifications and record of service

【资料】 zīliào ① means: 生产～ means of production; capital goods/ 生活～ means of livelihood (或 subsistence); consumer goods ② data; material: 参考～ reference material/ 搜集～ gather material; collect data/ ～处理 data processing ◇ ～室 reference room

【资望】 zīwàng seniority and prestige

【资用】 zīyòng <物> available ◇ ～功 available work/ ～假说 working hypothesis

【资源】 zīyuán natural resources; resources: ～丰富 abound (或 be rich) in natural resources/ 开发～ tap (或 exploit) natural resources/ 中国的妇女是一种伟大的人力～。Women form a great reserve of labour power in China.

【资质】 zīzhì natural endowments; intelligence

【资助】 zīzhù aid financially; subsidize

## 赀 zī ① estimate: 所费不～ incur a considerable or great expense ② 见"资" zī ①

## 缁 zī <书> black

## 滋 zī ① grow; multiply: ～蔓 grow and spread/ ～事 create (或 stir up) trouble/ 繁～ multiply profusely ② more: 为害～甚 cause greater havoc than ever ③ <方> spurt; burst: 水管裂缝了,直往外～水。Water is spurting from the crack in the pipe./ 电线～火。Sparks are spurting out from the electric wire.

【滋补】 zībǔ nourishing; nutritious: ～食品 nourishing food; nourishment/ ～气血药 tonics for building up vital energy and nourishing the blood/ 人参是～身体的名药。Ginseng is well known for its tonic effect.

【滋蔓】 zīmàn <书> grow and spread; grow vigorously: 湖中水藻～。Algae grow and spread quickly in the lake.

【滋润】 zīrùn ①moist: ～的土地 moist soil ②moisten: 雨露～禾苗壮。Moistened by rain and dew, young crops grow strong.
【滋生】 zīshēng ①multiply; breed; propagate: 防止蚊蝇～prevent the breeding of flies and mosquitoes ②cause; create; provoke: ～事端 cause trouble; create a disturbance
【滋味】 zīwèi taste; flavour: 这个菜很有～。This dish tastes good./ 尝尝艰苦生活的～ have a taste of hard life
【滋芽】 zīyá 〈方〉 sprout; germinate
【滋养】 zīyǎng ①nourish: ～身体 be nourishing ②nutriment; nourishment: 丰富的～ rich nutriment ◇ ～品 nourishing food; nutriment; nourishment
【滋阴】 zīyīn 〈中医〉 method of treating *yin* deficiency by reinforcing body fluid and nourishing the blood
【滋长】 zīzhǎng grow; develop: 防止～骄傲自满情绪 guard against arrogance and conceit/ 长期的和平环境容易～和平麻痹思想。A long period of peace is apt to engender a false sense of security.

孳 zī multiply; propagate
【孳生】 zīshēng multiply; breed; propagate
【孳孳】 zīzī 见"孜孜" zīzī

辎 zī an ancient covered wagon
【辎重】 zīzhòng 〈军〉 impedimenta; supplies and gear of an army; baggage

趑 zī
【趑趄】 zījū 〈书〉 ①walk with difficulty; plough one's way ②hesitate to advance

锱 zī an ancient unit of weight, equal to one fourth of a *liang* (两)
【锱铢必较】 zī-zhū bì jiào haggle over every penny; dispute over every detail

龇 zī 〈口〉 bare; show: ～着牙 bare one's teeth
【龇牙咧嘴】 zīyá-liězuǐ ①show one's teeth; look fierce ②contort one's face in agony; grimace in pain

鲻 zī 〈动〉 mullet

髭 zī moustache

## zǐ

子 zǐ ①son; child: 父～ father and son/ 独生～ an only son/ 母～候车室 waiting room (as in a railway station) for mothers with babies ②person: 男～ male person; man/ 女～ female person; woman ③ancient title of respect for a learned or virtuous man: 荀～ Master Xun (313?-238 B.C.) ④seed: 瓜～儿 melon seed/ 结～儿 bear seed; go to seed ⑤egg: 鸡～儿 hen's egg/ 鱼～ roe ⑥young; tender; small: ～鸡 chick/ ～姜 tender ginger ⑦something small and hard: 棋～儿 chessman; piece/ 枪～儿 bullet/ 算盘～儿 abacus bead/ 石头～儿 small stone; pebble ⑧copper coin; copper: 一个～儿都不值 not worth a copper/ 一个～儿也没有 penniless ⑨〈量〉〔用于能用手指掐住的一束细长的东西〕: 一～儿挂面 a bundle of fine dried noodles/ 一～儿毛线 a hank of knitting wool ⑩viscount ⑪the first of the twelve Earthly Branches

子 zi ①〔名词后缀〕: 帽～ cap; hat/ 旗～ flag/ 胖～ fat person; fatty/ 推～ hair-clippers; barber's clippers ②〔个别量词后缀〕: 这档～事 this matter; this business/ 我一下～想不起他的名字。I just can't recall his name. 或 His name escapes me for the moment.

【子畜】 zǐchù young animal; newborn animal
【子代】 zǐdài 〈生〉 filial generation: 第一～ the first filial generation
【子弹】 zǐdàn bullet; cartridge: 步枪～ rifle bullet/ 汽枪～ air-gun pellet/ 练习～ dummy cartridge ◇ ～带 cartridge belt; bandoleer/ ～箱 cartridge box
【子弟】 zǐdì sons and younger brothers; juniors; children: 纨袴～ profligate sons of the rich/ 职工～ children of the workers and staff (of a factory, etc.)/ 工农～ sons and daughters of workers and peasants
【子弟兵】 zǐdìbīng army made up of the sons of the people; our own army: 解放军是人民的～。The PLA is the people's own army.
【子房】 zǐfáng 〈植〉 ovary
【子妇】 zǐfù ①son and daughter-in-law ②daughter-in-law; one's son's wife
【子宫】 zǐgōng 〈生理〉 uterus; womb
◇ ～颈 cervix (of womb)/ ～颈炎 cervicitis/ ～帽 cervical cap/ ～切除术 uterectomy/ ～脱垂 metroptosis; prolapse of uterus/ ～外孕 ectopic (或 extrauterine) pregnancy
【子规】 zǐguī 〈动〉 cuckoo
【子爵】 zǐjué viscount ◇ ～夫人 viscountess
【子粒】 zǐlì 〈农〉 seed; grain; kernel; bean: ～饱满 full grains
【子棉】 zǐmián unginned cotton
【子母弹】 zǐmǔdàn 〈军〉 shrapnel; canister shot
【子母机】 zǐmǔjī 〈军〉 composite aircraft
【子母扣儿】 zǐmǔkòur snap fastener
【子目】 zǐmù specific item; subtitle
【子囊】 zǐnáng 〈植〉 ascus
【子女】 zǐnǚ sons and daughters; children
【子时】 zǐshí the period of the day from 11 p.m. to 1 a.m.
【子实】 zǐshí 〈农〉 seed; grain; kernel; bean
【子嗣】 zǐsì son; male offspring
【子孙】 zǐsūn children and grandchildren; descendants: ～后代 descendants; posterity; coming generations
【子午线】 zǐwǔxiàn 〈地〉 meridian (line): 本初～ the prime (或 first) meridian
【子午仪】 zǐwǔyí 〈天〉 meridian instrument
【子细】 zǐxì 见"仔细" zǐxì
【子痫】 zǐxián 〈医〉 eclampsia
【子虚】 zǐxū 〈书〉 fictitious; unreal: 事属～。It is sheer fiction.
【子婿】 zǐxù 〈书〉 son-in-law
【子叶】 zǐyè 〈植〉 cotyledon
【子夜】 zǐyè midnight
【子音】 zǐyīn 〈语〉 consonant

仔 zǐ (of domestic animals or fowls) young: ～猪 piglet; pigling/ ～鸡 chick
另见 zǎi; zī
【仔畜】 zǐchù newborn animal; young animal
【仔细】 zǐxì ①careful; attentive: ～分析 analyse carefully/ ～地研究文件 pore over a document/ 上课～听讲 listen attentively in class/ 她做事很～。She's very careful in everything she does. ②be careful; look out: 路很滑,～点儿。Watch your step! The road is very slippery. ③〈方〉 frugal; economical: 日子过得～ be frugal of one's expenses

姊 zǐ elder sister; sister
【姊妹】 zǐmèi elder and younger sisters; sisters

【姊妹篇】 zǐmèipiān companion volume (或 piece)

**籽** zǐ seed: 菜～儿 vegetable seed/ 棉～儿 cotton seed

【籽棉】 zǐmián unginned cotton

**梓** zǐ ①〈植〉 Chinese catalpa (*Catalpa ovata*) ② cut blocks for printing: 付～ send to the printers

【梓里】 zǐlǐ 〈书〉 native place; home town

**紫** zǐ purple; violet

【紫菜】 zǐcài 〈植〉 laver (*Porphyra* spp.)

【紫草】 zǐcǎo Asian puccoon; Chinese gromwell

【紫草茸】 zǐcǎoróng 〈化〉 shellac; lac

【紫癜】 zǐdiàn 〈医〉 purpura

【紫貂】 zǐdiāo 〈动〉 sable

【紫丁香】 zǐdīngxiāng (early) lilac

【紫绀】 zǐgàn 〈医〉 cyanosis

【紫河车】 zǐhéchē 〈中药〉 dried human placenta

【紫红】 zǐhóng purplish red

【紫花地丁】 zǐhuā dìdīng 〈植〉 Chinese violet

【紫胶】 zǐjiāo shellac; lac ◇～虫 lac insect

【紫金牛】 zǐjīnniú 〈植〉 Japanese ardisia (*Ardisia japonica*)

【紫堇】 zǐjǐn 〈植〉 corydalis

【紫禁城】 Zǐjìnchéng the Forbidden City (in Beijing)

【紫荆】 zǐjīng 〈植〉 Chinese redbud (*Cercis chinensis*)

【紫羚羊】 zǐlíngyáng bongo

【紫罗兰】 zǐluólán 〈植〉 violet; common stock

【紫茉莉】 zǐmòli 〈植〉 four-o'clock (*Mirabilis jalapa*)

【紫杉】 zǐshān 〈植〉 (Japanese) yew

【紫石英】 zǐshíyīng 〈矿〉 amethyst

【紫苏】 zǐsū 〈植〉 purple perilla (*Perilla frutescens* var. *crispa*)

【紫穗槐】 zǐsuìhuái 〈植〉 false indigo

【紫檀】 zǐtán 〈植〉 red sandalwood; padauk

【紫藤】 zǐténg 〈植〉 Chinese wistaria (*Wistaria sinensis*)

【紫铜】 zǐtóng red copper

【紫外线】 zǐwàixiàn 〈物〉 ultraviolet ray ◇～灯 ultraviolet lamp

【紫菀】 zǐwǎn 〈植〉 aster

【紫薇】 zǐwēi 〈植〉 crape myrtle

【紫药水】 zǐyàoshuǐ 〈药〉 gentian violet

【紫云英】 zǐyúnyīng 〈植〉 Chinese milk vetch (*Astragalus sinicus*)

【紫竹】 zǐzhú 〈植〉 black bamboo

**滓** zǐ 见"渣滓" zhāzǐ

**訾** zǐ 〈书〉 slander; calumniate

【訾议】 zǐyì 〈书〉 discuss the failings of others; criticize; impeach: 无可～ above criticism; unimpeachable

## zì

**字** zì ① word; character: ～义 meaning of a word/ 汉～ Chinese character ② pronunciation (of a word or character): 咬～清楚 pronounce every word clearly; have clear articulation ③ form of a written or printed character; style of handwriting; printing type: 篆～ seal character/ 黑体～ boldface; boldface type/ 柳～ style of calligraphy of Liu Gongquan (柳公权, 778-865 A.D.)/ 他写得一手好～。He writes a good hand. 或 He has good handwriting. ④ scripts; writings: 专藏～,不藏画 only collect scripts (或 writings), not paintings ⑤ receipt; written pledge: 立～为凭 give a written pledge/ 收到款子,写个～儿给他。Write him a receipt when you get the money from him. ⑥ a style (或 name) taken at the age of twenty, by which a man is sometimes called: 诸葛亮～孔明。Zhuge Liang styled himself Kongming. ⑦〈旧〉 (of a girl) be betrothed: 待～闺中 not be betrothed yet

【字典】 zìdiǎn dictionary: 查～ consult a dictionary

【字调】 zìdiào 〈语〉 tones of Chinese characters 参见"四声" sìshēng

【字号】 zìhao the name of a shop

【字盒】 zìhé 〈印〉 (type) mould

【字画】 zìhuà calligraphy and painting

【字汇】 zìhuì glossary; wordbook; lexicon

【字迹】 zìjī handwriting; writing: ～工整 neat writing/ ～模糊 illegible handwriting

【字句】 zìjù words and expressions; writing: ～通顺 coherent and smooth writing

【字据】 zìjù written pledge (e.g. receipt, IOU, contract, etc.)

【字里行间】 zìlǐ-hángjiān between the lines: 他的信～流露出畏难情绪。His letter reveals, between the lines, a certain fear of difficulty.

【字谜】 zìmí a riddle about a character or word

【字面】 zìmiàn literal: ～上的意思 literal meaning/ 从～上看 taken literally

【字模】 zìmú 〈印〉 (type) matrix: 冲压～ punched matrix ◇～雕刻机 matrix cutting machine

【字母】 zìmǔ letters of an alphabet; letter: 汉语拼音～ the Chinese phonetic alphabet/ 英语～ the English alphabet/ 大写～ a capital letter/ 按～顺序排列 be arranged in alphabetical order; be arranged alphabetically ◇～表 alphabet

【字幕】 zìmù captions (of motion pictures, etc.); subtitles: 中文～ Chinese subtitles (或 captions)

【字盘】 zìpán 〈印〉 case: 大写～ upper case/ 小写～ lower case

【字书】 zìshū wordbook; lexicon; dictionary

【字体】 zìtǐ ① form of a written or printed character; script; typeface ② style of calligraphy

【字条儿】 zìtiáor brief note

【字帖】 zìtiè copybook (for calligraphy)

【字眼】 zìyǎn wording; diction: 玩弄～ play with words/ 挑～儿 cavil at sb.'s choice of words; quibble

【字样】 zìyàng ① model of written characters ② printed or written words (which succinctly inform, instruct, warn, etc.): 封面上有"初稿"～。On the cover are the words "First Draft".

【字斟句酌】 zìzhēn-jùzhuó choose one's words with great care; weigh every word

【字纸】 zìzhǐ wastepaper with characters written or printed on it ◇～篓 wastepaper basket

**自** zì ① self; oneself; one's own: ～画像 self-portrait/ ～不量力 overestimate one's strength or oneself; not know one's own limitations/ ～打耳光 slap one's own face; contradict oneself ② certainly; of course: ～当努力 will certainly do one's best/ ～不待言 it goes without saying; be self-evident ③ from; since: ～即日起生效 become effective (as) from this date; with effect from (w.e.f.)/ ～数十元至几千元不等 ranging from tens to thousands of *yuan*/ ～古以来 since ancient times; from time immemorial/ ～幼 since childhood

【自爱】 zì'ài regard for oneself; self-respect

【自拔】 zìbá free oneself (from pain or evildoing); extricate oneself: 不能～ unable to extricate oneself

【自白】 zìbái make clear one's meaning or position; vindicate oneself

【自报公议】 zì bào gōng yì self-assessment and public discussion

【自暴自弃】 zìbào-zìqì be backward and have no urge to make progress; be resigned to one's backwardness; give oneself up as hopeless

【自卑】 zìbēi feel oneself inferior; be self-abased ◇ ～感 inferiority complex; sense of inferiority

【自备】 zìbèi provide for oneself: 在本食堂用饭请～碗筷。Will those who have their meals here please bring their own bowls and chopsticks.

【自变量】 zìbiànliàng 〈数〉 independent variable

【自便】 zìbiàn at one's convenience; as one pleases: 听其～。Let him do as he pleases./ 请～。Please do as you like.

【自裁】 zìcái 〈书〉 commit suicide; take one's own life

【自惭形秽】 zì cán xíng huì feel unworthy (of others' company); have a sense of inferiority or inadequacy

【自差】 zìchā 〈电〉 autodyne ◇ ～收音机 autodyne (radio receiver)

【自称】 zìchēng call oneself; claim to be; profess: ～内行 call oneself an expert; claim to be an old hand/ ～不知情 profess ignorance

【自成一家】 zì chéng yī jiā (in calligraphy, painting, sculpture, etc.) have a style of one's own; be unique in one's style

【自乘】 zìchéng 〈数〉 involution; squaring: 七～得四十九。The square of 7 is 49. 或 7 squared is 49.

【自持】 zìchí control oneself; restrain oneself; exercise self-restraint

【自吹自擂】 zìchuī-zìlèi blow one's own trumpet; crack oneself up

【自从】 zìcóng since: ～去年秋天到现在 from last autumn till now; since last fall

【自大】 zìdà self-important; arrogant ◇ ～狂 megalomania

【自得】 zìdé contented; self-satisfied: 悠然～ contentedly take one's ease; act in a leisurely, contented manner/ 洋洋～ complacent; smug

【自得其乐】 zì dé qí lè be content with one's lot

【自动】 zìdòng ① voluntarily; of one's own accord: ～参加 participate voluntarily/ ～帮忙 make a spontaneous offer of help/ ～交待 make a voluntary confession; confess of one's own accord/ 一切反动派都不会～退出历史舞台。No reactionary force will ever step down from the stage of history of its own accord. ② automatic: ～延长 (of a lease, etc.) be automatically extended
◇ ～步枪 automatic rifle/ ～扶梯 escalator/ ～换梭织机 automatic shuttle-changing loom/ ～绢网印花机 automatic screen printing machine/ ～控制 automatic control/ ～铅笔 propelling pencil/ ～饲喂器 〈牧〉 self-feeder/ ～线 transfer machine/ ～音量控制 automatic volume control/ ～饮水器 〈牧〉 automatic drinking bowl/ ～增益控制 〈电〉 automatic gain control/ ～装配线 automatic assembly line/ ～装填炮 autoloading gun

【自动化】 zìdònghuà automation: 工艺过程～ process automation/ 铁路编组站～ automation of a railway marshalling yard

【自渎】 zìdú 〈书〉 self-abuse; masturbation

【自发】 zìfā spontaneous: ～的斗争 spontaneous struggle/ 小资产阶级的无政府主义～倾向 the spontaneous petty-bourgeois tendency towards anarchism ◇ ～性 spontaneity

【自肥】 zìféi fatten oneself; enrich oneself by misappropriating funds or material; feather one's nest

【自费】 zìfèi at one's own expense: ～旅行 travel at one's own expense

【自封】 zìfēng ① proclaim (或 style) oneself: ～为诗人 proclaim oneself a poet ② confine oneself; isolate oneself: 故步～ stand still and refuse to make progress; be complacent and conservative

【自负】 zìfù ① be responsible for one's own action, etc.: 文责～。The author takes sole responsibility for his views. ② think highly of oneself; be conceited: 这个人很～。This person is rather conceited.

【自负盈亏】 zì fù yíng-kuī (of an enterprise) assume sole responsibility for its profits or losses

【自甘堕落】 zì gān duòluò wallow in degeneration; abandon oneself to vice

【自感应】 zìgǎnyìng 〈物〉 self-induction

【自高自大】 zìgāo-zìdà self-important; conceited; arrogant

【自告奋勇】 zì gào fènyǒng offer to undertake (a difficult or dangerous task); volunteer (to do sth. difficult): ～参加突击队 volunteer to join the shock team

【自割】 zìgē 〈动〉 autotomy

【自各儿】 zìgěr 〈方〉 oneself; by oneself: 我很忙，你～去，好吗？I'm busy. Would you go there by yourself?

【自耕农】 zìgēngnóng owner-peasant; land-holding peasant

【自供】 zìgòng confess ◇ ～状 confession

【自顾不暇】 zì gù bù xiá be unable even to fend for oneself (much less look after others); be busy enough with one's own affairs

【自汗】 zìhàn 〈中医〉 spontaneous perspiration (或 sweating)

【自豪】 zìháo have a proper sense of pride or dignity; be proud of sth.: 我们为社会主义祖国的伟大成就而～。We are proud of the great achievements of our socialist country. ◇ ～感 sense of pride

【自花不稔性】 zìhuā bùrěnxìng 〈植〉 self-sterility

【自花传粉】 zìhuā chuánfěn 〈植〉 self-pollination

【自毁】 zìhuǐ 〈军〉 self-destruction: 导弹～ missile self-destruction

【自己】 zìjǐ ① oneself: 生～的气 be angry with oneself/ ～动手 use one's own hands/ 打击别人，抬高～ sling mud at others so as to boost oneself/ 你～看看去！Go and see for yourself!/ 瓶子不会～倒下来，准是有人碰了它。The bottle couldn't have fallen down of itself. Someone must have knocked it over. ② closely related; own: ～弟兄 one's own brothers

【自己人】 zìjǐrén people on one's own side; one of us: 他是～。He's one of us./ 都是～，你别客气了。You're among friends, so make yourself at home.

【自给】 zìjǐ self-sufficient; self-supporting: 粮食～有余 be more than self-sufficient in grain ◇ ～经济 self-supporting (或 self-contained) economy/ ～率 degree of self-sufficiency

【自给自足】 zìjǐ-zìzú self-sufficiency; autarky

【自家】 zìjiā 〈方〉 oneself

【自荐】 zìjiàn recommend oneself (for a job); offer one's services

【自尽】 zìjìn commit suicide; take one's own life

【自净】 zìjìng 〈环保〉 self-purification

【自咎】 zìjiù blame oneself; rebuke oneself

【自救】 zìjiù save oneself; provide for and help oneself: 团结～ get united for one's own salvation/ 生产～ provide for and help oneself by engaging in production

【自居】 zìjū consider oneself to be; pose as: 以功臣～ pose as one who has rendered great service; give oneself the airs of a hero

【自决】 zìjué self-determination: 民族～ national self-determination ◇ ～权 right to self-determination

【自觉】 zìjué conscious; aware: 这种病初起时，患者每不～。Those suffering from the disease are often unaware of it in the early stages./ ～的共产主义战士 a politically conscious fighter for communism/ ～遵守纪律 conscientiously observe discipline ◇ ～性 (level of political) consciousness

【自觉自愿】 zìjué-zìyuàn voluntarily; willingly; of one's own free will

【自绝】 zìjué alienate oneself: ～于人民 alienate oneself from the people

【自掘坟墓】 zì jué fénmù dig one's own grave; work for one's own destruction

【自夸】 zìkuā sing one's own praises; crack oneself up

【自拉自唱】 zìlā-zìchàng ① accompany one's own singing ② hold forth all alone in defence of one's own views or proposals; second one's own motion

【自来】 zìlái from the beginning; in the first place; originally

【自来红】 zìláihóng born red: 没有～,只有改造红。No one is born red; one becomes red only through ideological remoulding. 或 No one is born with a proletarian world outlook; one acquires it only through ideological remoulding.

【自来火】 zìláihuǒ 〈方〉 ① matches ② cigarette-lighter; lighter

【自来水】 zìláishuǐ running water; tap water ◇ ～厂 waterworks

【自来水笔】 zìláishuǐbǐ fountain pen

【自理】 zìlǐ take care of or provide for oneself: 伙食～ make one's own eating arrangements/ 旅费～ pay one's own travelling expenses

【自立】 zìlì stand on one's own feet; support oneself; earn one's own living

【自力更生】 zìlì gēngshēng regeneration (或 reconstruction) through one's own efforts; self-reliance: ～重建家园 rebuild one's homeland through self-reliance (或 one's own efforts)/ 我们是主张～的。We stand for self-reliance.

【自力霉素】 zìlìméisù 〈药〉 mitomycin C

【自量】 zìliàng estimate one's own ability or strength: 不知～ overrate one's abilities

【自流】 zìliú ① (of water, etc.) flow automatically; flow by itself ② (of a thing) take its natural course; (of a person) do as one pleases: 听其～ let things drift along; let people act freely without leadership ◇ ～灌溉 〈农〉 gravity irrigation/ ～井 〈地〉 artesian well

【自留畜】 zìliúchù livestock for personal needs; privately owned livestock: 在牧区,人民公社社员可以有少量的～。In pastoral areas, commune members may keep a limited number of livestock for personal needs.

【自留地】 zìliúdì plot of land for personal needs; family plot; private plot

【自卖自夸】 zìmài-zìkuā praise the goods one sells; indulge in self-glorification; blow one's own trumpet

【自满】 zìmǎn complacent; self-satisfied: ～情绪 complacency; self-satisfaction/ 要认真学习一点东西,必须从不～开始。We cannot really learn anything until we rid ourselves of complacency.

【自明】 zìmíng self-evident; self-explanatory; obvious: 其理～。The principle involved is obvious./ 含义～,无须多说。This point is self-evident and needs no elaboration.

【自鸣得意】 zì míng déyì show self-satisfaction; be very pleased with oneself; preen oneself

【自鸣钟】 zìmíngzhōng striking clock; chime clock

【自命】 zìmìng consider oneself; regard oneself as: ～为历史学家 consider oneself a historian; profess to be a historian

【自命不凡】 zìmìng bù fán consider oneself no ordinary being; have an unduly high opinion of oneself; think no end of oneself

【自馁】 zìněi lose confidence; be discouraged

【自捻纱】 zìniǎnshā 〈纺〉 self-twisted yarn

【自拍机】 zìpāijī 〈摄〉 self-timer

【自喷井】 zìpēnjǐng 〈石油〉 flowing well; gusher well

【自喷期】 zìpēnqī 〈石油〉 flush stage; flowing life

【自欺欺人】 zì qī qī rén deceive oneself as well as others: 所谓通过"议会道路"实现社会主义,完全是～之谈。To proclaim that socialism can be realized through the "parliamentary road" is a gross deception.

【自遣】 zìqiǎn divert oneself from melancholy, etc.; cheer oneself up: 无以～ have no way to cheer oneself up (或 amuse oneself); have nothing to divert oneself with

【自戕】 zìqiāng 〈书〉 commit suicide; take one's own life

【自强不息】 zìqiáng bù xī make unremitting (或 unceasing) efforts to improve oneself; constantly strive to become stronger

【自轻自贱】 zìqīng-zìjiàn belittle oneself; lack self-confidence or self-respect

【自取灭亡】 zì qǔ mièwáng court (或 invite) destruction; take the road to one's doom

【自取其咎】 zì qǔ qí jiù bring blame on oneself; have only oneself to blame: 你这是～。You asked for it.

【自然】 zìrán ① natural world; nature: 改造～ transform nature/ 与～作斗争 struggle with nature; battle the elements/ ～条件 natural conditions ② naturally; in the ordinary course of events: ～地归于消灭 die out naturally/ 功到～成。Constant effort yields sure success./ 这病不用吃药,休息一两天～会好的。No medicine is necessary for this illness. With a couple of days of rest you'll be all right./ 你先别问,到时候～明白。Don't ask now. You'll understand in due course. ③ of course; naturally: 你第一次登台感到紧张是很～的。Naturally, you were keyed up when you went on the stage for the first time./ 只要努力,～会取得好成绩。If you work hard, you're bound to get good results.

◇ ～辩证法 dialectics of nature/ ～博物馆 museum of natural history/ ～规律 natural law/ ～环境 natural environment/ ～界 natural world; nature/ ～金属 native metal/ ～经济 natural economy/ ～科学 natural science/ ～类群 〈生〉 natural group/ ～力 natural forces/ ～区域 natural regions/ ～人 〈法〉 natural person/ ～数 natural number/ ～死亡 natural death/ ～铜 native copper/ ～现象 natural phenomena/ ～形态 natural form/ ～选择 〈生〉 natural selection/ ～灾害 natural calamity/ ～主义 naturalism/ ～资源 natural resources (或 wealth)

【自然】 zìran at ease; natural; free from affectation: 态度非常～ be quite at ease/ 她虽是初次演出,但是演得很～。Her acting was very natural although it was the first time she appeared on the stage./ 他不～地笑了一笑。He forced a smile.

【自然而然】 zìrán'érrán naturally; automatically; spontaneously; of oneself

【自然神论】 zìránshénlùn 〈哲〉 deism ◇ ～者 deist

【自燃】 zìrán 〈化〉 spontaneous combustion (或 ignition)

【自认晦气】 zì rèn huìqì accept bad luck without complaint; grin and bear it

【自如】 zìrú 〈书〉 freely; smoothly; with facility: 操纵～ operate with facility/ 旋转～ rotate or revolve freely/ 运用～ handle and use (a tool) with skill; wield skilfully

【自若】 zìruò 〈书〉 self-possessed; composed; calm and at ease: 神态～ appear calm and at ease; appear composed/ 临危不惧,谈笑～ talk and laugh imperturbably in face of danger

【自杀】 zìshā commit suicide; take one's own life

【自上而下】 zì shàng ér xià from above to below; from top to bottom: 军队中～的统一指挥 unified command from above in the army

【自身】 zìshēn self; oneself: ～难保 be unable even to fend for oneself/ ～思想革命化 revolutionization of one's thinking

【自生自灭】 zìshēng-zìmiè (of a thing) emerge of itself and perish of itself; run its course

【自食其果】 zì shí qí guǒ eat one's own bitter fruit; reap what one has sown

【自食其力】 zì shí qí lì support oneself by one's own labour; earn one's own living

【自始至终】 zì shǐ zhì zhōng from start to finish; from beginning to end

【自视】 zìshì consider (或 think, imagine) oneself: ～甚高 think highly of oneself; be self-important

【自恃】 zìshì be self-assured for having sth. or sb. to rely on; count on; capitalize on: ～有功 capitalize on one's achievements/ ～有靠山 count on sb.'s backing

【自是】 zìshì naturally; of course: 久别重逢，～高兴。It was of course a delight for them to meet again after such a long separation.

【自首】 zìshǒu ① (of a criminal) voluntarily surrender oneself; confess one's crime; give oneself up: 投案～ surrender oneself to the police or judicial department ② make a political recantation; surrender to the enemy: ～变节 recant and turn traitor ◇ ～书 confession

【自赎】 zìshú redeem oneself; atone for one's crime: 立功～ perform meritorious services to atone for one's crime

【自述】 zìshù an account in one's own words

【自私】 zìsī selfish; self-centred: ～自利是可鄙的。Selfishness is contemptible./ 毫无～自利之心的精神 the spirit of absolute selflessness

【自诉】 zìsù 〈法〉 private prosecution; action initiated by an injured party without the participation of the public prosecutor ◇ ～人 private party who prosecutes a case by himself; party who initiates a private prosecution

【自讨苦吃】 zì tǎo kǔ chī ask for trouble

【自体不育性】 zìtǐ bùyùxìng 〈动〉 self-sterility

【自投罗网】 zì tóu luówǎng hurl oneself willingly into the net; bite the hook

【自卫】 zìwèi ① defend oneself: ～能力 the capacity to defend oneself ② self-defence: ～反击 fight (或 strike) back in self-defence
◇ ～反击战 counterattack in self-defence/ ～军 self-defence corps/ ～行动 an act in self-defence/ ～原则 principle of self-defence/ ～战争 war of self-defence

【自为阶级】 zìwèijiējí class-for-itself

【自慰】 zìwèi console oneself: 聊以～ just to console oneself

【自刎】 zìwěn commit suicide by cutting one's throat; cut one's throat

【自问】 zìwèn ① ask oneself; examine oneself: 反躬～ examine oneself; examine one's conscience ② reach a conclusion after weighing a matter: 我～是花过不少力气的。I flatter myself that I have spared no pains./ 我～没有什么对不起他的地方。I don't remember ever doing him wrong.

【自我】 zìwǒ 〔用在双音动词前面，表示这个动作由自己发出，同时又以自己为对象〕 self; oneself: ～介绍 introduce oneself
◇ ～暗示 〈心〉 self-suggestion/ ～暴露 self-betrayal; self-exposure/ ～辩解 self-justification/ ～表现 self-expression/ ～吹嘘 self-glorification/ ～催眠 autohypnosis/ ～改造 self-remoulding/ ～观察 〈心〉 self-observation/ ～检查 self-examination; introspection/ ～教育 self-education/ ～批评 self-criticism/ ～牺牲 self-sacrifice/ ～欣赏 self-appreciation; self-admiration

【自我作古】 zì wǒ zuò gǔ be the first to do sth.; originate a method, etc.

【自习】 zìxí (of students) study by oneself in scheduled time or free time ◇ ～时间 time for individual study

【自下而上】 zì xià ér shàng from bottom to top; from below: ～的监督 supervision from below

【自相残杀】 zì xiāng cánshā (of persons within a group, party, etc.) kill each other; cause death to one another

【自相惊扰】 zì xiāng jīngrǎo alarm one's own group, etc.; create disturbance within one's ranks; raise false alarms

【自相矛盾】 zì xiāng máodùn contradict oneself; be self-contradictory: 他的话～。What he says is self-contradictory./ 你这不是～吗？Aren't you contradicting yourself?

【自卸卡车】 zìxiè kǎchē dump truck; tip truck

【自新】 zìxīn turn over a new leaf; make a fresh start: 改过～ correct one's errors and make a fresh start; turn over a new leaf

【自信】 zìxìn self-confident: 有～心 have self-confidence; be sure of oneself/ 我～能够完成这项任务。I'm sure I can fulfil the task.

【自行】 zìxíng ① by oneself: ～解决 settle (a problem) by oneself/ ～安排 arrange by oneself/ ～设计 make designs of one's own ② of oneself; of one's own accord; voluntarily: ～到来 come of itself/ 敌人是不会～消灭的。The enemy will not perish of himself. ③ 〈天〉 proper motion

【自行车】 zìxíngchē bicycle; bike: 骑～ ride a bicycle/ 骑～进城 go down town by bike
◇ ～架 bicycle stand/ ～竞赛 cycle racing/ ～棚 bicycle shed

【自行火炮】 zìxíng huǒpào 〈军〉 self-propelled gun

【自行其是】 zì xíng qí shì act as one thinks fit; go one's own way

【自修】 zìxiū ① (of students) study by oneself; have self-study ② study on one's own; study independently: ～法语 teach oneself French

【自诩】 zìxǔ 〈书〉 praise oneself; crack oneself up; brag

【自序】 zìxù ① author's preface; preface ② autobiographic note; brief account of oneself 又作"自叙"

【自选】 zìxuǎn 〈体〉 free; optional: ～动作 optional exercise/ ～手枪五十米赛 free pistol 50 m.

【自学】 zìxué study on one's own; study independently; teach oneself: 培养～能力 cultivate (或 foster) one's ability to study independently ◇ ～课本 teach-yourself books

【自寻死路】 zì xún sǐlù bring about one's own destruction

【自言自语】 zìyán-zìyǔ talk to oneself; think aloud; soliloquize

【自养生物】 zìyǎng shēngwù 〈生〉 autotroph

【自养植物】 zìyǎng zhíwù 〈植〉 autophyte; autotrophic plant

【自以为是】 zì yǐwéi shì consider oneself (always) in the right; regard oneself as infallible; be opinionated

【自缢】 zìyì 〈书〉 hang oneself

【自用】 zìyòng ① obstinately holding to one's own views; opinionated; self-willed: 刚愎～ obstinate; self-opinionated/ 愚而好～ ignorant and self-willed ② for private use; personal: ～物品 personal effects; personal belongings

【自由】 zìyóu ① freedom; liberty: 公民～权 civil liberties/ 中国公民有言论、通信、出版、集会、结社、游行、示威、罢工的～。Citizens of China enjoy freedom of speech, correspondence, the press, assembly, association, procession, demonstration and the freedom to strike. ② 〈哲〉 freedom: ～和必然 freedom and necessity ③ free; unrestrained: ～讨论 have a free exchange of views/ ～选择 be free to choose; have a free choice/ ～行动 act on one's own/ ～发表意见 express one's views unreservedly/ 决不能让资产

阶级思想～泛滥。Bourgeois ideas must not be allowed to spread unchecked.
◇ ～电子 free electron/ ～港 free port/ ～化 liberalization/ ～汇率 free exchange rate/ ～竞争 free competition/ ～联想〈心〉 free (或 uncontrolled) association/ ～恋爱 freedom to choose one's spouse/ ～贸易 free trade/ ～民〈史〉 freeman/ ～能〈物〉 free energy/ ～诗 free verse; unorthodox verse/ ～市场 free (或 open) market/ ～体操 free exercise; floor exercise; free callisthenics/ ～意志 free will/ ～泳 freestyle (swimming); crawl/ ～职业 profession/ ～职业者 professional/ ～资本主义 non-monopoly capitalism; *laissez-faire* capitalism/ ～资产阶级 non-monopoly bourgeoisie; liberal bourgeoisie

【自由兑换】 zìyóu duìhuàn 〈经〉 convertibility: 可以～的货币 convertible currency/ 不能～的货币 inconvertible currency

【自由放任】 zìyóu fàngrèn allowing unrestrained freedom; *laissez-faire* ◇ ～主义 *laissez-faire*

【自由散漫】 zìyóu-sǎnmàn slack; lax in discipline: ～现象 slackness (in discipline)/ 小资产阶级的～性 the petty bourgeoisie's individualistic aversion to discipline

【自由王国】 zìyóu wángguó 〈哲〉 realm of freedom: 人类的历史，就是一个不断地从必然王国向～发展的历史。The history of mankind is one of continuous development from the realm of necessity to the realm of freedom.

【自由主义】 zìyóuzhǔyì liberalism: ～的倾向 liberal tendencies/ 革命的集体组织中的～是十分有害的。Liberalism is extremely harmful in a revolutionary collective. ◇ ～者 liberal

【自由自在】 zìyóu-zìzài leisurely and carefree; free and unrestrained

【自由组合规律】 zìyóu zǔhé guīlǜ 〈生〉 law of independent assortment

【自育】 zìyù 〈动〉 self-fertile

【自圆其说】 zì yuán qí shuō make one's statement consistent; justify oneself: 这样解释能～吗? Is this a plausible explanation?/ 不能～ cannot offer a tenable argument; cannot justify oneself

【自怨自艾】 zìyuàn-zìyì ① repent and redress one's errors ② be full of remorse

【自愿】 zìyuàn voluntary; of one's own accord; of one's own free will: 出于～ on a voluntary basis; of one's free will/ ～参加山区建设 volunteer to work in a mountainous area/ ～互利的原则 the principles of voluntary participation and mutual benefit/ 按照群众的需要和～ in accordance with the needs and wishes of the masses

【自在】 zìzài free; unrestrained: 逍遥～ leisurely and carefree; free from trammels; at liberty to enjoy oneself

【自在】 zìzai comfortable; at ease: 主人太客气了，反而使他们有些不～。The host's assiduous attentions made them feel rather ill at ease./ 身体有点不～ feel a little out of sorts; not be quite oneself

【自在阶级】 zìzàijiējí 〈哲〉 class-in-itself

【自在之物】 zìzài zhī wù 〈哲〉 thing-in-itself

【自找】 zìzhǎo suffer from one's own actions; ask for it: 这是你～的嘛! You asked for it./ ～麻烦 be looking for trouble

【自知之明】 zìzhī zhī míng self-knowledge: 无～ lack of self-knowledge/ 人贵有～。It is important to know one's own limitations. 或 Self-knowledge is wisdom.

【自治】 zìzhì autonomy; self-government: 民族区域～regional national autonomy/ ～的权限 autonomous jurisdiction ◇ ～机关 organ of self-government/ (英联邦的) ～领 dominion/ ～区 autonomous region/ ～权 autonomy/ ～条例 regulations on the exercise of autonomy/ ～县 autonomous county/ ～州 autonomous prefecture

【自制】 zìzhì ① made by oneself: 这台铣床是我们厂～的。This milling machine was made in our own plant. ② self-control; self-restraint: 失去～ lose self-control

【自重】 zìzhòng ① conduct oneself with dignity; be self-possessed. ② dead weight: 车皮～ the dead weight of a wagon

【自主】 zìzhǔ act on one's own; decide for oneself; keep the initiative in one's own hands: 独立～ independently and with the initiative in one's own hands/ 不由～ cannot help (it); involuntarily/ 男女婚姻～。Men and women shall marry the partners of their choice.

【自传】 zìzhuàn autobiography

【自转】 zìzhuàn 〈天〉 rotation: 地球的～ the rotation of the earth ◇ ～轴〈天〉 axis of rotation

【自走式】 zìzǒushì self-propelled ◇ ～联合收割机 self-propelled combine harvester

【自尊】 zìzūn self-respect; self-esteem; proper pride: 伤了他的～心 injure his self-esteem; wound his pride ◇ ～感 sense of self-respect

【自作自受】 zìzuō-zìshòu suffer from one's own actions; as a man sows, so shall he reap: 这是你～。As you make your bed, so you must lie on it.

【自作聪明】 zì zuò cōngmíng think oneself clever (in making suggestions, etc.)

【自作主张】 zì zuò zhǔzhāng act on one's own; decide for oneself: 这件事我们得请示领导，不能～。We can't decide this matter for ourselves; we must ask the leadership for instructions.

**恣** zì throw off restraint; do as one pleases: 得以自～ be able to do as one likes (或 indulge oneself)

【恣肆】 zìsì 〈书〉 ① unrestrained; self-indulgent; wanton ② (of writing style) forceful and unrestrained; free and natural

【恣睢】 zìsuī 〈书〉 reckless; unbridled

【恣行无忌】 zì xíng wú jì act wilfully and unscrupulously; behave recklessly

【恣意】 zìyì unscrupulous; reckless; unbridled; wilful: ～妄为 behave unscrupulously/ ～践踏 wilfully trample on/ ～掠夺别国的资源 indulge in unbridled plunder of the resources of other countries

**渍** zì ① steep; soak; ret: ～麻 ret flax, jute, etc./ 白衬衫被汗水～黄了。The white shirt has yellowed with sweat. ② floodwater on low-lying land: 防洪排～ prevention of floods and drainage of floodwater ③ be soiled (with grease, etc.): 她每天擦机器，不让～一点油泥。She polishes the machine every day so that there's not a speck of dirt on it./ 烟斗里～了很多油子。The pipe is caked with tar. ④ 〈方〉 stain; sludge: 油～ oil sludge/ 茶～ tea stains

**眦** zì corner of the eye; canthus

## zōng

**宗** zōng ① ancestor: 列祖列～ successive generations of ancestors ② clan: 同～ of the same clan ③ sect; faction; school: 正～ orthodox school ④ principal aim; purpose: 开～明义 make clear the purpose and main theme from the very beginning ⑤ (in academic or artistic work) take as one's model ⑥ model; great master: 一代诗～ an outstanding figure among the poets of the time ⑦ 〈量〉: 一～心事 a matter that worries one/ 大～款项 a large sum of money/ 大～货物 a large quantity of goods ⑧ 〈旧〉 an

administrative unit in Xizang, roughly corresponding to the county ⑨ (Zōng) a surname
【宗祠】 zōngcí ancestral hall (或 temple)
【宗法】 zōngfǎ patriarchal clan system ◇ ～社会 patriarchal society
【宗匠】 zōngjiàng 〈旧〉 great master (in academic or artistic work)
【宗教】 zōngjiào religion: 公民有信仰～的自由和不信仰～、宣传无神论的自由。Citizens enjoy freedom to believe in religion and freedom not to believe in religion and to propagate atheism.
◇ (中世纪天主教审判异教徒的)～法庭 the Inquisition/ ～改革 religious reform/ ～戒律 religious taboo/ ～派别 religious sect/ ～信仰 religious belief/ ～仪式 religious rites; ritual
【宗庙】 zōngmiào ancestral temple (或 shrine) of a ruling house
【宗派】 zōngpài faction; sect
◇ ～斗争 factional strife/ ～活动 factional activities; sectarian activities/ ～主义 sectarianism; factionalism/ ～主义者 sectarian; factionalist
【宗师】 zōngshī 〈旧〉 master of great learning and integrity
【宗室】 zōngshì ① imperial (或 royal) clan ② imperial (或 royal) clansman
【宗仰】 zōngyǎng 〈书〉 hold in esteem: 海内～ be held in esteem throughout the country
【宗旨】 zōngzhǐ aim; purpose: 建党～ the aim of Party building/ 全心全意地为人民服务是我军的唯一～。To serve the people wholeheartedly is the sole purpose of our army.
【宗主国】 zōngzhǔguó suzerain (state); metropolitan state
【宗主权】 zōngzhǔquán suzerainty
【宗族】 zōngzú ① patriarchal clan ② clansman

## 综

zōng put together; sum up: ～上所述 to sum up
另见 zèng
【综观】 zōngguān make a comprehensive survey
【综合】 zōnghé ① synthesize: ～群众的意见 synthesize (或 sum up) the opinions of the masses ② synthetical; comprehensive; multiple; composite: ～的研究 a synthetical (或 comprehensive) study
◇ ～报导 comprehensive (或 composite) dispatch; news roundup/ ～报告 comprehensive report; summing-up report/ ～病征 syndrome/ ～大学 university/ ～规划 unified plan/ ～考察 comprehensive survey/ ～利用 comprehensive utilization; multipurpose use/ ～平衡 overall balance/ ～性工厂 multiple-producing factory/ ～语 〈语〉 synthetic language
【综计】 zōngjì sum up; add up: 合理化建议～有九个方面。To sum up, the rationalization proposals fall into nine categories.
【综括】 zōngkuò sum up: ～起来 to sum up; to state succinctly
【综述】 zōngshù summarize; sum up: 来稿～ a summary of readers' contributions

## 棕

zōng ① palm ② palm fibre; coir: ～绳 coir rope
【棕绷】 zōngbēng wooden bed frame strung with crisscross coir ropes
【棕榈】 zōnglǘ palm ◇ ～酸 palmitic (或 palmic) acid/ ～油 palm oil; palm butter
【棕毛】 zōngmáo palm fibre: ～蓑衣 palm rain cape
【棕壤】 zōngrǎng 〈农〉 brown earth
【棕色】 zōngsè brown ◇ ～森林土 〈农〉 brown forest soil
【棕树】 zōngshù palm
【棕熊】 zōngxióng 〈动〉 brown bear

## 踪

zōng footprint; track; trace: 跟～ follow the tracks of; trail
【踪迹】 zōngjì trace; track: 不留～ not leave a trace
【踪影】 zōngyǐng 〔多用于否定式〕 trace; sign: 毫无～ leaving without a trace

## 鬃

zōng hair on the neck of a pig, horse, etc.: 马～ horse's mane/ 猪～ pig's bristles/ ～刷 bristle brush

# zǒng

## 总

zǒng ① assemble; put together; sum up: 汇～ assemble; collect; gather together/ ～起来说 to sum up/ ～其成 assume overall command of a project and bring it to completion/ 把两笔帐～到一块算 settle the two accounts together ② general; overall; total: ～产量 total output/ ～趋势 general trend/ ～危机 general crisis/ ～开关 master switch/ ～根源 root cause/ 抓～ assume overall responsibility/ ～的说来 generally speaking; by and large/ 开总结会,算～帐 hold summing-up meetings for a general check-up ③ chief; head; general: ～编辑 editor in chief/ ～工程师 chief engineer/ ～店 head office (of a firm)/ ～部 general headquarters/ ～书记 secretary-general; general secretary/ ～头目 chief boss; chieftain ④ always; invariably: ～是站在斗争的第一线 always stand in the forefront of the struggle/ 正确的东西～是在同错误的东西作斗争的过程中发展起来的。What is correct invariably develops in the course of struggle with what is wrong. ⑤ anyway; after all; inevitably; sooner or later: 问题～是要解决的。The problem will be settled sooner or later./ 两个超级大国的激烈争夺,～有一天要导致世界大战。The fierce contention between the two superpowers is bound to lead to a world war some day./ 他～还是个孩子,哪能象大人那样有力气? After all, he's only a child. How can he possibly be as strong as a grown-up?
【总参谋部】 zǒngcānmóubù the Headquarters of the General Staff
【总参谋长】 zǒngcānmóuzhǎng chief of the general staff
【总成】 zǒngchéng 〈机〉 assembly
【总得】 zǒngděi must; have to; be bound to: ～想个办法 have got to find a way out/ 他今天～来一趟。He's bound to come today.
【总动员】 zǒngdòngyuán general (或 total) mobilization
【总督】 zǒngdū governor-general; governor; viceroy
【总额】 zǒng'é total: 存款～ total deposits/ 工资～ total wages
【总而言之】 zǒng ér yán zhī in short; in a word; in brief; to make a long story short
【总方针】 zǒngfāngzhēn general policy; general principle: 经济工作的～ the general policy guiding economic work/ 外交政策～ general principles of foreign policy
【总纲】 zǒnggāng general programme; general principles: 党章～ the general programme of the Party Constitution/ 中华人民共和国宪法～ the General Principles of the Constitution of the People's Republic of China
【总工会】 zǒnggōnghuì federation of trade unions: 中华全国～ All-China Federation of Trade Unions
【总攻】 zǒnggōng 〈军〉 general offensive
【总共】 zǒnggòng in all; altogether; in the aggregate: ～约五千人 about five thousand people in all/ 这个地区～有二百二十家工厂。There are altogether 220 factories in this area.
【总管】 zǒngguǎn manager

【总归】 zǒngguī anyhow; eventually; after all: 困难～是可以克服的。Difficulties can after all be overcome./ 事实～是事实。After all, facts are facts.

【总和】 zǒnghé sum; total; sum total: 无数相对的真理之～,就是绝对的真理。The sum total of innumerable relative truths constitutes absolute truth./ 对世界政治、经济的～进行具体的分析 make a concrete analysis of world politics and economics as a whole/ 各部分的～ summation of individual parts

【总后勤部】 zǒnghòuqínbù the General Logistics Department

【总汇】 zǒnghuì ① (of streams) come or flow together: ～入海 flow into the sea together ② confluence; concourse; aggregate: 人民是智慧的海洋，力量的～。The people are a sea of wisdom and the aggregation of strength./ 李时珍的《本草纲目》是当时中国药物学的～。*Compendium of Materia Medica* by Li Shizhen (1518-1593) was a comprehensive summary of all pharmacological knowledge accumulated in China up to his time.

【总机】 zǒngjī switchboard; telephone exchange

【总计】 zǒngjì ① 〈数〉 grand total ② amount to; add up to; total: ～一千元。It amounts to 1,000 *yuan*. 或 It adds up to 1,000 *yuan*./ 观众～有十万人。The audience totalled 100,000. 或 There were 100,000 spectators in all.

【总价】 zǒngjià total (price)

【总监】 zǒngjiān inspector general; chief inspector

【总角】 zǒngjiǎo 〈书〉 a child's hair twisted in a knot — childhood: ～之交 childhood friend

【总结】 zǒngjié ① sum up; summarize: ～经验 sum up one's experience/ ～工作 summarize one's work ② summary; summing-up: 作～ make a summary/ 哲学是关于自然知识和社会知识的概括和～。Philosophy is the generalization and summation of the knowledge of nature and society. ◇ ～报告 summary (或 final, concluding) report/ ～会 summing-up meeting

【总括】 zǒngkuò sum up: ～起来 to sum up; to state succinctly

【总揽】 zǒnglǎn assume overall responsibility; take on everything: ～大权 have overall authority; assume a dominant role

【总理】 zǒnglǐ premier; prime minister: 国务院～ the Premier of the State Council

【总领事】 zǒnglǐngshì consul general ◇ ～馆 consulate general

【总路线】 zǒnglùxiàn general line: 党在过渡时期的～ the Party's general line for the transition period

【总目】 zǒngmù comprehensive table of contents

【总平面图】 zǒngpíngmiàntú general layout

【总评】 zǒngpíng general comment; overall appraisal

【总谱】 zǒngpǔ 〈乐〉 score

【总数】 zǒngshù total; sum total

【总司令】 zǒngsīlìng commander in chief ◇ ～部 general headquarters

【总算】 zǒngsuàn 〈副〉 ① at long last; finally: 会议一再延期,现在～开成了。After several postponements the meeting has been held at last./ 他想来想去,最后～想出了一个好主意。He thought it over and over and finally hit upon a good idea. ② considering everything; all things considered; on the whole: 小孩子的字能写成这样，～不错了。For a child's handwriting, it's quite good.

【总体】 zǒngtǐ overall; total ◇ ～规划 overall plan/ ～战 general war; total warfare

【总统】 zǒngtǒng president (of a republic) ◇ ～府 presidential palace; the residence and/ or office of a president/ ～选举 presidential election/ ～制 presidential government

【总务】 zǒngwù ① general affairs ② person in charge of general affairs ◇ ～科 general affairs section/ ～司 general service department

【总则】 zǒngzé general rules; general principles

【总闸门】 zǒngzhámén 〈石油〉 master valve; master gate

【总帐】 zǒngzhàng general ledger

【总政治部】 zǒngzhèngzhìbù the General Political Department ◇ ～主任 Director of the General Political Department

【总之】 zǒngzhī in a word; in short; in brief

【总支】 zǒngzhī general branch: 党～ general Party branch/ 团～书记 secretary of the genreal Youth League branch

【总值】 zǒngzhí total value: 生产～ total output value/ 进(出)口～ gross import (export) value/ 国民生产～ gross national product (GNP)

【总指挥】 zǒngzhǐhuī ① commander in chief ② general director ◇ ～部 general headquarters

【总状花序】 zǒngzhuàng huāxù 〈植〉 raceme

**偬** zǒng 见"倥偬" kǒngzǒng

## zòng

**纵** zòng ① from north to south: 大运河～贯河北、山东、江苏、浙江四省。The Grand Canal flows southwards through the four provinces of Hebei, Shandong, Jiangsu and Zhejiang. ② vertical; longitudinal; lengthwise: ～剖面 vertical section ③ release; set free: 七擒七～ capture and release seven times ④ indulge; let loose; let oneself go: 放～ let sb. have his way; indulge/ 娇～ pamper (a child)/ ～声大笑 have a hearty laugh ⑤ jump up; jump into the air: 他向前一～,就把球接住了。He leaped forward and caught the ball. ⑥〈书〉 even if; though; even though: ～有千难万险，也挡不住英勇的勘探队员。Even though there are myriad hardships and hazards, they can't stop the dauntless prospectors.

【纵波】 zòngbō 〈物〉 longitudinal wave

【纵步】 zòngbù ① stride: ～向前走去 stride forward ② jump; bound: 他一个～跳过了小河。He crossed the brook in one big jump.

【纵断面】 zòngduànmiàn vertical section

【纵队】 zòngduì column; file: ～队形 column formation/ 一路～ column of files; single file/ 二路～ column of twos

【纵隔】 zònggé 〈生理〉 mediastinum ◇ ～炎 mediastinitis

【纵横】 zòng-héng ① in length and breadth; vertically and horizontally: ～数百里的山区 a mountainous area several hundred *li* in length and breadth/ ～交错的水渠 a crisscross network of irrigation channels ② with great ease; freely: 笔意～ write with great ease

【纵横捭阖】 zònghéng-bǎihé manoeuvre among various political groupings

【纵横驰骋】 zònghéng chíchěng (of an army) move about freely and quickly; sweep through the length and breadth of: 八路军在华北平原～，歼灭大量敌人。The Eighth Route Army swept through the length and breadth of the north China plain, wiping out large numbers of enemy troops./ 青年们可以在广阔的科学领域里～。The length and breadth of the whole realm of science is open for our youth to explore and conquer.

【纵横家】 Zònghéngjiā Political Strategists (in the Warring States Period, 475-221 B.C.)

【纵虎归山】 zòng hǔ guī shān let the tiger return to the mountain — cause calamity for the future

【纵火】 zònghuǒ set on fire; commit arson ◇ ～犯 arsonist

【纵酒】 zòngjiǔ drink to excess
【纵览】 zònglǎn look far and wide; scan: ～群书 read extensively
【纵目】 zòngmù look as far as one's eyes can see: ～四望 look far into the distance in all directions
【纵情】 zòngqíng to one's heart's content; as much as one likes: ～歌唱 sing to one's heart's content; sing heartily
【纵然】 zòngrán even if; even though: ～成功的希望不大,我们也要试试。We will try even if there isn't much hope of success.
【纵容】 zòngróng connive; wink at: 在某人～下 with the connivance of sb./ 受到～和庇护 be winked at and shielded
【纵射】 zòngshè 〈军〉 enfilade
【纵身】 zòngshēn jump; leap: ～一跳 jump into the air; jump up/ ～上马 leap onto a horse
【纵深】 zòngshēn 〈军〉 depth: 向～发展 develop in depth/ 对敌人的补给线进行～阻截 carry out a deep interdiction of enemy supply routes ◇ ～防御 defence in depth
【纵使】 zòngshǐ even if; even though
【纵视图】 zòngshìtú longtitudinal view
【纵谈】 zòngtán talk freely: ～国内外大好形势 talk freely about the excellent internal and external situation
【纵欲】 zòngyù give way to one's carnal desires; indulge in sensual pleasures
【纵坐标】 zòngzuòbiāo 〈数〉 ordinate

**粽** zòng 见"粽子"
【粽子】 zòngzi a pyramid-shaped dumpling made of glutinous rice wrapped in bamboo or reed leaves (eaten during the Dragon Boat Festival)

## zōu

**邹** Zōu a surname

**陬** zōu 〈书〉 ① corner ② foot of a hill

## zǒu

**走** zǒu ① walk; go: 一直往前～ go straight ahead/ ～很远的路 walk a long distance/ ～社会主义道路 take the socialist road/ ～群众路线 follow the mass line/ ～下主席台 step down from the rostrum/ ～在游行队伍的前列 march in the van of the procession/ ～遍全国 travel the length and breadth of the whole country/ ～前人没有～过的道路 break new paths; take paths never trodden before/ ～回头路 turn back; retrace one's steps/ ～弯路 take a roundabout route; make a detour/ ～一步看一步 take one step and look around before taking another — proceed without a plan, or with caution/ 孩子还不会～。The baby cannot walk yet./ 这船一小时～十五海里。The ship makes 15 knots. ② run; move: 奔～ run; rush about/ 钟不～了。The clock has stopped./ 这个表～得很准。This watch keeps good time./打得赢就打,打不赢就～。Fight when you can win, move away when you can't./ 你这步棋～坏了。You've made a bad move. ③ leave; go away: ～开! Get away! 或 Clear off!/ 我们该～了。It's time for us to leave. 或 We must be off now./ 他已经把蓝图拿～了。He's taken the blueprint away. ④ visit; call on: ～亲戚 call on relatives/ ～娘家 (of a married woman) visit her parents' home/ 他们两家～得很近。The two families often visit each other. ⑤ through; from: 咱们～这个门进去吧。Let's go in through this door. ⑥ leak; let out; escape: ～气了。The gas is leaking. 或 The air is escaping./ 说～了嘴 make a slip of the tongue; blurt something out ⑦ depart from the original; lose the original shape, flavour, etc.: 把原来的意思讲～了 fail to get across the original meaning/ 说话～题儿 speak beside the point; wander from the subject
【走笔】 zǒubǐ 〈书〉 write rapidly
【走步】 zǒubù 〈篮球〉 walk with the ball
【走刀量】 zǒudāoliàng 〈机〉 feed
【走道】 zǒudào ① pavement; sidewalk ② path; walk; footpath
【走道儿】 zǒudàor 〈口〉 walk: 小孩子刚会～。The baby has just learned to toddle.
【走调儿】 zǒudiàor out of tune: 她唱歌爱～。Her singing often gets out of tune.
【走动】 zǒudòng ① walk about; stretch one's legs: 坐了一整天了,出去～～吧。We've been sitting all day long. Let's go out for a stroll./ 病人能～了。The invalid is able to get about now. ② (of relatives and friends) visit each other: 他们两家关系不错,常常～。The two families are on good terms and often visit each other.
【走读】 zǒudú attend a day school ◇ ～生 day student; nonresident student
【走访】 zǒufǎng ① interview; have an interview with: 本报记者～了几位著名的小说家。Our reporter interviewed several famous novelists. ② pay a visit to; go and see
【走风】 zǒufēng let out a secret; leak out
【走钢丝】 zǒu gāngsī 〈杂技〉 wirewalking
【走狗】 zǒugǒu running dog; lackey; flunkey; stooge; servile follower
【走过场】 zǒu guòchǎng make a gesture to give the impression of doing sth.; go through the motions; do sth. perfunctorily or superficially
【走后门】 zǒu hòumén get in by the back door; secure advantages through pull or influence: 纠正"～"之类的不正之风 overcome such unhealthy tendencies as "entering by the back door"
【走火】 zǒuhuǒ ①〈电〉sparking ② (of firearms) discharge accidentally: 他一时不慎,枪～了。He wasn't careful and his rifle went off accidentally. ③ go too far in what one says; put sth. too strongly; overstate
【走江湖】 zǒu jiānghu wander from place to place and earn a living by juggling, fortune-telling, etc.; become a vagrant
【走廊】 zǒuláng corridor; passage; passageway: 河西～ the Hexi (或 Gansu) Corridor
【走漏】 zǒulòu ① leak out; divulge: ～风声 divulge a secret; leak information ② smuggling and tax evasion
【走路】 zǒulù walk; go on foot: 你们是坐车去还是～去? Will you go there by bus or on foot?/ 过去打运动战,～的时间常多于作战的时间。In mobile warfare, we used to spend more time in moving than in fighting.
【走马】 zǒumǎ gallop or trot along on horseback
【走马灯】 zǒumǎdēng a lantern with papercut figures of men, animals, etc. made to revolve when the lantern is lit: 人员不断更换,就象～似的。Personnel were shifted about as often as if they were on a merry-go-round.
【走马疳】 zǒumǎgān 〈医〉 noma; gangrenous stomatitis
【走马看花】 zǒu mǎ kàn huā look at flowers while riding on horseback — gain a superficial understanding through cursory observation 又作"走马观花"
【走南闯北】 zǒunán-chuǎngběi journey north and south; travel extensively
【走内线】 zǒu nèixiàn seek sb.'s favour by approaching his family members (esp. wife) or confidant; use private influence to achieve one's end; go through private channels

【走禽】 zǒuqín Cursores; cursorial birds
【走色】 zǒushǎi lose colour; fade
【走绳】 zǒushéng 〈杂技〉 ropedancing; ropewalking 又作"走索"
【走失】 zǒushī wander away; be lost; be missing: 一只羊～了。A sheep has wandered away from the flock./ 我们一起出去的,半路上他～了。We went out together and he got lost on the way.
【走时】 zǒushí 见"走运"
【走兽】 zǒushòu beast; quadruped; four-footed animal
【走水】 zǒushuǐ be on fire; catch fire
【走私】 zǒusī smuggle: ～的货物 smuggled goods
【走投无路】 zǒu-tóu wú lù have no way out; be in an impasse; come to the end of one's tether: 逼得～ be driven (或 pushed) to the wall
【走味】 zǒuwèi lose flavour: 茶叶～了。The tea has lost its flavour.
【走向】 zǒuxiàng ① run; trend; alignment: 矿脉的～ the run of the ore vein/ 海岸线～ the trend of the coastline/ 确定两国边界线的全部～ determine the entire alignment of the boundary line between the two countries/ 横断山脉是南北～的山脉。The Hengduan Mountains run from south to north. ② 〈地〉 strike: ～断层 strike fault/ ～节理 strike joint ③ move towards; head for; be on the way to: ～大治 move towards great order/ ～胜利 advance towards victory; march to victory/ ～反面 change (或 turn) into one's opposite/ ～死亡 head for one's doom; go down to one's doom/ 世界一定要～进步,～光明,而决不是～反动,～黑暗。The world will surely move towards progress and light, and definitely not towards reaction and darkness.
【走样】 zǒuyàng lose shape; go out of form; be different from what is expected or intended: 放上鞋楦免得鞋～。Use shoe trees to keep your shoes from losing shape./ 这事让他给说～了。His account presented a distorted picture of the matter.
【走运】 zǒuyùn be in luck; have good luck: 不～ have bad luck (或 fortune)/ 咱们真～! We're really in luck.
【走着瞧】 zǒuzheqiáo wait and see: 咱们～! We'll see (who's right).
【走资派】 zǒuzīpài capitalist-roader; person in power taking the capitalist road
【走卒】 zǒuzú pawn; cat's-paw; lackey; stooge
【走嘴】 zǒuzuǐ make a slip of the tongue; let slip an inadvertent remark

## zòu

**奏** zòu ① play (music); perform (on a musical instrument): ～国歌 play the national anthem/ 独～ (instrumental) solo/ 伴～ accompaniment/ 当贵宾进入宴会厅时,乐队开始～迎宾曲。The band struck up a tune of welcome when the distinguished guests entered the banquet hall. ② achieve; produce: ～功 achieve success ③ present a memorial to an emperor
【奏捷】 zòujié win a battle; score a success
【奏凯】 zòukǎi win victory; be victorious; triumph
【奏鸣曲】 zòumíngqǔ 〈乐〉 sonata: 小～ sonatina ◇ ～式 sonata form
【奏疏】 zòushū memorial to the throne
【奏效】 zòuxiào prove effective; be successful; get the desired result: 这药服了马上～。This medicine will have immediate efficacy./ 这个办法能～吗? Will this method work?
【奏乐】 zòuyuè play music; strike up a tune
【奏章】 zòuzhāng memorial to the throne
【奏折】 zòuzhé memorial to the throne (as written on paper folded in accordion form)

**揍** zòu ① 〈口〉 beat; hit; strike: 把他～一顿 beat him up/ 挨～ get a thrashing ② 〈方〉 smash; break: 他把碗给～了。He smashed the bowl./ 小心别把玻璃～了。Be careful not to break the glass.

## zū

**租** zū ① rent; hire; charter: ～三间房 rent three rooms/ ～一条小船 hire a boat/ ～一架飞机 charter a plane ② rent out; let out; lease: 这块地已经～给人了。This piece of land has been leased out./ 此屋招～。Room to let./ 出～连环画 lend picture-story books (for a small fee) ③ rent: 房～ house rent/ 地～ land rent (to a landlord)/ 收～ collect rent ④ land tax
【租船】 zūchuán chartering ◇ ～代理 chartering agent/ ～契约 charter party/ ～人 charterer/ ～市场 chartering market
【租佃】 zūdiàn (of a landlord) rent out land to tenants ◇ ～关系 tenancy relationship/ ～制度 tenancy system
【租户】 zūhù ① tenant (of a building or part of it); lessee; leaseholder ② hirer (of a thing)
【租界】 zūjiè concession (in former times, a tract of land in a Chinese port or city supposedly on lease to, but actually seized by, an imperialist power and put under its colonial rule)
【租借】 zūjiè rent; hire; lease ◇ ～地 leased territory; leasehold/ ～人 leaseholder; lessee; tenant; hirer
【租金】 zūjīn rent; rental: 这套房间每月～八元。The rent for this flat is eight *yuan* a month.
【租赁】 zūlìn rent; lease; hire: ～服装和道具 rent costumes and stage properties
【租钱】 zūqian 〈口〉 rent; rental
【租书处】 zūshūchù book rental
【租税】 zūshuì 〈旧〉 land tax and other levies
【租用】 zūyòng rent; hire; take on lease: ～家具 rent furniture/ ～礼堂 hire a hall ◇ ～人 leaseholder; tenant; lessee; hirer
【租约】 zūyuē lease: ～什么时候到期? When does the lease expire?
【租子】 zūzi 〈口〉 land rent; ground rent; rent

## zú

**足** zú ① foot; leg: 赤～ barefoot/ 鼎～而立 standing like a tripod — a tripartite balance of forces ② sufficient; enough; ample: 富～ plentiful; abundant; wealthy/ 丰衣～食 have ample food and clothing; be well-fed and well-clothed ③ full; as much as: 路上～～走了两个钟头。The journey took fully two hours./ 从这里到邮局～有二里路。It's a good two *li* from here to the post office. ④ 〔多用于否定式〕 enough; sufficient: 微不～道 not worth mentioning
【足赤】 zúchì pure gold
【足够】 zúgòu enough; ample; sufficient: ～用十个月的燃料 sufficient fuel to last ten months/ 有～的时间吗? Is there enough time?/ 我们对困难要有～的估计。We must take full account of our difficulties.
【足迹】 zújì footmark; footprint; track: 雪地上的～ footprints (或 tracks) in the snow/ 祖国各个角落都有地质勘探

队员的～。In every corner of our country there are footmarks left by our geological prospectors.

【足见】 zújiàn it serves to show; one can well perceive: 他的发言内容丰富，～他是作了认真准备的。His speech is substantial, which shows he took great pains to prepare it.

【足金】 zújīn pure gold; solid gold

【足球】 zúqiú ① soccer; football: 踢～ play soccer (或 football)/ 美国式～ American football/ 英国式～ soccer; association football ② football (the ball used in playing either soccer or American football) ◇ ～队 football team; eleven/ ～运动员 footballer

【足色】 zúsè (gold or silver) of standard purity

【足下】 zúxià a polite form of address between friends (used mostly in letters): ～以为如何？I wonder what you think of this.

【足以】 zúyǐ enough; sufficient: 你的话不～说服她。What you say isn't enough to convince her.

【足月】 zúyuè (of a foetus) born after the normal period of gestation; mature

【足智多谋】 zúzhì-duōmóu wise and full of strategems; resourceful

**卒** zú ① soldier; private: 士～ soldiers; the rank and file/ 小～ private; a mere pawn ② servant: 走～ underling; lackey ③ finish; end: ～其事 finish the job; wind up the business/ 聊以～岁 just to tide over the year ④ finally; at last: ～底于成 finally achieve success ⑤ die: 病～ die of illness/ 生～年月 dates of birth and death ⑥ pawn, one of the pieces in Chinese chess

【卒业】 zúyè 〈书〉 graduate; finish a course of study

**族** zú ① clan: 合～ all the members of a clan; the whole clan ② a death penalty in ancient China, imposed on an offender and his whole family, or even the families of his mother and wife ③ race; nationality: 汉～ the Han nationality ④ a class or group of things with common features: 水～ aquatic animals/ 语～ a family of languages/ 猫～ the cat tribe/ 碱土～ 〈化〉 alkaline earth family

【族权】 zúquán clan authority; clan power

【族人】 zúrén clansman

【族长】 zúzhǎng clan elder; the head of a clan

**镞** zú 〈书〉 arrowhead

## zǔ

**阻** zǔ hinder; block; obstruct: 拦～ block; hold back/ 劝～ dissuade sb. from; advise sb. against/ 通行无～ go through without hindrance/ 道路险～。The road is dangerous and difficult.

【阻碍】 zǔ'ài hinder; block; impede: ～交通 block the traffic/ 遇到～ meet with obstruction/ ～生产力的发展 hinder the development of the productive forces

【阻挡】 zǔdǎng stop; stem; resist; obstruct: 不可～的历史潮流 an irresistible historical trend/ 中国人民一定要解放台湾，这是任何力量也～不了的。The Chinese people are determined to liberate Taiwan and no force on earth can stop them from doing so. ◇ ～犯规〈篮球〉 blocking

【阻遏】 zǔ'è check; stem; stop

【阻隔】 zǔgé separate; cut off: 山川～ be separated by mountains and rivers

【阻击】 zǔjī 〈军〉 block; check: 我军以一部～南线之敌。Our army used part of its forces to check the enemy coming from the south. ◇ ～战 blocking action/ ～阵地 blocking position

【阻抗】 zǔkàng 〈电〉 impedance: 反射～ reflected impedance ◇ ～匹配 impedance matching

【阻拦】 zǔlán stop; obstruct; bar the way: 他决心要走，我们也不好～。As he was determined to go, we thought it better not to stop him.

【阻力】 zǔlì ① obstruction; resistance: 减少前进的～ reduce resistance to forward movement/ 冲破各种～ break through all kinds of obstructions ② 〈物〉 resistance; drag: 空气～ air resistance/ 迎面～ frontal resistance/ 摩擦～ friction drag

【阻挠】 zǔnáo obstruct; thwart; stand in the way; put a spoke in sb.'s wheel: 条约的履行受到了～。The execution of the treaty was obstructed./ ～两国关系正常化 stand in the way of the normalization of relations between the two countries

【阻尼】 zǔní 〈物〉 damping ◇ ～器 damper/ ～振荡 damped oscillation

【阻塞】 zǔsè block; obstruct; clog: 交通～。The traffic is held up. 或 There's a traffic jam./ 脏东西把管子～了。The pipe is clogged with dirt. ◇ ～振荡器 blocking oscillator

【阻援】 zǔyuán hold off (或 delay) enemy reinforcements

【阻止】 zǔzhǐ prevent; stop; hold back: ～事态的恶化 prevent the situation from deteriorating/ ～敌军前进 check the enemy's advance/ 任何反动势力都不能～人类历史的前进。No force of reaction can arrest the progress of human history.

**诅** zǔ

【诅咒】 zǔzhòu curse; swear; wish sb. evil; imprecate

**组** zǔ ① organize; form: 改～ reorganize; reshuffle ② group: 读报～ a newspaper-reading group ③ 〈量〉 set; series; battery: 两～发电机 two generators/ 一～邮票 a set of stamps

【组胺】 zǔ'àn 〈化〉 histamine

【组成】 zǔchéng form; make up; compose: ～统一战线 form a united front/ 水的～ the composition of water/ ～部分 component part; component/ 每五个人～一组。Every five persons constitute a group./ 主席团由一百四十八位代表～。The presidium consists of 148 delegates./ 党组织是由无产阶级先进分子～的。The Party organization is composed of the advanced elements of the proletariat.

【组稿】 zǔgǎo (of editors) commission authors to write on given topics; solicit contributions

【组歌】 zǔgē 〈乐〉 suite of songs

【组阁】 zǔgé form (或 set up, organize) a cabinet

【组合】 zǔhé ① make up; compose; constitute: 这本集子是由诗、散文和短篇小说三部分～而成的。This collection is made up of three parts: poems, essays and short stories./ 各种政治力量的重新～ a realignment of various political forces ② association; combination ③ 〈机〉 〈数〉 combination
◇ ～车床 combined lathe/ ～理论 〈数〉 combinatorial theory/ ～体 〈机〉 assembly/ ～钻床 combination drilling machine

【组件】 zǔjiàn 〈电〉 package; module: 微型～ micromodule; module

【组曲】 zǔqǔ 〈乐〉 suite

【组态】 zǔtài 〈物〉 configuration: 平衡～ configuration of equilibrium

【组织】 zǔzhī ① organize; form: ～劳力 organize a labour force; organize labour power/ ～一个登山队 form a mountaineering team/ ～一次座谈 organize a discussion/ ～

一次演出 get up a performance/ 把他们的积极性～到建设祖国的伟大事业中去 enlist their initiative in the great cause of reconstructing the nation/ 这篇文章～得很好。This article is well-organized. ② organization; organized system: 党团～ Party and Youth League organizations/ 群众～ mass organizations/ 给予～处分 take disciplinary measures against a member of an organization/ 党的～原则是民主集中制。The organizational principle of the Party is democratic centralism. ③ 〈纺〉 weave: 平纹～ plain weave/ 斜纹～ twill weave/ 缎纹～ satin weave ④ 〈生理〉 tissue: 结缔～ connective tissue/ 神经～ nerve (或 nervous) tissue

◇ ～胺 〈化〉 histamine/ ～法 rules of organization; organic law; constituent act/ ～关系 credentials showing membership in an organization; membership credentials/ ～疗法 tissue therapy; histotherapy/ ～生活 regular activities of an organization/ ～条例 organic rules/ ～委员 committee member in charge of organizational work/ ～委员会 organizing committee/ ～学 〈生理〉 histology/ ～液 〈生理〉 tissue fluid

**祖** zǔ ① grandfather: 外～ maternal grandfather ② ancestor: 远～ remote ancestors ③ founder (of a craft, religious sect, etc.); originator: 鼻～ the earliest ancestor; originator (of a tradition, school of thought, etc.) ④ (Zǔ) a surname

【祖辈】 zǔbèi ancestors; forefathers; ancestry

【祖传】 zǔchuán handed down from one's ancestors: ～秘方 a secret prescription handed down in the family from generation to generation

【祖坟】 zǔfén ancestral grave

【祖父】 zǔfù (paternal) grandfather

【祖国】 zǔguó one's country; homeland; native land; motherland; fatherland

【祖籍】 zǔjí original family home; ancestral home; the land of one's ancestors

【祖鲁语】 Zǔlǔyǔ Zulu (language)

【祖率】 zǔlǜ 〈数〉 the approximate ratio of the circumference of a circle to its diameter as calculated by Zu Chongzhi (祖冲之, 429-500), i.e. between 3.1415926 and 3.1415927

【祖母】 zǔmǔ (paternal) grandmother

【祖上】 zǔshàng ancestors; forefathers; forbears

【祖师】 zǔshī ① the founder of a school of learning, a craft, etc. ② the founder of a sect of Buddhism or Taoism

【祖孙】 zǔ-sūn grandparent and grandchild: ～三代 three generations

【祖先】 zǔxiān ancestry; ancestors; forbears; forefathers

【祖宗】 zǔzōng forefathers; ancestry; forbears ◇ ～崇拜 ancestor (或 ancestral) worship

【祖祖辈辈】 zǔzǔbèibèi for generations; from generation to generation: 我家～都是种地的。 Our family have been farmers for generations.

**俎** zǔ ① an ancient sacrificial utensil ② a kind of chopping block used in ancient times

【俎上肉】 zǔshàngròu 〈书〉 meat on the chopping block—a helpless victim

## zuān

**钻** zuān ① drill; bore: ～孔 drill a hole/ ～木取火 drill wood to make fire ② get into; go through; make one's way into: ～进密林深处 go deep into a forest/ 火车走这条线得～许多山洞。The train has to pass through quite a few tunnels on this railway line./ 月亮从云缝里～了出来。The moon broke through the clouds. ③ study intensively; dig into: ～书本 dig into books/ ～故纸堆 bury oneself in outdated writings/ ～业务 dig into one's job or a subject; work hard to perfect oneself professionally/ 有许多人～进去了，就有一点内行的味道了。 Quite a few have studied their trade and become quite professional.

另见 zuàn

【钻空子】 zuān kòngzi avail oneself of loopholes (in a law, contract, etc.); exploit an advantage: 不让对方～ leave no loopholes for the other side to exploit/ 被人钻了空子 be taken in; be tricked

【钻谋】 zuānmóu use pull to get what one wants

【钻牛角尖】 zuān niújiǎojiān ① take unnecessary pains to study an insignificant or insoluble problem; split hairs ② get into a dead end (或 a blind alley)

【钻圈】 zuānquān 〈杂技〉 jumping (或 plunging) through hoops

【钻探】 zuāntàn (exploration) drilling: 海底～ offshore drilling/ ～设备 drilling equipment ◇ ～工 driller/ ～机 drilling machine

【钻心虫】 zuānxīnchóng borer

【钻研】 zuānyán study intensively; dig into: ～马列主义理论 assiduously study Marxist-Leninist theory/ 为革命～技术 perfect one's skill for the revolution; master technique for the revolution/ 努力～业务 endeavour to gain professional proficiency

【钻营】 zuānyíng curry favour with sb. in authority for personal gain; secure personal gain

**躜** zuān ① jump up ② dash forward: 燕子～天儿。The swallow dashed (或 shot) through the air.

## zuǎn

**缵** zuǎn inherit

**纂** zuǎn ① 〈书〉 compile; edit: ～修 compile; edit/ 编～字典 compile a dictionary ② 〈方〉 a woman's hair worn in a knot at the nape; bun

## zuàn

**钻** zuàn ① drill; auger: 手摇～ hand drill; drill/ 风～ pneumatic drill ② diamond; jewel: ～戒 diamond ring/ 十九～的手表 a 19-jewel watch ③ bore; drill: 在木头上～个眼 bore a hole in wood

另见 zuān

【钻床】 zuànchuáng 〈机〉 drilling machine; driller: 龙门～ planer drilling machine

【钻杆】 zuàngǎn 〈石油〉 drill rod (或 pipe)

【钻机】 zuànjī 〈石油〉 (drilling) rig; drilling machine: 安装～ rig up/ 拆卸～ rig down/ 旋转～ rotary rig

【钻井】 zuànjǐng well drilling: 构造～ core drilling/ 海洋～ offshore drilling

◇ ～队 drilling crew (或 team)/ ～工人 driller/ ～记录 drill log

【钻具】 zuànjù 〈石油〉 drilling tool; drilling rig

【钻模】 zuànmú 〈机〉 (drill) jig: 分度～ indexing jig

【钻石】 zuànshí ① diamond ② jewel (used in a watch)

【钻塔】 zuàntǎ 〈矿〉 boring tower; derrick

【钻铤】 zuàntǐng 〈石油〉 drill collar

【钻头】 zuàntóu bit (of a drill): 装上～ brace a bit/ 卸下～ break out a bit/ 三牙轮～ three cone bit

【钻压】 zuànyā 〈石油〉 bit pressure; bit weight

**赚** zuàn 〈方〉 kid; deceive; hoax
另见 zhuàn

**攥** zuàn 〈口〉 hold; grip; grasp: 手里～着一把斧子 hold an axe in one's hand/ ～紧拳头 clench one's fist/ 一把～住他的手 clasp him by the hand

## zuǐ

**嘴** zuǐ ① mouth: 闭～ keep one's mouth shut/ ～上说说而已 pay lip service ② anything shaped or functioning like a mouth: 茶壶～ the spout of a teapot/ 瓶～儿 the mouth of a bottle/ 烟～儿 cigarette holder

【嘴巴】 zuǐba ①〈方〉 mouth: 张开～。Open your mouth. ②〈口〉〔多用于〕: 打～ slap sb. in the face; box sb.'s ears/ 挨了个～ get a slap in the face

【嘴笨】 zuǐbèn inarticulate; clumsy of speech

【嘴馋】 zuǐchán fond of good food

【嘴唇】 zuǐchún lip: 上(下)～ the upper (lower) lip/ 咬着～ bite one's lips

【嘴乖】 zuǐguāi 〈口〉 (of children) clever and pleasant when speaking to elders

【嘴尖】 zuǐjiān sharp-tongued; cutting in speech: 他这个人～,说的话真刺耳。He's sharp-tongued and what he says is often very biting.

【嘴角】 zuǐjiǎo corners of the mouth

【嘴紧】 zuǐjǐn tight-lipped; closemouthed; secretive

【嘴快】 zuǐkuài have a loose tongue

【嘴脸】 zuǐliǎn 〈贬〉 look; features; countenance: 揭露他们修正主义的丑恶～ expose their ugly revisionist features/ 他那副～真难看。He had a very nasty look on his face./ 社会上各种人物的～被区别得清清楚楚。 All sorts of people in society have been clearly shown up for what they are.

【嘴皮子】 zuǐpízi 〈口〉 lips (of a glib talker): 耍～ talk glibly/ 他那两片～可能说了。He has a ready tongue. 或 He can argue on any side of any question.

【嘴碎】 zuǐsuì loquacious; garrulous

【嘴甜】 zuǐtián ingratiating in speech; smooth-tongued; honeymouthed

【嘴稳】 zuǐwěn able to keep a secret; discreet in speech

【嘴硬】 zuǐyìng stubborn and reluctant to admit mistakes or defeats: 知道错了,就别～。You know you're wrong, so don't stubbornly insist that you aren't.

【嘴子】 zuǐzi ①〈方〉 anything shaped or functioning like a mouth: 山～ the tip of a foothill ②〈乐〉 mouthpiece (of a wind instrument)

## zuì

**最** zuì 〈副〉〔表示某种属性超过所有同类的人或事物〕: ～小 the smallest; the tiniest/ ～为积极 be the most active/ 速度～快 the fastest/ 政治上～有远见 be the most farsighted politically/ ～大的幸福 supreme happiness/ ～基本的条件 fundamental prerequisites/ 结成～广泛的国际统一战线 form the broadest possible international united front

【最初】 zuìchū initial; first: ～阶段 the initial stage/ ～的印象 first impressions/ ～的计划 the original plan; the first and earliest plan/ ～她不想来,后来改变了主意。At first she didn't want to come, but later she changed her mind.

【最大公约数】 zuìdà gōngyuēshù 〈数〉 greatest common divisor 又作"最大公因子"

【最低】 zuìdī lowest; minimum ◇ ～纲领 minimum programme/ ～价格 lowest (或 bottom) price

【最多】 zuìduō at most; maximum: 屋里～不过十个人。There were at most ten people in the room./ 这个礼堂～能容纳一千人。This hall can hold a maximum of one thousand people./ 这所学校学生～的时候有三千人。 The school's enrolment at its height reached 3,000./ 我～只能等半个小时。I can wait half an hour at the longest.

【最高】 zuìgāo highest; supreme; tallest: ～国家权力机关 the highest organ of state power/ 达到～峰 reach the climax (或 peak); reach a culminating point/ 创造历史上～纪录 hit an all-time high
◇ ～点〈统计〉peak/ ～纲领 maximum programme/ ～国务会议 the Supreme State Conference/ ～年产量 peak annual output/ ～权力 supreme power/ ～速度 maximum speed/ ～统帅 supreme commander/ ～限额 ceiling

【最高级】 zuìgāojí ① highest; summit: ～会谈 top-level talks; summit talks/ ～会议 summit conference ②〈语〉 the superlative degree

【最好】 zuìhǎo ① best; first-rate: ～的办法 the best way/ 质量～ best in quality/ ～的干部 first-rate cadres ② had better; it would be best: 你～今天把它搞完。 You'd better finish it today./ 我们～在天黑以前赶到目的地。It would be best if we could reach our destination before dark.

【最后】 zuìhòu final; last; ultimate: ～胜利 final victory/ ～解决问题 bring the issue to a final solution; settle the question once and for all/ 作～挣扎 make a last-ditch struggle/ 坐在～一排 sit in the last row/ 他们的建议～被采纳了。Their suggestion was eventually accepted./ ～,我想谈一下学习问题。Lastly, I would like to touch on the problem of study.
◇ ～条款 final provisions; final articles/ ～议定书 final protocol/ ～议事录 *procès-verbal final*

【最后通牒】 zuìhòu tōngdié ultimatum

【最惠国】 zuìhuìguó most-favoured-nation: 给以～待遇 accord (a country) most-favoured-nation treatment

【最佳】 zuìjiā 〈物〉 optimum ◇ ～数 optimum number/ ～谐振 optimum resonance

【最近】 zuìjìn ① recently; lately; of late: 我～很忙。I've been very busy recently./ ～几天 in the last few days/ ～的消息 the latest news; recent news/ ～一期的《红旗》杂志 the current issue of *Hong Qi* ② in the near future; soon: ～要上演许多新电影。Many new films will be released soon.

【最轻量级】 zuìqīngliàngjí 〈举重〉 bantamweight

【最小二乘法】 zuìxiǎo èrchéngfǎ 〈数〉 least square method

【最小公倍数】 zuìxiǎo gōngbèishù 〈数〉 lowest common multiple

【最终】 zuìzhōng final; ultimate: ～结果 the final outcome/ 党的～目的,是实现共产主义。The ultimate aim of the Party is the realization of communism.

**罪** zuì ① crime; guilt: 有～ guilty of a crime; guilty/ 轻～ misdemeanour/ 重～ felony/ 判～ condemn; pass sentence/ ～上加～ be doubly guilty/ 宣告无～ acquit sb. (of a crime); declare sb. innocent/ ～有应得 deserve the punishment ② fault; blame: 归～于人 lay the blame on others ③ suffering; pain; hardship: 受～ endure suffering; be in pain; have a hard time ④ put the blame on: ～已 bear the blame oneself; take the blame on oneself

【罪案】 zuì'àn details of a criminal case; case

【罪不容诛】 zuì bùróng zhū even death cannot atone for the offence; be guilty of crimes for which even death is insufficient punishment

【罪大恶极】 zuìdà-èjí be guilty of the most heinous crimes
【罪恶】 zuì'è crime; evil: ～多端 be guilty of all kinds of evil/ ～滔天 be guilty of monstrous crimes
【罪犯】 zuìfàn criminal; offender; culprit
【罪该万死】 zuì gāi wàn sǐ be guilty of a crime for which one deserves to die ten thousand deaths; be guilty of a crime for which even death cannot atone
【罪过】 zuìguò ① fault; offence; sin: 这是我的～。It's my fault./ 他有什么～要受这样的苦？What sin has he committed to deserve all this? ② 〈谦〉 thanks, but this is really more than I deserve
【罪魁】 zuìkuí chief criminal (或 culprit, offender); arch-criminal
【罪名】 zuìmíng charge; accusation: 偷窃的～ a charge of theft/ 罗织～ frame a case against sb.
【罪孽】 zuìniè wrongdoing that brings retribution; sin: ～深重 sinful
【罪人】 zuìrén guilty person; offender; sinner: 历史～ a person condemned by history
【罪行】 zuìxíng crime; guilt; offence: 他的～较轻。His offence is a minor one.
【罪责】 zuìzé responsibility for an offence: ～难逃 cannot escape the responsibility for the offence; cannot get away with it
【罪证】 zuìzhèng evidence of a crime; proof of one's guilt
【罪状】 zuìzhuàng facts about a crime; charges in an indictment: 反革命分子的～ the crimes of a counterrevolutionary/ 党八股的八大～ the eight indictments against stereotyped Party writing (或 Party jargon)

**醉** zuì ① drunk; intoxicated; tipsy: 烂～ be dead drunk/ 他喝～了。He's tipsy. 或 He's had a drop too much. ② (of some kinds of food) liquor-saturated; steeped in liquor: ～蟹 liquor-saturated crab
【醉鬼】 zuìguǐ drunkard; sot; inebriate
【醉汉】 zuìhàn drunkard; drunken man
【醉生梦死】 zuìshēng-mèngsǐ live as if intoxicated or dreaming; lead a befuddled life
【醉态】 zuìtài the state of being drunk; drunkenness
【醉翁之意不在酒】 zuìwēng zhī yì bù zài jiǔ the drinker's heart is not in the cup — have ulterior motives
【醉心】 zuìxīn be bent on; be wrapped up in: 他～于数学的研究。He's deeply engrossed in mathematical research./ ～名利 be infatuated with fame and gain
【醉醺醺】 zuìxūnxūn sottish; drunk; tipsy
【醉眼】 zuìyǎn 〈书〉 eyes showing the effects of drink: ～朦胧 drunken and bleary-eyed
【醉意】 zuìyì signs or feeling of getting drunk: 他已经有几分～了。He is a bit tipsy.

## zūn

**尊** zūn ① senior; of a senior generation: ～长 elders ② respect; venerate; honour: ～师爱生 respect the teacher and love the student ③ 〈敬〉〔旧时称跟对方有关的人或事物〕: ～夫人 your wife/ ～府 your residence/ ～姓大名？May I know your name? ④ 〈量〉: 一～佛像 a statue of a Buddha/ 五十～大炮 fifty artillery pieces ⑤ a kind of wine vessel used in ancient times
【尊称】 zūnchēng ① a respectful form of address; honorific title ② address sb. respectfully: 人们～他为郭老。People respectfully called him the venerable Guo.
【尊崇】 zūnchóng worship; revere; venerate
【尊贵】 zūnguì honourable; respectable; respected: ～的客人 an honoured guest
【尊敬】 zūnjìng ① respect; honour; esteem: 非常～他 have the greatest esteem for him ② 见"尊贵"
【尊严】 zūnyán dignity; honour: 国家～ national dignity/ 维护法律的～ guard the sanctity of the law
【尊长】 zūnzhǎng elders and betters: 目无～ with no regard for one's elders and betters
【尊重】 zūnzhòng respect; value; esteem: 互相～ respect each other/ ～少数民族的风俗习惯 respect the habits and customs of the minority nationalities/ ～群众的首创精神 value the initiative of the masses/ 一切知识分子，只要是在为人民服务的工作中著有成绩的，都应受到～。As long as they serve the people creditably, all intellectuals should be esteemed.

**遵** zūn abide by; obey; observe; follow: ～纪爱民 observe discipline and cherish the people/ ～医嘱 follow the doctor's advice
【遵从】 zūncóng defer to; comply with; follow: ～上级的指示 in compliance with the directives of the leadership/ ～全国人民的愿望 in deference to the desire of the people of the whole country/ ～老师的教导 follow the teacher's advice
【遵命】 zūnmìng 〈敬〉 comply with your wish; obey your command: ～办理 act in compliance with instructions
【遵守】 zūnshǒu observe; abide by; comply with: ～劳动纪律 observe labour discipline/ ～公共秩序 observe public order/ ～时间 be on time; be punctual/ ～法律 abide by the law/ ～并执行协议 comply with and carry out the agreement
【遵行】 zūnxíng act on; follow: ～一贯的原则 act according to one's consistent principles
【遵循】 zūnxún follow; abide by; adhere to: ～毛主席的革命路线 follow the revolutionary line of Chairman Mao/ 制定一个章程，使大家有所～ work out a set of rules so that people will have something to go by
【遵义会议】 Zūnyì Huìyì the Zunyi Meeting (the historic meeting in Zunyi, Guizhou Province, held in January 1935, which put an end to the domination of the "Left" opportunist line in the Party Central Committee and established Chairman Mao's leadership in the whole Party)
【遵照】 zūnzhào obey; conform to; comply with; act in accordance with: ～上级的命令 in obedience to orders from above/ ～党中央制定的政策办事 act in accordance with the policies formulated by the Party Central Committee

**樽** zūn a kind of wine vessel used in ancient times

**鳟** zūn trout: 虹～ rainbow trout

## zǔn

**撙** zǔn save: 每月～下一些钱 save some money every month
【撙节】 zǔnjié retrench; practise economy: ～开支 retrench; cut down expenses

## zuō

**作** zuō ①〔限用于某些词语〕do: 自～自受 suffer through one's own misdeeds; stew in one's own juice; lie in the

bed one has made ② workshop: 木工～ carpenters' workshop/ 洗衣～ laundry
另见 zuó; zuò

【作坊】 zuōfang workshop: 生产纺织品的～ a workshop for manufacturing textiles

【作弄】 zuōnòng tease; make a fool of; play a trick on; poke fun at

【作死】 zuōsǐ seek death; take the road to ruin; look for trouble: 天这么冷不穿棉衣,你～呀! Are you tired of life that you don't wear padded clothes in such cold weather?

【作揖】 zuōyī make a bow with hands folded in front

**嘬** zuō 〈口〉 suck: 小孩儿～奶。The baby is sucking its mother's breast.

## zuó

**作** zuó 〔限用于下列词语〕
另见 zuō; zuò

【作践】 zuójian 〈口〉 ① spoil; waste: ～东西 spoil things ② run sb. down; disparage: 他这不是故意～人吗? Didn't he say that just to run me down? ③ humiliate; insult

【作料】 zuóliao condiments; seasoning

【作兴】 zuóxīng 〈方〉 ① there's reason to; it's justifiable (或 permissible) to: 可不～骂人。It's not right to swear at people. ② perhaps; possibly; maybe: ～要下雨。Maybe it's going to rain.

**昨** zuó yesterday: ～晚 yesterday evening; last night

【昨儿】 zuór 〈口〉 yesterday 又作"昨儿个"

【昨天】 zuótiān yesterday

**琢** zuó
另见 zhuó

【琢磨】 zuómo turn sth. over in one's mind; ponder: ～问题 turn a problem over in one's mind/ ～出个办法 figure out a way (to do sth.)/ 这件事她～了很久。She pondered over the matter for a long time.
另见 zhuómó

## zuǒ

**左** zuǒ ① the left side; the left: ～上方 the upper left/ 向～转 turn to the left; turn left ② east: 山～ areas east of the Taihang Mountains, specifically Shandong Province ③ the Left: 思想极～ be ultra-left in one's thinking /凡有人群的地方,都有～、中、右。Wherever there are masses of people they are invariably divided into the Left, the middle and the Right. ④ queer; unorthodox; heretical: ～脾气 have a queer temperament ⑤ wrong; incorrect: 你想～了。You're not thinking in the right way. 或 You've got a wrong idea. ⑥ different; contrary; opposite: 意见相～ hold different views; be at variance ⑦ (Zuǒ) a surname

【左边锋】 zuǒbiānfēng 〈足球〉 outside left; left wing

【左边】 zuǒbian the left; the left (或 left-hand) side: 房子～有一棵榆树。There's an elm tree on the left of the house.

【左不过】 zuǒbuguò ① anyway; anyhow; in any event: 他说来说去,～是这么个意思。He put it this way and that, but anyway that's what it boils down to. ② only; merely; just: 你怎么啦?——没什么,～有点头痛。What's the matter with you? — Nothing serious. Just a slight headache.

【左道旁门】 zuǒdào-pángmén ① heretical sect; heterodox school ② heresy; heterodoxy

【左舵】 zuǒduò left standard rudder; left rudder: ～十度! Port 10 degrees!

【左锋】 zuǒfēng 〈篮球〉 left forward

【左顾右盼】 zuǒgù-yòupàn glance right and left: 他～,象是在找人。Casting his glances about, he seemed to be looking for somebody.

【左后卫】 zuǒhòuwèi 〈足球〉 left back

【左近】 zuǒjìn in the vicinity (或 neighbourhood); nearby: ～有邮局吗? Is there a post office in the vicinity?/ 他就住在～。He lives nearby.

【左轮】 zuǒlún revolver

【左面】 zuǒmiàn the left side; the left-hand side

【左内锋】 zuǒnèifēng 〈足球〉 inside left

【左派】 zuǒpài ① the Left; the left wing ② Leftist ◇ ～势力 Left forces; forces of the Left

【左撇子】 zuǒpiězi left-handed person; left-hander; lefty

【左迁】 zuǒqiān 〈书〉 demote

【左前卫】 zuǒqiánwèi 〈足球〉 left halfback; left half

【左倾】 zuǒqīng left-leaning; progressive; inclined towards the revolution

【"左"倾】 "zuǒ"qīng "Left" deviation: ～空谈 "Left" phrase-mongering ◇ ～机会主义 "Left" opportunism/ ～冒险主义 "Left" adventurism

【左手】 zuǒshǒu ① the left hand ② 见"左首"

【左首】 zuǒshǒu the left-hand side: 坐在我的～ sit on my left

【左袒】 zuǒtǎn 〈书〉 take sides with; be partial to

【左舷】 zuǒxián port

【左翼】 zuǒyì ① 〈军〉 left wing; left flank ② the left wing; the Left ◇ ～分子 Leftist; Left-winger/ ～文艺运动 the Left-wing movement in literature and art

【左右】 zuǒyòu ① the left and right sides: 主席台～,红旗迎风飘扬。Red flags are fluttering on both sides of the rostrum./ ～摇摆 vacillate now to the left and now to the right ② 〔用在数目字后面表示概数〕: 八点钟～ around eight o'clock/ 一个月～ a month or so/ 价值十元～。It's worth about 10 *yuan.* ③ master; control; influence: ～局势 be master of the situation/ 为人所～ be controlled by sb.; fall under sb.'s influence ④ those in close attendance; retinue: 屏退～ order one's attendants to clear out ⑤ anyway; anyhow; in any case: 我～闲着没事,就陪你走一趟吧。Anyway I'm free now. Let me go with you.

【左右逢源】 zuǒ-yòu féng yuán ① be able to achieve success one way or another ② gain advantage from both sides

【左右开弓】 zuǒ-yòu kāi gōng shoot first with one hand, then with the other; shoot first to one side, then to the other; use first one hand and then the other in quick succession

【左右手】 zuǒyòushǒu right-hand man; valuable assistant

【左右袒】 zuǒyòutǎn take sides with; be partial to

【左右为难】 zuǒ-yòu wéinán in a dilemma; in an awkward predicament

【左…右…】 zuǒ...yòu... 〔强调同类行为的反复〕: 左思右想 think from different angles; turn sth. over in one's mind/ 左劝右劝 try again and again to persuade sb./ 左一条清规,右一条戒律 one taboo after another/ 左一趟右一趟地去请他 go several times to invite him

【左证】 zuǒzhèng evidence; proof

【左支右绌】 zuǒzhī-yòuchù not have enough money to cover the expenses; be unable to cope with a situation; be in straitened circumstances

**佐** zuǒ ① assist: ～理 assist sb. with a task ② assistant

【佐餐】 zuǒcān be eaten together with rice or bread; go

with rice or bread
【佐药】 zuǒyào 〈医〉 adjuvant
【佐证】 zuǒzhèng evidence; proof

**撮** zuǒ 〈量〉〔用于成丛的毛发〕: 一～儿黑毛 a tuft of black hair
另见 cuō
【撮子】 zuǒzi 〈口〉 tuft (of hair)

## zuò

**坐** zuò ① sit; take a seat: 请～! Please sit down. 或 Please be seated./ 进来～～。Come in and sit down for a while./ 我们一听说有新任务,就～不住了。When we learnt that we'd been given a new task, we just couldn't sit still any longer. ② travel by (a plane, etc.): ～飞机去昆明 go to Kunming by plane ③ (of a building) have its back towards: 这所房子～北朝南。This house faces south. ④ put (a pan, pot, kettle, etc.) on a fire: 把壶～上 put the kettle on (the fire) ⑤ 见"座" zuò① ⑥ (of a building) sink; subside: 这个房子向后～了。This house is beginning to slope backwards. ⑦ (of rifles, guns, etc.) recoil; kick back: 这枝步枪的～劲儿不小。This rifle has a terrible kick. ⑧ be punished: 反～ be sentenced to the punishment meant for the person one has falsely accused ⑨〈书〉 because; for the reason that: ～此解职 be dismissed on this account
【坐标】 zuòbiāo 〈数〉 coordinate ◇ ～轴 coordinate axis
【坐禅】 zuòchán 〈佛教〉 sit in meditation
【坐吃山空】 zuò chī shān kōng sit idle and eat, and in time your whole fortune will be used up
【坐待】 zuòdài sit back and wait
【坐等】 zuòděng sit back and wait: ～胜利 sit back waiting for victory with folded arms
【坐地分赃】 zuò dì fēn zāng (of a ringleader, criminal, booty harbourer, etc.) take a share of the spoils without participating personally in the robbery
【坐垫】 zuòdiàn cushion
【坐骨】 zuògǔ 〈生理〉 ischium ◇ ～神经 sciatic nerve/ ～神经痛 sciatica
【坐观成败】 zuò guān chéng-bài wait to see what will come of another's venture; look on coldly; be a mere onlooker
【坐禁闭】 zuò jìnbì be placed in confinement (as a disciplinary measure)
【坐井观天】 zuò jǐng guān tiān look at the sky from the bottom of a well — have a very narrow view
【坐具】 zuòjù a thing to sit on; seat
【坐科】 zuòkē undergo professional training at an old-type opera school
【坐困】 zuòkùn be confined; be walled in; be shut up: ～金陵一年余 be confined within the walls of Jinling city for over a year/ ～愁城 be walled in by one's own worries
【坐牢】 zuòláo be in jail; be imprisoned
【坐冷板凳】 zuò lěngbǎndèng hold a title without any obligations of office; be kept waiting long for an assignment or an audience with a VIP
【坐力】 zuòlì 〈物〉 recoil: 无～炮 recoilless gun
【坐立不安】 zuò-lì bù ān feel uneasy whether sitting or standing; be fidgety; be on tenterhooks
【坐落】 zuòluò (of a building) be situated; be located: 我们工厂～在山脚下。Our factory is located at the foot of a hill.
【坐蓐】 zuòrù 〈书〉 confinement in childbirth; lying-in
【坐山雕】 zuòshāndiāo 〈动〉 cinereous vulture
【坐山观虎斗】 zuò shān guān hǔ dòu sit on top of the mountain to watch the tigers fight — watch in safety while others fight, then reap the spoils when both sides are exhausted
【坐商】 zuòshāng tradesman (as opposed to itinerant merchant); shopkeeper
【坐失良机】 zuò shī liángjī let slip a golden opportunity
【坐视】 zuòshì sit by and watch; sit tight and look on: ～不理 sit by idly and remain indifferent/ ～不救 sit back and watch without going to the rescue
【坐收渔利】 zuò shōu yúlì reap the spoils of victory without lifting a finger; profit from others' conflict; reap third party profit 又作"坐收渔人之利"
【坐探】 zuòtàn an enemy agent planted within one's own ranks
【坐位】 zuòwei ① a place to sit; seat: 留几个～ reserve some seats/ 排～ make seating arrangements/ 回到你的～上去。Go back to your place. ② a thing to sit on; seat: 给我搬个～儿来。Get (或 Fetch, Bring) me a seat.
【坐卧不宁】 zuò-wò bù níng be unable to sit down or sleep at ease; feel restless; be on tenterhooks 又作"坐卧不安"
【坐席】 zuòxí ① take one's seat at a banquet table ② attend a banquet
【坐享其成】 zuò xiǎng qí chéng sit idle and enjoy the fruits of others' work; reap where one has not sown
【坐药】 zuòyào suppository
【坐以待毙】 zuò yǐ dài bì sit still waiting for death; await one's doom; resign oneself to death
【坐以待旦】 zuò yǐ dài dàn sit up and wait for daybreak; remain awake till dawn
【坐月子】 zuò yuèzi 〈口〉 confinement in childbirth; lying-in
【坐镇】 zuòzhèn (of a commander) personally attend to garrison duty; assume personal command
【坐庄】 zuòzhuāng ① be a resident buyer of a business firm ② be the banker or dealer (in a gambling game)

**作** zuò ① do; make: ～功课 do one's homework/ ～报告 make a report; deliver a speech/ ～斗争 wage a struggle; combat/ ～结论 pass a verdict; reach a conclusion/ ～出决断 make a final decision/ ～长期打算 plan on a long-term basis ② rise; get up: 日出而～ get up at sunrise/ 枪声大～。Heavy firing broke out. ③ write; compose: ～诗 compose a poem/ ～书一封 write a letter/ ～画 paint a picture ④ writings; work: 遗～ a posthumous work/ 新～ a new work ⑤ pretend; affect: 装模～样 put on an act; behave in an affected way/ 故～怒容 pretend to be angry ⑥ regard as; take sb. or sth. for: 认贼～父 take the foe for one's father/ 把他看～英雄 regard him as a hero ⑦ feel; have: ～冷 feel a chill/ ～痒 have an itch ⑧ act as; be; become: ～口译 act as interpreter/ 人民当家～主人。The people are the masters of their country.
另见 zuō; zuó
【作案】 zuò'àn commit a crime or an offence: ～时被捕 be caught in the act; be caught red-handed
【作罢】 zuòbà drop; relinquish; give up: 双方意见不一,事情只好～。Since the two sides couldn't agree, the matter had to be dropped.
【作保】 zuòbǎo be sb.'s guarantor; go bail for sb.; sponsor sb.
【作弊】 zuòbì practise fraud; cheat; indulge in corrupt practices
【作壁上观】 zuò bìshàngguān stay behind the breastworks and watch others fight; be an onlooker; sit by and watch

【作别】 zuòbié 〈书〉 bid farewell; take one's leave: 与亲友～ take leave of one's relatives and friends

【作操】 zuòcāo do gymnastics; do callisthenics; do exercises

【作词】 zuòcí write words (for a song): 李红～ words by Li Hong

【作对】 zuòduì set oneself against; oppose: 他没有理由和你～。He has no reason to oppose you.

【作恶】 zuò'è do evil: ～多端 do all kinds of evil; be steeped in iniquity

【作伐】 zuòfá 〈书〉 act as matchmaker

【作法】 zuòfǎ ① way of doing things; course of action; practice: 这种～已经很普遍了。This has become a common practice./ 他现在的～是行不通的。His present course of action will get him nowhere./ 文章～ technique of writing; art of composition ② 〈旧〉 resort to magic arts

【作法自毙】 zuò fǎ zì bì make a law only to fall foul of it oneself; be hoist with or by one's own petard; get caught in one's own trap

【作废】 zuòfèi become invalid: 宣布～ declare invalid/ 过期～ become invalid after a specified date/ 宣布条约～ declare a treaty null and void

【作风】 zuòfēng style; style of work; way: 工作～ style of work/ ～正派 be honest and upright; have moral integrity/ 资产阶级生活～ bourgeois way of life; bourgeois life-style/ 推广民主～ develop a democratic style of work/ 实事求是的～a practical and realistic way of doing things/ 永远保持艰苦奋斗的～ always keep to the style of hard struggle and plain living

【作梗】 zuògěng obstruct; hinder; create difficulties: 这一定是有人从中～。Somebody must have been creating difficulties.

【作古】 zuògǔ 〈书〉〈婉〉 die; pass away

【作怪】 zuòguài do mischief; make trouble: 保守思想在他们头脑中～。Conservative ideas are doing mischief in their minds.

【作家】 zuòjiā writer ◇ ～协会 the Writers' Union

【作假】 zuòjiǎ ① counterfeit; falsify ② cheat; play tricks ③ behave affectedly

【作价】 zuòjià fix a price for sth.; evaluate: 合理～，公平交易 fair pricing and square dealing/ 旧水泵～五十元 appraise the old pump at 50 *yuan*

【作奸犯科】 zuòjiān-fànkē violate the law and commit crimes; commit offences against law and discipline

【作茧自缚】 zuò jiǎn zì fù spin a cocoon around oneself — get enmeshed in a web of one's own spinning

【作客】 zuòkè 〈书〉 sojourn: ～他乡 sojourn in a strange land ◇ ～思想 feeling of not belonging; guest mentality

【作乐】 zuòlè make merry; enjoy oneself; have a good time: 寻欢～ seek pleasure and make merry
另见 zuòyuè

【作乱】 zuòluàn stage an armed rebellion

【作美】 zuòměi 〔多用于否定〕 (of weather, etc.) help; cooperate; make things easy for sb.: 我们正想去郊游，天公不～，下起雨来了。We were just thinking of going on an outing when, as Heaven wasn't cooperative, it began to rain.

【作难】 zuònán ① feel embarrassed; feel awkward ② make things difficult for sb.

【作孽】 zuòniè 〈佛教〉 do evil; commit a sin

【作呕】 zuò'ǒu feel sick; feel like vomiting; be overcome by nausea: 令人～的气味 a sickening smell/ 令人～地吹捧 nauseatingly extol

【作陪】 zuòpéi help entertain the guest of honour; be invited along with the chief guest

【作品】 zuòpǐn works (of literature and art)

【作畦】 zuòqí 〈农〉 bedding ◇ ～机 bedder

【作曲】 zuòqǔ write music; compose: 王芳～ music by Wang Fang ◇ ～家 composer

【作色】 zuòsè show signs of anger; get worked up: 愤然～ flush with indignation

【作势】 zuòshì assume a posture; attitudinize

【作数】 zuòshù count; be valid: 怎么昨天说的，今天就不～了？How is it that what you said yesterday no longer counts today?/ 那条旧规定不～了。That old rule doesn't hold any longer.

【作祟】 zuòsuì ① (of ghosts, spirits, etc.) haunt ② make mischief; cause trouble; exercise evil influence: 这都是利己主义～。All this trouble is caused by selfishness.

【作态】 zuòtài pose; affect; strike an attitude: 我讨厌她的忸怩～。Her affectations annoy me.

【作威作福】 zuòwēi-zuòfú tyrannically abuse one's power; ride roughshod over others; act like a tyrant: 骑在人民头上～ ride roughshod over the people; lord it over the people

【作为】 zuòwéi ① conduct; deed; action: 从他的～可以看出他的态度。From his deeds we can discern his attitude. ② accomplish; do sth. worthwhile: 无所～ attempt nothing and accomplish nothing/ 知识青年在这里是可以大有～的。School graduates can do a lot here. ③ regard as; look on as; take for: ～借口 use sth. as an excuse/ ～靠山 look upon sb. as one's prop ④ as: ～国家干部，我们要把人民的利益放在第一位。As government cadres, we should place the interests of the people above everything else.

【作伪】 zuòwěi fake (works of art, cultural relics, etc.); make an imitation; forge

【作文】 zuòwén ① (of students) write a composition ② composition

【作物】 zuòwù crop: 高产～ high-yield crops

【作息】 zuò-xī work and rest: 按时～ work and rest according to schedule ◇ ～时间表 daily schedule; timetable; work schedule

【作业】 zuòyè ① school assignment: 做～ do one's assignment/ 家庭～ homework/ 改～ correct students' papers ② work; task; operation; production: 水下～ underwater operation/ 野外～ field work/ 农业主要～机械化 mechanization in all major processes of farm work
◇ ～班 work team/ ～计划 production plan/ ～区 operation area/ ～线 production line

【作用】 zuòyòng ① act on; affect: 外界事物～于我们的感官，在我们的头脑中形成印象。External things act on our sense organs and give rise to impressions in our brains. ② action; function: 化学～ chemical action/ 反～ reaction/ 心脏的～ the function of the heart ③ effect: 惯性～ inertial effect/ 副～ side effect/ 积极～ positive role/ 起带头～ play a vanguard role ④ intention; motive: 他那样说是有他的～的。He had an axe to grind when he said that.
◇ ～范围 sphere of action/ ～力 effort; applied force

【作乐】 zuòyuè 〈书〉 play music
另见 zuòlè

【作战】 zuòzhàn fight; conduct operations; do battle: 英勇～ fight heroically/ 大规模～ conduct large-scale operations/ 积极对敌～ active warfare against the enemy
◇ ～部队 combat (或 fighting) troops/ ～部署 operational preparations/ ～地图 battle map; operation map/ ～方案 battle plan; line of action/ ～方法 method of fighting; tactics in operations/ ～方式 mode of operations/ ～方针 concept of operations; operational principles; operational policy/ ～基地 operational base; base of operations/ ～技术 fighting technique/ ～命令 combat (或 operation) order/ ～区域 theatre of war/ ～线 battle line/ ～效能

fighting efficiency/ ～指挥部 operational headquarters
【作者】 zuòzhě author; writer: ～不详 by an anonymous author; authorship unknown
【作证】 zuòzhèng testify; give evidence; bear witness: 在法庭上～ bear witness in a lawcourt
【作主】 zuòzhǔ ① decide; take the responsibility for a decision: 我作不了主。I am not in a position to decide./ 这件事是他自己～办的。He did it on his own responsibility./ 只能作一半主 have only half the say ② back up; support: 只要我们做得对,党委会给我们～的。So long as we act correctly the Party Committee will back us up.
【作准】 zuòzhǔn ① 见"作数" ② valid; authentic ◇ ～文本 authentic text

## 柞

zuò oak (*quercus*)
【柞蚕】 zuòcán tussah ◇ ～丝 tussah silk
【柞栎】 zuòlì 〈植〉 toothed oak
【柞丝绸】 zuòsīchóu tussah silk; pongee

## 胙

zuò sacrificial meat (in ancient times)

## 座

zuò ① seat; place: 就～ take one's seat/ 满～ full house/ 请入～。Please be seated./ 剧场内～无虚席。The theatre had a full house. ② stand; pedestal; base: 花瓶～儿 vase stand/ 塑像～儿 pedestal for a statue ③〈天〉constellation: 大熊～ the Great Bear ④〈量〉〔多用于较大或固定的物体〕: 一～山 a mountain/ 一～桥 a bridge/ 一～铜像 a bronze statue
【座次】 zuòcì order of seats; seating arrangements
【座上客】 zuòshàngkè guest of honour; honoured guest
【座谈】 zuòtán have an informal discussion
【座谈会】 zuòtánhuì forum; symposium; informal discussion: 文艺～ forum on literature and art/ 新针疗法～ symposium on new acupuncture therapy
【座位】 zuòwèi seat; place: 这个体育馆有一万八千个～。The stadium seats 18,000.
【座右铭】 zuòyòumíng motto; maxim: "为人民服务"是我们的～。"Serve the people" is our motto.
【座钟】 zuòzhōng desk clock
【座子】 zuòzi ① stand; pedestal; base ② saddle (of a bicycle, motorcycle, etc.)

## 唑

zuò 见"咔唑" kǎzuò; "噻唑" sāizuò

## 做

zuò ① make; produce; manufacture: ～衣服 make clothes/ 这种糖是甜菜～的。This sugar is made from beets./ 这是你自己～的吗? Did you make this yourself? ② cook; prepare: ～饭 do the cooking; prepare a meal/ ～菜 cook a dish ③ do; act; engage in: ～好事 do good; do a good deed/ ～生意 do business; carry on trade/ ～好本职工作 do one's best at one's own job/ 从点滴的事情～起 start with little things/ 大事～不来,小事又不～ be unable to do big jobs and look down on small ones/ 照正确的意见去～ act upon correct views/ 去年全队社员共～了两万多个劳动日。The members of the team did a total of more than 20,000 workdays last year./ 我们正在～我们的前人从来没有～过的极其光荣伟大的事业。We are now engaged in a great and most glorious cause, never undertaken by our forefathers. ④ be; become: ～演员 become an actor or actress; go on the stage/ 后来她～保育员了。Later she became a child-care worker./ 今天开会由你～主席。You'll be the chairman at today's meeting. ⑤ write; compose: ～一首诗 write a poem ⑥ hold a family (或 home) celebration: ～生日 celebrate sb.'s birthday ⑦ be used as: 这篇文章可以～教材。This article may be used as teaching material. ⑧ form or contract a relationship: ～朋友 make friends with/ ～亲 (of two families) become relatives by marriage/ ～对头 set oneself against sb.
【做伴】 zuòbàn keep sb. company
【做到】 zuòdào accomplish; achieve: 说到～ be as good as one's word; abide by one's promise/ 我们应当～增产不增人。We should manage to increase production without taking on new hands./ 西方资产阶级～的,东方无产阶级也一定能够～,而且做得更好。What the bourgeoisie in the West has accomplished the proletariat in the East can also accomplish and do a better job of it.
【做东】 zuòdōng play the host; host sb.; act as host to sb.
【做法】 zuòfǎ way of doing or making a thing; method of work; practice: 惯常的～ the usual practice; the usual way of doing sth.
【做工】 zuògōng ① do manual work; work: 她在纺织厂～。She works in a textile mill. ② charge for the making of sth.: 这套衣服～十块钱。The charge for the tailoring of this suit was ten *yuan*. ③ workmanship: ～精美 of excellent workmanship
【做功】 zuògōng 〈剧〉 acting; business 又作"做工"
【做官】 zuòguān be an official; secure an official position: ～当老爷 act like high officials and overbearing bureaucrats; act as bureaucrats and overlords
【做鬼】 zuòguǐ play tricks; play an underhand game; get up to mischief
【做活儿】 zuòhuór work; do manual labour: 他们一块儿在地里～。They worked together in the fields.
【做绝】 zuòjué leave no room for manoeuvre: 把事情～ get things into an impasse; leave oneself no avenue of retreat; pass the point of no return/ 坏事～ perpetrate every kind of villainy
【做客】 zuòkè be a guest: 我昨天到一个老朋友家里去～。I was a guest at an old friend's yesterday.
【做礼拜】 zuò lǐbài 〈基督教〉 go to church; be at church
【做媒】 zuòméi be a matchmaker (或 go-between)
【做梦】 zuòmèng ① have a dream; dream: 做恶梦 dream a bad dream; have a nightmare/ 我们～也没有想到有今天。We never dreamt that we would be as we are today. ② have a pipe dream; daydream: 做美梦 cherish fond hopes/ 他岂不是在～吗? Isn't he just daydreaming?
【做人】 zuòrén ① conduct oneself; behave: 懂得如何～处世 know how to conduct oneself in society ② be an upright person: 重新～ turn over a new leaf
【做声】 zuòshēng make a sound (as when speaking, coughing, etc.): 别～! Keep quiet!
【做事】 zuòshì ① handle affairs; do a deed; act: ～不能只凭动机,不问效果。Actions shouldn't be guided solely by motive without any attention to effect./ 热心为群众～ be enthusiastic in rendering services to the masses ② work; have a job: 他在钢铁厂～。He works in an iron and steel mill.
【做寿】 zuòshòu celebrate the birthday (usu. of elderly people); hold a birthday party
【做文章】 zuò wénzhāng ① write an essay ② make an issue of: 他想抓住这件事情～。He tried to seize upon the matter and make an issue of it.
【做戏】 zuòxì ① act in a play ② put on a show; playact
【做一天和尚撞一天钟】 zuò yī tiān héshang zhuàng yī tiān zhōng go on tolling the bell as long as one is a monk — do the least that is expected of one; take a passive attitude towards one's work
【做贼心虚】 zuò zéi xīnxū have a guilty conscience: 他们推三阻四,正好暴露了他们～。In making so many excuses,

they revealed their own guilty conscience.

【做主】 zuòzhǔ 见"作主" zuòzhǔ

【做作】 zuòzuo affected; artificial: 他老是那么～。He's always affected. 或 He's never natural./ 她唱得还可以，就是演得太～。Her singing is all right, but her acting is overdone.

## 酢

zuò 见"酬酢" chóuzuò
另见 cù

## 凿

zuò ①〈书〉 certain; authentic; irrefutable: 确～ authentic; conclusive ② mortise
另见 záo

【凿空】 zuòkōng 〈书〉 forced; farfetched: ～之论 farfetched argument

【凿枘】 zuòruì 〈书〉 incompatible

【凿凿】 zuòzuò 〈书〉 true; certain; verified: 言之～ say sth. with certainty/ ～有据 with irrefutable evidence

# 附 录

# 汉字简化字和繁体字对照表

# The Original Complex Forms of Chinese Characters and Their Simplified Versions

## 第 一 表

### 不作简化偏旁用的简化字

本表共收简化字 352 个，按读音的拼音字母顺序排列。本表的简化字都不得作简化偏旁使用。

**A**

碍〔礙〕
肮〔骯〕
袄〔襖〕

**B**

坝〔壩〕
板〔闆〕
办〔辦〕
帮〔幫〕
宝〔寶〕
报〔報〕
币〔幣〕
毙〔斃〕
标〔標〕
表〔錶〕
别〔彆〕
卜〔蔔〕
补〔補〕

**C**

才〔纔〕
蚕〔蠶〕
灿〔燦〕
层〔層〕
搀〔攙〕
谗〔讒〕
馋〔饞〕
缠〔纏〕
忏〔懺〕
偿〔償〕
厂〔廠〕
彻〔徹〕
尘〔塵〕
衬〔襯〕
称〔稱〕
惩〔懲〕
迟〔遲〕
冲〔衝〕
丑〔醜〕
出〔齣〕
础〔礎〕
处〔處〕
触〔觸〕
辞〔辭〕
聪〔聰〕
丛〔叢〕

**D**

担〔擔〕
胆〔膽〕
导〔導〕
灯〔燈〕
邓〔鄧〕
敌〔敵〕
籴〔糴〕
递〔遞〕
点〔點〕
淀〔澱〕
电〔電〕
迭〔疊〕①
冬〔鼕〕
斗〔鬥〕
独〔獨〕
吨〔噸〕
夺〔奪〕
堕〔墮〕

**E**

儿〔兒〕

**F**

矾〔礬〕
范〔範〕
飞〔飛〕
坟〔墳〕
奋〔奮〕
粪〔糞〕
凤〔鳳〕
肤〔膚〕
妇〔婦〕
复〔復〕〔複〕
〔覆〕②

**G**

盖〔蓋〕
干〔乾〕③
〔幹〕
赶〔趕〕
个〔個〕
巩〔鞏〕
沟〔溝〕
构〔構〕
购〔購〕
谷〔穀〕
顾〔顧〕
刮〔颳〕
关〔關〕
观〔觀〕
柜〔櫃〕

**H**

汉〔漢〕
号〔號〕
合〔閤〕
轰〔轟〕
后〔後〕
胡〔鬍〕
壶〔壺〕
沪〔滬〕
护〔護〕
划〔劃〕
怀〔懷〕
坏〔壞〕
欢〔歡〕
环〔環〕
还〔還〕
回〔迴〕
伙〔夥〕④
获〔獲〕〔穫〕

**J**

击〔擊〕
鸡〔鷄〕
积〔積〕
极〔極〕
际〔際〕
继〔繼〕
家〔傢〕
价〔價〕
艰〔艱〕
歼〔殲〕
茧〔繭〕
拣〔揀〕
硷〔鹼〕
舰〔艦〕
姜〔薑〕
浆〔漿〕
桨〔槳〕
奖〔獎〕
讲〔講〕
酱〔醬〕
胶〔膠〕
阶〔階〕
疖〔癤〕
洁〔潔〕
借〔藉〕⑤
仅〔僅〕
惊〔驚〕
竞〔競〕
旧〔舊〕
剧〔劇〕
据〔據〕
惧〔懼〕
卷〔捲〕

**K**

开〔開〕
克〔剋〕
垦〔墾〕
恳〔懇〕
夸〔誇〕
块〔塊〕
亏〔虧〕
困〔睏〕

**L**

腊〔臘〕
蜡〔蠟〕
兰〔蘭〕
拦〔攔〕
栏〔欄〕
烂〔爛〕
累〔纍〕
垒〔壘〕
类〔類〕
里〔裏〕
礼〔禮〕
隶〔隸〕
帘〔簾〕
联〔聯〕
怜〔憐〕
炼〔煉〕
练〔練〕
粮〔糧〕
疗〔療〕
辽〔遼〕
了〔瞭〕
猎〔獵〕
临〔臨〕
邻〔鄰〕
岭〔嶺〕
庐〔廬〕
芦〔蘆〕
炉〔爐〕
陆〔陸〕
驴〔驢〕
乱〔亂〕

**M**

么〔麼〕⑥
霉〔黴〕
蒙〔矇〕〔濛〕
〔懞〕
梦〔夢〕
面〔麵〕
庙〔廟〕
灭〔滅〕
蔑〔衊〕
亩〔畝〕

**N**

恼〔惱〕
脑〔腦〕
拟〔擬〕
酿〔釀〕
疟〔瘧〕

**P**

盘〔盤〕
辟〔闢〕
苹〔蘋〕
凭〔憑〕
扑〔撲〕
仆〔僕〕
朴〔樸〕

**Q**

启〔啓〕
签〔籤〕
千〔韆〕
牵〔牽〕
纤〔縴〕〔纖〕
窍〔竅〕
窃〔竊〕
寝〔寢〕
庆〔慶〕
琼〔瓊〕
秋〔鞦〕
曲〔麯〕
权〔權〕
劝〔勸〕
确〔確〕

**R**

让〔讓〕
扰〔擾〕
热〔熱〕
认〔認〕

**S**

洒[灑]
伞[傘]
丧[喪]
扫[掃]
涩[澀]
晒[曬]
伤[傷]
舍[捨]
沈[瀋]
声[聲]
胜[勝]
湿[濕]
实[實]
适[適]
势[勢]
兽[獸]
书[書]
术[術]
树[樹]
帅[帥]
松[鬆]
苏[蘇][囌]
虽[雖]
随[隨]

**T**

台[臺][檯][颱]
态[態]
坛[壇][罎]
叹[嘆]
誊[謄]
体[體]
粜[糶]
铁[鐵]
听[聽]
厅[廳]
头[頭]
图[圖]
涂[塗]
团[團][糰]
椭[橢]

**W**

洼[窪]
袜[襪]
网[網]
卫[衛]
稳[穩]
务[務]
雾[霧]

**X**

牺[犧]
习[習]
系[係][繫]
戏[戲]
虾[蝦]
吓[嚇]
咸[鹹]
显[顯]
宪[憲]
县[縣]
响[響]
向[嚮]
象[像]⑦
协[協]
胁[脅]
亵[褻]
衅[釁]
兴[興]
须[鬚]
悬[懸]
选[選]
旋[鏇]

**Y**

压[壓]
盐[鹽]
阳[陽]
养[養]
痒[癢]
样[樣]
钥[鑰]
药[藥]
爷[爺]
叶[葉]
医[醫]
亿[億]
忆[憶]
应[應]
痈[癰]
拥[擁]
佣[傭]
踊[踴]
忧[憂]
优[優]
邮[郵]
余[餘]⑧
御[禦]
吁[籲]
郁[鬱]
誉[譽]
渊[淵]
园[園]
远[遠]
愿[願]
跃[躍]
运[運]
酝[醞]

**Z**

杂[雜]
赃[贓]
脏[臟][髒]
凿[鑿]
枣[棗]
灶[竈]
斋[齋]
毡[氈]
战[戰]
赵[趙]
折[摺]⑨
这[這]
征[徵]⑩
症[癥]
证[證]
只[隻][衹]
致[緻]
制[製]
钟[鐘][鍾]
肿[腫]
种[種]
众[衆]
昼[晝]
朱[硃]
烛[燭]
筑[築]
庄[莊]
桩[樁]
妆[妝]
装[裝]
壮[壯]
状[狀]
准[準]
浊[濁]
总[總]
钻[鑽]

# 第二表

## 可作简化偏旁用的简化字和简化偏旁

本表共收简化字 132 个和简化偏旁 14 个。简化字按读音的拼音字母顺序排列，简化偏旁按笔数排列。

**A**

爱[愛]

**B**

罢[罷]
备[備]
贝[貝]
笔[筆]
毕[畢]
边[邊]
宾[賓]

**C**

参[參]
仓[倉]
产[産]
长[長]
尝[嘗]
车[車]
齿[齒]
虫[蟲]
刍[芻]
从[從]
窜[竄]

**D**

达[達]
带[帶]
单[單]
当[當][噹]
党[黨]
东[東]
动[動]
断[斷]
对[對]
队[隊]

**E**

尔[爾]

**F**

发[發][髮]
丰[豐]⑪
风[風]

**G**

冈[岡]
广[廣]
归[歸]
龟[龜]
国[國]
过[過]

**H**

华[華]
画[畫]
汇[匯][彙]
会[會]

**J**

几[幾]
夹[夾]
戋[戔]
监[監]
见[見]
荐[薦]
将[將]
节[節]
尽[盡][儘]
进[進]
举[舉]

**K**

壳[殼]

**L**

来[來]
乐[樂]
离[離]
历[歷][曆]
丽[麗]
两[兩]
灵[靈]
刘[劉]
龙[龍]
娄[婁]
卢[盧]
虏[虜]
卤[鹵][滷]
录[録]
虑[慮]
仑[侖]
罗[羅][囉]

**M**

马[馬]
买[買]
卖[賣]
麦[麥]
门[門]
黾[黽]

**N**

难[難]
鸟[鳥]
聂[聶]
宁[寧]
农[農]

**Q**

齐[齊]
岂[豈]
气[氣]
迁[遷]
佥[僉]
乔[喬]
亲[親]
穷[窮]
区[區]

**S**

啬[嗇]
杀[殺]
审[審]
圣[聖]
师[師]
时[時]
寿[壽]
属[屬]
双[雙]
肃[肅]
岁[歲]
孙[孫]

**T**

条[條]

**W**

万[萬]
为[爲]
韦[韋]
乌[烏]
无[無]

**X**

献[獻]
乡[鄉]
写[寫]
寻[尋]

**Y**

亚[亞]
严[嚴]
厌[厭]
尧[堯]
业[業]
页[頁]
义[義]
艺[藝]
阴[陰]
隐[隱]
犹[猶]
鱼[魚]
与[與]
云[雲]

**Z**

郑[鄭]
执[執]
质[質]
专[專]

**简化偏旁**

讠[言]
饣[食]
𠃓[昜]
纟[糸]
収[臤]
𫇧[𤇾]
𫶧[臨]
只[戠]
钅[金]
𫠠[𦥯]
𠬤[睪]⑫
𢀖[巠]
亦[䜌]
呙[咼]

# 第三表

## 应用第二表所列简化字和简化偏旁得出来的简化字

本表共收简化字 1,754 个(不包含重见的字。例如"缆"分见"纟、𠂉、见"三部，只算一字)，以第二表中的简化字和简化偏旁作部首，按第二表的顺序排列。同一部首中的简化字，按笔数排列。

**爱**

嗳〔噯〕
嫒〔嬡〕
叆〔靉〕
瑷〔璦〕
暧〔曖〕

**罢**

摆〔擺〕〔襬〕
罴〔羆〕
䅈〔穲〕

**备**

惫〔憊〕

**贝**

贞〔貞〕
则〔則〕
负〔負〕
贡〔貢〕
呗〔唄〕
员〔員〕
财〔財〕
狈〔狽〕
责〔責〕
厕〔廁〕
贤〔賢〕
账〔賬〕
贩〔販〕
贬〔貶〕
败〔敗〕
贮〔貯〕
贪〔貪〕
贫〔貧〕
侦〔偵〕
侧〔側〕
货〔貨〕
贯〔貫〕
测〔測〕
浈〔湞〕
恻〔惻〕
贰〔貳〕
贲〔賁〕
贳〔貰〕
费〔費〕
郧〔鄖〕
勋〔勛〕
帧〔幀〕
贴〔貼〕
贶〔貺〕
贻〔貽〕
贱〔賤〕
贵〔貴〕
钡〔鋇〕
贷〔貸〕
贸〔貿〕
贺〔賀〕
陨〔隕〕
涢〔溳〕
资〔資〕
祯〔禎〕
贾〔賈〕
损〔損〕
贽〔贄〕
埙〔塤〕
桢〔楨〕
唝〔嗊〕
唢〔嗩〕
赅〔賅〕
圆〔圓〕
贼〔賊〕
贿〔賄〕
赆〔贐〕
赂〔賂〕
债〔債〕
赁〔賃〕
渍〔漬〕
惯〔慣〕
琐〔瑣〕
赉〔賚〕
匮〔匱〕
掼〔摜〕
殒〔殞〕
勚〔勩〕
赈〔賑〕
婴〔嬰〕
啧〔嘖〕
赊〔賒〕
帻〔幘〕
偾〔僨〕
铡〔鍘〕
绩〔績〕
溃〔潰〕
溅〔濺〕
赓〔賡〕
愦〔憒〕
愤〔憤〕
蒉〔蕢〕
赍〔賫〕
蒇〔蕆〕
䞍〔䝼〕
赔〔賠〕
赕〔賧〕
遗〔遺〕
赋〔賦〕
喷〔噴〕
赌〔賭〕
赎〔贖〕
赏〔賞〕
赐〔賜〕
赒〔賙〕
锁〔鎖〕
馈〔饋〕
赖〔賴〕
赪〔赬〕
碛〔磧〕
㱮〔殨〕
赗〔賵〕
腻〔膩〕
赛〔賽〕
䙌〔䙡〕
赘〔贅〕
撄〔攖〕
槚〔檟〕
嘤〔嚶〕
赚〔賺〕
赙〔賻〕
罂〔罌〕
镄〔鐨〕
箦〔簀〕
鲗〔鰂〕
缨〔纓〕
璎〔瓔〕
聩〔聵〕
樱〔櫻〕
赜〔賾〕
篑〔簣〕
濑〔瀨〕
瘿〔癭〕
懒〔懶〕
赝〔贋〕
豮〔豶〕
赠〔贈〕
鹦〔鸚〕
獭〔獺〕
赞〔贊〕
赢〔贏〕
赡〔贍〕
癞〔癩〕
攒〔攢〕
籁〔籟〕
缵〔纘〕
瓒〔瓚〕
臜〔臢〕
赣〔贛〕
趱〔趲〕
躜〔躦〕
戆〔戇〕

**笔**

滗〔潷〕

**毕**

荜〔蓽〕
哔〔嗶〕
筚〔篳〕
跸〔蹕〕

**边**

笾〔籩〕

**宾**

傧〔儐〕
滨〔濱〕
摈〔擯〕
嫔〔嬪〕
缤〔繽〕
殡〔殯〕
槟〔檳〕
膑〔臏〕
镔〔鑌〕
髌〔髕〕
鬓〔鬢〕

**参**

渗〔滲〕
惨〔慘〕
掺〔摻〕
骖〔驂〕
毵〔毿〕
瘆〔瘮〕
碜〔磣〕
䅟〔穇〕
糁〔糝〕

**仓**

伧〔傖〕
创〔創〕
沧〔滄〕
怆〔愴〕
苍〔蒼〕
抢〔搶〕
呛〔嗆〕
炝〔熗〕
玱〔瑲〕
枪〔槍〕
戗〔戧〕
疮〔瘡〕
鸧〔鶬〕
舱〔艙〕
跄〔蹌〕

**产**

浐〔滻〕
萨〔薩〕
铲〔鏟〕

**长**

伥〔倀〕
怅〔悵〕
帐〔帳〕
张〔張〕
枨〔棖〕
账〔賬〕
胀〔脹〕
涨〔漲〕

**尝**

鲿〔鱨〕

**车**

轧〔軋〕
军〔軍〕
轨〔軌〕
厍〔厙〕
阵〔陣〕
库〔庫〕
连〔連〕
轩〔軒〕
诨〔諢〕
郓〔鄆〕
轫〔軔〕
轭〔軛〕
匦〔匭〕
转〔轉〕
轮〔輪〕
斩〔斬〕
软〔軟〕
浑〔渾〕
恽〔惲〕
砗〔硨〕
轶〔軼〕
轲〔軻〕
轱〔軲〕
轷〔軤〕
轻〔輕〕
轳〔轤〕
轴〔軸〕
挥〔揮〕
荤〔葷〕
轹〔轢〕
轸〔軫〕
轺〔軺〕
涟〔漣〕
珲〔琿〕
载〔載〕
莲〔蓮〕
较〔較〕
轼〔軾〕
轾〔輊〕
辂〔輅〕
轿〔轎〕
晕〔暈〕
渐〔漸〕
惭〔慚〕
皲〔皸〕
琏〔璉〕
辅〔輔〕
辄〔輒〕
辆〔輛〕
堑〔塹〕
啭〔囀〕
崭〔嶄〕
裤〔褲〕
裢〔褳〕
辇〔輦〕
辋〔輞〕
辍〔輟〕
辊〔輥〕
椠〔槧〕
辎〔輜〕
暂〔暫〕
辉〔輝〕
辈〔輩〕
链〔鏈〕
翚〔翬〕
辏〔輳〕
辐〔輻〕
辑〔輯〕
输〔輸〕
毂〔轂〕
辔〔轡〕
辖〔轄〕
辕〔轅〕
辗〔輾〕
舆〔輿〕
辘〔轆〕
撵〔攆〕
鲢〔鰱〕
辙〔轍〕
錾〔鏨〕
辚〔轔〕

**齿**

龀〔齔〕
啮〔嚙〕
龆〔齠〕
龅〔齙〕
龃〔齟〕
龄〔齡〕
龇〔齜〕
龈〔齦〕
龉〔齬〕
龊〔齪〕
龌〔齷〕
龋〔齲〕

**虫**

蛊〔蠱〕

**刍**

诌〔謅〕
㑇〔㑳〕
邹〔鄒〕
㤘〔㥮〕
驺〔騶〕
绉〔縐〕
皱〔皺〕
趋〔趨〕

雏〔雛〕

**从**

苁〔蓯〕
纵〔縱〕
枞〔樅〕
怂〔慫〕
耸〔聳〕

**窜**

撺〔攛〕
镩〔鑹〕
蹿〔躥〕

**达**

㳠〔澾〕
闼〔闥〕
挞〔撻〕
哒〔噠〕
鞑〔韃〕

**带**

滞〔滯〕

**单**

郸〔鄲〕
惮〔憚〕
阐〔闡〕
掸〔撣〕
弹〔彈〕
婵〔嬋〕
禅〔禪〕
殚〔殫〕
瘅〔癉〕
蝉〔蟬〕
箪〔簞〕
蕲〔蘄〕
冁〔囅〕

**当**

挡〔擋〕
档〔檔〕
裆〔襠〕
铛〔鐺〕

**党**

谠〔讜〕
傥〔儻〕
镋〔钂〕

**东**

冻〔凍〕
陈〔陳〕
岽〔崬〕
栋〔棟〕
胨〔腖〕
鸫〔鶇〕

**动**

恸〔慟〕

**断**

簖〔籪〕

**对**

怼〔懟〕

**队**

坠〔墜〕

**尔**

迩〔邇〕
弥〔彌、瀰〕
祢〔禰〕
玺〔璽〕
猕〔獼〕

**发**

泼〔潑〕
废〔廢〕
拨〔撥〕
钹〔鏺〕

**丰**

沣〔灃〕
艳〔艷〕
滟〔灧〕

**风**

讽〔諷〕
沨〔渢〕
岚〔嵐〕
枫〔楓〕
疯〔瘋〕
飒〔颯〕
砜〔碸〕
飓〔颶〕
飔〔颸〕
飕〔颼〕
飗〔飀〕
飘〔飄〕
飙〔飆〕

**冈**

刚〔剛〕
㧏〔掆〕
岗〔崗〕
纲〔綱〕
㭎〔棡〕
钢〔鋼〕

**广**

邝〔鄺〕
圹〔壙〕
扩〔擴〕
犷〔獷〕
纩〔纊〕
旷〔曠〕
矿〔礦〕

**归**

岿〔巋〕

**龟**

阄〔鬮〕

**国**

掴〔摑〕
帼〔幗〕
腘〔膕〕
蝈〔蟈〕

**过**

挝〔撾〕

**华**

哗〔嘩〕
骅〔驊〕
烨〔燁〕
桦〔樺〕
晔〔曄〕
铧〔鏵〕

**画**

婳〔嫿〕

**汇**

㧟〔擓〕

**会**

刽〔劊〕
郐〔鄶〕
侩〔儈〕
浍〔澮〕
荟〔薈〕
哙〔噲〕
狯〔獪〕
绘〔繪〕
烩〔燴〕
桧〔檜〕
脍〔膾〕
鲙〔鱠〕

**几**

讥〔譏〕
叽〔嘰〕
饥〔饑〕
机〔機〕
玑〔璣〕
矶〔磯〕
虮〔蟣〕

**夹**

郏〔郟〕
侠〔俠〕
陕〔陝〕
浃〔浹〕
挟〔挾〕
荚〔莢〕
峡〔峽〕
狭〔狹〕
惬〔愜〕
硖〔硤〕
铗〔鋏〕
颊〔頰〕
蛱〔蛺〕
瘗〔瘞〕
箧〔篋〕

**戋**

刬〔剗〕
浅〔淺〕
饯〔餞〕
线〔綫〕
残〔殘〕
栈〔棧〕
贱〔賤〕
盏〔盞〕
钱〔錢〕
笺〔箋〕
溅〔濺〕
践〔踐〕

**监**

滥〔濫〕
蓝〔藍〕
尴〔尷〕
槛〔檻〕
褴〔襤〕
篮〔籃〕

**见**

苋〔莧〕
岘〔峴〕
觃〔覎〕
视〔視〕
规〔規〕
现〔現〕
枧〔梘〕
觅〔覓〕
觉〔覺〕
砚〔硯〕
觇〔覘〕
览〔覽〕
宽〔寬〕
蚬〔蜆〕
觊〔覬〕
笕〔筧〕
觋〔覡〕
觌〔覿〕
靓〔靚〕
搅〔攪〕
揽〔攬〕
缆〔纜〕
窥〔窺〕
榄〔欖〕
觎〔覦〕
觏〔覯〕
觐〔覲〕
觑〔覷〕
髋〔髖〕

**荐**

鞯〔韉〕

**将**

蒋〔蔣〕
锵〔鏘〕

**节**

栉〔櫛〕

**尽**

浕〔濜〕
荩〔藎〕
烬〔燼〕
赆〔贐〕

**进**

琎〔璡〕

**举**

榉〔櫸〕

**壳**

悫〔愨〕

**来**

涞〔淶〕
莱〔萊〕
崃〔崍〕
徕〔徠〕
赉〔賚〕
睐〔睞〕
铼〔錸〕

**乐**

泺〔濼〕
烁〔爍〕
栎〔櫟〕
轹〔轢〕
砾〔礫〕
铄〔鑠〕

**离**

漓〔灕〕
篱〔籬〕

**历**

沥〔瀝〕
坜〔壢〕
苈〔藶〕
呖〔嚦〕
枥〔櫪〕
疬〔癧〕
雳〔靂〕

**丽**

俪〔儷〕
郦〔酈〕
逦〔邐〕
骊〔驪〕
鹂〔鸝〕
酾〔釃〕
鲡〔鱺〕

**两**

俩〔倆〕
唡〔啢〕
辆〔輛〕
满〔滿〕
瞒〔瞞〕
颟〔顢〕
螨〔蟎〕
魉〔魎〕
懑〔懣〕
蹒〔蹣〕

**灵**

棂〔欞〕

**刘**

浏〔瀏〕

**龙**

陇〔隴〕
泷〔瀧〕
宠〔寵〕
庞〔龐〕
垄〔壟〕
拢〔攏〕
茏〔蘢〕
咙〔嚨〕
珑〔瓏〕
栊〔櫳〕
䶮〔龑〕
昽〔曨〕
胧〔朧〕
砻〔礱〕
袭〔襲〕
聋〔聾〕
龚〔龔〕
龛〔龕〕
笼〔籠〕
詟〔讋〕

**娄**

偻〔僂〕
溇〔漊〕
蒌〔蔞〕
搂〔摟〕
嵝〔嶁〕
喽〔嘍〕
缕〔縷〕
屡〔屢〕
数〔數〕
楼〔樓〕
瘘〔瘻〕
褛〔褸〕
窭〔窶〕
䁖〔瞜〕
镂〔鏤〕
屦〔屨〕
蝼〔螻〕
篓〔簍〕
耧〔耬〕
薮〔藪〕
擞〔擻〕
髅〔髏〕

**卢**

泸〔瀘〕
垆〔壚〕
栌〔櫨〕
轳〔轤〕
胪〔臚〕
鸬〔鸕〕
颅〔顱〕
舻〔艫〕
鲈〔鱸〕

**虏**

掳〔擄〕

**卤**

鹾〔鹺〕

**录**

箓〔籙〕

**虑**

滤〔濾〕
摅〔攄〕

**仑**

论〔論〕
伦〔倫〕
沦〔淪〕
抡〔掄〕
囵〔圇〕
纶〔綸〕
轮〔輪〕
瘪〔癟〕

**罗**

萝〔蘿〕
逻〔邏〕
猡〔玀〕
椤〔欏〕
锣〔鑼〕
箩〔籮〕

**马**

冯〔馮〕
驭〔馭〕
闯〔闖〕
吗〔嗎〕
犸〔獁〕
驮〔馱〕
驰〔馳〕
驯〔馴〕
妈〔媽〕
玛〔瑪〕
驱〔驅〕
驳〔駁〕
码〔碼〕
驼〔駝〕
驻〔駐〕
驵〔駔〕
驾〔駕〕
驿〔驛〕
驷〔駟〕
驶〔駛〕
驹〔駒〕
驺〔騶〕
骀〔駘〕
驸〔駙〕
驽〔駑〕
骂〔罵〕
蚂〔螞〕
笃〔篤〕
骇〔駭〕
骈〔駢〕
骁〔驍〕
骄〔驕〕
骅〔驊〕
骆〔駱〕
骊〔驪〕
骋〔騁〕
验〔驗〕
骏〔駿〕
骎〔駸〕
骑〔騎〕
骐〔騏〕
骒〔騍〕
骓〔騅〕
骖〔驂〕
骗〔騙〕
骘〔騭〕
骛〔騖〕

骚〔騷〕
骞〔騫〕
骜〔驁〕
蓦〔驀〕
腾〔騰〕
骝〔騮〕
骟〔騸〕
骠〔驃〕
骢〔驄〕
骡〔騾〕
羁〔羈〕
骤〔驟〕
骥〔驥〕
骧〔驤〕
**买**
荬〔蕒〕
**卖**
读〔讀〕
渎〔瀆〕
续〔續〕
椟〔櫝〕
觌〔覿〕
赎〔贖〕
犊〔犢〕
牍〔牘〕
窦〔竇〕
黩〔黷〕
**麦**
唛〔嘜〕
麸〔麩〕
**门**
闩〔閂〕
闪〔閃〕
们〔們〕
闭〔閉〕
闯〔闖〕
问〔問〕
扪〔捫〕
闱〔闈〕
闵〔閔〕
闷〔悶〕
闰〔閏〕
闲〔閑〕
间〔間〕
闹〔閙〕⑬
闸〔閘〕
钔〔鍆〕
阂〔閡〕
闺〔閨〕
闻〔聞〕
闼〔闥〕
闽〔閩〕
闾〔閭〕
闿〔闓〕
阁〔閤〕
阁〔閣〕
阀〔閥〕
润〔潤〕
涧〔澗〕
悯〔憫〕
阆〔閬〕
阅〔閱〕
阃〔閫〕
阄〔鬮〕⑬
阇〔闍〕
娴〔嫻〕
阏〔閼〕
阈〔閾〕
阉〔閹〕
阊〔閶〕
阍〔閽〕
阌〔閿〕
阋〔鬩〕⑬
阐〔闡〕
阎〔閻〕
焖〔燜〕
阑〔闌〕
裥〔襇〕
阔〔闊〕
痫〔癇〕
鹇〔鷳〕
阕〔闋〕
阒〔闃〕
搁〔擱〕
锏〔鐧〕
锎〔鐦〕
阙〔闕〕
阖〔闔〕
阗〔闐〕
榈〔櫚〕
简〔簡〕
谰〔讕〕
阚〔闞〕
蔺〔藺〕
澜〔瀾〕
斓〔斕〕
㘓〔囒〕
镧〔鑭〕
躏〔躪〕
**黾**
渑〔澠〕
绳〔繩〕
鼋〔黿〕
蝇〔蠅〕
鼍〔鼉〕
**难**
傩〔儺〕
滩〔灘〕
摊〔攤〕
瘫〔癱〕
**鸟**
凫〔鳧〕
鸠〔鳩〕
岛〔島〕
茑〔蔦〕
鸢〔鳶〕
鸣〔鳴〕
枭〔梟〕
鸩〔鴆〕
鸦〔鴉〕
䴓〔鳾〕
鸥〔鷗〕
鸨〔鴇〕
鸧〔鶬〕
窎〔窵〕
莺〔鶯〕
鸪〔鴣〕
捣〔搗〕
鸫〔鶇〕
鸬〔鸕〕
鸭〔鴨〕
鸯〔鴦〕
鸮〔鴞〕
鸲〔鴝〕
鸰〔鴒〕
鸳〔鴛〕
鸵〔鴕〕
袅〔裊〕
鸱〔鴟〕
鸶〔鷥〕
鸾〔鸞〕
䴔〔鵁〕
鸿〔鴻〕
鸷〔鷙〕
鸸〔鴯〕
䴕〔鴷〕
鸼〔鵃〕
鸽〔鴿〕
鸹〔鴰〕
鸺〔鵂〕
鸻〔鴴〕
鹈〔鵜〕
鹇〔鷳〕
鹁〔鵓〕
鹂〔鸝〕
鹃〔鵑〕
鹆〔鵒〕
鹄〔鵠〕
鹅〔鵝〕
鹑〔鶉〕
鹒〔鶊〕
䴖〔鶄〕
鹉〔鵡〕
鹊〔鵲〕
鹋〔鶓〕
鹌〔鵪〕
鹏〔鵬〕
鹐〔鵮〕
鹚〔鷀〕
鹕〔鶘〕
鹖〔鶡〕
䴗〔鶪〕
鹗〔鶚〕
鹘〔鶻〕
鹙〔鶖〕
鹜〔鶩〕
鹛〔鶥〕
鹤〔鶴〕
鹣〔鶼〕
鹞〔鷂〕
鹡〔鶺〕
鹧〔鷓〕
鹢〔鷁〕
鹥〔鷖〕
鹦〔鸚〕
鹨〔鷚〕
鹫〔鷲〕
鹩〔鷯〕
鹪〔鷦〕
鹬〔鷸〕
鹰〔鷹〕
鹯〔鸇〕
鹭〔鷺〕
䴙〔鸊〕
鹳〔鸛〕
**聂**
慑〔懾〕
滠〔灄〕
摄〔攝〕
嗫〔囁〕
镊〔鑷〕
颞〔顳〕
蹑〔躡〕
**宁**
泞〔濘〕
拧〔擰〕
咛〔嚀〕
狞〔獰〕
柠〔檸〕
聍〔聹〕
**农**
侬〔儂〕
浓〔濃〕
哝〔噥〕
脓〔膿〕
**齐**
剂〔劑〕
侪〔儕〕
济〔濟〕
荠〔薺〕
挤〔擠〕
脐〔臍〕
蛴〔蠐〕
跻〔躋〕
霁〔霽〕
鲚〔鱭〕
齑〔齏〕
**岂**
剀〔剴〕
凯〔凱〕
恺〔愷〕
闿〔闓〕
垲〔塏〕
桤〔榿〕
觊〔覬〕
硙〔磑〕
皑〔皚〕
铠〔鎧〕
**气**
忾〔愾〕
饩〔餼〕
**迁**
跹〔躚〕
**佥**
剑〔劍〕
俭〔儉〕
险〔險〕
捡〔撿〕
猃〔獫〕
验〔驗〕
检〔檢〕
殓〔殮〕
敛〔斂〕
脸〔臉〕
裣〔襝〕
睑〔瞼〕
签〔簽〕
潋〔瀲〕
蔹〔蘞〕
**乔**
侨〔僑〕
挢〔撟〕
荞〔蕎〕
峤〔嶠〕
骄〔驕〕
娇〔嬌〕
桥〔橋〕
轿〔轎〕
硚〔礄〕
矫〔矯〕
鞒〔鞽〕
**亲**
榇〔櫬〕
**穷**
䓖〔藭〕
**区**
讴〔謳〕
伛〔傴〕
沤〔漚〕
怄〔慪〕
抠〔摳〕
奁〔奩〕
呕〔嘔〕
岖〔嶇〕
妪〔嫗〕
驱〔驅〕
枢〔樞〕
瓯〔甌〕
欧〔歐〕
殴〔毆〕
鸥〔鷗〕
眍〔瞘〕
躯〔軀〕
**啬**
蔷〔薔〕
墙〔墻〕
嫱〔嬙〕
樯〔檣〕
穑〔穡〕
**杀**
铩〔鎩〕
**审**
谉〔讅〕
婶〔嬸〕
**圣**
柽〔檉〕
蛏〔蟶〕
**师**
浉〔溮〕
狮〔獅〕
蛳〔螄〕
筛〔篩〕
**时**
埘〔塒〕
莳〔蒔〕
鲥〔鰣〕
**寿**
俦〔儔〕
涛〔濤〕
祷〔禱〕
焘〔燾〕
畴〔疇〕
铸〔鑄〕
筹〔籌〕
踌〔躊〕
**属**
嘱〔囑〕
瞩〔矚〕
**双**
扨〔㩳〕
**肃**
萧〔蕭〕
啸〔嘯〕
潇〔瀟〕
箫〔簫〕
蟏〔蠨〕
**岁**
刿〔劌〕
哕〔噦〕
秽〔穢〕
**孙**
荪〔蓀〕
狲〔猻〕
逊〔遜〕
**条**
涤〔滌〕
绦〔縧〕
鲦〔鰷〕
**万**
厉〔厲〕
迈〔邁〕
励〔勵〕
疠〔癘〕
虿〔蠆〕
趸〔躉〕
砺〔礪〕
粝〔糲〕
蛎〔蠣〕
**为**
伪〔僞〕
沩〔溈〕
妫〔媯〕
**韦**
讳〔諱〕
伟〔偉〕
闱〔闈〕
违〔違〕
苇〔葦〕
韧〔韌〕
帏〔幃〕
围〔圍〕
纬〔緯〕
炜〔煒〕
祎〔禕〕
玮〔瑋〕
韨〔韍〕
涠〔潿〕
韩〔韓〕
韫〔韞〕
韪〔韙〕
韬〔韜〕
**乌**
邬〔鄔〕
坞〔塢〕
呜〔嗚〕
钨〔鎢〕
**无**
怃〔憮〕
庑〔廡〕
抚〔撫〕
芜〔蕪〕
呒〔嘸〕
妩〔嫵〕
**献**
谳〔讞〕
**乡**
芗〔薌〕
飨〔饗〕
**写**
泻〔瀉〕
**寻**
浔〔潯〕
荨〔蕁〕
挦〔撏〕
鲟〔鱘〕

**亚**
垩〔堊〕
垭〔埡〕
挜〔掗〕
哑〔啞〕
娅〔婭〕
恶〔惡〕〔噁〕
氩〔氬〕
壶〔壺〕
**严**
俨〔儼〕
酽〔釅〕
**厌**
恹〔懨〕
厣〔厴〕
靥〔靨〕
餍〔饜〕
魇〔魘〕
黡〔黶〕
**尧**
侥〔僥〕
浇〔澆〕
挠〔撓〕
荛〔蕘〕
峣〔嶢〕
哓〔嘵〕
娆〔嬈〕
骁〔驍〕
绕〔繞〕
饶〔饒〕
烧〔燒〕
桡〔橈〕
晓〔曉〕
硗〔磽〕
铙〔鐃〕
翘〔翹〕
蛲〔蟯〕
跷〔蹺〕
**业**
邺〔鄴〕
**页**
顶〔頂〕
顷〔頃〕
项〔項〕
顸〔頇〕
顺〔順〕
须〔須〕
颃〔頏〕
烦〔煩〕
顼〔頊〕
顽〔頑〕
顿〔頓〕
颀〔頎〕
颁〔頒〕
颂〔頌〕
倾〔傾〕
预〔預〕
庼〔廎〕
硕〔碩〕
颅〔顱〕
领〔領〕
颈〔頸〕
颇〔頗〕
颏〔頦〕
颊〔頰〕
颉〔頡〕
颍〔潁〕
颌〔頜〕
颋〔頲〕
滪〔澦〕
颐〔頤〕
蓣〔蕷〕
频〔頻〕
颓〔頹〕
颔〔頷〕
颖〔穎〕
颗〔顆〕
额〔額〕
颜〔顏〕
撷〔擷〕
题〔題〕
颙〔顒〕
颛〔顓〕
缬〔纈〕
濒〔瀕〕
颠〔顛〕
颟〔顢〕
颞〔顳〕
颡〔顙〕
嚣〔囂〕
颢〔顥〕
颤〔顫〕
巅〔巔〕
颥〔顬〕
癫〔癲〕
灏〔灝〕
颦〔顰〕
颧〔顴〕
**义**
议〔議〕
仪〔儀〕
蚁〔蟻〕
**艺**
呓〔囈〕
**阴**
荫〔蔭〕
**隐**
瘾〔癮〕
**犹**
莸〔蕕〕
**鱼**
鱽〔魛〕
渔〔漁〕
鲂〔魴〕
鱿〔魷〕
鲁〔魯〕
鲎〔鱟〕
蓟〔薊〕
鲆〔鮃〕
鲏〔鮍〕
鲅〔鮁〕
鲈〔鱸〕
鲇〔鮎〕
鲊〔鮓〕
䲟〔鮣〕
稣〔穌〕
鲋〔鮒〕
鲍〔鮑〕
鲐〔鮐〕
鲞〔鯗〕
鲝〔鮺〕
鲚〔鱭〕
鲛〔鮫〕
鲜〔鮮〕
鲑〔鮭〕
鲒〔鮚〕
鲔〔鮪〕
鲟〔鱘〕
鲗〔鰂〕
鲖〔鮦〕
鲙〔鱠〕
鲨〔鯊〕
噜〔嚕〕
鲡〔鱺〕
鲠〔鯁〕
鲢〔鰱〕
鲫〔鯽〕
鲥〔鰣〕
鲩〔鯇〕
鲣〔鰹〕
鲤〔鯉〕
鲦〔鰷〕
鲧〔鯀〕
橹〔櫓〕
氇〔氌〕
鲸〔鯨〕
鲭〔鯖〕
鲮〔鯪〕
鲰〔鯫〕
鲲〔鯤〕
鲻〔鯔〕
鲳〔鯧〕
鲱〔鯡〕
鲵〔鯢〕
鲷〔鯛〕
鲶〔鯰〕
藓〔蘚〕
䲡〔鰌〕
䲠〔鰆〕
鲿〔鱨〕
鳊〔鯿〕
鲽〔鰈〕
鳁〔鰮〕
鳃〔鰓〕
鳄〔鰐〕
镥〔鑥〕
鳅〔鰍〕
鳆〔鰒〕
鳇〔鰉〕
鳌〔鰲〕
[illegible]〔[illegible]〕
䲢〔鰧〕
鳒〔鰜〕
鳍〔鰭〕
鳎〔鰨〕
鳏〔鰥〕
鳑〔鰟〕
癣〔癬〕
鳖〔鱉〕
鳙〔鱅〕
鳛〔鰼〕
鳕〔鱈〕
鳔〔鰾〕
鳓〔鰳〕
鳘〔鰵〕
鳗〔鰻〕
鳝〔鱔〕
鳟〔鱒〕
鳞〔鱗〕
鳜〔鱖〕
鳣〔鱣〕
鳢〔鱧〕
**与**
屿〔嶼〕
欤〔歟〕
**云**
芸〔蕓〕
昙〔曇〕
叆〔靉〕
叇〔靆〕
**郑**
掷〔擲〕
踯〔躑〕
**执**
垫〔墊〕
挚〔摯〕
贽〔贄〕
鸷〔鷙〕
蛰〔蟄〕
絷〔縶〕
**质**
锧〔鑕〕
踬〔躓〕
**专**
传〔傳〕
抟〔摶〕
转〔轉〕
䏝〔膞〕
砖〔磚〕
啭〔囀〕
**讠**
计〔計〕
订〔訂〕
讣〔訃〕
讥〔譏〕
议〔議〕
讨〔討〕
讧〔訌〕
讦〔訐〕
记〔記〕
讯〔訊〕
讪〔訕〕
训〔訓〕
讫〔訖〕
访〔訪〕
讶〔訝〕
讳〔諱〕
讵〔詎〕
讴〔謳〕
诀〔訣〕
讷〔訥〕
设〔設〕
讽〔諷〕
讹〔訛〕
䜣〔訢〕
许〔許〕
论〔論〕
讼〔訟〕
讻〔訩〕
诂〔詁〕
诃〔訶〕
评〔評〕
诏〔詔〕
词〔詞〕
译〔譯〕
诎〔詘〕
诇〔詗〕
诅〔詛〕
识〔識〕
诌〔謅〕
诋〔詆〕
诉〔訴〕
诈〔詐〕
诊〔診〕
诒〔詒〕
诨〔諢〕
该〔該〕
详〔詳〕
诧〔詫〕
诓〔誆〕
诖〔詿〕
诘〔詰〕
诙〔詼〕
试〔試〕
诗〔詩〕
诩〔詡〕
诤〔諍〕
诠〔詮〕
诛〔誅〕
诔〔誄〕
诟〔詬〕
诣〔詣〕
话〔話〕
诡〔詭〕
询〔詢〕
诚〔誠〕
诞〔誕〕
浒〔滸〕
诮〔誚〕
说〔說〕
诫〔誡〕
诬〔誣〕
语〔語〕
诵〔誦〕
罚〔罰〕
误〔誤〕
诰〔誥〕
诳〔誑〕
诱〔誘〕
诲〔誨〕
诶〔誒〕
狱〔獄〕
谊〔誼〕
谅〔諒〕
谈〔談〕
谆〔諄〕
谉〔讅〕
谇〔誶〕
请〔請〕
诺〔諾〕
诸〔諸〕
读〔讀〕
诼〔諑〕
诹〔諏〕
课〔課〕
诽〔誹〕
诿〔諉〕
谁〔誰〕
谀〔諛〕
调〔調〕
谄〔諂〕
谂〔諗〕
谛〔諦〕
谙〔諳〕
谜〔謎〕
谚〔諺〕
谝〔諞〕
谘〔諮〕
谌〔諶〕
谎〔謊〕
谋〔謀〕
谍〔諜〕
谐〔諧〕
谏〔諫〕
谞〔諝〕
谑〔謔〕
谒〔謁〕
谔〔諤〕
谓〔謂〕
谖〔諼〕
谕〔諭〕
谥〔謚〕
谤〔謗〕
谦〔謙〕
谧〔謐〕
谟〔謨〕
谠〔讜〕
谡〔謖〕
谢〔謝〕
谣〔謠〕
储〔儲〕
谪〔謫〕
谫〔譾〕
谨〔謹〕
谬〔謬〕
谩〔謾〕
谱〔譜〕
谮〔譖〕
谭〔譚〕
谰〔讕〕
谲〔譎〕
谯〔譙〕
蔼〔藹〕
槠〔櫧〕
谴〔譴〕
谵〔譫〕
谳〔讞〕
辩〔辯〕
䜩〔讌〕
雠〔讎〕
谶〔讖〕
霭〔靄〕
**饣**
饥〔饑〕
饦〔飥〕
饧〔餳〕
饨〔飩〕
饭〔飯〕
饮〔飲〕
饫〔飫〕
饩〔餼〕
饪〔飪〕
饬〔飭〕
饲〔飼〕
饯〔餞〕
饰〔飾〕
饱〔飽〕
饴〔飴〕
饳〔飿〕
饸〔餄〕
饷〔餉〕
饺〔餃〕
饻〔餏〕
饼〔餅〕
饵〔餌〕

饶〔饒〕
蚀〔蝕〕
饹〔餎〕
饽〔餑〕
馁〔餒〕
饿〔餓〕
馆〔館〕
馄〔餛〕
馃〔餜〕
馅〔餡〕
馉〔餶〕
馇〔餷〕
馈〔饋〕
馊〔餿〕
馐〔饈〕
馍〔饃〕
馎〔餺〕
馏〔餾〕
馑〔饉〕
馒〔饅〕
馓〔饊〕
馔〔饌〕
馕〔饢〕

**𠃓**

汤〔湯〕
扬〔揚〕
场〔場〕
旸〔暘〕
饧〔餳〕
炀〔煬〕
杨〔楊〕
肠〔腸〕
疡〔瘍〕
砀〔碭〕
畅〔暢〕
钖〔鍚〕
殇〔殤〕
荡〔蕩〕
烫〔燙〕
觞〔觴〕

**纟**

丝〔絲〕
纠〔糾〕
纩〔纊〕
纡〔紆〕
纣〔紂〕
红〔紅〕
纪〔紀〕
纫〔紉〕
纥〔紇〕
约〔約〕
纨〔紈〕
级〔級〕
纺〔紡〕
纹〔紋〕
纬〔緯〕
纭〔紜〕
纯〔純〕
纰〔紕〕
纽〔紐〕
纳〔納〕
纲〔綱〕
纱〔紗〕
纴〔紝〕
纷〔紛〕
纶〔綸〕
纸〔紙〕
纵〔縱〕
纾〔紓〕
纼〔紖〕
咝〔噝〕
绊〔絆〕
线〔綫〕
绀〔紺〕
绁〔紲〕
绂〔紱〕
绋〔紼〕
绎〔繹〕
经〔經〕
绍〔紹〕
组〔組〕
细〔細〕
䌷〔紬〕
绅〔紳〕
织〔織〕
绌〔絀〕
终〔終〕
绉〔縐〕
绐〔紿〕
哟〔喲〕
绖〔絰〕
荮〔葤〕
荭〔葒〕
绞〔絞〕
统〔統〕
绒〔絨〕
绕〔繞〕
绔〔絝〕
结〔結〕
绗〔絎〕
给〔給〕
绘〔繪〕
绝〔絕〕
绛〔絳〕
络〔絡〕
绚〔絢〕
绑〔綁〕
莼〔蒓〕
绠〔綆〕
绨〔綈〕
绡〔綃〕
绢〔絹〕
绣〔綉〕
绥〔綏〕
绦〔縧〕
鸶〔鷥〕
综〔綜〕
绽〔綻〕
绾〔綰〕
绻〔綣〕
绩〔績〕
绫〔綾〕
绪〔緒〕
续〔續〕
绮〔綺〕
缀〔綴〕
绿〔綠〕
绰〔綽〕
绲〔緄〕
绳〔繩〕
绯〔緋〕
绶〔綬〕
绸〔綢〕
绷〔綳〕
绺〔綹〕
维〔維〕
绵〔綿〕
缁〔緇〕
缔〔締〕
编〔編〕
缕〔縷〕
缃〔緗〕
缂〔緙〕
缅〔緬〕
缘〔緣〕
缉〔緝〕
缇〔緹〕
缈〔緲〕
缗〔緡〕
缊〔緼〕
缌〔緦〕
缆〔纜〕
缓〔緩〕
缄〔緘〕
缑〔緱〕
缒〔縋〕
缎〔緞〕
辔〔轡〕
缞〔縗〕
缤〔繽〕
缟〔縞〕
缣〔縑〕
缢〔縊〕
缚〔縛〕
缙〔縉〕
缛〔縟〕
缜〔縝〕
缝〔縫〕
缡〔縭〕
潍〔濰〕
缩〔縮〕
缥〔縹〕
缪〔繆〕
缦〔縵〕
缨〔纓〕
缫〔繅〕
缧〔縲〕
蕴〔藴〕
缮〔繕〕
缯〔繒〕
缬〔纈〕
缭〔繚〕
橼〔櫞〕
缰〔繮〕
缳〔繯〕
缲〔繰〕
缱〔繾〕
缴〔繳〕
辫〔辮〕
缵〔纘〕

**収**

坚〔堅〕
贤〔賢〕
肾〔腎〕
竖〔竪〕
悭〔慳〕
紧〔緊〕
铿〔鏗〕
鲣〔鰹〕

**龷**

劳〔勞〕
茕〔煢〕
茔〔塋〕
荧〔熒〕
荣〔榮〕
荥〔滎〕
荦〔犖〕
涝〔澇〕
崂〔嶗〕
莹〔瑩〕
捞〔撈〕
唠〔嘮〕
莺〔鶯〕
萤〔螢〕
营〔營〕
萦〔縈〕
痨〔癆〕
嵘〔嶸〕
铹〔鐒〕
耢〔耮〕
蝾〔蠑〕

**𠂉**

览〔覽〕
揽〔攬〕
缆〔纜〕
榄〔欖〕
鉴〔鑒〕

**只**

识〔識〕
帜〔幟〕
织〔織〕
炽〔熾〕
职〔職〕

**钅**

钆〔釓〕
钇〔釔〕
钌〔釕〕
钋〔釙〕
钉〔釘〕
针〔針〕
钊〔釗〕
钗〔釵〕
钎〔釺〕
钓〔釣〕
钏〔釧〕
钍〔釷〕
钐〔釤〕
钒〔釩〕
钖〔鍚〕
钕〔釹〕
钔〔鍆〕
钬〔鈥〕
钫〔鈁〕
钚〔鈈〕
䥺〔釾〕
钪〔鈧〕
钯〔鈀〕
钭〔鈄〕
钙〔鈣〕
钝〔鈍〕
钛〔鈦〕
钘〔鈃〕
钮〔鈕〕
钞〔鈔〕
钢〔鋼〕
钠〔鈉〕
钡〔鋇〕
钤〔鈐〕
钧〔鈞〕
钩〔鈎〕
钦〔欽〕
钨〔鎢〕
铋〔鉍〕
钰〔鈺〕
钱〔錢〕
钲〔鉦〕
钳〔鉗〕
钴〔鈷〕
钺〔鉞〕
钵〔鉢〕
钹〔鈸〕
钼〔鉬〕
钾〔鉀〕
铀〔鈾〕
钿〔鈿〕
铎〔鐸〕
䥽〔鏺〕
铃〔鈴〕
铅〔鉛〕
铂〔鉑〕
铄〔鑠〕
铆〔鉚〕
铍〔鈹〕
钶〔鈳〕
铊〔鉈〕
钽〔鉭〕
铌〔鈮〕
钷〔鉕〕
铈〔鈰〕
铉〔鉉〕
铒〔鉺〕
铑〔銠〕
铕〔銪〕
铟〔銦〕
铷〔銣〕
铯〔銫〕
铥〔銩〕
铪〔鉿〕
铞〔銱〕
铫〔銚〕
铵〔銨〕
衔〔銜〕
铲〔鏟〕
铰〔鉸〕
铳〔銃〕
铱〔銥〕
铓〔鋩〕
铗〔鋏〕
铐〔銬〕
铏〔鉶〕
铙〔鐃〕
银〔銀〕
铛〔鐺〕
铜〔銅〕
铝〔鋁〕
铡〔鍘〕
铠〔鎧〕
铨〔銓〕
铢〔銖〕
铣〔銑〕
铤〔鋌〕
铭〔銘〕
铬〔鉻〕
铮〔錚〕
铧〔鏵〕
铩〔鎩〕
揿〔撳〕
锌〔鋅〕
锐〔鋭〕
锑〔銻〕
锒〔鋃〕
铺〔鋪〕
铸〔鑄〕
嵚〔嶔〕
锓〔鋟〕
锃〔鋥〕
链〔鏈〕
铿〔鏗〕
锏〔鐧〕
销〔銷〕
锁〔鎖〕
锄〔鋤〕
锅〔鍋〕
锉〔銼〕
锈〔銹〕
锋〔鋒〕
锆〔鋯〕
铹〔鐒〕
锔〔鋦〕
锕〔錒〕
锎〔鐦〕
铽〔鋱〕
铼〔錸〕
锇〔鋨〕
锂〔鋰〕
锧〔鑕〕
锘〔鍩〕
锞〔錁〕
锭〔錠〕
锗〔鍺〕
锝〔鍀〕
锫〔錇〕
错〔錯〕
锚〔錨〕
锛〔錛〕
锯〔鋸〕
锰〔錳〕
锢〔錮〕
锟〔錕〕
锡〔錫〕
锣〔鑼〕
锤〔錘〕
锥〔錐〕
锦〔錦〕
锨〔鍁〕
锱〔錙〕
键〔鍵〕
镀〔鍍〕
镃〔鎡〕
镁〔鎂〕
镂〔鏤〕
锲〔鍥〕
锵〔鏘〕
锷〔鍔〕
锶〔鍶〕
锴〔鍇〕
锾〔鍰〕
锹〔鍬〕
锿〔鎄〕
镅〔鎇〕
镄〔鐨〕
锻〔鍛〕
锸〔鍤〕
锼〔鎪〕
镎〔鎿〕

| | | | | | | | | |
|---|---|---|---|---|---|---|---|---|
| 镓[鎵] | 镏[鎦] | 𬭛[鐥] | 镬[鑊] | 搅[攪] | 铎[鐸] | 烃[烴] | 孪[孿] | **呙** |
| 镋[钂] | 镜[鏡] | 镨[鐠] | 镮[鐶] | 喾[嚳] | 萚[蘀] | 轻[輕] | 峦[巒] | 剐[剮] |
| 镔[鑌] | 镝[鏑] | 镧[鑭] | 镯[鐲] | 鲎[鱟] | 释[釋] | 氢[氫] | 娈[孌] | 涡[渦] |
| 镒[鎰] | 镛[鏞] | 镥[鑥] | 镲[鑔] | 黉[黌] | 箨[籜] | 胫[脛] | 恋[戀] | 埚[堝] |
| 𬭤[鍽] | 镞[鏃] | 镤[鏷] | 镳[鑣] | **𠬤** | **𢀖** | 痉[痙] | 栾[欒] | 㖞[喎] |
| 镑[鎊] | 镖[鏢] | 镢[鐝] | 镴[鑞] | 译[譯] | 劲[勁] | 羟[羥] | 挛[攣] | 莴[萵] |
| 镐[鎬] | 镚[鏰] | 镣[鐐] | 镶[鑲] | 泽[澤] | 刭[剄] | 颈[頸] | 鸾[鸞] | 娲[媧] |
| 镉[鎘] | 镗[鏜] | 镫[鐙] | 𫓹[钁] | 怿[懌] | 陉[陘] | 巯[巰] | 湾[灣] | 祸[禍] |
| 镊[鑷] | 𬭬[鐯] | 镪[鏹] | **𭕄** | 择[擇] | 泾[涇] | | 蛮[蠻] | 脶[腡] |
| 镇[鎮] | 镘[鏝] | 镰[鐮] | 峃[嶨] | 峄[嶧] | 茎[莖] | **亦** | 脔[臠] | 窝[窩] |
| 镍[鎳] | 镩[鑹] | 镱[鐿] | 学[學] | 绎[繹] | 径[徑] | 变[變] | 滦[灤] | 锅[鍋] |
| 镌[鎸] | 镦[鐓] | 镭[鐳] | 觉[覺] | 驿[驛] | 经[經] | 弯[彎] | 銮[鑾] | 蜗[蝸] |

**注:**

① 在迭和叠意义可能混淆时,叠仍用叠。

② 答覆、反覆的覆简化作复,覆盖、颠覆仍用覆。

③ 乾坤、乾隆的乾读 qián (前),不简化。

④ 作多解的夥不简化。

⑤ 藉口、凭藉的藉简化作借,慰藉、狼藉等的藉仍用藉。

⑥ 读 me 轻声。读 yāo (夭)的幺应作幺(么本字)。吆应作吆。麽读 mó (摩)时不简化,如幺麽小丑。

⑦ 在象和像意义可能混淆时,像仍用像。

⑧ 在余和馀意义可能混淆时,馀仍用馀。

⑨ 在折和摺意义可能混淆时,摺仍用摺。

⑩ 宫商角徵羽的徵读 zhǐ (止),不简化。

⑪ 四川省酆都县已改丰都县。姓酆的酆不简化为邦。

⑫ 睾丸的睾读 gāo (高),不简化。

⑬ 門字头的字,一般也写作門字头,如鬧、鬮、鬩写作閙、鬮、閲。因此,这些門字头的字可简化作门字头。但鬥争的鬥应简化作斗(见第一表)。

# 汉语拼音方案

# Scheme for the Chinese Phonetic Alphabet

## 一　字母表

| | | | | | | | |
|---|---|---|---|---|---|---|---|
| 字母: | Aa | Bb | Cc | Dd | Ee | Ff | Gg |
| 名称: | ㄚ | ㄅㄝ | ㄘㄝ | ㄉㄝ | ㄜ | ㄝㄈ | ㄍㄝ |
| | Hh | Ii | Jj | Kk | Ll | Mm | Nn |
| | ㄏㄚ | ㄧ | ㄐㄧㄝ | ㄎㄝ | ㄝㄌ | ㄝㄇ | ㄋㄝ |
| | Oo | Pp | Qq | Rr | Ss | Tt | |
| | ㄛ | ㄆㄝ | ㄑㄧㄡ | ㄚㄦ | ㄝㄙ | ㄊㄝ | |
| | Uu | Vv | Ww | Xx | Yy | Zz | |
| | ㄨ | ㄪㄝ | ㄨㄚ | ㄒㄧ | ㄧㄚ | ㄗㄝ | |

v 只用来拼写外来语、少数民族语言和方言。字母的手写体依照拉丁字母的一般书写习惯。

## 二　声母表

| | | | | | | | |
|---|---|---|---|---|---|---|---|
| b | p | m | f | d | t | n | l |
| ㄅ玻 | ㄆ坡 | ㄇ摸 | ㄈ佛 | ㄉ得 | ㄊ特 | ㄋ讷 | ㄌ勒 |
| g | k | h | | j | q | x | |
| ㄍ哥 | ㄎ科 | ㄏ喝 | | ㄐ基 | ㄑ欺 | ㄒ希 | |
| zh | ch | sh | r | z | c | s | |
| ㄓ知 | ㄔ蚩 | ㄕ诗 | ㄖ日 | ㄗ资 | ㄘ雌 | ㄙ思 | |

在给汉字注音的时候，为了使拼式简短，zh ch sh 可以省作 ẑ ĉ ŝ。

## 三　韵母表

| | i ㄧ 衣 | u ㄨ 乌 | ü ㄩ 迂 |
|---|---|---|---|
| a ㄚ 啊 | ia ㄧㄚ 呀 | ua ㄨㄚ 蛙 | |
| o ㄛ 喔 | | uo ㄨㄛ 窝 | |
| e ㄜ 鹅 | ie ㄧㄝ 耶 | | üe ㄩㄝ 约 |
| ai ㄞ 哀 | | uai ㄨㄞ 歪 | |
| ei ㄟ 欸 | | uei ㄨㄟ 威 | |
| ao ㄠ 熬 | iao ㄧㄠ 腰 | | |
| ou ㄡ 欧 | iou ㄧㄡ 忧 | | |
| an ㄢ 安 | ian ㄧㄢ 烟 | uan ㄨㄢ 弯 | üan ㄩㄢ 冤 |
| en ㄣ 恩 | in ㄧㄣ 因 | uen ㄨㄣ 温 | ün ㄩㄣ 晕 |
| ang ㄤ 昂 | iang ㄧㄤ 央 | uang ㄨㄤ 汪 | |
| eng ㄥ 亨的韵母 | ing ㄧㄥ 英 | ueng ㄨㄥ 翁 | |
| ong (ㄨㄥ)轰的韵母 | iong ㄩㄥ 雍 | | |

(1) “知、蚩、诗、日、资、雌、思”等七个音节的韵母用 i，即：知、蚩、诗、日、资、雌、思等字拼作 zhi, chi, shi, ri, zi, ci, si。

(2) 韵母ㄦ写成 er，用做韵尾的时候写成 r。例如：“儿童”拼作 ertong,“花儿”拼作 huar。

(3) 韵母ㄝ单用的时候写成 ê。

(4) i 行的韵母，前面没有声母的时候，写成：yi（衣），ya（呀），ye（耶），yao（腰），you（忧），yan（烟），yin（因），yang（央），ying（英），yong（雍）。

u 行的韵母，前面没有声母的时候，写成：wu（乌），wa（蛙），wo（窝），wai（歪），wei（威），wan（弯），wen（温），wang（汪），weng（翁）。

ü 行的韵母，前面没有声母的时候，写成：yu（迂），yue（约），yuan（冤），yun（晕）；ü 上两点省略。

ü 行的韵母跟声母 j, q, x 拼的时候，写成：ju（居），qu（区），xu（虚），ü 上两点也省略；但是跟声母 n, l 拼的时候，仍然写成：nü（女），lü（吕）。

(5) iou, uei, uen 前面加声母的时候，写成：iu, ui, un。例如 niu（牛），gui（归），lun（论）。

(6) 在给汉字注音的时候，为了使拼式简短，ng 可以省作 ŋ。

## 四　声调符号

| 阴平 | 阳平 | 上声 | 去声 |
|---|---|---|---|
| ˉ | ˊ | ˇ | ˋ |

声调符号标在音节的主要母音上，轻声不标。例如：

| 妈 mā | 麻 má | 马 mǎ | 骂 mà | 吗 ma |
|---|---|---|---|---|
| (阴平) | (阳平) | (上声) | (去声) | (轻声) |

## 五　隔音符号

a, o, e 开头的音节连接在其他音节后面的时候，如果音节的界限发生混淆，用隔音符号(')隔开，例如：pi'ao（皮袄）。

# 汉语拼音和威妥玛式拼法音节对照表

# Chinese Phonetic Alphabet and Wade System

| 汉语拼音 | 威妥玛拼法 | 汉语拼音 | 威妥玛拼法 | 汉语拼音 | 威妥玛拼法 |
|---|---|---|---|---|---|
| a | a | chuang | ch‘uang | fo | fo |
| ai | ai | chui | ch‘ui | fou | fou |
| an | an | chun | ch‘un | fu | fu |
| ang | ang | chuo | ch‘o | ga | ka |
| ao | ao | ci | tz‘ŭ(ts‘ŭ) | gai | kai |
| ba | pa | cong | ts‘ung | gan | kan |
| bai | pai | cou | ts‘ou | gang | kang |
| ban | pan | cu | ts‘u | gao | kao |
| bang | pang | cuan | ts‘uan | ge | kê,ko |
| bao | pao | cui | ts‘ui | gei | kei |
| bei | pei | cun | ts‘un | gen | kên |
| ben | pên | cuo | ts‘o | geng | kêng |
| beng | pêng | da | ta | gong | kung |
| bi | pi | dai | tai | gou | kou |
| bian | pien | dan | tan | gu | ku |
| biao | piao | dang | tang | gua | kua |
| bie | pieh | dao | tao | guai | kuai |
| bin | pin | de | tê | guan | kuan |
| bing | ping | deng | têng | guang | kuang |
| bo | po | di | ti | gui | kui |
| bu | pu | dian | tien | gun | kun |
| ca | ts‘a | diao | tiao | guo | kuo |
| cai | ts‘ai | die | tieh | ha | ha |
| can | ts‘an | ding | ting | hai | hai |
| cang | ts‘ang | diu | tiu | han | han |
| cao | ts‘ao | dong | tung | hang | hang |
| ce | ts‘ê | dou | tou | hao | hao |
| cen | ts‘ên | du | tu | he | hê,ho |
| ceng | ts‘êng | duan | tuan | hei | hei |
| cha | ch‘a | dui | tui | hen | hên |
| chai | ch‘ai | dun | tun | heng | hêng |
| chan | ch‘an | duo | to | hong | hung |
| chang | ch‘ang | e | ê | hou | hou |
| chao | ch‘ao | ê | eh | hu | hu |
| che | ch‘ê | ei | ei | hua | hua |
| chen | ch‘ên | en | ên | huai | huai |
| cheng | ch‘êng | eng | êng | huan | huan |
| chi | ch‘ih | er | êrh | huang | huang |
| chong | ch‘ung | fa | fa | hui | hui |
| chou | ch‘ou | fan | fan | hun | hun |
| chu | ch‘u | fang | fang | huo | huo |
| chua | ch‘ua | fei | fei | ji | chi |
| chuai | ch‘uai | fen | fên | jia | chia |
| chuan | ch‘uan | feng | fêng | jian | chien |

| 汉语拼音 | 威妥玛拼法 | 汉语拼音 | 威妥玛拼法 | 汉语拼音 | 威妥玛拼法 |
|---|---|---|---|---|---|
| jiang | chiang | lun | lun | pei | p‘ei |
| jiao | chiao | luo | luo | pen | p‘ên |
| jie | chieh | ma | ma | peng | p‘êng |
| jin | chin | mai | mai | pi | p‘i |
| jing | ching | man | man | pian | p‘ien |
| jiong | chiung | mang | mang | piao | p‘iao |
| jiu | chiu | mao | mao | pie | p‘ieh |
| ju | chü | me | me | pin | p‘in |
| juan | chüan | mei | mei | ping | p‘ing |
| jue | chüeh, chüo | men | mên | po | p‘o |
| jun | chün | meng | mêng | pou | p‘ou |
| ka | k‘a | mi | mi | pu | p‘u |
| kai | k‘ai | mian | mien | qi | ch‘i |
| kan | k‘an | miao | miao | qia | ch‘ia |
| kang | k‘ang | mie | mieh | qian | ch‘ien |
| kao | k‘ao | min | min | qiang | ch‘iang |
| ke | k‘ê, k‘o | ming | ming | qiao | ch‘iao |
| ken | k‘ên | miu | miu | qie | ch‘ieh |
| keng | k‘êng | mo | mo | qin | ch‘in |
| kong | k‘ung | mou | mou | qing | ch‘ing |
| kou | k‘ou | mu | mu | qiong | ch‘iung |
| ku | k‘u | na | na | qiu | ch‘iu |
| kua | k‘ua | nai | nai | qu | ch‘ü |
| kuai | k‘uai | nan | nan | quan | ch‘üan |
| kuan | k‘uan | nang | nang | que | ch‘üeh |
| kuang | k‘uang | nao | nao | | ch‘üo |
| kui | k‘ui | ne | nê | qun | ch‘ün |
| kun | k‘un | nei | nei | ran | jan |
| kuo | k‘uo | nen | nên | rang | jang |
| la | la | neng | nêng | rao | jao |
| lai | lai | ni | ni | re | jê |
| lan | lan | nian | nien | ren | jên |
| lang | lang | niang | niang | reng | jêng |
| lao | lao | niao | niao | ri | jih |
| le | lê, lo | nie | nieh | rong | jung |
| lei | lei | nin | nin | rou | jou |
| leng | lêng | ning | ning | ru | ju |
| li | li | niu | niu | ruan | juan |
| lia | lia | nong | nung | rui | jui |
| lian | lien | nou | nou | run | jun |
| liang | liang | nu | nu | ruo | jo |
| liao | liao | nü | nü | sa | sa |
| lie | lieh | nuan | nuan | sai | sai |
| lin | lin | nüe | nüeh | san | san |
| ling | ling | | nüo | sang | sang |
| liu | liu | | nio | sao | sao |
| long | lung | nuo | no | se | sê |
| lou | lou | o | o | sen | sên |
| lu | lu | ou | ou | seng | sêng |
| lü | lü | pa | p‘a | sha | sha |
| luan | luan | pai | p‘ai | shai | shai |
| lüe | lüeh | pan | p‘an | shan | shan |
| | lüo | pang | p‘ang | shang | shang |
| | lio | pao | p‘ao | shao | shao |

| 汉语拼音 | 威妥玛拼法 | 汉语拼音 | 威妥玛拼法 | 汉语拼音 | 威妥玛拼法 |
|---|---|---|---|---|---|
| she | shê | tun | t'un | yun | yün |
| shei | shei | tuo | t'o | za | tsa |
| shen | shên | wa | wa | zai | tsai |
| sheng | shêng | wai | wai | zan | tsan |
| shi | shih | wan | wan | zang | tsang |
| shou | shou | wang | wang | zao | tsao |
| shu | shu | wei | wei | ze | tsê |
| shua | shua | wen | wên | zei | tsei |
| shuai | shuai | weng | wêng | zen | tsên |
| shuan | shuan | wo | wo | zeng | tsêng |
| shuang | shuang | wu | wu | zha | cha |
| shui | shui | xi | hsi | zhai | chai |
| shun | shun | xia | hsia | zhan | chan |
| shuo | sho | xian | hsien | zhang | chang |
| si | sŭ, szŭ, ssŭ | xiang | hsiang | zhao | chao |
| song | sung | xiao | hsiao | zhe | chê |
| sou | sou | xie | hsieh | zhei | chei |
| su | su | xin | hsin | zhen | chên |
| suan | suan | xing | hsing | zheng | chêng |
| sui | sui | xiong | hsiung | zhi | chih |
| sun | sun | xiu | hsiu | zhong | chung |
| suo | so | xu | hsü | zhou | chou |
| ta | t'a | xuan | hsüan | zhu | chu |
| tai | t'ai | xue | hsüeh, hsüo | zhua | chua |
| tan | t'an | xun | hsün | zhuai | chuai |
| tang | t'ang | ya | ya | zhuan | chuan |
| tao | t'ao | yan | yen | zhuang | chuang |
| te | t'ê | yang | yang | zhui | chui |
| teng | t'êng | yao | yao | zhun | chun |
| ti | t'i | ye | yeh | zhuo | cho |
| tian | t'ien | yi | yi | zi | tzŭ(tsŭ) |
| tiao | t'iao | yin | yin | zong | tsung |
| tie | t'ieh | ying | ying | zou | tsou |
| ting | t'ing | yo | yo | zu | tsu |
| tong | t'ung | yong | yung | zuan | tsuan |
| tou | t'ou | you | yu | zui | tsui |
| tu | t'u | yu | yü | zun | tsun |
| tuan | t'uan | yuan | yüen | zuo | tso |
| tui | t'ui | yue | yüeh | | |

# 汉语拼音声母韵母和国际音标对照表

# Consonants and Vowels of the Chinese Phonetic Alphabet and their Corresponding International Phonetic Symbols

| 汉语拼音 | 国际音标 | 汉语拼音 | 国际音标 | 汉语拼音 | 国际音标 | 汉语拼音 | 国际音标 |
|---|---|---|---|---|---|---|---|
| b | [p] | s | [s] | ê | [ɛ] | ian | [ian] |
| p | [p‘] | zh | [tʂ] | er | [ər] | in | [in] |
| m | [m] | ch | [tʂ‘] | | | iang | [iaŋ] |
| f | [f] | sh | [ʂ] | ai | [ai] | ing | [iŋ] |
| d | [t] | r | [ʐ] | ei | [ei] | iong | [yŋ] |
| t | [t‘] | | | ao | [au] | ua | [ua] |
| n | [n] | y | [j] | ou | [əu] | uo | [uə] |
| l | [l] | w | [w] | an | [an] | uai | [uai] |
| g | [k] | | | en | [ən] | ui, uei | [uei] |
| k | [k‘] | ɑ | [a] | ang | [aŋ] | uan | [uan] |
| h | [x] | o | [o] | eng | [əŋ] | un, uen | [uən] |
| j | [tɕ] | e | [ə] | ong | [uŋ] | uang | [uaŋ] |
| q | [tɕ‘] | i | [i] | ia | [ia] | üe | [yɛ] |
| x | [ɕ] | u | [u] | ie | [iɛ] | üan | [yan] |
| z | [ts] | ü | [y] | iao | [iau] | ün | [yn] |
| c | [ts‘] | -i | [ɿ] [ʅ]* | iu, iou | [iəu] | | |

* [ɿ] 用于 z c s 后，[ʅ] 用于 zh ch sh r 后。

# 世界各国家、地区、首都(或首府)及货币名称表

# Countries, Regions, Capitals and Currencies

| 简 称 | 全 称 | 首 都(首府) | 货 币 | 地理位置(洲) |
|---|---|---|---|---|
| 阿尔巴尼亚 Albania | 阿尔巴尼亚社会主义人民共和国 the People's Socialist Republic of Albania | 地拉那 Tirana | 列克 Lek | 欧 |
| 阿尔及利亚 Algeria | 阿尔及利亚民主人民共和国 the Democratic People's Republic of Algeria | 阿尔及尔 Algiers | 阿尔及利亚第纳尔 Algerian Dinar | 非 |
| 阿富汗 Afghanistan | 阿富汗民主共和国 the Democratic Republic of Afghanistan | 喀布尔 Kabul | 阿富汗尼 Afghani | 亚 |
| 阿根廷 Argentina | 阿根廷共和国 the Argentine Republic | 布宜诺斯艾利斯 Buenos Aires | 阿根廷比索 Argentine Peso | 拉美 |
| 阿拉伯联合酋长国 the United Arab Emirates | 阿拉伯联合酋长国 the United Arab Emirates | 阿布扎比 Abu Dhabi | 迪拉姆 Dirham | 亚 |
| 阿曼 Oman | 阿曼苏丹国 the Sultanate of Oman | 马斯喀特 Muscat | 阿曼里亚尔 Rial Omani | 亚 |
| 埃及 Egypt | 阿拉伯埃及共和国 the Arab Republic of Egypt | 开罗 Cairo | 埃及镑 Egyptian Pound | 非 |
| 埃塞俄比亚 Ethiopia | 埃塞俄比亚 Ethiopia | 亚的斯亚贝巴 Addis Ababa | 埃塞俄比亚比尔 Ethiopian Birr | 非 |
| 爱尔兰 Ireland | 爱尔兰共和国 the Republic of Ireland | 都柏林 Dublin | 爱尔兰镑 Irish Pound | 欧 |
| 安道尔 Andorra | 安道尔公国 the Principality of Andorra | 安道尔 Andorra la Vella | 西班牙比塞塔和法国法郎 Spanish Peseta and French Franc | 欧 |
| 安的列斯群岛(荷属部分) Netherlands Antilles | 安的列斯群岛(荷属部分) Netherlands Antilles | 威廉斯塔德 Willemstad | 荷属安的列斯盾 Netherlands Antilles Guilder | 拉美 |
| 安哥拉 Angola | 安哥拉 Angola | 罗安达 Luanda | 宽扎 Kwanza | 非 |
| 安提瓜岛(英) Antigua | 安提瓜岛(英) Antigua | 圣约翰 St. John's | 东加勒比元 East Caribbean Dollar | 拉美 |
| 澳大利亚 Australia | 澳大利亚联邦 the Commonwealth of Australia | 堪培拉 Canberra | 澳大利亚元 Australian Dollar | 大洋洲及太平洋岛屿 |
| 奥地利 Austria | 奥地利共和国 the Republic of Austria | 维也纳 Vienna | 奥地利先令 Austrian Schilling | 欧 |
| 巴巴多斯 Barbados | 巴巴多斯 Barbados | 布里奇顿 Bridgetown | 巴巴多斯元 Barbados Dollar | 拉美 |

| 简 称 | 全 称 | 首 都(首府) | 货 币 | 地理位置(洲) |
|---|---|---|---|---|
| 巴布亚新几内亚<br>Papua New Guinea | 巴布亚新几内亚<br>Papua New Guinea | 莫尔兹比港<br>Port Moresby | 基那<br>Kina | 大洋洲及太平洋岛屿 |
| 巴哈马<br>the Bahamas | 巴哈马联邦<br>the Commonwealth of the Bahamas | 拿骚<br>Nassau | 巴哈马元<br>Bahamian Dollar | 拉美 |
| 巴基斯坦<br>Pakistan | 巴基斯坦伊斯兰共和国<br>the Islamic Republic of Pakistan | 伊斯兰堡<br>Islamabad | 巴基斯坦卢比<br>Pakistan Rupee | 亚 |
| 巴拉圭<br>Paraguay | 巴拉圭共和国<br>the Republic of Paraguay | 亚松森<br>Asunción | 巴拉圭瓜拉尼<br>Paraguayan Guarani | 拉美 |
| 巴勒斯坦<br>Palestine<br>附:(以色列)<br>(Israel) | 巴勒斯坦<br>Palestine | | | 亚 |
| 巴林<br>Bahrain | 巴林国<br>the State of Bahrain | 麦纳麦<br>Manama | 巴林第纳尔<br>Bahrain Dinar | 亚 |
| 巴拿马<br>Panama | 巴拿马共和国<br>the Republic of Panama | 巴拿马城<br>Panama City | 巴拿马巴波亚<br>Panamanian Balboa | 拉美 |
| 巴西<br>Brazil | 巴西联邦共和国<br>the Federative Republic of Brazil | 巴西利亚<br>Brasilia | 巴西克鲁赛罗<br>Brazilian Cruzeiro | 拉美 |
| 百慕大群岛(英)<br>Bermuda | 百慕大群岛(英)<br>Bermuda | 汉密尔顿<br>Hamilton | 百慕大元<br>Bermuda Dollar | 北美 |
| 保加利亚<br>Bulgaria | 保加利亚人民共和国<br>the People's Republic of Bulgaria | 索非亚<br>Sofia | 列弗<br>Lev | 欧 |
| 贝宁<br>Benin | 贝宁人民共和国<br>the People's Republic of Benin | 波多诺伏<br>Porto Novo | 非洲金融共同体法郎<br>CFAF (Franc de la Communauté Financière Africaine) | 非 |
| 比利时<br>Belgium | 比利时王国<br>the Kingdom of Belgium | 布鲁塞尔<br>Brussels | 比利时法郎<br>Belgian Franc | 欧 |
| 秘鲁<br>Peru | 秘鲁共和国<br>the Republic of Peru | 利马<br>Lima | 索尔<br>Sol | 拉美 |
| 冰岛<br>Iceland | 冰岛共和国<br>the Republic of Iceland | 雷克雅未克<br>Reykjavik | 冰岛克朗<br>Icelandic Krona | 欧 |
| 波多黎各岛(美)<br>Puerto Rico | 波多黎各岛(美)<br>Puerto Rico | 圣胡安<br>San Juan | 美元<br>United States Dollar | 拉美 |
| 波兰<br>Poland | 波兰人民共和国<br>the Polish People's Republic | 华沙<br>Warsaw | 兹罗提<br>Zloty | 欧 |
| 玻利维亚<br>Bolivia | 玻利维亚共和国<br>the Republic of Bolivia | 拉巴斯(政府所在地)<br>La Paz<br>苏克雷(法定首都)<br>Sucre | 玻利维亚比索<br>Bolivian Peso | 拉美 |
| 博茨瓦纳<br>Botswana | 博茨瓦纳共和国<br>the Republic of Botswana | 哈博罗内<br>Gaborone | 普拉<br>Pula | 非 |
| 伯利兹(英)<br>Belize | 伯利兹(英)<br>Belize | 贝尔莫潘<br>Belmopan | 伯利兹元<br>Belizean Dollar | 拉美 |

| 简 称 | 全 称 | 首 都(首府) | 货 币 | 地理位置(洲) |
|---|---|---|---|---|
| 不丹 Bhutan | 不丹王国 the Kingdom of Bhutan | 廷布 Thimphu | 努尔特鲁姆 Ngultrum | 亚 |
| 布隆迪 Burundi | 布隆迪共和国 the Republic of Burundi | 布琼布拉 Bujumbura | 布隆迪法郎 Burundi Franc | 非 |
| 朝鲜 Korea | 朝鲜民主主义人民共和国 the Democratic People's Republic of Korea | 平壤 Pyongyang | 圆 Won | 亚 |
| 赤道几内亚 Equatorial Guinea | 赤道几内亚共和国 the Republic of Equatorial Guinea | 马拉博 Malabo | 赤道几内亚埃奎勒 Equatorial Guinea Ekuele | 非 |
| 丹麦 Denmark | 丹麦王国 the Kingdom of Denmark | 哥本哈根 Copenhagen | 丹麦克朗 Danish Krone | 欧 |
| 德意志联邦共和国 the Federal Republic of Germany | 德意志联邦共和国 the Federal Republic of Germany | 波恩 Bonn | 德意志马克 Deutsche Mark | 欧 |
| 德意志民主共和国 the German Democratic Republic | 德意志民主共和国 the German Democratic Republic | 柏林 Berlin | 德意志民主共和国马克 Mark der Deutschen Demokratischen Republik | 欧 |
| 东帝汶 East Timor | 东帝汶民主共和国 the Democratic Republic of East Timor | 帝力 Dilly | | 亚 |
| 东萨摩亚(美) Eastern Samoa | 东萨摩亚(美) Eastern Samoa | 帕果-帕果 Pago Pago | 美元 United States Dollar | 大洋洲及太平洋岛屿 |
| 多哥 Togo | 多哥共和国 the Republic of Togo | 洛美 Lomé | 非洲金融共同体法郎 CFAF (Franc de la Communauté Financière Africaine) | 非 |
| 多米尼加岛(英) Dominica | 多米尼加岛(英) Dominica | 罗索 Roseau | 东加勒比元 East Caribbean Dollar | 拉美 |
| 多米尼加共和国 the Dominican Republic | 多米尼加共和国 the Dominican Republic | 圣多明各 Santo Domingo | 多米尼加比索 Dominican Peso | 拉美 |
| 厄瓜多尔 Ecuador | 厄瓜多尔共和国 the Republic of Ecuador | 基多 Quito | 苏克雷 Sucre | 拉美 |
| 法国 France | 法兰西共和国 the French Republic | 巴黎 Paris | 法国法郎 French Franc | 欧 |
| 法属波利尼西亚 French Polynesia | 法属波利尼西亚 French Polynesia | 帕皮提 Papeete | 太平洋结算法郎 CFPF | 大洋洲及太平洋岛屿 |
| 菲律宾 the Philippines | 菲律宾共和国 the Republic of the Philippines | 马尼拉 Manila | 菲律宾比索 Philippine Peso | 亚 |
| 斐济 Fiji | 斐济 Fiji | 苏瓦 Suva | 斐济元 Fiji Dollar | 大洋洲及太平洋岛屿 |
| 芬兰 Finland | 芬兰共和国 the Republic of Finland | 赫尔辛基 Helsinki | 芬兰马克 Finnish Markka | 欧 |
| 佛得角 Cape Verde | 佛得角共和国 the Republic of Cape Verde | 普腊亚 Praia | 佛得角埃斯库多 Cape Verde Escudo | 非 |

| 简　　称 | 全　　称 | 首　都(首府) | 货　　币 | 地理位置(洲) |
|---|---|---|---|---|
| 冈比亚<br>the Gambia | 冈比亚共和国<br>the Republic of the Gambia | 班珠尔<br>Banjul | 达拉西<br>Dalasi | 非 |
| 刚果<br>the Congo | 刚果人民共和国<br>the People's Republic of the Congo | 布拉柴维尔<br>Brazzaville | 非洲金融共同体法郎<br>CFAF (Franc de la Communauté Financière Africaine) | 非 |
| 哥伦比亚<br>Colombia | 哥伦比亚共和国<br>the Republic of Colombia | 波哥大<br>Bogotá | 哥伦比亚比索<br>Colombia Peso | 拉美 |
| 哥斯达黎加<br>Costa Rica | 哥斯达黎加共和国<br>the Republic of Costa Rica | 圣约瑟<br>San José | 哥斯达黎加科郎<br>Costa Rican Colon | 拉美 |
| 格林纳达<br>Grenada | 格林纳达<br>Grenada | 圣乔治<br>St. George's | 东加勒比元<br>East Caribbean Dollar | 拉美 |
| 古巴<br>Cuba | 古巴共和国<br>the Republic of Cuba | 哈瓦那<br>Havana | 古巴比索<br>Cuban Peso | 拉美 |
| 瓜德罗普岛(法)<br>Guadeloupe | 瓜德罗普岛(法)<br>Guadeloupe | 巴斯特尔<br>Basse Terre | 法国法郎<br>French Franc | 拉美 |
| 关岛(美)<br>Guam | 关岛(美)<br>Guam | 阿加尼亚<br>Agaña | 美元<br>United States Dollar | 大洋洲及太平洋岛屿 |
| 圭亚那<br>Guyana | 圭亚那合作共和国<br>the Co-operative Republic of Guyana | 乔治敦<br>Georgetown | 圭亚那元<br>Guyana Dollar | 拉美 |
| 圭亚那(法)<br>French Guiana | 圭亚那(法)<br>French Guiana | 卡宴<br>Cayenne | 法国法郎<br>French Franc | 拉美 |
| 海地<br>Haiti | 海地共和国<br>the Republic of Haiti | 太子港<br>Port-au-Prince | 古德<br>Gourde | 拉美 |
| 荷兰<br>the Netherlands | 荷兰王国<br>the Kingdom of the Netherlands | 阿姆斯特丹<br>Amsterdam<br>海牙　(政府所在地) The Hague (the seat of government) | 荷兰盾<br>Guilder (或 Florin) | 欧 |
| 洪都拉斯<br>Honduras | 洪都拉斯共和国<br>the Republic of Honduras | 特古西加尔巴<br>Tegucigalpa | 伦皮拉<br>Lempira | 拉美 |
| 吉布提<br>Djibouti | 吉布提共和国<br>the Republic of Djibouti | 吉布提<br>Djibouti | 吉布提法郎<br>Djibouti Franc | 非 |
| 吉尔伯特群岛(内部自治)<br>Gilbert Islands | 吉尔伯特群岛(内部自治)<br>Gilbert Islands | 塔拉瓦<br>Tarawa | 澳大利亚元<br>Australian Dollar | 大洋洲及太平洋岛屿 |
| 几内亚<br>Guinea | 几内亚共和国<br>the Republic of Guinea | 科纳克里<br>Conakry | 西里<br>Syli | 非 |
| 几内亚比绍<br>Guinea-Bissau | 几内亚比绍共和国<br>the Republic of Guinea-Bissau | 比绍<br>Bissau | 几内亚比索<br>Guinea Peso | 非 |
| 加拿大<br>Canada | 加拿大<br>Canada | 渥太华<br>Ottawa | 加拿大元<br>Canadian Dollar | 北美 |
| 加那利群岛(西)<br>Canary Islands | 加那利群岛(西)<br>Canary Islands | 拉斯帕耳马斯<br>Las Palmas | 西班牙比塞塔<br>Spanish Peseta | 非 |
| 加纳<br>Ghana | 加纳共和国<br>the Republic of Ghana | 阿克拉<br>Accra | 塞地<br>Cedi | 非 |

| 简 称 | 全 称 | 首 都(首府) | 货 币 | 地理位置(洲) |
|---|---|---|---|---|
| 加蓬<br>Gabon | 加蓬共和国<br>the Republic of Gabon | 利伯维尔<br>Libreville | 非洲金融共同体法郎<br>CFAF (Franc de la Communauté Financière Africaine) | 非 |
| 柬埔寨<br>Kampuchea | 民主柬埔寨<br>Democratic Kampuchea | 金边<br>Phnom Penh | 瑞尔<br>Riel | 亚 |
| 捷克斯洛伐克<br>Czechoslovakia | 捷克斯洛伐克社会主义共和国<br>the Czechoslovak Socialist Republic | 布拉格<br>Prague | 克朗<br>Koruna | 欧 |
| 津巴布韦(在白人种族主义者统治下)<br>Zimbabwe<br>(罗得西亚)<br>(Rhodesia) | 津巴布韦<br>Zimbabwe<br>(罗得西亚)<br>(Rhodesia) | 索尔兹伯里<br>Salisbury | 罗得西亚元<br>Rhodesian Dollar | 非 |
| 喀麦隆<br>Cameroon | 喀麦隆联合共和国<br>the United Republic of Cameroon | 雅温得<br>Yaoundé | 非洲金融共同体法郎<br>CFAF (Franc de la Communauté Financière Africaine) | 非 |
| 卡奔达<br>Cabinda | 卡奔达<br>Cabinda | 卡奔达<br>Cabinda | | 非 |
| 卡塔尔<br>Qatar | 卡塔尔国<br>the State of Qatar | 多哈<br>Doha | 卡塔尔里亚尔<br>Qatar Riyal | 亚 |
| 开曼群岛(英)<br>Cayman Islands | 开曼群岛(英)<br>Cayman Islands | 乔治敦<br>Georgetown | 开曼群岛元<br>Cayman Islands Dollar | 拉美 |
| 科摩罗<br>the Comoros | 科摩罗共和国<br>the Republic of the Comoros | 莫罗尼<br>Moroni | 非洲金融共同体法郎<br>CFAF (Franc de la Communauté Financière Africaine) | 非 |
| 科威特<br>Kuwait | 科威特国<br>the State of Kuwait | 科威特<br>Kuwait City | 科威特第纳尔<br>Kuwaiti Dinar | 亚 |
| 肯尼亚<br>Kenya | 肯尼亚共和国<br>the Republic of Kenya | 内罗毕<br>Nairobi | 肯尼亚先令<br>Kenya Shilling | 非 |
| 库克群岛(新)<br>the Cook Islands | 库克群岛(新)<br>the Cook Islands | 阿瓦鲁阿<br>Avarua | 新西兰元<br>New Zealand Dollar | 大洋洲及太平洋岛屿 |
| 莱索托<br>Lesotho | 莱索托王国<br>the Kingdom of Lesotho | 马塞卢<br>Maseru | 南非兰特<br>the South African Rand | 非 |
| 老挝<br>Laos | 老挝人民民主共和国<br>the People's Democratic Republic of Laos | 万象<br>Vientiane | 基普<br>Kip | 亚 |
| 黎巴嫩<br>Lebanon | 黎巴嫩共和国<br>the Lebanese Republic | 贝鲁特<br>Beirut | 黎巴嫩镑<br>Lebanese Pound | 亚 |
| 利比里亚<br>Liberia | 利比里亚共和国<br>the Republic of Liberia | 蒙罗维亚<br>Monrovia | 利比里亚元<br>Liberian Dollar | 非 |
| 利比亚<br>Libya | 阿拉伯利比亚人民社会主义民众国<br>the Socialist People's Libyan Arab Jamahiriya | 的黎波里<br>Tripoli | 利比亚第纳尔<br>Libyan Dinar | 非 |
| 列支敦士登<br>Liechtenstein | 列支敦士登公国<br>the Principality of Liechtenstein | 瓦杜兹<br>Vaduz | 瑞士法郎<br>Swiss Franc | 欧 |

| 简　　　称 | 全　　　称 | 首　都(首府) | 货　　　币 | 地理位置(洲) |
|---|---|---|---|---|
| 留尼汪岛(法)<br>Réunion | 留尼汪岛(法)<br>Réunion | 圣但尼<br>Saint-Denis | 法国法郎<br>French Franc | 非 |
| 卢森堡<br>Luxembourg | 卢森堡大公国<br>the Grand Duchy of Luxembourg | 卢森堡<br>Luxembourg | 卢森堡法郎<br>Luxembourg Franc | 欧 |
| 卢旺达<br>Rwanda | 卢旺达共和国<br>the Republic of Rwanda | 基加利<br>Kigali | 卢旺达法郎<br>Rwanda Franc | 非 |
| 罗马尼亚<br>Romania | 罗马尼亚社会主义共和国<br>the Socialist Republic of Romania | 布加勒斯特<br>Bucharest | 列伊<br>Leu | 欧 |
| 马达加斯加<br>Madagascar | 马达加斯加民主共和国<br>the Democratic Republic of Madagascar | 塔那那利佛<br>Tananarive | 马达加斯加法郎<br>Malagasy Franc | 非 |
| 马尔代夫<br>Maldives | 马尔代夫共和国<br>the Republic of Maldives | 马累<br>Male | 马尔代夫卢比<br>Maldivian Rupee | 亚 |
| 马耳他<br>Malta | 马耳他共和国<br>the Republic of Malta | 瓦莱塔<br>Valletta | 马耳他镑<br>Malta Pound | 欧 |
| 马尔维纳斯群岛（阿、英争议）<br>Islas Malvinas<br>（福克兰群岛）<br>(the Falkland Islands) | 马尔维纳斯群岛<br>Islas Malvinas<br>（福克兰群岛）<br>(the Falkland Islands) | 斯坦利港<br>Stanley | 福克兰镑<br>Falkland Islands Pound | 拉美 |
| 马拉维<br>Malawi | 马拉维共和国<br>the Republic of Malawi | 利隆圭<br>Lilongwe | 马拉维克瓦查<br>Malawi Kwacha | 非 |
| 马来西亚<br>Malaysia | 马来西亚<br>Malaysia | 吉隆坡<br>Kuala Lumpur | 林吉特<br>Ringgit | 亚 |
| 马里<br>Mali | 马里共和国<br>the Republic of Mali | 巴马科<br>Bamako | 马里法郎<br>Mali Franc | 非 |
| 马里亚纳群岛、加罗林群岛、马绍尔群岛(美托管)<br>Mariana Is., Caroline Is., and Marshall Is. | 马里亚纳群岛、加罗林群岛、马绍尔群岛(美托管)<br>Mariana Is., Caroline Is., and Marshall Is. | 塞班<br>Saipan | 美元<br>United States Dollar | 大洋洲及太平洋岛屿 |
| 马提尼克岛(法)<br>Martinique | 马提尼克岛(法)<br>Martinique | 法兰西堡<br>Fort-de-France | 法国法郎<br>French Franc | 拉美 |
| 毛里求斯<br>Mauritius | 毛里求斯<br>Mauritius | 路易港<br>Port Louis | 毛里求斯卢比<br>Mauritius Rupee | 非 |
| 毛里塔尼亚<br>Mauritania | 毛里塔尼亚伊斯兰共和国<br>the Islamic Republic of Mauritania | 努瓦克肖特<br>Nouakchott | 乌吉亚<br>Ouguiya | 非 |
| 美国<br>the United States | 美利坚合众国<br>the United States of America | 华盛顿<br>Washington | 美元<br>United States Dollar | 北美 |
| 美属维尔京群岛<br>Virgin Islands of the United States | 美属维尔京群岛<br>Virgin Islands of the United States | 夏洛特阿马利亚<br>Charlotte Amalie | 美元<br>United States Dollar | 拉美 |
| 蒙古<br>Mongolia | 蒙古人民共和国<br>the People's Republic of Mongolia | 乌兰巴托<br>Ulan Bator | 图格里克<br>Tugrik | 亚 |

| 简 称 | 全 称 | 首 都(首府) | 货 币 | 地理位置(洲) |
|---|---|---|---|---|
| 蒙特塞拉特岛(英) Montserrat | 蒙特塞拉特岛(英) Montserrat | 普利茅斯 Plymouth | 东加勒比元 East Caribbean Dollar | 拉美 |
| 孟加拉国 Bangladesh | 孟加拉人民共和国 the People's Republic of Bangladesh | 达卡 Dacca | 塔卡 Taka | 亚 |
| 缅甸 Burma | 缅甸联邦社会主义共和国 the Socialist Republic of the Union of Burma | 仰光 Rangoon | 缅元 Kyat | 亚 |
| 民主也门 Democratic Yemen | 也门民主人民共和国 the People's Democratic Republic of Yemen | 亚丁 Aden | 也门第纳尔 Yemeni Dinar | 亚 |
| 摩洛哥 Morocco | 摩洛哥王国 the Kingdom of Morocco | 拉巴特 Rabat | 摩洛哥迪拉姆 Moroccan Dirham | 非 |
| 摩纳哥 Monaco | 摩纳哥公国 the Principality of Monaco | 摩纳哥 Monaco-Ville | 法国法郎 French Franc | 欧 |
| 莫桑比克 Mozambique | 莫桑比克人民共和国 the People's Republic of Mozambique | 马普托 Maputo | 莫桑比克埃斯库多 Mozambique Escudo | 非 |
| 墨西哥 Mexico | 墨西哥合众国 the United States of Mexico | 墨西哥城 Mexico City | 墨西哥比索 Mexican Peso | 拉美 |
| 纳米比亚(前南非委任统治地,现为南非非法吞并) Namibia (西南非洲) (South-West Africa) | 纳米比亚 Namibia (西南非洲) (South-West Africa) | 温得和克 Windhoek | 南非兰特 the South African Rand | 非 |
| 南非(在白人种族主义者统治下) South Africa (阿扎尼亚) (Azania) | 南非 South Africa (阿扎尼亚) (Azania) | 比勒陀利亚 Pretoria | 南非兰特 the South African Rand | 非 |
| 南斯拉夫 Yugoslavia | 南斯拉夫社会主义联邦共和国 the Socialist Federal Republic of Yugoslavia | 贝尔格莱德 Belgrade | 南斯拉夫第纳尔 Yugoslav Dinar | 欧 |
| 瑙鲁 Nauru | 瑙鲁共和国 the Republic of Nauru | 瑙鲁 Nauru | 澳大利亚元 Australian Dollar | 大洋洲及太平洋岛屿 |
| 尼泊尔 Nepal | 尼泊尔王国 the Kingdom of Nepal | 加德满都 Kathmandu | 尼泊尔卢比 Nepalese Rupee | 亚 |
| 尼加拉瓜 Nicaragua | 尼加拉瓜共和国 the Republic of Nicaragua | 马那瓜 Managua | 科多巴 Córdoba | 拉美 |
| 尼日尔 the Niger | 尼日尔共和国 the Republic of the Niger | 尼亚美 Niamey | 非洲金融共同体法郎 CFAF (Franc de la Communauté Financière Africaine) | 非 |
| 尼日利亚 Nigeria | 尼日利亚联邦共和国 the Federal Republic of Nigeria | 拉各斯 Lagos | 奈拉 Naira | 非 |
| 纽埃岛(新) Niue Island | 纽埃岛(新) Niue Island | 阿洛菲 Alofi | 新西兰元 New Zealand Dollar | 大洋洲及太平洋岛屿 |

| 简　称 | 全　称 | 首　都(首府) | 货　币 | 地理位置(洲) |
|---|---|---|---|---|
| 挪威 Norway | 挪威王国 the Kingdom of Norway | 奥斯陆 Oslo | 挪威克朗 Norwegian Krone | 欧 |
| 诺福克岛(澳) Norfolk Island | 诺福克岛(澳) Norfolk Island | 金斯敦 Kingston | 澳大利亚元 Australian Dollar | 大洋洲及太平洋岛屿 |
| 皮特克恩岛(英) Pitcairn Island | 皮特克恩岛(英) Pitcairn Island | 亚当斯敦 Adamstown | 澳大利亚元 Australian Dollar | 大洋洲及太平洋岛屿 |
| 葡萄牙 Portugal | 葡萄牙共和国 the Portuguese Republic | 里斯本 Lisbon | 葡萄牙埃斯库多 Portuguese Escudo | 欧 |
| 日本 Japan | 日本国 Japan | 东京 Tokyo | 日元 Japanese Yen | 亚 |
| 瑞典 Sweden | 瑞典王国 the Kingdom of Sweden | 斯德哥尔摩 Stockholm | 瑞典克朗 Swedish Krona | 欧 |
| 瑞士 Switzerland | 瑞士联邦 the Swiss Confederation | 伯尔尼 Berne | 瑞士法郎 Swiss Franc | 欧 |
| 萨尔瓦多 El Salvador | 萨尔瓦多共和国 the Republic of El Salvador | 圣萨尔瓦多 San Salvador | 萨尔瓦多科郎 Salvadoran Colon、 | 拉美 |
| 塞拉利昂 Sierra Leone | 塞拉利昂共和国 the Republic of Sierra Leone | 弗里敦 Freetown | 利昂 Leone | 非 |
| 塞内加尔 Senegal | 塞内加尔共和国 the Republic of Senegal | 达喀尔 Dakar | 非洲金融共同体法郎 CFAF (Franc de la Communauté Financière Africaine) | 非 |
| 塞浦路斯 Cyprus | 塞浦路斯共和国 the Republic of Cyprus | 尼科西亚 Nicosia | 塞浦路斯镑 Cyprus Pound | 亚 |
| 塞舌尔 Seychelles | 塞舌尔共和国 the Republic of Seychelles | 维多利亚 Victoria | 塞舌尔卢比 Seychelles Rupee | 非 |
| 沙特阿拉伯 Saudi Arabia | 沙特阿拉伯王国 the Kingdom of Saudi Arabia | 利雅得 Riyadh | 沙特里亚尔 Saudi Riyal | 亚 |
| 上沃尔特 the Upper Volta | 上沃尔特共和国 the Republic of the Upper Volta | 瓦加杜古 Ouagadougou | 非洲金融共同体法郎 CFAF (Franc de la Communauté Financière Africaine) | 非 |
| 圣多美和普林西比 São Tomé and Príncipe | 圣多美和普林西比民主共和国 the Democratic Republic of São Tomé and Príncipe | 圣多美 São Tomé | 多布拉 Dobra | 非 |
| 圣赫勒拿岛和阿森松岛等(英) St. Helena, Ascension Island, etc. | 圣赫勒拿岛和阿森松岛等(英) St. Helena, Ascension Island, etc. | 詹姆斯敦 Jamestown | 英镑 Pound Sterling | 非 |
| 圣基茨—尼维斯—安圭拉(英) St. Kitts-Nevis-Anguilla | 圣基茨—尼维斯—安圭拉(英) St. Kitts-Nevis-Anguilla | 巴斯特尔 Basseterre | 东加勒比元 East Caribbean Dollar | 拉美 |
| 圣卢西亚岛(英) St. Lucia | 圣卢西亚岛(英) St. Lucia | 卡斯特里 Castries | 东加勒比元 East Caribbean Dollar | 拉美 |
| 圣马力诺 San Marino | 圣马力诺共和国 the Republic of San Marino | 圣马力诺 San Marino | 意大利里拉 Italian Lira | 欧 |

| 简 称 | 全 称 | 首 都(首府) | 货 币 | 地理位置(洲) |
|---|---|---|---|---|
| 圣皮埃尔岛和密克隆岛(法) St. Pierre and Miquelon Islands | 圣皮埃尔岛和密克隆岛(法) St. Pierre and Miquelon Islands | 圣皮埃尔 St. Pierre | 法国法郎 French Franc | 北美 |
| 圣文森特岛(英) St. Vincent | 圣文森特岛(英) St. Vincent | 金斯敦 Kingstown | 东加勒比元 East Caribbean Dollar | 拉美 |
| 斯里兰卡 Sri Lanka | 斯里兰卡共和国 the Republic of Sri Lanka | 科伦坡 Colombo | 斯里兰卡卢比 Sri Lanka Rupee | 亚 |
| 斯威士兰 Swaziland | 斯威士兰王国 the Kingdom of Swaziland | 姆巴巴纳 Mbabane | 里兰吉尼 Lilangeni(复数: 埃马兰吉尼 Emalangeni) | 非 |
| 苏丹 the Sudan | 苏丹民主共和国 the Democratic Republic of the Sudan | 喀土穆 Khartoum | 苏丹镑 Sudanese Pound | 非 |
| 苏里南 Surinam | 苏里南共和国 the Republic of Surinam | 帕拉马里博 Paramaribo | 苏里南盾 Surinam Guilder | 拉美 |
| 苏联 the Soviet Union | 苏维埃社会主义共和国联盟 the Union of Soviet Socialist Republics | 莫斯科 Moscow | 卢布 Rouble | 欧 |
| 所罗门群岛 Solomon Islands | 所罗门群岛 Solomon Islands | 霍尼亚拉 Honiara | 澳大利亚元 Australian Dollar | 大洋洲及太平洋岛屿 |
| 索马里 Somalia | 索马里民主共和国 the Somali Democratic Republic | 摩加迪沙 Mogadishu | 索马里先令 Somali Shilling | 非 |
| 泰国 Thailand | 泰王国 the Kingdom of Thailand | 曼谷 Bangkok | 泰铢 Thai Baht | 亚 |
| 坦桑尼亚 Tanzania | 坦桑尼亚联合共和国 the United Republic of Tanzania | 达累斯萨拉姆 Dar es Salaam | 坦桑尼亚先令 Tanzania Shilling | 非 |
| 汤加 Tonga | 汤加王国 the Kingdom of Tonga | 努库阿洛法 Nukualofa | 潘加 Pa'anga | 大洋洲及太平洋岛屿 |
| 特克斯群岛和凯科斯群岛(英) Turks and Caicos Islands | 特克斯群岛和凯科斯群岛(英) Turks and Caicos Islands | 大特克 Grand Turk | 美元 United States Dollar | 拉美 |
| 特立尼达和多巴哥 Trinidad and Tobago | 特立尼达和多巴哥共和国 the Republic of Trinidad and Tobago | 西班牙港 Port of Spain | 特立尼达和多巴哥元 Trinidad and Tobago Dollar | 拉美 |
| 突尼斯 Tunisia | 突尼斯共和国 the Republic of Tunisia | 突尼斯 Tunis | 突尼斯第纳尔 Tunisian Dinar | 非 |
| 图瓦卢(英) Tuvalu | 图瓦卢(英) Tuvalu | 富纳富提 Funafuti | 澳大利亚元 Australian Dollar | 大洋洲及太平洋岛屿 |
| 土耳其 Turkey | 土耳其共和国 the Republic of Turkey | 安卡拉 Ankara | 土耳其里拉 Turkish Lira | 亚 |
| 托克劳群岛(新) Tokelau Islands | 托克劳群岛(新) Tokelau Islands | 法考福 Fakaofo | 新西兰元 New Zealand Dollar | 大洋洲及太平洋岛屿 |
| 瓦利斯群岛和富图纳群岛(法) Wallis and Futuna | 瓦利斯群岛和富图纳群岛(法) Wallis and Futuna | 马塔乌图 Mata Utu | 太平洋结算法郎 CFPF | 大洋洲及太平洋岛屿 |

| 简　　称 | 全　　称 | 首　都(首府) | 货　　币 | 地理位置(洲) |
|---|---|---|---|---|
| 危地马拉<br>Guatemala | 危地马拉共和国<br>the Republic of Guatemala | 危地马拉<br>Guatemala City | 格查尔<br>Quetzal | 拉美 |
| 委内瑞拉<br>Venezuela | 委内瑞拉共和国<br>the Republic of Venezuela | 加拉加斯<br>Caracas | 博利瓦<br>Bolivar | 拉美 |
| 文莱(英)<br>Brunei | 文莱苏丹国(英)<br>the Sultanate of Brunei | 斯里巴加湾市<br>Bandar Seri Begawan | 文莱元<br>Brunei Dollar | 亚 |
| 乌干达<br>Uganda | 乌干达共和国<br>the Republic of Uganda | 坎帕拉<br>Kampala | 乌干达先令<br>Uganda Shilling | 非 |
| 乌拉圭<br>Uruguay | 乌拉圭东岸共和国<br>the Oriental Republic of Uruguay | 蒙得维的亚<br>Montevideo | 乌拉圭新比索<br>Uruguayan New Peso | 拉美 |
| 西班牙<br>Spain | 西班牙国<br>the Spanish State | 马德里<br>Madrid | 西班牙比塞塔<br>Spanish Peseta | 欧 |
| 西撒哈拉<br>Western Sahara | 西撒哈拉<br>Western Sahara | | | 非 |
| 西萨摩亚<br>Western Samoa | 西萨摩亚独立国<br>the Independent State of Western Samoa | 阿皮亚<br>Apia | 西萨摩亚塔拉<br>Western Samoa Tala | 大洋洲及太平洋岛屿 |
| 希腊<br>Greece | 希腊共和国<br>the Hellenic Republic | 雅典<br>Athens | 德拉克马<br>Drachma | 欧 |
| 锡金<br>Sikkim | 锡金<br>Sikkim | 甘托克<br>Gangtok | 印度卢比<br>Indian Rupee | 亚 |
| 象牙海岸<br>the Ivory Coast | 象牙海岸共和国<br>the Republic of the Ivory Coast | 阿比让<br>Abidjan | 非洲金融共同体法郎<br>CFAF (Franc de la Communauté Financière Africaine) | 非 |
| 新赫布里底(英、法)<br>New Hebrides | 新赫布里底(英、法)<br>New Hebrides | 维拉港<br>Vila | 澳大利亚元及法国法郎<br>Australian Dollar and French Franc | 大洋洲及太平洋岛屿 |
| 新加坡<br>Singapore | 新加坡共和国<br>the Republic of Singapore | 新加坡<br>Singapore | 新加坡元<br>Singapore Dollar | 亚 |
| 新喀里多尼亚(法)<br>New Caledonia | 新喀里多尼亚(法)<br>New Caledonia | 努美阿<br>Nouméa | 太平洋结算法郎<br>CFPF | 大洋洲及太平洋岛屿 |
| 新西兰<br>New Zealand | 新西兰<br>New Zealand | 惠灵顿<br>Wellington | 新西兰元<br>New Zealand Dollar | 大洋洲及太平洋岛屿 |
| 匈牙利<br>Hungary | 匈牙利人民共和国<br>the Hungarian People's Republic | 布达佩斯<br>Budapest | 福林<br>Forint | 欧 |
| 叙利亚<br>Syria | 阿拉伯叙利亚共和国<br>the Syrian Arab Republic | 大马士革<br>Damascus | 叙利亚镑<br>Syrian Pound | 亚 |
| 牙买加<br>Jamaica | 牙买加<br>Jamaica | 金斯敦<br>Kingston | 牙买加元<br>Jamaican Dollar | 拉美 |
| 也门<br>Yemen | 阿拉伯也门共和国<br>the Yemen Arab Republic | 萨那<br>San'a | 也门里亚尔<br>Yemeni Rial | 亚 |
| 伊拉克<br>Iraq | 伊拉克共和国<br>the Republic of Iraq | 巴格达<br>Baghdad | 伊拉克第纳尔<br>Iraqi Dinar | 亚 |

| 简 称 | 全 称 | 首 都(首府) | 货 币 | 地理位置(洲) |
|---|---|---|---|---|
| 伊朗<br>Iran | 伊朗<br>Iran | 德黑兰<br>Teheran | 伊朗里亚尔<br>Iranian Rial | 亚 |
| 意大利<br>Italy | 意大利共和国<br>the Italian Republic | 罗马<br>Rome | 意大利里拉<br>Italian Lira | 欧 |
| 印度<br>India | 印度共和国<br>the Republic of India | 新德里<br>New Delhi | 印度卢比<br>Indian Rupee | 亚 |
| 印度尼西亚<br>Indonesia | 印度尼西亚共和国<br>the Republic of Indonesia | 雅加达<br>Jakarta | 印度尼西亚卢比(通称盾)<br>Indonesia Rupiah | 亚 |
| 英国<br>Britain | 大不列颠及北爱尔兰联合王国<br>the United Kingdom of Great Britain and Northern Ireland | 伦敦<br>London | 英镑<br>Pound Sterling | 欧 |
| 英属维尔京群岛<br>British Virgin Islands | 英属维尔京群岛<br>British Virgin Islands | 罗德城<br>Road Town | 美元<br>United States Dollar | 拉美 |
| 约旦<br>Jordan | 约旦哈希姆王国<br>the Hashemite Kingdom of Jordan | 安曼<br>Amman | 约旦第纳尔<br>Jordan Dinar | 亚 |
| 越南<br>Viet Nam | 越南社会主义共和国<br>the Socialist Republic of Viet Nam | 河内<br>Hanoi | 盾<br>Dong | 亚 |
| 赞比亚<br>Zambia | 赞比亚共和国<br>the Republic of Zambia | 卢萨卡<br>Lusaka | 赞比亚克瓦查<br>Zambian Kwacha | 非 |
| 扎伊尔<br>Zaïre | 扎伊尔共和国<br>the Republic of Zaïre | 金沙萨<br>Kinshasa | 扎伊尔<br>Zaïre | 非 |
| 乍得<br>Chad | 乍得共和国<br>the Republic of Chad | 恩贾梅纳<br>Ndjamena | 非洲金融共同体法郎<br>CFAF (Franc de la Communauté Financière Africaine) | 非 |
| 智利<br>Chile | 智利共和国<br>the Republic of Chile | 圣地亚哥<br>Santiago | 智利比索<br>Chilean Peso | 拉美 |
| 中非帝国<br>the Central African Empire | 中非帝国<br>the Central African Empire | 班吉<br>Bangui | 非洲金融共同体法郎<br>CFAF (Franc de la Communauté Financière Africaine) | 非 |
| 中国<br>China | 中华人民共和国<br>the People's Republic of China | 北京<br>Beijing | 人民币元<br>Renminbi Yuan | 亚 |

(本表所据资料截止至 1978 年 7 月)

# 中国历史年代简表

# A Brief Chinese Chronology

| | | | |
|---|---|---|---|
| 夏 Xia Dynasty | | | 约前21世纪—约前16世纪 |
| 商 Shang Dynasty | | | 约前16世纪—约前11世纪 |
| 周 Zhou Dynasty | 西周 Western Zhou Dynasty | | 约前11世纪—前771 |
| | 东周 Eastern Zhou Dynasty | | 前770—前256 |
| | 春秋 Spring and Autumn Period | | 前770—前476 |
| | 战国 Warring States | | 前475—前221 |
| 秦 Qin Dynasty | | | 前221—前207 |
| 汉 Han Dynasty | 西汉 Western Han | | 前206—公元24 |
| | 东汉 Eastern Han | | 25—220 |
| 三国 Three Kingdoms | 魏 Wei | | 220—265 |
| | 蜀汉 Shu Han | | 221—263 |
| | 吴 Wu | | 222—280 |
| 西晋 Western Jin Dynasty | | | 265—316 |
| 东晋 Eastern Jin Dynasty | | | 317—420 |
| 南北朝 Northern and Southern Dynasties | 南朝 Southern Dynasties | 宋 Song | 420—479 |
| | | 齐 Qi | 479—502 |
| | | 梁 Liang | 502—557 |
| | | 陈 Chen | 557—589 |
| | 北朝 Northern Dynasties | 北魏 Northern Wei | 386—534 |
| | | 东魏 Eastern Wei | 534—550 |
| | | 北齐 Northern Qi | 550—577 |
| | | 西魏 Western Wei | 535—556 |
| | | 北周 Northern Zhou | 557—581 |
| 隋 Sui Dynasty | | | 581—618 |
| 唐 Tang Dynasty | | | 618—907 |
| 五代 Five Dynasties | 后梁 Later Liang | | 907—923 |
| | 后唐 Later Tang | | 923—936 |
| | 后晋 Later Jin | | 936—946 |
| | 后汉 Later Han | | 947—950 |
| | 后周 Later Zhou | | 951—960 |
| 宋 Song Dynasty | 北宋 Northern Song Dynasty | | 960—1127 |
| | 南宋 Southern Song Dynasty | | 1127—1279 |
| 辽 Liao Dynasty | | | 916—1125 |
| 金 Jin Dynasty | | | 1115—1234 |
| 元 Yuan Dynasty | | | 1271—1368 |
| 明 Ming Dynasty | | | 1368—1644 |
| 清 Qing Dynasty | | | 1644—1911 |
| 中华民国 Republic of China | | | 1912—1949 |
| 中华人民共和国 People's Republic of China | | | 1949 成立 |

# 化 学 元 素 表

# A Table of Chemical Elements

| 元素名称 中文 | 汉语拼音 | 英文 | 符号 | 原子序数 | 元素名称 中文 | 汉语拼音 | 英文 | 符号 | 原子序数 |
|---|---|---|---|---|---|---|---|---|---|
| 锕 | ā | actinium | Ac | 89 | 硅 | guī | silicon | Si | 14 |
| 锿 | āi | einsteinium | Es | 99 | 铪 | hā | hafnium | Hf | 72 |
| 砹 | ài | astatine | At | 85 | 氦 | hài | helium | He | 2 |
| 钯 | bǎ | palladium | Pd | 46 | (⿰钅罕) | hǎn | hahnium | Ha | 105 |
| 钡 | bèi | barium | Ba | 56 | 钬 | huǒ | holmium | Ho | 67 |
| 铋 | bì | bismuth | Bi | 83 | 镓 | jiā | gallium | Ga | 31 |
| 铂 | bó | platinum | Pt | 78 | 钾 | jiǎ | potassium | K | 19 |
| 钚 | bù | plutonium | Pu | 94 | 金 | jīn | gold | Au | 79 |
| 氮 | dàn | nitrogen | N | 7 | 锔 | jú | curium | Cm | 96 |
| 锝 | dé | technetium | Tc | 43 | 锎 | kāi | californium | Cf | 98 |
| 镝 | dī | dysprosium | Dy | 66 | 钪 | kàng | scandium | Sc | 21 |
| 碲 | dì | tellurium | Te | 52 | 氪 | kè | krypton | Kr | 36 |
| 碘 | diǎn | iodine | I | 53 | 铼 | lái | rhenium | Re | 75 |
| 铥 | diū | thulium | Tm | 69 | 镧 | lán | lanthanum | La | 57 |
| 氡 | dōng | radon | Rn | 86 | 铹 | láo | lawrencium | Lw | 103 |
| 锇 | é | osmium | Os | 76 | 铑 | lǎo | rhodium | Rh | 45 |
| 铒 | ěr | erbium | Er | 68 | 镭 | léi | radium | Ra | 88 |
| 钒 | fán | vanadium | V | 23 | 锂 | lǐ | lithium | Li | 3 |
| 钫 | fāng | francium | Fr | 87 | 钌 | liǎo | ruthenium | Ru | 44 |
| 镄 | fèi | fermium | Fm | 100 | 磷 | lín | phosphorus | P | 15 |
| 氟 | fú | fluorine | F | 9 | 硫 | liú | sulphur | S | 16 |
| 钆 | gá | gadolinium | Gd | 64 | (𬬻) | lú | rutherfordium | Rf | 104 |
| 钙 | gài | calcium | Ca | 20 | 镥 | lǔ | lutetium | Lu | 71 |
| 锆 | gào | zirconium | Zr | 40 | 铝 | lǚ | aluminium | Al | 13 |
| 镉 | gé | cadmium | Cd | 48 | 氯 | lǜ | chlorine | Cl | 17 |
| 铬 | gè | chromium | Cr | 24 | 镅 | méi | americium | Am | 95 |
| 汞 | gǒng | mercury | Hg | 80 | 镁 | měi | magnesium | Mg | 12 |
| 钴 | gǔ | cobalt | Co | 27 | 钔 | mén | mendelevium | Md | 101 |

续 表

| 元素名称 | | | 符号 | 原子 | 元素名称 | | | 符号 | 原子 |
|---|---|---|---|---|---|---|---|---|---|
| 中文 | 汉语拼音 | 英文 | | 序数 | 中文 | 汉语拼音 | 英文 | | 序数 |
| 锰 | měng | manganese | Mn | 25 | 钛 | tài | titanium | Ti | 22 |
| 钼 | mù | molybdenum | Mo | 42 | 钽 | tǎn | tantalum | Ta | 73 |
| 镎 | ná | neptunium | Np | 93 | 碳 | tàn | carbon | C | 6 |
| 钠 | nà | sodium | Na | 11 | 铽 | tè | terbium | Tb | 65 |
| 氖 | nǎi | neon | Ne | 10 | 锑 | tī | antimony | Sb | 51 |
| 铌 | ní | niobium | Nb | 41 | 铁 | tiě | iron | Fe | 26 |
| 镍 | niè | nickel | Ni | 28 | 铜 | tóng | copper | Cu | 29 |
| 钕 | nǚ | neodymium | Nd | 60 | 钍 | tǔ | thorium | Th | 90 |
| 锘 | nuò | nobelium | No | 102 | 钨 | wū | tungsten | W | 74 |
| 锫 | péi | berkelium | Bk | 97 | 硒 | xī | selenium | Se | 34 |
| 硼 | péng | boron | B | 5 | 锡 | xī | tin | Sn | 50 |
| 铍 | pí | beryllium | Be | 4 | 氙 | xiān | xenon | Xe | 54 |
| 钋 | pō | polonium | Po | 84 | 锌 | xīn | zinc | Zn | 30 |
| 钷 | pǒ | promethium | Pm | 61 | 溴 | xiù | bromine | Br | 35 |
| 镤 | pú | protactinium | Pa | 91 | 氩 | yà | argon | Ar | 18 |
| 镨 | pǔ | praseodymium | Pr | 59 | 氧 | yǎng | oxygen | O | 8 |
| 铅 | qiān | lead | Pb | 82 | 铱 | yī | iridium | Ir | 77 |
| 氢 | qīng | hydrogen | H | 1 | 钇 | yǐ | yttrium | Y | 39 |
| 铷 | rú | rubidium | Rb | 37 | 镱 | yì | ytterbium | Yb | 70 |
| 铯 | sè | cesium | Cs | 55 | 铟 | yīn | indium | In | 49 |
| 钐 | shān | samarium | Sm | 62 | 银 | yín | silver | Ag | 47 |
| 砷 | shēn | arsenic | As | 33 | 铀 | yóu | uranium | U | 92 |
| 铈 | shì | cerium | Ce | 58 | 铕 | yǒu | europium | Eu | 63 |
| 锶 | sī | strontium | Sr | 38 | 锗 | zhě | germanium | Ge | 32 |
| 铊 | tā | thallium | Tl | 81 | | | | | |